THE
RESTAURANT
GUIDE
2016

AA Lifestyle Guides

Published by AA Publishing, a trading name of AA Media Limited, whose registered office is Fanum House, Basing View, Basingstoke, Hampshire RG21 4EA. Registered number 06112600.

23rd edition published 2015
© AA Media Limited 2015

Please contact
Advertisement Sales: advertisingsales@theaa.com
Editorial Department: lifestyleguides@theaa.com
Hotel Services: hotelservices@theaa.com

Photographs in the gazetteer are provided by the establishments. Every effort has been made to trace copyright holders, and we apologise in advance for any unintentional omissions or errors. We would be pleased to apply any corrections in a following edition of this publication.

Typeset and repro by Servis Filmsetting Ltd, Stockport.

Printed in Italy by Printer Trento SRL

This directory is compiled by AA Lifestyle Guides; managed in the Librios Information Management System and generated by the AA establishment database system.

Restaurant descriptions have been contributed by the following team of writers: Hugh Morgan, Mike Pedley, Allen Stidwill, Andrew Turvil, Stuart Walton. Thank you also to Phil Bryant and Mark Taylor.

AA Lifestyle Guides would like to thank Julia Powers and Sean Callery for their help in the preparation of this guide.

Maps prepared by the Mapping Services Department of AA Publishing. Maps © AA Media Limited 2015.

Contains Ordnance Survey data © Crown copyright and database right 2015.

Information on National Parks in England provided by the Countryside Agency (Natural England).

Information on National Parks in Scotland provided by Scottish Natural Heritage.

Information on National Parks in Wales provided by The Countryside Council for Wales.

ISBN: 978-0-7495-7722-3

A05289

Contents

Welcome to the AA Restaurant Guide

Welcome to the 23rd edition of The AA Restaurant Guide. As ever, our team of AA hotel and restaurant inspectors have been travelling the length and breadth of the country, making anonymous visits to hundreds of establishments and awarding coveted AA Rosettes to the best of the UK's restaurants.

Up-and-comers

For another year, we've been thrilled with the quality of the UK dining scene. This year's guide includes 12 five-Rosette, 38 four-Rosette and 205 three-Rosette restaurants, the elite of what the country has to offer – that's 21 more than in 2015 – as well as more than 210 entirely new restaurants to the guide.

It's been a particularly strong year for the up-and-comers, with all four of the Restaurants of the Year chosen by our team of inspectors on their visits having opened within the past two or three years. Find them all on pages 14–15.

Keeping up the pace

That's not to say that the old favourites aren't keeping pace, however; Stephanie Sparrow spoke to Craig Bancroft and Nigel Haworth on their 30 years at Northcote, and found out how they've been refurbishing and investing to make sure they remain at the top of their game in our feature on page 28. Also putting in the long years is the winner of this year's Lifetime Achievement Award on page 12, while the winner of the AA Chefs' Chef Award on page 10, voted for by their peers, trails with a mere quarter-century of cooking to his name, 17 as a head chef. No slouches here.

Extra special

Everyone wants to feel like they're in safe hands when they're wining or dining, and we're no different. The AA Wine Awards (see page 16) single out three restaurants in the country that we feel have shown a real passion for and knowledge of wine, to curate wine lists that will add that special touch to any meal. We've also highlighted other restaurants with notable wine lists throughout the guide (🍷 NOTABLE WINE LIST).

Meanwhile, Mike Pedley can be found discussing how to cook the perfect steak on page 20, with help from David McIntyre at CUT and Nigel Boschetti at JW Steakhouse, and we're celebrating the third winner of the AA Food Service Award on page 13 – extra special isn't just about the food and drink.

Who's in the guide?

We make our selection by seeking out restaurants that are worth making a detour for – the best ingredients, expertly prepared, whether in skilled interpretations of classic dishes or modern, innovative flavour combinations. Some may be part of an upmarket hotel, others a small family-run business; what they all have in common is excellent food. To learn more about how the AA assesses restaurants for Rosette awards, see page 9.

Changing places

The transient nature of the hospitality industry means that chefs move around all the time, and restaurants may change hands. As any change at multi-Rosette level requires a new inspection to verify their award, some of these restaurants appear in the guide with their Rosette level unconfirmed.

Our inspections are ongoing throughout the year however, so once their award is confirmed it will be published in the restaurants section on theAA.com.

How to use the guide

1.

3.

4.
5.
6.

9.

10.

11.

12.

14.

16.

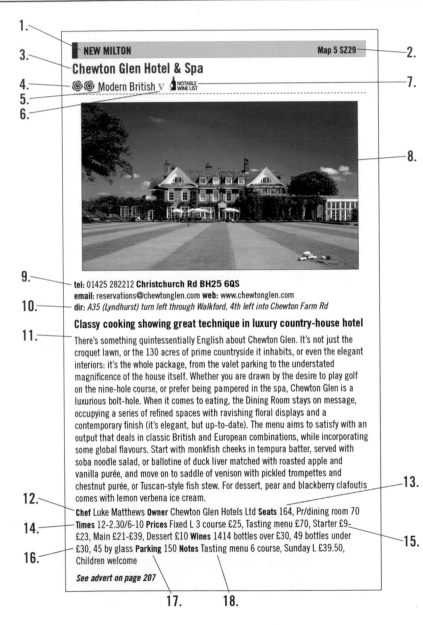

NEW MILTON   Map 5 SZ29

Chewton Glen Hotel & Spa

◉◉ Modern British V   NOTABLE WINE LIST

tel: 01425 282212 **Christchurch Rd BH25 6QS**
email: reservations@chewtonglen.com **web:** www.chewtonglen.com
dir: *A35 (Lyndhurst) turn left through Walkford, 4th left into Chewton Farm Rd*

Classy cooking showing great technique in luxury country-house hotel

There's something quintessentially English about Chewton Glen. It's not just the croquet lawn, or the 130 acres of prime countryside it inhabits, or even the elegant interiors: it's the whole package, from the valet parking to the understated magnificence of the house itself. Whether you are drawn by the desire to play golf on the nine-hole course, or prefer being pampered in the spa, Chewton Glen is a luxurious bolt-hole. When it comes to eating, the Dining Room stays on message, occupying a series of refined spaces with ravishing floral displays and a contemporary finish (it's elegant, but up-to-date). The menu aims to satisfy with an output that deals in classic British and European combinations, while incorporating some global flavours. Start with monkfish cheeks in tempura batter, served with soba noodle salad, or ballotine of duck liver matched with roasted apple and vanilla purée, and move on to saddle of venison with pickled trompettes and chestnut purée, or Tuscan-style fish stew. For dessert, pear and blackberry clafoutis comes with lemon verbena ice cream.

Chef Luke Matthews **Owner** Chewton Glen Hotels Ltd **Seats** 164, Pr/dining room 70
Times 12-2.30/6-10 **Prices** Fixed L 3 course £25, Tasting menu £70, Starter £9-£23, Main £21-£39, Dessert £10 **Wines** 1414 bottles over £30, 49 bottles under £30, 45 by glass **Parking** 150 **Notes** Tasting menu 6 course, Sunday L £39.50, Children welcome

See advert on page 207

17.   18.

2.

7.

8.

13.

15.

1. Location

Restaurants are listed in country and county order, then by town and then alphabetically within the town. There is an index by restaurant at the back of the guide and a similar one for the Central & Greater London sections on page 256.

2. Map reference

Each town or village is given a map reference – the map page number and a two-figure reference based on the National Grid. For example:
Map 5 SZ29
5 refers to the page number of the map section at the back of the guide
SZ is the National Grid lettered square (representing 100,000 sq metres) in which the location will be found
2 is the figure reading across the top and bottom of the map page
9 is the figure reading down at each side of the map page. For Central London and Greater London, there is a map section starting on page 260.

3. Restaurant name

Some details and prices may be omitted from an entry when the establishment has not supplied us with up-to-date information. This is indicated where an establishment name is shown in italics.

4. AA Rosette award

Restaurants are awarded one or more Rosettes, up to a maximum of five. See page 9.

5. Food style

A summary of the main cuisine type(s).

6. Vegetarian menu

V Indicates a vegetarian menu. Restaurants with some vegetarian dishes available are indicated under Notes (see 18, below).

7. Notable wine list

NOTABLE WINE LIST This symbol, where present, indicates a notable wine list (see pages 16–19).

8. Photograph(s)

Restaurants are invited to enhance their entry with up to two photographs.

9. Contact details

10. Directions

Short directions are given. London locations give the nearest station.

11. Description

Description of the restaurant and the food.

12. Chef(s) and owner(s)

The names of the chef(s) and owner(s) are as up-to-date as possible at the time of going to press, but changes in personnel often occur, and may affect both the style and quality of the restaurant.

13. Number of seats

Number of seats in the restaurant, followed by private dining room (Pr/dining room).

14. Daily opening and closing times

Daily opening and closing times, the days of the week when closed and seasonal closures. Some restaurants offer all-day dining. Note that opening times are liable to change without notice. It is wise to telephone in advance.

15. Prices

Prices are for fixed lunch (2 courses) and dinner (3 courses) and à la carte dishes. Note: Prices quoted are an indication only, and are subject to change. We ask restaurants questions about service charge and their responses appear here too.

16. Number of wines

Number of wines under and over £30, and available by the glass.

17. Parking details

On-site parking or nearby parking.

18. Notes

Additional information as supplied by the restaurants including, for example, availability of vegetarian dishes (not a full menu, see 6, above), Sunday lunch prices and policy towards children.

FURTHER INFORMATION

Food allergies

From December 2014, a new EU regulation came into force making it easier for those with food allergies to make safer food choices when eating out. There are 14 allergens listed in the regulation, and restaurants are required to list any of these that are used in the dishes they offer. These may be highlighted on the menus or customers can ask staff for full information.

Remember, if you are allergic to a food and are in any doubt speak to a member of the restaurant's staff. For further information see: www.food.gov.uk/science/allergy-intolerance

Smoking regulations

From July 2007 smoking was banned in all enclosed public places in the United Kingdom and Ireland. Internal communal areas must be smoke-free.

Facilities for disabled guests

The Equality Act 2010 provides legal rights for disabled people including access to goods, services and facilities, and means that service providers may have to consider making adjustments to their premises. For more information about the Act see www.gov.uk/government/policies/creating-a-fairer-and-more-equal-society or www.gov.uk/definition-of-disability-under-equality-act-2010.

The establishments in this guide should be aware of their obligations under the Act. We recommend that you phone in advance to ensure that the establishment you have chosen has appropriate facilities.

How the AA assesses for Rosette Awards

The AA's Rosette Award scheme was the first nationwide scheme for assessing the quality of food served by restaurants and hotels.

A consistent approach

The Rosette scheme is an award, not a classification, and although there is necessarily an element of subjectivity when it comes to assessing taste, we aim for a consistent approach throughout the UK. Our awards are made solely on the basis of a meal visit or visits by one or more of our hotel and restaurant inspectors, who have an unrivalled breadth and depth of experience in assessing quality. They award Rosettes annually on a rising scale of one to five.

What makes a restaurant worthy of a Rosette award?

For our inspectors, the top and bottom line is the food. The taste of a dish is what counts, and whether it successfully delivers to the diner the promise of the menu. A restaurant is only as good as its worst meal. Although presentation and competent service should be appropriate to the style of the restaurant and the quality of the food, they cannot affect the Rosette assessment as such, either up or down. The summaries below indicate what our inspectors look for, but are intended only as guidelines. The AA is constantly reviewing its award criteria, and competition usually results in an all-round improvement in standards, so it becomes increasingly difficult for restaurants to reach an award level. For more detailed Rosette criteria, please visit theAA.com.

☻ One Rosette

These are excellent restaurants that stand out in their local area featuring:
* Food prepared with care, understanding and skill
* Good quality ingredients
Around 45% of restaurants in this guide have one Rosette.

☻☻ Two Rosettes

The best local restaurants, which aim for and achieve:
* Higher standards
* Better consistency
* Greater precision apparent in the cooking
* Obvious attention to the quality and selection of ingredients
Around 45% of restaurants in this guide have two Rosettes.

☻☻☻ Three Rosettes

Outstanding restaurants demanding recognition well beyond their local area. The cooking will be underpinned by:
* Selection and sympathetic treatment of highest quality ingredients
* Consistent timing, seasoning and judgement of flavour combinations
* Excellent, intelligent service and a well-chosen wine list
Around 10% of restaurants in this guide have three Rosettes.

☻☻☻☻ Four Rosettes

Among the top restaurants in the UK, where the cooking demands national recognition and shows:
* Intense ambition
* A passion for excellence
* Superb technical skills
* Remarkable consistency
* Appreciation of culinary traditions combined with desire for exploration and improvement
* Cooking demanding national recognition
Thirty-eight restaurants in this guide have four Rosettes.

☻☻☻☻☻ Five Rosettes

Where the cooking stands comparison with the best in the world. These restaurants have:
* Highly individual cooking
* Breathtaking culinary skills
* Standards to which others aspire
* A knowledgeable and distinctive wine list
Twelve restaurants in this guide have five Rosettes.

AA Chefs' Chef 2015–16

© Adrian Franklin

Daniel Clifford

This year's AA Chefs' Chef Award goes to Daniel Clifford of Midsummer House Restaurant, Cambridge

Daniel Clifford's name has been synonymous with the award-winning Midsummer House restaurant in Cambridge for the past 17 years, but his culinary journey started more than a decade before that. Clifford's formative years as a trainee chef were spent learning his craft under some of the biggest names in celebrated restaurants in the UK and France. He claims the biggest influence was a stint with Jean Bardet in France, although time spent working for Simon Gueller at Rascasse in Leeds and Marco Pierre White at The Box Tree in Ilkley also helped to shape him into one of the UK's most respected and decorated chefs, with five AA Rosettes to his name.

Clifford went on to work at Howfield Manor Hotel and Restaurant in Kent and with David Cavalier at The Bell Inn in Buckinghamshire. With the backing of business partner Russell Morgan, founder and chairman of successful catering company The Crown Partnership, Clifford took over Midsummer House in 1998, his first head chef position. An inquisitive and ambitious chef, he was inspired by visits to Heston Blumenthal's The Fat Duck at Bray and Michel Bras in France.

Schooled in the classic techniques of French cooking, Clifford has embraced kitchen science, molecular gastronomy and innovative presentation, whilst still relying on the finest local and seasonal ingredients and making sure taste always comes first. The result is a highly individual style that has won him countless awards for such creative dishes as pot-roasted pigeon d'Anjou, chickpeas, apple and chamomile; and poached kumquat, tamarind yogurt sorbet, carrot and cardamom.

A chef who prefers the heat of the kitchen to the glare of the TV studio lights, Clifford made an exception to appear on BBC2's *Great British Menu*. He was well rewarded for it, as he won the banquet main course in 2012 and the banquet dessert round in 2013.

With five daughters, Clifford doesn't get that much spare time, but when he does get a rare day off, he likes nothing more than spending it by the river fishing for carp. Not that he will get much time off now, as he has just bought a farm in Essex, which he plans to convert into a wedding venue, cookery school and farm shop selling dishes he can't the put on the menu at Midsummer House. Apparently he makes a 'blinding' steak and kidney pudding – and who would argue with that?

On the menu

Beetroot baked on open coals,
quinoa, goat's cheese, mizuna

Barbecued Cumbrian lamb, courgette
and basil purée, 'Pommes Anna'

Poached kumquat, tamarind yogurt
sorbet, carrot and cardamom

Previous winners

AA Lifetime Achievement Award 2015–16

Robin Hutson

Robin Hutson has dedicated his entire working life to creating and developing luxurious and special places for people to stay. Leaving Brooklands Technical College with an OND in Hotel and Catering Operations, Hutson joined the Savoy Group's management training programme, working in all departments of Claridge's, Stones Chop House and the Berkeley Hotel before a year-long stint at Hotel du Crillon in Paris.

Returning to the UK, he became the Savoy Group's youngest-ever reception manager at The Berkeley, during which time he met his wife, Judy, to whom he has been married for 32 years and who is now responsible for the striking interiors at The Pig hotels.

Newly married, Hutson spent two years at the five-star Elbow Beach Hotel in Bermuda before being lured back to the UK with the offer of the GM role at Chewton Glen in Hampshire. He was eventually promoted to MD and spent eight influential years there, where he met like-minded sommelier Gerard Basset. The ambitious duo shared a vision of opening a more accessible and relaxed luxury hotel, a vision which came to pass with the opening of the first Hotel du Vin in Winchester in 1994. It was a groundbreaking concept for boutique hotels and became a highly successful and influential chain, which they sold ten years later for £66.5m.

Hutson's Midas touch continued when he went on to become executive chairman of the Soho House Group, during which time the group doubled in size and was eventually sold in 2008 for £105m. Not one to stand still, he then jumped at the chance to work with Jim Ratcliffe, who was developing the Lime Wood country house hotel in the New Forest, which opened in 2009. Hutson is now executive chairman of the group and has since developed Home Grown Hotels and The Pig hotel concept, a more contemporary take on the Hotel du Vin format, this time based more around kitchen garden produce or ingredients sourced within 15 miles of the kitchen.

With all of these hotels running on almost 100% occupancy and with food and beverage accounting for 60% of turnover, Hutson's achievements and creative genius speak for themselves. Highly regarded in the hospitality industry as one of the most innovative hoteliers, he remains totally hands-on in his businesses – a regular visitor to his own hotels, it's not unusual to see him in reception, or even working in the garden.

AA Food Service Award 2015–16

Belmond Le Manoir aux Quat' Saisons, Great Milton, Oxfordshire

Customer-facing staff in the UK restaurant industry do not generally get the recognition that they deserve, but this award acknowledges the vital role played by service teams across the country. From the 2,000-plus AA Rosette restaurants featured in the 2016 Restaurant Guide, the AA inspection team nominated the very best of the best, based on the following criteria:

- Consistently delivering excellent standards of restaurant service and hospitality
- Technical service skills and food and beverage knowledge of the highest standard
- Clear commitment to staff training and development

Since it opened in 1984, Belmond Le Manoir aux Quat' Saisons has become one of the UK's leading culinary lights, with service standards that not only match the exacting credentials expected by AA inspectors and consumers, but are internationally renowned in their own right.

Situated in the pretty Oxfordshire village of Great Milton, this 32 bedroom hotel and restaurant is a legendary gastronomic destination and home to its iconic chef/patron Raymond Blanc. Set in beautifully manicured grounds with a stunning two-acre vegetable and herb garden, the kitchen delivers outstanding cooking, with the levels of service given equal focus to ensure meticulous attention to detail and superlative fluency under the personal direction of general manager Philip Newman-Hall.

The service at Belmond Le Manoir aux Quat' Saisons is formal in style, yet engaging and personal, delivered by an immaculately presented and well-structured brigade. A separate team of sommeliers is in charge of the hotel's famous cellars, which are home to more than 1,000 different wines. It comes as no surprise that many of the restaurant team regularly achieve industry recognition for their skills in prestigious awards such as the Annual Awards of Service Excellence with the Royal Academy of Culinary Arts.

Product knowledge and technical skill impress in equal measure, reflecting the high level of training and development that is deep-rooted in Raymond Blanc's ethos of sharing his culinary knowledge. This commitment to teaching future generations has extended to The Raymond Blanc Cookery School, which opened in 1991.

'Impeccable' and 'faultless' are common descriptions for both our AA inspectors and consumers when recounting their service experience at Belmond Le Manoir aux Quat' Saisons, and it is this consistency of excellence that the award acknowledges.

The award's two runners-up were Jesmond Dene House, Newcastle-upon-Tyne and Paul Ainsworth at No. 6, Padstow.

AA Restaurants of the Year 2015–16

ENGLAND

HOUSE OF TIDES ❀❀❀
NEWCASTLE-UPON-TYNE page 526

Chef-patron Kenny Atkinson has enjoyed much success with his career, building up great experience in five-star properties such as The Chester Grosvenor, Mandarin Oriental London and Rockliffe Hall, with appearances on television shows such as *Great British Menu* to boot. Striking out on his own, Kenny decided to open his own restaurant back in his home city of Newcastle. Fifteen months on, House of Tides continues to flourish.

The listed building, dating back to the 16th century, is located right on the Quayside, and the rustic feel of the exterior is continued inside. Drinks and nibbles are served on the ground floor and the dining experience continues on the upper floor. There is a great deal of imagination shown with the menus and the marriage of produce, with the visual dishes incorporating a sense of theatre.

House of Tides achieved three AA Rosettes in January of this year. To establish a restaurant of this quality and calibre and gain such a reputation in a relatively short space of time is very impressive.

LONDON

TREDWELL'S ❀❀
LONDON page 406 NEW ENTRY

Tredwell's is the latest project from Marcus Wareing, offering an informal setting in which diners can enjoy his 'Modern London cooking'. Located in the heart of Theatreland, just off Seven Dials, with a footprint over three floors, it is flooded with natural light via large windows, pavement lights and a skylight, creating an airy and spacious feel. The interior features racing green leather banquette and booth seating, giving the restaurant a comfortable and welcoming feel.

The bar area situated on the lower ground floor does pre-dinner drinks, with a selection of cocktails created by Dav Eames on offer, and a global wine list. The site also features a spacious 'eat at bar' arrangement on the ground floor. In the main restaurant, meanwhile, the food is fun, inventive and original. Flavours are big and punchy, and include a variety of gluten-free and vegan-friendly dishes.

Tredwell's brings a refreshingly new concept to the Marcus Wareing stable and will be a well-received winner of this prestigious accolade.

AA Wine Awards 2015–16

The annual AA wine award, sponsored by Matthew Clark Wines, attracted a huge response from our AA recognised restaurants with over 1,300 wine lists submitted for judging. Three national winners were chosen – The Sun Inn, Dedham for England and Overall winner; Ubiquitous Chip, Glasgow for Scotland; and the Walnut Tree Inn, Abergavenny for Wales (see overleaf for details of the winners).

All 2,000 Rosetted restaurants in last year's guide were invited to submit their wine lists. From these the panel selected a shortlist of over 260 establishments who are highlighted in the guide with the Notable Wine List symbol ▲NOTABLE WINE LIST.

The shortlisted establishments were asked to choose wines from their list (within a budget of £80 per bottle) to accompany a menu designed by last year's winner, The Olive Tree at the Queensberry Hotel, Bath.

The final judging panel included Simon Numphud, Head of AA Hotel Services, Laurence Beere, Proprietor of The Queensberry Hotel and Nick Zalinski, Business Director of Matthew Clark Wines (our sponsor). The judges' comments are shown under the award winners overleaf.

Other wine lists that stood out in the final judging included Andrew Fairlie@Gleneagles in Auchterarder, Donnington Valley in Newbury, Park House in Cardiff, Pheasant Inn in Keyston and Chewton Glen in New Milton.

What makes a wine list notable?

We are looking for high-quality wines, with diversity across grapes and/or countries and style, the best individual growers and vintages. The list should be well presented, ideally with some helpful notes and, to reflect the demand from diners, a good choice of wines by the glass.

Things that disappoint the judges are spelling errors, wines under incorrect regions or styles, split vintages (which are still far too common), lazy purchasing (all wines from a country from just one grower or negociant) and confusing layouts. Sadly, many restaurants still do not pay much attention to wine, resulting in ill-considered lists.

To reach the final shortlist, we look for a real passion for wine, which should come across to the customer, a fair pricing policy (depending on the style of the restaurant), interesting coverage (not necessarily a large list), which might include areas of specialism, perhaps a particular wine area, sherries or larger formats such as magnums.

The Sun Inn, Dedham
– the winning wine selection

Menu	Wine Selection
Amuse – Crab lasagne, mousse and bisque, basil and ginger	2010 Riverbrook Riesling, Pyramid valley, Marlborough, New Zealand
Starter – Duck liver, poached and roasted, pickled rhubarb, shiitake mushrooms and candied walnuts	2012 Kerner, Cantina Produttori Valle Isarco, Alto-Adige, Italy
Fish course – Halibut, pan fried, leek, Shimeji mushroom, salt baked celeriac, Noilly Prat sauce and winter truffle	2013 Didi Novello, Tom Shobbrook, Barossa, South Australia
Main course – Venison loin, quince purée, smoked bacon, spiced red cabbage and Brussel sprouts	2000 Buccerchiale, Chianti Rufina Riserva, Fattoria Selvapiana
Cheese – Roquefort, pear, candied walnuts and celery	2007 Grandjo Late Harvest, Real Companhia Valha, Douro, Portugal
Dessert – English rhubarb, yogurt and vanilla mousse, puff pastry and rhubarb sorbet	Billecart-Salmon Rosé NV
Coffee and petit four	Marsala Superiore 10 year Old, Marco de Bartoli, Sicily

The AA Wine Awards are sponsored by Matthew Clark, Whitchurch Lane, Bristol, BS14 OJ2 Tel: 01275 891400
email: enquiries@matthewclark.co.uk web: www.matthewclark.co.uk

AA Wine Awards — the winners

THE SUN INN ❀❀
DEDHAM page 168

In the heart of Constable country, The Sun Inn's location may be quintessentially English, but the kitchen in this characterful 15th-century village inn looks to the sunny Mediterranean for its main inspiration. High-quality locally sourced produce rubs shoulders with imported Italian ingredients including cured meats, cheeses and oils, in straightforward, confident dishes; fresh crab crostini with aioli, Parma ham, olives and Mersea rock oysters; grilled salt marsh leg of lamb, roasted red and yellow beetroots, salsa verde; Old Spot pork loin, braised black cabbage and Spello lentils. The accessible, well-annotated wine list blends New World with Old, and bottles are arranged by style, such as 'rich and structured' or 'succulent and aromatic'. The bias may be on Italy and France, but bottles from England and the Southern Hemisphere keep things interesting.

Judges' comments: A cracking list that offers superb value throughout. Offers a great selection of wines by the glass and carafe. Its unconventional three-format approach was much admired, starting with the list in full, followed by a food and wine section, and finally the list presented again with full informative tasting notes. A super, quirky and highly personal list with great choices throughout that simply does not fail to engage you, this list oozes personality. The diverse range of really interesting wines reflects the multi-supplier approach that the business adopts.

WINNER FOR SCOTLAND

UBIQUITOUS CHIP ◎◎
GLASGOW page 645

A Glasgow institution since 1971, Ubiquitous Chip's enduring success is partly down to the fact that it has moved with the times, preferring to set its own agenda rather than follow the fashions. Ronnie Clydesdale's West End brasserie proudly flies the Scottish flag when it comes to produce, with a typical menu featuring a signature venison haggis; seared Islay scallops, crispy pig cheek, haricot bean, truffle tartare; Galloway roe deer haunch, roast squash, baby onions, smoked potato, hazelnuts and cocoa. Such imaginative dishes and well-defined flavours require a suitably vigorous and engaging range of wines and the list here is well-balanced, approachable and fairly priced. Whether it's the tried and tested 'Chip Recommends' or the wine flights, this is a list that reads as well as it drinks.

Judges' comments: A charming list full of personality and passion. Judges liked the small introduction to each section plus the 'Chip Recommends' that the list opens with, an interesting mix of personal choices. The extensive range of wines by the glass across a good price range also stood out.

WINNER FOR WALES

WALNUT TREE INN ◎◎◎
ABERGAVENNY page 687

Occupying a remote position on a crest of a hill just outside Abergavenny, this whitewashed former inn was a celebrated Italian restaurant for four decades under previous owners Franco and Ann Taruschio. Since 2008, it has been in the equally safe hands of Shaun Hill, widely regarded as one of the UK's greatest chefs. The no-frills, rustic interior is the perfect setting for Hill's finely-tuned, produce-driven dishes: lobster with lentil and coriander sauce; halibut with clams and mussels in a spiced broth; veal loin and kidneys with mustard sauce. The globe-trotting wine list opens with a mission statement that 'we list what we taste and like', and the simplicity and personality of the wines matches the food, with plenty of good drinking under £30 and a decent range offered by the glass and carafe.

Judges' comments: A great concise list that is very much built around the restaurant and Shaun's cooking. The simplicity of its three key sections Essential / Core / Classic resonated with all the judges. This list engages at all different levels, offers good value and gives short, punchy tasting notes with both personality and humour.

19

Raising the steaks

by Mike Pedley

Sidelined on the slightly boring end of the culinary spectrum for many years, steakhouses are a hot ticket at the moment. Of course, for many unreconstructed carnivores, those classic cuts of beef never really went away, but these days they have traded up from the status of a comforting fallback option to star billing in a gaggle of dedicated steakhouses across the UK.

Espoused by high-profile names such as Marco Pierre White and Wolfgang Puck, whose Park Lane joint is probably the slinkiest-looking steakhouse this side of the pond, steak has had a serious image makeover.

So why have sizzling slabs of beef become sexy and aspirational? Perhaps it's a reaction against all those mimsy froths, airs and espumas of the molecular gastronomy brigade, whose culinary fireworks may well titillate and entertain, but don't grab us in that visceral caveman way that only a charred and bloody piece of cow can manage. Perhaps there's also something trendily retro about steak and chips (triple-cooked, of course, these days), a whiff of the 70s that will evoke nostalgia in anyone old enough to remember the defunct Berni Inn chain. What's sure is that there's nothing subtle about a good steak, but when it's done right, charred and smoky outside, tender and juicy inside with that big beefy hit, it's hard to beat.

What's the beef?

Chefs have long made a virtue of provenance, and the same rules apply to steak: before the meat gets as far as the grill, it's important to consider where it's coming from, and how it has been aged. There are many different types of cattle across the world, and the animal's breed and factors such as where it was raised and what is was fed on all influence the quality of the meat and thus the end results on your plate. Cattle can be grass-fed, or raised with a mixture of grass feeding, hay and grains. The grains add fat to the diet so that gives the meat more marbling, which translates as rich, butter-soft meat. US beef tends to be started on grass then finished with grain – look for the USDA (US Department of Agriculture) certification: this is the body that carefully measures and certifies the quality and consistency of cattle across North America. Experts say that Kansas Black Angus is the gold standard for USDA beef and is consistently tender and delicious.

UK, European or Argentinean cattle tend to eat grass, so they have less marbling than USDA beef, and aren't as rich and fatty tasting as American cattle, but they have a more irony, distinctive flavour that reflects the pasture on which the cattle are grazed.

"Origin makes a significant difference – the USDA beef is corn fed, which gives the steak a soft, rich, buttery texture: however, the grass-fed Aberdeen Angus has a fuller, more in-depth flavour."

Nigel Boschetti, Executive Chef, JW Steakhouse

Making the cut

Broadly speaking, the front and rear ends of the animal do most of the work, so meat from here needs longer cooking to make it tender. This is why the best steaks come from the middle, where the muscles do less work and are consequently more tender. There's a baffling variety of steaks out there these days, so here's a guide to the most commonly seen cuts:

• Rump steak

This is a real steak eater's steak – a tender, good-quality everyday cut that has heaps more flavour than fillet for a lot less money. As the name suggests, it comes from the cow's backside and must be well hung for tenderness.

• Sirloin steak

A stalwart of the steak scene, the sirloin comes from the upper middle of the cow between the rib and the fillet, a part that doesn't work nearly as hard as, say, the shoulder, so it is very tender and well marbled with fat. It needs good butchery and preparation to make sure all the gristle is removed.

• T-bone & Porterhouse steak

There's not much difference between these two cuts. Both are huge slabs of meat that are 'double steaks' – sirloin on one side of the bone and fillet on the other, so you get the best of both worlds. On the downside, they cook at different rates so you have to accept the compromise. The T-bone comes from the thicker end of the spine, meaning you get more bone, less meat.

• Rib-eye steak

An old classic, rib-eye has become rather trendy with a new generation of steak aficionados. It comes from a cow's fore rib section and is marbled with a central piece of fat, which makes it very tender and gives it a full-bore, rich and beefy flavour.

> "The Japanese 100% pure Wagyu melts in your mouth, but it's very rich, like eating a pat of butter, so you only need a small piece. Once you try different types of beef and get to know your steak you can certainly tell the difference."

David McIntyre, Executive Chef, CUT

The Japanese Wagyu is a breed apart: it has a much higher percentage of fat, so it is prized for its exceptional tenderness, and in recent years, this type of steak has gone from being almost unknown to a common, if eye-wateringly expensive, feature on high-end menus; you're not meant to eat huge slabs of it, and the price alone is enough to discourage a Wagyu blowout – an 8oz rib-eye steak of gold-standard, true Japanese Wagyu will set you back £140 in Cut at 45 Park Lane, for example. Fans of UK-bred beef can even tuck into home grown 'McWagyu' cattle, which have been farmed by Blackford Farms in Perthshire since 2011.

How old should a steak be?

If steak is not hung to age it's much tougher, and it can be either wet aged or dry aged. Dry ageing means it's dried in the open (rather than wet aged in a bag), so that natural evaporation reduces the water content by 20 per cent or so, depending on how long it's aged for. You get a more concentrated flavour, but you can also expect it to cost more to make up for this weight loss. The Goodman steakhouses in London, for example, dry-age their meat on-site in a temperature controlled, dehumidified environment in order to bring out the full concentration of flavour. You're usually looking for a steak to have at least 21 days ageing under its belt, although fillet can be aged for a shorter period; 28 days is also common, and 35 days is generally considered to be about the limit of the optimum length.

> "Our USDA beef is aged for 35 days. Some people age beef up to 60 days – there's nothing wrong with that, but it will be too gamey for a lot of people. Here at CUT we wet-age our meat." David McIntyre

• Fillet steak and Chateaubriand

The fillet comes from the tenderloin inside the sirloin and is always pitched at the pricier end of the menu. This muscle does no work at all, so the steak is tender as butter, and devoid of fat; on the downside it doesn't have as much beefy flavour as other cuts. As it's so lean, fillet steak is a good one to perk up with a punchy sauce. The chateaubriand is a big hunk of meat taken from the larger end of the fillet, and is often dished up as a sharing steak for two.

It's worth remembering that steak's not all about the prime cuts mentioned above – there are various interesting and tasty cuts from more humble parts of the cow, and they are becoming quite trendy too:

• Bavette/flank steak

Well known to francophiles, this bistro-style steak has crossed the channel and caught on with inquisitive fans of cheaper cuts. It has a coarse, ropy grain and can be a bit chewy, but the upside is its great flavour. A punchy marinade or condiment will really bring it to life.

• Onglet steak

Tender (but not quite melt-in-the-mouth), ropy-textured and dark, garnet-red, onglet offers deep flavour with a hint of offal (it comes from near the liver and kidneys). It's the classic cut served as steak-frites in France.

• Featherblade

An old-fashioned, thrifty cut that has been rediscovered by curious foodies. Taken from the shoulder blade – ie potentially tough – it is a rich, hearty steak that is often braised or casseroled, but also works well when cooked rare. When it is cut with the grain it appears on menus as a flat-iron steak.

The dining room at JW steakhouse

SAUCES & TOPPINGS

BOURBON PEPPERCORN

BÉARNAISE

CREAMY HORSERADISH

RED WINE

PORT & STILTON

OSCAR

OLD BAY

AN ICONIC, ZESTY SEASONING FOR CRAB AND SHRIMP CREATED MORE
THAN 70 YEARS AGO IN THE US SEA PORT OF BALTIMORE. AROUND THE GLOBE
OLD BAY SEASONING HAS ACHIEVED A NEAR CULT-LIKE STATUS AMONG CRAB AND
SHRIMP AFICIONADOS. IT'S DISTINCTIVE RED COLOUR AND BOLD FLAVOUR
MAKE IT AN ESSENTIAL INGREDIENT IN OUR AUTHENTIC JUMBO
LUMP CRAB CAKES.

STEAK TEMPERATURES

BLACK AND BLUE

RARE

MEDIUM RARE

MEDIUM

MEDIUM WELL

WELL DONE

The right equipment

If you've ever wondered how chefs manage to cook a steak to stunning perfection compared to your less-than-perfect attempts at home, remember that the engine room of any steakhouse worthy of the name will have at its heart some serious chargrilling kit. It's also common in many restaurants these days to cook meat sous-vide – aka the 'boil in the bag' technique, where meat is poached in a vacuum-sealed bag in a water bath, which cooks the meat slowly to achieve a delicate texture, before finishing on the barbecue to give it that just-roasted, smoky depth of flavour from the bars of the grill.

But most true steakhouses achieve remarkable results with a distinctly low-tech approach – full-on heat. High temperature is crucial to achieving that perfect crusty-edged, browned steak, and it's all down to a bit of science known as the Maillard reaction, a chemical reaction in which sugars and amino acids in the meat react and create new and delicious compounds – it's the same reaction that occurs when you toast bread.

To get a Maillard reaction, the surface temperature of the steak needs to be around 350ºC – and that's where the charcoal grill or oven comes in. The JW Steakhouse on London's Park Lane uses a Montague Legend radiant grill with a cooking temperature of 650ºC on the top and bottom of the grilling surface, searing both sides of the meat quickly and evenly to seal in the juices, while Clive Davidson, chef-patron of The Champany Inn in Linlithgow – a mecca for beef – designed his own range and had it built to his specification to deliver the exact levels of heat he wants to seal and cook the prime cuts of Aberdeen Angus beef.

> "We cook on a charbroiler at 650°C to sear in the juices with a natural crust, then the really important part is resting it for 5–10 minutes, depending on the cut, before serving it." David McIntyre

You don't even have to go to a pukka steakhouse to get perfectly seared steak nowadays as there's an off-the-shelf piece of kit that fits the bill nicely: enter the Josper charcoal oven and grill. The heat of these enclosed indoor barbecues reaches 350ºC, and comes from all around rather than just underneath, so the meat colours evenly and intensifies the flavour. At around £12,000, they don't come cheap, but many restaurants that don't bill themselves as dedicated steakhouses, but still want to showcase the excellent meats they source from local farmers, are making the investment.

TIP: you'll sometimes see the term 'charbroiled' steak, or the cooking apparatus referred to as a 'broiler'. This is simply another (North American) word for a grill.

As you like it

The ideal steak is a matter of taste – it's how you like it, so even though the red-in-tooth-and-claw carnivores sneer at well-done beef, an awful lot of folk like it that way. Cooking it accurately is where the chef's skill lies. It's a game of temperatures that involves balancing a high external temperature with a lower internal temperature; getting it right ensures that the steak is tender and juicy on the inside, and seared brown and flavourful on the outside.

Whether you like your steak 'still mooing' or incinerated, the experts at JW Steakhouse have compiled a useful working guide to the appearance and eating characteristics of each category:

BLUE: seared at very high temperature so the steak is charred on the outside but deep red and cool inside. When pressed it will feel spongy with no resistance like raw meat.

RARE: outside is grey-brown, the inside dark red and barely warm with some juice flowing (core temperature 52°C).

MEDIUM RARE: nicely seared on the outside, warm and red in the centre with pink juices flowing. This is the recommended degree of cooking for most steaks (core temperature 55°C).

MEDIUM: the middle of the steak is hot and red with pink surrounding the centre and very little juice flowing. It feels firm and springy to the touch (core temperature 60°C).

MEDIUM WELL: slightly pink surrounding the centre (core temperature 60°C).

WELL DONE: the steak is grey-brown throughout and charred on the outside (core temperature 71°C).

No matter how you like your steak however, there's one final stage to go through before eating it – the resting. This should be for 5–10 minutes on a wooden or ceramic board, or a warm plate. You can loosely cover it in foil if you want to help retain the heat, but don't wrap it – this will make the meat sweat and undo your good work.

"Resting is one of the most important aspects of cooking a great steak: once cooked, the steak needs to relax, which in turn ensures all the juices and flavour are kept inside. Meat not rested long enough when cut will result in the juices pouring out from the steak, leaving it dry and tasteless. The bigger the cut, the longer the resting period." Nigel Boschetti

And that's how it's done.

The experts' choice

We spoke to Nigel Boschetti, Executive Chef at JW Steakhouse and David McIntyre, Executive Chef at CUT, both in Mayfair, about what they're looking for when they fancy a steak.

What is your favourite cut?

NIGEL My favourite cut is the Porterhouse as this gives you the best of both worlds, tender fillet and juicy sirloin, and shows the very best of USDA prime meat.

DAVID For me it has to be a rib-eye, which gives a great balance of fat marbling and lean meat. Fat to me means flavour, and the USDA prime Black Angus beef that we source from Creekstone Farms in Kansas is hard to beat.

What is your favourite sauce to go with it?

NIGEL Bourbon green peppercorn sauce is the best accompaniment to any steak, delicious undertones of bourbon with a great peppery kick

DAVID Personally I don't eat steak with a sauce as I don't want to dilute the flavour, but if I had to go for one it would be classic béarnaise – you can't beat something buttery to go with steak.

Building a legacy

by Stephanie Sparrow

The 30-year working partnership of Craig Bancroft and Nigel Haworth at Northcote may be one of the longest in the business, but they have secured a £7m refurbishment and a wave of new talent to ensure that they can look to the future rather than reflect on the past. Stephanie Sparrow talks to the far-sighted operators

Few hotels and restaurants, particularly those in a country-house setting, successfully combine tradition with confident modernity, but Northcote in Lancashire's Ribble Valley is determined to pull the trick off.

Design flourishes included in the £7m redevelopment and refurbishment of the 19th-century manor are a metaphor for the forward-thinking yet still homely hotel and restaurant. Cushions in fuchsia-coloured raw silk brighten up the serviceable, tweedy sofas, and a bold chandelier of crystal 'icicles' illuminates the 60-seat restaurant and its deep-buttoned hide chairs.

Three phases of building work and decoration have extended the kitchen and restaurant, and added a cookery school, a new staff wing and a cocktail bar. The Louis Roederer dining room has become a suite of private rooms with its own entrance (modelled on that of the label's château near Reims in France), courtyard and four bedrooms above, creating the flexibility of a standalone unit. The construction work culminated in the opening of the Garden Lodge in December 2014, boasting seven bedrooms and a master suite, although activity continues in the gardens where a pond and herb gardens are taking shape.

Northcote's glamorous comfort epitomises a Lancashire business that champions local food producers, and nurtures home-grown talent while also attracting acclaimed international chefs to its annual gastronomy festival, known as Obsession. Its new look coincides with Northcote's chef patron Nigel Haworth and director of wines Craig Bancroft celebrating 30 years at the business. In that time they have taken a six-bedroom hotel, where newly appointed chef Haworth despaired of the Formica-topped facilities ('I remember Nigel's first day in the kitchen,

because most of it went in a black bin bag,' says Bancroft), and transformed it into a 26-bedroom hotel with a £500,000 kitchen and four AA red stars.

From being manager and chef, the pair became business partners, buying Northcote for £380,000 in 1985. Along the way they have gathered national and international recognition, including four AA Rosettes, a Michelin star, and dozens of industry awards including the Special Award at the 2009 Cateys. Staff are encouraged to share the limelight, and so along with Great British Menu winner Howarth, Northcote boasts two other finalists (head chefs Lisa Allen and Aled Williams), a new master sommelier (Adam Pawlowski) and an up-and-coming advanced sommelier (Tamas Czinki). In late 2014 the property joined the Relais & Châteaux portfolio while retaining its membership of Pride of Britain. It has now fixed its sights on a fifth Rosette and a second Michelin star.

The redevelopment was made possible by the spring 2012 restructuring of Northcote Leisure Group (which owned the hotel, Ribble Valley Inns and catering at Ewood Park, home of local team Blackburn Rovers). Bancroft and Haworth are no longer major shareholders after selling some of their equity to local businesspeople and enthusiastic customers Richard and Lynda Matthewman. Matthewman is now chairman of Northcote Leisure Group, with Bancroft and Haworth remaining as managing directors.

'We needed to reinvest in Northcote to continue to put it up the ladder,' says Bancroft. He explains that plans had been hindered by the impact of the recession on the Ribble Valley Inns portfolio.

Left: Nigel Haworth in the kitchen; Above: Northcote Restaurant

L-R: Nigel Haworth and Craig Bancroft; master sommelier Adam Pawlowski; head chef Lisa Goodwin

'We really struggled, and so we had to go out and find an investor. They have given us a platform to be the best hotel restaurant, for me, in the North of England and to be mentioned in the same breath as Gidleigh, Whatley and Lucknam Park.'

The redevelopment has also created the potential for many different profit streams (hotel, restaurant, private dining, cookery school), operating from a comparatively small site of just 7.5 acres. 'We will be an extremely powerful entity,' says Howarth, 'because we have got a very small footprint. We don't have 10,000 acres, a golf course or spa to maintain, or any of that.'

Northcote now features on the Relais map of the UK, but its local following means that its business model differs from that of its national peers because food and beverage income is so dominant. Bancroft estimates that this constitutes around two-thirds of the £4.5m turnover, whereas other country houses are more likely to see that sort of proportion coming from accommodation.

"An oasis of food and wine excellence with genuine and outstanding hospitality."

'Where I struggle, compared to some of the luminaries, is that I can't demand the bedroom rate for Friday, Saturday, Sunday, which underpins everything enormously,' says Bancroft. 'But as our reputation grows, and our stock is bedded down even further, those days will arrive.'

The kitchen

This important income stream is reflected in the new kitchen area. Designed by Haworth and head chef Allen, the kitchen was completed in December 2013 and is twice the size of the original (the new preparation areas alone occupy much of the old kitchen space). Bancroft estimates that the final bill, including building alterations, came to around £500,000, with £380,000 going on equipment. The wide, bright spaces and the long L-shaped pass feel cool thanks to induction hobs in the main cooking suite. There is extensive use of CCTV in the prep areas and the pass, designed to give Chef an up-to-the-minute overview during service. Raw prep is carried out in a dedicated area close to a suite of coldrooms (previously housed outside), rather than in the main kitchen area, to avoid cross-contamination, whilst the Louis Roederer private dining rooms have their own work space in the kitchen too.

Further adding to the mix is the cookery school, which runs events three times a week, and can also be used for events at the Chef's Table. Its eight workstations, CCTV and a hydraulic table are separated from the main kitchen by plate-glass doors and give the appearance of a kitchen within a kitchen. Its side door opens onto one of the new courtyards and entertaining spaces that now encircle Northcote. Up to 14 guests can be accommodated at the Chef's Table, hosted by a dedicated chef and sommelier, while enjoying an overview of the pass.

After initial worries that the kitchen might be too big, Bancroft feels that the expansion is justified, particularly when afternoon

teas and private dining are included. 'You have a potential 340 covers if everything is full, and if we hadn't built a kitchen that has got the available space to mise-en-place, to prepare, and enough fridging to be able to roll the stock, and enough space for people to work in pockets and do various things, and to do the private dining while not interfering with the à la carte dining, and run a Chef's Table and a cook's school during the day, it would never work.'

It also demonstrates a commitment to the staff. 'If your income streams are so powerful in that kitchen area, you have got to invest in the people and give them a work environment in which they can execute to the highest possible level,' he says.

Northcote, which has run its own apprentice schemes for the past 25 years and also provides training loans, further emphasised its commitment to staff by building 'a welfare wing' in the same phase as the new kitchen. Its entrance is framed by the hotel's motto: 'An oasis of food and wine excellence with genuine and outstanding hospitality.' There are staff changing rooms, showers and lockers, a staff canteen serving three meals a day, a 'chill room' with television, and an extensive library of food and wine books. There are also computers for compulsory online training and plugs for personal devices. Staff are expected to read the customer reviews and comments displayed there, and charts showing who's who in the hotel.

'Our future'

The staff facilities fulfil a long-term ambition to be attractive recruiters in what Bancroft terms a 'geographically challenged area'. Northcote's rural location, on the fringes of the Ribble Valley, stops staff popping out to a coffee shop or the cinema as they might in London, particularly during the split shifts that Bancroft says he is trying to phase out.

'Apprenticeships and stages are a big factor in our future,' says Haworth, pointing out that the seven new student bedrooms in the roof of the staff wing will help the talent

TRAINING at Northcote

Encouragement and opportunities are part of Bancroft and Howarth's approach to employee development. 'It's in the DNA of the business,' says Bancroft.

Training loans are available, which do not have to be repaid in full if the employee remains for a year after completing the training. And all staff who complete the compulsory online training course in safety and hygiene are given a £10 voucher to spend at Ribble Valley Inns.

A sustainable approach to talent comes in the apprenticeships programme that Northcote has run with local colleges and Liverpool's L20 for the past 25 years. Students combine paid work with study, and Haworth organises visits to local fish markets and producers, and international catering schools to broaden their outlook.

'Courses are NVQ-led, but I go into the college to work with the staff and try to develop a style that will suit our staff,' he says.

Northcote currently has 12 chef apprentices, who are expected to progress in its kitchens or Ribble Valley Inns, which is where many of the head chefs started as Northcote sous chefs or apprentices.

Northcote paid for Adam Palowski's training as a master sommelier and funds monthly visits by a master of wine to enrich staff learning.

Management training is also encouraged. Hotel manager Craig Jackson, 27, who started as a weekend casual at 16, says that he benefitted from financial and practical support – work experience and time away from the business – while completing his degree in hospitality management and his Master Innholders Aspiring Leaders diploma.

'I am pretty much home-grown talent,' he says.

pipeline. These facilities, due to be finished by the end of the year, will extend the opportunities for placements or stages from catering schools here and abroad, and staff exchanges with long-standing contacts, such as Vila Joya in Albufeira, Portugal.

So, after three decades, what has sustained one of the longest partnerships in the industry? Both Haworth and Bancroft talk of their mutual respect for each other's skills, and a shared compulsion to build a legacy.

'I think the key is that we have been able to keep the passion for Northcote for 30 years. That has never waned, even when we have had really tough times. We have always been united and able to get through,' says Haworth.

They share a determination to make the most of the opportunities that have been created by the new look. 'My team is now targeting five Rosettes and the second star,' says Howarth. 'Development becomes more intrinsic, as we look at more details and finish to the dishes,' he says, adding that he is strengthening expertise in seasonal and even foraged ingredients.

'My son, Kirk, senior sous chef, will follow a line of development in keeping with our seasonal British programme

Below left: the new-look Northcote

> "We have got great facilities, and a great platform, and it's a wonderful time to be cooking in the UK,"

and mandate, and he will link in strongly with myself, Lisa and Aled.

'We have got great facilities, and a great platform, and it's a wonderful time to be cooking in the UK,' says Haworth. 'Maybe we can just grab that moment and achieve those goals.'

OBSESSION at Northcote

This year's Obsession food festival – the 15th running of the annual event – featured 27 chefs with 27 Michelin stars between them, including Jacob Jan Boerma from Restaurant De Leest, near Amsterdam. The 2015 festival ran over 15 nights earlier this year, from 23 January to 7 February.

Guest chefs fly in with a commis to run the kitchen with Howarth and stay at Northcote. Bancroft takes the opportunity to explore new wine pairings. He says that all staff learn from the discipline of the event, and Howarth, who first persuaded him that they should hold the festival to 'brighten up January', admits that it inspires him too.

'Technically there are lots of things you see that you can put in the memory banks,' says Howarth, citing Shaun Hergatt, from New York's Juni, as an example. 'Shaun took a lot of time to look at the presentation and textures and use a lot of subtle ingredients – like hibiscus flower with beetroot.' Such inspiration is translated into the Northcote vernacular – 'That's

one of the nice things Obsession does; it can refresh the palate but not change the direction.'

The profile benefits of Obsession are obvious, but despite sponsorship deals and guests paying around £150 a head, does it make any money? Bancroft is tight-lipped about the finance. 'It's a break-even business,' he says, 'but we never made any money at all for probably 12 years. It's much more a brokering of PR, training, enjoyment, good fun, and covering your costs.'

Names for the 2016 Obsession will not be revealed until autumn 2015. In the meantime, Bancroft is assessing the impact of having more bedrooms: he is excited to welcome new guests, but does not want to run lots of tables of two if this risks altering the 'house party' atmosphere created by local customers who bring groups of friends.

'They are the ones who have meant 100 covers-plus every single night of every single Obsession there has ever been,' he says.

Below: Yorkshire rhubarb & custard with shortbread crumble

TIMELESS ELEGANCE FROM VILLEROY & BOCH

The perfect contours and proportions of classical Roman architecture are the inspiration behind the design of La Classica and La Classica Contura. Sophisticated, modern and stylish, in premium bone porcelain.

SPONSORING THE AA AWARDS FOR 25 YEARS.

Villeroy & Boch are proud to have presented the AA Awards every year since their inception 25 years ago. Quality and inspiration are the defining qualities of a great restaurant. They are also the values that have made Villeroy & Boch, with its tradition of innovation dating back to 1748, the leading tableware brand in Europe. Dining with friends and family, and enjoying good food and drink together are special to all of us, and these occasions are made all the more special when served on beautiful tableware from Villeroy & Boch. Our distinctive and original designs have consistently set the pace for others to follow and provide the perfect setting chosen by many of the world's leading chefs to frame their award-winning creations. Villeroy & Boch offer a wide range of stunning designs to suit any lifestyle and décor, and create the perfect ambience for successful entertaining and stylish family living.

UK and Ireland customer services line: 0208-871-0011
line open Monday-Friday 9am-5pm

JOIN OUR 1748 CLUB

Subscribe to our FREE 1748 Club email newsletter, and you'll find it packed with:
• Recipes
• New products
• Exclusive Members' offers
• Top tips from our stylist
• Competitions
• Chef's corner
• Table style advice
• Product care
• How to guides
And much more besides. Just register online at **www.1748club.co.uk/newsletter**
Incidentally, our 1748Club web site was recently voted 'web site of the week' by a leading women's weekly magazine.

AA MEMBERS SAVE 10%

As an AA member you enjoy **10% off** when shopping online using this link:
www.theaa.com/rewards
In addition, members of the AA also receive **10% off** full price products in any of our Concession Stores on presentation of an AA membership card. For a list of stockists go to www.1748club.co.uk and click on Where Can I See.

Visit our community web site at:
www.1748club.co.uk

The top ten per cent

Each year all the restaurants in the AA Restaurant Guide are awarded a specially commissioned plate that marks their achievement in gaining one or more AA Rosettes. The plates represent a partnership between the AA and Villeroy & Boch – two quality brands working together to recognise high standards in restaurant cooking.

Restaurants awarded three, four or five AA Rosettes represent the top ten per cent of the restaurants in this guide. The pages that follow list those establishments that have attained this special status.

5 ROSETTES

LONDON

Marcus
Wilton Place
Knightsbridge
SW1
020 7235 1200

Restaurant Gordon Ramsay
68 Royal Hospital Road
SW3
020 7352 4441

Hibiscus
29 Maddox Street
Mayfair
W1
020 7629 2999

Sketch (Lecture Room & Library)
9 Conduit Street
W1
020 7659 4500

ENGLAND

BERKSHIRE
The Fat Duck
High Street
BRAY
SL6 2AQ
01628 580333

CAMBRIDGESHIRE
Midsummer House Restaurant
Midsummer Common
CAMBRIDGE
CB4 1HA
01223 369299

CUMBRIA
L'Enclume
Cavendish St
CARTMEL
LA11 6PZ
015395 36362

DEVON
Gidleigh Park
CHAGFORD
TQ13 8HH
01647 432367

NOTTINGHAMSHIRE
Restaurant Sat Bains with Rooms
Lenton Lane
Trentside
NOTTINGHAM
NG7 2SA
0115 986 6566

OXFORDSHIRE
Belmond Le Manoir aux Quat' Saisons
Church Road
GREAT MILTON
OX44 7PD
01844 278881

SURREY
Michael Wignall at The Latymer
London Road
BAGSHOT
GU19 5EU
01276 471774

SCOTLAND

CITY OF EDINBURGH
The Kitchin
78 Commercial Quay
Leith
EDINBURGH
EH6 6LX
0131 555 1755

4 ROSETTES
❀❀❀❀

LONDON

Restaurant Story
201 Tooley Street, SE1
020 7183 2117

Seven Park Place
by William Drabble
7–8 Park Place, SW1
020 7316 1600

Alain Ducasse at
The Dorchester
The Dorchester
53 Park Lane, W1
020 7629 8866

Alyn Williams at The Westbury
Bond Street, W1
020 7183 6426

Fera at Claridge's
Brook Street, W1
020 7107 8888

Le Gavroche Restaurant
43 Upper Brook Street, W1
020 7408 0881

The Greenhouse
27a Hay's Mews
Mayfair, W1
020 7499 3331

Hélène Darroze at
The Connaught
Carlos Place, W1
020 3147 7200

Murano
20–22 Queen Street, W1
020 7495 1127

Pied à Terre
34 Charlotte Street, W1
020 7636 1178

Pollen Street Social
8–10 Pollen Street, W1
020 7290 7600

The Square
6–10 Bruton Street
Mayfair, W1
020 7495 7100

Texture Restaurant
4 Bryanston Street, W1
020 7224 0028

The Ledbury
127 Ledbury Road, W11
020 7792 9090

LONDON, GREATER
Chapter One
Farnborough Common
Locksbottom, BROMLEY
BR6 8NF
01689 854848

ENGLAND

BERKSHIRE
The Waterside Inn
Ferry Road, BRAY
SL6 2AT
01628 620691

BRISTOL
Casamla Restaurant
38 High Street, Westbury
Village, Westbury-on-Trym
BRISTOL BS9 3DZ
0117 959 2884

BUCKINGHAMSHIRE
The Hand & Flowers
126 West Street
MARLOW SL7 2BP
01628 482277

CHESHIRE
Simon Radley at The
Chester Grosvenor
Eastgate, CHESTER
CH1 1LT
01244 324024

CORNWALL &
ISLES OF SCILLY
Restaurant Nathan Outlaw
6 New Road
PORT ISAAC PL29 3SB
01208 880896

GLOUCESTERSHIRE
Le Champignon Sauvage
24–28 Suffolk Road
CHELTENHAM GL50 2AQ
01242 573449

GREATER MANCHESTER
The French by Simon Rogan
Peter Street, MANCHESTER
M60 2DS
0161 236 3333

LANCASHIRE
Northcote
Northcote Road
LANGHO BB6 8BE
01254 240555

MERSEYSIDE
Fraiche
11 Rose Mount
Oxton, BIRKENHEAD
CH43 5SG
0151 652 2914

RUTLAND
Hambleton Hall
Hambleton
OAKHAM LE15 8TH
01572 756991

SURREY
Stovell's
125 Windsor Road
CHOBHAM GU24 8QS
01276 858000

SUSSEX, WEST
Matt Gillan at The Pass
Restaurant At South Lodge,
an Exclusive Hotel
Brighton Road
LOWER BEEDING RH13 6PS
01403 891711

WILTSHIRE
Whatley Manor Hotel and Spa
Easton Grey
MALMESBURY SN16 0RB
01666 822888

YORKSHIRE, NORTH
The Burlington Restaurant
BOLTON ABBEY
BD23 6AJ
01756 710441

CHANNEL ISLANDS

JERSEY
Bohemia Restaurant
The Club Hotel & Spa
Green Street
ST HELIER JE2 4UH
01534 880588

Ocean Restaurant at
The Atlantic Hotel
Le Mont de la Pulente
ST BRELADE JE3 8HE
01534 744101

SCOTLAND

CITY OF EDINBURGH
21212
3 Royal Terrace
EDINBURGH EH7 5AB
0131 523 1030

Restaurant Martin Wishart
54 The Shore, Leith
EDINBURGH EH6 6RA
0131 553 3557

HIGHLAND
Boath House
Auldearn
NAIRN IV12 5TE
01667 454896

PERTH & KINROSS
Andrew Fairlie@Gleneagles
The Gleneagles Hotel
AUCHTERARDER PH3 1NF
01764 694267

WALES

CEREDIGION
Plas Ynyshir Hall Hotel
EGLWYS FACH SY20 8TA
01654 781209

REPUBLIC OF IRELAND

DUBLIN
Restaurant Patrick Guilbaud
Merrion Hotel, 21 Upper
Merrion Street DUBLIN
01 6764192

WATERFORD
Cliff House Hotel
ARDMORE
024 87800

3 ROSETTES

⚜ ⚜ ⚜

LONDON

E1
Galvin La Chapelle
St. Botolph's Hall
35 Spital Square
020 7299 0400

E2
Town Hall Hotel
Patriot Square
020 7871 0461

EC1
The Clove Club
Shoreditch Town Hall
380 Old Street
020 7729 6496

Club Gascon
57 West Smithfields
020 7600 6144

EC2
1901 Restaurant
40 Liverpool Street
020 7618 7000

City Social
Tower 42
020 7877 7703

HKK
Broadgate West
88 Worship Street
020 3535 1888

Merchants Tavern
36 Charlotte Road
020 7060 5335

NW1
Odette's
130 Regent's Park Road
020 7586 8569

SW1
Adam Handling at Caxton
2 Caxton Street
St James Park, Westminster
020 7222 7888

Amaya
Halkin Arcade
Motcomb Street
020 7823 1166

Ametsa with Arzak Instruction
Halkin Street, Belgravia
020 7333 1234

Dinner by Heston Blumenthal
66 Knightsbridge
020 7201 3833

The Goring
Beeston Place
020 7396 9000

Koffmann's
The Berkeley, Wilton Place
020 7235 1010

Pétrus
1 Kinnerton Street
Knightsbridge
020 7592 1609

The Rib Room
Cadogan Place
020 7858 7250

Roux at Parliament Square
Parliament Square
020 7334 3737

**Thirty Six by Nigel Mendham
at Dukes London**
35 St James's Place
020 7491 4840

SW10
Medlar Restaurant
438 King's Road, Chelsea
020 7349 1900

SW11
London House
7–9 Battersea Square
Battersea Village
020 7592 8545

SW17
Chez Bruce
2 Bellevue Road
Wandsworth Common
020 8672 0114

SW3
The Five Fields
8–9 Blacklands Terrace
020 7838 1082

Outlaw's at The Capital
Basil Street, Knightsbridge
020 7591 1202

Rasoi Restaurant
10 Lincoln Street
020 7225 1881

SW4
Trinity Restaurant
4 The Polygon, Clapham
020 7622 1199

SW7
**Rivea London Bulgari
Hotel & Residences**
171 Knightsbridge
020 7151 1025

W1
Arbutus Restaurant
63–64 Frith Street
020 7734 4545

L'Autre Pied
5–7 Blandford Street
Marylebone Village
020 7486 9696

Brasserie Chavot
41 Conduit Street, Mayfair
020 7183 6425

Corrigan's Mayfair
28 Upper Grosvenor Street
020 7499 9943

CUT at 45 Park Lane
45 Park Lane
020 7493 4554

Dabbous
39 Whitfield Street, Fitzrovia
020 7323 1544

**Galvin at Windows
Restaurant & Bar**
London Hilton on Park Lane
22 Park Lane
020 7208 4021

Gauthier Soho
21 Romilly Street
020 7494 3111

Hakkasan Mayfair
17 Bruton Street
020 7907 1888

Kitchen Table
70 Charlotte St
020 7637 7770

Little Social
5 Pollen St
020 7870 3730

Locanda Locatelli
8 Seymour Street
020 7935 9088

Maze
London Marriott Hotel
10–13 Grosvenor Square
020 7107 0000

The Ritz Restaurant
150 Piccadilly
020 7300 2370

Roka Charlotte Street
37 Charlotte Street
020 7580 6464

Roka Mayfair
30 North Audley St
020 7305 5644

Sixtyone Restaurant
Great Cumberland Place
020 7958 3222

Sketch (The Gallery)
9 Conduit Street
020 7659 4500

Social Eating House
58–59 Poland Street
020 7993 3251

**Theo Randall at the
InterContinental**
1 Hamilton Place
Hyde Park Corner
020 7318 8757

Umu
14–16 Bruton Place
020 7499 8881

Wild Honey
12 Saint George St
020 7758 9160

W2
The New Angel Notting Hill
39 Chepstow Place
020 7221 7620

W4
Hedone
301–303 Chiswick High Road
020 8747 0377

W6
The River Café
Thames Wharf Studios
Rainville Road
020 7386 4200

W8
Kitchen W8
11–13 Abingdon Road
Kensington
020 7937 0120

Min Jiang
2–24 Kensington High Street
020 7361 1988

WC2
L'Atelier de Joël Robuchon
13–15 West Street
020 7010 8600

Clos Maggiore
33 King Street
Covent Garden
020 7379 9696

LONDON, GREATER
La Belle Époque
Sofitel London Heathrow
Terminal 5, Wentworth Drive
London Heathrow Airport
TW6 2GD
020 8757 7777

Bingham
61–63 Petersham Road
RICHMOND UPON THAMES
TW10 6UT
020 8940 0902

The Glasshouse
14 Station Parade
KEW TW9 3PZ
020 8940 6777

ENGLAND
BEDFORDSHIRE
Paris House Restaurant
London Road, Woburn Park
WOBURN MK17 9QP
01525 290692

BERKSHIRE
Hinds Head
High Street
BRAY SL6 2AB
01628 626151

L'Ortolan
Church Lane
SHINFIELD RG2 9BY
0118 988 8500

The Royal Oak Paley Street
Paley Street, Littlefield Green
MAIDENHEAD SL6 3JN
01628 620541

The Vineyard
Stockcross
NEWBURY RG20 8JU
01635 528770

BUCKINGHAMSHIRE
André Garrett at Cliveden
Cliveden Estate
TAPLOW SL6 0JF
01628 668561

The Artichoke
9 Market Square
Old Amersham
AMERSHAM HP7 0DF
01494 726611

The Coach
3 West Street
MARLOW SL7 2LS
01628 483013

Humphry's at Stoke Park
Park Road
STOKE POGES SL2 4PG
01753 717171

The Riverside Restaurant
Macdonald Compleat Angler
Marlow Bridge
MARLOW SL7 1RG
01628 484444

CAMBRIDGESHIRE
Restaurant Alimentum
152–154 Hills Road
CAMBRIDGE CB2 8PB
01223 413000

CHESHIRE
**1851 Restaurant at
Peckforton Castle**
Stone House Lane
PECKFORTON CW6 9TN
01829 260930

The Alderley Restaurant
Macclesfield Road
ALDERLEY EDGE SK9 7BJ
01625 583033

The Lord Clyde
36 Clarke Lane, Kerridge
MACCLESFIELD SK10 5AH
01625 562123

CORNWALL &
ISLES OF SCILLY
Driftwood
Rosevine
PORTSCATHO TR2 5EW
01872 580644

Hell Bay
BRYHER TR23 0PR
01720 422947

Hotel Tresanton
27 Lower Castle Road
ST MAWES TR2 5DR
01326 270055

Paul Ainsworth at No. 6
6 Middle Street
PADSTOW PL28 8AP
01841 532093

The Seafood Restaurant
Riverside
PADSTOW PL28 8BY
01841 532700

CUMBRIA
Hipping Hall
Cowan Bridge
KIRKBY LONSDALE LA6 2JJ
015242 71187

Gilpin Hotel & Lake House
Crook Road
WINDERMERE LA23 3NE
015394 88818

**Linthwaite House
Hotel & Restaurant**
Crook Road
WINDERMERE LA23 3JA
015394 88600

Rogan & Company Restaurant
The Square
CARTMEL LA11 6QD
015395 35917

The Samling
Ambleside Road
WINDERMERE LA23 1LR
015394 31922

Storrs Hall Hotel
Storrs Park
WINDERMERE LA23 3LG
015394 47111

DERBYSHIRE
Fischer's Baslow Hall
Calver Road
BASLOW DE45 1RR
01246 583259

The Peacock at Rowsley
Bakewell Road
ROWSLEY DE4 2EB
01629 733518

DEVON
**The Elephant Restaurant
and Brasserie**
3–4 Beacon Terrace
TORQUAY TQ1 2BH
01803 200044

The Horn of Plenty
Gulworthy
TAVISTOCK PL19 8JD
01822 832528

The Old Inn
DREWSTEIGNTON EX6 6QR
01647 281276

3 ROSETTES

❀❀❀

continued

DORSET

Summer Lodge Country House Hotel, Restaurant & Spa
Fore Street
EVERSHOT DT2 0JR
01935 482000

COUNTY DURHAM

The Orangery
Rockliffe Hall, Rockliffe Park
Hurworth-on-Tees
DARLINGTON DL2 2DU
01325 729999

GLOUCESTERSHIRE

The Beaufort Dining Room
Ellenborough Park
Southam Road
CHELTENHAM GL52 3NH
01242 545454

Buckland Manor
BUCKLAND WR12 7LY
01386 852626

The Feathered Nest Country Inn
NETHER WESTCOTE
OX7 6SD
01993 833030

Lords of the Manor
UPPER SLAUGHTER
GL54 2JD
01451 820243

Lower Slaughter Manor
LOWER SLAUGHTER
GL54 2HP
01451 820456

GREATER MANCHESTER

Manchester House Bar & Restaurant
Tower 12
18–22 Bridge Street
MANCHESTER M3 3BZ
0161 835 2557

HAMPSHIRE

36 on the Quay
47 South Street
EMSWORTH PO10 7EG
01243 375592

Avenue Restaurant at Lainston House Hotel
Woodman Lane, Sparsholt
WINCHESTER SO21 2LT
01962 776088

Hartnett Holder & Co
Beaulieu Road
LYNDHURST SO43 7FZ
023 8028 7167

JSW
20 Dragon Street
PETERSFIELD GU31 4JJ
01730 262030

The Montagu Arms Hotel
Palace Lane
BEAULIEU SO42 7ZL
01590 612324

HERTFORDSHIRE

Colette's at The Grove
CHANDLER'S CROSS
WD3 4TG
01923 807807

KENT

Apicius
23 Stone Street
CRANBROOK TN17 3HF
01580 714666

Thackeray's
85 London Road
ROYAL TUNBRIDGE WELLS
TN1 1EA
01892 511921

The West House
28 High Street
BIDDENDEN TN27 8AH
01580 291341

LANCASHIRE

The Freemasons at Wiswell
8 Vicarage Fold, Wiswell
WHALLEY BB7 9DF
01254 822218

LINCOLNSHIRE

Harry's Place
17 High Street, Great Gonerby
GRANTHAM NG31 8JS
01476 561780

Winteringham Fields
1 Silver Street
WINTERINGHAM DN15 9ND
01724 733096

MERSEYSIDE

The Dining Room at Hillbark
Royden Park
FRANKBY CH48 1NP
0151 625 2400

The Lawns Restaurant at Thornton Hall
Neston Road, THORNTON
HOUGH CH63 1JF
0151 336 3938

NORFOLK

Morston Hall
Morston, Holt
BLAKENEY NR25 7AA
01263 741041

The Neptune Restaurant with Rooms
85 Old Hunstanton Road
Old Hunstanton
HUNSTANTON PE36 6HZ
01485 532122

Roger Hickman's Restaurant
79 Upper St Giles Street
NORWICH NR2 1AB
01603 633522

Titchwell Manor Hotel
TITCHWELL PE31 8BB
01485 210221

NORTHAMPTONSHIRE

Rushton Hall Hotel and Spa
Rushton
KETTERING NN14 1RR
01536 713001

OXFORDSHIRE

Fallowfields Hotel and Restaurant
Faringdon Road, KINGSTON
BAGPUIZE OX13 5BH
01865 820416

The Kingham Plough
The Green
KINGHAM OX7 6YD
01608 658327

Macdonald Randolph Hotel
Beaumont Street
OXFORD OX1 2LN
01865 256400

Orwells
Shiplake Row, Binfield Heath
HENLEY-ON-THAMES
RG9 4DP
0118 940 3673

The Sir Charles Napier
Sprigg's Alley
CHINNOR OX39 4BX
01494 483011

Sudbury House
56 London Street
FARINGDON SN7 7AA
01367 241272

SHROPSHIRE

Fishmore Hall
Fishmore Road
LUDLOW SY8 3DP
01584 875148

Old Downton Lodge
Downton on the Rock
LUDLOW SY8 2HU
01568 771826

SOMERSET

Allium Restaurant at The Abbey Hotel
1 North Parade
BATH BA1 1LF
01225 461603

The Bath Priory Hotel, Restaurant & Spa
Weston Road
BATH BA1 2XT
01225 331922

The Dower House Restaurant
The Royal Crescent Hotel & Spa, 16 Royal Crescent
BATH BA1 2LS
01225 823333

Little Barwick House
Barwick Village
YEOVIL BA22 9TD
01935 423902

The Olive Tree at the Queensberry Hotel
Russel Street
BATH BA1 2QF
01225 447928

STAFFORDSHIRE
Swinfen Hall Hotel
Swinfen
LICHFIELD WS14 9RE
01543 481494

SUFFOLK
Lavenham Great House 'Restaurant with Rooms'
Market Place
LAVENHAM CO10 9QZ
01787 247431

The Packhorse Inn
Bridge Street, Moulton
NEWMARKET CB8 8SP
01638 751818

SURREY
Drake's Restaurant
The Clock House, High Street
RIPLEY GU23 6AQ
01483 224777

Langshott Manor
Langshott Lane
HORLEY RH6 9LN
01293 786680

SUSSEX, WEST
Amberley Castle
AMBERLEY BN18 9LT
01798 831992

Graveye Manor Hotel
Vowels Lane, West Hoathly
EAST GRINSTEAD RH19 4LJ
01342 810567

The Lickfold Inn
LICKFOLD GU28 9EY
01789 532535

Restaurant Tristan
3 Stan's Way, East Street
HORSHAM RH12 1HU
01403 255688

TYNE & WEAR
House of Tides
28–30 The Close
NEWCASTLE UPON TYNE
NE1 3RF
0191 230 3720

Jesmond Dene House
Jesmond Dene Road
NEWCASTLE UPON TYNE
NE2 2EY
0191 212 3000

WARWICKSHIRE
The Dining Room at Mallory Court Hotel
Harbury Lane, Bishop's Tachbrook, ROYAL LEAMINGTON SPA
CV33 9QB
01926 330214

Restaurant 23 & Morgan's Bar
34 Hamilton Terrace
ROYAL LEAMINGTON SPA
CV32 4LY
01926 422422

WEST MIDLANDS
Adam's
21a Bennetts Hill
BIRMINGHAM B2 5QP
0121 643 3745

Hampton Manor
Swadowbrook Lane
Hampton-in-Arden
SOLIHULL B92 0EN
01675 446080

Purnell's
55 Cornwall Street
BIRMINGHAM B3 2DH
0121 212 9799

Simpsons
20 Highfield Road
Edgbaston
BIRMINGHAM B15 3DU
0121 454 3434

Turners
69 High Street
Harborne
BIRMINGHAM B17 9NS
0121 426 4440

WILTSHIRE
The Bybrook at The Manor House Hotel
CASTLE COMBE SN14 7HR
01249 782206

The Harrow at Little Bedwyn
LITTLE BEDWYN SN8 3JP
01672 870871

The Park Restaurant
Lucknam Park Hotel & Spa
COLERNE SN14 8AZ
01225 742777

Red Lion Freehouse
East Chisenbury
PEWSEY SN9 6AQ
01980 671124

WORCESTERSHIRE
Brockencote Hall Country House Hotel
CHADDESLEY CORBETT
DY10 4PY
01562 777876

YORKSHIRE, NORTH
The Angel Inn
HETTON BD23 6LI
01756 730263

The Black Swan at Oldstead
OLDSTEAD YO61 4BL
01347 868387

Black Swan Hotel
Market Place
HELMSLEY YO62 5BJ
01439 770466

Judges Country House Hotel
Kirklevington Hall
YARM TS15 9LW
01642 789000

The Park Restaurant
4–5 St Peters Grove
Bootham
YORK YO30 6AQ
01904 640101

Samuel's at Swinton Park
Swinton
MASHAM HG4 4JH
01765 680900

Yorebridge House
BAINBRIDGE DL8 3EE
01969 652060

YORKSHIRE, WEST
Box Tree
35–37 Church Street
ILKLEY LS29 9DR
01943 608484

Design House Restaurant
Dean Clough
Arts & Business Centre
HALIFAX HX3 5AX
01422 383242

CHANNEL ISLANDS

JERSEY
Longueville Manor Hotel
ST SAVIOUR JE2 7WF
01534 725501

Ormer
7–11 Don Street
ST HELIER JE2 4TQ
01534 725100

SCOTLAND

ANGUS
Gordon's
Main Street
INVERKEILOR DD11 5RN
01241 830364

ARGYLL & BUTE
Airds Hotel and Restaurant
PORT APPIN PA38 4DF
01631 730236

AYRSHIRE, SOUTH
Glenapp Castle
BALLANTRAE KA26 0NZ
01465 831212

Lochgreen House Hotel
Monktonhill Road, Southwood
TROON KA10 7EN
01292 313343

DUMFRIES & GALLOWAY
Knockinaam Lodge
PORTPATRICK DG9 9AD
01776 810471

3 ROSETTES

❀ ❀ ❀

continued

DUNBARTONSHIRE, WEST

Martin Wishart at Loch Lomond
Cameron House on Loch Lomond, BALLOCH G83 8QZ
01389 722504

CITY OF EDINBURGH

Castle Terrace Restaurant
33–35 Castle Terrace
EDINBURGH EH1 2EL
0131 229 1222

Norton House Hotel & Spa
Ingliston
EDINBURGH EH28 8LX
0131 333 1275

Number One, The Balmoral
1 Princes Street
EDINBURGH EH2 2EQ
0131 557 6727

Plumed Horse
50–54 Henderson Street
Leith, EDINBURGH EH6 6DE
0131 554 5556

Pompadour by Galvin
Waldorf Astoria Edinburgh
The Caledonian
Princes Street
EDINBURGH EH1 2AB
0131 222 8975

Restaurant Mark Greenaway
69 North Castle Street
EDINBURGH EH2 3LJ
0131 226 1155

Timberyard
10 Lady Lawson St
EDINBURGH EH3 9DS
0131 221 1222

FIFE

The Cellar
24 East Green
ANSTRUTHER KY10 3AA
01333 310378

The Peat Inn
PEAT INN KY15 5LH
01334 840206

Road Hole Restaurant
The Old Course Hotel
Golf Resort & Spa
ST ANDREWS KY16 9SP
01334 474371

Rocca Restaurant
Macdonald Rusacks Hotel
Pilmour Links
ST ANDREWS KY16 9JQ
01334 472549

CITY OF GLASGOW

Cail Bruich
752 Great Western Road
GLASGOW G12 8QX
0141 334 6265

Hotel du Vin at One Devonshire Gardens
1 Devonshire Gardens
GLASGOW G12 0UX
0141 339 2001

HIGHLAND

Inverlochy Castle Hotel
Torlundy
FORT WILLIAM PH33 6SN
01397 702177

Station Road
The Lovat, Loch Ness
Loch Ness Side, FORT
AUGUSTUS PH32 4DU
01456 459250

The Torridon
By Achnasheen, Wester Ross
TORRIDON IV22 2EY
01445 791242

PERTH & KINROSS

Fonab Castle Hotel
Foss Road
PITLOCHRY PH16 5ND
01796 470140

STIRLING

Roman Camp Country House Hotel
CALLANDER FK17 8BG
01877 330003

SCOTTISH ISLANDS

MULL, ISLE OF

Tiroran House Hotel
TIRORAN PA69 6ES
01681 705232

SKYE, ISLE OF

Kinloch Lodge
Sleat
ISLEORNSAY IV43 8QY
01471 833214

Ullinish Country Lodge
STRUAN IV56 8FD
01470 572214

WALES

ANGLESEY, ISLE OF

Sosban & The Old Butcher's Restaurant
Trinity House
1 High Street
MENAI BRIDGE LL59 5EE
01248 208131

Ye Olde Bulls Head Inn
Castle Street
BEAUMARIS LL58 8AP
01248 810329

CONWY

Bodysgallen Hall and Spa
LLANDUDNO LL30 1RS
01492 584466

MONMOUTHSHIRE

Walnut Tree Inn
Llandewi Skirrid
ABERGAVENNY NP7 8AW
01873 852797

The Whitebrook
WHITEBROOK NP25 4TX
01600 860254

NEWPORT

Terry M at The Celtic Manor Resort
Coldra Woods
NEWPORT NP18 1HQ
01633 413000

PEMBROKESHIRE

The Grove
Molleston
NARBERTH SA67 8BX
01834 860915

POWYS

Llangoed Hall
LLYSWEN LD3 0YP
01874 754525

VALE OF GLAMORGAN

Restaurant James Sommerin
The Esplanade
PENARTH CF64 3AU
029 2070 6559

NORTHERN IRELAND

COUNTY ANTRIM

Galgorm Resort & Spa
136 Fenaghy Road, Galgorm
BALLYMENA BT42 1EA
028 2588 1001

BELFAST

EIPIC
36–40 Howard Street
BELFAST BT1 6PF
028 9033 1134

COUNTY DOWN

The Boathouse Restaurant
1a Seacliff Road
BANGOR BT20 5HA
028 9146 9253

COUNTY FERMANAGH

Lough Erne Resort
Belleek Road
ENNISKILLEN BT93 7ED
028 6632 3230

REPUBLIC OF IRELAND

COUNTY CLARE

Gregans Castle
BALLYVAUGHAN
065 7077005

COUNTY KILKENNY

The Lady Helen Restaurant
Mount Juliet Hotel
THOMASTOWN
056 7773000

AA GUIDES

WE KNOW BRITAIN

▶ THE BEST PLACES TO VISIT

▶ CLEAR TOWN PLANS AND MAPPING

▶ WRITTEN BY LOCAL EXPERTS

▶ RECOMMENDED PLACES TO EAT

▶ TRUSTED LISTINGS

THE AA GUIDE TO
Wales
WE KNOW BRITAIN

THE AA GUIDE TO
Lake District & Cumbria
WE KNOW BRITAIN
THE BEST PLACES TO VISIT ◀
TRUSTED LISTINGS ◀
WRITTEN BY LOCAL EXPERTS ◀
RECOMMENDED PLACES TO EAT ◀

THE AA GUIDE TO
Norfolk & Suffolk
with Cambridge
WE KNOW BRITAIN
THE BEST PLACES TO VISIT ◀
TRUSTED LISTINGS ◀
WRITTEN BY LOCAL EXPERTS ◀
RECOMMENDED PLACES TO EAT ◀

THE AA GUIDE TO
The Peak District

THE AA GUIDE TO
Cornwall
WE KNOW BRITAIN
THE BEST PLACES TO VISIT ◀
TRUSTED LISTINGS ◀
WRITTEN BY LOCAL EXPERTS ◀
RECOMMENDED PLACES TO EAT ◀
CLEAR TOWN PLANS AND MAPPING ◀

THE AA GUIDE TO
Durham & Northumberland
WE KNOW BRITAIN
THE BEST PLACES TO VISIT ◀
TRUSTED LISTINGS ◀
WRITTEN BY LOCAL EXPERTS ◀
RECOMMENDED PLACES TO EAT ◀
CLEAR TOWN PLANS AND MAPPING ◀

THE AA GUIDE TO
The Cotswolds
with Oxford & Stratford-upon-Avon

THE AA GUIDE TO
Yorkshire
WE KNOW BRITAIN
THE BEST PLACES TO VISIT ◀
TRUSTED LISTINGS ◀
WRITTEN BY LOCAL EXPERTS ◀
RECOMMENDED PLACES TO EAT ◀
CLEAR TOWN PLANS AND MAPPING ◀

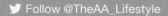 Follow @TheAA_Lifestyle

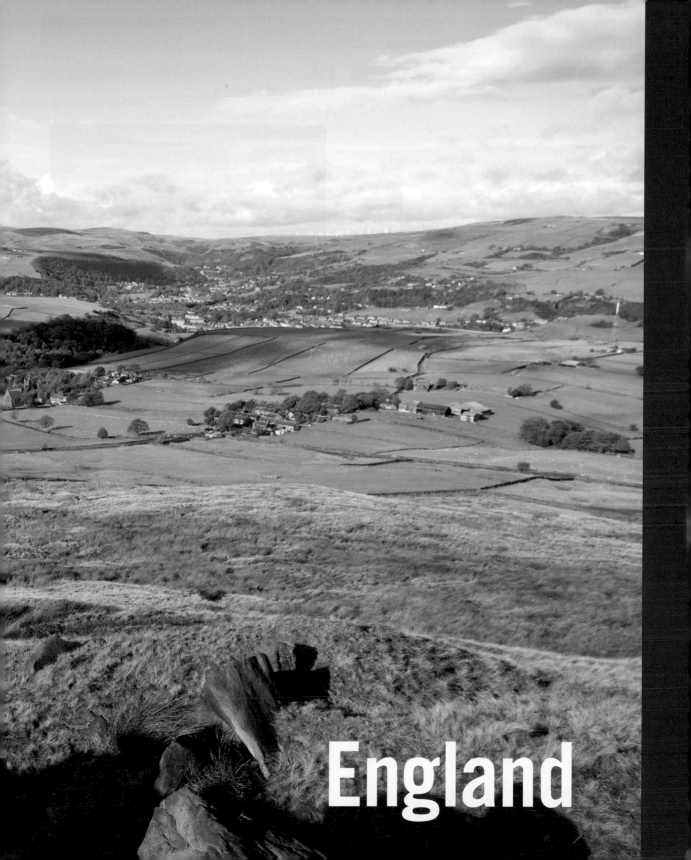

England

BEDFORDSHIRE

BEDFORD
Map 12 TL04

The Barns Hotel

◉ Modern British

tel: 01234 270044 **Cardington Rd MK44 3SA**
email: reservations@barnshotelbedford.co.uk **web:** www.barnshotelbedford.co.uk
dir: *M1 junct 13, A421, approx 10m to A603 Sandy/Bedford exit, hotel on right at 2nd rdbt*

Modern brasserie-style dining by the river

Samuel Whitbread of brewing fame was born here in the 18th century and today's pub-restaurant-and-hotel combo has plenty of old-world tranquillity about it. The WineGlass Restaurant is the main dining option with a bright and contemporary conservatory-style dining room that opens onto a terrace overlooking the River Great Ouse (there's pub grub in the Riverside Bar, too). The menu favours feel-good modern British combinations, so there might be a black pudding and pork Scotch egg to kick things off, the egg suitably runny, or curried seared scallops with creamed leeks. Main courses such as tender rump of lamb with roasted aubergine, fondant potato and a flavoursome jus show good sense and sound execution, or go for fish and chips with herby batter and 'crushed' peas. To finish, Valrhona white and dark chocolate mousse with salted caramel is properly fashionable. The wine list has a particularly good showing by the glass.

Chef Sean Waskett **Seats** 47, Pr/dining room 80 **Times** 12-2/6.30-9.30 **Prices** Fixed L 2 course £18-£32.50, Fixed D 3 course £24-£41, Starter £5.50-£8.50, Main £12.50-£24, Dessert £6-£8.50, Service optional **Wines** 12 bottles over £30, 26 bottles under £30, 34 by glass **Parking** 90 **Notes** Sunday L fr £17.50, Vegetarian available, Children welcome

The Bedford Swan Hotel

◉ British **v**

tel: 01234 346565 **The Embankment MK40 1RW**
email: info@bedfordswanhotel.co.uk **web:** www.bedfordswanhotel.co.uk
dir: *M1 junct 13, take A421 following signs to city centre (one way system). Turn left to The Embankment, car park on left after Swan statue*

Re-modelled 18th-century riverside hotel with inventive menu

Rooted into the town's life since the 18th century, the Bedford Swan now puts on a contemporary show after a swish makeover. Its River Room restaurant overlooks the River Ouse through elegant Georgian bow windows. There's the bonus of a waterside terrace on balmy days. Period charm still abounds in the exposed stone walls and burnished wooden tables that make an appealing setting for hearty British cooking with a creative edge. Scallops and pork are matched with andouille sausage, fiery harissa aïoli and sakura shoots to get things off the mark, ahead of a meaty combo involving lamb (cannon, grilled cutlets and confit pressed shoulder) with sautéed celeriac, shallot purée and minted red wine jus. Fish fans might find pan-fried stone bass with golden beetroot risotto and watercress 'bubbles'. For afters, honey adds richness to a crème brûlée with buttery shortbread.

Chef Jason Buck **Owner** BDL **Seats** 90, Pr/dining room 20 **Times** 12-3/6-10 **Prices** Prices not confirmed **Wines** 6 by glass **Parking** 90 **Notes** Sunday L, Children welcome

BOLNHURST
Map 12 TL05

The Plough at Bolnhurst

◉ Modern British

tel: 01234 376274 **Kimbolton Rd MK44 2EX**
email: reservations@bolnhurst.com **web:** www.bolnhurst.com
dir: *A14/A421 onto B660 for approx 5m to Bolnhurst village*

Classy modern seasonal menu in a lively Tudor pub

The Plough is a classic whitewashed 15th-century country inn which envelops you in a cocoon of Tudor beams and timbers, exposed stone walls, tiny windows, and welcoming open fires in its cosy bars. A move into the contemporary restaurant brings a striking contrast: the airy extension features lofty oak-beamed ceilings and a wall of full-length windows to flood the room with light. Fizzing with life at lunchtime, the mood mellows into a more intimate, candlelit vibe in the evening. Top-quality local produce is transformed into big-flavoured modern dishes on daily-changing menus that keep an eye on the seasons, opening in summer with Portland crab with Jersey Royal potatoes, spring onion salad and watercress oil. Next up, pork belly is cooked overnight for that melting texture, and matched with roast Bramley apple purée, creamed potato and crushed peas. For pudding, there's vanilla soufflé with strawberry sauce.

Chef Martin Lee **Owner** Martin & Jayne Lee, Michael Moscrop **Seats** 96, Pr/dining room 34 **Times** 12-2/6.30-9, Closed 27 Dec-14 Jan, Mon, D Sun **Prices** Prices not confirmed, Service optional **Wines** 60 bottles over £30, 76 bottles under £30, 15 by glass **Parking** 30 **Notes** Sunday L, Vegetarian available, Children welcome

FLITWICK
Map 11 TL03

Menzies Hotels Woburn Flitwick Manor

◉◉ British, Modern European

tel: 01525 712242 **Church Rd MK45 1AE**
email: flitwick@menzieshotels.co.uk **web:** www.menzieshotels.co.uk
dir: M1 junct 12, follow Flitwick after 1m turn left into Church Rd. Manor 200 yds on left

Classic British dishes in modern European style

A Georgian house in its own wooded Bedfordshire parkland, Flitwick began showing its country hotel paces in the 1980s. Tennis and croquet go on in the grounds, there is a honeymoon suite with its own sauna and kissing-baths, and a light-filled dining room that looks over the terrace and gardens. Classic British dishes with some modern European influence, served neatly and imaginatively, are the stock-in-trade. Among those making a strong impact are a starter of braised pig's cheek scattered with dried grapefruit and crumbled walnuts, alongside silky parsnip purée. Look out for a main offering of seasonal grouse, the breast and leg bursting with gamey flavour, helped along with caramelised roasted onion, sliced pear and yogurt, the whole topped with delicate onion rings, while fish may be cod with butternut squash, Savoy cabbage and spring onion. At dessert, it's hard to resist the allure of a snowball of banana parfait with chocolate mousse, chunks of peanut brittle and a ribbon of caramel. A seven-course tasting menu is the high-flying option.

Chef Steve Barringer **Owner** Topland Hotels **Seats** 26, Pr/dining room 20
Times 12-2/7-9.30 **Prices** Fixed L 2 course £19.50, Fixed D 3 course £40, Tasting menu £70, Service optional **Wines** 16 bottles over £30, 12 bottles under £30, 8 by glass **Parking** 75 **Notes** Sunday L £29.95, Vegetarian available, Children welcome

HENLOW
Map 12 TL13

The Crown

◉ Modern British **NEW**

tel: 01462 812433 **2 High St SG16 6BS**
email: info@thecrownpub.co.uk **web:** www.crownpub.co.uk
dir: A1 junct 10, A507 for 7m, rdbt A507/A659, turn right into Henlow. On right

Modernised village pub with inventive cooking

The busy pub on the main road through the village functions as a quintessential rural hostelry, full of enthusiastic local custom in both bar and dining room. Despite its modernisation with candy-coloured seating, a light decorative tone and the requisite exposed-brick columns, it retains its pub ethos, and boasts a young,

classically trained chef who is full of good up-to-date ideas. That might furnish a starter of hazelnut-crumbed pigeon breast with peppered goats' cheese mousse and beetroot textures, or another of seared scallops with caramelised leek, pea purée and smoked duck bacon. Main courses take a more traditional tack with meats such as herb-crusted rack of lamb and wild mushrooms, or maintain the inventive pace for fish, perhaps sea trout with crabmeat sauce, braised fennel and clams. Finish with roasted pear in puff pastry and tarragon cream, or apple and lemon posset with almond crumble and raspberry mousse.

Chef Karl Jaques **Owner** Paul, Janet & Kevin Wallman **Seats** 80, Pr/dining room 24
Times 7.30am-9.30pm, All-day dining, Closed 25 Dec **Prices** Starter £4.95-£9.95, Main £11.50-£19.95, Dessert £4.50-£7.95, Service optional **Wines** 13 bottles over £30, 28 bottles under £30, 15 by glass **Parking** 60 **Notes** Sunday L £11.50-£19.95, Vegetarian available, Children welcome

LUTON
Map 6 TL02

Adam's Brasserie at Luton Hoo Hotel, Golf & Spa

◉ Modern British

tel: 01582 734437 & 698888 **Luton Hoo Hotel, Golf & Spa,**
The Mansion House LU1 3TQ
email: reservations@lutonhoo.co.uk
dir: M1 junct 10a, A1081 towards Harpenden/St Albans. Hotel less than a mile on left

Brasserie cooking in smartened up stables

The extensive Luton Hoo Estate with its golf course and magnificent gardens is home to a luxe spa hotel and two dining options. You'll find Adam's Brasserie in the one-time stables, which operates as a country club and makes a good alternative to the more formal Wernher Restaurant. A host of films have been shot on the estate and the brasserie walls are adorned with familiar faces who have filmed here over the years. High ceilings and large windows give a sense of space, and some booth seating down one wall boosts the brasserie vibe. The menu fits the bill with a roster of feel-good dishes such as baked baby camembert with toasted home-made walnut bread and red onion marmalade, followed by red mullet with chorizo and black olive, or perhaps a steak or burger cooked on the grill.

Chef Kevin Clark **Owner** Elite Hotels **Seats** 90, Pr/dining room 280
Times 12-3/6-10, Closed D Sun **Prices** Starter £6.50-£11.50, Main £12.95-£26.50, Dessert £6.75-£9.75, Service optional **Wines** 30 bottles over £30, 16 bottles under £30, 12 by glass **Parking** 100 **Notes** Pre-open air cinema menu 2 course £19.50 (Aug-Sep), Sunday L £35, Vegetarian available, Children welcome

LUTON*continued*

Wernher Restaurant at Luton Hoo Hotel, Golf & Spa

◎◎ Modern European

tel: 01582 734437 & 698888 **The Mansion House LU1 3TQ**
email: reservations@lutonhoo.co.uk **web:** www. lutonhoo.co.uk
dir: *M1 junct 10a, A1081 towards Harpenden/St Albans. Hotel less than a mile on left*

Magnificent country estate with inventive modern cooking

The Wernher is the fine-dining option on the magnificent Luton Hoo Estate. The house has stately proportions and impeccable credentials – designed by Robert Adam and Sir Robert Smirke (of British Museum fame) and transformed at the turn of the 20th century by one of the richest men in the world. And 'Capability' Brown did the gardens. Today's luxe hotel hosts a couple of dining options, the lavish Wernher the pick of the bunch, with its marble panelling, ornate chandeliers and opulent fabrics. The team in the kitchen deliver bright modern European dishes using high quality ingredients. To start, pan-fried scallops might turn up in the company of roast langoustine and a fennel soubise, or roast venison and partridge terrine with mulled baby beetroot and a Guinness purée. Main course are equally inventive: pan-fried halibut, for example, with mustard and pancetta crust and confit pork belly. There's creativity among desserts, too, with warm beetroot and blackberry chocolate coulant served with a Merlot sorbet.

Chef Kevin Clark **Owner** Elite Hotels **Seats** 80, Pr/dining room 280
Times 12.30-2/7-10, Closed Jan, Mon-Tue **Prices** Fixed L 2 course £25-£47.50, Fixed D 3 course £42.50-£52.50, Tasting menu £62.50-£95, Service optional **Wines** 264 bottles over £30, 3 bottles under £30, 12 by glass **Parking** 316 **Notes** Speciality menu, 'Ladies Hoo Lunch' Wed with wine, Sunday L £35, Vegetarian available, Children welcome

See advert on page 47

WOBURN Map 11 SP93

Paris House Restaurant

◎◎◎ *– see opposite*

The Woburn Hotel

◎◎ Modern British, French

tel: 01525 290441 **George St MK17 9PX**
email: info@thewoburnhotel.co.uk **web:** www. thewoburnhotel.co.uk
dir: *5 mins from M1 junct 13. Follow signs to Woburn Hotel. In town centre at x-rds, parking to rear via Park St*

High-impact French cooking on the Woburn Estate

Dating from the 18th century and now providing high levels of style and comfort, The Woburn is at the entrance to the 3,000-acre Woburn Abbey Estate. Olivier's Restaurant, named after the head chef, is an eye-catching room, with comfortable button-back leather chairs at polished tables, wall sconces and a large round mirror above the mantelpiece. Olivier Bertho's cooking is rooted in the great French traditions but is very much of the present, so roast cod fillet, for instance, is served with brandade and chorizo and bean cassoulet. Combinations in dishes intrigue without seeming wacky, as seen in a palate-pleasing starter of a pan-fried scallop with lime syrup, crab cannelloni and crispy squid with garlic and chilli. Meat dishes are just as well thought out: pan-fried braised lamb with pistachio pesto, redcurrant jus and spices, say, or roast breast of guinea fowl with creamy mushroom sauce, thyme-flecked sweet potato purée and Savoy cabbage. Standards are well maintained in desserts too, as in strawberry trifle with sparkling wine jelly and elderflower syllabub cream.

Chef Olivier Bertho **Owner** Bedford Estates **Seats** 40, Pr/dining room 90
Times 12-2/6.30-9.30 **Prices** Starter £5.20-£9.95, Main £12.95-£19.75, Dessert £6.95-£11.95, Service optional **Wines** 21 bottles over £30, 21 bottles under £30, 17 by glass **Parking** 80 **Notes** Sunday L £20-£25, Vegetarian available, Children welcome

BERKSHIRE

ASCOT Map 6 SU96

The Barn at Coworth

◎ British

tel: 01344 876600 **Blacknest Rd SL5 7SE**
email: restaurants.CPA@dorchestercollection.com
dir: *M25 junct 13 onto A30 signed Egham/Bagshot until Wentworth Golf Club. Right at lights onto Blacknest Rd (A329) Hotel on left*

Converted barn with a local flavour

Polo is the game at Coworth Park, a lavish country hotel and spa which is part of the Dorchester group. There's a fine-dining restaurant, of course, but also this converted barn near the stables where you can tuck into some classy brasserie-style food. It looks great with its open-to-view kitchen, unbuttoned vibe and cheerful service team sporting orange polo tops, and there's a fabulous terrace, too, with gorgeous views over the grounds. There are some good local ingredients on the menu such as trout from the River Test, potted and served with horseradish crème fraîche and lamb's lettuce, or main-course Bramble Farm chicken with creamed potatoes, New Forest mushrooms, cabbage and bacon. There're also a posh burger and fish and chips. Among desserts, free-range egg custard tart might come with Yorkshire rhubarb in season.

Times 12.30-2.45/6-9.30

Bluebells Restaurant & Garden Bar

◉◉ Modern British

tel: 01344 622722 **Shrubbs Hill, London Rd, Sunningdale SL5 OLE**
email: info@bluebells-restaurant.co.uk
dir: From M25 junct 13, A30 towards Bagshot. Restaurant between Wentworth & Sunningdale

Stylish setting for ambitious contemporary cooking

Bluebells certainly stands out from the crowd with its sleek modern looks and upbeat, buzzy ambience. Shimmery voile curtains divide up a long dining room done out with stylish darkwood tables and chairs upholstered with pearl-white panels. The kitchen works a modern British groove, delivering labour-intensive dishes with multi-layered flavours, brought thoughtfully together with skill and a good eye for presentation. That old stager, chicken liver parfait, gets a kick from cubes of red Muscadet wine jelly, quince chutney, poached pear and toasted hazelnuts, while goats' cheese nuggets and sesame and parmesan shortbread add value to smoked Jerusalem artichoke velouté. Meticulously sourced ingredients are a hallmark of a main course partnering Blythburgh pork tenderloin with crispy pig's head, wilted kale, roasted garlic foam and potato fritters. Or you might opt for fish, in a take on cassoulet uniting monkfish with mussels, white beans, chorizo and saffron. Service remains expert, meticulous and relaxed all the way through to a finale of vanilla and praline crème brûlée with chestnut ice cream and vanilla macaroons.

Chef Adam Turley **Owner** John Rampello **Seats** 90, Pr/dining room 14
Times 12-2.30/6.30-9.45, Closed 25-26 Dec, 1-11 Jan, BHs, Mon, D Sun **Prices** Fixed L 2 course fr £17, Starter £8.50-£18, Main £17-£30, Dessert £8.50-£9.75 **Wines** 74 bottles over £30, 30 bottles under £30, 12 by glass **Parking** 100 **Notes** Sunday L, Vegetarian available, Children welcome

Macdonald Berystede Hotel & Spa

◉ British, European

tel: 01344 623311 **Bagshot Rd, Sunninghill SL5 9JH**
email: general.berystede@macdonald-hotels.co.uk **web:** www.berystede.com
dir: M3 junct 3/A30, A322 then left onto B3020 to Ascot or M25 junct 13, follow signs for Bagshot. At Sunningdale turn right onto A330

Ambitious brasserie cooking near Legoland and the racing

The Berystede is a handsome red-brick Victorian mansion handy for both Legoland and the racing at Ascot, depending on how you get your kicks. It's the image of a modern corporate hotel, with the usual spa and business facilities to please all-comers, yet it has character, plus the stylish Hyperion restaurant. Curvy banquettes and gleaming contemporary cutlery and glassware set the scene for inventive, up-to-date brasserie dishes that can look a little busy but deliver on flavour. Pan-fried scallops with black pudding, lardo, Brussels sprouts and chestnuts might start you off. Go on to something like wild turbot fillet with squid ink gnocchi, roasted salsify, samphire and smoked mussels, or onion ash-rolled venison loin with venison faggot, ceps, grelot onions and venison jus. Desserts are no less labour intensive, as in chocolate and peanut butter mousse with peanut butter and caramel ice cream and salted chocolate popcorn.

Times 12.30-2/7-9.45, Closed L Sat

Paris House Restaurant ❀❀❀

Modern British
tel: 01525 290692 **London Rd, Woburn Park MK17 9QP**
email: info@parishouse.co.uk
dir: M1 junct 13. From Woburn take A4012 Hockliffe, 1m out of Woburn village on left

Impeccable contemporary cooking in a reassembled timbered house

Pass through the grand gateway and cross the Duke of Bedford's deer park at his Woburn estate to reach this beautiful half-limbered Tudoresque building, originally constructed in Paris for the 1878 International Exhibition, then taken apart and reassembled here. The door is opened for guests as they arrive, while dining takes place in refined surroundings of elegance and charm, where front-of-house staff are professional and relaxed. Phil Fanning describes his style as retro French classic, which seems a bit narrow when he sources ingredients globally, adding his unique stamp to his output and taking an international approach. Dinner consists of a six-, eight- or ten-course tasting menu of boldly inventive ideas. It might start with mackerel, plums and thyme, with chilled buttermilk adding a temperature contrast – a dish of outstanding balance. Next up might be tom yum with steamed pork dumplings in light pastry with squid noodles, the waiter pouring the soup at table. Timings and techniques are spot on, and the cooking involves a high degree of invention. Perfectly executed Moroccan-style lamb tagine, for instance, comes with smoked tree bark with herbs, black-eyed peas and ras el hanout, and 'pot-au-feu' of halibut and clams spiked with hamachi is timed to the second. A plate of artisan cheeses is an optional extra, while thrillingly creative desserts can be a highlight. Pumpkin munchkin with condensed milk parfait, apple and preserved grapes, along with fruit jelly and a tuile in the shape of branches hung with flowers, is a stunner, while kombu (Japanese seaweed) is served with beetroot, chocolate and pistachios.

Chef Phil Fanning, Paul Lobban **Owner** Phil & Claire Fanning **Seats** 37, Pr/dining room 14 **Times** 12-2/7-9, Closed Xmas, Mon-Tue, D Sun **Prices** Service optional 12.5% **Wines** 120 bottles over £30, 4 bottles under £30, 20 by glass **Parking** 24 **Notes** Gourmand menu 6/8/10 course £39/£82/£99, Chef's table D £200, Sunday L £55, Vegetarian available, Children welcome

ASCOT *continued*

Restaurant Coworth Park

◉◉ Modern British 🍷 NOTABLE WINE LIST

tel: 01344 876600 **London Rd SL5 7SE**
email: restaurants.CPA@dorchestercollection.com **web:** www.coworthpark.com
dir: *M25 junct 13 onto A30 signed Egham/Bagshot until Wentworth Golf Club. Right at lights onto Blacknest Rd (A329) Hotel on left*

Modern classic dishes in a gleaming-white hotel

A gleaming-white balustraded Georgian house in the vicinity of the racecourse, Coworth is part of the Dorchester Collection. It's not all standing on West End ceremony, for the Barn is available for eating and rustic relaxation, but the main dining room piles on contemporary style with its pale pastel look, and trailing ceiling foliage of oversized copper oak leaves. The kitchen's output is similarly forward-thinking, with a plethora of modern classic dishes produced with scrupulous attention to detail. The now inseparable pairing of scallops and black pudding offers caramelised shellfish, texturally echoed by silky shallot purée, as an alternative to lightly spiced duck breast with beetroot and salt-baked turnips. Then comes perhaps an eloquent fish dish such as roasted turbot, given the bourguignon treatment with bacon, mushrooms and red wine, or else Scottish beef fillet with oxtail suet pudding and watercress purée. Yorkshire rhubarb with blood orange, cheesecake cream and a scattering of crumbs makes a simple enough deconstruction, or there may be tarte Tatin for sharing, made with Braeburns and sauced in Somerset cider brandy.

Times 12.30-3/6.30-9.30, Closed Mon, D Sun

BRACKNELL　　　　　　　　　　Map 5 SU86

Coppid Beech

◉ European, Pacific Rim

tel: 01344 303333 **John Nike Way RG12 8TF**
email: sales@coppidbeech.com **web:** www.coppidbeech.com
dir: *M4 junct 10 take Wokingham/Bracknell onto A329. In 2m take B3408 to Binfield at rdbt. Hotel 200yds on right*

Alpine atmosphere and modern food by the Thames

You may think that the Thames Valley is not known for its skiing and Alpine chalets, but that is because you haven't yet discovered the Coppid Beech. The smart modern hotel not only has the look of a Swiss chalet, but there's the chance to strap on the planks too as there's a dry-ski slope, an ice rink and toboggan run in the complex. With an appetite suitably sharpened by the year-round winter sports, move on to Rowans, the hotel's upscale dining option. It is an eye-catching space, with plush drapes and linen-clothed tables beneath a soaring timbered ceiling hung with crystal chandeliers as a backdrop to a menu that covers a fair amount of modern European territory. Start with wood pigeon en croûte served with beetroot carpaccio and orange and beetroot jus, followed by sirloin steak with mushrooms, parsnip purée, garlic spinach and marchand de vin sauce. Finish with a Thai-influenced coconut pannacotta with sweet-and-sour pineapple, and basil jelly.

Chef Paul Zolik **Owner** Nike Group Hotels Ltd **Seats** 120 **Times** 12-2/7-9.30, Closed L Sat, D Sun **Prices** Fixed D 3 course £27.50, Starter £4.50-£8.25, Main £12.50-£22.50, Dessert £6.25-£7.50 **Wines** 20 bottles over £30, 20 bottles under £30, 15 by glass **Parking** 350 **Notes** Sunday L, Vegetarian available, Children welcome

BRAY　　　　　　　　　　Map 6 SU97

Caldesi in Campagna

◉◉ Traditional Italian

tel: 01628 788500 **Old Mill Ln SL6 2BG**
email: campagna@caldesi.com
dir: *M4 junct 8/9, at rdbt exit A308 Bray/Windsor. Continue for 0.5m, left B3028 Bray village, right Old Mill Lane, restaurant in 400yds on right*

Refined Italian eatery with a smart patio garden

A taste of Italy in Berkshire – and an alternative to the other dining options in this particular village (shh... you know who) – the enterprising couple who run it also have a cafe and cookery school in London. Here, in an immaculate house on the edge of Bray, tables are dressed up for the business of fine dining, including those on the charming patio. Expect classic Italian stuff made with (mostly) British ingredients. Among antipasti, deep-fried courgette flowers are filled with ricotta and basil, seared Scottish scallops arrive with a Jerusalem artichoke cream, pancetta and some slivers of black truffle, and cured hams are shipped over from the motherland. Pasta courses include tagliolini with Cornish crab, and pappardelle with duck and a rich red wine and tomato ragù. Follow on with a classic cacciucco – seafood casserole – with squid, gurnard, clams and mussels, or pan-fried calves' liver with sage and an olive oil mash. Traditional desserts might include Sicilian lemon tart or a trio of pannacotta (basil, marinated berries and espresso).

Chef Gregorio Piazza **Owner** Giancarlo Caldesi **Seats** 50, Pr/dining room 12 **Times** 12-2.30/6.30-10, Closed Xmas for approx 5 days, Mon, D Sun **Prices** Fixed L 2 course £16.50, Tasting menu £85-£105, Starter £8.50-£16, Main £13.50-£28.50, Dessert £6.95-£13.50 **Wines** 110 bottles over £30, 15 bottles under £30, 18 by glass **Parking** 8 **Notes** Sunday L, Vegetarian available, Children welcome

The Crown

◉◉ British

tel: 01628 621936 & 788545 **High St SL6 2AH**
email: reservations@thecrownatbray.co.uk
dir: *M4 junct 8/9, follow signs for Maidenhead/Windsor. At rdbt take 3rd exit to Windsor, then left into Bray. 100mtrs on left after bridge*

Heston's proper pub

Devotees of the British pub can rest assured that the Crown is safe in Heston Blumenthal's hands. His third address in the village (after you-know-where and the Hinds Head up the road), this 16th-century village inn has been spruced up while keeping its cosy corners, open fires and chunky beams. It has history, too – they say Charles II used to pop by when visiting Nell Gwyn. There are real ales, a well-constructed wine list and a menu that owes much to pub traditions while showing the inimitable stamp of quality that goes with the Blumenthal name. King prawn cocktail is a classy version served with rye bread, Cornish mussels are flavoured by garlic, apple and cider, and if you just fancy a sandwich, there are the likes of an open salt beef version with dill pickles and shallots. Main courses might include fish and chips and a hamburger, or go for free-range pork belly with castelluccio lentils and hispi cabbage. Finish with rhubarb and custard.

Chef Matt Larcombe **Owner** Heston Blumenthal **Seats** 44 **Times** 12-2.30/6-9.30 **Prices** Starter £6.95-£9.25, Main £14.95-£28.95, Dessert £5.50-£7.50 **Wines** 26 bottles over £30, 17 bottles under £30, 13 by glass **Parking** 37 **Notes** Sunday L £18.50-£23.50, Vegetarian available, Children welcome

The Fat Duck

◉◉◉◉◉ *– see opposite*

The Fat Duck ✿✿✿✿✿

BRAY Map 6 SU97

Modern British V

tel: 01628 580333 **High St SL6 2AQ**
dir: *M4 junct 8/9 (Maidenhead) take A308 towards Windsor, turn left into Bray. Restaurant in centre of village on right*

Mind-boggling culinary creations old and new at Heston HQ

Heston and his team spent the first half of 2015 in Australia, spreading the culinary magic around in The Crown Melbourne Resort. Meanwhile, back in Bray, the building has had a complete overhaul, so although the physical aspect is still agreeably cottagey and informal, there's a shiny new kitchen and a re-vamped wine cellar in the background and a few more 'typically Heston' touches. Clearly the sabbatical has spurred Heston Blumenthal's tireless curiosity and willingness to push at the boundaries of convention, and a spell in the development kitchen has brought in a more psychological aspect to some dishes. The creator of the multisensory approach to cooking is no longer content with playing all sorts of tricks with your eyes, nose, ears and taste buds (the 'Sound of the Sea' for example, delivering aural stimulation alongside some fab kingfish, abalone and mackerel), Heston now wants to mess with your head, evoking nostalgia and exploring historic roots via heritage-inspired dishes, as typified in the 'eggs in verjus (c.1726), verjus in egg (c.2013)' idea. A foodie pilgrimage to Hestonworld has never come cheap – the entrance fee is £220 these days (plus the 12½% service charge), but for most, this is one of those bucket-list experiences that will stay with you forever. When you appreciate the work that goes into each dish – the craft, the passion, the time – the cost seems easier to justify, and the stellar staff can cope with eight or so languages to keep the international punters informed as they go along. What follows consumes you as much as you consume it. The nitro-poached aperitifs are still are a lot of fun to start, but a little different this time round – perhaps an espuma flavoured with vodka and lime sour, gin and tonic or tequila and grapefruit poached in liquid nitrogen at -196 degrees C, dissolving on your tongue to deliver an intense hit of clean, crisp flavour. The unique menu continues to evolve. Some of the signature 'classics' remain on show as that's what the punters have come for – three cheers for snail porridge with Ibérico Bellota ham and shaved fennel, but new things arrive to keep the interest of seasoned visitors -we won't ruin the surprise, suffice to say there are a few that make it certainly worth the revisit. The science and the innovation impresses, but most of all, it's the taste that lingers in the memory. There's theatrical presentation, too – take a bow 'Mad Hatters tea party' (as seen on TV), and sweet courses are a lot of fun, with 'Whisk (e) y wine gums' and a newer addition 'Like a Kid in a Sweet Shop' evoking childhood memories.

Chef Heston Blumenthal, Jonny Lake **Owner** Fat Duck Ltd
Seats 40 **Times** 12-2/7-9, Closed 2 wks at Xmas, Sun-Mon
Prices Tasting menu fr £220 **Wines** 500 bottles over £30, 13 by glass **Parking** Two village car parks **Notes** Tasting menu only, Children welcome

BRAY *continued*

Hinds Head

◉◉◉ *– see below*

The Riverside Brasserie

◉◉ Modern European

tel: 01628 780553 **Bray Marina, Monkey Island Ln SL6 2EB**
email: info@riversidebrasserie.co.uk
dir: *Off A308, signed Bray Marina*

Accomplished cooking by the Thames

If you like to make a grand entrance, why not arrive by boat? This hidden gem is tucked away beside the Thames in Bray Marina; the waterside decked terrace is perfect for alfresco dining, but if summer sets in with its customary severity and drives you indoors, the simple interior oozes understated class and an easygoing ambience. Full-length glass doors mean the river views are still there, while the chefs working in an open-to-view kitchen turn out straightforward yet skilfully cooked brasserie food. Chicken liver and foie gras parfait with onion marmalade and toasted brioche is a classic starter, done right, while splendid ingredients bring lustre to an uncomplicated main course comprising spanking fresh cod with crunchy choucroute, pea purée and crispy Parma ham. Elsewhere, there may be Romney Marsh lamb rump, cooked sous-vide for maximum tenderness, and served with green beans and Sicilian pesto. To finish, a great combo of sweet and salty flavours comes courtesy of a chocolate ganache and salted caramel tart served with milk ice cream.

Times 12-2.30/7-9.30, Closed Mon-Thu (Oct-Mar), L Fri (Oct-Mar)

Waterside Inn

◉◉◉◉ *– see opposite*

| CHIEVELEY | Map 5 SU47 |

Crab & Boar

◉◉ Modern British

tel: 01635 247550 **Wantage Rd RG20 8UE**
email: info@crabandboar.com **web:** www.crabandboar.com
dir: *M4 junct 13, towards Chieveley. Left into School Rd, right at T-junct, 0.5m on right. Follow brown tourist signs*

Singular seafood in rural Berkshire

Restaurants with rooms don't come much more singular in intent than the Crab & Boar, a thatched cottage in rural Berkshire where the guest rooms are decorated in homage to famous hotels around the world from Fiji to Scotland, while a warren of interlinked rooms make up the seafood restaurant. In case you've missed the theme, the walls are adorned with fishing scenes in bright colours, and the ceilings hung with laden nets. You could be in a little fishing village, were you not land-bound in Berkshire. Main courses do the freshness and vitality of their prime materials proud, by means of dishes such as sea bass with parmesan gnocchi, mushrooms and artichoke cream, turbot and lobster bouillabaisse with rock samphire, and well-timed scallops with a black pudding beignet and sweetcorn risotto, a dish only slightly unbalanced by over-assertive chorizo. Attention to detail is on reassuring show in starters like duck and foie gras terrine wrapped in Parma ham, with raisin purée and a crisp-fried quail's egg, and properly wobbly coconut pannacotta with pineapple granité and soft vanilla meringues.

Times 12-2.30/6-9.30, Closed D 25 Dec

Hinds Head ❀❀❀

| BRAY | Map 6 SU97 |

British ⚘ NOTABLE WINE LIST

tel: 01628 626151 **High St SL6 2AB**
email: info@hindsheadbray.com
dir: *M4 junct 8/9, at rdbt take exit to Maidenhead Central, next rdbt take exit Bray & Windsor, after 0.5m take B3028 to Bray*

Heston's modern take on old-English fare with bang-on flavours

When Heston Blumenthal took over Bray's village boozer in 2004 the intention was never to turn it into another branch of the Fat Duck, touting molecular fireworks along the lines of pork pie custard with real ale nitrogen vapour, but rather to offer traditional true-Brit cooking in keeping with the building's 15th-century heritage. Perhaps inevitably, mission creep has taken hold and the place has become a dining destination in itself. That said, you could just pop in for a pint of real ale from a local micro-brewery in the beamed bar, although the majority are clearly here for the menu of historic English tavern fare produced by Heston's research into the UK's culinary history (hash of snails, anyone?) and classy versions of gastro pub classics. Chef Janos Veres delivers well-crafted dishes that can be as simple as snacks (Devils on horseback or a Scotch egg, say) or an immaculate starter of hand-dived scallops with black pudding and curried cauliflower. Everything is presented with a touch of rustic flair and flavours are spot on. Main-course fillet of stone bass with crushed Jerusalem artichokes, cider butter sauce and mussels has a first-rate piece of fish at its heart, or you could opt for a heritage dish of oxtail and kidney pudding. To finish, 'wassailing' is a revived pudding of caramelised butter loaf with apple in a multitude of textures – or you might take refuge in the comforts of warm chocolate pudding with orange marmalade ice cream. Naturally, the wine list goes way, way beyond the sort of offerings you'd expect in a pub, with impeccably sourced bottles from small châteaux as well as gilt-edged vintages from around the globe.

Chef Janos Veres **Owner** Hinds Head Ltd **Seats** 100, Pr/dining room 22 **Times** 12-2.30/6.15-9.30, Closed 25-26 Dec, D 1 Jan, BHs, Sun **Prices** Fixed L 2 course fr £17.50, Tasting menu fr £65, Starter £7.50-£10.50, Main £15.95-£35, Dessert £7.95-£9.50 **Wines** 78 bottles over £30, 16 bottles under £30, 13 by glass **Parking** 40 **Notes** Tasting menu 6 course with 24hrs notice, Sunday L, Vegetarian available, Children welcome

Waterside Inn ❀❀❀❀

BRAY   Map 6 SU97

French

tel: 01628 620691 **Ferry Rd SL6 2AT**
email: reservations@waterside-inn.co.uk
dir: *M4 junct 8/9, A308 (Windsor) then B3028 to Bray. Restaurant clearly signed*

The Roux family's riverside restaurant four decades on

An old English pub by the banks of the River Thames caught the eye of a pair of French brothers who had made their name in London, and in 1972 they opened the Waterside Inn. Over 40 years later and it is still in the family. We're talking, of course about the Roux family, and it is Alain, son of Michel, who has taken on the mantle here by the river. Alain Roux didn't just turn up and expect his birthright, far from it; several years spent working in France and even more working his way up through the ranks here have made him the ideal man to carry this iconic restaurant into the 21st century. And that's exactly what he's done, partly by not changing it, for the Waterside is a bastion of classic French cooking, a luxury address offering the highest level of service you're likely to find anywhere (three cheers for Diego Masciaga who leads the team with charm and assurance). Things get off to a very good start with the valet parking, which makes you feel rather special from the off. That sense of being special will stay with you the whole visit. Things get even better if the weather allows drinks and canapés on the terrace by the water, but even if you're kept indoors, rest assured all is comfort and joy. The cuisine is based around French classical ways as you might expect, but there are modern touches threaded seamlessly through, with luxury ingredients in abundance. If you choose to stick with the à la carte over the gastronomique or exceptionnel menus, you might start with langoustine soufflé with an accompanying cassoulet of langoustines scented with truffles, or ravioli and 'diablotins' of Burgundy snails enriched with parsley and garlic, and served with a lemongrass-scented chicken bouillon. Move on to whole braised turbot partnered with lobster mousseline and a champagne and chive sauce, but note you'll need a willing accomplice for this one. Challandais duck is carved at the table with breath-taking precision (and served with a jus flavoured with Earl Grey tea and bergamot), or go for grilled rabbit fillets with celeriac fondant, glazed chestnuts and Armagnac sauce. Alain Roux is a master pâtissier, so prepare for a stunning dessert such as warm rhubarb soufflé. Prices are high, but that is no surprise (the valet parking was an early clue). The wine list, like everything else, is a thrilling and classy ride.

Chef Alain Roux **Owner** Alain Roux **Seats** 75, Pr/dining room 8 **Times** 12-2/7-10, Closed 26 Dec-29 Jan, Mon-Tue **Prices** Fixed L 2 course fr £49.50, Starter £37-£60, Main £53-£60, Dessert £32-£41 **Wines** 1000+ bottles over £30, 1 bottle under £30, 14 by glass **Parking** 20 **Notes** Tasting menu 6 course, Sun L 3/6 course, Sunday L £79.50-£160, Vegetarian available, Children 12 yrs+

COOKHAM
Map 6 SU88

The White Oak

European, British

tel: 01628 523 043 **The Pound SL6 9QE**
email: info@thewhiteoak.co.uk
dir: *M4 junct 8/9 onto A308(M) towards Maidenhead Central, continue towards Marlow. Right at lights Switchback Road South to Gardener Road. At rdbt 1st exit B4447 Switchback Road North to Cookham, right at mini-rdbt to The Pound*

Traditional pub cooking in Stanley Spencer country

The team behind the White Oak reopened it in 2008 as a modern dining pub. Set in Stanley Spencer's beloved Cookham, it has all the fashionable decorative amenities to be expected, including splashy contemporary artwork, bare tables and generous washes of natural light from a skylight and patio doors. The core of the operation is traditional pub cooking, including a Monday steak night, but with some latter-day technical ambition. That comes off well in a pressed leek terrine with whipped Roquefort and chopped walnuts, or perhaps a simple roasting of brill on the bone with chips and spinach, less so in a ragout of venison with puréed celeriac. Gird your loins at pudding stage for a hunk of lardy cake with salted whisky caramel. The chocolate mousse looks a bit of a splodge, but does have good depth of flavour.

Chef Clive Dixon, Adam Hague **Owner** Henry & Katherine Cripps **Seats** 80, Pr/dining room 14 **Times** 12-2.30/6.30-9.30, Closed D Sun (winter) **Prices** Fixed L 2 course £12, Fixed D 3 course £19, Starter £5-£12, Main £14-£19, Dessert £5-£9, Service optional 12.5% **Wines** 26 bottles over £30, 29 bottles under £30, 13 by glass **Parking** 32 **Notes** Tasting menu 5-7 course, Sunday L £14-£19, Vegetarian available, Children welcome

EAST GARSTON
Map 5 SU37

Queens Arms

British NEW

tel: 01488 648757 **RG17 7ET**
email: info@queenshotel.co.uk **web:** www.queensarmshotel.co.uk
dir: *From A338 into Shefford, then follow signs to East Garston. On right as you enter village*

Smart village inn with confident cooking

Part of a small group consisting of three inns, the Queens Arms is a traditional sort of place, where the decor recalls country pursuits and fires glow in the cooler months. Real ales are the mainstay of the bar, while the restaurant has plenty of 18th-century character and burnished wooden tables. The daily-changing menu runs to starters such as a coarse pork and apple terrine with a sticky onion marmalade and oat biscuits, followed by pan-seared stone bass with creamed potatoes and basil pesto, or slow-roasted featherblade of beef with dauphinoise potatoes. There is simple stuff like a home-made burger, too (just about everything is made in-house), and desserts include a classic crème brûlée served with shortbread. The wine list offers a good global spread and a decent choice by the glass. Comfortable bedrooms and a private dining room complete the picture.

Chef Andrew Rolfe **Owner** Ashley & Tracey Levett **Seats** 35 **Times** 12-2/6.30-9, Closed 25 Dec, D 26 Dec, 1 Jan **Prices** Starter £5.50-£9, Main £11-£24, Dessert £5.50, Service optional **Wines** 20 bottles over £30, 10 bottles under £30, 6 by glass **Parking** 25 **Notes** Sunday L £20-£24, Vegetarian available, Children welcome

FRILSHAM
Map 5 SU57

The Pot Kiln

British, European

tel: 01635 201366 **RG18 0XX**
email: info@potkiln.org
dir: *From Yattendon follow Pot Kiln signs, cross over motorway. Continue for 0.25m pub on right*

Confident country cooking in rural inn

This rural red-brick country inn is worth tracking down for its proper pubby vibe and unpretentious approach to modern British cooking. The owners, Mike and Katie Robinson, source their produce with a good deal of care, but what makes the Pot Kiln stand out from the herd is its passion for game. Mike is an outdoors man, and when he's not out shooting for the larder, he's on the telly a fair bit, usually banging the drum for British game. Start with a classic chicken liver and foie gras parfait with toasted brioche and chutney, or you might get stuck straight into a wild venison Scotch egg from the bar menu. Main-course beef cheeks are braised for 10 hours and served with mash, black cabbage and slow-cooked shallots, or there may be pan-fried hake with fennel rösti, roasted vine tomatoes, spinach and basil.

Chef Mike Robinson **Owner** Mike & Katie Robinson, Tom Dennis **Seats** 48 **Times** 12-2.30/7-9.30, Closed 25 Dec, Tue, D Sun **Prices** Starter £6.50-£10.50, Main £13-£21, Dessert £7-£12 **Wines** 45 bottles over £30, 17 bottles under £30, 12 by glass **Parking** 70 **Notes** Monthly food event nights, Sunday L £17-£19, Vegetarian available, Children welcome

HUNGERFORD
Map 5 SU36

Littlecote House Hotel

Modern British

tel: 01488 682509 **Chilton Foliat RG17 0SU**
web: www.warnerleisurehotels.co.uk
dir: *M4 junct 14, A338/A4 Hungerford, follow brown signs*

Appealing modern menu in an historic house

Littlecote has history: there's a Roman mosaic and the remains of a Roman settlement in the grounds, while the house itself is where Henry VIII met his third wife, Jane Seymour, and Cromwell's soldiers are billeted here in the Civil War. So well done for spotting where the top restaurant option – Oliver's Bistro – got its name. Here we fast-forward to the 21st century: the setting is slickly modern and minimalist, the kitchen turns out resolutely up-to-date, creative ideas that showcase local suppliers, and it's all supported by a globetrotting wine list. Confit duck terrine looks as pretty as a picture on a black slate, together with fig sorbet and cubes of brioche, while main-course confit pork belly is matched imaginatively with fondant potato, cauliflower purée, pancetta and Granny Smith apple. Fans of the fish and meat combo might find poached cod loin partnered by caramelised veal sweetbreads and chive mash. For pudding, try a simple but highly effective pairing of chocolate fondant with peanut ice cream and brittle.

Chef Matthew Davies **Owner** Warner Leisure Hotels **Seats** 40, Pr/dining room 8 **Times** 6.30-9, Closed Mon, L all week **Prices** Prices not confirmed, Service optional **Wines** 4 bottles over £30, 23 bottles under £30, 13 by glass **Parking** 200 **Notes** L only Oliver's Bistro 12-2, 2/3 course £17.50-£20.50, Sunday L, Vegetarian available, No children

The Olde Bell Inn

◎◎ Modern British

tel: 01628 825881 **High St SL6 5LX**
email: oldebellreception@coachinginn.co.uk **web:** www.theoldebell.co.uk
dir: M4 junct 8/9 follow signs for Henley. At rdbt take A4130 to Hurley, turn right to Hurley Village, 800yds on right

Classy, creative cooking in a smartly revamped coaching inn

There's no shortage of period character at the 12th-century Bell (very much an olde), with beams, fireplaces etc., but the place is by no means preserved in aspic. In fact, it's done out with a good deal of charm-of the rustic-chic variety-with chunky designer tables and some rather cool fixtures and fittings. There are six acres of fabulous grounds to get lost in, including a kitchen garden that provides plenty of good stuff for the table. The kitchen makes good use of regional produce and serves up some nifty dishes that show sound technical skill and, like the inn itself, a creative and rustic spin. A starter of pressed ham hock terrine comes with apple sauce and rye bread, while roasted quail is partnered with an apple and white cabbage remoulade. Next up, butter-roasted lamb with garlic and cream potato has at its heart a fine piece of meat, correctly cooked, or go for pan-fried plaice served in the classic way with lemon, capers and a nutty brown butter sauce. Sign off in style with an iced mango parfait with caramel popcorn crumb.

Times 12-2.30/6-9.30

Boulters Riverside Brasserie

◎◎ Modern British

tel: 01628 621291 **Boulters Lock Island SL6 8PE**
email: Info@boultersrestaurant.co.uk
dir: M4 junct 7 onto A4 towards Maidenhead, cross Maidenhead bridge, right at rdbt. Restaurant 0.5m on right

Modern brasserie dining by the river

The to-die-for Thames-side location overlooking Boulters Lock, where the river ambles past Maidenhead Bridge, is a very good reason to head to this buzzy, contemporary brasserie. There may be nothing but glass walls between diners and the river, but Boulters is not a place to let the food take a back seat while the views pull in the punters: the ground-floor fine-dining brasserie is flooded with light and looks stylishly neutral with its bare darkwood tables and wooden floors. The food fits the setting to a T – well-executed contemporary brasserie dishes wrought from quality local produce, all impeccably presented. Roast pumpkin and parmesan risotto gets a herby kick from marjoram and deeper earthy notes from truffle butter, while a main course delivers splendidly fresh baked cod with a cheese crust, fondant potato, wilted spinach and wholegrain mustard sauce. For dessert, only Valrhona's finest will do for a hot chocolate fondant with pistachio parfait.

Chef Daniel Woodhouse **Owner** The Dennis family **Seats** 70, Pr/dining room 12
Times 12-9.30, All-day dining, Closed D Sun **Prices** Fixed L 2 course £15.95, Starter £7.95-£8.95, Main £12.95-£18.95, Dessert £5.95-£8.50 **Wines** 33 bottles over £30, 30 bottles under £30, 18 by glass **Parking** 20 **Notes** Brunch 10-11.30am, High tea 3-5pm, Sunday L £19.95-£24.95, Vegetarian available, Children welcome

Fredrick's Hotel and Spa

◎◎ Modern British, French **NEW**

tel: 01628 581000 **Shoppenhangers Rd SL6 2PZ**
email: reservations@fredricks-hotel.co.uk **web:** www.fredricks-hotel.co.uk
dir: From M4 junct 8/9 take A404(M), then turning (junct 9a) for Cox Green/White Waltham. Left on to Shoppenhangers Rd, restaurant 400 mtrs on right

Modern dining at a classy spa hotel

Fredrick's has entered new ownership since last year's guide, but a determined attempt at continuity has resulted in nobody really being able to see the join. The building still looks endearingly as though it may have been put together by a dissenting committee of architects, but the spa facilities and interiors are as graceful and as classy as ever, and the dining room in royal blue and gold, with twinkling chandeliers and views over the gardens, is a treat. The same team remains at the kitchen helm too, producing an assiduously researched version of contemporary cooking. Home-smoked salmon tian comes with potato galette and dill pickle, and pork is put to good use in the form of rillettes and crackling salad with pickled apple. Meats come in pairs at main course: loin and belly of lamb, fillet and cheek of pork, breast and confit leg of duck, the last with Swiss chard, rhubarb and gingered mash. A trio of traditional grills offers the extra treat of duck-fat roasties. Populist desserts include chocolate fondant with salt caramel and yogurt sorbet.

Chef Craig Smith **Owner** Art Hotels **Seats** 60, Pr/dining room 20
Times 12-2/6.30-9.30, Closed L Sat, D Sun **Prices** Fixed L 2 course £20-£29, Fixed D 3 course £25-£39, Starter £6.50-£13.50, Main £15-£28.50, Dessert £6.50-£13.50, Service optional 12.5% **Wines** 40 bottles over £30, 20 bottles under £30, 12 by glass **Parking** 100 **Notes** Sunday L £20-£26.50, Vegetarian available

The Royal Oak Paley Street

◎◎◎ – see page 56

Donnington Valley Hotel & Spa

◎◎ Modern British ▮ NOTABLE WINE LIST

tel: 01635 551199 **Old Oxford Rd, Donnington RG14 3AG**
email: general@donningtonvalley.co.uk **web:** www.donningtonvalley.co.uk
dir: M4 junct 13, A34 towards Newbury. Take immediate left signed Donnington Hotel. At rdbt take right, at 3rd rdbt take left, follow road for 2m, hotel on right

Engaging modern cooking in a golfing and spa hotel

There's a lot going on at this ultra-modern hotel with its gym, pool, sauna and 18-hole golf course, plus state-of-the-art meeting facilities. It's also popular for weddings. This is a likeable, informal sort of place, not least the Wine Press restaurant: a large, light-filled, high-ceilinged, raftered room on two levels. There's much to like on the menu as well, with a kitchen turning out up-to-the-minute dishes alongside more conventional British fare. Pan-fried scallops are partnered by tomato and bean cassoulet, white pudding and pancetta crisps, before a main course of braised blade of beef with pancetta dauphinoise, wild mushrooms and fine beans. Pickled cucumber gives a welcome smack of acidity to poached salmon and herb roulade, and orange jus is a traditional contrast to confit duck leg with buttery mash and stem broccoli. Half a dozen well-chosen cheeses are possibilities, while the sweet of tooth could go for warm milk chocolate fondant with dark chocolate ganache and triple chocolate ice cream.

Chef Kelvin Johnson **Owner** Sir Peter Michael **Seats** 120, Pr/dining room 130
Times 12-2/7-10, Closed L 1 Jan **Prices** Fixed D 3 course fr £28, Starter £8-£12, Main £17-£28, Dessert £8-£18, Service optional **Wines** 321 bottles over £30, 49 bottles under £30, 36 by glass **Parking** 150 **Notes** Sunday L £19-£22, Vegetarian available, Children welcome

The Royal Oak Paley Street ❀❀❀

MAIDENHEAD Map 6 SU88

British, European ● NOTABLE WINE LIST

tel: 01628 620541 **Paley St, Littlefield Green SL6 3JN**
email: reservations@theroyaloakpaleystreet.com
web: www.theroyaloakpaleystreet.com
dir: *M4 junct 8/9. Take A308 towards Maidenhead Central, then A330 to Ascot. After 2m, turn right onto B3024 to Twyford. Second pub on left*

First-class modern British cooking in a spruced up country pub

Proving beyond doubt the dictum that you can't judge a book by its cover, the Royal Oak looks like your average whitewashed village pub. Indoors, it's good to see real ale on the hand-pumps and due respect paid to the beamed 17th-century charm of the place; there are flagstones on the floor, a fire in the hearth and colourful modern art on the walls. An appealingly upmarket country pub, then, but it is chef Michael Chapman's stellar performance in the kitchen that has put this modest little settlement on the foodie map. If proof were needed of the operation's success, a new extension to the restaurant doubled its size in 2012, opening into a delightful contemporary garden that makes an idyllic setting for pre-dinner drinks. The menus follow the seasons and are filled with things you'll want to eat, thus a summer's meal kicks off with seared mackerel with red pepper purée, confit fennel and a crunchy raw fennel salad. It may sound simple, but a main course showcasing new season spring lamb achieves that holy grail of bringing together earthiness and refinement, the cutlet barbecued to charred and smoky perfection, the rolled and braised breast

matched with an intense gravy, golden-crusted boulangère potatoes and top-class carrots and turnip. Dessert, too, is a seriously classy finale, the richness of a brown butter pannacotta counterpointed with chocolate mousse and banana sorbet. Everything else, from superb sun-dried tomato and olive breads to the stonking list of 500-odd wines with a good choice by the glass, is hard to fault. Informed, friendly service and attention to detail is the cherry on top.

Chef Michael Chapman **Owner** Nick Parkinson **Seats** 80, Pr/dining room 20 **Times** 12-2.30/6.30-9.30, Closed D Sun **Prices** Fixed L 2 course fr £19.95, Starter £6.50-£12, Main £14.50-£27, Dessert £6.50-£9.50 **Wines** 400 bottles over £30, 80 bottles under £30, 20 by glass **Parking** 70 **Notes** Sunday L, Vegetarian available, Children 3 yrs+

NEWBURY *continued*

Regency Park Hotel

◉ Modern European **V**

tel: 01635 871555 **Bowling Green Rd, Thatcham RG18 3RP**
email: info@regencyparkhotel.com **web:** www.regencyparkhotel.co.uk
dir: *M4 junct 13, follow A339 to Newbury for 2m, then take the A4 (Reading), the hotel is signed*

Good cooking in a modern spa hotel

Not far from Highclere Castle, which these days lives a double life as *Downton Abbey*, the Regency Park is a modern spa hotel in pleasant grounds, making up in interior style what it lacks on the outside. A spacious dining room with one whole wall of glass looking out on a garden cascade, the Watermark's dimmed lights and piped music bring soothing balm in the evenings. The cooking delivers with dishes that hit the spot; pinkly roasted wood-pigeon salad with quail's eggs, Parma ham, pine nuts and raisins is a nicely balanced assemblage for example. Main course could be precisely timed sea bass in saffron velouté, served with both herb gnocchi and spring onion risotto, and the star finisher is rich vanilla pannacotta with mulled winter fruits and a caramel biscuit.

Chef Christopher Shanks **Owner** Planned Holdings Ltd **Seats** 90, Pr/dining room 40 **Times** 12.30-2/7-10, Closed L Sat **Prices** Prices not confirmed, Service optional **Wines** 21 bottles over £30, 27 bottles under £30, 14 by glass **Parking** 200 **Notes** Sunday L, Children welcome

The Vineyard

◉◉◉ – *see below*

The Woodspeen – Restaurant and Cookery School

◉◉ Modern British **NEW**

tel: 01635 265070 **Lambourn Rd RG20 8BN**
email: hello@thewoodspeen.com
dir: *Phone for directions*

Unfussy modern food from a master practitioner

An old pub called the Five Bells has been reborn under the guidance of John Campbell, a chef well known in the county for his time spent winning awards and plaudits aplenty at the Vineyard in Stockcross. The Woodspeen is a restaurant with a swanky new cookery school attached in an adjacent period building (complete with a chef's table dining option). The building has been expanded with a natty glass-fronted extension that has a touch of Scandinavian style about it, complete with a soaring blond wood ceiling. The cooking does not quite present the culinary fireworks of JC's previous ventures, but that's part of the point, for this is a more relaxed and energetic venue. Start with Cornish mackerel with beetroots (golden and ruby) and horseradish in a fashionable partnership, or a simple wild mushroom risotto with aged parmesan. Follow with local venison of the highest order, or a halibut and chorizo dish that doesn't reach the same heights. There's plenty of talent in this kitchen, judging by a finisher of egg custard tart with clementine sorbet.

Chef John Campbell **Owner** John Campbell, Alastair Storey **Seats** 70 **Times** 12-2.30/6-9.30, Closed Xmas, New Yr, Mon, D Sun **Prices** Fixed L 2 course £18, Fixed D 3 course £24, Starter £7-£11, Main £15-£25, Dessert £8 **Wines** 211 bottles over £30, 51 bottles under £30, 13 by glass **Parking** 30 **Notes** Pre-theatre menu 6-6.30pm, Sunday L £7-£22, Vegetarian available, Children welcome

---

The Vineyard ◉◉◉

NEWBURY   Map 5 SU46

Modern French **V** ◈ NOTABLE WINE LIST
tel: 01635 528770 **Stockcross RG20 8JU**
email: general@the-vineyard.co.uk **web:** www.the-vineyard.co.uk
dir: *From M4 take A34 towards Newbury, exit at 3rd junct for Speen. Right at rdbt then right again at 2nd rdbt*

World-class wines and modern French cuisine in five-star splendour

Sorry to burst your bubble, but there's no vineyard at The Vineyard, although owner Sir Peter Michael's world-class Californian winery supplies some pretty amazing wines in a cellar that runs to a staggering 30,000 bottles. In fact, the super-slick operation is a stylish and sybaritic celebration of the world of wine and gastronomy, with side orders of spa pampering, luxurious accommodation and chic public areas. On the food front, chef Daniel Galmiche's classy, intelligent French cooking delivers breathtaking marriages of flavour and texture, and a lot of fun. All this happens in an elegant dining room, where a sweeping staircase sports a balustrade resembling a grapevine coiling between the two levels, tables are resplendent in white linen, and striking artwork jazzes up the walls. The menu concept is to choose four or five dishes then trust the expert sommelier to match each with a suitable wine. Alternatively, there are two tasting menus: the seven-course Judgement which pairs

dishes up with both Californian and French wines, or the Discovery with matching wines chosen from lesser-known parts of the world. Opening the show, pressed confit foie gras might be counterpointed with pear, cucumber and ginger, or pheasant and partridge terrine helped along by orange, radish and Brussels tops. Dishes owe their impact to top-class ingredients rather then left-field combinations or techno trickery – Cornish sea bass with Cévennes onions and lemongrass jus, say or corn-fed duck breast with Cheltenham beetroot and blackberry. Desserts also impress with their technique and creativity – perhaps vanilla and prune parfait with plums and almond biscuits. If you're confident enough to do your own wine matching, around 100 are available by the glass.

Chef Daniel Galmiche **Owner** Sir Peter Michael **Seats** 86, Pr/dining room 140 **Times** 12-2/7-9.30, **Prices** Prices not confirmed, Service optional **Wines** 2800 bottles over £30, 60 bottles under £30, 120 by glass **Parking** 100 **Notes** ALC 2/3 course £62/£72, Tasting menu 5/7 course, Sunday L, Children welcome

Cerise Restaurant at The Forbury Hotel

◉◉ Modern International

tel: 0118 952 7770 **26 The Forbury RG1 3EJ**
email: reception@theforburyhotel.co.uk **web:** www.theforburyhotel.co.uk
dir: *Phone for directions*

Switched-on brasserie cooking in a cherry-red basement

The Forbury is a boutique townhouse hotel that presents a sober face to the world, but once inside, aims to wow. Striking, sexy and sybaritic, the place is peppered with modern art, bold fabrics and wallpapers, and a centrepiece Italian chandelier with 86,000 glass beads running from top to bottom of the building. Not to be outdone in the style stakes, the Cerise Restaurant lives up to its name, with cherry-red the prevailing tone providing the backdrop to a lively menu of brasserie food, full of contemporary ideas and juxtapositions that make sense. Try mussel and cod fishcake with coriander and lime coulis, perhaps, then rump of West Country lamb pepped up with Moroccan spices and apricot and mint couscous, or roasted monkfish wrapped in the salty embrace of Parma ham, with peas, thyme and chorizo. Finally, all of the flavours and textures ring true in a zesty dessert involving pineapple carpaccio with lemongrass pannacotta and pineapple and black pepper sorbet. On warm days you can eat in the secret garden in the shade of a pomegranate tree.

Chef Michael Parke **Seats** 72, Pr/dining room 35 **Times** 12-2/7-10, Closed L Sat-Sun **Prices** Starter £9-£11.50, Main £14.50-£25, Dessert £8.50-£11.50, Service optional **Wines** 70 bottles over £30, 24 bottles under £30, 11 by glass **Parking** 18 **Notes** Vegetarian available, Children welcome

Forbury's Restaurant

◉ French, European 🍷 NOTABLE WINE LIST

tel: 0118 957 4044 **1 Forbury Square RG1 3BB**
email: forburys@btconnect.com
dir: *In town centre, opposite Forbury Gardens*

Refined, confident cooking in smartly contemporary venue

Cross the small terrace and enter the smart, warm and inviting interior of Forbury's, with its floor-to-ceiling windows, white-clothed tables, spotlights in the ceiling reflected in mirrors, and young, approachable and friendly staff. The kitchen is a forward-thinking sort of place, stamping its own distinctive style on dishes, turning out pig's cheek broth with root vegetables and roasted sweetbreads, then roast cod fillet with oxtail and mustard sauce and braised red cabbage. An international element is discernible along with variations on classics: tuna céviche, say, with pickled melon and fennel alongside ballotine of foie gras with Sauternes jelly, almonds and toasted brioche, followed by sea bass fillets with salsa verde, green beans and herb-crushed potatoes, or confit duck leg with cassoulet, celeriac mash, figs and marrowbone. Desserts can vary from good old English lemon posset to peanut butter parfait with salted butter caramel.

Chef Chris Prow **Owner** Xavier Le-Bellego **Seats** 80, Pr/dining room 16 **Times** 12-2.15/6-10, Closed 26-28 Dec, 1-2 Jan, Sun **Prices** Fixed L 2 course £15-£20, Fixed D 3 course £26, Tasting menu £68, Starter £7-£11.95, Main £17.95-£29, Dessert £7.95-£9.50, Service optional 12.5% **Wines** 185 bottles over £30, 19 bottles under £30, 12 by glass **Parking** 40 **Notes** Tasting menu 6 course, Vegetarian available, Children 6 yrs+

The French Horn

◉◉ Traditional French, British V

tel: 0118 969 2204 **Sonning RG4 6TN**
email: info@thefrenchhorn.co.uk **web:** www.thefrenchhorn.co.uk
dir: *From Reading take A4 E to Sonning. Follow B478 through village over bridge, hotel on right, car park on left*

Classical French dining on the Thames

The riverside setting is a treat rain or shine, but especially in the latter, when the dining room opens up onto the terrace to give views of all the live action on the Thames. The lounge bar ensures all-weather satisfaction, though, perhaps with ducks spit-roasting over the log fire. The family-run French Horn is full of old-school charm and the service is slick and well managed. The menu looks across the Channel for its inspiration, with a classically-minded repertoire, and high prices. A starter of Orkney scallops is a dish alive with vibrant colours-vivid green from the accompanying apples (from their own orchard) and crisp shards of local bacon-with the scallops themselves nicely caramelised. Next up, braised and roasted lamb split with a chive pancake is served with a mint and date sauce, or go for one of those Aylesbury ducks, with apple sauce, sage stuffing and a rich duck sauce. For dessert, rich raspberry soufflé shows the skill in the kitchen, with the sauce poured at the table.

Chef J Diaga **Owner** The Emmanuel family **Seats** 70, Pr/dining room 24 **Times** 12-2/7-9.30, Closed 1-4 Jan **Prices** Fixed L 2 course £21, Fixed D 3 course £28, Starter £10.25-£18, Main £20-£36.50, Dessert £8.90-£11.50 **Wines** 400 bottles over £30, 6 bottles under £30, 14 by glass **Parking** 40 **Notes** Sunday L £55.75, Children welcome

Holiday Inn Reading M4 Jct 10

◉◉ Modern British, Indian

tel: 0118 944 0444 **Wharfedale Rd, Winnersh Triangle RG41 5TS**
email: reservations@hireadinghotel.com **web:** www.hireadinghotel.com
dir: *M4 junct 10/A329(M) towards Reading (E), 1st exit signed Winnersh. Left at lights into Wharfedale Rd. Hotel on left, ajacent to Winnersh Triangle Station*

Imaginative modern cooking in a smart new Holiday Inn

It's probably fair to say that the hotel's rather utilitarian moniker wouldn't have you hot-footing it down the M4 for a dinner date, but those in the know are aware that this is a brand-new flagship for the group. Designed with an impressive level of contemporary flair, it's an airy structure with a spiral-shaped chandelier on the staircase, while the Caprice dining room sports smart linen, fresh flowers, and views of landscaped gardens through full-length windows. Led by a chef with a solid country house pedigree, the skilled kitchen team delivers well-thought-out menus of modern Mediterranean-inflected ideas built on well-sourced seasonal materials. Pan-fried king scallops with pea purée, pancetta and mint foam is the sort of dish you'd love to find all along the motorway network. Follow with a three-way serving of pork (pan-fried tenderloin, slow-cooked belly and braised cheeks) supported by baby turnips, sweet potato and cider sauce, or there could be monkfish with celeriac rösti, fennel, and tomato and star anise sauce. End with something like blackberry soufflé with clotted cream ice cream.

Chef Laurent Guyon **Owner** Meridian Reading Ltd **Seats** 120, Pr/dining room 20 **Times** 12-11, All-day dining **Prices** Fixed L 2 course £19.95, Fixed D 3 course fr £23.95, Starter £7.25-£8.50, Main £16.50-£24.95, Dessert £6.25-£7.75, Service optional **Wines** 7 bottles over £30, 63 bottles under £30, 14 by glass **Parking** 130 **Notes** Sunday L, Vegetarian available, Children welcome

Malmaison Reading

◉ Modern European, International

tel: 0118 956 2300 & 956 2302 **Great Western House, 18-20 Station Rd RG1 1JX**
email: reading@malmaison.com **web:** www.malmaison.com
dir: Next to Reading station

Enlivening brasserie cooking in a restyled railway hotel

By all accounts the oldest surviving railway hotel in the world, the early Victorian property is a real charmer and makes an ideal location for the Reading outpost of the Malmaison brand. The historic past of the old girl is recognised in some decorative touches, but this being a Mal, they're done very tastefully and the overall finish is glamorous and stylish. Settle into the Malbar for a pre-dinner cocktail or head straight into the restaurant with its bare-brick walls, exposed ducting and back-to-back bench seating recalling the old railway couchettes. The brasserie-inspired menu serves up fashionable plates and traverses the globe in search of feel-good flavours; prawn cocktail to start, say, or tuna tartare with an Asian spin, or a classic moules marinière. Move on to a Black Angus steak cooked on the grill, porcini risotto or a blinged-up burger.

Chef Jan Chmelicek **Owner** Malmaison **Seats** 64, Pr/dining room 22 **Times** 12-2.30/6-10.30, Closed L Sat, D 25 Dec **Prices** Fixed L 2 course £15.95-£19.95, Fixed D 3 course £19.95-£24.95, Tasting menu £59, Starter £5-£9.50, Main £12-£36, Dessert £6-£9 **Wines** 42 bottles over £30, 16 bottles under £30, 16 by glass **Parking** NCP across road **Notes** Wine D monthly £59, Sunday L £19.95-£24.95, Vegetarian available, Children welcome

Millennium Madejski Hotel Reading

◉◉ British, International

tel: 0118 925 3500 **Madejski Stadium RG2 0FL**
email: reservations.reading@millenniumhotels.co.uk **web:** www.millenniumhotels.co.uk
dir: 1m N from M4 junct 11. 2m S from Reading town centre

Modern British dishes in a glam football hotel

The Madejski Stadium, base of Reading Football Club, shares an ultra-modern complex with this swishly smart hotel. There's a champagne bar on entry, while Cilantro is the fine-dining restaurant, its refined feel defined by a display of wines, neatly clothed tables, banquettes, subtle lighting and sharp service. The menu runs to just a handful of choices per course, the better for the kitchen to concentrate its efforts. Dishes tend to be straightforward, with little flounce or flourish, seen in succulent fillet of beef with a selection of vegetables, a rich port-based jus and a textbook version of béarnaise. Fish might be represented by braised brill with no more than cauliflower purée and glazed carrots, and bookending main courses may be scallop céviche and gravad lax with caviar and green beans with chives, and strawberry cheesecake with matching sorbet and jelly, or caramelised apple layers with vanilla ice cream.

Times 7-10, Closed 25 Dec, 1 Jan, BHs, Sun-Mon, L all week

Mya Lacarte

◉ Modern British

tel: 0118 946 3400 **5 Prospect St, Caversham RG4 8JB**
email: eat@myalacarte.co.uk
dir: M4 junct 10, continue onto A3290/A4 signed Caversham. At Crown Plaza Hotel continue over Caversham Bridge, restaurant 3rd left

Carefully sourced British produce on the high street

Mya Lacarte aims to minimise its impact on the environment by sourcing materials as locally as possible, with some customers providing surplus garden produce. It's dedicated to healthy living, so the menu flags dairy- and gluten-free dishes as well as vegetarian, and the results on the plate are deeply satisfying. Starters can be as busy as pan-fried fillet of haddock with bubble-and-squeak, a poached egg, smoked bacon and pancetta and as simple as a pork Scotch egg with mustard mayonnaise. Choose from dishes of clearly defined, complementary flavours such as braised shin of beef with mustard-enhanced mash, baby vegetables and mushrooms, or a salad of roast winter vegetables with pine nuts, sunflower seeds, parmesan shavings and basil oil. Finish on deconstructed baked Alaska with basil ice cream.

Chef Aidan Channon **Owner** Matthew Siadatan **Seats** 35, Pr/dining room 12 **Times** 12-3/5-10.30, Closed 25-26 Dec, 1 Jan, Sun (excl occasions & functions) **Prices** Prices not confirmed, Service optional **Wines** 10 bottles over £30, 20 bottles under £30, 10 by glass **Parking** NCP **Notes** Vegetarian available, Children welcome

---

SHINFIELD Map 5 SU76

L'Ortolan

◉◉◉ — see page 60 and advert on page 61

L'Ortolan 🏵️🏵️🏵️

SHINFIELD   **Map 5 SU76**

Modern French **V** 🍾 NOTABLE WINE LIST

tel: 0118 988 8500 **Church Ln RG2 9BY**
email: info@lortolan.com **web:** www.lortolan.com
dir: *From M4 junct 11 take A33 towards Basingstoke. At 1st lights turn left, after garage turn left, 1m turn right at Six Bells pub. Restaurant 1st left (follow tourist signs)*

Consummate modern French style in a former vicarage

The red-brick 17th-century vicarage sits in the leafy embrace of mature trees in immaculately-kept grounds that feels a million miles from the hubbub of Reading and the hurly burly of the M4. L'Ortolan has been a fixture in the top flight of British gastronomic destinations for a generation, offering classical cuisine of a distinctly haute nature in a very serious fine-dining environment. Today, head chef Tom Clarke offers creative, dynamic contemporary cooking with its foundations firmly rooted in classical French cuisine. Via a host of menus including a gourmand option, lighter lunchtime tasting menu and clearly focused à la carte, expect visually stunning dishes of vim and vigour. It all starts with amuse-bouche such as spot-on whitebait in a light, crisp crumb, and some trendy paprika-flavoured popcorn. A first-course confit salmon allows the fish to take centre stage alongside pickled beetroot, horseradish in ice and powder form, and a swipe of liquorice-flavoured 'paint'. Move on to a perfectly cooked piece of stone bass with a creamy smoked potato purée and various textures of Jerusalem artichoke, or a busy plate of Gressingham duck with flavours of orange and ginger. There's a vegetarian version of the gourmand menu, too, which offers up some classy veggie dishes such as hen's egg and truffle ravioli with artichokes and salsify, and a pumpkin risotto with Amaretto crumb and sage butter. Among desserts, 'toffee apple' combines an apple parfait with Muscavado sponge, salted toffee and Calvados jelly, or go for bitter chocolate tart with olive and praline ice cream. The wine list is a class act, with organic and biodynamic options, and a sommelier on hand to help you through. There are wine flight options as well.

Chef Tom Clarke **Owner** Newfee Ltd **Seats** 58, Pr/dining room 22 **Times** 12-2/7-9, Closed 2 wks Xmas-New Year, Sun-Mon **Prices** Fixed L 2 course £28-£58, Fixed D 3 course £65, Tasting menu £42-£105 **Wines** 200 bottles over £30, 14 bottles under £30, 19 by glass **Parking** 30 **Notes** Chef's table, Children 3 yrs+

SLOUGH

Map 6 SU97

Hilton London Heathrow Airport Terminal 5

British, International

tel: 01753 686860 **Poyle Rd, Colnbrook SL3 0FF**
email: heathrowairportterminal5.info@hilton.com
dir: *M25 junct 14, exit onto Horton Rd signed Poyle, Datchet. At 2nd rdbt exit onto Poyle Rd, Heathrow Terminal 5 is 400mtrs on left*

Global flavours at Terminal 5

Open all day and located on the mezzanine level of this monolithic hotel by Terminal 5. The Gallery serves up views over the bustling lobby as well as offering a long menu that aims to impress with dishes that recall an altogether more pastoral existence. 'From the farm' comes orange- and thyme-crusted rack of Casterbridge lamb served with a potato gratin, spring vegetables and Grand Marnier jus, while 'From the field' there might be Thai vegetable curry with steamed fragrant rice. Start with a good, meaty terrine spiked with apricots served with a Cumberland jelly, or a Cornish crab falafel with beetroot houmous and a pomegranate and chilli salsa. The menu takes a global viewpoint (which seems appropriate in an airport), with a 'From the sea' main course featuring a nicely cooked steamed sea bass fillet perked up with Asian greens and black bean and chilli dressing. Finish with a deconstructed blueberry cheesecake.

Chef Marcus Gregs **Owner** Rishi Sachdev **Seats** 203 **Prices** Prices not confirmed **Wines** 20 bottles over £30, 18 bottles under £30, 22 by glass **Parking** 472 **Notes** Sunday L, Vegetarian available, Children welcome

Mr Todiwala's Kitchen

Modern Pan-Asian

tel: 01753 686860 & 766482 **Poyle Rd, Colnbrook SL3 0FF**
email: heathrowairportterminal5.info@hilton.com **web:** www.hilton.com/heathrowt5
dir: *M25 junct 14, at rdbt exit Horton Rd signed Poyle, Datchet. 2nd rdbt take 2nd exit onto Poyle Rd*

Uplifting Pan-Indian cooking at Heathrow's newest terminal

The spanking-new Hilton at Terminal 5 is a classic business-oriented airport hotel, but these days there is more of an effort to provide distinctiveness in such operations, not least by means of the eating options, which is where TV chef, author and product manufacturer Cyrus Todiwala (he of Café Spice Namaste) comes in. His Kitchen brings Pan-Indian style to the scene in a clinically white atmosphere of lime-washed floors and café-style furnishing, with a large wheeled elephant to greet you. Highly spiced, vividly seasoned food is the perfect antidote to corporate anonymity, and is delivered here in the form of tandoori-grilled scallops with their corals alongside hotly spiced peppers and tomato, crab sizzled in mustard seeds and chilli with grated coconut, and mains such as lamb shank bhuna with caramelised onions and yogurt, pomfret glazed in green coconut chutney and steamed in a banana leaf, and venison tikka singing with star anise and fennel. Crème brûlée is given thrilling aromatic uplift with saffron, cardamom and ginger.

Chef Cyrus Todiwala, Arun Dev **Owner** Shiva Hotels, Cyrus Todiwala **Seats** 70 **Times** 6-10.30, Closed Xmas, Sun **Prices** Prices not confirmed **Wines** 10 bottles over £30, 11 bottles under £30, 10 by glass **Parking** 480 **Notes** Vegetarian available, Children welcome

WHITE WALTHAM
Map 5 SU87

The Beehive
◉◉ British NEW

tel: 01628 822877 **Waltham Rd SL6 3SH**
email: reservations@thebeehivewhitewaltham.com
dir: *M4 junct 8/9, follow signs White Waltham. Located opposite cricket grounds*

Gimmick-free cooking in a village local

With the cricket ground opposite, The Beehive is the epitome of the English village pub. Filling the generous grassed space between the pub itself and the road are tables and benches-an ideal spot for shouting 'Howzat!'. The bar is very much for drinkers, while the restaurant area with leather chairs interspersed among the wooden dining furniture is decorated with an eclectic collection of artworks. A bar menu, daily changing lunch and dinner menus, and a specials board reveal season-driven, modern British dishes known for their gimmick-free, 'less is more' simplicity. If a starter of Dorset snails with garlic butter, Gorgonzola and grilled sourdough wouldn't be your choice, you'll easily find an alternative, such as English asparagus with poached egg, monk's beard, parmesan and pea shoots. Follow with calves' liver, cooked pink, with crisp bacon, soft and sweet melted onions and mash, or roast Cornish turbot with cockles, clams and purple sprouting broccoli. Yorkshire rhubarb trifle topped with vanilla custard, cream, almonds and berries looks especially scrumptious in its glass tumbler.

Chef Dominic Chapman **Owner** Dominic Chapman **Seats** 75
Times 12-2.30/6-9.30, Closed 25-26 Dec, D Sun **Prices** Starter £6.50-£9.95, Main £12.95-£19.95, Dessert £4.95-£6.50 **Wines** 14 bottles over £30, 12 bottles under £30, 12 by glass **Parking** 30 **Notes** Sunday L £18.95-£19.95, Vegetarian available, Children welcome

WINDSOR
Map 6 SU97

The Greene Oak
◉ Modern British

tel: 01753 864294 **Oakley Green SL4 5UW**
email: info@thegreeneoak.co.uk
dir: *Phone for directions*

Modern pub dining in a welcoming country inn

Very much a dining pub, the Greene Oak is a charming old place with bright, homely decor and cheerful staff who keep it all ticking along nicely. There are splashes of green paintwork to maintain a verdant theme, plus polished flagstones, rustic wooden tables and comfy banquettes scattered with colourful cushions. The kitchen makes good use of local seasonal ingredients to deliver a menu that continually evolves and is supported by daily specials, with the focus on gently contemporary British- and European-inspired ideas. A starter of salt-cod croquettes arrives in the company of pea purée, mint aïoli and a quail's egg, with main-course pan-roasted sea trout to follow, or a succulent confit pork belly in an earthy combo with trompette mushrooms and grain mustard sauce. End on a tropical note with coconut pannacotta, pineapple carpaccio and spiced pineapple sorbet. Terrace tables fill up fast on warm days.

Times 12-2.15/6-9.15

Macdonald Windsor Hotel
◉ Scottish, Modern British

tel: 01753 483100 **23 High St SL4 1LH**
email: gm.windsor@macdonaldwindsor.co.uk **web:** www.macdonaldhotels.co.uk
dir: *M4 junct 6 A355, take A332, rdbt 1st exit signed town centre. In 0.7m turn left into Bachelors Acre*

Scottish (and other) steak club opposite Windsor Castle

A contemporary townhouse hotel opposite the castle, offering ringside views of the changing of the guard, the Windsor is on hand to take in a good proportion of the tourist trade. Its dining room always had a yen for a Scottish accent, and the love-affair is now fully consummated in its transformation to the Scottish Steak Club. Not that all the steak is Scottish — some comes from the US, and there's Argentinian Black Angus too — but the charcoal-grilling of sirloins, rib-eyes and fillets has been refined to a high pitch, and all the traditional accompaniments are in evidence, including peppercorn, béarnaise, Diane, and Dunsyre Blue cheese sauces. Top and tail with a plate of dressed smoked salmon and deep-filled apple and cinnamon pie with clotted cream, and you'll be all set up for a wander along the ramparts.

Chef Sanobia Cutino **Owner** Macdonald Hotels **Seats** 70, Pr/dining room 24
Times 7am-10pm, All-day dining **Prices** Tasting menu £39.50-£45, Starter £6.50-£10.95, Main £11.50-£28.50, Dessert £3-£12.50, Service optional **Wines** 34 bottles over £30, 13 bottles under £30, 14 by glass **Parking** 30, Pre-booked and chargeable **Notes** ALC also Sun, Scottish Steak Club menu, Sunday L £14.95-£23, Vegetarian available, Children welcome

Mercure Windsor Castle Hotel
◉ Modern British

tel: 01753 851557 **18 High St SL4 1LJ**
email: h6618@accor.com **web:** www.mercure.com
dir: *M25 junct 13 take A308 towards town centre then onto B470 to High St. M4 junct 6 towards A332, at rdbt first exit into Clarence Rd, left at lights to High St*

British cooking in the vicinity of the Queen's residence

Sitting directly opposite the Royal Guildhall, with the Queen's Berkshire bolt hole on hand, the hotel named after the latter could hardly be better positioned. It's an originally Tudor building with a balcony and patriotic flagpoles, and a large dining room called 18. The kitchen's modern British fare includes the likes of scallops and cauliflower purée with baby carrots to start, and main courses such as cod with peperonata and chickpeas, corn-fed chicken with mushrooms in red wine sauce, or decent lamb chump with Anna potatoes and chunks of celeriac in a rich lamb jus, garnished with thoughtfully placed spots of purée. Rhubarb crumble looks endearingly homely, and comes with its own sorbet and a scattering of toasted almonds. The 'British' cheese selection is a good one, if Irish patrons will forgive the renationalising of Cashel Blue.

Times 12-2.30/6.30-9.45

Oakley Court Hotel

@@ Modern British V

tel: 01753 609988 **Windsor Rd, Water Oakley SL4 5UR**
email: guestrelations@oakleycourthotel.co.uk **web:** www.oakleycourt.co.uk
dir: M4 junct 6 to Windsor. At rdbt right onto A308. Hotel 2.5m on right

Creative modern European cooking amid Gothic extravagance

The Victorians left the British Isles strewn with a magnificent legacy of Gothic castles. Oakley Court is a prime example, with turrets, stepped gables and 37 acres of well-tended grounds. As you would expect in a hotel of this standing, there's golf, tennis and swimming on tap, or pampering in the treatment rooms. The half-panelled dining room, with its crisply clothed tables and formal service, is the place to head to for creative modern British cooking built on diligently-sourced local ingredients. The contemporary classic pairing of shellfish and pig is celebrated in an opener combining caramelised scallops with Ibérico ham, Cornish crab, and fresh peas, before a big-hearted main course partnering roast rib-eye with the robust flavours of confit oxtail, pan-fried ceps, Maxim potatoes and a meaty jus. Fish might be Loch Duart salmon served with a stew of clams and mussels, with smoked tomato butter and lemon chard potatoes. Finish with a white chocolate and peanut mousse with salted caramel, chocolate soil and peanut sugar.

Chef Damian Broom **Owner** Vinyl Space Ltd **Seats** 28 **Times** 6.30-9.30, Closed Xmas, New Year, Sun-Mon, L all week **Prices** Prices not confirmed **Wines** 29 bottles over £30, 14 bottles under £30, 10 by glass **Parking** 200 **Notes** Children 12 yrs+

Sir Christopher Wren Hotel and Spa

@ Modern British

tel: 01753 442400 **Thames St SL4 1PX**
email: wrens@sarova.co.uk **web:** www.sirchristopherwren.co.uk
dir: M4 junct 6, 1st exit from relief road, follow signs to Windsor, 1st major exit on left, turn left at lights

Modern cooking by the River Thames

Sir Christopher Wren is reputed to have overseen the completion of Windsor's Guildhall and to have worked on the Castle's State Rooms, and is honoured here by this Thames-side hotel consisting of several buildings clustered around a cobbled street. In the restaurant, where large windows and mirrors allow diners to enjoy the river traffic, the menu is an appealingly varied slate of contemporary ideas. Starters take in perfectly cooked scallops complemented by spicy tomato salsa and a balsamic reduction, accompanied by pea shoots, as well as a duo of duck terrine (foie gras and leg) with spiced plums and Grand Marnier dressing. To follow there might be lamb noisette in a herby broth with braised baby gem and fondant potato, or darne of salmon with marinated peppers, aubergine and courgette, lime-mashed potatoes and salsa verde. End with an attractive-looking pudding like a trio of pannacottas (vanilla, chocolate and strawberry).

Chef Aime Zbinden **Owner** Sarova Hotels **Seats** 65, Pr/dining room 100 **Times** 12.30-2.30/6.30-10 **Prices** Starter £6.50-£10.50, Main £15.50-£24.50, Dessert £6-£10, Service optional 15% **Wines** 20 bottles over £30, 35 bottles under £30, 10 by glass **Parking** 14, Pre-bookable only, Riverside train station **Notes** Pre-theatre D, Sunday L £20-£26, Vegetarian available, Children welcome

WOKINGHAM Map 5 SU86

Miltons Restaurant

@ British, European NEW

tel: 0118 989 5100 & 989 5166 **Cantley House Hotel, Milton Rd RG40 5QG**
email: info@miltonsrestaurant.co.uk **web:** www.miltonsrestaurant.co.uk
dir: Phone for directions

A rustic-chic modern barn brasserie

The Cantley House Hotel has been conjured out of a 17th-century barn, with Miltons as its eatery. It's a split-level space done in rustic chic, with wood-panelled dividers, walls in bleached slatted wood or naked brick, and a jumble of furniture at bare-topped tables. Modern brasserie food is the name of the game, with a seasonally changing menu of simple dishes that nonetheless have plenty to say for themselves. Grilled sardines with sweet red pepper escabèche is an appetising Mediterranean beginner, ham hock and foie gras terrine with pickled walnuts a nice balance of earthy and refined flavours. At main, precise timing and seasoning distinguishes pan-roasted lamb rump with excellent roasted veg, sauced with red wine and mustard seeds, while fish might be monkfish with gnocchi and shaved Serrano ham in a parsleyed parmesan emulsion. Sticky toffee pudding with cream takes a miraculously light approach to the old favourite, or else go for a few of the blue-riband British cheeses.

Chef Andreas Barauskas **Owner** Jon Scott-Maxwell **Seats** 60, Pr/dining room 34 **Times** 12.30-2.30/6.30-10 **Prices** Fixed L 2 course £9.95-£14.50, Fixed D 3 course £29, Starter £5.50-£8.50, Main £16.50-£22.50, Dessert £4.50-£6, Service optional 12.5% **Wines** 16 bottles over £30, 23 bottles under £30, 12 by glass **Parking** 70 **Notes** Sunday L £17.55-£22.50, Vegetarian available

BRISTOL

BRISTOL Map 4 ST57

The Avon Gorge Hotel

@ Modern British

tel: 0117 973 8955 **Sion Hill, Clifton BS8 4LD**
email: rooms@theavongorge.com **web:** www.theavongorge.com
dir: From S: M5 junct 19, A369 to Clifton Toll, over suspension bridge, 1st right into Sion Hill. From N: M5 junct 18A, A4 to Bristol, under suspension bridge, follow signs to bridge, exit Sion Hill

Splendid Clifton location and modern British cooking

Fans of Brunel's landmark suspension bridge couldn't ask for a better vantage point to take in his handiwork than this Victorian hotel's Bridge Café overlooking the gorge and the glorious bridge. Seats on the terrace are hotly contested on fine days, but the views are the same throughout the restaurant's floor-to-ceiling windows whatever the weather. Burgers (lamb with tomato and rosemary focaccia and cucumber and harissa yogurt, anyone?) and steaks with béarnaise or venison steak glazed with port, juniper and redcurrant, and timeless ideas such as Butcombe beer-battered fish and chips, broaden the appeal of an inventive, broadly modern British menu that kicks off with smoked duck terrine with home-made chutney and toasted brioche. Main-course fish options deliver herb-crusted pollock fillet with crayfish and saffron risotto and lemon oil, and to finish, there's a retro classic in the form of peach Melba.

Chef Marcus Bradley **Owner** Swire Hotels **Seats** 50, Pr/dining room 20 **Times** 12-4/6-10 **Prices** Prices not confirmed **Wines** 21 bottles under £30, 24 by glass **Parking** 25 **Notes** Sunday L, Vegetarian available, Children welcome

BRISTOL *continued*

Berwick Lodge

◎◎ Modern British

tel: 0117 958 1590 **Berwick Dr, Henbury BS10 7TD**
email: info@berwicklodge.co.uk **web:** www.berwicklodge.co.uk
dir: *M5 junct 17, A4018 (Westbury-on-Trym). At 2nd rdbt 1st left (Westbury-on-Trym). At next rdbt double back on dual carriageway (signed M5 (M4)). Left after brown Clifton RFC sign. At x-rds straight on, follow Berwick Lodge signs*

Bold contemporary dining in a boutique manor house

The Victorian gent who built this manor house back in the 1890s picked a good spot close to Bristol, and the house remains in open countryside to this day, with the M5 on hand to ease access for those new-fangled mechanised horseless carriages. Surrounded by 18 acres of gardens and woodland, the manor has a classically-inspired boutique finish in its bedrooms and public spaces, including the restaurant, Hattua, which is named after a Bronze Age World Heritage site in Turkey. It's a stylish and civilised spot. The kitchen turns out creative modern dishes which look impressive on the plate – lots of scattered flowers and micro-herbs – and flavours and textures are thoughtfully balanced. A meltingly tender piece of duck liver arrives with punchy rhubarb to cut through the delicious richness of the meat, plus some spicy ginger bread, and main-course cod comes in the trendy company of tender pork cheek. There's a tasting menu if you fancy the culinary works, and even a cookery school in the former stables where you can pick up a few tips.

Chef Paul O'Neill **Owner** S & F Arikan **Seats** 80, Pr/dining room 16
Times 12-2.30/6.30-10, Closed D Sun **Prices** Fixed L 2 course £23, Fixed D 3 course £26.50, Starter £10-£12, Main £19-£24, Dessert £9 **Wines** 350 bottles over £30, 30 bottles under £30, 13 by glass **Parking** 100 **Notes** Sunday L, Vegetarian available, Children welcome

BEST WESTERN Henbury Lodge Hotel

◎◎ Modern British

tel: 0117 950 2615 **Station Rd, Henbury BS10 7QQ**
email: info@henburyhotel.com **web:** www.henburyhotel.com
dir: *M5 junct 17/A4018 towards city centre, 3rd rdbt right into Crow Ln. At end turn right, hotel 200mtrs on right*

Country-house style at Edmund Burke's old place

Edmund Burke, statesman and philosopher, lived at Henbury when he was MP for Bristol, when the surrounding vista from his favourite window of the house was one of open fields. Bristol itself presses rather closer these days, but the house retains the appealing feel of a Georgian country mansion nonetheless, with its portico entrance, elegant interiors and a many-mirrored dining room, the Blaise restaurant, done in pale primrose. French windows lead to a terrace and walled garden, and the cooking has more than a little of the country-house style about it. Start with a sauté of chicken livers and smoked bacon in a salad with caramelised hazelnuts, prior to a well-judged main course of crisp-skinned haddock with two-tone carrots (yellow and purple), seared duck breast with roast plums in port, or the signature rabbit leg filled with black pudding and apple, wrapped in Parma ham, on leeks in grain mustard sauce. For dessert, there could scarcely be anything more comforting than a slab of luxuriously gooey treacle tart with mascarpone and an unusual but effective marmalade ice cream.

Chef Paul Bullard **Owner** Tim & Rosalind Forester **Seats** 22, Pr/dining room 12
Times 7-10, Closed Xmas-New Year, Sun, L all week **Prices** Fixed D 3 course £25.95-£29.95, Service optional 10% **Wines** 1 bottle over £30, 16 bottles under £30, 14 by glass **Parking** 20 **Notes** Vegetarian available, Children welcome

Bordeaux Quay

◎ Modern European

tel: 0117 943 1200 **V-Shed, Canons Way BS1 5UH**
email: info@bordeaux-quay.co.uk
dir: *Canons Rd off the A4, beyond Millennium Square car park*

Modern warehouse conversion covering all bases on the waterfront

This dynamic set up on Bristol's waterfront takes in a restaurant, brasserie, bar, deli, bakery and cookery school in a stylishly redeveloped dockland warehouse. The operation's eco-credentials bring a strong commitment to sustainability and sourcing local, preferably organic, materials. It brings them together in well-conceived, daily-changing menus of modern European ideas. The restaurant is on the first floor, with elegant table settings and fine wood alongside industrial pipe work, or you might opt for an alfresco meal on the terrace of the brasserie downstairs. Start with squid ink risotto with smoked haddock and a quail's egg, before moving on to salt marsh lamb (roasted and served with crispy bonbon, chermoula and fried polenta), or leek and saffron tart with Jerusalem artichokes, bitter leaves and toasted hazelnuts. To finish, pear tarte Tatin comes in the creative company of star anise and molasses parfait.

Chef Alex Murray, Andy Pole **Owner** Alex & Luke Murray **Seats** 90, Pr/dining room 28
Times 12-10.30, All-day dining, Closed Xmas **Prices** Fixed D 3 course £19.50, Starter £6.50-£10, Main £12.50-£22.50, Dessert £7.50-£9.50 **Wines** 40 bottles over £30, 40 bottles under £30, 30 by glass **Parking** Millennium Sq **Notes** Breakfast from 8am Mon-Fri, 9am Sat-Sun, Sunday L £13.50-£20.50, Vegetarian available, Children welcome

Casamia Restaurant

◎◎◎◎ – *see opposite*

Glass Boat Restaurant

◎◎ Modern French

tel: 0117 929 0704 **Welsh Back BS1 4SB**
email: bookings@glassboat.co.uk
dir: *Moored below Bristol Bridge in the old centre of Bristol*

Modern bistro fare on a glamorous barge

Given the name, you might feel short changed if it wasn't, but the venue is indeed a boat with vast expanses of glass giving views over the water. The 1920s barge once earned its crust along the Severn Estuary but is now moored up in the docks in the heart of the city, converted to a decidedly handsome restaurant with walnut floors, and a beautiful marble bar at the bow end. You may need your sea legs if the current is high, but the ambience is too glamorous to miss for the sake of a bit of bobbing about. The menu offers modern bistro fare with plenty of imagination, plying a course from chicken liver parfait with onion jam, or crispy frogs' legs with wild garlic risotto, to chicken suprême with celeriac, Savoy cabbage with lardons and honey-roasted swede. Seafood dishes are full of appeal too – perhaps a creamy bourride of monkfish and mussels. Finish with zesty lemon tart with crème fraîche. Theatre-goers can enjoy a good-value supper until 7pm.

Times 12-2.30/5.30-10.30, Closed 24-26 Dec, 1-10 Jan, L Mon, D Sun

Casamia Restaurant ✿✿✿✿

BRISTOL

Map 4 ST57

Modern British V

tel: 0117 959 2884 **38 High St, Westbury Village, Westbury-on-Trym BS9 3DZ**
email: info@casamiarestaurant.co.uk
dir: *Close to Westbury College Gatehouse*

Exciting progressive cooking following the seasons

Peter and Jonray Sanchez-Iglesias are so dedicated to the seasons that they change the decor of their restaurant to fit the mood of the time of year. This level of attention to detail and enthusiasm for culinary ways has taken the two brothers on a journey to the very top. They took over their parents' place in the middle of the noughties as an Italian restaurant serving a regular menu, but a passion for modern cooking styles and finely tuned technical abilities transformed it into one of the best restaurants in the UK. It all takes place behind a wrought iron gate that leads down a little alleyway to the restaurant where the dining room is tweaked to reflect the changing seasons. A homely and gently contemporary space gives no clue as to the culinary fireworks to follow in an all-encompassing dining experience where the kitchen staff join the waiters in delivering food to the tables, dishes are described with passion, and there's frequently a touch of theatre to the presentation. Ordering is a piece of cake as the set-up is a no-choice tasting menu, including a shorter set lunch version if required, and a special one for the lucky people sat at the chef's table. The menu descriptions give little away, but rest assured the full gamut of modern techniques are called upon, every flavour is precisely and explosively delivered, and it's all going to taste jolly nice. The ten or so courses of the winter menu might take you from a winter salad with goats' cheese via fallow deer with parsnip to a sweet finisher of blood orange and rosemary. Every one of the succession of dishes in various colours and styles looks positively glorious. From the spring menu, Cornish squid is served up with the gentle aromas of wild garlic, and salt marsh lamb in the company of a variety of zingy sea herbs, while the sweet courses confirm the technical know-how and sound judgement of the team in the kitchen (if variations of rhubarb is anything to go by). A wine flight ensures the balance and harmony of each dish is enhanced further.

Chef Peter & Jonray Sanchez-Iglesias **Owner** The Sanchez-Iglesias family **Seats** 40, Pr/dining room 6
Times 12-2/6-9.30, Closed Xmas, New Year, BHs, Sun-Mon
Prices Tasting menu £68-£125, Service optional **Wines** 34 bottles over £30, 12 bottles under £30, 10 by glass **Parking** On street **Notes** Children welcome

BRISTOL *continued*

Goldbrick House

Modern British

tel: 0117 945 1950 **69 Park St BS1 5PB**
email: info@goldbrickhouse.co.uk
dir: *M32, follow signs for city centre. Left side of Park St, going up the hill towards museum*

Modern brasserie cooking in an all-things-to-all-comers venue

You're not exactly stuck for choice when it comes to eating and drinking options at Goldbrick House. In a converted pair of conjoined Georgian townhouses, an informal all-day café/bar, a champagne and cocktail bar, a main restaurant and now the Orangery, a new extension, appear to have all bases covered. That last, formerly the Terrace, is a light-filled space with many windows and bright violet seating, while the main restaurant goes for a mustard-hued look, with Italian chandeliers and large gilt-framed mirrors. Christian Wragg has taken over in the kitchens, but maintains Goldbrick's modern brasserie style in starters such as lamb arancini in redcurrant dressing with minty salad, and mains that mine the heritage cookbook for beef bourguignon with whipped truffle mash, herbed chicken breast with gnocchi and roasted onions, or grilled lemon sole in shellfish broth topped with puff pastry. Fun specials include the de rigueur Scotch egg made with black pudding, and a Bloody Mary version of prawn cocktail, while a nostalgic return to childhood produces finishers like peanut butter crème brûlée with home-made Jammy Dodgers.

Chef Christian Wragg **Owner** Dougal Templeton, Alex Reilley, Mike Bennett **Seats** 200, Pr/dining room 40 **Times** 12-10.30, All-day dining, Closed 24-26 Dec, 1 Jan, Sun **Prices** Fixed L 2 course £12, Starter £5.25-£7.50, Main £9.95-£21.95, Dessert £4.50-£5.75 **Wines** 12 bottles over £30, 15 bottles under £30, 7 by glass **Parking** On street, NCP **Notes** Early D menu 5.30-6.45pm, Vegetarian available, Children welcome

Hotel du Vin Bristol

French NOTABLE WINE LIST

tel: 0117 9255577 **The Sugar House, Narrow Lewins Mead BS1 2NU**
email: info.bristol@hotelduvin.com **web:** www.hotelduvin.com
dir: *From M4 junct 19, M32 into Bristol. At rdbt take 1st exit & follow main road to next rdbt. Turn onto other side of carriageway, hotel 200yds on right*

Simple and successful brasserie cooking with first-rate wines

There's no shortage of period properties in Bristol, reflecting its time as a one-time powerhouse of Britain's trading empire, and the good folk at HdV found a good one in the form of this former sugar warehouse close to the waterfront. With its loft-style bedrooms, loungey bar and casual French-inspired bistro (which really does look the part, right down to faux nicotine stains on the ceiling), the Bristol address is buzzy and easy-going. Factor in the world class wine list, and you've got a compelling package. The bilingual menu deals in classic stuff such as steak tartare or French onion soup, and the kitchen tackles a Comté soufflé with considerable success. Among main courses, moules et frites and calves' liver and bacon are straight-up options, with duck shepherd's pie offering something a little off-piste. Excellent pastry helps a treacle tart hit the spot, and the impressive wine list isn't all about France.

Chef Marcus Lang **Owner** KSL **Seats** 85, Pr/dining room 72
Times 12-2.30/5.30-10.30, Closed L 31 Dec **Prices** Fixed L 2 course £16.95, Fixed D 3 course £19.95, Starter £6.50-£11.50, Main £14.95-£60, Dessert £6.95-£9.50 **Wines** 332 bottles over £30, 18 bottles under £30, 23 by glass **Parking** 8, NCP Rupert St **Notes** Sunday L £24.95, Vegetarian available, Children welcome

No.4 Clifton Village

Modern European

tel: 0117 970 6869 **4 Rodney Place, Clifton BS8 4HY**
email: bookings@no4cliftonvillage.co.uk **web:** www.no4cliftonvillage.co.uk
dir: *M5 junct 19, follow signs across Clifton Bridge. At mini rdbt turn onto Clifton Down Rd. Hotel 150yds on right*

Straightforward bistro cooking with garden views

The Rodney is a Georgian townhouse hotel in refined Clifton village, a little to the east of the Avon. In addition to its main dining room, it also offers this comfortably appointed bistro room overlooking a walled garden. With exposed stone walls, quirky pictures and a light-fixture that looks like a collection of jam jars, it makes an inspired setting for utterly straightforward bistro food that delivers plenty of punch. Start with toasted goats' cheese served with beetroot purée, walnuts and apple jelly, or smoked salmon with fennel salad and pineapple-chilli chutney. Mains might offer seasonal game such as pheasant with puréed cauliflower, salt-baked beetroot and sautéed spinach, or cod with sweet potatoes and bacon in balsamic vinaigrette. Gooseberry crunch cheesecake makes a change, or there could be classic pear frangipane tart with apple syrup and cream. Make up a party of 20 or more, and a barbecue menu is yours for the asking.

Chef David Jones **Owner** Hilary Lawson **Seats** 36, Pr/dining room 50
Times 6-10, Closed 25 Dec-2 Jan, Sun, L all week **Prices** Starter £4.50-£8, Main £9-£18, Dessert £4.50-£8 **Wines** 5 bottles over £30, 18 bottles under £30, 12 by glass **Parking** On street **Notes** Afternoon tea £15, Vegetarian available, Children welcome

The Ox

Modern British **NEW**

tel: 0117 922 1001 **The Basement, 43 Corn St BS1 1HT**
email: info@theoxbristol.com
dir: *Exit M32 towards City centre A38, Baldwin St B4053. Park at Princes St NCP. 100mtrs down from Bristol Register Office*

Steaks and more in an atmospheric basement

The Georgian Commercial Rooms has had many roles since its heyday as a gathering place for local business folk. There's a Wetherspoon pub occupying the ground floor these days, but head on down to the basement – a one-time bank vault – and you'll find a restaurant that is a cut above. The old boys of yesteryear would have admired the decor, with its oak panels, ox blood leather seats and murals – and surely they'd have appreciated the red blooded menu too, for the Ox focuses on steaks (rib-eye, sirloin, rib on the bone, fillet etc) all served with triple-cooked chips and a choice of sauce. There's a lot more besides, including trendy small plates of hickory-smoked ribs and squid salad, plus a charcuterie board to share, and alternative main courses run to fishcakes and veggie cannelloni. Finish with warm caramelised rice pudding with boozy prunes and apple compôte.

Chef Todd Francis **Owner** Nathan Lee, Kevin Stokes, Jason Mead **Seats** 80
Times 12-2.30/5-10.30, Closed Xmas, L Mon-Wed, Sat, D Sun **Prices** Fixed L 2 course £14, Starter £3.50-£7.50, Main £12.50-£28, Dessert £5-£8 **Wines** 36 bottles over £30, 11 bottles under £30, 8 by glass **Parking** NCP Prince St, NCP Trenchard **Notes** Sharing menu £32-£35, Early bird steak & wine Mon-Sat 5-7pm, Sunday L £12.50-£19, Vegetarian available, Children welcome

The Pump House

◉◉ Modern British 🍷 NOTABLE WINE LIST

tel: 0117 927 2229 **Merchants Rd, Hotwells BS8 4PZ**
email: info@the-pumphouse.com web: www.the-pumphouse.com
dir: A4 Clevedon to city centre, left before swing bridge

Thriving dockside pub-restaurant with a serious approach to food

Chef-proprietor Toby Gritten has made great use of the hydraulic pumping station down on the waterside where the docks meet the River Avon to create a buzzy gastro-pub and restaurant. You can eat downstairs in the pub part of the operation, outside by the water's edge, or head upstairs to the dinner-only mezzanine for a little more refinement and a little less hubbub. Gritten likes to bang the drum for local produce, including foraged materials, and doesn't cut corners, making everything from bread to chutneys in-house. Depending on the season, you might start with seared Bath chap with apple, celeriac and a fried quail's egg, or game terrine with forced rhubarb and chicory. This is robust and hearty stuff, but not without refinement. Main-course venison steak with root vegetables and smoked bone marrow is one way to go, but there's also the likes of roast gurnard with walnuts, parsley and brown shrimps. End on a lemon and lime theme with lemon croquette, kaffir lime leaves and sorbet, and toasted marshmallow.

Chef Toby Gritten Owner Toby Gritten, Dan Obern Seats 50
Times 12-3.30/6.30-9.30, Closed 25 Dec, Mon-Wed, L Thu, D Sun Prices Fixed L 2

course £15, Fixed D 3 course £17.50, Tasting menu £40-£56, Starter £4.50-£8.50, Main £15-£21.50, Dessert £5.50-£7.50, Service optional 10% Wines 138 bottles over £30, 47 bottles under £30, 24 by glass Parking 20 Notes Tasting menu 5/8 course, Sunday L £14-£18.50, Vegetarian available, Children welcome

riverstation

◉ Modern European 🍷 NOTABLE WINE LIST

tel: 0117 914 4434 & 914 5560 **The Grove BS1 4RB**
email: relax@riverstation.co.uk web: www.riverstation.co.uk
dir: On harbour side in central Bristol between St Mary Redcliffe church & Arnolfini

Buzzy riverside setting and switched-on brasserie food

Converted from a river police station (the clue's in the name), this lively eatery is glazed from top to bottom to make the most of the harbour views, whether you're in the buzzy café-bar at water level or the cool industrial-chic restaurant on the first floor. Inspiration is drawn from far and wide to create bright, up-to-date dishes rooted in good culinary sense. Thus maple-smoked Wagyu beef is matched with horseradish cream and a watercress, radish and asparagus salad, ahead of duck breast with panisse (fried chick-pea flour cake), spring greens and roasted peach. To finish, warm mascarpone and honey soufflé cheesecake with raspberry sorbet and a poppy seed tuile hits the spot. The kitchen is serious about its ingredients-churning its own butter, baking bread and smoking fish in-house-so you can rest assured that it's all based on top-notch seasonal materials.

Chef Toru Yanada Owner J Payne Seats 120, Pr/dining room 30
Times 12-2.30/6-10.30, Closed 24-26 Dec, D Sun Prices Fixed L 2 course fr £13.50, Fixed D 3 course fr £19, Starter £5.50-£8.50, Main £15.50-£20, Dessert £5.50-£6.50, Service optional Wines 38 bottles over £30, 25 bottles under £30, 15 by glass Parking Pay & display, parking opposite (meter) Notes Pre-theatre £10 Mon-Fri 6-7.15pm, Fixed D 2/3 course Mon-Fri, Sunday L £18-£22, Vegetarian available, Children welcome

BRISTOL *continued*

Second Floor Restaurant

◎◎ Modern European ▮NOTABLE WINE LIST

tel: 0117 961 8898 **Harvey Nichols, 27 Philadelphia St, Quakers Friars BS1 3BZ**
email: Reception.Bristol@harveynichols.com
dir: *Phone for directions*

Lively modern cooking on the top floor

Other Harvey Nics branches may rise higher (the second-floor home of the restaurant here is the top layer), but only Bristol's Broadmead store overlooks the old Dominican friary of Quakers Friars and the shopping entrepôt of Cabot Circus. Done in gentle umbers and beiges, the dining room is a supremely relaxing place, where the kitchen turns out a menu of lively modern British food. Tea-smoked Creedy Carver duck breast with roast beetroot, poached apple and beetroot jelly makes an attention-seeking opener, or you may be pleasantly surprised by the depth of flavour conjured out of potato and kale soup slicked with chorizo oil. A vegetarian main with broad appeal comes in the form of twice-baked Westcombe Cheddar soufflé with German-style schupfen noodles and pickled oyster mushrooms, or there could be roast sea bass with squid-ink linguini in a cucumber and horseradish emulsion sauce, topped with a crisp-fried oyster. Finish with rhubarb and custard, garnished with rhubarb jelly and mini macaroons, or a plate of West Country and Welsh cheeses with home-made oatcakes and chutney. There are some pretty good wines on offer too.

Chef Louise McCrimmon **Owner** Harvey Nichols **Seats** 60, Pr/dining room 10 **Times** 12-3/6-10, Closed 25 Dec, 1 Jan, Etr Sun, D Sun-Mon **Prices** Fixed L 2 course £17, Fixed D 3 course £20, Starter £7-£8.50, Main £20-£25, Dessert £5-£7 **Wines** 310 bottles over £30, 43 bottles under £30, 29 by glass **Parking** NCP/Cabot Circus car park **Notes** Sun brunch 11-4, Afternoon tea 3-5, Vegetarian available, Children welcome

The Spiny Lobster

◎ Mediterranean, Seafood

tel: 0117 973 7384 **128 Whiteladies Rd, Clifton BS8 2RS**
email: enquiries@rockfishgrill.co.uk
dir: *From city centre follow signs for Clifton, restaurant halfway along Whiteladies Rd*

Fish and seafood presented fresh and simple

Rebranded from its former incarnation as the Rockfish Grill, Mitch Tonks' seafood brasserie and fish market maintains a rigorous commitment to freshness and simplicity, using fish and shellfish mostly landed by the Brixham boats. The refurbished room sports racing-green buttoned banquettes, linen-clothed tables and piscine artwork, and willing, friendly staff make the formula a winning one. The simple approach with top-class materials slapped onto a charcoal-burning Josper grill works wonders with scallops roasted with citrus and cucumber, then mains such as hake served with romesco sauce, John Dory with tomato and basil, or lemon sole with anchovy and rosemary. Puddings stick to the straightforward brief with the likes of chocolate tart with honey and crème fraîche.

Times 12-2.30/6-10.30, Closed 25 Dec, 1 Jan, Sun-Mon

BUCKINGHAMSHIRE

AMERSHAM   Map 6 SU99

The Artichoke

◎◎◎ – *see opposite*

The Crown

◎ Modern British

tel: 01494 721541 **16 High St HP7 0DH**
email: reception@thecrownamersham.com **web:** www.thecrownamersham.com
dir: *M40 junct 2 onto A355, continue to Amersham. Onto Gore Hill, left into The Broadway*

Good eating in a modernised coaching inn

This 16th-century timber-framed coaching inn has brushed up nicely after a stylish makeover, and now presents an eclectic rustic-chic look to its 21st-century visitors, mixing ancient period character with a clean-cut modern style. There are Tudor beams, inglenook fireplaces and sloping floors, offset by trendy fabrics and chunky bare wood tables. The unfussy cooking aims for big-hearted natural flavours, serving seared scallops as an opener with crispy cauliflower and a punchy currant and peppercorn vinaigrette, or you might go for home-made balls of hot and crispy breadcrumbed brawn served with piccalilli. Main course brings a well-crafted take on chicken Kiev with truffle butter, braised wing, garlic purée, crispy potatoes and broccoli, while gilt head bream could get a full-flavoured accompaniment of lemon thyme salsify, wild mushrooms, samphire, pommes Anna and red wine jus. After all that richness, crème brûlée gets a lift from lemon verbena, rhubarb and champagne sorbet, and lemon and black pepper shortbread.

Chef Emma Carrier **Owner** Old Amersham Hotels **Seats** 24, Pr/dining room 36 **Times** 12-3/6-9.30 **Prices** Prices not confirmed **Wines** 32 bottles over £30, 23 bottles under £30, 10 by glass **Parking** 35 **Notes** Afternoon tea, Sunday L, Vegetarian available, Children welcome

Gilbey's Restaurant

◎◎ Modern British

tel: 01494 727242 **1 Market Square HP7 0DF**
email: oldamersham@gilbeygroup.com
dir: *M40 junct 2, A355 exit Beaconsfield/Amersham*

Imaginative modern cooking in a former school building

A former grammar school building dating from the 17th century is the setting for Gilbey's Old Amersham restaurant and serves its local clientele as a textbook reliable neighbourhood bistro. There are low ceilings, wood flooring and cheerful art on sky-blue walls to create an ambience of stylish, intimate rusticity, while the friendly staff contribute much to the congenial atmosphere that pervades the place. The kitchen makes a virtue of simplicity, working an intelligent vein of appealing modern British ideas that reflects the season's bounty, as in a summery lunch that gets going with a colourful and vibrantly-flavoured starter of seared scallops and crisp pancetta with artichokes, haricot beans, tomato and berries. Next up, the same inventive streak partners an appealingly purple-hued risotto of girolle mushrooms and red wine with radicchio, parmesan, rosemary oil and ciabatta crostini, or there might be rosemary and fennel-braised belly porchetta with crackling, balsamic Puy lentils, broad beans and chicory. To finish, dark chocolate and peanut butter parfait is served to good effect with banana mousse and crystallised chocolate.

Chef Adam Whitlock **Owner** Michael, Bill, Caroline & Linda Gilbey **Seats** 50, Pr/dining room 12 **Times** 12-2.30/6.45-9.45, Closed 23-28 Dec, D Sun **Prices** Fixed L 2 course £19.50, Fixed D 3 course £25.50, Starter £6.50-£12.95, Main £16.95-£27.50, Dessert £7.55-£11.50 **Wines** 21 bottles over £30, 17 bottles under £30, 8 by glass **Parking** On street & car park **Notes** Sunday L £21-£27.50, Vegetarian available, Children welcome

The Artichoke 🌸🌸🌸

AMERSHAM   Map 6 SU99

Modern European V 🍷 NOTABLE WINE LIST

tel: 01494 726611 **9 Market Square, Old Amersham HP7 0DF**
email: info@artichokerestaurant.co.uk
web: www.artichokerestaurant.co.uk
dir: *M40 junct 2. 1m from Amersham New Town*

Highly creative and technically impressive cooking with a local flavour

Proving the saying that it's an ill wind that blows no good, a fire put Laurie and Jacqueline Gear's restaurant out of action back in 2008, with two results. One was that they expanded into the next door building and reworked the whole interior design aesthetic with a decor combining the period charm of original 16th-century features (a huge open fireplace and oak beams) with designer chairs, walnut tables and modern art. The three dining areas now look contemporary and stylish and one is home to the open kitchen, bringing even more life and energy to the space. The blaze also led to Laurie putting in a game-changing stint at Réné Redzepi's Noma in Copenhagen. He returned to Amersham's market square fired up with new inspiration, and The Artichoke took off in a new culinary direction turning organic, free-range and foraged ingredients into dynamic, contemporary, full-on and expertly crafted food. There's a tasting menu (with wine flight), a veggie version, plus a carte that might begin with hop-smoked sea trout with malted grains, dill emulsion and beetroot sorbet. There's plenty going on in main courses too: an immaculately poached fillet of wild turbot might come partnered with sea jelly beans and aster, roasted Jerusalem artichoke and orange butter sauce.

Desserts are no less creative and appealing-Brillat Savarin cheesecake, perhaps, with Poire Williams eau-de-vie sorbet, pickled pear, sweet cicely and granola, or go for French and English farmhouse cheeses with hand-made crackers. The wine list is a class act, too, with its well-chosen bins covering the globe in style.

Chef Laurie Gear, Ben Jenkins **Owner** Laurie & Jacqueline Gear **Seats** 48, Pr/dining room 16 **Times** 12-3/6.30-11, Closed 1 wk Xmas & Apr, 2 wks Aug/Sep, Sun-Mon **Prices** Fixed L 2 course £24.50, Fixed D 3 course £48, Tasting menu £68, Starter £12.50-£14, Main £22.50-£24.50, Dessert £6.50-£8.50 **Wines** 246 bottles over £30, 5 bottles under £30, 13 by glass **Parking** On street, nearby car park **Notes** Tasting menu 7 course, L tasting menu 5 course £38, Children welcome

AYLESBURY
Map 11 SP81

Hartwell House Hotel, Restaurant & Spa

◉◉ Modern British NOTABLE WINE LIST

tel: 01296 747444 **Oxford Rd HP17 8NR**
email: info@hartwell-house.com **web:** www.hartwell-house.com
dir: 2m SW of Aylesbury on A418 (Oxford road)

Ambitious country-house cooking in a rococo stately home

Within 90 acres of parkland in the Vale of Aylesbury, Hartwell House is a majestic property with enough pomp to have served as home to an exiled claimant to the French throne (Louis XVIII, no less). The grand proportions and luxurious features make an ideal setting for an upscale country-house hotel, with the expected spa, meeting rooms and fine-dining restaurant. Decorated in pristine primrose, with ornate mirrors and swags, the dining room is a fine setting for Daniel Richardson's ambitious classically-minded modern cooking. The estate ensures a home-grown flavour to some dishes, but what doesn't come from the grounds is sourced with care and attention. Seafood normally crops up among well-constructed starters – perhaps pan-fried fillet of red mullet with chorizo and cannellini bean cassoulet and creamed leeks. Everything looks good on the plate and flavours are nicely handled. Main-course slowly-braised ox cheek bourguignon with Savoy cabbage, winter vegetables, delmonico potatoes and braising juices, is a real seasonal warmer, while the estate's orchard and hives are behind apple mousse with honeycomb, apple jelly and cinnamon ice cream.

Chef Daniel Richardson **Owner** Historic House Hotels/National Trust **Seats** 56, Pr/dining room 36 **Times** 12.30-1.45/7.30-9.45, Closed L 31 Dec **Prices** Fixed L 2 course £25, Fixed D 3 course £32-£62 **Wines** 325 bottles over £30, 11 bottles under £30, 15 by glass **Parking** 50 **Notes** Sunday L £28-£36, Vegetarian available, Children 6 yrs+

BEACONSFIELD
Map 6 SU99

Crazy Bear Beaconsfield

◉ British, International

tel: 01494 673086 **75 Wycombe End, Old Town HP9 1LX**
email: enquiries@crazybear-beaconsfield.co.uk **web:** www.crazybeargroup.co.uk
dir: M40 junct 2, 3rd exit from rdbt, next rdbt 1st exit. Over 2 mini-rdbts, on right

Bright modern menus in flamboyant setting

The word 'restraint' was not in the designers' brief when they converted this coaching inn dating from the 15th century into a flamboyant, English-themed restaurant (there's also a Thai option). The bling-laden look goes for extreme opulence as chandeliers and cream bench seating mingle with the red brick and oak beams of the original building. It's a fun, high-energy place, with a menu that covers a lot of ground, from classics to chargrilled meats and some lively modern global ideas. The set-up has its own farm shop that supplies the black pudding and crispy Old Spot bacon to go with seared Lyme Bay scallops. Main course sees pan-fried sea bass fillet matched with Mediterranean vegetables, a soft-boiled quail's egg and black olive potatoes. Dessert gilds the lily somewhat, partnering a well-executed Madagascan vanilla crème brûlée with raspberry sorbet, jelly and shortbread.

Chef Martin Gallon **Owner** Jason Hunt **Seats** 75, Pr/dining room 22 **Times** 12-12, All-day dining **Prices** Prices not confirmed **Wines** 180 bottles over £30, 30 bottles under £30, 20 by glass **Parking** 20, On street **Notes** Sunday L, Vegetarian available, Children welcome

The Jolly Cricketers

◉ Modern British

tel: 01494 676308 **24 Chalfont Rd, Seer Green HP9 2YG**
email: amanda@thejollycricketers.co.uk
dir: M40 junct 2, take A355 N, at rdbt 1st exit onto A40, next rdbt 2nd exit onto A355, turn right into Longbottom Ln, turn left into School Ln & continue into Chalfont Rd

Assured cooking in village pub with a cricketing theme

This is just the sort of traditional country pub you love to come across when tootling around the countryside. The Jolly Cricketers ticks all the boxes with its cosy, low-ceilinged bar, cricket-themed pictures, a warm-hearted and congenial atmosphere (four-legged friends are welcome too), a range of real ales and a sensibly concise menu of crowd-pleasing modern dishes. Devilled Cornish crab with melba toast gets things off to a flying start, or you might go for the earthier flavours of rabbit and ham terrine with carrot and vanilla purée. A main course of Cornish hake baked with a lemon and parsley crust and served with potato gnocchi, chorizo and cucumber hits all the right notes, otherwise traditionalists need look no further than pot-roasted rump of beef with carrots, pancetta and creamed potatoes. End with vanilla pannacotta with poached champagne rhubarb and rhubarb sorbet.

Chef Matt Lyons **Owner** A Baker & C Lillitou **Seats** 36, Pr/dining room 22 **Times** 12-2.30/6.30-9, Closed 25-26 Dec **Prices** Starter £6-£10.50, Main £12.75-£23.50, Dessert £6-£7.50, Service optional 10% **Wines** 21 bottles over £30, 16 bottles under £30, 16 by glass **Parking** 10, On street **Notes** Sunday L, Vegetarian available, Children welcome

BRILL
Map 11 SP61

The Pointer

◉◉ Modern British NEW v

tel: 01844 238339 **27 Church St HP18 9RT**
email: info@thepointerbrill.co.uk
dir: M40 junct 9, A41 Aylesbury, right onto B4011, left towards Brill, 20mtrs on left

Relaxed 18th-century dining pub with modern fare

This hilltop village is worth visiting for its location alone, but if you also take in its stylish bar/restaurant you'll double your enjoyment. A once-sleepy pub, it has been expertly opened up to display to best advantage hefty oak beams, old stone walls and other original features. The restaurant, with scrubbed wooden tables, overlooks a small garden and is reached by walking past the open kitchen. From here comes a modern British line-up that makes good use of the rare breed pigs and English Longhorn cattle that owner David Howden raises with a local farmer. Try therefore, as a lunchtime starter, Pointer Farm pork croquettes with crispy pork salad, sweet mustard dressing, or from the same source, a dinner main course of beef fillet with shallot jam, roasted carrots, burnt onions and creamed potatoes. As a fish alternative, consider roast Scottish cod loin with crushed Jersey Royals, new season's greens and crab bisque. Finish with sticky date pudding, caramelised banana and toffee parfait.

Chef Mini Patel **Owner** David & Fiona Howden **Seats** 25 **Times** 12-2.30/6.30-9, Closed 1 wk Jan, 1 wk Aug, Mon, D Sun **Prices** Starter £6-£8, Main £13-£20, Dessert £6-£7, Service optional **Wines** 19 bottles over £30, 17 bottles under £30, 18 by glass **Parking** 5 **Notes** Sunday L £18-£27, Children welcome

BUCKINGHAM

Map 11 SP63

Villiers Hotel

◉ Modern British

tel: 01280 822444 **3 Castle St MK18 1BS**
email: reservations@villiershotels.com **web:** www.villiers-hotel.co.uk
dir: *Town centre – Castle Street is to the right of Town Hall near main square*

Straightforward brasserie cooking in the medieval quarter

The Villiers has a smartly kitted-out restaurant overlooking a courtyard with a relaxed and informal atmosphere. Don't expect too many surprises on the menu in terms of outré combinations or obscure ingredients as the kitchen concentrates on tried-and-tested dishes. Thus, pan-fried fillet of sea bass with potato purée and garden greens might be an alternative main course to pan-fried calves' liver with bubble-and-squeak, pancetta and mustard sauce. More innovative dishes are just as well handled, seen in a gently flavoured starter of mushroom, leek and spinach risotto with goats' cheese mousse and mushroom velouté, followed by slow-cooked breast of lamb with piperade, goats' curd, aubergine, polenta and pine nuts, all components adding up to a satisfying whole. End with one of the enjoyable puddings, such as pistachio baked Alaska with candied pistachios.

Chef Paul Stopps **Owner** Oxfordshire Hotels Ltd **Seats** 70, Pr/dining room 150
Times 12-2.30/6-9.30 **Prices** Fixed L 2 course £14–£18, Fixed D 3 course £23–£25,
Starter £4.75–£7.95, Main £10.50–£20.50, Dessert £6.95–£7.75, Service optional
10% **Wines** 17 bottles over £30, 32 bottles under £30, 13 by glass **Parking** 52
Notes Sunday L £18–£23, Vegetarian available, Children welcome

BURNHAM

Map 6 SU98

Burnham Beeches Hotel

◉ Modern British, European

tel: 01628 429955 **Grove Rd SL1 8DP**
email: burnhambeeches@corushotels.com **web:** www.corushotels.com
dir: *Off A355, via Farnham Royal rdbt*

Classically-minded cooking in an early Georgian hotel

A grand Georgian pile in ten acres of pretty grounds, Burnham Beeches is a popular wedding venue, but it is worth checking out the restaurant called Gray's. This consists of two formal interlinked rooms, one rich with oak panels, with tables dressed up in white linen. There are daylight views into the garden through well-proportioned Georgian windows. The kitchen favours sound classical thinking, delivering gently modern dishes that won't scare the horses. Start with a salad of home-smoked chicken breast with crispy pancetta and a soft-poached quail's egg, or pan-fried scallops with creamed leeks and poached baby leeks. Main-course honey-roasted breast of Gressingham duck is an attractively presented plate, the meat nice and pink, with an accompanying croquette and port sauce. Finish with a Yorkshire rhubarb and ginger cheesecake, or the selection of British cheeses.

Times 12-2/7-9.30

CADMORE END

Map 5 SU79

The Tree at Cadmore

◉ Indian, Continental **NEW**

tel: 01494 881183 **Marlow Rd HP14 3PF**
email: cadmore@treehotel.co.uk **web:** www.cadmore.treehotel.co.uk
dir: *M40 junct 5 towards Stokenchurch, right onto Marlow Rd, then left after 2m*

European and Indian cuisine in a rustic setting

The Tree is a bit of a hybrid. It's a hotel, for a start, with bedrooms in the modern country vein, but it's also a dining pub with a menu that covers European and Indian bases. The bar/restaurant is a charmingly rustic space, with wooden beams and exposed brickwork, watched over by an eager uniformed service team. Pan-

seared scallops with apple salsa and bacon powder is a thoroughly modern European option among starters, or head east for maas ke sholey (marinated lamb cooked in the tandoor and served with mint chutney). This is not fusion food as each cuisine stands on its own merits. Among main courses, whole tandoori poussin catches the eye, delicately spiced and arriving with pulao rice and curry sauce on the side, while European options might include wild mushroom risotto or confit pork belly with mustard-braised Savoy cabbage and mash. Finish with an Alphonse mango samosa.

Chef Amit Kumar **Seats** 80 **Times** 12-9.30, All-day dining **Prices** Starter £5.45–£6.95,
Main £10.95–£15.95, Dessert £4.95–£5.95, Service optional **Wines** 2 bottles over
£30, 20 bottles under £30, 7 by glass **Parking** 30 **Notes** Sunday L £12.95–£17.95,
Vegetarian available, Children welcome

CUBLINGTON

Map 11 SP82

The Unicorn

◉◉ Modern, Traditional British

tel: 01296 681261 **12 High St LU7 0LQ**
email: theunicornpub@btconnect.com **web:** www.theunicornpub.co.uk
dir: *2m N of A418 (between Aylesbury & Leighton Buzzard). In village centre*

The kind of pub every village should have

This red-brick 17th-century inn is much more than a bar serving real ales and a restaurant serving real food, for it meets the needs of the local community too. It has a shop, opens for coffee mornings and afternoon teas on Friday and Saturday and breakfast on Saturday morning and serves bar snacks all day. Head for the restaurant for the full works and to sample the high standards of a sure-footed kitchen. Interesting ways with seafood can be seen in crab cakes with mango salsa, pea shoots and beurre blanc, then pan-fried sea trout with ratatouille and saffron confit potatoes. Meat is deftly handled too: pheasant sausage with apricot and fig compôte and hazelnut emulsion, for example, followed by a duo of lamb (confit shoulder and rack) with fondant potato and pea and carrot purée. Don't pass on puddings such as chocolate marquise with caramelised oranges or plum frangipane tart with clotted cream.

Chef Christopher George **Owner** Mr S D George **Seats** 60, Pr/dining room 30
Times 12-2.30/6.30-9, Closed D Sun **Prices** Fixed D 3 course £16.95–£21.95,
Service optional **Wines** 5 bottles over £30, 23 bottles under £30, 10 by glass
Parking 20 **Notes** Breakfast Sat, Sunday L £12.50–£19.95, Vegetarian available,
Children welcome

GERRARDS CROSS

Map 6 TQ08

The Bull Hotel

Modern British

tel: 01753 885995 **Oxford Rd SL9 7PA**
email: bull@sarova.co.uk **web:** www.sarova.com
dir: M40 junct 2 follow Beaconsfield on A355. After 0.5m 2nd exit at rdbt signed A40 Gerrards Cross for 2m. The Bull on right

Classy hotel restaurant on the high street

The old Bull started life in 1688, serving travellers on the road between London and Oxford, and has morphed over from a simple coaching inn into a swish four-star hotel with tip-top facilities. Its Beeches restaurant has a smart contemporary look involving boldly-patterned carpets, tones of burgundy and cream, unclothed tables and a Mediterranean-accented menu that keeps abreast of the times. Consider ham hock terrine with home-made piccalilli, griddled sourdough bread and beetroot pearls to start. Follow with something like cod loin with Swiss chard, parsley purée, sautéed parsley root, beetroot carpaccio and chorizo crisp, or pork fillet and braised belly with black pudding, apple purée and red wine sauce. Puddings can be as true Brit as Cox's apple tart with rhubarb crumble ice cream and toffee apple, or as Gallic as chocolate fondant with Chantilly cream.

Times 12-2.30/7-9, Closed L Sat

GREAT MISSENDEN

Map 6 SP80

Nags Head Inn & Restaurant

British, French

tel: 01494 862200 & 862945 **London Rd HP16 0DG**
email: goodfood@nagsheadbucks.com **web:** www.nagsheadbucks.com
dir: N from Amersham on A413 signed Great Missenden, left at Chiltern Hospital onto London Rd (1m S of Great Missenden)

Charming pub with ambitious Anglo-French cooking

Originally three 15th-century cottages, then a coaching inn, the Nags Head is now a stylishly modernised gastro-pub, with an open fire in the old inglenook under oak beams, and dining areas with a Roald Dahl theme (he was a regular and there's a museum devoted to him nearby). Contemporary Anglo-French cuisine is the attraction, with the kitchen adding its own endlessly inventive-and totally persuasive-touches to dishes. Starters can be as straightforward as a plate of home-smoked fish with lemony coriander butter and tomato chutney and as complicated as pan-fried foie gras on milk bread with red onion and pear jam along with mi-cuit foie gras shavings on rocket. Ever successful main courses follow a similar route, among them fillet of stone bass with green beans and a simple Noilly Prat cream, and roast breast of guinea fowl with a pheasant sausage, liver mousse

feuilleté and thyme jus. To end, sticky toffee pudding seems a fixture, and there might be vanilla crème brûlée as well.

Nags Head Inn & Restaurant

Chef Claude Paillet, Alan Bell **Owner** Alvin, Adam & Sally Michaels **Seats** 60 **Times** 12-2.30/6.30-9.30, Closed 25 Dec **Prices** Fixed L 2 course £16.50, Fixed D 3 course £22, Starter £5.95-£13.95, Main £12.95-£25.95, Dessert £5.95-£6.95, Service optional **Wines** 95 bottles over £30, 31 bottles under £30, 19 by glass **Parking** 35 **Notes** Sunday L £13.95-£16.95, Vegetarian available, Children welcome

LONG CRENDON

Map 5 SP60

The Angel Restaurant

Modern British, International V NOTABLE WINE LIST

tel: 01844 208268 **47 Bicester Rd HP18 9EE**
email: info@angelrestaurant.co.uk
dir: M40 junct 7, beside B4011, 2m NW of Thame

Confident cooking in 16th-century coaching inn

This one-time coaching inn dates from the 16th century and retains plenty of period charm. It's more restaurant with rooms than country pub these days. There is a cosy bar for a pre-dinner drink, plus dining areas filled with original features and a smart conservatory. There are outdoor tables, too, on the heated terrace. The cooking is broadly modern British with a good many Asian influences adding a notion of Pacific Rim to proceedings. Daily specials appear on a blackboard and fish is very much a favourite ingredient in the kitchen. Citrus-cured gravad lax is a starter perked up with crispy fried squid and pickled kohlrabi, with another pairing honey- and soy-glazed duck breast with steamed bok choy and plum and ginger sauce. But there's also chargrilled fillet of beef with classic accompaniments, and desserts such as warm treacle tart with honeycomb ice cream or limoncello pannacotta with rhubarb compôte.

Chef Trevor Bosch **Owner** Trevor & Annie Bosch **Seats** 75, Pr/dining room 14 **Times** 12-2.30/7-9.30, Closed D Sun **Prices** Fixed L 2 course £10.95, Starter £5.25-£8.50, Main £10.50-£29.50, Dessert £6.25-£6.75, Service optional **Wines** 60 bottles over £30, 40 bottles under £30, 12 by glass **Parking** 30 **Notes** Sunday L £19.95-£24.95, Children welcome

MARLOW

Map 5 SU88

The Coach

– see opposite

Danesfield House Hotel & Spa

◉◉ British ▮NOTABLE WINE LIST

tel: 01628 891010 **Henley Rd SL7 2EY**
email: reservations@danesfieldhouse.co.uk **web:** www.danesfieldhouse.co.uk
dir: *M4 junct 4/A404 to Marlow. Follow signs to Medmenham and Henley. Hotel is 3m outside Marlow*

Classy, classical dining in a majestic house

Danesfield House is nothing short of magnificent: a 1901 white mansion with a castellated roof in beautifully maintained grounds. Flawless service means guests are pampered from the moment they arrive, an experience endorsed by indulgently luxurious surroundings. The Great Hall is just that-a soaring room hung with tapestries above panelling-the swimming pool has frescoed walls, and the restaurant has a relaxingly neutral decor, with floor-length undercloths on circular tables, upholstered chairs and a moulded ceiling. There's nothing too rarefied about the cooking, which comes out of the contemporary British mould. The odd luxury appears-lobster linguine with shellfish cream, say-but the kitchen generally takes a down-to-earth approach. Potted shrimps, game terrine and scallops with sauce vièrge are all there for the asking, and might be followed by cod fillet with spicy lentils, fondant potato and meat jus, or, in season, pheasant breast saltimbocca with green beans, chestnut mash and sage jus. Pastry is clearly made by an expert, so focus on a tart for dessert: pear frangipane with matching purée, say, or lemon with blackberry sorbet.

Chef Billy Reid **Seats** 84, Pr/dining room 14 **Times** 12-2.30/6.30-9.30, Closed BHs **Prices** Fixed L 2 course fr £28, Starter £8.95-£16.50, Main £13-£30, Dessert £8.50-£13 **Wines** 235 bottles over £30, 15 bottles under £30, 30 by glass **Parking** 100 **Notes** Sunday L, Vegetarian available, Children welcome

The Hand & Flowers

◉◉◉◉ – *see page 74*

The Riverside Restaurant

◉◉◉ – *see page 75*

Sindhu by Atul Kochhar

◉◉ Modern Indian **NEW** v

tel: 01628 405405 **Macdonald Compleat Angler, Marlow Bridge SL7 1RG**
email: info@sindhurestaurant.co.uk
dir: *M4 junct 8/9 or M40 junct 4. A404 to rdbt, take Bisham exit, 1m to Marlow Bridge, hotel on right*

Indian cuisine with traditional roots and contemporary variations

Opened in November 2014, this is Macdonald Hotels' second restaurant within its Compleat Angler on the River Thames by Marlow Weir. A riverside terrace takes full advantage of this lovely spot. Among Sindhu's hallmarks are formal service from uniformed staff and readily offered wine advice by a sommelier. Atul is one of Britain's most critically acclaimed chefs, renowned for his take on modern Indian cuisine, and for his strong stand on sustainable fishing, always using responsibly sourced fish in his restaurants. Knowing where to start could prove tricky, but try karara kekda, a crisp soft-shell crab with spiced squid and passionfruit chilli chutney. Highly recommended too is erachi Chettinad, tandoor-grilled rack of lamb with vegetable polenta and spices from Tamil Nadu. Equally desirable are murgh makhani, which is tandoor-smoked chicken with creamy tomato and fenugreek sauce, and pan-roasted stone bass with coconut meen moilee sauce and fork-crushed potato with mustard seeds. Like everything that emanates from Atul's kitchens, desserts work well and bhapi doi, a rose yogurt cheesecake, is no exception.

Chef Gopal Krishnan **Owner** Atul Kochhar **Seats** 58 **Times** 12-3/6-11, Closed Mon, L Tue, D Sun **Prices** Fixed L 2 course £18.50, Tasting menu £48, Starter £10-£28, Main £16-£24, Dessert £6-£7.50 **Wines** 40 bottles over £30, 20+ bottles under £30, 10 by glass **Parking** 100 **Notes** Sunday L £25, Children welcome

The Coach ◉◉◉

MARLOW	Map 5 SU88

British, French **NEW**
tel: 01628 483013 **3 West St SL7 2LS**
dir: *Phone for directions*

Big-hearted cooking in Tom Kerridge's second pub

The mock-Tudor timbered inn in the centre of town is unassuming enough, but interest is perked up when you learn that it's Tom Kerridge's second pub. The place is just down the road from the celebrated Hand & Flowers mothership, but while the H&F has morphed into a foodie destination that's booked solid, months in advance, The Coach doesn't take bookings, so you just have to turn up early doors, with fingers crossed. It's a cosy, compact, pubby-enough sort of space dominated by the L-shaped pewter bar (park here for close-up views of the pass), with elbow-to-elbow tables, and an open kitchen complete with a meat fridge and rôtisserie on display. It's a busy, buzzy spot, with chefs pitching in to help the switched-on, chatty staff get dishes out to the tables. Head chef Nick Beardshaw was Kerridge's sous-chef at the Hand & Flowers, so you can expect food in a similar vein, big on flavour and made with top-class ingredients handled with real skill. Divided between meat and 'no meat' dishes, the menu reads like a roster of uncomplicated modern pub ideas, starting with a rice-free mushroom 'risotto'

inspired by Claude Bosi (of Hibiscus fame), or you might get off the mark with a more visceral crispy pig's head with piccalilli. The same big-hearted, contemporary British tone informs main courses: take beautifully-rendered pork belly with crisp crackling and velvety mash offset by the acidity of pickled cabbage; steak and ale pie with moresome suet pastry cooked in the rotisserie; or subtly-spiced line-caught cod with roast cauliflower and peanuts. For pudding, top-class pastry skills are in evidence in a hot chocolate tart with hazelnut ice cream.

Chef Nick Beardshaw, Tom Kerridge **Owner** Tom & Beth Kerridge **Seats** 40 **Times** 12-2.30/6-10.30, Closed 25 Dec **Prices** Starter £5, Main £12.50, Dessert £6.50 **Wines** 14 bottles over £30, 6 bottles under £30, 20 by glass **Notes** Sunday L, Vegetarian available, Children welcome

The Hand & Flowers ✿✿✿✿

MARLOW   Map 5 SU88

British, French
tel: 01628 482277 **126 West St SL7 2BP**
email: contact@thehandandflowers.co.uk
dir: *M40 junct 4/M4 junct 8/9 follow A404 to Marlow*

Big flavours and traditional techniques in an outstanding gastro inn

Popping into the Hand & Flowers just for a pint would be a bit like driving around the Silverstone racetrack in a Citroen 2CV – a wasted opportunity. For a decade now Tom and Beth Kerridge's pub has been turning out food that has garnered praise, headlines and a host of awards. Not your everyday pub then. One of the many compelling attributes of the H&F is how comfortably the place sits with its pub past, with a satisfying lack of pretension all round and, given the outstanding food that follows, the place is uncannily relaxed and friendly. It still looks like a pub from the outside, with a proper pub sign and colourful hanging baskets at certain times of the year, and there is still a sense of rusticity within. Look a little closer and you might notice the attention to detail that has gone into making it look so humble – interesting artworks, precise table settings and the professionalism underlying the cheerfulness of the service team. Tom has made an impact on our TV screen in recent years, ever since his triumph on the BBC's *Great British Menu* in 2010, and his relatively direct approach to cooking and passion for robust flavours has hit home. The menu has an unaffected British flavour and there's smoking, pickling, salt-curing, blowtorching and all sorts going down in the kitchen. The lack of a tasting menu proves the direct and unpretentious nature of the place, with the à la carte menu supported by an amazingly good value no-choice set lunch option. There's a Sunday lunch menu, too, where treacle-cured Chateaubriand of Stokes Marsh Farm beef with Yorkshire pudding, roast potatoes and red wine sauce may just well prove to be the best you've ever had. The simplicity only extends so far, for the technical accomplishment of this kitchen delivers refinement, too. Take a soup of lovage flavoured with Bramley apple, for example, which comes with smoked eel and ham and cheese tortellini, or another starter that partners roast English onion tart with an étuvée of alliums, smoked butter and salt-cured pork.

Among main courses, the Essex lamb 'bun' may sound humble but delivers powerful and complex layers of flavour, while Cornish line-caught cod is matched with a black grape sauce and is served with endive gratin, hazelnuts and ham hock butter. Finish with something as simple as chocolate and ale cake, which is of course quite brilliant.

Chef Tom Kerridge **Owner** Tom & Beth Kerridge **Seats** 54 **Times** 12-2.45/6.30-9.45, Closed 24-26 Dec, D Sun, 1 Jan **Prices** Fixed L 2 course £15, Starter £9.50-£15.50, Main £27-£38, Dessert £9.50 **Wines** 107 bottles over £30, 16 bottles under £30, 17 by glass **Parking** 20 **Notes** Sunday L £38.50, Vegetarian available, Children welcome

MARLOW *continued*

The Vanilla Pod

◉◉ British, French V ⚑ NOTABLE WINE LIST

tel: 01628 898101 **31 West St SL7 2LS**
email: contact@thevanillapod.co.uk
dir: *From M4 junct 8/9 or M40 junct 4 take A404, A4155 to Marlow. From Henley take A4155*

Intelligently constructed dishes in central townhouse

The culinary bar is set high in this well-heeled Thames-side stretch of the stockbroker belt, with stellar competition all around. Happily, The Vanilla Pod has the hand of chef-proprietor Michael Macdonald on the tiller to deliver a sure-footed take on modern British cooking with its roots clearly in the French classics. The setting is a handsome townhouse where TS Eliot once lived, thoroughly refurbished with a chic contemporary look in tones of brown and cream, and the hum of conversation and clued-up service to add to the upbeat feel of the place. Not surprisingly, given the restaurant's name, vanilla is something of a leitmotif, and it might turn up in a starter of seared scallops with truffle-infused butternut squash purée and apple foam. The kitchen extracts clear, robust flavours from top-class ingredients in main courses such as loin of venison with pear and fondant potato, and puddings could press the eponymous pod into service once again in a classic vanilla crème brûlée with butterscotch jelly, condensed milk purée and popcorn ice cream.

Chef Michael Macdonald **Owner** Michael & Stephanie Macdonald **Seats** 28, Pr/dining room 8 **Times** 12-2/7-10, Closed 24 Dec-3 Jan, Sun-Mon **Prices** Prices not confirmed, Service optional **Wines** 80 bottles over £30, 12 bottles under £30, 10 by glass **Parking** West St car park **Notes** ALC 3 course £45, Tasting menu 8 course, Children welcome

---

STOKE POGES
Map 6 SU98

Humphry's at Stoke Park

◉◉◉ *– see page 76*

Stoke Place

◉◉ Modern European ⚑ NOTABLE WINE LIST

tel: 01753 534790 & 560216 **Stoke Green SL2 4HT**
email: enquiries@stokeplace.co.uk **web:** www.stokeplace.co.uk
dir: *M4 junct 6, A355, right at 1st lights to A4 Bath Rd. At 1st rdbt take 2nd exit onto Stoke Rd. B416 to Stoke Green. Hotel 200mtrs on right*

Thoughtfully conceived cooking in pace-setting Poges

Just south of the thriving gastronomic hotbed of Stoke Poges, Stoke Place is a red-brick mansion house in extensive tranquil grounds, where the Seasons restaurant was relaunched in 2014. An unclothed, pastel-hued look in sage green and stone is now preferred, with shelves of objets and parkland views to ponder. Thoughtfully conceived dishes on large plates that avoid over-garnishing are the norm, and there is plenty of modernist ingenuity in evidence. A dumpling of spiced Cornish lamb on sheep's cheese, alongside a salad of braised tongues, is a bravura opener, or there may be scallops and shrimps with cobnut praline and Gentleman's Relish. Dishes include tricky items like pancetta-wrapped monkfish in clam dressing and bergamot sabayon; rabbit ballotine with black pudding and girolles lacks nothing in earthy savour. A deconstruction of banoffee has a scattered biscuit base, fine banana ice cream and a fugitive hint of liquorice.

Chef Jonathan Stephens **Owner** Mr & Mrs Dhillon **Seats** 50, Pr/dining room 30 **Times** 12-2.30/7-9.30, Closed 24 Dec-9 Jan **Prices** Prices not confirmed **Wines** 235 bottles over £30, 41 bottles under £30, 18 by glass **Parking** 120 **Notes** Sunday L, Vegetarian available, Children welcome

---

The Riverside Restaurant ◉◉◉

MARLOW
Map 5 SU88

Modern British
tel: 01628 484444 & 405406 **Macdonald Compleat Angler, Marlow Bridge SL7 1RG**
email: compleatangler@macdonald-hotels.co.uk
web: www.macdonaldhotels.co.uk/compleatangler
dir: *M4 junct 8/9 or M40 junct 4. A404 to rdbt, take Bisham exit, 1m to Marlow Bridge, hotel on right*

Modern classic dishes on Izaak Walton's riverside

The Riverside is part of an upscale 18th-century hotel named after Izaak Walton's indispensable reference, *The Compleat Angler* (1653), written in and around the Thames at Marlow. It makes the most of its location with a lovely conservatory room overlooking the water, recently refurbished in sharp contemporary style with linen-swathed tables, buttoned banquettes and professionally formal service from uniformed staff and a helpful sommelier. Cleverly worked modern cooking is the attraction here, with interesting combinations of top-drawer materials forming the backbone of attractively presented dishes. The menu aims for urbane simplicity rather than showy gestures, and leads off with a classy ham hock and foie gras terrine with pea mousse, raisin purée and pea shoots-or there might be a modern classic presentation of crab ravioli in langoustine bisque.

Next up, a contemporary deconstructed take on fish and chips brings delicate slow-cooked cod with crunchy scraps of batter, silky split-pea purée, parsley 'tartare' and crisp chips, while more visceral compositions might include loin of Highland lamb and its sweetbreads with crushed minted peas, or beef fillet with 'umami crunch', creamed Dijon potatoes and caramelised shallots. Dessert brings a fine specimen of lemon tart, the crisp shortcrust pastry packed with creamy, zesty filling and partnered with crystallised stem ginger, luscious mascarpone sorbet and dried rose petals, or you might bow out with a well-judged trio of blackberry parfait, toffee apple purée and crème fraîche sorbet. If you fancy soaking up those river views on a budget, the lunch market menu offers a wallet-friendly option, and when the sun plays ball, alfresco dining on the waterside terrace is a truly idyllic moment.

Chef Michael Lloyd **Owner** Macdonald Hotels **Seats** 90, Pr/dining room 120 **Times** 12.30-2/7-10 **Prices** Fixed L 2 course £23.50, Tasting menu £60, Starter £9-£12, Main £22.50-£28, Dessert £8-£13 **Wines** 120 bottles over £30, 16 bottles under £30, 17 by glass **Parking** 100 **Notes** Sunday L £39, Vegetarian available, Children welcome

Humphry's at Stoke Park @@@

STOKE POGES   Map 6 SU98

Modern British

tel: 01753 717171 & 717172 **Park Rd SL2 4PG**
email: info@stokepark.com
web: www.humphrysrestaurant.co.uk
dir: *M4 junct 6 or M40 junct 2, take A355 towards Slough, then
B416. Stoke Park in 1.25m on right*

Innovative contemporary country-club cuisine

The thousand luxuriant acres of Stoke Park were turned into
Britain's first country club in 1908, the domed and pillared
mansion house at its centre surveying some of the grandest golf
the nation had to offer. Since then, the place has weathered the
storms of fashion, playing host to pro-am tournaments and
concerts of popular beat music, as well as providing regular
locations for a portfolio of British cinema from James Bond to
Bridget Jones. The interiors are splendidly preserved, and there is
no hiding of decorative lights under architectural bushels, least of
all in the magnificent marble-pillared, deep-piled dining room,
arrayed in sunny pastel yellow and named in honour of Humphry
Repton, who did the gardens. Attentive service retains a degree of
pomp in relaxed circumstance. Chris Wheeler makes it his mission
to ensure that your culinary memories of Stoke Park will live long,
and achieves it with innovative dishes that mobilise the full range
of contemporary technique, while maintaining respect for the
prime materials. That's clear straight away from a first course of
lobster poached in tarragon butter, its flesh moist and sweet,
served alongside spiced yogurt croquettes with lemon-dressed
micro-saladings. That could be succeeded by a majestic treatment

of pinkly roasted duck breast topped with a lobe of seared foie
gras, with a little fondant potato, some parsnip purée and cherry
jus. The six-course tasting menu, plus incidentals, offers a
breathtaking tour of the territory, including sea bass on leek,
butternut and sorrel risotto, and cannon of lamb with ale-braised
'osso buco', concluding with raspberry soufflé and cheesecake
ice cream.

Chef Chris Wheeler **Owner** Roger King **Seats** 50, Pr/dining room
146 **Times** 12-2.30/7-10, Closed 24-26 Dec, 1st wk Jan, Mon, L Tue
Prices Fixed L 2 course £25, Fixed D 3 course £65, Tasting menu
£50-£80 **Wines** 95 bottles over £30, 10 bottles under £30, 12 by
glass **Parking** 400 **Notes** ALC L only, Tasting menu 5/7 course also
avail with wine, Sunday L, Vegetarian available, Children 12 yrs+

TAPLOW
Map 6 SU98

André Garrett at Cliveden
❀❀❀ – see below

WADDESDON
Map 11 SP71

The Five Arrows
❀❀ Modern European

tel: 01296 651727 **High St HP18 0JE**
email: reservations@thefivearrows.co.uk **web:** www.waddesdon.org.uk
dir: On A41 in Waddesdon. Into Baker St for car park

Contemporary dining on the Rothschild estate

The Five Arrows in question are the family emblem of the Rothschilds, each arrow representing one of the five sons who was sent off to establish banking houses in Europe's financial capitals. The rest, as the saying goes, is history. The small Victorian hotel stands at the gates of Waddesdon Manor, and other than a mock-Tudor flourish here and there, has none of the airs and graces of the grand French château-style stately home. The restaurant sports a smartly contemporary look with unclothed darkwood tables and Rothschild wine-related prints on the walls, and a refreshingly relaxed ambience. The repertoire displays a commendable seasonal focus that delivers bright contemporary ideas, starting with a ballottine of chicken and black pudding matched with honey-poached cranberries, cauliflower purée, celery and lemon oil. Next up, the Waddesdon Estate supplies the venison (pan-fried loin and braised haunch) that comes with the hearty accompaniments of herb mash, braised red cabbage, girolles, and redcurrant jus, and for pudding there's hazelnut and vanilla iced parfait with caramelised hazelnuts and hazelnut tuile.

Chef Karl Penny **Owner** Rothschild Waddesdon Ltd **Seats** 60, Pr/dining room 30
Times 12-2.15/6.30-9.15, Closed D 25-26 Dec, 1 Jan **Prices** Prices not confirmed
Wines 53 bottles over £30, 39 bottles under £30, 22 by glass **Parking** 30
Notes Sunday L, Vegetarian available, Children welcome

WOOBURN COMMON
Map 6 SU98

Chequers Inn
❀❀ British, French

tel: 01628 529575 **Kiln Ln, Wooburn HP10 0JQ**
email: info@chequers-inn.com **web:** www.chequers-inn.com
dir: M40 junct 2, A40 through Beaconsfield Old Town towards High Wycombe. 2m from town left into Broad Ln. Inn 2.5m on left

French-influenced modern cooking in an old coaching inn

A former 17th-century coaching inn, the Chequers reveals its antiquity via chunky oak beams and flagstoned floors in the bar, but, as the more contemporary finish in the lounge and restaurant suggests, this place has moved with the times. It's still a pub, mind you, with real ales and bar snacks, although it is the chic restaurant that sets it apart. The Anglo-French cooking shows modern touches and delivers compelling flavour combinations. A starter of cured mackerel, for example, is partnered with horseradish pannacotta and apple, radish and orange vinaigrette, and there's a bit of luxury, too, in the form of seared foie gras with raisins marinated in port, cocoa nibs and fig chutney. A main course dish of lamb – saddle and crispy belly – arrives with pea relish, goats' cheese mash and mint jus, while a fishy main might be plaice with chargrilled baby gem, ricotta gnocchi, pickled black grapes and curry cream sauce. Desserts are no less creative: try blueberry cheesecake with confit lemon and crème fraîche sorbet.

continued

André Garrett at Cliveden ❀❀❀

TAPLOW
Map 6 SU98

Modern British, French ᵛ 🍷 NOTABLE WINE LIST
tel: 01628 668561 **Cliveden Estate SL6 0JF**
email: info@clivedenhouse.co.uk **web:** www.clivedenhouse.co.uk
dir: M4 junct 7, A4 towards Maidenhead, 1.5m, onto B476 towards Taplow, 2.5m, hotel on left

Stunning dishes in a stately home with a racy past

English mansions don't come much more stately than Cliveden, where luxury and style are guaranteed following a sixteen-month major refurbishment that has transformed the public spaces, suites and bedrooms and restored the house to its former glory. The dining goes on in the former Terrace Dining Room, with its sparkly crystal chandeliers, velour banquettes, silk drapes and views over parterre gardens to the Thames. André Garrett has taken to this luxurious setting like a duck to water, using razor-sharp technique to deliver exquisitely presented contemporary country-house dishes fashioned from ingredients of remarkable quality. The results are served up via a carte or eight-course tasting menu (there's an impressive veggie version too) if the whole table is up for that option, plus a weekday lunchtime market menu that constitutes very good value indeed considering the high-toned setting. Choosing from the carte, you might consider butter-poached lobster matched with grilled leeks,

the bittersweet tang of Seville orange and a luxuriant champagne sabayon to be an appropriately decadent starter. Next might be venison saddle partnered by a boulangère-style treatment of braised shoulder, pickled red cabbage, puréed quince and cardamom, or a sexed-up take on classic Dover sole Véronique, the fish served with verjus butter sauce, salted grapes, grilled lettuce and chicken juices. To conclude, desserts seduce with a lush pavé of Valrhona's superb Araguani dark chocolate paired with aerated milk chocolate, Beaujolais syrup and thyme ice cream. The wine list is suitably oligarchic, with excellent advice on hand from the sommelier if required.

Chef André Garrett **Owner** SRE Hotels **Seats** 78, Pr/dining room 60
Times 12.15-2.30/7-9.45, **Prices** Fixed L 3 course £32-£70, Fixed D 3 course £70, Tasting menu £95 **Wines** 575 bottles over £30, 8 bottles under £30, 10 by glass **Parking** 60 **Notes** Tasting menu L £85, Sunday L £50, Children welcome

WOOBURN COMMON *continued*

Chef Pascal Lemoine **Owner** PJ Roehrig **Seats** 60, Pr/dining room 60
Times 12-2.30/7-9.30, Closed D Sun, 25 Dec, 1 Jan **Prices** Fixed L 2 course fr
£13.95, Fixed D 3 course fr £27.95, Starter £6.95-£10.95, Main £13.95-£27.95,
Dessert £6.50-£8.50, Service optional **Wines** 11 bottles over £30, 27 bottles under
£30, 11 by glass **Parking** 50 **Notes** Afternoon tea £12.95, Sunday L £22.95-£27.95,
Vegetarian available, Children welcome

CAMBRIDGESHIRE

BALSHAM   Map 12 TL55

The Black Bull Inn

◉ Modern British

tel: 01223 893844 **27 High St CB21 4DJ**
email: info@blackbull-balsham.co.uk **web:** www.blackbull-balsham.co.uk
dir: *From S: M11 junct 9, A11 towards Newmarket, follow Balsham signs. From N: M11
junct 10, A505 signed Newmarket (A11), onto A11, follow Balsham signs*

Thatched country pub with creative team in the kitchen

Topped by a mop of thatch and with a fabulous garden and terrace, The Black Bull
Inn has its own-brewed real ale on tap and a choice of eating spaces from the
tucked-away nooks around the bar to a barn with a lofty vaulted ceiling and chunky
solid oak tables. Choose from a bar menu of simple, gutsy classics, the celebrated
pie board, or a more inventive carte. Start, perhaps, with pan-fried pigeon breast
with beetroot, lardons, pine nuts and balsamic-dressed rocket. Move on to braised
lamb shank with Parmentier potatoes, pearl barley, root vegetables and mint jus, or
pancetta-wrapped monkfish tail with curried clam cream and vanilla mashed
potato. Finish with an inventive clementine and star anise tarte Tatin with
pomegranate seeds and crème anglaise.

Chef Andrew Price **Owner** Alex Clarke **Seats** 60, Pr/dining room 60 **Times** 12-2/6.30-9
Prices Starter £5-£10, Main £9-£24, Dessert £3-£10, Service optional **Wines** 16
bottles over £30, 38 bottles under £30, 22 by glass **Parking** 20 **Notes** Tasting menu,
Pudding Club, Sunday L £5-£30, Vegetarian available, Children welcome

CAMBRIDGE   Map 12 TL45

BEST WESTERN PLUS Cambridge Quy Mill Hotel

◉◉ Modern European, British, French

tel: 01223 293383 **Church Rd, Stow-Cum-Quy CB25 9AF**
email: info@cambridgequymill.co.uk **web:** www.cambridgequymill.co.uk
dir: *Exit A14 at junct 35, E of Cambridge, onto B1102 for 50yds. Entrance opposite church*

Confident cooking in a former watermill

At the heart of this extended contemporary hotel and health club complex set in 11
acres of riverside meadows, is the original watermill, which was built in 1830.
Situated in the miller's house, and overlooking the waterwheel and mill race, the

refurbished Mill House restaurant makes the most of this feature, while putting on
a distinctly contemporary country inn look. By night it is an intimate place with
open fires and candlelight, cool jazz floating in the background, and a friendly,
upbeat ambience. The skilled kitchen team's intelligent contemporary cooking takes
full account of East Anglian produce allied with spot-on accuracy of timing and
thoughtful composition to make an impact. The menu keeps a keen eye on the
seasons, uniting roast venison with parsnip ketchup, apple and hazelnuts, while
butter-poached pheasant breast might arrive with its slow-cooked leg, pumpkin,
granola and pickled pear. Fishy ideas run to roasted halibut with baby gem, salt-
baked shallots, wild mushrooms and bacon, and for dessert, perhaps plum, vanilla
and almond tart with plum ripple ice cream.

Chef Andrew Walker **Owner** David Munro **Seats** 48, Pr/dining room 80
Times 12-2.30/7-9.45, Closed 25 Dec, L Mon-Fri **Prices** Fixed L 2 course £15, Starter
£7.50-£9.50, Main £16.50-£28, Dessert £6.50-£12, Service optional **Wines** 25
bottles over £30, 35 bottles under £30, 14 by glass **Parking** 90 **Notes** Complimentary
bread & amuse bouche with all ALC, Sunday L £20-£25, Vegetarian available,
Children welcome

Hotel du Vin Cambridge

◉ French Bistro

tel: 01223 227330 **15-19 Trumpington St CB2 1QA**
email: info.cambridge@hotelduvin.com **web:** www.hotelduvin.com
dir: *M11 junct 11 Cambridge S, pass Trumpington Park & Ride on left. Hotel 2m on right
after double rdbt*

Classic bistro dining in the city centre

Hotel du Vin's Cambridge outpost follows the chain's typical concept of a retro
French bistro, all reclaimed wooden floors, banquettes, unclothed wooden tables,
candlelight, an open-to-view kitchen and references to wine all around. The place is
normally humming, and well-drilled staff deliver authentic, well-executed bistro
staples that seem to have been around for centuries. Steak tartare, prawn cocktail,
chicken liver parfait and scallops with sauce vierge-the list goes on-before main
courses of roast chicken with pommes frites, moules frites or a steak from the grill:
perhaps rib-eye or fillet. Good-quality rustic bread, served with unsalted butter, is
part of the package, puddings run to rich chocolate mousse with Chantilly cream,
or tarte au citron, and the wine list is outstanding.

Chef Gareth Davies **Owner** KSL **Seats** 82, Pr/dining room 32 **Times** 12-2.30/6-10
Wines 300 bottles over £30, 58 bottles under £30, 25 by glass **Parking** Valet parking
service **Notes** Brunch 4 course £24.95, Sunday L fr £24.95, Vegetarian available,
Children welcome

Hotel Felix

◎◎ Modern British, Mediterranean

tel: 01223 277977 **Whitehouse Ln, Huntingdon Rd CB3 0LX**
email: help@hotelfelix.co.uk **web:** www.hotelfelix.co.uk
dir: M11 junct 13. From A1 N take A14 turn onto A1307. At City of Cambridge sign turn left into Whitehouse Ln

Intricate and inventive modern cooking in a boutique hotel

This lovely bow-fronted Victorian mansion is home to a sleek boutique hotel which artfully combines elegant period features with a contemporary sheen. The Graffiti restaurant sports abstract modern art on battleship-grey walls, burnished darkwood floors, and unclothed tables, while the large terrace is a crowd puller for alfresco aperitifs and fair weather dining. Like the décor, the food is vibrant and sets off along a modern British road with plenty of sunny Mediterranean flavours along the way. It gets off the blocks with a creative juxtaposition of mackerel tartare with celeriac pannacotta, pickled candied beetroot, horseradish cream and smoked sourdough bread. Next out, ballotine of cod shares a plate with salt cod and leek brandade, roasted cauliflower and cauliflower cheese purée, and lemon and caper brown butter, while game season might see roast haunch of venison matched with kohlrabi fondant, rainbow chard, parsley root purée and whisky sauce. The inventive flair is maintained in an enterprising finale of lemon olive oil cake with lemon yoghurt sorbet, raspberry, white chocolate and lavender.

Chef Jose Graziosi **Owner** Jeremy Cassel **Seats** 45, Pr/dining room 60 **Times** 12–2/6.30–10 **Prices** Fixed L 2 course £14.50, Starter £5.95–£11.95, Main £14.95–£21.95, Dessert £5.75–£10.50 **Wines** 20 bottles over £30, 22 bottles under £30, 19 by glass **Parking** 90 **Notes** Afternoon tea, Sunday L fr £14.50, Vegetarian available, Children welcome

Midsummer House

◎◎◎◎◎ – see page 80 and advert on page 81

Restaurant Alimentum

◎◎◎ – see page 82

Restaurant 22

◎ Modern European

tel: 01223 351880 **22 Chesterton Rd CB4 3AX**
email: enquiries@restaurant22.co.uk
dir: M11 junct 13 towards Cambridge, turn left at rdbt onto Chesterton Rd

Accomplished cooking in an elegant little restaurant

The converted Victorian townhouse near Jesus Green conceals a discreetly elegant and comfortable dining room done out in shades of fawn, brown and beige. The menu follows a monthly-changing, set-price formula of three courses with a sorbet following the starter, which might be pheasant linguine with toasted pine nuts and sage crisps, or haddock, clam and almond chowder. The cooking is driven by market-fresh ingredients, and dishes are distinguished by a lack of frill and flounce. Consistently accomplished main courses have included griddled swordfish steak, accurately timed, with caper and marjoram sauce, rösti and roast baby vegetables, and a labour-intensive ballotine of three birds wrapped in pancetta served with pearl barley, curly kale and a Calvados reduction. The December menu might feature roast fallow deer with an unusual dark chocolate and sprout salad, a bonbon and sweet potato fondant, and close with Christmas pudding and chocolate fondant with spiced pumpkin ice cream.

Chef Chris Kipping **Owner** Armando & Sharon Tommaso **Seats** 26, Pr/dining room 14 **Times** 7–9.45, Closed 25 Dec & New Year, Sun-Mon, L all week **Prices** Prices not confirmed, Service optional **Wines** 26 bottles over £30, 52 bottles under £30, 6 by glass **Parking** On street **Notes** Vegetarian available, Children 10 yrs+

The Anchor Inn

◎ Modern British

tel: 01353 778537 **Bury Ln, Sutton Gault CB6 2BD**
email: anchorinn@popmail.bta.com **web:** www.anchor-inn-restaurant.co.uk
dir: Signed off B1381 in Sutton village, 7m W of Ely via A142

Local flavours in Fen country

Right out in the sticks, a few miles from Ely, the Anchor was built some 365 years ago to put up the workers digging the canals that drained the Fens – the New Bedford River flows past the pub as a reminder of their handiwork. The heritage of the building looms large when you get inside, with its oak panels, quarry tiles and hefty beams, while the smell of wood smoke from one of the log-burners is an evocative addition in the cooler months. Although very much a pub (with real ales at the pumps), food is the star attraction, with a menu packed with British-inspired contemporary stuff such as seared king scallops with chicken wings and a powerful horseradish purée, or G&T-cured salmon. A porcine main course combines tenderloin with confit belly, veggies have options too, and much of the seafood comes from the North Norfolk coast.

Chef Maciej Bilewski **Owner** Black Rock Inns **Seats** 70 **Times** 12–3.30/7–11 **Prices** Fixed L 2 course £14.95, Starter £6–£12, Main £13–£26, Dessert £6–£12, Service optional **Wines** 12 bottles over £30, 38 bottles under £30, 10 by glass **Parking** 16 **Notes** Sunday L fr £12.95, Vegetarian available, Children welcome

See advert on page 83

Midsummer House ❀❀❀❀❀

Modern British **V** 🍷 NOTABLE WINE LIST

tel: 01223 369299 **Midsummer Common CB4 1HA**
email: reservations@midsummerhouse.co.uk
web: www.midsummerhouse.co.uk
dir: *Park in Pretoria Rd, then walk across footbridge. Restaurant on left*

Stellar cooking from a chef at the top of his game

In a city used to topping league tables, Midsummer House does its bit to make Cambridge an essential stopover on any culinary tour of the country. Daniel Clifford took over this Victorian villa on common land by the river (where cows do actually freely roam as if they own the place) back in 1998 and set about creating the divertingly handsome, dynamic and high-powered restaurant we see today. It is an exceedingly civilised series of spaces done out with good taste in fashionably neutral shades with a warmth that is enhanced by the service team who make a visit seamless, easy and fun. The place has been improved and upgraded year-on-year, which reflects Daniel's single-minded approach to constant improvement. The conservatory looks over the pretty garden and there's a small bar upstairs with a terrace looking out over the River Cam. A window gives a view into the kitchen without allowing the action to distract too much. The menus are of the tasting variety – five-, seven- and ten-course options – with the shorter version offered at lunch in the week and in the private dining room (it's worth mentioning at this point that there's a rather glam first-floor private dining room). Whichever of the menus you go for, whether your decision is made by appetite or budget, rest assured that the kitchen has done everything to ensure there are plenty of thrills along the way. With a background at the top end of classical dining, combined with a creative mind and astounding technical abilities, Clifford delivers flavour combinations that hit the mark again and again, with outstanding ingredients and everything looking gorgeous on the plate. First up might be smoked haddock with pickled onion and grilled cheese in a clever partnership that brings the best out of the immaculate produce, followed by beetroot baked over hot coals and matched with quinoa and goats' cheese. Braised pork cheeks arrive tender and packed with flavour, and roasted scallops with an accompanying tartare, Jerusalem artichokes and some black truffle. If pot roasted chicken, leeks and mushrooms sounds humble, rest assured it is not. There's a lot of ground to cover if you've gone for the ten-courses, but it is so well judged that you don't want it to end. Adding a cheese course from the trolley before dessert is one way of keeping things going. The sweet courses (two of them) might include a stunning chocolate dome or an exotic poached kumquat number with tamarind yogurt sorbet, carrot and cardamom. The wine list, like everything here, is a class act.

Chef Daniel Clifford **Owner** Midsummer House Ltd **Seats** 45, Pr/dining room 16 **Times** 12-1.30/7-9, Closed 2 wks Xmas, Sun-Mon, L Tue **Prices** Prices not confirmed **Wines** 759 bottles over £30, 23 bottles under £30, 21 by glass **Parking** On street **Notes** Tasting menu 5/7/10 course £47.50/£82.50/£105, Children welcome

MIDSUMMER HOUSE

Midsummer House is located in the heart of historic Cambridge. This Victorian Villa encapsulates Daniel Clifford's vision for culinary perfection and is home to some seriously stylish food.

Daniel Clifford's quest for culinary perfection has taken the restaurant to another level over the past 13 years; his cooking has a modern-focus which is underpinned by classical French technique offering seriously sophisticated food with dishes arriving dressed to thrill.

Upstairs there is a private dining room, and a sophisticated bar and terrace for alfresco drinks with river views. Our private dining room is the perfect location for small weddings, lavish birthday celebrations, simple family gatherings or corporate entertaining.

Midsummer Common, Cambridge CB4 1HA
Tel: 01223 369299 • Fax: 01223 302672
Website: www.midsummerhouse.co.uk • **Email:** reservations@midsummerhouse.co.uk

Restaurant Alimentum ✿✿✿

Modern European 🍷 NOTABLE WINE LIST

tel: 01223 413000 **152-154 Hills Rd CB2 8PB**
email: reservations@restaurantalimentum.co.uk
web: www.restaurantalimentum.co.uk
dir: *Opposite Cambridge Leisure Park*

Impeccable ingredients and classy, contemporary cooking

If your Latin's a bit rusty, the name of this operation in a modern building near the city's leisure park, means 'food', and the place comes with bags of contemporary swagger. It has seats upholstered in red at black-lacquered tables, scarlet padded walls and smoked glass, plus an open-to-view kitchen giving a window onto chef-proprietor Mark Poynton and his brigade at work. Poynton puts ethics and sustainability at the top of the agenda when it comes to sourcing his ingredients, while the kitchen follows a broadly modern European path of diverting originality. The set-price lunch and early-evening menu offers storming value, and trading upwards, there's a carte, a seven-course 'Taste of Alimentum' and a ten-course 'Surprise' menu, all keeping step with the seasons. This produces starters such as duck foie gras mousse with passionfruit, walnut and spring onion to leaven its richness, or a dish of grilled plaice with langoustine, fennel, cucumber and seaweed that armchair gourmets might recognise from the chef's appearance on the *Great British Menu*. Tight-lipped menu descriptions belie the complexity and multi-layered flavours in dishes: a straightforward-sounding main course of beef fillet with snails and red wine, for instance, is a tried-and-true marriage

of complementary flavours. Fish is treated inventively, with butternut squash, chorizo, apple and samphire bringing explosions of distinct flavours to roast halibut fillet cooked with pinpoint accuracy. It's all beautifully presented, too, through to show-stealing puddings that might unite apple caramel and vanilla with an Arctic roll theme, or a thought-provoking combo of barbecue orange parfait with mojito and liquorice. The judiciously curated wine list covers the principal French regions before moving on to the rest of Europe and the New World.

Chef Mark Poynton **Owner** Mark Poynton **Seats** 62, Pr/dining room 30 **Times** 12-2.30/6-10, Closed 24-30 Dec, BHs, L 31 Dec **Prices** Fixed L 2 course £20.50, Fixed D 3 course £26.50, Tasting menu £72, Starter £15, Main £23, Dessert £15 **Wines** 206 bottles over £30, 9 bottles under £30, 24 by glass **Parking** NCP Cambridge Leisure Centre (3 min walk) **Notes** Tasting menu 'surprise' 10 course £85, Sunday L, Vegetarian available, Children welcome

FORDHAM
Map 12 TL67

The White Pheasant
◉◉ British, European

tel: 01638 720414 **21 Market St CB7 5LQ**
email: whitepheasant@live.com **web:** www.whitepheasant.com
dir: A14 to Newmarket, A142 Ely junct, follow signs Fordham. Situated on rdbt, junct Station Rd

Gastro-pub run by an accomplished chef

After setting out on his culinary career by training at the White Pheasant in 2005, Calvin Holland has returned in triumph as its new chef-proprietor following a spell spent honing his craft in some pretty whizzo kitchens. The place ticks all the right boxes for a switched-on modern foodie pub with its simply decorated interior, log fires and plain wood tables, but the cooking sets it a cut above the average. The kitchen has impeccable supply lines to the best materials from local producers, bolstered by freshly caught fish and seasonal game, and the technical nous to extract full-on flavours from it all. Duck might provide the meat for a starter, served as a crispy croquette, with its liver in a smooth parfait, home-made pickles to cut the richness, and a teriyaki sauce. Main course could see seared rump of lamb partnered with a terrine of shoulder meat and potatoes, crispy sweetbreads, peas

and beans, and at the end, lemon drizzle cake comes with lemon curd, violet meringue and ginger beer sorbet.

The White Pheasant

Chef Calvin Holland **Owner** Gary & Andrea Holland **Seats** 50
Times 12-2.30/6.30-9.30, Closed Mon, D Sun **Prices** Service optional **Wines** 17 bottles over £30, 22 bottles under £30, 10 by glass **Parking** 25 **Notes** Tasting menu £79 for 2 people, Sunday L £15.95-£22.95, Vegetarian available, Children welcome

HINXTON
Map 12 TL44

The Red Lion Inn
◉ Modern British

tel: 01799 530601 **32 High St CB10 1QY**
email: info@redlionhinxton.co.uk **web:** www.redlionhinxton.co.uk
dir: M11 junct 10, at rdbt take A505 continue to A1301 signed Saffron Walden/Hinxton for 0.75m & follow signs for Hinxton. From S: M11 junct 9, towards A11, left onto A1301. Left to Hinxton

Complex modern cookery in a Tudor village inn

The timbered Tudor inn wears its age on its sleeve, with an appealing rustic look both on the pinkish outside and on the beamed and brick-walled interior. Unclothed tables with plenty of space between make for a relaxed feel, and the team do their versatile best to keep everyone happy, both the traditional pub-food customers and the seekers after modern British localist gastronomy. There's much to enjoy in dishes that are often technically quite complex, such as braised pig's cheek with

continued

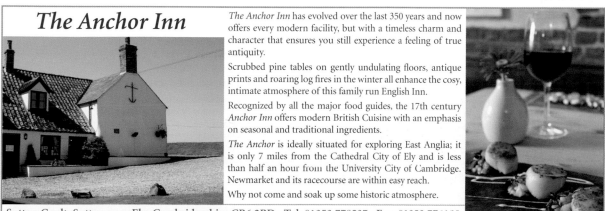

The Anchor Inn

The Anchor Inn has evolved over the last 350 years and now offers every modern facility, but with a timeless charm and character that ensures you still experience a feeling of true antiquity.

Scrubbed pine tables on gently undulating floors, antique prints and roaring log fires in the winter all enhance the cosy, intimate atmosphere of this family run English Inn.

Recognized by all the major food guides, the 17th century *Anchor Inn* offers modern British Cuisine with an emphasis on seasonal and traditional ingredients.

The Anchor is ideally situated for exploring East Anglia; it is only 7 miles from the Cathedral City of Ely and is less than half an hour from the University City of Cambridge. Newmarket and its racecourse are within easy reach.

Why not come and soak up some historic atmosphere.

Sutton Gault, Sutton near Ely, Cambridgeshire CB6 2BD • Tel: 01353 778537 • Fax: 01353 776180
Website: www.anchor-inn-restaurant.co.uk • Email: anchorinn@popmail.bta.com

HINXTON *continued*

root veg purée, caramelised apple, leek crisps and tomato jus, and mains like truffled turbot with moules marinière, steamed leeks and gnocchi, or maple-glazed goose breast with parsnip variations in horseradish jus, decorated with a blood orange tuile. Home-made ice creams and sorbets, or cheeses with tomato chutney, are simpler alternatives to rather over-involved desserts such as caramelised lemon tart with honey, pistachio praline, mango coulis and a cider and lime sorbet.

Chef Jiri Wolker **Owner** Alex Clarke **Seats** 60 **Times** 12–2/6.30–9 **Prices** Starter £5–£10, Main £9–£24, Dessert £3–£10, Service optional **Wines** 16 bottles over £30, 38 bottles under £30, 22 by glass **Parking** 43 **Notes** Pudding Club, Sunday L £5–£30, Vegetarian available, Children welcome

---

HUNTINGDON
Map 12 TL27

The Abbot's Elm
◉◉ Modern European

tel: 01487 773773 **Abbots Ripton PE28 2PA**
email: info@theabbotselm.co.uk **web:** www.theabbotselm.co.uk
dir: A1(M) junct 13 onto A14 towards Huntingdon. At 1st rdbt straight on (A141 Spittals Way). Left at 2nd rdbt signed Abbots Ripton. 3m in village centre

Thatched inn with confident cooking

A fire a couple of years ago badly damaged this 17th-century pub, but once again the thatch is spruce and the external walls are a warm shade of pinky terracotta. The owners, John and Julia Abbey, took the opportunity to modernise the interior a bit – nothing jarring – keeping the soul of the place, and adding a bit of a contemporary sheen. With exposed oak rafters and a large brick fireplace, The Abbot's Elm has surely never looked so good. There's a lounge bar serving real ales, a cosy snug, a smart restaurant, plus three bedrooms and a cookery school where chef-patron Julia passes on her wisdom and experience. There's a beer garden, too. Expect classy pub classics and sandwiches in the bar (or garden), while the restaurant ups the ante with the likes of seared scallops and red mullet with a crab and scallop sauce. There are classical leanings to the output, with the flavours hitting the mark. Main-course breast of Tiddenham duck arrives perfectly pink, for example, served with its confit leg, dauphinoise potatoes and juniper sauce.

Chef Julia Abbey **Owner** John & Julia Abbey **Seats** 54 **Times** 12–2.15/6–9.30, Closed D Sun **Prices** Fixed L 2 course £13.95, Fixed D 3 course £22.50, Tasting menu £49.50, Starter £4.75–£9.50, Main £8.75–£22.50, Dessert £6.50–£6.95 **Wines** 35 bottles over £30, 23 bottles under £30, 29 by glass **Parking** 50 **Notes** Sunday L £17.95–£22.50, Vegetarian available, Children welcome

---

The Old Bridge Hotel
◉◉ Modern British 🍷 NOTABLE WINE LIST

tel: 01480 424300 **1 High St PE29 3TQ**
email: oldbridge@huntsbridge.co.uk **web:** www.huntsbridge.com
dir: From A14 or A1 follow Huntingdon signs. Hotel visible from inner ring road

Notable cooking and exceptional wines from an old favourite

The Old Bridge, at one time a bank, combines the function of busy inn, boutique-style hotel and popular, light and airy restaurant overlooking the patio. The kitchen combines Mediterranean and modern British styles with the occasional nod towards the Far East, with seasonality driving its output. One attractively presented and colourful starter is precisely seared scallops served on twigs of rosemary with squash, borlotti beans, capers, sage and chilli, forming a well-considered amalgam of flavours and textures. An alternative might be chicken and shrimp naan roll with sweet chilli dipping sauce and daikon, before main courses such as moist and

tender saddle of venison accompanied by potato and beetroot boulangère, artichokes and rosemary sauce, or fillet of bass with crushed new potatoes, purple-sprouting broccoli and another well-wrought sauce, this time salsa verde. Complimentary freshly baked bread is appreciated, and skilfully made puddings could run to chocolate marquise flavoured with salted caramel served with pistachio ice cream and peanut brittle. The extensive wine list is a delight, and there's also a wine shop on site.

Chef Jack Woolner **Owner** J Hoskins **Seats** 100, Pr/dining room 60
Times 12–2/6.30–10 **Prices** Prices not confirmed, Service optional **Wines** 300 bottles over £30, 75 bottles under £30, 35 by glass **Parking** 60 **Notes** Sunday L, Vegetarian available, Children welcome

---

KEYSTON
Map 11 TL07

Pheasant Inn
◉◉ Modern British, European 🍷 NOTABLE WINE LIST

tel: 01832 710241 **Loop Rd PE28 0RE**
email: info@thepheasant-keyston.co.uk
dir: 0.5m off A14, clearly signed, 10m W of Huntingdon, 14m E of Kettering

European-influenced cooking full of fresh ideas

A whitewashed thatched village inn some 12 miles outside Huntingdon, the Pheasant is unmistakably a country cousin of that town's Old Bridge. Inside, it's been allowed to maintain its centuries-old identity, with simple furniture under the oak beams. The dining room, done in hunting-print wallpaper with high-backed chairs at unclothed tables, plays host to European-influenced cooking that's full of fresh ideas, much of it sourced from the Pheasant's own kitchen garden. Crown Prince squash makes a hearty soup, garnished with a slick of crème fraîche, or there could be a portion of smoked haddock to start, topped with a poached egg, in tarragon-parmesan sauce. Main courses look to Italy for inspiration for the shellfish risotto and cavolo nero that accompany sea trout, or to France for a classically mandarin-sauced serving of duck-breast and confit leg-with rösti, red cabbage and beetroot. Pub classics will warm the cockles of the bangers and mash brigade. Finish with tremulous pannacotta, served with poached pear and rhubarb sorbet.

Chef Simon Cadge **Owner** Simon Cadge, Gerda Koedijk **Seats** 80, Pr/dining room 30
Times 12–2/6.30–9.30, Closed 2–15 Jan, Mon, D Sun **Prices** Fixed L 2 course fr £14.95, Fixed D 3 course fr £29.95, Tasting menu fr £55, Starter £5.95–£9.95, Main £11.95–£21.95, Dessert £5.95–£7.95, Service optional **Wines** 50 bottles over £30, 25 bottles under £30, 12 by glass **Parking** 40 **Notes** Sunday L £15.95–£25, Vegetarian available, Children welcome

---

LITTLE WILBRAHAM
Map 12 TL55

Hole in the Wall
◉◉ Modern British

tel: 01223 812282 **2 High St CB21 5JY**
email: hello@holeinthewallcambridge.co.uk
dir: A14 junct 35. A11 exit at The Wilbrahams

Classic country inn with sound seasonal cooking

In a pretty village near Cambridge, this 16th-century inn has bags of character, with open fires, low beams in the ceilings and good-natured atmosphere. Pop in for a drink or join the faithful admirers for a meal: it's easy to see why it is such a popular place, with more than a hint of the cosmopolitan about the daily-changing menu. Scallops are partnered by chorizo and served with cauliflower purée and a novel but effective pickled raisin sauce, and onion and black truffle risotto is perfectly timed to bring out its clear, robust flavours. Often innovative sauces and accompaniments add an extra dimension to sound, well-timed ingredients: a spicy caramel jus adds a touch of sweetness to first-rate roast duck, with rösti, chicory and pickled cucumber, while cod fillet is accompanied by curried granola and raisin agrodolce. Dishes are neatly and appetisingly presented, particularly puddings of lemon and Earl Grey posset, and spiced plum crumble with custard.

Chef Alex Rushmer **Owner** Alex Rushmer **Seats** 75, Pr/dining room 40
Times 12-2/7-9, Closed 2 wks Jan, Mon, L Tue, D Sun **Prices** Fixed L 2 course £18, Fixed D 3 course £30, Tasting menu £45-£55 **Wines** 10 by glass **Parking** 30
Notes Sunday L £26-£30, Vegetarian available, Children welcome

MELBOURN
Map 12 TL34

The Sheene Mill
◉◉ Modern, Traditional British **NEW**

tel: 01763 261393 **39 Station Rd SG8 6DX**
email: enquiries@thesheenemill.com web: www.thesheenemill.com
dir: *M11 junct 10 onto A505 towards Royston. Right to Melbourn, pass church on right, on left before old bridge*

Confident modern cooking in a stylish mill

The 16th-century mill house no longer works the River Mel as it once did, but the waterway and pond are reminders of its former life. Today's Sheene Mill is a

restaurant and wedding venue that serves the local community in an altogether different way but is most certainly an asset in every sense. There are glorious gardens, a spa and stylish bedrooms, while the restaurant is an elegant space watched over by an engaging service team. The kitchen takes a contemporary approach and shows attention to detail in the execution of modern British dishes. Rock oyster beignets arrive as a starter with chilli and parsley salsa and cucumber jelly, for example, and mackerel cannelloni is a clever construction pointed up by home-made piccalilli. Everything looks good on the plate and high quality regional produce makes its mark throughout. Slow-cooked belly of pork with braised Puy lentils, black pudding bonbon and sautéed wild mushrooms is a rustic-chic main course option, with pineapple and star anise tarte Tatin among some creative desserts.

The Sheene Mill

Chef Ivor Morgan **Owner** Adam Jordan, Serena Saunders **Seats** 120, Pr/dining room 60 **Times** 12-3/6-9.30, Closed 26 Dec, 1 Jan **Prices** Fixed L 2 course £18, Fixed D 3 course £22, Starter £5.95-£12.50, Main £9.95-£29.95, Dessert £3.50-£9.50, Service optional 10% **Wines** 31 bottles over £30, 18 bottles under £30, 11 by glass **Parking** 50 **Notes** Afternoon tea £18, Sunday L £19.95-£28.95, Vegetarian available, Children welcome

See advert below

BEST WESTERN PLUS Orton Hall Hotel & Spa

Modern British

tel: 01733 391111 **The Village, Orton Longueville PE2 7DN**
email: reception@ortonhall.co.uk **web:** www.bw-ortonhallhotel.co.uk
dir: *Off A605 E, opposite Orton Mere*

Grand old building with well-crafted menu

With a heritage as the former home of the Marquess of Huntly, the old hall doesn't lack for period charm, and that certainly goes for the main restaurant, bedecked with burnished oak panels and mullioned windows. The 20-acre estate boasts a swish spa and former stables turned into an atmospheric pub, but the Huntly Restaurant catches the eye. It's a refined room with smartly dressed tables and a formal service style (drinks in the bar beforehand, for example). The cooking is broadly modern British, with starters such as a terrine of chicken and spicy pork, served with a winter apple chutney, followed by a main of poached Scottish salmon with a smoked haddock velouté and caper and parsley potatoes. To finish there might be glacé cherry and almond parfait with lemon biscuits.

Chef Kevin Wood **Owner** Abacus Hotels **Seats** 34, Pr/dining room 40
Times 12.30-2/7-9.30, Closed 25 Dec, L Mon-Sat **Prices** Fixed D 3 course £30-£40.95, Service optional **Wines** 10 bottles over £30, 37 bottles under £30, 6 by glass **Parking** 200 **Notes** Sunday L fr £18.95, Vegetarian available, Children welcome

Bull Hotel

Modern European, British

tel: 01733 561364 **Westgate PE1 1RB**
email: rooms@bull-hotel-peterborough.com **web:** www.peelhotels.co.uk
dir: *Off A1, follow city centre signs. Hotel opposite Queensgate Shopping Centre. Car park on Broadway adjacent to library*

Modernised classic dishes in a 17th-century coaching inn

This one-time coaching inn dates from the 17th century and still displays its period credentials out front. There's a contemporary swagger inside, though, not least in the brasserie-style restaurant out back. With its creamy neutrality and darkwood tables, the informal and cheerful vibe is matched by the spiffy staff dressed in trendy black with matching aprons. The menu deals in classic flavours and combinations, comfort food for the 21st century. Chicken liver parfait with balsamic onions and toasted onion bread is a typical first course, or there's the slightly more racy devilled sardine sandwich with tomato and apple chutney. Main-course roast rump of lamb with a fondant potato and Mediterranean-inspired flavours (olives, sun-blushed tomatoes and garlic) hits the spot, or go for chargrilled sirloin steak with parsley mash and Portobello mushrooms. Finish with a hot chocolate fondant with pistachio ice cream and sesame wafer.

Chef Jason Ingram **Owner** Peel Hotels plc **Seats** 80, Pr/dining room 200
Times 12-2/6.30-9.45, Closed L Sat **Prices** Fixed D 3 course £24.50, Starter £5.50-£7.50, Main £12.95-£21.95, Dessert £5.95-£6.95, Service optional **Wines** 3 bottles over £30, 20 bottles under £30, 8 by glass **Parking** 100 **Notes** Brunch, Afternoon tea, Sunday L, Vegetarian available, Children welcome

The George Hotel & Brasserie

Modern British

tel: 01480 812300 **High St, Buckden PE19 5XA**
email: mail@thegeorgebuckden.com **web:** www.thegeorgebuckden.com
dir: *Off A1, S of junct with A14*

Popular brasserie with well-judged dishes

The heyday of The George may have seemed long gone, but the vision of the Furbank family brought the old coaching inn back to life in 2003 as they created a venue with a cool and contemporary demeanour while respecting the integrity of the old building. The charming period exterior with its grand columns still exudes old-world solidity, but inside it is opened-up, relaxed and rather stylish. The same forethought and good sense went into the dining option, with the brasserie providing an easy-going environment but not stinting on quality. The chef's Italian background is evident in the menu, which delivers feel-good flavours based on quality ingredients (including some stuff they grow themselves). Smoked haddock risotto is helped along with a hint of curry spices and matched with cauliflower tempura, followed perhaps by a simple, comforting main of slow-cooked blade of beef with velvety mash, carrots and beans. Apple and frangipane tart with Calvados ice cream or morello cherry clafoutis with mascarpone cream end things indulgently.

Chef José Graziosi **Owner** Richard & Anne Furbank **Seats** 60, Pr/dining room 30
Times 12-2.30/7-9.30 **Prices** Prices not confirmed, Service optional **Wines** 42 bottles over £30, 70 bottles under £30, 18 by glass **Parking** 25 **Notes** Sunday L, Vegetarian available, Children welcome

Bell Inn Hotel

Modern British, French V

tel: 01733 241066 **Great North Rd PE7 3RA**
email: reception@thebellstilton.co.uk **web:** www.thebellstilton.co.uk
dir: *A1(M) junct 16, follow Stilton signs. Hotel in village centre*

Contemporary cooking in rambling old coaching inn

This coaching inn in a charming village on the Great North Road dates from 1642. Gentle updating and gentrification have added a high level of 21st-century comforts while retaining stone walls, mullioned windows, blazing fires and beams; a large courtyard entices in good weather. The kitchen moves with the times and turns out bright ideas in the contemporary mode. Pulled pork and apple terrine with piccalilli and a deep-fried egg has a good balance of flavours among starters, or there might be broad bean risotto in garlic and parsley butter topped with seared scallops. Main courses run to roast chicken breast, succulent and full of flavour, with tarragon sauce, baby vegetables and dauphinoise, or loin of cod on tomato and basil sauce with butternut squash risotto and wilted spinach. Presentation is a forte, seen in a dessert of peanut butter parfait with hot toffee sauce garnished with slices of marinated plums.

Chef Robin Devonshire **Owner** Liam McGivern **Seats** 60, Pr/dining room 20 **Times** 12-2/7-9.30, Closed 25 Dec, BHs, L Mon-Sat, D Sun **Prices** Fixed D 3 course £29.95-£35.15, Starter £5.35-£7.10, Main £9.95-£19.25, Dessert £5.65, Service optional **Wines** 8 bottles over £30, 31 bottles under £30, 11 by glass **Parking** 30 **Notes** Sunday L £15.95-£18.95, Children welcome

WANSFORD
Map 12 TL09

The Haycock Hotel

⊛ Modern British

tel: 01780 782223 & 781124 **London Rd PE8 6JA**
email: phil.brette@thehaycock.co.uk **web:** www.thehaycock.co.uk
dir: In village centre accessible from A1/A47 intersection

Bright, modern cooking in historic inn

This 16th-century coaching inn on the River Nene has been offering up hospitality for travellers for several hundred years and shows no sign of giving up the ghost. Part of the Macdonald group, the 21st-century Haycock matches the period charm of days gone by with the anticipated modern touches, so there are meeting rooms, WiFi and the like, but also a rather nifty dining option. The restaurant has shifted out of the conservatory and into a cosy room not lacking traditional features. The kitchen is not averse to the occasional contemporary touch and modern cooking technique, so carpaccio of venison might come with a horseradish pannacotta and parmesan wafer, and a main course fillet of beef is served with an oxtail barley risotto and merlot reduction. There's evident ambition on show, although not everything reaches the same heights. For dessert, chocolate and pear brûlée is served with a brandy snap biscuit.

Times 12-2.30/6.30-9.30, Closed D Sun, 24 & 31 Dec

WISBECH
Map 12 TF40

Crown Lodge Hotel

⊛ Modern, Traditional

tel: 01945 773391 **Downham Rd, Outwell PE14 8SE**
email: office@thecrownlodgehotel.co.uk **web:** www.thecrownlodgehotel.co.uk
dir: 5m SE of Wisbech on A1122, 1m from junct with A1101, towards Downham Market

Simple modern setting and a broad menu

A modern hotel that is kitted out to host conferences and meetings, Crown Lodge is a useful local resource with a spacious bar and restaurant that cover several bases. On the banks of Welle Creek at Outwell, the hotel is also somewhat of a hotspot for squash, with courts to hire and bookable coaching sessions. The flexible approach to dining means you can go for simple things like fish and chips or a burger, but there's also a more ambitious carte. This offers a starter of roast loin of lamb with sweetbreads and braised Puy lentils, and another that wraps local asparagus in filo pastry and dresses it with lemon and thyme. Move on to whole grilled plaice, or pan-fried kangaroo steak with wasabi-infused mash, and you'll find plenty of choice for dessert with everything from classic crème brûlée to hearty sticky toffee pudding up for grabs.

Chef Jamie Symons **Owner** Mr W J Moore **Seats** 40, Pr/dining room 100 **Times** 12-2.30/6-10, Closed 25-26 Dec, 1 Jan **Prices** Prices not confirmed, Service optional **Wines** 4 bottles over £30, 52 bottles under £30, 10 by glass **Parking** 50 **Notes** Sunday L, Vegetarian available, Children welcome

CHESHIRE

ALDERLEY EDGE
Map 16 SJ87

The Alderley Restaurant

⊛⊛⊛ – see page 88

BROXTON
Map 15 SJ45

Carden Park Hotel, Golf Resort & Spa

⊛ Modern British

tel: 01829 731000 **Carden Park CH3 9DQ**
web: www.cardenpark.co.uk
dir: A41 signed Whitchurch to Chester, at Broxton rdbt turn on to A534 towards Wrexham. After 2m turn into Carden Park Estate

Nostalgic country estate cooking

Standing in a rolling expanse of Cheshire countryside, much of which is championship golf acreage, through which the winding approach road leads, Carden Park is a lavishly scaled country estate not far from Chester. If you look hard, you'll see its Jacobean core, but the views from Redmond's dining room over the formal gardens to the Welsh mountains beyond are enough to be going on with. Country-house cooking with a nostalgic air is the drill, embracing ginger-crumbed goats' cheese mousse with beetroot purée and a parmesan wafer, before a trio of lamb – a faggot of braised shoulder, roast rump and chargrilled cutlet – with sticky red cabbage, wilted spinach and fondant potato, or roast salmon on warm Niçoise with a fried egg and hollandaise. Finish with flapjack-based coconut and raspberry delice with coconut ice cream and raspberry sauce, or tangerine tart and orange sorbet.

Times 12.30 2.30/7-10, Closed L Mon-Sat, D Sun

BURWARDSLEY
Map 15 SJ55

The Pheasant Inn

⊛ British, European

tel: 01829 770434 **Higher Burwardsley CH3 9PF**
email: info@thepheasantinn.co.uk **web:** www.thepheasantinn.co.uk
dir: A41 from Chester towards Whitchurch. After 6m turn left for Tattenhall. In village signs for Burwardsley. Top of hill left at PO

Crowd-pleasing modern pub dining

Looking smart after a recent spruce up, The Pheasant is an attractive proposition with well-kept real ales lining up at the bar, no-nonsense modern pub cooking, and comfy rooms to stay over. The wide-ranging menu features a healthy showing of local produce and pleases both traditionalists seeking pub classics done well (home-made pies and gravy, or beer-battered haddock and chunky chips with mushy peas and tartare sauce, say) or those looking for more contemporary ideas. These include crispy ox cheek with celeriac and horseradish remoulade, candied beetroot and smoked bacon, ahead of pheasant 'saltimbocca' with sauerkraut, sweetcorn, and apple and sage fritters. Desserts deliver comfort in the form of sticky toffee pudding with salted caramel sauce and rum and raisin ice cream, or creamy rice pudding with lavender shortbread and blackberry jam.

Chef Matt Leech **Owner** Sue & Harold Nelson **Seats** 120 **Times** 12-9.30, All-day dining **Prices** Starter £5-£7.50, Main £8.95-£19.95, Dessert £5.25-£8.95, Service optional **Wines** 13 bottles over £30, 27 bottles under £30, 12 by glass **Parking** 60 **Notes** Sunday L £12.95, Vegetarian available, Children welcome

The Alderley Restaurant ❀❀❀

ALDERLEY EDGE   Map 16 SJ87

Modern British V

tel: 01625 583033 **Macclesfield Rd SK9 7BJ**
email: reservations@alderleyedgehotel.com
web: www.thealderleyedgehotel.com
dir: *A538 to Alderley Edge, then B5087 Macclesfield Rd*

Dynamic modern British cooking amid the Cheshire smart set

Manchester's movers and shakers, such as the wealthy industrialist who built this Victorian Gothic pile, have always gravitated towards the des-res village of Alderley Edge, although these days its residents are more likely to kick a ball for a living. The conservatory restaurant hogs pole position for views over lush grounds and gardens, offering a splendid retro setting with swagged-back curtains, chandeliers, artwork and crisp napery on well-spaced tables, while well-informed and amiable staff keep the wheels turning smoothly. Chef Sean Sutton conjures up exciting modern British food brimming with locally-sourced ingredients, all composed with a happy marriage of flavours and textures, and delivered via a trio of multi-course tasting menus in support of the carte. Roasted scallops with crisp pancetta and a workout of apple textures is an attention-grabbing opener, as is ballotine of rabbit with foie gras cream, its richness balanced by soused cherries and crumbled amaretti biscuits. Fishy compositions unite baked hake with pumpkin purée, wild mushrooms and grilled leeks, while fillet and crispy-crumbed cheek of Cheshire beef with caramelised shallots, purées of onion and potato, Bovril carrots, and a rich beefy sauce will bring a smile from carnivores. Desserts are as well

thought out, impressively constructed and attractive as the rest of the show: a zippy mojito-themed pairing of lime espuma and mint granita sits high on the refreshing spectrum. But when it comes to choc-fest satisfaction, top Parisian chocolatier Cluizel provides the wherewithal for a luxuriant chocolate crémeux, ganache and brownie matched with passionfruit textures and honeycomb. Cheese lovers should not pass on the superb listing of artisan English cheeses. There's also a brasserie with a separate menu.

Chef Sean Sutton **Owner** J W Lees (Brewers) Ltd **Seats** 80, Pr/ dining room 130 **Times** 12-2/7-10, Closed 1 Jan, L 31 Dec, D 25-26 Dec **Prices** Fixed L 2 course £22.95, Tasting menu £36.95-£76.50, Starter £11.95-£12.95, Main £22.95-£23.50, Dessert £10.95, Service optional **Wines** 300 bottles over £30, 19 bottles under £30, 16 by glass **Parking** 82 **Notes** Sunday L fr £27.95, Children welcome

ABode Chester

◉◉ Modern British **V**

tel: 01244 405820 & 347000 **Grosvenor Rd CH1 2DJ**
email: restaurant@abodechester.co.uk **web:** www.abodechester.co.uk
dir: *Phone for directions*

Confident contemporary cooking and stellar views

The Cheshire outpost of the Abode hotel group occupies a shiny, modern rotunda overlooking Chester Racecourse. Like the others in the group, Michael Caines Restaurant is the main dining option, and here it's up on the fifth floor with stellar views over the castle, racecourse and lush countryside. There's a contemporary finish to the space, with stylish fixtures and fittings such as rather glam light fittings. The service team are a well-drilled bunch. The menus-carte, tasting and table d'hôte among them-take a classical approach with contemporary touches along the way. Ham hock terrine comes with an excellent piccalilli and thyme and rosemary focaccia, while a single (and sizable) scallop is partnered with truffled celeriac purée and raisin vinaigrette. Main courses bring slow-cooked venison with sauerkraut, or pan-fried fillet of stone bass with tomato fondue and shellfish bisque. For dessert, there's the likes of pistachio soufflé with the nut also flavouring the accompanying crème anglaise and ice cream.

Chef Ian Hird **Owner** Andrew Brownsword **Seats** 78, Pr/dining room 18
Times 12-2.30/6-9.45 **Prices** Fixed L 2 course £10, Fixed D 3 course £22.95, Tasting menu £65, Starter £8.50-£15, Main £10.50-£25.50, Dessert £8.95, Service optional 12% **Wines** 33 bottles over £30, 17 bottles under £30, 9 by glass **Parking** 36 **Notes** Sunday L £10-£25, Children welcome

BEST WESTERN PREMIER Queen Hotel

◉◉ British **NEW**

tel: 01244 305000 **City Rd CH1 3AH**
email: queenhotel@feathers.uk.com **web:** www.feathers.uk.com
dir: *Follow signs for Railway Station. Hotel is opposite*

Modern brasserie style in an old railway hotel

The Queen, a Victorian railway hotel, has been rising to the stately occasion since the days of steam locomotives, and continues to pile on the style in the modern city. Handy of course for the station and not far from the cathedral, it has now been given an eye-popping interior design to shake out any cobwebs, with much use of loudly patterned fabrics. There are three restaurants, the principal one being a sleek wood-floored space with unclothed tables, kitchen views, mirrored pillars and gold voile curtains to divide the expansive space. The cooking style is modern brasserie, with the kitchen treating quality ingredients with respect in vigorously flavoured dishes. A trio of scallops sitting individually on cushions of creamy brown shrimp risotto looks the part, and may be the curtain-raiser to herb-crusted lamb rump, served with champ in a forthright rosemary jus. Indulgence arrives in the form of a finale of treacle frangipane tart with egg custard ice cream, made with eggs from a local Cheshire farm.

Chef Alan Davies **Owner** Feathers Hotel Group **Seats** 54, Pr/dining room 16
Times 6-10 **Prices** Fixed D 3 course £30, Starter £6-£12, Main £17-£25, Dessert £5.50-£8, Service optional **Wines** 5 bottles over £30, 27 bottles under £30, 6 by glass **Parking** 153 **Notes** Vegetarian available, Children 8 yrs+

La Brasserie at The Chester Grosvenor & Spa

◉◉ Modern, European

tel: 01244 324024 **Eastgate CH1 1LT**
email: restaurants@chestergrosvenor.co.uk
dir: *A56 follow signs for city centre hotels. On Eastgate St next to the Eastgate clock*

Top-end brasserie dining at landmark hotel

Offering commendable support to its superstar sibling – Simon Radley at The Chester Grosvenor – the brasserie at this landmark hotel is no shrinking violet. With all the swagger of an authentique Parisian outfit, La Brasserie has black-leather banquettes, wooden floors, shimmering brass and a giant hand-painted glass skylight, plus a menu that builds on the classic repertoire with confidence. A first course dish called 'Piglet' turns out some tender pork belly in the company of a squid cassoulet, or go for the simplicity of Severn and Wye smoked salmon. Veal T-bone steak is cooked to delicious smokiness in the Josper grill and comes with Italian ham, artichokes, figs and chestnuts. The Josper is put to good use throughout, with Welsh dry-aged beef cooked over sustainably sourced wood from Kent. Seafood gets a look-in, too, with the likes of Atlantic cod and sea bass cooked as you like and served with a choice of sauces. That leaves desserts such as a terrific Grosvenor chocolate cheesecake with raspberry ice.

Chef Simon Radley, Howard Edwards, Duncan Highway **Owner** Grosvenor **Seats** 80
Times 12-2.30/5.30-10.30, Closed 25 Dec **Prices** Fixed L 2 course fr £19.50, Fixed D 2 course fr £25, Starter £7.95-£13.95, Main £16.95-£29.95, Dessert £6.25-£8.95, Service optional **Wines** 13 bottles over £30, 18 bottles under £30, 31 by glass **Parking** NCP attached to hotel **Notes** Champagne Sun 3 course £35, All day menu Sat-Sun, Sunday L fr £35, Vegetarian available, Children welcome

The Chef's Table

◉◉ Modern British **NEW**

tel: 01244 403040 **Music Hall Passage CH1 2EU**
email: info@chefstablechester.co.uk
dir: *M53 junct 12 onto A56 to city centre. Delamere St onto Northgate St then onto St Werburgh St. 500 yds to right is Music Hall passage*

Bold flavours and modern cooking close to the cathedral

At the end of a narrow alley between a dress shop and a globally known coffee house, Chef's Table announces 'Seasonal Food. Second-hand Books. Eclectic Music. Original Art'. The compact and bijou interior contains a bar, beyond which you can see the goings-on in the kitchen. When the sightseeing or shopping are done, disappear down the alley, take a seat and consult one of the clipboards listing the weekly-changing dishes. For an all-day brunch, maybe an Isle of Man crab sandwich, a roast lamb rump salad or a Hebridean black pudding tattie scone. Two- or three-course, fixed-price lunches are served until 3pm. In the evening, start with clear-flavoured fresh squid in its own ink, saffron aïoli, chorizo purée and monk's beard agretti, and follow with roast rack of lamb with pistachio, confit tomatoes, broad beans, oca du Peru, carrots and even nasturtiums. Roast monkfish aromatic curry with crab samosa and black rice could be an alternative. To finish, try poached rhubarb, rhubarb ripple and bubble gum ice cream, candyfloss and toasted almonds.

Chef Liam McKay **Owner** Liam McKay, Thomas Hughes **Seats** 24
Times 12-2.30/6-9, Closed Xmas, New Yr, Sun-Mon **Prices** Fixed L 2 course £15, Starter £5.75-£8.25, Main £14.95-£21.95, Dessert £5.50-£7.50 **Wines** 6 bottles over £30, 10 bottles under £30, 15 by glass **Parking** Chester Market NCP **Notes** Brunch menu, Vegetarian available, Children welcome

CHESTER *continued*

Grosvenor Pulford Hotel & Spa

⚜ Mediterranean, European

tel: 01244 570560 **Wrexham Rd, Pulford CH4 9DG**
email: enquiries@grosvenorpulfordhotel.co.uk **web:** www.grosvenorpulfordhotel.co.uk
dir: *M53/A55 at junct signed A483 Chester/Wrexham & North Wales. Left onto B5445, hotel 2m on right*

The flavours of the Med in a smart hotel

The sprawling red-brick hotel has a swish spa, luxe bedrooms, and pretty gardens for a stroll or photos (it's a big hit on the local wedding scene), but the main dining option of Ciro's Brasserie really stands out with its classical theme recalling ancient Rome via arches, murals and stucco paintwork. Note that the service team do not wear togas. If it all sounds a little 'theme-y', rest assured it is actually rather charming and fits the bill with its Italian and broadly Mediterranean-inspired menu. Chicken liver parfait with plum and apple chutney and toasted brioche is one way to begin, or go for ravioli filled with oak-smoked salmon and creamed leeks. Main courses are equally well crafted and well considered: Ciro's bouillabaisse, for example, packed with fresh seafood, or blade of beef braised for six hours and served with horseradish creamed potatoes and roasted root vegetables.

Chef Richard Pierce, Paul Prescott **Owner** Harold & Susan Nelson **Seats** 120, Pr/dining room 200 **Times** 12-2/6-9.30 **Prices** Starter £5.95-£8.95, Main £9.95-£28.95, Dessert £6.50-£8.95, Service optional **Wines** 16 bottles over £30, 30 bottles under £30, 12 by glass **Parking** 200 **Notes** Afternoon tea £14.95, Sunday L £12.95, Vegetarian available, Children welcome

Restaurant 1539

⚜ Modern British

tel: 01244 304611 & 304610 **Chester Race Company Limited, The Racecourse CH1 2LY**
email: restaurant1539@chester-races.com
dir: *Located in Chester racecourse, access via main car park entrance or by foot from Nun's Road*

Brasserie cooking for racing enthusiasts

Part of the Chester racecourse complex, 1539 was given a cool half-million's worth of upgrade in 2014, allowing patrons to take in the racing (or the nightclub beat in the evenings) in even finer style than hitherto. The full-drop windows of the restaurant are still a major feature, and if your heart isn't given to equestrianism, swivel round for an ambient view into the kitchen. It produces up-to-the-minute brasserie cooking with verve and accuracy, ranging from ham hock terrine with crushed peas and bacon in mustard dressing, to mains like well-timed roast cod with a brown shrimp risotto in red wine reduction, or honey-roast breast and confit

leg of duck with braised red cabbage in orange and port jus. Desserts court the popular vote with dark chocolate tart and salted caramel, or a version of Eton Mess made with spiced orange.

Chef Ian Penn **Owner** Chester Race Company **Seats** 160, Pr/dining room 60 **Times** 12-9.30, All-day dining, Closed D Sun **Prices** Starter £4.95-£11.25, Main £11.75-£32.50, Dessert £5.25-£8.75, Service optional **Wines** 40 bottles over £30, 20 bottles under £30, 14 by glass **Parking** 60 **Notes** Sunday L £15.39-£19.50, Vegetarian available, Children welcome

Rowton Hall Country House Hotel & Spa

⚜ Modern British

tel: 01244 335262 **Whitchurch Rd, Rowton CH3 6AD**
email: reception@rowtonhallhotelandspa.co.uk **web:** www.rowtonhall.co.uk
dir: *M56 junct 12, A56 to Chester. At rdbt left onto A41 towards Whitchurch. Approx 1m, follow hotel signs*

Modern and classic menus in a Georgian manor

A grand house with plenty of Georgian period charm and eight acres of grounds, these days Rowton is a big hit on the wedding and conference circuit, with all the usual facilities. It is home to the Langdale restaurant, with its oak-panelled walls and smart linen-clad tables. There's evident classic French culinary influence on the menu and plenty of seasonal British produce on show, while the kitchen is not averse to modern culinary techniques. Start with a sous-vide-cooked loin and leg of rabbit, served with spiced carrot and vanilla foam, for example, or their home-cured gravad lax with a salad of baby chard and beetroot. Main-course rump of lamb might come with minted pea and broad bean cassoulet, plus baby fondants and rosemary jus. Desserts run to blueberry and passionfruit cheesecake with mini passionfruit jellies.

Times 12-2/7-9.30

Simon Radley at The Chester Grosvenor

⚜⚜⚜⚜ *– see opposite*

The Sticky Walnut

⚜⚜ Modern European

tel: 01244 400400 **11 Charles St CH2 3AZ**
dir: *5 mins from Chester train station*

Well-presented high quality seasonal dishes and rustic charm

With its shop front exterior and rough-and-ready rustic vibe, The Sticky Walnut is a neighbourhood restaurant for the 21st-century-unpretentious, chilled-out and serious about the end product. It is spread over two floors, with chunky wooden tables, blackboards and an open kitchen. On the plate is some seriously good stuff based on excellent seasonal ingredients. There's a broadly European spin to much of the menu and both concept and execution are pretty much bang on. First course chicken liver pâté with apple and pear chutney and buttery toasted focaccia delivers complementary flavours and shows refinement in its presentation. Or choose squab pigeon breast with quince, salsify, caraway and meat juices, before a main course of fillet of brill matched with pumpkin and parmesan risotto and sautéed wild mushrooms. Meaty mains bring full-bore flavours, perhaps braised beef shin with truffle chips and onion purée. With cracking desserts like a deconstructed lime cheesecake with pecan butter biscuits and chocolate sorbet, this is a kitchen that delivers real impact in a relaxed, modern manner.

Chef Gary Usher **Owner** Gary Usher **Seats** 50 **Times** 12-3/6-10, Closed 25-26 Dec **Prices** Starter £6-£10, Main £14-£22, Dessert £5-£7 **Wines** 10 bottles over £30, 20 bottles under £30, 11 by glass **Parking** Car park nearby **Notes** Sunday L £16-£20, Vegetarian available, Children welcome

Simon Radley at The Chester Grosvenor ❁ ❁ ❁ ❁

CHESTER   Map 15 SJ46

Modern French V 🍷 NOTABLE WINE LIST

tel: 01244 324024 & 895618   **Eastgate CH1 1LT**
email: hotel@chestergrosvenor.co.uk
web: www.chestergrosvenor.co.uk
dir: *A56 follow signs for city centre hotels. On Eastgate St next to the Eastgate clock*

Cooking of grand excitement in Chester's crown jewel hotel

The Chester Grosvenor resonates with the kind of antiquity that can make an American tourist go weak at the knees, and it has the sort of finish that will impress even the most ardent international traveller. It is part of the Duke of Westminster's Grosvenor group of properties and has not lacked investment over the years, and in 2015 the hotel celebrated 150 years of service. The partly black-and-white timbered exterior dates from the Elizabethan era, since which period the place has been a prime address in this historic Roman city, but it has been added to over the years to create a façade that reflects the passage of time. The sheer grace of the old girl is evident when you cross the threshold, where elegant public rooms await, not to mention a swanky spa. The Arkle Bar and Lounge is a must-visit venue named after a racehorse that won the Cheltenham Gold Cup three times consecutively in the 1960s (and was owned by a Grosvenor of course), while La Brasserie recreates Paris in the west of England. The star attraction is the Simon Radley restaurant, which has dignified grandeur in spades, with its classical proportions and on-point service team. The food is contemporary but not overtly so-no smoke and mirrors-with restraint and good judgement ensuring the first-rate ingredients are allowed to shine. With a tasting menu and three-course signature option, there are a few ways to go, but you can't go wrong if you stick with the à la carte. Begin, say, with a dish described as 'avocado prawn', which is rather more dynamic and exciting than the original-torched obsiblue crevette, Devon cock crab and langoustine. Or how about 'five spice'? This is a fashionable partnership of lacquered pork jowl and king scallop, plus enoki mushrooms, puffed rice and honeycomb. Among main courses, there's evidence of an appreciation of French classical ways in the likes of 'roots and shoots', which sees braised wild turbot matched with frogs' leg, West Country snails and creamed parsley root. There's similar Francophilia in a dessert called 'salade rouge' (almond blancmange, rhubarb, sweet beets and blood orange) and a crémeux made with estate chocolate and hazelnut praline. The wine list more than holds its own in such esteemed company.

Chef Simon Radley, Ray Booker **Owner** Grosvenor **Seats** 45, Pr/dining room 14 **Times** 6.30-9, Closed 25 Dec, 1 wk Jan, Sun-Mon, L all week (ex Dec) **Prices** Fixed D 3 course fr £75, Tasting menu £59-£99 **Wines** 819 bottles over £30, 41 bottles under £30, 24 by glass **Parking** Car park attached to hotel (£10 24hrs) **Notes** ALC £50-£75, Tasting menu (also vegetarian) 8 course, Children 12 yrs+

CREWE
Map 15 SJ75

Crewe Hall

◉ Modern European

tel: 01270 253333 & 259319 **Weston Rd CW1 6UZ**
email: crewehall@qhotels.co.uk **web:** www.qhotels.co.uk
dir: *M6 junct 16 follow A500 to Crewe. Last exit at rdbt onto A5020. 1st exit next rdbt to Crewe. Crewe Hall 150yds on right*

Contemporary brasserie in a 17th-century stately home

When it comes to making a good first impression, the Jacobean Crewe Hall can't fail to excite, with its grandeur more reminiscent of a stately home than a mere hotel. The magnificent interiors remain, with its vast spaces rich with period character and filled with lavish furniture, but there's nothing stuffy about the place, and that especially goes for the Brasserie, housed in a modern wing of the building, with its open-plan layout and buzzy atmosphere. The menu takes inspiration from far and wide, with tikka spicing in a first-course pressing of lamb belly (with Indian-inspired accompaniments), and soy and honey enriching slow-cooked onglet steak among main courses. There's simplicity in a fish dish of pan-fried stone bass with hollandaise sauce, a pasta option of home-made pappardelle with goats' cheese, and steaks cooked on the grill. Finish with a fashionably modern warm bitter chocolate construction with chocolate soil and yogurt sorbet.

Chef Brian Spark **Owner** QHotels **Seats** 120 **Times** 12-3/6-10 **Prices** Fixed L 2 course fr £12.50, Starter £3.50-£7, Main £12-£22.50, Dessert £5-£9.50, Service optional **Wines** 25 bottles over £30, 18 bottles under £30, 12 by glass **Parking** 500 **Notes** Sunday L £15.50-£18.50, Vegetarian available, Children welcome

KNUTSFORD
Map 15 SJ77

Belle Epoque

◉◉ Modern French **NEW**

tel: 01565 633060 **60 King St WA16 6DT**
email: info@thebelleepoque.com **web:** www.thebelleepoque.com
dir: *Phone for directions*

Contemporary brasserie cooking in a glam 1907 building

As its name suggests, this restaurant occupies a 1907 building full of period character, and its culinary direction has a suitably cross-Channel accent. In the rather glam dining room, crimson leather seats, mosaic floors, timber-clad walls, and art nouveau fireplaces make an impressive backdrop for the kitchen's repertoire of modern and classic brasserie dishes. The place has been run by the same family for over 40 years, so supply lines to local farmers and artisan producers are well established, and the kitchen uses thoroughbred produce to good effect. This is evident in a starter of hot-smoked salmon that comes with cauliflower purée, caviar and samphire, while main course stars lamb fillet and breast alongside celeriac purée, kale, parmesan crisps and fondant potatoes. Fish cookery is equally well executed, perhaps serving pan-fried skate wing with Morecambe Bay shrimps, fondant potatoes and brown butter sauce. At dessert, you won't be disappointed by a modern take on rhubarb and custard, the rhubarb served poached, as a sorbet, and a jelly 'cannelloni' wrapped around silky crème pâtissière.

Chef Kevin Lynn **Owner** Matthew Mooney **Seats** 60, Pr/dining room 80 **Times** 12-3/5.30-9.30, Closed L Sat, D Sun **Prices** Fixed L 2 course £14.95, Fixed D 2 course £14.95, Tasting menu £30-£39.95, Starter £6.95-£10.95, Main £12.95-£24.95, Dessert £7.95, Service optional **Wines** 60 bottles over £30, 40 bottles under £30, 10 by glass **Parking** Car park nearby **Notes** Fixed D before 7.30pm, Tasting menu 5/8 course, Sunday L, Vegetarian available, Children 7 yrs+ L/D

Cottons Hotel & Spa

◉ International, British

tel: 01565 650333 **Manchester Rd WA16 0SU**
email: cottons.dm@shirehotels.com **web:** www.restaurant-and-bar.co.uk/knutsford/
dir: *On A50, 1m from M6 junct 19*

Appealing British menus in modern surroundings

Indulge in a spa treatment before a blowout in the sleekly designed restaurant at Cottons, a large, modern hotel at the edge of town. The menu is an appealing brasserie-style package, with ideas drawn from British culinary tradition. Start with oak-smoked Severn and Wye salmon, served with beetroot and horseradish crème fraîche, or share a 'taste of Cheshire' plate of cured meats and seasonal salads. Chargrilled steaks (aged for 28 days) come with confit tomato and fries, and sandwiches are up for grabs during the day. Among main courses, fish curry with a spicy coconut cream sauce arrives with basmati rice and naan bread, and Wainwright ale-battered haddock is served with thick-cut chips, mushy peas and tartare sauce. Comforting desserts include warm treacle tart with Pedro Ximénez and clotted cream, or chocolate and hazelnut brownie with roasted peanut ice cream.

Chef Adrian Sedden **Owner** Shire Hotels **Seats** 80, Pr/dining room 30 **Times** 11.30-9.30, All-day dining **Prices** Fixed D 3 course £25.95, Starter £6.50-£10.50, Main £11.95-£29.50, Service optional **Wines** 15 bottles over £30, 34 bottles under £30, 18 by glass **Parking** 120 **Notes** Afternoon tea, Early bird menu, Supper events, Sunday L £15.95-£23.95, Vegetarian available, Children welcome

Mere Court Hotel & Conference Centre

◉ Mediterranean, Modern British

tel: 01565 831000 **Warrington Rd, Mere WA16 0RW**
email: sales@merecourt.co.uk **web:** www.merecourt.co.uk
dir: *A50, 1m W of junct with A556, on right*

Arts and Crafts style and creative modern cooking

Dating from the turn of the 20th century, Mere Court is an Arts and Crafts house with plenty of period swagger – carved wood, metalwork and stained glass included. With seven acres of lush gardens and a lake, this country-house hotel has bags of appeal. The oak-panelled Arboretum Restaurant is an elegant spot, with lake views, and is the setting for some upbeat modern European cooking. Fillet of cold-smoked salmon comes in a first course with soft-boiled quail's eggs, beetroot fondant and dill mayonnaise, while main courses might include breast of Gressingham duck with its confit of leg meat turned into a Scotch egg, plus parsnip mash and caramelised chicory. Desserts are similarly creative: white peach parfait, for example, with caramel-roasted white nectarine and peach crisps.

Times 12-2/6.30-9.30

The Mere Golf Resort & Spa

◉◉ International

tel: 01565 830155 **Chester Rd, Mere WA16 6LJ**
email: reservations@themereresort.co.uk **web:** www.themereresort.co.uk
dir: *M6 junct 19 or M56 junct 7*

Modern Brit brasserie cooking at a Cheshire resort

A golfing resort and health spa not far from Knutsford, the Mere is a must for Cheshire's denizens of the fairways. It's also a good location for accomplished brasserie dining, which takes place in the open-plan Browns, named after a former luminary of the Mere, Max Brown. Linen tablecloths and relatively formal service are slightly at odds with the overall tone, but the food makes some good modern statements. Start perhaps with smoked salmon and salmon rillettes with horseradish cream, beetroot and watercress. Deeply flavoured oxtail roulade with creamed parsnip and a potato scone makes a more robust opener, as a prelude to the likes of well-seasoned grilled John Dory with apple, mussels and pancetta, or slow-cooked venison rump with baby turnips, spiced pear and carrot purée in redcurrant and rosemary sauce. Finish with sticky toffee pudding in butterscotch sauce with vanilla ice cream, or a selection of cheeses with tomato chutney.

Times 12.30-4/6-9.30

LYMM
Map 15 SJ68

The Church Green British Grill
◉◉ Modern British

tel: 01925 752068 & 748231 **Higher Ln WA13 0AP**
email: reservations@thechurchgreen.co.uk
dir: *M6 junct 20 follow signs for Lymm along B5158 after 1.5m turn right at T-junct onto A56 towards Altrincham, on right after 0.5m*

A fresh take on traditional grill cookery in a Cheshire village

Chef-patron Aiden Byrne will be a familiar face to *MasterChef* fans, and known through his food to anybody who has eaten in recent years at some of London's premier addresses, Tom Aikens and the Dorchester Grill included. There is no metropolitan ostentation in Lymm, but a village pub that's all bare brick and bare wood, with a conservatory section allowing enjoyment of the extensive garden. The culinary focus harks back to traditional British grill cooking, with excellent prime materials and touches of modern technique adding lustre. It is not all steaks, covetable though they are. Pheasant breast and pork belly crop up too, the former regally partnered with smoked foie gras, charred kale and hazelnut risotto. Fish shows up well, as in olive-oiled salmon with a robust fresh Niçoise salad. Topping and tailing it all might be a serving of home-made black pudding with a crisply poached egg (quite a feat) and caper and rocket salad, or crab beignets with green chilli jam, and comfort-pud finales like Bakewell tart with black cherry and Amaretto ice cream.

Chef Aiden Byrne **Owner** Aiden & Sarah Byrne **Seats** 50 **Times** 12-9.30, All-day dining, Closed 25 Dec **Prices** Tasting menu £60-£70, Starter £6-£9.50, Main £9.50-£34, Dessert £6.50-£7.50, Service optional **Wines** 27 bottles over £30, 31 bottles under £30, 15 by glass **Parking** 25 **Notes** Tasting menu 5/8 course, Sunday L £15, Vegetarian available, Children welcome

---

MACCLESFIELD
Map 16 SJ97

The Lord Clyde
◉◉◉ – see below

The Lord Clyde ◉◉◉

MACCLESFIELD
Map 16 SJ97

Modern British
tel: 01625 562123 **36 Clarke Ln, Kerridge SK10 5AH**
email: hello@thelordclyde.co.uk
dir: *A523 Silic Rd take B5090 Bollington Rd. 1st right onto Clarke Ln*

Brilliantly innovative country-pub food from a South African émigré

A stone-built inn on a quiet country lane in Cheshire feels like an odd destination for a boy from Cape Town, albeit one whose culinary ambitions matured early, and whose journey brought him here via Copenhagen's Noma, Le Manoir aux Quat' Saisons and the Fat Duck. Such is Ernst van Zyl, a prodigiously talented chef who has spread his wings here to dazzling effect. Against a contemporary rustic backdrop of chunky wood tables, tiled floor and a smattering of modern artwork, The Lord Clyde successfully exercises the dual function of local pub and dining destination, with polished but engaging service in the restaurant. Menu specifications are shorthand notes of their principal ingredients, and the distinctively presented dishes are fizzing with innovative energy. The first foray might be a single, perfectly caramelised, plump scallop on a bed of sticky braised oxtail, the textures offset with parsley root crisps and walnut biscuits, or else an assemblage of sweetbreads, cabbage, button mushrooms and pear. Most things are conceived as two pairs, as though on a dance card, so a main course of pork and Jerusalem artichoke, quince and broccoli, offers the Parma-wrapped fillet matched with the smokiness of Jerusalems, the al dente broccoli with sweetly poached quince. Monkfish is cooked at 48°C, not a degree more or less, and then partnered with parsley root, palourde clams and beetroot. These are combinations to induce reflection as well as delight. Ingenuity at dessert might produce a disassembled cheesecake of banana with banana biscuit, crunchy honeycomb and parmesan, salted peanuts and powdered peanut butter, a brilliantly designed dish where every element has earned its place. Incidentals maintain the cracking pace-don't miss the little sack of sourdough bread with smoking butter, sea salt and beef dripping.

Chef Ernst van Zyl **Owner** Sarah Richmond, Ernst van Zyl **Seats** 24 **Times** 12-2.30/6.30-9, Closed Sun, L Mon **Prices** Tasting menu £30-£75, Starter £6-£12, Main £14-£25, Dessert £6-£8.50 **Wines** 15 bottles over £30, 38 bottles under £30, 12 by glass **Parking** 7 **Notes** Tasting menu 5 course (Tue), 7/10 course with wine £80/£110, Vegetarian available, Children welcome

MACCLESFIELD *continued*

The Shrigley Hall Hotel, Golf & Country Club

 Modern British V

tel: 01625 575757 **Shrigley Park, Pott Shrigley SK10 5SB**
email: shrigleyhall@thehotelcollection.co.uk **web:** www.thehotelcollection.co.uk
dir: Exit A523 at Legh Arms towards Pott Shrigley. Hotel 2m on left before village

Modern British cooking in a stately Georgian hotel

Built in 1825 for William Turner MP, in the days when second homes were less controversial, Shrigley hasn't lost an iota of its grandeur over the past two centuries-the painted domed ceiling above the grand staircase is not to be missed. A spacious, elegant room overlooking the grounds, with the distant Peaks as backdrop, the Oakridge dining room goes for the swagged-curtains-and-chandeliers look to match the classical culinary approach. Poached and roasted pork fillet with carrot purée, wilted spinach, and red wine and oregano sauce turns up as a main course, as might chicken roulade with leeks and wild mushrooms, prune purée and red wine jus. Bookending those are the likes of chicken liver parfait with red onion jam and brioche, or a more with-it goats' cheese pannacotta with sun-blushed tomatoes, gem lettuce and black olive bread, and favourite puddings such as raspberry Bakewell tart with ripple parfait.

Chef Mark Adley **Owner** The Hotel Collection **Seats** 130, Pr/dining room 20
Times 7-9.30, Closed L all week **Prices** Prices not confirmed, Service optional
Wines 25 bottles over £30, 15 bottles under £30, 6 by glass **Parking** 250
Notes Children welcome

NANTWICH
Map 15 SJ65

Rookery Hall Hotel & Spa

Modern British

tel: 01270 610016 **Main Rd, Worleston CW5 6DQ**
email: rookeryhall@handpicked.co.uk **web:** www.handpickedhotels.co.uk/rookeryhall
dir: B5074 off 4th rdbt, on Nantwich by-pass. Hotel 1.5m on right

Old-school comforts in an imposing Cheshire mansion

Rookery Hall was built in 1816 by the owner of a Jamaican sugar plantation whose wealth is evident in the sumptuous interior. There's a splendid oak staircase, and the public rooms are beautifully proportioned and now tastefully decorated and furnished, with conference facilities in a purpose-built extension. The main dining room is panelled, with an embossed barrel ceiling, marble fireplaces and stylishly set tables. The kitchen deploys tip-top ingredients and adds its own refined style to dishes, producing highly wrought, successful combinations. Notable starters have included crisp pork belly with pea purée, caramelised Granny Smiths and Maxim potatoes, and white crab meat with tomato confit, red pepper and avocado sorbet. Sound technique and accuracy are hallmarks of main courses too, seen in breast of Yorkshire grouse with creamed potato, bread purée, cabbage and bacon fricassée, watercress cream and wood sorrel, and monkfish in curry sauce with sauté potatoes, broccoli and crispy almond flakes. Extras like canapés are well up to scratch, as are puddings like prune and almond tart, its pastry lightly flaky, with Armagnac ice cream.

Chef Michael Batters **Owner** Hand Picked Hotels **Seats** 90, Pr/dining room 160
Times 12-2/7-9.30, Closed L Mon-Sat **Prices** Prices not confirmed, Service optional
Wines 81 bottles over £30, 9 bottles under £30, 12 by glass **Parking** 100
Notes Sunday L, Vegetarian available, Children welcome

PECKFORTON
Map 15 SJ55

1851 Restaurant at Peckforton Castle

– see opposite

PUDDINGTON
Map 15 SJ37

Macdonald Craxton Wood Hotel

Modern British V

tel: 0151 347 4000 & 347 4016 **Parkgate Rd, Ledsham CH66 9PB**
email: events.craxton@macdonald-hotels.co.uk
web: www.macdonaldhotels.co.uk/craxtonwood
dir: From M6 take M56 towards N Wales, then A5117/A540 to Hoylake. Hotel on left 200yds past lights

Smart British cooking and top-notch ingredients

Just a short drive from Chester, this grand-looking hotel is surrounded by 27 acres of peaceful woodland. It's a stylish and relaxed sort of place, with a restaurant done out in muted mauve colours and round-backed padded dining chairs upholstered in striped fabric. The Josper grill comes into its own for main-course meats – rump of Highland lamb, beef sirloin, pork cutlets, all served with traditional accompaniments and a choice of sauces – but the cooking has a lot more going for it. The kitchen has compiled an enterprising, all-embracing menu and turns out some fashionably imaginative dishes, such as starters of black pudding Scotch egg with mustard mayonnaise, apple, watercress and bacon, braised pig's cheek with scallops, squash and date purée, and salads such as crayfish tail Caesar with bacon. Quality produce, confidently handled is at the heart of the operation, seen in main courses of crispy pork belly with cranberries, chestnuts and Savoy cabbage, and cod fillet with seared scallops and crispy chicken wing.

Chef Mark Burke **Owner** Macdonald Hotels **Seats** 100, Pr/dining room 12
Times 12-3/6-10, Closed L Mon-Sat **Prices** Fixed D 3 course £29.95, Starter £6.50-£10, Main £14-£29, Dessert £7.50-£9, Service optional **Wines** 32 bottles over £30, 28 bottles under £30, 12 by glass **Parking** 300 **Notes** Sunday L £19.95-£24.95, Children welcome

---

SANDIWAY
Map 15 SJ67

Nunsmere Hall Hotel

British, European

tel: 01606 889100 **Tarporley Rd, Oakmere CW8 2ES**
email: reservations@nunsmere.co.uk **web:** www.nunsmere.co.uk
dir: M6 junct 18, A54 to Chester, at x-rds with A49 turn left towards Tarporley, hotel 2m on left

Traditional European cooking in the old Brocklebank place

The palatial red-brick mansion not far from Chester was built at the dawn of the 20th century, its first occupant being the chairman of the Brocklebank shipping line, Sir Aubrey. With an ornamental lake out front, and much panelled magnificence within, it continues to look the part. Salute the nautical heritage with a drink in the Captain's Bar, then glide in state to a berth in the Crystal dining room, where pictures of polo-players adorn the walls and long drapes frame the garden view. The cooking keeps things firmly anchored in European traditions, opening with crab salad on sun-dried tomato toast, or a blue cheese soufflé with poached pear in honey-mustard dressing. After this, beef arrives lavishly in two guises-slow-roast sirloin and braised shin-on green bean fricassée with wine-pickled shallots and fluffy chips. Salmon is cooked sous-vide and served with bok choy in port syrup, and dessert might be firm vanilla pannacotta with poached rhubarb, or lemon tart and raspberry sorbet.

Chef Craig Malone **Owner** Prima Hotels Ltd **Seats** 60, Pr/dining room 80 **Times** 12-2/7-9.30 **Prices** Prices not confirmed **Wines** 66 bottles over £30, 32 bottles under £30, 15 by glass **Parking** 80 **Notes** Sunday L, Vegetarian available, Children welcome

---

TARPORLEY
Map 15 SJ56

Macdonald Portal Hotel Golf & Spa
Modern British

tel: 01829 734100 **Cobblers Cross Ln CW6 0DJ**
email: general.portal@macdonald-hotels.co.uk **web:** www.macdonaldhotels.co.uk/the portal
dir: Off A49 in village of Tarporley

Classic and modern cuisine amid three golf courses

The Portal comes with not one but three golf courses to choose from, so don't forget the irons. There are spa treatments on hand too, and a restaurant that has panoramic views of the fairways and the Cheshire countryside beyond. Comfortable leather banquette seating and unclothed tables make for an unfussy look, and the

cooking follows suit with a foundation of classic steaks and grills supporting forays into the modern British style. The repertoire takes in haggis fritter with a poached egg and hot-spiced tomato relish, and mains such as well-timed square-cut cod fillet in a herb crust with salty kale and samphire and puréed cauliflower, or honey-glazed duck breast with dauphinoise, roast pumpkin and pak choi in anise sauce. Finish with hot chocolate fondant, served with white chocolate mousse and banana ice cream, or one of the generously loaded cheese slates.

Owner Macdonald Hotels **Seats** 100, Pr/dining room 45 **Times** 12-3/6-9.30 **Prices** Fixed D 3 course £25, Service optional **Wines** 69 bottles over £30, 16 bottles under £30, 19 by glass **Parking** 200 **Notes** Sunday L, Vegetarian available, Children welcome

1851 Restaurant at Peckforton Castle ❀❀❀

PECKFORTON
Map 15 SJ55

Modern British, French
tel: 01829 260930 **Stone House Ln CW6 9TN**
email: info@peckfortoncastle.co.uk **web:** www.peckfortoncastle.co.uk
dir: 15m from Chester, situated near Tarporley

An abundance of fresh, innovative energy

Peckforton is a manifestation in stone of how far the Victorians were prepared to go in the way of architectural nostalgia. This feudal castle complete with an array of ramparts and turrets was actually completed in 1851. It is now a luxury hotel and wedding venue, and while the temptation may have been to offer traditional English cooking to fit the surroundings, Mark Ellis has loftier ambitions. Officially, the cooking is moving in an even more contemporary direction than it was, though it may be difficult for the non-expert diner to spot the differences. There has been fresh, innovative energy in abundance here in recent years. A chicken starter has all sorts of things done to it, the wing compressed, the skin crunched, and comes with an egg yolk, along with the ritzier accoutrements of foie gras and truffle oil, the last mingling with the released yolk to make an instant sauce. Mallard liver is whipped up with ham and attended by wild legumes in horseradish snow. The origins, by no means all immediately local, of main-course principals are proudly stated in

dishes that run from Cornish brill simmered at 44°C in Pinot Noir, its bourguignon garnishes transformed into roasted grelots, smoked bacon emulsion and parsley gel, to loin and shoulder of Derbyshire venison with parsnips and loganberries. The desserts have postmodern brand-names such as Nevado, composed of variously tormented ingredients such as whipped white chocolate and torched banana, or the fascinating Taste of the Caribbean that comprises coconut parfait with rum jelly, lime sorbet and pineapple (a reimagined Piña Colada in all but name).

Chef Mark Ellis **Owner** The Naylor family **Seats** 60, Pr/dining room 165 **Times** 6-8.45, Closed L Mon-Sat **Prices** Prices not confirmed, Service optional 10% **Wines** 39 bottles over £30, 27 bottles under £30, 10 by glass **Parking** 100 **Notes** Sunday L, Vegetarian available, Children welcome

WARMINGHAM
Map 15 SJ76

The Bear's Paw
◉ Modern European, British

tel: 01270 526317 **School Ln CW11 3QN**
email: info@thebearspaw.co.uk web: www.thebearspaw.co.uk
dir: *M6 junct 17, A534, A533 signed Middlewich & Northwich. Continue on A533, left into Mill Ln, left into Warmingham Ln. Right into Plant Ln, left into Green Ln*

Northwestern cooking in a modernised village pub

A Victorian pub in the timbered idiom, the Bear's Paw is to be found in a village not far from Sandbach. It's been given a modern makeover inside, with lots of light wood, plenty of space, and library shelves adding a touch of refinement to the dining room. Local farmers and trawlers are called upon to supply the kitchen with quality North Western produce, with cheeses and ice creams also sourced from within a tightly drawn radius. It all ends up on a lengthy menu of modern country-inn cooking, taking in a generous fishcake of poached salmon and smoked haddock garnished with curly kale, beetroot purée and a perfectly timed soft-poached egg among beginners. This could be followed by the likes of calves' liver with crisp-fried haggis, caramelised onion purée, Chantenay carrots and creamy mash in an earthy lentil jus. The crème brûlée with honeycomb is a little over-sweet, so perhaps finish with a textbook rendition of Black Forest gâteau, or Bakewell tart with blackcurrant sorbet.

Chef Scott Cunningham **Owner** Harold & Susan Nelson **Seats** 150 **Times** 12-9.30, All-day dining **Prices** Starter £5.50-£7.50, Main £8.95-£22.95, Dessert £4.50-£9.95, Service optional **Wines** 17 bottles over £30, 26 bottles under £30, 12 by glass **Parking** 75 **Notes** Sunday L £12.50, Vegetarian available, Children welcome

WARRINGTON
Map 15 SJ68

BEST WESTERN Fir Grove Hotel
◉ Modern British **NEW**

tel: 01925 267471 **Knutsford Old Rd WA4 2LD**
email: firgrove@bestwestern.co.uk web: www.bw-firgrovehotel.co.uk
dir: *M6 junct 20, follow signs for A50 to Warrington for 2.4m, before swing bridge over canal, turn right & right again*

Opulent room for contemporary dining

There's an Italian theme going down at the Fir Grove Hotel, with business facilities including the Venetian Conference Centre and a bar called Sculptures in reference to the copious pieces of art that are dotted around the place. The dining option is the Capri Restaurant-keeping to the theme-and it is a plush and elegant space with depictions of historic statues looking down on diners. The kitchen does not show such obsession for Italy, though, but rather takes a contemporary Modern British approach, while there's a decidedly sunny, Mediterranean spin to the output. Duck terrine, poached rhubarb, gingerbread crumb is a thoroughly modern combination, followed by a well-timed cod loin with creamed potatoes and crispy

pieces of chorizo. To finish, stem ginger and lime posset is served with a nicely crumbly piece of shortbread. Service is by a young and brisk team.

Chef David Phythian **Owner** Topland **Seats** 50, Pr/dining room 50 **Times** 12-3/6.30-9.30, Closed Sun **Prices** Prices not confirmed **Wines** 8 by glass **Parking** 52 **Notes** Vegetarian available, Children welcome

WILMSLOW
Map 16 SJ88

Stanneylands Hotel
◉◉ Modern British

tel: 01625 525225 **Stanneylands Rd SK9 4EY**
email: sales@stanneylandshotel.co.uk web: www.stanneylandshotel.co.uk
dir: *From M56 at airport turn off, follow signs to Wilmslow. Left into Station Rd, onto Stanneylands Rd. Hotel on right*

Classically-based cooking in a stylish Cheshire hotel

Despite being over the county border in Cheshire, Wilmslow has long been a gentrified refuge from nearby Manchester and the airport, which makes Stanneylands a good bet for the business traveller, as well as those seeking an escape from urban bustle. Way back in the 18th century, it was a simple farmhouse, but gradual evolution has transformed it into a stylish country hotel with a traditional oak-panelled ambience and crisp formality in both the table linen and the service tone. The temptations of modernity are resisted in favour of a classically based repertoire that produces a nicely runny omelette Arnold Bennett topped with watercress, and then sea trout with broad beans, samphire and champ in thermidor sauce, or roast breast of duck with crisp-fried spinach and a morello sauce, along with an arancino of the confit leg meat and sage. An enormous bowl of under seasoned mash brings us down to earth with a clunk, but a seasonal summer dessert that works strawberries into a mini Pavlova, pannacotta and sorbet is a cheering idea.

Chef Andrew Grundy **Owner** Prima Hotels Ltd **Seats** 60, Pr/dining room 120 **Times** 12-2.30/7-9.45 **Prices** Fixed L 2 course £14.95, Fixed D 3 course £31.95, Tasting menu £50, Starter £5.45-£8.95, Main £15.75-£26.50, Dessert £7.50-£10, Service optional **Wines** 66 bottles over £30, 32 bottles under £30, 15 by glass **Parking** 110 **Notes** Afternoon tea £15, Sunday L £24.95, Vegetarian available, Children welcome

CORNWALL & ISLES OF SCILLY

BODMIN
Map 2 SX06

Trehellas House Hotel & Restaurant
◉ British, French

tel: 01208 72700 **Washaway PL30 3AD**
email: enquiries@trehellashouse.co.uk web: www.trehellashouse.co.uk
dir: *Take A389 from Bodmin towards Wadebridge. Hotel on right 0.5m beyond road to Camelford*

Bright Cornish cooking at an inn with a past

Trehellas House has come full circle from its early days as the Washaway, the inn to a landed estate, via a period in the Victorian era as a courthouse serving the judicial circuit, to a modern-day country hotel, its guest rooms spread between the inn itself and the coach house. A low-slung greystone building between Bodmin and Wadebridge, with a beamed, slate-flagged dining room, it makes a homely setting for some bright Cornish cooking that mixes innovation and tradition. Potted St Ives crab with gravad lax and melba toast might be the curtain-raiser for slow-roast lamb shank with crushed minted potatoes and ratatouille in thyme jus, or sea bass with spinach in caper butter sauce. Finish with nutty apple and apricot crumble, served with rhubarb ice cream, or a selection of local cheeses with celery, grapes and chutney. The hotel's proximity to Camel Valley makes that vineyard's benchmark Cornish fizz the obvious aperitif.

Times 12-2/6.30-9

BOSCASTLE
Map 2 SX09

The Wellington Hotel

◉◉ Modern British, French

tel: 01840 250202 **The Harbour PL35 0AQ**
email: info@wellingtonhotelboscastle.com **web:** www.wellingtonhotelboscastle.com
dir: *A30, A395 at Davidstowe follow Boscastle signs. B3266 to village. Right into Old Rd*

Creative contemporary cooking in popular fishing village

A coaching inn since the 16th-century, The Wellington was renamed after that business in Belgium in 1815. The views over the harbour have hardly changed in that time, and the building itself stands strong with seeming indifference to the passage of time – it's even got a castellated tower. The restaurant follows the theme (it's called Waterloo) and has plenty of charm with its chandeliers and linen-clad tables, and there's also a traditional bar with real ales and dishes written up on blackboards. The kitchen team seek out regional produce to pepper the restaurant menu. A first-course smoked chicken terrine with pear and honeycomb is a creative construction, or go for the no-less inventive Cornish mussels with curry butter and parsnips. There's plenty of Cornish seafood on show, including a fine piece of cod, cooked just right, and served in a main course with variations of parsnip, vanilla cream, and a crab and basil combo. Finish with a plum tart with poached plums, Armagnac and almonds.

Chef Kit Davis **Owner** Cornish Coastal Hotels Ltd **Seats** 25, Pr/dining room 20 **Times** 6-9, Closed Sun-Mon, L all week **Prices** Fixed D 3 course £35-£40, Service optional **Wines** 10 bottles over £30, 25 bottles under £30, 7 by glass **Parking** 15 **Notes** Vegetarian available, Children welcome

BRYHER (ISLES OF SCILLY)
Map 2 SV81

Hell Bay

◉◉◉ *– see below*

CALLINGTON
Map 3 SX36

Langmans Restaurant

◉◉ Modern British

tel: 01579 384933 **3 Church St PL17 7RE**
email: dine@langmansrestaurant.co.uk
dir: *From the direction of Plymouth into town centre, left at lights and second right into Church St*

Imaginative tasting menu using regional ingredients

This restaurant offers finely-crafted regional food in an unassuming venue in the Cornish near east, between the moorlands of Bodmin and Dart. A seven-course tasting menu is the drill, full of imaginative dishes building on well-honed classical technique. Start perhaps with a partridge breast on spelt risotto, followed by a bacon-enriched soup of butternut squash garnished with a scallop. Fish comes next, perhaps sea bass in a green array of samphire, spinach and fennel, and then a choice of main meats, fallow deer in red wine with dauphinoise, chanterelles and sprout-flowers, or sirloin in Madeira with grelots and smoked mash. A digestive pause will do nicely before the Cornish and West Country cheeses appear, prior to two desserts. A chocolate version of the B52 cocktail shot might precede apple crumble and custard. Game nights in season are a particular highlight.

Chef Anton Buttery **Owner** Anton & Gail Buttery **Seats** 24 **Times** 7.30-close, Closed Sun-Wed, L all week **Prices** Tasting menu £42.50, Service optional **Wines** 45 bottles over £30, 50 bottles under £30, 11 by glass **Parking** Town centre car park **Notes** Tasting menu 7 course, Vegetarian available

Hell Bay ◉◉◉

BRYHER (ISLES OF SCILLY)
Map 2 SV81

Modern British v
tel: 01720 422947 **TR23 0PR**
email: contactus@hellbay.co.uk **web:** www.hellbay.co.uk
dir: *Access by boat from Penzance, plane from Exeter, Newquay or Land's End*

Assured cooking in a Scilly Isles hideaway

As you arrive on the ferry from St Mary's or Tresco, the cove at the western end of Bryher is actually a rather idyllic spot, and not nearly as infernal as it sounds, although it does incur the wrath of the Atlantic from time to time. Inhabited by a mere 80-odd souls, tiny Bryher really is that place to 'get away from it all'. This rugged, gently hilly island offers little other than unspoiled gorse-clad beauty, crystal-clear seas and sandy beaches to draw seekers of serenity to the white-fronted, low-slung, modern hotel hunkered down in its concealing cove. Large windows in the restaurant look over tussocks of windswept grasses to the rock-strewn shore and the sea. It's a simply decorated, light-filled room, hung with Cornish artworks as a backdrop to Richard Kearsley's confident, seasonally-driven cooking. Local materials are as good as it gets-seafood such as crab and lobster is caught off the island itself, and local farmland supplies much of the fresh produce, while mainland Cornwall contributes meats and artisan cheeses. Daily-changing menus are carefully balanced between European tradition and modernity, so a dinner may start out with halibut gravadlax with sauce gribiche, fennel and potato crisp. Stick with seafood at main, and it could be pan-roasted wild sea bass fillet with a broth of saffron, mussels and herbs, or if meat is more your thing, braised shoulder and roasted loin of lamb might come with Anna potatoes, peas, broad beans and rosemary, or haunch of West Country venison with turnip gratin, red cabbage and chocolate jus. Desserts provide a memorable finish, with tiramisù presented as a terrine with caramel ice cream.

Chef Richard Kearsley **Owner** Tresco Estate **Seats** 70, Pr/dining room 12 **Times** 12-2/7-9.30, Closed 2 Nov-17 Mar **Prices** Fixed D 3 course £42.50, Service optional **Wines** 20 bottles over £30, 30 bottles under £30, 11 by glass **Notes** Children welcome

Falmouth Hotel

◉ British V

tel: 01326 312671 **Castle Beach TR11 4NZ**
email: reservations@falmouthhotel.com **web:** www.falmouthhotel.com
dir: *A30 to Truro then A390 to Falmouth. Follow signs for beaches, hotel on seafront near Pendennis Castle*

Seasonal cooking in a great white seafront hotel

Nothing becomes a seaside town like a great white hotel, lording it over the waters from the headland. The eponymous Falmouth went up in the 1860s as the Great Western Railway extended into Cornwall. It did its duty in both wars, and between times, has hosted the crowned heads and pop sensations of the day. The elegant dining room has sweeping views over the bay and a menu that works its way round the seasonal calendar in both British and international modes. Many dishes obligingly come in two sizes, so that you might start imaginatively with roasted ling fillet wrapped in Parma ham in a sweetcorn and potato chowder with prawns and a near-bushel of fresh parsley, while main course might be a rump cut of superb local lamb on well-executed potato rösti. Good pastry is the hallmark of zesty lemon tart, which comes with raspberry coulis and clotted cream.

Chef Mark Aldred **Owner** Richardson Hotels **Seats** 150, Pr/dining room 40
Times 12-2/6.45-8.45 **Prices** Prices not confirmed, Service optional **Wines** 15 bottles over £30, 15 bottles under £30, 7 by glass **Parking** 65 **Notes** Wed L 2/3 course £12/£15, Sunday L, Children welcome

The Greenbank Hotel

◉◉ Modern British

tel: 01326 312440 **Harbourside TR11 2SR**
email: reception@greenbank-hotel.co.uk **web:** www.greenbank-hotel.co.uk
dir: *Approaching Falmouth from Penryn, take left along North Parade. Follow sign to Falmouth Marina and Greenbank Hotel*

Crowd-pleasing menu with panoramic estuary views

The house that grew up into the Greenbank Hotel has occupied this prime spot on the Fal estuary since 1640, and 2015 saw another burst of renovation, with the restaurant receiving a top-to-toe facelift. The splendid view, however, remains unchanged: full-length windows fold back to open the space up to a panorama that sweeps across the harbour. As well as the refurb, it was all change in the kitchen too, with a new head chef taking the helm to deliver a please-all roster of classics (fish and chips, burgers and steaks) and modern European dishes that take Cornish produce as a starting point. Expect uncluttered starters such as potted ham hock with home-made piccalilli, followed by well-thought-out mains starring fish from local day boats-pan-roasted hake fillet, say, with crab and chorizo risotto, samphire and pomegranate. If the mood calls for something meatier, braised beef cheeks are matched with celeriac dauphinoise, cauliflower and red wine sauce. Desserts take the comforting route of sticky toffee pudding with white chocolate fudge, toffee sauce and clotted cream.

Chef Nick Hodges **Owner** Greenbank Hotel (Falmouth) Ltd **Seats** 80, Pr/dining room 16 **Times** 12-9.15, All-day dining **Prices** Fixed L 2 course £15.95, Fixed D 3 course £35, Starter £6-£9, Main £11-£21, Dessert £6-£10, Service optional **Wines** 27 bottles over £30, 38 bottles under £30, 14 by glass **Parking** 60 **Notes** Afternoon tea, Sunday L, Vegetarian available, Children welcome

The Royal Duchy Hotel

◉◉ Modern British

tel: 01326 313042 **Cliff Rd TR11 4NX**
email: reservations@royalduchy.co.uk **web:** www.brend-hotels.co.uk
dir: *On Cliff Rd, along Falmouth seafront*

Well-judged cooking and Falmouth Bay views

With palm trees framing splendid sea views across the bay towards Pendennis Castle from its alfresco terrace, the Royal Duchy Hotel certainly has that Riviera touch. The stately Pendennis Restaurant features plush furnishings, crisp white linen-clad tables, chandeliers, a tinkling grand piano and gracious, unobtrusive service that all work together to create a sense of occasion. Gently contemporary cooking is the order of the day, based on simple combinations that reflect the seasons. Thus a summer's meal sets out with ham hock terrine partnered by pea pannacotta and sweet mustard vinaigrette, followed by a main course showcasing superb roast loin of with new potatoes, seasonal vegetables and lamb nage. Fish lovers might be treated to pan-fried bream and scallops with olive crushed potatoes, ratatouille and sauce vièrge. For dessert, try warm ginger cake with candied carrot and mascarpone, or coconut rice pudding with mango sorbet and purée.

Times 12.30-2/6-9, Closed L Mon-Sat

St Michael's Hotel and Spa

◉◉ Modern Mediterranean, British

tel: 01326 312707 **Gyllyngvase Beach, Seafront TR11 4NB**
email: info@stmichaelshotel.co.uk **web:** www.stmichaelshotel.co.uk
dir: *Follow signs for seafront & beaches*

Seductive sea views and compelling contemporary cooking

There's a stylishly upmarket vibe at this seaside hotel, with a hip-looking bar and a nautically themed restaurant done out in shades of blue, as if to bring the sea indoors. Floor-to-ceiling windows give inspiring views over four acres of sub-tropical gardens to a beach and Falmouth Bay. The kitchen buys solely from local producers, and its passion for cooking is palpable in well executed, succulent seared scallops, served with celeriac purée, delicate vanilla dressing and apple and hazelnut salad, and game and bacon terrine with pickled mushrooms and onion chutney. The brigade clearly understands ingredients and how to balance them out, seen in bitter chocolate jus for perfectly timed seared venison steak, with parsnips, red cabbage and silky mash, and in a crab fritter and smoked haddock and mussel chowder for baked hake fillet. The momentum carries into desserts: perhaps peanut butter parfait with moreish chocolate sorbet and chunks of banana, and lemon and blackberry posset with mascarpone cream.

Chef James Knight-Pacheco **Owner** Nigel & Julie Carpenter **Seats** 80, Pr/dining room 25 **Times** 12-2.30/6.30-9.30 **Prices** Tasting menu £31.95-£37.95, Starter £6.95-£9.50, Main £13.95-£24, Dessert £6.95-£8.95, Service optional **Wines** 14 bottles over £30, 32 bottles under £30, 17 by glass **Parking** 30 **Notes** Sunday L £15.95-£21.50, Vegetarian available, Children welcome

The Fowey Hotel

◉◉ Modern European

tel: 01726 832551 **The Esplanade PL23 1HX**
email: reservations@thefoweyhotel.co.uk **web:** www.richardsonhotels.co.uk
dir: A30 to Okehampton, continue to Bodmin. Then B3269 to Fowey for 1m, on right bend left junct then right into Dagands Rd. Hotel 200mtrs on left

Focused cooking and soothing harbour views

If you're ambling the town's narrow streets of crooked houses and shops tumbling towards the River Fowey estuary and fancy making a pitstop to dine on excellent local produce, including fish and seafood landed practically on the doorstep, keep an eye out for the handsome Victorian hotel amid landscaped gardens with sweeping views across the water. Its restaurant-Spinnakers-basks in those splendid briny vistas, while the kitchen delivers an upbeat repertoire of simple classic combinations. Fowey mussels in a creamy, saffron-infused fricassée with celeriac and tomato sets the ball rolling, followed by a three-way serving of West Country lamb, comprising seared loin, rolled breast and sweetbreads in the company of fondant potato, wilted greens, carrot purée, purple sprouting broccoli and a mint and balsamic jus. To finish, a correctly wobbly yogurt pannacotta is matched with poached rhubarb and its jelly, and orange syrup.

Times 12-3/6.30-9

Cormorant Hotel & Restaurant

◉◉ Modern British, Mediterranean V

tel: 01726 833426 **PL23 1LL**
email: relax@cormoranthotel.co.uk **web:** www.cormoranthotel.co.uk
dir: A390 onto B3269 signed Fowey. In 3m left to Golant, through village to end of road, hotel on right

Mediterranean modernism on the Fowey estuary

The Cormorant occupies a roost above the estuary, which spreads out before it in both directions, as a seat on the sunny terrace confirms. It's only a short woodland walk to Fowey itself, should the urge grab you, but the air of refined relaxation in the hotel makes it hard to leave. A pastel-hued dining room with linen-clad tables is the soothing setting for painstakingly detailed cooking that has reset its compass in the direction of Mediterranean shores. That might translate into chargrilled mackerel with pepper and fennel escabèche, prawn fritters and tomato gel, or chicken terrine with butternut purée, roasted hazelnuts and something the menu calls 'pickled smijis', possibly renamed shimeji mushrooms. Cornish produce is in abundant evidence throughout, from glorious shellfish to pollock with lemon mash and sautéed bok choy, or a pork assiette comprised of roast loin, confit belly and black pudding, served with a dollop of sweet potato purée. At dessert, things go Caribbean with pineapple Tatin and coconut ice cream, or distinctly homely for apple and pear crumble with vanilla ice and thyme caramel.

Chef Dane Watkins **Owner** Mary Tozer **Seats** 30 **Times** 12-2/6.30-9.30, Closed L Nov-Feb (some days) **Prices** Fixed D 3 course £32.50-£40, Tasting menu £55, Starter £6-£11, Main £16-£24, Dessert £7-£10, Service optional **Wines** 25 bottles over £30, 46 bottles under £30, 6 by glass **Parking** 20 **Notes** Tasting menu 6 course, Brasserie menu, Sunday L £14-£28, Children 12 yrs+ D

Rosewarne Manor

◉◉ Modern British

tel: 01209 610414 **20 Gwinear Rd TR27 5JQ**
email: enquiries@rosewarnemanor.co.uk **web:** www.rosewarnemanor.co.uk
dir: A30 Camborne West, A3047 towards Connor Downs, left into Gwinear Rd. 0.75m to Rosewarne Manor

Ambitious cooking in renovated 1920s manor

After a period when this grand 1920s building had fallen into neglect, the current owners have resurrected Rosewarne as a venue with a keen eye to the weddings and functions market, and with good food to boot. The modern British repertoire is driven by seasonality and local sourcing, and the confident cooking delivers well-defined flavours. The menu gives little away in terms of description or cooking methods, so you will need to quiz the helpful staff about what, exactly, is involved at each stage. You might set the ball rolling with Cornish blue cheese pannacotta, matched inventively with apple textures and gingerbread, then progress to an unusual assemblage of pork belly with dark chocolate, cauliflower and apple, or there could be a fashionable fish and meat combo involving line-caught sea bass with beef shin, Savoy cabbage and beurre noisette. To finish, egg custard tart with lemon curd and pistachio crumb might catch the eye, or you could round things off on a savoury note with the excellent artisan Cornish cheeses.

Chef Phil Thomas, Craig Tuxworth **Owner** Cyril & Gill Eustice **Seats** 90, Pr/dining room 12 **Times** 12-2.30/6-9, Closed 2 wks New Year, Mon-Tue **Prices** Fixed L 2 course £12.50-£24, Fixed D 3 course £18.90-£30, Tasting menu £45, Starter £4.95-£6.95, Main £7.95-£19.95, Dessert £3.50-£6, Service optional **Wines** 2 bottles over £30, 22 bottles under £30, 11 by glass **Parking** 50 **Notes** Tasting menu 6 course, Sunday L £9.95, Vegetarian available, Children welcome

New Yard Restaurant

◉◉ New English

tel: 01326 221595 **Trelowarren Estate, Mawgan TR12 6AF**
email: newyard@trelowarren.com **web:** www.newyardrestaurant.co.uk
dir: 5m from Helston

Modern Cornish cooking on a historic estate

The New Yard Restaurant has been carved out of the former stable yard of the Trelowarren Estate, which comprises 1,000 acres of woodland and pasture leading down to the Helford River. Outside, the yard itself feels more like a Mediterranean courtyard with its pair of magnificent olive trees, while the interior has a distinctive look, sporting a chequered floor, arched windows, log fires, unclothed wooden tables and an open-plan kitchen. The punchy, far-reaching menu has ranged from tempura calamari with chilli jam to rump of lamb with spicy yogurt, sweet potato and baby carrots, and the brigade pulls out all the stops to produce generally

continued

HELSTON *continued*

uncomplicated dishes that are big on flavour. Carpaccio with rocket and parmesan, or crab with pumpkin, macaroni and parmesan, is a prelude to pork belly, of superb quality, accompanied by smoked cheek in a subtle sauce, queen scallops, cauliflower and samphire, or John Dory Véronique with samphire and spinach. Puddings are well worth exploring, judging by white chocolate mousse with a raspberry and lemon version of Eton Mess and raspberry sorbet.

Chef Chris Philliskirk **Owner** Sir Ferrers Vyvyan **Seats** 50 **Times** 12-2.15/6.30-9, Closed Jan, Mon (mid Sep-Spring BH), D Sun **Prices** Starter £6-£8, Main £10.50-£17, Dessert £1.75-£9, Service optional **Wines** 8 bottles over £30, 19 bottles under £30, 6 by glass **Parking** 20 **Notes** Breakfast Fri-Sun, Vegetarian menu on request, Sunday L, Children welcome

---

▌ LIZARD   Map 2 SW71

Housel Bay Hotel

◉ Modern British **V**

tel: 01326 290417 & 290917   **Housel Cove TR12 7PG** email: info@houselbay.com **web:** www.houselbay.com **dir:** *A30 from Exeter, exit Truro and take A34/A394 to Helston & A3083 to Lizard*

Regional cooking on a Lizard clifftop

Perched on a blustery clifftop on the Lizard, Housel Bay is a late Victorian hotel that retains a generous complement of original features, including a choice of dining rooms looking out through flat and bay windows over the gardens and the Channel. The walls are crowded with pictures and ephemera, staff engage diners with charm and efficiency, and the kitchen does its bit with a modern British repertoire that exhibits some Italian influence. This is evident in a full-flavoured first course of oxtail ravioli with mushrooms and spinach, dressed in truffle oil and parmesan. Fine Cornish fish (seafood has its own menu) might include seared haddock with crayfish, pea purée and an underpowered beurre blanc, or there may be slow-cooked shoulder of lamb with Greek salad, and plenty of vegetarian choices. Finish with orange and passionfruit tart, classic tiramisù, or a slate of regional cheeses.

Chef Alberto Franchetti **Owner** Mr & Mrs Mesropians **Seats** 70 **Times** 12-2/6.45-9, Closed 24 Dec-mid Jan **Prices** Starter £5.50-£9, Main £14.95-£26.95, Dessert £5-£6.50, Service optional **Wines** 6 bottles over £30, 20 bottles under £30, 12 by glass **Parking** 25 **Notes** ALC 2/3 course £27/£32, Sunday L £16.95-£19.95, Children welcome

---

▌ LOOE   Map 2 SX25

Trelaske Hotel & Restaurant

◉◉ Modern British

tel: 01503 262159 **Polperro Rd PL13 2JS** email: info@trelaske.co.uk **web:** www.trelaske.co.uk **dir:** *B252 signed Looe. Over Looe bridge signed Polperro. 1.9m, hotel signed on right*

Local produce in verdant Cornwall

In a rural location between Looe and Polperro, this small-scale hotel is surrounded by four acres of peaceful grounds. In the spacious restaurant, where large curtained windows look over the grounds, Hazel Billington is a charming and efficient hostess, whole Ross Lewin runs the stoves. His daily-changing menus are dictated by availability and clearly illustrate his respect for ingredients. His dishes are intelligently composed and never overworked, to allow flavours to sparkle. Take a starter of duck liver, fig and pistachio terrine, the hint of sweetness from the fruit a perfect foil for the bold meaty flavour, the nuts adding some crunch. An alternative might be crabmeat with pink grapefruit and rösti before beautifully timed roast salmon fillet with rolls of cucumber stuffed with a creamy mint and cumin filling, or equally straightforward well-timed loin of lamb with mint and lemon stuffing, ratatouille and lamb jus. Vegetables (from the garden) get the thumbs up for their stunningly fresh flavours, as do breads, while

puddings hit the same consistently high standards: perhaps vanilla pannacotta, or summer pudding.

Chef Ross Lewin **Owner** Ross Lewin, Hazel Billington **Seats** 40 **Times** 12-2/7-9, Closed 22-26 Dec, Jan, L Mon-Sat **Prices** Fixed D 3 course £33.50, Service optional **Wines** 10 bottles over £30, 22 bottles under £30, 8 by glass **Parking** 60 **Notes** Sunday L £21.50, Vegetarian available, Children 5 yrs+

▌ LOSTWITHIEL   Map 2 SX15

Asquiths Restaurant

◉◉ Modern British

tel: 01208 871714 **19 North St PL22 0EF** email: info@asquithsrestaurant.co.uk **dir:** *Opposite St Bartholomews church*

Minimal fuss, maximum flavours

Its black and white decor, some exposed stone walls, modern artwork, smartly set clothed tables and elegant and approachable staff, combine to create positive impressions of this restaurant opposite the church. Food is taken seriously too, as confirmed by a glance at the sensibly short menu, with the kitchen turning out thoughtfully composed, accurately prepared dishes with little fuss on the plate. Confit duck and beetroot pastilla has been an effective combination, teamed up with silky pomegranate molasses and couscous, with an alternative perhaps of kedgeree with a Scotch egg and pea cream. Fish gets a decent showing, maybe a well-timed roast hake fillet given an Indian slant from curried cauliflower and a courgette bhaji along with potato purée. Or go for full-bodied haunch of venison with Puy lentils braised with smoked bacon, hogs pudding croquette and butternut squash purée. Culinary skills don't waver at pudding stage: try elegantly presented caramelised stout pannacotta with cinnamon crumbs and apple cannoli, or plum Tatin with rosemary ice cream.

Chef Graham Cuthbertson **Owner** Graham & Sally Cuthbertson **Seats** 28, Pr/dining room 10 **Times** 7-9, Closed Xmas, Jan, Sun-Mon, L all week **Prices** Starter £6-£7, Main £14-£17, Dessert £6-£7.50, Service optional **Wines** 4 bottles over £30, 36 bottles under £30, 6 by glass **Parking** Car park at rear **Notes** Vegetarian available, Children welcome

---

▌ MARAZION   Map 2 SW53

Mount Haven Hotel & Restaurant

◉◉ Modern British

tel: 01736 710249 **Turnpike Rd TR17 0DQ** email: reception@mounthaven.co.uk **web:** www.mounthaven.co.uk **dir:** *From centre of Marazion, up hill E, hotel 400yds on right*

Accomplished modern cooking in family-run hotel

St Michael's Mount soaring out of the sea forms a dramatic backdrop at this boutique hotel near the South West Coast Path. Inside, the furnishings and decor are a mixture of Eastern and Western artefacts, while a team of holistic therapists is on hand for mind, body and spirit treatments. What's on offer in the restaurant, with its boarded floor, pot plants and patterned banquettes, is of a thoroughly contemporary British flavour, with the kitchen showing an unassuming respect for its ingredients. Panko-crusted ham hock and black pudding terrine, given a gentle punch from piccalilli, has been a deeply flavoured starter, with roast scallops with crisp pork belly and sweetcorn purée another thoughtfully composed first course. Seafood is a strong suit among mains-perhaps roast hake fillet accompanied by crab risotto, or whole plaice with tartare sauce, herbed new potatoes and salad-while meat-eaters could choose perhaps pork chop with mustard mash, kale and caramelised onion jus. Properly wobbly pannacotta with caramelised figs is an effective finale, or go for treacle tart.

Chef Nathan Williams **Owner** Orange & Mike Trevillion **Seats** 50 **Times** 12-2.30/6.30-9, Closed 20 Dec-8 Feb **Prices** Fixed L 2 course fr £14.50,

Starter £5-£8, Main £12.50-£27, Dessert £1.50-£8, Service optional **Wines** 20 bottles over £30, 20 bottles under £30, 19 by glass **Parking** 32 **Notes** Sunday L £10-£18.50, Vegetarian available, Children welcome

MAWGAN PORTH
Map 2 SW86

The Scarlet Hotel
◉◉ Modern European

tel: 01637 861800 **Tredragon Rd TR8 4DQ**
email: stay@scarlethotel.co.uk **web:** www.scarlethotel.co.uk
dir: A39, A30 towards Truro. At Trekenning rdbt take A3059, follow Newquay Airport signs. Right after garage signed St Mawgan & Airport. Right after airport, right at T-junct signed Padstow (B3276). At Mawgan Porth left. Hotel 250yds on left

Southwestern clifftop cooking in a soothing eco-hotel

The Scarlett has impeccable eco credentials, but there is no evangelical zeal when it comes to spreading the word, for first and foremost this place is about more hedonistic pleasures-wining, dining and some serious pampering. So the pool is chemical free, the spa treatments take place in treatment tents, but this hotel up on the cliffs has a super-stylish contemporary finish-miles of glass, exterior staircases and trendy furnishings. The restaurant gets the view (wear sunglasses and you'll appreciate it to the max) and the team in the kitchen keep things focused on the West Country. Pan-fried gurnard rocks up with a jumble of stir-fried squid flavoured with chilli and ginger, while terrine of confit Cornish chicken comes in the company of celeriac remoulade and pickles. Next up, tender braised ox cheek forms the bedrock of an impressive main course (with potato and bacon terrine and white port sauce), and, to finish, white chocolate mousse is surrounded by a honeycomb shell, joined by pistachio cake and griottine cherries. The European-only wine list (thinking of the carbon footprint) has lots of organic and biodynamic options.

Chef Tom Hunter **Owner** Red Hotels Ltd **Seats** 70, Pr/dining room 20 **Times** 12.30-2.15/7-9.30, Closed 3-31 Jan, L 25 & 31 Dec **Prices** Fixed L 3 course £22.50-£25, Fixed D 3 course £43.50, Starter £7-£14, Main £14-£22, Dessert £6-£10, Service optional **Wines** 69 bottles over £30, 19 bottles under £30, 39 by glass **Parking** 37, In village **Notes** ALC menu L only, Sunday L, Vegetarian available, Children 13 yrs+

MAWNAN SMITH
Map 2 SW72

Budock Vean – The Hotel on the River
◉ Traditional British V

tel: 01326 252100 **TR11 5LG**
email: relax@budockvean.co.uk **web:** www.budockvean.co.uk
dir: From A39 follow tourist signs to Trebah Gardens. 0.5m to hotel

On point flavours in a traditional country house

Cornwall's benign climate has played its part in creating the 65 acres of sub-tropical gardens that surround Budock Vean, but it is the inspired vision of the owners that has created an organically-managed landscape of woodlands, gardens and golf course on the banks of the Helford River. The hotel aims to maintain the tranquillity with its traditional attitude towards hospitality, which extends to a jacket-and-tie dress code for men at dinner (or one or other during school holidays). The elegant restaurant is the setting for a menu that aims to satisfy rather than dazzle, so high-quality Cornish produce is treated with simplicity and respect in dishes such as spiced West Country chicken breast with poached pear, followed by pan-fried fillet of John Dory (from local waters) with wild mushrooms and chive-butter sauce. A dessert of banoffee pie with chocolate ice cream and honeycomb hits the sweet spot.

Chef Darren Kelly **Owner** The Barlow family **Seats** 100, Pr/dining room 40 **Times** 12-2.30/7.30-9, Closed 3 wks Jan, L Mon-Sat **Prices** Starter £9.43-£21.15, Main £18.20-£37.75, Dessert £7.20, Service optional **Wines** 41 bottles over £30, 49 bottles under £30, 7 by glass **Parking** 100 **Notes** 4 course D £40, L menu served in Cocktail Bar, Sunday L £20.50, Children welcome

MEVAGISSEY
Map 2 SX04

Trevalsa Court Hotel
◉ Modern British

tel: 01726 842460 **School Hill, Polstreth PL26 6TH**
email: stay@trevalsa-hotel.co.uk **web:** www.trevalsa-hotel.co.uk
dir: From St Austell take B3273 to Mevagissey. Pass sign to Pentewan. At top of hill left at x-rds. Hotel signed

Clifftop hotel with a modern menu and good seafood

This is a handsome house built of granite and slate, with some period touches within, including in the smart restaurant. If the weather is kind, a table on the terrace with views across Mevagissey Bay is worth its weight in gold, but fear not, for the view is pretty mint from inside the restaurant, too, particularly if you bag a table by the window. There's a decidedly sub-tropical feel hereabouts – check out the pretty garden – but what appears on the menu is grounded in the local environment, with a decent showing of seafood (crab, lobster and oysters are generally available with a bit of notice). Start with crispy pig's cheek, fennel and apple risotto before a main course of grey mullet perked up with some pickled vegetables, plus squid, mussels, pomegranate and parsley mash. There's also burger, steak or fish cooked on the grill, and desserts such as autumn berry crumble with elderflower and thyme ice cream.

Chef Adam Cawood **Owner** John & Susan Gladwin **Seats** 26 **Times** 12.30-3/6.30-9, Closed Dec-Jan, L Some days (seasonal) **Prices** Fixed L 2 course fr £14.50, Starter £5.50-£8.50, Main £14.50-£22.50, Dessert £5.50-£8.50, Service optional **Wines** 7 by glass **Parking** 20 **Notes** Afternoon tea, Sunday L £14.50-£19.50, Vegetarian available, Children welcome

MULLION
Map 2 SW61

Mullion Cove Hotel
◉◉ Modern British

tel: 01326 240328 **TR12 7EP**
email: enquiries@mullion-cove.co.uk **web:** www.mullion-cove.co.uk
dir: A3083 towards The Lizard. Through Mullion towards Mullion Cove. Hotel in approx 1m

Sea views and accomplished modern cooking

This solidly built white property on the Lizard Peninsula sits on the top of cliffs, giving uninterrupted sea and coast views. The restaurant is a reassuringly traditional and smart environment, with professional and friendly service. The kitchen is committed to local suppliers, with day boats providing seafood: perhaps whole grilled plaice with baby potatoes, seasonal greens and citrusy caper butter. Otherwise there might be another main course of roast breast and confit leg of guinea fowl, the meat of superb quality and perfectly cooked, served with carrots, parsnip purée, kale and Calvados velouté. Seafood platters are offered with 24 hours' notice, and an international element is evident in some dishes, for example a flavourful starter of seafood laksa (clams, squid, mullet and prawns) with pickled vegetables. More mainstream perhaps is another starter of Exe mussels cooked with cider, cream and shallots, and the kitchen's industry is put to good effect in puddings such as chocolate mousse with chocolate 'soil' and damson and liquorice sorbet.

Chef Fiona Were **Owner** Matthew Grose **Seats** 60 **Times** 12-2/6.30-8.45, Closed L Mon-Sat **Prices** Fixed D 3 course £35-£50, Service optional **Wines** 51 bottles over £30, 44 bottles under £30, 16 by glass **Parking** 45 **Notes** Sunday L £15-£22, Vegetarian available, Children 7 yrs+

NEWQUAY
Map 2 SW86

Silks Bistro and Champagne Bar

◉ Modern British

tel: 01637 839048 & 872244 **Atlantic Hotel, Dane Rd TR7 1EN**
email: info@atlantichotelnewquay.co.uk **web:** www.atlantichotelnewquay.co.uk
dir: From M5 southbound junct 31, take A30 at Newquay sign. Follow signs Fistral Beach.
Hotel at top of Dane Rd

Modern bistro cooking with a champagne bar attached

Built in 1892 in 10 acres of headland, the Atlantic overlooks the golden crescent of
Fistral Beach, Cornwall's surfing central. This is no gloomy Victorian haunt, though,
for inside it is filled with daylight. The focal point is its bright, modern Silks Bistro
and Champagne bar, with zebra-patterned bar stools, and sunburst-styled cafe
chairs at linen-swathed tables. In the evenings, candlelight softens the scene as
the sun descends into the ocean. Starters such as ham hock and parsley terrine
with home-made piccalilli or Newlyn crab cakes with lemon and sweet chilli mayo
pave the way for comfort-oriented mains. These might be battered fish (whatever's
fresh on the day) with proper chips, lemon and tartare sauce, or a hearty plate of
confit belly pork with cassoulet and apple coulis. Puddings continue the feel-good
mood via dark chocolate brownie with toffee sauce and vanilla ice cream.

Chef Aaron Janes **Owner** Lorraine Stones **Seats** 100, Pr/dining room 24 **Times** 12-9,
All-day dining **Prices** Fixed D 3 course £25-£28, Starter £5.50-£10.50, Main £9.95-
£17.95, Dessert £5.95-£6.95, Service optional **Wines** 9 bottles over £30, 22 bottles
under £30, 9 by glass **Parking** Car park adjacent **Notes** Sunday L £11.95-£19.50,
Vegetarian available, Children welcome

PADSTOW
Map 2 SW97

The Metropole

◉ Modern British

tel: 01841 532486 & 0800 005 2244 **Station Rd PL28 8DB**
email: reservations@the-metropole.co.uk **web:** www.the-metropole.co.uk
dir: M5/A30 past Launceston, follow signs for Wadebridge and N Cornwall. Then take A39
and follow signs for Padstow

Harbour side restaurant with an assured team in the kitchen

This Victorian hotel has commanding views over the foodie town and Camel
Estuary, and where better to enjoy them but over a meal in the Harbour Restaurant,
with large windows and high-backed upholstered dining chairs at clothed tables on
the carpeted floor. The kitchen is driven by local supplies-fish landed in the nearby
harbour, for instance-and plays a with-it tune, producing starters of seared
scallops with celeriac, apple purée and hog's pudding alongside blue cheese and
leek bread-and-butter pudding with apple, apricot and rocket. Salmon fillet stars in
a main course with sauté potato, confit tomato, celeriac, fine beans and beurre
blanc, or there may be roast chicken breast with dauphinoise potatoes, Savoy
cabbage, carrot purée and thyme jus. End in the comfort zone with lemon and
thyme-glazed treacle tart with blackberries and lemon curd ice cream.

Chef Michael Corbin **Owner** Richardson Hotels **Seats** 70, Pr/dining room 30
Times 6.30-9, Closed L Mon-Tue, Thu-Sat **Prices** Fixed L 2 course fr £9.50, Fixed D 3
course £32.95, Starter £6.50-£11, Main £15.95-£20.95, Dessert £7-£10, Service
optional **Wines** 7 bottles over £30, 24 bottles under £30, 9 by glass **Parking** 50
Notes Sunday L £12.95-£15.95, Vegetarian available, Children welcome

Paul Ainsworth at No. 6

◉◉◉ *– see opposite*

St Petroc's Hotel and Bistro

◉ Traditional, Mediterranean

tel: 01841 532700 **4 New St PL28 8EA**
email: reservations@rickstein.com **web:** www.rickstein.com
dir: From Lawns car park on New St, head down hill. Establishment 100yds on right

Informal bistro dining from Rick Stein's stable

The bistro is an informal and relaxing sort of place, with simple tables and chairs
on worn wooden floorboards, modern paintings on plain white walls, and
professional service from attentive staff. There's a cosy bar and a pleasant lounge
for pre-dinner drinks and a courtyard and garden for alfresco meals. With Rick
Stein at the helm, it comes as no surprise that seafood is the main business, with
the kitchen deploying top-quality raw materials to produce dishes of imagination
and flair, from well-timed grilled scallops with truffle butter, or salt-cod fritters with
aïoli, to grilled lemon sole with brown shrimps and mushrooms, or roast tronçon of
turbot with sauce vierge. Steaks from the grill are a feature too, another meaty
option perhaps tender, deeply-flavoured venison au poivre nicely balanced by salt-
baked beetroot and horseradish. End if you can with the bitter-sweet tastes of
dense chocolate and marmalade tart with raspberry sorbet, or perhaps warm apple
and cider cake.

Chef Nick Evans **Owner** R & J Stein **Seats** 54, Pr/dining room 12
Times 12-2/6.30-9.30, Closed 25-26 Dec, D 24 Dec **Prices** Fixed L 2 course £18,
Starter £5.95-£9.95, Main £15.95-£29, Dessert £6.75-£8.50, Service optional
Wines 12 bottles over £30, 13 bottles under £30, 12 by glass **Parking** Lawns car
park up hill **Notes** Vegetarian available, Children welcome

Paul Ainsworth at No. 6

PADSTOW   Map 2 SW97

Modern British V

tel: 01841 532093 **6 Middle St PL28 8AP**
email: enquiries@number6inpadstow.co.uk
web: www.number6inpadstow.co.uk
dir: *A30 follow signs for Wadebridge then sign to Padstow*

Defining contemporary cooking in a pint-sized townhouse

Down one of Padstow's narrow streets, just back from the harbour, Paul Ainsworth's townhouse restaurant has been a major player here since 2006, and since 2010 he's had a second address down the road called Rojano's on the Square-empire building must be in the water round these parts. Paul has built a reputation for creating contemporary food that is focused on the regional produce that makes Cornwall such a culinary destination these days, while exposure on TV via the BBC's The *Great British Menu* has done him no harm. The restaurant occupies three diminutive spaces on the ground floor and another upstairs, with the Georgian charm of the spaces intact, some well-chosen arty pieces on the shelves and lit alcoves, and dark-wood tables that might be a wee bit close together for some. The cooking is modern inasmuch as all sorts of new-fangled ideas are embraced along the way, from cooking techniques to flavour combinations, but there is level-headedness, too, with the ingredients given the opportunity to make an impression on their own merits. Porthilly oysters are hard to ignore at the best of times, and doubly so here, where they are served crisp-fried and matched with cured pork, green apple and fennel, or go for another seafood opener that delivers torched mackerel in a Med-inspired dish with celeriac remoulade, coppa ham and

cucumber. Next up, cod and crab combine in a main course that shows off the best of the West, while full-flavoured venison arrives with 'pain au pudding' and yeast-glazed celery root. To finish, there's the 'fairground tale' (the dish that wowed the judges at the Beeb), or a Cornish 'trifle' with blood orange and saffron. There's also an inventive children's menu and set lunch option.

Chef Paul Ainsworth **Owner** Paul Ainsworth **Seats** 46, Pr/dining room 10 **Times** 12-2.30/6-10, Closed 24-26 Dec, 14 Jan-4 Feb, Sun-Mon (excl BH Sun), L 1 May **Prices** Fixed L 2 course £19, Starter £12-£14, Main £28-£38, Dessert £11-£24, Service optional **Wines** 75 bottles over £30, 18 bottles under £30, 16 by glass **Parking** Harbour car park and on street **Notes** Children 4 yrs+

PADSTOW continued

The Seafood Restaurant

@@@ – see below

Treglos Hotel

@ Traditional English v

tel: 01841 520727 Constantine Bay PL28 8JH
email: stay@tregloshotel.com web: www. tregloshotel.com
dir: At St Merryn x-rds take B3276 towards Newquay. In 500mtrs right to Constantine Bay, follow brown signs

Modern Cornish cooking at a smart family hotel

An upscale, family-run hotel overlooking Constantine Bay near Padstow, the Treglos is a late Victorian house converted into a hotel in the 1930s. Wallis Simpson stayed here during the brief reign of Edward VIII, and the sparkling-white frontage and smart interiors certainly look as though they're geared for the glitterati. The dining room is done in maroon and leafy green, with discreet artworks and ceramics here and there, and the menus take a modern approach, with specials built around a solid core repertoire. Proceedings might get under way with a serving of pigeon in delicious blueberry jus, garnished with beetroot purée, potato crisps and pea shoots. This is merely a curtain-raiser for mains such as seafood stew in bouillabaisse sauce with wilted bok choy and saffron aïoli, or tenderloin pork medallions in cider sauce with black pudding and champ. At the end comes flawlessly rendered lemon tart, served with a dollop of incisive lemon curd and the gentling influence of mint crème fraîche.

Chef Gavin Hill Owner Jim & Rose Barlow Seats 100
Times 12-2.30/6.45-8.45, Closed 30 Nov-10 Feb Prices Prices not confirmed, Service optional Wines 8 by glass Parking 40 Notes Sun L by arrangement £10/£30, Afternoon tea £5.25, Children 3 yrs+

PENZANCE
Map 2 SW43

The Bay@Hotel Penzance

@@ Modern British, French

tel: 01736 366890 & 363117 Britons Hill TR18 3AE
email: eat@thebaypenzance.co.uk web: www.thebaypenzance.co.uk
dir: From A30 take exit to Penzance at Tesco rdbt. 3rd right onto Britons Hill. Hotel on right

Appealing modern food, sea views and a stylish setting

As well as magnificent views over rooftops to Mount's Bay, the Bay Brasserie offers plenty to catch the eye indoors, since monthly-changing exhibitions of local artists' work are a draw in the light and airy contemporary space. The kitchen sources its materials from the West Country, with all of the fresh fish and shellfish hauled in from Cornish ports to appear in mains such as roast cod fillet with squid and vegetable compôte and seaweed salsa, or grilled brill with brown shrimps, tomato and samphire. Cornish lobster needs 24 hours' notice and comes grilled with garlic and herbs or thermidor sauce. The wide-ranging modern English menu also gives fans of local meat plenty to get their teeth into – perhaps pan-fried pigeon breast with figs, chard and Pernod jus, while roast rump of lamb gets the full-bore support of onions and anchovy, smoked aubergine and potato cake. Baked dark chocolate and cardamom tart with crème fraîche sorbet, or artisan West Country cheeses with pickled grapes and home-made oat biscuits could provide the finale.

The Seafood Restaurant @@@

PADSTOW
Map 2 SW97

Traditional, International Seafood v ♦ NOTABLE WINE LIST
tel: 01841 532700 Riverside PL28 8BY
email: reservations@rickstein.com web: www.rickstein.com
dir: Follow signs for Padstow town centre, onto Station Rd signed Harbour car park, restaurant opposite

Padstein ahoy! Delights from around the globe

The Rick Stein phenomenon started here on Padstow's quayside back in 1975. Quite apart from Stein's culinary globetrotting for the BBC, his domain now extends to eight restaurants stretching from Cornwall to Australia. Global influences garnered from exploration of the world's cuisines all have their bit to say in the Seafood Restaurant's menu, providing a glow of the Med here, a kick of Asian fire and spice there, as well as classics that you just don't mess with-Dover sole, for example, grilled whole and served à la meunière or with nutty brown beurre noisette. Telly exposure has certainly been good for business: fizzing with life through the year, the flagship is an expansive space of blond wood, white walls, colourful splashes of contemporary art, and linen-dressed tables spread around a central altar of shellfish and crustacea. Stir-fried salt and pepper squid is a simple starter handled with skill-lightly charred, perfectly seasoned and revved up with chilli, ginger and spring onions. Elsewhere,

Stein's Spanish travels inform an opener of grilled scallops partnered with Ibérico ham, pimentón and Pardina lentils. Mains keep things simple, too, as when a fillet of red mullet with mushrooms, sun-dried tomatoes and rocket proclaims its seasonal freshness in ringing tones, or a tronçon of turbot is roasted on the bone and served with a well-made hollandaise. Those in search of more far-flung exotica could take an Indonesian seafood curry of monkfish, pollock, squid and prawns, and to finish, perhaps rum and chestnut mousse with hazelnut meringue. Rather like the boss, the expansive, well-thought-out wine list travels the world to bring home good ideas from every continent.

Chef Stephane Delourme Owner Rick & Jill Stein Seats 120
Times 12-2.30/6.30-10, Closed 25-26 Dec, D 24 Dec Prices Starter £14.50-£26.50, Main £19.50-£55, Dessert £8.90-£9.50, Service optional Wines 181 bottles over £30, 34 bottles under £30, 46 by glass Parking Pay & display opposite Notes Fixed L 3 course summer menu £40, winter menu £31, Children 3 yrs+

Chef Ben Reeve Owner Yvonne & Stephen Hill Seats 60, Pr/dining room 12
Times 12-2.30/17-9.30, Closed 1st 2 wks Jan Prices Starter £6.95-£8.95, Main
£14-£24, Dessert £7.25-£9.50, Service optional Wines 31 bottles over £30, 23
bottles under £30, 13 by glass Parking 12, On street Notes Sunday L £13.50,
Vegetarian available, Children welcome

Ben's Cornish Kitchen

@@ British

tel: 01736 719200 West End, Marazion TR17 OEL
email: ben@benscornishkitchen.com
dir: On coast road opposite St Michael's Mount

Contemporary cooking on the Cornish coast

Seagulls wheel about the thriving little village of Marazion, just outside Penzance,
in a coastal scene that may strike a chord with followers of *Doc Martin*. Behind its
shop front façade, the Kitchen extends over two wooded floors furnished with plain
tables and raffia chairs, with some local artworks for sale. Contemporary-styled
cooking with a classical background features dishes that are perfectly married
constructs, with prime ingredients receiving due prominence. In starters, that could
mean a dual role for cured and crisp-fried beef with watercress, pungent
horseradish and a sourdough croûton, or a twice-baked cheese soufflé with soused
pear and spiced pecans. Then mains bring on milky-textured cod with crushed root
veg, mussels and spinach, or intensely flavoured braised lamb shoulder with
frankly stunning pearl barley risotto and crunchy broccoli in salsa verde. Tropical
elements add up to an irresistible dessert of coconut pannacotta with dried
pineapple, lime-macerated mango, spiced caramel and mint sugar. Cheeses are a
sound Anglo-French selection that comes with home-made biscuits and damson
jelly. Oh, and don't miss the excellent breads.

Chef Ben Prior Owner Ben Prior Seats 40, Pr/dining room 25
Times 12-2/7-9, Closed Sun-Mon Prices Fixed L 2 course £17, Starter £6-£9, Main
£12-£20, Dessert £6-£8, Service optional Wines 65 bottles over £30, 65 bottles
under £30, 25 by glass Parking Across the road Notes Vegetarian available,
Children welcome

The Coldstreamer Inn

@ Modern British

tel: 01736 362072 Gulval TR18 3BB
email: info@coldstreamer-penzance.co.uk web: www.coldstreamer-penzance.co.uk
dir: 1m NE of Penzance on B3311, right turn into School Ln in Gulval, opposite church

Big local flavours in a Cornish village inn

The Coldstreamer is a traditionally run village inn a mile outside Penzance, its
participation in the life of the local community extending not just to feeding and
watering Gulval and the environs, but showcasing the work of local artists too, a
month at a time. Eating takes place in both the bar and a dedicated dining area
with foursquare wooden furniture and rough stone walls. Local produce naturally
features prominently in menus that offer an uncomplicated style of country-inn
cooking with the emphasis on big, belting flavours. Start with chunky fishcakes of
salmon, fennel and lemon, then sensitively timed pork loin with brittle crackling,
red cabbage and punchy dauphinoise, or a whole plaice with fine beans and tomato
in pesto dressing. Pudding could be as light as yoghurt pannacotta with honey-
roast figs and blackberry sorbet, if you're not quite up to the sticky toffee and
butterscotch route.

Chef Darren Broom Owner Richard Tubb Seats 40 Times 12-3/6-9, Closed 25 Dec
Prices Prices not confirmed, Service optional Wines 24 bottles under £30, 9 by glass
Parking Village square Notes Sunday L, Vegetarian available, Children welcome

Harris's Restaurant

@ Modern European, French, British

tel: 01736 364408 46 New St TR18 2LZ
email: contact@harrissrestaurant.co.uk
dir: Located down narrow cobbled street opposite Lloyds TSB & the Humphry Davy statue
on Market Jew St

Clearly focused, unfussy food just off the high street

The Harris family have been running their restaurant for over 30 years, its success
down to professionally prepared and freshly cooked quality produce (local meats,
seafood from Newlyn, for instance), with the kitchen taking an unshowy,
straightforward line. It's an unpretentious, engaging restaurant on a cobbled side
street in the centre. Seafood makes up the bulk of starters, with meat dishes
getting a fair showing among mains. Kick off with grilled scallops with a simple
herb dressing, or cornets of smoked salmon stuffed with white crabmeat, and
proceed to impeccably timed Dover sole grilled with butter and chives, or sole
goujons with tartare sauce. Committed meat-eaters could go for pheasant breast
stuffed with mushrooms and apple wrapped in filo, and all comers could end with
a satisfying pudding like treacle tart, or crème brûlée.

Chef Roger Harris Owner Roger & Anne Harris Seats 40, Pr/dining room 20
Times 12-2/7-9.30, Closed 3 wks winter, 25-26 Dec, 1 Jan, Sun-Mon Prices Starter
£7.50-£8.95, Dessert £7.95-£9.50 Wines 28 bottles over £30, 17 bottles under £30,
8 by glass Parking On street, local car park Notes Seasonal opening times,
Vegetarian available, Children 5 yrs+

PORTHLEVEN
Map 2 SW62

Kota Restaurant with Rooms

@@ British, Pacific Rim

tel: 01326 562407 Harbour Head TR13 9JA
email: kota@btconnect.com web: www.kotarestaurant.co.uk
dir: B3304 from Helston into Porthleven, Kota on harbour head opposite slipway

Seafood-based fusion food on a Cornish harbour

Perched on the waterfront in a picturesque Cornish harbour town, Kota takes its
name from the Maori word for seafood, the linguistic reference giving a clue to one
element of chef-patron Jude Kereama's ethnicity. In a spacious beamed room with a
tiled floor and unclothed tables, an inspired spin on marine-based fusion food wins
many converts. Lively pairings such as Falmouth scallops and pork belly with
parsnips and apple and ginger dressing, or a trio of crab presentations (fresh,
spring roll and tempura-battered claw) in chilli-tamarind mayo, give way to brightly
spiced, generous main dishes like an array of hake, king prawn, scallop and crispy
squid in red pepper, ginger and chilli sauce. The meat brigade might look to rump
and shoulder of lamb with beetroot, kale and aubergine, dressed with redcurrant
jelly and soy jus. Finish up with West Country cheeses and home-made chutneys, or
baked lemon mascarpone with lemon curd, ginger crunch and mango sorbet.

Chef Jude Kereama Owner Jude & Jane Kereama Seats 40 Times 6-9, Closed Jan-Feb,
Sun-Mon, L all week Prices Fixed D 3 course £21.50, Starter £6.95-£9.25, Main
£13.95-£21, Dessert £5.95-£9.50, Service optional 10% Wines 7 bottles over £30,
30 bottles under £30, 13 by glass Parking On street Notes Vegetarian available,
Children welcome

■ PORT ISAAC   Map 2 SW98

Outlaws Fish Kitchen

◉◉ Modern British, Seafood

tel: 01208 881183 & 880237   **1 Middle St PL29 3RH**
email: fishkitchen@outlaws.co.uk
dir: *Phone for directions*

Stunning seafood in a casual setting

'The sea and fishermen dictate our daily menu', declares Nathan Outlaw, a sentiment that ensures freshness and shows due respect to the hard labour that brings the ingredients to the table. Mr Outlaw is a big fish in Cornwall – and on telly these days – with a number of restaurants across the county (plus one in London), the pick of which is Restaurant Nathan Outlaw itself (see entry). The Fish Kitchen is a different kettle of fish, being a rustic little place right on the harbour, with sea views and an easy-going vibe. Inside are whitewashed walls, unclothed tables and a keen service team. The deal is multiple small plates, and what a fab bunch they are too. The menu is straight and true when it comes to the fruits of the sea, so a smoked haddock Scotch egg with curry sauce oozes in all the right places, and seafood and bean stew shows spot-on technique and delivers sparkling flavours. Crispy ling with roasted garlic mayonnaise and pickled carrot and green chilli packs a delightful punch, and, for dessert, there is baked rice pudding with rhubarb and gingerbread. Every seaside town should have one.

Chef Simon Davies, Deano Medlen **Owner** Nathan Outlaw Restaurants Ltd **Seats** 25 **Times** 12-3/6-9.30, Closed Jan, Xmas, Sun-Mon (Oct-Jun) **Prices** Starter £6.50-£22, Dessert £6-£7, Service optional **Wines** 14 bottles over £30, 5 bottles under £30, 6 by glass **Parking** 2 car parks – top of village **Notes** To share – 5 course L £19.50, 10 course D £39.50, Vegetarian available, Children welcome

Restaurant Nathan Outlaw

◉◉◉◉ *– see opposite*

■ PORTLOE   Map 2 SW93

The Lugger

◉◉ European

tel: 01872 501322 **TR2 5RD**
email: reservations.lugger@ohiml.com **web:** www.luggerhotel.com
dir: *A390 to Truro, B3287 to Tregony, A3078 (St Mawes Rd), left for Veryan, left for Portloe*

Enterprising cooking by the harbour

Dating from the 16th century, now a luxury hotel, The Lugger overlooks the sea and tiny harbour of this picturesque Roseland Peninsula village, with a terrace outside the smart restaurant for summer dining. Local ingredients are the kitchen's linchpin, particularly seafood, which might appear as moules marinière, or crab salad, followed by cod fillet with caper and lemon butter. Elsewhere, look for contemporary treatments of maple-glazed pork belly with a scallop and cauliflower cream, and pigeon with beetroot and pomegranate salad, then pheasant breast with basil polenta, dried tomatoes and game chips, and saddle of venison with bitter chocolate jus, spinach and dauphinoise potatoes. Cornish cheeses are alternatives to puddings like orange pannacotta with poached rhubarb.

Times 12.30-2.30/7-9

■ PORTSCATHO   Map 2 SW83

Driftwood

◉◉◉ *– see below*

Driftwood ❀❀❀

■ PORTSCATHO   Map 2 SW83

Modern European
tel: 01872 580644 **Rosevine TR2 5EW**
email: info@driftwoodhotel.co.uk **web:** www.driftwoodhotel.co.uk
dir: *5m from St Mawes off the A3078, signed Rosevine*

Accomplished cooking in a stunning coastal setting

This elegant boutique bolt-hole perches on the clifftop above the rugged coastline around Gerrans Bay where diners are treated to a Cornish vista through the huge windows. It is a supremely relaxing spot, done out with an understated beachcomber-chic look – a predominantly white room with pale wood floors and linen-draped tables. Head chef Chris Eden is a Cornishman whose pride in his region drives him to use the best ingredients his home territory can offer and bring it together in intelligently designed compositions. The food aims high and hits the mark with a well-constructed dish of cider-glazed Saddleback pork belly with roasted shallots and apple confit providing counterpoints of sweetness and acidity, crunchy crackling and edible Nasturtium flowers. There's real flair in selecting ingredients for their striking originality, well-judged partnerships and how they work together on the palate, witness a main course of immaculately-handled, sea-fresh hake, partnered by taramasalata, palourde clams, dainty kale crisps and broccoli. More earthy ingredients are dealt with no less adroitly: roast partridge and its confit leg meat, for instance, with pearl barley, ceps, pancetta and elderberries. All of the peripheral items, from superb fruit and walnut bread to a stunningly-crafted amuse of pea foam, onion jelly, crispy bacon and mushroom dust, are first class. This is also true of a carefully constructed dessert of spiced pineapple matched with a toasted coconut meringue and a palate-cleansing lemongrass and lime sorbet.

Chef Christopher Eden **Owner** Paul & Fiona Robinson **Seats** 34 **Times** 6.30-9.30, Closed early Dec-early Feb, L all week (ex Thu-Sat, Jun-Sep) **Prices** Fixed D 3 course £55, Tasting menu £80-£90, Service optional **Wines** 50 bottles over £30, 14 bottles under £30, 10 by glass **Parking** 20 **Notes** Vegetarian available, Children 6 yrs+

Restaurant Nathan Outlaw ❀❀❀❀

Modern British, Seafood **NEW** V

tel: 01208 880896 **6 New Rd PL29 3SB**
email: rno@nathan-outlaw.com
dir: *M5/A30/A39 towards Wadebridge, B3267 through St Teath, B3267 on to Port Isacc*

Refined multi-course seafood dining from a modern master

Like many a canny contemporary chef, Nathan Outlaw's not shy of spreading his name far and wide and building the Outlaw brand via appearances in the BBC's *Great British Menu* and other armchair foodie slots on the telly, but the celeb stuff doesn't get in the way of cooking fish in a masterly manner. His empire now encompasses venues in London and here in Port Isaac, where the serious business goes on in his new full-works, namesake flagship. The new premises sit at the top end of the village, with unsullied views out to sea and an understated minimal look involving neutral tones, local art, and chunky wooden tables. Nothing distracts from the creative and intelligent work that leaves the kitchen. The concept behind this operation is to let the top-class Cornish materials speak eloquently for themselves, helped along, naturally, with high-flying technique and an innate sense of what works with what. Choosing what to eat is easy: since most diners see this as something of a foodie pilgrimage, there's just fish and seafood, delivered in an eight-course tasting menu and a set lunch option, plus veggie alternatives to both. First off, sweet cured monkfish is matched with a saffron aïoli and smoked almonds in a dish that kicks off proceedings in fine style, before raw scallops partnered with preserved herring, onion and chilli. It all looks beautiful on the plate and the quality of the ingredients is never in doubt, with the flavours leaving a lasting impression as one dish follows another. Next up, moist and delicate lemon sole comes with a crispy breaded oyster, Jerusalem artichoke purée and wild garlic, followed by crab pointed up with lightly pickled sliced asparagus, asparagus mousse and sourdough crisps to scoop it all up with. Turbot is roasted to perfection and served with a bacon crust, charred cauliflower, peppery watercress purée, with sliced razor clams bringing a subtle taste of the sea — a divine combination, and everything is there for a reason. Follow on with a cheese course — Camembert-like Tunworth goats' cheese layered millefeuille-style with crisp fennel and served with various textures of earthy beetroot, and candied pine nuts. Finally, a brace of desserts: juniper crème brûlée atop a layer of rhubarb jam, which pairs thrillingly with blood orange segments and orange granité, and dark chocolate tart with passionfruit purée and coconut sorbet. If you're seeking a more unbuttoned alternative, try the seafood small plates in Outlaw's Fish Kitchen.

Chef Nathan Outlaw, Chris Simpson **Owner** Nathan Outlaw Restaurants Ltd **Seats** 24 **Times** 12-2/7-9, Closed Xmas, Jan, Sun-Tue, L Wed-Thu **Prices** Tasting menu £99 **Wines** 163 bottles over £30, 1 bottle under £30, 12 by glass **Parking** Adjacent to restaurant **Notes** Fixed L 4 course £49, Children 12 yrs+

Rose-in-Vale Country House Hotel

◉◉ Modern, Traditional British

tel: 01872 552202 **Mithian TR5 0QD**
email: reception@roseinvalehotel.co.uk **web:** www.roseinvalehotel.co.uk
dir: *Take A30 S towards Redruth. At Chiverton Cross rdbt take B3277 signed St Agnes. In 500mtrs turn at tourist info sign for Rose-in-Vale. Into Mithian, right at Miners Arms, down hill*

Modern country cooking in a Cornish valley

The Rose-in-Vale Hotel is a real hideaway, a gorgeous creeper-clad Georgian manor house tucked into the tranquil village of Mithian on the north Cornish coast. Recent refurbishment has given its Valley Restaurant a clean-lined contemporary look to go with the pastoral views, and formal-yet-friendly service keeps everything on track. The kitchen is a hive of activity with a clear sense of purpose, making everything in-house from top-class local produce and keeping its seasonal menus refreshed with daily specials. Gently-updated country-house ideas set off with pressed pork with velvety celeriac purée, haricot beans, pickled baby carrots and watercress, or perhaps pan-seared scallops with smoked bacon crumbs and pea purée. Main courses draw on local fish landed at St Agnes — crispy-skinned sea bass is partnered with tiger prawn tortellini, fennel purée and potato terrine — but there may also be a two-way serving of local duck, involving breast and a spring roll packed with confit meat, matched with potato fondant, dates and julienned vegetables. To finish, lemon pannacotta appears alongside pistachio sponge and blackcurrant sorbet.

Chef James & Tom Bennett, Scott Pascoe **Owner** James & Sara Evans **Seats** 80, Pr/dining room 12 **Times** 12-2/7-9, Closed 2 wks Jan, L Mon-Wed (winter) **Prices** Starter £6-£10, Main £12-£25, Dessert £6-£10, Service optional **Wines** 20 bottles over £30, 25 bottles under £30, 7 by glass **Parking** 50 **Notes** Sunday L, Vegetarian available, Children 12 yrs+

Austell's

◉◉ Modern British

tel: 01726 813888 **10 Beach Rd PL25 3PH**
email: brett@austells.co.uk
dir: *From A390 towards Par, 0.5m after Charlestown rdbt at 2nd lights turn right. Left at rdbt. Restaurant 600yds on right*

Sophisticated dining near the beach

In an unassuming setting on a parade of shops on the road to Carlyon Bay, Austell's is a simple, uncluttered spot, with wooden floors and artwork on plain walls. The split-level layout fosters a convivial mood, while diners on the raised area can watch and chat with the team at work in the open-plan kitchen. There are no corners cut here: seasonality drives the menus so new dishes pop up regularly, and everything is made in-house, from breads (perhaps mustard bread served with nutty rapeseed oil) to home-churned herb butter. Mediterranean accents add zing to a menu that always offers generous helpings of Cornish produce — local ham hock comes in a terrine with pea risotto, smoked Granny Smith apple purée, port and truffle dressing and a prmesan wafer, followed by pan-fried sea bass fillet and seared scallops with dauphinoise potato, carrot purée, green beans wrapped in pancetta, and a delightful pea velouté. For dessert, black cherry compôte is a perfect foil for a decadently gooey chocolate brownie, with honeycomb, frosted pecans and cherry ice cream adding further interest.

Chef Brett Camborne-Paynter **Owner** Brett Camborne-Paynter **Seats** 48 **Times** 12-2/6-9, Closed 1-15 Jan, Mon, L Tue-Sat **Prices** Fixed D 3 course fr £27.50, Starter £5.50-£8.95, Main £16.50-£19.95, Dessert £5.50-£8.50, Service optional **Wines** 18 bottles over £30, 29 bottles under £30, 12 by glass **Parking** 30 **Notes** Sunday L £14.95-£19.95, Vegetarian available, Children welcome

Boscundle Manor

◉◉ Modern British

tel: 01726 813557 **Boscundle PL25 3RL**
email: reservations@boscundlemanor.co.uk **web:** www.boscundlemanor.co.uk
dir: *Phone for directions*

Country hotel with a local flavour

The 18th-century manor that stands today benefits from the kind of facilities that lure the 21st-century traveller, so expect spa treatments, an indoor pool and a smart restaurant. The hotel is in five acres of grounds, within easy striking distance of the Eden Project, and its restaurant is very much a draw in its own right. The dining room is done out in a traditional and decidedly romantic manner, with candlelight, mellow pinky-red colour tones, and tables dressed up in white linen. The chef sources much of the produce from the local environment, and everything is made in-house, from bread to ice cream. The à la carte menu is a satisfying blend of classical technique and contemporary touches, with flavours working in harmony. A first course dish of pan-seared scallops sees the bivalves perfectly caramelised and served with roasted butternut squash risotto, crispy pancetta and cumin oil (a winning combination), and for main course there might be breast of honey-glazed duck with potato fondant and a cranberry and orange sauce.

Times 6.30-9, Closed L all week

Carlyon Bay Hotel

◉ Modern, Traditional British

tel: 01726 812304 **Sea Rd, Carlyon Bay PL25 3RD**
email: reservations@carlyonbay.com **web:** www.carlyonbay.com
dir: *From St Austell, follow signs for Charlestown. Carlyon Bay signed on left, hotel at end of Sea Rd*

Simple traditions on the St Austell clifftop

Surveying the rugged Cornish coast from its clifftop perch above St Austell, the creeper-curtained Carlyon Bay Hotel is an imposing presence above the bay. Within its 250 acres of grounds you'll find a full complement of spa and leisure facilities, including its own championship golf course. Taking care of the gastronomic side of things is the aptly-named Bay View Restaurant, where huge windows allow maximum exposure to the sea views, and everything is smartly turned out, from the linen-swathed tables to the amicable, black-and-white-uniformed staff. The kitchen tacks a pretty traditional course, keeping things simple and relying on the quality and provenance of its ingredients to win plaudits. Cornish mussels with cider, cream and garlic is a good way to start, then follow with roast rump of new season's lamb with pea purée, creamed potato, and rosemary and redcurrant sauce. To finish, vanilla pannacotta gets a lift from tangy poached rhubarb and crunchy pistachio.

Times 12-2/7-9.30

The Cornwall Hotel, Spa & Estate

◉ Modern British v

tel: 01726 874050 & 874051 **Pentewan Rd, Tregorrick PL26 7AB**
email: enquiries@thecornwall.com **web:** www.thecornwall.com
dir: *A391 to St Austell then B3273 towards Mevagissey. Hotel approx 0.5m on right*

Enticing modern cooking in a stylish manor house

When you need to seek sanctuary from the frazzling effects of the modern world, this luxurious Victorian country house with a spa and woodland holiday homes in 43 acres of tranquil grounds should do the job. On the fine dining side of the equation, the Arboretum Restaurant in the old White House part of the hotel is a classy, contemporary space done out in a fashionably muted palette. The menu here treads an uncomplicated modern path, keeping step with the seasons and making good use of regional ingredients. Get things going with the timeless comfort of chicken liver parfait with fig chutney and brioche, followed by pan-roasted cod with crispy ham, crushed potatoes, mange-tout and white wine sauce. For more casual eating, there's Acorns Brasserie and the Parkland Terrace, whose views over the Pentewan Valley make it a fine spot for a pre-dinner cocktail.

Owner Bell Isle Hotels Management Ltd **Seats** 40, Pr/dining room 16 **Times** 12.30-2.30/6.30-9.30 **Prices** Starter £6.50-£10, Main £14-£23, Dessert £6.50-£14.50, Service optional **Wines** 15 bottles over £30, 18 bottles under £30, 9 by glass **Parking** 100 **Notes** Sunday L £15.95-£21.95, Children welcome

ST IVES

Map 2 SW54

Carbis Bay Hotel

◎ International

tel: 01736 795311 **Carbis Bay TR26 2NP**
email: info@carbisbayhotel.co.uk **web:** www.carbisbayhotel.co.uk
dir: A3074, through Lelant. 1m, at Carbis Bay 30yds before lights turn right into Porthrepta Rd to sea & hotel

Contemporary cooking and panoramic views

The family that run the hotel also own the sandy beach that is only 90 seconds away, and the view over pristine sand and the sea is breathtaking. The 19th-century property perched on the hillside has, in the form of the Sands Restaurant, a dining option that means there's no need to head into nearby St Ives in search of something good to eat. David Sharland (who formerly worked with Rick Stein) brings his culinary expertise to the Sands Restaurant with its glorious sea views and contemporary finish (there's also the new Beach Club down by the water's edge). There's plenty of seafood up for grabs with the likes of seared scallops with variations of apple or monkfish tails with crayfish fritter and crab remoulade, but meaty options hit the spot, too, such as a starter of chicken satay with sticky chilli peanuts and caramelised pineapple. Finish with dark chocolate mousse served with a cherry and Disaronno ice cream.

Chef David Sharland, Tom Avery **Owner** Messrs M W & S P Baker **Seats** 150, Pr/dining room 40 **Times** 12-3/6-9.30 **Prices** Service optional **Wines** 45 bottles over £30, 35 bottles under £30, 21 by glass **Parking** 100 **Notes** Sunday L £15.95-£18.95, Vegetarian available, Children welcome

The Garrack

◎ Modern British

tel: 01736 796199 **Burthallan Ln TR26 3AA**
email: garrackhotel@btconnet.com **web:** www.garrack.com
dir: Exit A30 for St Ives, then from B3311 follow brown signs for Tate Gallery, then brown Garrack signs

Enterprising menus and sea views

Both the restaurant and conservatory at this hotel in its own private garden offer uninterrupted sea views over St Ives. The room itself has been given a stylish contemporary look, with high-backed leather seats and lamps on the tables. Pan-fried scallops with crispy-coated black pudding, silky celeriac purée and roast pepper emulsion is a starter of vibrant, well-defined flavours. Follow with beautifully cooked slow-roast belly pork with crisp crackling, bubble-and-squeak and thyme-speckled cider jus, with rhubarb compôte by way of counterpoint. The kitchen reaches out to global cuisines to add variety – tempura crayfish tails, say, with sweet chilli dipping sauce and mango and chilli salsa, then pink duck breast in an orange reduction with wontons, spiced pears and butternut squash roasted with beetroot. Bread is baked in-house, and pastry is consistently good, seen in pear frangipane tart with Amaretto ice cream.

Chef Adam James, Tom Swan, Mark Forster **Owner** Andrew Baragwanath **Seats** 52 **Times** 6.30-9 **Prices** Starter £5.50-£9.50, Main £12.95-£21, Dessert £5.95-£6.50, Service optional **Wines** 5 bottles over £30, 31 bottles under £30, 10 by glass **Parking** 20 **Notes** Sunday L £8.95-£16.50, Vegetarian available, Children welcome

Porthminster Beach Restaurant

◎◎ Modern Mediterranean, Pacific Rim v

tel: 01736 795352 **TR26 2EB**
email: pminster@btconnect.com
dir: On Porthminster Beach, beneath the St Ives Railway Station

Seafood-led fusion cookery on the beach at St Ives

In a region with no shortage of places to eat with an accompanying sea view, the landmark white building surveying Porthminster Beach stands head and shoulders above much of the competition. With its tiled floors and decked terrace, there's a Mediterranean feel to the place, while an Aussie chef makes sure that the spanking-fresh local fish and seafood is subjected to a globetrotting array of fusion influences. Crispy-fried salt-and-spice squid is served with an Asian salad and a zippy citrus miso, while main-course John Dory fillets are pan fried and partnered with tempura prawns, jasmine rice, chilli ponzu and lime. Or there may be Indonesian-style monkfish curry with mussels, prawns, coconut and tamarind. There are good meat dishes too – Thai-style duck curry, perhaps, with aubergine, bok choy, crispy noodles and beansprout salad. To finish, poached pear cuts the richness of chocolate crème brûlée with chocolate cinder biscuit and lavender-scented white chocolate.

Chef Mick Smith, Ryan Venning **Owner** Jim Woolcock, David Fox, Roger & Tim Symons, M Smith **Seats** 60 **Times** 12-3.30/6-9.30, Closed 25 Dec, Mon (winter) **Prices** Starter £4.95-£10.95, Main £11-£28.95, Dessert £4.95-£7.50, Service optional **Wines** 16 bottles over £30, 26 bottles under £30, 9 by glass **Parking** 300yds (railway station) **Notes** Children welcome

The Queens

◎ Modern British

tel: 01736 796468 **2 High St TR26 1RR**
email: info@queenshotelstives.com **web:** www.queenshotelstives.com
dir: A3074 to town centre. With station on right, down hill to High St

Upmarket seasonal gastro-pub fare near the harbour

Behind the flower-planted frontage of this pub is a mixture of wooden tables and chairs on a boarded floor, a bar with a white marble top, sofas and armchairs for lolling and an open fire. It's all quite trendy and modern while retaining a traditional feel, so all comers are happy, as they will be with the appealingly interesting cooking. Ideas are plucked from a variety of sources, so fish goujons with taramasalata is as likely to feature among starters as crispy pork with a quail's egg and parsnip purée. Well-considered main courses are of our day too: herb-roasted hake, flaky and moist, for instance, is served with tempura samphire, green bean and quinoa salad and crushed potatoes, and loin of lamb with shepherd's pie, greens and carrot purée. Don't pass on puddings, among them apple, raisin and cinnamon crumble.

Chef Matt Perry **Owner** Neythan Hayes **Seats** 50 **Times** 12.30-2.30/6.30-9, Closed 25 Dec, L Mon (Nov-Mar) **Prices** Starter £6-£9, Main £9-£16, Dessert £3-£6, Service optional **Wines** 3 bottles over £30, 20 bottles under £30, 12 by glass **Parking** Station car park **Notes** L menu all mains £10 or under, Sunday L £11, Vegetarian available, Children welcome

ST IVES continued

Seagrass Restaurant

◉ Modern Seafood

tel: 01736 793763 **Fish St TR26 1LT**
email: info@seagrass-stives.com
dir: *On Fish Street opposite the Sloop pub*

Splendid seafood straight from the bay

Its location on Fish Street is a serendipitous address for this exciting relative newcomer to the St Ives foodie scene; Seagrass has already made quite a splash with its modern seafood-orientated cooking. Tucked away just off the seafront, a secretive doorway leads up to the rather cool, stylish first-floor restaurant, where the focus is firmly on top-class seasonal Cornish produce. The kitchen cuts no corners here, making everything – breads, stocks, ice cream-from scratch, and maintaining strong supply lines to local fishermen to ensure the shellfish that make up the platters of fruits de mer are plucked fresh from the bay. Make a start with pan-fried Cornish scallops with cucumber, lime and avocado, then move on to salted cod loin, matched enterprisingly with seafood cannelloni, roast tomato velouté, peas, samphire and crispy sea lettuce, and round off with pink grapefruit tart with candied walnuts and crème fraîche.

Chef Stephen Block **Owner** Scott & Julia Blair **Seats** 32 **Times** 6-9.30, Closed 26 Dec, 1-2 Jan, Sun-Mon (Nov-Apr ex BH), L Autumn/winter seasonal opening, D 25 Dec **Prices** Fixed D 3 course £19.95, Starter £5.95-£9.95, Main £11-£23.95, Dessert £5.95-£9.75, Service optional 10% **Wines** 11 bottles over £30, 23 bottles under £30, 11 by glass **Parking** The Sloop car park **Notes** Oyster & shells menu, Vegetarian available, Children welcome

---

ST MAWES   Map 2 SW83

Hotel Tresanton

◉◉◉ – *see opposite*

ST MELLION   Map 3 SX36

St Mellion International Resort

◉◉ Modern International

tel: 01579 351351 **PL12 6SD**
email: stmellion@crown-golf.co.uk web: www.st-mellion.co.uk
dir: *On A388 about 4m N of Saltash*

Accomplished cosmopolitan cooking in large golfing resort

St Mellion looks remarkably like a modern block of flats plonked down beside a lake. It's surrounded by 450 acres with extensive sports and leisure facilities, including two golf courses, tennis courts and no fewer than three pools. The culinary focus is the An Boesti restaurant, a spacious room with a striking colour scheme of black and white. The kitchen steers a course between the traditional and more modern concepts, so beef Wellington is as likely to be on the menu as loin of lamb with rhubarb, garlic confit and potatoes mashed with rosemary, with a fish option of perhaps seared sea bass fillet with potato purée, samphire, courgettes and sultana beurre blanc. Dishes are appreciated for their well-judged combinations and precise timings. Roast chicken wings appear as a starter with Thai mushrooms, limed cucumber and butternut squash alongside ham hock terrine with coriander yogurt, pickled ginger and shallots. A seven-course tasting menu is also on offer, and as well as a selection of Cornish cheeses, a pleasing conclusion may be cappuccino crème brûlée with cinnamon doughnuts.

Chef Mark Brankin **Owner** Crown Golf **Seats** 60, Pr/dining room **Times** 6.30-9.30, Closed Xmas, New Year, Mon-Tue (off season), L all week **Prices** Prices not confirmed, Service optional **Wines** 7 by glass **Parking** 750 **Notes** Sunday L, Vegetarian available, Children 4 yrs+

TALLAND BAY   Map 2 SX25

Talland Bay Hotel

◉◉ Traditional International

tel: 01503 272667 **Porthallow PL13 2JB**
email: info@tallandbayhotel.co.uk web: www.tallandbayhotel.co.uk
dir: *Signed from x-rds on A387 between Looe & Polperro*

Extensive menu and eccentric artefacts

The hotel named after the bay has bundles of boutique personality. Situated just up from the coastal path, with Looe and Polperro within rambling distance, it's full of eccentric artefacts, staggeringly jazzy furniture fabrics, and the commanding maritime views that extend from the dining room's windows. The extensive menu matches the mood, with dishes that offer a tour of traditional international dishes and look good, avoiding the latter-day tendency to skimpiness. A crisped pork schnitzel with shaven fennel and apple purée in grain mustard dressing is a robust enough starter, for all that it could handle more seasoning, which oversight shouldn't be a problem with salt-and-pepper squid in sweet chilli with peanuts. With the sea right before you, fish dishes are a strong suit, as is the case with crisp-grilled sea bass in orange and rosemary butter. A Greek theme brings on versions of kleftiko and moussaka, and desserts go for classic simplicity in the shape of thin-based lemon tart with intense blackcurrant sorbet, or a cheesecake take on Eton Mess.

Chef Nick Hawke **Owner** Ms A V Rees **Seats** 40, Pr/dining room 24 **Times** 12-2.30/6.30-9.30 **Prices** Starter £5.95-£11.25, Main £12.95-£25.95, Dessert £7.95-£9.95 **Wines** 9 by glass **Parking** 23 **Notes** Sunday L £21.50-£25, Vegetarian available, Children welcome

---

TRESCO (ISLES OF SCILLY)   Map 2 SV81

New Inn

◉ Modern, Traditional

tel: 01720 422849 & 422867 **TR24 0QQ**
email: newinn@tresco.co.uk web: www.tresco.co.uk
dir: *Ferry or light plane from Land's End, Newquay or Exeter; 250yds from harbour (private island, contact hotel for details)*

Unfussy cooking in a lively pub

The plane/boat or boat/boat choices only increase the sense of anticipation on the journey to Tresco, and the charms of this family-owned island will win you over. It's unique. The waterside New Inn is right at the heart of this small community, and that's because it's a proper pub combining traditional hospitality with a bit of beachcomber cool. It's a case of ordering at the bar (remember your table number) and then tucking into simple dishes that are based around island produce (everything else has to be brought in by sea, don't forget). Kick off with potted ham hock with Tribute ale chutney and move onto megrim sole, a classy burger, or surf 'n' turf (Bryher lobster with chargrilled steak). There are daily specials, a short but inspiring wine list, and desserts such as malted pannacotta with chocolate sauce and honeycomb. Regular live music keeps the atmosphere buoyant.

Chef Alan Hewitt **Owner** Mr Robert Dorrien-Smith **Seats** 80, Pr/dining room 20 **Times** 12-2/6.30-9 **Prices** Starter £6-£9, Main £14-£30, Dessert £2.10-£8, Service optional **Wines** 15 bottles under £30, 14 by glass **Parking** Car free island **Notes** Sunday L £11-£14, Vegetarian available, Children welcome

TRURO
Map 2 SW84

The Alverton Hotel

◉ Modern British, European

tel: 01872 276633 **Tregolls Rd TR1 1ZQ**
web: www.thealverton.co.uk
dir: *From Truro bypass take A39 to St Austell. Just past church on left*

Grand hotel with upscale brasserie dining using local ingredients

Built in 1830 and designed by the same chap who gave us Truro Cathedral, The Alverton is an impressive construction of granite with manicured gardens and a swish interior – a big hit with wedding planners. Food and drink is a major part of the appeal, whether that's lunch, afternoon tea, cocktails or an evening meal in the upmarket brasserie. There is plenty of period charm and a slick, contemporary finish to the place. The menu takes a modern European path with a good showing of Cornish ingredients. There's an upscale prawn cocktail, while pan-fried scallops with pea purée, crispy angel hair noodles and pancetta dust shows no lack of invention. Wild sea bass gets the pan-fried treatment, too, with crab and saffron risotto, or go for roast loin of venison with wild mushrooms, smoked aubergine purée and a red wine sauce. Finish with lemon tart with thyme crème fraîche or Cornish cheeses.

Times 12-2/5.30-9.30

Hooked Restaurant & Bar

◉ Modern British, Seafood

tel: 01872 274700 **Tabernacle St TR1 2EJ**
email: inthecity@hookedcornwall.com
dir: *100yds off Lemon Quay*

Lively spot for modern seafood cookery

Formerly known as Indaba Fish, this smart Truro venue on a quiet street in the city centre has moved up a gear, with a modern brasserie look of uncovered tables and floor against voguishly exposed brickwork. There's a palpable sense of new energy about the place, but continuation under the same ownership has ensured consistency where it counts. Seafood is the leading suit, with tapas dishes available daytime and evening (tempura squid and chilli jam, scallop and black pudding with apple chutney, dill-cured salmon and cream cheese). The main menu incorporates chorizo-stuffed monkfish in pastry with root mash and tarragon sauce, Goan-style seafood curry with jasmine rice and a crab bhaji, and good old fish and chips with mushy peas and tartare. Desserts are intricately worked creations on the themes of orchard fruits, chocolate and nuts, or 'Cream Tea', which comprises clotted cream brûlée, Earl Grey parfait and rose jelly.

Chef Robert Duncan **Owner** Stephen Shepherd **Seats** 40, Pr/dining room 24 **Times** 12-2.30/5.30-9.30, Closed Sun **Prices** Fixed L 2 course fr £13.95, Fixed D 3 course fr £16.95, Starter £3-£8.50, Main £10.50-£28.95, Dessert £2.50-£7.95, Service optional **Wines** 6 bottles over £30, 24 bottles under £30, 12 by glass **Parking** Car park opposite **Notes** Pre-theatre menu 5.30-6.45 Mon-Sat 2/3 course £13.95/£16.95, Vegetarian available, Children welcome

Hotel Tresanton ❀❀❀

ST MAWES
Map 2 SW83

British, Mediterranean
tel: 01326 270055 **27 Lower Castle Rd TR2 5DR**
email: info@tresanton.com
dir: *On the waterfront in town centre*

Bright modern cooking in super-stylish seafront hotel

The Tresanton has been in the hospitality business since its post-War days as a club for local yachties, but things took a different tack when Olga Polizzi reinvented the place with a dose of cool seaside boutique chic back in 1997. It's still looking good, with the whiff of the sea in the air, jaunty nautical style and Mediterranean-inspired luminosity. The place is set discreetly back above the narrow, seafront lane, and once you walk through the secluded entrance, the cluster of smartly revamped former cottages is revealed at the top of the pathway, as are sweeping views out to sea and towards Falmouth from its sun-trap terrace (an idyllic spot for afternoon tea, with Cornish clotted cream, naturally). The restaurant, with its vanilla-painted tongue-and-groove walls, and blue seats at pristine, white linen-clad tables on mosaic-tiled floors, is a delightful setting for sparkily confident modern British and Med-inspired cooking that gives star billing to locally-landed fish and seafood and prime West Country meats. There are comfort classics such as fish and chips with crushed peas and tartare sauce, otherwise a silky Jerusalem artichoke soup with vegetable crisps might get the ball rolling, or squid with smoked paprika aïoli and lemon. A fishy main could transport you to the Riviera via sun-drenched fish soup full of langoustine tails, mussels, crab and John Dory with the classic accompaniment of croûtons, spicy rouille and gruyère. Meaty ideas may deliver Terras Farm duck with roast potatoes, carrots, celeriac and parsnips. For dessert, plum crumble is partnered with vanilla ice cream, or there's the indulgence of a dark chocolate marquise with nougat ice cream and caramelised hazelnuts.

Chef Paul Wadham **Owner** Olga Polizzi **Seats** 60, Pr/dining room 45 **Times** 12.30-2.30/7-9.30, Closed 2 wks Jan **Prices** Fixed L 2 course £22, Starter £8-£14, Main £16-£26, Dessert £7-£9, Service optional **Wines** 51 bottles over £30, 16 bottles under £30, 8 by glass **Parking** 30 **Notes** Sunday L, Vegetarian available, Children 6 yrs+ D

TRURO *continued*

Tabb's

◎◎ Modern European

tel: 01872 262110 **85 Kenwyn St TR1 3BZ**
email: info@tabbs.co.uk
dir: *Down hill past train station, right at mini rdbt, 200yds on left*

Skilful contemporary cooking a short stroll from the city centre

Tabb's occupies a white corner building that looks for all the world like a private house. Inside is a gently soothing colour scheme of lilac and lemon, with a black-tiled floor, comfortable high-backed chairs and a friendly, relaxing atmosphere helped along by attentive front-of-house staff. The kitchen's a busy place, producing everything in-house, from a complimentary soup (perhaps deeply flavoured mushroom) to petits fours, and it turns out some commendably labour-intensive dishes. Pigeon breast is partnered by a soft-boiled egg, black pasta and sun-dried tomato dressing, for instance, and another starter might be rich smoked haddock chowder flavoured with lemongrass, ginger and chilli oil. Combinations are sensibly thought through: beautifully tender roast pork belly is accompanied by couscous gently spiked by harissa along with black olives, green lentils, battered courgettes and sauté potatoes, and grilled hake fillet by Provençal-style leeks and mushrooms and Jerusalem artichoke velouté. Puddings run to tonka bean pannacotta with strawberry sorbet given a kick of black pepper, and chocoholics can get their fix from hot chocolate fondant with cream cheese ice cream.

Chef Nigel Tabb **Owner** Nigel Tabb **Seats** 30 **Times** 12-2/5.30-9.30, Closed 25 Dec, 1 Jan, 1 wk Jan, Sun-Mon, L Sat **Prices** Fixed L 2 course £19.50, Fixed D 3 course £25, Starter £7.25-£10.50, Main £15.75-£20.50, Dessert £7.50, Service optional **Wines** 17 bottles over £30, 30 bottles under £30, 15 by glass **Parking** 200yds **Notes** Tapas L £12, Pre-theatre menu 5.30-6.45pm bookings only, Vegetarian available, Children welcome

VERYAN
Map 2 SW93

The Quarterdeck at The Nare

◎◎ Traditional British

tel: 01872 500000 **Carne Beach TR2 5PF**
email: stay@narehotel.co.uk **web:** www.quarterdeckrestaurant.co.uk
dir: *From Tregony follow A3078 for approx 1.5m. Left at Veryan sign, through village towards sea & hotel*

Smart beachside setting for stylish modern food

The more casual of the Nare Hotel's dining options, The Quarterdeck, is a shipshape, yachtie-themed setting of polished teak, gingham seats and square rails. The sea view through vast full-length windows is pretty special, and you get it whether you're out on the idyllic terrace breathing in the salty air, or indoors on a typically severe English summer's day. The kitchen produces confident modern dishes bursting with big bold flavours – pan-seared scallops are partnered with braised pork cheek, potato and truffle terrine, parsnip purée and sauced with a cider reduction, followed by a big, rich dish of roasted grouse matched with foie gras, creamy polenta, date purée, poached pear and caramelised shallots. Fish and shellfish from the local waters are a strong point too – perhaps a luxurious duo of pan-fried turbot and lobster medallion with carrot and lime purée, honeycomb and beurre blanc. A finale of apple pie millefeuille highlights strong technical skills, the crisp pastry layered with apple pie mousse and served with spheres that burst in the mouth to reveal luscious vanilla cream.

Chef Richard James **Owner** Toby Ashworth **Seats** 60
Times 12.30-2.30/7-9.30, Closed 25 Dec, D 31 Dec **Prices** Starter £7.50-£10, Main £13-£39, Dessert £7.50-£10, Service optional **Wines** 150 bottles over £30, 50 bottles under £30, 19 by glass **Parking** 60 **Notes** Afternoon tea, Vegetarian available, Children welcome

WATERGATE BAY
Map 2 SW86

Fifteen Cornwall

◎ Italian

tel: 01637 861000 **On The Beach TR8 4AA**
email: restaurant@fifteencornwall.co.uk
dir: *M5 to Exeter & join A30 westbound. Exit Highgate Hill junct, following signs to airport and at T-junct after airport, turn left & follow road to Watergate Bay*

Italian cooking, Jamie-style, on the beach

Jamie Oliver's Cornish outpost has a sea view that presents an ever-changing colour tone of blue and green, while the interior is more than appealing when darkness has descended. The guiding principle of the place remains to give young people a solid grounding in kitchen skills and experience, and it has been a roaring success. It all takes place in a large, contemporary space with floor-to-ceiling windows serving up that seascape, and although it's an easy-going place, it's no surfer hangout. The classy fixtures and fittings and not-so-low prices mean this is a destination eatery, not necessarily somewhere you'd grab a bite after a day on the beach. There's even a tasting menu. The food follows the Italian principles beloved by Mr Oliver, and the kitchen delivers some good stuff. Creamy burrata with Italian black figs and hazelnuts is one way to begin, or go for a plate of pasta such as radiatore (yes, they look like old school radiators) with Pre Pen Farm ragu and pecorino. Main courses can deliver pan-fried turbot with peperonata.

Chef Andy Appleton **Owner** Cornwall Food Foundation **Seats** 120, Pr/dining room 10 **Times** 12-2.30/6.15-9.15 **Prices** Prices not confirmed, Service optional **Wines** 15 by glass **Parking** In front of restaurant & on site P&D **Notes** Tasting menu D 5 course, ALC L only, Vegetarian available, Children 12 yrs+ D

CUMBRIA

ALSTON
Map 18 NY74

Lovelady Shield Country House Hotel

◎◎ Modern British

tel: 01434 381203 **CA9 3LF**
email: enquiries@lovelady.co.uk **web:** www.lovelady.co.uk
dir: *2m E of Alston, signed off A689 at junct with B6294*

Refined modern dining in intimate country house

Hands-on owners greet guests at their white Georgian property in three acres of secluded gardens on the bank of the River Nent. Within are all the trappings of a country-house hotel, including a cocktail bar, a library, a lounge with log fires and a dining room with a restful decor, swagged curtains and wall lights casting a soft glow. Eating here is a treat, with a wide-ranging menu that can set diners dithering. Starters might include saffron-infused crab arancini with tomato compôte and basil pesto or carpaccio with horseradish crème fraîche, hazelnuts, orange and goats' cheese. Main courses too are not without a degree of complexity, bringing out layers of flavours and textures: lamb shank, for instance, is braised in spicy tomato sauce and accompanied by a pick of rump, a bhaji and rice, and roast cod fillet by pancetta sauce, anchovy and sunblush tomato pangritata (ask the staff to elucidate) and lemon and thyme risotto. A skilled pastry cook is behind puddings such as tarte Tatin with ginger custard, and there's a selection of local cheeses for the savoury of tooth.

Chef David Haynes **Owner** Peter & Marie Haynes **Seats** 30
Times 12-2/7-8.30, Closed L Mon-Sat **Prices** Prices not confirmed, Service optional **Wines** 100 bottles over £30, 50 bottles under £30, 11 by glass **Parking** 20 **Notes** D 4 course £49.50, Tasting D 7 course £59.50, Sunday L, Vegetarian available, Children 7 yrs+

AMBLESIDE

Map 18 NY30

The Old Stamp House Restaurant

@@ Modern British **NEW** v

tel: 015394 32775 **Church St LA22 OBU**
email: oldstamphouse@outlook.com
dir: Follow A591 into Ambleside from either direction & enter one way system. Church St accessed from Lake Rd, right after the Royal Oak

Contemporary cooking in Wordsworth's old place

It's not widely known that William Wordsworth was Cumbria's 'Distributor of Stamps' back in the first half of the 19th century, and this is where he plied his trade. Ryan Blackburn has turned this historic building into a restaurant that reflects the great poet's love of the county, with evident passion for regional produce on show. A warren of subterranean spaces, with whitewashed walls and slate floors, simple wooden tables and artworks depicting the local landscape, make for a charmingly rustic setting. The organic and foraged ingredients on show, plus a fondness for contemporary cooking techniques, make this is a thoroughly modern sort of restaurant. Prices are fair given the craft and creativity, with the fixed-price lunch a veritable bargain. Things kick off with excellent bread before first-course smoked Furness wood pigeon with beetroot turned out fashionably in an array of textures, plus celeriac purée and pickled cherries. Next up, Whitehaven turbot, cooked just right, or Alston Moor red grouse with Scottish girolles and truffle jus. Finish with a dazzling Amaretto parfait.

Chef Ryan Blackburn **Owner** Ryan & Craig Blackburn **Seats** 30, Pr/dining room 8 **Times** 12.30-1.30/6-9, Closed Xmas, Sun-Mon **Prices** Fixed L 2 course £18.50, Tasting menu £35-£55, Starter £7.50-£12, Main £18-£25, Dessert £7-£9.50, Service optional **Wines** 25 bottles over £30, 15 bottles under £30, 6 by glass **Parking** On street **Notes** Children welcome

Waterhead Hotel

@ Modern British

tel: 015394 32566 **Lake Rd LA22 0ER**
email: waterhead@englishlakes.co.uk **web:** www.englishlakes.co.uk
dir: A591 into Ambleside, hotel opposite Waterhead Pier

Vibrant brasserie cooking on the edge of Windermere

The poems and paintings of Tennyson and Turner have immortalised the splendid Lakeland landscapes framing Windermere, and the Waterhead has a ringside seat to take it all in, just a short stroll from the bustle of Ambleside. The view from the Bar and Grill restaurant is timeless, but the venue itself sports a thoroughly modern boutique look with funky purple LED lighting to go with its up-to-date brasserie dishes. Start with duck liver parfait with red onion jelly and toasted treacle and walnut bread. Follow with pan-fried tuna steak with fondant potatoes, seasonal veggies and béarnaise sauce, or look to the grill for slabs of Cumbrian beef, or a trendy burger of pulled pork shoulder with honey and bourbon barbecue sauce, sweet potato wedges and crispy fried onions. Coconut and raspberry pannacotta with shaved coconut and raspberry purée is a good way to finish.

Times 7-9.30, Closed Xmas, New Year (only open to residents), L Mon-Sat

APPLEBY-IN-WESTMORLAND

Map 18 NY62

Appleby Manor Country House Hotel

@ Modern British v

tel: 017683 51571 **Roman Rd CA16 6JB**
email: reception@applebymanor.co.uk **web:** www.applebymanor.co.uk
dir: M6 junct 40/A66 towards Brough. Take Appleby turn, then immediately right. Continue for 0.5m

Peaceful rural views and modern country-house cooking

The outlook over Appleby Castle and the Eden Valley towards the fells of the Lake District is a real pastoral treat, and this Victorian sandstone house was put up by someone with an eye for a view. The hotel's newest addition is the 1871 Bistro, named in honour of the year the house went up, and it delivers some breezy feel-good dishes in a charming rustic room with French windows opening on to the garden. The main restaurant takes a more refined approach to proceedings, with tables dressed up in white linen and oak panels on the walls. There's a good amount of regional produce on the menu and the kitchen delivers some smart, upscale food. Double-baked crab soufflé with a seafood velouté is one way to begin, or there might be seared Solway scallops with black pudding and pancetta. Next up, duo of wild mallard (roast breast and slow-cooked leg) is a fine bird, well cooked, and served with vegetable fondants and black cherry sauce. For dessert, try perhaps a lemon tart with Earl Grey sorbet, raspberry syrup and ginger crumble.

Chef Chris Thompson **Owner** The Dunbobbin family **Seats** 100, Pr/dining room 20 **Times** 12-2/7-9, Closed 24-26 Dec **Prices** Starter £7.95-£10.95, Main £14.95-£22.95, Dessert £4.95-£7.95, Service optional **Wines** 10 bottles over £30, 38 bottles under £30, 10 by glass **Parking** 60 **Notes** Sunday L £12.95-£20, Children welcome

BARROW-IN-FURNESS

Map 18 SD26

Abbey House Hotel

@ Traditional British, French **NEW**

tel: 01229 838282 & 0844 826 2091 *(Calls cost 7p per minute plus your phone company's access charge)* **Abbey Rd LA13 0PA**
email: enquiries@abbeyhousehotel.com **web:** www.abbeyhousehotel.com
dir: From A590 follow signs for Furness General Hospital & Furness Abbey. Hotel approx 100yds on left

Stylish spot for contemporary hotel dining

The grand red-brick house stands in 14 acres of countryside and gardens not too far from all the Lakeland action, and it's kitted out for swanky weddings and conferences. It's also home to the rather charming and gently contemporary Oscar's restaurant. The house was originally built for a bigwig at Vickers shipyard and much of the period character remains, not least in the restaurant, where the grandeur of the space is matched by tasteful contemporary colour tones and modern designer fittings. There's nothing stuffy about the place, with a relaxed (but professional) approach all round. The kitchen turns out modern dishes based on a good amount of regional produce. Gravad lax is a simple enough starter, but here it is perked up with an oyster beignet, pickled beetroot and basil crème fraîche, while main-course cannon of lamb is tender and full of flavour. Finish with a decent version of tarte Tatin with home-made fig ice cream and cinnamon syrup. There's a stylish cocktail bar, too.

Chef James Lowery **Owner** Kilroe **Seats** 80, Pr/dining room 24 **Times** 10-10, All-day dining **Prices** Starter £3.50-£8.45, Main £10.50-£21.95, Dessert £6-£7.95, Service optional **Wines** 8 bottles over £30, 16 bottles under £30, 6 by glass **Parking** 200 **Notes** Sunday L £10.95-£26.35, Vegetarian available, Children welcome

BARROW-IN-FURNESS *continued*

Clarence House Country Hotel & Restaurant

◉◉ British, International

tel: 01229 462508 **Skelgate, Dalton-in-Furness LA15 8BQ**
email: clarencehsehotel@aol.com **web:** www.clarencehouse-hotel.co.uk
dir: *A590 through Ulverston & Lindal, 2nd exit at rdbt & 1st exit at next. Follow signs to Dalton, hotel at top of hill on right*

Modern British versatility in an orangery setting

The white-fronted hotel in Dalton-in-Furness, not far from Barrow, is perfectly poised between sandy beaches and the lush green acres of Lakeland. A dining room designed like an orangery, with windows on three sides, affords covetable views over the St Thomas Valley, and terrace tables make the best of the sun. The menus are defined by that resourcefully versatile reach that has come to be the hallmark of the modern British idiom, offering Chinese-style slow-roasted duck in plum sauce with cashews and pomegranate to start, or a tian of Cornish crab set in avocado, tomato and basil. For main, there may be grilled salmon garnished with crisp pancetta and a pea and mint risotto, or roast chump of Cumbrian lamb with provençale accompaniments of aubergine, confit peppers and tapenade. A grill section offers various steaks and chops with a choice of sauces. Friday night is carvery night.

Times 12-2/7-9, Closed D Sun

▌**BASSENTHWAITE**　　　　　　　　　　　　**Map 18 NY23**

Armathwaite Hall Country House & Spa

◉◉ British, French **V**

tel: 017687 76551 **CA12 4RE**
email: reservations@armathwaite-hall.com **web:** www. armathwaite-hall.com
dir: *From M6 junct 40/A66 to Keswick then A591 towards Carlisle. Continue for 7m and turn left at Castle Inn*

Fine dining with lake views

Standing in 400 acres of grounds bordering Bassenthwaite Lake, Armathwaite boasts all of the hoped-for open fires, rich fabrics and acres of oak panelling, and a facelift has brought all the mod cons expected in a 21st-century hotel, including a spa. The Lake View Restaurant is a lovely high-ceilinged room with oak panelling, rich golds and reds and comfortable chairs at formally set tables. Attentive staff are sprucely turned out – as you'd expect of a restaurant with a smart dress code. The kitchen steers a course to keep traditionalists and modernists happy, sending out starters like slow-braised belly of Cumberland pork with buttered spinach and black pudding. Main course might be local game – soy-infused loin of Cartmel venison, say, with marinated red cabbage, sweet potato, pak choi and black pepper jus. For dessert, try perhaps the apple and cinnamon spring roll with vanilla crumble and ice cream and Granny Smith apple purée.

Chef Kevin Dowling **Owner** The Graves family **Seats** 80, Pr/dining room
Times 12.30-1.45/7.30-9 **Prices** Prices not confirmed, Service optional **Wines** 6 by glass **Parking** 100 **Notes** Fixed D 5 course £46.95, Sunday L, Children welcome

The Pheasant

◉ Modern British

tel: 017687 76234 **CA13 9YE**
email: info@the-pheasant.co.uk **web:** www.the-pheasant.co.uk
dir: *M6 junct 40, take A66 (Keswick and North Lakes). Continue past Keswick and head for Cockermouth. Signed from A66*

Interesting contemporary cooking led by Cumbrian ingredients

Dating from the 17th century, this long, low-slung building has a charming, atmospheric bar and a beamed bistro as well as the more formal (think stiff white napery) Fell Restaurant. The kitchen relies on local sources for its ingredients and, while its roots may lie in the great classical techniques and repertoire, it clearly keeps its finger on the culinary pulse to come up with thoroughly contemporary ideas. It's a busy place too, baking bread, making canapés, pickling grapes and picking sorrel, the last two going into a starter of spiced goats' cheese along with shallots, candied walnuts and celery. If combinations sound overwrought, dishes seem to work, such as perfectly cooked, tender duck breast with chorizo, mushrooms, braised romaine lettuce, butternut squash, pearly barley and bacon crisp and truffled hollandaise. Fish might be fillet of cod with shellfish risotto, red pepper velouté and samphire. Puddings are a strength: consider rich dark chocolate terrine cut by griottine cherries and sour cherry ice cream.

Times 12-2.30/7-9, Closed 25 Dec, Mon, L Tue-Sat, D Sun

Ravenstone Lodge

◉ British

tel: 01768 776629 **CA12 4QG**
email: enquiries@ravenstonelodge.co.uk **web:** www.ravenstonelodge.co.uk
dir: *5m N of Keswick on A591*

Unfussy but imaginative country-house cooking

A country-house hotel on a human scale, the buildings that make up Ravenstone used to be the mews and coach house for the big house across the way. They're not playing second fiddle, though, for this place has plenty going on, including a bar and bistro in the former stables. The main restaurant – the Coach House – is smartly turned out and the team in the kitchen takes good, regional ingredients and doesn't muck about with them too much. There's some good cooking on show, though, and no shortage of good ideas. A starter of mackerel escabèche comes with celeriac remoulade and pickled Chantenay carrots and desserts extend to warm apple tarte Tatin with vanilla ice cream and caramel sauce. In between might come main courses that can be as comforting as roast breast of chicken with celeriac dauphinoise, Savoy cabbage with bacon and wild mushroom jus, or as refined as grilled fillet of brill with basil gnocchi and Cumbrian crab.

Times 6.30-9

Borrowdale Gates Hotel

Modern British V

tel: 017687 77204 & 0845 833 2524 *(The only charge for this call will be your phone company's access charge)* **CA12 5UQ**
email: hotel@borrowdale-gates.com web: www.borrowdale-gates.com
dir: *B5289 from Keswick, after 4m turn right over bridge to Grange. Hotel 400yds on right*

Skilful modern country-house dining with Lakeland views

The fells and rugged countryside of the Borrowdale Valley running down to Derwent Water form a diverting backdrop to dining in this classic Lakeland country house. Pack a copy of one of Wainwright's famous guides and a yomp up Scafell Pike or Catbells should set you up for dinner. The kitchen has ramped up its efforts recently, turning out a confident take on modern British dishes cooked with skill and an eye to local and seasonal materials. Start with a surf and turf combo of crispy pork belly, tiger prawn and chorizo bonbon pointed up with ginger, lemongrass and chilli dressing. Proceed to honey-roasted breast of wild mallard glazed with poached plums, served with a crispy vegetable wonton, celeriac purée, leeks and bacon. End with a dessert that matches the comfort of chocolate fondant with pistachio ice cream.

Chef Christopher Standhaven **Owner** Colin Harrison **Seats** 50
Times 12-3/6.30-8.45, Closed Jan **Prices** Fixed D 3 course fr £41, Service optional **Wines** 19 bottles over £30, 38 bottles under £30, 8 by glass **Parking** 35
Notes Sunday L fr £21.50, Children welcome

Hazel Bank Country House

British **NEW**

tel: 017687 77248 **Rosthwaite CA12 5XB**
email: info@hazelbankhotel.co.uk web: www.hazelbankhotel.co.uk
dir: *A66 Keswick, follow B5289 signed Borrowdale, turn left before Rosthwaite over humpback bridge*

Daily-changing set menu in gorgeous Lakeland valley

If you are aiming to get away from it all, it may be comforting to know that it's very hard to get a mobile signal in the village of Rosthwaite in the gorgeous Borrowdale Valley, where this classic stone-built Lakeland house sits amid four acres. A beckside walk is one attraction, and a full-dress linened dining room looks out over grounds where red squirrels are known to scamper. The drill is a daily-changing four-course menu, with a cheeseboard as optional extra. Spring might bring on a short-pastried warm goats' cheese tart with caramelised red onion marmalade to begin, followed by a tranche of seared monkfish in lemon oil with minted peas. Then comes Lakeland beef for main, served with charlottes roasted in the skins, and parsnip purée topped with smoked black pudding crumble, in thyme-scented red wine jus. Things come to rest with a featherlight chocolate brownie, Belgian truffle and white chocolate ice cream.

Chef David Jackson **Owner** Garry & Donna Macrae **Seats** 20 **Times** 7-8, Closed Dec-Jan, L all week **Prices** Prices not confirmed, Service optional **Wines** 25 bottles over £30, 55 bottles under £30, 6 by glass **Parking** 12 **Notes** Vegetarian available, Children 14 yrs+

Leathes Head Hotel

British

tel: 017687 77247 **CA12 5UY**
email: reservations@leatheshead.co.uk web: www.leatheshead.co.uk
dir: *3.75m S of Keswick on B5289, set back on the left*

Modern country-house cooking and glorious views

Tucked away in the heart of the beautiful Borrowdale Valley, the Leathes Head was built in Edwardian times as a gentleman's residence, and is full of original character. It's a lovely spot with three acres of gardens plus rolling fells and meandering rivers all around. A new head chef has reinvigorated the kitchen's output, showing real passion for locally-grown and reared produce in daily-changing menus of smartly turned out contemporary ideas that let the ingredients shine. Dishes exhibit three-dimensional flavours and juxtapositions that make sense. Ham hock terrine is pointed up with mustard mayonnaise, sherry vinegar jelly and a crispy deep-fried quail's egg, while local Herdwick hogget is showcased in a main course involving cutlets, roasted shoulder and kidney with white bean purée, fondant potato and a glossy rosemary jus. Fish-wise, there might be sea trout with smoked crushed potatoes, purple sprouting broccoli and wild garlic mayonnaise. For dessert, the citrussy hit of lemon parfait is counterpointed with the intensity of praline and caramelised popcorn.

Chef Daniel Hopkins **Seats** 24 **Times** 6.30-8.30, Closed mid Nov-mid Feb **Prices** Fixed D 2 course fr £28.95, Service optional **Wines** 23 bottles over £30, 31 bottles under £30, 10 by glass **Parking** 15 **Notes** Fixed D 4 course £39.50, Vegetarian available, Children 9 yrs+

Lodore Falls Hotel

Modern British V

tel: 017687 77285 & 0800 840 1246 **CA12 5UX**
email: lodorefalls@lakedistricthotels.net web: www.lakedistricthotels.net/lodorefalls
dir: *M6 junct 40, A66 to Keswick, B5289 to Borrowdale. Hotel on left*

Plush lakeside dining using local ingredients

The situation by Derwentwater and the eponymous falls provides a suitably Lakeland vista, with good views over the water to distant hills from the dining room. Its outside tables are a big hit in the warmer months. The Lake View Restaurant has plush, traditional furnishings and pristine white tablecloths, and is the setting for some good modern dishes. Opening the batting could be a brilliantly crisp-skinned fillet of gilt-head bream on soba noodles, seasoned with wasabi and yuzu. A sorbet, perhaps pink champagne, precedes the main course, which may be breast of locally-shot pheasant with wilted Savoy cabbage, a loose carrot and swede purée and thyme-roasted potatoes, in a rich jus boosted with port, or sea bass with crushed potato and crab in brandied lobster cream sauce. A fine dark chocolate fondant with crushed pistachios and whisky marmalade ice cream is well worth the wait.

Chef Colin Gannon **Owner** Lake District Hotels **Seats** 120, Pr/dining room 24 **Times** 12-2/6.30-9.15 **Prices** Fixed L 2 course £14.95, Fixed D 3 course £35 **Wines** 16 bottles over £30, 32 bottles under £30, 12 by glass **Parking** 90 **Notes** Pudding Club 2nd Thu of month D 4 course & dessert £42.50, Sunday L £14.95-£19.95, Children welcome

BRAITHWAITE

Map 18 NY22

The Cottage in the Wood

◉◉ Modern British V

tel: 017687 78409 **Whinlatter Pass CA12 5TW**
email: relax@thecottageinthewood.co.uk web: www.thecottageinthewood.co.uk
dir: *M6 junct 40, A66 signed Keswick. 1m after Keswick take B5292 signed Braithwaite, hotel in 2m*

Sound food in sight of the fells

The Lakeland writer A W Wainwright reckoned that the northwestern fells were the most delectable in the whole district, and there they are, right before your eyes in the view from this 17th-century coaching inn. Despite its faintly fairy tale name, it's a distinctively contemporary place, with spacious, airy rooms and a restaurant called Mountain View for its majestic prospect. The kitchen maintains an established commitment to sound regional produce in modern British dishes full of sharply honed flavours, as seen in a starter where apricot and vanilla purée and pistachio biscotti are the accompaniments to a virtuoso terrine of Cartmel Valley duck, wrought from chunks of liver, smoked breast and confit leg wrapped in Cumbrian air-dried ham. Next up, the focus is on gold-standard Skrei cod from the east coast, but its accoutrements of chorizo, fondant potato, cauliflower textures and romesco sauce bring a lively taste of the Mediterranean. That sun-drenched aromatic twist surfaces again in a dessert of deconstructed lemon meringue comprising Sicilian lemon curd, sorbet and marshmallows with mini meringues.

Chef Christopher Archer **Owner** Liam & Kath Berney **Seats** 40
Times 12.30-2/6-9, Closed Jan, Sun-Mon **Prices** Fixed L 2 course fr £22, Tasting menu £55-£65, Service optional **Wines** 40 bottles over £30, 12 bottles under £30, 8 by glass **Parking** 16 **Notes** Fixed D 5 course £55 (groups of 6+), Children 10 yrs+ D

CARLISLE

Map 18 NY35

Crown Hotel

◉ Modern British

tel: 01228 561888 **Station Rd, Wetheral CA4 8ES**
email: info@crownhotelwetheral.co.uk web: www.crownhotelwetheral.co.uk
dir: *M6 junct 42, B6263 to Wetheral, right at village shop, car park at rear of hotel*

Modern British cooking in a village hotel

This white Georgian hotel, updated to meet 21st-century requirements, is in a picturesque village a few miles out of Carlisle close to Hadrian's Wall. The Conservatory Restaurant, overlooking the landscaped gardens, has a striking raftered ceiling, red quarry tiles on the floor and round-backed padded dining chairs at polished wooden tables. The kitchen favours a largely modern British approach and gives dishes their own distinctive identity. Cauliflower, both puréed and pickled, adds extra dimensions to pan-fried scallops with Parma ham, and venison carpaccio is interestingly teamed with Blue Whinnow cheese, pickled walnuts and mushroom pâté. Spirited ways with main courses have seen perfectly

cooked curried monkfish with chilli and caper dressing and spiced aubergine, and a mead reduction for Goosnargh duck breast with spicy red cabbage, baby turnips and roast potatoes. For pudding, look no further than glazed lemon tart with lemon ice cream, or pear tarte Tatin with mulled fruit and vanilla cream.

Crown Hotel

Chef Paul Taylor **Owner** David Byers **Seats** 80, Pr/dining room 120
Times 12-2.30/7-9.30, Closed L Sat **Prices** Prices not confirmed, Service optional **Wines** 8 bottles over £30, 36 bottles under £30, 14 by glass **Parking** 70
Notes Sunday L, Vegetarian available, Children welcome

CARTMEL

Map 18 SD37

Aynsome Manor Hotel

◉ Modern, Traditional British

tel: 015395 36653 **LA11 6HH**
email: aynsomemanor@btconnect.com web: www.aynsomemanorhotel.co.uk
dir: *M6 junct 36, A590 signed Barrow-in-Furness towards Cartmel. Left at end of road, hotel before village*

Traditional country-house dining with a daily-changing menu

The old manor is now a charming small country-house hotel in the untouched Vale of Cartmel with views south to the Norman priory, meadows and woods. Log fires burn in the lounge, while the restaurant features panelling, a moulded ceiling, oak furnishings and an intimate atmosphere. The cooking shows accurate timings, judiciously considered combinations and clear flavours, seen in starters of guinea fowl and leek terrine wrapped in Cumbrian ham served with apricot and sultana chutney, and mussels steamed with garlic, parsley, cream and white wine. Main courses on the short, daily-changing menus might include rich, gamey venison loin in damson and gin jus plated with a sage and onion-flavoured polenta cake. Seasonal vegetables are served separately, and classic lemon tart with whipped cream and fruit compôte is a memorable finish.

Chef Gordon Topp **Owner** Christopher & Andrea Varley **Seats** 28
Times 7-8.30, Closed 25-26 Dec, 2-28 Jan, L Mon-Sat, D Sun (ex residents)
Prices Fixed L 3 course £18.95-£19.50, Fixed D 3 course fr £29.50, Service optional **Wines** 20 bottles over £30, 45 bottles under £30, 6 by glass **Parking** 20
Notes Sunday L, Vegetarian available, Children 5 yrs+

L'Enclume

◉◉◉◉◉ – see opposite

Rogan & Company Restaurant

◉◉◉ – see page 118

L'Enclume ✿✿✿✿

CARTMEL   Map 18 SD37

Modern British **V** 🍷 NOTABLE WINE LIST

tel: 015395 36362 **Cavendish St LA11 6PZ**
email: info@lenclume.co.uk **web:** www.lenclume.co.uk
dir: *Follow signs for A590 W, turn left for Cartmel before Newby Bridge*

A world-class dining experience in a little Cumbrian village

Perfectly in tune with the Lake District village surroundings, L'Enclume looks at first sight like the solid 700-year-old blacksmith's forge it once was (the name is French for 'anvil') – but in the hands of Simon Rogan it has morphed into a world-class culinary destination. On the inside, things aren't much different: the sparse interior is all whitewashed walls with minimal adornment, polished stone floors and unclothed tables. If you want to put up for the night, the operation comprises classy bedrooms in three buildings around the village. Most kitchens these days claim to supply their kitchens from the local larder, but few achieve the level of control over the ingredients' provenance that is achieved here: much of what's on your plate will have been picked a short while ago at Rogan's six-acre organic farm nearby, or foraged from the local countryside. What he doesn't produce himself is sourced from trusted local suppliers – now that's what you call 'cuisine de terroir'! The service team are on hand to help with the multi-course (we're talking double figures here) menus, dealing with the inevitable queries on their more idiosyncratic contents, giving advice with charm and professionalism. With inventive cooking of this ilk, the kitchen needs its gadgets, but everything is done here for a reason rather than mere effect, and respect for the produce remains amid the high-tech treatments. Humour and technical brilliance are there from the off in the canapés – 'oyster pebbles' are soft meringues filled with oyster cream; smoked eel with ham fat arrives surrounded by hay under a smoke-filled cloche, before the meal proper starts with white turnip with 'Marans hen's egg' and nasturtium leaves, a dish of explosive flavours. The colours on the plate make a startling impact, quite beautiful at times, and the flavour combinations are uniformly clever, as in the onion ash, lovage and wood sorrel that accompany minuscule potatoes. Elsewhere, lightly-smoked venison comes with crystallised balls of charcoal oil, mustard mayonnaise and strands of fennel, while turbot is grilled over spruce and matched with salsify, a single plump mussel, shellfish oil and sea vegetables. Sweet courses might deliver green strawberries with pea-sized globes of apple marigold custard and beech leaves, or meadowsweet with cherries, cider and flowers and iced tea. Matching wine to flavours such as this is a challenge that the sommelier team approach with passion, championing lesser-seen grape varieties, biodynamic wines, and always keen to support English producers. If you can't make it to Cumbria, by the way, then the Rogan empire has spread its wings to the The Midland Hotel in Manchester, where there's a brace of dining options – The French and Mr Cooper's House and Garden – and has found its latest home in Fera within that grandest of old dames, Claridge's.

Chef Simon Rogan, Mark Birchall, Tom Barnes **Owner** Simon Rogan, Penny Tapsell **Seats** 50, Pr/dining room 10 **Times** 12-1.30/6.30-9.30, Closed L Mon-Tue **Prices** Prices not confirmed, Service optional **Wines** 220 bottles over £30, 12 by glass **Parking** 7, On street **Notes** Fixed L 6 course £45, Fixed D 18-20 course £120, Children 10 yrs+ D

CROSTHWAITE

Map 18 SD49

The Punchbowl Inn at Crosthwaite

⊚⊚ Modern British

tel: 015395 68237 **Lyth Valley LA8 8HR**
email: info@the-punchbowl.co.uk **web:** www.the-punchbowl.co.uk
dir: A590 then A5074 signed Bowness/Crosthwaite. Inn within 3m on right

Fashion-conscious Cumbrian dishes in the damson-rich Lyth Valley

A small country house in the verdant Lyth Valley, where the damsons are nonpareil, The Punchbowl stands next to the parish church of St Mary. It's one of Lakeland's homelier places, run with great civility but without any overly starched formality. A slate-topped bar and modern rustic furniture give the place a fresh look, and the dining room is decorated with interesting pictures and furnished with stylish high-backed chairs. A substantial menu of modern Cumbrian food shows plenty of fashion-conscious technique, as when venison tartare starts proceedings dressed in juniper, hazelnuts, blue cheese, capers and a smoked egg yolk. Mains show off some fine principals, perhaps roast loin and leg croquette of rabbit, with crayfish mousse, apricots and chard, or brill with butternut squash, potato rösti, and smoked salmon and caper butter. Those fabulous damsons might turn up in a posset for pudding, accompanied by lemon jelly and pink peppercorn meringue, or whizzed up as a garnish for the adventurous Anglo-French cheese selection, which also comes with pear chutney and candied walnuts.

Chef Scott Fairweather **Owner** Richard Rose **Seats** 50, Pr/dining room 16 **Times** 12-9, All-day dining **Prices** Starter £4.95-£9.95, Main £14.50-£19.95, Dessert £6.95-£9.95, Service optional **Wines** 74 bottles over £30, 33 bottles under £30, 14 by glass **Parking** 40 **Notes** Sunday L £14.95, Vegetarian available, Children welcome

ELTERWATER

Map 18 NY30

Langdale Hotel & Spa

⊚⊚ Modern British

tel: 015394 37302 & 38080 **The Langdale Estate LA22 9JD**
email: purdeys@langdale.co.uk **web:** www.langdale.co.uk
dir: M6 junct 36, A591 or M6 junct 40, A66, B5322, A591

Modern Lakeland food by a tumbling waterfall

An environmentally sensitive hotel to the south of Lake Windermere, the Langdale blends into its beckside surroundings with stone construction, neutral interior tones of brown and grey, and a view of a tumbling waterfall through a picture window in the bar. The gastronomic action is in Purdey's dining room, and is a gently modernised version of Lakeland cooking that aims for subtle potency rather than garish innovation. Oak-smoked salmon is served warm and accompanied by the de

Rogan & Company Restaurant ❀❀❀

CARTMEL

Map 18 SD37

Modern British
tel: 015395 35917 **The Square LA11 6QD**
email: reservations@roganandcompany.co.uk
dir: From M6 junct 36 follow signs for A590. Turn off at sign for Cartmel village

Tirelessly inventive pastoral cooking the Rogan way

After a dozen years in Cartmel Simon Rogan is heralded as one of the UK's finest chefs with restaurants in London and Manchester to spread the word. Rogan & Company may be the second-string venue in Cartmel, but it could hold its own anywhere in the country. The two-storey Lakeland house of roughcast stone and undoubted charm is surrounded by a rolling landscape divided by dry-stone walls, with Cartmel Priory an impressive backdrop. Its riverside location is a winner too. The à la carte menu reflects Rogan's approach – although he is not at the stoves of course – and supremely good produce lies at the heart of everything (much of it from his farm down the valley). It is dynamic, contemporary stuff, but such that it allows the ingredients to win the day. Raw beef with pickled kohlrabi is a typical first course and a case of simplicity done with style, with sweet tomato jam and toast by way of accompaniments, or go for salmon marinated in dill and served on buckwheat blinis and dressed with sea herbs and beetroot sabayon. Among main courses, a stellar veggie option might be roast sweetheart cabbage with teriyaki sauce, Wiltshire truffle and hot wasabi mayonnaise, while omnivores can go for haunch of red deer with smoked potatoes, hay-baked celeriac and creamed kale. Desserts are no less enticing judging by the caramel tart which arrives with mascarpone ice cream and coffee crumb, or the fried apple pie with butterscotch and Cornish clotted cream. British and continental cheeses are kept in tip-top condition and you might want to take them up on the suggestion of an accompanying glass of Taylor's Vintage Port (1985).

Chef Simon Rogan, Ashley Bennett **Owner** Simon Rogan, Penny Tapsell **Seats** 40, Pr/dining room 10 **Times** 12-2.30/6.30-9, Closed Sun, L Mon **Prices** Starter £6-£9, Main £12.50-£22.50, Dessert £7 **Wines** 30 bottles over £30, 18 bottles under £30, 12 by glass **Parking** On street **Notes** Vegetarian available, Children welcome

rigueur beetroot and a horseradished potato mousse, or there may be pigeon breast with pine kernels and textures of onion. The two-tier technique of poaching and roasting works wonders with chicken, traditionally teamed with wild mushrooms and truffled gnocchi in tarragon jus, while fish could be fine seared stone bass with samphire and asparagus, as well as a crisply battered oyster. A custard slice with pear sorbet, hazelnut crumble and honeycomb has a distant ring of afternoon tea to it, as does the spin on Jaffa Cakes, which comes with orange crème brûlée and a chocolate tuile.

Times 6.30-9.30, Closed L ex groups (booking essential)

GLENRIDDING   Map 18 NY31

The Inn on the Lake

◉◉ Modern European

tel: 017684 82444 **Lake Ullswater CA11 0PE**
email: innonthelake@lakedistricthotels.net **web:** www.lakedistricthotels.net
dir: M6 junct 40, A66 Keswick, A592 Windermere

Modern cooking on the shore of Ullswater

The hotel is a prime piece of Lakeland real estate within 15 acres of grounds surrounding Ullswater. The lake makes pretty much the perfect backdrop and there are panoramic views from just about every public space. There are lots of refuelling options, from lunch in the Orangery, afternoon tea, and the pub-style Ramblers Bar in the grounds, but the main culinary action takes place in the Lake View Restaurant. The elegant dining room is decorated with natural shades of lilac and fawn, with decorative touches and pictures of the local landscape. The kitchen makes good use of regional ingredients to produce dishes of modernity and creativity. First course seared king scallops, for example (cooked just right) arrive in the company of textures of cauliflower and black pudding fritter, dressed with a pancetta foam, and there's an Asian spin to a main course of cured salmon with crispy salt and pepper squid and Thai broth. Desserts run to the likes of dark chocolate delice or a tarte Tatin made with Cox's apples.

Times 12-2/7-9

GRANGE-OVER-SANDS   Map 18 SD47

Clare House

◉ Modern British

tel: 015395 33026 **Park Rd LA11 7HQ**
email: info@clarehousehotel.co.uk **web:** www.clarehousehotel.co.uk
dir: Off A590 onto B5277, through Lindale into Grange, keep left, hotel 0.5m on left past Crown Hill & St Paul's Church

Country-house cookery overlooking the bay

The Read family has been running Clare House since the late 1960s, and their care and attention is evident at every turn. The beautiful, immaculately tended gardens have a feeling of seclusion from the swirling tourist traffic of the town, and the traditional decor complements the fine views over the bay. Well-spaced tables dressed in crisp linen, attended by smartly turned-out staff, are the order of the day, and while the cooking cleaves to an essentially traditional style, the presentation is as contemporary as can be. That accounts for chicken liver parfait with scrumpy jelly arriving in a Kilner jar. Butter-roasted hake is given resonance with Puy lentils, bacon and herbs, wild mushrooms and a meaty beer sauce, while roast rib-eye comes with balsamic-roasted potatoes and Madeira sauce. To finish there could be a well-executed pear frangipane tart with vanilla ice cream.

Chef Andrew Read, Mark Johnston **Owner** Mr & Mrs D S Read **Seats** 36
Times 12-2.30/6.30-7.30, Closed mid Dec-end Mar **Prices** Service optional **Wines** 1 bottle over £30, 26 bottles under £30, 3 by glass **Parking** 16 **Notes** Fixed D 5 course £38, Light L menu Mon-Sat, Sunday L £19-£24, Vegetarian available, Children welcome

---

GRASMERE   Map 18 NY30

The Dining Room

◉◉ Modern British ᵥ

tel: 015394 35217 **Oak Bank Hotel, Broadgate LA22 9TA**
email: info@lakedistricthotel.co.uk **web:** www.lakedistricthotel.co.uk
dir: N'bound: M6 junct 36 onto A591 to Windermere, Ambleside, then Grasmere. S'bound: M6 junct 40 onto A66 to Keswick, A591 to Grasmere

Stylish modern cooking in Lakeland country house

The old Victorian Oak Bank Hotel has lots of Lakeland charm, with pretty gardens that run down to the River Rothay and decor that is smart and comfortable. The Dining Room restaurant – equally comfortable and refined, with a conservatory extension – is perhaps surprisingly, then, among all this civilised conformity, the setting for some ambitious and creative food. Chef Darren Comish clearly has an eye for presentation and enticing combinations, never outlandish, but most certainly contemporary in their execution. A first course, for example, might consist of home-cured gravadlax with a perky lemongrass pannacotta, a caesar cream wrapped in cucumber and roasted melon – a dish with a good deal going on, a good deal of which is brilliant. Next up, a tasting plate of rare breed pork has among its treasures a succulent cheek and mini black pudding boudin, or go for a fishy option in the form of pan-roasted salt cod with spiced couscous, curry nut crumble and curry velouté. And for dessert, how about a chocolate-fest, including chocolate tart and pistachio cake?

Chef Darren Comish **Owner** Glynis & Simon Wood **Seats** 30
Times 12.30-1.30/6.30-8.30, Closed 20-26 Dec, 2-21 Jan, 7-18 Aug, 1-5 May
Prices Fixed L 2 course £22.95-£24.70, Fixed D 3 course £39.50-£42, Tasting menu £55-£60, Service optional **Wines** 14 bottles over £30, 47 bottles under £30, 7 by glass **Parking** 14 **Notes** Fixed D menu 5 course £39.50-£47.45, Sunday L £22.95-£24.70, Children 10 yrs+

Rothay Garden Hotel

◉◉ Modern British ᵥ

tel: 01539 435334 **Broadgate LA22 9RJ**
email: stay@rothaygarden.com **web:** www.rothaygarden.com
dir: From N: M6 junct 40, A66 to Keswick, then S on A591 to Grasmere. From S: M6 junct 36 take A591 through Windermere/Ambleside to Grasmere. At N end of village adjacent to park

Well-balanced modern dishes in a contemporary conservatory

On the edge of Grasmere, this thoroughly (and expensively) refurbished Victorian hotel sits in a couple of acres of riverside gardens, with the panoramic sweep of the Lakeland fells as background. The country house chintz was chucked long ago, and dining goes on in a thoroughly modern conservatory-style room with restful views of the gardens and spa centre – a classy and bright setting that's just right for gently updated country house cooking offering comfort, interest and satisfaction. A starter of seared scallops and barbecued pork belly is enhanced with sweet potato purée and piquant spiced apple, or there could be grilled sea bass with shellfish risotto, lemongrass foam and leek julienne. Next up, the focus is on Lakeland lamb, served as roast rump and shepherd's pie with carrot purée, parsnip and potato rösti, green beans and rosemary jus, or roast venison with dauphinoise potato, Drambuie jus, braised red cabbage and roast pear might catch the eye. The finishing flourish is a well-risen raspberry soufflé with crème anglaise.

Chef Andrew Burton, A Kneeshaw **Owner** Chris Carss **Seats** 60 **Times** 12-1.30/7-9 **Prices** Fixed L 3 course £21.50, Fixed D 3 course £39.50, Service optional **Wines** 12 by glass **Parking** 38 **Notes** Sunday L fr £21.50

The Golden Fleece

◉ Modern British **NEW**

tel: 01228 573686 **Rule Holme CA6 4NF**
email: info@thegoldenfleececumbria.co.uk **web:** www.thegoldenfleececumbria.co.uk
dir: M6 junct 44 onto A689 signed Brampton. 1m past airport located on left

Upgraded old inn with polished gastro-pub cooking

Refurbishment has transformed this white two-storey inn into the eye-catching combination of bar and restaurant with rooms it is today. Log fires and beams in low ceilings remain in place, and the three dining areas have more of a feeling of an inn than a formal restaurant, although tables are smartly set and kindly staff wear their own livery. The menu neatly encapsulates both pub elements and more refined offerings. Ale-battered cod and chips, lamb hotpot and chargrilled steaks are all possibilities, alongside tender pink slices of loin of venison on rösti with a copper pot of game casserole, red wine jus and seasonal vegetables, or roast monkfish tail in Thai-style broth with jasmine rice. Topping and tailing these are light-textured cheese soufflé with a refreshing herb salad, and burnt Cambridge cream (a precursor of crème brûlée) with berry compôte and amaretti biscuit.

Chef Robert Cowan **Owner** Robert Cowan **Seats** 70, Pr/dining room 30 **Times** 12-9, All-day dining, Closed 1-8 Jan **Prices** Tasting menu £49, Starter £5.50-£11, Main £12-£21, Dessert £5.50-£6, Service optional **Wines** 2 bottles over £30, 33 bottles under £30, 12 by glass **Parking** 100 **Notes** Sunday L £11.50-£12.50, Vegetarian available, Children welcome

BEST WESTERN PLUS Castle Green Hotel in Kendal

◉◉ Modern British

tel: 01539 734000 **Castle Green Ln LA9 6RG**
email: reception@castlegreen.co.uk **web:** www.castlegreen.co.uk
dir: M6 junct 37, A684 towards Kendal. Hotel on right in 5m

Innovative Cumbrian cooking with views of the fells

Kendal is the gateway to the Lakes, featuring what's left of a castle that was once the ancestral home of Katherine Parr, as well as this very much intact charming country house that's now a spa hotel. A £250,000 splashout on the Greenhouse restaurant and bar means a stylish makeover, with a boldly patterned carpet and walls crowded with little pictures, while the panoramic views over the fells and into the kitchen are undisturbed. Innovative Cumbrian food pours forth from first one and then the other, producing starters such as glazed beef cheeks with watercress risotto and a slow-cooked egg yolk in ale jus, prior to hazelnut-crusted halibut with salsify and artichokes in a nutty velouté, or loin and shoulder of lamb with onion purée, pumpkin and curd cheese. A grilled 10oz saddleback pork chop with sauté potatoes and sweetcorn salsa is a house speciality, and proceedings close with local cheeses served with green tomato chutney, or something like semolina, coconut and marmalade cake with corn flake ice cream and yogurt.

Chef Justin Woods **Owner** James & Catherine Alexander **Seats** 80, Pr/dining room 250 **Times** 12-2/6-10 **Prices** Prices not confirmed **Wines** 8 bottles over £30, 32 bottles under £30, 7 by glass **Parking** 200 **Notes** Tasting menu 3/5 course, Afternoon tea, Vegetarian available, Children welcome

Morrels

◉ Modern British

tel: 017687 72666 **34 Lake Rd CA12 5DQ**
email: info@morrels.co.uk
dir: Between market square & Keswick Theatre by the lake

Light-filled modern brasserie

The Victorian house situated between the Theatre by the Lake and Keswick Market has been repurposed into a combination of self-catering apartments with a contemporary restaurant on hand, for when the self-catering impulse falters. In a light-filled ambience of uncovered tables and floor, a menu of modern brasserie cooking pushes many of the right buttons. Fishcakes of Cajun-style blackened salmon and chorizo, dressed with mint and dill yogurt, are a palate-priming starter, as are haggis spring rolls with hoisin dip. Mains offer plenty of Lakeland meats – sizable sirloins with chunky chips and sauce Diane, fell-bred lamb with bubble-and-squeak – as well as forthright fish preparations such as monkfish parcelled in prosciutto with tomato, clam and garlic linguini. Finish with a raspberry ripple-themed Eton Mess, or a warm chocolate brownie served with white chocolate and marshmallow sauce.

Chef Karl Link, David Lamont **Owner** The Freeman & Link families **Seats** 56 **Times** 5.30-close, Closed 5-16 Jan, Mon, L all week **Prices** Fixed D 2 course £21.95, Starter £4.95-£7.50, Main £12-£19.50, Dessert £5.95-£6.50, Service optional **Wines** 8 bottles over £30, 28 bottles under £30, 9 by glass **Notes** Sun D 2/3 course £14.50/£17.95, Sunday L, Vegetarian available, Children 5 yrs+

Swinside Lodge Country House Hotel

◉◉ Modern, Traditional British **V**

tel: 017687 72948 **Grange Rd, Newlands CA12 5UE**
email: info@swinsidelodge-hotel.co.uk **web:** www.swinsidelodge-hotel.co.uk
dir: M6 junct 40, A66, left at Portinscale. Follow to Grange for 2m ignoring signs to Swinside & Newlands Valley

Seasonal set menu amid the brooding fells

A small white-fronted country house in the Newlands Valley, Swinside makes a good job of seeming to be miles from anywhere, despite the nearness of Keswick. Surrounded by brooding fells, its own modest but well-kept gardens look positively friendly, and that's certainly the tone maintained within, where a hands-on approach by the owners makes everyone feel at home. Clive Imber cooks a daily-changing four-course menu. It might begin with a soup such as richly satisfying vine tomato and basil intervening between an impactful fish starter, comprising gravad lax, roast salmon, and crab and horseradish remoulade in beetroot dressing, and a main course of duck breast with potato gratin, sweet shallots and spice-roasted plum sauced in red wine. At the end, there's a choice of desserts, perhaps a traditional sponge pudding such as ginger, or a more adventurous dark chocolate pavé and white chocolate mousse with Kirsch-drenched cherries and lots of passionfruit. If you've room, there is always a fine Anglo-French cheese slate, as well as good breads and envelopingly rich petits fours.

Chef Clive Imber **Owner** Mike & Kath Bilton **Seats** 18 **Times** 7.30-10.30, Closed Dec-Jan, L all week **Prices** Prices not confirmed, Service optional **Wines** 54 bottles over £30, 18 bottles under £30, 10 by glass **Parking** 12 **Notes** Fixed D 4 course £45, Children 12 yrs+

Hipping Hall

◉◉◉ – see opposite

Pheasant Inn

◉ Modern British NEW

tel: 015242 71230 **Casterton LA6 2RX**
email: info@pheasantinn.co.uk **web:** www.pheasantinn.co.uk
dir: *M6 junct 36, A590 towards Kirby Lonsdale. At rdbt take 2nd exit A65 towards Skipton. At next rdbt take 2nd exit A65 to Skipton. Turn left onto A683 to Casterton, Barbon & Sedbergh*

Unpretentious dining in an old coaching inn

An 18th-century coaching inn with a proper bar complete with real ales and snug, the Pheasant Inn also boasts traditional bedrooms and a wood-panelled restaurant. It's a family-run place, operated with enthusiasm by a couple of generations of Wilsons. When it comes to eating, grab a table by the fire in the bar, or head on through to the slightly more refined restaurant – whichever you prefer, as the menu is the same throughout. Expect dishes that reflect the easy-going pub setting but don't lack ambition. A starter of braised pig's cheek with Bury black pudding and caramelised apples is soft, sweet and tender in all the right places, or go for shallot tarte Tatin with glazed goats' cheese. Follow with lightly battered king prawns with hand-cut chips, or a Med-inspired baked fillet of turbot, and finish with a spot-on crème brûlée.

Chef Duncan Wilson **Owner** The Wilson family **Seats** 40 **Times** 12-2/6-9, Closed 25-26 Dec **Prices** Starter £4.95-£7.95, Main £12.95-£17.95, Dessert £5.50-£8.95 **Wines** 7 bottles over £30, 26 bottles under £30, 8 by glass **Parking** 32 **Notes** Sunday L, Vegetarian available, Children welcome

The Sun Inn

◉◉ Modern British ᵥ

tel: 015242 71965 **6 Market St LA6 2AU**
email: email@sun-inn.info **web:** www.sun-inn.info
dir: *From A65 follow signs to town centre. Inn on main street*

Friendly old inn with local ingredients and plenty of flavour

Gentle strolls along the River Lune to soak up the celebrated 'Ruskin's View' across the valley, as immortalised by J M W Turner, are one good reason to visit the historic market town of Kirkby Lonsdale on the borders of the Lake District and the Yorkshire Dales. But anyone with foodie inclinations should also schedule a pitstop in the white-painted 17th-century Sun Inn, a proper pub with oak beams, log fires and real ales in the convivial bar, and a smart contemporary dining room. There's a serious commitment to using the best local ingredients, and reliable hands in the kitchen to conjure full-flavoured dishes. Start with suckling pig pointed up with blood orange gel, caramelised red chicory, deep-fried black pudding and crispy crackling, followed by a bouillabaisse-style fish stew of gurnard, squid, home-smoked mussels and fennel, all topped with croûtons and a punchy red pepper rouille. To finish, a chocolate and mint-themed workout delivers a diverting array of textures including mousse, gel, foam and chocolate Genoese cake.

Chef Sam Carter **Owner** Lucy & Mark Fuller **Seats** 36 **Times** 12-5/6.30-9, Closed L Mon **Prices** Fixed D 3 course £31.95, Service optional **Wines** 13 bottles over £30, 45 bottles under £30, 7 by glass **Parking** On street & nearby car park **Notes** Sunday L £23.95-£25.95, Children welcome

Hipping Hall ✿✿✿

KIRKBY LONSDALE   Map 18 SD67

Modern British ᵥ 🏵 NOTABLE WINE LIST

tel: 015242 71187 **Cowan Bridge LA6 2JJ**
email: info@hippinghall.com **web:** www.hippinghall.com
dir: *8.5m E of M6 junct 36 on A65*

Accomplished modern cooking with national parks on either hand

The word 'hipping' refers to an old term for stepping stones, which allowed a dry crossing of the wonderfully named Broken Beck (the wee stream running through the grounds). The hall has been on this site for centuries and has a timeless appeal, and for a place with the moniker 'hall' it is relatively modest, but charming nonetheless. Standing between the Lake District and the Yorkshire Dales within its own mature garden, Hipping Hall has a real asset in its restaurant. Oli Martin is the new man in the kitchen and he's serving up impressively contemporary and considered plates of food. It all takes place in an elegant but not OTT room. Things get off to a flyer with amuse-bouche including lamb jerky with a sweet jelly and edible flowers, and some excellent breads. From the à la carte and tasting menus come dishes of refinement and creativity. A starter of Cartmel rabbit (tender loin and confit leg meat) shows acute technical skills, while another sees black garlic flavouring a savoury pannacotta, served with wild rice and alliums. Spot-on wild sea bass stars in a main course with salt-baked celeriac purée, monk's beard and shrimp butter, or go for a meat option such as rib of Lakeland beef with pied bleu mushrooms. Among desserts, chocolate sphere arrives looking stunning on the plate, with shavings of truffle, caramel and a mandarin sorbet. One to watch.

Chef Oli Martin **Owner** Andrew Wildsmith **Seats** 32 **Times** 12-2/7-9, Closed L Mon-Fri **Prices** Fixed L 3 course fr £29.50, Fixed D 3 course fr £55, Tasting menu fr £65, Service optional **Parking** 20 **Notes** Sunday L fr £29.50, Children 12 yrs+

LUPTON
Map 18 SD58

Plough Inn
◎ Modern British

tel: 015395 67700 **Cow Brow LA6 1PJ**
email: info@theploughatlupton.co.uk **web:** www.theploughatlupton.co.uk
dir: *M6 junct 36 onto A65 signed Kirkby Lonsdale*

Smart contemporary looks and savvy pub food

Enjoying a new lease of life since the team behind The Punchbowl Inn in Crosthwaite carried out a major makeover, the Plough sports a clean-lined contemporary look without sacrificing the best of its pubby character. It's a classy act with tasteful colours, leather sofas, and a Brathay slate-topped bar set against the cosiness of wooden floors, beams, real fires and the like. The place hasn't lost track of what a good, up-to-date inn should be so there are real ales alongside a wide-ranging roster of please-all British cooking. Home-made pork pies are a speciality here, served with piccalilli and salad, and you can follow that with two-day braised beef brisket with parsley mash, Savoy cabbage, crispy bone marrow and proper gravy. For dessert, vanilla pannacotta comes with damson compôte and Jammy Dodger shortbread.

Chef Matt Adamson **Owner** Paul Spencer **Seats** 120, Pr/dining room 8 **Times** 12-9, All-day dining **Prices** Starter £4.50-£12, Main £9.95-£24.95, Dessert £4.95-£7.95, Service optional **Wines** 14 bottles over £30, 28 bottles under £30, 10 by glass **Parking** 40 **Notes** Sunday L £12.95, Vegetarian available, Children welcome

NEAR SAWREY
Map 18 SD39

Ees Wyke Country House
◎ Modern, Traditional British

tel: 015394 36393 **LA22 0JZ**
email: mail@eeswyke.co.uk **web:** www.eeswyke.co.uk
dir: *On B5285 on W side of village*

Homely Lakeland cooking where Beatrix Potter took her hols

Beatrix Potter spent her holidays in this white Georgian house, and it isn't hard to see the appeal. Surrounding by shelving grounds and the timeless tranquillity of the Lakes, it's on a small enough scale to create a feeling of togetherness among guests, reinforced by a four-course dinner menu served at a single start time. A pair of choices is offered at most stages, beginning perhaps with seared scallops and a balsamic-dressed salad of shoots and cress, before a fixed fish dish such as cayenne-peppered haddock. If you want to stick with fish, main course could be beautifully fresh sea bass in the East Asian company of spring onions, chilli, garlic and ginger, while meat might comprise noisettes of local lamb in red wine jus. The sticky toffee pudding displays a lighter touch than is customary, but still comes with hot butterscotch sauce.

Times 7.30-close

Sawrey House Hotel
◎ Modern British **NEW**

tel: 015394 36387 **LA22 0LF**
email: enquiries@sawreyhouse.com **web:** www.sawreyhouse.com
dir: *From Ambleside A593 S, left at Clappersgate onto B5286 towards Hawkshead then take B5285 towards Sawrey/Ferry. Hotel 1.5m on right*

Classic Lakeland house with locally-sourced cooking

The location is pure Lakeland, the stone-built Victorian country house looking out over three acres of its own gardens towards Esthwaite Water and the forest of Grizedale, plus it is next to Beatrix Potter's Hill Top Farm. Those luscious views are to be enjoyed from the linened dining room, where globally-inspired, locally-sourced cooking displays plenty of thought, imagination and technical skill. Textures of on-

trend beetroot — mousse, jelly and gel — are the accompaniments to a starter of home-cured salmon garnished with its crisped dried skin, or there could be parsnip soup with an onion bhaji and curry foam. At main course stage, pedigree Cumbrian meats star, perhaps venison saddle or lamb in three guises, the roast rump, confit belly and haggis with boulangère potatoes in red cabbage consommé. Finish with nougat glacé in caramel sauce, served with poached pear, marinated berries and apple sorbet.

Chef Ashley Wood **Owner** David Bulmer **Seats** 20
Times 12-2.30/6.30-8.30, Closed 24-26 Dec **Prices** Fixed L 2 course £18.95, Fixed D 3 course £34.95, Starter fr £7, Main fr £16, Dessert fr £7, Service optional **Wines** 2 bottles over £30, 10 bottles under £30, 5 by glass **Parking** 15, On street **Notes** Sunday L £24.95, Vegetarian available, Children 12 yrs+

NEWBY BRIDGE
Map 18 SD38

Lakeside Hotel Lake Windermere
◎◎ Modern British

tel: 015395 30001 **Lakeside LA12 8AT**
email: sales@lakesidehotel.co.uk **web:** www.lakesidehotel.co.uk
dir: *M6 junct 36 follow A590 to Newby Bridge, straight over rdbt, right over bridge. Hotel within 1m*

Lakeside modern dining with a choice of restaurants

The Lakeside sits, as you might expect, right on the water's edge at the southern shore of Lake Windermere, surrounded by wooded slopes. It started out as a coaching inn in the 17th century, and is now a substantial building, with a lakeside terrace, spa and pool and a brasserie as well as the Lakeview restaurant looking over boats bobbing on the water. Main courses on the interesting menu show that the kitchen has a thoroughly modern outlook, among them halibut fillet with haggis, ceps and mushroom cappuccino, and breast and drumstick of squab pigeon with dates and boulangère potatoes. The bulk of materials are sourced locally, plus seafood from Scotland and Cornwall, going into appealingly assembled starters of white crabmeat with bulgar wheat, avocado and tomato confit, and the full-on flavours of shin of beef with celeriac, beetroot and green mustard. The seasonally-changing menu might conclude with zingy desserts like rhubarb soufflé with eucalyptus parfait and pink grapefruit, or dark chocolate mousse with butterscotch, chocolate soil and double-milk ice cream.

Times 12.30-2.30/6.45-9.30, Closed 23 Dec-16 Jan

Whitewater Hotel
◎ Modern, Traditional British **V**

tel: 015395 31133 **The Lakeland Village LA12 8PX**
email: enquiries@whitewater-hotel.co.uk **web:** www.whitewater-hotel.co.uk
dir: *M6 junct 36 follow signs for A590 Barrow, 1m through Newby Bridge. Right at sign for Lakeland Village, hotel on left*

Punchy modern British cooking by the River Leven

The hotel occupies a substantial grey stone building, a cotton mill in the Victorian period, in a rural setting beside the fast-flowing River Leven. The restaurant itself overlooks the river, a welcoming room with exposed stone walls and high-backed maroon and grey leather-look seats at fully dressed tables. The menus are built around a modern British repertoire with some international influences. To start might be a warm salad of red mullet with Niçoise vegetables, tapenade and sardine vinaigrette, or flavour-packed oxtail and smoked ham hock terrine, served in a neat cylinder with pickled vegetables and horseradish dressing. Main courses are given an extra dimension by sauces: a glossy, rich red wine jus for accurate and moist pan-fried monkfish tail in a pleasingly piquant crust of chorizo and rosemary, and one of Madeira and summer truffle for fillet of beef with wild mushrooms and young vegetables. For pudding, look no further than prune and pistachio parfait.

Chef Pascal Tabard **Owner** Heritage Resorts **Seats** 50, Pr/dining room 20
Times 7-9, Closed L all week **Prices** Prices not confirmed, Service optional **Wines** 12
by glass **Parking** 30 **Notes** Children welcome

RAVENGLASS   Map 18 SD09

The Pennington Hotel

◉ British

tel: 0845 450 6445 *(The only charge for this call will be your phone company's access charge)* **CA18 1SD**
email: info@penningtonhotels.com **web:** www.penningtonhotels.com
dir: *M6, junct 36 to A590 Barrow, right Greenodd A5092, joining A595 Muncaster/ Ravenglass. Located in village centre*

Fashionable dishes in a Tudor coaching inn

The venerable black and white hotel wears its age on its sleeve, having started out as a coaching inn in the Tudor era. A latter-day wash and brush-up has put it once more at the centre of life in its picturesque village, with Muncaster Castle for company. Culinary modernism is the order of the day in the light, relaxing dining room, where many of the fashionable treatments are on show in a repertoire that runs from salmon cured in beetroot and gin with horseradish crème fraîche and lime jelly to belly and fillet of pork with black pudding, buttered kale and apple soup. Seafood is imaginatively handled, as when halibut arrives with a crab beignet, asparagus and herbed gnocchi in lemon cream sauce, and it all concludes with desserts that score highly for novelty, such as Pina Colada cheesecake with pineapple compôte and coconut popcorn.

Chef Kath Steward, Helen Todd **Owner** Iona Frost-Pennington **Seats** 36, Pr/dining room **Times** 12-2.30/7-9 **Prices** Fixed L 2 course £17.95-£26.95, Fixed D 3 course £27.50-£37.50, Starter £8.95-£12.95, Main £12.95-£24.95, Dessert £6.95-£9.95, Service optional **Wines** 14 bottles over £30, 16 bottles under £30, 8 by glass **Parking** 20 **Notes** Sunday L £9.95, Vegetarian available, Children welcome

ROSTHWAITE   Map 18 NY21

Scafell Hotel

◉ Modern British **NEW**

tel: 017687 77208 **CA12 5XB**
email: info@scafell.co.uk **web:** www.scafell.co.uk
dir: *M6 junct 40 to Keswick on A66. Take B5289 to Rosthwaite*

British dining with an international twist

Surrounded by peaks and the lush greenery of the Borrowdale Valley, the Scafell Hotel is ideal for those seeking to maximise time spent in the great outdoors. It's ideally situated if one or other of walking, climbing and fishing are your favoured pastimes, while there's no mobile phone signal to offer external distractions. The Riverside Bar and lounge bar offer informal dining possibilities, with the main restaurant a more formal option with its linen-clad tables and confidently executed British menu. Salmon is cured in-house and matched with avocado and tomato salsa, while another starter sees flaked crab with linguine given a nicely judged hit of chilli. Main-course herb-crusted shoulder and noisette of lamb is partnered with Thai-style vegetables, and pan-roasted monkish comes in a Mediterranean-style combination of confit plum tomatoes, red peppers and red onions. Finish with a light and fluffy mousse of chocolate, Tia Maria and mocha.

Chef Paul Wilson **Owner** Miles Jessop, Andrew Nelson **Seats** 65
Times 12-2.30/6.30-9, Closed L Mon-Sat **Prices** Starter £5.25-£7.50, Main £16.95-£21.95, Dessert £5.25-£7.95, Service optional **Wines** 35 bottles over £30, 57 bottles under £30, 11 by glass **Parking** 100 **Notes** Sunday L £18.95, Vegetarian available, Children welcome

SEASCALE   Map 18 NY00

Sella Park House Hotel

◉ Traditional British

tel: 0845 450 6445 *(The only charge for this call will be your phone company's access charge)* & 01946 841601 **Calderbridge CA20 1DW**
email: info@penningtonhotels.com **web:** www.penningtonhotels.com
dir: *From A595 at Calderbridge, follow sign for North Gate. Hotel 0.5m on left*

Local supplies and a modern approach

Six acres of lovely gardens running down to the River Calder make this historic 16th-century manor house a popular venue for tying the knot, but you don't have to be heading for a wedding to see what the kitchen can do. There's no faulting the splendid seasonal Cumbrian produce it hauls in as the basis of its up-to-date cooking: vegetables, fruit and herbs are plucked fresh from the kitchen garden at nearby Muncaster Castle, and great care is taken in tracking down the best local meat and fish. The Priory Restaurant makes a traditional setting for ideas that run the gamut from a tried-and-tested pairing of local hand-dived scallops and home-made black pudding lifted by crisp sage and quince jelly, to a main course of Goosnargh duck breast with butternut squash and orange purée, braised red cabbage and spicy duck jus. For dessert, apple tarte Tatin rounds things off nicely.

Chef Jon Fell **Owner** Iona Frost-Pennington **Seats** 34, Pr/dining room 40
Times 12-3/6-9 **Prices** Starter £5-£8.95, Main £12-£24, Dessert £6.50-£8.50, Service optional **Wines** 14 bottles over £30, 16 bottles under £30, 6 by glass **Parking** 30 **Notes** Sunday L £9.95-£19.95, Vegetarian available, Children welcome

TEMPLE SOWERBY   Map 18 NY62

Temple Sowerby House Hotel & Restaurant

◉◉ Modern British

tel: 017683 61578 **CA10 1RZ**
email: stay@templesowerby.com **web:** www.templesowerby.com
dir: *7m from M6 junct 40, midway between Penrith & Appleby, in village centre*

Boldly modern cooking overlooking the garden in Eden

Occupying a median point between Penrith and Appleby in the appropriately named Eden Valley, one of northern Cumbria's loveliest spots, Temple Sowerby is home to the impressive early Georgian house of the same name. With sandstone columns framing the view over the walled garden, high-backed patterned chairs and bundles of fresh flowers, the place has all the charm of a smart family-run country hotel. The kitchen specialises in a boldly modern style, the suavely presented dishes showing plenty of European influence, extending even to India in a starter of tandoori shoulder and smoked rump of lamb with lentil dhal and an onion bhaji, or Thailand for scallop mousse with coconut prawns in satay sauce. The compass needle judders back to Europe for mains such as halibut with lemony pearl barley in red wine, or sublime ale-braised beef cheek with smoke-cured sirloin in intense braising juices. Top it all off with a hot toddy winter dessert featuring whisky pannacotta and single-malt jelly, lemon and ginger doughnuts and ginger ice cream.

Chef Ashley Whittaker **Owner** Paul & Julie Evans **Seats** 24, Pr/dining room 24
Times 7-9, Closed 8 days Xmas, L all week **Prices** Fixed D 3 course fr £43, Service optional **Wines** 10 bottles over £30, 30 bottles under £30, 7 by glass **Parking** 20 **Notes** Vegetarian available, Children 12 yrs+

WATERMILLOCK
Map 18 NY42

Macdonald Leeming House
◎◎ Modern British

tel: 01768 486674 **CA11 OJJ**
email: leeminghouse@macdonald-hotels.co.uk **web:** www.macdonald-hotels.co.uk
dir: *M6 junct 40, continue on A66 signed Keswick. At rdbt follow A592 towards Ullswater, at T-junct turn right, hotel 3m on left*

Ambitious country-house cooking on the shores of Ullswater

The 200-year-old manor is an impressive-looking property, with eye-catching cast-iron stanchions supporting a first-floor balcony. Its location is pretty impressive too, as it's in 22 acres of grounds with direct access to Ullswater, where it has a private fishing licence. For the full-on Lakeland dining experience, head for the elegant Regency Restaurant, where floor-to-ceiling windows, hung with heavy red drapes and plush pelmets, give views to the lake and fells beyond. The menus are reassuringly familiar, with some contemporary twists to established ideas. Pressed confit duck leg, for instance, is partnered by poached plums and red wine syrup, and smoked salmon terrine by herby lemon butter, pink peppercorns and fennel salad. Dishes are well executed and attractively presented, seen in main courses of flavoursome slices of roast loin of Highland lamb with rösti, carrot purée, crushed peas and rosemary jus, and baked plaice fillets with sauté potatoes, broccoli and béarnaise. End on an international note with lemongrass pannacotta with mango milkshake, or gingerbread parfait with caramelised pineapple and Malibu syrup.

Times 12-2/6.45-9

Rampsbeck Country House Hotel
◎◎ Modern British **V**

tel: 017684 86442 **CA11 OLP**
email: enquiries@rampsbeck.co.uk **web:** www.rampsbeck.co.uk
dir: *M6 junct 40, A592 to Ullswater, T-junct turn right at lake's edge. Hotel 1.25m, on lake side*

Smart modern cooking in a refined lakeside setting

The white-painted villa sits on a hillside overlooking Ullswater, with 18 acres all to itself, including a piece of valuable shoreline. It delivers a country-house experience which meets expectations in terms combining old-world luxury with some contemporary comforts, while the culinary output from the kitchen really catches the eye. There are acres of burnished panels, antiques and ornate ceilings throughout the 18th-century house, and smart lounges where it's easy to lose an hour or two. The dining room itself has all the period details, plus neatly laid tables and a menu with its roots in classical French cooking. But this is bright, modern stuff, presented with a good deal of style. Pan-fried red mullet, for example, comes with a salt-cod mousse, black olive purée and a red pepper crisp in a starter that has evident Mediterranean leanings. Follow on with fillet of English rose veal served with a warm salad of mixed beans, and for dessert finish with a modern take on a

classic combination of flavours: carrot cake with chocolate soil, yogurt sorbet and candied carrot.

Rampsbeck Country House Hotel

Chef Ben Wilkinson **Owner** Blackshaw Hotels Ltd **Seats** 40, Pr/dining room 16
Times 12-1.45/7-9 **Prices** Fixed D 3 course fr £32, Tasting menu £50.95-£68.95,
Service optional **Wines** 43 bottles over £30, 47 bottles under £30, 7 by glass
Parking 30 **Notes** Sunday L fr £32, Children 10 yrs+

WINDERMERE
Map 18 SD49

Beech Hill Hotel
◎ Modern British **V**

tel: 015394 42137 **Newby Bridge Rd LA23 3LR**
email: reservations@beechhillhotel.co.uk **web:** www.beechhillhotel.co.uk
dir: *M6 junct 36, A591 to Windermere. Left onto A592 towards Newby Bridge. Hotel 4m from Bowness-on-Windermere*

Appealing modern cooking on the shores of Windermere

After canapés and pre-dinner drinks you can soak up the dramatic views over Lake Windermere to the fells beyond from Burlington's Restaurant. The menu's altogether more catholic than that usually found in such a context, embracing a crispy haggis cake on crushed carrots and turnips topped with a fried egg, and dill-battered sea bass fillet sauced with rouille served with saffron potato purée and tender-stem broccoli. Cumbrian produce is used to good effect, and the kitchen clearly has a solid grounding in the French classics, but adds its own spin on dishes. Morecambe Bay shrimps go into a risotto with dill and parmesan, to be followed perhaps by passionfruit-glazed crispy duck confit served with honey-roast parsnips and carrots. Allow ten minutes for a soufflé – blackcurrant, say, with blueberry sorbet – or order something chilled like mandarin crème brûlée.

Chef Christopher Davies **Owner** Mr F Richardson **Seats** 130, Pr/dining room 90
Times 7-9, Closed L all week (ex party booking), D 25 Dec **Prices** Fixed D 3 course fr
£34.95, Service optional **Wines** 25 bottles over £30, 25 bottles under £30, 8 by glass
Parking 60 **Notes** Fixed D 5 course £39.95, Children welcome

Cedar Manor Hotel & Restaurant
◎◎ Modern British

tel: 015394 43192 **Ambleside Rd LA23 1AX**
email: info@cedarmanor.co.uk **web:** www.cedarmanor.co.uk
dir: *From A591 follow signs to Windermere. Hotel on left just beyond St Mary's Church at bottom of hill*

Peaceful small hotel with impressive seasonal cooking

Built of grey stone in 1854, the manor occupies a peaceful spot in attractive gardens, complete with eponymous cedar, on the outskirts of Windermere. It's a small-scale hotel, with a modern look, while the restaurant is well appointed, with leather-look chairs at neatly set tables; well-trained but unbuttoned staff keep the ball rolling. Seasonality leads the kitchen, with its reliance on Lakeland produce, and the cooking is marked out by its technical precision and, given the quintessentially English surroundings, by its wide-ranging scope. Thus, pavé of salmon is marinated in ginger and served with robust wasabi mayonnaise, some pickled vegetables and leaves, and another starter combines the pungency of aubergine, onion and potato bhajis with mint chutney and a coriander and onion dip. Main courses are in similar vein — Moroccan lamb tagine with herby couscous, for instance — although pink-roast duck breast has appeared in autumn with seasonal fruits, sautéed pumpkin and a perfect rendition of dauphinoise. Incidentals like breads and a complimentary soup are well reported, as are puddings such as chocolate millefeuille.

Chef Roger Pergl-Wilson **Owner** Caroline & Jonathan Kaye **Seats** 22, Pr/dining room 10 **Times** 6.30-8.30, Closed Xmas & 6-25 Jan, L all week **Prices** Fixed D 3 course £39.50-£42.95, Service optional **Wines** 11 bottles over £30, 26 bottles under £30, 7 by glass **Parking** 12 **Notes** Vegetarian available, Children 12 yrs+

Gilpin Hotel & Lake House

❀❀❀ – see page 126

Holbeck Ghyll Country House Hotel

❀❀ Modern British V ◈ NOTABLE WINE LIST

tel: 015394 32375 **Holbeck Ln LA23 1LU**
email: stay@holbeckghyll.com **web:** www.holbeckghyll.com
dir: 3m N of Windermere on A591, right into Holbeck Lane (signed Troutbeck), hotel 0.5m on left

Classical Lakeland cooking overlooking Windermere

Sitting proud above the shimmering expanse of Lake Windermere, Holbeck Ghyll enjoys panoramic views of the pikes and fells in the distance, and the long drive up to the front door emphasises the feeling that you are entering another world. Inside, the house is consummately stylish, it's art nouveau signature decor beautifully maintained, and an air of a peaceable retreat reigns supreme. A new private dining room, the Segrave, is named after one of the previous holders of the water speed record, set in the 1930s, but the oak-panelled main restaurant has bundles of charm in itself. Confident country-house cookery, with a strong classical foundation, discreetly offset with a little French-inspired modernity is the deal here, opening with confit duck terrine with pear, green beans and brioche, while main course stars roasted wild turbot supported by creamed leeks, crisp ham and red wine sauce. A dessert of vanilla bavarois with blackcurrant and liquorice sorbet is

given textural variety with the crunch of brandy snap, honeycomb and a shard of blackberry meringue.

Holbeck Ghyll Country House Hotel

Chef David McLaughlin **Owner** Stephen Leahy **Seats** 50, Pr/dining room 20 **Times** 12.30-2/7-9.30 **Prices** Fixed L 2 course £35-£55, Fixed D 3 course £75, Tasting menu £95, Service optional **Wines** 270 bottles over £30, 29 bottles under £30, 13 by glass **Parking** 50 **Notes** Sunday L £35-£55, Children 8 yrs+

Lindeth Howe Country House Hotel & Restaurant

❀❀ Modern British V

tel: 015394 45759 **Lindeth Dr, Longtail Hill LA23 3JF**
email: hotel@lindeth-howe.co.uk **web:** www.lindeth-howe.co.uk
dir: 1m S of Bowness onto B5284, signed Kendal and Lancaster. Hotel 2nd driveway on right

Imaginative modern cooking in verdant setting chez Beatrix Potter

There may not be any shortage of delightful Lakeland hotels, nor of any overlooking Lake Windermere, but this is a classic country house with a unique pedigree – it was once home to Beatrix Potter, who wrote a couple of her tales here. So after consuming the delicious views of the lake and mountains beyond, and exploring the verdant grounds, it is back for dinner in the handsomely turned-out dining room. The kitchen team is passionate about regional produce, seeking out first-class ingredients and serving up a menu of contemporary and creative dishes. It all looks as pretty as a picture on the plate and everything is there for a reason. Poached salmon fillet takes centre stage in a starter with broad beans, tomato and pickled samphire, followed by roast corn-fed chicken ballotine with chervil mousse, black garlic mash, carrot purée and a light jus. To finish, warm blackberry clafoutis is matched with tonka bean ice cream, and black pepper and berry jelly.

Chef Robert Taylor **Owner** Lakeinvest Ltd **Seats** 70, Pr/dining room 20 **Times** 12-2/6.30-9 **Prices** Prices not confirmed, Service optional **Wines** 8 by glass **Parking** 50 **Notes** Fixed D 5 course £49.50, Table d'hôte menu £46.50, Sunday L, Children 7 yrs+

Linthwaite House Hotel & Restaurant

❀❀❀ – see page 127

Gilpin Hotel & Lake House 🌹🌹🌹

WINDERMERE   **Map 18 SD49**

Modern British V

tel: 015394 88818 **Crook Rd LA23 3NE**
email: hotel@thegilpin.co.uk **web:** www.thegilpin.co.uk
dir: *M6 junct 36 take A590/A591 to rdbt N of Kendal, then B5284 for 5m*

Dynamic contemporary cooking in fabulous family-run hotel

This Edwardian house in 22 acres of peaceful gardens, moors and woodland near Windermere is the very essence of a tranquil and luxurious getaway. Gilpin Lodge has been run by the Cunliffes since 1988, when they turned the place into a country-house hotel done out with a good deal of style and not an iota of chintz. Its original features (built in 1901) remain, but the impression within is of timeless contemporary luxury and comfort. There's also Lake House a short drive away in its own 100 acres, which offers six more beautiful bedrooms, a lakeside vista and spa. After his moment in the TV limelight when he won BBC2's *Chefs on Trial*, Hrishikesh Desai is the new man directing the kitchen's efforts and eating here remains, as ever, a highlight of a stay. The cooking is thrillingly contemporary, but clearly focused at the same time. There are plenty of creative ideas and preparations on show, everything looks wonderful on the plate, and the ingredients are second to none. Sea-fresh Kyle of Lochalsh scallops with crisp haddock brandade fritters, saffron-scented pickled carrots, and tomato and cumin vinaigrette is a storming opener, followed by an uncontroversial main course full of the joys of Spring: tender, pink new season lamb loin with a shepherd's pie

of rich minced lamb served in a potato skin and supported by asparagus, wild garlic, crushed peas and broad beans. For pudding, gin and tonic sorbet and blackberry coulis (the latter poured in at the table) are the accompaniments to an exemplary blackberry soufflé. You're welcome to check out the globetrotting bins in the walk-in wine cellar, and the staff run the show with charm and professionalism.

Chef Hrishikesh Desai **Owner** The Cunliffe family **Seats** 60, Pr/dining room 20 **Times** 12-2/6.30-9.30, **Prices** Fixed L 3 course £30-£35, Tasting menu fr £85, Service optional **Wines** 139 bottles over £30, 13 bottles under £30, 15 by glass **Parking** 40
Notes Fixed D 4 course £58, Sunday L fr £35, Children 7 yrs+

WINDERMERE *continued*

Macdonald Old England Hotel & Spa

◎◎ Traditional British, European

tel: 015394 87890 **23 Church St, Bowness LA23 3DF**
email: sales.oldengland@macdonald-hotels.co.uk **web:** www.macdonaldhotels.co.uk
dir: *Through Windermere to Bowness, straight across at mini-rdbt. Hotel behind church on right*

Stylish modern dining and stunning lake views

There is something rather wonderful about dining with a view over water, and with its lakeside setting, the Number 23 Church Street Restaurant at the Macdonald Old England serves up a very nice one indeed. It's Lake Windermere, of course, that you'll see through the floor-to-ceiling windows (or better still the terrace), but there're plenty of other good reasons to come here. The Victorian mansion is much extended these days and includes a spa amongst its many attractions. The restaurant has a good deal to offer, from steaks cooked on the grill, through to some gently contemporary dishes based on top quality regional ingredients. You might start with a ballotine of confit duck leg with honey-pickled vegetables, or a twice-baked cheese soufflé with a fricassée of roasted butternut squash. Those steaks – rib-eye, perhaps – come with plum tomatoes, field mushrooms and hand-cut chips, or go for grilled fillet of grey mullet with fennel purée and poached potatoes. For dessert, chocolate and stem ginger tart with ginger ice cream shows a lightness of touch.

Times 6.30-9.30, Closed L all week

Miller Howe Hotel

◎◎ Modern British **v** 🍷 NOTABLE WINE LIST

tel: 015394 42536 **Rayrigg Rd LA23 1EY**
email: info@millerhowe.com **web:** www.millerhowe.com
dir: *M6 junct 36. Follow the A591 bypass for Kendal. Enter Windermere, continue to mini rdbt, take left onto A592. Miller Howe is 0.25m on right*

Romantic lakeside setting and polished country-house cooking

Miller Howe must be the yardstick by which other country-house hotels are judged, with its emphasis on guests' comfort, luxury fixtures and fittings, five and a half acres of landscaped grounds and stunning views over Lake Windermere to Langdale Pikes beyond. The restaurant, spread over three rooms, with its lime-green colour scheme and wooden floor, is split-level to ensure most guests can enjoy the lake views. 'Modern British with a twist' is the self-described cooking style, and the kitchen devises relatively short but punchy menus. Seasonality leads, with home-grown and wild produce in evidence, while presentation is precise and colourful and techniques are unerringly correct. Expect starters along the lines of prawns in shellfish bisque with black pudding, mandarin purée and segments, coriander and crushed nuts, a tour de force of flavours and textures. No less impressive are main courses of pink-roast rump of lamb with glazed sweetbreads, courgette purée, tomatoes and sheep's curd milk or more straightforward John Dory with asparagus, sorrel and brown butter hollandaise. Every effort seems to be thrown at desserts, among them a textbook blackcurrant soufflé with hot chocolate sauce and a Parma Violets macaroon.

Chef Matthew Horsfall **Owner** Martin & Helen Ainscough **Seats** 80, Pr/dining room 30
Times 12.30-1.45/6.45-8.45 **Prices** Fixed L 2 course £22.50, Service optional
Wines 100 bottles over £30, 50 bottles under £30, 12 by glass **Parking** 40
Notes Fixed D 4 course £47.50, Sunday L £30, Children welcome

Linthwaite House Hotel & Restaurant ✿✿✿

WINDERMERE   Map 18 SD49

Modern British
tel: 015394 88600 **Crook Rd LA23 3JA**
email: stay@linthwaite.com **web:** www.linthwaite.com
dir: *A591 towards The Lakes for 8m to large rdbt, take 1st exit (B5284), 6m, hotel on left. 1m past Windermere golf club*

Adventurous contemporary cooking with captivating Lakeland views

Built as a private residence in the Edwardian era, Linthwaite House is in an unbeatable location set in more than 14 acres of wooded grounds, offering stupendous views from its hillside setting of Lake Windermere and the surrounding fells. The interior has been given a luxury gloss in both decoration and furnishings, but there's no pretension or stuffiness here. The restaurant has a polished wooden floor, neat upholstered seating and blinds and curtains at the windows – and fab Lakeland views. The daily-changing dinner menu follows a three-course, set-price format with around half a dozen choices per course. Chris O'Callaghan's cooking is in the contemporary mode, based on refined classical techniques, and a glance at the menu shows that he's no slouch when it comes to adopting ideas from around the globe to suit each dish. A starter of venison tartare, for instance, is accompanied by wasabi mayonnaise and confit egg yolk, and another, of seared tuna steak, is flavoured with soya and coriander and plated with avocado. Dishes are tried and tested to ensure their different components make happy marriages, so the forthright flavours of steak-and-kidney pudding with roast sirloin steak and swede baked with cinnamon make a deeply satisfying main course. Fish crops up in the form of perhaps roast cod fillet, perfectly timed, with cavolo nero purée, hazelnut orzo, artichoke and prunes, while halibut is given an Indian treatment: crusted in curry and served with spicy lentil purée, sweet potato saag aloo, yogurt and mint. Puddings make an impact too, both on the palate and the eye: perhaps pineapple upside-down cake with cardamom and lime ice cream.

Chef Chris O'Callaghan **Owner** Mike Bevans **Seats** 64, Pr/dining room 16
Times 12.30-2/7-9.30, Closed Xmas & New Year (ex residents) **Prices** Fixed L 2 course £14.95, Fixed D 3 course £52, Tasting menu £62-£82 **Wines** 25 bottles over £30, 25 bottles under £30, 14 by glass **Parking** 40 **Notes** Sunday L £24.95, Vegetarian available, Children 7 yrs+ D

WINDERMERE *continued*

Porto

◉ Modern British

tel: 015394 48242 **3 Ash St, Bowness LA23 3EB**
email: info@porto-restaurant.co.uk **web:** www.porto-restaurant.co.uk
dir: *Take A5074 from Windermere down hill into Bowness-on-Windermere*

Eclectic modern cookery in a stylish town-centre venue

On a cobbled street in the heart of Bowness-on-Windermere, Porto is well placed to cater to a healthy proportion of the seasonal Lakeland crowds. It's a low-roofed white-fronted old house with seating on two floors, a heated roof terrace and a summer garden, the main room rather dramatically done up in red and gold with mirrors, black napery and crystal light fixtures. Staff are brisk and efficient, and know their onions when it comes to both the menu and the wine list. A voguishly eclectic mix of European and Asian influences amid more obviously straightforward fare indicates a kitchen aiming to please, and dishes are neatly and painstakingly presented. First up could be a classic twice-baked Cumbrian cheddar soufflé, offset by the sharpness of a white wine and chive sauce, cherry tomatoes and rocket. Mains run a gamut of thematic explorations, from the salmon version that incorporates seared Loch Duart fillet with a mini fish pie and fishcake to the bluntly named 'pig plate', at which you may feed on slow-cooked belly, pulled pork bubble-and-squeak and pigs in blankets, garnished with apple purée and a creamy mustard sauce. Proceedings end on a crowd-pleasing note with chocolate ganache cake, salted caramel, popcorn and richly flavoured vanilla ice cream.

Chef David Bewick **Owner** Faye Ramsey **Seats** 68, Pr/dining room 50
Times 12-2/6-9, Closed 24-26 Dec, 2nd wk Jan-2nd wk Feb, Tue **Prices** Prices not confirmed, Service optional **Wines** 10 bottles over £30, 20 bottles under £30, 7 by glass **Notes** Vegetarian available, Children welcome

The Ryebeck

◉◉ Modern British **NEW** v

tel: 015394 88195 **Lyth Valley Rd LA23 3JP**
email: info@ryebeck.com **web:** www.ryebeck.com
dir: *Phone for directions*

Imaginative modern cooking by the shining expanse of Windermere

Formerly known as Fayrer Garden, The Ryebeck is an appealingly isolated country house on a raised bank overlooking the shining expanse of Windermere, one of the greatest vistas the English national parks have to offer. The same dedicated team has run it for many years, so it's a well-oiled operation, with an informal conservatory dining room, where unclothed tables enjoy views over the lake. The modern British food displays a good mix of technical skills, mobilised in thoughtful and imaginative marriages of flavours and high visual impact. Pressed rabbit is rich and satisfying, offset with the sweetness of a langoustine and textured carrot in a sturdy game stock reduction, or there may be salt-cod tartare, dressed with dill mayonnaise, shallots and an egg yolk. One cut of pork is hardly ever enough nowadays, and here saddleback arrives as fillet, crisped cheek and brined belly, along with celeriac, kale and a purée of black pudding, while fish options include a pairing of cod and sticky chicken wing with a potato dumpling in fish broth. Chocolate and orange then work their magic together in a dense delice with fast-melting blood-orange sorbet.

Owner Andrew Wildsmith **Seats** 52 **Times** 12.30-4/6.30-8.45 **Prices** Fixed D 3 course £39.50, Tasting menu £47, Service optional **Wines** 19 bottles over £30, 21 bottles under £30, 9 by glass **Parking** 30 **Notes** Tasting menu 7 course, Afternoon tea, Children 6 yrs+

The Samling

◉◉◉ – *see opposite*

Storrs Hall Hotel

◉◉◉ – *see opposite*

DERBYSHIRE

BAKEWELL   Map 16 SK26

Piedaniel's

◉ Traditional French, European

tel: 01629 812687 **Bath St DE45 1BX**
dir: *From Bakewell rdbt in town centre take A6 Buxton exit. 1st right into Bath St (one-way)*

Bistro cooking done with personal warmth and charm

The half-timbered exterior and wood-beamed ceilings inside lend plenty of character to Piedaniel's, which is to be found near Bakewell's town hall chambers. It's run with great personal warmth and charm by a husband-and-wife team, and keeps the town supplied with reliable bistro cooking that doesn't go too far down the modernist road. Starters encompass a simple salad of smoked chicken and roast cherry tomatoes dressed in white truffle oil, or perhaps a saffron-fragranced take on moules marinière. Main courses nail their colours to the mast of hearty prime cuts – confit duck leg, lamb shank, beef fillet topped with red onion marmalade in wild mushroom casserole – while fish gets a look-in in the form of cod crusted in lemon and parsley, sauced with white Burgundy. Finish with brioche-and-butter pudding in Grand Marnier custard, or proper crêpes Suzette.

Chef E Piedaniel **Owner** E & C Piedaniel **Seats** 50, Pr/dining room 16
Times 12-2/7-10, Closed Xmas & New Year, 2 wks Jan, 2 wks Aug, Sun-Mon
Prices Prices not confirmed **Wines** 10 by glass **Parking** Town centre **Notes** Vegetarian available, Children welcome

The Samling 🌸🌸🌸

Modern British, European V
tel: 015394 31922 **Ambleside Rd LA23 1LR**
email: info@thesamlinghotel.co.uk **web:** www.thesamlinghotel.co.uk
dir: *M6 junct 36, A591 through Windermere towards Ambleside. 2m. 300yds past Low Wood Water Sports Centre just after sharp bend turn right into hotel entrance*

Experimental British cooking in a winsome Windermere retreat

The immaculate white-painted house overlooking Lake Windermere provides a classic Lakeland vista. It's a gloriously peaceful spot within 67 acres of grounds with the bucolic panorama best taken in from the terrace with a glass of something in your hand. The interior is simply smart and stylish. Country-house dining doesn't get much more modern than what's on offer in the Samling's restaurant. There's a development kitchen where dishes are created and refined, and a kitchen garden that uses progressive growing techniques and even exchanges seeds with the best restaurants in the world to grow first-class produce. The kitchen makes use of these fine home-grown ingredients alongside judiciously sourced stuff (see the list of suppliers on the menu) to deliver cutting-edge cuisine via tasting and à la carte menus. Presentation is eye-catching and modern cooking techniques abound. Start with a nitro terrine of foie gras with walnuts, ceps and moss, or the playfully named 'snail trail', which combines veal sweetbreads with red wine-braised snails, garlic purée and horseradish 'snow'. 'Pork sandwich' is a main course consisting of roasted loin of Middlewhite with red cabbage, onion and a truffle cream sauce, while roasted monkfish is rolled in squid ink and served with lobster bisque and chestnut mushroom duxelle. There's no less creativity and imagination in desserts such as Black Forest gâteau with textures of cherry, chocolate and vanilla, or another that combines chocolate and hazelnuts with hits of Amaretto, frangelico and Baileys. Well-kept British and European cheeses arrive at the tableside in a trolley. The wine list is a serious piece of work that covers the best of the world's regions.

Chef Ian Swainson **Owner** Mr Danson **Seats** 22, Pr/dining room 8
Times 12-2/6.30-9.30, **Prices** Tasting menu £65-£100, Service optional
Wines 198 bottles over £30, 26 bottles under £30, 22 by glass **Parking** 20
Notes Fixed L 5 course £45-£85, Prestige menu 10 course £100, Sunday L, Children welcome

Storrs Hall Hotel 🌸🌸🌸

Modern British V
tel: 015394 47111 **Storrs Park LA23 3LG**
email: enquiries@storrshall.com **web:** www.storrshall.com
dir: *On A592 2m S of Bowness, on Newby Bridge road*

Ambitious Lakeland cooking with views over the fells

A location on the shore of Lake Windermere sets off the two-tiered sparkling-white Georgian villa that is Storrs Hall to perfection. The house stands amid 17 acres of manicured grounds, its deep windows generously taking in the classic Lakeland view of shining water and brooding fells. Inside, the decor aims for strong colour contrasts rather than bland pastels, with apple green and aubergine the theme in the Tower Bar, so named as the bar itself was fashioned from materials salvaged from Blackpool Tower. The main dining room looks out over the gardens with their giant stone urns and immaculate topiary, and makes a relaxing setting for Conor Toomey's ingenious modern Lake District cooking. Evenings bring on the choice of a three-course carte with extras or a nine-stage taster menu full of vaulting ambition. Clean fresh flavours distinguish a starter of soused Cornish mackerel, with diverting accompaniments of vividly colourful cucumber ice cream, and a horseradish emulsion sauce textured with peanuts and sesame seeds. Main course could be a tribute to local pork from Huntsham Farm, dry-aged for 55 days, the belly moist and tender with crisped fat layer, together with a wonton of pulled meat with strips of mooli, and smoothly puréed quince. The viscous sherry jus adds a resonant bass-note to the whole dish. Fish might well receive the Mediterranean treatment, such as in a tranche of pearly cod poached in Arbequina olive oil, alongside a boudin of scallops and Jerusalem artichokes, while a vegetarian dish combines roast garlic gnocchi with parsley root purée, leek crisps and pickled shimejis. Innovation is maintained through to desserts such as frozen lemon custard with yuzu crémeux and fennel pollen ice cream, garnished with shards of crumbled meringue and an assertively flavoured powder of green tea.

Chef Conor Toomey **Owner** Storrs Hall **Seats** 82, Pr/dining room 40
Times 12.30-2/7-9.30, **Prices** Fixed L 2 course fr £19.50, Fixed D 3 course £52, Tasting menu £65 **Wines** 28 bottles over £30, 9 bottles under £30, 8 by glass
Parking 50 **Notes** Themed evenings, Afternooon tea, Sunday L £19.50-£26.50, Children welcome

Cavendish Hotel

◉◉ Modern British **V**

tel: 01246 582311 **Church Ln DE45 1SP**
email: info@cavendish-hotel.net **web:** www.cavendish-hotel.net
dir: *M1 junct 29 follow signs for Chesterfield. From Chesterfield take A619 to Bakewell, Chatsworth & Baslow*

Classic and offbeat modern dishes à la Chatsworth

If it begins to seem as though you can't move on the Chatsworth Estate without walking into another centre of culinary excellence – but who's complaining? The Cavendish is a stone-built hotel (once the Peacock Inn) acquired in 1830, its present incarnation recreated to a historic template by the Devonshires, using some of their own furnishings. The Gallery is a low-ceilinged dining room done in robin's-egg blue, or there's a Garden Room for more informal dining. A roll call of modern classics such as seared scallops with black pudding and pea purée, roast pigeon breast with couscous, and loin and haunch of venison with celeriac and beetroot in chocolate jus utilises much of the pedigree produce of the estate. But the beaten track is also profitably abandoned for the likes of tandoori monkfish cheek with pumpkin purée, butternut squash cake with wilted greens and spiced lentils, and pecan pie with blackberries and salted brown butter ice cream. If you're more of a stickler for tradition, the artisan English cheeses are of the gold standard, and there's apple crumble and vanilla ice cream too.

Chef Mike Thompson **Owner** Chatsworth Estates **Seats** 50, Pr/dining room 18 **Times** 12-2.30/6.30-10, Closed D 25 Dec **Prices** Fixed L 2 course £35, Fixed D 3 course £45 **Wines** 35 bottles over £30, 21 bottles under £30, 11 by glass **Parking** 40 **Notes** Kitchen table £85, Sunday L £27.50, Children welcome

Fischer's Baslow Hall

◉◉◉ *– see opposite*

The Devonshire Arms at Beeley

◉◉ Modern British 🍷 NOTABLE WINE LIST

tel: 01629 733259 **Devonshire Square DE4 2NR**
email: enquiries@devonshirebeeley.co.uk **web:** www.devonshirebeeley.co.uk
dir: *6m N of Matlock & 5m E of Bakewell, located off B6012*

Serious eating and drinking on the Chatsworth estate

A night or two in one of the guest rooms at The Devonshire would allow you to say you'd stayed at Chatsworth, sort of, as this stone-built village inn is situated in the heart of the estate. A little to the east of the River Derwent, it's a soothing and uplifting spot for a stay, the more so as its chef-proprietor takes as impeccably constructive an approach to the business of drinking – expect cask-conditioned ales and a terrific wine list – as to contemporary pub cooking. Dishes combine diverse ingredients successfully, as when salt-baked beetroot comes in a winter starter with lemon thyme ricotta, pomegranate, molasses and basil, while what might be a simple seafood chowder of hake and shrimps is enriched with buttermilk, and adorned with samphire, purple potato, sweetcorn and cornbread. Mains use local meats to worthwhile effect, perhaps for estate venison in a truffled-up bourguignon with wild mushrooms and pancetta. Mrs Hill's lemon tart is the owner's mum's recipe, while lime parfait with coconut foam and papaya is probably his own.

Chef Alan Hill, Joseph Aram **Owner** Duke of Devonshire **Seats** 60, Pr/dining room 14 **Times** 12-9.30, All-day dining **Prices** Starter £6.95-£13, Main £11.95-£17.50, Dessert £5-£7, Service optional **Wines** 14 by glass **Parking** 30 **Notes** Sunday L £13.95, Vegetarian available, Children welcome

The Samuel Fox Country Inn

◉◉ Modern British

tel: 01433 621562 **Stretfield Rd S33 9JT**
email: enquiries@samuelfox.co.uk **web:** www.samuelfox.co.uk
dir: *M1 junct 29, A617 towards Chesterfield, onto A619 towards A623 Chapel-en-le-Frith. B6049 for Bradwell, restaurant on left on leaving Bradwell*

Hearty Peak District sustenance with a modern touch

The stone-built Peak District inn near the Pennine Way and the Derbyshire spa towns is named after the Victorian steel magnate who invented the folding ribbed umbrella. It's been cannily made over with a fresh modern look and plenty of daylight from big windows washes through the open-plan white-walled restaurant and bar. Bradwell locals know the latter as a prime source of real ales, and the kitchen cooks a modernist version of pub food that's full of generous, hearty appeal. Breads of the day, variously flavoured with treacle or with Henderson's relish and onion, make an encouraging prelude to starters such as pig's trotter and ham with a slow-cooked egg and crispy potato in anchovy sauce, or a sturdy broth composed of kohlrabi with brown shrimps and sea lettuce. Seasonal game is a winner, perhaps roast breast and braised leg of pheasant with cabbage in Madeira, or there may be poached lemon sole with cavolo nero and Jerusalem artichokes. Finish with chocolate parfait, served with coffee sorbet and a burnt clementine.

Chef James Duckett **Owner** Johnson Inns **Seats** 40 **Times** 12-2.30/6-9, Closed 2-18 Jan, Mon-Tue, L Wed-Thu, D 25-26 Dec, 1 Jan **Prices** Starter £5-£9.50, Main £10-£20, Dessert £5-£10.50, Service optional **Wines** 3 bottles over £30, 33 bottles under £30, 19 by glass **Parking** 15 **Notes** Sunday L £5-£20, Vegetarian available, Children welcome

BEST WESTERN Lee Wood Hotel

◉ British

tel: 01298 23002 **The Park SK17 6TQ**
email: reservations@leewoodhotel.co.uk **web:** www.leewoodhotel.co.uk
dir: *M1 junct 24, A50 towards Ashbourne, A515 to Buxton. From Buxton town centre follow A5004 Long Hill to Whaley Bridge. Hotel approx 200mtrs beyond University of Derby campus*

Conservatory dining in the Peak District

Refurbished style exudes from every pore of Lee Wood, a Georgian grey stone manor house near the spa town of Buxton in the Peak District. Dining goes on in an expansive conservatory room with fronds of hanging foliage overhead and refreshing views of the grounds all about. The young service team runs the show with admirable efficiency, delivering modern brasserie cooking that scores some hits. A meal might run from roast chicken and wild mushroom terrine with soused vegetables, potato salad and beetroot mayonnaise, to a main course of pork with black pudding purée and sautéed potatoes in cider oil dressing. The assiette of desserts may well be the high point of the show.

Chef Simon Gould **Owner** Mr J C Millican **Seats** 150, Pr/dining room 10 **Times** 12-2/5.30-9.15 **Prices** Fixed L 2 course £17.50-£25, Fixed D 3 course £25-£30, Starter £5.95-£7, Main £15.95-£28.50, Dessert £6-£8.50, Service optional **Wines** 6 bottles over £30, 22 bottles under £30, 7 by glass **Parking** 40 **Notes** Pre-theatre menu, Sunday L £11.95, Vegetarian available, Children welcome

Fischer's Baslow Hall 🌸🌸🌸

BASLOW   Map 16 SK27

Modern European **V**

tel: 01246 583259 **Calver Rd DE45 1RR**
email: reservations@fischers-baslowhall.co.uk
web: www.fischers-baslowhall.co.uk
dir: From Baslow on A623 towards Calver. Hotel on right

Meticulously-sourced modern country-house cooking near Chatsworth

Max and Susan Fischer bought Baslow Hall in the heady days of the country-house movement in 1988. It's a fine Edwardian house, built in the style of a Stuart manor with protruding wings and mullioned windows, reached by a winding driveway lined with mature chestnut trees, not far from the Chatsworth Estate and the Derbyshire town of Bakewell, famed for its eponymous pudding. The gathered drapes and peeps of the garden make the dining room a picture of elegance, and the service team brings polished attentiveness to the whole experience. Rupert Rowley's supply lines begin in Baslow's own kitchen garden, but all the sourcing is meticulous, and ingredients are treated with the respect they deserve, so if it all feels and looks impeccably modern, the underlying principles are tried-and-true. That applies equally to a game starter of hay-baked partridge with Jerusalem artichokes and pearl barley, as to the Thai styling of satay-sauced langoustines with mango and coconut. Fish cookery is sensitive and accurate, pairing seared scallops with chargrilled baby gem on the tasting menu. Mains showcase pedigree meats such as classic saddle of hare in blood sauce with caramelised quince purée and chicory, or fore-rib and smoked cheek of local beef,

offset with the earthiness of wild mushrooms and the sweetness of caramelised onions. A trolley of fine British cheeses awaits the savoury toothed, but most will find it hard to skip the playfully inventive desserts such as a chocolate tree trunk with sap-green lime sorbet filling and mint 'moss', or the festive treat of Christmas pudding soufflé anointed with BenRiach Speyside Scotch and accompanied by Pedro Ximenez ice cream.

Chef Rupert Rowley **Owner** Mr & Mrs M Fischer **Seats** 55, Pr/dining room 38 **Times** 12-1.30/7-8.30, Closed 25-26 & 31 Dec **Prices** Fixed L 2 course fr £20.15, Fixed D 3 course fr £72, Tasting menu fr £80, Starter £16-£18, Main £25-£30, Dessert £8.50-£11, Service optional **Wines** 110 bottles over £30, 20 bottles under £30, 6 by glass **Parking** 20 **Notes** Taste of Britain L £60/£100, wknd L 2/3 course £32/£38, Sunday L, Children 5/8yrs+ L/D

Casa Hotel

◉◉ Modern European

tel: 01246 245990 & 245999 **Lockoford Ln S41 7JB**
email: cocina@casahotels.co.uk **web:** www.casahotels.co.uk
dir: *M1 junct 29 to A617 Chesterfield/A61 Sheffield, 1st exit at rdbt, hotel on left*

Celebrate all things Spanish in a lopsided 'pomo' hotel

Casa gives Chesterfield a chunk of architectural modernity – love it or loathe it – with a Spanish theme. The Cocina restaurant is entirely in keeping, a large über-chic space with pale wood, white chairs and floor-to-ceiling windows. The menu is as likely to appeal to grazers as to trenchermen, with a sizeable selection of salads and tapas running from a board of Spanish charcuterie to a croquette of hake, cheese and chives with tartare dressing. Elsewhere, the menu is a tranche of bright, modern ideas. Among successful starters are seared scallops with black pudding purée, truffle butter and apple jelly and crisps, and carpaccio with horseradish cream, red pepper coulis, watercress and pork crackling. The Josper grill comes into its own for steaks with a choice of sauces, and there might be paella, or venison hotpot with Savoy cabbage, swede purée and roasting juices. The early-evening menu is a snip, and puddings include retro rice pudding with home-made blueberry jam.

Chef Andrew Wilson **Owner** Steve Perez **Seats** 100, Pr/dining room 200 **Times** 12-4/6-10, Closed L Mon-Sat **Prices** Prices not confirmed, Service optional **Wines** 31 bottles over £30, 34 bottles under £30, 12 by glass **Parking** 200 **Notes** Early bird menu 6-7pm Mon-Fri, 5.30-6.30pm Sat, Sunday L, Vegetarian available, Children welcome

Peak Edge Hotel at the Red Lion

◉◉ Modern British V

tel: 01246 566142 **Darley Rd, Stone Edge S45 0LW**
email: sleep@peakedgehotel.co.uk **web:** www.peakedgehotel.co.uk
dir: *M1 junct 29, A617 to Chesterfield. At rdbt take 1st exit onto A61, at next rdbt 2nd exit onto Whitecotes Ln, continue onto Matlock Rd (A632) then Darley Rd (B5057)*

Inventive cooking in a Georgian inn next to a brand-new hotel

A new-build stone edifice on the border of the Peak District National Park, the family-owned hotel is handy for the historic houses of Chatsworth and Haddon Hall, as well as the old Derbyshire market towns. Not all is pristine, box-fresh modernity, though, for next door to the new building is the Red Lion, a Georgian coaching inn that is the venue for the hotel's bar and bistro. With the markets and moors to source from, not to mention salad vegetables from its own back garden, there is plenty for the kitchen to go at, and the results are offered in the form of inventive contemporary British dishes. First up might be an assemblage of baked oats, slow-cooked parsnip, egg yolk, pink grapefruit and lettuce, before main courses perform spins on bubble-and-squeak, fillet steak on the bone with horseradish in oxtail bourguignon, and sea bass with pak choi, radishes and oysters. It's all designed to

stimulate the imagination as well as the taste buds, and concludes in like manner with toasted coconut cream, mango, basil sorbet and red chilli, or reimagined Bakewell tart with almond milk ice cream and raspberry jelly.

Chef Daniel Laycock **Owner** Damian & Jo Dugdale **Seats** 80 **Times** 12-9.30, All-day dining **Prices** Prices not confirmed, Service optional **Wines** 16 bottles over £30, 27 bottles under £30, 9 by glass **Notes** Afternoon tea, Sunday L, Children welcome

Hotel Van Dyk

◉ Modern British V

tel: 01246 810219 **Worksop Rd S43 4TD**
email: info@hotelvandyk.co.uk **web:** www.hotelvandyk.co.uk
dir: *M1 junct 30, towards Worksop, at rdbt 1st exit, next rdbt straight over. Through lights, hotel 100yds on right*

Sugar-white hotel with appealing modern British cooking

The white-fronted Van Dyk stands on the A619 not far from Chesterfield. Amid the surrounding ruggedness, it looks a little like a sugar-frosting confection, which only adds to its idiosyncratic character. Inside, it's geared up for weddings and business, and the public rooms are all contemporary elegance. That said, there's a hint of old-school formality about the Bowden dining room, with swagged curtains, trio of chandeliers, and a baby grand piano as white as the building itself. Modern northern cooking is the bill of fare, with dishes founded on sound culinary logic. Open with pancetta-wrapped figs stuffed with feta in honey and thyme glaze, as a prelude to roast monkfish in shellfish bisque with saffron mash and parsnip crisps, or chicken and rabbit ballotine with marinated peach and baby carrots. A full vegetarian menu includes the likes of butternut squash stuffed with chestnuts and cranberries in port jus.

Chef Ben Richardson **Owner** Gail & Peter Eyre **Seats** 89, Pr/dining room 14 **Times** 12-9.30, All-day dining **Prices** Starter £4.99-£8.99, Main £10.99-£24.99, Dessert £5.99-£7.49, Service optional **Wines** 7 bottles over £30, 28 bottles under £30, 13 by glass **Parking** 120 **Notes** Sun D last orders 7.30pm, Sunday L £10.99-£14.99, Children welcome

The Black Cow

◉ Modern British

tel: 01332 824297 **The Green, Dalbury Lees DE6 5BE**
email: enquiries@theblackcow.co.uk **web:** www.theblackcow.co.uk
dir: *From Derby A52 signed Ashbourne, Kirk Langley; turn into Church Lane, then Long Lane, follow signs to Dalbury Lees*

Real ales and pub favourites opposite the village green

Don't be fooled by the name: The Black Cow is a bright white beast bedecked in pink and purple flower baskets, lording it over the village green in the south Derbyshire village of Dalbury Lees. Everything inside looks the modernised country pub part, with a big stone fireplace, framed pictures on emulsion-coated walls, and bookshelf-effect wallpaper in the dining area. International pub favourites form the backbone of the kitchen's output, with reliable satisfaction to be had from Thai-style salmon fishcakes and chilli dip, or chicken Caesar, for beginners. Follow on with ale-battered cod with mushy peas, or velvety-tender braised lamb shank with red onion marmalade and creamy mash in rosemary and garlic jus. Head for sticky toffee or apple and blueberry crumble for dessert, while a plethora of real ales from breweries such as Jennings, Dancing Duck and Mr Grundy add class to the drinking options.

Chef Jazwant Singh **Owner** Mark & Sean Goodwin **Seats** 30, Pr/dining room 25 **Times** 12-2/6-9 **Prices** Prices not confirmed, Service optional **Wines** 1 bottle over £30, 17 bottles under £30, 8 by glass **Parking** 12, On street **Notes** Sunday L, Vegetarian available, Children welcome

DARLEY ABBEY
Map 11 SK33

Darleys Restaurant
@@ Modern British V

tel: 01332 364987 **Haslams Ln DE22 1DZ**
email: info@darleys.com **web:** www.darleys.com
dir: A6 N from Derby (Duffield road). Right in 1m into Mileash Ln, to Old Lane, right, over bridge. Restaurant on right

Modern British cooking by the water's edge

A table on the terrace is a treat in good weather, but don't make Darleys a fair-weather friend. It looks okay on the inside, too, you see, with stylish contemporary tones of brown and cream, white linen on the tables and a grown-up feel all round. This converted silk mill, right by the River Derwent, is the setting for some bright, modern cooking, with a kitchen team making good use of regional produce. Nori-wrapped Loch Duart salmon is a thoroughly contemporary way to start a meal, with crispy squid, ginger and soy, while another first course has fun with goats' cheese and pineapple. Main course fillet of Derbyshire beef with layers of potato and mushrooms and a shallot purée shows respect for classical ways. Another main course combines sustainable Icelandic cod with smoked bacon polenta and clam sauce, and, when it comes to dessert, there's plenty of creativity on show in a mini lemon cake with Swiss meringue and red berry lollipop parfait.

Chef Jonathan Hobson, Mark Hadfield **Owner** Jonathan & Kathryn Hobson **Seats** 70
Times 12-2/7-9.30, Closed BHs, 1st 2 wks Jan, D Sun **Prices** Fixed L 2 course fr
£19.95, Tasting menu fr £50, Starter £7.20-£9.50, Main £19.95-£24.50, Dessert
£7.95-£9.15, Service optional **Wines** 33 bottles over £30, 64 bottles under £30, 18
by glass **Parking** 9 **Notes** Sunday L fr £25, Children welcome

DERBY
Map 11 SK33

Masa Restaurant
@ Modern European

tel: 01332 203345 **The Old Chapel, Brook St DE1 3PF**
email: enquiries@masarestaurantwinebar.com
dir: 8m from M1 junct 25. Brook St off inner ring road near BBC Radio Derby

Modern brasserie dishes in a converted chapel

The 200-year-old building that houses Masa used to be a chapel, and if that isn't entirely obvious from the outside, it certainly becomes apparent when you cross the threshold and see the voluminous galleried space within. The stylish contemporary restaurant is up in the gallery, with a lounge bar occupying the ground floor, and the lawned front garden and rear patio available for outdoor imbibing. The restaurant deals in brasserie-style dishes via a sensibly concise carte and terrific value set menu (lunchtime and mid-week evenings). Start with an attractively presented ham hock and guinea fowl ballotine, served with red onion marmalade and pickled girolles, and move on to pan-fried sea bass sitting on tagliatelle, or trio

of pork in the fruity company of apple compôte, blackberries and glazed pear. Finish with lemon and lime crème brûlée or date sponge with tonka bean ice cream.

Times 12-2/6-9, Closed Mon-Tue

FROGGATT
Map 16 SK27

The Chequers Inn
@ Modern British

tel: 01433 630231 **S32 3ZJ**
email: info@chequers-froggatt.com **web:** www.chequers-froggatt.com
dir: On A625 between Sheffield & Bakewell, 0.75m from Calver

Rustic Peak District inn with hearty modern dishes

The Tindalls' country inn is a model of Peak District charm, fashioned as it is from a row of Georgian cottages in the Hope Valley. Equipped inside with farmhouse furniture, including old oak settles, and hung with a multitude of framed pictures, it's the kind of place where you can buy a jar of home-made chutney or marmalade to see you on your way. The menu steers a deft course between stalwart dishes to support the inn trade and more modern offerings that nonetheless retain the emphasis on hearty sustenance. Open with grilled mackerel in fennel tea with a salad of mandarin and watercress, ahead of braised pork belly accompanied by a scallop, squid and chorizo in black cider sauce, or monkfish parcelled in Parma ham, with crab arancini and winter roots in veal jus. The giddy pace is sustained into desserts such as chocolate delice with cherry textures and creamed tonka bean cannelloni.

Chef Carl Riley **Owner** Jonathan & Joanne Tindall **Seats** 90
Times 12-2.30/6-9.30, Closed 25 Dec **Prices** Starter £7.50-£8.50, Main £12.95-£18.95, Dessert £5.95-£6.50, Service optional **Wines** 3 bottles over £30, 34 bottles under £30, 10 by glass **Parking** 50 **Notes** Sunday L £13.95, Vegetarian available, Children welcome

GRINDLEFORD
Map 16 SK27

The Maynard
@@ Modern British

tel: 01433 630321 **Main Rd S32 2HE**
email: info@themaynard.co.uk **web:** www.themaynard.co.uk
dir: M1/A619 into Chesterfield, onto Baslow, A623 to Calver right into Grindleford

Anglo-French magic à la Peak District

If Grindleford sounds like the made-up location of a Miss Marple mystery, The Maynard suits it to perfection. Its stone-built majesty rises out of the Derwent Valley as a manifestation of Peak boutique, a tranquil country mansion in Derbyshire's national park. A terrace for catching the sunset makes a good starting place for dinner, which takes place in a relaxing contemporary room done in slate-grey and hung with original artworks. Appealingly mixing modern British thinking with classical French influence, the dishes are exquisitely presented and work with the grain of their fine components rather than disguising them with technical trickery. Lightly sautéed breast of wood-pigeon opens the show, served with braised baby leeks and puréed butter beans in port reduction. This is followed by accurately timed sea bass dressed in lemon, with Jersey Royals and a summer salad of peas and rocket, or 'chicken cooked two ways', confit leg and poached and roasted breast (so three ways, really), with lemon spinach and colcannon in tarragon sauce. Finish with a multi-faceted coconut tasting, its chocolate mousse and sphere of sponge cake the highlights.

Chef Mark Vernon **Owner** Jane Hitchman **Seats** 50, Pr/dining room 140
Times 12-2/7-9, Closed L Sat **Prices** Prices not confirmed, Service optional **Wines** 7 by glass **Parking** 60 **Notes** Sunday L, Vegetarian available, Children welcome

The Mill Wheel

◎ Modern British

tel: 01283 550335 **Ticknall Rd DE11 7AS**
email: info@themillwheel.co.uk **web:** www.themillwheel.co.uk
dir: *M42 junct 2, A511 to Woodville, left onto A514 towards Derby to Hartshorne*

Unpretentious cooking in a 17th-century mill

The 24-foot water wheel is still in place to provide a connection to the 17th-century building's past life – in fact, the bar has been designed around it. Today's country inn has married period details with a contemporary finish to offer stylish spaces to suit your mood – leather sofas, patio garden or beamed restaurant. The menu offers up light lunches and baguettes during the day (the latter served until early evening), plus a main menu at lunch and dinner that keeps things relatively simple. Start with chicken liver parfait flavoured with thyme, or creamy garlic mushrooms on bruschetta, followed by braised beef bourguignon with horseradish mash or pot-roasted pheasant breast. Steaks are cooked on the grill and served with classic accompaniments, with a traditional burger and pie of the day in support. Finish with lime and ginger cheesecake.

Chef Adrian Vince **Owner** Colin & Jackie Brown **Seats** 52 **Times** 12-2.15/6-9.15 **Prices** Fixed L 2 course £6.50, Starter £3.95-£6.50, Main £8.95-£19.95, Dessert £3.95-£4.95, Service optional **Wines** 1 bottle over £30, 15 bottles under £30, 9 by glass **Parking** 50 **Notes** Champagne breakfast 4 course £19.95, Sunday L fr £9.95, Vegetarian available, Children welcome

George Hotel

◎◎ Modern British V

tel: 01433 650436 **Main Rd S32 1BB**
email: info@george-hotel.net **web:** www.george-hotel.net
dir: *In village centre on junction of A625/B6001*

Novel ideas from a hard-working Peak District kitchen

The 500-year-old stone-built hotel looks like a little castle, with its turreted frontage and mullioned windows. Its interiors have been carefully planned to do nothing to obscure the impression of dignified venerability, the hefty stones of the walls offset by wooden floors and simple furniture in the smartly attired dining room. The hard-working kitchen, makes many of the foundation elements of the menu in-house, including breads, pasta and preserves. Most of the rest is sourced from trusted Peak District suppliers, perhaps for a starter of potted beef with the chef's own piccalilli and potato crisps, or there might be soused mackerel, accompanied by the sharp-edged flavours of beetroot, horseradish and a jelly of Granny Smiths. For main, it could be wild boar with blackberries, served with its own sausage and wild mushroom rösti, or sea bream and sweet potato with leeks two ways (caramelised purée and steamed baby ones). Dessert ideas are both novel and enticing, for example rice pudding soufflé with orange and ginger jam, honeycomb, and the entertaining contradiction of a hot toddy sorbet.

Chef Helen Prince **Owner** Eric Marsh **Seats** 45, Pr/dining room 70 **Times** 12-2.30/6.30-9, Closed D 25 Dec **Prices** Fixed L 2 course £15.85-£29.65, Fixed D 3 course £19.30-£36.95 **Wines** 13 bottles over £30, 26 bottles under £30, 11 by glass **Parking** 45 **Notes** Early bird menu Mon-Fri 6.30-7.30pm, Sunday L £20-£25, Children welcome

The Plough Inn

◎ Modern British

tel: 01433 650319 **Leadmill Bridge S32 1BA**
email: sales@theploughinn-hathersage.co.uk **web:** www.theploughinn-hathersage.co.uk
dir: *1m SE of Hathersage on B6001. Over bridge, 150yds beyond at Leadmill*

Sustaining modern dishes in a Tudor riverside inn

In a thoroughly restorative setting, the stone-built 16th-century Plough sits in nine acres of grounds that slope gently down to the River Derwent. There's a warm welcome whatever the season, whether out in the courtyard by the babbling brook or before the log fire in winter, and the dining room is always turned out in best bib and tucker. The same might be said of the cooking, which mixes modern global and homely local to generate its appeal. A starter might be smoked bacon velouté with a black pudding toastie, or mackerel with fennel salad dressed in orange and pomegranate. Follow with sustaining main courses like beef and Guinness pie with honey-roast parsnips and mash, or monkfish with a lobster beignet and wild rice in shellfish cream. Wild mushroom and artichoke pizzetta in tomato and olive fondue is a possible vegetarian option. Given the location, a faithful version of classic Bakewell pudding is only to be expected.

Chef Robert Navarro **Owner** Robert & Cynthia Emery **Seats** 40, Pr/dining room 24 **Times** 11.30-9.30, All-day dining, Closed 25 Dec **Prices** Fixed L 2 course £15-£19, Starter £6-£10, Main £14-£25, Dessert £6-£7, Service optional **Wines** 22 bottles over £30, 23 bottles under £30, 20 by glass **Parking** 40 **Notes** Sunday L £14-£24, Vegetarian available, Children welcome

Santo's Higham Farm Hotel

◎ Modern International

tel: 01773 833812 **Main Rd DE55 6EH**
email: reception@santoshighamfarm.co.uk **web:** www.santoshighamfarm.co.uk
dir: *M1 junct 28, A38 towards Derby, then A61 to Higham, left onto B6013*

Italian-influenced cooking in a Derbyshire farmstead hotel

Santo Cusimano runs a highly individual rural retreat. With the rolling Amber Valley all about, it's in a prime slice of Derbyshire walking country, and has been fashioned from an old farmstead. The dining room is designed to soothe the senses, with an air of soft-focus pastel charm, comfortable bucket chairs and smart table settings. Menus mobilise plenty of pedigree local produce, as well as thoroughbred items like steamed Shetland mussels in garlic cream. Given the owner's provenance, Italian influences are never distant, perhaps for parmesan risotto that comes with salt-baked kohlrabi and truffled celeriac purée, or mains such as leg of corn-fed chicken stuffed with wild mushrooms and spinach, alongside a stew of butter beans and pancetta in red wine sauce. The chargrilled local beef has been aged on the bone for 28 days. For dessert, there's pannacotta and candied pistachios, plus more offbeat proposals, such as sticky ginger cake with pineapple and passionfruit salsa and Pina Colada ice cream.

Chef Cameron Smith Owner Santo Cusimano Seats 50, Pr/dining room 34
Times 12-3/7-9.30, Closed BHs, L Mon-Sat, D Sun Prices Starter £5-£7.50, Main
£14.50-£24.50, Dessert £5-£6.50 Wines 13 bottles over £30, 37 bottles under £30,
6 by glass Parking 100 Notes Sunday L £9.95-£15.95, Vegetarian available,
Children welcome

HOPE
Map 16 SK18

Losehill House Hotel & Spa
◎◎ Modern British V

tel: 01433 621219 Lose Hill Ln, Edale Rd S33 6AF
email: info@losehillhouse.co.uk web: www.losehillhouse.co.uk
dir: A6187 into Hope. Take turn opposite church into Edale Rd. 1m, left & follow signs
to hotel

Glorious Peak District views and interesting contemporary cooking

Losehill House, built in 1914 in the Arts and Crafts style, is in a secluded spot in
the Peak District National Park and has stunning views, also appreciated from the
Orangery Restaurant, a light-filled, comfortable room with a contemporary look. The
kitchen rounds up Peak District produce and uses it to good effect in its modern,
creative style, adding novel and intriguing elements to many dishes. Rolled lamb
leg, for instance, is accompanied by leek ash, camomile gel and turnips, and fillet
of mackerel by carrot ketchup, carrot purée and sultanas – and those are just
starters. Confident techniques and good judgement result in appreciated main
courses of local venison loin with pommes Anna, beetroot, leeks and cocoa nib
crumb, and grilled lemon sole on the bone with a simple lemon sauce, buttered
spinach and turnips. Invention marks out desserts: consider chocolate pudding
with white chocolate mousse, blackcurrant sorbet and dark chocolate soil, or
orange cheesecake with a raspberry bubble, orange jelly and raspberry sorbet.

Chef Darren Goodwin Owner Paul & Kathryn Roden Seats 50, Pr/dining room 30
Times 12-2.30/6.30-9 Prices Fixed L 3 course £22-£24, Fixed D 3 course £39.50,
Tasting menu £49.50, Service optional Wines 36 bottles over £30, 12 bottles under
£30, 6 by glass Parking 25 Notes Taste of Losehill 7 course, Sunday L £27.50,
Children welcome

MATLOCK
Map 16 SK35

Stones Restaurant
◎◎ Modern British V

tel: 01629 56061 1c Dale Rd DE4 3LT
email: info@stones-restaurant.co.uk
dir: Phone for directions

Modern Mediterranean-influenced dining with a riverside terrace

Stones may be an intimate basement venue, but it has the best of both worlds on
fine days thanks to a tiled sun terrace perched above the River Derwent. Fully
refurbished after a fire, there's a new conservatory to go with a sophisticated
brasserie-style decor that works a mix of subtle earthy tones, with simple art,
wooden floors, and seats upholstered with designer fabric to match a
Mediterranean-inflected menu of contemporary modern British dishes. Well-judged
combinations get under way with a deliciously-scented wild mushroom and spring
onion risotto with parmesan and truffle oil. The fish of the day is worth a punt at
main course stage, particularly when it is a fine slab of salmon matched with lemon
crushed potatoes, creamed leeks and caper velouté, or there might be roasted pork
fillet with butternut squash purée, fondant potato, apple gel and crisp pancetta.
Dessert is a simple but effective play of well-thought-through textures and tastes
involving lemon macaroon, roasted pineapple and raspberry mascarpone.

Chef Kevin Stone Owner Kevin Stone, Jade Himsworth, Katie Temple Seats 50, Pr/
dining room 16 Times 12-2/6.30-9, Closed 26 Dec, 1 Jan, Sun (some), Mon, L Tue
Prices Fixed L 2 course £18-£20, Fixed D 3 course £32-£41.50, Tasting menu
£48.50, Service optional Wines 22 bottles over £30, 13 bottles under £30, 9 by glass
Parking Matlock train station Notes Sunday L £22-£25, Children welcome

MELBOURNE
Map 11 SK32

The Bay Tree
◎◎ Modern British

tel: 01332 863358 4 Potter St DE73 8HW
email: enquiries@baytreerestaurant.com
dir: From M1(N) junct 23A or junct 24 (S) take A453 to Isley Walton, turn right & follow
signs to Melbourne town centre

Riotously colourful dishes in a dashing room

The stone façade of what was once a bunch of shops on a hill prepare you for the
different levels of the place inside, but not quite for the dashing blue and lilac
decorative job, with tables in unclothed limed ash and bundles of artificial flora.
A similar cat-and-mouse game is played by the menus, which adopt the modern
technique of making dishes sound quite straightforward, making their arrival
all the more astonishing. Beetroot salad is served carpaccio-style, with
accompaniments of asparagus, walnuts, apple and Roquefort tossed in balsamic
vinaigrette, a riot of colour. Even chicken liver parfait is vividly offset by bright red
onion confit. Artichoke hearts with tomato centres are the flanking attendants to a
piece of artichoke-crusted baked sea bass with peas, while the pink lamb rack is
all adazzle with tomato fondue and black olive jus. Chocolate ganache tart set with
raspberries has a tart-matching coulis and whipped cream to hold the dish
together, while cardamom rice pudding comes with Armagnac prunes.

Chef Rex Howell Owner R W Howell Seats 60 Times 10.30-3/6.30-10.30, Closed 25 &
31 Dec, BHs, Mon-Tue, D Sun Prices Fixed L 2 course £22.50-£27.50, Fixed D 3
course £27.50 Wines 6 by glass Parking On street Notes Champagne breakfast £22
Wed-Sat, Sunday L £24.50, Vegetarian available, Children welcome

MORLEY
Map 11 SK34

The Morley Hayes Hotel
◎◎ Modern British

tel: 01332 780480 Main Rd DE7 6DG
email: enquiries@morleyhayes.com web: www.morleyhayes.com
dir: 4m N of Derby on A608

Appealingly eclectic cooking on a converted farm estate

Morley Hayes near Derby has been a farm estate and an orphanage in its time, but
has been run as a dynamic hotel since the 1980s, and with its golf complex,
conference facilities and wedding venue, it has most bases covered. The Dovecote,
its principal dining room, is to be found on the raftered first floor of a separate
former farm building, overlooking the golf course and surrounding countryside. The
kitchen keeps abreast of contemporary trends, offering a roster of unpretentious
modern dishes, with influences from home and around the globe adding vibrancy
and colour. Crispy pork terrine with black pudding and rhubarb purée may whet the
appetite for roast loin of local lamb given a Moroccan spin with lamb kofta,
couscous and smoked aubergine, or you might head east for five spice-roasted duck
with sweet potato purée, pak choi, carrots and soy sauce dressing. Finish with
classic apple tart Tatin with clotted cream ice cream, or ginger beer rum baba with
rhubarb compôte and vanilla cream.

Chef Nigel Stuart Owner Robert & Andrew Allsop, Morley Hayes Leisure Ltd
Seats 100, Pr/dining room 24 Times 12-2/7-9.30, Closed 27 Dec, 1 Jan, L Sat, Mon
Prices Fixed L 2 course fr £17.95, Fixed D 3 course £21.95, Starter £7.50-£9.50,
Main £16.75-£20.50, Dessert £6.95-£8.95, Service optional Wines 22 bottles over
£30, 30 bottles under £30, 12 by glass Parking 250 Notes Champagne breakfast
£22.95, Sunday L £26.45, Vegetarian available, Children welcome

ROWSLEY
Map 16 SK26

The Peacock at Rowsley
◎◎◎ – see page 136 and advert on page 137

The Peacock at Rowsley ❀❀❀

ROWSLEY   Map 16 SK26

Modern British V

tel: 01629 733518 **Bakewell Rd DE4 2EB**
email: reception@thepeacockatrowsley.com
web: www.thepeacockatrowsley.com
dir: A6, 3m before Bakewell, 6m from Matlock towards Bakewell

Winning modern combinations, Derbyshire-style

There is scarcely any aspect of The Peacock that doesn't give evidence of the drive to create an utterly classy all-round operation. It's a sturdy-looking 17th-century mansion built of Derbyshire stone in just the right dimensions to make for a country-house hotel on the human scale. The interiors by India Mahdavi are deeply comfortable, from the relaxing lounge to a stone-walled bar hung with oil paintings that makes a very cosy retreat on a winter night – the more so for its generous range of stock, including a run of grappas. The main dining room looks out on the well-tended gardens, and makes a restful setting for Dan Smith's modern British cooking. Having done a stint with Tom Aikens in London, Smith has absorbed a sound understanding of combinational technique, now brought to bear on the northern larder, and the results are striking. A texturally lively salad of both types of artichoke, hazelnuts and crisp smoked quail's eggs in a cold herb dressing offers a perfectly considered array of flavours, while unabashed regional notes are sounded in a starter serving of grouse breast with a sausage roll, beetroot ketchup and fried sprout leaves. Winning combinations distinguish main dishes such as lemon sole with snails on a root veg and bacon ragout with parsley gnocchi in red wine, a dish full of forthright, pitch-perfect

seasoning, or there may be venison loin with smoked mash, cavolo nero, walnuts and elderberries in a sauce of lapsang souchong. Top-gear chocolate from Cluizel goes into a gâteau to beat the band, served with breakfast cereal sorbet, peanuts and honeycomb, or consider a reworking of pain perdu, served with Barkham Blue cheese and a fig poached in red wine.

Chef Daniel Smith **Owner** Rutland Hotels **Seats** 40, Pr/dining room 20 **Times** 12-2/7-9, Closed D 24-26 Dec **Prices** Prices not confirmed, Service optional **Wines** 44 bottles over £30, 11 bottles under £30, 23 by glass **Parking** 25 **Notes** Sunday L, Children 10 yrs+

The Peacock at Rowsley

The Peacock at Rowsley is cosy, chic boutique hotel, originally a manor house in the heart of the Peak District National Park and very close to Haddon Hall and Chatsworth House. Perfect for a countryside break with comfortable bedrooms including four posters and one of the best hotel suites in the region. Our award winning restaurant serves a delicious fine dining menu, crafted by Head Chef Dan Smith. Dan worked with notable chefs such as Tom Aikens before joining *The Peacock* seven years ago. The atmospheric bar with open fire is a very convivial place to meet for lunch, dinner or just for a drink – with its own menu of freshly cooked local food. Sunday lunch at *The Peacock* is a local favourite. The hotel is famed for its excellent fly fishing on the Derbyshire Wye and river Derwent.

The Peacock at Rowsley, Derbyshire DE4 2EB • **Tel:** 01629 733518 • **Fax:** 01629 732671
Website: www.thepeacockatrowsley.com • **Email:** reception@thepeacockatrowsley.com

DEVON

AXMINSTER
Map 4 SY29

Fairwater Head Hotel

Modern British

tel: 01297 678349 **Hawkchurch EX13 5TX**
email: info@fairwaterheadhotel.co.uk **web:** www.fairwaterheadhotel.co.uk
dir: *A358 into Broom Lane at Tytherleigh, follow signs to Hawkchurch & hotel*

Modern classic dishes in a rural Devon retreat

An appealing grey stone building covered in climbing foliage, Fairwater Head enjoys panoramic views over the Axe Valley, only five miles from the old carpet town of Axminster. Three acres of manicured lawns and attractive interiors contribute to the restful rural ambience, and the Greenfields dining room boasts smart table linen and friendly, informal service. Devon produce of flawless pedigree flows forth from the kitchen, worked into an extensive choice of modern classic dishes with a refreshing absence of extraneous lily-gilding. Expect wild mushroom risotto with rocket and parmesan, home-cured gravad lax, or chicken liver parfait with onion marmalade in port reduction to start, followed up by sea bass with crushed new potatoes in chive velouté, or lamb rump with dauphinoise and ratatouille. Finish with textbook lemon tart in raspberry coulis with lime sorbet, or crème brûlée wittily served in a cup and saucer. West Country cheeses with home-made chutney are welcome temptations too.

Chef Tony Golder **Owner** Adam & Carrie Southwell **Seats** 60, Pr/dining room 18 **Times** 12-2/7-9, Closed Jan, L Mon-Tue, Thu-Fri **Prices** Tasting menu fr £39.50, Starter £4.75-£6.50, Main £10.95-£19.45, Dessert £6-£8, Service optional **Wines** 6 bottles over £30, 62 bottles under £30, 12 by glass **Parking** 40 **Notes** Sunday L fr £10.95, Vegetarian available, Children welcome

BAMPTON
Map 3 SS92

The Swan

Modern, Traditional British **NEW**

tel: 01398 332248 **Station Rd EX16 9NG**
email: info@theswan.co **web:** www.theswan.co
dir: *Please phone for directions*

Stylish pub with contemporary grub

The Swan is a proper pub where locals prop up the bar and real ales, wine and food are all given the attention they deserve. But it's a smart sort of place, too, where the original features of the 15th-century building have been maintained and an

opened-up contemporary finish has been brought into play. Warm colours, lots of solid oak, a few sofas, it's the kind of place it's very easy to while away a few hours in. Food is very much part of the picture and it is good local stuff, cooked simply and delivered in a fashionable rustic style. Potted ham hock with piccalilli and soda bread is just-so, a classic combination to warm the cockles, or go for River Exe mussels in a Thai-style coconut sauce. Among main courses slow-cooked sticky pork belly and beer-battered fish and chips show the way, and there are 28-day-aged steaks (rib-eye maybe) and modish beef and chilli burger.

The Swan

Chef Paul Berry **Owner** Paul & Donna Berry **Seats** 60, Pr/dining room 20 **Times** 12-2/6-9.30, Closed 25 Dec **Prices** Starter £4.50-£8, Main £10.95-£16.95, Dessert £5.50-£7.50, Service optional **Wines** 10 bottles over £30, 30 bottles under £30, 40 by glass **Parking** Opposite, 100 spaces **Notes** Sunday L £9.50-£11.50, Vegetarian available, Children welcome

BEESANDS
Map 3 SX84

The Cricket Inn

Modern British

tel: 01548 580215 **TQ7 2EN**
email: enquiries@thecricketinn.com **web:** www.thecricketinn.com
dir: *From Kingsbridge follow A379 towards Dartmouth, at Stokenham mini-rdbt turn right for Beesands*

Seafood specialities at historic Inn

Smack on the seafront overlooking the shingle beach, with stunning views across Start Bay, The Cricket enjoys an unrivalled location. It retains every last ounce of its identity as a former fisherman's pub, with maritime memorabilia in the bar, as well as photographs of the village in olden times, but the dining area is done in light bright white in the Maryland manner, with a ship's wheel among the decorative touches. Blackboard menus advertise what has been freshly drawn from the bay, backed up by stalwarts such as scallops and chorizo on saffron risotto, and whole lobsters done thermidor. A bowl of creamy crab soup is smooth and satisfying, and the unimpeachable freshness of the shellfish is celebrated in simple mains such as king prawn linguine with confit tomatoes, fennel, chilli, garlic and ginger. Baked Alaska is all the rage right now, and comes with orange meringue and mango.

Chef Scott Heath **Owner** Nigel & Rachel Heath **Seats** 65, Pr/dining room 40 **Times** 12-2.30/6-8.30, Closed 25 Dec **Prices** Starter £5.50-£9, Main £11-£25, Dessert £4.50-£6, Service optional **Wines** 2 bottles over £30, 26 bottles under £30, 12 by glass **Parking** 30 **Notes** Sunday L £11-£18, Vegetarian available, Children welcome

BIGBURY-ON-SEA
Map 3 SX64

The Oyster Shack
◉ Seafood **NEW**

tel: 01548 810876 & 810934 **Stakes Hill TQ7 4BE**
email: bigbury@oystershack.co.uk
dir: A379 Modbury to Kingsbridge road, B3392 to Bigbury, left at St Anns Chapel, signed to Oyster Shack 1m on left

Waterside spot for simple seafood dining

The name itself suggests the casual nature of the place and the warm greeting ensures everything gets off on the right foot. Eating super-fresh seafood is the name of the game, and it's all the better if you sit outside under the sail-like awning. In fact, well-considered protection and a relatively benign micro-climate make it possible to eat outdoors for a large chunk of the year, but all is well inside, too, with a relaxed vibe and fishermen's theme. Giant blackboards reveal what's on offer from crabs and lobsters (by weight), to fishy plates such as whole roasted gurnard with anchovy butter. Start with oysters a host of ways (grilled with blue cheese and smoked bacon, say), and follow with a fruits de mer or a staggeringly good fillet of hake with roasted pepper, chorizo and mussels. Finish with cherry and chocolate brownie, and drink beer, cider or something from the short (and mostly white) wine list.

Chef Andy Richardson **Owner** Chris Yandell **Seats** 60 **Times** 12-3/6-9, Closed 25 Dec, 2-31 Jan, D Sun (Nov-24 Mar) **Prices** Fixed L 2 course £12, Fixed D 3 course £14, Starter £6.50-£9.50, Main £12.95-£21.50, Dessert £6-£6.75, Service optional **Wines** 4 bottles over £30, 18 bottles under £30, 5 by glass **Parking** 25 **Notes** All day dining 7 days/wk in summer, Sunday L, Vegetarian available, Children welcome

BRIXHAM
Map 3 SX95

Quayside Hotel
◉ Modern British

tel: 01803 855751 **41-49 King St TQ5 9TJ**
email: reservations@quayside.co.uk **web:** www.quaysidehotel.co.uk
dir: From Exeter take A380 towards Torquay, then A3022 to Brixham

The freshest seafood by the harbour

A good deal of the fish eaten in the best restaurants in the country is landed at Brixham, but you don't have to head out of the town to sample what comes out of the chilly local waters. The restaurant at the Quayside Hotel majors in seafood and what reaches the menu depends on what has been caught – skate, black bream, pollock, turbot and more, it's a piscine lottery. Judging by a beautiful piece of cod, cooked just right (baked with herb crust and served with tomato salsa), the kitchen knows how to treat this prime product with respect. There are non-seafood options as well, such as minestrone soup, grilled sirloin steak, veggie risotto and banoffee iced parfait for dessert, but there's no bigger draw than the plateau de fruits de mer. It all takes place in a candlelit dining room with harbour views and a refreshing lack of pretence.

Times 6.30-9.30, Closed L all week

BURRINGTON
Map 3 SS61

Northcote Manor
◉◉ Modern British V

tel: 01769 560501 **EX37 9LZ**
email: rest@northcotemanor.co.uk **web:** www.northcotemanor.co.uk
dir: M5 junct 27 towards Barnstaple. Left at rdbt to South Molton. Follow A377, right at T-junct to Barnstaple. Entrance after 3m, opposite Portsmouth Arms railway station and pub. (NB do not enter Burrington village)

Tranquil country-house setting and well-sourced modern British food

The old stone manor, dating from the early 1700s, occupies 20 or so acres of lush Devon countryside, and is these days a classy county-house hotel with an impressive restaurant. It has a reassuringly traditional finish, with upscale fixtures and fittings, plus a service team who match the charm of the setting. The dining room has the expected refinement and formality, with pristine tables and a period feel. The menu makes good use of seasonal, regional ingredients, and there's a good showing of West Country game and seafood. Start with a succulent terrine of ham hock matched with apple chutney and honey-roasted parsnip purée, followed by line-caught mullet and seared scallops, partnered by silky pommes purée and butternut squash (served braised and as a purée), all finished with a fresh herb dressing. Meat fans might go for a tournedos of free-range Devon Red Ruby beef with dauphinoise potatoes, woodland mushrooms, carrots and Madeira gravy, and for pud there's apple tarte Tatin with blackberry crumble, clotted cream and butterscotch sauce.

Chef Richie Herkes **Owner** J Pierre Mifsud **Seats** 34, Pr/dining room 50 **Times** 12-2/7-9 **Prices** Prices not confirmed, Service optional **Wines** 22 bottles over £30, 34 bottles under £30, 9 by glass **Parking** 30 **Notes** Sunday L, Children welcome

CHAGFORD
Map 3 SX78

Gidleigh Park
◉◉◉◉◉ – see page 140

DARTMOUTH
Map 3 SX85

The Dart Marina Hotel
◉ Modern British V

tel: 01803 832580 **Sandquay Rd TQ6 9PH**
email: reception@dartmarinahotel.com **web:** www.dartmarina.com
dir: A3122 from Totnes to Dartmouth. Follow road which becomes College Way, before Higher Ferry. Hotel sharp left in Sandquay Rd

Confident modern cooking in contemporary riverside hotel

The hotel is perfectly positioned to deliver views of the River Dart and the wooded hills across the water, with the eponymous marina providing further distraction via its ever-changing flotilla. This is a contemporary paradise with neutral colour tones, tasteful and trendy furniture and a swish spa, and it's also home to the River Restaurant. Views of the river are guaranteed through floor-to-ceiling windows, while the menu also does its bit to provide a sense of place by featuring regional produce. Local crab finds its way into tortellini, dressed with red pepper and crab foam, and seared pigeon breast arrives with fig Tatin and a port and hazelnut vinaigrette. Among main courses, sea bream is served with an Asian spin and braised beef is cooked bourguignon-style and partnered with horseradish pommes purée. Modern desserts include Alunga chocolate and hazelnut mousse with hazelnut gel and candied hazelnut.

Chef Peter Alcroft **Owner** Richard Seton **Seats** 86 **Times** 12-2/6-9, Closed 23-26 & 30-31 Dec, L Mon-Sat **Prices** Starter £6.95-£9.95, Main £15.95-£29.95, Dessert £6.95-£11.50, Service optional **Wines** 38 bottles over £30, 26 bottles under £30, 20 by glass **Parking** 100 **Notes** Sunday L £18.95, Children welcome

Gidleigh Park ❀ ❀ ❀ ❀ ❀

CHAGFORD   Map 3 SX78

Modern European V 🍷 NOTABLE WINE LIST

tel: 01647 432367 **TQ13 8HH**

email: gidleighpark@gidleigh.co.uk **web:** www.gidleigh.com

dir: *From Chagford Sq turn right at Lloyds TSB into Mill St, after 150yds right fork, across x-rds into Holy St. Restaurant 1.5m*

Stunning contemporary cooking in idyllic wonderful Dartmoor isolation

When it comes to quintessentially English settings, they don't come much more bucolic than Gidleigh Park. The approach from the village of Chagford down winding lanes and the similarly long driveway raises the level of anticipation with every passing furlong. The magnificent Arts and Crafts-style half-timbered mansion stands in pretty manicured gardens surrounded by soaring trees, with the River Teign flowing through the grounds. The sense of tranquillity and escape is enhanced by the wild Dartmoor landscape that surrounds this luxurious haven of civilisation. From the public spaces to the bedrooms, the hotel has a smart and stylish finish. Gidleigh's reputation has in part been made by its outstanding restaurant. The series of interlinked wood-panelled rooms make for serious and refined spaces, where well-drilled staff ensure all needs are met. Michael Caines has been in charge of the kitchen at Gidleigh for more than 20 years creating a restaurant of unerring confidence and bravura while overseeing various other operations and appearing on television. Showing respect for classical ways and embracing contemporary creativity, Caines and his team offer refined modern European dishes based on spectacularly good ingredients, many of which are sourced from the kitchen garden or come from the region's top producers, growers and suppliers. Via à la carte, signature tasting menu and a set lunch option, expect deliciously exciting platefuls that deliver spot-on flavours. From the carte, foie gras terrine with Sauternes jelly, quince and sultana purée reveals Caines' roots in classical French cuisine, but there's usually a modern take, something special that lifts each dish up a notch or two into the sought-after 'wow factor' territory. Another first course shows how the kitchen is not adverse to seeking out contemporary partnerships, such as wasabi cream and honey and soy vinaigrette that accompanies Loch Duart salmon, with the addition Oscietra caviar and salmon and cucumber jelly. The technical virtuosity on show is never less than impressive. Among main courses, the renowned partnership of duck and orange gets a shot in the arm with a Cornish duckling arriving flavoured with star anise and in the company of orange-braised chicory and an orange-scented sauce. The region's waters play their part, too, providing the turbot and scallops that come with leeks, wild mushrooms and chive butter sauce. Desserts also combine classical and contemporary thinking – hot prune and Armagnac soufflé, say, served with an ice cream of the same, while a 'plate of orange' is a delightful melange of mandarin confit, tartlet of orange, orange mousse and orange sorbet. Artisan cheeses arrive on a trolley and include the best local stuff with some European heavyweights. The wine list is a stunning piece of work with more than 1,300 bins (and 13,000 bottles in the cellars). If you're staying for a while be sure to try the afternoon tea.

Chef Michael Caines MBE **Owner** Andrew & Christina Brownsword **Seats** 52, Pr/dining room 22 **Times** 12-2/7-9.45, **Prices** Fixed L 2 course fr £45, Service optional **Wines** 1190 bottles over £30, 10 bottles under £30, 16 by glass **Parking** 45 **Notes** Signature menu 8 course £143, ALC 3 course £118, Children 8 yrs+ D

The Seahorse

◉◉ Mediterranean, Seafood

tel: 01803 835147 **5 South Embankment TQ6 9BH**
email: enquiries@seahorserestaurant.co.uk
dir: *Phone for directions*

Bountiful fresh seafood by the Dart estuary

Hard to miss in the bustling strip along the Dart waterfront, Mitch Tonks's Seahorse is some kind of flagship for his burgeoning empire of seafood restaurants. Subdued lighting and comfortable banquette seating make the place an inviting evening venue, while big windows let in the Devon light on summer days. The menu evolves rapidly, and is always based, as is only proper, on the day's specials. With a bounty of fresh fish and shellfish virtually on the doorstep, it's easy to see what the attraction is. Mussels cultured in nearby Elberry Cove, summer crustacea and seasonal veg from the vicinity and from markets just across the Channel add lustre to menus that take in risotto of mixed seafood, bream fillet steamed in paper with garlic, rosemary and chilli, roast turbot fillet with chive butter and — for the seafood refuseniks — osso buco. Many of the dishes are cooked over an open charcoal fire, used for anything from monkfish to rump steak. Lemon sorbet mixed with elderflower fizz makes a distinguished finale.

Chef Mat Prowse, Mitch Tonks **Owner** Mat Prowse, Mitch Tonks **Seats** 40
Times 12-2.30/6-9.30, Closed 25 Dec, 1 Jan, Mon, L Tue, D Sun **Prices** Prices not confirmed, Service optional **Wines** 80 bottles over £30, 20 bottles under £30, 6 by glass **Parking** On street **Notes** Vegetarian available, Children welcome

The Nobody Inn

◉ Modern British

tel: 01647 252394 **EX6 7PS**
email: info@nobodyinn.co.uk **web:** www.nobodyinn.co.uk
dir: *From A38 turn off at top of Haldon Hill, follow signs to Doddiscombsleigh*

Sophisticated dining in popular country inn

It's worth the drive along narrow twisting lanes to reach this gem of a 17th-century thatched inn, with its blackened beams, low ceilings, inglenook and rustic furniture. It's a winner in many ways, with bedrooms, a hefty wine list, collections of whiskies and cheeses and sophisticated eating. The team in the kitchen is evangelical about tracking down local produce and using it to create stylish modern dishes. Panko-crumbed squid comes with chilli mayonnaise, and game terrine with apple chutney, candied hazelnuts and apple jelly. Dishes are intelligently assembled and ingredients are treated carefully. For example, roast pheasant breast, succulent and full of flavour, is served with confit leg, fondant potato, braised red cabbage and gravy, and steak and ale pie with horseradish mash and seasonal vegetables. There's a fish of the day, and puddings extend to caramel pannacotta with gingerbread, and apple tarte fine with custard and Calvados cream.

Owner Susan Burdge **Seats** 80, Pr/dining room 24 **Times** 6.30-9, Closed 1 Jan, Sun-Mon, L all week **Prices** Starter £4.95-£8.95, Main £11.95-£22.95, Dessert £2.95-£6.95, Service optional **Wines** 102 bottles over £30, 102 bottles under £30, 30 by glass **Parking** 30 **Notes** Vegetarian available, Children welcome

The Old Inn

◉◉◉ *— see page 142*

Plantation House

◉◉ Modern British ⱽ

tel: 01548 831100 **Totnes Rd PL21 9NS**
email: info@plantationhousehotel.co.uk **web:** www.plantationhousehotel.co.uk
dir: *Phone for directions*

Simple but convincing country cooking in the Erme valley

The South Hams below Dartmoor is one of Devon's most covetable regions, and the generations of clergymen who once lived in the Georgian rectory overlooking the River Erme must have felt particularly blessed. Now an elegant boutique hotel, it exudes character, with high-windowed views over stunning gardens at the front, heavy bucket chairs in twisted wicker at solid dark wood tables, and attractive soft furnishings in both dining rooms. A south-facing terrace for summer aperitifs adds to the appeal, as does the cooking, which is full of genuine passion for prime materials that are given simple but powerfully convincing treatments. After a swig of truffled wild garlic and nettle soup, it's on with a beautifully rendered dish of shellfish in a Thai broth of chilli, lime, ginger, lemongrass and coconut. Crackly-skinned duck makes a majestic main, served with well-seasoned dauphinoise in Merlot jus, while fish might be grilled turbot on a potato and chive cake in lime hollandaise. Dessert may be cardamom pannacotta with gingered rhubarb syrup and matching sorbet, or crème brûlée with blood orange and rosé wine jelly.

Chef Richard Hendey, John Raines **Owner** Richard Hendey **Seats** 28, Pr/dining room 16 **Times** 7-9, Closed L all week **Prices** Fixed D 3 course £36-£39.50 **Wines** 27 bottles over £30, 25 bottles under £30, 6 by glass **Parking** 30 **Notes** 4/5 course D £36/£39.50, Breakfast 7.30-9.30, Children welcome

ABode Exeter

◉◉ Modern British, French

tel: 01392 319955 **Cathedral Yard EX1 1HD**
email: tables@abodeexeter.co.uk **web:** www.abodeexeter.co.uk
dir: *Town centre, opposite cathedral*

Classy cooking chez Michael Caines

Michael Caines made his name in Devon cooking at Gidleigh Park and opened up the first ABode on this site back in 2000. The group has expanded since and gone from strength-to-strength. Just about all the bases are covered here in Cathedral Yard, where the charming hotel occupies a prime spot in the city with a buzzy tavern, café/grill, cocktail bar and the main event, the fine-dining Michael Caines Restaurant set in a handsome room with lots of original features and a smart contemporary finish. There are plenty of regional ingredients on the menu (carte, tasting and an excellent value set lunch option) and the carefully executed dishes are based on a sound classical footing. Start with crab ravioli, say, with grapefruit, ginger and coriander, or a warm salad of Devon quail with smoked bacon, quail's egg and caramelised hazelnuts. Main-course roasted hake is a fine piece of fish, cooked just right, served with River Exe mussels, creamed leeks and saffron sauce. Finish with banana and chocolate parfait.

Chef Michael Caines, Nick Topham **Owner** Andrew Brownsword **Seats** 65, Pr/dining room 80 **Times** 12-2.30/6-9.30 **Prices** Fixed L 2 course £14.95, Fixed D 3 course £22.95, Tasting menu £65, Starter £7.95-£16.95, Main £8.95-£23.95, Dessert £7.95 **Wines** 83 bottles over £30, 27 bottles under £30, 11 by glass **Parking** Car park Mary Arches St **Notes** Afternoon tea £15, Sunday L £17.95-£22.95, Vegetarian available, Children welcome

EXETER continued

Barton Cross Hotel & Restaurant

Traditional British, French V

tel: 01392 841245 & 841584 **Huxham, Stoke Canon EX5 4EJ**
email: bartonxhuxham@aol.com web: www.thebartoncrosshotel.co.uk
dir: 0.5m off A396 at Stoke Canon, 3m N of Exeter

Reliably good, well-judged food in thatched hotel

At Barton Cross, a 17th-century thatched longhouse in a delightful rural spot just a few miles from Exeter, low beams and cob walls abound, and while the galleried restaurant looks like it could do service as a medieval banqueting hall, there's nothing archaic about what arrives on the plate. The kitchen deals in straightforward Anglo-European cooking, sending out a gutsy ham hock terrine matched with caramelised apple and red onion chutney, alongside smoked salmon risotto spiked with dill and lemon. Main course sees well-timed beef fillet in a herb crust served with fondant potato, roasted shallot, and sun-blushed tomato and basil sauce. Fish is handled deftly-perhaps fillet of sea bass with tangerine butter and chargrilled fennel, or pan-fried monkfish with coconut and curry sauce. The enterprising desserts run to iced mint and chocolate parfait with hazelnut wafers.

Chef Nicholas Beattie **Owner** Brian Hamilton **Seats** 50, Pr/dining room 26 **Times** 12.30-2.30/6.30-11.30, Closed L Mon-Thu **Prices** Fixed D 3 course £29.50, Starter £5-£6.50, Main £14-£16.50, Dessert £5, Service optional **Wines** 30 bottles over £30, 60 bottles under £30, 10 by glass **Parking** 50 **Notes** Children welcome

EXMOUTH

Map 3 SY08

Les Saveurs

Modern French, International

tel: 01395 269459 **9 Tower St EX8 1NT**
email: lessaveurs@yahoo.co.uk
dir: A376 to Exmouth, left at rdbt. Right at next rdbt onto Rolle St. Tower St on right

French fish cookery and more near the Exe estuary

On a pedestrianised street near both the centre and the beach, Les Saveurs is everything you could wish for in a small neighbourhood restaurant. It offers a relaxing atmosphere generated by courteous and unobtrusive staff, a pale decor, with some exposed-brick walls, and fine cooking. The kitchen's focus is on seafood, although meat-eaters will find plenty to appeal, from black pudding with a poached egg on green beans, potatoes and sun-blushed tomatoes to a main course of roast rump of lamb with a mushroom and Madeira sauce and dauphinoise potatoes. Otherwise go for pan-fried scallops, accurately timed, with pea purée and minted mussel velouté, followed by crisp-skinned fillet of gilt head bream on chive mash with an exemplary sauce Américaine, or the contemporary pairing of cod fillet and chorizo with lentils and lemon and thyme sauce. Puddings reflect the chef's French credentials, among them snow eggs, given a kick with Baileys custard and caramel.

Chef Olivier Guyard-Mulkerrin **Owner** Olivier & Sheila Guyard-Mulkerrin **Seats** 30, Pr/ dining room 30 **Times** 7-10.30, Closed Nov-Apr advance bookings only, Sun-Mon (ex by special arrangement), L all week **Prices** Prices not confirmed, Service optional **Wines** 10 bottles over £30, 19 bottles under £30, 5 by glass **Parking** On street/ council offices **Notes** Vegetarian available, Children 10 yrs+

The Old Inn ❀❀❀

DREWSTEIGNTON

Map 3 SX79

Modern European
tel: 01647 281276 **EX6 6QR**
email: enquiries@old-inn.co.uk
dir: A30 W, exit Cheriton Bishop, Drewsteignton, Castle Drogo, turn left at Crockenwell, follow signs to Drewsteignton. A38 to A382 Bovey Tracy, Mortonhampstead, turn right at Sandy Park, continue past Castle Drogo, follow signs to Drewsteignton

Well-judged modern cooking in a Dartmoor village inn

Chef-patron Duncan Walker moved from the northeast half a lifetime ago to work with Shaun Hill at Gidleigh Park, and put down deep roots in the Dartmoor region. His delightful restaurant with rooms occupies a whitewashed, 17th-century former coaching inn in a chocolate box village on the fringes of the moor. There's a cosy lounge with squashy sofas by a wood burner and a brace of tail wagging retrievers to welcome guests, and a pair of smartly inviting dining rooms with bare oak tables and claret and sage-green walls hung with art, but refreshingly free from designer pretentions. The icing on the cake is a trio of cosy bedrooms so you can stay over and give the uncluttered modern European menu and concise, well-chosen wine list a full workout. And with just 17 diners to cater for, you can expect focused cooking of pin-sharp accuracy. Walker is a chef who has that magic touch, achieving big flavours from harmonious combinations of top-quality ingredients, whether it's a starter of sautéed calves' sweetbreads with olive potato cake, brown butter and capers, or a well-judged marriage of spiced pork belly with sautéed scallops and sesame. Beautifully fresh regional produce is treated with respect, allowing the principal component to shine, in main courses like roast loin of Dartmoor lamb with fondant potato and rosemary, while fish-based mains might see a spanking-fresh grilled fillet of sea bass partnered with saffron pasta, mussels and watercress. Desserts are equally accomplished, perhaps a celebration of seasonal fruit in a warm plum tart with cinnamon ice cream, or a technically flawless blackcurrant soufflé rising impressively to the occasion with liquorice ice cream.

Chef Duncan Walker **Owner** Duncan Walker **Seats** 17, Pr/dining room 10 **Times** 12-2/7-9, Closed Sun-Tue, L Sun-Thu **Prices** Fixed L 3 course £29.50, Fixed D 3 course £49 **Wines** 24 bottles over £30, 21 bottles under £30, 4 by glass **Parking** Village square **Notes** Service flexible, pre book, tables 6 or more by arrangement, Children 12 yrs+

Map 3 SX77

Rock Inn

◉ Modern British, European

tel: 01364 661305 & 661556 **TQ13 9XP**
email: info@rock-inn.co.uk **web:** www.rock-inn.co.uk
dir: From A38 at Drum Bridges, onto A382 to Bovey Tracey. In 2m take B3387 towards Haytor for 3.5m, follow brown signs

Modern classic dishes at a Dartmoor inn

The rustic inn on the eastern flank of Dartmoor was built in the 1820s, along with the row of cottages it sits in, to serve workers in the granite quarries. It retains plenty of its pre-Victorian air, with flagged floors, mighty stone walls and beams providing a welcoming backdrop to the modern European culinary style on show in the candlelit dining room. Parma-wrapped scallops with cauliflower purée is a modern standby but well-executed for all that, and another of today's classic combinations is celebrated in grilled Ragstone goats' cheese with beetroot variations. At main, there's plenty satisfaction to be had from flavourful duck breast with dauphinoise and an eloquent spiced jus, or from Indian-seasoned monkfish in a yogurt and turmeric sauce. Finish with properly rich dark chocolate delice and orange sorbet, or a platter of West Country cheeses and home-made chutney.

Times 12-2.15/6.30-9, Closed 25-26 Dec

Map 4 ST10

The Deer Park Country House Hotel

◉◉ Modern British

tel: 01404 41266 **Weston EX14 3PG**
email: admin@deerparkcountryhotel.co.uk **web:** www.deerparkcountryhotel.co.uk
dir: Phone for directions

Modern cooking in boutique country house

This 18th-century Georgian mansion set in 80 acres of glorious grounds is a quintessentially English set-up brought into the 21st century with a sprinkle of boutique style and great food served in an elegant dining room to seal the deal. The kitchen is diligent in its sourcing of local produce, going no further than its own garden for fresh seasonal fruit and veg, and bringing it all together in confidently-cooked modern ideas. Begin with watercress soup, salt cod beignet and aïoli, although the River Exe mussels with white wine and garlic cream is another diverting starter. Follow, perhaps, with roasted rump of grass-fed Devon lamb, smoked aubergine, wild garlic and sweetbread. Fish might appear in a well-considered composition such as a trio of bream, salmon and hake with broad bean and potato salad and sauce vierge. Finish with a moreish dessert of dark chocolate brownie with hazelnut praline and salted caramel ice cream, or maybe pick from a selection of perfectly kept West Country cheeses.

Chef Andrew Storey **Owner** Deer Park Hotel Ltd **Seats** 45, Pr/dining room 30
Times 12-2.30/6.30-9.30 **Wines** 17 bottles over £30, 29 bottles under £30, 7 by glass **Parking** 60 **Notes** Sunday L £22-£29, Vegetarian available, Children welcome

The Holt Bar & Restaurant

◉◉ Modern British

tel: 01404 47707 **178 High St EX14 1LA**
email: enquiries@theholt-honiton.com
dir: At west end of High St

Imaginative, impressive cooking in a local pub

With a range of its ales dispensed at the bar, The Holt looks like any other high-street pub from the outside, while the interior has a more contemporary look, with its mixture of seats and sofas and rustic tables and chairs. The main dining area is upstairs: open-plan, with a wooden floor, simple decor, candlelight, and pleasant, efficient service. Food is a serious commitment here and standards are consistently high, with the menu a happy blend of the traditional and more à la mode. Dishes are hardly shy and retiring – the food has plenty of clout – but show clarity of thought and skilled execution. Salmon is smoked in-house for a traditional starter with rye toast, or there may be a tart of artichoke, olives and feta. Following on might be well-timed breast and confit leg of duck, served with ultra-crunchy roasties and Savoy cabbage, or smoked haddock rarebit conjured into a main course with champ, celeriac and leeks. Finish with chocolate cloud cake in fudge sauce with preserved berry meringues.

Chef Angus McCaig, Billy Emmett, Will Scott **Owner** Joe & Angus McCaig **Seats** 50 **Times** 12-2/6.30-10, Closed 25-26 Dec, Sun-Mon **Prices** Starter £5.50-£7, Main £13.50-£17, Dessert £5.50-£6.50, Service optional **Wines** 6 bottles over £30, 25 bottles under £30, 6 by glass **Parking** On street, car park 1 min walk **Notes** Vegetarian available, Children welcome

Map 3 SS54

The Olive Room

◉◉ Modern British NEW

tel: 01271 867831 & 879005 **56 Fore St EX34 9DJ**
email: info@thomascarrchef.co.uk **web:** www.thomascarrchef.co.uk
dir: A361 into Ilfracombe, through lights into High St. At end fork left into Fore St, continue straight down, pass no entry signs, on left hand side

Clever modern cooking from a rising star

After honing his skills in the kitchens of Restaurant Nathan Outlaw and Michael Caines's Coach House at Kentisbury Grange, Thomas Carr's cooking is on a roll, and he has set up shop in the dining room of the Georgian Olive Branch Guest House. The setting is smartly contemporary with leather chairs, unclothed tables and modern art on brick walls, and with just 25 covers to cook for, you can expect focused and accurate cooking of Devon's fine produce. Spanking-fresh line-caught fish landed daily at the harbour appears in a starter of Lundy plaice served with a crispy oyster, brown shrimps, and an invigorating cucumber dressing, followed by well-timed lamb loin paired with a fritter of shoulder meat, plus bubble-and-squeak, charred broccoli, a fried egg, roast garlic and rosemary. With this sort of creativity, you probably won't be surprised to see vegetables and spices turning up in a dessert of carrot cake cheesecake – with orange curd providing a creamy, citrus hit – and cinnamon ice cream.

Chef Thomas Carr, John Cairns **Owner** Thomas Carr **Seats** 18 **Times** 6-9, Closed Sun, L all week **Prices** Tasting menu £55, Starter £7-£10, Main £17-£21, Dessert £7-£8, Service optional **Wines** 2 bottles over £30, 15 bottles under £30, 8 by glass **Parking** NCP Fore St **Notes** Vegetarian available, Children welcome

ILFRACOMBE *continued*

The Quay Restaurant

◉ Modern, Traditional British, European

tel: 01271 868090 **11 The Quay EX34 9EQ**
email: info@11thequay.co.uk
dir: *Follow signs for harbour and pier car park. Restaurant on left before car park*

Classic brasserie menu on the harbour front

Perched on the harbour front of this north Devon coastal town, The Quay is a place with a strong sense of identity. Adorned with original artworks by Damien Hirst at his more docile, the Atlantic Room with its vaulted ceiling is a bright and breezy setting for internationally inspired brasserie classics. Crab claws in garlic mayonnaise, native oysters, or mussels from the Exe given the marinière treatment all make the most of the location, while tuna may appear Thai-style or Niçoise. For main, there are one or two more obviously contemporary ideas, such as roasted cod with pancetta and peas in mussel cream, amid the boeuf bourguignon and mash, or lamb cutlets and mint sauce. Finish with any of a number of chart-topping desserts – tiramisù, lemon posset, chocolate fondant, Eton Mess – or West Country cheeses and pear chutney.

Chef Henry Sowden **Owner** Damien Hirst **Seats** 45, Pr/dining room 26
Times 12-2.30/6-9, Closed 25-26 Dec, 2 wks Jan **Prices** Prices not confirmed, Service optional **Wines** 10 bottles over £30, 19 bottles under £30, 10 by glass **Parking** Pier car park 100yds **Notes** Vegetarian available, Children welcome

Sandy Cove Hotel

◉ Modern British

tel: 01271 882243 **Old Coast Rd, Combe Martin Bay, Berrynarbor EX34 9SR**
email: info@sandycove-hotel.co.uk **web:** www.sandycove-hotel.co.uk
dir: *A339 to Combe Martin, through village towards Ilfracombe for approx 1m. Turn right just over brow of hill marked Sandy Cove*

Simple cooking, local produce, views to die for

The sprawling Sandy Cove Hotel sits on a clifftop with stunning views over the sea and the wild landscape of Exmoor. The best of both worlds. The restaurant is positioned to maximise the vista, with large windows, or if you're really lucky the weather will allow a table on the deck. The hotel itself has a swimming pool with a sliding roof (so indoor or outdoor), and the decor is contemporary. The menu keeps things gently modern, too, with local seafood and steaks from nearby farms, and sticks to familiar and successful combinations. Start with a Thai fishcake, for example, with an accompanying sweet chilli dip, before moving on to roast breast of duck with a fondant potato, red cabbage and a red wine sauce. For dessert, lemon tart gives a good hit of citrus acidity, and is served with a raspberry sorbet.

Times 12-2/6.30-9

ILSINGTON Map 3 SX77

Ilsington Country House Hotel

◉◉ Modern European

tel: 01364 661452 **Ilsington Village TQ13 9RR**
email: info@ilsington.co.uk **web:** www.ilsington.co.uk
dir: *A38 to Plymouth, exit at Bovey Tracey. 3rd exit from rdbt to Ilsington, then 1st right, hotel on right in 3m*

Great Dartmoor views and confident cooking

A substantial white property, Ilsington is surrounded by 10 acres of gardens within Dartmoor National Park. Decorated and furnished along the lines of a quality country-house hotel, with guests' comfort foremost, the restaurant, with well-spaced tables on a boldly patterned carpet, gives wonderful views of rolling hills

from a wall of floor-to-ceiling windows. The diverse menu showcases the kitchen's technical skills as it takes a Pan-European route to produce divertingly appealing dishes. Take a starter of seared mackerel fillets, accompanied by chilli and tomato couscous, a chorizo and pea pancake, leeks and Avruga oil, or duck breast, which is plated with hogs pudding, beetroot, roasted courgettes and blackberry gastrique. Accompaniments complement the main ingredient without swamping it, seen in main courses of roast chicken with a maple and mustard gel, pommes Anna, pea purée, mushrooms, confit tomato and smoked beetroot, and pavé of hake with sauce nero, chorizo and chickpea cassoulet and Bombay-style potatoes. Finish with the multiple flavours of cinnamon pannacotta with strawberry and elderflower jelly, a rice pudding fritter and honeycomb.

Chef Mike O'Donnell **Owner** The Hassell family **Seats** 75, Pr/dining room 70
Times 12-2/6.30-9, Closed L Mon-Sat **Prices** Fixed D 3 course fr £36, Starter £5.50-£8.95, Main £9.50-£18.95, Dessert £6.50-£7.50 **Wines** 12 bottles over £30, 32 bottles under £30, 7 by glass **Parking** 60 **Notes** Sunday L £18-£21.50, Vegetarian available, Children welcome

KENTISBURY Map 3 SS64

Kentisbury Grange

◉◉ Modern British

tel: 01271 882295 **EX31 4NL**
email: reception@kentisburygrange.co.uk **web:** www.kentisburygrange.com
dir: *From Barnstaple take A3125. At rdbt take 2nd exit onto A39 to Burrington through Shirwell & Arlington. After Kentisbury Ford, follow signs for hotel for approx 0.75m*

Creative modern cooking in a stylish old coach house

This country-house hotel is placed firmly at the boutique end of the spectrum, with decor that is a little bit luxurious but deliberately lived-in. The Coach House restaurant is just that (a former 17th-century coach house), a short scrunch across the gravel from the hotel, and it looks peachy with its rustic-chic oak tables, banquette seating and contemporary artworks. The ingredients are sourced from nearby, including crabs from Lundy Island and ducks from the farm next door. A first course dish of sea bream featuring a superbly cooked piece of fish, red pepper jam, saffron and shellfish sauce and olives is a refined and well-judged combination, or go for the chef's take on a lobster cocktail with smoked Exe mussels. A main course of Waytown fillet of beef comes with Jacob's ladder (short-rib) fritter and roasted shallots, mushroom ketchup and chips. The cheeseboard flies the flag for Devon, while desserts run to lemon tart with frozen yogurt, lemon curd and meringue.

Chef Thomas Hine **Owner** Mark Cushway **Seats** 54, Pr/dining room 22 **Times** 12-2/6-9 **Prices** Fixed L 2 course £14.95, Fixed D 3 course £35, Tasting menu £55 **Wines** 34 bottles over £30, 41 bottles under £30, 12 by glass **Parking** 70 **Notes** Sunday L £14.95-£19.95, Vegetarian available, Children welcome

KINGSBRIDGE Map 3 SX74

Buckland-Tout-Saints

◉ Modern British **V**

tel: 01548 853055 **Goveton TQ7 2DS**
email: enquiries@bucklandtoutsaints.co.uk **web:** www.tout-saints.co.uk
dir: *Turn off A381 to Goveton. Follow brown tourist signs to St Peter's Church. Hotel 2nd right after church*

Classic country-house dining with regional accent and period decor

A picture-perfect William and Mary-era house in four acres of gardens and woodland sets the scene for a classy country-house package. The interior is refined and packed with period details such as wood panelling and grand fireplaces, not least in the Queen Anne Restaurant, with one room replete with burnished Russian pine, the other with duck egg blue paintwork. The scene is dressed with white linen and fresh flowers. The kitchen turns out bright modern British cooking with a good showing of regional ingredients. There might be Salcombe crab to start, for example, in a modern dish with pineapple chutney, goats' curd and brown crab purée. Next up, roast rump of lamb with wild garlic and pearl barley risotto, or roasted tail of monkfish with curried lentils and golden raisin purée. Dessert follows the Pan-European pathway, with the likes of vanilla pannacotta perked up with cinnamon beignets and poached raspberries.

Chef Ted Ruewell **Owner** Eden Hotel Collection **Seats** 40, Pr/dining room 40 **Times** 12-2/7-9, Closed 2-17 Jan **Prices** Fixed L 2 course fr £18, Fixed D 3 course fr £35, Starter £9-£11, Main £24.50-£26.50, Dessert £9, Service optional **Wines** 30 bottles over £30, 30 bottles under £30, 10 by glass **Parking** 70 **Notes** Sunday L £18-£22, Children welcome

---

KNOWSTONE
Map 3 SS82

The Masons Arms
◉◉ Modern British

tel: 01398 341231 **EX36 4RY**
email: enqs@masonsarmsdevon.co.uk
dir: Signed from A361, turn right once in Knowstone

Strong contemporary cooking in the lush western countryside

A genuinely delightful thatched medieval country inn that maintains strong links to excellent local growers and suppliers, The Masons also manages to retain the atmosphere of a village pub. Deep in the lush countryside on the border between Devon and Somerset, it is surrounded by rolling hills, and is full of cheer on winter evenings when the fire crackles, and in summer too for an outdoor meal. The celestial ceiling mural in the dining room has to be seen to be believed. Mark Dodson once cooked under Michel Roux at Bray, which might explain the flair and precision evident in the dishes here. Good strong contemporary thinking informs a starter of wood pigeon breasts, flash-fried and tender, accompanied by puréed beetroot and pine nuts in blueberry jus, while the main-course pairing of local beef fillet and oxtail in its truffled, Madeira-rich juices continues to be a triumph of timing and seasoning. Fish could be something almost as robust, perhaps sea bass alongside Jerusalem artichoke purée, butter beans and flageolets with smoked garlic in red wine jus, and dessert closes things with a fitting flourish in the form of lemon mascarpone mousse with passionfruit syrup, or an apple trio with Granny Smith sorbet.

Chef Mark Dodson, Jess Thorne **Owner** Mark & Sarah Dodson **Seats** 28 **Times** 12-2/7-9, Closed 1st wk Jan, Feb half term, 1 wk Aug BH, Mon, D Sun **Prices** Fixed L 2 course £20, Starter £9.25-£12.50, Main £18.70-£26.50, Dessert £8.50-£9.75, Service optional **Wines** 41 bottles over £30, 17 bottles under £30, 9 by glass **Parking** 10 **Notes** Sunday L, Vegetarian available, Children 5 yrs+ D

LIFTON
Map 3 SX38

Arundell Arms
◉◉ Modern British V

tel: 01566 784666 **Fore St PL16 0AA**
email: reservations@arundellarms.com **web:** www.arundellarms.com
dir: Just off A30 in Lifton, 3m E of Launceston

Traditional Anglo-French cooking with contemporary detailing

Wedged in the narrow interstice between the western edge of Dartmoor and the Cornish border, in some of the southwest's most appealing countryside, the Arundell Arms sits on the main road through its little village. What looks like a rural pub on the outside is an elevated country hotel within, with lavish traditional furnishings and a large dining room with tall windows looking over the grounds at the back. The kitchen offers a traditionally based Anglo-French repertoire founded on quality materials, with some contemporary detailing adding interest. First off could be a grilled John Dory fillet on creamed lentils with brown shrimps and a scallop fritter,

or classic sautéed lamb's kidneys with onion purée in grain mustard sauce, the overtures possibly to pork tenderloin with chicken mousseline in a sauce of Cornwall's Rattler cider. There's a gentle richness to the impact of dishes, seen in Aylesbury duck with dauphinoise and rhubarb in peppercorn sauce, and most temptingly of all in dark chocolate terrine with marinated orange and Amaretto ice cream.

Chef Steven Pidgeon **Owner** Adam Fox-Edwards **Seats** 70, Pr/dining room 24 **Times** 12-2.30/7-10, Closed D 24-26 Dec **Prices** Fixed L 2 course fr £19.50, Tasting menu £47.50, Starter £9.50-£12.50, Main £19.50-£25, Dessert £8.95-£15.50, Service optional **Wines** 5 bottles over £30, 5 bottles under £30, 7 by glass **Parking** 70 **Notes** Sunday L £19.50-£25, Children welcome

---

LYNMOUTH
Map 3 SS74

Rising Sun Hotel
◉ British, French

tel: 01598 753223 **Harbourside EX35 6EG**
email: reception@risingsunlynmouth.co.uk **web:** www.risingsunlynmouth.co.uk
dir: M5 junct 23 (Minehead). Take A39 to Lynmouth. Opposite the harbour

Modern British cooking in a convivial harbourside inn

Given its atmospheric location by the harbour and 14th-century walls, it's not surprising that the Rising Sun once had associations with smugglers. Today the place positively rocks with good vibrations. There's a bar that is just that – a proper pub, packed, lively and full of beans – and an oak-panelled dining room that doesn't want for atmosphere either. The food strikes a good balance between hearty generosity and contemporary combinations, with plenty of seafood dishes as you might hope in this setting. Start with a modern classic – seared king scallops with cauliflower cream and crisp pancetta, or an 'old favourite' such as chicken livers enriched with baby onions, pancetta and a balsamic and Madeira sauce (with brioche to soak up the juices). Next up, a generous portion of wild sea bass with samphire and a bouillabaisse sauce, or chargrilled rib-eye with field mushrooms and twice-cooked chips, and finish with a well-made crème brûlée.

Times 7-9, Closed L all week

PLYMOUTH
Map 3 SX45

Artillery Tower Restaurant
◉ Modern British

tel: 01752 257610 **Firestone Bay, Durnford St PL1 3QR**
dir: 1m from city centre & rail station

Bistro food in a Tudor gunnery tower

Those on the lookout for a more singular venue than Georgian coaching inns might set their sights on the 16th-century circular gunnery tower on the Plymouth waterfront, which once set its own sights on enemy shipping in Firestone Bay. Grip the handrail tight as you climb the spiral staircase. Arched windows that once served as gun emplacements in three-foot walls surround the dining space, where simple modern bistro food is the drill. Expect Mediterranean fish soup and harissa to start, or game terrine in cider sauce, as lead-ins to substantial main dishes of peppered venison loin with cranberry and orange compôte, duck breast and confit leg with quince, or roasted pollock with crab gratin and spinach, sauced in white wine. Finish with chocolate nemesis and chocolate sorbet, or wait the 20 minutes for freshly baked cherry frangipane tart with Amaretto ice cream.

Chef Peter Constable **Owner** Peter & Debbie Constable **Seats** 26, Pr/dining room 16 **Times** 12-2.15/7-9.30, Closed Xmas, New Year, Sun-Mon, L Sat **Prices** Prices not confirmed, Service optional **Wines** 5 bottles over £30, 20 bottles under £30, 6 by glass **Parking** 20, Evening only **Notes** Vegetarian available, Children welcome

PLYMOUTH *continued*

Barbican Kitchen

◉ Modern V

tel: 01752 604448 **Plymouth Gin Distillery, 60 Southside St PL1 2LQ**
email: info@barbicankitchen.com **web:** www.barbicankitchen.com
dir: *On Barbican, 5 mins walk from Bretonside bus station*

Convincing brasserie food from the Tanner brothers

The renowned Plymouth Gin distillery is home to the Tanner brothers' second dining option in the city, and entering past the huge vats gives a reminder of the esteemed history of the building. You can take a tour if you want. The Barbican Kitchen spreads over two floors and packs a visual punch with its bold colours and contemporary prints (purple and lime chairs and Banksy no less), plus there's an open kitchen to add to the youthful, energetic vibe. The menu is a feel-good foray into contemporary tastes with a West Country flavour. There are burgers and steaks, even beer-battered fish and chips (its accompanying peas 'smashed'), but this is a kitchen that can also turn out rolled lamb shoulder with goats' cheese crumb and salsa verde, or a Chateaubriand for two. Start with chicken liver parfait with apple and cider chutney, and finish with a zesty lemon tart accompanied by raspberry sorbet.

Chef Martyn Compton, Christopher & James Tanner **Owner** Christopher & James Tanner **Seats** 100, Pr/dining room 22 **Times** 12-2.30/6-9.30, Closed 25-26 & 31 Dec, Sun **Prices** Fixed L 2 course £12.95, Fixed D 3 course £15.95, Starter £4.50-£7.95, Main £12.50-£24.95, Dessert £5.95-£6.95, Service optional **Wines** 5 bottles over £30, 25 bottles under £30, 13 by glass **Parking** Drakes Circus, Guildhall **Notes** Fixed 2/3 course L menu pre-theatre, Children welcome

BEST WESTERN Duke of Cornwall Hotel

◉ Modern British, European

tel: 01752 275850 & 275855 **Millbay Rd PL1 3LG**
email: enquiries@thedukeofcornwall.co.uk **web:** www.thedukeofcornwall.co.uk
dir: *City centre, follow signs 'Pavilions', hotel road is opposite*

Modern cooking with West Country produce in a Victorian hotel

With its imperious Gothic exterior and impressive Victorian proportions within, the Duke of Cornwall deserves the epithet 'landmark'. You ain't gonna miss it. The restaurant is suitably refined and formal, with its chandelier, patterned carpet and tables dressed with fresh flowers and white linen. The kitchen works a modern European repertoire with a decent showing of West Country ingredients. Pulled Creedy Carver duck might turn up in a warm salad among first courses, with

another option being caramelised red onion and goats' cheese tart topped with an abundance of salad leaves. Main course medallion of venison is a good piece of meat, nicely cooked, accompanied by celeriac purée and château potatoes, while honey-roast duck breast is partnered with sauerkraut. To finish, white chocolate pannacotta is served in a glass with mixed summer berries and crushed almonds.

Chef Kevin Scargill **Owner** W Combstock, J Morcom **Seats** 80, Pr/dining room 30 **Times** 7-10, Closed 26-31 Dec, L all week **Prices** Fixed D 3 course £21.50, Starter £6-£6.75, Main £14.95-£19.95, Dessert £5-£5.95 **Wines** 8 by glass **Parking** 40, Also on street **Notes** Vegetarian available, Children welcome

The Greedy Goose

◉◉ Modern British **NEW**

tel: 01752 252001 **Prysten House, Finewell St PL1 2AE**
email: enquiries@thegreedygoose.co.uk
dir: *Exit A38 Marsh Mills. Follow Embankment Rd onto Gdynia Way. At Cattedown rdbt, take Exeter St to Royal Parade. 2nd left at rdbt*

Contemporary cooking in a venerable Barbican house

Tucked away in the oldest part of Plymouth, the historic Barbican district, ancient beams and stone walls are a testament to this building's antiquity. The restaurant sports a sleek look, with smart, claret-hued, high-backed chairs at polished wood tables, contemporary art on the walls, and arched leaded windows lending a church-like feel to the romantic ambience. The up-to-date cooking is built on seasonal West Country produce, producing a starter of pan-fried scallops with crispy black pudding fritters and celeriac purée, or perhaps a trio of duck liver parfait, rillettes and crackling with pear pickle and brioche. Creedy Carver duck also stars in a main course, supported by red cabbage, caramelised parsnips, fondant potatoes and rich gravy, while local boats supply the goodies for a multi-layered dish comprising plaice fillets with sea spinach, crisp Exmouth mussels, seaweed gnocchi, citrus-pickled fennel and mussel bisque. To finish, nougat and white chocolate parfait comes with raspberry sorbet, or there may be the nursery comforts of bread-and-butter pudding with spiced custard and Devon clotted cream.

Chef Ben Palmer **Owner** Ben Palmer, Francesca McBean **Seats** 50, Pr/dining room 30 **Times** 12-2.30/6-close, Closed 25 Dec, Sun-Mon **Prices** Fixed L 2 course £17, Fixed D 3 course £20, Tasting menu £50-£90, Starter £6-£10, Main £13-£28, Dessert £5-£8 **Wines** 43 bottles over £30, 33 bottles under £30, 12 by glass **Parking** Pay & display next to restaurant **Notes** Tasting menu 6 course, Vegetarian available, Children 4 yrs+

Langdon Court Hotel & Restaurant

◉◉ Traditional British, French V

tel: 01752 862358 **Adams Ln, Down Thomas PL9 0DY**
email: enquiries@langdoncourt.com **web:** www.langdoncourt.com
dir: *signed from A379 at Elburton rdbt*

Impressive regional cooking at a Tudor manor house

The South Hams district of Devon is one of the county's prize assets, and in Langdon Court the area has a country-house hotel fully worthy of it. A 16th-century manor house, it has played host to royal personages and their consorts all the way from Henry VIII and Catherine Parr to Edward VII and the actress Lillie Langtry. A home for sick children to convalesce in style, it returned to private ownership and hotel duties in 1960. Local farm supplies and the Devon catch make their way to the kitchen, where a dynamic approach has seen the cooking continue on an impressive upward trajectory. Ideas flow thick and fast: an Indian approach to scallops sees them teamed with saag aloo and a cauliflower bhaji, while the Japanese note sounds in a version of gravad lax cured in sake with wasabi crème fraîche. Fish for main might be pollock fillet with clams and leeks in cider, or there could be herb-crusted local lamb provençal. A hugely successful banana version of tarte Tatin comes with rich toffee ice cream.

Chef Jamie Rogers **Owner** Emma & Geoffrey Hill **Seats** 36, Pr/dining room 92 **Times** 12-3/6.30-9.30 **Prices** Fixed L 2 course £16, Fixed D 3 course £20, Tasting menu £49-£65, Starter £7-£12, Main £17-£25, Dessert £7.95-£9, Service optional **Wines** 26 bottles over £30, 26 bottles under £30, 8 by glass **Parking** 60 **Notes** Breakfast £15, Sunday L £12-£20, Children welcome

Rhodes@The Dome

🌸 Modern British

tel: 01752 266600 **Barbican PL1 2NZ**
email: info@rhodesatthedome.co.uk **web:** www.rhodesatthedome.co.uk
dir: On Plymouth Hoe

Modern bistro dining beneath the dome

Have a drink in the bar in the eponymous dome, with Smeaton's Tower above and the whole of Plymouth Sound before you, with a menu here running from brunch and tapas to cream teas, or head for the stylishly chic restaurant for the full works. Gary Rhodes brings his own stamp to proceedings, producing bistro-style menus and distinctively flavoured, unfussy dishes. A hash cake of corned beef, potato and onion, served with a poached egg and chive hollandaise, is typical of his output. To follow might come seared sea bream, perfectly timed, with spring onions, leeks, mushrooms and pak choi, all subtly spiked with ginger, and exemplary sauté potatoes. Variety might be extended by the likes of punchy chicken spring rolls with hoisin and bang-bang sauce, and to cap a meal try cappuccino pannacotta with grated bitter chocolate and clotted cream.

Chef Gary Rhodes, Paul Webber **Owner** Rhodes@The Dome Ltd **Seats** 150, Pr/dining room 25 **Times** 12-2.30/5.30-10, Closed 26 Dec, D 25 Dec **Prices** Starter £5-£8, Main £12-£29, Dessert £5.50, Service optional **Wines** 7 bottles over £30, 33 bottles under £30, 8 by glass **Parking** On street **Notes** Sunday L £12.95-£18.95, Vegetarian available, Children welcome

Rock Salt Café and Brasserie

🌸🌸 Modern British

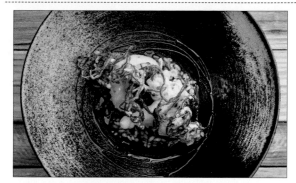

tel: 01752 225522 **31 Stonehouse St PL1 3PE**
email: info@rocksaltcafe.co.uk **web:** www.rocksaltcafe.co.uk
dir: Located between Brittany ferry port & Royal William Yard

Informal all-day eatery with confident cooking

Open all day and all week from breakfast until late, this former pub with its slate-tiled exterior and easy-going seasidey vibe strikes a relaxed pose but takes the food seriously. There's attention to detail in the likes of smoked salmon and scrambled egg with sourdough toast at breakfast, or a lunchtime king prawn laksa. This is a kitchen that can turn out a classy butter-roasted guinea fowl for lunch, alongside an open sandwich with steak, onion jam and fried egg. If you settle down in the evening for the full three courses you might go from potted shrimps with crayfish, pickles and toast to braised Cornish brill with fennel and anchovies, finishing with a dessert of vanilla pannacotta with passionfruit and honeycomb. It all takes place in a cheery setting of blond wood and tasteful neutral colours, and the service is suitably on the ball.

Chef David Jenkins, Joe Turner **Owner** Steve & David Jenkins **Seats** 60, Pr/dining room 25 **Times** 9am-10pm, All-day dining, Closed 24-26 Dec, 1-8 Jan **Prices** Fixed D 3 course £28, Tasting menu £45, Starter £3.95-£9.95, Main £9.95-£21.95, Dessert £5.50-£7.50, Service optional **Wines** 6 bottles over £30, 24 bottles under £30, 6 by glass **Parking** On street **Notes** Sunday L fr £13.95, Vegetarian available, Children welcome

---

Treby Arms

@@ Modern European

tel: 01752 837363 **Sparkwell PL7 5DD**
email: trebyarms@hotmail.co.uk
dir: *A38 Plympton turn off towards Langage & Dartmoor Zoological Park, signed Sparkwell*

Modern cooking of a high order from the 2012 *MasterChef* champ

The trim-looking Treby Arms with its whitewashed front stands in the Dartmoor village of Sparkwell, not far from major routes, but far enough for tranquillity. A small bar with log-fire caters for drinkers, but the greater part of the operation is turned over to dining, as you would expect from a place run by a *MasterChef The Professionals* champion. Anton Piotrowski has overseen an upsurge in business since his triumph. Stake your claim early, and be rewarded with locally-sourced, energetic modern cookery of a high order. First up might be a slab of meaty terrine served on a board, and composed of suckling pig and black pudding, garnished with mandarin, pickles and toasted brioche. Dishes can on occasion be a little over contrived, as when a small fillet of John Dory appears alongside a courgette flower stuffed with scallop and shrimp mousse and a king prawn wrapped in a jacket of pork crackling. Herb-rolled venison loin with confit onion, red cabbage and carrots looks more the part. Elegant desserts include a meringue globe encasing lemon curd and matching sorbet.

Chef Anton Piotrowski **Owner** Anton & Clare Piotrowski **Seats** 60
Times 12-3/6-9.30, Closed 25-26 Dec, 1 Jan, Mon **Prices** Service optional 12.5%
Wines 19 bottles over £30, 28 bottles under £30, 11 by glass **Parking** 14, Village hall opposite **Notes** Sunday L fr £16.95, Vegetarian available, Children welcome

---

The Jack In The Green Inn

@@ Modern British V

tel: 01404 822240 **EX5 2EE**
email: info@jackinthegreen.uk.com
dir: *3m E of M5 junct 29 on old A30*

A creative powerhouse in a Devon country pub

Even when busy – which it frequently is – The Jack never loses its cool, for this place is run with charm and generosity by Paul Parnell and his team. It looks and feels like a pub, with no airs and graces, just a satisfying mix of old and new throughout its series of atmospheric rooms. The kitchen is passionate about Devon produce and composes a menu awash with high quality ingredients that reflect the landscape and waters in this beautiful part of the country. There's a refined contemporary polish to the kitchen's output, for everything is presented with style, but flavour is always king. A savoury 'crème brûlée' made with chicken liver and wild morel mushrooms with celeriac and truffle is an up-to-date way to start, followed by a well-thought-out main course of five spice-scented Creedy Carver duck breast pointed with the tart note of griottine cherries, plus sweet potato fondant and pak choi. To finish, there's a zingy confection of lemon posset, lime pannacotta, mint and tequila granita and salted lemon ice cream.

Chef Matthew Mason **Owner** Paul Parnell **Seats** 80, Pr/dining room 60
Times 12-2/6-9, Closed 25 Dec-5 Jan **Prices** Fixed L 3 course £25, Tasting menu £25, Starter £5.50-£9.50, Main £9.95-£27.50, Dessert £6.50-£8.95, Service optional **Wines** 60 bottles over £30, 40 bottles under £30, 12 by glass **Parking** 120
Notes Sunday L £21.50-£26.50, Children welcome

Soar Mill Cove Hotel

@@ Modern British

tel: 01548 561566 **Soar Mill Cove, Marlborough TQ7 3DS**
email: info@soarmillcove.co.uk **web:** www.soarmillcove.co.uk
dir: *A381 to Salcombe, through village follow signs to sea*

Top-notch West Country produce and fab sea views

This family-run hotel is in a lovely location, with the cove below and uninterrupted sea views. A host of facilities, from a heated indoor seawater swimming pool, gym and sauna to tennis and snooker, plus a champagne bar, mean you may not want to leave the hotel. Another plus is this restaurant, done out in pale blue with floor-to-ceiling windows catching the fabulous view, and turning out consistently accomplished cooking. The kitchen has its roots in the classical techniques and gives its own modern spin to its output. Thus, sautéed scallops are partnered by melting crab thermidor and sautéed leeks. Timings are carefully judged and presentation is a strength, seen in a main course of roast chicken breast wrapped in bacon with Madeira jus accompanied by earthy girolles, parsnip purée and a tartlet of caramelised shallots. A fish option might bring on roast monkfish in ham with wild mushrooms, spinach and red wine sauce. Breads are made in-house, and well-executed puddings may stretch to silkily textured lemon and lime posset with vibrant raspberry coulis and home-made shortbread.

Chef I Macdonald **Owner** The Makepeace family **Seats** 60
Times 10.30-5/6-9, Closed Jan **Prices** Prices not confirmed, Service optional
Wines 21 bottles over £30, 25 bottles under £30, 6 by glass **Parking** 25
Notes Vegetarian available, Children welcome

Saunton Sands Hotel

@ Traditional, Modern British V

tel: 01271 890212 & 892001 **EX33 1LQ**
email: reservations@sauntonsands.com **web:** www.sauntonsands.com
dir: *Exit A361 at Braunton, signed Croyde B3231, hotel 2m on left*

Imaginative and complex cooking beside a beach

The location alone is a draw at this long white art deco hotel, as it overlooks a three-mile stretch of unspoiled sandy beach. It's a popular holiday destination, with a spa and pool and the beach on the doorstep, with rural and seaside pursuits nearby. Watch the sun set from the terrace or soak up the maritime views from the stylish restaurant with its original 1930s chandeliers. The kitchen is impassioned about using only West Country produce and turns out some stimulating dishes in the contemporary mould. The daily-changing menu might open with a complex but effective starter of soused mackerel with smoked mussels, curried mayonnaise, fennel and apple salad, fennel pollen and salted honeycomb, and proceed to pork belly with braised faggot, morcilla, pommes mousseline, quince purée and a cider and sage jus. A fish main-course option might be fillet of bream imaginatively paired with crab and ginger hash, served with braised chicory and shellfish bisque and espuma. Puddings include salted caramel tart with banana ice cream.

Chef D Turland, B Snelling **Owner** Brend Hotels **Seats** 200, Pr/dining room 20
Times 12.30-2/6.45-9.30 **Prices** Fixed L 2 course £19.95, Fixed D 3 course £36, Starter £8-£9.95, Main £16.95-£29.95, Dessert £6-£7.95, Service optional **Wines** 53 bottles over £30, 54 bottles under £30, 15 by glass **Parking** 140 **Notes** Sunday L, Children welcome

SHALDON
Map 3 SX97

ODE dining
◉◉ British

tel: 01626 873977 **21 Fore St TQ14 ODE**
email: contact@odetruefood.com
dir: Cross bridge, 1st right into Shoreside, directly left into car park

Top-quality local and organic produce in coastal village

This small restaurant, in a Georgian house in an estuary village, gets its name not from anything poetic but more prosaically from its postcode. Ethically sourced and organic produce is the name of the game here, with the kitchen delivering refined and ambitious dishes. Starters can range from salted and slow-cooked cod with granola and bay leaf cream to sugar-cured duck breast with a salad of pickled turnips and pears. Both accuracy and a flair for successful combinations are apparent in the handful of main courses: perhaps a winter offering of guinea fowl with squash, braised lentils and shiitaki mushrooms, or steamed sea bass in a rosemary crumb with crispy pork, Savoy cabbage, a blini and cider sauce. Artisan cheeses, served with house-made walnut toast and chutney, are all from the West Country. Otherwise, end with one of the imaginative puddings: walnut and date tart with vanilla and Earl Grey cream, or burnt cream with apple jelly and a rosemary scone. The owners also run a café and micro-brewery.

Chef Tim Bouget **Owner** Tim & Clare Bouget **Seats** 24 **Times** 7-9.30, Closed 25 Dec, BHs, Sun-Tue, L all week **Prices** Fixed D 3 course £25-£42.50, Service optional **Wines** 10 bottles over £30, 10 bottles under £30, 5 by glass **Parking** Car park 3 mins walk **Notes** Wed reduced price/menu 2/3 course £25/£30, Vegetarian available, Children 8 yrs+

SIDMOUTH
Map 3 SY18

Hotel Riviera
◉◉ Modern British

tel: 01395 515201 **The Esplanade EX10 8AY**
email: enquiries@hotelriviera.co.uk **web:** www.hotelriviera.co.uk
dir: From M5 junct 30 take A3052 to Sidmouth. Situated in centre of The Esplanade

Modern British dining in Regency Sidmouth

The name may suggest Cannes or Las Vegas, but Devon has its very own version of seaside grandeur, and the spotless bow-fronted Riviera is a prime example of it. The future Queen Victoria was brought on holiday here as a little girl, in the days when Sidmouth was all the rage. Tables on an outdoor terrace make the most of the summer weather, and a menu of gently modernised British cooking has something to cater for most tastes. Kick off with duck and blueberry terrine, served with spiced pear and toasted walnut and raisin bread, or perhaps a simple plate of Loch Fyne smoked salmon. Mains encompass bistro-style paupiette of lemon sole stuffed with salmon mousse alongside lemon couscous, as well as roast rack of local lamb with ratatouille, herbed mash and thyme jus. Finish off with with the likes of egg custard tart with nutmeg ice cream and blackcurrant coulis.

Chef Martin Osedo **Owner** Peter Wharton **Seats** 85, Pr/dining room 65
Times 12.30-2/7-9 **Prices** Fixed L 2 course £25, Fixed D 3 course £38, Starter £10.50-£14, Main £16-£32, Dessert £6.50-£10.50, Service optional **Wines** 45 bottles over £30, 31 bottles under £30, 10 by glass **Parking** 26 **Notes** Fixed L 4 course £29.50, D 5 course £42, Sunday L, Vegetarian available, Children welcome

The Salty Monk
◉◉ Modern British V

tel: 01395 513174 **Church St, Sidford EX10 9QP**
email: saltymonk@btconnect.com **web:** www.saltymonk.co.uk
dir: From M5 junct 30 take A3052 to Sidmouth, or from Honiton take A375 to Sidmouth, 200yds on right opposite church in village

Gentle modern British food in a former salt house

The name is not a reference to a seafaring friar, but rather the building's 16th-century role as a store for the salt the monks' traded at Exeter Cathedral. These days, Andy and Annette Witheridge run the place as a charming restaurant with rooms with an inviting garden and courtyard patio for outdoor dining on balmy days. The Garden Room restaurant (open for dinner and Sunday lunch) makes a suitably smart yet understated backdrop for Andy's unpretentious cooking, which brings together top-notch regional ingredients with disarming simplicity, underpinned by sound technique. To begin, Capricorn goats' cheese pannacotta is pointed up with apricot and lentil relish, or there might be braised pork cheek set in its own jelly with home-made piccalilli and melba toast. Main course is an imaginative pairing of confit duck tartlet with slow-roasted belly pork, champ potatoes and a light porky jus bringing it all together. To finish, a classic lemon tart comes hot from the oven with clotted cream.

Chef Annette & Andy Witheridge, Scott Horn **Owner** Annette & Andy Witheridge **Seats** 45 **Times** 12-1.30/6.30-9, Closed 1 wk Nov & Jan, L Mon-Wed **Prices** Prices not confirmed, Service optional **Wines** 22 bottles over £30, 47 bottles under £30, 14 by glass **Parking** 20 **Notes** Tasting menu 7 course, Sunday L, Children welcome

The Victoria Hotel
◉ Traditional

tel: 01395 512651 **The Esplanade EX10 8RY**
email: reservations@victoriahotel.co.uk **web:** www.victoriahotel.co.uk
dir: At western end of The Esplanade

Turn-of-the-century splendour beside the sea

The Victoria's old-world charm and dignity isn't exactly the fashion these days. There's a doorman to usher you inside the handsome building, gents have to put on their jackets and ties in the dining room, and a pianist tinkles away at the ivories. For some, that's just the ticket. The setting at the end of the town's impressive Georgian esplanade is alluring, with the expansive bay offered up in all its shimmering glory. The formal restaurant has pastel tones and spiffy table settings, and what appears on the plate is generally classically minded and based on local ingredients. Devonshire chicken liver parfait with toasted brioche and piccalilli is one way to begin, or confit of salmon with pickled cucumber, beetroot, and vanilla mayonnaise. Main-course fillet of turbot might follow on, or rack of pork with celeriac purée and black pudding, and, for dessert, perhaps a chocolate tart.

Times 1-2/7-9

Find out more about how we assess for Rosette awards on page 9

The Laughing Monk

◉ Modern British

tel: 01803 770639 **Totnes Rd TQ6 0RN**
email: thelaughingmonk@btconnect.com
dir: A38 & follow signs towards Dartmouth, 700yds past Dartmouth Golf Club take right turn to Strete. Restaurant on left just past church

Resourceful and interesting cooking in the South Hams

The South West Coast Path runs practically outside the front door of this converted old school, and both Slapton and Blackpool Sands are a mere mile or so away. The place has been given a bit of a refurb, and offers a light-filled, airy space with an impressive inglenook and a cheery atmosphere. The kitchen makes enviable use of Devon's resources and turns out carefully composed dishes, often with stimulating touches. Crab and prawn cocktail, for instance, is served with guacamole and lime mayonnaise, and crisp salt-and-pepper squid with Asian salad and sweet chilli dressing. Seafood figures prominently, from roast monkfish and prawns with rösti and pepper confit to sea bass fillet in pancetta with pea purée, roast asparagus and tomato vinaigrette. Carnivores are not overlooked: there might be roast rump of lamb with fondant potato, ratatouille and black raisin sauce. Caramelised apple crumble with custard is a good way to end.

Chef Ben Handley **Owner** Ben & Jackie Handley **Seats** 60 **Times** 6.30-9, Closed Xmas, Jan, Sun-Mon, L all week **Prices** Starter £6-£10, Main £14-£30, Dessert £6-£9 **Wines** 6 bottles over £30, 23 bottles under £30, 5 by glass **Parking** 4, On street **Notes** Early supper menu Tue-Fri, Vegetarian available, Children welcome

Bedford Hotel

◉ British

tel: 01822 613221 **1 Plymouth Rd PL19 8BB**
email: enquiries@bedford-hotel.co.uk **web:** www.bedford-hotel.co.uk
dir: M5 junct 31, A30 (Launceston/Okehampton). Then A386 to Tavistock, follow town centre signs. Hotel opposite church

Confident modern cooking in a Gothic hotel

The Gothic building with its castellated walls certainly makes an impression – which is what that style is all about – but those walls were never intended to keep out invaders. This place has always been about hospitality, and so it remains today. There's no lack of character and charm within, including the restaurant with its moulded ceilings and panelled walls. So far, so traditional. The kitchen takes a more contemporary position, but a reassuringly gentle one. A first-course potted rabbit is one way to begin, or go for salmon ballotine in the more modern company of pickled beetroot and wasabi mayonnaise. Devon venison bourguignon is a flavoursome main course, as is a well-judged dish of duck and chorizo. Desserts such as egg custard or treacle tart with Devon clotted cream show off good technical skills, and there are West Country cheeses if you still have room.

Chef Mike Palmer **Owner** Warm Welcome Hotels **Seats** 55, Pr/dining room 30 **Times** 12-2.30/7-9, Closed 24-26 Dec **Prices** Fixed L 2 course £15-£20, Fixed D 3 course £25-£35, Starter £5.50-£8.50, Main £11.50-£22, Dessert £5-£7.50, Service optional **Wines** 4 bottles over £30, 38 bottles under £30, 11 by glass **Parking** 48 **Notes** Sunday L £21.95, Vegetarian available, Children welcome

The Horn of Plenty

◉◉◉ – see opposite

Thurlestone Hotel

◉ British

tel: 01548 560382 **TQ7 3NN**
email: enquiries@thurlestone.co.uk **web:** www.thurlestone.co.uk
dir: A38 take A384 into Totnes, A381 towards Kingsbridge, onto A379 towards Churchstow, onto B3197 turn into lane signed to Thurlestone

Stunning sea views and well-judged cooking using regional produce

The view across the golf course and sub-tropical gardens to the sea and distant horizon is a cracker (especially from the terrace), and with its proximity to Salcombe, the Thurlestone is a south Devon hotspot. With a spa and all mod cons, there's plenty to keep you occupied, rain or shine. The Margaret Amelia restaurant is another star attraction, with its formal table setting and glorious views through the floor-to-ceiling picture windows. The menu makes good use of the region's produce in dishes that have classical foundations. Cornish blue cheese pannacotta is an inventive opener, or go for half a grilled lobster. Next up, a sorbet (lemon, maybe) followed by a main course, such as confit of belly pork with crackling, champ, Calvados raisins and Bramley apple purée. For dessert, white chocolate crème brûlée with a compôte of summer berries and shortbread biscuit hits the spot.

Times 12.30-2.30/7.30-9, Closed 2 wks Jan, L Mon-Sat

Corbyn Head Hotel

◉ Modern, Traditional

tel: 01803 213611 **Torbay Rd, Sea Front TQ2 6RH**
email: info@corbynhead.com **web:** www.corbynhead.com
dir: Follow signs to Torquay seafront, turn right on seafront. Hotel on right with green canopies

Seafront hotel with imaginative and accomplished cooking

Bang on the seafront, with views over the bay, this white hotel with green awnings above the windows is a blaze of colourful flowers in summer. It's an ideal holiday destination, with an outdoor pool; it also has conference facilities and is a popular wedding venue. It's no poser to guess where the Harbour View Restaurant got its name. The dining area is a pretty room done out in shades of pink, while the kitchen sets itself high standards and turns out dishes in an ambitious, contemporary style. Among starters, ham hock and black pudding terrine is deeply flavoured and tasty, cut by gooseberry relish, or there might be crab and salmon roulade with pickled shredded vegetables and sesame dressing. Main courses are commendably restrained – confit duck leg with vegetable stir-fry and peppercorn sauce, for instance – and fish is a strength, judging by pan-fried cod fillet, of superb quality, fleshy and succulent, with saffron sauce and creamed leeks. End with indulgent clotted cream rice pudding with blueberry compôte.

Times 12-2/7-9, Closed L Mon-Sat

The Elephant Restaurant and Brasserie

◉◉◉ – see opposite

The Horn of Plenty ❀❀❀

Modern British
tel: 01822 832528 **Gulworthy PL19 8JD**
email: enquiries@thehornofplenty.co.uk **web:** www.thehornofplenty.co.uk
dir: *From Tavistock take A390 W for 3m. Right at Gulworthy Cross. In 400yds turn left, hotel in 400yds on right*

Confident contemporary cooking and glorious valley views

Set on the fringes of the Dartmoor National Park, The Horn of Plenty is a country-house hotel on a human scale, offering views to die for across the Tamar Valley and the kind of cosseting luxury that feels like home (if only home were like this!). It was built in the 19th century for a mine captain, and there's plenty of Regency period charm inside and out, plus five acres of landscaped gardens and wild orchards. The dining room — it feels more like a hotel dining room than a restaurant, but not in a bad way — has daylight views and a satisfying intimacy, watched over by a soothing service crew who banish any hint of stuffiness. Headed up by Scott Paton, the team in the kitchen are a progressive bunch, who deliver sharp, contemporary food celebrating locally grown and reared produce (including seasonal stuff from the hotel's own garden). Dishes exhibit a fine-tuned precision with three-dimensional flavours and juxtapositions that make sense. Spot the respect for classical French roots in a starter of seared veal sweetbreads and punchy braised ox cheek with wild garlic purée, served atop a sweet blini base, then taste those flavour-smacking Asian notes in a main course of pan-roast fillet of turbot with Thai-scented vegetable purée and crab and ginger tortellini, all offset by a sharp lime emulsion. There are good skills on show in meat-based ideas too — perhaps a tender pork neck fillet matched with pork-stuffed agnolotti, hazelnuts, smoked bacon and braised gem lettuce. Finish with a skilfully executed composition involving mango mousse with intense compressed mango, coconut sorbet and passionfruit curd.

Chef Scott Paton **Owner** Julie Leivers, Damien Pease **Seats** 60, Pr/dining room 16 **Times** 12-2.15/7-10.15 **Prices** Fixed L 2 course £19.50, Fixed D 3 course £49.50, Tasting menu £65, Service optional **Wines** 34 bottles over £30, 29 bottles under £30, 11 by glass **Parking** 25, On street **Notes** Sunday L £19.50-£24.50, Vegetarian available, Children welcome

The Elephant Restaurant and Brasserie ❀❀❀

Modern British
tel: 01803 200044 **3-4 Beacon Ter TQ1 2BH**
email: info@elephantrestaurant.co.uk
dir: *Follow signs for Living Coast, restaurant opposite*

Ambitious contemporary cooking from a Devon food hero

On a rising street above the harbour, not far from the secluded Beacon Cove where local lass Agatha Christie used to go swimming as a girl, The Elephant has for many years been a kind of beacon in itself. A double-fronted place in a former townhouse, it's split over two levels. On the ground floor is a breezy, informally run, year-round Brasserie with a simpler but inspired menu of modern food, but the culinary stops are pulled out in the first-floor Room, open from late spring to early autumn. Here, an ambitious contemporary tasting menu is served in a pastel-hued period ambience, with clothed tables and perfectly informed service. Simon Hulstone is something of a Devon food hero, and an integral part of the Elephant's output these days is sourced from the establishment's own 69-acre smallholding in the south of the county. Wild and foraged ingredients feature prominently too, as in the starter of Brixham crab with pickled turnip and samphire, and a croquette of crab and lovage. A dish of cucumber sorbet melting into a bowl of tomato consommé is an essay in summer freshness, and the astonishing follow-up is beetroot Tatin caramelised with red wine, served with smoked blueberries and a snow of Vulscombe goats' cheese, the whole scented with lemon thyme. Main course could be opalescent cod with lardo ibérico and dill pollen in verjus, or perhaps local lamb with ceps, grelot onions and yin yang beans. The desserts line-up includes a sabayon dish of summer berries topped with Korean mint ice cream, and an olive-oiled chocolate mousse with blackberry sorbet, candied pistachios and a decorative frill of wood-sorrel. Fine breads and petits fours underscore the painstaking attention to detail.

Chef Simon Hulstone **Owner** Peter Morgan, Simon Hulstone **Seats** 75, Pr/dining room 12 **Times** 12-2/6.30-9, Closed 1st 2 wks Jan, Sun-Mon **Prices** Tasting menu £55 **Wines** 24 bottles over £30, 30 bottles under £30, 8 by glass **Parking** Opposite restaurant **Notes** Vegetarian available, Children 12 yrs+

TORQUAY *continued*

Grand Hotel

◉ Modern European

tel: 01803 296677 **Torbay Rd TQ2 6NT**
email: reservations@grandtorquay.co.uk **web:** www.grandtorquay.co.uk
dir: *M5 junct 31, follow signs for Torquay. At the Penn Inn rdbt follow signs for seafront*

Grand-hotel dining on the English Riviera

Occupying a prime position on Torquay's seafront, the Grand certainly has presence, built in Victorian times and expanding as the popularity of the English Riviera grew. Behind the impressive Victorian façade are art deco features and over 130 bedrooms. The main dining option is the 1881 Restaurant (in honour of the year the hotel opened), with its genteel formality in keeping with its august past (Agatha Christie spent her honeymoon here). The menu sticks to traditional ideas with just enough contemporary thrust to satisfy both schools. Start with celeriac and apple soup, or dressed crab salad fired up with wasabi, and move onto pan-fried sea bass with king prawns and pearl barley. There are steaks cooked on the grill, and, for dessert, lemon posset comes with shortbread, candied lemons and berry compôte.

Times 12.30-3/6.30-9.30, Closed L Mon-Sat

The Headland Hotel

◉ Modern, Traditional

tel: 01803 295666 **Daddyhole Rd TQ1 2EF**
email: info@headlandtorquay.com **web:** www.headlandtorquay.com
dir: *Phone for directions*

Confident cooking and a sea view

This Victorian villa originally built for royalty (the Romanov's of Russia, no less) has a prime spot overlooking the best the English Riviera has to offer in the form of the promised headland and the sparkling blue sea (some of the time at least). There are two acres of pretty gardens to explore, a heated outdoor pool and an elegant restaurant named after those famous regal former residents. The sea-facing dining room has grand proportions, a great view and a traditional finish. The kitchen turns out well-crafted dishes based on good quality ingredients. Start with a smooth and lightly whipped liver parfait with beetroot chutney and toasted brioche, followed by grilled sea bass with mussels, samphire and a full-flavoured white wine and dill cream.Desserts can be as comforting as a chocolate brownie wheel, accompanied by hot chocolate sauce and whipped cream.

Times 6.30-8.30

The Imperial Hotel

◉ Modern British

tel: 01803 294301 **Park Hill Rd TQ1 2DG**
email: imperialtorquay@thehotelcollection.co.uk **web:** www.thehotelcollection.co.uk
dir: *M5 to Exeter, A380 then A3022 to Torquay. Park Hill Rd off Torwood St/Babbacombe Rd, just N of New Harbour*

Superb views and careful, unpretentious cooking

The Imperial's Victorian founders couldn't have chosen a better spot for their hotel, whose clifftop position has wide-ranging views over the bay and Channel. The Regatta Restaurant is housed in a pleasant, spacious room with a sense of grandness, and it is worth getting here before sunset for the full experience. The kitchen chooses its ingredients diligently, making good use of fish and local produce, and turns out well-considered, carefully timed dishes. It has a flair for presentation, too, without over-complicating what appears on the plate. Home-made Brixham fishcake is a well-executed starter, served with pea shoot salad, or go for a pressing of ham hock accompanied by a pear poached in red wine. Next up, rump of highland lamb with spiced aubergine caviar and rosemary-flavoured potato fondant, and to finish, go for cherry pannacotta.

Chef Jacek Gorney **Owner** The Hotel Collection **Seats** 170, Pr/dining room 350 **Times** 7-9.30, Closed L all week **Prices** Prices not confirmed, Service optional **Wines** 15 bottles over £30, 47 bottles under £30, 18 by glass **Parking** 110, NCP town centre **Notes** Vegetarian available, Children welcome

Orestone Manor

◉◉ Modern, European V

tel: 01803 328098 **Rockhouse Ln, Maidencombe TQ1 4SX**
email: info@orestonemanor.com **web:** www.orestonemanor.com
dir: *A379 to Shaldon. Follow road through, hotel signed on left (beware sharp turn)*

Capable cooking in boutique manor house

This handsome Georgian manor house peeps out invitingly from landscaped grounds over Lyme Bay. Family-run, and with just 11 stylish bedrooms, Orestone exudes a civilised, personable charm combined with the serious attitude to gastronomy you'd expect from a hotel owned by a pair of chefs. The main restaurant is a traditional space with wooden floors and linen-swathed tables that makes the most of its views of gardens and sea. It is a suitably upmarket setting with uniformed staff offering correctly formal service for the kitchen's ambitious à la carte menus. Classic French-accented technique allied to top-quality local produce delivers a refined starter of beetroot carpaccio with Vulscombe goats' cheese, red pepper jelly, pine nuts and apple and elderflower syrup. If the nearness of the briny puts you in the mood for fish, pan-fried brill fillet arrives with poached celery, wild mushrooms, smoked garlic mash, clams and ceps cream. For dessert, yogurt pannacotta pairs effectively with passionfruit coulis, mangosteen and hazelnuts, or go for a savoury finish with artisan West Country cheeses.

Chef Tom Ward, Neil & Catherine D'Allen **Owner** Neil & Catherine D'Allen **Seats** 55, Pr/dining room 22 **Times** 12-2.30/6.30-9.30, Closed 3-30 Jan **Prices** Fixed L 2 course £19, Fixed D 3 course £25, Tasting menu £47, Starter £5.50-£12, Main £12-£25, Dessert £6.50-£7.50, Service optional **Wines** 22 bottles over £30, 45 bottles under £30, 12 by glass **Parking** 38 **Notes** Tasting menu at wknds or by arrangement, Sunday L £12.50, Children welcome

TOTNES
Map 3 SX86

The Riverford Field Kitchen
@ Modern British, Organic

tel: 01803 762074 **Riverford TQ11 0JU**
email: fieldkitchen@riverford.co.uk
dir: *From A38 Buckfastleigh, take A384 to Totnes. Left to Riverford Organics*

Vegetables take a starring role at this organic Devon farm

If you've sampled the veg boxes, or maybe just seen the vans busying along your road heading to someone else's doorstep, you'll have an idea of what to expect here. This is the hub of the Riverford brand (they have five farms around the country now), delivering organically grown fruit and veg across the land. At Wash Barn you can take a look around the farm, stock up on supplies, or hunker down at communal tables for some good and hearty organic food. It's a fixed deal of whatever is on-the-money that day, with lots of ace organic vegetable and salad accompaniments. Start with a salad packed with beetroot, pickled kohlrabi and Millstone cheese, walnuts and radish sprouts – a winning combination. Next up, a main course of barbecue chicken flavoured with paprika and served up with an array of side dishes – carrots with fennel, rainbow chard with lemon and garlic, potatoes and roasted red peppers, and more. To finish, try an egg custard tart with gooseberry compôte.

Chef Rob Andrew **Owner** Guy Watson **Seats** 72 **Times** 12.30-3/7-11.30, Closed D Sun **Prices** Fixed L 3 course fr £23.50, Fixed D 3 course fr £27.50, Service optional **Wines** 2 bottles over £30, 16 bottles under £30, 7 by glass **Parking** 30 **Notes** Sunday L fr £23.50, Vegetarian available, Children welcome

TWO BRIDGES
Map 3 SX67

Two Bridges Hotel
@ Modern British

tel: 01822 892300 **PL20 6SW**
email: enquiries@twobridges.co.uk **web:** www.twobridges.co.uk
dir: *8m from Tavistock on B3357, hotel at junct with B3312*

Dartmoor coaching inn with modern British food

The hotel began life in 1792 as the Saracen's Head coaching inn, but was later renamed in honour of the pair of ancient bridges that span the twin sources of the river here. It's a white-fronted building of obvious venerability, with a prettily appointed dining room named Tors, after the local topographical features depicted in the stained-glass panels. Here, a gentle style of British modernism is practised, which might run to goats' cheese tortellini in tomato consommé, ahead of cheek, loin and belly of local pork in maple syrup with broccoli and walnuts. Chicken liver parfait has its richness offset by pickled veg, while a main-course seafood array provides hake, crayfish and little fishcakes with braised baby gem and mustard mash. Finish with crème brûlée and rhubarb sorbet, or boozed-up spotted dick with whisky custard and vanilla ice cream. West Country cheeses come with fig chutney.

Times 12-2/6.30-9.30

What makes the perfect steak?
Find out on page 20

WOOLACOMBE
Map 3 SS44

Watersmeet Hotel
@@ Traditional British, European

tel: 01271 870333 **Mortehoe EX34 7EB**
email: info@watersmeethotel.co.uk **web:** www.watersmeethotel.co.uk
dir: *M5 junct 27. Follow A361 to Woolacombe, right at beach car park, 300yds on right*

Punchy modern dishes and stunning sunsets

This sparkling-white meringue of a building stands above the bay at Mortehoe on the north Devon coast, with views across to the birders' island paradise of Lundy. The waves smashing on to the rocks below offer a beguiling vista that often has guests just sitting and gazing. The westerly situation makes for alluring sunsets too. Factor in accurately cooked, punchy modern dishes as well, and the Watersmeet is a sure-fire winner. An enterprising fixed-price menu may lead you from smoked pigeon breast with a game sausage, Savoy cabbage purée and salt-baked beetroot to well-seasoned and carefully timed plaice fillets in herb sauce with diced fried potatoes and bacon and hazelnut dressing, or perhaps a serving of Exmoor sirloin with mini-steak and tongue pudding and truffled mash. Simple but boldly flavoured desserts encompass the likes of apple and vanilla delice with blackcurrant sorbet, or a pairing of pannacotta and zabaglione with plum compôte. If sweet stuff isn't your thing, there are thoroughbred West Country cheeses, served with pickled celery.

Chef John Prince **Owner** Mrs James **Seats** 56, Pr/dining room 18 **Times** 12-2/6.30-9 **Prices** Prices not confirmed, Service optional **Parking** 40 **Notes** Sunday L, Vegetarian available, Children 8 yrs+

DORSET

BEAMINSTER
Map 4 ST40

BridgeHouse
@@ Modern European

tel: 01308 862200 **3 Prout Bridge DT8 3AY**
email: enquiries@bridge-house.co.uk **web:** www.bridge-house.co.uk
dir: *From A303 take A356 towards Dorchester. Turn right onto A3066, 200mtrs down hill from town centre*

Up-to-date cooking in a 13th-century building

There's a sense of refinement to BridgeHouse, where the original heritage of the building (all 700 years of it) is respected and maintained, but a sheen of modernity prevents any feeling of stuffiness. It's a class act. That goes for its Beaminster Brasserie, too, which consists of three areas: a slightly more formal panelled and candlelit main room with an Adam fireplace, a conservatory and the terrace overlooking the walled garden. Similarly, the kitchen strikes a good balance between creativity and reassuring classical thinking, with a good amount of regional produce bringing a sense of place. West Bay crab from down the road turns up in an orientally-inspired first course with samphire spring rolls and bonbons, plus pickled cucumber and sweet chilli. Main course roasted local partridge is a more classical (or classical European) offering with dauphinoise potatoes, braised Savoy cabbage, lardons, baby onions and wild mushrooms. There's a sure hand in the kitchen, with flavours hitting the mark throughout. To finish, warm pistachio cake is perked up by its accompanying poached pear, nifty ginger beer gel and blackberry ice cream.

Chef Stephen Pielesz **Owner** Mark & Joanna Donovan **Seats** 45, Pr/dining room 45 **Times** 12-2/7-9 **Prices** Fixed L 2 course £14-£30, Fixed D 3 course £28-£49, Starter £6.50-£10.95, Main £14.50-£22.50, Dessert £6.50-£14.50 **Wines** 18 bottles over £30, 29 bottles under £30, 8 by glass **Parking** 20 **Notes** Sunday L £15.50-£45, Vegetarian available, Children welcome

BEST WESTERN The Connaught Hotel

◎◎ Modern British

tel: 01202 298020 **30 West Hill Rd, West Cliff BH2 5PH**
email: reception@theconnaught.co.uk **web:** www.theconnaught.co.uk
dir: *Follow Town Centre West & BIC signs*

Traditionally based British cooking in a grand seaside hotel

The Connaught, as befits its name, is a rather grand old beast, ruling the roost on Bournemouth's West Cliff, with pristine sandy beaches stretching below it. It offers sumptuous prospects all round, and its principal dining room, Blakes, overlooks the hotel's own gardens, where candlelit outdoor tables are a delightful feature on balmy southern evenings. Inside, a curtain divides the room at less busy sessions, the better to create a sense of intimacy, and the lightly formal tone makes an agreeable ambience for carefully considered, traditionally based British dishes. Seared scallops are presented in a delicate bouillabaisse broth with various textural treatments of fennel. That might be followed by roast breast and confit leg of pheasant with Maris Piper mash, pancetta and baby onions in red wine, or seared bream in a saffron-scented nage of mussels. Celebrate the domestic fruit season with a dessert that combines roasted plums and plum and sloe berry sorbet with silky buttermilk pannacotta. If you're having cheese instead, seek out the local Dorset varieties on the trolley.

Chef Ben Nicol **Owner** Franklyn Hotels Ltd **Seats** 80, Pr/dining room 16 **Times** 6.30-9, Closed L all week (private lunches by arrangement) **Prices** Starter £6-£6.95, Main £15-£27.50, Dessert £6-£6.95 **Wines** 25 bottles over £30, 24 bottles under £30, 13 by glass **Parking** 66 **Notes** Pre-theatre menu must pre-book, Vegetarian available, Children welcome

Bournemouth Highcliff Marriott Hotel

◎◎ Modern British

tel: 01202 557702 **St Michael's Rd, West Cliff BH2 5DU**
email: reservations.bournemouth@marriotthotels.co.uk **web:** www.highcliffgrill.co.uk
dir: *Take A338 dual carriageway through Bournemouth, then follow signs for International Centre to West Cliff Rd, then 2nd right*

Up-to-date cooking in a colourful clifftop hotel restaurant

As the name pretty much shouts out, it's on a high clifftop overlooking the lush golden sands of Bournemouth beach, and is a majestic old seaside hotel in the grandest vein, with imperious sea views as standard. The dining room has been hauled into the modern era with a stripped-down but colourful look, featuring unclothed tables amid striped and spotted upholstery in candy colours. Up-to-date ingredients and techniques, backed by the provender of local suppliers, distinguish the extensive menus. Smoked mutton 'bacon' with beer-pickled wild mushrooms and onions, zizzed up with horseradish, is an assertive opener, rabbit terrine with date and orange pastilla and pickled carrots perhaps a little overwhelmed by its accompaniments. A partnership of brown crabmeat and quinoa makes an interesting discovery in the context of a main dish of fried hake, while local rose veal comes as roast loin and braised shin with salt-baked celeriac, curly kale and apple. Finish with a rhubarb and custard spin, the former poached and jellied, the latter set into a pannacotta garnished with honeycomb.

Chef Matthew Budden **Owner** Marriott International **Seats** 80, Pr/dining room 14 **Times** 1-3/6-9.30, Closed L Mon-Sat, D Sun (winter) **Prices** Starter £7.50-£9.50, Main £14.50-£29.50, Dessert £4.50-£10 **Wines** 27 bottles over £30, 20 bottles under £30, 11 by glass **Parking** 100 **Notes** Taste of Dorset menu 2/3 course £20/£25, Afternoon tea, Sunday L £15-£20, Vegetarian available, Children welcome

The Crab at Bournemouth

◎◎ Seafood

tel: 01202 203601 **Exeter Rd BH2 5AJ**
email: info@crabatbournemouth.com **web:** www.crabatbournemouth.com
dir: *Follow signs to BIC, restaurant opposite*

Seafood specialist on the Bournemouth seafront

The very essence of a seafront venue, The Crab is part of the pristine white-fronted Park Central Hotel, but functions very much as a restaurant in its own right. Recent refurbishment brings a new layout and refitted bar and dining room, and the prevailing tone is of crabshell and sandy hues against a background of dark wood. The seafood theme is reflected in colourful charger plates, but mainly in the menus, where a cornucopia of fresh fish and shellfish spills forth. Preparations are never less than appetising, whether you're starting with John Ross smoked salmon, Caesar risotto and a poached egg, or seared scallops with truffled butternut purée and pancetta. A half-lobster makes a magnificent main, or go large for the whole thing, thermidored, garlic-buttered, or even with Thai-style coconut dressing. Otherwise, there are sea bass with clams, mussels and crab in bouillabaisse, or crab-crusted sole with crayfish potato crush and olive jus. Finish with dark chocolate tart and passionfruit sorbet. A set menu supplements the carte, and there's a namesake sibling restaurant at Chieveley in Berkshire.

Chef Nick Hope **Owner** Julie Savage **Seats** 80 **Times** 12-2.30/5.30-10 **Prices** Fixed L 2 course £16.95, Fixed D 3 course £20.95, Starter £6.95-£10.95, Main £14.50-£42.95, Dessert £5.95-£8.50 **Wines** 18 bottles over £30, 24 bottles under £30, 19 by glass **Parking** BIC **Notes** Pre-theatre 3 course 5.30-7pm £20.95, Sunday L £20.95, Vegetarian available, Children welcome

Cumberland Hotel

◎◎ British

tel: 01202 290722 & 556529 **27 East Overcliff Dr BH1 3AF**
email: kwood@cumberlandbournemouth.co.uk **web:** www.cumberlandbournemouth.co.uk
dir: A35 towards East Cliff & beaches, right onto Holdenhurst Rd, straight over 2 rdbts, left at junct to East Overcliff Drive, hotel on seafront

Modern brasserie food and poolside barbecues art deco-style

Sitting proud above Bournemouth Bay, the Cumberland is a beautifully preserved specimen of British art deco, built in 1937. It rises in orderly geometric snowy-white tiers with covered balconies and a sign in elegant period lettering, and retains all its key features inside, with judiciously done recent additions. The Mirabelle Restaurant offers standard hotel cuisine with accompaniment from a grand piano as white as the building itself, while a more obviously contemporary menu is the drill in the Ventana Grand Café, which opens on to a swimming pool with lido seating, where barbecues and cocktails are the order of many a summer day. Otherwise, expect lively brasserie dishes like salmon fishcake with spinach and sorrel sauce, followed by braised oxtail with champ and cabbage cooked with bacon and cumin, or the house fish pie with a portion of garlic soda bread. Gourmet burgers won't lack for takers, and nor will the likes of sherry-lashed, Swiss roll-based trifle to finish. Cheese plates show off Dorset's finest. Steak nights and Fish Fridays help to keep the crowds rolling in.

Chef Mateusz Nowatkowski **Owner** Kevin Wood **Seats** 90, Pr/dining room 40 **Times** 12-10, All-day dining, Closed 25 Dec, L 26 Dec, D 31 Dec **Prices** Starter £5-£8, Main £10-£27, Dessert £5-£7, Service optional **Wines** 4 bottles over £30, 24 bottles under £30, 8 by glass **Parking** 55, On street **Notes** Afternoon tea £12.95, Sunday L £12.95-£19.95, Vegetarian available, Children welcome

The Green House

◎◎ Modern British

tel: 01202 498900 **4 Grove Rd BH1 3AX**
email: info@thegreenhousehotel.com **web:** www.thegreenhousehotel.co.uk
dir: Phone for directions

Resourceful cooking built on eco-friendly produce

'The greenest hotel in the UK,' claims The Green House, a striking-looking, centrally located property converted and run on sustainable principles. There are beehives on the roof, and the Arbor (Latin for 'tree' to underline its green credentials) Restaurant deals in only organic, Fair Trade and farm-assured, mostly local produce. The seasonally-changing menu might open in summer with pan-fried salmon with spiced puy lentils and coconut foam or truffled gnocchi, peas and English feta. Main courses can then include Mendip Hills lamb loin and tongue, confit onion and potato terrine or glazed pork cheek with wholegrain mustard potato cake and baby vegetables. Local hand-made cheeses, accompanied by home-cooked biscuits and chutney, are a savoury alternative to puddings like summer berry soup with creamy strawberry parfait combined with meringue.

Chef Andrew Hilton **Owner** City Eco Hotel Ltd **Seats** 38, Pr/dining room 70 **Times** 12-14.30/5.30-9.30 **Prices** Fixed L 2 course fr £17, Starter £4.50-£6.50, Main £11.50-£21, Dessert £5.50-£9.50, Service optional 12.5% **Wines** 14 bottles over £30, 16 bottles under £30, 9 by glass **Parking** 30 **Notes** Pre-theatre 3 course £20, Sunday L £20, Vegetarian available, Children welcome

Hermitage Hotel

◎ Traditional British V

tel: 01202 557363 **Exeter Rd BH2 5AH**
email: info@hermitage-hotel.co.uk **web:** www.hermitage-hotel.co.uk
dir: Follow A338 (Ringwood-Bournemouth) & signs to pier, beach & BIC. Hotel directly opposite

Seafront hotel with ambitious and thoughtful cooking

The Hermitage couldn't be in a better location, opposite the beach and pier and a few minutes from the centre. Its restaurant is a large, high-ceilinged room with white linen on properly laid tables where service is on the correct side, with staff formally attired. The interesting menus offer variety aplenty, as they must with residents eating here perhaps every evening. Starters are along the lines of seared scallops with chorizo, cauliflower purée and minted pea dressing, while main courses include steaks, seared duck breast with beetroot jus, fondant potato and wilted spinach, or whole Dover sole. Flavour combinations are straightforward and effective, seen in potted ham hock cut by piccalilli and a pickled duck egg, and crisp-skinned pan-fried fillet of bream in chive butter accompanied by clams and mussels, confit tomatoes and new potatoes. Puddings don't disappoint either: go for clementine and honeycomb parfait with caramelised orange, or even crêpe Suzette.

Chef Seth Le Noury **Owner** Mr P D Oram **Seats** 120, Pr/dining room 50 **Times** 10-2/6.15-9 **Prices** Starter £6.50-£8.95, Main £17.95-£25.95, Service optional **Wines** 8 by glass **Parking** 60 **Notes** Sunday L £16.45-£19.45, Children welcome

Menzies Hotels Bournemouth / Carlton

◎ Modern, Traditional British

tel: 01202 552011 **East Overcliff BH1 3DN**
email: carlton@menzieshotels.co.uk **web:** www.menzieshotels.co.uk
dir: M3/M27, follow A338 (Bournemouth). Follow signs to town centre & East Overcliff. Hotel is on seafront

Traditional cooking in a grand old seaside hotel

Sitting proud on the East Cliff above Bournemouth's golden sands and the bay, the Carlton is an old smoothie of a seaside hotel, with its grandiose pilastered hallway and poolside seats under the tropical vegetation. Frederick's restaurant, named after one of the former owners, suits the mood with its regal purple-red upholstery and swagged curtains. A discreet top layer of modern garnishing doesn't attempt to disguise the traditional British underlay to the menus, so expect smoked salmon and quail's eggs, or rich, well-seasoned crab and lobster bisque with Armagnac cream, to start. Main course brings on quality meats such as honey-glazed pork fillet wrapped in pancetta with walnut and pepper dressing, and the short dessert selection includes zesty lemon tart and clotted cream.

Chef Richard Allsopp **Owner** Topland Hotels **Seats** 120, Pr/dining room 180 **Times** 12.30-2/7-9.45 **Prices** Fixed D 3 course £26.95, Starter £7-£10.50, Main £16.50-£28.50, Dessert £5.95-£8.50, Service optional **Wines** 7 bottles over £30, 27 bottles under £30, 8 by glass **Parking** 76 **Notes** Sunday L £16.95-£22.95, Vegetarian available, Children welcome

BOURNEMOUTH *continued*

West Beach

Modern, Seafood

tel: 01202 587785 **Pier Approach BH2 5AA**
email: enquiry@west-beach.co.uk **web:** www.west-beach.co.uk
dir: *100yds W of the pier*

Classy seafood dishes next to the beach

Virtually on the beach and with a sunny terrace almost within touching distance of the waves, you might be forgiven for thinking you were eating in a Spanish resort rather than a fish restaurant on the Jurassic Coast. Floor-to-ceiling picture windows make the most of the sea views and the recently refurbished Beachcomber-style interior is bright and contemporary with pastel shades and bleached wood. Young, smiley staff add to the relaxed, unpretentious vibe of the restaurant with its open-to-view kitchen adding a degree of theatre. The freshest seafood simply cooked is the deal here and you might set out with a light and crisp tempura squid with a mixed radish salad. It could be followed by a spankingly fresh Weymouth wild sea bass fillet served with mixed shellfish cooked in a crab bisque.

Chef Marcin Pacholarz **Owner** Andrew Price **Seats** 90 **Times** 12-3.30/6-10, Closed 25 Dec, D 26 Dec, 1 Jan **Prices** Starter £6-£10, Main £14-£23, Dessert £6-£9, Service optional **Wines** 32 bottles over £30, 27 bottles under £30, 15 by glass **Parking** NCP 2 mins **Notes** Tasting menu, Pre-theatre 2 course £14.95, Sunday L, Vegetarian available, Children welcome

Riverside Restaurant

Seafood, International

tel: 01308 422011 **West Bay DT6 4EZ**
email: neilriverside@hotmail.com **web:** www.riverside-restaurant.com
dir: *A35 Bridport ring road, turn to West Bay at Crown rdbt*

Long-standing harbourside fish restaurant

When the Watsons acquired this harbourside restaurant no less than 50 years ago, they were continuing a local tradition that stretched back to Victorian days, of serving pearly-fresh fish and seafood from the day's catch with views over the sea. In the 19th century, a humble awning was extended over the spot, whereas now you sit in refreshing splendour behind picture windows, the better to enjoy the prospect. The cooking keeps things as simple as the prime materials require: traditional fish soup with garlicky rouille, grilled lemon sole seasoned with sea salt and lemon, brill in sorrel sauce, whole plaice on the bone. There are occasional forays into the modern cookbook, for seared scallops with truffled celeriac purée, or turbot with banana shallots, mushrooms and pancetta, and these are perfectly sound, but hardly anything beats a seafood platter. Not a fish fan? Then try the crackled pork belly with smoked garlic mash in red wine. Finish with apricot pannacotta and shortbread.

Chef A Shaw, E Webb, N Larcombe **Owner** Mr & Mrs A Watson **Seats** 80, Pr/dining room 30 **Times** 12-2.30/6.30-9, Closed 30 Nov-12 Feb, Mon (ex BHs), D Sun **Prices** Fixed L 2 course £22, Starter £4.95-£10.75, Main £12.95-£30, Dessert £4.95-£6.60, Service optional **Wines** 10 bottles over £30, 45 bottles under £30, 12 by glass **Parking** Public car park 40 mtrs **Notes** Flxed L 1 course £6.95, Sunday L, Vegetarian available, Children welcome

Captains Club Hotel and Spa

Modern European

tel: 01202 475111 **Wick Ferry, Wick Ln BH23 1HU**
email: enquiries@captainsclubhotel.com **web:** www.captainsclubhotel.com
dir: *Hotel just off Christchurch High St, towards Christchurch Quay*

Riverside brasserie dining of appealing simplicity

Opened in 2006, the Captains Club is a glass-fronted boutique hotel by the river Stour, an enticing location that allows it to benefit from strong local support. An open-plan flow leads from cocktail bar to lounge to restaurant, with a water-feature to echo the riverside setting, and the kitchen's appealingly simple, straightforward approach to modern brasserie fare is fully in keeping with the surroundings. A slice of pig's cheek and apple terrine is big on flavour and comes with a sharp-shooting pea and radish salad, while classic seafood specialities such as moules marinière or whole dressed crab won't lack for subscribers. Stick with fish into main, and it could be nicely timed sea bass with lobster mash, samphire and asparagus in dill sauce, or else opt for lamb rump with beetrooted dauphinoise in red wine. Veggie possibilities include an Indian-spiced cauliflower risotto with coconut and coriander, and the dessert crowd-pleasers take in textbook crème brûlée with a chocolate chip cookie, or vanilla cheesecake (deconstructed, natch) with blood orange jelly.

Chef Andrew Gault **Owner** Platinum One Hotels Ltd **Seats** 100, Pr/dining room 120 **Times** 11.30-10, All-day dining **Prices** Service optional **Wines** 64 bottles over £30, 40 bottles under £30, 12 by glass **Parking** 41 **Notes** Sunday L £25-£30, Vegetarian available, Children welcome

The Jetty

◉◉ Modern British

tel: 01202 400950 **95 Mudeford BH23 3NT**
email: dine@thejetty.co.uk
dir: A35/A337 to Highcliffe. Right at rdbt, hotel & restaurant 1.5m on left

Sleek venue with sharp, unfussy cooking

A dashing contemporary construction of glass and wood, The Jetty has impeccable carbon-neutral credentials and sea views to die for. In the grounds of the Christchurch Harbour Hotel, it's a short stroll to the water's edge where some impressive modern British cooking is up for grabs, with seafood to the fore. The culinary output is headed up by Alex Aitken, who also oversees the other restaurant in the hotel (the Upper Deck), and provenance is everything here. Grab a table on the terrace if you can (and if the weather allows), but floor-to-ceiling windows give everyone a glimpse of the glorious view over Mudeford Quay. The kitchen turns out contemporary dishes taking inspiration from far and wide, so seared tuna gets a Japanese twist with avocado and wasabi ice cream (just the right punchiness), and there's a classical European approach to a fabulous fillet of sea bass with lemon butter sauce. There are meaty options such calves' liver with truffle sausage, and desserts run to a summery New Forest strawberry creation.

Chef Alex Aitken **Owner** Christchurch Restaurants Ltd **Seats** 70 **Times** 12-2.30/6-10 **Prices** Fixed L 2 course £18.95, Fixed D 3 course £22.95, Tasting menu £55, Starter £7.50-£11.95, Main £16.95-£28.50, Dessert £5-£8.50 **Wines** 82 bottles over £30, 21 bottles under £30, 14 by glass **Parking** 40 **Notes** Mini gastro menu 4 course £25, Sunday L £29.95, Vegetarian available, Children welcome

The Lord Bute & Restaurant

◉ British, Mediterranean

tel: 01425 278884 **179-181 Lymington Rd, Highcliffe on Sea BH23 4JS**
email: mail@lordbute.co.uk **web:** www.lordbute.co.uk
dir: Follow A337 to Lymington, opposite St Mark's churchyard in Highcliffe

Consistent cooking in a former castle entrance lodge

What is now an eye-catching boutique hotel was once the entrance lodge to Highcliffe Castle, for a year or two in the 1760s serving as home to the eponymous Lord Bute, one of Britain's lesser-known prime ministers. It's superbly placed for access to the golden beaches and blustery clifftops of the Dorset coast, and has been remade in delightful modern style within, its classical dining room boasting an orangery extension, and on-the-ball, well-drilled service to boot. A loyal local following can't resist the jazz nights, and the long residency of chef Kevin Brown has ensured continuity in the cooking. A broad range of menu choice encompasses modern classic offerings such as seared scallops with black pudding and white bean purée in beurre blanc, herb-crusted lamb loin with asparagus, wilted spinach

and a tarragon-spiked red wine sauce, lemon-coated cod in saffron seafood broth, and well-executed passionfruit pannacotta with matching sorbet in caramel sauce.

Chef Kevin Brown **Owner** S Box & G Payne **Seats** 95 **Times** 12-2/7-9.30, Closed Mon, L Sat, D Sun **Prices** Service optional **Wines** 13 bottles over £30, 35 bottles under £30, 10 by glass **Parking** 50 **Notes** Sunday L £24.95, Vegetarian available, Children welcome

Upper Deck Bar & Restaurant

◉ Modern British

tel: 01202 400954 **95 Mudeford BH23 3NT**
email: christchurch.restaurant@harbourhotels.co.uk **web:** www.christchurch-harbour-hotel.co.uk/upper-deck
dir: A35/A337 to Highcliffe. Right at rdbt, hotel & restaurant 1.5m on left

Chic waterside restaurant for local produce and stunning views

Whichever of the two restaurants at this classy hotel you choose, good views over the water are guaranteed, as is a fine showing of regional produce. Chef-patron Alex Aitken is the man behind it all and you are in safe hands with his dedication to keeping everything fresh, seasonal and local. The Upper Deck is pretty swanky, featuring a sleek and contemporary bar and an upmarket seasidey vibe, or there's the terrace for fine days. It's a quality set up. The cooking takes a modern British route through contemporary tastes, so there are French and British preparations, a few Asian flavours here and there, and, given the setting, plenty of locally-landed fish. Terrine of ham hock, lentils and game comes in the fashionable company of piccalilli to cut through the richness, or there might be Thai fish broth packed with the catch of the day. Main course fillet of lemon sole stuffed salmon mousse and served with mashed potato is one way to follow on, or there are steaks cooked on the grill, and crème brûlée for dessert.

Chef Alex Aitken **Owner** Harbour Hotels Group **Seats** 95, Pr/dining room 20 **Times** 12-2.30/6-9.45 **Prices** Prices not confirmed **Wines** 30 bottles over £30, 30 bottles under £30, 12 by glass **Parking** 100 **Notes** Sunday L, Vegetarian available, Children welcome

■ **CORFE CASTLE** Map 4 SY98

Mortons House Hotel

◉◉ Modern British

tel: 01929 480988 **49 East St BH20 5EE**
email: stay@mortonshouse.co.uk **web:** www.mortonshouse.co.uk
dir: In village centre on A351

Clean-lined modern cooking with East Asian notes

Mortons is a beautifully maintained Elizabethan manor of the 1590s on the Isle of Purbeck, within sight of Corfe Castle. All dark oak panelling and low-hanging beams inside, it wears its traditionalism on its sleeve. The same menu is offered in the main restaurant as in the less formal 'bistro' room, and there's a terrace for summer lunches. Clean-lined contemporary simplicity is the contrasting mood of the food, with tight technique and prime materials of obvious quality inspiring confidence. An openness to East Asian tastes brings a teriyaki-sesame dressing to seared salmon seasoned with Dorset's own wasabi as an opener. This could be the prelude to fillet and braised cheek of pork with fondant celeriac and rustic white bean cassoulet fragrant with rosemary, or sea bass with crab and tomato in a Thai-seasoned sauce of lemongrass and galangal. Sharp citric flavours illuminate Tuscan-style orange cake with lemon curd and mascarpone ice cream, and refreshment is also the keynote of chilled rice pudding served in cherry soup.

Chef Ed Firth **Owner** Mrs Woods, Mr & Mrs Clayton **Seats** 60, Pr/dining room 22 **Times** 12-1.45/7-9 **Prices** Service optional **Wines** 17 bottles over £30, 25 bottles under £30, 6 by glass **Parking** 40 **Notes** Sunday L £13-£24.50, Vegetarian available, Children 5 yrs+

EVERSHOT

Map 4 ST50

The Acorn Inn

◉ British

tel: 01935 83228 **28 Fore St DT2 0JW**
email: stay@acorn-inn.co.uk **web:** www.acorn-inn.co.uk
dir: From A37 between Yeovil & Dorchester, follow Evershot & Holywell signs, 0.5m to inn

Wessex country pub with a traditional approach

Plumb in the middle of Thomas Hardy's favourite stretch of England, the 16th-century coaching inn makes an appearance in *Tess of the d'Urbervilles* as the Sow and Acorn. In its earliest days, the landlord brewed his own ales with river-water from the Frome, and while things have moved on a touch since then, there's still a skittle alley, and the main dining area boasts a carved stone fireplace and terracotta tiles. To start, grilled local goats' cheese in orange dressing may be a safer bet than the more ambitious truffled gnocchi, but there's nothing wrong with correctly cooked plaice on the bone with triple-cooked chips and caper butter, and it's worth the wait for a slow roasting of pork belly, served with appled mash in Madeira jus. The chocolate fondant is styled 'melt-in-the-middle' in supermarket fashion, but is a superior sponge with unctuous oozy filling, accompanied by brilliantly intense salted caramel ice cream.

Chef Guy Horley **Owner** Red Carnation Hotels **Seats** 45, Pr/dining room 35
Times 12-2/7-9 **Prices** Starter £5-£8, Main £11-£23, Dessert £6-£12, Service optional **Wines** 16 bottles over £30, 26 bottles under £30, 39 by glass **Parking** 40
Notes Sunday L £12-£15, Vegetarian available, Children welcome

George Albert Hotel

◉ Modern British

tel: 01935 483430 **Wardon Hill DT2 9PW**
email: enquiries@gahotel.co.uk **web:** www.georgealberthotel.co.uk
dir: On A37 (between Yeovil & Dorchester). Adjacent to Southern Counties Shooting Ground

Well-balanced modern dishes at a new hotel

The George Albert is a new-build hotel that opened its doors in 2010, in an interestingly remote spot on the A37 between Yeovil and Dorchester. Despite the box-freshness of it all, a determined attempt to create a traditional feel brings monogrammed carpets and starched table linen to Kings Restaurant, where direct modern dishes presented without smoke and mirrors both look and taste good. Seared scallops with leeks and mash in creamy mussel chowder is a beguiling opener, if you can resist the appeal of good old ham hock terrine and piccalilli. Main courses bring all their components together in well-balanced harmony, as in the quince purée, parsnip mash, fondant potato and baconed cabbage that come with duck breast in port jus, or grilled grey mullet with pak choi in lime butter. To finish, there may be sweet passionfruit pannacotta with mango sauce and pineapple.

Times 12-2.30/6.30-9

Summer Lodge Country House Hotel, Restaurant & Spa

◉◉◉ – see below

Summer Lodge Country House Hotel, Restaurant & Spa ◉◉◉

EVERSHOT

Map 4 ST50

Modern British
tel: 01935 482000 **Fore St DT2 0JR**
email: summerlodge@rchmail.com **web:** www.summerlodgehotel.com
dir: 1m W of A37 halfway between Dorchester & Yeovil

Assured modern cooking in peaceful surroundings

It may be on the main road through the pretty village of Evershot but once you turn into the drive of this elegant country-house hotel it's as if you're miles from anywhere, such is the sense of tranquillity emanating from Summer Lodge. And with four acres of gardens, an indoor pool, spa and all-weather tennis court, there's every reason to stick around. The pretty Grade II listed Georgian dower house has a Victorian extension designed by architect and local literary giant, Thomas Hardy. Offering a touch of refinement and a wonderfully soothing service style, Summer Lodge is a delightfully old-school place with an interior design that has not been affected by passing fashions. The restaurant with its swagged curtains and plush table settings radiates the feel of an English rose garden, while a light-flooded conservatory extension gives views of the real thing. Steven Titman and his team deliver menus rooted in classical good sense, introducing contemporary ideas with a light touch. A starter of Dorset rose veal carpaccio with crispy sweetbreads, watercress aïoli

and horseradish pannacotta really shows what this kitchen is capable off – deliciously focused and creative food. Another first course combines Lyme Bay scallops with Jerusalem artichoke purée, home-cured bacon and confit garlic. Top-notch regional ingredients feature throughout, such as the lamb (roasted loin and braised shoulder) in a main course with Savoy cabbage and a rosemary jus, the shoulder meat made into a mini 'shepherd's pie', or go for John Dory with shellfish ravioli and lobster Cognac sauce. Finish with warm Dorset apple cake with stem ginger ice cream and cinnamon foam. Like everything else, the wine list is a class act.

Chef Steven Titman **Owner** Bea Tollman **Seats** 60, Pr/dining room 20
Times 12-2.30/7-9.30, **Prices** Fixed L 3 course £19.50-£26, Tasting menu £75, Starter £13-£19, Main £22-£30, Dessert £11-£13, Service optional **Wines** 1450 bottles over £30, 15 bottles under £30, 25 by glass **Parking** 60 **Notes** Tasting menu 8 course, Surprise menu D 6 course £65/£120, Sunday L £39, Vegetarian available, Children welcome

FARNHAM

Map 4 ST91

Museum Inn

◉◉ Modern, Traditional British

tel: 01725 516261 **DT11 8DE**
email: enquiries@museuminn.co.uk **web:** www.museuminn.co.uk
dir: *12m S of Salisbury, 7m N of Blandford Forum on A354. Signed from A354 Salisbury Blandford Forum Rd*

Ambitious cooking with a solid country-pub foundation

Victorian archaeologist General Augustus Pitt-Rivers was responsible for the Oxford museum collection that bears his name, and for extending the partly thatched Museum Inn, the core of which dates back to the 17th century. A brick-built fireplace and wood-faced bar make for a welcoming pub scene, where ploughman's lunches and sandwiches are the drill, but things get a touch more ambitious if you take a seat at one of the distressed wood tables for a meal. While there is a solid pub foundation to proceedings with moules marinière or ham hock terrine with red onion chutney and toast, there are also excursions over the Channel for pheasant Normandy-style, braised in local cider, or into Med territory for aubergine and feta schnitzel on red pepper coulis. Fish specials from the day-boats are chalked on the board, and a section of standards offers the comforting likes of smoked haddock and salmon fish pie with gruyère-gratinated mash, or honey-mustard glazed ham and chips. Dessert might well be Italian chocolate torta, or rice pudding ritzed up with passionfruit.

Chef Simon Trepess **Owner** Cirrus Inns **Seats** 69, Pr/dining room 40 **Times** 12-2.30/6.30-9.30, Closed 25 or 26 Dec **Prices** Starter £5.50-£7.95, Main £11.95-£23.95, Dessert £6.50-£9 **Wines** 35 bottles over £30, 22 bottles under £30, 18 by glass **Parking** 14 **Notes** Sunday L £14.50-£16.50, Vegetarian available, Children welcome

LYME REGIS

Map 4 SY39

The Mariners

◉ British, International

tel: 01297 442753 **Silver St DT7 3HS**
email: enquiries@hotellymeregis.co.uk **web:** www.hotellymeregis.co.uk
dir: *S onto B3261 from A35, on left opposite right turn to the Cobb*

Updated old coaching inn with local seafood and more

The former coaching inn dates back to the 17th century and looks the part with its pink-washed façade and period charm. It's looking spruce inside these days, made over with a contemporary finish that matches old and new with a keen eye. There are views from the back over the town and out to sea, which are particularly good from the garden filled with chunky wooden tables on which to sit and ponder. The restaurant with its light and bright feel is the setting for some breezy modern food with a good showing of local seafood. Among starters, for example, might be Lyme Bay scallops with crispy pancetta, butternut squash purée and watercress pesto, or go for an earthy dish of wild mushrooms on toasted brioche. Main-course roasted Cornish hake is served with local crab fritters and shellfish paella, while a meaty main might be confit of Creedy Carver duck leg. Finish with a Baileys crème brûlée.

Chef Steve Rainey **Owner** Jerry Ramsdale **Seats** 36 **Times** 12-2/6.30-9, Closed D 25 Dec **Prices** Prices not confirmed, Service optional **Wines** 3 bottles over £30, 27 bottles under £30, 9 by glass **Parking** 20, Car park 200mtrs **Notes** Sunday L, Vegetarian available, Children welcome

MAIDEN NEWTON

Map 4 SY59

Le Petit Canard

◉ Modern British, French

tel: 01300 320536 **Dorchester Rd DT2 0BE**
email: le-petit-canard2@btconnect.com **web:** www.le-petit-canard.co.uk
dir: *In centre of Maiden Newton, 8m W of Dorchester*

Honest, accomplished cooking in pretty village restaurant

The location in a cottagey terrace building – once a coaching inn by all accounts – and the traditional, homely decor is not exactly the cutting-edge of restaurant design, but no matter, for this is a delightful place run with passion by Gerry and Cathy Craig. The tables are neatly laid with linen cloths and topped with flowers and candles, and the original features of the property – wooden beams and some exposed stonework – add to its charm. Gerry's cooking does not try to reinvent the wheel, but neither is it stuck in the past. Seared scallops with celeriac purée, for example, is a gently modish construction, or go for the bresaola with rocket, olive oil and parmesan shavings. Main-course roast breast of duck comes with a plum and ginger sauce, and loin fillet of local wild venison with pear chutney, while dessert might be a textbook crème brûlée.

Chef Gerry Craig **Owner** Gerry & Cathy Craig **Seats** 28 **Times** 12-2/7-9, Closed Mon, L all week (ex 1st & 3rd Sun in month), D Sun **Prices** Fixed D 3 course £34-£36.95, Service optional **Wines** 8 bottles over £30, 22 bottles under £30, 6 by glass **Parking** On street, village car park **Notes** Sunday L £25, Vegetarian available, Children 12 yrs+

Harbour Heights

◉◉ Modern European

tel: 01202 707272 **73 Haven Rd, Sandbanks BH13 7LW**
email: enquiries@harbourheights.net web: www.fjbhotels.co.uk
dir: *From A338 follow signs to Sandbanks, restaurant on left past Canford Cliffs*

Spectacular views and modern bistro food

The teak-decked alfresco terrace of this 1920s art deco beauty is the place to be to soak up the views across Poole harbour when the sun shines, but a 21st-century boutique facelift (this is Sandbanks after all) makes the glossy Harbar Bistro an equally inviting prospect when the weather drives you inside to enjoy the vista through its floor-to-ceiling picture windows. With a French chef at the helm, you can expect a menu of modern European food full of enticing seasonal ideas built with top-quality local ingredients. Check out the fresh fish counter, laden with the day's catch from Poole Quay, to steer you towards a main course starring a pavé of cod supported by butter bean, pea and chorizo fricassée and sherry emulsion. Otherwise, start with pan-fried pigeon breast with Puy lentils and sloe gin syrup, followed, perhaps, by venison loin with fondant potato, caramelised onion, wilted spinach, chestnut purée, and Vin Santo and hazelnut jus. Wrap things up with pear and almond tart with vanilla ice cream.

Chef Loic Gratadoux **Owner** FJB Hotels **Seats** 90, Pr/dining room 120
Times 12-2.15/7-9.15 **Prices** Fixed L 2 course £18.50-£22.50, Fixed D 3 course £29.50, Starter £6.50-£12.50, Main £16.50-£59.50, Dessert £6.50-£9.50 **Wines** 69 bottles over £30, 43 bottles under £30, 13 by glass **Parking** 50 **Notes** Sunday L £22.50-£29, Vegetarian available, Children welcome

The Haven

◉◉ Modern British V

tel: 01202 707333 **161 Banks Rd, Sandbanks BH13 7QL**
email: reservations@havenhotel.co.uk web: www.fjbhotels.co.uk/haven
dir: *Follow signs to Sandbanks Peninsula; hotel next to Swanage ferry departure point*

Delightful Poole Bay views and confident modern cooking

Dating from the 1880s, this large white hotel is right on the water's edge at the southern end of Sandbanks. La Roche restaurant considerately has its tables tiered, giving more than just window seats a sea view; the room has the feel of a relaxed brasserie, helped along by friendly but informed staff, and two large fish tanks divert the eye. The kitchen buys the best regional produce for the time of year and devises menus with much of interest without confining itself to the fruits of the sea. Start, for instance, with nicely wobbly pannacotta subtly hinting of ginger, with toasted pumpkin seeds, a parmesan crackle and butternut squash purée adding textural and flavour contrasts. Dishes are never too elaborate: a pressing of duck with apple chutney, say, then a well-thought-out main course of pavé of salmon with curried lentils, salt-cod fritters and raita, or sautéed calves' liver with potato purée and onion sauce. Crème brûlée with banana and passionfruit sorbet and poached pineapple is an ambitious, effective pudding.

Chef Jason Hornbuckle **Owner** Mr J Butterworth **Seats** 80, Pr/dining room 156
Times 12-2.30/7-9.30 **Prices** Fixed L 2 course fr £24.50, Fixed D 3 course £32, Starter £7.90-£14.50, Main £18.50-£32, Dessert £7.50-£12 **Wines** 59 bottles over £30, 38 bottles under £30, 19 by glass **Parking** 90 **Notes** Sunday L £24.50-£32, Children welcome

Hotel du Vin Poole

◉ Modern British, French

tel: 01202 785578 **Mansion House, Thames St BH15 1JN**
web: www.hotelduvin.co.uk
dir: *A350 into town centre follow signs to Channel Ferry/Poole Quay, left at bridge, 1st left is Thames St*

Bistro cooking in an elegant Georgian house

Hotel du Vin's Poole outpost is a bit of a landmark just off the quayside, a creeper-covered Georgian mansion. In common with the other branches, it's been renovated to a high standard, with a bar, a wine-tasting room and a buzzy bistro-style restaurant with a wooden floor, bentwood chairs, banquettes, unclothed tables, wine memorabilia and casual but clued-up staff. As expected, the kitchen deals in crowd-pleasing brasserie staples from over the Channel, all cooked just so. Start perhaps with crab toasts with sliced radish and black pepper mayonnaise, escargots in classic garlic and herb butter, or onion soup, and proceed to steak frites, pink-roast rump of lamb with broccoli and boulangère potatoes with chorizo, or sole meunière. Puddings are as Gallic as the rest of the package, among them Paris-Brest and tarte au citron, although bread-and-butter pudding flavoured with rum and banana may please patriots.

Chef Darren Rockett **Owner** Hotel du Vin/SLK **Seats** 85, Pr/dining room 48
Times 12.30-2/5.30-10.30 **Prices** Fixed L 2 course £16.95, Fixed D 3 course £19.95, Starter £5.95-£12.95, Main £13.95-£29.75, Dessert £6.95-£8.95 **Wines** 10 by glass **Parking** 12, NCP (available until 11pm) **Notes** Pre-theatre 1 course wine & coffee £12.95, Sunday L £24.95, Vegetarian available, Children welcome

SHAFTESBURY
Map 4 ST82

La Fleur de Lys Restaurant with Rooms
◉◉ Modern French

tel: 01747 853717 **Bleke St SP7 8AW**
email: info@lafleurdelys.co.uk **web:** www.lafleurdelys.co.uk
dir: Junct A350/A30

West Country cooking in a former boarding-school

The former girls' boarding-school that the owners took on in 1991 needed a lot of remedial attention, and has become one of the area's favourite dining destinations, a creeper-covered restaurant with rooms that has something of the feel of a country inn. Smartly linened-up tables are the order in the dining room, where lemon-yellow and exposed stone walls produce a relaxing atmosphere. Fixed-price menus offer an accommodating range of choice, with West Country supplies to the fore. Start with sautéed scallops in zesty lime crumb, served with a cherry tomato and spring onion salad dressed in yogurt, lime and chilli, or a bowl of hearty broth composed of wild mushrooms, pearl barley and leeks. The main business arrives in the form of hake with king prawns and samphire in coriander sauce, or breast of guinea-fowl with roast parsnips, sauced with grain mustard. Dessert could be as simple as a seasonal cornucopia of strawberries and raspberries with clotted cream, or as highfalutin as a dark chocolate box filled with fudge ice cream, macerated orange and candied nuts in Amaretto sauce.

Chef D Shepherd, M Preston **Owner** D Shepherd, M Preston, M Griffin **Seats** 45, Pr/dining room 12 **Times** 12-2.30/7-10.30, Closed 3 wks Jan, L Mon-Tue, D Sun **Prices** Fixed D 3 course £35-£42, Starter £7.50, Main £17.50, Dessert £7, Service optional **Wines** 50 bottles over £30, 50 bottles under £30, 8 by glass **Parking** 10 **Notes** Sunday L £17.50-£33, Vegetarian available, Children welcome

SHERBORNE
Map 4 ST61

Eastbury Hotel
◉◉ Modern British V

tel: 01935 813131 **Long St DT9 3BY**
email: enquiries@theeastburyhotel.com **web:** www.theeastburyhotel.co.uk
dir: 5m E of Yeovil, follow brown signs for Eastbury Hotel

Cosmopolitan cooking in utterly English surroundings

In the heart of one of Dorset's most picturesque towns, the Eastbury offers a hint of country-estate living without the need to head for the hills. It's all on a compact scale, to be sure, with a single attractive acre of walled garden to potter about in, but lacks nothing in either tranquil charm or warm hospitality. An outdoor terrace is an inviting adjunct to the conservatory dining room, and much of the kitchen's raw material comes from the Eastbury garden and its beehives. Despite the utterly English surroundings, the menu is unabashed about looking both eastwards for soy-glazed pig's cheek with aduki beans in yuzu dressing, or smoked salmon with lime and nori, and southwards for a main dish of Creedy Carver duck breast, accompanied by cassoulet of confit leg and sausage, slow-cooked gizzards, charred leeks and sweet onion. Skrei cod is seasoned with sumac, weighted with lardo, and dressed with coriander yogurt. Gird your loins for substantial desserts such as caramelised banana cake and peanut ice cream, or rhubarb mascarpone cheesecake with rhubarb sorbet.

Chef Matthew Street **Owner** Mr & Mrs P King **Seats** 40, Pr/dining room 12 **Times** 12-2/6.30-9 **Prices** Fixed D 3 course £23.50-£41, Tasting menu £55, Service optional **Wines** 23 bottles over £30, 48 bottles under £30, 6 by glass **Parking** 20 **Notes** Tasting menu 7 course, Sunday L, Children welcome

The Green
◉◉ Modern British, European

tel: 01935 813821 **3 The Green DT9 3HY**
email: info@greenrestaurant.co.uk
dir: A30 towards Milborne Port, at top of Greenhill turn right at mini rdbt. Restaurant on left

Creative modern dishes in picture-postcard property

The Green, in a Grade II listed building, is a popular and busy restaurant with a lively atmosphere. The kitchen sets its sights on local and ethically sourced raw materials and produces palate-pleasing dishes that are high on interest and low on fuss. Moist and succulent chargrilled scallops come with a cylinder of black pudding and a dressing of leaves drizzled in sea buckthorn oil, toasted pine kernels adding some crunch, while another starter might be a simple serving of seasonal asparagus with brioche crumbs and parmesan. Quality ingredients and high technical skills are evident throughout: pink-roast rack of lamb, juicy and of super-meaty flavour, for instance, accompanied by an onion and potato cake and rich tarragon jus, and fillet of Cornish hake with roasted tomatoes and lemon butter. There are delicious and imaginative desserts along the lines of ginger sticky toffee pudding, of clear toffee and ginger flavours, enhanced by subtle lime leaf ice cream and Grand Marnier sauce.

Chef Alexander Matkevich **Owner** Alexander Matkevich **Seats** 40, Pr/dining room 24 **Times** 12-2.30/7-9.30, Closed Sun-Mon **Prices** Fixed L 2 course £17.95-£20, Fixed D 3 course £20-£35, Starter £6-£12, Main £14.95-£25, Dessert £6.50-£9, Service optional **Wines** 12 bottles over £30, 30 bottles under £30, 8 by glass **Parking** On street, car park **Notes** Vegetarian available, Children welcome

The Kings Arms
◉ Modern British

tel: 01963 220281 **Charlton Herethorne DT9 4NL**
email: admin@thekingsarms.co.uk **web:** www.thekingsarms.co.uk
dir: From A303 follow signs for Templecombe & Sherborne onto B3145 to Charlton Horethorne

Hard-working kitchen in a modernised country inn

Sarah and Tony Lethbridge's stone-built country inn looks rather imposing for a village hostelry, but that is what it has been since it was first licensed way back in the Regency era. Behind that grand façade, the place has been given a thoroughly modern makeover, though not to the detriment of its original charm. There's the usual choice of informal bar eating, or a dedicated dining room, the latter attractively done in wood tones against white walls, with arched panelled mirrors to deepen the space. Sarah Lethbridge heads up the kitchen operation, capitalising on much pedigree West Country produce, as well as drying and curing meats in-house, and making her own breads and ice creams. The style of cooking is unconstrained by national boundaries, bolstering a first course of smoked haddock croquettes with a thick Thai-spiced velouté (scented with coconut and coriander) or serving French-influenced duck leg confit with dauphinoise and Russian kale, alongside a fricassée of wild mushrooms and broad beans. Lusciously rich crème brûlée has its brittle crisp top cleverly echoed with intense wafer-thin ginger biscuits, with a garnish of caramelised plums.

Chef Sarah Lethbridge **Owner** Sarah & Tony Lethbridge **Seats** 120, Pr/dining room 70 **Times** 12-2.30/7-close, Closed 25 Dec **Prices** Prices not confirmed, Service optional **Wines** 18 bottles over £30, 40 bottles under £30, 13 by glass **Parking** 30 **Notes** Sunday L, Vegetarian available, Children welcome

STUDLAND
Map 5 SZ08

THE PIG on the Beach
◎◎ Modern British NEW v

tel: 01929 450288 **The Manor House, Manor Rd BH19 3AU**
email: info@thepigonthebeach.com **web:** www.thepighotel.com
dir: A338 from Bournemouth, follow signs to Sandbanks ferry, cross on ferry, then 3m to Studland

Garden-to-table cooking in a shabby-chic seaside manor

Part of a mini chain of quirky boutique hotels offering switched-on contemporary cooking, this little piggy sits on the coast overlooking the sandy sweep of Studland Bay. The turreted manor house is bang up-to-date these days, with the foodie side of the operation taking place in a Victorian-style greenhouse dining room decked out with shabby-chic looks. Food miles matter here, and the '25-mile menu' speaks for itself: fruit, veg and herbs are plucked fresh daily from the walled kitchen garden, a coop of chickens and quails supplies eggs, foraged ingredients play their part, as does locally-landed fish and seafood. A main course of South Coast hake with plump Dorset cockles, foraged Alexander, sea beets and Hampshire salami shows the style. Fans of local meat might find pork belly, smoked in-house and matched with olives, tomatoes and spring onions. Bookending this, an opener of grilled cuttlefish with braised veal tongue, rocket, roasted garlic and lemon crème fraîche, and for pudding, hazelnut and cocoa meringue is filled with yogurt cream and partnered by pressed pears and caramel sauce.

Chef Andy Wright **Owner** Home Grown Hotels **Seats** 70, Pr/dining room 12 **Times** 12-2.45/6.30-10 **Prices** Starter £6-£12, Main £12-£25, Dessert £6-£8, Service optional 12.5% **Wines** 40 bottles over £30, 20 bottles under £30, 20 by glass **Parking** 30 **Notes** Sunday L, Children welcome

WIMBORNE MINSTER
Map 5 SZ09

Les Bouviers Restaurant with Rooms
◎◎ French

tel: 01202 889555 **Arrowsmith Rd, Canford Magna BH21 3BD**
email: info@lesbouviers.co.uk **web:** www.lesbouviers.co.uk
dir: 1.5m S of Wimborne on A349, turn left onto A341. In 1m turn right into Arrowsmith Rd. 300yds, 2nd property on right

Francophile cooking in an elegant restaurant with rooms

A modern, even suburban-looking house in over five acres of land complete with stream and lake is where the Cowards run their restaurant with rooms. The setting for James Coward's elaborate cooking is tastefully decorated and furnished, the restaurant done out in shades of claret and gold, with contemporary artwork hanging on the walls. Cheese soufflé with watercress and horseradish sauce is something of a signature starter, or there might be a salad of local wood pigeon with sautéed tongue and beetroot chutney. Classic Dover sole meunière might appear among main courses, but more typical of the adventurous style is loin of veal with sautéed calves' sweetbreads, tomato confit, buttered spinach and a wild mushroom sauce, or brill on Puy lentils in saffron sauce with chorizo, courgettes and sun-blushed tomato. Innovative elements are introduced to puddings: chocolate and meringue ice cream for warm dark chocolate fondant, and crème brûlée flavoured with lemongrass, lemon and thyme.

Times 12-2.15/7-9.30, Closed D Sun

Number 9
◎◎ Modern British, Seafood

tel: 01202 887557 **West Borough BH21 1LT**
email: no9wimborne@aol.com
dir: 150 yds from The Square before Tivoli Theatre, on West Borough

Modern European food near the Tivoli Theatre

The late 18th-century townhouse not far from the Tivoli Theatre and the main square has become a supremely stylish restaurant with rooms for the modern age. It is designed with today's clean, uncluttered lines and gentle colour palette in mind, as is evidenced by a dining room that features plain walls and unclothed tables flooded with daylight from the French windows. Greg Etheridge cooks to a modern European template, offering a pre-theatre menu for Tivoli-goers, with seafood and fish a notably strong suit. A Niçoise salad of fine chargrilled tuna looks the part, with pinkly meaty fish, crunchy green beans and garlicky olives in two colours. This might be followed majestically by a whole baked sea bass stuffed with lemon and oregano, robustly served with chorizo mash and crunchy seasonal veg. Meat could be a venison steak, served with red cabbage and dauphinoise in a juniper- and rosemary-scented red wine jus, with zesty lemon posset garnished with berry compôte and sugared almonds to finish. A winter spin on Eton Mess adds figs and cinnamon apple to crushed pistachio meringue.

Chef Greg Etheridge **Owner** Roy & Linda Tazzyman **Seats** 50, Pr/dining room 30 **Times** 12-2.30/6-9.30, Closed Xmas, BH Mon, D Mon **Prices** Starter £5.95-£7.95, Main £14.95-£24.95, Dessert £4.95-£8.50, Service optional **Wines** 3 bottles over £30, 18 bottles under £30, 9 by glass **Parking** On street or car park **Notes** Pre-theatre menu, Sunday L £12.50-£18.95, Vegetarian available, Children welcome

WYKE REGIS
Map 4 SY67

Crab House Café
◎ British, Seafood

tel: 01305 788867 **Ferrymans Way, Portland Rd DT4 9YU**
email: info@crabhousecafe.co.uk **web:** www.crabhousecafe.co.uk
dir: A354 along Westwey once onto Portland Rd continue for just under a mile, at rdbt take 2nd exit for restaurant

Fresh seafood in a laid-back beach hut

Situated in a spruced up wooden hut overlooking Chesil Beach, the Crab House Café has natural charms aplenty. Simplicity and freshness is the name of the game, with oysters coming from their own beds out front and everything sourced from within a 40-mile radius. Rustic pub-style benches outside are a treat in the warmer months of the year, but it's all well and good if you've got to eat inside, with an open-to-view kitchen and easy-going attitude. Kick off with some oysters either au naturel or with combos of pesto/parmesan and bacon/cream. A starter of queenie scallops comes topped with a paprika-flavoured gratin and an asparagus purée, or go for Thai fishcakes with sweet chilli sauce. The fresh crabs are hard to ignore – with Chinese spicing perhaps – or go for another main course such as roasted skate with chorizo and spring onions. Finish with a crème brûlée served in a coffee mug.

Crab House Café

Chef Nigel Bloxham, Adam Foster **Owner** Nigel Bloxham **Seats** 40 **Times** 12-2/6-9, Closed mid Dec-Jan, Mon-Tue (ex 8 wks in summer), D Sun (Oct-Mar) **Prices** Starter £3.50-£10.50, Main £12.50-£27, Dessert £5-£9.50, Service optional **Wines** 18 bottles over £30, 31 bottles under £30, 13 by glass **Parking** 40 **Notes** Sunday L, Vegetarian available, Children welcome

COUNTY DURHAM

BARNARD CASTLE
Map 19 NZ01

The Morritt Country House Hotel & Spa
◉◉ Modern French **NEW**

tel: 01833 627232 **Greta Bridge DL12 9SE**
email: relax@themorritt.co.uk **web:** www.themorritt.co.uk
dir: *From M1 (east) exit at junct 57 onto A66 westbound. From M6 (west) exit at junct 40 onto A66 eastbound. Follow signs to Greta Bridge*

Full of character, a popular meeting place

The arrival of transport by mail coach in the 18th century saw this former farm develop into an overnight stop for travellers between London and Carlisle. Charles Dickens probably stayed here in 1839 while researching *Nicholas Nickelby*, which is why there's a Dickens Bar displaying two murals themed on his works, one created in 2012 to commemorate the 200th anniversary of the author's birth. Also displayed are works by local artist John Gilroy, who produced iconic Guinness advertising posters for 35 years. The wooden-walled and floored fine-dining restaurant is named after him. Following an amuse-bouche, two people might start by sharing wood-pigeon with smoked yogurt, blueberry ketchup, spelt and sweet cicely, then continue in separate directions, one with pan-fried halibut, mussels, saffron potato, salsify and puréed kale, the other with Marley's beef rump cap with braised cheek, horseradish mayo, Jersey Royals and spinach purée. Among the desserts is rhubarb and custard anglaise with beurre noisette. Wines span the alphabet from Cabernets to Viogniers, although few are by the glass.

Chef Lee Stainthorpe **Owner** Barbara Anne Johnson, Peter Phillips **Seats** 60, Pr/dining room 50 **Times** 12-3/6-9, Closed Mon, L Tue-Sat **Prices** Fixed D 3 course £39, Service optional **Wines** 24 bottles over £30, 36 bottles under £30, 10 by glass **Parking** 30 **Notes** Sunday L £16-£19, Vegetarian available, Children welcome

BILLINGHAM
Map 19 NZ42

Wynyard Hall Hotel
◉◉ Modern British v

tel: 01740 644811 **Wynyard TS22 5NF**
email: reception@wynyandhall.co.uk **web:** www.wynyandhall.co.uk
dir: *A19 onto A1027 towards Stockton. At rdbt 3rd exit B1274 (Junction Rd). At next rdbt 3rd exit onto A177 (Durham Rd). Right onto Wynyard Rd signed Wolviston. Left into estate at gatehouse*

Accomplished cooking in a lavish country mansion setting

Wynyard Hall was certainly built to impress: the vast Victorian pile sits in 150 acres of grounds with its own lake, and as you'd expect these days in one of the northeast's top country-house hotels, a full complement of spa pampering and wedding facilities. Inside, oil paintings, marble, mahogany and stained glass combine in a display of jaw-dropping opulence, a style that continues in the Wellington Restaurant. Food can sometimes play second fiddle in such surroundings, but the imaginative, contemporary cooking more than matches the setting. To start, there's a terrine of ham hock with a crispy pork bonbon, apple purée and a sourdough crisp, while main course brings together inventive interplays of taste and texture in a duo of slow-cooked pork belly and cheek supported by broccoli and potato fondant, or you could go for pan-roasted cod with cauliflower couscous and a warm bacon and sherry vinaigrette. Elegance and comfort are key again in a finale of crème brûlée with Garibaldi biscuits and pistachio ice cream.

Chef Adam Heggarthy **Owner** Allison Antonopoulos **Seats** 80, Pr/dining room 30 **Times** 12-3/7-9.30 **Prices** Service optional **Wines** 51 bottles over £30, 30 bottles under £30, 10 by glass **Parking** 200 **Notes** Traditional/Gentleman's afternoon tea £19.95/£24.95, Sunday L £18.50-£25, Children welcome

DARLINGTON
Map 19 NZ21

Headlam Hall
◉◉ Modern British, French

tel: 01325 730238 **Headlam, Gainford DL2 3HA**
email: admin@headlamhall.co.uk **web:** www.headlamhall.co.uk
dir: *8m W of Darlington off A67*

Country mansion with unpretentious menu

This handsome house was built at the beginning of the 17th century and retains much of its period charm. It's been extended over the centuries and boasts a modern spa among its best assets these days, while the restaurant is a draw in its own right. The eating takes place in a series of rooms including an elegant panelled dining room with swagged curtains and burnished dark wood tables, and the more contemporary orangery. The kitchen delivers gently modern dishes based on classic combinations. Shetland mussels with white wine, cream and garlic is a straightforward opener that hits the mark, or go for a pressed terrine of game with caramelised cauliflower purée and a grapefruit salad to cut through its inherent richness. Next up, slow-cooked shank of mutton arrives with roast root veg, creamy mash and mint jus, while a fish option might be grilled fillet of salmon with tempura king prawn and lemon cream. Finish with dark chocolate tart with white chocolate ice cream, or a selection of local cheeses.

Chef Derek Thomson **Owner** J H Robinson **Seats** 70, Pr/dining room 30 **Times** 12-2.30/7-9.30, Closed 25-26 Dec **Prices** Fixed L 2 course fr £17, Starter £8-£9.50, Main £18-£25, Dessert £6-£9, Service optional **Wines** 20 bottles over £30, 38 bottles under £30, 10 by glass **Parking** 80 **Notes** Sunday L £25, Vegetarian available, Children welcome

DARLINGTON *continued*

The Orangery

◉◉◉ – *see below*

Bistro 21

◉ Modern British V

tel: 0191 384 4354 **Aykley Heads House, Aykley Heads DH1 5TS**
email: admin@bistrotwentyone.co.uk
dir: *Off B6532 from Durham centre, pass County Hall on right & Dryburn Hospital on left. Turn right at double rdbt into Aykley Heads*

Upbeat bistro cooking in a former farmhouse

Satisfyingly free of airs and graces, this place stays true to its bistro moniker by combining a vibrant and easy-going atmosphere with simple, straightforward food with a bit of oomph. The converted former farmhouse over two floors has stripped wooden floors and whitewashed walls, plus a snug bar with a barrel-vaulted ceiling, and nabbing a table on the terrace is a treat when the weather is up to the job. The kitchen matches local ingredients with regional preparations and some global flavours in dishes that come under the modern British banner. Start with a pressed ham terrine with pickled veg, or a soufflé rich with gruyère and leeks, before moving on to a perfectly cooked piece pan-fried cod with chargrilled squid and red pepper vinaigrette. There are daily specials, classic Sunday lunches, excellent veggie options, and private dining options. Finish with raspberry cheesecake and vanilla-baked peaches.

Chef Rauri McKay **Owner** Terence Laybourne **Seats** 65, Pr/dining room 30 **Times** 12-2/5.30-10, Closed 25 Dec, 1 Jan, D Sun **Prices** Fixed L 2 course fr £16, Fixed D 3 course fr £19, Starter £7.50, Main £17.50, Dessert £6.50 **Wines** 6 bottles over £30, 18 bottles under £30, 9 by glass **Parking** 11 **Notes** Early D menu, Sunday L £18.50-£21.50, Children welcome

Honest Lawyer Hotel

◉ Modern British

tel: 0191 378 3780 **Croxdale Bridge, Croxdale DH1 3SP**
email: enquiries@honestlawyerhotel.com **web:** www.honestlawyerhotel.com
dir: *A1 junct 61*

Something for everybody in a modern city hotel

The Honest Lawyer is a modern hotel offering the chance of all-day dining in the bar, with table service in the bright and welcoming restaurant. The kitchen sources its materials from within 20-miles of the hotel and has devised a wide-ranging brasserie-style menu with plenty to tempt. Start with the full-on flavours of baked scallops with pancetta lardons and leeks in a creamy fish sauce, accompanied by a brioche topped with parmesan and herbs, or corned beef hash with black pudding, brown sauce and a fried egg. Main courses are equally varied, taking in a trio of lamb (tender roast rump, cutlet and haggis spring roll), with honey and whisky sauce a good contrast, served with dauphinoise potatoes, as well as, say, grilled smoked cod loin on paella (prawns, chicken, chorizo and mussels). End with a familiar dessert like knickerbocker glory or sticky toffee pudding.

Chef Harry Bailie **Owner** John Sanderson **Seats** 45, Pr/dining room 60 **Times** 12-9.30, All-day dining **Prices** Prices not confirmed **Wines** 2 bottles over £30, 27 bottles under £30, 7 by glass **Parking** 150 **Notes** Sunday L, Vegetarian available, Children welcome

---

The Orangery ◉◉◉

Modern British

tel: 01325 729999 **Rockliffe Hall, Rockliffe Park, Hurworth-on-Tees DL2 2DU**
email: enquiries@rockliffehall.com **web:** www.rockliffehall.com
dir: *A1(M) junct 57, A66(M), A66 towards Darlington, A167, through Hurworth-on-Tees. In Croft-on-Tees left into Hurworth Rd, follow signs*

Creative contemporary dishes in an ornate dining room

Like many a Georgian country mansion, Rockliffe Hall is all about sport and leisure these days, with its 18-hole golf course, spa pampering and a trio of restaurants. Chief among these is The Orangery, a superb space with slender wrought-iron columns supporting a glass roof, and a laid-back mood helped along by mellow piano music floating in from the hall. After a couple of years of musical chairs in the kitchen, things have settled down with Richard Allen now heading up the team to deliver contemporary five-course 'land' and 'sea'-themed tasting menus, plus veggie and three-course à la carte options. Local sourcing is still key – much of the produce comes from the house's 365-acre estate – and it's all presented in imaginative juxtapositions of flavour, texture and temperature. The 'Land & Sea' taster kicks off with a vibrantly-coloured salad of beetroot textures (fresh, a macaroon, remoulade and powder) with truffled goats' cheese and a crisp goats' cheese bonbon, then a beautiful piece of turbot comes with brown crab meat lifted with lemon, saffron foam, quinoa, tapioca, broccoli purée and a squid ink cracker. Next up, duck liver parfait is partnered with Pata Negra ham, compressed pear, peanut butter and chocolate, while pork gets a posh (and highly labour intensive) surf 'n' turf workout – crispy belly and richly sticky braised cheek allied with tender poached langoustine, lobster foam and chorizo purée, all brought together with a honey and five spice sauce. Finish with a high-impact dessert of ginger cake with granola, rhubarb meringue, black butter and fresh basil. The cheeseboard displays some notable British specimens. There are also five-course pescetarian and veggie tasters, as well as a seven-course 'surprise' option.

Chef Richard Allen **Owner** Rockliffe Hall **Seats** 60, Pr/dining room 20 **Times** 6.30-9.30, Closed L all week, D Sun-Mon **Prices** Fixed D 3 course £55, Tasting menu £75, Service optional **Wines** 600 bottles over £30, 3 bottles under £30, 35 by glass **Parking** 300 **Notes** Vegetarian available, Children welcome

Ramside Hall Hotel

International

tel: 0191 386 5282 **Carrville DH1 1TD**
email: mail@ramsidehallhotel.co.uk **web:** www.ramsidehallhotel.co.uk
dir: A1(M) junct 62, A690 to Sunderland. Straight on at lights. 200mtrs after rail bridge turn right

Carnivore heaven in golf-oriented hotel

Sprawling outwards from a largely Victorian house, Ramside was beefed up in the late 20th century with massive conference and banqueting facilities, two 18-hole championship golf courses, and 2015 saw the opening of a glossy spa and health club. The crowd-pleasing culinary options run from straightforward carvery dishes to the menu in the brasserie-style Rib Room, a steakhouse and grill which is a temple to slabs of locally-reared 28-day aged beef. Just choose your cut (a peckish pair might go halves on a 30oz tomahawk rib-eye) which then arrives with roasted mushrooms, braised onions and a choice of classic sauces. Non-carnivores could go for grilled sea bass with braised fennel and herb velouté. Preceding this there might be confit belly pork with black pudding and toffee apple, and to finish, comfort-oriented puddings such as a retro knickerbocker glory or baked Alaska.

Times 7am-10pm, All-day dining

HUTTON MAGNA Map 19 NZ11

The Oak Tree Inn

Modern British

tel: 01833 627371 **DL11 7HH**
email: claireross67@hotmail.com
dir: 7m W on A66 from Scotch Corner

Confident, creative cooking in a converted village inn

Run by husband-and-wife team Alastair and Claire Ross, The Oak Tree is just the sort of unassuming village inn you'd like to come across when touring the elemental Pennine landscapes. Locals drop in for a chat and a pint, but the towering piles of cookery books show where the heart of the operation lies. Whitewashed stone and panelled walls, beams, sofas at an open fire and, in the restaurant, high-backed chairs at unclothed tables make a cosy backdrop for Alastair's skilfully-cooked modern British dishes. Main courses keep a clear focus on the main ingredient: top-class Scarborough cod is partnered with steamed Shetland mussels, parsnip purée and curry, while best end of lamb might be supported by giant couscous, merguez sausage and cumin. Elsewhere, dishes are interesting without being overloaded with flavours, as seen in a warm salad of smoked duck and black pudding with a well-balanced honey and mustard dressing. Expect excellent home-baked breads, and the ice creams to accompany desserts, such as the salted caramel that comes with hot chocolate fondant, are also made on the premises.

Chef Alastair Ross **Owner** Alastair & Claire Ross **Seats** 20, Pr/dining room 20 **Times** 6.30-9.30, Closed 24-27 & 31 Dec, 1-2 Jan, Mon, L all week **Prices** Starter £5.50-£9.50, Main £19.50-£25, Dessert £6.95-£8.95, Service optional **Wines** 14 bottles over £30, 47 bottles under £30, 8 by glass **Parking** 3, On street **Notes** Vegetarian dishes & children's portions by prior arrangement, Children welcome

---

REDWORTH Map 19 NZ22

Redworth Hall Hotel

British

tel: 01388 770600 **DL5 6NL**
email: redworthhallreservations@thehotelcollection.co.uk
web: www.thehotelcollection.co.uk
dir: From A1(M) junct 58 take A68 towards Corbridge. At 1st rdbt take A6072 towards Bishop Auckland. At next rdbt take 2nd exit (A6072). Hotel on left

Modern British cooking in a 17th-century manor

It's a grand looking place – positively stately – dating from the back end of the 17th century and constructed in homage to the earlier Jacobean style. The galleried Great Hall harks back to days of magnificent parties, while today's visitor is as likely to be here for a wedding, a beauty treatment, or the nearby golf courses. The 1774 Restaurant is worth a punt, though, with its classical elegance and posh table settings. The kitchen offers up a gently contemporary repertoire with some good ideas and nothing to scare the horses. Start with chicken and ham terrine, served on a slate, with piccalilli to cut through the richness and some toasted pesto bruschetta. Among main courses, braised blade of beef is served on champ and comes with a red onion tarte Tatin. For dessert, chocolate torte has an accompanying jug of pouring cream.

Owner The Hotel Collection **Seats** 200, Pr/dining room 240 **Times** 12-2/6-9.45, Closed D 25 Dec **Prices** Fixed L 2 course fr £17.95, Fixed D 3 course fr £25 **Wines** 14 bottles over £30, 49 bottles under £30, 29 by glass **Parking** 220 **Notes** Afternoon tea 2-4.30pm, Sunday L fr £17.95, Vegetarian available, Children welcome

---

ROMALDKIRK Map 19 NY92

The Rose & Crown

Modern British, Continental

tel: 01833 650213 **DL12 9EB**
email: hotel@rose-and-crown.co.uk **web:** www.rose-and-crown.co.uk
dir: 6m NW of Barnard Castle on B6277

Classically-based cuisine in a lovely old inn

You know you're on to a good thing as soon as you arrive in Romaldkirk: not one, but three village greens complete with Saxon church, village pump and stocks, bracket The Rose & Crown. The 18th-century inn is steeped in tradition, yet bang up-to-date where it matters. With its oak settles and antique chairs, the creaky bar is the sort of place you dream of finding for a pint of Black Sheep by a sizzling log fire — you're welcome to eat here, but at dinner, many guests go for the romantic candlelit vibe of the elegant oak-panelled dining room, where dinner menus are built on local, seasonal produce and inspired by classic and contemporary trends. Slow-braised pressed pork belly with black pudding and a crispy poached egg to give textural contrast shows the style, while main course might be pot-roasted shoulder of local

continued

ROMALDKIRK *continued*

lamb and chorizo with pearl barley, carrot, onion and celery brunoise, sobrasada foam and root vegetable crisps. Creative ideas such as ginger pannacotta with poached rhubarb and hazelnut praline close proceedings.

Chef Dave Hunter **Owner** Thomas & Cheryl Robinson **Seats** 24
Times 12-2.30/6.30-9, Closed 23-27 Dec **Prices** Fixed L 3 course fr £17, Fixed D 3 course fr £35, Tasting menu fr £50, Starter £7-£9, Main £13-£24, Dessert £5-£8, Service optional **Wines** 22 bottles over £30, 34 bottles under £30, 10 by glass **Parking** 25 **Notes** Sunday L, Vegetarian available, Children 7 yrs+ D

SEAHAM
Map 19 NZ44

The Ozone Restaurant
◉ Asian Fusion

tel: 0191 516 1400 **Seaham Hall Hotel, Lord Byron's Walk SR7 7AG**
email: hotel@seaham-hall.com
dir: *Leave A1018 onto A19 at rdbt take 2nd exit onto B1285/Stockton Rd. Turn left at Lord Byron Walk in 0.3m turn right*

Asian flavours in a glamorous five-star hotel

Seaham Hall's sleek Ozone Restaurant pulls in the day spa sybarites for its stimulating Pan-Asian food, but locals are also wise to what's on offer, so diners are as likely to be wearing suits as lounging in robes and slippers. Floor-to-ceiling windows and a wraparound outdoor terrace open up heavenly garden views as a backdrop to the light and zingy fusion food sent from the open kitchen. Confit duck pancake with hoi sin sauce, crisp lettuce and cucumber makes a suitably clean-lined starter, or crispy squid with coriander and sweet chilli might appeal, ahead of main-courses such as Thai prawn curry or tempura cod with roast peanuts and Thai shallot and apple salad. For dessert, coconut pannacotta with roasted pineapple keeps things suitably oriental.

Chef Simon Bolsover **Owner** Seasons Plc **Seats** 60 **Times** 11-5/6-9, Closed 25 Dec **Prices** Starter £6, Main £12.50, Dessert £6, Service optional **Wines** 4 bottles over £30, 7 bottles under £30, 11 by glass **Parking** 200 **Notes** Sunday L, Vegetarian available, Children welcome

---

Seaham Hall – Byron's Bar & Grill
◉◉ Modern British

tel: 0191 516 1400 **Seaham Hall Hotel, Lord Byron's Walk SR7 7AG**
email: hotel@seaham-hall.co.uk **web:** www.seaham-hall.co.uk
dir: *A19 at 1st exit signed B1404 Seaham and follow signs to Seaham Hall*

Modern grill dining in luxury hotel

The late 18th-century Seaham Hall now trades as a state-of-the-art spa hotel with luxurious treatment rooms and a brace of stimulating eating options. After complete refurbishment in 2013, the space formerly known as the White Room

restaurant is reborn as Byron's Bar & Grill, a swish contemporary space with a glossy sheen, velour banquettes, darkwood flooring and marble-topped tables. The kitchen has kicked the erstwhile fine-dining approach into touch and now delivers a crowd-pleasing menu aiming unashamedly at the hearts of carnivores, although well-sourced fish – herb-crusted cod with bacon, Savoy cabbage and carrots, for example – provides meat-free alternatives. Expect the likes of devilled crispy whitebait with caper and parsley mayonnaise to start, followed by top-quality cuts of 28-day aged beef from the grill – a rib-eye steak with balsamic-glazed onions, confit tomatoes and hand-cut chips, say. Desserts take a similarly uncomplicated approach with the likes of rum baba or chocolate fudge brownie.

Seaham Hall – Byron's Bar & Grill

Chef Simon Bolsover **Owner** Seaham Hall Management Ltd **Seats** 46, Pr/dining room 100 **Times** 11-9.30, All-day dining **Prices** Fixed L 2 course £18.50, Fixed D 3 course £30, Starter £8-£12, Main £22-£30, Dessert £7-£9, Service optional **Wines** 148 bottles over £30, 22 bottles under £30, 11 by glass **Parking** 120 **Notes** Sunday L £14.95-£30, Vegetarian available, Children welcome

---

ESSEX

BRENTWOOD
Map 6 TQ59

Marygreen Manor Hotel
◉ Modern European **V**

tel: 01277 225252 **London Rd CM14 4NR**
email: info@marygreenmanor.co.uk **web:** www.marygreenmanor.co.uk
dir: *M25 junct 28, onto A1023 over 2 sets of lights, hotel on right*

Enterprising modern food in a Tudor mansion

Dating from the early 16th century, when it was built by a courtier of Catherine of Aragon, the manor is a perfect example of a half-timbered building, the restaurant an impressive-looking room with a profusion of oak wall and ceiling timbers and carved stanchions. Classy ingredients are carefully handled by a kitchen that combines them sympathetically to create some stimulating dishes. Start with veal sweetbreads with onions, spinach, rhubarb and radish, or lobster with leeks, ceps and lobster foam, before grilled Dover sole with beurre noisette and capers, or beef fillet with cauliflower purée, mushrooms and pak choi. Vegetarians have a separate menu, and desserts have included banana pudding with caramel fudge sauce and vanilla ice cream, or raspberry and chocolate tart.

Chef Majid Bourote **Owner** Mr S Bhattessa **Seats** 80, Pr/dining room 85
Times 12.30-2.30/7.15-10.15, Closed L Mon, D Sun, BHs **Prices** Prices not confirmed
Wines 72 bottles over £30, 51 bottles under £30, 12 by glass **Parking** 100
Notes Tasting menu 6 course, Sunday L, Children welcome

CHELMSFORD
Map 6 TL70

County Hotel
◉ Modern European

tel: 01245 455700 **29 Rainsford Rd CM1 2PZ**
email: kloftus@countyhotelgroup.co.uk **web:** www.countyhotelgroup.co.uk
dir: Off Chelmsford ring road close to town centre and A12 junct 18

British and Mediterranean flavours in town-centre hotel

A conveniently short stroll from the railway station and town centre, the County Hotel is done out in a cheery modern style, as typified in the County Kitchen restaurant, where oak floors and leather seats in summery pastel hues of mustard, mint and tangerine add colour to neutral contemporary decor. Uncomplicated modern European cooking using local materials is the kitchen's stock in trade, starting along the lines of venison and confit pheasant terrine with celeriac remoulade and toasted walnut bread; mains might bring fillet steak with potato rösti, butternut squash purée, curly kale and red wine jus, or a burst of Mediterranean warmth in the form of Ligurian fish stew. For dessert, there could be dark chocolate fondant with clotted cream ice cream.

Times 12-2.30/6-10, Closed L Sat

COGGESHALL
Map 7 TL82

Baumann's Brasserie
◉◉ French, European

tel: 01376 561453 **4-6 Stoneham St CO6 1TT**
email: food@baumannsbrasserie.co.uk **web:** www.baumannsbrasserie.co.uk
dir: A12 from Chelmsford, exit at Kelvedon into Coggeshall. Restaurant in centre opposite clock tower

Gutsy cooking in buzzy brasserie

Originally launched by legendary restaurateur Peter Langan, chef-patron Mark Baumann's buzzy brasserie has been a fixture on the local dining scene for almost 30 years. The setting may be a 16th-century timbered house, and continental-style

pavement tables hint at a classic French bistro, but there's nothing stuck in the past about Baumann's inventively-tweaked French and British dishes. Inside, the mood is laid-back and cosmopolitan and the one-off decor is akin to an eclectic art gallery done out with antique linen-clothed tables. Smart, on-the-money food is the deal here, delivered via no-nonsense menus that follow the seasons rather than the vagaries of culinary trends. Beetroot tarte Tatin with chive-whipped goats' cheese and sugar-roasted chestnuts makes a cracking starter, then you might continue with something from the daily fish menu – fillet of monkfish, for example, gets the robust flavours of Thai red curry crust and king prawns in garlic and ginger. It all ends on a high note with an excellent traditional marmalade steamed sponge with vanilla custard.

Times 12-2/7-9.30, Closed 2 wks Jan, Mon-Tue

COLCHESTER
Map 13 TL92

The North Hill Hotel
◉◉ Modern British

tel: 01206 574001 **51 North Hill CO1 1PY**
email: info@northhillhotel.com **web:** www.northhillhotel.com
dir: Follow directions for town centre, down North Hill, hotel on left

Traditional bistro fare plus coffee and cake

A short trot from the high street of England's oldest town, The North Hill presents two faces to the world, one a traditional half-timbered medieval look, the other of yellow-painted brickwork. The diversity continues indoors, with a range of pared-down spaces, including a reclaimed 15th-century hall house repurposed into the hotel's function room. Unclothed lightwood tables lend a Nordic touch to the Green Room bistro, where the produce of East Anglia is celebrated with gusto, from Mersea oysters to Red Poll beef and extra-virgin rapeseed oil for the dressings. The cooking is traditional bistro fare, and none the worse for that, beginning with seafood specialities such as dressed crab and citrus mayonnaise, or a salmon and crayfish fishcake in chervil dressing. There are days when only sausages and mash in onion gravy will do, but if you're after something glitzier, look to lemon and garlic lamb with new potato crush and spinach in salsa verde. Coffee and cake is an all-day treat, the daily-changing specials including carrot and walnut, or chocolate and red wine cake.

Chef John Riddleston **Owner** Rob Brown **Seats** 90, Pr/dining room 30
Times 12-2.30/6-9.30 **Prices** Fixed L 2 course £9.50-£16, Fixed D 3 course £19-£38.50, Starter £4.50-£7.50, Main £10-£24, Dessert £4.50-£7, Service optional
Wines 14 bottles over £30, 34 bottles under £30, 14 by glass **Parking** NCP opposite
Notes Pre-theatre 10% discount (Mercury), Thu catch with drink £10, Sunday L £10-£24, Vegetarian available, Children welcome

COLCHESTER *continued*

Stoke by Nayland Hotel, Golf & Spa

◉◉ Modern British

tel: 01206 262836 & 265843 **Keepers Ln, Leavenheath CO6 4PZ**
email: restaurant@stokebynayland.com **web:** www.stokebynayland.com
dir: *From A134, pass through the village of Nayland, ignoring signs to Stoke-by-Nayland.*
Continue on A134, shortly after Hare & Hounds turn right on to B1068 signed Stoke-by-
Nayland Golf Club. In approx 1.5m right

Complex contemporary cooking overlooking the golf

This purpose-built hotel complex comes complete with spa, high-tech gym, function
rooms and two championship-level golf courses. It's family-owned and sets high
standards of customer care. The Lakes Restaurant is the serious dining option, a
bright and airy room with sliding glass doors giving panoramic views. The
enterprising kitchen assembles some ambitiously successful dishes (available as à
la carte only), seen in the clearly defined, full-on flavours of hake fillet with pork
crackling, white pudding, broccoli, potato mashed with bacon and mustard, and
blood orange, and another main course of chicken breast roasted with smoked
garlic served with coconut Dhal, romanesco, mango pickle, tomato chilli oil and
sweet-and-sour potatoes. Starters are equally eclectic, among them rum-cured
salmon with lime purée, mint syrup ice, rum marshmallow and fizz, although there
may also be more orthodox chicken liver parfait with apricot and sultana jam.
Desserts deliver the goods in the shape of bread-and-butter pudding with raisin
compôte and blue cheese and white chocolate ice cream, and a palate-challenging
doughnut stuffed with sticky toffee bacon served with spiced coffee sugar, milk,
maple walnut ice cream and pancetta.

Chef Alan Paton **Owner** The Boxford Group **Seats** 100, Pr/dining room 60
Times 12.30-2.30/6.30-10 **Prices** Fixed D 3 course £29, Starter £5.25-£7, Main
£10.50-£18.75, Dessert £5-£6.95, Service optional **Wines** 9 bottles over £30, 40
bottles under £30, 14 by glass **Parking** 350 **Notes** Sunday L £12.50-£19.50,
Vegetarian available, Children welcome

DEDHAM Map 13 TM03

milsoms

◉ Modern International

tel: 01206 322795 **Stratford Rd CO7 6HN**
email: milsoms@milsomhotels.com **web:** www.milsomhotels.com
dir: *7m N of Colchester, just off A12. Follow signs to Dedham then brown signs*

Global food in a fuss-free contemporary setting

The old creeper-covered house in its neat garden may look like a bastion of
traditional values, but this place offers a little piece of boutique glamour in a pretty
Essex village. The bar and brasserie strike a contemporary pose, the latter with its
split-level dining room opening out onto a beautiful (and large) terrace, the sun
kept at bay by a sail-like awning, and heaters for when the air is chilly. The menu –
which is available all day – sticks to the modern message and offers everything
from posh lunchtime sandwiches to steaks and burgers cooked on the grill. An
international flavour sees pumpkin samosa alongside Asian duck tacos among first
courses, and mains such as slow-cooked lamb shank with elephant beans and feta,
or a thick-cut Scottish hake number with chorizo, pepper and chickpea stew. Finish
with spiced apple crumble cheesecake.

Chef Sarah Norman, Ben Rush **Owner** The Milsom family **Seats** 80, Pr/dining room
30 **Times** 12-9.30, All-day dining **Prices** Starter £5.75-£11.50, Main £11.95-£29.95,
Dessert £5.95, Service optional **Wines** 26 bottles over £30, 38 bottles under £30,
20 by glass **Parking** 80 **Notes** Brunch, Sunday L, Vegetarian available,
Children welcome

The Sun Inn

Rustic Italian, Modern British NOTABLE WINE LIST

tel: 01206 323351 **High St CO7 6DF**
email: office@thesuninndedham.com **web:** www.thesuninndedham.com
dir: *In village centre opposite church*

A taste of Italy in a village inn

The setting may be in the heart of Constable country, but The Sun Inn's culinary leanings have a distinctly sunny Mediterranean soul. The place is a proper 15th-century village inn, revamped to sit well with modern sensibilities, but not at the expense of its character: there are open fires, doughty timbers and panelling, backed by friendly service and a good range of real ales. Food is taken seriously, combining fresh locally-sourced produce and quality Italian ingredients, such as cured meats, cheeses and oils, in uncomplicated, well-executed dishes. The kitchen is led by an Italian chef, so antipasti are on offer – perhaps a platter of bresaola, Neapolitan salami and Mersea oysters – or take a starter of duck hearts with white onion, sage, broad beans and home-made bread to mop up the juices. A simple main course of top-notch hand-dived scallops with lentils and samphire, is proof that less really can be more, while the Mediterranean theme winds things up in a dessert of elderflower pannacotta with poached apricots.

Chef Ugo Simonelli **Owner** Piers Baker **Seats** 70
Times 12-2.30/6.30-9.30, Closed 25-26 Dec, 3-4 Jan **Prices** Fixed L 2 course £12-£18, Fixed D 3 course £15-£20, Starter £5-£8.50, Main £9.50-£24, Dessert £6-£9, Service optional **Wines** 44 bottles over £30, 46 bottles under £30, 20 by glass **Parking** 15 **Notes** Breakfast Fri-Sun, Sunday L £15-£24, Vegetarian available, Children welcome

Le Talbooth

Modern British, European NOTABLE WINE LIST

tel: 01206 323150 **Stratford Rd CO7 6HN**
email: talbooth@milsomhotels.com **web:** www.milsomhotels.com/letalbooth
dir: *6m from Colchester follow signs from A12 to Stratford St Mary, restaurant on the left before village*

Classy creative cooking and lovely riverside setting

At the heart of Constable country, the setting is quintessentially English: a former toll house by the River Stour dating from Tudor times that oozes period character. Whatever the weather throws at you, alfresco dining is on the cards thanks to an impressive sail canopy above the waterside terrace. The Milsom family have run this East Anglian stalwart for over half a century, so the whole operation ticks over with well-drilled precision. Inside, the look is slick and contemporary, and the kitchen stays abreast of culinary trends while paying attention to the seasons and local materials. Pan-roasted skate wing served with razor clams, smoked shallots and lardo is a thoughtfully composed idea backed by top-quality ingredients and accurate cooking. Next up, pot-roast sea bass fillet is partnered with seared squid,

saffron tagliatelle, spinach and pickled cockles, or if meat is called for, you might try venison saddle with thyme-infused polenta, blackberries, kale and red wine jus. An inventive apple-themed dessert brings a classic tarte Tatin, sorbet, apple and sage doughnut and poached blackberries.

Chef Andrew Hirst, Ian Rhodes **Owner** The Milsom family **Seats** 80, Pr/dining room 34 **Times** 12-2/6.30-9, Closed D Sun (Oct-Apr) **Prices** Fixed L 2 course £25, Starter £12.75-£18.50, Main £19.50-£33, Dessert £8.75-£9.75, Service optional **Wines** 250 bottles over £30, 46 bottles under £30, 19 by glass **Parking** 50 **Notes** Sunday L £36, Vegetarian available, Children welcome

GESTINGTHORPE · Map 13 TL83

The Pheasant

British

tel: 01787 465010 & 461196 **Audley End CO9 3AU**
web: www.thepheasant.net
dir: *Phone for directions*

Traditional country-pub cooking on the north Essex border

A smartly spruced-up 500-year-old country inn, The Pheasant sits on the road between Sudbury and Halstead on the north Essex border. Its trimly beamed ceilings are exactly what you expect to see, and dining goes on in a trio of interconnecting rooms adorned with plenty of greenery. Any suggestion of undue complexity is sidestepped in menus that build on the traditional country-pub repertoire, supplemented by a specials board. Battered tiger prawns with garlic mayonnaise for dipping feature alongside grilled goats' cheese in sweet chilli dressing, before the main attraction arrives in the shape of local farm sausages with creamy mash and onion gravy, or duck breast with orange and fennel salad. Most things come with hand-cut chips, including the half-pound sirloins, and there are sticky toffee pudding in caramel sauce, or cider-laced apple crumble with real custard bringing up the rear.

Chef James Donoghue **Owner** James & Diana Donoghue **Seats** 40, Pr/dining room 16 **Times** 12-3/6.30-9 **Prices** Prices not confirmed, Service optional **Wines** 5 bottles over £30, 21 bottles under £30, 7 by glass **Parking** 25 **Notes** Sunday L, Vegetarian available, Children welcome

GREAT TOTHAM · Map 7 TL81

The Bull & Willow Room at Great Totham

Modern, Traditional British

tel: 01621 893385 & 894020 **2 Maldon Rd CM9 8NH**
email: reservations@thewillowroom.co.uk **web:** www.thebullatgreattotham.co.uk
dir: *Exit A12 at Witham junct to Great Totham*

A 16th-century village inn with high-toned dining

There's no lack of distractions at The Bull. Cabaret tribute nights featuring the work of Robbie Williams and Dame Shirley Bassey are just the start of it. The 16th-century village inn has come roaring into the modern world, not least by means of an uncommonly posh eating area, the Willow Room, kitted out with a panelled bar, double-layered napery and chandeliers. Smartly attired staff keep things ticking over out front, while the kitchen produces a repertoire of mixed and modernised pub classics and forays into the contemporary. Crisp-fried duck's egg with truffle-dressed Russian salad is an interesting starter, while mains might bring on well-timed John Dory with warm potato and olive salad, pancetta and watercress, or breast of Barbary duck, the leg meat parcelled in tortellini, with puréed quince and creamed cabbage in blackberry jus. There's much to choose from, and most of it makes a big impact, through to rich summer berry pannacotta with mint sorbet, or chocolate fondant with pistachio ice cream. A three-meat mixed roast with Yorkshire pudding is the star of the Sunday lunch offering.

Chef Luke Stevens **Owner** David Milne **Seats** 75, Pr/dining room 20
Times 12-2.30/5-9.45 **Prices** Prices not confirmed, Service optional **Wines** 19 bottles over £30, 46 bottles under £30, 9 by glass **Parking** 80 **Notes** Fixed D Mon-Fri, Menus/prices change 8-10 wks, Sunday L, Vegetarian available, Children welcome

GREAT YELDHAM   Map 13 TL73

The White Hart

◉◉ British, European

tel: 01787 237250 **Poole St CO9 4HJ**
email: mjwmason@yahoo.co.uk **web:** www.whitehartyeldham.com
dir: *On A1017, between Halstead & Haverhill*

Intricate modern British cooking in Tudor surroundings

Dating back to the early Tudor era, The White Hart is a classic timbered country inn set in extensive grounds, the kind of period property that understandably does a roaring wedding trade. Within its walls are all the oak panelling, heavy beams and exposed brickwork you could wish for, as well as sofas that invite pre-dinner lolling. Crisp white napery and quality tableware confer distinctive class on the dining room, where the intricately composed British cooking is inflected with some European accents. A daring pairing of seared scallops and smoked duck breast, with shallot purée, pickled onion, grapefruit and radish is full-to-bursting with flavours, while citrus-cured trout comes with Cromer crab and a mousse of smoked salmon. At main, salt marsh lamb is given star billing, the belly stuffed with haggis alongside a pink noisette and a kidney, as well as rosemary polenta and wild mushrooms, a strong jus unifying all the components. In conclusion, there could be strawberry cheesecake with matching jelly and sorbet and a white chocolate and Amaretto mousse.

Chef Wu Zhenjang, K White **Owner** Matthew Mason **Seats** 44, Pr/dining room 200 **Times** 12-3/6-12, Closed 25 Dec eve, Mon, L Tue **Prices** Starter £6.95-£12.95, Main £16.95-£24.95, Dessert £5.95-£10.95, Service optional **Wines** 19 bottles over £30, 21 bottles under £30, 8 by glass **Parking** 50 **Notes** Sunday L £8.95-£18.95, Vegetarian available, Children welcome

HARWICH   Map 13 TM23

The Pier at Harwich

◉◉ Modern British, Seafood

tel: 01255 241212 **The Quay CO12 3HH**
email: pier@milsomhotels.com **web:** www.milsomhotels.com
dir: *A12 to Colchester then A120 to Harwich Quay*

Spankingly fresh seafood and harbour views

Right on the quayside with views of bobbing boats and an ever-changing seascape, the Pier provides the opportunity to sample super-fresh seafood in a manner that suits your mood. The ground-floor Ha'Penny Bistro is the casual option, with first-rate fish and chips and an outside terrace if the weather is up to the job, but it's the Harbourside Restaurant upstairs that is the real catch of the day. With glorious views and dressed to impress (white linen tablecloths, original nautically-themed artworks), the main dining room is the setting for a menu that extends to a refined tiger prawn ravioli with a punchy shellfish sauce, followed by pan-fried halibut, cooked simply and accurately and matched with spinach and hollandaise sauce. Chargrilled Dedham Vale steaks are served up as an alternative to the fishy options (with skinny fries and traditional accompaniments), but Harwich crab, lobsters fresh out of the salt-water tanks and skate wing with capers and parsley butter make for stiff competition. Finish off with roasted fig and almond pudding, or crème caramel with Turkish salad and a pistachio and sesame snap.

The Pier at Harwich

Chef John Goff **Owner** The Milsom family **Seats** 80, Pr/dining room 16 **Times** 12-2/6-9.30, Closed Mon-Tue **Prices** Fixed L 2 course fr £20, Starter £8.50-£11.95, Main £19.50-£30, Dessert £7.25, Service optional **Wines** 48 bottles over £30, 26 bottles under £30, 12 by glass **Parking** 12, On street **Notes** Sunday L, Vegetarian available, Children welcome

HOCKLEY   Map 7 TQ89

The Anchor Riverside Pub and Restaurant

◉ Modern British **NEW**

tel: 01702 230777 **Ferry Rd, Hullbridge SS5 6ND**
email: info@theanchorhullbridge.co.uk
dir: *Phone for directions*

Modern British food in an appealing waterside location

Shortly before the road ends at (or in!) the River Crouch is this thoroughly modern gastro-pub, with full-height windows looking over the water. The Riverside Orangery opens up in summer and, understandably, is a big hit, but if the weather's kind you may prefer to sit outside in the extensive gardens with something grilled, a salad or just a sandwich. Divided up by screens and wine walls, and with four spacious booths, the restaurant is designed for lingering over a decent three-course meal. Try roasted hand-dived scallops with crispy suckling pig and apple purée, followed by tandoori-roast monkfish with masala potatoes and spinach, or duck cottage pie with wild mushrooms, pumpkin jam and chestnut's. Custard tart with grated nutmeg makes for a good dessert, but you might go for British cheeses with biscuits, pickled onions, grapes and piccalilli or have both.

Chef Daniel Watkins **Owner** CK Property Investments **Seats** 160 **Times** 12-3/6-9.30, Closed 25 Dec **Prices** Fixed L 2 course £15.95-£16.95, Fixed D 3 course £17.95-£18.95, Starter £6-£8.50, Main £13-£22.50, Dessert £5.50-£7.50, Service optional **Wines** 12 bottles over £30, 25 bottles under £30, 18 by glass **Notes** Sunday L £13.95-£16.95, Vegetarian available, Children welcome

MANNINGTREE
Map 13 TM13

The Mistley Thorn

Modern British, Mediterranean

tel: 01206 392821 **High St, Mistley CO11 1HE**
email: info@mistleythorn.co.uk
dir: *From A12 take A137 for Manningtree & Mistley*

Seafood-strong California cool on the Stour estuary

Chef-patron Sherri Singleton, who hails from California, has created a little gem of a place in an old coaching inn in the centre of village, a short stroll from the harbour. There's a lot going on here (smart bedrooms, a cookery school, deli and wine store), but the super-fresh seafood served in the restaurant really catches the eye. Georgian details remain in the bar and restaurant, and neutral colours keep it light, bright and contemporary. It's not an exclusively seafood menu, so you might start with seared pigeon breast with roasted squash and move onto rib-eye of Red Poll beef. Look out for the specials menu offering the catch of the day – grilled whole lemon sole with seaweed butter and hand-cut chips, maybe, or cider-cured sea trout with sea vegetables and shellfish sauce. Fans of oysters are in the right place, so kick off with half-dozen West Mersea rocks as they come or fried in a batter made with Aspall cider. Finish with lemon, almond and polenta cake.

Chef Sherri Singleton, Karl Burnside **Owner** Sherri Singleton, David McKay **Seats** 75, Pr/dining room 28 **Times** 12-2.30/6.30-9.30 **Prices** Fixed L 2 course £10.95-£14.95, Starter £5.25-£7.95, Main £10.95-£20.95, Dessert £5.50-£6.95, Service optional **Wines** 4 bottles over £30, 34 bottles under £30, 17 by glass **Parking** 7 **Notes** Sunday L £12.95-£16.95, Vegetarian available, Children welcome

SOUTHEND-ON-SEA
Map 7 TQ88

Holiday Inn Southend

Traditional British

tel: 01702 543001 **77 Eastwoodbury Crescet SS2 6XG**
email: restaurantmgr@hisouthend.com **web:** www.1935rooftoprestaurant.com
dir: *Entrance to Southend Airport*

Slick modern dining with aeroplanes in the background

If you're a plane spotting foodie both of your interests can be indulged in one fell swoop at the fifth-floor 1935 Restaurant overlooking the aviation action at Southend Airport. Naturally enough, soundproofing is of the highest order, and there's a real sense of occasion in the slick contemporary space when you look through the full-length glass windows and the runway lights put on a show in the evening. The kitchen deals in unpretentious classic and modern ideas, taking off with game terrine wrapped in pancetta with toasted brioche and red onion marmalade, followed by a three-way serving of duck – leg, breast and confit – matched with beetroot mash, cavolo nero and berry sauce. Elsewhere, there are straight-up steaks from the grill, or fish, in the form, perhaps, of pan-fried hake with pappardelle vegetables, crushed new potatoes and dill cream sauce. Finish with pecan cheesecake with salted caramel ice cream.

Chef Michael Walker **Owner** London Southend Airport Ltd **Seats** 82, Pr/dining room 12 **Times** 12-2.30/6-10 **Prices** Fixed L 2 course £16.95-£19.35, Starter £4.95-£8.95, Main £9.95-£25.95, Dessert £4.50-£5.95, Service optional **Wines** 5 bottles over £30, 21 bottles under £30, 10 by glass **Parking** 226 **Notes** Afternoon tea £15.95/£21.95, Sunday L £12.95-£19.35, Vegetarian available, Children welcome

The Roslin Beach Hotel

British

tel: 01702 586375 **Thorpe Esplanade, Thorpe Bay SS1 3BG**
email: info@roslinhotel.com **web:** www.roslinhotel.com
dir: *On Thorpe Esplanade 2.5m past Southend Pier towards Shoeburyness*

Well-conceived dishes in a buzzy seaside setting

If you do like to be beside the seaside, The Roslin Beach Hotel is for you. It's a popular place and its position looking out across the road to the sea is part of its appeal. With tables outside on the sea-facing heated terrace, and those indoors shielded by glass, it feels seasidey whatever the weather. And it's rather smart, too. Tables are dressed up in white linen and there's quite a buzz about the place when it's busy. There's a good showing of local seafood on the menu and some of the meat (duck, beef) comes from the owners' farm in Hampshire. Start with locally-caught whitebait with tartare sauce, or gin and tonic smoked salmon, or goats' curd with fig caponata and oatcakes. Among main courses, steaks cooked on the grill are a big hit, but there is also fresh grouse with pickled red cabbage, chestnuts and wild mushroom ravioli. For dessert, try a vanilla and bourbon pannacotta with raspberry 'bombs'.

Times 12-2.45/6-9.30

STANSTED MOUNTFITCHET
Map 12 TL52

Linden House

Modern European

tel: 01279 813003 **1-3 Silver St CM24 8HA**
email: stay@lindenhousestansted.co.uk **web:** www.lindenhousestansted.co.uk
dir: *M11 junct 8 towards Newport on A120, on right after windmill*

Contemporary cooking in a stylish restaurant with rooms

Spruced up with a touch of boutique style, Linden House has designer bedrooms and a bar and restaurant that positively hum when it's busy (which it frequently is). But it isn't all style over substance. The kitchen crew has put together a modern menu of bright ideas, and the service team do their work with a great level of engagement. Seared local wood pigeon with Kentish cobnuts and pan-fried wild mushrooms is a real country dish with a bit of finesse, while vegetarians might be drawn to carpaccio of beetroot with goats' cheese dusted in paprika and dressed with a sweet basil oil. Among main courses, seven-hour pork (slow-cooked collar) sits alongside mixed grill of fish with smoked garlic mayonnaise and hand-cut fat chips, plus Hereford steaks cooked on the grill. Desserts are a comforting bunch ranging from sticky toffee pudding to maple pannacotta with caramelised pineapple.

Chef Matthew Hill **Owner** Karl & Sarah Foster **Seats** 50 **Times** 12-3/6-9.30 **Prices** Fixed L 2 course fr £15, Service optional **Wines** 37 bottles over £30, 23 bottles under £30, 11 by glass **Parking** Pay & display 100yds **Notes** Breakfast, Afternoon tea, Sunday L £15-£18, Vegetarian available, Children welcome

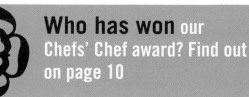
Who has won our **Chefs' Chef award? Find out on page 10**

STOCK

Map 6 TQ69

The Hoop
◉ Modern British

tel: 01277 841137 **High St CM4 9BD**
email: thehoopstock@yahoo.co.uk
dir: A12 Billericay Galleywold junct, on B1007

Assured modern cooking in an old pub

The building was converted to an ale house some 450 years ago and remains in that line of business to this day. The wooden-boarded Hoop has an atmospheric pub on the ground floor – acres of beams, draught ales at the bar – and an upstairs restaurant that is opened up to the rafters to create a slightly more refined setting amid the exposed oak. The kitchen turns out modern food that wouldn't look out of place on the menu of a thrusting big-city brasserie. Chickpea fritters, for example, as a starter with dukkah spice, pomegranate and mango yogurt, or pheasant tempura with a game gravy to dip them into. Main courses might deliver brined belly of pork with seared scallops and winter cabbage, or slow-roasted Creedy Carver duck leg with black pudding and smoked sausage. Finish with bread-and-butter pudding with candied orange and white chocolate ice cream.

Chef Phil Utz **Owner** Michelle Corrigan **Seats** 40 **Times** 12-2.30/6-9, Closed Beer festival wk, 1st wk Jan, Mon, L Sat, D Sun **Prices** Tasting menu fr £60, Starter £5.95-£8.95, Main £11.95-£27.95, Dessert £5.95-£8.95, Service optional 10% **Wines** 11 bottles over £30, 33 bottles under £30, 14 by glass **Parking** Village hall **Notes** Sunday L £25, Vegetarian available, Children welcome

TENDRING

Map 7 TM12

The Fat Goose
◉ Modern British

tel: 01255 870060 **Heath Rd CO16 0BX**
email: eat@fat-goose.co.uk
dir: A120 to Horsley Cross, follow B1035 to Tendring/Thorpe-le-Soken. 1.5m on right

Confident cooking in a charming former pub

The family-run Fat Goose is the kind of place where the kitchen bakes its own bread and local ingredients figure large on the menu. It's a restaurant, not a pub, but it still has an easy-going vibe and it's quite possible to while away a few hours here. The interior blends old and new with aplomb, so expect slate floors, exposed beams and well-spaced wooden tables, and a warming wood-burning stove in the cooler months. The menu ploughs a bistro-like furrow, with twice-baked smoked haddock and cheddar soufflé, followed by a home-made burger (minced from rib-eye, rump and chuck) with hand-cut chips, or pan-roasted haunch of venison with a potato and herb rösti. There's also a daily specials board, plus an extremely good fixed-price menu midweek. For dessert there might be vanilla pannacotta with vanilla and blueberry compôte, or glazed lemon tart with a dark chocolate ganache. There's a children's menu, too.

Chef Philip Hambrook-Moore **Owner** Philip Hambrook-Moore **Seats** 50 **Times** 12-2.30/6.30-9.30, Closed Mon **Prices** Fixed L 2 course fr £13, Fixed D 3 course fr £16, Starter £4.95-£8.50, Main £11.75-£18.95, Dessert £3-£5.50, Service optional **Wines** 7 bottles over £30, 30 bottles under £30, 10 by glass **Parking** 50 **Notes** Sunday L £11.50-£17, Vegetarian available, Children welcome

GLOUCESTERSHIRE

ALMONDSBURY

Map 4 ST68

Aztec Hotel & Spa
◉ Modern British

tel: 01454 201090 **Aztec West BS32 4TS**
email: quarterjacks@shirehotels.com **web:** www.aztechotelbristol.com
dir: M5 junct 16/A38 towards city centre, hotel 200mtrs on right

Eclectic globally-inspired modern menu in a vibrant room

A hotel with the full remit of spa activities and business facilities, the Aztec also has a restaurant and bar which is worth a visit. It's a contemporary space with a Nordic feel, with a high-vaulted ceiling, rustic stone fireplace, polished wooden floors, leather seating and bold modern abstract art. The menu takes a broad sweep through global culinary culture, with British 28-day aged beef cooked on the chargrill a bit of a speciality. You might start with crispy duck with an accompanying coriander salad and pickled ginger, or home-made oxtail soup, the meat slow-cooked for five hours. Main courses take a similar international route, so tiger prawn linguine with chilli and garlic stands alongside Wainwright ale-battered haddock with thick-cut chips, mushy peas and lemon and tartare sauce. Those steaks include Chateaubriand for two, and there's also a steak sandwich on toasted focaccia, with desserts running to warm chocolate brownie with raspberry ripple ice cream.

Times 12.30-2/7-9.30, Closed L Sat, D 25-26 Dec

ALVESTON

Map 4 ST68

Alveston House Hotel
◉ Modern European

tel: 01454 415050 **Davids Ln BS35 2LA**
email: info@alvestonhousehotel.co.uk **web:** www.alvestonhousehotel.co.uk
dir: On A38, 3.5m N of M4/M5 interchange. M5 junct 16 N'bound or junct 14 S'bound

Attractive Georgian hotel with traditionally based menu

A Georgian hotel with a small portico entrance, set within walled gardens with a restaurant to one side, Alveston House is well worth the short drive out from Bristol. The gardens with their ornamental lily pond are a pleasant spot for a drink, and inside the place is done in calming pastel shades, not the nerve-twanging primary colours favoured by many a boutique hotel. Carriages, the dining room, is all light lemon and cream, a restful neutral backdrop to the gently modernised British and European fare on offer. Steamed Fowey mussels marinière, or a tartlet of asparagus, leeks and peas with herb salad, could be the curtain-raisers to bacon-wrapped cod with baby greens, sundried tomatoes and olives, or rump and kidney of lamb with red cabbage and mashed potato in grain mustard jus. Finish indulgently with chocolate, almond and hazelnut torte and crème fraîche, or more lightly with lemon tart, mango sorbet and raspberries. Coffee comes with home-made shortbread.

Chef Ben Halliday **Owner** Julie Camm **Seats** 75, Pr/dining room 40 **Times** 12-1.45/7-9.30 **Prices** Fixed L 2 course fr £20, Fixed D 3 course fr £25, Starter £5.75-£7.50, Main £15.50-£24.75, Dessert £5.75-£7.25, Service optional **Wines** 6 bottles over £30, 27 bottles under £30, 6 by glass **Parking** 60 **Notes** Sunday L £18.50-£22.50, Vegetarian available, Children welcome

---

ARLINGHAM Map 4 SO71

The Old Passage Inn

◉◉ Seafood, Modern British

tel: 01452 740547 **Passage Rd GL2 7JR**
email: oldpassage@btconnect.com **web:** www.theoldpassage.com
dir: *M5 junct 13/A38 towards Bristol, 2nd right to Frampton-on-Severn, over canal, bear left, follow to river*

Seafood specialities overlooking a bend in the Severn

In a prominent position on the bank of the River Severn, The Old Passage is a white-painted restaurant with rooms. It's popular with walkers and cyclists, with tracks along the river, and the Severn bore is another attraction. The restaurant, a simply designed room with a tiled floor and striking artwork on its plain walls, is another draw. The kitchen's focus is on seafood, all accurately cooked, with fish roasted (wild turbot fillet counterbalanced by oxtail, served with braised pak choi, celeriac purée and girolles), poached (hake with saffron and tarragon butter, potato, fennel and tomato) and fried (good old beer-battered cod with chips and tartare sauce). Lobster comes natural, grilled or thermidor, and starters range from fish soup with the usual trimmings to seared scallops interestingly served with crispy pork terrine, apple purée and rum-soaked raisins. As much thought and effort goes into a meat main course – perhaps roast breast and confit leg of pheasant with vegetables – and to puddings such as raspberry mousse with raspberry and champagne jelly and white chocolate sorbet.

Chef Mark Redwood **Owner** Sally Pearce **Seats** 60, Pr/dining room 12
Times 12-2/7-9.30, Closed 25-26 Dec, Mon, D Sun, Tue-Wed (Jan-Feb) **Prices** Starter £9.25-£13.25, Main £18.25-£34, Dessert £7.85-£9.60, Service optional **Wines** 29 bottles over £30, 16 bottles under £30, 15 by glass **Parking** 40 **Notes** ALC menu only, Sunday L, Vegetarian available, Children L only

---

BARNSLEY Map 5 SP00

Barnsley House

◉◉ Modern European

tel: 01285 740000 **GL7 5EE**
email: info@barnsleyhouse.com **web:** www.barnsleyhouse.com
dir: *4m N of Cirencester on B4425 between Cirencester & Burford*

Uncomplicated country cooking overlooking the kitchen garden

Dating from the late 17th century, Barnsley House combines the functions of hotel, spa and skincare treatment centre and restaurant, the last being decorated in gentle neutral tones, with lightwood tables. This is named the Potager, after the ornamental and vegetable garden designed in the 1950s by Rosemary Verey which it overlooks. The kitchen eschews fancy flourishes in favour of an unfussy, straightforward approach to bring out distinctive flavours, using fresh produce from the garden. Perfectly cooked lamb sweetbreads in a noteworthy jus are served with no more than morels and garden chard, or there might be smoked haddock and pea risotto. An Italian influence is evident in some dishes: a starter of Vincisgrassi, for instance, based on an 18th-century recipe for baked pasta with Parma ham, porcini mushrooms and truffles. End with a fruity pudding such as passionfruit tart with tangy lime syrup and mascarpone, or roasted figs with Venetian-style rice pudding.

Chef Graham Grafton **Owner** Calcot Health and Leisure **Seats** 40, Pr/dining room 14
Times 12-2.30/7-9.30 **Prices** Fixed L 2 course £26, Starter £7-£13, Main £14-£28, Dessert £7.50 **Wines** 40 bottles over £30, 20 bottles under £30, 10 by glass **Parking** 25 **Notes** Sunday L, Vegetarian available, Children 12 yrs+ D

The Village Pub

◉ Modern, Traditional British v

tel: 01285 740421 **GL7 5EF**
email: info@thevillagepub.co.uk **web:** www.thevillagepub.co.uk
dir: *B4425 from Cirencester to Bibury*

Reworked British (and French) pub classics

Getting away from it all to a country inn for a night or two, like this Cotswold gem just outside Cirencester, is a sure-fire way to recharge the batteries. The place is done up with an eye to comfort throughout, and there's a nice idiosyncrasy to the combination of swagged drapes and bare floorboards. Reworked classic pub dishes are the foundation of the appeal, but there are forays further afield too for the likes of fennel-cured salmon with apple and fennel remoulade, or baked red pepper with tomato and halloumi. Appetising snacks such as smoked mackerel pâté or Scotched black pudding quail's eggs are a good way to start, and might lead on to whole plaice in beurre noisette, or pot-roast brisket with red cabbage, beetroot and dauphinoise. Afterwards, there's steamed ginger pudding, or chocolate St-Emilion, as well as a specials list of home-made ice creams.

Chef Graham Grafton **Owner** Richard Ball **Seats** 60 **Times** 12-2.30/6-9.30
Prices Starter £7-£12, Main £11-£30, Dessert £6, Service optional **Wines** 5 bottles over £30, 16 bottles under £30, 3 by glass **Parking** 24 **Notes** Sunday L £8-£30, Children welcome

BOURTON-ON-THE-WATER

Dial House

◉◉ Classical French, Modern **NEW** v

tel: 01451 822244 **High St GL54 2AN**
email: info@dialhousehotel.com **web:** www.dialhousehotel.com
dir: Take A429 Cirencester Rd into Bourton. Dial House is set back from High St

High-calibre contemporary cooking in classy surrounds

This small-scale hotel occupies one of this popular village's oldest houses, built in the 18th century from honeyed Cotswold stone. Inside, the place has large stone fireplaces as reminders of its antiquity, and an all-round feeling of quality and elegance that continues through to a stylish dining room. The kitchen delivers finely-tuned Anglo-French cooking via a quartet of 5-course menus with themes ranging from Ocean, Earth, Indulgence and Garden, plus an 8-course extravaganza, each supported by a wine flight presented by a relaxed and knowledgeable sommelier. The 'Indulgence' option opens with luxurious smoked Périgord foie gras (served theatrically in a smoke-filled cloche) with brioche crumb and a cep reduction, followed by Portland crab in a bravura display of finely-worked emulsion and a roast crab meat reduction, its richness offset by apple and sorrel. Next comes Brittany asparagus with egg yolk emulsion and gel, morel essence and summer flowers, then fish: brill cooked sous-vide and matched with potato espuma and black truffle. Finally, a Valrhona Guanaja chocolate crémeux with avocado textures and olive oil powder.

Chef Paul Nicholson **Owner** Elaine & Martyn Booth **Seats** 30, Pr/dining room 16 **Times** 12-2/7-9 Closed 1st wk Jan **Prices** Tasting menu £79-£89 **Wines** 45 bottles over £30, 25 bottles under £30, 15 by glass **Parking** 15 **Notes** Fixed D 5 course £55-65, Afternoon tea £22 No children

BUCKLAND   Map 10 SP03

Buckland Manor

◉◉◉ *– see below*

CHELTENHAM   Map 10 SO92

The Beaufort Dining Room Ellenborough Park

◉◉◉ *– see opposite*

Le Champignon Sauvage

◉◉◉◉ *– see page 176*

The Cheltenham Park Hotel

◉ Modern International

tel: 01242 222021 **Cirencester Rd, Charlton Kings GL53 8EA**
email: cheltenhampark@thehotelcollection.co.uk **web:** www.thehotelcollection.co.uk
dir: On A435, 2m SE of Cheltenham near Lilley Brook Golf Course

Classic and contemporary dining beside a lake

Whether you have had a winner or lost your shirt on the horses at nearby Cheltenham racecourse, the Lakeside Restaurant of this smart country hotel is the place to end the day with a meal of celebration or consolation. The bright and airy space is flooded with light from walls of floor-to-ceiling windows overlooking the gardens and lake, and cheerfully kitted out with tangerine, burgundy, and grey high-backed seats at bare darkwood tables – a setting that sits well with the uncomplicated, please-all repertoire of classic and gently modern cooking. The kitchen sources its materials

Buckland Manor ◉◉◉

BUCKLAND   Map 10 SP03

British ⚑ NOTABLE WINE LIST

tel: 01386 852626 **WR12 7LY**
email: info@bucklandmanor.com **web:** www.bucklandmanor.co.uk
dir: 2m SW of Broadway. Take B4632 signed Cheltenham, then take turn for Buckland. Hotel through village on right

Confident modern cooking in a grand country house

Classic Cotswold country-house hotels don't come much more impressive than Buckland Manor. This mighty stone manor house was built in the 13th century next to the village church and has 10 acres of grounds. The finish on the inside is impressive, too, with period details all present and correct – wooden panels, mullioned windows, stone fireplaces – and the place is filled with fine furniture. It's the kind of place where formality is observed (jackets in the dining room please, gents). The restaurant matches the rest of the house in the looks department, with its white-painted panels, portraits on the walls and elegantly dressed tables setting the tone. The kitchen, though, headed-up by Will Guthrie, offers something rather more contemporary. Via tasting menus at lunch and dinner, a fixed price à la carte and good-value set lunch option, the chef and his team deliver pin-sharp modern British food that is creative and extremely well judged (nothing too outlandish to send shockwaves

through the genteel dining room). Halibut is smoked on the premises and arrives in a first course with dressed crab and candied beetroot, while among main-course loin of Dumbleton Estate venison might be partnered with spiced red cabbage, smoked pancetta and juniper berry sauce. Classic thinking is generally the foundation of each dish, but technique and clever twists elevate the food to a higher level. For dessert, rhubarb and pistachio crumble soufflé is surely worth the wait, served with an accompanying orange custard and pistachio cream, or go for thyme pannacotta with a fig poached in red wine, liquorice meringue and pear sorbet.

Chef Will Guthrie **Owner** Andrew & Christina Brownsword **Seats** 40, Pr/dining room 14 **Times** 12.30-2/7-9, **Prices** Fixed L 2 course fr £21.50, Fixed D 3 course fr £65, Tasting menu fr £85 **Wines** 400 bottles over £30, 17 bottles under £30, 15 by glass **Parking** 20 **Notes** Tasting menu 7 course, Sunday L £31.50-£35.50, Vegetarian available, Children 8 yrs+

diligently and delivers well-executed dishes along the lines of chicken liver parfait with fruit chutney and melba toast, followed by braised shoulder of lamb with gratin potatoes, spinach, asparagus and roasted parsnips. End in comfort mode with sticky toffee pudding with butterscotch sauce and clotted cream.

Chef Sourabh Gupta **Owner** The Hotel Collection **Seats** 180, Pr/dining room 22 **Times** 7-9.30, Closed L all week **Prices** Prices not confirmed **Wines** 14 bottles over £30, 47 bottles under £30, 18 by glass **Parking** 170 **Notes** Vegetarian available, Children welcome

The Curry Corner

◉◉ Bangladeshi, Indian

tel: 01242 528449 **133 Fairview Rd GL52 2EX**
email: info@thecurrycorner.com
dir: From A40 turn right into Hewlett Rd, at mini-rdbt turn left

Genuine Bangladeshi flavours, superbly cooked

On the edge of Cheltenham's main shopping area, The Curry Corner occupies a Georgian townhouse-style property behind a white façade. It's been given a chic, contemporary look, with ruby-red wall coverings set off by carvings. Well-dressed tables are decently spaced, and lighting and music add to the ambience, as do the relaxed and friendly staff. Genuine Bangladeshi home cooking is the theme, so spices are flown in from far-flung countries like India, Morocco and Turkey, with fresh produce sourced locally. This policy, combined with high technical skills and good judgement, results in dishes that zing with layers of flavours, from starters of prawn luchi puri (in tomato curry) and shingara (spiced shredded lamb in crisp pastry) to main courses such as melt-in-the-mouth duck breast in orange-based curry sauce, and tender hot chilli lamb. Breads, vegetables and chutneys are all of a standard, as are attractively presented desserts like gulab jamon and coconut sorbet.

Times 12-2/5.30-11.30, Closed 25 Dec, Mon (open some BHs), L Fri

The Daffodil

◉ British, European

tel: 01242 700055 **18-20 Suffolk Pde, Montpellier GL50 2AE**
email: eat@thedaffodil.com
dir: S of town centre, just off Suffolk Rd, near Cheltenham Boys' College

Chargrilled specialities in a gorgeous art deco cinema

Once Cheltenham's first cinema, opening in 1922 in the days when such venues were as ostentatious as ocean-liners (check those sweeping staircases), The Daffodil makes a stunning restaurant venue. Art deco touches abound, including the majestic light fixtures, and a pair of kissing seats (an undivided double seat for canoodlers) is preserved in what was once the circle. The open kitchen with its charcoal oven is the centre of attention nowadays, and the chargrilled dishes are not to be missed. Calves' liver is tenderly textured and comes in classic fashion with brittle streaky bacon, fondant potato and mint butter, and the steaks are among the dazzling ornaments of the town's dining scene. Fish might be sea bass with clams and cockles in Indian-spiced sauce. Start as you mean to go on with assertive black pudding and scallops, served with pea purée and truffle honey. The talking-point dessert is pineapple carpaccio with coconut ice cream and honey baba in lime and chilli syrup.

Chef Tom Rains **Owner** Mark Stephens, James McAlpine **Seats** 140 **Times** 12-3/6-10, Closed 25-26 Dec, 1-7 Jan, Sun **Prices** Fixed L 2 course fr £13.95, Fixed D 3 course fr £35, Tasting menu fr £50, Starter £6.50-£12.50, Main £13.50-£26, Dessert £5.95-£14.95 **Wines** 29 bottles over £30, 17 bottles under £30, 29 by glass **Parking** On street, NCP **Notes** Fixed price menu Mon-Sat until 7.30pm, Vegetarian available, Children welcome

The Beaufort Dining Room Ellenborough Park ❀❀❀

CHELTENHAM	Map 10 SO92

Modern British 🍷 NOTABLE WINE LIST
tel: 01242 545454 **Southam Rd GL52 3NH**
email: info@ellenboroughpark.com **web:** www.ellenboroughpark.com
dir: A46 right after 3m onto B4079, merges with A435, 4m, over 3 rdbts, left onto Southam Lane, right onto Old Road, right onto B4632, hotel on right

High-gloss cooking in a luxurious Tudor mansion

If you have had a good day on the gee-gees at Cheltenham racecourse, you might consider blowing your winnings in this grandee of the English country-house scene – as a guest you can even make use of the private track from the course to the hotel. Ellenborough Park is a blue-blooded 16th-century stately home brimming with unreconstructed period grandeur and the sort of add-ons you expect these days – a glitzy spa, 21st-century business facilities, hyper-classy bedrooms, and two restaurants, a brasserie and the top-end option, the splendid Beaufort Dining Room. In this haven of ornately-carved oak panels, stained-glass windows in stone mullions, bone china, and equestrian paintings, head chef David Kelman produces carefully-crafted, refined and classically-based cooking that comes with a high level of technical gloss and plenty of contemporary vivacity and sparkle. For starters, he serves a precisely-made pressing of chicken with an egg yolk cooked at 62 degrees, summer vegetables, crispy chicken skin and an ambrosial chicken broth, or pan-fried scallops, cooked to gleaming perfection, in a well-judged match with carrot and golden raisin salsa, wasabi mayonnaise and coriander shoots. Following on, immaculately-timed roast beef fillet is teamed with silky smooth foie gras, garlic and thyme potatoes, carrots, Portabello mushroom purée and red wine jus. Fish gets similar careful treatment – perhaps pan-fried sea bass fillet embellished with caper and dill butter, baby spinach and white asparagus. As for dessert, iced rhubarb and custard parfait is given texture by ginger crumb and a luscious poached rhubarb and custard milkshake. The wine list runs to over 500 bins, including superstar producers and boutique wines from all around the globe.

Chef David Kelman **Seats** 60, Pr/dining room 20 **Times** 7-10, Closed Mon, L Tue-Sat, D Sun **Prices** Fixed D 3 course £55, Service optional **Wines** 510 bottles over £30, 25 bottles under £30, 12 by glass **Parking** 130 **Notes** Sunday L, Vegetarian available, Children welcome

Le Champignon Sauvage 🌹🌹🌹🌹

Modern French

tel: 01242 573449 **24-28 Suffolk Rd GL50 2AQ**
email: mail@lechampignonsauvage.co.uk
dir: *S of town centre, on A40, near Cheltenham College*

Cooking from the heart in a civilised setting

The restaurant's name is a clear pointer to the classical French culinary direction of David and Helen Everitt-Matthias's stellar Cheltenham operation. The Champignon has been a fixture in the premier league of the UK's gastronomic scene since 1987, and they have never missed a service. Now that's what you call staying power, and time hasn't in the least dimmed their enthusiasm for the job. The cornerstone of David's ethos is that a chef belongs in the kitchen, so when you go there – and go there you should, as this is a place every foodie should have on their bucket list – you can be sure that the chef himself will be at the stoves rather than in a TV studio or managing his empire. Helen continues to preside over the dining room with unflappable graciousness in a calm space where decor and ambience are utterly without pretension, just soothingly neutral shades jazzed up with an eclectic collection of modern artworks. David's cooking may be rooted in the classics but that doesn't mean he's not experimenting tirelessly. He describes his food as mixing terroir and modern French – and don't forget that the Champignon was in the vanguard of restaurants that started to replace luxury ingredients with foraged and more humble produce. So expect a showing of wild ingredients from the Cotswolds' woods and hedgerows to feature in a gutsy, full-bore style of cooking. Clarity of flavour defines a starter of miso-glazed hake, its savoury notes boosted by chrysanthemum and seaweed dashi, sesame and sea vegetables. Cod with grated mandarin, clams, black radish and a clam jus thickened with walnut oil shows an unerring eye for flavour combination, while a splendid terrine brings layers of maize-fed chicken (confit and tender breast) and salt-baked kohlrabi, counterpointed by sweet quince jelly and silky kohlrabi purée. At main course stage, houmous, anchovy emulsion, feta bonbons and chickpeas add a lively hit of salt to perfectly-timed pink Cinderford lamb. Aromatic herb and spices confer individualism on a thrilling dessert of caramelised mango with Thai-spiced cream and a Thai green curry sorbet fizzing with notes of lime and coriander. For a more traditionally decadent finale, a sauce of butterscotch and beurre noisette is hidden within an intense chocolate mousse topped with rich dark chocolate ganache and served with milk ice cream. The outstanding 20-page wine list is an exciting tour de France, with a nod to the New World, and all at eminently reasonable prices.

Chef David Everitt-Matthias **Owner** Mr & Mrs D Everitt-Matthias **Seats** 40 **Times** 12.30-1.30/7.30-8.45, Closed 10 days Xmas, 3 wks Jun, Sun-Mon **Prices** Prices not confirmed, Service optional **Parking** Public car park (Bath Rd) **Notes** ALC 2/3 course £48/£59, 4 course with cheese & dessert £69, Children welcome

CHELTENHAM *continued*

The Greenway Hotel & Spa

◉◉ Modern British, French V 🍷NOTABLE WINE LIST

tel: 01242 862352 **Shurdington GL51 4UG**
email: info@thegreenway.co.uk **web:** www.thegreenwayhotelandspa.com
dir: *3m S of Cheltenham on A46 (Stroud) & through Shurdington*

Refined modern cooking in the Cotswolds

An impeccable Elizabethan manor house of considerable charm, The Greenway has all the initial attributes needed to make a fine country-house hotel, with glorious grounds, original features and the like. Add to those the 21st-century embellishments of a swish spa, elegant bedrooms and a brace of dining options, and you have a place ready to impress the modern day visitor. The Orchard Brasserie is a stylish venue with a cool and contemporary finish, while the main fine-dining Garden Restaurant aims to impress with its take on refined, modern British cooking (with definite evidence of classical French ways). Start with ballotine of rabbit in the company of beetroot 'textures' and a raisin sauce, or scallops with curried lentils and cod cheeks. Main-course might deliver a fillet of pan-seared sea bream with crushed new potatoes and tomato confit, or twice-cooked belly of pork partnered with dauphinoise potatoes. For dessert, expect the likes of orange pannacotta with raspberry sorbet or dark chocolate marquise with honeycomb and passionfruit sorbet.

Chef Robin Dudley **Owner** Sir Peter Rigby **Seats** 60, Pr/dining room 22 **Times** 12-2.30/7-9.30 **Wines** 200 bottles over £30, 40 bottles under £30, 11 by glass **Notes** ALC 3 course £49.50, Sunday L £24.50-£29, Children welcome

Hotel du Vin Cheltenham

◉ British, French, European

tel: 01242 588450 **Parabola Rd GL50 3AQ**
email: info.cheltenham@hotelduvin.com **web:** www.hotelduvin.com
dir: *M5 junct 11, follow signs for city centre. At rdbt opposite Morgan Estate Agents take 2nd left, 200mtrs to Parabola Rd*

Bistro dining in Cheltenham's restaurant quarter

The restaurant at the Cheltenham branch of this popular hotel chain follows the usual bistro look of wooden floor, unclothed tables, banquettes and a wine related theme of empty bottles, prints and memorabilia. A difference here is a large spiral staircase leading from the bar down to the bustling restaurant, where helpful staff keep the wheels turning. The menu goes along the expected bistro route, while the kitchen employs premium ingredients and produces carefully cooked, compelling dishes. Kick off with chicken liver parfait with raisin chutney and sourdough toast before roast rump of lamb dressed with chorizo and pesto served with broccoli and boulangère potatoes. Finish in true French style with lemon tart and raspberry sorbet. Plenty of wines are available by the glass from the exceptional list.

Chef Paul Mottram **Owner** KSL **Seats** 92, Pr/dining room 32 **Times** 12-2/6.30-10.30 **Prices** Service optional 10% **Wines** 300 bottles over £30, 70 bottles under £30, 20 by glass **Parking** 23 **Notes** Sun brunch 4 course 12-4pm, Sunday L £24.99, Vegetarian available, Children welcome

Lumière

◉◉ Modern British V 🍷NOTABLE WINE LIST

tel: 01242 222200 **Clarence Pde GL50 3PA**
email: info@lumiere.cc **web:**
dir: *Town centre, near bus station*

High-octane modern cooking from skilled chef

Behind an unassuming façade is a cool, contemporary restaurant designed with the comfort and well-being of diners in mind, run by an amenable front-of-house team. The kitchen makes everything in-house, from canapés to petits fours, and comes up with some cutting-edge ideas founded on classical notions. Pollock fillet has been presented with bacon, clams, samphire and kombu to make a vividly tasting starter, and equally persuasive has been mozzarella and chorizo with apple, smoked watermelon, avocado and pistachios. If the menu descriptions of main courses make them sound busy, the original combinations pay dividends on the palate: duck breast with a spring roll, say, and chicory, carrot and orange, or bass fillet with oxtail, girolles, salsify and cauliflower. Innovation runs into puddings, among them perhaps dark chocolate delice with bourbon cheesecake and brown bread ice cream. Alternatively, go for the selection of English and Welsh cheeses.

Chef Jon Howe **Owner** Jon & Helen Howe **Seats** 25 **Times** 12-1.30/7-9, Closed 2 wks winter, 2 wks summer, Sun-Mon, L Tue-Thu **Prices** Fixed L 3 course £28, Fixed D 3 course £55, Tasting menu £60-£75 **Wines** 70 bottles over £30, 14 bottles under £30, 17 by glass **Parking** On street **Notes** Tasting menu 7/9 course, Children 8 yrs+

Monty's Brasserie

◉◉ Modern British, Seafood V

tel: 01242 227678 & 238811 **St Georges Rd GL50 3DZ**
email: info@montysbraz.co.uk **web:** www.montysbraz.co.uk
dir: *M5 junct 11, follow signs to town centre. At lights (TGI Fridays) turn left onto Gloucester Rd. Straight on, at lights turn right onto St Georges Rd, Monty's 0.75m on left*

Smart seasonal brasserie cooking in stylish Grade II listed hotel

Monty's is part of the Grade II listed George Hotel, built, like much of the spa town, in the Georgian era. It's a modern and lively brasserie, with a bare-boarded floor, brown leather-look seats at unclothed tables, plain walls and a cheerful atmosphere. The seasonally-changing menu is exactly right for the place, and what the kitchen does supremely well with sound ingredients, adding a degree of complication to dishes without pushing them into a taste too far. Crab, cod and dill fishcakes, for instance, come with crushed peas, parsley purée, pickled onions and lemon and caper mayonnaise, and that's just a starter. Roast partridge might appear in season, stuffed with apricots and cranberries, served with red wine jus, braised leg, pickled pears and fondant potato. The appeal is broadened by the likes of Thai crispy duck with chilli and sesame dipping sauce, then seared harissa-spiced salmon fillet with ras el hanout dressing, chilli and lemon couscous and cauliflower beignets. To top things off might be sticky toffee pudding with rum and raisin ice cream.

Chef Marcus Hobbs **Owner** Jeremy Shaw **Seats** 40, Pr/dining room 32 **Times** 12-2/6-10, Closed 25-26 Dec **Prices** Fixed L 2 course £14.50, Fixed D 3 course £17, Starter £6.50-£10, Main £14-£26, Dessert £6-£8 **Wines** 17 bottles over £30, 25 bottles under £30, 7 by glass **Parking** 30 **Notes** Fixed D Sun-Thu 6-7pm, Sunday L £18-£22, Children welcome

The Kings

◎◎ Modern British V

tel: 01386 840256 **The Square, High St GL55 6AW**
email: info@kingscampden.co.uk web: www.kingscampden.co.uk
dir: *In centre of town square*

Uncomplicated British cooking on the square

A bow-windowed Georgian townhouse in Cotswold stone, The Kings stands proud on the town-centre square, a playful lock of foliage climbing up one side. The interiors have been done in contemporary style, the open fireplace in the dining room strewn with candles, the tables unclothed, and a predominant colour-scheme of cool lemon offset by dark brown. British modernism is the kitchen's guidepost, but without the undue complication that can plague this style. First up, wood pigeon breast is partnered with shallot cream, poached grapes and celery, or there might be a creative salad of goats' curd with roast apple purée, walnuts and honey dressing. Main-course stone bass is timed spot-on and served with coco beans, brown shrimps, broccoli purée and lemon oil, while local meat fans might head for rump and crispy shoulder of Lighthorne lamb alongside celeriac, wild garlic, sheep's curd and hazelnut. In conclusion, bitter dark chocolate mousse and cocoa nib tuile are paired with the contrasting sharpness of blood orange sorbet.

Chef Ben Tynan **Owner** Sir Peter Rigby **Seats** 45, Pr/dining room 20
Times 12-2.30/6.30-9.30 **Prices** Fixed L 2 course £13.50, Fixed D 3 course £32.50, Service optional **Wines** 25 bottles over £30, 22 bottles under £30, 10 by glass **Parking** 12 **Notes** Sunday L £18.50-£22.50, Children welcome

The Seagrave Arms

◎◎ Modern British **NEW**

tel: 01386 840192 **Friday St GL55 6QH**
email: enquiries@theseagravearms.com web: www.seagravearms.com
dir: *A44 Oxford/Evesham, exit Broadway & follow B4632 towards Stratford-upon-Avon*

Cotswolds heartland village inn

Stone-built and four-square, the 400-year-old Seagrave is, both inside and out, a Cotswolds inn of considerable character. In this neck of the woods don't be too surprised to find its dining rooms have a huntin', shootin' and fishin' theme. In fact, it's more than a theme since game in season (Salperton Shoot partridge, for instance) and locally-caught fish are often on the menu. You don't, of course, have to own a pair of green wellies to enjoy the modern British cooking, although classic undertones are still discernible. Prove it by selecting dishes such as rabbit and Morteau sausage pie with cider gravy, well complemented by pickled mustard seeds, then slow-cooked, dry-aged beef rib with chips (The Seagrave's chips won a national award in 2015, by the way), carrots and smoked garlic purée, wrapping up with apple tart and vanilla ice cream. For a fish alternative, perhaps Cornish monkfish with beetroot, turnip, parsnip and pear cider sauce. A good selection of wines by the glass includes a sparkling white from Nyetimber's South Downs vineyard.

Chef Newstead Sayer **Owner** Newstead Sayer, Hannah Brown **Seats** 30
Times 12-2.30/6-9.30 **Prices** Starter £5.50-£13, Main £12-£20, Dessert £6-£8
Wines 17 bottles over £30, 20 bottles under £30, 12 by glass **Parking** 11
Notes Sunday L £15-£16, Vegetarian available, Children welcome

Three Ways House

◎ Modern British

tel: 01386 438429 **Chapel Ln, Mickleton GL55 6SB**
email: reception@puddingclub.com web: www.threewayshousehotel.com
dir: *On B4632, in village centre*

More than just desserts at the home of the Pudding Club

You can take it for granted that the Cotswolds home of the famous Pudding Club won't be serving up any foams, froths or drizzles. As its name hints, the club is famous for championing Great British Puddings, but there's a lot more to appreciate here before we get to dessert. The Victorian hotel has oodles of period character, although the restaurant bucks the trend with a more contemporary look involving stripy seats and cool blue walls. As you might expect, the food is punchy, big-hearted British stuff, put together with a flag-waving dedication to local raw materials. Pressed turkey and bacon terrine with cranberry compôte is a typical starter, followed by roast pork fillet with black pudding mash and roasted garlic. And so to pudding, which just has to be a selection of steamed puds-sticky toffee and date, chocolate, and syrup sponge, anyone? – with lashings of custard.

Chef Mark Rowlandson **Owner** Simon & Jill Coombe **Seats** 80, Pr/dining room 70
Times 12-2.30/7-9.30, Closed L Mon-Sat **Prices** Fixed D 3 course fr £39, Service optional **Wines** 12 bottles over £30, 31 bottles under £30, 13 by glass **Parking** 37, On street **Notes** Pudding Club places £37, Sunday L £23.25-£26.75, Vegetarian available, Children welcome

Jesse's Bistro

◎◎ Modern British

tel: 01285 641497 & 07932 150720 **14 Blackjack St GL7 2AA**
email: info@jessesbistro.co.uk web: www.jessesbistro.co.uk
dir: *In town centre between the parish church & Roman Museum, behind Jesse Smith the Butchers*

Resourceful international cooking behind the butchers

Tucked into a brick-paved back alley in the town centre, with a butcher's shop out front, the bistro is a hospitable venue that's currently going from strength to strength. Inside, the old beamed interior has been done up in understated modern style, with russet walls and a tiled floor, and a resourceful menu that garnishes its foundation of solid British tradition with excursions to the Mediterranean and east Asia. First up might be a serving of Serrano ham with salami, figs and pine nuts in sherry dressing, or perhaps a well-risen twice-baked cheese soufflé with poached pear and caramelised walnuts. Chinese paces are shown for a seafood main of Duart salmon and tiger prawns in soy and ginger broth, with crispy noodles, brown rice and bok choy, or there might be Gatcombe lamb rack and braised belly with bubble-and-squeak and baby turnips. There is impressive precision in the seasoning and timing of dishes, and an understanding of how to please the crowds at meal's end, when something like dark chocolate cheesecake with malted-milk Malteser ice cream comes into play.

Chef David Witnall, Andrew Parffrey **Owner** Watermoor Meat Supply **Seats** 55, Pr/dining room 12 **Times** 12-3/7-10, Closed Sun, D Mon **Prices** Fixed L 2 course £19-£25, Fixed D 3 course £25-£37.50, Starter £6.50-£11.50, Main £12.50-£32.50, Dessert £7-£9, Service optional **Wines** 35 bottles over £30, 25 bottles under £30, 15 by glass **Parking** Old station car park **Notes** Vegetarian available, Children welcome

CLEARWELL — Map 4 S050

Tudor Farmhouse Hotel & Restaurant

◉◉ Modern British

tel: 01594 833046 **High St GL16 8JS**
email: info@tudorfarmhousehotel.co.uk **web:** www.tudorfarmhousehotel.co.uk
dir: Off A4136 onto B4228, through Coleford, turn right into Clearwell, hotel on right just before War Memorial Cross

Old and new ideas in the Forest of Dean

The name reveals all, although the charm-laden grey stone building in the Forest of Dean looks a little more grand country cottage than former farmstead. Old furnishings, heavy beams and exposed-stone walls make an impressive frame for the more modern accoutrements of the dining room, which is kept plentifully supplied by a kitchen garden, and by trips to gather wild ingredients. A heartening spin is put on some old pub favourites for starters such as corned beef hash with beans and brown sauce, or potted shrimps on toast, but then there are more extravagant flights into the realms of honey-roast parsnip soufflé with blue cheese crumble and a sesame tuile. Mains look beyond British shores for the likes of Moroccan-spiced rump and braised shoulder of lamb with toasted couscous, preserved lemon, apricot and almonds, while the oxtail-and-fish modern classic is given an outing here with plaice, sprout tops and burnt cucumber in red wine. The signature dessert is an invitingly rich malted chocolate cake with stout ale ice cream and malted honeycomb.

Times 12-2/6.30-9, Closed 2-5 Jan

The Wyndham Arms Hotel

◉ Modern British

tel: 01594 833666 **GL16 8JT**
email: stay@thewyndhamhotel.co.uk **web:** www.thewyndhamhotel.co.uk
dir: Exit B4228. Hotel in village centre on B4231

Polished gastro-pub fare in old village inn

Clearwell is a picturesque village near Offa's Dyke Path between the Wye Valley and the Forest of Dean, and this characterful old inn is at its centre. Local ales and cider are dispensed in the rustic-style bar, and meals are served in the stone-walled, vaulted restaurant. The pub keeps Gloucestershire Old Spot pigs (and sells its own takeaway sausages and burgers), which turn up in pork and ham hock terrine, and as roast loin with apple and potato mash and cider cream. Elsewhere, starters can take in home-smoked duck breast with raspberry vinaigrette, or sardine escabèche in a salad with crayfish and citrus dressing, with pubby main courses like grilled gammon steak with fried eggs and chips, or more classically-orientated pan-fried fillet of sea bass with barigoule sauce and saffron-flavoured potatoes.

Times 12-2/6.30-9, Closed 1st wk Jan, L some days in winter, D some Sun

COLEFORD — Map 4 S051

The Miners Country Inn

◉ Modern **NEW** v

tel: 01594 836632 **Chepstow Rd, Sling GL16 8LH**
email: admin@theminerssling.co.uk **web:** www.theminerssling.co.uk
dir: Phone for directions

Top-quality ingredients in West Country oriented pub food

Look for signs to the tiny village of Sling in the Forest of Dean, and be rewarded with an enviably located family-run dining pub. Garden seating allows for indulgent views of the surrounding countryside on balmy days, while the bar fills up with happy locals. Beamed ceilings and stone floors come as standard, and the restaurant towards the back is simply but tastefully decorated, with smiling staff adding to the sense of relaxation. Trencherman's portions of pub food stand out for the unimpeachable quality of their West Country ingredients. Fishcakes with tomato and chilli jam are a promising start, and there's properly chunky ham hock terrine with pineapple pickle and a fried quail's egg. Roll on with ale-battered haddock, a mighty fine pie of chicken, leek and ham, or even the more poshed-up venison rack with purple potatoes in chocolate sauce, and it's all good. Chips are triple-cooked giants, and there's new-fangled chocolate-chilli ice cream with the chocolate and pistachio brownie.

Chef Steven Jenkins **Owner** Steven Jenkins, Sam Hughes **Seats** 50
Times 12-3/4.30-11 **Prices** Fixed L 2 course £9.95, Starter £2.95-£6.95, Main £7.95-£20, Dessert £4.50-£6.50, Service optional **Wines** 2 bottles over £30, 10 bottles under £30 **Parking** 40 **Notes** Mon D pot luck half price menu, Sat D 2 steaks & wine £28.95, Sunday L £7.95-£12.15, Children welcome

CORSE LAWN — Map 10 S083

Corse Lawn House Hotel

◉◉ British, French v | NOTABLE WINE LIST

tel: 01452 780771 **GL19 4LZ**
email: enquiries@corselawn.com **web:** www.corselawn.com
dir: 5m SW of Tewkesbury on B4211, in village centre

Extensive menus in an appealing rural setting

The red-brick house dates from the Queen Anne period of the early 18th century and stands on the village green in front of a large pond that once had the job of cleaning up both coach and horses. It's a lovely spot. The hotel has been run by the Hine family since 1978 and continues to be operated with old-school charm. There's a traditionally decorated bistro (no tablecloths) and a smart restaurant (tablecloths) with the latter serving up a classic modern British menu that makes good use of trusted local supply lines. A simple starter of grilled Cornish sardines (not so local, but lovely and fresh) with tapenade and tomato vinaigrette shows the way, and there are more Mediterranean flavours in a fish soup with all the trimmings. Next up might be pan-fried fillet of pollock with with samphire and saffron sauce, or roast haunch of venison partnered with celeriac and a blueberry sauce. A zingy lemon posset tart makes for a fine finale, and there are cheeses served from the trolley.

Chef Martin Kinahan **Owner** The Hine family **Seats** 50, Pr/dining room 28
Times 12-2/7-9.30, Closed 24-26 Dec **Prices** Fixed L 2 course £16.50-£22.50, Fixed D 3 course £21.50-£33.50, Starter £6.95-£12.95, Main £14.95-£22.95, Dessert £5.95-£10.95, Service optional **Wines** 220 bottles over £30, 80 bottles under £30, 10 by glass **Parking** 60 **Notes** Sunday L £21.50-£25.50, Children welcome

DAYLESFORD
Map 10 SP22

Daylesford Farm Café
◉ Modern British

tel: 01608 731700 **GL56 0YG**
email: thefarm@daylesfordorganic.com
dir: *From Cheltenham take A40 & A436 through Stow-on-the Wold, follow signs to Daylesford farmshop*

Organic produce cooked with flair in converted barn

On the Gloucestershire farmland that spawned a mini-empire, the Daylesford Farmshop and Café is a little slice of foodie heaven, where shelves are stacked with organic goodies from seafood to vegetables, from bread to meat, to supplement a cookery shop and the Café. The setting is a smartly converted barn with a New England finish and an open-to-view kitchen. The Café is busy at lunchtimes (it's also open for 'supper' on Friday and Saturday evenings), so arrive early to avoid disappointment. The food makes a virtue of simplicity, with ingredients allowed to shine. A first-course chicken liver parfait served in a Kilner jar has fabulous depth of flavour and comes with home-made ciabatta, or go for barley risotto with steamed celeriac, cavolo nero and pumpkin seed pesto. Venison pappardelle with woodland mushrooms and parmesan is a memorable pasta dish, and the finishing flourish could be deeply rich chocolate nemesis with vanilla ice cream.

Times 12-3/7-9.30, Closed 25-26 Dec, 1 Jan, D Mon-Thu, Sun

EBRINGTON
Map 10 SP14

The Ebrington Arms
◉◉ Modern British

tel: 01386 593223 **GL55 6NH**
email: reservations@ebringtonarms.co.uk **web:** www.theebringtonarms.co.uk
dir: *From Chipping Campden take B4035 towards Shipston-on-Stour, left to Ebrington*

Classic village inn with a modern menu

Still very much a pub, and right in the heart of the village by the green, The Ebrington Arms has served its community for several hundred years. The honey-coloured property dates from the 17th century, which is evident from the copious oak beams and flagged floors, and, if you arrive in the cooler months, a roaring fire awaits. It may be a classic pub in the best sense, but the menu takes a contemporary line, with the kitchen turning out bright dishes based on seasonal, local ingredients. There are daily specials and pub classics, too. Ham hock terrine with raisin purée and beef dripping brioche is one way to begin, or dive into Cornish crab cake with garlic aïoli and chilli and coriander salsa. Next up, salt-baked celeriac with cider-braised onions, pearl barley and onion ash is a creative veggie dish, or go for stout-braised ox cheek with creamed potatoes, carrots and kale. There's craft and creativity among desserts, too, with the likes of plum clafoutis with vanilla ice cream.

Times 12-2.30/6-9.30, Closed 25 Dec

GLOUCESTER
Map 10 SO81

Hatton Court
◉ Classic British, French **NEW** v

tel: 01452 617412 **Upton Hill, Upton St Leonards GL4 8DE**
email: res@hatton-court.co.uk **web:** www.hatton-court.co.uk
dir: *Phone for directions*

Modern British repertoire in creeper-covered country house

A country-house hotel not far from the M5, Hatton Court is smothered with climbing foliage, its little windows barely peeping through the green. It was once named the Tara Hotel, and the name survives in the dining rooms, the more formal of which is kitted out with linen-clad tables, wood panelling and full-drop windows at one end.

Here, the modern British repertoire is enthusiastically rehearsed, beginning with a clutch of scallops in a light, coriandery curry emulsion with the requisite cauliflower purée and a scatter of raisins. Main might be a pair of pork cuts, the loin and cheek, with some black pudding done up in a cabbage leaf, or perhaps red snapper with vanilla mash, braised red chicory and pea purée in sweetcorn velouté. Desserts offer some fanciful ideas too, in the way of a tropical lattice with passionfruit and guava ice pops and passionfruit fool, if sticky toffee pudding and butterscotch isn't your bag.

Chef Mike Hall **Owner** Darren Hiscox **Seats** 75, Pr/dining room 50 **Times** 12-10, All-day dining **Prices** Fixed L 2 course £12, Fixed D 3 course £25-£40, Tasting menu £49, Starter £7-£10, Main £18-£25, Dessert £8-£11, Service optional 12.5% **Wines** 30 bottles over £30, 12 bottles under £30, 8 by glass **Parking** 100 **Notes** Afternoon tea fr £10, Sunday L £15.95-£21.95, Children welcome

The Wharf House Restaurant with Rooms
◉ Modern European

tel: 01452 332900 **Over GL2 8DB**
email: enquiries@thewharfhouse.co.uk **web:** www.thewharfhouse.co.uk
dir: *From Over rdbt take A40 westbound to Ross-on-Wye, 1st right in 50 yds*

Appealing cooking in a former lockhouse by the Severn

The Wharf House overlooks a canal basin (it's owned by the Herefordshire and Gloucestershire Canal Trust), and there are plenty of watery walks nearby, either along the towpath or by the River Severn. Eating out on the terrace may be a possibility, while the restaurant is an inviting prospect, designed along clean, uncluttered lines with modern oak furniture on a parquet floor. 'We strive to work with the best of local suppliers,' declares the menu, and the produce is subjected to modern treatments, often continental. Herrings are marinated in dill and served with avocado and melon, and carpaccio is plated with fiery horseradish, celery and rocket. Among main courses, venison loin is rolled in walnuts and accompanied by rich redcurrant and chocolate sauce, Savoy cabbage sprinkled with sesame, and chips, and there's normally a fish of the day and a couple of vegetarian options. End with straightforward crème brûlée.

Chef David Penny **Owner** H & G Canal Trust **Seats** 40 **Times** 12-3/6-close, Closed 22 Dec-8 Jan, Sun-Mon **Prices** Fixed L 2 course £18.99, Fixed D 2 course £18.99, Tasting menu £45.99-£52.99, Starter £5.99-£8.99, Main £9.99-£22.99, Dessert £4.99-£12.99 **Wines** 21 bottles over £30, 27 bottles under £30, 7 by glass **Parking** 32 **Notes** Vegetarian available, Children welcome

LOWER SLAUGHTER
Map 10 SP12

Lower Slaughter Manor
◉◉◉ — *see opposite*

The Slaughters Country Inn
◉◉ Modern British

tel: 01451 822143 **GL54 2HS**
email: info@theslaughtersinn.co.uk **web:** www.theslaughtersinn.co.uk
dir: *Exit A429 at 'The Slaughters' sign, between Stow-on-the-Wold & Bourton-on-the-Water. In village centre*

Contemporary classic dishes in a Cotswold country hotel

Formerly known as Washbourne Court, this 17th-century house, once an Eton crammer, long ago banished all thought of swishing canes for the distinctly lovelier prospect of welcoming guests to the kind of haven of relaxation they might hope for from a hotel on a bank of the River Eye in a peaceful Cotswolds village. The riverside terrace is a plum spot for lunch or aperitifs, while memories linger on in the name only of Eton's Restaurant, a stylish venue with fine table appointments and smartly attentive service. Expect a modern British menu that uses an exciting mix of ingredients, in a starter of Hereford salt beef terrine, with mustard mayonnaise and pickled vegetables, alongside, contemporary classics. Mains could be grilled sea bream, with artichoke, green beans, shrimps and a lemon butter sauce, or some honey-glazed Creedy Carver duck breast, with carrots, fennel and a hazelnut and rocket salad. Finish with dark chocolate mousse and pistachio granola, served with caramel ice cream.

Chef Chris Fryer **Owner** Mr & Mrs Brownsword **Seats** Pr/dining room 30 **Times** 12-3/6.30-9, Closed L Mon-Sat **Prices** Prices not confirmed, Service optional **Wines** 15 bottles over £30, 10 bottles under £30, 8 by glass **Parking** 40 **Notes** Afternoon tea, Sunday L, Vegetarian available, Children welcome

---

MORETON-IN-MARSH   Map 10 SP23

Manor House Hotel
◉◉ Modern British V

tel: 01608 650501 **High St GL56 0LJ**
email: info@manorhousehotel.info **web:** www.cotswold-inns-hotels.co.uk/manor
dir: Off A429 at south end of town

Classy modern cooking in a 16th-century gem

On the High Street of the tourist honeypot of a village, this Cotswold-stone hotel dates from the reign of Henry VIII, when he bequeathed it to the Dean and Chapter of Westminster. Careful renovation and updating have brought it squarely into the 21st century while retaining original features – a priest hole, for one – while the Mulberry Restaurant is a carpeted room with generously spaced, dressed tables, comfortable dining chairs and on-the-ball staff. The kitchen demonstrates sound talent and produces appealing dishes without over-complicating things. Foams sometimes embellish starters: redcurrant for venison and game terrine with prune and whisky purée, lemon for another starter of crab exotically flavoured with chilli, coconut, ginger and coriander, served with avocado mousse and Bloody Mary jelly.

Well-considered main courses have included a taste of pork (slow-roast belly, braised cheek, pancetta-wrapped tenderloin, all accurately timed), with Calvados sauce, garlicky mash, broad beans and marinated apple, and pan-fried fillets of sole with prawns and scampi, shallot sauce, chive-crushed potatoes and curly kale. End with something like strawberry sponge with sherry ice cream and custard.

Chef Nick Orr **Owner** Michael & Pamela Horton **Seats** 55, Pr/dining room 120 **Times** 12-2.30/7-9.30, Closed L Mon-Sat **Prices** Fixed D 3 course £39, Tasting menu £60, Service optional 10% **Wines** 20 bottles over £30, 20 bottles under £30, 12 by glass **Parking** 32 **Notes** Tasting menu 8 course, Sunday L £19.95-£22.50, Children 8 yrs+

Redesdale Arms
◉ British

tel: 01608 650308 **High St GL56 0AW**
email: info@redesdalearms.com **web:** www.redesdalearms.com
dir: On A429, 0.5m from rail station

Relaxed dining in historical Cotswold inn

Dating from the 17th century, this inn has been sympathetically updated to give it a more contemporary edge while retaining original features like thick oak floorboards. There are two dining rooms, one in a rear conservatory, the other overlooking the high street. A glance at the menu shows a kitchen seaming the modern British vein. Ham hock terrine with a hint of cheese has a good depth of flavour, attractively presented on a slate with piccalilli and crisp breads, and may precede tail of Cornish monkfish, accurately timed and seasoned, vibrant anchovy salsa a good foil, served with dauphinoise potatoes. End with something like white chocolate and raspberry crème brûlée with crisp, light and flaky almond twists.

Times 12-2.30/6.30-9

Lower Slaughter Manor ❀❀❀

LOWER SLAUGHTER   Map 10 SP12

Modern British V
tel: 01451 820456 **GL54 2HP**
email: info@lowerslaughter.co.uk **web:** www.lowerslaughter.co.uk
dir: Off A429, signed 'The Slaughters'. 0.5m into village on right

Contemporary cooking in an elegant Cotswolds hotel

The magnificent honey stone manor house has stood in the village since the middle of the 17th century and has lost none of its appeal over the centuries. It stands in pretty, well-maintained gardens where you can play croquet on the lawn or simply take a wander to pass the time. The interior brings a gentle contemporary finish to the period spaces, especially in the Sixteen58 restaurant where neutral colours help create a soothing and unpretentious setting for some modern dining. It all starts in one of the elegant lounges, where canapés are served, and you can always head back to the comfort of the sofas for a coffee or night cap if you wish. Nick Chappell has taken charge of the kitchen and he delivers modern and creative dishes via tasting and table d'hôte menus. Begin with confit salmon combined with the flavours and textures of beetroot, passionfruit and coconut, or another where roasted quail and butternut squash is rich with the aroma of truffles. Beef sirloin stars in a main course alongside ox cheeks braised in stout until meltingly tender, while

another partners poached fillet of turbot with squid, choucroute and soy. There's no less original thinking going on at dessert stage, where textures of caramel come in the aromatic company of lemongrass and lime leaf ice cream, and salted chocolate mousse arrives with a little cake made from chocolate and rapeseed oil. If you fancy ending on a savoury note, try the truffled Tunworth cheese served with a crumpet, honey and fig.

Chef Nick Chappell **Owner** Brownsword Hotels **Seats** 48, Pr/dining room 24 **Times** 12.30-2/7-9.30, **Prices** Fixed L 2 course £20.50-£27, Fixed D 3 course fr £65, Tasting menu fr £85, Service optional **Wines** 180 bottles over £30, 19 bottles under £30, 9 by glass **Parking** 30 **Notes** Afternoon tea, Sunday L £30.50-£37, Children welcome

MORETON-IN-MARSH *continued*

White Hart Royal Hotel

◉ Traditional British

tel: 01608 650731 **High St GL56 OBA**
email: whr@bulldogmail.co.uk **web:** www.whitehartroyal.co.uk
dir: *In town centre*

Modern cooking in a Cotswold coaching inn

Some 370 years ago, Charles I took shelter here after the battle of Marston Moor, and it's not a huge leap of imagination to picture what the place was like back then, with no shortage of period features as reminders of the heritage of the building. Refurbishment has been respectful of all that history, delivering spaces that have original charm alongside a few gently contemporary touches. The Courtyard restaurant – outside tables are a fair-weather treat – is a linen-free zone, the darkwood tables and bold colours creating a smart-casual space that will do for a special occasion or for when no excuse is needed. The menu takes a modern, brasserie-style tack in starters such as barbecue pulled pork croquette with Cajun-spiced baby corn and chipotle purée, or pan-seared scallops with curried lentil salad. Move on to main-course confit chicken thighs with rösti potatoes and desserts such as pistachio crème brûlée.

Times 11-10, All-day dining

NAILSWORTH   Map 4 ST89

Wild Garlic Restaurant and Rooms

◉◉ Modern British V

tel: 01453 832615 **3 Cossack Square GL6 0DB**
email: info@wild-garlic.co.uk **web:** www.wild-garlic.co.uk
dir: *M4 junct 18. A46 towards Stroud. Enter Nailsworth, turn left at rdbt and then an immediate left. Restaurant opposite Britannia Pub*

Bountifully inventive modern cooking in garlic country

So prolific is wild garlic around these parts that, not only have the Beardshalls named their stylish restaurant with rooms after it, but in 2015 they inaugurated a competitive garlic-hunting event as a red-letter day in the Nailsworth calendar. Some of it may turn up in a falafel with matching mayonnaise, a little taster of the bountifully inventive modern cooking on offer here. Cotswold tapas are one of the options, but it's on the main menus that the kitchen really shows its paces. Start with creamed goats' cheese and celeriac cannelloni in warm walnut dressing, or a grilled mackerel with smoked potato salad and shellfish sauce. Move on to shoulder of lamb with salt-baked parsnips, burnt onion and gremolata, or roasted brill with artichokes, wild mushrooms and spinach in red wine reduction. Local Woefuldane cheeses are enthusiastically supported, perhaps in a Gewürztraminer-laced fondue with sourdough rye bread, if you find yourself shying away from the likes of deep-fried rice pudding with poached Asian fruits in coconut sauce.

Chef Matthew Beardshall **Owner** Matthew Beardshall **Seats** 42
Times 12-2.30/7-9.30, Closed Mon-Tue, D Sun **Prices** Tasting menu £55, Starter £8.50-£9.50, Main £15.50-£27.50, Dessert £4.95-£6.95, Service optional **Wines** 22 bottles over £30, 32 bottles under £30, 12 by glass **Parking** NCP, parking on street **Notes** Tasting menu 6 course with wine £80, Sunday L £12.95-£15.95, Children welcome

NETHER WESTCOTE   Map 10 SP22

The Feathered Nest Country Inn

◉◉◉ *– see opposite*

NEWENT   Map 10 SO72

Three Choirs Vineyards

◉ Modern British, European

tel: 01531 890223 **GL18 1LS**
email: ts@threechoirs.com **web:** www.three-choirs-vineyards.co.uk
dir: *2m N of Newent on B4215, follow brown tourist signs*

Up-to-the-minute cooking on a pedigree wine estate

Three Choirs was off and running in the English wine renaissance long before others had even started planting, and has a solid reputation for producing fresh, aromatic wines. The estate also incorporates this hotel, where barbecues on the Vine Room terrace are a regular feature, and the dining room deals in up-to-the-minute cooking that draws inspiration from other European wine-producing countries. Roast courgette and lemon risotto might precede a laden sharing platter of seafood, or something like black-eyed bean cassoulet with cumin mushrooms and pilaff. Top-gear meats are carefully sourced, as for cannon of lamb in salsa verde with roast garlic and pomme purée, while 21-day aged local beef fillet comes with all the expected trimmings, down to a peppercorned whisky sauce. Finish with white chocolate crème brûlée and raspberry shortbread, or the evergreen sticky toffee pudding and custard.

Chef Margot Heski **Owner** Three Choirs Vineyards Ltd **Seats** 50, Pr/dining room 20 **Times** 12-2/7-9, Closed Xmas, 1st 2 wks Jan **Prices** Fixed L 2 course fr £18, Fixed D 3 course fr £22, Starter £6.75-£8.95, Main £17.50-£28, Dessert £8-£9, Service optional **Wines** 10 bottles over £30, 24 bottles under £30, 14 by glass **Parking** 50 **Notes** Sunday L £21-£24.50, Vegetarian available, Children welcome

STOW-ON-THE-WOLD   Map 10 SP12

The Kings Head Inn

◉ British

tel: 01608 658365 **The Green, Bledington OX7 6XQ**
email: info@kingsheadinn.net **web:** www.kingsheadinn.net
dir: *On B4450, 4m from Stow-on-the-Wold*

Refined pub fare in an atmospheric village inn

Picture this: a mellow stone Cotswolds pub looking on to a village green with ducks playing in a meandering brook; inside is a classic bar with wobbly floors – wobblier still after a few pints of Hook Norton – heart-warming log fires, head-skimming beams and an unbuttoned dining room kitted out with solid oak tables on a flagstone floor. All in all, a textbook example of a switched-on village pub where a perfect ratio is struck between food and drink: the place is still the local boozer, while the cooking is a definite notch or two above your average pub. A menu in the modern British idiom showcases local free-range and organic materials, starting with Tamworth ham hock and spinach terrine with artichoke salad and brioche, then perhaps wood pigeon tart with carrot purée, wild mushrooms, rocket and blue cheese. Finish with treacle tart with malt ice cream and raspberry sauce.

Times 12-2/6.30-9, Closed 25-26 Dec

The Feathered Nest Country Inn 🌹🌹🌹

NETHER WESTCOTE   Map 10 SP22

Modern British

tel: 01993 833030 **OX7 6SD**
email: info@thefeatherednestinn.co.uk
web: www.thefeatherednestinn.co.uk
dir: On A424 between Burford & Stow-on-the-Wold, signed

A gem of a country pub in a beautiful Cotswold village

Creating the perfect country inn is a difficult alchemy indeed, and many fail in the quest to balance drinking with eating, but Tony and Amanda Timmer at The Feathered Nest have struck gold in an Area of Outstanding Natural Beauty. Since opening the revamped inn in 2010, the seriousness of their intentions is plain to see, with respect for the drinking traditions matched by a culinary output that is positively starry. There's pretty accommodation, too, if you fancy staying the night. The Cotswold-stone building looks good inside and out, with an interior that might be described as contemporary country-chic (check out the bar stools made from saddles, the real fires in the winter, and the views from the terrace and garden out back). When it comes to matters of service, the level of professionalism is above and beyond that of the average inn. The kitchen brings regional ingredients into the equation, confirming the sense of place, and providing the icing on the cake. Expect a modern British menu that fizzes with good ideas and appealing combinations such as Asian-inspired first courses of octopus and pork belly, a contemporary surf 'n' turf with pak choi, miso glaze and sesame seeds, and cod cheek escabèche fired up with chilli and coriander. A beef starter with snail cannelloni and Périgord truffles owes more to French classicism, as do main

courses of veal with creamed potatoes and heritage carrots, or quail served up with a little tart and duck liver. The charcoal grill delivers up simple steaks done really well, and when it comes to dessert, finish on a creative high with Valrhona chocolate ganache with goats' milk ice cream. The wine list deserves your full attention.

Chef Kuba Winkowski **Owner** Tony Timmer **Seats** 60, Pr/dining room 14 **Times** 12-2.30/6.30-9.30, Closed 25 Dec, Mon, D Sun **Prices** Prices not confirmed, Service optional **Wines** 215 bottles over £30, 29 bottles under £30, 19 by glass **Parking** 45 **Notes** Sunday L, Vegetarian available, Children welcome

STOW-ON-THE-WOLD *continued*

Number Four at Stow Hotel & Restaurant

◎◎ British, European

tel: 01451 830297 **Fosseway GL54 1JX**
email: reservations@hotelnumberfour.co.uk **web:** www.hotelnumberfour.co.uk
dir: *Situated on A424 Burford Road, at junct with A429. Hotel entrance on A424*

Stylish modern restaurant serving classic food

When you're looking for a bolt-hole in the heart of the Cotswolds offering flawless service and fabulous food, Number Four should fit the bill. The whitewashed 17th-century building is home to a chic boutique hotel that gets everything pitch perfect, from the opulent contemporary look to the sort of prescient service that anticipates guests' needs. The culinary side of the equation takes place in the oldest part of the house, where the classy Cutler's Restaurant offers a neutral palette of coffee and cream, unclothed tables and striking artworks as a backdrop to uncontroversial British and European dishes. The chef gets his raw materials from a well-chosen network of suppliers and brings it all together in tried-and-true combinations. Try caramelised scallops with a silky purée of cauliflower and cumin to start. Mains stick to similarly straightforward, well-conceived pairings of flavour and texture, such as roast saddle of Cotswold lamb with gratin dauphinoise, or perhaps pan-fried cod with wild mushrooms and potato gnocchi. Apricot parfait with pistachio and polenta cake wraps things up in fine style.

Chef Brian Cutler **Owner** Caroline & Patricia Losel **Seats** 50, Pr/dining room 40 **Times** 12-2/7-9, Closed Xmas, D Sun **Prices** Fixed L 2 course £16.50, Starter £6-£13, Main £16.50-£25, Dessert £5.50-£7.50, Service optional **Wines** 15 bottles over £30, 15 bottles under £30, 10 by glass **Parking** 50 **Notes** Sunday L £28.50-£32.50, Vegetarian available, Children welcome

The Porch House

◎◎ Modern British

tel: 01451 870048 **Digbeth St GL54 1BN**
email: book@porch-house.co.uk **web:** www.porch-house.co.uk
dir: *Phone for directions*

Historic inn with a classy modern menu

Claiming to be the oldest inn in England, the original building has been dated to AD 947, and from then on, every century has done its bit to create the atmospheric construction that exists today. A 21st-century refurbishment has matched the undoubted period charm with a rustic-chic contemporary finish, and it's looking good. The bar is stocked with real ales, while the restaurant turns out some impressive modern British dishes. Twice-baked cheddar soufflé with leeks in grain mustard sauce packs a good flavour punch, or there may be smoked haddock with a poached egg and parsleyed crushed potatoes in hollandaise. After those, Cotswold lamb rump is impressively tender for the cut, served with Jerusalem artichokes and green beans in a light lamb jus. Among desserts there might be rich chocolate mousse served warm with a sharp counterpoint of raspberry sorbet. There are sandwiches and sharing boards, too, alongside bar staples like grilled pork chops and sirloin steaks with a choice of sauces.

Times 12-2.30/6.30-9.30, Closed L Mon-Sat (Conservatory open), D Sun (Conservatory open)

Wyck Hill House Hotel & Spa

◎◎ Modern British

tel: 01451 831936 **Burford Rd GL54 1HY**
email: info.wyckhillhouse@bespokehotels.com **web:** www.wyckhillhousehotel.co.uk
dir: *A429 for Cirencester, pass through 2 sets of lights in Stow-on-the-Wold, at 3rd set of lights bear left signed Burford, then A424 signed Stow-on-the-Wold, hotel 7m on left*

Stylish contemporary cooking in smart Cotswolds hotel

With 100 acres of fabulous grounds, green-and-pleasant views over the undulations of the Cotswold Hills and Windrush Valley, chic antique-strewn lounges, an oak-panelled bar, and a glitzy spa, Wyck Hill House is a place to pamper yourself in. On the food front, there's a classy restaurant with a conservatory surveying the estate, where light floods in on cream-painted tongue and groove walls, and plushly-upholstered seats at white-linen tables on bare floorboards. It's a suitably elegant backdrop for meals with a contemporary British tone and a fondness for regional produce. You might set out with game terrine helped along by fig chutney, black pudding biscotti and apple balsamic, and move on to main courses put together with fine-tuned precision, perhaps a full-bore partnership of Herefordshire beef with an ox cheek pithivier, dauphinoise potatoes, cep marmalade and Madeira jus. A lot of work goes into puddings, too: good old rhubarb and custard might get a contemporary makeover, the creamy vanilla custard made with duck eggs and counterpointed by the tang of poached rhubarb and rhubarb sorbet.

Chef Mark Jane **Owner** City & Country Hotels Ltd **Seats** 50, Pr/dining room 120 **Times** 12.30-2/7-9.30 **Prices** Fixed L 2 course £15.95, Fixed D 3 course £29.95, Starter £6.95-£8.50, Main £14.95-£23.50, Dessert £5.95-£8.95, Service optional **Wines** 21 bottles over £30, 26 bottles under £30, 11 by glass **Parking** 120 **Notes** Sunday L £19.95, Vegetarian available, Children welcome

The Bear of Rodborough

◎ Traditional British **NEW**

tel: 01453 878522 **Rodborough Common GL5 5DE**
email: info@bearofrodborough.info **web:** www.cotswold-inns-hotels.co.uk/index.aspx
dir: *M5 junct 13, A419 to Stroud. Follow signs to Rodborough. Up hill, left at top at T-junct. Hotel on right*

Thoroughgoing British modernism in a (sort of) library

On Rodborough Common not far from Stroud, this Cotswold hotel with its own vineyard is a handsome white-fronted beast, its identity emphasised by two stuffed bears in reception. A stone-walled dining room called the Library is more trompe d'oeil design feature than actual rows of volumes, but does enjoy ravishing countryside views and a menu of thoroughgoing British modernism. The kitchen sometimes overdoes the complexity, so not every element of a dish registers convincingly, but there are definite successes. These include tandoori-spiced mackerel with a salad of tomato, red onion and fennel, and mains such as lamb rump and sausage in tomato fondue with aubergine and yogurt dressing, or roast cod with curly kale in celery cream sauce. Dessert might be pleasantly aromatic jasmine and green tea delice with pistachio sponge and passionfruit sorbet, or cardamom-laced chocolate mousse with hazelnut parfait.

Chef Felix Prem **Owner** Cotswold Inns & Hotels Ltd **Seats** 70, Pr/dining room 50 **Times** 12-2.30/7-9.30, Closed L Mon & Sat **Prices** Service optional 10% **Wines** 18 bottles over £30, 36 bottles under £30, 8 by glass **Parking** 100 **Notes** Sunday L £13.95-£19.95, Vegetarian available, Children welcome

Burleigh Court Hotel

◉ British, Mediterranean

tel: 01453 883804 **Burleigh, Minchinhampton GL5 2PF**
email: burleighcourt@aol.com **web:** www.burleighcourthotel.co.uk
dir: 2.5m SE of Stroud, off A419

Country-house cooking in the Golden Valley

Built in the early years of the 19th century, Burleigh Court is an imposing, three-storey house of ivy-clad Cotswold stone, standing in three acres of luxuriant grounds overlooking the Golden Valley. The interiors are done in fine Georgian style, with an oak-panelled lounge and a dining room in lilac hung with equestrian scenes, with swagged curtains opening on to the relaxing garden view. The cooking takes a gentle country-house tone to fit the circumstances, pairing rainbow trout fillet with Parma ham and marinated vegetables for an opener that might lead on to mallard breast with a parcel of confit, alongside butternut squash and red cabbage in five spice jus, or sea bream with chargrilled veg and buttered spinach, sauced in tomato and chilli. Finish with rhubarb clafoutis, clotted cream and shortbread, or baked chestnut and vanilla cheesecake with marinated fruits.

Chef Adrian Jarrad **Owner** Louise Noble **Seats** 34, Pr/dining room
Times 12-2/7-9, Closed Xmas **Prices** Fixed L 2 course £20, Starter £5.75-£10.50,
Main £15.95-£22.50, Dessert £7.50-£9.75, Service optional **Wines** 8 bottles over £30, 8 bottles under £30, 8 by glass **Parking** 28 **Notes** Afternoon tea, Sunday L £26.50, Vegetarian available, Children welcome

---

TETBURY   Map 4 ST89

Calcot Manor

◉◉ Modern British

tel: 01666 890391 **Calcot GL8 8YJ**
email: reception@calcotmanor.co.uk **web:** www.calcotmanor.co.uk
dir: M4 junct 18, A46 towards Stroud. At x-roads junct with A4135 turn right, then 1st left

Charming 14th-century Cotswold retreat with vibrant modern cuisine

The days when Calcot Manor was a lowly farmhouse are long gone: it is now a design-led boutique-style country-house hotel for 21st-century sybarites with pampering on the agenda. A fabulous health spa takes care of the body, while the contemporary rustic-chic of the luminous Conservatory Restaurant panders to the palate. The kitchen takes a strong stance on sourcing locally for its repertoire of modern British dishes, and flavours have real punch, helped along by a wood-burning oven that adds an authentically rustic Mediterranean edge. The wide-ranging menu has all bases covered, whether you just want to graze on nibble-sized portions of venison carpaccio with parmesan, blackberries, green chillies and candied chestnuts, or go for the full three-course format. Should you prefer the latter, you might set out with turbot tartare with horseradish cream, lobster bisque

and crispy potatoes, then look to the wood oven for organic beef from the Calcot estate, with béarnaise sauce, French beans and artichokes, and end with dark chocolate and salted caramel mousse with orange peel sorbet and candied nuts.

Chef Michael Benjamin **Owner** Richard Ball **Seats** 100, Pr/dining room 16
Times 12-2/7-9.30, Closed D 25 Dec **Prices** Fixed L 2 course £19, Starter £10-£14,
Main £16-£36, Dessert £8, Service optional **Wines** 59 bottles over £30, 26 bottles under £30, 24 by glass **Parking** 150 **Notes** Sunday L £21-£26, Vegetarian available, Children welcome

---

The Close Hotel

◉◉ Modern British

tel: 01666 502272 **8 Long St GL8 8AQ**
email: info@theclose-hotel.com **web:** www.theclose-hotel.com
dir: From M4 junct 17 onto A429 to Malmesbury. From M5 junct 14 onto B4509

Creative cooking in a 16th-century house

Although it's situated in the town, The Close Hotel has the feel of a country-house hotel. It's a handsome pile dating from the 16th century, and within there are period details and a finish of refined, contemporary elegance. There are two dining options in the form of a brasserie and fine-dining restaurant. Any sense of old-school solidity has been avoided by painting the wall panels in a fashionable shade of blue/grey and by keeping the tables free of heavy linen (the Adam ceiling remains to impress traditionalists). The modern British menu strikes the right balance in this setting, with the dishes showing craft and creativity. A first-course goose liver parfait comes with an assiette of rhubarb to alleviate any richness (even an ice cream), plus a slice of pain d'épices. Main courses,such as steamed halibut with broccoli purée and scallop mousse,are equally impressive. Desserts like the hot banana soufflé served with hazelnut ice cream confirm that this is a kitchen on song.

Chef David Brown **Owner** Cotswold Inns & Hotels Ltd **Seats** 54, Pr/dining room 26
Times 12-3/6.30-9.30 **Prices** Prices not confirmed **Wines** 11 bottles over £30, 20 bottles under £30, 6 by glass **Parking** 18 **Notes** Sunday L, Vegetarian available, Children welcome

---

Hare & Hounds Hotel

◉◉ Modern British V

tel: 01666 881000 **Westonbirt GL8 8QL**
email: reception@hareandhoundshotel.com **web:** www.cotswold-inns-hotels.co.uk
dir: 2.5m SW of Tetbury on A433

Charming Cotswold hotel with confident team in the kitchen

The Beaufort Restaurant is the culinary heart of this Cotswold-stone hotel just outside Tetbury. It's a handsome room, with an unusual hammer-beam ceiling, wooden floors and leaded bay windows overlooking the garden. The menu is a roll-call of pretty nifty ideas that are amply met by what appears on the plate. A main course of sautéed halibut fillet, for instance, is accompanied by toasted coconut, curried Puy lentils and sweet potato, and haggis croquette gives an extra taste dimension to tender loin of venison with wine-poached pears, carrots and port jus. Starters generally follow the contemporary route of cured salmon with beetroot carpaccio and salsa verde, and beef salad with watercress sauce, horseradish cream and parmesan crisps. A good range of canapés served in the bar gets things off to a good start, and an impressive line-up of cheeses can cap off a meal, or there might be a pudding such as the intriguing combination of dark chocolate and black olive tart with black olive coulis and pistachio ice cream.

Chef David Hammond **Owner** Cotswold Inns & Hotels Ltd **Seats** 60, Pr/dining room
10 **Times** 7-9.30, Closed L Mon-Sat **Prices** Fixed D 3 course £39, Tasting menu £55
Wines 18 bottles over £30, 40 bottles under £30, 12 by glass **Parking** 40
Notes Tasting menu 8 course, Sunday L £18.95-£21.95, Children welcome

continued

Ronnie's of Thornbury

◉◉ Modern European

tel: 01454 411137 **11 St Mary St BS35 2AB**
email: info@ronnies-restaurant.co.uk
dir: *Phone for directions*

Modern European cooking in a 17th-century schoolhouse

Tucked away in an unlikely location in the town's shopping precinct, Ronnie's was an instant hit with locals when it opened in 2007. It's easy to see why: whether you pop in for brunch or dinner, the mood is easy-going, and the modern European cooking keeps things local, seasonal and to the point. The 17th-century building wears its contemporary look well: stone walls, beamed ceilings, wooden floors and neutral hues are pointed up by paintings and photos by West Country artists. Ronnie Faulkner's team will send you away happy if you turn up to kick start the day with coffee and eggs Benedict, or round it off with an intelligent, precisely cooked dinner. That might open with lasagne of braised ox cheek with wild mushrooms, before the main business brings on pork tenderloin with mustard mash and Savoy cabbage in cider jus, or lightly spiced smoked haddock kedgeree. Tempting desserts include vanilla cheesecake with tropical fruit salad and passionfruit sorbet, or you could go for a savoury finish with the splendid array of English artisan cheeses.

Chef Pawel Walkiewicz **Owner** Ron Faulkner **Seats** 45 **Times** 12-3/6-10, Closed 25-26 Dec, 1-8 Jan, Mon, D Sun **Prices** Fixed L 2 course fr £10, Tasting menu fr £45, Starter £7.25-£10.85, Main £13.30-£22.95, Dessert £6.50-£12 **Wines** 30 bottles over £30, 33 bottles under £30, 12 by glass **Parking** Car park **Notes** Daily menu 2/3 course £10/£13, Tasting menu 6 course, Sunday L £21-£25, Vegetarian available, Children welcome

Thornbury Castle

◉◉ Modern British, European

tel: 01454 281182 **Castle St BS35 1HH**
email: info@thornburycastle.co.uk **web:** www.thornburycastle.co.uk
dir: *M5 junct 16, N on A38. 4m to lights, turn left. Follow brown historic castle signs. Restaurant behind St Mary's church*

Heritage and modernity side by side in a Tudor castle

Construction work on the castle was well under way in the early 16th century when its intended occupant, Edward Stafford, became one of the many Tudor notables to find himself parting company with his head on the orders of Henry VIII. Thornbury isn't quite the full medieval fortress, more a castellated country house, but is not a whit less grandiose for that. Canopy beds, old tapestries and armour help set the tone, and the hexagonal Tower dining room with its arrow-slits feels secure against the marauding hordes. Supplied in part from Thornbury's own gardens (and vineyard), the menu is in the vein of modern British pastoral, with invention and heritage running side by side. Tomato and shallot tart with pickled samphire and Cerney Ash goats' cheese establishes the mood, or there may be wood-pigeon with roasted beetroot and celeriac in caper dressing. Mains may look further afield for roast skrei (Norwegian migratory cod) with crispy oysters, or Devon sea bass with lobster ravioli, but herb-crusted Uley Fields hogget with peas and polenta brings us home to Gloucestershire.

Chef Mark Veale **Owner** LFH **Seats** 72, Pr/dining room 22 **Times** 11.45-2/7-9.30 **Prices** Prices not confirmed, Service optional **Wines** 7 by glass **Parking** 50 **Notes** ALC 2/3 course £42/£50, Sunday L, Vegetarian available, Children welcome

Lords of the Manor

◉◉◉ – *see opposite*

Wesley House

◉◉ Modern European

tel: 01242 602366 **High St GL54 5LJ**
email: enquiries@wesleyhouse.co.uk **web:** www.wesleyhouse.co.uk
dir: *In centre of Winchcombe*

Impressive modern cooking in a period house

Wesley House occupies a half-timbered property built in the 15th century for a merchant, so it's difficult to miss on the High Street. An inglenook, venerable beams and stone walls all feature in the main restaurant, and there's also a modern and stylish conservatory with rural views. Good-quality produce is the key to the kitchen's success as it works around a modern European repertory. Cured sea trout, for instance, is served atop well-gauged horseradish cream garnished with pickled beetroot, making a successful starter, or there might be carpaccio with piquillo peppers and rocket. A mastery of techniques is on show in soft, tender and crisp-skinned breast of corn-fed chicken with rich thyme sauce, peas, broad beans and sauté potatoes. Equally unfussy is another main course of roast sea bream with chorizo, cauliflower and paprika butter. Breads and canapés are spot on, and desserts round things off very nicely: perhaps vanilla pannacotta with a meringue nest of summer berries.

Wesley House

Times 12-2/7-9, Closed Mon, D Sun

See advert on page 188

Wesley House Wine Bar & Grill

European

tel: 01242 602366 **High St GL54 5LJ**
email: enquiries@wesleyhouse.co.uk
dir: *In the centre of Winchcombe*

Trend-setting brasserie next door to Wesley House

'Wine Bar & Grill' is a pretty accurate description of what Wesley House's next-door neighbour is all about. It's a laid-back sort of place, with a welcoming atmosphere and some quirky touches, with a bistro feel to the downstairs area. The menu is built on bistro lines too, with a Mediterranean focus. A starter of thinly sliced chorizo topped with slices of tender squid dressed with harissa mayonnaise may be followed perhaps by traditional beer-battered fish and chips with crushed peas and tartare sauce, or more contemporary smoked chicken, beetroot and pine nut salad with blue cheese dressing. A tapas sharing board for two, consisting of cured meats, cheese and fish, is a good idea. To end, try praline and olive oil cake, of moist sponge, with toffee ice cream.

Times 12-2/6-10, Closed 25-26 Dec, 1 Jan, Sun-Mon

See advert on page 188

Lords of the Manor ❀❀❀

UPPER SLAUGHTER   **Map 10 SP12**

Modern British 🍷 NOTABLE WINE LIST

tel: 01451 820243 **GL54 2JD**
email: reservations@lordsofthemanor.com **web:** www.lordsofthemanor.com
dir: *Follow signs towards The Slaughters 2m W of A429. Hotel on right in centre of Upper Slaughter*

Finely crafted French-inflected cooking in a magical Cotswold hotel

Upper Slaughter seems timeless, an unspoilt, bucolic place, and one of the country's few Thankful Villages, marking the fact that all its men returned alive from the horrors of the trenches. Grandest of all the glorious honey-coloured Cotswold stone buildings that make up the parish is Lords of the Manor, a former rectory dating from the 17th century that backs on to eight acres of green and pleasant grounds. The interior has the best of both worlds: original features and chic furnishings. The restaurant is a formal spot dressed up for the business of fine dining, where well-drilled staff strike a good balance between formality and friendliness. Head chef Richard Picard-Edwards'combines elements of French classical cooking with more contemporary ideas to create a menu that suits the style of the hotel, with attractive plating to make a good first impression. It's the flavours that live in the memory, though, such as a first-course velouté of smoked haddock, with cauliflower and spinach, or the

fashionable pairing of tarragon-glazed chicken wings with bacon custard and pickled salsify. Main courses are similarly inventive: Salisbury Plain venison, perhaps, as loin and ragoût, served with pickled red cabbage, crosnes and sloe gin sauce, or braised lardo-glazed turbot with oxtail and roast turbot consommé. The same degree of technical virtuosity is on display when it comes to dessert, with Yorkshire rhubarb and ginger soufflé rising to the occasion, and that old favourite tiramisù forming the inspiration for a coffee, mascarpone and almond sponge number. A seven-course tasting menu takes you through the greatest hits, while the wine list is an epic piece of work that fearlessly covers the globe.

Chef Richard Picard-Edwards **Owner** Empire Ventures Ltd **Seats** 50, Pr/dining room 30 **Times** 12-2.30/7-9.30, Closed L Mon-Sat **Prices** Fixed D 3 course £72.50, Tasting menu £85, Service optional **Wines** 400 bottles over £30, 95 bottles under £30, 15 by glass **Parking** 40 **Notes** ALC menu £72.50, Sunday L £35, Vegetarian available, Children 7 yrs+

WOTTON-UNDER-EDGE
Map 4 ST79

Tortworth Court Four Pillars Hotel

Modern British

tel: 01454 263000 **Tortworth GL12 8HH**
email: tortworth@four-pillars.co.uk **web:** www.four-pillars.co.uk
dir: *M5 junct 14. Follow B4509 towards Wotton. Turn right at top of hill onto Tortworth Rd, hotel 0.5m on right*

Upmarket brasserie-style menu in striking Victorian mansion

A magnificent Victorian mansion, Tortworth Court is surrounded by 30 acres of grounds including an arboretum. Sympathetic renovation and modernisation in the 1990s have brought all the amenities of a 21st-century hotel, and it's a popular venue for conferences, weddings and other functions, while Moreton's, the main restaurant, has retained the original oak panelling, ornate arches and mpressive fireplace of what used to be the library. The kitchen takes a something-for-everyone approach, an appealing mix of upmarket brasserie-type fare. Dinner could kick off with partridge breast with spicy poached pears, or mussels in saffron and parsley broth, and proceed to hake fillet roasted in chorizo, served with chickpeas and new potatoes, or classic navarin of lamb with boulangère potatoes spiked with rosemary. Puddings are a mixed bunch too, taking in lemon posset with mulled berries, and tarte Tatin with cinnamon-flavoured custard.

Times 12-2.30/6.30-10, Closed L Sat

GREATER MANCHESTER

ALTRINCHAM
Map 15 SJ78

Earle by Simon Rimmer

Modern European

tel: 0161 929 8869 **4 Cecil Rd, Hale WA15 9PA**
email: info@earlerestaurant.co.uk
dir: *M56 junct 7 onto A556 towards Altrincham, follow signs to Hale*

Vibrant modern cooking in village brasserie

Telly chef Simon Rimmer's buzzy contemporary brasserie is an effortlessly stylish spot. Herringbone wood panelling and floors, bare-brick walls and unclothed wooden tables look the part, and you may see the man himself at the stoves in the open-to-view kitchen. A simple approach sees classic comfort dishes alongside bright modern ideas peppered with global accents, with all the right boxes ticked for locally-sourced and seasonal ingredients. Get going with confit treacle-cured salmon with spring onion and pickled ginger, and follow with an on-trend dish like pulled pork shoulder with spiced red cabbage and whipped potato, or roasted cod given a Middle Eastern spin with baba ganoush, saffron potatoes and tabbouleh salad. Finish with ginger sponge with salted caramel sauce and stem ginger ice cream, or a plate of local artisan cheeses with home-made biscuits and carrot chutney.

Chef Simon Rimmer **Owner** Simon Rimmer **Seats** 65, Pr/dining room 14
Times 12-2/5.30-9.30, Closed 25-26 Dec, 1 Jan, L Mon **Prices** Starter £4.50-£9.50, Main £13-£26, Dessert £6.50-£8.50, Service optional **Wines** 17 bottles over £30, 20 bottles under £30, 10 by glass **Parking** Station car park **Notes** Sunday L £13-£21, Vegetarian available, Children welcome

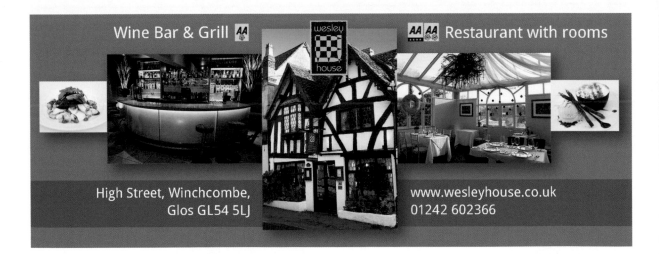

BURY   Map 15 SD81

Red Hall Hotel

◉ Modern British **NEW**

tel: 01706 822476 **Manchester Rd, Walmersley BL9 5NA**
email: contact@oscarsattheredhall.co.uk **web:** www.oscars.red-hall.co.uk
dir: *Phone for directions*

Crowd-pleasing food and countryside views

Set in Lancashire's verdant pastures, just a stone's throw from Bury, this modern hotel occupies converted farm buildings basking in views that are clearly popular as a stage set for wedding parties. After recent refurbishment, the conservatory-style restaurant now goes by the name of Oscar's, and looks rather swish with its contemporary silver and grey tones and bare darkwood tables on herringbone parquet floors. The modern British menu covers a lot of ground, from grills and comfort-food classics to an opener of cigar-like rolls of tuna sashimi filled with dressed white crab meat and pointed up with pickled shallots, tomato concasse and cucumber. Asian accents appear again at mains, when five spice and honey are used to flavour roast duck breast matched with a croquette of confit leg meat, fondant potato, braised leeks, pak choi and celeriac purée, and black cherry jus. At the end, caramelised lemon tart comes with almond macaroons and raspberries.

Chef Andrew Robinshaw **Owner** Tim Kilroe **Seats** 45 **Times** 12-2.30/5.30-9.30 **Prices** Fixed L 2 course fr £12.95, Starter £6.50-£7.95, Main £10.95-£24.95, Dessert £5.95-£7.95, Service optional **Wines** 27 bottles over £30, 25 bottles under £30, 6 by glass **Parking** 60 **Notes** Fizzy Fri – sharing platter + prosecco £20, Sunday L £13.95-£17.95, Vegetarian available, Children welcome

DELPH   Map 16 SD90

The Old Bell Inn

◉ Modern British

tel: 01457 870130 **5 Huddersfield Rd OL3 5EG**
email: info@theoldbellinn.co.uk **web:** www.theoldbellinn.co.uk
dir: *From M62 junct 22, follow A672 to Denshaw junct signed Saddleworth. Left onto A6052 signed Delph. Through village left at x-rds, 150yds on left*

Up-to-date food with an imaginative edge

This solid 18th-century coaching inn has successfully made the transition to a smart 21st-century operation without losing its soul. Before we get to the table, a gin-based aperitif is in order, since the selection runs to a mind-boggling 230 bottles; thus fortified, the restaurant's high-backed seats and darkwood floors make a suitably contemporary setting for the kitchen's hearty and imaginative modern food. There's much emphasis on local components and plenty to tempt – a velouté of smoked haddock comes in a mini bottle to pour over a Lancashire cheese and leek fishcake paired with a warm leek pannacotta, followed by the porky pleasures of slow-roasted belly, braised shoulder, marinated fillet and sticky rib with cabbage and sweet potato. Fish dishes are worth checking out too – perhaps baked sea bass fillet with braised celery, shellfish risotto and bisque. The creative approach runs through to a dessert of rhubarb and ginger cheesecake with granola nougat and rhubarb sorbet.

Chef Mark Pemberton **Owner** Philip Whiteman **Seats** 65 **Times** 12-9.30, All-day dining **Prices** Prices not confirmed, Service optional **Wines** 5 bottles over £30, 24 bottles under £30, 10 by glass **Parking** 21 **Notes** Signature menu £25-£30, Pre-theatre menu, Sunday L, Vegetarian available, Children welcome

The Saddleworth Hotel

◉ Modern European

tel: 01457 871888 **Huddersfield Rd OL3 5LX**
email: enquiries@thesaddleworthhotel.co.uk **web:** www.saddleworthhotel.co.uk
dir: *A62, located between A6052 & A670*

Modern British cooking showing wit and skill

The Saddleworth feels like an assiduous attempt to create a country inn for the modern era. Built of stone, and sitting amid landscaped gardens and woodland with sweeping views over the Lancashire moorland, it's not far from Oldham but feels pleasingly remote from anywhere. The location makes it a popular choice for weddings, and the dramatic decor of Bakers Restaurant, where sparkling glassware gleams against black table linen, exercises its own allure. The opening salvo is some witty little snacking items (including a cucumber mojito and beans on toast). Then the six-course tasting menu ploughs a fascinating furrow through the modern British repertoire, from scallops and cauliflower scented with espresso and adorned with cobnuts and parmesan, through rabbit tortellini with truffled baby artichokes, and turbot with foraged sea flora in shellfish broth, to local free-range pork belly with aubergine purée and celery and Stilton gnocchi. Dessert could be an almond sponge with variations of pear and raspberry.

Times 12-2/7-9.30

MANCHESTER   Map 16 SJ89

ABode Manchester

◉◉ Modern European, British **V**

tel: 0161 247 7744 **107 Piccadilly M1 2DB**
email: tables@abodemanchester.co.uk **web:** www.michaelcaines.com
dir: *in city centre, 2 mins walk from Piccadilly station*

Compelling modern cooking in stylish central hotel

On a prime chunk of real estate, this luxury hotel has been converted from a cotton warehouse built in 1898, evidence of which can be seen in the original walnut staircase, tiling and wrought ironwork. The Michael Caines Restaurant is a two-tier room, next to the Champagne Bar, with a glossy designer-led contemporary look and an upmarket vibe. The cooking is exciting and innovative, resting squarely on the classical repertoire. An auspicious amuse-bouche gets the palate ringing before such starters as beautifully made, wafer-thin ravioli stuffed with rich crabmeat in shellfish bisque, topped with tiny pieces of pink grapefruit and ginger for contrast, or a gutsy dish of ox tongue with carrots, a bone marrow galette, and horseradish ice cream. Ambitions are amply met in well-judged main courses: super-fresh and perfectly timed hake fillet under crispy chicken skin in chicken broth with parsnips, or pork fillet with butternut squash, boulangère potatoes and smoked paprika. Puddings alone are worth a visit here, among them the signature chocolate orange confit mousse with orange sorbet and dark chocolate ice cream, and prune and Armagnac soufflé with matching ice cream.

Chef Robert Cox **Owner** Brownsword Hotels **Seats** 80, Pr/dining room 26 **Times** 12-2.30/6-10, Closed Sun-Mon **Prices** Fixed L 3 course £15-£24.75, Fixed D 3 course £22.95, Tasting menu £60-£95, Starter £9.50-£16.50, Main £19-£25, Dessert £8.95-£10 **Wines** 71 bottles over £30, 19 bottles under £30, 11 by glass **Parking** NCP opposite **Notes** Fixed L 4/5 course £20/£25, Children welcome

The French by Simon Rogan

◉◉◉◉ *– see page 190*

The French by Simon Rogan 🌹🌹🌹🌹

MANCHESTER   Map 16 SJ89

Modern British V 🍷 NOTABLE WINE LIST

tel: 0161 236 3333 **Peter St M60 2DS**
email: midlandsales@qhotels.co.uk
web: www.qhotels.co.uk
dir: M602 junct 3, follow Manchester Central Convention Complex signs, hotel opposite

A cutting-edge revolution for The French

The Midland first opened its doors to an admiring public back on 5th September 1903 and its French restaurant has been the fine-dining player in the city for as long as anyone can remember. Hitting the headlines again in 2013, the restaurant was given a new lease of life under one of the UK's most talented and exciting chefs – step forward The French by Simon Rogan. If you're looking to move with the times, that's the way to do it! The first thing they did was chuck out the chintz to create a room that better reflected Mr Rogan's style, which means a more natural and casual look with light green on the walls, a carpet that is designed to look like floorboards and tables that aren't ashamed of being made of wood. They didn't trash the place though, for this was a respectful makeover that maintained the best original features such as the ornate plasterwork, while the stylish contemporary chandeliers maintain a sense of glamour. The kitchen is headed up by the prodigiously talented Adam Reid, charged with delivering the Rogan style of cuisine that is both cutting edge, respectful of the old ways, and most importantly of all focused on the actual ingredients. The passion, curiosity, skill and sheer drive of Simon Rogan is evident from what arrives on the plate, while his own Cumbrian farm provides a good deal of what features on the menu (and what isn't from his own land is from trusted suppliers). Six- and ten-course tasting menus are the way to go, with a three-course option during the day. Marans egg yolks are smoked and arrive in one course with yellow turnip, truffles and a broth of mushrooms, followed by more delicious smokiness in the form of the ox in coal (tartare-style rump), and then a breaded oyster and butternut squash with bacon, buttermilk and mint. Every element contributes to the dish as a whole, and the innate flavours are never lost in the mix. Pickled red cabbage is partnered with a cream made with Beenleigh Blue cheese (from Devon), violet mustard, linseeds and walnuts, while we've got Reg to thank (apparently) for the duck that arrives with roasted parsnips, cavolo nero and Old Tom vinegar. Among sweet courses, beetroot and blackberry combine with sheep's milk and chestnuts, and quince and pears are united with the flavours of ginger and butterscotch. As we go to press the restaurant is closing for a short while for a refurbishment to add a lounge area and improve the loos.

Chef Adam Reid, Simon Rogan **Owner** QHotels **Seats** 55 **Times** 12-1.30/6.30-9, Closed Xmas, Sun-Mon, L Tue **Prices** Prices not confirmed, Service optional **Wines** 118 bottles over £30, 5 bottles under £30, 17 by glass **Parking** NCP behind hotel **Notes** 6/10 course L/D fr £65/fr £85, Children 8 yrs+

MANCHESTER *continued*

Greens

◉ Modern Vegetarian V

tel: 0161 434 4259 **43 Lapwing Ln, West Didsbury M20 2NT**
email: greensdidsbury@gmail.com
dir: *Between Burton Rd & Palatine Rd*

Veggie Mancunian star draws crowds for top flavours

TV chef Simon Rimmer's restaurant is a lively place, drawing crowds with exciting vegetarian cooking. Darkwood tables and chairs, with some banquettes, boarded and tiled floors, some funky wallpaper and spotlights dangling from the ceiling all create a positive impression. Clearly-flavoured cooking is the hallmark of the kitchen, with ideas picked up from around the globe to produce a menu that bursts with bright and appealing dishes. Hits among starters include carrot and sweet potato soup spiked with ginger and chilli, and rich Roquefort, pecan and tarragon cheesecake cut by spicy tomato chutney. Garnishes and sauces give extra depth to dishes, seen in main courses of a generous, well-made spinach, feta and pistachio pie in filo with tomato and cinnamon sauce, and Lancashire cheese and basil sausages with mustard mash, beer gravy and tomato ketchup chutney. Simon's talents extend to puddings along the lines of treacle tart with Earl Grey cream, and textbook lemon tart with raspberry sauce.

Chef Simon Rimmer **Owner** Simon Connolly, Simon Rimmer **Seats** 84
Times 12-2/5.30-10, Closed 25-26 Dec, 1 Jan, L Mon **Prices** Fixed L 2 course £12, Fixed D 3 course £15, Starter £4.50-£7, Main £12.50-£13.50, Dessert £4.95-£6, Service optional **Wines** 7 bottles over £30, 24 bottles under £30, 7 by glass **Parking** On street **Notes** Sun all day menu, Sunday L £13-£15, Children welcome

Harvey Nichols Second Floor Restaurant

◉◉ Modern European ▮ NOTABLE WINE LIST

tel: 0161 828 8898 **21 New Cathedral St M1 1AD**
email: secondfloor.reservations@harveynichols.com
dir: *Just off Deansgate, town centre. 5 min walk from Victoria Station, on Exchange Sq*

Chic global cuisine with views of the city centre

The Harvey Nics restaurant at the Manchester store is to be found on the second floor, and has the house style familiar from Dublin to Knightsbridge, with the signature emphasis on chic. The leather and wire seats are a triumph of comfort over visual aesthetics, and the pale pastel palette does nothing to detract from the bird's-eye views of the city-centre's heritage architecture. Once, the presumption was all for regional French offerings, but the team in the kitchen cook on-trend renditions of global reference dishes, dressing seared tuna with wasabi, carrot and ginger, garnishing a starter portion of rabbit with sweetcorn purée and pancetta, and then spreading their wings at main course to produce precision-timed lemon sole with wild mushroom risotto and artichoke barigoule, or turning out lamb in three guises – braised shoulder, rump and sweetbreads – alongside smooth, herb-flecked mash. To finish, there could be properly fragile vanilla pannacotta with rhubarb and ginger, or the crowd-wowing show-stopper of silky chocolate mousse, espresso espuma and hazelnut shortbread.

Times 12-3/6-9.30, Closed 25-27 Dec, Etr Sun, D Sun-Mon

Macdonald Manchester Hotel

◉ Modern British, Scottish

tel: 0161 272 3200 **London Rd M1 2PG**
email: general.manchester@macdonald-hotels.co.uk web: www.macdonaldhotels.co.uk/our-hotels/north-england/manchester/
dir: *Opposite Piccadilly Station*

City-centre temple to pedigree beef

Handy for collapsing into if you've just been disgorged from the rail network at Piccadilly station, the Macdonald is an imposing presence on the city-centre landscape, the kind of modern hotel that looks like an office block until you get inside and find spa facilities, stylish comfort and a deep-windowed eating space with its kitchen on view. Prime slabs of pedigree beef from Scotland, the US and Argentina get star billing, aged for three weeks and treated to all the traditional trimmings, whether you want a melting lump of fillet or a tastily spiced burger. Start with fishcakes in caper mayo, or Stornoway black pudding Scotch egg with home-made piccalilli. If it sounds like a vegetarian's nightmare, fear not; sweet potato, goats' cheese and red onion tart may help matters. Then fill any remaining spaces with caramel peanut parfait or lemon cheesecake.

Chef Mat Lloyd **Owner** Macdonald Hotels **Seats** 140 **Times** 5-10, Closed L all week **Prices** Fixed D 3 course £16.50, Starter £4.50-£9.50, Main £7-£28, Dessert £3-£7.50 **Wines** 24 bottles over £30, 17 bottles under £30, 13 by glass **Parking** 85, NCP **Notes** Sunday L fr £21.50, Vegetarian available, Children welcome

Malmaison Manchester

◉ Modern British, American, International

tel: 0161 278 1000 **Piccadilly M1 3AQ**
email: manchester@malmaison.com web: www.malmaison.com
dir: *From M56 follow signs to Manchester, then to Piccadilly*

Modern comfort food in the city centre

A prime piece of heritage industrial architecture, Manchester's Malmaison is a former linen warehouse plumb in the city centre, not far from Piccadilly station. The interior scene is all boutique to the max, with eye-catching decorative flourishes in a soothing low-lit ambience. Cocktails and upscale brasserie food draw in the buzziest of crowds, and staff cope well with the demand. In the Smoak Bar Grill, the kitchen is open to view, and produces efficient, often surprising versions of modern comfort food, not least the range of steaks that are done on the Josper charcoal grill. Creamed brie with a wine-poached pear and candied pecans is an attractive opener, while mains run to confit duck with Puy lentils and garlic mash, or calves' liver and pancetta with roasted onions. Chicken tikka with all the Indian trimmings is a crowd-pleaser. Round things off with a vanilla-fragrant crème brûlée.

Chef Kevin Whiteford **Owner** Malmaison **Seats** 85, Pr/dining room 10
Times 12-2.30/6-11, Closed L 31 Dec, D 25 Dec **Prices** Starter £5-£9.50, Main £14-£20, Dessert £6.95 **Wines** 20 bottles over £30, 12 bottles under £30, 21 by glass **Parking** NCP 100 mtrs **Notes** Sun brunch, Sunday L £19.95, Vegetarian available, Children welcome

Manchester House Bar & Restaurant

◉◉◉ – see page 192

MANCHESTER *continued*

Mr Cooper's House and Garden by Simon Rogan

◉◉ International

tel: 0161 932 4128 **The Midland Hotel, Peter St M60 2DS**
email: info@mrcoopershouseandgarden.co.uk
dir: *From M6 junct 19 join M56. Follow signs city centre (A5103). Follow signs Manchester Central Convention Complex/Bridgewater Hall onto Medlock St. Through lights onto Lower Mosley St. Pass Bridgewater Hall on right, hotel facing you*

Cool and contemporary dining

The sister restaurant to the high-flying The French is named in honour of a coach-making family whose home and gardens were based on this site in the 19th century, and, true to its name, there's a tree in the middle of the dining room. This is the more casual dining option in the hotel, but seeing as this is Simon Rogan's version of casual dining, the culinary output is a cut above the norm. The cool and contemporary venue consists of a number of spaces with a clubby library area with leather-swathed booths and a main room with plants and that 35-foot tree. The menu takes a slightly more global approach than might be expected from Mr Rogan, with his usual attention to detail and passion for provenance, seasonality and flavour. Pork belly with peanut emulsion and black pudding is a starter with winning flavour combinations, followed by confit duck fritter or sea bass with stir-fried corn and a sweet-and-sour sauce. Finish with white chocolate cake with a pineapple and cardamom compôte.

Chef Gareth Jones **Owner** Simon Rogan, QHotels **Seats** 150
Times 12-2/5-10, Closed 25-26 Dec, 1 Jan **Prices** Fixed L 2 course fr £15, Fixed D 3 course fr £23, Starter £5-£11, Main £13.50-£22.50, Dessert £6.50-£7.50 **Wines** 30 bottles over £30, 20 bottles under £30, 12 by glass **Parking** NCP Manchester Central
Notes Sunday L, Vegetarian available, Children welcome

The Rose Garden

◉ Modern British, European **NEW**

tel: 0161 478 0747 **218 Burton Rd, West Didsbury M20 2LW**
email: info@therosegardendidsbury.com
dir: *Phone for directions*

European bistro food with urban boho credentials

Didsbury is one of Manchester's more stylish quarters, and The Rose Garden suits it to a T. It could be mistaken for a contemporary art space, with its minimal gleaming-white ambience enlivened with punches of glaring colour in purple and citrus from paint or lighting. White moulded swivel chairs at laminate wipe-clean tables, not to mention the pacy, on-point service, contribute to an urban boho atmosphere, and the modern European bistro food does the rest. Slices and chunks of softly braised octopus form the centrepiece of a salad of heritage tomato, onion, fennel, croûtons and chilli, and might precede a creative juxtaposition of turbot fillet and snails with wilted baby gem in seaweed-salty spring vegetable nage. More seafood, in the form of squid salsa, is inveigled into a main of pork belly and pineapple, and herbal fragrance lends character to desserts such as chocolate and rosemary delice with Italian meringue and a walnut tuile.

Chef William Mills **Owner** William Mills, Emma Caress **Seats** 58
Times 6-9.30, Closed 25-26 Dec, 1 Jan, L Mon-Sat **Prices** Fixed D 3 course £20.95, Starter £6.95-£10.95, Main £14.95-£21.95, Dessert £6.50, Service optional 10%
Wines 11 bottles over £30, 10 bottles under £30, 9 by glass **Parking** On street
Notes Sunday L £17.95-£20.95, Vegetarian available, Children welcome

Manchester House Bar & Restaurant ◉◉◉

MANCHESTER   Map 16 SJ89

Modern British V 🍷 **NOTABLE WINE LIST**

tel: 0161 835 2557 **Tower 12, 18-22 Bridge St M3 3BZ**
email: restaurant@manchesterhouse.uk.com
dir: *Located on Bridge St, on edge of Spinning Fields. Entrance is in Tower 12 behind Waitrose*

Buzzy new address for contemporary dining

Things have settled down on Manchester's dining scene after BBC2's *Restaurant Wars* treated viewers to the spectacle of Simon Rogan's The French and Aiden Byrne's operation in Manchester House battling to bring high-end dining to the city. It's a see-and-be-seen sort of spot, so if you'd like to preface the experience with a cocktail and a gander at the Mancunian beau monde, the lift whizzes you up to the 12th floor of Spinningfields' Tower 12 for a sharpener with cityscape views. Then slide back down to the second floor, where Byrne's restaurant – a rather glam, urban, industrial-style venue with a clubby mood – puts the chefs right in the heart of the action in an open kitchen. If you're planning a Saturday evening visit, be aware that the 12-course tasting menu is the only option, but the rest of the time the carte leads the way, with the taster available if the whole table is up for it, and there's a dedicated non-meat taster and carte for veggies. There's a definite regional flavour to the cooking,

with a reworked classic here and there – roasted langoustine served with grilled pumpkin consommé and black pudding tortellini is a typical first course requiring a lot of technical know-how, or perhaps squab pigeon with cherries, pistachio and violet mustard. Next up, complex main-course numbers might involve John Dory baked in celeriac and served with truffled chicken consommé, or veal fillet partnered by baby globe artichoke, smoked foie gras mousse and braised veal shin. Otherwise, straight-up Belted Galloway rib-eye and fillet steaks will sort out unreconstructed carnivores. For dessert, there's Manchester tart or the pretty-as-a-picture chocolate and violet millefeuille.

Chef Aiden Byrne **Owner** Living Ventures & Aiden Byrne **Seats** 78, Pr/dining room 8 **Times** 12-2.30/7-9.30, Closed 1st 2 wks Jan, 2 wks summer, Sun-Mon
Prices Prices not confirmed **Wines** 193 bottles over £30, 26 bottles under £30, 12 by glass **Notes** Children welcome

Sweet Mandarin

◉ Chinese V

tel: 0161 832 8848 **19 Copperas St M4 1HS**
email: lisa@sweetmandarin.com
dir: *Top end of High Street opposite Old Smithfield Fish Market façade in Northern Quarter*

Wildly popular Chinese family restaurant run by honoured sisters

The Tse sisters, who run what has become one of the most popular Chinese restaurants for miles around, were awarded MBEs for their services to food in the 2014 New Year Honours list. From humble family beginnings in 1950, Sweet Mandarin has expanded its remit to take in a cookery school, outside catering, a recipe book and a line of products. The foundation for it all is the relaxed and comfortable glass-fronted venue itself, where, against a backdrop of red screens and lanterns, a mix of traditional and less familiar Chinese dishes is offered. Expect chicken and sweetcorn soup, mixed platters of hors d'oeuvres, and well-rendered main dishes like freshly shredded, moistly flavourful Peking duck, Manchurian beef fillet in a sauce of black peppers and onions sizzled on the skillet at your table. Look out for Shanghai-spiced king prawns, and the original General Tse's wok-braised sweet-and-sour tofu cooked with peppers, onions and pineapple.

Chef Lisa Tse **Owner** Helen Tse **Seats** 85 **Times** 5-11, Closed 25-26 Dec, Mon, L all week **Prices** Prices not confirmed **Wines** 1 bottle over £30, 13 bottles under £30, 7 by glass **Parking** Shudehill car park **Notes** Children welcome

---

MANCHESTER AIRPORT   Map 15 SJ88

BEST WESTERN PLUS Pinewood on Wilmslow

◉ Modern, Traditional NEW

tel: 01625 529211 **180 Wilmslow Rd SK9 3LF**
email: pinewood.res@pinewood-hotel.co.uk **web:** www.pinewood-hotel.co.uk
dir: *Phone for directions*

Contemporary setting for modern brasserie dining

This good-looking red-brick hotel with a splendid garden has a decidedly contemporary finish within and is a popular wedding and conference venue. It's also home to the thoroughly modern One Eighty restaurant, a sleek looking space with darkwood tables (no stuffy linen here) and fashionably muted colour tones. The menu is equally on the money, maintaining the brasserie attitude and revealing keen creativity in the kitchen. There's well-judged execution in the smoking of scallops which arrive with celeriac and apple purée, while duck liver pâté is served with warm brioche and spiced apple and pear chutney. Main courses include a glammed up burger (brioche bun, Applewood cheese, dry-cured bacon and onion marmalade) and a veggie open lasagne with wild mushrooms and spinach. There are sharing platter, steaks with triple-cooked chips, and desserts such as a retro banana split.

Chef Colin Starkey **Owner** James Alexander **Seats** 80 **Times** 12-4/6-9 **Prices** Tasting menu £60, Starter £4.50-£8, Main £10.50-£23, Dessert £5.95-£7.25, Service optional **Wines** 13 bottles over £30, 30 bottles under £30, 15 by glass **Notes** Seasonal menu £6.95-£19.95, Tasting menu 6 course, Sunday L £16.95, Vegetarian available, Children welcome

---

OLDHAM   Map 16 SD90

The White Hart Inn

◉◉ Modern British V

tel: 01457 872566 **51 Stockport Rd, Lydgate OL4 4JJ**
email: bookings@thewhitehart.co.uk **web:** www.thewhitehart.co.uk
dir: *M62 junct 20, A627, continue to end of bypass, then A669 to Saddleworth. Enter Lydgate turn right onto Stockport Rd. White Hart Inn 50yds on left*

Confident contemporary cooking in a moorland inn

You're not far from the centre of Oldham in The White Hart, but when you're settled into this rambling old village inn on the fringes of the moors, the city feels a good way off. The convivial bar will sort you out with a fine pint of real ale, and the cooking is right on the money, delivering big seasonal flavours from well-sourced ingredients, whether you're in the traditional, rustic-styled brasserie or the more contemporary-looking restaurant. A seven-course tasting option shows the team at the stoves has both confidence and ambition, while the seasonal menu sets out heartily with pan-roasted cod with Puy lentils and Alsace bacon, followed by a main course displaying a keen eye for harmonious flavours and lively textural contrasts: lamb rump with goats' curd, raw courgette, braised and puréed shallots, onion ash and chilli oil. Elsewhere, monkfish with wild garlic, heritage potatoes and clams might catch the eye, and for pudding, a reworked old favourite sees rhubarb (poached and gel) matched with duck egg custard and a ginger biscuit.

Chef Mike Shaw **Owner** Charles Brierley **Seats** 50, Pr/dining room 32 **Times** 12-2.30/6-9.30, Closed 26 Dec, 1 Jan **Prices** Fixed L 2 course £13.50, Tasting menu £32-£50, Starter £6-£11.50, Main £12-£26.50, Dessert £6.50-£7.50, Service optional **Wines** 70 bottles over £30, 70 bottles under £30, 10 by glass **Parking** 75 **Notes** Tasting menu 7 course, 2 for 1 D 5 course £39.50, Sunday L £22.50, Children welcome

---

ROCHDALE   Map 16 SD81

Nutters

◉ Modern British V   ▨ NOTABLE WINE LIST

tel: 01706 650167 **Edenfield Rd, Norden OL12 7TT**
email: enquiries@nuttersrestaurant.com
dir: *From Rochdale take A680 signed Blackburn. Edenfield Rd on right on leaving Norden*

Personality-laden modern British food at a Gothic manor house

When you arrive at the hefty Victorian Gothic manor with the large red and white sign above the door declaring 'Nutters', there's no mistaking that you're entering the world of Andrew Nutter. A television personality and larger-than-life character, Mr Nutter's restaurant is a family affair (mum and dad work here too), with the grand old house done out in a contemporary manner. The menu takes a modern British path, with plenty of flavours from Asia added to the mix, and regional ingredients providing a sense of place. Among starters, slow-roasted Dingley Dell pork belly is infused with Chinese flavours, while main courses might include pan-seared hake with ginger beer-battered scallop and tarragon hollandaise, or Goosnargh chicken served two ways (Parma ham-wrapped roulade and mini Kiev). Finish with dark and white chocolate cheesecake with Oreo crumb and honeycomb.

Chef Andrew Nutter **Owner** The Nutter family **Seats** 143, Pr/dining room 100 **Times** 12-2/6.30-9.30, Closed 1-2 days after both Xmas & New Year, Mon **Prices** Fixed L 2 course fr £16.50, Tasting menu fr £42, Starter £4.80-£9.50, Main £15.60-£23.50, Dessert £5.20-£7.80, Service optional **Wines** 95 bottles over £30, 93 bottles under £30, 10 by glass **Parking** 100 **Notes** Gourmet menu 6 course £42, Afternoon tea £15-£23.50, Sunday L £23.50, Children welcome

ROCHDALE *continued*

The Peacock Room

◉◉ Modern British

tel: 01706 368591 **Crimble Hotel, Crimble Ln, Bamford OL11 4AD**
email: crimble@thedeckersgroup.com **web:** www.thedeckersgroup.com
dir: *M62 junct 20 follow signs for Blackburn, left onto B6222 (Bury road) contine for 1m Crimble Lane on left*

Art deco design and smart contemporary food

The Peacock Room is a fitting name for this flamboyantly decorated restaurant. Huge gold sculptures of the fowl on the door handles, a mirrored ceiling hung with chandeliers, cornicing picked out in gold, and plush seats on a busily patterned carpet all contribute to the exuberant style, while the birds parade the grounds. Dishes themselves are never over elaborate, the kitchen delivering quail breast with a spicy quail's egg, sweetcorn purée and morels, then butter-poached lemon sole with a fricassee of baby vegetables and time-honoured parsley sauce. Prime ingredients are the norm, and combinations give satisfying results, so foie gras joins ham hock in a terrine, served with poached apples and gingerbread, and poached fillet of halibut is accompanied by snail fricassée, pea purée, green vegetables and smoked butter sauce. Committed meat-eaters could opt for roast cannon of beef fillet with oxtail fritters, foie gras, confit potatoes and celeriac. No need to dither over a pudding when there's a quartet of desserts to order: praline parfait, orange crème brûlée, mango trifle and chocolate delice.

Chef Robert Walker **Owner** The Deckers Hospitality Group **Seats** 80
Times 12-2.30/6.30-10, Closed Mon-Tue, L Sat, D Sun **Prices** Fixed L 2 course £13.50-£17.50, Fixed D 3 course £19.50-£23.50, Starter £5.05-£9.55, Main £15.95-£23.95, Dessert £4.50-£10 **Wines** 30 bottles over £30, 71 bottles under £30, 6 by glass **Parking** 120 **Notes** Sunday L £21.50-£27.25, Vegetarian available, Children welcome

---

WIGAN   Map 15 SD50

Macdonald Kilhey Court Hotel

◉ Modern British

tel: 01257 472100 **Chorley Rd, Standish WN1 2XN**
email: general.kilheycourt@macdonald-hotels.co.uk **web:** www.macdonaldhotels.co.uk
dir: *M6 junct 27, through village of Standish. Take B5239, left onto A5106, hotel on right*

Peaceful garden views and sound cooking

Built towards the end of the 19th century, Kilhey Court is a solid red-brick building in landscaped grounds with a lake (plenty of photo opportunities for weddings). It has a self-contained meeting and events centre, and a comfortable, carpeted restaurant in a large, split-level conservatory overlooking the gardens. The modern British menu is biased towards classical ideas. To start may be fishcakes with caper mayonnaise, or tagliatelle tossed with mushrooms, sage, garlic and shavings of hard cheese. Grilling is a popular cooking medium, resulting in whole lemon sole, say, with a selection of vegetables, or there may cannon of lamb in red wine jus with seasonal greens and potatoes fried with garlic and parsley. Zesty, velvety lemon tart is a good example of the beast, raspberry coulis providing contrast.

Chef Stephen Newhouse **Owner** Macdonald Hotels **Seats** 80, Pr/dining room 22
Times 12.30-2.30/6.30-9.30, Closed L Sat **Prices** Service optional **Wines** 13 by glass **Parking** 300 **Notes** Afternoon tea, Sunday L fr £18.95, Vegetarian available, Children welcome

---

Wrightington Hotel & Country Club

◉ Modern International

tel: 01257 425803 **Moss Ln, Wrightington WN6 9PB**
email: info@bennettsrestaurant.com **web:** www.bennettsrestaurant.com
dir: *M6 junct 27, 0.25m W, hotel on right after church*

Unfussy cooking and top-notch leisure facilities

This modern hotel, with extensive conference, leisure and wedding facilities, is on the edge of Wigan within peaceful countryside. A recent makeover gives Bennett's Restaurant a stylishly elegant look, but a relaxed atmosphere and brisk young staff soon dispel any notion of formality. 'Lancashire Classics' puzzlingly includes a multinational main course of prawn tempura in panko breadcrumbs with Caesar salad topped with parmesan and olives, with a mix of the traditional and contemporary found elsewhere. A smoked salmon parcel enclosing mousseline of prawn, cod and salmon, served with lemon crème fraîche, could be followed by accurately seared duck breast with blackberry jus and cabbage sautéed with bacon. Desserts end positively with perhaps lemon parfait with lemon cream, or rhubarb and plum syllabub.

Times 6-9.30, Closed Sun, L all week

WORSLEY
Map 15 SD70

Grenache
@@ Modern British, French

tel: 0161 7998181 **15 Bridgewater Rd, Walkden M28 3JE**
email: info@grenacherestaurant.co.uk
dir: *Off Bridgewater Road B5232*

Revamped basement restaurant with French classical technique

The restaurant named after a red grape variety flourishes in the frankly unlikely Manchester suburb of Walkden, mixing it with the kebabs and burgers of the vicinity. New ownership in July 2014 brought a revamp to the basement dining room, which is now two-toned in magenta and white, with abstract artworks and hospitable staff. The cooking leans towards a French axis, with classical technique underlying the modern combinations. The unctuous smoothness of a pressed foie gras terrine gains all the textural counterpoint it needs from a salad of cobnuts, granola, greengages and grapes, the fruity elements perhaps surpassing the need for a further, rather bitter damson and red wine chutney. Then it could be herb-crusted halibut with well-made scallop tortellini and various ways with cauliflower – a fish's best friend these days – or perhaps roasted rump and braised shoulder of lamb with pesto mash and ratatouille in rosemary jus. A slice of gloriously rich treacle tart comes with clotted cream ice cream, with some macerated raspberries to keep up the vitamin count. Incidentals are all up to the mark.

Chef Mike Jennings **Owner** Mike Jennings **Seats** 40 **Times** 12.30-2.30/5.30-close, Closed Mon-Tue, D Sun **Prices** Fixed D 3 course fr £23.95, Tasting menu fr £45, Starter £6.95-£11.50, Main £16.50-£24.95, Dessert £6.50-£7.95, Service optional **Wines** 25 bottles over £30, 35 bottles under £30, 16 by glass **Parking** On street **Notes** Sunday L £19.95-£23.95, Vegetarian available, Children welcome

HAMPSHIRE

ALRESFORD
Map 5 SU53

Pulpo Negro
@@ Spanish, Mediterranean **NEW**

tel: 01962 732262 **28 Broad St SO24 9AQ**
email: Info@pulponegro.co.uk
dir: *Phone for directions*

Spanish tapas in the English countryside

Alresford – famous for its watercress, steam railway and clear-running chalk streams – has rather improbably added a sunny slice of the Med to its quintessentially English appeal with the arrival of new kid on the block, Pulpo Negro. Chef-patron Andres Alemany (who originally hails from Barcelona) knows his huevos flamencos (Andalusian flamenco eggs) from his pig's trotter croquetas. There's a smart-casual, modern feel-good vibe about the place, with its floorboards, café-style chairs, pews and wooden tables, while dangling Edison-style lighting flirts with fashion. Counter-style seats and traditional tiles fronting the open kitchen add subtle nods to Spain. However, the appealing tapas menu speaks with a broad Spanish accent; take succulent, full-flavoured secreto (shoulder) Ibèrica to slow-cooked Ibèricus tomatoes bursting with sweetness, or spicy Alejandro chorizo teamed with local watercress to an individual piquillo pepper tortilla. Top ingredients are a given, and simple but skilled handling delivers flavours of attitude. The finish, crèma Catalana to Spanish cheeses, while well-selected Spanish wines (alongside a good showing of sherry and gin) send all home happy. Alfresco pavement tables out front are a sunny-day top call too.

Chef Andres Alemany **Owner** Andres & Marie-Lou Alemany **Seats** 80 **Times** 12-3/6-11, Closed 1 Jan, Sun-Mon (ex L BH) **Prices** Fixed L 2 course £14 **Wines** 17 bottles over £30, 23 bottles under £30, 25 by glass **Parking** On street **Notes** Tapas menu, Vegetarian available, Children 5 yrs+

ALTON
Map 5 SU73

The Anchor Inn
@@ British

tel: 01420 23261 **Lower Froyle GU34 4NA**
email: info@anchorinnatlowerfroyle.co.uk **web:** www.anchorinnatlowerfroyle.co.uk
dir: *From A31, turn off to Bentley*

Impressive and wide-ranging cooking at village inn

The Anchor, dating from the 16th century, has all the elements of a traditional country inn down to its low beams, walls full of pictures and press cuttings, wooden tables and a double-sided bar. It's a popular place, attracting people not just for drinks in the bar but with a wide-ranging menu assembled by a kitchen that clearly has high levels of culinary skill and integrity. Pub stalwarts of sausage and mash are on the menu, but so too is an excellent rack of lamb, served pink in its own juices, with crispy breaded shoulder, pea purée and pommes Anna. Inventive treatments extend to a garlic and thyme sauce for pan-fried fillet of pollock, accompanied by mussels, clams and samphire, and starters of guinea fowl terrine with date and thyme purée, or a purée of avocado, chilli and lime for crab mayonnaise. Desserts are best-sellers, judging by the number on offer, among them pannacotta topped with crumbled nuts served with poached rhubarb.

Times 12-2.30/6.30-9.30, Closed 25 Dec, D 26 Dec, 1 Jan

ANDOVER
Map 5 SU34

Esseborne Manor
@@ Modern British

tel: 01264 736444 **Hurstbourne Tarrant SP11 OER**
email: info@esseborne-manor.co.uk **web:** www.esseborne-manor.co.uk
dir: *Halfway between Andover & Newbury on A343, just 1m N of Hurstbourne Tarrant*

Confident modern cooking in bucolic country house

In a delicious spot designated an Area of Outstanding Natural Beauty, Esseborne is a dignified Victorian country house on a human scale. The owners have not attempted to wash away all vestiges of the past. There's a traditional finish within – classy rather than chintzy – with an elegant restaurant that is the very model of refined good taste. There's a good chance that if what you eat doesn't come from the garden in the grounds, it won't have travelled very far. Chef Dennis Janssen creates modern dishes that sparkle, showing good technical skills and creativity. It's not all whizz-bang, though, and there is evident classical thinking going on. Pigeon features in a first course with black pudding and cauliflower, with the zippy flavours of cumin and capers, or go for a fashionable combination of ham hock terrine with piccalilli and gingerbread. Main course cod with ox cheek and salsify delivers satisfying flavours, or go for a classic wild mushroom risotto. There's a tasting menu, too, plus contemporary desserts such as an apple and toffee pressing with walnut cake and goats' cheese ice cream.

Chef Dennis Janssen **Owner** Ian Hamilton **Seats** 35, Pr/dining room 80 **Times** 12-2/7-9.30 **Prices** Fixed L 2 course £15, Tasting menu £55-£70, Starter £5-£7.50, Main £13-£22, Dessert £5-£7.50, Service optional **Wines** 33 bottles over £30, 57 bottles under £30, 12 by glass **Parking** 40 **Notes** Afternoon tea £15, Sunday L £24, Vegetarian available, Children welcome

ANDOVER *continued*

The Plough Inn

◉◉ Modern British V

tel: 01264 720358 **Longparish SP11 6PB**
email: eat@theploughinn.info
dir: *M3 junct 8, A303 towards Andover then B3048 for Longparish*

Adventurous cooking in a rustic Hampshire pub

Looking for a break from the traffic-clogged stretches of the A303, you might happen upon Longparish nearby, an unmolested Hampshire village that boasts a creeper-clad country pub in The Plough. Serving the locals since the 1720s, it's run these days by London refugee James Durrant, who retains the rustic look of the place with its exposed brickwork, log-burning fires and a snug worthy of the name. The cooking has gradually diverged into two menus, so that the fish and chips and meat pie trade need not feel neglected, but those in the market for something more adventurous are catered for too. First up might be roasted squash with goats' cheese, wild mushrooms and toasted walnuts, before mains head off in the directions of tenderly braised pig's cheek with salt-baked beetroot, smoked mash, spring onions and mint, or a regally served whole grilled plaice in brown shrimp, caper and raisin vinaigrette. Salty caramel continues to rule the roost for afters, appearing here in an ice cream to go with potent chocolate marquise and a more shy and retiring caramel jelly.

Chef James Durrant **Owner** James & Louise Durrant **Seats** 52
Times 12-2.30/6-9.30, Closed Mon, D Sun **Prices** Starter £5-£9.50, Main £12.50-£24, Dessert £7.50-£8.50, Service optional **Wines** 19 bottles over £30, 14 bottles under £30, 11 by glass **Parking** 25 **Notes** Sunday L, Children welcome

■ **BARTON-ON-SEA** Map 5 SZ29

Pebble Beach

◉ British, French, Mediterranean

tel: 01425 627777 **Marine Dr BH25 7DZ**
email: mail@pebblebeach-uk.com **web:** www.pebblebeach-uk.com
dir: *Follow A35 from Southampton onto A337 to New Milton, turn left onto Barton Court Av to clifftop*

Upbeat brasserie cooking with a clifftop sun terrace

A clifftop perch gives this modern bar and brasserie a sweeping vista across Christchurch Bay to the Needles and the Isle of Wight. Inside, it is a buzzy split-level venue where high stools at the oyster bar allow you to catch the action in the open-plan kitchen. With a sublime view, plus an irresistible alfresco terrace to bring in the punters, lesser restaurants might slack off in the food department, but with head chef Pierre Chevillard directing culinary efforts, there's a clear Gallic accent in the kitchen's output. Fish and seafood are strong suits – perhaps a Breton-style fish soup with croûtons, garlic mayonnaise and gruyère cheese, followed by grilled sea bass fillet glazed with parmesan, and served with fennel, and orange butter sauce. Meats might encompass wild boar, slow-cooked with juniper and red wine and matched with sautéed wild mushrooms, and truffle oil-scented potato mousseline, and proceedings end with lemon crème brûlée and fresh raspberries.

Chef Pierre Chevillard **Owner** Michael Caddy **Seats** 90, Pr/dining room 8
Times 11-2.30/6-11, Closed D 25 Dec, 1 Jan **Prices** Prices not confirmed, Service optional **Wines** 2 bottles over £30, 52 bottles under £30, 16 by glass **Parking** 20
Notes Sunday L, Vegetarian available, Children welcome

■ **BASINGSTOKE** Map 5 SU65

Audleys Wood

◉◉ Modern British

tel: 01256 817555 & 0845 072 7405 *(Calls cost 7p per minute plus your phone company's access charge)* **Alton Rd RG25 2JT**
email: audleyswood@handpicked.co.uk **web:** www.handpickedhotels.co.uk/thesimondsroom
dir: *M3 junct 6. From Basingstoke take A339 towards Alton, hotel on right*

Local ingredients cooked with classical flair in a grand setting

This striking property was built as a private residence in the 1880s, in seven acres of grounds and woodland, and comes with all the trappings of a luxury country-house hotel. The main restaurant is the grand Simonds Room, the walls covered with heavy oak panelling hung with framed tapestries, with an imposing fireplace and ornate carved oak cornicing. A classical vein runs through the menu of otherwise modern British ideas. Fillet of halibut, for instance, gets the bonne femme treatment in a main course, served with Jerusalem artichoke, and copybook boulangère potatoes accompany a tender, flavourful cut of venison, served rare, along with silky-smooth red cabbage purée. Starters include an up-to-the-minute dish of lightly poached marinated mackerel fillet, served with al dente goats' cheese and potato cannelloni and a pickled clam, the plate dotted with drops of golden and red beetroot purée. The same beautiful balance is seen in deconstructed lemon meringue pie: a crumble base topped by parfait, droplets of curd adding tartness, with individually sculpted pieces of meringue and vanilla ice cream.

Times 7-9, Closed Sun-Mon, L all week

Oakley Hall Hotel

◉◉ Modern British

tel: 01256 783350 **Rectory Rd, Oakley RG23 7EL**
email: enquiries@oakleyhall-park.com **web:** www.oakleyhall-park.com
dir: *M3 junct 7, follow Basingstoke signs. In 500yds before lights turn left onto A30 towards Oakley, immediately right onto unclass road towards Oakley. In 3m left at T-junct into Rectory Rd. Left onto B3400. Hotel signed 1st on left*

Classically based cooking with Jane Austen connections

Jane Austen enthusiasts will have fun spotting references to Oakley Hall in her work. As a young woman, she was a frequent visitor, and its then matriarch, Mrs Bramston, found her way into the role of Lady Bertram in *Mansfield Park*. All new in 2014 was the Glasshouse restaurant, which takes its inspiration and name from Oakley's original such structure, designed by landscape gardener Edward Milner in 1850. It's open all day every day, and as well as breakfasts and afternoon tea, is the setting for classically-based British menus that draw many of their raw materials from the kitchen garden. Thai-spiced butternut soup with coriander oil vies with rabbit and pheasant terrine and quince chutney for starters, before mains follow on with well-handled prime cuts such as duck breast with dauphinoise in redcurrant sauce, hake fillet with king prawns and samphire on crab velouté, and traditional sirloin with roast cherry tomatoes and wild mushroom sauce. Chocoholics won't go unrewarded at dessert, but if you're looking for something lighter, consider poached pear in red wine syrup with cinnamon ice cream.

Chef Justin Mundy **Owner** Jon Huxford **Seats** 100, Pr/dining room 300
Times 12-2/6.30-9.30 **Prices** Starter £6.50-£8.50, Main £14.50-£24.95, Dessert £6.75-£9.50, Service optional **Wines** 87 bottles over £30, 11 bottles under £30, 8 by glass **Parking** 100 **Notes** Afternoon tea £22.95, Sunday L £21.95-£27.50, Vegetarian available, Children welcome

The Wellington Arms

◉◉ Modern British

tel: 0118 982 0110 **Baughurst Rd RG26 5LP**
email: hello@thewellingtonarms.com **web:** www.thewellingtonarms.com
dir: *M4 junct 12 follow Newbury signs on A4. At rdbt left signed Aldermaston. Through Aldermaston. Up hill, at 2nd rdbt 2nd exit signed Baughurst, left at T-junct, pub 1m on left*

Top pub food crafted from the most local of local produce

The Wellington Arms is a dining pub with a capital D. A good deal of what you eat will have found its way into the kitchen from the garden, and what isn't home-grown or home-reared won't have travelled very far. Jason King and Simon Page are passionate about what they do, and this is reflected in their quest to be as sustainable as possible. The old pub has scrubbed up very nicely indeed and looks as sharp as a pin these days: it is rustic, charming and spruce. There's a fire indoors on cooler days and, with its tiled floor and wooden tables, it's definitely at the rustic-chic end of the spectrum. Blackboards reveal what lies ahead. Twice-baked Marksbury cheddar soufflé sits on braised leeks, finished with a little cream and parmesan, or there might be fine duck liver and organic port parfait with home-made pickled shallots and chargrilled toast. Follow on with Grange Farm rib-eye with hand-cut chips and red wine jus, or baked fillet of cod (from Brixham) with oven-dried tomatoes, black olives and crushed anya potatoes, and finish with chocolate squidgy pudding with espresso ice cream.

Chef Jason King **Owner** Simon Page, Jason King **Seats** 40, Pr/dining room 18 **Times** 12-3/6-9.30, Closed D Sun **Prices** Fixed L 2 course fr £16, Starter £7-£14, Main £12-£24, Dessert £3.50-£8.50 **Wines** 45 bottles over £30, 21 bottles under £30, 9 by glass **Parking** 25 **Notes** Sunday L, Vegetarian available, Children welcome

Beaulieu Hotel

◉ British

tel: 023 8029 3344 **Beaulieu Rd SO42 7YQ**
email: beaulieu@newforesthotels.co.uk **web:** www.newforesthotels.co.uk
dir: *On B3056 between Lyndhurst & Beaulieu. Near Beaulieu Road railway station*

Modern British cooking in the New Forest

Built of warm red bricks, the former coaching inn is in its own landscaped grounds within open heathland on the edge of the village. It's a smartly appointed sort of place, guests' comfort of primary concern, the traditionally styled dining room no exception. Service might be on the formal side, but staff know what they're doing. The kitchen's a busy place, baking bread daily in-house and relying on local and therefore seasonal ingredients. Tea-smoked pigeon and apple salad with beetroot sorbet is something of a signature starter, and might be followed by properly timed, crisp-skinned pan-fried sea bass interestingly complemented by chorizo, olives and

pepper relish, or Hampshire lamb cooked two ways served with bubble-and-squeak and pea purée. Pastry work is clearly a forte, judging by a light and fresh base for velvety lemon tart with a novel basil and champagne sorbet.

Chef Michael Mckell **Owner** New Forest Hotels **Seats** 60, Pr/dining room 80 **Times** 5.30-9.30, Closed L all week **Prices** Prices not confirmed, Service optional **Wines** 8 bottles over £30, 30 bottles under £30, 8 by glass **Parking** 60 **Notes** Vegetarian available, Children welcome

The Master Builder's at Buckler's Hard

◉ Modern British NEW

tel: 01590 616253 **Buckler's Hard SO42 7XB**
email: enquiries@themasterbuilders.co.uk **web:** www.themasterbuilders.co.uk
dir: *From M27 junct 2 follow signs to Beaulieu. Turn left onto B3056, then 1st left, hotel in 2m*

Unpretentious modern cooking and river views

The master builder's commemorated in the name of this cosily rustic 18th-century hotel once built ships for Nelson's fleet on the grassy areas running down to the River Beaulieu. Part of the Beaulieu Estate, the place is handy for New Forest walks and the petrolhead pleasures within the National Motor Museum. When a pitstop is required, the place offers the pubby Yachtsman's Bar and brasserie-style dining in the Riverview Restaurant. With those tranquil watery views as a backdrop, you can expect sound modern British cooking based on well-sourced local ingredients – home-made linguine with Dorset crab, lemon and thyme oil as a starter, then a ballotine of local pheasant pointed up with tart blackberry jus and matched with roast root vegetables, buttery kale and mash. For dessert, there's a deconstructed take on Millionaire's shortbread, or you might go for a savoury finish with a plate of impeccably local cheeses.

Chef Edward Cracknell **Owner** Hillbrooke Hotels **Seats** Pr/dining room 40 **Times** 12-3/7-9.30 **Prices** Fixed L 2 course £18.75-£29.75, Starter £6-£9, Main £17.50-£48.90, Dessert £7-£7.50 **Wines** 34 bottles over £30, 20 bottles under £30, 12 by glass **Parking** 60 **Notes** Sunday L £19.95-£23.50, Vegetarian available, Children welcome

The Montagu Arms Hotel

◉◉◉ – see page 108

Monty's Inn

◉ Traditional British NEW

tel: 01590 614986 & 612324 **Palace Ln SO42 7ZL**
email: reservations@montaguarmshotel.co.uk
dir: *M27 junct 2, follow signs to Beaulieu*

Comforting English food in a 17th-century hotel

If you're not up for the full-dress gastronomic blowout in the smart 17th-century Montagu Arms Hotel's Terrace Restaurant, Monty's Inn will sort you out with hearty, unpretentious food that doesn't try to punch above its weight. The place goes for a clubby look involving wood-panelled walls, wooden floors and unclothed tables – a posh country pub setting that chimes with a crowd-pleasing menu that opens with a home-made local pork Scotch egg with spiced apple sauce and dressed rocket. The coast isn't too far off, so fish is well represented by pan-roasted sea bass with lemon fondant potatoes, broccoli, shallot purée, crispy mussels and red wine jus, while meaty mains could offer ginger beer-glazed roast duck breast with a leg meat spring roll, bok choy and duck fat potatoes. For pudding, there's dark chocolate mousse with cherry sorbet.

Chef Robert McClean **Owner** Greenclose **Seats** 50 **Times** 12-2.30/6.30-9.30, Closed D 24-26 Dec, 1 Jan **Prices** Starter £5.75-£10.95, Main £11.75-£21.95, Dessert £1.95-£5.50, Service optional **Wines** 11 bottles over £30, 18 bottles under £30, 8 by glass **Parking** 40 **Notes** Sunday L £13.95, Vegetarian available, Children welcome

BRANSGORE
Map 5 SZ19

The Three Tuns
British, European

tel: 01425 672232 **Ringwood Rd BH23 8JH**
email: threetunsinn@btconnect.com **web:** www.threetunsinn.com
dir: On A35 at junct for Walkford/Highcliffe follow Bransgore signs, 1.5m, restaurant on left

Appealing varied menu in a traditional thatched inn

Picture this: a picture-postcard 17th-century thatched gem deep in the New Forest National Park which is a delight in summer, festooned with flowers, and cosy in winter, with blazing log fires warming the low beamed bar and dining areas. That's The Three Tuns, which draws foodies and forest visitors for its charm and character, its buzzy atmosphere, the glorious sun-drenched garden, and an eclectic menu that lists pub classics alongside adventurous modern British gastro-pub dishes. Using game from surrounding estates, locally-shot venison, farm meats and fish delivered to door, the seasonal menu kicks off with a robust Sicilian fish soup full of chunks of sea bass and red mullet and the Mediterranean flavours of fennel, peppers and tomatoes. Follow with Landes chicken roasted with garlic and paired with snails, fondant potato, tomato salad and rocket pesto. To finish, chocolate mousse comes with hazelnut macaroons and popping candy for a bit of fun.

Chef Colin Nash **Owner** Nigel Glenister **Seats** 60, Pr/dining room 50
Times 12-2.15/6-9.15, Closed 25-26 & 31 Dec, D 5 Nov **Prices** Prices not confirmed, Service optional **Wines** 3 bottles over £30, 24 bottles under £30, 11 by glass **Parking** 50 **Notes** Sunday L, Vegetarian available, Children welcome

BROCKENHURST
Map 5 SU30

The Balmer Lawn Hotel
Modern British

tel: 01590 623116 & 625725 **Lyndhurst Rd SO42 7ZB**
email: info@balmerlawnhotel.com **web:** www.balmerlawnhotel.com
dir: Take A337 towards Brockenhurst, hotel on left after 'Welcome to Brockenhurst' sign

Fine dining at grand New Forest hotel

Now that shooting the wildlife is off the agenda, this imposing pavilion-style Victorian hunting lodge in a charming New Forest setting trades as a friendly, family-run operation aimed more at pampering or business with its excellent spa, sports and conference facilities. Beresford's restaurant is the fine-dining option, an impressive, grandly-proportioned space recently made over in a decluttered contemporary style – wooden flooring and high-backed seats at unclothed darkwood tables. Expect modern cooking with a healthy showing of prime-quality,

The Montagu Arms Hotel ❀❀❀

BEAULIEU
Map 5 SU30

Modern European **NOTABLE WINE LIST**
tel: 01590 612324 **Palace Ln SO42 7ZL**
email: reception@montaguarmshotel.co.uk **web:** www.montaguarmshotel.co.uk
dir: From M27 junct 2 take A326 & B3054 for Beaulieu

Refined country-house cooking with a modern touch

With the famous motor museum on hand and the New Forest all around, The Montagu Arms has a lot going for it in the location stakes. It's a brick-built country house of the 17th century, its final wing added only in the 1920s, clad in climbing foliage and with an old-fashioned inn sign out front, as though ironically belying the sumptuous country-hotel comforts within. Had it come to a land invasion in the last war, The Montagu stood ready as a firing position for the Home Guard. The Terrace Restaurant, a wood-panelled room with attractive views over the gardens, is the focus of Matthew Tomkinson's high-flying culinary production. Special dinners for shoot parties are a feature, and much of the organically-grown produce is sourced from the hotel's own well-maintained kitchen garden. Anglo-French dishes of refined panache show some innovative touches, but with commendable restraint. A starter serving of slow-cooked oxtail in lasagne with celeriac purée and horseradish cream is an enterprising idea, and even the now familiar combination of scallops and cauliflower purée emerges as something interesting again, with its garnish of julienned apple and a velouté scented with coriander and cumin. Great depth of impact is conjured from prime materials such as Lymington sea bass in home-cured ham with red wine sauce, or Welsh lamb with a falafel and roast aubergine. A truffled breast of free-range chicken has plenty to say for itself too, along with its dauphine potatoes and fondue of Tunworth cheese. Fine English and French farmhouse cheeses roll round on the trolley as a possible extra to a dessert such as praline soufflé with chocolate ice cream, or zestily upstanding shortbread-based lemon meringue pie with poached orange and a bright green basil sorbet.

Chef Matthew Tomkinson **Owner** Greenclose Ltd, Mr Leach **Seats** 60, Pr/dining room 32 **Times** 12-2.30/7-9.30, Closed Mon, L Tue **Prices** Fixed L 2 course £25, Fixed D 3 course £75, Tasting menu £95, Service optional **Wines** 24 bottles over £30, 4 bottles under £30, 16 by glass **Parking** 50 **Notes** D 3 course ALC £70, Sunday L £29.50-£34.50, Vegetarian available, Children 11 yrs+

often local, materials – perhaps confit rabbit rillettes with plum ketchup and home-made pumpernickel bread, followed by roast saddle of lamb with beetroot mash, roasted butternut squash purée and curly kale, or 28 day-matured Hampshire steaks from the grill with confit tomatoes, fat chips, mushrooms and watercress. Inventive endings run to 'textures of milk and honey' or classics like treacle tart with clotted cream.

Chef Chris Wheeldon **Owner** Mr C Wilson **Seats** 80, Pr/dining room 100 **Times** 12.30-2.30/7-9.30 **Prices** Fixed L 2 course £9.95-£15.95, Starter £6.50-£12, Main £15-£32, Dessert £6.50-£8 **Wines** 30 bottles over £30, 20 bottles under £30, 10 by glass **Parking** 100 **Notes** Sunday L £9.95-£24.95, Vegetarian available, Children welcome

Careys Manor Hotel & Senspa

◉◉ Modern British

tel: 01590 623551 **Lyndhurst Rd SO42 7RH**
email: zengarden@senspa.co.uk **web:** www.thezengarden.co.uk
dir: M27 junct 2, follow Fawley/A326 signs. Continue over 3 rdbts, at 4th rdbt right lane signed Lyndhurst/A35. Follow A337 (Lymington/Brockenhurst)

Imaginative cooking in the New Forest

Careys Manor, the original building dating from 1888, is in a delightful spot in the New Forest. It has three eateries: a French bistro, the Thai Zen Garden, and the cream of the crop, the Manor Restaurant, where the skilled kitchen team applies some culinary wizardry to fresh seasonal produce. Seared pigeon breast with red wine reduction, sweet potato and cumin purée and rocket sounds mainstream enough, but an alternative may be butter-poached sea trout with seaweed-marinated mooli and cucumber dressing. Technical precision is evident throughout, and combinations thoughtful. Thus, confit pork belly comes with black pudding purée, potato gratin and a sage jus, and slices of roast Dorset rump of veal are plated on spinach and accompanied by pommes Anna, caramelised onion purée and rich thyme-infused gravy. Fish gets a decent showing: perhaps glazed salmon fillet creatively partnered by saffron gratin with kale, caper and raisin purée, prawn shavings and lemon butter. Bread and extras get nods of approval, and desserts are as well made as everything else, among them perhaps honey parfait with raspberry sorbet.

Times 12-2.30/7-10, Closed D Mon

THE PIG

◉◉ British V 🍷NOTABLE WINE LIST

tel: 01590 622354 **Beaulieu Rd SO42 7QL**
email: info@thepighotel.com **web:** www.thepighotel.com
dir: M27 junct 2, follow A326 Lyndhurst, then A337 Brockenhurst onto B3055 Beaulieu Road. 1m on left up private road

Home-grown and foraged food in a New Forest hotel

The Pig truly is a restaurant with rooms for our times, where cocktails are served in old jam jars and you can get a massage in the old potting shed. Surrounded by the

wilds of the New Forest, the main passion is for home-grown and foraged ingredients, and there's no playing to the gallery here – check out the walled kitchen garden, the wood-fired oven and the 25-mile policy for ingredients on the menu. It's a buzzy place with a retro interior, and the Victorian greenhouse dining room provides an informal setting for the serving of rustic dishes with the focus on flavour. There's simple and careful execution in a starter of Sopley Farm asparagus with pickled quail's eggs, pancetta and a deeply-flavoured lemon dressing. Follow that with rump of Hampshire lamb (a fine piece of meat, too) with broad beans, peas and baby onions, or pollock with Hampshire chorizo and cockles. The careful and considered cooking continues with a dessert of Cox's apple tart with cider apple and Dorset clotted cream ice cream.

Chef James Golding **Owner** Robin Hutson **Seats** 85, Pr/dining room 14 **Times** 12-2.30/6.30-9.30 **Prices** Starter £5-£8, Main £14-£18, Dessert £7 **Wines** 59 bottles over £30, 38 bottles under £30, 14 by glass **Parking** 40 **Notes** Sunday L £16-£17, Children welcome

Rhinefield House

◉◉ Modern British

tel: 01590 622922 & 0845 072 7516 *(Calls cost 7p per minute plus your phone company's access charge)* **Rhinefield Rd SO42 7QB**
email: rhinefieldhouse@handpicked.co.uk **web:** www.handpickedhotels.co.uk/rhinefieldhouse
dir: A35 towards Christchurch. 3m from Lyndhurst, turn left to Rhinefield, 1.5m to hotel

Modern cooking in a stunning Victorian mansion

Rhinefield cropped up on Wordsworth's poetic gazetteer in the 1790s, though he didn't live to see the present magnificence spring up in the late Victorian era. A Tudor-Gothic hybrid architecturally, the interiors are awash with finely crafted mouldings, copperwork and beautiful examples of the lavatorialist's art, plus Grinling Gibbons carvings, ceilings by Fragonard, and a room modelled on the Alhambra. James Whitesmith steps manfully up to the plate in these surroundings to captivate what remains of your attention with some eye-catching modern cooking. Scallops with sea trout mousse and pickled baby carrots in sauce vierge might set the pace, and be succeeded by cod in Caesar sauce with clams and almonds, or rack of lamb with dauphinoise and rhubarb under a froth of sheep's milk. Dishes can sometimes feel a little over-engineered – you can have all the froths and foams in the world, but getting pork to crackle properly is just as important – but there is no lack of conceptual energy nonetheless. Desserts might include a raspberry version of crème brûlée with raspberry texture variations, served with rhubarb and ginger ice cream.

Chef James Whitesmith **Owner** Hand Picked Hotels **Seats** 58, Pr/dining room 12 **Times** 12-5/7-10 **Prices** Fixed D 3 course £37, Starter £10.50-£12.50, Main £18.50-£28.50, Dessert £11-£15, Service optional **Wines** 151 bottles over £30, 14 bottles under £30, 18 by glass **Parking** 150 **Notes** Sunday L £24.95, Vegetarian available, Children welcome

Find out more about how we assess for Rosette awards on page 9

BROCKENHURST *continued*

The Zen Garden Restaurant

Thai

tel: 01590 623219 & 623551 **The SenSpa, Careys Manor Hotel, Lyndhurst Rd SO42 7RH**
email: zengarden@senspa.co.uk
dir: *A337 from Lyndhurst signed Lymington, Brockenhurst, within Careys Manor Hotel*

Vibrant Thai cooking in a spa hotel

If you go down to the woods today you're in for a big surprise, for within the SenSpa at Careys Manor Hotel in the New Forest is a smart Thai eatery. The Zen Garden Restaurant certainly makes a style statement with its gold columns, bamboo ceiling and darkwood tables and chairs, and the kitchen takes an ethical approach by sourcing local and organic materials for the traditional menus. Classic tom yam soup kick-starts the palate with its sour, fiery and fragrant cocktail of tiger prawns, mushrooms, chilli, lemongrass, galangal and kaffir lime leaves, or you might get going with crispy fried soft-shelled crab with garlic and pink peppercorn sauce. Main-course wok-seared beef comes with red curry paste, beans, red cabbage, tumicuni ginger and chilli, and proceedings end with a sharp, cleansing dessert of pineapple carpaccio with agave syrup, fresh basil and coconut ice cream.

Times 12-2.30/7-10, Closed D Mon

BROOK   Map 5 SU21

The Bell Inn

Modern British

tel: 023 8081 2214 **SO43 7HE**
email: bell@bramshaw.co.uk **web:** www.bellinnbramshaw.co.uk
dir: *M27 junct 1 onto B3079, hotel 1.5m on right*

Attractively presented modern cooking at a New Forest inn

There can't be many places that can claim to have continued in the ownership of the same family since George III was on the throne, as The Bell can boast. It's in a picturesque New Forest village not far from Lyndhurst, and is a bit more than a simple country inn in that it lays claim to a pair of golf courses. The interior looks the modernised rustic part, with blackboard menus and log fires in winter, and plenty of gracefully presented local produce on offer. A serving of seared scallops with pickled cauliflower and tea-soaked raisins might kick things off, as the preamble to loin, confit belly and crisped hock of local pork, served with mash, greens and pineapple purée. Finish with smoothly textured, sharply zesty lemon cream garnished with crunchy meringue, candied lemon and yogurt sorbet. A fine selection of cheeses from independent producers, served with biscuits and chutney, is a heartening sight.

Chef James Burger **Owner** The Crosthwaite Eyre family **Seats** 60, Pr/dining room 40 **Times** 12-3/6.30-9.30 **Prices** Starter £5.95-£7.50, Main £12.50-£23.50, Dessert £5.95-£8.95, Service optional **Wines** 21 bottles over £30, 22 bottles under £30, 13 by glass **Parking** 40 **Notes** Sunday L £9.95-£29.95, Vegetarian available, Children welcome

BURLEY   Map 5 SU20

Moorhill House Hotel

Modern, Traditional British

tel: 01425 403285 **BH24 4AG**
email: moorhill@newforesthotels.co.uk **web:** www.newforesthotels.co.uk
dir: *Exit A31 signed Burley Drive, through village, turn right opposite cricket pitch*

Well-executed British dishes at a New Forest hotel

Penetrating deep into the ancient woodland of the New Forest is as good a start as any for a few days away, or even just a meal, and Moorhill's location, near the pretty village of Burley, admirably fits the bill. Sitting in its own handsome gardens, it's done out in light, attractive country house style within, with log fires for the toasting of toes in winter. In the newly refurbished dining room, straightforward but well-executed British dishes are Ben Cartwright's forte, so expect to start with devilled sardines on fennel-seed toast with cherry tomato and basil compote. Move on to slow-roast pork belly with glazed apple and sautéed Savoy cabbage, sauced with the famous local Burley cider, or grilled haddock with chorizo and chickpea cassoulet. Cockle-warming puddings include a spiced rum parfait with ginger biscuits and coffee sauce, and black treacle and almond tart with orange ice cream.

Times 5.30-9.30, Closed L Mon-Sat

CADNAM   Map 5 SU21

Bartley Lodge Hotel

Traditional British

tel: 023 8081 2248 **Lyndhurst Rd SO40 2NR**
email: bartley@newforesthotels.co.uk **web:** www.newforesthotels.co.uk
dir: *M27 junct 1, A337, follow signs for Lyndhurst. Hotel on left*

Elegant surroundings for country-house cooking

The Grade II listed Bartley Lodge has eight acres of precious Hampshire countryside all to itself, with a croquet on the lawn and an indoor swimming pool among its attractions. The 18th-century house has hung onto many original features, and there's a relaxed and professional attitude all round. The 'flexible dining' approach means the menu is available throughout the hotel, which extends to the Crystal Restaurant with its elegant centrepiece chandelier and delicate Wedgwood blue and gold colour scheme, or the cosy bar. The menu deals in feel-good flavours and simple presentations, so you might start with wild and button mushrooms with bacon and cheese on bruschetta, following on with something as homely as lasagne or Ringwood ale-battered fish and chips, or opt for the more ambitious ballotine of sea trout with horseradish mash and a caviar and leek cream. Finish with a lime and mango pannacotta.

Chef Stephen Sutton **Owner** New Forest Hotels **Seats** 60, Pr/dining room 90 **Times** 5.30-9.30 **Prices** Prices not confirmed, Service optional **Wines** 8 bottles over £30, 32 bottles under £30, 8 by glass **Parking** 90 **Notes** Sunday L, Vegetarian available, Children welcome

DOGMERSFIELD
Map 5 SU75

Four Seasons Hotel Hampshire

◉◉ British v

tel: 01252 853000 & 853100 **Dogmersfield Park, Chalky Ln RG27 8TD**
email: reservations.ham@fourseasons.com **web:** www.fourseasons.com/hampshire
dir: M3 junct 5 onto A287 Farnham. After 1.5m take left to Dogmersfield, hotel 0.6m
on left

Fine-tuned contemporary cooking in a grand Georgian manor

In keeping with the upscale brand's house style, you'll be treated like royalty and
pampered to within an inch of your life in this grand red-brick Georgian mansion.
Set within the expansive acreages of the Dogmersfield Estate, there's a spa, of
course, plus handsome period features – a sweeping staircase, ornate plasterwork
and glitzy chandeliers. The dining options include a bistro and café, but the main
event is the Seasons restaurant, a light-filled space with French windows and an
upscale, gently contemporary sheen. The team in the kitchen keeps things
seasonal, drawing on the estate and nearby suppliers to deliver well-crafted and
dynamic modern European-accented food. You might start with a soft-boiled duck's
egg with girolles, glazed asparagus and a glossy duck emulsion, followed by roast
beef tenderloin paired with oxtail-filled rigatoni, crispy potato, organic mushrooms
and bordelaise sauce. Fishy mains could be pan-seared turbot with brown butter,
spinach and basil purée and bouillabaisse jus. For a satisfying finish, go for
something like crème brûlée infused with Hampshire lavender.

Chef James Dugan **Owner** Four Seasons Hotels & Resorts **Seats** 100, Pr/dining room
24 **Times** 6-10.30, Closed Mon, L Tue-Sat, D Sun **Wines** 75 bottles over £30, 15 by
glass **Parking** 100 **Notes** Sunday L £55, Children 8 yrs+ D

DROXFORD
Map 5 SU61

Bakers Arms

◉ Traditional British

tel: 01489 877533 **High St SO32 3PA**
email: adam@thebakersarmsdroxford.com
dir: Off A32

Favourites and fancier in a homely Hampshire pub

The Bakers Arms is a whitewashed pub in a small village with a warmly welcoming
atmosphere generated by hands-on young staff, an open fire, ceiling beams, rugs
on floors of parquet, stone and concrete and dark half-panelling. The regularly-
changing menu (with favourites like sausage and mash with onion gravy remaining
constant) concentrates on great British traditions with forays further afield – pub
grub this is not. Beautifully made smoked ham hock terrine is served with vibrant
ale and onion chutney, to be followed by crisp-skinned pan-fried sea bass fillet, of
melt-in-the-mouth consistency, on couscous with roast vegetables and coriander
oil, or pan-fried kidneys with pancetta and horseradish mash. Unusually for a pub,
desserts – among them perhaps orange and lemon cake with clotted cream, or
white chocolate and raspberry cheesecake – are listed with recommended
pudding wines.

Chef Adam Cordery **Owner** Adam & Anna Cordery **Seats** 45
Times 11.45-3/6-11, Closed D Sun **Prices** Fixed L 2 course fr £15, Fixed D 2 course fr
£15, Starter £5.50-£8.50, Main £11-£20, Dessert £6, Service optional **Wines** 12
bottles over £30, 23 bottles under £30, 13 by glass **Parking** 30 **Notes** Sunday L £15,
Vegetarian available, Children welcome

EMSWORTH
Map 5 SU70

Fat Olives

◉◉ British, Mediterranean

tel: 01243 377914 **30 South St PO10 7EH**
email: info@fatolives.co.uk
dir: In town centre, 1st right after Emsworth Square, 100yds towards the Quay.
Restaurant on left with public car park opposite

Locally-inspired inventive modern cooking near the quay

A 17th-century fishermen's cottage just a few steps from the quayside of pretty
Emsworth harbour supplies the setting for Lawrence and Julia Murphy's smart
brasserie, which ticks all the right boxes for the faithful foodies who have kept it
buzzing for over a decade. The stripped-out interior of cream walls, bare wooden
floors and unclothed tables is as unvarnished and honest as the food. Lawrence
lets the excellent raw materials do the talking, helped by a judicious hand to ensure
spot-on accuracy, and a gentle whiff of the Mediterranean. The menu is an
appetising fusion of modern, well thought through ideas. It might take in roast
breast and confit leg of quail with chorizo-spiked cassoulet, then move on to
perfectly-timed silver mullet with Puy lentils, neatly balanced by the tartness of
salsa verde. Or you might be tempted by a more Brit-influenced and resolutely local
plate of South Downs pork loin teamed with a faggot, quince, and trotter sauce. At
the end, vanilla pannacotta comes with raspberry coulis and crunchy oat biscuits.

Chef Lawrence Murphy **Owner** Lawrence & Julia Murphy **Seats** 25
Times 12-2.30/7-9.30, Closed 1 wk Xmas, 1 wk Mar, 2 wks Jun, Sun-Mon
Prices Fixed L 2 course fr £18.50, Starter £6.25-£10.95, Main £15.75-£23.50,
Dessert £6.75-£7.95, Service optional **Wines** 23 bottles over £30, 24 bottles
under £30, 8 by glass **Parking** Opposite restaurant **Notes** Vegetarian available,
Children 8 yrs+

36 on the Quay

◉◉◉ see page 202

FAREHAM
Map 5 SU50

Solent Hotel & Spa

◉ Modern British, European

tel: 01489 880000 **Rookery Av, Whiteley PO15 7AJ**
email: solent@shirehotels.com **web:** www.shirehotels.com
dir: M27 junct 9, hotel on Solent Business Park

Sound brasserie cooking in a relaxed atmosphere

The Shire group's contemporary spa hotel in Whiteley near Fareham has been fine-
tooled for relaxation, whether your preferred element be pool, massage table or
dining room. The last is a compact space at the far end of the bar, with smartly
clothed tables, low lighting and candles. A glass wine store reflects the heartening
prospect of a serious wine list. The cooking takes a brasserie approach, with
international classics, pasta dishes, steaks from the chargrill, and seasonal daily
specials. Grainy-textured mushroom soup topped with fried mushrooms and pea
shoots gets things off to a hearty start, or there may be tiger prawns and chilli dip,
or smoked salmon with beetroot and horseradish crème fraîche. Crisp-skinned sea
bass for main is timed well and comes with a warm Niçoise salad, while sticky
toffee pudding in hot treacle sauce with vanilla ice cream won't lack for takers at
the finish.

Chef Peter Williams **Owner** Shire Hotels **Seats** 130, Pr/dining room 40 **Times** 12-9.30,
All-day dining, Closed L Sat **Prices** Fixed L 2 course £19.95, Starter £2.75-£8.95,
Main £11.95-£59, Dessert £6.25-£13.50, Service optional **Wines** 15 by glass
Parking 200 **Notes** All day menu, Sunday L £19.95-£21.95, Vegetarian available,
Children welcome

FARNBOROUGH
Map 5 SU85

Aviator

◎◎ Modern European V

tel: 01252 555890 **Farnborough Rd GU14 6EL**
email: brasserie@aviatorbytag.com **web:** www.aviatorbytag.com
dir: *A325 to Aldershot, continue for 3m. Hotel on right*

Aviation-themed brasserie dining from the charcoal grill

The TAG timepiece manufacturer's aviation-themed hotel has landed on the Hampshire-Surrey border, in the vicinity of the celebrated air show at Farnborough. Enjoy the aerial action from the Sky Bar, but don't forget to schedule a layover in the Brasserie, where stars of the silver screen watch over proceedings. The drill is uncomplicated modern brasserie food centred on a repertoire of classic cuts of steak, done on the charcoal grill and served with béarnaise, bordelaise or peppercorn sauces. If your tastes extend to the very meaty, you might start with a portion of jugged hare and horseradish mash, but a gentler run-up is provided by shellfish in chickpea velouté, or goats' cheese and potato terrine with red onion purée and apple. Non-charcoaled mains include lemon sole with kohlrabi and pickled samphire, and the safe landing is achieved by means of blackberry mousse on cinnamon sponge with vanilla ice cream.

Chef Adam Fargin **Owner** TAG **Seats** 120, Pr/dining room 8 **Times** 12-2/6.30-10.30 **Prices** Fixed L 3 course £23, Fixed D 3 course £35, Tasting menu fr £65, Starter £7-£10, Main £16.50-£24, Dessert £8 **Wines** 44 bottles over £30, 18 bottles under £30, 16 by glass **Parking** 169 **Notes** Tasting menu with wine £95, Sunday L £25, Children welcome

HAMBLE-LE-RICE
Map 5 SU40

The Bugle

◎ Modern British

tel: 023 8045 3000 **High St SO31 4HA**
email: manager@buglehamble.co.uk
dir: *M27 junct 8 to Hamble-Le-Rice. In village follow signs to foreshore*

Traditional and modern fare in an ancient riverside inn

Having stood here in one incarnation or another for around 700 years, as ferry-house, cab-hire office and rural inn, The Bugle is staying put, despite an attempt to have it demolished a few years ago. Its carefully restored interiors with their solid brickwork, bare floorboards, low ceilings and beams are exactly what a country inn should look like, while the kitchen offers a clever mix of pub stalwarts and modern dishes that are in tune with present-day requirements. Fish and chips, Sunday roasts and sandwiches will keep traditionalists happy, while the gastro brigade delight in the likes of pressed rabbit and prune terrine with pickled turnip to start, followed by bream fillet with potato salad, creamed leeks and kale, or braised lamb with confit shallots and parsnip purée in rosemary jus. Extras include a tempting bubble-and-squeak cake, and finishers are rewarded with honey-spiced pear with pistachio ice cream and honeycomb, or dark chocolate terrine with boozy cherries and clotted cream.

Chef James Harrison **Owner** Ideal Leisure Ltd **Seats** 28, Pr/dining room 12 **Times** 12-2.30/6-9.30, Closed 25 Dec **Prices** Fixed L 2 course £15, Starter £5-£11.50, Main £12-£23, Dessert £5-£8, Service optional 10% **Wines** 14 bottles over £30, 26 bottles under £30, 12 by glass **Parking** Foreshore car park 50 yds **Notes** Sun prix fixe 2/3 course £16/£20, Sunday L £12-£14, Vegetarian available, Children welcome

36 on the Quay ◎◎◎

EMSWORTH
Map 5 SU70

Modern British, European

tel: 01243 375592 & 372257 **47 South St PO10 7EG**
email: info@36onthequay.co.uk **web:** www.36onthequay.co.uk
dir: *Last building on right in South St, which runs from square in centre of Emsworth*

Cooking of long-standing excellence on the harbour side

It's fair to say that Ramon and Karen Farthing put Emsworth on the map when they opened here what feels like a generation ago. Anticipating the present trend for venues with sea vistas well in advance, they created a chic restaurant with rooms (and one-bedroom cottage) from a 17th-century house on the quayside, the view of peaceably drifting boats a thoroughly relaxing backdrop to proceedings in the smartly attired dining room. Tables are got up in their best whites for a performance that takes the business of fine dining and drinking with serious enthusiasm. Tutored wine evenings are a regular feature. Ramon's cooking has developed in harmony with current fashion, and is presented in the form of a principal prix-fixe with four choices at each stage (three at lunch), or a five-course taster that, unusually, comes at a lower outlay than the carte. All the excitement of modern technique is here, as may be seen from a starter that teams hazelnut-crumbed seared scallops with fermented and roasted carrot in sea buckthorn dressing, or makes a spaghetti of kohlrabi, beans and shallots to go with a serving of lobster in lemon verbena-scented stock. Main courses depart from the beaten track with rabbit loin and leg rillettes, which come with salt-baked turnip, honey and mead gel and broad beans, while even the more classical treatment of roast aged sirloin with wild mushrooms is given a new spin with pumpkin in various guises — pickled, puréed and toasted seeds. British artisan cheeses with salted almonds and fruit are the alternative to one of the inventive desserts, which take in pear terrine with granola parfait, spiced biscuits, damson cream and a foam of pear liqueur.

Chef Ramon Farthing, Gary Pearce **Owner** Ramon & Karen Farthing **Seats** 45, Pr/dining room 12 **Times** 12-2/7-9.30, Closed 1st 2/3 wks Jan, 1 wk end May & Oct, 25-26 Dec, Sun-Mon **Prices** Prices not confirmed, Service optional **Wines** 7 by glass **Parking** Car park nearby **Notes** Tasting menu complete tables only 8 course, ALC menu £57.95, Vegetarian available, Children welcome

HAYLING ISLAND
Map 5 SU70

Langstone Hotel

◉◉ Modern British

tel: 023 9246 5011 **Northney Rd PO11 0NQ**
email: info@langstonehotel.co.uk **web:** www.langstonehotel.co.uk
dir: *From A27 signed Havant/Hayling Island follow A3023 across roadbridge onto Hayling Island & take sharp left on leaving bridge*

Creative spins on modern brasserie classics with views of the harbour

The Langstone is a contemporary hotel on the north shore of Hayling Island, enjoying sweeping views towards Chichester Harbour, easily accessed from Portsmouth. There are vivid colour schemes all over the show, except in the restaurant, where the neutral palette of beiges and light browns is discreet enough not to upstage the marine views through a curving wall of pillared windows. There is up-to-date brasserie cooking of real flair here, with some creative spins on modern classic ideas such as goats' cheese and beetroot, the latter element appearing in salt-baked, sweet-pickled, grilled and raw guises, along with goats' cheese mousse and a distant waft of elderflower. Mains run to curried cod with pearl barley and grilled leeks, or a bravura take on duck and cherries, with succulent breast and rillettes of the leg-meat, as well as a slice of potato terrine. A speciality steak menu woos traditionalists, while nothing could be more popular now than fairground treats to finish, as witness a texturally satisfying dish of peanut parfait covered in popcorn and chocolate peanuts.

Chef James Parsons **Owner** BDL Hotels **Seats** 120, Pr/dining room 120
Times 12.30-2/6.30-9.30 **Prices** Prices not confirmed, Service optional **Wines** 17 bottles over £30, 24 bottles under £30, 7 by glass **Parking** 220 **Notes** Sunday L, Vegetarian available, Children welcome

HIGHCLERE

The Yew Tree

◉◉ Modern British NEW

tel: 01635 253360 **Hollington Cross RG20 9SE**
email: info@theyewtree.co.uk **web:** www.theyewtree.co.uk
dir: *1m S of Highclere Village*

English classic cooking in a classic English pub

Here is a classic English country inn in a ravishing setting not far from Highclere Castle. Outdoor tables in the garden come with their own seafood bar in the summer months, and inside makes a comforting retreat on cold nights, with low-beamed ceilings, tartan upholstery and many little nooks. Traditional English cooking is the order of the day, overlaid with some flourishes from the modern repertoire. Cod and salmon fishcakes are gently seasoned with chilli and dressed in mango mayonnaise, potted beef comes with cornichons and melba toast, and local asparagus in season is topped with poached eggs and hollandaise. Roast lamb loin is spectacularly full of flavour, enhanced by chargrilled veg and a gutsy, garlicky salsa verde, while fish might be sparkling-fresh chalk-stream trout with new potatoes. A roll call of 'The Usual Suspects' will keep the fish-and-chips and burger brigade content. Cherry Bakewell is as good as it gets outside Derbyshire, matched with vanilla cream and cherry coulis, or there's lemon posset given savoury edge with walnut and rosemary biscotti.

Chef Simon Davis **Owner** Cirrus Inns **Seats** 68, Pr/dining room 12
Times 12-2.30/6.30-9.30 Closed D 25-26 Dec, 1 Jan **Prices** Starter £6-£11, Main £11-£28, Dessert £6-£8 **Wines** 45 bottles over £30, 17 bottles under £30, 14 by glass **Parking** 30 **Notes** Sushi night Thu, Sunday L £15-£18, Vegetarian available, Children welcome

LYMINGTON
Map 5 SZ39

The Elderflower Restaurant

◉◉ Modern British NEW

tel: 01590 676908 **4A Quay St SO41 3AS**
email: info@elderflowerrestaurant.co.uk
dir: *M27 junct for A337 Lyndhurst. At rdbt take 1st exit A31, follow A337 then B3054 Captains Row, left onto Nelson Pl then left onto Quay Rd*

Inspirational cooking full of bright ideas

Andrew and Marjolaine Du Bourg have set about bringing a new dimension of classy Anglo-French dining to Georgian Lymington. With flower baskets adorning the frontage on a cobbled street, and a low-ceilinged beamed interior with linened tables, they have created a restaurant with rooms that fits the character of the building as well as exploring the conceptual range of the modern British kitchen. Indian technique is brought productively into play for a starter of curried mussels with smoked tapioca, spiced cauliflower purée and shallot bhajis, while a clump of samphire adds a salty hit. Next up might be Jurassic Coast veal – the loin, liver and panko-crumbed sweetbreads – which comes with a casserole of chanterelles and butter beans and fried kale in an ingenious crayfish bisque. Other inspirationally bright ideas include trout with celeriac remoulade, clementine and mustard, and confit mallard leg with port-glazed beetroot and pickled squash in sour cherry jus. Crème brûlée gets a twist with puréed chestnut worked into the custard, alongside sherry-soaked raisins, clove ice cream and ginger crumb.

Chef Andrew Du Bourg **Owner** Andrew & Marjolaine Du Bourg **Seats** 40
Times 12-2.30/6.30-9.30, Closed Last wk Jan, Mon, D Sun **Prices** Tasting menu fr £42, Starter £7-£10.50, Main £15.50-£26, Dessert £7-£10.50 **Wines** 39 bottles over £30, 51 bottles under £30, 6 by glass **Parking** Quay car park **Notes** Sun champagne breakfast, Market tapas dishes £3.50-£8, Sunday L £3.50-£8.50, Vegetarian available, Children welcome

Stanwell House Hotel

◉◉ Modern European

tel: 01590 677123 **14-15 High St SO41 9AA**
email: enquiries@stanwellhouse.com **web:** www.stanwellhouse.com
dir: *M27 junct 1. follow signs to Lyndhurst into Lymington centre & High Street*

Modern seafood and bistro cookery at a historic address

General James Wolfe spent his last night in England at Stanwell, his cousin's home, before departing for the hostilities in Quebec in 1759. After a spell in the Victorian age as a young ladies' finishing-school, it became a hotel around the end of the last war. Enjoying the healthful airs of one of Hampshire's best-loved coastal towns, the restaurant, fronting the high street, is devoted to seafood specialities given the cosmopolitan treatment. Expect to start with a crab and pink grapefruit cocktail, or mackerel on toast with elderflower, gooseberries and shallots. Move on to a majestic pairing of fried red mullet and braised chicken wing, with stir-fried noodles, Asian coleslaw and carrot and ginger purée. A secondary dining option, the Bistro, offers the likes of hearty game consommé with crispy duck, and a comprehensive main course of pork cuts, including a smoked potato and black pudding croquette, in Calvados jus. What could be more alluring to finish than a spin on Pina Colada, comprising coconut parfait, Szechuan-spiced pineapple and a generous hand with the rum?

Times 12-3/6-10

The Glasshouse

@@ Modern British

tel: 023 8028 6129 & 8028 3677 **Pikes Hill, Romsey Rd SO43 7AS**
email: enquiries@theglasshousedining.co.uk **web:** www.theglasshousedining.co.uk
dir: *M27 junct 1, A337 towards Lyndhurst. In village, with police station & courts on right, take 1st right into Pikes Hill*

Contemporary-style restaurant with well-judged cooking

On the outskirts of Lyndhurst, this hotel, a Georgian dower house, has had a thoroughly contemporary makeover, creating a hugely stylish environment. The flexible menu covers a lot of ground, from bar nibbles and light bites to burger with chunky chips as well as more ambitious fare, such as a well-conceived starter of quail three ways (poached breast, confit leg and a mini Scotch egg) with a herb salad, creamed leeks and Albufera sauce, all elements complementing each other to make a most enjoyable dish. A piscine opener is crisp sea bass fillet with a warm vegetable salad and sunblush tomato in olive dressing. The kitchen generally mines the modern British vein, seen in seared veal tongue with spicy blackberry ketchup, sticky baby onions and watercress, and effectively pairing a main course of seared salmon fillet with a dressing of lime, basil and sour cream and serving it with smoked haddock and potato brandade. Puddings run the gamut from berry millefeuille with raspberry coulis to rich double-layered chocolate pavé balanced by milk sorbet.

Chef Darren Appleby **Owner** New Forest Hotels **Seats** 40, Pr/dining room 10
Times 12-2.30/5.30-9.30 **Prices** Fixed L 2 course £15.50-£18.50, Fixed D 3 course £18.50-£25.50, Starter £6.95-£7.95, Main £12.90-£19.95, Dessert £5.50-£7.50, Service optional **Wines** 16 bottles over £30, 26 bottles under £30, 2 by glass **Parking** 60 **Notes** Sunday L £15.50-£18.50, Vegetarian available, Children 12 yrs+

Hartnett Holder & Co

@@@ – *see opposite and advert on page 206*

Verveine Fishmarket Restaurant

@@ Seafood **NEW**

tel: 01590 642176 **98 High St, Lymington SO41 0QE**
email: info@verveine.co.uk
dir: *A337, B3058, Church Hill. Left onto High St, 200 mtrs on right*

Ultra-modern village seafood cookery

Three miles west of Lymington, the village of Milford on Sea is home to David Wykes' seafood restaurant, which doubles upfront as a fishmonger. At the back is the intimate, elegant dining room, reached by passing the kitchen, from which chef himself often emerges to bring your dish to table. Inspiration comes from the process approach of contemporary cooking, with in-house smoking, bain-marie cooking and dehydrating in evidence, and a vein of wit runs through it all. Choose your fish, then match it with one of the accompaniment options from the blackboard. A chunk of monkfish given the Madras treatment arrives with spiced carrot purée, plump raisins and sous-vide potato. Other possibilities are founded on East Asian seasonings, chorizo and pickled peppers, or slow-cooked pork cheek with burnt apple. Scallops with their corals to start come in a laver bread, oat and pancetta porridge (inspired by Fat Duck's snail porridge), dressed in 50-year-old balsamic, while dessert looks to Roald Dahl's Violet Beauregarde for a blueberry study incorporating pannacotta, sorbet, tuile, foam, and even some fresh berries. Throw in granary fig bread to start and picturesquely creative canapés to complete a terrific meal.

Chef David Wykes **Owner** David Wykes **Seats** 32 **Times** 12-2/6.30-10, Closed 25 Dec-18 Jan, Sun-Mon **Prices** Fixed L 2 course fr £17, Tasting menu £42-£135, Starter £8.95-£13.50, Dessert fr £8.50, Service optional **Wines** 24 bottles over £30, 27 bottles under £30, 6 by glass **Parking** On street, car park 200 mtrs **Notes** Vegetarian available, Children welcome

Chewton Glen Hotel & Spa

@@ Modern British V NOTABLE WINE LIST

tel: 01425 282212 **Christchurch Rd BH25 6QS**
email: reservations@chewtonglen.com **web:** www.chewtonglen.com
dir: *A35 (Lyndhurst) turn left through Walkford, 4th left into Chewton Farm Rd*

Classy cooking showing great technique in luxury country-house hotel

There's something quintessentially English about Chewton Glen. It's not just the croquet lawn, or the 130 acres of prime countryside it inhabits, or even the elegant interiors: it's the whole package, from the valet parking to the understated magnificence of the house itself. Whether you are drawn by the desire to play golf on the nine-hole course, or prefer being pampered in the spa, Chewton Glen is a luxurious bolt-hole. When it comes to eating, the Dining Room stays on message, occupying a series of refined spaces with ravishing floral displays and a contemporary finish (it's elegant, but up-to-date). The menu aims to satisfy with an output that deals in classic British and European combinations, while incorporating some global flavours. Start with monkfish cheeks in tempura batter, served with soba noodle salad, or ballotine of duck liver matched with roasted apple and vanilla purée, and move on to saddle of venison with pickled trompettes and chestnut purée, or Tuscan-style fish stew. For dessert, pear and blackberry clafoutis comes with lemon verbena ice cream.

Chef Luke Matthews **Owner** Chewton Glen Hotels Ltd **Seats** 164, Pr/dining room 70
Times 12-2.30/6-10 **Prices** Fixed L 3 course £25, Tasting menu £70, Starter £9-£23, Main £21-£39, Dessert £10 **Wines** 1414 bottles over £30, 49 bottles under £30, 45 by glass **Parking** 150 **Notes** Tasting menu 6 course, Sunday L £39.50, Children welcome

See advert on page 207

Hartnett Holder & Co 🌹🌹🌹

British, Italian 🍷 NOTABLE WINE LIST

tel: 023 8028 7167 & 8028 7177   **Beaulieu Rd SO43 7FZ**
email: info@limewood.co.uk **web:** www.limewood.co.uk
dir: *A35 through Ashurst for 4m, then left in Lyndhurst signed Beaulieu, 1m to hotel*

Italian family cooking in a sophisticated New Forest hotel

In the heart of the New Forest, a mile and a half out of Lyndhurst, Lime Wood is a boutique country-house hotel in a painstakingly and lovingly renovated Regency mansion. The interior has gained a gloss of glamour without being in the least pretentious or stuffy, with antique and bespoke furniture and hand-picked artwork and objets d'art. With luxury bedrooms, some cottages in the forest, extensive grounds and a posh spa, guests may not wish to leave the hotel, especially when the restaurant, an eye-catching room with button-back leather seats, is a collaboration between Lime Wood's own Luke Holder and Angela Hartnett, she of Murano and telly celeb fame. The kitchen aims to produce food that's 'fresh, foraged and not fiddled with', built on produce from the gardens, forest and local farmers, based on British traditions with, understandably, a strong element of Italian cuisine. Begin with vitello tonnato with capers, parsley and lemon, a simple salad of young vegetables with goats' cheese, pumpkin seeds and honey dressing, or a pasta dish: such as game ravioli with crispy kale and sweet-and-sour jus. This straightforward, even understated, approach brings out clear, clean flavours, with components complementing rather than muddying each other. Beef cheek comes with no more than risotto milanese, and pork belly with

parsley root and apple remoulade. Technical standards never fluctuate, seen in tender, moist pot-roast pheasant with black cabbage and root vegetables, and in griglia misto di pesce, of pinpoint accuracy, with chickpeas and prawns infused with saffron. For dessert, wave the Tricolore with tiramisù, or sgonfiotto with rhubarb and custard. An antique wooden table in the kitchen seats up to 10 for those who'd like to witness the team at work.

Chef Angela Hartnett, Luke Holder **Owner** Lime Wood Group
Seats 70, Pr/dining room 16 **Times** 12-11, All-day dining
Prices Fixed L 2 course £19.50, Tasting menu £55, Starter £8.50-£14.50, Main £9-£50, Dessert £7-£16 **Wines** 609 bottles over £30, 31 bottles under £30, 14 by glass **Parking** 60 **Notes** Tavolo Della Cucina 5 course £55, Sunday L £37.50, Vegetarian available, Children welcome

HARTNETT HOLDER & CO

Hartnett Holder & Co is a relaxed, stylish and comfortable upscale restaurant - full of character, yet unpretentious. Angela Hartnett and Lime Wood's Luke Holder, with their team, create locally sourced English dishes with a respectful nod to the seasons and to Italian culinary ideologies. This collaboration is reflected in their fresh, confident approach ensuring that this is "fun dining, not fine dining".

Hartnett and Holder's food is out-and-out British yet comes with the much loved Italian approach to eating - where sharing and provenance is everything. Expect a menu of Italian influenced forest dishes with English classics, pulling together both chef's much admired signature styles. Sample dishes include pizzetta with quail egg, taleggio and spinach, whole wild turbot (for two) with fennel, basil & preserved lemon or gnocchi with veal bolognaise.

Lime Wood, Beaulieu Road, Lyndhurst, Hampshire SO43 7FZ
Tel: 02380 287177   Website: www.hhandco.co.uk   Email: info@hhandco.co.uk

CHEWTON GLEN

HAMPSHIRE

Always a special occasion...

New Forest | Hampshire | England BH25 6QS
Telephone 01425 282212 | reservations@chewtonglen.com
www.chewtonglen.com

NORTHINGTON
Map 5 SU53

The Woolpack Inn
⊛ Classic British **NEW**

tel: 01962 734184 **Totford SO24 9TJ**
email: info@thewoolpackinn.co.uk **web:** www.thewoolpackinn.co.uk
dir: *From Basingstoke take A339 towards Alton. Under motorway, turn right (across dual carriageway) onto B3036 signed Candovers & Alresford. Pub between Brown Candover & Northington*

Pretty country inn with gently modernised food

In a tiny hamlet within the pretty Candover Valley, this Grade I listed flint and brick inn dates back to the late 19th Century, when it was used by travellers using the Drovers Trail between Alresford and Stockbridge. It has retained its traditional country pub feel with open fires, flagstoned floors and real ales, although these days the emphasis is as much on food, which is available throughout. A combination of traditional British pub dishes and European influences makes for an appealing menu that might kick off with cod and chorizo kebabs with tomato salsa and aïoli. Slow-cooked lamb, spiced chickpeas and mint yogurt looks to the Middle East for inspiration, with Pimm's jelly and vanilla cream making for a summery finale. The pub also has an outdoor kitchen which comes into its own on the Sunday 'pizza night'.

Chef Matt Gisby **Owner** The Woolpack Operating Co Ltd **Seats** 50, Pr/dining room 14 **Times** 12-2.30/6.30-9, Closed D 25 Dec **Prices** Starter £5-£8, Main £11.50-£19.50, Dessert £6.50 **Wines** 25 bottles over £30, 22 bottles under £30, 12 by glass **Parking** 40 **Notes** Sunday L £11.50-£15.95, Vegetarian available, Children welcome

OLD BURGHCLERE
Map 5 SU45

The Dew Pond Restaurant
⊛ British, European

tel: 01635 278408 **RG20 9LH**
dir: *Newbury A34 South, exit Tothill. Follow signs for Highclere Castle, pass castle entrance on right, down hill & turn left signed Old Burghclere & Kingsclere, restaurant on right in approx 0.25m*

Classical cooking not far from the setting for *Downton Abbey*

Just off the A34 between Newbury and Winchester, The Dew Pond was once a pair of 16th-century drovers' cottages, now welded into a very chic, pastel-hued country restaurant, not far from Highclere Castle (aka *Downton Abbey* off the telly). In two interlinked rooms connected by an arch, the cooking is founded on classical principles with the sort of personal overlay that has won many local devotees. An exemplary soufflé of Keen's cheddar with rocket and spring onion cream sauce is an accomplished opener, and might be followed by roasted sea bream with grilled tiger prawns, ratatouille and saffron potatoes, or a crowded plate of softly braised suckling pig belly with tenderloin and peppery black pudding, baby leeks, and Granny Smith purée in Calvados. At close of business, there may be an unevenly caramelised lemon tart with blackcurrant sorbet and meringue, or that old standby, sticky toffee with praline ice cream.

Chef Keith Marshall **Owner** Keith Marshall **Seats** 45, Pr/dining room 30 **Times** 7-9.30, Closed 2 wks Xmas & New Year, 2 wks Aug, Sun-Mon, L served by appointment only **Prices** Prices not confirmed, Service optional **Wines** 50 bottles over £30, 50 bottles under £30, 15 by glass **Parking** 20 **Notes** ALC 3 course £36, Vegetarian available, Children welcome

OTTERBOURNE
Map 5 SU42

The White Horse
⊛ Modern, Traditional British

tel: 01962 712830 **Main Rd SO21 2EQ**
email: manager@whitehorseotterbourne.co.uk
dir: *M3 junct 12/A335 1st exit at 1st rdbt & 2nd exit at next 2 rdbts, via Otterbourne Hill into Main Rd. Restaurant on left*

Modern pub grub done right

When you come down from a hike along the lofty spine of the South Downs – the western end of the South Downs Way is at nearby Winchester – you couldn't ask for a more fortifying pitstop. After a top-to-toe refurb by the team behind The White Star in Southampton and The Bugle in Hamble, this run-down village boozer now looks every inch the modern dining pub with its wooden and quarry-tiled floors, bare beams, cheerful heritage hues, and mismatched vintage tables. The mood is unbuttoned and family-friendly, while the kitchen is driven by an enthusiasm for local ingredients, served up in a straightforward contemporary vein. This might translate as fried squid with smoked paprika aïoli, followed by beef shin suet pudding paired with seared fillet, braised red cabbage and mash. Puddings take a similarly comfort-oriented route – perhaps Bramley apple syrup sponge with custard.

Times 12-2.30/6-9.30

PETERSFIELD
Map 5 SU72

JSW
⊛⊛⊛ – *see opposite*

Langrish House
⊛⊛ Modern British

tel: 01730 266941 **Langrish GU32 1RN**
email: frontdesk@langrishhouse.co.uk **web:** www.langrishhouse.co.uk
dir: *A3 onto A272 towards Winchester. Hotel signed, 2.5m on left*

Vigorous modern British cooking at a South Downs house with a past

Langrish House has been home to the Talbot-Ponsonby family for seven generations, and when you see the gorgeous 17th-century mansion in 14 acres of undulating Hampshire countryside it is no surprise that they have never moved on. Frederick's restaurant immortalises an off-the-wall Victorian great uncle who enjoyed the odd game of tennis – very odd, in fact, as he insisted on wearing a skirt. It is a cosy, traditional spot, or for a memorably romantic meal, you could dine in the low-lit intimacy of the old vaults below, which were dug by Royalist prisoners in the Civil War. As far as the food is concerned, it is fast forward to modern times for menus of straightforward up-to-date ideas. Kick off with the likes of roast wood pigeon pointed up with apple and ginger purée, pickled radish, beetroot and wild mushrooms, before moving on to wild sea bass with crushed Jersey Royals, crab, baby leeks and shellfish sauce. Winding up proceedings is a creative combo of honey parfait with popcorn, banana sorbet and toasted marshmallow.

Chef Nathan Marshall **Owner** Mr & Mrs Talbot-Ponsonby **Seats** 18, Pr/dining room 80 **Times** 12-2/7-9.30, Closed 27 Dec-10 Jan **Prices** Fixed L 2 course £18.95, Starter £6.50-£9.50, Main £16.50-£22, Dessert £6.50-£10 **Wines** 26 bottles over £30, 19 bottles under £30, 11 by glass **Parking** 100 **Notes** Sunday L £18.95-£21.95, Vegetarian available, Children 7 yrs+

The Old Drum

🌸 Modern British

tel: 01730 300544 **16 Chapel St GU32 3DP**
email: info@theolddrum.co.uk **web:** www.theolddrum.co.uk
dir: *Phone for directions*

A refreshingly modern approach in a town-centre inn

Less of the 'old', if you don't mind. The whitewashed inn may have stood here a few centuries, but its decorative styling – both outside, with the newly landscaped gardens, and in, where there are now five guest rooms – has determinedly moved with the times. Tiled floors and unclothed tables create the right mood of informality for the refreshingly modernised pub food on offer. There's rabbit pie with home-made pickle to start, or a veggied-up Scotch egg made with Puy lentils in curry sauce with mango chutney, before main courses come steaming in with twice-cooked beef Jacob's ladder and oxtail, served with salt-baked carrots and crème fraîche mash. Fish ideas are good too, perhaps pairing pollack with a saffron brandade of the salted fish, alongside parsnip purée and kale in red wine sauce. A combination of ginger cake and salted caramel ice cream affogato then pushes all the right dessert buttons.

Chef Simon Hartnett **Owner** Simon & Suzi Hawkins **Seats** 45
Times 12-2/6-9.30, Closed 1st wk Jan, D Sun **Prices** Prices not confirmed, Service optional **Wines** 11 bottles over £30, 19 bottles under £30, 10 by glass
Parking Adjacent car park **Notes** Sunday L, Vegetarian available, Children welcome

The Thomas Lord

🌸 Modern British

tel: 01730 829244 **High St, West Meon GU32 1LN**
email: info@thethomaslord.co.uk
dir: *M3 junct 9, A272 towards Petersfield, right at x-rds onto A32, 1st left*

Inventive country pub cooking

Named after the founder of Lord's Cricket Ground, who lies in the nearby churchyard, The Thomas Lord is a proper pub with fine local ales (the place is under the same ownership as Upham Brewery near Winchester) and no-one turns up their nose at visiting canines. The place has a shabby-chic charm, kitted out with rustic scrubbed pine tables, well-worn oak parquet floors, church pews and a Chesterfield sofa; on the food front, everything is made in-house, the garden supplies seasonal goodies, and the majority of materials come from small-scale local producers and farmers. The kitchen deals in country-pub classics and some more inventive ideas, starting with dressed Portland crab paired with brown crab custard, treacle bread and kohlrabi remoulade. Mains show off prime materials in the form of tender belly and fillet of pork, layered with black pudding and delivered with peas, broad beans, cauliflower purée, candied fennel, smoked apple purée and crackling. For afters, there's a choc fest of warm chocolate mousse in a chocolate tuile, aerated chocolate, brownie, salt caramel and buttermilk ice cream.

Chef Fran Joyce **Owner** Upham Ales **Seats** 70 **Times** 12-2.30/6-9.30, Closed D 25-26 Dec, 1 Jan **Prices** Fixed L 2 course £16, Fixed D 3 course £20, Starter £5.50-£8, Main £11.50-£18, Dessert £5.50-£8.50, Service optional 10% **Wines** 16 bottles over £30, 21 bottles under £30, 10 by glass **Parking** 20 **Notes** Sunday L £11.50-£16, Vegetarian available, Children welcome

JSW 🌸🌸🌸

PETERSFIELD Map 5 SU72

Modern British **v**
tel: 01730 262030 **20 Dragon St GU31 4JJ**
email: jsw.restaurant@btconnect.com
dir: *A3 to town centre, follow one-way system to College St which becomes Dragon St, restaurant on left*

Dynamic contemporary cooking in a made-over old inn

Book a table here and it's yours all evening, with plenty of distance between you and your neighbour. Jake Saul Watkins – the man who put the JSW into JSW – is a singular kind of chef-patron, and he's created a restaurant where the customer actually gets to feel rather special. That may sound a little old school, but dining here is anything but that. The 17th-century one-time coaching inn has been spruced up inside and out, with terrace tables out back and a simple and smart contemporary finish within. There is no shortage of original character in the shape of copious light-coloured oak beams, while neutral colours, immaculately laid tables and high-backed leather chairs set the tone. Four tasteful bedrooms await upstairs if you fancy stopping over. The menu focuses on high-quality British ingredients, but there's a willingness to go farther afield in search of excellence; France, for example, is the source for chickens, duck and guinea fowl. The best way to get a handle on Mr Watkins' abilities is to go for one of the tasting menus (five, seven or nine courses), while there's also a fixed-price carte and good-value midweek lunch option. This kitchen makes everything in-house, from bread (expect a basket including walnut rolls) to ice cream. To begin, fresh-as-a-daisy scallops are cooked on the plancha and arrive with thin shavings of apple and fennel, plus a salted lemon gel. Next up, slow-cooked duck is served pink and comes with a brace of purées (hay-baked parsnip purée and salted orange). The impressive technical skill continues into desserts such as a booze-inspired one with 'get smashed' stout, gin and tonic and Pimm's.

Chef Jake Watkins **Owner** Jake Watkins **Seats** 58, Pr/dining room 18
Times 12-1.30/7-9.30, Closed 2 wks Jan, May & summer, Mon-Tue, D Sun **Prices** Fixed L 2 course £25-£29.50, Tasting menu £45-£95 **Wines** 492 bottles over £30, 36 bottles under £30, 9 by glass **Parking** 19 **Notes** Tasting menu L/D 5/7 course, ALC 2/3 course £32.50/£49.50, Sunday L £32.50-£95, Children 6 yrs+

Portsmouth Marriott Hotel

Modern British

tel: 023 9238 3151 **Southampton Rd PO6 4SH**
web: www.portsmouthmarriott.co.uk
dir: *M27 junct 12, keep left to lights, turn left. Hotel on left*

Lively hotel restaurant near the marina

A sizable chunk of 20th-century real estate, looking for all the world like an office block, the Portsmouth Marriott is rather more bright and breezy once you get inside. The Sealevel restaurant occupies a vast atrium-like area that has the proportions of a cathedral, but a decidedly contemporary sheen. There's a lively lounge bar occupying the space alongside the dining area, which possesses an easy-going brasserie-style finish. The kitchen is singing to the same tune, delivering modern British favourites such as seared king scallops with cauliflower beignets and apple purée, or another starter of twice-baked cheese soufflé. Move on to garlic- and rosemary-flavoured butterfly chicken, or stuffed sea bass with sauce vièrge, and finish with a classic crème brûlée with a perfectly caramelised topping, or a winter trifle with crushed meringue and shortbread. The hotel is handy for Gunwharf Quays and the Spinnaker Tower.

Chef Martyn Tod **Seats** 70 **Times** 12-3/6.30-10 **Prices** Starter £5-£8, Main £14.50-£18.50, Dessert £6-£9, Service optional **Wines** 4 bottles over £30, 26 bottles under £30, 19 by glass **Parking** 196 **Notes** Sunday L £12.95-£15.95, Vegetarian available, Children welcome

Restaurant 27

Modern European **V**

tel: 023 9287 6272 **27a South Pde PO5 2JF**
email: info@restaurant27.com
dir: *M27 junct 12, take M275 to A3, follow A288 South Parade, left Burgoyne Rd*

Vivid cooking based on thought-provoking combinations

A little way off the seafront in Southsea, the whitewashed building with its black hanging sign may look a little like a storage-shed, but appearances can be deceptive. Inside is a smartly appointed, high-ceilinged dining room with unclothed dark tables, chairs upholstered in leafy-green, and plenty of natural light from high windows. It makes an engaging setting for chef-proprietor Kevin Bingham's contemporary food that tries out some thought-provoking combinations in the dual form of a fixed-price carte with four choices per course, or six-course tasting menus that showcase the range of the kitchen's abilities. Flavours are vivid and captivating, as when silky haddock and prawn velouté is garnished with a raviolo of orange and pine nuts, and marinated foie gras gains in intensity from its accompaniments of Granny Smith apple, honey and ginger. At main course, a multicultural approach sees 'umami duck' juxtaposed with Ibérico chorizo and feta, or there could be sea bass with smoked pancetta in scallop and clam chowder. The signature take on cherry Bakewell may be a shock to Derbyshire purists, while the crème brûlée is sharpened with blackcurrant and star anise.

Chef Kevin Bingham, Annie Smith, Matt Barnes **Owner** Kevin & Sophie Bingham **Seats** 34 **Times** 12-2.30/7-9.30, Closed Xmas, New Year, Mon-Tue, L Wed-Sat, D Sun **Prices** Fixed D 3 course £44, Tasting menu £39-£50, Service optional **Wines** 30 bottles over £30, 23 bottles under £30, 9 by glass **Parking** On street **Notes** Tasting menu 7 course Wed-Thu/8 course Fri-Sat, Sunday L £29-£39, Children welcome

The Three Tuns

Modern British

tel: 01794 512639 **58 Middlebridge St SO51 8HL**
email: manager@the3tunsromsey.co.uk
dir: *A27 bypass on A3030*

Classy pub cooking with lashings of period charm

Middlebridge Street is sufficiently hidden from Romsey's hurly-burly that The Three Tuns counts as something of a retreat. Acquired by the team behind Winchester's Chesil Rectory, it has been sympathetically remodelled rather than given the scruff-of-the-neck approach, and retains its olden-times charm, with winter fires, dark beams and slate floors, exposed brickwork, and stuffed birds in glass cases. An extensive menu of pub classics aims to please all comers, Sunday roasts of beef or chicken with all the trimmings are an ever-popular draw, while a bowl of curried parsnip soup and crusty bread a godsend on a chilly day. Meaty things are dependably satisfying, as for chunky ham hock terrine with piccalilli and pea shoots, or mains such as braised lamb shoulder in pan juices with fondant potato and puréed carrots. If it's fish you're after, there will be much rejoicing over devilled whitebait with aïoli, followed perhaps by grilled mackerel with courgettes and spring onions in salsa verde. Proceedings conclude with stickily glazed, citrussy treacle tart and vanilla ice cream, or chocolate marquise with salted caramel ice cream.

Chef Damian Brown, Declan Bungay **Owner** M Dodd, D Brown **Seats** 35 **Times** 12-2.30/6-9, Closed 25-26 Dec **Prices** Starter £5.50-£7, Main £11.95-£13.95, Dessert £5.95, Service optional **Wines** 7 bottles over £30, 19 bottles under £30, 11 by glass **Parking** 14, On street **Notes** Sunday L fr £12.95, Vegetarian available, Children welcome

The White Horse Hotel & Brasserie

Modern British

tel: 01794 512431 **19 Market Place SO51 8ZJ**
web: www.thewhitehorseromsey.co.uk
dir: *M27 junct 3, follow signs for Romsey, right at Broadlands. In town centre*

Brasserie dining on a site noted for hospitality since the 12th century

The White Horse has a past. Its timber framing dates back to the mid-15th century, and it's possible that some sort of inn stood here to provision visitors to the Abbey a good 300 years before that. At the heart of operations is a brasserie-styled dining room done in pastel shades, the walls crowded with wildlife pictures, and with two windowed sides looking on to the terrace and courtyard. The menu lives up to the brasserie classification, with a British-based roll call of dishes inflected with some European technique. Well-defined flavours shine forth from quality prime materials, and presentations are clean and appealing. A piece of finely timed salmon is partnered with seared foie gras and cumined lentils for an effective opener, while mains run to wild mushroom and leek lasagne with a fried duck egg, herb-crusted cod in butternut velouté, and chargrilled loin and braised neck of local lamb with a purée of haricots in balsamic jus. Go Spanish at dessert stage with soft-centred churros and toasted almonds, accompanied by tart raspberry sorbet.

The White Horse Hotel & Brasserie

Chef Nick O'Hallaran **Owner** Mr Jonathan Nuttall **Seats** 85, Pr/dining room 40 **Times** 12-3/6-10 **Prices** Fixed L 2 course fr £16, Starter £6.95-£11.50, Main £13-£36, Dessert £6.95-£7.95 **Wines** 32 bottles over £30, 17 bottles under £30, 11 by glass **Parking** Car park nearby **Notes** Afternoon tea £18.50-£45, Sunday L £19.50-£22, Vegetarian available, Children welcome

See advert on page 212

| ROTHERWICK | Map 5 SU75 |

Tylney Hall Hotel

◉◉ Traditional British **v**

tel: 01256 764881 **Ridge Ln RG27 9AZ**
email: sales@tylneyhall.com **web:** www.tylneyhall.co.uk
dir: M3 junct 5, A287 to Basingstoke, over junct with A30, over rail bridge, towards Newnham. Right at Newnham Green. Hotel 1m on left

Victorian house with Gertrude Jekyll gardens and a grand dining room

Tylney Hall is for occasions when only the whole country-house hotel, fine-dining experience will do. The Grade II listed Victorian red-brick pile sits in 66 acres of parkland with gardens designed by Gertrude Jekyll, and the interior is none too shabby either, with its oak panelling and rococo plasterwork. The surroundings

---

scream classical country-house dining, and the Oak Room restaurant duly delivers the goods in a setting involving oak panels, a domed ceiling, and opulent swagged drapes — all accompanied by a tinkling grand piano. What arrives on the plate is a gently updated take on the classics, with splashes of modernity here and there. A seared fillet of sea bream is accompanied by fennel in coriander and ginger for a southeast Asian flourish, prior to something like tender-as-anything venison loin with potato and pumpkin gratin and confit root veg in a sparse but intense port reduction. Chocolate orange tart, its opulently thick filling offset by delicate flaky pastry, orange purée and mascarpone ice cream, brings down the curtain.

Tylney Hall Hotel

Chef Stephen Hine **Owner** Elite Hotels **Seats** 80, Pr/dining room 120 **Times** 12.30-2/7-10 **Prices** Fixed L 2 course fr £19.95, Starter fr £10.50, Main fr £20.50, Dessert fr £8.50, Service optional **Wines** 350 bottles over £30, 5 bottles under £30, 10 by glass **Parking** 150 **Notes** Sunday L fr £32.95, Children welcome

See advert on page 213

| SOUTHAMPTON | Map 5 SU41 |

BEST WESTERN Chilworth Manor

◉ Modern British

tel: 023 8076 7333 **Chilworth SO16 7PT**
email. sales@chilworth-manor.co.uk **web:** www.chilworth-manor.co.uk
dir: 1m from M3/M27 junct on A27 Romsey Rd N from Southampton. Pass Chilworth Arms on left, in 200mtrs turn left at Southampton Science Park sign. Hotel immediately right

Brasserie-style cooking in a grand Edwardian hotel

A grand Edwardian pile in charming grounds, Chilworth Manor is these days a classy hotel with all mod cons — swish spa, well kitted out meeting rooms and a smart restaurant. There's no shortage of period elegance in the restaurant, with its oak panels and tables dressed in white linen cloths, but the menu takes a slightly less formal approach to proceedings. This is upmarket brasserie-style cooking, with a menu that contains regional ingredients and global influences. Start with pan-seared scallops with parsnip purée and a dressing combining apples and roasted hazelnuts, and follow on with Owtons of Hampshire saddle of venison with fondant potato and a fig and juniper berry sauce. There is a burger, too, and monkfish wrapped in nori. Finish with a fun dessert such as iced prosecco and rhubarb parfait with spiced ginger biscuits and a bag of delicious custard doughnuts.

Chef Chris Keel **Owner** Chilworth Manor Ltd **Seats** 80, Pr/dining room 150 **Times** 12-1.45/7-9.30, Closed L Sat **Prices** Fixed L 2 course fr £14.95, Fixed D 3 course £26-£34, Starter £6-£9, Main £12-£19, Dessert £6-£8, Service optional **Wines** 2 bottles over £30, 27 bottles under £30, 11 by glass **Parking** 250 **Notes** Sunday L £17.95, Vegetarian available, Children welcome

THE WHITE HORSE
HOTEL & BRASSERIE

"Small things make perfection but perfection is no small thing"

Sir Henry Royce

Set in the heart of Romsey, The White Horse has been a coaching inn for almost 600 years.
The 2 AA rosette awarded Brasserie & Grill is a wonderful place to enjoy every occasion from a romantic dinner for two to a robust family lunch, during the summer months the courtyard offers a perfect retreat for al fresco dining. A stay here with us is a time to unwind – relax in one of our individually designed bedrooms, enjoy a cocktail in our delightful bar or even sample one of our delicious afternoon teas in the historic Tudor or Palmerston lounges. The hotel is also fully licensed for wedding ceremonies and offers the most romantic and intimate venue for your wedding day. **Historic charm meets modern classic chic.**

Market Place, Romsey, Hampshire SO51 8ZJ
AA ★★★★ **T** 01794 512431 **F** 01794 517485 **E** thewhitehorse@twhromsey.com
RESTAURANT Hotel **www.thewhitehorseromsey.com**

SOUTHAMPTON *continued*

Botleigh Grange Hotel

◎ Traditional British

tel: 01489 787700 **Grange Rd, Hedge End SO30 2GA**
email: enquiries@botleighgrange.com **web:** www.botleighgrange.com
dir: *On A334, 1m from M27 junct 7*

Modern British classics in a stylish spa hotel

A gleaming white spa hotel not far from Southampton, Botleigh Grange has been around since the mid-17th century, yet the place looks pristinely maintained and box-fresh inside, with the Hampshire's dining room bathed in daylight from a glass-domed ceiling, and swagged curtains to frame the garden view. An expansive menu of modern British classics is on offer. The poshing of Scotch eggs (with black pudding and a quail's egg here) is right on trend, and fried cakes of either crab or sweet potato and corned beef hash make good starters. After those might come a chicken breast bound in Parma ham and filled with sun-dried tomatoes and feta in red pepper sauce, or blackened salmon with garlicky crushed potatoes and avocado-mango salsa, before a finale of orange and lemon posset with vanilla shortbread.

Chef Stephen Lewis **Owner** Botleigh Grange Hotel Ltd **Seats** 100, Pr/dining room 350 **Times** 7-9.30, Closed L Mon-Sat **Prices** Fixed D 3 course fr £29.95, Starter £5.95-£7.95, Main £13.95-£24.95, Dessert £6.50-£8.95 **Wines** 16 bottles over £30, 29 bottles under £30, 10 by glass **Parking** 300 **Notes** Gourmet break 6 course, Sunday L £14.95-£17.95, Vegetarian available, Children welcome

Mercure Southampton Centre Dolphin Hotel

◎ Modern International

tel: 023 8038 6460 **34-35 High St SO14 2HN**
email: H7876@accor.com **web:** www.mercure.com
dir: *A33 follow signs for Docks & Old Town/IOW ferry, at ferry terminal turn right into High Street, hotel 400yds on left*

Historic hotel with crowd-pleasing menu

Formerly a 17th-century coaching inn boasting the likes of Jane Austen, Queen Victoria and Admiral Nelson among its former guests, several million pounds and a takeover from the Mercure chain later, this is a striking and characterful place to stay and to eat. In the Signature Restaurant, contemporary tones abound and it all looks suitably contemporary and unstuffy – darkwood tables, plenty of period character, and a menu that doesn't stray far from traditional, brasserie-style comforts. Baked ramekin of Hampshire pear with Stilton cream and watercress salad might precede steak and kidney pie, half a roast poussin with bubble-and-squeak and bread sauce, or a Casterbridge steak from the grill.

Chef Tibor Suli **Owner** Longrose Buccleuch **Seats** 80 **Times** 12-2.30/7-9.45 **Prices** Prices not confirmed **Wines** 8 bottles over £30, 24 bottles under £30, 12 by glass **Parking** 80 **Notes** Vegetarian available, Children welcome

White Star Tavern, Dining and Rooms

◎◎ British

tel: 023 8082 1990 **28 Oxford St SO14 3DJ**
email: reservations@whitestartavern.co.uk **web:** www.whitestartavern.co.uk
dir: *M3 junct 14 onto A33, towards Ocean Village*

Confident modern dishes in a local hotspot

Bringing a touch of boutique style to Southampton, the White Star – named for the shipping line who commissioned the Titanic – has cool designer bedrooms, a bar/pub that can turn out a nifty cocktail, and a restaurant that delivers feel-good dishes with a local flavour. There's a satisfying blend of period details and contemporary touches in the dining room, and an easy-going attitude that hits the spot. The place is open for breakfast, serves sandwiches until 5pm, and offers classy pub classics such as local beer-battered fish with triple-cooked chips. But this kitchen also produces some strident modern stuff that fits really well with the brasserie-style attitude. Starters include blow-torched smoked salmon with cucumber pickle and crumbed quail's egg, or seared scallops with cauliflower textures and black pudding. Among main courses, cod loin comes with a chestnut crust alongside artichoke purée and dauphinoise potatoes, and Wiltshire partridge with the leg meat in an accompanying raviolo, plus parsnip purée and sticky red cabbage. Finish with Bakewell tart with clotted cream ice cream and drunken cranberries.

Times 12-2.30/6-9.30, Closed 25-26 Dec

▍STOCKBRIDGE   Map 5 SU33

The Greyhound on the Test

◉◉ Modern British

tel: 01264 810833 **31 High St SO20 6EY**
email: info@thegreyhoundonthetest.co.uk **web:** www.thegreyhoundonthetest.co.uk
dir: *9m NW of Winchester, 8m S of Andover. Off A303*

Upmarket town inn with up-to-date food and local fishing rights

This classily refurbished inn, or restaurant with rooms if you like, has a garden that runs down to the River Test with its own fishing beat, so it's well-and-truly on the map for anglers. But The Greyhound has no shortage of appeal, from upmarket, sumptuous bedrooms to a restaurant with that opened-up, country-chic vibe. Lots of original beams, a mismatched array of chunky wooden tables and warm neutral tones give the place a breezy, relaxed feel, with candles bringing a warm glow all day. The menu is a thoroughly up-to-date affair with regional produce at its heart; witness a starter of Broughton buffalo carpaccio with celeriac remoulade and pine nuts. At main course stage, super-fresh monkfish and scallops are served raw, céviche-style with finely shaved fennel, mooli radish and lime, or if you fancy something more visceral, the grill might supply best end of lamb, haggis and faggots with sweet-and-sour carrots and crushed olives. You're sure to go home happy after dark chocolate brownie with chocolate mousse, cherries and amaretti.

Chef Neil Cooper **Owner** Lucy Townsend **Seats** 52, Pr/dining room 20
Times 12-4/7-9, Closed 25-26 Dec, D Sun (winter), 31 Dec-1 Jan **Prices** Fixed D 3 course £13.95-£18.95, Tasting menu £20-£55 **Wines** 32 bottles over £30, 27 bottles under £30, 12 by glass **Parking** 20 **Notes** Sunday L, Vegetarian available, Children welcome

The Peat Spade Inn

◉ Modern British

tel: 01264 810612 **Village St, Longstock SO20 6DR**
email: info@peatspadeinn.co.uk **web:** www.peatspadeinn.co.uk
dir: *M3 junct 8, A303 W approx 15m, then take A3057 Stockbridge/Andover*

Rustic cooking with a French feeling and fly-fishing in the vicinity

Close to the fly-fishing nerve-centre that is Stockbridge, The Peat Spade at Longstock in the Test Valley is a stolid-looking red-brick country inn, perfectly positioned to offer angling and a range of other rural sporting pursuits. Close-set tables add to the dining-room buzz, and the decor is handsome deep red with clusters of pictures. Rustic cooking with more than a soupçon of French influence proves abidingly popular, seen here in the form of fried chicken livers on sourdough toast with charred sweetcorn in peppercorn sauce to start. Then come mains like accurately timed baked cod in a bouillabaisse of Portland shellfish with saffron gnocchi, fennel, samphire and aïoli that some may judge falls short of its garlicky duty, or venison loin with wild mushrooms, lentils and spiced bread purée. The modernist trail is then followed for desserts such as white chocolate pannacotta with raspberry sorbet and chocolate doughnuts in passionfruit coulis.

Chef Nathan Gebert **Owner** Upham Pub Company **Seats** 49, Pr/dining room 12
Times 12-2.30/6.30-9.30, Closed 25 Dec, D 26 Dec, 1 Jan **Prices** Starter £7-£9.50, Main £17-£35, Dessert £7-£9, Service optional **Wines** 13 bottles over £30, 24 bottles under £30, 10 by glass **Parking** 19 **Notes** Pre-booking strongly recommended, Daily menu, Sunday L £12-£15, Vegetarian available, Children welcome

The Three Cups Inn

◉ Modern, Traditional English

tel: 01264 810527 **High St SO20 6HB**
email: manager@the3cups.co.uk **web:** www.the3cups.co.uk
dir: *Phone for directions*

Old coaching inn with a modern menu

Dating back to the 1500s, this coaching inn is still very much a pub, offering regularly-changing local ales. It's also a dining destination with low-ceilinged dining room and an orangery extension out back with full-width doors opening up to the garden (eating outside is a fair-weather option). There are en suite bedrooms, too. The kitchen makes good use of local foodstuffs, with local game in season, plus lunchtime snacks and Sunday roasts. From the main restaurant menu, chicken, mushroom and tarragon terrine is perked up with wilted pak choi and soy jus, while among main courses pan-fried calves' liver comes nice and pink with accompanying beetroot dauphinoise, cabbage with pancetta, Chantenay carrots and a red wine jus. Bread is made on the premises and, for dessert, there is a well-made banana and peanut cheesecake with a dark chocolate sauce.

Chef Ian Hamilton **Owner** Mrs L Tickle **Seats** 50, Pr/dining room 20
Times 12-2.30/6.30-9.30, Closed 25-26 Dec **Prices** Prices not confirmed, Service optional **Wines** 10 bottles over £30, 16 bottles under £30, 12 by glass **Parking** 15 **Notes** Sunday L, Vegetarian available, Children welcome

▍WINCHESTER   Map 5 SU42

Avenue Restaurant at Lainston House Hotel

◉◉◉ – *see opposite*

The Black Rat

◉ Modern British

tel: 01962 844465 & 841531 **88 Chesil St SO23 0HX**
email: reservations@theblackrat.co.uk
dir: *M3 junct 9/A31 towards Winchester & Bar End until T-junct. Turn right at lights, restaurant 600yds on left*

Culinary modernism with a traditional pub ambience

A white-fronted former pub on the edge of town, The Black Rat retains the atmosphere of open fires, chunky tables and exposed brick, while setting its sights firmly on culinary modernism. It's now most definitely a restaurant. At the moment, the kitchen's ambitious cooking is rather hit-and-miss, with oddball combinations of ingredients and techniques. When they do, there's much to admire, as in a vibrantly colourful fish stew of bream, ling and gurnard with aïoli and saffron noodles, or grilled monkfish tail with cauliflower purée and grape couscous in verjus. Meat could be fine Elwy lamb with goats' curd and hay-baked turnips, and white chocolate cheesecake is an impressive finale, let down slightly by the accompanying chicory mousse and beetroot granola.

Chef Ollie Moore **Owner** David Nicholson **Seats** 40, Pr/dining room 16
Times 12-2.15/7-9.30, Closed 2 wks Etr, 2 wks Oct/Nov, 2 wks Xmas & New Year, L Mon-Fri **Prices** Fixed L 2 course £25.95, Starter £9-£11.50, Main £19.50-£22.50, Dessert £7.95-£9.95, Service optional **Wines** 6 by glass **Parking** Car park opposite **Notes** Fixed L Sat-Sun only, Sunday L £25.95-£28.95, Vegetarian available, No children

The Chesil Rectory

@@ Modern British

tel: 01962 851555 **1 Chesil St SO23 OHU**
email: enquiries@chesilrectory.co.uk
dir: *S from King Alfred's statue at bottom of The Broadway, cross small bridge, turn right, restaurant on left, just off mini rdbt*

Modernised British dishes in a medieval house

A beautiful half-timbered building dating back to 1450, The Chesil Rectory is the oldest house in Winchester. From the street you enter through a low door – the first of many original features – to be greeted in the cooler months by a roaring log fire warming a brilliantly preserved interior with low ceilings and beams, charming inglenook fireplaces, exposed brickwork and wooden floors, and a quirky collection of taxidermy. The kitchen puts a gently modernised spin onto classic British dishes, bolstered by some that have nothing to do with the native repertoire, as in a starter of creamy white onion risotto with crispy shallots and burnt onion ash. A main course fillet of cod delivers exceptional plump and sea-fresh fish, well-timed and tender, with brown shrimps in chive butter, crushed potatoes and broccoli, or spring might see a pairing of loin and belly of pork with spätzle and the commendably seasonal accompaniments of asparagus and wild garlic pesto. Finish with an apple tarte fine with salted caramel sauce and Calvados ice cream.

Chef Damian Brown **Owner** Mark Dodd, Damian Brown **Seats** 75, Pr/dining room 14 **Times** 12-2.20/6-9.30, Closed 25-26 Dec, 1 Jan **Prices** Fixed L 2 course £15.95, Fixed D 3 course £19.95, Starter £5.95-£9.50, Main £13.95-£19.50, Dessert £6.95-£8.50, Service optional **Wines** 42 bottles over £30, 25 bottles under £30, 13 by glass **Parking** NCP Chesil St adjacent **Notes** Fixed menu Mon-Sat 12-2.20/6-7, Sun 6-9, Sunday L £21.95-£26.95, Vegetarian available, Children 12 yrs+ D

Holiday Inn Winchester

@ British, French

tel: 01962 670700 **Telegraph Way, Morn Hill SO21 1HZ**
email: info@hiwinchester.co.uk **web:** www.hiwinchester.co.uk
dir: *M3 junct 9, A31 signed Alton, A272 & Petersfield. 1st exit at rdbt onto A31, 1.6m, take 1st exit into Alresford Rd, left into Telegraph Way*

Ambitious cooking at an out-of-town hotel

The Winchester Holiday Inn is large purpose-built hotel quietly located on the edge of the South Downs National Park. The Morn Hill Brasserie on the lower ground floor is a coolly modern space where black tables and light upholstered chairs make quite a design statement. The kitchen goes to some pains to source local produce and has its own contemporary take on the British and French repertoires. Start with the earthy flavours of mushroom ravioli with wilted spinach and thyme foam, or foie gras and partridge terrine with fig chutney. High culinary standards elevate the cooking well above that normally seen in hotel chains, evident in loin of Hampshire venison, cooked to pink, accompanied by celeriac and potato purée, carrots and port jus, a masterly combination, and cod fillet imaginatively partnered by mussel and vegetable soup along with mash and sautéed spinach. Conclude with citrus tart with lemon curd and orange sorbet.

Chef Robert Quehan **Owner** Zinnia Hotels **Seats** 128, Pr/dining room 200 **Times** 12-2/6.30-9.30 **Prices** Prices not confirmed, Service optional **Wines** 17 bottles over £30, 34 bottles under £30, 10 by glass **Parking** 170 **Notes** Sunday L, Vegetarian available, Children welcome

Avenue Restaurant at Lainston House Hotel @@@

WINCHESTER   Map 5 SU42

Modern British V
tel: 01962 776088 **Woodman Ln, Sparsholt SO21 2LT**
email: enquiries@lainstonhouse.com **web:** www.lainstonhouse.com
dir: *2m NW off B3049 towards Stockbridge, junct with Woodman Ln*

Creative modern cooking in 17th-century country-house hotel

Originally a 17th-century hunting lodge, Lainston House is a charming and cosseting country-house hotel embraced in 63 acres of parkland just a few miles from Winchester. The setting is a rural idyll, with four of those acres earning their keep as a kitchen garden supplying seasonal fruit, veg and herbs, and there's a dining area smack in the centre, with a wood-fired oven for summer barbecues. Taking its name from the mile-long stretch of lime trees glimpsed through its windows, the Avenue Restaurant offers a traditional setting of burnished wood panels and burgundy leather seats in which to dine. Head chef Olly Rouse's contemporary cooking shows first-rate technical know-how and a firm grasp of how tastes and textures work together; visual impact plays its part too, but the ingredients remain the star of the show. Well-structured starters might match octopus with a Mediterranean roll call of chorizo, pine nut, basil and green olive, while an equally well-thought-through, if more left-field idea, is quail supported by cauliflower, an anchovy beignet and celeriac chutney. Main courses bring more thought-provoking juxtapositions of flavour, but everything is here for a reason, whether it's a supporting cast of sweetcorn, shiitake mushrooms, dandelion and pear providing explosions of distinct flavours to accompany perfectly-timed pink duck, or halibut in a productive coalition with bulgur wheat, baby gem, cashew and pomelo. British cheeses are an alternative to innovative desserts such as dark chocolate pavé with coffee beans and a yogurt and vanilla set foam, or pears poached in orange blossom. A bountiful cellar comes up with a globetrotting array of bottles to suit most tastes and budgets.

Chef Olly Rouse **Owner** Exclusive Hotels & Venues **Seats** 60, Pr/dining room 120 **Times** 12-2/7-9, Closed 25-26 & 31 Dec, L Sat, D 24 Dec **Prices** Fixed D 3 course £32.50-£35, Tasting menu £75 **Wines** 120 bottles over £30, 30 bottles under £30, 9 by glass **Parking** 100 **Notes** ALC 3 course £55, Afternoon tea £26, Sunday L £25-£35, Children welcome

WINCHESTER *continued*

Hotel du Vin Winchester

◉◉ Traditional British, French ■ NOTABLE WINE LIST

tel: 01962 841414 **14 Southgate St SO23 9EF**
email: info@winchester.hotelduvin.co.uk **web:** www.hotelduvin.com
dir: *M3 junct 11, follow signs to Winchester town centre, located on left*

Classic French bistro fare in the first HdV

Here was where the Hotel du Vin (HdV) adventure all began, in the group's first and smallest boutique hotel-cum-wine bar-cum-bistro. It's an attractive townhouse dating from the very outset of the Georgian era, not far from the magnificent cathedral. The house decorative style of wooden floors, unclothed tables and cream walls hung with a multitude of pictures is the ambience here too, and the food is gently modernised classic French bistro fare. Expect to start with chicken liver parfait or French onion soup or, for something a little more enterprising, such as a successful presentation of seared scallops with artichoke and pistachio purée and pancetta vinaigrette. Mains take in satisfyingly crackled pork belly with mustardy dauphinoise and a sauce incorporating Agen prunes, or there are various cuts of fine 28-day dry-aged beef. Dishes of the day are worth a look, and meals end with the likes of caramel parfait with candied pecans, date-stuffed baked apple, or good old Black Forest gâteau. Brunches and afternoon tea bolster the daytime repertoire and, as throughout the HdV group, there is an adventurous, extensive list of French-led fine wines.

Chef Michael Chapman **Owner** KSL **Seats** 65, Pr/dining room 48
Times 12-2.30/5.30-10 **Prices** Fixed L 2 course £16.95, Fixed D 3 course £19.95, Service optional 10% **Wines** 250 bottles over £30, 50 bottles under £30, 20 by glass **Parking** 40, NCP Tower St **Notes** Sunday L fr £24.95, Vegetarian available, Children welcome

Marwell Hotel

◉◉ Modern European

tel: 01962 777681 **Thompsons Ln, Colden Common, Marwell SO21 1JY**
email: info@marwellhotel.co.uk **web:** www.marwellhotel.co.uk
dir: *B3354 through Twyford. 1st exit at rdbt (B3354), left onto B2177 signed Bishop Waltham. Left into Thompsons Ln after 250yds, hotel on left*

Contemporary-styled traditional dishes next door to the zoo

A pastoral retreat in the manner of an African safari lodge, Marwell is set in wooded grounds next door to the area's wildlife park, so the odd screech of a monkey shouldn't strike the surreal note that it would elsewhere in Hampshire. Full-drop windows in the oak-beamed dining room look out over the countryside, and the kitchen matches the mood with cooking that applies modern styling to mostly traditional dishes. Pairing scallops with cauliflower purée pretty much counts as a tradition these days; here they're forthrightly seasoned, and come with balled apple and ink-dyed tempura for a well-balanced opening foray. Menu specifications need watching a little more carefully, but most things are present and correct in a main course of minted lamb rump with a potato cake and celeriac purée. A chocolate fondant made with 70% gear is a stimulating finish, its fabulous riches offset with humble honeycomb and a faintly citric yogurt sorbet.

Times 5.30-10, Closed 25 Dec

Running Horse Inn

◉◉ Modern International, British

tel: 01962 880218 **88 Main Rd, Littleton SO22 6QS**
email: info@runninghorseinn.co.uk **web:** www.runninghorseinn.co.uk
dir: *B3049 out of Winchester 1.5m, turn right into Littleton after 1m, Running Horse on right*

Innovative flavour-packed cooking in informal upgraded inn

A revitalised village inn, with real ales dispensed at the bar, the Running Horse is a relaxed and informal dining environment, with a wood-burning stove in a brick fireplace, some banquette seating, wooden tables and a mixture of artwork adorning the walls. The menu is an enticing read, and the kitchen delivers some stimulating dishes that are full of flavour. Cauliflower pannacotta with capers in a Cajun-spiced parmesan crust is skilfully made and tasty starter, offered alongside home-cured gravad lax with cucumber noodles, sour cream and sherry dressing. 'Lighter Bites' are possibilities, among them omelette Arnold Bennett, while main courses run the gamut from sirloin steak with bordelaise sauce and the usual accompaniments, through Thai green chicken urry with basmati rice to more contemporary ideas like pork belly with a black pudding crumb, buttered leeks, garlic mash and thyme cream. Daily specials extend the range even further, and desserts follow the well-trodden path of crème brûlée and sticky toffee pudding with salted caramel sauce.

Chef Stewart Hellsten **Owner** Upham Pub Co **Seats** 60 **Times** 12-2.30/6.30-9.30 **Prices** Prices not confirmed, Service optional **Wines** 18 bottles over £30, 22 bottles under £30, 13 by glass **Parking** 40 **Notes** Sunday L, Vegetarian available, Children welcome

The Wykeham Arms

◎◎ Modern British

tel: 01962 853834 **75 Kingsgate St SO23 9PE**
email: wykehamarms@fullers.co.uk **web:** www.wykehamarmswinchester.co.uk
dir: S out of city along Southgate St. Take 3rd turning L into Canon St, inn on R at end

Rustic, historic pub with contemporary tucker

A coaching inn since the mid-1700s, The Wykeham Arms is situated in the historic heart of the city, close to the cathedral and the 14th-century college, and the place has steadfastly managed to avoid getting a contemporary makeover. It really looks the part, its walls covered with pictures that reflect the past, large mirrors and copious bric-a-brac. With rustic wooden tables, chunky original floorboards and a lively atmosphere, it's an archetypal English inn. When it comes to culinary output, things take a contemporary turn. There are simpler options listed as 'Home Comforts' on the menu — beer-battered South Coast haddock — but this is a kitchen that can turn out a starter as fashionable as boneless chicken wings with BBQ emulsion and blue cheese sauce. A bang-on piece of sea bream stars in a main course with a seared scallop, salt-baked celeriac and wild mushrooms, while another partners roasted venison loin with red cabbage ketchup and cocoa gnocchi (the classic flavours delivered in a creative manner). Finish with peanut butter parfait with strawberry jelly and toast ice cream.

Times 12-3/6-9.30, Closed D 25 Dec

WOODLANDS   Map 5 SU31

Woodlands Lodge Hotel

◎ Modern British

tel: 023 8029 2257 **Bartley Rd, Woodlands SO40 7GN**
email: reception@woodlands-lodge.co.uk **web:** www.woodlands-lodge.co.uk
dir: M27 junct 2, rdbt towards Fawley, 2nd rdbt right towards Cadnam. 1st left at White Horse Pub onto Woodlands Road, over cattle grid, hotel on left

Kitchen garden produce at a New Forest hotel

When we say this hotel is 'in the New Forest', we mean it. The ancient woodland can be accessed directly from the Lodge's gardens, making it the perfect spot for a walking break. Former service as a hunting lodge is reflected in the name of Hunters restaurant, where an elegant lightness of tone prevails, with chairs and wall panels in delicate forest green to match the view from the swagged windows. A south-facing walled garden supplies vegetables and soft fruits, and all meats are reared locally. It serves capably rendered modern British dishes with plenty of verve, starting perhaps with Lymington scallops and pork belly with butternut purée and parsnip crisps, and proceeding to sea bass en papillote with garlic butter, or a version of that triumphantly returned bistro classic, boeuf bourguignon, served with horseradish mash. Finish off with brioche-and-butter pudding, or Baileys torte with vanilla ice cream and (no, really) more of those parsnip crisps.

Chef John Oyard **Owner** Robert Anglaret **Seats** 30, Pr/dining room 35
Times 12-2.30/7-9 **Prices** Fixed D 3 course fr £30, Service optional **Wines** 7 bottles over £30, 29 bottles under £30, 5 by glass **Parking** 80 **Notes** Sunday L fr £17.50, Vegetarian available, Children welcome

---

YATELEY   Map 5 SU86

Casa Hotel & Marco Pierre White Restaurant

◎ French, British

tel: 01252 873275 & 749142 **Handford Ln GU46 6BT**
email: info@wheelerscamberley.com **web:** www.wheelerscamberley.com
dir: M3 junct 4a, follow signs for town centre. Hotel signed

Comforting Anglo-French dining

A sprawling hotel that can sort out your wedding and conference needs, the Casa is home to a Marco Pierre White restaurant, under the Wheeler's umbrella. The restaurant takes over two areas with wooden beams and a real fire to bring a warm glow, and the tables wear white linen cloths to inject a little refinement to proceedings. The menu is classic MPW, that is to say a little bit French, a little bit British, with plenty of things you actually want to eat. King scallops with cauliflower purée is a modern classic, here the bivalves cooked just right, or you might kick off with the comforting familiarity of a prawn cocktail. Move on to pan-roasted breast of guinea fowl with green beans, fondant potato and fine jus — a French brasserie dish of heart and soul — while Wheeler's venison pie with parsnip purée is another deeply satisfying option. Cambridge burnt cream and sticky toffee pudding are typical desserts.

Times 12-2.30/6.30-9.30

HEREFORDSHIRE

EWYAS HAROLD   Map 9 SO32

The Temple Bar Inn

◎◎ Modern British NEW

tel: 01981 240423 **HR2 0EU**
email: phillytemplebar@btinternet.com **web:** www.thetemplebarinn.co.uk
dir: From Pontrilas (A465) take B4347 to Ewyas Harold. 1m left into village. 0.1m on right

Renovated village pub with top-notch grub

The recent refurbishment by local craftsmen of this Victorian village watering hole has been a true labour of love. Still a proper pub complete with a pool table, well-kept real ales, oak beams, flagstones and a blazing fire, it's an inviting spot with a friendly atmosphere and accomplished cooking that goes way beyond average gastro-pub offerings. The old stables now house a simple dining room with local artists' work on whitewashed walls, chunky oak tables and sturdy beams. The approach is relatively straightforward, but there are some well-honed modern ideas on the concise, weekly-changing menu, and they are realised with sharp technical ability. Tomato and basil vinaigrette is a vibrant foil to prawn and crab ravioli, while main-course duck breast is supported by a golden potato cake layered with pork fat and black pudding. Otherwise, you might take refuge in the robust comforts of fillet steak with rolled beef shin and suet pudding, creamed potato, kale and crispy bone marrow, and end with fig cake with a brandy snap and vanilla ice cream.

Chef Mike Brindley **Owner** Peter & Phillippa Jinman **Seats** 30, Pr/dining room 45
Times 12-2.30/7-9, Closed 25 Dec, 1 wk Jan/Feb, 1 wk Nov, D Sun-Tue **Prices** Starter £5.50-£8, Main £12-£22, Dessert £5.95-£8, Service optional **Wines** 5 bottles over £30, 14 bottles under £30, 5 by glass **Parking** 12 **Notes** Brunch Sat 11-1pm, Sunday L £13, Vegetarian available, Children welcome

HEREFORD
Map 10 SO53

Castle House
◎◎ Modern British

tel: 01432 356321 Castle St HR1 2NW
email: info@castlehse.co.uk web: www.castlehse.co.uk
dir: City centre, follow brown signs to Castle House Hotel

Culinary voyages into modern Britain within sight of Hereford Castle

The house began life as a conjoined pair of elegant villas lording it over Castle Street during the Regency of George IV. In the 19th century, two became one, their staircases fusing into one majestic sweep, and the entire edifice embarked on its grand hotel career in the 1940s. Beautifully maintained today, it's owned by a local farmer whose produce finds its way on to the unmistakably modern British menus. The principal dining room overlooks the Hereford Castle moat, and is the refined setting for culinary voyages such as grilled mackerel with horseradish gnocchi, beetroot and white chocolate adding a sweet element, followed perhaps by duck breast with sweet potato, green beans, pickled fennel and raspberry vinaigrette. Reversing the fish and meat order might produce braised neck of lamb and courgette lasagne sauced with salsa verde, then roast sea bass fillet with spiced lentils, vanilla-roasted butternut squash, langoustine and pear purée. Vegetarian dishes think outside the box for something like a compression of sweet potatoes and courgettes with roasted shallots and cauliflower, spinach and white wine sauce. Then what else to finish with but white chocolate and dill parfait with pickled cucumber?

Chef Claire Nicholls Owner David Watkins Seats 40 Times 12-2/6.30-9.30
Prices Starter £5-£9, Main £12-£26, Dessert £7-£8, Service optional Wines 57 bottles over £30, 41 bottles under £30, 9 by glass Parking 12 Notes Tasting menu 7 course, Sunday L, Vegetarian available, Children welcome

See advert opposite

Holme Lacy House Hotel
◎◎ Modern British

tel: 01432 870870 Holme Lacy HR2 6LP
email: holmelacy@bourne-leisure.co.uk web: www.warnerleisurehotels.co.uk
dir: B4399 at Holme Lacy, take lane opposite college. Hotel 500mtrs on right

Quality dining in the Wye Valley

Set in the Wye Valley, Holme Lacy House is a listed Georgian mansion in 20 acres of parkland (note the topiary), with an interior boasting ornate ceilings in the lounges, a grand central staircase, and the oak-panelled Orchard Restaurant with its grand fireplace. The menu offers much to interest the palate and the eye, and ingredients are well chosen, with starters like langoustine risotto with tomato fondant and parmesan crisps, and pork faggot with shallot purée, crispy leeks and cider-roast apple. Main courses make an impact too, with nothing too fancy or gimmicky: moist, flavourful roast chicken breast, for instance, served on cabbage, accompanied by confit leg, baby carrots, boulangère potatoes and a well-made jus, or a well-conceived fish alternative of roast halibut fillet with citrus-braised mussels, fennel and dauphinoise potatoes. End with a fruity pudding like pineapple tart with pineapple and Malibu sorbet and coconut mousse, or perhaps the 'quartet of chocolate', or alternatively a plate of top-notch local cheeses.

Chef Douglas Elliman Owner Bourne Leisure Seats 50 Times 6-9, Closed L all week
Prices Prices not confirmed, Service optional Wines 11 bottles over £30, 26 bottles under £30, 11 by glass Parking 200 Notes Vegetarian available, No children

KINGTON
Map 9 SO25

The Stagg Inn and Restaurant
◎◎ Modern British V

tel: 01544 230221 Titley HR5 3RL
email: reservations@thestagg.co.uk
dir: Between Kington & Presteigne on B4335

Impeccable regional cooking in an old drovers' inn

Standing at the junction of two drovers' roads, the Stagg is a country inn on a medieval base with Victorian embellishments. It does everything country inns should, offering accommodation to all (not just drovers), refreshing drinkers in the bar with local ales and good wines, and – the absolute essential these days – a menu of regionally sourced, impeccably presented British food that works some modern technique into deeply rooted traditional ideas. Hearts and livers of duck with mushrooms on toast is one, richly satisfying way to start, while a mackerel fillet comes with smoked bone marrow and pickled cucumber. Locally farmed meats are a joy: rump steak, ox cheek with smoked tongue, shoulder and chop of lamb with caramelised shallots, pheasant with white truffle and parsnip purée. There's room for fish too though, perhaps sea bass with salt-and-pepper squid, and desserts offer an array of seasonal fruits, as well as treats like Pedro Ximénez sherry cheesecake with prunes and coffee ice cream, or there's a trolley freighted with West Country and Welsh cheeses.

Chef S Reynolds, M Handley Owner Steve & Nicola Reynolds Seats 70, Pr/dining room 30 Times 12-2/6.30-9, Closed 2 wks Jan-Feb, 1st 2 wks Nov, Mon-Tue Prices Fixed D 3 course £21.50-£26, Starter £6.50-£9.90, Main £16.90-£24.90, Dessert £7-£8.50, Service optional Wines 8 by glass Parking 22 Notes Sunday L, Children welcome

LEDBURY

Map 10 SO73

Feathers Hotel

◉ Modern British

tel: 01531 635266 **High St HR8 1DS**
email: mary@feathers-ledbury.co.uk **web:** www.feathers-ledbury.co.uk
dir: M50 junct 2. Ledbury on A449/A438/A417. Hotel on main street

Dynamic modern cooking in Tudor style

The heavily timbered Feathers has been wetting whistles and filling stomachs since Shakespeare's day, and it looks as though it intends to stay put. It's a wonderful slice of Tudor England, its oak-panelled venerability thrown into relief by a modern brasserie named after the hop variety Fuggles, and an upmarket dining room, Quills, where dynamic, brightly seasoned modern dishes rule the roost. Look for the likes of lamb kidneys in smoked paprika and sherry cream to start, or scallops with pork scratchings and apple, prior to well-rendered turbot on crab and spring onion risotto with courgette ribbons in shellfish sauce. Sirloins and fillets of local beef are a big draw, as are sweet things such as an ingenious bread-and-butter pudding made with pain au chocolat, served with salt caramel ice cream and chocolate sauce – an absolute treat.

Chef Susan Isaacs **Owner** David Elliston **Seats** 55, Pr/dining room 60
Times 12-2/6.30-9.30 **Prices** Fixed D 3 course fr £27.50, Starter £5.25-£12.50, Main £12.50-£27.50, Dessert £6.25-£10 **Wines** 42 bottles over £30, 97 bottles under £30, 12 by glass **Parking** 30 **Notes** Sunday L, Vegetarian available, Children welcome

Verzon House

◉ Modern British **NEW**

tel: 01531 670381 **Trumpet HR8 2PZ**
email: info@verzonhouse.com **web:** www.verzonhouse.com
dir: M50 junct 2, left at rdbt, follow A438 to Hereford, located on right

Stylish and contemporary restaurant with rooms

A restaurant with rooms that strikes a good balance between rustic charm and contemporary style, Verzon House feels very much of our time. There is evident attention paid to the details, whether that's the quirky designer items dotted about the place or the careful sourcing of ingredients undertaken by the kitchen team. The trendy bar is the place to go if you fancy a nifty cocktail. The restaurant – or Kitchen as they call it – has period appeal and a rustic-chic finish (chunky wooden tables, mix-and-match chairs, neutral colours), and offers a menu packed with regional produce. The Josper grill works its magic on Hereford beef – 28-day aged sirloin, say, cooked as requested and served with triple-cooked chips – or a Middlewhite pork chop with a cider glaze. Start with summer vegetable gnocchi or a tartare of Cornish mackerel, and finish with tonka bean rice pudding. Afternoon tea and local ales add to the appeal of the place.

Chef Callum McDonald **Owner** Kate & William Chase **Seats** 50, Pr/dining room 20
Times 12-2.30/6.30-9.30 **Prices** Fixed L 2 course £18, Starter £6-£11, Main £14-£50, Dessert £7-£7.50, Service optional **Wines** 42 bottles over £30, 29 bottles under £30, 11 by glass **Parking** 35 **Notes** Afternoon tea £15, Sunday L £20-£25, Vegetarian available, Children welcome

LEINTWARDINE

Map 9 SO47

The Lion

◉ Modern British

tel: 01547 540203 & 540747 **High St SY7 0JZ**
email: enquiries@thelionleintwardine.co.uk **web:** www.thelionleintwardine.co.uk
dir: On A4113. At bottom of High Street by bridge

Seasonal modern pub cooking on the Teme

Keen anglers should cast their rods in the direction of this village pub on the upper Teme, a tributary of the River Severn, where trout and grayling are abundant. Others will just appreciate the authentic air of a country inn, where old beams and inviting leather sofas play their homely part. The lounge bar and an attractive garden are supplementary dining spaces to an elegant restaurant, and the seasonally-changing contemporary food is squarely in the modern manner. Start with goats' cheese and spinach ravioli in truffled cream sauce with crispy leeks, as a possible overture to turbot with garlicky razor clams and chorizo-butter bean cassoulet, local beef fillet with dauphinoise, or a faithful rendering of hearty coq au vin. Pudding might be something sturdily British like a treacle and ginger suet sponge with custard. Light bites such as tomato and mozzarella bruschetta should satisfy the snackers.

Chef Paul Halmshaw **Owner** Mr & Mrs W Watkins **Seats** 50, Pr/dining room 20
Times 12-2.30/6-9.30, Closed 25 Dec **Prices** Starter £5-£8, Main £13-£24, Dessert £5-£9 **Wines** 12 bottles over £30, 27 bottles under £30, 10 by glass **Parking** 20 **Notes** Sunday L £13.95-£19.95, Vegetarian available, Children welcome

The Chase Hotel

◉ British, Modern European

tel: 01989 763161 **Gloucester Rd HR9 5LH**
email: res@chasehotel.co.uk **web:** www.chasehotel.co.uk
dir: *M50 junct 4 onto A449. Take A40 towards Gloucester, turn right at rdbt into Ross-on-Wye. Hotel on left 0.25m*

Georgian country-house hotel with stylish restaurant

Every bit the contemporary dining room, Harry's Restaurant is named after the owner's grandson, rather than an homage to the iconic Venetian bar. Set in a large Georgian mansion with 11 acres of grounds, its modern shades of cream, tan and black, up-to-date furnishings and silk drapes blend quite happily with the room's original high ceilings, ornate plasterwork and tall windows. The modern European comfort-orientated menu ranges widely, offering something for everyone, built on fresh, quality local ingredients. Things like slow-braised belly pork with black pudding, apple purée and crackling, Puy lentils and creamed potato line up alongside those that speak of sunnier climes – perhaps monkfish wrapped in pancetta and served with silverskin onions, mushrooms and red wine jus. Desserts follow the theme, with a true Brit sticky toffee pudding competing for favour against an almond and apricot tart with Amaretto syllabub.

Chef Andrew Clark **Owner** Camanoe Estates Ltd **Seats** 70, Pr/dining room 300 **Times** 12-2/6-9.30, Closed 24-27 Dec **Prices** Starter £6-£10, Main £11-£23, Dessert £6-£9, Service optional **Wines** 12 bottles over £30, 33 bottles under £30, 13 by glass **Parking** 75 **Notes** Sunday L £22.50, Vegetarian available, Children welcome

Glewstone Court Country House Hotel

◉◉ Modern, Traditional British

tel: 01989 770367 **Glewstone HR9 6AW**
email: info@glewstonecourt.com **web:** www.glewstonecourt.com
dir: *From Ross Market Place take A40/A49 (Monmouth/Hereford) over Wilton Bridge. At rdbt left onto A40 (Monmouth/S Wales), after 1m turn right for Glewstone. Hotel 0.5m on left*

West Country produce in an attractive Wye Valley Georgian hotel

The Homewoods have done an exemplary job turning this Georgian rural retreat with portico entrance and deep windows into the model of a warmly welcoming country hotel. Its two acres of grounds have the lush Wye Valley for backdrop, the interiors are simply but elegantly appointed, with candelabra on the dining tables, and the cooking, which casts its net wide for inspiration, is now on a strong upswing. Delicately constructed mushroom ravioli made of sheer pasta are meatily enhanced with chorizo and a salad of shredded chicken, lobster cocktails come with Bloody Mary gel, and salmon is cured in maple syrup and orange and served with a beetroot blini. Among main courses, things go Moroccan for the spiced lamb samosa, and apricot and pomegranate tabbouleh, that come with braised lamb rump, or there may be red snapper in sauce vièrge. A signature take on banoffee produces cookie dough, caramel parfait and fudge, along with banana ice cream and chocolate shreds, for a triumphant finale. You can tell the Eton Mess is particularly posh, as it comes with Pimm's jelly and a minty tuile.

Chef Vicky Lyons **Owner** Gary & Karen Homewood **Seats** 70, Pr/dining room 45 **Times** 12-2/7-10, Closed 27-28 Dec, D 24-26 Dec **Prices** Tasting menu £40, Starter £6-£11, Main £16-£22, Dessert £7, Service optional **Wines** 16 bottles over £30, 29 bottles under £30, 14 by glass **Parking** 28 **Notes** Sunday L £12-£25, Vegetarian available, Children welcome

Orles Barn

◉ British, European NEW

tel: 01989 562155 & 07747 187786 **Wilton HR9 6AE**
email: reservations@orles-barn.co.uk **web:** www.orles-barn.co.uk
dir: *From Wilton rdbt take slip road between BP Garage & A40 to Monmouth. 200 yds on left*

Genteel spot for imaginative modern menus

This red-brick building with 17th-century origins has been turned into a genteel restaurant with rooms. The internal spaces are elegant and gently contemporary, suiting the relaxed and soothing mood of the place, and they can even sort out your wedding day with the help of a marquee in the pretty garden. When it comes to wining and dining, the restaurant offers contemporary British dishes in a traditionally refined space with pistachio-coloured walls and well-spaced tables. Kick off with pink and gamey pigeon breast, served with salted turnips, turnip purée and a punchy blackberry jus, followed by sea bass with orange and fennel salad, or a fashionable trio of pork with crackling sticks. For dessert, spiced carrot cake comes with a carrot and toffee sauce, and blackberry and apple parfait with honey ice cream, while a plate of five local cheeses is a savoury alternative.

Chef Richard Hoskins **Owner** Kerry Oloman, Richard Hoskins **Seats** 70 **Times** 12-2/6.30-9 **Prices** Fixed L 2 course £16.50, Fixed D 3 course £21.15-£38.50, Tasting menu £65, Starter £4.95-£9.95, Main £11.25-£18.50, Dessert £4.95-£9.95, Service optional **Wines** 1 bottle over £30, 18 bottles under £30, 7 by glass **Parking** 12 **Notes** Sunday L £16.50-£19.95, Vegetarian available, Children welcome

Wilton Court Restaurant with Rooms

◉◉ Modern British

tel: 01989 562569 **Wilton Ln HR9 6AQ**
email: info@wiltoncourthotel.com **web:** www.wiltoncourthotel.com
dir: *M50 junct 4 onto A40 towards Monmouth at 3rd rdbt turn left signed Ross-on-Wye then take 1st right, hotel on right*

Intelligent modern cookery on the Wye riverside

A riverside setting on the Wye makes for much natural diversion at Wilton Court. Swans glide, otters splash, kingfishers swoop, and the air is full of birdsong. Wilton itself partly dates back to around 1500 and was once the local magistrate's court. What is now the Riverview dining room rang to the handing down of sentences, while the Mulberry Restaurant is where the intelligent modern British food is allowed free rein. Full-flavoured soups are a smart bet – perhaps roast tomato and chilli, or celeriac with potato dumplings and bacon foam – or you may opt to start with a vivid risotto of smoked haddock and peas. Then it's local meats to the fore in mains such as mustard- and herb-crumbed lamb loin with dauphinoise and ratatouille, or pedigree Hereford beef fillet on a big roasted mushroom, with champ and a sauce of pink peppercorns. West Country and Welsh cheeses (the border is a mere five miles away) get a listing of their own, or there are sweet indulgences like white chocolate parfait with dark chocolate milkshake and a brownie.

Chef Rachael Williams **Owner** Roger & Helen Wynn **Seats** 40, Pr/dining room 12 **Times** 12-2.30/6.30-9.15, Closed 1st 2 wks Jan **Prices** Fixed L 2 course £16.95, Fixed D 3 course £32.50, Tasting menu £52.50, Starter £5.25-£9.25, Main £14.95-£24.50, Dessert £6.95-£7.50, Service optional **Wines** 8 bottles over £30, 37 bottles under £30, 9 by glass **Parking** 25 **Notes** Tasting menu 7 course (complete tables only), Sunday L £16.95-£19.95, Vegetarian available, Children welcome

HERTFORDSHIRE

BERKHAMSTED
Map 6 SP90

The Gatsby

Modern European

tel: 01442 870403 **97 High St HP4 2DG**
email: thegatsby@live.co.uk
dir: M25 junct 20/A41 to Aylesbury in 3m take left turn to Berkhamsted following town signs. Restaurant on left on entering High St

Movies and brasserie cooking in a retooled art deco cinema

The Rex cinema opened in 1938 and closed 50 years on. The good news is the cinema returned to business in 2004 with the addition of The Gatsby restaurant the next year. This stylish modern brasserie occupies a handsome art deco space with darkwood tables and plenty of pictures of the golden age of British cinema. The menu takes inspiration from far and wide and shows a good degree of ambition. A starter of chargrilled artichoke and Swiss chard risotto, for example, might have caught Fellini's interest while the smoked fish kedgeree with soft boiled egg and Chiltern eye might have been down Hitchcock's street. Next up, fillet of halibut is served with a moules marinière sauce, lamb tagine is enriched with almonds and dates, and roast Barbary duck breast is dressed with a blackberry and anise sauce. Finish with treacle tart with candied pecans or a classic tarte Tatin with rum and raisin ice cream.

Chef Matthew Salt **Owner** Nick Pembroke **Seats** 65
Times 12-2.30/5.30-10.30, Closed 25-26 Dec **Prices** Fixed L 2 course £14.95, Fixed D 3 course £20.90, Starter £6.95-£9.25, Main £14.95-£28.95, Dessert £7.95-£8.95, Service optional **Wines** 25 bottles over £30, 27 bottles under £30, 16 by glass **Parking** 10 **Notes** Pre cinema menu Mon-Sat 12-2.30 & 5.30-6.30, Sunday L £15.95, Vegetarian available, Children welcome

BISHOP'S STORTFORD
Map 6 TL42

Down Hall Country House Hotel

Modern British **NEW**

tel: 01279 731441 **Hatfield Heath CM22 7AS**
email: info@downhall.co.uk **web:** www.downhall.co.uk
dir: Take A414 towards Harlow. At 4th rdbt follow B183 towards Hatfield Heath, keep left, follow hotel sign

Brasserie-style menu in a grand house

The house originally dates from the 1300s, but its impressively grand Italianate exterior shows the mark of a Victorian makeover. The surrounding landscape – 110 acres all to itself – helps to enhance the sense of getting away from it all, and explain why this venue is such a hit with the wedding and conference brigade. The dining options include a terrace serving up bar snacks in the summer, with afternoon tea up for grabs in one of the elegant lounges, but the main event is the Grill Room restaurant. With period details such as ornate cornices and white-painted columns, the dining room has a vibe reminiscent of an upmarket French brasserie. The kitchen delivers unruffled stuff such as Coln Valley smoked salmon with bacon and lentils, followed by corn-fed chicken breast with wild mushroom risotto or rib-eye steak with classic accompaniments. Finish with an equally classic lemon tart.

Chef Robert Haynes **Owner** Down Hall Hotel Ltd **Seats** 60, Pr/dining room 200 **Times** 12.30-2/6.30-9.30, Closed 24 & 31 Dec, L Sat **Prices** Fixed L 2 course fr £25.95, Fixed D 3 course fr £32.50 **Wines** 19 bottles over £30, 19 bottles under £30, 8 by glass **Parking** 120 **Notes** Sunday L fr £24.50, Vegetarian available, Children welcome

CHANDLER'S CROSS
Map 6 TQ09

Colette's at The Grove

– see page 222

The Stables Restaurant at The Grove

Modern British

tel: 01923 807807 & 296015 **WD3 4TG**
email: restaurants@thegrove.co.uk
dir: M25 junct 19, A411 towards Watford. Hotel on right

Creative modern cooking in George Stubbs' favourite stables

The original stable block of the Georgian mansion, where George Stubbs spent hours at his easel, has been given a modern makeover under its rafters and is now the informal eatery at The Grove. The open-to-view kitchen is equipped with a wood-fired oven and chargrill, but the menu has a lot more going for it than pizzas and steaks. Imaginative starters have run from chicken liver and foie gras brûlée to beetroot and goats' cheese tarte Tatin with truffled honey. Seafood gets a good airing, from aromatic crab cake to well-timed roast pollack with cockles, pancetta and Jerusalem artichoke purée, and quality produce is apparent throughout. Try roast Banham chicken with Savoy cabbage and chestnuts, say, or roast shoulder of salt marsh lamb with parsley creamed potatoes, mushrooms, roast garlic and confit shallots. Dark chocolate tart and Baileys crème brûlée are popular puddings.

Chef Christopher Mouyiassi **Owner** Ralph Trustees Ltd **Seats** 120, Pr/dining room 16 **Times** 12-3/6-9.30, Closed 25 Dec, D 31 Dec **Prices** Starter £7-£12, Main £14-£30, Dessert £6-£13, Service optional **Wines** 11 bottles over £30, 10 bottles under £30, 10 by glass **Parking** 300 **Notes** Sunday L £16-£19.50, Vegetarian available, Children welcome

DATCHWORTH
Map 6 TL21

The Tilbury

Modern British

tel: 01438 815550 **Watton Rd SG3 6TB**
email: info@thetilbury.co.uk
dir: A1(M) junct 7, A602 signed Ware & Hertford. At Bragbury End right into Bragbury Lane to Datchworth

Village gastro-pub doing Datchworth proud

The food at The Tilbury headed upwards a notch or two after a new chef took the culinary helm in 2014. Lucky Datchworth, then, as it has a gastro-pub that balances being a good local watering hole and a place to eat seriously good food. Quality first and foremost drives the kitchen's output, starting with carefully-sourced produce, much of it British, and much of it local. Keeping things classic, a pub menu lists the likes of cottage pie or fish and chips with mushy peas and tartare sauce. Flip it over and it's clear that this kitchen can move things up a gear, sending out a starter of chicken terrine with bacon jam and sweetcorn purée, followed by a robust plate of pork belly and loin with ham and squeak balls, bacon greens and apple sauce. Fishy ideas could see pan-fried turbot paired with girolles, baby onions, kale and mash. Pudding could be a classy cylinder of white chocolate parfait coated with pistachio crumbs and served with olive oil cake.

Chef Chas Wheeler **Owner** James & Tom Bainbridge, Nicola Brown **Seats** 70, Pr/dining room 36 **Times** 12-2.30/6-9.30, Closed Closed some BHs, Mon, D Sun **Prices** Fixed L 2 course £15-£17, Starter £5.50-£8.50, Main £12-£22.50, Dessert £5-£7.50, Service optional **Wines** 15 bottles over £30, 20 bottles under £30, 11 by glass **Parking** 40 **Notes** Sunday L £21-£25, Vegetarian available, Children welcome

ELSTREE
Map 6 TL19

Laura Ashley The Manor
Modern British NEW

tel: 020 8327 4700 **Barnet Ln WD6 3RE**
email: elstree@lauraashleyhotels.com **web:** www.lauraashleyhotels.com
dir: From A1 take A411 from Stirling Corner. From M25 either junct 19 or 23

Country-house dining and Laura Ashley styling

The Laura Ashley empire does much more than purvey floral-print furnishings to the discerning. Its hotel operation includes this 16th-century manor house restyled in plenty of contemporary beige, the panelling given a light cream look throughout. Setting off the mullioned windows in the Cavendish dining room, it makes for a cheering ambience in which to eat some well-considered country-house cooking. Purées abound, apple for the ham knuckle terrine, and the expected cauliflower for scallops in a lively currant and peppercorn dressing. Main courses explore the possibilities of gentle slow cooking for braised beef with glazed baby onions, mushrooms and creamy mash, or potato-crusted sea bass with Brussels sprouts and pea purée. Finish with the sensational trifle, a treat all the way from its crushed amaretti topping to its cherry compôte foundation.

Chef Stephanie Malvoisin **Owner** Laura Ashley Hotels **Seats** 40, Pr/dining room 40 **Times** 12.30-2/7-9.30, Closed L Sat **Prices** Fixed L 2 course £19.95, Fixed D 3 course £35 **Wines** 33 bottles over £30, 11 bottles under £30, 12 by glass **Parking** 100 **Notes** Afternoon tea £20.95, Sunday L £24.95, Vegetarian available, Children welcome

FLAUNDEN
Map 6 TL00

Bricklayers Arms
British, French

tel: 01442 833322 & 831722 **Black Robin Ln, Hogpits Bottom HP3 0PH**
email: goodfood@bricklayersarms.com
dir: M25 junct 20, A451 towards Chipperfield. Into Dunny Ln, 1st right into Flaunden Ln. 1m on single track

Traditional country inn with well-crafted Anglo-French cooking

The Bricklayers was built in the 18th century and is now a cheery gastro-pub with a cosy atmosphere, rustic oak beams, a log fire and a brick bar, offering plenty of tables in the garden and on the terrace. Food is a serious commitment, with the kitchen sourcing locally and paying due respect to the seasons and complementing the menus with daily fish and vegetarian specials. 'English and French fusion' is the self-described style, so expect to find eggs Benedict to start alongside venison terrine with pear chutney. Among main courses, haunch of venison is cooked in red wine and redcurrants and topped with glazed onions and mushrooms, another full-on meat alternative is ox cheek in ale and honey served with champ. The fish of the day may bring on haddock and red mullet pie in saffron cream, and puddings may run to thin apple tart with vanilla ice cream.

Chef Claude Paillet, Alan Bell, Martin West **Owner** Alvin & Sally Michaels **Seats** 95, Pr/dining room 50 **Times** 12-2.30/6.30-9.30, Closed 25 Dec **Prices** Fixed L 2 course £16.50, Fixed D 3 course £21.50, Starter £6.45-£9.45, Main £11.95-£25.95, Dessert £4.75-£7.45, Service optional **Wines** 96 bottles over £30, 34 bottles under £30, 16 by glass **Parking** 40 **Notes** Sunday L, Vegetarian available, Children welcome

Colette's at The Grove

CHANDLER'S CROSS
Map 6 TQ09

Modern European V NOTABLE WINE LIST

tel: 01923 807807 **WD3 4TG**
email: info@thegrove.co.uk **web:** www.thegrove.co.uk
dir: M25 junct 19, follow signs to Watford. At 1st large rdbt take 3rd exit. 0.5m, entrance on right

Avante-garde cooking on a grand country estate

It's hard to believe you're within the radius of the M25 in this grand Georgian mansion built for the Earls of Clarendon in 300 acres of prime Hertfordshire countryside. Today's incarnation is a luxurious country hotel, where an air of finely drilled professionalism prevails throughout and all the expected temptations to satisfy the 21st-century visitor are to hand. That means a championship golf course, indulgent spa, and contemporary old-meets-new decor. The range of dining options peaks in Colette's, where Russell Bateman's avante-garde culinary genius is given free rein. Bateman has worked with several of the big names of contemporary Anglo-French gastronomy – Gordon Ramsay, Marc Veyrat and Marcus Wareing – and he's on a mission to dazzle. It all starts with the raw materials of course, many from the estate's organic walled garden. If the whole table is up for it, there are five- or nine-course taster menus (including a vegetarian version), but if you prefer to retain control over what you eat, choose from the à la carte Haiku menu – dishes cross from one to the other anyway. A starter of diver-caught scallops and oyster is offset with the flavours of celeriac, apple and coastal herbs, or the richness of Landes foie gras might be leavened by prunes, plum and brioche. Main course focuses on the distinctive qualities of Wagyu beef rump, which arrives in a picturesque medley with spring onion cannelloni, black garlic, shiitake mushrooms and watercress. Dessert brings intense Inaya chocolate with subtle undertones of Provençal olive oil and salt. There's a less formal eating option in the Stables, where the great equestrian painter George Stubbs produced much of his work.

Chef Russell Bateman **Owner** Ralph Trustees Ltd **Seats** 40, Pr/dining room 24 **Times** 6.30-9.30, Closed Sun-Mon (ex BHs), L all week **Prices** Tasting menu £75-£85, Service optional **Wines** 8 bottles over £30, 4 bottles under £30, 24 by glass **Parking** 300 **Notes** ALC 3 course £65, Vegetarian tasting menu 8 course, Children 16 yrs+

Beales Hotel

 Modern British

tel: 01707 288500 & 288518   **Comet Way AL10 9NG**
email: outsidein@bealeshotels.co.uk **web:** www.bealeshotels.co.uk
dir: *On A1001 opposite Galleria Shopping Mall – follow signs for Galleria*

Anglo-Med magic in a striking modern hotel

The Hatfield Beales is a striking piece of contemporary design, from its jungle-gym outer packaging to its self-assertively patterned interiors, hung with works by Hertfordshire University students. Not for Beales the monotonous monochrome surfaces of elsewhere; if they could squeeze on a repeating motif, it's got one. The dining room looks unexpectedly small for a hotel, which creates its own aura of exclusivity, and some tables even have couches so you can loll through dinner. The cooking is a mix of modern British classics and Mediterranean magic, with goats' cheese pannacotta in warmly spiced tomato salsa, or a slim slice of chicken and ham terrine in mustard vinaigrette. This sets up the taste buds for mains such as crisp-fried sea bass with accurately timed saffron risotto and diced chorizo, or perhaps a rib eye steak of local beef with onion rings and peppercorn sauce. A dessert glass of slightly slushy papaya and dragon fruit parfait with excellent passionfruit sorbet is a thing of two halves, so raspberry and white chocolate tart with clotted cream and almond brittle may be the better bet.

Chef Scott Whitehead **Owner** Beales Ltd **Seats** 60, Pr/dining room 300
Times 12-2.30/6-10 **Prices** Prices not confirmed, Service optional **Wines** 11 by glass
Parking 126 **Notes** Vegetarian available, Children welcome

Chez Mumtaj

French, Asian

tel: 01727 800033 **Centurian House, 136-142 London Rd AL1 1PQ**
email: info@chezmumtaj.com **web:** www.chezmumtaj.com
dir: *Please phone for directions*

Franco-Asian fusion food in opulent surroundings

Chez Mumtaj emanates class and style, with its panelled walls and comfortable cream leather-look banquettes at correctly set clothed tables, and an open-to-view kitchen. As the name suggests, the style is a culinary hybrid: what the restaurant itself describes as 'haute cuisine in modern French-Asian dining', with classical techniques applied to tip-top produce. The long menu may open with the signature dish of bird's nest quail Scotch egg – the egg encased in truffle, foie gras and

minced chicken, coated in breadcrumbs within crispy kataifi pastry and served with wasabi remoulade – or soft-shelled crab in chilli and garlic tempura with spicy marmalade. Best end of lamb rogan josh sounds familiar enough, and there may also be a main course of seared fillets of sea bass with Keralan-style velouté, garlicky okra, smoked aubergine and chickpea caviar, chive butter, and lemon and chilli rice. End with the more Western-sounding mango and orange crème brûlée.

Chez Mumtaj

Chef Chad Rahman **Owner** Chad Rahman **Seats** 100, Pr/dining room 16
Times 12-2.30/6-11, Closed 25 Dec, Mon **Prices** Prices not confirmed **Wines** 21 bottles over £30, 26 bottles under £30, 14 by glass **Parking** On street & car park nearby **Notes** Tasting menu, Early bird D menu, Sunday L, Vegetarian available, Children welcome

See advert on page 224

St Michael's Manor

Modern British, European **V**

tel: 01727 864444 **Fishpool St AL3 4RY**
email: reservations@stmichaelsmanor.com **web:** www.stmichaelsmanor.com
dir: *Off Hight St onto George St. Past Cathedral into Fishpool St. Hotel at end*

Accomplished British cooking with lakeside views

A handsome Georgian mansion standing in five acres of beautiful landscaped gardens, complete with lake, and close to the magnificent cathedral, St Michael's Manor provides the setting for food with clear flavours and top-class provenance. The culinary side of things takes place in the classy orangery-style Lake restaurant, whose windows allow you to contemplate those sumptuous gardens and the water. An ambitious new chef took the reins in 2014, propelling the kitchen's seasonal modern British cuisine on an upwards trajectory. Take your pick between a fortnightly-changing two- or three-course menu of uncomplicated brasserie-style ideas, or trade up to the carte. This delivers a main course matching spiced tenderloin of pork and crispy pork cheek with mango and wilted pak choi. Fish is also handled with aplomb – perhaps steamed sea bass with Dorset crab crushed potatoes, sauce vièrge and herb salad. Before that, pan-fried scallops are pointed up with chorizo-flecked mayonnaise and cauliflower. For afters, wrap things up with a vibrant combo of coconut pannacotta with mango and lime.

Chef Simon Johnston **Owner** Sheila Newling Ward **Seats** 130, Pr/dining room 22
Times 12-2/7-9.30, Closed L 31 Dec, D 25 Dec **Prices** Prices not confirmed **Wines** 39 bottles over £30, 40 bottles under £30, 8 by glass **Parking** 80 **Notes** ALC menu 2/3 course £26/£34, Sunday L, Children welcome

ST ALBANS *continued*

Sopwell House

◉ Modern British, French

tel: 01727 864477 **Cottonmill Ln, Sopwell AL1 2HQ**
email: enquiries@sopwellhouse.co.uk **web:** www.sopwellhouse.co.uk
dir: *M25 junct 22, A1081 St Albans. At lights left into Mile House Ln, over mini-rdbt into Cottonmill Ln*

Smart dining in Mountbatten's former country home

The estate dates from Tudor times, though the present house is Georgian, having been leased to the late Earl Mountbatten as a country residence in the last century. It makes a splendid stately hotel, equipped with spa and wedding facilities, with dining divided among conservatory, brasserie and restaurant, depending on your style. The last is a glamorous, high-ceilinged setting for modern cooking of great vigour. Crab tian with avocado, pink grapefruit and lemon purée brings new pizazz to an old classic, or there may be potted salt beef with a crisp-cooked quail's egg and horseradish crème fraîche. Main courses are built on solid culinary logic, partnering grilled trout with lobster linguini and seafood broth, while honey-roast duck comes with braised red cabbage and truffled chive mash. Sides include hearty leek and potato gratin, and desserts won't lack for takers when there's chocolate truffle and pistachio ice cream on offer.

Chef Mark Sutherland, Gopi Chandra **Owner** Abraham Bejerano **Seats** 100, Pr/dining room 320 **Times** 12-2/7-9.30, Closed Mon-Tue, L Thu & Sat, D Sun **Prices** Fixed L 3 course £29-£35, Fixed D 3 course £35, Starter £9.75-£12.75, Main £22-£28, Dessert £6-£9.50 **Wines** 32 bottles over £30, 20 bottles under £30, 14 by glass **Parking** 300 **Notes** L/D offer £55/£65 for 2 with wine, Sunday L £29, Vegetarian available, Children welcome

THOMPSON@Darcy's

◉◉ Modern British V

tel: 01727 730777 **2 Hatfield Rd AL1 3RP**
email: info@thompsonatdarcys.co.uk **web:** www.thompsonatdarcys.co.uk
dir: *M25 junct 22, A1081 London Rd to St Albans. At major x-rds right onto St Albans High St, 2nd right onto Hatfield Rd*

Classy contemporary cooking with interesting combinations

Phil Thompson's name is above the door of his restaurant in a row of part-boarded cottages in the centre of town. Having won plaudits at Auberge du Lac down the road, Thompson has struck out on his own in this smartly done out address with local artworks hanging on the walls (for sale if you fancy one) and a stylish contemporary finish. The menu shows classical leanings and plenty of interesting combinations, with the dishes arriving at the table looking fine and dandy. There are set lunch and midweek evening menus (great value) alongside the carte, while Sunday evening is 'Lobster & Steak Night'. A starter of port-marinated foie gras

boudin shows off the skill and confidence of this kitchen, with perfect balance of flavours, followed by chargrilled Dingley Dell pork rib-eye partnered with its confit shoulder (plus poached plums and gingerbread crumb). Finish with fromage frais pannacotta with poached Yorkshire rhubarb and delicious little custard doughnuts. A terrific addition to the Hertfordshire dining scene.

THOMPSON@Darcy's

Chef Phil Thompson **Owner** Phil Thompson **Seats** 90, Pr/dining room 70 **Times** 12-2.30/6-9 **Prices** Fixed L 2 course £16.50, Fixed D 3 course £23, Tasting menu £49-£55, Starter £10.50-£14, Main £21-£32, Dessert £4.50-£12.50, Service optional 10% **Wines** 36 bottles over £30, 21 bottles under £30, 16 by glass **Parking** 0.5m away (signed) **Notes** Tasting menu 6 course, Lobster & steak night Sun eve, Sunday L £25-£29.50, Children welcome

TRING
Map 6 SP91

Pendley Manor Hotel

◉◉ Traditional British

tel. 01442 891891 **Cow Ln HP23 5QY**
email: sales@pendley-manor.co.uk **web:** www.pendley-manor.co.uk
dir: M25 junct 20, A41 (Tring exit). At rdbt follow Berkhamsted/London signs. 1st left signed Tring Station & Pendley Manor

Handsome manor house with modern cooking

Although Pendley's history stretches back a 1,000 years and gets it a mention in the Domesday Book, the current incarnation is part Victorian neo-Tudor, built in 1872 after a fire destroyed the original, and part modern annexe, built to extend significantly its events and conference capacity. The Victorian section offers period grandeur in spades, particularly in the Oak Restaurant where oak flooring, lofty ceilings, colourful patterned wallpaper, and swagged-back drapes at vast bay windows make for an imposing setting. The cooking, however has its feet firmly in the 21st century: 'ham, eggs, chips, peas and ketchup' brings those components together in a rather more refined version than the greasy spoon classic, or you might set out with seared scallops with lobster potato cake, pea salad, plum tomato and lemon verbena sauce. At main course stage, butter-poached halibut fillet is teamed to good effect with chive mash, caramelised veal sweetbreads, gem lettuce, morels, green beans and a chicken stock lifted with sherry vinegar. Finally, peanut parfait arrives with dark chocolate mousse and caramel sauce.

Chef Martin White **Owner** Craydawn Pendley Manor **Seats** 75, Pr/dining room 200 **Times** 12.30-2.30/7-9.30, Closed L Sat **Prices** Prices not confirmed, Service optional **Wines** 13 bottles over £30, 33 bottles under £30, 7 by glass **Parking** 150 **Notes** Sunday L, Vegetarian available, Children welcome

WELWYN
Map 6 TL21

Auberge du Lac

◉◉ French, European, British V

tel. 01707 368888 **Brocket Hall Estate, Brocket Rd AL8 7XG**
email: auberge@brocket-hall.co.uk
dir: A1(M) junct 4, B653 to Wheathampstead. In Brocket Ln take 2nd gate entry to Brocket Hall

Refined contemporary cooking in a lakeside hunting lodge

The pretty red-brick Auberge a short stroll from the big house (the magnificent Brocket Hall) used to be a hunting lodge, but these days it has far more leisurely pursuits in mind. Standing by the eponymous lake amidst the 543-acre estate, Auberge du Lac doesn't want for charm, with its 18th-century façade and soothing waterside setting. A table outside is a real treat when the weather allows. Within, all is soothing sophistication, with the tables dressed in pristine white linen. The cooking has its roots in classical French tradition, but a cornucopia of British ingredients and an eye for contemporary culinary goings-on mean the kitchen turns out bright and creative dishes. Pan-roasted Orkney scallops come as a first course in the fashionable company of black pudding and textures of cauliflower, followed by braised pork belly flavoured with five spice and served with a sesame coated spare rib (plus a broccoli purée and pak choi). Finish with hazelnut, coffee and chocolate dacquoise. The wine list doesn't stint when it comes to offering up stellar French bottles.

Chef Marcus McGuinness **Owner** CCA International **Seats** 70, Pr/dining room 32 **Times** 12-2.30/7-9.30, Closed 27 Dec-17 Jan, Mon, D Sun **Prices** Prices not confirmed **Wines** 14 by glass **Parking** 50 **Notes** ALC fixed 3 course £60, Tasting menu 6/9 course £69/£79, Sunday L, Children 12 yrs+

Tewin Bury Farm Hotel

◉◉ Modern British V

tel. 01438 717793 **Hertford Road (B1000) AL6 0JB**
email: restaurant@tewinbury.co.uk **web:** www.tewinbury.co.uk
dir: A1(M) junct 6 (signed Welwyn Garden City), 1st exit A1000. 0.25m to B1000 Hertford Rd. Hotel on left

Up-to-the-minute modern cookery on a working farm

A complex of barns on a working farm has been skilfully converted into this characterful modern hotel and restaurant with conference facilities; it's a sought-after venue for weddings too. The restaurant is in what used to be a chicken shed, now a handsome room with a beamed ceiling above rafters, mustard-yellow banquettes, a boarded floor and bare-topped wooden tables. Many of the kitchen's raw materials are produced on-site, with the rest assiduously sourced: Dingley Dell pork from Suffolk, for instance, seen in a gutsy main course of slow-cooked belly with a crisp cake of head meat in red wine jus with apple purée, celeriac gratin and curly kale. The rest of the menu is a slate of highly original, well-executed ideas, from white bean and chorizo soup to smoked and poached salmon rillettes with nori and a salad of fennel, red endive and orange. The thoughtful approach continues with main courses like spot-on, firm-fleshed fillet of hake with clam chowder, spinach and new potatoes. Glazed orange tart is a rich, creamy way to finish, offset by liquorice ice cream.

Owner Vaughan Williams **Seats** 60, Pr/dining room 30 **Times** 12-2.30/6.30-9.30, Closed D 25 & 31 Dec **Prices** Fixed L 2 course £17.50, Starter £6.50-£7.95, Main £13.95-£23.95, Dessert £6.50-£9.25, Service optional **Wines** 13 bottles over £30, 19 bottles under £30, 12 by glass **Parking** 400 **Notes** All day dining on Sun 8am-8.30pm, Sunday L £24.95, Children welcome

WELWYN *continued*

The Waggoners

🏵 French

tel: 01707 324241 **Brickwall Close, Ayot Green AL6 9AA**
email: laurent@thewaggoners.co.uk
dir: *A1(M) junct 6 to B197, right into Ayot and 1st left Brickwall Close*

Contemporary French cooking in lovely village inn

With its venerable beams, inglenook fireplace and convivial ambience, the setting is that of a rather romantic, quintessentially English 17th- century inn, albeit with a nod to 21st-century tastes in the restaurant. But all is not what it seems: the effusive greeting from The Waggoners' hands-on French owners serves as a heads-up to the distinctly Gallic leanings of the menu. There are seasonal influences drawn from the wider European cuisine, thus a summer meal opens with smoked duck salad with spiced apple chutney, watercress and radish and grain mustard dressing, or perhaps gazpacho with the added bonus of crayfish, avocado and grilled peppers. Following on, pan-fried sea bream is matched with saffron and fennel compôte and sauce vièrge, and things end on an impeccably summery note courtesy of a vanilla pannacotta with strawberry compôte and basil.

Chef Paul Ribbands **Owner** Laurent & Aude Brydniak **Seats** 65, Pr/dining room 35 **Times** 12-2.30/6.30-9, Closed D Sun **Prices** Fixed L 2 course £14.50-£17.50, Fixed D 3 course fr £19.95, Tasting menu fr £30, Starter £6-£10.50, Main £13-£24, Dessert £6-£7, Service optional **Wines** 40 bottles over £30, 60 bottles under £30, 22 by glass **Parking** 70 **Notes** Sunday L £18-£28, Vegetarian available, Children welcome

The Wellington

🏵 Modern British

tel: 01438 714036 **High St AL6 9LZ**
email: info@wellingtonatwelwyn.co.uk **web:** www.wellingtonatwelwyn.co.uk
dir: *A1(M) junct 6, on High Street in Welwyn village across from St Mary's Church*

Village inn with an appealing menu

Going strong since 1352, The Wellington, on Welwyn's pretty high street, is an old coaching inn which takes a contemporary approach to the business of hospitality. A makeover a few years ago has opened up the place, seen the addition of some rather cool bedrooms, and put the focus firmly on the gastro side of the pub spectrum. It looks good with its rustic-chic exposed brick walls, real fires and bar stocked with proper beers. The menu keeps things simple and unpretentious, so you might choose to tuck into a hearty beef and Wellington ale pie. If you're up for the full works, however, you might start with crispy duck and hoi sin dumpling, or go for one of the daily specials such as crab and tarragon bonbons with samphire, radish, cucumber and tarragon oil. Next up, a fillet burger, fish pie, or something a little more adventurous such as braised ox cheek with an oxtail lollipop.

Chef John Beardsworth **Owner** Christopher Gerard **Seats** 90 **Times** 12-10, All-day dining **Prices** Prices not confirmed **Wines** 10 bottles over £30, 40 bottles under £30, 30 by glass **Parking** 40 **Notes** Sunday L, Vegetarian available, Children welcome

---

WILLIAN Map 12 TL23

The Fox

🏵🏵 Modern British

tel: 01462 480233 **SG6 2AE**
email: info@foxatwillian.co.uk
dir: *A1(M) junct 9 towards Letchworth, 1st left to Willian, The Fox 0.5m on left*

Creative and accomplished cooking in a smart local pub

If you lived in a pretty village with just the one pub, you'd hope for it to be a stylish gastro-pub such as The Fox. It ticks all the boxes with its proper bar bristling with well-kept real ales, a smart contemporary open-plan dining room hung with original artwork beneath a glazed atrium ceiling, and a skilled kitchen whose ambition goes way beyond pub grub staples. Under the same ownership as The White Horse in Brancaster Staithe, supply lines to fish and seafood from the Norfolk coast are strong, so mussels from the beds next to its seaside sibling, served with cider and pancetta cream and freshly-baked bread might open the show, followed by roasted suprême of coley with Parma ham and potato terrine, Savoy cabbage, broad beans, crayfish, and chive beurre blanc. Meaty mains run to pan-fried venison loin with suet pudding, creamed celeriac, roasted beetroot and redcurrant jus.

Chef Sherwin Jacobs **Owner** Anglian Country Inns, The Nye family **Seats** 70 **Times** 12-2/6.30-9.15, Closed D Sun **Prices** Fixed L 2 course £15, Starter £4.95-£8.95, Main £11.95-£19.95, Dessert £4.95-£7.95 **Wines** 13 bottles over £30, 28 bottles under £30, 15 by glass **Parking** 40 **Notes** Sunday L, Vegetarian available, Children welcome

ISLE OF WIGHT

SEAVIEW Map 5 SZ69

Priory Bay Hotel

🏵 Modern British

tel: 01983 613146 **Priory Dr PO34 5BU**
email: enquiries@priorybay.co.uk **web:** www.priorybay.co.uk
dir: *B3330 towards Seaview, through Nettlestone. (Do not follow Seaview turn, but continue 0.5m to hotel sign)*

Attractive Regency dining room and creative menu

Since the 14th century, medieval monks, Tudor farmers and Georgian gentry have all contributed their bit of character to this sumptuous country-house retreat. Buffered from the modern world by a 70-acre estate of gardens, woodlands and even its own beach, the enticing package also comes with a brace of dining options. The Priory Oyster brasserie deals in gutsy dishes along the lines of duck livers on toast with caramelised onions, ahead of fillet and belly of local lamb with sautéed potatoes, kale and wild garlic, or you could trade up to the elegant Regency-style Island Room restaurant with its gilded plasterwork and floor-to-ceiling windows giving views across to the Solent. The fine-dining menu is built on local seafood, game and fresh and foraged produce from the gardens and woodlands, and takes in the likes of line-caught sea bass with seaweed, or garden beans in pork broth, and elderberries with Isle of Wight cream to finish.

Chef Darren Williams **Owner** Mr R & Mr J Palmer **Seats** 60, Pr/dining room 50 **Times** 12.30-2.15/6.30-9.30 **Prices** Starter £6-£8, Main £11-£22, Dessert £5-£11 **Wines** 60 bottles over £30, 25 bottles under £30, 12 by glass **Parking** 50 **Notes** Blind tasting menu, Priory afternoon tea, Sunday L £14.95-£22, Vegetarian available, Children welcome

VENTNOR
Map 5 SZ57

The Leconfield

◉ Traditional British V

tel: 01983 852196 **85 Leeson Rd, Upper Bonchurch PO38 1PU**
email: enquiries@leconfieldhotel.com **web:** www.leconfieldhotel.com
dir: *Situated Upper Bonchurch on A3055, 1m from Ventnor, 2m from Shanklin opposite turning, Bonchurch Shute*

Homely cooking overlooking the Channel

On the south-facing side of the Isle of Wight, the picture-perfect Leconfield hotel is covered with climbing foliage. It sits above the village of Bonchurch looking out over the Channel, with inspiring views from the Seascape dining room and the conservatory. With service nicely pitched between formal and relaxed, and glass-topped tables on wicker supports, it's the setting for carefully wrought cooking that has a reassuring touch of the homely to it. A bowl of broccoli and Stilton soup delivers the right savoury, salty hit, or there may be mushrooms sautéed in smoked garlic and served on toasted brioche, followed by poached salmon in caper and lemon butter with puréed spinach, or slow-cooked leg of lamb on parsnip mash with redcurrant gravy. A rum-laced chocolate pot comes with matching ice cream and a sweet-and-sour berry compôte to make a satisfying array of flavours. Home-made breads add to the welcome sense of being looked after.

Chef Cheryl Judge **Owner** Paul & Cheryl Judge **Seats** 26 **Times** 6.30-close, Closed 24-26 Dec, 3 wks Jan, L all week (ex by prior arrangement) **Prices** Fixed D 3 course £25-£35, Service optional **Wines** 3 bottles over £30, 30 bottles under £30, 3 by glass **Parking** 14 **Notes** Children 16 yrs+

The Pond Café

◉ Modern European

tel: 01983 855666 & 856333 **Bonchurch Village Rd, Bonchurch PO38 1RG**
email: reservations@robert-thompson.com
dir: *A3055 to Leeson Rd follow Bonchurch signs until village turn off*

Intimate little venue with an eclectic menu

In the tranquil environs of Bonchurch, The Pond is a simple set-up as the café designation indicates, with candles and intimate proportions adding a romantic charm, and there's an outdoor terrace for those balmier days. The menu offers a pleasing array of rustic Italian dishes and simple stone-baked pizza – anchovies, oregano and capers, anyone? Beef from the island provides the main component for a classic carpaccio served with shaved parmesan and – more unusually – pickled and raw beetroot. Given the proximity to the briny all around, fish has to be a good bet, and here it is in the form of grilled plaice with salsa verde, lentils and sun blushed tomatoes, or there could be roasted local pigeon with pancetta and cavolo nero. At the end, there's lemon tart with mascarpone sorbet, or pears poached in mulled wine, partnered with zabaglione and crunchy almonds.

Times 12-2.30/6-9.30

The Royal Hotel

◉◉ Modern British V

tel: 01983 852186 **Belgrave Rd PO38 1JJ**
email: enquiries@royalhoteliow.co.uk **web:** www.royalhoteliow.co.uk
dir: *On A3055 (coast road) into Ventnor. Follow one-way system, left at lights into Church St. At top of hill left into Belgrave Rd, hotel on right*

Contemporary cooking in a rcharmingly old-fashioned setting

The Royal is a handsome slice of Regency grandeur amid sub-tropical gardens on the Isle of Wight's southeastern coast, a spot that unblushingly styles itself 'the Madeira of England'. Inside, is a classic English tableau fully loaded with fancy plasterwork ceilings, crystal chandeliers, parquet floors and decorative ironwork. The Appuldurcombe Restaurant is an elegant grande dame too, with its swagged drapes and oil paintings, and the kitchen rises to the occasion with panache, delivering food that belongs firmly in the 21st century. The island's own Gallybagger cheese opens proceedings in a soaring soufflé, together with caramelised cauliflower purée, while main course teams poached and roasted chicken breast with crispy wings, baked onion, purée and florets of broccoli and chicken sauce. Fish is always a good bet here, perhaps brill fillet with hand-dived scallops, vanilla purée, foraged sea herbs and pickled raisins, while desserts aim to cosset with the likes of baked almond ricotta cheesecake with rhubarb, and ginger baked Alaska with rhubarb consommé and compôte.

Chef Steven Harris **Owner** William Bailey **Seats** 140, Pr/dining room 40 **Times** 12-1.45/6.45-9, Closed 2 wks Jan or 2 wks Dec, L Mon-Sat **Prices** Fixed L 2 course £15, Fixed D 3 course £40, Tasting menu £50, Service optional **Wines** 30 bottles over £30, 59 bottles under £30, 8 by glass **Parking** 50 **Notes** Sunday L £24-£30, Children 3 yrs+

YARMOUTH
Map 5 SZ38

The George Hotel

◉◉ Modern British, Mediterranean

tel: 01983 760331 **Quay St PO41 OPE**
email: info@thegeorge.co.uk **web:** www.thegeorge.co.uk
dir: *Between castle & pier*

Modern British elegance looking over the sea

Yarmouth is the oldest town on the Isle of Wight, razed by marauding French on two occasions, but rising phoenix-like to tell the tale. Squeezed in between the dinky little castle and the pier, The George is an elegant 17th-century townhouse turned boutique hotel with two dining venues. Isla's Restaurant and Conservatory both capitalise on the location with commanding views over manicured lawns to the sea, with large abstract artworks against a neutral backdrop of taupe and beige. A meal in the elegant, stone-toned Isla's Restaurant ranges widely over the island larder, progressing perhaps from an amuse of asparagus, peas, almond granola and mushroom ketchup, through well-timed seared hand-dived Orkney Island scallops with Isle of Wight pancetta, romanesco, compressed apple and lemon verbena, to roast rack and braised shoulder of lamb, crushed minted peas, wild garlic, pea purée, purple sprouting broccoli and lamb jus. Finish with a superb poached rhubarb pannacotta with rhubarb and ginger jelly, rhubarb sorbet and a sumac and rhubarb essence.

Chef Dan Inniss-Fitzhugh **Owner** Dame Dianne Thompson **Seats** 70, Pr/dining room 18 **Times** 12-3/6-9.30 **Prices** Starter £6-£9, Main £14.50-£22.50, Dessert £7, Service optional **Wines** 30 bottles over £30, 18 bottles under £30, 15 by glass **Parking** The Square **Notes** Afternoon tea, Sunday L, Vegetarian available, Children welcome

KENT

Eastwell Manor

◉◉ British, European

tel: 01233 213000 **Eastwell Park, Boughton Lees TN25 4HR**
email: enquiries@eastwellmanor.co.uk **web:** www.eastwellmanor.co.uk
dir: *From M20 junct 9 take 1st left (Trinity Rd). Through 4 rdbts to lights. Left onto A251 signed Faversham. 0.5m to sign for Boughton Aluph, 200yds to hotel*

Broadly-based modern cooking in a grand manorial pile

With its vast grounds and immaculate gardens, Eastwell is very much the manorial pile, practically a stately home indeed, partly smothered in climbing greenery, and full of magnificent, well-appointed interiors. The lounge, bar and Manor dining room all gaze out over the lawns, and the last is equipped with a large open fireplace for atmospherics. If it all looks quintessentially Garden of England, there is no automatic allegiance to traditional British ways in the cooking, which casts its net wide for inspiration. So a sturdily constructed terrine of ham hock and foie gras, accompanied by pickled veg and truffled mayonnaise, might be followed by a roasted fillet of stone bass that comes on vegetable stir-fry with pak choi and Thai-spiced purée. Another route might be to open with hot-smoked salmon rillettes, fennel and cucumber, and proceed to braised rump of Romney Marsh lamb with wild garlic, smoked yogurt and pine nuts in tapenade jus. A fixed-price menu offers slightly simpler dishes, while desserts aim to seduce with a serving of marinated strawberries and mousse, or chocolate fondant with malted milk and brandy ice cream.

Chef Byron Hayter **Owner** Turrloo Parrett **Seats** 80, Pr/dining room 80
Times 12-2.30/7-10 **Prices** Fixed L 2 course £18.50, Fixed D 3 course £35, Tasting menu £65-£85, Service optional 10% **Wines** 163 bottles over £30, 123 bottles under £30, 14 by glass **Parking** 120 **Notes** Gourmet champagne evenings, Sunday L, Vegetarian available, Children welcome

Soufflé Restaurant

◉ Modern European

tel: 01622 737065 **31 The Green ME14 4DN**
email: soufflerestaurant@hotmail.co.uk
dir: *M20 junct 7 follow Maidstone signs, bear left towards Bearsted straight over at rdbt, towards Bearsted Green at next mini-rdbt, continue for approx 1.5m to the green. Restaurant on left, turn left just before Soufflé sign & park at rear of restaurant*

Updated classics in a friendly and relaxed family-run restaurant

With its quintessentially green and pleasant setting on Bearsted's pretty green, Soufflé is an irresistible prospect, particularly when balmy weather allows alfresco dining on the canopied front terrace. Inside, the 16th-century house is a tangle of low, oak-beamed ceilings and beamed, whitewashed walls; the building was originally a bakery and still has the cast-iron oven set into a bare-brick wall. Nick Evenden cooks while his wife Karen takes care of front of house to ensure a friendly and relaxed ambience. It's clearly a formula that works: Soufflé has been a stalwart of the local foodie scene for 15 years, luring in the diners with intelligent cooking that puts a creative spin on classic ideas. Chicken and mushroom terrine with tarragon and mayonnaise dressing sets the ball rolling, followed by baked fillet of pollack topped with tomato fondue and herb crust, with white wine sauce; white chocolate mousse with oranges and Suzette sauce wraps things up in fine style.

Times 12-2/7-9.30, Closed Mon, L Sat, D Sun

The West House

◉◉◉ – *see opposite*

The Mulberry Tree

◉◉ Modern British

tel: 01622 749082 & 741058 **Hermitage Ln ME17 4DA**
email: info@themulberrytreekent.co.uk
dir: *B2163 turn into Wierton Rd straight over x-rds, 1st left East Hall Hill*

Precise, skilful, modern cooking, full of the flavours of Kent

Lost among the back lanes of deepest Kent, The Mulberry Tree's clean-lined modern looks certainly come as a surprise. Inside, the expansive dining area is done out in a light contemporary style – wooden floors, bare wooden tables, and strikingly patterned designer wallpapers. On a mild summer's evening the tranquil garden patio is the place to be. Well-tuned modern British food is what tempts diners off the beaten track; expect European accents, and staunchly local ingredients from a kitchen that not only bangs the drum for Kent's peerless produce (local suppliers all duly name-checked on the menu), but also tends a kitchen garden and rears its own Kentish Middlewhite pigs and chickens in a two-acre field behind the restaurant. Skilfully woven flavours and precise timings are the hallmarks of a dinner starting with smoked ham hock and parsley terrine, chicken liver parfait, piccalilli and black pepper crackers, followed by fall-apart tender pork belly with fondant potatoes, apple and kohlrabi salad and apple purée. To finish, vanilla pannacotta comes with almond crumble and a rhubarb-fest of jelly, sorbet and compôte.

Chef Mark Pearson **Owner** Karen Williams, Mark Jones **Seats** 70, Pr/dining room 16
Times 12-2/6.30-9.30, Closed 26 Dec, Mon, D Sun **Prices** Fixed L 2 course £15.95, Fixed D 3 course £18.95, Starter £6.95-£10.95, Main £15.95-£22.95, Dessert £6.50-£7.95, Service optional **Wines** 30 bottles over £30, 31 bottles under £30, 54 by glass **Parking** 60 **Notes** Sunday L £20.95-£23.95, Vegetarian available, Children welcome

CANTERBURY
Map 7 TR15

ABode Canterbury

◉◉ Modern European

tel: 01227 766266 & 826678 **High St CT1 2RX**
email: reservations@abodecanterbury.co.uk **web:** www.abodecanterbury.co.uk
dir: Phone for directions

Modern European eating boutique-style

Not far from the cathedral, the Canterbury ABode is a half-timbered building of obvious venerability that retains its ancient beams inside a structure that has been decoratively refashioned for the boutique crowd. A champagne bar and a tavern are among the amenities, as is the County Restaurant, where modern European cooking is brought off with panache. Dishes combine lightness and intensity, and certainly look the part, as when barbecued mackerel appears in a neat line-up with pickled vegetables and avocado purée, or wild mushroom risotto arrives with a parmesan crisp sticking out of it amid a ruffle of white wine foam. Dishes are also capable of striking the more robust note for braised beef featherblade with horseradish mash in red wine jus, while fish could be steamed hake with herbed quinoa and chorizo foam. Chocolate heaven delivers pretty much what the tin promises, with an omnium gatherum of ganache, brownie and soil, as well as praline ice cream, or there may be rhubarb and ginger cheesecake with ginger biscuit base and rhubarb sorbet.

Times 12-2.30/5.30-9.30, Closed D Sun

BEST WESTERN Abbots Barton Hotel

◉ Modern British **NEW**

tel: 01227 760341 **New Dover Rd CT1 3DU**
email: info@abbotsbartonhotel.com **web:** www.abbotsbartonhotel.com
dir: A2 (N/S) A2050(S) Canterbury city centre, A28 (E/W) A2 Dover. Located in New Dover Rd

A ten-minute stroll from the cathedral and medieval city

Built in the mid-19th century as a large private house, this early example of Victorian Gothic architecture has been a hotel since 1927. To the front, separating the hotel from a road, lies a two-acre expanse of lawns and tree-lined gardens. Although a second restaurant is mooted, diners currently eat in The Fountain Restaurant, whose modern British menu likes to declare Garden of England provenance in dishes such as duo of Romney Marsh lamb with dauphinoise potato, pea purée, and apple and mint relish, Alkham Valley Old Spot pork belly with soy and ginger marinade, and from an Orpington (which used to be in Kent) farm, seasonal vegetable platter dressed with extra-virgin Kentish rapeseed oil. The home made breads are excellent. Finish with salted caramel and milk chocolate parfait.

Chef William Britton **Owner** Abbots Barton Hotel Ltd **Seats** 50, Pr/dining room 20 **Times** 7-9.30, Closed 25 & 31 Dec **Prices** Fixed D 3 course £24, Starter £7.25-£7.75, Main £18.75-£20.75, Dessert £7.25-£8.75, Service optional **Wines** 14 bottles over £30, 42 bottles under £30, 13 by glass **Parking** 40 **Notes** Vegetarian available, Children welcome

The West House ◉◉◉

BIDDENDEN
Map 7 TQ83

Modern European **V**
tel: 01580 291341 **28 High St TN27 8AH**
email: thewesthouse@btconnect.com
dir: Junct of A262 & A274. 14m S of Maidstone

Vanguard cooking in a charming Kentish village

The setting is Old England at its purest, a 16th-century Flemish weaver's cottage on the high street of a Kentish wine village, but Graham and Jackie Garrett's restaurant with rooms is very much a 21st-century operation. Graham learned his craft in the kitchens of such luminaries as Nico Ladenis and Richard Corrigan, and he has done the TV chef thing (always a good move for boosting your restaurant's public profile). The media exposure hasn't gone to his head and he's happiest in the kitchen, driven by the pursuit of wringing every molecule of flavour from a larder stocked with impeccable local and ruthlessly seasonal materials. The full panoply of modern, cutting-edge cooking methods is deployed to achieve masterful balance of texture and flavour, ensuring that each ingredient is shown off to its best advantage. Starters can be as intense and contemporary as a steamed brioche bun filled with hare and boosted by chocolate sauce and horseradish, or a more subtle combination of scorched marinated mackerel fillet with hibiscus,
warm oyster and cucumber. Main courses aim to nail big, clearly-defined flavours in dishes such as roast haunch of Sika deer with mashed swede, wild mushrooms and 'twiglets', while fish might appear in an entertaining 'rockpool' presentation, with grilled fillets of wild halibut appearing alongside cockles, squid ink sponge and dashi broth, or a robust composition involving roast hake with grilled squid, pickled chilli, lime and aïoli. Desserts might take 'milk and honey' as a theme and make jelly, mousse, nuggets and crisps, together with buttermilk sorbet, or revert to childhood confectionery in an homage to a 'Crunchie' of white chocolate and honeycomb parfait with dark chocolate sorbet.

Chef Graham Garrett, Ben Crittenden **Owner** Jackie & Graham Garrett **Seats** 32 **Times** 12-2/7-9.30, Closed 24-26 Dec & 1 Jan, Mon, L Sat, D Sun **Prices** **Wines** 54 bottles over £30, 28 bottles under £30, 22 by glass **Parking** 7 **Notes** 6 course £60 (£90 with wine), Sunday L £35-£60, Children welcome

CANTERBURY *continued*

The Dove Inn

◉ Modern British, Continental

tel: 01227 751360 **Plum Pudding Ln, Dargate ME13 9HB**
email: doveatdargate@hotmail.com
dir: *6m NW of Canterbury. A299 Thanet Way, turn off at Lychgate service station*

Attractive food-focused country pub

The Dove is a cosy and friendly village gastro-pub dating from the 18th century. A wood-burning stove in a stone fireplace adds a cheery, welcoming glow in the bar, with its polished wooden furniture, panelling and boarded floor. The kitchen toes the contemporary British line and produces dishes that are short on flummery and big on flavour. Seared scallops paired with black pudding and bacon chips, served with pea velouté, or chicken liver parfait with red onion jam are what to expect among starters, followed by roast hake fillet on potato purée with sautéed new potatoes, chorizo and wilted chard or, in season, roast leg of guinea fowl with black pudding mash, greens and a red wine jus. Gourmet wine dinners are run here, and the short menus may conclude with cherry Bakewell tart with berry compôte and cherry brandy ice cream.

Chef Benjamin Johnson **Owner** Christopher & Benjamin Johnson, Dorota Jacyno **Seats** 36, Pr/dining room 12 **Times** 12-2.30/6-9, Closed Mon, L Tue, seasonal, D Sun-Mon **Prices** Tasting menu £55-£75, Starter £7-£12, Main £13.50-£27, Dessert £6-£12 **Wines** 10 bottles over £30, 20 bottles under £30, 12 by glass **Parking** 15, On street **Notes** Gourmet & wine evenings £55-£70, Sunday L £20-£25, Vegetarian available, Children welcome

The Goods Shed Restaurant

◉ British

tel: 01227 459153 **Station Road West CT2 8AN**
email: restaurant@thegoodsshed.co.uk
dir: *Adjacent to Canterbury West train station*

Farmers' market menu at the railway station

The permanent farmers' market that opened next to Canterbury West station in 2002 was a great idea. It has helped to showcase a generation of British artisan farm produce, as well as offering an on-site restaurant elevated above the market floor. Chunky wood tables with views through majestic arched windows over the comings and goings below are an inspired setting for cooking using that market produce to the full, the selections changing with every service. Start with scallops thermidor, or a crab and tarragon 'risotto' of bulgar wheat, before main courses that go the distance with pedigree meats like 24-day aged rib eye in Colston Bassett Stilton butter, or rack of lamb with prunes and pine nuts. Fish might be hake with curried mussels, and dessert a satisfyingly tart Bramley apple crème brûlée with cinnamon shortbread. Hearty breakfasts incorporate bubble-and-squeak in among all the usual suspects, and are served up to 10.30am.

Chef Rafael Lopez **Owner** Susanna Sait **Seats** 80
Times 12-2.30/6-9.30, Closed 25-26 Dec, 1-2 Jan, Mon, D Sun **Prices** Starter £6-£11, Main £13.50-£23, Dessert £6.50-£9 **Wines** 10 bottles over £30, 27 bottles under £30, 10 by glass **Parking** 40 **Notes** Banquet menu £38, Sunday L, Vegetarian available, Children welcome

CRANBROOK   Map 7 TQ73

Apicius

◉◉◉ – *see opposite*

DARTFORD   Map 6 TQ57

Rowhill Grange Hotel & Utopia Spa

◉◉ Modern European **V**

tel: 01322 615136 **Wilmington DA2 7QH**
email: admin@rowhillgrange.com **web:** www.alexanderhotels.co.uk
dir: *M25 junct 3, take B2173 towards Swanley, then B258 towards Hextable. Straight on at 3 rdbts. Hotel 1.5m on left*

Soothing modernised dishes in Kentish rural tranquillity

A substantial 18th-century manor in acres of grounds that include a pond, Rowhill Grange is now an upmarket boutique hotel. It's high in the comfort factor, with furnishings and decor, as well as service, of a high standard. RG's is the serious dining option, where the modern British style encompasses a range of bright ideas with some interesting combinations. Roast hare (a welcome appearance) is served with textures of cauliflower and beer onions, for instance, and roast scallops with a scallop cracker, confit leek and leek ash mayonnaise. Main courses run to the full-blooded flavours of braised oxtail and kidney suet pudding with caramelised onion gravy as well as local venison with figs, dauphinoise and purple-sprouting broccoli. Fish, meanwhile, crops up as roast skate wing fashionably paired with pork belly and accompanied by red wine salsify and Swiss chard, with puddings along the lines of light and fluffy rhubarb soufflé with ginger ice cream, and mandarin parfait with almond milk ice cream.

Chef Chris Mann **Owner** Peter & Deborah Hinchcliffe **Seats** 100, Pr/dining room 16 **Times** 12-2.30/7-9.30 **Prices** Fixed L 2 course £20, Starter £8-£12.50, Main £20-£29, Dessert £7.50-£9.50 **Wines** 38 bottles over £30, 20 bottles under £30, 11 by glass **Parking** 300 **Notes** Sunday L £24-£32, Children 16 yrs+ D

DEAL   Map 7 TR35

Dunkerleys Hotel & Restaurant

◉◉ Modern British

tel: 01304 375016 **19 Beach St CT14 7AH**
email: ddunkerley@btconnect.com **web:** www.dunkerleys.co.uk
dir: *Turn off A2 onto A258 to Deal – situated 100yds before Deal Pier*

Seafood-based menu in a long-running seafront hotel

Run with down to earth friendliness for over a quarter of a century by Ian and Linda Dunkerley, this relaxed and homely seafront hotel in Deal has hit on a winning formula. The place exudes a jauntily inviting air, with its flagpoles and flower-baskets, and the newly refurbed dining room looks the part, with smart white linen and high-backed chairs; on a fine day, the Kentish sunshine might tempt you out on to the terrace. Fuss-free dishes bring fresh local materials together in well-balanced combinations, and in Deal, seafood has got to be the main deal, getting the show on the road with the likes of seared scallops with Bramley apple and sloe gin purée. The main event might star roast sea bass fillet with carrot and star anise purée and shaved fennel, or a whole Dover sole grilled with parsley butter. If you want to get you teeth into something meaty, there's roast rack of herb-crusted lamb with ratatouille and bordelaise potatoes, and to finish, perhaps cinnamon crème brûlée with praline ice cream.

Times 12-2.30/7-9.30, Closed Mon, D Sun

The Marquis at Alkham

◉◉ Modern British · NOTABLE WINE LIST

Map 7 TR34

tel: 01304 873410 **Alkham Valley Rd, Alkham CT15 7DF**
email: reception@themarquisatalkham.co.uk **web:** www.themarquisatalkham.co.uk
dir: M20 continue to A2. Take A260 exit & turn on to the Alkham Valley Rd

Creative cooking and boutique chic deep in the Kent countryside

It may look a little like the traditional country pub it once was from the outside (albeit a rather posh one), but cross the threshold and it becomes apparent that The Marquis at Alkham has morphed into a restaurant with rooms – modern art, stylish furnishings and boutique bedrooms make a fine impression. The smart restaurant offers a carte and two tasting menus (one aimed at the best of Kentish produce), which deliver modern plates of food based on classic flavour combinations. Kick off with ham hock terrine partnered with tomato and apple chutney and toasted brioche, or textures of beetroot with goats' curd and smoked hazelnuts. Among main courses, leg of guinea fowl is cooked slowly au vin, and arrives with dauphinoise potatoes, red cabbage and green beans, or go for fillet of local cod with purple potatoes, a langoustine, and hollandaise sauce. Desserts are a refined and comforting bunch, from lemon tart with chewy meringue and raspberry sorbet, to raspberry soufflé with white chocolate ice cream and crunchy pieces of honeycomb.

Chef Andrew King **Owner** Tony Marsden, Hugh Oxborrow **Seats** 60, Pr/dining room 20 **Times** 12-2.30/6.30-9.30, Closed L Mon **Prices** Prices not confirmed **Wines** 88 bottles over £30, 32 bottles under £30, 9 by glass **Parking** 26 **Notes** Sunday L, Vegetarian available, Children 8 yrs+

Wallett's Court Country House Hotel & Spa

◉◉ Modern British

tel: 01304 852424 **West Cliffe, St Margaret's-at-Cliffe CT15 6EW**
email: dine@wallettscourt.com **web:** www.wallettscourthotelspa.com
dir: M2/A2 or M20/A20, follow signs for Deal (A258), 1st right for St-Margaret's-at-Cliffe. Restaurant 1m on right

Family-owned country hotel with cosmopolitan menu

The straggling ruin the Oakleys first looked over in 1975 led them to think you'd have to be mad to buy it. Forty years later, they still own the place and have lavished buckets of TLC on it. The dining room with its beamed ceiling and uneven floor retains all its antique character, though, and as befits a hotel that offers facilities for glampers among its attractions, there are some tables in the great outdoors too. Fixed-price dinner menus take a cosmopolitan approach to local materials, kicking off with garden gazpacho enriched with goats' cheese and sour cream, or wood pigeon in apple and beetroot port jus, prior to rump of Romney Marsh lamb in a richly flavoured broth with summer greens and radishes, or a full-dress lobster thermidor with a salad of courgette flowers. Meals end with plenty of seasonal fruit, perhaps in cherry pancakes with almond ice cream, rice pudding with black grapes and Bramley apple sorbet, or a raspberry version of Eton Mess, rechristened 'neat and tidy', its elements carefully separated out and arranged on a slab.

Chef Michael Fowler **Owner** Gavin, Lea & Chris Oakley **Seats** 60, Pr/dining room 40 **Times** 12-2.30/7-9, Closed 25-26 Dec **Prices** Fixed L 2 course £16.95-£18, Fixed D 3 course £42-£45, Tasting menu £55-£65, Service optional **Wines** 18 bottles over £30, 25 bottles under £30, 17 by glass **Parking** 50 **Notes** Tasting menu on request, Afternoon tea £10-£25, Sunday L £20-£25, Vegetarian available, Children welcome

Apicius ◉◉◉

Map 7 TQ73

Modern European
tel: 01580 714666 **23 Stone St TN17 3HF**
dir: In town centre, opposite Barclays Bank, 50yds from church

Imaginative star quality in a small high-street venue

The name references a Roman gourmet and all-round bon viveur, and modern epicures in the know set the SatNav for the high street address of this high-flying restaurant in an unassuming Kentish village. The location may seem incongruous, but it does mean that chef-patron Timothy Johnson has a wealth of the best regional ingredients from the hills and coast of Sussex and Kent practically on his doorstep. With its frontage of weatherboards and large windows, the setting is simple and charming, an intimate room done out with linen-swathed tables and framed menus from stellar restaurants on whitewashed walls. It's not a good idea to turn up on spec, as tables are booked well ahead for weekend dining. The flip side of that coin is that with only 30 covers to cater for, the kitchen can concentrate on delivering cooking of pinpoint accuracy. Dishes are broadly modern European in scope, with bright, bold flavours and interesting juxtapositions of flavour and texture; compressed pickled cucumber, Granny Smith apples and pomegranate as a counterpoint to marinated and poached salmon say. Francophile leanings and robust, thrilling flavours are a hallmark of main courses – slow-roast and shredded shoulder of lamb, for example, with boulangère potatoes, roast garlic, tomatoes, black olives and artichokes. Fish is cooked with flair, too: pan-fried sea bream, with braised chicory and fennel, tomatoes and garlic and citrus jus. International flavours and lively ideas come together in well-constructed desserts such as passionfruit rice pudding with coconut pannacotta, pineapple sorbet and pomegranate or iced goats' cheese parfait with roast almonds, compressed kumquats, caraway and cumin notes from kummel liqueur jelly, and black olives.

Chef Timothy Johnson **Owner** Timothy Johnson, Faith Hawkins **Seats** 30 **Times** 12-2/7-9, Closed 2 wks Xmas-New Year, 2 wks summer, Mon-Tue, L Sat, D Sun **Prices** Fixed L 2 course fr £28, Fixed D 3 course fr £41 **Wines** 19 bottles over £30, 11 bottles under £30, 10 by glass **Parking** Public car park at rear **Notes** Sunday L £28-£35, Vegetarian available, Children 8 yrs+

EGERTON
Map 7 TQ94

Frasers

◉◉ Modern British

tel: 01233 756122 **Coldharbour Farm TN27 9DD**
email: lisa@frasers-events.co.uk **web:** www.frasers-events.co.uk
dir: *Phone for directions*

Seasonal eating on an industrious Kentish farm

The House of Fraser is a pretty reliable bet when it comes to quality products, and Adam and Lisa-Jane Fraser are descendants of that Victorian enterprise, keeping up that reputation on their Kentish farm estate. The operation has mushroomed into a large-scale agricultural enterprise supplying many local pubs and turning out its own breads and preserves. A hotel and cookery school are part of the set up, along with a barn-style dining room with high ceilings and exposed timbers, which hosts regular gourmet evenings, and there's a regular seasonal menu on offer too. Proceedings open with a smoked haddock Scotch egg with pickled cucumber and lemon mayonnaise, before moving on to pan-fried chicken suprême partnered by confit garlic-infused crushed potatoes, purple sprouting broccoli, wild garlic pesto and toasted pine nuts, or perhaps citrus and herb-crusted rack of Romney lamb with lyonnaise potatoes, carrots and leeks, and a red wine reduction. To finish, there are Kentish cheeses on hand for those determined to resist the allure of pear and frangipane tart with Amaretto ice cream.

Chef Alan Egan **Owner** Lisa-Jane & Adam Fraser **Seats** 30, Pr/dining room 50 **Times** 12.30-3/6.30-9, Closed L subject to private functions, D subject to private functions **Prices** Tasting menu £55-£75, Starter £6.95-£9.50, Main £15.95-£25.50, Dessert £7-£8.50, Service optional **Wines** 6 bottles over £30, 20 bottles under £30, 5 by glass **Parking** 30 **Notes** Brunch, Afternoon tea, Vegetarian available, Children welcome

FAVERSHAM
Map 7 TR06

Read's Restaurant

◉◉ Modern British ▬ NOTABLE WINE LIST

tel: 01795 535344 **Macknade Manor, Canterbury Rd ME13 8XE**
email: enquiries@reads.com
dir: *From M2 junct 6 follow A251 towards Faversham. At T-junct with A2 (Canterbury road) turn right. Hotel 0.5m on right*

Refined modern British cooking in an elegant Georgian manor

Chef-patron David Pitchford's Georgian manor house has long been a Kentish destination for those in the know. Set in lush grounds, which provide much of the fresh produce used in the kitchen, it feels like a remote country retreat, and is run with the kind of friendly, grown-up affability we hope to find in such places. Old-school refinement is the name of the game, the dining rooms done out with elegant, understated style and flooded with light from floor-to-ceiling sash windows. Read's was doing modern British cooking before many others had cottoned on to it, the dishes carefully composed and based on sound culinary tradition. Haddock fishcakes arrive in a crispy crumb shell with zingy home-made tomato ketchup, followed by a super-fresh pan-fried fillet of locally-caught hake with braised coco beans, salsify and a dry vermouth sauce. A short wait for dessert is amply rewarded with an apricot soufflé, cooked to order and matched with rich and creamy vanilla ice cream slotted into the centre of the soufflé to melt and mingle. A splendid wine list completes the picture.

Chef David Pitchford **Owner** David & Rona Pitchford **Seats** 50, Pr/dining room 30 **Times** 12-2.30/7-10, Closed BHs, Sun-Mon **Prices** Fixed L 3 course £26, Fixed D 3 course £60, Tasting menu £60, Service optional **Wines** 100 bottles over £30, 45 bottles under £30, 18 by glass **Parking** 30 **Notes** Tasting menu 7 course, Vegetarian available, Children welcome

FAWKHAM GREEN
Map 6 TQ56

Brandshatch Place Hotel & Spa

◉◉ Modern British

tel: 01474 875000 & 0845 072 7395 *(Calls cost 7p per minute plus your phone company's access charge)* **Brands Hatch Rd DA3 8NQ**
email: brandshatchplace@handpicked.co.uk **web:** www.handpickedhotels.co.uk/brandshatchplace
dir: *M25 junct 3/A20 West Kingsdown. Left at paddock entrance/Fawkham Green sign. 3rd left signed Fawkham Rd. Hotel 500mtrs on right*

Witty modern brasserie cooking near Brands Hatch

The hotel isn't entirely about motor racing, not when this handsome Georgian manor house, now part of the Hand picked Hotels group, stands ready to receive those avid for sophisticated dining and spa treatments, or for wandering in sumptuous grounds. There may be a hint of distantly roaring turbo engines in the dining room, but it mingles harmoniously with the discreet classical music played. Modern brasserie cooking of engaging informality and wit is the theme – how about a 'Battenberg' of salmon and cod with caviar and cucumber dressing? – and dishes reflect a concentrated degree of attention. The visual dazzle of poached mackerel in its setting of rhubarb jelly, radish and red-vein sorrel makes a bold opening statement, and there is much to enjoy in a main course pig medley that encompasses earthy ham hock, well-trimmed belly and a croquette of the cheek, alongside puréed onion and rib-sticking mash in red wine. A red wine reduction also turns up with the must-have baked Alaska, offsetting the sweetness of its meringue shell.

Chef Carl Smith **Owner** Hand Picked Hotels **Seats** 60, Pr/dining room 110 **Times** 12-2/7-9.30 **Prices** Fixed D 3 course £39, Starter £9.95-£12.50, Main £19.95-£26.95, Dessert £8.50-£9.95, Service optional **Wines** 92 bottles over £30, 8 bottles under £30, 18 by glass **Parking** 100 **Notes** Sunday L £23.50, Vegetarian available, Children welcome

FOLKESTONE
Map 7 TR23

Rocksalt Rooms

◉◉ Modern British

tel: 01303 212070 **2 Back St CT19 6NN**
email: info@rocksaltfolkestone.co.uk **web:** www.rocksaltfolkestone.co.uk
dir: *M20 junct 13, follow A259 Folkestone Harbour, then left to Fish Market*

Fabulous harbour side setting and a local flavour

Rocksalt's kitchen team has a passion for provenance, so they are perfectly placed to grab the freshest seafood from local boats, as well as Kent-and Sussex-bred meats and herbs and vegetables plucked fresh from farms under the same ownership as the restaurant. It's a great building sitting quite literally on the harbour with a curving terrace cantilevered out over the water, a huge sliding glass wall to capitalise on the view over the harbour and open sea beyond, and a classy, well-designed interior with oak floors, dark timber tables and leather banquettes. The menu has seafood at its heart, but there's also hay-baked rump of Romney Marsh lamb with anchovy potatoes or prime slabs of steak to keep carnivores happy. Start with smoked coley with creamy mash and a poached egg, and move on to poached cod fillet with samphire and celeriac and mussel broth, or roast thornback ray wing with hedgerow green garlic sauce. For dessert, there's baked egg custard tart with blackcurrant sorbet or buttermilk pudding with blood orange.

Chef Simon Oakley **Owner** Mark Sargeant, Josh De Haan **Seats** 100, Pr/dining room 24 **Times** 12-3/6.30-10 **Prices** Prices not confirmed **Wines** 14 by glass **Parking** On street, pay & display car park **Notes** Sunday L, Vegetarian available, Children welcome

GRAFTY GREEN
Map 7 TQ84

Who'd A Thought It
◎◎ Modern British V

tel: 01622 858951 **Headcorn Rd ME17 2AR**
email: joe@whodathoughtit.com **web:** www.whodathoughtit.com
dir: *M20 junct 8, A20 towards Lenham. 1m take Grafty Green turn, follow brown tourist signs for 4.5m*

Modern classic cooking in an unassuming Kentish village

A champagne and oyster bar with rooms in a Kentish village not far from the M20 has a definite sector of the market firmly cornered, and the racy opulence with which every last corner of it has been designed will convince any waverers. Guest rooms equipped for pole-dancing and hot-tubbing should blow away any cobwebs, while the zebra-print upholstery in the main restaurant looks a treat against the buttoned padding of the walls and flamboyant chandeliers. A menu of modern classics — scallops with cauliflower purée, beetroot and goats' cheese salad with candied walnuts and celery shoots, cider-braised pork belly with red cabbage, damsons and crackling — is brought off with persuasive aplomb, and prime ingredients are excellent. Witness a thyme-infused breast of corn-fed chicken with pearl barley and bacon risotto, served with charred baby onions and buttered cabbage. Shellfish platters and thermidor will please seafood purists, as will sticky toffee pudding with butterscotch sauce and salted caramel ice cream, or a by-the-book crème brûlée singing with vanilla.

Chef Tim Ward **Owner** Joe Mallett **Seats** 50 **Times** 11.30-9.30, All-day dining, Closed 1 Jan **Prices** Fixed L 2 course £12, Fixed D 3 course £29, Starter £5-£23, Main £15-£50, Dessert £5-£12, Service optional **Wines** 80 bottles over £30, 23 bottles under £30, 14 by glass **Parking** 45 **Notes** Sunday L £9-£13, Children welcome

LENHAM
Map 7 TQ85

Chilston Park Hotel
◎◎ Modern British

tel: 01622 859803 & 0845 072 7426 *(Calls cost 7p per minute plus your phone company's access charge)* **Sandway ME17 2BE**
email: chilstonpark@handpicked.co.uk **web:** www.handpickedhotels.co.uk/chilstonpark
dir: *M20 junct 8*

Splendid Georgian mansion with elegant restaurant

Chilston Park has been home to a steady procession of nobility and prominent Kentish families through the centuries. Nowadays, the Georgian mansion does business as an upscale country-house hotel tucked away down leafy lanes in the Garden of England. Secluded in 22 acres of sublime landscaped gardens and parkland, its interior brims with enough period authenticity, antiques and oil paintings that you might be inspired to dress as Jane Austen's Mr Darcy or Elizabeth Bennet for dinner in the unique, sunken Venetian-style Culpeper's restaurant. Here ornate plasterwork ceilings, a grand fireplace and fancy crystal chandeliers certainly build a sense of occasion. The kitchen deals in a style of modern British cooking that is clearly rooted in the classics but has no hesitation in sending out some inventive combinations. Goats' cheese mousse with butternut purée and toasted seeds might open the bidding, before a well-timed tranche of halibut arrives with saffron cocotte potatoes and marsh samphire in a citrus-spiked red wine emulsion. Proceedings conclude with a well-made apple and quince tart and milk sorbet.

Chef Rohan Nevins **Owner** Hand Picked Hotels **Seats** 45, Pr/dining room 20 **Times** 7-9.30, Closed L Mon-Sat **Prices** Fixed D 3 course £39, Tasting menu £60-£90, Starter £8.50-£10.50, Main £22-£28.50, Dessert £8.50-£12.50, Service optional **Wines** 60 bottles over £30, 15 bottles under £30, 18 by glass **Parking** 100 **Notes** Seasonal gourmet menu, Sunday L £25, Vegetarian available, Children welcome

MAIDSTONE
Map 7 TQ75

Fish on the Green
◎◎ British, French

tel: 01622 738300 **Church Ln, Bearsted Green ME14 4EJ**
dir: *N of A20 on village green*

Refreshingly simple fish and seafood in a Kentish village

The title says it all: the pretty village green setting is English to the core, while the restaurant occupying a converted stable block near the original coaching house, the Oak on the Green, deals in the finest piscine produce. Fish on the Green has netted a strong local fan base — and what's not to like about its fresh, unpretentious interior of whitewashed brick hung with fishy-themed paintings, the smartly-turned-out and clued-up staff, and, of course, the excellent fish and seafood on the menu? Super-fresh materials are treated simply, setting out with pan-fried crab cakes with crayfish salsa and coriander shoots, or potted crab flavoured with nutmeg and lemon butter. Next up, pan-fried wild sea bass fillet is paired with the Mediterranean flavours of roasted fennel, black olive tapenade and red pepper sauce, and if you just don't fancy fish, something like confit free-range pork belly with seared scallops, sweetcorn purée, black pudding mash and sage jus should fit the bill. Finish with blueberry and frangipane tart with blueberry compôte and clotted cream.

Chef Peter Baldwin **Owner** Alexander Bensley **Seats** 50 **Times** 12-2.30/6.30-10, Closed Xmas, Mon (some), D Sun (some) **Prices** Fixed L 2 course £16.95, Starter £7.25-£11.75, Main £18.25-£27.75, Dessert £6.95 **Wines** 9 bottles over £30, 20 bottles under £30, 8 by glass **Parking** 50 **Notes** Vegetarian available, Children welcome

MARGATE
Map 7 TR37

The Ambrette
◎ Modern Indian

tel: 01843 231504 **44 King St CT9 1QE**
email: info@theambrette.co.uk
dir: *A299/A28, left into Hawley St B2055. Restaurant on right corner King St*

Modern Anglo-Indian food based on local prime produce

At both his restaurant in Rye and here in Margate, Dev Biswal combines modern British and Indian flavours into something which could be described as modern Indian food, but is probably best labelled Anglo-Indian. The decor is more Anglo than Indian, minimally decorated and filled with wooden tables and chairs. The presentation of dishes is more akin to European food as well. However you choose to define it, the combination is a winning one, with bags of flavour and a good amount of Kentish produce on show (the provenance is written up on the menu). A starter of wood pigeon smoked with cloves and marjoram comes with a rosemary and cinnamon-spiced peach, game pâté, pigeon roulade and a garlic and tomato chutney. Among the main courses, slow-cooked leg of mallard is served with spiced courgette, cauliflower purée and a sauce flavoured with lime leaves and lemongrass.

Chef Dev Biswal **Owner** Dev Biswal **Seats** 52 **Times** 11.30-2.30/5.30-9.30 **Wines** 15 bottles over £30, 20 bottles under £30, 16 by glass **Parking** 10 **Notes** Pre-theatre menu until 6.30 & after 9pm, Sunday L £10.95-£20.95, Vegetarian available, Children welcome

MARGATE *continued*

Sands Hotel
⊛⊛ Modern European **NEW**

tel: 01843 228228 & 07794 336063 **16 Marine Dr CT9 1DH**
email: info@sandshotelmargate.co.uk **web:** www.sandshotelmargate.co.uk
dir: *A28 to Marine Drive. B2051 in Margate*

Contemporary dining with a sea view

A breath of fresh air on the Margate seafront, Sands Hotel offers a contemporary experience while maintaining a sense of place with sweeping views of the sea. The view can be enjoyed from the appropriately named Bay Restaurant, and there's even a fun ice cream parlour serving home-made flavours made with milk and cream from a local herd of Guernsey cows. Ryan Tasker heads up the restaurant and turns out impressive modern food based on first-class regional ingredients. There are classical foundations to many of the dishes, but there's no shortage of creativity either; salmon rillettes, for example, with crème fraîche jelly and pickled cucumber and fennel, or glazed duck breast with candied swede and charred chicory (dressed with a spiced honey jus). The fresh fish offering changes depending on the catch of the day, and cheeses such as Ashmore and Canterbury Cobble hail from Kent. The sweet-toothed can end on a high with butterscotch pannacotta with glazed banana and chocolate sauce. Dining on the terrace is a fair-weather treat.

Chef Ryan Tasker **Owner** Nick Conington **Seats** 56, Pr/dining room **Times** 12-2/7-9
Prices Fixed L 2 course £15, Starter £6-£12, Main £11.50-£24, Dessert £6.50,
Service optional **Wines** 12 bottles over £30, 26 bottles under £30, 9 by glass
Parking Car park 100 yds **Notes** Jazz & seasonal offers, Sunday L £11.50-£15.95,
Vegetarian available, Children welcome

ROCHESTER
Map 6 TQ76

Topes Restaurant
⊛⊛ Modern British

tel: 01634 845270 **60 High St ME1 1JY**
email: julie.small@btconnect.com **web:** www.topesrestaurant.com
dir: *M2 junct 1, through Strood High St over Medway Bridge, turn right at Northgate onto High St*

An atmospheric gem in historic Rochester

On a corner of Rochester's Dickensian High Street, with the castle and cathedral visible through side windows, Topes occupies a building spanning the 15th to 17th centuries and could be a set for a period drama with its frontage of wonky, sagging timbers – in fact the place gets a mention in Dickens' last novel, *The Mystery of Edwin Drood*. Inside it's a romantic, cosy space with dark linenfold panels and carved black ceiling beams, far from gloomy and medieval – the patina of age is relieved by light colours, an uncluttered modern decor, and the mood is relaxed. Chef-proprietor Chris Small's cooking taps into the current appetite for ingredient-led, unpretentious dishes with forthright flavours. Excellent Kentish produce underpins a starter of king scallops, truffled cauliflower purée, boudin noir and bacon, and chanterelle cream, before main course brings herb-crusted Romney Marsh lamb rump, matched with a faggot of braised shoulder, sweet potato fondant, Savoy cabbage, cobnuts, bacon and Jerusalem artichoke purée. A rich and indulgent finale of sticky date pudding, butterscotch sauce and tonka bean ice cream wraps things up in fine style.

Chef Chris Small **Owner** Chris & Julie Small **Seats** 55, Pr/dining room 16
Times 12-2.30/6.30-9, Closed Mon-Tue, D Sun **Prices** Fixed L 2 course £19.50, Fixed D 3 course £25, Starter £7-£10, Main £16-£22, Dessert £6.95-£8.45, Service optional **Wines** 19 bottles over £30, 35 bottles under £30, 10 by glass
Parking Public car park **Notes** Sunday L £19.50-£25, Vegetarian available, Children welcome

SANDWICH
Map 7 TR35

The Lodge at Prince's
◉◉ Modern British

tel: 01304 611118 **Prince's Dr, Sandwich Bay CT13 9QB**
email: j.george@princesgolfclub.co.uk **web:** www.princesgolfclub.co.uk
dir: M2 onto A299 Thanet Way to Manston Airport, A256 to Sandwich, follow sign to golf course

Golf-centric hotel with modern brasserie

The Lodge occupies a substantial purpose-built property of white walls and red roofs and combines the function of conference facilities and golf links. Another reason for a visit is to sample the innovative cooking in the brasserie-style restaurant, a coolly elegant space in shades of pale blue/grey, with a lightwood floor and a wood-burning stove. Fashionable foams are a favoured device in some starters – one of bacon for seared scallops with belly pork, cauliflower and vanilla purée and shallots, for instance – and the rest of the menu is a slate of nippy ideas. Sea trout tartare is served with apple, fennel and gin and tonic sorbet, and could be followed by properly rested saddle of venison with chestnuts, figs, braised red cabbage and fondant potato, with a game faggot adding an extra dimension. A fish main course on the short menu may be fillet of sea bass with the luxury of lobster tortellini along with samphire and seaweed. Puddings do the trick, especially the light and delicate vanilla and coconut pannacotta with lime sorbet.

Chef Ricky Smith **Owner** Mr M McGuirk **Seats** 55, Pr/dining room 20 **Times** 12-2.30/6.30-9 **Prices** Prices not confirmed, Service optional **Wines** 10 bottles over £30, 30 bottles under £30, 8 by glass **Parking** 100 **Notes** Sunday L, Vegetarian available, Children welcome

SITTINGBOURNE
Map 7 TQ96

Hempstead House Country Hotel
◉ Traditional European

tel: 01795 428020 **London Rd, Bapchild ME9 9PP**
email: info@hempsteadhouse.co.uk **web:** www.hempsteadhouse.co.uk
dir: 1.5m from town centre on A2 towards Canterbury

Modern and classical cooking in a Victorian hotel

Lakes Restaurant at this country-house hotel and spa gets its name from the family who built the original property in the mid-19th century. Elaborate swagged drapes hang at the large windows looking out to the grounds, chandeliers add a bit of glitter, and upholstered dining chairs are pulled up to formally set tables. The kitchen takes its cue from the contemporary British repertoire, with seasonality and local produce to the fore. Scallop and apple tartare, for instance, comes with cider and lemon vinaigrette pearls, and venison carpaccio with saffron and yogurt dressing and beetroot chutney. Ambitious, well-rounded main courses run to an assiette of lamb-shepherd's pie, braised neck and breaded cutlet-on a celeriac cake with kale, and gurnard fillet on spicy lentil stew served with razor clams and sautéed pickled samphire. Close with chocolate and pistachio fondant with mint chocolate ice cream, or rhubarb custard tart.

Times 12-2.30/7-10, Closed D Sun (non residents)

TENTERDEN
Map 7 TQ83

The Swan Wine Kitchen
◉ European

tel: 01580 761616 **Chapel Down Winery, Small Hythe Rd TN30 7NG**
email: booking@swanchapeldown.co.uk
dir: B2082 between Tenterden and Rye

Winning winery with contemporary menu

One of the big guns in English wine production, Chapel Down Winery offers guided tours and tastings and a shop packed with goodies to take home. The striking building of oak and galvanised steel is also home to The Swan Wine Kitchen, an expansive space with lots of natural wood and a contemporary finish. There's a bar and terrace, too, with lovely views over the Kent countryside. The kitchen in the Kitchen makes good use of local ingredients to produce dishes with modern European leanings and offering fashionable pairings. Start with some whipped goats' cheese in a salad, or smoked duck ham fired up with chicory and blood orange. Among main courses, flank of beef arrives with roasted heritage carrots and smoked carrot purée, while another combines cod caught off the Kent coast with cauliflower couscous, capers and raisins. Finish with peanut butter and chocolate cheesecake, and, given the setting, drink something English.

Chef Josh Felstead **Owner** Pete Cornwell **Seats** 65, Pr/dining room 18 **Times** 12-3/6-9, Closed D Sun-Wed **Prices** Fixed L 2 course £17.95, Fixed D 3 course £19.95, Starter £6.50-£8.50, Main £13-£22, Dessert £6.50-£8 **Wines** 16 bottles over £30, 8 bottles under £30, 7 by glass **Parking** 100 **Notes** Gathering menu 2/3 course Mon-Fri 12-3 advance booking req, Sunday L £24.50, Vegetarian available, Children welcome

TUNBRIDGE WELLS (ROYAL)
Map 6 TQ53

Hotel du Vin Tunbridge Wells
◉ French, British

tel: 01892 526455 **Crescent Rd TN1 2LY**
email: reception.tunbridgewells@hotelduvin.com **web:** www.hotelduvin.com
dir: Follow town centre to main junct of Mount Pleasant Rd & Crescent Rd/Church Rd. Hotel 150yds on right just past Phillips House

French bistro food and a monster wine list

A Grade II listed Georgian mansion is home to HdV's operation in Tunbridge Wells, built of local sandstone and enjoying views of the ornamental gardens in Calverley Park at the back. When proceedings may start either in the Dom Pérignon Lounge or the Burgundy Bar, it's hard to miss the point, and the enormous wine lists remain an integral part of the attraction of this hotel chain. The cooking continues on a solid French bistro basis, offering scallops in sauce vièrge, or chicken liver parfait on sourdough toast, to start, then sole meunière with brown shrimps, pedigree 28-day aged rib-eye with skinny chips and textbook béarnaise, or the more obviously Anglo comfort-food likes of 'shepherd's pie' made with duck. Vegetarian mains include parsnip and beetroot Tatin, or spelt risotto with chanterelles. To close, treacle tart is a moistly satisfying rendition, served with clotted-cream ice cream.

Chef Jimmy Worrall **Owner** Hotel du Vin Ltd **Seats** 80, Pr/dining room 84 **Times** 12-2.30/5.30-10 **Prices** Fixed L 2 course £16.95, Fixed D 3 course £40-£60, Starter £5.95-£12.95, Main £14.95-£30, Dessert £7.95-£9.95 **Wines** 16 by glass **Parking** 30, NCP **Notes** Pre-theatre meal offer on selected nights, Sunday L £24.95, Vegetarian available, Children welcome

The Kentish Hare

◉◉ Modern British **NEW**

tel: 01892 525709 **95 Bidborough Ridge, Bidborough TN3 0XB**
email: enquiries@thekentishhare.com
dir: *From A26 London Rd, take B2176 Bidborough Ridge. 0.9m to restaurant*

Dynamic modern cooking in a rejuvenated pub

Chris and James Tanner have their brotherly fingers in all sorts of pies from the southwest to Kent, where they have reopened what was a closed-down pub earmarked for conversion into flats as a dynamic, splendidly refurbished contemporary restaurant with a summer terrace and a large topiary hare out front. Smart table-settings and exposed beams create the right kind of contrast, and the open pass to the kitchen acknowledges today's impulse to break down boundaries. Dishes that are squarely in the modern manner are produced as if newly minted, as with a starter of seared scallops, wafer-thin cauliflower slices, pine nuts and raisins in curry oil, which might presage a main course of deftly crackled pork belly in a neat block like a vanilla slice, accompanied by goats cheese fondue and pickled mushrooms. An alternative route might be via chicken liver parfait with candied walnuts and pear jelly to smoked haddock risotto with leeks and a poached egg in grain mustard sauce. Finish with chocolate ganache with a liquid caramel centre (à la Rolo), served with salted popcorn and milk sorbet.

Chef C & J Tanner, Sam Spratt **Owner** Tanners South-East Ltd **Seats** 40 **Times** 12-2.30/6-9.30, Closed 1st week Jan, Mon **Prices** Fixed L 2 course £18-£21, Fixed D 3 course £22-£25, Starter £5.95-£10.95, Main £12.95-£27.95, Dessert £5.95-£7.50 **Wines** 9 bottles over £30, 18 bottles under £30, 23 by glass **Parking** 24 **Notes** Vegetarian available, Children welcome

The Spa Hotel

◎◉ Modern, Traditional British

tel: 01892 520331 **Mount Ephraim TN4 8XJ**
email: reservations@spahotel.co.uk **web:** www.spahotel.co.uk
dir: *On A264 leaving Tunbridge Wells towards East Grinstead*

Country-house dining beneath crystal chandeliers

Famously one of the UK's spa towns, Tunbridge Wells has no shortage of buildings built in the 18th century to capitalise on that particular boom business. There's a spa here of course in this fine-looking mansion, but it's a 21st-century version offering full pampering and restorative services. The house has 14 acres of grounds, so there's nature's therapy available for free. There's a brasserie on site (Zagatos), while the main Chandelier Restaurant with its grand proportions and elegant finish provides something rather more refined. Begin with a raviolo with a richly satisfying lobster filling and a foamy shellfish sauce on top, or a salad of wood pigeon, quail's egg and air-dried ham. Main course fillet of red mullet is served with fregola pasta enriched with mussels, clams, scallops and squid. Among meat options, rump of Cornish lamb comes in the company of risotto packed with wild garlic and broad beans. Among desserts, dark chocolate fondant is soft and yielding in the all the right places and is partnered with a substantial chunk of honeycomb and tonka bean ice cream.

Times 12.30-2/7-9.30, Closed L Sat

Thackeray's

◎◎◎ *– see opposite*

The Swan

◎◉ Modern British

tel: 01732 521910 **35 Swan St ME19 6JU**
email: info@theswanwestmalling.co.uk
dir: *M20 junct 4 follow signs for West Malling, left into Swan St. Approx 200yds on left*

Seasonal modern brasserie food in a stylish setting

The Swan has been feeding and watering West Malling since it was built as a coaching inn in the 15th century. In January 2015, a stylish refurbishment of the entire ground floor introduced curvaceous seats, exposed brickwork and talking-point light fixtures. The acquisitive modern British manner informs brasserie-style menus that build on Kentish farm produce with influences from far and wide. Spiced chickpea fritters with spring onion and feta in tamarind dressing might be one way to start, the razor-sharp seasonings of sea bass céviche in fennel, orange and coriander an equally tempting one. Mains get as grand as a roast rack of lamb for two to share, accompanied by mini shepherd's pies, while the grill produces variously sauced steaks, or spatchcocked chicken with a salad of sweetcorn and cashews. An Anglo-Welsh cheese selection with truffle honey is at least as powerful a lure to finish as the plentiful chocolate offerings, or a tarte Tatin made with Pink Lady apples and served with Calvados ice cream.

Chef Lee Edney **Owner** Swan Brasserie Ltd **Seats** 90, Pr/dining room 28 **Times** 12-3.30/5.30-10, Closed 1 Jan, D Sun **Prices** Fixed L 2 course fr £16.50, Fixed D 3 course fr £20, Starter £6-£9.50, Main £13-£25, Dessert £6-£7 **Wines** 60 bottles over £30, 32 bottles under £30, 17 by glass **Parking** Long-stay car park **Notes** All day fixed menu 2 course, Sunday L, Vegetarian available, Children welcome

The Sportsman

◎◉ Modern British

tel: 01227 273370 **Faversham Rd, Seasalter CT5 4BP**
email: contact@thesportsmanseasalter.co.uk
dir: *On coast road between Whitstable & Faversham, 3.5m W of Whitstable*

Bracing freshness and absence of pretension in a Kentish pub

The Sportsman, a few miles out of Whitstable, has a distinctly rustic, unpretentious look, with scuffed floorboards, plain walls hung with pictures above half-panelling, and flowers and curtains a nod to refinement. The kitchen, too, has a down-to-earth, no-frills approach, using top-quality local produce and making everything in-house, including butter. Start with an appetiser of fresh-as-possible oyster topped with warm chorizo before a first course of to-die-for soda bread smeared with soft cheese topped with home-smoked mackerel with dice of apple jelly and a grating of horseradish, or pork terrine. Apart from high levels of technical skills, the kitchen has a profound sense of what goes with what in dishes of remarkably clear flavours. Stunningly fresh braised brill fillet on tender leeks is topped with mussels and bacon and accompanied by creamy mash, and roast saddle of lamb with no more than mint sauce and seasonal vegetables. End with unpasteurised cheese or a copybook example of apple soufflé – well risen, light and airy – with salted caramel ice cream.

Chef Stephen Harris, Dan Flavell **Owner** Stephen & Philip Harris **Seats** 50 **Times** 12-2/7-9, Closed 25-26 Dec, 1 Jan, Mon, D Sun **Prices** Tasting menu £45-£65, Starter £7.95-£11.95, Main £19.95-£23.95, Dessert £7.95-£8.95, Service optional **Wines** 18 bottles over £30, 33 bottles under £30, 10 by glass **Parking** 20 **Notes** Sunday L, Vegetarian available, Children welcome

WROTHAM

Map 6 TQ65

The Bull

◉◉ Modern British

tel: 01732 789800 **Bull Ln TN15 7RF**
email: info@thebullhotel.com **web:** www.thebullhotel.com
dir: *Between M20 & M26 junct. In centre of village*

Contemporary cooking in old village inn

An enthusiastic landlord has transformed a 600-year-old country inn into a destination restaurant and hotel, with the dining room of some style, done out in shades of pink, with blinds and curtains at the windows, a lightwood floor, wood-burners adding focus, and a mix of wooden and leather-look chairs at unclothed wooden tables. These are pitch-perfect surroundings in which to sample some

dynamic cooking. Seaweed pesto and goats' cheese cream add interesting elements to impressively braised lamb shoulder with minted Puy lentils, soused beetroot and peas, and another innovative main course has been seared cod fillet with fennel whitebait, truffled spinach, celeriac dauphinoise and almond-flavoured cauliflower purée. Starters have included smoked salmon fishcakes with pea purée and a salad of citrus fruit, peas and mint – a well-conceived dish – and more mainstream chicken liver parfait with caramelised onions. The kitchen puts its shoulder behind puddings too: copybook honey pannacotta with peach purée and apricots, for instance, or chocolate and almond cake with candied fennel and a poached pear.

The Bull

Chef Rob McLean **Owner** Martin Deadman **Seats** 60, Pr/dining room 12
Times 12-2.30/6-9 **Prices** Starter £7-£7.50, Main £13-£27, Dessert £6.50-£8.50,
Service optional 10% **Wines** 28 bottles over £30, 29 bottles under £30, 9 by glass
Parking 30 **Notes** Sunday L £13.50, Vegetarian available, Children welcome

---

Thackeray's ❀❀❀

TUNBRIDGE WELLS (ROYAL)

Map 6 TQ53

Modern French, European v
tel: 01892 511921 **85 London Rd TN1 1EA**
email: reservations@thackerays-restaurant.co.uk
dir: *A21/A26, towards Tunbridge Wells. On left 500yds after the Kent & Sussex Hospital*

Glossy modern French cooking at the novelist's home

Facing the common is a white-weatherboarded double-fronted house, built in around 1660, where visitors to the spa would have stayed in the 18th century. A century or so later it was the home of the author of *Vanity Fair*, hence the name for this stylish restaurant. The main dining room is softly lit under its low ceiling, with brown banquettes and comfortable chairs on its boarded floor; outside is the Japanese terrace garden, where an outdoor heating system means it's in use all year round. Richard Phillips prides himself on sourcing only top-quality raw materials from within Kent and Sussex and deploys them intelligently and imaginatively, his contemporary French style based on the classical repertory and techniques. He pulls off some astoundingly appealing dishes, such as ballotine of quail breasts served with confit and fried leg, winter truffles, truffled mayonnaise, butternut squash, sautéed duck liver and sweet wine glaze, and spiced langoustines and confit pork belly are plated appropriately

with onion bhaji, lime, mango, pine nuts and parsnip foam. If these sound complex, a meticulous sense of proportion ensures all elements work together. Among the handful of main courses might be fillet of halibut, perfectly timed, with vanilla-infused bisque, parmesan gnocchi, broccoli purée, fennel and courgettes, with a well-judged meat option of perhaps roast duck breast with braised leg, creamy mash, red cabbage, fine beans with bacon, and sherry glaze. Dishes make an impact on the eye as well as on the palate: just look at (before eating it) pear tarte Tatin with chocolate sauce and vanilla ice cream, or light and fluffy raspberry soufflé with vanilla sauce.

Chef Richard Phillips, Shane Hughes **Owner** Richard Phillips **Seats** 70, Pr/dining room 16 **Times** 12-2.30/6.30-10.30, Closed Mon, D Sun **Prices** Fixed L 2 course £17.95, Starter £10.95-£15.95, Main £25.95-£29.50, Dessert £11.95 **Wines** 140 bottles over £30, 17 bottles under £30, 20 by glass **Parking** On street in evening, NCP **Notes** Sunday L £29.50, Children welcome

LANCASHIRE

BLACKBURN
Map 18 SD62

The Clog & Billycock

Traditional British

tel: 01254 201163 **Billinge End Rd, Pleasington BB2 6QB**
email: enquiries@theclogandbillycock.com
dir: M6 junct 29/M65 junct 3. Follow signs to Pleasington

Celebrating northern gastronomy in a Lancashire village inn

Nigel Haworth's pint-sized Ribble Valley pub empire includes this efficiently modernised inn in the village of Pleasington near Blackburn. Bench seating supplements the jumble of furniture, while big windows let in plenty of light on the boutiquey interiors, where stone tiles and framed pictures of local food heroes are the order of the day. As at the other venues in the group, a redeveloped version of traditional northern fare produces some novel ideas, founded on thoroughgoing celebration of the region's gastronomic heritage. A starter of Scotch egg made with black pudding comes with straw potatoes and mustard mayonnaise served in an eggbox, while mains run to herb-crusted lamb cutlets with hedgerow fruit jelly, or signature dishes such as hotpot, fish pie, and devilled chicken with dripping chips. You'll rarely find a better bowl of trifle than here, made with proper custard, a lovely, slightly sticky jelly, and fresh raspberries.

Times 12-2/5.30-8.30

The Millstone at Mellor

Modern British

tel: 01254 813333 **Church Ln, Mellor BB2 7JR**
email: info@millstonehotel.co.uk **web:** www.millstonehotel.co.uk
dir: 4m from M6 junct 31 follow signs for Blackburn. Mellor is on right 1m after 1st set of lights

Smart village inn with feel-good menu

The Millstone is owned by Thwaites Brewery (also of this parish) whose ales can be found at the pumps (Lancaster Bomber, for example, or their golden ale, Wainwright). It's not all about beer, though, for this old coaching inn with its rustic bar and handsome dining areas also deals in feel-good menus that offer up pub classics, lunchtime sandwiches, locally-sourced steaks cooked on the grill, and quite a few global flavours. Begin with a charcuterie board to share, with home-cured meats, pickles and various oils, or go for duck spring rolls with plum sauce. Main courses can be as traditional as home-made burger or breaded chicken with garlic and herb butter, or check out the daily seasonal specials to see what's up for grabs. Those steaks are aged for 28 days – flat iron, maybe, or 8oz rib-eye – and come with flat-cap mushroom, baked tomato and thick-cut chips. Among desserts, sticky toffee pudding and chocolate fondant show the style, while the cheese slate stays true to the British Isles.

Chef Anson Bolton **Owner** Thwaites Inns of Character **Seats** 90, Pr/dining room 20 **Times** 12-9.30, All-day dining, Closed D 25-26 Dec, 1 Jan **Prices** Starter £5-£9, Main £10-£26, Dessert £6-£8, Service optional **Wines** 9 bottles over £30, 32 bottles under £30, 9 by glass **Parking** 45, On street **Notes** Sunday L £17-£20, Vegetarian available, Children welcome

BURROW
Map 18 SD67

The Highwayman

Traditional British

tel: 01524 273338 **LA6 2RJ**
email: enquiries@highwaymaninn.co.uk
dir: M6 junct 36 to A65 Kirkby Lonsdale, off A683

Modern Lancashire pub food chez Haworth

One of the four limbs of Nigel Haworth's Ribble Valley Inns, The Highwayman is up in the far north of Lancashire, near Kirkby Lonsdale. The atmosphere here is determinedly rural, with foursquare wooden tables and an open fire, for all that it looks so box-fresh. As at the other inns, pictures of local suppliers hang about the place, and the cooking single-mindedly pursues a celebration of the county's produce. A twice-baked cheese soufflé made with Sandham's Lancashire, dressed with a heap of peppery leaves, is a robust starter. Mains include the house fish pie, lamb hotpot, and battered haddock with beef-dripping chips, and there are excellent showcases for individual farm produce, such as lamb's liver and kidneys with streaky bacon, spring onion mash and onion gravy (a proper hearty dish). Portions remain heroic to the end, when a large wedge of almond tart turns up steeped in lemon and wild honey, garnished with clotted cream and strawberry jam.

Chef Bruno Birbeck **Owner** Nigel Haworth, Craig Bancroft, Richard Matthewman **Seats** 120 **Times** 12-2/5.30-8.30 **Prices** Fixed L 2 course fr £12.50, Fixed D 3 course fr £15, Starter £5-£6.25, Main £12-£26, Dessert £3.75-£8.50, Service optional **Wines** 5 bottles over £30, 28 bottles under £30, 11 by glass **Parking** 45 **Notes** Fixed L/D Tue-Thu, Sunday L £17.50-£21, Vegetarian available, Children welcome

CLITHEROE
Map 18 SD74

The Assheton Arms

Contemporary Seafood **NEW**

tel: 01200 441227 **Downham BB7 4BJ**
email: info@asshetonarms.com **web:** www.seafoodpubcompany.com/the-assheton-arms
dir: Phone for directions

Outstandingly fresh seafood in an untouched conservation village

Originally a farmhouse that brewed beer, this pub was renamed in honour of the contribution Ralph Assheton, Lord Clitheroe, made to the 1939-45 war effort. Although decidedly inland, its ownership by Joycelyn Neve's Seafood Pub Company guarantees excellent Fleetwood-landed fish and seafood, although your dining choice extends way beyond what a trawler can net. Thus, while one possible starter is devilled crab, salmon and brown shrimp salad, another might be steamed Korean buns with crispy duck and spring onions. Mains too offer plenty of variety, such as hake fillet with udon noodles and crispy seaweed, Goan king prawn curry, toro pie filled with slow-cooked beef and chorizo, and Szechuan spiced chicken with egg-fried rice. For something light to follow, try passionfruit and blackberry mess with baby meringues. Wines are mostly New World, with a reasonable number by the glass.

Chef Louise Kinsella **Owner** Joycelyn Neve, Andrew McLean **Seats** 90, Pr/dining room 12 **Times** 12-9, All-day dining **Prices** Starter £4.95-£7.50, Main £10.95-£23.95, Dessert £2.95-£6.50, Service optional **Wines** 24 bottles over £30, 30 bottles under £30, 13 by glass **Parking** 16 **Notes** Sunday L £13.50, Vegetarian available, Children welcome

GISBURN
Map 18 SD84

Stirk House Hotel

Modern, Traditional

tel: 01200 445581 **BB7 4LJ**
email: reservations@stirkhouse.co.uk **web:** www.stirkhouse.co.uk
dir: M6 junct 32, W of village, on A59. Hotel 0.5m on left

Modern Lancashire cooking in a Tudor manor

The majestic scenery of the Ribble Valley and the Forest of Bowland provide a wild Lancashire backdrop for the weathered stone walls of 16th-century Stirk House. The stone manor house has been revamped in tasteful contemporary style, and offers all you could ask for to wind down, work out, do business or get hitched. Original plasterwork ceilings and an ornate fireplace add character to the restaurant, where friendly staff are keen to please and well-briefed on the menu. The cooking keeps things classic and straightforward and relies on splendid Lancashire produce. Smooth chicken liver parfait comes with red pepper chutney and toasted sourdough bread, followed by herb-crusted baked cod with roasted cherry tomatoes, green beans and garlic oil, or there may be roast pork wrapped in prosciutto with wholegrain mustard mash and cider cream sauce. Rounding things off, there's apricot Bakewell tart with stem ginger ice cream.

Chef Chris Dobson **Owner** Paul Caddy **Seats** 40, Pr/dining room 50
Times 12.30-2.30/7-9, Closed Xmas **Prices** Service optional **Wines** 9 bottles over £30, 23 bottles under £30, 9 by glass **Parking** 300 **Notes** Sunday L £16.95-£19.95, Vegetarian available, Children welcome

LANCASTER
Map 18 SD46

Lancaster House

Traditional British

tel: 01524 844822 **Green Ln, Ellel LA1 4GJ**
email: reception.lancaster@englishlakes.co.uk **web:** www.englishlakes.co.uk
dir: 3m from Lancaster city centre. From S: M6 junct 33, head towards Lancaster. Continue through Galgate village, turn left up Green Ln just before Lancaster University

Regional brasserie cooking in a Lancashire event hotel

A little to the west of the M6, and practically on the doorstep of the Lake District, Lancaster House is an events and leisure hotel with up-to-the-minute spa facilities and all the organisational precision to make anything from a conference to a wedding go swimmingly. Foodworks is the promising name of the restaurant, where a relaxed, hang-loose brasserie feel predominates, with unclothed tables and a bar at one end, ornate light fittings and mural graphics of flat-capped folk going about their Lancashire business. Despite the Cantonese name, Damien Ng is Lancashire born and bred, and cooks a seasonal menu of readily understandable brasserie fare such as starters of scallops and black pudding with pancetta, or duck liver parfait with plum purée and poppy seed toast. To follow, try the likes of chargrilled swordfish with cherry tomato relish and noodles fried in sesame oil, chilli and soy, or minted lamb hotpot with silverskin onions, pickled beetroot and buttered kale, an impeccable regional classic. Finish with plum frangipane tart and Amaretto custard.

Chef Damien Ng **Owner** English Lakes Hotels **Seats** 90, Pr/dining room 150
Times 12.30-2.30/7-9.30 **Prices** Fixed L 2 course £15-£28, Starter £4.50-£7.25, Main £12.95-£22.95, Dessert £5.95-£6.25, Service optional **Wines** 6 bottles over £30, 39 bottles under £30, 10 by glass **Parking** 130 **Notes** Please phone to check L openings, Sunday L £13.50-£16.50, Vegetarian available, Children welcome

LANGHO
Map 18 SD73

Northcote

– see page 240 and advert on page 241

LEYLAND
Map 15 SD52

BEST WESTERN PREMIER Leyland Hotel

Modern British **NEW**

tel: 01772 422922 **Leyland Way PR25 4JX**
email: leylandhotel@feathers.uk.com **web:** www.feathers.uk.com
dir: M6 junct 28, turn left, hotel 1st on left

Modern hotel dining with a local flavour

A modern purpose-built hotel with a decor that treads a line between opulence and chintz, the Leyland impresses with its range of facilities aimed at the corporate and wedding markets. Staff are neatly turned out and ensure everything goes to plan. The Four Seasons dining room occupies a lavishly decorated octagonal space, with neo-classical sculptures, rich colours and well-spaced, well-dressed tables. The kitchen offers up classically-inspired dishes with contemporary touches and a decent showing of regional produce. Confit pork belly, for example, comes with apple balsamic and deconstructed piccalilli to cut through its richness, with main courses serving up locally-sourced steaks or cannon of lamb with buttered leeks and herby mash. Dessert include a classic crème brûlée with a cherry biscotti or a rhubarb crumble tart, and the cheeseboard stays true to Lancashire.

Chef Stuart McNorton **Owner** Feathers Hotel Group **Seats** 80, Pr/dining room 20
Times 6.30-9.30, Closed Xmas, 31 Dec, L all week **Prices** Starter £6-£7, Main £15-£25, Dessert £4-£9, Service optional **Wines** 5 bottles over £30, 27 bottles under £30 **Parking** 100 **Notes** Vegetarian available, Children welcome

LYTHAM ST ANNES
Map 18 SD32

Bedford Hotel

Modern British

tel: 01253 724636 **307-313 Clifton Drive South FY8 1HN**
email: reservations@bedford-hotel.com **web:** www.bedford-hotel.com
dir: From M55 follow signs for airport to last lights. Left through 2 sets of lights. Hotel 300yds on left

Clearly- focused cooking in seaside resort hotel

The Bedford is a welcoming, family-run Victorian hotel with lots going on, from spa and gym to coffee shop, all within a short stroll of the town's famous golf course and its genteel seafront. The Cartland Restaurant has plenty of period charm, with decorative plasterwork, warm pastel tones, black-and-white prints of film stars and neatly laid tables. The cooking keeps things straightforward, steering sensibly clear of left-field flavours and making good use of Lancashire produce. Venerable Lancashire cheesemaker Sandham's provides the wherewithal for an air-light soufflé, with caramelised red onion marmalade and a balsamic reduction providing the sweet-and-sour counterpoints. Next up, sea bass fillet is seared to perfection and matched with vine tomato and basil fondue, saffron potatoes and crisp leeks. The good ideas and careful execution continue at dessert stage with orange cheesecake topped with candied ginger.

Times 10-5/6.30-8.30

Northcote 🌸🌸🌸🌸

Modern British V   NOTABLE WINE LIST

tel: 01254 240555 **Northcote Rd BB6 8BE**
email: reception@northcote.com **web:** www.northcote.com
dir: *M6 junct 31, 9m to Northcote. Follow Clitheroe (A59) signs. Hotel on left before rdbt*

Luxe Victorian manor with benchmark regional cooking

The Victorian manor house cocooned amid rolling acres on the edge of the Ribble Valley near Blackburn has steadily risen in the world since Nigel Haworth and Craig Bancroft invented it as a country hotel many years ago. In 2014, it was welcomed into the prestigious international Relais & Château group, which feels only right as the near 18 months of refurbishment and renovation the place has undergone has given the place a truly luxurious feel, with new guest rooms, a dedicated space for the cookery school and an updated restaurant. While the old fireplace and ornate mouldings are retained, the room has been extended, its various sections connected by arches, with windows looking out over the newly landscaped herb garden. Tables are smartly dressed and set with Riedel glassware, and staff maintain the deft, friendly, helpful tone that makes a visit to Northcote a pleasure. Lisa Allen's cooking has something to do with that too. After a period of maternity leave, she has returned with renewed creative energy, and the cooking is as assured as ever. Many claim to be celebrating localism these days, but the commitment to Lancashire produce that has always been the foundation of Haworth's vision here is one of blazing conviction. Much of the produce comes from Northcote's own extensive kitchen gardens, but regional game, seafood and the inimitable Lancashire cheese all feature prominently too. The five-course Gourmet Menu is designed to give a comprehensive illustration of the style. Smoked eel and Morecambe Bay shrimps are the stunning double-act in an opening take on Caesar salad, which is followed by another marine pairing, this time of salmon belly and tempura scallop with laverbread and an ozone-fresh array of sea greens. A bowl of clear Scotch broth with pearled veg and barley presents a logistical challenge that will need all your ingenuity with the cutlery to set about its piece of salt marsh lamb wrapped in puff pastry. The main course is sublime wheat-fed guinea-fowl breast with a casserole of the leg meat, damson prunes and clumps of rice. After a suitable pause, dessert looks over the county boundary for Yorkshire's incomparable rhubarb, which makes a regal setting for a white chocolate ball of vanilla custard, alongside a little rhubarb and ginger jelly. Superb cheeses come with home-made wafers and fruit and walnut loaf. Incidentals and in-betweenies are little masterpieces of ingenuity, such as the 'tumbleweed' canapé of a mushroom wrapped in kataifi pastry.

Chef Nigel Haworth, Lisa Allen **Owner** Nigel Haworth, Craig Bancroft, Richard Matthewman **Seats** 70, Pr/dining room 60 **Times** 12-2/7-9.30, Closed Food & Wine Festival **Prices** Fixed L 2 course £21-£30, Fixed D 3 course £40-£90, Tasting menu fr £85 **Wines** 359 bottles over £30, 31 bottles under £30, 12 by glass **Parking** 60 **Notes** Fixed gourmet D 5 course £60, Seasonal L 3 course £27.75, Sunday L £40, Children welcome

Northcote

dedicated to perfection

Michelin-starred restaurant and country-house hotel Northcote has cemented its reputation as the go-to destination for luxury travel and dining in the UK.

Following eighteen months of extensive renovations and refurbishment – which included a new-look restaurant, twelve new bedrooms, a cookery school, a chef's table and *The Louis Roederer Private Dining Rooms*, Northcote kicked off 2015 with the launch of the hughly anticipated *Garden Lodge*, an impressive new building of 7 bedrooms and a master suite, ideal for groups of up to 16 Gourmands.

The iconic Northcote is the country-house hotel of choice for discerning diners and seasoned travellers around the UK. An oasis of food and wine served with Northern hospitality from a highly talented team.

Northcote Road, Langho, Blackburn, Lancashire BB6 8BE
Tel: 01254 240555 • **Website:** www.northcote.com • **Email:** reception@northcote.com

LYTHAM ST ANNES *continued*

BEST WESTERN Glendower Hotel

◉ Modern British **NEW**

tel: 01253 723241 **North Promenade FY8 2NQ**
email: info@glendowerhotel.co.uk **web:** www.glendowerhotel.co.uk
dir: *From M55 follow signs for Lytham St Annes then signs for Promenade*

Brasserie dining in a seafront hotel

A Victorian seafront hotel just along from the pier, the Glendower is home to Coast, a contemporary restaurant with a brasserie vibe and a local flavour. The refurbished space doesn't lack for natural light in the daylight hours with large bay windows offering good views over the beach, while staff are a helpful bunch. The kitchen turns out modern British dishes that deliver a twist on classic regional fare. Cottage pie, for example, arrives as a first course topped with truffle foam, or go for the more Euro-centric grilled sardine with tomato concasse and sautéed ratte potatoes. Calves' liver is served as a main course with textures of onion and a buttery champ, or try fillet of black bream with ratatouille and chorizo. Sirloin steak, chicken leg, gammon and salmon are cooked on the grill, and desserts include a modern interpretation of carrot cake.

Chef Craig Brown **Owner** The Haworth family **Seats** 70, Pr/dining room 40 **Times** 6-9.30 **Prices** Fixed D 3 course £15-£25, Starter £5-£7.50, Main £15-£17.50, Dessert £5-£7.50 **Wines** 5 bottles over £30, 18 bottles under £30, 8 by glass **Parking** 40 **Notes** Sunday L £12.95-£14.95, Vegetarian available, Children welcome

Clifton Arms Hotel

◉◉ British

tel: 01253 739898 **West Beach, Lytham FY8 5QJ**
email: welcome@cliftonarms-lytham.com **web:** www.cliftonarms-lytham.com
dir: *On A584 along seafront*

Fun contemporary cooking in a genteel Lytham hotel

The present red-brick building dates from the early Victorian era, and arose on the site of what was a small inn as Lytham ascended to the status of Lancashire gentility. It's a refined spot for an upmarket hotel, all the more so for being not a million miles from the hectic hurly-burly of Blackpool. Chic table settings with good napery and floral adornments look the part against the neutral hues of the main dining room, where the kitchen delivers contemporary Anglo-French cooking that keeps a weather eye on the seasons. An autumn menu might kick off with chicken liver and foie gras parfait with truffle-buttered toast and Madeira jelly. Mains might include a generous tranche of carefully timed halibut with langoustines and saffron mash in a sweet-sour port reduction, or slow-cooked belly and cheek of Old Spot pork with pease pudding, puréed Bramley and pickled carrots. Dessert presentations are fun: imagine a spooky grassy knoll with a crooked tree growing out of the top, and you've pictured something like the chocolate soil, pistachio sponge and yogurt offering.

Chef Justin Jerome **Owner** David Webb **Seats** 60, Pr/dining room 140 **Times** 12-2.30/6.30-9 **Prices** Starter £6, Main £15.50-£20.95, Dessert £5, Service optional **Wines** 11 bottles over £30, 29 bottles under £30, 13 by glass **Parking** 50 **Notes** Sunday L £25, Vegetarian available, Children welcome

Greens Bistro

◉ Modern British

tel: 01253 789990 **3-9 St Andrews Road South, St Annes-on-Sea FY8 1SX**
email: info@greensbistro.co.uk
dir: *Just off St Annes Sq*

Lancashire bistro cooking in a bright basement

A basement bistro venue on a backstreet in Lytham – Blackpool's posher cousin a little way down the coast – Greens is the sort of place that every small town should have. For a subterranean room, it looks bright and airy, with ornate high-backed chairs in light wood at smartly clothed tables and deep green carpeting. The cooking is straightforward bistro fare based on pedigree Lancashire produce, including the county's famous cheese, which goes classically into a twice-baked soufflé, served with warm tomato salsa and rocket salad. Ribble sea bass is a treat for main, a thick tranche served with rösti and foraged samphire in saffron sauce. Meat might be lamb shoulder in rosemary-laced juices with a dollop of mashed maris pipers. Finish with a good brûlée and strawberries in summer, or apple crumble with rhubarb ripple ice cream when the orchard fruits come on stream.

Chef Paul Webster **Owner** Paul & Anna Webster **Seats** 38 **Times** 6-10, Closed 25 Dec, BHs, 1 wk summer, Sun-Mon, L all week **Prices** Fixed D 3 course £19.20, Starter £4.95-£6.50, Main £14-£17.95, Dessert £4.95-£5.25, Service optional **Wines** 2 bottles over £30, 18 bottles under £30, 7 by glass **Parking** On street **Notes** Vegetarian available, Children welcome

MORECAMBE	Map 18 SD46

The Midland

◉ Modern British **NEW**

tel: 01524 424000 **Marine Road West LA4 4BU**
email: themidland@englishlakes.co.uk **web:** www.englishlakes.co.uk/hotels/midland
dir: *A589 towards Morecambe, follow seafront signs, left on B5321 (Lancaster Rd) then Easton Rd, left into Central Drive. Right at rdbt on seafront. Left to hotel entrance*

Modern Lancashire cuisine in an art deco hotel

An art deco gem, The Midland was built by the London, Midland and Scottish Railway in 1933 in the 'streamline modern' style, and it's looking good since a refurbishment in 2008. Fabulous views of Morecambe Bay are guaranteed come rain or shine, and there's nowhere better to enjoy them than from the hotel's Sun Terrace Restaurant with its wall of glass. There's a sharp modernity to the restaurant that suits the space, with a contemporary finish and neat white tablecloths to ensure everything is right and proper. Likewise, the menu meets contemporary expectations with its focus on regional ingredients and fashionable flavour combinations. Scallops are roasted just so and served with cauliflower purée, crispy bacon and pistachio crumb, and main courses are big on the feel-good factor. Try slow-cooked blade of beef, rib-eye steak, or poached plaice with ham fritter and red wine syrup. Finish with dark chocolate and rosewater cheesecake or a cracking array of British cheeses.

Chef Michael Wilson **Owner** English Lakes Hotels, Resorts and Venues **Seats** Pr/dining room 24 **Times** 12.30-2/6.30-9.30, Closed Xmas & New Year **Prices** Fixed L 2 course £21.50, Starter £4.95-£9.25, Main £13.95-£23.95, Dessert £5.95-£8.95, Service optional **Wines** 26 bottles over £30, 36 bottles under £30, 9 by glass **Notes** Sunday L £17.95-£21.95, Vegetarian available, Children welcome

RILEY GREEN
Map 18 SD62

The Royal Oak

Traditional British **NEW** v

tel: 01254 201445 **Blackburn Old Rd PR5 OSL**
email: royaloak@dininginns.co.uk
dir: *M65 junct 3 towards Walton le Dale, right at T-junct*

Unpretentious pub with confident cooking

Just a short distance from the Hoghton Tower in a beautiful part of Lancashire, this roadside inn has a proper pub atmosphere with traditional touches of open fires, stone walls and church pews. A welcoming buzz and Thwaites ales on tap add to the unpretentious, relaxed vibe and new owners Chris and Mike Rawlinson have traded up when it comes to its food offering. Whether you grab a table in the bar or the dining area, the modern British dishes are straightforward but cooked with confidence and flair. Hoi sin-glazed short rib beef with salt and pepper squid, pickled cucumber, chilli and coriander salad and wasabi mayonnaise is a typical starter, followed by pan-fried hake, cavolo nero, capers, tartare sauce and hand-cut chips. To end, chocolate brownie might be paired with caramelised banana, Chantilly and vanilla ice cream.

Chef Chris Rawlinson **Owner** Chris & Mike Rawlinson **Seats** 75 **Times** 12-2.30/5.30-9 **Prices** Starter £4.95-£8.95, Main £10.95-£19.95, Dessert £4.59-£6.95 **Wines** 18 bottles over £30, 34 bottles under £30, 9 by glass **Parking** 100 **Notes** Sunday L £11.95, Children welcome

THORNTON
Map 18 SD34

Twelve Restaurant and Lounge Bar

Modern British

tel: 01253 821212 **Marsh Mill Village, Marsh Mill-in-Wyre, Fleetwood Road North FY5 4JZ**
email: info@twelve-restaurant.co.uk **web:** www.twelve-restaurant.co.uk
dir: *A585 follow signs for Marsh Mill Complex. Turn right into Victoria Rd East, entrance 0.5m on left*

Stimulating modern cooking in contemporary setting

Virtually under the sails of an 18th-century windmill, Twelve has an ultra-modern, stripped-down sort of look, with exposed air ducts and beams, brick walls, slate flooring, sleek designer furniture and pop art on the walls. Chef-proprietor Paul Moss works in association with regional producers and suppliers, and his bold cooking style is as contemporary as the surroundings. Poached breast of quail with a quail sausage (actually mousse in pancetta), served with light blue cheese gnocchi and textures of pear, is a highly worked starter of clear and clean flavours, as is goats' cheese pannacotta with caramelised walnuts, pickled beetroot and red chard. Main courses are a blend of up-to-date concepts and more traditional ideas. So haunch of venison, with chocolate, beetroot and salsify, might be offered alongside a deconstructed version of fish pie – accurately poached cod fillet with

pieces of bacon topped with grilled mash, the plate dotted with green vegetables, all hitting the palate buttons – or 'three bits of pig' (belly, head and fillet) with crackling and apple gel. End with a stylish pudding like vanilla parfait with coffee ice cream and vodka gel.

Twelve Restaurant and Lounge Bar

Chef Paul Moss **Owner** Paul Moss, Caroline Upton **Seats** 90 **Times** 12-3/6.30-12, Closed 1st 2 wks Jan, Mon, L Tue-Sat **Prices** Fixed D 3 course £23.45-£24.95, Starter £5.95-£10.50, Main £18.50-£24.95, Dessert £5.95-£8.95, Service optional **Wines** 18 bottles over £30, 38 bottles under £30, 12 by glass **Parking** 150 **Notes** Sunday L £17.95-£23.45, Vegetarian available, Children welcome

See advert on page 244

WHALLEY
Map 18 SD73

The Freemasons at Wiswell

– see page 245

The Three Fishes

British

tel: 01254 826888 **Mitton Rd, Mitton BB7 9PQ**
email: enquiries@thethreefishes.com
dir: *M6 junct 31, A59 to Clitheroe. Follow Whalley signs, B6246, 2m*

Village inn celebrating Lancashire food heroes

The flagship of the Ribble Valley Inns group run by Nigel Haworth and Craig Bancroft of Northcote fame is dedicated to celebrating Lancashire's larder. It's a buzzing spot with cheery service and a wide-ranging menu of no-nonsense modern pub ideas and old-favourites done right – fish and chips, for example, is line-caught haddock with dripping-cooked chips and marrowfat peas. Its head chef, well-versed in Haworth's philosophy of 'keeping it local', is making a fine job of delivering muscular regional flavours, thus Butler's Lancashire cheese supplies the oomph in a twice-baked soufflé with beetroot relish and cheese sauce, while North Sea cod stars in a main course with seaweed potatoes, brown shrimps and crispy mussels. At the end, good pastry skills are evident in a Bramley apple tart served with vanilla ice cream and caramel.

Chef Ian Moss **Owner** Craig Bancroft, Nigel Haworth, Richard Matthewman **Seats** 140 **Times** 12-2/5.30-8.30 **Prices** Fixed L 2 course fr £12.50, Fixed D 3 course fr £15, Starter £3.75-£8.50, Main £10.50-£24.50, Dessert £3.75-£8.50, Service optional **Wines** 5 bottles over £30, 29 bottles under £30, 11 by glass **Parking** 70 **Notes** Fixed L/D 2/3 course Mon-Thu, Sunday L £17.50-£21, Vegetarian available, Children welcome

WHITEWELL

Map 18 SD64

The Inn at Whitewell

◉ Modern British

tel: 01200 448222 **Forest of Bowland, Clitheroe BB7 3AT**
email: reception@innatwhitewell.com **web:** www.innatwhitewell.com
dir: *From S: M6 junct 31 Longridge follow Whitewell signs. From N: M6 junct 33 follow Trough of Bowland & Whitewell signs*

Traditional rural inn with wide-ranging feel-good food

Overlooking the River Hodder, with stunning views of the Forest of Bowland, this handsome 16th-century inn is a gem of stone floors and ancient beams, open fires, antique furniture and prints. You can eat in the bar areas or in the more formal restaurant. Either way, you'll be spoiled for choice on a diverse menu that encompasses grilled black pudding with cheese mash and apple purée, and a main course of lamb shoulder slowly roasted with rosemary and garlic served with hotpot potatoes, caramelised onions and carrot purée. Much of the produce is local and the kitchen has a confident touch, turning its hands to spicy fried squid in chilli lime and soy dressing with carrot and ginger salad, then seared salmon fillet with smoked haddock, spinach, potato chowder and pea purée, or chargrilled beef sirloin with the usual trimmings. End with one of the traditional puddings or home-made ice cream.

Times 12-2/7.30-9.30

WREA GREEN

Map 18 SD33

The Spa Hotel at Ribby Hall Village

◉◉ Modern, Traditional

tel: 01772 674484 **Ribby Hall Village, Ribby Rd PR4 2PR**
web: www.ribbyhall.co.uk/spa-hotel
dir: *M55 junct 33 follow A585 towards Kirkham & brown tourist signs for Ribby Hall Village. Straight across 3 rdbts. Village 200yds on left*

Cooking with real flair in a smart spa hotel

As its name makes clear, there are some pretty swanky spa facilities at this classy adult-only retreat in 100 acres of Lancashire countryside. The Brasserie is another string to its bow, and with its recently completed Orangery extension, the light-bathed venue now offers plenty of room in a clean-lined space done out with orange and lime leather seats at unclothed tables. Smart modern food with a good showing of regional ingredients on the menu and a decidedly modern British approach is the deal here. Start with barbecued salmon, served up with pickled white asparagus, samphire, caviar, and potato mousse, or go for glazed pig's cheek offset by burnt apple, blackberries and parsley purée. Dishes can be complex, but the kitchen has the skills to deliver balanced flavours, as seen in an impressive main course starring suckling pig in the form of roast loin and a croquette of braised shoulder with black pudding, salt-baked celeriac, apple textures and caramelised sprouts. For dessert, there's a faultless tarte Tatin of red wine-poached pears with vanilla ice cream.

Chef Michael Noonan **Owner** W & G Harrison Ltd t/a Ribby Hall Village **Seats** 46 **Times** 12-2/6-9 **Prices** Prices not confirmed, Service optional **Wines** 26 bottles over £30, 52 bottles under £30, 13 by glass **Parking** 100 **Notes** Booking advisable, Vegetarian available, No children

WRIGHTINGTON
Map 15 SD51

Corner House
Modern British

tel: 01257 451400 **Wrightington Bar WN6 9SE**
email: info@cornerhousewrightington.co.uk
dir: *4m from Wigan. From M6 junct 27 towards Parbold, right after motorway exit, by BP garage into Mossy Lea Rd. On right after 2m*

Contemporary hostelry with pub classics and more

The Corner House dates from the 1830s and stands out on Wrightington Bar with its white and blue paint job and creepers neatly trimmed around the windows. It's bright, colourful and contemporary on the inside, opened up in the modern way and with real ales at the pumps, but first and foremost it's a dining destination. The kitchen neatly meets the expectations of those after some traditional pub grub, while satisfying those seeking something a little more unpredictable. So you might start with an old classic (prawn cocktail) or a modern one (Goosnargh chicken liver parfait with onion marmalade and toasted brioche), and move on to fish and chips or tender braised ox cheek with a rich, glossy port jus. Steaks are cooked on the grill and arrive with mushrooms stuffed with brie, onion ring and chips, while, for dessert, crème brûlée comes with a home-made cookie.

Chef Ross Lawson **Owner** Ross Lawson, Helen Hunter **Seats** 60
Times 12-2.30/5-8.30, Closed 26 Dec, Mon (ex BHs) **Prices** Prices not confirmed **Wines** 9 bottles over £30, 26 bottles under £30, 8 by glass **Parking** 80 **Notes** L fr £4.95, Sunday L, Vegetarian available, Children welcome

LEICESTERSHIRE

CASTLE DONINGTON
For restaurant details see East Midlands Airport

EAST MIDLANDS AIRPORT
Map 11 SK42

BEST WESTERN PREMIER Yew Lodge Hotel & Spa
British

tel: 01509 672518 **Packington Hill DE74 2DF**
email: info@yewlodgehotel.co.uk web: www.yewlodgehotel.co.uk
dir: *M1 junct 24. Follow signs to Loughborough & Kegworth on A6. On entering village, 1st right, after 400yds hotel on right*

International cooking near East Midlands airport

At the heart of Yew Lodge is the original Georgian house with its views down Packington Hill, though the full panoply of spa and conference facilities it boasts today is attuned to modern requirements, as befits its latter-day proximity to East Midlands Airport. The Orchard restaurant presents an attractively traditional look, with double-clothed tables and plenty of natural light from deep windows. The menu takes a modern European approach, with occasional forays east for the likes of stir-fried noodles with Chinese greens and baby corn, or seared sea bass in Thai broth. Otherwise, expect grilled haloumi on a tart topped up with courgette, aubergine and peppers, before pulled pork with black pudding and apple-sultana salsa, or perhaps seared salmon with its own croquette in Caesar sauce. Desserts include carrot cake with crème fraîche sorbet, or summer berry Pavlova with ginger cream and lime granita.

Times 12-2/6.30-9.30, Closed L Sat

The Freemasons at Wiswell

WHALLEY
Map 18 SD73

Modern British NOTABLE WINE LIST
tel: 01254 822218 **8 Vicarage Fold, Wiswell BB7 9DF**
email: steve@freemasonswiswell.co.uk
dir: *A59, located on the edge of Whalley village near Clitheroe*

Exciting virtuoso cooking in a relaxed village inn

This chocolate-box village has become a hot-spot foodie destination in recent years thanks to the high-flying cooking of chef-patron Steven Smith. Converted from three small cottages, one of which was a freemasons' lodge, the place is decked out with antique furniture, rugs on the floor, an open fire and even a stag's head. It all adds up to a welcoming, warm and convivial atmosphere. Steven Smith worked in some of the North's top kitchens before going solo, so he knows exactly how to use Lancashire's finest produce as the basis for inventive, technically-accomplished dishes. He can take the humble spud as the starting point for an opener whose array of flavours and textures delivers real wow factor, the potatoes cooked in bacon dashi stock partnered with a crispy hen's egg, wild 'hen of the woods' mushrooms and deeply flavoured Ibérico ham. Main course showcases wild hare: the saddle, roasted and smoked over pine, is brought to the table in a pot, releasing a waft of fragrant smoke, and plated with loin tartare, roast and puréed parsnips, apple purée,

Stilton and shaved chocolate and a dazzling Grand Huntsman sauce. Fish, meanwhile, might appear as plain and simple as the catch of the day grilled with lemon and brown butter and accompanied by potted Southport shrimps and chips, or roast loin of cod with a risotto of squid, Jerusalem artichoke, hazelnuts, chorizo and yuzu. Knockout presentation is a forte too, all the way through to a dessert starring Michel Cluizel's unctuous single estate chocolate matched with caramelised banana, rum gel, raisins, fresh passionfruit, and brown butter ice cream.

Chef Steven Smith, Hywel Griffith **Owner** Steven Smith **Seats** 70, Pr/dining room 14 **Times** 12-2.30/5.30-9, Closed 2 Jan for 2 wks, Mon-Tue **Prices** Fixed L 2 course £15, Fixed D 3 course £15, Tasting menu £70, Starter £8.95-£16.95, Main £16.95-£35, Dessert £8.95-£12.95, Service optional **Wines** 108 bottles over £30, 56 bottles under £30, 30 by glass **Parking** In village **Notes** Fixed L/early supper 3 course seasonal menu, Sunday L £25, Vegetarian available, Children welcome

EAST MIDLANDS AIRPORT *continued*

The Priest House Hotel

◎◎ Modern British

tel: 01332 810649 & 0845 072 7502 *(Calls cost 7p per minute plus your phone company's access charge)* **Kings Mills DE74 2RR**
email: thepriesthouse@handpicked.co.uk
web: www.handpickedhotels.co.uk/thepriesthouse
dir: *M1 junct 24, onto A50, take 1st slip road signed Castle Donington. Right at lights, hotel in 2m*

Confident modern cooking in a riverside country house

Once standing in the vicinity of mills that ground flint for Derby porcelain, the Priest's House survived a fire in the 1920s that destroyed much else around it. Close by the River Trent, its location perfectly fits it for the role of contemporary country-house hotel. A stylish restaurant in neutral tones looks on to a small courtyard, and is decorated with naturally inspired abstract artworks on the stone walls. The kitchen brims with confidence as it sets about furnishing the place with statement examples of modern British cooking. Combinations could be as intuitive as beef carpaccio and horseradish sorbet with pickled turnip, or as off-the-wall as crispy squid, watermelon, dried olives and pumpkin seeds, both highly accomplished openers. Dishes are complex, which always raises the stakes, as when lemon sole is stuffed with crab and served with butternut squash gnocchi in pine nut dressing, but breast of duck with confit leg bonbon, hazelnuts and a skirlie cake oddly doesn't seem greater than the sum of its parts. The bravura dessert is excellent chocolate marquise with a chocolate cylinder of pistachio mousse.

Chef David Humphreys **Owner** Hand Picked Hotels **Seats** 34, Pr/dining room 100 **Times** 12-2.30/7-9.30, Closed L Mon-Sat, D Sun **Prices** Fixed D 3 course £39, Service optional **Wines** 76 bottles over £30, 19 bottles under £30, 19 by glass **Parking** 100 **Notes** Sunday L £24.95, Vegetarian available, Children welcome

KEGWORTH

For restaurant details see East Midlands Airport

LEICESTER
Map 11 SK50

Hotel Maiyango

◎ Modern International

tel: 0116 251 8898 **13-21 St Nicholas Place LE1 4LD**
email: reservations@maiyango.com **web:** www.maiyango.com
dir: *M1 junct 21, A5460 for 3.5m. Turn right onto A47 round St Nicholas Circle onto St Nicholas Place*

Fab decor and creative contemporary cooking

Bringing a dose of boutique razzle-dazzle to the centre of Leicester, Hotel Maiyango has a cocktail bar on the top floor where you can gaze out over the rooftops. The restaurant is a good looker, too, sporting a stylish North African/Middle Eastern look, with ornate lamps, contemporary chairs and rustic booths decorated with hanging fabrics. The menu draws inspiration from far and wide and is particularly strong when it comes to creating interesting veggie options (maris piper and cumin whip with squash fritter, for example, followed by ricotta and parmesan ravioli with baby plum tomato stew). Main course steamed wild sea bass is served Asian-style with spiced coconut laksa and a chilli and mint relish, while Gressingham duck breast with confit leg fritter is a dish rooted in European tradition. Finish with a vegan green tea jelly with apple sorbet and chilli sugar.

Chef Salvatore Tassari **Owner** Aatin Anadkat **Seats** 55, Pr/dining room 80 **Times** 12-3/6.30-9.30, Closed 25 Dec, 1 Jan, L Sun-Mon **Prices** Fixed L 2 course fr £18.50, Fixed D 3 course fr £32, Tasting menu £35-£45, Service optional **Wines** 19 bottles over £30, 35 bottles under £30, 12 by glass **Parking** NCP **Notes** Brunch, Vegetarian available, Children welcome

LONG WHATTON
Map 11 SK42

The Royal Oak

◎ Modern British

tel: 01509 843694 **26 The Green LE12 5DB**
email: enquiries@theroyaloaklongwhatton.co.uk **web:** www.theroyaloaklongwhatton.co.uk
dir: *Phone for directions*

Skilful modern cooking in a smartly modernised village inn

No longer a pub starved of love and attention, the 21st-century incarnation of The Royal Oak is a thriving gastro-pub in the contemporary manner. The facelift undertaken over the last few years has resulted in a smart interior, the addition of some natty bedrooms, and a focus on food. That said, real ale is all part of the plan, and a few 'pub classics' remain on the menu to ensure the place remains part of the community (a proper pub in other words). The kitchen buys local where possible and turns out lively stuff such as chicken liver parfait with red onion jam, or Cullen skink arancini to start. There are sharing platters filled with goodies, and impressive main courses such as grilled fillet of hake with caper and tarragon butter, served with a ham hock bubble-and-squeak and confit egg yolk. To finish, tiramisù with Kahlúa eggnog and cinnamon-infused compôte.

Chef James & Charles Upton, Shaun McDonnell **Owner** Alex & Chris Astwood **Seats** 45 **Times** 12-2.30/5.30-9.30, Closed D Sun **Prices** Service optional **Wines** 5 bottles over £30, 28 bottles under £30, 12 by glass **Parking** 30 **Notes** Early doors menu Mon-Fri 5.30-6.30, Sunday L £17.25-£21.50, Vegetarian available, Children welcome

MELTON MOWBRAY
Map 11 SK71

Stapleford Park

◎◎ Modern French, British 🍷 NOTABLE WINE LIST

tel: 01572 787000 & 787019 **Stapleford LE14 2EF**
email: reservations@stapleford.co.uk **web:** www.staplefordpark.com
dir: *A1 to Colsterworth onto B676, signed Melton Mowbray. In approx 9m turn left to Stapleford*

Aspirational cooking in a grand old Leicestershire house

Stapleford's lineage can be traced back to medieval times, the estate being owned by successive generations of the Earls of Harborough for nearly 500 years. Parts of the house itself are of great age, while other bits have been treated to a modernising makeover, the Old Wing having been given a fresher look as recently as 1633. It all comes to a head in the riotously opulent dining room, with its high moulded ceiling, classical paintings and Grinling Gibbons mantelpiece. Impeccable staff keep the elevated tone buoyant, and the cooking aims high too. Preparations tend to the refined rather than belligerently modern, so expect smoked mackerel pâté with celeriac remoulade and sourdough toast, or rabbit rillettes with soused carrots and sultanas, to start, and then perhaps breast of corn-fed chicken with Toulouse sausage and cassoulet, the plate adorned with a swipe of vivid carrot purée. Finish with crisp-based almond and amaretti tart, served with Amaretto-laced coffee ice cream, or with fine British cheeses. Home-made breads arrive in four versions, variously flavoured with cheese, herbs and seeds.

Chef Martin Furlong **Owner** Shuif Hussain **Seats** 70, Pr/dining room 180 **Times** 11.30-2.30/6-9.30, Closed exclusive use days **Prices** Starter £9-£12, Main £19-£31, Dessert £9.50-£15 **Wines** 300 bottles over £30, 4 bottles under £30, 10 by glass **Parking** 120 **Notes** Tasting menu 7 course, Themed monthly gourmet eve £99, Sunday L £27.50, Vegetarian available, Children welcome

NORTH KILWORTH
Map 11 SP68

Kilworth House Hotel & Theatre
◉◉ Modern British **V**

tel: 01858 880058 **Lutterworth Rd LE17 6JE**
email: info@kilworthhouse.co.uk **web:** www.kilworthhouse.co.uk
dir: A4304 towards Market Harborough, after Walcote, hotel 1.5m on right

Modern country-house cooking in a heritage hotel

A top-to-toe restoration overseen by the eagle eyes of English Heritage means period authenticity runs seamlessly through this Italianate 19th-century mansion. Only two families lived in it for 120 years, before it became an upmarket country-house hotel in the noughties with all the plush style, fittings and furniture you'd expect in a venue of this standing (including, these days, an open-air theatre in the grounds). The Wordsworth Restaurant is the fine-dining option, amid a truly remarkable confection of stained-glass windows, rich red patterned wallpaper and burnished antique tables beneath a lanterned dome of elaborate plasterwork and twinkling chandeliers. A posh setting indeed, but the kitchen team rises to the occasion with a repertoire of classic country-house cooking brought gently up to date. Try pork belly with tomato red chard, tarragon and langoustine for starters, while main course partners sea trout with brown shrimps, samphire and sea herbs, or game season could see roast quail matched with creamed spelt, chanterelle mushrooms and walnuts. Desserts take in ideas like passionfruit mousse and sorbet with caramelised banana.

Chef Carl Dovey **Owner** Mr & Mrs Mackay **Seats** 70, Pr/dining room 130
Times 12-2.30/7-9.30 **Prices** Fixed L 2 course fr £22.50, Tasting menu £49, Starter £6.75-£9.95, Main £14.95-£24.95, Dessert £7.50, Service optional **Wines** 44 bottles over £30, 35 bottles under £30, 10 by glass **Parking** 140 **Notes** Theatre menu in season 3 course £28, Tasting menu Wed-Sat, Sunday L £24.95-£28.95, Children welcome

QUORN
Map 11 SK51

Quorn Country Hotel
◉ Modern British

tel: 01509 415050 **Charnwood House, 66 Leicester Rd LE12 8BB**
email: sales@quorncountryhotel.co.uk **web:** www.quorncountryhotel.co.uk
dir: M1 junct 23/A6 towards Leicester, follow signs for Quorn

Modern British flavours in a stylish country hotel

With manicured gardens and oak-panelled interiors, the Quorn Country Hotel has a 17th-century house at its heart, which has been much extended over the years. The restaurant, Shires, is a useful spot to know about in this neck of the woods, just outside Loughborough, with its formal table settings and professional service team. The menu takes a modern British path, and doesn't stray too far into the outer reaches. You might start with a ham hock terrine with piccalilli and parsnip purée, or seared scallops in the familiar company of cauliflower purée and bacon. Main-course salmon — cooked just right — is partnered with a pea croquette, bubble-and-squeak cake and dressed with a prawn and lemon beurre blanc, or go for breast of Barbary duck with redcurrants and rosemary. Finish with something like lime cheesecake with lemon curd and a brandy snap filled with crème fraîche.

Times 12-2/7-9, Closed L Sat

WYMESWOLD
Map 11 SK62

Hammer & Pincers
◉◉ Modern European **V**

tel: 01509 880735 **5 East Rd LE12 6ST**
email: info@hammerandpincers.co.uk
dir: Phone for directions

Innovative modern global cooking with contemporary art

The village restaurant on the Leicestershire-Nottinghamshire border has bags of personality, its toolbox name being only the start of it. Having trained at The Savoy, the owners know a thing or two about hospitality in the grand manner, but the mood here is decidedly more cutting-edge, evident not least in the regular displays of contemporary artworks that are the product of a collaboration with a German art foundation. Innovative modern global cooking is most popularly experienced in the form of a grazing menu, but there is a more conventional format for three-coursers. Begin with vigorously spiced curry-roast scallops with cumined cauliflower purée and Indian accoutrements, including a pakora, mango chutney and a scattering of poppadoms. That could be followed by pork fillet roasted in smoked paprika and garlic with chorizo and aïoli, or Moroccan-accented salmon chermoula wrapped in brik pastry on apricot and pistachio tabouleh. This is Stilton country, so a serving of Cropwell Bishop with quince paste might look just as appealing as honey and rosemary rice pudding, served with chunks of pear poached in red wine.

Chef Daniel Jimminson **Owner** Daniel & Sandra Jimminson **Seats** 46
Times 12-2/6-9, Closed Mon, D Sun **Prices** Tasting menu £45-£65, Service optional **Wines** 18 bottles over £30, 26 bottles under £30, 16 by glass **Parking** 40
Notes Sunday L £14-£20, Children welcome

LINCOLNSHIRE

GRANTHAM
Map 11 SK93

Harry's Place
◉◉◉ – see page 248

HORNCASTLE
Map 17 TF26

Magpies Restaurant with Rooms

◉◉ British, European

tel: 01507 527004 **73 East St LN9 6AA**
web: www.magpiesrestaurant.co.uk
dir: *A158 into Horncastle, continue at lights. On left opposite Trinity Centre*

Bright, contemporary cooking in the Lincolnshire Wolds

In a terrace of 200-year-old cottages, Magpies has a romantic style of decor of duck-egg blue, with mirrors, modern light fittings, candlelit white-clothed tables and drapes over the bay windows. Some global influences are discernible on the menus, with chef-proprietor Andrew Gilbert making his personal mark on his output with a high degree of originality without going over the top. Slow-roast pork belly, moist and flavoursome, has appeared as a starter spiced up with star anise accompanied by tortellini sauced with apple, garlic and Yarg, and crisp salt-and-pepper crackling. Roast loin of cod as a main course gets the Eastern treatment, served in hoi sin sauce with a spicy vegetable spring roll, chilli-spiked Chinese leaves and rösti, or there may be fillet of venison stuffed with figs and macadamias served with sweet potato terrine, savoury Savoy cabbage and bread sauce. Canapés get the ball rolling, and to cap a meal might be a trio of desserts: chocolate mousse, espresso crème brûlée and dark chocolate fondant.

Chef Andrew Gilbert **Owner** Caroline Gilbert **Seats** 34
Times 12-2/7-9.30, Closed 26-30 Dec, 1-8 Jan, Mon-Tue, L 24 & 31 Dec, Sat
Prices Fixed L 2 course £20, Fixed D 3 course £47, Service optional **Wines** 72 bottles over £30, 72 bottles under £30, 11 by glass **Parking** On street **Notes** Magpie menu 3 course D Wed-Thu & Sun £25, Sunday L £20-£25, Vegetarian available, Children welcome

HOUGH-ON-THE-HILL
Map 11 SK94

The Brownlow Arms

◉ British

tel: 01400 250234 **High Rd NG32 2AZ**
email: armsinn@yahoo.co.uk web: www.thebrownlowarms.com
dir: *Take A607 (Grantham to Sleaford road). Hough-on-the-Hill signed from Barkston*

Country-pub cooking in an elegant village inn

A Lincolnshire village inn that has come up in the world, The Brownlow is as elegantly appointed as an interiors magazine country house, with tapestry-backed chairs and gilt-framed mirrors in a panelled dining room. Attentive, friendly service puts everyone at their ease though, and the menu stays within the familiar territory of classic country-pub cooking. Devilled lamb's kidneys in a puff pastry basket make a robust opener, or there might be battered tiger prawns dressed Thai-style in lime, coriander and green chilli. The Asian note might be struck again in a main of sesame-crusted duck with pak choi and a little rhubarb tart, or there may be a fish assemblage of plaice, salmon and scallops, served with crushed peas in lemon and chive beurre blanc. A successful dessert is the griottine cherry frangipane tart, with creamy praline parfait and frangelico ice cream. Cheeses are served with grapes and membrillo.

Times 12-2.30/6.30-9.30, Closed 25-26 Dec, Mon, L Tue-Sat, D Sun

Harry's Place ◉◉◉

GRANTHAM
Map 11 SK93

Modern French
tel: 01476 561780 **17 High St, Great Gonerby NG31 8JS**
dir: *1.5m NW of Grantham on B1174*

Outstanding quality in a restaurant built for ten

The quaint former farmhouse on the main road through Great Gonerby has been Harry's Place (or more accurately, Harry and Caroline Hallam's place) for nearly 30 years. This husband-and-wife team run the show from top to bottom, with Caroline an engaging presence out front and Harry in the kitchen cooking up a storm. With only 10 tables they are able to ensure everything goes swimmingly, so booking a table well in advance is advisable, especially at weekends. There's a cosy old-fashioned feel to the dining room with the diners generating a contented hum. The menu is short and focused offering two starters, two mains and two desserts, plus a cheese course at the end if you're still going. Harry's cooking is rooted in classical ways and he shows little interest in following fashion and current trends and you can expect beautifully and simply constructed dishes that provide full-on flavours and deep satisfaction. First courses can be as straightforward as celeriac soup, the veg grown around these parts, or as refined as Orkney king scallops lightly seared and served in a spicy marinade with a scallop stock reduction, plus a julienne of red pepper and orange. Follow with fillet of wild turbot (with a sauce flavoured with white wine and Pernod), or fillet of Aberdeen Angus beef partnered with a relish of tomatoes, olives and capers, and a red wine and Armagnac sauce. If vegetarians give advance warning all will be well. Desserts might include a cherry brandy jelly served with yogurt and black pepper, or a hot apricot soufflé. That cheese course includes an array of first class British and French options, from Hampshire's Tunworth to Burgundy's Époisses.

Chef Harry Hallam **Owner** Harry & Caroline Hallam **Seats** 10
Times 12.30-3/7-9, Closed 2 wks from 25 Dec, 2 wks Aug, Sun-Mon
Prices Starter £9.50-£22.50, Main £39.50, Dessert £8, Service optional **Wines** 19 bottles over £30, 2 bottles under £30, 4 by glass **Parking** 4 **Notes** Vegetarian meal on request at time of booking, Vegetarian available, Children 5 yrs+

LACEBY
Map 17 TA20

BEST WESTERN Oaklands Hall Hotel

⚫ Modern British

tel: 01472 872248 **Barton St DN37 7LF**
email: reception@oaklandshallhotel.co.uk **web:** www.oaklandshallhotel.co.uk
dir: *Phone for directions*

Eye-catching, inventive food in a Victorian mansion

The stolid-looking balustraded red-brick mansion, built in 1877, sits in the heart of five acres of landscaped parkland between the Wolds and the Humber, not far from Grimsby. It's a pleasant spot for the full country-house experience, which these days often means a combination of Victorian architectural brio with understated interior styling in the modern idiom. What might once have been called the dining room is, more entertainingly, the Comfy Duck Bistro, a place of unclothed tables, minimal wall adornment, and chairs in alternating beige and blue. Modern food stylings are the norm, with eye-catching presentations of inventive modern British comfort food. A pork pie with salad cream (both home-made) comes with roasted chestnuts as one way to start, while walnut-crumbed pressed smoked salmon is partnered with apple and salted cucumber. Mains comprise multiple technical components – such as duck leg confit with a ham and foie gras croquette, herb-crusted cod with shellfish cannelloni – or else appear in variant guises, as for braised neck and roast rack of lamb with provençal veg, capers and powdered olives. An on-trend dessert is lemon and poppyseed cake with white chocolate cream, salt-baked pineapple and a coconut tuile.

Chef Steven Bennett, Alasdair Eccles **Owner** Nigel Underwood, John Lawson **Seats** 80, Pr/dining room 25 **Times** 11.30-2.30/5-9.30, Closed 26 Dec, D 25 Dec **Prices** Starter £4.50-£7.95, Main £9.95-£19.95, Dessert £4.50-£9.95 **Wines** 5 bottles over £30, 36 bottles under £30, 14 by glass **Parking** 100 **Notes** Sun D special offer , Steak night Thu, Sunday L £11.95-£19.95, Vegetarian available, Children welcome

LINCOLN
Map 17 SK97

Branston Hall Hotel

⚫ Modern British

tel: 01522 793305 **Branston Park, Branston LN4 1PD**
email: info@branstonhall.com **web:** www.branstonhall.com
dir: *On B1188, 3m S of Lincoln. In village, hotel drive opposite village hall*

Ambitious cooking with lake and parkland views

Branston Hall's 88 acres of mature parkland and lakes provide a tranquil buffer zone between the gracious Victorian country house and the frazzling effects of the modern world. It is a handsome old pile, with lofty decorative gables, pinnacle chimneys and interiors that evoke a more gentle pace of life. The Lakeside dining room follows the restful theme, with views over the park, and a culinary style which adds gently modernised twists to the classical country house repertoire – pulled pork, for example, in a composition with Orkney scallops, pease pudding, quail's egg and bacon. At main course stage, Gressingham duck breast is partnered by spiced pumpkin purée, fried kale, Agen prunes and a rich orange and pomegranate sauce. To finish, there's a millefeuille of peanut mousse and chocolate pannacotta with caramel sauce.

Times 12-2/7-9.30

The Old Bakery

⚫⚫ Modern British, Italian

tel: 01522 576057 **26-28 Burton Rd LN1 3LB**
email: enquiries@theold-bakery.co.uk **web:** www.theold-bakery.co.uk
dir: *From A46 follow directions for Lincoln North then follow brown signs for The Historic Centre*

Restaurant with rooms in a converted bakery

In the Uphill district of this undulating city, very near the cathedral and castle, Ivano and Tracey de Serio's restaurant with rooms is a distinctly homely place, with the feel of a farmhouse kitchen in the tiled dining room. A dresser furnished with produce baskets and a wine rack overlook proceedings, and the kitchen turns out a fairly lengthy menu of modern British food that has most of the technical tricks of today's culinary fashion at its disposal. Pork chine terrine, served with apples stewed in ginger beer, saffron piccalilli and pickled cucumber, is a beguiling mixture of messages to begin, while main courses are multi-layered, richly sauced affairs, running from, say, roast rack of lamb in a deeply flavoured tomato reduction with lovage-infused potatoes and roasted beetroot and aubergine to the market fish of the day. A five-course taster menu offers a comprehensive tour, and desserts include white chocolate and pistachio ganache with vanilla pannacotta and delicately flavoured star anise ice cream.

Chef Ivano de Serio **Owner** Alan & Lynn Ritson, Tracey & Ivano de Serio **Seats** 65, Pr/dining room 15 **Times** 12-1.30/7-9, Closed 26 Dec, 1-16 Jan, 1st wk Aug, Mon, L Tue-Wed, D Sun **Prices** Fixed L 2 course £14.50, Tasting menu £44-£55, Starter £6.50-£13.50, Main £14.95-£26, Dessert £5.50-£12.95, Service optional **Wines** 70 bottles over £30, 40 bottles under £30, 9 by glass **Parking** On street, public car park 20mtrs **Notes** Tasting menu 7/10 course, 5/8 course with wine £53-£65, Sunday L £19.95, Vegetarian available, Children welcome

Tower Hotel

⚫ Modern

tel: 01522 529999 **38 Westgate LN1 3BD**
email: tower.hotel@btclick.com **web:** www.lincolntowerhotel.com
dir: *Next to Lincoln Castle*

Fashionable textures in the cathedral quarter

In the Bailgate district of the cathedral quarter, the Tower benefits from all the charm that medieval Lincoln has to offer. Maintaining a high standard of hospitality, it's the sort of place that's very much driven by its catering operation, where the aim to please is written in menus that courteously negotiate today's various special diets. The backbone of it all is finely detailed, up-to-date cooking, heralded by the arrival of a basket of home-made breads and flavoured butters. Gels, dusts and purées in profusion give evidence of an understanding of fashionable textural variety. The range might open with a smoked haddock 'Scotch egg' with pea coulis and lemon gel, proceed to pork belly braised for 36 hours, served with champ, sage custard and Bramley apple gel, and conclude triumphantly with shortbread-crumbed cinnamon brûlée with anise-roasted plum and clementine gel.

Chef Darren Rogan **Owner** P Creasey **Seats** 48 **Times** 12-5/6-9.30, Closed 25-26 Dec, 1 Jan **Prices** Prices not confirmed, Service optional **Wines** 5 bottles over £30, 20 bottles under £30, 8 by glass **Parking** NCP opposite **Notes** Sunday L, Vegetarian available, Children welcome

LINCOLN *continued*

Washingborough Hall Hotel

◉◉ Modern British

tel: 01522 790340 **Church Hill, Washingborough LN4 1BE**
email: enquiries@washingboroughhall.com **web:** www.washingboroughhall.com
dir: *B1190 into Washingborough. Right at rdbt, hotel 500yds on left*

Modern cooking in Georgian country house

Set in three acres of lovely grounds at the heart of a sleepy Lincolnshire village, and with a garden to provide herbs for the kitchen, Washingborough Hall delivers all you would hope for in a Georgian manor house earning its living as a small but switched-on country-house hotel. The smart Dining Room restaurant exudes quietly understated class with its restrained heritage colours, unclothed tables, pale wooden floors, ornate marble fireplace and floor-to-ceiling Georgian windows overlooking the garden – a suitably unshowy setting for unpretentious modern cooking that aims to soothe rather than challenge. Gently inventive contemporary ideas are underpinned by Lincolnshire produce and keep a keen eye on the seasons, starting with a twice-baked local goats' cheese soufflé with tomato chilli jam, followed by rack of lamb with mustard potato gratin and pan juices. Fish is handled with a similar lack of fuss – perhaps poached paupiette of sole with pea purée and crispy bacon. To finish, try a lemon posset with honeyed nectarines and hazelnut biscuit.

Times 12-2/6.30-9

▮ LOUTH   Map 17 TF38

Brackenborough Hotel

◉ Modern British

tel: 01507 609169 **Cordeaux Corner, Brackenborough LN11 0SZ**
email: reception@brackenborough.co.uk **web:** www.oakridgehotels.co.uk
dir: *Hotel located on main A16 Louth to Grimsby Rd*

Inventive bistro dining in a rural setting

Just outside the historical town of Louth, this small hotel (24 rooms) is within beautifully maintained lawns and gardens and has lovely country views. Its Bistro Bar, split into two areas, the bar to the front, the bistro in a rear conservatory extension, is a popular dining venue. The menu might be a crowd-pleaser, but the kitchen puts a great deal of effort and imagination into well-constructed, often unusual dishes. Start with chicken liver and Calvados parfait, rich and smooth, with quince and apple purée and toasted walnut bread, or wild mushroom béarnaise with a slow-cooked egg, and go on to roast chicken breast with celeriac and pea risotto with parmesan and truffle shavings, or grilled plaice fillets with beurre blanc, triple-cooked chips and mushy peas. Wind things up with treacle tart and ginger ice cream.

Chef Bill Britten **Owner** Ashley Lidgard **Seats** 78, Pr/dining room 120
Times 11.30-2.30/5-9.30 **Prices** Prices not confirmed, Service optional **Wines** 36 bottles over £30, 47 bottles under £30, 11 by glass **Parking** 80 **Notes** 2 people 2 course with wine £33, Sunday L, Vegetarian available, Children welcome

▮ MARKET RASEN   Map 17 TF18

The Advocate Arms

◉ Modern European, British

tel: 01673 842364 **2 Queen St LN8 3EH**
email: info@advocatearms.co.uk **web:** www.advocatearms.co.uk
dir: *Located just off Market Place, High Street*

Confident cooking in a town-centre restaurant with rooms

This 18th-century restaurant with rooms in the centre of town has a contemporary finish and aims to impress with its boutique-style attitude and opened-up interior. The space is cleverly divided up with glass panels to distinguish between the buzzy bar and lounge and the brasserie-style dining area. The former is the place to head to for a pint, coffee or something to eat off the bar menu, while breakfast is also served seven days a week. The main restaurant's output is broadly modern British, with some inventive combinations and plenty to satisfy traditionalists. Start with a terrine made with confit belly pork served with crackling, apple purée and baby leek, and follow with pan-fried sea bass partnered with mango and crab salsa, confit potato and a minty pea purée. There are steaks – rib-eye, fillet and sirloin – served with trad accompaniments, and desserts such as a trendy little number combining coffee semi-fredo with stem ginger flapjack, coffee sabayon and popcorn.

Chef Josh Kelly **Owner** Darren Lince **Seats** 65, Pr/dining room 16 **Times** 7am-9.30pm, All-day dining, Closed D Sun (last orders 6.30) **Prices** Starter £4.50-£8.75, Main £11.95-£24.95, Dessert £5.50-£8.95, Service optional **Wines** 10 bottles over £30, 32 bottles under £30, 12 by glass **Parking** 6, Short walk **Notes** Sunday L, Vegetarian available, Children welcome

▮ SCUNTHORPE   Map 17 SE81

Forest Pines Hotel & Golf Resort

◉ Modern British

tel: 01652 650770 **Ermine St, Broughton DN20 0AQ**
email: forestpines@qhotels.co.uk **web:** www.qhotels.co.uk
dir: *M180 junct 4, towards Scunthorpe on A18. Continue straight over rdbt, hotel on left*

Sustainable seafood in a country-house hotel

Say the name 'Grimsby' and the port's fishing heritage immediately springs to mind. The fine-dining restaurant at the swish Forest Pines Hotel & Golf Resort a few miles inland in the North Lincolnshire countryside is called Eighteen57 in honour of the year Grimsby's main fish dock opened. Its interior follows a snazzy piscine theme involving blue mosaic-tiled walls, and pictures, reliefs and murals celebrating the maritime world. Produced by a kitchen that has an eye to sustainability in its sourcing policy, local fish and seafood feature prominently, but by no means exclusively on an enticing modern repertoire, so a meaty starter of potted pork hock with cider jelly, crackling, and ginger and wholegrain mustard clotted cream might precede braised ox cheek with confit garlic mash and seasonal vegetables. On the fish front, citrus batter puts a creative spin on haddock with triple-cooked chips and pea purée, while pudding brings lemon tart with gin, cucumber and tonic granita.

Chef Paul Montgomery **Owner** QHotels **Seats** 70 **Times** 6.30-10 **Prices** Prices not confirmed, Service optional 10% **Wines** 7 by glass **Parking** 400 **Notes** Sunday L, Vegetarian available, Children welcome

San Pietro Restaurant Rooms

◎◎ Modern Mediterranean **NEW**

tel: 01724 277774 **11 High Street East DN15 6UH**
email: info@sanpietro.uk.com **web:** www.sanpietro.uk.com
dir: *Situated in Grade II listed Windmill at x-rds of Brigg Rd & Station Rd*

Stylish spot for creative cuisine

Pietro Catalano, who hails from Sicily, has created a restaurant with rooms that combines the best of Italian hospitality with a touch of boutique swagger. There are swanky bedrooms with stylish decor and a luxe finish, and a restaurant and bar (with a separate entrance to the hotel) that provides a sophisticated setting for menus that deliver contemporary British cuisine with some Italian influences. The former windmill makes for an appealing venue, done out with exposed brick walls, pretty designer wallpapers and sparkling chandeliers. There's evident ambition in the kitchen's output if a first course dish of ballotine of rabbit and foie gras is anything to go by, with its accompanying trio of pear (jelly, poached and velouté), plus some smoked loin and a pistachio biscuit. A fashionable partnership of turbot and crispy pork belly is up next, with tempura prawns and romanesco purée, or go for loin, daube and boudin of venison with sour cherry jus. The complexity continues into desserts such as 'toast and marmalade' sponge, which is served with brown bread ice cream and orange crème anglaise.

Chef Pietro Catalano, Chris Grist **Owner** Pietro & Michelle Catalano **Seats** 80, Pr/ dining room 14 **Times** 12-1.45/6-9.30, Closed 25-26 Dec, Sun, L Mon **Prices** Fixed L 2 course £14.95, Fixed D 3 course £27.50, Tasting menu £49.50, Service optional **Wines** 58 bottles over £30, 52 bottles under £30, 13 by glass **Parking** 22 **Notes** ALC 2/3 course £31.95/£38.50, Vegetarian available, Children welcome

---

SLEAFORD Map 12 TF04

The Bustard Inn & Restaurant

◎ Modern British

tel: 01529 488250 **44 Main St, South Rauceby NG34 8QG**
email: info@thebustardinn.co.uk
dir: *A17 from Newark, turn right after B6403 to Ancaster. A153 from Grantham, after Wilsford, turn left for South Rauceby*

Sensitively refurbished old inn in peaceful village

The bar, with an open fireplace, flagstones and real ales, is the hub of this Grade II listed inn. It's possible to eat in here as well as the restaurant, where tapestry chairs are pulled up to wooden tables, walls are bare stone and the floor is of porcelain tiles. There are 'classics' on the menu such as fish and chips, but look elsewhere for more adventure and to see what the kitchen is really capable of. Two ways with beef (fillet and rillette), for instance, are accompanied by Madeira sauce, a fricassée of greens, pommes Anna and wild mushrooms, and pan-fried sea bass fillet with crispy Parma ham, pesto mash and ratatouille. Starters tick all the right boxes too, taking in carefully grilled red mullet fillets with parmesan polenta and tomato fondue, and deep-fried squid with Thai noodles and sweet chilli dip, while puddings include apple crumble tart with blackberry ripple ice cream.

Chef Phil Lowe **Owner** Alan & Liz Hewitt **Seats** 66, Pr/dining room 12
Times 12-2.30/6-9.30, Closed 1 Jan, Mon, D Sun **Prices** Starter £5.50-£11.95, Main £10.95-£26.50, Dessert £5.75-£6.95, Service optional **Wines** 15 bottles over £30, 28 bottles under £30, 11 by glass **Parking** 18, On street **Notes** Light L menu 2/3 course £12.50/£17, Sunday L £14.50-£25, Vegetarian available, Children welcome

---

STAMFORD Map 11 TF00

The Bull & Swan at Burghley

◎ Traditional British

tel: 01780 766412 **High St, St Martins PE9 2LJ**
email: enquiries@thebullandswan.co.uk **web:** www.thebullandswan.co.uk
dir: *A1 onto Old Great North Rd, left onto B1081, follow Stamford signs*

Fuss-free cooking using regional produce in historical inn

The old stone inn used to be a staging post for coaches on the Great North Road and is nowadays an informal dining pub. Within are beams, stone walls, rugs on darkwood floors and caramel-coloured leather dining chairs. Regional produce is the backbone, with meat and vegetables from the nearby Burghley Estate, and the kitchen balances up-to-date ideas with the more traditional. Ham hock and foie gras terrine, with apple and celery salad and complementary piccalilli purée, has a nice balance of flavours, or there might be smoked eel risotto with leeks and watercress velouté. Main courses embrace gammon steak with chips, egg and pineapple as well as the wilder reaches of pressed belly pork with cheek and black pudding tortellini, and sea bass fillet with seaweed, mussel cream, mash and kale. End with a satisfying pudding like cranberry jam roly-poly with custard.

Times 12-2.30/6-9

The George of Stamford

◎ Traditional British **v** ☙ NOTABLE WINE LIST

tel: 01780 750750 **71 St Martins PE9 2LB**
email: reservations@georgehotelofstamford.com **web:** www.georgehotelofstamford.com
dir: *From A1(N of Peterborough) turn onto B1081 signed Stamford and Burghley House. Follow road to 1st set of lights, hotel on left*

Historical institution treasured for its traditional values and cooking

History seeps from the pores of every mellow stone of this venerable coaching inn, which once fed and watered passengers from the 40 coaches that stopped here each day on the Great North Road. The oak-panelled restaurant is a magnificent room with an old-world feel, and its menus are steadfastly traditional too: trolleys do the rounds, delivering the signature dish of roast sirloin of English beef, carved at the table. But it's not all about heritage dining, as modernists are kept happy with pan-fried sea bass matched with herb risotto and sunblushed tomato, or perhaps an up-to-date riff on lamb, comprising roast loin, liver and kidney, and deep-fried sweetbreads. Then it's time for the trolleys again, this time to deliver a traditional ending of cheeses and sweets.

Chef Chris Pitman, Paul Reseigh **Owner** Lawrence Hoskins **Seats** 90, Pr/dining room 40 **Times** 12.30-2.30/7.30-10.30 **Prices** Prices not confirmed, Service optional **Wines** 113 bottles over £30, 41 bottles under £30, 25 by glass **Parking** 110 **Notes** Walk in L menu, Sunday L, Children 10 yrs+

STAMFORD *continued*

No.3 The Yard

◉ British, European

tel: 01780 756080 **3 Ironmonger St PE9 1PL**
email: info@no3theyard.co.uk
dir: *Phone for directions*

Classic bistro cooking in a conservatory restaurant

It's well worth seeking out The Yard, tucked away as it is behind buildings on Ironmonger Street in this charming old town. French windows in the ground-floor conservatory open on to a secluded courtyard and pretty garden, and there's more space upstairs, where monochrome photographs on brick walls show past times in Stamford. Rich and flavourful goats' cheese risotto studded with cubes of thyme-roasted beetroot gets things off to a flying start, or there might be sautéed prawns thermidor. The kitchen looks towards Europe for its inspiration, so among main courses expect a classic rendition of pan-fried breast of Barbary duck with roast potatoes, seasonal greens and a correctly viscous orange sauce. An alternative might be creamy fish pie with seasonal samphire, and desserts are a class act too, among them pear frangipane tart, its pastry crisp and golden, or chocolate fondant.

Chef Tim Luff **Owner** Simon McEnery **Seats** 55, Pr/dining room 14
Times 11.30-2.30/6-9.30, Closed Mon, D Sun **Prices** Fixed L 2 course £14.50, Fixed D 3 course £19.50, Starter £5.95-£7.50, Main £13-£22.50, Dessert £4-£7.50, Service optional **Wines** 17 bottles over £30, 41 bottles under £30, 16 by glass **Parking** Broad St **Notes** Sunday L £18.50-£22.50, Vegetarian available, Children welcome

The William Cecil

◉ Modern British

tel: 01780 750070 **High St, St Martins PE9 2LJ**
email: enquiries@thewilliamcecil.co.uk **web:** www.thewilliamcecil.co.uk
dir: *Exit A1 signed Stamford & Burghley Park. Continue & hotel 1st building on right on entering town*

Stylishly modernised Georgian hotel restaurant with creative menu

The hotel is an interesting amalgam of three Georgian houses built at different times, originally named after one of William Cecil, Lord Burghley's descendants, Lady Anne, but now restored to the Elizabethan statesman himself. Just off the approach road to Stamford, it's a clever blend of old and new inside, the panelling done in lighter colours, with booth seating and a laminate floor in the restaurant. The kitchen team sources locally in the best modern way, and has more than a touch of creative flair at its disposal. That can be seen in a starter of hazelnut-crusted foie gras parfait with truffled cucumber salad and brioche toast, which might be followed by lemon sole and crayfish tails in champagne butter sauce with colcannon, or a meat dish such as Gressingham duck breast and celeriac gratin with a reduction sauce incorporating elderflower and pomegranate. Finish with richly filled chocolate tart, white chocolate honeycomb and vanilla clotted cream.

Times 12-3/6-9

Winteringham Fields ❁❁❁

WINTERINGHAM	Map 17 SE92

Modern British, European
tel: 01724 733096 **1 Silver St DN15 9ND**
email: reception@winteringhamfields.co.uk **web:** www.winteringhamfields.co.uk
dir: *Village centre, off A1077, 4m S of Humber Bridge*

Thrilling cooking on the Humber estuary

Chef-patron Colin McGurran will be a familiar face for aficionados of the BBC's *Great British Menu*, so if you're inspired to try his artistry first-hand you'll need to set the GPS for the wilds of Lincolnshire near the Humber estuary. This is not where you'd expect to find a top-flight restaurant with rooms, perhaps, but Winteringham has long been a destination for culinary excellence. The place has its own farm producing honey, free-range eggs, and seasonal fruit, veg and herbs. What doesn't come from Winteringham's fertile soil is sourced diligently from local suppliers and Grimsby's quayside. In a plush dining room recently reworked with slinky velour curtains, stag's head wallpaper, and tartan-upholstered seats at linen-swathed tables, you can enjoy fascinating, techno-driven assaults on the expectations. Dinner takes the shape of seven- or nine-course Surprise menus that take you on a gastronomic rollercoaster through oyster bavarois served in its shell with sea bass, chives, cucumber and salmon roe, then a playful presentation of tomato gazpacho, delivered inside a mini vine tomato and helped along by basil pesto and feta cheese. Next comes melt-in-the-mouth confit salmon with cabbage purée and dill oil, followed by beef fillet with cubes of beef cheek topped with a deeply meaty jelly and boosted further still by bone marrow kuzu sauce, caramelised onion and buckwheat. A palate-blasting lime and pineapple bomb clears the way for a finale of egg custard tart with honeycomb and yogurt sorbet. If you prefer to choose what to eat, lunchtimes offer a four-course à la carte. A rarefied list of commendably well-chosen wines has plenty to suit the challenging style of the food.

Chef Colin McGurran **Owner** Colin McGurran **Seats** 60, Pr/dining room 12
Times 12-1.30/7-9, Closed 2 wks Xmas, last 2 wks Aug, Sun-Mon **Prices** Fixed L 3 course fr £39.95, Tasting menu £69-£79, Service optional **Wines** 20 by glass **Parking** 20 **Notes** Menu surprise 7/9/11 course £69/£79/£89, Vegetarian available, Children welcome

WINTERINGHAM — Map 17 SE92

Winteringham Fields

❀❀❀ – see opposite

WOOLSTHORPE — Map 11 SK83

Chequers Inn

❀ Modern British

---

tel: 01476 870701 **Main St NG32 1LU**
email: justinnabar@yahoo.co.uk **web:** www.chequersinn.net
dir: *From A1 exit A607 towards Melton Mowbray follow heritage signs for Belvoir Castle*

17th-century inn with impeccable modern regional cooking

A beautifully preserved inn from the Stuart era, the Chequers stands cheek by jowl with Belvoir Castle in a pastoral spot where Lincs meets Leics and Notts. The matching of old and new in the decor is a test of many an old country inn, and the Chequers has it just right, with brasserie-style tables and banquettes against imposing stone walls in the dining room, while the pub itself retains its rustic ambience with a big old fireplace and low ceilings to contain the happy babble. There are cask ales and scrumpy, around three dozen wines by the glass, and a menu of impeccably forward-thinking British food built from local supplies. Start with a chicken and stuffing terrine with red onion marmalade and toasted brioche, or Long Clawson Stilton and onion tart. Fish might be a rosette of plaice with brown shrimps and crayfish in saffron velouté, while game season turns up pheasant with pearl barley risotto and roasted roots. For veggies, butternut and aubergine tagine with spiced couscous should appeal. Conclude with dark chocolate and hazelnut marquise and confit kumquats.

Times 12-3/5.30-11, Closed D 25-26 Dec, 1 Jan

London

Index of London Restaurants

This index shows Rosetted restaurants in London in alphabetical order, followed by their postal district or location and plan/map references. Page numbers precede each entry.

Index of London Restaurants

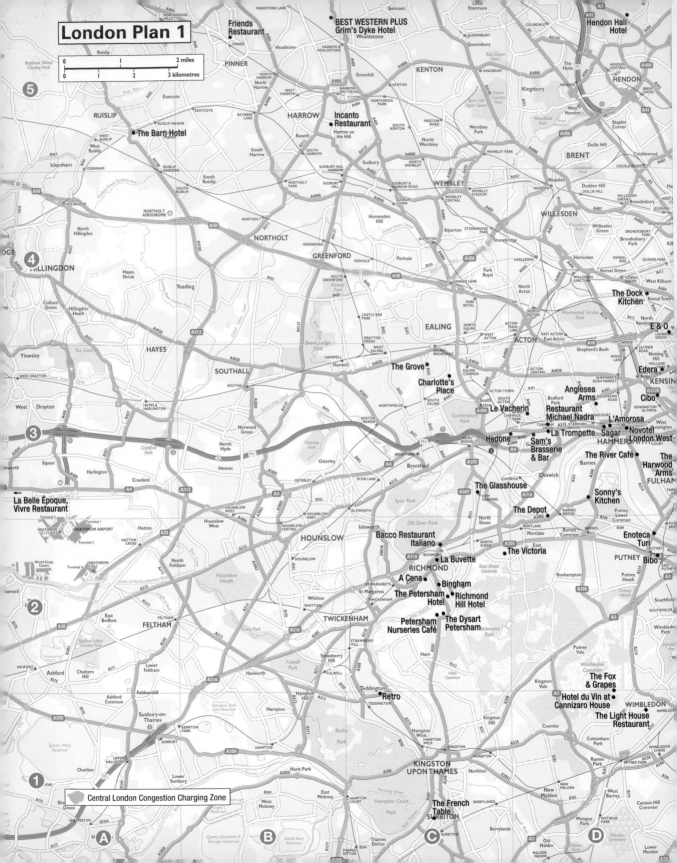

London Plan 1

2 miles
3 kilometres

⑤ ④ ③ ② ①

Ⓐ Ⓑ Ⓒ Ⓓ

Friends Restaurant

BEST WESTERN PLUS Grim's Dyke Hotel

Hendon Hall Hotel

PINNER

KENTON

HENDON

Incanto Restaurant

HARROW

BRENT

RUISLIP

The Barn Hotel

WEMBLEY

WILLESDEN

HILLINGDON

NORTHOLT

GREENFORD

The Dock Kitchen

E & O

EALING

Edera

ACTON

Cibo

The Grove

Anglesea Arms

Charlotte's Place

Restaurant Michael Nadra

L'Amorosa

HAYES

Le Vacherin

La Trompette

Sagar

Novotel London West

SOUTHALL

Hedone

HAMMER

Sam's Brasserie & Bar

The River Café

The Harwood Arms

FULHAM

The Glasshouse

Sonny's Kitchen

La Belle Époque, Vivre Restaurant

The Depot

Enoteca Turi

HEATHROW AIRPORT

Bacco Restaurant Italiano

The Victoria

Bibo

PUTNEY

La Buvette

RICHMOND

A Cena

Bingham

The Petersham Hotel

Richmond Hill Hotel

HOUNSLOW

TWICKENHAM

Petersham Nurseries Café

The Dysart Petersham

FELTHAM

The Fox & Grapes

Retro

Hotel du Vin at Cannizaro House

WIMBLEDON

The Light House Restaurant

KINGSTON UPON THAMES

The French Table

SURBITON

⬤ Central London Congestion Charging Zone

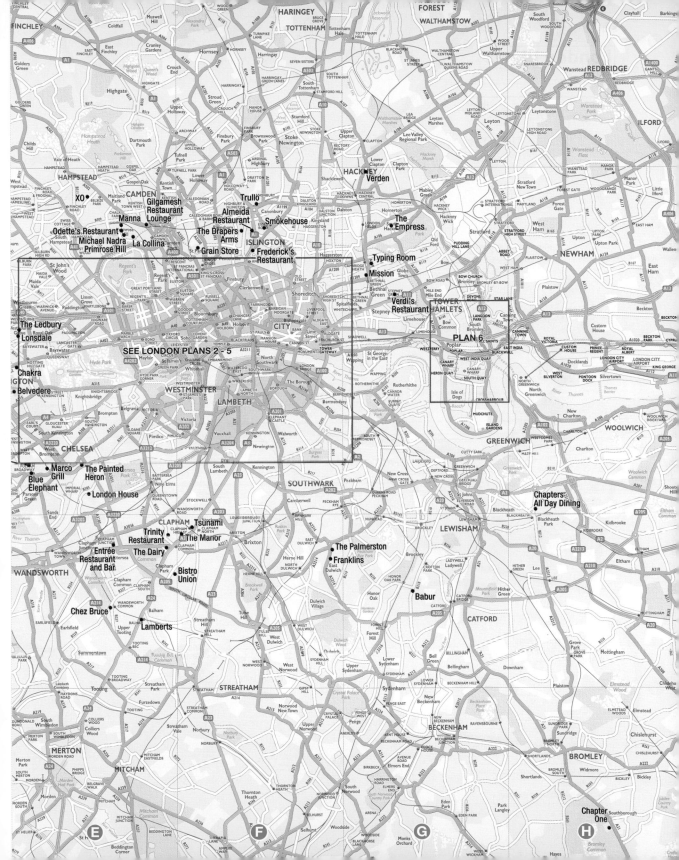

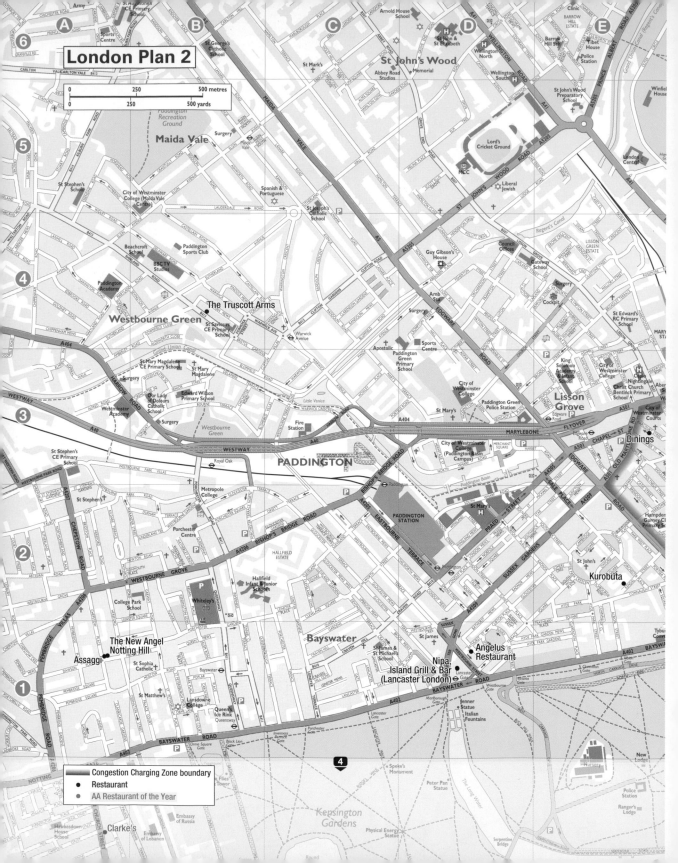

London Plan 2

0 —— 250 —— 500 metres
0 —— 250 —— 500 yards

A **B** **C** **D** **E**

6

5

4

3

2

1

Maida Vale

St John's Wood

Westbourne Green

● The Truscott Arms

PADDINGTON

Little Venice

Lisson Grove

● Dinings

Bayswater

● Kurobuta

● The New Angel
Notting Hill

● Assaggi

● Angelus Restaurant

● Nipa,
Island Grill & Bar
(Lancaster London)

Kensington Gardens

● Clarke's

Congestion Charging Zone boundary
● **Restaurant**
● **AA Restaurant of the Year**

4

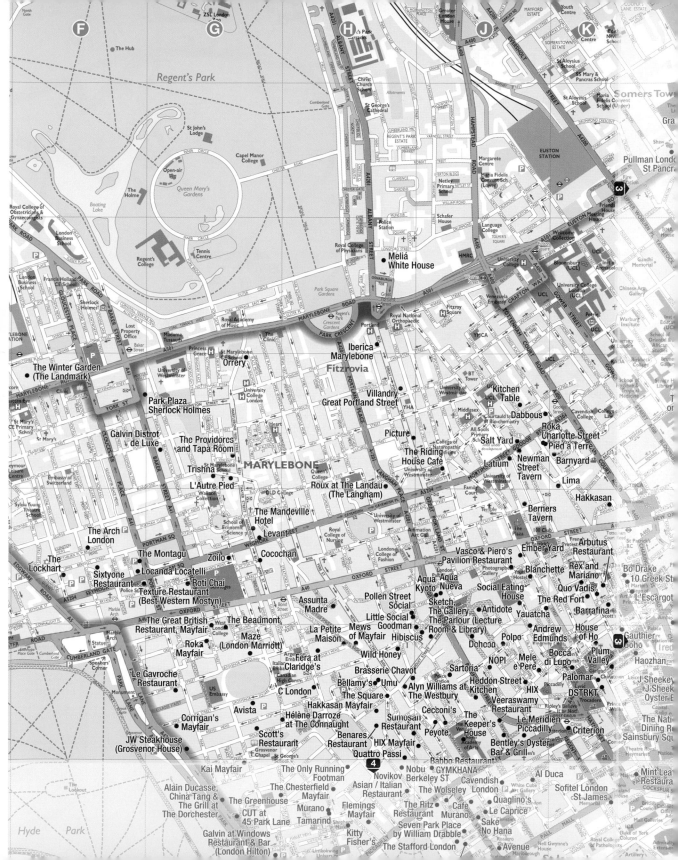

London Plan 3

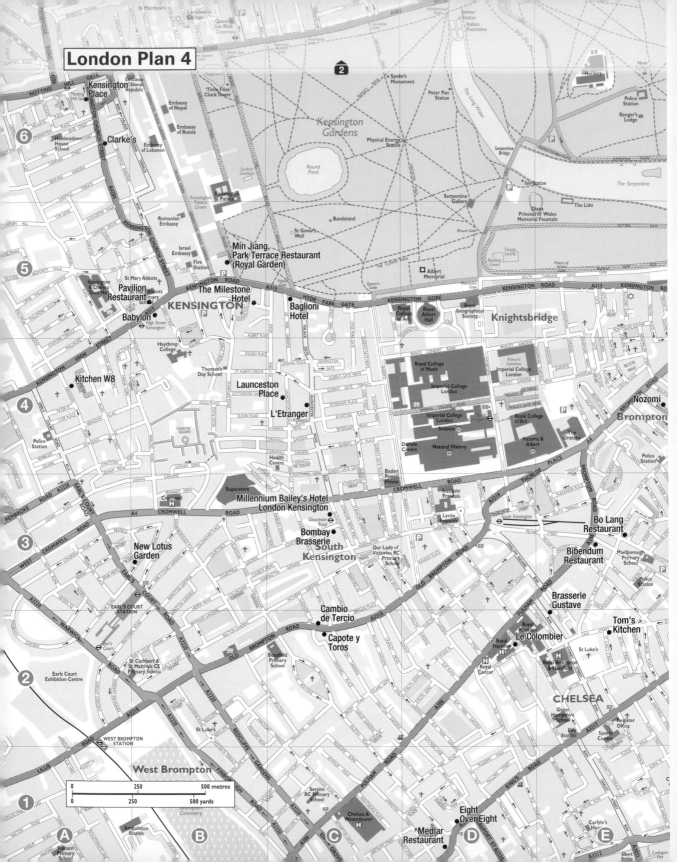

London Plan 4

NOTTING HILL GATE

Kensington Place

Embassy Slovak Republic

Embassy of Nepal

Embassy of Russia

Clarke's

Embassy of Lebanon

Hawkesdown House School

6

Romanian Embassy

Kensington Gardens

Speke's Monument

Peter Pan Statue

The Long Water

Physical Energy Statue

Round Pond

Serpentine Bridge

Serpentine Gallery

Isis Statue

The Serpentine

Diana Princess of Wales Memorial Fountain

The Lido

Police Station

Ranger's Lodge

Israel Embassy

Fire Station

5

Min Jiang, Park Terrace Restaurant (Royal Garden)

Kensington Palace

St Govor's Well

Bandstand

Albert Memorial

Mount Gate

Tennis Courts

Bowling Green

Prince of Wales Drive

Pavilion Restaurant

Kensington & Chelsea Town Hall

St Mary Abbots

The Milestone Hotel

KENSINGTON

Baglioni Hotel

Royal College of Art

Royal Albert Hall

Royal Geographical Society

Knightsbridge

Babylon

Heythrop College

Thomas's Day School

Launceston Place

L'Etranger

Royal College of Music

Prince's Gardens

Imperial College London

Kitchen W8

4

Police Station

St Alban's Grove

Imperial College London

Science

Royal College of Art

Victoria & Albert

The Oratory

Nozomi

Brompton

Darwin Centre

Natural History

Police Station

Baden Powell House

Institute Français

CROMWELL ROAD

Lycée Français

Superstore

Cromwell

Millennium Bailey's Hotel London Kensington

CROMWELL ROAD

Gloucester Road

Bombay Brasserie

South Kensington

Our Lady of Victories RC Primary School

Bo Lang Restaurant

Bibendum Restaurant

Marlborough Primary School

Police Station

3

New Lotus Garden

EARL'S COURT STATION

Earl's Court

Brasserie Gustave

Cambio de Tercio

Royal Marsden

Le Colombier

Tom's Kitchen

Capote y Toros

Royal Marsden

Royal Brompton & Harefield

St Luke's

Boursfield Primary School

Royal Cancer

St Cuthbert & St Matthias CE Primary School

2

Earls Court Exhibition Centre

CHELSEA

Great Hampshire School

Register Office

Fire Station

Sports Centre

St Luke's

WEST BROMPTON STATION

West Brompton

Servite RC Primary School

Chelsea & Westminster

Eight Over Eight

Medlar Restaurant

Carlyle's House

| 0 | 250 | 500 metres |
| 0 | 250 | 500 yards |

Brompton Cemetery

Ambulance Station

1

A   B   C   D   E

Fulham Primary School

Albert Bridge

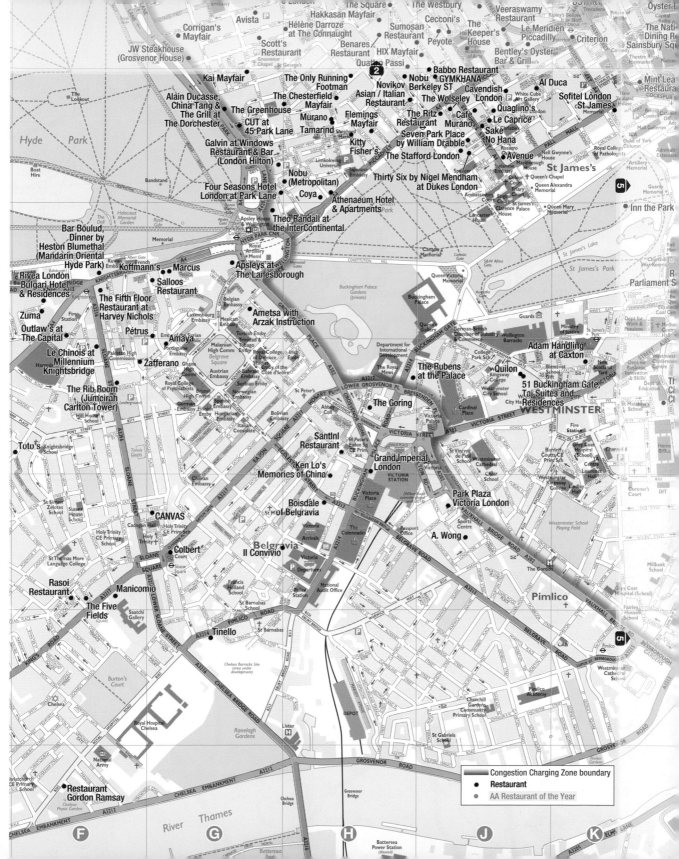

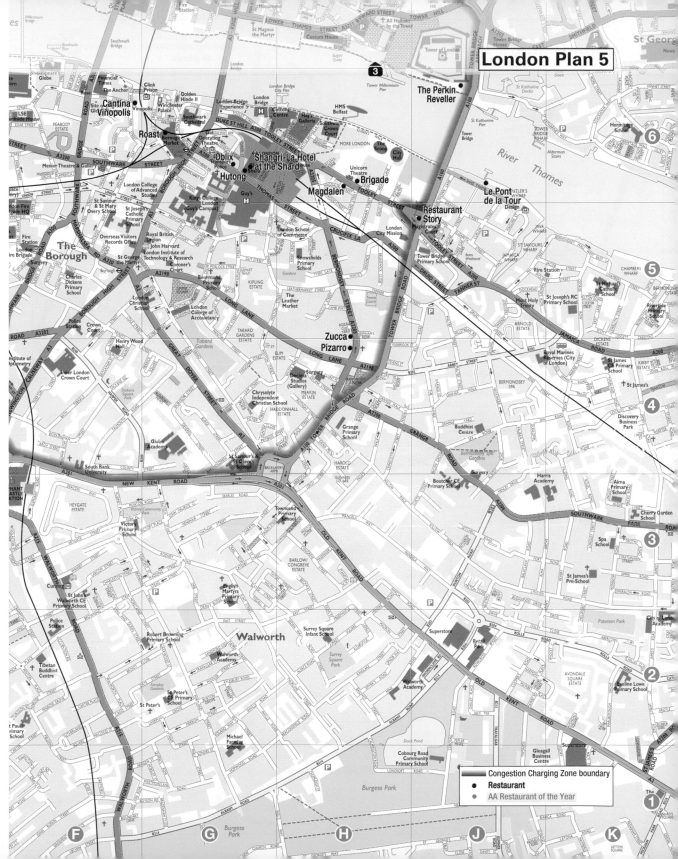

London Plan 5

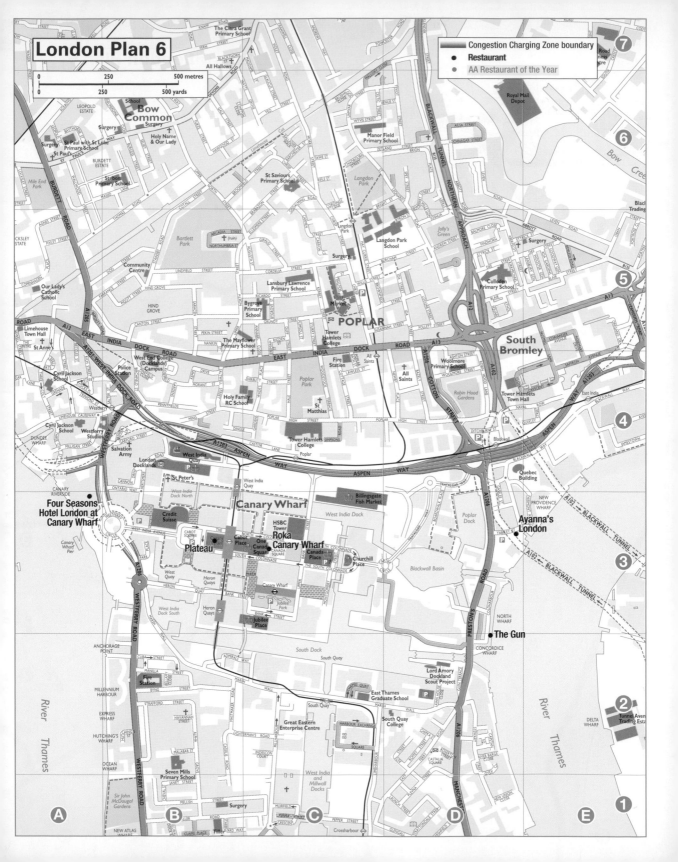

LONDON

Restaurants are listed below in postal district order, commencing east, then north, then south and west. Detailed plans 2-6 (pages 260–70) show the locations of restaurants with AA Rosette Awards within the Central London postal districts. If you do not know the postal district of the restaurant you want, please refer to the index preceding the street plans (pages 256–9) for the entry and map pages. The map plan reference for each restaurant also appears within its directory entry.

LONDON

LONDON E1

Café Spice Namasté
PLAN 3 J1

Indian

tel: 020 7488 9242 **16 Prescot St E1 8AZ**
email: binay@cafespice.co.uk
dir: *Nearest station: Tower Gateway (DLR), Aldgate, Tower Hill*

Vibrant modern Indian cooking in Whitechapel

This longstanding Indian restaurant may be set in an imposing red-brick Victorian block, but its colourful interior is far more Mumbai than Whitechapel. Here, vibrantly-painted walls and colourful fabrics are matched by friendly service headed by the effervescent Pervin Todiwala, while husband Cyrus's refined, confidently spiced, inventive modern cooking draws on his Parsee roots and the best of seasonal British ingredients. From menus with detailed notes, perhaps start with street-food style dahi saev batata poori (explosive mouthfuls of crisp, wafer-thin puffed poories filled with crushed potato, spiced yogurt, and tamarind and date chutney, sprinkled with chickpea vermicelli and fresh coriander). Specials up the ante – perhaps sea-fresh line-caught cod fillet for the main event, marinated with tamarind, crushed pepper, yogurt and garlic, then chargrilled and served with coconut curry sauce. Otherwise, try a traditional Parsee-style chicken curry (murgh ni curry nay papaeto): rich and exotic with spiced attitude and cooling coconut in equal parts.

Chef Cyrus Todiwala **Owner** Cyrus & Pervin Todiwala **Seats** 120 **Times** 12-3/6.15-10.30, Closed Xmas, BHs, Sun, L Sat **Prices** Fixed L 2 course £30-£70, Fixed D 3 course £35-£70, Tasting menu £70, Starter £5.75-£9.50, Main £14.50-£19.50, Dessert £5.50-£7.95 **Wines** 11 bottles over £30, 17 bottles under £30, 7 by glass **Parking** On street, NCP **Notes** Vegetarian available, Children welcome

Galvin Café à Vin
PLAN 3 H3

French, Italian

tel: 020 7299 0404 **35 Spital Square E1 6DY**
email: info@galvinrestaurants.com
dir: *Nearest station: Liverpool St*

Bustling City wine cafe with good bistro cooking

The dress-down sibling of the frères Galvin's La Chapelle, shares the same space in revamped St Botolph's Hall, and simple modern Anglo-French bistro cooking is the deal here. The 'vin' part of the equation is covered by interesting, often biodynamic, organic or natural wines on offer in a variety of measures. A flexible approach lets you eat and drink at the burnished zinc bar, at a table in the pint-sized interior, or on the heated and covered garden terrace. With the emphasis on hang-loose informality, the place is popular at lunchtimes and early evening, when a value prix-fixe with a pair of choices at each course might offer confit pork belly with fregola, then cod with smoked tomato passata and monk's beard. Otherwise, set off with snails à la bourguignon from the wood-fired oven, follow with something like dry-aged Saddleback pork chop with apple sauce and sautéed potatoes and finish with apple tarte Tatin with crème fraîche. Cheeses are from Spitalfields specialists Androuet.

Chef Jack Boast, Jeff Galvin **Owner** Chris & Jeff Galvin **Seats** 75, Pr/dining room 12 **Times** 11.30-10.30, All-day dining, Closed 25-26 Dec, 1 Jan, D 24 Dec **Prices** Fixed L 2 course fr £16.50, Starter fr £5.50, Main £14.50-£21.50, Dessert £6.50-£7.50 **Wines** 15 bottles over £30, 12 bottles under £30, 17 by glass **Parking** On street, Spital Sq **Notes** Fixed D 6-7pm, Sunday L £16.50-£19.95, Vegetarian available, Children welcome

Galvin La Chapelle
PLAN 3 H3

– *see page 272*

Jago
PLAN 3 J3

Mediterranean **NEW**

tel: 020 3818 3241 **68-80 Hanbury St E1 5JL**
email: info@jagorestaurant.com
dir: *Nearest station: Liverpool St, Aldgate East*

Appealing modern cooking in E1

In keeping with its location just off Brick Lane in this increasingly fashionable part of London, Jago occupies the ground floor of a former factory now housing creatives and IT entrepreneurs, many of whom use this light and informal restaurant as their staff canteen. Chef Louis Solley used to work for Ottolenghi, which explains the vibrant Middle Eastern-meets-Mediterranean cuisine on offer. Sticking rigidly to the seasons, a springtime meal might kick off with incredibly fresh sardines on toast accompanied by a mélange of marinated tomatoes, celery, parsley and lemon juice. A typical main course of rich, slow-cooked veal cheek goulash with orzo pasta and sour cream is simply presented but big on flavour. It might be followed by a perfectly balanced vanilla pannacotta with poached rhubarb. A vibrant, Eurocentric wine list offers plenty of choices by the glass.

Chef Louis Solley **Owner** Hugo Thurston, Louis Solley, Vinny Burke **Seats** 68, Pr/dining room 18 **Times** 12-3/6-9.30, Closed BHs, Sun **Prices** Starter £6-£9, Main £9.50-£16, Dessert £6 **Wines** 33 bottles over £30, 11 bottles under £30, 27 by glass **Parking** car park nearby **Notes** Breakfast Mon-Fri 8-11am, Vegetarian available, Children Sat only

Galvin La Chapelle ✿✿✿

LONDON E1   **PLAN 3 H3**

French 🍷 NOTABLE WINE LIST

tel: 020 7299 0400 **St. Botolph's Hall, 35 Spital Square E1 6DY**
email: info@galvinrestaurants.com
web: www.galvinrestaurants.com
dir: *Nearest station: Liverpool St*

Victorian school chapel with classic and modern French cooking

The brothers Galvin have a gem of a location here, the one-time chapel of St Botolph's girls' school, with its marble pillars and roof open to the rafters some 30 metres up. A mezzanine level of shiny steel is like a 21st-century interloper amid the reverential grandeur of the space, and it's worth getting a table up there for the interesting perspective it affords. The space is filled with generously sized tables (wearing pristine white linen tablecloths), and is watched over by an attentive and well-drilled team. The à la carte menu waves a metaphorical tricolore in evident admiration of French classical preparations – as is the Galvin way – with enough contemporary touches and fine UK ingredients to form an entente cordiale. There's no shortage of luxury and indulgence here, with lasagne of Dorset crab (a Galvin signature dish) alongside risotto of Périgord truffles with Jerusalem artichokes and wood sorrel. Home-cured organic salmon is a lighter option. Among main courses, vegetarians (or anyone for that matter) can indulge in roast Italian aubergine with miso glaze, served with hazelnuts and pied de mouton mushrooms, or there is fillet of wild sea bass marinière, artichokes and mussels on hand for fish fans. With a willing accomplice, Chateaubriand can be yours, a superb piece of

Cumbrian beef, partnered with creamed spinach, potato millefeuille and confit garlic. The menu gourmand offers the opportunity to go the whole hog, from that lasagne of Dorset crab to an apple tarte Tatin with Normandy crème fraîche. Another dessert might be the more exotic lychee soufflé with rose lychee sorbet and raspberry coulis. The wine list doesn't ignore the rest of the world, but it comes into its own with the French big guns.

Chef Jeff Galvin, Eric Jolibois **Owner** Chris & Jeff Galvin **Seats** 110, Pr/dining room 16 **Times** 12-2.30/6-10.30, Closed 25-26 Dec, 1 Jan, D 24 Dec **Prices** Fixed L 2 course fr £24, Fixed D 3 course fr £29, Tasting menu fr £70, Starter £9.50-£21.50, Main £26.50-£32.50 **Wines** 282 bottles over £30, 18 bottles under £30, 17 by glass **Parking** On street, NCP **Notes** Fixed price D 6-7pm, Tasting menu 7 course with wine £142, Sunday L fr £34.50, Vegetarian available, Children welcome

LONDON E1 *continued*

Lyle's Tea Building
PLAN 3 J4

◉◉ Modern British **NEW** v

tel: 020 3011 5911 **56 Shoreditch High St E1 6JJ**
email: reservations@lyleslondon.com
dir: *Nearest station: Liverpool St, Shoreditch High St*

Shoreditch hot-ticket for on-trend pared-back dining and vibe

In his first solo venture here at bustling Shoreditch High Street's iconic Tea Building, chef James Lowe's impeccable pared-back style, reasonable prices and Lyle's coolly casual warehouse good looks have made it a 'must-go-to' outfit right from the off. The room is uncompromising white, with painted brick walls and pillars and low-hanging lights and a functional on-trend vibe. Huge arched windows dominate the street-side wall and its small bar. The atmosphere is uptempo and current, while service is informal yet switched on. Hip it may be, but the food certainly delivers on the hype and expectation, via a daily roster that offers a selection of small and larger plates at lunch and a five-course, no-choice fixed-price menu at dinner. Prime produce and seasonality are key, including some lesser-used more gutsy cuts and innovative combinations. Take a pairing of warm beetroot, smoked eel and peppy horseradish, for instance, while lamb's hearts, broccoli leaves and anchovy has even more oomph. A stunningly light treacle tart comes with milk ice cream to cut through the sweetness.

Chef James Lowe **Owner** James Lowe, John Ogier **Seats** 48
Times 12-2.30/6-10.30, Closed BHs, Xmas, New Year, Sun **Prices** Starter £5.90-£9, Main £12-£18, Dessert £5-£7 **Wines** 30 bottles over £30, 7 bottles under £30, 10 by glass **Notes** Fixed D 5 course £39, Children welcome

Marco Pierre White Steak & Alehouse
PLAN 3 H3

◉ Modern European v

tel: 020 7247 5050 **East India House, 109-117 Middlesex St E1 7JF**
email: info@mpwsteakandalehouse.org
dir: *Nearest station: Liverpool St*

Quality City steakhouse in a bright basement setting

This MPW-branded eatery offers a brasserie-style roster of dishes with timeless English appeal sexed up with accents from France and Italy. The operation occupies a well-lit basement tucked away from the bustle of Bishopsgate, done out with a classic brasserie look involving white tablecloths, burgundy leather seats, darkwood flooring, and walls lined with JAK cartoons (Mail on Sunday fame). As its name suggests, meat is the mainstay, running from Scottish steaks (take your pick from rib-eye to fillet to a 24oz Boston chop for two — with the usual choice of sauces) to the likes of calves' liver and dry-cured bacon, while non-carnivores could go for a rare tuna steak à la Sicilienne. Expect well-sourced ingredients and unshowy cooking, but factor in necessary side-order triple-cooked chips and veg, while desserts offer the thumb-sucking comforts of Bakewell tart or sticky toffee pudding. Throw in well-selected wines and good cocktails and all bases are covered.

Chef Stefan Brodin **Owner** James & Rachael Robertson **Seats** 86, Pr/dining room 24
Times 12-3/5.30-10.30, Closed 25 Dec, 1 Jan **Prices** Fixed L 3 course £23.50-£39.50, Fixed D 3 course £23.50-£39.50, Starter £7-£12.75, Main £16.50-£54, Dessert £7.50-£9.50 **Wines** 55 bottles over £30, 19 bottles under £30, 13 by glass **Parking** On street after 7pm **Notes** Afternoon tea, Sunday L, Children welcome

St John Bread & Wine
PLAN 3 J3

◉ British

tel: 020 7251 0848 **94-96 Commercial St E1 6LZ**
email: reservations@stjohnbreadandwine.com
dir: *Nearest station: Liverpool St, Aldgate East*

Gutsy British cooking in Spitalfields

The name sums up the back-to-basics approach to dining in this operation across the street from Spitalfields Market. The younger, smaller sibling of St John is a wonderfully utilitarian, canteen-like space, with whitewashed walls, old wooden furniture and an open-to-view kitchen and bakery, and the focus — like the original — is on the trademark nose-to-tail British food. Expect unfussy and robust dishes, driven by flavour and quality seasonal produce, including those lesser-known cuts and ingredients: where else could you see pig's head stew, or blood cake and duck egg on the menu? There's no truck with three-course convention either, just small and larger plates so sharing is encouraged. Start with devilled duck hearts on home-made toast, or skate cheeks with tartare sauce, and proceed to pheasant and trotter pie. Breads are exceptional, and for pud, there's the likes of Eccles cake and Lancashire cheese, or date loaf and butterscotch sauce.

Times 9am-11pm, All-day dining, Closed 24 Dec-1 Jan

Super Tuscan
PLAN 3 H3

◉ Italian

tel: 020 7247 8717 **8A Artillery Passage E1 7LJ**
email: info@supertuscan.co.uk
dir: *Nearest station: Liverpool St*

Italian enoteca dining in a hang-loose atmosphere

The cheery Italian enoteca in Spitalfields continues to go from strength to strength, its ambience of parquet floor, exposed brick walls and mixture of booth and bar seating a hang-loose setting for inspired classic Italian home cooking and characterful wines. Antipasti sharing platters of salamis and/or cheeses, or burrata with San Daniele ham, are the obvious ways to pique the appetite. Clipboard menus then offer the likes of arancini risotto balls made smoky with plenty of paprika, moreish broccoli heads fried in olive oil and anchovy batter, and heritage pasta dishes like mushroom tortelloni in cream sauce. Sturdier tastes are sated by wonderful meats such as roast kid pre-cooked in milk, the cooking liquor used to make a richly comforting sauce, or chargrilled veal chop with rosemary-spiked potatoes. Finish with melting chocolate and almond sponge cake, served with quality vanilla ice cream.

Chef Nick Grossi **Owner** Nick Grossi **Seats** 30 **Times** 12-2.30/5.30-10, Closed Xmas, New Year, Sun, L Sat **Prices** Starter £4-£7.95, Main £10.95-£20, Dessert £4.50-£9.95, Service optional **Wines** 32 bottles over £30, 31 bottles under £30, 14 by glass **Notes** Vegetarian available, Children welcome

LONDON E1 *continued*

Upstairs at The Ten Bells

PLAN 3 J3

◉◉ Seasonal Modern British

tel: 07530 492986 **First Floor, 84 Commercial St E1 6LY**
email: reservations@tenbells.com
dir: *Nearest station: Shoreditch High St*

In-place Spitalfields gaff for cool, inspired dining

Originally set up as a pop-up by Isaac McHale of the Young Turks chefs' collective, this permanent reincarnation above the high-octane former 'Jack the Ripper' pub is as cool as they come. Hip, pared-back and shabby-chic, the dining room is a trendy confection of mismatched darkwood furniture, scuffed floorboards, retro chandeliers, floor-standing candelabra and edgy contemporary art. The backing track, buzz from downstairs bar and low lighting ride perfectly with the inspiring modern seasonal cooking, marked by flair and layers of flavour, with well-considered dishes delivered with finesse without being overworked. Take a 'wow' dessert of the sweetest roast pineapple, for instance, cleverly teamed with goats' milk rice pudding, yogurt 'crumb' and skilfully balanced madras sorbet. Ex-Ledbury chef Giorgio Ravelli's compact yet appealing carte starts out with fashionable snacks such as buttermilk chicken and pine salt. The mains feature knockout combos like succulent rolled lamb breast and sweetbreads, accompanied by sweet sandy carrots, caraway and salted lemon. Relaxed and informed service fits the bill, as do the reasonable prices and the excellent wines from France and Italy.

Chef Giorgio Ravelli **Owner** Patrick Fawley **Seats** 45, Pr/dining room 15
Times 12-2.30/6-10.30, Closed Mon, D Sun **Prices** Fixed L 3 course £25, Fixed D 3 course £25, Starter £7-£12, Main £14-£30, Dessert £5-£7, Service optional **Wines** 23 bottles over £30, 11 bottles under £30, 7 by glass **Parking** White's Row car park **Notes** Early bird 3 course £25, Sunday L £14-£25, Vegetarian available, Children welcome

Verdi's Restaurant

PLAN 1 G4

◉ Traditional Italian NEW

tel: 020 7702 7051 **237 Mile End Rd, Stepney Green E1 4AA**
email: info@gverdi.uk
dir: *Nearest station: Stepney Green*

Regional Italian home cooking in a converted Georgian pub

Housed in a former pub dating back to the Georgian period, this is now home to the Orsini family who originate from Parma, as did the composer who lends his name to this buzzy Italian restaurant. Soft shades of green create a calming ambience and photos of family and local landmarks are dotted over the walls of the long, narrow room, which leads to the partially open kitchen at the far end. The simplicity of the room and decor is reflected by the no-frills home-cooking, which is mostly influenced by the Emilia-Romagna region of Italy; this is honest food with big flavours. A starter of risotto di seppia with calamari genuinely tastes of the sea and might precede a generous main course of braised rabbit with pine nuts, olives, raisins and rosemary. For pudding, try perhaps a traditional tiramisù.

Chef Mirella Pau **Owner** M Skelton **Seats** 45, Pr/dining room 20
Times 12-2.30/6-10.30, Closed 25 Dec, 1 Jan **Wines** 1 bottle over £30, 18 bottles under £30, 3 by glass **Notes** Sunday L £15-£25, Vegetarian available, Children welcome

Wright Brothers Spitalfields

PLAN 3 J3

◉◉ Modern British Seafood NEW

tel: 020 7377 8706 **8/9 Lamb St, Old Spitalfields Market E1 6EA**
email: spitz@thewrightbrothers.co.uk
dir: *Nearest station: Liverpool St*

The Wright stuff comes to Spitalfields

The latest addition to the expanding Wright Brothers operation brings sea-to-plate fish and seafood cookery to the bustling environs of Spitalfields Market. A pair of rooms done in dressed-down urban chic – exposed brickwork, industrial light-fittings, bar-stool dining for those with good balance – is equipped with a crustacean tank, with more of an aquarium going on downstairs, and some outdoor tables to boot. It's busy-busy too, emphasising that big-city diners have never lost their dedication to fresh fish cookery. Start with a simple but effective dish of seared octopus, served in a fancy pan with chunks of chorizo and broad beans, or crab and scampi with curried mayonnaise and pickled pear. Fish mains are object lessons in freshness and timing, their seasonings apposite, perhaps biting lemon and chilli with sea bass, or sweet grapes in classic lemon sole Véronique. There are meats too, such as duck with blood orange, and unashamedly populist desserts, such as caramel-centred chocolate pot, or green apple parfait with a cinnamon doughnut and crème fraîche ice cream. However, pairings of Scottish cheeses and malt whisky are a powerful distraction from the sweet stuff.

Chef Richard Kirkwood **Owner** The Wright Brothers **Seats** Pr/dining room 40 **Times** 12-10.30, All-day dining, Closed BHs **Prices** Starter £7-£14.75, Main £16.50-£28.50, Dessert £4.50-£8 **Wines** 52 bottles over £30, 9 bottles under £30, 21 by glass **Parking** On street **Notes** Wknd brunch 10am-3pm, Sunday L, Vegetarian available, Children welcome

LONDON E2

Brawn

PLAN 3 K5

◉◉ Traditional European 🍷 NOTABLE WINE LIST

tel: 020 7729 5692 **49 Columbia Rd E2 7RG**
email: enquiries@brawn.co
dir: *Nearest station: Liverpool St, Bethnal Green*

Smart, honest cooking in trendy East London

Aside from the vibrant Columbia Road Sunday flower market, Brawn (sibling to Covent Garden's Terroirs) is arguably this edgier quarter of East London's main draw. Set among a run of interesting artisanal shops, the corner-sited restaurant is a fittingly hard-edged and pared-back neighbourhood outfit. The trendy warehouse-like interior of white-painted brickwork, high ceilings and dangling lamps is divided across a pair of rooms separated by a dinky bar. Plain-wood tables and retro wooden chairs foster the chilled look, while the staff are both smiley and informed. The European-focused daily-changing menu (provincial French and Italian with input from Spain) is driven by seasonality and provenance, and the cooking follows a simple path to deliver big-hearted flavours. Three-course formality is dispensed with here in favour of a selection of small plates for sharing. Piggy treats might take in namesake brawn or rillettes, to prime charcuterie, while gutsy offerings like duck gizzards line up alongside the more conventional, such as a summery risotto of girolles, English peas and parmesan. Top-drawer sourdough and superb wines – from biodynamic and organic producers – demand additional applause.

Chef Owen Kenworthy **Owner** Ed Wilson **Seats** 70 **Times** 12-3/6-11, Closed Xmas, New Year, BHs, L Mon, D Sun **Prices** Starter £7-£13, Main £12-£55, Dessert £5-£6 **Wines** 98 bottles over £30, 33 bottles under £30, 14 by glass **Parking** On street **Notes** Sunday L fr £28, Vegetarian available, Children welcome

Mission
PLAN 1 G4

British, Italian **NEW**

tel: 020 7613 0478 **250 Paradise Row E2 9LE**
email: hello@missione2.com
dir: *Nearest station: Bethnal Green*

Chic dining underneath the arches

Apart from the giveaway shape of the ceiling, nothing else here shouts 'railway arch' at you. To Network Rail it's Arch 250 carrying the tracks into Liverpool Street station, but to its patrons it's a stunning place to eat and drink, with liberal use of dark wood for the tables and around the walls, wine seductively displayed in backlit cabinets, and a palm tree spreading its fronds over the bar. London E2 has changed hugely, as has the nature of the food that the area's upwardly mobile population enjoys. The menu pitches accordingly, with starters of oxtail tagliatelle, octopus with potato and parsley, and duck hearts with bacon. As a main course, mackerel is served with fennel and rhubarb, gnudi (ricotta cheese pasta) with peas and mint, and sea trout and brown shrimp with white sprouting broccoli. California's 'young producers' feature among the carefully chosen wines.

Chef James De Jong **Owner** Michael & Charlotte Sager-Wilde **Seats** 62, Pr/dining room 40 **Times** 12-10.30, All-day dining **Prices** Starter £7-£10, Main £13-£16, Dessert £5-£6 **Wines** 150 bottles over £30, 2 bottles under £30, 20 by glass **Notes** Wknd brunch, Daily dish L £9 Mon-Fri, Sharing menu £38, Vegetarian available, Children welcome

Typing Room
PLAN 1 G4

— *see below*

LONDON E5

Verden
PLAN 1 G4

Modern European **NEW**

tel: 020 8986 4723 **181 Clarence Rd, Clapton E5 8EE**
email: info@verdenE5.com
dir: *Nearest station: Hackey Central, Hackney Downs, Clapham*

Corner pub turned smart wine bar and restaurant

We're used to an X marking where to find treasure. Here it's a big white V on the apex wall of this wedge-shaped, former East End boozer, as its architecture still reveals. Inside, however, no traces remain of its proletarian past, for it's all attractively minimalist, with some unusual lighting fitments, and a lower-ground-floor kitchen where you can see your meal being prepared. As well as taking its wines very seriously, Verden bills itself as specialising in the 'world's best' salamis, smoked and cured meats, and hard, soft, goats', washed and blue cheeses, all offered in 40g mix-and-match portions for a tasting board. If it's dinner you're after, though, the small economically worded à la carte menu is changed weekly. Octopus carpaccio is a good place to start, thin slices blended with a heady sauce, coriander leaves and a delicate mayo. Follow with flavoursome stuffed saddle of rabbit with spring vegetables for textural contrast, with rich, well-balanced salted caramel chocolate pot to close proceedings. The restaurant also offers a 'feasting menu' for large parties.

Chef Tom Fraser **Owner** Tom Bell, Edward Wyand **Seats** 70, Pr/dining room 40 **Times** 12-3/6-late, Closed 24-26 Dec, 1 Jan, Mon, L Tue-Thu **Prices** Starter £6-£10, Main £12-£17, Dessert £1.50-£6 **Parking** On street **Notes** Wknd brunch 11-5pm, Tue steak night, Vegetarian available, Children welcome

Typing Room

LONDON E2 PLAN 1 G4

British, Modern European **v NEW**
tel: 020 7871 0461 **Town Hall Hotel, Patriot Square E2 9NF**
email: reservations@typingroom.com
dir: *Nearest station: Bethnal Green*

A newcomer with pizzazz and high-fashion cooking

2014 was a big year for Lee Westcott, with the opening of the Typing Room signalling his arrival on the London restaurant scene. He's headed up joints for Jason Atherton, worked alongside Tom Aikens, tackled stages at Per Se in New York and Noma in Copenhagen, and now he's the man in the limelight, and 2015 is looking like it's going to be a very good year indeed. Bethnal Green's grand old Edwardian town hall has been a boutique hotel for a few years now and there are no prizes for guessing the function the area the restaurant occupies served in the old order. The long-gone typists wouldn't recognise the place with its open kitchen (a calm oasis of efficiency) and pale wood and natural colour tones, with unclothed marble-topped tables and contemporary images all adding to the clean-cut vibe. Service hits the spot too. Expect a menu of intricate, meticulously engineered dishes, combining colour, texture and temperature and delivering natural good looks on the plate. Tasting menus of five and seven courses lead the way, kicking off with a series of 'snacks' such as some magnificent things with crispy chicken skin, before raw beef that simply melts in the mouth. Another course recalls the Med with a sea bass/octopus/braised red peppers combo, before a stunning piece of Ibérico pork arrives served up with chervil root purée. Among sweet courses a dessert (called 'treats') of squeaky fresh summer berries combines with rich chocolate ice cream, yogurt and wonderful wafers of heavenly meringue for a seasonal winner. Breads are a course in their own right, coffee is top drawer, and the accompanying wine list is a fine piece of work.

Chef Lee Westcott, Greg Clarke **Owner** Peng Loh **Seats** 36 **Times** 12-2.30/6-10, Closed 24-26 Dec, 1 Jan, Sun-Mon, L Tue **Prices** Fixed L 2 course £24, Tasting menu £60-£75, Service optional 12.5% **Wines** 85 bottles over £30, 8 bottles under £30, 13 by glass **Parking** Opposite (meter) **Notes** Children welcome

LONDON E9

The Empress

PLAN 1 G4

◉◉ Modern British

tel: 020 8533 5123 **130 Lauriston Rd, Victoria Park E9 7LH**
dir: *Nearest station: Cambridge Heath, Mile End*

Laid-back crowd-pleaser with simple, feisty dishes

This classic Victorian tavern fits right into its buzzy Victoria Park location, with the bones of the old building intact and a contemporary makeover that has kept the feel of a public house. Red Chesterfields, fashionable retro light fittings and bare-brick walls are suitably à la mode, while the all-round relaxed attitude keeps the punters coming back (it feels like a local). When it comes to matters of food, the kitchen (headed-up by an ex L'Ortolan man) delivers a simple but far from simplistic repertoire. This is honest stuff made with good quality ingredients. A starter of tender chargrilled octopus, for example, comes with sobrasada (a Spanish sausage) and olives, while another combines ricotta cheese and beetroot with sesame and seaweed. Move on to pork belly with its crispy skin and meltingly soft meat, served with spelt risotto and garlic purée, or cod with fregola and salsa verde. Among desserts, a suitably wobbly vanilla pannacotta arrives with rhubarb and candied almonds, and chocolate mousse with burnt honey ice cream.

Chef Elliott Lidstone **Owner** Michael Buurman **Seats** 49
Times 12-3.30/6-10.15, Closed 25-26 Dec, L Mon (ex BHs) **Prices** Starter £5.20-£9.50, Main £12-£26.50, Dessert £3.60-£6 **Wines** 24 bottles over £30, 42 bottles under £30, 16 by glass **Parking** On street **Notes** Brunch Sat-Sun 10-12, Sunday L £12-£16, Vegetarian available, Children welcome

LONDON E14

Four Seasons Hotel London at Canary Wharf

PLAN 6 A3

◉ Italian, International V

tel: 020 7510 1858 & 7510 1999 **46 Westferry Circus, Canary Wharf E14 8RS**
email: restaurant.quadrato.caw@fourseasons.com
web: www.fourseasons.com/canarywharf
dir: *Nearest station: Canary Wharf*

Ambitious Italian cooking by the Thames

The ten-storey white hotel with its uniform square windows sits among the higher-rise buildings on Canary Wharf, with the river flowing past right in front. A terrace overlooking the pool for fine-weather dining is an unexpected bonus, while contemporary Italian chic reigns in the Quadrato restaurant, both in the pillared design and in the cooking, which can be seen coming together behind a glass viewing-screen. Simplicity is the watchword in a meal that might run from crab cavatelli sprinkled with lemon zest, through veal escalope milanese with tomato relish, and come to rest with properly boozy, espresso-ey tiramisù. There are more ambitious dishes though, such as a starter of salmon marinated in gin, served with apple and Earl Grey purée, followed perhaps by beef fillet with a tart of red onion, carrot and orange in peppercorned single malt sauce, and then Brillat-Savarin cheesecake with beetroot-marinated pear. Side dishes are extra.

Chef Paolo Belloni **Owner** Four Seasons Hotels & Resorts **Seats** 90
Times 12-3/6-10.30 **Prices** Prices not confirmed, Service optional **Wines** 110 bottles over £30, 8 bottles under £30, 35 by glass **Parking** 26 **Notes** Brunch £45, Sunday L, Children welcome

The Gun

PLAN 6 D2

◉ Modern British

tel: 020 7515 5222 **27 Coldharbour E14 9NS**
email: info@thegundocklands.com
dir: *Nearest station: South Quay DLR, Canary Wharf*

Gutsy British food in an historic waterside pub

Renovated a decade ago after a fire gutted the 250-year-old inn which once hosted Lord Nelson's trysts with Lady Emma Hamilton, this former dockers' boozer now wears the spruced-up look of a modern gastro pub. The Thames-side terrace with views across the water of the O2 Arena, along with an upbeat atmosphere and big-hearted cooking draw in the crowds from nearby Canary Wharf. There's a smart dining room in the main bar at the front, cosy snugs at the back, and it's all decked out with wooden and slate floors, naval-related art on white walls, and white linen on the tables. Top-quality, seasonal ingredients are at the heart of it all, setting out with confit wild boar collar with celeriac remoulade and burnt apple purée ahead of roasted fillet of cod with lemon ricotta ravioli, samphire and caper beurre blanc. An indulgently rich dark chocolate mousse with confit oranges wraps things up in fine style.

Times 12-3/6-10.30, Closed 25-26 Dec

Plateau

PLAN 6 B3

◉◉ Modern French V 🍷 NOTABLE WINE LIST

tel: 020 7715 7100 **4th Floor, Canada Place, Canada Square, Canary Wharf E14 5ER**
email: plateaureservations@danddlondon.com
dir: *Nearest station: Canary Wharf DLR*

Sophisticated, contemporary fine dining in futuristic landscape

Try to bag a table in the wall of windows to take in the incredible view over Canary Wharf from this fourth-floor restaurant. As is to be expected in this part of town, it's in a modern building, with a minimalist décor of white futuristic swivel chairs at marble-topped tables, large curving stainless-steel floor lamps and an open-plan kitchen. The culinary style is rooted in the great French repertory, but haute cuisine this isn't. Marinated seared scallops, for instance, beautifully arranged on a glass dish, are served with cucumber marinated in squid ink, radish and amaranth, and may appear alongside another starter of more traditional honeyed ham and parsley terrine with sauce gribiche. Innovative main courses are just as well considered and properly timed: roast loin of rabbit in Parma ham stuffed with kidneys accompanied by a croquette of shoulder, braised baby gem lettuce and barigoule of artichokes, say, or roast monkfish with osso buco sauce, veal tongue and pipérade. A skilful pastry cook is behind a crisp pastry case for salted caramel and chocolate tart with raspberry coulis.

Chef Daniel McGarey **Owner** D & D London **Seats** 120, Pr/dining room 30
Times 12-2.30/6-10.30, Closed 25 Dec,1 Jan, Sun **Prices** Fixed L 2 course £25, Fixed D 3 course £30, Tasting menu £55-£75, Starter £7.50-£64.50, Main £16.50-£35, Dessert £6-£11.50 **Wines** 400 bottles over £30, 30 bottles under £30, 24 by glass **Parking** 500 **Notes** Tasting menu 6 course, Brasserie Sat L 2/3 course £32/£35, Children welcome

Roka Canary Wharf
PLAN 6 C3

◎◎ Japanese ▮ NOTABLE WINE LIST

tel: 020 7636 5228 **1st Floor, 40 Canada Square E14 5FW**
email: infocanarywharf@rokarestaurant.com
dir: Nearest station: Canary Wharf

Top-flight Japanese cooking in Canary Wharf

A cool, ultra-modern interior of natural woods befits the setting in Canada Square, with the soaring skyline of Canary Wharf providing the backdrop. As at its counterparts in Aldwych, Charlotte Street and Mayfair, contemporary Japanese robatayaki cuisine is the deal, based on the robata grill (diners sitting alongside can watch the chefs silently working), with first-class fresh produce the kitchen's stock-in-trade. From the grill come scallop skewers with wasabi and shiso, and beef fillet with chilli and spring onions. Seafood maki rolls (the likes of freshwater eel with avocado and cucumber) and sashimi (fatty tuna or squid) make good openers, while set-price brunches and a tasting menu are good ways in to the cuisine. To conclude a meal from the carte is a page of desserts, among them dark chocolate and green tea pudding with crunchy jivara and pear ice cream, and banana ice cream with salted cocoa crumble and apple bamboo. Clued-up, helpful staff are on hand to explain unfamiliar menu terms.

Chef Libor Dobis **Owner** Rainer Becker, Arjun Waney **Seats** 105, Pr/dining room 14 **Times** 11.45-3/5.30-11, Closed 25-26 Dec, 1 Jan **Prices** Prices not confirmed **Wines** 152 bottles over £30, 13 by glass **Parking** Canada Sq car parks **Notes** Sun brunch menu options £42/£54/£66, Vegetarian available, Children welcome

█ LONDON EC1

The Bleeding Heart
PLAN 3 D3

◎◎ Modern French

tel: 020 7242 2056 **Bleeding Heart Yard, Off Greville St EC1N 8SJ**
email: bookings@bleedingheart.co.uk
dir: Nearest station: Farringdon, Chancery Lane

Discreet and romantic Hatton Garden favourite

Taking its name from the Dickensian cobbled courtyard where 17th-century 'It girl' Lady Elizabeth Hatton was killed by her jealous lover, this bastion of French cooking has character and atmosphere in spades. The cellar restaurant is a popular spot for business lunches, but with bags of Gallic charm courtesy of a slick front-of-house team, and intimate, warm-toned looks – low-beamed ceilings, panelling, wine-themed prints, white linen and burgundy leather seating – the place is an equally good bet for a romantic dinner. The kitchen deals in modish, unapologetically French fare built on a sound base of British produce. Start with ballottine of confit duck and chicken with pistachio, saffron jelly and apple and raisin chutney, followed by an assiette comprising suckling pig and crackling with an apricot and sage faggot, a crispy pig's trotter cromesquis, fondant potato and Bramley apple sauce. To finish, the decadence of dark chocolate delice and caramel honeycomb is tempered by fresh mandarin and orange coulis. A stand-out wine list runs to over 450 bottles, including wines from their own Hawkes Bay estate.

Chef Julian Marshall **Owner** Robert & Robyn Wilson **Seats** 110, Pr/dining room 40 **Times** 12-3/6-10.30, Closed Xmas & New Year (10 days), Sat-Sun (Bistro open Sat) **Prices** Fixed L 2 course £21, Fixed D 3 course £30, Starter £7-£13, Main £14-£29, Dessert fr £6.95 **Wines** 360 bottles over £30, 40 bottles under £30, 23 by glass **Parking** 20 evening only, NCP nearby **Notes** Vegetarian available, Children 7 yrs+

Le Café du Marché
PLAN 3 E3

◎ Traditional French

tel: 020 7608 1609 **Charterhouse Mews, Charterhouse Square EC1M 6AH**
dir: Nearest station: Barbican

Gallic cooking in a classically converted warehouse

When the urge for Gallic gastronomy strikes, you'll find this true taste of France tucked down a tiny cobbled alley just off Charterhouse Square. The place drips classic cross-Channel country auberge style with its bare-brick walls, French posters, jazz pianist and candlelit starched linen-dressed tables set in a rustic-chic converted Victorian warehouse. The scene thus set, you can expect unreconstructed French provincial dishes on an uncomplicated two- or three-course fixed price menu – honest, peasant cooking built on the sound foundations of fresh, well-sourced materials – in short, food that has stood the test of time. Start with classic fish soup down with croûtons, rouille and grated gruyère, and progress to pan-fried venison with cauliflower purée, apricot chutney and port sauce, or two might share a grilled leg of Pyrenean milk-fed lamb with flageolet beans and Madeira sauce. Finish with a chocolate and caramel bavarois, or the splendid selection of French cheeses.

Chef Simon Cottard **Owner** Anna Graham-Wood **Seats** 120, Pr/dining room 65 **Times** 12-2.30/6-10, Closed Xmas, New Year, Etr, BHs, Sun, L Sat **Prices** Prices not confirmed **Parking** Next door (small charge) **Notes** Vegetarian available, Children welcome

The Clove Club
PLAN 3 H5

◎◎◎ – see page 278

Club Gascon
PLAN 3 E3

◎◎◎ – see page 278

Le Comptoir Gascon
PLAN 3 E3

◎ Traditional French

tel: 020 7608 0851 **61-63 Charterhouse St EC1M 6HJ**
email: info@comptoirgascon.com
dir: Nearest station: Farringdon, Barbican, St Paul's

Gutsy French dishes near Smithfield Market

The casual, bustling, petite bistro-deli sibling of heavyweight Club Gascon, Comptoir deals in the gutsy food of southwest France, delivering simple market-driven cooking with full-on flavours: duck gets its own section, arriving classically, in the shape of confit or magret, or on-trend burgers, or you mighty go for a traditional Toulousain cassoulet. If you're not up for web-footed fodder, seared cod, baby gem and chorizo, wild garlic sauce is well executed, and desserts – like lemon tart or a classic chocolate fondant – keep things simple yet show acute technical ability in their making. The decor fits the bill with its modern-rustic vibe; exposed brickwork and ducting, dinky elbow-to-elbow wooden tables, small velour-covered chairs and wines tantalising from their shelves, while the miniscule deli counter – with displays of breads, conserves, pastries and the like – offers supplies to take away. Well-chosen wines are from southwest France... where else?

Chef Pascal Aussignac **Owner** Vincent Labeyrie, Pascal Aussignac **Seats** 35 **Times** 12-2.30/7-10, Closed 25 Dec-1 Jan, BHs, Sun-Mon **Prices** Starter £5-£7.50, Main £6.50-£27.50, Dessert £4.50-£9 **Wines** 19 bottles over £30, 13 bottles under £30, 11 by glass **Parking** NCP 50 mtrs **Notes** Vegetarian available, Children welcome

The Clove Club 🏵️🏵️🏵️

LONDON EC1   PLAN 3 H5

Modern British V

tel: 020 7729 6496 **Shoreditch Town Hall, 380 Old St EC1V 9LT**
email: hello@thecloveclub.com
dir: *Nearest station: Old St*

Magical culinary mystery tour in an old town hall

Built in 1865, the old Shoreditch Town Hall ceased to be a local government building in the 1960s, and it now houses arts venues and this rather chic, trend-conscious eatery. In step with the hipster-central location, the place goes for a pared-back look – white walls, wooden floors and tables, and a tiled open pass – and booking a table is a novel experience: go for lunch, and the time-honoured system of paying for what you have just eaten is in force, but admittance to dinner is via a pre-paid ticket system – yes, that's right, you pay up front and if you fail to turn up, tough luck, although you might be able to sell on your ticket to someone else if cancellation is unavoidable. What you get is a choice of either a five- or nine-course taster, preceded by a fusillade of 'snacks' to get the taste buds standing to attention, all bursting with new-fangled and revived forgotten ingredients, an eccentric edge and plenty of fun. How about smoked wild Irish trout with watercress, kelp and cherry blossom as an intriguing opener? Subsequent courses raise eyebrows as well as expectations – try raw Orkney scallop with brown butter, sudachi (a sour Japanese citrus fruit), and Périgord truffle, or blood pudding with chicory and Braeburn apple foam. When meat turns up, it's in an almost mainstream idea matching rose veal with cep duxelles, wild garlic sauce and a crisp potato galette. Amalfi lemonade with Sarawak pepper ice cream clears the palate for a finale on a strawberries and cream theme, involving creamy pannacotta, a galette, strawberry jam and honey ice cream. Pre-selected wine pairings only add to the sense of a magical mystery tour.

Chef Isaac McHale, Tim Spedding **Owner** Isaac McHale, Daniel Willis, Johnny Max Smith **Seats** 43 **Times** 12-4/6-12, Closed Xmas, New Year, Sun, L Mon **Prices** Fixed L 3 course £35, Starter £6.50-£17, Main £19.50-£35, Dessert £5.50-£8 **Wines** 85 bottles over £30, 2 bottles under £30, 18 by glass **Notes** Fixed price L 5 course £65, D 6/9 course £65/£95, Children welcome

Club Gascon 🏵️🏵️🏵️

LONDON EC1   PLAN 3 E3

Modern French V ■ NOTABLE WINE LIST

tel: 020 7600 6144 & 7600 1961   **57 West Smithfields EC1A 9DS**
email: info@clubgascon.com
dir: *Nearest station: Barbican, Farringdon, St Paul's*

Innovation and excitement from southwest France

Pascal Aussignac's avante-garde take on the cooking of southwest France remains as vibrant and exciting as it did when Club Gascon first opened back in 1998, and he's still turning up at the stoves every day rather than devoting all his time to the ever-growing Gascon empire in London. Right by Smithfield Market in what was once the Lyons' teashop, the mothership is a grand, high-ceilinged space of marble walls, oak floors, exuberant sheaves of flowers, and blue banquettes at closely set tables. Staff are clued up and keen as mustard, and there's a sommelier to guide the way through the 400-plus varieties from the southern-French wine list. Aussignac may take his spiritual inspiration from his homeland's southwest, particularly the Gascony region, but this is highly-evolved, technical cooking that is a long way from the goose-fat-and-garlic peasant cuisine of its roots. The entry-level option is a two-course set lunch, which is a snip. Trading upwards, there's a five-course seasonal Le Marché menu or a carte of tapas-sized dishes in five themed clusters, from La Route du Sel to Les Pâturages, with a half-dozen variations on foie gras getting star billing. Imported produce ensures authenticity in compositions that range from an almost mainstream cappuccino of black pudding, lobster and asparagus, to a more radical pairing of seared and braised hare with tulip, green quinoa and watercress. Choosing from the L'Océan section could bring on scallop and eel 'Tatin' with leeks and bordelaise sauce, while the foie gras department supplies the liver with 'chocobar' gingerbread and crazy salt. The style continues into puddings such as crispy meringue pebbles with pear emulsion, rhubarb and praline dust.

Chef Pascal Aussignac **Owner** P Aussignac & V Labeyrie **Seats** 40 **Times** 12-2/6.30-10, Closed Xmas, New Year, BHs, Sun, L Sat **Prices** Fixed L 2 course £26.50, Tasting menu £26.50-£65, Starter £12-£18, Main £14-£27, Dessert £8-£14 **Wines** 400 bottles over £30, 30 bottles under £30, 15 by glass **Parking** NCP opposite restaurant **Notes** Tasting menu 5 course £100 with wine, Children welcome

LONDON EC1 *continued*

Hix Oyster & Chop House
PLAN 3 E3

@ Modern British V

----

tel: 020 7017 1930 **36-37 Greenhill Rents, Cowcross St EC1M 6BN**
email: chophouse@restaurantetcltd.co.uk
dir: *Nearest station: Farringdon*

Accomplished ingredient-led Brit cooking in chilled-out Clerkenwell

Mark Hix's first outfit in a now burgeoning portfolio, it perfectly embraces its Smithfield setting. Wooden floors, tiled walls, darkwood and whirring ceiling fans characterise the cool, pared-down space, pepped-up by leather seating, white linen, edgy artwork and a jazz soundtrack.The kitchen takes a similar unfussy approach, the updated British cooking reflecting the Hix credo for quality local, seasonal ingredients (with producers duly name-checked) treated with simplicity, respect and flair. Wild ingredients play their part, as does fish (take sea aster served with sparkling-fresh steamed Torbay hake fillet and Morecambe Bay shrimp), though meats are the main draw; think Boccadon Farm veal chop with sage butter or perhaps well-marbled steaks like South Devon ruby red fillet. It also lives up to its other billing, with great oysters like Blackwater wild or Maldon pearls. Round-off with home-spun desserts (perhaps Wye Valley rhubarb and Bramley apple pie), plus great wines, Brit-brew beers and ciders, and interesting cocktails.

Chef Jamie Guy **Owner** Mark Hix **Seats** 65 **Times** 12-close, All-day dining, Closed 25-26 Dec, BHs, L Sat **Prices** Fixed L 2 course £19.50, Fixed D 3 course £24.50, Starter £6.95-£10.75, Main £17.50-£75, Dessert £1-£12 **Wines** 56 bottles over £30, 13 bottles under £30, 17 by glass **Parking** On street (meter) **Notes** D served from 5.30pm, Sunday L £23.95-£27.95, Children welcome

----

Malmaison Charterhouse Square
PLAN 3 E3

@@ French, European

----

tel: 020 7012 3700 **18-21 Charterhouse Square, Clerkenwell EC1M 6AH**
email: athwaites@malmaison.com **web:** www.malmaison.com
dir: *Nearest station: Barbican*

Modern classic brasserie dishes in best boutique surroundings

The London Malmaison occupies a former nurses' home on the edge of Clerkenwell, not far from the Barbican arts complex. Like other hotels in the group, it's done out in best boutique fashion, with dramatic crimson and purple interiors, a sultrily lit bar and a brasserie in deep brown tones. The order of the day is lively modern British dishes with interesting variations here and there. The fritto misto starter comes with sweet chilli and lemon aïoli dips, while creamed brie has a wine-poached pear and salted and candied pecans. For main, it could be chicken tikka with chutney, raita and naan, lamb forestière, or a chunky smoked haddock fishcake with spinach and poached egg in hollandaise. For something a little off the beaten path, consider sea bass with chorizo in mussel and tomato dressing. There are fine steaks too, dry-aged for 28 days, with a sauce range including piquant blue cheese butter. Crowd-wowing desserts include a spectacular ice cream sundae, or sticky toffee pudding with pecan caramel sauce.

Times 12-2.30/6-10.30, Closed 23-28 Dec, L Sat

The Modern Pantry
PLAN 3 E4

@@ Modern Fusion

----

tel: 020 7553 9210 **47-48 St John's Square, Clerkenwell EC1V 4JJ**
email: enquiries@themodernpantry.co.uk
dir: *Nearest station: Farringdon, Barbican*

Creative fusion food in a trendy part of town

Set in two listed Georgian townhouses on St John's Square, this breezy all day eatery splits between an airy cafe (and traiteur) on the ground floor and a light and sleek first-floor restaurant that pulls together period features with clean contemporary looks. It's an intimate, relaxed backdrop for a lively trek through the world of fusion cooking. Kiwi chef-proprietor Anna Hansen has been at the vanguard of this culinary style since the early 90s, so you can expect influences from all around the globe, delivered in inspired combinations and stimulating contrasts of flavour and texture. Roam from seared diver-caught scallops with squid ink risotto, hijiki (an Asian sea vegetable, in case you were wondering – even the most clued-up gastronome will be stumped by some of the items on the menu), and a relish of beetroot and moromi, to roast cod with baked cauliflower, mustard and bacon sauce, mole rojo crumbs, and a pomegranate and fennel salad. For dessert, poached cranberries and gingerbread crumb add a novel spin to tonka bean pannacotta.

Chef Anna Hansen, Robert McLeary **Owner** Anna Hansen **Seats** 110, Pr/dining room 60 **Times** 12-10.30, All-day dining, Closed Xmas, New Year, Aug BH **Prices** Fixed L 2 course £22.50, Starter £6-£9.20, Main £16.50-£21.50, Dessert £2.80-£7.50 **Wines** 61 bottles over £30, 14 bottles under £30, 13 by glass **Parking** On street (meter) **Notes** Brunch menu Sat-Sun, Sunday L, Vegetarian available, Children welcome

----

The Montcalm London City at The Brewery
PLAN 3 G4

@ Traditional British

----

tel: 020 7614 0100 **52 Chiswell St EC1Y 4SB**
email: reservations@themontcalmlondoncity.co.uk
web: www.themontcalmlondoncity.co.uk
dir: *Nearest station: Liverpool St, Barbican, Moorgate*

Smart hotel with a taste of Britain on the menu

It was on this spot where Samuel Whitbread built up one of the UK's foremost beer brands, and part of his one-time Georgian brewery has been converted into this swanky hotel. There are a couple of dining options in situ, with the Jug Hare keeping to the pub theme by offering a traditional bar meals, while the Chiswell Street Dining Rooms takes a more genteel stance, with its elegant light-coloured panelled interior and stylish leather seats (all entirely in keeping with the Georgian setting). The all-day menu deals in modern classics such as a posh burger, while the main carte offers up a little more refinement in the form of celeriac velouté with pig's cheek, scrumpy mustard and choucroute, and a main course dish of pan-fried cod with confit chicken wings. Desserts are a sophisticated bunch including blood orange tart with heather honey and stem ginger ice cream.

Chef Peter Fitz-Dreyer **Owner** Montcalm London Hotels Ltd **Seats** 70, Pr/dining room **Times** 11.45-3.30/5.45-11, Closed Xmas, New Year, BHs, Sat-Sun **Prices** Starter £6.50-£15.50, Main £14.50-£28, Dessert £7-£8.50, Service optional 12.5% **Wines** 8 bottles over £30, 12 bottles under £30, 20 by glass **Parking** The Barbican car park **Notes** Pre/post-theatre 5.30-6.30/10-10.45pm, Vegetarian available, Children welcome

LONDON EC1 *continued*

Moro
PLAN 3 D4

Islamic, Mediterranean

tel: 020 7833 8336 **34-36 Exmouth Market EC1R 4QE**
email: info@moro.co.uk
dir: *Nearest station: Farringdon, Angel*

Lively Moorish and Spanish cuisine in a long-stayer

It may be about to turn 20, but Moro still has bags of contemporary verve and vigour. Sam and Samantha Clark's Moorish food takes its cue from Spain via North Africa to the eastern Mediterranean, a popular formula with regulars who spill out onto pavement tables in fine weather. Indoors it's a sparsely-furnished, high-decibel venue where you can perch at the bar washing down tapas with splendid sherries and Iberian wines, or sink into a harem-style bolster cushion at one of the closely-packed tables. Friendly, well-briefed staff keep it all nicely together, while inventive menus deliver vibrant, colourful dishes of generosity and big flavours. Try palourde clams in an invigorating herby broth of peas and salsa verde, then gold-standard Norwegian Skrei cod matched with tangy barberries, sweet herbs and chickpeas. Finish with a citrus blast of yogurt cake with pistachios and pomegranate.

Times 12-2.30/6-10.30, Closed Xmas, New Year, BHs, D Sun

St John
PLAN 3 E3

British

tel: 020 7251 0848 **26 St John St EC1M 4AY**
email: reservations@stjohnrestaurant.com
dir: *Nearest station: Farringdon*

Nose-to-tail eating at its best

St John has become something of a pilgrimage spot for anyone claiming foodie credentials. Set up in 1994 by Fergus Henderson and Trevor Gulliver in a former Georgian smokehouse by Smithfield Market, the 'nose-to-tail' eating philosophy championing unglamorous, lesser-used cuts has turned on a generation of chefs to the robust, gutsy style, but few come close to achieving St John's unvarnished, no-nonsense simplicity. A wrought-iron staircase leads up from the bare-bones ground-floor bar and bakery counter to a utilitarian, canteen-like dining room – a stark-white space with a high-decibel vibe, permanently busy with white-apron-clad staff whizzing between the open kitchen and punters packed in elbow-to-elbow at ranks of white-paper-clothed tables. The long-running roast bone marrow with parsley salad is a surefire starter, followed by a rustic plate of braised rabbit with Savoy cabbage and green herb sauce. It's not all about the meat though – how about skate with monk's beard and capers? Desserts are equally comfort-spun, from the signature Eccles cake and Lancashire cheese, to buttermilk pudding with poached rhubarb.

Times 12-3/6-11, Closed Xmas, New Year, BHs, L Sat, D Sun

Smiths of Smithfield, Top Floor
PLAN 3 E3

Modern British

tel: 020 7251 7950 **67-77 Charterhouse St EC1M 6HJ**
email: reservations@smithsofsmithfield.co.uk
dir: *Nearest station: Farringdon, Barbican, Chancery Lane*

Terrific views, buzzy City-suit vibe and spot-on ingredients

Each of the four floors at SOS (a former Grade II listed meat warehouse now eating and drinking emporium) has its own distinctive style. There's something for everyone, from the high-octane ground floor to the first-level cocktail bar or second-floor brasserie-style Dining Room, while the big hitter is the Top Floor. Smack opposite Smithfield Market, it offers show-stopping rooftop views (with the Shard at centre stage) from its long, light-filled room through full-drop sliding glass doors and dream-ticket decked terrace. Also the culinary champion, the Top Floor's kitchen deals in ingredients of quality and provenance in light, modern, refined dishes of flair and flavour. Rare-breed beef steaks fittingly play a starring role (perhaps succulent 28-day dry-aged South Devon sirloin), though fish doesn't play a small part – witness sparkling-fresh pan-fried halibut served with warm tartare sauce, vanilla mash and spinach. For dessert, finish with wobbly buttermilk pannacotta perfection, pepped up by honey-roast quince. White linen, funky dining chairs, semi-circular leather banquettes and unstuffy service are spot on, while wines are a serious bunch.

Chef Tony Moyse **Seats** 80, Pr/dining room 30 **Times** 12-3.30/6.30-11, Closed 25-26 Dec, 1 Jan, Sun, L Sat **Prices** Starter £8-£16, Main £17-£30, Dessert £7-£8 **Wines** 148 bottles over £30, 14 bottles under £30, 15 by glass **Parking** NCP Snowhill **Notes** Sunday L, Vegetarian available, Children welcome

LONDON EC2

L'Anima
PLAN 3 H4

Italian

tel: 020 7422 7000 **1 Snowden St, Broadgate West EC2A 2DQ**
email: info@lanima.co.uk
dir: *Nearest station: Liverpool St*

Southern Italian cooking with a sense of style

Understated but self-assured style is the prevalent mood at L'Anima. An expansive room with the dimensions of an assembly-hall has textured reddish-brown walls and a long windowed frontage, with white leather seating at smartly linened tables. The clean-lined look extends to the cooking too, which uses the traditional four-stage menu format to offer a repertoire of classic southern Italian regional dishes from Calabria, Puglia and the islands, presented with contemporary flair. Home-made pasta is excellent, perhaps in the garganelli tubes that form the basis for a ragù of wild boar and pistachios, while fragrant saffron risotto is adorned with roast squab and Grana Padano. Mains might offer Sardinian shellfish stew or rabbit agrodolce, and there is the odd modernist flourish, as for cod marinated in liquorice and chilli, with burned baby gem and red onion purée. Bookending it all come sterling antipasti such as truffled pounded beef, or crab with apple, and unmissable dolci along the lines of monte bianco, a mountainous creation of meringue, chestnuts and vanilla cream in a sauce of mixed berries.

Chef Francesco Mazzei **Owner** Peter Marano **Seats** 120, Pr/dining room 15 **Times** 11.45-3/5.30-11, Closed BHs, Sun, L Sat **Prices** Fixed L 3 course £35-£125, Fixed D 3 course £35-£125, Starter £14.50-£32, Main £16.50-£38, Dessert £7-£15.50 **Wines** 200 bottles over £30, 6 bottles under £30, 11 by glass **Parking** On street **Notes** Open table offer 3 course with glass of wine £35, Vegetarian available, Children welcome

L'Anima Café
PLAN 3 H4

◉ Italian **NEW**

tel: 020 7422 7080 **10 Appold St EC2A 2AP**
email: info@lanimacafe.co.uk
dir: *Nearest station: Liverpool St*

Southern Italian soul food

Fans of Francesco Mazzei's classy Italian joint near Liverpool Street station don't have far to go in search of its more informal cousin – L'Anima Café is part of the same substantial office block, just a short walk from the original. The sizable, open-plan space consists of a deli with imported produce and meals to go, a lively bar for all-day dining and an easy-going restaurant that reflects Mazzei's passion for the flavours of Southern Italy. It's cool, casual and contemporary. Kick off with grilled calamari with a flavoursome pappa al pomodoro, or creamy Puglian burrata with roast peppers and anchovies. There's a wood-fired oven so the pizza is a good bet (the Aglio with smoked garlic and sun-dried tomatoes, say), or go for the wonderfully earthy flavours of rabbit stew. With top-notch pasta and desserts such as pannacotta with blueberries and grappa, plus regional Italian wines, L'Anima Café is one to know about.

Chef Lula Terraneo **Owner** Peter Marano **Seats** 160, Pr/dining room 20 **Times** 11.30-11, All-day dining, Closed BHs, D Sun **Prices** Starter £9.75-£12, Main £8.50-£18.50, Dessert £4.75-£7 **Wines** 7 bottles over £30, 5 bottles under £30, 13 by glass **Notes** Wknd brunch, Sunday L £35, Vegetarian available, Children welcome

Boisdale of Bishopsgate
PLAN 3 H3

◉ Traditional British, French, Scottish

tel: 020 7283 1763 **Swedeland Court, 202 Bishopsgate EC2M 4NR**
email: manager@boisdale-city.co.uk
dir: *Nearest station: Liverpool St*

Cooking showcasing Scotland's best produce

Tucked away down a Dickensian alley near Liverpool Street station, Boisdale's City branch occupies an atmospheric vaulted basement with black leather booth seating, its scarlet walls hung with monochrome photos of celebs, and to reinforce the city slicker vibe, there's a champagne and oyster bar and live jazz most nights. The cooking is simple, classic stuff founded on thoroughbred Scottish meats and seafood, so starters predictably include smoked salmon – perhaps with dressed crab, pickled vegetables and orange dressing – the range broadened by the likes of sautéed sweetbreads with maple-glazed bacon and mint hollandaise. Main courses tend to be safe bets: prime steaks with béarnaise, say, or guinea fowl with potato dumplings, wild garlic, morel mushrooms and Parmesan and sage velouté. Finish with bread and butter pudding with orange marmalade and Glenfiddich custard. Boisdale also has outposts in Belgravia and Canary Wharf.

Chef Sam Njenga **Owner** Ranald Macdonald **Seats** 100 **Times** 11-3/6-9.30, Closed Xmas, 31 Dec, BHs, Sun, L Sat **Prices** Starter £6.75-£15, Main £13.75-£37.50, Dessert £6.50 **Wines** 121 bottles over £30, 9 bottles under £30, 24 by glass **Parking** Middlesex St **Notes** Vegetarian available, Children welcome

City Social
PLAN 3 H2

❀❀❀ – see below

City Social ❀❀❀

LONDON EC2
PLAN 3 H2

Modern British, European
tel: 020 7877 7703 **Tower 42 EC2N 1HQ**
email: reservations@citysociallondon.com
dir: *Nearest station: Liverpool St*

High-flying cooking in a high-rise city tower

The gherkin, the cheese grater, the walkie-talkie...not an avante-garde menu choice but rather the view out of the window, for City Social is on the 24th floor of tower 42 (the old Nat West Tower). Following on the successes of Jason Atherton's Pollen Street Social, Little Social and Social Eating House, City Social delivers high-end food that displays classical inspiration alongside a touch of contemporary dynamism. The interior designer went for a swish art deco look with a shimmering ceiling and rosewood panelling, with a couple of original Warhols to offer competition to the stunning metropolitan landscape the other side of the floor-to-ceiling windows. There's a city-slicker bar serving up cocktails and a seriously impressive range of spirits, plus ample bar snacks if you're not up for the full works. Staff look natty in their Savile Row suits and the service throughout is top drawer. Executive Chef Paul Walsh is adept at getting maximum flavour out of dishes that reveal Pan-European and modern British roots and arrive dressed for our times.

Pig's trotter and ham hock partner up in panko-covered rissoles with Lancashire black pudding and apple purée, while another classic combo of mackerel, beetroot and goats' cheese also hits the spot. There are pasta/risotto options and steaks cooked over charcoal, but this being Jason Atherton's gaff, expect a risotto of ceps with crispy veal sweetbreads and flavoursome steaks sourced from the Lake District. Pheasant from the Yorkshire Moors stars in a main course with rainbow chard and caramelised red onion, and Cornish sea bass comes with a deep-fried oyster and oyster velouté. There's comfort to be found among desserts, too, with the likes of pistachio soufflé and chocolate sorbet up for grabs. The excellent wine list has plenty for big hitters.

Chef Paul Walsh, Jason Atherton **Owner** Jason Atherton & Restaurant Associates **Seats** 90, Pr/dining room 24 **Times** 12-2.45/6-10.30, Closed 25 Dec, 1 Jan, BHs, Sun **Prices** Prices not confirmed, Service optional 12.5% **Wines** 209 bottles over £30, 5 bottles under £30 **Parking** Finsbury Circus NCP **Notes** Tasting menu at Chef's Table, Private dining menu fr £65, Vegetarian available, Children welcome

LONDON EC2 *continued*

Coq d'Argent
PLAN 3 G2

◉◉ French

tel: 020 7395 5000 **1 Poultry EC2R 8EJ**
email: coqdargent.co.uk
dir: *Nearest station: Bank*

French cuisine and rooftop terraces with Square Mile views

A stylish, modern, sharp-suit confection it maybe, but its dream-ticket rooftop terraces and City views (from the eight floor of the No 1 Poultry building) make it a year-round hot ticket. Sunny tables, pretty planting and even manicured lawns provide the alfresco seduction, while indoors, a sophisticated restaurant and more relaxed Bar and Grill (lunchtime food/lively evening bar) are divided by a reception area. The curving, glass-fronted restaurant itself — with leather seating and wood veneer — comes properly dressed for the accomplished, big-flavoured French cooking. Menus boast bags of luxury for those City high rollers; from oysters, lobster or caviar to deep-wallet mains like fillet of beef Rossini teamed with pan-fried foie gras, sautéed mushrooms, a Madeira sauce and black truffle. Otherwise, for lighter options, check out the likes of roasted sea bream fillet served with an étuvée of artichoke, fennel and salsify in olive oil. Desserts, from classic vanilla crème brûlée to a warm, super-light ginger bread sponge slice (with stem ginger and cinnamon ice cream) likewise impress, while the wine list is a serious mover and service professional without being snooty.

Times 11.30-3/6-10, Closed BHs, L Sat, D Sun

Duck & Waffle
PLAN 3 H2

◉◉ British, European

tel: 020 3640 7310 **110 Bishopsgate EC2N 4AY**
email: duckandwaffle@sushisamba.com
dir: *Nearest station: Liverpool St*

Mesmerising views 24/7

Heron Tower (aka 110 Bishopsgate) is home to Duck & Waffle, and those high-flying allusions are appropriate given the restaurant is on the 40th floor and offers spectacular views of the capital. As you might expect, it's a pointedly modern space open to city slickers and night owls 24 hours a day. Rock up first thing for a Belgian waffle known as the 'Full Elvis' (peanut butter and jelly), or an English breakfast made with high-quality British ingredients, or anytime for the trademark duck & waffle (crispy leg confit, fried duck egg, mustard maple syrup). Small plates are the way to go (bigger plate options are available), with the likes of 'East End Eels' — excellent smoky fish with samphire and horseradish — and a luxe yellowfin tuna dish with foie gras. A Spanish-style torrejas dessert comes with cinnamon ice cream and is made for sharing, or you can go for orange posset with Aperol granité and keep it all to yourself. With ace cocktails and a serious wine list (with matching prices), Duck & Waffle is a fun place that has a keen eye on quality control.

Chef Daniel Doherty **Owner** Samba Brands Management **Seats** 260, Pr/dining room 18 **Times** 12-12, All-day dining **Prices** Starter £9-£16, Main £17-£40, Dessert £4-£11 **Wines** 199 bottles over £30, 1 bottle under £30, 15 by glass **Notes** Open 24 hrs, Breakfast, Wknd brunch, Late night menu, Sunday L £9-£17, Vegetarian available, Children welcome

Eyre Brothers
PLAN 3 H4

◉◉ Spanish, Portuguese

tel: 020 7613 5346 **70 Leonard St EC2A 4QX**
email: eyrebros@btconnect.com
dir: *Nearest station: Old St Exit 4*

Big, enticing Iberian flavours in the City

Off the beaten track in the City's northern hinterland, this urban-cool outfit looks the authentic Iberian business with its masculine darkwood floors, deep-brown soft leather banquettes, curvy wooden seats, and crisp white tablecloths. A long wooden counter beneath black and white photos of jazz musicians and chalkboards listing gutsy tapas dishes looks onto an open kitchen. Here David Eyre's cooking draws inspiration from across the Iberian Peninsula, delivering full-on flavours wrought from top-class produce treated with integrity and skill. An opener of salt-cod brandade with black olives, capers, basil, a soft-boiled egg and crunchy garlic toast evokes the flavours of the Mediterranean, followed by Basque-style hake and clams in a full-flavoured broth of fresh parsley, green peas and diced potato. If the sizzle of the charcoal grill proves too tempting, you might go for a grilled fillet of acorn-fed Ibérico pork marinated with pimentón pepper, thyme and garlic, and served with patatas pobres — potatoes roasted with green peppers, onion, garlic and white wine. Finish with hot caramel and spiced quince tart with vanilla ice cream.

Chef David Eyre, Joao Cleto **Owner** Eyre Bros Restaurants Ltd **Seats** 85 **Times** 12-3/6.30-10.30, Closed Xmas-New Year, BHs, Sun, L Sat **Prices** Starter £6-£12, Main £14-£23, Dessert £2-£6 **Wines** 44 bottles over £30, 29 bottles under £30, 16 by glass **Parking** On street **Notes** Vegetarian available, Children welcome

HKK
PLAN 3 H4

◉◉◉ – *see opposite*

Manicomio, City
PLAN 3 F2

◉ Modern Italian

tel: 020 7726 5010 **Gutter Ln EC2V 8AS**
email: gutterlane@manicomio.co.uk
dir: *Nearest station: St Paul's*

Contemporary Italian with a cool City vibe

The shimmering glass building that houses Manicomio was designed by Norman Foster and it certainly looks the business — this is the City of London after all. There's a lot going on here with a ground-floor level cafe-bar/takeaway (open from breakfast), a little terrace screened from the street and a slick and stylish Italian restaurant upstairs. There might be a little more refinement in the restaurant — linen on the tables, for example — but there's nothing stuffy about the place. The modern output includes creative antipasti such as organic salmon crudo with hay-smoked aubergine and a selection of Venetian-style cichetti. Move on to a pasta course along the lines of rainbow kale and ricotta ravioli, or ox cheek and tail pappardelle. Among fish main courses, grilled swordfish is served with sprouting broccoli and Taggiasche olives, while a meat option might be Rhug Estate chicken roasted in buttermilk. Finish with steamed blood orange pudding.

Chef Tom Salt **Owner** Andrew & Ninai Zarach **Seats** 95, Pr/dining room 60 **Times** 11.45-3/6-10, Closed 1 wk Xmas, Sat-Sun **Prices** Starter £8.75-£11, Main £14.75-£26.50, Dessert £7.50-£8.50 **Wines** 101 bottles over £30, 33 bottles under £30, 14 by glass **Parking** On street (meter) **Notes** Vegetarian available, Children welcome

Merchants Tavern
PLAN 3 H4

◉◉◉ – *see opposite*

HKK ✿✿✿

LONDON EC2	PLAN 3 H4

Modern Chinese V

tel: 020 3535 1888 **Broadgate West, 88 Worship St EC2A 2BE**
email: reservations@hkklondon.com
dir: *Nearest station: Liverpool St, Shoreditch High St*

First-class Chinese cooking with borrowings from the West

Part of the glamorous global Hakkasan stable, this new-wave Chinese cuts a dash with its modern, minimalist, clean-lined looks – all mushroom-coloured banquettes, black chairs with slate-blue cushions and a glass-walled kitchen. Chef Tong Chee Hwee's creative take on contemporary Chinese cooking comes up with some striking creations, revitalising old ideas with Western twists and liberal use of in-vogue, sous-vide cooking techniques. Of course, it all relies on produce of outstanding quality, much of it organic and sourced from around the UK, and perhaps predictably, given the city-slicker location, the experience doesn't come cheap. Dinner takes the shape of 10- and 15-course tasting extravaganzas loaded with luxurious ingredients, and veggies are invited to the party with dedicated meat-free alternatives. Typifying the East-meets-West style, the 15-course taster might kick off with roasted poulet de Bresse with foie gras leavened by a trenchant mandarin confit, while other highlights are the 'dim sum trilogy' (perhaps a crunchy vermicelli-wrapped, deep-fried lobster tail, a foie gras sweet bun, and soft spicy lamb in a tomato dim sum skin). Fish and seafood courses take in the likes of grilled lobster with garlic and Parmesan, or baked Chilean sea bass in black truffle sauce, while meat lovers are treated to the signature seared Rhug Farm organic lamb with lotus leaf rice, or jasmine tea-smoked Wagyu beef. Desserts pursue the fusion theme productively with ideas such as green apple jelly with black pepper ice cream as a precursor to caramelised pear with ginger and pear cream and puff pastry. Those without a bonus to blow could come for the 4-course set lunch, with meat, seafood and vegetarian options.

Chef Tong Chee Hwee **Owner** Hakkasan Group **Seats** 63, Pr/dining room 14 **Times** 12-2.30/6-9.45, Closed BHs (some), Sun **Prices** Tasting menu £48-£98, Starter £8-£16, Main £10-£28.80, Dessert £8 **Wines** 128 bottles over £30, 2 bottles under £30, 26 by glass **Parking** NCP, on street **Notes** Fixed L 4 course £29, Children welcome

Merchants Tavern ✿✿✿

LONDON EC2	PLAN 3 H4

Modern European

tel: 020 7060 5335 & 7033 1879 **36 Charlotte Rd EC2A 3PG**
email: booking@merchantstavern.co.uk
dir: *Nearest station: Liverpool St, Old St, Shoreditch High St*

Classy, flavour-packed cooking in a converted warehouse

The Merchants Tavern might be in Shoreditch but it sure as hell ain't no dive bar. This partnership between Angela Hartnett, chef Neil Borthwick and the folks behind the Canteen group is bang-on trend with its urban-rustic appeal and the classy seasonal cooking of Mr B. The place has bags of style but soul, too, with a log-burning stove in the bar area, sexy curved banquettes and a kitchen counter if you want to get some close-up cooking action. Time spent with the likes of Michel Bras in the South of France and some top addresses in the UK has given Borthwick a killer instinct when it comes to getting flavour on the plate, and he's created a menu that combines classical technique and a sense of Britishness. Staying around the fire in the bar and tucking into snacks such as smoked cod's roe on sourdough accompanied by a cocktail or draught Camden beer is an appealing option, but there's no ignoring the temptation of the restaurant. There are small plates and sharing platters such as a stunning plum-soaked pork neck with forgotten carrots (or rather slow-cooked to maximise flavour) and an apple and date écrasée, or go for a braised ox cheek and tongue dish that you can keep all to yourself. The quality of the ingredients shine: the super-fresh tuna in céviche form, say, or the scallops in another starter with crushed pumpkin and pickled chanterelles. The climax of a meal may well be dessert if a silky chocolate tart with a stellar salted almond ice cream is anything to go by. The wine list shows the same level of pizzazz and good taste, with plenty of options by the glass and carafe.

Chef Neil Borthwick **Owner** A Hartnett, N Borthwick, D Lake, P Clayton-Malone **Seats** 85, Pr/dining room 22 **Times** 12-3/6-11, Closed 25-26 Dec, 1 Jan **Prices** Fixed L 2 course £16-£20, Tasting menu £50-£100, Starter £7.50-£10, Main £15-£22, Dessert £7.50-£12 **Wines** 53 bottles over £30, 7 bottles under £30, 22 by glass **Parking** NCP Great Eastern St **Notes** Sunday L, Vegetarian available, Children welcome

LONDON EC2 *continued*

Miyako

PLAN 3 H3

⚜ Japanese V

tel: 020 7618 7100 **ANdAZ London, 40 Liverpool St EC2M 7QN**
email: london.restres@andaz.com
dir: *Nearest station: Liverpool St*

Authentic Japanese dining within the ANdAZ London hotel

Beside Liverpool Street Station, Miyako is within the ANdAZ London hotel, although it has its own entrance on to the street where queues form at lunchtime for takeaway boxes. The restaurant itself has a cool, uncluttered look, thanks to large windows, walls veneered in pale wood and bamboo, and black-lacquered tables and chairs. Traditional Japanese cuisine is the order of the day, with spankingly fresh ingredients cooked just so. The wide-ranging menu takes in sushi (perhaps raw sliced sea bream atop glutinous rice), sashimi (among them tuna with pickled ginger and wasabi) and tempura (say, soft-shelled crab in thin, crisp batter). A bento box is a good introduction to the cuisine, and among the specials may be miso soup with scallops, salmon, sea bass and vegetables, and – dinner only – seafood hoiruyaki consisting of sea bass, scallops, salmon and shiitaki and oyster mushrooms. Finish with a selection of fresh fruit or something more exotic like light, lemony yuzu mousse on a sesame biscuit.

Chef Kosei Sakamoto **Owner** Hyatt **Seats** 30 **Times** 12-10.30, All-day dining, Closed Xmas, New Year, Sat-Sun **Prices** Prices not confirmed **Wines** 4 bottles over £30, 3 bottles under £30, 9 by glass **Parking** NCP London Wall **Notes** Children welcome

1901 Restaurant

PLAN 3 H3

⚜⚜⚜ – *see below*

SUSHISAMBA London

PLAN 3 H2

⚜⚜ Japanese, Brazilian, Peruvian 🍾 NOTABLE WINE LIST

tel: 020 3640 7330 **110 Bishopsgate EC2N 4AY**
email: guestrelations@sushisamba.com
dir: *Nearest station: Liverpool St*

Trendy Japanese-meets-South American cuisine with capital views

Not the most famous of London's new skyscrapers, but Heron Tower is certainly up there in the culinary stakes. Also home to Duck & Waffle (floor 40), the 38th and 39th floors play host to this restaurant, and there's a super-fast external glass elevator to whizz you up there. The views are spectacular, naturally, enjoyed through floor-to-ceiling windows, and a bamboo-covered ceiling in the starkly modern space alludes to the cuisine on offer. Japan, Brazil and Peru provide the inspiration for a menu that deals in small grazing plates of Asian and South American fusion food. High-quality ingredients are a feature, not least the Kobe beef, which you can have cooked on a hot stone (ishiyaki) or sizzled on the robata grill. Flavours are spot on in options such as yellowtail tiradito with jalapeño and lemongrass, and the hot stuff is as equally on the money (lamb chop with red miso and lime, say). There's straight-up sushi, too, and desserts such as chocolate banana cake.

Chef Claudio Cardoso **Owner** Samba Brands Management **Seats** Pr/dining room 40 **Times** 11.30-mdnt, All-day dining **Prices** Starter £10-£17, Main £14-£45, Dessert £9-£12 **Wines** 189 bottles over £30, 1 bottle under £30, 13 by glass **Notes** Vegan & gluten free menus, Vegetarian available, Children welcome

1901 Restaurant ⚜⚜⚜

LONDON EC2

PLAN 3 H3

British V

tel: 020 7618 7000 **40 Liverpool St EC2M 7QN**
email: london.restres@andaz.com **web:** www.andazdining.com/1901
dir: *Nearest station: Liverpool St*

Modern British cooking in hotel's former ballroom

From the outside the ANdAZ London may look like a Victorian railway hotel (built in 1884 for just that purpose), but cross the threshold and you enter a slick and contemporary space. There are a host of eating and drinking options, including a wood-panelled pub, with the pick of the bunch being the 1901 Restaurant. Old meets new in a pristine white space, with soaring columns, contemporary furniture, frescoes and faux back-lit windows under a magnificent stained-glass skylight. The menus – tasting, à la carte and set option – are built on first-rate British produce and offer creative contemporary dishes. The source of the main ingredient is listed on the menu, thus crab from Devon comes dressed in a first course with some soft-shell crab by way of textural contrast, plus little fruity hits of grapefruit and blackberry. Another starter is based around parsnips (from Kent) in velouté form, served with duck fritter and chestnut pannacotta. Among main courses, poached and cured Cornish salmon arrives with beetroot and a pepper sponge, while we have Wales to thank for the rack and belly of lamb which is partnered with onion rösti and pickled sharon fruit. The craft and creativity continues into desserts such as a posh version of carrot cake with burnt orange segments, mascarpone and orange sorbet, or baked vanilla cheesecake with poached pear, salted caramel popcorn and Williams pear sorbet. The selection of British cheeses catches the eye – Dorstone from Herefordshire, say, or Beenleigh Blue ewe's cheese from Devon. Afternoon tea is a real treat, taken in the impressive main dining room, and including an array of sandwiches and cakes, and even a tea-based cocktail or three.

Chef Hameed Farook **Owner** Hyatt **Seats** 100 **Times** 12-2.30/6.30-10, Closed Xmas, New Year, BHs, Sun **Prices** Starter £12-£16, Main £20-£30, Dessert £10-£12 **Wines** 235 bottles over £30, 16 bottles under £30, 50 by glass **Parking** NCP London Wall **Notes** Tasting menu 6 course, Afternoon tea, Children welcome

LONDON EC3

Caravaggio
PLAN 3 H2

Modern Italian

tel: 020 7626 6206 **107-112 Leadenhall St EC3A 4AF**
email: caravaggio@etruscarestaurants.com **web:** www.caravaggiorestaurant.co.uk
dir: *Nearest station: Aldgate, Fenchurch St, Liverpool St*

Smart City Italian in former banking hall

There's a hint of 1930s ocean liner about this dapper Square Mile Italian, the former banking hall retaining something of its grand art deco past, with ornate lofty ceilings, splendid light fittings, mellow marble and an imposing staircase leading up to a trump-card mezzanine gallery. The pace is full-on at lunch when the City suits turn up for the pleasing mix of traditional and more contemporary regional Italian cooking, while the evenings are more chilled. This is food of simplicity, generosity and flavour. Take a classic pasta dish like spaghetti, brimming with the sweet, fresh flavour of a San Murano tomato sauce and buffalo mozzarella, or big-hearted grilled calves' liver paired with luganiga sausage, Italian pancetta and a potato rösti, or even stuffed rabbit leg with Chantenay carrots, baby artichokes and a light parmesan sauce. Desserts fit the mould – think tiramisù to Amalfi lemon cake – while wines are a serious Italian bunch.

Chef Faliero Lenta **Owner** Enzo & Piero Quaradeghini **Seats** 150
Times 12-3/6.30-10, Closed Xmas, BHs, Sat-Sun **Prices** Fixed L 2 course £17.50,
Fixed D 3 course £23, Starter £7-£15, Main £17-£22.50, Dessert £6.25-£7.50
Wines 120 bottles over £30, 30 bottles under £30, 14 by glass **Parking** On street
Notes Vegetarian available, Children welcome

Chamberlains Restaurant
PLAN 3 H2

Modern British, Seafood

tel: 020 7648 8690 **23-25 Leadenhall Market EC3V 1LR**
email: info@chamberlainsoflondon.com **web:** www.chamberlainsoflondon.com
dir: *Nearest station: Bank, Monument*

Super-fresh fish in the heart of the City

With long-established Billingsgate fishmongers Chamberlain & Thelwell behind this classy City operation, you can be sure that the fish and seafood here is as fresh as it comes. Spread over three floors amid the Victorian splendour of Leadenhall Market, Chamberlains buzzes with the power-lunch crowd who drop in from the nearby Gherkin and Lloyd's. There's an all-weather terrace beneath the market's glass roof, while huge windows in the lively ground-floor dining room and more intimate mezzanine make for good people-watching, and wood floors, comfy caramel leather seats and white linen keep things light and contemporary; for a more casual vibe (with a separate menu), head down to the bar and brasserie in the brick vaulted basement. Sea-fresh seafood is what to expect in a menu that mixes classics (lobster bisque or skate wing with nut brown butter) with more modern thinking, setting out with silky butternut squash velouté with foie gras beignet, ahead of cod fillet with couscous, confit shallot, black cabbage and balsamic jus; meat options could run to roast grouse with turnips, crispy potatoes and rosehip jus.

Chef Andrew Jones **Owner** Chamberlain & Thelwell, Andrew Jones **Seats** 100, Pr/
dining room 55 **Times** 12-2.30/5.30-9.30, Closed Xmas, New Year & BHs, Sat
Prices Fixed L 2 course £24.50, Fixed D 3 course £29.50, Tasting menu £49.50,
Starter £9.75-£14.50, Main £16.50-£39.75 **Wines** 76 bottles over £30, 18 bottles
under £30, 13 by glass **Notes** Vegetarian tasting menu £45, Sunday L £21.50-
£27.50, Vegetarian available, Children welcome

LONDON EC3 *continued*

The Perkin Reveller

PLAN 5 J6

◎◎ British

tel: 020 3166 6949 **The Wharf, The Tower of London EC3N 4AB**
email: info@perkinreveller.co.uk
dir: *Nearest station: Fenchurch St, Tower Hill*

Seasonal British cooking and stunning Thames views

Don't be put off by the wacky name (a merry character from Chaucer's *The Cook's Tale*) as this restaurant with show-stopping views of Tower Bridge and the brooding walls of the Tower of London is no touristy pitstop. Light, contemporary and hard-edged, the glass-walled dining space comes kitted out with solid pale-wood furniture (including long refectory-style tables) set on dark slate-tiled flooring. Of its two bars, one is located in the adjoining tower gatehouse, with its haunting, romantic atmosphere. The kitchen's not stuck in the past though, instead celebrating modern British cooking of flair and panache with a light touch, fashioned from premium seasonal produce. Well-dressed plates might take in signature salt marsh lamb three ways (succulent rump, melt-in-the-mouth slow-cooked shoulder, and crisp fried tongue) served with swede fondant, while desserts could deliver a light, moist carrot cake teamed with marmalade ice cream. The outdoor terrace is a must on a sunny day, and the place is also open for breakfast and afternoon tea.

Times 11.30-3.30/5.30-10.30, Closed 24-26 Dec, D Sun

Restaurant Sauterelle

PLAN 3 G2

◎◎ Modern European, French

tel: 020 7618 2483 **The Royal Exchange EC3V 3LR**
email: pawelk@danddlondon.com
dir: *Nearest station: Bank*

Confident contemporary cooking in a landmark building

Dining up on the mezzanine floor amid the Victorian pomp of the historic Royal Exchange certainly adds wow factor to proceedings at glossy Sauterelle. Looking down through glazed arches onto a soaring atrium courtyard glistening with high-end boutiques and jewellers, and surrounded by expense account Square Milers, a more glammed-up setting is harder to imagine. The ambience is impeccably chic, service is slickly professional, and the cooking inspired by modern European thinking. A starter of seared Isle of Skye scallops with cauliflower mousseline, oyster leaves and toasted olives delivers a light, contemporary touch, clean, fresh flavours and well-dressed presentation. Main courses bring medallions of excellent firm, fresh and well-timed monkfish on top of a bed of delicate Sicilian red prawn risotto, or a gamey combo of red-legged partridge with braised Savoy cabbage, crisp Ventrèche bacon and pomegranate that chimes perfectly with both the calendar and blue-blooded surroundings. At dessert, coffee and hazelnut combine decadently in a classic Opéra gâteau, offset by a dark chocolate ball filled with tart cherry coulis.

Times 12-2.30/6-9.30, Closed BHs, Xmas, New Year, Etr, Sat-Sun

LONDON EC4

Apex Temple Court Hotel

PLAN 3 D1

◎ European NEW

tel: 020 3617 0060 & 3004 4141 **1-2 Serjeants' Inn, Fleet St EC4Y 1LL**
email: chambers@apexhotels.co.uk web: www.apexhotels.co.uk
dir: *Nearest station: Blackfriars, Temple, Chancery Lane*

European-accented food in a slick hotel setting

Whether you're suited and booted for business or exploring the City's heritage, this swanky modern hotel is located in a handy spot in the historic Serjeant's Inn within the Inner Temple legal district. The Chambers Restaurant provides a suitably sleek, contemporary setting for some modern European food with strong Italophile leanings. To start, runny yolk inside a crisp-coated hen's egg adds creaminess to black pudding and a white bean and chorizo casserole, while main course oxtail ragù with home-made herb gnocchi is full of wintry comfort. Further comforting ideas come sizzling from the grill, in the shape of dry-aged Aberdeen Angus steaks – take your pick from rib-eye or fillet – while fish dishes run to roasted sea bass with Jerusalem artichoke, pan-fried Lyonnaise-style with butter and parsley. For pudding, how about a textbook, oozing chocolate fondant with candied orange peel and vanilla ice cream?

Chef Mirko Musini Owner Apex Hotels Ltd Seats 78, Pr/dining room 42
Times 12-2.30/6-10 Prices Starter £6.50-£12.50, Main £14.25-£32, Dessert £5.75-£9 Wines 28 bottles over £30, 16 bottles under £30, 12 by glass Notes Pre-theatre 2/3 course with Prosecco £16.50/£19.50, Vegetarian available, Children welcome

Barbecoa

PLAN 3 F2

◎ Modern

tel: 020 3005 8555 **20 New Change Passage EC4M 9AG**
dir: *Nearest station: St Paul's*

Jamie Oliver's buzzing BBQ joint

Expect a backing track of high-energy chatter and throbbing music at Jamie O and Adam Perry Lang's rammed-to-the-rafters City temple to meat, flame and smoke. It's a cool glass-sided venue that offers show-stopping views of St Paul's Cathedral while wrapping itself around a semi-open kitchen. Macho features – polished stone floor and brickwork – mix with low-slung leather banquettes, funky dangling lighting and wine display cabinets. Cooking by fire, smoke and charcoal is the thing, which means some flashy bits of kit like robata grills, tandoor ovens, Texan pit smokers and wood-fired ovens. Impeccably sourced British and Irish meats are prepared in the ground-floor butcher's shop. Tuck into signature dry-aged steaks like rump or T-bone, or try grilled lamb rack or pulled pork shoulder, perhaps with pukka duck-fat chips, while desserts might take in baked vanilla cheesecake with roasted peaches and star-turn Bellini sorbet. A posse of friendly staff help keep the party rolling.

Times 11.30-11, All-day dining

Bread Street Kitchen

PLAN 3 F2

◎◎ Modern British, European

tel: 020 3030 4050 **10 Bread St EC4M 9AJ**
email: info@breadstreetkitchen.com
dir: *Nearest station: Mansion House*

Vibrant, City-cool brasserie from the Gordon Ramsay stable

The name suggests a homely wholefood co-operative, but the reality is a cavernous, high-decibel, high-octane city-slicker operation, courtesy of Gordon Ramsay Holdings. The huge first-floor restaurant seems to extend as far as the eye can see, a soaring, warehouse-like space that mixes retro and modern looks with art deco references and the feel of a film set from Fritz Lang's *Metropolis*. Check out the exposed industrial ducting, a wall of full-length glass, black and white chequerboard floors, gold and green banquettes, and classic cafe-style black marble or darkwood tables, plus a mezzanine wine gallery with thousands of bottles in green glass cabinets. Battalions of servers dressed in black ricochet to and fro, all friendly, engaging and on the ball, delivering quick-fire dishes from a lengthy all-day roster (including breakfast weekdays). Try potted salt brisket with grain mustard and piccalilli, then steamed sea bream with braised leeks, brown shrimps, sea purslane and shellfish dressing, or something meaty along the lines of Dingle Dell pork chop or Herdwick lamb cutlets from the Josper grill. End with chocolate fondant with mint chip ice cream.

Times 11-3/5.30-11

The Chancery
PLAN 3 D2

◉◉ Modern European

tel: 020 7831 4000 **9 Cursitor St EC4A 1LL**
email: reservations@thechancery.co.uk
dir: *Nearest station: Chancery Lane*

Intimate, fine-tuned dining in legal land

This bijou restaurant secreted away in a side street off the eponymous lane draws in a crew of suited and booted professionals from the nearby worlds of law and finance. Mirrors and globe pendant lights add a hint of art deco style, otherwise it's all modish shades of grey and cream offset by modern abstract art, dark wood floors, black leather seats and banquettes and white linen-swathed tables – an effortlessly urbane look that suits its smart clientele. Chef Graham Long deals in immaculately presented, inventive modern European dishes, starting out strongly with an open ravioli of suckling pig shoulder with bacon and cider velouté. Next up, an intelligently composed main course brings together immaculately timed poached Cornish cod with lemon-infused prawns, roasted Jerusalem artichokes, fromage frais and wasabi, or you might go for roast guinea fowl with Morteau sausage roll, Savoy cabbage, parsley root and thyme jus gras. A richly indulgent chocolate fondant with walnut ice cream and 'crunchy stuff' hits the spot at dessert, and a well-chosen wine list rounds off a class act.

Chef Graham Long **Owner** Zak Jones **Seats** 50, Pr/dining room 30
Times 12-2.30/6-10.30, Closed Xmas, Sun, L Sat **Prices** Fixed L 2 course fr £39.50, Fixed D 3 course fr £46.50, Tasting menu fr £68 **Wines** 52 bottles over £30, 8 bottles under £30, 6 by glass **Parking** On street **Notes** Tasting menu 7 course, Vegetarian available, Children welcome

Chinese Cricket Club
PLAN 3 E1

◉ Chinese

tel: 020 7438 8051 **Crowne Plaza London – The City, 19 New Bridge St EC4V 6DB**
email: loncy.ccc@ihg.com
dir: *Nearest station: Temple, St Paul's, Blackfriars*

Classy Chinese in a modern City hotel

Chinese Cricket Club is named in honour of the original national Chinese cricket team, which played its first international match in 2009. The restaurant is a sponsor of the Oval, and much cricketing memorabilia decorate the walls. The kitchen combines modern techniques with traditional and authentic flavours of the Szechuan cuisine, updating it to the 21st century. Prawn and pork sui mai, from the dim sum list, come as four light and fluffy dumplings packed with minced pork and prawn with a dipping sauce of chilli and tamarind. Follow on with tender beef tenderloin with black pepper and spring onions and a soy-based sauce with a serving of noodles. The wide-ranging menu also takes in fish and shellfish – perhaps fried sea bass with sweet-and-sour sauce, and scallops with black beans – while desserts are mainly Western, although basil ice cream hinting of wasabi comes with dark chocolate tart.

Times 12-2.30/6-10, Closed Xmas & Etr, L 10 Jan

Diciannove
PLAN 3 E1

◉◉ Italian

tel: 020 7438 8052 & 7438 8055 **Crowne Plaza London – The City, 19 New Bridge St EC4V 6DB**
email: loncy.refettorio@ihg.com **web:** www.refettorio.com
dir: *Nearest station: Blackfriars*

Slick Italian cookery in gleaming contemporary style

The slick Italian operation at the heart of the Crowne Plaza City branch looks like the upscale café of a smart contemporary art gallery, all gleaming uncovered surfaces, striped upholstery, and a bar lit in throbbing sunny yellow, at which you may choose to sit. The menu is structured in the classic Italian fashion, for those who have room enough and time for an intermediate pasta dish – say casarecce tubes with n'duja sausage and olives – between their antipasto and their main. A variously sized anything-and-everything platter, Il Supremo, may be the smart start, offering burrata, zucchini fritti, calamari, fennel salami, Tuscan prosciutto and more, much more. At main, rose veal is succulent and tender, and comes with rosemary fried potatoes, asparagus and gremolata, or there could be well-handled fish such as roast halibut on braised leeks and capers. Finish in sublime simplicity with a bowl of warm amarena cherries, ricotta and sweet pistachios, classic espresso-laced affogato, or with benchmark Italian cheeses, and don't miss the stunning home-baked rosemary focaccia with olive oil and balsamic.

Times 12-2.30/6-10.30, Closed Xmas, 24-30 Jan, Etr & BHs, Sun, L Sat

Lutyens Restaurant
PLAN 3 E2

◉◉ Modern European ⬥ NOTABLE WINE LIST

tel: 020 7583 8385 **85 Fleet St EC4Y 1AE**
email: info@lutyens-restaurant.com
dir: *Nearest station: Chancery Lane, St Paul's, Blackfriars*

Accomplished modern brasserie cooking in stylish setting

The elegant Lutyens-designed building that was once home to Reuters and the Press Association now bears the Conran stamp in its cool pastel tones, pale wood, white linen and pixellated marble floors. The seductive operation takes in a city-slicker wine bar with a stellar listing of fine wines, the restaurant and raw bar (for oysters, tartare, carpaccios and céviche), private dining rooms in the basement and a members' club. Chef Henrik Ritzen's light-touch cooking is rooted in classic French technique but there are subtle hints of his Nordic roots. This is seen in a simple and elegant starter of smoked eel with beetroot, Gourmande pear and bitter leaves that relies on the sheer quality of the raw materials for its effect, or a main-course involving haunch of venison teamed with pickled walnut purée, roasted celeriac and grey leg chanterelles. Fish is handled with equal skill – perhaps partnering poached monkfish with cockles, swede, lettuce and Jamón Ibérico de Bellota. Dessert brings spiced quince soufflé with stem ginger ice cream.

Chef Henrik Ritzen **Owner** Peter Prescott, Terence & Vicki Conran **Seats** 120, Pr/dining room 26 **Times** 12-3/6-10, Closed Xmas & BHs, Sat-Sun **Prices** Fixed L 2 course fr £23.50, Fixed D 3 course fr £30, Starter £8-£14, Main £14-£39, Dessert £6-£9 **Wines** 514 bottles over £30, 37 bottles under £30, 40 by glass **Parking** On street after 7pm, NCP **Notes** Vegetarian available, Children welcome

LONDON EC4 *continued*

28-50 Wine Workshop & Kitchen

PLAN 3 D2

◉◉ French, European

tel: 020 7242 8877 **140 Fetter Ln EC4A 1BT**
email: info@2850.co.uk
dir: *Nearest station: Chancery Lane*

Serious about wine, serious about food

Wine steals the show at 28-50, the digits referencing the latitude range within which the world's vineyards are planted. It's a relaxed, uptempo basement affair (from the team behind Texture) and comes kitted out in a dark-green and dark-green colour scheme, with wine the theme at every turn (displays of bottles, pictures, corks and boxes). Floorboards, exposed brick, porthole mirrors and knowledgeable service add to the on-cue vibe. Simple French bistro-inspired fare is the name of the game, wrought from premium produce and accessibly priced. Witness succulent rump of lamb served with panisse (chickpea fritter), exemplary ratatouille and basil, or perhaps top-dollar sirloin (28-day aged US grain-fed beef) teamed with braised shallots, watercress and classic béarnaise. And then there are the fairly priced wines, with 30 served by the glass, carafe or bottle on the every-day selection. Alternatively, take your pick from the Collector's List with some starry vintages and more wallet-busting prices. (There's a second branch in Marylebone.)

Times 12-2.30/6-9.30, Closed Xmas, New Year, BHs, Sat-Sun

Vanilla Black

PLAN 3 D2

◉◉ Modern Vegetarian **V**

tel: 020 7242 2622 **17-18 Tooks Court EC4A 1LB**
email: vanillablack@btconnect.com
dir: *Nearest station: Chancery Lane*

Classy vegetarian cookery in a hidden London location

Tucked away in a little alley just off Chancery Lane, the upmarket sheen of Andrew Dargue and Donna Conroy's slick restaurant says straight away that the place is a million miles from the lentil bake school of vegetarian cookery. A mix of muted contemporary colours blends with dark pine floorboards, antique framed photos and prints, and rustic pine tables, while statement circular lightshades add a hint of art deco. And what arrives on the plate lives up to the setting: interesting, innovative dishes that combine high-quality ingredients, up-to-the-minute technique and a sound approach to texture and flavour contrasts. The rich creaminess of brie ice cream is balanced cleverly with fresh blackberries, globules of tart blackberry coulis, pickled spring onions, and a crisp quinoa cracker. Next up, double-baked Ribblesdale goats' cheese pudding is paired with smoked potato croquette, pineapple pickle and poached hen's egg, and the creativity keeps on coming with a baked black treacle sponge with cardamom milk, mandarin and parkin crumb in a creative finale of comforting christmassy flavours with exotic Middle Eastern notes.

Chef Andrew Dargue **Owner** Andrew Dargue & Donna Conroy **Seats** 45
Times 12-2.30/6-10, Closed 2 wks Xmas & New Year, BH Mons, Sun **Prices** Fixed L 2 course £19.50, Fixed D 3 course £41.75 **Wines** 48 bottles over £30, 14 bottles under £30, 10 by glass **Parking** On street (meter) or NCP **Notes** Children welcome

The White Swan Pub & Dining Room

PLAN 3 D3

◉ Modern British

tel: 020 7242 9696 **108 Fetter Ln EC4A 1ES**
email: info@thewhiteswanlondon.com
dir: *Nearest station: Chancery Lane*

City gastro-pub with classy first-floor restaurant

The panelled ground-floor bar and mezzanine balcony of this smart Holborn pub – sibling of The Gun – heave with a boisterous crew of suited-and-booted drinkers unwinding after a hard day in the office. The bar menu offers appealing contemporary gastropub fodder, but if you want to dine in more refined surroundings, the top-floor dining room is the place to go. It's a soberly turned-out space with windows on two sides, a mirrored ceiling, curvy leather seating, white linen-clad tables and a patterned-wood floor. The kitchen turns out appropriately up-to-date, well-flavoured dishes with an eye on presentation and seasonal produce. Thus, an autumnal dinner starts with artichoke and ceps velouté, poured at the table around a wild rabbit Scotch quail's egg, before Yorkshire red-legged partridge arrives in the company of chestnuts, chanterelles and game chips. To finish, there's damson soufflé with ginger and vanilla ice cream.

Chef Chris Cooper **Owner** Tom & Ed Martin **Seats** 52, Pr/dining room 52
Times 12-3/6-10, Closed Xmas, 1 Jan, BHs, Sat-Sun (ex private parties)
Prices Starter £6.50-£11, Main £14-£23, Dessert £6 **Wines** 40 bottles over £30, 35 bottles under £30, 23 by glass **Parking** On street & NCP (Hatton Garden)
Notes Vegetarian available, Children welcome

▍ LONDON N1

Almeida Restaurant

PLAN 1 F4

◉◉ French

tel: 020 7354 4777 **30 Almeida St, Islington N1 1AD**
email: almeida-reservations@danddlondon.com
dir: *Nearest station: Angel, Highbury & Islington*

Honest French cooking opposite the theatre

A little walk from the hustle and bustle of Islington's busy centre rewards with good honest French food in a contemporary setting. The eponymous theatre is opposite. In the airy room, dressed in fashionable contemporary neutrality, large windows look out onto the street where parasols are set along the pavement for eating outside in the warmer months. White linen tablecloths adorn the tables at the back of the space, whilst up front is a tad less formal; both areas, though, hum with a heartfelt Gallic bonhomie. The food carries its French allegiances lightly, with some standout seasonal British ingredients taking centre stage. Cornish crab ravioli comes with buttered lettuce and beurre blanc in a well-crafted first course, followed by Denham Estate venison à la bourguignon with gratin dauphinoise which is brim full of flavour. Finish with a textbook crème brûlée à la vanille and a warm madeleine.

Times 12-2.30/5.30-10.30, Closed 26 Dec, 1 Jan, L Mon, D Sun

The Drapers Arms

PLAN 1 F4

◉ British

tel: 020 7619 0348 **44 Barnsbury St N1 1ER**
email: info@thedrapersarms.com
dir: *Nearest station: Highbury & Islington, Angel*

Real gastropub serving no-nonsense modern British food

Secreted away in the well-heeled backstreets of Islington, the Drapers Arms is a buzzy neighbourhood meeting and eating place that sits comfortably at the gastropub end of the spectrum, but without the pretensions that the term sometimes implies. The airy high-ceilinged room has a lived-in look featuring scuffed floorboards, old mismatched chairs and bare tables around the central bar. Drop in for a pint and you'll find an impressive range of real ales on tap, and a chalkboard list of gutsy bar food to go with it. But it's worth honing your appetite to tackle the menu of no-nonsense seasonal British cooking. A starter of grilled ox heart with green sauce and watercress pulls no punches, then duck breast with Muscat grapes and red cabbage follows in a similarly fuss-free vein. Pudding lands smack in the comfort zone with a rib-sticking combo of gingerbread pudding accompanied by whipped cream and crunchy oats.

Chef Gina Hopkins **Owner** Nick Gibson **Seats** 80, Pr/dining room 55
Times 12-3.30/6-10, Closed 25-26 Dec **Prices** Starter £6.50-£8, Main £12.50-£17.50, Dessert £6.50-£7, Service optional 12.5% **Wines** 30 bottles over £30, 39 bottles under £30, 16 by glass **Parking** On street **Notes** Sunday L £12.50-£17.50, Vegetarian available, Children welcome

Fifteen London – The Restaurant
PLAN 3 G5

Modern British

tel: 020 3375 1515 **15 Westland Place N1 7LP**
email: reservations@fifteen.net
dir: *Nearest station: Old St*

Turning lives around by means of vibrant seasonal cooking

Sailing into its second decade of operations, the original incarnation of Jamie Oliver's philanthropic restaurant enterprise continues to draw in the punters, though with a completely new look and style. The former warehouse has been completely refurbished to give it more of a neighbourhood vibe and gone is the Italian menu and instead the deal is a range of smaller and larger plates for sharing, all based on prime seasonal ingredients and delivering big, fresh flavours. So you might start with devilled egg and smoked anchovy, duck ham and quince, or beef and barley buns and horseradish, moving on to cockles, pig's cheek, butter beans and laverbread, and braised lamb shoulder with purple sprouting broccoli and new season garlic. The place still continues in its original purpose though – to take in young unemployed people and prepare them for a career in the kitchen – so you can feel good about yourself as you feast on rotisserie Norfolk chicken with violet artichokes and lovage mayo.

Chef Robin Holmgren **Owner** Jamie Oliver Foundation **Seats** 65
Times 12-2.45/6-10.45, Closed 25 Dec, 1 Jan **Prices** Fixed L 2 course £19, Tasting menu fr £55, Starter £8-£12, Main £17-£28, Dessert £4-£8 **Wines** 25 bottles over £30, 9 bottles under £30, 23 by glass **Parking** On street & NCP **Notes** Tasting menu 5 course with wine £75, Sunday L £16-£19, Vegetarian available, Children welcome

Frederick's Restaurant
PLAN 1 F4

Modern British

tel: 020 7359 2888 **106-110 Islington High St, Camden Passage, Islington N1 8EG**
email: dine@fredericks.co.uk
dir: *Nearest station: Angel*

Popular dining spot among Islington's antique shops

Built in 1789 as a pub, and rebuilt in 1834, Frederick's has been a stalwart of the Islington dining scene since the late 1960s and is still going strong. It's an attractive space, its brick walls hung with abstracts; a recent addition has been the Club Room, a contemporary private dining room. Its appeal lies in its broadly based menu and consistently high-quality cooking. Straightforwardly pleasing starters might take in crab and avocado salad with cucumber jelly, and prawns fried with garlic butter. Among main courses, monkfish gets the bourguignon treatment, served with Charlotte potatoes, while in season may come roast breast of guinea fowl with an onion tart, pepper and cumin purée and purple-sprouting broccoli. Chocoholics could end with rich chocolate fondant cut by cinnamon ice cream, while others could go for something like three ways with rhubarb.

Chef Adam Hilliard **Owner** Nick Segal **Seats** 150, Pr/dining room 40
Times 12-2.30/5.45-11.30, Closed Xmas, New Year, BHs, Sun (ex functions) **Prices** Fixed L 2 course fr £15.50, Fixed D 3 course fr £19, Starter £6.50-£13.50, Main £12-£30, Dessert £7-£10.50 **Wines** 125 bottles over £30, 20 bottles under £30, 25 by glass **Parking** NCP Business Design Centre, on street **Notes** Sat brunch, Vegetarian available, Children welcome

Grain Store
PLAN 1 F4

Modern, European

tel: 020 7324 4466 **Granary Square, 1-3 Stable Square, King's Cross N1C 4AB**
email: eat@grainstore.com
dir: *Nearest station: King's Cross*

Classy globe-trotting fare in an industrial landscape

The latest venture from chef Bruno Loubet and the Zetter Group's Michael Benyan, the Grain Store in newly trendy King's Cross blurs the boundary between kitchen and dining room in one massive industrial-looking space. There are ducts snaking across the high ceiling, chunky wooden tables, exposed brickwork and an all-round urban-cool vibe. There's a buzzy bar, too, for a cocktail or something off the all-day menu. The main menu combines the classic cooking of Monsieur Loubet's French roots with something altogether more globe-trotting. Mushroom and duck liver pâté with celeriac remoulade and mulled wine jelly harks of the old country, or go for another starter of mackerel tartare with seaweed and cucumber, green apple purée and pickled redcurrants. Vegetables get top billing (often listed first among ingredients) with grilled leeks and an apple and pickled walnut salsa partnering a gloriously tender confit of pork belly. There's plenty of craft and creativity in desserts, too, such as chocolate and peanut delice, which arrives in the company of slices of eucalyptus- and mint-poached pineapple.

Times 12-2.30/6-10.30, Closed 24-26 Dec, D Sun

Smokehouse
PLAN 1 F4

International

tel: 020 7354 1144 **63-69 Canonbury Rd, Islington N1 2DG**
email: info@smokehouseislington.co.uk
dir: *Nearest station: Highbury & Islington*

Meat meets fire in an Islington pub

One of a quartet of London pubs forming the Noble Inns group, the Smokehouse is an old Islington boozer that has seen new life as a temple to the simple, primeval principle of subjecting hunks of meat to fire and woodsmoke. In the yard at the back are three giant smokers, fuelled by sustainable English oak, as is detailed on a blackboard above the open kitchen. Neil Rankin doesn't much mind where the culinary influence comes from, as long as smoke can play a part, so expect chunks of French classicism alongside east Asian sizzle and bite – Korean spicy rice cake with mussels, main-course smoked duck with kimchi and potato cake. There is no precious primping here and flavours are primed to explode, as when a lobe of seared foie gras in a reduction of red wine and bourbon is offset by a crisp-shelled apple fritter and a runny duck egg. Following that, short rib bourguignon arrives as though from the barbecue in heaven, its sealed smoky potency supported by a bone-thickened red wine sauce, creamy mash, bacon lardons, girolles and deep-fried shallot rings. There are non-meat dishes, such as roasted aubergine curry, or grilled mackerel with radishes, peanuts and green chilli, but there may be a feeling that shunning the meats is missing the point. If you've room for afters, a hunk of white chocolate cheesecake comes with a properly puckering shot of lemon sorbet as refresher. Book well ahead, for the Smokehouse is playing to packed houses. An extensive list of craft beers is not the least part of the explanation.

Chef Neil Rankin **Owner** Scott & Maria Hunter **Seats** 50 **Times** 6-10, Closed 24-26 Dec, L Mon-Fri **Prices** Starter £7-£11, Main £13.50-£18, Dessert £6.50-£8 **Wines** 17 bottles over £30, 22 bottles under £30, 11 by glass **Parking** On street **Notes** Sat brunch, Sunday L £16.50-£18, Vegetarian available, Children welcome

LONDON N1 *continued*

Trullo
PLAN 1 F4

◉◉ Italian

tel: 020 7226 2733 **300-302 St Paul's Rd N1 2LH**
email: enquiries@trullorestaurant.com
dir: *Nearest station: Highbury & Islington*

Upbeat modern Italian cooking near Highbury Corner

Just off Highbury Corner, Trullo is a cracking little place, a vibrant, friendly and affordable neighbourhood eatery with pared-back bistro looks, well-worn floorboards, black bentwood chairs, paper table coverings and an animated atmosphere. It's a suitably rustic and bustling setting for honest, ingredients-driven modern Italian cooking. Expect good seasonal materials, top-drawer pasta that is hand-rolled minutes before service, a charcoal grill for adding an aromatic note to fish and meat, all presented in a switched-on menu that changes not just with the seasons but with every sitting. Antipasti run to full-bore ideas such as ox tongue with agretti and anchovy, then follow with pasta – the signature pappardelle with beef shin ragù is a fine example of hearty Italian comfort food done well. The charcoal grill adds a smoky edge to sea bass served with a lively salad of purple beetroot, lamb's lettuce and pistachios, or the oven might offer up rabbit leg braised with pancetta and shallots, and matched with baked cannellini beans. Finish with excellent almond tart and poached rhubarb.

Chef Conor Gadd, Tim Siadatan **Owner** Jordan Frieda, Tim Siadatan **Seats** 40, Pr/dining room 30 **Times** 12.30-2.45/6-10.15, Closed 25 Dec-3 Jan, some BHs, D Sun **Prices** Starter £7-£10.50, Main £14-£22, Dessert £5-£7.50, Service optional **Wines** 40 bottles over £30, 11 bottles under £30, 11 by glass **Parking** On street **Notes** Large table menus £25-£45, Sunday L £17-£35, Vegetarian available, Children welcome

LONDON NW1

La Collina
PLAN 1 E4

◉ Modern Italian

tel: 020 7483 0192 **17 Princess Rd, Chalk Farm NW1 8JR**
email: info@lacollinarestaurant.co.uk
dir: *Nearest station: Chalk Farm, Camden Town*

Classy neighbourhood Italian for honest, simple cooking

La Collina is a relaxed and authentic neighbourhood Italian for the boho-chic residents of Primrose Hill, its discreet black frontage slotted into an elegant terrace. Inside, the place is simplicity itself: cream walls without adornment, dark pine floors, black leather seats and white tablecloths, and a small bar in the corner, all flooded with light from large sash windows. A cast-iron spiral staircase coils down to the basement, where you get a ringside seat for the tiny open kitchen – the domain of chef Diana Rinaldo who sends out homespun regional, ingredient-led dishes offering a pleasing mix of tradition and more modish thinking. A starter of home-made pappardelle with cep mushroom sauce is just what Italian food is all about: simple, seasonal and fresh. Next up, spanking fresh sea bass fillets are flavoured with tomatoes, thyme, and white wine, and to finish, the house tiramisù is a paragon of its ilk. All-Italian wines, and friendly Latin service add to the appeal.

Chef Diana Rinaldo **Owner** Patrick Oberto, Diana Rinaldo **Seats** 40 **Times** 12-2.30/6-10.30, Closed Xmas wk, L Mon **Prices** Fixed L 2 course £14.50, Starter £7-£10.50, Main £13.50-£21.50, Dessert £5-£7 **Wines** 35 bottles over £30, 25 bottles under £30, 7 by glass **Parking** Free after 6pm & weekends **Notes** Vegetarian available, Children welcome

The Gilbert Scott
PLAN 3 B5

◉◉ British

tel: 020 7278 3888 **Renaissance St Pancras Hotel, Euston Rd NW1 2AR**
email: reservations@thegilbertscott.co.uk
dir: *Nearest station: St Pancras*

Versatile cooking in Gilbert Scott's majestic St Pancras hotel

Arguably Britain's finest railway hotel when it opened in 1873 as an amenity to St Pancras station, the meticulously restored Midland (now the Renaissance) is once more a London landmark, now witnessing the then unthinkable business of trains that run continuously to the continent. A masterpiece of Gothic Revival, from its magnificent portico entrance to a sweeping double staircase that is broad enough to allow two crinolined ladies to pass each other without unseemly collision, it's the kind of venue that has to be seen to be believed. Dimmed lights and candles create a thrilling ambience in the gorgeous cocktail bar, and the dining room is patrolled by staff whose long aprons match the seating. Traditional and contemporary dishes of imagination and flair complete the alluring picture. Expect roasted beetroot with ricotta, fried onion and beetroot aïoli; beautifully judged Cornish plaice on the bone with mussels, sweet tomatoes and basil; sturdy, well-filled pies such as rabbit, prawn and mushroom. There are indulgeable desserts like toffee cheesecake with salted caramel ice cream, or Lord Mayor's trifle, a concoction of blackberries and coconut sponge.

Times 12-3/5.30-11

Gilgamesh Restaurant Lounge
PLAN 1 E4

◉ Pan-Asian

tel: 020 7428 5757 & 7428 4922 **The Stables Market, Chalk Farm Rd NW1 8AH**
email: reservations@gilgameshbar.com
dir: *Nearest station: Chalk Farm, Camden Town*

Pan-Asian dishes in a psychedelic re-creation of ancient Babylon

The exotic maelstrom that is Camden's Stables Market is good preparation for a meal here, for Gilgamesh is no ordinary venue. Be prepared for interiors inspired by the excesses of Babylon (the ancient Mesopotamian city, not a nightclub in Ilford). This amounts to hand-carved wooden furniture, extravagant fabrics, a lapis lazuli inlaid 50-metre bar, ornate walls of beaten bronze panels, marble pillars, palm trees, vast windows and nightclub-esque psychedelic lighting. The menu takes its inspiration from the East, serving up a Pan-Asian panoply of ideas: dim sum, sushi, Malaysian curries and more. Start with crispy squid with garlic chips and a sweet-and-sour dipping sauce, or salmon céviche, and move onto rack of organic lamb breaded with oriental herbs and served with an Asian dressing, or beef Penang. Desserts can be as Asian-inspired as an exotic tropical fruit bowl, or as indulgently European as milk chocolate fondant with praline and vanilla ice cream.

Times 12-2.30/6-12

Meliá White House

PLAN 2 H4

◉◉ Spanish, Mediterranean

tel: 020 7391 3000 **Albany St, Regent's Park NW1 3UP**
email: melia.white.house@melia.com web: www.melia-whitehouse.com
dir: *Nearest station: Great Portland St, Regent's Park, Warren St*

Inventive Spanish cooking in an art deco hotel

The Iberian-owned art deco hotel pays homage to its national cuisine in the elegant Spanish restaurant, L'Albufera. Close to Regent's Park, and an easy stroll from Oxford Street, it is a glossy space, all polished wooden floors, black-clothed tables and cream upholstered chairs as a backdrop to vibrant cooking that walks a line between traditional and modern Spanish schools. Materials are sourced from the homeland for maximum authenticity (a requirement here, since the place is well frequented by Spanish visitors) so Serrano ham is carved from a trolley for traditionalists, otherwise grilled octopus with black olive chimichurri dressing and crunchy salsify, or spicy Spanish sausage cooked in cider with lavender are the sort of starters to expect. Paella comes in various forms — a black squid ink version with clams and monkfish, say — while mains could be slow-cooked suckling pig with paprika and garlic-mashed potatoes, mange-tout and thyme jus. For dessert, perhaps lemon posset topped with almond crumble and passionfruit foam, or finish instead with Spanish cheeses served with quince jelly.

Chef Gines Lorente Barcelona, David Aguado **Owner** Melia White House (Biosphere Hotel Co) **Seats** 62, Pr/dining room 14 **Times** 7-10.30, Closed Sun, BHs, L all week **Prices** Fixed D 3 course £25, Starter £8-£19, Main £16-£22, Dessert £6-£9 **Wines** 21 bottles over £30, 8 bottles under £30, 10 by glass **Parking** On street **Notes** Buffet L only in The Place, Vegetarian available, Children welcome

Michael Nadra Primrose Hill

PLAN 1 E4

◉◉ Modern European

tel: 020 7722 2800 **42 Gloucester Av NW1 8JD**
email: primrose@restaurant-michaelnadra.co.uk
dir: *Nearest station: Chalk Farm, Camden Town*

Global cuisine right by the canal

Following a highly successful Chiswick opening, Nadra has headed to north London for his second restaurant. The canal-side location incorporates a brick tunnel, once used by barge horses, now hosting a row of dining tables, and there is a garden area and martini bar, so something to suit all comers. Nadra cooks on-the-money reference dishes of global cuisine, a reach that extends from tuna tartare and salmon céviche with chilli-pickled cucumber and salmon crackling, through Ibérico presa (shoulder steak) and belly, wild mushrooms and mash in Madeira jus, to an apple and pear version of kataifi, the Greek shredded pasta dish, accompanied by pistachio praline and ice cream and a dollop of wild thyme honey. Intriguing flavours pour forth from each dish, the fish options especially inspired — sea bass comes with siu mai-style prawn dumplings and bok choy in lemongrass-spiked crab bisque. The six-course tasting menu is excellent value, and includes a sorbet course served with a slug of Grey Goose vodka.

Chef Michael Nadra **Owner** Michael Nadra **Seats** 100, Pr/dining room 40 **Times** 12-2.30/6-10, Closed 24-26 Dec, 1 Jan **Prices** Fixed L 2 course £21-£29, Fixed D 3 course £37-£45, Starter £10-£13, Main £21-£26, Dessert fr £8 **Wines** 150 bottles over £30, 25 bottles under £30, 16 by glass **Parking** On street **Notes** Tasting menu 6 course, L 20% discount ALC menu, Sunday L £21-£34, Vegetarian available, Children welcome

Odette's Restaurant

PLAN 1 E4

◉◉◉ – *see below*

Odette's Restaurant ◉◉◉

LONDON NW1   PLAN 1 E4

Modern British V
tel: 020 7586 8569 **130 Regent's Park Rd NW1 8XL**
email: info@odettesprimrosehill.com
dir: *Nearest station: Chalk Farm*

Confident modern British cooking in a local favourite

Welsh celeb chef Bryn Williams took over this leafy Primrose Hill favourite back in 2008 and has since brought it right up to date, yet it still retains the charm of a neighbourhood outfit, albeit with ambition worthy of any postcode. Fair-weather pavement tables out front under a striped awning and a charming little courtyard garden out back are an added magnet for the prosperous local beau monde and add to the feel-good factor, bolstered by the friendly and unstuffy service. Inside there's a smart finish of cool pastel shades and exposed brick, with walls enlivened by cartoons. Black banquettes and matching modern chairs, polished-wooden tables, parquet-style flooring and dangling globe lighting all fit with the stylish, urbane good looks without losing that intimate neighbourhood vibe. There's no less ambition about the kitchen's modern British output, the enterprise far outstripping that of a humble neighbourhood gaff. Balanced, creative combinations, intelligent sourcing (including a sprinkling of Welsh ingredients, say,

Carmarthen ham combining with sweet pear and mooli in a marinated scallop starter), pretty presentation and delicate, subtle flavours resonate in light modern dishes. The repertoire's delivered via fashionable tasting menu (including a veggie offering and a bespoke version if you're sat at the Kitchen Table downstairs), an amazing value weekday lunch, plus an intelligently compact carte that offers five options at each turn. Off the carte, expect mains like fabulous Goosnargh duck breast served with a tarte fine of smoked bacon and mushrooms, blood orange and crushed turnips, or perhaps melting Welsh lamb pepped up with spiced aubergine, artichokes and wild garlic. To close, pistachio cake, apple terrine and green apple sorbet, or the signature Odette's 'jaffa cake' with orange cream and marmalade that smacks of childhood memories.

Chef Bryn Williams, Jamie Randall **Owner** Bryn Williams **Seats** 70, Pr/dining room 10 **Times** 12-2.30/6-10, Closed 25-26 Dec, 1 Jan **Prices** Fixed L 2 course £13, Fixed D 3 course fr £20, Tasting menu £52-£80, Starter £7-£12, Main £17-£24, Dessert £6-£9 **Wines** 36 bottles over £30, 16 bottles under £30, 16 by glass **Parking** On street **Notes** Tasting/Vegetarian menu 6/10 course, Sunday L £26-£32, Children welcome

LONDON NW1 *continued*

Pullman London St Pancras

PLAN 3 A5

Modern European

tel: 020 7666 9000 & 7666 9038 **100-110 Euston Rd NW1 2AJ**
email: h5309@accor.com **web:** www.accorhotels.com/5309
dir: *Nearest station: King's Cross, Euston, St Pancras Int*

International menu in a contemporary railway hotel

Those old enough to remember the days of steam might know that the Golden Arrow was a luxury boat train linking London with Dover, and this sleek hotel restaurant (part of the French Accor group) continues the cross-channel link by refuelling Eurostar travellers at St Pancras International, five minutes off. But that's as far as the belle epoque connection goes: this is a clean-cut 21st-century space constantly thrumming with activity. An open kitchen and Josper grill turn out an eclectic repertoire of uncomplicated modern European dishes such as Gloucester ham hock and leek terrine served with piccalilli and onion bloomer bread. Since this is an operation that seeks out quality produce, salt marsh lamb is sourced from Foulness Island and partnered with béarnaise sauce, tomato and basil salad and fine beans. To finish, salted caramel chocolate tart is nicely accompanied by vanilla custard ice cream.

Chef Michael Penn **Owner** Accor UK **Seats** 92 **Times** 12-2.30/6-11, Closed L Sat-Sun **Prices** Prices not confirmed **Wines** 46 bottles over £30, 12 bottles under £30, 310 by glass **Notes** Vegetarian available, Children welcome

St Pancras Grand Brasserie

PLAN 3 B6

Modern, Northern European

tel: 020 7870 9900 **St Pancras International NW1 9QP**
email: stpg@searcys.co.uk
dir: *Nearest station: King's Cross, St Pancras*

Feel-good flavours at the Eurostar terminal

With its shimmering belle epoque finish (courtesy of designer Martin Brudnizki), this brasserie within St Pancras station is aptly named. Adjacent to 'Europe's longest' Champagne Bar, the Grand Brasserie is a compelling option whether or not you're heading for mainland Europe. The menu combines French and British classics in an entente cordiale of feel-food Pan-European flavours. Kick off with potted shrimps with sourdough bread, or a smoked duck salad perked up with Roquefort, or splash out for half-a-dozen oysters with a glass of fizz. Among main courses, bubble-and-squeak enriched with Montgomery cheddar risotto is a creative take on an old favourite, with steak frites and lobster thermidor keeping up the best of Gallic tradition. There are posh burgers, too, and fish and chips, and daily specials such as Thursday's beef bourguignon with creamy mash. Desserts run to Earl Grey crème brûlée or apple and blackberry strudel.

Chef Jack Norman, Andy Horsman **Owner** Searcys/WSH **Seats** 160, Pr/dining room 14 **Times** 11am-11.30pm, All-day dining, Closed 25 Dec **Prices** Fixed L 2 course £15-£20, Fixed D 2 course £15-£20, Starter £5-£10, Main £10-£25, Dessert £4-£7 **Wines** 39 bottles over £30, 29 bottles under £30, 24 by glass **Notes** Sunday L £15-£20, Vegetarian available, Children welcome

The Winter Garden

PLAN 2 F3

British, Mediterranean

tel: 020 7631 8000 & 7631 8230 **222 Marylebone Rd NW1 6JQ**
email: restaurants.reservation@thelandmark.co.uk **web:** www.wintergarden-london.com
dir: *Nearest station: Marylebone*

Classical cooking under a soaring glass roof

The Winter Garden is open all day for breakfast, lunch, afternoon tea and dinner, and the mood changes as does the hour (and the weather), for this dining room is in the heart of the eight-storey glass-covered atrium that forms the central focus of The Landmark Hotel. A grand railway hotel of the old school, it is these days an upscale address and its atrium is an impressive spot to sit and tuck into some classically-minded modern European food. Start, for example, with crab and sweetcorn cannelloni or roasted wood pigeon with a foie gras ballotine, spiced figs and pistachio. Denham Estate venison might feature among main courses as pan-fried loin and a separate pie (with salsify and Cumberland chutney), while a fish option might be wild halibut with mild curried gnocchi and trompette mushrooms. Desserts are equally well put together with sticky toffee pudding cranking up the comfort factor, and iced tarragon parfait showing the inventive streak runs right through.

Chef Gary Klaner **Owner** Khun Jatuporn Sihanatkathakul **Seats** 90 **Times** 7am-10.30pm, All-day dining **Prices** Prices not confirmed, Service optional **Wines** 25 by glass **Parking** 40, On street **Notes** Champagne brunch, Theatre/Opera D, Afternoon tea, Sunday L, Vegetarian available, Children welcome

LONDON NW3

Manna

PLAN 1 E4

International Vegan

tel: 020 7722 8028 **4 Erskine Rd, Primrose Hill NW3 3AJ**
email: inquires@mannav.com
dir: *Nearest station: Chalk Farm*

Long-running neighbourhood vegetarian in leafy Primrose Hill

A forerunner of gourmet vegetarian and vegan dining when it opened in the 60s, Manna is still going strong with regard to ethical principles and organic values. The attractive shop front in a residential street in well-heeled Primrose Hill opens on to a rather up-to-date decor with wooden floors and furniture given a touch of class with designer wallpaper featuring silhouetted trees and birds and silver wreath-style light fittings. Carefully sourced produce is turned into vibrantly colourful dishes that are in step with the times, taking inspiration from far and wide. The menu globetrots from Greek-style spanikopita tart with a salad of fennel, rocket, preserved lemon and dill salad, to a main course of wild mushroom ragù with chestnut polenta, seared kale, beetroot and horseradish slaw and parsnip crisps. For dessert, there's a light vegan take on sticky toffee pudding with vanilla ice cream and caramel sauce.

Owner R Swallow, S Hague **Seats** 50 **Times** 12-3/6.30-11, Closed Xmas & New Year, Mon, L variable **Prices** Tasting menu £14-£22, Starter £7-£8, Main £14-£15, Dessert £7-£8 **Wines** 8 by glass **Parking** On street **Notes** Sunday L £14-£40, Children welcome

XO

PLAN 1 E4

Pan-Asian

tel: 020 7433 0888 **29 Belsize Ln NW3 5AS**
email: xo@rickerrestaurants.com
dir: *Nearest station: Swiss Cottage, Belsize Park*

Asian variety act in well-heeled Belsize Park

This outpost of Will Ricker's stable of trendy bar-restaurants brings a touch of big-city cool to the upscale 'village' of leafy Belsize Park. The slick space is dressed up in shades of black, scarlet and lime green with grey leather banquettes, black-painted wooden chairs, darkwood flooring, flower-patterned ironwork and angled wall mirrors so you can check out who's in the house as you graze through the menu of voguish Pan-Asian dishes. The kitchen's repertoire is designed for sociable sharing and takes in everything from dim sum (prawn har gau dumplings or chilli salt squid to get the taste buds standing to attention) to sashimi, sushi and tempura (such as black cod with yuzu aïoli). Among more substantial offerings, chicken is revved up with spicy sambal and a zingy, lime-dressed salad of coriander, bean sprouts, chopped peanuts and red chillies. Eye-catching cocktails, well-chosen wines and up-tempo music round off a polished package.

Times 12-3/6-11, Closed 25-26 Dec, 1 Jan

LONDON NW4

Hendon Hall Hotel

PLAN 1 D5

Modern, Traditional British

tel: 020 8457 2200 & 0845 072 7448 *(Calls cost 7p per minute plus your phone company's access charge)* **Ashley Ln, Hendon NW4 1HF**
email: hendonhall@handpicked.co.uk **web:** www.handpickedhotels.co.uk/hendonhall
dir: *Nearest station: Hendon Central*

Historic North London mansion with contemporary cooking

The impressive North London mansion dates from the 16th century and has earned a crust as a hotel since 1911. Nowadays, the place has a light contemporary look that blends well with a host of period features, including crystal chandeliers, a grand staircase and handsomely-proportioned rooms. Named after the 18th-century actor and manager of the eponymous Drury Lane theatre, who once owned the hall, the fine dining Garrick Restaurant works an upmarket modern look with contemporary art on the walls and smart russet and gold high-backed chairs at formally-laid tables. The kitchen continues to score palpable hits with its up-to-date cooking, setting out with a well-made terrine of confit duck, guinea fowl and foie gras matched creatively with red wine pear purée and parsnip. Next up, roast fillet of hake comes with capers and leek fondue, and jus noisette. The modern, creative thinking continues at dessert stage too with a well-thought-out composition of flavours and textures involving whipped lemon curd, meringue, citrus jelly and lemonade granita.

Times 12.30-2.30/6.30-9.30

LONDON SE1

The Anchor & Hope

PLAN 5 E5

British

tel: 020 7928 9898 **36 The Cut SE1 8LP**
email: anchorandhope@btconnect.com
dir: *Nearest station: Southwark, Waterloo*

Thrilling gastro-pub with big-hearted cooking

This tumultuous Waterloo gastro-pub is a roaring success – roaring being the operative word when it is rammed and you're in the high-decibel bar with a pint of real ale waiting your turn for a table in the eating area (you can't book to eat, except for Sunday lunch). The Anchor & Hope still looks and feels like a pub with its pared-back, no-frills interior – oxblood walls hung with modern art, and well-worn wooden tables and mismatched chairs. The food suits the mood of the place: flannel-free, unpretentious dishes built on quality seasonal ingredients. The menu changes each session, and descriptions rarely go beyond a handful of words, so forget three-course formality and just order whatever grabs your attention – warm snail and bacon salad or grilled razor clams might get the juices flowing, followed by roast Swaledale beef rump with dripping potatoes and horseradish. Otherwise three of you (or a greedy pair) could sign up for roast kid's leg 'saltimbocca' with chips and aïoli. Puds stay on message, perhaps raspberry Bakewell tart with clotted cream.

Times 12-2.30/6-10.30, Closed BHs, 25 Dec-1 Jan, L Mon, D Sun

Brigade

PLAN 5 H6

British

tel: 0844 346 1225 *(Calls cost 7p per minute plus your phone company's access charge)*
The Fire Station, 139 Tooley St SE1 2HZ
email: info@thebrigade.co.uk
dir: *Nearest station: London Bridge*

Turning up the heat in an old fire station

Named not only for the team in the kitchen, but also the firemen who once worked out of this grand red-brick former fire station, Brigade offers an upbeat, high-decibel vibe in an airy contemporary space with high ceilings, leather chairs and banquettes, and black tables, and the lively atmosphere is helped along by the sounds, sights and smells of the central open kitchen (perch at the counter for a close-up view of the action). Expect uncomplicated modern food driven by fresh, seasonal produce, much of it sourced from local suppliers and markets such as nearby Borough Market. Scotch egg with beetroot piccalilli and fennel and green apple slaw is a sound opening gambit, followed by a summery British take on seafood bouillabaisse with saffron and garlic rouille, or take the comfort route with a burger made from rump steak and shredded oxtail and finish with bitter chocolate tart with marmalade ice cream.

Times 12-3/5.30-10, Closed Sun, L Sat

LONDON SE1 *continued*

Cantina Vinopolis

PLAN 5 F6

Modern Mediterranean · NOTABLE WINE LIST

tel: 020 7940 8333 **1 Bank End SE1 9BU**
email: cantina@vinopolis.co.uk
dir: *Nearest station: London Bridge*

Dining underneath the arches at the South Bank's wine emporium

The soaring arches of a Victorian railway viaduct near London Bridge Station make an impressive cathedral-like space for worshipping the grape in its multifarious forms. Part of the Vinopolis complex, Cantina is the place to head for Mediterranean-accented dining in a modish setting of oak tables and leather banquettes beneath cavernous vaulted brick ceilings, with the rumble of overhead trains as an evocative soundtrack. It's run by staff who are passionate about food and wine, and in case you had forgotten that this is a temple to good wines, there are displays of bottles and a splendid list to jog the memory. Expect straight-talking ideas along the lines of duck foie gras terrine with home-made bread, followed by pheasant served with potato fondant, braised black cabbage, green lentils and vegetable stew, or if you fancy fish, perhaps lemon sole with spinach, new potatoes, capers and passionfruit marinière. Stay with the wine theme and treat yourself to a glass of something sticky to go with prune and almond tart served with vanilla ice cream.

Chef Moges A Wolde **Owner** Claudio Pulze **Seats** 200, Pr/dining room 100
Times 12-3/6-10.30, Closed Xmas, BHs, L Mon-Wed, D Sun **Prices** Fixed L 2 course £25.95, Fixed D 3 course £29.95, Starter £6.75-£10.50, Main £11.25-£21.50, Dessert £6.25-£8.50 **Wines** 112 bottles over £30, 49 bottles under £30, 26 by glass **Parking** On street **Notes** Sunday L £15-£19.95, Vegetarian available, Children welcome

Chino Latino London

PLAN 5 G5

Modern Pan-Asian V

tel: 020 7769 2500 **18 Albert Embankment SE1 7SP**
email: london@chinolatino.co.uk **web:** www.chinolatino.co.uk
dir: *Nearest station: Vauxhall*

Asian and Latin American spice and fire on the South Bank

Pan-Asian food with Latin inflections is the best-of-both-worlds approach at this rocking international chain that has pitched its London tent in the Park Plaza hotel complex on the South Bank, not far from Vauxhall station. A cocktail bar to be seen in, where the fiery Latino potions come with lashings of chilli and crushed mint, a sushi bar, and a sexy main dining room all in black, offset with light panels in

shimmering cherry, add up to a potently heady style mix. The food delivers too, with exquisitely presented dishes bursting with freshness, heat and umami. A maki roll of soft-shelled crab, avocado and Japanese rice comes with tomato-chilli mayo, or you might kick off with chicken, foie gras and shiitake shu mai in teriyaki sauce. Main courses mix and match the house influences, as when duck breast is dressed in both miso marinade and aji Amarillo yellow chilli, while bracing seafood flavours feature in the shape of a pairing of yuzu-gratinated lobster and king crab with chilli-garlic hollandaise. The eye-catching finisher is a chocolate dome of salted banana toffee, served with vanilla ice cream.

Chino Latino London

Chef Werner Seebach **Owner** Park Plaza Hotels **Seats** 85
Times 12-2.30/6-10.30, Closed L Sat-Sun **Prices** Fixed L 2 course £14.50, Fixed D 3 course £48-£50, Tasting menu fr £48, Starter £4-£12, Main £10-£25, Dessert £6-£7.50 **Wines** 29 bottles over £30, 18 bottles under £30, 12 by glass **Parking** Q park Waterloo station **Notes** Children welcome

See advert on opposite page

H10 London Waterloo Hotel

PLAN 5 E5

European

tel: 020 7928 4062 **284-302 Waterloo Rd SE1 8RQ**
email: h10.london.waterloo@h10hotels.com **web:** www.hotelh10londonwaterloo.com
dir: *Nearest station: Waterloo, Lambeth North*

Spanish hotel cooking with views of Waterloo

The Waterloo H10 could almost be London's newly built, lopsided answer to Manhattan's Flatiron Building, such is its streamlined angular look. Its principal eating space is Three O Two, which looks like an airport café, with unclothed tables in neat rows, plenty of daylight in the day, and uplighters raking the white net curtains in the evenings. Spanish is the chosen gastronomic accent, so expect classic tapas, as well as octopus and potato salad, rabbit and chicken paella, and ritzy main dishes like beef fillet with Menorcan Mahón cheese, garlic cream and a reduction sauce of Somontano wine. Pork cheeks with raisins and Parmentier potatoes, sauced in manzanilla sherry, are juicy and flavourful. Generously laden Catalan suquet seafood stews comprise salmon, squid, clams and mussels, and the dessert temptations take in variations on rice pudding, as well as nicely rich vanilla cheesecake.

Chef David Ovejo **Owner** H10 Hotels **Seats** 100, Pr/dining room 50
Times 6.30-10.30, Closed L all week (ex events) **Prices** Fixed D 2 course £15-£30, Starter £2.30-£19.60, Main £14.90-£26.30, Dessert £5.10-£9.50 **Wines** 9 bottles over £30, 37 bottles under £30, 16 by glass **Parking** NCP Library St or Elephant & Castle **Notes** Vegetarian available, Children welcome

Hutong
PLAN 5 G6

◉◉ Northern Chinese

tel: 020 3011 1257 **Level 33 The Shard SE1 9RY**
email: hutongreservations@aqua-london.com
dir: *Nearest station: London Bridge*

Top-end Chinese dining on the 33rd floor

Hutong pays homage to the cuisine of Northern China, the cooking based on the Shandong cuisine that was served up in the Imperial Palaces of old Peking. It's not exactly located in a palace as such, but a shrine to London's international standing, for it's located on the 33rd floor of The Shard. Yes, the view is stunning, particularly at night with the shimmering lights below, and it goes without saying there's maximum glass to enable everyone to get full impact. The room is a bit of a looker itself, with red lanterns and an open-to-view wood-fired oven where the ducks – a big part of the menu – can be seen cooking and drying. The kitchen turns out some classy dim sum at lunchtime, but the carte is also available lunch and dinner. Start with spiced razor clams or Szechuan peppered cuttlefish before tucking into the classic Peking duck, served in two waves – the crispy skin with pancakes and hoi sin sauce, then the meat with onions, peppers and chilli in a rich, flavoursome sauce. Fried prawns with jasmine tea leaves is a typically impressive main course, and there are sweet custard buns for dessert.

Times 12-3/6-11, Closed 25 Dec, 1 Jan

Magdalen
PLAN 5 H6

◉◉ British, European

tel: 020 7403 1342 **152 Tooley St SE1 2TU**
email: info@magdalenrestaurant.co.uk
dir: *Nearest station: London Bridge*

Vibrantly flavoured and thoughtful cooking near London Bridge

Magdalen, on a corner site hard by London Bridge, is a classy place, with burgundy-coloured walls hung with contemporary artwork, bentwood chairs at white-clothed tables covered with paper liners and a darkwood floor. Dishes are marked by their simplicity and judicious combinations (which belies the kitchen's technical skill and careful choice of ingredients), so clear flavours are allowed to speak for themselves. Perfectly timed, tender pieces of cuttlefish are cooked in ink and simply accompanied by whole chickpeas with a squeeze of lemon and a sprinkling of parsley, and chopped suckling pig comes with spiced clementines and toast. Main courses follow a similar mould: one beautifully presented dish is rare, melt-in-the-mouth roast haunch of venison with braised red cabbage and a gratin of potatoes and Gubbeen (an Irish cheese), or there is baked sea bass fillet with fennel, chard and anchovy dressing. Puddings make an impact too – perhaps decadent, dense chocolate pot, its richness cut by preserved cherries, or classic tarte Tatin.

Chef James & Emma Faulks, David Abbott **Owner** Roger & James Faulks **Seats** 90, Pr/dining room 30 **Times** 12-2.30/6.30-10, Closed Xmas, BHs, Sun, L Sat **Prices** Fixed L 2 course £16.50, Starter £7.50-£12.50, Main £15-£27.50, Dessert £6-£7 **Wines** 58 bottles over £30, 15 bottles under £30, 12 by glass **Parking** On street **Notes** Vegetarian available, Children welcome

Oblix
PLAN 5 G6

◉ American

tel: 020 7268 6700 **Level 32, The Shard, 31 St Thomas St SE1 9RY**
email: info@oblixrestaurant.com
dir: *Nearest station: London Bridge*

Steaks and more 32 floors up

If it's not a little trite to say so, the views are terrific. This is the 32nd floor of The Shard after all, and the Oblix takes up the entire space with its slick, brasserie vibe, open kitchen, cool lounge bar, luxe cocktails and live music (they have their own house band – really). When it comes to food, the grill and Josper oven are the stars of the show, with veal chop and gremolata and Wagyu tenderloin waiting to provide a satisfying hit of protein. It's not all about the red stuff, though, for this is a kitchen that turns out nifty starters such as grilled diver-caught scallops with lime and tamarind cream or wood-fired roasted beets with rye bread and goats' curd. Among main courses, too, there are alternatives to the meaty offerings, with barbecue black cod with coriander salsa catching the eye. Finish with a pecan nut and chocolate bar with bourbon ice cream, and then hit the bar. It's a seriously glamorous spot.

Owner Rainer Becker **Seats** 100 **Times** 12-3/6-11, Closed 25 Dec **Prices** Starter £8.50-£19.50, Main £14.50-£92, Dessert £2.50-£10.50 **Notes** Deli L £29, Wknd brunch £58 (champagne on arrival), Vegetarian available, Children welcome

LONDON SE1 *continued*

The Oxo Tower Restaurant

PLAN 3 D1

◉◉ Modern, Traditional British V ◈ NOTABLE WINE LIST

tel: 020 7803 3888 **8th Floor, Oxo Tower Wharf, Barge House St SE1 9PH**
email: oxo.reservations@harveynichols.com **web:** www.harveynichols.com
dir: Nearest station: Blackfriars, Waterloo, Southwark

Captivating views and impressive food

Up on the eighth floor of the old Oxo building, this bar, brasserie and restaurant combo overlooks the river and St Paul's Cathedral, a world-class vista which never fails to impress, day or night. A table on the outdoor terrace is a prized possession indeed (when the weather's right, of course), but it's impressive enough from behind the vast wall of glass in a smart, neutral space, where well turned-out staff keep things ticking over with suave professionalism. The cooking is broadly focused on modern European preparations, spiced with a bit of globetrotting into Asian territory. Seared tuna with Granny Smith apple, radish and dandelion salad relies on deep-red, sashimi-grade tuna of exceptional quality for its impact, while main-course roast monkfish comes with a squid ink popadom, red pepper coulis and radishes, or there might be fillet of beef with girolles, parmesan gnocchi and spiced golden raisin purée. To finish, strawberry and champagne millefeuille with wild strawberry sorbet is a vibrant ode to summer. Do allow some time to peruse the exceptional wine list.

Chef Jeremy Bloor **Owner** Harvey Nichols **Seats** 150 **Times** 12-3/6-11.30, Closed 25 Dec, D 24 Dec **Prices** Starter £12.50-£22.50, Main £21-£40, Dessert £8.50-£29.50 **Wines** 700 bottles over £30, 11 bottles under £30, 17 by glass **Parking** On street, NCP **Notes** Children welcome

Park Plaza County Hall London

PLAN 5 C5

◉ Modern Italian

tel: 020 7021 1919 & 7021 1800 **1 Addington St SE1 7RY**
email: ppchres@pphe.com **web:** www.parkplazacountyhall.com
dir: Nearest station: Waterloo, Westminster

Italian favourites in Thames-side landmark building

This snazzy modern hotel is next to County Hall on the South Bank, so right in the heart of the central London action. L'Italiano restaurant is on a mezzanine level, looking down on the buzzy first-floor bar, and it has got bags of style. There's a great view of the capital through the large wall of glass. At the heart of the culinary action is a wood-fired oven, which given the Italian focus of the place, means great pizzas (picante, perhaps, with salami, red onion and chill, or rustica with Parma ham and artichokes). But there's lots more going on. Beef carpaccio is a good version, or you might start with deep-fried squid with lemon mayonnaise. Pasta and risotto are traditional choices such as lasagne or seafood linguine, but there's also slow-roasted pork belly and whole sea bass poached in a light, spicy broth. Desserts are a familiar bunch: pannacotta with wild berries, or tiramisù.

Chef Mark Dancer **Owner** Park Plaza Hotels **Seats** 104, Pr/dining room 50 **Times** 5.30-10.15, Closed L all week **Prices** Prices not confirmed **Wines** 12 bottles over £30, 18 bottles under £30, 13 by glass **Parking** U Park Ltd **Notes** Vegetarian available, Children welcome

Park Plaza Westminster Bridge London

PLAN 5 C5

◉◉ Modern French

tel: 020 7620 7200 **SE1 7UT**
email: ppwlres@pphe.com **web:** www.parkplaza.com
dir: Nearest station: Westminster, Waterloo

Traditionally focused French brasserie dining near the Eye

At the opposite end of Westminster Bridge to the Houses of Parliament is the central London branch of the Park Plaza group, handy for a spin on the London Eye before you dine. A succession of designer spaces opens up, the dining options centring on a French venue called Brasserie Joël, a monochrome space with a large tree in the middle and funky music filling the air. A mix of traditional and lightly modernised French dishes brings plenty of lustre to a menu formatted in true brasserie style, and there's more of an awareness of seasonality than you might expect in a big city hotel. Old-fashioned things are done well enough to distinguish a starter of foie gras terrine with pain d'épices and delightfully sticky fig chutney, with perhaps rabbit in mustard cream and buttery mash, or Black Angus onglet and fries, to follow. Seafood is rendered with confident accuracy, as for grilled tiger prawns and scallops with butternut risotto and pea shoots, and proceedings end on a spectacular note with lemon tart and meringue flambée.

Times 12-2/5.30-10.30, Closed L Sat

Find out more about how we assess for Rosette awards on page 9

Pizarro

PLAN 5 H4

Traditional Spanish

tel: 020 7378 9455 **194 Bermondsey St SE1 3TQ**
email: management@pizarrorestaurant.com
dir: Nearest station: Bermondsey, Borough, London Bridge

Spanish cooking at its best in foodie Bermondsey

José Pizarro bangs the drum for authentic Spanish cocina in his TV appearances and cookbooks so head for his buzzy self-titled restaurant in newly-trendy Bermondsey to try his take on modern Spanish cuisine. It's a roomy, open-plan space that combines traditional Iberian touches – whole hams hanging at a Spanish tile-frieze bar, warm textures of wood – with a stripped back aesthetic that appeals to local hipsters. Choose between booth seats, a long communal table, a long marble counter looking out of the window, or perch on a ringside seat by the open kitchen. Don't expect the fiddly, molecular cooking that has made several Spanish chefs world famous: the kitchen deals in top-notch ingredients put together in simple, unfussy combinations. Tender grilled octopus matched with creamy, paprika-infused potato and egg caviar gets the taste buds revved up for a punchy main course of venison stew with chestnuts and earthy black trompette mushrooms, or there might be roast Segovian suckling pig with cranberry sauce. Finish with a riff on chocolate – mousse, buñuelo, ice cream and truffle.

Chef José Pizarro **Owner** José Pizarro **Seats** 75, Pr/dining room 10
Times 12-3/6-11, Closed 4 days Xmas **Prices** Prices not confirmed, Service optional
Wines 20 bottles over £30, 15 bottles under £30, 27 by glass **Parking** On street, NCP car park **Notes** Sunday L, Vegetarian available, Children welcome

Le Pont de la Tour

PLAN 5 J6

Modern French

tel: 020 7403 8403 **The Butlers Wharf Building, 36d Shad Thames SE1 2YE**
email: lepontres@danddlondon.com
dir: Nearest station: Tower Hill, London Bridge

Great views and assured French cooking

The name translates as Tower Bridge, and that's what lies before you, a solid-gold view framed by the city skyscrapers, and you get it whether you're dining out on the planter-lined riverside terrace, or indoors taking in the scene through a sweep of floor-to-ceiling windows. The setting is chic, with linen tablecloths and brass-edged mirrored columns evoking the gracious lines of art deco style in 1930s Paris, and correctly paced service hits all the right notes. Expect well-executed food that is rooted in the French classics, where seafood is always a strong suit (various types of oysters or a plateau de fruits de mer) and luxury ingredients come thick and fast. Start with roasted wood pigeon with confit leg tortellini, celeriac and pear, followed by pan-fried John Dory partnered by bone marrow, sauté squid and sauce bordelaise. Sticking with the Gallic theme, Valrhona milk chocolate mousse is served with salted caramel ice cream. If your wallet can stand the strain, the place is well known for its cracking wine list

Chef Tom Cook **Owner** Des Gunewardena **Seats** 140, Pr/dining room 24
Times 12-3/6-11 **Prices** Fixed L 2 course fr £20, Fixed D 3 course fr £25, Tasting menu fr £55, Starter £11-£16.50, Main £19.50-£38, Dessert £7.50-£13, Service optional 12.5% **Wines** 150 bottles over £30, 20 bottles under £30, 35 by glass **Parking** On street, car park **Notes** Sunday L £20-£25, Vegetarian available, Children welcome

Restaurant Story

PLAN 5 J5

– see page 298

Roast

PLAN 5 G6

British V

tel: 020 300 6611 **The Floral Hall, Borough Market, Stoney St SE1 1TL**
email: info@roast-restaurant.com **web:** www.roast-restaurant.com
dir: Nearest station: London Bridge

Great British produce overlooking Borough Market

There's no doubting the foodie credentials of the location, right in the heart of Borough Market, even if the place is more of a tourist attraction these days. The one-time Floral Hall is a cracking setting for a restaurant, perched above the market with views across London taking in St Paul's Cathedral. There's a bar serving up seasonal cocktails, and a top-notch Scotch egg if you're feeling peckish. The restaurant is the setting for some British-focused food, sourced with due diligence, and in true market fashion, it's open for breakfast. Maldon sweetcorn and smoked haddock chowder is a starter packed full of flavour, or go for gamekeeper's terrine with cranberry compôte. Next up, pan-fried fillet of Cornish sole is a generous serving, with accompanying smoked sea trout and chive butter sauce. For dessert, there's chocolate and clementine trifle, or an excellent Dorset blueberry and almond tart with yogurt cream.

Chef Marcus Verberne **Owner** Iqbal Wahhab **Seats** 120
Times 12-3.45/5.30-11, Closed 25-26 Dec, 1 Jan, D Sun **Prices** Prices not confirmed
Wines 310 bottles over £30, 20 bottles under £30, 21 by glass **Parking** NCP Kipling St **Notes** Sunday L, Children welcome

RSJ, The Restaurant on the South Bank

PLAN 5 D6

Modern European

tel: 020 7928 4554 **33 Coin St SE1 9NR**
email: tom.king@rsj.uk.com
dir: Nearest station: Waterloo

Pleasingly unfussy food and notable Loire wines

The neighbourhood has changed rather dramatically since this stalwart of the South Bank's dining scene set up shop in 1980. Its long-standing appeal is down to its French and Italian-inspired menus that are guaranteed to pack in the pre- and post-theatre and concert crowds, while the specialist Loire Valley wine list (handpicked by the owner who's been visiting France for 'research purposes' for over 30 years) is a show-stopper in itself and it is all served up in an unpretentious vibe, with a mellow decor of wooden floors, neutral tones and simple blond-wood chairs. In the kitchen, unfussy food is elevated by intelligent flavour combinations and sound cooking – Cornish mackerel fillet with pickled red cabbage and watercress is a fresh and vibrant opener, followed by roasted hake with buttery crushed Jersey Royals lifted with lemon and chives, and a punchy sauce viérge. Pear and pine nut tart with home-made basil ice cream brings down the curtain.

Times 12-2.30/5.30-11.30, Closed Xmas, 1 Jan, Sun, L Sat

Restaurant Story ❀❀❀❀

LONDON SE1   **PLAN 5 J5**

Modern British **V** ❦ NOTABLE WINE LIST

tel: 020 7183 2117 **201 Tooley St SE1 2UE**
email: dine@restaurantstory.co.uk
web: www.restaurantstory.co.uk
dir: *Nearest station: London Bridge, Tower Hill*

White-hot opening from a rising global talent

Anyone wanting to get a handle on what is occurring in the world of contemporary dining should head on over to Tooley Street to see what's going down at Tom Sellers' place. Don't bother going on the spur of the moment though, for bookings are open a month ahead and the place fills up fast. Restaurant Story was opened in 2013 and the modern wood-and-glass structure near Tower Bridge quickly became one of the must-visit destinations in the capital. Tom Sellers learned his trade in some stellar kitchens including Tom Aikens here in London, Thomas Keller at Per Se in New York and René Redzepi's Noma in Copenhagen. There aren't many dining rooms that are as on trend as this vaguely Nordic-style space of elemental surfaces, open-to-view kitchen and hip designer chairs, with enough space between tables to ensure every customer feels valued. Everything here tells a story, including the cocktails which are inspired by (and credited to) members of the team — Campari with bittered vermouth and black olive soda, say. The menu arrives inside an old book (sticking to the theme) and is a tasting version with seven- or ten-course options, called Half Story and Full Story respectively, with a shorter mid-week lunch if you don't fancy going the whole hog. Most people, though, having secured a table and aware of the high praise, go the whole hog. It all starts with the signature 'bread and dripping'

(a 'candle' made of beef dripping which you dip a sourdough roll into as it melts) and a succession of small 'snacks'. Creativity and ingenuity abounds throughout and everything is rooted in something from Tom's own story (or journey if you will). Every dish looks stunning on the plate: sometimes playful, sometimes simple, and always intriguing. The menu evolves rather than changes with any regularity, but then again these ideas take time to get right. Scallops are a perfect match for cucumber and dill ash, raw beef arrives with apple and Wiltshire truffle, and the richness of foie gras has a perfect foil in the form of passionfruit and nasturtium. Among sweet courses there's harmony in a plate of pumpkin, burnt clementines and cardamom, while 'almond and dill' uses dill oil and dill salt to stunning effect. Every dish on the menu has a recommended drink to accompany it, and it might not be wine — rum softened with cucumber and dill to go with that scallop number, for example.

Chef Tom Sellers **Owner** Tom Sellers **Seats** 40
Times 12-5/6.30-9.30, Closed 2 wks Aug, 2 wks Xmas, Sun-Mon **Prices** Fixed L 3 course fr £45 **Wines** 147 bottles over £30, 4 bottles under £30, 11 by glass **Parking** On street
Notes Fixed menu L Tue-Sat 7 course £80, D 6/10 course £75/£95, Children welcome

LONDON SE1 *continued*

Shangri-La Hotel at The Shard
PLAN 5 G6

◉ Modern European v NEW

tel: 020 7234 8008 & 7234 8000 **31 St Thomas St SE1 9QU**
email: ting.slln@shangri-la.com **web:** www.ting-shangri-la.com
dir: *Nearest station: London Bridge*

East meets West halfway up The Shard

Renzo Piano's Shard is home to the London branch of the international Shangri-La hotel group, or at least the 34th to the 52nd floors are. On 52, as they say, is the Gong cocktail bar, but you won't ascend quite as far into the mists to find the Ting fusion restaurant, which is on 35. Full-drop windows to torment the acrophobic throw all London before you, in a long room with fretwork-encased steel pillars and wine shelves. The menu hovers between Asian and European modes, more in a state of ambivalence than of fusion, but the cooking packs dynamic punch all the same. A brace of whopping scallops dressed in yuzu, mandarin and ginger is adorned with turned carrot, prior to a pinkly roasted serving of Rhug lamb loin, which comes with erengi mushrooms, apple and shiso in soy and sake dressing. Mirabelle plum crumble takes a surprisingly rustic approach, its chunky oat topping concealing sharp-flavoured fruit, with a matching sorbet and some vanilla cream to throw it into relief.

Chef Emil Minev **Owner** Shangri-La Hotel at The Shard, London **Seats** 95 **Times** 12-2.30/6-11.15 **Prices** Fixed L 2 course £29, Tasting menu fr £55, Starter £14-£19, Main £20-£38, Dessert £8-£12 **Wines** 218 bottles over £30, 16 by glass **Parking** 15, NCP London Bridge **Notes** Tasting menu 4 course £95 with wine, Children welcome

Skylon
PLAN 5 C6

◉ Modern British v

tel: 020 7654 7800 **Royal Festival Hall, Southbank Centre SE1 8XX**
email: skylonreservations@danddlondon.com
dir: *Nearest station: Waterloo Station*

Smart riverside dining at the Royal Festival Hall

Knock-out Thames-side views and its setting inside the Royal Festival Hall ensure that Skylon rocks. A real looker, the Southbank set up incorporates a hotspot centrepiece bar, swish grill and stellar restaurant. The triple-height space is dominated by a vast wall of windows waterside to offer those show-stopping views. The restaurant turns heads too, with striking chandelier-style lighting, soaring pillars, dramatic flower displays and low-slung contemporary seating, while a soothing colour palette and white linen relaxes the high-energy vibe. The restaurant kitchen speaks with a simple modern-British accent and pinch of panache without cheffy showboating, for example in an opener of melt-in-the-mouth smoked Lincolnshire eel teamed with crispy bacon potato cake and sweet sea kale salad. On the other hand, roasted wild sea bass is popped up with Swiss chard and a lightly spiced mussel casserole, while a signature cherry crème brûlée tart with basil sorbet and cherry salad is the way to finish. The slick service is sunny natured, while the wine list could grace any top-flight establishment.

Chef Adam Gray **Owner** D & D London **Seats** 100, Pr/dining room 33 **Times** 12-2.30/5.30-10, Closed 25 Dec, D Sun **Prices** Prices not confirmed **Wines** 260 bottles over £30, 16 bottles under £30, 18 by glass **Notes** Pre-theatre menu, Fixed menu 2/3 course £42/£48, Sunday L, Children welcome

Union Street Café
PLAN 5 E6

◉◉ Italian, Mediterranean

tel: 020 7592 7977 & 7592 1701 **47-51 Great Suffolk St SE1 0BS**
email: unionstreetcafe@gordonramsay.com
dir: *Nearest station: Southwark*

Ramsay's new warehouse-styled urban-chic Italian

David Beckham may have pulled out of backing this new venture with his pal Gordon Ramsay at the last moment, but it didn't do the opening's media frenzy any harm. The casual, urban-chic warehouse sheen makes it a big hit with the thirtysomethings, while switched-on casually clad staff fit the bill too. Trendy background music, funky lighting, buffed concrete, striking artwork and fashionable leather seating, keep it right on white-linen-free vogue, with an elevated open kitchen and cool vibe to boot. The cooking is Italian from chef Davide Degiovanni, and menus (in Italian) change daily to keep things fresh driven by the best market produce. Skilled simplicity and a confident light modern touch keep the food high on flavour. Take the crispiest fritto rammed with the freshest salt cod and teamed with silky peppers and vibrant salsa verde to open, while pasta might feature big-hit flavoured tagliatelle with rabbit, caciocavallo (cheese) and olives, or wobbly pannacotta perfection with 'wow' Yorkshire rhubarb compôte at dessert. The basement bar has an equally casual-chic, arty vibe, and the cocktails are a big draw.

Chef Davide Degiovanni **Owner** Gordon Ramsay Holdings Ltd **Seats** 125, Pr/dining room 18 **Times** 12-3/6-11, Closed 25-27 Dec, 1 Jan **Prices** Fixed L 2 course £19, Starter £7-£10, Main £19-£26, Dessert £6-£9 **Wines** 116 bottles over £30, 23 bottles under £30, 20 by glass **Parking** NCP, Ewer St **Notes** Events menu 3/4 course £35/£45, Sunday L £19-£45, Vegetarian available, Children welcome

Zucca
PLAN 5 H4

◉◉ Modern Italian v

tel. 020 7378 6809 **184 Bermondsey St SE1 3TQ**
email: reservations@zuccalondon.com
dir: *Nearest station: London Bridge*

Vibrant, compelling modern Italian cooking and a lively atmosphere

Chef-patron Sam Harris is one of a long line of River Café chefs who has gone on to do his own thing, serving up skilfully executed modern Italian cooking with the focus on tip-top seasonal ingredients in his upbeat Bermondsey eatery. It's a wide-open space full of light and activity thanks to a long wall of floor-to-ceiling windows, minimalist grey and white contemporary decor, and the buzz of cheffy goings-on behind the open kitchen counter. The compact menu changes daily, and the pricing is commendably reasonable for food of this quality. Antipasti are designed for sharing, and might open with namesake zucca fritti (zucca meaning pumpkin in Italian) or perhaps squid bruschetta, while splendid own-made pasta features rope-like corda pasta with pork and fennel ragu. Main course matches roast mallard with a tangy salmoriglio sauce, nutty farro grains and borlotti beans, while desserts include a lush vanilla pannacotta with poached apple and caramel. Super home-baked breads, informed service and some cracking Italian wines all add up to a class act.

Chef Sam Harris **Owner** Sam Harris **Seats** 64, Pr/dining room 10 **Times** 12-3/6-10, Closed 25 Dec, 1 Jan, Etr, Mon, D Sun **Prices** Starter £4.95-£13.95, Main £8-£18.95, Dessert £2.50-£10, Service optional **Wines** 141 bottles over £30, 11 bottles under £30, 12 by glass **Parking** On street **Notes** Sunday L £4.95-£18.95, Children welcome

Chapters All Day Dining

PLAN 1 H3

◉◉ Modern British

tel: 020 8333 2666 **43-45 Montpelier Vale, Blackheath Village SE3 0TJ**
email: chapters@chaptersrestaurants.co.uk **web:** www.chaptersrestaurants.com
dir: *Nearest station: Blackheath*

Blackheath Village eatery buzzing all day long

With a super location overlooking the heath from its alfresco pavement tables or through floor-to-ceiling windows, Chapters (relaxed sibling of big-hitting big-brother restaurant Chapter One) is an all-round hot ticket. Fashionable good looks (floorboards, banquettes, exposed brick, mirrors, dangling globe lights and a zinc-topped bar) pull in an appreciative young and young-at-heart crowd to the two-floored dine-all-day outfit at the heart of trendy Blackheath Village. It covers all the bases, from breakfast to weekend brunch, morning coffee to modern brasserie classics at lunch and dinner. Throw in daily specials, a fixed-price lunch option, kids' dishes, well-chosen wines (with plenty by glass or pichet) and accessible prices and everyone's happy. Conjured from quality ingredients, well-presented, clean-flavoured dishes might take in slow-roasted belly of Gloucestershire Old Spot pork with colcannon, caramelised apple and a cider velouté, or perhaps smoked haddock fishcake with creamed spinach, beurre blanc sauce and frisée salad, while from the Josper grill there might be rib-eye steak or Kentish double Barnsley lamb chop. Comfort desserts (Eton Mess, baked vanilla cheesecake) round off an accomplished, neighbourhood-restaurant act.

Times 8am-11pm, All-day dining, Closed 2-3 Jan

Franklins

PLAN 1 F2

◉ Seasonal British

tel: 020 8299 9598 **157 Lordship Ln, East Dulwich SE22 8HX**
email: info@franklinsrestaurant.com
dir: *Nearest station: East Dulwich*

Hearty British cooking on East Dulwich high street

British produce is celebrated zealously at Franklins, an exemplary neighbourhood eatery that combines the virtues of a pubby bar and a buzzy bistro at the rear that's all exposed brick, bare floorboards, big Victorian mirrors, and paper-clothed tables with an open view into the kitchen. The place takes an unbuttoned, no-nonsense approach, producing food from the more visceral end of the modern British spectrum in its concise, daily-changing menus with seasonal ideas based on simple combinations that make perfect sense. There are gutsy starters such as haslet – a meatloaf of chopped pork and offal – with home-made piccalilli, followed by straight-up platefuls of lamb's kidneys with Swiss chard and mustard, or hearty, no-frills ideas such as red leg partridge with butternut squash and bacon. Caramelised apple and almond frangipane tart keeps pudding firmly in the comfort zone.

Times 12-12, All-day dining, Closed 25-26 & 31 Dec, 1 Jan

The Palmerston

PLAN 1 F2

◉ Modern British, European

tel: 020 8693 1629 **91 Lordship Ln, East Dulwich SE22 8EP**
email: info@thepalmerston.co.uk
dir: *Nearest station: East Dulwich*

Modern cooking in a traditional East Dulwich pub

This classic Victorian corner pub in East Dulwich is an inviting prospect with its clubby wood panelling, racing-green leather banquettes and mismatched, scrubbed-wood tables and chairs – the ideal setting, in fact, for some switched-on contemporary pub cooking. A quick glance over the menu shows that this kitchen prizes seasonal British produce and has its heart in French and Mediterranean cuisine, so you can expect honest dishes full of robust flavours. Home-cured salt cod fritters with spiced tomato sauce and aïoli make a straight-talking opener, or you might kick off with smoked eel with beetroot, damson jelly, horseradish and mustard cress. Next up, grilled rabbit leg comes with a punchy stew of braised ganxet beans, chorizo, kale and salt-baked celeriac, and for pud, an inventive take on the trifle theme brings terrific English pink winter rhubarb with Swiss roll, amaretti and sherry.

Chef Jamie Younger, Robert Willcox **Owner** Jamie Younger, Paul Rigby, Remi Olajoyegbe **Seats** 70, Pr/dining room 26 **Times** 12-2.30/7-12, Closed 25-26 Dec, 1 Jan **Prices** Fixed L 2 course £14, Starter £7-£10, Main £16-£21, Dessert £6-£9 **Wines** 40 bottles over £30, 20 bottles under £30, 30 by glass **Parking** On street **Notes** Light menu 3-6pm, Sunday L £16-£18, Vegetarian available, Children welcome

Babur

PLAN 1 G2

◉◉ Modern Indian

tel: 020 8291 2400 **119 Brockley Rise, Forest Hill SE23 1JP**
email: mail@babur.info **web:** www.babur.info
dir: *Nearest station: Honor Oak Park*

Modern Indian cuisine in a cool brasserie-style setting

Babur is not hard to spot: just look for the life-size tiger prowling the roof. A quick glance through the plate glass frontage confirms that this is a long way from an average curry house. Inside the look is classy and modern: walnut veneer, exposed brickwork and limestone flooring meets brown-leather banquettes and industrial ducting — throw in a gallery of striking ethnic artworks and funky pendant lighting and the place really comes to life. The cooking has impact too, delivering an entertaining and adventurous canter through the contemporary Indian idiom, while wines are spice-friendly and the menu includes recommendations to match each main course. Quality ingredients — many not widely encountered in Indian cooking — and judicious spicing are graced with well-dressed presentation. Chargrilled monkfish tikka in spiced coconut broth is a lively starter, followed by meltingly tender spice-crusted shoulder of lamb with beetroot rice, or there might be rabbit, pot-roasted with mustard and ginger. Finish with an East-meets-West dessert of saffron and pistachio praline kulfi.

Chef Jiwan Lal **Owner** Babur 1998 Ltd **Seats** 72 **Times** 12-2.30/6-11.30, Closed 26 Dec, L 27 Dec, D 25 Dec **Prices** Tasting menu £32.95-£35.95, Starter £6.75-£8.50, Main £13.95-£17.95, Dessert £5.25-£6.95, Service optional **Wines** 12 bottles over £30, 38 bottles under £30, 13 by glass **Parking** 15, On street **Notes** Vegetarian tasting menu £29.95-£32.95, Sunday L £7.95-£13.95, Vegetarian available, Children welcome

See advert below

LONDON SW1

Adam Handling at Caxton
PLAN 4 K4

◎◎◎ — see below

Al Duca
PLAN 4 J6

◎ Modern Italian 🍷 NOTABLE WINE LIST

tel: 020 7839 3090 **4-5 Duke of York St SW1Y 6LA**
email: alduca@btconnect.com
dir: *Nearest station: Green Park*

Buzzy, fairly priced Italian in St James's

This upmarket and rather romantic Italian is tucked away in a discreet St James's street behind Fortnum & Mason. The smart contemporary decor — tiled floor, white linen on tables, toffee-brown and black leather seats — fits the posh location. Add a buzzy ambience and sensible pricing and it's clear why the place is perennially popular, although knowledgeable staff and a spot-on all-Italian wine list also play their part. The repertoire of uncomplicated classic and gently-modernised Italian dishes built on top-class ingredients has stood the test of time. Start with risotto with clams and saffron, followed by pan-fried fillet of cod with chickpeas and fresh tomatoes, or pan-fried pork belly with celeriac mash, sautéed Savoy cabbage and raisins. Finish with a textbook tiramisù or chocolate and almond cake with pistachio ice cream.

Chef Giovanni Andolfi **Owner** Cuisine Collection, Claudio Pulze **Seats** 56 **Times** 12-11, All-day dining, Closed Xmas, BHs, Sun **Prices** Prices not confirmed **Wines** 160 bottles over £30, 20 bottles under £30, 13 by glass **Parking** Jermyn St, Duke St **Notes** Pre/post-theatre 2/3 course £16.50/£19.50, Vegetarian available, Children welcome

Amaya
PLAN 4 G4

◎◎◎ — see opposite

Ametsa with Arzak Instruction
PLAN 4 G5

◎◎◎ — see opposite

Adam Handling at Caxton ❀❀❀

LONDON SW1
PLAN 4 K4

Modern European, British 🍷 NOTABLE WINE LIST

tel: 020 7222 7888 **2 Caxton St, St James Park, Westminster SW1H 0QW**
email: reservations@sterminshotel.co.uk **web:** www.caxtongrill.co.uk
dir: *Nearest station: Victoria, St James's Park*

Confident modern cooking in a luxury hotel

The eponymous Mr Handling was a runner-up in the BBC's *MasterChef: The Professionals* in 2013, while 2014 saw the publication of his first book. After an excellent few years, this talented chef has his name above the door here at the luxurious St Ermin's Hotel, with Adam Handling at Caxton offering a mix of creative contemporary cooking and staggeringly good steaks (the restaurant used to be called the Caxton Grill). It all takes place in a fashionable space done-out in shades of cream and grey, with a modern artworks and lots of designer touches — decidedly smart-casual. A tasting menu gives chef free rein to impress with an array of modern techniques and inspired flavour combinations, but there are thrills to be had on the à la carte, too, as well as those steaks cooked in the Josper oven (Scottish Buccleuch beef aged for 40 days and served with watercress, chips and a choice of sauce). Melt-in-the-mouth salmon with a light and creamy mousse comes with sweet-and-sour wasabi gels, while another starter partners piglet belly with octopus and a soy consommé. Another consommé makes an impression among main courses, a tea version this time, served with breast and legs of quail, plus sweetcorn purée and popcorn. Desserts are no less inventive, including the freebie number such as apple sorbet with G&T jelly that precedes the main event (a beautiful looking damson parfait with sour plums, perhaps). There's an outdoor terrace overlooking the courtyard where champagne cocktails and a menu of European and Asian bento boxes are up for grabs, while the bar has a fine collection of whiskies.

Chef Adam Handling, Sylvan Chevereau **Owner** Amerimar **Seats** 72, Pr/dining room 10 **Times** 12-2/6-10.30, Closed L Sat-Sun, 26 & 31 Dec **Prices** Tasting menu £70-£110, Starter £9-£18, Main £16-£50, Dessert £9.50 **Wines** 65 bottles over £30, 18 bottles under £30, 29 by glass **Parking** Valet parking **Notes** Vegetarian available, Children welcome

Amaya ✿✿✿

LONDON SW1   PLAN 4 G4

Modern Indian
tel: 020 7823 1166 **Halkin Arcade, Motcomb St SW1X 8JT**
email: amaya@realindianfood.com
dir: *Nearest station: Knightsbridge, Hyde Park, Sloane Sq*

Fine Indian cuisine with plenty of kitchen theatre

This high-gloss contemporary Indian operation has just celebrated a decade of wowing the well-heeled denizens of Knightsbridge with its ground-breaking tapas-style cooking. In fitting with the posh Halkin Arcade address, Amaya looks sleek and well-turned-out, with a glazed atrium ceiling, leather chairs at rosewood tables, brightly-coloured modern artwork from Kerala and Bengal on the walls, terracotta statuary and the all-important open-to-view kitchen. Here the cooking is based on three methods: the tandoor clay oven, tawa (flat griddle) and sigri (charcoal grill). Ingredients are of the first order, dishes are accurately timed, spicing and seasoning are spot on, and complex marinades and infused oils build layers of flavour. The format is flexible enough to suit most occasions: if you're a bit pushed for time or have a job to get back to, a lunchtime platter should fit the bill, but a more leisurely approach allows you to surrender to the rhythm of the kitchen by grazing through a succession of grilled, seared and tandoor-roasted dishes. These arrive in waves as and when they are ready, and it all changes so frequently that you won't know exactly what's on the menu until you turn up. First up, perfectly-seared scallops arrive in their shells with an aromatic coconut jus, then that old stager, chicken tikka, comes like you've never had it before, in succulent chunks packed with flavour and clearly-defined spices. The signature chargrilled Madagascan jumbo prawn delivers intricately-spiced chunks of sweet flesh, while elsewhere, there are a few curries and biryanis up for grabs – perhaps gosht nihari – lamb osso buco slow-cooked with mace and cardamom, before the curtain comes down on a textbook orange brûlée.

Chef Karunesh Khanna **Owner** R Mathrani, N & C Panjabi **Seats** 99, Pr/dining room 14 **Times** 12.30-2.15/6.30-11.30 **Prices** Fixed L 2 course £22.50, Tasting menu £60-£85, Starter £8-£27, Main £23-£38.50, Dessert £8.50-£10 **Wines** 93 bottles over £30, 20 by glass **Parking** NCP **Notes** Fixed D 6 course £80-£115, Sunday L, Vegetarian available, Children 3 yrs+

Ametsa with Arzak Instruction ✿✿✿

LONDON SW1   PLAN 4 G5

New Basque 🍷 NOTABLE WINE LIST
tel: 020 7333 1234 **Halkin St, Belgravia SW1X 7DJ**
email: ametsa.thehalkin@comohotels.com **web:** www.ametsa.co.uk
dir: *Nearest station: Hyde Park Corner*

Flavourburst Basque cuisine for a new age

If there is one regional cuisine that has risen from obscurity to epitomise everything that is exciting in the contemporary world of gastronomy, it has to be 'New Basque cuisine'. Nowadays, everyone is hot-footing it to the pintxo bars and stellar foodie destinations of San Sebastián such as Arzak, where the eponymous father-and-daughter team marry molecular techniques with the region's earthy flavours and splendid organic materials. As the rather unwieldy name implies, neither of these culinary explorers is actually in the kitchen of the London export on a day-to-day basis, but a team that has done time in the Spanish mothership interprets the style faithfully. The restaurant is located in the super-cool Halkin, a minimalist style-slave mecca, and its dining room looks futuristically pristine in brilliant white, with an impressive ceiling fashioned from 7,000 golden glass test tubes filled with spices. An à la carte menu supports the tasting menu, both packed with first-class ingredients, many of which are sourced from these shores. The craft and technique of the kitchen are evident from the off in a starter of seared scallops with squid ink sponge, enoki mushrooms, mojo sauce and truffle vinaigrette – a delicate plate of swipes and vivid colours. Next comes John Dory of exceptional quality with crisp tempura spheres of beetroot sauce, followed by beef fillet paired with green chillies dipped in port and red pepper gel, purées of onion, pea and mint and sea hawthorn sauce. Things end in the same vein at dessert, when clove custard with toasted milk and pineapple ice cream sounds like a car crash of a dish, but turns out to be a clever combination of finely judged flavours.

Chef Sergio Sanz **Owner** Halkin by COMO **Seats** 60, Pr/dining room 24 **Times** 12-2/6.30-10.30, Closed 24-26 Dec, 1 Jan, Sun, L Mon **Prices** Fixed L 2 course fr £27.50, Tasting menu £105-£154, Starter £16-£32, Main £26-£39, Dessert £12.50-£13.50 **Wines** 126 bottles over £30, 13 by glass **Parking** On street (after 6pm) **Notes** Fixed L 4 course £52, L Tasting menu £52-£68, Vegetarian available, Children welcome

LONDON SW1 *continued*

Avenue

PLAN 4 J6

◉ Modern British

tel: 020 7321 2111 **7-9 St James's St SW1A 1EE**
email: avenuereservations@danddlondon.com
dir: *Nearest station: Green Park*

Buzzy modern restaurant and bar with its heart in New York

The address may be quintessentially English, but the re-launched Avenue has been transformed into a stylish American gaff. Okay, there are elements of its voguish past, with its high ceilings and eclectic modern art, but today's soundtrack is Manhattan glam. The long bar sets a classy tone, while the restaurant spreads out behind around a centrepiece 'wine-glass' chandelier and decanting bar, instantly confirming wine as a key player. The big-city-cool look comes with semi-circular banquettes, trendy low-back chairs and funky 'tilting' lamps, while service is equally switched on. The kitchen delivers a take on modern American fare with a light, fresh, clean-flavoured touch characterised by a pinch of spice. Take signatures like clam chowder (served in hollowed-out sourdough with littleneck clams and paper bag 'crumbled' bay crackers) or desserts like 'donut holes' (with cinnamon sugar, raspberry jam and bourbon chocolate). In between, perhaps sea-fresh stone bass mains (with old bay spice pepping up a spring vegetable succotash) to Black Angus hamburgers or grain-fed beef steaks.

Times 12-3/5.45-11, Closed 25-26 Dec, 1 Jan, BHs, Sun, L Sat

A. Wong

PLAN 4 J3

◉◉ Chinese

tel: 020 7828 8931 **70 Wilton Rd, Victoria SW1V 1DE**
email: info@awong.co.uk
dir: *Nearest station: Victoria*

Exploring China's vast culinary range

Andrew Wong has brought a modern gastronomic sensibility to his regional Chinese operation in Victoria. Pointing out that China has 14 national borders, he aims to present a kaleidoscope of its food traditions, in the contemporary structure of bar and table seating, with a table in the kitchen for those who want to see it all happening. The showpiece is a 10-course tasting menu, which arcs gracefully from a 63-degree green tea egg on shredded filo with burning cinnamon bark, to a Shaanxi pulled lamb burger with Xinjiang pomegranate salad, and chilli-barbecued pineapple with Beijing street yogurt and Szechuan pepper ice cream. Dim sum are a long way from the high-street Cantonese: preserved vegetables and peanuts in chilli oil on Chengdu tofu; a pork-prawn dumpling topped with crackling; slivers of sesame-buttered chicken in satay. More substantial main dishes are stunning too; Scotch beef rump on rice noodle stir-fry, say, or braised abalone with shiitake mushrooms. East Asian flavours remain proudly assertive in desserts such as dragon fruit poached in star anise with an iced coconut dumpling and pandan jelly.

Chef Andrew Wong **Owner** Andrew Wong **Seats** 65, Pr/dining room 12
Times 12-2.30/5.30-10.30, Closed Xmas, Sun, L Mon **Prices** Prices not confirmed
Parking On street **Notes** Vegetarian available, Children welcome

Bar Boulud

PLAN 4 F5

◉◉ French, American 🍷 NOTABLE WINE LIST

tel: 020 7201 3899 **Mandarin Oriental Hyde Park, 66 Knightsbridge SW1X 7LA**
email: barboulud@mohg.com
dir: *Nearest station: Knightsbridge*

Very classy bistro cooking from superstar chef

Lyon via New York, Daniel Boulud is a big name stateside and his London restaurant doesn't lack for glitz and glamour. This is bistro food, albeit high cost bistro food with a bit of New York swagger, and it is a winning formula judging by the contented buzz in the room. Tables are turned, staff whizz about...it is terrific fun. The long zinc-topped bar is a cool spot to linger, and there's a charcuterie counter overlooking the open kitchen, or you might prefer to sink into one of the red leather banquettes in one of the interconnected dining rooms. The menu speaks French with English translations and offers up high-quality ingredients, prettily presented. An array of charcuterie, terrines and pâtés served with pickles and mustards is a great way to start, if you want to share. Or you might fancy the classy sausages (the spicy lamb merguez, perhaps with mint tabouleh and pepper stew). Main-course coq au vin or sea bass cooked a la plancha are classy rustic-chic main courses, and for dessert, pomme Bretonne or gâteau Basque await. Burgundy and the Rhône are the stars of the stellar wine list.

Chef Dean Yasharian, Daniel Boulud **Owner** Daniel Boulud **Seats** 168, Pr/dining room 20 **Times** 12-11, All-day dining **Prices** Prices not confirmed **Wines** 500 bottles over £30, 6 bottles under £30, 27 by glass **Parking** NCP Sloane St **Notes** Sunday L, Vegetarian available, Children welcome

Boisdale of Belgravia

PLAN 4 H3

◉ Traditional British v

tel: 020 7730 6922 **15 Eccleston St SW1W 9LX**
email: info@boisdale.co.uk
dir: *Nearest station: Victoria*

A bit of Scotland imported to London

A combination of jazz venue, bar and restaurant, Boisdale of Belgravia is spread over a number of rooms in a handsome townhouse, with a clubby decor and red walls hung with a profusion of pictures. As at its sibling in Bishopsgate, the cooking is built on fine Scottish produce, skilfully and accurately worked. Seared scallops with haggis and saffron-mashed potatoes are a happy blend of flavours, an alternative to another starter of seasonal asparagus with a poached duck egg and truffle vinaigrette. Top-quality Aberdeenshire steaks with a choice of sauces may vie for attention with the luxury of grilled lobster with garlic and parsley butter, although a gutsy dish of sautéed lamb's sweetbreads and braised kidneys, served with mustard and tarragon sauce, mash, and Savoy cabbage mixed with bacon, may be an option too.

Chef Colin Wint **Owner** Mr R Macdonald **Seats** 140, Pr/dining room 40
Times 12-3/6-11.15, Closed Xmas, New Year, Etr, BHs, Sun, L Sat **Prices** Fixed L 2 course £17.80, Fixed D 2 course £17.80, Starter £6.50-£19, Main £13.75-£28.50, Dessert £6.50-£8.50 **Wines** 172 bottles over £30, 27 bottles under £30, 22 by glass **Parking** On street, Belgrave Sq **Notes** Children welcome

Café Murano

PLAN 4 J6

◎◎ Northern Italian

tel: 020 3371 5559 **33 St James's St SW1A 1HD**
email: reception@cafemurano.co.uk
dir: *Nearest station: Green Park*

Celebrated chef Angela Hartnett's relaxed new St James's Italian

Little sister to grown-up Murano, this Angela Hartnett newcomer is anything but a 'café', rather a sophisticated, albeit relaxed, St James's take on a 'pop-in-every-day' Italian. It comes with in-place credentials and pizzazz, and service doesn't miss a beat. The snazzy, voguish, art deco-esque slim room is a looker from its marble-topped bar (decked out for bar dining) to wooden floors, brown leather banquettes and eye-catching lighting and mirrors. The cooking — under Hartnett's protégé Sam Williams — is equally on-cue, embracing that relaxed 'Murano' theme, with a northern Italian menu of simple, rustic (if refined, well-executed and presented) lightly portioned dishes conjured from top-notch produce. Witness classics like cichetti (big-hit truffle arancini) to freshly-made signature pasta, perhaps wonderful pappardelle with the meaty kick of a hogget ragu and olives. Fish might feature sparkling-fresh cod teamed with earthy castelfiorito lentils and a vibrant salsa verde. Desserts, such as prune and almond bake with lemon cream, hold-up afters form, likewise peripherals such as fabulous focaccia, while cracking Italian wines (and cocktails) also tempt. The set menu is particularly good value.

Chef Sam Williams **Owner** Angela Hartnett **Seats** 85, Pr/dining room 22 **Times** 12-2.45/5.30-10.45, Closed 25-26 Dec, D 24 & 31 Dec **Prices** Fixed L 2 course £18, Fixed D 3 course £22, Starter £8.50-£12, Main £16.50-£23, Dessert £5.50-£7 **Wines** 37 bottles over £30, 10 bottles under £30, 13 by glass **Notes** Fixed D 10-11pm, Sharing menu Sun £33 pp, Sunday L, Vegetarian available, Children welcome

CANVAS at Chelsea

PLAN 4 G3

see page 306

Le Caprice

PLAN 4 J6

◎ Modern European V

tel: 020 7629 2239 & 7016 5220 **Arlington House, Arlington St SW1A 1RJ**
email: reservations@le-caprice.co.uk
dir: *Nearest station: Green Park*

Renowned Mayfair favourite

There's an ageless feeling to this iconic Mayfair favourite just behind The Ritz. The predominantly black and white colour scheme remains in place, as do smart linen-covered tables, crockery stamped with the restaurant's own logo, and David Bailey's monochrome photographs of young-looking celebs on the walls. Plenty of staff deliver the goods from the pan-European menu with a bias towards comfort food. Creamy risotto with butternut squash, finely chopped cobnuts and melted taleggio is a fine rendition, while main courses are often the highlight: perhaps neat slices of Glencoe venison, meltingly tender, with creamed Savoy cabbage and an attention-grabbing plum tarte Tatin. Some ideas are pulled in from the East — seen in monkfish and prawn tikka masala with saffron pilaf, for instance — and among puddings might be chocolate mousse with orange ice cream.

Chef Andy McLay **Owner** Caprice Holdings **Seats** 86 **Times** 12-12, All-day dining, Closed 25-26 Dec, L 1 Jan, D 24 Dec **Prices** Prices not confirmed **Wines** 110 bottles over £30, 6 bottles under £30, 29 by glass **Parking** On street, NCP **Notes** Wknd brunch menu, Sunday L, Children welcome

Cavendish London

PLAN 4 J6

◎◎ British

tel: 020 7930 2111 **81 Jermyn St SW1Y 6JF**
email: info@thecavendishlondon.com web: www.thecavendishlondon.com
dir: *Nearest station: Green Park, Piccadilly*

Lively cooking in a smart hotel behind Fortnum and Mason

Among the gentlemen's outfitters and boutique emporia of Jermyn Street, the Cavendish lurks opposite the back entrance of Fortnum and Mason. The location is as chic as can be then, and the hotel interiors rise to the occasion with a plethora of striking modern paintings, and a first-floor dining room that may look out on St James's, but conjures in its name — Petrichor — the scent of freshly moistened earth after the first rains. Staff are acutely attentive and professional, as befits the ethos. The kitchen draws on thoroughbred suppliers for materials such as Wicks Manor pork, perhaps served as a croquette of the cheek meat, alongside a trio of garlic purées — white, black and wild green. After that, it may be fillets of salmon given extra depth with an accompaniment of crushed potatoes laced with smoked haddock and a vivid green pea velouté. Dessert produces the upstanding zestiness of lemon and orange posset with citrus salad, a tuile of popping candy and a scattering of tiny basil leaves.

Times 12-2.30/5.30-10.30, Closed 25-26 Dec, 1 Jan, L Sat-Sun & BH Mon

Céleste at The Lanesborough

PLAN 4 G5

see page 306

Le Chinois at Millennium Knightsbridge

PLAN 4 F4

◎ Chinese

tel: 020 7201 6330 **17 Sloane St, Knightsbridge SW1X 9NU**
email: lechinois@millenniumhotels.co.uk web: www.millenniumhotels.com/knightsbridge
dir: *Nearest station: Knightsbridge, Victoria*

Lengthy Chinese menu in a glam setting

The Millennium is a modern Sloaneland hotel aimed at the style-conscious, plumb in the vicinity of all the couture label shopping you could want. Rather than settle for another rendition of modern British, the principal dining room takes as its template the renowned Hua Ting restaurant at the Orchard Hotel in Singapore. Dark wood and plum-coloured light pillars, as well as a row of birdcage light fittings, make a bright backdrop to the refined Cantonese-based cooking on offer, which veers between textbook traditionalism and newer ideas. Open with a palate-priming bowl of Szechuan-style hot-and-sour lobster soup, or salt-and-pepper soft-shelled crab. Head-turning main dishes include sautéed prawns glazed in honey and lemon, steamed whole sea bass with preserved vegetables and shredded pork, and venison sizzling in ginger and spring onions on a hot stone plate. Chinese sweets such as red bean pancakes are a safe bet to finish on.

Chef Anthony Kong **Owner** Millennium Hotels **Seats** 65 **Times** 12-10.30, All-day dining **Prices** Prices not confirmed **Wines** 30 bottles over £30, 8 bottles under £30, 14 by glass **Parking** 8, Chargeable , NCP Pavilion Rd **Notes** Sunday L, Vegetarian available, Children welcome

CANVAS at Chelsea

LONDON SW1 PLAN 4 G3

Modern European
tel: 020 7823 4463 **1 Wilbraham Place, Belgravia SW1X 9AE**
email: info@canvasatchelsea.com
dir: Nearest station: Sloan Sq

Dynamic modern cooking in Chelsea

The Rosette award for this establishment has been suspended due to a change of chef. Reassessment will take place in due course under the new chef. In a quiet street not far from Sloane Square, having moved from Marylebone, the new basement location looks dapper with its pastel tones and splashes of black and red (from luxe leather seats). There's an oak-clad cocktail bar which is the place to head for if you like the sound of a caramelised passionfruit martini, or a classic white lady. The place has quite a buzz about it at busy times. The menu takes the tasting route, but with a difference in as much as you get to pick which of the 16 or so items you fancy — build your own tasting menu with options between five and a dozen courses. The wine list has some top-drawer stuff from around the world and care and attention has gone into making sure the wines match the food (take a wine flight and see for yourself). The vibrant nature of the cooking is evident from the off when an amuse-bouche black pudding ravioli with horseradish foam arrives. There are classic foundations to dishes such as a cod and pig's cheek number, but also a lightness of touch and a well-managed creativity. Duck and orange is familiar enough, but here it arrives as perfectly cooked breast, flavour-packed confit leg and the orange element as a sort of marmalade, plus corn in various forms and some baby gem — stunning. The attractive presentation and inventiveness continues into a dessert of crisp sablé biscuit topped with lemon cream, a lemony olive oil emulsion and a caramel disk. There's a chef's table and private dining area, too, while service is slick and friendly from start to finish.

Chef Ruben Aguilar Bel **Owner** Nick Wood, Phil Porter **Seats** 50, Pr/dining room 12 **Times** 12-2.30/5.30-9.30, Closed BHs, Mon-Tue, L Wed, D Sun **Prices** Fixed L 2 course £21-£23, Tasting menu £60-£70, Starter £15.50-£17.50, Main £21-£33, Dessert £10.50-£15.50 **Wines** 179 bottles over £30, 3 bottles under £30, 21 by glass **Parking** On street, Wilbraham Place **Notes** Pre-theatre meal offer 5.30-6.45pm, Sunday L £23-£27, Vegetarian available, Children welcome

Céleste at The Lanesborough

LONDON SW1 PLAN 4 G5

British, French
tel: 020 7333 7254 & 7333 7645 **Hyde Park Corner SW1X 7TA**
email: info@lanesborough.com
web: http://www.lanesborough.com/eng/restaurant-bars/celeste/
dir: *Nearest station: Hyde Park Corner*

Outstanding modern French cooking in ultra-luxe hotel

The Rosette award for this establishment has been suspended due to a change of chef. Reassessment will take place in due course under the new chef. A grand old mansion on Hyde Park Corner, The Lanesborough offers a world-class level of luxury and service pitched straight at celebs and oligarchs. But if you're not up for stratospherically priced rooms — personal butler included — you can get a taste of the hotel's plush glamour by booking a table at Céleste (formerly Apsleys), the opulent Venetian-style restaurant, where a glass-domed ceiling lights up blue and white friezes resembling delicate Wedgwood china, a trio of shimmering chandeliers, deep carpets, and tables resplendent with top-class crystal and silverware. After a volte-face in culinary direction, modern French cuisine is now the kitchen's thing, cooked with top-level skill under the aegis of Eric Frechon, a French super-chef at the top of his game. Day-to-day delivery of the Frechon style is down to the flair and talent of head chef Florian Favario who's been brought in from Frechon's stellar Epicure restaurant in the Parisian Le Bristol hotel. Céleste pairs a French kitchen and über-professional front-of-house team with resolutely British materials underpinning the first-class menu: Cornish turbot, say, poached in lemongrass butter with bok choi, carrot and ginger purée and fresh herb jus, while Welsh Lamb — grilled chops, roast saddle and braised sweetbreads — could appear alongside courgette, Israeli couscous and home-made harissa. Desserts are a bravura display of technical proficiency — perhaps Guanaja chocolate mousse, coffee ice cream and caramelised cashew praline.

Chef Florian Favario **Seats** 100, Pr/dining room 14 **Times** 12.30-2.30/7-10.30 **Prices** Prices not confirmed **Wines** 27 by glass **Parking** 25 **Notes** Tasting menu 5/7 course, Vegetarian available, Children welcome

LONDON SW1 *continued*

The Cinnamon Club

PLAN 5 A4

◉◉ Modern Indian 🏆 NOTABLE WINE LIST

tel: 020 7222 2555 **The Old Westminster Library, 30-32 Great Smith St SW1P 3BU**
email: info@cinnamonclub.com
dir: *Nearest station: Westminster, St James Park*

Inventive Indian food in a grand listed building

Former public buildings tend to make good venues, particularly ones built with a bit of empire pomp. Such is the old Westminster Library, with its handsome façade and galleried interior (including some shelves stacked with books in homage to days gone by). Tables are neatly laid, nicely spaced apart, and there's a high-end feel all round. On offer is some well-worked, classy modern Indian cooking that combines Asian and European techniques to deliver bang-on flavours. Bengali-style cod cakes with kasundi mustard, shrimp and coriander mayonnaise, for example, is a starter showing fine balance of flavours, the cake packed with fish, the cooking skills flying high. Ingredients are top quality, too, such as a generous main-course portion of chargrilled halibut with Kashmiri fennel, ginger sauce and curry leaf quinoa, while roasted loin of Oisin red deer might turn up with fenugreek potatoes, Indore korma and wild venison pickle. There are daily specials and desserts which tend more to the European perspective, such as lemon tart with bergamot sorbet and iced lemon mousse.

Chef Vivek Singh, Rakesh Ravindran **Owner** Indian Restaurant Ltd **Seats** 130, Pr/dining room 60 **Times** 12-2.45/6-10.45, Closed BHs (some), Sun, D 25 Dec **Prices** Fixed L 2 course £22, Fixed D 3 course £24, Tasting menu £75-£150 **Wines** 305 bottles over £30, 18 bottles under £30, 19 by glass **Parking** Abingdon St **Notes** Tasting menu 7 course, Pre-theatre 2/3 course £22/£24, Vegetarian available, Children welcome

Colbert

PLAN 4 G3

◉ French V

tel: 020 7730 2804 **50-52 Sloane Square, Chelsea SW1W 8AX**
email: info@colbertchelsea.com
dir: *Nearest station: Sloane Sq*

Paris comes to Sloane Square

Inspired by the grand boulevard cafés of Paris, the Colbert sits smack on Sloane Square and bustles with a wonderful feel-good vibe from breakfast to late evening, and is a good call for watching the world go by both inside and out. It's kitted out in a timeless art deco pastiche; think burgundy leather banquettes, wood panelling, chessboard floor and tightly packed tables, while walls come crammed with colourful Francophile posters and prints, and all is overseen by an energetic waiting team donning waistcoats and long white aprons. Owned by the same team behind the famous Wolseley, the Colbert runs like clockwork, with a lengthy all-day menu that doesn't talk three-course formality. Grab eggs Benedict or croque monsieur to top-dollar Beluga caviar, or steak tartare to sea-fresh lemon sole goujons with tartare, or crank up the ante with Chateaubriand for two – there's something for every occasion. The essence of the cooking is clean simplicity, defined by premium ingredients and flavour without cheffy grandstanding. Blackboard specials (bouillabaisse perhaps) bolster output, while the bar gets rammed and street-side alfresco tables are a hot ticket.

Chef Maarten Geschwindt **Owner** Corbin & King **Times** 8am-11.30pm, All-day dining **Wines** 50 bottles over £30, 8 bottles under £30, 37 by glass **Notes** Cover charge £1.75 L/D in dining rooms, Sunday L £19.75, Children welcome

Dinner by Heston Blumenthal

PLAN 4 F5

◉◉◉ – *see below*

Dinner by Heston Blumenthal ◉◉◉

LONDON SW1

PLAN 4 F5

British
tel: 020 7201 3833 **66 Knightsbridge SW1X 7LA**
email: malon-dinnerhb@mohg.com **web:** www.dinnerbyheston.com
dir: *Nearest station: Knightsbridge*

A culinary history lesson from Heston

Heston's history-themed sequel to The Fat Duck occupies a capacious space backing on to Hyde Park within the swanky Mandarin Oriental Hotel. His fascination with our culinary heritage has always played second fiddle to the molecular science stuff, so this is his chance to travel back to the past and delve into 500 years of historic British cooking. Despite the name, dinner is not actually by Heston, but by executive chef Ashley Palmer-Watts, who developed the menu with his Fat Duck mentor. As befits the Knightsbridge postcode, the setting is upscale, glossy and understated, with dark wood tables, neutral tones, lots of leather and fun detail in the porcelain jelly mould light fittings. The glassed-in kitchen takes centre stage, so you can watch the action at the Josper grill and see whole pineapples turning on clockwork rotisseries. Each dish on the menu is given a date of its approximate arrival on the culinary scene, ranging from 1390 to 1940. But this is not all about the past: the history angle is

a peg on which to hang some very 21st-century ideas, thus 'savoury porridge' is a first course dating from 1660, but delivers a very of-the-moment blend of crisp-crumbed frogs' legs with oats cooked in stock, chanterelles, garlic, parsley and fennel, while the 'Meat Fruit' (c. 1500) has pretty much been the signature dish from day one. And who'd have thought the Victorians would tuck into main-course roast sea bass with mussel and seaweed ketchup, salmon roe and sea rosemary? For dessert, go back to the late-Georgian era for tipsy cake with spit-roast pineapple. If the prices look a bit alarming, set lunch offers two choices per course.

Chef Ashley Palmer-Watts **Owner** Mandarin Oriental Hyde Park **Seats** 149, Pr/dining room 10 **Times** 12-2.30/6.30-10.30, **Prices** Fixed L 3 course £38, Starter £16.50-£18.50, Main £28-£42, Dessert £12-£14.50 **Wines** 500 bottles over £30, 25 by glass **Parking** Valet parking, NCP **Notes** Vegetarian available, Children welcome

51 Buckingham Gate, Taj Suites and Residences · PLAN 4 J4

◉ Modern Mediterranean **NEW**

tel: 020 7769 7766 **SW1E 6AF**
email: kona.london@tajhotels.com **web:** www.taj51buckinghamgate.co.uk
dir: *Nearest station: St James Park, Victoria*

Southern European menu in opulent surroundings

Butler service comes as standard to anybody booking a suite at the Taj group's elegant historic premises near the Palace. You'd expect nothing less. The welter of dining options includes Kona, a chic parquet-floored room adorned with smoked mirrors and an eclectic display of artworks, where the culinary inspiration is southern European. Foie gras with damsons and Marcona almonds seems a suitably opulent starting point in the surroundings, but so does a bowl of velvety lobster bisque with a quenelle of white crabmeat and crème fraîche. At main course, there is no stinting on quality of prime materials for sea bass with squid and chorizo, or pinkly tender cannon and bolognaise of Cotswold lamb, served with well-made polenta and pesto. Finish with a brioche tart of caramelised apple with hazelnut crumble and cinnamon ice cream, or a thyme-poached plum with lemon sponge, lemon mint sorbet and candied pistachios.

Chef David Tilly, Thomas Cruise **Owner** Taj Hotels and Resorts **Seats** 44, Pr/dining room 12 **Times** 7-10.30, Closed Sun, L all week **Prices** Tasting menu £50, Starter £6-£10, Main £12-£34, Dessert £7-£9 **Wines** 63 bottles over £30, 13 bottles under £30, 8 by glass **Notes** Tasting menu 7 course, Vegetarian available, Children 5 yrs+

The Goring · PLAN 4 H4

◉◉◉ — *see below*

The Goring ◉◉◉

LONDON SW1 · PLAN 4 H4

Traditional British ᵛ 🍷 NOTABLE WINE LIST

tel: 020 7396 9000 **Beeston Place SW1W 0JW**
email: diningroom@thegoring.com **web:** www.thegoring.com
dir: *Nearest station: Victoria*

A century-old family-run hotel with classical and modern cooking

The Goring family has owned this grand hotel since its opening in 1910. It was to be the last new London hotel in the reign of Edward VII. A century and a bit later, it remains proudly within the family, and is still frequented by the international notability. It's only a short saunter to Buckingham Palace, so has always been very handy for when those garden-party invites come through. The Goring is run with impeccable old-school civility, but it doesn't rest on its style laurels. This is clear from the lounge-bar livery of red-hot burgundy and mustard, although the dining room aims to soothe with accents of regal gold and white. Shay Cooper has worked assiduously to achieve the elusive balance between classical reassurance and modernist freshness that suits a place like The Goring, and the results are impressive. You might start with a favourite dish of the late Queen Mother: eggs Drumkilbo, a grand luxe crab cocktail with grated egg and cucumber, garnished with lobster claw, dots of caviar and apple jelly. So far, so nostalgic, but main courses might bring curry-spiced Romney Marsh lamb with roast cauliflower, duck with stuffed prunes and chervil root, or a showcase of concentrated flavour in a golden-crusted tranche of roast cod with baby fennel, buttered leeks and a deep-fried oyster. At the finishing line, there are plenty of old favourites, including an utterly reliable brandy-sauced Christmas pudding in December. There's much to delight bright young things too, such as sea buckthorn in the baked Alaska, and a chocolate ganache accompanied by barley malt caramel and popcorn ice cream.

Chef Shay Cooper **Owner** The Goring family **Seats** 70, Pr/dining room 50 **Times** 12-2.30/6-10, Closed L Sat **Prices** Fixed L 3 course fr £42.50, Fixed D 3 course fr £52.50 **Wines** 450 bottles over £30, 5 bottles under £30, 22 by glass **Parking** 7 **Notes** Pre-theatre 2 course £35, Sunday L, Children welcome

Grand Imperial London

PLAN 4 H4

◉ Cantonese, Chinese V

tel: 020 7821 8898 **The Grosvenor, 101 Buckingham Palace Rd SW1W 0SJ**
email: reservations@grandimperiallondon.com
dir: *Nearest station: Victoria*

Upscale Chinese dining in a Victorian setting

Classic and modern Cantonese cooking in a grand Victorian building is the USP of the Grand Imperial. The two elements combine very well indeed in the stylish and refined restaurant with the room's splendid proportions and period details enhanced by some smart oriental touches. There's a dim sum menu at lunchtime, with some impressive upscale options such as chicken sui mai with black truffle, or a black cod dumpling with saffron. There's a dim sum option among first courses on the carte, too, or else you might kick off with crispy duck salad or golden king prawns with wasabi mayo. Soups such as a beef broth with mushroom are an option before main courses of baked black cod with miso, deep-fried duck with lemon sauce, or pork ribs with barbecue and honey sauce. Set menus can make ordering a breeze, and there's a swanky tasting version, too.

Chef Rand Cheung **Owner** Grand Imperial & Guoman Hotels **Seats** 140, Pr/dining room 26 **Times** 12-10.45, All-day dining, Closed 25-26 Dec **Prices** Prices not confirmed **Wines** 60 bottles over £30, 10 bottles under £30, 12 by glass **Parking** NCP **Notes** Meal deals, Sunday L, Children welcome

House of Ho

PLAN 2 K1

◉ Modern Vietnamese

tel: 020 7287 0770 **55-59 Old Compton St, Soho W1D 6HR**
email: info@houseofho.co.uk
dir: *Nearest station: Piccadilly Circus*

Buzzy Vietnamese joint with a fusion flavour

Bobby Chinn is quite the star in Asia with TV shows, books and a restaurant in Hanoi to his name, and now he's in Old Compton Street with a lively, buzzy place that fits right into the Soho scene. Tables are close together, cocktails rule, and the food is a mix of traditional and contemporary Vietnamese. There are evident influences from France as the two countries' food cultures are very much entwined (former colony and all), plus Bobby's time in London, Egypt and San Francisco. From the 'Light & Raw' section comes duck 'a la banana' blossom salad or spicy salmon tartare, while 'Hot & Grilled' delivers barbecue baby back ribs with a light Asian slaw. Sharing is the way to go, with apple-smoked pork belly with braised cabbage and chicken potato curry coming in generous portions. Finish with lemon-scented crème brûlée.

Times 12-close, All-day dining, Closed 25 Dec, New Year

Il Convivio

PLAN 4 G3

◉◉ Modern Italian

tel: 020 7730 4099 **143 Ebury St SW1W 9QN**
email: ilconvivio@etruscarestaurants.com **web:** www.ilconvivio.co.uk
dir: *Nearest station: Victoria, Sloane Sq*

Smart, friendly modish Italian in Belgravia

A family-owned Italian, set on swanky Ebury Street in a trim Georgian townhouse, Il Convivio is an evergreen favourite of the smart Belgravia set. Its name is inspired by Dante's poem, which translates as 'a meeting over food and drink', and lines from his poems are inscribed on the red and cream walls of the grown-up, yet relaxed, split-level space. Cream leather seating, white linen and wood flooring set the scene, and, while tables upfront overlook the street, the light-filled conservatory area at the back – with fully retractable roof for alfresco dining – is the top call. The predominantly Italian wine list shows serious intent from the off, while the kitchen doesn't hold back either, with modern renditions of classic combinations underpinned by quality Italian and British seasonal produce. Witness homemade pasta, like limoncello tagliolini combined with palourde clams, broccoli, datterini tomato tartare and Sardinian bottarga, while, from the bank-manager-friendly fixed-price lunch menu, perhaps 'sparkling-fresh' pan-fried sea trout served with crushed maris pipers, black olives and 'sweet' sun-dried tomatoes. Finish on a high, with an innovatively presented pistachio pannacotta with orange marmalade, open cannoli tuile and ricotta ice cream.

Chef Cedric Neri **Owner** Piero & Enzo Quaradeghini **Seats** 65, Pr/dining room 14 **Times** 12-3/6-11, Closed Xmas, New Year, BHs, Sun **Prices** Fixed L 2 course £17.50, Fixed D 3 course £29, Starter £8.50-£21, Main £17.50-£24, Dessert £6-£9.50 **Wines** 142 bottles over £30, 28 bottles under £30, 14 by glass **Parking** On street **Notes** Vegetarian available, Children welcome

LONDON SW1 *continued*

Inn the Park
PLAN 5 A5

🌸 British

tel: 020 7451 9999 **St James's Park SW1A 2BJ**
email: reservations@innthepark.com
dir: *Nearest station: St James's Park, Charing Cross, Piccadilly*

Honest, seasonal British cooking in the heart of a London park

In a fantastic location by the lake in St James's Park beneath a verdant canopy of stately plane trees, this curving wooden building is just the spot to enjoy Central London's park life in a happy, bustling atmosphere. Thanks to full-length walls of sliding glass, the interior is a striking, light-flooded space with a clean-lined, Scandinavian-feeling decor of tubular steel chairs, tooled black leather banquettes and apricot-topped tables. But it's the covered wooden terrace that is the hot ticket when warm weather strikes and you're in the market for fresh, impeccably seasonal British produce prepared with pleasing simplicity. Grilled squid, maple-cured bacon and blistered tomatoes is a bright and cheerful dish bursting with the feel of summer, followed by whole Cornish megrim sole partnered with crab vinaigrette and crushed new potatoes with diced tomato, green herbs and white crabmeat, or you might go for honey-glazed, herb-fed chicken with smoked potatoes, broad beans, peas and bacon.

Chef Craig Milnes **Owner** Oliver Peyton **Seats** 140 **Times** 12-11, Closed 25 Dec, D Sun (Oct-Apr) **Prices** Starter £6-£9, Main £12-£19, Dessert £6 **Wines** 10 bottles over £30, 15 bottles under £30, 13 by glass **Parking** On street **Notes** Breakfast, Afternoon tea, Sunday L £16, Vegetarian available, Children welcome

Ken Lo's Memories of China
PLAN 4 H3

🌸 Chinese

tel: 020 7730 7734 **65-69 Ebury St SW1W 0NZ**
email: moc@londonfinedininggroup.com
dir: *Nearest station: Victoria*

Classy Chinese dishes at a long-standing Belgravia venue

A generation of well-heeled Belgravia custom has trooped through the sumptuous upscale restaurant created by the late Kenneth Lo, one of modern Chinese gastronomy's early movers and shakers in the capital. Oriental screen dividers, smartly clothed tables and a bottle-store create a fine-dining ambience for classy Chinese cooking from all the regions. A gargantuan menu in the classical idiom features delights such as Pekingese guo-tie fried dumplings filled with chicken, garlic, ginger and spring onion with a vinegary dipping sauce, as well as pepperpot fish soup, luxurious stir-fried lobster with noodles. Look out for guo da chicken in omelette batter sauced in rice vinegar and garlic, iron-plate sizzling dishes of salmon or beef, and sides such as Yangchow fried rice with shrimp, chicken and peas. Fixed-price set menus offer a traditional way of experiencing the range, and there is even the odd tempting dessert such as spun-sugar glazed apple and banana with vanilla ice cream.

Times 12-2.30/6-11, Closed 25-26 Dec

Koffmann's
PLAN 4 G5

🌸🌸🌸 – *see below*

Marcus
PLAN 4 G5

🌸🌸🌸🌸🌸 – *see opposite*

Koffmann's 🌸🌸🌸

LONDON SW1   PLAN 4 G5

French 🍷 NOTABLE WINE LIST

tel: 020 7235 1010 **The Berkeley, Wilton Place SW1X 7RL**
email: koffmanns@the-berkeley.co.uk
dir: *Nearest station: Knightsbridge, Hyde Park Corner*

Top-grade regional French cooking from a virtuoso

Within The Berkeley, with its own entrance, Koffmann's is a light and spacious restaurant with a decor of pale neutral shades offset by large flower displays and comfortable chairs and banquettes at formally set tables, appropriately plush surroundings for the inspired cooking of culinary legend Pierre Koffmann. His seasonally-inspired menus focus on the cuisine of his native southwest France, based on top-drawer produce and first-class technical execution, delivered by formal and attentive staff with a genuine approach to hospitality. Crab salad is a beautifully presented starter, its accompaniments of avocado and grapefruit adding richness and acidity in equal measure, forming a simple but much appreciated dish. Hot foie gras with Sauternes sauce and chicory is a classic idea, while other starters push the boundaries to add variety: Thai-spiced seared scallops, for instance, or bolognese-style squid. Aficionados will not be disappointed to see a signature dish of pig's trotter stuffed with sweetbreads and morels and full-blooded beef cheeks braised in red wine. If there's an element of comfort food to such dishes,

the style is more notable for its lack of frills and flounces, so flavours are bright and clear. Sole poêlée grenobloise, taken off the bone at table speedily and precisely, the fish of exceptional quality with melt-in-the-mouth finish, comes with no more than fresh and zingy tomato, caper and parsley butter along with château potatoes and broccoli, and grilled lobster with herb butter. The attention to detail is unwavering. Breads are excellent, canapés too, and pastry is made by a master, seen in tarte au citron and pear frangipane tart, while chocoholics will not be let down by light but rich dark chocolate mousse.

Chef Pierre Koffmann **Owner** Pierre Koffmann **Seats** 120, Pr/dining room 16 **Times** 12-2.30/6-10.30, **Prices** Fixed L 2 course fr £22.50, Fixed D 3 course fr £28, Tasting menu £80-£100, Starter £12-£16, Main £22-£29, Dessert £9-£15 **Wines** 260 bottles over £30, 6 bottles under £30, 16 by glass **Parking** Knightsbridge car park **Notes** Pre-theatre menu 2/3 course £24/£28, Sunday L £22.50-£26, Vegetarian available, Children welcome

Marcus ✿✿✿✿✿

LONDON SW1   **PLAN 4 G5**

Modern European, British **V** ⚬ NOTABLE WINE LIST

tel: 020 7235 1200 **Wilton Place, Knightsbridge SW1X 7RL**
email: reservations@marcuswareing.com
web: www.marcus-wareing.com
dir: *Nearest station: Knightsbridge, Hyde Park Corner*

Impeccable benchmark contemporary cooking

Viewers of BBC's *MasterChef: The Professionals* might have noticed a more mellow Marcus Wareing on their screens in the 2014 series. A little less scary. It's TV, not real life, but the change to a more reflective and compassionate position arrived at the same time as he dropped his surname from the designation of his eponymous restaurant in 2014; a sign of the times, maybe, and an indication that his profile has reached a place where the single name identifier is all that is needed. Marcus – the man – has been involved with The Berkeley for over a decade, with the relaunch in 2014 cementing his restaurant's place as one of the foremost dining opportunities in London. A chunky piece of Knightsbridge real estate that would be worth gazillions on the open market, the hotel itself is a luxurious five-star outfit that makes an ideal location for a restaurant that reaches such heady heights of achievement. Marcus – the restaurant – has the sort of genteel refinement you might expect at this level (and at these prices), so plenty of space between the immaculately set tables, and a few striking contemporary artworks to shake up the discreetly elegant interior. The engaging service team work tirelessly (and seemingly effortlessly) to ensure that every element of the experience meets the exacting standards set. Wareing has three restaurants in his group, which is modest by the standards of today's new entrepreneurial breed of chefs, and means he's able to play close attention to his flagship address, while the kitchen is headed-up by Mark Froydenlund. Lunchtimes offer a tantalising opportunity via a menu that, if not quite a bargain, is very good value at this level, but having gone to the trouble of securing a table, the boat is surely there to be pushed out. The combination of superb ingredients, measured and creative thinking and precise execution results in compelling stuff from the carte and tasting menu such as a foie gras starter that deftly uses blood orange to cut through its richness, or another that matches veal sweetbreads with flavours and textures of pear and almond. Everything looks spectacular on the plate, but elegantly so – there's no grandstanding here, for everything is on the plate for a reason. Herdwick mutton makes a welcome appearance, with calçot (a type of spring onion from northern Spain) and radicchio, while a fish option combines turbot and Dorset snails in a captivating partnership. Desserts can be deconstructions of classic dishes, where the flavours are already proven winners, but there's always a level of surprise and excitement – white chocolate, damson and sarsaparilla, for example. The cheese trolley is not bettered anywhere in the country and is hard to resist, while the wine list of over 1,000 bins has all the big guns alongside some more unusual options.

Chef Marcus Wareing, Mark Froydenlund **Owner** Marcus Wareing Restaurants Ltd **Seats** 90, Pr/dining room 16
Times 12-2.30/6-10.45, Closed 5-7 Jan, Sun, L 8 Jan
Prices Prices not confirmed **Wines** 950 bottles over £30, 13 by glass **Parking** NCP, on street, valet **Notes** Children welcome at lunch only

LONDON SW1 *continued*

Mint Leaf Restaurant & Bar

PLAN 5 A6

Modern Indian

tel: 020 7930 9020 **Suffolk Place, Haymarket SW1Y 4HX**
email: reservations@mintleafrestaurant.com **web:** www.mintleafrestaurant.com
dir: *Nearest station: Piccadilly, Charing Cross*

Inspired modern Indian food at a seductive West End address

A contemporary Indian eaterie to grace the West End, the Mint Leaf is on a corner of one of the side-streets off Haymarket. Its interiors are svelte and seductive, a dimly lit mood prevailing in the dramatic cocktail bar and the main restaurant, where angled spotlights enhance the varnished tabletops and quality glassware, as well as the colourful, assertively spiced dishes. The menu teems with original and inspired preparations, from lime- and garlic-marinated tiger prawns in mango salsa, or beetroot and potato cake with papaya chutney, to mains such as sea bass steamed in a banana leaf with ginger, coriander and coconut, or the sublimely fiery duck and pepper stir-fry with red onions, curry leaves, garlic, star anise and black cardamom. Vegetarian dishes are full of imagination too, for example stuffed peppers with spiced potato, corn and aubergine, dressed with tomato and coriander chutney. Finish with blueberry kulfi, served with a warm compôte of summer berries.

Chef Rajinder Pandey **Owner** Out of Africa Investments **Seats** 144, Pr/dining room 66 **Times** 12-3/5.30-11, Closed 25-26 Dec, 1 Jan, L Sat-Sun **Prices** Prices not confirmed **Wines** 100 bottles over £30, 17 bottles under £30, 13 by glass **Parking** NCP, on street **Notes** Pre-theatre menu 5-7pm 2/3 course £13.95/£17.95, Vegetarian available, Children welcome

Osteria Dell'Angolo

PLAN 5 A4

Italian

tel: 020 3268 1077 **47 Marsham St SW1P 3DR**
email: osteriadell_angolo@btconnect.com
dir: *Nearest station: St James's Park, Westminster*

Italian classics in the heart of Westminster

The kitchen of this contemporary Italian in the heart of Westminster near to the Houses of Parliament has its finger firmly on the regional pulse of Tuscan cuisine. After a glass of prosecco in the smart darkwood bar, take a seat in the dining room where butch burgundy leather contrasts with white linen and the Mediterranean warmth of a yellow and amber colour scheme. Well-sourced artisan produce from Italy and splendid true-Brit materials work together in dishes such as grilled Cornish squid filled with Swiss chard, capers, pine kernels, stracciatella Pugliese cheese and black olives, while home-made gnocchi are stuffed with goats' cheese and served with wild mushrooms, pumpkin and sage sauce. Full-flavoured mains run to roast monkfish with osso buco sauce, sautéed radicchio, and toasted almond and red wine sauce, or grilled Galloway beef fillet with turnip tops and a timbale of borlotti beans and leeks.

Chef Massimiliano Vezzi **Owner** Claudio Pulze **Seats** 80, Pr/dining room 22 **Times** 12-3/6-10.30, Closed Xmas, New Year, last 2 wks Aug, BHs, Sun, L Sat **Prices** Fixed L 2 course £17.50, Starter £7.50-£12, Main £13-£25, Dessert £5.50-£9 **Wines** 200 bottles over £30, 8 bottles under £30, 12 by glass **Parking** 6 **Notes** Vegetarian available, Children welcome

Park Plaza Victoria London

PLAN 4 J3

Italian

tel: 020 7769 9771 **239 Vauxhall Bridge Rd SW1V 1EQ**
email: reservations@tozirestaurant.co.uk **web:** www.tozirestaurant.co.uk
dir: *Nearest station: Victoria*

Venetian sharing plates in a contemporary space

The Fiat 500 at the entrance of the TOZI Restaurant & Bar of the swanky Park Plaza is a clue to what lies ahead. Venetian cicchetti is the name of the game, those fashionable sharing plates of punchy Italian flavours, and it all takes place in a snazzy modern room with an open kitchen and full-length windows. With lots of natural wood and neutral colours, this is a classy and chilled-out environment with a bar that can turn out a nifty Bellini or spritz. Veal ravioli with girolles shows that the kitchen can cook, as the dish provides a nicely judged delicate earthiness, and there is soft-shelled crab, too, with red chilli and parsley sauce. There are good meats such as wild boar salami from Umbria, and aged Parma ham, plus pizetta and piadina cooked in the wood-fired oven. Berries and limoncello millefoglie is a well-balanced finish.

Chef Maurilio Molteni **Owner** Park Plaza Hotels **Seats** 100, Pr/dining room 20 **Times** 12-10.30, All-day dining **Prices** Tasting menu £40-£50, Starter £3.75-£12.50, Main £7.25-£23, Dessert £5.75 **Wines** 48 bottles over £30, 13 bottles under £30, 12 by glass **Notes** Sunday L, Vegetarian available, Children welcome

Pétrus

PLAN 4 G5

– *see opposite*

Quaglino's

PLAN 4 J6

European NEW

tel: 020 7930 6767 **16 Bury St SW1Y 6AJ**
email: quaglinos@danddlondon.com
dir: *Nearest station: Green Park, Piccadilly Circus*

Glamorous brasserie dining on the cruise-ship scale

A star is reborn. Quaglino's is too much of a legend of London dining to fade away for long and, under its present ownership, has come roaring back out of the traps. Once the favoured watering-hole of such as Evelyn Waugh and the future Edward VIII, it's a masterpiece of art deco style on the cruise-ship scale, complete with a golden-lit descending entrance staircase to tempt out your inner Gloria Swanson. Tables fan out around a horseshoe-shaped bar counter, and the smart set dines on turbo-charged brasserie food, thoroughbred wines and the coolest cocktails. Flavours and seasonings need to assert themselves in this context, and they shine from the plate: soused charred mackerel with mustard onion compôte and vodka dill pickle won't get forgotten in a hurry. Mains offer trimly presented meats such as roast breast and croquetted leg of pheasant with cabbage and pear in truffled jus, or perhaps a whole sea bass for sharing, served on saffron pilaf and beurre blanc. A profiterole makeover sees a ball of cracked choux filled with salted caramel, but still doused in chocolate sauce by the waiter as of old.

Chef Mickael Weiss **Seats** Pr/dining room 36 **Times** 12-3/5.30-11 **Prices** Fixed L 3 course £30, Fixed D 3 course £30, Starter £8.25-£11.50, Main £13-£39.50, Dessert £2.50-£7.50 **Wines** 113 bottles over £30, 9 bottles under £30, 20 by glass **Notes** Brunch menu, Fixed D 5.30-7pm

Quilon

PLAN 4 J4

Indian **NOTABLE WINE LIST**

tel: 020 7821 1899 **41 Buckingham Gate SW1E 6AF**
email: info@quilonrestaurant.co.uk **web:** www.quilon.co.uk
dir: *Nearest station: St James's Park, Victoria*

Upmarket decor and traditional and contemporary Indian cuisine

Quilon has the sort of designer-led, ultra-modern interior that looks as if it had money thrown at it, with a predominantly gold colour scheme, some wooden latticed screens and comfortable chairs and banquettes. It's no surprise to know that a parliamentary division bell rings here when MPs need to vote. The cooking concentrates on the cuisine of India's southwest coastal region, mixing traditional and more progressive recipes, with tip-top materials the backbone of the kitchen's output. Masala dosai filled with 'tempered' potatoes and vegetables is subtly spiced with ginger, garlic and turmeric, served with rich and flavoursome sambar, while seafood broth spiked with coriander is an authentic dish of the area. Main courses are well up to snuff too, among them roast quail stuffed with minced meat flavoured with chilli, ginger, onion and spices served with mustard sauce, and equally judiciously spiced baked black cod. The kitchen pays the same care and attention to rice and breads, there's a decent showing of vegetarian dishes, and desserts may run to caramelised banana pudding with parfait.

Quilon

Chef Sriram Aylur **Owner** Taj International Hotels **Seats** 90, Pr/dining room 16 **Times** 12-2.30/6-11, Closed 25 Dec **Prices** Prices not confirmed **Wines** 130 bottles over £30, 4 bottles under £30, 16 by glass **Parking** On street, NCP **Notes** Sunday L, Vegetarian available, Children welcome

---

Pétrus ❀❀❀

LONDON SW1

PLAN 4 G5

Modern French **v**
tel: 020 7592 1609 **1 Kinnerton St, Knightsbridge SW1X 8EA**
email: petrus@gordonramsay.com
dir: *Nearest station: Knightsbridge, Hyde Park, Sloane Sq*

Immaculate modern French cooking from the Ramsay stable

Restaurant Gordon Ramsay in Royal Hospital Road may well be the flagship of Mr Ramsay's empire, but Pétrus runs it a very close second when it comes to delivering dynamic modern French food in a smart and luxurious setting. The dining room is based around a feature walk-in glass wine store, which has a functional purpose and aesthetic appeal. It's a sophisticated space with neutral creamy colours perked up by a rich reds (a splash of pétrus perhaps?), and the well-spaced tables dressed up for the business of fine dining. The service team are entirely on message. The kitchen is headed up by new man Neil Snowball, and there's good reason to be very optimistic indeed about the future of Pétrus. Via a tasting menu, à la carte and set lunch version, the chef and his team deliver contemporary dishes that fizz with excitement and technical accomplishment. A starter of Cheltenham beetroot terrine, for example, elevates the humble veg to star status, along with fresh goats' curd, shaved fennel with buttermilk, and a scattering of horseradish snow – impressive stuff. Next up, it's the turn of wood pigeon to steal the show, in the classic company of Alsace bacon and Puy lentils, plus endive perked up with blood orange, or go for fillet of Cornish brill with cuttlefish and ceps bolognaise. A dessert of seared pineapple with smoked coconut and a lime sorbet tastes as good as it looks, while chocolate lovers might prefer to lose themselves in the chocolate sphere. The wine list is full of heavyweight contenders and includes a page dedicated to Pétrus starting at a little over three grand.

Chef Neil Snowball **Owner** Gordon Ramsay Holdings Ltd **Seats** 55, Pr/dining room 8 **Times** 12-2.30/6.30-10.30, Closed 22-26 Dec, Sun **Prices** Fixed L 3 course £37.50, Fixed D 3 course £75, Tasting menu £95 **Wines** 428 bottles over £30, 2 bottles under £30, 27 by glass **Parking** On street (free after 6.30pm)/NCP Park Towers **Notes** Chef's menu 5 course, Children welcome

LONDON SW1 *continued*

The Rib Room
PLAN 4 F4

@@@ *– see below*

Roux at Parliament Square
PLAN 5 B5

@@@ *– see opposite*

The Royal Horseguards
PLAN 5 B6

@@ Modern British

tel: 020 7451 9333 & 7451 0390 **2 Whitehall Court SW1A 2EJ**
email: 1212royalhorseguards@guoman.co.uk web: www.guoman.co.uk
dir: *Nearest station: Embankment, Charing Cross*

Enterprising cooking near Whitehall

Aficionados of black-and-white thrillers might spot the reference to Scotland Yard's long-gone phone number – Whitehall 1212 – which lives on in One Twenty One Two, the fine-dining restaurant of this regal Victorian Thames-side hotel (the rozzers were once neighbours). The grand old pile was home to the Secret Service in World War I, and now makes an upmarket base for London's central attractions. Its posh restaurant comes kitted out with plushly-upholstered crimson banquettes and seats, and white linen on the tables, and deals in appealing modern brasserie-style food with its roots in French classics. Expect starters such as Old Spots pork belly with braised pineapple, port jus and bitter cress, or wood pigeon with smoked potato mash, bok choy and mulled wine jus. Move on to venison loin with Lyonnaise potatoes, sprouts, chestnuts and English ham, or straightforward grills – beef rib, perhaps with a choice of classic sauces. To finish, perhaps a pineapple variant of

tarte Tatin jazzed up with caramel, spiced passionfruit sauce and coconut crunch ice cream.

Chef Ryan Matheson **Owner** GLH Hotels Management (UK) Ltd **Seats** 100, Pr/dining room 24 **Times** 12-3/5.30-10 **Prices** Tasting menu £65-£110, Starter £8-£14, Main £16-£30, Dessert £8-£10 **Wines** 33 bottles over £30, 2 bottles under £30, 9 by glass **Parking** Q park Trafalgar Sq **Notes** Table d'hôte menu L/D 2/3 course £22/£25, Pre-theatre menu, Sunday L £35, Vegetarian available, Children welcome

The Rubens at the Palace
PLAN 4 H4

@@ Modern British

tel: 020 7834 6600 **39 Buckingham Palace Rd SW1W OPS**
email: bookrb@rchmail.com web: www.redcarnationhotels.com
dir: *Nearest station: Victoria*

Traditionally styled hotel dining opposite the Palace

Occupying a prime spot opposite Buckingham Palace Mews, The Rubens has been a hotel since 1912, when it became the obvious choice for debutantes and notables attending functions at the Palace. Restored to a distinctly Edwardian opulence, it's peopled with conscientious, attentive staff, its main restaurant being the Library, where dining goes on amid glass-fronted bookshelves, with busy-patterned seating on upright armchairs. The menu attempts a medley of nostalgic numbers and modern pop hits, opening with a powerfully flavoured Arbroath smokie fishcake with a poached egg in chive butter, alongside the prawn and crayfish cocktails, Caesar salad, and smoked salmon. Buccleuch steaks form the centrepiece, perhaps Chateaubriand for two, or a hefty rib-eye on the bone, matched with truffled macaroni cheese and creamed spinach in peppercorned Cognac sauce, though every accompaniment is charged extra. By contrast, fried hake with salsify and sea

The Rib Room @@@

LONDON SW1
PLAN 4 F4

Modern British
tel: 020 7858 7250 **Cadogan Place SW1X 9PY**
email: reservations@theribroom.co.uk web: www.theribroom.co.uk
dir: *Nearest station: Knightsbridge*

Old stalwarts and seasonal modernity in a Sloaneland hotel

Enter from the lobby and approach the reception desk leading to the bar and, on a raised section, to the restaurant area. This has had money thrown at it, as might be expected in a luxury hotel occupying a premier chunk of Knightsbridge real estate. Tables are traditionally appointed, with small flower arrangements and quality tableware, there are leather banquettes, dark wood blinds on the windows and a preponderance of wood creating a clubby, aged effect. Seats outside are provided for the (many) smokers among the international clientele. Waiting staff are correct but friendly and efficient and can describe dishes in detail. Given the restaurant's name, it comes as a bit of a surprise to find a modern menu that packs in quite a variety, with more than ribs and steaks (although chargrilled sirloin of dry-aged beef, served with slow-cooked cheek, buttered carrots and watercress purée is there for the asking). Among the imaginative, well-thought-out starters are Scottish lobster with cured salmon in wasabi dressing with pickled cucumber, radishes and a quail's egg,

and seared foie gras with a peach and sherry reduction, chicken wings and chicory. Prime cuts and top-end ingredients are the norm, and main courses are as well conceived and technically accurate as the rest. Roast duck breast is served with leg in a crisp potato shell, beautifully caramelised salsify, pear purée and colourful beetroot and broad beans, all set off by a light and flavoursome sauce. Fish choices might extend to fillet of wild halibut on clam chowder with seaweed, broccoli and roast baby onions, and desserts can be as rich as layers of salted caramel, pistachio cream and dense chocolate mousse topped with honeycomb and pistachio crumbs, served with milk ice cream.

Chef Ian Rudge **Owner** Michele Caggianese **Seats** 120, Pr/dining room 20 **Times** 12-2.45/6.30-10.45, **Prices** Fixed L 2 course £28-£49, Fixed D 3 course fr £58, Starter £15-£33.50, Main £26-£70, Dessert £8.50-£12 **Wines** 439 bottles over £30, 11 bottles under £30, 29 by glass **Parking** 78 **Notes** Sunday L fr £55, Vegetarian available, Children welcome

beets is straight from the modern repertoire. Finish with banana profiteroles and chocolate sauce, or crème brûlée and shortbread.

Times 7.30-10.30, Closed 24-27 Dec, L all week

Sake No Hana
PLAN 4 J6

Modern Japanese V NOTABLE WINE LIST

tel: 020 7925 8988 **23 Saint James's St SW1A 1HA**
email: reservations@sakenohana.com
dir: Nearest station: Green Park, Piccadilly Circus

Sophisticated Japanese cooking in a smart part of town

An escalator delivers you to the first-floor dining room where a smiling team await in the glossy black foyer to lead you into the dining room. It's a big, striking L-shaped space with a giant wooden lattice ceiling, linear bamboo columns and full-length windows hung with long screens reminiscent of tatami mats – it could only be a Japanese restaurant. There's a sushi counter, where a skilled team do their stuff, and a menu that encompasses contemporary and traditional dishes made with top quality ingredients. Among smaller bites, octopus is cooked sous-vide until meltingly tender and served with a sesame dressing, sea bass comes sashimi style with a chilli ponzu dressing, while the charcoal grill chips in with teriyaki-glazed lamb cutlets or corn-fed chicken with a sauce rich with chilli, ginger and garlic. There are sushi rolls like the one filled with fatty tuna and avocado, or another with king crab, seared salmon and nashi pear. Set signature menus are a good bet and there's a stylish cocktail and sake bar on the ground floor.

Chef Hideki Hiwatashi **Owner** Hakkasan Ltd **Seats** 100, Pr/dining room 32 **Times** 12-3/6-11, Closed 25 Dec, 1 Jan, Sun **Prices** Starter £4-£16, Main £11.50-£37, Dessert £5-£8.50 **Wines** 8 by glass **Parking** NCP **Notes** Fixed L 4 course fr £29, D 6 course fr £39. UMAI Sat £37, Children welcome

Salloos Restaurant
PLAN 4 G5

Pakistani

tel: 020 7235 4444 **62-64 Kinnerton St SW1X 8ER**
dir: Nearest station: Knightsbridge

Authentic Pakistani cooking in a discreet Knightsbridge mews

Salloos is a pukka, family-run Pakistani outfit that has gone quietly about its business in a corner mews house just across from The Berkeley Hotel since 1976. In the intimate first-floor dining room, warm tones of chocolate brown and flame-orange blend with latticework-screened windows, crystal chandeliers and contemporary artwork, while the atmosphere is traditional and the service politely formal. Consistently sound Pakistani cooking is the kitchen's strength – the chef has been here almost 40 years, so confident spicing is assured in well-tuned Mughlai cuisine fashioned from quality ingredients on a repertoire that sees little change. Salloos is renowned for its tandooris, so kick off with a top-class minced lamb seekh kebab, and follow with house specialities such as tandoori lamb chops or a Khyber region chicken karahi: de-boned chicken cooked in an iron wok with tomatoes, ginger, green chillies and fresh coriander.

Chef Abdul Aziz **Owner** Mr & Mrs M Salahuddin **Seats** 65 **Times** 12-11, All-day dining, Closed Xmas, Sun **Prices** Starter £6-£12.25, Main £16-£20, Dessert £6.50 **Wines** 37 bottles over £30, 11 bottles under £30, 2 by glass **Parking** Kinnerton St car park (meter) **Notes** Vegetarian available, Children 8 yrs+

Roux at Parliament Square ❀❀❀

LONDON SW1
PLAN 5 B5

Modern European V
tel: 020 7334 3737 **Parliament Square SW1P 3AD**
email: roux@rics.org
dir: Nearest station: Westminster

High-flying candidate on Parliament Square

In a rather handsome Georgian building, designed by Alfred Waterhouse of London's Natural History Museum fame, and home to the Royal Institution of Chartered Surveyors, this restaurant offers a touch of refinement with the Roux endorsement. Part of the broader Roux family, the kitchen here is headed up by Steve Groves, a prodigious talent in his own right. In a couple of elegant dining rooms decorated with timeless simplicity and an absence of chintz, the chef and his team deliver vibrant plates of classically-inspired food that show plenty of contemporary flair. Start upstairs in the cocktail bar if you've time and sip on a blue martini before heading into the restaurant. Choose between the tasting, à la carte and set menu options. The high quality of the produce is evident from the off with an earthy first course of veal sweetbreads with grilled hearts, turnips and tarragon mustard, or the more genteel roast Scottish langoustine partnered with prawn tortellini and coastal vegetables. Flavours are well-judged and presentation impresses throughout.

Ibérico pork chop is served as a main course with textures of onion, while hogget of Herdwick lamb with smoked tomato and wild garlic. A fish main course might be Brixham brill with brown crab and the subtle aroma of lemongrass. Among desserts, Yorkshire rhubarb and vanilla soufflé looks amazing on the plate, with rhubarb sorbet, vanilla custard and shortbread crumble, or go for three scoops of ice cream or sorbet from the day's selection. British and French cheeses are perfectly kept and make a tantalising finale. The wine list focuses on the French big guns without ignoring the rest of the world.

Chef Steve Groves **Owner** Restaurant Associates **Seats** 56, Pr/dining room 10 **Times** 12-2/6.30-10, Closed Xmas, New Year, BHs, Sat-Sun **Prices** Prices not confirmed **Wines** 4 bottles under £30, 24 by glass **Parking** NCP Semley Place **Notes** Children welcome

LONDON SW1 *continued*

Santini Restaurant
PLAN 4 H4

◉ Traditional Italian

tel: 020 7730 4094 & 7730 8275 **29 Ebury St SW1W ONZ**
email: santini@santinirestaurant.com **web:** www.santinirestaurant.com
dir: *Nearest station: Victoria*

Faithful Italian cooking in ritzy surroundings

Santini has been a glamorous Belgravia darling since the early 1980s, much in demand with the glitterati for its romantic alfresco terrace discreetly bordered by glass screens, potted Mediterranean herbs and olive trees, and an airy pastel-hued interior with marble floors, leather banquettes and low-slung chairs. The traditional values of a family-run Italian restaurant underpin this glossy set-up, and Latin style runs all the way from the waiters to the wine list. Impeccably sourced seasonal ingredients treated with a light touch are at the centre of things, starting with the likes of fried courgette flowers stuffed with mozzarella and herbs; if you prefer to start with classic pasta, you can't get much more simple and authentic than cappellini with fresh tomato and basil. Main courses take in poached sea bass with lentils and herb and balsamic dressing, or grilled beef fillet with Barolo butter, with — what else? — classic tiramisú to finish.

Chef Christian Gardin **Owner** Mr G Santin **Seats** 65, Pr/dining room 30
Times 12-3/6-11, Closed Xmas, 1 Jan, Etr Sun-Mon **Prices** Starter £10-£24, Main £15-£40, Dessert £8-£15 **Wines** 62 bottles over £30, 1 bottle under £30, 18 by glass **Parking** Meter (no charge after 6.30pm) **Notes** Pre-theatre menu, Sunday L, Vegetarian available, Children welcome

Seven Park Place by William Drabble
PLAN 4 J6

◉◉◉◉ *— see opposite*

Sofitel London St James
PLAN 4 K6

◉ French, British

tel: 020 7968 2900 **6 Waterloo Place SW1Y 4AN**
email: thebalcon.london@sofitel.com **web:** www.sofitelstjames.com
dir: *Nearest station: Piccadilly Circus*

A touch of French style on Pall Mall

The hotel is an imposing piece of London real estate in an upmarket part of town, and The Balcon restaurant is suitably capacious and stylish (and rather glamorous with it). It's done out in the grand Parisian manner with double-height ceiling, soaring columns, a show-stopping duo of matching spiral staircases, plus a charcuterie and champagne bar. The menu ploughs a brasserie furrow with British and French influences along the way, and some excellent British ingredients on show. There are tarts and tartines (Welsh rarebit, for example) and superb charcuterie from Trealy Farm in Monmouthshire and Mas le Rouget in Cantal (south-central France). Start with a salad — perhaps roasted and pickled beetroots with Roquefort, candy walnuts and frisée — follow on with Label Anglais chicken cooked on the rotisserie, or beer-braised ox cheeks, and finish with a lemon pudding with lemon sauce.

Times 11-11, All-day dining

The Stafford London
PLAN 4 J6

◉◉ Modern, Traditional British, European

tel: 020 7518 1124 & 7493 0111 **16-18 St James's Place SW1A 1NJ**
email: info@thelyttelton.com **web:** www.thelyttelton.com
dir: *Nearest station: Green Park*

Luxurious hotel dining in exclusive location

Tucked away in a discreet street near Green Park, The Stafford is a luxurious St James's address that is worth tracking down. Its legendary American Bar is a world-class cocktail spot, but if it is something more sustaining you're after, the Lyttelton restaurant occupies the former dining and drawing rooms of the eponymous family. It's an intimate, elegant setting that screams 'five stars' with its panelled ceilings, soft-focus hues of ivory, lavender and grey, bespoke artworks and chandeliers. The kitchen takes top-notch British produce as its starting point, subjects it to contemporary treatments and comes up with ambitious dishes glowing with Mediterranean colour. A quail millefeuille pointed up with summer truffle and sun-dried tomato makes a bright, attractive lead-in to a classy main course of perfectly-timed grilled brill with vegetable spaghetti and champagne and caviar beurre blanc. At the end, blueberries add a creative twist to Bakewell tart with ginger and almond ice cream. The wine list runs to over 600 bins with a Master of Wine sommelier to help navigate the way.

Chef Carlos Martinez **Owner** B H L **Seats** 52, Pr/dining room 44
Times 12-2.30/6-10, Closed D 25 Dec **Prices** Fixed L 2 course £19.12, Starter £12.50-£19, Main £25.50-£36, Dessert £9.50-£12.50, Service optional 12.5% **Wines** 340 bottles over £30, 5 bottles under £30, 11 by glass **Parking** NCP on Arlington Street **Notes** Pre-theatre menu 5.30-7pm 2/3 course £19.12/£24.12, Sunday L £19.12-£24.12, Vegetarian available, Children welcome

Thirty Six by Nigel Mendham at Dukes London
PLAN 4 J6

◉◉◉ *— see page 318*

Seven Park Place by William Drabble ❀❀❀❀

LONDON SW1   **PLAN 4 J6**

Modern French 🍷 NOTABLE WINE LIST

tel: 020 7316 1600 **7-8 Park Place SW1A 1LP**
email: info@stjameshotelandclub.com
web: www.stjameshotelandclub.com
dir: *Nearest station: Green Park*

Assured French cooking in a riotously decorated club

The eponymous chef whose name hangs above the door of his pocket-sized restaurant within the celeb-haunt St James's Hotel and Club is a prodigious talent. Drabble took over the reins at Aubergine in Chelsea following Gordon Ramsay's departure, and he stayed for a decade to firmly re-establish the place in the foodie premier league – a stellar signing for the St James's. This is an attractively small-scale operation and with just 26 diners in an adjoining pair of intimate dining rooms to cook for, the kitchen is hardly overstretched, ensuring that timings, textures and flavours are fine-tuned. With its opulent tones of brown, black and gold, the decor is certainly swish, and occupies a place at the opposite pole of the ubiquitous beige minimalism of modern restaurants, being a riot of geometric patterning in carpets and upholstery, with broad swathes of art deco-ish foliage snaking up walls punctuated with striking artworks. A foundation of assured French classicism keeps Drabble's cooking on track as it roams between familiar and new territory without ever losing its way. Menus come liberally-sprinkled with high-end ingredients, as in a simple but flavour-packed opener of poached Dorset blue lobster tail with roasted cauliflower, cauliflower purée, black trompette mushrooms and lobster butter sauce, or a partnership of roasted quail with crispy veal sweetbreads and marinated foie gras pointed up with a warm orange and hazelnut dressing. Next up, an assiette of pork is a highly technical workout that demonstrates the understated finesse of Drabble's cooking, comprising unctuous braised cheek, slow-cooked belly, a braised head croquette and fillet with black pudding, broad beans and an intensely porky jus – this is cooking of exquisite concentration and intensity. If your fancy turns to fish, there might be griddled sea bass fillet matched with an oyster beignet, salsify, smoked garlic hollandaise and red wine and rosemary jus. At the end, an assiette of chocolate is a masterclass comprising mousse, parfait, ice cream, and caramel and white chocolate pannacotta, or you might take a plate of Paxton and Whitfield cheeses. Considering the level of cooking on offer, you can eat here at an astonishingly keen price if you go for the set-price lunch menu, but it's obviously the carte and dégustation menus that hold greatest excitement, and if you get seduced by the excellent globetrotting wine list, consider the budget well and truly blown.

Chef William Drabble **Seats** 34, Pr/dining room 40
Times 12-2/7-10, Closed Sun-Mon **Prices** Fixed L 2 course fr £25.50, Fixed D 3 course fr £61, Tasting menu fr £72 **Wines** 257 bottles over £30, 16 bottles under £30, 11 by glass **Parking** On street and NCP **Notes** Fixed 6 course menu gourmand, Vegetarian available, Children welcome

LONDON SW1 *continued*

Tinello

PLAN 4 G2

◉◉ Italian

tel: 020 7730 6327 & 7730 3663 **87 Pimlico Rd SW1W 8PH**
email: info@tinello.co.uk
dir: *Nearest station: Sloane Sq*

Classy Italian cooking in stylish restaurant

Run by brothers Federico and Max Sali and backed by their mentor, celeb chef Giorgio Locatelli, you're in good hands at Tinello. The place lives up to its posh Belgravia location with a classy, rather masculine decor of bare bricks, dark oak floors and brown banquettes at linen-swathed tables beneath low-slung brass lampshades. It strikes a discreet and serious pose to go with straightforward modern Italian cooking built on a clear dedication to superb ingredients. There are 'small eats' – roast bone marrow with celery, capers and rocket salad, say, or you might launch straight into skilfully-made pasta from the seasonal repertoire: a classic pairing of herb pappardelle with duck ragù, or spaghetti with gurnard and black olives. Main courses take an equally gimmick and fuss-free line. A splendid slab of perfectly-timed roast Cornish cod with sliced razor clams and cannellini beans is a pitch-perfect combination, or you might enjoy the meaty delights of chargrilled quail with the simple accompaniments of sautéed broccoli, almonds and chilli. Finish with pannacotta with intensely-flavoured preserved amarena cherries.

Chef Federico Sali **Owner** Giorgio Locatelli **Seats** 75, Pr/dining room 25 **Times** 12-2.30/6.15-10.30, Closed BH Mon, Sun **Prices** Starter £1.95-£10, Main £15-£24.50, Dessert £4.75-£8.50, Service optional **Wines** 189 bottles over £30, 50 bottles under £30, 23 by glass **Parking** On street, single yellow from 6.30pm **Notes** Vegetarian available, Children welcome

Zafferano

PLAN 4 F4

◉◉ Modern Italian 🍷 NOTABLE WINE LIST

tel: 020 7235 5800 **15 Lowndes St SW1X 9EY**
email: zafferano@londonfinedininggroup.com
dir: *Nearest station: Knightsbridge*

Refined but authentic Italian cooking in Knightsbridge

Zafferano has always held its head high among the upper echelons of the UK's contemporary Italians, ever since Giorgio Locatelli opened the place back in 1995. The output may have wobbled with each new change of guard in the kitchen, but the cooking still inspires confidence. In the well-heeled environs of Knightsbridge you have to look the part, and the bare brickwork, rustic stone floors, stripy banquettes and exuberant explosions of fresh flowers still give off all the right discreetly elegant messages. The kitchen gives classic dishes a sophisticated spin without losing sight of the basic principle of simplicity, and superb ingredients remain at the heart of it all, starting with antipasti like cured bresaola beef with rocket and goats' cheese dressing. Pasta dishes here are something special – perhaps veal osso buco ravioli with gremolata, or paccheri tubes with aubergine, nduja sausage and salted ricotta. Secondi could be pot-roasted monkfish with sautéed chard and pine nuts and sultana sauce, or classic chicken paillard. To finish, honey pannacotta might be paired with white grape compôte.

Chef Daniele Camera **Owner** A-Z Restaurants-London Fine Dining Group **Seats** 140, Pr/dining room 26 **Times** 12-11.30, All-day dining, Closed 25 Dec **Prices** Fixed L 2 course £22.50, Starter £12.50-£21.50, Main £15.50-£41, Dessert £8-£10 **Wines** 600 bottles over £30, 5 bottles under £30, 6 by glass **Parking** NCP behind restaurant **Notes** Vegetarian available, Children welcome

Thirty Six by Nigel Mendham at Dukes London ❀❀❀

LONDON SW1   PLAN 4 J6

Modern British
tel: 020 7491 4840 **35 St James's Place SW1A 1NY**
email: thirtysix@dukeshotel.com web: www.dukeshotel.com
dir: *Nearest station: Green Park*

Precise and non-technological modern British cooking

Tucked away on the cusp of Mayfair and St James's, Dukes is as discreetly located as it's possible for an upscale hotel to be in this part of London. From the moment you pass through the flagged entrance, it's clear you've entered a world of high-class hospitality, the interiors agleam with serious investment, and staff on high professional alert throughout. The cocktail and champagne bars are worth tarrying in, and the small, classically styled dining room, named after the address (and freighted with numerological significance, if that's your thing), is consecrated to the refreshingly straightforward, uncomplicated culinary vision of Nigel Mendham. Chef doesn't buy into the mad-professor school, so you won't get doused in liquid nitrogen, but instead plays to the strengths of classic combinations and technique brought off with aplomb. This is evident in an opening crab cocktail that embraces white meat, avocado purée and pink grapefruit for a balanced preparation that works, as also in a pork terrine matched with Granny Smith apple

and a langoustine. Meats of outstanding quality crop up at main in the form of salt marsh lamb with goats' curd, smoked aubergine, burnt onion and a delicately cumined croquette, while fish could be John Dory with cauliflower, almonds and coriander. Texture is hugely important in desserts these days, as witness an assemblage of peanut parfait with caramelised banana, peanut brittle and banana sherbet, as also the textured apple variations that come with blackberry sorbet and cardamom cream. Well-chosen British artisan cheeses with tomato chutney and apple compôte are another cause for celebration. A seven-course taster drawn from the main menu, with optional wine flight, gives a comprehensive indication of Mendham's range.

Chef Nigel Mendham **Seats** 36 **Times** 12-2.30/6-9.30, Closed L Mon, D Sun **Prices** Fixed L 2 course £25, Fixed D 3 course £35-£60, Tasting menu £75-£105, Starter £12-£19, Main £15-£29, Dessert £10-£18 **Wines** 62 bottles over £30, 2 bottles under £30, 13 by glass **Parking** Holiday Inn, Britannia car park **Notes** Tasting menu 6 course, Early bird menu 3 course £31/£36, Sunday L £35-£45, Vegetarian available, Children welcome

LONDON SW3

Bibendum Restaurant
PLAN 4 E3

@ @ British, French NOTABLE WINE LIST

tel: 020 7581 5817 **Michelin House, 81 Fulham Rd SW3 6RD**
email: reservations@bibendum.co.uk
dir: Nearest station: South Kensington

Modern classics at a Chelsea institution

The landmark Michelin building merits a visit for the iconic art nouveau tiled wall friezes and mosaic floors of the ground-floor oyster bar. But the first-floor dining room has a special magic, particularly on bright days when the Michelin man stained-glass windows light up an amazingly luminous space. This is a bastion of Frenchness, starting with the smooth Gallic service that imparts an air of quiet refinement to the place. A new head chef took over the reins in April 2015, but fear not: traditional French dishes still rub along nicely with modern British ideas on the re-jigged menu. You might start with Burgundy snails – after all they have been fixtures for 28 years – otherwise, consider Bath chap with chicory, radish and capers, ahead of a tranche of turbot with béarnaise sauce, or two might share a guinea fowl roasted with butter, thyme and lemon. To finish, perhaps an Armagnac baba with prunes and vanilla ice cream.

Chef Peter Robinson **Owner** Sir Terence Conran, Simon Hopkinson, Michael Hamlyn **Seats** 80 **Times** 12-2.30/7-11, Closed 24-26 Dec, 1 Jan **Prices** Starter £8.50-£15.50, Main £16.50-£34, Dessert £3-£12, Service optional 12.5% **Wines** 786 bottles over £30, 14 bottles under £30, 22 by glass **Parking** On street **Notes** Sun D 3 course £33.50, Sunday L £33.50, Children welcome

Bo Lang Restaurant
PLAN 4 E3

@ Chinese

tel: 020 7823 7887 **100 Draycott Av SW3 3AD**
email: reservations@bolangrestaurant.co.uk
dir: Nearest station: South Kensington

Enterprising dim sum in Chelsea

This is the Chelsea hangout for lovers of dim sum, a dimly lit space with grey leather sofas, charcoal velvet chairs, wooden-topped tables, cut-out wooden screens and a load of lanterns dangling from the ceiling. The short menu is helpfully divided into sections (dim sum steamed, dim sum baked/fried, main courses and so on). Standards are high, and dishes never less than interesting. Three rolls of honey-glazed rib wrapped in puff pastry, tender shui mai of chicken minced with black truffle, and soft-shelled crab with chilli and lime have all been mentioned in dispatches. No less accomplished are main courses: stir-fried diced beef in rich black bean and pepper sauce, slivers of chicken with noodles and cashew nuts, and baby pak choi steamed with garlic and goji berries all make an impact. There's even a short choice of desserts, among them frozen lemongrass and ginger yogurt.

Times 12-11.30, All-day dining

Brasserie Gustave
PLAN 4 E2

@ @ French NEW

tel: 020 7352 1712 & 7352 9510 **4 Sydney St SW3 6PP**
email: info@brasserie-gustave.com
dir: Nearest station: South Kensington

Classic French cuisine in an upmarket brasserie

The Gustave in question is Monsieur Eiffel, and with classic French posters on the bright yellow walls, rich red leather banquettes and chairs, and French music playing over the sound system, this place could hardly be more Gallic. The service fits the bill, too, with the waiting staff uber-efficient and smartly attired. The bilingual menu continues the theme by featuring classic brasserie fare. Roasted bone marrow comes with a teaspoon to make sure you get every last delicious smidgeon, plus parsley and gherkin salad and a powerful red wine sauce, while duck foie gras terrine is combined with ham hock and artichokes. Gilt head bream arrives with perfectly crispy skin and soft flesh in a main course with aubergine purée and confit tomatoes (a real taste of the Med), or go for confit duck leg with homemade pickled white cabbage (choucroute). The classic influences continue into well-made desserts such as chocolate fondant with hazelnut ice cream, or a tarte Tatin for two.

Chef Laurence Glayzer **Owner** Ismayil Malikov **Seats** 50, Pr/dining room 16 **Times** 11.30-2.30/6-10.30, Closed Mon, L Tue **Prices** Fixed L 2 course fr £19.50, Fixed D 3 course fr £22.50, Tasting menu fr £39, Starter £7-£16, Main £16-£39, Dessert £5.50-£9.50 **Wines** 126 bottles over £30, 13 bottles under £30, 12 by glass **Parking** On street **Notes** Brunch menu £14.50, Pre-theatre menu £19.50, Sunday L £23.50-£28.50, Vegetarian available, Children welcome

Le Colombier
PLAN 4 D2

@ Traditional French

tel: 020 7351 1155 **145 Dovehouse St SW3 6LB**
email: lecolombier1998@aol.com
dir: Nearest station: South Kensington

Classic authentic French bistro in Chelsea

Tucked away on a buzzy corner just off the Fulham Road beside the Royal Marsden Hospital, long-running Le Colombier is the epitome of the old-school neighbourhood French restaurant. The front conservatory – bathed in sunlight and leafy fronds – is a fine-weather hot ticket, while inside the main dining room in an equally sunny confection of cream and blue tones, set against polished floorboards and classic white linen and accompanied by helpings of entente cordiale served up by a host of formally clad French staff. Thus, this is not a place for faddish cooking, so expect unfussy, unashamedly classic French brasserie-style dishes (most so familiar they hardly need their translations). Take openers like duck liver terrine, perhaps, served with fig jam, or mains like steak tartare with frites, fillet of beef with béarnaise, or wild sea bass fillet served with lemon-spiked olive oil, spinach and potatoes. Desserts are similarly vintage too; from a decadent tarte Tatin to crêpe Suzette or crème brûlée, while the serious all-French wine list is the perfect accomplice.

Chef Philippe Tamet **Owner** Didier Garnier **Seats** 70, Pr/dining room 28 **Times** 12-3/6.30-10.30 **Prices** Fixed L 2 course fr £18.50, Starter £6.90-£14.50, Main £19.20-£32, Dessert £7.90 **Wines** 195 bottles over £30, 32 bottles under £30, 10 by glass **Parking** On street (meter) **Notes** Sunday L fr £23, Vegetarian available, Children 10 yrs+

LONDON SW3 *continued*

Eight Over Eight

PLAN 4 D1

◉ Pan-Asian

tel: 020 7349 9934 **392 King's Rd SW3 5UZ**
email: eightovereight@rickerrestaurants.com
dir: *Nearest station: Sloane Sq, South Kensington*

Pan-Asian cooking in a cool, buzzy Chelsea favourite

The King's Road branch of Will Ricker's oriental fusion trio (also E&O and XO), Eight Over Eight is a fashionable assemble of bar and understatedly sexy restaurant. Effortlessly cool, the corner-sited, high-ceilinged outfit is flush with light from huge windows by day and large dangling oriental-style lights by night. Wide floorboards, paper-clothed tables, slick banquettes and black lacquered chairs complete the on-trend, up tempo vibe. But it's not all style over substance, with well-conceived Pan-Asian grazing plates the kitchen's raison d'être. All the classics appear on a well-honed roster, from dim sum to classy sushi and sashimi, through to pukka tempura (like soft-shelled crab and zesty jalapeno), Asian salads, curries (think high-octane dry red barramundi with green beans) and specials like black cod and sweet miso. And it's all prepared with skill and presented with plenty of style to match the surroundings and switched-on service. Eye-catching Asian-influenced cocktails are a good way to kick-off proceedings.

Times 12-3/6-11, Closed 24-29 Dec, Etr

The Five Fields

PLAN 4 F3

◉◉◉ – *see below*

Manicomio

PLAN 4 F3

◉ Modern Italian

tel: 020 7730 3366 **85 Duke of York Square, Chelsea SW3 4LY**
email: info@manicomio.co.uk
dir: *Nearest station: Sloane Sq*

Bustling modern Italian just off Sloane Square

Built as the military asylum of the Duke of York barracks, Manicomio presents a cool, calming image, with its planked floor, wall banquettes and vivid artwork. Contemporary Italian cooking is the draw, with many ingredients imported from the Motherland: perhaps speck d'Aosta in a starter with mozzarella and baby artichokes, and lentils from Umbria to accompany roast hake fillet, parsley pesto and spinach. The menu is evenly divided between fish and meat, the latter extending to chargrilled quail skewered with chicken livers on polenta with vin cotto sauce, followed by a winter main course of grilled sirloin with bone marrow, braised ox cheek and roast squash. Finish with the tiramisù or treacle and lemon tart.

Chef Tom Salt **Owner** Ninai & Andrew Zarach **Seats** 70, Pr/dining room 30 **Times** 12-3/6.30-10.30, Closed Xmas & New Year, D Sun (Jan-Feb) **Prices** Fixed L 2 course fr £23.50, Fixed D 3 course fr £27.50, Starter £8.50-£10.75, Main £15.75-£25.75, Dessert £5.75-£7.75 **Wines** 78 bottles over £30, 23 bottles under £30, 18 by glass **Parking** On street **Notes** Pre-theatre menu, Sunday L, Vegetarian available, Children welcome

The Five Fields ◉◉◉

LONDON SW3

PLAN 4 F3

Modern British v NEW
tel: 020 7838 1082 **8-9 Blacklands Ter SW3 2SP**
email: info@fivefieldsrestaurant.com
dir: *Nearest station: Sloane Sq*

Colourful contemporary cooking in a smart dining room

The name refers to the area back in the middle of the 18th century when cartographer John Rocque mapped the ever-expanding city of London, and chef-patron Taylor Bonnyman has created a singular kind of restaurant in what is now an area of prime real estate. The designers have gone for an upscale finish of soothing neutrality, with tones of cream and caramel and a signature cocoa plant motif among the many creative touches if you look closely enough. The professional nature of the service feels just right in this setting. Bonnyman and his head chef, Marguerite Keogh, have at their disposal their own kitchen garden in East Sussex growing much of the vegetables, herbs and salads for the table. This passion for provenance is evident from the menu where dishes are described using today's fashionable brevity. The food is attractively presented, creative and full of deeply satisfying flavours. 'Crab and Octopus', for example, combines the fresh seafood, cooked just right, with compressed melon, a salsa verde and delicately placed herbs and flowers to deliver an impressive first course. Next up, 'Old Spot Pig' consists of spectacularly tender loin in a Med-style combo, and 'Cornish Turbot' arrives with laverbread, razor clams and blackberries. The freshness of the produce shines out once again in a dessert called 'Orchard', which is as pretty as a picture and delivers the likes of figs, plums, raspberries and more, enhanced by a light sponge and vanilla-scented crème anglaise. Go for the tasting menu if the rest of your table are up for the ride, and give due consideration to the wine list and cocktails.

Chef Taylor Bonnyman, Marguerite Keogh **Owner** Taylor Bonnyman **Seats** 40, Pr/dining room 10 **Times** 6.30-10, Closed Xmas, 2 wks Jan, Sun-Mon **Prices** Fixed D 3 course £50-£55, Tasting menu £75-£80, Service optional 12.5% **Wines** 435 bottles over £30, 15 bottles under £30, 15 by glass **Parking** On street, NCP 150 yds **Notes** No high chairs or child menu, Children welcome

Nozomi

PLAN 4 E4

◉ Contemporary Japanese

tel: 020 7838 1500 & 7838 0181 **14-15 Beauchamp Place, Knightsbridge SW3 1NQ**
email: enquiries@nozomi.co.uk
dir: *Nearest station: Knightsbridge*

Contemporary Japanese cooking in slick setting

The fashionable good looks of the front bar of this contemporary Japanese make it a darling of the see-and-be-seen crowd, though for foodies the real draw is the dining room behind. This is a rather more soothing space with cream walls and leather seating, subdued lighting, and black-clad waiting staff combining with a trendy backing track to create an upbeat, modern space for some equally in-vogue cooking. Authentic contemporary Japanese cuisine is the deal, with the long menu covering a lot of ground. A selection of sushi is a good way to start – perhaps turbot and salmon nigiri – or choose from an extensive list of maki rolls and temaki, or small dishes such as soft-shelled crab with spicy red pepper sauce, or grilled eel in unagi sauce. Not surprisingly in this postcode, luxuries are strewn liberally around, among them whole tempura lobster with ponzu and daikon, pan-fried foie gras marinated in whisky, and chargrilled Wagyu beef steaks.

Times 12-3/6.30-11.30, Closed L Mon

Outlaw's at The Capital

PLAN 4 F5

◉◉◉ – *see below*

Rasoi Restaurant

PLAN 4 F3

◉◉◉ – *see page 322*

Restaurant Gordon Ramsay

PLAN 4 F1

◉◉◉◉ – *see page 323*

Tom's Kitchen

PLAN 4 E2

◉◉ British, French

tel: 020 7349 0202 **27 Cale St, South Kensington SW3 3QP**
email: info@tomskitchen.co.uk
dir: *Nearest station: South Kensington, Sloane Sq*

First-class brasserie food from top-class chef

With its utilitarian good looks, Tom's kitchen fizzes with life and bonhomie. The ethos is there for all to see: 'food for everyone and anyone' it says engraved on a piece of slate, and that's a fair statement, just as long as that 'someone' can pay seventeen quid for fish and chips. But this is Chelsea (just around the corner from Tom's flagship restaurant) and the prices are not unreasonable, and perhaps most important of all, the quality is high. Covering three floors of this handsome townhouse, there's a space to suit your mood, and it is the all-day, ground-floor brasserie where most of the action takes place at tightly packed wooden tables. Spicy crabcake, perked up with a tomato salsa and packed with a goodly amount of crab, shows the way, or go for something along the lines of baked scallops with garlic and lemon. Top-notch produce is sourced with due diligence throughout. Chicken, leek and bacon pie is a real cracker, and desserts run to apple and blackberry crumble with toasted almond ice cream. There's a second branch in Somerset House in the West End.

Times 12-3.30/6-10.30, Closed 25-26 Dec, D 24 Dec

Outlaw's at The Capital ◉◉◉

LONDON SW3   PLAN 4 F5

British, Seafood v 🍷 NOTABLE WINE LIST

tel: 020 7591 1202 **Basil St, Knightsbridge SW3 1AT**
email: outlaws@capitalhotel.co.uk web: www.capitalhotel.co.uk
dir: *Nearest station: Knightsbridge*

The best of Cornish seafood in London

If you have been meaning – like any self-respecting foodie should – to pay a visit to Nathan Outlaw's Cornish flagship, but just can't find the time to make it down to the wild West Country, his London venture might offer easier access to the famed first-rate seafood cooking. Ensconced in the ultra-smart, five-star heaven of The Capital, a splendid boutique townhouse hotel just around the corner from Harrods, Outlaw's restaurant occupies an understated art deco-esque space with blond wood panelling, paintings of seahorses, wall mirrors and unclothed tables. The highly knowledgeable service team takes a more unbuttoned approach than is often the case in London restaurants at this level. With his burgeoning empire down in Cornwall, and a big move for the mothership from Rock to Port Isaac in 2015, Outlaw can't be regularly at the stoves here, so his right-hand man, Pete Biggs, heads up the kitchen, ensuring that the emphasis remains to let top-class Cornish materials speak eloquently for themselves, helped along, naturally, with high-flying

technique. Seafood risotto sounds like a workaday starter, but here it acquires benchmark status, with impeccably-handled mussels, scallops, octopus and prawns delivering bursts of clearly-defined flavours. Or you might start with paprika-cured brill with dill yogurt, smoked almonds and peppers. Mains focus on a humble fillet of plaice, albeit of exceptional quality, helped along by potato terrine, braised leeks, crispy crumbed lobster 'scampi' and a lobster bisque of head-spinning depth of flavour. Dessert also dazzles when it arrives with the fragrance of lime from a syrup and lime zest grated over poached pear with dark chocolate mousse and stem ginger ice cream. Bargain hunters should head straight for the remarkable value of the set lunch deal.

Chef Nathan Outlaw, Pete Biggs **Owner** Mr D Levin **Seats** 35, Pr/dining room 24 **Times** 12-2/6.30-10, Closed Sun **Prices** Fixed L 2 course £22, Fixed D 3 course £55, Tasting menu £75 **Wines** 37 by glass **Parking** 8 **Notes** Tasting menu 5 course, BYO wine Thu, Children welcome

LONDON SW4

Bistro Union
PLAN 1 E2

@@ British

tel: 020 7042 6400 **40 Abbeville Rd, Clapham SW4 9NG**
email: eat@bistrounion.co.uk
dir: *Nearest station: Clapham South*

True-Brit food in neighbourhood bistro

The casually-dressed sibling of Adam Byatt's high-flying Trinity operation is the sort of easy-going neighbourhood eatery we'd all like on our patch. Its simple, pared-back decor and relaxed vibes sit well with the local clientele in the trendy Abbeville Village postcode. You can perch on wooden stools at the bar with your cutlery and menu in individual drawers under the counter, choosing something like pickled quail's eggs or salt cod fritters with aïoli from a bar menu of on-trend nibbles hand-written onto a roll of brown paper. The food is in the day-to-day hands of Karl Goward who comes from Fergus Henderson's St John Bread and Wine, so you can expect a no-nonsense approach with a nod to the 'nose-to-tail' eating style. What leaves the kitchen is creative, fun, and built with British-led ingredients – ox tongue is smoked in house and comes in the vibrant company of beetroot, horseradish and pickled walnuts. Mains could bring roast mallard with lentils, roast squash and black mustard. Hearty puds include ginger parkin with salt caramel sauce.

Chef Karl Goward, Adam Byatt **Owner** Adam Byatt **Seats** 40
Times 12-3/6-10, Closed 24-27 Dec, 1-2 Jan **Prices** Starter £4-£7, Main £11-£18, Dessert £2-£6 **Wines** 24 bottles over £30, 16 bottles under £30, 13 by glass **Parking** On street **Notes** D Sun 6-8pm 3 course £27, Wknd brunch, Sunday L, Vegetarian available, Children welcome

The Dairy
PLAN 1 E2

@@ Modern British V

tel: 020 7622 4165 **15 The Pavement, Clapham SW4 0HY**
email: bookings@the-dairy.co.uk
dir: *Nearest station: Clapham Common*

Relaxed bar-bistro serving innovative modern food

Its central Clapham location – looking out over the common just a few paces from the tube – isn't The Dairy's only draw, as this relaxed, on-cue outfit is home to some seriously fine cooking at accessible prices. From the outside it looks unremarkable, but step inside and you'll find it a friendly, welcoming and popular place, with a dinky bar up front and a bistro behind with a pared-back look of recycled and reclaimed furniture and fittings, flag-stoned floors and an open kitchen. The cooking is clever and innovative, producing well-crafted dishes that are light and colourful with clean flavours and modern presentation. Some of the seasonal ingredients used come from The Dairy's own urban garden. Kick off with some fresh sourdough bread with home-made smoked bone marrow butter, then choose a selection of small plates from the varied menu. You might begin with a plate of potted salmon with Guinness soda bread, or some slices of excellent salumi, moving on to garden-fresh peas with celery, mint and fried bread, and perhaps sea-fresh West Coast lemon sole teamed with maple pancetta and ember oil buttermilk. For dessert, how about Lincolnshire rhubarb (nicely tart) with contrasting sweet hibiscus meringue, pumpkin seeds and rhubarb ice cream?

Chef Robin Gill **Owner** Robin & Sarah Gill, Matt Wells **Seats** 40 **Times** 12-11, All-day dining, Closed Xmas, Mon, L Tue, D Sun **Prices** Fixed L 3 course £25, Tasting menu £45, Starter £5.50-£9.50, Main £9-£10.50, Dessert £6-£6.50 **Wines** 48 bottles over £30, 12 bottles under £30, 8 by glass **Notes** Sunday L £45, Children welcome

Rasoi Restaurant @@@

LONDON SW3
PLAN 4 F3

Modern Indian V ◆NOTABLE WINE LIST

tel: 020 7225 1881 **10 Lincoln St SW3 2TS**
email: info@rasoirestaurant.co.uk
dir: *Nearest station: Sloane Sq*

Chelsea townhouse with ground-breaking Indian cooking

Vineet Bhatia's restaurant in a swish Chelsea townhouse down a smart little street off the King's Road is one of the leading lights among nouveau Indian eateries in the capital. With its tiled path and window-box, it looks like an upscale private home, particularly as you have to ring a bell to get in, but once you're through the door, it's all very chic, with silk wall hangings, designer wallpapers, Indian artefacts and antiques, and the heady aroma of eastern spices in the air. The new-wave style of cooking is delivered via menus that are structured in the western three-course format (helpful staff are on hand to decode the often baffling descriptions), with seven-course prestige and vegetarian taster deals on offer, the former with the option of pre-selected wine matches. You can expect a palate-tingling treat that fizzes with originality: toasted sesame and ginger work their magic on cod, partnered in an inventive opening salvo with spring onion khichdi (a south Asian dish of rice and dhal), fennel pollen ice cream and cashew nut salsa, or there might be

Malabari lamb boti baked in a banana leaf and served with a tandoori lamb chop and pomegranate raita. Global cuisines are cross-fertilised productively in main courses such as quinoa-crusted sea bass spiked with chilli and lime and asparagus couscous, tomato and beetroot tadka sauce and crab chutney, or grilled lamb fillet with cinnamon-scented lamb jus, sun-dried tomato upma and a blue cheese seekh kebab. Vegetarian dishes are equally precise and refined creations – perhaps street food-inspired chaats of samosa, dahi bhalla ice cream, spinach tikki and tomato chutney. Intriguing desserts include the signature chocolate samosa with rose petal and vanilla ice cream.

Chef Vineet Bhatia **Owner** Vineet & Rashima Bhatia **Seats** 35, Pr/dining room 14 **Times** 12-2.30/6-10.30, Closed Xmas, New Year, BHs, Mon, L Sat **Prices** Fixed L 2 course £24-£29, Fixed D 3 course £66-£76, Tasting menu £79-£89, Starter £21-£26, Main £33-£51, Dessert £12-£22 **Wines** 300 bottles over £30, 10 bottles under £30, 10 by glass **Parking** On street **Notes** Tasting menu 7 course with wine, Sunday L £24-£36, Children welcome

Restaurant Gordon Ramsay 🌹🌹🌹🌹🌹

LONDON SW3	PLAN 4 F1

French, European **V** 🍷 NOTABLE WINE LIST

tel: 020 7352 4441 **68 Royal Hospital Rd SW3 4HP**
email: reservations@gordonramsay.com
dir: *Nearest station: Sloane Sq*

The mothership of the Gordon Ramsay empire

The restaurant first opened its doors in 1998 to signal the launch of the Gordon Ramsay brand, which now extends to a dozen or so addresses in London, a brace apiece for France and Italy, a smattering of locations across Asia and the Middle East, and venues across the pond from Las Vegas to New York. The Royal Hospital Road location has a reputation as a dining destination that extends further back than even Ramsay's tenure, while its position in a quiet part of Chelsea adds to the sense of exclusivity. Clare Smyth took charge of the kitchen in 2008 and is now chef-patron. The dining room is compact – just 45 or so seats – and if at first glance it looks a little crowded, the tables are cleverly arranged to allow maximum privacy. There's a sophisticated finish to the space, with lilac shades and a smattering of art deco influence, plus tables that are set with precision and relative simplicity. The service team is headed-up by Jean-Claude Breton, who has remained in the Ramsay fold since the Aubergine days, with his charming manner making every guest feel like a regular visitor. The fixed-price lunch menu is almost half the price of the carte, making it a good option for anyone looking to keep the costs down, while at the other end of the spectrum the Prestige and Seasonal Inspiration menus offer the opportunity to go the whole hog. Ramsay's place has long been grounded in French classical ways, and so it continues under Clare Smyth's guidance, but there are some more contemporary flourishes on show these days. From the à la carte menu comes a fashionable first course based around baked Cheltenham beetroot, where clementines and pink grapefruit, hazelnuts and smoked goats' curd combine in an attractive ensemble, or there's the no-holds-barred luxury of sautéed foie gras with roast veal sweetbreads, carrot purée and almond foam, all finely offset with the astringency of Cabernet Sauvignon vinegar. Next comes suckling pig (crispy belly, roasted loin and a spicy sausage made from the shoulder meat), or a dish that conveys the essence of the sea: Cornish turbot, baked on the bone en papillotte and plated at the table with its accompaniments of seaweed, palourde clams, sea beet, an exquisite wild chervil sauce and charred hispi cabbage. Everything looks picture-perfect on the plate, right through to a signature dessert of trenchant lemonade parfait with a spun honeycomb tuile, bergamot gel and sheep's milk sorbet. Cheese lovers will not be able to ignore the passing trolley. When it comes to matters of wine, expect a truly memorable list with the world's best producers present and correct, with sommelier Jan Konetzki and his team to help you through it.

Chef Gordon Ramsay, Clare Smyth **Owner** Gordon Ramsay Holdings Ltd **Seats** 45 **Times** 12-2.15/6.30-10.15, Closed 1 wk Xmas, Sat-Sun **Prices** Fixed L 3 course £55, Fixed D 3 course £95, Tasting menu £135-£195 **Wines** 1300 bottles over £30, 5 bottles under £30, 22 by glass **Notes** ALC 3 course £95, Tasting menu 7 course, Children welcome

LONDON SW4 *continued*

The Manor
PLAN 1 F2

◉ Modern British **NEW** v

tel: 020 7720 4662 **148 Clapham Manor St SW4 6BX**
email: reservations@themanorclapham.co.uk
dir: *Nearest station: Clapham North, Clapham Common*

Inventive cooking in side-street bistro

South of the Thames is no longer the land that taxi drivers shun, with Clapham in particular now highly desirable. Tucked along one of its tree-lined side streets of Victorian terraces, just past St Peter's parish church, is The Manor, converted in 2014 from a long-established tapas bar. The decor is simple (loos excepted), which makes it easy to concentrate instead on the far more important job of studying the part-seasonal, part-daily changing menu. And well thought out they are, too, with hardly a dish that could be described as familiar. For example, try a starter of 'Mavie' skate and smoked roe, followed by barbecued lamb ribs, heart and sweetbreads, and dessert of salted almond mousse with Guinness bread parfait, banana and chocolate. Equally interesting alternatives feature Galician octopus, honey-smoked asparagus with mead, and suckling pig belly, although not, of course, on the same plate.

Chef Dean Parker **Owner** Robin Gill **Seats** 55 **Times** 12-3/6-10, Closed 21-29 Dec, 1 Jan, Mon, L Tue, D Sun **Prices** Tasting menu £42 **Wines** 30 bottles over £30, 7 bottles under £30, 10 by glass **Parking** On street **Notes** Tasting menu 7 course, Children welcome

Trinity Restaurant
PLAN 1 E2

◉◉◉ – *see below*

Tsunami
PLAN 1 F2

◉ Japanese

tel: 020 7978 1610 **5-7 Voltaire Rd SW4 6DQ**
email: clapham@tsunamirestaurant.co.uk
dir: *Nearest station: Clapham North, Clapham High St*

Cool minimalism and Japanese fusion food

This original branch of the two Tsunami outlets (the other is on Charlotte Street in the West End) has been making waves in Clapham's hinterland for a dozen years and still gets rammed with crowds of thirty-somethings eager for first-class sushi and sashimi and slick modern Japanese fusion food. A confection of grey, black and gold hues – including faux crocodile-skin banquettes, an open-to-view kitchen and clubby cocktail bar – hits all the fashionable notes, while pavement-side tables offer alfresco dining. Okay, the open-planned space may be hard-edged and high-decibel, but it's really sociable, with the kitchen delivering fresh, skilful, smart-looking classic-meets-contemporary dishes designed for sharing and grazing. Witness unagi (freshwater eel) and foie gras nigiri to seafood tempura, or mains like top-dollar grilled black cod in sweet miso, to truffle rib-eye, while crossover desserts could feature a lemongrass and lime pannacotta.

Chef Ken Sam **Owner** Ken Sam **Seats** 90 **Times** 12.30-3.30/5.30-11, Closed 24-26 Dec, 1 Jan, L Mon-Fri **Prices** Fixed L 2 course £15, Starter £4.65-£12.50, Main £7.90-£28, Dessert £4-£6.50 **Wines** 36 bottles over £30, 13 bottles under £30, 19 by glass **Parking** On street **Notes** Fixed D 5 course £37/£42, Sunday L £7.50-£15, Vegetarian available, Children welcome

Trinity Restaurant ◉◉◉

LONDON SW4 PLAN 1 E2

British, European v
tel: 020 7622 1199 **4 The Polygon, Clapham SW4 0JG**
email: dine@trinityrestaurant.co.uk
dir: *Nearest station: Clapham Common*

Dynamic modern cooking in Clapham

In the old town, a short walk from Clapham Common tube, Adam Byatt's restaurant brings some modern-day verve to SW4. There is no need for the lucky locals to head north in search of culinary thrills with this gem on their doorstep, and non-locals need only jump on the Northern Line (it's well worth the trip). The contemporary dining room is watched over by a slick service team who are all wised-up about the menu and maintain a confident air throughout proceedings. You might have seen Adam on the BBC's *Great British Menu*. There's a tasting menu and carte available lunch and dinner, plus a good-value lunch, while the Sunday lunch menu includes 40-day aged Dexter beef with Yorkshire pudding. The kitchen combines classic and modern ideas in dishes that impress with their invention and satisfy with their relative simplicity. Crispy trotters make an impressive opener, with zingy sauce gribiche and cider mayonnaise, or go for a plate of house-cured meats served with salt-baked quince. Everything looks fine and dandy on the plate, with

a refinement that doesn't detract from the central element. A main course osso buco stays true to the spirit of the original, while adding a contemporary touch or two, and another option might be baked lemon sole with mussels and charred leeks. The adroit technical skills in this kitchen are on show again at dessert stage, with a salted caramel and chocolate cremosa delivering precisely balanced flavours, or in a cheesecake made with vacherin and white chocolate. The wine list matches the food very well.

Chef Adam Byatt **Owner** Angus Jones, Adam Byatt **Seats** 61, Pr/dining room 12 **Times** 12.30-2.30/6.30-10, Closed 24-27 Dec, 1-2 Jan, L Mon, D Sun **Prices** Fixed L 2 course fr £22, Tasting menu £55-£70, Starter £6-£14, Main £18-£30, Dessert £6-£10 **Wines** 220 bottles over £30, 22 bottles under £30, 16 by glass **Parking** On street **Notes** Sunday L £32, Children welcome

LONDON SW5

Cambio de Tercio
PLAN 4 C2

◉◉ Spanish **V**

tel: 020 7244 8970 **163 Old Brompton Rd SW5 0LJ**
email: cambiodeterciogroup@btconnect.com
dir: *Nearest station: Gloucester Rd*

Vibrant modern Spanish cooking in a setting to match

With tapas joints Capote y Toros and Tendido Cero, owner Abel Lusa has created a 'Little Spain' enclave on this bend in Old Brompton Road. In flagship Tercio, folding full-length glass windows open the place up to the street for a Mediterranean vibe, and there's a G&T bar with over 80 gins to tackle. Inside it has a dark, intimate, sexy Spanish feel – black slate floors and big and bold hues of mustard yellow and deep fuchsia pink hung with striking modern artworks. The modern Spanish food is equally colourful and good looking, ranging from traditional tapas done right, to innovative signature dishes with a homage to the legendary El Bulli here and there. Oxtail caramelised in red wine matched with apple and lemon-thyme air is a star turn, while more substantial mains run to Basque-style hake casserole with parsley sauce, razor clams, mussels and cockles, or grilled skate with crunchy pig's trotters, Burgos morcilla terrine and orange vinaigrette. Desserts keep the creativity on stream with the likes of crispy Cuban mojito in a caramel ball.

Chef Alberto Criado **Owner** Abel Lusa **Seats** 90, Pr/dining room 18 **Times** 12-2.30/6.30-11.30, Closed 2 wks at Xmas, New Year **Prices** Tasting menu £45, Starter £3.75-£23.50, Main £19.75-£28, Dessert £7.50-£14.50 **Wines** 300+ bottles over £30, 15 bottles under £30, 6 by glass **Parking** 10, Paid parking **Notes** Sunday L £24-£27, Children welcome

Capote y Toros
PLAN 4 C2

◉ Spanish **V**

tel: 020 7373 0567 **157 Old Brompton Rd SW5 0LJ**
email: cambiodeterciogroup@btconnect.com
dir: *Nearest station: South Kensington, Gloucester Rd*

Authentic tapas plus interesting specialities

A few doors away from sibling Cambio de Tercio, Capote y Toros describes itself as a tapas, ham and sherry bar. It has vivid decor with photographs of matadors and hams hanging from the ceiling above the bar. Live flamenco music and a friendly team providing attentive levels of service add to the laid-back sense of fun. More than 100 sherries and a patriotic wine list play a part too. Ask the staff about how much and what to order and jump in. Soft and tender chorizo cooked in fino, Galician-style octopus with potato and paprika, five pork meatballs with oloroso sauce and patatas bravas should see you right, being of exceptional quality and all cooked exactly as they would be back home. Don't overlook the specialities, among them loin of venison with baked apple and Pedro Ximénez sauce, and home-made cod sausage with peppers and vegetables. Among the puddings, try perhaps tipsy Spanish bread pudding with amontillado.

Chef Luis Navacerrada Lanzadera **Owner** Abel Lusa **Times** 6-11.30, Closed Xmas, Sun-Mon, L all week **Prices** Starter £4.50-£23, Main £5.25-£10.50, Dessert £6-£8 **Wines** 110 bottles over £30, 35 bottles under £30 **Parking** On street **Notes** Children welcome

New Lotus Garden
PLAN 4 B3

◉ Chinese

tel: 020 7244 8984 **15 Kenway Rd SW5 0RP**
email: jiang.hubert@gmail.com
dir: *Nearest station: Earl's Court*

Neighbourhood Chinese that really hits the spot

Down a residential street in Earl's Court, the white-painted New Lotus Garden is a little powerhouse of Pekinese and Cantonese cooking. This is the domain of Hubert Jiang and it's only little and rather humble, but that's a good thing, and the warm red décor gives a comforting glow. The menu is long and doesn't really stand out from the crowd, but execution is good and the flavours sing out. Start with salt and pepper asparagus, or succulent barbecue spare ribs, or mussels in black bean sauce. There are dim sum dishes, too, plus crispy aromatic duck and soups like a classic chicken and sweetcorn version. Among main courses, twice-cooked belly of pork with preserved vegetables hits the spot, or try the spicy crispy shredded beef. Vegetarians get a decent amount of choice with things like aubergines braised in black bean sauce, and there is a good range of noodle dishes.

Times 12-2.30/5-11.30, Closed 24-26 Dec

LONDON SW6

Blue Elephant
PLAN 1 E3

◉ Thai **V**

tel: 020 7751 3111 **The Boulevard, Imperial Wharf, Townmead Rd SW6 2UB**
email: london@blueelephant.com
dir: *Nearest station: Imperial Wharf*

Lavish riverside setting for upmarket Thai dining

The Blue Elephant pulls in an international crowd to the plush Thames-side Imperial Wharf development. The multi-level space has an extravagant decor inspired by the Saran Rom palace in Bangkok. With its mini rainforest of luxuriant foliage, Thai artefacts of carved and painted wood, orchids on dark wood tables and a gilded bar modelled on the Royal Barge of Thailand, it's over the top, but enjoyably so. The lengthy menu is divided into Thai cooking of 'the past', 'today' and 'tomorrow', plus a couple of tasting options and a vegetarian section. Start in the present with 'paper prawns' – tiger prawns wrapped in rice-paper stuffed with minced chicken and crushed peanuts, with a home-made plum sauce for dipping – followed by steamed whole sea bass with organic lemongrass, fresh lime juice, Thai pickled garlic and crushed chillies. Service is charming and authentic and there's also a riverside alfresco terrace.

Chef Nooror Somany **Owner** Blue Elephant International Group **Seats** 150, Pr/dining room 8 **Times** 12-2.30/7-10.30, Closed 25-28 Dec, 1 Jan, L Mon-Fri **Prices** Prices not confirmed **Wines** 100 bottles over £30, 5 bottles under £30, 13 by glass **Parking** Car park next to Imperial Wharf tube station **Notes** Sun brunch, Sunday L, Children welcome

LONDON SW6 *continued*

The Harwood Arms
PLAN 1 E3

◉◉ British V

tel: 020 7386 1847 **27 Walham Grove, Fulham SW6 1QR**
email: admin@harwoodarms.com
dir: *Nearest station: Fulham Broadway*

Supplier-led British cooking in smart gastro-pub

On an unassuming backstreet in trendy Fulham, the stylish Harwood Arms is one of Britain's top gastro-pubs, all the more so as it remains true to its roots as a cracking community local – Tuesday night is quiz night, there's a raft of real ales on tap, and the overall vibe is relaxed and informal. With Brett Graham of The Ledbury and The Pot Kiln's Mike Robinson as owners, you've a right to have high expectations. And they are duly met. Inside you could almost forget you're in London with photos of outdoor country pursuits hung on grey and cream walls, and rustic wooden tables. On the menu, first class, carefully-sourced English produce is cooked with confidence; Berkshire rabbit faggots, for example, with split peas, smoked bacon and pickled mushrooms is a robust way to start, before moving on to Old Spots pork belly with root vegetable broth and ribs glazed in ginger beer, or wild sea bass with cauliflower, oat-crusted mussels and preserved lemon. And neither do desserts miss a beat: baked stem ginger custard with honeycomb ice cream is an unerringly satisfying finale.

Chef Alex Harper **Owner** Trieamain Harwood Ltd **Seats** 60
Times 12-3/6.30-9.30, Closed 24-28 Dec, 1 Jan, L Mon **Prices** Fixed L 2 course £20-£33.50, Fixed D 3 course £39.50, Tasting menu £45-£90 **Wines** 183 bottles over £30, 14 bottles under £30, 20 by glass **Parking** On street **Notes** Sunday L, Children welcome

Marco Grill
PLAN 1 E3

◉◉ British Grill

tel: 020 7915 2929 **M&C Hotels at Chelsea FC, Stamford Bridge, Fulham Rd SW6 1HS**
email: info@marcogrill.com
dir: *Nearest station: Fulham Broadway*

Steakhouse and brasserie-style dishes at Stamford Bridge

Yes, it is that Marco who is the man behind this glossy steakhouse operation, so rest assured that the beef is supported by MPW's signature style of tried-and-tested brasserie dishes, and it is all driven by top-class ingredients, sharply-defined flavours and classy execution. The place may be in Chelsea football ground, but this is a world a long, long way from the pies and hotdogs that fuel the footie fans: a chic decor brings together charcoal-grey walls, smoked mirrors, low-level lighting, and leather banquettes and velour seats at linen-swathed tables. Melt-in-the-mouth tuna carpaccio is matched with the punchy flavours of coriander shoots and ginger, then as top-class 35-day aged steaks are the main culinary thrust here, a rib-eye is seared to perfection and delivered with triple-cooked chips and a textbook béarnaise. Otherwise go for a Gallic brasserie classic – perhaps roast rack of lamb with Mediterranean vegetables, gratin dauphinoise and sauce paloise. Puddings are a strong suit, as in a chocolate mousse duo encased in a dark chocolate dome with raspberry sauce.

Chef Roger Pizey **Owner** C.F.C **Seats** 70 **Times** 6-10.30, Closed 2 wks Jul-Aug, Sun-Mon, L all week **Prices** Tasting menu £65, Starter £8-£12, Main £12-£26, Dessert £5.50-£7.50 **Wines** 20 bottles over £30, 7 bottles under £30, 8 by glass **Parking** 10 **Notes** Steak club Thu, Vegetarian available, Children welcome

Baglioni Hotel
PLAN 4 C5

◉ Modern Italian

tel: 020 7368 5700 **60 Hyde Park Gate, Kensington Rd, Kensington SW7 5BB**
email: brunello.london@baglionihotels.com **web:** www.baglionihotels.com
dir: *Nearest station: High St Kensington*

Modern Italian cooking in swish hotel

The Baglioni's Brunello restaurant is an open-plan bar-lounge and stylish dining room with plush seating, rich fabrics, chandeliers and charming and attentive staff, mostly Italian. Ingredients are diligently sought out, many from the motherland, to re-create the modern Italian cooking style, as in a richly flavoured starter of caponata and burrata cheese drizzled with olive oil, and smoked swordfish with exotic fruit salad in a grape reduction. Pasta dishes are given their due – perhaps pappardelle with veal ragù and broad beans – and main courses have included pink and succulent veal chop with creamy mash and sautéed spinach, and chargrilled prawns and squid with baby seasonal vegetables. There's a great range of home-made breads, and among dolci might be vanilla cheesecake with cherry sorbet.

Chef Stefano Impera **Owner** Baglioni Hotels **Seats** 70, Pr/dining room 60
Times 12.30-3/5.30-11 **Prices** Prices not confirmed **Wines** 4 bottles under £30, 8 by glass **Parking** 2, On street Kensington Rd/De Vere Gardens **Notes** Pre-theatre menu 5.30-7pm all wk £25-£29, Sunday L, Vegetarian available, Children welcome

Bombay Brasserie
PLAN 4 C3

◉◉ Indian

tel: 020 7370 4040 **Courtfield Close, Courtfield Rd SW7 4QH**
email: info@bbrestaurant.co.uk
dir: *Nearest station: Gloucester Rd*

Long-running, stylish address with modern Indian cooking

It's hard to believe that the Bombay has been feeding London with authentic, carefully crafted Indian food for over 30 years, but so it is. The Kensington location ensures a lot of plutocratic custom, but the place has always had wide appeal. There are two stylish dining rooms, one of deep-pile banquettes under statement chandeliers, the other a lighter conservatory-roofed space. The food is presented in an elegant contemporary western manner, its spices and seasonings guaranteed to make the palate sit up and take notice. Start with crisp-fried spinach in evanescently thin batter, dressed with date and tamarind chutney and yogurt, or with cakes of shredded duck meat stuffed with red onions in yogurt and mint. Those might be followed by corn-fed chicken tikka marinated in cardamom, coriander and garlic, masala sea bass with mushrooms, or a majestic seafood platter that includes, among other items, prawns with green mango, soft-shelled crab and tandoori monkfish. Keep on going to dessert stage, and don't miss the almond and date pudding, with fennel and cracked pepper sauce and rose ice cream.

Chef Prahlad Hegde **Owner** Taj International Hotels **Seats** 185, Pr/dining room 16
Times 12-2.30/6.30-11.30, Closed 25 Dec, L Mon **Prices** Fixed L 3 course fr £24, Fixed D 3 course £44-£90, Starter £7-£12, Main £16-£25 **Wines** 97 bottles over £30, 7 bottles under £30, 18 by glass **Parking** Millennium Gloucester Hotel next door **Notes** Sat-Sun buffet L £31, Sunday L, Vegetarian available, Children welcome

L'Etranger

PLAN 4 C4

◉◉ French, Japanese NOTABLE WINE LIST

tel: 020 7584 1118 & 7823 9291 **36 Gloucester Rd SW7 4QT**
email: etranger@etranger.co.uk
dir: *Nearest station: Gloucester Rd*

A Franco-Japanese handshake in chic South Ken surroundings

The Franco-Japanese fusion focus of L'Etranger might have felt like a passing fad when the place opened many years ago, and yet it has proved enduringly popular, and has a tenacious local following among the well-heeled of South Kensington. It's dressed to impress, the walls cut with a mirrored panel offset with fronds of greenery, dark glass tables and an oak floor. Staff are smart in every sense of the term, and the food looks as stylishly fine-tuned as befits a marriage of French chic and Japanese precision. Marinated mackerel with mooli and Granny Smith is a bracing way to begin, or there may be truffled miso quail with mustard ice cream, or traditional sashimi platters. Main courses add yuzu foam to sea bass and shiitakes with raisin purée, or add a vivid splash of parsley chlorophyll to Grade 9 wagyu sirloin. Lunch is a simpler, more obviously western affair – perhaps foie gras terrine with port jelly and pain d'épices, then cod and squid with chorizo. Finish with textured variations on chocolate and pear, or light cheesecake with fig compôte.

Chef Jerome Tauvron **Owner** Ibi Issolah **Seats** 64, Pr/dining room 20 **Times** 12-3/5.30-11, Closed 26-27 Dec **Prices** Fixed L 2 course £19.50, Fixed D 3 course £26.50-£77, Tasting menu £75, Starter £6.50-£14.50, Main £12.50-£50, Dessert £7.50-£12.50 **Wines** 1400 bottles over £30, 60 bottles under £30, 12 by glass **Parking** NCP **Notes** Degustation 6 course £75, Pre/post-theatre 3 course menu, Sunday L £7.50-£25, Vegetarian available, Children welcome

Millennium Bailey's Hotel London Kensington

PLAN 4 C3

◉ Italian

tel: 020 7331 6308 & 7331 6301 **140 Gloucester Rd SW7 4QH**
email: olives.baileys@millenniumhotels.com **web:** www.olivesrestaurant.co.uk
dir: *Nearest station: Gloucester Rd*

Uncomplicated Italian food in South Ken

The elegantly restored Victorian townhouse hotel in upmarket South Kensington is handy for the museums as well as some serious shopping. Arched windows and sweeping staircases confer a sense of bygone magnificence on the scene, but the main dining room, Olives, a long narrow room with unclothed tables and pastel-shaded upholstery, goes for a pared-down look, the better to offset the uncomplicated Italian cooking on offer. The classically structured menu format takes in antipasti such as porchetta with fennel and chilli relish, intermediates such as pumpkin gnocchi with balsamic beef and shaved parmesan, and main items like breast and confit leg of duck with beetroot salad and mash, or seared tuna with apple and pesto. Pre-theatre menus are efficiently dispensed to those with a curtain-up deadline. Finish with the utter simplicity of coffee-flavoured crème caramel, or pineapple carpaccio infused with vanilla.

Chef Davide di Croce **Owner** Millennium & Copthorne **Seats** 70 **Times** 12-10.30, All-day dining **Prices** Prices not confirmed **Notes** Vegetarian available, Children welcome

Rivea London Bulgari Hotel & Residences

PLAN 4 F5

◉◉◉ *– see below*

Rivea London Bulgari Hotel & Residences ◉◉◉

LONDON SW7

PLAN 4 F5

Modern French, Italian Riviera NOTABLE WINE LIST
tel: 020 7151 1025 & 7151 1010 **171 Knightsbridge SW7 1DW**
email: reservations@rivealondon.com **web:** www.rivealondon.com
dir: *Nearest station: Knightsbridge*

Franco-Italian cooking in relaxed and stylish surroundings

Alain Ducasse is one of the heavyweights of French cooking and a master of haute cuisine, but he also has restaurants all over the world that reflect his passion for more simple and humble things. Here at the dazzling Bulgari Hotel is Rivea London, a venue dedicated to the flavours of the Riviera, with the tastes of Italy and France combining to create dynamic and classic plates for sharing. The dishes really punch above their weight. Take the sweeping staircase downstairs to be met with a vision of art deco glamour and colour tones reminiscent of Provence, with polished service befitting the postcode. When it comes to simplicity, quality of produce is all, and judging by a superb red mullet (cooked just-so) with confit-style tomatoes and a scattering of black olives and capers, this is a kitchen that knows how to buy as well as cook. The dishes come out of the kitchen as and when they are ready in an order unknown to the customer. Green asparagus and parmesan is light and delicate, marinated sea bream delivers a lively hit of citrusy acidity, and there are pasta options such as ravioli filled with artichoke and borage. The first-class produce continues to shine in a dish of rib and saddle of lamb, or another where turbot arrives in the company of root vegetables and muscat grapes. There's evident technical skill right the way through to a classic chocolate tart served up with malted ice cream. The wine list has lots of interesting options from Italy and France.

Chef Alexandre Nicolas **Seats** 80, Pr/dining room 12 **Times** 12-2.30/6.30-10.30, **Prices** Fixed L 3 course fr £35, Starter £6-£13, Main £12-£23, Dessert £6-£8 **Wines** 200 bottles over £30, 5 bottles under £30, 15 by glass **Parking** NCP Pavillion Rd **Notes** Sunday L fr £35, Vegetarian available, Children welcome

LONDON SW7 *continued*

Zuma
PLAN 4 F5

◉◉ Modern Japanese

tel: 020 7584 1010 **5 Raphael St, Knightsbridge SW7 1DL**
email: info@zumarestaurant.com
dir: *Nearest station: Knightsbridge*

Buzzy modern Japanese in fashionable Knightsbridge

An effortlessly cool playground of the beau monde, Knightsbridge's high-energy trend-setting Zuma (now a global brand) is every bit a top-call for lovers of contemporary Japanese food and slick design. Its über-chic interior has that minimal Zen-like high gloss, with striking contemporary textures of blond wood, polished granite, steel and glass and the comforts of fashionable cream leather seating. The vibe is high octane, buoyed by the buzzing front bar-lounge offering 40 different sakes. But, whether you dine in the main restaurant, at the sizzling robata grill or calmer sushi counter, the precision cooking is defined by superb fresh ingredients, clear flavours, eye-catching presentation and slick service. Graze through a lengthy roster of in-vogue sharing plates; perhaps crispy fried squid pepped up by green chilli and lime, or, from the robata, succulent pork skewers (stickily glazed) with lively mustard miso, while classics like vegetable tempura and signatures like marinated black cod (wrapped in hoba leaf) find their place too. Desserts, such as yuzu cheesecake with raspberry granité and black sesame, bridge the East-West divide, while sushi is exemplary. Okay, prices might alarm your financial advisor, but the high quality and up tempo vibe are priceless.

Chef Bjoern Weissgerber **Owner** Rainer Becker, Arjun Waney **Seats** 175, Pr/dining room 14 **Times** 12-3/6-11, Closed 25 Dec **Prices** Prices not confirmed **Parking** On street **Notes** Vegetarian available, Children welcome

---

LONDON SW10

Medlar Restaurant
PLAN 4 D1

◉◉◉ *– see below*

The Painted Heron
PLAN 1 E3

◉ Modern Indian

tel: 020 7351 5232 **112 Cheyne Walk SW10 0DJ**
email: thepaintedheron@btinternet.com
dir: *Nearest station: South Kensington*

First-rate modern Indian near the river

This upscale Chelsea Indian is a thoroughly modern affair with its clean-lined interior done out with black leather upholstered chairs, white linen-clothed tables and understated neutral hues. The cooking is equally smart and modern, underpinned by seasonality and well-judged spicing, and making use of produce not often encountered on Indian menus: in game season there's partridge with spicy minced lamb sauce, or perhaps mallard with root vegetable mash and curry sauce. Elsewhere, starters tickle the fancy with home-smoked monkfish tikka with carom seeds or perhaps chargrilled lamb chops with nutmeg flowers, while main courses cater to traditionalists with an 'Indian Railways' mutton curry. The dessert list closes with an East-meets-West fusion of sticky gulab jamun with passionfruit mousse or pistachio and pear cup cake with chai cream and mango samosa. There are plenty of spice-friendly wines too, and cigar smokers have the luxury of their own lounge out back.

Chef Yogesh Datta **Owner** Yogesh Datta **Seats** 70 **Times** 12-3/6-11, Closed Xmas, 1 Jan **Prices** Starter £7-£9.50, Main £13.50-£20, Dessert £4-£5 **Wines** 38 bottles over £30, 21 bottles under £30, 16 by glass **Parking** On street **Notes** Tasting menu 6 course whole table min 2 people, Sunday L, Vegetarian available, Children welcome

---

Medlar Restaurant ❀❀❀

LONDON SW10
PLAN 4 D1

Modern European ⬥ NOTABLE WINE LIST
tel: 020 7349 1900 **438 King's Rd, Chelsea SW10 0LJ**
email: info@medlarrestaurant.co.uk
dir: *Nearest station: Sloane Sq, Earl's Court, Fulham Broadway*

Fashionable Chelsea spot for cooking of gutsy potency

If you're hoofing it from the tube, Medlar is about 20 minutes from either Sloane Square or Fulham Broadway. This has been one of Chelsea's more talked-about dining spots since it opened. The place looks box-fresh, with Lincoln-green banquette seating against mirror panels in one section, leading to a back room done in crisp white with a foliate pattern in thin green tracery on the walls. There's a feeling of spacious freshness, which might lead you to expect an ethereal approach to the food, but Joe Mercer Nairne's food has gutsy, earthy substance. He specialises in taking often humble ingredients and less common cuts and subjecting them to treatments that bring out all their intrinsic flavour, in dishes that are easy to understand but still full of commanding potency. Take a starter serving of thinly sliced breast of lamb, pair it with tempura-battered baby artichokes and dress it with aïoli to create an instant classic. Even a more obvious seafood dish, such as crab raviolo with brown shrimps and samphire on leek fondue in rich bisque has new resonance struck from it. Offal is favoured, winningly so in a main dish of grilled ox tongue with truffled macaroni gratin, cauliflower, walnuts and glazed shallot, while meats such as duck breast and venison loin have all their innate intensity conjured forth, the latter perhaps with a spiced pastilla, carrot and swede crush and hispi cabbage in a belting Cabernet Sauvignon sauce. The dessert list, by contrast, is put together on the principle that old favourites make the best finale: pear frangipane with clotted cream, chocolate marquise with peanut ice cream, crème brûlée.

Chef Joe Mercer Nairne **Owner** Joe Mercer Nairne, David O'Connor **Seats** 85, Pr/dining room 28 **Times** 12-3/6.30-10.30, Closed Xmas, 1 Jan **Prices** Fixed L 2 course £22.50, Fixed D 3 course £46 **Wines** 500+ bottles over £30, 45 bottles under £30, 28 by glass **Parking** On street (may be difficult during lunch) **Notes** Prix fixe menu, Sat L 2/3 course £25/£30, Sunday L £20-£35, Vegetarian available, Children welcome

LONDON SW11

Entrée Restaurant and Bar
PLAN 1 E2

@@ Modern European

tel: 020 7223 5147 **2 Battersea Rise, Battersea SW11 1ED**
email: info@entreebattersea.co.uk
dir: Nearest station: Clapham Junction, Clapham Common

Buzzing neighbourhood restaurant and bar

It's easy to see why this smart but relaxed venue – complete with bijou low-lit cocktail bar and jazz piano on the lower floor and atmospheric dining room above – is such a big hit with the Battersea/Clapham set. There's an on-cue open kitchen, while wooden floors, black leather banquettes and unclothed tables create a laid-back fashionable tone. Thoughtfully presented food – on a regularly changing menu – comes prepared from fresh, seasonal, quality Brit ingredients, with the cooking influenced by France. Ambition is apparent yet it's skilfully restrained, with light, refined, eye-catching dishes the kitchen's forte. Take a duo of lamb (succulent rump and full-flavoured shoulder) teamed with a Med-inspired combo of tomato, chargrilled courgette and olive and pommes purées, or for fish lovers, perhaps sea bass, the fillet seared and served with braised baby gem, crushed new potatoes and cauliflower. Do save room for desserts like a classy bitter chocolate delice with pistachio ice cream and a wow-inducing blood orange purée to cut through the richness. Relaxed small-plate dining is offered in the bar.

Times 12-4/6-10.30, Closed 1 wk Xmas, Mon, L Tue-Fri, D Sun

London House
PLAN 1 E3

@@@ – see below

LONDON SW12

Lamberts
PLAN 1 E2

@@ Modern British

tel: 020 8675 2233 **2 Station Pde, Balham High Rd SW12 9AZ**
email: bookings@lambertsrestaurant.com
dir: Nearest station: Balham

Top-notch produce treated with respect in a smart, modern setting

Just a minute's stroll from the tube station, this smart eatery makes the idea of a foray into Balham a more inviting prospect than might otherwise be the case. The compact space wears an inoffensively neutral modern look with mustard yellow walls, chocolate brown banquettes, bare darkwood tables and dark hardwood flooring – nothing to stand out from many an urban brasserie, perhaps, but it is apparent when the food arrives that the place is driven by a passion for sourcing top-class ingredients, and a chef who knows how to make their flavours shout out loud. There's certainly much more going on than the dishes' minimal menu descriptions would suggest: confit trout with potato salad and watercress bursts with subtle notes, while a main course of Herdwick lamb with peas, wilted gem lettuce and mash gains lustre from the sheer quality of the produce. For dessert, a textbook chocolate fondant mingles wickedly with stout ice cream.

Chef Matthew Harris **Owner** Mr Joe Lambert **Seats** 50
Times 12.30-2.30/6-10, Closed 25 Dec, BHs (except Good Fri), Mon, D Sun
Prices Fixed L 2 course £12-£15, Fixed D 3 course £20-£24, Starter £7-£10, Main £13-£20, Dessert £6-£9 **Wines** 33 bottles over £30, 25 bottles under £30, 13 by glass **Parking** On street **Notes** Sunday L £24-£28, Vegetarian available, Children welcome

London House @@@

LONDON SW11
PLAN 1 E3

Modern European

tel: 020 7592 8545 & 7592 7952 **7-9 Battersea Square, Battersea Village SW11 3RA**
email: londonhouse@gordonramsay.com
dir: Nearest station: Clapham Junction

Refined cooking with the focus on flavour

They used to consume oysters on this spot back in the day when they were the food of the people (1780 it says on the gable), and today this prominent corner spot on Battersea Square is in fine fettle as part of the Gordon Ramsay empire, for he's brought a touch of uptown glamour to SW11. There's a classy lounge bar looking like a funky gentlemen's club, where you can sit in front of a flame-effect fire and enjoy a cocktail mixed by the talented team behind the copper-topped bar. The restaurant areas are smart and contemporary, with splashy modern artworks and plenty of room between the tables. The kitchen is headed up by Dublin-born Anna Haugh, and her food has refinement without an excess of fine-dining baggage. The menu du jour is the entry level option (available lunchtime and early evening), while the carte offers a sensible six or so options per course, and the tasting menu is consigned to history. Anna has worked at some high-end addresses around the world and she's clearly found inspiration along the way, with high quality British ingredients forming the foundation of the menu. Scottish girolles, for example, find their way into a velouté which is by turns rich and light, with pink pistachios bringing texture and the accompanying mixed seed bread served in a dinky terracotta flower pot. Among main courses, a perfectly steamed plaice comes in the Mediterranean-inspired company of parmesan arancini and tapenade purée with Cumbrian beef matched with a stellar broad bean purée and gnocchi made with the braised cheek. Winning flavour combinations and technical proficiency continue in a chocolate tart with lavender ice cream and honeycomb caramel. The wine list offers plenty of enticing options by the glass.

Chef Anna Haugh-Kelly **Owner** Gordon Ramsay Holdings Ltd **Seats** 63
Times 12-3/6-10, Closed Mon (ex BHs), L Tue-Wed **Prices** Fixed L 2 course £22.50-£32.50, Fixed D 3 course £28-£40, Service optional 12.5% **Wines** 180 bottles over £30, 22 bottles under £30, 13 by glass **Parking** On street **Notes** Vegetarian available, Children welcome

LONDON SW13

Sonny's Kitchen
PLAN 1 D3

◉◉ Modern British, French

tel: 020 8748 0393 & 8741 8451 **94 Church Rd, Barnes SW13 0DQ**
email: manager@sonnyskitchen.co.uk
dir: *Nearest station: Barnes*

Popular and highly regarded neighbourhood restaurant

Sonny's, part restaurant, part food store, has clearly hit on a winning formula, since the lucky residents of Barnes have kept the place buzzing towards its third decade. The unassuming frontage in a parade of shops opens into a surprisingly roomy split-level space with a neutral designer-chic decor of almost Scandinavian minimalism involving textures of wood, leather, ceramic tiles, glass bricks and white walls hung with art. The kitchen deals in inventive modern European food with sunny Mediterranean accents, delivering precise flavours and textures in a well-composed starter of chargrilled spatchcock quail with quinoa, pomegranate, pistachio and raisins, or you might get going with steamed Cornish cockles with lemon and olive oil. Main course brings an exemplary slab of roast cod, timed to perfection and matched with pea purée and potato and ham galette, while meatier offerings run to the likes of slow-cooked veal cheek with hand-made strozzapreti pasta, girolles and smashed peas. It all ends on a satisfying note with a warm chocolate fondant with milk ice cream and a squidgy-centred pistachio macaroon.

Chef James Holah **Owner** Rebecca Mascarenhas, Phil Howard **Seats** 100, Pr/dining room 18 **Times** 12-2.30/6.30-10.30, Closed Xmas, New Year **Prices** Fixed L 2 course fr £17.95, Fixed D 3 course fr £19.95, Starter £3.25-£8.50, Main £13-£29.50, Dessert £6-£9.50 **Wines** 36 bottles over £30, 24 bottles under £30, 20 by glass **Parking** On street **Notes** Brunch Sat-Sun 10-12, Sunday L £25, Vegetarian available, Children welcome

LONDON SW14

The Depot
PLAN 1 D3

◉ Modern European, British

tel: 020 8878 9462 **Tideway Yard, 125 Mortlake High St, Barnes SW14 8SN**
email: info@depotbrasserie.co.uk
dir: *Nearest station: Barnes Bridge*

Popular, relaxed, neighbourhood brasserie by the river

Built in 1901 and smartly converted from Barnes Council refuse depot's stables and coach house in 1986, The Depot pulls in the crowds with its knockout riverside views and a crowd-pleasing European brasserie-style food. It's a good-looking venue with a skeleton rowing boat hanging above herringbone parquet floors, rustic painted tables, brightly-patterned banquettes and simple wooden chairs set against warm mustard and coffee-coloured walls. Foie gras and ham hock terrine with dandelion, walnut and shallot salad and toasted brioche starts things off, followed by roast brill fillet with lemon butter, baby artichoke, samphire, potato and pea fricassée, or you might keep it classic with a chargrilled bavette with chips and garlic béarnaise. It all finishes comfortably with a pot of Venezuelan chocolate with salted caramel mousse and shortbread. Fixed-price options and bar and children's menus help keep the locals returning.

Times 12-3.30/6-10

The Victoria
PLAN 1 C2

◉◉ Modern British **NEW**

tel: 020 8876 4238 **10 West Temple Sheen SW14 7RT**
email: bookings@thevictoria.net **web:** www.thevictoria.net
dir: *Nearest station: Mortlake*

Great all-rounder by the park

A short stroll from Richmond Park, The Victoria describes itself as a public house, dining room and hotel, and the truth is it fulfils each role with aplomb. In a residential street with a primary school next door, the lucky locals seem to appreciate what they have on their doorstep. The bar stocks real ales, the conservatory restaurant opens onto a terrace, and the rooms are bright and contemporary. Co-owned by chef Paul Merrett – as seen on TV – the kitchen's modern British output impresses with its ambition and execution. A first course Loch Duart salmon sashimi is dependent on the quality of the fish, and this one is spot on, topped with shallot and chilli crunch and served with ketjapmanis (an Indonesian sauce) and pickled cucumbers. Among main course options, chargrilled leg of lamb comes with Middle Eastern accompaniments, South Devon rib-eye steak arrives with béarnaise sauce and 'thrice cooked' chips, and pan-roasted rainbow trout is partnered with cockles, bacon and monk's beard. Finish with dark chocolate shortbread with milk chocolate mousse and nut brownie ice cream.

Chef Paul Merrett **Owner** Greg Ballamy, Paul Merrett **Seats** 70, Pr/dining room 45 **Times** 12-2.30/6-10 **Prices** Fixed L 2 course fr £17, Fixed D 2 course fr £17, Starter £6-£8.50, Main £13.50-£21, Dessert £4-£7, Service optional 12.5% **Wines** 40+ bottles over £30, 26 bottles under £30, 25 by glass **Parking** 18 **Notes** Fixed L/D Mon-Fri only, Brunch Sat 11-3pm, Sunday L £24-£28, Vegetarian available, Children welcome

LONDON SW15

Bibo
PLAN 1 D2

◉ Modern Italian

tel: 020 8780 0592 **146 Upper Richmond, Putney SW15 2SW**
email: info@biborestaurant.com
dir: *Nearest station: East Putney*

Relaxed, high-energy East Putney Italian with bags of pedigree

Rebecca Mascarenhas, London restaurateur with the Midas touch when it comes to neighbourhood outfits (think Kitchen W8, Sonny's, etc.), launched this cracking local Italian back in March 2014 and it hit the ground running. Head chef Chris Beverley has pedigree too (ex Theo Randall at The InterContinental and Chez Bruce) and it shows on the menu and plate. In classic Italain style, and, with a strong regional accent, simple seasonal combinations allow prime ingredients to shine. Pasta is a forte, perhaps spot-on taglierini nero teamed with octopus and pepped up by chilli and garlic, while mains, like sparkling-fresh sea bream, deliver brilliantly with squeaky-fresh asparagus and spinach. Desserts (pannacotta with poached rhubarb), in-house breads, all-Italian wines and sunny service maintain stellar form. The fashionable pared-back surroundings fit the neighbourhood billing, with street-side terrace and bar up front (and all-day small-plate dining), while the two-tiered dining room behind comes with vibrant Bruce McLean prints, and the upper-level with conservatory-style overhead windows. Otherwise, white-washed brickwork, small waxed-oak tables, banquettes or café-style chairs and high decibels complete the on-cue look.

Chef Chris Beverely **Owner** R Mascarenhas **Seats** 70
Times 12-2.30/6-10.30, Closed 24-26 Dec, BHs, L Good Fri, D Etr Sun **Prices** Starter £6-£10.50, Main £13-£18.50, Dessert £5.50-£7.50, Service optional 12.5% **Wines** 62 bottles over £30, 16 bottles under £30, 12 by glass **Parking** On street **Notes** L dish of day Mon-Fri 1 course £10, Sunday L £25, Vegetarian available, Children welcome

Enoteca Turi

PLAN 1 D2

◉ Modern Italian

tel: 020 8785 4449 **28 Putney High St SW15 1SQ**
email: info@enotecaturi.com
dir: *Nearest station: Putney, Putney Bridge*

Regional Italian food and wine in Putney

Occupying its corner plot since 1990, EnotecaTuri is an Italian restaurant of heart and soul. Run by the same family for all that time, the focus remains on regional Italian flavours, with the menu highlighting the origins of each dish (Piedmont, Puglia, etc.). It's the kind of place that buzzes with life when it's busy, which is often the case. The wine is another element that makes it stand out from the crowd, with more than 300 bins offering some really interesting stuff, sorted by region with matches for every dish. The menu doesn't lack for refinement, but the focus is on high quality, seasonal ingredients. Among antipasti, braised cuttlefish might come with chickpea purée and deep-fried pasta, or grilled fillet of mackerel with fennel and blood orange salad and a citrus dressing. Next up, a duck dish with a punchy sauce flavoured with liver, served with polenta gnocchi and cavolo nero.

Chef Michele Blasi **Owner** Mr G & Mrs P Turi **Seats** 85, Pr/dining room 18 **Times** 12-2.30/7-10.30, Closed 25-26 Dec, 1 Jan, Sun, L BHs **Prices** Fixed L 2 course fr £18.50, Fixed D 3 course fr £34.50 **Wines** 300 bottles over £30, 15 bottles under £30, 13 by glass **Parking** Putney Exchange car park, on street **Notes** Vegetarian available, Children welcome

LONDON SW17

Chez Bruce

PLAN 1 E2

◉◉◉ – *see below*

LONDON SW19

The Fox & Grapes

PLAN 1 D2

◉ Traditional British

tel: 020 8619 1300 **9 Camp Rd, Wimbledon SW19 4UN**
email: reservations@foxandgrapeswimbledon.co.uk
dir: *Nearest station: Wimbledon*

Country pub charms by the Common

On the edge of Wimbledon Common, The Fox & Grapes has the feel of a country pub, but a smart one, mind you, for this is SW19. The opened-up interior has beams and parquet floors and still has the attitude of an upscale inn – real ales at the pumps, smart bedrooms upstairs – while offering food that offers a slick take on some old favourites. Avocado prawn cocktail is a starter with bags of retro appeal, but there's also the more contemporary cured salmon with pickled kohlrabi and horseradish yogurt. Among main courses, a fashionably pimped-up burger is present and correct (topped with Ogleshield cheese), and there's a Middle Eastern spin to partridge flavoured with ras el hanout and served with chickpeas and preserved lemons. The Butcher's Board lists the various cuts of steak on offer, and, to finish, there might be treacle tart with stem ginger ice cream.

Chef Lee Barnett **Owner** Jolly Fine Pubs **Seats** 90 **Times** 12-3/6-9.30, Closed 25 Dec **Prices** Prices not confirmed, Service optional 12.5% **Wines** 33 bottles over £30, 16 bottles under £30, 11 by glass **Parking** On street (free) **Notes** Sunday L, Vegetarian available, Children welcome

---

Chez Bruce ◉◉◉

LONDON SW17

PLAN 1 E2

Modern 🍷 NOTABLE WINE LIST

tel: 020 8672 0114 **2 Bellevue Rd, Wandsworth Common SW17 7EG**
email: enquiries@chezbruce.co.uk
dir: *Nearest station: Wandsworth Common, Balham*

Supremely accomplished cooking in a neighbourhood stalwart

Bruce Poole's unostentatious and dynamic cooking has taken his venue opposite Wandsworth Common from top-of-the-range neighbourhood eatery to a destination on the gastronomic satnav. Poole has been quite a mover and shaker on the London restaurant scene over the last 20 years, branching out with The Glasshouse in Kew and La Trompette in Chiswick, and even finding the time to write a signature cookbook. The Wandsworth mothership has always gone discreetly about its business with a studied absence of showboating; a purple frontage opens into a white-walled room hung with tasteful art and furnished with linen-clad tables on herringbone parquet floors, and staff run it with unflappable aplomb and keen attention. It's a setting that suits Poole's unfussy but highly classy cooking to perfection, and the menu clearly revels in the bright, sunny flavours of southern France and the wider Mediterranean. Try openers such as poached lamb's tongues with crushed Jersey Royal potatoes, hispi cabbage and morels, or cod brandade with mussels, crisp egg and wild garlic, all built from ingredients that taste supremely of themselves. Next up, perhaps seafood cassoulet with red mullet, chorizo, octopus, salsa verde and fennel, or excursions eastwards for imam bayildi with spiced chickpea pastilla, yogurt and coriander, and into the heritage cookbook for a serving of côte de boeuf with chips and béarnaise. To finish, there's textbook crème brûlée, or clever takes on old favourites such as an ethereal millefeuille filled with rhubarb and vanilla and served with the citrus double-whammy of blood orange sorbet and lemon curd. Otherwise, bow out on a savoury note with an array of hummingly ripe cheeses from the board.

Chef Bruce Poole, Matt Christmas **Owner** Bruce Poole, Nigel Platts-Martin **Seats** 75, Pr/dining room 16 **Times** 12-2.30/6.30-10, Closed 24-26 Dec, 1 Jan **Prices** Fixed L 2 course £24.50-£29.50, Fixed D 3 course fr £47.50 **Wines** 750 bottles over £30, 30 bottles under £30, 15 by glass **Parking** On street, station car park **Notes** Sunday L, Vegetarian available, Children L only

Hotel du Vin at Cannizaro House
PLAN 1 D1

◉◉ Modern British, European

tel: 020 8879 1464 **West Side, Wimbledon Common SW19 4UE**
email: info@cannizarohouse.com **web:** www.cannizarohouse.com
dir: *Nearest station: Wimbledon*

British modernism in a lavish Wimbledon mansion

The acquisition of Cannizaro House is something of a key-change for the Hotel du Vin group. Its hotels are always highly individual buildings with personality and history to spare, but not as eye-poppingly posh as this late-Georgian mansion in parkland next to Wimbledon Common. In the Victorian era, it welcomed such glitterati as Alfred Lord Tennyson and Oscar Wilde. A glassed-in frontal extension shelters a swirly-carpeted bar and informal dining space, the Orangerie, while further inside, there's a lounge in sultry deep purple. The main restaurant goes for an old-school look with a chandelier in dripping crystal, gilt-framed mirrors, tables in full linen, and – what else? – a pink flamingo motif in the wallpaper. The British modernist repertoire is given a thorough outing, with all the expected technical tricks and reference ingredients. Seared tuna with an egg yolk and Shetland black potato, or chicken and chorizo terrine with puffed saffron rice, piquillo peppers and lemon purée, make bold opening statements. European traditions are creatively tweaked, as when whipped duck rillettes with Agen prunes are given a pain d'épices dressing, or fermented truffle lights up a main-course risotto enriched with mascarpone as well as parmesan. Low cooking temperatures preserve the moist texture of salmon that comes with red cabbage variations, while pork collar is complemented by crisped stuffing, romanesco, and tart green apple purée. Sundays offer traditional roasts with all the trimmings. Meals conclude either with pedigree Neal's Yard cheeses, or one of the ingeniously constructed desserts, such as spiced morello cherry crumble with walnut snow, or chocolate marquise with sugared hazelnuts, pistachio cake, truffle ice cream and cocoa soil.

Chef Christian George **Owner** Hotel du Vin **Seats** 60, Pr/dining room 120
Times 12–2.30/7–9.30 **Prices** Fixed L 2 course £24.50, Fixed D 3 course £29.50, Tasting menu £50–£85, Starter £12–£14, Main £25–£28, Dessert £8–£13 **Wines** 63 bottles over £30, 32 bottles under £30, 15 by glass **Parking** 55 **Notes** Sunday L £27.50–£32.50, Vegetarian available, Children welcome

The Light House Restaurant
PLAN 1 D1

◉ British, International

tel: 020 8944 6338 **75–77 Ridgway, Wimbledon SW19 4ST**
email: info@lighthousewimbledon.com
dir: *Nearest station: Wimbledon*

Cheerful neighbourhood restaurant with appealing cooking

The Light House is a beacon of uncomplicated, fresh seasonal cooking just a short stroll from Wimbledon Common and the village. Done out with wood, leather and neutral hues, and hung with cheerful artworks, it's an upbeat, bright and breezy space whose contemporary feel is in-line with the friendly well-informed service. Appealing menus of fresh, modern-bistro style dishes are on offer, with plenty of sunny, Mediterranean flavours cooked up in the open kitchen, where choice produce is handled with skill to bring out distinctive flavours. Chicken liver and tarragon pâté with apricot chutney and toast gets things off to a flying start, or there could be harissa mackerel with aubergine and tahini dip and piquillo peppers. Next out, steamed hake with Jersey Royals, peas, spinach and champagne butter sauce is a delightful light, fresh and seasonal summery dish. And who could fail to be won over by puddings like vanilla yogurt pannacotta with cherry compôte.

Chef Chris Casey **Owner** Mr Finch, Mr Taylor **Seats** 80, Pr/dining room 12
Times 12–2.45/6–10.30, Closed 24–26 Dec, 1 Jan, D Sun **Prices** Fixed L 2 course fr £14.95, Starter £5.95–£12.50, Dessert £5.50–£6.50 **Wines** 61 bottles over £30, 24 bottles under £30, 19 by glass **Notes** Fixed D 2/3 course Mon–Thu 6–7.30pm £18.95/£22.95, Sunday L, Vegetarian available, Children welcome

Alain Ducasse at The Dorchester
PLAN 4 G6

◉◉◉◉ – **see opposite**

Alyn Williams at The Westbury
PLAN 2 H2

◉◉◉◉ – **see page 334**

Andrew Edmunds
PLAN 2 J1

◉ Modern European

tel: 020 7437 5708 **46 Lexington St, Soho W1F OLW**
dir: *Nearest station: Oxford Circus, Piccadilly Circus*

Evergreen, rustic, Soho favourite

The tiny ground-floor dining room of this bistro stalwart is one of the West End's most intimate and romantic venues. With its simple rustic decor – wood floors and church pews, elbow-to-elbow tables with paper tablecloths, all low-lit by candles in wine bottles – it has an old Soho feel of a Dickensian tavern. The kitchen takes an equally uncomplicated and honest approach, producing seasonal, ingredients-driven dishes on a daily-changing handwritten menu that has its feet firmly in the modern European idiom. Slow-cooked octopus and chorizo in tomato sauce with Gordal olives and capers arrives straight from the Iberian tapas repertoire, followed by a splendid slab of snow-white wild halibut partnered simply with buttered new potatoes, spinach, and a zingy home-made tartare sauce. Carnivores might be tempted by roast spatchcock grouse with duck-fat potatoes, watercress, and bread sauce, while puddings bring the nursery comforts of warm treacle tart with cream.

Chef Bob Cairns **Owner** Andrew Edmunds **Seats** 60
Times 12–3.30/5.30–10.45, Closed Xmas, Etr **Prices** Starter £3.50–£11.50, Main £11–£25, Dessert £5–£8 **Wines** 140 bottles over £30, 60 bottles under £30, 6 by glass **Notes** Sunday L, Vegetarian available, Children welcome

Antidote
PLAN 2 J2

◉◉ Modern European

tel: 020 7287 8488 **12a Newburgh St W1F 7RR**
email: contact@antidotewinebar.com
dir: *Nearest station: Oxford Circus*

Relaxed restaurant and wine bar with food and wine of pedigree

Trendily tucked away in a cobbled, 'off-the-radar' lane behind Carnaby Street, Antidote offers the perfect fix for organic/biodynamic wine lovers and foodies alike. A makeover and re-launch in March 2014 grabbed the attention, not least because Mikael Jonsson (aka, Chiswick's Hedone) owned up to being its consultant. Upstairs, above its bustling wine bar, the dining room is a relaxed oasis, with a fashionable pared-back look of grey walls, floorboards, funky silver bistro chairs, wooden tables and dangling Edison-style light bulbs. Chef Chris Johns provides the colour (alongside cheery French service) and takes on Jonsson's ethos for perfection and carefully-sourced ingredients with aplomb. Thus simplicity reigns on changing set-course menus of light, delicate, understated, clear-flavoured, 'pretty' dishes. Standouts might include sparkling Cornish turbot teamed with wonderful rainbow chard, monk's beard and a light shellfish emulsion, while succulent guinea fowl might come served with green asparagus, cracking wild garlic and spinach purée and spot-on sauce vin jaune. A rich, high-gloss dark chocolate moelleux is another winner, with passionfruit ice cream the perfect partnership. Sourdough bread (from Hedone's kitchen) is to die for, while the wine list is a corker.

Chef Mikael Jonsson, Chris Johns **Owner** Thierry Bouteloup, Guillaume Siard **Seats** 45
Times 12–2.30/6–10.30, Closed Xmas, BHs, Sun **Prices** Fixed L 2 course fr £19, Tasting menu £40, Starter £8–£12, Main £20–£30, Dessert £7–£11, Service optional 12.5% **Wines** 188 bottles over £30, 5 bottles under £30, 13 by glass **Parking** On street **Notes** Fixed D 4 course £40, Tasting menu wknds only 7 course, Vegetarian available, Children welcome

Alain Ducasse at The Dorchester ✖✖✖✖

LONDON W1   **PLAN 4 G6**

Contemporary, Modern French **V**

tel: 020 7629 8866 **The Dorchester, 53 Park Ln W1K 1QA**
email: alainducassereservations@alainducasse-dorchester.com
dir: *Nearest station: Hyde Park Corner, Marble Arch*

Unashamedly classical French haute cuisine

From Las Vegas to Qatar, Monsieur Ducasse's name is synonymous with glamorous locations and modern French cooking. But the man is an innovator, too, whose almost academic passion for classical French cuisine and creative mind have resulted in an empire that spans the globe. What better location for his main London outpost than the Dorchester? The hotel, which has hosted the country's great and good since the 1930s, has a host of dining possibilities, but the shining star carries the name of Alain Ducasse. The dining room is positively serene and stylish enough without leaving a lasting impression, but there's plenty of space between the impeccably set tables. The discreet service suits the mood of the place; on hand precisely when you need them. Jocelyn Herland is the man charged with delivering the Ducasse-inspired repertoire via the seasonally changing, bilingual carte, tasting and set lunch menus, while, if you're lucky enough to arrive in season, there might be one dedicated to black truffles. Begin with an amuse-bouche of three textures of salsify (foam, braised and creamed), and five different breads that showcase the baking skills in the kitchen. The importance of temperature is shown to good effect in a preserved duck foie gras starter, where maximum flavour is achieved, and the accompanying white and black grapes provide just the right amount of acidity and sweetness. A perfectly cooked piece of halibut stars in a main course, with winkles, cockles and razor clams cooked marinière style, with two sauces, one of which is poured by the waiter at the table. First-rate produce figures all the way through, such as a rib and belly of Denbighshire pork (served with aubergine and vrai jus), and into desserts such as one with chocolate brought over from Paris and made into a praline and creamy number with flavour notes from sweet to bitter. An assortment of French cheeses arrives in perfect condition with country bread and condiments, but there's also the option of Colston Bassett Stilton if you want to keep to this side of the Channel. The wine list is a heavyweight contender by any standards, with more than 1,000 bins to choose from and a team of sommeliers on hand to guide you through the maze.

Chef Jocelyn Herland, Angelo Ercolano, Jean Philippe Blondet **Owner** The Dorchester Collection **Seats** 82, Pr/dining room 30 **Times** 12-1.30/6.30-9.30, Closed 1-7 Jan, 3-6 Apr, 9 Aug-1 Sep, 26-30 Dec, Sun-Mon, L Sat **Prices** Fixed L 3 course £60-£95, Fixed D 3 course fr £95, Tasting menu £135-£180 **Wines** 18 by glass **Parking** 20 **Notes** Tasting menu 7 course, D 4 course £105, Seasonal menu £180, Children 10 yrs+

Alyn Williams at The Westbury ✿✿✿✿

LONDON W1	PLAN 2 H2

French, European V ⬧ NOTABLE WINE LIST

tel: 020 7183 6426 **Bond St W1S 2YF**
email: alynwilliams@westburymayfair.com
web: www.alynwilliams.com
dir: *Nearest station: Oxford Circus, Piccadilly Circus, Green Park*

Innovation, top-flight skills and heaps of glamour

The gleaming Westbury hotel is a ritzy five-star address where doormen usher you inside and a host of drinking and dining options await. The pièce de résistance among the culinary alternatives is the one with Alyn Williams' name above the door, a chef whose pedigree is unquestionable after many years in the kitchens of Gordon Ramsay and Marcus Wareing, and here he continues to lead diners along the path of highly-refined, French-accented contemporary cooking. Since 2011, he has consolidated his reputation here by turning out creative and dynamic food. It all takes place in an ample room that lives up to the swish Mayfair address by way of a luxe decor of burnished wooden panels, mature shades of brown and cream, huge mirrors and a carpet that actually sparkles. The pristine tables are well spaced around the room, with formal service to match the sophisticated mood. Things get off to a very good start indeed when the amuse-bouche and bread basket arrive, with venison tartare served on parmesan crisps, topped with tomato chutney, and first-rate breads, including sourdough with onion seeds and Italian yeast-free carta di musica crispbread. Alyn's cooking may well have its foundations in classical French tradition, with some Pan-European influences along the way, but there's individuality in his output, especially when it comes to his inventive and inspired visual presentations. A first course dish of roasted Orkney scallops looks stunning on the plate, with watermelon, ricotta, balsamic and quinoa in supporting roles, or there could be Mersea crab with Jersey Royals, English asparagus and low-salt Malossol caviar. Main courses are painstakingly assembled to deliver remarkable clarity of flavour – take tender English veal with slow-cooked brisket and heritage carrots adding texture and colour, plus confit potatoes, and a fine-tuned veal jus bringing it all together, or glazed pigeon with white asparagus, given an Eastern spin with dukkah spice and turmeric yogurt. There's impressive balance of sweetness in a dessert of caramelised apple with Madagascan vanilla ice cream and hits of lemon thyme, or you might bow out with a trio of aerated white chocolate, candied fennel and lime. The wine list has an impressive global reach, and there is even a choice of beers chosen to match the food. If the pricing of the carte and tasting menus is a bit rich for your blood, the three-course set lunch option offers staggering value for cooking of this class.

Chef Alyn Williams **Owner** Cola Holdings Ltd **Seats** 65, Pr/dining room 20 **Times** 12-2.30/6-10.30, Closed 1-17 Jan, 18 Aug-4 Sep, Sun-Mon **Prices** Fixed L 3 course £30, Tasting menu fr £70 **Wines** 450 bottles over £30, 10 bottles under £30, 15 by glass **Parking** 20 **Notes** Fixed ALC 3 course £60, Tasting menu 7 course with wine £130, Children welcome

LONDON W1 *continued*

Aqua Kyoto
PLAN 2 J2

◉◉ Japanese

tel: 020 7478 0540 **240 Regent St W1B 3BR**
email: reservation@aqua-london.com
dir: *Nearest station: Oxford St*

Classy Japanese food in super-cool rooftop setting

From the smart lobby entrance, you're whisked by lift to the 5th floor and the über-chic world of Aqua. The super-sexy Spirit cocktail bar is up first; it's shared by twin restaurants Aqua Nueva (Spanish tapas) and this modern Japanese outfit, and covers the top floor of the former Dickins & Jones building. There's great rooftop views from the terrace, while, like everything else here, Kyoto's ultra-designed dining room shimmers with contemporary style and teems with beautiful people, especially in the evenings when it becomes a high-energy 'destination' (lunch is quieter). Moody black, red and gold complement the theatre of a sunken centrepiece sushi bar, charcoal grill and jaw-dropping lantern-style light fitting. It's not design over substance: the cooking deserves serious attention, while friendly staff are happy to advise on the menus. Visually striking, well-constructed dishes and top-drawer ingredients are the thing; take king crab tempura with crab miso, or perhaps twice-cooked crispy pork belly with langoustine and yuzu pepper to high-rolling Wagyu beef with garlic ponzu and grape icicles. Otherwise there's cracking sushi and sashimi, fashionable wines and super cocktails.

Times 12-3/6-11.15, Closed 25-26 Dec, BHs, D Sun

Aqua Nueva
PLAN 2 J2

◉◉ Spanish

tel: 020 7478 0540 **5th Floor, 240 Regent St W1B 3BR**
email: reservation@aqua-london.com
dir: *Nearest station: Oxford Circus*

Fashionable restaurant for Spanish wines and top-notch tapas

A lift whizzes you up from ground-floor street life to jet-set high life on the fifth floor, where a huge bull's head sculpture looms from a dimly-lit corridor, and you emerge in the nightclubby bling of the super cool Aqua Spirit cocktail bar. Slurp a cocktail with the beau monde then move into the slick restaurant, a designer-led space hung with thousands of wooden spindles. Two roof terraces and a Cava bar add to the upbeat vibe. This is the sort of place where people come to see and be seen as much as for the contemporary renditions of tapas based on top-end Spanish ingredients, so take your pick from a bilingual menu full of good-sounding ideas. Old favourites abound, from salt-cod croquettes to morcilla blood sausage with roasted peppers, or lamb shoulder confit. Otherwise, a 3-course format might start with ox cheek cannelloni with tomato confit, potato purée and guacamole, then continue with black cuttlefish rice with aïoli, and conclude with coffee sponge with Amaretto jelly.

Times 12-3/6-11.30, Closed Xmas, New Year, BHs, Sun

Arbutus Restaurant
PLAN 2 K2

◉◉◉ – *see below*

Arbutus Restaurant ◉◉◉

LONDON W1
PLAN 2 K2

Modern French
tel: 020 7734 4545 **63-64 Frith St W1D 3JW**
email: info@arbutusrestaurant.co.uk
dir: *Nearest station: Tottenham Court Rd*

Adventurous cooking with interesting combinations off Soho Square

The urban-chic, gun-metal frontage of Anthony Demetre and Will Smith's Soho operation hasn't dated since its opening in 2006, nor has the uncomplicated, modern and inventive cooking style – in fact, Arbutus was in the vanguard of restaurants espousing the now ubiquitous use of more humble cuts of meat and slow-cooking methods. You could go no further than the bar and park at one of the high stools to dine at the counter, or push on into the main dining room. This has a pared-back, minimalist look with wooden floors, plain walls hung with artwork and photographs, and a picture window giving on to Frith Street, from where passers-by eyeball what's on the plates. Good value for money has always been the mantra here, and daily-changing menus run from a reasonably-priced carte (given the West End location), to bargain-basement working lunch and pre-theatre menus. A signature starter of warm crisp pig's head with potato purée, black radish and pistachios attests to a fondness for the sort of peasant ingredients that

wouldn't look out of place in an old-school French country auberge. Elsewhere, dishes impress with the quality of their ingredients and their sensible but interesting compositions; a summer starter of Devon crab with guacamole, peanuts, melon and peas, for instance, and a main course of roast cod fillet with boneless chicken wings, sweetcorn purée, Jersey Royals and moreish chicken juices. For pudding, there's rum baba with pineapple sorbet, Chantilly cream and seven-year-old Havana Club rum sloshed on at the table. The good value ethos extends to the wine offering: all the bottles on the 50-strong Eurocentric list are also available by the 250ml carafe, so diners can mix and match.

Chef Anthony Demetre, Patrick Leano **Owner** Anthony Demetre, Will Smith **Seats** 75 **Times** 12-2.30/5-11.30, Closed 25-26 Dec, 1 Jan **Prices** Fixed L 3 course fr £19.95, Fixed D 3 course fr £20.95, Starter £7.50-£16.50, Main £18.50-£28.50, Dessert £6.50-£9.50 **Wines** 40 bottles over £30, 10 bottles under £30, 50 by glass **Notes** Pre-theatre D 5-6.30pm 3 course £19.95/£20.95, Sunday L, Vegetarian available, Children welcome

LONDON W1 *continued*

The Arch London
PLAN 2 F2

Modern British **NEW**

tel: 020 7725 4825 **50 Great Cumberland Place W1H 7FD**
email: hunter486@thearchlondon.com **web:** www.thearchlondon.com
dir: *Nearest station: Marble Arch*

Vibrant cooking near Marble Arch

Just a short stroll from Marble Arch, The Arch is spread over seven Georgian townhouses. It's a charming hotel, tastefully furnished and decorated, with a glam-looking restaurant of leather banquettes, plush seats and dark-topped wooden tables on chrome supports. All-day pizzas are possibilities, but there's much imagination at play here to enjoy. A stone oven comes into its own with some main courses, from game pie to whole sea bass with orange and rosemary butter; a steak from the grill is another option, with a handful of other mains, among them fish stew with saffron aïoli, and breaded veal escalope on a bed of spinach topped with a well-timed fried egg along with anchovies and caper butter. Successful starters include steak tartare, and carpaccio with tapenade, parmesan and rocket, while among the enjoyable puddings are cappuccino pannacotta with coffee crumble, chocolate ice cream and banana foam.

Chef Gary Durrant **Owner** AB Hotels **Seats** Pr/dining room 40 **Times** 12-10.30, All-day dining **Prices** Fixed L 2 course £19, Starter £7.50-£12.50, Main £12.50-£26, Dessert £6-£8.50 **Wines** 30 bottles over £30, 10 bottles under £30, 9 by glass **Parking** NCP 2 mins **Notes** Express menu (L & pre-theatre), Afternoon tea, Breakfast, Sunday L £24-£27, Vegetarian available, Children welcome

Assunta Madre
PLAN 2 H2

Italian Seafood **NEW**

tel: 020 3230 3032 **9-10 Blenheim St W1S 1LJ**
email: info@assuntamadre.com
dir: *Nearest station: New Bond St*

Authentic Italian seafood dishes in the West End

Sibling to the original Assunta Madre in Rome, this popular Italian is named after one of the fishing boats owned by proprietor Giovanni Micalusi, himself an ex-fisherman. Not surprisingly, the freshest seafood and fish, much of it flown in from Italy every day, is the deal here and there's even a display fish tank near the board displaying photos of Micalusi with visiting film stars. The time-honoured combination of brick walls and exposed beams provides a classic trattoria backdrop to a meal that might begin with vermicelli alle vongole veraci – a pasta dish packed with clams – followed by pescespade in guazzetto comprising slices of swordfish in a light tomato and olive sauce. A simple and well-made cherry tart is a typical dessert. The Italian-only wine list features plenty of desirable bottles with price tags to match.

Chef Mario Bruno **Owner** Giovanni Micalusi **Seats** 80, Pr/dining room 20 **Times** 12-12, All-day dining **Prices** Starter £20-£100, Main £25-£40, Dessert £8-£10 **Wines** 100+ bottles over £30, 10 by glass **Parking** NCP nearby **Notes** Sunday L, Vegetarian available, Children welcome

Athenaeum Hotel & Apartments
PLAN 4 H6

Modern British

tel: 020 7499 3464 **116 Piccadilly W1J 7BJ**
email: info@athenaeumhotel.com **web:** www.athenaeumhotel.com
dir: *Nearest station: Hyde Park Corner, Green Park*

Old-school Mayfair cooking of substance and luxury

Charles Dickens found himself frankly impressed by the interiors of what was then Hope House when it was first built in the mid-19th century, and the place continues to astonish today. For years, it was the number one destination for showbiz glitterati, welcoming everyone from Cary Grant to Donny Osmond to its Mayfair location overlooking Green Park. A vertical garden clambering up the outside is a feature, while the dining room pours on the style with mirrored walls, pillars and table tops for checking your look. You'll need your appetite too, as the cooking is determinedly old-school in its luxiness and substantiality. So expect caviar-topped lobster on spinach mousse in a bowl of salty bisque, and then roast quail stuffed with goose liver and wrapped in pancetta, with dauphinoise and confit garlic in red wine jus. It's as though Escoffier had never left London. Dessert might be a cherry and lavender tart with excellent pastry though rather shy filling, accompanied by vanilla ice cream.

Times 12.30-2.30/5.30-10.30

L'Autre Pied
PLAN 2 G3

– *see opposite*

Avista
PLAN 1 C2

Italian

tel: 020 7596 3399 & 7629 9400 **Grosvenor Square W1K 2HP**
email: reservations@avistarestaurant.com **web:** www.avistarestaurant.com
dir: *Nearest station: Bond St*

Authentic Italian cooking in Grosvenor Square

Fashioned from three grand townhouses overlooking Grosvenor Square Gardens, the Mayfair Millennium has been a hotel since the 1960s. The Georgian façade with its neo-classical Doric columns gives plenty of indication of the grandeur to be found within, but the Avista dining room is all light contemporary elegance, aubergine and mustard hues offset by exposed brick walls, with views over the gardens and into the finishing kitchen. Modernised Italian food is the bill of fare, kicking off with hearty spinach gnocchetti and rabbit ragu encircled by a cordon of parmesan sauce, or perhaps ginger-marinated salmon with red onion and coconut compôte and green apple foam. An ingenious presentation of main-course duck produces pink breast and boned leg-meat wrapped in the sage-seasoned skin, alongside orange-spiked carrot purée, while cod is blackened in squid-ink, and served with broad beans and samphire in shellfish sauce. Desserts tend towards big robust flavours too, as when hazelnut fondant comes with truffled ice cream, and pannacotta has a refreshing fruit salad for company, along with basil meringue and lychee sorbet.

Chef Arturo Granato **Owner** Millennium & Copthorne Hotels **Seats** 75, Pr/dining room 12 **Times** 12-2.30/6-10.30, Closed 1 Jan, Sun, L Sat **Prices** Fixed L 2 course £23, Fixed D 3 course £29, Tasting menu £75, Starter £11.50-£19.50, Main £19-£29.50, Dessert £7.50-£11.50 **Wines** 73 bottles over £30, 4 bottles under £30, 11 by glass **Parking** On street, NCP **Notes** Vegetarian available, Children welcome

Babbo Restaurant

PLAN 4 J6

Modern Italian NEW

tel: 020 3205 1099 **39-40 Albemarle St W1S 4JQ**
email: reservations@babborestaurant.co.uk web: www.babborestaurant.co.uk
dir: *Nearest station: Green Park*

Italian family hospitality in Mayfair

Babbo aims for a compromise position between Mayfair elegance and Italian family hospitality, so while there are chandeliers and a showcase of venerable wines, the walls are crammed with framed family photographs of grinning kids, babies being nuzzled, or mamma and papa in their Sunday best. The cooking keeps things on a tight domestic leash, but using fine aged ingredients from the top drawer. There are Tuscan ribollita or burrata with tomato and basil, as well as deep-fried calamari with artichoke chips. Those might be followed by a refined pasta dish such as tagliatelle with cacio cheese and broad beans, and then main dishes that apply a little Frenchified gloss for grilled salmon and shrimps in herbed velouté, or pigeon with potato millefeuille and foie gras. Desserts are as ambrosial as is proper: look no further than a pear frangipane tart with cinnamon ice cream.

Chef Carlo Scotto **Owner** Kia Joroobschian **Seats** 56, Pr/dining room 14
Times 12-3/6-11, Closed L Sun **Prices** Fixed L 2 course fr £25, Tasting menu fr £120, Starter £9.50-£16.80, Main £22-£44, Dessert £7.50-£8.50, Service optional 12.5%
Wines 162 bottles over £30, 1 bottle under £30, 13 by glass **Notes** Vegetarian available, Children welcome

L'Autre Pied

LONDON W1

PLAN 2 G3

Modern European V
tel: 020 7486 9696 **5-7 Blandford St, Marylebone Village W1U 3DB**
email: info@lautrepied.co.uk
dir: *Nearest station: Bond St, Baker St*

Exciting contemporary cooking off Marylebone High Street

L'Autre Pied may be the dressed-down sister of Pied à Terre, but don't go thinking you might slouch along in trainers and trackie bottoms. Just off Marylebone High Street, in the heart of the well-heeled and ever-chic 'village', the other Pied is an equally classy act that draws in a strong following for its unpretentious, lively buzz, switched-on service and stylish, French-inspired contemporary menus. The room is a looker too, in an elegant and unobtrusively stylish way, with its textured flower motifs on the walls, rosewood tables, brown leather chairs and cherry-red banquettes, and exuberant flower arrangements. Andrew McFadden's cooking goes from strength to strength as he comes up with exciting new ideas for his repertoire. Examples include a starter of flame-grilled mackerel with horseradish milk, apple tapioca, celery and miso, and a main course of Berkshire lamb with red pepper ketchup, violet artichoke, burnt aubergine and spinach. This is a kitchen firing on all cylinders, with precision techniques applied to first-class produce. Fish is timed to the second in well-composed main courses such as roast sea bass fillet with grilled leek, fennel and squid, or poached cod served with ruby grapefruit, brassicas and quinoa. The momentum is well maintained in artfully contrived puddings, among which might be coconut rice pudding with sweet cheese, sake and lime, or a chocolate cremeux with honeycomb, pistachio and tonka beans. Food to ooh and aah over, indeed, and it comes in formulas to suit most moods and budgets – the whole table might explore the nine-course taster (there's a veggie version too), and if it's value you want, look no further than the stonkingly well-priced lunch and pre-theatre option.

Chef Andrew McFadden **Owner** David Moore **Seats** 53, Pr/dining room 16
Times 12-2.45/6-10.45, Closed 4 days Xmas, 1 Jan, D Sun **Prices** Fixed L 2 course £24, Tasting menu £65-£75, Starter £11.50-£18.50, Main £28-£30, Dessert £10-£14 **Wines** 200 bottles over £30, 6 bottles under £30, 10 by glass **Notes** Pre-theatre dinner 6-7pm 2/3 course £24/£29, Sunday L £35, Children welcome

LONDON W1 *continued*

Barnyard
PLAN 2 K3

◉ Farmhouse

tel: 020 7580 3842 **18 Charlotte St W1T 2LZ**
email: info@barnyard-london.com
dir: *Nearest station: Goodge St*

Country cool with plenty of flavour on Charlotte Street

With corrugated iron on the walls, an abundance of chunky planks of wood and staff dressed as farm hands, the theme runs deep, but this place is the brainchild of Ollie Dabbous, and there's substance to the style. It looks great, with a cool, rustic bar and tables up on a mezzanine level. Sharing is the name of the game, with the menu full of full-flavoured stuff with broad appeal and the comfort factor. Dishes are listed in sections which reflect a country-style honesty – 'pig', 'cow' and 'chicken', plus 'egg', 'vegetables & sides' and 'pudding'. Lard on toast is decidedly old school, but this is a 21st-century version, while chicken in a bun is another plate that needs no introduction. Barbecued grain-fed short rib with home-made pickle, mustard and black treacle sums up what this place is all about – great ingredients cooked to maximise flavour and served in a straight-up, no-nonsense manner. Finish with a classic lemon posset with marjoram.

Times 12-3/5-10.30, Closed 25-26 Dec, Etr BH, D Sun

Barrafina
PLAN 2 K2

◉ Spanish

tel: 020 7813 8016 **54 Frith St W1D 4SL**
email: jose@barrafina.co.uk
dir: *Nearest station: Tottenham Court Rd*

Classic Spanish tapas at a marble counter in Soho

In a city that hasn't always got time to linger over dining, tapas is often the answer, and while the term has been elasticated nowadays to cover anything that comes in undersized portions, the original Spanish article remains the bedrock. With a new branch open from April 2014 on Adelaide Street, Charing Cross, Barrafina is a prime exponent of the genre. A long marble counter facing an open kitchen is the setting for vigorous, piquant, often gorgeous mouthfuls of strong savoury satisfaction, such as pimientos de Padrón, Ibérico de Bellota, prawn and piquillo tortilla, octopus with capers, chicken in romanesco, chorizo with potato and watercress, or baby gem salad with anchovies and smoked bacon. It's all served efficiently and with dispatch, though the no-bookings policy means you may have to wait your turn. What better opportunity to kick back with a glass of manzanilla? If you've time, finish with canonical tarta de Santiago, or a mouthful of gum-coating turrón.

Times 12-3/5-11, Closed BHs

The Beaumont
PLAN 2 G1

◉ British, American **NEW** v

tel: 020 7499 9499 & 7499 1001 **8 Balderton St, Mayfair W1K 6TF**
email: info@colonygrillroom.com **web:** www.colonygrillroom.com
dir: *Nearest station: Bond St*

Appealing old-fashioned brasserie dining in art deco style

On the south side of Oxford Street, not far from Selfridges, The Beaumont is a burnished slice of Mayfair elegance that offers a bedroom designed by Antony Gormley that sits rather uncomfortably on the front of the building. In the Colony Grill Room restaurant, gorgeous art deco style prevails, the walls hung with caricature portraits of literati and the lighting on mood setting. Bow-tied waiters bring you appealing brasserie food such as potted Morecambe Bay shrimps with brown bread and butter, omelette Arnold Bennett, and servings of caviar. You can unblushingly dine on gammon and pineapple once again in London, or there may be neatly manicured lamb cutlets with béarnaise and a side order of rosemary-roasted

pumpkin. Who remembers steak Diane? Veal Pojarski? Here they are, alongside more voguish touches such as fried chicken in buttermilk with spiced remoulade. Sumptuously layered trifle crammed with fruit and lashed with amontillado sherry makes a satisfying finish.

Chef Christian Turner **Owner** Corbin & King **Seats** 100, Pr/dining room 40 **Times** 7am-mdnt, All-day dining **Prices** Starter £3.95-£23.75, Main £6.75-£39.50, Dessert £6.25-£9, Service optional 12.5% **Wines** 100+ bottles over £30, 14 bottles under £30, 45 by glass **Parking** Private garage **Notes** Wknd brunch 7-11.30am, Sunday L £26, Children welcome

Bellamy's
PLAN 2 H1

◉ French

tel: 020 7491 2727 **18-18a Bruton Place W1J 6LY**
email: gavin@bellamysrestaurant.co.uk
dir: *Nearest station: Green Park, Bond St*

Classy brasserie just off Berkeley Square

Resolutely Mayfair, with its mews setting just off Berkeley Square, its effortlessly classy good looks and slickly professional service, Bellamy's epitomises the chic, timeless French brasserie genre. Dark-green leather banquettes, pale-yellow walls (lined with vibrant French posters and mirrors), white linen and staff in bow ties and waistcoats add to the authentic look, while the classic brasserie cooking is conjured from premium seasonal produce. Simple, ungimmicky, clear-flavoured dishes are the kitchen's raison d'être, with menus written in franglais and sporting luxury at every turn – foie gras terrine, oysters, or caviar to start, Dover sole or Castle Mey beef entrecote to follow. Otherwise, try poached sea-fresh skate Grenobloise (set atop spinach and served with croûtons, capers and a buttery lemon sauce), and finish with a classic tarte Tatin. Fabulous all-French wines and an interconnecting oyster bar and food store complete the experience.

Chef Stephane Pacoud **Owner** Gavin Rankin and Syndicate **Seats** 70 **Times** 12-2.30/7-10.30, Closed Xmas, New Year, BHs, Sun, L Sat **Prices** Fixed L 2 course £19.75, Fixed D 3 course £24.75, Starter £6.50-£15.50, Main £17.50-£30, Dessert £7.50 **Wines** 63 bottles over £30, 5 bottles under £30, 19 by glass **Parking** On street, NCP **Notes** Vegetarian available, Children welcome

Benares Restaurant
PLAN 2 H1

◉◉ Modern Indian v

tel: 020 7629 8886 & 7514 2805 **12a Berkeley Square W1J 6BS**
email: reservations@benaresrestaurant.co.uk
dir: *Nearest station: Bond St, Green Park*

Innovative new-wave Indian on Berkeley Square

Atul Kochhar's high-rolling Mayfair thoroughbred is a world apart from traditional curry house expectations. His portfolio takes in venues in Marlow, Kent and Dubai as well as stints on P&O cruise ships, and writing a slew of cookbooks, but his attention is most closely focused on this upscale address on Berkeley Square. A broad staircase sweeps up to the stylish first-floor bar and dining room, complete with chef's table, and the whole place purrs with the sheen of a glitzy nightclub. Well-drilled staff take a serious approach, and Kochhar's crossover Anglo-Indian cooking always excites with its groundbreaking ideas, sharp technique and gorgeous presentation. Start with a lamb shami kebab and tandoori cutlet with mint and tamarind relish and baby radish for a palate-priming overture. Move on to South Indian seafood kofta balls in tomato and ginger sauce with poriyal vermicelli, or tandoori-spiced quail supreme with wild mushroom biryani, quail's egg and pineapple raita. The East-meets-West style concludes with a cheesecake-style rasmalai with chocolate ice cream, crunchy chocolate balls and ground pistachios.

Chef Atul Kochhar **Owner** Atul Kochhar **Seats** 120, Pr/dining room 36 **Times** 12-2.30/5.30-11, Closed 25-26 Dec, 1 Jan, Sun **Prices** Fixed L 2 course fr £29, Fixed D 3 course fr £35, Tasting menu fr £82, Starter £11-£25, Main £24-£34, Dessert £8.50-£12 **Wines** 300 bottles over £30, 10 bottles under £30, 17 by glass **Parking** On street **Notes** Fixed menu until 6.30pm, Children before 7pm

Bentley's Oyster Bar & Grill
PLAN 2 J1

🌸 British, Irish 🍷 NOTABLE WINE LIST

tel: 020 7734 4756 **11-15 Swallow St W1B 4DG**
email: reservations@bentleys.org **web:** www.bentleys.org
dir: *Nearest station: Piccadilly Circus*

Lovingly restored seafood bar and restaurant in London's Piccadilly

Though celebrating its 100th birthday in 2016, the illustrious oyster bar (tucked-away between Piccadilly and Regent Street) is still a top-call for seafood, thanks to its adoption by celebrated restaurateur Richard Corrigan. Enjoy a drink at the champagne bar before pulling up a stall in the adjoining Oyster Bar, or grab a table out front on the posh covered Terrace for top-draw oysters and classic seafood. It's a highly popular, feel-good rendezvous, while upstairs, the Grill restaurant takes a more formal, sophisticated approach, with striking William Morris wallpaper, blue leather chairs, 'creaky' floorboards and original artworks. Start with a light seafood céviche with avocado, poppy lime and scallions if opting out of the oyster route, and perhaps continue with pan-fried turbot served with grilled calcots and sweet and tangy caper-raisin sauce. Portioning is light and prices lean toward West End grabby, but ingredients are excellent, service slick and wines a superb bunch. Desserts range from classics to the more modern chilli and ginger pineapple with coconut parfait. A few meat options (aka rack of lamb) from the wood-fired grill keep carnivores onside.

Chef Richard Corrigan, Michael Lynch **Owner** Richard Corrigan **Seats** 70, Pr/dining room 60 **Times** 12-3/5.30-11, Closed 25 Dec, 1 Jan, L Sat (Grill only) **Prices** Fixed L 2 course £25, Fixed D 3 course £29, Starter £12-£75, Main £24-£44, Dessert £6-£8.50 **Wines** 100 bottles over £30, 5 bottles under £30, 24 by glass **Notes** Pre-theatre menu 2/3 course £26/£29, Sunday L £19, Vegetarian available, Children welcome

Berners Tavern
PLAN 2 J2

🌸🌸 Contemporary British 🍷 NOTABLE WINE LIST

tel: 020 7908 7979 **10 Berners St W1T 3NP**
email: bernerstavern@editionhotels.com **web:** www.bernerstavern.com
dir: *Nearest station: Oxford Circus*

Modern brasserie dining in a room of untavern-like opulence

The pillared entrance in Fitzrovia tells you what to expect from Ian Schrager's London Edition hotel, and one look at the Berners Tavern dining room confirms it. You won't be surprised to hear it's nothing like a tavern, but is instead a huge palatial space with a magnificent, subtly lit moulded plaster ceiling, ovoid chandelier, and walls crowded with an eclectic mix of pictures, from landscape to still-life to architectural interiors (there's something for everyone). Jason Atherton oversees the cooking, which emerges through sliding glass doors at one end, and is in the master's contemporary brasserie style. Restyled classics such as lobster and prawn cocktail, or a compendious starter of chicken liver and foie gras parfait with a jointed quail in sherry caramel, get things going. Main dishes are multi-faceted too, producing Gruyère-crusted cod with braised clams and leeks, gnocchetti and sprouting broccoli, or try almost homely roast chicken breast with bacon and mash in coq au vin sauce with smoked garlic salsa verde. Rhubarb trifle and lemon thyme ice cream, topped with crumbled meringue, arrives in a jar.

Chef Phil Carmichael, Jason Atherton **Seats** 114, Pr/dining room 14 **Times** 12-3/6-10.30 **Prices** Prices not confirmed **Wines** 330 bottles over £30, 25 bottles under £30, 19 by glass **Parking** On street, NCP & car park **Notes** All day menu, Sunday L, Vegetarian available, Children welcome

Blanchette
PLAN 2 J2

🌸 Modern, Traditional French Tapas v

tel: 020 7439 8100 **9 D'Arblay St, Soho W1F 8DR**
email: info@blanchettesoho.co.uk
dir: *Nearest station: Oxford Circus*

Hip French bistro dining in the hinterland of Soho

Opened by three brothers from across the Channel, Blanchette strives to deliver a soupçon of authentic bistro-style French cuisine served as sharing plates. The setting suits the urban cool motif found in this part of town – a little bit rough round the edges, with a retro and recycled finish and breezy, casual attitude. The charcuterie and cheese selections show what this place is all about – meaty stuff such as saucisse seche from the Rhône-Alpes region and coppa from Corsica, plus Bleu des Basques and Fourme d'Ambert among the fromage. The kitchen can cook up some good things in support, with a plate of octopus with burnt clementine, fennel and pistachio, or another that combines confit duck leg with chilli and star anise. There are veggie options (roasted beetroots with pickled girolles, Fleur de Maquis cheese and tarragon dressing), and sweet courses such as passionfruit vacherin.

Chef Tam Storrar **Owner** Maxime, Yannis & Malik **Seats** 54, Pr/dining room 14 **Times** 12-3/5.30-11 **Prices** Fixed L 2 course £35-£45, Fixed D 2 course £35-£45, Starter £3-£6, Main £6-£10, Dessert fr £5.95 **Wines** 17 bottles over £30, 7 bottles under £30, 15 by glass **Parking** Car park, Poland St **Notes** Charcuterie & cheese platters when kitchen closed, Sunday L, Children welcome

LONDON W1 continued

Bocca di Lupo

PLAN 2 K1

◉ Italian ⚜ NOTABLE WINE LIST

tel: 020 7734 2223 & 7734 7128 **12 Archer St W1D 7BB**
email: info@boccadilupo.com
dir: Nearest station: Piccadilly Circus

Regional Italian sharing plates in the heart of Soho

High-energy, high-octane and great fun, Bocca di Lupo rocks. Though open since 2008, this feel-good contemporary trattoria is still smack on trend. It's a relaxed, hip outfit where the interior cuts a dash of glamour. Grab a stool at the long marble bar's 'chef's counter' to enjoy the culinary theatre, or head into the restaurant area proper, with its polished wood tables, brown leather seating, large aristocratic-looking paintings and feature lighting. The menu doesn't talk the full three courses, instead the lengthy, daily-changing roster – defined by simplicity and flavour – comes as small or large plates, while everything is regionally name-checked, likewise the corking Italian wines. Expect pukka tagliolini with squid ragú or homemade lamb sausage and earthy lentils, and don't overlook salads like a headlining radish, celeriac, pomegranate, pecorino and truffle dressing assemble. Desserts, like gelato – from their own ice cream parlour, 'Gelupo' opposite – or perhaps a pear and hazelnut tart hit all the right notes.

Chef Jacob Kenedy **Owner** Jacob Kenedy, Victor Hugo **Seats** 75, Pr/dining room 32 **Times** 12.15-3.45/5.15-10.45, Closed Xmas **Prices** Starter £6-£10, Main £12-£26.50, Dessert £3-£9 **Wines** 140 bottles over £30, 15 bottles under £30, 20 by glass **Parking** NCP Brewer St **Notes** Pre-theatre 1 course menu, Sunday L, Vegetarian available, Children welcome

Bó Drake

PLAN 3 A2

◉ Korean, Mexican **NEW**

6 Greek St W1D 4DE
email: contact@bodrake.co.uk
dir: Nearest station: Picadilly Circus, Oxford Circus

Bustling on-trend Soho Korean-Mexican outfit

Tucked away at the top-end of Greek Street, Bó Drake is made for Soho; an of-the-moment, no-reservation new-wave Korean-Mexican outfit delivering slow cooked and smoky barbeque street-food flavours at wallet-friendly prices in small but hip surroundings. A big bar for counter-dining dominates proceedings, while elbow-to-elbow tables, exposed ducting, concrete grey walls and dangling lighting deliver that on-trend pared-back vibe. Eating together is the way ahead here; try brisket bao (melting 12-hour smoked beef brisket with peppy mustard barbecue relish served in a bao (soft rice-flour bun), its flavours cut through with the crunch and freshness of cucumber and fried lotus root. Otherwise, go for Bo ssäm (succulent pulled pork, smoky and with spicy attitude), accompanied by dipping sauces of spring onion oil, ssamjiang (fiery soy bean Korean sauce) and kimchi (fermented vegetables) that you lettuce-wrap together to offer mouthfuls of fiery, smoky, sweet, salty meatiness that dances on the palate. Staff have plenty of knowledge and enthusiasm, while cocktails, beer and spirits lead the way over wines.

Chef Heath MacDonald **Owner** Jan Lee **Seats** 55 **Times** 12-2.30/5.30-11, Closed Xmas, New Year, Sun **Prices** Prices not confirmed **Wines** 8 bottles under £30 **Parking** On street **Notes** Vegetarian available, Children welcome

Brasserie Chavot

PLAN 2 H1

◉◉◉ – see below

Brasserie Chavot ◉◉◉

LONDON W1

PLAN 2 H1

Modern French
tel: 020 7183 6425 **41 Conduit St, Mayfair W1S 2YF**
email: reservation@brasseriechavot.com
dir: Nearest station: Bond St, Green Park

Classy brasserie from a French master

After a decade spent serving the hautest of cuisine at The Capital, Eric Chavot's place in London's gastronomic Hall of Fame is assured. Before that, his illustrious CV reads like a gazetteer of stellar kitchens, taking in stints with Raymond Blanc at Le Manoir aux Quat' Saisons, with Koffman at La Tante Claire, and at Marco-Pierre White's Harveys. After a couple of years out of London, he returned in 2013 to set up shop in Brasserie Chavot, ditching the cloches and straitjacketed formality of his previous fine-dining operation in order to return to the roots of French cuisine. That's not to say his new operation is a place you'd consider slouching into in T-shirt and trainers: attached to the swanky Westbury Hotel, the room is every inch the deluxe Parisian brasserie with its art nouveau-style mosaic floor, mirrors, dark wood panels, chandeliers and deep red leather banquettes and chairs. The menu remains true to brasserie classics, but Chavot's technique raises the cooking to a higher plane. Honest, old-school dishes such as snails in parsley and garlic butter, or tartare de salmon (the menu speaks franglais) are done very well indeed. It's all in the detail. Main course confit de canard is as good a rendition of this peasant classic as you're likely to encounter, the rich, crisp-skinned leg meat collapsing off the bone, while fish gets similarly unaffected treatment in dishes such as roast cod with lentils and lardons. There's a grill section, too, offering tiger prawns with harissa or grilled poussin with garlic and confit lemon. Desserts are an equally classic bunch, among them Ile flottante or rum baba. The wine list majors in French regions with a few global interlopers.

Chef Eric Chavot **Owner** Eric Chavot **Seats** 76 **Times** 12-2.30/6-10.30, **Prices** Fixed L 2 course fr £32 **Wines** 129 bottles over £30, 6 bottles under £30, 14 by glass **Parking** Mayfair Parking **Notes** Vegetarian available, Children welcome

Cecconi's
PLAN 2 J1

◎◎ Traditional Italian

tel: 020 7434 1500 **5a Burlington Gardens W1S 1EP**
dir: *Nearest station: Piccadilly Circus, Oxford Circus*

Swanky Mayfair address for top-class seasonal Italian cooking

Cecconi's works a glossy Mayfair look with its discreet dark glass frontage. Black-suited waiters swish in and out bearing trays of aperitifs and cicchetti (Venetian tapas) to the pavement tables; inside, the vibe is low-lit, old-school glamour – a magnet for the well-heeled international crew raising the decibels at green-leather high stools round the marble-topped island bar. All around are linen-clad tables, mirrored walls, blue velour banquettes and black-and-white diagonal-striped marble floors. Waiters are real pros, working the room with professional slickness but still chatty and friendly, and they know the all-day menu inside out. The trump card here is dedication to top-class seasonal produce, prepared simply to deliver clear, full-on flavours. Kickstart the taste buds with the cicchetti – ox tongue and salsa verde, say – then move on to pasta of unimpeachable class: crab ravioli in a delicate tomato and fish stock broth with fresh basil and tomatoes. Main course brings an intensely-flavoured casserole of baked cod with clams, mussels and capers, or you might go meaty with a simple pairing of lamb cutlet and caponata.

Times 7am-1am, All-day dining, Closed Xmas, New Year

The Chesterfield Mayfair
PLAN 4 H6

◎◎ Traditional British

tel: 020 7491 2622 **35 Charles St, Mayfair W1J 5EB**
email: bookch@rchmail.com **web:** www.chesterfieldmayfair.com
dir: *Nearest station: Green Park*

Cosseting luxury, Mayfair style

A rather fine Georgian property jam-packed with antiques and run with a touch of old-school charm, The Chesterfield offers traditional comforts in a well-to-do postcode. The restaurant, Butlers, keeps to the programme with its decor of rich, warm colours, light wooden panels and patterned carpet, while the service is suitably formal and precise. The kitchen draws inspiration from British culinary traditions, with a few modern touches and simple flavour combinations. A first-course suckling pig's cheek croquette looks pretty on the plate, joined by a sliver of black pudding and sweetcorn purée, while another puts Orkney king scallops in the fashionable company of chicken wings (plus girolles, pea purée and cobnuts). Move on to a spiced-up line-caught sea bass with curried mussels or a Dedham Vale steak cooked on the grill, and finish with an English strawberry tart topped with a scoop of powerful peppermint crisp ice cream. There's a pre-theatre menu if you're in a hurry to catch a show (or simply after a good deal) and afternoon tea is served in the conservatory.

Chef Ben Kelliher **Owner** Red Carnation Hotels **Seats** 65, Pr/dining room 40
Times 12-2.30/5.30-10, Closed L Sat-Sun **Prices** Fixed L 2 course fr £24, Fixed D 3 course fr £26, Starter £9-£18, Main £19-£39, Dessert £9-£13 **Wines** 60 bottles over £30, 12 bottles under £30, 20 by glass **Parking** NCP 5 mins **Notes** Pre-theatre menu, Afternoon tea, Vegetarian available, Children welcome

China Tang at The Dorchester
PLAN 4 G6

◎◎ Classic Cantonese

tel: 020 7629 9988 **53 Park Ln W1K 1QA**
email: reservations@chinatanglondon.co.uk
dir: *Nearest station: Hyde Park Corner*

Glamorous Cantonese cooking in five-star Park Lane surroundings

There are basements and basements. Needless to say, the basement of The Dorchester is not a bad place to be, in fact, it looks incredible, and its home to China Tang. The bar is opulent and old school, the restaurant itself a celebration of refined Chinoiserie with contemporary fish-themed Asian art and art-deco mirrored columns. There's a reassuring confidence and professionalism to the service team. The menu won't be unfamiliar to anyone used to eating Cantonese food in the UK, but there are more than enough luxury items to act as a reminder that this is the Dorchester. Soft-shelled crab fried with egg yolk shows this to be a kitchen that doesn't waste time with unnecessary embellishments, likewise the salt-and-pepper squid. There is classic lobster braised in bouillon, plus whole suckling pig if you give 24-hour's notice, but equally there's the humble lamb brisket cooked in a clay pot. Desserts such as warm chocolate pudding with vanilla ice cream can have a Western flavour, and dim sum is served all day.

Times 12-12, All-day dining, Closed 25 Dec

C London
PLAN 2 H1

◎◎ Italian

tel: 020 7399 0500 **23-25 Davies St W1K 3DE**
email: london@crestaurant.co.uk
dir: *Nearest station: Bond St*

Venetian elegance and celeb spotting in Mayfair

Formerly named (and still known to its faithful as) Cipriani, C London is sibling to Venice's famous Harry's Bar and is beloved by the international glitterati. Don't be surprised if the paparazzi are waiting outside as you arrive at the glass-fronted restaurant with its revolving door, such is its popularity on the celeb circuit. Once inside, meeter-greeters from a battalion of white-jacketed, slickly professional staff commence the charm offensive no matter what your status, and the large, snazzy dining room looks appealing with its impeccable art-deco styling complete with Murano glass chandeliers. It's certainly not all style over substance – the straightforward classic Italian cooking is founded on tip-top produce and doesn't disappoint. Take sea-fresh Dover sole simply partnered by zucchini, or from the grill, moist, full-flavoured corn-fed chicken with lovely crispy skin, served simply with mixed vegetables. Breads are fabulous, a Bellini aperitif is almost a requisite, and for dessert you might choose something like lemon meringue pie from the 'selection of home-made cakes'. Factor in a buzzing atmosphere, 15% service and prices that are certainly determined with the celebrity in mind.

Times 12-3/6-11.45, Closed 25 Dec

LONDON W1 *continued*

Cocochan

PLAN 2 G2

◉ Chinese, Japanese

tel: 020 7486 1000 **38-40 James St, Marylebone W1U 1EU**
email: info@cocochan.co.uk **web:** www.cocochan.co.uk
dir: *Nearest station: Bond St*

Pan-Asian fusion cooking in vibrant West End setting

If you hanker after the cuisines of Thailand, Vietnam, China, Japan and Korea, head over to this address near Oxford Street. It's modern and colourful interior consists of mirrored lattice work and bamboo tables, plus an outside terrace. The menu offers a pan-Asian panoply that includes creative dim sum such as chicken croquettes with yuzu mayo and crispy aromatic duck rolls, alongside classic sushi and sashimi (spicy tuna and spring onion ura maki, say, or salmon sashimi). There are small snacks and salads along the lines of chicken thigh teriyaki skewers and confit duck salad with watermelon, and full-on main courses that run to stir-fried tiger prawn sambal and red duck curry with pineapple and bamboo shoots. Desserts include the exotic sounding yuzu cheesecake with kumquat compôte, and the more European-centric chocolate fondant.

Chef Yuka Aoyama **Owner** Hrag Darakjian **Seats** 80, Pr/dining room 35 **Times** 12-12, All-day dining, Closed 25 Dec **Prices** Tasting menu fr £40, Starter £4-£16, Main £13-£27, Dessert £4.50-£7 **Wines** 40 bottles over £30, 15 bottles under £30, 15 by glass **Parking** On street **Notes** Sharing menu £35-£40, Bento box L min £13.50, Sunday L £25-£45, Vegetarian available, Children welcome

Corrigan's Mayfair

PLAN 2 G1

◉◉◉ – *see opposite and advert below*

Corrigan's Mayfair ❀❀❀

LONDON W1   PLAN 2 G1

British, Irish **V** 🍷 NOTABLE WINE LIST

tel: 020 7499 9943 **28 Upper Grosvenor St W1K 7EH**
email: reservations@corrigansmayfair.com
web: www.corrigansmayfair.com
dir: *Nearest station: Marble Arch*

Finely crafted gutsy cuisine and top service in Mayfair

Richard Corrigan brings together impeccable hospitality and excellent food in equal measure in his swanky flagship just off Park Lane. When he's in celeb chef mode on the telly, he comes across as a jovial, straight-talking chap but this dining room is as buffed-up and glossy as you'd expect in the blue chip Mayfair postcode. There's a real feel of old school grandeur, tempered by playful touches (note the ostrich lamps) to lighten up the gentlemen's club luxury of burnished wood, shimmering copper wall panels, plush grey leather seats and banquettes in the art deco-style dining room. If you prefer to perch centre stage and slurp down half a dozen Carlingford oysters, park at one of the high stools along the marble-topped bar. The front-of-house team are as slick as they come and the food is grounded in honest-to-goodness gutsiness and robustness, allied to the pin-sharp techniques of haute cuisine, whether you go for the six-course taster, the keenly-priced lunchtime market menu, or the carte. A clever starter of home-made pheasant sausage wrapped in bacon delivers gamey depth, leavened by the textures of artichoke purée and crisps and pickled damsons. Main-course sirloin of Hereford beef is a splendid slab of protein, expertly hung and aged for well-developed flavour, timed to perfection in the kitchen and served with snail persillade, wilted spinach, sweet onion purée, and a flavoursome jus, but if you want spuds with it, be prepared to stump up extra for double-cooked chips or mash. Fish is handled with aplomb, too – steamed brill with minestrone and kale salsa, perhaps – and for dessert, ginger custard is poured into a spot-on rhubarb crumble soufflé at the table.

Chef Richard Corrigan, Alan Barrins **Owner** Richard Corrigan
Seats 85, Pr/dining room 30 **Times** 12-3/6-10, Closed Xmas, BHs,
L Sat **Prices** Fixed L 2 course £25, Tasting menu £75, Starter £9-
£24, Main £18-£38, Dessert £7.50-£11 **Wines** 13 by glass
Parking On street **Notes** Tasting menu 6 course, Seasonal market
menu L, Sunday L £29-£48, Children welcome

LONDON W1 *continued*

Coya
PLAN 4 H6

◎◎ Modern Peruvian

----

tel: 020 7042 7118 **118 Piccadilly, Mayfair W1J 7NW**
email: info@coyarestaurant.com
dir: *Nearest station: Hyde Park Corner*

Peruvian cooking and bags of style

With three open kitchens, a céviche counter, an open charcoal grill, and a pisco bar stocking trendy infusions and over 40 tequilas, Coya is a hive of Peruvian-inspired activity. It's seriously cool. The kitchen delivers classy plates of food that are rich with South American flavours and a contemporary swagger. The strong visual impact of the restaurant extends to the food, too, such as a classic plate of that céviche – sea bass, cut with precision and sparklingly fresh, with red onions, sweet potato and white corn. The ingredients are spot-on throughout, such as a plate of octopus cooked on the Josper grill and partnered with Peruvian olives. The meat cookery is equally impressive; corn-fed baby chicken, for example, with aji panca (a dark red pepper) and coriander, or lamb chops with crushed aubergines. The signature dessert is the corn sundae, consisting of sweetcorn ice cream and popcorn, or go for the salted caramel ganache with blood orange and pisco. The tasting menu is a good option (at a price).

Times 12-2.45/6-10.45

Criterion
PLAN 2 K1

◎ Modern British, European

----

tel: 020 7930 0488 **224 Piccadilly W1J 9HP**
email: reservations@criterionrestaurant.com
dir: *Nearest station: Piccadilly Circus*

Well-produced brasserie fare in spectacular-looking restaurant

Byzantium comes to Piccadilly Circus with the Criterion's spectacular interior, a large, long room of marble, mosaics, gold and mirrors. The kitchen deals in modern British brasserie-style cooking based on the great French traditions. Expect starters of mussels, served in a pot, cooked in a well-made creamy cider-based sauce with garlic and shallots, or ham hock and black pudding terrine with apple purée and pickled vegetables. Accurate timing and sound technique are evident in main courses: pink, juicy and tender lamb chop accompanied by smooth mashed potato and broccoli, and pan-fried salmon fillet (from Loch Duart) with beetroot and horseradish purée, samphire and chive beurre blanc. Breads – and butter – are made in-house, and a creative talent is behind such puddings as brioche and Calvados baba with custard foam and blackberry sorbet, or orange posset with spicy poached clementines and lemon verbena gratin.

Chef Artan Hasa **Owner** Mr I Sopromadze **Seats** 160 **Times** 12-2.30/5-11, Closed 25 Dec **Prices** Fixed L 2 course £20-£28, Fixed D 3 course £25-£35, Starter £8-£12, Main £18-£34, Dessert £8-£12, Service optional 12.5% **Wines** 110 bottles over £30, 15 bottles under £30, 10 by glass **Parking** Brewer St, Leicester Sq NCP **Notes** Breakfast, Afternoon tea, Sunday L, Vegetarian available, Children welcome

----

CUT at 45 Park Lane
PLAN 4 G6

◎◎◎ – *see below*

CUT at 45 Park Lane ✿✿✿

LONDON W1
PLAN 4 G6

Modern American
tel: 020 7493 4554 & 7493 4545 **45 Park Ln W1K 1BJ**
email: reservations.45L@dorchestercollection.com
web: www.dorchestercollection.com
dir: *Nearest station: Hyde Park Corner, Green Park*

Californian steak maestro's high-gloss Mayfair temple of beef

Compared to chefs who go by just one name – Heston or Raymond, for example – Wolfgang Puck may not be a household name in the UK, but this Austrian chef and restaurateur is a big deal Stateside. His Beverly Hills Spago played its part in defining Californian cuisine, and now he runs a global empire, including several joints under the CUT banner. The Park Lane postcode is a heads-up that you're not going to be eating on a budget – that, plus the location in a swanky hotel under the Dorchester brand. You only have one chance to make a first impression and the long, narrow ground-floor restaurant pulls it off thanks to an über-glam decor of striking contemporary chandeliers, swathes of curtain, burnished wooden panels and a cosmopolitan, high-end vibe. This may seem a touch OTT for what is essentially a steakhouse, but here the top-grade beef is treated with reverence. So it should be, since it comes from all over the world to your plate: Black Angus from Creekstone Farms in Kansas, South Devon Angus from the West Country, and Wagyu from Queensland in Australia. But it's not all about beef. Fish eaters can set off with tuna tartare with wasabi aïoli, ginger and togarashi crisps and there are also non-meaty main courses such as Dover sole meunière with preserved lemon and parsley. But onto the steaks: whatever prime cut your wallet can bear, it will be cooked to perfection and come with an array of sauces from béarnaise to Argentinian chimichurri. Desserts are no mere afterthought: dark Valrhona chocolate soufflé with crème fraîche and hazelnut gianduja ice cream is an unctuous, decadent finale.

Chef David McIntyre, Wolfgang Puck **Owner** Dorchester Collection **Seats** 70, Pr/dining room 12 **Times** 12-2.45/6-10.45, **Prices** Prices not confirmed **Wines** 600 bottles over £30, 10 bottles under £30, 20 by glass **Notes** Sun brunch 11-3.30pm, Vegetarian available, Children welcome

Dabbous
PLAN 2 J3

🌸🌸🌸 – see below

Dehesa
PLAN 2 J1

🌸 Spanish, Italian

tel: 020 7494 4170 **25 Ganton St W1F 9BP**
email: info@dehesa.co.uk
dir: *Nearest station: Oxford Circus*

First-rate tapas in Soho

Dehesa comes from the same stable as Salt Yard and Opera Tavern and, like them, is a charcuterie and tapas bar dedicated to the cuisines of Spain and Italy. It's a small place and it's easy to see why it gets so busy: quality ingredients are handled professionally, following authentic recipes, to bring the flavours of those two countries to life in London. Bar snacks of house-cured duck breast, or jamón Ibérico, with a glass of fino make pleasing partners, or select from the full list of unfussy hot and cold dishes. Venetian-style sardines with sautéed onions, sultanas and pine nuts, and piquant salt-cod croquettes with sauce romesco are among the fish options, with tender confit pork belly with rosemary-scented cannellini beans, and fried lamb cutlet with broad beans, chilli and mint among the meat. You might not need extra vegetables like patatas fritas, but leave room for tempting puddings like chocolate cake with cappuccino ice cream.

Chef Giancarlo Vatteroni **Owner** Simon Mullins, Ben Tish **Seats** 40, Pr/dining room 12 **Times** 12-3/5-11, Closed 24-26 & 31 Dec, 1 Jan **Prices** Prices not confirmed **Wines** 70 bottles over £30, 17 bottles under £30, 24 by glass **Parking** NCP **Notes** Sunday L, Vegetarian available, Children welcome

Dinings
PLAN 2 E3

🌸🌸 Japanese, European

tel: 020 7723 0666 **22 Harcourt St W1H 4HH**
dir: *Nearest station: Edgware Rd, Marylebone*

Pint-sized basement room doing dazzling Japanese tapas

Exquisitely-crafted miniatures are a Japanese strong point, so the concept of Japanese tapas shows the savvy culinary synergy going on here at Dinings, where the creative kitchen fuses Japanese and modern European dishes into some extremely productive ideas. There's still a bonsai-sized traditional sushi bar on the ground floor where just six diners get to share elbow-to-elbow space, up close and personal with the chefs, but it is down in the utilitarian basement that a city-chic clientele turns up to be led through the hot, sour, sweet and savoury spectrum. Concrete floors, walls painted blue and cream, bare tables and leatherette seating amount to a pretty spartan setting, but you're not here for the interior design: check out the blackboard specials, then tackle the lengthy menu in the true tapas spirit by sharing a bunch of small dishes. Pan-fried padron peppers with garlic and shichimi pepper, tar-tar chips (home-made potato crisps filled with avocado, seafood, meat, vegetables and sauces) and – heading upmarket – seared Wagyu beef with chilli miso is a typical trio.

Times 12-2.30/6-10.30, Closed Xmas, 31 Dec-1 Jan, Sun

Dabbous 🌸🌸🌸

LONDON W1
PLAN 2 I3

Modern British
tel: 020 7323 1544 **39 Whitfield St, Fitzrovia W1T 2SF**
email: info@dabbous.co.uk
dir: *Nearest station: Goodge St*

Ingenious modern dining under bare lightbulbs

The waiting list to get in here has been known to stretch from here to eternity, a sure sign that Ollie Dabbous has his finger on one of the various heating pulses of fashionable London dining. It isn't just that nobody minds the brutalist industrial styling of the interior, where air-con ducts are on show, and behind the metal mesh screens, bare lightbulbs are poised as though for an interrogation; they positively relish it as the mood of the moment. If you want chandeliers, go to The Ritz. In the basement here is Oskar's Bar, where a DJ plays and the cocktails incorporate homemade syrups and infusions. Dabbous's food is spun from gathered wild ingredients, including many not previously thought edible, and culinary technique that is intent on making everything new. Seasonings are thought-provoking from the off, as witness a starter of goose meat cured with fenugreek, or the glazed pig cheek main that's scented with clover and sage and comes with hispi cabbage. Despite the complicated treatments, there is also an engaging simplicity to the dishes, a difficult trick to pull off. Coddled egg with mushrooms and smoked butter evokes layers of earthy flavour from its humble components, as do the favoured broths in which main ingredients repose – squid, radishes and toasted buckwheat, or cod with wild garlic and seaside herbs. Japanese notes are struck for a main dish of barbecued pigeon (or celeriac and hazelnuts in the veggie version) with miso quince, while desserts are often imbued with botanical aromatics, such as the rose petals, fennel pollen and sorrel that come with yogurt sorbet. Warm beer cake with clotted cream is the manly alternative.

Chef Ollie Dabbous **Owner** Ollie Dabbous **Seats** 36 **Times** 12-2.15/6.30-9.30, Closed 1 wk Etr, 2 wks Aug, 1 wk Xmas, Sun **Prices** Tasting menu £64-£73, Service optional 12.5% **Wines** 110 bottles over £30, 10 bottles under £30, 16 by glass **Notes** Fixed L/D 4 course £32/£52, Tasting menu whole tables only

LONDON W1 *continued*

DSTRKT

PLAN 2 K1

◉ ◉ Modern American

tel: 020 7317 9120 **9 Rupert St W1D 6DG**
email: reservations@dstrkt.co.uk
dir: *Nearest station: Piccadilly Circus*

Nightclub-style dining at the cutting edge

With a name that looks like it's written in Klingon, this restaurant/nightclub hybrid is high on concept, but determined to prove that being seen with beautiful people and eating well don't have to be mutually incompatible endeavours. It all happens down a dark staircase in a cavernous, high-decibel witches' grotto in black and gold, interlaced with botanical forms. Georgi Yaneff, an American chef of major repute, brings a forceful West Coast sense of sass with him, boldly melding continental cuisines with Pan-Asian modes into a gigantic global fusion. Starters are sized for pick'n'mixing: flash-fried cubes of tuna are topped with soy foam and supported by avocado purée, while a single tentacle of grilled octopus is matched with an earthy caramelised chickpea purée, fresh peas and preserved orange. At main-course stage, ostrich skewers come with a mustard and Guinness dipping sauce, and grilled lamb cutlets arrive with lamb pancetta, smoky aubergine purée and piquillo pepper coulis. Finish with caramelised apple frangipane tart with apple purée and ice cream and Cognac cream.

Times 6pm-3am, Closed Sun-Mon, L all week

Ember Yard

PLAN 2 J2

◉ ◉ Spanish, Italian **NEW** 🍷 **NOTABLE WINE LIST**

tel: 020 7439 8057 **60-61 Berwick St W1F 8SU**
email: info@emberyard.co.uk
dir: *Nearest station: Oxford Circus*

Hot spot for chargrilled and smoked Italian and Spanish tapas

Ember Yard is the latest in the chain of up tempo tapas outfits (from the guys behind Salt Yard, Dehesa and Opera Tavern) that have been trending in the capital in recent years. The smart modern look is right on cue; on street level there are leather banquettes, high tables and chairs, and the de rigueur open kitchen (this version with high-stall dining at the pass), while dangling lighting and colourful modern art helps ticks the relevant style boxes. Downstairs there's a cool bar and further dining, though it's the poor relation in the atmosphere stakes. The food comes inspired by Spain (the Basque country in particular) and Italy, and is smoked or cooked simply on a Basque-style wood and charcoal grill. Sharing platters of classy charcuterie and cheeses are sourced from peerless suppliers like everything else, otherwise start with chargrilled cuttlefish with a sweet hit from honey-roasted butternut squash and citrus-packed gremolata, and don't miss the melt-in-the-mouth chargrilled Ibérica presa (shoulder), served with whipped jamón butter. Finish in style with moist vanilla and almond cake, ricotta and juicy loquats. Switched-on service hits the spot, likewise the Spanish-Italian wines and house cocktails.

Chef Maria Elia **Owner** Simon Mullins **Seats** 120, Pr/dining room 18 **Times** 12-12, All-day dining, Closed 25-26 Dec **Prices** Prices not confirmed, Service optional 12.5% **Notes** Vegetarian available, Children welcome

L'Escargot

PLAN 3 A2

◉ ◉ French, Mediterranean

tel: 020 7439 7474 & 7494 1318 **48 Greek St W1D 4EF**
email: bc@lescargotrestaurant.co.uk **web:** www.lescargotrestaurant.co.uk
dir: *Nearest station: Tottenham Court Rd, Leicester Sq*

French bistro cookery at an old Soho stager

The dear old Snail of Soho has seen some changes since its inception in 1927, and the pattern continued in 2014. New owners have transformed the place room by room, and a new man, Oliver Lesnik, arrived to head up the kitchen. The Escargot's many firm friends need have no fear that some wrenching gear-change in the style is under way; the kitchen continues to produce sleekly worked renditions of classic French bistro food for an appreciative audience. Bilingual menus open with pork and veal terrine grande-mère, onion soup slicked with gruyère, and baked haddock with quail's eggs, before launching off into fortifying comfort-food territory for devilled sweetbreads in mustard, lobster thermidor, coq au vin, and grilled veal cutlet with lemon and thyme. Rest assured that snails, oysters and caviar still ornament the menu, and that you won't be deprived of a crème brûlée, a Grand Marnier soufflé, or even a startlingly trendy némésis au chocolat, at the end of it all.

Chef Oliver Lesnik **Owner** Brian Clivaz **Seats** 80, Pr/dining room 60 **Times** 11am-11.30pm, All-day dining, Closed 25-26 Dec, 1 Jan **Prices** Fixed L 2 course fr £17.50, Fixed D 3 course fr £21, Starter £6-£18, Main £12-£34, Dessert £5-£8 **Wines** 80 bottles over £30, 12 bottles under £30, 12 by glass **Parking** NCP Chinatown, on street parking **Notes** Fixed L & D 2/3 course pre/post-theatre, Sunday L £10-£25, Vegetarian available, Children 10 yrs+

Fera at Claridge's

PLAN 2 H1

◉ ◉ ◉ ◉ – *see opposite*

Fera at Claridge's ❀❀❀❀

Modern British V ⚑ NOTABLE WINE LIST

tel: 020 7107 8888 **Brook St W1K 4HR**
email: reservations@feraatclaridges.co.uk
web: www.feraatclaridges.co.uk
dir: *Nearest station: Bond St, Green Park*

Dynamic modern cooking courtesy of Simon Rogan

Claridge's is London's art deco gem, revamped in the 1920s and surviving intact due to good sense and good luck. It's never been a place resistant to the passage of time though, for at the five-star level it doesn't do to stand still. If ever there was a demonstration of this desire to remain at the forefront, it is the arrival of Fera. With a host of AA rosettes under his belt at L'Enclume in Cumbria and The French in Manchester, Mr Rogan is the UK's culinary hot ticket, and Fera at Claridge's is a restaurant to stir heart and soul. British designer Guy Oliver has created a space which has maintained the artistic spirit of the place while conveying a sense of the natural world in the chosen colour palette, burnished walnut tables and murals. A culinary journey chez Rogan starts with the ingredients themselves and a great deal of what will appear before you will have come from his farm in the Lake District, and what has been sourced from elsewhere will come from his band of trusted suppliers. This passion for the produce results in a genuine freedom of expression, where inspiration and creativity meet prodigious technical ability. Choose from the carte or tasting menu (note the set lunch is a cracking deal), and expect the flavours to linger long in the memory. It all starts with a series of 'snacks', or rather delightful little nibbles such as rabbit and lovage beignet, or potato and cheese espuma with duck hearts. A first course proper of tender roasted English quail arrives with fennel, wood sorrel and various texture of onions, plus a runny quail's egg. Sweetbreads star in another first course with goats' curd, land seaweed (also known as saltwort) and verjus that delivers clear and simple flavours to stunning effect. The clever layering of flavours and superb produce continues to create the hallowed 'wow' factor in dishes such as one of dry-aged Middlewhite pork with sensational meat, carrots to savour, black pudding and mulled cider sauce, or another that matches a superb piece of monkfish with mussels, salsify and sea herbs. Among the sweet courses, sheep's yogurt sorbet and roasted white peach is a winner, and salted chocolate cream with jasmine and caramel might be even better. The wine list is a treasure trove of interesting things.

Chef Simon Rogan, Dan Cox **Owner** Simon Rogan **Seats** 94, Pr/dining room 12 **Times** 12-2/6.30-10, **Prices** Fixed L 2 course fr £25, Tasting menu fr £95, Starter £14-£27, Main £20-£36, Dessert £12, Service optional 12.5% **Wines** 500 bottles over £30, 7 bottles under £30, 17 by glass **Parking** On street, NCP **Notes** No high chairs available, Children welcome

LONDON W1 *continued*

Flemings Mayfair
PLAN 4 H6

❀ Modern European

tel: 020 7499 0000 **Half Moon St, Mayfair W1J 7BH**
email: thegrill@flemings.co.uk web: www.flemings-mayfair.co.uk
dir: *Nearest station: Green Park*

Luxury hotel with top-notch steaks and more

This luxury boutique hotel in well-heeled Mayfair has an entirely appropriate glossy restaurant, with a striking rich colour scheme of red, brown and gold, a soft swirly-patterned carpet and comfortable dining chairs and button-back banquettes. TV chef Rosemary Shrager has had some input, with half a dozen dishes on the menu attributed to her. These include smoked duck with chicory marmalade, hazelnuts and beetroot, and halibut fillet with cockles and mussels, salsify and lobster essence. Otherwise, the main thrust is on steaks from the grill with a choice of sauces: say, rib-eye with mustard and tarragon butter. The rest of the menu is a relatively humble bunch, although produce is of the best quality and high levels of technical skill are clear. Start with smoked salmon with watercress dressing, capers and lemon, go on to chicken or beef burger or the fish of the day. Conclude with pears poached in white wine with chocolate sauce.

Times 12-2/5.30-10, Closed L Sat-Sun

Four Seasons Hotel London at Park Lane
PLAN 4 G6

❀❀ International, British, Italian ᴠ

tel: 020 7319 5206 **Hamilton Place, Park Ln W1J 7DR**
email: amaranto.lon@fourseasons.com web: www.fourseasons.com/london/dining
dir: *Nearest station: Green Park, Hyde Park Corner*

Carefully crafted Italian grand-hotel dining

The Four Seasons stands opposite the InterContinental at Hyde Park Corner, united in modern grandeur in a distinctly plutocratic node of central London. When it comes to dining, the Amaranto restaurant is the reference point. The dining room, and its accompanying lounge and bar, are done in a mix of black lacquer and smouldering crimson, and the place opens up to an attractive garden area with outdoor tables. Well-sourced and carefully crafted Italian dishes mostly reject today's obsessive technical complexity in favour of the fundamental simplicity for which everyone turns to Italian food. Open proceedings with inspired antipasti such as culatello and melon, or burrata with broad beans and raw artichoke. Beautifully silky sheer pasta encases finely textured rabbit for a ravioli dish with a counter-intuitive garnish of langoustines and a scattering of fragrant tarragon. Next is a deftly executed dish of fried calamari on tomato and rocket salad dressed with pesto and wedges of lime, or grilled veal chop with sauté potatoes. A retooled tiramisù is garnished with a salted tuile set with cocoa nibs.

Chef Adriano Cavagnini **Owner** Four Seasons Hotels & Resorts **Seats** 58, Pr/dining room 10 **Times** 12-2.30/6.30-10.30 **Prices** Prices not confirmed **Wines** 200 bottles over £30, 200 by glass **Parking** 10 **Notes** Tasting menu 6 course, Fixed L 2/3 course, Sunday L, Children welcome

Galvin at Windows Restaurant & Bar
PLAN 4 G6

❀❀❀ – *see below*

Galvin at Windows Restaurant & Bar ❀❀❀

LONDON W1   PLAN 4 G6

Modern French
tel: 020 7208 4021 **London Hilton on Park Ln, 22 Park Ln W1K 1BE**
email: reservations@galvinatwindows.com
dir: *Nearest station: Green Park, Hyde Park Corner*

Modern European cooking in the sky

Restaurants in the sky are common in London these days, with various City venues outdoing each other in reaching for the clouds. The Park Lane Hilton was ahead of the pack in these stakes, its 28th-floor Windows restaurant having long been one of its most seductive features. The eye can never be jaded enough to tire of views like this, with Canary Wharf, the London Eye, Buckingham Palace, the green expanse of Hyde Park and the arch of distant Wembley Stadium all clearly visible. Needless to say, it's worth holding out for a window table. Chris Galvin's continuing residency here, with Korean-born head chef Joo Won (not to be confused with his namesake, the actor) at the stoves, adds all the culinary lustre the place deserves. Start with a little cocktail razzmatazz in the bar, before gliding through to the dining room for some inspired modern European cooking. The vein of high-powered French bistro style originally brought in by Galvin is just still discernible in dishes like the ballotine of foie gras with marinated prunes, orange purée and

pain d'épices, and mains such as sea bass with fennel and an oyster in jus gras, but there are excursions further afield these days. A vegetarian opener combines onion bhajis and curried cauliflower purée with a soft-boiled egg in vivid green spinach emulsion, and a Spanish treatment of roast cutlet and crisped brawn of Ibérico pork comes with peppery-hot jus diablo. Desserts keep up the pace by means of dark chocolate fondant with praline and a sorbet of yogurt and dill, or nougat parfait, caramelised banana, Muscovado meringues and black pepper ice cream. Cheeses come from the Bayswater specialist, Buchanan's.

Chef Joo Won, Chris Galvin **Owner** Hilton International **Seats** 130 **Times** 12-2.30/6-10.30, Closed BHs, 26 Dec, 9 Apr, 7 May, L Sat, D Sun, 25 Dec **Prices** Fixed L 2 course £26, Tasting menu £99-£199, Starter £20, Main £40, Dessert £15 **Wines** 248 bottles over £30, 36 bottles under £30, 31 by glass **Parking** NCP **Notes** Tasting menu 6 course, Dégustation menu, Sunday L £45, Vegetarian available, Children welcome

Galvin Bistrot de Luxe
PLAN 2 G3

French 🍷 NOTABLE WINE LIST

tel: 020 7935 4007 **66 Baker St W1U 7DJ**
email: info@galvinrestaurants.com **web:** www.galvinrestaurants.com
dir: *Nearest station: Baker St*

Well-crafted French cooking in stylish bistro

Serving up classic bistro food for a decade now, Chris and Jeff Galvin's place on Baker Street has an authenticity and bonhomie that reflects their genuine love of the genre – this is no pastiche. It really does feel like you're in Paris, with fans spinning on the ceiling, acres of mahogany and a whole load of mirrors. The staff look the business too, in their white aprons, black bow ties and waistcoats. An addition to the dining room this year is a salon privé where up to 12 people can be cossetted away and receive a bespoke menu. There's a prix-fixe menu available lunchtime and early or late evening, or dive into the carte and expect first class ingredients and a modern touch or two. Terrine of corn-fed chicken and foie gras comes with sauce gribiche, and snails in classic bourguignon style, or start with a more contemporary heritage ruby beetroot salad with quinoa, nuts and seeds. Move on to duck cassoulet or a risotto of wild mushrooms and truffle, and finish with blood orange soufflé with marmalade ice cream. The wine list is brimful with French classics.

Chef Chris Galvin, Tom Duffill **Owner** Chris & Jeff Galvin **Seats** 110, Pr/dining room 22 **Times** 12-2.30/6-10.30, Closed 25-26 Dec, 1 Jan, D 24 Dec **Prices** Fixed L 3 course fr £21.50, Fixed D 3 course fr £23.50, Starter £7.50-£14.50, Main £17.50-£27.50, Dessert £6.50-£12 **Wines** 147 bottles over £30, 12 bottles under £30, 18 by glass **Parking** On street, Portman Sq car park **Notes** Prix fixe D 6-7pm, Sunday L fr £29, Vegetarian available, Children welcome

Gauthier Soho
PLAN 3 A1

— *see below*

Le Gavroche Restaurant
PLAN 2 G1

— *see page 350*

Gauthier Soho 🌹🌹🌹

LONDON W1
PLAN 3 A1

French V NOTABLE WINE LIST
tel: 020 7494 3111 & 7851 9382 **21 Romilly St W1D 5AF**
email: info@gauthiersoho.co.uk
dir: *Nearest station: Leicester Sq*

Outstanding modern French cooking in the heart of Soho

There's something of a private dining club ambience about Alexis Gauthier's intimate restaurant, a feeling that is enhanced by the requirement to ring the doorbell to gain access to the Regency townhouse. Once inside, the hurly-burly of Soho street life fades away in two restaurant rooms occupying the ground and first-floor spaces, and two private dining rooms that take up the second floor. Since the kitchen lives down in the basement, the staff must be some of the fittest in London as they yo-yo up and down, but they take it all in their stride, remaining impeccably turned out and unfailingly friendly and helpful. White walls and tablecloths, beige chairs, mirrors, and splashes of colour from fresh flowers and artworks all add up to a bright and cheery setting for Gauthier's intricate modern French cooking. He is an instinctive cook who relies on his intuition and taste buds, and the results can be stunningly good. The menus follow a set-price formula, with two or three courses at lunch, up to five at dinner, priced according to number taken. An intricately-marbled first course game terrine of foie gras, quail, partridge and duck is helped along by impeccably-sourced seasonal fruits and veg, peppered game jelly and toasted sourdough. Top-drawer ingredients are imaginatively mixed and matched, treated with a high level of technical skill, and sent out dressed to thrill. Loin and rack of venison is served with red wine-poached Williams pear, caramelised pumpkin and truffled celeriac purée, while halibut is given a boost by its accompanying fennel fondant, confit tomato, Meyer lemon and sauce vièrge. Sure-footedness continues through to a classic Grand Marnier soufflé with bitter orange marmalade and a matching sorbet.

Chef Gerard Virolle, Alexis Gauthier **Owner** Gerard Virolle, Alexis Gauthier **Seats** 60, Pr/dining room 32 **Times** 12-2.30/6.30-10.30, Closed Xmas, BHs, Sun, L Mon **Prices** Fixed L 2 course £18, Tasting menu £65-£75, Starter £12-£13.50, Main £12-£13.50, Dessert £12-£13.50 **Wines** 150 bottles over £30, 30 bottles under £30, 20 by glass **Parking** On street, NCP Chinatown **Notes** ALC fixed L/D menu, Deluxe L 3 course with wine £40, Children welcome

Le Gavroche Restaurant ❀❀❀❀

LONDON W1   **PLAN 2 G1**

French

tel: 020 7408 0881 **43 Upper Brook St W1K 7QR**
email: bookings@le-gavroche.com
dir: *Nearest station: Marble Arch*

Unwavering commitment to classical French gastronomy

For nearly half a century Le Gavroche has been synonymous with classic French cuisine while also playing a crucial role in helping to give the UK its own culinary identity. That's down to the amazing chefs who have passed through the kitchen over the years, learned the classic ways, tasted the perfectionism, and gone their own way. Situated in a smart Mayfair basement since 1981 (having moved from Lower Sloane Street where it opened in 1967), the room avoids contemporary neutrality and sticks to a refined and graceful look that seems entirely in keeping. The service remains a highlight of a visit – charming, precise and pretty much telepathic. Michel Roux Jr took over running the place in 1991 (from his father Albert) and presided over the restaurant's move into the 21st century. It went rather well. Le Gavroche has never been in better health as it delivers haute cuisine to the modern world. A lighter touch and a few contemporary ideas along the way has made it stronger, and it is proof that there is still a demand for formal dining. A tasting menu – menu exceptionnel – is indeed an exceptional offering (including an impressive vegetarian version), while the à la carte menu is a bilingual treat with prices that may induce a sharp intake of breath. Yes, it is expensive, but the quality is undoubted and the experience second to none. There's an Asian spin to an assiette of king crab and a straight down the line classicism in a lobster mousse that comes with caviar and a champagne butter sauce. The technical flair on show never ceases to impress and the composition of each plate is hard to fault. Turbot is roasted on the bone and arrives with heritage carrots and radish, plus another light creamy sauce (chives this time), while a meat course might be roast Goosnargh duck served with its crispy legs, beetroot Tatin and port jus. The dessert stage should not be missed under any circumstances, not when apricot and Cointreau soufflé is up for grabs, or the set coconut and white chocolate cream with mango and lime salad. The cheese course sticks to British and French artisan varieties and presents them in perfect condition, and the monumental wine has the world's best wines and a decent spread at the lower price range. There's a private table for up to six people called the Chef's Library.

Chef Michel Roux Jnr **Owner** Le Gavroche Ltd **Seats** 60, Pr/dining room 6 **Times** 12-2/6-10, Closed Xmas, New Year, BHs, Sun, L Sat **Prices** Prices not confirmed, Service optional 12.5% **Wines** 2500 bottles over £30, 25 bottles under £30, 25 by glass **Parking** NCP Park Lane **Notes** Tasting menu 8 course, Fixed L menu, Vegetarian available, Children welcome

LONDON W1 *continued*

Goodman PLAN 2 J1

British, American NOTABLE WINE LIST

tel: 020 7499 3776 **26 Maddox St W1S 1QH**
email: reservations@goodmanrestaurants.com
dir: *Nearest station: Oxford Circus*

American-style Mayfair steakhouse serving prime cuts

Dark banquettes and booth seating, photographs hanging on the walls and a wooden floor create a clubby, intimate atmosphere at this upmarket steakhouse based on the New York prototypes. All the meat (USDA Angus or grass-fed in the Lake District) is dry-aged on-site in a temperature-controlled, dehumidified environment and cooked on charcoal to impart a slightly smoky flavour. Select from the various cuts on the menu, from fillet, through bone-in sirloin to porterhouse, the last priced per 100 grammes, and it will be cooked as requested and served with béarnaise, pepper or Stilton sauce. Wide-ranging starters take in Caesar salad and the luxury of lobster cocktail or pan-fried foie gras with roasted figs, oyster mushrooms and truffled honey. Puddings are no afterthought: consider honeycomb parfait with banana sorbet, or cookie sundae with chocolate and caramel sauce.

Chef Phil Campbell **Owner** Mikhail Zelman **Seats** 95 **Times** 12-10.30, All-day dining, Closed Xmas, New Year, BHs, Sun **Prices** Starter £7.50-£40, Main £15-£45, Dessert £7-£12 **Wines** 290 bottles over £30, 7 bottles under £30, 30 by glass **Parking** On street **Notes** Children welcome

The Great British Restaurant, Mayfair PLAN 2 G1

British

tel: 020 7741 2233 **North Audley St W1K 6WE**
email: reservations@eatbrit.com
dir: *Nearest station: Bond St, Marble Arch*

Classic British food at accessible prices in Mayfair

This easygoing little place strikes a pleasantly incongruous note in the gilt-edged neighbourhood around Grosvenor Square. As part of a revamp, the Great British has added a takeaway fish and chip counter (not many of those in Mayfair), and the decor is modelled on a simple fish and chip cafe, but poshed up with a touch of Mayfair polish. As the name makes clear, the kitchen champions much-loved British fare, with well-sourced materials underpinning menus of retro comfort classics which sit alongside some more modern, clear-flavoured dishes. Stick with something traditional like shepherd's pie or standout fish and chips, or go for a more up-to-date Devon cod loin served with a parsley crust, mussels and samphire. Top and tail that with crispy squid with roast garlic and parsley mayonnaise, and a luscious pud like hot chocolate fondant with salted caramel ice cream and cinder toffee, or apple and blackberry crumble with proper custard.

Chef Pete Taylor **Owner** George Hammer, Jamie Jones, Pete Taylor **Seats** 45, Pr/dining room 14 **Times** 12-3/5.30 10.30, Closed Xmas, New Year & BHs, D Sun **Prices** Starter £6-£22, Main £10-£20, Dessert £4.50-£7 **Wines** 4 bottles over £30, 8 bottles under £30, 7 by glass **Parking** On street **Notes** Wknd brunch 9-3, Sunday L fr £14.50, Vegetarian available, Children welcome

The Greenhouse PLAN 4 H6

— *see page 352*

The Grill at The Dorchester PLAN 4 G6

British

tel: 020 7317 6531 **Park Ln W1K 1QA**
email: thegrill.TDL@thedorchester.com **web:** www.thedorchester.com
dir: *Nearest station: Hyde Park Corner*

Top quality eating at a world-class hotel

There's a been a Grill room at the Dorchester since 1931 and today's new look version has a classic appearance that harks back to those days, but not without a touch of contemporary glamour. A hand-blown Murano glass chandelier makes a fine centrepiece and fits in perfectly with the shimmering and elegant room. The menu is rightly focused on the grill itself, with, for example, a strikingly good veal chop cooked just right, and perfectly rested, arriving with a creamy mushroom sauce, or go for peppered organic Aberdeen Angus prime rib, or Scottish salmon steak with béarnaise. The grill works its magic on some first-course scallops, too, served with an autumn salad and rich truffle dressing, with other options up for grabs including chicken Caesar salad or duck foie gras with red onion chutney. Finish with a zesty lemon tart, or wait for 20 minutes and try one of the soufflés (Sicilian pistachio, for example, with salted caramel). Sunday roasts are carved to order – Large White pork belly cooked for seven hours, say, or organic Aberdeen Angus beef.

Chef Christophe Marleix **Owner** Dorchester Collection **Seats** 62 **Times** 12-1.30/6.30-10.30 **Prices** Fixed L 3 course fr £39, Starter £12-£19, Main £29-£52, Dessert £13-£14 **Wines** 400 bottles over £30, 4 bottles under £30, 11 by glass **Parking** 20 **Notes** Sunday L £48, Vegetarian available, Children welcome

GYMKHANA PLAN 4 J6

Modern Indian **NEW** v

tel: 020 3011 5900 **42 Albermarle St W1S 4JH**
email: info@gymkhanalondon.com
dir: *Nearest station: Green Park*

Exciting modern Indian food in a Raj-era club setting

It may be designed to look like a colonial-era Indian gentlemen's club with its dark oak panelling, marble tables in rattan-trimmed booths, swishing ceiling fans, monochrome sporting photos and boar's head on the wall, but there's nothing retro about this restaurant's inventive new-wave Indian cooking. It's a lively spot, buzzing with the hum of diners oohing and aaahing over the powerful flavours that the kitchen coaxes from top-class British produce. Soft-shelled crab Jhalmuri is deep-fried in crunchy spiced batter and matched with puffed rice, samphire and coriander, while an expertly spiced kid goat methi keema is rich, comforting and fragrant with fenugreek leaves (hardcore foodies have the option to add its brains to the equation). Elsewhere, wild boar vindaloo, or wild muntjac biryani with pomegranate and mint raita catch the eye, while game lovers might go for quail seekh kebab with pickled green chilli chutney. Dessert is a perfect fusion of Anglo-Indian ideas: zingy rhubarb chutney atop a sweet ras malai cheese dumpling soaked in cardamon-infused milk with crushed pistachios and almonds.

Chef Rohit Ghai, Karam Sethi **Owner** JKS Restaurants **Seats** 90, Pr/dining room 39 **Times** 12-2.30/5.30-10.30, Closed Xmas, Sun **Prices** Fixed L 2 course £25, Tasting menu £65, Starter £5-£18, Main £14-£48, Dessert £6-£9 **Wines** 169 bottles over £30, 14 bottles under £30, 14 by glass **Parking** Albemarle St **Notes** Fixed D 4 course £35, Pre-theatre menu, Children before 7pm

The Greenhouse ❀❀❀❀

LONDON W1   **PLAN 4 H6**

French, European **V** 🍾 NOTABLE WINE LIST

tel: 020 7499 3331 **27a Hay's Mews, Mayfair W1J 5NY**
email: reservations@greenhouserestaurant.co.uk
dir: *Nearest station: Green Park, Bond St*

Gastronomic delights in a discreet Mayfair location

A succession of top-class chefs including Brian Turner and Gary Rhodes have headed up the kitchen at The Greenhouse over the decades, ensuring its place in the upper echelons of the UK's culinary experiences. Today's incumbent, Arnaud Bignon, doesn't let the side down with his refined, hyper-focused interpretation of the modern French idiom. The Mayfair mews location speaks of discreet, high-end pleasures, approached via a decked pathway lined with bamboo plants, box hedges, bay trees, sculptures and little fountains. This lovely, tranquil garden setting makes you wish alfresco dining were an option. Inside, instead, the connection to nature is firmly established with views of the garden from the serenely stylish dining room, where restful shades of beige and ivory are offset by modern dark wood floors, avocado-coloured leather banquettes and chairs, tables dressed in their finest white linen, and a feature wall with a filigree display of tree branches to emphasise the garden theme. Extremely professional yet very friendly service plays its part in creating an oasis of calm and refinement. Bignon cooks from the heart, starting with the best ingredients money can buy and combining techniques old and new to produce dishes with clean, precise flavours that look beautiful on the plate. After a spectacular array of canapés (fennel and aniseed macaroon, tuna and melon wrapped in nori) to get the taste buds a-tingle, and some fabulous fresh breads (chorizo and cheese, sourdough and a baguette) proceedings get under way with a signature starter of Cornish crab with curry mayonnaise and creamy cauliflower purée, lifted by mint jelly and Granny Smith apple foam. This delightful dish is light, fresh, beautifully balanced and full of textural contrasts. Next up, a four-bone rack of Burgaud Estate lamb is butchered with consummate skill, roasted to perfection with a layer of nori seaweed to boost its savoury depth, and matched inventively with blackened cucumber, sweet black garlic purée and yogurt. Desserts continue to play on influences from around the globe, using matcha green tea powder to flavour pannacotta and bavarois, and in an off-the-wall pairing with wafers of lime meringue, lemon cream and dill sorbet, while the cheese trolley comes loaded with pedigree, perfectly ripened items from France and the UK. Running to 111 pages and with Mayfair pricing, the staggering wine list may require help from the knowledgeable sommelier – and perhaps a little advice from the bank manager too.

Chef Arnaud Bignon **Owner** Marlon Abela Restaurant Corporation
Seats 60, Pr/dining room 12
Times 12-2.30/6.30-11, Closed Xmas, BHs, Sun, L Sat
Prices Fixed L 2 course fr £35, Fixed D 3 course fr £95, Tasting menu £110-£125, Starter fr £30, Main fr £50, Dessert fr £18
Wines 3300 bottles over £30, 22 bottles under £30, 27 by glass
Parking On street **Notes** Children welcome

LONDON W1 *continued*

Hakkasan
PLAN 2 K2

◉◉ Modern Chinese

tel: 020 7927 7000 **8 Hanway Place W1T 1HD**
email: reservation@hakkasan.com
dir: *Nearest station: Tottenham Court Rd*

New-wave Chinese cooking in a see-and-be-seen basement setting

Discretely hidden from the maddening crowds just off Tottenham Court Road and Oxford Street, this original Hakkasan still rocks (there's a sister restaurant in Mayfair). Descend to the moody basement and you're immediately captivated by the effortlessly cool, modern Chinoiserie design and night-clubby vibe: think darkwood latticing, black and gold traditionally drawn panels, and low-slung leather seating, plus a backlit cocktail bar and open kitchen. To match the up tempo vibe, an innovative repertoire of new-wave meets classic Cantonese dishes covers all bases, and everything is exquisitely presented. You might start with some first-rate dim sum (XO scallop dumplings perhaps) or jasmine tea smoked organic pork ribs from the 'small eat' section of the menu, before moving on to something like stir-fried Chilean sea bass with white truffle and black bean sauce, or maybe sweet-and-sour Duke of Berkshire pork with pomegranate. Desserts lean heavily on the West: witness a deconstructed apple tarte Tatin with blackberry, almond and vanilla. A heavyweight wine list and an exciting cocktail selection completes the picture.

Chef Tong Chee Hwee **Owner** Tasameem Group **Seats** 210, Pr/dining room 20 **Times** 12-3.15/5.30-11.15, Closed 25 Dec **Prices** Fixed L 3 course £40-£45, Fixed D 3 course £55-£128, Tasting menu £35, Starter £8-£23.50, Main £19.30-£61, Dessert £7.50-£13.50 **Wines** 400 bottles over £30, 2 bottles under £30, 10 by glass **Parking** NCP Great Russell St **Notes** Sunday L £48-£58, Vegetarian available, Children welcome

Hakkasan Mayfair
PLAN 2 H1

◉◉◉ – *see below*

Haozhan
PLAN 3 A1

◉ Modern Peking, Cantonese

tel: 020 7434 3838 **8 Gerrard St W1D 5PJ**
email: info@haozhan.co.uk
dir: *Nearest station: Trafalgar Sq, Piccadilly Circus, Leicester Sq*

Chinatown star serving exciting modern Chinese food

Haozhan stands out from the opposition in the heart of Chinatown by virtue of its simple contemporary looks and a creative kitchen that puts a modern spin on Chinese regional dishes to come up with some truly original dishes. Statement lampshades hang above simple black wooden tables and a wall of illuminated green and black, and the buzzy ambience is a testament to the popularity of its cooking. A broad-minded roster of dim sum dishes bolsters an already extensive menu, so start with steamed dumplings of spanking-fresh scallops and spinach, then look beyond the comfort of staples such as aromatic crispy duck for the full-bore flavours of a spicy Szechuan hotpot of intestines. Elsewhere, steamed chicken with wolfberry and tong gui herbs vies for attention with casserole of beef brisket and turnips. End with something like tapioca cream with fresh mango and grapefruit.

Chef Heng Thiang **Owner** Jimmy Kong **Seats** 80 **Times** 12-11.30, All-day dining, Closed 25 Dec **Prices** Fixed D 3 course £14-£28, Starter £3.50-£32.80, Main £6.80-£30, Dessert £4-£4.80, Service optional 12.5% **Wines** 18 bottles over £30, 44 bottles under £30, 13 by glass **Parking** Chinatown **Notes** Tasting menu for 2, Pre-theatre menu fr £16.50, Vegetarian available, Children welcome

---

Hakkasan Mayfair ◉◉◉

LONDON W1 PLAN 2 H1

Chinese ♦ NOTABLE WINE LIST

tel: 020 7907 1888 & 7355 7701 **17 Bruton St W1J 6QB**
email: mayfairreservation@hakkasan.com
dir: *Nearest station: Green Park*

Upmarket Chinese cooking in luxury surroundings

The aspirational Hakkasan brand reaches around the globe from the US to the Emirates to Mumbai – there's even a Shanghai outpost to bring the new-wave Cantonese cuisine back home these days. Back here in Blighty, its Mayfair branch sets a suitably exclusive tone with a doorman at the entrance, welcoming meet-and-greeters inside, and a slinky decor that's all latticed screens, marble floors, comfortable banquettes, burnished wooden panels and moody lighting. Staff are slick, friendly and on the ball – and they need to be, given the number of covers spread over its two perpetually heaving floors. As befits the high-rolling surrounds, the menu is dripping with top-end ingredients and luxuries, with prices to match, among them grilled Wagyu beef with enoki mushrooms and soya and garlic dipping sauce, Peking duck with Beluga caviar, and braised Japanese abalone with goose feet and sea cucumber. The rest of the menu offers a roll call of interesting, often unusual and original dishes that's a far cry from the usual Chinese staples, and the cooking is distinguished by its accurate timing, well-conceived combinations and accurate spicing and seasoning. Traditionalists can open with platters of exemplary dim sum or salt-and-pepper squid with sweet chilli sauce, while pace-setting piscine mains take in the likes of roasted silver cod sauced with champagne and honey, or steamed mini New Zealand lobster wrapped in glass vermicelli with rice wine and chilli and garlic sauce. Meatier fare could see steamed pork belly matched with gai lan and dried seafood sauce. Desserts can be highlights, taking their inspiration from the Western repertoire such as a luscious chocolate marquise with kumquat and caramelised macadamia nuts.

Chef Tong Chee Hwee, Koon Chuen Liang **Owner** Tasameem **Seats** 220, Pr/dining room 14 **Times** 12-3.15/6-11.15, Closed 24-25 Dec, L 26 Dec, 1 Jan **Prices** Starter £8-£23.50, Main £18-£61, Dessert £7.50-£13.50 **Wines** 400 bottles over £30, 10 bottles under £30, 9 by glass **Parking** NCP **Notes** Afternoon menu 3.15-5pm, Vegetarian available, Children welcome

LONDON W1 *continued*

Heddon Street Kitchen

PLAN 2 J1

⊚ European, International **NEW** v

tel: 020 7592 1212 **3-9 Heddon St, Regent Street Food Quarter W1B 4BD**
email: heddonstreetkitchen@gordonramsay.com
dir: *Nearest station: Green Park, Oxford Circus*

Buzzy brasserie in the heart of the West End

Part of Gordon Ramsay's impressive London empire, this sleek brasserie just off Regent Street has brought an unmistakable slice of New York to the edge of Mayfair. Set across two floors, it's loud, buzzy and lively – a fun place aimed at the younger crowd, more than those looking for a quiet business meal. The seasonal menu is an eclectic mix combining hot and cold starters, salads, grills and main courses, with the emphasis on comfort dishes, accurately cooked or assembled. A simple starter of rigatoni with tomatoes, aubergines, buffalo mozzarella and pecorino might precede a main course of roasted cod, crushed potatoes, artichoke, salted capers, red wine and lemon sauce. An oozing chocolate fondant with salted caramel and Amaretto ice cream is a typical dessert. The wine list should appeal to all budgets and there's a cracking cocktail list too.

Chef Maria Tampakis **Owner** Gordon Ramsay **Seats** Pr/dining room 12
Times 11.30am-11pm, All-day dining, Closed 25 Dec **Prices** Starter £6.50-£12, Main £12.50-£34, Dessert £7-£10.50 **Wines** 110 bottles over £30, 15 bottles under £30, 41 by glass **Parking** NCP **Notes** Brunch, Breakfast, Pre-theatre 2/3 course £22/£26

Hélène Darroze at The Connaught

PLAN 2 H1

⊚⊚⊚⊚ *– see opposite*

Hibiscus

PLAN 2 J1

⊚⊚⊚⊚⊚ *– see page 356*

HIX

PLAN 2 J1

⊚⊚ British

tel: 020 7292 3518 **66-70 Brewer St W1F 9UP**
email: reservations@hixsoho.co.uk
dir: *Nearest station: Piccadilly Circus*

A celebration of British ingredients

A giant wooden door and understated red neon sign are the only clues that this is a Mark Hix outfit, and, the Soho mothership of his restaurant empire, paying homage to the modern British brasserie and Brit Art alike. The dining room has an art deco feel, with reeded glass panels, white-tiled floor, big mirrors and leather seating. Tables come tightly packed, while the long silver-topped bar is set up for dining, ramping up the decibels and atmosphere. But it's the eclectic collection of mobiles dangling from the ceiling (by celebrated artists like Damien Hirst), plus neons and artworks on walls that really add personality and verve. Hix's patriotic brasserie fare supports seasonality and British regional fare, including some lesser-used ingredients such as alexanders maybe partnering fabulous steamed fillets of St

Mary's Bay red mullet and knockout Morecambe Bay shrimps. The cooking isn't tricksy, preferring to focus on the simple treatment of prime produce, as in the wonderfully tart Yorkshire rhubarb with creamy saffron custard to finish. Though carte prices are high, the fixed-price option is easier on the wallet. The bustling, clubby Mark's Bar downstairs is the place for cocktails and fashionable small-plate food.

Times 12-12, All-day dining, Closed 25-26 Dec, 1 Jan

HIX Mayfair

PLAN 2 J1

⊚⊚ Traditional British v ⍟ NOTABLE WINE LIST

tel: 020 7518 4004 **Albemarle St, Mayfair W1S 4BP**
email: hixmayfair@roccofortehotels.com **web:** www.roccofortehotels.com
dir: *Nearest station: Green Park*

Modern cooking, traditional ingredients, contemporary art

The dining at Brown's Hotel has undergone a fair few manifestations in recent years, but the present one, under the aegis of in-demand modern Britishist Mark Hix, is undoubtedly one of the most inspired. Against a backdrop of work by British artists of various generations – Tracey Emin and Bridget Riley among them – Hix's menus are given dazzling execution by the team in the kitchen. Hix himself drops in to give the occasional workshop on such essentials as carving. Thoroughbred British produce and foraged materials pour forth on menus that take in Dorset snails with Cumbrian black pudding and bacon, crispy Goosnargh duck with chickweed and marinated cherries, and a salad of vibrantly coloured Dorset Blue lobster with sea purslane. These fine prime ingredients are treated with respect, not muddled into a crowd of supporting characters, so that main courses such as chargrilled Torbay sole, and roast mallard with gamekeeper's pie and spiced red cabbage, make perfect sense. So does an apple pie made with juicy, aromatic Cox's and served with real custard.

Chef Mark Hix, Lee Kebble **Owner** Rocco Forte Hotels **Seats** 80, Pr/dining room 70 **Times** 12-3/5.30-11 **Prices** Fixed L 2 course £27.50, Fixed D 3 course £32.50-£35, Starter £6.95-£17.95, Main £17.50-£42.50, Dessert £6.95-£7.95 **Wines** 280 bottles over £30, 2 bottles under £30, 18 by glass **Parking** Valet/Burlington St **Notes** Pre-theatre 5.30-7.30pm Mon-Sat, Sunday L, Children welcome

Hélène Darroze at The Connaught ✿ ✿ ✿ ✿

LONDON W1   **PLAN 2 H1**

French V

tel: 020 3147 7200 & 3147 7108 **Carlos Place W1K 2AL**
email: helenedarroze@the-connaught.co.uk
web: www.the-connaught.co.uk
dir: *Nearest station: Bond St, Green Park*

Complex cooking from a French star in a British institution

The venerable old Connaught has been synonymous with old-school luxury since Queen Victoria ruled an empire on which the sun never set. The historic dining room exudes all the expected clubby grandeur, but when Hélène Darroze arrived in 2008 the place took a more cross-Channel view of things. Paris-based designer India Mahdavi reworked the interior with a more feminine, contemporary look using swirly patterned fabrics that soften and complement the original burnished oak panelling and delicate plasterwork ceilings, while Riedel wine glasses, silver cutlery and gleaming cloches all feed into the feeling of luxury. The battalion of front-of-house staff, too, has been shipped in almost exclusively from across the water, and strikes a pleasing balance between the impeccable correctness of tone and relaxed confidence that suit this style of high-end dining operation. For those unfamiliar with her CV, Hélène Darroze is a protégée of French super-chef Alain Ducasse, and her cooking is rooted in the earthy dishes of her native southwestern France, but the overall impression is of well-crafted, dynamic, modern food that all looks like a work of art on the plate. Diners are given a novel way of choosing what they want to eat using a solitaire board with a food item written on each marble to cross-reference with the menu of a dozen or so dishes and arrive at the five-, seven- or nine-course options that suit their mood (and budget). Things begin impressively with an idea inspired by a trip to Vietnam, starring Guy Grieve's Mull scallops with amaranth and shiso leaves, borage flowers, shellfish jelly and sauce. Given the chef's origins in the Landes region, foie gras will undoubtedly feature somewhere, on this occasion in a composition with eel, girolles and coco bean sauce, while a main course of Rhug Estate venison arrives in the company of Medjool dates, pumpkin, a Brussels sprout, nasturtium leaves and a deliciously rich date and liquorice sauce. Spot-on precision and the best possible raw materials are the key, all the way through to refined and creative desserts: artisan French chocolatier Olivier de Loisy provides the chocolate for a fabulous parfait teamed with bourbon vanilla ice cream, coriander, and miniature praline cakes. A biblical wine list of blue-blooded bottles offers fantastic choice at correspondingly high prices. As the place is a special occasion destination (for normal mortals), diners are presented with a personalised copy of the menu at the end.

Chef Hélène Darroze **Owner** Maybourne Hotel Group **Seats** 60, Pr/dining room 20 **Times** 12-2/6.30-10, Closed Jan, Aug, Sun-Mon **Prices** Fixed L 2 course £30, Fixed D 3 course £52, Tasting menu £155 **Wines** 735 bottles over £30, 25 by glass **Parking** South Audley car park **Notes** Fixed 4/5/7 course £45/£92/£125, Tasting 9 course, Children welcome

Hibiscus ✿ ✿ ✿ ✿ ✿

LONDON W1   PLAN 2 J1

Modern French **V** 🍾 NOTABLE WINE LIST

tel: 020 7629 2999 **29 Maddox St, Mayfair W1S 2PA**
email: enquiries@hibiscusrestaurant.co.uk
dir: *Nearest station: Oxford Circus, Marble Arch*

Top-class modern French cooking from a master of his art

Claude Bosi has French culinary traditions running through his DNA. After a childhood spent at his parents' restaurant in Lyon (France's food 'capital') he spent time with super-chef Alain Ducasse, then crossed over la Manche to do his bit in transforming Ludlow into a foodie hotspot at the original Hibiscus. Its Mayfair incarnation is a discreet, rather dignified space, revamped in 2013 to give the place a more contemporary face, with muted tones and modern artworks, pale oak floors, tables dressed up in brilliant white cloths, and a magnificent floral display in the centre of the room. Always one to plough his own furrow, Bosi's menu format is slightly quirky: there's no carte as such, just a shopping list of prime seasonal ingredients. You pick what you like the sound of, and then choose how many courses (three, six or eight) you (and your bank manager) feel up to, and the kitchen does the rest. If that sounds too radical, the three-course lunchtime menu (with half a bottle of wine, coffee and petits fours thrown in) is terrific value for food of this level and suits those who have offices to get back to or shops to hit. The style is modern French, the dishes full of thrilling avant-garderie and speculative, sometimes slightly worrying combinations, but you are in the very safe hands of a chef at the peak of his powers and unlikely to encounter anything that is less than stunningly successful. Expect to be served artfully constructed dishes that are swooningly pretty but never lack punch. A summer's lunch starts with tartare of Scottish langoustines with sauce vièrge — but this is Claude Bosi's take on that classic sauce, the orthodox tomatoes replaced with strawberries — controversial, you may think, but it works. Some stunning ideas come in small parcels, as when delicate ravioli are filled with spring onion and lime, then doused with a heavenly king prawn consommé at the table. Mains bring together combinations that meld together as a whole while maintaining the integrity of each individual element — an immaculately handled piece of John

Dory, for example, topped with earthy girolles and succulent diced Morteau sausage, all helped along by Lancashire mead sauce and a contrasting salted lime gel. Or try top-class crispy-skinned duck breast with subtle barbecue and cumin notes beside confit kumquats, burnt tomato purée, carrots and a mint and coriander-spiked jus. The meal ends with dazzling desserts: a 'tart' of razor-thin chocolate leaves layered with a powerful chocolate mousse is served with basil ice cream and star anise brittle, and a dome of olive oil and kaffir lime parfait is encased in white chocolate and partnered with ripe mango. Matching wine to such adventurous flavours is a bit tricky, so let the pros guide you — or consider splashing out on wine flights.

Chef Claude Bosi **Owner** Claude Bosi **Seats** 48, Pr/dining room 18 **Times** 12-2.30/6.30-10.30, Closed 24-26 Dec, 1 Jan, 1 wk Etr, Sun-Mon **Prices** Fixed L 3 course £35-£40, Fixed D 3 course £90, Tasting menu £100-£120 **Wines** 345 bottles over £30, 4 bottles under £30, 20 by glass **Parking** On street **Notes** Tasting menu D only 3/6/8 course, Children welcome

LONDON W1 *continued*

Ibérica Marylebone

PLAN 2 H4

Modern Spanish

tel: 020 7636 8650 **195 Great Portland St W1W 5PS**
email: reservations@ibericarestaurants.com **web:** www.ibericarestaurants.com
dir: *Nearest station: Great Portland St, Regent's Park*

An authentic taste of Spain in the heart of Marylebone

With a particular focus on the Asturias region of northern Spain, Ibérica occupies a sizable corner plot in Fitzrovia/Marylebone border country. There's a decidedly Ibérian feel to the interior, with a marble-topped bar in the double-height space, plus tiles, huge lanterns and a deli section with hanging hams. A mezzanine level adds even more tables. Tapas and pinchos are the name of the game, and there is an authenticity to the output. A simple plate of asparagus; manchego and onion confit on a truffle oil toast is a classy little toastie, the cheese soft and melting, the aroma of truffle nicely judged. There are all the anticipated cured meats, too, and croquettes such as a classic ham version served in a generous portion. Twice-cooked lamb comes with an almond purée and tomatoes and pepper from El Bierzo (near Léon), while cuttlefish and prawns star in a risotto made with black rice and served with a zingy aïoli. Desserts run to apple tart with crema catalana, and there are Spanish wines and sherries to help you on your way.

Chef Nacho Manzano, Luis Contreras, César García **Owner** Iberica Food & Culture Ltd **Seats** 100, Pr/dining room 30 **Times** 11.30-11, All-day dining, Closed 25-26 Dec & BHs, D Sun **Prices** Starter £6-£22, Main £4-£190, Dessert £4-£5 **Wines** 61 bottles over £30, 19 bottles under £30, 34 by glass **Notes** Vegetarian available, Children welcome

JW Steakhouse

PLAN 2 G1

American

tel: 020 7499 6363 & 7399 8400 **Park Ln W1K 7TN**
email: info@jwsteakhouse.co.uk **web:** www.jwsteakhouse.co.uk
dir: *Nearest station: Marble Arch*

Prime steaks and cocktails on Park Lane

There is and ever shall be a reliable market for prime steak. Offer the luxe surroundings of a Park Lane hotel, and few would pass up the opportunity. The expansive JW brings steakhouse dining, American style, to the Grosvenor House, in an ambience of black and white ceramic floor tiles and parquet, darkwood dressers, and a big blackboard menu offering all the permutations of cuts, sauces, cooking degrees and provenance. There's a cocktail bar on hand to wet your whistle, before getting stuck into the protein. The beef is all thoroughbred USDA-approved gear, from Josper-grilled New York strip steak in béarnaise, with superb hand-cut chips and organic salad, to the house Tomahawk rib-eye, for which the indispensable partner is Tomahawk Vineyard Napa Valley Cabernet Sauvignon. Start with a bowl of earthy, creamy truffled wild mushroom

soup, and finish with a gooey-centred, freshly baked chocolate brownie and vanilla ice cream, and it's hard to know what more you could wish for.

Times 12-2.30/6-10.30

Kai Mayfair

PLAN 4 G6

Modern Chinese NOTABLE WINE LIST

tel: 020 7493 8988 **65 South Audley St W1K 2QU**
email: reservations@kaimayfair.co.uk
dir: *Nearest station: Marble Arch*

Vibrant Chinese cooking in opulent Mayfair setting

Spread over two floors, this swanky Chinese restaurant is decorated in rich hues, with arty Chinese photographs on the walls. Kai aims to show the diversity of Chinese cuisine and the cooking is noted for its accurate timing, judicious use of spicing and seasoning, and its subtle combination of flavours and textures. You could take refuge in the comfort of classics such as crispy duck and sweet-and-sour pork, but why not get off to a flying start with deep-fried soft-shelled crab, in a crisp batter spiked with garlic, chilli and shallots, and pointed up with green mango julienne, or a decadent fusion idea pairing pan-fried foie gras with caramelised cashews, white pepper, spring onions, its richness cut with grapes and passionfruit dressing? Next up, top-class Ibérico pork loin comes with bean and shrimp crumble, Washington apple compôte and Granny Smith jelly. The menu opens unusually with a page of desserts, showing how seriously they are taken here, and Amadei chocolate fondant with pistachio ice cream, crumbs and powder shows the creative approach.

Times 12-2.15/6.30-10.45, Closed 25-26 Dec, 1 Jan

The Keeper's House

PLAN 2 J1

Modern British

tel: 020 7300 5881 **Royal Academy of Arts, Burlington House, Piccadilly W1J 0BD**
email: keepershouse@peytonandbyrne.co.uk
dir: *Nearest station: Piccadilly Circus*

Appealing European cooking in the Royal Academy

Tucked away in one corner of the courtyard, The Keeper's House was installed in the 19th century as a grace-and-favour apartment for the resident steward of the Royal Academy collections. A strikingly attractive restaurant has been fashioned from it, the recessed rooms imitating those of the galleries upstairs, with bare contemporary light fittings and jade-green walls hung with small casts of classical reliefs. As well as inspiring cocktails and English wines, there's a menu of spruce European cooking. Start boldly with snail ravioli, or a bowl of refreshing gazpacho with red pepper sorbet, and then consider the likes of roast lamb saddle with tomato ragoût and gnocchi, turbot and prawns with kale and glazed pumpkin, or pedigree sirloin aged for four weeks and dressed with bone marrow and browned onions. Round things off with a serving of rhubarb rice pudding and matching sorbet, or brown bread mousse. It's members only until 4pm, and then all are welcome.

Chef Valerio Deplano **Owner** Oliver Peyton **Seats** 65, Pr/dining room 45 **Times** 12-3/5.30-10, Closed Sun **Prices** Fixed L 2 course £24.50, Fixed D 3 course £27.50-£53, Starter £7-£15, Main £12.50-£25.50, Dessert £8-£12.50 **Wines** 46 bottles over £30, 12 bottles under £30, 15 by glass **Parking** On street **Notes** Pre-theatre menu 5.30-7pm 2/3 course £19/£24, Vegetarian available, Children welcome

Kitchen Table

PLAN 2 J3

– *see page 358*

LONDON W1 *continued*

Kitty Fisher's
PLAN 4 H6

❀❀ Modern British NEW

tel: 020 3302 1661 **10 Shepherd Market W1J 7QF**
dir: *Nearest station: Green Park*

Robust British cooking in stylish surroundings

Named after the courtesan who once 'entertained' her gentlemen in this characterful Mayfair building, Kitty Fisher's is certainly compact, although that hasn't stopped a tidal wave of glowing reviews since it opened its doors without fanfare at the end of 2014. Closely packed tables and stools at the bar offer diners two options in this low-lit, atmospheric, Bohemian-style restaurant with red velvet banquettes, retro light fittings and candles. The modern British food is driven by what's available at the market on the day, with the wood-fired grill being the workhorse of the kitchen. Dishes are deceptively simple and reliant on the very best ingredients, as demonstrated in a starter of breaded Cornish mussels wild garlic mayonnaise. It might be followed by precisely cooked, well-rested lamb cutlets served with a punchy and well-balanced sauce of anchovy, mint and parsley. An intense chocolate mousse accompanied by poached rhubarb, crème fraîche and a sprinkling of toasted hazelnuts is one satisfying way to finish.

Chef Tomos Parry **Owner** Tom Mullion, Oliver Milburn, Tim Steel **Seats** 38 **Times** 12-2.30/6.30-9.30, Closed Sun, L Sat **Prices** Starter £3-£12, Main £17-£30, Dessert £6-£12, Service optional **Wines** 19 bottles over £30, 4 bottles under £30, 9 by glass **Parking** On street, NCP Shepherd St **Notes** Vegetarian on request, Galician Steak min 2 share £80, Children welcome

Latium
PLAN 2 J3

❀❀ Italian

tel: 020 7323 9123 **21 Berners St W1T 3LP**
email: info@latiumrestaurant.com
dir: *Nearest station: Goodge St, Oxford Circus, Tottenham Court Rd*

Regional Italian cooking with ravioli a speciality

Chef-patron Maurizio Morelli's smart Fitzrovia restaurant is named after the ancient title of the Italian region of Lazio, so you can expect to enjoy the authentic Roman flavours as well as seasonal ideas from around the country. Imported produce ensures authenticity, and the kitchen makes everything else, including pasta and bread each day. The intimate setting features stone mosaics and arty Italian photography to liven up a sober backdrop of black leather banquettes set against neutral walls. Ravioli fans will be pleased to find a menu devoted to the medium, offering pasta parcels stuffed with oxtail in celery sauce, or a selection of fish ravioli with sea bass bottarga. Elsewhere, the kitchen delivers the goods in the shape of comforting chicken tortellini in chicken broth, followed by roast monkfish with a silky chickpea and rosemary sauce, Swiss chard and fried celeriac. To finish, there's a creative winter season take on pannacotta, flavoured with chestnut and matched with pear poached in red wine. The impressive wine list is an all-Italian affair.

Chef Maurizio Morelli **Owner** Maurizio Morelli, Claudio Pulze **Seats** 50 **Times** 12-3/5.30-10.30, Closed 24-26 Dec, Etr Sun & Mon, L Sun & BHs **Prices** Fixed L 2 course £16.50-£29.50, Fixed D 3 course £35.50 **Wines** 100 bottles over £30, 25 bottles under £30, 14 by glass **Parking** On street, NCP **Notes** Pre-theatre menu 2/3 course £16.50/£22.50, Vegetarian available, Children welcome

Kitchen Table

LONDON W1
PLAN 2 J3

Modern British V

tel: 020 7637 7770 **70 Charlotte St W1T 4QG**
email: kitchentable@bubbledogs.co.uk
dir: *Nearest station: Goodge St*

Sitting at the counter, chatting with the chefs

It is just possible, of course, that you might want to book a restaurant table somewhere to thrash out the details of a contract, or catch up with an old friend. This isn't it. Kitchen Table is much more the kind of place you come not just to concentrate intensely on what you're eating, but to chat to the chefs about it while they're getting it ready. Nineteen inquisitive souls are berthed around two sides of the culinary action in a gently lit, almost after-hours kind of ambience. Around a dozen or more daily-changing dishes — really, who's counting? — will come your way, labelled by their main ingredients, which have themselves come the way of the kitchen according to what trusted suppliers have told them is good that day. Guest chefs happen in for one night only. It's an open-ended kind of a thing, a poster-child for new London dining. A menu might go something like this: Oyster; Chicken; Scallop; Monkfish; Sole; Truffle; Asparagus; Duck; Goat; Rhubarb; Orange; Caramel. And that's pretty much all you need to know in advance of the arrival of each

explosively creative dish. One or two items are stalwarts of the repertoire, such as the crispy chicken skin with rosemary mascarpone and bacon jam, while others come and go. Roe deer on a bed of shredded onion simmered in yogurt with slivered raw chestnuts and elderberries, burrata with damson purée, the curiously intense pear sponge with svelte liquorice ice cream are all deeply memorable morsels. Occasionally, the slight air of the science laboratory creates expectations that aren't quite fulfilled on the palate, but overall the aim is true, and the scattergun approach means there's always something new to talk about.

Chef James Knappett **Owner** James Knappett, Sandia Chang **Seats** 19 **Times** 6-11, Closed Sun-Mon, L all week **Prices** Tasting menu £88 **Wines** 50 bottles over £30, 8 by glass **Parking** On street **Notes** No children

Levant
PLAN 2 G2

Lebanese, Middle Eastern

tel: 020 7224 1111 **Jason Court, 76 Wigmore St W1U 2SJ**
email: reservations@levant.co.uk
dir: *Nearest station: Bond St*

The scents and flavours of the Middle East

Levant brings the authentic flavours of the Middle East to Wigmore Street, along with an exotic decor of rich fabrics, carved wood, candlelight and lamps, with a fun atmosphere – even belly dancers in the evening and live music at weekends. Choose a succession of grazing-sized plates to share, starting perhaps with soujok (spicy Armenian sausage with tomatoes, parsley and garlic), or deep-fried squid with sumac. Freshly cooked meat dishes are succulent and full of flavour, from a skewer of grilled minced lamb with herbs, onions and spices to a pastry case of chicken, onions and pine nuts. Vegetarians get a good deal, with tabouleh and grilled haloumi, served with tomatoes, green olives and mint, among the options, and you could finish with a platter of Baklava, fresh fruit and Turkish delight.

Times 12-3am, All-day dining, Closed 25-26 Dec, L 1 Jan

Lima
PLAN 2 K3

Modern Peruvian

tel: 020 3002 2640 **31 Rathbone Place, Fitzrovia W1T 1JH**
email: enquiry@limalondon.com
dir: *Nearest station: Goodge St, Tottenham Court Rd*

Buzzy, contemporary setting for a genuine taste of Peru

This glass-fronted restaurant, named after Peru's capital, brings that country's contemporary cuisine to the West End. It's a neatly decorated place, with a pale coffee colour scheme, large mirrors, unusual light fittings and bright canvases on the walls; downstairs is a bar and an additional dining area. Service is from warm and pleasant staff who happily provide descriptions of the dishes, as well they might, as even the English translations can need elucidation (anyone for Amazonian fish with seaweed brown butter, annatto, white kiwicha and cacao Amazonia?). Excellent Peruvian ingredients are the backbone, all handled confidently and skilfully. Start with slices of raw scallops with velvety yellow pepper purée and fresh-tasting ground and dried muña mint corn, or perhaps a simple salad of radishes, red potato, avocado and passionfruit. Tender and juicy duck breast escabèche may follow, with roast Andean potatoes and cylinders of red and purple mash, or warm salmon céviche with plantain majado, aji limo pepper and ginger. Palate-bursting flavours are also evident in puddings like cactus mousse with crisp wafers of rocoto peppers, meringue and coconut.

Chef Robert Ortiz, Virgilio Martinez **Owner** Gabriel Gonzalez, Virgilio Martinez, Jose Luis **Seats** 60, Pr/dining room 25 **Times** 12-2.30/5.30-10.30, Closed Xmas, D Sun **Prices** Prices not confirmed, Service optional 12.5% **Wines** 31 bottles over £30, 9 bottles under £30, 12 by glass **Parking** On street **Notes** Pre-theatre 2/3 course 5.30-6pm £20/£23 pre-bkg recommended, Sunday L, Vegetarian available, Children welcome

Little Social
PLAN 2 H2

– *see below*

Locanda Locatelli
PLAN 2 G2

– *see page 360*

Little Social

LONDON W1   PLAN 2 H2

French, Modern European **NOTABLE WINE LIST**
tel: 020 7870 3730 **5 Pollen St W1S 1NE**
email: reservations@littlesocial.co.uk
dir: *Nearest station: Oxford Circus*

Backstreet Parisian bistro chic chez Atherton

There seems to be nothing stopping Jason Atherton these days, as his growing restaurant group adds character and style to central London dining. Pollen Street Social's cousin is right opposite the original, hidden behind a discreet black frontage. Inside, it's indisputably little from side to side, but extends back as far as the eye can see. The place was cannily chosen for a homage to Parisian backstreet bistro eating, since that is what it most physically resembles, with its oxblood banquettes, tables of antique elm, ornately framed pictures and Michelin maps. Additional bar-stool dining accentuates the cultural point, as does the busy babble of keen custom that throngs the place much of the time. Presentations are simple, emphasising the quality of prime materials, aiming for straightforwardness rather than complexity. Great satisfaction comes from a starter of roast breast and confit leg of quail with sautéed foie gras and peach compôte, and in a dish of smoked eel with beetroot and horseradish cream. Bistro fans expect cheaper cuts of meat crammed with flavour, and there can be nothing more satisfying than a braised ox cheek with roast marrowbone and horseradished mash, but even the fish dishes have a substantial air to them, as for example sea bass BLT-style with Portobello mushrooms and sauce bois boudran. Desserts are mostly from the classic Gallic cookbook, though not without a London overlay. So hot chocolate moelleux is partnered by almond and sea-salt ice cream, and there are maple-glazed, apple-filled doughnuts sprinkled with cinnamon sugar, served with real crème anglaise. Bread looks like traditional baguette, but comes in sourdough guise with smoked butter.

Chef Cary Docherty **Owner** Jason Atherton **Seats** 55, Pr/dining room 8 **Times** 12-2.30/6-10.30, Closed 25-26 Dec, 1-2 Jan, BHs, Sun **Prices** Fixed L 2 course £21, Starter £9.50-£15.50, Main £16-£33, Dessert £7.50-£16 **Wines** 60 bottles over £30, 3 bottles under £30, 23 by glass **Parking** Burlington car park, Cavendish Sq **Notes** Exclusive hire, Prix fixe menu, Vegetarian available, Children welcome

LONDON W1 *continued*

The Lockhart

PLAN 2 F2

◉ American **NEW**

tel: 020 3011 5400 **22-24 Seymour Place W1H 7NL**
email: info@lockhartlondon.com
dir: *Nearest station: Marble Arch*

America's Deep South off Edgware Road

A boarded floor, simple wooden tables and chairs, old railway benches, antique sideboards and walls of exposed whitewashed brick give an unassuming look to this restaurant off Edgware Road. Big windows create a light and airy feel, with the bar downstairs in the basement. The cuisine of the southern states of the USA is the theme, which translates into homely cooking that packs a punch in terms of flavour. Try catfish gumbo – tender rice with okra, pork sausage and bright white flakes of fish – or wedge salad with bacon, chopped egg and buttermilk ranch dressing. Move on to ribs in a BBQ reduction with tomato and cucumber salad, or skate wing in a lightly spiced crab dressing with charred broccoli. Equally authentic are puddings such as the chocolate chess or lemon icebox pies.

Chef Brad McDonald **Owner** Chris & Gwen Wren **Seats** 55, Pr/dining room 30
Times 12-3/6-10, Closed 24-25 Dec **Prices** Starter £8-£12, Main £16-£23, Dessert £7 **Wines** 30+ bottles over £30, 5 bottles under £30, 10 by glass **Parking** On street **Notes** Sun brunch, Sunday L £12-£22, Vegetarian available, Children welcome

The Mandeville Hotel

PLAN 2 G2

◉ Modern British

tel: 020 7935 5599 **Mandeville Place W1U 2BE**
email: info@mandeville.co.uk **web:** www.mandeville.co.uk
dir: *Nearest station: Bond St, Baker St*

Brasserie food in a stylish boutique hotel

What is now known as Marylebone village has always been an oasis of civility for those prepared to venture a block or two north of the busy Oxford Street, and a boutique hotel like The Mandeville suits the district to a T. Understated contemporary decor and a calming ambience are the hallmarks, while the cumbersomely named Reform Social and Grill emulates the London gentlemen's club, albeit one where women are allowed. Unclothed tables and bottle-green banquettes set the tone, and the food follows on with plenty of hang-the-diet protein in the form of steaks and quality burgers. A starter of chunky roast chicken terrine and smooth chicken liver pâté mobilises the best of both worlds, and a Josper-grilled lobster burger with chips is an interesting variant. Otherwise, expect braised ox cheeks with horseradish mash, or 'seaside pie' made with smoked haddock, coley, cockles and samphire, before getting down to the serious end of things with jam roly-poly or sticky toffee pudding.

Chef Sergio Neale **Seats** 90, Pr/dining room 12 **Times** 12-3/7-11 **Prices** Prices not confirmed **Parking** NCP nearby **Notes** Vegetarian available, Children welcome

Locanda Locatelli ◉◉◉

LONDON W1

PLAN 2 G2

Italian ⌕ NOTABLE WINE LIST
tel: 020 7935 9088 **8 Seymour St W1H 7JZ**
email: info@locandalocatelli.com **web:** www.locandalocatelli.com
dir: *Nearest station: Marble Arch*

Fabulous top-class Italian cooking of daring simplicity

Back in action and firing on all cylinders after a much-publicised explosion in the neighbouring Churchill Hotel's basement closed its doors for four months in early 2015, Giorgio Locatelli's glamorous venue is once again in the business of bringing the best of Italy to London. If you've seen him on the telly, or maybe browsed his cookbooks, you really should get round to eating his food, for while the place may not be at the budget end of Italian dining in the capital, it is about as good as it gets. It's a slinky designer room, all parquet floors, textured wooden walls, ivory leather bucket chairs, diaphanous drapes and booths divided by etched-glass screens, and the front-of-house team deserve a special mention for their smart and informed service. The cooking has traditional Italian values at its core – freshness and simplicity – and there's a peasant heartiness to it, alongside a dash of contemporary panache. Antipasti kick things off as they mean to go on, perhaps a classic ox tongue with green sauce, while pasta dishes – perhaps ravioli packed with pheasant and served with rosemary jus, or homely orecchiette ('little ears') with turnip tops, chilli, garlic and anchovies – are a benchmark by which all others are measured. Main-course slow-cooked suckling pig with mashed potato and caramelised Granny Smith apples delivers deep comfort, or go for wild sea bass fillet baked in a salt and herb crust. Desserts can be an exemplary tiramisù, or a take on Eton Mess with Amalfi lemon cream and sorbet. To cap it all off, the wine list is a virtuoso performance, with plenty of choice by the glass.

Chef Giorgio Locatelli **Owner** Plaxy & Giorgio Locatelli **Seats** 70, Pr/dining room 50 **Times** 12-3/6-11, Closed 24-26 Dec, 1 Jan **Prices** Starter £9-£20, Main £13.50-£32.50, Dessert £6.75-£12.50, Service optional **Wines** 576 bottles over £30, 30 bottles under £30, 18 by glass **Parking** NCP adjacent (meter) **Notes** Sunday L, Vegetarian available, Children welcome

Maze
PLAN 2 G1

❀❀❀ – see below

Mele e Pere
PLAN 2 J1

❀ Italian

tel: 020 7096 2096 **46 Brewer St, Soho W1F 9TF**
email: info@meleepere.co.uk
dir: Nearest station: Piccadilly Circus

Dynamic Italian basement venue

'Apples and Pears' looks a riot of colour and conviviality on its Soho corner. At ground-floor level is a café area, but the main dining goes on downstairs in a dynamic, russet-walled basement room centred on a well-stocked bar with counter seating and a formidable collection of specialist vermouths. Italian sharing plates are the principal draw to start, with San Daniele ham and gnocchi, deep-fried squid and smoked aïoli, or beef carpaccio with pecorino among the offerings. Then it's braised veal shin with wild mushrooms and polenta, or grilled bream and gremolata, with perhaps an intermediate pasta dish or risotto to bridge the gap. It's all done with infectious panache, warm-heartedness and due despatch if you're off to the theatre afterwards. Lingerers, meanwhile, may well just be setting about a maraschino cherry sundae with blackcurrant and vanilla ice creams, or mascarpone cheesecake with white chocolate and wild berries.

Chef A Mantovani **Owner** P Hughes, A Mantovani **Seats** 90 **Times** 12-11, All-day dining, Closed 25-26 Dec, 1 Jan, Etr Sun-Mon **Prices** Fixed D 3 course £19.50, Starter £8, Main £29, Dessert £6 **Wines** 51 bottles over £30, 25 bottles under £30, 16 by glass **Parking** NCP **Notes** Pre-theatre menu until 7pm £16.50-£19.50, Vegetarian available, Children welcome

Le Meridien Piccadilly
PLAN 2 J1

❀ Modern British V

tel: 020 7734 8000 **21 Piccadilly W1J 0BH**
email: piccadilly.terrace@lemeridien.com **web:** www.lemeridienpiccadilly.com
dir: Nearest station: Piccadilly Circus

Grills and a lot more at a top-end hotel

Le Meridien, among the capital's top-end hotels, occupies a prime site on one of central London's most famous thoroughfares. Within is a series of vast public rooms, with the impressive Terrace Grill and Bar a futuristic atrium-style space with a curved glass ceiling, columns and darkwood tables; a terrace looking over Piccadilly is a possibility for alfresco dining. In this context, it's no surprise that the kitchen deploys prime ingredients – Carlingford oysters, Denham Estate venison (served as carpaccio), native lobster (paired with anchovy and shallot butter), and Red Poll beef steaks. Although grills – all accurately timed – abound, from lamb rack to lemon sole, a contemporary approach is taken for some dishes. For instance, chicken and duck liver parfait with beetroot and spiced oranges could be followed by a steamed sea bass parcel with mussels in Pernod. In-house bread is excellent, and among puddings could be banoffee sundae with home-made vanilla ice cream or retro knickerbocker glory.

Chef Michael Dutnall **Seats** 80 **Times** 12-2.30/5.30-10.30 **Prices** Fixed L 3 course fr £25, Fixed D 3 course fr £25, Starter £7-£12, Main £17-£38, Dessert £9, Service optional **Wines** 42 bottles over £30, 5 bottles under £30, 11 by glass **Notes** Chef's table 5 course £99 (max 10 people), Sun brunch £54, Children welcome

Maze ❀❀❀

LONDON W1	PLAN 2 G1

French, Asian V

tel: 020 7107 0000 & 7592 1350 **London Marriott Hotel, 10-13 Grosvenor Square W1K 6JP**
email: maze@gordonramsay.com
dir: Nearest station: Bond St

Franco-Japanese rapprochement in uplifting surroundings

Gordon Ramsay's Maze is in prime position on Grosvenor Square, with the United States embassy looming in the background for company. The stolid red-brick building may look more like a government department than somewhere exciting to eat, but outward appearances count for nothing. All the bases of modern restaurant dining are covered, from the elegant table that can accommodate a private party eager to observe the kitchen at its work, to a bar fitted out with decorative rolls of steel mesh, to the expansive principal dining room, where creamy upholstery and a swirly-patterned carpet create an uplifting setting for executive chef Matt Pickop's resourceful menus, deftly realised by Alsace-born head chef Alex Thiebaut. A strong east Asian element marks much of the output, to the extent of a dedicated sushi menu, and the amalgam of the main carte is a productive fusion of French and Japanese thinking. Beef tataki with smoked ponzu, pickled mooli and shiso is a long way from home, but Arctic king crab with a pork cracker and wasabi in Granny Smith consommé inaugurates a rapprochement between east and west. By the time you get to cannon of lamb with Jersey Royals in mint sauce, you could be eating in the greatest country pub in London, but if the hankering for the diamond-bright seasonings and defined edges of Asian cooking is still strong, consider pork belly with smoked bacon and tiger prawns in miso broth. Prime materials, from yellowfin tuna to fillet and braised cheeks of beef adorned with bone marrow and spring turnips, are of the finest, and intriguing presentations continue through to the final offerings of truffled brie with frozen grapes, apricot olive oil cake with pinenut ice cream, or white chocolate cheesecake with lychees and pink peppercorns.

Chef Alex Thiebaut, Matthew Pickop **Owner** Gordon Ramsay Holdings Ltd **Seats** 94, Pr/dining room 90 **Times** 12-3/5.30-11, **Prices** Tasting menu £75, Starter £14-£17.50, Main £14-£17.50, Dessert £9.50-£12 **Wines** 600 bottles over £30, 10 bottles under £30, 23 by glass **Parking** On street **Notes** Fixed L/D 4 course £33, Children welcome

LONDON W1 *continued*

Mews of Mayfair PLAN 2 H1

◉ Modern British **V**

tel: 020 7518 9388 **10-11 Lancashire Court, New Bond St, Mayfair W1S 1EY**
email: info@mewsofmayfair.com
dir: *Nearest station: Bond St*

Fashionable setting for modern brasserie cooking

The fashionable Mayfair set converge on this stylish bar and restaurant, delightfully hidden from the maddening Bond Street crowds on a narrow cobbled alleyway. With its terrace tables and roll-back doors, on a warm day it feels more Mediterranean than West End. The lively street-level cocktail bar and cool basement lounge make a glam statement, while the first-floor brasserie is a light, airy space decorated in pastel tones, with cream leather banquettes, exposed floorboards and chunky wooden tables, and a relaxed, easy vibe. The kitchen delivers a please-all brasserie roster of seasonal dishes driven by prime, responsibly sourced produce. There are comfort classics like fish and chips (with mushy peas and tartare) alongside the likes of Cornish cod with parsley crumb and a fabulous crab mash, or perhaps 35-day dry-aged steaks (South Devon rib-eye maybe) cooked on the Josper grill. Well-made desserts continue the theme, such as banoffee pie or treacle tart.

Chef Michael Lecouteur **Owner** James Robson, Robert Nearn **Seats** 70, Pr/dining room 28 **Times** 12-3.30/6-11.30, Closed 25 Dec, D Sun **Prices** Starter £6.50-£14, Main fr £9.50, Dessert £6-£12 **Wines** 81 bottles over £30, 7 bottles under £30, 16 by glass **Parking** On street, NCP **Notes** Sunday L £18-£40, Children welcome

The Montagu PLAN 2 F2

◉◉ Modern British **V**

tel: 020 7299 2037 **Hyatt Regency London, The Churchill, 30 Portman Square W1H 7BH**
email: montagu.hrlondon@hyatt.com
dir: *Nearest station: Marble Arch*

Modern comfort food in smart West End venue

The swanky five-star hotel has many riches, not least Locanda Locatelli which has its own entrance and a life of its own. The hotel's Montagu restaurant has plenty to offer, too, with a menu of smart, modern British ideas and views over Portland Square. There are liveried doormen out front and elegant proportions within. An open kitchen ensures a buzz in the room and the food takes an up-beat brasserie approach with grills, lunchtime specials and comforting puddings. You might start with a ham hock, pistachio and chestnut terrine, in the company of a Cumberland sauce, or an upmarket prawn cocktail with avocado. Main-course fillet of Sussex black bream comes with a scallop céviche and a potato and Jerusalem artichoke millefeuille, or there's a beer-battered cod served in the traditional manner. Banoffee pie with honey ice cream competes for attention with chocolate and raspberry delice among desserts, and there are the artisan British cheeses, too.

Chef Felix Luecke **Owner** Hyatt Regency London-The Churchill **Seats** 60 **Times** 12-10.45, All-day dining **Prices** Fixed L 2 course £23, Fixed D 3 course £28, Tasting menu £45, Starter £6-£12.50, Main £16.50-£38, Dessert £6.50 **Wines** 41 bottles over £30, 4 bottles under £30, 14 by glass **Parking** 18 **Notes** Chef's table 5/7 course £75/£95, Wknd brunch £49/£65, Sunday L £65, Children welcome

Murano PLAN 4 H6

◉◉◉◉ – *see opposite*

Newman Street Tavern PLAN 2 J3

◉ Seasonal British

tel: 020 3667 1445 **48 Newman St W1T 1QQ**
email: reservations@newmanstreettavern.co.uk
dir: *Nearest station: Goodge St*

Revamped Fitzrovia pub with a passion for ingredients

This trendily zhooshed-up boozer is smack on-cue with today's modern pub-restaurant scene. Okay, so food may be at the top of the agenda, but seasonality, provenance and produce quality are admirably king, and you can still grab a pint in the uptempo bar alongside pukka bar snacks and breakfast. Upstairs the place divides seamlessly into a charming, quieter restaurant with a colour scheme of warm pastel shades, while foodie pictures make a bold statement of intent on one wall. It's a bright space with tall sash-and-cord windows, darkwood tables and period chairs jauntily jazzed up with gaily-coloured upholstered seats. The cooking is defined by simple handling and big flavour. Take pig's cheek scrumpets with 'kicking' mustard mayo to open, or mains like a daily special of melt-in-the-mouth venison loin teamed with fondant potato, wilted spinach and a peppery jus. Wobbly pannacotta perfection served with wonderfully tart champagne rhubarb is a great finale, while wines punch above their weight, including a strong by-glass and carafe range.

Chef Peter Weeden **Owner** James McLean **Seats** 140 **Times** 12-11, All-day dining, Closed D Sun **Prices** Starter £6-£13.50, Main £13.50-£21, Dessert £2-£6.50 **Wines** 63 bottles over £30, 10 bottles under £30 **Parking** On street **Notes** Wknd brunch menu from 10am, Sunday L £13.50-£19, Vegetarian available, Children welcome

Nobu PLAN 5 H6

◉◉ Japanese

tel: 020 7447 4747 **Old Park Ln W1K 1LB**
email: london@noburestaurants.com web: www.noburestaurants.com
dir: *Nearest station: Hyde Park Corner, Green Park*

Top-end Japanese dining with views over Hyde Park

From Miami to Milan, globetrotting foodies are never too far away from a Nobu. Here, overlooking Hyde Park, is where in 1997 Londoners' first got a glimpse of Nobu Matsuhisa's brand of Japanese precision and South American spice. It was staggeringly fashionable and super-cool back then, and – do you know what? – it can still hold its own. They come, they look cool, they nibble. The prices were eye-watering back then, now the place just seems as expensive as everywhere else. The quality remains high, the seafood sparklingly fresh – the tuna, halibut and sea urchin linger long in the memory. South American street food is the inspiration for anticucho spicy salmon skewer, or tea-smoked lamb, and there are straight-up Japanese dishes such as sushi and sashimi. There are luxury ingredients such as an indulgent Wagyu and foie gras gyoza with spicy ponzu, and the pretty much iconic black cod with miso. It all looks beautiful on the plate and the staff are extremely helpful. Desserts maintain the fusion theme – Fuji apple crumble, for example – and there are cocktails and sake, too.

Chef Mark Edwards **Owner** Nobuyuki Matsuhisa **Seats** 160, Pr/dining room 40 **Times** 12-2.15/6-10.15, Closed 25 Dec, 1 Jan **Prices** Starter £9-£25, Main £16-£42, Dessert £3.90-£11.50 **Wines** All bottles over £30, 8 by glass **Parking** Car park nearby **Notes** Pre-theatre Bento box £35, Fixed L 5 course, D 7 course, Sunday L, Vegetarian available, Children welcome

Murano ❀❀❀❀

Modern European, Italian influence
tel: 020 7495 1127 **20-22 Queen St W1J 5PP**
email: muranorestaurant@angela-hartnett.com
dir: *Nearest station: Green Park*

Classy showcase for Italian-led contemporary cooking

After cutting loose from the Ramsay empire, Angela Hartnett's career trajectory has headed ever upwards, and she now heads up her own mini-constellation of restaurants. Back in 2008, her elegant Mayfair flagship weighed in as a serious contender among London's upscale Italian dining establishments, but these days the kitchen takes its influences from a wider sweep of the Continent. The setting is a fresh, light-filled room whose Mayfair postcode is reflected in the upscale decor: the namesake Venetian glass stars in spiffy chandeliers, above white leather seats, crisp table linen, fluted art deco-style columns and sheaves of fresh flowers. For culinary voyeurs, a swanky chef's table offers the expected window onto the kitchen, while the super-professional, smartly groomed and attired service team make everyone feel special with their effortless cordiality. The menus clearly reflect Hartnett's Italian-influenced upbringing, and prime Italian ingredients and preparations are very much on show. A stunningly fresh and simple composition of sea bream céviche with creamy avocado, chilli, coriander and citrus compôte is a first course with decidedly contemporary credentials. Follow with Cornish sea trout with caramelised fennel, crushed Jersey Royals and cucumber yogurt – and those excellent ideas come from the remarkably wallet-friendly set lunch option. Trade up to the flexible carte, which leaves you to choose whether to stick at two courses or do the whole five, and you might set out with a hearty pairing of pan-fried scallops and confit duck leg with almond purée, apples and dates, the timing spot on, the flavours deftly handled. Given Hartnett's grasp of the subtleties of Italian food, it would be a mistake to pass on the pasta, with the likes of pheasant agnolotti with white onion purée, rosemary jus and black truffle on offer, or crab ravioli with almond pesto and grilled spring onions. At main course stage, fish is expertly handled – perhaps sea bass with white bean purée, octopus and charred romanesco – or there could be a comfort-oriented pairing of crispy pork belly with celeriac purée, king prawns, grapes and crispy tempura kale. Desserts are equally stimulating, with a pistachio and olive oil cake with blackberries and milk ice cream sitting alongside a classic Amalfi lemon tart. The impressive wine list naturally features well-chosen Italian growers, with France also well represented, and the expert Italian sommelier also allows in the odd bottle from the New World.

Chef Angela Hartnett, Pip Lacey **Owner** Angela Hartnett
Seats 46, Pr/dining room 12 **Times** 12-3/6.30-11, Closed Xmas, Sun **Prices** Fixed L 2 course fr £28, Fixed D 3 course fr £65, Starter fr £15, Main fr £35, Dessert fr £15 **Wines** 745 bottles over £30, 7 bottles under £30, 21 by glass **Parking** Carrington St NCP **Notes** Fixed D 4/5 course £75/£85, Vegetarian available, Children welcome

Nobu Berkeley ST

PLAN 4 H6

◉◉ Japanese, Peruvian V 🍷 NOTABLE WINE LIST

tel: 020 7290 9222 **15 Berkeley St W1J 8DY**
email: berkeleyst@noburestaurants.com
dir: *Nearest station: Green Park*

Super-cool Mayfair hot-spot for great Japanese food

The Nobu brand spans the globe from the Bahamas to Beijing, its glossy Berkeley Street outpost still drawing in the Mayfair fashionistas who come for the see-and-be-seen buzz of the ground-floor bar, before winding up the spiral staircase to the cool minimalist David Collins-designed restaurant. It's a high-energy, high-decibel space where black-clad staff play their part in keeping the up tempo vibe going, and are clued-up enough to brief diners on the ins and outs of the menu. Nobu's trademark roster of spanking-fresh sushi and sashimi and Latino-accented fusion cooking continues to develop productively. Traditionalists can head straight for the sushi bar, or for a bit of fun DIY dining with chefs supervising your efforts around a sunken hibachi grill. Whichever path you take, expect first-rate ingredients, exquisite presentation, and the cleanness and precision of Japanese cooking. Open with soft-shelled crab kara-age with ponzu, or a hybrid whitefish sashimi with aji amarillo (yellow chilli) salsa, then move on to the signature black cod with miso or rib-eye anticucho skewers.

Chef Mark Edwards **Owner** Nobuyuki Matsuhisa, Robert de Niro **Seats** 180 **Times** 12-2.30/6-1am, Closed 25 Dec, 1 Jan, L Sun (ex Mother's Day) **Prices** Tasting menu £85-£95 **Wines** 200 bottles over £30, 10 by glass **Parking** Mayfair NCP **Notes** Tasting menu 6 course, Bento box L £38-£48, Children welcome

NOPI

PLAN 2 J1

◉ Mediterranean

tel: 020 7494 9584 **21-22 Warwick St W1B 5NE**
email: contact@nopi-restaurant.com
dir: *Nearest station: Oxford Circus, Piccadilly Circus*

A buzzing atmosphere and creative cooking with flavour to the fore

Owner Yotam Ottolenghi's cooking is built on the sun-drenched cuisines of the Middle East, North Africa and the Mediterranean with some global input. This translates as a menu packed with creativity and bursting with punchy flavours, served in an all-white brasserie-style space with white marble floors, white-topped tables edged with brass and Levantine-style hemispherical brass ceiling lights. Down in the basement are two large communal tables with ringside seats for the action in the open-to-view kitchen. Whichever you choose, the vibe is a chatty hubbub of people enjoying themselves while tucking into dishes made for sharing; if ingredients sound alien ask the clued-up staff for explanation. Kick off with cod, crispy pancetta, pistachio and lovage vichyssoise, or go veggie with roasted aubergine, feta, coriander pesto and walnut. Main course brings twice-cooked baby chicken with lemon myrtle salt and chilli sauce, and desserts such as caramel and roasted peanut ice cream, chocolate sauce and peanut brittle come with equally vigorous flavours.

Chef Yotam Ottolenghi, Ramael Scully **Owner** Yotam Ottolenghi **Seats** 100 **Times** 12-2.45/5.30-10.15, Closed D Sun **Prices** Starter £8.90-£13.90, Main £19.90-£24.90, Dessert £4.90-£9, Service optional 12.5% **Wines** 53 bottles over £30, 2 bottles under £30, 28 by glass **Notes** Pre-theatre menu 2/3 course £21.50/£24.50, Sunday L, Vegetarian available, Children welcome

Novikov Asian Restaurant

PLAN 4 H6

◉ Chinese, Pan Asian

tel: 020 7399 4330 **50a Berkeley St W1J 8HA**
dir: *Nearest station: Charing Cross, Green Park*

Style-conscious Pan-Asian dining in Mayfair

The Asian Room of Russian restaurateur Arkady Novikov's see-and-be-seen Mayfair food palace offers a palate-tingling mix of Japanese, Chinese, Thai and Malaysian dishes, running from top-drawer sushi and sashimi to dim sum and sizzling fish and meat from the charcoal teppan grill. A private jet menu secures the place's position on the oligarchs' speed dial listings, while normal mortals in the slick brasserie-style space can watch the busy team of chefs behind a glass wall among mounds of super-fresh produce resembling an Asian street market. They send out skilfully-made prawn 'money bag' dumplings and crispy salt and pepper squid to get the taste buds standing to attention. Elsewhere, there's grilled baby chicken with miso or steamed sea bass with ginger and soy, while an East-meets-West fusion of mango tiramisù keeps things lively at dessert stage. There's also an Italian venue downstairs.

Times 12-4/5.30-12, Closed 25 Dec, D 24 Dec

Novikov Italian Restaurant

PLAN 4 H6

◉ Italian

tel: 020 7399 4330 **50a Berkeley St W1J 8HA**
email: reservations@novikovrestaurant.co.uk
dir: *Nearest station: Green Park*

Plutocratic Italian cooking and dazzling displays

The Novikov complex, fronted by street-level security guards, includes an Italian room with striped walls in the vast basement, where cornucopian displays dazzle on arrival. There are towers of oranges in baskets, wine barrels crowded with grappa bottles and iced seafood, and floor-to-ceiling refrigerated cabinets containing enough antipasti to provision the nuclear bunker of a small town. Chefs beaver away behind a glass screen producing creditable renditions of uncontroversial Italian food. Fritto misto could do with crisper coatings perhaps, but the cured meats, including venison and Sardinian wild boar prosciutto, are excellent. Unimpeachably fresh sea bream has come all the way from the Med, and is dressed in Capezzana olive oil, and there are wood-fired oven and Josper grill offerings such as lamb cutlets in mint sauce. Pannacotta with mixed berries in syrup is the real creamy deal, or forsake Italy altogether for green tea brûlée with guava sorbet.

Times 12-12, All-day dining, Closed 25 Dec, D 24 Dec

10 Greek Street

PLAN 3 A2

◉◉ Modern British, European

tel: 020 7734 4677 **W1D 4DH**
email: info@10greekstreet.com
dir: *Nearest station: Charing Cross, Tottenham Court Rd*

Modern-day Soho bistro with flexible approach

It pays to understand the drill at number 10. Bookings are taken for lunches only. In the evenings, it's first come first served, so if you're not quite ready to eat at 5.30, you may have to put yourself on the list, leave your mobile number and await the call. It's well worth it, as the lively modern European cooking, served in surroundings that look like a Soho bistro reinvented for the present age, has plenty to say for itself. Fish dishes in two sizes, such as gurnard with Jerusalem artichokes and black pudding, or mackerel chermoula with pomegranate and pistachio, indicate a flexible approach. They hold the line between starters such as octopus carpaccio with chicory, fennel and blood orange, and meat main courses like venison with sprout tops and a parsnip and juniper pancake, or Middle-White pork with romanesco, pinenuts and puréed raisins. Finish with affogato, or pecan pie with maple and stout ice cream. All-day tapas such as crumbed goats' cheese and honey or mussel fritters raise the bar for central London snacking options.

Chef Cameron Emirali, Todd Higgs **Owner** Luke Wilson, Cameron Emirali **Seats** 30, Pr/dining room 12 **Times** 12-2.30/5.30-10.45, Closed Xmas, Sun & some BHs **Prices** Starter £6-£10, Main £14-£21, Dessert £6-£7, Service optional **Wines** 10 bottles over £30, 21 bottles under £30, 20 by glass **Parking** China Town, NCP Upper St Martins Lane **Notes** Vegetarian available, Children welcome

The Only Running Footman
PLAN 4 H6

◉ Traditional British

tel: 020 7499 2988 **5 Charles St, Mayfair W1J 5DF**
email: manager@therunningfootmanmayfair.com
dir: Nearest station: Green Park

Smart Mayfair pub with commitment to great food

It looks like a pub, which indeed it is, but there's more than meets the eye to The Only Running Footman. The distinctive red-brick corner building in Mayfair has a ground-floor bar where you can have a drink and pick something off the all-day bar menu (from a sandwich to chargrilled Longhorn rib-eye steak), plus a smarter and quieter upstairs restaurant, where closely-packed tables are done-out in crisp white linen and all is a little more refined. (There's also a chef's table in a separate room which doubles up as a cookery school.) Upstairs you might start with sautéed Cornish squid and chorizo salad, followed by pan-fried sea bass with caramelised salsify and sauce vièrge, finishing off with a berry Pavlova or cheeses from the Bath Cheese Company with pear chutney and pain aux fruits.

Chef Eddie Kouadio, Peter Pereira **Owner** Barnaby Meredith **Seats** 30, Pr/dining room 40 **Times** 12-2.30/6.30-10, Closed D 25 Dec **Prices** Prices not confirmed **Wines** 49 bottles over £30, 28 bottles under £30, 12 by glass **Parking** On street **Notes** Chef's table £80, Sunday L, Vegetarian available, Children welcome

Orrery
PLAN 2 G3

◉◉ Modern French

tel: 020 7616 8000 **55-57 Marylebone High St W1U 5RB**
email: orreryreservation@danddlondon.com
dir: Nearest station: Baker St, Regent's Park

Stylish, elegant restaurant above designer store

The Orrery may be a Marylebone old-timer, but it cuts a contemporary swagger with its classy good looks, polished service and skilful, modern take on classical French cuisine. On the first floor above the Conran store, the long, narrow room is a fashionably clean-lined space, filled with light from its large arched windows and ceiling skylight. Pastel tones blend with pale wood, mirrors and white linen, while a glass wine cellar signals a dazzling list. Menus are driven by prime ingredients and seasonality, and come dotted with luxuries (attracting the odd supplement here and there), with dishes showing a lightness of touch, matched by refined presentation. Fish delivers strongly, perhaps a seafood ravioli opener in a rich lobster bisque, while to follow, sea-fresh turbot is served with braised celery and gnocchi and complemented by a fabulous mussel velouté. There's no let up at dessert stage either: witness honey-glazed poached pineapple with a light-as-a-feather pistachio sponge and yogurt sorbet. An intimate bar, summer roof terrace and street-level epicerie add further appeal.

Times 12-2.30/6.30-10.30, Closed 1 Jan, 26-27 Dec

Palomar
PLAN 2 K1

◉◉ Middle Eastern **NEW**

tel: 020 7439 8777 **34 Rupert St W1D GDN**
email: info@thepalomar.co.uk
dir: Nearest station: Piccadilly Circus, Leicester Sq

Authentic Middle Eastern cuisine in Soho

In the throbbing heart of theatreland, this bijou restaurant has become one of the most talked about new openings in recent months, picking up awards and glowing reviews from food critics. Inspired by the modern eateries of Jerusalem, the front of the restaurant has a 16-seat zinc-topped bar where diners can eat while watching the chefs in the open-plan kitchen. Alternatively, the intimate dining area at the rear has an understated but elegant decor with darkwood panelling and royal blue leather banquette seating. The cooking looks to the Levant, North Africa and southern Spain for inspiration and the sunny flavours have broad appeal. A quirkily named and beautifully presented 'Octo-houmous' sees octopus cooked over charcoal served with chickpea masabacha and cherry tomato confit. Main courses deliver the likes of corn-fed chicken cooked in buttermilk with Jerusalem spices and teamed with rainbow chard and freekeh (roasted wheat grain). Desserts are equally diverting – perhaps a rose-scented malabi (a Middle Eastern classic) with raspberry coulis and coconut meringue pistachio crunch.

Chef Tomer Amedi **Owner** Zoe & Layo Paskin **Seats** 50 **Times** 12-2.30/5.30-11, Closed 25-26 Dec, D Sun **Prices** Tasting menu fr £55, Starter £6-£9, Main £9.50-£18, Dessert £7-£7.50 **Wines** 29 bottles over £30, 7 bottles under £30, 12 by glass **Parking** Q park Chinatown **Notes** Sunday L, Vegetarian available, Children welcome

Park Plaza Sherlock Holmes
PLAN 2 F3

◉ British, Modern European

tel: 020 7486 6161 **108 Baker St W1U 6LJ**
email: info@sherlockholmeshotel.com **web:** www.sherlockholmeshotel.com
dir: Nearest station: Baker St

Modern grill near the home of Holmes

The Baker Street address is bang on the money for an operation bearing the fictional sleuth's name, but the place eschews the Edwardian period theme in favour of a slick contemporary boutique hotel look. Holding centre stage in the open-plan space of Sherlock's Bar & Grill is the kitchen team, hard at work over charcoal grills and a wood-burning oven in the open-to-view kitchen. The please-all Mediterranean-accented menu offers a bit of everything from modern and classic ideas to pizzas – aubergine, sweet pepper and goats' cheese, say – from that wood oven. Grilled king scallops with baba ghanoush and crispy bread set the ball rolling, then hot off the charcoal grill comes crispy Gressingham duck breast with caramelised figs, or there could be a seared tuna steak with ratatouille. For pudding, chocolate tart with Cornish clotted cream should press all the right comfort buttons.

Times 12-2.30/6-10.30, Closed D Sun, BHs

LONDON W1 *continued*

La Petite Maison

PLAN 2 H1

◉◉ French, Mediterranean

tel: 020 7495 4774 **54 Brooks Mews W1K 4EG**
email: info@lpmlondon.co.uk
dir: Nearest station: Bond St

The flavours of the Midi in Mayfair

Modelled on and named after its sister restaurant in Nice, the light, open-plan, sunny room exudes a breezily Mediterranean vibe transposed to an ultra-posh postcode. The Riviera-cool look takes in creamy walls with wrap-around windows, and an up tempo, see-and-be-seen atmosphere. A battalion of skilful staff preside over closely-set tables, while the cooking shows a light modern touch, keeping things simple and fresh, driven by top-notch produce in a procession of skilfully delivered dishes designed for sharing. The sun-drenched flavours of the Côte d'Azur and its Italian neighbours over the border in Liguria turn up in a starter of salt-cod croquettes with oven-roasted pepper relish, or the likes of pissaladière tart of onions and anchovies, or burrata cheese with tomatoes and basil. Main course delivers turbot with a rich barigoule stew of artichokes, chorizo, white wine and olive oil, or you might go for pasta – home-made tagliolini with clams, say – while two could share a whole roasted black-leg chicken with foie gras. The Gallic focus runs through to a finale of exemplary vanilla crème brûlée.

Chef Raphael Duntoye **Owner** Raphael Duntoye, Arjun Waney **Seats** 85
Times 12-3/6-11, Closed 25-26 Dec **Prices** Prices not confirmed **Wines** 16 by glass
Parking On street **Notes** Vegetarian available, Children welcome

Peyote

PLAN 2 J1

◉ Mexican

tel: 020 7409 1300 **13 Cork St, Mayfair W1S 3NS**
email: info@peyoterestaurant.com
dir: Nearest station: Green Park

Modern Mexican food good for sharing in Mayfair

That it's named after a cactus native to the Chihuahuan desert is a pointer to this restaurant's Mexican theme, and indeed it has called on some of that country's finest chefs to give London modern interpretations of its cuisine. It's been given an ultra-modern, stylish makeover, over two levels, with closely set wooden tables and artistic skulls making a bold design statement. Well-informed staff are on hand to offer guidance through the menu of mainly tasting-sized platters for sharing, so it's sensible to come in a group and order a variety. Ensalata de nopales (cactus salad), hot, fresh and spicy, sums up the style, along with lobster céviche subtly flavoured with chilli, and soft-shelled crab tacos. Dishes are distinctly flavoured without being swamped, seen in main courses of veal chop with onion and jalapeño salsa, and sea bass with pineapple sauce spiked with coriander. Finish by trying churros with chocolate sauce or play safe with whisky crème brûlée.

Chef Stamatios Loumousiotis **Owner** Tarun Mahrotri **Seats** 110, Pr/dining room 12
Times 12-3/6-1, Closed Xmas, New Year, Sun, L Sat **Prices** Prices not confirmed
Wines 88 bottles over £30, 7 bottles under £30, 11 by glass **Notes** Vegetarian available, Children welcome

Picture

PLAN 2 H3

◉◉ Modern European V

tel: 020 7637 7892 **110 Great Portland St W1W 6PQ**
email: info@picturerestaurant.co.uk
dir: Nearest station: Oxford Circus

Top-call for small-plate dining with a touch of pedigree

This happening outfit's name reflects its setting in the shadow of the BBC, yet it is anything but a corporate diner and has a refreshingly cool neighbourhood vibe. There are classy credentials from the off, as it is set up by three talented young deserters from the acclaimed Arbutus/Wild Honey stable (a manager and two chefs). The stylishly stark long room presses all the so-now buttons, with grey-washed walls, floorboards, retro furnishings and warehouse-style bulkhead lighting, while a rear atrium allows daylight to flood in. The food is also more cheffy than its trendy brown-paper menus, tea-towel napkins, accessible pricing, or casually dressed staff (switched-on and cheery) might suggest. The kitchen deals in fresh, clean, prettily dressed, fashionable 'small plates' spiked with flavour and flair and put together with skill and confidence. Take ravioli of Italian greens pepped up by ricotta and chilli, while succulent 28-day aged beef gets the 'Picture' treatment teamed with heritage carrots, Swiss chard and a hit of cumin. Desserts might feature vanilla pannacotta topped with wonderful champagne rhubarb and zingy gingerbread 'crisps'. Well-selected wines are offered by the glass, carafe or bottle.

Chef Alan Christie, Colin Kelly **Owner** Tom Slegg, Alan Christie, Colin Kelly **Seats** 55
Times 12-2.30/6-10.30, Closed Xmas, BHs, Sun **Prices** Tasting menu £30-£35
Wines 12 bottles over £30, 14 bottles under £30, 21 by glass **Parking** On street
Notes Tasting menu 6 course, Food menu all dishes £4-£9, Children welcome

Pied à Terre

PLAN 2 J3

◉◉◉◉ – *see opposite*

Plum Valley

PLAN 2 K1

◉ Chinese

tel: 020 7494 4366 **20 Gerrard St W1D 6JQ**
dir: Nearest station: Leicester Sq

Contemporary Cantonese cooking and cool decor in Chinatown

There's a cool confidence to Plum Valley, standing out on Gerrard Street with its sleek black frontage. Like a lot of the restaurants in Chinatown, there are multiple rooms and stairs to be negotiated, but unlike a lot of the opposition, it's got a dark, contemporary finish. Service is brisk. The kitchen has kicked MSG into touch and instead gets the best out the ingredients by handling them with skill and respect. The mainstay of the menu is classic Cantonese stuff, with plenty of familiar dishes and some perky modern stuff, too. Vietnamese vegetable spring rolls are as crisp and golden as you might hope, while veggies might opt for spicy tofu in a light batter. There's a dim sum platter and main courses such as braised lobster with ginger and spring onion (at the pricier end of the spectrum), or braised pork belly with rice wine and sweet vinegar, or even pan-fried ostrich.

Times 12-11.30, All-day dining, Closed 25 Dec

Pollen Street Social

PLAN 2 J2

◉◉◉◉ – *see page 368*

Pied à Terre ❁❁❁❁

Modern French, European V NOTABLE WINE LIST

tel: 020 7636 1178 **34 Charlotte St W1T 2NH**
email: info@pied-a-terre.co.uk
dir: *Nearest station: Goodge St*

Art on a plate in one of London's finest

A big hitter on the London dining scene since the early 1990s, David Moore's Pied à Terre built its reputation very quickly and has managed to maintain its place at the top table ever since, which is not an easy task. Great chefs have come and gone, and a fire even put the place out of action for a while back in the mid noughties, but it goes on evolving and improving. The smart and contemporary main dining room has had a refurbishment to refresh the space, while the stylish private bar is a little haven of tranquillity amid the Charlotte Street hubbub. There's a private dining room, too. The service is charismatic and professional. Head chef Marcus Eaves – who joined from sister restaurant L'Autre Pied in 2011 – offers a host of menus including a great value set lunch (one of the capital's best), seven- and ten-course tasting menus and a fixed-price carte. Whichever way you go, even if it's the cheaper set lunch option, outstanding contemporary food awaits. Start with a fabulous quail number, where the breasts are roasted until pink and tender, the leg arrives crispy and succulent, and a little Kiev is a nice touch (the dish is finished off with hazelnut dressing and shallot and Douglas Fir purée). Another first course sees poached and roasted lemon sole in the company of red prawns, Meyer lemon (a native of China), black olives and pine nuts. During truffle season expect to be offered the option of adding even more va-va-voom to your dish. Suckling pig belly is served as a main course with glazed trotters, and cod is poached in dashi and partnered with watercress, wakame and borage. Rib of Limousin veal with fregola sarda, tardivo (radicchio) and broad beans has a supplement to the standard à la carte price. Every dish arrives looking absolutely beautiful, not least desserts such as orange and vanilla crème caramel with golden raisins and ginger ice cream, or the Valrhona chocolate mousse with its accompanying peanut ice cream and Pedro Ximenez jelly. Vegetarians will find the veggie version of the tasting menu one of the most compelling in the capital offering the likes of spinach and celeriac lasagne with wild garlic, parsley and lovage. The rooftop garden guarantees a steady supply of herbs. The wine list is a fine piece of work with wine flight options and plenty of advice on hand if you require it.

Chef Marcus Eaves **Owner** David Moore, Mathieu Yermond **Seats** 40, Pr/dining room 14 **Times** 12-2.45/6-11, Closed 2 wks Xmas & New Year, Sun, L Sat **Prices** Fixed L 2 course fr £27.50, Fixed D 3 course fr £80, Tasting menu fr £105 **Wines** 750 bottles over £30, 20 bottles under £30, 25 by glass **Parking** Cleveland St **Notes** ALC 2/3 course menu £65/£80, Children welcome

Pollen Street Social ✿✿✿✿

LONDON W1   PLAN 2 J2

Modern British V

tel: 020 7290 7600 **8-10 Pollen St W1S 1NQ**
email: reservations@pollenstreetsocial.com
dir: *Nearest station: Oxford Circus*

Sophisticated cooking in Atherton's buzzy flagship

Jason Atherton is a chef at the top of his game, and following the familiar trajectory of superstar cheffery (he's been part of the Ramsay phenomenon, after all). Much of his energy is aimed at empire building (Social Eating House, Little Social, City Social, Berners Tavern, plus restaurants in Singapore, Hong Kong and Shanghai, at the latest count), but you can be reassured that he's not taking his eye off the ball in the Mayfair flagship, where the kitchen is still firing on all cylinders. Despite the 'social' moniker, which might conjure images of working men's clubs in readers of a certain age, this operation is as trendy as they come, with an open kitchen (glass-fronted to reduce noise but keeping the visual theatre), a bar area with a sexy cocktail list, and the famous dessert bar that allows the sweet of tooth to pop in and head straight for pud without any of the savoury preamble. Assuming, however, that you're here for more than drinks or pudding, there's an eight-course tasting menu, the à la carte, a dedicated vegetarian menu, and a set lunch offering an accessible entry point. The airy main dining room's decor is classy but far from intimidating — it's a neutral, contemporary urban space, with the familiar look of wooden floors, linen-clothed tables and white walls broken up by modern British artworks — very much more of-the-moment than the 'contemporary bistro offering deformalised fine dining', which is how Atherton describes the place. Foodies queue at the door because he has a knack for creating deconstructed masterpieces, with pace-setting invention and riveting combinations of taste and texture. His dishes look pretty amazing on the plate, too. Ingredients from top British farmers are subjected to modern techniques, with bags of contemporary ideas and clever twists and turns along the way. For instance, a risotto-like starter is actually tiny, rice-sized pieces of line-caught Devon squid cooked in cauliflower-flavoured cream, with roasted squid juices, ink rice and sea herbs. Main-course Lake District lamb delivers remarkable intensity of flavour in a melt-in-the-mouth rack, crumbed sweetbreads and a heavenly shepherd's pie, helped along by braised lettuce, girolles and mustard seeds. Whether you decamp to the dessert bar or stay at your table, a finale of chocolate marquise, praline, milk mousse and honey ice cream is sure to knock your socks off.

Chef Jason Atherton **Owner** Jason Atherton **Seats** 52, Pr/dining room 14 **Times** 12-2.45/6-10.45, Closed BHs, Sun **Prices** Fixed L 2 course £28.50, Tasting menu £89, Starter £14.50-£16, Main £29.50-£36.50, Dessert £9.50-£10.50 **Wines** 800 bottles over £30, 8 bottles under £30, 20 by glass **Parking** On street, car park Mayfair, Park Lane **Notes** Tasting menu 8 course, Children welcome

LONDON W1 continued

Polpo

PLAN 2 J1

◉ Italian

tel: 020 7734 4479 & 7287 1152 **41 Beak St W1F 9SB**
dir: Nearest station: Piccadilly Circus

Bustling Venetian-style bacaro in the heart of Soho

An ultra casual take on the bacaros of Venice, Polpo is almost too cool for its own good, with the diminutive outfit constantly rammed and tables hard to come by. You can't book in the evenings, so expect to queue beside the bar with its high stools for dining (even this feels part of the fun though). The decor is pared-back and distressed, all elbow-to-elbow tables, dangling light bulbs, exposed-brick and floorboards. So what's all the fuss about? It's Italian-style tapas (cicchetti) ordered from brown-paper menus (doubling as placemats) and sent out quick-fire by the kitchen as affordably priced small plates to graze on. It's authentic, simple, bold-flavoured stuff hewn from more modest cuts: think spicy pork and fennel meatballs with a good anise note, cod cheeks with lentils and piquant salsa verde, or perhaps grilled mortadella with celeriac and apple slaw. Italian wines come by glass (tumblers in this case), carafe and bottle, while a basement Campari bar kicks off at 5.30pm. There are sibling Polpo's in Covent Garden, Chelsea, Smithfield and Notting Hill.

Chef Jason Wass **Owner** Russell Norman, Richard Beatty **Seats** 60 **Times** 12-11, All-day dining, Closed 25-26 Dec, 1 Jan **Prices** Prices not confirmed **Wines** 12 bottles over £30, 15 bottles under £30, 18 by glass **Notes** Cicchetti – small plates based on Venitian bacaros, Vegetarian available, Children welcome

The Providores and Tapa Room

PLAN 2 G3

◉ International Fusion ▮ NOTABLE WINE LIST

tel: 020 7935 6175 **109 Marylebone High St W1U 4RX**
email: anyone@theprovidores.co.uk
dir: Nearest station: Bond St, Baker St, Regent's Park

Twin-faceted venue for inventive fusion cooking

The Tapa Room on the ground floor, named after the Rarotongan tapa cloth hanging on the wall, is an all-day café and restaurant, but to experience in full New Zealander Peter Gordon's cooking – some of the most exciting and innovative fusion food in the capital – head upstairs to Providores. Dishes can pile on the ingredients in unlikely-sounding combinations, but the results never fail to stimulate the palate. How about a lively starter of seared yellowfin tuna with papaya, carrots, cucumber salad, lime chilli dressing, toasted nori sauce, peanuts and sesame? Main courses can seem a tad calmer in comparison. Beef pesto is a signature dish – tender and tasty fillet with pesto and a salad of chard, courgettes and beetroot with olives – and there might be crispy pork belly with dashi-braised sprouts, Puy lentils, apple and peanut butter flavoured with lemongrass. End with what the menu calls 'pumpkin pie – sort of' and see what comes.

Chef Peter Gordon **Owner** P Gordon, M McGrath **Seats** 38
Times 12-2.30/6-10, Closed 25-26 Dec **Prices** Prices not confirmed **Wines** 122 bottles over £30, 7 bottles under £30, 20 by glass **Notes** Fixed D 2-5 course £33-£63, Sat-Sun Brunch menu, Vegetarian available, Children welcome

Quattro Passi

PLAN 2 H1

◉◉ Italian, Mediterranean **NEW**

tel: 020 3096 1444 **34 Dover St W1S 4NG**
email: info@quattropassi.co.uk
dir: Nearest station: Green Park

Classy Italian in the heart of Mayfair

The West End may seem a long way from the Amalfi coast location of his other restaurant, but Antonio Mellino captures the essence of Southern Italy in his sleek Mayfair establishment. No expense has been spared in the elegant dining room with its high quality leather banquettes, marble floors and chandeliers, with waiting staff equally well-attired and polished. Top-notch ingredients, many of them imported directly from Italy, home-made pasta and solid technical skills are the foundations of the kitchen, with the owner's son Antonio manning the stoves. Dishes are straightforward but attractively presented. Super-fresh piscine produce is treated with respect in no-frills dishes such as a starter of chargrilled octopus served on a warm bed of grilled fennel and courgette arrives with a rich celeriac cream. For main course, a well-judged and precisely cooked dish of scialatielli pasta with pumpkin, cuttlefish, prawns and mint is a harmonious combination. Desserts are no less impressive: for example the pastiera Napoletana is as rich as it is elaborate.

Chef Antonio Mellino **Owner** Antonio Mellino **Seats** 80, Pr/dining room 45
Times 12-3/6.30-10.30, Closed Sun **Prices** Fixed L 2 course fr £26, Starter £10-£18, Main £25-£35, Dessert £8-£10 **Wines** 300 bottles over £30, 6 bottles under £30, 20 by glass **Parking** Berkeley Sq **Notes** Vegetarian available, Children welcome

Quo Vadis

PLAN 2 K2

◉◉ Modern British

tel: 020 7437 9585 **26-29 Dean St W1D 3LL**
email: reception@quovadissoho.co.uk
dir: Nearest station: Tottenham Court Rd, Leicester Sq

Smart British cooking at a Soho institution

Safe in the capable hands of the Hart brothers, Quo Vadis has an illustrious culinary history. Jeremy Lee leads the line with his take on British cuisine; a little bit modern, certainly, but also recalling heartier times. The art deco building has some tables outside if you fancy a cigarette and a slice of Soho life, but it's looking pretty fine inside these days, with tan leather banquettes, modern art on the walls, and original stained-glass windows, wall mirrors and wooden floors in appreciation of the building's heritage. There's a cocktail bar, private rooms, and even a bakery turning out some quality stuff. Squid with puntarella, fennel and bergamot is a simple starter with a spot-on sweet-and-sour hit, followed perhaps with a dish of beautifully tender and pink venison, with roasted apples and cranberries. Desserts run to an indulgent apple, almond, mincemeat and crumble tart sitting in a pool of crème anglaise. The service team are a friendly bunch, adding greatly to the charm of the place.

Chef Jeremy Lee **Owner** Sam & Eddie Hart **Seats** 72, Pr/dining room 32
Times 12-3/5.30-11, Closed BHs (except Good Fri), D Sun **Prices** Fixed L 2 course £18.50, Fixed D 3 course £21.50, Starter £7-£12.50, Main £15-£26, Dessert £6.50-£8.50 **Wines** 110 bottles over £30, 11 bottles under £30, 11 by glass **Parking** On street or NCP **Notes** Theatre fixed menu, Sunday L £7-£26, Vegetarian available, Children welcome

LONDON W1 *continued*

The Red Fort

PLAN 2 K2

Indian V

tel: 020 7437 2525 **77 Dean St, Soho W1D 3SH**
email: info@redfort.co.uk
dir: *Nearest station: Leicester Sq, Tottenham Court Rd*

Authentic modern Indian in the heart of Soho

This stylish red-fronted Indian has a surprisingly restrained demeanour for bustling Soho, with its white linen, smartly attired staff, leather seating and walls of inlaid sandstone and Mogul arch motifs. Opened back in 1983, it was one of the early modern Indian restaurants, and today continues to deliver a mix of classic Mogul court cooking and more contemporary dishes, successfully combining fine British produce with authentic sub-continental flavours, albeit at fairly hefty prices. From the open kitchen at the rear, expect a traditional Hyderabadi bhuna gosht (chunks of Herdwick lamb with a rich, aromatic spicing hit of ginger, black pepper, coriander seed and red chilli simply served with a cooling peach raita), while for seafood lovers, there's Samundari rattan (a Neptune's supper of scallops, squid, stone bass and king prawn in a spicy fennel, coconut and carom sauce). Below stairs, the more trendy Zenna Bar is the place to head for after-work cocktails and lighter bites.

Chef M A Rahman **Owner** Amin Ali **Seats** 84 **Times** 12-3/5.30-11.30, Closed L Sat-Sun **Prices** Fixed L 2 course £15-£25, Fixed D 3 course £18-£59, Starter £7-£12, Main £18-£42, Dessert £7-£8 **Wines** 173 bottles over £30, 29 bottles under £30, 11 by glass **Parking** NCP Brewer St **Notes** Tasting menu 4 course, Fixed pre-theatre D, Children welcome

Rex and Mariano

PLAN 2 K2

British, Italian, Mediterranean NEW

tel: 020 7437 0566 **2 St Anne's Court W1F 0AZ**
email: info@rexandmariano.com
dir: *Nearest station: Tottenham Court Rd*

Simply cooked seafood in a utilitarian venue

Fish and seafood is the name of the game at this bare-bones, industrial canteen-like eatery. Between them, Rex Goldsmith of the Chelsea Fishmonger, and Sicilian Mariano Li Vigni, have the contacts to haul in the best piscine produce from the UK and the Med, and when the gear is this good, there's no point faffing about with it. The open kitchen turns out super-simple dishes full of Mediterranean warmth — so simple that much of it isn't even cooked: oysters with classic dressings of lemon, Tabasco or vinaigrette; sea bass céviche with coriander, yuzu, red onion and tiger's milk; tuna tartare with avocado, chilli and chives; salmon carpaccio with olive oil, lemon, tomato and basil. When heat is applied, it comes from the grill in dishes like megrim sole with lemon butter or plump Sicilian prawns with lemon, red chilli, parsley and olive oil.

Chef Chris Piorkowski **Owner** Misha Zelman, Ilya Demichev, George Bukhov **Times** noon-22.30, All-day dining, Closed Xmas, New Yr, BHs **Prices** Prices not confirmed **Wines** 5 bottles over £30, 10 bottles under £30, 13 by glass **Parking** NCP Soho/China Town **Notes** Children welcome

The Riding House Café

PLAN 2 J3

Modern European

tel: 020 7927 0840 **43-51 Great Titchfield St W1W 7PQ**
email: info@ridinghousecafe.co.uk
dir: *Nearest station: Oxford Circus*

Buzzy all-day brasserie near Oxford Street

Handy for a pit stop if you're hitting the Oxford Street shops, The Riding House Café is a big, high-decibel, hyper-trendy all-day operation with a modern, urban brasserie vibe. Large art deco windows curve all the way round, making it a see-and-be-seen sort of place. Head for a swivel seat at the white-tiled island bar for a close up gander at the action in the open kitchen, or park at the long refectory table; if you don't do communal dining, there are classic marble topped tables and a separate more traditional space with panelled walls and a quieter, more intimate mood. A flexible menu of small plate options and modern brasserie dishes is the order of the day at lunch and dinner (don't forget to factor in the necessity for side orders),so you might start with cod tongues with deep-fried pickles, split peas, and pommes paille, then follow with well-timed venison haunch with winter greens, celeriac purée and blackberry sauce, and wind things up with chocolate fondant and malted milk ice cream.

Chef Paul Daniel **Owner** Adam White **Seats** 115, Pr/dining room 14 **Times** 12-3.30/6-10, Closed 25 Dec **Prices** Prices not confirmed **Wines** 15 bottles over £30, 15 bottles under £30, 20 by glass **Parking** On street **Notes** Sunday L, Vegetarian available, Children welcome

The Ritz Restaurant

PLAN 4 J6

– see opposite

Roka Charlotte Street

PLAN 2 J3

– see opposite

Roka Mayfair

PLAN 2 G1

– see page 372

Roti Chai

PLAN 2 G2

Modern Indian

tel: 020 7408 0101 **3 Portman Mews South W1H 6AY**
email: infowala@rotichai.com
dir: *Nearest station: Bond St, Marble Arch*

Vibrant Indian street food close to Oxford Street

Roti Chai is a restaurant of two halves that takes its inspiration from the street stalls, roadside and railway cafés of the Indian sub-continent. The ground-floor Street Kitchen is a bright, casual canteen-style venue serving homely 'street food', while the basement Dining Room deals in more refined nouveau Indian cooking. The look is part industrial — exposed ducting and spotlights and black-painted breezeblock walls — mixed with smart contemporary darkwood floors, chunky oak tables, black leather seats, and railway carriage references in wall-mounted luggage racks and brass-framed, smoked mirrors. Staff are all young, keen, and well-briefed on the menus. Expect a vibrant, modern take on Indian flavours wherever you sit. Bengali crab and fishcakes with onion seeds and cumin gets things under way in the Dining Room, followed by a posh version of classic saagwala gosht — slow-cooked Elwy Valley Welsh lamb in a smooth and spicy spinach sauce. For dessert, chai brûlée puts a twist on an old friend by flavouring it with cardamom, cloves and cinnamon.

Times 12-11.45, All-day dining

The Ritz Restaurant ❀❀❀

LONDON W1 PLAN 4 J6

British, French V ❦ NOTABLE WINE LIST
tel: 020 7300 2370 **150 Piccadilly W1J 9BR**
email: dining@theritzlondon.com **web:** www.theritzlondon.com
dir: *Nearest station: Green Park*

Arresting dining in sumptuous formal restaurant

Tailcoated waiters serving cloche-covered plates of luxurious food to the privileged elite: dining at The Ritz is a timewarp experience akin to winding back the clock to the dawn of the 20th century. It's a special place, so why not go for broke and start with a glass of bubbly in the art deco Rivoli Bar to steady the nerves for the extravagant opulence of the dining room – a space to rival Versailles Palace, with its rich Louis XVI-inspired decor of murals, painted ceilings, statues and glittering chandeliers reflecting from mirrored walls. An army of waiting staff (four sommeliers, no less) pulls off a correctly polite performance with theatrical classic tableside service that avoids any hint of stuffiness. Auguste Escoffier would find no fault with the whole show, including the classically-inspired menu, although the odd Gallic eyebrow might be raised at executive chef John Williams' own distinctively contemporary reworkings, such as the celeriac, walnut and salted grapes that accompany grouse. Given the surroundings and the prices, luxury ingredients abound. But it's not all about lobster and caviar (although the crustacean stars in a main course with carrot fondant, ginger and lime): one starter matches soft and creamy veal sweetbreads with truffles and puréed parsnip, and Dover sole is pointed up with wild mushrooms and champagne sauce, while posh beef tournedos might slum it with ox cheek and celeriac. At dessert stage, a light and perfectly risen exotic fruit soufflé comes with banana and rum ice cream, or you could invoke the spirit of Escoffier and bow out with crêpes Suzette for two, flambéed theatrically at the table.

Chef John T Williams MBE **Owner** The Ritz Hotel (London) Ltd **Seats** 90, Pr/dining room 60 **Times** 12.30-2/5.30-10, **Prices** Fixed L 3 course £49, Fixed D 3 course £59, Tasting menu £95, Starter £18-£24, Main £37-£40, Dessert £14-£16 **Wines** 450 bottles over £30, 19 by glass **Parking** 10, NCP **Notes** Menu surprise 6 course £95, 'Live at the Ritz' menu £95, Sunday L £49-£79, Children welcome

Roka Charlotte Street ❀❀❀

LONDON W1 PLAN 2 J3

Contemporary Japanese
tel: 020 7580 6464 **37 Charlotte St W1T 1RR**
email: infocharlottestreet@rokarestaurant.com
dir: *Nearest station: Goodge St, Tottenham Court Rd*

Stylish robata cookery full of freshness and umami

London loves stylish Japanese dining, and scarcely more so than among the media folk of Charlotte Street, an area that has long been a barometer of restaurant trends in the capital, though the group has other branches at Canary Wharf, Mayfair and Aldwych. Sit up at the counter for robata grill specials that are made to order before your eyes, or out front behind the potted plants if you want to get some sun. On Sundays, there's the extra option of being served with champagne throughout lunch on a tempting fixed-price deal. The food itself is marked by all the sizzling freshness and umami of the national tradition, but with plenty of dynamic modern pairing, on menus written up in transliterated Japanese as well as English. Raw salmon, avocado and asparagus garnished with tobiko (flying-fish roe) make for a stimulating maki roll, while yellowtail tuna appears in a tartare with lemon, ginger and chilli and a sesame rice cracker. Nigiri sushi and sashimi are exemplary, and the tempura items are properly crisp and dry in the coating, perhaps for soft-shelled crab with a dressing of roasted chilli. The appetite thus fired up, it's time for the robata offerings – sea bass with yuzu-dressed shiso and ginger salad, Portobello mushrooms in sesame oil, smoked duck breast with barley miso and kumquats, pure-breed Wagyu with tsukemono (pickled vegetables). For those with the time, the tasting menus represent a fine introduction to the genre. Dessert might be a monogrammed block of dark chocolate and green tea sponge with pear ice cream and a Jivara tuile, or a strawberry and honey version of chawan mushi with a ginger and almond biscuit.

Chef Hamish Brown **Owner** Rainer Becker, Arjun Waney **Seats** 90 **Times** 12-3.30/5.30-11.30, Closed 25 Dec **Prices** Tasting menu £79 **Parking** On street, NCP in Brewers St **Notes** Champagne Sun lunch +£25, Vegetarian available, Children welcome

LONDON W1 *continued*

Roux at The Landau
PLAN 2 H4

◉◉ Modern European, French V 🏆 NOTABLE WINE LIST

tel: 020 7636 1000 **Portland Place W1B 1JA**
email: reservations@thelandau.com **web:** www.thelandau.com
dir: *Nearest station: Oxford Circus*

Highly polished modern cuisine à la Roux

The Roux dining room at the elegant Langham Hotel opposite the BBC building is a haven of traditional values. If things have gone dressed-down and laid-back elsewhere, here the elevated tone of the panelled oval room does justice to the highly polished cooking of the Roux ethos. Chris King is its vicar on earth, and having worked at Le Gavroche, not to mention for New York hotshot Thomas Keller, may be presumed a confident hand on the tiller. Attentive timing and precise balance distinguish a first-course trio of caramelised scallops with braised pork jowl, chickpea purée and cracked spices, ahead of a serving of richly flavoured milk-fed lamb and kidneys, accompanied by buckwheat salad and diced feta. A creamy, lemon-spiked sauce arrives almost as an afterthought. Gigha halibut appears in a Japanese study, with miso-glazed white asparagus, Tokyo turnips and grapefruit. Comice pear soufflé with lightly poached whole pear is an essay in airy delicacy, the dish given depth by the kid-glove insertion at the table of a bitter chocolate sorbet.

Chef Chris King **Owner** Langham Hospitality Group **Seats** 100, Pr/dining room 18 **Times** 12.30-2.30/5.30-10.30, Closed BHs, Sun, L Sat **Prices** Fixed L 3 course £35-£45, Fixed D 3 course £35-£45, Tasting menu £65-£115, Starter £9-£24.50, Main

£19.50-£56, Dessert £9.25-£15 **Wines** 200 bottles over £30, 12 bottles under £30, 20 by glass **Parking** On street, NCP **Notes** Children welcome

Salt Yard
PLAN 2 J3

◉◉ Italian, Spanish

tel: 020 7637 0657 **54 Goodge St W1T 4NA**
email: info@saltyard.co.uk
dir: *Nearest station: Goodge St*

Top-notch tapas just off Tottenham Court Road

Spain and Italy unite harmoniously in this buzzy restaurant in fashionable Fitzrovia. The ground-floor bar is a top place for a glass of prosecco or cava, or a nifty Bellini and some charcuterie. But if you're here for a while, and looking for something more substantial, head downstairs to the main dining room, with its leather banquette seating and views into the kitchen. The winning combination of two great European nations results in an appealing mix of feel-good flavours and ideas. Salt-cod croquetas with bravas sauce are an irresistible classic, but there might be the less commonly seen marmitako of tuna (a Basque stew), or confit of Gloucestershire Old Spots pork belly with rosemary-scented cannellini beans. The idea is to share, tapas-style, and the mix of the familiar and creative works a treat. There are good technical skills on show, too: crispy baby squid, for example, cooked perfectly, and served with a perky squid ink aïoli and baby chard, or the chargrilled chorizo with chickpea, cumin and garlic.

Times 12-3/5.30-11, Closed BHs, 10 days Xmas, Sun

Roka Mayfair ❀❀❀

LONDON W1
PLAN 2 G1

Modern Japanese
tel: 020 7305 5644 **30 North Audley St W1K 6ZF**
email: infomayfair@rokarestaurant.com
dir: *Nearest station: Bond St*

Dazzling robata grill cuisine in Mayfair

The robata grill is quite rightly the pulsing heart of Roka's uber-cool Mayfair operation, so bag a ringside seat to watch the chefs in the engine room that drives the high-energy buzz in this drop-dead cool eatery. Walls of floor-to-ceiling glass ensure that the see-and-be-seen factor is sky high, all around are exotic hardwoods and industrial textures of steel, concrete and copper, and the super-slick service team play their part in keeping the atmosphere at boiling point. Charcoal-grilled main courses also provide the soul of the contemporary Japanese fusion menu, which takes the fashionable route of sharing plates, with dishes whizzed to the table as soon as they are ready. There's also a roster of sushi and sashimi for traditionalists, and a brace of tasting menus — whichever floats your boat, you can rest assured that it's all made with real skill using top-notch fresh and flavourful ingredients. The 'Roka News' section showcases new ideas, such as the foie gras with plum wine-infused black breadcrumbs that opens the show with a bang, or you might go

for classic soft-shelled crab tempura pointed up with a spicy roasted chilli dressing. Next up, black cod is marinated in yuzu miso and seared to perfection on the barbecue, while meat fans might head straight for lamb cutlets with Korean spices. The craft and creativity carries on into desserts as well, with green tea providing the centre within a well-crafted chocolate fondant served with the harmonious flavour of pear ice cream. An extensive list with tasting notes means sake fans are in for a treat too. Roka also has branches in Canary Wharf and Fitzrovia.

Chef Luca Spiga **Owner** Rainer Becker, Arjun Waney **Seats** 113 **Times** 12-3.30/5.30-11.30, **Prices** Tasting menu £55-£79 **Wines** 100 bottles over £30, 3 bottles under £30, 13 by glass **Notes** Sunday L, Vegetarian available, Children welcome

Sartoria

PLAN 2 J1

Italian

tel: 020 7534 7000 & 3195 9794 **20 Savile Row W1S 3PR**
email: sartoriareservations@danddlondon.com
dir: *Nearest station: Oxford Circus, Green Park, Piccadilly Circus*

Smart setting for modern Italian cooking

Taking its name from the Italian for tailor's shop, Sartoria is an impeccably well-dressed operation in the heart of our home-grown centre of bespoke suiting in Savile Row. The chic interior oozes understated class with a nod to the world of couture in its scissor motifs. Switched-on, polished service comes courtesy of staff dressed to look the part. The menu straddles classic and contemporary Italian cooking with a leaning towards the regional Milanese style. Cappelletti ('little hat') pasta stuffed with goats' cheese bob around in a rich, piping hot chicken broth with spinach and parmesan, ahead of sea bream with white beans, semi-dried tomatoes and fresh mint. Meaty offerings might run to fillet of lamb with artichoke, pine nuts and wild plums, while the dolci department comes up with traditional Napoli cake made with spelt, ricotta, candied fruit and orange blossom water.

Chef Lukas Pfaff **Owner** D & D London **Seats** 100, Pr/dining room 48
Times 12-3/5.30-11, Closed 25-26 Dec, 1 Jan, Etr Mon, Sun (open for private parties only), L Sat **Prices** Fixed L 2 course £25, Fixed D 3 course £30, Starter £9-£19, Main £17-£37, Dessert £6-£12 **Wines** 119 bottles over £30, 23 bottles under £30, 13 by glass **Parking** On street **Notes** Vegetarian available, Children welcome

Scott's Restaurant

PLAN 2 G1

Seafood v NOTABLE WINE LIST

tel: 020 7495 7309 **20 Mount St W1K 2HE**
dir: *Nearest station: Bond St, Green Park*

Bags of style and first-rate seafood

This Mayfair stalwart has been a magnet for the glitterati looking for a fishy feast since the year dot. Inside, it's a clubby art deco charmer with mosaics, huge mirrors, oak-panelled walls, leather seats, and impressive modern British artworks to provide a talking point when the celeb count is low. Those really wanting to see and be seen perch at the onyx-topped oyster bar with a glass of bubbly — those bivalves might include Lindisfarne rocks or West Mersea natives — while the classic brasserie menu starts off with the likes of shellfish bisque or octopus carpaccio with chilli, spring onion and coriander. The produce is top class and the cooking precise. Among mains, halibut fillet with crab tortellini and shellfish butter, or pan-fried skate wing with caper butter might appeal, while rump of lamb with Jerusalem artichokes, fregola and mint will assuage die-hard carnivores. For dessert, it's comfort all the way from Bakewell pudding with almond ice cream to a whole steamed treacle sponge with custard for two.

Chef Dave McCarthy **Owner** Caprice Holdings **Seats** 160, Pr/dining room 40
Times 12-10.30, All-day dining, Closed 25-26 Dec, D 24 Dec **Prices** Starter £8.50-£36, Main £18.75-£82, Dessert £4.50-£10 **Wines** 195 bottles over £30, 3 bottles under £30, 25 by glass **Parking** On street **Notes** Sunday L, Children welcome

Sixtyone Restaurant

PLAN 2 F2

– see below

Sixtyone Restaurant ❀❀❀

LONDON W1	PLAN 2 F2

British, French v

tel: 020 7958 3222 **Great Cumberland Place W1H 7PP**
email: reservations@sixtyonerestaurant.co.uk **web:** www.sixtyonerestaurant.co.uk
dir: *Nearest station: Marble Arch*

Boldly flavoured cuisine amid southern Marylebone glitz

Sixtyone is part and parcel of the boutique Montcalm Hotel, but functions very much as a stand-alone operation, helmed by Anglo-French chef Arnaud Stevens, who brings a pedigree CV to the job after working under several of the capital's headline names (including Gordon Ramsay, Richard Corrigan and Jason Atherton). A pause in the champagne bar next door for a glass of bubbles sets a suitably high-rolling mood for a dining room which glows with the sort of sheen that doesn't come cheap. You'll meet a sleek palette of cream and caramel leather with banquette seating and big mirrors, unclothed tables and quality glassware, with structured service in the old-school manner. Any hint of upscale anonymity, though, is banished by the big, bold flavours that emerge from the kitchen: dishes may be presented in the deconstructive fashion, but there are no mimsy froths and foams here, since Stevens's cooking has its roots in the hearty peasant dishes of southern France. Seasonal menus are built on artisan supplies, and deliver high-impact with meaty starters such as 'pig on toast' offset with pear and pecans. At main, Herdwick lamb shoulder might be partnered with carrot, onion and pickled garlic, or beef fillet counterpointed with the bitter edge of puntarelle chicory, and aubergine boosted with a savoury hit of miso. Vegetarian dishes don't stint on forthright richness either: try marinated beetroot salad with Cashel Blue and walnuts, then salt-baked carrot with smoked spelt and wild garlic. For dessert, perhaps a divertingly reimagined take on a tiramisù theme, or an inventive confection involving Braeburn apple, almond ice cream and the Christmas-cake flavours of speculoos biscuits.

Chef Arnaud Stevens **Owner** Searcys **Seats** 70, Pr/dining room 16
Times 12-2.30/5.30-10.30, Closed 25-26 Dec, D Sun **Prices** Fixed L 2 course £18, Fixed D 3 course £22, Tasting menu £35-£61, Starter £8-£11, Main £17-£28, Dessert £7-£9 **Wines** 140 bottles over £30, 9 bottles under £30, 14 by glass **Notes** Sunday L £18, Children welcome

LONDON W1 *continued*

Sketch (The Gallery)
PLAN 2 J1

◎ ◎ ◎ – *see opposite*

Sketch (Lecture Room & Library)
PLAN 2 J1

◎ ◎ ◎ ◎ ◎ – *see page 376*

Sketch (The Parlour)
PLAN 2 J1

◎ ◎ Modern European

tel: 020 7659 4500 **9 Conduit St W1S 2XG**
email: info@sketch.uk.com **web:** www.sketch.london
dir: *Nearest station: Oxford Circus, Green Park, Bond St*

Eccentric, arty setting for casual dining and drinking

This Parisian-esque salon's sexy boudoir look may appear a little Laurence Llewelyn-Bowen, with its quirky array of Louis XV antique chairs, sofas and divans, atmospheric lighting and bold retro colours and objets d'art, but it all fits the bill perfectly. The Parlour is the entry-level option at Sketch, the funky collaboration between French super-chef Pierre Gagnaire and Mourad 'Momo' Mazouz that spans various eating and drinking spaces (see also Lecture Room & Library and The Gallery) in this arty, theatrical and glam Mayfair playpen. An all-day café to see and be seen, The Parlour serves breakfast, afternoon tea and informal comfort food (from noon) before morphing into a lively evening cocktail bar (members only after 9pm). Enjoy haddock soufflé or croque monsieur to larger plates like chicken cocotte or steak and pommes sautés. Desserts and cakes are to die for, as in 'royal peach' (sweet wine-poached peach with Kirsch mousseline, rose ice cream and almond and redcurrant sponge cake), and first-class macaroons like rose and raspberry or lemon.

Chef Pierre Gagnaire, Herve Deville **Owner** Mourad Mazouz **Seats** 50 **Times** noon-1am, All-day dining, Closed Xmas, 1 Jan **Prices** Starter £9.50-£15, Main £12-£24, Dessert £2-£5.50 **Wines** 23 bottles over £30, 4 bottles under £30, 12 by glass **Parking** NCP Soho **Notes** Sunday L £14, Vegetarian available, Children welcome

Social Eating House
PLAN 2 J2

◎ ◎ ◎ – *see page 377*

The Square
PLAN 2 H1

◎ ◎ ◎ ◎ – *see page 378*

Sumosan Restaurant
PLAN 2 H1

◎ ◎ Japanese Fusion

tel: 020 7495 5999 **26B Albermarle St, Mayfair W1S 4HY**
email: info@sumosan.com
dir: *Nearest station: Green Park*

Glossy backdrop for first-class contemporary Japanese cooking

The glossy contemporary interior – a large open-plan room in dark shades, with padded purple panels on brown walls, pale wood floors, and deeply-lacquered exotic tiger-striped macassar wood tables – is a suitably high-end modern backdrop for the up-to-date Japanese cooking that draws in crowds of international jet-setters and well-heeled denizens of Mayfair. The vibe is bustling and always on the boil as well-briefed, uniformed staff work the room, whisking the kitchen's output of precisely-cooked, immaculately-presented dishes built on top-class ingredients efficiently to their destination. To get things rolling, there's spot-on crispy salt and pepper squid, or excellent sushi – yuwaku roll with king crab, super-fresh raw tuna, wasabi mayonnaise, spring onion, sesame seeds and bottarga-type fish roe, say – prepared by chefs at an open marble-topped counter, as well as sashimi dishes and teppan grilling The wide-ranging menu runs to fusion ideas such as steamed Chilean sea bass with orange sauce, or lamb chops furikaki presented in a salty, nutty, crunchy coating of sesame seeds, almonds, and spices.

Times 12-3/6-11.30, Closed 26 Dec, New Year, L Sat-Sun

Tamarind
PLAN 4 H6

◎ ◎ Indian

tel: 020 7629 3561 **20 Queen St, Mayfair W1J 5PR**
email: manager@tamarindrestaurant.com
dir: *Nearest station: Green Park*

Classy, contemporary Indian cooking with a European touch

Discreetly tucked away in a quiet Mayfair street, Tamarind was in the vanguard of design-led new-wave Indians when it opened in 1995. The expansive basement still works a glamorous contemporary chic with shimmery hues of bronze and black leather, and linen-clad tables tended by formally dressed, charming staff. The cooking takes its cue from the rich Mogul dishes of the Indian north-west, which makes ample use of the tandoor, but the kitchen likes to experiment and keeps things fresh by tossing modern European ideas into the mix, using top-drawer ingredients enhanced by subtle spicing. A light-touch starter of seafood salad brings steamed shrimps, tilapia, squid and black olives with a fennel and ginger dressing, ahead of a remarkably tender Hyderabadi lamb shank with a velvety sauce of turmeric, yogurt and freshly-ground spices. Elsewhere there may be a creative partnership of sea bass fillet with fine beans, raw mango and a tamarind and tomato sauce, and to finish, tandoori-grilled spiced pineapple is drizzled with honey and matched with rose ice cream. A six-course tasting menu has been introduced featuring signature dishes from Tamarind's repertoire.

Chef Peter Joseph **Owner** Indian Cuisine Ltd **Seats** 90
Times 12-2.45/5.30-11, Closed 25-26 Dec, 1 Jan, L Sat **Prices** Fixed L 2 course £21.50, Fixed D 3 course £68, Tasting menu £65, Starter £8-£14.95, Main £19.75-£24.75, Dessert £7-£8.50 **Wines** 162 bottles over £30, 3 bottles under £30, 16 by glass **Parking** NCP **Notes** Pre-theatre D £35 5.30-6.45pm & 10-10.45pm, Sunday L £32, Vegetarian available, Children 5 yrs+

Sketch (The Gallery) ❀❀❀

LONDON W1   **PLAN 2 J1**

Modern European ▲ NOTABLE WINE LIST

tel: 020 7659 4500 **9 Conduit St W1S 2XG**
email: info@sketch.uk.com **web:** www.sketch.london
dir: *Nearest station: Oxford Circus, Green Park, Bond St*

Modern brasserie cooking, but not as we know it

Among the various dining options at Mayfair's Sketch, where neither the design jobs nor the culinary adventuring stand still, The Gallery is the 'gastro-brasserie'. It's an extravagantly spacious room done in defiant candyfloss-pink, which plays rotating host to a series of contemporary artists, much as the fourth plinth in nearby Trafalgar Square does. The present incumbent is David Shrigley, over 200 of whose gnomic cartoons are laid up in neat rows on the walls, but who also has his vicarious say on the menu in the form of what might become known as sashimi Shrigley, composed of raw red tuna, frosted grapes, salted daikon and avocado. If it's brasserie cooking, it's not as we know it, but then there's plenty of that going on elsewhere. Try crabmeat with squid and veal brawn in cucumber consommé, garnished with a gougère of salt-cod brandade, before moving on to duck à l'orange, structured as a sequence that begins with the breast served with red cabbage and celeriac in sauce bigarade, and then the crisped thigh with croquette potatoes and piquillo peppers. If you can manage an in-betweenie in the Italian fashion, consider morel ravioli with a hint of coffee, served with Swiss chard and spring onion gratin. The sides — onion rings, creamed spinach, steamed veg — look positively trad in the context, but order is restored when dessert brings on a cheesecake and sorbet of speculoos (the

Belgian shortcrust Christmas biscuit), along with clementine compôte, or perhaps pannacotta with bubblegum ice cream, lemon foam and a strawberry marshmallow to match the banquettes. Patisserie indeed is one of Pierre Gagnaire's specialities, and not to be missed.

Chef Pierre Gagnaire, Herve Deville **Owner** Mourad Mazouz
Seats 150 **Times** 12-2/6.30pm-2am, Closed Xmas, New Year, BHs, L all week **Prices** Starter £14-£27, Main £21-£45, Dessert £6-£11
Wines 85 bottles over £30, 9 bottles under £30, 15 by glass
Parking On street, NCP **Notes** Vegetarian available, Children welcome

Sketch (Lecture Room & Library) ✿✿✿✿✿

LONDON W1 **PLAN 2 J1**

Modern European V NOTABLE WINE LIST

tel: 020 7659 4500 **9 Conduit St W1S 2XG**
email: info@sketch.uk.com **web:** www.sketch.london
dir: *Nearest station: Oxford Circus, Green Park, Bond St*

Multiform dishes of exhaustive complexity

Behind the façade of a Grade II listed townhouse in Mayfair lurks something a little surprising. Built at the back end of the 18th century, the place may look at first glance like a bastion of traditional values, but within you'll find a venue as avant-garde as any in the capital. With an approach to interior design that doesn't so much push the envelope as shred the envelope into a million tiny pieces and use it as a decorative feature, Sketch is a one off. The Gallery restaurant's design is currently (they like to change it every year) by Turner prize nominee David Shrigley. Head up the stairs, though, and you'll find the main dining space – the Lecture Room & Library. The domain of French super-chef Pierre Gagnaire since 2003, this star attraction is a dining room that sets the pulses racing, with its lavish red, pink, orange and gold colour scheme, padded leather walls and gigantic vases. Like a Victorian salon seen through the eyes of Lewis Carroll, it's a suitably esoteric spot for some ground-breaking cuisine. The menu – à la carte and tasting – reveals dishes of complexity and imagination, with descriptions that consist of a lot of words that can be difficult to take in, but trust in the skill of this kitchen. 'Cod – brown shrimp – caviar' is the simple headline of one starter, with a list of ingredients and preparations below that prepare you for what is to come – a beautiful plate of complementary flavours, appealing textures and visual impact. Native cod 'demi-sel' is combined with a brown shrimp jelly and pumpkin velouté, plus sardine rillettes

and black blini, and a delicate egg mimosa. If a whole roasted Dover sole meunière sounds simple enough, rest assured it is not, for it comes with banana mousseline and green curry, a cider reduction and more, while Bresse chicken stars in another main course with chicken liver gâteau, orange paste, Tokyo turnips and crispy chicken thigh. Prices are sky high, but then again this is food that has been worked into something far more than the sum of its parts, and note there is a gourmet rapide lunch by way of a relatively low entry point. When it comes to dessert, a soufflé may well be the way to go, such as a chocolate version partnered with pistachio parfait, rice pudding and grapefruit confit, or go for the full assiette, or Neil's Yard cheeses. The wine list is up to the job of finding something to suit the dynamic food.

Chef Pierre Gagnaire, Johannes Nuding **Owner** Mourad Mazouz
Seats 50, Pr/dining room 24
Times 12-2.30/6.30-11, Closed 18-29 Aug, 23-30 Dec, 1 Jan, BHs, Sun-Mon, L Sat **Prices** Fixed L 2 course £35, Tasting menu £95-£110, Starter £38-£49, Main £49-£55, Dessert £17-£28
Wines 730 bottles over £30, 70 bottles under £30, 20 by glass
Parking NCP Soho, Cavendish Sq **Notes** Tasting & vegetarian tasting menu 6 course, Children welcome

LONDON W1 *continued*

Texture Restaurant

PLAN 2 F2

@@@@ – *see page 379*

Theo Randall at the InterContinental

PLAN 4 G5

@@@ – *see page 380*

Trishna

PLAN 2 G3

@@ Modern Indian v

tel: 020 7935 5624 **15-17 Blandford St W1U 3DG**
email: info@trishnalondon.com
dir: *Nearest station: Bond St, Baker St*

The distinctive flavours of south-west India brought to Marylebone

A real gem of a restaurant in the heart of chic Marylebone village, Trishna takes a minimalist line with its decor in two dining rooms done out with oak floors and tables, painted brickwork, mirrored walls, and hues of cream and duck-egg blue. On sunny days, floor-to-ceiling windows open onto the street. The kitchen celebrates the coastal cuisine of south-west India in fresh, flavour-packed contemporary dishes, although equal attention is given to meat and vegetarian ideas, and it's all built on well-sourced British seasonal produce. Nandu Varuval – crispy soft-shelled crab deep-fried in tempura batter spiked with green chilli and garlic, and matched with white crab chutney – makes a cracking starter, followed by a Keralan tiger prawn curry distinctively flavoured with coconut and fresh curry leaves. Carnivores could go for duck seekh kebab then tandoori lamb chops with chilli, ginger and mooli radish, or guinea fowl tikka with masoor lentils, star anise and fennel. Desserts end creatively with carrot halva and samosa with masala chai ice cream.

Chef Karam Sethi, Rohit Ghai **Owner** Karam Scthi **Seats** 65, Pr/dining room 12 **Times** 12-2.45/6-10.30, Closed 24-27 Dec, 1-3 Jan **Prices** Fixed L 2 course £17-£18.50, Fixed D 3 course £28, Tasting menu £45-£60, Starter £7-£10.50, Main £16-£22.50, Dessert £6.50-£9.50 **Wines** 150 bottles over £30, 15 bottles under £30, 14 by glass **Parking** On street, NCP **Notes** L bites 2-5 course £18.50-£33.50, Tasting menu 5/7 course, Sunday L £18.50-£60, Children welcome

Umu

PLAN 2 H1

@@@ – *see page 381*

Looking for a London restaurant by name?
Use the index on pages 256–59

Social Eating House @@@

LONDON W1

PLAN 2 J2

Modern British v NOTABLE WINE LIST
tel: 020 7993 3251 **58-59 Poland St W1F 7NS**
email: reservations@socialeatinghouse.com
dir: *Nearest station: Oxford Circus*

Vintage chic and classy cooking with flavours galore

It may be part of Jason Atherton's ever-expanding group of restaurants, but the chef-patron here in Soho's Poland Street is actually Paul Hood. This partnership has resulted in an engaging restaurant that fits nicely into Soho with a pared-back vintage decor and lively contemporary bistro menu that is most definitely a cut above the competition. It's dark, trendy and atmospheric. Covering three storeys, there's a first-floor bar called the Blind Pig and a chef's bar that can seat up to 15 at any one time, while the ground-floor restaurant buzzes from lunch to dinner. The kitchen does not bamboozle or seek to showboat, but delivers gently sophisticated plates that show restrained modernity and focus on flavour. This food is good to eat. There are sharing jars aimed to accompany a pre-meal snifter, such as the trendy combination of shrimp and grits with green chilli slaw. Roasted foie gras with confit duck leg, grape molasses and gingerbread brings a bit of French classical refinement to proceedings, while wild mushrooms are delivered 'from a bag' and served with ceps purée on toast. Among main courses, Cornish sea bass is glazed in kombu (an Asian seaweed) and arrives with spelt and mushroom tea, and salt marsh lamb from Kent is served as rump and confit neck with miso caramel and pale aubergine. The bistro vibe of the place is enhanced by steaks cooked over charcoal (35-day aged Cumbrian Black Angus rib-eye, say) partnered with duck fat chips and a classic sauce. The menu reveals the distances each ingredient has travelled to get here. And when it comes to dessert, lemon meringue pie has never been so sexy.

Chef Paul Hood **Owner** Paul Hood, Jason Atherton **Seats** 75, Pr/dining room 8 **Times** 12-2.30/6-10.30, Closed 25-26 Dec, BHs, Sun **Prices** Fixed L 2 course £19, Tasting menu £55, Starter £9.50-£12.50, Main £17-£35.50, Dessert £7.50 **Wines** 140 bottles over £30, 9 bottles under £30, 25 by glass **Parking** Q park, Poland St **Notes** Chef's experience £110, Children welcome

The Square ✿✿✿✿

LONDON W1   **PLAN 2 H1**

Modern French V

tel: 020 7495 7100 **6-10 Bruton St, Mayfair W1J 6PU**
email: reception@squarerestaurant.com
dir: *Nearest station: Bond St, Green Park, Oxford Circus*

World-class cooking from a long-running Mayfair star

The Square celebrates its quarter century this year, and has never budged from the top-flight of London's places to eat. Many a hot spot restaurant has come and gone in that time, and those that wish to emulate such high-flying achievement might like to consider how Philip Howard has stayed at the top of the pile from day one. Howard is one of the UK's most talented chefs, and although he's been on the Great British Menu he has never gone down the route of constant TV cheffery. The Square has never tried to be hip or chase the fickle attentions of celebs; the room itself was never intended to wow fashionistas. It's a grown-up, gently contemporary space with roomy, generously-spaced tables dressed up in pristine linen cloths, abstract art on pearlescent walls and sober, polished parquet floors – all in keeping with the exclusive Mayfair postcode and giving off all the right messages to make it clear you're in a top-end set-up with serious intent. Head chef Gary Foulkes leads the kitchen team, delivering contemporary, very haute and distinctly French cooking with the emphasis on flavour rather than flashy technique. If you're not on an expense account, the set lunch is a remarkably accessible entry point, while the whole table can sign up to a blow-out via the tasting menu with wine flight. Lasagne of Dorset crab with shellfish cappuccino and champagne foam is a signature dish from the lunchtime menu that delivers on all levels, while a faultlessly seasonal main course brings the autumnal delights of grouse, the breast and croustillant of the leg tender and rich with flavour, served with crushed celeriac, bacon, the contrasting textures of sticky damsons, cauliflower purée and pomegranate seeds. Impeccable ingredients are, of course, key to the cooking, with a devotion for provenance and seasonality. Thus the carte might offer up the deep winter comforts of crisp pork jowl with home-made sausage, carrot and swede, Bramley apple and vacherin Mont d'Or cheese. Exceptional technical ability and intelligent thinking continue at dessert, when wild bay leaf ice cream is slipped into the centre of a perfect damson soufflé. The service team are a bunch of real pros, with a friendly and expert sommelier to navigate the way through a French-dominated wine list running to 68 pages and encompassing 1,500 bins packed with amazing stuff, with a particularly remarkable showing from Burgundy.

Chef Philip Howard, Gary Foulkes **Owner** N Platts-Martin, Philip Howard **Seats** 75, Pr/dining room 18
Times 12-2.30/6.30-10.30, Closed 24-26 Dec, 1 Jan, L Sun, BHs
Prices Fixed L 2 course fr £32.50, Fixed D 3 course £90, Tasting menu fr £115 **Wines** 14 by glass **Parking** NCP on Grosvenor Hill
Notes ALC 3 course £90, Tasting menu with matching wine £175, Children welcome

Texture Restaurant ❀❀❀❀

LONDON W1   PLAN 2 F2

Modern European V

tel: 020 7224 0028 **4 Bryanston St W1H 7BY**
email: info@texture-restaurant.co.uk
web: www.texture-restaurant.co.uk
dir: *Nearest station: Marble Arch, Bond St*

Creative and dynamic cooking with Icelandic soul

The friendship and professional relationship between an Icelandic chef and a French sommelier began at Le Manoir aux Quat' Saisons and has blossomed into a fruitful partnership. The fact that the chef (Agnar Sverrisson) is a prodigious talent and that sommelier (Xavier Rousset) was the youngest Master Sommelier in the world when he was 23, perhaps meant their association was always going to lead to great things. Since opening here on the ground floor of a smart Georgian hotel, they've opened three '28°–50°' wine bars across the capital (or Wine Workshop & Kitchen, as they call them). It is just off Oxford Street in Texture Restaurant, though, that the success of the partnership can be measured. The gloriously proportioned space consists of a Champagne Bar to the front (with a slick decor of leather seats and striking artworks), serving up a cracking 110 different champagnes, including around five available by the glass and all the big names (at big-name prices). There are champagne cocktails too. The restaurant itself has a slight Scandinavian feel with lots of light wood, plenty of room between tables, and some original plasterwork confirming the heritage of the building. Whether you go for the à la carte or tasting menu (versions available lunch and dinner), or the cheaper set lunch menu, expect pin-sharp cooking and a lightness of touch. There's an evident Scandinavian undercurrent to the kitchen's modern European output and the savoury courses have a distinct lightness (but most definitely not of flavour) due to the chef's preference to minimise cream and butter in those courses. Start with new season's English beetroots with goats' cheese, pistachios and a refreshing 'snow', or a dish of Scottish scallops where the accompanying flavours of coconut, ginger, lime leaf and lemongrass are deftly judged. Next up, Cornish monkfish arrives with super-fresh shellfish, fregola and pickled vegetables, and organic duck breast with Seville oranges, celeriac and bulgar wheat. The creativity and technical skill in the kitchen ensures flavours hit the mark and the outstanding quality ingredients don't get in each other's way. For dessert, baby English Brogdale pears get a work-out in an inventive dish with a complementary cardamom ice cream, or go for a similar exploration of new season Yorkshire rhubarb with honey ice cream. There are fish and vegetarian versions of the tasting menu, plus a bespoke vegetarian à la carte. The wine list is as good as you might hope for given the provenance of the co-owner, with good advice on hand and those champagnes to get stuck into.

Chef Agnar Sverrisson **Owner** Xavier Rousset, Agnar Sverrisson **Seats** 52, Pr/dining room 16 **Times** 12-2.30/6.30-10.30, Closed 2 wks Xmas, 2 wks Aug, 1 wk Etr, Sun-Mon **Prices** Prices not confirmed **Wines** 600 bottles over £30, 6 bottles under £30, 30 by glass **Parking** NCP Bryanston St **Notes** Scandinavian fish tasting menu £78, Children welcome

LONDON W1 *continued*

Vasco & Piero's Pavilion Restaurant

PLAN 2 J2

◉ Modern Italian

tel: 020 7437 8774 **15 Poland St W1F 8QE**
email: eat@vascosfood.com
dir: *Nearest station: Oxford Circus*

Seasonal Umbrian cooking in hospitable Soho favourite

This stalwart of the Soho dining scene has been plying its trade in a low-key corner building since 1989. Authentic cooking from the Umbrian region of Italy is the name of the game and you don't need to be one of the glitterati who frequently drop by to receive a warm welcome. Warm colours and subtle lighting add to the authentic Mediterranean ambience and many of the quality ingredients are imported from Italy, although sauces and, of course, pasta are hand-made. The handwritten menu changes after each serving, so you can take seasonality for granted and look forward to great things in the truffle season. Rustic, home-style cooking delivers clear flavours in a starter of spaghettini with calamari, garlic and black ink sauce, followed by a fillet of sea bass served with a herb dressing, steamed vegetables and new potatoes. Among meatier fare, there might be roast shoulder of pork with cannellini beans and crispy kale, or calves' liver and onions with sautéed cabbage, and to finish, there's a textbook tiramisù.

Chef Vasco Matteucci **Owner** Tony Lopez, Paul & Vasco Matteucci **Seats** 50, Pr/dining room 36 **Times** 12-3/5.30-10, Closed BHs, Sun, L Sat **Prices** Fixed L 2 course £16.50, Fixed D 2 course £16.50, Starter £6.50-£10.50, Main £14.50-£24.50, Dessert £4.50-£6.50 **Wines** 35 bottles over £30, 19 bottles under £30, 12 by glass **Parking** NCP car park opposite **Notes** Tasting menu on request, Vegetarian available, Children 5 yrs+

Veeraswamy Restaurant

PLAN 2 J1

◉◉ Indian

tel: 020 7734 1401 **Mezzanine Floor, Victory House, 99 Regent St W1B 4RS**
email: info@realindianfood.com
dir: *Nearest station: Piccadilly Circus*

Stylish sub-continental cooking in Britain's oldest Indian restaurant

The granddaddy of all Indian restaurants in Britain, this lavishly elegant first-floor venue just off Regent Street threw open its doors in the year of the General Strike. It has served London durably and stylishly all through the generations, introducing adventurous palates to the cooking of the various regions of the sub-continent, from the humblest street-snacks to the grand dishes of the Raj culinary repertoire. The rich reds and oranges of the decorative scheme seem to reflect the vivid spicing of dishes such as crab cakes vibrant with ginger, lime and chilli, or Keralan prawn curry with green apple. Scallop moilee is a popular starter, its gingery aromatics a preparatory boost to the taste buds, but there are also tried-and-true classics such as Kashmiri rogan josh (very much a signature dish here), the soft shank meat enhanced with crimson cockscomb flowers and saffron, Malabar lobster curry with coconut and green mango, and biryani variations. Favoured sweets include benchmark gulab jamun, as well as seductive caramelised banana kulfi. Impeccable service enhances the experience.

Times 12-2.30/5.30-11.30, Closed D 25 Dec

Theo Randall at the InterContinental ❀❀❀

LONDON W1   PLAN 4 G5

Italian **v**

tel: 020 7318 8757 **1 Hamilton Place, Hyde Park Corner W1J 7QY**
email: reservations@theorandall.com web: www.theorandall.com
dir: *Nearest station: Hyde Park Corner, Green Park*

Exciting and authentic Italian cooking in landmark hotel

The super-luxe surrounds of Park Lane's InterContinental Hotel might seem utterly disconnected from rustic Italian regional cuisine, but Theo Randall's restaurant joins the dots between the two worlds. It's a light and airy room with an understated look – cool, neutral tones, artwork and mirrors on the walls, darkwood chairs at white-clothed tables, and an unbuttoned ambience (there's even a kids' menu). Randall set up his Mayfair operation after 17 years at the legendary River Café, so you can expect the same ingredients-led, bold and earthy cooking, built on a bedrock of fresh produce, often flown in from small artisan producers in the name of authenticity. The results are impressive, delivering big mouthfuls of flavours from even simple-sounding dishes – gold-standard Punta d'Anca bresaola cured beef, for instance, with radicchio, aged balsamic, parmesan and pine nuts. Don't be tempted to skip the freshly-made pasta dishes when there's the likes of cappelletti ('little hats') stuffed with slow-cooked veal and pancetta and served with chanterelle and porcini mushrooms up for grabs. Main courses go straight to the heart of what makes Italian food unique. Chargrilled Hereford beef sirloin is served simply with a seasonal 'fritto misto' of squash and Jerusalem and globe artichokes pointed with chilli and parsley. Good use is made of the wood-fired oven, from roasted wild black bream with slow-cooked fennel, spinach, Datterini tomatoes, capers and parsley, to roast guinea fowl on bruschetta stuffed with Parma ham, mascarpone and thyme, partnered by Swiss chard and mushrooms. Top-level pastry skills make for exemplary tarts – prune, almond and Vecchia Romagna brandy, perhaps – otherwise bow out with pannacotta with rhubarb, orange and Moscato wine.

Chef Theo Randall **Owner** Intercontinental Hotels Ltd, Theo Randall **Seats** 124, Pr/dining room 24 **Times** 12-3/5.45-11, Closed 25-26 Dec, New Year, BHs, Sun, L Sat **Prices** Fixed L 2 course £27, Fixed D 3 course £33-£80, Tasting menu £65, Starter £11-£19, Main £25-£38, Dessert £6-£8 **Wines** 147 bottles over £30, 1 bottle under £30, 13 by glass **Notes** Sharing menu £60, Children's menu £8-£16, Children welcome

Umu

LONDON W1　　　　　　　　　　　　**PLAN 2 H1**

Japanese **NOTABLE WINE LIST**

tel: 020 7499 8881 **14-16 Bruton Place W1J 6LX**
email: reception@umurestaurant.com
web: www.umurestaurant.com
dir: *Nearest station: Green Park, Bond St*

Kaiseki dining in low-lit high style

Traditional Japanese fine dining has been one of the unlikelier success stories of the London restaurant scene in the most recent generation. While a smart Mayfair address such as Umu is unlikely to lack for Japanese business custom, its constituency has always been wider than that. Supporters are prepared to pay handsomely for food of such lightness and bracing freshness, and the inimitable stylishness with which the package is achieved. Enter the push-button sliding door and find a greeting called out to you in the best tradition of Japanese hospitality, the wood-toned interiors imitating an upmarket Kyoto kaiseki place, with multi-ethnic waiting staff swishing slickly about the crepuscularly lit space. The advertised tranquillity, it's fair to say, is fairly regularly sacrificed to the babble of a busy city restaurant. Bento-box lunches and various set menus remove the need to agonise over the extensive main menu, the former opening with a precisely assembled salad before going on with a selection of sashimi, wasabi and shoyu, chargrilled chicken with mushroom and spring onion, cured bream in seaweed, and simmered duck with sea aubergine. The carte may be more terra incognita, with its chargrilled Welsh eel, grade 11 Wagyu tataki in sesame-ponzu, and game of the day, accompanied by sake-laced foie gras purée in matcha green tea sauce. Kaiseki menus deliver a world of umami, sharp-edged spice, sparkling-fresh fish and gold-standard meats. At the end, there may be something as simple as a fruit platter finished with grated yuzu, or poached and fresh pear with chutney, beetroot and tofu cream. There are no fewer than 160 sakes to choose from or, if none of those suit, 800 or so pedigree wines.

Chef Yoshinori Ishii **Owner** Marlon Abela Restaurant Corporation **Seats** 64, Pr/dining room 12 **Times** 12-2.30/6-11, Closed Xmas, New Year, BHs, Sun, L Sat **Prices** Prices not confirmed **Wines** 860 bottles over £30, 25 by glass **Parking** On street, NCP Hanover Hill **Notes** Kaiseki menu £115, Vegetarian available, Children welcome

LONDON W1 *continued*

Villandry Great Portland Street

PLAN 2 H3

French, European

tel: 020 7631 3131 **170 Great Portland St W1W 5QB**
email: greatportlandstreet@villandry.com
dir: *Nearest station: Great Portland St, Oxford Circus*

Appealingly simple cooking in a foodie emporium

Thanks to new owners who have given the place a smart refurb, Villandry has voguish good looks. Billing itself as a grand café, it's an on-trend all-day food emporium, combining a café-bar with takeaway, a shop and patisserie counter, the 'red room' full of wines to drink in or take home, and a more formal restaurant at the rear. The flexible nature of the place means you can grab breakfast (eggs Benedict, say), have coffee and a pastry (salted caramel and walnut tart perhaps), moules frites with wine, or a full blown meal in the restaurant. Here, simple, sunny natured, French-Mediterranean dishes are prepared with a lightness of touch from seasonal produce. Tuck into something like cod with a high-impact chorizo crust, with wilted spinach, white beans and fresh tomatoes, or big-hearted Galloway fillet steak (28-day dry-aged) with chips and béarnaise. Dessert might deliver a pukka classic like apple tarte Tatin or warm chocolate fondant.

Chef Eddie Pérez **Owner** Philippe Le Roux **Seats** 120, Pr/dining room 50
Times 12-3/6-10.30, Closed 25-26 Dec, D Sun **Prices** Fixed D 3 course £19, Starter £6-£14, Main £13.50-£23.50, Dessert £2-£10 **Wines** 32 bottles over £30, 11 bottles under £30, 15 by glass **Parking** Devonshire St, Gt Portland St, Bolsover St **Notes** Brunch menu, Afternoon tea, Sunday L £5.60-£20.50, Vegetarian available, Children welcome

Wild Honey

PLAN 2 H1

– see below

The Wolseley

PLAN 4 J6

Traditional European v

tel: 020 7499 6996 **160 Piccadilly W1J 9EB**
email: reservations@thewolseley.com
dir: *Nearest station: Green Park*

Bustling landmark brasserie stylishly serving all day

They describe themselves as a 'café-restaurant in the grand European tradition', which is exactly what it feels like, particularly the 'grand' part. A doorman ushers you inside, The Ritz is a near neighbour, and there are soaring pillars and marble floors, but there's nothing stuffy about The Wolseley. This place fair fizzes with energy. Staff rush about, customers chatter, and that's the case all day long, from breakfast, brunch, lunch and afternoon tea, through to evening meals. Start with a timeless brasserie classic such as avocado vinaigrette, or a coarse terrine of venison and pigeon (served with a beetroot chutney and toast), followed by lemon sole St Germain with tartare sauce, a simple steak, or schnitzel. Desserts carry on in the same classic vein with baked vanilla cheesecake and banana split. Breakfast is a large choice from full English to grilled kipper with mustard butter, and the all-day concept fits the bill whether you're after savoury satisfaction or a sweet treat.

Chef Lawrence Keogh **Owner** Chris Corbin, Jeremy King **Seats** 150, Pr/dining room 12
Times 7am-mdnt, All-day dining **Prices** Prices not confirmed **Wines** 44 bottles over £30, 7 bottles under £30, 37 by glass **Parking** NCP Arlington St **Notes** Afternoon tea, Sunday L, Children welcome

Wild Honey

LONDON W1

PLAN 2 H1

Modern European
tel: 020 7758 9160 **12 Saint George St W1S 2FB**
email: info@wildhoneyrestaurant.co.uk
dir: *Nearest station: Oxford Circus, Bond St*

Modernist cooking in wood-panelled Mayfair

Anthony Demetre and Will Smith achieved a minor revolution in London gastronomy when they opened Frith Street's Arbutus in the noughties, swiftly followed in 2007 by the present venue. The contrast between pared-down Soho minimalism in the former and the more classical wood-panelled ambience of Wild Honey, with its view of St George's church opposite and its proximity to the ringing tills of Bond Street, makes for a nice equilibrium. Against the stolid wood, the crimson banquettes and mustard-yellow chairs, together with a display of enigmatic photography, add buoyancy to the decor, and as at many such places, a seat at the counter offers the best way of feeling intimately involved with the way the place runs. Jamie McCallum now heads the kitchen, which is gradually diverging from the traditionally founded French mode of hitherto, in the direction of more speculative modern brasserie food. Warm potato velouté is garnished with a poached egg, but also with pink grapefruit jam, while smoked eel may be lacquered in an Asian spice mix and served with kohlrabi, pickled mushrooms and mango chutney. At main course, pedigree prime materials are their exalted addresses, Angus beef from Creekstone, Kansas, venison from the Denham Estate, turbot from Cornish waters, the last honour-guarded with cockles and winkles, as well as roast endive zested with Sicilian orange. That steak, as is often the way, receives the least modernist treatment, turning up with wild mushrooms and crisp, buttery pommes Anna. A quartet of diners might order up a freshly made apple Tatin for dividing among them, but if you prefer to hog a dessert to yourself, try the warm chocolate tart with spiced orange, bergamot and rice pudding ice cream.

Chef Anthony Demetre, Jamie McCallum **Owner** Anthony Demetre, Will Smith
Seats 65 **Times** 12-2.30/6-10.30, Closed 25-26 Dec, 1 Jan, Sun **Prices** Fixed L 3 course £29.50, Tasting menu fr £75, Starter £10-£19, Main £24-£38, Dessert £7-£12 **Wines** 45 bottles over £30, 6 bottles under £30, 50 by glass **Parking** On street **Notes** Early supper menu 3 course £39, Vegetarian available, Children welcome

Yauatcha
PLAN 2 J2

◉◉ Modern Chinese

tel: 020 7494 8888 **15 Broadwick St W1F 0DL**
email: reservations@yauatcha.com
dir: Nearest station: Tottenham Court Rd, Piccadilly, Oxford Circus

New-wave Chinese cooking in a cool Soho address

An amazingly colourful array of pâtisserie opens the show in Yauatcha's ground-floor 'tea house', but down in the basement dining room things are lively and loud. There's a long, illuminated fish tank (its occupants are not on the menu), a black ceiling studded with a firmament of star-like lights, candle lights flickering in crucifix-shaped alcoves in bare brick walls, and low-slung turquoise banquettes lining elbow-to-elbow darkwood tables. Staff are well versed in the extensive menu, which impresses with its excellent ingredients and exciting blend of traditional Cantonese favourites and more intriguing contemporary compositions. Venison puffs are Wellington-style flaky pastry dim sum with notes of hoi sin, chilli and sesame, while traditionalists might stick with prawn and chicken shui mai dumplings. Larger plates also deliver exhilarating flavours, as seen in a dish of stir-fried scallops with lotus root, or for meat fans, there may be hakka-style pork belly with cloud ear mushrooms. Not normally a high point of the oriental repertoire, the creative fusion-style desserts here are a real treat.

Times 12-11.45, All-day dining, Closed 24-25 Dec

Zoilo
PLAN 2 G2

◉◉ Argentine

tel: 020 7486 9699 **9 Duke St W1U 3EG**
email: info@zoilo.co.uk
dir: Nearest station: Bond St

Authentic flavours of Argentina and an easy-going atmosphere

South American cuisine may well be flavour of the month right now, but that's for a very good reason. This previously un-mined cooking-style has a lot to offer, the authentic, full-on version available at Zoilo inspired by the regions of Argentina, from Patagonia to Mendoza. Over two floors in classy Duke Street, another big part of its appeal is the rustic, easy-going vibe, with exposed brick walls and darkwood tables, plus basement counter seats right in front of the open kitchen. It's contemporary and buzzy and fun. The wine list is 100% Argentinian, with carafe options on most bins. Sharing is the name of the game, so get ready for satisfying plates such as crab on toast with humita and pickled turnips or sweetbreads with onions, hazelnuts and preserved lemons. There are empanadas, too, with fillings such as braised beef skirt, potatoes, onions and olives, or a veggie version with spinach, goats' cheese raisins and pine nuts. Asado (flank steak with celeriac and bone marrow) is a classic, and to finish, there might be milk cake with passionfruit sorbet and toasted almonds.

Chef Diego Jacquet **Owner** Diego Jacquet, Alberto Abbate **Seats** 48, Pr/dining room 10 **Times** 12-2.30/5.30-10.30, Closed Xmas, Sun **Prices** Fixed L 2 course £9.95, Starter £3.50-£7.95, Main £6.95-£23.95, Dessert £5.95-£8.95 **Wines** 46 bottles over £30, 8 bottles under £30, 23 by glass **Parking** On street **Notes** Vegetarian available, Children welcome

Angelus Restaurant
PLAN 2 D1

◉◉ Modern French ▮ NOTABLE WINE LIST

tel: 020 7402 0083 **4 Bathurst St W2 2SD**
email: info@angelusrestaurant.co.uk
dir: Nearest station: Lancaster Gate, Paddington Station

Classy French brasserie with vibrant cooking

A former pub which was transformed into a classy Parisian-style brasserie by renowned sommelier, Thierry Tomasin, Angelus Restaurant continues to impress with its luxe, art nouveau-inspired finish and ambitious, modern French cooking. It looks smart with its darkwood panelling and red leather banquettes, and with its wine list offering up some seriously good drinking, this is a place worth knowing about. The kitchen turns out some rather ambitious stuff, rooted in French tradition perhaps, but with plenty of bright, modern ideas on show. Fried and poached scallops, for example, might come in a first course with dehydrated scallop roe and langoustine foam, while another starter serves up duck liver in a luscious crème brûlée alongside caramelised almonds and toasted bread. For main course, coq au vin comes with smoked mash, and pan-fried gurnard with chargrilled white asparagus, caper butter and a crab beignet. The bright, modern ideas continue into dessert stage with the likes of compressed English apples and pears partnered with salted caramel and a ginger and oat crumble.

Chef Pierre Needham **Owner** Thierry Tomasin **Seats** 40, Pr/dining room 22 **Times** 10am-11pm, All-day dining, Closed 23 Dec-4 Jan **Prices** Fixed L 2 course £22, Tasting menu £75, Starter £10-£17, Main £19-£32, Dessert £9-£13 **Wines** 600 bottles over £30, 20 bottles under £30, 4 by glass **Parking** On street **Notes** Brunch menu, Sunday L £22-£27, Vegetarian available, Children welcome

Island Grill & Bar
PLAN 2 D1

◉◉ Modern European

tel: 020 7551 6070 **Lancaster Ter W2 2TY**
email: eat@islandrestaurant.co.uk **web:** www.islandrestaurant.co.uk
dir: Nearest station: Lancaster Gate

Polished brasserie-style cooking with Hyde Park views

Island Grill & Bar is on the ground floor of the hotel with views through its tall windows over the busy road to Hyde Park opposite. It's been given an appealingly bright and modern look that matches the brasserie-style menu. Diehard carnivores can settle on something from the grill – perhaps a steak with béarnaise or pork cutlets – but there are far more diversions on the far-reaching menu. Fillet of salmon, for instance, is served in a saffron-infused consommé with spinach, potato and brown shrimps, and roast spring chicken, moist and tasty, in a rich jus with cavolo nero and classic Sarladaise potatoes. Starters are a mixed bunch of equally skilfully prepared dishes, from dressed crab and avocado with a salad of cucumber and mint to Chinese-style pork belly with noodles and melon and cucumber salad with chilli, lime and coriander. For pudding, who could resist honeycomb pannacotta made with the hotel's own honey?

Chef Darren Marshall **Owner** Khun Jatuporn Sihanatkathakul **Seats** 68 **Times** 7am-10.30pm, All-day dining **Prices** Fixed L 2 course £9.50, Fixed D 3 course £12.50, Starter £4.95-£8.95, Main £11.25-£23.95, Dessert £5-£6.50 **Wines** 9 bottles over £30, 15 bottles under £30, 7 by glass **Parking** Hotel or on street **Notes** Fixed D served until 7pm, Sunday L £17.50, Vegetarian available, Children welcome

LONDON W2 *continued*

Kurobuta
PLAN 2 E2

◉◉ Japanese

tel: 020 3475 4158 **17-20 Kendal St, Marble Arch W2 2AW**
email: info@kurobuta-london.com
dir: *Nearest station: Marble Arch, Edgeware Rd*

On-trend Japanese fusion cooking

The man at the culinary reins of this upbeat Japanese fusion operation is Scott Hallsworth, former head chef at Nobu, so there's no question about his familiarity with the genre. Inspired by Japan's izakaya taverns, the interior goes for a stripped-down look of white walls and wooden benches, and a trendy soundtrack adds to the high-decibel vibe. A vibrant opener of salmon gravad lax and avocado tartare with dill mayonnaise, crunchy rice crackers and a citrussy hit of yuzu zest has the taste buds all standing to attention in readiness for a pair of fluffy steamed buns filled with full-flavoured barbecued pork belly and a thick, sticky soy and chopped peanut dressing. The à la mode robata grill provides tea-smoked lamb with smoky nasu and Korean miso, or on the lighter side, there's crisp-coated squid kara-age with a punchy green jalapeño dipping sauce. Desserts don't let you down either. Yuzu tart puts an oriental spin on an old western favourite with a topping of soft meringue on a lush citrus filling.

Times 9am-11.30pm, All-day dining

The New Angel Notting Hill
PLAN 2 A1

◉◉◉ – *see below*

Nipa
PLAN 2 D1

◉◉ Traditional Thai

tel: 020 7551 6039 **Lancaster London Hotel, Lancaster Ter W2 2TY**
email: nipa@lancasterlondon.com
dir: *Nearest station: Lancaster Gate*

Precise Thai cooking in an authentic setting overlooking Hyde Park

It may only be on the first floor of the tower block that is the Lancaster London Hotel, but there's still a cracking view from this Thai restaurant over treetops and Hyde Park. The dining room has wooden panels and carvings, tables are topped with Thai orchids, and the prevailing impression is one of refinement. With a panoramic window to make the best of the view, and an attentive service team on hand, Nipa is worth knowing about. Begin with a fine version of a classic appetiser (chargrilled chicken with peanut sauce and cucumber relish), or go for selection, and move on to a soup such as a sterling version of tom yum koong, fired up with chilli, lemongrass and lime. Among main courses, crisp-fried salmon with minced prawn shows excellent balance of flavours, or go for a spicy green coconut curry filled with chicken and Thai aubergines. Set menus prevent the need to make difficult decisions, and, for dessert, mango sticky rice with coconut cream is spot on.

Chef Sanguan Parr **Owner** Lancaster London **Seats** 55 **Times** 5-10.30, Closed L all week **Prices** Fixed D 3 course £17.50-£20, Tasting menu £25, Starter £11-£24, Main £12-£30 **Wines** 21 bottles over £30, 10 bottles under £30, 13 by glass **Parking** Paddington **Notes** 4 course D £35-£40, Khantok menu 5-7pm £25, Vegetarian available, Children welcome

The New Angel Notting Hill ◉◉◉

LONDON W2
PLAN 2 A1

Modern European NEW v
tel: 020 7221 7620 **39 Chepstow Place W2 4TS**
email: info@thenewangel-nh.co.uk
dir: *Nearest station: Notting Hill Gate*

Celeb chef back in town at neighbourhood-cum-destination venture

TV foodie programmes, like French Leave plus an appearance as a contestant on shows like *I'm a Celebrity... Get Me Out of Here!* may have brought chef-restaurateur John Burton-Race wider public recognition and notoriety, but it was his highly-acclaimed cooking at L'Ortolan in Berkshire (in the late 80s and 90s) and subsequently at his eponymous named restaurant at London's Landmark Hotel around the millennium that showed his impeccable talent at the stove. He later took Dartmouth's iconic Carved Angel to further critical acclaim, re-branding it the New Angel. Returning to London after 12 years, he opened this neighbourhood-cum-destination outfit in trendy Notting Hill in spring 2014, with his long-time protégé Stephen Humphries as head chef. The restaurant's good looks are light, stylish and modern, with a brass-topped bar up front and warming neutral tones of beige and brown enhanced by statement wallpaper, mirrors, in-vogue seating and white linen. The kitchen's modern European output fits the bill, underpinned by classical French influence and played out with matching light modern spin (take an opener terrine of foie gras teamed with apricot purée, almonds and split green beans in truffle honey with toasted brioche). The roster of prime and luxury ingredient-led, seasonal menus all deliver intricately presented, pretty dishes of high skill, finesse and clean flavour, backed by slick, charming, professional yet unstuffy service. Okay, the style is quite French and decadent and doesn't try to be cutting edge, but there's certainly a classy touch and bags of flair. Take sparkling-fresh pan-fried John Dory fillets partnered by a Devonshire crab-stuffed courgette flower, sea vegetables, ratte potatoes and a fathoms-deep tasting shellfish cream. A superbly balanced delice of chocolate and raspberry teamed with white chocolate ice cream turns heads too, while excellent breads, amuse-bouche (perhaps fish soup with rouille and crouton), a tantalising cheese trolley and petits fours all hit top form also, while wines are French-led with good by-glass action.

Chef Stephen Humphries **Owner** John Burton-Race **Seats** 55, Pr/dining room 55 **Times** 12-2.30/6-10.30, Closed 1 wk Xmas, 2 wks Aug, Sun-Mon **Prices** Fixed L 2 course fr £28, Fixed D 3 course fr £56, Tasting menu fr £77 **Wines** 250 bottles over £30, 40 bottles under £30, 20 by glass **Parking** On street, Princes Sq **Notes** Children welcome

LONDON W4

Hedone   PLAN 1 D3

@@@ – *see below*

Restaurant Michael Nadra   PLAN 1 D3

@@ Modern European

tel: 020 8742 0766 **6/8 Elliott Rd, Chiswick W4 1PE**
email: chiswick@restaurant-michaelnadra.co.uk
dir: *Nearest station: Turnham Green*

Classy modern cooking in Chiswick

It may look much like any other small neighbourhood outfit from outside, squirreled away just off the bustling High Road, but Restaurant Michael Nadra is a classy stalwart of the Chiswick dining scene. Burnished, tightly-packed wooden tables, black leatherette banquettes and chairs and black slate flooring create a cool yet intimate, urbane vibe in its cosy U-shaped dining room. Likewise, the kitchen's appealing Pan-European fixed-price repertoire offers bags of interest, the cooking displaying classical underpinning (think melting sautéed foie gras combined with the balanced sharpness of poached Yorkshire rhubarb, nasturtium leaves and a warm mini brioche loaf to accompany), though ultimately it is defined by intelligent composition, clean flavours, careful execution and a light modern touch that looks pretty on the plate. Witness also classy mains, perhaps with a Mediterranean lilt like top-drawer slow-roasted Ibérico presa teamed with wonderfully tender suckling pig belly, crisp crackling, braised chicory, fennel salad and pickled grapes that deliver sweet explosions on the palate. Desserts, like pineapple carpaccio with lime, chilli, ginger crumble and coconut ice cream, hold up form too. There's a sister Restaurant Michael Nadra in Primrose Hill.

Chef Michael Nadra **Owner** Michael Nadra **Seats** 55
Times 12-2.30/6-10, Closed Xmas, 1 Jan, D Sun **Prices** Fixed L 2 course fr £21, Fixed D 3 course fr £37, Tasting menu £48-£59 **Wines** 130 bottles over £30, 15 bottles under £30, 16 by glass **Parking** On street **Notes** Tasting menu 6 course, Sunday L £21-£27, Vegetarian available, Children welcome

---

Follow The AA online

twitter: @TheAA_Lifestyle
facebook: www.facebook.com/TheAAUK

Find us on **Facebook**

Hedone @@@

LONDON W4   PLAN 1 D3

Modern European
tel: 020 8747 0377 **301-303 Chiswick High Rd W4 4HH**
email: Aurelie@hedonerestaurant.com
dir: *Nearest station: Chiswick Park, Gunnnersbury*

Chiswick temple to superb produce cooked with flair

Mikael Jonsson is a singular kind of chef who came to the restaurant business relatively late in life and has created one of the capital's most compelling dining experiences. Born in Sweden, he chose to open on Chiswick High Road, and the rest, as they is history. There's a relaxed Scandinavian charm to the room, with the open kitchen acting as the beating heart of the place. Mikael was a food blogger for a while before jumping in the deep end and his main passion is for ingredients. The menus even evolve through the service so you might not get exactly the same dish as your neighbour. At lunchtime choose from a four-course menu, tasting option, or the full monty 'carte blanche', with the four-course option dropped in the evening. The home-baked sourdough bread is as good as you'll find anywhere. Start with poached Cornish rock oysters – plump, juicy and faultlessly cooked – matched with a delicate apple foam, while a single hand-dived scallop cooked in its own juices needs no more than a hint of salt and dried seaweed powder to intensify its natural flavours. Follow on with liquid parmesan ravioli with onion consommé, mild horseradish and pancetta in an inventive dish, the pasta beautifully made and the flavours nicely judged, while next up might come roasted breast and leg of squab with silky-smooth smoked potatoes, a deeply-flavoured blackcurrant purée, a vivid green purée made from rocket and lemongrass, and a foie gras sauce. Among sweet courses, fresh English blueberries arrive with an intense blueberry syrup, topped with a tiny crisp meringue and a beautifully made lemon and rosemary sorbet, and then a warm chocolate mousse is served with powdered raspberry, passionfruit jelly and Madagascan vanilla ice cream.

Chef Mikael Jonsson **Owner** Mikael Jonsson **Seats** Pr/dining room 16
Times 12-2.30/6.30-9.30, Closed Sun-Mon, L Tue-Wed **Prices** Prices not confirmed

LONDON W4 *continued*

Sam's Brasserie & Bar

PLAN 1 D3

◉ Modern European, International

tel: 020 8987 0555 **11 Barley Mow Passage, Chiswick W4 4PH**
email: info@samsbrasserie.co.uk **web:** www.samsbrasserie.co.uk
dir: *Nearest station: Chiswick Park, Turnham Green*

Buzzy all-day brasserie in a factory conversion

It's easy to see the appeal of this easy-going neighbourhood eatery just off Chiswick High Road. The large, open-plan space divides between a cool-looking bar (exposed girders and bare brickwork are a nod to the place's past as a paper factory) and a dining area with a loft-style urban edge in its chunky wood tables, open-to-view kitchen and mezzanine level. Chatty staff dressed in long aprons keep things ticking over nicely, and menus printed on paper table mats offer something for all-comers, starting with a well-made ham hock and prune terrine with celeriac remoulade, then a splendid chargrilled steak of swordfish served with caponata. Meaty mains could bring lamb rump with smoked celeriac purée, cavolo nero and green olive tapenade. Finish with a textbook chocolate fondant with black cherries and mascarpone ice cream. Two- and three-course set menus deliver top value for the bargain hunter.

Chef Mark Baines **Owner** Sam Harrison **Seats** 100 **Times** 9am-10.30pm, All-day dining, Closed 24-26 Dec **Prices** Prices not confirmed **Wines** 18 bottles over £30, 36 bottles under £30, 22 by glass **Parking** On street & car park **Notes** Fixed L Mon-Fri, Early bird D Sun-Thu before 7.30pm, Sunday L, Vegetarian available, Children welcome

La Trompette

PLAN 1 D3

◉◉ Modern European 🍷 NOTABLE WINE LIST

tel: 020 8747 1836 **5-7 Devonshire Rd, Chiswick W4 2EU**
email: reception@latrompette.co.uk
dir: *Nearest station: Turnham Green*

Relaxing and mellow mood for a creative French repertoire

The three-strong amalgamation of Wandsworth's Chez Bruce, Kew's Glasshouse and La Trompette is one of London's classiest, most quality-conscious small restaurant groups. Here in Chiswick, the mood is as mellow and relaxing as at the other venues, with a broad glass frontage opening to a terrace from an expansive room with well-spaced tables, pale banquette seating and abstract artworks in bold primaries. The culinary repertoire reflects the group's house style, which is a creative outgrowth of French cuisine bourgeoise with cosmopolitan leanings. Crisp-fried mackerel with grilled baby squid comes with pickled cucumber and bonito cream, as one alternative to the more classical likes of foie gras parfait with spiced pear chutney. At main, there are pedigree meats such Ayrshire beef – grilled rib-eye and short rib with scorched onions in red wine – as well as earthily treated fish like black bream, which turns up with crushed butternut squash, cavolo nero, walnut

pesto and the eponymous trompettes. Finish with a crème fraîche tart piled with clementine and medjool dates, or cast an eye over the superb French cheeseboard.

Chef Rob Weston **Owner** Nigel Platts-Martin, Bruce Poole **Seats** 88, Pr/dining room 16 **Times** 12-2.30/6.30-10.30, Closed 24-26 Dec, 1 Jan **Prices** Fixed L 2 course £24.50, Fixed D 3 course £47.50 **Wines** 483 bottles over £30, 63 bottles under £30, 16 by glass **Parking** On street **Notes** Sunday L £32.50, Vegetarian available, Children welcome

Le Vacherin

PLAN 1 D3

◉◉ French

tel: 020 8742 2121 **76-77 South Pde W4 5LF**
email: info@levacherin.com
dir: *Nearest station: Chiswick Park*

French classics in smart, relaxed neighbourhood bistro

This neighbourhood bistro certainly conjures the mood and looks of cross-Channel dining with its polished wood floors, brown leather banquettes at linen-swathed tables and mirror-friezes on cream walls hung with French-themed posters. Gastro anoraks might know that Le Vacherin is named after a French Alpine cheese and a light-as-air dessert consisting of a meringue crust filled with Chantilly cream and fruit, so the classic French cooking comes as no surprise. The kitchen excels at doing simple things well; you might find beignets of frog's legs with sauce gribiche alongside grilled red mullet paired with peas, broad beans and saffron aïoli, while a main-course roast rump of Hereford beef is partnered by bone marrow, watercress, pommes allumettes and bordelaise sauce. If you are after a real hit of rustic authenticity, how about an assiette of duck, comprising magret, leg, gizzards and foie gras with Puy lentils? For dessert, pear and almond tart with raspberry ripple ice cream should send you home with a smile. The prix-fixe menu is particularly good value in any language.

Chef Malcolm John **Owner** Malcolm & Donna John **Seats** 72, Pr/dining room 36 **Times** 12-2.30/6-11, Closed BHs, L Mon **Prices** Fixed L 2 course £18.50, Fixed D 3 course £22.50, Starter £7.50-£14, Main £14.95-£26.50, Dessert £5.50-£13.50 **Wines** 200 bottles over £30, 15 bottles under £30, 12 by glass **Parking** On street (meter) **Notes** Fixed price menu until 7pm, Steak & wine £9.95 before 8pm, Sunday L £25, Vegetarian available, Children welcome

LONDON W5

Charlotte's Place

PLAN 1 C3

◉◉ Modern European, British

tel: 020 8567 7541 **16 St Matthews Rd, Ealing Common W5 3JT**
email: restaurant@charlottes.co.uk
dir: *Nearest station: Ealing Common, Ealing Broadway*

Splendid seasonal food in a neighbourhood gem

This sparkling neighbourhood bistro has impeccable ethical credentials, sourcing its materials from like-minded local suppliers and working in tune with the seasons to ensure there's always something to catch the interest on its breezy modern menus. The setting suits the food: an unpretentious yet stylish blend of black leather seats at unclothed darkwood tables on well-trodden wooden floors, all framed by plain cream walls hung with colourful prints. Top-notch pastry skills distinguish a splendid tart of line-caught mackerel matched with a lively accompaniment of olives, peppers, parmesan, anchovy and balsamic. A Mediterranean warmth infuses a main course of well-timed hake teamed with braised octopus, sautéed potatoes, chorizo and croûtons cooked in chorizo oil, all rounded off with a punchy salsa verde; meat comes in for robust treatment – perhaps onglet skirt steak with bone marrow fritter, celeriac, roast onions and sauce bordelaise. In summer, English raspberries are showcased fresh and as a coulis to go with a wobbly pannacotta pointed up with mint, Moscato d'Asti jelly and a Breton biscuit.

Chef Lee Cadden Owner Alex Wrethman Seats 54, Pr/dining room 30
Times 12-3/6-9.30, Closed 26 Dec, 1 Jan, D 25 Dec Prices Fixed L 2 course £19.95,
Fixed D 3 course £34.95 Wines 141 bottles over £30, 38 bottles under £30, 7 by
glass Parking On street Notes Early D 6-7pm 3 course with aperitif £26.95, Sunday
L £22.95-£26.95, Vegetarian available, Children welcome

The Grove
PLAN 1 C3

◉ Classic British, French NEW

tel: 020 8567 2439 **The Green, Ealing W5 5QX**
email: info@thegrovew5.co.uk
dir: *Nearest station: Ealing Broadway*

European brasserie dishes opposite the Ealing film studios

A brick-built block of an old pub, just off Ealing Broadway and opposite the old film
studios, The Grove features an outdoor terrace as well as a lively interior furnished
with rough wooden tables, bare floors and deep charcoal-grey walls. It is
permanently abubble with convivial atmosphere, its bustling kitchen on view from
the dining room. European brasserie cooking done with care and flair scores many
hits for the likes of fried lamb's sweetbreads with minted pea purée and wild garlic,
Spanish charcuterie and manchego boards with olives and home-baked bread, and
robust main dishes such as roasted hake on crushed new potatoes in caper beurre
noisette. Sticklers for tradition will welcome garlicky pork sausages with mash in
thyme gravy, beer-battered haddock and mushy peas, or the 28-day aged Angus
rib-eye with green peppercorn sauce. Finish with a properly bracing lemon tart and
raspberry sorbet.

Chef Marek Ciskal Owner Metropolitan Pub Co, Greene King Seats 80
Times 12-4/6-10 Prices Starter £5-£8, Main £11.50-£19.50, Dessert £5-£6.50
Wines 8 bottles over £30, 34 bottles under £30, 19 by glass Parking On street,
shopping centre multi-story Notes Questors Theatre 20% food discount pre/post-
theatre, Sunday L £13.50-£18, Vegetarian available, Children welcome

LONDON W6

L'Amorosa
PLAN 1 D3

◉ Italian, Mediterranean, British NEW

tel: 020 8563 0300 **278 King St, Ravenscourt Park W6 0SP**
email: bookings@lamorosa.co.uk
dir: *Nearest station: Ravenscourt Park*

Local Italian with plenty to tempt

This neighbourhood restaurant on Hammersmith's main drag has a man with
pedigree at the stoves, in the shape of ex-Zafferano head chef Andy Needham, a
skilled interpreter of the modern Italian style who has scaled back his output to a
more comfort-oriented level. The setting is smart-casual – darkwood floors, classy
polished wood tables, buttoned brown leather banquettes and cream-painted walls
hung with modern art – with a mezzanine, plus a few pavement tables for balmy
days. A starter plate of pumpkin ravioli delivers pitch-perfect pasta with rich
gorgonzola sauce and crispy deep-fried sage, followed by sea-fresh roast cod with
chickpeas, samphire and salsa verde, while meaty mains could see a classic
combination of osso buco braised veal shin with tangy gremolata and
saffron risotto. Pear and almond tart with mascarpone cream makes a fine finale,
with timeless tiramisù also in the running.

Chef Andy Needham Owner Andy Needham Seats 40
Times 12-2.30/6-10, Closed Xmas 1 wk, BHs, Mon, D Sun Prices Fixed L 2 course fr
£15.50, Starter £6-£9, Main £12-£26, Dessert £6-£12, Service optional 12.5%
Parking Free parking after 5pm & wknds Notes Sunday L £8-£25, Vegetarian
available, Children welcome

Anglesea Arms
PLAN 1 D3

◉ Modern British

tel: 020 8749 1291 **35 Wingate Rd, Ravenscourt Park W6 0UR**
dir: *Nearest station: Ravenscourt Park, Goldhawk Rd, Hammersmith*

Superior cooking in a pioneering gastro-pub

The Anglesea Arms was one of the pioneering London gastro-pubs, and after a
relaunch in June 2014, it's as popular today as it ever has been. There's an oak-
panelled front bar with real ales, church pew seats and a buzzy, laid-back
atmosphere and a skylit dining area with an open kitchen, and an appealing, well-
thought-out menu brimming with interesting ideas, while technical accuracy and
well-judged combinations mark out the cooking. A seared mackerel fillet with a cod
and truffle fritter and beetroot and watercress salad with lemon dressing is a
perfect summery opener, followed by the porcine pleasure of Gloucester Old Spots
pork belly, pointed up inventively with roast peach, spinach and lentils; if you're in
the mood for fish, there might be hake with girolle mushrooms, samphire, radishes
and broad beans. Finish with almond milk pannacotta with cherry sorbet and
compôte, or warm chocolate and ale cake with ale caramel sauce and cereal milk
ice cream.

Chef Philip Harrison Owner George & Richard Manners Seats 37
Times 12.30-3/6-10, Closed 24-26 Dec, L Mon-Thu (excl BH) Prices Starter £6-£11,
Main £10-£18, Dessert £6, Service optional 12.5% Wines 23 bottles over £30, 25
bottles under £30, 16 by glass Parking On street, pay & display (free at wknds)
Notes Sunday L £6-£18, Vegetarian available, Children welcome

Novotel London West
PLAN 1 D3

◉ Modern British

tel: 020 8741 1555 **1 Shortlands W6 8DR**
email: H0737@accor.com web: www.novotellondonwest.co.uk
dir: *Nearest station: Hammersmith*

Modern comfort food in a contemporary hotel

This is the kind of modern hotel that can satisfy the needs of business folk in need
of meeting space or accommodation, or families with children looking for
somewhere to cut loose in West London. When it comes to eating, it's a 24/7 kind of
place, with the Artisan Grill restaurant being the hub of the culinary output. The
modern space with a glass façade offers views of the hotel's comings and goings,
and the menu does its best to cover most bases. The eponymous grill turns out
steaks in familiar formats, and there's also all the comfort of traditional steak and
kidney pie in a rich gravy with colcannon, or mussels marinière with chips. Desserts
continue to raise the comfort factor with something like chocolate fondant, which
has a light sponge and oozing liquid centre.

Times 12-2.30/5.30-10.30, Closed L Sat-Sun

The River Café
PLAN 1 D3

◉◉◉ – *see page 388*

The River Café 🌸🌸🌸

LONDON W6   **PLAN 1 D3**

Italian
tel: 020 7386 4200 **Thames Wharf Studios, Rainville Rd W6 9HA**
email: info@rivercafe.co.uk
dir: *Nearest station: Hammersmith*

Outstanding Italian cooking from a riverside icon

As it heads for its 30th birthday, it is interesting to note that not a great deal has changed at The River Café in three decades, and that is because everything was absolutely spot on from day one. Culinary fads have come and gone, but everything this place stands for has stood the test of time. The food here is timeless because it has always been about fantastic ingredients (which never come cheap, as the prices attest), ruthless seasonality and big flavours — an ethos that has spawned a generation of alumni who have gone on to become household names in their own right, pre-eminently Jamie Oliver and Hugh Fearnley-Whittingstall. That 'café' tag remains as tongue-in-cheek as ever, although there is an unbuttoned, unrestauranty mood to the minimalist, light-filled room with its cherry-pink wood burning oven and waterside views that is a long way from the hushed tones of 'faine daining', and children are just as welcome as the movers and shakers and glitterati. The daily menus offer an Italophile's tour through the traditional four courses, setting out with antipasti of chargrilled squid with fresh red chilli and rocket, perhaps, followed by primi based on impeccable pasta — the likes of rigatoni with langoustines and parmesan and pecorino cheese, or pappardelle with beef fillet slow-cooked in a sauce of Chianti, sage and tomato. Main courses let the excellence of their prime ingredients do the talking: turbot is wood-roasted with Sicilian tomatoes and served with anchovies, agretti and lemon, while chargrilled marinated lamb leg is partnered by wood-roasted pumpkin, braised turnip tops and fresh horseradish. Awaiting at the end, perhaps pannacotta with grappa and rhubarb, or thoroughbred Italian cheeses.

Chef Joseph Trivelli, Ruth Rogers, Sian Owen **Owner** Ruth Rogers **Seats** 120, Pr/dining room 18 **Times** 12.30-3/7-11, Closed 24 Dec-1 Jan, BHs, D Sun **Prices** Prices not confirmed **Wines** 230 bottles over £30, 14 by glass **Parking** 29, Valet parking evening & wknds, pay & display **Notes** Sunday L, Vegetarian available, Children welcome

LONDON W6 *continued*

Sagar
PLAN 1 D3

@ Indian Vegetarian V

tel: 020 8741 8563 **157 King St, Hammersmith W6 9JT**
email: info@sagarveg.co.uk
dir: *Nearest station: Hammersmith, Ravenscourt Park*

Cracking-value South Indian vegetarian dining

Among the shop fronts of Hammersmith's main drag, you might take Sagar to be just another modern-looking high-street curry house. But behind the full-drop glass frontage, the place has an almost Scandinavian feel with pale wood floors, chairs, tables and walls – the give away is alcoves holding Hindu deities and artefacts. Expect well-crafted dishes, smartly attired service and wallet-friendly prices. The roster focuses on South Indian staples such as crisp paper-thin dosas (rice and lentil pancakes with various fillings) and uthappams (lentil 'pizzas'), while a starter of Kancheepuram idli delivers fluffy rice and lentil steamed dumplings with fresh coconut chutney. The lengthy output takes in Bombay chowpati (street snacks) like crispy puri, plus all-inclusive thali platters and simple curries such as brinjal bhaji – aubergine and green pepper cooked in fresh tomato with South Indian spices. Sagar also has branches in Covent Garden and Fitzrovia.

Chef S Sharmielan **Owner** S Sharmielan **Seats** 60
Times 12-3/5.30-10.45, Closed 25-26 Dec **Prices** Fixed L 2 course £7.20-£14.30, Fixed D 3 course £10.15-£17.85, Starter £2.25-£5.55, Main £4.95-£8.75, Dessert £2.95-£3.55, Service optional **Wines** 911 bottles under £30, 8 by glass **Parking** On street **Notes** Children welcome

LONDON W8

Babylon
PLAN 4 B5

@@ Modern British

tel: 020 7368 3993 **The Roof Gardens, 99 Kensington High St W8 5SA**
email: babylon@roofgardens.virgin.com **web:** www.roofgardens.virgin.com
dir: *Nearest station: High St Kensington*

South London skyline views and modern British cooking

There's no shortage of restaurants boasting skyline views in the capital these days, but Babylon has something different to offer as well – views over the famous rooftop gardens one floor below. With a chic finish and a wall of glass serving up those views, plus tables on a terrace, Babylon is a seventh-floor hotspot for modern British dining. The menu deals in classic combinations with a contemporary spin here and there. Start, for example, with an open lasagne made with smoked chicken and leeks, while treacle-cured salmon and smoked Gigha halibut is an option if you fancy something a little lighter. Next up, scallop and squid comes with black tagliolini and roasted rump of lamb with aligot potato gnocchi and a mushroom and Madeira reduction. Desserts show plenty of ambition, too, judging by baked lemon cheesecake with jasmine latte foam, ginger custard and dulce de leche ice

cream, or an almond financier with salted caramel, passionfruit cream and Granny Smith purée.

Babylon

Times 12-2.30/7-10.30, Closed D Sun

See advert opposite

Belvedere
PLAN 1 E3

@@ British, French

tel: 020 7602 1238 **Abbotsbury Rd, Holland House, Holland Park W8 6LU**
email: sales@belvedererestaurant.co.uk **web:** www.belvedererestaurant.co.uk
dir: *Nearest station: Holland Park*

Modern brasserie-style dishes in upscale Holland Park

A dream-ticket location in lovely Holland Park – surrounded by primped lawns, flower gardens and fountain, and the odd peacock or two – ensures Belvedere is a year-round hit. Dating back to the 17th century and once the summer ballroom of Holland House, the dining room is a real looker too. High ceilings and bags of art deco glitz with giant shell-like lampshades, bevelled mirrors, parquet flooring and cloister-style windows bring the va-va-voom, while white linen and modern leather seating provide the comforts. A marble staircase sweeps up to a mezzanine and a much-sort-after terrace overlooking the gardens, and a slinky bar adds further kudos. The room and setting may be the real draw, but the accomplished Anglo-French brasserie cooking certainly plays its part. Take the freshest Cornish pollack served on curly kale and crushed new potatoes with star-turn shrimp beurre noisette, or succulent roast lamb rump with classic pommes boulangère, haricots verts and rosemary jus. A top-value jour menu delivers all the glam at lunch and early evening without gold-card pricing.

Chef Gary O'Sullivan **Owner** Jimmy Lahoud **Seats** 90
Times 12-2.30/6-10.30, Closed 26 Dec, 1 Jan, D Sun **Prices** Prices not confirmed **Wines** 120 bottles over £30, 12 bottles under £30, 12 by glass **Parking** Council car park **Notes** Wknds L menu 3 course £27.50/£29.50 (summer), Sunday L, Vegetarian available, Children welcome

LONDON W8 *continued*

Clarke's
PLAN 4 A6

◎◎ Modern British, Mediterranean

tel: 020 7221 9225 **124 Kensington Church St W8 4BH**
email: restaurant@sallyclarke.com
dir: *Nearest station: Notting Hill Gate*

Full-on flavours chez Sally

Sally Clarke's eponymous restaurant is on two levels: a light-filled ground-floor room and a larger basement with an open-to-view kitchen. Her cooking is founded on the best, freshest produce available in the markets each day, which means the menu changes at each session, and focuses on the integrity of that produce. Vegetables, herbs and salad leaves are often brought from Sally's own garden, the last going into a typical, clear-tasting starter with mozzarella, pears and blood orange with citrus dressing, or a heartier one of rare-roast duck breast and grilled heart with balsamic and beetroot dressing. Main-course meats and fish are often chargrilled or roasted to bring out the maximum flavour: a large veal chop, precisely grilled, for instance, with well-chosen vegetables, or roast monkfish tail with anchovy salsa verde, baked artichoke and désirée potatoes. Imaginative puddings could run to rhubarb trifle or chocolate tart, its pastry light and crisp.

Chef Sally Clarke **Owner** Sally Clarke **Seats** 90, Pr/dining room 30
Times 12.30-2.30/6.30-10, Closed 8 days Xmas & New Year, 2 wks Aug, Sun
Prices Fixed L 2 course £25, Fixed D 3 course £39, Starter £7.50-£13, Main £19-£29, Dessert £7.50-£8.50 **Wines** 80 bottles over £30, 10 bottles under £30, 8 by glass **Parking** On street **Notes** Breakfast, Vegetarian available, Children welcome

Kensington Place
PLAN 4 A6

◎◎ British

tel: 020 7727 3184 **201-209 Kensington Church St W8 7LX**
email: kensingtonplace@danddlondon.com **web:** www.kensingtonplace-restaurant.com
dir: *Nearest station: Notting Hill Gate*

Bustling seafood brasserie next door to the fishmonger's

The long-running glass-fronted brasserie on Church Street is a component part of London's restaurant heritage. It set the pace for a new brisk informality in high-end dining when it opened in 1987, and the mood has been sustained into the 21st century with a seafood-based menu, the orientation emphasised by the fishmonger next door. In an atmosphere of infectious buzz, with a checkerboard tiled floor and a large communal table for the sociably inclined, the various catches of the day receive their due credit. Main dishes take in sea bream on pearl barley with beech mushrooms and turnips, a distinctly filling partnership of roast hake with a smoked haddock fishcake and garlic sausage, or good old beer-battered fish and chips with tartare sauce. Kick things off with a textbook fish soup, served with rouille, croutons and gruyère, and happiness is assured. Meatheads might prefer a main such as braised suckling pig with black pudding and a pasty of smoked ham hock, while all

are reunited for populist desserts like sponge-topped dark chocolate mousse with peanut praline and milk ice cream.

Kensington Place

Chef Daniel Loftin **Owner** D & D London **Seats** 110, Pr/dining room 40
Times 12-3/6.30-10.30, Closed 24-25 Dec, 1 Jan, BHs, L Mon, D Sun **Prices** Prices not confirmed **Wines** 50 bottles over £30, 13 bottles under £30, 28 by glass **Parking** On street **Notes** Sunday L, Vegetarian available, Children welcome

Kitchen W8
PLAN 4 A4

◎◎◎ – *see opposite*

Launceston Place
PLAN 4 C4

see page 392

The Milestone Hotel
PLAN 4 B5

◎◎ Modern British ♦ NOTABLE WINE LIST

tel: 020 7917 1000 **1 Kensington Court W8 5DL**
email: bookms@rchmail.com **web:** www.milestonehotel.com
dir: *Nearest station: High St Kensington*

Unreconstructed haute cuisine in patterned luxury

The old cast-iron London milestone that stands next to the hotel explains its name. Home to what was called as a lunatic asylum in the Victorian era, it's a stolid red-brick corner edifice in affluent Kensington, with traditionally styled interiors that don't give any quarter in piling on all the flounce and vividly patterned luxury you could ask for. Formal service in the lead-windowed Cheneston dining room extends to a commis chef on hand to carve from the roast-of-the-day trolley, and the bulk of the carte's business is painstakingly rendered versions of the haute cuisine of yesteryear. A prawn and crayfish cocktail with brown bread and lemon is spanking-fresh and richly dressed, and might precede fried tenderloin and slow-roasted belly of Dingley Dell pork, which has perfect crackling, well-seasoned potato galette and a fortifying jus. Finish with a chocolate study that combines a smooth dark parfait, deeply rich mini brownies, a crisp tuile and butterscotch sauce. Incidentals offer a nod to modernism with foaming appetisers and pre-desserts, the latter perhaps lemon curd mousse under yogurt froth.

Chef Alexandras Diamantis **Owner** Red Carnation Hotels **Seats** 30, Pr/dining room 8
Times 12-3/5.30-11 **Prices** Prices not confirmed **Wines** 200 bottles over £30, 10 bottles under £30, 12 by glass **Parking** NCP Young St off Kensington High St **Notes** Vegetarian available, Children welcome

Min Jiang
PLAN 4 B5

◎◎◎ – *see page 393 and advert on page 394*

Park Terrace Restaurant

PLAN 4 B5

@ @ Modern Seasonal

tel: 020 7361 1999 **Royal Garden Hotel, 2-24 Kensington High St W8 4PT**
email: reservations@parkterracerestaurant.co.uk web: www.parkterracerestaurant.co.uk
dir: *Nearest station: High St Kensington*

Sophisticated modern British cuisine overlooking Kensington Gardens

With its leafy views over Kensington Gardens, the upscale Royal Garden Hotel's location takes some beating as a central London base, and its aptly-named Park Terrace comes with those views through floor-to-ceiling windows the full length of the room. On the ground floor just off the swanky, marble-floored foyer, it is the more casual dining option (the other being glamorous Min Jiang, up on the 10th floor). The contemporary decor cleverly reflects the park-life theme, with a natural colour palate, wood veneer and large black-and-white images of trees. Steve

Munkley's modern British cooking is light, clear-flavoured and uncomplicated, and shows a strong commitment to local British suppliers and seasonality. Seared sesame-crusted tuna is matched with a palate-sharpening Bloody Mary sorbet, followed by chargrilled T-bone of halibut, crispy cod's cheek, Lyonnaise potatoes, asparagus and tartare sauce, and to finish, there's prune and Cognac double-baked soufflé with brandy cream. Service is smartly attired, clued-up and friendly, while the value lunch keeps the Kensington locals on-side.

Park Terrace Restaurant

Chef Steve Munkley **Owner** Goodwood Group **Seats** 90, Pr/dining room 40 **Times** 12-10.30, All-day dining **Prices** Fixed L 2 course £16.50, Fixed D 3 course £37.50, Service optional **Wines** 70 bottles over £30, 6 bottles under £30, 13 by glass **Parking** 200 **Notes** Pre-theatre menu, Afternoon tea, Lounge menu, Sunday L £21-£26, Vegetarian available, Children welcome

See advert on page 395

Kitchen W8 @@@

LONDON W8

PLAN 4 A4

Modern British
tel: 020 7937 0120 **11-13 Abingdon Rd, Kensington W8 6AH**
email: info@kitchenw8.com
dir: *Nearest station: High St Kensington*

Exciting modern cooking in a neighbourhood star

The smart black façade and awning hint that you're in for something a bit special at Kitchen W8, and expectations are borne out by the equally slick interior: striking art on the walls, good-looking upholstered chairs at linen-swathed tables, and an overall feel of well-designed class. It's a pretty cool and upmarket neighbourhood restaurant (well, this is Kensington after all) as envisaged by the partnership of Philip Howard (holder of 4 Rosettes at The Square in Mayfair) and Rebecca Mascarenhas (of Sonny's in Barnes), whose aim is to produce knockout food and keep the prices down – the latter objective is achieved by set lunch and early dinner deals that offer some of the best value eating in the capital. This menu is a treasury of bright modern ideas, ingredients are of the first order, and the amount of effort that goes on in the kitchen is clear. Deeply satisfying starters might include barbecued glazed quail with rhubarb, spiced bread, pickled turnips and foie gras, or thin slices of smoked eel partnered with grilled mackerel, golden beetroot and

sweet mustard. At main course stage, ideas such as slow-poached cod with razor clams, herb farfalle, chorizo, sea kale and cider, and Ibérico pork chop sauced with a sherry reduction alongside smoked celeriac, charred pear and bacon dauphine show a real flair for how flavours and textures work together. For dessert, perhaps Yorkshire rhubarb with crème fraîche custard, blood orange and stem ginger, or a pavé of chocolate and beurre noisette with hazelnuts and salt caramel doughnuts. The intelligent wine list has around 20 choices by the glass and 250ml carafe and on Sunday there is an amnesty on corkage for BYO-ers.

Chef Mark Kempson **Owner** Philip Howard, Rebecca Mascarenhas **Seats** 75 **Times** 12-2.30/6-10, Closed 25-26 Dec, BHs **Prices** Fixed L 2 course £20, Fixed D 3 course £25, Tasting menu £60, Starter £8.95-£15.95, Main £19.95-£27.50, Dessert £5.95-£8.50 **Wines** 110 bottles over £30, 10 bottles under £30, 14 by glass **Parking** On street, NCP High St **Notes** Fixed D 6-7pm 2/3 course £22/£25, Sunday L £28-£32.50, Vegetarian available, Children welcome

Launceston Place

LONDON W8   **PLAN 4 C4**

Modern European 🍷 NOTABLE WINE LIST

tel: 020 7937 6912 **1a Launceston Place W8 5RL**
email: launcestonplace@danddlondon.com
dir: *Nearest station: Gloucester Rd, High St Kensington*

Dynamic modern cooking in a genteel Kensington mews

The Rosette award for this establishment has been suspended due to a change of chef. Reassessment will take place in due course under the new chef. Launceston Place has long had a reputation as a destination for good food, but right now it's enjoying a place at the top table. With Tim Allen at the stoves, this leafy part of South Ken has a restaurant that can hold its own with the best the capital has to offer. The location on the corner of an upmarket mews (just about everything is upmarket around here), looks ordinary enough, consisting of four Victorian houses that could be mistaken for a jazzed-up boozer or a smart neighbourhood joint. But once you're over the threshold, and the first-class service team swings into action, it's clear there's nothing ordinary about Launceston Place. The interior design is certainly in keeping with the postcode, with the series of spaces done out in shades of grey with splashes of colour coming from the modern artworks on the walls. The carte (market menu) and tasting option are packed with prime British ingredients that arrive at the table looking absolutely top drawer, which is also the case for dishes from the very good value set lunch option. A starter of quail consists of two breasts topped with truffles and crab apple (looking like fish scales), while two quails eggs arrive hidden under a cloche – the big reveal delivering a smoky hit of hay. Add to that some corn in various textures and a hit of acidity from verjus, and we're off to a flyer. A main course English veal rump, with three ravioli filled with truffled cream cheese, smoked grelot onions and some tête de veau doesn't need any theatre to show its class. Another course matches fillet of plaice with linguine and a crab sauce with sea purslane. There's no let-up in the intensity of flavours and technical virtuosity when it comes to the sweet stages either, not if raspberry delice with aerated white chocolate and a silky smooth quenelle of white chocolate ice cream is anything to judge by. Another dessert offers a refined hit of citrus in the form of a bergamot soufflé and its accompanying lemon curd ice cream. Head sommelier Agustin Trapero and his team have put together an exceptional wine list that champions smaller producers and has a particularly cracking selection from Burgundy.

Owner D & D London **Seats** 50, Pr/dining room 10
Times 12-2.30/6-10, Closed Xmas, New Year, Etr, Mon, L Tue
Prices Fixed L 3 course fr £30, Fixed D 3 course fr £55, Tasting menu fr £70, Starter £21, Main £30, Dessert £12 **Wines** 352 bottles over £30, 4 bottles under £30, 15 by glass **Parking** On street, car park off Kensington High St **Notes** ALC prices for L only, Market menu 3 course £55, Sunday L fr £35, Vegetarian available, Children welcome

Min Jiang 🏵🏵🏵

LONDON W8   PLAN 4 B5

Chinese

tel: 020 7361 1988 **2-24 Kensington High St W8 4PT**
email: reservations@minjiang.co.uk **web:** www.minjiang.co.uk
dir: *Nearest station: High St Kensington*

Stylish and authentic Chinese cuisine overlooking Hyde Park

Seen from up on the 10th floor of the swanky Royal Garden Hotel, the splendid views across the treetops of Hyde Park and Kensington Gardens to the city skyscrapers spearing the skyline are worth the price of a lunch at Min Jiang. That magnificent cityscape is no longer such a draw after dark, of course, but the strikingly stylish dining room featuring blue-and-white Chinese porcelain, red lacquered walls hung with black-and-white photos, and tables swathed in crisp white linen is none too shabby a sight, and the service is proficient and ready with guidance on the ins and outs of the menu. Whatever the time of day, the food doesn't take a backseat to the surroundings. Upscale Chinese cuisine in five-star hotels is not always the best idea (the risk is that you find yourself eating sweet-and-sour pork at about ten times what it would cost in Chinatown), but here, authenticity in ingredients, seasonings and timings is assured. Dim sum make a fine introduction, including fried cuttlefish cake with sweet basil and lemongrass, and pan-fried lobster buns, all perfectly textured and feather-light. Fans of Beijing duck should consider the kitchen's take on this classic, the wood-fired meat served in a series of imaginative presentations. Otherwise, go for main items such as steamed sea bass with preserved turnip and dried shrimp in soy sauce, or venison fillet in cumin and pepper sauce, with a side dish perhaps of egg fried rice with blue swimmer crab and asparagus. There are great desserts too, as a creative modern approach here produces jackfruit cheesecake with caramelised cashews and pandan ice cream, or poached black sesame dumplings.

Chef Weng Han Wong, Steve Munkley **Owner** Goodwood Group **Seats** 100, Pr/dining room 20 **Times** 12-3/6-10.30, **Prices** Starter £7-£15, Main £12-£62.50, Dessert £6.50-£14.50, Service optional **Wines** 133 bottles over £30, 4 bottles under £30, 15 by glass **Parking** 200 **Notes** Dim Sum Menu, Vegetarian available, Children welcome

LONDON W8 *continued*

Pavilion Restaurant
PLAN 4 B5

◉◉ Modern British **NEW**

tel: 020 7221 2000 & 7993 7170 **96 Kensington High St W8 4SG**
email: reservations@kensingtonpavilion.com
dir: *Nearest station: High St Kensington*

A glitzy Kensington club with cooking to match

A restaurant open to all in a very Kensington private members' club has all the cachet one could hope for. It has its own little florist at the entrance, and a bakery and deli counter within. This all takes place in a dramatically glitzy series of spaces, with a swirling white staircase descending into the lounge, bar seating in screaming lemon, and a covered patio area for fair-weather dining. Adam Simmonds (once of Danesfield House, Buckinghamshire) takes up the kitchen reins here, overseeing a sizeable brigade producing resourceful, ingenious modern British cookery of the latest vintage. First up could be a deeply satisfying serving of smoked eel with beetroot and a high-octane caper and raisin purée, or else a something-for-everyone assemblage of pork belly, langoustine, home-made black pudding, smoked pineapple and lardo. Outstanding fish might include poached halibut with hay-baked celeriac, pickled onion and Granny Smith in beurre blanc. One glance at the meat displays is enough to inspire confidence in the steaks, which come with such accoutrements as whipped bone marrow and truffle salad, or there may be venison with its own sausage in 70% Guanaja chocolate. Dessert might include tarte Tatin or pear and cinnamon rice pudding with pear sorbet.

Chef Adam Simmonds **Times** 12-2.30/6.30-10 **Prices** Fixed L 2 course £20.50, Starter £7.50-£11.95, Main £13.95-£32.50, Dessert £7-£8 **Wines** 77 bottles over £30, 20 bottles under £30, 12 by glass **Notes** Breakfast, Children 12 yrs+

Use the maps on pages 260–70

LONDON W9

The Truscott Arms
PLAN 2 B4

◉◉ Modern British **NEW** 🍷 NOTABLE WINE LIST

tel: 020 7266 9198 **55 Shirland Rd, Maida Vale W9 2JD**
email: joinus@thetruscottarms.com **web:** www.thetruscottarms.com
dir: *Nearest station: Warwick Ave*

Classy made-over pub with contemporary flavour

The Truscott Arms has been done up with a designer's eye for matching old and new, so the five-storey Victorian property kept all of its charm while being brought lovingly into the 21st century. It operates as a proper pub, with one of the ground-floor rooms offering up London ales, the main restaurant upstairs, and an outside terrace with funky coloured tables and chairs. Genuine effort is made to give the menu a regional flavour and sourcing and sustainability are taken seriously. Start with veal sweetbreads flavoured with lavender honey or some Wye Valley asparagus with morels, almonds and bergamot. Among main courses, South Downs lamb (neck and tongue) are partnered with a host of fresh British vegetables, and halibut gets a lovely smoky flavour from its accompanying smoked clams. There's a tasting menu with accompanying wine flight, too. Finish with an egg with Bartlett (or Williams) pear and perry sorbet, or a wild strawberry number with meringues and black pepper crumble.

Chef Aidan McGee **Owner** Andrew & Mary Jane Fishwick **Seats** 52, Pr/dining room 34 **Times** 12-4/6-11, Closed Mon-Tue **Prices** Fixed L 2 course £22, Fixed D 3 course £34 **Wines** 151 bottles over £30, 79 bottles under £30, 32 by glass **Parking** On street **Notes** Sunday L £12-£18, Vegetarian available, Children welcome

LONDON W10

The Dock Kitchen
PLAN 1 D4

Modern International

tel: 020 8962 1610 **Portobello Docks, 342/344 Ladbroke Grove W10 5BU**
email: reception@dockkitchen.co.uk
dir: *Nearest station: Ladbroke Grove, Kensal Rise, Kensal Green*

Appealingly eclectic cooking by the canal

A one-time pop-up outfit – at Tom Dixon's furniture design gallery – The Dock Kitchen sits snug by the Grand Union Canal and has become a Ladbroke Grove fixture. The long, narrow dining space has a chilled-out warehouse vibe, complete with central open kitchen and floor-to-ceiling windows offering waterway views. Otherwise, exposed brick and dangling lamps provide the on-trend looks, while Dixon's furniture gets public exposure via funky wooden chairs and bare metal tables. Stevie Parle's kitchen showcases global flavours and ingredients inspired by his travels, with influences as far and wide as the Med, Middle East or South America. Take a spicy attitude Mexican birria (stew) of top-drawer monkfish, cod and octopus served with a Mexican winter salad and corn tortillas, or perhaps Chinese pork knuckle (for two) teamed with grilled leeks, cucumber pickle, ground peanuts and jasmine. Finish with a moist, textbook pistachio and nutmeg cake and saffron yogurt or Amalfi lemon tart. The alfresco terrace is another crowd pleaser.

Times 12-2.30/7-9.30, Closed Xmas, BHs, D Sun

LONDON W11

E&O
PLAN 1 D4

Pan-Asian

tel: 020 7229 5454 **14 Blenheim Crescent, Notting Hill W11 1NN**
email: eando@rickerrestaurants.com
dir: *Nearest station: Notting Hill Gate, Ladbroke Grove*

East Asian grazing plates for the Notting Hill cognoscenti

The concept may not have changed much at this west London outpost of Will Ricker's era-defining Pan-Asian grazing-plate venue (the others being Eight Over Eight and XO), but E&O still rocks and is trend-central with the Notting Hill hangers-out and fashionistas. The decor may be a bit scuffed these days, but the high-octane vibe (ramped-up by a lively front bar) puts the experience-factor in overdrive. The chocolate brown and cream colour palette is on trend, with leather seating, louvered screening, oversized oriental-style lighting and paper-clothed tables. The young-at-heart pack the place for the fashionable, well-conceived Pan-Asian cuisine alongside some great cocktails. All the classics are here; sushi and sashimi (perhaps a spicy tuna roll) or tempura (avocado and sweet potato), while top-dollar back cod with sweet miso cranks up the ante, and a lychee and mango green curry the spice attitude. Alfresco street-side tables are a fair-weather top-call also.

Times 12-3/6-11, Closed 25-26 Dec, 1 Jan, Aug BH

Edera
PLAN 1 D3

Modern Italian

tel: 020 7221 6090 **148 Holland Park Av W11 4UE**
email: roberto@edera.co.uk
dir: *Nearest station: Holland Park*

Well-liked neighbourhood Italian in leafy Holland Park

Decked out on tiered levels, with blond-wood floors, light walls hung with big mirrors and linen-dressed tables, this minimally-styled Holland Park eatery pulls in a well-heeled crowd for its fashionable Sardinian-accented Italian cooking. Pavement tables fill early on warm sunny days despite traffic passing close by. The kitchen certainly knows its stuff, keeping things simple and straightforward, allowing the excellent ingredients to speak for themselves. There is much that is

familiar from the Italian mainland, bolstered by a daily specials list featuring the likes of chargrilled sea bream with courgettes and basil oil, and baked salted sea bass with potato salad, but the chef is Sardinian, so there might be spaghetti with grey mullet roe, plus Sicilian cannoli for pudding.

Chef Carlo Usai **Owner** A-Z Ltd/Mr Pisano **Seats** 70, Pr/dining room 20 **Times** 12-11, All-day dining, Closed 25-26 & 31 Dec **Prices** Prices not confirmed **Wines** 13 by glass **Parking** On street parking **Notes** Black truffle menu all year, White truffle menu in season, Children welcome

The Ledbury
PLAN 1 E4

@@@@ – see page 398

Lonsdale
PLAN 1 E4

Modern British

tel: 020 7727 4080 **48 Lonsdale Rd W11 2DE**
email: info@thelonsdale.co.uk
dir: *Nearest station: Notting Hill, Ladbroke Grove*

Trendy Notting Hill lounge bar dining

Tucked away on a residential street, this hip Notting Hill/Westbourne Grove hangout is an uptempo evenings-only affair. The lively front bar gets rammed on busy nights, with cocktails and fizz de rigueur before moving on to the equally funky lounge-style dining area behind. Red mock-croc, low-backed banquettes, darkwood tables, gold walls and a centrepiece light feature deliver a low-lit nightclub vibe for a backing track of trendy music, youthful service and high decibels. The equally well-dressed but straightforward cooking is driven by quality ingredients and suits the mood; perhaps haunch of venison with juniper and chocolate sauce or pan-roasted sea bass with a fricassée of mussels, samphire and sorrel. Steaks from the Lake District (35-day hung) and starters such as black figs with Gervic goats' cheese fit the bill.

Times 6-12, Closed 25-26 Dec, 1 Jan, Sun-Mon, L all week

LONDON W14

Cibo
PLAN 1 D3

@@ Italian

tel: 020 7371 2085 & 7371 6271 **3 Russell Gardens W14 8EZ**
email: ciborestaurant@aol.com
dir: *Nearest station: Olympia, Shepherd's Bush*

W14's friendly and highly individual Italian flagship

The epitome of the authentic neighbourhood Italian, long-serving Cibo is still a big hit with the savvy Holland Park-ers. Unassumingly tucked away in a little parade of shops and eateries, the modern glass-fronted venue is unexpectedly arty and shabby-chic inside; a 'one-off' with its wacky nude reliefs and huge mirrors dominating walls, and colourful ceramic vases lining the service bar. White linen proves the perfect backcloth for oversized, equally colourful dining plates, while sunny-natured Italian staff and all-Italian wines transport you straight to their homeland. Breads – from carta di musica to focaccia – and nibbles like olives and mini pizzas raise expectation from the off. Pasta is the real deal too – perhaps ravioli filled with well-flavoured duck in a wild mushroom sauce, while starters like marinated roast peppers, courgettes and aubergines, teamed with creamy mozzarella shout of the Mediterranean too. This is classically simple, skilful Italian cooking showing due respect of prime ingredients, flavour and precision. Mains like sparkling grilled swordfish simply served alongside baby tomatoes, olives and capers, and desserts (classics such as pannacotta and tiramisù) are equally convincing classics.

Chef Piero Borrell **Owner** Gino Taddei, C Pertini **Seats** 50, Pr/dining room 14 **Times** 12.15-3/6.15-10.30, Closed Xmas, Etr BHs, Sun, L Sat **Prices** Fixed L 2 course £19.50, Starter £8-£13, Main £13-£24, Dessert £5.50-£8 **Wines** 26 bottles under £30, 4 by glass **Parking** On street **Notes** Vegetarian available, Children welcome

LONDON WC1

The Montague on the Gardens

PLAN 3 B3

@ British

tel: 020 7612 8416 & 7612 8412 **15 Montague St, Bloomsbury WC1B 5BJ**
email: aarapi@rchmail.com **web:** www.montaguehotel.com
dir: *Nearest station: Russell Sq, Holborn, Tottenham Court Rd*

Stylish hotel bistro with modern comfort classics

The bowler-hatted doorman at the entrance is a clue that this is a classy boutique hotel, on a quiet street around the corner from the British Museum. Its Blue Door Bistro is a welcoming and informal dining room, decorated on three sides by a frieze depicting London in around 1850. There's mahogany panelling, with contemporary wall lights and good use of mirrored glass and flowers on clothed dining tables. Simplicity is the kitchen's byword, producing starters such as a signature bowl of chicken noodle soup, and a portion of smoked salmon with beetroot salad and horseradish cream. Quality produce is treated with good judgement, seen in main courses like haddock fillet in crisp and golden beer batter, served with mushy peas, chips and notably good tartare sauce, and ham-wrapped chicken breast accompanied by olives, green beans and cherry tomatoes. End with an upbeat dessert like pear and chocolate tart.

Chef Martin Halls **Owner** Red Carnation Hotels **Seats** 40, Pr/dining room 100 **Times** 12.30-2.30/5.30-10.30 **Prices** Fixed L 2 course fr £25, Fixed D 3 course fr £28, Starter £6-£11, Main £14-£38, Dessert £6-£10 **Wines** 61 bottles over £30, 25 bottles under £30, 24 by glass **Parking** On street, Bloomsbury Sq **Notes** Pretheatre 2/3 course £16.50/£19.50, Sunday L £14-£38, Vegetarian available, Children welcome

Otto's French Restaurant

PLAN 3 C4

@@ Classic French **NEW**

tel: 020 7713 0107 **182 Gray's Inn Rd WC1X 8EW**
email: enquiries@ottos-restaurant.com
dir: *Nearest station: Chancery Lane*

Classic French cooking with old school service

Otto Albert Tepassé worked for years in notable Gallic establishments both in London and France, but he opened his eponymous restaurant close to Chancery Lane in 2011. Small, intimate and owner-run, this resolutely old-school French restaurant feels like it has been here for decades, mainly due to the appreciative regulars who flock here and the timeless decor, complete with culinary gadgets used for classic dishes still prepared at the table. As befits a traditional French restaurant, the wine list is hefty in both range and price and the food displays confident cooking skills, high quality ingredients and the type of heavy saucing you rarely encounter this side of the Channel. Fresh ravioli of snails marinated in Chablis served with bordelaise red wine sauce with bone marrow, Bayonne ham and mushrooms makes for a rich start to a meal, particularly if followed by the showstopping canard de Rouen à la pressé, finished off at the table by Otto himself. Leave room for classic tarte Tatin and crème anglaise.

Chef Luca Puzzoli **Owner** Otto Tepassé, Elin Hansen **Seats** 45, Pr/dining room 30 **Times** 12-3/6-10, Closed Xmas, BHs, Sun, L Sat **Prices** Fixed L 2 course fr £24 **Wines** 200 bottles over £30, 20 bottles under £30, 10 by glass **Parking** On street **Notes** Children 8 yrs+

The Ledbury ✿✿✿✿

LONDON W11   **PLAN 1 E4**

British, French **V** 🍾 **NOTABLE WINE LIST**

tel: 020 7792 9090 **127 Ledbury Rd W11 2AQ**
email: info@theledbury.com
dir: *Nearest station: Westbourne Park, Notting Hill Gate*

Imaginative cooking from a supremely talented chef

Brett Graham started his career working in a fish restaurant in
Newcastle, New South Wales, where the Hunter River meets the
Pacific Ocean. He's been a shining star in the UK's culinary
firmament for over a decade now, with The Ledbury well and truly
established as one of London's top dining destinations. It looks
rather exclusive from the outside, with its smart frontage guarded
by an array of plantings that shield anyone sitting on the small
terrace from the street action (which is generally fairly low-key
anyway). The room feels bigger than it really is thanks to the
judicious use of mirrors, with the well-dressed tables spread
evenly around the contemporarily neutral space – creamy pastel
shades, modern artworks and shimmering chandeliers. A balance
is struck between professionally formal service and a softer more
approachable manner, which is perhaps what you might expect
with an Australian in charge. Choose from the carte, tasting menu
and set lunch option, and expect stunningly attractive plates of
divertingly contemporary and compelling food. The à la carte menu
is set up to encourage four courses (at a fixed price). You might
start with an inspired 'first' of Chantilly of oyster with a tartare of
sea bream and frozen English wasabi, or white beetroot baked in
clay, flavoured with caviar salt and served with smoked and dried
eel. 'Second' offers up rabbit shoulder with lentil cream and
chanterelles, or roast scallops seductively partnered with pumpkin,
mandarin and ginger. Moving on to 'third', fillet of sea brass
arrives with brassicas, seaweed and sake, while Herdwick lamb
comes with salt-baked kohlrabi and fiery padron peppers. There's
no less invention and acute technical skill evident in 'fourth' (or
dessert), with a thrilling brown sugar tart with stem ginger ice
cream, or another that combines an olive oil cake with blood
orange, white chocolate and tea. If you're already feeling full,
divert your eyes from the cheese trolley for it will surely seduce you.
The excellent wine list favours France while embracing the entire
world, and also includes a range of sake and non-alcoholic
cocktails – do make use of the excellent sommelier. The set lunch
menu isn't cheap, but it is a useful entry point if you want to try
Brett's food for pretty much half the price of the carte.

Chef Brett Graham **Owner** Nigel Platts-Martin, Brett Graham,
Philip Howard **Seats** 55 **Times** 12-2/6.30-9.45, Closed 25-26 Dec,
Aug BH, L Mon-Tue **Prices** Tasting menu £115 **Wines** 819 bottles
over £30, 10 bottles under £30, 16 by glass **Parking** Talbot St
Notes Fri-Sun evening tasting menu only, 4 course L/D £50/£95,
Sunday L £85, Children welcome

LONDON WC1 *continued*

Rosewood London
PLAN 3 C3

◉◉ Modern European

tel: 020 3747 8620 & 3747 8621 **252 High Holborn WC1V 7EN**
email: mirrorroom@rosewoodhotels.com **web:** www.rosewoodhotels.com/london
dir: *Nearest station: Holborn*

British heritage cookery in a magnificently restored building

Once the headquarters of the Pearl Assurance company, the magnificent building on High Holborn was begun on the eve of the Great War, and gradually took shape over half a century. In consultation with English Heritage, its fine façades, original banking halls and grand staircase have been restored to glory, and the entrance into a domed courtyard would have been suitable for the horse-drawn carriages of the Georgian era. It's a fitting venue for a Rosewood hotel, the old East Banking Hall with its soaring marble pillars now seeing service as a modernistically grand restaurant, with bars at either end for counter dining. A brasserie menu of traditional British dishes that have been gently coaxed into the present day offers the likes of Dublin Bay prawns in mayonnaise, Marie Rose shellfish cocktail with avocado, or fried squid with Gentleman's Relish to start. Majestic follow-ups follow, such as roast beef rib, served with a fine, deeply flavoured gravy and crisp onion rings, or perfectly timed, garlic-buttered grilled lobster with sea vegetables and chips. There is the odd surprise – a shrimp burger with jalapeño tartare – but the essential repertoire contains nothing that would have baffled Mrs Beeton. Baked rice pudding with a blob of blackcurrant jam, sherried-up trifle, or banana with custard, are the pleasantest ways of harking back.

Chef Amandine Chaignot **Owner** Rosewood Hotel London **Seats** 70, Pr/dining room 20 **Times** 12-2.30/6.30-10 **Prices** Fixed L 2 course £28, Fixed D 3 course £35, Starter £12-£22, Main £19-£29, Dessert £7-£12 **Wines** 350 bottles over £30, 4 bottles under £30, 16 by glass **Parking** 12 **Notes** Afternoon tea, Sunday L £40, Vegetarian available, Children welcome

■ LONDON WC2

L'Atelier de Joël Robuchon
PLAN 3 A2

◉◉◉ – *see below*

Balthazar
PLAN 3 B1

◉ French, European

tel: 020 3301 1155 **4-6 Russell St WC2B 5HZ**
email: info@balthazarlondon.com
dir: *Nearest station: Covent Garden*

All-day French brasserie fare and a high-energy atmosphere

Just off the Covent Garden piazza, the London offshoot of the legendary New York brasserie has played to packed houses ever since it opened in 2013. It's a real looker, a large, high-ceilinged room decked out with mosaic floors, darkwood panelling, art deco lighting, red-leather banquettes and giant antique mirrors. And with an army of sunny natured staff, a swanky bar, and a constant turnover of animatedly enthusiastic diners, the place really rocks. It's an all-day affair, buzzing from breakfast through to lunch, afternoon tea and dinner with menus delivering a crowd-pleasing line-up of classic French brasserie fare, from snails with garlic butter to salad Niçoise and moules frites, as well as a more up-to-date roasted stone bass with artichoke purée, smoked aubergine, baby fennel, and a tomato, basil and olive dressing. Desserts are exemplary renditions of comfort classics like crème brûlée or apple tarte Tatin.

Chef Robert Reed **Owner** Keith Minally **Seats** 175, Pr/dining room 60 **Times** 7.30am-mdnt, All-day dining, Closed 25 Dec **Prices** Fixed D 3 course fr £25, Starter £6-£11, Main £16-£33.50, Dessert £7-£10 **Wines** 100 bottles over £30, 20 bottles under £30 **Parking** NCP Parker St **Notes** Fixed D only 5-6.30pm & 10-11pm, Vegetarian available, Children welcome

---

L'Atelier de Joël Robuchon ◉◉◉

LONDON WC2
PLAN 3 A2

Modern French v
tel: 020 7010 8600 **13-15 West St WC2H 9NE**
email: info@joelrobuchon.co.uk
dir: *Nearest station: Leicester Sq, Covent Gdn, Tottenham Court Rd*

Innovative dining from a French master-chef in a glam setting

For those unfamiliar with the name, Monsieur Robuchon is a global culinary superstar who has spread his glamorous chain of Atelier-branded restaurants from France via London and Las Vegas to the mega-cities of the Far East. 'Atelier' means workshop and the London operation on the fringes of Covent Garden is as much like a workshop as Harrods is like, well, a corner shop. This is an achingly cool and glamorous venue with two dining areas and Le Salon Bar and Terrace for drinkies and snacks up on the roof. If you're in the mood for a bit of buzz around you, go for L'Atelier on the ground floor with its counter seats at the open kitchen, otherwise the more conventional table seating in the monochrome first-floor restaurant offers more intimacy. Staff field questions with great charm (advice on the bilingual menus may well be required) and the Franco-Mediterranean dishes, spiked here and there with exotic notes, come in either small tasting plate format, a traditional carte, or multi-

course tasting menus. The small plate listing might offer black cod with Malabar pepper sauce, pak choi and coconut foam, or minced pig's trotters with black truffles, while mains from the carte tend to be more mainstream ideas from the modern French repertoire – poached turbot with Portland clams, say, or seared venison loin with apple and grapefruit chutney. Spectacular desserts might take the form of a sphere of mandarin mousse and sorbet with a cinnamon 'cloud' and shortbread. It doesn't come cheap, but set lunch and pre- and post-theatre menus relieve some of the pain, while veggie alternatives will impress non-meat eaters.

Chef Xavier Boyer **Owner** Joel Robuchon **Seats** 43
Times 12-3/5.30-11, Closed Aug BH, 25 Dec, 1 Jan **Prices** Fixed L 2 course £31-£45, Tasting menu £95-£214 **Wines** 250 bottles over £30, 4 bottles under £30, 16 by glass **Parking** Valet parking service **Notes** Pre-theatre 2/3/4 course (with wine), Sunday L £36-£64, Children welcome

LONDON WC2 *continued*

Barrafina
PLAN 3 B1

◎◎ Modern Spanish NEW

tel: 020 7440 1456 & 7440 1450 **10 Adelaide St WC2N 4HZ**
email: jose@barrafina.co.uk
dir: *Nearest station: Charing Cross, Leicester Sq*

Vibrant spot for stunning tapas

The first Barrafina opened in Soho in 2007 with the second arriving on a busy corner in Covent Garden in 2014. It was worth the wait. Tapas is the name of the game and the place is cool, lively and packed to the rafters. The no booking policy means queues are likely (just like the very best places in Barcelona!) and the deal is you sit on a stool at the marble counter and tuck into small plates that are full of flavour and vitality. There are daily specials galore, superb cured meats and lots of things you've maybe not tried before. The crab croquetas should not be missed, there's milk-fed lamb's brains, fabulously fresh hake cooked on the plancha, deeply satisfying arroz de marisco, classic tortilla – the cooking is spot-on, the produce first class. Note the cost can creep up if you get carried away with the choices. Sweet courses offer no less satisfaction, and to drink there are excellent sherries and Spanish wines. The Hart brothers also run Fino and Quo Vadis.

Chef Nieves Barragán Mohacho **Owner** Sam & Eddie Hart **Seats** 29, Pr/dining room 32 **Times** 12-3/5-11, Closed Xmas, New Yr **Prices** Prices not confirmed, Service optional 12.5% **Wines** 10 bottles under £30, 21 by glass **Notes** Vegetarian available, Children welcome

Christopher's
PLAN 3 C1

◎ Contemporary American

tel: 020 7240 4222 **18 Wellington St, Covent Garden WC2E 7DD**
email: reservations@christophersgrill.com
dir: *Nearest station: Embankment, Covent Garden*

Lively Stateside eating in an elegant Covent Garden room

The long-running Christopher's, an American eatery on the fringes of Covent Garden, can hardly ever have looked so elegant as it has since its refurb in early 2013. High, elaborately corniced ceilings tower over the expansive main room, where chairs in grey and lemon are offset by purple drapes, not to mention stylishly attired staff. The kitchen turns out a menu of lively Stateside food, including the likes of blackened salmon and jambalaya risotto, BBQ-rubbed tip steaks of USDA beef, and pork belly with creamed corn and plantain blinis, with perhaps a side of Boston baked beans, or mac and cheese, optionally ritzed up with lobster. More off-piste dishes work well too, as in caramelised scallops with chorizo in orange-cardamom dressing, or an Italianate sea bass main course, served with roasted figs, ricotta and prosciutto, before all are reunited for gooey chocolate and peanut butter tart with salty caramel ice cream.

Times 12-3/5-11.30, Closed Xmas, 1 Jan

Cigalon
PLAN 3 D2

◎ French

tel: 020 7242 8373 **115 Chancery Ln WC2A 1PP**
email: bookings@cigalon.co.uk
dir: *Nearest station: Chancery Lane, Temple*

Provençal-style cooking in legal land

A former auction house in Chancery Lane makes for a surprisingly sunny setting during daylight hours, thanks mainly to its atrium-like glass ceiling, while olive trees and an abundance of warming Mediterranean colours inside allude to the fact that Cigalon focuses on the cuisine of Southern France and Corsica. There's even a soundtrack of chirpy birdsong and cicada. The chefs in the open-to-view kitchen make good use of the grill to create Provençal-inspired dishes such as grilled lamb

saddle with smoked anchovies and Swiss chard, or loin of venison with sage gnocchi and wild mushrooms. It's simple, full-flavoured stuff. A starter of chicken liver terrine comes with pickled veg to cut through the richness, while another sees cannelloni filled with beef from the Camargue (enriched with a red wine and bone marrow sauce). For dessert, tuck into dark chocolate tart with orange blossom ice cream. Baranis is their basement bar.

Chef Julien Carlon **Owner** Vincent Labeyrie **Seats** 60, Pr/dining room 8 **Times** 12-2.15/5.45-10, Closed Xmas, New Year, BHs, Sat-Sun **Prices** Fixed L 2 course £21.50, Fixed D 3 course £34.50, Starter £7.50-£13.50, Main £12-£22, Dessert £7-£8.50 **Wines** 83 bottles over £30, 20 bottles under £30, 10 by glass **Parking** On street **Notes** Vegetarian available, Children welcome

Clos Maggiore
PLAN 3 B1

◎◎◎ – *see opposite*

The Delaunay
PLAN 3 C2

◎ European

tel: 020 7499 8558 **55 Aldwych WC2B 4BB**
email: reservations@thedelaunay.com
dir: *Nearest station: Holborn, Covent Garden*

Brasserie dining in the grand European tradition

The Delaunay, like its ever-popular Piccadilly sibling, The Wolseley, was conceived in the style of the grand café-restaurants of central Europe, making a vibrant, glamorous spot, great for people watching, with slick, well-pitched service and an extensive all-day dining repertoire. Swish darkwood panelling, marble surfaces, linen-clothed tables and brass lighting set a classy tone, and the kitchen sends out an eclectic roll-call of things you actually want to eat – classic European comfort food rather than cheffy stuff chasing the latest trend. Start with sautéed pierogi dumplings with cottage cheese, sage, onion and paprika butter, then sea trout with summer vegetables and sorrel beurre blanc. If you're up for something more substantial, go for Hungarian Goulash or Wiener schnitzel, and don't think of skipping dessert when there's apple and gooseberry strudel or white and dark Bavarian chocolate cream up for grabs. The Counter – with a separate entrance – offers a takeaway service, including fabulous pâtisserie.

Times 11.30-mdnt, All-day dining

Les Deux Salons
PLAN 3 B1

◎◎ French

tel: 020 7420 2050 **40-42 William IV St WC2N 4DD**
email: info@lesdeuxsalons.co.uk
dir: *Nearest station: Charing Cross, Leicester Sq*

Authentic French brasserie menu in the heart of theatreland

A revamp at Les Deux Salons in 2014 has added a coffee shop and all-day dining area on the ground floor (complete with two large communal tables). There's a little more refinement upstairs, with white linen on the tables and rather more space between the tables. The French-focused repertoire extends to entrées such as a simple plate of first-rate charcuterie, an artisanal black pudding served with a fried egg, and snail and bacon pie. Next up, the Josper oven provides the prime protein in the shape of bavette steak and frites and 300 grams of côtes de veau with truffle honey, or alternatively go for a lighter option such as lemon sole meunière. A sharing option might be rack of Welsh lamb with fondant potato, confit garlic and rosemary jus. Finish in classic brasserie style with ile flottante or the tart of the day. The lunchtime and early evening prix-fixe menu is particularly useful in this part of town.

Chef Barry Tonks **Owner** Prescott and Conran **Seats** 160, Pr/dining room 34 **Times** 12-11, All-day dining, Closed 25-26 Dec, 1 Jan, D Sun **Prices** Fixed L 2 course £17, Fixed D 3 course £20, Starter £4.95-£12.50, Main £14.50-£30, Dessert £3.95-£6.95 **Wines** 37 bottles over £30, 11 bottles under £30, 28 by glass **Parking** On street **Notes** Sunday L, Vegetarian available, Children welcome

Clos Maggiore 🏵️🏵️🏵️

LONDON WC2   **PLAN 3 B1**

French, Mediterranean V 🍷 NOTABLE WINE LIST

tel: 020 7379 9696 **33 King St, Covent Garden WC2E 8JD**
email: enquiries@closmaggiore.com **web:** www.closmaggiore.com
dir: *Nearest station: Covent Garden, Leicester Sq*

An intimate oasis in the heart of Covent Garden

Clos Maggiore is probably best known for its charming courtyard garden, and when the retractable roof is opened up to reveal the sky – blue, black or somewhere in-between – it's easy to imagine you're in Provence or Tuscany. But it's more than just London's alfresco gem, for Marcellin Marc and his team deliver persuasive modern French cuisine that also takes inspiration from the broader Mediterranean region. If you can't secure a table in the courtyard, or the roof is closed due to inclement weather, Clos Maggiore still has much to offer, and still feels soothingly romantic – soft lighting, smarty set tables and an elegant sheen. Pre- and post-theatre menus are useful additions given this is Covent Garden and a host of shows are on within a short walk, while there's a tasting menu if you intend sticking around (including an excellent vegetarian version). The à la carte menu offers a good choice at this level of attainment. Start with tortellini luxuriously filled with Maine lobster, scallop and king prawn, served with a roasted langoustine, or an equally indulgent roasted duck foie gras with crisp confit duck leg, its richness cut by forced rhubarb and Minus 8 vinegar from Canada. If you'd prefer something lighter, go for a salad of seasonal green leaves and herbs with black truffle vinaigrette. Among main courses, Welsh lamb (rack and slow-cooked shank) stars in a dish with fennel, asparagus and macerated golden raisins, while pan-roasted Cornish sea bass arrives with morels and broad bean étuvée. The craft and creativity continues with desserts such as peanut butter and frangelico parfait with black sesame sponge and a fromage frais sorbet flavoured with cranberries. The impressive wine list has around 2,500 choices, including a mind-blowing variety of champagnes.

Chef Marcellin Marc **Owner** Tyfoon Restaurants Ltd, Paul Corrett **Seats** 70, Pr/dining room 23 **Times** 12-2.30/5-11, Closed 24-25 Dec **Prices** Fixed L 2 course £24.50, Tasting menu fr £55, Starter £6.90-£16.50, Main £17.50-£32.50, Dessert £6.90-£8.90 **Wines** 1900 bottles over £30, 10 bottles under £30, 21 by glass **Parking** On street, NCP **Notes** Pre/post-theatre menu, Tasting menu 5 course, Sunday L £29.50-£45, Children L only

LONDON WC2 *continued*

Great Queen Street

PLAN 3 B2

◉ British, European

tel: 020 7242 0622 **32 Great Queen St WC2B 5AA**
email: greatqueenstreet@googlemail.com
dir: *Nearest station: Covent Garden, Holborn*

Best of British in a bustling eatery

Younger stablemate of Waterloo's Anchor & Hope, Great Queen Street occupies a long pub-like room with a bar down one side and an open kitchen at the back. It's a busy, high-decibel place with an easy-going, friendly and completely unpretentious vibe; its elbow-to-elbow wooden tables are constantly being turned, and mismatched chairs fit with the back-to-basics ethos. Wines are served in tumblers and specials are chalked-up, while the twice-daily-changing menu deals in quality produce where seasonality, sourcing and provenance are king. Intelligently simple, unfussy Brit fare with gutsy, big flavours is the kitchen's preference. There's no three-course formality, with dishes laid out in ascending price order, so mix-and-match with small plates — cured, marinated sardines and panzanella, say — and larger dishes like lamb neck fillet with bobby beans, mint and tomatoes, or shin of beef with peas.

Times 12-2.30/6-10.30, Closed last working day in Dec-1st working day in Jan, BHs, D Sun

The Ivy

PLAN 3 A1

◉ British, International ᵥ

tel: 020 7836 4751 **1-5 West St, Covent Garden WC2H 9NQ**
dir: *Nearest station: Leicester Sq*

Old and new brasserie cooking at a theatreland institution

A long-running old stager on a corner site in the heart of London theatreland, The Ivy has seen stars of stage, screen and Westminster come and go within its hallowed portals. Following a thorough transformation, this well-known celebrity haunt has seen a once-cramped bar become a spacious 20-seater counter that's now centre stage to the proceedings. The Ivy requires booking well ahead, and if you can break off from the star-gazing for five minutes, you'll notice that Asian flavours have been introduced to the menus alongside ancient and modern brasserie dishes. You might choose to graze and share a tempura rock shrimp and squid with chilli tofu mayonnaise, but the compass-needle has always tended towards more traditional fare. Steak tartare and the various roasts, grills and hamburgers are what keep the crowds returning. To finish, there could be baked vanilla cheesecake, or a Pimm's Royale jelly with strawberry sorbet.

Chef Gary Lee **Owner** Caprice Holdings **Seats** 100, Pr/dining room 60 **Times** noon-mdnt, All-day dining, Closed 25-26 Dec, 1 Jan **Prices** Starter £8-£14, Main £14-£40, Dessert £6-£9 **Wines** 109 bottles over £30, 5 bottles under £30, 18 by glass **Parking** Valet service **Notes** Pre/post-theatre menu, Children welcome

J. Sheekey & J. Sheekey Oyster Bar

PLAN 3 B1

◉ Seafood ᵥ

tel: 020 7240 2565 **32-34 St Martin's Court WC2N 4AL**
dir: *Nearest station: Leicester Sq*

Renowned theatreland fish restaurant

Very much a London legend, this enduring and much-loved seafood restaurant in the heart of theatreland began life as a seafood stall in the 19th century. J Sheekey expanded the business into adjoining properties and it has been a haunt of the

great and the good ever since, including theatrical types who ply their trade on the surrounding boards. Inside is a warren of snug wood-panelled dining rooms, plus a seafood and oyster bar, and a menu listing relatively straightforward fish and shellfish dishes prepared from superb quality raw ingredients. Start with a classic Catalan-inspired dish of razor clams with chorizo and broad beans, or a choice of oysters if you want to keep it simple, followed by a superb cod fillet on buttered leeks with meaty Isle of Mull mussels and wilted sea aster. A-listers might go for Oscietra with blinis and sour cream (£100 for 30g), but everyone else can take comfort in a plum and almond tart.

Chef James Cornwall **Owner** Caprice Holdings **Seats** 114
Times 12-3/5.30-12, Closed 25-26 Dec, 1 Jan, D 24 Dec **Prices** Starter £9.50-£14.75, Main £15.75-£49.50, Dessert £7.50-£9.50 **Wines** 83 bottles over £30, 3 bottles under £30, 30 by glass **Parking** On street, NCP **Notes** Wknd fixed menu £26.50, Children welcome

Kaspar's Seafood Bar & Grill

PLAN 3 C1

◉◉ Seafood

tel: 020 7836 4343 **The Savoy, Strand WC2R OEU**
email: savoy@fairmont.com **web:** www.fairmont.com/savoy
dir: *Nearest station: Embankment, Covent Garden, Charing Cross*

Super-fresh seafood and more in a stunning art deco setting

First off, Kaspar refers to a fictitious cat that 'joins' tables of 13 to stop them being tables of 13, which is a tradition at The Savoy that goes way back (no doubt to a particularly superstitious maître d'). The dining room looks impressive — it's the old River Room spot — with a central seafood bar and art deco-inspired fixtures and fittings such as gold and black patterned tiling, decorative glass panels and unusual light fittings. The menu has meaty options like a posh burger and steaks cooked on the grill, but seafood is the focus of the kitchen's output. Green pea soup is poured at the table over two seafood dumplings, while another starter of wild sea bass céviche with confit octopus brings a South American flavour. There are fruit de mers platters, a host of smoked and cured fish options, and main courses along the lines of a simple dish of Scottish salmon with a seafood nage. Desserts offer interesting combinations such as vanilla cake with roasted pineapple and lemon and mascarpone verrine with almond streusel, while the wine list has a good range by the glass and carafe.

Chef Holger Jackisch **Owner** Fairmont **Seats** 114, Pr/dining room 12 **Times** 12-11.30, All-day dining **Prices** Fixed L 2 course £25-£35, Fixed D 3 course £28-£38, Starter £9-£21, Main £16-£38, Dessert £9 **Wines** 40 bottles over £30, 40 by glass **Parking** 20 **Notes** Fixed D pre-theatre only 5-6.30pm, Vegetarian available, Children welcome

Kopapa

PLAN 3 B2

◉◉ Fusion

tel: 020 7240 6076 **32-34 Monmouth St, Seven Dials, Covent Garden WC2H 9HA**
email: information@kopapa.co.uk
dir: *Nearest station: Covent Garden*

Culinary Covent Garden alchemy from a master of fusion cuisine

Trendily informal, the bustling Seven Dials' sister to Kiwi fusion maestro Peter Gordon's Providores, Kopapa rocks. Elbow-to-elbow tables, big Kiwi artworks, fashionable seating and a so-now bar for dining and cocktails, Kopapa is the complete ticket. Its smart good looks — backed up by youthful, switched-on service, a high-energy vibe and innovative cuisine — prove an irresistible magnet for the savvy Covent Garden crowds. On the menu, its globetrotting fusion food comes showcased via the now familiar small plate, large plate, sharing formula, and delivered all day from breakfast (weekend brunch), lunch and dinner. Witness a not-to-be-missed crispy tempura 'pocket' filled with high-kicking spiced dhal inari that comes counterbalanced by caramelised coconut and cooling pickled green papaya 'spaghetti', or perhaps try pan-fried scallops with sweet chilli sauce and crème fraîche. Elsewhere, larger offerings might feature succulent lamb rump satay with a taro root rösti, pak choi, rosemary, miso and peanut sauce. Desserts (like coffees) are top drawer too: perhaps a tropical-esque alphonso mango and coconut pannacotta served in a sublime kiwi gazpacho. Interesting cocktails, and global wines come with a nod to New Zealand.

Chef Peter Gordon **Owner** Peter Gordon, Adam Willis, Brandon Allan, Michael McGrath **Seats** 66 **Times** 12–11, All-day dining **Prices** Fixed D 2 course £18.95-£21.95, Starter £6.50–£9.50 **Wines** 25 bottles over £30, 12 bottles under £30, 21 by glass **Parking** On street **Notes** Pre-theatre menu until 7pm Mon-Sat, Sun 9.30pm, Vegetarian available, Children welcome

Lima Floral

PLAN 3 B1

◉◉ Modern Peruvian **NEW**

tel: 020 7240 5778 **14 Garrick St WC2E 9BJ**
email: enquiry@limafloral.com
dir: *Nearest station: Leicester Sq*

A blast of Peruvian sunshine in theatreland

Joining its elder sibling, Lima Fitzrovia, Peruvian cuisine hot-foots it to the corner of Floral Street in Covent Garden theatreland. It offers a blast of South American vivacity amid bright blue columns, an abstract mural dominating the room from one end, with a brick-walled, low-lit bar downstairs where pisco cocktails and piqueos (Peruvian tapas) are the order of the day. First-class, ethnically unimpeachable ingredients go into sharply executed dishes that are colourful and carefully balanced as well as original. Tiger's milk is a zesty citrus marinade for producing sea bream céviche, which comes with thick avocado purée, crisp-dried onions and toasted puffed cancha corn. More corn, whizzed up this time, comes with chicken chalaca for main, served with gentle aji panca chilli sauce, and given textural interest with purple potato 'paper' and slivers of raw asparagus. Peru pretty much invented the potato, so expect lots of it, as well as a similar tuber, olluquito, which comes here with suckling pig. To finish, fine Palo Blanco chocolate is turned into a rich mousse, topped with crunchy oats and garnished with tiny shards of honeycomb and nasturtiums.

Chef Virgilio Martinez, Robert Ortiz **Owner** Gabriel & Jose Luis Gonzalez **Seats** 60, Pr/dining room 12 **Times** 12.30-2.30/5.30-10.30, Closed Xmas, New Year, D Sun **Prices** Fixed L 2 course £17.50, Fixed D 3 course £19.50, Starter £9–£12, Main £19-£28, Dessert £4 **Wines** 27 bottles over £30, 8 bottles under £30, 13 by glass **Parking** On street **Notes** Vegetarian available, Children welcome

Massimo Restaurant & Bar

PLAN 5 B6

◉ Modern, Traditional Italian

tel: 020 7998 0555 **10 Northumberland Av WC2N 5AE**
email: tables@massimo-restaurant.co.uk
dir: *Nearest station: Embankment, Charing Cross*

Grand Roman style in the West End

Set in the glitzy Corinthia Hotel (though with its own street entrance), Massimo's low-lit dining room is a show-stopper, thanks to its flamboyant David Collins' Studio design. The opulent art deco styling is a jaw-dropper, with lines of soaring candy-striped Corinthian columns, hovering globe lighting, sleek mahogany,

intricate mosaics and striking artworks, and acres of plush leather seating and tables dressed in their best whites. Though eponymous chef Massimo Riccioli no longer presides over proceedings, you'll still find bold-flavoured, authentic regional Italian cooking, albeit with premium ingredients for an international jet-setter audience. The menu covers all the bases in traditional Italian format. Try home-made cacao pasta teamed with wild boar ragù, or a well-balanced assemble of slow-cooked cod with escarole (endive-esque), zingy caper and black olives, while a flourless chocolate cake with Amaretto ice cream might feature in the finale. Wines are a cracking Italian-dominated bunch, and the hotel-style service is switched on and unreservedly friendly. The cool oyster bar is the place to begin.

Chef Andrea Cirino **Owner** Corinthia Hotel London **Seats** 140, Pr/dining room 20 **Times** 12–3/5.30–11, Closed Sun **Prices** Fixed L 3 course £30, Fixed D 3 course £30, Starter £8–£15, Main £12–£28, Dessert £8–£10 **Wines** 22 by glass **Parking** Car park **Notes** Vegetarian available, Children welcome

Mon Plaisir

PLAN 3 B2

◉ Traditional French

tel: 020 7836 7243 **19-21 Monmouth St WC2H 9DD**
email: monplaisirrestaurant@googlemail.com **web:** www.monplaisir.co.uk
dir: *Nearest station: Covent Garden, Leicester Sq*

A Francophile's delight in theatreland

Impervious to fads and fashion and about as French as they come this side of the Channel, Mon Plaisir – claiming to be London's oldest French restaurant – is a popular, nostalgic haven of joie de vivre. The original front dining room has changed little since the 1940s (unapologetically Parisian bistro), while beyond there's a series of lighter, cosy rooms (including a bar and mezzanine-style loft) decked out with French posters and memorabilia, as well as more modern abstracts and mirrors. The menu mixes the times, too; country terrine is jazzed up with artichoke chutney, before heading to the Med for a main course of sea bass fillet with potato, olive and basil cake and sauce vierge. Elsewhere there are timeless classics such as snails with garlic and parsley butter, or coq au vin. Close-set tables, resolutely French service and regional wines and cheeses add to the authenticity and upbeat vibe.

Chef Francois Jobard **Owner** Alain Lhermitte **Seats** 100, Pr/dining room 25 **Times** 12-2.30/5.45-11.15, Closed Xmas, New Year, BHs, Sun **Prices** Fixed L 2 course £14.95, Fixed D 3 course £15.95-£24.95, Starter £5.95-£12.95, Main £15.95-£19.95, Dessert £5.50-£9.95 **Wines** 50 bottles over £30, 21 bottles under £30, 20 by glass **Notes** Fixed D pre-theatre 2/3 course, Menu du Mois 2/3 course, Vegetarian available, Children welcome

LONDON WC2 *continued*

The National Dining Rooms
PLAN 3 A1

◉ British

tel: 020 7747 2525 **Sainsbury Wing, The National Gallery, Trafalgar Square WC2N 5DN**
email: ndr.reservations@peytonandbyrne.co.uk
dir: *Nearest station: Charing Cross*

Simple, seasonal cooking in a prime spot

The Peyton and Byrne team have bagged a dream location for this sleek modern all-day operation. Overlooking Trafalgar Square from the National Gallery, the place would never struggle to fill its tables, but there's a lot more to the cooking than a simple pit-stop when you're checking out the art. The unfussy modern British repertoire is built on well-sourced materials and keeps an keen eye on the seasons, starting with a Cornish crab salad with Jersey Royals, gem leaves, wild herbs and cocktail sauce that has 'springtime' written all over it. Main course could be a superior take on an old friend – slow-cooked gammon with peppered pineapple, chips, a quail's egg with crisp pancetta and home-made brown sauce – or you might trade up to John Dory with lentils, salsify, horseradish and Savoy cabbage. It all ends with a fun 'broken' lemon pie with crisp pastry atop the lemon curd filling and peaks of soft meringue all around.

Times 10-8.30, All-day dining, Closed 24-26 Dec, 1 Jan, D Sat-Thu

The Northall
PLAN 5 B6

◉◉ Modern British ᵛ

tel: 020 7321 3100 **Corinthia Hotel London, 10a Northumberland Av WC2N 5AE**
email: northallenquiry@corinthia.com **web:** www.thenorthall.co.uk
dir: *Nearest station: Charing Cross, Embankment*

Celebrating British produce in five-star style

Corinthia Hotels' Whitehall outpost is very much the jewel in its crown, a splendid piece of metropolitan Victoriana close to the river, handy for just about anything you might want to do in central London. The internal spaces are vast, with daylight pouring in through full-drop windows on to the magic of glinting modern chandeliers, bravura floral displays and a marble island bar. Among the dining options, The Northall is dedicated to all things British, with the produce of artisan growers and breeders showcased in the modern national culinary style. Cumbrian beef tartare is finely shredded, bound with well-seasoned mayonnaise, surrounded by wasabi, pickled girolles and breadsticks and topped with an egg yolk. Impeccable seafood cookery produces a main course of seared sea bass with confit octopus and razor clams, an ingenious 'risotto' made of riced saffron potato, and assertive garlic velouté. Lamb is aristocratic Herdwick, served with caramelised shallot purée in minted jus. Savoury notes in desserts, often a minefield, are mobilised well for rosemary parfait with fig carpaccio, lemon verbena curd and honeycomb.

Chef Garry Hollihead **Owner** Corinthia Hotel London **Seats** 185, Pr/dining room 30 **Times** 12-3/5.30-11 **Prices** Fixed L 3 course £30, Fixed D 3 course £30, Tasting menu £45-£75, Starter £7-£15, Main £12-£41, Dessert £8-£12 **Wines** 16 bottles over £30, 16 by glass **Parking** Valet parking **Notes** 3 course with champagne, Sunday L, Children welcome

The Opera Tavern
PLAN 3 C1

◉◉ Spanish, Italian

tel: 020 7836 3680 **23 Catherine St, Covent Garden WC2B 5JS**
email: info@operatavern.co.uk
dir: *Nearest station: Covent Garden*

High-impact tapas dishes in operaland

Plumb in the middle of Covent Garden, opposite the Drury Lane Theatre and close enough to the Opera House to make it to your box on time, the Tavern is a classic old London pub at its architectural heart, repurposed for today's tastes as an upscale, two-storeyed tapas joint. On the ground floor, the charcoal grill dominates proceedings in an atmosphere of hustle and bustle, while the chandeliered dining room upstairs offers a marginally more sedate setting. You could go three-course if you're an old stickler, but little dishes are the principal bill of fare. They pack quite an impact: a truffle-buttered, panko-crumbed scallop with braised peas and prosciutto has a lot going for it, as does impeccably Spanish roasted salt hake with saffron-almond sauce and beans. Superb meats are treated with respect, as for Ibérico loin with morcilla and a purée of pickled apricots, or beef shin with girolles, smoked anchovies and salsa verde. Pink prosecco jelly with raspberries and meringue ice cream is one of the lighter ways to conclude.

Chef Jamie Thickett, Ben Tish **Owner** Simon Mullins, Sanya Morris, Ben Tish **Seats** 75 **Times** 12-3/5-11.30, Closed 25-26 Dec, 1 Jan, some BHs, D Sun **Prices** Starter £3-£12, Main £4-£12, Dessert £4.50-£6.50 **Wines** 24 by glass **Notes** Fixed tapas menus 3 course over 7 people £35-£40, Vegetarian available, Children welcome

Orso
PLAN 3 C1

◉ Modern Italian

tel: 020 7240 5269 & 7845 6474 **27 Wellington St WC2E 7DA**
email: info@orsorestaurant.co.uk
dir: *Nearest station: Covent Garden*

Regional Italian food in a lively basement

Since 1975, savvy crowds have been flocking downstairs to this relaxed, all-day Covent Garden Italian tucked away in an expansive basement that was once an orchid warehouse. The place buzzes with conversation, clinking glasses and unstuffy, quick-fire service. It is all classic Italian from the herringbone-patterned wood floors, white tiled columns, terracotta walls and black-and-white photos, with their nod to Milan of the '50s, through to crowd-pleasing menus showcasing simple regional Italian cooking. A concise handful of pasta dishes offers the likes of tagliatelle with braised lamb, rosemary and tomato, while mains bring Tuscan 'cacciucco' – a seafood stew with hake, king prawns, cuttlefish, mussels, chilli and tomato – or slow-roasted crispy pork belly with cavolo nero and roast potatoes. At dessert, rhubarb makes a zingy foil to a textbook creamy vanilla pannacotta with candied fennel. A fixed-price pre-theatre option and all-Italian wine list add to the all-round appeal.

Chef Paolo Belcastro **Owner** Tim Healey, Lawrence Hartley **Seats** 90 **Times** 12-12, All-day dining, Closed 25 Dec **Prices** Fixed L 2 course £16.75, Fixed D 3 course £19.50, Starter £5.50-£12.50, Main £11.95-£26.50, Dessert £5.50-£9 **Wines** 20 bottles over £30, 16 bottles under £30, 16 by glass **Notes** Pre/post-theatre 2/3 course £16.75/£19.50, Sunday L, Vegetarian available, Children welcome

Roka Aldwych
PLAN 3 C2

◉◉ Contemporary Japanese NEW

tel: 020 7294 7636 **71 Aldwych WC2B 4HN**
email: infoaldwych@rokarestaurant.com
dir: *Nearest station: Temple, Holborn*

Impressive robatayaki specialities – and more

The hub of this latest recruit to the four-strong Roka stable is the centrally located robata grill. This is the focus of the cooking and of the restaurant layout as diners can sit and watch the chefs earnestly preparing their food. Roka is characterised by top-drawer ingredients, with the freshest of fresh seafood, to-the-second timings and artful presentation. The speciality is robatayaki: contemporary-style Japanese barbecued food. Examples are skewers of chicken with spring onions and tender smoked duck breast, charred on the outside, pink inside, with barley, miso and sticky, intense kumquat paste, or black cod marinated in yuzu miso with home-made hajikami. Sushi are good bets too, such as Wagyu gunkan (beef sushi with Oscietra caviar, spring onions and ginger) – as are hotpots, perhaps lamb with crab and wasabi tobiko. Puddings are the real thing and include Japanese pancakes with banana, toffee and black sugar syrup, and cherry blossom ice cream accompanying almond crème brûlée.

Chef Hamish Brown **Owner** Rainer Becker **Times** 12-3.30/5.30-11.30, Closed 25 Dec **Prices** Tasting menu £79 **Notes** L menu £27, Vegetarian available, Children welcome

Savoy Grill
PLAN 3 C1

◉◉ British, French V

tel: 020 7592 1600 **1 Savoy Hill, Strand WC2R OEU**
email: savoygrill@gordonramsay.com
dir: *Nearest station: Charing Cross*

Classically-inspired cooking at a Premier League address

The Savoy's iconic Grill has always been the place to see and be seen, and its drop-dead gorgeous looks have been buffed up further in the zillion-pound makeover of the hotel. The handsome, low-lit art deco room inspires with its walnut panelling, mirrors and plush banquettes set beneath glittering chandeliers. The cooking is international, with classic foundations – there's even a roster of Escoffier signature dishes, from which a glazed omelette Arnold Bennett makes a comforting starter. The fish and shellfish section might offer lobster thermidor or Dover sole (grilled or meunière), while top-dollar grills from the wood-fired charcoal oven take in British steaks – a 40-day aged rump steak with marrowbone and shallot sauce fits the bill for main course. Elsewhere, there are 'roasts, braises and pies', such as steak-and-ale pudding or beef Wellington with horseradish cream. Dessert brings forth pineapple tarte Tatin with coconut ice cream. Naturally, none of this is cheap and there's a £2 cover charge to factor in. However, the simpler lunch option delivers good value. A heavyweight wine list raises the bill skywards.

Chef Andy Cook **Owner** Gordon Ramsay Group **Seats** 98, Pr/dining room 40 **Times** 12-3/5.30-11 **Prices** Fixed L 2 course £26, Fixed D 3 course £28, Starter £8-£16, Main £18-£42, Dessert £7-£10 **Wines** 300 bottles over £30, 20 by glass **Notes** Pre-theatre 2/3 course, Escoffier signature 4 course, Sunday L, Children welcome

Spring
PLAN 3 C1

◉◉ European NEW

tel: 020 3011 0116 & 3011 0115 **New Wing, Somerset House, Lancaster Place WC2R 1LA**
email: reservations@springrestaurant.co.uk
dir: *Nearest station: Temple, Covent Garden, Charing Cross*

Classy cooking in a light and elegant dining room

After winning much acclaim at the rustic glasshouse restaurant of Petersham Nurseries, Skye Gyngell has brought her trademark style – simply, if classily treated seasonal ingredients and flavour – to the grander stage of Somerset House. The luminous, high-ceilinged space is punctuated by striking globe chandeliers and artworks, soaring pillars and arched windows, while staff as sunny natured as the surroundings help create a relaxed ambience. The regularly-changing Mediterranean menu (with Italian the predominant accent) delivers good-looking plates of seasonal fair, backed by skilful execution and deft combinations that allow flavours to shine. A knockout starter of squid with chilli oil and mashed broad beans shows a kitchen that knows what works with what, while generous mains triumph with a pairing of grilled lamb and asparagus, boosted by a clear-flavoured lovage salsa verde. The lightest black treacle cake proves a classy number among appealing desserts, and is cleverly teamed with citrus curd, warming candied ginger and zesty clementine. Though prices might alarm your financial adviser, a fixed-price lunch option eases the bottom line.

Chef Skye Gyngell **Seats** 100 **Times** 12-2.30/6-10.30, Closed D Sun **Prices** Fixed L 2 course £25.50, Starter £12-£16, Main £16-£34, Dessert £8-£12 **Wines** 72 bottles over £30, 6 bottles under £30, 20 by glass **Parking** On street, NCP **Notes** Sunday L £25.50-£29.50, Vegetarian available, Children welcome

Terroirs
PLAN 3 B1

◉◉ Mediterranean, European

tel: 020 7036 0660 **5 William IV St, Covent Garden WC2N 4DW**
email: enquiries@terroirswinebar.com
dir: *Nearest station: Covent Garden, Charing Cross*

French provincial cooking with flavours to the fore

Terroirs is split over two levels: a ground-floor wine bar and a downstairs restaurant. You can eat what you like where you like. Provincial French cooking, with a nod towards the Mediterranean, is the style, based on quality fresh produce. Kick off with a dish of charcuterie – perhaps duck rillettes – and progress to a selection of 'small plates', which is a decent choice that includes, say, brawn with sauce gribiche and toast, prawns cooked in sherry, chilli and garlic or Bayonne ham with celeriac remoulade. Dishes are never over-complicated or ostentatiously novel, so flavours are forthright, which is as true of the handful of plats du jour as it is of the rest of the output. Among successes are lamb chops with anchovy, capers and chard, and roast partridge with lentils and salsa verde, while the fish dish of the day could be gilt head bream fillet with Jerusalem artichokes and wild mushrooms. An impressive line-up of well-kept cheeses awaits as a finale, with a short list of puddings extending perhaps to pannacotta flavoured with orange and Campari.

Chef Ed Wilson **Owner** Ed Wilson, Oli Barker, Eric Narioo **Seats** 120, Pr/dining room 40 **Times** 12-11, All-day dining, Closed Xmas, New Year, Etr, BHs, Sun **Prices** Starter £4.50-£12.75, Main £15.25-£18, Dessert £5.50-£7 **Wines** 200 bottles over £30, 30 bottles under £30, 18 by glass **Notes** Fixed 1 course L £10, Vegetarian available, Children welcome

LONDON WC2 *continued*

Tredwell's

PLAN 3 B1

@ @ Modern British **NEW**

tel: 020 3764 0840 **4a Upper St Martin's Ln, Covent Garden WC2H 9NY**
email: hello@tredwells7dials.com
dir: *Nearest station: Leicester Sq*

Contemporary comfort food, Marcus Wareing-style

The latest outpost in Marcus Wareing's burgeoning empire opened its doors in the Seven Dials heart of theatreland in autumn 2014. Tredwell's (theatre buffs may spot the reference to the butler in Agatha Christie's *The Seven Dials Mystery*) spreads over three floors with a basement cocktail bar and two airy, retro-looking dining rooms lit by large windows, done out with racing-green leather banquettes and buzzing with a high-decibel West End vibe. The menu describes itself as 'modern London cooking' which translates as good-quality Brit ingredients sexed up with globetrotting flavours, aimed squarely at the comfort zone and backed by a multinational wine list. A starter of light and creamy chicken liver mousse is served in a Kilner jar with a layer of bacon jam, while main-course sea bass arrives with silky carrot purée and earthy lentils. Meaty ideas take in the likes of braised lamb belly with aubergine and tomato curry or pork chops with baked celeriac, while pain perdu with maple ice cream and crispy bacon provides a sweet and salty conclusion.

Chef Andy Ward **Owner** Marcus Wareing **Seats** 180, Pr/dining room 30 **Times** 12-3/5-11, Closed 25-26 Dec, 1 Jan **Prices** Fixed L 2 course £17, Starter £5-£8.50, Main £9-£26, Dessert £3-£6 **Wines** 40 bottles over £30, 4 bottles under £30, 15 by glass **Parking** Townsave Shelton St **Notes** Pre-theatre 2/3 course £17/£20, All day dining Thu-Sun, Sunday L £16.50-£18.50, Vegetarian available, Children welcome

Map 6 TQ29

Savoro Restaurant with Rooms

@ Modern European, British

tel: 020 8449 9888 **206 High St EN5 5SZ**
email: savoro@savoro.co.uk **web:** www.savoro.co.uk
dir: *M25 junct 23 to A1081, continue to St Albans Rd, at lights turn left to A1000*

Contemporary good looks and well-judged menus

This building a few paces off the High Street once housed an inn, a bakery and a tea shop, and is now a restaurant with rooms. Behind a rather quaint-looking shop front, the interior has been given a cool, contemporary look. 'Simple execution of good technique' is the kitchen's mantra, with everything made in-house. A terrine of foie gras and duck confit is partnered by pickled apricots, apple and chervil and pain d'épice, and seared scallops by pea purée and macadamia nuts. Menus encompass the familiar as well as the more adventurous: grilled rib-eye with béarnaise, say, whole sea bass stuffed with herbs, or chicken danoise with rhubarb compôte, pickled cucumber, Parisienne potatoes and chicken jus. Puddings are no afterthought when among them might be lemon crème brûlée with raspberries and ginger shortbread.

Chef Andi Andersen, Pritesh Bangera **Owner** Jack Antoni, Dino Paphiti **Seats** 100, Pr/dining room 50 **Times** 12-3/6-11, Closed 1 Jan, 1 wk New Year **Prices** Fixed L 2 course fr £14.95, Fixed D 3 course fr £29.95, Starter fr £6.95, Main fr £17, Dessert fr £6 **Wines** 30 bottles over £30, 30 bottles under £30, 12 by glass **Parking** 6, On street **Notes** Early eve menu Mon-Thu 2 course £14.95, Sunday L, Vegetarian available, Children welcome

Chapter One

PLAN 1 H1

@ @ @ @ – *see opposite*

Map 6 TQ39

Royal Chace Hotel

@ Modern British

tel: 020 8884 8181 **162 The Ridgeway EN2 8AR**
email: reservations@royalchacehotel.co.uk **web:** www.royal-chace.com
dir: *3m from M25 junct 24, 1.5m to Enfield*

Imaginative cooking in an elegant setting with rural views

There's some bright, modern cooking going on at this large hotel that caters for weddings and conferences, and it's a useful spot to know about in the outer-reaches of North London. There are pretty gardens – good for those wedding photos – and some rather splendid function spaces, while The Kings Restaurant puts the venue on the culinary map. It's a rather elegant room with a large skylight and a swish finish (linen cloths, fresh flowers, that sort of thing), and what comes out of the kitchen is some smart modern British fare. Seared hand-dived scallops might come with a white fish and Puy lentil mousse, a trendy golden raisin purée and crustacean broth, or how about Gressingham duck confit with sweet pickled candy beetroot and foie gras ravioli? Main-course delivers the likes of a trio of Saddleback pork, and dessert a Hertfordshire rhubarb fool with toffee popcorn and sesame crisp.

Times 12-9.30, All-day dining, Closed D Sun

Chapter One

Modern European V

tel: 01689 854848 **Farnborough Common, Locksbottom BR6 8NF**
email: info@chaptersrestaurants.com
web: www.chaptersrestaurants.com
dir: *On A21, 3m from Bromley. From M25 junct 4 onto A21 for 5m*

Strikingly refined cooking in an out-of-town hotspot

Located in an old Tudor house on a main road that links up with the M25 a few miles away, Chapter One is a world-class restaurant in the most unexpected of places, but it all makes perfect sense once you've crossed the threshold. Andrew McLeish has been executive chef since 2000 and has turned this little corner of suburban Kent into one of Greater London's premier dining destinations. The finish within is smart and stylish in the modern manner, which means lots of neutral shades of coffee and cream and tables set with precision. One of the stand-out features of Chapter One has been its relative value for money, with a three-course lunchtime menu du jour that is nothing short of a steal, and a tasting menu and à la carte that constitute remarkable value at this level. A new brasserie menu is served in a more relaxed setting, and offers the likes of USDA steaks cooked on the Josper grill. Service is consistently professional and charming. Expect pin-sharp contemporary dishes that look stunning on the plate and have their roots in classic European cooking. A risotto richly flavoured with morels and wild garlic is a classy first course, while another dish of yellowfin tuna shows a broader global inspiration with its accompanying wasabi mayonnaise and pickled shimeji mushrooms. Technical know-how and considered flavour combinations are also a feature of main courses. A Med-inspired pan-roasted Scottish salmon dish, for example, comes in the company of artichokes, olives and aubergines. The Josper grill is put to good use again, this time for Ibérico pork, which is partnered with tender braised cheek, smoked potato purée and a carrot and apple compôte. The desserts are equally creative and refined: peanut and chocolate tart, say, with banana sorbet and salted caramel, or another construction that reimagines rhubarb and custard. Sunday lunch is another bargain (you could spend more in a local pub), with air-hung sirloin of beef roasted just right and offered up with roasted potatoes, red cabbage and red wine jus. The wine list is exceedingly well put together, with the bottles tantalisingly visible from the bar and restaurant safely secured behind glass in their temperature and humidity controlled 'cellar'. Make use of the sommelier and chances are you'll drink something interesting from the list which is helpfully put together by style rather than geographical location.

Chef Andrew McLeish **Owner** Selective Restaurants Group
Seats 120, Pr/dining room 55
Times 12-2.30/6.30-10.30, Closed 2-4 Jan **Prices** Fixed L 3 course £19.95, Tasting menu fr £55, Starter £6.50-£9.70, Main £17-£22, Dessert £6.45-£8.25 **Wines** 20 bottles over £30, 20 bottles under £30, 13 by glass **Parking** 90 **Notes** Brasserie menu light L Mon-Sat 12-3pm, Sunday L £22.95, Children welcome

HADLEY WOOD

Map 6 TQ29

West Lodge Park Hotel

Modern British

tel: 020 8216 3900 **Cockfosters Rd EN4 OPY**
email: westlodgepark@bealeshotels.co.uk web: www.bealeshotel.co.uk
dir: *On A111, 1m S of M25 junct 24*

Polished cooking in a parkland setting

The restaurant at this imposing white mansion takes its name from the portraitist Mary Beale, an ancestor of the owners, whose works hang on the walls. This is a stylish room, given a contemporary look, with well-spaced tables and light streaming in from huge windows looking over the surrounding parkland, and there's summer dining on the terrace. The kitchen team makes good use of local produce and cooks in a confidently unfussy style. Game terrine balanced by home-made tomato and onion chutney is an impressive starter, and there could be a more contemporary pairing of seared scallops and oxtail sauce with cauliflower purée. Main courses run from boeuf bourguignon through Madras chicken curry to accurately cooked sea bass fillets with lemon butter, croquette potatoes, carrots and spinach. To finish a soufflé — perhaps spicy apple and sultana with blackberry custard — is well worth the 20-minute wait.

Chef Wayne Turner **Owner** Beales Ltd **Seats** 92, Pr/dining room 110 **Times** 12.30-2/7-9.30 **Prices** Starter £6.50-£12.50, Main £16.50-£26.50, Dessert £6.50-£10.50, Service optional **Wines** 57 bottles over £30, 44 bottles under £30, 14 by glass **Parking** 75 **Notes** Sunday L £28-£33, Vegetarian available, Children welcome

HARROW ON THE HILL

Incanto Restaurant

PLAN 1 B5

Modern European ⬥ NOTABLE WINE LIST

tel: 020 8426 6767 **The Old Post Office, 41 High St HA1 3HT**
email: info@incanto.co.uk web: www.incanto.co.uk
dir: *M4 junct 3 at Target rdbt, follow signs A312 Harrow. Continue through South Harrow, turn right at Roxeth Hill, turn left at top of hill*

Ambitious contemporary cooking in a modest, modern setting

The one-time Victorian post office is delivering an altogether more sybaritic package to the local community these days in the shape of Incanto, a deli, café and restaurant with a modern European spin. The deli-café is to the front, where you can fuel up with a ciabatta sandwich or salad, or stock up with some goodies to take home, but the main action takes place in the restaurant to the rear. It's a bright, split-level space with a glass skylight and an unfussy finish — modern art, darkwood tables, and neutral colours. The tasting menu allows for a full-on examination of the kitchen's talents, while the vegetarian version is no slouch either. From the carte, expect creative starters such as poached cod and langoustine with manchego gnocchi and winter truffle, or a pork belly and eel dish with pork croquette and piccalilli emulsion. Next up, corn-fed chicken breast is partnered with chorizo porridge and charred hisbi cabbage, and roasted stone bass with salt-baked celeriac and heritage potatoes. Finish with 'many ways of chocolate and honeycomb', or a modern take on a classic apple pie with cinnamon ice cream.

Incanto Restaurant

Chef Peter Howarth **Owner** David & Catherine Taylor **Seats** 64, Pr/dining room 30 **Times** 12-2.30/6.30-10.30, Closed 24-26 Dec, 1 Jan, Etr Sun, Mon, D Sun **Prices** Fixed L 2 course £21.95-£26.95, Fixed D 3 course £24.95, Tasting menu £46-£65, Starter £8-£10, Main £16-£22, Dessert £7.50-£9.95 **Wines** 77 bottles over £30, 19 bottles under £30, 9 by glass **Parking** On street **Notes** Sunday L £7-£22, Vegetarian available, Children welcome

HARROW WEALD

BEST WESTERN PLUS Grim's Dyke Hotel

PLAN 1 B5

British, European

tel: 020 8385 3100 **Old Redding HA3 6SH**
email: reservations@grimsdyke.com web: www.grimsdyke.com
dir: *3m from M1 between Harrow & Watford*

Modern British cooking in a country setting

The former home of Sir William Gilbert of 'and Sullivan' fame, Grim's Dyke is a rather grand house standing in 40 acres of grounds, including primped gardens and natural woodland. The hotel has made good use of the capacious features of the house, not least in Gilbert's Restaurant, which occupies the space that was once the great man's billiard room. Traditional decor remains in keeping with the building, the formal tone maintained by the uniformed service team. The kitchen displays evident affection for English classics such as fish and chips and Lancashire hotpot, but there's a lot more going on here, expanding into the modern British repertoire which itself entails some global flavours and broader European influences. Ham hock terrine with piccalilli and toast, or a crispy oriental duck salad are two possibilities when it comes to first courses, followed perhaps by calves' liver, creamed potato and razor thin shards of crispy pancetta. There is a classic roast option for Sunday lunch, and desserts such as a tangy lemon tart.

Times 12.30-2/7-9.30, Closed 24 Dec, 1 Jan, L Sat, D 25-26 Dec

HEATHROW AIRPORT (LONDON)

La Belle Époque

PLAN 1 A3

⬥⬥⬥ – *see opposite*

Vivre Restaurant

PLAN 1 A3

◉ International

tel: 020 8757 5027 & 8757 7777 **Sofitel London Heathrow, Terminal 5, Wentworth Dr, London Heathrow Airport TW6 2GD**
email: vivre@sofitelheathrow.com
dir: *M25 junct 14, follow signs to Terminal 5*

Assured international cooking from an open-to-view kitchen

The Heathrow Sofitel boasts more decent eating than many an airport hotel. Head for Terminal 5 and walk through. As an alternative to the fine French goings-on in La Belle Époque, Vivre is the place to repair for a more informal dining experience. It's an open-plan room full of vibrantly colourful contemporary design, the kitchen team on view at their wokking, pizza-throwing and grilling, and service that aims to put everyone at their ease. The large menu changes seasonally, but is built around a core of stalwarts cooked with assurance. Among the international offerings of note are tempura-battered king prawns with tonkatsu sweet chilli dip and a crunchy salad, mildly spiced Indian butter chicken with a side of spinach, served with the full monty of naan bread, poppadums and fluffy basmati rice, and French-style glazed apple frangipane tart with light puff pastry, served with rip-roaringly rich clotted cream ice cream.

Times 6-10.30, Closed L all week

■ KESTON

Map 6 TQ46

Herbert's

◉◉ British, International

tel: 01689 855501 **6 Commonside BR2 6BP**
email: info@thisisherberts.co.uk
dir: *M25 junct 4, follow A21 Bromley*

Ambitious modern fare and a relaxing atmosphere

A white property on Keston Common is the home of Herbert's, an oak-floored space with oval-backed chairs at wooden-topped tables and a warm and relaxing atmosphere. The team in the kitchen cooks in the modern European mode and devise menus with headings such as 'stream and sea' and 'four legs (or two)'. Imaginative starters may run to prawns in white wine with gremolata, or pheasant ballotine with mushroom and beetroot dressing. Ingredients are well chosen and handled confidently so flavours are clear. Pork belly, served with apple sauce, red cabbage and pommes purée, is the sort of mainstream main course to expect, and fish is properly treated, seen in pan-fried mackerel partnered by pancetta, accompanied by cockle dressing, roast onions and new potatoes, and cod fillet given a kick from Madeira jus accompanied by ham hock mash. Finish with a comforting dessert like cinnamon-flavoured rice pudding with poached plums, or lemon curd tart with crème fraîche ice cream and passionfruit coulis.

Chef Angela Herbert-Bell **Owner** Angela Herbert-Bell **Seats** 52, Pr/dining room 32 **Times** 12-3/6.30-10, Closed Mon, D Sun **Prices** Fixed L 2 course £14.50-£19.50, Fixed D 3 course £21.50-£40, Starter £4.50-£11.50, Main £10.50-£25.50, Dessert £4.50-£6.50 **Wines** 12 bottles over £30, 12 bottles under £30, 10 by glass **Parking** Free car park 1min walk away **Notes** Breakfast menu Tue-Fri, Wknd brunch, Sunday L £19.95-£22.95, Vegetarian available, Children welcome

---

La Belle Époque ◉◉◉

■ HEATHROW AIRPORT (LONDON)

PLAN 1 A3

French

tel: 020 8757 7777 **Sofitel London Heathrow, Terminal 5, Wentworth Dr, London Heathrow Airport TW6 2GD**
email: labelleepoque@sofitelheathrow.com **web:** www.sofitel.com
dir: *M25 junct 14, follow signs to Terminal 5*

Airport hotel dining of inventiveness and complexity

Experience may not lead you to expect anything more than bland international cuisine from airport hotels, but the Sofitel group has created something quite special at its Heathrow property. The building itself is a remarkable piece of modernist styling, reached by a covered walkway from Terminal 5. It seems fitting that the newest terminal should boast a cutting-edge venue such as La Belle Époque. A changing of the guard at the stoves brings in Mayur Nagarale this year, but the mode of cooking stands firm in the contemporary Anglo-French camp (menus are written in both languages). Dishes are constructed of neatly contrasting components, as when a parcel of Cornish mackerel en papillote is teamed with salt-cod croquettes and cucumber 'kimchi' with a dressing of horseradish and lemongrass crème fraîche, or that new favourite starter, wood pigeon, roasted in a nest of hay, turns up with a truffled egg yolk, roasted leeks and baby onions. Mains take in a wealth of choice from Szechuan-spiced trotters with boudin blanc, a ham hock raviolo, shiitakis and pak choi, to hake in a paprika-panko coat, served with ratatouille and crab and sea purslane tortellini in crab beurre blanc. There is a lot going on in these dishes, and yet the kitchen keeps its eye firmly on the ball. Bouillabaisse is a miso-laced version teeming with sea bass, John Dory, razor clams, scallops and langoustine, and there is plenty of heartening inventive labour in the vegetarian offerings too. A trio of mini-soufflés — cep, spring onion and spinach — requires careful oversight, or there could be an ingeniously assembled millefeuille of artichoke, peppers, fennel and wild mushrooms with onion marmalade.

Chef Mayur Nagarale **Owner** Surinder Arora **Seats** 88, Pr/dining room 20 **Times** 12-2.30/6-10, Closed Xmas, BHs, Sun, L Sat **Prices** Tasting menu £55, Starter £8.50-£11.50, Main £21.50-£33, Dessert £8.50-£11.50 **Wines** 236 bottles over £30, 6 bottles under £30, 16 by glass **Parking** 400 **Notes** Vegetarian available, Children welcome

KEW

The Glasshouse

PLAN 1 C3

◉◉◉ – see below

PINNER

Friends Restaurant

PLAN 1 B5

◉ Modern British

tel: 020 8866 0286 **11 High St HA5 5PJ**
email: info@friendsrestaurant.co.uk web: www.friendsrestaurant.co.uk
dir: *M25 junct 17 then via Northwood to Pinner. 2 mins walk from Pinner tube station*

Heartwarming French bistro fare in an old timbered house

Occupying a 400-year-old timbered building, chef-patron Terry Farr's restaurant feels like it's in a village but this is Betjeman's suburban Metro-Land, with the train to central London just a couple of minutes' walk away. The decor is intimate and rather romantic, with a low-beamed ceiling and contemporary black leather seats at white linen tables. After more than two decades in business, local supply lines are strong, while top-grade meat and fish comes from Smithfield and Billingsgate markets. The menu deals in tried-and-true French bistro cooking jazzed up with sound modern thinking. Open the show with wood pigeon accompanied by cauliflower purée, pancetta lardons and balsamic, moving on to Shetland sea trout helped by the kick of lemongrass and ginger with fondant potato and samphire. At the end, the tang of orange sauce proves the perfect foil to the rich comfort of bread-and-butter pudding.

Friends Restaurant

Chef Terry Farr **Owner** Terry Farr **Seats** 40, Pr/dining room 30 **Times** 12-3/6.30-10, Closed 25-26 Dec, 1 Jan, BHs, Mon, D Sun **Prices** Fixed L 2 course £20.50, Fixed D 3 course £35, Starter £7.50-£9.50, Main £18.50-£25, Dessert £7.50-£8.50 **Wines** 31 bottles over £30, 28 bottles under £30, 12 by glass **Parking** Nearby car parks **Notes** Sunday L £29.50, Vegetarian available, Children welcome

---

The Glasshouse ❀❀❀

KEW

PLAN 1 C3

Modern International ⚑ **NOTABLE WINE LIST**

tel: 020 8940 6777 **14 Station Pde TW9 3PZ**
email: info@glasshouserestaurant.co.uk
dir: *Just outside Kew Gardens underground station*

French-based cooking of exemplary consistency in a modern setting

The Glasshouse has hit on a winning formula that keeps this classy neighbourhood eatery perennially rammed with lucky Kew residents. First and foremost, of course, there's the food: what's not to like about seasonally driven modern European cooking built upon the solid foundations of classical French cuisine bourgeoise that makes its impact without any need to resort to culinary flimflam? Then there's the setting, a light-flooded, unbuttoned and slickly neutral contemporary space with full-drop plate glass windows that stand out in the parade of shops near Kew Gardens tube station. Conscientious and clued-up staff are the icing on the cake, with Berwyn Davies leading the kitchen brigade's efforts in producing simple and sumptuous openers such as warm octopus with periwinkles, given extra depth by fennel cream, radish and citrus fruits, or a gutsy pig's head terrine leavened by a bitter endive salad, clementine and honey mustard dressing. Main courses bring a similarly accomplished layering of flavours and textures in dishes that might bring together sea-fresh poached skate with Cornish crab, supported by monk's beard, crushed sweet potato and lemon beurre blanc. Meatier ideas include rack and slow-cooked belly of lamb accompanied by padrón peppers, mustard gnocchi and rosemary, or another two-way serving, say, duck breast and its braised leg matched with honey-roasted parsnips, sprout tops and Madeira jus. Dessert also achieve a level of refinement that only comes with top-level technical ability – a dark chocolate and orange mousse with hazelnut dacquoise and burnt orange ice cream shows a firm grasp of how flavours work together, or you might bow out on a classic note with an exemplary tarte Tatin with vanilla ice cream.

Chef Berwyn Davies **Owner** Nigel Platts-Martin, Bruce Poole **Seats** 60 **Times** 12-2.30/6.30-10.30, Closed 24-26 Dec, 1 Jan **Prices** Fixed L 2 course £24.50-£27.50, Fixed D 3 course £45 **Wines** 459 bottles over £30, 9 bottles under £30, 13 by glass **Parking** On street (meter) **Notes** Sunday L £22.50-£32.50, Vegetarian available, Children welcome

RICHMOND UPON THAMES

Bacco Restaurant Italiano

PLAN 1 C2

Italian

tel: 020 8332 0348 **39-41 Kew Rd TW9 2NQ**
email: bookings@bacco-restaurant.co.uk
dir: *A316 towards Richmond Station or town centre, 2 min walk from tube*

Family hospitality and traditional Italian cooking

This smart independent Italian next to the Orange Tree Theatre has built a loyal local fan base, who come for its lively vibe and straight-talking contemporary cooking. There's a decked terrace out on the pavement, and when the weather's not on your side, two distinct dining areas take in a wall of all-Italian wines running along one side, and it is all done out in an up-to-date style with bare floorboards, colourful artwork, and convivial elbow-to-elbow tables. Among starters, you might encounter king prawns with sautéed Sardinian fregola and sun-dried tomatoes, and pasta is freshly made in-house every day, appearing as twisted tubes of casarecce with slow-cooked wild boar ragú. Mains deliver basil and lemon-roasted cod with caponata, or perhaps calves' liver in sage butter. Traditional tiramisù is always a good way to finish, or there's vanilla pannacotta with mango coulis.

Chef Vito Fanara **Owner** Stefano Bergamin **Seats** 50, Pr/dining room 27 **Times** 12-2.30/5.45-11, Closed Xmas, New Year, BHs, D Sun **Prices** Fixed D 3 course £18.50, Starter £7.50-£9.50, Main £16.50-£25, Dessert £5-£6.50 **Wines** 20 bottles over £30, 30 bottles under £30, 16 by glass **Notes** Sunday L, Vegetarian available, Children welcome

Bingham

PLAN 1 C2

@@@ – *see below*

La Buvette

PLAN 1 C2

French, Mediterranean V

tel: 020 8940 6264 **6 Church Walk TW9 1SN**
email: info@labuvette.co.uk
dir: *3 mins from train station, opposite St Mary Magdalene Church, off main High St on corner of Tesco Metro*

Cheery bistro serving French classics and more

If the sun is shining on Richmond upon Thames, La Buvette's courtyard tables come into their own, but this place is a winner all-year-round when it comes to classic, bistro-style dining. It's a real neighbourhood joint, down a leafy walkway off the main high street, with closely packed tables and a menu of familiar dishes backed up by daily specials. A starter of rabbit and pork terrine with onion marmalade is one way to kick off, or go for scallops in a flavour-packed plateful with broad beans, bacon and persillade. Main-course braised shin of pork comes with black pudding and hispi cabbage, and there's roast salmon with crushed new potatoes and sorrel cream sauce. There's steak, too, in the form of chargrilled onglet, served rare, with garlic butter, chips and salad, and a plate of artisan French cheeses if you've room. Dessert delivers old favourites such as crème brûlée and a charlotte made with Yorkshire rhubarb.

Chef Buck Carter **Owner** Bruce Duckett **Seats** 50 **Times** 12-3/5.45-10, Closed 25-26 Dec, 1 Jan, Good Fri, Etr Sun **Prices** Fixed L 2 course £16.50, Fixed D 3 course £22, Starter £5.75-£9.50, Main £13.50-£18, Dessert £5.25-£6.75 **Wines** 21 bottles over £30, 13 bottles under £30, 16 by glass **Parking** NCP Paradise Rd **Notes** Sunday L, Children welcome

Bingham @@@

RICHMOND UPON THAMES

PLAN 1 C2

Modern British NOTABLE WINE LIST

tel: 020 8940 0902 & 8940 8009 **61-63 Petersham Rd TW10 6UT**
email: info@thebingham.co.uk **web:** www.thebingham.co.uk
dir: *On A307, near Richmond Bridge*

Peerless produce cooked with intelligent simplicity beside the river

Fashioned from a pair of knocked-together Georgian townhouses, the Bingham delivers the chic boutique bolt hole experience in spades. Overlooking the Thames, just a short and scenic stroll along the towpath from the centre of Richmond, the place has a look taken straight out of a glossy interior design magazine: nothing jars, from the unchallenging neutral palette to the glamorous teardrop chandeliers and cleverly recessed lights casting a soft glow over velvety banquettes, pale gold chairs, art deco-style mirrors and silk curtains in the sleek dining rooms. A glamorous spot, then, but happily, the place is not a case of style over substance when it comes to the culinary output, which relies on impeccable, sustainably produced ingredients, mostly from the local area, for its effect. Of course, someone has to turn this peerless produce into food and the kitchen here takes a light touch approach – no faffing about with jellies and foams, just handling it all with respect and restraint to bring out sharply-defined flavours and textures. Things start with a no-nonsense pairing of scallops and cured pork belly matched inventively with endive and lime caramel, or there might be an intriguing juxtaposition of quail with butternut squash, quinoa and tarragon. Main-course fish comes in a well-judged and harmonious composition involving wild brill with octopus, chorizo, red pepper confit and on-trend black garlic purée, all made to look deceptively simple by top-class technical skills. After that, a richly-flavoured caramel mousse with a freshly-baked milk biscuit and milk sorbet illustrates why less is often more. A skilled and friendly service team dispels any hint of pretentiousness and offers helpful advice on the excellent wine list.

Chef Andrew Cole **Owner** Ruth & Samantha Trinder **Seats** 40, Pr/dining room 90 **Times** 12-2.30/6.30-10, Closed D Sun **Prices** Fixed L 2 course £15, Fixed D 3 course £30, Tasting menu £55, Starter £7-£12, Main £13-£25, Dessert £5-£8 **Wines** 190 bottles over £30, 8 bottles under £30, 14 by glass **Parking** 19, Town centre **Notes** Sunday L £38, Vegetarian available, Children welcome

RICHMOND UPON THAMES *continued*

The Dysart Petersham
PLAN 1 C2

◉◉ Modern British V

tel: 020 8940 8005 **135 Petersham Rd, Petersham TW10 7AA**
email: enquiries@thedysartpetersham.co.uk **web:** www.thedysartpetersham.co.uk
dir: *By pedestrian gate to Richmond Park in centre of Petersham*

Fantastic ingredients used creatively in an Arts and Crafts setting

The decor at The Dysart is kept neutrally simple the better to show off the 1904 Arts and Crafts building's original leaded windows and wooden window frames. The oak bar is even older, bought in 1850 from decommissioned French warships. The building faces south over Richmond Park, so sunshine streams in on bright days, and a low-key jazz soundtrack floats around the elegant room. Kenneth Culhane is a confident cook whose experimental approach delivers some fascinating, intricately detailed dishes full of subtle interplays of taste and texture. How about roast quail, with dehydrated Petersham nettles, fermented chilli, fresh peas for starters, or charred mackerel with kombu-braised daikon, ginger and champagne? A classical training is evident in precise mains made with top-class ingredients; witness a three-way serving of Middlewhite pork (loin, belly and nut-crusted gammon) partnered with velvety Cévennes onion purée, radicchio, and black truffle mustard, or perhaps wild sea bass with lemon celeriac, and a spiced kaffir lime and green chilli sauce. It all ends strongly with an air-light burnt honey custard with Chablis apple.

Chef Kenneth Culhane **Owner** Mr & Mrs W N Taylor **Seats** 50, Pr/dining room 40 **Times** 11.30-3/5.30-11.30, Closed 25 Dec, D Sun **Prices** Fixed L 2 course fr £18.50, Fixed D 3 course fr £22.50, Tasting menu fr £60, Starter £7.50-£15.50, Main £15.95-£26.95, Dessert £7-£9.50, Service optional **Wines** 120 bottles over £30, 37 bottles under £30, 15 by glass **Parking** 30 **Notes** Sun L Prix fixe 3 course £34, Sunday L, Children 10 yrs+ D

The Petersham Hotel
PLAN 1 C2

◉◉ British, European V

tel: 020 8939 1084 & 8940 7471 **Nightingale Ln TW10 6UZ**
email: restaurant@petershamhotel.co.uk **web:** www.petershamhotel.co.uk
dir: *From Richmond Bridge rdbt A316 follow Ham & Petersham signs. Hotel in Nightingale Ln on left off Petersham Rd*

Classic cookery overlooking a bend of the Thames

Built on the side of Richmond Hill in 1865, The Petersham is master of all it surveys, which takes in a stretch of the Thames and its surrounding meadows, the view best enjoyed from the terrace. Sports fans note: it's not too far from the rugby at Twickenham either. The dining room capitalises on the location with its own views over the river bend, and with comfortable banquette seating and smartly dressed tables, a sense of high-toned relaxation is assured. Choose from the great value set menu and you'll find classic combinations, starting with the likes of chicken liver parfait with a range of heritage beetroots and pink onions, followed by Dingley Dell pork loin with creamed potatoes, pancetta and Agen prunes. Trade up to the carte and the opener might be roast poussin with pearl barley, celeriac and artichokes, followed by a tranche of wild sea bass with smoked shrimps, baked pasta, braised leeks and sea purslane. Desserts include rice pudding beignets with chocolate sauce, or classic tarte Tatin with caramel ice cream.

Chef Adebola Adeshina **Owner** The Petersham Hotel Ltd **Seats** 70, Pr/dining room 26 **Times** 12.15-2.15/7-9.45, Closed 25-26 Dec, 1 Jan, D 24 Dec **Prices** Fixed L 2 course £22.95, Fixed D 3 course £26.95, Starter £8-£16, Main £16-£34, Dessert £8-£16 **Wines** 93 bottles over £30, 34 bottles under £30, 8 by glass **Parking** 45 **Notes** Degustation menu 5 course £95, Sunday L fr £34.50, Children welcome

Petersham Nurseries Café
PLAN 1 C2

◉ Modern British, Italian

tel: 020 8940 5230 **Church Ln, Petersham Rd TW10 7AB**
email: info@petershamnurseries.com
dir: *Adjacent to Richmond Park & Petersham Meadows. Best accessed on foot or bicycle along the river*

Fresh, vibrant cooking from garden to plate

This ramshackle glasshouse café in a garden centre is a true one-off, self-consciously rustic, unfussy, shabby-chic, and great fun (cheerful, certainly, but far from cheap). The place is a dress-down affair that's magical on sunny days, when it feels more Tuscany than Richmond, with its dirt floor, mismatched tables and chairs and leafy surrounds. The kitchen builds its modern Italian-accented menus on the seasonal bounty of fresh produce that flows from the garden, including edible flowers and herbs straight from the walled potager. The results are colourful plates of lively flavours such as a whole poussin with fennel and rosemary, chargrilled celeriac, violet potatoes and watercress salsa, or monkfish with Castelluccio lentils, anchovies, preserved tomatoes and fashionable barba di frate greens. Bookending this, perhaps risotto with pheasant and radicchio, and for pud, Yorkshire rhubarb and almond tart with rhubarb ice cream.

Chef Damian Clisby **Owner** Franceso & Gael Boglione **Seats** 120, Pr/dining room 20 **Times** 12-2, Closed Etr Sun, 25 Dec, Mon (ex BHs), D all week **Prices** Fixed L 2 course fr £23, Starter £10-£15, Main £19-£30, Dessert £5-£8 **Wines** 83 bottles over £30, 6 bottles under £30, 8 by glass **Parking** Town Centre, Paradise Rd or The Quadrant **Notes** Supper Club 15 evenings/yr £75, Vegetarian available, Children welcome

RUISLIP

The Barn Hotel
PLAN 1 A5

◉◉ Modern French **v**

tel: 01895 636057 **West End Rd HA4 6JB**
email: info@thebarnhotel.co.uk web: www.thebarnhotel.co.uk
dir: *A40 onto A4180 (Polish War Memorial) exit to Ruislip. 2m to hotel entrance at mini-rdbt before Ruislip tube station*

Assertive modern cooking at a Middlesex boutique hotel

An expansive modern boutique hotel handy for inward-bound travellers at Heathrow, The Barn might sound rather agricultural, but stands in fact in three acres of attractive landscaped gardens, and has all the business facilities you might need. A Jacobethan effect has been created in the dark-panelled dining room, Hawtrey's, where classical music plays, and the scene is set with chandeliers, spotlit oil paintings, and painstaking descriptions of the dishes as they're delivered. Chef Vic Ramana cooked his way around the Indian Ocean before arriving in Middlesex, and there's a refreshing breadth of appeal to the menus. Langoustine in squid ink tortellini with pak choi is a dramatic starter, and big, convincing flavours distinguish potted duck with cranberry jelly and pickled veg, as well as slow-cooked pork belly with black pudding crushed potatoes, an onion bhaji and raisin purée. An assertive approach to fish sees roast brill and calamari offset with red pepper tapenade, a ragoût of mange-tout and clam-flavoured foam. Technically impressive desserts include a chocolate sponge roll filled with pistachio parfait, served with clearly defined Baileys ice cream.

Chef Vic Ramana **Owner** Pantheon Hotels & Leisure **Seats** 44, Pr/dining room 20 **Times** 12-2.30/7-10.30, Closed L Sat, D Sun **Prices** Prices not confirmed **Wines** 9 by glass **Parking** 50 **Notes** Sunday L, Children welcome

SURBITON

The French Table
PLAN 1 C1

◉◉ Modern French **v** 🍷NOTABLE WINE LIST

tel: 020 8399 2365 **85 Maple Rd KT6 4AW**
email: enquiries@thefrenchtable.co.uk
dir: *5 min walk from Surbiton station, 1m from Kingston*

Modern French goings-on in a twinned restaurant and bakery

Restaurant and boulangerie sit side by side in a leafy quarter of Surbiton, French Table and French Tarte joined at the hip. In case you hadn't quite grasped the point, a row of little tricolors hangs in front of the baker's premises, and a paradise of pastries, breads and cakes awaits. Next door, they're settling into pale green banquettes at smartly clothed tables for a repertoire of appealing modern French cooking that absorbs touches of north Africa, in the likes of roasted vegetable pastilla in harissa oil, and Italian tradition, though to a lesser extent than it used to. Partridge breast with girolles in foie gras sauce could be the opulent opener to cod with salmon and ginger mousse and a lobster beignet, or Herdwick lamb crumbed in goats' cheese with potato and beetroot gratin in sage sauce. The drill is a lunchtime prix-fixe and evening carte, now supplemented by a five-course taster, running from langoustine miso soup to a dessert assiette, perhaps incorporating thyme pannacotta in cinnamon syrup, or passionfruit tart with white chocolate and ginger ice cream.

Chef Eric Guignard **Owner** Eric & Sarah Guignard **Seats** 48, Pr/dining room 32 **Times** 12-2.30/7-10.30, Closed 25-26 Dec, 1-3 Jan, Sun-Mon **Prices** Fixed L 3 course £23.50, Tasting menu fr £45 **Wines** 62 bottles over £30, 35 bottles under £30, 10 by glass **Parking** On street **Notes** Tasting menu Tue-Sat D with wine £75, Children welcome

TEDDINGTON

Retro
PLAN 1 C1

◉◉ French **v**

tel: 020 8977 2239 **114-116 High St TW11 8JB**
email: retrobistrot@aim.com
dir: *A313 Teddington High St*

Le retro-cooking véritable de la France

When le patron named the place Retro, he meant it. The high-street bistro consists of a pair of rooms furnished with bentwood chairs at little unclothed tables, and a display of artworks on bare brick. That said, any starkness is thrown into relief by purple wallpaper on some walls, gathered drapes and chandeliers, and by voluble Gallic warmth in the service approach. The core of the menu is classic French bistro cookery, tracing a lineage from foie gras terrine, apple chutney and brioche to vanilla-rich crème brûlée, via the likes of guinea-fowl with carrots Vichy and potato fondant in red wine. Discreet modernisation of the repertoire can be productive too, as when a clutch of scallops turns up on grainy sweetcorn purée with crisped bacon, followed perhaps by confit pork belly with spiced apple and pickled white cabbage, or a roasting of halibut with baby spinach in mussel cream. Chocomaniacs will go gaga for the glorious soufflé with its matching double-choc ice cream and sauce, while others set soberly about a quintet of cheeses.

Chef François Fayd'Herbe de Maudave **Owner** Vincent Gerbeau **Seats** 110, Pr/dining room 50 **Times** 12-3.30/6.30-11, Closed Xmas, 1 Jan, BHs, D Sun **Prices** Fixed L 2 course £12.95, Fixed D 3 course £19.95-£22.50, Starter £6.20-£18, Main £13.50-£27.50, Dessert £7-£7.95 **Wines** 56 bottles over £30, 30 bottles under £30, 26 by glass **Parking** On street **Notes** Fixed D 2/3 course min price applies Mon-Thu, max Fri-Sat, Sunday L, Children welcome

TWICKENHAM

A Cena
PLAN 1 C2

◉ Modern Italian

tel: 020 8288 0108 **418 Richmond Rd TW1 2EB**
email: acenarichmond@gmail.com
dir: *100yds from Richmond Bridge*

Reliable Italian cooking near Richmond Bridge

On the Twickenham side of Richmond Bridge, A Cena is an informal neighbourhood bistro-style Italian that reliably comes up with the goods, dishing up comforting, authentic cooking that follows the seasons and is big on flavour. A Spring meal opens with a stimulating partnership of pan-fried Cornish mackerel fillet with grilled cucumber salad, while main course brings pan-roasted lamb rump matched with a vibrantly minty salsa verde, braised tomato with onions and buttery smashed cannellini beans. There's pasta too, of course – perhaps fusilli with a cacciatore sauce of rabbit braised with vegetables, tomato, white wine and herbs. For pudding, torta di Verona is a moreesome, tiramisù-like confection of light sponge soaked in bitter-sweet Amaretto liqueur and Marsala, layered with gooey mascarpone and served with blueberries and roasted almonds. Cheeses and wines all speak with an Italian accent.

Chef Nicola Parsons **Owner** Justine Kemsley **Seats** 55 **Times** 12-2/7-10, Closed Xmas & BHs, L Mon, D Sun **Prices** Starter £2.95-£10, Main £7-£23.50, Dessert £4.50-£6 **Wines** 60 bottles over £30, 13 bottles under £30, 16 by glass **Parking** On street **Notes** Fixed L 3 course pre-rugby £50, Express L Tue-Sat £10, Sunday L £21-£25, Vegetarian available, Children welcome

MERSEYSIDE

BIRKENHEAD
Map 15 SJ38

Fraiche
◉◉◉◉ – see page 415

FRANKBY
Map 15 SJ28

The Dining Room at Hillbark

@@@ – see page 416

Hillbark Grill

@@ Modern British NEW

---

tel: 0151 6252400 **Royden Park CH48 1NP**
dir: *M53 junct 3, A552 (Upton), right onto A551 (Arrowe Park Rd). 0.6m at lights, left into Arrowe Brook Rd. 0.5m on left*

Oak-panelled grill cookery

Built in the 1890s for the Hudson soap family, precursor to Lever Brothers, the house was moved and painstakingly reassembled piece by piece in its current location at the turn of the 1930s. Incorporating a fireplace once belonging to Sir Walter Raleigh, another by Robert Adam, and stained-glass by William Morris, it's an architectural treasure not to be missed. While the full-dress menu is served in The Dining Room, the Grill is a good bet too for traditional British fare in an oak-panelled ambience. Grilled whole Dover sole in caper butter is sublimely fresh, for all that it could do with a little neater trimming, while other options include steaks, chops, burgers, and duck breast with cherries and watercress. A pair of veggies might share a large goats' cheese and beetroot tart, served with gnocchi and wild mushrooms. Veg and sauces are charged extra. Starter could be as simple as Caesar, or as artfully composed as scallops with smoked eel on risotto, adorned with apple purée and squid-ink crackers. Finish with tonka pannacotta, pistachio crumble and blackberries.

Chef Ashley Moran **Owner** Contessa Hotels **Seats** Pr/dining room 30 **Times** 12-10.30, All-day dining, Closed Tue-Wed **Prices** Starter £6-£10, Main £13-£57, Dessert £6-£10, Service optional 12.5% **Wines** 600 bottles over £30, 3 bottles under £30, 560 by glass **Parking** 160 **Notes** Sunday L £24, Vegetarian available, Children welcome

---

LIVERPOOL
Map 15 SJ39

Albina Restaurant

@ Traditional British NEW

---

tel: 0151 932 9460 **55 Coronation Rd, Crosby L23 5RE**
email: crosby@albina.co.uk
dir: *Follow A565 to lights at Stamps Bar. Left onto Coronation Rd*

History meets gastronomy in outer Liverpool suburb

The concept in this wood floored, bare brick-walled Crosby restaurant is rather novel: British food through the ages. The year the recipe for each dish was first published is noted on the menu so, for example, among the starters are potted Southport shrimp (1797), crispy lamb's tongue (1679), and house black pudding (1660). The oldest main course, allegedly from 1390, is macrows, an old word for macaroni with Northumbrian Chevington cheese. By contrast, Mrs Kirkham's fish pie can be traced back only to 2014. Lamb cutlets wrapped in sausage meat were, of course, a 19th-century favourite, and Arthur Kenny-Herbert's chicken curry was a dish this British-Indian army officer included in *Culinary Jottings for Madras*, published in 1878. The nostalgic theme continues with desserts such as lemon jelly with mead and whipped cream, and jam roly-poly. The malty beer bread with mustard butter is an added delight.

Chef Steven Burgess **Owner** Alex McElhoney **Seats** 52 **Times** 12-3/8-11, Closed 26-28 Dec, 1 Jan, Mon, L Tue-Sat **Prices** Starter £4-£6.50, Main £10-£16.50, Dessert £3-£8, Service optional **Wines** 5 bottles over £30, 17 bottles under £30, 10 by glass **Parking** On street **Notes** Small plates menu Tue-Thu & before 7pm Fri-Sat, Sunday L £15-£18, Vegetarian available, Children welcome

The Art School Restaurant, Liverpool

@@ Modern International NEW v

tel: 0151 230 8600 **1 Sugnall St L7 7DX**
email: eat@theartschoolrestaurant.co.uk **web:** www.theartschoolrestaurant.co.uk
dir: *Up Leece St then Hope St, follow A5039 around to back of Liverpool Philharmonic, taking 1st road on right. Restaurant on this road, and is only door on Sugnall St*

Confident modernist cooking in a new city-centre venue

Local food hero Paul Askew, who has lately been the creative force behind some of Liverpool's high-achieving hotels and restaurants, opened The Art School in September 2014. From the city-centre site of a Victorian home for destitute children, a typically dynamic and exciting space has been conjured, the main restaurant looking like a stage set, with its combination of dark wood, veined slate, glass roof, and chairs in fashionable raspberry-red. A fish tank window affords kitchen views. Askew has brought thoroughgoing British culinary modernism to Liverpool, and takes things a stage further here. Dishes are carefully composed, full of imaginative juxtapositions, and confidently rendered. A fat butter-seared scallop sits regally amid smoked pork loin, caramelised celeriac purée and a slew of golden raisins in Sauternes and garlic vinaigrette. These are just a prelude to properly trimmed red-legged partridge with a mini Cox's apple tart, a parmesaned cabbage parcel and quince paste for a fine autumnal main course. Fish could be a hake fillet robustly supported by morcilla and Brussels sprouts. A well-executed pear and apricot frangipane tart makes a fitting finale with its accompaniments of white chocolate mascarpone and limoncello syrup.

Chef Paul Askew **Owner** Paul Askew **Seats** 50 **Times** 12-2.30/5-9.30, Closed 25-26 Dec, 1 Jan, Sun-Mon **Prices** Fixed L 2 course fr £22.50, Fixed D 3 course fr £29, Tasting menu £89-£108.50 **Wines** 248 bottles over £30, 22 bottles under £30, 13 by glass **Parking** On street **Notes** Pre-theatre menu, Children welcome

Fraiche ✿✿✿✿

Modern French, European V

tel: 0151 652 2914 **11 Rose Mount, Oxton CH43 5SG**
email: contact@restaurantfraiche.com
dir: M53 junct 3 towards Prenton. In 2m left towards Oxton. Fraiche on right

Cutting-edge cooking on the Wirral peninsula

Chef-patron Marc Wilkinson's idiosyncratic Wirral restaurant is certainly a one-off: with just five tables to cater for (and a new chef's table in a glass room), he can give full rein to his cutting-edge culinary creativity. Of course, he could squeeze far more tables into the compact dining room (and reduce the waiting time for queues of foodies clamouring to bag one) but prefers to plough his own furrow, thinking through every aspect of the experience, from the decor of the decidedly understated room itself (conceived to reflect the topography of the local shoreline), to the soundtrack and accompanying images projected onto the walls, to choreographing the well-drilled, attentive and knowledgeable service team, who are happy to talk you through the intricacies of each dish as it arrives at the table – a rather useful bonus since descriptions are minimal. Even the location, in the leafy conservation village of Oxton, rather than across the Mersey amid Liverpool's regenerated dockside glamour, speaks of a man who has no wish to court celebrity. Wilkinson says he is obsessed with food and the science of how we perceive flavours and textures. The results of his tireless research and discoveries are six-course menus that unfold at a leisurely pace; classical French foundations inform ingredients, techniques and the visually arresting presentation of the dishes, although produce is often transformed into dusts, powders, gels and foams. A trio of perfectly-sculpted appetisers paves the way for what is to follow: turnip greens with goats' curd and crushed cocoa; a cloud of apple foam with apple gel and borage flowers and leaves adding bitter freshness; horseradish pannacotta with finely-shredded bresaola beef and hazelnut. Then the meal proper gets under way with a thought-provoking opener matching diced scallop with compressed avocado, wasabi leaf, grapefruit gel, a buttermilk sphere and salty pumpkin seeds. Main courses bring roast turbot with various preparations of cauliflower (roasted, pickled, puréed), a squid ink crisp, fried capers and gherkin purée, while charcoal-grilled rib-eye of beef is boosted by cep cream, textures of celeriac and crisps of potato and spinach. Sweet courses draw things to conclusion, with a final flourish of techno wizardry displayed in ideas including lemongrass pannacotta with sour cherry foam, fizzy grapes with mint, lemon sponge filled with lemon curd, sorrel and candied lemon zest, and green tea set cream shrouded within a film of raspberry jelly, plus roasted white chocolate cream and lemon verbena. The 300-bin list meets the challenge of matching wines to food of this ilk, and wine flights are highly recommended as huge effort goes into pairing unusual choices to each dish.

Chef Marc Wilkinson **Owner** Marc Wilkinson **Seats** 16, Pr/dining room 20 **Times** 12-1.30/7-close, Closed 25 Dec, 1 Jan, 2 wks Aug, Mon-Tue, L Wed-Thu **Prices** Prices not confirmed, Service optional **Wines** 260 bottles over £30, 30 bottles under £30, 8 by glass **Parking** On street **Notes** Tasting menu L £38/D £85, Sunday L, Children 8 yrs+

LIVERPOOL *continued*

The London Carriage Works
◉◉ Modern European ⬥ NOTABLE WINE LIST

tel: 0151 705 2222 **40 Hope St L1 9DA**
email: eat@hopestreethotel.co.uk **web:** www.thelondoncarriageworks.co.uk
dir: *Follow cathedral & university signs on entering city, at the centre of Hope St between the two cathedrals*

Regionally-focused menu in a trendy hotel conversion

The stripped-back interior of the one-time carriage workshop is a very modern sort of dining room, with decorative shards of floor-to-ceiling glass and lots of exposed bricks, plus large windows to give a view of the street action. There's plenty of room between the lightwood tables and the young service team are attentive. The menu makes much of provenance and there's a satisfying regional flavour to the menu.

Grilled fillet of Menai mackerel might kick things off, or breast of Lakeland wood pigeon with a beetroot and green peppercorn sauce. There are sharing platters, too, with vegetarian, seafood and meaty options, plus salads such as one with marinated herring fillets and new potatoes. Main-course assiette of Blackface Suffolk lamb consists of loin, shoulder and kidney, or go for roast breast of Gressingham duck with jasmine tea, pink grapefruit and root ginger jus. Desserts run to Sicilian lemon and raspberry tart – good and zesty – with raspberry sorbet and sesame tuile, and there's a good selection of British cheeses.

Chef David Critchley **Owner** David Brewitt **Seats** 100, Pr/dining room 50
Times 12-3/5-10, Closed D 25 Dec **Prices** Fixed L 2 course £17.50, Fixed D 3 course £22.50, Tasting menu £62.50-£110, Starter £5-£14, Main £11.50-£28, Dessert £5-£10, Service optional 10% **Wines** 125 bottles over £30, 45 bottles under £30, 21 by glass **Parking** On street, car park opposite **Notes** Breakfast, Afternoon tea, Pre-theatre menu, Sunday L £17.50-£22.50, Vegetarian available, Children welcome

Malmaison Liverpool
◉ Modern British

tel: 0151 229 5000 **7 William Jessop Way, Princes Dock L3 1QZ**
email: liverpool@malmaison.com **web:** www.malmaison.com
dir: *Located on Princes Dock near the Liver Building*

Modern brasserie food on the Princes Dock

Right on the water's edge, with the Liver Birds as near neighbours, the Liverpool Mal is in the heart of the action. It's a purpose-built hotel with the brands trademark luxe bedrooms, some of which pay homage to Liverpool legends. The double-height brasserie references the industrial heritage of the city, and the docks in particular, with a stripped-down, industrial look of exposed bricks and pipework. Modern brasserie cooking is the name of the game, with plenty of global flavours on

The Dining Room at Hillbark ❁❁❁

FRANKBY	Map 15 SJ28

Modern British ⱽ ⬥ NOTABLE WINE LIST
tel: 0151 625 2400 **Royden Park CH48 1NP**
email: enquiries@hillbarkhotel.co.uk **web:** www.hillbarkhotel.co.uk
dir: *M53 junct 3, A552 (Upton), right onto A551 (Arrowe Park Rd). 0.6m at lights left into Arrowe Brook Rd. 0.5m on left*

Textural surprises and bold presentations

So committed were the Victorians to imagining themselves architecturally back into the medieval era that it's tempting to imagine them addressing each other in Chaucerian English. The Hudson soapflake family commissioned this impeccable replica of a timber manor house in 1891. It was moved, bit by carefully labelled bit, to its present location between the wars, and has a great deal to show for itself, including a fireplace before which Sir Walter Raleigh once warmed himself. The surroundings demand cooking that makes a striking statement. Enter Richard Collingwood, whose cooking style is as firmly in the contemporary groove as can be. Counter-intuitive ingredient pairings, textural surprises and bold presentations all come as standard, and the results are hard to argue with. A portion of veal sweetbread acquires the company of a chicken wing to start, the forthright Indian spices in the accompanying granola emphasised by dates and tamarind. The Japanese way with crab

adds miso and pickled mooli, but for a true touch of the unexpected, a bundle of braised dulse (red seaweed). Main courses accord their prime ingredients star billing, but with a cast of unusual extras in each case, whether for monkfish with celeriac, salsify and oyster emulsion, or the oxidised pear, liquoriced carrots and blood pudding that come with suckling pig. They're the kinds of dishes that make you want to try everything, which is where the eight-course taster may come in handy. Dessert could be olive oil cake with pistachios, lemon and yogurt, but even the cheese option is transformed into a dish, as when Stilton is teamed with cranberries, amaretti and raspberry vinegar.

Chef Richard Collingwood **Owner** Contessa Hotels **Seats** 36, Pr/dining room 30
Times 12-10, All-day dining, Closed Sun-Mon **Prices** Fixed L 2 course £18.50, Fixed D 3 course £60, Tasting menu £90 **Wines** 600 bottles over £30, 3 bottles under £30, 560 by glass **Parking** 160 **Notes** Afternoon tea £25 (with champagne £33), Children welcome

show. Fritto misto recalls sunnier climes, with the tempura of squid, tiger prawn and courgette served up with a lemon aïoli and sweet chilli sauce, or there's a classic Caesar salad available as either a starter or main course. Steak frites is another old favourite, served with a red wine and shallot sauce, while chicken tikka with a masala sauce shows the global reach of the kitchen. Finish with pear tarte Tatin with Calvados mascarpone.

Times 12-2/6.30-10.30, Closed L Sat

60 Hope Street Restaurant

🏵 Modern British V

tel: 0151 707 6060 60 Hope St L1 9BZ
email: info@60hopestreet.com web: www.60hopestreet.com
dir: From M62 follow city centre signs, then brown tourist signs for cathedral. Hope St near cathedral

Confident modern cooking near the cathedrals

In a handy spot, close to the Philharmonic Hall and the two cathedrals, this popular Georgian townhouse restaurant still pulls in the crowds 15 years down the line. The ground-floor dining room goes for a smart, contemporary big-city look, with a stripped-back decor of wooden floors and bare-brick walls, but remains a reassuringly friendly place to eat, and a metal staircase leads to a relaxed basement bistro. Simple, seasonal British food with a Mediterranean glow is the deal, starting with the comfort and fun of crisply-fried ham hock terrine with egg, chips and béarnaise sauce, followed by pan-fried salmon with a cassoulet of Spanish white beans and chorizo. Otherwise, go for something like roast rump of Cumbrian lamb with duck fat potatoes, parsnips and carrots and mint jus, and finish with pear and almond tart with dulce de leche ice cream.

Chef Neil Devereux Owner Colin & Gary Manning Seats 90, Pr/dining room 40 Times 12-2.30/5-10.30, Closed 26 Dec, 1 Jan Prices Fixed L 2 course £19.95, Fixed D 3 course £24.95, Starter £6.95-£13.95, Main £12.95-£29.95, Dessert £5.95-£9.95, Service optional Wines 60 bottles over £30, 9 bottles under £30, 6 by glass Parking On street Notes Pre-theatre 5-7pm, Sunday L, Children welcome

PORT SUNLIGHT Map 15 SJ38

Leverhulme Hotel

🏵🏵 Modern International

tel: 0151 644 6655 & 644 5555 Central Rd CH62 5EZ
email: enquiries@leverhulmehotel.co.uk web: www.leverhulmehotel.co.uk
dir: From Chester: M53 junct 5, A41 (Birkenhead) in approx 4m left into Bolton Rd, on at rdbt, 0.1m right into Church Drive. 0.2m hotel on right. From Liverpool: A41 (Chester), 2.7m, 3rd exit at 3rd rdbt into Bolton Rd (follow directions as above)

Locally-sourced natural flavours amid art deco philanthropy

The whiter-than-white interiors of the Leverhulme are fitting for a building that has its origins in cleanliness. One of the Edwardian era's great philanthropists, Lord

Leverhulme, opened the place in 1907 as a cottage hospital for soapworks employees at his Port Sunlight garden village, and who wouldn't find their health restored amid such exquisite art deco surroundings? Maintaining the ethical standards in which its history is steeped, the hotel now boasts a dining venue called Twenty-Eight Miles, which is the distance, as the crow flies from Port Sunlight, within which most of the supplies are garnered. The menu is a celebration of natural bounty with the likes of Hedgerow Platter (pigeon terrine, blackberry jelly, pickled mushrooms), Wirral Rock Pool (crayfish in bisque with an egg yolk simmered at 62 degrees), cod loin in a borrowed coat of chicken skin with caramelised onion purée, and a dessert array of sweet vegetables – pea pannacotta, carrot and vanilla purée, beetroot jelly and honeyed parsnip.

Times 12-2.30/6-10

SOUTHPORT Map 15 SD31

Bistrot Vérité

🏵🏵 French

tel: 01704 564199 7 Liverpool Rd, Birkdale PR8 4AR
dir: Phone for directions

Traditional French cooking in Birkdale village

Marc and Michaela Vérité's place has an unaffected charm that is the very essence of a neighbourhood bistro. The neighbourhood may well be Birkdale village, but the focus of the menu is classic French fare, albeit with contemporary finesse and lots of local Lancashire ingredients. The tables are closely packed, the staff are chatty, keen and clued-up, and the place generates a contented buzz much of the time. Start perhaps with a daily special such as baked crab thermidor jazzed up with some crispy samphire and croûtes. Next up, roast haunch of red deer is a modern number with a tasting of pear and fois gras cromesquis, finished with a deeply flavoursome red wine jus, or go for Scottish mussels in marinière mode. 'Le steaks' include rib-eye, fillet and the mighty Chateaubriand for two (served with frites, salad and a choice of classic sauce). Finish with tarte Tatin or rhubarb and custard millefeuille. The wine list is mostly French and includes a decent house wine by the glass or carafe.

Chef Marc Vérité Owner Marc & Michaela Vérité Seats 45 Times 12-1.30/5.30-late, Closed 1 wk Feb & 1 wk Aug, Sun-Mon Prices Starter £5-£12, Main £10-£27, Dessert £6.25, Service optional Wines 12 bottles over £30, 29 bottles under £30 Parking Birkdale station Notes Vegetarian available, Children welcome

Gusto Trattoria

🏵 Modern Italian

tel: 01704 544255 58-62 Lord St PR8 1QB
email: info@gustotrattoria.co.uk
dir: Located centre Southport

A taste of Italy in Southport

Gusto is a trattoria with a nice line in cheerful bonhomie and some good and proper Italian cooking. The two rooms are looked over by the charming service team and the open kitchen adds to the buzz of the place. The food does not attempt to reinvent the wheel, just to do things properly. The pizzas are very good – the 'boscaiola', for example, with ham and mushrooms, or the 'Gusto', fired up with anchovies and chilli. Vegetali parmigiana is a first course filled with the flavours of the Med, or go for polpette piccanti (meatballs in a spicy Arrabiata sauce). Pasta is made in-house and should not be ignored: pappardelle al carciofo, maybe, which is cooked perfectly, or try the gnocchi al pesto. Desserts such as frutta caramellata and home-made tiramisù hit the spot, too, and it all comes at a very reasonable price.

Chef Giorgio Lamola Owner Giorgio Lamola Seats 38 Times 12-3/5-10, Closed Mon (excl BH) Prices Prices not confirmed, Service optional Parking On street Notes Open all day Sat-Sun 12-10, Vegetarian available, Children welcome

SOUTHPORT continued

Vincent Hotel

◉◉ British, European, Japanese

tel: 01704 883800 **98 Lord St PR8 1JR**
email: manager@thevincenthotel.com **web:** www.thevincenthotel.com
dir: M58 junct 3, follow signs to Ormskirk & Southport

Skilful cooking in a stylish hotel

The V-Café and Sushi Bar at this stylish contemporary hotel is the place to be in the evening, when lights are dimmed and candles are lit. Tables are closely packed and floor-to-ceiling windows look onto bustling Lord Street, where there are tables for alfresco dining. The menu roams around Britain and Europe before arriving in Japan with some platters of authentic sushi and sashimi, maki and temaki, with a section of 'gringo sushi for non-fish-lovers' – roasted crispy duck and mango maki for example, or barbecue pulled pork maki. Choosing from the European side of the fence, you might start with uncomplicated classics along the lines of duck liver parfait with toasted brioche, or smoked haddock and salmon fishcake with tartare sauce and endive salad. A main course suprême of cod matched with spring onion mash and brown shrimp beurre noisette stands out for its freshness, accurate cooking and balanced combinations. Those with a taste for rhubarb could finish with the tart vegetable served as ice cream and compôte with custard foam and spicy ginger crumb.

Chef Andrew Carter **Owner** Paul Adams **Seats** 85, Pr/dining room 12 **Times** 7.30am-9.30pm, All-day dining **Prices** Starter £3.95-£9.95, Main £12.95-£25.95, Dessert £6.50-£14.95, Service optional 10% **Wines** 8 bottles over £30, 12 bottles under £30, 5 by glass **Parking** 50, Valet parking **Notes** Fixed D 3 course Sun-Thu, Sunday L £13.95, Vegetarian available, Children welcome

THORNTON HOUGH   Map 15 SJ38

The Lawns Restaurant at Thornton Hall

◉◉◉ – see opposite

WALLASEY   Map 15 SJ29

Canteen

◉ Modern British, European **NEW**

tel: 0151 6383633 **45 Wallasey Rd CH45 4NN**
email: bookings@canteenrestaurant.co.uk
dir: Liscard town centre, approx 1.5m from Wallasey/Liverpool tunnel. 100 mtrs from Boot public house

Competitively priced brasserie-style food

From the street the premises look rather unassuming, more shop-front than restaurant, but don't be deterred. The long, simply styled room you'll enter is decorated in black, grey and silver, with a small bar near the entrance and a young, friendly serving team. A straightforward one-, two- or three-course fixed-price menu lists traditional and modern dishes, or you can opt for a steak. Well-balanced flavours are brought out in starters of home-made chicken liver parfait with red onion marmalade, and sticky chipolatas with honey and wholegrain mustard. Turning to the mains, choices include slow-roasted, home-cured pork belly with Chinese five spice, Asian slaw and sweet chilli, and marinated smoked fish kedgeree risotto with a free-range egg. For vegetarians, there's gnocchi with pumpkin, feta and pine nuts. Children's dishes include ice cream and a fruit shoot.

Chef Alan Wycherley **Owner** Alan & Diane Wycherley **Seats** 25 **Times** 5-9, Closed BHs, 26 Dec, 1 Jan, Sun-Mon, L all week **Prices** Fixed D 3 course £13.95-£19.45, Service optional **Wines** 2 bottles over £30, 16 bottles under £30, 5 by glass **Parking** On street, car park in adjacent street **Notes** Vegetarian available, Children welcome

NORFOLK

ALBURGH   Map 13 TM28

The Dove Restaurant with Rooms

◉◉ Modern, Traditional European V

tel: 01986 788315 **Holbrook Hill IP20 0EP**
email: info@thedoverestaurant.co.uk **web:** www.thedoverestaurant.co.uk
dir: On South Norfolk border between Harleston & Bungay, by A143, at junct of B1062

Classic cooking in charming restaurant with rooms

Robert and Conny Oberhoffer have been running their restaurant with rooms for 15 years, although it's been in Robert's family since 1980. The restaurant is a prettily decorated room, long and thin, with two rows of dining tables on a lightwood floor, the scene for some classy honest-to-goodness cooking. Hits among starters include home-made pork and game terrine with onion chutney, and potted smoked mackerel pâté with piri-piri sauce. Typical of the straightforward style of main courses is venison casserole with creamed potatoes, red cabbage and ham, and roast whole sea bass finished with a balsamic reduction served with peppers, capers and sun-dried tomatoes. Breads are made in-house, as are puddings of Valrhona chocolate terrine with meringue, whipped cream and mango coulis, and cherry and confectioner's custard flan with home-made ice cream.

Chef Robert Oberhoffer **Owner** Robert & Conny Oberhoffer **Seats** 60 **Times** 12-2/7-9, Closed Mon-Thu, L Fri-Sat, D Sun **Prices** Prices not confirmed, Service optional **Wines** 1 bottle over £30, 31 bottles under £30, 5 by glass **Parking** 20 **Notes** Sunday L, Children welcome

BARNHAM BROOM   Map 13 TG00

Barnham Broom

◉ Modern British, European

tel: 01603 759393 **Honingham Rd NR9 4DD**
email: enquiry@barnhambroomhotel.co.uk **web:** www.barnham-broom.co.uk
dir: A11/A47 towards Swaffham, follow brown tourist signs

Contemporary cooking overlooking the golf course

Set within 300 acres of peaceful Norfolk countryside and landscaped grounds, this luxury hotel boasts two golf courses, plus a gym, indoor pool and spa facilities. There are two bars and The Brasserie, a modern, open-plan restaurant looking out to the greens. Catering for the diversity of its diners, the kitchen keeps dishes straightforward and there is a focus on showcasing Norfolk produce. The seasonal menu might kick off with an attractively presented dish of seared scallops teamed with chorizo and cauliflower purée. Grilled steaks feature among main courses, with a choice of marinades and sauces, with such classical alternatives as breast of chicken with fondant potato, Savoy cabbage and smoked bacon or roasted cod on braised fennel with saffron potatoes and chive and white wine sauce. Indulgent desserts include hazelnut parfait with mango salsa and chocolate sauce.

Chef Nigel Brown **Owner** Barnham Broom **Seats** 100, Pr/dining room 50 **Times** 12.30-2/7-9.30, Closed L Mon-Sat **Prices** Fixed L 2 course fr £15.95, Fixed D 3 course fr £27.50, Starter £5.45-£6.95, Main £10.95-£22.95, Dessert £5.95 **Wines** 27 bottles over £30, 29 bottles under £30, 9 by glass **Parking** 500 **Notes** Afternoon tea £12.95, Sunday L, Vegetarian available, Children welcome

The Lawns Restaurant at Thornton Hall ⚘⚘⚘

THORNTON HOUGH   Map 15 SJ38

Modern European V

tel: 0151 336 3938 **Neston Rd CH63 1JF**
email: reservations@thorntonhallhotel.com
web: www.lawnsrestaurant.com
dir: *M53 junct 4 onto B5151 & B5136, follow brown tourist signs (approx 2.5m) to Thornton Hall Hotel*

Forceful modernist cooking in an all-action hotel

There is a distinct feeling at Thornton Hall that it would be a shame to go there and loll about doing nothing. One of the hotel's many packages is Smart Boot Camp, a regime designed to hone your fitness and get your weight down by means of everything from boxing lessons to a snow cave. There's more golf than you can shake a niblick at, and at the heart of the appeal, a chandeliered dining room done in daringly dark tones, though with bay windows looking out over the lawns acknowledged in its name. A new executive chef, Matthew Worswick, has stepped in, though the kitchen brigade is still headed by the same personnel as before, and the cooking style hasn't lost its modernist energy. Dishes aim to make an impact partly through forceful and unusual combinations – start with a pairing of cod and a sticky chicken wing with Vichy carrots and smoked yogurt, and move on to ox cheek and an oxtail faggot in soy and coffee – and partly through clear references to culinary tradition of one source or another. That latter produces a first course of partridge in autumnal livery with pear, chestnuts and date purée, or home-smoked salmon à la japonaise with pickled cucumber and wasabi. Robust treatments for fish include the salted milk crumble and smoked almonds that accompany gurnard, or the Jerusalem artichokes, sprout tops and bacon with sea bream. For those who manage to resist the allurements of the cheese trolley, desserts take a botanical approach to ice creams, burdock root with chocolate delice and marquise, fennel with pistachio cake. The six-course tasting menu resolves all indecision.

Chef Matt Worswick **Owner** The Thompson family **Seats** 45, Pr/dining room 24 **Times** 12-2.30/7-9.30, **Prices** Fixed L 2 course fr £18, Tasting menu £75-£120, Starter £10-£14, Main £20-£27, Dessert £8-£10, Service optional **Wines** 100 bottles over £30, 27 bottles under £30, 18 by glass **Parking** 250 **Notes** Tasting menu Mon-Sat, Sunday L, Children welcome

BLAKENEY
Map 13 TG04

The Blakeney Hotel

Modern British V

tel: 01263 740797 **The Quay NR25 7NE**
email: reception@blakeneyhotel.co.uk **web:** www.blakeneyhotel.co.uk
dir: From A148 between Fakenham & Holt, take B1156 to Langham & Blakeney

Accomplished modern cooking in a quayside hotel

Those who like to be by the sea need look no further: this hotel is in a perfect spot on the quay, with magnificent views over the estuary to Blakeney Point. Well-sourced raw materials underpin the operation, while a sure-footed handling of ingredients gives dishes layers of flavours. Seared pigeon breast, for instance, comes with a salad of cracked wheat, hazelnuts and pistachios in mint and quince dressing, and a stew of peppers, chickpeas and orange is the accompaniment for squid seared with chorizo. To follow, roast breast of guinea fowl in bacon gets the familiar partners of roast roots, potato gratin and bread sauce. Well-timed grilled Dover sole comes on pommes Anna with pickled vegetables and caper and lemon butter. Puddings are in the mould of sherry trifle and lemon tart.

Chef Martin Sewell **Owner** Emma Stannard **Seats** 100, Pr/dining room 80 **Times** 12-2/6.30-9, Closed 25-27 Dec, D 24 & 31 Dec **Prices** Fixed D 3 course fr £29, Service optional **Wines** 25 bottles over £30, 75 bottles under £30, 16 by glass **Parking** 60 **Notes** ALC 3 course £29-£38.50, No high chairs after 6.45pm, Sunday L, Children welcome

Morston Hall

– see below

BRANCASTER STAITHE
Map 13 TF74

The White Horse

Modern, Traditional British

tel: 01485 210262 **PE31 8BY**
email: reception@whitehorsebrancaster.co.uk **web:** www.whitehorsebrancaster.co.uk
dir: On A149 (coast road) midway between Hunstanton & Wells-next-the-Sea

Seafood-led cooking on the Norfolk coastal marshes

The big skies of north Norfolk are always balm to the soul, and are all the better for being viewed over platefuls of fantastic regional produce. The White Horse has bagged itself a truly gorgeous coastal location, with sweeping views from its spacious conservatory dining room, or better still, from the decked terrace on balmy days, taking in tidal salt marshes complete with fishing boats and mussel growers going about their business. In a location such as this, diners are bound to have fish and seafood in mind, and the kitchen isn't about to argue, bringing together fantastic regional produce in its imaginative menus. Brancaster's finest mussels reliably turn up in the classic company of garlic, parsley, white wine and cream, while mains can be as timeless as fish and chips with minted mushy peas, or come in a contemporary idea such as pan-roasted sea bass with squid ink risotto, parsley root and on-trend crispy chicken skin. Local meat fans might find roast venison loin with game hotpot, parsnips, Savoy cabbage and cocoa nib jus.

Chef Fran Hartshorne **Owner** Clifford Nye **Seats** 100 **Times** 12-2/6.15-9 **Prices** Starter £5.95-£9, Main £12.95-£16.50, Dessert £5.50-£6.95, Service optional **Wines** 16 bottles over £30, 26 bottles under £30, 14 by glass **Parking** 85 **Notes** Sunday L £12.95-£16.50, Vegetarian available, Children welcome

Morston Hall

BLAKENEY
Map 13 TG04

Modern British, European V NOTABLE WINE LIST

tel: 01263 741041 **Morston, Holt NR25 7AA**
email: reception@morstonhall.com **web:** www.morstonhall.com
dir: On A149 (coast road) between Blakeney & Stiffkey

Seven-course dinner menu on the alluring north Norfolk coast

Morston stands on the A149 coastal road across alluring north Norfolk, in the vicinity of a cluster of historic houses, including the royal residence at Sandringham. It's a handsome enough house in itself, dating back to the Jacobean period, with generous glassed-in spaces at the front to take advantage of the maritime vistas. The Blackistons run the place with personable warmth and easy-going charm, and a considerateness that extends to plenty of room between tables in the dining areas, from the main restaurant to the orangery and conservatory. More than a little of the Lakeland ethos in which Galton Blackiston cut his teeth a generation ago is evident here. Dinner is a fixed tasting menu of seven courses, with optional wine pairings, and beginning, as is the Cumbrian tradition, with a soup of tomato consommé or smoked haddock velouté with chervil. Next up could be a plump raviolo of ox cheek with sautéed spinach in beef tea, before a distinctly original vegetable course, which may be a serving of cabbage jelly with buttermilk and Morston's home-cured

pancetta. Fish might be skate wing, its traditional brown butter sauce reduced to powder alongside a classic sauce vièrge, and then local roe deer in game jus, with a serving of dauphinoise and thyme-baked beetroot. An intermediate refresher course, perhaps grapefruit in champagne, provides the bridge to brown sugar tart with blood orange sorbet, or cheeses and black treacle bread if you prefer. The wine choices to go with these dishes bear all the hallmarks of thoughtful selection based on testing and tasting, beginning with André Colonge's strawberryish Fleurie with the ox cheek, and concluding with a glass of Taylor's 10-year-old Tawny port with the cheeses.

Chef Galton Blackiston **Owner** T & G Blackiston **Seats** 50, Pr/dining room 30 **Times** 12.15-3/7.15-close, Closed Xmas 3 days, 3 wks Jan, L Mon-Sat (ex party booking) **Prices** Tasting menu £67, Service optional **Wines** 130 bottles over £30, 14 bottles under £30, 12 by glass **Parking** 40 **Notes** Champagne tea £27, Afternoon tea £18.50, Sunday L £37, Children welcome

COLTISHALL
Map 13 TG21

Norfolk Mead Hotel

◉ Modern British

tel: 01603 737531 **Church Ln NR12 7DN**
email: info@norfolkmead.co.uk **web:** www.norfolkmead.co.uk
dir: From Norwich take B1150 to Coltishall village, go right with petrol station on left, 200 yds church on right, go down driveway

Cooking with a local flavour in a charming small country-house hotel

This handsome old house in the heart of the beautiful Norfolk Broads is looking dapper after new owners refurbished the place in recent years with a contemporary, country-chic look. The smart restaurant follows the theme, seamlessly blending period features with an uncluttered style – white walls punctuated with abstract artwork, wooden floors and unclothed tables decorated with simple flower arrangements. Windows look over pretty gardens – perfect for a pre- or post-prandial stroll down to the River Bure. On the food front, the kitchen hauls in the finest, freshest local ingredients for its attractively presented modern British cooking. Start with a lime chicken and prawn skewer with pea crème brûlée, followed by a skilfully executed duo of pan-fried halibut and crispy chicken thigh served with polenta, watercress purée, cavolo nero and chicken butter sauce. Vanilla pannacotta with prosecco-poached rhubarb rounds things off nicely.

Chef Anna Duttson, Sam Bayton **Owner** James Holliday, Anna Duttson **Seats** 40, Pr/dining room 22 **Times** 12-2.30/6.30-9, Closed L Mon-Sat **Prices** Fixed D 3 course £33-£35, Service optional **Wines** 22 bottles over £30, 31 bottles under £30, 8 by glass **Parking** 45 **Notes** Afternoon tea £15, Sunday L £26.50-£28.50, Vegetarian available, Children welcome

CROMER
Map 13 TG24

The Grove Cromer

◉◉ Modern British

tel: 01263 512412 **95 Overstrand Rd NR27 ODJ**
email: enquiries@thegrovecromer.co.uk **web:** www.thegrovecromer.co.uk
dir: Into Cromer on A149, right at 1st mini rdbt into Cromwell Rd. At double mini rdbt straight over into Overstrand Rd, 200mtrs on left

Polished and passionate cooking on the coast

A private path leads through woodland to the beach from this north Norfolk hotel, a substantial white Georgian house partly covered in creepers. There's an indoor pool and self-catering accommodation in converted barns in the grounds. In the restaurant, with its polished boarded floor and curtains and blinds over the windows giving garden views, staff make a real effort to engage with guests, contributing to a warm and intimate atmosphere. The kitchen team turns out dishes that sing with clear, fresh flavours without piling on the layers. Scallops are given a novel accompaniment of a paprika-spiked risotto of parsnips, peas and lime, while local quail comes with wilted kale (from the garden) and poached pears. Main courses are also carefully considered: seasonal roast pheasant with fondant potatoes and blackberry jus, for instance, and pan-seared sea bass fillet with prawn and mussel velouté and chive mash. Five Norfolk cheeses with quince jelly are an alternative to desserts along the lines of chocolate and marmalade bread-and-butter pudding.

Chef Michael West **Owner** The Graveling family **Seats** 48, Pr/dining room 30 **Times** 12-2/6-9, Closed Jan (phone to check), L Mon-Sat (winter) **Prices** Fixed L 2 course £19.95, Starter £5.95-£9.95, Main £9.95-£19.95, Dessert £5.95, Service optional **Wines** 30 bottles over £30, 9 bottles under £30, 10 by glass **Parking** 15 **Notes** Breakfast £12.95, Sunday L £19.95-£24.95, Vegetarian available, Children welcome

Sea Marge Hotel

◉◉ Modern British

tel: 01263 579579 **16 High St, Overstrand NR27 OAB**
email: seamarge@mackenziehotels.com **web:** www.mackenziehotels.com
dir: A140 to Cromer, B1159 to Overstrand, 2nd left past Overstrand Church

Haute cuisine in a seaside village hotel

On the edge of the village of Overstrand, not far from Cromer, the Sea Marge is a family-run Edwardian hotel of great charm. Its terraced lawns sit just above the coastal path, with marine views from the panelled dining room, Frazer's, where pastel hues and linen-clad tables create a restful ambience. The kitchen does a skilful job of incorporating touches of British modernism into what are essentially traditional haute cuisine dishes. First up might be a pairing of seared scallops with crab and langoustine ravioli, garnished with saffron-scented baby veg, in creamy shellfish broth. This is very much fish and seafood territory, so a main course of beetroot-marinated salmon with potato cake in salsa verde might appeal next, but there could also be smoked chicken breast with a little chicken cottage pie and a ball of cabbage and bacon in a sauce of café au lait. Toffee apple crumble tart with clotted cream-based cinnamon ice cream perhaps lacks the persuasive flavour shown in the chocolate and ginger terrine with salted caramel ice cream.

Chef Rene Ilupar **Owner** Mr & Mrs Mackenzie **Seats** 80, Pr/dining room 40 **Times** 12-2/6.30-9.30 **Prices** Fixed D 3 course £21, Starter £4.95-£8, Main £9.25-£21, Dessert £4.95-£7.95, Service optional **Wines** 4 bottles over £30, 24 bottles under £30, 7 by glass **Parking** 50 **Notes** Full afternoon tea, Sunday L, Vegetarian available, Children welcome

The White Horse Overstrand

◉◉ Modern European, British

tel: 01263 579237 **34 High St, Overstrand NR27 OAB**
email: enquiries@whitehorseoverstrand.co.uk **web:** www.whitehorseoverstrand.co.uk
dir: From A140, before Cromer, turn right onto Mill Rd. At bottom turn right onto Station Rd. After 2m, bear left onto High St, White Horse Overstrand on left

Great Norfolk produce cooked with flair

In a pretty village a short walk to the sea, this Victorian inn pulls in the punters, with a bar (real ales and its own menu), a games room, garden and guest accommodation as well as the restaurant in a converted barn, given a sleek modern look within flint walls and oak ceiling trusses. The kitchen's a hive of industry, making everything on the premises, from excellent breads to ice creams, and putting its hands to a range of ambitious, assertively flavoured dishes. Confit pork belly with sweet potato mousse, baked beans and apple and cider purée is a nicely balanced starter, an alternative to mussels in Thai-style broth finished with lemongrass and coriander. Smoked ham hock rillettes and beetroot jam add depth to a main course of pavé of cod with roast ratte potatoes and mushrooms, and another well-considered main could be pork fillet with Brussels sprouts creamed with pancetta, onion jus and roast parsnips. Puddings seem to consist of trios, among them maybe vanilla pannacotta with apple fritters and white chocolate buttons.

Chef Nathan Boon **Owner** Darren Walsgrove **Seats** 80, Pr/dining room 40 **Times** 12-3/6-9.30, Closed D 25 Dec **Prices** Starter £6-£8, Main £11-£20, Dessert £6, Service optional **Wines** 3 bottles over £30, 20 bottles under £30, 8 by glass **Parking** 6, On street **Notes** Sunday L £12, Vegetarian available, Children welcome

GREAT BIRCHAM · Map 13 TF73

The Kings Head Hotel

◉ Modern British

tel: 01485 578265 **PE31 6RJ**
email: info@thekingsheadhotel.co.uk **web:** www.the-kings-head-bircham.co.uk
dir: A148 to Hillington through village, 1st left Bircham

Classic and modern food in an revamped old inn

The Kings Head is an old inn which has had an injection of boutique styling and operates as a country-house hotel, with colourful bedrooms, conference facilities and a bar stocked with real ales. The team in the kitchen covers a lot of bases, so you can pop into the bar for posh scampi and chips or head into the restaurant with its gently contemporary decor and tuck into something a little more creative. There's a pleasing lack of stuffiness all round. The kitchen makes good use of Norfolk's plentiful larder, so there might be a starter of smoked Norfolk ham (served with honey-mustard dressing and pickled veg) followed by roast loin of local pork, or go for a fishy main such as grilled filet of bream with Med-style accompaniments. Everything looks good on the plate, including a fashionable dessert of salted caramel and chocolate tart.

Chef Nicholas Parker **Owner** Craig Jackson **Seats** 80, Pr/dining room 30 **Times** 12-2/6-9 **Prices** Service optional **Wines** 8 bottles over £30, 46 bottles under £30, 14 by glass **Parking** 25 **Notes** Sunday L £20, Vegetarian available, Children welcome

GREAT YARMOUTH · Map 13 TG50

Andover House

◉◉ Modern British

tel: 01493 843490 **28-30 Camperdown NR30 3JB**
email: info@andoverhouse.co.uk **web:** www.andoverhouse.co.uk
dir: Opposite Wellington Pier, turn onto Shadingfield Close, right onto Kimberley Terrace, follow onto Camperdown. Property on left

Breezily contemporary cooking in townhouse

A touch of boutique styling has been sprinkled over the white-painted Victorian terrace that is Andover House, and these days it's a rather cool hotel, restaurant and bar, with a spruce look of fashionable muted pastel tones and a distinct lack of chintz. The restaurant is filled with blond wood with nary a tablecloth in sight and is a bright and breezy environment for the cooking, which fits the bill to a T. There's a daily specials board in support of the à la carte menu. The cooking treads a contemporary path and there are plenty of global flavours on show: first-course crispy beef and spring onion salad with a sweet chilli and pimento dressing, for example, or a vegetarian main course tajine. It's back to Europe for a pasta starter – linguini with pan-fried squid, chorizo, ginger, chilli and lime – and main-courses such as tournedos Rossini or rack of English spring lamb with ratatouille,

Parmentier potatoes, minted pears and rosemary jus. For dessert, the tasting plate removes any indecision.

Chef Sandra Meirovica **Owner** Mr & Mrs Barry Armstrong **Seats** 37, Pr/dining room 18 **Times** 6-9.30, Closed Xmas, L all week **Prices** Starter £4-£6, Main £12-£20, Dessert £5-£7, Service optional **Wines** 17 bottles under £30, 9 by glass **Parking** On street **Notes** Vegetarian available, Children 13 yrs+

Imperial Hotel

◉ Modern British

tel: 01493 842000 **North Dr NR30 1EQ**
email: reception@imperialhotel.co.uk **web:** www.cafecrurestaurant.co.uk
dir: Follow signs to seafront, turn left. Hotel opposite waterways

Modern brasserie classics in a grand old seaside hotel

Successive generations of the Mobbs family have been running the grand old Imperial since the 1930s, when one of the attractions that lifted it above the common run of seaside hotels was that guests were seated at separate tables. Its physiognomy has changed somewhat in modern times with the addition of a glassed-in terrace for watching the tide roll in, and the Café Cru restaurant, where frosted glass panels divide the seating booths as though to demonstrate that separate tables are still the elevated norm. Classic dishes from the present-day brasserie repertoire are the stock-in-trade, opening perhaps with lime and chilli scallops and smoked pancetta with minted pea purée, and following on with pesto-crusted cannon of local lamb with puréed parsnip and balsamic courgette ribbons in red wine and rosemary, or sea bass with a risotto of beetroot, mushrooms and Merlot. Finish exotically with spiced coconut rice pudding and caramelised pineapple.

Chef Simon Wainwright **Owner** Mr N L & Mrs A Mobbs **Seats** 60, Pr/dining room 140 **Times** 12-2/6.30-10, Closed 24-28 & 31 Dec, L Sat, Mon, D Sun **Prices** Starter £5-£9, Main £12-£25, Dessert £6.50-£9, Service optional **Wines** 10 bottles over £30, 30 bottles under £30, 12 by glass **Parking** 45 **Notes** Sunday L £17-£23, Vegetarian available, Children welcome

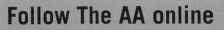

GRIMSTON
Map 12 TF72

Congham Hall Country House Hotel
◉◉ Modern British, European

tel: 01485 600250 **Lynn Rd PE32 1AH**
email: info@conghamhallhotel.co.uk **web:** www.conghamhallhotel.co.uk
dir: *6m NE of King's Lynn on A148, turn right towards Grimston. Hotel 2.5m on left (do not go to Congham)*

Creative contemporary cooking in charming Georgian house

The Georgian house was built in the 1780s by a wealthy merchant from King's Lynn, which is about the time that the nearby royal residence of Sandringham House was constructed. If an invite to the latter is not forthcoming, fear not, for Congham Hall can provide plenty of cossetting luxury, with gorgeous gardens, a swish spa and a restaurant that has genuine Georgian charm. The dining room has French windows looking on to the garden and pristine, linen-clad tables. There's a herb garden in the grounds with an amazing 400 varieties finding their way to the table, plus a kitchen garden and orchards, and what ingredients don't hail from the grounds are sourced with care from the local environs. The cooking is gently modern and shows allegiance to both the crown and our European partners. Start, perhaps, with a tart of local feta, leek and artichoke, or a duck and chicken liver terrine with garden chutney. For main course, a trio of local pheasant or roasted fillet and liver of Sandringham beef, and for dessert, hot chocolate fondant with popcorn ice cream.

Times 12-2/7-9

HEACHAM
Map 12 TF63

Heacham Manor Hotel
◉ Modern European

tel: 01485 536030 & 579800 **Hunstanton Rd PE31 7JX**
email: info@heacham-manor.co.uk **web:** www.heacham-manor.co.uk
dir: *On A149 between Heacham & Hunstanton. Near Hunstanton rdbt with water tower*

Fine local produce by the Norfolk coast

The wide-open skies of Norfolk's fabulous coast make Heacham Manor an attractive prospect; the place even comes with its own coastal golf course if you're a player. Originally built as an Elizabethan manor, the hotel has been brought smartly up-to-date by complete renovation in recent years, and its airy conservatory-style Mulberry Restaurant is reason enough to pay a visit. The kitchen's output is simple, staunchly seasonal and driven by a sincere belief in local sourcing — salt marsh lamb comes from Wells-next-the-Sea, and the locally-landed fish and seafood racks

up very few food miles on its way to the table. Goats' cheese cheesecake with red onion marmalade and mizuna leaf salad gets things off the blocks, followed by Gressingham duck breast teamed with grain mustard mash, Savoy cabbage, celeriac purée, and blackberry jus. At the end, rhubarb compôte provides a tangy foil to crème brûlée with fennel seed biscotti.

Times 12-2.30/6.30-9

HETHERSETT
Map 13 TG10

Park Farm Hotel
◉ Modern British

tel: 01603 810264 **NR9 3DL**
email: enq@parkfarm-hotel.co.uk **web:** www.parkfarm-hotel.co.uk
dir: *6m S of Norwich on B1172*

Unfussy modern cooking in a spa hotel

The hotel, with spa and conference facilities, is in a rural location surrounded by 200 acres of countryside. The restaurant, looking over the gardens, is an open-plan-style room with ceiling spotlights, tall-backed padded chairs at clothed tables and potted plants dotted about. The kitchen has a comprehensive outlook, turning out starters of tempura red mullet fillet with lemon and lime salsa, and tender pigeon breast on confit garlic mash with cranberry and onion chutney, pea purée and port jus. Ingredients are of good quality and timings accurate, seen in nicely presented main courses of baked halibut fillet on fennel purée with wasabi mash, diced smoked salmon, braised chicory and pickled raspberries, and partridge roasted with bacon and thyme served on rösti with baby vegetables and red wine sauce. For a fitting finale try hazelnut and Muscovado tart topped with clotted cream on a mixed berry coulis.

Times 12-2/7-9.30

HOLT
Map 13 TG03

The Lawns
◉ Modern European

tel: 01263 713390 **26 Station Rd NR25 6BS**
email: info@lawnshotelholt.co.uk **web:** www.lawnshotelholt.co.uk
dir: *A148 (Cromer road). 0.25m from Holt rdbt, turn left, 400yds along Station Rd*

Populist cooking in a Georgian townhouse

A small hotel dating from Georgian times, The Lawns offers a number of dining options: bar, conservatory, restaurant and south-facing garden. It's a warm and friendly place, reflected in a menu of largely comfortingly reassuring dishes pinned on East Anglian produce. Thai-style beef curry with coconut rice and prawn crackers is about as exotic as things get; more typical are main courses of beer-battered haddock with chips, or braised oxtail with bubble-and-squeak and root vegetables. Bookending them might be prawn and crayfish cocktail, or sautéed pigeon breast with chorizo, red cabbage and mini roast potatoes, and resourceful puddings of Tunisian sticky orange cake with Chantilly cream, or plum crumble cheesecake with raspberry coulis.

Chef Leon Brookes, Adam Kobialka **Owner** Mr & Mrs Daniel Rees **Seats** 60
Times 12-2/6-9 **Prices** Prices not confirmed, Service optional **Wines** 2 bottles over £30, 32 bottles under £30, 13 by glass **Parking** 18 **Notes** Sunday L, Vegetarian available, Children welcome

HOLT *continued*

The Pheasant Hotel & Restaurant

🏵 Modern, Traditional

tel: 01263 588382 & 588540 **Coast Rd, Kelling NR25 7EG**
email: enquiries@pheasanthotelnorfolk.co.uk **web:** www.pheasanthotelnorfolk.co.uk
dir: *On A149 coast road, mid-way between Sheringham & Blakeney*

Modern British coastal cooking and afternoon tea

With the stretching beaches and marshland of the north Norfolk coast on hand, The Pheasant is plumb in one of the country's most fashionable resort areas. A white-faced building with portico entrance, it's had a bit of a rejig in the dining department, with landscape pictures now adorning a bright, informal room furnished with bare tables, but the cooking continues its modern British mission, with seafood still a strong suit. Expect a smokehouse platter to start, laden with salmon, prawns and mackerel, pickled veg and tartare, or classic scallops with local black pudding, before pork belly with clapshot and burnt orange purée, or sea trout on leek velouté with charred chicory. The finisher might be banana loaf with a matching fritter and malt ice cream. Afternoon teas, with scones and crustless sandwiches piled on cake stands, are an abiding part of The Pheasant's appeal.

Chef Erling Rugsten **Owner** Mr G Widdowson **Seats** 78, Pr/dining room 30
Times 12-2/6-9 **Prices** Fixed L 3 course £23, Tasting menu £45-£55, Starter £7-£9.50, Main £14.50-£24.50, Dessert £6.10-£8.70, Service optional **Wines** 17 bottles over £30, 34 bottles under £30, 23 by glass **Parking** 50 **Notes** Sunday L £20-£26, Vegetarian available, Children welcome

HUNSTANTON
Map 12 TF64

Caley Hall Hotel

🏵 Modern British ᵥ

tel: 01485 533486 **Old Hunstanton Rd PE36 6HH**
email: mail@caleyhallhotel.co.uk **web:** www.caleyhallhotel.co.uk
dir: *Located on A149, Old Hunstanton*

Well-judged menus on the Norfolk coast

Built around a manor dating from 1648, Caley Hall is a short walk to the wide beaches on The Wash, a twitcher's paradise. Its restaurant, in a former stable block, is a relaxing-looking room with a tartan carpet and high-backed leather-look

seats at well-spaced tables. It's a popular place, part of the attraction the consistently precise cooking of quality East Anglian produce. The short menu is unlikely to rock any boats, starting with crayfish cocktail in Marie Rose sauce with avocado purée and tomato confit, followed by beef braised in red wine and rosemary served with celeriac mash, carrots and greens. Look to the specials for more vim: perhaps seared scallops with cauliflower purée, bacon crisps, sorrel and shallot butter, then three ways with pork (slow-cooked belly, herb-crusted fillet, fried liver) with a thyme jus, potato terrine and roasted baby parsnips. Finish with peanut butter parfait with salted peanut brittle, a truffle and griottes.

Chef Shayne Wood **Owner** Caley Hall Hotel Ltd **Seats** 80 **Times** 12-9, All-day dining, Closed 21-26 Dec, 10-22 Jan **Prices** Starter £5-£9, Main £13-£21.50, Dessert £6.50-£7.50, Service optional **Wines** 23 bottles under £30, 6 by glass **Parking** 50 **Notes** Sunday L £10.95-£20.95, Children welcome

The Neptune Restaurant with Rooms

🏵 🏵 🏵 *– see opposite*

KING'S LYNN
Map 12 TF62

Bank House

🏵 Modern British

tel: 01553 660492 **King's Staithe Square PE30 1RD**
email: info@thebankhouse.co.uk **web:** www.thebankhouse.co.uk
dir: *Follow signs to Old Town and onto quayside, through floodgate, hotel on right opposite Custom House*

Gently modernised British cooking on the quayside

The Georgian townhouse hotel on the south quayside amid the town's cultural district (the Corn Exchange Theatre and Arts Centre are close by) is a far jollier prospect as a hotel than when it was a bank. Such is the cheering insolence of the conversion that what was the bank manager's office is now the bar. A trio of smart dining rooms have polished tables, candlelight and music, and trade in gently modernised traditional British fare. Start with a slab of Parma-wrapped pork belly terrine and sticky carrot chutney, or double-baked goats' cheese soufflé with Puy lentils, before pressing on to fried ray in cockle butter with crispy seaweed and saffron potatoes, or a 9oz steak in peppercorn sauce. Desserts do their best to look the part and are a little over-zealous in their garnishing, but the principals, perhaps lemon tart and raspberry sorbet, are good enough to stand alone.

Chef Stuart Deuchars **Owner** Jeannette & Anthony Goodrich **Seats** 100, Pr/dining room 40 **Times** 12-9, All-day dining **Prices** Starter £5.25-£7.50, Main £11.25-£19.50, Dessert £3.50-£6.25, Service optional **Wines** 12 bottles over £30, 32 bottles under £30, 15 by glass **Parking** On quayside or Baker Lane car park **Notes** Pre-theatre 2 course £15, Fresh fish Friday menu, Sunday L fr £13.50, Vegetarian available, Children welcome

The Legacy Duke's Head Hotel

◉ Modern International **NEW**

tel: 01553 774996 **5-6 Tuesday Market Place PE30 1JS**
email: reception@dukesheadhotel.com web: www.legacy-hotels.co.uk
dir: *From A10/A47/A17 enter King's Lynn via South Gates rdbt. Hotel opposite Corn Exchange.*

Period charm and seasonal menus

The hotel occupies a prime spot on the town's main square, its sky blue frontage and period features making a fine first impression. The interior designers have done a cracking job at keeping its old-world charm and meeting contemporary tastes, so the place feels traditional but in no way stuck in the past. There's a contemporary bistro-style restaurant called Gryffens and a fine-dining option, Turners Restaurant. Sitting behind a wall of glass, the latter is an elegant space with well-dressed tables and, once again, that feeling of old meeting new. The kitchen brings classical and modern ideas to the table, with the fixed-price seasonal menu offering up a mini Greek salad or potted crayfish with pickled cucumber among first courses. Move on to pan-fried duck breast (cooked just right) with boulangère potatoes and a punchy blackcurrant sauce, and finish with lemon and thyme pannacotta.

Chef Shane Wagg **Owner** Surya Hotels **Seats** 60, Pr/dining room 40
Times 12-3/6.30-9.30 **Prices** Prices not confirmed, Service optional **Parking** 40
Notes Sunday L, Vegetarian available, Children welcome

LODDON Map 13 TM39

The Loddon Swan

◉ Modern British **NEW**

tel: 01508 528039 **23 Church Plain NR14 6LX**
email: info@theloddonswan.co.uk web: www.theloddonswan.co.uk
dir: *Phone for directions*

Quality cooking in a revamped country inn

Close to the stunning River Chet, this former 18th-century coaching inn reopened in 2012 after a comprehensive refurbishment under new owners, who have retained the traditional country charm while bringing it into the 21st century. Relaxed and informal, you can eat in the bar or restaurant overlooking the patio garden, which is an additional dining option in the summer. While much is made of local sourcing of ingredients, the menu mixes modern British dishes with Mediterranean classics, offering chargrilled steaks alongside slow-roasted tomato ragout, gnocchi, olives, crispy chickpeas and pesto-dressed leaves. Equally impressive dishes range from a starter of pressed lamb shoulder, with peas, mint, broad bean and radishes to a main course of slow-braised Heckingham beef cheek, fondant potato, roasted shallot and red wine jus. To finish, try lemon curd tart, basil meringues and raspberry gel.

Chef Jason Wright **Owner** Andrew Freeland **Seats** 70, Pr/dining room 30
Times 12-2.30/6.30-9, Closed D Sun (Jan-Apr) **Prices** Starter £5.25-£6.50, Main £12.95-£16.95, Dessert £5.50-£7.25 **Parking** 15 **Notes** Sunday L £17.95-£22.95, Vegetarian available, Children welcome

---

The Neptune Restaurant with Rooms ❀❀❀

HUNSTANTON Map 12 TF64

Modern European **V**
tel: 01485 532122 **85 Old Hunstanton Rd, Old Hunstanton PE36 6HZ**
email: reservations@thonoptunc.co.uk web: www.theneptune.co.uk
dir: *On A149*

Precision-tuned cooking in a smartly converted Norfolk inn

A creeper-covered 18th-century coaching inn with a model sailing ship prominently displayed in a front window has been updated into the Mangeolles' restaurant with rooms not far from the beach. The modern look of the pint-sized restaurant contrasts nicely with the period features, with a plain boarded floor, original artwork hung above the half-panelled walls and high-backed wicker chairs at white-clothed tables with flowers. Kevin Mangeolles' cooking goes from strength to strength. His menus run to just a handful of choices per course, all built on local and seasonal produce, and there's nothing pretentious or gimmicky about his style, with no unnecessary garnishes or fuss. Roast quail impresses not only for its accurate timing but for the intelligent accompaniments of sultanas, sweetcorn purée and Savoy cabbage to make a memorable starter. Various influences are at work to suit each dish, seen in another starter of sake-poached salmon fillet with radish, oyster mayonnaise and puffed wild rice. Main courses are equally memorable, among them lightly cooked fillet of wild turbot with the eloquent but subtle flavours of aubergine purée, salsify, kale and Pink Fir potatoes, and the full-on flavours of roast loin and braised haunch of hare with celeriac, wild mushrooms, carrots and creamed potatoes. Breads are made in-house, canapés are stars in their own right and a pre-dessert, perhaps of fruit jelly topped with mascarpone, arrives before the real McCoy, which include smooth, rich coconut and ginger pannacotta with zesty mango sorbet, and milk chocolate bavarois with dark chocolate sorbet and blueberry compôte.

Chef Kevin Mangeolles **Owner** Kevin & Jacki Mangeolles **Seats** 24
Times 12-1.30/7-9, Closed Jan, 2 wks Nov, 26 Dec, Mon, L Tue-Sat (ex by arrangement) **Prices** Fixed D 3 course £56, Tasting menu £72, Service optional
Wines 70 bottles over £30, 20 bottles under £30, 14 by glass **Parking** 6, On street
Notes Sunday L £29 £35, Children 10 yrs+

NORTH WALSHAM
Map 13 TG23

Beechwood Hotel

◎◎ Modern British V

tel: 01692 403231 **20 Cromer Rd NR28 OHD**
email: info@beechwood-hotel.co.uk web: www.beechwood-hotel.co.uk
dir: *From Norwich on B1150, 13m to N Walsham. Left at lights, next right. Hotel 150mtrs on left*

Charming hotel with good local ingredients on the menu

Hospitality is top of the agenda at this charming hotel, with hands-on owners and lots of staff ensuring that guests are well looked after. There's a small bar (although drinks and canapés are also served in the garden in summer), a lounge with overstuffed upholstery and a traditionally appointed restaurant. The kitchen sources most ingredients from within 10 miles of the hotel and works around a contemporary British repertory in its own individualistic style. Dinner could open with a successful marriage of rich butternut squash and onion velouté with apple foam, or warm smoked salmon with a caper and potato croûton and sherry vinaigrette. Proceed to the Asian flavours of duck leg croquette with beetroot and star anise sorbet, pickled beetroot and honey and soya dressing. Fish might be represented by Lowestoft-landed cod fillet with a ragout of cannellini beans, mushrooms and red peppers, spring vegetables and crispy leeks. Finish with vanilla crème brûlée with pineapple and mango compôte.

Chef Steven Norgate **Owner** Don Birch, Lindsay Spalding **Seats** 60, Pr/dining room 20 **Times** 12-1.45/7-9, Closed L Mon-Sat **Prices** Fixed D 3 course fr £40, Service optional **Wines** 50 bottles over £30, 26 bottles under £30, 11 by glass **Parking** 20 **Notes** Sunday L £26, Children welcome

NORWICH
Map 13 TG20

BEST WESTERN Annesley House Hotel

◎◎ Modern

tel: 01603 624553 **6 Newmarket Rd NR2 2LA**
email: annesleyhouse@bestwestern.co.uk web: www.bw-annesleyhouse.co.uk
dir: *On A11, close to city centre*

Easy-going modern British cooking outside the city walls

Annesley began life as a trio of private houses built on the eve of the Victorian age, conjured into one century later by an enterprising hotelier. Standing just outside the old city walls, its landscaped gardens add a country-house feel, and an old vine supplies sweet red grapes to garnish the cheese plates. In the bright conservatory dining room, with its uncovered tables and floor, an easy-going version of British modernist cuisine is offered, and scores many convincing hits. A pair of scallops comes with curried apple, capers and sultanas and the requisite purée of celeriac, while more traditional smoked salmon is served warm with a quail's egg and fennel salad. Dishes are carefully attended to for timing, as is the case in roast guinea fowl with confit garlic and braised baby gem, and in the complex construction that

is seared tenderloin and crisped belly of pork with a little portion of ham hock lasagne in grain mustard sauce. Today's favourite dessert components of chocolate, salted caramel and nuts are piled on to a tart for afters.

Chef Steven Watkin **Owner** Mr & Mrs D Reynolds **Seats** 30 **Times** 12-2/6-9, Closed Xmas & New Year, L Sun **Prices** Prices not confirmed, Service optional **Wines** 10 bottles under £30, 7 by glass **Parking** 29 **Notes** Pre-theatre menu from 6pm by arrangement, Vegetarian available, Children welcome

Brasteds

◎◎ Modern European

tel: 01508 491112 **Manor Farm Barns, Fox Rd, Framingham Pigot NR14 7PZ**
email: enquiries@brasteds.co.uk web: www.brasteds.co.uk
dir: *A11 onto A47 towards Great Yarmouth, then A146. After 0.5m turn right onto Fox Rd, 0.5m on left*

Exciting skilful cooking in a stylish barn conversion

In the village of Framingham Pigot, four miles from the city centre, Brasteds occupies a converted barn, a charming room of raftered ceiling, oak floor and brick walls. Chris 'Buzz' Busby is a skilful and confident chef, compiling seasonally-changing menus that are big on canny ideas, all based on impressive Norfolk produce. Dishes are not without a degree of complexity, but sure-footed experience brings everything together. Starters might be poached ray wing with grape gel, steamed clams and a chorizo and truffle cream, or a terrine of smoked chicken, foie gras and Parma ham with grilled garlic snails and tomato and chive caviar. Main courses are generally in the same vein, although classic bouillabaisse might also make an appearance. Accurately sautéed sea bass, for instance, is plated with creamed potato, artichoke purée spiked with chervil, sticky red cabbage and lemon butter sauce, while lamb fillet gets the Wellington treatment, accompanied by confit of shoulder, minted pea and potato crumble and a rich jus. Welsh rarebit is on offer alongside puddings of cherry Bakewell tart with cherry sorbet and caramelised cherries.

Times 12-2.30/7-10, Closed Sun-Wed, L Sat, Thu

The Maids Head Hotel

◎ Modern British

tel: 01603 209955 **Tombland NR3 1LB**
web: www.maidsheadhotel.co.uk
dir: *A147 to north of the city. At rdbt for A1151, signed Wroxham, follow signs for Cathedral and Law Courts along Whitefriars. Hotel is approx 400 mtrs on right along Palace St*

Simple modern cooking in Britain's oldest hotel

The brick-built hotel in the city centre lays claim to being the UK's oldest, having been feeding and watering East Anglian travellers for a sterling 800 years. It stands next to the cathedral for company of due venerability, although the Jacobean bar is a relative stripling in the context. Dining goes on in a glassed-in courtyard with a quarry-tiled floor and simple wooden tables, and the menus keep things fairly simple too, albeit in the modern British idiom. Expect to start with the likes of Cromer crab mousse with tomato gel, seaweed salad and avocado oil, before progressing to a Parma-wrapped breast of corn-fed chicken with bubble-and-squeak, roasted beetroot and a jus of cider and thyme, or seared sea bass on mussel and courgette risotto with buttered leeks in white wine sauce. Dessert might be a verrine of strawberries and Greek yogurt, accompanied by strawberry ice cream.

Chef Magic Pomierny **Owner** The Maids Head Hotel Ltd **Seats** 70, Pr/dining room 130 **Times** 12-3/6.30-9.30 **Prices** Fixed D 3 course £25-£28, Tasting menu £49.50-£69.50, Starter £6.50-£7.95, Main £13.95-£26, Dessert £4.50-£6.95, Service optional **Wines** 11 bottles over £30, 31 bottles under £30, 40 by glass **Parking** 60 **Notes** Fixed D 5 course with wine £49, Pre/post-theatre menu, Sunday L £9.95-£15.95, Vegetarian available, Children welcome

The Old Rectory

◉◉ Modern British V

tel: 01603 700772 **103 Yarmouth Rd, Thorpe St Andrew NR7 0HF**
email: enquiries@oldrectorynorwich.com **web:** www.oldrectorynorwich.com
dir: *From A47 southern bypass onto A1042 towards Norwich N & E. Left at mini rdbt onto A1242. After 0.3m through lights. Hotel 100mtrs on right*

Georgian rectory hotel with a local flavour

Creepers cover the large Georgian house, giving the impression the garden is attempting to reclaim the land – but the red-brick former rectory is here to stay, built to last back in the day and thriving in the 21st century as a country hotel. The dining room has a traditional finish, a room of generous proportions and period details, and is the setting for candlelit dinners (afternoon tea is also available). The daily-changing menu has a good showing of regional produce and keeps to a sensibly manageable choice of three dishes per course. Starters of partridge, pork and prune terrine or lime-marinated organic salmon fillet with grapefruit, pickled vegetables and orange dressing are typical of the output. Among main courses, baked fillet of cod is served with saffron mash, leeks, peas and roasted tomato dressing, and Gressingham duck might feature as leg confit served with baked Jersey Royals, roast Puy lentils and a selection of vegetables. Puddings may bring on white chocolate and vanilla tart with rhubarb.

Chef James Perry **Owner** Chris & Sally Entwistle **Seats** 18 **Times** 7-9, Closed Xmas, New Year, Sun-Mon, L all week **Prices** Fixed D 3 course £30-£35, Service optional **Wines** 6 bottles over £30, 16 bottles under £30, 5 by glass **Parking** 16 **Notes** Children welcome

Roger Hickman's Restaurant

◉◉◉ – see below

St Benedicts Restaurant

◉ Modern British, French

tel: 01603 765377 **9 St Benedicts St NR2 4PE**
email: stbenedicts@rafflesrestaurants.co.uk
dir: *Just off inner ring road. Turn right by Toys-R-Us, 2nd right into St Benedicts St. Restaurant on left by pedestrian crossing*

Imaginative accomplished cooking in the heart of Norwich

This popular city-centre restaurant has been going strong for more than 20 years. A blond-wood floor, pale wooden tables and chairs and pale blue tongue-and-groove panelling all combine to give it a light, airy feel, a convivial place in which to enjoy some consistently accomplished cooking based on indigenous produce. Starters of duck rillettes with home-made plum chutney, and hot-smoked salmon with green beans, red onion and crayfish set the standards. The main courses have a good balance of flavours without being over-complicated: slow-cooked crispy duck, say, with mustard sauce, caramelised apple, bubble-and-squeak and glazed carrots, or well-timed grilled sea bass fillet with pea purée, Jerusalem artichokes and waxy new potatoes. End with one of the moreish desserts like dark chocolate delice with raspberries, or lemon buttermilk pudding with candied zest.

Chef Nigel Raffles **Owner** Nigel & Jayne Raffles **Seats** 42, Pr/dining room 24 **Times** 12-2/6-10, Closed 25-31 Dec, Sun-Mon **Prices** Prices not confirmed **Wines** 8 by glass **Parking** On street, car parks nearby **Notes** Prix fixe menu 6-7pm Tue-Sat 2 course £10, Vegetarian available, Children welcome

Roger Hickman's Restaurant ◉◉◉

| NORWICH | Map 13 TG20 |

Modern British 🍾 **NOTABLE WINE LIST**
tel: 01603 633522 **79 Upper St Giles St NR2 1AB**
email: info@rogerhickmansrestaurant.com
dir: *In city centre, from A147 at rdbt into Cleveland Rd, 1st left into Upper St Giles St*

A haven of high-achieving British food with French underpinnings

The location down a quiet cul-de-sac in the fashionable St Giles district, not far from the cathedral, serves notice that Roger Hickman's place is conceived as something of a haven from urban bustle, as opposed to a noisy brasserie. It looks like a proper restaurant inside, with plain wooden floors, walls adorned with colourful original artworks, and tables dressed in full-length linens, set with high-calibre appointments and stemware. It's a split-level space naturally disposed into sections, run by professional, clued-up staff, who announce each arriving dish with accurate decorum, and are ready with suggestions should they be required. Hickman's style is clearly modern British, with a range of interesting techniques and some evidence of classical French underpinning, offered in the form of fixed-price menus that rise to a seven-course taster with optional wine matches. Dishes look dazzling, and have the impact on the palate to back it up, even for something as relatively simple as a warm artichoke salad dressed with yogurt and dukkah-spiced crumbs. The blowtorched mackerel is something of a signature starter, with its baby beetroots and horseradish, and fish treatments are impressive throughout, as for a main course of perfectly timed sea bream, which comes with tempura-battered salt cod, sweet shallots and leek. Traditional preparations for meats include partridge in winter array with cabbage, chestnuts, parsnips and mash, or venison with braised red cabbage, celeriac and kale. Reimaginings of old-school desserts are all the rage, but work to great effect here, perhaps for lemon meringue pie, which gains apple, almonds and Calvados, or the raspberry trifle that's singing with aromatic vanilla and enriched with burnt honey. Offbeat wine choices include Australia's challengingly named Spitting Spider (maybe don't look at the label, arachnophobes).

Chef Roger Hickman **Owner** Roger Hickman **Seats** 40 **Times** 12-2.30/7-10, Closed 1 wk Jan & Aug, Sun-Mon **Prices** Fixed L 2 course fr £20, Fixed D 3 course fr £44, Tasting menu fr £60 **Wines** 95 bottles over £30, 14 bottles under £30, 12 by glass **Parking** On street, St Giles multi-storey **Notes** Pre-theatre menu £20/£24. L tasting menu £35, Vegetarian available, Children welcome

NORWICH *continued*

St Giles House Hotel

◉◉ Modern British

tel: 01603 275180 **41-45 St Giles St NR2 1JR**
email: reception@stgileshousehotel.com **web:** www.stgileshousehotel.com
dir: *A11 into central Norwich. Left at rdbt signed Chapelfield Shopping Centre. 3rd exit at next rdbt. Left onto St Giles St. Hotel on left*

Classic and modern dishes in an architectural gem

You could punctuate your perusal of Norwich city centre's retail opportunities with a pitstop in St Giles House for coffee, a massage, cocktails or something more gastronomically satisfying in the SGH Bistro. The grand Edwardian pile is worth a gander in its own right – beyond its magnificent pillared façade is a palatial interior of marble floors, oak panelling and elaborate plaster ceilings, all sharpened with a stylish contemporary makeover. The SGH Bistro mingles art deco-inspired lines with sleek modern looks as a setting for the kitchen's appealing repertoire of uncomplicated, up-to-date cooking. Clearly defined flavours leap out from every skilfully rendered dish, be it roast pigeon served with foie gras, shallot and a tart cherry sauce, or a main course of lightly-spiced roast monkfish delivered in a mussel and herb broth with spiced butter, a crispy potato cake and bok choy. To finish, it's worth the wait for a freshly-cooked apple tarte Tatin with cinnamon ice cream. Smartly turned out in black, the front-of-house team are a polished act who keep everything running smoothly.

Chef Ellery Powell **Owner** Ensco 1035 Ltd **Seats** 50, Pr/dining room 48 **Times** 11-10, All-day dining **Prices** Fixed D 3 course £32.50, Starter £7-£8.50, Main £18-£24, Dessert £6.50-£7.50, Service optional **Wines** 23 bottles over £30, 37 bottles under £30, 19 by glass **Parking** 30 **Notes** Afternoon tea £13.50, Sunday L £17.50-£21.50, Vegetarian available, Children welcome

Stower Grange

◉ Modern British

tel: 01603 860210 **40 School Rd, Drayton NR8 6EF**
email: enquiries@stowergrange.co.uk **web:** www.stowergrange.co.uk
dir: *Norwich ring road N to ASDA supermarket. Take A1067 (Fakenham road) at Drayton, right at lights into School Rd. Hotel 150yds on right*

Country-house dining with simplicity and style

The ivy-covered country house in its own wooded grounds a few miles out of Norwich is a charming family-run hotel. Friendly upbeat staff exude a mood of great warmth, and the traditional decorative styling of the place feels fully in keeping. Gathered drapes frame the garden view in the comfortably furnished dining room, where contemporary cooking based on quality ingredients aims to satisfy rather than startle. Begin then with a grilled mackerel, simply adorned with peas, lemon and cucumber, or a voguish pigeon breast starter with a salad of pomegranate, hazelnuts and watercress. Fish continues to show well at main course stage, in the form of crisp-skinned sea bass with wild mushrooms, beetroot and puréed onions, while the game season brings on roast pheasant with orange-spiked cabbage. Finish with apple and pecan pie and clotted cream ice cream, or white chocolate and raspberry cheesecake.

Times 12-2.30/6.30-9.30, Closed 26-30 Dec, D Sun

The Sugar Hut

◉ Thai

tel: 01603 766755 **4 Opie St NR1 3DN**
email: lhongmo@hotmail.co.uk
dir: *City centre next to Castle Meadow & Castle Mall car park*

Vibrant Thai food near the castle

Leelanooch Hongmo's expanding empire now incorporates this venue near the castle. The ethos throughout combines the famed courtesy of Thai service with a menu dealing in the sweet, hot-and-sour currents of classic cooking from that country. A yellow and blue colour scheme offsets the black-clad staff to a T, and the food is as bracing and vibrant as you would hope. Khanom jeep – dumplings of steamed marinated minced pork and prawns, deep-fried in wonton pastry – are a good way to set about things, or you could kick start the palate with lime-sharp tom yam gung soup. Main course curries – fiery beef gang ped red curry, for example – are the real deal, while roast duck with seaweed and tamarind sauce offers an excursion beyond the usual Thai staples. Good pad Thai, drunken noodles, or fried rice with crabmeat provide a fragrant accompaniment.

Times 12-2.30/6-10.30, Closed Sun, L Mon

Thailand Restaurant

◉ Thai

tel: 01603 700444 **9 Ring Rd, Thorpe St Andrew NR7 0XJ**
email: siamkidd@aol.com
dir: *From Southern bypass, follow airport signs. Located at top of hill past Sainsbury's*

True flavours of Thailand in busy out-of-town restaurant

Plants and colourful hanging baskets add some dash to the exterior of this well-established restaurant. Inside, the decor is as busy on the eye as the bamboo-framed upholstered seats are as busy with customers: drapes over the windows, statues in niches, friezes on the ceiling beams and lots of greenery. What marks out the cooking is the sourcing of authentic ingredients, the accurate use of spicing and seasoning and spot-on timing to replicate the true flavours of Thailand's cuisine in the suburbs of Norwich. From the long menu comes namoo – deep-fried minced pork within a bread base served with plum and chilli sauce – alongside the more commonplace chicken satay, followed by tender spare ribs marinated in curry sauce, beef musaman – braised steak stewed with red curry paste, roasted peanuts and new potatoes – and prawns stir-fried with garlic in oyster sauce and coriander. Finish with a refreshing sorbet or tuck in to bananas in creamy coconut milk sauce.

Times 12-3/6-10, Closed 25 Dec, L Sat-Sun

SHERINGHAM
Map 13 TG14

Dales Country House Hotel

@@ British, European

tel: 01263 824555 **Lodge Hill, Upper Sheringham NR26 8TJ**
email: dales@mackenziehotels.com **web:** www.mackenziehotels.com
dir: On B1157, 1m S of Sheringham. From A148 Cromer to Holt road, take turn at entrance to Sheringham Park. Hotel 0.5m on left

Smart modern cooking in rural Norfolk

With the big skies of the north Norfolk coast close by, and Humphry Repton's Sheringham Park gardens next door a riot of rhododendrons and azaleas in the season, there's plenty to keep you busy until dinner calls at the Dales Country House Hotel. The step-gabled Victorian mansion has period charm in spades, although the cooking in Upchers restaurant takes a rather more contemporary European view of things. Lamb kofta with spiced aubergine caviar, cucumber and mint raita and Madras foam might open the show. With the briny so near, fish and seafood is always going to be a good bet for mains – perhaps a fillet of sea bass with herby crushed potatoes, wilted greens, fennel purée and caper and tomato sauce. Local meat plays its part too, often appearing in two-way servings such as roast smoked breast and poached leg of guinea fowl served with fondant potato, mushroom purée and smoked pancetta jus. To finish, maybe cappuccino crème brûlée with chocolate truffle bonbons or Norfolk cheeses with apricots and orange chutney.

Chef Rene Ilupar **Owner** Mr & Mrs Mackenzie **Seats** 70, Pr/dining room 40
Times 12-2/7-9.30 **Prices** Service optional **Wines** 6 bottles over £30, 26 bottles under £30, 7 by glass **Parking** 50 **Notes** Afternoon tea, Sunday L £17.95, Vegetarian available, Children welcome

SNETTISHAM
Map 12 TF63

The Rose & Crown

@ British

tel: 01485 541382 **Old Church Rd PE31 7LX**
email: info@roseandcrownsnettisham.co.uk **web:** www.roseandcrownsnettisham.co.uk
dir: From King's Lynn take A149 N towards Hunstanton. After 10m into Snettisham to village centre, then into Old Church Rd towards church. Hotel 100yds on left

Consistently popular village inn with hearty cooking

The stone-built whitewashed country inn stands in a north Norfolk village a little way from King's Lynn. Inside is all twisty passageways and low beams, with a crackling fire to warm the winter away, and the full array of hand-pumped ales, flagged floors and hearty cooking. It isn't unknown for locals to dine here three or four times a week, which should tell you something, and what they return for are fried sardines in arrabbiata sauce, crisp-skinned salmon in seafood chowder, and sterling meat dishes from the environs, such as pigeon with a black pudding and mushroom tart and sprouting broccoli, or duck breast with bubble-and-squeak and green beans in red wine jus. House classics include exemplary fish and chips and Lincolnshire sausages and mash in a gravy of Adnams bitter. Finish with eggnog pannacotta, served with a poached pear and biscotti.

Chef Jamie Clarke **Owner** Anthony & Jeanette Goodrich **Seats** 160, Pr/dining room 30
Times 12-9, All-day dining **Prices** Starter £5.25-£7.25, Main £10.25-£18.50, Dessert £3.50-£6.50, Service optional **Wines** 12 bottles over £30, 32 bottles under £30, 15 by glass **Parking** 70 **Notes** Sunday L fr £13.95, Vegetarian available, Children welcome

STALHAM
Map 13 TG32

The Ingham Swan

@@ Modern European

tel: 01692 581099 **Sea Palling Rd, Ingham NR12 9AB**
email: info@theinghamswan.co.uk **web:** www.theinghamswan.co.uk
dir: A419 follow signs for Ingham. Next to church

14th-century thatched foodie inn with daily-changing menu

Originally part of Ingham priory, the 14th-century Swan survived Henry VIII's attempts to demolish it, and still presents the timeless face of a thatched chocolate box inn to the 21st-century world. Like many a country pub, the old place has traded up these days – if you fancy a pint, there's a cosy bar serving Woodforde's ales, but the driving force is the stylish rustic restaurant where exposed Norfolk flint walls, oak parquet floors, beams and an inglenook are overlaid with modern art. Daily-changing menus are built on local materials handled skilfully and without fuss to deliver a repertoire offering plenty to tempt. Seared pigeon breast with earthy wild mushroom and truffle oil risotto, crispy pancetta and swede purée is strong opener, followed by a confidently cooked main course of pan-fried wild sea bass with crispy Cromer crab cakes, buttered local asparagus, samphire and watercress velouté. The kitchen continues to deliver the goods right through to a seriously impressive pudding showcasing seasonal rhubarb as sorbet, poached, and in a pannacotta with vanilla, and ginger syrup.

Chef Daniel Smith **Owner** Daniel Smith **Seats** 55 **Times** 12-2/6-9, Closed 25-26 Dec
Prices Fixed L 2 course £16.50, Fixed D 3 course £28, Tasting menu £55, Starter £6.95-£9.50, Main £14.50-£25.95, Dessert £6.95-£9.50, Service optional **Wines** 27 bottles over £30, 21 bottles under £30, 9 by glass **Parking** 12, On street
Notes Sunday L £22.50-£28, Vegetarian available, Children welcome

THETFORD
Map 13 TL88

Elveden Café Restaurant

@ Traditional British

tel: 01842 898068 **London Rd, Elveden IP24 3TQ**
email: lucy.wright@elveden.com
dir: On A11 between Newmarket & Thetford, 100 mtrs from junct with B1106

Fresh seasonal cooking in a busy farm shop

The 10,000 acres of the Guinness estate in Norfolk are the base for a modern agricultural enterprise, supplying a formidable annual tonnage of fresh produce to East Anglia and beyond, with a raftered farm shop at its heart. The all-day café it incorporates is a bright, open space with granite tables and a wall of deep windows. At lunchtimes, it hosts quite a press of enthusiastic regular business, but service remains attentive and focused, and the weekend pre-Christmas party nights are a blast. A weekly-changing menu of sensitively cooked seasonal dishes, precisely seasoned and neatly presented, might open with smoked salmon and prawn potato cakes in mango-chilli dressing, and continue with braised pig's cheek on celeriac purée with smoked mash, or pan-roasted Loch Duart salmon on pasta with artichokes and peas in a vivid, sharp watercress sauce. Finish with a bravura version of lemon meringue pie, served with clotted cream and seasonal berries.

Times 9.30-5, Closed 25-26 Dec, D all week

THURSFORD
Map 13 TF93

The Old Forge Seafood Restaurant

Seafood

tel: 01328 878345 **Fakenham Rd NR21 0BD**
email: sarah.goldspink@btconnect.com **web:** www.seafoodnorthnorfolk.co.uk
dir: *On A148*

Rustic seafood cooking in a historic former forge

The whitewashed former coaching station and forge used to be a resting place for pilgrims heading to Walsingham, and even merits a name-check in *The Pilgrim's Progress*. A sympathetic refurbishment means beams, York stone floor and even the original iron hooks where the horses were shod are in evidence in the cosy, buzzy restaurant. It's all about the seafood here, and why not, when you can get it in fresh every day from nearby Blakeney and Wells-next-the-Sea? Expect good, honest, rustic cooking, often with Spanish influences and using spices grown in The Old Forge's garden. There might be sizzling tiger prawns in the Spanish way, served with chunks of bread, lobster grilled with garlic and parsley butter, or a zarzuela of fish – another Spanish dish with white fish and shellfish cooked in white wine, cream and tomatoes, served in a large paella-style pan.

Chef Colin Bowett **Owner** Colin & Sarah Bowett **Seats** 28 **Times** 6.30-10, Closed Mon, L all week **Prices** Prices not confirmed, Service optional **Wines** 1 bottle over £30, 12 bottles under £30, 5 by glass **Parking** 12 **Notes** Opening times vary (phone to check), no late bkgs Jan-Feb, Vegetarian available, Children 5 yrs+

TITCHWELL
Map 13 TF74

Titchwell Manor Hotel

– see below

WIVETON
Map 13 TG04

Wiveton Bell

British, European

tel: 01263 740101 **The Green, Blakeney Rd NR25 7TL**
email: wivetonbell@me.com **web:** www.wivetonbell.co.uk
dir: *1m S of Blakeney on the Holt road*

Flying the regional flag in a north Norfolk country inn

An authentic Georgian country pub on the village green next to a fine old church, the Bell is near Blakeney and the salt marshes of north Norfolk. Done up in light and airy modern fashion, it's perfectly placed to capitalise on the pick of regional seasonal produce, which of course includes fine seafood from local boats. There's also work by local artists on display to orient you even more securely. The cooking has a pleasingly traditional air about it, so you might begin with smoked haddock

Titchwell Manor Hotel

TITCHWELL
Map 13 TF74

Modern European
tel: 01485 210221 **PE31 8BB**
email: margaret@titchwellmanor.com **web:** www.titchwellmanor.com
dir: *On A149 (coast road) between Brancaster & Thornham*

Lively modernist cooking at a family-run coastal hotel

The Snaith family's pride and joy since 1988 has a seriously good kitchen. Of course, they were canny enough to spot the potential of the area when they set about converting this Victorian farmhouse, which enjoys unbroken views across marshland to the North Sea. The interiors all have a brightness and freshness to them and dining goes on across two spaces. It's a supremely relaxing setting for Eric Snaith's lively modernist cooking. A skill with novel combinations produces a first course of roasted quail with watermelon, Alsace bacon and peas, which builds up to a cumulatively sweet but balanced dish, or there may be mackerel dressed in soy, shallots and lime with a touch of caviar. At main, there are fine locally-reared and-landed meats and fish, the latter perhaps flawlessly timed hake with rainbow chard, pearl barley and a sauce based on wine-stewed matelote with apple. The bells-and-whistles option is the seven-course Conversation taster, which will strike up many a happily animated dialogue by means of dishes such as Norfolk lamb with

parsley root purée, olive and preserved lemon, with a cheese offering such as brie de meaux mousse with gingerbread, leading on to a pre-dessert lollipop flavoured with lemon and lovage. Daring technique is in consistent evidence through to the finale of barbecued pineapple with coconut and burnt meringue.

Chef Eric Snaith **Owner** Margaret & Ian Snaith **Seats** 80
Times 12-5.30/6.30-9.30, **Prices** Tasting menu £55-£65, Starter £6-£12, Main £11-£28, Dessert £7-£10, Service optional **Wines** 54 bottles over £30, 40 bottles under £30, 9 by glass **Parking** 50 **Notes** Tasting menu D 5/8 course, Sunday L £17-£29, Vegetarian available, Children welcome

and horseradish fishcake with a poached egg, and go on with pork belly slow-cooked for 12 hours, served with cider-braised apple, fennel fritters and champ. There are also precisely cooked classics such as beer-battered fish and chips, or puff-pastried partridge pie with roasted roots. Bringing up the rear might be an Eton Mess made with winter fruits, or orange and star anise blancmange with candied orange.

Chef Jamie Murch **Owner** Berni Morritt, Sandy Butcher **Seats** 60
Times 12-2.15/6-9.15, Closed 25 Dec **Prices** Starter £6.95-£8.95, Main £12.95-£21.95, Dessert fr £7.95 **Wines** 6 bottles over £30, 22 bottles under £30, 13 by glass **Parking** 5, Village green 50yds away **Notes** Sunday L £15.95-£26.95, Vegetarian available, Children welcome

WYMONDHAM
Map 13 TG10

Number Twenty Four Restaurant
◉ Modern British

tel: 01953 607750 **24 Middleton St NR18 0AD**
web: www.numbcr24.co.uk
dir: Town centre opposite war memorial

Comfortable, homely venue with appealing cooking

Hewn out of a row of Georgian cottages in the Norfolk market town whose pronunciation newcomers are bound to get wrong, the Griffins' comfortably furnished restaurant has a small but homely feel, with standard lamps and dressers, ruched curtains and neatly folded napkins. The cooking keeps things within realistic bounds for such appealing offerings as mild goats' cheese and cauliflower tart on rocket and pine nut salad, followed by seared sirloin with grain mustard mash, flat mushrooms and kale in rumbustious ale gravy, or grilled halibut with more mash in a sauce of white wine, capers and crayfish. The veggie main course could be roasted squash cannelloni with mascarpone and sage in amontillado cream. A stonkingly rich, soft-textured chocolate mousse cake served warm with maple and walnut ice cream and chocolate sauce is a grand finale.

Chef Jonathan Griffin **Owner** Jonathan Griffin **Seats** 60, Pr/dining room 55
Times 12-2/7-9, Closed 26 Dec, 1 Jan, Mon, L Tue, D Sun **Prices** Fixed L 2 course £16.95-£21.45, Fixed D 3 course £27.50-£35.70, Service optional **Wines** 3 bottles over £30, 30 bottles under £30, 7 by glass **Parking** On street opposite, town centre car park **Notes** Sunday L £16.95-£18.95, Vegetarian available, Children welcome

NORTHAMPTONSHIRE

DAVENTRY
Map 11 SP56

Fawsley Hall
◉◉ Modern British

tel: 01327 892000 & 0845 072 7482 **Fawsley NN11 3BA**
email: info@fawsleyhall.com **web:** www.fawsleyhall.com
dir: A361 S of Daventry, between Badby & Charwelton, hotel signed (single track lane)

Assertive modern British cooking in a grand setting

Plantagenets, Tudors and Georgians all had a go at Fawsley Hall over the centuries, resulting in the beguiling architectural mishmash we see today. It screams 'grand', with oak panels, stone arches and the fabulous Equilibrium dining room, where a 25-foot-high beamed ceiling and huge inglenook, flagstone floor and flickering candlelight create a real sense of occasion. That said, the number of covers is kept low, so that a proper feeling of intimacy pervades the place, and the kitchen deals in imaginative 21st-century ideas with clever flavour combinations and impeccable ingredients. Start perhaps with pressed Landes foie gras with apricot granola and sour apples, or yellowfin tuna sashimi pointed up by lime oil, pressed tomatoes, wasabi rouille and basil caviar. Main courses might offer seared halibut with vegetable tajine, confit squid, chickpeas and lemon oil, or a pairing of smoked belly pork with langoustines, supported by cocotte potatoes, carrot purée and sorrel and watercress sauce. Desserts stay creative with the likes of poached pear with pickled walnuts, and Roquefort ice cream.

Times 7-9.30, Closed Xmas, New Year, Sun-Wed, L all week

KETTERING
Map 11 SP87

Kettering Park Hotel & Spa
◉ Modern British

tel: 01536 416666 **Kettering Parkway NN15 6XT**
email: kpark.reservations@shirehotels.com **web:** www.ketteringparkhotel.com
dir: Off A14 junct 9 (M1 to A1 link road), hotel in Kettering Venture Park

International classics in a characterful hotel restaurant

A member of the Shire spa hotels group, Kettering Park belies its location in a business park by having a degree of charming personality about it. The restaurant boasts a real open fire in winter for a start, and is a multi-tiered room with an appealing look of the modern brasserie, with views over the gardens at the back. The menu deals in the international stalwarts of today, but turned out with proficiency and style, and there is a buffet featuring a selection of local produce, from Melton Mowbray pies to Leicestershire cheeses. Kick start the taste buds with a salad of winter greens, goats' cheese, beetroot, roasted hazelnuts and pomegranate, before a comforting main course of pan-roasted chicken breast with parsnip mash, crispy bacon, shallots in red wine and mushrooms. Finish with warm treacle tart jazzed up with clotted cream and a sherry reduction.

Chef Jamie Mason **Owner** Shire Hotels **Seats** 90, Pr/dining room 40
Times 12-1.45/7-9.30, Closed Xmas, New Year (ex residents & pre-booked), L Mon-Sat **Prices** Service optional **Wines** 27 bottles over £30, 49 bottles under £30, 16 by glass **Parking** 200 **Notes** Sunday L £19.50, Vegetarian available, Children welcome

Rushton Hall Hotel and Spa
◉◉◉ – see page 432

NASSINGTON
Map 12 TL09

The Queens Head Inn

◉◉ Modern British

tel: 01780 784006 **54 Station Rd PE8 6QB**
email: info@queensheadnassington.co.uk **web:** www.queensheadnassington.co.uk
dir: A1(M) N exit Wansford, follow signs to Yarwell & Nassington

Inviting riverside inn with treats from the grill

Standing on the banks of the River Nene in the postcard-pretty village of Nassington, The Queens Head is a delightful mellow stone inn with a relaxed vibe and a solid line in muscular modern cooking built on locally-sourced ingredients. The 200-year-old hostelry still functions as a pub if you fancy a jar, but it is food that really drives the action these days. When you have a serious piece of kit such as a charcoal-fired Josper grill and oven in the kitchen, it makes sense to focus on unfussy meat and fish dishes sizzled to perfection on the flames. If you're up for some serious meat action, the steaks are impeccably sourced, and even extend to a rib-eye of Wagyu beef. Otherwise, you might take on hickory-smoked rump of lamb with rosemary croquettes, wild garlic, Chantenay carrots and wine jus, and end with salted caramel doughnuts with maple-glazed peanuts, ginger powder and orange ice cream.

Chef Erran Buckingham **Owner** Complete Hotels Ltd **Seats** 40, Pr/dining room 70 **Times** 12-2.30/6-9 **Prices** Prices not confirmed, Service optional **Wines** 6 bottles over £30, 23 bottles under £30, 14 by glass **Parking** 45 **Notes** Sunday L, Vegetarian available, Children welcome

---

NORTHAMPTON
Map 11 SP76

The Hopping Hare

◉ Modern British **NEW** V

tel: 01604 580090 **18 Hopping Hill Gardens, Duston NN5 6PF**
email: info@hoppinghare.com **web:** www.hoppinghare.com
dir: M1 junct 16. A4500 to Northampton 5m, past Northamptom Saints Rugby Ground, left into Argyle St, 200 yds left A428 (Harlestone Rd). 2m on left

Ambitious cooking in a contemporary setting

The Hopping Hare is a 21st-century venue: the bar is of the lounge variety and offers a stylish place to drink and meet up, while the restaurant bit is informal and atmospheric. Factor in boutique-style bedrooms and you have a place that chimes with the times. The culinary output includes pub classics, some impressive grazing boards filled with cheeses, salmon pastrami and such like, and extends to ambitious modern British dishes. An example is a starter of pan-fried pigeon breast with Jerusalem artichoke purée, sticky honey-glazed chestnuts and black pudding crumb. There are French classical influences on show in dishes like a main course pan-fried Gressingham duck breast with confit leg, sautéed Savoy cabbage and Earl Grey jus, and a dessert of pineapple and star anise tarte Tatin. Desserts are a strong suit in fact, judging by lavender and honey pannacotta with vanilla-poached pink rhubarb and ginger beer sorbet.

Chef Jennie Bowmaker **Owner** David & Joy George **Seats** 80 **Times** 12-2.30/5.30-9.30 **Prices** Fixed L 2 course fr £16.95, Starter £5.75-£6.50, Main £11.95-£25, Dessert £4.95-£6, Service optional **Wines** 10 bottles over £30, 25 bottles under £30, 9 by glass **Parking** 40, On street **Notes** Sunday L £16.50-£19.50, Children welcome

---

Rushton Hall Hotel and Spa ❀❀❀

KETTERING
Map 11 SP87

Modern British
tel: 01536 713001 **Rushton NN14 1RR**
email: enquiries@rushtonhall.com **web:** www.rushtonhall.com
dir: A14 junct 7, A43 to Corby then A6003 to Rushton, turn after bridge

Modern cookery contrasting with stately old surroundings

If you like your country-house hotels on the Downton Abbey scale, look no further than Rushton Hall, a sprawling stately home with magnificent 16th-century façade standing on what was once known as a 'gentle eminence'. In the Tudor period, it was owned by the Tresham family, who were very much on the Roman side of the confessional divide, to the extent of engagement in the Gunpowder Plot and paid the price for it in all sorts of ways. Drinks are taken in the cavernous splendour of the Great Hall, then it's on to the dining room, where tables are impeccably dressed, service is from silver trays, and even the background music is charmingly dated. Adrian Coulthard offers a style of investigative British cooking rather at odds with the surroundings, dishes wrought from many elements, with textural variations a constant watchword. First off might be pressed confit duck with smoked breast and livery parfait, dressed with fig jam, or there could be poached, smoked and gin-cured salmon with tonic water sorbet and fennel. For all the multifarious nature of these compositions, everything is carefully considered, as

is certainly the case in a main course of monkfish with crisped brandade, pickled veg salad and asparagus, the plate dotted with pieces of light lemon sponge. Meat might be seared loin of venison with suet pudding and chillied swede in chocolate. The variations approach is sustained in desserts such as barbecued pineapple with iced and parfait presentations of the fruit and a coconut sorbet.

Chef Adrian Coulthard **Owner** Tom & Valerie Hazelton **Seats** 40, Pr/dining room 60 **Times** 12-1/7-9, Closed L Mon-Sat **Prices** Fixed D 3 course £55, Service optional **Wines** 50 bottles over £30, 36 bottles under £30, 16 by glass **Parking** 140 **Notes** Fixed L 3 course Sun, ALC 3 course £55, Sunday L £30, Vegetarian available, Children 10 yrs+ D

The Talbot Hotel

◉ British

tel: 01832 273621 **New St PE8 4EA**
email: talbot@bulldogmail.co.uk web: www.thetalbot-oundle.com
dir: *A605 Northampton/Oundle at rdbt exit Oundle A427 – Station Road turn onto New Street*

Classic and modern comfort food in an ancient hostelry

If The Talbot looks ancient, that's maybe because its stone façades, mullioned windows and grand timber staircase were recycled from Fotheringhay Castle in the 17th century. Nowadays it does a brisk trade as a hotel, coffee house and eatery, aka the restaurant, where bare tables and classy cutlery work well in the modern, minimalist-yet-comfy space (you are welcome to eat wherever you like, including the paved courtyard and garden). A menu of contemporary comfort-oriented dishes covers a lot of ground, starting with crab linguine ramped up with dill, lemon, chilli crème fraîche and shaved truffle, followed by a home-baked, shortcrust pastry-topped steak, ale and mushroom pie with thick-cut chips. Otherwise, go for something more up-to-date like roast lamb rump with Moroccan-spiced couscous and chickpea salsa and finish with fig and almond tart sauced with honey ice cream.

Chef David Simms **Owner** Bulldog Hotel Group **Seats** 48, Pr/dining room 64
Times 12-2.30/6.30-9.30 **Prices** Starter £5-£9, Main £12-£20, Dessert £5-£7, Service optional **Wines** 9 bottles over £30, 30 bottles under £30, 16 by glass
Parking 30 **Notes** Sunday L £12-£28, Vegetarian available, Children welcome

Roade House Restaurant

◉ Modern British

tel: 01604 863372 **16 High St NN7 2NW**
email: info@roadehousehotel.co.uk
dir: *M1 junct 15 (A508 Milton Keynes) to Roade, left at mini rdbt, 500yds on left*

Much-loved village restaurant with rooms

A family-run restaurant with rooms in a snoozy Northamptonshire village, the Roade House sits within easy reach of the M1 and the high-octane thrills of Silverstone racetrack. The traditional beamed dining room is done out with bentwood seats at white linen-clothed tables and restful neutral tones, making a calm setting for chef-patron Chris Kewley's confident cooking. The straight-talking menu aims for robust flavours and takes its inspiration from far and wide, so a perfectly-executed smoked haddock risotto might sit alongside a salad of Swedish salt herring with rye bread and mustard sauce. Main course delivers roast breast of guinea fowl together with its confit leg meat, apple and Calvados sauce and potato gratin, or there could be blackened salmon fillet with aïoli sauce and apricot and pistachio couscous. Completing the appealing picture, there's honey pannacotta with roast figs for pudding.

Chef Chris Kewley **Owner** Mr & Mrs C M Kewley **Seats** 50, Pr/dining room 16
Times 12-2/7-9.30, Closed 1 wk Xmas, BHs, L Sat, Mon, D Sun **Prices** Fixed L 2 course £20.50-£21, Starter £5.75-£8, Main £16-£24, Dessert £5.50-£6.50, Service optional **Wines** 20 bottles over £30, 20 bottles under £30, 6 by glass **Parking** 20
Notes Sunday L £21-£24.50, Vegetarian available, Children welcome

Narrow Boat at Weedon

◉ Modern, Traditional British

tel: 01327 340333 **Stowe Hill, A5 Watling St NN7 4RZ**
email: info@narrowboatatweedon.co.uk web: www.narrowboatatweedon.co.uk
dir: *M1 junct 16 follow signs to Flore. At A5 junct turn south towards Towcester. Located on Grand Union Canal*

Canalside eatery serving classic and modern fare

The place is not an actual narrowboat, but plenty of them moor up for this popular dining inn's modern British cooking. Easy to find on the A5, it's an enticing spot for alfresco meals in summer with watery views and fields all around, while the kitchen caters to all comers with menus taking in everything from pub classics – home-made pies, burgers made from top-grade beef, say – to stone-baked pizzas, and more up-to-date ideas in the restaurant. Start with pressed ham hock with minted pea purée, a ham and cheese bonbon and English mustard mayo before going on to main business such as pan-seared duck breast with a cottage pie of confit leg meat with baby veg and red wine jus. The finale is a reworking of the good old rhubarb and custard theme: custard pannacotta with the rhubarb element appearing as ice cream, poached and jelly with ginger biscotti.

Chef Daniel Turner **Owner** Richard & Karen Bray **Seats** 100, Pr/dining room 40
Times 12-2.30/6-10, Closed 26 Dec **Prices** Prices not confirmed, Service optional 10% **Wines** 4 bottles over £30, 25 bottles under £30, 20 by glass **Parking** 40
Notes Sunday L, Vegetarian available, Children welcome

Whittlebury Hall

◉◉ Modern British, European

tel: 01327 857857 & 0845 400 0002 *(Calls cost 7p per minute plus your phone company's access charge)* **NN12 8QH**
email: reservations@whittleburyhall.co.uk web: www.whittleburyhall.co.uk
dir: *A43/A413 towards Buckingham, through Whittlebury, turn for hotel on right (signed)*

Contemporary and creative fine dining and motor racing

Whittlebury Hall, a plush neo-Georgian hotel with a Rolls Royce of a spa, lies just a Ferrari's roar away from Silverstone. The much-loved Formula 1 commentator Murray Walker lends his name to its sophisticated fine-dining restaurant, where some of his celebrated gaffes are immortalised on the walls, together with F1 memorabilia. While the slick front-of-house team ensures diners can relax in the slow lane, the kitchen shifts into top gear with its modern British cooking underpinned by finely-tuned classical techniques. A starter entitled 'ham, egg and chips' grabs the attention, delivering ham hock and Serrano ham with truffled scrambled egg and golden raisin jus, while line-caught sea bass with garlic, sauce basquaise, mussels and grapes turns up at main course stage. Meatier offerings might run to veal sirloin with lentils, celeriac root, pied bleu mushrooms and baby turnips, and for pudding, a take on millefeuille is served with raspberries, with champagne and lemon sorbet.

Times 7-9.30, Closed selected dates at Xmas, 31 Dec, Sun-Mon, L all week

NORTHUMBERLAND

BAMBURGH
Map 21 NU13

Waren House Hotel
◉◉ Modern British

tel: 01668 214581 **Waren Mill NE70 7EE**
email: enquiries@warenhousehotel.co.uk **web:** www.warenhousehotel.co.uk
dir: Exit A1 on B1342, follow signs to Bamburgh. Hotel located close to Budle Bay, approx 2m from A1

Local supplies for country-house cooking

Near the coast by Bamburgh Castle and Lindisfarne Island, Waren House is a Georgian mansion set in six acres of landscaped grounds with sea views. Everything cries out classic country-house style, from the grandfather clock and log fires to the oil paintings and soothing blue-and-gold hues of its Grays Restaurant, where burnished tables and gleaming glassware reflect the candlelight at dinner. Tradition is the watchword in the kitchen, too, starting with diligent sourcing of the region's finest ingredients, which are brought together in a broadly modern British style. Pan-seared scallops are matched with creamed cauliflower, pea shoots, raisins and a mildly curry-spiced dressing, followed by a well-conceived main course partnering cumin-braised pork belly with cabbage and apple, cider jelly, puffed crackling, and a honeyed apple sauce. Fish cookery is handled with aplomb, perhaps roast pavé of halibut with crab and lemon crumble, buttered samphire and brown crab velouté. Dark chocolate fondant with a richly oozing centre is a good way to finish, particularly as it comes with white chocolate sorbet, crème fraîche, and chocolate streusel.

Chef Steven Owens **Owner** Mr & Mrs Laverack **Seats** 30 **Times** 6-8.45 **Prices** Starter £8.45-£9.95, Main £16.95-£24, Dessert £6.50-£9.95, Service optional **Wines** 65 bottles over £30, 120 bottles under £30, 8 by glass **Parking** 15 **Notes** Vegetarian available, Children 14 yrs+

BERWICK-UPON-TWEED
Map 21 NT95

Magna
◉ Indian

tel: 01289 302736 & 306229 **39 Bridge St TD15 1ES**
email: oliul.khan@gmail.co.uk
dir: A1 Berwick next to the old bridge

Skilled tandoori cooking and local ingredients

Since firing up the tandoor in 1982, Magna has earned a reputation for top-notch Indian cooking. It occupies a rather grand Victorian building close to the original bridge over the Tweed, and inside bright red chairs add a cheery glow to the space. The menu has plenty of familiar curry-house standards up for grabs, but the thing that sets the place apart is its use of local meats (including game) and locally-grown vegetables. Start with tandoori barbecued prawns, marinated for 72 hours and then served on finely sliced onion on a sizzling-hot skillet, or maybe a mixed platter of Sylheti hors d'oeuvres. Main courses include various ways with horeen (venison), perhaps tender strips marinated and cooked in tomato, onion and plenty of fresh chilli, or go for a green Bengal dish, meat or seafood cooked with spinach, green pepper, green beans and peas.

Chef Oliul Khan **Owner** The Khan family **Seats** 85, Pr/dining room 40
Times 12-2/5-11.30 **Prices** Fixed D 2 course £16.95-£34.95, Starter £3.95-£8.95, Main £7.95-£15.95, Dessert £3.45-£4.95 **Wines** 2 bottles over £30, 16 bottles under £30, 6 by glass **Parking** 60 **Notes** Sunday L, Vegetarian available, Children welcome

BLANCHLAND
Map 18 NY95

The Lord Crewe Arms Blanchland
◉ Traditional British **NEW**

tel: 01434 675469 **The Square DH8 9SP**
email: enquiries@lordcrewearmsblanchland.co.uk
web: www.lordcrewearmsblanchland.co.uk
dir: Phone for directions

Age-old hospitality 21st-century style

One of a kind, for how many inns have a 14th-century loo? Built for the residents of Blanchland Abbey in the 1100s, this wonderfully historic inn has served everyone from monks to lead miners. It seems unlikely that the latter, after a long, hard day under ground, would have been much interested in the inn's architecture, not even the vaulted stone crypt, now an atmospheric bar. Upstairs is the Bishop's Dining Room which clearly intends to make a regular customer of you by offering such appealing dishes as potted crab on toast with brown crab mayonnaise, Boccadon Farm veal rump, roasted Loch Duart salmon, and chargrilled flat-iron steak. Finish with Alnwick rum and nut tart, or rhubarb fumble. On Sundays lunch is self-selected sharing platters. Headed 'Glug, Glug, Glug!', the 50-strong wine list offers eight by the glass.

Chef Simon Hicks **Owner** Calcot Health & Leisure Ltd **Seats** 40, Pr/dining room 14 **Times** 12-2.30/6-9 **Prices** Starter £4.45-£7.75, Main £12.25-£22.73, Dessert fr £4.25, Service optional **Wines** 26 bottles over £30, 25 bottles under £30, 11 by glass **Parking** 30 **Notes** Sunday L £18-£24, Vegetarian available, Children welcome

CHATHILL
Map 21 NU12

Doxford Hall Hotel & Spa
◉◉ Modern British **V**

tel: 01665 589700 **NE67 5DN**
email: info@doxfordhall.com **web:** www.doxfordhall.com
dir: 8m N of Alnwick just off A1, signed Christon Bank & Seahouses. B6347 then follow signs for Doxford

Modern treatments of local supplies

Doxford Hall impresses on all counts. For a start, the grounds are simply stunning, with manicured lawns and flowerbeds, plus a yew tree maze (plans offered at reception). Then there's the building itself, dating from the early 19th century and lavishly upgraded to meet 21st-century needs including a swimming pool, library, bar and restaurant. The last is a splendid room with chandeliers in ornate ceilings, a stone fireplace, deep-red walls and pillars. The menus, too, reflect 21st-century dining expectations. Seared scallops with two croquettes of slowly cooked pig's cheek and celeriac remoulade is a starter of intense, distinct flavours, as is rabbit and Parma ham rillette with beetroot and truffled mayonnaise. Combinations are assessed diligently: roast loin of lamb with a copper pan of braised meat topped with a cobbler along with a spoonful of pea and onion fricassée and a glossy sauce, for instance, or curried fish pie and a soft-boiled duck's egg accompanying roast fillet of hake. Puddings are well up to snuff too, among them moist lemon cake with matching iced parfait and lemony caramel sauce.

Chef Mark Young **Owner** Robert Parker **Seats** 60, Pr/dining room 200
Times 12-2/6.30-9.30 **Prices** Fixed L 2 course £25, Starter £7.95-£9.95, Main £16.50-£25.95, Dessert £6.50-£8.50, Service optional **Wines** 25 bottles over £30, 47 bottles under £30, 15 by glass **Parking** 100 **Notes** Afternoon tea, Sunday L £24.95, Children welcome

CORNHILL-ON-TWEED
Map 21 NT83

Tillmouth Park Country House Hotel
Modern British

tel: 01890 882255 **TD12 4UU**
email: reception@tillmouthpark.force9.co.uk **web:** www.tillmouthpark.co.uk
dir: A698, 3m E from Cornhill-on-Tweed

Seasonal cooking in a splendid mansion

Close to the Scottish border, this splendid Victorian mansion is surrounded by 15 acres of landscaped grounds. It's a peaceful and atmospheric place to stay, with all the stained glass, oak panelling, real fires, comfy sofas and oil paintings you'd expect in a property of this vintage. Entry to the elevated Library Dining Room – with candlelit tables and views over the grounds – is via a beautiful wooden staircase around the edge of the tower. The kitchen turns out classically-based modern British food with menus driven by the best of local produce. Goats' cheese pannacotta with semi-dried cherry tomatoes and basil compôte starts things off, followed by a well-made risotto of Eyemouth smoked haddock turbocharged with fresh chilli and lemon. Hot chocolate fondant with vanilla ice cream is another classic done well to bring things to a close.

Chef Piotr Dziedzic **Owner** Tillmouth Park Partnership **Seats** 40, Pr/dining room 20 **Times** 7-9, Closed 26-28 Dec, Jan-Mar, L all week **Prices** Starter £4.95-£7.50, Main £13-£22.50, Dessert £5.85-£6.95, Service optional **Wines** 18 bottles over £30, 31 bottles under £30, 7 by glass **Parking** 50 **Notes** Vegetarian available, Children welcome

HEXHAM
Map 21 NY96

Barrasford Arms
Modern, Traditional British

tel: 01434 681237 **NE48 4AA**
email: contact@barrasfordarms.co.uk **web:** www.barrasfordarms.co.uk
dir: A69 at Acomb onto A6079 towards Chollerton. Turn left at church and follow signs to Barrasford

Modern English cooking in a genuine country inn

Not far from the heritage landmark of Hadrian's Wall, surrounded by the undulating grandeur of the Northumberland hills, the Barrasford Arms is an authentic country inn with ivy climbing over its façade. A suite of three dining rooms is kitted out with rustic furniture, the walls hung with pictures of the place in bygone days. Tony

Binks works to a modern English template, with the emphasis firmly placed on regional supplies and big flavours. Ham hock terrine with pease pudding and toast is a characteristically earthy start, but if you're after something lighter, a twice-cooked cheddar soufflé should fit the bill. Moving on, there may be full-flavoured grilled sea bass in lobster sauce with crunchy spring cabbage, or tenderest lamb shank in red wine, garlic and rosemary, served with a cloud of fluffy champ. Finish with a slice of plum and almond tart with vanilla sauce, or a lemon posset scattered with summer berries.

Chef Tony Binks **Owner** Tony Binks **Seats** 60, Pr/dining room 10 **Times** 12-2/6.30-close, Closed 25-26 Dec, BHs, Mon (Nov-Mar), L Mon, D Sun **Prices** Fixed L 2 course £13, Fixed D 3 course £27.50, Service optional **Wines** 1 bottle over £30, 19 bottles under £30, 7 by glass **Parking** 30 **Notes** Sunday L £12-£17.50, Vegetarian available, Children welcome

Langley Castle Hotel
Modern British

tel: 01434 688888 **Langley NE47 5LU**
email: manager@langleycastle.com **web:** www.langleycastle.com
dir: From A69 S on A686 for 2m. Hotel on right

Thrilling modern food in a genuine castle

Built in 1350 during the reign of Edward III, Langley's walls are seven feet thick and the castellated towers look over a 10-acre estate. You might be expecting a traditional restaurant with beams, heavy fabrics and exposed stone walls, which is exactly what you get, but the divertingly contemporary cuisine is a real bonus. The Josephine Restaurant is a traditional space watched over by a professional service team, while Daniel Grigg's menu is creative and modern. Via a table d'hôte and tasting menu, expect dishes rooted in classical good sense and made with high quality ingredients, but also some cutting edge techniques and bold ideas. Start, perhaps, with the playfully named 'liver, bacon and onion', which is in fact foie gras ganache with jamón Ibérico and various textures of onion. Main courses deliver the same level of refinement: Cartmel Valley venison, say, with sauerkraut, pulses and chocolate, or a fine piece of Isle of Gigha halibut with English samphire, razor clams and chorizo. Finish with 'a taste of chocolate' (tart, powder and crisp) served with iced parsnip.

Chef Daniel Grigg **Owner** Dr S Madnick **Seats** 48, Pr/dining room 28 **Times** 12-2.30/6.30-9 **Prices** Fixed L 3 course £25.50, Fixed D 3 course £49.50, Tasting menu £65, Service optional **Wines** 21 bottles over £30, 33 bottles under £30, 10 by glass **Parking** 57 **Notes** Sunday L £25.50, Vegetarian available, Children welcome

HEXHAM *continued*

Slaley Hall

◉ Modern & Classic British

tel: 01434 673350 **Slaley NE47 0BX**
web: www.qhotels.co.uk
dir: *A1 from S to A68 link road follow signs for Slaley Hall. From N A69 to Corbridge then take A68 S and follow signs to Slaley Hall*

Old and new in a grand Northumbrian manor

From its elevated position, the imposing Edwardian pile of Slaley Hall looks out over 1,000 acres of parkland, and beyond to the wild and rugged Northumberland countryside. There's plenty going on at Slaley — luxury accommodation, two championship golf courses, a spa and fitness centre, and three dining venues. Duke's Grill is the top dining option, a bay-windowed dining room done in tasteful Edwardiana, with wing-backed chairs in claret upholstery, lit framed pictures and mirrors, and an air of unruffled calm. The cooking balances old and new, setting out with a simple but effective combo of fried duck's egg with Stornoway black pudding, crispy pancetta and truffle dressing. Next up, prime cuts of meat and fish are cooked on the Josper grill — perhaps a whole rack of Ingram Valley lamb for two to share, or monkfish wrapped in Bayonne ham and delivered with squid céviche.

Times 6.30-9.45, Closed L all week

LONGHORSLEY   Map 21 NZ19

Macdonald Linden Hall, Golf & Country Club

◉◉ Modern British

tel: 01670 500000 **NE65 8XF**
email: lindenhall@macdonald-hotels.co.uk web: www.macdonaldhotels.co.uk/lindenhall
dir: *7m NW of Morpeth on A697 off A1*

Appealing mainstream cooking in a grand Georgian manor

The late-Georgian manor house of Linden Hall sits in 450 acres of park and mature woodland amid uplifting views of the Cheviots and wild Northumberland landscapes. As one might expect, a hotel of this standing comes with its own championship golf course and a full complement of spa and health and fitness facilities to sharpen the appetite. At its culinary heart is the upscale Dobson Restaurant, a plush venue done out in warm autumnal tones of russet and brick-red, with linen-clothed tables and relaxed, professional service. It makes a suitably refined setting for well-conceived dishes based on carefully-sourced raw materials. Tried-and-tested themes aim to comfort rather than challenge diners, so ham hock terrine is accompanied by mustard mayonnaise, then main course brings roasted corn-fed chicken breast stuffed with sunblushed tomato mousse and matched with sweet potato fondant, braised red cabbage and red wine jus. Otherwise, there may be braised pork belly with vegetable dauphinoise, caramelised apple and cider jus. To finish, there's a classic lemon meringue pie with raspberry sorbet.

Chef Jerome Cogne **Owner** Macdonald Hotels **Seats** 78, Pr/dining room 40
Times 12.30-2/6.30-9.30 **Prices** Fixed D 3 course fr £36, Starter £6-£9.50, Main £6.25-£23.50, Dessert £7-£10.95, Service optional **Wines** 82 bottles over £30, 17 bottles under £30, 14 by glass **Parking** 300 **Notes** Afternoon tea, Sunday L £15.50-£18.50, Vegetarian available, Children welcome

---

MATFEN   Map 21 NZ07

Matfen Hall

◉◉ Modern British

tel: 01661 886500 **NE20 0RH**
email: info@matfenhall.com web: www.matfenhall.com
dir: *A69 signed Hexham, leave at Heddon-on-the-Wall. Then B6318, through Rudchester & Harlow Hill. Follow signs on right for Matfen*

Dinner in the library at an ancestral home

Ancestral home of the Blacketts since the reign of George II, the hall we see at Matfen today is a creation of the Victorian era. Only 15 miles out of Newcastle, but wrapped in 300 acres of rolling northern parkland, it's an oasis of pastoral calm, with all the modern amenities from spa treatments to golf. The library, still replete with shelves of old volumes, does duty as the dining room, and has taken to the role well, with plenty of natural light by day and a romantic air in the evenings. The contemporary menus make a neat counterpoint to the surroundings, offering a crab salad with pea purée, crab pannacotta and the jolt of chilli jam to start, and then fantastic local beef tournedos under a bone marrow crust with braised leeks in a sauce of the sublimely fruity Magic Ale brewed by nearby High House Farm. Fish could be seared stone bass with rainbow chard, kale and samphire in bouillabaisse. A well-executed glazed lemon tart with raspberry sorbet makes a fine finish.

Chef Paul Blakey **Owner** Sir Hugh & Lady Blackett **Seats** 52, Pr/dining room 30
Times 12.30-3/6.45-9.15, Closed L Mon-Sat **Prices** Starter £6.50-£13.95, Main £17.50-£33, Dessert £6.50-£9.95, Service optional **Wines** 44 bottles over £30, 34 bottles under £30, 9 by glass **Parking** 200 **Notes** Afternoon tea £16.95, Sunday L £22.95, Vegetarian available, Children welcome

---

MORPETH   Map 21 NZ18

Eshott Hall

◉◉ British, European

tel: 01670 787454 **Eshott NE65 9EN**
email: info@eshotthall.co.uk web: www.eshotthall.co.uk
dir: *Eshott signed from A1. N of Morpeth*

Ambitious cooking of Northumbrian produce

Between Morpeth and Alnwick, Eshott Hall is a compact boutique hotel in a handsome Georgian property, its front covered with wisteria, within lovely gardens and woodland. It makes a perfect base from which to explore the Northumberland National Park and end the day with dinner in the elegantly appointed restaurant, with its moulded plasterwork on the walls, a soothing gold colour scheme and a fire in cooler weather. Full advantage is taken of the natural bounties of the area, with some vegetables and fruit from the hotel's kitchen garden. Pork belly wonton with apple jelly and crackling, and Craster smoked salmon with Seahouses crab, celeriac remoulade and watercress salad are the sort of lively starters to expect. Main courses maintain the style, seen in well-crafted dishes of seasonal roast saddle of venison with braised ox cheek, pommes Anna, baby shallots and veal jus, and halibut fillet with an accomplished tarragon cream sauce, heritage potato, roast squash and fennel. End on a sweet note such as tiramisù mousse with coffee and vanilla cream.

Chef Chris Haddock **Owner** Rev Robert Parker **Seats** 30, Pr/dining room 30
Times 12-2.30/6-8.30, Closed private functions **Prices** Fixed L 2 course fr £21.75, Fixed D 3 course fr £39, Service optional **Wines** 12 bottles over £30, 20 bottles under £30, 14 by glass **Parking** 60 **Notes** Sunday L £21.75-£29, Vegetarian available, Children welcome

NOTTINGHAMSHIRE

FARNDON
Map 17 SK75

Farndon Boathouse

Modern British, European, International

tel: 01636 676578 **Off Wyke Rd NG24 3SX**
email: info@farndonboathouse.co.uk
dir: *From A46 rdbt (SW of Newark-on-Trent) take Fosse Way signed Farndon. Turn right into Main St signed Farndon. At T-junct turn right into Wyke Lane, follow Boathouse signs*

Up-to-date brasserie cooking in a riverside setting

The leafy banks of the meandering River Trent make an interesting contrast to the contemporary exposed ducting, industrial-style lighting, stone floors and glazed frontage of the stylish Boathouse. The kitchen is driven by the guiding principles of sourcing locally and seasonally, and using modern cooking techniques such as sous-vide to squeeze every molecule of flavour from the ingredients. Uncomplicated contemporary brasserie dishes run the gamut from starters such as in-house-smoked duck breast with marinated feta cheese, compressed melon and lamb's lettuce, and cashew crumb, to seared sea bass with home-made pesto and parmesan gnocchi, squash purée and roast tomatoes; meaty ideas are along the lines of pan-fried pheasant breast with potato terrine, crispy ham, confit garlic and peas and roasting juices. Finish with the home comforts of sticky toffee pudding with milk ice cream and caramel sauce.

Chef Dan Garner **Owner** Dan Garner, Nathan Barton **Seats** 120 **Times** 12-3/6-9.30 **Prices** Fixed L 2 course fr £14.95, Fixed D 3 course £17.95-£30, Starter £3-£11.95, Main £11.95-£25, Dessert £4.95-£6.50, Service optional **Wines** 20 bottles over £30, 10 bottles under £30, 18 by glass **Parking** 18 **Notes** Early bird menu L & 6-7pm, Sunday L £9.95-£19.95, Vegetarian available, Children welcome

GUNTHORPE
Map 11 SK64

Tom Browns Brasserie

Modern International

tel: 0115 966 3642 **The Old School House, Trentside NG14 7FB**
email: info@tombrowns.co.uk **web:** www.tombrowns.co.uk
dir: *A6097, Gunthorpe Bridge*

From Victorian learning to modern brasserie cooking

We may not be in Rugby, but the homage to Thomas Hughes' plucky Victorian schoolboy denotes the fact that this large riverside building on the Trent was a place of education in the 19th century. Not that it bears much evidence of the academic now, with its elegant grey-toned, laminate-floored interior and tables for open-air dining. The other part of the name tells you to anticipate up-to-date cooking with strong impact, presented with a certain degree of informality. A compendious first-course gathering of seared Shetland scallops, Ibérico chorizo, sweet potato and butter bean purée is intriguingly garnished with a strip of dried sweet potato dusted with icing sugar. The labour-intensive follow-up could be superb pork belly accompanied by Savoy cabbage, apple and vanilla purée, and potato and sage terrine in mustard jus, a riot of flavours that just holds together, or perhaps fillets of sea bass with an array of artichokes, beetroot, gnocchi and salsa verde. Triumphant finale may be light-pastried chocolate and orange millefeuille with a burst of explosive flavour from blood orange sorbet.

Times 12-2.30/6-9.30, Closed D 25-26 Dec

NEWARK-ON-TRENT
Map 17 SK85

Kelham House Country Manor Hotel

Traditional English, French **NEW**

tel: 01636 705266 **Main St, Kelham NG23 5QP**
email: enquiries@kelhamhouse.co.uk **web:** www.kelhamhouse.co.uk
dir: *On A617 between Southwell & Newark*

Contemporary cooking in a grand country manor

The handsome red-brick house with grand gables and glorious gardens dates from the early 20th century and makes for a fine setting for a country-house hotel; it's unsurprisingly popular for wedding and functions. The restaurant is called Kitchen Garden and it's an elegant and contemporary space – as is the whole venue – with neat tables and fine-dining appeal. The modern output runs to a savoury take on crème brûlée with a Devon crab version with crisp parmesan topping, while another starter combines guinea fowl and smoked bacon in a terrine with home-made piccalilli. Among main courses, Scottish fillet steak comes with wild mushroom cream, and spiced Cornish monkfish with green olive dressing. Desserts such as strawberry pannacotta with Earl Grey sorbet are equally contemporary. Prices are very reasonable, particularly at lunchtime, and there's a smart modern bar offering simple food and a terrace.

Chef Marc Jakubic **Owner** Jon-Paul & Charlotte Davies **Seats** 25, Pr/dining room 25 **Times** 12-3/6.30-9.30 **Prices** Fixed L 2 course £9.95-£12.95, Fixed D 3 course £24.95-£29.95, Starter £4.95-£8.95, Main £12.95-£25, Dessert £6.95-£8.95 **Wines** 4 bottles over £30, 8 bottles under £30, 4 by glass **Parking** 150 **Notes** Sunday L £21.95, Vegetarian available, Children welcome

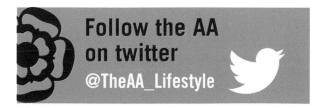

Hart's Restaurant

◉◉ Modern British

tel: 0115 988 1900 & 911 0666 **Standard Hill, Park Row NG1 6GN**
email: ask@hartsnottingham.co.uk **web:** www.hartsnottingham.co.uk
dir: At junct of Park Row & Ropewalk, close to city centre

Smart contemporary cooking from a skilled team

Next to the boutique hotel of the same name, Hart's Restaurant is owned by Tim Hart, who also owns Hambleton Hall Hotel in Oakham, Rutland. With its contemporary good looks and booth seating, it's a welcoming restaurant with an approachable, daily-changing menu of neatly-devised dishes in the modern British style. The kitchen's with-it approach is seen in main courses of corn-fed chicken breast, which is poached in chicken and mushroom stock for maximum tenderness and served with spelt and chicken risotto enriched with Madeira, cream, Parmesan and lemon, or there might be roast cod with spiced lentils, orange-glazed salsify, curly kale and lemon and hazelnut dressing. Bookending them is a starter of pan-fried sea bass with tart escabèche-style fennel and carrot counterpointing a creamy parsley purée, or a more robust pairing of braised lamb's tongue with rosemary and garlic purée, crosnes and baby gem lettuce, and to finish, poached Yorkshire rhubarb is matched with kaffir lime-flavoured pannacotta and pistachio brittle. Tim Hart compiled the interesting wine list, which is arranged by style.

Chef Daniel Burridge **Owner** Tim Hart **Seats** 80, Pr/dining room 100
Times 12-2/6-10.30, Closed 1 Jan, L 31 Dec, D 25-26 Dec **Prices** Fixed L 2 course £15.95, Fixed D 3 course £24, Starter £5.95-£12.95, Main £15.50-£25.50, Dessert £7.15-£8.50 **Wines** 6 by glass **Parking** 15, Mount Street NCP (discounted), on street **Notes** Pre-theatre menu 2/3 course £18/£23, Sunday L £23, Vegetarian available, Children welcome

MemSaab Restaurant

◉◉ Indian NEW

tel: 0115 957 0009 **12-14 Maid Marian Way NG1 6HS**
email: contact@mem-saab.co.uk
dir: 5 mins walk from Nottingham Castle. Opposite Park Plaza Hotel

Vibrant northern Indian cooking in a big city-centre venue

There is no shortage of Indian food in the centre of Nottingham, so to stand out from the crowd you have to do something special. MemSaab achieves this and

more, impressively so in a gigantic venue of 200 covers. There is a real vibrancy about the place, extending from the cohort of loyal supporters to the lively northern Indian and Punjabi cooking, where even the most familiar dishes are cooked with finely detailed accuracy and presented with care. Tender salmon tikka are redolent of fenugreek and marinated in yogurt lit up with garam masala. A signature starter comes in the form of tandoori ostrich, roasted in garlic and red chilli. Meats benefit from the tenderising influence of slow cooking, as when lamb shank falls obligingly from its bone into cardamom-laced sauce, accompanied by spinach-topped masala mash, while king prawns are marinated in onion-seeded yogurt and chargrilled with peppers. Proving that restaurant fashion hasn't passed the Indian constituency by, there's a taster trio of desserts, comprised of sticky gulab jamun, bread-and-butter pudding, and a shot glass of phirni, a saffron milk pudding garnished with pistachios.

Chef Majid Ashraf **Owner** Amita Sawhney **Seats** 200, Pr/dining room 60
Times 5.30-10.30, Closed 25 Dec, L all week **Prices** Starter £4.95-£9.95, Main £8.95-£21.95, Dessert £4.95-£5.65, Service optional 10% **Wines** 11 bottles over £30, 34 bottles under £30, 12 by glass **Parking** NCP Mount St, NCP St James St **Notes** Early D menu 2 course, Vegetarian available, Children welcome

Park Plaza Nottingham

◉ Pan-Asian

tel: 0115 947 7444 & 947 7200 **41 Maid Marian Way NG1 6GD**
email: nottingham@chinolatino.co.uk **web:** www.chinolatino.eu
dir: A6200 (Derby Rd) into Wollaton St. 2nd exit into Maid Marian Way. Hotel on left

East Asian food gets the Latin treatment

The Nottingham branch of the Park Plaza offers just about all cons describable as mod, including a restaurant and bar complex, Chino Latino, trading on the fashionable association of Latin American and East Asian culinary traditions. There's a strong Japanese streak to the set menus, which take in offerings such as crispy duck with umeboshi plums in sake sauce, or prawn tempura with wasabi peas, supported by a range of bespoke bento box options. At the Latino end of the spectrum, beef picanha with chorizo polenta and aji panca (Peruvian red pepper) should get the taste buds sitting up and taking notice. Chinese and Thai currents join the flow too, the latter incorporating dry panang curry with 'crinkled' vegetables, while some dishes creatively mix it all, perhaps chicken tamarind with smoked chipotle sweet potato, figs and coriander. Trendsetting desserts include chocolate-pistachio tempura in ginger syrup, and mango cheesecake with matching salsa.

Chef Paul Thacker **Owner** Park Plaza Hotels **Seats** 70, Pr/dining room **Times** 12-10.30, All-day dining, Closed Xmas, Sun **Prices** Fixed D 2 course £25-£35, Tasting menu fr £45, Starter £4.50-£16, Main £14-£29, Dessert £5-£13 **Wines** 28 bottles over £30, 7 bottles under £30, 11 by glass **Parking** 30, Hotel chargeable. On street, NCP **Notes** 4 course L £10.95, Vegetarian available, Children welcome

Restaurant Sat Bains with Rooms

◉◉◉◉◉ – see opposite

Restaurant Sat Bains with Rooms ❀❀❀❀❀

NOTTINGHAM   Map 11 SK53

Modern British V ⚲ NOTABLE WINE LIST

tel: 0115 986 6566 **Lenton Ln, Trentside NG7 2SA**
email: info@restaurantsatbains.net
web: www.restaurantsatbains.com
dir: *M1 junct 24, A453 for approx 8m. Through Clifton, road divides into 3 – take middle lane signed 'Lenton Lane Industrial Estate', then 1st left, left again. Follow brown Restaurant Sat Bains sign*

Analytical dining from a quicksilver creative intellect

If you're staying overnight you'll find a note in your room listing the staff who you might encounter during the course of your visit. It's a nice touch. There was a time when during a night out there was little chance of meeting anyone other than the front-of-house team, but these days, with all the possibilities for close-up action with the guys and gals in white, you never know who you're going to meet. Make a reservation for the Chef's Table or Kitchen Bench if you want to see them in action, not to mention the whites of their eyes. Sat Bains is just the sort of guy to credit his team, a big-hearted man with an exceptional talent, and the nous to create a restaurant that excels in every department. The former Victorian farmhouse and its outbuildings have been converted with style to create a restaurant with rooms that meets the exacting standards of Sat and Amanda Bains. It is refined and elegant, with bedrooms that would pass muster in any five-star address, and a dining room that is dominated by statement artworks on a grand scale. When it's time to eat, prepare to be met by a menu with colour charts to help guide your way, the idea to reveal the balance of flavours in each dish – sweet, sour, salt, bitter and umami. What is on offer has been prepared with precision and unerring skill, with every taste, texture and temperature put under the microscope (not literally, but almost...), so you are taken to places you don't usually go when seated at a dining table. Choose between the seven- and ten-course tasting menus. Dish descriptions are minimalist, the dishes themselves are anything but; duck egg, peas and mint sounds like a happy partnership, and indeed it is, spectacular even, a vivid green ice cream of tantalising sweetness arriving with a perfectly poached egg and a thin shard of bread. Follow that with a scallop creation which combines seared and raw bivalves, each beautiful specimens, with variations in texture provided by nuts and seeds and cauliflower and vanilla purée, and then a crab 'satay' which is full of surprises and outstanding flavours. There's a 'crossover' dish that arrives after the savoury courses to ease you into desserts such as a seemingly simple construction of chocolate, coffee and olive oil that delivers a perfect chocolate mousse, intense coffee gel and whizzy olive oil jelly. If you feel inspired by your visit, book an early return via a place on the Kitchen Workshop, where you can pick up some tricks of the trade. Gourmet vegetarians should be knocking down the door for their bespoke dishes that have undergone the same vigorous R&D process as the main menu. The exceptional wine list has a colour-coding system all of its own, highlighting acidity, fruit, mineral, oak and non-fruit, with lots of things to drink that you've quite possibly never come across before.

Chef Sat Bains **Owner** Sat & Amanda Bains **Seats** 40, Pr/dining room 14 **Times** 12-1/6-9.45, Closed 2 wks Jan, 1 wk May, 2 wks Aug, Sun-Mon, L all week **Prices** Prices not confirmed **Wines** 30 by glass **Parking** 22 **Notes** L 7 course £75, D 7/10 course £85/£95, Chef's table £99, Children 8 yrs+

NOTTINGHAM *continued*

World Service
◉◉ Modern British

tel: 0115 847 5587 **Newdigate House, Castle Gate NG1 6AF**
email: info@worldservicerestaurant.com **web:** www.worldservicerestaurant.com
dir: *200mtrs from city centre, 50mtrs from Nottingham Castle*

Sharp cooking and idiosyncratic surroundings

Renaissance-styled Newdigate House was built in 1675, but what leaves its kitchen since it became home to World Service is distinctly contemporary work. The idiosyncratic interior mines a colonial vein, the warm orange and copper hues of the main dining room offset with oriental artefacts: Buddha heads, Indian statuary and objets d'art in glass cases. It all combines to create a laid-back Zen ambience, but the staff are super-slick, smartly-suited and sharp on the uptake, while bassy background beats add a funky urban edge to proceedings. If the restaurant's name isn't enough of a hint, the cooking has a gentle East-meets-West theme, although western influences hold sway. This is a kitchen that thinks about textures, putting an imaginative spin on to classic ideas, as seen in a starter matching braised ox tongue with gremolata and parmesan – a clever twist on classic carpaccio – followed by accurately-timed sea bass served with Korean sticky rice cakes, spring onion and bok choy. Carnivores might go for rump and shoulder of local lamb with potato terrine, butternut squash purée and shallot rings. At the end, banana parfait with banoffee caramel and palm sugar sorbet keeps the good ideas coming.

Times 12-2.15/7-10, Closed 26 Dec, 1-7 Jan, D Sun (ex Dec & BH Sun)

■ **OLLERTON** Map 16 SK66

Thoresby Hall Hotel
◉◉ British, International

tel: 01623 821000 & 821008 **Thoresby Park NG22 9WH**
email: thoresbyhall@bourne-leisure.co.uk **web:** www.warnerleisurehotels.co.uk
dir: *Phone for directions*

Classic grill menu overlooking Humphry Repton's gardens

The principal restaurant at Thoresby has undergone a restyling. Now known as the Blue Grill, it has a more informal feel, despite the blue silk damask wall coverings, and is equipped with a grill menu that embraces today's range of pedigree beef – Wagyu, USDA and local – as well as pork cutlets and breasts of corn-fed chicken. Steamed lobsters are on hand for the surf-and-turf platters. There are neat inventive touches alongside the hunks of protein, with Asian-spiced cauliflower and pak choi accompanying the braised pig's cheek, or perhaps a main-course salad of roast pigeon with parsnip purée, scorched spring onions and hazelnuts. Extensive listings of sides and sauces make for much happy mixing and matching, and by the sweet stage, the kitchen aims to twang your nostalgia strings with sharing platters of fairground treats – candyfloss, marshmallows, ice cream cones, doughnuts and toffee apples. It all takes place, a little incongruously, in a huge

palatial Victorian hall built amid gardens by Repton and parkland laid out by 'Capability Brown'.

Chef Mark Maris, Gary Griffiths **Owner** Warner Leisure Hotels **Seats** 50, Pr/dining room 50 **Times** 12-2/6.30-9, Closed D Mon, Wed **Prices** Starter £6-£12, Main £14.95-£39.95, Dessert £6.50-£16, Service optional **Wines** 15 by glass **Parking** 140 **Notes** Afternoon tea, Sunday L fr £22.95, Vegetarian available, Children 21 yrs+

OXFORDSHIRE

■ **ASTON ROWANT** Map 5 SU79

Lambert Arms
◉ Modern British

tel: 01844 351496 **London Rd OX49 5SB**
email: info.lambertarms@bespokehotels.com **web:** www.bespokehotels.com/lambertarms
dir: *M40 junct 6, at T-junct right towards Chinnor (B4009), back under motorway. 1st left to Postcombe/Thame (A40)*

Timbered coaching inn a stone's throw from the M40

The black-and-white Lambert Arms is at the foot of the Chiltern Hills (an Area of Outstanding Natural Beauty), yet only 500 metres from junction 6 of the M40. The former coaching inn is geared up to meet the needs of the business community, with meeting rooms, gym and outdoor spaces for events and such. But food plays its part, too, with the culinary output covering all the bases from pub classics to more refined and ambitious stuff. Eat in the bar or the relaxed, traditionally decorated dining room. The kitchen crafts well-constructed dishes that deliver on flavour; confit duck terrine, for example, served with rosemary bread and spiced carrot, or Bibury rainbow trout with chorizo and chargrilled veg. Aged rib-eye steak (served on a wooden board) and hand-made burgers play to the gallery. Finish with a comforting plum and almond tart.

Chef Christopher Coates **Owner** Bespoke Hotels **Seats** 46, Pr/dining room 60 **Times** 12-2.30/6.30-9 **Prices** Fixed L 2 course £12.50, Starter £5-£7.50, Main £11.95-£21.50, Dessert £5-£8.50, Service optional **Wines** 3 bottles over £30, 16 bottles under £30, 12 by glass **Parking** 80 **Notes** Sunday L £12-£22, Vegetarian available, Children welcome

■ **BANBURY** Map 11 SP44

BEST WESTERN PLUS Wroxton House Hotel
◉ Modern British

tel: 01295 730777 **Wroxton St Mary OX15 6QB**
email: reservations@wroxtonhousehotel.com **web:** www.wroxtonhousehotel.com
dir: *From M40 junct 11 follow A422 (signed Banbury, then Wroxton). After 3m, hotel on right*

Modern brasserie dishes in a thatched hotel restaurant

The stone-built Wroxton House is a honey-stone beauty in a photogenic thatched village near Banbury. Its restaurant occupies what was a terraced row of cottages, and is all oak beams and columns with an inglenook fireplace. Table settings are smart, service is a matter of well-judged formality, and the kitchen team, headed by Steven Mason-Tocker, turns out thoughtfully composed modern brasserie dishes founded on classic combinations. A starter might be poached cod, served with crayfish risotto in chorizo oil, or more simply a bowl of butternut and sweet potato soup. Duck for main course comes two ways – roast breast and confit leg – with wilted kale and puréed carrots in blackcurrant sauce, while fish might be gilthead bream with new potato, spinach and chorizo salad. Finish with pear frangipane tart and clotted cream. English and French cheeses come with outstanding home-made chutney.

Chef Steve Mason-Tocker **Owner** John & Gill Smith **Seats** 60, Pr/dining room 80 **Times** 12-2/7-9, Closed L Mon-Sat **Prices** Service optional **Wines** 7 bottles over £30, 35 bottles under £30, 10 by glass **Parking** 70 **Notes** Sunday L £21.95, Vegetarian available, Children welcome

The Three Pigeons Inn

Contemporary British NEW

tel: 01295 275220 **3 Southam Rd OX16 2ED**
email: manager@thethreepigeons.com **web:** www.thethreepigeons.com
dir: *M40 junct 11, left A422, left A361. Inn on left at lights on corner of Southam Rd & Castle St*

Charming town inn with modern rustic cooking

This old red-brick inn has been servicing the needs of the community since the 17th century. Today's incumbents took over in 2011 and brought the place back to life. It's surely never looked so good. Great care has been made to maintain the integrity of the building and its atmospheric interior, with the contemporary rustic-chic finish bringing the place into the modern era. There's a light-filled dining room extension (the Winter Garden), panelled bar, cosy bedrooms and a smart courtyard garden. The menu offers modern British dishes such as a pretty tian of oak-smoked salmon, crayfish and avocado, followed by a hearty but refined main course combining venison haunch with black pudding, plus rosemary and thyme dauphinoise, blueberry coulis and a cauliflower and almond purée. For dessert, apple crumble with crème anglaise competes with a pear poached in hot chocolate. Expect attentive service from the young team.

Owner Tina & Paul Laird **Seats** 40, Pr/dining room 20 **Times** 12-3/6-9, Closed D Sun, 25-26 Dec, 1 Jan **Prices** Fixed L 2 course £15.95, Fixed D 3 course £19.95, Starter £5.95-£9.25, Main £11.95-£26.95, Dessert £5.50-£9.50, Service optional **Wines** 4 bottles over £30, 20 bottles under £30, 11 by glass **Parking** 11 **Notes** Sunday L £12.95, Vegetarian available, Children welcome

The White Horse

Traditional British, French NEW

tel: 01295 812440 **2 The Square, Kings Sutton OX17 3RF**
email: julie@whitehorseks.co.uk
dir: *Phone for directions*

Award-winning cooking in appealing village pub

This old pub has been given a makeover that, while creating a clean, modern look, still ensures you are reminded of its past. Clearly popular, for which the friendly staff must take much credit, it has received regional food accolades for its British and European cooking. Typical is a starter of crispy pig's head with pancetta, black pudding, rhubarb and pistachio, breast and leg of Loomswood duck with carrot, cumin and lentil dahl as a main, and lemon cheesecake with stem-ginger ice cream to finish. Fillet of sea bream is one of several fish options, and for vegetarians there's pea, broad bean and barley risotto. A good choice of moderately priced wines includes a balanced mix from both the Old and New Worlds.

Chef Hendrik Dutson **Owner** Julie Groves, Hendrik Dutson **Seats** 40, Pr/dining room 7 **Times** 12-2.30/6-9, Closed Mon (ex BHs), D Sun **Prices** Fixed L 2 course £10-£13, Tasting menu fr £39.95, Starter £5.95-£7.10, Main £10.95-£23, Dessert £4.50-£5.95, Service optional **Wines** 3 bottles over £30, 29 bottles under £30, 21 by glass **Parking** 14 **Notes** Steak night Tue fr £14.95, Sunday L £10.50-£14.95, Vegetarian available, Children welcome

---

BURFORD Map 5 SP21

The Bay Tree Hotel

Modern British

tel: 01993 822791 **Sheep St OX18 4LW**
email: info@baytreehotel.info **web:** www.cotswold-inns-hotels.co.uk/baytree
dir: *A40 or A361 to Burford. From High St turn into Sheep St, next to old market square. Hotel on right*

Elizabethan inn with modern classic menu

Queen Elizabeth I's Great Baron of the Exchequer once lived here, and if it was good enough for him, it's good enough to be a modern country inn. Built in Cotswold stone, and festooned with purple wisteria, it's a stylishly appointed place with a dining room all dressed up in candelabra and linen, and a menu of modern-classic English food. That can only mean scallops on cauliflower purée, and it's a reliable version, with light caramelisation bringing out the sweetness of the shellfish. Mains range from roasted trout and samphire in crab bisque and lemon beurre blanc to capably handled rack of suckling pig with creamed leeks and cider-apple gel. A loosely textured chocolate and blood orange tart with candied peel makes up in flavour what it lacks in structural integrity, or try banana bread millefeuille with salted caramel and banana sorbet.

Times 12-2/7-9.30

The Bull at Burford

Modern French, Traditional British

tel: 01993 822220 **105 High St OX18 4RG**
email: info@bullatburford.co.uk **web:** www.bullatburford.co.uk
dir: *On A40 between Cheltenham & Oxford, in town centre*

Confident cooking in a former coaching inn

The High Street of Burford is rich with historic buildings, including The Bull, which first opened its doors in 1610 as a coaching inn. The façade maintains the period character, of course, but inside there's a little more leeway to bring in a contemporary touch or two. There's still charm and traditional features aplenty, but there's a satisfying modernity, too, with the restaurant offering up bare Cotswold-stone walls, age-blackened beams, original artwork, and butterscotch-hued seats at linen-swathed tables. The kitchen turns out bright, contemporary stuff, inflected with modern European ideas. Among starters, lemon and parsley fishcake comes with Provençal vegetables and a tomato and thyme sauce, for example, and a fish platter is filled with the likes of salmon tartare, herring salad and gravadax. A main course pan-seared fillet of Bibury trout is served with an accompanying pea and asparagus risotto, while sirloin steak comes with a choice of classic sauces. Desserts might deliver a baked Vienna cheesecake with caramelised peaches and passionfruit sorbet.

Chef Peter Juszkiewicz **Owner** Mr & Mrs J-M Lauzier **Seats** 40, Pr/dining room 12 **Times** 12-2.30/7-9.30 **Prices** Fixed L 2 course £12.45, Fixed D 3 course £14.95, Starter £5.95-£9.75, Main £9.95-£27.95, Dessert £6.95-£8.45, Service optional **Wines** 36 bottles over £30, 39 bottles under £30, 12 by glass **Parking** 6, On street **Notes** Sunday L, Vegetarian available, Children welcome

BURFORD *continued*

The Lamb Inn

◎◎ Modern British V

tel: 01993 823155 **Sheep St OX18 4LR**
email: info@lambinn-burford.co.uk
dir: *Exit A40 into Burford, down hill, take 1st left into Sheep St, hotel last on right*

Anglo-French modernism in the old weavers' homes

The Lamb came to light from what was originally a row of weavers' cottages dating back to the reign of Henry V. It has the full complement of a wisteria-clad front and stone-flagged bar, and an elegant dining room done in shimmering fuchsia, overlooking the terrace and courtyard. Fixed-price menus, including an eight-course taster with optional wine choices, indicate an ambitious approach to dining, and the mood is modern. Starters include an ingenious spin on a club sandwich, fashioned from wood pigeon, duck liver and figs, as an alternative to the more familiar likes of scallops and cauliflower, or beetroot carpaccio and goats' cheese. Multi-layered main courses are carefully thought through, producing satisfying compositions such as roast pheasant with black cabbage, sweetcorn purée and a boudin of the confit leg, or stone bass with crab, quinoa, salted fennel and sun-dried tomato gel. A labour of deconstruction transforms Black Forest gâteau into a densely rich chocolate cake with cherry jelly and mascarpone sorbet, or there could be a terrine of mulled pears in cocoa syrup and vanilla cream.

Chef Peter Galeski **Owner** Cotswold Inns & Hotels Ltd **Seats** 40, Pr/dining room 20 **Times** 12-2.30/7-9.30 **Prices** Fixed L 2 course £20, Fixed D 3 course £42, Tasting menu £58 **Wines** 60 bottles over £30, 40 bottles under £30, 12 by glass **Parking** Care of The Bay Tree Hotel **Notes** Tasting menu 8 course with dégustation wines, Sunday L £20-£25, Children welcome

---

CHECKENDON   Map 5 SU68

The Highwayman

◎ Modern, Traditional British

tel: 01491 682020 **Exlade St RG8 0UA**
dir: *Exlade St signed off A4074 (Reading/Wallingford road), 0.4m*

Nice mix of menus in a welcoming country local

A hike on the wooded Chiltern Hills nearby should bring on a keen appetite for The Highwayman's good honest cookery. Tucked away in a secluded hamlet, the setting is a rambling 16th-century inn done out with exposed brickwork and beams and a wood-burner in a huge inglenook. Fine ales are on tap in the pubby bar, and all bases are covered in the food department by steaks from the grill, home-made pies – wild boar with sage and apple, perhaps – and if you're in the market for something more contemporary, a carte with plenty of seasonal focus. Game pâté with pickled vegetables is a great way to start, followed by roast pork belly with black pudding faggot, barley, turnips, apple jelly and mustard jus. Round off with treacle tart with ginger and honey ice cream or a rhubarb duo of Pavlova and coulis.

Chef Paul Burrows **Owner** Paul Burrows **Seats** 55, Pr/dining room 40 **Times** 12-2.30/6-10, Closed 26 Dec, 1 Jan, Mon, D Sun **Prices** Prices not confirmed, Service optional **Wines** 5 by glass **Parking** 30 **Notes** Sunday L, Vegetarian available, Children welcome

---

CHINNOR   Map 5 SP70

The Sir Charles Napier

◎◎◎ – *see below*

The Sir Charles Napier ◎◎◎

CHINNOR   Map 5 SP70

Modern British, European ⚜ NOTABLE WINE LIST

tel: 01494 483011 **Sprigg's Alley OX39 4BX**
email: info@sircharlesnapier.co.uk
dir: *M40 junct 6, B4009 to Chinnor. Right at rdbt to Sprigg's Alley*

Resourceful blend of old and new in a beautiful country inn

Just to mark your card, it was Sir Charles who, with colonial thoroughness, relieved the besieged Sindh province (in what is now Pakistan) on behalf of the British Empire in 1842. Julie Griffiths' inn, named after the Victorian general, is more noted for relieving the besieged appetites of residents of nearby Chinnor, and the many who come from further afield, with menus of vigorous modern British cooking, courtesy of head chef Anthony Skeats. The ambience is as neatly fused of old and new as is the cooking, stretches of exposed brickwork interspersed with artistically adorned walls, enveloping sofas, and tables outside under the trees in the beautifully kept gardens. Dishes throw the net wide for inspiration, subjecting scallops to a refreshing Spanish treatment with gazpacho, a smoky note from charred tomato and a sweeter one from red pepper purée. Endive marmalade and burnt onions provide the counterpointing notes to seared foie gras in another starter, and the next stop on the journey might be a main-course pairing of confit leg and yuzu-glazed breast of Goosnargh duck with cumined carrot, or a distinctly more French-sounding sea bass with haricots blancs, trompettes de mort mushrooms and violet artichokes in hazelnut vinaigrette. Exceptional rose veal comes with a sweetbread boudin, big morels and zesty gremolata. Sides might include an on-trend dish of buttered purple kale, while puddings up the stakes once more for parsnip and macadamia sponge with maple syrup and rosemary ice cream, or the shamelessly indulgent chocolate, salt caramel and peanut terrine with lime ice cream to bring it into focus. British and French cheeses are all top-drawer gear too. A superlative wine list, opening with imaginative selections by the glass, completes an accomplished picture.

Chef Anthony Skeats **Owner** Julie Griffiths **Seats** 75, Pr/dining room 45 **Times** 12-3.30/6.30-10, Closed 25-27 Dec, Mon, D Sun **Prices** Fixed L 2 course £17.50-£19.50, Fixed D 2 course £19.50, Tasting menu £65, Starter £10.50-£15.50, Main £21.50-£28.50, Dessert £8.50, Service optional 12.5% **Wines** 10 by glass **Parking** 60 **Notes** Sunday L, Vegetarian available, Children welcome

The Chequers

◎ British

tel: 01608 659393 **Church Rd, Churchill OX7 6NJ**
email: reservations@thechequerschurchill.com
dir: *Phone for directions*

Modern pub grub done right

A village pub with a stag's head behind the bar and a focus on food, The Chequers has been done up with a bit of individuality and doesn't look quite the same as everywhere else. That attention to detail and keen eye extends to the menu. There's nothing fancy or fussy about the culinary output, but time has been taken to seek out good quality ingredients such as British charcuterie and oysters from the south coast. Snails and mushrooms arrive on toast, rich with parsley and garlic, while main courses include steaks such as flat iron and rib-eye served with chips cooked in duck fat. Alternatively go for breaded lemon sole with fennel slaw and brown shrimps. To finish, rhubarb mess and banoffee pot are modern takes on classic puds.

Chef Dominic Blake **Owner** Sam & Georgie Pearman **Seats** 40, Pr/dining room 12 **Times** 12-3/6-9.30, Closed D Sun **Prices** Starter £2-£9, Main £8-£45, Dessert £4-£6 **Wines** 31 bottles over £30, 10 bottles under £30, 10 by glass **Parking** 15 **Notes** Sunday L £16-£18, Vegetarian available, Children welcome

Wild Thyme Restaurant with Rooms

◎◎ Modern British

tel: 01608 645060 **10 New St OX7 5LJ**
email: enquiries@wildthymerestaurant.co.uk **web:** www.wildthymerestaurant.co.uk
dir: *A44 Evesham, through Market Place. On left opposite Sainsbury's car park*

Contemporary style and a regional flavour

Grade II listed and 400 years old, Wild Thyme is located in a building that doesn't want for character. The interior of this smart little restaurant with rooms (just 35 covers and three bedrooms) has original features on show, but the place feels bright and contemporary just the same. That's down to the easy-going look of exposed stone walls and white-painted woodwork, with the wooden tables left unclothed. There's modern art, too, matching the modernity of the kitchen's output. Chef-patron Nick Pullen seeks out top-notch seasonal regional produce and turns out smart, contemporary British food that deals in intelligent flavour combinations, revealing a respect for classical culinary traditions. A double-baked goats' cheese soufflé arrives in the company of gold beetroots, hazelnuts and red onion marmalade, and Cornish mackerel with parsnip purée, shiitake mushrooms and crispy pancetta. Among main courses, local rabbit stars three ways in one dish as puff pastry pie, steamed loin and wonton (served with wild mushrooms, Puy lentils and winter roots). For dessert, there's the likes of crispy apple tart with rosemary ice cream, or a riff on rhubarb with crumble, quince brulée and ice cream.

Chef Nicholas Pullen **Owner** Nicholas & Sally Pullen **Seats** 35, Pr/dining room 14 **Times** 12-2/7-9, Closed Sun-Mon **Prices** Fixed L 2 course £18, Starter £6-£10, Main £14-£25, Dessert £6.50-£11.50, Service optional **Wines** 21 bottles over £30, 19 bottles under £30, 10 by glass **Parking** Public car park 3 min walk **Notes** Vegetarian available, Children welcome

The Unicorn Inn

◎ Modern British **NEW**

tel: 01869 338838 **Market Place OX15 0SE**
email: info@unicorndeddington.co.uk **web:** www.unicorndeddington.co.uk
dir: *Phone for directions*

Robust flavours in traditional village pub setting

In the heart of the village, this refurbished 17th-century former coaching inn has been given a new lease of life under dynamic new owners. A cosy bar warmed by a real fire reels in discerning drinkers with the promise of local real ales and a carefully selected wine list, while diners flock to the relaxed restaurant with its exposed stone walls and open kitchen. Chef-patron Johnny Parke's modern British cooking is prepared with good technique and plenty of flair. A well-presented starter of chicken and duck liver parfait, pistachio, poached rhubarb and toast could be followed by roast fillet of stone bass, buttered potato, Swiss chard, artichoke and Ibérico ham. Round things off with the home-made raspberry Bakewell tart and salted caramel ice cream. When the sun shines, tables on the attractive rear terrace are highly prized.

Chef Johnny Parke **Owner** Johnny Parke, Chris Brewster **Seats** 60, Pr/dining room 16 **Times** 12-2.30/6.30-9.30, Closed 1 Jan, D 25 Dec **Prices** Fixed L 2 course £12, Starter £5-£9, Main £13-£21, Dessert £5.50-£8, Service optional **Wines** 8 bottles over £30, 23 bottles under £30, 11 by glass **Parking** Market car park **Notes** Fixed L Mon-Fri only, Sunday L £14-£16, Vegetarian available, Children welcome

The Eagle

◎◎ Modern European

tel: 01367 241879 **Little Coxwell SN7 7LW**
email: eaglelittlecoxwell@gmail.com **web:** www.eagletavern.co.uk
dir: *A420, follow signs for 1m to Little Coxwell village*

Modern pub food with continental influences

Built at the beginning of the last century to serve the farming community around Little Coxwell, a comely village in the Vale of the White Horse, The Eagle is a rather grand architectural affair for a village local. Inside certainly looks the part, with its plain wood tables and open fires. An air of warmth and tranquillity prevails, staff establishing an easy rapport with diners, and the menu of reworked pub food is strong on continental influences. First off might be a dish of potted rabbit adorned with pickled carrot, mustard seeds and prune chutney, a starter guaranteed to get the taste buds sitting up and taking notice, or there could be a savoury take on crème brûlée made from Oxford Blue cheese with rhubarb sorbet. At main, star-of-the-show cod is pan-roasted and served in creamy shellfish bisque with buttery leeks and saffron potatoes, while local lamb comes with asparagus and minted sheep's yogurt. Grape strudel with raspberry sorbet and crème anglaise is a successful new spin on an old favourite.

Chef Marcel Nerpas **Owner** Marcel Nerpas **Seats** 28 **Times** 12-2.30/5.30-11, Closed Mon, D Sun **Prices** Prices not confirmed, Service optional **Wines** 4 bottles over £30, 21 bottles under £30, 8 by glass **Parking** On street **Notes** Sunday L, Vegetarian available, Children welcome

Sudbury House

◎◎◎ *– see page 444*

FARINGDON *continued*

The Trout at Tadpole Bridge

◉ Modern, Traditional British

tel: 01367 870382 **Buckland Marsh SN7 8RF**
email: info@troutinn.co.uk **web:** www.troutinn.co.uk
dir: *A415 from Abingdon signed Marcham, through Frilford to Kingston Bagpuize. Left onto A420. 5m, right signed Tadpole Bridge. Or M4 (E'bound) junct 15, A419 towards Cirencester. 4m, onto A420 towards Oxford. 10m, left signed Tadpole Bridge*

Classy inventive cooking in a traditional Thames-side inn

The 17th-century stone inn in an idyllic spot on the upper reaches of the Thames, with berthing for up to six boats and a waterside garden, has the expected rural charm of open fires and beams. It hasn't forgotten it's a pub, with real ales dispensed at the bar, but the main attraction is a menu sparkling with bright ideas. Sourcing is a strength (Hereford beef, Kelmscott pork, for instance) and dishes are created to bring out forthright and often bold flavours. Fishcakes with buttered spinach and tartare sauce is a signature starter, and rabbit and quail pâté with fig chutney is typical. Apricot and rosemary jus gives a lift to pink-roast rack of lamb with dauphinoise and red cabbage purée, an alternative to confit rabbit Wellington with roasted salsify, garlicky spinach and port sauce. Invention doesn't tail off among desserts: there may be limoncello jelly, or mango and vodka cheesecake.

Chef Kevin Jones **Owner** Helen & Gareth Pugh **Seats** 50, Pr/dining room 40
Times 12-2/7-9, Closed 25-26 Dec **Prices** Fixed L 2 course £12.50, Fixed D 3 course £16, Starter £5-£11, Main £11.95-£23.95, Dessert £6.50-£8, Service optional
Wines 68 bottles over £30, 50 bottles under £30, 11 by glass **Parking** 40
Notes Sunday L £14.95-£16.95, Vegetarian available, Children welcome

---

FYFIELD
Map 5 SU49

The White Hart

◉◉ Modern British

tel: 01865 390585 **Main Rd OX13 5LW**
email: info@whitehart-fyfield.com
dir: *A420 Oxford-Swindon, 7m S of Oxford A34*

Traditionally-based British food with a minstrels' gallery

Built as a chantry house at the tail-end of the Plantagenet era, The White Hart was sold to St John's College following the enforced closure of such establishments under the Tudors. It still wears its age on its sleeve, however, with a minstrels' gallery looking down on the three-storeyed hall with its inglenooks and flagstones. You can eat just about anywhere, including the gallery, choosing from a menu of traditionally-based British food with some contemporary flourishes along the way. Pink-cooked pigeon turns up with caramelised onions and toasted pine kernels on puff pastry for an impressive beginner, while mains run to well-timed fish such as salmon, served with homely accompaniments like fish fingers or a copper pan of fish pie, and meats such as pheasant with boxty potato cake and winter veg. Steaks are top-drawer: 28-day aged rib-eyes in béarnaise with proper chips. Sharing boards of fish, meze or antipasti are another popular option. Dessert could be a study in cherry, with purée, tuile, sorbet and Kirsch-soaked fruit to accompany pistachio cake, or pineapple Tatin with coconut sorbet in lemongrass syrup.

Chef Mark Chandler **Owner** Kay & Mark Chandler **Seats** 65, Pr/dining room 32
Times 12-2.30/7-9.30, Closed Mon (ex BHs), D Sun **Prices** Fixed L 2 course fr £17, Starter £6.50-£9, Main £15-£24, Dessert £6.50-£7.50, Service optional **Wines** 28 bottles over £30, 26 bottles under £30, 11 by glass **Parking** 60 **Notes** Chef's tasting menu on request, Sunday L £23-£26, Vegetarian available, Children welcome

---

Sudbury House ◉◉◉

FARINGDON
Map 5 SU29

Modern British **NEW** v

tel: 01367 241272 **56 London St SN7 7AA**
email: restaurant56@sudburyhouse.co.uk **web:** www.sudburyhouse.co.uk
dir: *M40 junct 9, A34 Swindon, follow A420 towards Swindon/Oxford*

Imaginative cooking with a sense of fun

Sudbury House sits in nine acres of pleasant grounds on the fringes of the Cotswolds – handy for doing business in Oxford and Swindon, as well as for visits to Cheltenham and Blenheim Palace. Its Restaurant 56 occupies the original Georgian wing of the house, where an elegant sweeping staircase, crystal chandelier and chequerboard floor in its own entrance hall make a classy first impression. The place was once home to Sir William Glock, an erstwhile BBC Controller of Music, but these days the harmonious symphonies are of the culinary variety, composed and orchestrated by Andrew Scott, who has spent time in some pedigree kitchens (Simon Rogan's L'Enclume and heading up the team at Mallory Court, to name but two). Antiques, sculptures, original artworks on deep red walls and opulent fabrics set an upmarket tone in the dining room, but pleasant and helpful staff dispel any hint of stuffiness. On the food front, all is on trend with a tasting menu and à la carte offered at dinner, plus a keenly-priced three-course lunch. Everything is underpinned by top-class seasonal produce and the cooking displays real flair with Scott's precise technique combining entertainingly with a sense of fun. A multi-layered opener serves up mackerel – charred and hot-smoked parfait – with earthy heritage beets, yuzu adding a citrus note and a kick of iced wasabi, while main-course mallard comes in another well-executed duo (roast breast and confit leg) with plenty of supporting flavours and textures – cranberry sauce, walnuts, shallot and spiced red cabbage – brought into play. A clever dessert of warm pistachio cake with zippy orange curd, marmalade ice cream and mascarpone also earns top marks.

Chef Andrew Scott **Owner** Roger Hancox **Seats** 28, Pr/dining room 14
Times 12-2.30/6.30-9.30, Closed Sun-Mon **Prices** Fixed L 2 course £20-£25, Tasting menu £60-£80, Starter £12-£18, Main £26-£30, Dessert £9-£12, Service optional **Wines** 23 bottles over £30, 12 bottles under £30, 11 by glass **Parking** 70 **Notes** Afternoon tea, Children 12 yrs+

GORING
Map 5 SU68

The Leatherne Bottel
◉◉ British, French

tel: 01491 872667 **Bridle Way RG8 OHS**
email: leathernebottel@aol.com
dir: *M4 junct 12 or M40 junct 6, signed from B4009 towards Wallingford*

Anglo-French cooking by the Thames

The Bottel floats serenely on the Thames with the Chilterns as a backdrop. If you're arriving by your own launch, you can step straight on to the sun-dappled or windswept terrace, depending on the season. It's a lovely spot, and the place is a dining destination of long repute, weathering the vicissitudes of culinary fashion without getting stuck in any ruts. The accent is Anglo-French, perfectly seen in a meal that follows a petit Crottin goats' cheese, roast fig and chestnut purée with beef Wellington, a beautifully moist recollection of the victory at Waterloo, complete with a porty reduction but rather uneven pastry. Lighter fish dishes might include seared turbot with shallot gratin in smoked haddock chowder, and meals come to a satisfying conclusion with something like a pear poached in Pinot Noir served with clotted cream and toasted almonds. The radio blaring out from the kitchen can make one wish all the more wistfully that someone would step up to the plate and give us something on the grand piano that stands in the centre of the dining room.

Times 12-2/7-9, Closed D Sun

The Miller of Mansfield
◉◉ British **NEW** v

tel: 01491 872829 & 07702 853413 **High St RG8 9AW**
email: reservations@millerofmansfield.com **web:** www.millerofmansfield.com
dir: *M40 junct 7, S on A329 towards Benson, A4074 towards Reading, B4009 towards Goring. Or M4 junct 12, S on A4 towards Newbury, 3rd rdbt onto A340 to Pangbourne. A329 to Streatley, right at lights onto B4009 into Goring*

Stylish country inn with contemporary menus

An 18th-century coaching inn made over to chime with our times, The Miller has boutique bedrooms, a stylish bar with real ales and real fires, and a restaurant offering impressive sharp modern British output. The views over rolling countryside add to the charm of the place, and the Thames is only a short stroll away. The restaurant's flickering candles on smart oak tables set the mood for menus that deliver classically-minded dishes with contemporary undertones. A starter of warm salmon bradan rost comes with hot and creamy horseradish mayonnaise and a sweet and sticky syrup of mirin and soy, while another might be a refined button mushroom soup with black truffle and pickled mushrooms. Gigha halibut arrives slow cooked in a main course with charred leeks, Jerusalem artichoke purée and a red wine sauce enriched with smoked bacon. Finish with tonka bean pannacotta with pistachio cake and blackberries (fresh, gel and meringue). An excellent value set lunch option catches the eye, and there are classy bar snacks and sandwiches too.

Chef Nick Galer **Owner** Nick & Mary Galer **Seats** 60, Pr/dining room 12
Times 12-2.30/6.30-9.30 **Prices** Fixed L 2 course £12.50, Tasting menu £45-£65, Starter £5.75-£7.50, Main £10.50-£22.50, Dessert £5.50-£6.50, Service optional **Wines** 26 bottles over £30, 13 bottles under £30, 17 by glass **Parking** 2 **Notes** Sunday L fr £15, Children welcome

GREAT MILTON
Map 5 SP60

Belmond Le Manoir aux Quat' Saisons
◉◉◉◉◉ *– see page 446*

HAILEY
Map 11 SP31

The Lamb Inn
◉◉ Traditional British **NEW** v

tel: 01993 708792 **Steep Hill, Crawley OX29 9TW**
email: lambcrawley@yahoo.co.uk **web:** www.lambcrawley.co.uk
dir: *Phone for directions*

Smartly presented contemporary food in a convivial atmosphere

A whitewashed Georgian inn at the heart of a peaceful Cotswold village not far from Witney, The Lamb has been given a strong makeover for the present day by Matt and Rachel Weedon. They have retained the comforting country-pub ambience in the bar, with roughcast stone walls, low oak beams and a crackling winter fire, but nudged the supplementary dining area into modernity with a salmon colour scheme. There is an air of warm conviviality throughout, and the cooking is smartly presented with much flair and thought, homemade breads arriving swaddled in a little cloth bag. Hot-smoked salmon cut chunkily and served warm with beetroot cubes and apple purée might almost be an old-fashioned pub dish, but then main course brings loin and faggot of venison with braised red cabbage and parsnip-vanilla purée in a sweetly viscous chocolate gravy, or perhaps lemon sole roasted on the bone with brown shrimps, sprouting broccoli and cep sauce. Dessert comes in a mason jar containing blood orange posset, citrus meringue and orange sorbet in tart blood orange soup.

Chef Matt Weedon **Owner** Matt & Rachel Weedon **Seats** 40, Pr/dining room 20
Times 11-3/6-11, Closed 2 wks Jan, Mon, D Sun (winter only) **Prices** Starter £6.50-£9, Main £18-£23, Dessert £6.50-£9, Service optional **Wines** 4 bottles over £30, 17 bottles under £30, 10 by glass **Parking** 16 **Notes** Sunday L £27, Children welcome

HENLEY-ON-THAMES
Map 5 SU78

The Baskerville
◉ Modern British **NEW** v

tel: 0118 940 3332 **Station Rd, Lower Shiplake RG9 3NY**
email: enquiries@thebaskerville.com **web:** www.thebaskerville.com
dir: *2m S of Henley in Lower Shiplake. Exit A4155 into Station Rd, inn signed*

Red-brick pub with the focus on food

This Baskerville is a handsome beast, a contemporary kind of inn that offers beer and bar snacks, comfortable rooms, and a restaurant that produces serious modern British grub. There's a traditional finish to the interior with lots of natural wood, warm colours and country-style furniture. The kitchen's ambitious output extends to European-influenced options such as a starter of crispy fried salt and pepper squid or the more modern British sounding pan-seared wood pigeon with sloe gin jelly and pickled wild mushrooms. There are lots of good ideas and sound combinations among main courses, too: an oriental-inspired slow-cooked pork belly dish, say, or Gressingham duck breast with a marmalade glaze (served with truffled mash and blackberry jus). Pub classics like steak, ale and mushroom pie and Sunday roasts play to the gallery, with desserts offering comfort in the form of plum and finger crumble. A table in the garden is a warm weather option.

Chef Marc Price **Owner** Allan & Kathleen Hannah **Seats** 58, Pr/dining room 12
Times 12-9.30, All-day dining, Closed 1 Jan, D Sun **Prices** Fixed L 2 course £16, Fixed D 3 course £20, Starter £6-£11, Main £14-£23.50, Dessert £6-£8, Service optional **Wines** 27 bottles over £30, 32 bottles under £30, 17 by glass **Parking** 15, Also at Shiplake Station **Notes** Sunday L, Children welcome

Belmond Le Manoir aux Quat' Saisons @@@@@

GREAT MILTON	Map 5 SP60

Modern French V 🍷 NOTABLE WINE LIST

tel: 01844 278881 **Church Rd OX44 7PD**
email: manoir.mqs@belmond.com
web: www.belmond.com/lemanoir
dir: *M40 junct 7 follow A329 towards Wallingford. After 1m turn right, signed Great Milton and Le Manoir aux Quat' Saisons*

Benchmark French cooking of rare excellence

It's a little over 30 years since Raymond Blanc took a chance on this little manor house in Great Milton. The amount of love, energy and hard work directed at the place over those years is immeasurable, but the result is clear for all to see, for Le Manoir aux Quat' Saisons is beautiful inside and out, and what it offers by way of hospitality is as good as you'll find anywhere in the UK. Whether you come for a once in a lifetime dinner to celebrate a special occasion, or are lucky enough to be a regular customer, the service you receive will live long in the memory. Now part owned by the Belmond group, Le Manoir remains a truly singular place. The manor looks immaculate with its old stone walls covered in creepers and the garden primped and manicured to pretty perfection. Leave time to explore the rest of the grounds, with its Japanese tea garden, striking statues and English water garden, and take a wander around the vegetable garden where much of what you eat is grown. The house itself more than passes muster – the comfort-factor is set at ten – and every room in the place looks elegant and refined, with the conservatory dining room at its best during daylight hours when the garden view can be best appreciated. The arrival of a series of amuse-bouche (curried vegetable bonbon, say) and the array of fabulous breads (eight in total) signals the start of a meal that is rooted in classical French ways. The bilingual menus include tasting versions and an à la carte that change with the seasons and reflect the superb supply lines that have been developed over the years by Raymond and Gary Jones, his long-serving right-hand man at the stoves. The ingredients shine throughout, such as a superb piece of salmon, prepared mi-cuit, and partnered with apples in various textures and lemon verbena, or the wild mushrooms and white Alba truffle that find their way into a risotto. There's nothing here to confound or confuse, but the precision and technical proficiency of the kitchen never fails to impress. Examples include a main-course roasted loin of Rhug Estate venison lavishly served up with a smattering of truffles and a silky celeriac purée, or a fish dish that combines Cornish sea bass with a light seafood broth and sea vegetables with a hit of citrusy yuzu. A dessert of Manjari chocolate and raspberry crumble delivers an astonishing balance of sweetness and sharpness, and looks positively stunning on the plate. The cheese trolley is hard to resist. The wine list has been trimmed in recent years to meet the changing demands of their customers, but it continues to offer a stellar array of top-drawer options at prices that might well make your eyes water.

Chef Raymond Blanc, Gary Jones **Owner** Mr R Blanc & Belmond **Seats** 100, Pr/dining room 50 **Times** 12-2.30/7-10, **Prices** Prices not confirmed, Service optional **Wines** 650 bottles over £30, 40 by glass **Parking** 60 **Notes** Fixed L 5 course Mon-Fri, 7 course, D 6/9 course, Sunday L, Children welcome

The Cherry Tree Inn

◉ Modern British

tel: 01491 680430 **Main St, Stoke Row RG9 5QA**
email: enquiries@thecherrytreeinn.co.uk **web:** www.thecherrytreeinn.co.uk
dir: *On A4155 from Henley-on-Thames exit B481 to Sonning Common. Follow Stoke Row signs, turn right for inn*

Popular old inn serving good, honest food

This old brick and flint inn is in an Area of Outstanding Natural Beauty at one of the highest points in the Chilterns. A makeover has given the interior a stripped-back look, with rugs on polished wooden floorboards and plain wooden tables, chairs and benches. This is the sort of pub that every village should have, not just for its ales and atmosphere but for the quality of its modern British cooking. Perfectly roast local pigeon comes with a salad of beetroot, pine nuts and rocket enhanced by raspberry dressing to make a particularly effective starter. Sauces and gravies never fail to impress among main courses: one of star anise jus for confit duck leg with fondant potato and red cabbage, a rich red wine reduction for tender organic roast chicken breast with root vegetable mash, roast parsnips and kale. The kitchen's no slouch when it comes to puddings either: try caramel pannacotta with berry compôte.

Chef Will Shaw **Owner** Douglas & Lolly Green **Seats** 60, Pr/dining room 12
Times 12-3/6.30-9.30 **Prices** Starter £4.95-£7.95, Main £10.50-£19.95, Dessert
£5.50-£6 **Wines** 12 bottles over £30, 12 bottles under £30, 8 by glass **Parking** 30
Notes Breakfast, Sunday L £4.95-£15, Vegetarian available, Children welcome

Hotel du Vin Henley-on-Thames

◉ European

tel: 01491 848400 **New St RG9 2BP**
email: info.henley@hotelduvin.com **web:** www.hotelduvin.com
dir: *M4 junct 8/9 signed High Wycombe, take 2nd exit and onto A404 in 2m. A4130 into Henley, over bridge, through lights, up Hart St, right onto Bell St, right onto New St, hotel on right*

French bistro specials in a Georgian brewery

Hotel du Vin always chooses impressive buildings, and the Henley branch is no exception: a Thames-side Georgian property that was the HQ of Brakspears brewery. The Bistro here is just that, with the eye-catching good looks of its Gallic counterparts, with lots of wood, comfortable seating, soft lighting and framed pictures on the walls. Well-drilled but casual staff add to the convivial atmosphere. Bistro classics plus a few less standard dishes are what to expect, as at the other branches, all cooked just as they should be. Perfectly steamed moules marinière or chicken liver parfait with raisin chutney and sourdough bread get things off to a promising start before steak frites, sole meunière with caper and brown shrimp beurre noisette or Toulouse sausage and mash. Treacle tart may not be particularly French but it makes a good conclusion, and there's always perennial crème brûlée.

Times 12-2.30/5.30-10

Orwells

◉◉◉ – *see below*

The Kingham Plough

◉◉◉ – *see page 448*

Orwells ◉◉◉

Modern British
tel: 0118 940 3673 **Shiplake Row, Binfield Heath RG9 4DP**
email: eat@orwellsatshiplake.co.uk
dir: *A4155 to Binfield Heath, take Plough Lane to Shiplake Row, restaurant on left*

Creativity and classics in a Georgian country pub

There may well be a local or two sipping pints at the bar, or out in the garden in the summer, but first and foremost Orwells is a rather splendid restaurant. The white-painted country pub has been in the hands of two dynamic young chefs since 2010 – Ryan Simpson and Liam Trotman – and they've tapped into local supply lines and contemporary culinary thinking to deliver a menu fizzing with creative ideas and exciting combinations. It all takes place in an understated, rustic setting, with the bones of the old country pub there for all to see. There is a tasting menu if you can persuade the whole table to join you on the journey, with a wine flight if you fancy going the whole hog, and at the other end of the spectrum, the fixed-price lunch is a bit of a bargain. Ryan and Liam have their own smallholding down the road, so a supply of seasonal veg, fruits and herbs help provide a focus for the kitchen, with everything else sourced with due diligence. A starter off the à la carte menu might

combine muntjac venison with langoustines in a fashionable pairing with pickled mushrooms, capers and scallions, while another makes a cannelloni out of beetroot and goats' curd. Everything looks pretty as a picture on the plate. There are luxury ingredients such as Wagyu beef, served in a main course with Périgord truffles and compelling combinations like monkfish and duck with brassicas and hazelnuts. Desserts can nearly steal the show – lemon tart with cream cheese sorbet, say, or cardamom pannacotta with flavours of ginger, blood orange and rum.

Chef Ryan Simpson, Liam Trotman **Owner** Ryan Simpson, Liam Trotman **Seats** 60,
Pr/dining room 20 **Times** 11.30-3/6.30-9.30, Closed 2 wks beg Jan, 1 wk Jun, 2
wks beg Sep, Mon-Tue, D Sun **Prices** Fixed L 2 course £15, Fixed D 3 course
£24.95, Tasting menu £65, Starter £8.50-£12.50, Main £18-£28.50, Dessert
£8.50, Service optional **Wines** 125 bottles over £30, 29 bottles under £30, 37 by
glass **Parking** 40 **Notes** Tasting menu with/without wines, Sunday L £29.95-
£34.95, Vegetarian available, Children welcome

KINGHAM *continued*

The Wild Rabbit

see opposite

KINGSTON BAGPUIZE
Map 5 SU49

Fallowfields Hotel and Restaurant

⊛⊛⊛ – *see opposite*

MILTON COMMON
Map 5 SP60

The Oxfordshire

⊛ Modern British

tel: 01844 278300 **Rycote Ln OX9 2PU**
email: info@theoxfordshire.com web: www.theoxfordshire.com
dir: *From S M40 junct 7 onto A370 towards Thame. Hotel on right in 2m*

Modern British cooking in golfing hotel

A round on the championship golf course is high on many guests' agenda at this new-build hotel in the Chilterns, while others with less energetic priorities will head straight for a spot of pampering in the classy spa. Whether you're here for sport or luxury, the Sakura restaurant has sweeping views of the course and countryside from its picture windows as a backdrop to a broad-ranging menu of modern dishes spiked with global influences. Kick off with monkfish nuggets with saffron aïoli, then roasted sea bass with lemon, fennel, basil and roasted red pepper butter, or rump of lamb with ratatouille, sweet potato fondant and minty salsa verde. Unreconstructed carnivores are sorted out with straight-up grilled steaks served with a choice of classic sauces, grilled tomatoes, watercress and triple-cooked chips. How about spotted dick with vanilla custard to finish?

Times 6-9.30, Closed Xmas, New Year, D Sun

MURCOTT
Map 11 SP51

The Nut Tree Inn

⊛⊛ Modern European V ⏽ NOTABLE WINE LIST

tel: 01865 331253 **Main St OX5 2RE**
dir: *M40 junct 9. A34 towards Oxford, take 2nd exit for Islip. At Red Lion pub turn left, then 3rd right signed Murcott*

Confident cooking in a pretty village inn

You can prop up the bar with a jar of real ale in this whitewashed and thatched 15th-century inn surveying the village pond deep in the Oxfordshire countryside, but the food is the big draw now that chef-proprietor Mike North's skilful modern European cooking has turned the inn into a local foodie destination. Refurbished in spring 2015, the place has retained its structure of stone walls and gnarled beams, a venerable backdrop for contemporary dishes that are unfussy, precise and assured, and designed to tease maximum flavour from exemplary ingredients. A salad of the Nut Tree's own garden roots in balsamic vinaigrette with vegetable crisps is an appealing simple opener to proceedings. Follow with wild mushroom fricassée with parmesan and rosemary croquette, roast saddle and faggot of lamb in sauce vierge, with an array of provençale veg, including puréed aubergine, or an Indian-spiced treatment of cod garnished with almonds and raisins. Bringing up the rear could be warm chocolate fondant with orange ice cream, or a plate of artisan cheeses.

Chef Michael & Mary North **Owner** Michael & Imogen North **Seats** 70, Pr/dining room 36 **Times** 12-2.30/7-9, Closed 2 wks from 27 Dec, Mon, D Sun **Prices** Fixed L 2 course £18, Fixed D 2 course £18, Tasting menu £55, Starter £7.50-£14, Main £17.50-£33, Dessert £7.50-£8.50, Service optional **Wines** 102 bottles over £30, 19 bottles under £30, 11 by glass **Parking** 30 **Notes** Sunday L £17.50-£26, Children welcome

The Kingham Plough ⊛⊛⊛

KINGHAM
Map 10 SP22

Modern British

tel: 01608 658327 **The Green OX7 6YD**
email: book@thekinghamplough.co.uk web: www.thekinghamplough.co.uk
dir: *B4450 from Chipping Norton to Churchill, 2nd right to Kingham. Left at T-junct, Plough on right*

Modernised country food in a family-friendly inn

Sitting on a tranquil country road, the old stone-built inn has amply articulated the vision of a family-friendly village pub with top-notch dining conceived by the owners when they set up here in 2007. The restaurant looks like the dining room of a farmhouse with its rough stone walls, beamed ceiling and rustic furniture, and staff are clued up about the output from the kitchen. Chef proprietor Emily Watkins had her eyes opened to what can be achieved with fine ingredients during her stint in Heston's team in The Fat Duck, but there's no molecular wizardry going on here, instead she offers a modernising take on country food. She brings together home-smoked Bath chaps with Wye Valley asparagus and a poached egg all pointed up with a light grain mustard vinaigrette, or perhaps making braised oxtail and tongue into a witty first-course sandwich on fried bread slathered with horseradish cream, and served with fiery pickled radishes. Main course showcases a stunning piece of spanking-fresh cod topped with a crust of mussel and sea lettuce, accompanied by seaweed and potato dumplings, mussels and foraged sea vegetables and a punchy mussel broth. Meatier appetites might head for loin and steamed pudding of hogget with carrots roasted in thyme, or a clever pigeon Wellington with rainbow chard and creamy mash. Dessert is a crisp pastry tart filled with rich chocolate ganache packed with salted peanuts, accompanied by home-made peanut butter ice cream and salted caramel, or else blood orange trifle with sherry, sweet cream and honeycomb. Superbly ripened local cheeses come with home-made quince jelly, oatcakes and hazelnut fruit bread.

Chef Emily Watkins, Ben Dulley **Owner** Emily Watkins & Miles Lampson **Seats** 54, Pr/dining room 20 **Times** 12-2/6.30-9, Closed 25 Dec, D Sun **Prices** Starter £8-£12, Main £15-£24, Dessert £6-£8 **Wines** 42 bottles over £30, 14 bottles under £30, 7 by glass **Parking** 30 **Notes** Sunday L £16-£20, Vegetarian available, Children welcome

The Wild Rabbit

Modern British NEW

tel: 01608 658389 **Church St OX7 6YA**
email: theteam@thewildrabbit.co.uk **web:** www.thewildrabbit.co.uk
dir: *Phone for directions*

Spiffy country pub from the Daylesford folk

The Rosette award for this establishment has been suspended due to a change of chef. Reassessment will take place in due course under the new chef. The good people at Daylesford organic farm have a lot of fingers in a lot of pies, what with the famed delivery service and deli, cookery school, Cotswold cottages to rent, a range of women's clothing and accessories, and even a French vineyard and château. Now you can add a classy country pub with rooms to the list. The 18th-century inn of mellow Cotswold stone has been revitalised by the team and turned into a delicious spot with a winning combination of country charm and contemporary style. There's a proper bar with exposed stone walls and a roaring log fire, offering up draught ales, trendy spirits and well-chosen wines, and a dining area that keeps to the spirit of rustic neutrality. The kitchen team have their own garden on hand to provide a good amount of the fresh stuff, and given the provenance of the owners, there's a good deal of attention paid to the quality of everything that turns up on the plate. But don't go thinking this is rustic, rough-and-ready stuff, for this kitchen sends out rather sophisticated platefuls. Take a starter of crab and scallop ravioli, for example, sitting in a punchy crab bisque and delivering a gentle hit of lemongrass, or a main course that combines a perfectly cooked tranche of cod with artichokes and a fab warm oyster. There's a Josper oven turning out steaks such as the 10oz flat iron, served with hand-cut chips and a rocket and parmesan salad, and a bar and terrace menu that serves some simpler stuff. Spiced apple crumble soufflé is a dessert that rises to the occasion with accompanying hot blackberry sauce and ice cold apple sorbet.

Chef Antony Parkin **Owner** Lady Bamford **Seats** 50, Pr/dining room 16 **Times** 12-2.30/7-9.30, Closed D Sun **Prices** Starter £9.50-£14.50, Main £16.50-£30, Dessert £8.50-£9, Service optional 10% **Wines** 24 bottles over £30, 12 bottles under £30, 14 by glass **Parking** 20 **Notes** Sunday L £22, Vegetarian available, Children welcome

Fallowfields Hotel and Restaurant ❀❀❀

Modern British V

tel: 01865 820416 **Faringdon Rd OX13 5BH**
email: stay@fallowfields.com **web:** www.fallowfields.com
dir: *A34 (Oxford Ring Rd) take A420 towards Swindon. At junct with A415 left for 100yds then turn at mini rdbt. Hotel on left after 1m*

Imaginative reworkings of traditional English dishes

A generation ago, nobody would have conceived of the neighbouring villages of Southmoor and Kingston Bagpuize, near Abingdon, as a fine-dining destination, but such is the brave new world of British gastronomy. This modern boutique country hotel is equipped with grounds including a sleek croquet lawn, a productive kitchen garden, orchards, and acres of grazing ground for livestock. Dining room windows look out on some of it through gathered curtains, and the pastel ambience makes a restful setting for the contemporary English food, which is delivered by knowledgeable staff from a kitchen headed up since September 2014 by the prodigiously talented Mark Potts. Imaginative reworkings of popular favourites are his speciality, resulting in starters such as soup and a sandwich of Coronation crab, a quail-based full English breakfast with mushroom ketchup, or a simple serving of new season's asparagus with a poached egg yolk and a slew of morels. Main courses offer stupendous prime materials – nose-to-tail Fallowfields pork, fillet and glazed cheek of Cornish cod with Muscat grapes, venison from the Marlborough estate, bedded on red cabbage shreds, with vanilla-scented parsnip purée and the sweet note of pear. The vegetarian tasting menu is an aromatic delight from wild mushroom and charred artichoke start to white chocolate and passionfruit cheesecake finish. Roast pork and crackling in cider jus is an irresistible Sunday lunch draw. Herb-garden fragrances add character to desserts, lemon sorrel accompanying lemon meringue cheesecake, lavender ice cream a prune and Armagnac soufflé, and meadowsweet ice cream and leaves of wood sorrel for rhubarb and custard millefeuille. Thoroughbred English cheeses come with home-made biscuits. The suggested wine pairings with each dish are worth following.

Chef Mark Potts **Owner** Anthony & Peta Lloyd **Seats** 42, Pr/dining room 14 **Times** 12-2.30/7-9.30, Closed Mon-Tue **Prices** Fixed L 2 course £30, Tasting menu £59, Starter £11-£20, Main £22-£30, Dessert £9-£11 **Wines** 70 bottles over £30, 20 bottles under £30, 14 by glass **Parking** 50 **Notes** Tasting menu 7 course must be taken by the whole table, Sunday L £30-£35, Children welcome

OXFORD
Map 5 SP50

Bear & Ragged Staff
◎ Modern British NEW

tel: 01865 862329 **Appleton Rd, Cumnor OX2 9QH**
email: enquiries@bearandraggedstaff.com
dir: *A420 to Cumnor, left at mini rdbt towards Appleton*

Trend-conscious cooking and contemporary design

A stone-built country inn in the village of Cumnor, not far from Oxford, the Bear offers an appealing mixture of traditional atmosphere, with comfy sofas facing the roaring fire, and contemporary design. The latter tendency comes in the form of masses of artwork on cool green walls in the dining room, offsetting the roughcast stone, and in the forward-thinking menus of trend-conscious British food. Grilled mackerel with mussels, potato salad, puréed spinach and spring onion dressing gets things off to a fine start, and might be followed by braised pig's cheek and belly with celeriac fondant in apple jus. A more traditional French note is sounded in fried lamb's kidneys with pancetta in sherry dressing, or in classic coq au vin. Then stay on the French track for dark chocolate and orange soufflé with Grand Marnier Chantilly, or book a passage back home with the likes of rhubarb and custard tart and elderflower crème fraîche.

Chef Scot Simpson **Owner** Mark Greenwood **Seats** 60 **Times** 12-9.30, All-day dining **Prices** Starter £5-£10, Main £12-£19, Dessert £6-£7.50 **Wines** 15 bottles over £30, 30 bottles under £30, 20 by glass **Parking** 30 **Notes** Breakfast menu, Sunday L £12-£14, Vegetarian available, Children welcome

Cotswold Lodge Hotel
◎ British, European NEW

tel: 01865 512121 **66a Banbury Rd OX2 6JP**
email: info@cotswoldlodgehotel.co.uk web: www.cotswoldlodgehotel.co.uk
dir: *A40 Oxford ring rd onto A4165 Banbury Rd signed city centre/Summertown. Hotel 2m on left*

Straight-talking modern food in a Victorian mansion

This stately Victorian villa is replete with period style, all high ceilings, sweeping staircases and expansive bay windows, but a light contemporary facelift has leavened the 19th-century chintz. Dining takes place in its Restaurant 66A (that's the address on the busy Banbury Road), an understated space with darkwood floors and tables. The kitchen deals in contemporary food with clear European accents, turning out a pressed game terrine of guinea fowl, duck, rabbit, pistachios and leeks, countered by a lively quince chutney, among starters. For mains, pan-fried lamb might come with samphire, turnips, Parmentier potatoes, apricots and rosemary jus, while fish dishes could see seared gurnard partnered with kohlrabi, pak choi, and tomato butter sauce. End with rhubarb and stem ginger pannacotta with pineapple carpaccio and orange sorbet, or bow out on a savoury note with a plate of Oxfordshire cheeses.

Chef Paul Haysom **Owner** Mr & Mrs Peros **Seats** 50, Pr/dining room 120 **Times** 12-2.30/6.30-10 **Prices** Fixed L 2 course £12.25, Starter £5-£10.50, Main £10.95-£18.75, Dessert £6.25-£9.50, Service optional **Wines** 4 bottles over £30, 19 bottles under £30, 6 by glass **Parking** 40 **Notes** Sunday L £12.50-£15.50, Vegetarian available, Children welcome

Gee's Restaurant
◎ Mediterranean

tel: 01865 553540 **61 Banbury Rd OX2 6PE**
email: info@gees-restaurant.co.uk
dir: *N off A4165, from city centre right onto Banbury Rd, located just past Bevington Rd*

Med-influenced brasserie cooking in a glasshouse

The long-running Gee's continues to delight townies and gownies alike on the northern edge of the city centre. Not the least attraction is the glasshouse setting, where silvery-green potted olive trees and lightweight café-style furniture in a room flooded with natural light are an uplifting prospect on a bright day. Weekend brunches and inexpensive lunch deals remain popular, as does the Med-influenced modern brasserie cooking. A newly installed wood-fired oven turns out pizzetti and sharing ribs of beef, while a charcoal grill does its stuff to steaks, burgers and chops of lamb, pork or venison, served with creamed spinach. Crab mayonnaise or artichoke fritters are good starters, while fish-lovers may be tempted by the prospect of a whole sea bass dressed in the simple homespun of lemon and parsley. Finish with blood orange tart, or a serving of prune ice cream glooped with treacly Pedro Ximenez sherry.

Times 12-10.30, All-day dining

Macdonald Randolph Hotel
◎◎◎ *– see opposite*

Malmaison Oxford
◎ Modern British, French

tel: 01865 268400 **3 Oxford Castle, New Rd OX1 1AY**
email: oxford@malmaison.com web: www.malmaison.com
dir: *M40 junct 9 (signed Oxford/A34). Follow A34 S to Botley Interchange, then A420 to city centre*

Crowd-pleasing food in the old prison canteen

Thanks to the Mal designers, Oxford's old slammer is now leading a reformed life as a classy hotel, with seductive bedrooms in the cells and a moodily-lit brasserie in the former basement canteen. Cast-iron staircases and arched doorways are an atmospheric reminder of its past, but the feel is now pure 21st-century chic, while the cooking is a little bit French, a little bit British, and a little bit global. The feel-good results are starters like ahi (yellowfin) tuna tartare with avocado, pickled ginger, soy and lime dressing and wasabi, alongside chicken liver parfait and classic prawn cocktail. Moules marinières will sort out the Francophiles, while steaks and burgers seared on the grill, or pan-fried sea bass with chorizo, black olives, new potatoes and mussel vinaigrette all have their place on the please-all roster. And for dessert, perhaps a Valrhona chocolate soufflé.

Chef Marcin Worzalla **Owner** KSL **Seats** 100, Pr/dining room 35 **Times** 12-2.30/6-10.30 **Prices** Fixed L 2 course £19.95, Fixed D 3 course £24.95, Starter £5.50-£10, Main £13-£37, Dessert £6-£9 **Wines** 45 bottles over £30, 10 bottles under £30, 18 by glass **Parking** 30, Must pre book £28.50, Worcester St, Westgate **Notes** Sunday L £19.95-£24.95, Vegetarian available, Children welcome

Mercure Oxford Eastgate Hotel

Modern British

tel: 01865 248695 **73 High St OX1 4BE**
email: h6668-fb1@accor.com **web:** www.thehightableoxford.co.uk
dir: *A40 follow signs to Headington & city centre, over Magdalen Bridge, stay in left lane, through lights, left into Merton St, entrance to car park on left*

Vibrant brasserie in an historic building

The 17th-century building doesn't want for period charm with its mullioned windows and sandstone façade, but on the inside it's rather swanky in the contemporary manner — well-designed fixtures and fittings and a decidedly cool restaurant called the High Table Brasserie & Bar. Old regulars such as C.S. Lewis and J.R.R. Tolkien wouldn't recognise the place. It's a large open-plan space with whitewashed walls, white-tiled flooring, bare wooden tables and grey banquette seating; a perfect setting for its menu of British and Mediterranean-influenced food. Start with a single salmon fishcake served with a micro herb salad, follow on with a home-made burger with chips fried in duck fat, or roasted Cornish bass with braised Puy lentils, celeriac and pear remoulade. To finish, expect something like sticky toffee pudding with clotted cream ice cream and caramel sauce. And note it's close to all the city-centre action.

Times 12-2.30/6-9.30

The Oxford Kitchen

Modern British **NEW** v

tel: 01865 511149 **215 Banbury Rd, Summertown OX2 7HQ**
email: hello@theoxfordkitchen.co.uk
dir: *Centre of Summertown. 5 min from A40 on Banbury Road*

Seriously good cooking and contemporary verve

Rubbing shoulders with high-end boutiques and stylish delis along busy Banbury Road, The Oxford Kitchen is a switched-on modern venue that is establishing itself as a foodie landmark. Inside, you'll find a pared-back decor of tiled and blond wood floors, industrial pendant lamps above darkwood booths, and exposed brick walls punctuated by colourful prints of Warhol's soup cans, and the welcome from smartly-uniformed staff is warm. The kitchen cooks to a broadly modern British template that has clear roots in classic French thinking, opening the show with an impressive Creedy Carver duck composition involving smoked breast, confit and parfait, with hazelnuts and poached quince to leaven the richness. A perfectly tuned main of Cornish stone bass with roasted cauliflower, golden raisins, almonds and curry displays commendable lightness of touch, or a more robust duo of beef fillet and braised ox cheek with potato purée, watercress, black truffle, and red wine essence might appeal. Harmonious flavour combinations continue at dessert, with an on-trend trifle with poached figs, almond sponge and Amaretto cream.

Chef John Footman **Owner** Samantha Davies, Steve Quinn **Seats** 80, Pr/dining room **Times** 12-2.30/6-9.30, Closed 1st 2 wks Jan, D Sun **Prices** Fixed L 2 course £15.50, Fixed D 3 course £18.50, Tasting menu £49-£70, Starter £7-£15, Main £15.50-£28, Dessert £6.50-£9 **Wines** 22 bottles over £30, 24 bottles under £30, 11 by glass **Parking** Car park opposite **Notes** Sunday L £16.50-£17.50, Children welcome

Macdonald Randolph Hotel

OXFORD Map 5 SP50

Traditional British
tel: 01865 256400 **Beaumont St OX1 2LN**
email: foodservice.randolph@macdonald-hotels.co.uk
web: www.macdonaldhotels.co.uk
dir: *M40 junct 8, A40 towards Oxford, follow city centre signs, leads to St Giles, hotel on right*

Adventurous cookery in grand city-centre hotel

A liveried commissionaire welcomes guests to this landmark city-centre hotel, a substantial building on a corner site. It's as well known to television viewers as it is to locals, thanks to Inspector Morse, with his watering hole named in his honour (the Morse Bar). Conference and wedding facilities are all part of the package, with the restaurant like a baronial hall, its walls adorned with the crests of Oxford colleges and double-aspect full-length windows looking over Beaumont Street and the Ashmolean Museum. Service is on the formal side, which befits a Victorian institution with much oak panelling and vaulted ceilings. The cooking, though, is firmly in the 21st century, built on traditional British values, with some thrillingly stimulating ideas. Rabbit terrine, for instance, is partnered by grilled saddle and served with Puy lentils, parsnips, dressed sprout leaves, cider jelly, black pudding and pork crackling to make an imaginative

and enjoyable starter, or there might be a more straightforward platter of smoked salmon with the traditional garnishes. Quality ingredients are carefully sourced, and a high degree of technical expertise is evident throughout. Witness main courses of fillet of monkfish and hand-picked crab, accompanied by compressed cucumber, gnocchi, charred broccoli and essence of crab, and the carnivore's delight of a tasting of Scottish beef (seared fillet, cheeks braised for 24 hours and a trencher of dry-aged beef) with green beans, wild mushrooms, onion rings, two sauces (béarnaise and one of red wine) and not just truffled creamed potatoes but triple-fried chips as well. Anyone with room after that could go for the multi-layered flavours of poached rhubarb with chilled ginger rice pudding, pink champagne and honeycomb, or the selection of native cheeses with tomato chutney.

Chef Simon Bradley **Owner** Macdonald Hotels **Seats** 90, Pr/dining room 30 **Times** 12.30-2.30/6.30-10, Closed L Mon-Fri **Prices** Tasting menu fr £60, Starter fr £12.50, Main fr £30, Dessert fr £12.50 **Wines** 120 bottles over £30, 20 bottles under £30, 15 by glass **Parking** 50, Chargeable (pre-booking essential) **Notes** Pre-theatre menu 2 course with wine £23.95, Sunday L £23.95-£29.95, Vegetarian available, Children welcome

OXFORD continued

Oxford Thames Four Pillars Hotel

◉ Modern International NEW

tel: 01865 334444 Henley Rd, Sandford-on-Thames OX4 4GX
email: thames@four-pillars.co.uk web: www.oxfordthameshotel.co.uk
dir: Exit A4074 signed Sandford-on-Thames. Right at T-junct/mini rdbt. Hotel 0.5m on left on Henley Road

Straightforward dining in a stylish spot with with river views

Set in 30 acres of parkland running down to the river, and with the full complement of spa, leisure and conference facilities, the smart Oxford Thames hotel makes a tranquil base just a short drive from the 'city of dreaming spires'. Its contemporary River Room restaurant overlooks the grounds and takes care of the gastronomic side of the equation with a please-all menu that has its share of classic dishes – from moules marinières to beer-battered haddock and chips – with some modern ideas, too. The kitchen goes the extra mile, making everything from ice cream to breads plus smoking fish and meats on the premises. Chicken liver parfait with pear chutney and toasted focaccia makes a sound starter, followed by a straight-up grilled rib-eye steak with chunky chips. To finish, there's home-made lemon tart with clotted cream and a lime and lemon reduction.

Chef Claudio Costea **Owner** Starwood Capital **Seats** 150, Pr/dining room 50
Times 7-9.30, Closed 25 & 31 Dec, L Mon-Sat **Prices** Starter £6.95-£9.95, Main £13.95-£22, Dessert £6.95-£9.95, Service optional **Wines** 14 bottles over £30, 35 bottles under £30, 19 by glass **Parking** 150 **Notes** Sunday L £15.95-£19.95, Vegetarian available, Children welcome

---

▮ STADHAMPTON   Map 5 SU69

The Crazy Bear

◉◉ Modern British

tel: 01865 890714 Bear Ln OX44 7UR
email: enquiries@crazybear-stadhampton.co.uk web: www.crazybeargroup.co.uk
dir: M40 junct 7, A329. In 4m left after petrol station, left into Bear Lane

Rebooted Tudor inn with brasserie classics and more offbeat stuff

We often say that the modern conversion of an English Tudor inn has been carried out so as carefully to preserve its original character, but the epithet 'crazy' (unknown in the sense of 'mad' in Tudor English) is the clue that a different approach, to put it mildly, has been adopted here. Pink cushioned walls, a leopard-print carpet, big steel mirrors and a kind of herringbone overhead wine store set the scene for what's on offer in the English arm of the operation (see entry below for the Asian room). It's an exhaustively long list of contemporary brasserie food, with lots of push-button classics, such as tuna tartare and wasabi mayo, scallops and black pudding with pea purée, and chicken and mushroom pie with triple-cooked chips, mingling in among the more offbeat likes of squid pil-pil with pancetta, coriander and chilli, or crispy pork belly and smoked eel with baby beets and horseradish cream. You could even kickstart an evening with honey-glazed Old Spot whizzers, if you knew what they were, and ensure contentment at the end with a white chocolate cone of hazelnut semi-fredo.

Chef Martin Picken **Owner** Jason Hunt **Seats** 40, Pr/dining room 140 **Times** 12-10, All-day dining **Prices** Fixed L 2 course £19.50, Starter £7.50-£12.50, Main £11.95-£24.75, Dessert £8.50-£11.50 **Wines** 235 bottles over £30, 21 bottles under £30, 20 by glass **Parking** 100 **Notes** Sunday L, Vegetarian available, Children welcome

Thai Thai at The Crazy Bear

◉◉ Modern Thai

tel: 01865 890714 The Crazy Bear, Bear Ln OX44 7UR
email: enquiries@crazybear-stadhampton.co.uk
dir: M40 junct 7, A329. In 4m left after petrol station, left into Bear Lane

Southeast Asian cooking in a Tudor village inn

The original incarnation of the expanding Crazy Bear group occupies a Tudor inn in a rural Oxfordshire village. As well as a modern British dining room, it also boasts a head-turning Thai restaurant with crimson velvet beams, scatter-cushions and tables that give the thrown-together impression of brass platters balanced on boxes. If it all looks at first like a concept that has run away with itself, the extensive menus are replete with authentically fresh, hot, bracing southeast Asian dishes. There are forays beyond the Thai borders, for Peking duck rolls dipped in hoi sin, salt-and-pepper Japanese tofu with spring onions and habanero chillies, and stunning vegetarian compositions such as Penang aubergine with lychees, cherry tomatoes and grapes. The core of the repertoire, though, is accurately seasoned, palate-priming Thai classics, from pork satay to vermicelli glass noodles with black mushrooms, duck breast red curry with pineapple to steamed red snapper in a firestorm of chillies, galangal, lemongrass, lime leaves, garlic, coriander and lemon juice. Finish with bitter chocolate soup.

Chef Chalao Mansell **Owner** Jason Hunt **Seats** 30, Pr/dining room 140
Times 12-3/6-12, Closed L Sun **Prices** Starter £7.50-£14.50, Main £11.95-£19.50, Dessert £7.50-£11.50 **Wines** 235 bottles over £30, 21 bottles under £30, 20 by glass **Parking** 100 **Notes** Vegetarian available, Children welcome

---

▮ SWINBROOK   Map 10 SP21

The Swan Inn

◉◉ Modern British

tel: 01993 823339 OX18 4DY
email: info@theswanswinbrook.co.uk web: www.theswanswinbrook.co.uk
dir: A40 towards Cheltenham, turn left to Swinbrook

Historic village inn with locally-sourced ingredients

The wisteria-clad 16th-century Swan is the quintessential village pub, with an apple orchard to the rear and the Windrush River running by. It's owned by the Dowager Duchess of Devonshire, the last of the Mitford sisters, and there is interesting family memorabilia around the place as well as oak beams and flagstone floors, overlaid with a country-chic boutique style. The cooking stays abreast of the times thanks to a kitchen that sources seasonal ingredients with care (traceability is a big deal here), and knows how to turn it into some skilfully rendered dishes – pork and game terrine with celeriac remoulade and toast, for example, followed by a whole local partridge with glazed parsnips, braised red cabbage and thyme and chestnut gravy, or a tried-and-tested pub favourite such as braised faggots with swede mash, red onion and ale and sage gravy.

Chef Matthew Laughton **Owner** Archie & Nicola Orr-Ewing **Seats** 70
Times 12-2/7-9, Closed 25-26 Dec **Prices** Starter £5-£9.50, Main £13.50-£24, Dessert £6-£7.50 **Wines** 17 bottles over £30, 18 bottles under £30, 8 by glass **Parking** 12, On road **Notes** Sunday L fr £16.50, Vegetarian available, Children welcome

TOOT BALDON
Map 5 SP50

The Mole Inn
◉ Modern European

tel: 01865 340001 **OX44 9NG**
email: info@themoleinn.com
dir: *5m S of Oxford, restaurant 15 mins from M40 junct 7*

Country pub with globally-inspired cooking

In a quiet village on the outskirts of Oxford, The Mole Inn is everything a country inn should be. A mix of stone walls, original beams and terracotta tiled floors, this charming pub is adorned with framed mirrors and is run by a casual but professional team. Chef-patron Gary Witchalls and his team focus on simple but enjoyable Mediterranean-influenced dishes mixed with more familiar pub favourites. A starter of devilled lamb's kidneys with chargrilled ciabatta might be followed by rump of lamb, pea and mint mash, grain mustard cabbage and roast garlic. More globally-influenced dishes could include grilled natural smoked haddock, curry creamed leeks, curly kale and coriander mash, and Cafe de Paris butter. To finish, what could be better than chocolate and orange cheesecake, walnut ice cream and raspberry sip? A small conservatory to one side makes a pleasant summer retreat.

Chef Gary Witchalls **Owner** Gary Witchalls **Seats** 70 **Times** 12-2.30/7-9.30, Closed 25 Dec **Prices** Fixed L 2 course £19.50, Fixed D 3 course £25, Starter £6.95-£7.95, Main £14.50-£18.50, Dessert £6.95, Service optional **Wines** 7 bottles over £30, 24 bottles under £30, 8 by glass **Parking** 40 **Notes** Sunday L £14.95-£15.95, Vegetarian available, Children welcome

WANTAGE
Map 5 SU38

The Star Inn
◉◉ Modern British

tel: 01235 751873 **Watery Ln, Sparsholt OX12 9PL**
email: info@thestarsparsholt.co.uk **web:** www.thestarsparsholt.co.uk
dir: *Phone for directions*

Reinvented inn with accomplished food

This solid 300-year-old inn in the quintessentially English village of Sparsholt has had a stylish makeover since being taken over by a local resident. Inside, all is decluttered and open plan with chunky wooden furniture and plain white walls beneath venerable blackened beams, and the food has a suitably modern accent. The kitchen sets great store by local produce and the cooking gets straight to the point: an impressive starter balances the richness of foie gras and duck liver parfait with pear chutney and granola, and it comes with a buttery home-made brioche bun. Mains partner pan-fried halibut with sweet millet, purple sprouting broccoli, samphire, and a buttermilk cream sauce laden with squid, mussels and cockles. Elsewhere, loin of new season's lamb is served with its sweetbreads, peas, broad beans, scorched baby gem lettuce and salsa verde. Dessert takes mango as a theme to play with, serving it in an iced parfait with nougat, and as a purée, powder and frozen carpaccio with rose sorbet.

Times 12-2/6.30-9, Closed 2nd wk Jan for 2 wks, Mon, D Sun

WATLINGTON
Map 5 SU69

The Fat Fox Inn
◉ British, French

tel: 01491 613040 **13 Shirburn St OX49 5BU**
email: info@thefatfoxinn.co.uk **web:** www.thefatfoxinn.co.uk
dir: *M40 junct 6 onto B4009 S for 2.5m. On right in village*

Rustic, unfussy country-pub food

The Fat Fox lurks in a small market town on the edge of the Chilterns, and is a proper old country inn with an inglenook fireplace and wood-burning stove. A pleasingly jumbly look in the restaurant offers a mix of tables and seating against a lobster-shell colour scheme, and on the menu is hearty portions of generally rustic, unfussy food presented with just the right amount of modern tweaking – so expect there to be venison in the Scotch egg – Pub favourites such as mussels in Thai green curry, or chicken liver parfait with sharp chutney, pique the appetite for robustly constituted main dishes like a mash-topped trad fish pie made with haddock, salmon and king prawns, served with seasonal greens, venison stew with mashed swede, or a real steak-and-kidney suet pudding, with fig frangipane to finish.

Chef Mark Gambles **Owner** John Riddell **Seats** 26, Pr/dining room **Times** 12-3/6.30-10, Closed L 25 Dec, 1 Jan **Prices** Fixed L 2 course £12-£22, Fixed D 3 course £19-£31, Starter £4-£8, Main £8-£18, Dessert £5 **Wines** 2 bottles over £30, 21 bottles under £30, 12 by glass **Parking** 20 **Notes** Breakfast £10.50, Sunday L £13-£15, Vegetarian available, Children welcome

WESTON-ON-THE-GREEN
Map 11 SP51

The Manor Restaurant
◉◉ Modern European

tel: 01869 350621 **Northampton Rd OX25 3QL**
email: house@themanorweston.co.uk **web:** www.westonmanor.co.uk
dir: *M40 junct 9, exit A34 to Oxford then 1st exit on left signed Weston-on-the-Green/ Middleton Stony B4030. Right at mini rdbt, hotel 400yds on left*

Grand period room and modern cooking

Dating back some 900 years, The Manor certainly doesn't lack period character. A grand pile in glorious gardens, these days the house operates as a swish hotel with elegant bedrooms and a restaurant in the 11th-century Baron's Hall. As far as dining rooms go, this one is rather special, with a 30 foot high ceiling, acres of panels and a giant chandelier. The room has been dressed for the business of fine dining with crisp white linen and sparkling glassware, while the kitchen turns out some bright, modern food via tasting or à la carte menus. A fashionable surf 'n' turf combo turns up amongst the starters – Native lobster cooked a la plancha, with chicken wing, leek purée and a truffle-flavoured sauce – while main course brings forth spiced Herdwick mutton with pickled grapes and ratte potatoes. Flavours hit the mark in a dessert of Yorkshire rhubarb sorbet with fromage blanc and almonds.

Times 12-2.30/7-9

WITNEY
Map 5 SP31

Old Swan & Minster Mill
◉ Traditional British

tel: 01993 774441 **Old Minster OX29 0RN**
email: reception@oldswanandminstermill.com **web:** www.oldswanandminstermill.com
dir: Exit A40 signed Minster Lovell, through village right T-junct, 2nd left

Charming country pub by the River Windrush

The quintessentially Cotswolds village of Minster Lovell makes the perfect history-steeped setting for the Old Swan, a smart country inn with rooms next door in the more contemporary surrounds of Minster Mill. Inside, all is beams, flagstones and lots of cosy spaces to tuck yourself away in. There are real ales to keep the drinkers happy, while unpretentious food draws in folk from further afield. There's a local flavour to the menu (including produce grown in the kitchen garden) which sees daily specials sitting alongside pub classics. A fishcake of salmon, wholegrain mustard and spring onion makes a diverting opener, teamed with citrus crème fraîche, while cannon of new season lamb comes with almond stuffing, button mushrooms, and wild garlic and rosemary jus. For pudding, blackcurrant sorbet makes a well-judged counterpoint to an intense dark chocolate torte. On a fine day, the riverside garden is a treat.

Chef David Mwiti **Owner** The DeSavary family **Seats** 110, Pr/dining room 55 **Times** 12.30-3/6.30-9 **Prices** Prices not confirmed, Service optional **Wines** 33 bottles over £30, 19 bottles under £30 **Parking** 70 **Notes** Sunday L, Vegetarian available, Children welcome

The Restaurant at Witney Lakes Resort
◉ Modern European

tel: 01993 893012 & 893000 **Downs Rd OX29 0SY**
email: restaurant@witney-lakes.co.uk
dir: 2m W of Witney town centre, off B4047 Witney to Burford road

Popular brasserie cooking in a resort hotel

The sprawling modern resort in west Oxfordshire caters for iron-pumpers, niblick-swingers and the nuptial trade, as well as offering contemporary brasserie cooking in a destination restaurant that has acquired a dedicated local following. Regular champagne evenings and gourmet Thursdays are all part of the drill, and there are tables on a lakeside terrace in the sunnier months, but the core attraction is a menu of consistently dependable modern classic dishes. Opening with game terrine and pickled pear with sourdough toast, you might go on to gilt head bream in sauce vierge, or ox cheek and kidney suet pudding. In among these are one or two more speculative offerings, such as baby squid with chickpeas, chorizo and aïoli, while two of you might sign up for a rendition of sinew-stiffening cassoulet. Fifteen minutes' wait at dessert stage is rewarded with a chocolate fondant, served with salted caramel ice cream, or opt instead for a selection of local cheeses.

Chef Sean Parker, Owen Little **Owner** Sean Parker **Seats** 75 **Times** 12-3/6.30-9, Closed 25 & 31 Dec, 1 Jan, L Sat, D Sun-Mon **Prices** Fixed L 2 course £15-£18, Starter £5-£6, Main £12-£18, Dessert £5-£8, Service optional 10% **Wines** 9 bottles over £30, 38 bottles under £30, 11 by glass **Parking** 400 **Notes** Afternoon tea, Themed evenings, Live music, Sunday L £17-£21, Vegetarian available, Children welcome

WOODCOTE
Map 5 SU68

Woody Nook at Woodcote
◉ Modern British **V**

tel: 01491 680775 **Goring Rd RG8 0SD**
email: info@woodynookatwoodcote.co.uk
dir: Opposite village green

International flavours and top-notch Australian wines

Opposite the village green and cricket pitch, creeper-hung Woody Nook couldn't look more English, with its leaded windows, beams in low ceilings and spindle-back chairs at plain wooden tables. In fact, it's named after and showcases wines from the owners' winery in Margaret River, Western Australia. The menu has an international slant, with an ingenious kitchen turning out starters such as arancini stuffed with sun-dried tomatoes and mozzarella in puttanesca sauce and crab flavoured with ginger, citrus, coriander and chilli and sauced with rouille. Mains sound more familiar to 21st-century ears: ham-wrapped monkfish tail, say, with fettuccine sauced with tomato and basil, and chargrilled beef fillet with peppercorn sauce, fondant potato, mushrooms and tomatoes. End with exotic pineapple carpaccio with coconut ice cream and rum and ginger sauce or the admirable selection of cheese with apple, grape and celery chutney.

Chef Stuart Shepherd **Owner** Jane & Peter Bailey **Seats** 50 **Times** 12-2.30/7-9.30, Closed Xmas, Mon-Tue, D Sun **Prices** Fixed L 2 course £15.95, Fixed D 3 course £22.70, Starter £7.25-£13.95, Main £15.95-£22.95, Dessert £6.75, Service optional **Wines** 8 by glass **Parking** 25 **Notes** Sunday L £17.95-£24.70, Children welcome

WOODSTOCK
Map 11 SP41

The Feathers Hotel
◉◉ Modern British

tel: 01993 812291 **Market St OX20 1SX**
email: enquiries@feathers.co.uk **web:** www.feathers.co.uk
dir: From A44 (Oxford to Woodstock), 1st left after lights. Hotel on left

Modern British cooking in a colourfully boutiqued hotel

A brick-built inn in a Cotswold market town not far from Oxford, The Feathers has long been a local fixture. There can be no doubt about its having been coaxed into the boutique hotel era when you get inside. Get a load of those eye-popping colours: rooms turned out in appetising collisions of lime and cherry, a dining room with raspberry-red banquettes and a mixture of bold graphic and abstract artworks. A copiously stocked gin bar is in the record-books for having the most varieties on offer. Thoroughly modern British cooking is the order of the day, with organics and locals among the menu ingredients, as well as seafood from the distant coasts. That last might be on-trend seared scallops with pickled fennel and roasted scallop roe, full of sea-fresh appeal and natural sweetness, while mains bring along cod in tomato-herb dressing with bubble-and-squeak. A meatier route might produce braised pig's cheek with pearl barley in thyme sauce, then roast rump, smoked shoulder and curried sweetbreads of lamb. If you missed a G&T earlier, it could turn up as dry flakes decorating a lemony crème brûlée.

Chef Piotr Galeski **Owner** Empire Ventures Ltd **Seats** 40, Pr/dining room 24 **Times** 12-2.30/7-9 **Prices** Fixed L 2 course £14.95-£24.95, Tasting menu £55-£75, Starter £7-£11.50, Main £14.50-£25, Dessert £8.50-£11.95 **Wines** 80 bottles over £30, 10 bottles under £30, 16 by glass **Parking** On street **Notes** Sunday L £24.95-£29.95, Vegetarian available, Children welcome

Macdonald Bear Hotel

@@ Modern, Traditional British

tel: 01993 811124 **Park St OX20 1SZ**
email: general.bear@macdonald-hotels.co.uk **web:** www.macdonaldhotels.co.uk/bear
dir: M40 junct 9 follow signs for Oxford & Blenheim Palace. A44 to town centre, hotel on left

Accomplished modern cooking in medieval hotel

This former coaching inn, its façade covered in creeper, has its origins in the Middle Ages, evident in thick stone walls, oak beams and open fireplaces. Gentle updating has added a high comfort factor throughout the hotel, while the restaurant has been traditionally decorated and furnished in keeping with its original features. The kitchen clearly has its fingers on the pulse of today's tastes. Plump, lightly caramelised scallops are offset by buttery chorizo salsa and charred leeks, to be followed perhaps by seared loin of Highland venison with figs, celeriac, smoked Jerusalem artichoke and port jus. Fish gets a decent airing among main courses: for instance, accurately timed pan-seared fillet of wild brill accompanied by baby squid, sweetcorn and creamed potato. The kitchen's attention to detail extends to canapés, and puddings can be a visual delight: deeply flavoured dark chocolate tart, say, with cherry salsa and noteworthy pistachio ice cream, or passionfruit curd with raspberry sorbet.

Times 12.30-2.30/7-9.30

WOOTTON   Map 11 SP41

The Killingworth Castle

@ Modern British

tel: 01993 811401 & 01386 593223 **Glympton Rd OX20 1EJ**
email: reservations@thekillingworthcastle.com
dir: M40 junct 9, 2m outside Woodstock on Glympton Road, on edge of Wootton

Modern pub cooking in a reborn country inn

This inn has been an integral part of the community since the 1630s, and when Jim and Claire Alexander (who also run the Ebrington Arms near Chipping Campden) took over in 2012, the old place got the investment it needed to move into the 21st century. They've done a sterling job with the interior, keeping all its earthy charms and period character, and they even stock their own beers under the Yubberton brand (alongside regular regional guests). But the kitchen's output really makes the place stand out – imaginative stuff that isn't overly fussy. A starter of shallot tarte Tatin is enriched with whipped goats' cheese and truffle honey, while another features crispy chicken wings with salt and vinegar mash and a trendy morel powder. Among main courses, peppered loin of venison 'pastrami' is a clever idea, or go for a comforting dish of slow-braised Old Spots cheeks. End on a high with millionaire shortbread parfait.

Chef Phil Currie, Nathan Bowles **Owner** Jim & Claire Alexander **Seats** 68, Pr/dining room 20 **Times** 12-2.30/6-9, Closed 25 Dec **Prices** Fixed L 2 course fr £15, Fixed D 3 course fr £19, Starter £6-£8, Main £13-£22, Dessert £6-£8, Service optional **Wines** 22 bottles over £30, 40 bottles under £30, 10 by glass **Parking** 40 **Notes** Early bird for 2 Mon-Thu 6-7pm £29, Monthly food night, Sunday L £13.50-£15.50, Vegetarian available, Children welcome

---

RUTLAND

CLIPSHAM   Map 11 SK91

The Olive Branch

@ British, European V

tel: 01780 410355 **Main St LE15 7SH**
email: info@theolivebranchpub.com **web:** www.theolivebranchpub.com
dir: 2m from A1 at Stretton junct, 5m N of Stamford

Charming village dining inn firing on all cylinders

The Olive Branch ticks all of the boxes for an exemplary village dining pub. First and foremost it is still a pub, with stone walls, real fires and beams, serving a fine pint of local ale, as well as making their own mulled wine, sloe gin and fruity cocktails flavoured with foraged berries and herbs. It's clear, then, that this is a kitchen with a passion for seasonal and local stuff, for food that is big on flavour and fits the easy-going atmosphere of the great British pub. Daily-changing menus and blackboards offer everything from classic fish and chips to pan-seared scallops with black pudding and quince, and a main-course haunch of venison with juniper fondant potato, braised red cabbage and roast parsnips that brims with rich flavours and hearty intentions. Finish with lemon verbena meringue pie with raspberry sorbet.

Chef Sean Hope **Owner** Sean Hope, Ben Jones **Seats** 45, Pr/dining room 20 **Times** 12-2/6.30-9.30, Closed D 25 Dec, 1 Jan **Prices** Fixed L 2 course £16.95, Fixed D 3 course £29.50, Starter £6.25-£9.95, Main £14-£24.50, Dessert £4.95-£12.50, Service optional **Wines** 60 bottles over £30, 20 bottles under £30, 16 by glass **Parking** 15 **Notes** Sunday L £25.50, Children welcome

---

LYDDINGTON   Map 11 SP89

The Marquess of Exeter

@ Modern European

tel: 01572 822477 **52 Main St LE15 9LT**
email: info@marquessexeter.co.uk **web:** www.marquessexeter.co.uk
dir: M1 junct 19, A14 to Kettering, then A6003 to Caldecott. Right into Lyddington Rd, 2m to village

Welcoming village inn with appealing menus

Successfully balancing its pub, restaurant and hotel personalities, The Marquess of Exeter has plenty of character and charm. The bedrooms are smart and contemporary, the bar has a roaring fire and exposed stone walls, while the restaurant is an equally unpretentious and attractive space. The chef-patron has experience at top end places and even worked as private chef to Elton John for a couple of years, so expect well-crafted dishes (but no histrionics). Salt and chilli cuttlefish with Thai salad show globe trotting tendencies, but equally you might go for black pudding fritters with home-made piccalilli. It's all good honest stuff with broad appeal. Herb-crusted rack of lamb is cooked just right, served with dauphinoise potatoes and marinated shallots, and fish and chips plays to the gallery. There are sharing dishes such as rib of Derbyshire beef and, for dessert, vanilla pannacotta shows sharp technical skills.

Times 12-2.30/6.30-9.30, Closed 25 Dec

OAKHAM
Map 11 SK80

Barnsdale Lodge Hotel
Modern British

tel: 01572 724678 **The Avenue, Rutland Water, North Shore LE15 8AH**
email: enquiries@barnsdalelodge.co.uk web: www.barnsdalelodge.co.uk
dir: *Turn off A1 at Stamford onto A606 to Oakham. Hotel 5m on right. (2m E of Oakham)*

Simple British cooking at an ancestral family seat

The Noel family have lived at Barnsdale since the accession of George III, and they aren't going anywhere soon. To one side of the Earl of Gainsborough's Exton estate, it's a handsome country seat on the north shore of Rutland Water, with a conservatory dining room decorated in somewhat idiosyncratic style. Surveying the patio gardens, it's festooned with parasols and animal objets d'art, and plays host to simple modern British menus featuring the produce of the vegetable garden and of a plethora of local suppliers. A meal might follow an inspired and satisfying course from seared scallops with orange and fennel salad and watercress, through accurately timed marinated rump of local lamb with Chantenay carrots and garlic and rosemary dauphinoise, to a final sweet treat of reticently flavoured honey and yogurt pannacotta with warm poached figs. Very fine breads add to the overall sense of quality.

Times 12-2.15/6.30-9.30

Hambleton Hall
– see opposite

UPPINGHAM
Map 11 SP89

The Lake Isle
British, French

tel: 01572 822951 **16 High St East LE15 9PZ**
email: info@lakeisle.co.uk web: www.lakeisle.co.uk
dir: *M1 junct 19 to A14 Kettering, at rdbt take A43 signed Corby then A6003 to Rockingham/Uppingham. Continue to pedestrian lights Uppingham, right onto High St, Lake Isle on right after the square*

Georgian townhouse hotel with confident cooking

An 18th-century property is the setting for this restaurant with rooms in the market town of Uppingham. In the restaurant, a double-fronted glass façade looks over the High Street. It has panelling, wine corks and foodie pictures on the walls and unclothed wooden tables, with well-oiled service from amenable front-of-house staff. The kitchen puts a lot of creative effort to add interest and variety, pulling in ideas – and ingredients – from wherever. Crispy panko-crumbed scallops are served with pork belly, curry crème, butternut squash, peanuts and herbs in a starter of multiple flavours and textures, following suit with a main course of pan-fried duck breast with balsamic-infused baby beets, cippolini onions, chicory and polenta studded with feta and walnuts. Oriental influences are apparent occasionally, for example in grilled fillet of sea bass with Japanese mushrooms, toasted cucumber, prawn and sesame fishcakes and wasabi. Puddings return to base in the shape of pot au chocolat with mini doughnuts, or sticky plum, port and ginger compôte with rice pudding parfait.

Chef Stuart Mead **Owner** Richard & Janine Burton **Seats** 40, Pr/dining room 16 **Times** 12-2/7-9, Closed 1 Jan, BHs, L Mon, D Sun **Prices** Starter £5-£9, Main £13.50-£24.50, Dessert £7-£8.50, Service optional **Wines** 80 bottles over £30, 30 bottles under £30, 15 by glass **Parking** 6, P&D car park adjacent **Notes** Sunday L £16.50-£22.50, Vegetarian available, No children

WING
Map 11 SK80

Kings Arms Inn & Restaurant
Modern British

tel: 01572 737634 **13 Top St LE15 8SE**
email: info@thekingsarms-wing.co.uk web: www.thekingsarms-wing.co.uk
dir: *1m off A6003, between Oakham & Uppingham*

Enterprising supplier-led cooking in a traditional inn

Stone walls, beams and flagstones are reminders that this village inn dates from the 17th century. Real ales are dispensed in the bar, where comfortable seating is arranged around an open fire, and there's an informal and friendly dining room. 'Good food takes time to source, prepare and serve' trumpets the menu, and the kitchen is evangelical about all three, with everything delivered from within about 30 miles and even charcuterie and ketchup made in-house. Such integrity is amply demonstrated by what appears on the plate. Farmhouse pâté is deeply flavoured, topped with sautéed onions and mushrooms on a slice of toast, making a satisfying starter, and there could be a bold assembly of smoked eel (from the pub's smokehouse), black pudding, pancetta and apple sauce. Main courses are equally strong: pheasant hotpot with accurately timed green vegetables, say, or sea bass fillet with crab and fennel risotto and a tempura oyster. Portions tend to be generous but puddings are not to be missed, judging by vanilla and lavender pannacotta cut by Kirsch-soaked cherries.

Chef James Goss **Owner** David & James Goss **Seats** 32, Pr/dining room 20 **Times** 12-2.30/6.30-9, Closed L Mon, D Sun **Prices** Starter £7-£12, Main £16-£32, Dessert £6-£24, Service optional **Wines** 30 bottles over £30, 20 bottles under £30, 33 by glass **Parking** 20 **Notes** Sunday L £10.50-£13, Vegetarian available, Children welcome

Hambleton Hall 🌸🌸🌸🌸

OAKHAM   **Map 11 SK80**

British V 🍷 NOTABLE WINE LIST

tel: 01572 756991 **Hambleton LE15 8TH**
email: hotel@hambletonhall.com **web:** www.hambletonhall.com
dir: 8m W of A1 Stamford junct (A606), 3m E of Oakham

Superb fine dining in majestic country-house hotel

The house was built by a chap who made his fortune in the brewery trade and rather fancied a place to stop over when enjoying the excellent fox hunting in this part of the country. That was in the 1880s. He picked a good spot that happened to be made even better when Rutland Water reservoir was opened in 1976. A country-house hotel since 1979, Hambleton Hall is a handsome place that is small enough for visitors to feel at home (and very hard to leave). The gardens nearest to the house are neatly manicured and wouldn't look out of place in front of a stately home, while the broader grounds offer some pleasant spaces to wander. The public spaces on the inside benefit from generous Victorian proportions and are rich with original features, while the stylish decor and period furniture add to the pervading sense of exclusivity and luxury. Canapés in the bar is an exceedingly good way to begin — a tasting of sea bream, say, with saffron mayonnaise — before heading into one of the two dining rooms with an elegant and traditional finish (oil paintings, plush fabrics and glinting chandeliers). Views over the garden and down to the reservoir are a bonus. The kitchen has been headed up by Aaron Patterson since 1992, which means that he's perfected his regional supply lines to ensure the quality of the ingredients couldn't be higher. Bread is baked in their own bakery down the road. Via

tasting and à la carte menus the chef and his team deliver dishes that are rooted in classical good sense while taking in developments of contemporary cooking. An animated first course of red mullet with chorizo and minestrone sets the pace; a superb piece of fish with warm heritage baby tomatoes and a raviolo filled with chorizo, while the accompanying flavour-packed minestrone consommé is poured at the table. Follow that with loin and slow-cooked belly of lamb matched with pearl barley and dumplings, or pan-fried sea bass with a tomato and artichoke risotto. Everything looks picture-perfect on the plate and the balance of flavours and precise cooking means both style and substance are assured. A dessert of terrine of pear and mulled wine is a lesson in technical know-how. The smart-looking service team are a delight from start to finish. The wine list contains lots of interesting things from producers large and small.

Chef Aaron Patterson **Owner** Mr T Hart **Seats** 60, Pr/dining room 20 **Times** 12-2/7-9.30, **Prices** Fixed L 2 course fr £26.50, Fixed D 3 course fr £68, Tasting menu fr £80 **Wines** 20 bottles under £30, 10 by glass **Parking** 40 **Notes** ALC 3 course £68, Sunday L, Children welcome

SHROPSHIRE

BRIDGNORTH
Map 10 SO79

The Old Vicarage Hotel
◉◉ British, European

tel: 01746 716497 **Hallow, Worfield WV15 5JZ**
email: admin@oldvicarageworfield.com **web:** www.oldvicarageworfield.com
dir: *Off A454, approx 3.5m NE of Bridgnorth, 5m S of Telford on A442, follow brown signs*

Classic combinations in a conservatory-style hotel dining room

The Old Vicarage, a solid-looking red-brick property, is in a peaceful village near Bridgnorth within two acres of grounds. Its Orangery Restaurant is housed in a substantial conservatory tacked on at the back, a spacious, light-filled room in a neutral colour scheme and seats upholstered in yellow and orange fabrics at formally laid tables. The kitchen's ambitions run high and it confidently delivers dishes of multiple flavours and textures. Foie gras goes into crème brûlée, the topping adding an unusual but complementary sweetness to the pâté, served with delicate brandy jelly and apple compôte garnished with broad beans and girolles, an alternative to less complex smoked salmon ballotine with beetroot and apple. Main courses can be as familiar as fillet of beef on red wine jus with carrots and purées of shallots and potatoes, and as contemporary as fillet of cod with smoked ham hock adding a successful salty contrast, accompanied by braised pears and baby gem. Ambition runs in puddings such as gooey, rich chocolate coulant with sweet and crisp churros and honey-and-nut nougat.

Times 12-2.30/7-9.30, Closed L Mon-Tue, Sat-Sun (by reservation only), D 24-26 Dec

GRINSHILL
Map 15 SJ52

The Inn at Grinshill
◉◉ Modern British

tel: 01939 220410 & 07730 066451 **The High St SY4 3BL**
email: info@theinnatgrinshill.co.uk **web:** www.theinnatgrinshill.co.uk
dir: *7m N of Shrewsbury towards Whitchurch on A49*

Remote destination for contemporary pub cooking with show-kitchen

In the lee of Grinshill itself, with a railway station only a village away, The Inn is a smartly renovated remote country hostelry with half-a-dozen bedrooms. It manages the not always easy trick of pulling in both local custom for hand-pumped ales, and destination foodies for its stylish contemporary restaurant with show-kitchen. A gleaming-white decor with pictures printed high on the ceiling beams is the setting for friendly, efficient service and confident modernised pub cooking. Scotch eggs is made here with salt cod and a deliciously runny centre, dressed with a swoosh of saffron aïoli, or go for pine-smoked duck with caramelised orange in a chicory and pine nut salad. A hunk of pork fillet is wrapped in pancetta, and the accompaniments all do their bit; potato fondant done in red wine, puréed celeriac, kale with bite, apple gel, Calvados sauce. A wine- and cinnamon-poached pear with mincemeat ice cream is well worth trying. A well-chosen wine list accompanies.

Times 12-2.30/6.30-9.30, Closed Mon, D Sun

IRONBRIDGE
Map 10 SJ60

Restaurant Severn
◉◉ British, French

tel: 01952 432233 **33 High St TF8 7AG**
dir: *Travelling along High St pass Restaurant Severn on right, to mini rdbt, take 3rd exit onto Waterloo St, continue 50mtrs to car park on left*

Country cooking beside the Ironbridge gorge

Eric and Beb Bruce's small neighbourhood restaurant blends in unobtrusively with the terrace of souvenir and tea shops facing Abraham Darby's World Heritage cast-iron bridge. Inside, however, sunny yellow walls, bare wooden floors, unclothed tables and high-backed toffee leather chairs make for an intimate brasserie look. The supply lines to local producers are good in these parts, and full advantage is taken of the local larder, supplemented by home-grown organic seasonal materials from their own smallholding. Classical French influences are evident in starters such as a smooth chicken liver and malt whisky parfait served with red onion marmalade and melba toast, while mains plough a similarly simple and unfussy furrow, partnering medallions of Shropshire venison saddle with braised red cabbage, and Cognac and sun-dried cranberry sauce. Puddings are Beb Bruce's domain – perhaps dark Belgian chocolate delice with chocolate cannelloni – or you might be tempted by a platter of Shropshire cheeses served with home-made chutney and Beb's spiced bread.

Chef Eric & Beb Bruce **Owner** Eric & Beb Bruce **Seats** 30
Times 12-2/6.30-8.30, Closed BHs, Mon-Tue, L Wed-Sat, D Sun **Prices** Fixed D 3 course £27.95-£29.95, Service optional **Wines** 15 bottles over £30, 30 bottles under £30, 6 by glass **Parking** On street & car park opposite **Notes** Sun L once mthly, Gourmet evenings mthly 4 course £29.95, Sunday L, Vegetarian available, Children Sun L only

LUDLOW
Map 10 SO57

The Charlton Arms
◉ Modern British **NEW**

tel: 01584 872813 **Ludford Bridge SY8 1PJ**
email: reservations@thecharltonarms.co.uk **web:** www.thecharltonarms.co.uk
dir: *A49, turn onto B4361, Charlton Arms 1.9m on left just before bridge*

Classic food by the river

On Ludford Bridge and a short walk from historic Ludlow Castle, Cedric and Amy Bosi's smart, modernised stone-built pub has a lovely tiered terrace overlooking the River Teme. It's an ideal spot to enjoy a pint of locally-brewed Shropshire ale or select one of the conscientiously-sourced wines. Inside, the airy dining area is relaxed and informal with scrubbed wooden floorboards and mismatched chairs. The menu focuses on classy renditions of British pub classics with a Gallic twist, perhaps starting with wild boar terrine and pickled vegetables or Cornish crab and gruyère quiche with caramelised chicory. It might be followed by whole sea bream with white beans and bacon or chicken Kiev, skinny fries and caramelised onion ketchup. Comforting desserts include sticky toffee pudding, salted caramel and lime sorbet or almond milk pannacotta with pistachio crumb and fig.

Chef Christopher O'Halloran **Owner** Cedric & Amy Bosi **Times** 12-3/6-9.30, Closed D 25-26 Dec, 1 Jan **Prices** Starter £5-£9, Main £10-£18.50, Dessert £4-£7 **Wines** 6 bottles over £30, 18 bottles under £30, 8 by glass **Notes** Sunday L fr £12.95, Vegetarian available, Children welcome

The Clive Bar & Restaurant with Rooms
◉◉ Modern British

tel: 01584 856565 & 856665 **Bromfield SY8 2JR**
email: info@theclive.co.uk **web:** www.theclive.co.uk
dir: *2m N of Ludlow on A49, near Ludlow Golf Club, racecourse & adjacent to Ludlow food centre*

Assured regional cooking in Clive of India's former residence

The name memorialises Major-General Robert Clive (he of India), who once lived in this brick-built house on the Earl of Plymouth's estate. Just outside Ludlow, in the village of Bromfield, it became a pub for estate workers in recent times, and has been imaginatively refurbished to form the present day restaurant with rooms. West Country produce abounds on the seasonally-informed menus, which feature a stunning opener of Dorset crab ravioli, the white meat sharing its pasta parcel with a soft-poached quail's egg, accompanied by a salad of preserved lemon and fennel dressed in lemon purée. That might be succeeded by Herefordshire beef fillet with potato galette, creamed spinach and honey-roast carrots, a triumphantly traditional marriage of local ingredients in a rich bourguignon sauce, or perhaps sea bass with roasted salsify and sweet button onions in saffron vinaigrette. To finish comes a pretty textbook rendering of Bakewell tart, given contemporary twists with creamy apricot ice cream and a little pouring jug of Seville orange syrup, or there's a good selection of local cheeses served with fruit chutney.

Chef Krisztian Balogh **Owner** Ludlow Food Centre **Seats** 90 **Times** 12-3/6.30-10, Closed 25-26 Dec **Prices** Prices not confirmed, Service optional **Wines** 19 bottles over £30, 36 bottles under £30, 9 by glass **Parking** 80 **Notes** Sunday L, Vegetarian available, Children welcome

Dinham Hall Hotel

◉◉ Modern British

tel: 01584 876464 **By The Castle SY8 1EJ** **email:** info@dinhamhall.com **web:** www.dinhamhall.com **dir:** Town centre, off Market Place, opposite Ludlow Castle

Ambitious modern British cooking opposite the castle

This three-storey house dates from the Georgian period and stands in the town centre opposite the castle. Open fires in the lounge are a welcoming touch in winter, there's a pretty terrace for summer dining, and the restaurant itself is in two sections, one under a large skylight, the other in the original building. The kitchen's an enthusiastic place, building its output on a solid bedrock of local suppliers and turning its hands to starters such as sweet, well-timed seared scallops served with deeply flavoured black truffle and roast pumpkin as well as a more familiar-sounding salad of black pudding, smoked bacon and Jersey Royals. Moving on, you may come across fillet of silver mullet with pickled spring vegetables, saffron and coriander. Another option may be pink, tender and succulent venison steak, from Mortimer Forest, with a textbook version of red wine sauce, accompanied by braised endive, pumpkin purée, sautéed mushrooms and roast potatoes. Finish with a classic tiramisù or pistachio and griottine cherry crème brûlée with cherry sorbet.

Chef Wayne Smith **Owner** Metzo Hotels Ltd **Seats** 36, Pr/dining room 60 **Times** 12.30-2.30/6.30-9.30, Closed L Mon **Prices** Fixed L 2 course £12.95, Fixed D 3 course £29.95-£34.95, Service optional 10% **Wines** 20 bottles over £30, 50 bottles under £30, 8 by glass **Parking** 16, On street **Notes** Sunday L £24.95, Vegetarian available, Children 7 yrs+

The Feathers Hotel

◉ British, European

tel: 01584 875261 **The Bull Ring SY8 1AA** **email:** enquiries@feathersatludlow.co.uk **web:** www.feathersatludlow.co.uk **dir:** From A49 follow town centre signs to centre. Hotel on left

Gentle modern British cooking in a venerable much-timbered inn

'That prodigy of timber-framed houses,' Pevsner called it, and it isn't hard to see what he meant. The place was converted to an inn by a Royalist veteran of the Civil

War in around 1670, though its oldest parts hark back to the reign of James I. It has been sensitively decorated throughout to retain its true identity, as witness the dining room, where dark brown upholstery and crisp white linen blend in with the roughcast stone walls and venerable beams. Stuart Forman essays a gentle take on the modern British idiom. He partners scallops with the components of a BLT and vanilla mayonnaise to start, then adding a wild mushroom and tarragon mousse to saddle of rabbit with green beans in hazelnut butter, or pan-roasted halibut on fennel slaw with purple potatoes in lemon oil. Proceedings close with Valrhona fondant and pistachio ice cream, or with artisan cheeses, served with membrillo and walnut bread.

Chef Stuart Forman **Owner** Ceney Developments **Seats** 50, Pr/dining room 30 **Times** 7-9, Closed L all week **Prices** Fixed D 3 course £39.95-£42, Service optional **Wines** 14 bottles over £30, 23 bottles under £30, 10 by glass **Parking** 36 **Notes** Vegetarian available, Children welcome

Fishmore Hall

◉◉◉ – see page 460

Old Downton Lodge

◉◉◉ – see page 460

Overton Grange Hotel and Restaurant

◉ Modern British

tel: 01584 873500 **Old Hereford Rd SY8 4AD** **email:** info@overtongrangehotel.com **web:** www.overtongrangehotel.com **dir:** M5 junct 5. On B4361 approx 1.5m from Ludlow towards Leominster

Edwardian country house with modern British dishes

The white and red-brick-faced Edwardian country house is classic in style both outside and in, where panelled walls and squashy sofas in front of log fires make a thoroughly inviting impression. A conservatory dining room overlooks the surrounding farmland and gardens, and service from smartly suited staff is very obliging. A thoroughgoing excursion into modern British territory is mounted by the kitchen, and some things work well. After a starter perhaps of game ravioli in girolle velouté, crisp-skinned sea bass with clams, earthy mushrooms, fondant potato and asparagus is impressively well-timed, and glazed lemon tart with raspberry sorbet and crunchy meringue garnish ends things on a high. The show-stopping main course on the tasting menu might be roast organic guinea fowl done three ways, including a confit of the leg.

Chef Wayne Smith **Owner** Metzo Properties **Seats** 40, Pr/dining room 24 **Times** 12-2.30/7-9.30 **Prices** Fixed L 3 course £29.50-£32.50, Fixed D 3 course £34.95-£42.50, Tasting menu £59.50 **Wines** 12 by glass **Parking** 50 **Notes** Sunday L £29.95, Vegetarian available, Children 6 yrs+

Find out more about how we assess for Rosette awards on page 9

Fishmore Hall ❀❀❀

Modern European v

tel: 01584 875148 **Fishmore Rd SY8 3DP**
email: reception@fishmorehall.co.uk **web:** www.fishmorehall.co.uk
dir: *A49 from Shrewsbury, follow Ludlow & Bridgnorth signs. 1st left towards Bridgnorth, at next rdbt left onto Fishmore Rd. Hotel 0.5m on right after golf course*

Renovated country house with high-impact, thoughtful cooking

Situated just outside the foodie mecca of Ludlow, Fishmore surveys the undulating acres of Shropshire farmland and landscape, with the Clee Hills in the distance and the castle's towers poking above the trees. The fine Georgian mansion was in a pretty bad way until 2007, when its present owners got to work on transforming it into the sleek boutique operation we see today. An orangery extension forms the venue for the dining operation, named Forelles after the variety of pear trees in the garden. Neutral decor and minimalist artworks establish a gentle background, and tables are dressed to impress, with smart napery and quality glassware. Head chef Andrew Birch is a confident exponent of the modern European style, his dishes founded on pedigree materials sourced from within a 30-mile radius (apart from seafood, of course, which comes from Brixham and Skye) and delivered via a three-course carte and six- or nine-course tasting menus that are an exhilarating exploration of flavour and texture. There's plenty of impact to keep the palate jangling in a starter of pig's head croquette with smoked eel, beetroot, apple, and mustard purée. Birch can do delicate too, as witnessed in a well-balanced idea involving seared scallops with cauliflower purée, coriander, and cumin velouté. Next up, hake gets a robust outing in the company of bacon, seasonal morels, onion and mustard sauce, while Goosnargh duck breast is served alongside purple sprouting broccoli, chicory, pickled red cabbage and pepper sauce. Wickedly rich finishers bring banana mousse with hazelnuts and caramel crémeux, and set chocolate custard with orange purée and Kirsch cream.

Chef Andrew Birch **Owner** Laura Penman **Seats** 40, Pr/dining room 20 **Times** 12.30-2.30/7-9.30, Closed Mon, L Tue, D Sun, BHs **Prices** Fixed L 2 course £20-£39, Fixed D 3 course £49, Tasting menu £65-£75, Service optional **Wines** 52 bottles over £30, 16 bottles under £30, 12 by glass **Parking** 36 **Notes** Tasting menu 6/9 course, Vegetarian 2/3/6/9 course, Sunday L £20-£25, Children welcome

Old Downton Lodge ❀❀❀

Modern British **NEW** v

tel: 01568 771826 & 770175 **Downton on the Rock SY8 2HU**
email: bookings@olddowntonlodge.com **web:** www.olddowntonlodge.com
dir: *From Ludlow take A49 to Shrewsbury. Left to Knighton A4113, left to Downton. Old Downton Lodge after 3m*

Impressively creative cooking in an interesting multi-era setting

Another star has joined Ludlow's gastronomic firmament, in the form of Old Downton Lodge, a rural restaurant with rooms consisting of a fascinating mixture of buildings — medieval, half-timbered, Georgian — around a courtyard filled with herbs and flowers. The sitting room/ bar has been converted from the old stables, with the original stalls now part of the seating, while the restaurant, which dates from Norman times, has the feel of a medieval great hall, with a rich tapestry of a woodland hunting scene hanging on its stone walls, a metal chandelier, and chairs with a coat of arms motif at slate-topped, candlelit wooden tables all feeding into the Middle-Ages vibe. Dinner comprises set-price five- or seven-course, daily-changing menus, and it's all built on local, home-grown and foraged produce of the highest order. Head chef Karl Martin's cooking has an inherent simplicity and clever balance, kicking off with an impressive amuse of rich brown crab custard with mango purée and coriander to pave the way for asparagus mousse with vibrant ramson purée, mushrooms, feta and croûtons. Juxtaposing fruit and meat is a favoured tactic in main courses: intensely-flavoured part-dried grapes to counterpoint the richness of beautifully timed, crispy-skinned duck breast served with wild chervil, chicory, baked and puréed celeriac, or perhaps greengages with fillet and collar of pork, peas, gem lettuce and garlic flowers. These are highly original compositions where everything is there for a good reason, and the results are impressive all the way through to pudding, when a tricksy reworking of rhubarb trifle brings a Kilner jar layered with rhubarb (poached and jelly) with diced sponge and aerated custard foam, preceded, perhaps, by a pre-dessert like strawberries with gin, lime and vanilla.

Chef Karl Martin **Owner** Willem & Pippa Vlok **Seats** 25, Pr/dining room 45 **Times** 6-9, Closed Xmas, Sun-Mon **Prices** Tasting menu £40-£75, Service optional **Wines** 26 bottles over £30, 12 bottles under £30, 7 by glass **Parking** 20 **Notes** No children

MARKET DRAYTON
Map 15 SJ63

Goldstone Hall
◎◎ Modern British

tel: 01630 661202 **Goldstone Rd TF9 2NA**
email: enquiries@goldstonehall.com **web:** www.goldstonehall.com
dir: *4m S of Market Drayton off A529 signed Goldstone Hall Hotel. 4m N of Newport signed from A41*

Modern British ideas in a manor-house hotel

The Georgian house is handsome enough – with traditional features and an elegant interior – but the two stand-out elements to Goldstone Hall are its magnificent gardens and ambitious restaurant. The kitchen garden is a major part of the operation, providing fresh, seasonal produce for the table, and it's a good idea to make time to explore the grounds. Dining takes place in either a grandly panelled dining room with an Arts and Crafts fireplace, or in the more informal Orangery. The kitchen turns out bright, modern dishes while avoiding jumping on the bandwagon of every contemporary fashion (foams are avoided, for example), and the flavours of these carefully sourced (and home-grown) ingredients are given room to make an impression. Excellent amuse-bouche gets things off to a flying start, as do the excellent home-made breads. Then try crab and ginger salad, say, with confit fennel and lemon, followed by slow-cooked beef with bubble-and-squeak, Shropshire Blue bonbon and confit cabbage. Finish with a simple and well executed lemon tart with raspberry sorbet.

Chef Steven Blackshaw **Owner** John Cushing **Seats** 60, Pr/dining room 14 **Times** 11-3/7-10 **Prices** Starter £7-£12, Main £12-£29.50, Dessert fr £8.95, Service optional **Wines** 30 bottles over £30, 70 bottles under £30, 15 by glass **Parking** 70 **Notes** Garden L menu, Sunday L fr £32, Vegetarian available, Children welcome

MUCH WENLOCK
Map 10 SQ69

Raven Hotel
◎◎ Modern British

tel: 01952 727251 **30 Barrow St TF13 6EN**
email: enquiry@ravenhotel.com **web:** www.ravenhotel.com
dir: *10m SW from Telford on A4169, 12m SE from Shrewsbury. In town centre*

Ambitious cooking in a 17th-century coaching inn

The former coaching inn has held court in Much Wenlock since the 17th century and remains in the same line of business to this day. The place still has period charm, with venerable beams, log fires and hand-pulled ales available in the bar. On the dining front, though, things are a little more contemporary, positively 21st-century in fact. The kitchen makes excellent use of the plentiful (and top quality) produce available in this neck of the woods, and the menu turns them into smart, modern European constructions. It all takes place in a traditional room with a huge fireplace and more of those beams. A starter soup shows the ambition in the kitchen, with a slow-roast celeriac version topped with chorizo beignet and parmesan emulsion. Main course might bring forth a surf and turf number, pairing roast fillet of Mortimer Forest venison with lobster, plus haricot blanc, pancetta and lobster espuma. There's a tasting menu, too, serving up 68°C loin of cod. Desserts run to Granny Smith pannacotta with warm apple cake and apple ice cream, and the cheese selection is first class.

Chef Jason Hodnett **Owner** Kirk Heywood, Sheila Hartshorn **Seats** 40, Pr/dining room 14 **Times** 12-2.30/6.45-9.30, Closed 25-26 Dec **Prices** Prices not confirmed, Service optional **Wines** 10 bottles over £30, 48 bottles under £30, 12 by glass **Parking** 30 **Notes** Sunday L, Vegetarian available, Children welcome

MUNSLOW
Map 10 SO58

Crown Country Inn
◎◎ Modern British

tel: 01584 841205 **SY7 9ET**
email: info@crowncountryinn.co.uk **web:** www.crowncountryinn.co.uk
dir: *On B4368 between Craven Arms & Much Wenlock*

Classy modern cooking in old village inn

In an Area of Outstanding Natural Beauty, the Crown has some history behind it: it dates from Tudor times and was first licensed in 1790. The first-floor restaurant, a courtroom in the 17th century, is a beamed, cottagey-looking room with an impressive open fireplace. The kitchen follows the 'Local to Ludlow' precept, thus sourcing its ingredients within the locality, and produces food in the up-to-the-minute culinary style. That might take in a reworking of breakfast for black pudding croquettes with Boston beans, bacon and 'fried bread', or involve adding pea pesto, prosciutto and pickled fennel to scallops, for starters. Inspired main courses offer plenty of variety, from tapenade-crusted salmon with olive oil mash and creamed leeks In beurre rouge, to braised Bridgnorth brisket with butter bean fricassée, roast roots, pickled walnuts and polenta fritters. Desserts are a roll call of creatively tweaked favourites, orange crème brûlée with cranberry ice cream rubbing shoulders with banana parfait and caramel popcorn in toffee sauce. If sugar isn't your thing, there's an extensive list of pedigree British cheeses to ponder, served with home-made chutney.

Chef Richard Arnold **Owner** Richard & Jane Arnold **Seats** 65, Pr/dining room 42 **Times** 12-2/6.45-8.45, Closed some days during Xmas, Mon, D Sun **Prices** Starter £6-£9, Main £16-£22, Dessert £6.50, Service optional **Wines** 2 bottles over £30, 29 bottles under £30, 5 by glass **Parking** 20 **Notes** Sunday L £20-£24, Vegetarian available, Children welcome

NORTON
Map 10 SJ70

The Hundred House
◉◉ British, French

tel: 01952 580240 **Bridgnorth Rd TF11 9EE**
email: reservations@hundredhouse.co.uk **web:** www.hundredhouse.co.uk
dir: *Midway between Telford & Bridgnorth on A442. In village of Norton*

Quirky charm meets skilled modern cuisine

Run by the Phillips family since the mid-1980s, The Hundred House is brimful of character and personality, a breath of fresh air in a world of corporate blandness. The rather handsome Georgian coaching inn has stylish bedrooms which fall into the boutique end of the spectrum by contemporary classifications, a bar serving some pretty nifty pub grub, and a brasserie and restaurant producing some classy dishes based on tip-top regional ingredients. A first course of griddled scallops is served with a risotto cake and stir-fried vegetables, with another offering a plate of meze including falafel and aubergine purée. Next up, a main course of roast rack of Shropshire lamb with creamed garlic mash, or chicken breast stuffed with ricotta, spinach and pine nuts. Desserts can deliver all the comfort of a hot treacle tart with home-made custard, or sticky toffee pudding with vanilla ice cream, or go for the English cheeses with home-made chutney and biscuits.

Chef Stuart Phillips **Owner** Mr H Phillips, Mr D Phillips, Mr S G Phillips **Seats** 80, Pr/dining room 34 **Times** 12-2.30/6-9.30, Closed D 25 Dec **Prices** Fixed L 2 course £18.90-£37.90, Fixed D 3 course £25.85-£44.85, Tasting menu £50-£75, Starter £5.95-£12.95, Main £12.95-£24.95, Dessert £6.95, Service optional 10% **Wines** 9 bottles over £30, 36 bottles under £30, 12 by glass **Parking** 60 **Notes** Gourmet evenings, Sunday L £17.95-£20.95, Vegetarian available, Children welcome

OSWESTRY
Map 15 SJ22

Pen-y-Dyffryn Country Hotel
◉◉ Modern British

tel: 01691 653700 **Rhydycroesau SY10 7JD**
email: stay@peny.co.uk **web:** www.peny.co.uk
dir: *3m W of Oswestry on B4580*

Locally based cooking on the cusp of England and Wales

An enterprising construction company built the rectory, church and village school here in 1840 for £1,260 all in – quite a bargain. We can only shudder at the planning procedures that would be provoked today by the fact that the church is on the Welsh side of the border and the rectory, now a country hotel, on the English. With sweeping views over the valley, it's a relaxing place indeed, traditionally furnished in country-house style, with table linen, floral decorations and candles gracing the dining room, not to mention some fetching near-abstract paintings suggestive of the local landscape. David Morris's cooking is firmly in the modern Anglo-Welsh idiom, with organic materials and upstanding flavours on show. King scallops in verjus cream with tomato, basil and spinach delivers appetising sweetness and fragrance, and may be succeeded by well-seasoned lamb rump with a meat-stuffed tomato, creamed cabbage and pancetta. Fish could be a pairing of halibut and crab with red pepper risotto. The finale might be a properly vanillary crème brûlée strewn with raspberries.

Chef David Morris **Owner** M J M & A A Hunter **Seats** 25 **Times** 6.45-11, Closed 20 Dec-21 Jan, L all week **Prices** Fixed D 3 course £33-£40, Service optional **Wines** 40 bottles over £30, 40 bottles under £30, 6 by glass **Parking** 18 **Notes** Vegetarian available, Children 3 yrs+

Sebastians
◉◉ International, French

tel: 01691 655444 **45 Willow St SY11 1AQ**
email: sebastians.rest@virgin.net **web:** www.sebastians-hotel.co.uk
dir: *From town centre turn into Willow St signed Selatyn. Hotel on left in 400yds*

Skilled French cooking in boutique venue

Mark and Michelle Fisher's boutique restaurant with rooms purrs along with the well-polished professionalism that comes with over 20 years of practice. The building is a 16th-century inn, full of cossetting beamed character, but not stuck in the past. A comfy lounge with sofas and a roaring fire is an appealing spot for drinks and canapés, before moving on to the oak-panelled, apricot-hued dining room with its Orient Express-themed artwork, high-backed, tobacco leather chairs and crisp white linen. Monthly-changing set-price dinner menus take you through three courses of well-crafted, Gallic-influenced ideas, with an appetiser to set the ball rolling, and a sorbet before mains, or for tighter budgets there's a great value mid-week market menu. Start with well-made game terrine served with brioche and Cumberland sauce, followed by roasted leg and loin of lamb matched with wild mushroom pearl barley risotto and roast garlic purée, or a rich bouillabaisse of fish, shellfish and potatoes poached in saffron and fennel. Desserts might revert to British comfort mode with steamed marmalade pudding with Drambuie custard.

Chef Mark Fisher **Owner** Mark & Michelle Fisher **Seats** 45 **Times** 6.30-9.30, Closed 25-26 Dec, 1 Jan, Etr Mon, Sun-Mon, L all week **Prices** Fixed D 3 course £22.50, Service optional **Wines** 18 bottles over £30, 31 bottles under £30, 7 by glass **Parking** 6, On street **Notes** 5 course D £44.50, Vegetarian available, Children 12 yrs+

Wynnstay Hotel
◉◉ British

tel: 01691 655261 **Church St SY11 2SZ**
email: info@wynnstayhotel.com **web:** www.wynnstayhotel.com
dir: *In town centre, opposite church*

Modern classics in a Georgian setting complete with bowling-green

The Wynnstay has stood proud in the heart of town since it began life as a coaching inn in the early Georgian era. The hotel is a classic example of its ilk, a handsome red-brick edifice, fronted by a grand portico, but there are also modern spa and gym facilities spread around a centrepiece crown bowling green. The Four Seasons restaurant has upped its game since a new head chef took the helm in 2015, producing an appealing style of modern British cooking based on reinvented versions of dishes taken from the Wynnstay's 1960s menus. Ham hock terrine with a soft poached egg, asparagus and pea shoots is helped along by a piquant wholegrain mustard dressing, or you might start with a classic French onion soup with a gruyère croûte. Main-course sea bass is handled with aplomb and matched with sautéed potatoes, peas and chorizo, or if you're in the mood for meat, there could be the retro delights of pan-seared Gressingham duck breast à l'orange. Dessert brings a textbook crème brûlée with shortbread.

Chef Jamie Deery **Owner** Mr N Woodward **Seats** 50, Pr/dining room 200 **Times** 12-2.30/6-9.30 **Prices** Fixed L 2 course £13.50, Fixed D 3 course £13.50-£25, Starter £6.50-£9, Main £14.95-£25.95, Dessert £6.50-£8, Service optional **Wines** 27 bottles over £30, 45 bottles under £30, 11 by glass **Parking** 80 **Notes** Sunday L £13.50-£16.50, Vegetarian available, Children welcome

SHIFNAL

Map 10 SJ70

Park House Hotel

◉ Modern European

tel: 01952 460128 **Park St TF11 9BA**
email: reception02@parkhousehotel.net **web:** www.parkhousehotel.net
dir: *From M54 junct 4 take A464 through Shifnal; hotel 200yds after railway bridge*

Modern cooking in singular market town hotel

Two 17th-century country houses — one red-brick, one faced with white stucco — have been pasted seamlessly together to make Park House, an upmarket venue in a pleasant Shropshire market town. Period oak panelling and ornate plasterwork combine with a dramatic contemporary colour scheme to provide a classy backdrop in the brasserie-style Butlers restaurant. The kitchen doesn't try to reinvent the wheel here, focusing on good quality local produce in a repertoire of comfort classics — the likes of sirloin steak with blue cheese or peppercorn sauces, fish pie, or beer-battered haddock and proper chips — and straightforward modern European ideas. Spiced lamb terrine with flatbread and pear chutney leads the way, followed by a piggy plate of pork loin and a pulled pork bonbon with fondant potato and smoky red wine jus. At the end, coconut pannacotta is offset with astringent poached blackberries and crunchy honeycomb.

Times 12-10, All-day dining

SHREWSBURY

Map 15 SJ41

Albright Hussey Manor Hotel & Restaurant

◉◉ Modern British

tel: 01939 290571 **Ellesmere Rd, Broad Oak SY4 3AF**
email: info@albrighthussey.co.uk **web:** www.albrighthussey.co.uk
dir: *2.5m N of Shrewsbury on A528, follow signs for Ellesmere*

Confident modern cooking in a fascinating Tudor house

The Subbiani family's Tudor hotel is one of the more architecturally arresting 16th-century English buildings. It may look rather crudely extended to the untutored eye, but the two entirely unmatching wings — one brown-timbered, the other taller half of stone-faced brick — were built only 35 years apart. The place is stocked with fascinating antiques, both martial and domestic, the guest rooms have canopy beds, and dining takes place in a beamed room with mullioned windows and a pleasing coral-pink colour scheme. Confident contemporary cooking is the day's order, starting perhaps with gently spiced ham hock terrine dressed with raisin relish and baby gem and apple salad, or home-cured salmon with beetroot, before mains such as crisply seared sea bass with scallops and vegetable 'spaghetti' in a rich beurre blanc containing sorrel, or medallion of local beef with oxtail ravioli, fondant potatoes and spinach. Finish with proudly risen Amaretto soufflé laced with honey, accompanied by intensely flavoured matching ice cream.

Chef Michel Nijsten **Owner** Franco, Vera & Paul Subbiani **Seats** 80, Pr/dining room 40 **Times** 12-2.15/7-10 **Prices** Fixed L 2 course £15-£20, Fixed D 3 course £25-£35, Tasting menu £50-£70, Starter £5.95-£11, Main £14-£23, Dessert £6.50-£9, Service optional **Wines** 25 bottles over £30, 35 bottles under £30, 14 by glass **Parking** 100 **Notes** Sunday L, Vegetarian available, Children welcome

Drapers Hall

◉◉ Modern, Traditional

tel: 01743 344679 **10 Saint Mary's Place SY1 1DZ**
email: goodfood@drapershallrestaurant.co.uk **web:** www.drapershallrestaurant.co.uk
dir: *From A5191 (St Mary's St) on one-way system into St Mary's Place*

Updated classic cooking in a medieval dining room

Dating back to 1485, Draper's Hall restaurant with rooms is situated in one of the oldest buildings in the heart of Shrewsbury and offers the chance to dine in a lovingly restored period building. The place bursts with moody medieval character, with grand inglenook fireplaces, old wooden beams, ancient floors and wood-panelled walls hung with gilt-framed, artworks and mirrors. But this is no creaky museum: it's all overlaid with a funky modern edge, with beige tartan wool chairs at white-clothed tables and music playing softly in the background to add to the civilised ambience. When it comes to the menu, tried-and-tested combinations benefit from some gently updated touches. Crispy-skinned sea bass is served with saffron potatoes, green beans, and spinach wilted in wine adding a sharp edge to cut through a rich bisque-like bouillabaisse sauce. Bookending this, there's chicken liver parfait with caramelised orange, onion marmalade and sourdough toast to start, and to wrap things up, a well-crafted dessert of lemon tart with basil ice cream.

Chef Nigel J Huxley **Owner** Nigel & Sharon Huxley **Seats** Pr/dining room 20 **Times** 11-3.30/6-9.30, Closed L Mon, D Sun **Prices** Fixed L 2 course £14, Fixed D 3 course £30-£35, Starter £5-£15, Main £14-£30, Dessert £5-£15, Service optional **Wines** 40 bottles over £30, 24 bottles under £30, 16 by glass **Notes** Sunday L, Vegetarian available, Children welcome

Henry Tudor House Restaurant and Bar

◉ Modern British NEW

tel: 01743 361666 **Henry Tudor House, Barracks Passage SY1 1XA**
email: hello@henrytudorhouse.com
dir: *Phone for directions*

Modern British food in medieval building

The HTH is among the market town's oldest half-timbered buildings, although its interior is a pleasing mix of the traditional, modern and the downright whimsical. For example, while the restaurant walls display the obligatory old oak beams, there's a Parisian-style zinc bar-top bathed in ever-changing coloured light, and elegant chandeliers in the blue-tiled conservatory shine out through delicate iron birdcages. Whether you want a hearty stew, a delicate soufflé or something between the two, there will be something to suit from the all-day menu's range of classics, or from the more elaborate evening selection. Begin maybe with cured mackerel, rhubarb, radish and ginger ponzu dressing, move on to a tasty rabbit pie with lardo, peas and carrots, or baked red mullet with Mediterranean vegetables, then what better than peaches and cream with vanilla pannacotta, charred peaches and champagne.

Chef Chris Conde **Owner** Clare & Graham Jenkins **Seats** 45, Pr/dining room 18 **Times** 12-9.30, All-day dining, Closed 25-26 Dec, 1 Jan **Prices** Fixed L 3 course £13, Starter £5-£8, Main £10-£19.50, Dessert £6.50-£14 **Parking** On street, NCP **Notes** Tasting menu 7/9 course, Sunday L £12-£19, Vegetarian available, Children welcome

Lion & Pheasant Hotel

◉◉ British V

tel: 01743 770345 **49-50 Wyle Cop SY1 1XJ**
email: info@lionandpheasant.co.uk **web:** www.lionandpheasant.co.uk
dir: *From S & E: pass abbey, cross river on English Bridge to Wyle Cop, hotel on left. From N & W: follow Town Centre signs on one-way system to Wyle Cop. Hotel at bottom of hill on right*

Classic modern brasserie cooking in a townhouse hotel

This was a coaching inn back in the 16th century and the period façade still fits right in on Wyle Cop. It's a different picture inside, where contemporary style takes over, but in a restrained, easy-on-the-eye New England manner. Neutral tones and tongue-and-groove-panelling combine with the ancient beams and natural brick to create a very engaging space built for the business of hospitality. There are boutique bedrooms, a rather cool bar with a real fire and some cocktails, and a smart but relaxed restaurant that focuses on British ingredients. The menu shows a modern British spin to classic, brasserie-style combinations. Dill-cured gravad lax, for example, with horseradish crème fraîche, beetroot and capers is a simple enough dish, the flavours all pulling together, or there might be white onion soup with smoked cheese beignets. Main-course whole roasted partridge comes with

continued

SHREWSBURY *continued*

confit potato, trompettes and a nicely intense jus, and slow-roasted belly of pork with mustard mash and braised red cabbage and glazed carrots.

Chef David Martin **Owner** Jim Littler **Seats** 35, Pr/dining room 45 **Times** 12-2.30/6-9.30, Closed 25-26 Dec **Prices** Prices not confirmed, Service optional **Wines** 105 bottles over £30, 70 bottles under £30, 14 by glass **Parking** 14, NCP opposite **Notes** Sunday L, Children welcome

Porter House SY1

◉ Modern British, International, American **v**

tel: 01743 358870 **15 St Mary's St SY1 1EQ**
email: info@porterhousesy1.co.uk **web:** www.porterhousesy1.co.uk
dir: *In Shrewsbury town centre, on the one-way system, almost opposite St Mary's Church*

Trendy brasserie food with upscale burgers a speciality

The place used to be known as Mad Jack's, in homage to a Georgian roustabout, but has had an image makeover and gone distinctly saner, with a 21st-century monochrome look, all white walls and charcoal-grey furniture under the atrium ceiling. Local sourcing is a given, with Shropshire beef a particularly proud boast. It turns up, along with a little Wagyu for luxury, in the form of upscale burgers and 28-day aged steaks cooked on the grill, while the rest of the menu maintains the pace with trendy preparations such as New Orleans fish pie, pulled pork burrito and fajitas. It all creates a breezy mid-Atlantic feel in unassuming Shrewsbury, through to a slate of hipster desserts like triple chocolate brownie. Brunchers, start your taste buds with one of the Bloody something hangover cocktails, before moving on to a steak sandwich with slaw.

Chef Greg Huxford **Owner** Ann & Danny Ditella **Seats** 60, Pr/dining room 45 **Times** 10-9.30, All-day dining, Closed 25-26 Dec **Prices** Fixed L 2 course £12-£20, Fixed D 3 course £15-£30, Starter £5.50-£7, Main £12-£27, Dessert £5.50-£6.50, Service optional 10% **Wines** 14 bottles over £30, 37 bottles under £30, 30 by glass **Parking** Town centre **Notes** Sunday L £12-£25, Children welcome

█ **TELFORD** Map 10 SJ60

Chez Maw Restaurant

◉◉ Modern British **v**

tel: 01952 432247 **Ironbridge TF8 7DW**
email: info@thevalleyhotel.co.uk **web:** www.chezmawrestaurant.co.uk
dir: *M6/M54 from junct 6 take A5223 to Ironbridge for 4m. At mini island right, hotel 80yds on left*

Modern British cooking in a hotel near the Iron Bridge

Right on the bank of the Severn in the UNESCO World Heritage Site of Ironbridge, barely a rivet's throw from the eponymous first iron construction in the world, the Valley Hotel was once owned by Arthur Maw and his family, suppliers of ceramic tiles to the nobility. Hence the name of its restaurant, which is quite as fully occupied in supplying modern British cooking to a discerning local present-day clientele. A broad range of choice brings an array of different reference-points on to the menus, so starter might be a salmon and spring onion fishcake with chana Dhal in coconut-coriander cream sauce, or a spiced poached pear with dolcelatte mousse, melon and candied walnuts, before the main attraction arrives in the form of honey-glazed confit duck leg with celeriac, red cabbage and orange and onion marmalade in Madeira jus. A Chinese approach to fish sees sea bream accompanied by pak choi in sweet-and-sour dressing. Finish with chocolate and

peanut delice and chocolate ice cream, or carrot, date and sultana cake with mascarpone sorbet and orange syrup.

Chef Barry Workman **Owner** Philip & Leslie Casson **Seats** 50, Pr/dining room 30 **Times** 12-2/7-9.30, Closed 26 Dec-2 Jan, L Sat-Sun **Prices** Starter £5-£8, Main £13-£23, Dessert £6-£8, Service optional **Wines** 2 bottles over £30, 37 bottles under £30, 7 by glass **Parking** 100 **Notes** Children welcome

Hadley Park House

◉ Modern British

tel: 01952 677269 **Hadley Park TF1 6QJ**
email: info@hadleypark.co.uk **web:** www.hadleypark.co.uk
dir: *M54 junct 5, A5 (Rampart Way), at rdbt take A442 towards Hortonwood, over double rdbt, next rdbt take 2nd exit, hotel at end of lane*

Locally based cooking at a well-maintained Georgian manor

The origins of Hadley Park remain shrouded in mystery, but it seems likely to have been built in the mid-Georgian era, the 1770s perhaps. An august red-brick manor house in a couple of acres of lovely gardens, it makes a target venue for summertime country weddings. The conservatory extension dining room in the form of Dorrells is dedicated to the elegant pursuit of regionally sourced modern British cooking. Dishes are well-conceived, with a tendency to big, rich flavours, as in a starter of black pudding Scotch egg with pancetta crisps and mushroom ketchup, the sort of thing you could happily set about at breakfast, and mains like honey-glazed pork belly with peppery potato rösti in a shiny red wine jus. The showcase dessert is a layered parfait of white chocolate and raspberry, served with textural variations on raspberry – dried, gel and sorbet. Good home-made breads are a credit to the kitchen too.

Times 12-2/6.30-9.30, Closed 25-26 Dec D

█ **UPTON MAGNA** Map 10 SJ51

Basils at The Haughmond

◉ Modern British

tel: 01743 709918 **SY4 4TZ**
email: contact@thehaughmond.co.uk
dir: *Phone for directions*

Multi-component dishes in a country inn

A classic roadside country inn, The Haughmond's interior feels bright and contemporary, with its chunky wooden beams painted white and fashionable pastel shades on the walls, but there are still local ales at the pumps and the likes of steak and oxtail pie available in the bar/brasserie. The main dining room, Basils, deals in fine dining on Friday and Saturday evenings, with tables dressed for the part. The fixed price dégustation menu offers a choice of three or four courses, the choice being a fish main, a meat main or both. Start with cream of broccoli soup enriched with truffle and a deep-fried duck egg and move on to fillet of mackerel with a trio of cucumber preparations (grilled, ketchup and jelly). The meaty main might be marinated loin of venison with an oxtail fritter and salt-baked celeriac, and, for dessert, warm chocolate fondant plays the comfort card.

Chef Martin Board **Owner** Melanie & Martin Board **Seats** 20, Pr/dining room 20 **Times** 12-3/5.30-11, Closed Mon **Prices** Tasting menu £35-£55, Starter £5-£8, Main £9-£19, Dessert £5-£9, Service optional **Wines** 2 bottles over £30, 12 bottles under £30, 12 by glass **Parking** 30 **Notes** Dégustation menu 4-6 course, Sunday L £10-£18, Vegetarian available, Children welcome

SOMERSET

AXBRIDGE
Map 4 ST45

The Oak House
◎◎ Modern British

tel: 01934 732444 **The Square BS26 2AP**
email: info@theoakhousesomerset.com **web:** www.theoakhousesomerset.com
dir: *M5 junct 22 onto A38 north, turn right to Axbridge, signed*

Adventurous combinations in a stylish restaurant with rooms

Parts of the Oak House date from the 11th century, while the elegant façade has a more Georgian-style appearance, and once over the threshold a stylish mix of old and new confirms that this restaurant with rooms leans towards the boutique end of the design spectrum. The bar stocks bottled ciders to provide a sense of place, while the restaurant deals in feel-good flavours and fashionable pairings. Steaks are cooked on the grill — 10oz rib-eye, say — and arrive with triple-cooked chips, field mushroom and tomato, plus a choice of sauces from béarnaise to Stilton. Starters include a seafood cocktail (crab, crayfish and prawns) or a tasting of pork which includes a pulled pork bonbon and Bramley apple purée. Spiced monkfish is an alternative to the red meat, accompanied by onion bhaji and textures of beetroot and sweet potato, while a non-meat option might be chestnut gnocchi with hickory-smoked egg yolk. For dessert, 'chocolate orange' is another contemporary construction with chocolate soil, honeycomb and orange powder.

Chef James Challis **Owner** Oakhouse Hotels Ltd **Seats** 40 **Times** 12-2/6-9 **Prices** Starter £2.95-£7.95, Main £12.95-£22.95, Dessert £6.50-£8.75, Service optional **Wines** 6 bottles over £30, 22 bottles under £30, 15 by glass **Parking** 100mtrs **Notes** Sunday L £16.50-£19.50, Vegetarian available, Children welcome

BATH
Map 4 ST76

Allium Restaurant at The Abbey Hotel
◎◎◎ – *see page 466*

Bailbrook House Hotel
◎◎ Modern British **v NEW**

tel: 01225 855100 **Eveleigh Av, London Road West BA1 7JD**
email: sales.bailbrook@handpicked.co.uk **web:** www.bailbrookhouse.co.uk
dir: *M4 junct 18/A46, at bottom of long hill take slip road to city centre. At rdbt take 1st exit, London Rd. Hotel 200mtrs on left*

Satisfying cooking in a boutique country house

Set in 20 acres of parkland with views marching away to the Bath skyline, Bailbrook is a handsome Georgian country mansion done out in classy contemporary boutique style. Its Cloisters Restaurant is the fine-dining option, an intimate split-level space divided by wrought iron rails, with stone vaulted ceilings and chic medieval-style light fittings. Switched-on staff do their bit to foster a pleasant and relaxed experience, and the up-to-date country-house cooking aims to please rather than push any boundaries. Satisfaction is certainly achieved with a simple pairing of crab tortellini and bisque, or you might start with wood pigeon breast with pickled shiitake mushrooms and smoked bacon lardons, all set off with a walnut vinaigrette. Main-course cannon of lamb gets a pine nut and herb crust, and is partnered with a potato pressing, caramelised shallots, carrots and a glossy rosemary jus. Flavours counterpoint well in fish dishes such as halibut fillet with pea and bacon fricassée, Jersey Royals and girolles, and dessert might be a rich chocolate fondant with pistachio ice cream.

Chef Jonathan Machin **Owner** Hand Picked Hotels **Seats** 64, Pr/dining room 14 **Times** 12.30-2/7-9.30, Closed L Mon-Sat **Prices** Fixed L 3 course £27.95, Fixed D 3 course £39, Starter £7-£14, Main £19-£34, Dessert £9-£14 **Wines** 78 bottles over £30, 17 bottles under £30, 16 by glass **Parking** 100 **Notes** Sunday L £19.95-£27.95, Children welcome

The Bath Priory Hotel, Restaurant & Spa
◎◎◎ – *see page 466*

The Chequers
◎◎ Modern British

tel: 01225 360017 **50 Rivers St BA1 2QA**

email: info@thechequersbath.com **web:** www.thechequersbath.com
dir: *City centre near The Royal Crescent and The Circus*

Thrilling cooking in a Georgian gastro-pub

A short walk from the Georgian grandeur of Royal Crescent and The Circus, The Chequers has been in the business of providing drink and victuals since 1776. Nowadays, it wears the pared-back look of a switched on modern gastro-pub, with a calming pale colour scheme and much wood in evidence, from its herringbone parquet floor to tartan-cushioned church pews and plain tables, and sunshine streams in through large windows. Food is the core of the operation, with a serious kitchen sourcing all ingredients locally and making everything from scratch. Start with that old stager, salt and pepper squid with garlic aioli, if you like, but why not step outside the box of pub classics with something like seared scallops with smoked pork belly, cauliflower, candied lime and cumin velouté? A labour-intensive main course sees super-fresh lemon sole partnered with a crab bonbon and bisque, fennel, samphire, saffron potatoes and marinated tomato, or perhaps venison haunch with smoked garlic dauphinoise, red cabbage and blackberries. End on a high with burnt custard flavoured with mango, passionfruit and coconut.

Times 12-2.30/6-9.30, Closed 25 Dec

Allium Restaurant at The Abbey Hotel ✿✿✿

BATH   Map 4 ST76

Modern British
tel: 01225 461603 **1 North Pde BA1 1LF**
email: reservations@abbeyhotelbath.co.uk **web:** www.abbeyhotelbath.co.uk
dir: *M4 junct 18/A46 for approx 8m. At rdbt right onto A4 for 2m. Once past Morrisons stay in left lane & turn left at lights. Over bridge & right at lights. Over rdbt & right at lights. Hotel at end of road*

Stunning modern brasserie cooking in a Georgian hotel

Ian and Christa Taylor's classy Georgian townhouse hotel looks par for the course in Bath with its elegant 18th-century façade, but once you're through the pedimented portico, the place puts on a distinctly 21st-century face with its cool, clean-lined boutique style. The front terrace is a trump card for people watching on fine days, and modern art fans will find much to catch the eye inside, including one of Warhol's Marilyns to contemplate over pre- or post-dinner cocktails in the Artbar (there are 60-odd variations on the Gin & Tonic theme, for starters). The Allium Brasserie is the culinary focus of the operation, where purple velour seats, bare darkwood tables and bleached wood floors combine in a minimally cool big-city setting. The brasserie tag is deceptive here, since Chris Staines's fine-tuned contemporary cooking reworks classics with a fertile imagination, raising the bar well above the usual brasserie genre with creative global accents and skilful execution. Every element has been carefully considered in a confident starter of poached loin of veal matched, unusually, with tuna tartare, crisp radish and gem lettuce, artichoke hearts, lemon gel and tuna mayonnaise. Main course is a similarly multi-layered construction centred on perfectly-cooked stone bass embellished with salt-cod brandade, calamari, sea purslane and a deeply-flavoured dressing of tomato, orange, lemon and pink grapefruit that delivers explosions of distinct, vibrant flavours. Roast rump of lamb might be enlivened with the Mediterranean pizzazz of basil fregola, smoked ricotta and beetroot chutney. The same understanding of flavour contrasts makes desserts magical too – a textbook crème brûlée with a wafer-thin caramelised crust is matched with lightly-poached cherries with their gel and sorbet, and an almond frangipane cake.

Chef Chris Staines **Owner** Ian & Christa Taylor **Seats** 60, Pr/dining room 14 **Times** 12-3/5.30-9, **Prices** Fixed L 2 course fr £17.50, Fixed D 3 course fr £23.50, Starter £3.50-£9.50, Main £15-£24.50, Dessert £5-£7.50, Service optional **Wines** 82 bottles over £30, 4 bottles under £30, 16 by glass **Parking** Manvers St, Southgate Centre (charge made) **Notes** Fixed L/D 12-7, Afternoon tea, Sunday L £16-£18, Vegetarian available, Children welcome

The Bath Priory Hotel, Restaurant & Spa ✿✿✿

BATH   Map 4 ST76

Modern European, British v 🍷 NOTABLE WINE LIST
tel: 01225 331922 **Weston Rd BA1 2XT**
email: info@thebathpriory.co.uk **web:** www.thebathpriory.co.uk
dir: *Adjacent to Victoria Park*

Impeccable modern cooking in a gorgeously decorated house

The Gothic Regency grandeur of Bath Priory fits right in to the city's sweeping architectural landscape. Once you're over the threshold, though, the experience is more akin to a country-house hotel, with its luxurious and elegant interiors, four acres of glorious grounds and swanky spa – it is hard to imagine the city centre is only a short walk away. The restaurant, with its refined decor and views out over the manicured garden, is another string to the Priory's bow, with the kitchen headed up by Sam Moody. The hotel's kitchen garden provides plenty of the fruits, vegetables and herbs for the table, ticking the seasonal and local boxes, which suits Moody's style of gently contemporary cuisine. A tasting menu gives opportunity to put the kitchen through its paces. From the à la carte, a seared, creel-caught langoustine is served alongside confit pork belly, 'ketchup' and fennel, while another starter pairs roast Dorset veal sweetbreads with fresh black truffle, bitter leaves and finished with veal jus. Truffles may well crop up in main courses, too, where they're mixed with butter to enrich Cornish hake (partnered with salt brisket, sweet onion confit and ceps velouté). A meaty main course might be roast loin of Salisbury venison with artichoke and bacon gratin and an Armagnac sauce. Well-judged flavours and careful execution are features of desserts such as one that combines crispy pear with a cinnamon fritter, or another that matches salted caramel fondant with butterscotch and banana sorbet. The lunch menu is a tempting offer, especially on a warm summer's day, and the wine list is a fine piece of work with a global reach and good options by the glass.

Chef Sam Moody **Owner** Mr A Brownsword **Seats** 64, Pr/dining room 64 **Times** 12.30-2.30/6.30-9.30, **Prices** Fixed L 2 course £19.95, Fixed D 3 course £80, Tasting menu £90-£99, Starter £21.50, Main £38.50, Dessert £20, Service optional **Wines** 495 bottles over £30, 18 bottles under £30, 14 by glass **Parking** 40 **Notes** Tasting menu D 7 course, Menu surprise 11 course, Sunday L £30, Children 12 yrs+

BATH *continued*

The Circus Café and Restaurant

Modern British

tel: 01225 466020 **34 Brock St BA1 2LN**
email: ali@allgolden.co.uk
dir: *From West side of The Circus turn into Brock St, 2nd building on right heading towards the Royal Crescent*

Impressive upmarket cooking near the Royal Crescent

In a prime location between The Circus and Royal Crescent stands this upmarket all-day eatery, done out in a soothing shade of green, with modern art on the walls under a moulded ceiling. The monthly-changing menu is based on fine West Country produce and the kitchen team take inspiration from such culinary British greats as Jane Grigson and Joyce Molyneux. Start with a Med-inspired octopus dish with roasted peppers, and a caraway and coriander sauce, or a zesty undyed smoked haddock carpaccio. Among main courses, loin of venison is cooked as requested and arrives with parsnip purée and a red wine sauce enriched with Venezuelan chocolate, and calves' liver is served pink with a piquant sherry and grain mustard gravy. There's always a fish option, and among puddings might be warm rice pudding with honey-coated figs and cardamom, or a sorbet flavoured with Campari and grapefruit.

Chef Alison Golden, Máté Andrasko **Owner** Alison Golden **Seats** 50, Pr/dining room 32 **Times** 10am-mdnt, All-day dining, Closed 3 wks from 24 Dec, Sun **Prices** Fixed L 2 course £15, Starter £6.50-£6.90, Main £16.30-£18.70, Dessert £4.70-£6.50, Service optional **Wines** 11 bottles over £30, 20 bottles under £30, 6 by glass **Parking** On street, NCP Charlotte St **Notes** ALC D, Vegetarian available, Children 10 yrs+

The Combe Grove Manor Hotel

British, European

tel: 01225 834644 **Brassknocker Hill, Monkton Combe BA2 7HS**
email: combegrovemanor@thehotelcollection.co.uk **web:** www.thehotelcollection.co.uk
dir: *Exit A36 at Limpley Stoke onto Brassknocker Hill. Hotel 0.5m up hill on left*

Well-judged and inventive country-house cooking

A beautifully proportioned Georgian manor of mellow stone with 69 acres of gardens and woodland, Combe Grove boasts a driving range, tennis, a health club and both indoor and outdoor pools. There's also a brasserie and The Georgian Room restaurant, where pale blue walls, white-painted half-panelling and swagged curtains give a fresh and calming look. Consistently high standards from the kitchen are what to expect, with quality apparent in the raw materials. A warm Scotch egg with crispy bacon, grilled tomatoes and London (home-made brown) sauce is a novel starter, rather like a mini breakfast, but more typical of the style is smoked haddock brandade with a quail's egg and curried mayonnaise. Main courses are generally updated versions of tried-and-tested combinations: perhaps tender haunch of venison with rich chocolate sauce accompanied by sweet potato purée, beetroot game chips and juniper-flavoured cabbage, or pan-fried fillet of red mullet with chorizo, saffron arancini, parsnip purée and pak choi. Incidentals like bread get nods of approval as do puddings like orange and cardamom crème brûlée.

Times 12-2/7-9.30

The Dower House Restaurant

– see below

The Dower House Restaurant

BATH   **Map 4 ST76**

Modern British V

tel: 01225 823333 **The Royal Crescent Hotel & Spa, 16 Royal Crescent BA1 2LS**
email: info@royalcrescent.co.uk **web:** www.royalcrescent.co.uk
dir: *From A4, right at lights. 2nd left onto Bennett St. Continue into The Circus, 2nd exit onto Brock St*

Stimulating modern dishes in a luxury hotel

The Dower House Restaurant is in the acre of garden behind the luxury hotel in the centre of Bath's iconic crescent from which it takes its name. As expected in a hotel of this calibre, it's refined, elegant and comfortable, with flowers on well-spaced tables, a carpeted floor, soft furnishings of blue and gold and French windows opening on to the garden – perfect in summer. Service is on the formal side, with uniformed staff knowledgeable and willing, while a sommelier is on hand to help with choosing wines. Head chef David Campbell describes his style as a 'modern take on classic favourites', which modestly overlooks the high degree of creativity and imagination – as well as labour – of his cooking. Smoked trout, for instance, comes with variations on cucumber, horseradish pannacotta, samphire and caviar, a vibrant start to a meal. Dishes are complex without being ostentatious, with no attempt to pile on ingredients for the sake of novelty or innovation. Ibérico ham comes with a slow-cooked egg, leeks, Wiltshire truffles and, a playful touch, duck-fat soldiers. It could be followed by a well-considered theme on pork: loin of suckling pig, soft and deeply flavoured, with crisp-skinned belly and a spicy croquette accompanied by soya-glazed shiitaki, pak choi and a sesame-flavoured jus. Timings are of pinpoint accuracy, as ever seen to best effect in fish: perhaps fillet of Cornish sea bass with crispy mussels, cauliflower cheese and mussel velouté, a main course of well-defined flavours. Breads are must-haves, as are amuse-bouche and pre-desserts served before the real thing: perhaps peach parfait with scorched poached fruit, warm rosemary sponge and pistachio brittle, all elements enhancing without swamping each other.

Chef David Campbell **Owner** Topland (Royal Crescent Hotel) Ltd **Seats** 60, Pr/dining room 20 **Times** 7-9.30, Closed L all week **Prices** Prices not confirmed, Service optional **Wines** 200 bottles over £30, 18 bottles under £30, 10 by glass **Parking** 17, Charlotte St (charge for on site parking) **Notes** Pre-theatre menu, Tasting menu, Children welcome

BATH *continued*

The Hare & Hounds

◉ Modern British

tel: 01225 482682 **Lansdown Rd BA1 5TJ**
email: info@hareandhoundsbath.com **web:** www.hareandhoundsbath.com
dir: *M4 to A46 Bath for 4m, right A420 Bristol. After 0.8m take left to Bath Racecourse for 1.5m, then left towards Bath. Hare & Hounds on left in 2.5m*

Impressive committed cooking with glorious views

A mile and a half north of Bath, The Hare & Hounds is an enticing bolt-hole away from the city's bustle, with glorious views from its hilltop location. Huge leaded windows look over the terrace and catch the views in the neat interior, where wood proliferates: tables, chairs, panelling and floor. Relaxed and informal it may be, but the kitchen has a serious commitment to food and draws on top-grade produce. Starters include a slab of exemplary duck terrine, served with hazelnut salad and fig chutney, and crab and cod fishcakes with mango and chilli salsa. Main courses run the gamut from beer-battered haddock with chips and tartare sauce, through twice-baked cheese soufflé with pear and watercress salad and braised chicory, to full-blooded braised ox cheek with bourguignon garnish plus potato creamed with horseradish and root vegetables. Desserts are a strong suit too: try salted caramel tart with mandarin gel.

Times 12-3/5.30-9

Jamie's Italian

◉ Modern Italian

tel: 01225 432340 **10 Milsom Place BA1 1BZ**
email: bath.office@jamiesitalian.com
dir: *From A4 follow signs to city centre. Opposite Jolly's department store*

Jamie's winning way with real Italian food

The formula is a simple one: find a nice building (a Georgian one in the case of Jamie's Bath branch), fit it out with a trendy rustic look and run it with a wholesome lack of formality. The format clearly works, judging by the queues that build at busy times (bookings are taken for large groups only). This popularity brings a sure fire buzz to both floors of the place, matched by the energy and enthusiasm of the staff. As elsewhere in the chain, fresh, rustic Italian dishes are what the kitchen deals in, built on well-sourced raw materials. Sharing planks of excellent cured meats, Italian cheeses, pickles and vegetables make a popular opener. Then it's on to pasta, which is made fresh each day — porcini fettuccini , say, or a main-course of chicken milanese. End on Arctic Swiss roll with a chocolate mascarpone centre and butterscotch sauce.

Chef Eric Bernard **Owner** Jamie's Italian **Seats** 180 **Times** 12-11, All-day dining, Closed 25-26 Dec **Prices** Starter £3.95-£6.95, Main £10.95-£22.95, Dessert £4.95-£5.25, Service optional **Wines** 16 by glass **Parking** Podium car park Walcot St (A3039) **Notes** Vegetarian available, Children welcome

Macdonald Bath Spa

◉◉ Modern British **v**

tel: 01225 444424 **Sydney Rd BA2 6JF**
email: sales.bathspa@macdonald-hotels.co.uk
web: www.macdonald-hotels.co.uk/bathspa
dir: *From A4 follow city centre signs for 1m. At lights left signed A36. Turn right after pedestrian crossing, left into Sydney Place. Hotel 200yds on right*

Well-judged menu in grand Georgian hotel

The city of Bath has been about spa treatments and self-indulgence since Roman times, and the Bath Spa hotel keeps the tradition alive with an array of hydro-therapy facilities for 21st-century sybarites. Its majestic Georgian façade sets a grand tone, and it all looks over landscaped gardens. The classy Vellore Restaurant is in the original ballroom, with a high-domed ceiling, pillars and all round stately air. There's also a canopied outdoor terrace, plus engaging staff and a helpful sommelier keep things on track. The kitchen extracts the best from carefully-sourced ingredients, delivering well-conceived and unfussy dishes. Grilled mackerel comes with compressed cucumber cannelloni filled with crab and horseradish cream, or the seasonal approach may bring wild garlic soup with truffle oil. Next up, saddle of Highland lamb with an olive stuffing arrives with velvety sweetbreads, rosemary polenta and red pepper piperade, or there might be roast cod with salt-cod brandade, asparagus, vanilla raisins and confit chicken wing. To finish, chocolate marquise is served with lavender ice cream and cherries.

Chef Andrew Britton **Owner** Macdonald Hotels **Seats** 80, Pr/dining room 120 **Times** 12-10, All-day dining, Closed L Mon-Sat **Prices** Prices not confirmed **Wines** 140 bottles over £30, 20 bottles under £30, 12 by glass **Parking** 160 **Notes** Sunday L, Children welcome

Marlborough Tavern

◎◎ Modern British

tel: 01225 423731 **35 Marlborough Buildings BA1 2LY**
email: info@marlborough-tavern.com **web:** www.marlborough-tavern.com
dir: *200mtrs from W end of Royal Crescent, on corner of Marlborough Buildings*

Seasonal cooking and proper beer

Just a short stroll from the iconic Royal Crescent, this straight-talking foodie pub still functions as a watering hole with a pleasingly unstuffy vibe and local ales and ciders on tap for the drinkers. The decor mixes retro wooden tables with panels painted in heritage hues, while lively modern menus offer a daily-changing roster that could be as simple as home-made burgers or fish and chips, or at the more gastro end, a five-course tasting menu with matching wines. The latter sets out with a riff on the various colours and flavours of beetroot matched with goats' cheese pannacotta, poached fig and toasted walnut, progressing via scallops with confit pork belly, celeriac purée and hazelnut butter. Next comes a main course of tarragon and mustard-crusted Red Ruby beef fillet with creamy smoked garlic mash, wild mushrooms, crispy shallot rings and port and thyme jus. Toffee apple cake with salted caramel, cider brandy ice cream, brings proceedings to a close. Bag a table in the lovely courtyard garden when weather allows.

Times 12-2.30/6-10, Closed 25 Dec, D Sun

Menu Gordon Jones

◎◎ Innovative British **NEW** v

tel: 01225 480871 **2 Wellsway BA2 3AQ**
email: info@menugordonjones.co.uk
dir: *5 mins from city centre up Wells Rd (A367), restaurant in corner of road opposite local shops*

Avante-garde cooking from a rising star

The local dining scene in Bath is not short of gastronomic excitement, but this newcomer has certainly made a splash. Gordon Jones has form in Bath, having run the kitchen in the Royal Crescent Hotel. Now he's doing his own thing in an unassuming little spot with foodies beating a path to the door. It's no good being in a hurry: the deal is no-choice, five- and six-course surprise menus that change from one day to the next, so settle in and let Jones's clever, off-the-wall combinations work their magic. A starter of 'mushroom cappuccino' (cep mousse, smoked milk foam and parmesan madeleine), might be followed by a carnival of flavours and textures delivered in eye-catching compositions, among them perhaps cured sea trout with popcorn, marmalade purée, cucumber, cauliflower couscous, oca de Peru tubers, capers and mayonnaise. Then squab pigeon may arrive with wheat berries, spinach, mushroom, onion, crispy 'brick' bread and chervil root. Desserts follow the multi-layered approach, perhaps teaming toffee apple mousse with a cinnamon doughnut, white chocolate shards and blackcurrant sorbet.

Chef Gordon Jones **Owner** Gordon & Armi Jones **Seats** 22
Times 12.30-2/7-9, Closed 35 days a year (variable), Sun-Mon **Prices** Tasting menu £40-£60, Service optional **Wines** 22 bottles over £30, 10 bottles under £30, 6 by glass **Parking** On street **Notes** Tasting menu L 5 course, D 6 course, Sunday L, Children 12 yrs+

The Olive Tree at the Queensberry Hotel

◎◎◎ — see page 470

Woods Restaurant

◎ Modern British, French

tel: 01225 314812 & 422493 **9-13 Alfred St BA1 2QX**
email: woodsinbath@gmail.com
dir: *Phone for directions*

Contemporary bistro cooking in a Georgian setting

First opening its doors in 1979, Woods has stood the test of time, showing perhaps that quality lasts. It's a very 'Bath' setting, occupying the ground floor of five Georgian townhouses, and the comfortable bistro look is pretty much timeless. They're not adverse to change, though, with a bar menu a useful addition to the repertoire. The cooking is broadly European, with French and Italy to the fore, and a British flavour here and there. A first course dish of grilled Whitelake goats' curd with red pepper confit, crushed hazelnuts and vanilla honey is a vibrant construction, or go for home-cured peppered salmon with beetroot yogurt and baby curd. Confit of chicken leg with peas, Dijon mustard and a herby cream sauce is a bistro classic, or there might be Brixham crab linguine with a red Thai curry sauce and baby coriander. Finish with New York-style cheesecake with raspberry sauce.

Times 12-2.30/5-10, Closed 25-26 Dec, D Sun

CASTLE CARY
Map 4 ST63

The Pilgrims

◉◉ Modern British V

tel: 01963 240597 **Lovington BA7 7PT**
email: jools@thepilgrimsatlovington.co.uk **web:** www.thepilgrimsatlovington.co.uk
dir: On B3153, 1.5m E of lights on A37 at Lydford

Impeccable West Country produce in a stone-built village inn

The name honours those brave souls who passed this way in centuries gone by on their quest to find King Arthur's tomb. How times change: the stone-built inn has been reinvented these days as a welcoming restaurant with rooms, run with cheerful bonhomie by the Mitchisons – Sally taking care of front of house and Jools running the kitchen with the eminently sound ethos that the most important quality in a chef is restraint. The place is a hive of activity, and a showcase for excellent local suppliers, thus Lyme Bay crabmeat forms the flavour-packed filling for crisp-crumbed deep-fried crab cakes with bagnarotte sauce, followed by an exemplary slab of fresh turbot, whose sheer quality is allowed to do the talking alongside the simple accompaniments of asparagus, white sprouting broccoli, Jersey Royals and saffron crème fraîche. Meatier fare runs to pork in a blanket – full-flavoured tenderloin stuffed with Toulouse sausage, alongside black pudding and prunes macerated in cider brandy. Dessert is a simple but effective pear frangipane tart with vanilla ice cream.

Chef Julian Mitchison **Owner** Julian & Sally Mitchison **Seats** 25
Times 12-3/7-11, Closed Sun-Mon (ex BHs & L last Sun of month), L Tue-Thu
Prices Starter £6-£9, Main £14-£25, Dessert £6-£8, Service optional **Wines** 7
bottles over £30, 21 bottles under £30, 15 by glass **Parking** 40 **Notes** Sunday L £15-£25, Children welcome

CHEW MAGNA
Map 4 ST56

The Pony & Trap

◉◉ Modern British

tel: 01275 332627 **Knowle Hill BS40 8TQ**
email: info@theponyandtrap.co.uk
dir: Take A37 S from Bristol. After Pensford turn right at rdbt onto A368 towards Weston-Super-Mare. In 1.5m right signed Chew Magna & Winford. Pub 1m on right

Stonking modern pub food in a country cottage inn

Chef Josh Eggleton is becoming quite a household name these days after his storming 2014 telly performance on the *Great British Menu*. Away from the limelight, he is to be found at the stoves in The Pony & Trap, a revitalised 200-year-old country cottage pub in lush Chew Valley countryside. The classic pubby bar is an appealing venue with its no-nonsense bare wooden tables, or you could trade up to the restaurant with its slate floors, white linen and countryside views. Wherever you sit, the menu stays the same: big-hearted food from a chef who bangs the drum for local produce, and shows an innate feel for what works with what. A summer's lunch kicks off with chilled courgette soup poured around crab mayonnaise and pointed up with wild chive oil and wood sorrel. Next, a piggy plateful of rare breed pork chop, pulled pork shoulder, home-made 'hodge podge' black pudding, crackling and cauliflower purée hits the spot. For pudding, there's a refreshing key lime pie with lemongrass sorbet.

Chef Josh Eggleton **Owner** Josh Eggleton **Seats** 60 **Times** 12-2.30/6.30-9.30
Prices Starter £7.50-£9, Main £10.50-£22, Dessert £4-£6.50, Service optional
Wines 14 bottles over £30, 45 bottles under £30, 26 by glass **Parking** 40
Notes Tasting menu 7 course, Sunday L £16-£18.50, Vegetarian available,
Children welcome

The Olive Tree at the Queensberry Hotel ◉◉◉

BATH
Map 4 ST76

Modern British V 🍷 **NOTABLE WINE LIST**
tel: 01225 447928 **Russel St BA1 2QF**
email: reservations@olivetreebath.co.uk
web: www.olivetreebath.co.uk
dir: 100mtrs from the Assembly Rooms

Confident modern British cooking in a Georgian townhouse hotel

At the Queensberry Hotel, Laurence and Helen Beere have created one of Bath's most appealing addresses. The finish within is a winning combination of traditional and contemporary, creating civilised spaces that seem almost timeless, with a major revamp taking place as we write. The Olive Tree restaurant is down in the basement, but none the worse for it, and has long been one of the city's top dining venues. The kitchen – headed up by Chris Cleghorn – is particularly sensitive to dietary requirements with a bespoke dairy- and gluten-free menu, where you might start with duck liver (poached and roasted) with pickled rhubarb, shiitaki mushrooms and candied walnut and move on to halibut with braised chicory and sweet potato purée. There's an impressive vegetarian menu, too. The à la carte offers similarly contemporary dishes and shows evidence of a genuine commitment to West Country produce. Flavour combinations are well considered and classically inspired – crab lasagne, for example, with a crab mousse and bisque, followed by a main course loin of venison with quince purée, smoked bacon and spiced red cabbage. Desserts also hit the mark, delivering the comfort of hot chocolate fondant with pistachio ice cream and zingy exotic flavours via a mango soufflé with lemongrass and mango sorbet. The lively wine list contains much that catches the eye.

Chef Chris Cleghorn **Owner** Mr & Mrs Beere **Seats** 60, Pr/dining room 30
Times 12-2/7-10, Closed L Mon-Thu **Prices** Fixed L 2 course £21, Starter £9.50-£14.50, Main £19-£26.50, Dessert £8.25-£9.50 **Wines** 320 bottles over £30, 17
bottles under £30, 34 by glass **Parking** On street (meter) **Notes** Sunday L £21-£26, Children welcome

COMBE HAY
Map 4 ST75

The Wheatsheaf Combe Hay
Modern British V

tel: 01225 833504 **BA2 7EG**
email: info@wheatsheafcombehay.com **web:** www.wheatsheafcombehay.com
dir: *A367 towards Shepton Mallet, left at park & ride rdbt, follow signs Combe Hay Village*

Popular country inn with accomplished cooking

'Contemporary rustic chic' is how the proprietors describe the style of their 16th-century pub in large gardens overlooking the village, borne out by sofas in front of an inglenook, bare wooden tables on the boarded floor and vibrant artwork on plain walls, some half-panelled, some of rough stone. The kitchen has a generally modern British outlook and adds a dash of ingenuity to its dishes, turning out starters like wild rabbit ravioli with carrot and star anise, and seared scallops with fennel purée and a matching bhaji. Quality is clear at every turn, and the kitchen delivers successful main courses with the minimum of fuss: breast of guinea fowl, for instance, is poached in Sauternes and partnered by truffled mash and wild mushroom cassoulet. Fillet of brill is given an added zing from chorizo-crushed potatoes and watercress pesto. Meals end cheerfully with the likes of treacle tart, or chocolate delice with exotic fruit salad.

Chef Eddy Rains **Owner** Ian Barton **Seats** 55 **Times** 12-2/6.30-9, Closed Xmas, 1st wk Jan, Mon, D Sun **Prices** Fixed L 2 course £15.50, Fixed D 3 course £22.50, Starter £7-£10, Main £13-£25, Dessert £6-£10, Service optional 10% **Wines** 113 bottles over £30, 33 bottles under £30, 13 by glass **Parking** 100 **Notes** Sunday L £19.50-£24.50, Children welcome

CORTON DENHAM
Map 4 ST62

The Queens Arms
Modern British

tel: 01963 220317 **DT9 4LR**
email: relax@thequeensarms.com **web:** www.thequeensarms.com
dir: *A303 exit Chapel Cross signed South Cadbury & Corton Denham. Follow signs to South Cadbury. Through village, after 0.25m turn left up hill signed Sherborne & Corton Denham. Left at top of hill, pub at end of village on right*

Enterprising West Country cooking in a charming country pub

A mellow stone 18th-century inn amid buxom hills on the Somerset-Dorset border, The Queen's Arms is an inviting prospect. Inside, things just get better and better. There are local ciders and ales on tap, those with muddy boots and dogs are not shown the door, a wood-burning stove provides the heat, and the mismatched furniture has a nicely lived-in feel. The kitchen comes up trumps thanks to an appealing menu of skilful pub classics and sharply executed restaurant-style dishes. A glance at the menu shows a clear love for local produce and a creative mind, starting with pan-roasted scallops with tempura soft-shelled-crab, salsa rossa and Serrano ham. Main course loin and braised haunch of locally-shot venison goes down a treat with shallot and garlic purée, salsify, pommes Anna, chargrilled broccoli and a rich, sweet date jus. Or there could be pan-fried John Dory with chicken and smoked bacon mousse, oyster and Pernod velouté, brown shrimps and spinach gnocchi. For dessert, lemon meringue tart is allied with cherry sorbet.

Chef Ben Abercombie **Owner** Jeanette & Gordon Reid **Seats** 78, Pr/dining room 45 **Times** 12-3/6-10, Closed D 1 Jan **Prices** Prices not confirmed, Service optional **Wines** 19 bottles over £30, 25 bottles under £30, 21 by glass **Parking** 20 **Notes** Meal deal film offer £12.50, Sunday L, Vegetarian available, Children welcome

DULVERTON
Map 3 SS92

Tarr Farm Inn
Modern British

tel: 01643 851507 **Tarr Steps, Liscombe TA22 9PY**
email: enquiries@tarrfarm.co.uk **web:** www.tarrfarm.co.uk
dir: *6m NW of Dulverton. Off B3223 signed Tarr Steps, signs to Tarr Farm Inn*

Gently tweaked country cooking on the River Barle

In the heart of Exmoor, in 40 acres of its own, Tarr Farm is a Tudor inn standing immediately above the Tarr Steps bridge over the river Barle. A hub for the shooting and fishing brigades, it's a good place to find traditional English cooking given a gentle tweak of modernity. There's a palpable sense that each dish knows what it's about, as when glazed spatchcocked quail comes with potato salad for a full-flavoured opener, or when a bounty of shellfish – clams and prawns as well as mussels – go into classic marinière. Fish shows up well at main too, for grilled John Dory and crayfish bonne femme with orange-soaked raisins, while rump of moorland lamb arrives with dauphinoise, shallots and confit garlic in Madeira jus. All a perfectly creamy pannacotta needs to offset it is the sharpness of a slew of stewed blueberries, and simple satisfaction is assured.

Chef Christopher Bury **Owner** Hilary Lester **Seats** 50, Pr/dining room 20 **Times** 12-3/6.30-12, Closed 1-10 Feb **Prices** Starter £4.95-£7.95, Main £11.95-£22.50, Dessert £4.50-£6.50, Service optional **Wines** 58 bottles over £30, 42 bottles under £30, 12 by glass **Parking** 40 **Notes** Sunday L £4.95-£16.95, Vegetarian available, Children 10 yrs+

Woods Bar & Dining Room
Modern British, French

tel: 01398 324007 **4 Banks Square TA22 9BU**
email: woodsdulverton@hotmail.com
dir: *From Tiverton take A396 N. At Machine Cross take B3222 to Dulverton. Establishment adjacent to church*

Locally-sourced cooking in a rural Somerset inn

On the edge of Exmoor, Woods is a pub cunningly disguised on the outside to look like a café. The interior scene is cheered with a log fire in winter, and wooden partitions roughly divide the place between the drinking of local ales and the eating of locally-sourced food. There are light lunches and bar snacks in the daylight hours, and in the evenings the kitchen takes wing with intricately worked modern British cooking. Start with a tart of seasonal woodcock, garnished with prosciutto and puréed dates in Madeira sauce, ahead of roast ling fillet with mussels, clams, almonds, bacon and broccoli. Or try a protean trio of lamb – shoulder, loin and faggot – with Jerusalem artichoke purée, cavolo nero, spiced onion fondue and thyme sauce. At meal's end, it could be classic sticky toffee pudding with clotted cream, or a choice from home-made ice cream and sorbet flavours such as liquorice, white peach, and apple and star anise.

Times 12-2/7-9.30, Closed 25 Dec

EXFORD
Map 3 SS83

Crown Hotel

◉ Modern British

tel: 01643 831554 **Park St TA24 7PP**
email: info@crownhotelexmoor.co.uk **web:** www.crownhotelexmoor.co.uk
dir: *From Taunton take A38 to A358. Turn left at B3224 & follow signs to Exford*

Good full-flavoured cooking in a handsome coaching inn

The 17th-century Crown sits at the heart of pretty Exford Village, in three acres of grounds surrounded by countryside and moorland – huntin', shootin' fishin' territory, where horses clip-clop by and every other vehicle seems to be a 4x4. Naturally, then, this is a dog- and horse-friendly establishment, where the bar (complete with stag's head) makes an appealingly rustic spot for a pre-dinner drink, or you could tuck into hearty pub classics. But in the elegant dining room the kitchen cranks things up a notch or two. Free-range and organic local meat and fish get a good showing in full-flavoured dishes cooked with flair and precision. First out is pan-fried scallops with pancetta and cauliflower and pea purée, followed by crispy-skinned confit duck leg with Savoy cabbage, fondant potato, roasted root vegetables and port sauce. Raspberry pannacotta with a zingy exotic fruit salad and lime sorbet brings it all to a satisfying close.

Chef Raza Muhammad **Owner** Mr C Kirkbride, S & D Whittaker **Seats** 45, Pr/dining room 20 **Times** 6.45-9.15, Closed L all week **Prices** Prices not confirmed, Service optional **Wines** 20 bottles over £30, 12 bottles under £30, 19 by glass **Parking** 30 **Notes** Sunday L, Vegetarian available, Children welcome

HINTON CHARTERHOUSE
Map 4 ST75

Homewood Park Hotel & Spa

◉◉ British

tel: 01225 723731 **Abbey Ln BA2 7TB**
email: info@homewoodpark.co.uk **web:** www.homewoodpark.co.uk
dir: *6m SE of Bath on A36, turn left at 2nd sign for Freshford*

Impressive culinary artistry in ten acres of parkland

A few miles outside Bath, Homewood came to prominence during the first wave of the country-hotel movement in the 1980s. Its 10 acres of parkland and immaculate gardens surround an elegant house that's a Georgian-Victorian amalgam, done in contemporary chic with unclothed tables and rustic-looking upholstery in the dining room. The chef takes the modern British bull by the horns for dishes that are presented with impressive artistry and allow the quality of each component to shine out. That can be seen straight away in an opening serving of glazed pig's cheek with cheddar pommes purée and chard, a finely judged dish that could easily be halfway to a main. When main course itself arrives, it could be crisp-skinned sea bream, briefly seared and served with baby squid and samphire in assertive lemongrass foam, or maybe rack and braised shank of lamb with minted pea purée and shallots. Abandon all obligation to choose at dessert stage with an assiette comprising blackberry parfait, white chocolate mousse, almond marshmallow and various froths and berries, presented with painstaking precision.

Times 12-2.30/6.30-9.30

HOLCOMBE
Map 4 ST64

The Holcombe Inn

◉ British, International, French

tel: 01761 232478 **Stratton Rd BA3 5EB**
email: bookings@holcombeinn.co.uk **web:** www.holcombeinn.co.uk
dir: *From Bath or Shepton Mallet take A367 (Fosse Way) to Stratton. Follow inn signs*

Welcoming country inn with classic and modern menu

A little to the south of Bath, but out in the soft-focus Somerset countryside, The Holcombe is a textbook country inn. Behind the white façade lies a warmly welcoming place with winter fires, local ales and amicable staff. Regional ingredients, including the produce of its own garden, supply the menus of mostly traditional fare, where traditional is understood to include some of the modern classic dishes of the past generation. Scallops with cauliflower and spiced aubergine, or salt-and-pepper squid with salad and aïoli, are well-turned-out starters, while the main business might extend to noisette and braised neck of lamb with vegetable tagine and quinoa. Stick with fish for main, and you could be in for herb-crusted cod alongside dauphinoise and sprouting broccoli in a dressing of tomato and basil. Desserts get creative with a raspberry and nougat parfait choc ice to accompany Valrhona brownie and candied hazelnuts.

Chef Dan Kings **Owner** Julie Berry **Seats** 65 **Times** 12-2.30/6.30-9, Closed D 25-26 Dec **Prices** Service optional **Wines** 9 bottles over £30, 30 bottles under £30, 16 by glass **Parking** 30 **Notes** Breakfast on booking, Sunday L £12.95-£14.95, Vegetarian available, Children welcome

HUNSTRETE
Map 4 ST66

THE PIG near Bath

◉◉ Modern British **NEW** v

tel: 01761 490490 **Hunstrete House, Pensford BS39 4NS**
email: info@thepignearbath.com **web:** www.thepighotel.com
dir: *On A368, 8m from Bath*

Hyper-local food in a switched-on country house

At first sight, The Pig appears to be the archetypal English country-house hotel set in beautiful Mendips countryside, a splendid Georgian mansion within tranquil acres where deer roam free. Inside, however, the style is shabby-chic instead of chintz, the mood is chilled and hip rather than starchy, and the whole operation has food at its heart. The kitchen sources its materials from within a 25-mile radius, with much of the produce covering far less ground, brought in fresh from The Pig's greenhouses and gardens or foraged from fields and woods. There's nothing fancy going on here, no froths or gels, just combinations that make perfect sense, as in a starter of monkfish cheek and scallops with spinach and peas, or a classic main-course trio of chargrilled 35-day aged rib-eye with well-made béarnaise and triple-cooked chips. Desserts continue to toe the local, seasonal line, offering forced rhubarb – poached and in a fluffy mousse – with buttermilk sorbet. The setting is a Victorian-style greenhouse dining room, after cocktails served in jam jars in the bar.

Chef Kamil Oseka **Owner** Home Grown Hotels Ltd **Seats** 90, Pr/dining room 22 **Times** 12-2.30/6.30-9.30 **Prices** Starter £6-£8, Main £11-£22, Dessert £3.50-£7 **Wines** 100 bottles over £30, 60 bottles under £30, 20 by glass **Parking** 50 **Notes** Sunday L, Children welcome

LOWER VOBSTER
Map 4 ST74

The Vobster Inn
◉◉ British, European

tel: 01373 812920 **BA3 5RJ**
email: info@vobsterinn.co.uk web: www.vobsterinn.co.uk
dir: *4m W of Frome, between Wells & Leigh upon Mendip*

Traditional pub food with a Spanish, Italian and French twist

Surrounded by the patchwork fields and rolling hills of greenest Somerset, Lower Vobster is home to this friendly rural pub with rooms. Diving lessons at the nearby quay are a lure, and in the true spirit of country hospitality, the place is host to all manner of special offers and quiz nights. The chef-proprietor's Spanish heritage is reflected in the tapas and main courses such as pork belly with fabada asturiana, but things modulate into the Italian quite smoothly too, for well-judged crab and chilli linguine, or smoked haddock risotto topped with a poached egg. Nibble on Catalan-style tomato bread to get the taste buds working, before setting about a starter such as fried Loire goats' cheese dressed with the inn's own honey, or French onion soup served with red pepper bruschetta. Underpinning the whole show is a solid vein of traditional British pubbery, from rollmops with tracklements to steak and chips, and plaice with brown shrimps. The appealing dessert range takes in apple and plum crumble with double cream, as well as chocolate pannacotta with peach sorbet.

Chef Rafael F Davila **Owner** Rafael F Davila **Seats** 40, Pr/dining room 40 **Times** 12-3/6.30-11, Closed 25 Dec, Mon (check at BHs), D Sun **Prices** Fixed L 2 course £10, Starter £5.50-£8.50, Main £9.95-£18.50, Dessert £5.95, Service optional **Wines** 12 by glass **Parking** 60 **Notes** Sunday L fr £11.50, Vegetarian available, Children welcome

MIDSOMER NORTON
Map 4 ST65

BEST WESTERN PLUS Centurion Hotel
◉ Modern British

tel: 01761 417711 & 412214 **Charlton Ln BA3 4BD**
email: enquiries@centurionhotel.co.uk web: www.centurionhotel.co.uk
dir: *Phone for directions*

Golfing hotel with careful, confident cooking

This modern family-run hotel, with a health club and swimming pool, has had a bit of a makeover. The restaurant, overlooking the hotel's own nine-hole golf course, remains an inviting space, with a bright conservatory extension. The atmosphere here is relaxed and welcoming, with helpful and friendly service, while the carefully assembled menus are full of appealing options. A platter of cured meats with mozzarella and sun-dried tomatoes is one way to begin, or go for seared scallops fashionably partnered by bacon with avocado. Traditionalists could follow on with a steak from the grill and a choice of sauces. Moroccan-style lamb with rice is another possibility for meat-eaters, with something like wild mushroom and squash ravioli for vegetarians. All comers can conclude with one of the choose-me puddings such as an assiette of Yorkshire rhubarb, or caramelised pear rice pudding.

Chef Sean Horwood **Owner** L&F Jones Holdings Ltd **Seats** 60, Pr/dining room 120 **Times** 12-2/6-9.30, Closed 25-26 Dec, D Sun **Prices** Fixed D 3 course £25, Starter £6-£8, Main £12-£25, Dessert £6-£11 **Wines** 9 bottles over £30, 19 bottles under £30, 7 by glass **Parking** 100 **Notes** Sunday L £21-£31, Vegetarian available, Children welcome

MILVERTON
Map 3 ST12

The Globe
◉ Modern British

tel: 01823 400534 **Fore St TA4 1JX**
email: adele@theglobemilverton.co.uk web: www.theglobemilverton.co.uk
dir: *M5 junct 26 onto A38, then B3187 to Milverton*

Hearty country-pub cooking

The Globe is still very much a pub. You won't be ostracised for just wanting to prop up the bar, but it's a strong food destination too. The stolid stone-built façade with stepped window surrounds sets more of a period tone than the modernised interior of the main dining room, with its gathered drapes and contemporary artworks. The food is up-to-date country-pub fare, from fried chicken livers in sherry cream sauce, or cheddar and chive soufflé with walnut salad, to start. Move on to hearty main dishes such as enticingly gamey roast pheasant with smoked bacon and parsnip purée in a redcurrant sauce that stops usefully short of being too sweet. Sundays bring on traditionally garnished roasts – beef topside, lamb leg, pork – with roasties and Yorkshire, while Somerset apple cake with matching compôte and cream takes care of the pudding business.

Chef Mark Tarry, Kaan Atasoy **Owner** Mark & Adele Tarry **Seats** 50 **Times** 12-3/6-11.30, Closed L Mon, D Sun **Prices** Starter £6.50-£7.95, Main £10.95-£18.95, Dessert £5.95-£6.95, Service optional **Wines** 2 bottles over £30, 25 bottles under £30, 10 by glass **Parking** 3 **Notes** Sunday L fr £10.95, Vegetarian available, Children welcome

MONKSILVER
Map 3 ST03

The Notley Arms Inn
◉ Classic British

tel: 01984 656095 **Front St TA4 4JB**
email: notleyarmsinn@hotmail.com web: www.notleyarmsinn.co.uk
dir: *From A358 at Bishop's Lydeard onto B3224. After 5m turn right onto B3188 to Monksilver*

Stimulating well-flavoured cooking in village inn

A refurb has given a bright, fresh look to this whitewashed village inn. There are chesterfields at an open fire and a mix of dining chairs and pew-style seating at sturdy wooden tables; attentive staff genuinely engage with customers, adding to the enjoyable experience. The kitchen makes a virtue of its location by using local produce, and turns out some eloquently flavoured dishes, among them starters of ham hock terrine with mustard mayonnaise, pressed apples and pickled mushrooms, and goats' cheese mousse with candied walnuts and beetroot and celery salad. Dishes are assembled in the modern idiom and well executed: seared sea bass fillet, for instance, with a subtle saffron sauce, Bombay potatoes and buttery spinach, and confit duck leg with sticky red cabbage, curly kale and five spice sauce. Some pub stalwarts like fish and chips might be added to the mix, and to finish there may be smooth and silky lemon tart with raspberry sauce and passionfruit sorbet.

Chef Barrie Tucker **Owner** Simon & Caroline Murphy **Seats** 55 **Times** 12-2.30/6-9.30 **Prices** Starter £5-£8, Main £7-£20, Dessert £4-£8 **Wines** 7 bottles over £30, 25 bottles under £30, 12 by glass **Parking** 20 **Notes** Breakfast, Afternoon tea, Sunday L, Vegetarian available, Children welcome

NORTH WOOTTON
Map 4 ST54

Crossways

◉ Modern British

tel: 01749 899000 **Stocks Ln BA4 4EU**
email: enquiries@thecrossways.co.uk **web:** www.thecrossways.co.uk
dir: Exit M5 junct 22 towards Shepton Mallet, 0.2m from Pilton

Classy country inn with local ingredients and a Mediterranean twist

A thoroughly contemporary kind of inn these days, the 18th-century Crossways looks much the same as it always has from the outside, but a 21st-century makeover within has opened-up the place, bringing soothing neutrally-toned modernity. There's a splash of terracotta in the floor-tiles of the dining area, though, (after all, the place is Italian owned). It's the kind of place where you can eat what you want where you want, and there's a children's menu, too. The chef, who isn't Italian as it happens, makes a big play for local and regional ingredients, with Somerset's finest on show, but there's a Mediterranean spin to proceedings. Sautéed tiger prawns with sweet chilli, chorizo garlic, coriander and cream is a splash of southern sunshine and comes with the excellent home-made bread. Follow on with roasted breast of pheasant with its leg cooked confit, or honey-glazed ham with triple-cooked chips from the Pub Classics section. To finish, banana and walnut bread is the star of a busy dessert menu.

Chef Barney Everett **Owner** Mr M & Mr A Ambrosini **Seats** 100, Pr/dining room 86 **Times** 12-2/6-9 **Prices** Service optional **Wines** 2 bottles over £30, 24 bottles under £30 **Parking** 120 **Notes** Sunday L £8.45-£16.45, Vegetarian available, Children welcome

OAKHILL
Map 4 ST64

The Oakhill Inn

◉ Modern British

tel: 01749 840442 **Fosse Rd BA3 5HU**
email: info@theoakhillinn.com **web:** www.theoakhillinn.com
dir: On A367 between Stratton-on-the-Fosse & Shepton Mallet

Modernised British cooking in an old stone inn

An ancient stone-built inn with hanging baskets is a realisation of many people's idea of old England, and The Oakhill looks the part. With the Mendip hills as backdrop, the place has plenty to divert the eye inside too, not least the open kitchen, in which diners can now enjoy the theatre of food preparation. The food itself edges more firmly into modern British territory than hitherto, although devotees of pub classics such as bubble-and-squeak topped with a poached egg, or fish and chips with mushy peas, have not been abandoned. Otherwise, look to ox cheek terrine with red onion compôte in balsamic, and then roast cod with leeks, mussels and new potatoes in fish soup. Sides include the nowadays indispensable dauphinoise, and a satisfying conclusion is reached with desserts that major on chocolate and toffee, but also find room for tarte Tatin.

Chef Neil Creese **Owner** JC & AJ Digney **Seats** 30 **Times** 12-3/6-9, Closed 25-26 Dec **Prices** Fixed L 2 course £13.50, Starter £5.95-£6.95, Main £9.95-£18.95, Dessert £5.95, Service optional **Wines** 7 bottles over £30, 24 bottles under £30, 10 by glass **Parking** 12 **Notes** Sunday L £9.95-£15.95, Vegetarian available, Children welcome

PORLOCK
Map 3 SS84

The Oaks Hotel

◉ Traditional British

tel: 01643 862265 **TA24 8ES**
email: info@oakshotel.co.uk **web:** www.oakshotel.co.uk
dir: From E of A39, enter village (road narrows to single track) then follow hotel sign. From W: down Porlock Hill, through village, hotel sign on right

Traditional cooking in the Exmoor National Park

On the edge of the village, this small hotel occupies an imposing Edwardian property with glorious views of Porlock Bay from the reception rooms and restaurant, with its wrap-around windows. Antiques, pictures and fresh flowers proliferate, and log fires add a homely and comforting touch. The cooking tends towards the unpretentious and traditional. The daily-changing four-course menu might open with a tartlet, its pastry soft and crumbly, of cherry tomatoes, goats' cheese and pine nuts before a fish course: perhaps hot smoked haddock mousse. Sauces are a strong suit: one of cheesy fennel for sea-fresh fillet of John Dory, port and redcurrant for roast fillet of Exmoor venison, accompanied by garden-fresh vegetables. Breads are made each morning, and puddings include an excellent passionfruit custard tart, and lemon and raspberry roulade.

Times 7-8, Closed Nov-Mar, L all week

SHEPTON MALLET
Map 4 ST64

Charlton House Spa Hotel

◉◉ Modern British

tel: 01749 342008 & 0844 248 3830 (Calls cost 7p per minute plus your phone company's access charge) **Charlton Rd BA4 4PR**
email: enquiries.charltonhousehotel@bannatyne.co.uk **web:** www.bannatyne.co.uk
dir: On A361 towards Frome, 1m from town centre

Contemporary cooking in a smart country house

A grand stone manor on the edge of Shepton Mallet, Charlton House is a country-house hotel with the full complement of amenities, from plush spa, pretty grounds and business facilities. It's no surprise that it's a hit on the wedding scene. The interiors successfully combine period charm and contemporary style. The restaurant has gone for a traditional finish, with swagged curtains and formal tables settings, watched over by a slick, professional service team. A menu of modern British dishes includes flavours from beyond the European borders, so steamed tiger prawn with a coconut and green curry foam sits alongside carpaccio of scallop with raspberry and black pepper jelly among main courses. Next up, quail is wrapped in pancetta and roasted, and arrives in the company of thyme mash and roast swede, while fish options might include roast cod with pickled kohlrabi or a salmon number with quinoa and bok choy. For dessert, rhubarb trifle with Chantilly offers home comforts, with Asian flavours arriving again in the form of a rice pudding with chilli and lychee sorbet.

Chef Michael Sharp **Owner** Bannatyne Hotels Ltd **Seats** 60, Pr/dining room 80 **Times** 12.30-2.15/7-9.15 **Prices** Fixed L 2 course £14.95, Fixed D 3 course £36.95, Service optional **Wines** 22 bottles over £30, 25 bottles under £30, 9 by glass **Parking** 70 **Notes** Sunday L £19.95-£24.95, Vegetarian available, Children welcome

The Thatched Cottage Inn

◉ Modern British, European

tel: 01749 342058 **Thatched Cottage, 63-67 Charlton Rd BA4 5QF**
email: enquiries@thatchedcottageinn.com **web:** www.thatchedcottageinn.com
dir: 0.6m E of Shepton Mallet, at lights on A361

Smart old inn with an industrious kitchen

The 17th-century Thatched Cottage Inn has the advertised covering on its roof and the thoroughly chocolate-box appearance you would expect given its name. The interior looks the part too, gently updated without harming the intrinsic charm of its wooden beams and panelling, and vast stone fireplaces, while the kitchen pulls in the fans of straightforward modern cooking based on good local produce. Just about everything is cooked in-house from scratch, whether it's spiced crab cakes with home-made tartare sauce or classic ham hock terrine with piccalilli and sourdough toast. A well-thought-out main course brings pan-roasted chicken breast with wilted spinach, pommes Anna and wild mushroom jus, or there might be slow-roasted pork belly with sage mash, apple purée, braised red cabbage and cider jus. Dessert winds proceedings up with a classic sticky toffee pudding served with caramel sauce and honeycomb ice cream.

Times 12-2.30/6.30-9.30

SOMERTON
Map 4 ST42

The Devonshire Arms

◉ Modern British

tel: 01458 241271 **Long Sutton TA10 9LP**
email: mail@thedevonshirearms.com **web:** www.thedevonshirearms.com
dir: Off A303 onto A372 at Podimore rdbt. After 4m, left onto B3165, signed Martock and Long Sutton

Good, honest cooking by the village green

This Georgian former hunting lodge turned restaurant with rooms looks over the green in a pretty village in the heart of the Somerset Levels. Inside, the place has a smart contemporary look involving unclothed darkwood tables and hues of burgundy and grey. It's a convivial hub where people pop in for a jar of the village's own ale or cider in the bar, or for a full meal in the restaurant, while on a fine day, alfresco dining is on the cards in the courtyard and walled garden. Expect big-hearted cooking that seeks to comfort rather than to challenge, with a good showing of local produce brought together in well-considered combinations – crab and tomato tartlet, followed by guinea fowl breast with truffle mousse, local pancetta, mash spring greens and herb jus, and for pudding, perhaps treacle tart with lemon curd and home-made buttermilk ice cream.

Chef Max Pringle **Owner** Philip & Sheila Mepham **Seats** 40, Pr/dining room 16 **Times** 12-2.30/7-9.30, Closed 25-26 Dec **Prices** Starter £5.95-£10.95, Main £12.95-£19.95, Dessert £5.95-£8.95, Service optional 10% **Wines** 9 bottles over £30, 20 bottles under £30, 9 by glass **Parking** 6, On street **Notes** ALC menu served D, Sunday L £12.95-£14.50, Vegetarian available, Children welcome

TAUNTON
Map 4 ST22

Augustus

◉ European **NEW** v

tel: 01823 324354 **3 The Courtyard, St James St TA1 1JR**
email: info@augustustaunton.co.uk
dir: M5 junct 25. Town centre, next to cricket ground

Refined simplicity in a Taunton courtyard

The repeated shrilling of the phone serves notice of the popularity of Richard Guest's courtyard restaurant in the town centre. Book early to avoid disappointment (no, really). The pared-down contemporary look – uncovered tables and floor, whitewashed walls with a few pictures – ensures there are no distractions from the modern brasserie style of the food, which adds an element of refinement to essentially simple dishes. A warm salad of solferino-balled vegetables accompanies beautifully caramelised scallops to begin, or there could be a textbook presentation of traditional gnocchi with taleggio and rosemary cream. For main, straightforward fish dishes such as turbot with greens in mustard sauce, or John Dory with courgettes and tomato, allow their star performers to shine, while a bowl of rabbit saddle and roasted roots is a paradigm of rustic satisfaction. Crisp-shelled treacle tart with ginger ice cream has perhaps more sugar than you're braced for; otherwise, go for lemon posset with summer fruit compôte.

Chef Richard Guest **Owner** Cedric Chirossel, Richard Guest **Seats** 28 **Times** 10-3/6-9.30, Closed 25 Dec, 1 Jan, Sun-Mon **Prices** Starter £5-£9.95, Main £9.95-£21, Dessert £5-£6.95, Service optional **Wines** 74 bottles over £30, 36 bottles under £30, 14 by glass **Parking** On street **Notes** Children welcome

The Mount Somerset Hotel & Spa

◉◉ British v

tel: 01823 442500 **Lower Henlade TA3 5NB**
email: info@mountsomersethotel.co.uk **web:** www.mountsomersethotel.co.uk
dir: M5 junct 25, A358 towards Chard/Ilminster, right in Henlade (Stoke St Mary), left at T-junct. Hotel 400yds on right

Soundly conceived British modernism with peacocks

Ensconced in the bucolic tranquillity of Lower Henlade, The Mount is a pristine white Regency manor house in four acres. It fairly piles on the style all the way from its ornamental fountain and strutting peacocks to the Somerset dining room, where decorative panels and an ornate chandelier lord it over an ocean of white linen. West Country produce finds its way on to menus of soundly conceived, rather than wildly experimental, British modernism, in the symmetrical format of four options per course. Cauliflower purée be gone, as the scallops arrive with goats' cheese, pineapple and avocado aïoli, while venison, red cabbage and parsnips are resized into an appetising starter. Beef reared on Exmoor is aged for 28 days before the fillet is roasted and served with pink fir potatoes braised in duck fat. Fish might be Cornish turbot in vivid saffron nage with a crab and ginger raviolo. To finish, cheeses of the southwest are the specialist subject, if your tastes don't sweetly extend to pear and almond cream tart with an ice cream of Somerset cider brandy.

Chef Stephen Walker **Owner** Eden Hotel Collection **Seats** 60, Pr/dining room 50 **Times** 12-2/7-9.30 **Prices** Fixed L 2 course £17.50, Fixed D 3 course £35, Starter £9.95-£13.95, Main £23.95-£28.95, Dessert £9.95-£12.95, Service optional **Wines** 56 bottles over £30, 30 bottles under £30, 10 by glass **Parking** 100 **Notes** Sunday L £18.95-£22.50, Children welcome

TAUNTON continued

The Willow Tree Restaurant

◉◉ Modern British

tel: 01823 352835 3 Tower Ln, Off Tower St TA1 4AR
email: willowtreefood@hotmail.co.uk
dir: 200yds from Taunton bus station

Pin-sharp cooking in a 17th-century townhouse

Chef-patron Darren Sherlock's intimate neighbourhood restaurant occupies a beamed 17th-century house tucked away down a little lane beside a stream in the heart of town. With a waterside terrace and a smartly-furnished cottagey interior – artwork on the walls and high-backed chairs at clothed tables – it's an inviting setting for some distinctively precise, thoughtful cooking. Top-class ingredients, including locally-reared meats and fish from Newlyn's day boats help to give it the maximum impact with the minimum of fuss. You might start with a smoked haddock and leek tartlet with a slow-cooked, truffled egg yolk and parsley dressing before main courses that give those pedigree meats and fish star billing, whether it's pan-fried monkfish and scallops with 'linguine' of carrot and celeriac, home-made tarragon pasta and creamy lobster sauce, or roast rump of lamb with pommes Anna, ratatouille-style vegetables and black olive jus. Baking skills are evident in excellent home-made breads, and thought and workmanship are behind even straightforward-sounding desserts like bread-and-butter pudding with vanilla ice cream.

Chef Darren Sherlock Owner Darren Sherlock, Rita Rambellas Seats 25 Times 6.30-9, Closed Jan, Aug, Sun-Mon, Thu, L all week Prices Fixed D 3 course £27.95-£32.95, Service optional 10% Wines 20 bottles over £30, 27 bottles under £30, 6 by glass Parking 20 yds, 300 spaces Notes Vegetarian available, Children 10 yrs+

TINTINHULL
Map 4 ST41

Crown & Victoria

◉ British

tel: 01935 823341 Farm St BA22 8PZ
email: info@thecrownandvictoria.co.uk web: www.thecrownandvictoria.co.uk
dir: W'bound off A303 follow signs for Tintinhull

Good honest cooking in a lovely village pub

This is the kind of country pub that spurs urbanites to up sticks and make a move to a rural idyll. It's a proper pub, for a start, with a changing rota of ales at the bar and a serious approach to food. There's a fabulous garden too, and a large conservatory dining room which can hold its own against the worst of the weather. The kitchen keeps things as local as possible, seeking out organic and free-range ingredients to treat with simplicity and integrity. A bowl of celeriac and Bramley apple soup is just the ticket, simple and well-made, enriched with toasted walnuts and Blue Vinney cheese. Main course might be well-timed roast cod in lemongrass velouté, with creamy, garlicky dauphinoise and a side-dish of veg, and the conclusion could be hot chocolate fondant with salt caramel centre and pistachio ice cream.

Times 12-2.30/6.30-9.30, Closed D Sun

WELLS
Map 4 ST54

Ancient Gate House Hotel

◉ Modern Italian

tel: 01749 672029 20 Sadler St BA5 2SE
email: info@ancientgatehouse.co.uk web: www.ancientgatehouse.co.uk
dir: 1st hotel on left on cathedral green

Italian home cooking by the old West Gate

The hotel is so named as it incorporates nothing less than the Great West Gate that once formed part of the little city's medieval fortifications. Housed within it for the past 40 years has been Rugantino's, flying the flag for Italian home cooking. The lengthy menus deal in numerous favourites, from well-wrought pasta dishes such as linguine carbonara, and spaghetti del mare generously teeming with scallops, prawns, clams and crab, to main-course showstoppers like chicken breast stuffed with salsiccia and pine nuts with truffled mushroom cream sauce. Simple fish preparations are a good bet, for example sea bass with fennel and puréed red pepper. To finish, there are treats such as pannacotta and berry compôte, or white chocolate cheesecake and raspberry sorbet.

Chef Jamie Cundill Owner Nicholas & Jonathan Rossi Seats 40, Pr/dining room 20 Times 12-2.30/6-10, Closed 25-29 Dec Prices Fixed L 2 course £10.90-£13.90, Fixed D 3 course £25-£30, Starter £3.25-£8.50, Main £9.50-£21.50, Dessert £5.50-£6.50 Wines 6 bottles over £30, 27 bottles under £30, 9 by glass Parking On street Notes Tasting menu, Pre/post cathedral concert menu, Sunday L £13.90-£19.90, Vegetarian available, Children welcome

BEST WESTERN PLUS Swan Hotel

◉◉ Modern British

tel: 01749 836300 Sadler St BA5 2RX
email: info@swanhotelwells.co.uk web: www.swanhotelwells.co.uk
dir: A39, A371, on entering Wells follow signs for Hotels & Deliveries. Hotel on right opposite cathedral

An ancient inn with creative full-flavoured contemporary cooking

Hard by the cathedral, the Swan started life as a coaching inn and is now a sizable hotel with a health suite. One of its attractions is the quality of the food in the restaurant, a pleasant room with antiques, panelling and upholstered dining chairs at properly laid tables. The menu offers only a handful of choices per course but it's been assembled with some ingenuity to produce scope. Broccoli soup is a good rendition, deeply flavoured and served with cheese nuggets, or there might be seared Brixham scallops with grilled chorizo and white bean purée. Sirloin steak with well-made béarnaise seems to be a fixture, but other main courses include an accurate interpretation of lamb (from Launceston) kleftiko with couscous, and cod fillet in a herby crab crust served with pea and clam soup, leeks and mashed potato. There's a decent selection of breads, and desserts might run to crème brûlée or an unusual chocolate and beetroot torte with raspberry crème fraîche.

Chef Adam Kennington Owner Kevin Newton Seats 50, Pr/dining room 90 Times 12-2/7-9.30 Prices Fixed L 2 course £19.50-£24.50, Fixed D 3 course £27-£32, Service optional Wines 14 bottles over £30, 21 bottles under £30, 7 by glass Parking 30 Notes Sunday L £17.95-£19.95, Vegetarian available, Children welcome

Goodfellows

@@ Mediterranean, European

tel: 01749 673866 **5 Sadler St BA5 2RR**
email: goodfellows@btconnect.com **web:** www.goodfellowswells.co.uk
dir: Town centre near Market Place

Creative fish restaurant with a café attached

Look for the plum-coloured façade in the centre of town, and you can't go far wrong. If it's first thing in the morning, breakfast is on hand in the café, or you might have a Danish and cappuccino for elevenses. Otherwise, sign up for some distinguished seafood cookery in the adjoining restaurant, where fish is handled with confidence and care by a small, intensely focused brigade at work in the central open kitchen. There's a six-course tasting menu that reads like a shopping list (perhaps Crayfish, Salmon, Crab, Turbot, Scallops, Coconut), while the three-course format begins with poached ballotine of salmon with couscous salad and spicy tomato coulis, followed by a sunny southern composition of seared tuna loin with saffron-braised fennel, Mediterranean vegetables and tapenade. Meat eaters might go for a venison haunch steak with roasted root vegetables, confit potato, and prunes soaked in Armagnac. Don't skip dessert – the on-site pâtisserie means puddings and bread are ace, so end with iced almond parfait with fresh strawberries and strawberry coulis.

Chef Adam Fellows **Owner** Adam & Martine Fellows **Seats** 35, Pr/dining room 20
Times 12-2/6.30-9.30, Closed 25-27 Dec, 1 Jan, Sun, D Tue **Prices** Fixed L 2 course £20, Tasting menu fr £48, Starter £6-£14, Main £11-£24, Dessert £7-£9.50, Service optional **Wines** 19 bottles over £30, 24 bottles under £30, 6 by glass **Notes** Tasting menu 5 course, Seafood menu, Vegetarian available, Children welcome

The Old Spot

@@ Italian, French

tel: 01749 689099 **12 Sadler St BA5 2SE**
email: theoldspotwells@googlemail.com
dir: On entering Wells, follow signs for Hotels & Deliveries. Sadler St leads into High St, Old Spot on left opposite Swan Hotel

Confident cooking with regional ingredients

Back in the 1990s, Ian Bates was working in some of London's hottest addresses, and now it is the lucky people of Wells who get the benefit of all his experience. Hanging baskets outside suggest the mellow tone within, and indeed it is an easy-going place where the focus is on good food and good company. Chef also trained with the French master Michel Guérard, so there's a Gallic influence on show, but, most of all, it's all about the fabulous (and seasonal) produce of the southwest. Celeriac and apple soup is packed with flavour and arrives topped with walnut crumbs and pesto, or another starter is a Mediterranean-inspired octopus salad with green olives, preserved lemon and basil. Roast guinea fowl surfaces among courses, partnered with cauliflower purée, fondant potato and Madeira sauce, or try roast cod with olive oil mash, peppers and chorizo. Sunday lunch turns out a cracking roast chicken. For dessert, custard tart with Yorkshire forced rhubarb shows good pastry skills.

Chef Ian Bates **Owner** Ian & Clare Bates **Seats** 50 **Times** 12.30-2.30/7-9.30, Closed 1 wk Xmas, Mon-Tue, D Sun **Prices** Fixed L 2 course fr £15.50, Starter £5.50-£10.50, Main £12.50-£22, Dessert £6-£8.50 **Wines** 33 bottles over £30, 30 bottles under £30, 12 by glass **Parking** On street, Market Sq **Notes** Sunday L £22.50-£24.50, Vegetarian available, Children welcome

WESTON-SUPER-MARE   **Map 4 ST36**

The Cove

@ Modern British

tel: 01934 418211 **Marine Lake, Birnbeck Rd BS23 2BX**
email: info@thc-cove.co.uk
dir: From Grand Pier on Royal Parade N onto Knightstone Rd. Left into Birnbeck Rd. Restaurant on left

Cool seaside brasserie with Mediterranean influence

Bucket-and-spade Weston-super-Mare is trading up these days, and this smartly revamped bistro-style restaurant on the seafront near Birnbeck Pier fits in admirably with the town's new image. The outdoor terrace perched above the water is the place to be on a balmy day, while full-length picture windows make for a light-flooded space where everyone still gets a view of the bay, and chunky pale wooden tables combine with oak floors in a pared-back contemporary look that wouldn't look out of place in a big city. Spanking-fresh fish and seafood landed by dayboats in Newlyn and Brixham is the mainstay of an unpretentious, Mediterranean-accented menu that starts with the likes of steamed Cornish mussels with smoked bacon, kale and cider sauce, followed by poached sea bream fillet with Bombay potatoes, spinach and spiced cream. There's plenty to keep carnivores happy too – perhaps confit duck leg with Toulouse sausage and mash.

Chef Richard Tudor, Gemma Stacey **Owner** Heath Hardy, Gemma Stacey **Seats** 65 **Times** 12-9.30, All-day dining, Closed 25 Dec, Mon-Tue (Nov-Feb) **Prices** Fixed L 3 course £14.50, Fixed D 3 course £19.50, Starter £3.50-£8, Main £8.50-£17.50, Dessert £3.95-£6, Service optional **Wines** 2 bottles over £30, 30 bottles under £30, 6 by glass **Parking** On street/car park **Notes** Sunday L £10.95, Vegetarian available, Children welcome

WINCANTON
Map 4 ST72

Holbrook House
◉◉ Modern British

tel: 01963 824466 **Holbrook BA9 8BS**
email: enquiries@holbrookhouse.co.uk **web:** www.holbrookhouse.co.uk
dir: *From A303 at Wincanton, turn left on A371 towards Castle Cary & Shepton Mallet*

Diverting modern cooking in a house with a history

Close by the intersection of Somerset, Dorset and Wiltshire, Holbrook is a handsome Georgian manor house on an estate that can trace its history back to the 13th century – guests can study the records of its venerable lineage. Set amid acres of woodland and clad in red creeper, it makes a classic country-house hotel, complete with spa treatments and a health club, and a gifted chef leads the kitchen team. There are many different spots for pre-dinner drinks, so don't rush, but take in the consummate professionalism of surroundings where staff are knowledgeable about the menus and there's a serious wine list to contemplate. Start with a finely-wrought wild mushroom risotto with Jerusalem artichoke velouté and crisps, followed by precise flavours all working together in mains of line-caught wild sea bass with crab tortellini, carrot and tarragon gratin and vermouth and chive broth. At dessert, an ethereal caramel soufflé comes with chocolate sauce and vanilla ice cream.

Times 12.30-2/7-9, Closed L Mon-Thu, D Sun

YEOVIL
Map 4 ST51

Little Barwick House
◉◉◉ – *see below*

The Yeovil Court Hotel & Restaurant
◉◉ Modern European

tel: 01935 863746 **West Coker Rd BA20 2HE**
email: unwind@yeovilhotel.com **web:** www.yeovilhotel.com
dir: *2.5m W of town centre on A30*

Modern hotel with stimulating brasserie cooking

The entire ground floor of this low-slung white hotel on the outskirts of town is dedicated to eating, drinking and relaxing. There are public areas, a cosy bar and a dramatic-looking restaurant with unusual blinds over the windows and black chairs contrasting with white-clothed tables. It's a popular place, attracting guests with its interesting menus and skilful cooking. Seared scallops are partnered by pancetta and served with pea purée and shellfish oil, and may be followed by slices of roast pheasant with no more than lardons, spinach and potatoes. Various cultures are raided to extend variety: gnocchi with spinach and walnuts in creamy blue cheese sauce, for instance, then red snapper with couscous, peppers, spicy tomatoes, olives and rocket. A separate Classic menu lists such dishes as cottage pie and beer-battered hake with the customary accompaniments. Puddings might extend to pineapple jelly with mango sorbet and coconut and lime syrup, which makes a refreshing conclusion.

Times 12-1.45/7-9.30, Closed 26-30 Dec, L Sat

Little Barwick House ◉◉◉

YEOVIL
Map 4 ST51

Modern British ⧠ NOTABLE WINE LIST

tel: 01935 423902 **Barwick Village BA22 9TD**
email: reservations@barwick7.fsnet.co.uk **web:** www.littlebarwickhouse.co.uk
dir: *Turn off A371 Yeovil to Dorchester opposite Red House rdbt, 0.25m on left*

Simple but powerful dishes amid West Country heritage

Tim and Emma Ford's Georgian dower house is one of the most serene and self-effacing gems of the West Country, offering an enchanting, quintessentially English idyll. The soothing country decor is elegant without drowning in antiques and chintz, and the front-of-house approach is perfectly pitched – this is very much a family concern, with everyone pulling their weight, particularly son Oliver, who now keeps Tim on his toes in the kitchen. Rock-solid consistency defines the cooking here – there's no attempt to impress with the latest ephemeral trends, no foams, dusts or techno-trickery, just classically-based ideas that are carefully thought through and executed with great technique. It's the kind of location in which you would expect a fair proportion of local produce, and Tim Ford's connections with the area's food network come up with the goods, setting out with a simple trio of perfectly pan-fried local scallops matched with Jerusalem artichoke purée and crispy pancetta. Game is always up for grabs in season, as witnessed in a main course of roasted grouse with gaufrette potatoes, bread sauce and grouse sauce, which achieves the same impact of potency through simplicity. If you fancy fish, the region's boats supply splendid sea bass, which arrives perfectly timed with crisped-up skin, fennel and champagne sauce. After that, top-class baking skills provide a splendid finale: puff pastry tart filled with Bramley and russet apples and pear, balanced with a wicked caramel sauce and greengage sorbet. Wine lovers should note that the cellar goes way, way beyond what might be expected from such a small-scale restaurant with rooms: an exceptional global selection has something for everyone from connoisseurs to tipplers.

Chef Timothy Ford **Owner** Emma & Timothy Ford **Seats** 40
Times 12-2/7-9, Closed New Year, 2 wks Jan, Sun-Mon, L Tue **Prices** Fixed D 3 course £47.95, Service optional **Wines** 177 bottles over £30, 24 bottles under £30, 42 by glass **Parking** 25 **Notes** Vegetarian available, Children 5 yrs+

STAFFORDSHIRE

LEEK   Map 16 SJ95

Three Horseshoes Inn

◉◉ Modern British, Thai

tel: 01538 300296 **Buxton Rd, Blackshaw Moor ST13 8TW**
email: enquiries@threeshoesinn.co.uk **web:** www.threeshoesinn.co.uk
dir: M6 junct 15 or 16 onto A500. Exit A53 towards Leek. 2m from town centre

Grills and much more in a Peak District country inn

The stone-built inn overlooked by lowering gritstone outcrops in the southern stretches of the Peak District does a good job of covering many bases. It's a country pub, a smart rural hotel and a chic brasserie and grill all in the one package. The original oak beams in the brasserie and grill are offset by contemporary styling, with an open-to-view kitchen augmenting the dynamic atmosphere. The odd Southeast Asian dish appears on the menu among the western stuff, so that chicken, rabbit and pigeon terrine must take its chances amid the excitements of three Thai ways with crab (spring roll with tamarind, in noodle salad, and crabcake) to start, followed by Penang red curry on pineapple fried rice, or a steak from the Inka charcoal grill served with beef dripping chips, roasted tomato, herb butter, roasted mushroom and your choice of sauces. Intensive labours pay off in a dessert that offers white chocolate and raspberry in the various manifestations of trifle, cheesecake, doughnut and Eton mess.

Chef Mark & Stephen Kirk **Owner** Bill, Jill, Mark & Stephen Kirk **Seats** 50, Pr/dining room 150 **Times** 6.30-9, Closed 24-26 Dec, L Mon-Sat **Prices** Tasting menu £49.95, Starter £7.50-£8.50, Main £15.50-£22, Dessert £6.50-£7.50 **Wines** 47 bottles over £30, 67 bottles under £30, 10 by glass **Parking** 100 **Notes** Tasting menu 8 course, Sunday L £9.95-£19, Vegetarian available, Children welcome

LICHFIELD   Map 10 SK10

Netherstowe House

◉ Modern British V

tel: 01543 254270 **Netherstowe Ln WS13 6AY**
email: reception@netherstowehouse.com **web:** www.netherstowehouse.com
dir: A38 onto A5192, 0.3m on right into Netherstowe Ln. 1st left, 1st right down private drive

Local produce presented well in a boutique setting

With origins in the 12th century, Netherstowe is a characterful house that has been given the boutique treatment. It's not got one of those stark, modern interiors, however, boasting instead an altogether more genteel and refined finish. There are two dining options in the hotel. First off, The Steak Cellar Restaurant is a moodily-lit basement brasserie serving up 28-day aged beef from local farms, while the alternative is the fine-dining option, where the tables are dressed in white linen. There's passion for provenance and food miles throughout (locations and distances appear on the menu), and the fine-dining output is modern and attractively presented. Start with Staffordshire beef tartare with a confit duck's egg yolk and move on to a main course such as braised shoulder of Bretby lamb, served with its hay-smoked loin, or a fish dish of pan-roasted Cornish hake with wild nettle and spinach risotto. Finish with a pistachio and olive oil cake.

Chef Stephen Garland **Owner** Ben Heathcote **Seats** 30, Pr/dining room 14 **Times** 12-2.30/6-9, Closed New Year, D Sun **Prices** Fixed L 2 course £16, Fixed D 3 course £40, Service optional **Wines** 75 bottles over £30, 27 bottles under £30, 9 by glass **Parking** 50 **Notes** Brunch, Afternoon tea, Sunday L £24.95-£29.95, Children 12 yrs+

Swinfen Hall Hotel

◉◉◉ – see below

Swinfen Hall Hotel ◉◉◉

LICHFIELD   Map 10 SK10

Modern British
tel: 01543 481494 **Swinfen WS14 9RE**
email: info@swinfenhallhotel.co.uk **web:** www.swinfenhallhotel.co.uk
dir: 2m S of Lichfield on A38 between Weeford rdbt & Swinfen rdbt

Opulent country-house cooking in a Georgian mansion

The Four Seasons restaurant at Swinfen Hall Hotel is a formal affair with oak panels and a hand-painted ceiling, plus food that impresses with classic combinations, attention to detail and well-judged modernity. The half-acre Victorian garden provides its bounty for the kitchen and what isn't home grown is sourced with quality in mind. A first-course Staffordshire wood pigeon arrives as pink breast and tender confit leg, with a swipe of butternut squash purée, cannellini beans and raisins in a sweet sherry reduction, while another serves up beetroot from the garden in a fashionable paring with hot and cold goats' curd. Main courses continue in the same vein, with Gressingham duck (breast and crisp leg) partnered with heritage carrots in various forms including a delicious terrine, and pan-fried fillet of stone bass with caramelised garlic, anchovies and red chard. Finish with a pistachio frangipane tart or some excellent British cheeses (or both). There's a tasting menu option, too, offering seven or so courses, including a truly inspiring veggie version

offering the likes of shoestring-wrapped duck egg with vegetables from the garden, soused shallots and capers. Afternoon tea, Sunday lunches and summertime dining on the terrace all add to Swinfen's appeal.

Chef Paul Proffitt **Owner** Helen & Vic Wiser **Seats** 45, Pr/dining room 20 **Times** 12.30-2.30/7.30-9.30, Closed 26 Dec, 1 Jan, Mon, D Sun **Prices** Tasting menu £70-£100, Service optional **Wines** 97 bottles over £30, 38 bottles under £30, 10 by glass **Parking** 80 **Notes** ALC D 3 course £48, Vegetarian tasting menu £65, Sunday L £28-£36, Vegetarian available, Children welcome

The Moat House

◉◉ Modern British

tel: 01785 712217 **Lower Penkridge Rd, Acton Trussell ST17 0RJ**
email: info@moathouse.co.uk **web:** www.moathouse.co.uk
dir: *M6 junct 13 towards Stafford, 1st right to Acton Trussell, hotel by church*

Confident, creative cooking by a canal

A family-run hotel with conference and banqueting facilities, The Moat House is indeed moated, a part-timbered manor dating from the 14th century. Its Orangery Restaurant is bright and airy, with well-spaced tables, upholstered chairs and views over the canal; service is on the formal side, and there's a sommelier to advise on wines. The kitchen's a busy place, judging by the time and effort it puts into its output. The seasonally-changing carte might open with the luxury of lobster and crab ravioli with chervil tuber purée (the kitchen must have its own forager), fennel choucroute and sauce armoricaine, or more straightforward asparagus velouté with duck yolk and mushroom brioche soldiers. Main courses can be complex too but equally satisfying: attractively presented pork tenderloin with peanut-crusted belly, an oriental-style sauce, king prawn, carrot and star anise purée and pak choi, or lemon sole not just given the meunière treatment but served with scallops, parsley root and chard. End with one of the inventive puddings such as Turkish delight cheesecake with colourful rose water gel and chocolate sorbet.

Chef Matthew Davies, James Cracknell **Owner** The Lewis Partnership **Seats** 120, Pr/dining room 150 **Times** 12-2/6.30-9.30, Closed 25 Dec **Prices** Prices not confirmed, Service optional **Wines** 61 bottles over £30, 87 bottles under £30, 16 by glass **Parking** 200 **Notes** Tasting menu, Early doors menu, Sunday L, Vegetarian available, Children welcome

SUFFOLK

Brudenell Hotel

◉◉ Modern British, European

tel: 01728 452071 **The Parade IP15 5BU**
email: info@brudenellhotel.co.uk **web:** www.brudenellhotel.co.uk
dir: *A12/A1094, on reaching town, turn right at junct into High St. Hotel on seafront adjoining Fort Green car park*

Sunny brasserie cooking in a beachfront hotel

This privately-owned hotel is virtually on Aldeburgh's beach at the end of town. In the restaurant, windows to one side give wide views over the terrace to the shingle and the sea. Tables are arranged on different levels in the large open-plan room, dramatically decorated, with pale oak floors, lightwood tables and leather-look chairs. Smartly dressed staff are casual but careful, creating a relaxed and friendly atmosphere. Naturally enough, seafood tops the bill, freshly delivered along with free-range meat each morning. Whole dressed crab with salad, new potatoes and lemon mayonnaise, lobster with tarragon mayonnaise and potato salad, and perfectly cooked plaice fillets with chunky tartare sauce, petits pois and fries are all possibilities. Or break the mould and opt for asparagus and goats' cheese tart, its pastry crisp and light, with pesto, or potted duck and pork with cornichons and toast, before pink saddle of lamb with wild rice, kale, shallots and a tomato and basil jus. Either way, finish with sherry trifle – exactly how trifle should be – or rhubarb fool.

Times 12-2.30/6-9

Regatta Restaurant

◉ Modern British

tel: 01728 452011 **171 High St IP15 5AN**
email: rob.mabey@btinternet.com
dir: *Middle of High St, town centre*

Buzzy bistro, local seafood the stars

A nautical-themed mural and piscine prints leave no doubt that fresh local seafood, often landed on the beach, is the main thrust of the Mabeys' restaurant on the High Street. It's a cheery, relaxed sort of place, with brown leather-look banquettes and upholstered dining chairs at plain wooden tables, and a blackboard of daily specials padding out the carte. Oak-smoked salmon (from the smokery in the back garden) is appealingly partnered by Thai-style cucumber salad as a starter, contesting for attention with perhaps crayfish cocktail with basil and lemon. Dishes are timed just so and sensibly composed without swamping the main event, so griddled scallops are served on pea purée with crispy bacon, and, for meat-eaters, breast of chicken on roast sweet potatoes with piri-piri sauce and chips. Round things off with apple sorbet with a shot of Calvados, or malted bread-and-butter pudding with salted caramel sauce.

Chef Robert Mabey **Owner** Mr & Mrs R Mabey **Seats** 90, Pr/dining room 30 **Times** 12-2/6-10, Closed 24-26 & 31 Dec, 1 Jan **Prices** Fixed L 2 course fr £15, Fixed D 3 course fr £18, Starter £4.50-£9.50, Main £12-£22, Dessert £4.50-£8.50 **Wines** 6 bottles over £30, 30 bottles under £30, 12 by glass **Parking** On street **Notes** Gourmet evenings, Vegetarian available, Children welcome

Wentworth Hotel

◉◉ Traditional British V

tel: 01728 452312 **Wentworth Rd IP15 5BD**
email: stay@wentworth-aldeburgh.com **web:** www.wentworth-aldeburgh.com
dir: *From A12 take A1094 to Aldeburgh. In Aldeburgh straight on at mini rdbt, turn left at x-rds into Wentworth Rd. Hotel on right*

Family-run hotel with impeccable traditional cooking

Owned by the same family since 1920, the Wentworth has the deeply traditional feel of a smart country-house hotel with the bonus of splendid sea views from its peaceful spot on Aldeburgh's beachfront. Rich crimson walls hung with portraits, crisp napery and swagged-back drapes set the tone in the restaurant, where the kitchen turns out an appealing medley of English classics and gently updated dishes with a warm Mediterranean accent. As you'd hope, it's all anchored with local produce: meats from Suffolk farms, fish landed on the beach that morning. Techniques are sound and tried-and-tested combinations seek to comfort rather than to challenge, starting, perhaps, with home-made fishcakes with sweet chilli dressing, while main courses run the gamut from slow-cooked pork belly with butternut squash purée, Savoy cabbage, mashed potato and apple sauce, to grilled hake fillet with pesto mash, roast Mediterranean vegetables and tomato coulis. Among desserts, try red wine-poached pear with cinnamon ice cream and gingerbread or the thumb-sucking comfort of bread-and-butter pudding with custard.

Chef Jason Shaw **Owner** Michael Pritt **Seats** 100, Pr/dining room 22 **Times** 12-2.30/6-9 **Prices** Fixed L 2 course fr £13, Fixed D 3 course £15.90-£25, Starter £4.50-£9.50, Main £10-£32, Dessert £5-£7.95, Service optional **Wines** 21 bottles over £30, 53 bottles under £30 **Parking** 35 **Notes** Early supper 2/3 course £13/£17, Sunday L £21.50, Children welcome

The White Lion Hotel

◉ British, French

tel: 01728 452720 **Market Cross Place IP15 5BJ**
email: info@whitelion.co.uk **web:** www.whitelion.co.uk
dir: M25 junct 28 to A12 onto A1094, follow signs to Aldeburgh at junct on left. Hotel on right

Modern brasserie dining on the seafront

Sitting in prime beachfront splendour by the shingle banks of Aldeburgh's strand, The White Lion is the famous Suffolk festival town's oldest hotel. Inside, the place sports a fresh contemporary look, done out with cheery colours that let you know you're at the seaside. Unpretentious brasserie dining is the deal here, built on fine Suffolk ingredients – in fact, sourcing doesn't get more local than the fish landed a few steps away on the beach. If you can resist the temptations of haddock in Adnams beer-batter with chips and chunky tartare sauce, Cajun-spiced chicken breast with celeriac remoulade and sun-dried tomatoes is a fine main course. Bookending this are tempura king prawns with guacamole, mango and chilli dressing to start, and a moresome finale of flourless dark chocolate torte with popcorn praline and honeycomb ice cream.

Times 12-3/5.30-10

BROME   Map 13 TM17

BEST WESTERN Brome Grange Hotel

◉ Traditional British

tel: 01379 870456 **Norwich Rd, Nr Diss IP23 8AP**
email: info@bromegrangehotel.co.uk **web:** www.bromegrangehotel.co.uk
dir: 2m S of Diss on A140 between Ipswich & Norwich

Former coaching inn with carefully presented classic cooking

It's easy to imagine horse-drawn carriages sweeping into the central courtyard of this 16th-century former coaching inn, with plenty of period details remaining inside and out. It's a sprawling series of buildings with red pantiles on the roof and four acres of gardens. The restaurant is a traditional affair with lots of character – beams, fireplaces, leaded windows and wooden panelling – and leads into a conservatory. The service team are a cheerful bunch. The menu takes a broadly classical approach with some sound thinking going on and an eye for presentation. Start with a smoked salmon roulade, brought to the table with an accompanying sunflower and honey loaf, and move on to roast loin of cod in the sensible company of dill butter and sauté potatoes. To finish, bread-and-butter pudding is perfectly moist and comes flavoured with dates and orange.

Chef Satish Pagi **Owner** Brian & Kelly Keane **Seats** 60, Pr/dining room 28 **Times** 12-2/6.30-9, Closed D 25 Dec **Prices** Prices not confirmed, Service optional **Wines** 2 bottles over £30, 24 bottles under £30, 10 by glass **Parking** 120 **Notes** Sunday L, Vegetarian available, Children welcome

Find out more about how we assess for Rosette awards on page 9

BURY ST EDMUNDS   Map 13 TL86

The Angel Hotel

◉◉ Modern British

tel: 01284 714000 **Angel Hill IP33 1LT**
email: staying@theangel.co.uk **web:** www.theangel.co.uk
dir: From A134, left at rdbt into Northgate St. Continue to lights, right into Mustow St, left into Angel Hill. Hotel on right

Med-influenced brasserie dining in creeper-covered hotel

With a prime position overlooking the cathedral and the old abbey walls, The Angel meets all expectations of a quintessential Georgian coaching inn. Its brickwork façade is suitably handsome and curtained with creepers, and inside, the generous Georgian spaces have been overlaid with a contemporary boutique look, especially in The Eaterie, where artworks, bare pale wood tables, high-backed chairs and a statement chandelier make for a pleasingly up-to-date setting. The kitchen shows equally 21st-century sensibilities in its repertoire of Mediterranean-influenced brasserie food, sourcing top-notch local produce and bringing it all together in appealing flavour combinations with no unnecessary embellishment. Start with grilled quail with panzanella salad, or ox cheek braised in red wine matched with white onion and garlic risotto, then follow on with peppered leg of lamb with a salad of sautéed new potatoes, warm green beans, red onion and pecorino cheese. Finish with chocolate fondant with pistachio ice cream, or a true Brit classic such as sticky toffee pudding with vanilla ice cream.

Chef Arron Jackson **Owner** Robert Gough **Seats** 85, Pr/dining room 16 **Times** 12-9.45, All-day dining **Prices** Fixed L 2 course £13.95, Starter £6-£9.95, Main £13.50-£25.50, Dessert £5.95-£8.95 **Wines** 41 bottles over £30, 18 bottles under £30, 33 by glass **Parking** On street **Notes** Sunday L £17.95-£24.95, Vegetarian available, Children welcome

BEST WESTERN Priory Hotel

◉ Modern British, International

tel: 01284 766181 **Mildenhall Rd IP32 6EH**
email: reservations@prioryhotel.co.uk **web:** www.prioryhotel.co.uk
dir: From A14 junct 43 take Bury St Edmunds W slip road. Follow signs to Brandon. At mini-rdbt turn right. Hotel 0.5m on left

A peaceful setting for cooking with the surprise factor

On the approach road into town, the Priory sits in near-pastoral tranquillity within its original priory walls and lawns, a place of seclusion from Bury's hurly-burly. A peaceful atmosphere reigns throughout, including in the Garden Room restaurant, which looks out over the green, and offers soft lighting and a comforting feeling of being looked after by endlessly helpful staff. The kitchen aims for the surprise element in dishes that pull in inspiration from all over the known world, starting with spicy rabbit rissole dressed in Marsala. That might be the forerunner of duck breast in an east Asian mood, marinated in soy, mirin and yuzu, and bedded on soba noodles with pak choi in coriander and chilli broth. A dessert composition involving popcorn crumbs and caramel gel has a rather over-set tonka-bean pannacotta: try orange and almond tart with clotted cream instead.

Chef Matthew Cook **Owner** Peter Hobday **Seats** 72, Pr/dining room 28 **Times** 12-2/6.30-10 **Prices** Fixed L 2 course £15, Fixed D 3 course £18, Starter £4.75-£5.95, Main £11-£16.95, Dessert £4.95 **Wines** 2 bottles over £30, 26 bottles under £30, 9 by glass **Parking** 60, On street **Notes** Sunday L, Vegetarian available, Children welcome

continued

BURY ST EDMUNDS *continued*

Clarice House

◉ Modern European

tel: 01284 705550 **Horringer Court, Horringer Rd IP29 5PH**
email: bury@claricehouse.co.uk **web:** www.claricehouse .co.uk
dir: *From Bury St Edmunds on A143 towards Horringer and Haverhill, hotel 1m from town centre on right*

Well-crafted, contemporary cooking at a spa retreat

Health and fitness are top of the agenda at this impressive neo-Jacobean mansion in a parkland setting, with a spa, swimming pool, gym and health and beauty salon. So there's no excuse for not shedding the calories gained in the restaurant, where leather-upholstered chairs at bare wooden tables stand on the blue carpet and chandeliers hang from the ceiling. The menus steer a broadly European course, with appetising starters ranging from a warm salad of pigeon breast with carrot purée and parsnip crisps to smoked salmon Welsh rarebit. Main courses are a mixed bag, taking in burger with fries as well as the healthier option of steamed snapper fillet with steamed vegetables, prawns and ginger and soy sauce. Devil-may-care diners could end with sticky toffee pudding with caramel sauce and vanilla ice cream.

Chef Steve Winser **Owner** The King family **Seats** 70, Pr/dining room 20
Times 12-2/7-9, Closed 25-26 Dec, 1 Jan **Prices** Starter £5.50-£8, Main £11-£25, Dessert £6, Service optional **Wines** 5 bottles over £30, 14 bottles under £30, 10 by glass **Parking** 110 **Notes** Sunday L, Vegetarian available, Children welcome

The Grange Hotel

◉ Modern British

tel: 01359 231260 **Barton Rd, Thurston IP31 3PQ**
email: info@grangecountryhousehotel.com **web:** www. grangecountryhousehotel.com
dir: *A14 junct 45 towards Gt Barton, right at T-junct. At x-rds left into Barton Rd to Thurston. At rdbt, left after 0.5m, hotel on right*

Modern British classics in Tudor-style country house

Like many another country house, The Grange did its bit in the last war, acting as a makeshift army hospital. The surroundings could hardly be more suited to aid recovery, the peaceful village of Thurston being home to a late Victorian house timbered in the Tudor style. It retains its period appeal, with an oak-panelled dining room setting the stage for informal modern British food. That latter-day classic, ham hock terrine with piccalilli shows up well, with delicately judged sea bass to follow, accompanied by Lyonnaise potatoes and braised fennel in caper butter. Seared cod is tenderly swaddled in Parma ham and served with chorizo and wilted greens in tomato velouté, or there could be lamb rump with ratatouille in port jus, before the voice of sweet temptation calls out in the tones of dark chocolate tart with white chocolate crème brûlée and pistachio ice cream.

Chef Darren Marchant **Owner** Sortpad Ltd **Seats** 32, Pr/dining room 40
Times 12-2/7-9, Closed 1 Jan **Prices** Starter £5.95-£8.25, Main £13.95-£19.95, Dessert £6.50-£9.95, Service optional **Wines** 15 bottles over £30, 20 bottles under £30, 11 by glass **Parking** 60 **Notes** Classic afternoon tea £14.65, Sparkling cream tea £18.95, Sunday L £9.95-£18.95, Vegetarian available, Children welcome

The Leaping Hare Restaurant & Country Store

◉◉ Modern British

tel: 01359 250287 **Wyken Vineyards, Stanton IP31 2DW**
email: info@wykenvineyards.co.uk
dir: *8m NE of Bury St Edmunds, 1m off A143. Follow brown signs at Ixworth to Wyken Vineyards*

Vineyard restaurant with accomplished modern cooking

The Leaping Hare occupies a splendid 400-year-old barn, with a high beamed and raftered ceiling and polished wooden floor, on a 1,200-acre farm complete with a flock of Shetland sheep and Red Poll cattle, plus a vineyard. What the farm doesn't provide is grown or farmed locally too, often within five miles, with fish landed at Lowestoft. The kitchen follows a straightforward, uncomplicated route along classical lines, so expect starters of River Deben moules marinière, and roast pigeon breast with pancetta and artichoke and garlic purée. Accomplished main courses are distinguished by accurate timings and clearly discernible flavours, seen in a hearty dish of game and ale steamed pudding, served with mash and roasted root vegetables, and roast rack of estate lamb and confit shoulder with roast garlic jus, pommes Anna and purple-sprouting broccoli. Fish isn't entirely overlooked – there might be smoked salmon fillet with celery hearts and white beans with chorizo – and puddings end on an upbeat note with, say, ginger, passionfruit and white chocolate trifle.

Chef Jon Ellis **Owner** Kenneth & Carla Carlisle **Seats** 55 **Times** 12-2.30/7-9, Closed 2 wks Xmas, D Sun-Thu **Prices** Fixed L 2 course £18.95, Starter £6.95-£9.95, Main £13.95-£25.95, Dessert £6.95, Service optional **Wines** 6 bottles over £30, 11 bottles under £30, 13 by glass **Parking** 50 **Notes** Fri D 3 course £29.95, Sunday L £13.95-£35.95, Vegetarian available, Children welcome

Maison Bleue

◉◉ Modern French

tel: 01284 760623 **30-31 Churchgate St IP33 1RG**
email: info@maisonbleue.co.uk
dir: *A14 junct 43 (Sugar Beet, Central exit) to town centre. Follow signs to the Abbey Gdns, Churchgate St is opposite cathedral*

Traditional and modern French seafood dishes

The Maison continues to fly the tricolour for proudly French seafood cuisine in a quiet side-street off the bustling heart of medieval Bury St Edmunds. From the crisply professional French service to the smartly attired tables and a menu that runs from well-laden plateau de fruits de mer (book at least 48 hours ahead for that) to outstanding cheeses, it may be difficult to remind yourself you're in Suffolk. The place is teemingly popular, indicating that the taste for unreconstructed Gallic cooking never went away, though there is certainly no shyness about exploring the modern manner either. Start with a quenelle of poached chicken and blue cheese mousse accompanying a caramelised scallop garnished with truffle, or perhaps marinated langoustines with baby carrots and sprout leaves. The main deal arrives in the shape of sea bass with smoked onions in pumpkin velouté, or poached halibut with creamed mooli in Japanese dressing. There are meat dishes too for non-conformists – the beef featherblade is a cut above – and treats such as a study in chocolate and cherry to finish.

Chef Pascal Canevet **Owner** Pascal & Karine Canevet **Seats** 65, Pr/dining room 35
Times 12-2/7-9, Closed Jan, 2 wks summer, Sun-Mon **Prices** Fixed L 2 course £19.50, Fixed D 3 course fr £34.50, Starter £7.95-£13.50, Main £17.95-£28.50, Dessert £7.95, Service optional **Wines** 12 by glass **Parking** On street
Notes Vegetarian available, Children welcome

Pea Porridge

@@ Modern Bistro

tel: 01284 700200 **28-29 Cannon St IP33 1JR**
email: enquiries@peaporridge.co.uk
dir: Off A14 towards town, in Northgate St turn left into Cadney Lane. Restaurant opposite Old Cannon Brewery

Technically accomplished cooking of upbeat modern ideas

Two cottages dating from 1820 have been converted into this refreshingly unpretentious restaurant of three rooms with wooden floors, pine tables, exposed brick, beams and a baker's oven (the premises used to be a bakery). Guests are greeted warmly and nothing is too much trouble for the friendly front-of-house staff. 'Simplicity' is the kitchen's buzzword, which denies the level of thought and expertise that goes into the cooking. Snails sautéed with bone marrow, bacon, parsley, capers and garlic has been an imaginative starter of lovely clear flavours, an alternative to something like full-on lightly curried lamb's sweetbreads with kohlrabi and baby spinach. Timings are spot on and main courses can be masterpieces of contrasting flavours: loin of muntjac deer, lightly cooked and rare, as requested, with butternut squash purée, beetroot, fondant potato and raisins spiked with harissa, or fillet of sea bream with spicy aubergine and tomato stew, brown shrimps and salsa verde. Puddings make just as much impact when there's champagne pannacotta with rhubarb, say, or tarte Tatin.

Chef Justin Sharp **Owner** Justin Sharp **Seats** 46, Pr/dining room 20 **Times** 12-2.30/6.30-10, Closed 2 wks Sep, 2 wks Xmas, Sun-Mon, L Tue **Prices** Prices not confirmed, Service optional **Wines** 15 bottles over £30, 25 bottles under £30, 9 by glass **Parking** On street **Notes** Vegetarian available, Children welcome

The White Horse

@ Modern British

tel: 01284 735760 & 07778 996666 **Rede Rd, Whepstead IP29 4SS**
dir: 5m from Bury St Edmunds, 2m off A143 Bury/Haverhill

Well-crafted, unfussy cooking in country gastro-pub

Stylishly made over in recent years, this mustard-yellow village inn now sits comfortably at the gastro-pub end of the spectrum, but without losing any of the features one hopes for – the interior is a series of smart and cosy rooms with a copper-sheathed bar serving Suffolk ales, and there are exposed beams, a huge inglenook, country-style tables and chairs, artwork on the walls, and soothing Farrow & Ball colour schemes. The kitchen here appreciates the value of top-class local ingredients, follows the seasons keenly, and cuts no corners, making everything from scratch (including their own bangers – how about pork, paprika and sun-dried tomato sausages?). The blackboard menu lists joyously simple ideas: country pâté with home-made chutney and French bread, followed by a North African-influenced slow-braised shoulder of Ickworth lamb with tomatoes and black olives. Finish with baked apricot cheesecake, or how out on a savoury note with a plate of East Anglian cheeses.

Chef Gareth Carter **Owner** Gary & Di Kingshott **Seats** 50, Pr/dining room 25 **Times** 12-2/7-9.30, Closed 25-26 Dec, D Sun **Prices** Starter £5.95-£7.95, Main £10.95-£16.95, Dessert £5.95, Service optional **Wines** 7 bottles over £30, 18 bottles under £30, 8 by glass **Parking** 30 **Notes** Sunday L £20-£25, Vegetarian available, Children welcome

The George

@@ Modern British

tel: 01787 280248 **The Green CO10 8BA**
email: thegeorgecavendish@gmail.com **web:** www.thecavendishgeorge.co.uk
dir: A1092 into Cavendish, The George next to village green

Med-inflected cooking in characterful inn

The handsome timbered George dates from the 16th century and is rooted into the fabric of its ancient Suffolk village. These days, as is often the case, it's more of a restaurant with rooms than a village boozer – apart from a few bar stools there's not much pubbiness left; there are beams and bare-brick walls, but the understated Farrow & Ball neutral shades and classy cream seats combine in a tastefully made-over, thoroughly modern interior. The man cooking up a storm in the kitchen is chef-patron Lewis Bennet, who deals in no-nonsense modern comfort food with big, bold Mediterranean inflected flavours that keep a keen eye on the seasons. You might start with ballotine of quail partnered with foie gras parfait, poached grapes and truffled mushroom toast, and follow with roast duck breast supported by Jerusalem artichoke puree, wild mushroom duxelle and baked new potatoes, or turbot fillet with saffron and spinach risotto, crab mousse and squid ink. Pudding could be a deliciously summery elderflower pannacotta with wild rose jelly.

Times 12-2/6-9.30, Closed 25 Dec, 1 Jan, D Sun

The Froize Freehouse Restaurant

@ British, European

tel: 01394 450282 **The Street IP12 3PU**
email: dine@froize.co.uk
dir: On B1084 between Woodbridge & Orford

Popular inn with cracking menu

Converted from a brace of red-brick gamekeepers' cottages, The Froize is a welcoming Suffolk inn that is in fine shape after a contemporary makeover, and the mood is dressed-down and relaxed. Chef-proprietor David Grimwood is a local lad who likes to bang the drum for local materials, so his food taps into the current appetite for ingredients-led, honest-to-goodness dishes with clean-cut flavours – it's all so driven by what's in season locally that there are no menus at lunch, just blackboards with the day's specials. This is food straight from the heart – roast shoulder of locally-reared Old Spots pork is served with proper pan juice gravy, fresh apple sauce, crisp crackling and stuffing, or there might be slow-cooked hare with chestnuts, ceps and blackberry brandy. Starters could see Orford crab cakes pointed up with sweet chilli sauce, whilst desserts are comfort classics along the lines of marmalade bread-and-butter pudding.

Chef David Grimwood **Owner** David Grimwood **Seats** 48, Pr/dining room 20 **Times** 12-2/7-close, Closed Mon (ex BHs) **Prices** Service optional **Wines** 14 bottles under £30, 14 by glass **Parking** 40 **Notes** Sunday L £16-£25, Vegetarian available, Children welcome

DUNWICH

Map 13 TM47

The Ship at Dunwich

◉ Modern British

tel: 01728 648219 **St James St IP17 3DT**
email: info@shipatdunwich.co.uk **web:** www.shipatdunwich.co.uk
dir: *From N: A12, exit at Blythburgh onto B1125, then left to village. Inn at end of road. From S: A12, turn right to Westleton. Follow signs for Dunwich*

Locally-based cooking in an ideally located coastal pub

Climbing foliage in the form of a trident is the distinguishing outer feature of the red-brick pub in an East Anglian coastal village surrounded by wild heathland and nature reserves, with a beach on hand and Southwold nearby. It's got the lot, including an expansive garden with an ancient fig tree. Foursquare rustic furniture inside and a courtyard for sunny outdoor dining set the tone for a menu that takes in pork, apricot and pistachio terrine with pickled courgette, or salmon cured in Adnams' vodka and beetroot, to start, with follow-ups of chicken breast served with a pearl barley risotto of butternut, bacon and sage, or leg of local lamb with lamb cobbler, carrot and swede mash, and braised red cabbage in rosemary gravy. Your reward for finishing up your greens may well be chocolate nut torte with boozy blackberries, or there are fine East Anglian cheeses and home-made chutney.

Times 12-3/6-9

FRESSINGFIELD

Map 13 TM27

Fox & Goose Inn

◉◉ Modern British

tel: 01379 586247 **Church Rd IP21 5PB**
email: foxandgoose@uk2.net
dir: *A140 & B1116 (Stradbroke) left after 6m – in village centre by church*

Village restaurant and bar with modern cooking

Hard by the medieval church, Fressingfield's timber-framed Tudor guild hall serves the local community as the village inn. The pub part of the equation pulls a fine pint of real ale and sports a spruced-up modern look with old beams, open fires, church pews at pale wood tables, and slate and quarry tile floors. Like many a country pub these days, food is high on the agenda, and if you want something more ambitious than well-crafted pub classics, head upstairs to the beamed restaurant for creative modern cooking driven by Suffolk's abundant larder. Smoked salmon confit with apple and lemongrass consommé, coriander cress and coconut is the sort of opener that shows a kitchen aiming higher than the average pub offerings. Mains include beef fillet with dauphinoise foam, roasted cauliflower, kale, sauté potatoes and red wine sauce, or slow-cooked hake with oyster mushrooms, potato gnocchi, shaved fennel, mushroom ketchup and lobster sauce. Finish with warm treacle and hazelnut tart with marinated prunes and vanilla ice cream.

Chef P Yaxley, M Wyatt **Owner** Paul Yaxley **Seats** 70, Pr/dining room 35
Times 12-2/7-8.30, Closed 25-30 Dec, 2nd wk Jan for 2 wks, Mon **Prices** Fixed L 2 course fr £14.95, Fixed D 3 course fr £32, Tasting menu £45-£70, Service optional **Wines** 14 bottles over £30, 38 bottles under £30, 11 by glass **Parking** 15 **Notes** Tasting menu 8 course, Sunday L £19.50-£23.95, Vegetarian available, Children 9 yrs+ D

HINTLESHAM

Map 13 TM04

Hintlesham Hall Hotel

◉◉ Modern European V

tel: 01473 652334 **George St IP8 3NS**
email: reservations@hintleshamhall.com **web:** www.hintleshamhall.com
dir: *4m W of Ipswich on A1071*

Polished cooking in top-ranking country-house hotel

Hintlesham Hall is a beautifully proportioned building of three wings, the façade a 1720 addition to the 16th-century core. The interior is equally impressive, with all the elements expected in a grand country-house hotel, from oil paintings to antiques. The Salon dining room is truly stunning, with ruched drapes at the windows, an ornate fireplace, and portraits on white walls contrasting with a red carpet. The kitchen works around a slate of contemporary ideas and displays a level of originality not commonly seen in such surroundings. Pan-fried scallops are served with butternut squash purée, a salted sesame tuile and tarragon dressing, and venison haunch carpaccio could come with onion and goats' cheese croquettes, watercress essence and a port reduction. Main courses show restraint to allow clearly defined flavouring: seared medallions of monkfish are accompanied by tiger prawns and a shellfish reduction, and slow-cooked pork belly, tenderloin and cheeks are helped along by star anise sauce. Dessert might bring pear and green tea sorbet with melon and passionfruit sauce.

Chef Alan Ford **Owner** Has Modi **Seats** 80, Pr/dining room 80 **Times** 12-2/7-9.30 **Prices** Prices not confirmed, Service optional **Wines** 100 bottles over £30, 64 bottles under £30, 9 by glass **Parking** 80 **Notes** Sunday L, Children 12 yrs+ D

INGHAM
Map 13 TL87

The Cadogan Arms

◉ Traditional British

tel: 01284 728443 **The Street IP31 1NG**
email: info@thecadogan.co.uk **web:** www.thecadogan.co.uk
dir: A134, 4m from Bury St Edmunds

Well-executed dishes in stylish gastro-pub

Flexibility is the name of the game in this smartly revamped former coaching inn; whether you just want a jar of real ale in the bar (the inn has its own micro-brewery), a grazing board to snack on, or a full-blown meal, The Cadogan will sort you out. The decor is stylish with subdued lighting, upholstered sofas and chairs, and the kitchen cooks with an eye to the seasons and local producers. The menu includes pub classics such as fish and chips, burgers and steaks and if you fancy something that shows more ambition, you might start with Cromer crab and smoked salmon doughnuts with saffron mayonnaise, followed by Blythburgh pork fillet with apple, celery, walnuts and gnocchi. Puddings can be as timeless as treacle tart with clotted cream, or as creative as apple and cinnamon brioche ravioli.

Chef Michael Bell **Owner** David Marjoram **Seats** 72
Times 12-2.30/6-9.30, Closed 25-26 Dec **Prices** Starter £4.50-£18, Main £11.50-£18, Dessert £6, Service optional **Wines** 8 bottles over £30, 37 bottles under £30, 12 by glass **Parking** 39 **Notes** Sunday L £11.50-£16.50, Vegetarian available, Children welcome

IPSWICH
Map 13 TM14

BEST WESTERN Claydon Country House Hotel

◉ Modern British **V**

tel: 01473 830382 **16-18 Ipswich Rd, Claydon IP6 OAR**
email: enquiries@hotelsipswich.com **web:** www.hotelsipswich.com
dir: A14, junct 52 Claydon exit from rdbt, 300yds on left

Modern British cooking close to Ipswich

Two old village houses were joined seamlessly together to form this friendly, small-scale hotel to the northwest of Ipswich. The Victorian-style restaurant overlooks the gardens through a conservatory extension, although the classic look has been given a gentle update by ditching the cloths on its darkwood tables and adding high-backed leather chairs. Staff are smartly turned out to create a professional, welcoming vibe, and the kitchen draws on splendid locally-sourced produce as the bedrock of its unfussy European-accented modern British dishes. Expect starters along the lines of seafood risotto with rocket and parmesan, while mains could turn up roast rack of lamb with chive mash, wilted greens, and red wine and rosemary glaze. End with a warm Belgian chocolate muffin with chocolate sauce and vanilla ice cream.

Chef Frankie Manners **Owner** Mr Khurram Saeed **Seats** 40, Pr/dining room 85
Times 12-2/7-9.30 **Prices** Fixed D 3 course £24.95, Service optional **Wines** 5 by glass **Parking** 80 **Notes** Sunday L £9.95-£16.95, Children welcome

Mariners

◉ French, Mediterranean

tel: 01473 289748 **Neptune Quay IP4 1AX**
email: info@marinersipswich.co.uk
dir: Accessed via Key St. Follow brown tourist signs to waterfront

Honest Gallic brasserie fare afloat in Ipswich

A French brasserie on a Belgium gunboat in Ipswich... you've got to love it! Moored on Neptune Quay, the boat dates from 1899, but once you're on board, you could well be in Paris, and that could be the Seine through the window rather than Ipswich Marina. The brainchild of local hero, Regis Crepy ('local' via France), owner of The Great House in Lavenham, Mariners is no gimmick. There's a decidedly classy finish to the brasserie-style decor, with polished original brass, chandeliers, lots of burnished wood and tables laid with white linen cloths. Kick-off with a well put together carpaccio of beef with whole grain mustard sauce and green leaves, or a Mediterranean soup with the traditional accompaniments. Main-course grilled fillet of halibut with chive and shrimp sauce competes for your attention with a 36-hour-roasted belly of pork confit. Finish with French apple tart with vanilla ice cream and crème anglaise.

Times 12-2.30/7-9.30, Closed Jan, Sun-Mon

Milsoms Kesgrave Hall

◉ Modern International

tel: 01473 333741 **Hall Rd, Kesgrave IP5 2PU**
email: reception@kesgravehall.com **web:** www.kesgravehall.com
dir: A12 N of Ipswich/Woodbridge, rdbt onto B1214

Boutique global modernism in the Suffolk woods

Hiding in woodland near a little village to the east of Ipswich, Kesgrave Hall is no monument to twee rusticity, but a sparkling-white boutique hotel with a portico and veranda seating out front. The Brasserie dining room is fitted with an up-to-the-minute open kitchen and plain wooden tables. A quirk of the system is that you write down your food order and take it to the bar for service, which seems to run smoothly. An extensive menu of global modernism kicks off with starters in two sizes – 'ample' or 'generous' – for the likes of Wagyu carpaccio with pickled kohlrabi and truffled crème fraîche. Spot-on timing elevates a main course of wild salmon with samphire, asparagus and broad beans into the big league, or there may be guinea fowl in tomato consommé with Savoy cabbage and pancetta crisps. Go trad for afters with apple and sultana crumble and vanilla ice cream.

Times 12-9.30, All-day dining

IPSWICH *continued*

Salthouse Harbour Hotel

◉◉ Modern British

tel: 01473 226789 **No 1 Neptune Quay IP4 1AX**
email: reservations@salthouseharbour.co.uk **web:** www.salthouseharbour.co.uk
dir: *A14 junct 53, A1156 to town centre & harbour, off Key St*

On song brasserie flavours on the harbourside

A harbourside warehouse makeover in sea-salted red brick with eye-popping interior collisions of lime-green and violet, the Salthouse is a hotel for the style-hungry of the 21st century. Sub-Pollock abstracts and inscriptions of italic food terminology on matt black walls are only the half of it; the brick-walled Eaterie is adorned with art objects, waterfront views and relaxed service. They serve stylish brasserie food with look-at-me flavours. Cured trout with fennel and pickled beetroot, or a sauté of wild mushrooms with parmesan and truffle on sourdough toast, are precursors to today's favoured main-course proteins of duck breast, pork belly, and cod, the last appearing in Spanish guise with butter beans, spinach and chorizo. If you're looking for something a little off-piste, they'll happily spatchcock a poussin for you. A gin and tonic arrives a little later than is conventional, in a dessert of apple and Hendrick's jelly, with cucumber sorbet and lime granita, while the braised pineapple is alive with chilli. Old-school reassurance is on hand in the form of sticky toffee pudding.

Chef Chris McQuitty **Owner** Robert Gough **Seats** 70 **Times** 12-10, All-day dining **Prices** Fixed L 2 course £14, Starter £6-£10, Main £14-£22, Dessert £6.50-£8.95 **Wines** 42 bottles over £30, 23 bottles under £30, 31 by glass **Parking** Fore St, Duke St, along waterfront **Notes** Breakfast £15, Afternoon tea £16, Sunday L £20-£25, Vegetarian available, Children welcome

---

▮ IXWORTH
Map 13 TL97

Theobalds Restaurant

◉◉ Modern British

tel: 01359 231707 **68 High St IP31 2HJ**
dir: *7m from Bury St Edmunds on A143 (Bury to Diss road)*

Seasonal modern British food in a beamed Tudor room

Simon and Geraldine Theobald's restaurant certainly has staying power. Converted from a whitewashed Tudor inn in 1981, the place still pulls in the punters with its consistency, attention to detail and simple charm. Ancient beams abound and tables are dressed in pristine white. Every chef and his aunt claims to cook in tune with the seasons these days, but Simon was in the forefront of this sea change in British cooking in the 1980s, and the principle shines brightly in his repertoire. A five-course taster now bolsters the monthly-changing carte, so February's offerings might bring the warmth and comfort of a twice-baked cheddar cheese soufflé with a crisp cheesy top, followed by roast breast and braised leg of Gressingham duck with caramelised apples, golden sultanas and port wine sauce. Locally reared meats and East Anglian fish are the mainstays, and the quality of raw materials is indisputable. Desserts aim to indulge by means of brioche bread-and-butter pudding with prune and Armagnac ice cream, or invigorate with caramelised lemon tart with matching sorbet.

Chef Simon Theobald **Owner** Simon & Geraldine Theobald **Seats** 42, Pr/dining room 16 **Times** 12.15-1.30/7-9, Closed 10 days in spring/summer, Mon, L Tue-Thu, Sat, D Sun **Prices** Fixed L 2 course £23.50, Fixed D 3 course £28.50, Tasting menu £36.50, Service optional **Wines** 16 bottles over £30, 34 bottles under £30, 7 by glass **Parking** On street **Notes** Fixed L Fri, Fixed D Tue-Sat, Sunday L £27.50, Vegetarian available, Children 8 yrs+ D

▮ LAVENHAM
Map 13 TL94

Lavenham Great House 'Restaurant with Rooms'

◉◉◉ – *see opposite*

The Swan

◉◉ Modern, Traditional British ᴠ

tel: 01787 247477 **High St CO10 9QA**
email: info@theswanatlavenham.co.uk **web:** www.theswanatlavenham.co.uk
dir: *From Bury St Edmunds take A134 (S) for 6m then take A1141 to Lavenham*

Modernist cooking beneath a medieval minstrels' gallery

The asymmetrical timbered white building on the main street through the medieval East Anglian village of Lavenham gives evidence of its own great age. Dating back to the 15th century, it's an endearing maze of crannies and beams within, beautifully maintained and bursting with character. There's informal dining in the Brasserie, but the main restaurant is the Gallery. Here the high vaulted ceiling and minstrels' gallery, and polished and attentive service from smartly uniformed staff add to the sense of occasion. The modernism of the cooking is productively at odds with the venerability of its surroundings, opening perhaps with truffled goats' cheese and lightly pickled beets in pea shoot salad, and progressing to cod with spiced lentils and tempura sprouting broccoli, guinea fowl breast with gingered potato rösti and cumin-spiced pumpkin purée or, for vegetarians, an open lasagne of Mediterranean veg with chargrilled halloumi and pesto. An exhaustive deconstruction of tiramisù results in vanilla pannacotta, coffee meringue, vanilla foam, hazelnut crumb and coffee jelly, and very pleasing it is too. A list of 'British' cheeses includes Ireland's Ardrahan – oops.

Chef Justin Kett **Owner** Thorpeness & Aldeburgh Hotels **Seats** 90, Pr/dining room 32 **Times** 12-2.30/7-9.30 **Prices** Fixed L 2 course £16.95, Fixed D 3 course £29.50, Starter £9, Main £22.50, Dessert £8-£11, Service optional **Wines** 111 bottles over £30, 32 bottles under £30, 11 by glass **Parking** 50 **Notes** Breakfast fr £13.95, Sunday L £26.95, Children 5 yrs+

LONG MELFORD
Map 13 TL84

Long Melford Swan
®® Modern, Contemporary British NEW V

tel: 01787 464545 Hall St CO10 9JQ
email: info@longmelfordswan.co.uk web: www.longmelfordswan.co.uk
dir: *Phone for directions*

Confident modern cooking in stylish village restaurant

Slap bang in the middle of the high street in Long Melford, this elegant restaurant with rooms has undergone a complete refurbishment in recent months. With feature wallpaper, pastel colours and a large patio offering alfresco dining opportunities, quality oozes from every corner of this friendly, family-run operation, where service is cheerful and efficient. In the kitchen, the ambitious young team conjure some innovative combinations from tip-top ingredients and although the style is broadly modern British, influences look far beyond the doorstep. This global creativity is demonstrated in a flavour-packed starter of duck consommé, pork and prawn dumplings, chilli, ginger and pak choi. The flair and dexterity of the kitchen is equally evident in a main course of free-range pork loin teamed with chargrilled monkfish cheek, oyster mushroom, cider and mustard velouté and Ibérico ham. For those with more conservative palates, classic moules marinère is served in two sizes and simply grilled steaks and fish. Banana parfait makes for a satisfying conclusion.

Chef Oliver Macmillan, Tom Bushell **Owner** Lorna Pissarro, Oliver, Iain & Andrew Macmillan **Seats** 50, Pr/dining room 8 **Times** 12-2.30/6-9 **Prices** Fixed L 2 course £15.95, Starter £6.50-£11, Main £14-£38, Dessert £5-£8.50, Service optional **Wines** 30 bottles over £30, 35 bottles under £30, 18 by glass **Parking** On street **Notes** Sunday L fr £18.95, Children welcome

LOWESTOFT
Map 13 TM59

The Crooked Barn Restaurant
®® Modern British

tel: 01502 501353 Ivy Ln, Beccles Rd, Oulton Broad NR33 8HY
email: aa@ivyhousecountryhotel.co.uk web: www.ivyhousecountryhotel.co.uk
dir: *A146 into Ivy Lane*

Locally-based cooking in a thatched barn

On the banks of Oulton Broad, in 20 acres of grounds, the Ivy House Country Hotel has an ace up its sleeve in the form of The Crooked Barn Restaurant. The hotel's destination eatery is located in a 16th-century barn which has an abundance of character with the ceiling exposed to the rafters. There's plenty of room within for the smartly set tables, dressed in white linen and generously spaced around the room, plus views over the pretty garden. The kitchen makes excellent use of the region's produce in dishes that smack of Pan-European eclecticism. Start with a modern combo such as pan-fried scallops with parsnip purée and crispy bacon, or go for the globally-inspired home-cured salmon with tempura king prawns with cucumber and sweet chilli dip. Main-course fillet of beef is served in a classical manner with dauphinoise potatoes, honey-roasted vegetables and cracked black pepper sauce, while fillet of plaice is filled with a crayfish mousse and partnered with potato galette and a creamy saffron sauce. Finish with hot chocolate fondant.

Times 12-1.45/7-9.30, Closed 19 Dec-6 Jan

Lavenham Great House 'Restaurant with Rooms' ®®®

LAVENHAM
Map 13 TL94

Modern French
tel: 01787 247431 Market Place CO10 9QZ
email: info@greathouse.co.uk web: www.greathouse.co.uk
dir: *In Market Place (turn onto Market Lane from High Street)*

Modern French cooking in a medieval building

Despite a Georgian façade, the Great House was actually built in the 14th and 15th centuries by a family of textile barons. It's not all about Tudor timbers though, for the dining room has been given a calm and soothing, thoroughly modern look, combining age-old dark oak floorboards and sturdy brick inglenooks with panelled walls painted in soft tones, and comfy chairs upholstered in classy sage and midnight-blue leather. Despite the quintessentially English setting, this is an outpost of la belle France, evident in the slick, all-French front-of-house team, through to the skilled cooking, which is rooted in the great French repertoire. Creative flair suffuses the menu, starting with a pressing of white crab meat partnered with butternut squash chutney, grilled langoustine and mint and coriander vinaigrette, through to a main course starring roast saddle of lamb with a delicate pea pannacotta, pea shoot salsa, buttered Charlotte potatoes and lemongrass and oregano jus. Fish dishes, too, are characterised by vibrant flavours brought together in harmonious, multi-layered combinations, perhaps roast monkfish with red onion and walnut marmalade, Roquefort cheese cream spiced with Pyrenean espelette peppers, and glazed balls of Williams pear. To finish, a classic rum baba is filled with crème pâtissière and gets extra va-va-voom with confit pineapple and Pina Colada sorbet.

Chef Régis Crepy **Owner** Mr & Mrs Crepy **Seats** 40, Pr/dining room 15 **Times** 12-2.30/7-9.30, Closed Jan & 2 wks summer, Mon, L Tue, D Sun **Prices** Fixed L 2 course fr £19.50, Fixed D 3 course £35, Starter £9.95-£16, Main £18.50-£29.95, Dessert £6.95, Service optional **Wines** 65 bottles over £30, 75 bottles under £30, 10 by glass **Parking** Market Place **Notes** Sunday L £35, Vegetarian available, Children welcome

MILDENHALL
Map 12 TL77

The Bull Inn
Modern British

tel: 01638 711001 **The Street, Barton Mills IP28 6AA**
email: reception@bullinn-bartonmills.com web: www. bullinn-bartonmills.com
dir: *Off A11 between Newmarket & Mildenhall, signed Barton Mills. Hotel by Five Ways rdbt*

Funkiness in abundance in a multi-purpose pub

The Bull styles itself as a crossbreed amalgam of cosy B&B, boutique hotel and modern-day coaching inn, and was the AA's official Funkiest B&B of the Year last season, an attribute which is unmistakable from one glance at the menu. Brie fritters in berry coulis, smoked salmon Caesar, or ham and leek terrine with a beetroot-pickled egg make assertive openers to the main event, which might be a laden burger with optional garlic prawn skewer, or perhaps halibut with a backing trio of scallops in apple and vanilla Madeira jus. If you're prepared to forsake the 500-year-old dining rooms for the bar or the great outdoors, the repertoire extends to pub classics such as chicken curry or sausages and mash. Finish with Baileys' and Amaretto cheesecake with coffee ice cream.

Chef Cheryl Hickman, Shaun Jennings **Owner** Cheryl Hickman, Wayne Starling **Seats** 60, Pr/dining room 30 **Times** 12-9, All-day dining, Closed 25 Dec **Prices** Prices not confirmed, Service optional **Wines** 16 bottles over £30, 24 bottles under £30, 11 by glass **Parking** 60 **Notes** Sunday L, Vegetarian available, Children welcome

See advert opposite

NEWMARKET
Map 12 TL66

Bedford Lodge Hotel
Modern International

tel: 01638 663175 **Bury Rd CB8 7BX**
email: info@bedfordlodgehotel.co.uk web: www.bedfordlodgehotel.co.uk
dir: *From town centre take A1304 towards Bury St Edmunds, hotel 0.5m on left*

Classy and inventive dishes near the famous racecourse

This extended one-time Georgian hunting lodge has a prime position near the racecourse and enough top-end facilities to satisfy a modern epicure. There are spa treatments aplenty, the hotel is a big hit for weddings and business get-togethers, and there's a rather spruce restaurant called Squires, named in honour of a notorious former owner of the house. The split-level dining room has a comfortable finish and lots of local artworks to give a sense of place. The menu is packed with enticing dishes with decidedly modern British leanings and some creative combinations. Start with corn-fed chicken and ham hock with pickled mushrooms, cauliflower purée, caper berries and shallot crisps, or perhaps honey-glazed duck with fondant potato, sprouting broccoli, cherries and almond praline. A busy main course showcasing red mullet comes with fresh herbs and lemon, a crab bonbon, Jerusalem artichoke, beetroot, crayfish velouté and white radish. Finish with a fun 'sweet shop' dessert comprising strawberry and bubble gum pannacotta, banana marshmallow, candyfloss, orange sherbet and macaroons, all exploding with colour, texture and sound effects.

Chef James Fairchild **Owner** Review Hotels Ltd **Seats** 60, Pr/dining room 150 **Times** 12-2/7-9.30, Closed L Sat **Prices** Fixed L 2 course £24.50, Fixed D 3 course £28.50, Starter £7-£10, Main £18.50-£29, Dessert £8-£10 **Wines** 93 bottles over £30, 30 bottles under £30, 16 by glass **Parking** 120 **Notes** Sunday L £20.50-£28.50, Vegetarian available, Children welcome

The Packhorse Inn
– see page 490

Tuddenham Mill
Modern British v NOTABLE WINE LIST

tel: 01638 713552 **High St, Tuddenham St Mary IP28 6SQ**
email: info@tuddenhammill.co.uk web: www.tuddenhammill.co.uk
dir: *M11 junct 9 towards Newmarket, then A14 exit junct 38 in direction of Norwich. Turn right at Herringswell road*

Imaginative cooking of unusual ingredients in a converted watermill

The mill still looks as if it could put in a hard day's work, but look more closely and you'll see it's had a makeover. The riverside setting is positively serene and the contemporary decor within matches those views with original features and a clean, modern look. The water-wheel has been encased in glass to form a fine feature in the bar, while the restaurant has heavy oak beams and views over the millpond. The bright, contemporary-style cooking features local and regional produce in creative dishes that utilise lots of modern culinary techniques. From the carte, for example, organic salmon is cooked at 40 degrees and comes with plum emulsion and crispy rice, with another starter pairing a crispy skinned chicken wing with squash purée and roasted peanuts. These clever constructions are soundly thought through and carefully executed. Main-course hake has a well-judged cumin coating, served with Norfolk coppa with a flavourful leek and clam ragu, and another pairs lamb rump with its barbecued shoulder, soured red cabbage and mint. Desserts are no less creative: parsnip cake with celery ice and parsnip toffee, for example (a cracking combo), or lemon curd with goats' milk, hazelnut and mint oil.

Tuddenham Mill

Chef Lee Bye **Owner** Agellus Hotels **Seats** 54, Pr/dining room 18 **Times** 12-2.15/6.30-9.15 **Prices** Fixed L 2 course £15.50, Fixed D 3 course £19.50, Tasting menu £42, Starter £6.50-£10.50, Main £16.95-£25, Dessert £7-£9, Service optional **Wines** 149 bottles over £30, 29 bottles under £30, 13 by glass **Parking** 40 **Notes** Sunday L £19.50-£24.50, Children welcome

---

ORFORD
Map 13 TM45

The Crown & Castle
@@ Italian, British V NOTABLE WINE LIST

tel: 01394 450205 **IP12 2LJ**
email: info@crownandcastle.co.uk **web:** www.crownandcastle.co.uk
dir: *Off A12, on B1084, 9m E of Woodbridge*

Very good eating in a chic old Suffolk inn

There has been a hostelry on this site for 800 years and the tradition of hospitality is in particular good heart in the 21st century. It's co-owned by Ruth Watson (she's also executive chef) who was TV's Hotel Inspector once upon a time, and the combination of stylish bedrooms and an easy-going, rustic-chic restaurant is a winning one. There's genuine character to the spaces within, where beams, unclothed wooden tables and comfortable burgundy-velvet cushioned chairs and benches help create a relaxed vibe. The place is still an inn popular with the locals up for a pint, but it's also something of a foodie destination. The daily-changing menu has an Italian accent these days, featuring the fashionable Venetian small plates, cicchetti, alongside flavour-driven dishes that showcase the region's excellent ingredients. Grilled octopus with nduja sausage and potato salad is one way to kick off a meal, followed perhaps with duck breast with warm borlotti beans and morels, or a proper shortcrust steak and kidney pie. Finish with zabaglione or treacle tart.

Chef Ruth Watson, Charlene Gavazzi **Owner** David & Ruth Watson, Tim Sunderland **Seats** 60, Pr/dining room 10 **Times** 12.15-2.45/6.30-9.45 **Prices** Starter £5.50-£9.95, Main £15.95-£25, Dessert £6.95 **Wines** 65 bottles over £30, 66 bottles under £30, 16 by glass **Parking** 17, Market Sq, on street **Notes** Pre-concert supper (prior booking essential), Sunday L £23-£28, Children 8 yrs+ D

SIBTON

Map 13 TM36

Sibton White Horse Inn

Modern British

tel: 01728 660337 **Halesworth Rd IP17 2JJ**
email: info@sibtonwhitehorseinn.co.uk web: www.sibtonwhitehorseinn.co.uk
dir: *From A12 in Yoxford take A1120 signed Sibton & Peasenhall. 3m, in Peasenhall right opposite butcher's shop. White Horse 600mtrs*

Charming Tudor pub with modern global cooking

In the heart of Suffolk at its sleepiest, among villages full of candy-coloured cottages, though only a few minutes' drive from the A12 and Saxmundham, the White Horse is a beamed Tudor inn dating back to the 16th century. The place is reliably abuzz with local custom, chatter and laughter filling the low-ceilinged, quarry-tiled rooms. The kitchen team draw on regional produce to craft menus that display the global influences of modern cooking, but don't take off on a one-way trip to La-La Land either. Tea-smoked salmon makes a diverting starter, the deeply fragrant fish set off with grape and walnut salad and horseradish crème fraîche. That might be followed by pot-roast breast of first-class Gressingham duck with dauphinoise, roast baby onions and pak choi — a lovely balance of weight and flavour — or sea bass with Asian-spiced sticky rice and sweet chilli jam. Pear and pistachio millefeuille with mulled wine sorbet rounds things off in style.

Chef Gill Mason, James Finch **Owner** Neil & Gill Mason **Seats** 40, Pr/dining room 18 **Times** 12-2/6.30-9, Closed Xmas, L Mon **Prices** Fixed L 2 course £13-£22, Fixed D 3 course £23.50-£32.50, Starter £6-£7, Main £11.75-£20, Dessert £5-£7, Service optional **Wines** 3 bottles over £30, 29 bottles under £30, 8 by glass **Parking** 35 **Notes** Sunday L £11.75-£13.25, Vegetarian available, Children 6 yrs+ D

SOUTHWOLD

Map 13 TM57

Sutherland House

Modern British, Seafood

tel: 01502 724544 **56 High St IP18 6DN**
email: enquiries@sutherlandhouse.co.uk web: www.sutherlandhouse.co.uk
dir: *A1095 into Southwold, on High St on left after Victoria St*

Neighbourhood fish restaurant with diligent sourcing

The original parts of the building date from the 15th century, with the Georgians and Victorians chipping in along the way, to create a period house of genuine charm. There are wooden beams from ships that fought in the battle of Sole Bay (and that was in 1672!) and ornate ceilings, coving and real fireplaces throughout. The fixtures and fittings cut a more contemporary dash, giving a decidedly chic finish. Likewise, the cooking impresses with its modern ambitions, passion for seafood, and loyalty to local ingredients (fruit and veg come from their own

The Packhorse Inn

NEWMARKET

Map 12 TL66

Modern British
tel: 01638 751818 **Bridge St, Moulton CB8 8SP**
email: info@thepackhorseinn.com web: www.thepackhorseinn.com
dir: *A14 junct 39 onto B1506. After 1.5m turn left at x-rds onto B1085 (Moulton Rd). In Moulton, left into Bridge St*

Classy modern pub food in a stylishly reinvented country inn

A local businessman took over Moulton's old village pub in 2013, gave the place a cool and classy new look to meet 21st-century expectations, and installed Chris Lee at the stoves to come up with the culinary goods. The result balances the pub's original rustic charm with an upscale country-chic style, and although gentrified with a hefty dose of metropolitan-chic style, the bar still serves as the local pub with a relaxed attitude and welcoming approach. The focus on food however is unquestionable. Inside, a tasteful cream and aubergine palette sits well with bare bricks, trompe l'oeil panelled wallpaper, and bare-boarded floors strewn with rugs. The kitchen takes first-rate, well-sourced local materials as the starting point for seasonal menus that mix gently updated pub favourites — chicken liver parfait with toasted brioche and melon chutney, perhaps, ahead of scampi with braised lettuce, minted peas and fries — with more ambitious modern European ideas. Starters might include a tried-and-tested trio of scallops roasted with cumin and partnered with black pudding and cauliflower, or try out some canny on-trend touches like the deconstructing of a 'BLT' with rabbit loin, bacon jelly and confit tomato. Main courses can hit you with big, assertive flavours via a duo of loin and braised shin of Ampton Estate venison with boulangère potatoes and parsnips, or coax more subtle flavour combinations from brill partnered with artichoke, endives and truffled potato. To finish, pudding could be a fashionably retro reworking of bananas and custard or a comforting peanut butter and jam parfait with raspberry sorbet. Otherwise, go for a savoury finish with a plate of Anglo-French cheeses with port jelly.

Chef Chris Lee **Owner** Phillip & Amanda Turner **Seats** 65, Pr/dining room 32 **Times** 12-2.30/7-9.30, Closed D 25 Dec **Prices** Starter £3-£12, Main £10-£35, Dessert £3-£10, Service optional 10% **Wines** 74 bottles over £30, 36 bottles under £30, 18 by glass **Parking** 30 **Notes** Sunday L £14-£20, Vegetarian available, Children welcome

allotment, and there's a local flavour all round – 'food yards', as they say). Start with Debden mussels in classic marinière style, or English snails with a parmesan and asparagus soufflé. Main-course roasted cod loin comes with champ, clams and brown shrimps, and a meaty option might be 28-day aged fillet steak with sweet potato skinny fries. Dessert stage might deliver bread-and-butter pudding with a brûlée topping and vintage marmalade ice cream, or lemon and ginger cheesecake with candied lemon.

Chef Jed Tejada **Owner** Andy & Kinga Rudd **Seats** 50, Pr/dining room 60 **Times** 12-2.30/7-9, Closed 25 Dec, 2 wks Jan, Mon **Prices** Starter £5.50-£11, Main £18-£24, Dessert £5.50-£7, Service optional **Wines** 10 bottles over £30, 20 bottles under £30, 10 by glass **Parking** 1, On street **Notes** Sunday L £10-£24, Vegetarian available, Children welcome

Swan Hotel

◉◉ Modern British

tel: 01502 722186 **High St, Market Place IP18 6EG**
email: swan.hotel@adnams.co.uk **web:** www.adnamshotels.co.uk
dir: A1095 to Southwold. Hotel in town centre. Parking via archway to left of building

Smart British cooking at Adnams' flagship hotel

Just in front of the Sole Bay brewery, the epicentre of the Adnams' empire's Southwold operations, is the Swan – a handsome bay-fronted hotel occupying pole position among the boutiques. Inside, its 17th-century origins are revealed: there are wall panels, 18th-century oil paintings and gilt chandeliers, but time has not stood still, so it is all jazzed up with smart contemporary looks. As one would hope from the seaside town's brewer, main publican, wine merchant and hotelier, its flagship restaurant has well-established supply lines to prime local materials, which are deployed in confident, full-flavoured cooking. Pumpkin and walnut tart is matched with a poached duck egg and grain mustard sabayon, or you might start with that time-honoured duo of seared scallops and home-made black pudding, partnered with celeriac purée, apple and walnuts. Main course brings a big-hearted dish of venison loin with herb mash, root vegetables and fig purée, sauced with port and orange. For pudding, there's real lightness of touch and big flavour in a fig and almond sponge.

Times 12-2.30//-9.30

■ STOKE-BY-NAYLAND　　　　Map 13 TL93

The Angel Inn

◉ Modern British **NEW**

tel: 01206 263245 & 07748 484619 **Polstead St CO6 4SA**
email: info@angelinnsuffolk.co.uk **web:** www.angelinnsuffolk.co.uk
dir: From A134 onto Bear St (B1087), 2m on right in Stoke-by-Nayland

A timbered Tudor pub goes modern British

A timbered Tudor inn in Constable country has a lot going for it in the heritage stakes. Known as The Angel since the late 18th century, it's a charming hostelry with quarry-tiled floors, exposed red-brick walls and a double-height ceiling in the dining area with oak beams and the original well. A herb garden supplies the kitchen with its aromatics, which help to distinguish the confident modern British cooking on offer. Fish dishes are nicely considered and well timed, from a slate-plated starter of seared scallops and tempura squid with chorizo dressing, to mains such as sea bass with saffron potatoes in seaweed butter. There are quality meats too, like saddle and confit leg of rabbit with smoked pancetta and butter bean ragout. Veggies might opt for chickpea and bean curry on saffron pilaf, while little angels (aka kids) get their own menu. At close of business, the vanilla pannacotta is properly fragile and comes with lime-poached strawberries.

Chef Mark Allen **Owner** Exclusive Inns Ltd **Seats** 60, Pr/dining room 10 **Times** 12-2.30/6-9.30 **Prices** Fixed L 2 course £12.50-£13.95, Fixed D 3 course £21-£28, Tasting menu £45-£65, Starter £5.25-£9.75, Main £10.50-£21, Dessert £5.50-£8.25 **Wines** 12 bottles over £30, 14 bottles under £30, 10 by glass **Parking** 20 **Notes** Fish & Fizz Fri, Sunday L £13.95-£21.95, Vegetarian available, Children welcome

The Crown

◉◉ Modern British ▮ NOTABLE WINE LIST

tel: 01206 262001 **CO6 4SE**
email: info@crowninn.net **web:** www.crowninn.net
dir: Stoke-by-Nayland signed from A12 & A134. Hotel in village off B1068 towards Higham

Boutique hotel and village inn serving modern British food

Perfectly placed for exploring Constable country – the soaring tower of nearby St Mary's Church is immortalised in the artist's works – and with unspoilt views across the peaceful Box Valley, the classy 16th-century Crown has been spruced up with style and panache, morphing into a classy boutique inn with the addition of 11 swish bedrooms. The rambling beamed bar and dining areas sport a smart contemporary look, with cockle-warming log fires, cosy corners, and an in-house wine shop. Monthly-changing modern British menus, supplemented by daily fish dishes – landed by local fishing boats working from the Blackwater Estuary – on the chalkboard, reflect the seasons and show flair, imagination, and sound use of quality local ingredients. A summer's dinner sets out with guinea fowl terrine with bacon, garlic toast and apricot chutney, then the kitchen's confident creative spirit continues with pan-fried rainbow trout fillet with cauliflower and almond puree, wilted gem lettuce, a fried egg and thick-cut chips. For pudding, a deliciously retro Black Forest gâteau comes with fresh cherries.

Chef Dan Hibble **Owner** Richard Sunderland **Seats** 125, Pr/dining room 14 **Times** 12-2.30/6-9.30, Closed 25-26 Dec **Prices** Fixed L 2 course £15, Starter £5.25-£7.50, Main £12-£21, Dessert £4-£6.50, Service optional **Wines** 244 bottles over £30, 76 bottles under £30, 32 by glass **Parking** 49 **Notes** Sunday L, Vegetarian available, Children welcome

What makes the perfect steak?
Find out on page 20

SUDBURY
Map 13 TL84

The Case Restaurant with Rooms

Modern British

tel: 01787 210483 **Further St, Assington CO10 5LD**
email: restaurant@thecaserestaurantwithrooms.co.uk
web: www.thecaserestaurantwithrooms.co.uk
dir: *Located on A134 between Sudbury & Colchester. 0.5m past Newton Golf Club*

Characterful Suffolk inn with brasserie-style menu

This charming country inn has bags of character, with low beams and exposed brick in the bar area and a cosy little restaurant with a wood-burning stove, darkwood tables and ceiling beams. Host-led hospitality is the key to its success as well as the quality of the contemporary brasserie-style cooking. Start off with one of the appealing first courses: perhaps a king prawn version of Caesar salad, or duck, orange and Grand Marnier pâté with caper berries. The kitchen displays a great deal of flair in its creations and in their presentation and keeps things relatively straightforward, evident in main courses of poached fillet of plaice stuffed with salmon mousse accompanied by baby vegetables and new potatoes, and roast shoulder of lamb on a bed of red cabbage and apple with redcurrant jus and mint-crushed potato. Puddings hit the mark in the shape of French apple tart with custard.

Times 6.30-9, Closed L Mon-Sat, D Sun

THORPENESS
Map 13 TM45

Thorpeness Hotel

Modern British

tel: 01728 452176 **Lakeside Av IP16 4NH**
email: info@thorpeness.co.uk **web:** www.thorpeness.co.uk
dir: *A1094 towards Aldeburgh, take coast road N for 2m*

Simple but sound cookery next to golf course

The heathland golf course adjacent to the sea was opened in 1922 and has brought golfers to the region ever since, while the hotel offers R & R to all – there's lots to do hereabouts where a love of the fairways and greens is not required. The restaurant serves up views over the third tee in a traditional and roomy setting (there's also a wood-panelled bar and a terrace with a watery vista). The daily-changing menu keeps things relatively simple, so you might start with tender ham hock with home-made remoulade and granary toast, or lemon and dill fishcake with chunky tartare sauce. Move on to pan-fried rib-eye with hand-cut chips and classic trimmings, or Thorpeness fish pie with cheesy mash and greens. Among desserts, milk chocolate profiteroles come filled with white chocolate cream and tangy lemon tart is served with lemon sorbet and raspberry coulis.

Chef Adam Thompson **Owner** T A Hotel Collection **Seats** 80, Pr/dining room 30 **Times** 12.30-3/7-9.30, Closed L Mon-Sat **Prices** Prices not confirmed **Wines** 3 bottles over £30, 27 bottles under £30, 15 by glass **Parking** 80 **Notes** Sunday L, Vegetarian available, Children welcome

Who has won our
Food Service Award?
See page 13

WESTLETON
Map 13 TM46

The Westleton Crown

Modern British V

tel: 01728 648777 **The Street IP17 3AD**
email: info@westletoncrown.co.uk **web:** www.westletoncrown.co.uk
dir: *A12 N, turn right for Westleton just after Yoxford. Hotel opposite on entering village*

Vibrant modern cooking in an ancient inn

This hotel, restaurant and pub, between Aldeburgh and Southwold, has its roots in the 12th century. Real ales are pulled in the bar, with its log fire and beams, while diners make their way to the cosy parlour with its brick inglenook, or the Garden Room conservatory extension, a light-filled room with chunky wooden furniture, a tiled floor and a wall of folding doors opening on to the garden. 'Hearty yet sophisticated' cooking is the kitchen's aim, with the former apparent in chicken, leek and black pudding terrine with mustard dressing, then sirloin steak with all the trimmings. The kitchen never takes its eye off the ball in terms of timing or blending different elements into a successful whole. Asparagus with crispy bacon shavings, a herb-crumbed duck egg and aïoli is a starter with distinct, deep flavours, and might be followed by a nicely balanced main course of crisp-skinned fried sea trout fillet with asparagus, crushed potato and hollandaise. Ambition doesn't falter among puddings: expect chocolate and pistachio cake with chocolate sorbet and cherries.

Chef Robert Mace **Owner** Agellus Hotels Ltd **Seats** 85, Pr/dining room 50 **Times** 12-2.30/6.30-9.30 **Prices** Starter £5.50-£8.95, Main £14.25-£24.50, Dessert £6-£8.95, Service optional **Wines** 23 bottles over £30, 21 bottles under £30, 9 by glass **Parking** 50 **Notes** Afternoon tea, Sunday L £12.50-£27.95, Children welcome

WOODBRIDGE
Map 13 TM24

The Crown at Woodbridge

Modern European

tel: 01394 384242 **2 Thoro'fare IP12 1AD**
email: info@thecrownatwoodbridge.co.uk **web:** www.thecrownatwoodbridge.co.uk
dir: *A12 follow signs for Woodbridge onto B1438, after 1.25m from rdbt turn left into Quay Street & hotel on right, approx 100 yds from junct*

Intelligent contemporary cooking with East Anglia's fine produce

A no-expense-spared facelift relaunched The Crown as a stylish 21st-century inn back in 2009. The look is decidedly boutique, combining 16th-century features with a fresh, contemporary design ethos in four dining areas. One has glowing paprika red walls, another is done out in cool shades of grey and features an etched glass mural screen, while a Windermere skiff hangs above the glass-roofed bar. The kitchen raids the Suffolk larder for its unfussy, big-hearted modern cooking. Local fish and seafood make a good showing on a wide-ranging menu, firstly in a duo of seared scallops with crispy pig's cheek jazzed up with jalapeño pepper-spiked gribiche and sauced with cider and caramel, followed by grilled skate wing with sautéed new potatoes, purple sprouting broccoli, and cockle and caper butter. Desserts can be as classic as good old sticky toffee and date pudding with vanilla ice cream, or get creative with complex confections such as rhubarb and blood orange jelly with ginger pannacotta, rhubarb and ginger sorbet and gingerbread.

Chef Luke Bailey **Owner** Thorpeness & Aldeburgh Hotels **Seats** 60, Pr/dining room 20 **Times** 12-2.30/6-9, Closed D 25 Dec (available for residents only) **Prices** Fixed L 2 course £15, Fixed D 3 course £20, Starter £6.50-£19.50, Main £12-£26, Dessert £3.50-£8, Service optional **Wines** 58 bottles over £30, 31 bottles under £30, 26 by glass **Parking** 30 **Notes** Afternoon tea, Brunch, Sunday L £6-£25, Vegetarian available, Children welcome

Seckford Hall Hotel

@@ Modern European, British

tel: 01394 385678 **IP13 6NU**
email: reception@seckford.co.uk **web:** www.seckford.co.uk
dir: *Hotel signed on A12 (Woodbridge bypass). Do not follow signs for town centre*

Modern country house cooking in a Tudor mansion

Approached by a sweeping drive through well-preened grounds, this blue-blooded Tudor pile impresses from the off with its creeper-curtained brick façade, soaring chimneys and carved-oak front door. Seckford is a country-house hotel for the 21st century, with a swish interior that successfully blends its regal past with modern-day comforts. The 1530 restaurant embodies the style, with carved linenfold panelling set against a sleek minimalist backdrop. A new line-up in the kitchen follows a culinary style that is classical country house with a contemporary sensibility, offering starters like ham hock and parsley terrine with a crispy quail's egg and pickles, followed by mains that take in roast pork tenderloin with fondant potato, Savoy cabbage, and a dried ham and cider sauce, or fishy ideas such as pan-roasted cod with wild garlic, pommes Anna, purple sprouting broccoli, shallots and red wine jus. Desserts might bring the old-school comforts of lemon meringue, or seek inspiration from the continent for a vanilla pannacotta with cherries, and an Amaretto and almond tuile.

Chef Ian Kyle **Owner** Mr & Mrs Pankhurst **Seats** 85, Pr/dining room 150 **Times** 12.30-1.45/7-9.30 **Prices** Fixed L 2 course fr £13.50, Starter £6.95-£8.50, Main £11.50-£20.95, Dessert £6.50-£8.50, Service optional **Wines** 11 by glass **Parking** 100 **Notes** Sunday L £23, Vegetarian available, Children welcome

---

YAXLEY Map 13 TM17

The Auberge

@@ Traditional, International

tel: 01379 783604 **Ipswich Rd IP23 8BZ**
email: aubmail@the-auberge.co.uk **web:** www.the-auberge.co.uk
dir: *5m S of Diss on A140*

Well-crafted dishes in a medieval Suffolk inn

The ancient beams, panelling and exposed brickwork dating back to medieval times are clear evidence that this was a public house for many centuries, but its name serves notice that it is now reincarnated as a modern restaurant with rooms. The room is still darkly intimate; tables are crisply laid with linen, embellished with bowls of fresh lemons, limes and chillies and lit by candles. As the name would suggest, French influences underpin the cooking, but the kitchen relies on good supply lines to local materials for modern, skilfully rendered food that makes a virtue of simplicity. Start perhaps with smoked haddock fishcakes with pea shoots and lime and thyme mayonnaise, or a twice-baked three-cheese soufflé, before moving to slow-roasted pork belly with Aspall cider, crackling, and caramelised Pink Lady apples, or one of the speciality steaks – rib-eye, perhaps, with garlic and balsamic butter or pink peppercorn sauce. Puddings go unashamedly for the populist vote, with a pyramid of dark chocolate and nuts served with Cointreau ice cream, or cappuccino cheesecake.

Chef John Stenhouse, Mark Bond **Owner** John & Dee Stenhouse **Seats** 60, Pr/dining room 20 **Times** 12-2/7-9.30, Closed Sun, L Mon **Prices** Fixed L 2 course £17-£18.50, Fixed D 3 course £25-£27, Starter £8-£11.50, Main £15-£21, Dessert £6.95, Service optional **Wines** 22 bottles over £30, 28 bottles under £30, 13 by glass **Parking** 25 **Notes** Vegetarian available, Children welcome

---

YOXFORD Map 13 TM36

Satis House Hotel

@@ Modern British

tel: 01728 668418 **Main Rd IP17 3EX**
email: enquiries@satishouse.co.uk **web:** www.satishouse.co.uk
dir: *Off A12 between Ipswich & Lowestoft. 9m E Aldeburgh & Snape*

International bistro style with literary credentials

The Georgian manor house lent its name to the decaying mausoleum in which Miss Havisham entombed herself in *Great Expectations*, but survived the encounter with its life-affirming charm intact. A rural retreat in three acres of its own parkland, it makes a covetable country-house hotel these days, done up in a style that wouldn't have unduly startled Dickens, though the floral-wallpapered dining room daringly dispenses with carpet and cloths. The cooking style has more than a hint of French bistro to it, with peppery duck terrine, onion marmalade and ciabatta toast to start, followed by skewered monkfish robustly marinated in rosemary, fennel and lemon, or slow-roasted duck leg on white bean cassoulet. Other traditions receive their due too though, in yellow jungle curry with coconut rice, or Chianti-braised hare in pappardelle. Sunday lunch enshrines the old traditions, with roast loin of pork or beef topside for the taking, accompanied by goose-fat roasties and hearty gravy. Round it all off with a rhubarb spin on Eton Mess, or an indeterminately 'boozy' pannacotta with blackberries.

Chef David Little **Owner** David Little, Kevin Wainwright **Seats** 60, Pr/dining room 30 **Times** 12-2.30/6.30-9.30, Closed L Mon-Fri **Prices** Fixed L 2 course £18, Fixed D 3 course £23, Starter £6-£12, Main £13-£25, Dessert £7, Service optional **Wines** 20 bottles over £30, 30 bottles under £30, 8 by glass **Parking** 25 **Notes** Fixed L Sat only, Fixed D Sun-Thu (pre-book), Sunday L £14, Vegetarian available, Children welcome

---

SURREY

BAGSHOT Map 6 SU96

The Brasserie at Pennyhill Park

@@ Modern International

tel: 01276 471774 & 478569 **Pennyhill Park Hotel & The Spa, London Rd GU19 5EU**
email: enquiries@pennyhillpark.co.uk
dir: *M3 junct 3, through Bagshot, left onto A30. 0.5m on right*

Relaxed and airy brasserie with punchy contemporary cooking

The Brasserie is the more informal and relaxed alternative to Pennyhill Park's trailblazing Latymer. This large, colourful, stone-walled room, with bright banquettes and lots of windows, overlooks the pool and the huge spa complex. It makes a swish setting for some lively modern cooking, and the kitchen accordingly puts a fresh spin on the brasserie repertoire, aiming for punchy, tightly-defined flavours in creations that are contemporary without being outlandish. Poached crab roulade is matched with cured trout and basil jelly. Main courses bring the comfort of classic grilled steaks, or you might strike out towards more enterprising dishes – perhaps braised shoulder and loin of lamb teamed with haricot bean fricassée, spring cabbage, smoked celeriac purée and lamb caper jus, or pollack fillet baked in squid ink with pearl barley, pak choi, tapioca crisp, shiitaki mushrooms and coconut jus. To finish, lime parfait is a zingy counterpoint to strawberry marshmallow and sorbet.

Chef Steve Hubbert **Owner** Danny Pecorelli **Seats** 120 **Times** 12.30-2/6-10, Closed L Sat **Prices** Fixed L 2 course £25, Fixed D 3 course £40, Starter £6.50-£10.50, Main £16.50-£32.50, Dessert £6.50-£11 **Wines** 62 bottles over £30, 16 bottles under £30, 12 by glass **Parking** 200 **Notes** Sunday L £37, Vegetarian available, Children welcome

BAGSHOT *continued*

Michael Wignall at The Latymer

◉◉◉◉◉ *– see opposite*

– see opposite

CAMBERLEY Map 6 SU86

Macdonald Frimley Hall Hotel & Spa

◉◉ British, European

tel: 01276 413100 **Lime Av GU15 2BG**
email: general.frimleyhall@macdonald-hotels.co.uk **web:** www.macdonaldhotels.co.uk/
frimleyhall
dir: *M3 junct 3, A321 follow Bagshot signs. Through lights, left onto A30 signed Camberley & Basingstoke. To rdbt, 2nd exit onto A325, take 5th right*

Gentle modernist cooking at the home of Coal Tar Soap

The expansive handsome mansion not far off the M3 was once home to William Valentine Wright, the man who gave Britain Coal Tar Soap. Its immaculate preservation is a tribute to those halcyon pre-handwash days, the exterior half-covered in climbing ivy, the entrance dominated by a grand oak staircase. The Linden restaurant, by contrast, goes for a smart-casual look, with unclothed tables, garden views and an intimate candlelit ambience in the evenings. A streamlined modern menu showcases the gentler side of British modernism, juxtaposing pressed corn-fed chicken terrine with rhubarb three ways and gingerbread, or perhaps a simple bowl of creamed wild garlic soup, before main-course choices that take in fried hake fillet with truffled potato crush in lemon butter, or baked guinea fowl with a croquette of rosemary polenta in wild mushroom jus. Thoroughbred Scottish steaks are a popular feature, as are the intriguing desserts, which include chocolate and cherry cheesecake with popping chocolate soil, and 'torn' lemon sponge with crème fraîche sorbet. Quality cheeses come with cherry tomato chutney, figs and walnuts.

Chef Michael Ball **Owner** Macdonald Hotels **Seats** 55, Pr/dining room 25
Times 12.30-2/7-9.30 **Prices** Fixed D 3 course £32.50-£48 **Wines** 72 bottles over £30, 28 bottles under £30, 12 by glass **Parking** 75 **Notes** Sunday L £19-£25, Vegetarian available, Children welcome

CHIDDINGFOLD Map 6 SU93

The Swan Inn

◉◉ British, International

tel: 01428 684688 **Petworth Rd GU8 4TY**
email: info@theswaninnchiddingfold.com **web:** www.theswaninnchiddingfold.com
dir: *M25 junct 10, A3 to Milford junct. At rdbt 1st exit onto A283, left at lights. At next rdbt 2nd exit, 5m to Swan Inn*

Wide-ranging menus in a former coaching inn

While it has a bar with an inglenook and hops hanging from beams, The Swan is a popular destination restaurant, and its appeal is understandable. Unfussy decor sets the scene, all chunky wooden furniture, lots of bare brick, wooden floors and walls hung with a profusion of pictures. Outside is a three-tier terraced garden for alfresco dining. The kitchen pulls in ideas from a variety of sources without losing its British roots. Beefburger with chips and tomato chutney might appear alongside chermoula-marinated chicken breast with lemony yogurt dressing, roasted chickpeas and a sweet potato and spinach salad, or classic lamb's kidneys turbigo with mash, onion rings and runner beans. Dishes are carefully considered in terms of balance, so seared foie gras comes with the contrast of apple purée, a spicy red wine reduction and caramelised sherry vinegar, and another starter of Maryland crab cakes with sweet chilli salsa. End on a fruity note: perhaps pineapple sorbet, or caramelised lemon tart with confit orange and zesty lime sorbet.

Chef Graham Digweed, Aarron Foster **Owner** Annemaria & Stuart Boomer Davies
Seats 40, Pr/dining room 40 **Times** 12-3/6.30-10 **Prices** Starter £5-£12.25, Main £11.75-£19.95, Dessert £4.50-£6.50 **Wines** 22 bottles over £30, 29 bottles under £30, 15 by glass **Parking** 35 **Notes** Sunday L £11.75-£19.95, Vegetarian available, Children welcome

CHOBHAM Map 6 SU96

Stovell's

◉◉◉◉ *– see page 496*

– see page 496

DORKING Map 6 TQ14

Mercure Box Hill Burford Bridge Hotel

◉ British, European

tel: 01306 884561 **Burford Bridge, Box Hill RH5 6BX**
email: h6635@accor.com **web:** www.mercure.com
dir: *M25 junct 9, A245 towards Dorking. Hotel within 5m on A24*

Light and contemporary hotel cooking on the North Downs

At the foot of Box Hill in the sumptuous North Downs countryside, the Burford Bridge is proud of its location. Comprising a cluster of buildings including an old tithe-barn with original beams, it's been done in light contemporary style inside, including a monochrome bar with comfy sofas, and a white-walled dining room called the Emlyn, which has elegant curved banquette seating in gentle lilac. Light and contemporary describes the culinary approach too, which makes a good showing of starter dishes such as chunky pork terrine with pickled mushrooms and apple jelly, and mains like crisp-skinned seared chicken breast with charred onion, bread sauce and a good meaty jus, braised salmon with asparagus in champagne sauce, or vegetable cannelloni with smoked cheese and roasted vine tomatoes. A happy ending is assured with a textbook rendition of tiramisù, or pear frangipane tart with crème anglaise.

Times 12-2.30/7-9.30, Closed D Sun

Michael Wignall at The Latymer ✿✿✿✿✿

BAGSHOT	Map 6 SU96

Modern European V NOTABLE WINE LIST

tel: 01276 471774 **London Rd GU19 5EU**
email: enquiries@pennyhillpark.co.uk
web: www.exclusivehotels.co.uk
dir: *M3 junct 3, through Bagshot, left onto A30. 0.5m on right*

Stunningly-crafted contemporary cooking in a luxurious hotel

The creeper-covered Victorian manor at the heart of the 123-acre Pennyhill estate was built as a family home for a businessman of some regard, and has grown into a high-powered hotel and spa. The grounds include elegant gardens, wild woodland, a less wild golf course and even a rugby pitch where the England Rugby Union team trains. The spa is so swish it has its own swimming pool (one of eight!) with underwater music and there are pampering treatments on offer such as chocolate and vanilla body therapy (yum). Pennyhill has every base covered, with an impressive brasserie dining option and glorious afternoon teas taken in the Ascot Bar or out on one of the terraces. Everything is set up for pure indulgence and relaxation, and something would be amiss is there wasn't a serious dining option. There is: Michael Wignall at The Latymer is one of the top restaurants in the country. The dining room is split between two elegant spaces with oak panels and stained-glass windows, with a contemporary and smart finish, watched over by an effortlessly dynamic service team. Chef is a bit of an adrenalin junky outside the 'office', and snowboarding, wakeboarding and downhill mountain biking are doubtless welcome distractions from the intensity of the kitchen. Producing food this good takes 100% commitment, focus and perfectionism. The Drawing Room is the best place to start (with something to your taste in your hand), while deciding whether to go for the ten-course tasting menu, seven-course option or three courses off the fixed-price carte (particularly great value at lunchtime). Expect dishes of precision, creativity and verve. The canapés set the standard from the off: for example Japanese truffle dumpling (wow) or chicken liver parfait with Madeira jelly served on a crab biscuit (double wow). A starter of lightly salted cod shows superb technique, brilliant ingredients, and, most of all, respect for the first-class produce. The cod is poached in single estate olive oil and partnered with a roasted scallop, Ibérico lardo, textures of cauliflower and charcoal emulsion in a combination that positively inspires. Nothing is out of place in a stunning-looking main course of Lancashire suckling piglet, enriched with honey and mustard and matched with salt-baked swede, Tomme de Savoie, pak choi and golden enoki mushrooms. A dessert called 'yeast' delivers wonderful flavours and textures, not least the soft milk skin that accompanies the parfait and chocolate caramel, or go for a 'rhubarb' option with caramelised white chocolate and burnt butter crumble. The wine list matches the food in ambition and attainment.

Chef Michael Wignall **Owner** Exclusive Hotels & Venues
Seats 50, Pr/dining room 16 **Times** 12.30-2/7-9.45, Closed 1-14 Jan, Sun-Mon (open Sun BHs but closed following Tue), L Tue, Sat, D Sun-Mon **Prices** Fixed L 3 course £41, Tasting menu £94-£110 **Wines** 300 bottles over £30, 20 by glass **Parking** 500 **Notes** Tasting menu 7/10 course, Children 12 yrs+

Stovell's ❁❁❁

Modern European

tel: 01276 858000 **125 Windsor Rd GU24 8QS**
email: enquiries@stovells.com **web:** www.stovells.com
dir: *M25 junct 11. Join A317 then take A320 towards Chobham, A319 turn right Windsor Road*

Exhilarating modern food in a Tudor farmhouse

Fernando and Kristy Stovells' move in 2012 from catering to the celeb circuit of London's private clubs to renovating a 500-year-old Tudor farmhouse in deepest Surrey must have been something of a culture shock, but clearly a welcome one, since their self-named restaurant bears all the hallmarks of a passionate enthusiasm for food. Retaining its physiognomy of gnarled old age, it's all head-skimming ceilings and whitewashed brick walls punctuated by gnarled black beams inside, with roaring fires in an original inglenook in winter. There are contemporary-styled pictures of mushrooms to look at, and a rose-red Ibérico ham waiting on its slicer for the starter orders – all very coy, but with serious culinary intent. The pairing of unusual flavours and textures is clearly a passion, requiring an arsenal of skills to prepare and luckily there's genuine technical ability in the kitchen from this husband-and-wife team, supported by some serious kit, including a robata grill and wood-fired oven, so what is promised is delivered on the plate. There's skill and creativity from the off in an exhilarating virtuoso opening dish of caramelised hand-dived Kirkwall Bay scallops, served on a bed of ground corn grits, together with an impeccable lone shrimp, and melt-in-the-mouth pork jowl with a deep, piggy flavour that takes the dish to a higher plane. Luxury also beckons in a starter of warm aromatic foie gras with burnt grelot onions, toasted cobnuts, hay tea dressing and pennywort. Next up, more porcine pleasure, this time in the form of a pressing made from various cuts of suckling pig, with a supporting cast of crispy crackling, cauliflower purée, prunes dressed with bone-dry manzanilla sherry, and a head-spinning jus. A wood-fired clay oven does its bit too, chargrilling a big old rib of beef for two over vine cuttings from nearby Hush Heath vineyard, or adding smoky savour to a mixed grill of milk-fed kid served with morels, corn bread, 'land seaweed' and verjus. Impressive desserts are peppered with good ideas – a light-as-air baked dark chocolate mousse arrives on a fudgy salted caramel base revved up with Pedro Ximenez sherry and partnered with banana ice cream – or finish on a savoury note with perfectly ripened artisan cheeses. Service comes courtesy of a young, knowledgeable team and a first-rate sommelier. Incidentally, if you fancy a G&T for an aperitif, the Stovells distil their own organic gin made with sustainably foraged botanicals and a hint of Chobham honey.

Chef Fernando & Kristy Stovell **Owner** Fernando & Kristy Stovell **Seats** 60, Pr/dining room 14 **Times** 12-3.30/6-10.30, Closed Mon, L Sat, D Sun **Prices** Fixed L 2 course £16.50-£34.50, Fixed D 3 course £42-£53, Tasting menu fr £65 **Wines** 87 bottles over £30, 16 bottles under £30, 14 by glass **Parking** 20 **Notes** Tasting menu with wine £100, Vegetarian available, Children welcome

DORKING *continued*

Two To Four

◎◎ Modern European

tel: 01306 889923 **2-4 West St RH4 1BL**
email: two_to_four@hotmail.co.uk **web:** www.2to4.co.uk
dir: *M25, exit at Leatherhead junct, follow signs to town centre*

Modern cooking in a thriving neighbourhood venue

Occupying a period building in the town centre, this is the sort of friendly and welcoming neighbourhood restaurant we would all like on our manor. The decor goes in for a smart-casual look with unclothed tables, creaky floors and a blackboard specials menu that underlines the informal tone. First-class ingredients are the name of the game in a repertoire of uncomplicated modern European-style dishes; much of the meat is sourced from within a five-mile radius, and organic produce is used liberally. Seared scallops with artichoke purée, toasted hazelnuts and honey truffle vinaigrette is one way to start, while main courses take in roasted pork chop with parsnip mash, braised red cabbage and red wine jus, or perhaps pan-fried fillet of black bream with black olives, anchovy mayonnaise, Serrano ham and lemon gel, all realised with technical verve and presented with a modern flourish. For dessert, bread-and-butter pudding could be jazzed up with the addition of banana and peanut, and served with peanut butter ripple ice cream.

Times 12 2.30/6.30-10, Closed Xmas, Mon (subject to change)

Find out more about how we assess for Rosette awards on page 9

EGHAM Map 6 TQ07

The Estate Grill at Great Fosters

◎◎ Modern British

tel: 01784 433822 **Stroude Rd TW20 9UR**
email: reception@greatfosters.co.uk **web:** www.greatfosters.co.uk
dir: *A30 (Bagshot to Staines) right at lights by Wheatsheaf pub into Christchurch Rd. Straight on at rdbt (pass 2 shop parades on right). Left at lights into Stroude Rd. Hotel 0.75m on right*

Ingredient-led contemporary cooking with British artworks

The Estate Grill, with its chapel-like beams and displays of contemporary British artworks, is the brasserie here at Great Fosters. The chefs have a commitment to sourcing prime seasonal ingredients from regional suppliers, including Old Spots's pigs reared in the grounds, supplemented by kitchen garden and greenhouse produce, and honey from the apiary, as well as Cumbrian fell-bred lamb and Label Anglais chicken from Essex. It all works its way into dishes such as excellent smoked pork with langoustines, apple and turnip, or beef tartare with a duck egg and potato mousse to start. Then try whole plaice with capers and parsley or 28-day aged rib-eye steak with béarnaise, creamy mash and truffle shavings for main. Sharing platters are possibilities — charcuterie to start and a selection of estate-reared pork for main — and meals end with winning puddings like ginger-flavoured rhubarb mousse with ice cream and parkin, and treacle tart with pear and chamomile sorbet.

Chef Marc Hardiman **Owner** Great Fosters (1931) Ltd **Seats** 44, Pr/dining room 20 **Times** 12.30-2.30/6.30-9.30 **Prices** Fixed L 2 course £24.50, Starter £8-£16, Main £21-£36, Dessert £9 **Wines** 80 bottles over £30, 10 bottles under £30, 15 by glass **Parking** 200 **Notes** Sunday L £35, Vegetarian available, Children welcome

GODALMING
Map 6 SU94

La Luna

◎◎ Modern Italian 🍷 NOTABLE WINE LIST

tel: 01483 414155 **10-14 Wharf St GU7 1NN**
email: info@lalunarestaurant.co.uk **web:** www.lalunarestaurant.co.uk
dir: *In town centre, at junct of Wharf St & Flambard Way*

Stylish modern Italian venue

There's a satisfying modernity to La Luna, a place which deals in Italian dishes that are both familiar and a cut above. The space is on the sophisticated side, with fashionable muted earthy tones to the fore, and the service team go about their business with charm and confidence. The bilingual menu follows a traditional format, so things kick off with antipasti such as a plate of charcuterie to share, or smoked tuna tartare served with semi-dried cherry tomatoes and pickled artichoke hearts. Next up, a primi piatti of first-rate pasta or risotto; paccheri with monkfish and Gaeta olives and capers, for example, or squid ink risotto with seared scallop and gremolata. Then it's on to the main event, such as baked sea bream with herby new potatoes and smoked aubergine purée, or Shackleford pork fillet with smoked ham and a potato and Jerusalem artichoke millefoglie. There is a good value lunch menu, plus a tasting version with wine flight. For dessert there might be Sicilian blood orange tart or chocolate and orange tiramisù.

Chef Valentino Gentile **Owner** Daniele Drago **Seats** 58, Pr/dining room 24 **Times** 12-2/7-10, Closed 2 wks Aug, BHs, Sun-Mon **Prices** Fixed L 2 course fr £14.75, Tasting menu £85, Starter £5.25-£10.95, Main £11.95-£21.50, Dessert £6.95, Service optional **Wines** 141 bottles over £30, 37 bottles under £30, 8 by glass **Parking** Public car park behind restaurant **Notes** Tasting menu 7 course with wine, Vegetarian available, Children welcome

GUILDFORD
Map 6 SU94

The Mandolay Hotel

◎ Modern European **NEW**

tel: 01483 303030 **36-40 London Rd GU1 2AE**
email: info@guildford.com **web:** www.guildford.com
dir: *M25 junct 10, follow A3 (S) for 7m. At rdbt 3rd exit onto London Rd for 1m*

Inventive European-accented cooking in a smart setting

The restaurant of this smart hotel and conference centre certainly looks swish and up-to-date with its leather booth seating, bare darkwood tables, oak floors and low-hanging lights, and the kitchen delivers a menu of suitably contemporary European food built on a bedrock of British produce. Creativity suffuses the menus, from a well-balanced terrine of smoked chicken, spinach and foie gras served with white

truffle mayonnaise and sourdough toast, to an excellent monkfish tail wrapped in confit duck and Parma ham and partnered by hot cubes of beetroot, pea emulsion and a sesame and honey dressing. For unrepentant carnivores, the grill offers prime slabs of 28-day aged steak with twice-cooked chips, balsamic shallots, cherry vine tomatoes, watercress and classic sauces such as Café de Paris butter. Finish in the comfort zone with an exemplary sticky toffee pudding with butterscotch sauce and vanilla ice cream.

Chef Thomas Kingston **Owner** Stephen & William Hay **Seats** 60, Pr/dining room 300 **Times** 12-10, All-day dining **Prices** Fixed L 2 course £17-£25, Fixed D 3 course £20-£35, Starter £5-£10, Main £13-£29, Dessert £6-£12, Service optional **Wines** 16 bottles over £30, 23 bottles under £30, 17 by glass **Parking** 25, GLive car park **Notes** Pre-theatre menu, Afternoon tea, Sunday L £12-£30, Vegetarian available, Children welcome

HASLEMERE
Map 6 SU93

Lythe Hill Hotel & Spa

◎◎ Modern British, French

tel: 01428 651251 **Petworth Rd GU27 3BQ**
email: lythe@lythehill.co.uk **web:** www.lythehill.co.uk
dir: *1m E of Haslemere on B2131*

Inspired British modernism in a 15th-century farmhouse

The listed ancient farmhouse dates back to the near-end of the Plantagenet era in 1475, and some of the guest rooms retain architectural features from those times. The oak-panelled dining room at the front is of the same age, while the supplementary room, though of distinctly more modern provenance, overlooks the attractive grounds and ornamental lake. The kitchen team continues to deliver the house style of innovative modern British dishes interlaced with populist classics, but with a slightly more pared-down look, which is all to the good. Charred mackerel is served with tartare sauce, mandarin gel, black olives and fennel, or you might start with pan-seared king prawns with an Asian salad and Thai broth. Main course stars seared beef fillet with black truffle-flavoured Anna potatoes, bone marrow bonbons, turnip, cep soil and bordelaise sauce; if you're in the mood for fish, there could be seared salmon with olive crushed potatoes with fine beans, tomato coulis and sauce vièrge. For dessert, there's a well-conceived and executed trio of chocolate ganache, caramelised banana and peanut mousse.

Times 12-2.30/7-9.30

HORLEY

For restaurant details see Gatwick Airport (London), (Sussex, West)

OCKLEY
Map 6 TQ14

Bryce's The Old School House
◎ Modern British, Seafood

tel: 01306 627430 **The Old School House, Stane St RH5 5TH**
email: fish@bryces.co.uk
dir: From M25 junct 9 take A24, then A29. 8m S of Dorking on A29

Enterprising seafood in a smart country inn

Serving up south Coast seafood in the Surrey countryside for over 20 years now, Bryce's is a restaurant and country pub with a lot going on. Once upon a time it was a boys' boarding school and the beamed restaurant served time as its gym, but these days you can expect to tuck into seafood landed at Shoreham Harbour or bought at Billingsgate. Trio of Devon crab comes as a pan-fried cake, quenelle of mousse and twice-baked soufflé, or try their home-cured gravad lax with dill and mustard sauce. Among main courses, red snapper gets an Eastern flavour with bok choy, soy, ginger and sesame dressing, while fillets of plaice are stuffed with smoked salmon and chive mousse and served with champagne sauce. There's a bar menu too with scampi, fish pie and the like, plus a vegetarian menu and steaks as an alternative to all the fishy things.

Times 12-2.30/7-9.30, Closed 25 Dec, 1 Jan, Mon (Nov & Jan-Feb), D Sun (Nov & Jan-Feb)

OTTERSHAW
Map 6 TQ06

Foxhills
◎◎ Modern, Traditional British

tel: 01932 704471 **Stonehill Rd KT16 OEL**
web: www.foxhills.co.uk
dir: From M25 junct 11 take A320 to Woking. At 2nd rdbt take last exit Cobham Rd, right into Foxhills Rd, follow until T-junct, left into Stonohill Rd

Contemporary cooking of vaulting ambition

Named in honour of the parliamentarian Charles James Fox, this late Georgian manor house was built by George Basevi, architect of the Fitzwilliam Museum in Cambridge and London's Belgrave Square. Now a resort hotel offering golf, tennis, squash and swimming, it's also very handy for Heathrow. As to eating, Nineteen is a golfer's resort for informal dining, the Summerhouse is open in the appropriate months, but the Manor room is where the main action is. With views over the balustraded lawns, the prospect is set fair for contemporary, ingredient-led cooking of vaulting ambition. A pasta starter combines the open lasagne and cannelloni principles for a richly earthy oxtail formula with baby leeks and beetroot, while langoustine could be ponzued and chaperoned by compressed pickled watermelon, carrot, and pork crackling. Stone bass is also crisp-skinned, and comes with wafer-thin cauliflower and vine fruit, and there is further intrigue in a preparation of quail with truffled macaroni, pear, burnt leek and mushroom ketchup. Rhubarb crumble arrives in a tumbler, its crumb top covering layers of jelly and pannacotta.

Chef Alan O'Kane **Owner** Marc Hayton **Seats** 100 **Times** 12-2.30/6.30-9 **Prices** Prices not confirmed **Wines** 96 bottles over £30, 23 bottles under £30, 17 by glass **Parking** 200 **Notes** ALC menu £60, Fixed L £32, Fixed D £36, Sunday L, Vegetarian available, Children welcome

REDHILL
Map 6 TQ25

Nutfield Priory Hotel & Spa
◎◎ Modern British

tel: 01737 824400 **Nutfield RH1 4EL**
email: nutfieldpriory@handpicked.co.uk **web:** www.handpickedhotels.co.uk/nutfieldpriory
dir: On A25, 1m E of Redhill, off M25 junct 8 or M25 junct 6, follow A25 through Godstone

New classic dishes in a Victorian Gothic house

Standing in 12 acres on Nutfield Ridge, the Priory is a piece of classic Victorian neo-Gothic, finished in the 1870s as a homage to Pugin's Westminster. Despite the restfulness of the setting, it's not far from Gatwick, ideally placed to embrace the weary air-traveller. A dining room named Cloisters feels just right in the circumstances, its mullioned windows offering expansive views over the grounds and lake. Roger Gadsden is clear about his intentions: to recreate classic dishes, as well as adding some new ones. Duck rillettes thus come tricked out with beetroot arancini and Puy lentils, or you might start with Asian-spiced pollack, with crisp-fried mussels and citrus-dressed samphire. Chateaubriand of 35-day dry-aged beef for two will prove hard to resist for the high rollers, but there are also fine, vibrantly pink duck with truffled mash, creamed hispi cabbage and bacon in oloroso sauce, or spicy monkfish with butternut squash purée. Keen interest is maintained through to the many-layered desserts, which may include raspberry delice with elderflower granita, lemon curd, elderflower custard and brilliant pink peppercorn meringue.

Chef Roger Gadsden **Owner** Hand Picked Hotels **Seats** 60, Pr/dining room 60 **Times** 12.30-2/7-9.30 **Prices** Fixed L 2 course fr £25, Fixed D 3 course fr £39, Tasting menu fr £65, Starter £10.95-£15.95, Main £19.50-£32, Dessert £10.50-£13.50, Service optional **Wines** 84 bottles over £30, 11 bottles under £30, 26 by glass **Parking** 100 **Notes** Sunday L, Vegetarian available, Children welcome

REIGATE
Map 6 TQ25

The Dining Room
◎◎ Modern British V

tel: 01737 226650 **59a High St RH2 9AE**
dir: M25 junct 8/A217 follow one way system into High St. Restaurant on left

Stimulating cooking on the High Street

Tony Tobin may be well known to armchair chefs from his frequent telly appearances, but his TV chef status hasn't stopped him heading up the brigade at his first-floor restaurant on the High Street. It has been a hit with foodies since 1993 with its easy-on-the-eye looks, a cracking value fixed-price deal to pull in the lunchtime punters at lunchtime, as well as a carte of bright contemporary ideas. Celeriac and apple risotto with smoked quail's breast and a poached quail's egg, or seared scallops with Thai potato croquette, green mango and chilli syrup might appear among starters. Mains are all about pedigree materials: pan-roasted fillet of turbot, say, in a punchy surf 'n' turf duo with braised oxtail, potato fondant, baby gem lettuce and a complementary kick from lemon oil, or beef fillet matched with cauliflower and potato dauphinoise, spinach, and truffle dressing. The inventive approach extends to puddings such as tonka bean and white chocolate mousse with chocolate soil, wattle seed ice cream and coffee jelly.

Chef Tony Tobin **Owner** Tony Tobin **Seats** 75, Pr/dining room 28 **Times** 12-2/7-10, Closed Xmas, BHs, L Sat, D Sun **Prices** Prices not confirmed **Wines** 70 bottles over £30, 20 bottles under £30, 10 by glass **Parking** On street, car park **Notes** Tasting menu, Sunday L, Children welcome

RIPLEY

Map 6 TQ05

The Anchor

◉◉ Modern British

tel: 01483 211866 **High St GU23 6AE**
email: info@ripleyanchor.co.uk **web:** www.ripleyanchor.co.uk
dir: M25 junct 10 onto A3 towards Guildford, exit at junct for Ripley

Relaxed dining pub with a side order of pedigree

Though sibling to its renowned mother-ship restaurant Drake's just over Ripley village's bustling High Street, The Anchor is no pretentious gastro-pub annexe, but is rather a relaxed, friendly dining pub in the modern idiom with a dusting of pedigree. Okay, Drake's head chef Mike Wall-Palmer has moved across to man the stoves, but The Anchor delivers simple dining-pub fare with a touch of creativity and panache using quality produce. Dishes cover all the bases with a light modern touch, for example so 'now' snacks like crispy pollack croquettes with seaweed mayo, and mains such as sea-fresh cod fillet with piquant chorizo purée and mushrooms. Afters hold form, perhaps caramelised apple custard (brûlée perfection) with intense-flavoured Granny Smith sorbet and 'wafers'. The Grade II listed property itself (former almshouses) comes as well dressed as the food, with voguish good looks and hard surfaces. It has fashionable darkwood furniture, slate floors and Venetian blinds melded around original features, while armchairs by the log-burner add cosier, warming touches. Well-selected wines (and local ales) plus lovely in-house sourdough confirm its class.

The Anchor

Chef Michael Wall-Palmer **Owner** Drakes and Mealings **Seats** 38, Pr/dining room 8 **Times** 12-2.30/6-9.30, Closed Mon **Prices** Fixed L 2 course fr £15, Starter £6-£9, Main £12-£19, Dessert fr £6, Service optional **Wines** 49 bottles over £30, 26 bottles under £30, 10 by glass **Parking** 14 **Notes** Sunday L, Vegetarian available, Children welcome

Drake's Restaurant ❀❀❀

RIPLEY

Map 6 TQ05

Modern British ᴠ ◆NOTABLE WINE LIST
tel: 01483 224777 **The Clock House, High St GU23 6AQ**
email: info@drakesrestaurant.co.uk
dir: M25 junct 10, A3 towards Guildford. Follow Ripley signs. Restaurant in village centre

Fascinating modern cookery in a landmark Georgian house

Steve and Serina Drake's restaurant is not a hard place to track down among the timbered houses in this well-heeled Surrey village – just look for the Georgian redbrick house with its landmark clock and gorgeous walled garden, which really comes into its own for aperitifs in summer. Refurbishment has refined the look of the place, with a light, understated feel offset by the rustic wood of doors and window frames. Steve Drake set up shop in Ripley in 2004 after training with the sort of world-class chefs that go by just one name – Nico, Marco, Roux to name but a few. Learning his craft under the aegis of such classicists, you might expect his culinary style to follow broadly similar lines, but you would be wrong: this is an eclectic mind at work, driven first and foremost by considerations of flavour. There are some unusual juxtapositions at play here – just look at the stark menu descriptions (venison, Lapsang Souchong, parsley and orange purée, for example) – but confidence, technical wizardry and good judgement mean that they work brilliantly together and each leaves a clear impression on the palate. Choose between two to four courses on the carte, otherwise 'Discovery' and 'Journey' are the two whole-table taster options, the latter opening intriguingly with cauliflower, hazelnut and caper berry, before Jerusalem artichoke alongside veal sweetbreads, watercress and cep biscuit. After a fish course such as brill with cucumber ketchup, lemon thyme and kohlrabi, it might be pheasant with apple cannelloni, celeriac and Wiltshire truffle. A pre-dessert, perhaps of rhubarb and custard, prepares the way for the grand finale uniting pear, cinnamon and hibiscus.

Chef Steve Drake **Owner** Steve & Serina Drake **Seats** 40
Times 12-2/7-9.30, Closed 1 wk Jan, 2 wks Aug, 1 wk Xmas & after Etr, Sun-Mon, L Tue **Prices** Fixed L 3 course £28-£30 **Wines** 245 bottles over £30, 9 bottles under £30, 12 by glass **Parking** 2, 2 local car parks **Notes** Discovery menu £80, Journey menu £60, ALC 3 course £60, Children welcome

Drake's Restaurant

@@@ – *see opposite*

STOKE D'ABERNON   Map 6 TQ15

Woodlands Park Hotel

@@ Modern European

---

tel: 01372 843933 **Woodlands Ln KT11 3QB**
email: woodlandspark@handpicked.co.uk
web: www.handpickedhotels.co.uk/woodlandspark
dir: *A3 exit at Cobham. Through town centre & Stoke D'Abernon, left at garden centre into Woodlands Lane, hotel 0.5m on right*

Formal dining in a grand Victorian country house

Money was clearly no object for William Bryant, son of one of the founders of the match company, when he built this magnificent pile in 1885. It's set in landscaped grounds and gardens and has the sort of interior you'd expect, and the squishy sofas of the Great Hall are great for people watching. The Oak Room, the main dining option, is just that, its walls panelled, its ceiling of intricate oak, with comfortable leather chairs and professional but unbuttoned service. The kitchen aims to please its clientele by giving a contemporary tweak to traditional ideas, and a grounding in the classical repertoire is evident. Start with duck liver ballotine, its richness cut by sweet wine jelly, or leek and potato velouté with the luxury of black truffle shavings. Main courses make an impact without being overwrought: fillet and braised shoulder of lamb with goats' curd, roasted aubergine and caramelised cippolini onions, say, or pan-fried monkfish with spicy Puy lentils and tomato ragout. End with a textbook cherry clafoutis with clotted cream ice cream.

Chef Alec Mackins **Owner** Hand Picked Hotels **Seats** 35, Pr/dining room 150 **Times** 12-2.30/7-9.30, Closed L Mon-Sat **Prices** Prices not confirmed, Service optional **Wines** 15 by glass **Parking** 150 **Notes** Sunday L, Vegetarian available, Children welcome

---

WARLINGHAM   Map 6 TQ35

India Dining

@@ Modern Indian **NEW**

---

tel: 01883 625905 **6 The Green CR6 9NA**
email: info@indiadining.co.uk
dir: *From M25 junct 6 follow signs Caterham then Warlingham*

Contemporary Indian cuisine in a cool setting

Surprising as it may seem, unassumingly sat overlooking the village green in leafy Warlingham, Indian Dining is no ubiquitous flock-wallpapered curry house but, is in fact, a classy thoroughbred that takes a wholly modern approach to both cuisine and decor. From a stylish cocktail bar up front, to black leatherette banquettes and matching chairs, polished-wood tables and highly contemporary artworks and

lighting, there's urbane good looks at every turn. The authentic Pan-Indian cooking takes an equally creative, modern and upmarket approach, the menus intelligently condensed to allow quality and consistency to shine, while the kitchen is admirably committed to sustainable and organic produce. Pretty plates have that clean haute cuisine glow and deliver balance but spicy attitude. Take monkfish tikka to open, cooked in the tandoor, its peppy spicing not overwhelming the sparkling fresh fish and cooled by a cucumber riatha. Mains – like Bengali sea bass jhol – follow suit, accompanied by tangy-sweet lemon rice, while peripherals like poppadoms, chutney's and breads are equally top dollar. For meat lovers there's a Hyderbadi lamb biriyani and even sirloin chilli, while to finish, perhaps a passionfruit brûlée or chocolate fondant await.

Chef Asad Khan, Habibul Rahaman **Owner** Asad Khan **Seats** 69 **Times** 12-2.30/5.30-11, Closed 1 Jan **Prices** Tasting menu £39.95, Starter £5.95-£12.95, Main £9.95-£26.95, Dessert £4.95-£9.95, Service optional 12.5% **Wines** 20 bottles over £30, 32 bottles under £30, 12 by glass **Parking** On street, car park nearby **Notes** 2 dine 2 course with wine £29.95, Sunday L £15.95-£19.95, Vegetarian available, Children welcome

---

WEYBRIDGE   Map 6 TQ06

Brooklands Hotel

@@ British, European

---

tel: 01932 335700 **Brooklands Dr KT13 0SL**
email: brasserie@brooklandshotelsurrey.com **web:** www.brooklandshotelsurrey.com
dir: *Phone for directions*

Striking modern hotel where British motor-racing began

This thrillingly modern structure is built on a grand scale overlooking the first purpose-built car racing circuit in the world, opening back in 1907. You get a great view of the track while slurping a cocktail in the stylish art deco-inspired bar, before heading into the 1907 Restaurant, where cool colour tones of charcoal and aubergine and darkwood surfaces give a moody club-like vibe to the space. There's a creative modern brasserie feel to the food, with the kitchen team keen to deploy adventurous cooking techniques in dishes that arrive dressed to thrill. Pan-fried scallops come with glazed pork belly, cauliflower purée and golden raisins, followed by pink and tender rump of lamb with Israeli couscous, smoked aubergine purée, and pomegranate seeds adding little tart explosions, or you might look to the grill for a straight-up steak – 28-day aged rib-eye, say, with the usual accompaniments and sauces. End on a dessert on a tiramisù theme with a contrasting bitter chocolate sorbet, or apricot parfait, tart and compôte with rosemary sorbet.

Chef Norman Farquharson **Owner** Brooklands Hotel **Seats** 120, Pr/dining room **Times** 12.30-2.30/6.30-10 **Prices** Prices not confirmed, Service optional **Wines** 12 by glass **Parking** 120 **Notes** Sunday L, Vegetarian available, Children welcome

---

EAST SUSSEX

ALFRISTON
Map 6 TQ50

Deans Place

◉◉ Modern British ꝟ

tel: 01323 870248 **Seaford Rd BN26 5TW**
email: mail@deansplacehotel.co.uk **web:** www.deansplacehotel.co.uk
dir: *Off A27, signed Alfriston & Drusillas Zoo Park. Continue south through village*

Modern country cooking on the edge of the South Downs

On the southern fringe of the South Downs National Park, and once part of an extensive farming estate, Deans Place has been a hotel of one sort or another for the past century. Scarcely can it have been quite such an alluring prospect as it is today, its elegant modern decor making a refreshing backdrop to the Victorian gardens and charming riverside location. The principal dining area, recently refurbished, is The Dining Room, with the full-dress experience of fine table linen and glassware, while weekday lunches are served in the Terrace and Bar, with its gentle views over the croquet lawn. A distinctive style of updated country cooking is on offer in many formats: grills, seafood, vegetarian, and the principal dinner menu. That last might open with smoked haddock chowder and quail's eggs, or scallops with a tempura-battered oyster, and then move to local lamb with olive gnocchi, goats' cheese and romesco sauce, or sea bass with parsnip-vanilla purée, lemon potatoes and bok choy in vermouth cream. Finish with chocolate and bayleaf tart on pistachio anglaise.

Chef Stuart Dunley **Owner** Steyne Hotels Ltd **Seats** 74, Pr/dining room 50
Times 12.30-3/6.30-9.30 **Prices** Prices not confirmed, Service optional **Wines** 25 bottles over £30, 47 bottles under £30, 10 by glass **Parking** 100 **Notes** Sunday L, Children welcome

BATTLE
Map 7 TQ71

Powder Mills Hotel

◉◉ Modern British ꝟ

tel: 01424 775511 **Powdermill Ln TN33 0SP**
email: jcowpland@thepowermills.com **web:** www.powdermillshotel.com
dir: *M25 junct 5, A21 towards Hastings. At St Johns Cross take A2100 to Battle. Pass abbey on right, 1st right into Powdermills Ln. 1m, hotel on right*

Appealing modish cooking near the 1066 battlefield

Powder Mills was once the site of a major gunpowder making operation (good stuff, apparently, which helped defeat Napoleon), but these days it is about a tranquil a setting as you can imagine. The pretty Georgian house stands in 150 acres of glorious Sussex countryside with lush parkland, woods and a seven-acre fishing lake. It's the kind of place where country pursuits are on offer and the owner's Springer Spaniels sometimes welcome new arrivals. Wining and dining takes place in the Orangery Restaurant with its bright and traditional demeanour (wicker chairs, linen-clad tables and marble floor). The kitchen turns out broadly contemporary dishes with a good showing of regional ingredients to ensure a local flavour. Start with wild mushroom and tarragon soup enriched with truffle Chantilly, or smoked pigeon breast with Madeira jelly and balsamic pearls. Move on to a main course that partners Gressingham duck breast with ravioli made from the confit leg meat, plus cauliflower purée and roasted salsify. Finish with pistachio soufflé with a pistachio and thyme ice cream.

Chef Callum O'Doherty **Owner** Mrs J Cowpland **Seats** 90, Pr/dining room 16
Times 12-2/7-9 **Prices** Fixed L 3 course £19.95, Fixed D 3 course £29.95, Starter £6.50-£8.50, Main £15.95-£21.95, Dessert £6.95-£8.50 **Wines** 4 by glass **Parking** 100 **Notes** Library & conservatory menus, Sunday L £24.95, Children 10 yrs+

BODIAM
Map 7 TQ72

The Curlew Restaurant

◉◉ Modern British ꝟ 🍷 NOTABLE WINE LIST

tel: 01580 861394 & 861202 **Junction Rd TN32 5UY**
email: enquiries@thecurlewrestaurant.co.uk
dir: *A21 south turn left at Hurst Green signed Bodiam. Restaurant on left at end of road*

Modern country-inn fare near the Castle

The white-faced Curlew is perched on what was the old coaching-route from Hastings to London, not far from Bodiam's 14th-century moated castle. A relaxed countrified atmosphere prevails, with a roaring log-burner and a fresh, open look to the decor, striped armchairs in the lounge, chocolate banquettes in the dining area. The industrious culinary approach extends to thoughtful appetisers such as a pork beignet with apricot jam, and a menu of modern country-inn fare showcasing Sussex produce follows. Mackerel comes both scorched and in céviche, rootily dressed with beet and horseradish, while duck liver and foie gras parfait has both gingerbread and salted pineapple for sweet and savoury company. They could be followed by pinkish pine-smoked venison with spiced red cabbage, blackberries, and light clumps of sesame-scented granola, or a double-act of cinnamon and anise chicken with monkfish. Chop and chips is a trencherman's main that needs no explanation, and the chocolate fondant is a flawless rendition, served with hazelnut ice cream, but clementine mousse with spiced fruitcake and egg nog is the truly thought-provoking way to finish.

Chef Michael Mealey **Owner** Mark & Sara Colley **Seats** 64
Times 12-2.30/6.30-9.30, Closed Mon **Prices** Fixed L 2 course £20, Fixed D 3 course £25, Tasting menu £65, Starter £8-£12.50, Main £19.50-£24.50, Dessert £8.50-£9 **Wines** 66 bottles over £30, 13 bottles under £30, 19 by glass **Parking** 16 **Notes** Sunday L £38-£42, Children welcome

BRIGHTON & HOVE
Map 6 TQ30

Chilli Pickle
Regional Indian

tel: 01273 900383 **17 Jubilee St BN1 1GE**
email: info@thechillipickle.com **web:** www.thechillipickle.com
dir: *From the Steine (A23) right into Church Lane & right into Jubilee St. Next to myhotel Brighton, opposite Library*

Vibrant Indian flavours in buzzy venue

The Chilli Pickle has gone from strength to strength since it moved into capacious premises on a pedestrianised square in the regenerated North Laine quarter. Its full-length glass walls create the impression of dining alfresco whatever the weather, offering ringside seats for Brighton's ever-colourful street life. The interior works a contemporary rustic look with chunky wooden tables, blond-wood floors, and vivid splashes of blue and yellow to jazz up the almost Scandinavian minimalism of the place. The menu gives sub-continental clichés and curry house standards a swerve, dealing in smartly reworked thalis, dosai and Indian street-food-inspired dishes at lunchtime – fried coconut and coriander balls coated in potato and served with smoked red pepper, for example, ahead of Rajasthani mutton shoulder curry. At dinner, the kitchen cranks things up a gear, making good use of a brace of tandoors to produce the likes of a whole sea bream coated in green peppercorn chutney served with lemon rice and coconut chutney, or you could go all-out with a platter involving tandoor-roasted chicken, quail, clove-smoked venison, and spiced lamb chop.

Chef Alun Sperring **Owner** Alun & Dawn Sperring **Seats** 115
Times 12-3/6-10.30, Closed 25-26 Dec **Prices** Fixed D 3 course £27.95, Starter £4.50-£8.50, Main £10.75-£18.95, Dessert £5.80-£5.90, Service optional **Wines** 6 bottles over £30, 18 bottles under £30, 12 by glass **Parking** NCP Church St **Notes** King Thali menu £13.50, Mon £10, Sunday L £10.75-£18.95, Vegetarian available, Children welcome

What makes the perfect steak?
Find out on page 20

The Foragers
Modern European

tel: 01273 733134 **3 Stirling Place BN3 3YU**
email: info@theforagerspub.co.uk **web:** www.theforagerspub.co.uk
dir: *A2033 Sackville Rd, left Stirling Place, restaurant 200m on left*

Foraged ingredients and more in a popular Hove pub

This buzzy backstreet pub tucked away behind Hove's main drag hums with a casual upbeat vibe. Refreshingly free of designer gastro pretensions, the dining area goes for a likeable shabby-chic look: simple pine-topped pub tables set against funky shades of turquoise and fuchsia pink, and a large mural in blocks of vivid paintbox colours inspired by a Brazilian favela scene that turns the brightness factor up to 11. This, however, has nothing whatsoever to do with the culinary theme, which celebrates splendid seasonal Sussex produce. As its name suggests, the kitchen likes to use wild and foraged ingredients, so wood pigeon breast might start the show, together with sautéed Portobello mushrooms and parsnip puree, before a main course of tender duck breast with confit leg, potato fondant, red cabbage purée and orange jus. Dessert could be an intriguing and eclectic trio of ginger parkin with local Flower Marie cheese, and rosemary and hogweed seed honey.

Times 12-3/6-10

The Ginger Dog
Traditional British NEW

tel: 01273 620990 **12-13 College Place BN2 1HN**
email: gingerdog@gingermanrestaurants.com
dir: *College Place Eastbound, turn right opposite Brighton College*

Robust pub cooking à la McKellar

Ben McKellar's Ginger group incorporates what was a run-down corner pub in Kemptown village, now given the trademark makeover with clean white walls and bright pink banquettes in the main dining area, but retaining a more traditional feel in the bar. British pub food full of peasanty robustness and a rough-and-ready way with Mediterranean touches suits Brighton's mood to a nicety. Begin with a pairing of seared squid and breadcrumbed pig's trotter in smoked paprika pesto to get the taste buds fired up, or perhaps a bowl of velvety celeriac soup with truffled croûtons and a splash of Muscat vinegar. Main courses are earthy and filling, with nothing precious about them, so expect a chickpea and aubergine stew under roast hake, or roast lamb rump with a sugared pastilla, rainbow chard, giant couscous and pomegranate. If orange posset and meringue still sounds a little light after all that, go for cherry clafoutis with almond cream and cherry sorbet, scented with meadowsweet.

Chef Nick Cain **Owner** Ben McKellar **Seats** 45, Pr/dining room 22
Times 12-2/6-10, Closed 25 Dec **Prices** Fixed L 2 course £15-£20, Fixed D 3 course £25-£40, Starter £6.50-£9, Main £14-£21, Dessert £6.50-£8.50 **Wines** 27 bottles over £30, 23 bottles under £30 **Parking** On street **Notes** 2 course 12-2pm & 6-7pm £12.50, Sunday L £14.50-£15, Vegetarian available, Children welcome

The Gingerman Restaurant

◉◉ Modern British

tel: 01273 326688 **21a Norfolk Square BN1 2PD**
email: gingerman@gingermanrestaurants.com
dir: *A23 to Palace Pier rdbt. Turn right onto Kings Rd. At art-deco style Embassy building turn right into Norfolk Sq*

Dynamic modern British cooking near the seafront

Just up from the seafront on the cusp of Brighton & Hove, at least before the two became municipally one, The Gingerman was the original venue in an expanding local portfolio of Ginger thisses and thats. It began 2015 with a refurb, in which creamy neutrality was startled up with lime-green and brown flocked upholstery in floral art nouveau patterns. Cheeringly constant is the commitment to dynamic modern British cooking with an inventive slant, notably incorporating touches of the Maghreb tradition. Maple-glazed pigeon breast with pine nuts and dates vies for first-course attention with salmon 'pastrami' served with caramelised parsnip and labneh, as well as an egg yolk. Mains push the envelope further for vegetarian duck egg curry with a dosa, lemon pickle and green chutney, or there may be an anatomist's approach to beef — tongue and cheek as well as fillet — garnished with charred onion and parsley root in hearty braising juices. A soufflé for two is a pleasure, perhaps rhubarb with rhubarb and custard ice cream.

Chef Ben McKellar, Mark Charker **Owner** Ben & Pamela McKellar **Seats** 32 **Times** 12.30-2/7-10, Closed 2 wks from New Year's eve, Mon **Prices** Fixed L 2 course £15-£32, Fixed D 3 course £37, Service optional 12.5% **Wines** 14 bottles over £30, 23 bottles under £30, 14 by glass **Parking** Regency Sq NCP **Notes** Sunday L, Vegetarian available, Children welcome

The Grand Brighton

◉◉ Modern British, Seafood

tel: 01273 224300 **97-99 King's Rd BN1 2FW**
email: reservations@grandbrighton.co.uk
dir: *On A259 (seafront road between piers) adjacent to Brighton Centre*

Seafood specialities in the stylishly remodelled Grand

Turn your back on the stunning Italianate Victorian design at this seafront landmark and enter the cool, clean lines of the GB1 restaurant, with its lightwood floor, neat leather-look and bentwood chairs at plain tables, and high stools pulled up to a huge circular bar. Seafood is the thing here, with a menu as bright and contemporary as the surroundings. If platters of oysters, crab or prawns, herby fish soup or fish fingers (actually panko-coated whitebait) in a bap with fries don't appeal, go for more exotic scallops marinated in sashimi with asparagus, vanilla and chervil. All seafood is locally landed, simply treated and timed just so. Moist, crisp-skinned whole sea bass, for instance, is garnished with scallops, sauced with caper butter and accompanied by green beans. What's available depends on the catch, and you can choose a sauce like tartare or garlic butter. Meat-eaters are not ignored by any means, with a selection of grills on offer, and desserts are as well handled as the rest: perhaps multi-flavoured lime pannacotta with chocolate frangipane cake, a pistachio cone and a dollop of mascarpone, all as pretty as a picture.

Chef Alan White **Seats** 90, Pr/dining room **Times** 12.30-4/5-10 **Prices** Fixed L 2 course fr £13.95, Starter £6.50-£8.50, Main £12-£35, Dessert £5.50-£12.50 **Wines** 25 bottles over £30, 22 bottles under £30, 10 by glass **Parking** Behind hotel **Notes** Midwk menu 2 course with wine £45, Sunday L £16.95, Vegetarian available, Children welcome

Hotel du Vin Brighton

◉ Traditional British, French

tel: 01273 718588 **2-6 Ship St BN1 1AD**
email: info@brighton.hotelduvin.com **web:** www.hotelduvin.com
dir: *A23 to seafront, at rdbt right, then right onto Middle St, bear right into Ship St, hotel at sea end on right*

Upmarket bistro cooking off the seafront

The Brighton branch of the chain, just off the seafront, has all the expected Francophile touches, its walls adorned with wine and spirit posters and risqué pictures, leather-look banquettes running back to back down the centre, and small wooden tables (easily pushed together by nifty staff for larger groups). A glance at the menu shows that this is more than your average bistro fare, with potted crab with caper berries and egg salad followed by ox cheek bourguignon, alongside chicken terrine and bouillabaisse. Evidently the kitchen orders great-quality raw materials, often locally, and treats them with care and respect at the stoves. A simple starter of salmon ballotine with herbed fromage blanc might precede main-course chicken Dijonnaise, moist and full of flavour, with mousseline potatoes. Momentum doesn't falter at the final stretch, with light and tasty pistachio parfait with chocolate ice cream, the plate dotted with thick caramel sauce.

Chef Rob Carr **Seats** 100, Pr/dining room 90 **Times** 12-2/7-10 **Prices** Prices not confirmed **Wines** 12 by glass **Parking** The Lanes NCP **Notes** Sunday L, Vegetarian available, Children welcome

The Little Fish Market

◉◉ Modern Fish

tel: 01273 722213 **10 Upper Market St BN3 1AS**
email: thelittlefishmarket@gmail.com
dir: *Just off Western Rd Upper Market St past Co-op. Restaurant on right*

Top-drawer fish and shellfish specialities

The upswing that Brighton & Hove's food scene has been on lately was given a major boost with the arrival of Duncan Ray, who has stints at The Fat Duck and Pennyhill Park at Bagshot, Surrey under his belt. Simplicity itself is the decorative watchword of the venue, its two ample windows framing an understated space next door to the Old Market Theatre. The à la carte menu has been replaced by a five-course taster (three at lunch) which majors on fish but won't disoblige if you're hell-bent on something meaty as well. First up could be trout terrine served with a crisped quail's egg and watercress, followed smartly by a serving of truffle-scented salt-baked celeriac. Principal fish dishes are top-drawer, full of freshness and sharply defined flavours: sea bass with crab mayonnaise, fennel and pink grapefruit, or turbot in bouillabaisse with cockles, are typical. Shellfish are creatively inveigled into the meat options, an oyster with beef short rib, langoustine with pork belly. It all concludes with richly rewarding desserts such as banana parfait with chocolate and butterscotch accompaniments.

Chef Duncan Ray **Owner** Duncan Ray **Seats** 22 **Times** 12-2/7-9.30, Closed 1 wk Mar, 2 wks Sep, Xmas, Sun-Mon, L Tue-Fri **Prices** Fixed L 2 course fr £20, Tasting menu fr £50, Service optional **Wines** 10 bottles over £30, 6 bottles under £30, 14 by glass **Parking** On street **Notes** Vegetarian available, Children 12 yrs+

Terre à Terre

◉ Modern Vegetarian V

tel: 01273 729051 **71 East St BN1 1HQ**
email: mail@terreaterre.co.uk **web:** www.terreaterre.co.uk
dir: *Town centre, close to Brighton Pier & The Lanes*

Trendsetting vegetarian cooking from the rhyming dictionary

The throbbing purple frontage gives notice of the vibrant approach to trendsetting vegetarian cooking on which Terre à Terre embarked in the 1990s. In an expansive room that opens out to a small terrace at the back, the menu specifications are at least as voluminous as the surroundings. A streak of Brighton irony runs through it all: Eats Beets and Cheese involves buckwheat potato crumble and sheep's milk ricotta, soused honey carrots, sherry shallot purée and much more. The rhyming dictionary is mined for mains such as easy-peasy calabrese, and better batter with lemony Yemeni relish. Aubergine dengaku bakeo ito primo ingrodient in sake, before throwing a welter of other Japanese seasonings at it — white miso, wasabi, yuzu, the lot. With such an adventurous menu, the food may occasionally fall a little short of the expectations raised, but you can't go far wrong closing on a booze-shotted affogato.

Chef A Powley, P Taylor **Owner** A Powley, P Taylor **Seats** 110 **Times** 12-10.30, All-day dining, Closed 25-26 Dec **Prices** Fixed L 3 course £28-£30, Fixed D 3 course £28-£30, Starter £5.95-£9, Main £13.95-£14.95, Dessert £6.40-£8.90, Service optional **Wines** 14 bottles over £30, 40 bottles under £30, 14 by glass **Parking** NCP, on street **Notes** Terre à Verre menu — tapas, chips & wine carafe for 2 £39.95, Children welcome

Twenty Four St Georges

◉◉ Modern European

tel: 01273 626060 **24-25 St Georges Rd, Kemp Town Village BN2 1ED**
email: reservations@24stgeorges.co.uk **web:** www.24stgeorges.co.uk
dir: *A23 Brighton, left onto Edward St to Eastern Rd, right onto College Place, left onto St George's Rd*

Creative cooking in relaxed neighbourhood venue

Tucked away in the quiet end of Kemp Town village, just back from the seafront, chef-proprietors Dean Heselden and Jamie Everton-Jones have been quietly carving themselves a niche in the local foodie scene. The dining room is a relaxed and unshouty space, and the culinary deal includes well-executed dishes with an emphasis on local, seasonal produce — as you might hope when the splendid bounty of the Sussex coast and South Downs is on the doorstep. A starter of lobster cannelloni with Sussex blue cheese, tarragon, lemon gel and apple sets the tone, before a main course starring free-range chicken — breast and ballotine with chorizo stuffing — with a truffled croquette, oyster mushrooms, spring greens and Rioja jus. Fish might appear in the shape of pan-fried brill with Parmentier potatoes, seasonal vegetables, squid, and cider and tarragon sauce. Desserts range from chocolate and orange sponge with a crunchy piece of honeycomb, and the tang of mango bavarois and sorbet, to lemon drizzle cake with rhubarb ice cream, poached rhubarb, caramelised apple and meringue tuile.

Chef Dean Heselden **Owner** Jamie Everton-Jones, Dean Heselden **Seats** 52, Pr/dining room 12 **Times** 6-9.30, Closed 25-26 Dec, 1-2 & 11-19 Jan, Sun-Mon, L Tue-Fri **Prices** Tasting menu £59, Starter £6.95-£8.95, Main £12.50-£23.95, Dessert £6.95-£7.95, Service optional **Wines** 29 bottles over £30, 21 bottles under £30, 8 by glass **Parking** On street voucher **Notes** Vegetarian available, Children welcome

CAMBER
Map 7 TV91

The Gallivant
◉◉ Modern, Traditional British

tel: 01797 225057 **New Lydd Rd TN31 7RB**
email: mark@thegallivanthotel.com **web:** www.thegallivanthotel.com
dir: *M29 junct 10 to A2070, left Camber Road before Rye. Hotel located on left in Camber Village*

Local meats and seafood with New England style

Overlooking the Camber shoreline near Rye, The Gallivant has its heart in New England, where that laid-back eastern seaboard style translates as oceans of space, light wood, café furniture and a feeling that you might have stepped accidentally onto a small cruise-liner. Sourcing from within a 30-mile radius is an especially good idea when the radius takes in impeccable bay seafood, Sussex charcuterie and salt marsh lamb. The kitchen sensibly keeps things simple, offering a brasserie menu that opens with half-pints of prawns, and oysters in shallot vinegar, as well as sharing boards of shellfish or meaty stuff like rillettes, chorizo and Scotch egg. Once you get into the main menu, there are classics such as devilled crab with melted cheese and soldiers, then catch of the day with hollandaise or salsa verde, or rump and ribs of local beef in red wine, and that all-important salt marsh lamb, served with truffle-oiled green beans, garlic aubergine and buttery mash. Sides include a salad of caramelised orange and fennel, and the closer could be warm chocolate doughnuts with thick cream for dunking.

Times 12-3/6-9.30, Closed L Mon-Wed

EASTBOURNE
Map 6 TV69

The Grand Hotel
◉◉ Modern, Classic ☷ NOTABLE WINE LIST

tel: 01323 412345 **King Edwards Pde BN21 4EQ**
email: reservations@grandeastbourne.com **web:** www.grandeastbourne.com
dir: *Western end of seafront, 1m from Eastbourne station*

Grand seafront hotel with confident modern cooking

Built in 1875, Eastbourne's Grand Hotel — the 'White Palace' to its friends — embodies glorious Victorian Empire pomp like few other British seaside hotels. The grande dame of the seafront has hosted some famous faces over the years including Winston Churchill, Charlie Chaplin, Elgar, and Debussy who composed *La Mer* on his hols here in 1905. Naturally, the old girl has had a facelift to keep her 21st-century guests sweet, but some things don't change, such as that fine institution of afternoon tea, served in the marble-columned majesty of the Great Hall. The fine dining Mirabelle restaurant is an equally ritzy old-school setting, but there's nothing passé about the kitchen's contemporary take on flavour combinations and textures. When the silver cloches are lifted, the plates beneath reveal modern European thinking: to start, a crabmeat, tomato and saffron brûlée with soused cucumber, pickled ginger and toasted brioche, followed by slow-braised shin of beef with creamed potatoes, Tête de Moine cheese, and goulash sauce. A Granny Smith apple crumble with Calvados ice cream and custard makes a fine finale.

The Grand Hotel

Chef Keith Mitchell, Gerald Roser **Owner** Elite Hotels **Seats** 50
Times 12.30-2/7-10, Closed 2-16 Jan, Sun-Mon **Prices** Fixed L 2 course fr £22, Fixed D 3 course fr £43.50, Tasting menu £63-£95, Service optional **Wines** 221 bottles over £30, 24 bottles under £30, 11 by glass **Parking** 70 **Notes** Fixed L/D supplements added to price, Tasting menu 5 course, Sunday L, Vegetarian available, Children 12 yrs+

See advert opposite

Langham Hotel
◉ Modern British

tel: 01323 731451 **43-49 Royal Pde BN22 7AH**
email: neil@langhamhotel.co.uk **web:** www.langhamhotel.co.uk
dir: *A22 follow signs for seafront Sovereign Centre, take 3rd exit onto Royal Pde. Hotel on corner Royal Pde & Cambridge Rd*

Old-fashioned courtesies and a versatile menu

The Ladies' Lunch Club at the Langham has become so popular of late that, in a touch of 'anything goes', well-behaved gentlemen are now admitted on occasion. The bracing seafront of dear old Eastbourne fits this sparkling-white hotel like a glove, the marine views a treat from the conservatory dining room. Old-fashioned courtesies abound, even in the face of whole hungry coach-parties. The kitchen doesn't just stick to heritage Englishry, although you can go from potato and herb soup to sirloin and chips, with syrup sponge and custard to finish, if you've a mind. In between, though, there are wood pigeon salad with pickled mushrooms and roasted beetroot, nori-wrapped monkfish with spiced mussels, and cinnamon-infused fruity lamb tagine with orange, prunes and apricots. Things end on an upbeat with good pastry work in a pear frangipane tart, served with honey and ginger ice cream.

Chef Michael Titherington **Owner** Neil & Wendy Kirby **Seats** 24 **Times** 12-2.30/6-9.30
Prices Prices not confirmed, Service optional **Wines** 1 bottle over £30, 29 bottles under £30, 15 by glass **Parking** On street **Notes** Sunday L, Vegetarian available, Children welcome

FOREST ROW

Map 6 TQ43

Ashdown Park Hotel & Country Club

◉◉ Modern British ♦ NOTABLE WINE LIST

tel: 01342 824988 **Wych Cross RH18 5JR**
email: reservations@ashdownpark.com web: www.ashdownpark.com
dir: *A264 to East Grinstead, then A22 to Eastbourne. 2m S of Forest Row at Wych Cross lights. Left to Hartfield, hotel on right 0.75m*

Grand hotel dining in an upmarket country house

Ashdown Park is a magnificent Victorian pile in acres of grounds with a lake and golf course; it has an indoor pool, spa and extensive sporting facilities. Everything within bears the stamp of luxury, and the Anderida Restaurant (which takes its name from an old Roman word for 'hunting ground') is a grand room, with sconces on half-panelled walls and tall windows hung with heavy drapes. The cooking is based on the classical repertoire, with the kitchen overlaying its creative contemporary take on dishes. Scallops are roasted and served atop cauliflower risotto with ceps purée and vichyssoise crumb to make an enjoyable starter. Main courses may seem a tad complex, but flavours work well together: beef fillet, for instance, served pink, comes with mozzarella quiche, broad beans, pork texture, artichoke purée and truffled mushrooms. Whole Dover sole meunière with new potatoes and buttered greens will appeal to those who prefer plainer food, while desserts follow the multi-flavoured route of tonka bean pannacotta with orange sponge, honey and saffron cream, pistachios, banana confit and lime meringue.

Ashdown Park Hotel & Country Club

Chef Andrew Wilson **Owner** Elite Hotels **Seats** 120, Pr/dining room 160
Times 12-2/7-9.30 **Prices** Fixed L 2 course £18.50, Fixed D 3 course £42.50, Tasting menu £89, Starter £9-£10.95, Main £19-£36.50, Dessert £9.50-£16.50, Service optional **Wines** 250 bottles over £30, 16 bottles under £30, 12 by glass **Parking** 120 **Notes** Tasting menu 8 course, Sunday L £29, Vegetarian available, Children welcome

See advert on page 508

HASTINGS & ST LEONARDS
Map 7 TQ80

Bannatyne Spa Hotel Hastings

◎ Modern British **NEW**

tel: 0844 248 3836 *(Calls cost 5p per minute plus your phone company's access charge)* &
0344 248 3836 **Battle Rd TN38 8EA**
email: enquiries.hastingshotel@bannatyne.co.uk **web:** www.bannatyne.co.uk
dir: *M25 junct 5, A21 (Hastings). At 5th rdbt 2nd exit (Hastings/Filmwell). After 2 rdbts right (Folkestone/A259/Battle/A2100). Left at A2100/The Ridge Way. At 2nd rdbt right to hotel*

Imaginative cooking in a conservatory restaurant

In 38 acres of formal gardens and woodland, this large and solid-looking hotel with extensive spa and health club facilities has as its hub a colourful bar and a sizable conservatory restaurant. Cooking is a serious business here, and the kitchen turns out an interesting range of dishes. Get things going with a properly made roulade of duck confit and foie gras, with classic celeriac remoulade and the sweet contrast of caramelised plums, or that hallowed trio of seared scallops with black pudding and cauliflower purée. Move on to a triple helping of lamb – pink loin, confit shoulder and sautéed sweetbreads – all properly timed and rich-tasting, with a selection of vegetables and red wine sauce. A fish offering normally appears on the concise menu – perhaps pan-fried salmon fillet on peas à la France with saffron potato and mange-tout – and desserts are a strength, among them passionfruit pannacotta with mango, lemongrass and ginger soup.

Chef Hrvoje Loncarevic **Owner** Bannatyne Hotels Ltd **Seats** 68, Pr/dining room 18
Times 12.30-2.30/6.30-9.30 **Prices** Fixed L 2 course £14.50, Fixed D 3 course £30-£44 **Wines** 22 bottles over £30, 22 bottles under £30, 14 by glass **Parking** 150
Notes Sunday L £15.50-£19, Vegetarian available, Children welcome

LEWES
Map 6 TQ41

Jolly Sportsman

◎ Modern British, European

tel: 01273 890400 **Chapel Ln, East Chiltington BN7 3BA**
email: info@thejollysportsman.com
dir: *From Lewes A275, East Grinstead road, left onto the B2116 Offham, 2nd right into Novington Lane. In approx 1m first left Chapel Lane*

Country-chic rural pub with big-hearted food

Along a narrow lane between Lewes and Plumpton, with fields extending on every hand, the Sportsman could hardly be more rurally situated. Garden seating is a

must in summer, but the interior is welcoming too, with its country-chic look, all bare wooden boards for floors and tables, and a rather intimate room near the kitchen done in deep red, with low-hanging lights looking like frayed straw hats. Sturdy presentations of locally-sourced rustic food are the day's order, ranging from truffled boudin blanc with artichokes and chanterelles in butter sauce to mains such as turbot on samphire and pea fricassée with a spinach and red pepper croquette, or braised hare in port with Agen prunes, red cabbage and mash. Summer brings a refreshing finale of strawberry Pavlova with matching sorbet and jelly, or there may be tropical fruit fool. An impressive wine list of 150 bins is a heartening feature.

Times 12-3/6.30-10, Closed 25 Dec, Mon (ex BHs), D Sun

RYE
Map 7 TQ92

Mermaid Inn

◎◎ British, Traditional French **v**

tel: 01797 223065 **Mermaid St TN31 7EY**
email: info@mermaidinn.com **web:** www.mermaidinn.com
dir: *A259, follow signs to town centre, then into Mermaid St*

Atmospheric medieval inn with classic and modern menu

The cellars at the Mermaid Inn date from the 12th century, the inn itself from a mere 1420, so it is only 600 years old. In a town filled with spellbinding period buildings, this old inn has lots of historic charm and atmosphere. Check out the giant inglenook fireplace in the bar with its priest's hole, and the linenfold panels in the restaurant. The food takes an Anglo-French path and there are some

appealingly contemporary dishes on the menu. You might start with the youthful salt and pepper squid (from the south coast) with sweet chilli and coriander, or the more Francophile pressed duck leg terrine with toasted brioche, fruit chutney and watercress salad. Main course might serve up braised shoulder of Romney Marsh lamb (local ingredients get a good showing here) with chestnut mushrooms, baby onions, parsley creamed potatoes and pancetta. Finish with winter berry soufflé with orange crème anglaise and white chocolate ice cream.

Mermaid Inn

Chef Benjamin Fisher **Owner** J Blincow, G Kite **Seats** 64, Pr/dining room 14 **Times** 12-2.30/7-9.30 **Prices** Prices not confirmed **Wines** 15 bottles over £30, 22 bottles under £30, 15 by glass **Parking** 26 **Notes** Sunday L, Children welcome

Webbes at The Fish Café

◉ Modern British

tel: 01797 222226 **17 Tower St TN31 7AT**
email: info@thefishcafe.com
dir: *100mtrs before Landgate Arch*

Local seafood in an informal converted warehouse

A converted brick-built warehouse constructed in 1907 is now home to Webbe's at The Fish Café, a modern seafood restaurant that cooks in step with contemporary tastes. The place has a stylish look to show off the old warehouse's character – exposed brickwork, high ceilings and fish-related artwork all feed in to the buzz of the ground-floor dining room. The piscine produce comes from local boats working out of Rye and Hastings, and the chefs at work in the open-plan kitchen take a straight-up approach with it. Pan-fried cuttlefish with chorizo, sautéed potatoes and rocket and parsley salad is a vibrant starter, ahead of pan-fried wild sea bass fillets with suitably seasonal wild garlic, asparagus, new potatoes and mussel and chive sauce. Meat eaters won't feel left out with the likes of ox cheek with garlic and herb mash, caramelised onions and red wine jus. Finish with fennel seed pannacotta with orange compôte and sorbet.

Chef Paul Webbe, Matthew Drinkwater **Owner** Paul & Rebecca Webbe **Seats** 52, Pr/dining room 60 **Times** 11.30-2.30/6-9.30, Closed 24 Dec-10 Jan **Prices** Starter £6-£8.50, Main £12.50-£18, Dessert £6.50, Service optional **Wines** 10 by glass **Parking** Cinque Port St **Notes** Sunday L, Vegetarian available, Children welcome

TICEHURST Map 6 TQ63

Dale Hill Hotel & Golf Club

◉ Modern European

tel: 01580 200112 **TN5 7DQ**
email: info@dalehill.co.uk **web:** www.dalehill.co.uk
dir: *M25 junct 5/A21. 5m after Lamberhurst turn right at lights onto B2087 to Flimwell. Hotel 1m on left*

Imaginative modern European menu in a golfing hotel

With its duo of 18-hole courses, golf may be the signature dish at this hotel and country club in a fabulous location high on the Sussex Weald, but for non-players, uplifting views over the hills of East Sussex, a heated indoor pool and gym, and a brace of dining options are reasons enough to come. Of the two restaurants, the expansive fine-dining Wealden Restaurant is the star attraction, and it comes – perhaps inevitably – with vistas of the 18th green. Modern European cooking is par for this particular course, and it appears in some appetising ideas. You might tee off with pan-fried scallops with crisp pig's cheeks, celeriac purée and chestnut pesto, and follow on with a Barnsley lamb chop with watercress, confit shallots, pommes frites and bordelaise sauce, or wild mushroom tagliatelle with parmesan and truffle oil. Finish with pistachio and white chocolate mousse with pomegranate foam and lemon sorbet.

Chef Mark Carter **Owner** Mr & Mrs Paul Gibbons **Seats** 60, Pr/dining room 24 **Times** 12-2.30/6.30-9, Closed L Mon-Sat, D 25 Dec **Prices** Fixed D 3 course fr £29, Service optional **Wines** 8 bottles over £30, 29 bottles under £30, 7 by glass **Parking** 220 **Notes** Sunday L £15-£19, Vegetarian available, Children welcome

UCKFIELD Map 6 TQ42

Buxted Park Hotel

◉◉ Modern European V

tel: 01825 733333 & 0845 072 7412 *(Calls cost 7p per minute plus your phone company's access charge)* **Buxted TN22 4AY**
email: buxtedpark@handpicked.co.uk **web:** www.handpickedhotels.co.uk/buxtedpark
dir: *From A26 (Uckfield bypass) take A272 signed Buxted. Through lights, hotel 1m on right*

Creative modern British cooking in a pristine Palladian mansion

Buxted is the full country-house package, a graceful white Palladian mansion rising above immaculately laid gardens, with a pillared portico entrance and deep windows. It was built in the early Georgian era for Thomas Medley, who had made a fortune as a port shipper during Britain's periodic hostilities with France. A striking layout in the dining room features a mix of booth and table seating, with lilac upholstery against a pristine white backdrop. The dynamic kitchen produces an entertaining and carefully composed version of the modern British style. Seared scallops with apple curry sauce, julienned vegetables and crispy leeks opens the way for a main course starring a two-way serving of duck – crisp-skinned breast and a 'cigar' of confit meat – matched with Savoy cabbage with bacon, cream and marjoram, apple and star anise sauce and rich duck jus. A straightforward approach to desserts brings a gentle finale of dark chocolate fondant with mint ice cream, or classic vanilla crème brûlée.

Chef Steve Cole **Owner** Hand Picked Hotels **Seats** 40, Pr/dining room 120 **Times** 12-2/7-9.30 **Prices** Fixed L 2 course fr £16, Fixed D 3 course fr £39, Starter £12.50-£16, Main £23.50-£33.95, Dessert £6.50-£10.50, Service optional **Wines** 95 bottles over £30, 5 bottles under £30, 18 by glass **Parking** 100 **Notes** Dégustation 7 course with/without wine, Sunday L £25.95, Children welcome

UCKFIELD *continued*

East Sussex National Golf Resort & Spa

◎◎ Modern British, French

tel: 01825 880088 **Little Horsted TN22 5ES**
email: ops@eastsussexnational.co.uk **web:** www.eastsussexnational.co.uk
dir: *M25 junct 6, A22 signed East Grinstead & Eastbourne. Straight on at rdbt junct of A22 & A26 (Little Horsted). At next rdbt right to hotel*

Well-executed modern cooking and golf

There's a lot on offer at this modern hotel: more than 100 guest rooms, a health club and spa, two championship-level golf courses and conference and wedding facilities. Another reason for a visit is a meal in the vast Pavilion Restaurant looking over the greens and the South Downs. The menu is concise but still packs plenty of choice. Start, perhaps, with a nicely presented plate of salmon and samphire with mayonnaise, or the earthier flavours of rabbit and leek terrine with pistachios, carrot and sourdough bread. Dishes are composed to bring out upfront flavours without being gimmicky or ostentatious: pink and tender venison loin complemented by juniper sauce served with salsify, red cabbage, broccoli and violet potatoes, for instance, or brill fillet on a red wine jus with cockles, spinach and curried parsnip purée. Puddings are the real deal too, among them smooth chocolate tart, its pastry crumbly, with salted caramel ice cream and lime, or fig and almond cake with toffee sauce.

Chef Mark Burton **Owner** East Sussex National Ltd **Seats** 90
Times 12-2.30/7-9, Closed L Sun **Prices** Starter £6-£11, Main £14-£23, Dessert £7-£12, Service optional **Wines** 14 by glass **Parking** 500 **Notes** Vegetarian available, Children welcome

Horsted Place

◎◎ Modern British

tel: 01825 750581 **Little Horsted TN22 5TS**
email: hotel@horstedplace.co.uk **web:** www.horstedplace.co.uk
dir: *From Uckfield 2m S on A26 towards Lewes*

Unpretentious country-house cooking in Victorian Gothic masterpiece

When you're in the mood for a hit of Victorian Gothic splendour, Horsted Place delivers in spades: the house was built in 1850 by George Myers, with Pugin taking care of the details. It sits in 1,000 acres of verdant Sussex countryside with, oh yes, two championship golf courses, a tennis court and croquet on the lawn. Inside is as ornate as is to be expected, with well-spaced tables dressed in floor-length linen, and pictures of landscapes and horses in the dining room. Despite a few modernist tweaks, the country-house cooking does nothing to frighten those horses, but sticks to tried-and-true combinations, achieved with assured technical ability. Chargrilled baby squid appear with braised fennel, mange-tout and aïoli dressing, while a main course brings beef fillet with shallot and potato rösti, creamed leeks, girolles, green beans and red wine sauce. On the fish front, there might be pan-seared stone bass fillet with olive oil mash, provençal tomato and gremolata. Finish with limoncello cake with vanilla pannacotta and brandy-roasted peach.

Chef Allan Garth **Owner** Perinon Ltd **Seats** 40, Pr/dining room 80
Times 12-2/7-9.30, Closed 1st wk Jan, L Sat **Prices** Fixed L 2 course £18.95, Starter £9.50, Main £22, Dessert £9, Service optional **Wines** 74 bottles over £30, 24 bottles under £30, 9 by glass **Parking** 50 **Notes** Breakfast, Afternoon tea £19.50, Sunday L £28.50, Vegetarian available, Children 7 yrs+

WESTFIELD Map 7 TQ81

The Wild Mushroom Restaurant

◎◎ Modern British

tel: 01424 751137 **Woodgate House, Westfield Ln TN35 4SB**
email: info@wildmushroom.co.uk
dir: *From A21 towards Hastings, left onto A28 to Westfield. Restaurant 1.5m on left*

Modern British cooking in a charming converted farmhouse

A converted 19th-century farmhouse surrounded by countryside just a short drive from Hastings, Paul and Rebecca Webbe's restaurant is part of a mini-empire that includes Webbe's at The Fish Café in Rye and Rock-a-nore in Hastings Old Town. The restaurant takes up the whole of the ground floor, with a conservatory bar overlooking a small garden at the rear. There are original features like flagged floors and low beams, and a smart country feel to the place, helped along by the friendly service. Sharp, contemporary cooking is the name of the game, with ingredients shipped in locally from trusted suppliers and due heed paid to the seasons. There are set lunch, à la carte and tasting menus to choose from, with canapés, an amuse-bouche and home-made breads all part of the package. Pork and wild mushroom rillette served with toasted granary bread and home-made piccalilli is a switched on starter, with slow-cooked ox cheek with garlic mash and Shiraz jus a hit among main courses.

Chef Paul Webbe, Christopher Weddle **Owner** Mr & Mrs P Webbe **Seats** 40
Times 12-2.30/7-10, Closed 25 Dec, 2 wks at New Year, Mon-Tue, D Sun **Prices** Fixed L 2 course fr £17.95, Starter £7-£9, Main £14-£22, Dessert £7.50-£9, Service optional **Wines** 6 by glass **Parking** 20 **Notes** Tasting menu 6 course, Sunday L fr £35, Vegetarian available, Children welcome

WILMINGTON
Map 6 TQ50

Crossways
◉◉ Modern British

tel: 01323 482455 **Lewes Rd BN26 5SG**
email: stay@crosswayshotel.co.uk **web:** www.crosswayshotel.co.uk
dir: *On A27, 2m W of Polegate*

Country-house dining in relaxed restaurant with rooms

Crossways is a four-square white-painted Georgian restaurant with rooms with a small, traditional dining room with patterned wallpaper, drapes and pelmets adorning the windows. Everything is on an intimate scale, with the operation run like a private home, and indeed the owners are very much in evidence. The appeal lies in the standard of the cooking and in the interesting monthly-changing four-course menu. Mango salsa is a good foil for duck terrine wrapped in pancetta, or start with a seafood pancake. Soup normally follows before the main course, where a straightforward approach brings out the flavours of quality ingredients: perhaps five lamb cutlets, roasted to pink, with a copybook version of port, redcurrant and rosemary sauce and seasonal vegetables, or, in season, roast breast of local pheasant with a shallot, bacon and chestnut sauce. There's always a fish dish of the day, and puddings include Swiss roll with raspberries and cream.

Chef David Stott **Owner** David Stott, Clive James **Seats** 24
Times 7.30-8.30, Closed 24 Dec-24 Jan, Sun-Mon, L all week **Prices** Prices not confirmed, Service optional **Wines** 11 bottles over £30, 28 bottles under £30, 10 by glass **Parking** 20 **Notes** 4 course D £42.50, Vegetarian available, Children 12 yrs+

WEST SUSSEX

ALBOURNE
Map 6 TQ21

The Ginger Fox
◉ Modern British, European

tel: 01273 857888 **Muddleswood Rd BN6 9EA**
email: gingerfox@gingermanrestaurants.com
dir: *On A281 at junct with B2117*

English and Euro cooking on the South Downs

The Brighton-based Ginger group of restaurants and refashioned pubs has a bolt-hole in the country, on the A281 with commanding views of Devil's Dyke and the South Downs National Park. A stripped-down interior look with herringbone parquet and slate floors, chunky tables, and wood-burners in both restaurant and bar complements the beer-garden and raised beds where the Fox's own vegetables are grown. The menu mixes hearty English staples with modern European thinking, producing a rabbit croquette with foie gras, carrots and celeriac remoulade to start, then beef cheek with bone marrow and truffled mash, or sea bass with an oyster beignet, braised leeks and parsley root purée in red wine. A rarebit savoury made with Sussex ale is an alternative to the likes of pistachio cake with chocolate sorbet, or a rhubarb study that combines poached fruit with cheesecake and sorbet.

Chef Ben McKellar, James Dearden **Owner** Ben & Pamela McKellar **Seats** 50, Pr/dining room 24 **Times** 12-2/6-10, Closed 25 Dec **Prices** Prices not confirmed, Service optional **Wines** 18 bottles over £30, 25 bottles under £30, 20 by glass **Parking** 60 **Notes** Fixed L 2 course Mon-Fri until 7pm, Sunday L, Vegetarian available, Children welcome

AMBERLEY
Map 6 TQ01

Amberley Castle
◉◉◉ *– see page 512*

ARUNDEL
Map 6 TQ00

The Town House
◉◉ Modern V

tel: 01903 883847 **65 High St BN18 9AJ**
email: enquiries@thetownhouse.co.uk **web:** www.thetownhouse.co.uk
dir: *Follow A27 to Arundel, onto High Street, establishment on left at top of hill*

Classy bistro cooking facing Arundel Castle

You may not be in Arundel Castle itself, but sitting in the dining room of this Regency townhouse beneath the superb gilt carved Renaissance ceiling transported from Florence, you could almost imagine you were sitting down for dinner with the Duke of Norfolk. Sitting on a town-centre hill facing the castle, this smart restaurant with rooms is a place of enormous charm, its intimate dining room brought into the 21st century with high-backed black chairs, wooden floors and mirrors with funky striped frames, and the cooking is up-to-date stuff too. The kitchen takes the best of Sussex produce as the foundation for a menu of simple bistro dishes. Seared pigeon breast with pearl barley and wild garlic risotto is a faultlessly-executed starter, followed by roasted venison fillet with spinach, button mushrooms, baby onions, crisp roast potatoes and bacon jus. It's all very carefully timed and presented with aplomb, and a dessert of pannacotta with poached rhubarb and a sablé biscuit brings the curtain down on a high note.

Chef Lee Williams **Owner** Lee & Kate Williams **Seats** 24
Times 12-2.30/7-9.30, Closed 2 wks Etr, 2 wks Oct, Xmas, Sun-Mon **Prices** Fixed L 2 course fr £17.50, Fixed D 3 course fr £29.50, Service optional **Wines** 57 bottles over £30, 29 bottles under £30, 8 by glass **Parking** On street or nearby car park **Notes** Children welcome

BOSHAM
Map 5 SU80

The Millstream Hotel & Restaurant
◉◉ Modern British

tel: 01243 573234 **Bosham Ln PO18 8HL**
email: info@millstreamhotel.com **web:** www.millstreamhotel.com
dir: *4m W of Chichester on A259, left at Bosham rdbt. After 0.5m right at T-junct signed to church & quay. Hotel 0.5m on right*

Stylish inventive cooking in a charming quiet setting

Built of red brick and flint, the building was originally three 17th-century workmen's cottages, and has since earned a crust as a charming hotel. On a balmy evening, the fabulous lawned gardens with ducks quacking along the millstream make an idyllic spot for drinks, or you could join the yachtie crew in the convivial bar. The kitchen stays abreast of modern trends while keeping traditionalists happy with crowd-pleasing menus that bring new dishes each day. Starters can be as classic as warm chicken terrine with Caesar salad and grilled sourdough, or might push the boundaries a touch with the likes of smoked haddock and leek tart with a crispy egg yolk and crème fraîche. Quality is clear in the raw materials, and combinations

continued

BOSHAM *continued*

are intelligently thought through, so fillet of sea bass is partnered by shellfish bisque, crab beignets and Jersey Royals, and fillet of beef by truffle mash, morels, and smoked bone marrow. Puddings are worth exploring: perhaps basil pannacotta with strawberry jelly and champagne granita.

Chef Neil Hiskey **Owner** The Wild family **Seats** 60, Pr/dining room 40 **Times** 12.30-2/6.30-9 **Prices** Fixed L 2 course fr £22.50, Fixed D 3 course fr £35.50, Tasting menu fr £55, Service optional **Wines** 28 bottles over £30, 34 bottles under £30, 13 by glass **Parking** 40 **Notes** Tasting menu with wine 6 course, Pre-theatre menu, Sunday L £23-£27.50, Vegetarian available, Children welcome

---

| CHICHESTER | Map 5 SU80 |

Crouchers Country Hotel & Restaurant

◉◉ Modern British

tel: 01243 784995 & 07887 744570 **Birdham Rd PO20 7EH**
email: crouchers@btconnect.com **web:** www.croucherscountryhotel.com
dir: *From A27 Chichester bypass onto A286 towards West Wittering, 2m, hotel on left between Chichester Marina & Dell Quay*

Imaginative cooking in stylish hotel

During its two decades as a stalwart of the Chichester area's dining scene, Crouchers has traded ever upwards from a simple B&B to a smart modern hotel with an inviting wine bar and stylish oak-beamed restaurant looking over open green countryside near to Dell Quay and the marina. This well-run operation is popular because of its lack of airs and graces, and a kitchen that takes a serious approach to its work. That means bringing out the best from splendid locally-sourced raw materials to produce well-composed, imaginative modern ideas, as witnessed in a starter of lobster and salmon ravioli served with lobster bisque and parmesan snow. The main course brings skilfully handled duck breast, served pink with crispy skin,

together with a spring roll stuffed with confit duck and red onion marmalade, partnered by pak choi and a yuzu and wasabi dressing. Desserts maintain the high standards, as shown by the well-balanced flavours and textures of tonka bean cassonade with cocoa jelly, milk foam, amaretti crumbs and almond ice cream.

Times 12-2.30/7-9.30

Earl of March

◉ Modern British

tel: 01243 533993 & 783991 **Lavant Rd PO18 0BQ**
email: info@theearlofmarch.com
dir: *On A286, 2m N of Chichester towards Midhurst, on the corner of Goodwood Estate*

Classy cooking in revamped old pub

Just a short drive out of Chichester, the Earl of March is an 18th-century coaching inn with a rural aspect looking out over the South Downs. There's a small patio garden where you can soak up the view, but most of the action takes place inside, where the pub has been opened up to create a large dining area. A snug bar area has a real fire and sofas. The service team are a chatty bunch. The menu includes old favourites such as beer-battered haddock with hand-cut chips alongside brasserie staples such as sole meunière, while starters might include a richly flavoured wild mushroom soup or seared scallops with black pudding and watercress emulsion. Desserts are a feel-good lot such as sticky toffee pudding with bourbon ice cream, or a crumble of pear, blackberry and almond.

Chef Giles Thompson, Adam Howden **Owner** Giles & Ruth Thompson **Seats** 60, Pr/dining room 16 **Times** 12-2.30/5.30-9.30 **Prices** Fixed L 2 course £19.50, Fixed D 3 course £21.50, Starter £6.50-£12.50, Main £15.50-£23, Dessert £7, Service optional **Wines** 42 bottles over £30, 33 bottles under £30, 24 by glass **Parking** 30 **Notes** Pre-theatre/Early bird menu 2/3 course, Sunday L £19.50-£25, Vegetarian available, Children welcome

---

Amberley Castle ◉◉◉

| AMBERLEY | Map 6 TQ01 |

Modern British V 🍷NOTABLE WINE LIST
tel: 01798 831992 **BN18 9LT**
email: info@amberleycastle.co.uk **web:** www.amberleycastle.co.uk
dir: *Off B2139 between Storrington & Houghton*

Refined, contemporary cooking in a one-off historical setting

There are quite a few hotels in the UK with 'castle' in their names, but few can compete with Amberley when it comes to living up to expectations – it's a 900-year-old Norman castle with a twin-towered gatehouse complete with a portcullis, and battlements built to rebuff invaders sweeping over the South Downs. Goodness, it's impressive. Within its hefty stone walls, the public rooms have kept to the spirit of the antiquity of the place while adding a sense of contemporary luxury. The main dining room, the Queen's Room, has a 12th-century barrel-vaulted ceiling, open fireplace, murals, muskets and tapestries, and tables laid for the business of fine dining. The kitchen – headed up by Robby Jenks – meets 21st-century expectations, drawing on the best of British and European culinary traditions to create modern dishes that show creativity and craft. Flavours hit the mark, not least in a first-course lamb's sweetbread ravioli with its accompanying lamb jus, or a squab pigeon in the earthy company of mushrooms, Madeira and truffles. Tender slow-

cooked pork is perked up with fiery chorizo, lemon and capers, plus dinky pieces of popcorn, and cod arrives with mussels and salsify, delicately flavoured with saffron. Dessert is likely to be an imaginative offering such as one bringing together passionfruit and gorgonzola, or another that combines rhubarb and apple with mascarpone and apple blossom. There's a tasting menu where the chef is given free rein to impress, and the hotel is a great place to enjoy afternoon tea if you can fit it in. The wine list matches the setting, rampaging through Europe and the New World to deliver some classic bins and new discoveries, with the sommelier on hand to advise.

Chef Robby Jenks **Owner** Andrew Brownsword **Seats** 56, Pr/dining room 12 **Times** 12-2/7-9, **Prices** Fixed L 2 course fr £25.50, Starter fr £17.50, Main fr £37, Dessert fr £10.50, Service optional **Wines** 171 bottles over £30, 11 bottles under £30, 15 by glass **Parking** 40 **Notes** Sunday L fr £30.50, Children 8 yrs+

Halliday's

◉◉ Modern British

tel: 01243 575331 **Watery Ln, Funtington PO18 9LF**
email: hallidaysdinners@aol.com
dir: 4m W of Chichester, on B2146

Quality local produce cooked with flair

Halliday's occupies three flint-fronted thatched cottages dating from the 13th century, now divided into two eating areas with a small bar in between. Everything is made in-house with a good deal of finesse, from breads to petits fours, and chef Andy Stephenson goes that extra mile when it comes to sourcing first-rate produce from the local area, including home-smoking and foraging in the woodland. His sound technical abilities bring to life the sunny Mediterranean flavours in a seasonal summer menu, beginning with sautéed squid with chorizo, red wine, rocket and griddled ciabatta, or a croustade of roasted tomato, red onion and mozzarella with wild marjoram. Among meaty main courses, local rump of lamb teamed with baked aubergine, tomato, and basil oil is a bit of a treat, while fish from the south coast might include wild black bream with shaved fennel, pink peppercorns and blood oranges. To finish, the chef's grounding in the great French traditions is evident in an exemplary vanilla crème brûlée, whose richness is matched with a vibrant passionfruit sorbet and buttery shortbread.

Chef Andrew Stephenson **Owner** Mr A & Mrs J Stephenson **Seats** 26, Pr/dining room 12 **Times** 12-2.15/7-10.15, Closed 1 wk Mar, 2 wks Aug, Mon-Tue, L Sat, D Sun **Prices** Fixed L 2 course fr £16.50, Fixed D 3 course fr £27.50, Starter £6.50-£10.25, Main £17.50-£22, Dessert £6.50-£8, Service optional **Wines** 26 bottles over £30, 36 bottles under £30, 8 by glass **Parking** 12 **Notes** Sunday L £24, Vegetarian available, Children welcome

Richmond Arms

◉ Eclectic

tel: 01243 572046 **Mill Rd, West Ashling PO18 8EA**
email: richmondarms@gmail.com
dir: Phone for directions

Inspired global cooking at the foot of the Downs

The whitewashed Richmond is one of the glories of West Ashling, a peaceful village at the foot of the South Downs, only five minutes from Chichester. Locals pack the bar for real ales and snacks, and the kitchen sets to work producing locally-based food in an ambience of winter fires and candles on scrubbed unclothed tables. Daily specials are written up on the blackboard, and there's a wood-fired oven for authentic Sussex pizzas. Indeed, the extensive menus look far and wide for inspiration, from wood-roast aubergine with goats' curd, poppadoms and 'tandoori honey', to mains such as braised fallow venison shank in sweet Persian spices with nutty couscous, and grilled sea bass with a sweetcorn fritter and gingered squash in coconut and macadamia sambal. A dessert based on the B52 shooter recipe, featuring Kahlúa brûlée, Baileys' ice cream and Grand Marnier froth, certainly packs a punch.

Chef William Jack **Owner** William & Emma Jack **Seats** 36, Pr/dining room 60 **Times** 12-3/6-11, Closed Mon-Tue, D Sun **Prices** Prices not confirmed, Service optional **Parking** 9, On street **Notes** Sunday L, Vegetarian available, Children welcome

The Royal Oak Inn

◉◉ Modern British, European

tel: 01243 527434 **Pook Ln, East Lavant PO18 0AX**
email: info@royaloakeastlavant.co.uk **web:** www.royaloakeastlavant.co.uk
dir: From Chichester take A286 towards Midhurst, 2m to mini rdbt, turn right signed East Lavant. Inn on left

Imaginative modern menu in a charming village inn

This 200-year-old pub strikes a neat balance between its various functions. As the village inn, it fits the bill if you're looking for a pint of real ale, a table by the fire, or a seat out on the terrace to enjoy Sussex views. As a restaurant with rooms, food is reassuringly high on the agenda. The kitchen's output has a modern flavour with lots of British and European ideas, and daily specials chalked up on the blackboard, and it's all served up in a satisfyingly rustic interior with exposed brick walls, beams, leather-look chairs and wooden tables. A starter of pork and apricot ballotine with spiced apricot compôte and toasted sourdough raises the bar well above pub grub level, and main courses are just as intelligently put together. Succulent roast breast of guinea fowl comes with crisp potato rösti, wilted greens with pancetta and a punchy wild mushroom jus, and a trio of pork comprising belly, tenderloin and black pudding bonbons is matched with carrot and anise purée, purple sprouting broccoli and red wine jus.

Chef James Dean **Owner** Charles Ullmann **Seats** 55 **Times** 10-3/6-10.30 **Prices** Starter £6.50-£12.95, Main £15.90-£27.90, Dessert £6.95-£8.95, Service optional **Wines** 54 bottles over £30, 26 bottles under £30, 20 by glass **Parking** 25 **Notes** Pre-theatre menu from 5.30pm, Sunday L, Vegetarian available, Children welcome

See advert on page 514

CHICHESTER *continued*

The Ship Hotel

◉ Modern British

tel: 01243 778000 **57 North St PO19 1NH**
email: enquiries@theshiphotel.net **web:** www.theshiphotel.net
dir: *From A27 follow signs for town centre and Chichester Festival Theatre. Restaurant signed from Northgate rdbt*

Modern brasserie cooking in a boutique city-centre hotel

In the heart of historic Chichester, The Ship presents a sober, red-brick Georgian face to the world, but inside it's another story altogether. The designers have been unleashed, and the place is now a riot of boutique style. Murray's Restaurant is a split-level dining room that works a classy colonial look with palm trees, touchy-feely fabrics, exposed floorboards and unclothed dark wood tables. Brasserie-style menus tick the right boxes, opening with the likes of game terrine with cranberry relish and chargrilled sourdough bread, or scallops and belly pork with celeriac and apple purée and pancetta crumb. To follow, there are straight-up slabs of beef from the grill, or comforting old favourites such as steak and kidney pudding, while fish might be halibut with saffron fondant potatoes, celeriac, fennel remoulade and roasted beetroot. Simple but effective finishers include classic apple tarte Tatin with cinnamon and pecan ice cream, or chocolate ganache with orange oil and spices.

Chef Adam Young **Owner** Chichester Hotel Company LLP **Seats** 120, Pr/dining room 48 **Times** 10-10, All-day dining **Prices** Fixed L 2 course £17.50-£19.50, Fixed D 3 course £19.95-£24.50, Tasting menu £40-£85, Starter £5.50-£8.25, Main £12.50-£24.95, Dessert £6, Service optional **Wines** 6 bottles over £30, 20 bottles under £30, 12 by glass **Parking** 25 **Notes** Pre-theatre prix fixe plus full ALC, Sunday L £19.50-£24.50, Vegetarian available, Children welcome

---

CHILGROVE　　　　　　　　　　　　　　　　　**Map 5 SU81**

The White Horse

◉ British, European **NEW**

tel: 01243 519444 **High St PO18 9HX**
email: info@thewhitehorse.co.uk **web:** www.thewhitehorse.co.uk
dir: *From London, A3 to Portsmouth. Take A272 to Petersfield then right towards Pulens Ln B2199. At end turn left. After 3m, right onto B2146. Take B2141 into Chilgrove. On left. From Chichester, take road to Lavant, follow signs Chilgrove. On right*

Quirky pub restaurant with plenty of ambition

In the heart of the Sussex countryside on the fringes of the spectacular South Downs, this stylish pub is warmly inviting and boasts plenty of quirky touches, right down to sheepskin throws on the high-backed benches and deer skulls, some of which sport sunglasses and scarves. Whether you dine in the restaurant or outside in the courtyard, a meal here showcases some modern British cooking of considerable poise and confidence, with pub classics sitting shoulder to shoulder with more fine-dining dishes. Start with goats' cheese and honey mousse with pistachio crumb, red pepper coulis and herb oil, before a generously proportioned warm salad of roasted guinea fowl with wild mushrooms, Parma ham and new potatoes. Impressive pastry skills are evident in a white chocolate and raspberry crème brûlée. Service from relaxed and friendly staff is informal and personable.

Chef Robert Armstrong **Owner** Cirrus Inns **Seats** 100, Pr/dining room 25 **Times** 12-3/6-9, Closed D 25 Dec, 1 Jan **Prices** Starter £5-£8.75, Main £12.95-£26.95, Dessert £5.95-£7.50 **Wines** 100+ bottles over £30, 19 bottles under £30, 17 by glass **Parking** 50 **Notes** Sat-Sun all day dining, Sunday L £12.95-£14.50, Vegetarian available, Children welcome

The Felbridge Hotel & Spa

◉◉ Modern British

tel: 01342 337700 **London Rd RH19 2BH**
email: info@felbridgehotel.co.uk **web:** www.felbridgehotel.co.uk
dir: *From W: M23 junct 10, follow signs to A22. From N: M25 junct 6. Hotel on A22 at Felbridge*

Inventive modern food in a spa hotel

The Felbridge Hotel had a swish makeover back in 2007 making it fighting fit for the modern market. There's a snazzy spa, for a start, and a brace of dining options, the pick of the bunch being the Anise restaurant. There's an upmarket sheen to the room, with tones of brown and cream, and the tables are set for the business of fine dining. This is a kitchen turning out bright, contemporary food, with a keen eye on the provenance of the ingredients, a good amount of which comes from the south east. Modern techniques are used to maximise flavour and visual impact. A starter dish of scallops sees the bivalves partnered with mussels, chorizo, peas and wild rice, with the flavour of saffron deftly handled. Another first course puts Sussex ham hock centre stage, with pineapple, fennel and pistachio. Main-course breast of duck comes with parsnips, rhubarb and hazelnuts in a dazzling construction, and, for dessert, there's humour in the naming of 'Gone Nuts', which has baklava and almond pannacotta amongst its little treasures.

The Felbridge Hotel & Spa

Times 6-10, Closed L all week

See advert below

Gravetye Manor Hotel

◉◉◉ – *see page 516*

Gravetye Manor Hotel ✿ ✿ ✿

EAST GRINSTEAD   Map 6 TQ33

Modern British V 🍷 NOTABLE WINE LIST

tel: 01342 810567 **Vowels Ln, West Hoathly RH19 4LJ**
email: info@gravetyemanor.co.uk **web:** www.gravetyemanor.co.uk
dir: *From M23 junct 10 take A264 towards East Grinstead. After 2m take B2028 to Haywards Heath. 1m after Turners Hill fork left towards Sharpthorne, immediate 1st left into Vowels Lane*

Modernist cooking, an Elizabethan mansion and heritage gardens

The Elizabethan mansion was built by one Richard Infield as a little something for his new bride. Their initials appear above the garden entrance, and if you're lucky, you may find yourself staying in the bedroom that boasts a wood carving of the pair, still united in connubial bliss after 400 years. A century ago, the place was owned by the great Victorian landscaper William Robinson, who laid out its acres of grounds in the style we still see today. Gravetye played an integral part in the country-hotel movement of the 1980s, and has moved with the times, for example now offering a vegan menu option, centred perhaps on open kohlrabi lasagne with forest mushrooms and chard in tarragon oil and Madeira jus. George Blogg oversees the kitchen plus a one-acre produce garden too, supplying very nearly all the fruit and veg menu requirements in summer. A modernist style rules the roost, exploring novel combinations and textural contrasts. So the menu opens with treacle-cured sea trout and beetroot remoulade, with further flavour hits from oyster mayonnaise, fried capers and salmon caviar. Mains pull out the stops for too-rarely seen seared loin of hare with a faggot of the leg-meat, a tartlet of braised chicory and

blackberries. Fish cooking is precise and inspired, as in butter-seared brill fillet with hand-rolled malted macaroni in dramatic black, confit chicken wings and an emulsion sauce of leeks. An almond study to finish comes in the form of buttery frangipane tart topped with plums poached in mulled port, alongside almond ice cream, or there may be passionfruit soufflé with Thai basil-scented matching coulis and coconut ice cream.

Chef George Blogg **Owner** Jeremy & Elizabeth Hosking **Seats** 40, Pr/dining room 20 **Times** 12-2/6.30-9.30, **Prices** Fixed L 2 course fr £25, Tasting menu fr £85, Starter £17-£22, Main £29-£34, Dessert £12-£15 **Wines** 5 bottles under £30, 17 by glass **Parking** 25 **Notes** 4 course D £35, All day menu 10am-10pm, Afternoon tea, Sunday L fr £35, Children 7 yrs+

GATWICK AIRPORT (LONDON)   Map 6 TQ24

Arora Hotel Gatwick

Modern British **NEW**

tel: 01293 597701 & 530000 **Southgate Av, Southgate RH10 6LW**
email: gatwick@arorahotels.com
dir: M23 junct 10 then A2011 to Crawley. At 1st rdbt take 2nd exit towards town centre. At 2nd rdbt take 1st exit towards County Mall. Straight over at both sets of lights & County Mall should be on right. Under railway bridge, hotel on right

Sharp cooking in a smart hotel eatery

Despite its name, this smart modern hotel is in Crawley town centre, with the airport just a short bus trip away. However, there's no hurry to jet off when the place offers excellent fitness and business facilities, and the Grill restaurant is worth a visit in its own right. It's an airy open-plan room with clean-lined contemporary looks and an appetising, up-to-date menu that rings with seasonal flavours built from diligently sourced British produce. Parma ham and saffron risotto give an Italian spin to slow-cooked pork cheeks, while a slab of seared cod from the nearby south coast is matched with peas, fondant new potatoes and red wine jus. Straight-up steaks or a two-way serving of pork belly with crackling and caramelised onion purée keep the carnivores happy, and for pudding, baked vanilla cheesecake is partnered by sherry-glazed fig, glazed Victoria plums and blackberry sorbet.

Chef Tony Staples **Owner** Arora Hotels **Seats** 70, Pr/dining room 15
Times 12-2.30/6-10, Closed L Sat-Sun **Prices** Fixed D 3 course £19-£45, Starter £5.50-£12, Main £9.50-£24, Dessert £4.50-£8.50, Service optional 12.5% **Wines** 6 bottles over £30, 17 bottles under £30, 8 by glass **Parking** 210 **Notes** Vegetarian available, Children welcome

Langshott Manor

– see below

Sofitel London Gatwick

British, French

tel: 01293 567070 & 555000 **North Terminal RH6 0PH**
email: h6204-re@accor.com **web:** www.sofitel.com
dir: M23 junct 9, follow to 2nd rdbt. Hotel straight ahead

Smart brasserie cooking by the North Terminal

An impressive central atrium makes a massive impact at this smart hotel in a hefty new building in close proximity to Gatwick's North Terminal. Around this central space are three dining options: a café, Chinese restaurant, and La Brasserie, where the two rosettes are duly lodged. La Brasserie has a rather upscale finish, given the moniker, with neatly laid tables and prominent modern artworks. The menu takes a modern British path, with lots of good ideas and a sure hand at the stove. Start with a terrine of rabbit, ham hock and foie gras, for example, which is packed with flavour and comes in the company of a croquette, pickled carrot and punchy Pernod purée. Next up, sea bass fillet is cooked in a vacuum to maximise the flavour and precision, and is cooked just-so, with the flavours of lemon and dill well judged, plus a warm Pink Fir potato salad, lardons and citrus salad. The dessert menu offers a satisfying blueberry cheesecake with white chocolate sorbet and blueberry gel.

Times 6.30-10.30, Closed L all week

Langshott Manor

GATWICK AIRPORT (LONDON)   Map 6 TQ24

Modern European **v**
tel: 01293 786680 **Langshott Ln RH6 9LN**
email: admin@langshottmanor.com **web:** www.langshottmanor.com
dir: From A23 take Ladbroke Rd, off Chequers rdbt to Langshott, after 0.75m hotel on right

Dynamic contemporary cooking at an Elizabethan manor

Steeped in history as only an Elizabethan manor can be, Langshott is grand enough to have its own water-filled moat and resident ducks. All herringbone-patterned brick and mullioned windows outside, the interior decor is a mixture of rustic and plush, the occasional exposed brick fireplace offset with regal drapes and seductive views over the formally laid-out gardens. The terrace makes a sublime spot for afternoon tea. Splashes of vivid colour throw the period ambience of the Mulberry dining room into relief, not least from Phil Dixon's brightly presented, dynamic modern cooking. As is the way these days, a large helping of the fresh produce – fruits, vegetables and herbs – comes from the hotel's own kitchen garden, and much else is sourced in the locality. Tasting menus supplement the carte, which combines techniques both old and new for dishes such as a starter of wild duck en croûte with carrot, orange and bacon, or a lobster salad dressed in chicken cream with caviar and apple. Fish cookery is sensitively handled, as for a braised fillet of turbot seasoned with parsley root and mustard in chicken jus, and meats are of the most exclusive provenance – perhaps Limousin beef fillet with breaded ox tongue, artichoke and hazelnuts. Hare, once all but forgotten by ambitious chefs, is making a comeback all over, appearing here with cauliflower and truffled jus, and wild boar turns up with celeriac and pear. The inventive energy is maintained through desserts like pecan soufflé with squash and dulce de leche coffee ice cream, although a more traditional tack is taken with rum-soaked baba, which arrives with poached pineapple and guava sorbet. Artisan cheeses are served with pear and tomato chutney and pickled walnut bread.

Chef Phil Dixon **Owner** Peter & Deborah Hinchcliffe **Seats** 55, Pr/dining room 22
Times 12-2.30/7-9.30, **Prices** Fixed L 3 course £35, Fixed D 3 course £49.50, Tasting menu £75-£105 **Wines** 56 bottles over £30, 6 bottles under £30, 16 by glass **Parking** 25 **Notes** Sunday L £29.50, Children welcome

The Goodwood Hotel

◉◉ Contemporary British

tel: 01243 775537 **PO18 0QB**
email: reservations@goodwood.com **web:** www.goodwood.com
dir: Off A285, 3m NE of Chichester

Ambitious cooking on the Goodwood Estate

The luxury hotel, complete with health club and spa, is at the heart of the 12,000-acre Goodwood Estate, with the home farm, certified as organic, providing the kitchens of its various restaurants with pork, lamb and beef. The main dining option, the 18th-century Richmond Arms, is an elegant setting for finely honed contemporary British cooking, offering well-conceived dishes with flashes of French flair. Seared scallops come in a fashionable pairing with crispy chicken wing, charred spring onions, sweet and savoury bacon jam, and wild garlic buds. Or you might start with a tried-and-tested combination of chicken liver parfait with pear chutney and toasted brioche. Main course serves up that splendid Goodwood lamb with hay-baked beetroot and carrots, sorrel leaf, and charred asparagus, or there could be estate-reared Saddleback pork with aubergine, olive and baby vegetables. Fish options may include roast fillet of halibut with crayfish, sumac gnocchi, grapefruit, burnt cauliflower and sea herbs. Flavourings and seasonings remain crystal clear throughout, all the way to a dessert of peanut parfait and brittle with cherry sorbet.

Chef Mark Forman **Owner** The Goodwood Estate Company Ltd **Seats** 85, Pr/dining room 120 **Times** 12.30-2.30/6.30-10.30, Closed L Mon-Sat **Prices** Starter £6.50-£8.50, Main £15-£26, Dessert £7.75-£10 **Wines** 50 bottles over £30, 29 bottles under £30, 12 by glass **Parking** 150 **Notes** Sunday L £24-£30, Vegetarian available, Children welcome

Jeremy's at Borde Hill

◉◉ Modern European, Mediterranean

tel: 01444 441102 **Balcombe Rd RH16 1XP**
email: reservations@jeremysrestaurant.com **web:** www.jeremysrestaurant.com
dir: 1.5m N of Haywards Heath, 10mins from Gatwick Airport. From M23 junct 10a take A23 through Balcombe

Confident flavoursome cooking in idyllic garden setting

It is hard to imagine a more idyllic setting for summer dining than this contemporary restaurant in the quintessentially English Borde Hill Gardens. Jeremy's occupies a stylishly converted stable block overlooking the Victorian walled garden (which comes up trumps with fresh herbs and seasonal produce) and a dreamy south-facing terrace basking in the Sussex sun. Indoors, it's a wide-open, bright space with wooden floors, smart high-backed leather chairs and modern art on the walls. Chef-patron Jeremy Ashpool has a well-established network of small local producers to supply the best ingredients the bounteous Sussex larder has to offer, and knows how to extract the best from them. Expect big, bold flavours and colourful platefuls of thoroughly modern, vibrant, Mediterranean-inflected food, starting with grilled sea bass with red pepper, smoked aubergine purée and chargrilled fennel. Next up, rump and belly of South Downs lamb stars in a main course with smoked sheep's cheese, confit potatoes, carrots and tarragon jus. For dessert, bitter dark chocolate pavé is matched with white chocolate popcorn and salted caramel ice cream.

Jeremy's at Borde Hill

Chef Jimmy Gray, Jeremy Ashpool **Owner** Jeremy Ashpool **Seats** 55 **Times** 12-3/7-9.30, Closed after New Year for 7 days, Mon, D Sun **Prices** Fixed L 2 course £18, Fixed D 3 course £22, Tasting menu £40-£70, Starter £8-£12, Main £16-£26 **Wines** 19 bottles over £30, 16 bottles under £30, 18 by glass **Parking** 15, Overspill car park **Notes** Tasting menu 6 course, Fixed D midwk, Sunday L £26-£32, Vegetarian available, Children welcome

Restaurant Tristan

◉◉◉ – *see opposite*

Wabi

◉◉ Modern Japanese V

tel: 01403 788140 **38 East St RH12 1HL**
email: reservations@wabi.co.uk
dir: Corner Denne Rd & East St

Trendy venue for top-class Japanese in Horsham's restaurant quarter

There's no trace of Wabi's former life as a street-corner boozer: stylish to the hilt, the ground floor is a trendy, upbeat cocktail bar with copper pendant lights hanging from the raftered roof, a modern waterfall curtain behind the mixologists, plus a sushi bar/grill counter. Up on the first floor, the restaurant has a more minimal, cool and calming Zen garden vibe, with tatami-screened booths above spotlit beds of white pebbles, and darkwood everywhere. Japanese flavours are clearly the kitchen's primary inspiration, but that doesn't rule out input from the modern European idiom, while impeccable ingredients are sourced locally. If the menu terminology is alien, knowledgeable staff will penetrate the language barrier, and it's all designed for a sociable, tapas-style sharing approach. Get going with crispy chilli squid kara-age in crisp and light tempura batter, paired with mirin-sweetened daikon pickle and chilli dipping sauce, or roast duck bun with spicy peanut soy, red onions and chilli. For a knockout dish of head-spinning flavours, try tea-smoked lamb chops with smoky Japanese aubergine and spicy Korean red miso sauce.

Chef Lubomir Kovar **Owner** Paul Craig **Seats** 90, Pr/dining room 14 **Times** 12-2.30/6-10.30, Closed BHs **Prices** Prices not confirmed, Service optional 12.5% **Wines** 7 bottles over £30, 8 bottles under £30, 8 by glass **Parking** Car park **Notes** Fixed L/D 6 course £33-£45, Children welcome

LICKFOLD

Map 6 SU92

The Lickfold Inn

@@@ – see page 520

LODSWORTH

Map 6 SU92

The Halfway Bridge Inn

@ Modern British

tel: 01798 861281 **Halfway Bridge GU28 9BP**
email: enquiries@halfwaybridge.co.uk **web:** www.halfwaybridge.co.uk
dir: From Petworth on A272 towards Midhurst, 3m on right

Classic and modern pub fare in renovated old inn

This classy 18th-century roadside inn makes an inviting pitstop after a hike on the South Downs Way or a leisurely perusal of Petworth's antique emporia and Mr Turner's paintings in its famous stately home. Renovated from top to bottom with a cosy yet smartly-contemporary look, muted tones are set against dark beams, exposed brickwork, herringbone parquet floors, wood burners and roaring fires. The ambience is friendly and unbuttoned, while the kitchen deals in pub classics given a contemporary tweak, and with emphasis on local, seasonal materials. Kick off with potted game terrine with a classic duo of Cumberland sauce and melba toast, and follow with another rib-sticking idea – twice-cooked pork belly, rolled and stuffed with garlic and herbs, alongside bubble-and-squeak, and pear and cider sauce. To finish, cherry and almond frangipane tart comes with excellent vanilla and tonka bean ice cream.

Chef Gavin Rees **Owner** Sam & Janet Bakose **Seats** 55, Pr/dining room 16
Times 12-2.30/6-10 **Prices** Starter £6.50-£12.50, Main £12.50-£29, Dessert £6.50-£8, Service optional **Wines** 10 bottles over £30, 27 bottles under £30, 24 by glass
Parking 30 **Notes** Sunday L £15.95-£17.50, Vegetarian available, Children welcome

LOWER BEEDING

Map 6 TQ22

The Camellia Restaurant at South Lodge, an Exclusive Hotel

@@ British v NOTABLE WINE LIST

tel: 01403 891711 **Brighton Rd RH13 6PS**
email: enquiries@southlodgehotel.co.uk
dir: On A23 left onto B2110. Turn right through Handcross to A281 junct. Turn left, hotel on right

Vigorously original cooking in South Lodge's traditional dining room

Visitors to the handsome Victorian mansion hotel in the Sussex countryside have the option either of watching the kitchen at work in The Pass, or of gazing out over the inevitably more tranquil prospect of the grounds in The Camellia room. This is the traditional dining space, with its half-panelled oak beneath boldly floral wallpaper, although the cooking doesn't revert to country-house safety, choosing a vigorously original approach. A starter serving of crabmeat comes with roasted beetroot, clementine and watercress, while main courses offer their central components plenty to think about in the way of offbeat accompaniments. Loin and breast of lamb are partnered by salsify and spiced lentils in a striking passionfruit sauce, while stone bass arrives on a fatty jus gras with celeriac, romanesco and a carrot and coconut purée. Things settle a little for desserts such as plum Bakewell with marzipan ice cream, or classic Tatin for two, but cheese comes as a 'creation', perhaps a portion of Tunworth in a gougère with beetroot, manuka honey and fennel.

Chef Richard Mann **Owner** Exclusive Hotels & Venues **Seats** 100, Pr/dining room 140
Times 12-2.30/7-10 **Prices** Fixed L 2 course £19.50, Fixed D 3 course £37.50, Starter £9-£14, Main £24-£30, Dessert £10-£22 **Wines** 179 bottles over £30, 14 bottles under £30, 193 by glass **Parking** 200 **Notes** Sunday L £31, Children welcome

Restaurant Tristan @@@

HORSHAM

Map 6 TQ13

Modern British, French NOTABLE WINE LIST
tel: 01403 255688 **3 Stan's Way, East St RH12 1HU**
email: info@restauranttristan.co.uk
dir: Phone for directions

Clever, creative cooking in a historic beamed building

The 16th-century building in a pedestrianised street in the heart of old Horsham looks pretty historic, but chef-patron Tristan Mason's food is certainly of-the-moment stuff. Within, the setting blends ancient and modern elements with great effect: a striking beamed vaulted ceiling, wall timbers and bare floorboards sit alongside a contemporary decor of cream-painted walls broken up with designer floral wallpaper, pale wood tables simply set with olive-green place mats and crisp linen napkins. As is often the way with this kind of innovative, creative, technically skilful cooking, menus dispense with any description other than listing the components of each composition, but whether you go for three, four, six or eight courses, you can be sure that the full gamut of taste categories, textural contrasts and temperatures will be brought into play. Clever stuff, then, but this isn't just about techno flim-flam: having trained with Marco Pierre White, Mason's ideas are solidly grounded in classic French technique. An impressive, highly-detailed starter might see radish, apple and alexanders lined up to leaven the richness of crab, or a satisfyingly gooey duck egg (cooked at 64 degrees) matched with smoked turbot and burnt leek. Fish and meat combinations are favoured: Ventrèche bacon, say, brought in to add a salty hit to line-caught sea bass with chervil root and truffle. Elsewhere, beautifully cooked meat dishes might explore the textures and flavours of lamb, kid and goat, while partridge could arrive alongside pear and chestnut. Things are brought to a close with tour de force desserts involving, perhaps, a soaring rhubarb soufflé helped along by crème fraîche, liquorice and hibiscus, or an intriguing marriage of butternut pannacotta with wattleseed and sorrel.

Chef Tristan Mason **Owner** Tristan Mason **Seats** 40
Times 12-2.30/6.30-9.30, Closed Sun-Mon **Prices** Tasting menu £65-£80
Wines 30 bottles over £30, 16 bottles under £30, 20 by glass **Notes** L 3/4 course £25/£30, D 4 course £45, Tasting 6/8 course, Vegetarian available, Children 10 yrs+

LOWER BEEDING *continued*

Matt Gillan at The Pass Restaurant at South Lodge, an Exclusive Hotel

@ @ @ @ — *see opposite*

The Leconfield

@ Modern British

tel: 01798 345111 **New St GU28 0AS**
email: reservations@theleconfield.co.uk **web:** www.theleconfield.co.uk
dir: *Phone for directions*

Creative energy in a lively and popular restaurant

Petworth may be known for antiques but this red-brick former pub is firmly rooted in the 21st-century dining idiom. The Leconfield's lively ground-floor restaurant, with its bar and light, neutral decor of oak slab tables, bleached oak floors and caramel leather banquettes is all very cosmopolitan, and it opens on to a secluded cobbled courtyard that's perfect for balmy days. All sorts of ideas find their way on to the menus, from a lively starter of fennel gravad lax paired with salmon rillettes, quail's egg, and apple and endive salad, to a main course starring a spanking-fresh fillet of grey mullet with saffron potato, leek chowder, fish soup, and wild garlic croûtons; local meat fans might go for a fillet mignon of Storrington pork with grapes and Pommery mustard, pommes boulangère, asparagus and black pudding crumble. To finish, there's a spot-on wobbly vanilla pannacotta with a compôte of seasonal berries and a crunchy almond tuile.

The Leconfield

Chef David Craig-Lewis **Owner** Nicola Jones **Seats** 60, Pr/dining room 30
Times 12-3/6-9.30, Closed Mon, D Sun **Prices** Fixed L 2 course £25, Fixed D 3 course £30, Starter £12-£17, Main £19-£30, Dessert £9-£15 **Wines** 7 by glass **Parking** On street, car park **Notes** Fixed D early evening, Sunday L £25-£30, Vegetarian available, Children welcome

The Lickfold Inn @ @ @

British **NEW** v
tel: 01789 532535 **GU28 9EY**
email: dine@thelickfoldinn.co.uk
dir: *Signed from A272, 6m E of Midhurst. From A285, 6m S of Haslemere, follow signs for 'Lurgashall Winery', continue to Lickfold*

Thrilling, innovative cooking in a resurrected country inn

Rescued from a period of dereliction when it languished in the West Sussex backwoods near the Petworth House estate, The Lickfold Inn is not only up and running again, but the knight in shining armour behind its rescue is none other than Tom Sellers, whose thrilling cooking has made a big splash on the London dining scene in his much-lauded Restaurant Story. Sellers learned his craft in some of the world's top kitchens (René Redzepi's legendary Noma in Copenhagen, plus stints with Tom Aikens and at Thomas Keller's Per Se in New York) so culinary fireworks are clearly on the agenda. The pub side of things is an inviting spot for a jar of local ale to wash down superior versions of bar snacks like Scotch eggs, pork pies or charcuterie platters among open fires and ancient timbers, but the elegant upstairs dining room is where culinary matters get serious. The kitchen (fitted out with state-of-the-art gear) is run on a day-to-day basis by Graham Squire, who sends out some very sharp cooking built on the finest local materials brought together in intriguing, unorthodox alliances that really work. The terse menu kicks off with tender top-class smoked duck breast accompanied by its offal, a silky watercress emulsion, fresh watercress and alexanders. Left-field combinations are a hallmark of the style, as in a main course that partners immaculately-cooked halibut with a silky purée of caramelised cauliflower with subtle yeasty undertones (think Marmite!), cauliflower fondant, sea beets and sloes, while meaty mains might see pork belly matched with burnt pear and mead. Dessert reverts to a more mainstream vein with a rich custard tart layered with figs and damsons.

Chef Tom Sellers, Graham Squire **Owner** Montague Investments **Seats** 40
Times 12-3/6-9, Closed 25 Dec, Mon, D Sun **Prices** Fixed L 2 course £19, Starter £8-£12, Main £23-£32, Dessert £7-£8 **Wines** 109 bottles over £30, 11 bottles under £30, 10 by glass **Parking** 20 **Notes** Sunday L £25, Children welcome

Matt Gillan at The Pass Restaurant at South Lodge, an Exclusive Hotel ❀❀❀❀

LOWER BEEDING   Map 6 TQ22

Modern British **V** 🍷 NOTABLE WINE LIST

tel: 01403 891711 **Brighton Rd RH13 6PS**
email: enquiries@southlodgehotel.co.uk
web: www.southlodgehotel.co.uk
dir: *From A23 turn left onto B2110 & then right through Handcross to A281 junct. Turn left, hotel on right*

Ringside seats for a culinary firework display

If you like your meals to be a bit of a performance, South Lodge has taken the chef's table concept to its logical conclusion and inserted a whole restaurant into the kitchen. For the uninitiated, the pass is the part of the kitchen where the head chef gives the final okay to dishes before waiting staff whisk them away. It's decked out in modernist style with lime green and cream leather seats at tables along the edge of the pass, with the industrial stainless steel of the kitchen as a backdrop and – reality television addicts take note – plasma screens to zoom in on the action out of view. If you're hoping for a Ramsay-esque shouty, sweary experience, you'll be disappointed: head chef Matt Gillan and his team work in near silence, in a serene and well-organised environment. This is the key to pulling off dishes that mobilise all the tricks of the contemporary gastronomic trade. The format is multi-course tasting menus with a vegetarian version, and if making a decision is just too much hard work, go for the 12-course surprise menu. There's a lot more going on in each course than the terse, three-word descriptions imply, but rest assured that it's full of lively invention, built on first-class ingredients that work together and are sent out dressed to thrill. Things start with an egg in crisp potato strands with watercress, spring onion and French-fried shallots, prior to Sardinian fregola with crab, celery and toasted rice, while the fish course matches sea bass simply with black pudding and white beans. Meaty ideas see venison (a seared square and a crunchy croquette of confit meat) partnered with leeks and elderberries, both poached and as a jelly. Traditionalists might breathe a sigh of relief when the selection of artisan cheese provides a break from such high-tech endeavours, before desserts burst forth with further complexes of flavour, from lavender custard and jelly with poached blueberries and violet sorbet, to lemon granita with toasted oats and a soft, fudgy

honeycomb. If you're going for broke, the optional wine flights matched to the dishes are worth the extra outlay and provide a globetrotting voyage of vinous discovery. Alternatively, flights of juices infused with herbs, vegetables and herbs offer non-alcoholic flavour revelations. The Camellia Restaurant is the hotel's more mainstream dining option, providing contemporary renditions of country-house cooking in the Victorian mansion's panelled dining room.

Chef Matt Gillan **Owner** Exclusive Hotels & Venues **Seats** 26 **Times** 12-2/7-9, Closed 1st 2 wks Jan, Mon-Tue **Prices** Tasting menu £85-£95 **Wines** 185 bottles over £30, 16 bottles under £30, 11 by glass **Parking** 200 **Notes** Fixed L 4/6/8 course £27.50-£57.50, D 6/8 course £65/£75, Sunday L £37.50-£57.50, Children 12 yrs+

ROWHOOK
Map 6 TQ13

The Chequers Inn
◉ British

tel: 01403 790480 RH12 3PY
email: thechequersrowhook@googlemail.com
dir: From Horsham A281 towards Guildford. At rdbt take A29 signed London. In 200mtrs left, follow Rowhook signs

Ambitious modern cooking in village inn

The Chequers may well have been around since the 15th century, but it has stayed in tune with modern tastes. It is a proper village local, and with flagstones, oak beams, chunky wooden tables, welcoming open fires and a battery of well-kept real ales on handpump – what's not to like? Chef-proprietor Tim Neal clearly loves to haul in the best Sussex ingredients he can find, some of them supplied as locally as from the pub's garden, as well as foraged goodies and game in season. There are no pretensions or gimmicks, just bang-on-the-money modern ideas, from pan-fried scallops with parsnip and vanilla purée, to crispy confit duck with Puy lentil and merguez ragoût, spinach and French beans. If you're up for fish, there may be crispy hake fillet with curried mussel and leek cream, new potatoes and buttered spinach, and you could end with sticky toffee pudding with caramel sauce and vanilla ice cream.

Chef Tim Neal Owner Mr & Mrs Neal Seats 40 Times 12-2/7-9, Closed 25 Dec, D Sun Prices Starter £5.50-£9.95, Main £9.50-£23.50, Dessert £4.95-£6.50, Service optional Wines 7 bottles over £30, 26 bottles under £30, 8 by glass Parking 40 Notes Sunday L £5.95-£16.75, Vegetarian available, Children welcome

RUSPER
Map 6 TQ23

Ghyll Manor
◉ Traditional British

tel: 0330 123 0371 & 01293 871571 High St RH12 4PX
email: reception@ghyllmanor.co.uk web: www.ghyllmanor.co.uk
dir: M23 junct 11, A264 signed Horsham. Continue 3rd rdbt, 3rd exit Faygate, follow signs for Rusper, 2m to village

Country-house cooking amid 40 acres of prime Sussex countryside

A timbered manor house in 40 acres of picture-perfect Sussex countryside, Ghyll Manor is an obvious candidate for a retreat from the hurly-burly of the southeast. Inside, an appealing mixture of period features and modern styling creates a harmonious impression, and there's a terrace overlooking the gardens for summer aperitifs. This is country-house cooking that has its finger on the pulse of current tastes, without going all out for gasp-inducing avante-garderie. Beetroot-cured salmon with pickled fennel and cucumber is a modern classic dish, without question, but other starters are more traditional, perhaps ham hock terrine with Bramley apple compôte, before main courses arrive to deliver slow-roasted pork cheeks with white beans and chorizo, or rosemary-scented chicken breast with lentils, mushrooms and smoked bacon. Finish up with bread-and-butter pudding, or a passionfruit parfait garnished with toasted meringue.

Times 12-2/6.30-9.30

SIDLESHAM
Map 5 SZ89

The Crab & Lobster
◉◉ Modern British

tel: 01243 641233 Mill Ln PO20 7NB
email: enquiries@crab-lobster.co.uk web: www.crab-lobster.co.uk
dir: A27 S onto B2145 towards Selsey. At Sidlesham turn left onto Rookery Ln, continue for 0.75m

Switched-on modern menu in a waterside restaurant with rooms

The 17th-century, white-painted pub is these days more upscale restaurant with rooms than boozer, and it's looking spruce from top to bottom. On the edge of the Pagham Harbour nature reserve, The Crab & Lobster offers smart bedrooms and a stylish restaurant that aims to impress with its fine-dining ambitions. The period features of the building remain to bring character to the spaces, while the furnishings take a more contemporary line. The kitchen team delivers upscale modern British food that looks good on the plate and delivers bang-on flavours. Potted rabbit with toasted brioche and shallot marmalade is a classy first course, and there is a good showing of seafood, too, with the likes of Selsey crab cakes with mango, sesame and chilli jam. Main courses can be as populist as loin of beer-battered hake with hand-cut chips and tartare sauce (a swish fish and chips indeed), or as refined as Jerusalem artichoke and Oxford Blue risotto with artichoke crips and parsley oil. Finish with apple and rhubarb parfait.

Chef Sam Bakose, Clyde Hollett Owner Sam & Janet Bakose Seats 54 Times 12-2.30/6-10 Prices Fixed L 2 course £21.50, Starter £7.50-£13.50, Main £16.50-£31, Dessert £6.95-£8.95, Service optional Wines 28 bottles over £30, 25 bottles under £30, 25 by glass Parking 12 Notes Sunday L £16.95-£18.95, Vegetarian available, Children welcome

TANGMERE
Map 6 SU90

Cassons Restaurant
◉◉ Modern British

tel: 01243 773294 Arundel Rd PO18 0DU
email: cassonsresto@aol.com
dir: On Westbound carriageway of A27, 400mtrs from Tangmere rdbt

Good eating near Goodwood

Chef-patronne Viv Casson has run a successful restaurant across the water in France, so you can expect clear Gallic culinary influences to her work. The setting is a couple of farm cottages beside the A27 handily close to Goodwood, and, more importantly, perfectly placed to haul in local supplies from the nearby coast and the South Downs. Inside, the place has a rustic simplicity that gains character from the huge inglenook and low-beamed ceilings, while the modern menu takes in straightforward, classically influenced ideas as well as some more daring forays into innovative territory. Super-fresh crab from nearby Selsey appears with sweetcorn mousse, lime mayonnaise, lemon gel and potato 'glass' to get things off the mark, ahead of more of that excellent locally-caught seafood – fillets of bass and turbot teamed with samphire, sautéed potatoes and sauce vierge. Things get quite avante-garde at dessert, when good technical skills bring together a composition involving tangy lemon curd ice cream wrapped in vibrant rhubarb sorbet, with milk chocolate 'aero', rhubarb compôte and crumble.

Chef Viv Casson Owner Viv & Cass Casson Seats 36, Pr/dining room 14 Times 12-2/7-10, Closed between Xmas & New Year, Mon, L Tue, D Sun Prices Fixed L 2 course £17, Starter £8-£11, Main £23, Dessert £8-£11, Service optional Wines 41 bottles over £30, 33 bottles under £30, 6 by glass Parking 30 Notes Gourmet & special events, Sunday L £22.50-£28.50, Vegetarian available, Children welcome

TILLINGTON
Map 6 SU92

The Horse Guards Inn
Traditional British

tel: 01798 342332 **Upperton Rd GU28 9AF**
email: info@thehorseguardsinn.co.uk **web:** www.thehorseguardsinn.co.uk
dir: On A272, 1m west of Petworth, take road signed Tillington. Restaurant 500mtrs opposite church

Enterprising pub cooking near Petworth House

On the edge of Petworth Park, opposite the parish church, The Horse Guards is a relaxed, friendly and informal pub dating back 350 years, with open fires, plain wooden tables and seats, beams and a boarded floor. It's very much a foodie destination, the attraction a menu that changes daily, depending on what's been bought or foraged locally or dug up from the garden. Wide-ranging, contemporary ideas include starters of straightforward game terrine with rowan jelly, and more complex smoked eel with a potato cake, treacle, bacon, beetroot and horseradish. Main courses are equally varied, from a mainstream pairing of pork loin cutlet with apple sauce and gravy, served with fondant potato, celeriac purée and kale, to the vibrant flavours of mussels steamed in chilli, lemongrass, coconut milk and coriander. Diehards can opt for a pudding like steamed treacle suet sponge with custard, and there might also be chocolate, cherry and pistachio torte.

Chef Mark Robinson **Owner** Sam Beard, Michaela Hofirkova **Seats** 55, Pr/dining room 18 **Times** 12-2.30/6.30-9 **Prices** Starter £5.50-£8, Main £10-£22, Dessert £5-£8, Service optional **Wines** 33 bottles over £30, 15 bottles under £30, 14 by glass **Parking** On street **Notes** Sunday L £12-£16, Vegetarian available, Children welcome

TROTTON
Map 5 SU82

The Keepers Arms
British, Mediterranean

tel: 01730 813724 & 07506 693088 **Love Hill, Terwick Ln GU31 5ER**
email: sharonmcgrath198@btinternet.com
dir: A272 towards Petersfield after 5m, restaurant on right just after narrow bridge. From Midhurst follow A272 for 3m, restaurant on left

Upmarket country pub with appealing menu

The red tile-hung exterior of this 17th-century country inn is an inviting prospect on its perch above the A272, with a lovely garden and terrace that have plenty of alfresco appeal, and once inside, it is a gem of a pub. There's a proper friendly bar with a range of well-kept real ales, and the whole space has been opened out and given an easy-on-the-eye decluttered modern look, without sacrificing the inherent character in its plentiful beams and timbers. The stylish dining room looks out over the South Downs and aims for a contemporary hunting lodge look involving blond-wood tables, warm colours and funky tartans. Go for pubby classics from the chalkboards, or trade up to the carte of easy-eating contemporary ideas, and start with chicken liver and port parfait, followed by pan-fried sea bass fillet with truffle oil, crushed new potatoes, spinach and vanilla butter, and finish with chocolate fondant.

Times 11-3/6.30-9.30

TURNERS HILL
Map 6 TQ33

AG's Restaurant at Alexander House Hotel

see page 524

Reflections at Alexander House
Modern British V

tel: 01342 714914 **Alexander House Hotel, East St RH10 4QD**
email: admin@alexanderhouse.co.uk **web:** www.alexanderhouse.co.uk
dir: 6m from M23 junct 10, on B2110 between Turners Hill & East Grinstead

Modern brasserie cooking in an elegant spa hotel

The setting is impressive inside and out: 120 acres of gardens, woodland and parkland surround a handsome 17th-century mansion which has had a thoroughly modern makeover, moving it into boutique territory. Spa enthusiasts will be delighted by the restorative facilities at Alexander House, but there's also a buzzy brasserie – Reflections – to lift the spirits still further (the fine-dining option is AG's Restaurant). Expect sleek chocolate-coloured leather banquettes, slate floors and subtle grey and peach tones on the walls, plus there's a champagne bar and tables in the courtyard for eating outdoors. Start with something like terrine of foie gras and ham hock with sourdough toast, fritter and apricots, or gazpacho with avocado and cucumber, moving on to a classic beer-battered fish and chips or a more adventurous Telmara duck breast with gooseberry compôte and crisp radish salad. Banana parfait with toffee sauce and caramelised bananas makes for a richly indulgent pud, but then so does traditional warm sticky toffee pudding with rum and raisin ice cream.

Chef Darrel Wilde **Owner** Peter & Deborah Hinchcliffe **Seats** 70, Pr/dining room 12 **Times** 12-3/6.30-10 **Prices** Prices not confirmed **Wines** 25 bottles over £30, 5 bottles under £30, 12 by glass **Parking** 100 **Notes** Children welcome

TYNE & WEAR

GATESHEAD
Map 21 NZ26

Eslington Villa Hotel
Modern British

tel: 0191 487 6017 **8 Station Rd, Low Fell NE9 6DR**
email: home@eslingtonvilla.co.uk **web:** www.eslingtonvilla.co.uk
dir: Off A1(M) exit for Team Valley Trading Estate. Right at 2nd rdbt along Eastern Av. Left at car show room, hotel 100yds on left

Reliable modern cooking in a Victorian villa

Originally built for a Victorian industrialist and set in a couple of acres of immaculately tended gardens, today's hotel retains bags of period features, allied with contemporary verve and character. It's run with a genuine sense of bonhomie by Nick and Melanie Tulip, and its popularity as a wedding venue isn't hard to fathom. Dining goes on mainly in a conservatory extension with tiled floor and commanding views over the lawns, as well as in the interior room behind it. Start with an imaginative composition of blue cheese pannacotta with beetroot purée, apple and toasted peanuts, then move on to a well-executed main course pairing of pork fillet and shoulder with black pudding and potato bake and red cabbage. At the end, a purée of roast apple works well as a counterpoint to baked cheesecake with cinnamon ice cream and mini doughnuts.

Chef Jamie Walsh **Owner** Mr & Mrs N Tulip **Seats** 80, Pr/dining room 30 **Times** 12-2/5.30-9.45, Closed 25-26 Dec, 1 Jan, BHs **Prices** Fixed L 2 course £14.95, Fixed D 3 course £28.50, Service optional **Wines** 9 bottles over £30, 36 bottles under £30, 8 by glass **Parking** 30 **Notes** Early bird D 2/3 course £14.95/£17.95 from 5.30-6.45pm, Sunday L £17.25-£20.75, Vegetarian available, Children welcome

NEWCASTLE UPON TYNE — Map 21 NZ26

artisan

◉ Modern British

tel: 0191 260 5411 **The Biscuit Factory, 16 Stoddart St, Shieldfield NE2 1AN**
email: info@artisannewcastle.com
dir: *Phone for directions*

Contemporary dining in a stylish commercial art gallery

The Biscuit Factory is the UK's largest art, craft and design gallery, and there's craft of the culinary kind on show in the venue's artisan restaurant (so cool it's all written in lower case). The restaurant occupies an urban space with exposed brickwork, chunky wooden tables and shades of steely blue, with a 25-foot wall of glass showing off the sculptural displays in the adjacent gallery. The menu instils a sense of place with it regional bias, but there's certainly no lack of refinement on show in contemporary-minded dishes that look good on the plate. Start with warm salad of smoked haddock, with Puy lentils and horseradish cream, and follow on with rib-eye with 'thrice' cooked chips and a classic sauce, or fillet of North Sea cod in the company of a posh truffled mash. There's an early-evening menu, too, and desserts run to hot chocolate fondant with passionfruit sorbet.

Chef Andrew Wilkinson **Owner** Ramy Zack **Seats** 70, Pr/dining room 24 **Times** 12-2/5.30-9, Closed 25-26 Dec & 1 Jan, D Sun **Prices** Fixed L 2 course fr £15, Fixed D 3 course fr £24, Starter £6.50-£8.50, Main £17.50-£60, Dessert £5.50-£8.50, Service optional **Wines** 10 bottles over £30, 20 bottles under £30, 8 by glass **Parking** 20, On street **Notes** Sunday L £15.95-£18.95, Vegetarian available, Children welcome

Blackfriars Restaurant

◉ Modern, Traditional British

tel: 0191 261 5945 **Friars St NE1 4XN**
email: info@blackfriarsrestaurant.co.uk web: www.blackfriarsrestaurant.co.uk
dir: *Take only small cobbled road off Stowell St (China Town). Blackfriars 100yds on left*

Modern brasserie cooking in the old Dominican refectory

People have eaten well on this historic site since the 13th century, when it was the refectory for monks at the Dominican friary in the heart of medieval Newcastle. Exposed stonework, venerable timbers, wood panelling and floors and carved wooden chairs make for a suitably atmospheric setting, and the kitchen deals in gutsy modern and classic brasserie dishes, establishing its fondness for local materials on place mats mapping out regional food producers. Buttered lobster and crab with home-made pasta, tomato and oyster leaf kicks off with big flavours,

AG's Restaurant at Alexander House Hotel

TURNERS HILL — Map 6 TQ33

British, French **v**
tel: 01342 714914 **East St RH10 4QD**
email: admin@alexanderhouse.co.uk
dir: *6m from M23 junct 10, on B2110 between Turners Hill & East Grinstead*

Inspired modern British cooking in boutique surroundings

The Rosette award for this establishment has been suspended due to a change of chef. Reassessment will take place in due course under the new chef. The red-brick manor house set in 120 acres on the Sussex-Surrey border, not far from Gatwick, is an interesting hotchpotch. It has a battlemented turret at one end and an arrow-slit window for that essential touch of the medieval, as well as ranks of tall industrial-looking chimneys. The mixture deepens inside, where a contemporary boutique look has been laid over the original framework, with assertive psychedelic colours – lime green seats at the bar, unapologetic purple in the lounge – amid a pared-back, uncluttered feel. The principal dining room, AG's (there's also a banquetted brasserie called Reflections), is altogether more muted, and makes a good foil to the modern British food. In these landlocked parts, a bracing blast of sea air is a welcome note, arriving in the form of sliced caramelised scallops with cockles and clams, spears of samphire and an oyster-infused emulsion sauce.

Cooking techniques add depth, as when hay-smoked rib of beef is roasted on open coals, and teamed with the cheek glazed in whisky, with accompaniments of beer and cheddar gnocchi. Alternatively, monkfish tail could be poached in red wine and served à la bourguignon, with pommes soufflé. The show-stopping dessert is a fallen-tree creation in chocolate, garnished with a freshening lime sorbet and 'mushrooms', but bundles of textural and flavour complexity are delivered too in iced lemon curd with dill meringue and olive oil jelly. Incidentals, from breads to petits fours, are all consistently superb.

Chef Darrel Wilde **Owner** Alexander Hotels Ltd **Seats** 30, Pr/dining room 18 **Times** 12-2.30/7-9.30, Closed L Mon-Sat **Prices** Fixed D 3 course £65, Tasting menu £85 **Wines** 140 bottles over £30, 10 bottles under £30, 15 by glass **Parking** 100 **Notes** Tasting menu with wine 8 course, Sunday L £24-£30, Children 7 yrs+

followed by seared venison with butternut squash purée, red cabbage and chocolate sauce. North Sea fish gets a good outing, in the shape, perhaps, of pan-fried cod with chorizo and white bean stew and tomato and dill dressing, while crowd-pleasing desserts include sticky toffee pudding with banana ice cream and salted butter caramel.

Blackfriars Restaurant

Chef Dan Duggan **Owner** Andy & Sam Hook **Seats** 80, Pr/dining room 50 **Times** 12-2.30/5.30-12, Closed Good Fri & BHs, D Sun **Prices** Prices not confirmed **Wines** 14 bottles over £30, 31 bottles under £30, 8 by glass **Parking** Car park next to restaurant **Notes** Fixed menu 5.30-7pm, Sunday L, Vegetarian available, Children welcome

Café 21 Newcastle

◉ Modern British V

tel. 0191 222 0766 **Trinity Gardens, Quayside NE1 2HH** **email:** enquiries@cafetwentyone.co.uk **dir:** From Grey's Monument, S to Grey St & Dean St towards Quayside, left along the Quayside, 3rd left into Broad Chare. 1st right then 1st left into Trinity Gdns, restaurant on right

Brasserie buzz on the Newcastle quayside

The spacious, glass-fronted brasserie, with its polished wooden floor, leather banquettes and neatly clothed tables, remains as buzzy as ever, with slick and smooth service ensuring that all is as it should be. Part of the attraction is the ambitious cooking, with the longish menu an appealing mix of modern British brasserie-style dishes. Cheddar and spinach soufflé, perfectly cooked and nicely presented, is a great way to start, and there might be scallops grilled with chilli and garlic, or foie gras terrine. Main courses offer variety aplenty, from skewered tiger prawns on coconut curry risotto, through grilled calves' liver with bacon and onions, to roast cod fillet with boulangère potatoes, brown shrimps and red wine sauce. Crusty white bread is appreciated, and puddings can be a highlight, among them chocolate and salted caramel macaroons, and passionfruit soufflé with chocolate sorbet.

Chef Chris Dobson **Owner** Terry Laybourne **Seats** 130, Pr/dining room 44 **Times** 12-2.30/5.30-10.30, Closed 25-26 Dec, 1 Jan, Etr Mon, D 24 Dec **Prices** Fixed L 2 course £17.50, Fixed D 3 course £22, Starter £7.60-£15.50, Main £16-£29.80, Dessert £6.80-£8.80 **Wines** 40 bottles over £30, 29 bottles under £30, 15 by glass **Parking** NCP/Council **Notes** Fixed L/D 2/3 course Mon-Sat D 5.30-7pm, Sunday L £18.50-£22, Children welcome

Hotel du Vin Newcastle

◉◉ British, French

tel: 0191 229 2200 **Allan House, City Rd NE1 2BE** **email:** reception.newcastle@hotelduvin.com **web:** www.hotelduvin.com **dir:** A1 junct 65 slip road to A184 Gateshead/Newcastle, Quayside to City Rd

French brasserie fare in designer hotel with superb wine list

As ever with this chain, the building itself is a feature, in this case the converted red-brick Edwardian warehouse of the Tyne Tees Steam Shipping Company. Its riverside location gives the hotel commanding views of the city's many bridges, and the centre is just moments away. In keeping with other branches, the restaurant has the look of a French bistro, with its darkwood floor and wooden-topped tables; patio doors open on to a courtyard for alfresco eating and drinking. Trademark French brasserie fare is the deal, prepared from fresh seasonal produce, with starters taking in simple onion soup to more ambitious pan-seared scallops with artichoke and pistachio purée and pancetta vinaigrette. Old faithful boeuf bourguignon and moules frites show up among main courses, the range extended by the likes of well-presented roast halibut fillet nicely complemented by a robust langoustine bisque. Light and moist Black Forest gâteau is a good example of the beast.

Times 12-2.30/5.30-10

House of Tides

◉◉◉ – *see page 526*

Jesmond Dene House

◉◉◉ – *see page 526*

Malmaison Newcastle

◉ French, British

tel: 0191 245 5000 & 0844 693 0658 *(Calls cost 7p per minute plus your phone company's access charge)* **104 Quayside NE1 3DX** **email:** newcastle@malmaison.com **web:** www.malmaison.com **dir:** A1 junct 65 to A184 signed Gateshead/Newcastle. Follow signs for city centre, then for Quayside/Law Courts. Hotel 100yds past Law Courts

Brasserie dining with bright modern food by the quay

The urban-cool boutique chain has taken a quayside warehouse as the starting point for its Newcastle outpost. It is kitted out with the trademark look of the 'Mal' brand: boudoir-chic shades of crimson, deep purple and plum, and textures of wood, leather, velvet and chrome. Get things rolling with a cocktail and views of the Gateshead Millennium Bridge in the low-lit bar, then move into the brasserie for no-nonsense, globetrotting contemporary takes on the classic repertoire. A fritto misto of tempura-style squid, tiger prawn and courgette is one way to start, then stay on an Asian path, with seared, sesame-crusted ahi tuna matched with bok choy and miso dressing. Otherwise, mains could take you Stateside for gourmet burgers or New York strip steaks seared on the grill, before ending back in Europe with a Valrhona chocolate soufflé with vanilla ice cream.

Times 12-2.30/6-11

House of Tides ✹✹✹

AA RESTAURANT OF THE YEAR FOR ENGLAND 2015–16

Modern British v

tel: 0191 230 3720 **28-30 The Close NE1 3RF**
email: info@houseoftides.co.uk
dir: *Phone for directions*

Dynamic innovation on the Newcastle quayside

Kenny Atkinson hit the ground running when he set up in this former merchant's townhouse on the historic Newcastle harbourside in February 2014. With the Tyne Bridge arching in the background, it's a prime position in a city bursting with culinary dynamism. The action unfolds over two storeys: a ground floor with original 16th-century flagstones and coffee-coloured banquette seating, and a main dining area above, with venerable supporting beams, wooden floor and spotlit pictures. Atkinson oversees a young, focused and enthusiastic team, and his culinary vision is right on the cutting edge with dishes that are innovative, but founded on classical techniques and good sense. A winter opener based on cod cheeks brings a wealth of richness to bear on the fish with truffled celeriac velouté, hazelnuts, trompettes and chive snippings, or perhaps Wester Ross cured salmon, Whitby crab and brown shrimps in apple and jasmine. Modern meat thinking brings the dual poaching-and-roasting method to strikingly flavoured chicken, a main course full of interest from its partnerings of caramelised apple, crisp-fried kale, parsnips, chestnuts and smoked bacon. Highland venison appears in full traditional fig with dauphinoise, red cabbage and Brussels sprouts, but sea bream gains some new friends in butternut squash, crosnes, wild mushrooms and parmesan. Irresistible combinations illuminate the dessert choices, from dark chocolate mousse with clementine gel, whisky ice cream and butterscotch to vanilla cheesecake with mulled wine jelly, pear, cinnamon and ginger. Imaginative canapés and excellent breads fill in the all-important peripheral details, and there is a well-constructed wine list arranged by style, opening with an inspired selection by the glass.

Chef Kenny Atkinson **Owner** Kenny & Abbie Atkinson **Seats** 50, Pr/dining room 22 **Times** 12-2/6-10, Closed 2 wks Xmas-New Year, Sun-Mon, L Tue, Sat **Prices** Fixed L 2 course £20, Fixed D 3 course £45, Tasting menu £35-£65 **Wines** 55 bottles over £30, 23 bottles under £30, 15 by glass **Parking** 70, £1.20/hr, free after 6pm **Notes** Children 9 yrs+

Jesmond Dene House ✹✹✹

Modern British, European 🍷 NOTABLE WINE LIST

tel: 0191 212 3000 **Jesmond Dene Rd NE2 2EY**
email: info@jesmonddenehouse.co.uk **web:** www.jesmonddenehouse.co.uk
dir: *From city centre follow A167 to junct with A184. Turn right towards Matthew Bank. Turn right into Jesmond Dene Rd*

Imaginative modern cooking in an Arts and Crafts stately home

Sitting in a tranquil wooded valley, Jesmond Dene House has the feel of a grand country house, yet is actually within the city limits of Newcastle. Its original Georgian architect, John Dobson, designed much of the old city centre, but the present incarnation of the house dates largely from the 1870s, when it was made over in the Arts and Crafts style. There are two dining areas: the former music room and the light and bright garden room, with its lovely fair-weather terrace. The well-oiled service deserves special plaudits for fostering a pleasing lack of stuffiness all round. Head chef Michael Penaluna stocks his larder with the pick of local, seasonal materials and is adept at letting the flavours speak for themselves. There is refinement, creativity and skill in the execution of dishes, delivered via menus offering five choices at each stage (there's also a 10-course taster with a veggie version, where all the stops are pulled out). A starter of crab dumplings comes fired up with hot-and-sour sauce, shiitaki mushrooms and pomelo, while main-course monkfish is handled with aplomb and matched with delicately flavoured wild garlic linguine, razor clams and mussels. Those in search of more assertive flavours might take loin of Northumberland venison with parsnip, quince and cocoa foam. It all ends with a 'wow' via a signature dessert: a sphere of dark chocolate that melts before your eyes to reveal gingerbread ice cream on a disc of shortbread with salted caramel, or there might be apple tarte fine with vanilla cream and cider sorbet. All the incidentals, from appetisers to pre-dessert, combine to make this an all-round classy experience.

Chef Michael Penaluna **Owner** Peter Candler, Tony Ganley, Terry Bayliff, Paul Morrisey **Seats** 80, Pr/dining room 24 **Times** 12-2/7-9.30, **Prices** Fixed L 2 course £22, Tasting menu £75, Starter £12.50-£14.50, Main £19.50-£35, Dessert £6-£10.50 **Wines** 120 bottles over £30, 25 bottles under £30, 18 by glass **Parking** 64 **Notes** Tasting menu 10 course, Sunday L £25-£28, Vegetarian available, Children welcome

Vujon

◉ Indian

tel: 0191 221 0601 **29 Queen St, Quayside NE1 3UG**
email: mahtab@vujon.com
dir: *Phone for directions*

Fine dining Indian style at the trendy quayside

Set in the fashionable quayside area, Vujon has been the smart place to go for new-wave Indian cuisine since the 1990s. A stylish contemporary-looking dining room and switched-on service are the backdrop to a creative mix of classic and up-to-date Indian dishes. Spicing is expert and can be delicate, particularly in a main course of boneless pheasant tarkari, cooked in a mildly spicy sauce that shows its French origins from the Pondicherry region, while fusion dishes such as Jaipur-style pan-seared venison fillet, scented with cloves and served with spicy tomato and chilli jam, appear among old favourites along the lines of lamb saag gosht and chicken tikka masala. Rice and naan breads are exemplary, and the tandoor naturally plays its part too, turning out grilled tiger prawns marinated in chilli, lemongrass, kaffir lime and garlic. Super-sweet gulab jamun dumplings soaked in rose and cardamon syrup make for a classic finale.

Times 12-2/5.30-11.30, Closed 25 Dec, L Sun

WARWICKSHIRE

ALCESTER
Map 10 SP05

Number 50

◉ Modern British

tel: 01789 762764 **50 Birmingham Rd B49 5EP**
email: info@numberfifty.co.uk
dir: *From town centre towards Birmingham & M42. Restaurant is opposite Alcester Grammar School*

Unfussy cooking in a friendly modern bistro

A 17th-century cottage on the outside, Number 50 opens on to a scene of clean-cut contemporary style that mixes up ancient oak beams with cream-washed walls hung with modern art, and leather chairs at darkwood tables and slate placemats. The place has a strong local fan base, and no wonder: the vibe exudes the relaxed, friendly bustle of a well-loved neighbourhood eatery. The kitchen deals in cooking to suit the surroundings – unpretentious modern British dishes that are big on flavour, cooked accurately and without fuss, using a rock-solid base of locally-sourced produce. Set-price menus offer great value, setting out with seared scallops with green pea pannacotta, pea purée and crispy pancetta, while main-course roasted duck breast gets the spicy Szechuan treatment and is matched with potato terrine and liquorice jus. To finish, a simple classic is given a novel spin: rhubarb crumble soufflé comes with custard ice cream.

Chef Chris Short, Neil Peers **Owner** Chris Short **Seats** 50
Times 10-2.30/6.30-10, Closed Mon-Tue, L Sat, D Sun **Prices** Fixed L 2 course £13.50, Fixed D 3 course £19.50, Starter £6.50-£8, Main £10.95-£25, Dessert £6.50-£8, Service optional **Wines** 13 bottles over £30, 26 bottles under £30, 9 by glass **Parking** 19 **Notes** Sunday L £9.25-£12.95, Vegetarian available, Children welcome

ALDERMINSTER
Map 10 SP24

Ettington Park Hotel

◉◉ Modern, Traditional British ⱽ

tel: 01789 450123 & 0845 072 7454 *(Calls cost 7p per minute plus your phone company's access charge)* **CV37 8BU**
email: ettingtonpark@handpicked.co.uk **web:** www.handpickedhotels.co.uk/ettingtonpark
dir: *M40 junct 15/A46 towards Stratford-upon-Avon, then A439 into town centre onto A3400 5m to Shipston. Hotel 0.5m on left*

Confident contemporary cooking in a Gothic mansion

A magnificent example of mid-Victorian Gothic architecture, Ettington Park stands in 40 acres of grounds in the picturesque Stour Valley (the river runs through the estate). The interior is in keeping with the style, all antiques and walls hung with paintings; look out too for a number of friezes. The Oak Room restaurant takes its name from its panelled walls under a moulded ceiling. Staff are friendly and well drilled and deliver some surprisingly – given the surroundings – contemporary cooking. A deconstructed club sandwich is something of a signature starter, a successful amalgam of flavours consisting of chicken tortellini, tomato confit and aïoli, bacon foam, quail's eggs, little gem and breadcrumbs. If dishes seem to pile on the ingredients they nonetheless come off: witness a main course of seared scallops wrapped in smoked bacon served with apple and fennel coleslaw, deep-fried brie and cranberry sauce. An exotic element is sometimes seen – curry-crusted loin of monkfish with dhal and an aubergine and onion bhaji – and puddings continue the labour-intensive approach, among them an attractive assiette of chocolate (millefeuille, cannelloni and lime-flavoured ganache).

Chef Adrian Court **Owner** Hand Picked Hotels **Seats** 50, Pr/dining room 80
Times 12-2/7-9.30, Closed L Mon-Fri **Prices** Fixed D 3 course £39.50-£44.50, Tasting menu £75-£110, Starter £11.50-£14.50, Main £27-£31, Dessert £9-£14, Service optional **Wines** 76 bottles over £30, 15 bottles under £30, 12 by glass **Parking** 80 **Notes** Sunday L £19.95-£24.95, Children welcome

ANSTY
Map 11 SP48

Macdonald Ansty Hall

◉ British

tel: 024 7661 2888 **Main Rd CV7 9HZ**
email: ansty@macdonald-hotels.co.uk **web:** www.macdonald-hotels.co.uk/anstyhall
dir: *M6/M69 junct 2 through Ansty village approx 1.5m*

Tried-and-tested modern dishes not far from Stratford

Whether you're up in the area for the cultural enlightenment of the Shakespeare trail, or doing business in nearby Brum, Ansty Hall makes a rather classy base. The handsome, red-brick 17th-century mansion house sits in eight acres of landscaped grounds amid the rolling farmland and thatched cottages of Warwickshire. Within, all is elegantly furnished and replete with period character, not least in the classy Shilton dining room, where lavishly-draped sash windows offer views of the surrounding landscape. Tables are clothed in their best white linen, and the emphasis is firmly on British food wrought from good-quality seasonal produce, cooked without pretension and served without undue fanfare and fuss. Ham hock and leek terrine with chilled pease pudding gets things off the mark, followed by braised ox cheeks with toasted root vegetables and mash. Warm hazelnut and walnut sponge with home-made Muscovado ice cream and sweet pickled plums makes for a great finale.

Chef Paul Kitchener **Owner** Macdonald Hotels **Seats** 60, Pr/dining room 40
Times 12.30-2.30/6.30-9.30, Closed D 25 Dec **Prices** Starter fr £5.50, Main fr £15.50, Dessert fr £6, Service optional **Wines** 12 by glass **Parking** 100 **Notes** Sunday L £20-£30, Vegetarian available, Children welcome

ARMSCOTE
Map 10 SP24

The Fuzzy Duck
◉ Seasonal Modern British

tel: 01608 682635 **Ilmington Rd CV37 8DD**
email: info@fuzzyduckarmscote.com **web:** www.fuzzyduckarmscote.com
dir: M40 junct 15

Creative modern food in a swish gastro-pub

This upmarket gastro-pub with boutique bedrooms is looking pretty swanky these days after a makeover that made the most of the original character of the place (it's been doing the business as a coaching inn since the 18th century) and injected a bit of contemporary style. There's a serious approach to food and a pleasing lack of pretention. The modern British menu reads like a dream with lots of local ingredients on show and no lack of imagination or creativity. Hand-dived scallops come with confit duck, summer turnip and smoked hazelnuts in a thoroughly modern dish that strikes a good balance, and that might be followed by Scottish venison with heritage carrots, sweet cicely purée, blackcurrant and a potato fondant. A meat-free main course might be pearl barley risotto with mushrooms, duck yolk and truffle. Desserts such as stout and chestnut pudding have no less appeal and invention as witnessed in the accompanying cherry sorbet, stout ice cream and pork scratchings (yes, that's right, pork scratchings).

Chef Joe Adams **Owner** Tania & Adrian Slater **Seats** 35, Pr/dining room 20 **Times** 12-2.30/6.30-9, Closed Mon, D Sun **Prices** Fixed L 2 course £15, Service optional 10% **Wines** 22 bottles over £30, 21 bottles under £30, 11 by glass **Parking** 15, On street **Notes** Sunday L £14.95-£16.95, Vegetarian available, Children welcome

BRANDON
Map 11 SP47

Mercure Coventry Brandon Hall Hotel & Spa
◉ International

tel: 024 7654 6000 **Main St CV8 3FW**
email: h6625@accor.com **web:** www.mercure.com
dir: A45 towards Coventry S. After Peugeot-Citroen garage on left, at island take 5th exit to M1 South/London (back onto A45). After 200yds, immediately after Texaco garage, left into Brandon Ln, hotel after 2.5m

Confident, unfussy cooking in a smart manor-house hotel

Set in 17 acres of green-and-pleasant Warwickshire countryside, Brandon Hall is a smartly-revamped 19th-century manor that has something for everyone, whether you're in the area for business, or enjoying a spot of down time in the spa and fitness centre. Tones of chocolate and green predominate in the smart, contemporary-styled Clarendon restaurant, while service is as keen as mustard and the kitchen follows the seasons, drawing on conscientiously-sourced supplies for its straight-and-true menu of uncomplicated ideas. Well-made ham hock terrine is served with apple and celeriac salad and home-made piccalilli, or you could kick off with sautéed wild mushrooms in creamy white wine sauce on toasted brioche. Mains can be as straightforward as a 28-day aged rib-eye steak with herb-roasted field mushrooms, plum tomatoes, chips and pesto hollandaise, or there might be cod fillet with Dorset crab risotto and lobster sauce. For pudding, a chocolate fondant releases the requisite hot sauce when cut open, and comes with raspberry ripple ice cream and marshmallows.

Times 7am-9.30pm, All-day dining, Closed L Sat

EDGEHILL
Map 11 SP34

Castle at Edgehill
◉◉ Modern British NEW

tel: 01295 670255 **Main St OX15 6DJ**
email: enquiries@castleatedgehill.co.uk **web:** www.castleatedgehill.co.uk
dir: 4m from M40 junct 10 or 7m from M40 junct 11

Bright contemporary cooking in a Georgian castle

Built in 1742 to mark the centenary of the battle of Edgehill (the first major battle of the English Civil War), the Castle entered the hospitality game when it was converted to a pub in 1822. There are spectacular views to be had from its elevated position and plenty of character within, with original stone walls, wood panels and real fires. The terrace and garden are an enticing prospect in warm weather. The restaurant has a charming ambience – candlelit at night – and an informal attitude. Expect creative modern cooking from a kitchen team that show their mettle with the likes of spot-on scallops with saffron flavoured fennel, celeriac purée and spicy chorizo, or another starter that combines venison carpaccio with candied beetroot and honeyed parsnips. There might be venison among main course, too, pink and tender loin, served with feisty pieces of jerky, while a fishy main course is fillet of Cornish turbot with parsley root remoulade and trumpet mushrooms. Finish with a good looking (and fine tasting) baked Brillat-Savarin cheesecake.

Chef Matthew Ayers **Owner** Mark & Claire Higgs **Seats** 60, Pr/dining room 24 **Times** 12-2.30/6-9.30, Closed D Sun (Oct-Apr) **Prices** Fixed L 2 course £18-£25, Fixed D 3 course £25-£50, Tasting menu £35-£60, Starter £5-£14, Main £13-£30, Dessert £4-£9, Service optional **Wines** 8 bottles over £30, 16 bottles under £30, 8 by glass **Parking** 22 **Notes** Afternoon tea (must pre-book), Sunday L £10-£30, Vegetarian available, Children welcome

HENLEY-IN-ARDEN
Map 10 SP16

The Bluebell
◉◉ British

tel: 01564 793049 **93 High St B95 5AT**
email: info@bluebellhenley.co.uk
dir: M40 junct 4, A3400 (Stratford Rd) to Henley-in-Arden

Exciting globally-influenced food in a Tudor coaching inn

The Bluebell occupies a half-timbered coaching inn dating from the Tudor period on Henley's uncommercialised High Street. Within are uneven flagged floors, beams in the low ceilings, lots of white plaster, draught beers in the bar and an enterprising restaurant menu that pulls in the punters. The kitchen taps into local supply lines for its produce and travels further afield for some ideas, so expect Moroccan-style lentils with roast, spiced neck fillet of lamb along with a shallot, anchovy and parsley salad, and a cassoulet of orzo, cockles and vegetables with roast fillet, juicy and moist, of stone bass. Dishes are intelligently thought out and technique is never in doubt. A lovely, rich celeriac and pear velouté is served with a ramekin of crisp and cheesy gougères, and a pressing of duck and foie gras is enhanced by spicy plum purée and a helping of baby onions and beans. Home-baked sourdough bread gets rave notices, and desserts are well regarded: perhaps apricot, cranberry and sultana brioche-and-butter pudding with white chocolate ice cream.

Chef Duncan Mitchell **Owner** Leigh & Duncan Taylor **Seats** 46, Pr/dining room 10 **Times** 12-2.30/6-9.30, Closed Mon (ex BHs), D Sun **Prices** Starter £6-£12, Main £14-£25, Service optional **Wines** 8 bottles over £30, 14 bottles under £30, 13 by glass **Parking** 20 **Notes** Afternoon tea £18, L menu fr £10, Sunday L £25, Vegetarian available, Children welcome

LEA MARSTON
Map 10 SP29

Lea Marston Hotel & Spa
◉◉ Modern British

tel: 01675 470468 **Haunch Ln B76 0BY**
email: info@leamarstonhotel.co.uk **web:** www.leamarstonhotel.co.uk
dir: *From M42 junct 9/A4097 signed Kingsbury Hotel, 2nd turning right into Haunch Lane. Hotel 200yds on right*

Modern seasonal cooking in a golf and spa hotel

The modern Lea Marston Hotel sits in the tranquil Warwickshire countryside buffered by 54 acres of grounds, and is handy for doing business or exploring all that the rejuvenated centre of Birmingham has to offer. There's a spa, of course, to sort out the de rigueur 21st-century pampering requirements, as well as a golf course and a good eating option in the shape of The Adderley Restaurant. Decked out in shades of aubergine and greys, it's a swish, low-lit and romantic space with an unbuttoned vibe. The kitchen deals in unpretentious contemporary ideas, with a clear focus on seasonal, local ingredients – pink and tender pigeon is balanced thoughtfully by raspberry vinaigrette and orange salad and makes a fine precursor to wild sea bass with scallops, peas and vanilla foam. Otherwise, you might go for confit rump of lamb with fondant potato, chickpea and chorizo cassoulet, and red wine jus. Finish with a wobbly coconut pannacotta partnered with pineapple and vanilla salsa and cardamom ice cream.

Chef Richard Marshall **Owner** The Blake family **Seats** Pr/dining room 120 **Times** 1-3/7-9, Closed L Mon-Sat, D Sun **Prices** Fixed D 3 course £29.50, Starter £4.95-£12.50, Main £18.95-£22.95, Dessert £5.95-£6.95, Service optional **Wines** 6 bottles over £30, 23 bottles under £30 **Parking** 220 **Notes** Afternoon tea £14.95, Sunday L £16.95, Vegetarian available, Children welcome

LEAMINGTON SPA (ROYAL)
Map 10 SP36

The Brasserie at Mallory Court
◉◉ Modern British V

tel: 01926 453939 & 330214 **Harbury Ln, Bishop's Tachbrook CV33 9QB**
email: thebrasserie@mallory.co.uk
dir: *M40 junct 13 N'bound left, left again towards Bishop's Tachbrook, right onto Harbury Ln after 0.5m. M40 junct 14 S'bound A452 to Leamington, at 2nd rdbt left onto Harbury Ln*

Casual brasserie dining in an elegant hotel

As well as the main dining room, Mallory Court also boasts a more contemporary looking brasserie a short stroll from the main house. No mere adjunct to the main action, this is a fine venue in its own right, with glass-topped wicker tables, soothing neutral decor, and a backdrop of gentle jazz – a nice counterpoint to the formal refinement of the principal restaurant – A proper sectioned-up brasserie menu is offered, covering a range from ham and potato croquette with piccalilli, through beef medallions in Madeira sauce, to chocolate marquise and pistachio ice cream. Dishes are given careful consideration, so that skilful technique produces a tempura-battered soft-shelled crab with pungent aïoli, as well as intensely flavourful chicken rillettes with green beans. A layered dessert in a glass is always fun, and may consist here of blueberry and apple compôte topped with blueberry and vanilla pannacotta, granola, and apple sorbet. Or sign up for a selection of five pedigree cheeses from England, Ireland and France.

Chef Jim Russell **Owner** Sir Peter Rigby **Seats** 80, Pr/dining room 24 **Times** 12-2.30/6.30-9.30, Closed D Sun **Prices** Fixed L 3 course £19.50, Fixed D 3 course £19.50, Starter £4.95-£8.75, Main £12.50-£19, Dessert £4.95-£5.95, Service optional **Wines** 39 bottles over £30, 34 bottles under £30, 12 by glass **Parking** 100 **Notes** Sunday L £15-£22.50, Children welcome

The Dining Room at Mallory Court Hotel
◉◉◉ – *see page 530*

Queans Restaurant
◉ Modern European

tel: 01926 315522 **15 Dormer Place CV32 5AA**
email: laura@queans-restaurant.co.uk
dir: *Phone for directions*

Charming restaurant with well-sourced menu

You'd never guess from her cheerful and welcoming demeanor that chef-proprietor Laura Hamilton works alone in the kitchen – there are no outward signs that she feels any pressure! This is a delightful establishment with a good deal of genteel charm, where a smartly neutral decor meets an appealing menu of unpretentious dishes based on high-quality regional produce. You might start with a vegetarian tart such as one filled with roasted beetroot and butternut squash, served with an accompanying walnut salad, or maybe a brie and hazelnut bake with a smoky bacon jam. Clearly a dab hand at vegetarian cookery, chef can also turn out some impressive meat and fish options, too, such as a main-course grilled whole black bream (marinated in coriander and lime mustard), or roast loin of lamb with caramelised onion and fig stuffing. Finish with strawberry and pink champagne cheesecake. Somehow Laura finds the time to produce her own ice cream which is sold locally (and here, of course).

Times 12-2.30/6-10, Closed L Sat-Tue, D Sun-Mon

Restaurant 23 & Morgan's Bar
◉◉◉ – *see page 530*

SHIPSTON ON STOUR
Map 10 SP24

The Red Lion
◉ Traditional British

tel: 01608 684221 **Main St, Long Compton CV36 5JS**
email: info@redlion-longcompton.co.uk **web:** www.redlion-longcompton.co.uk
dir: *5m S on A3400*

Well-presented modern pub food in a traditional country inn

Settle into a settle by the inglenook fireplace on a winter's evening and prepare to be regaled by tales of the Long Compton witches, or the history of the Neolithic Rollright stone circle nearby. In an area drenched in ancient folklore, not far from Shipston-on-Stour, The Red Lion is a textbook country inn, down to the real ales, log-fired dining room and locally-based seasonal cooking. The bill of fare is amped-up pub food, with the emphasis on eye-catching presentations and unimpeachable raw materials. A meal might progress from smoked haddock and sweetcorn chowder to chargrilled Barnsley lamb chop with crushed cannellini beans, maple-roasted shallots and rosemary jus, or from pork and chicken terrine with Bramley apple chutney to pesto-crusted salmon with spinach in garlicky provençale dressing. Look to the blackboard for daily specials, and make room for lemon and ginger cheesecake with lime syrup to close the deal.

Chef Sarah Keightley **Owner** Cropthorne Inns **Seats** 70, Pr/dining room 20 **Times** 12-2.30/6-9, Closed 25 Dec **Prices** Fixed L 2 course fr £13.50, Fixed D 3 course fr £16.50, Starter £5.50-£7.50, Main £13-£20, Dessert £6-£7.50, Service optional **Wines** 2 bottles over £30, 24 bottles under £30, 10 by glass **Parking** 70 **Notes** Prix-fixe 2/3 course £12.50-£15.50 Mon-Fri L & 6-7pm, Sunday L fr £14, Vegetarian available, Children welcome

The Dining Room at Mallory Court Hotel ❀❀❀

LEAMINGTON SPA (ROYAL)　　　　　　　　　**Map 10 SP36**

Modern British v ❦ NOTABLE WINE LIST

tel: 01926 330214 **Harbury Ln, Bishop's Tachbrook CV33 9QB**
email: reception@mallory.co.uk **web:** www.mallory.co.uk
dir: M40 junct 13 N'bound. Left, left again towards Bishop's Tachbrook. 0.5m, right into Harbury Ln. M40 junct 14 S'bound, A452 for Leamington. At 2nd rdbt left into Harbury Ln

Stunning seasonal cookery with views of rolling Warwickshire

The mishmash of architectural and interior styling to be found inside Mallory Court means the place could effectively only be late-Victorian, when such pastiche came to a head. Hiding behind its thickly climbing creepers, it looks faintly Georgian from the outside, while the oak-panelled dining room and main house are done in the style of Lutyens. It all makes for a restful country-house experience not far out of Royal Leamington Spa, with Paul Foster's conscientiously crafted cooking one of its chief enticements. Against a backdrop of rolling Warwickshire, dishes showcase pedigree seasonal produce, much of it coming from the hotel's own kitchen garden. A starter of charred leeks and brown shrimps with onion and black garlic is a simple but effective prelude to main dishes like brill fillet with potato agnolotti and gem lettuce in chicken jus, or saddle and braised neck of local lamb with goats' curd and roasted crosnes. When all the stops are pulled for more complex dishes, the results can be stunning. An opening combination of rare-cooked salmon and white crabmeat is garnished with diced cucumber, little croûtons and puréed avocado, before being anointed with seafood bisque at the table, before beef sirloin turns up with Wagyu brisket, roasted celeriac, tiny caramelised onions, creamy mash and Belper Knolle cheese (a Swiss cow's-milk job flavoured with garlic and rolled in black pepper), the whole scattered with shavings of Périgord truffle. Dessert seals the deal with high-impact dishes such as a chocolate cone of salt caramel with orange cake, malted milk sorbet and an emulsion sauce based on olive oil, or perhaps passionfruit curd in white chocolate with sorrel granita. A separate vegetarian menu is equally full of invention.

Chef Paul Foster **Owner** Sir Peter Rigby **Seats** 56, Pr/dining room 14 **Times** 12-1.45/6.30-8.45, Closed L Sat **Prices** Fixed L 2 course £27.50, Fixed D 3 course £47.50-£65, Tasting menu £70, Service optional **Wines** 200 bottles over £30, 25 bottles under £30, 12 by glass **Parking** 100 **Notes** Tasting menu 7 course, Sunday L £39.50, Children welcome

Restaurant 23 & Morgan's Bar ❀❀❀

LEAMINGTON SPA (ROYAL)　　　　　　　　　**Map 10 SP36**

Modern European

tel: 01926 422422 **34 Hamilton Ter CV32 4LY**
email: info@restaurant23.co.uk
dir: M40 junct 13 onto A452 towards Leamington Spa. Follow signs for town centre, just off Holly Walk, next to police station

Accomplished modern cookery in a handsome Victorian building

The white-painted building that houses Restaurant 23 & Morgan's Bar is a handsome one which fits in well with its Georgian and Regency neighbours in Leamington Spa, but it actually dates from the Victorian period. The portico entrance and neat paint job make for an inviting frontage. Once you're across the threshold things get rather more 21st century with some contemporary design elements in the bar including splashes of bold colours on the armchairs and sofas. Stick around for a classic cocktail or one of the house's own, and note afternoon tea is also a popular affair. The patio offers alfresco opportunities. The restaurant itself combines old and new to create a sophisticated space that suits the fine-dining approach in the kitchen, while the service could be a little more on the ball. The kitchen's output matches the modern mood with dishes offered via à la carte and tasting menus (there's a great value set lunch menu, too). A meal begins with a little freebie nibble such as an oxtail and potato number with horseradish foam (served in smart glass) and excellent home-made rolls. Cornish crab salad is an attractive looking first course, with chilli, mango and brown crab croquettes, while main course barbecue monkfish is partnered with Cumbrian ham and new season asparagus. Alternatively, dry-aged fillet of beef comes with triple-cooked chips and béarnaise sauce, and the vegetarian option might be butternut squash and tallegio pithivier. Finish with an indulgently rich chocolate delice with roasted pear and popcorn ice cream, or the somewhat lighter vanilla pannacotta with poached Yorkshire rhubarb and gingerbread crumb.

Chef Peter Knibb **Owner** Richard Steeves **Seats** 60, Pr/dining room 16 **Times** 12-2/6.15-9.45, Closed 26 Dec, 1 Jan, Sun-Mon **Prices** Fixed D 3 course £45-£51.50, Tasting menu fr £70 **Wines** 200 bottles over £30, 26 bottles under £30, 11 by glass **Parking** On street opposite **Notes** Afternoon tea Tue-Sat 3-5pm, Tasting menu with wine £110, Vegetarian available, Children welcome

STRATFORD-UPON-AVON
Map 10 SP25

The Arden Hotel
◉◉ Modern British

tel: 01789 298682 **Waterside CV37 6BA**
email: enquiries@theardenhotelstratford.com **web:** www.theardenhotelstratford.com
dir: M40 junct 15 follow signs to town centre. At Barclays Bank rdbt left onto High St, 2nd left onto Chapel Lane (Nash's House on left). Hotel car park on right in 40yds

Enterprising modern cooking opposite the theatre

Directly facing the theatre complex of the Royal Shakespeare Company, The Arden has been coping with the tides of business generated by the Swan of Avon for many a long year. Overseas tourists and school parties of A-level students alike have trooped through its dining room, though these days a modern brasserie with big picture windows looking out over the river is the order of the day. Outdoor tables and a champagne bar play their parts in rising to the occasion, as does the enterprising contemporary cooking on offer from a skilled team. A favoured starter is the pot-roast pigeon with Scotch quail's egg, oyster mushrooms and quinoa, a modern reference dish if ever there was one. Mains take in the likes of roast cod with coco beans, spicy squid, chargrilled courgette, roast pepper and brandade, or duck breast with a little pie of the confit leg, braised chicory and orange purée. On-trend rhubarb gets a dessert look-in when it turns up in a moist cake strongly flavoured with orange and a crunchy garnish of almond brittle.

Times 12-3/5-9.30

The Billesley Manor Hotel
◉◉ Modern European V

tel: 01789 279955 **Billesley, Alcester B49 6NF**
email: billesleymanor.reservations@thehotelcollection.co.uk
web: www.thehotelcollection.co.uk
dir: M40 junct 15, A46S towards Evesham. Over 3 rdbts, right for Billesley after 2m

Traditional cooking in Tudor manor house

Set in 11 acres of primped and preened grounds in deepest Shakespeare country, Billesley Manor is a charming mellow-stone Elizabethan country mansion dating from the time of the Bard. A further attraction for those on the Shakespeare trail is a library reputedly used by the literary legend himself, but for those with culinary rather than literary matters in mind, the classic oak-panelled Stuart Restaurant is a more relevant venue. It is the quintessential English country-house setting-all plushly-upholstered comfort and formal service – and the kitchen has no intention of rocking this particular boat, sending out classically-inspired dishes with a nod to modern trends and presentation, and a keen eye on seasonal ingredients. A rich terrine of confit chicken and foie gras with quince jelly and pork scratchings gets things off to a flying start, ahead of cod fillet served atop curried lentils, and framed by baby samphire and minted yogurt. Standards remain high through to dessert – a well-made chocolate fondant with lush triple chocolate ice cream.

Chef Marc Ward **Owner** The Hotel Collection **Seats** 42, Pr/dining room 100 **Times** 12.30-2/7-9.30 **Prices** Prices not confirmed, Service optional **Wines** 16 bottles over £30, 46 bottles under £30, 26 by glass **Parking** 100 **Notes** Children welcome

The Falcon Hotel
◉ British, European NEW

tel: 01789 279953 **Chapel St CV37 6HA**
email: reception.falcon@sjhotels.co.uk **web:** www.sjhotels.co.uk
dir: From M40 junct 15 follow A46/A429 signs to Stratford. At rdbt take 1st exit A3400. Next rdbt take 1st exit onto High St

Uncomplicated cooking in town centre

Beyond the impressive black-and-white, half-timbered façade of this 16th-century former residence lie oak-beamed public areas with leaded windows, while to the rear are modern bedrooms. While hardly necessary to mention that Stratford was Shakespeare's birthplace, it does serve to introduce Will's Place, the hotel's opulent dining room, where the menu, although short, lists enough modern British dishes to satisfy most tastes. Start perhaps with an attractive starter of crisply crumbed boiled egg with sautéed wild mushrooms and a sherry dressing, before moving on to well-presented and executed slow-roasted pork belly served with sticky red cabbage, fondant potato, pickled apples, apple purée, seared scallop and 'natural' jus. Desserts take a keep-it-simple approach with, for instance, warm treacle tart with clotted cream and a raspberry garnish. Traditional afternoon tea is served in the beautiful courtyard garden throughout the spring and summer.

Chef Phil Bailey **Owner** SJ Hotels **Seats** 80, Pr/dining room 18 **Times** 6-9.30 **Prices** Starter £4.95-£9.95, Main £9.95-£21.95, Dessert £5.95-£8.95 **Wines** 6 bottles over £30, 18 bottles under £30, 10 by glass **Parking** 120 **Notes** Pre-theatre D, Vegetarian available, Children welcome

Macdonald Alveston Manor
◉ Modern British

tel: 01789 205478 **Clopton Bridge CV37 7HP**
email: events.alvestonmanor@macdonald-hotels.co.uk
web: www.macdonald-hotels.co.uk/alvestonmanor
dir: 6m from M40 junct 15, (on edge of town) across Clopton Bridge towards Banbury

Classically based cooking in a charming Tudor manor

A Tudor manor house only a few minutes' walk from the centre of the Shakespeare action in Stratford, Alveston brims with old-school charm. When you've wearied of minimalism in glass and steel, the gnarled oak beams and mullioned windows of the Manor dining room suddenly look luxurious. Traditional service from table-side trays is the vehicle for the subtly modernised British dishes that emerge from a classically rooted kitchen. The limitless variations on Scotch egg see another twist, with a breadcrumbed smoked mackerel pâté outer casing to a runny egg, the plate swiped with horseradish cream for good measure. Next up might be a pair of fine lamb cutlets alongside a pasty of minced lamb and pearl barley, with braised red cabbage and mash, or salmon fillet with crushed potato in herbed broth. Finish with a benchmark rendition of cherry Bakewell blobbed with clotted cream.

Chef Paul Harris **Owner** Macdonald Hotels **Seats** 110, Pr/dining room 40 **Times** 6-9.30, Closed L all week **Wines** 15 bottles under £30, 15 by glass **Parking** 120 **Notes** Pre-theatre menu, Sunday L £19.95, Vegetarian available, Children welcome

Mercure Stratford-upon-Avon Shakespeare Hotel
◉ American, Italian

tel: 01789 294997 **Chapel St CV37 6ER**
email: h6630@accor.com **web:** www.mercure.com
dir: Follow signs to town centre. Round one-way system, into Bridge St. At rdbt turn left. Hotel 200yds on left

New York Italian food in Shakespeare country

At the heart of the action in Bardsville, UK, the hotel named after the local genius is an appropriately antique-looking place with full timbering and venerable beamed interiors. When it comes to dining, the hotel bursts its moorings and fast-forwards a few centuries for Marco's New York Italian, in a room smartly accoutred with well-upholstered chairs at clothed tables, as well as a swish bar and terrace dining. Pastas, hand-made pizzas, burgers, steaks, ribs and seafood cover all conceivable bases, and the dishes are simple and straightforward but deliver in terms of quality and flavour. Expect garlic and lemon prawns with rustic toast to start, or meatballs in penne, followed by a sterling burger topped with crispy prosciutto and mozzarella, olive-oiled grilled salmon on rocket, or sirloin fiorentina. Hit the high notes at dessert with affogato, tiramisù, or classic New York vanilla cheesecake.

Times 12-10, All-day dining

STRATFORD-UPON-AVON *continued*

The Stratford

◉ British

tel: 01789 271000 **Arden St CV37 6QQ**
email: thestratfordreception@qhotels.co.uk **web:** www.qhotels.co.uk
dir: A439 into Stratford. In town follow A3400/Birmingham, at lights left into Arden
Street, hotel 150yds on right

Creative, well-presented cooking in contemporary hotel dining room

The sprawling Stratford hotel with its mod cons and state-of-the-art business
facilities is also home to Quills Restaurant, a thoroughly contemporary place with a
menu that shows a good degree of creativity. The part-wood-panelled walls give a
sense of maturity to the space, joined by tones of purple, red and cream to maintain
that urbane hotel-dining feel. The youthful service team set a pleasing, relaxed
tone. The kitchen likes to deal in contemporary combinations and shows a keen eye
for presentation. A scallop starter comes with pork belly 'nuggets', apple and
rehydrated sultanas in a dish with a good balance of sweetness and sharpness, or
go for chilled watermelon gazpacho with cured ham. The main course rump of lamb
gets a Mediterranean spin in the company of feta, broad beans, peas and mint from
the garden. For dessert, warm carrot cake comes with cardamom custard and stem
ginger ice cream.

Chef Adam Lawrenson **Owner** QHotels **Seats** 70, Pr/dining room 120
Times 5.30-9.30, Closed L all week **Prices** Starter £5-£11, Main £13.50-£22.50,
Dessert £6-£8 **Wines** 12 bottles over £30, 18 bottles under £30, 16 by glass
Parking 90 **Notes** Pre-theatre menu, Vegetarian available, Children welcome

The Welcombe Hotel Spa & Golf Club

◉◉ Modern British, French

tel: 01789 295252 **Warwick Rd CV37 0NR**
email: welcombe@menzieshotels.co.uk **web:** www.menzieshotels.co.uk
dir: M40 junct 15, A46 towards Stratford-upon-Avon, at rdbt follow signs for A439. Hotel
3m on right

Updated county-house cuisine in elegant Victorian hotel

If not exactly the Palace of Versailles, the formal garden out front of this splendid
Victorian house is mightily impressive and brings a stately presence to the
Jacobean-style property. With 157 acres of grounds all to itself, there's plenty of
space to wander (or take your wedding photos), and lots of opportunities within for
pampering in the spa. Conference and events are regular happenings here. The
restaurant matches the setting with its grandeur, with period features such as oak
panels and huge windows looking out over the grounds combining with plush decor
(swagged curtains, patterned carpet and formally laid tables). Start with a pre-
dinner drink in the lounge and eat alfresco if the weather is up to snuff. The menu
offers a contemporary take on classic country-house cuisine, so smoked salmon
comes with a whizzy lemon jelly and pan-seared scallops are served with black
pudding, celeriac and onion rösti and parsnip and vanilla purée. Follow with cod
wrapped in pancetta with red wine jus or rib-eye steak with triple-cooked chips,
and finish with blood orange cheesecake.

Chef Gary Lissemore **Owner** Topland No 14 **Seats** 70, Pr/dining room 150
Times 12.30-2/7-10, Closed L Sat **Prices** Fixed L 2 course £20, Fixed D 3 course £35,
Service optional **Wines** 10 bottles over £30, 10 bottles under £30, 8 by glass
Parking 150 **Notes** Afternoon tea £18-£30, Pre-theatre D menu from 5.30pm,
Sunday L £19-£25, Vegetarian available, Children welcome

WARWICK   Map 10 SP26

Ardencote Manor Hotel & Spa

◉◉ Modern British V

tel: 01926 843111 **The Cumsey, Lye Green Rd, Claverdon CV35 8LT**
email: hotel@ardencote.com **web:** www.ardencote.com
dir: Off A4189. In Claverdon follow signs for Shrewley & brown tourist signs for Ardencote
Manor, approx 1.5m

Confident, creative cooking by a lake

Dating from 1863, this substantial building, set in more than 100 acres beside a
lake, is now a luxury boutique hotel. Extensive facilities include a gym, two
swimming pools, beauty treatments and a nine-hole golf course. Add these together
with The Lodge Restaurant, a high-ceilinged room with a stone fireplace, and
guests hardly need to leave the hotel. The kitchen delivers an array of bright,
contemporary ideas, with enthusiastic combinations providing some gutsy flavours.
An assiette of duck, for instance, consists of confit leg, glazed tongue, foie gras,
brioche macaroon and salted grapes, and another starter comprises ray fillet
poached in brown butter, shrimps, béarnaise sauce, nasturtium, sea lettuce and
poached egg yolk. Main courses receive similar treatments, from the full-on meaty
flavours of poached beef fillet with oxtail, smoked marrow, consommé and morels to
a piscine offering such as turbot fillet with crab, courgettes, vanilla, pea tapioca
and fennel. Puddings can be equally complex and none the worse for it: perhaps
wild strawberries with vanilla sponge, clotted cream pannacotta and mint-
infused sugar.

Chef Ian Buckle **Owner** Mr Huckerby **Seats** 65 **Times** 12.30-2/7-10, Closed Mon-Tue, L
Wed-Sat, D Sun **Prices** Fixed L 3 course £19.95-£25, Fixed D 3 course £30-£45,
Starter £5.50-£8.95, Main £14.50-£19.95, Dessert £6.50-£8.95 **Wines** 37 bottles
over £30, 38 bottles under £30, 12 by glass **Parking** 350 **Notes** Sunday L £15.95-
£19.95, Children welcome

Tailors Restaurant

◉◉ Modern British NEW V

tel: 01926 410590 **22 Market Place CV34 4SL**
email: info@tailorsrestaurant.co.uk
dir: M40 junct 15. Follow A429 to Warwick, left into Swan St, 300mtrs on right in square

Technically skilled deconstructions of the British heritage

Looking for inspiration for the name of their market square venue in the heart of
historic Warwick, the partners considered its former incarnations. Tailors it is (and
was for nearly a century). It's a pint-sized room centred on an old brick fireplace,
decorated with framed images of local buildings, furnished with high-backed
chairs at uncovered tables. There is an adventurousness in a menu that arcs back
through British heritage to the heroic age of corned beef and prawn cocktails.
Dishes are complex, with many elements and much technical skill. That seafood
cocktail consists of prawns and brown shrimps, its Marie Rose dressing deep-fried
in a breadcrumb coating, with red pepper purée and a gel of preserved lemon, a
conceptual triumph. At main course, loin of fine local pork comes with a spring roll
of the braised rib, toasted almonds, apricot and bitter coffee jelly, or there could be
hot-smoked salmon with chestnut raviolo, goats' curd, sprouts and puréed
caramelised radicchio. Black Forest gâteau comes in for deconstruction too, its
warm ganache encased in soft crumb, with freeze-dried sour cherries and smooth
buttermilk ice cream boozed with Kirsch.

Chef Mark Fry, Dan Cavell **Owner** Mark Fry, Dan Cavell **Seats** 28
Times 12-2/6.30-9.15, Closed Xmas, Sun-Mon **Prices** Fixed L 2 course £16.50, Fixed
D 3 course £39.50-£52, Tasting menu fr £62.50, Service optional **Wines** 19 bottles
over £30, 28 bottles under £30, 11 by glass **Notes** Tasting menu L fr £32.50,
Children L only

WELLESBOURNE
Map 10 SP25

The Moncreiffe

◉◉ British

tel: 01789 842424 **Walton Hall, Walton CV35 9HU**
email: waltonreservations@thehotelcollection.co.uk
web: www.thehotelcollection.co.uk/hotels/walton-hall-warwickshire/
dir: *M40 junct 13 N'bound, M40 junct 15 S'bound, A429 Cirencester. 1.5m drive through Wellesbourne village*

Ambitious modern cooking in smart Warwickshire hotel

The setting may be a handsome Queen Anne house in 65 acres of green and pleasant Warwickshire countryside, but diners at Walton Hall can look forward to accomplished displays of technical skill in the kitchen's modern British cooking. Handy for pootling around in Shakespeare country, Walton Hall comes complete with lush gardens and a lake, gently updated interiors and conforms to 21st-century country-house form with its fitness and pampering facilities and dog-friendly attitude. The Moncreiffe dining room goes for a classically elegant look involving gold leaf, fancy plasterwork and grand crystal chandeliers, while the kitchen delivers carefully crafted ideas. Pea and ham soup is familiar enough, but is updated here by pouring the soup around pulled ham hock and a quenelle of crème fraîche. That sets the tone for a well-constructed main course of lamb, matched inventively with barley, garlic, fennel, lemon and goats' cheese. Desserts tend towards classic ideas, as seen in a combo of fresh strawberries and strawberry sorbet with fresh mint, basil and balsamic, or chocolate tart with pistachio ice cream and cherries.

Times 7-9.30

Walton Hotel

◉ Modern British NEW

tel: 01789 842424 **The Orangery, Walton CV35 9HU**
email: waltonreservations@thehotelcollection.co.uk
web: www.thehotelcollection.co.uk/waltonhotel
dir: *M40 junct 13 N'bound, M40 junct 15 S'bound, A429 Cirencester. 1.5m drive through Wellesbourne village*

Modern European dining in a contemporary hotel

A contemporary hotel which shares 65 acres of verdant Warwickshire countryside with The Moncreisse, Walton Hall (part of the same group), the Walton Hotel has conference facilities and all mod cons. It's also home to The Orangery Restaurant, a brasserie with a fine-dining finish and views out over the Victorian garden, plus a terrace to make the best of sunny days. This adaptable kitchen offers a vibrant Southeast Asian-style salad with peanuts, watermelon and a nam jim dressing, and also produces a twice-baked goats' cheese soufflé with a Waldorf salad and candied walnuts. Among main courses, pork belly is braised for six hours and served with crispy cheek and cider jus, or there's all the simplicity and comfort of beer-battered cod. Desserts are a Pan-European bunch such as a classic lemon tart or pannacotta with strawberry salad. There's afternoon tea and a more casual dining option, too.

Chef Adam Bateman **Owner** The Hotel Collection **Seats** 110, Pr/dining room 30 **Times** 6.30-9.30 **Prices** Service optional **Wines** 14 bottles over £30, 42 bottles under £30, 16 by glass **Notes** Sunday L £18.95-£22.95, Vegetarian available, Children welcome

WEST MIDLANDS

BALSALL COMMON
Map 10 SP27

Nailcote Hall

◉ Modern European

tel: 024 7646 6174 **Nailcote Ln, Berkswell CV7 7DE**
email: info@nailcotehall.co.uk web: www.nailcotehall.co.uk
dir: *On B4101 towards Tile Hill/Coventry, 10 mins from NEC/Birmingham Airport*

Flambéed steaks and modern cooking

Built on the eve of the Civil War, Nailcote is a stately home on a modest scale, with 15 acres of grounds containing what are reputedly some of England's oldest yew trees. Weddings, golf and aromatherapy are on the agenda these days, as is a bright interior styling approach with bold colours and patterns in the public rooms, and gnarled beams against white walls in the traditionally framed Oak Room restaurant. Old-school service extends to tableside steak-flambéing, but otherwise the mood is modern, for contemporary classics such as scallops with puréed roasted cauliflower and Clonakilty black pudding, and appealing main dishes like Gressingham duck breast with pak choi, sauce bigarade and an underlay of crunchy barley, or herb-crusted sea bass with red pepper and creamed leeks. For dessert, rhubarb and custard is reimagined as a parfait, topped with tangy apricot and ginger sorbet.

Chef Daniel Topa **Owner** Richard Cressman **Seats** 50, Pr/dining room 300 **Times** 12-2.30/7-9.30, Closed L Sat **Prices** Fixed L 2 course £19.50, Fixed D 3 course £29.50, Starter £6.25-£7.95, Main £12.95-£25.95, Dessert £6.25-£12.50, Service optional **Wines** 10 bottles over £30, 10 bottles under £30, 12 by glass **Parking** 150 **Notes** Fixed L Mon-Fri only, Vegetarian available, Children welcome

BIRMINGHAM
Map 10 SP08

Adam's

◉◉◉ *– see page 534*

Carters of Moseley

◉◉ Modern British NEW v

tel: 0121 449 8885 & 449 2962 **2c Wake Green Rd, Moseley B13 9EZ**
email: enquiries@cartersofmoseley.co.uk
dir: *B4217 Wake Green Rd off A435 Alcester Rd. On St Mary's Row slip road just past St Mary's Church*

Modern British food interpreted with simplicity and skill

The unassuming location amid a parade of shops of Brad Carter's neighbourhood restaurant belies its ambition. In a pared-down modern bistro setting with button-backed banquettes, pictures of cassette tapes, and a spy-window into the kitchen, a dynamic intelligence is at work. Simplicity and restraint are the keys to Carter's interpretation of the modern British style, resulting in balanced dishes executed with convincing skill. Fixed-price menus tend to the lighter at lunch, perhaps for a soft-cooked duck's egg with butterscotch cap mushrooms in chicken gravy, followed by a tranche of roast cod in seaweed butter with a bundle of marine flora – sea-aster, sea-cabbage and samphire. In the evening, the repertoire extends to hay-seared venison 'sashimi' with apple and smoked celeriac, sea bass with fermented garlic, and beef cheek with truffled polenta and a king oyster. The combination of rusticity and refinement is central to the appeal, through to Yorkshire rhubarb cake with almond milk, or goats' milk mousse with blood orange and fennel. You'll need a will of iron to resist a feather-light rendition of sticky toffee pudding, served in a Tate & Lyle Golden Syrup tin with Madagascar vanilla ice cream.

Chef Brad Carter **Owner** Brad Carter, Holly Jackson **Seats** 35 **Times** 12-2/6.30-9.30, Closed Mon-Tue **Prices** Fixed L 3 course £28-£42, Tasting menu £49-£70, Service optional 12.5% **Wines** 30 bottles over £30, 23 bottles under £30, 10 by glass **Parking** 4, 12 spaces outside **Notes** Tasting menu 6 course, Sunday L £28-£42, Children 8 yrs+

BIRMINGHAM *continued*

Circle Restaurant Birmingham Hippodrome

Modern British **NEW**

tel: 0844 338 9000 *(Calls cost 7p per minute plus your phone company's access charge)* & 0121 689 3181 **B5 4TB**
email: restaurantreservations@birminghamhippodrome.com
dir: *Phone for directions*

Show-stopping food for theatregoers

Pre-theatre dining doesn't get much closer to curtain-up than at this large, open-plan restaurant on the second floor of the Hippodrome. In the centre of Birmingham's shopping area, the majority of diners here are theatregoers and you can even save your dessert for during the interval, which is a uniquely quirky touch. A contemporary room with crisp-white walls dotted with vibrant artwork and background music (show tunes, naturally), service is friendly and the modern British cooking is confident. Seared tuna with green beans, lemon, black olives and confit tomatoes is one way to start, perhaps followed by a well-balanced main of Staffordshire pork belly fillet, crackling, bok choi, crispy potatoes, pineapple and curry oil. A well-presented and zesty Pina Colada pannacotta with pineapple, coconut and mint syrup is one of several enjoyable desserts available.

Chef Chris Bratt-Rose **Owner** Birmingham Hippodrome Theatre Trust **Seats** 95, Pr/dining room 25 **Times** 12-2/5.30-7.30, Closed Non-performance days, Sun-Mon (usually), L Tue, Thu-Fri (usually) **Prices** Fixed L 2 course £28.50-£29.50, Fixed D 3 course £34.50-£35.50, Service optional **Wines** 8 bottles over £30, 21 bottles under £30, 10 by glass **Parking** Arcadian car park, Bromsgrove St **Notes** Vegetarian available, Children welcome

Hotel du Vin Birmingham

British, French **NOTABLE WINE LIST**

tel: 0121 200 0600 **25 Church St B3 2NR**
email: info@birmingham.hotelduvin.com **web:** www. hotelduvin.com
dir: *M6 junct 6/A38(M) to city centre, over flyover. Keep left & exit at St Chads Circus signed Jewellery Quarter. At lights & rdbt take 1st exit, follow signs for Colmore Row, opposite cathedral. Right into Church St, across Barwick St. Hotel on right*

Bistro dining in converted former eye hospital

Hotel du Vin's Birmingham branch occupies an imposing 1884 red-brick building, at one time the city's eye hospital, in the right-on Jewellery Quarter. Sip an aperitif on one of the deeply comfortable sofas in the Bubble Lounge Bar or head downstairs for a pint in the vaulted Pub du Vin before dining in the stylish restaurant, with its Gallic-inspired decor of bare floorboards, panelled walls hung with sconces and pictures, and round-backed wooden chairs at polished tables. As in the rest of the group, the menu here focuses on French bistro classics with some British favourites thrown in, all cooked comme il faut and served by switched-on, friendly staff. Kick off with correctly timed Comté cheese soufflé or seared scallops with sauce vierge before tucking into one of the plats principaux: roast cod fillet with braised Puy lentils, button onions and pancetta, say, or beef bourguignon on the bone. End with that English favourite of treacle tart with clotted cream ice cream or cross the Channel for tarte au citron.

Chef Greg Pryce **Owner** KSL **Seats** 85, Pr/dining room 108 **Times** 12-2/6-10 **Prices** Fixed L 2 course £16.95, Starter £5.95-£9.95, Main £13.95-£29.50, Dessert £6.95 **Wines** 220 bottles over £30, 62 bottles under £30, 21 by glass **Parking** NCP Livery St **Notes** Sun brunch 4 course, Sunday L £24.95, Vegetarian available, Children welcome

Adam's ❀❀❀

BIRMINGHAM   Map 10 SP08

Modern British **V**
tel: 0121 643 3745 **21a Bennetts Hill B2 5QP**
email: info@adamsrestaurant.co.uk
dir: *Located in Birmingham City Centre, 2 mins walk from New Street Station*

Dynamic contemporary cooking in the city centre

The Adam in question is Adam Stokes, a chef with bags of experience at the top of the culinary firmament, and now he has his name above the door. He's taken a former sandwich shop in a ground-zero city-centre spot just around the corner from New Street Station and a short stroll from the finance quarter, and turned the space into a rather refined contemporary room done out with faux marble, neutral hues and glistening globe lights. With just 26 lucky diners to cater for – a greedy chef could have squeezed in many more – you can be sure that timings are pin-sharp, attention to detail is impressive, and the service team are 100% on the ball. Adam says 'my aim is not to baffle, but to excite and enthuse', which he readily achieves, for this dynamic, modern cooking makes perfect sense, and is balanced, creative and beautiful on the plate. It all comes in five- or nine-course tasters (the latter being the only option on Friday and Saturday nights), plus a decent value three-course lunchtime option, which is a very good entry point. The five-course tasting menu might start with a dish of cod with roasted cauliflower and smoked haddock, the fish spankingly fresh and cooked spot-on, followed by another refined and intelligent dish of ceps with rhubarb and hazelnut. The evident technical skills in the kitchen remain consistently high throughout, as seen in a course which matches mallard breast with plum, beetroot and turnip, or in a brace of desserts, the first of which combines the flavours of green tea with lime and goats' curd, the second a good-looking medley of milk chocolate, clementine, shiso and lemon. As we went to press, plans were afoot to move to a new premises.

Chef Adam Stokes **Owner** Adam & Natasha Stokes **Seats** 26 **Times** 12-2/7-9.30, Closed 2 wks summer, 3 wks Xmas, Sun-Mon **Prices** Fixed L 3 course fr £32, Tasting menu £50-£80 **Wines** 84 bottles over £30, 6 bottles under £30, 19 by glass **Parking** On street **Notes** Tasting menu 5/9 course, Children welcome

Lasan Restaurant

⚫ Indian

tel: 0121 212 3664 & 212 3665 **3-4 Dakota Buildings, James St, St Paul's Square B3 1SD**
email: info@lasan.co.uk
dir: *Near city centre, adjacent to Jewellery Quarter*

Contemporary Indian cooking in the Jewellery Quarter

Entirely on-message for the trendy Jewellery Quarter, Lasan is a contemporary Indian restaurant with loads of style and a vibrant atmosphere. The split-level dining room has as a contemporary demeanour that neatly avoids curry-house cliché without trying too hard to be something it isn't. The menu takes a broad sweep across the sub-continent to deliver a menu that offers regional authenticity alongside modern fusion touches. Start with batair, which is a quail number with some punchy marinades, or an onion and spinach pakora served with spiced mango and lentil chutney. Main courses run to mahi machli (salmon with tomato and red pepper purée) and a sharing platter for two consisting of spiced chicken sheek, lamb chops, tandoori salmon and spiced potato cakes. Herefordshire beef cheek is braised overnight to deliver a wonderfully tender and delicately spiced dish, and, to finish, Bombay Mess is a creative take on an English classic.

Chef Aktar Islam, Gulsher Khan **Owner** Jabbar Khan **Seats** 74
Times 12-2.30/6-11, Closed 25-26 Dec, 1 Jan, L Sat **Prices** Tasting menu £49.95, Starter £5.45-£22.95, Main £18.95-£26.95, Dessert £2.50-£6.95 **Wines** 14 bottles over £30, 12 bottles under £30, 7 by glass **Parking** On street **Notes** Sunday L, Vegetarian available, Children 10 yrs+

Malmaison Birmingham

⚫ Modern, Traditional

tel: 0121 240 5000 **1 Wharfside St, The Mailbox D1 1RD**
email: birmingham@malmaison.com **web:** www.malmaison.com
dir: *M6 junct 6, follow the A38 (city centre), via Queensway underpass. Left to Paradise Circus, 1st exit Brunel St, right T-junct, Malmaison directly opposite*

Buzzy setting and smart brasserie-style cooking

Maybe not the prettiest building you'll ever see, but a landmark nonetheless, the Mailbox is a former Royal Mail sorting office which has been turned into a swanky shopping centre with a host of dining and drinking options. The Malmaison team have brought their brand of boutique swagger to the place. The brasserie, with its floor-to-ceiling windows and dark and moody contemporary finish, is a relaxed and lively spot offering a menu of globally inspired contemporary dishes. Kick off with moules marinière or sticky Thai-style chicken wings, and move on to a steak cooked on the grill (Black Angus New York strip). With the likes of Goan tiger prawn curry and a slate of burgers up for grabs, this place is all about 21st-century comfort food. The Malbar comes into its own in the evening when cocktails and champagne bring in the crowds.

Chef Brian Neath **Owner** Malmaison **Seats** 120, Pr/dining room 20
Times 12-2.30/6-10.30 **Prices** Starter £5-£9.50, Main £12-£36 **Wines** 26 bottles over £30, 16 bottles under £30, 26 by glass **Parking** 300, Mailbox car park chargeable **Notes** Fixed 2/3 course, Sunday L £19.95-£24.95, Vegetarian available, Children welcome

Opus Restaurant

⚫⚫ Modern British

tel: 0121 200 2323 **54 Cornwall St B3 2DE**
email: restaurant@opusrestaurant.co.uk **web:** www.opusrestaurant.co.uk
dir: *Close to Birmingham Snow Hill railway station in the city's business district*

Smart city favourite for modern British cooking

Opus has bags of big-city attitude and a cosmopolitan vibe that suits its location in the city's financial quarter. An eye-catching, full-length, girder-framed glass frontage references Brum's industrial heritage, while inside it's a stylish setting: darkwood floors, linen-clothed tables, olive green suede and black leather banquette seating, and jazzy wallpapers to relieve the muted palette. The cooking has broad appeal thanks to daily-changing menus that follow the seasons with a beady eye. Top-quality British produce anchors the whole operation, and it's all brought together in straightforward modern treatments — you'll find nothing fussy, over-complex or speculative in either composition or presentation of dishes. From the great-value market menu, a rich ballotine of chicken and wild mushrooms is offset by the summery lightness of broad bean and artichoke salad with watercress dressing, while roasted cod is partnered by crushed blue potatoes, and a spicy purée and crunchy tempura of cauliflower. If you're after something meaty, the carte might offer cottage pie poshed up with Wagyu beef and partnered by crushed root vegetables and spring greens.

Chef Ben Tornront **Owner** Ann Tonks, Irene Allan **Seats** 85, Pr/dining room 32
Times 12-4/6-mdnt, Closed between Xmas & New Year, BHs, L Sat, D Sun
Prices Fixed L 2 course £14, Fixed D 3 course £16, Starter £6.50-£12.50, Main £12.50-£26, Dessert £6.50-£8.50 **Wines** 33 bottles over £30, 30 bottles under £30, 9 by glass **Parking** On street **Notes** Tasting menu 5 course, Kitchen table menu 5 course £75, Sunday L £25, Vegetarian available, Children welcome

Purnell's

⚫⚫⚫ – *see page 536*

Simpsons

⚫⚫⚫ – *see page 536*

Turners

⚫⚫⚫ – *see page 538*

Purnell's ❀❀❀

Modern British 🍷 NOTABLE WINE LIST

tel: 0121 212 9799 **55 Cornwall St B3 2DH**
email: info@purnellsrestaurant.com
dir: *Close to Birmingham Snow Hill railway station & junct of Church St*

Superbly accomplished and inventive cooking

Glynn Purnell's eponymous restaurant occupies a corner site in the second city's financial district not far from St Philip's Cathedral. It's been converted from a red-brick Victorian warehouse, with no expense spared, tones of mushroom and blue giving a cool and classy look. A recent introduction is Purnell's living room offering bite-sized plates for sharing, what Glynn calls 'Brummie tapas'. Expect adventurous dishes along the lines of beetroot mousse with escabèche of vegetables and horseradish crumble or a fish of the day with coconut, coriander and carrots. Elsewhere is a choice of set-price menus, with wine flights optional extras, the one at lunchtime offering, say, curry-cured salmon with mango chutney, pickled cauliflower and coriander, then duck breast with port-infused turnips and cabbage, concluding with pistachio macaroon with orange curd, poached rhubarb and frozen mascarpone. The cooking is bold and dynamic, with Glynn treating his top-grade ingredients with a sense of excitement, and every component is intelligently chosen to give bursts of flavours. The winter menu may start off with a poached egg yolk with Alsace bacon and a 'Brummie cake' and go on to a vegetable dish of sweetcorn, tomato, beetroot and carrot, before red mullet fillets with truffled pommes dauphine, bordelaise and parsley. Technical accomplishment and an eye for attractive presentation are hallmarks, seen in meat dishes such as veal cheek glazed in treacle and sesame-creamed mustard, and in slow-cooked Wiltshire lamb with a basil emulsion. An intermediate blue cheese cracker may precede puddings such as a crumble of lemon, dates, pine nuts and honey, and mint choccy chip.

Chef Glynn Purnell **Owner** Glynn Purnell **Seats** 45, Pr/dining room 12 **Times** 12-1.30/7-9, Closed 1 wk Etr, 2 wks end Jul-early Aug, Xmas, New Year, Sun-Mon, L Sat **Prices** Fixed L 3 course £32, Tasting menu £65-£85 **Wines** 222 bottles over £30, 24 bottles under £30, 19 by glass **Parking** On street, Snow Hill car park nearby **Notes** Tasting menu 6/12 course, Wine tasting fr £60, Vegetarian available, Children 10 yrs+

Simpsons ❀❀❀

Modern British V 🍷 NOTABLE WINE LIST

tel: 0121 454 3434 **20 Highfield Rd, Edgbaston B15 3DU**
email: info@simpsonsrestaurant.co.uk
dir: *1m from city centre, opposite St George's Church, Edgbaston*

Outstanding beautifully-presented cooking in Edgbaston favourite

Chef-patron Andreas Antona was in the vanguard of Brum's gastronomic renaissance back in 2004 with his classy restaurant with rooms in a white Georgian house in the genteel, leafy suburb of Edgbaston. In summer 2015 the place had a top-to-toe refurb to extend the main dining area and spruce up the already impeccably tasteful space, with its conservatory extension looking over the landscaped garden – a spot that comes into its own for alfresco dining under large parasols in balmy weather. Directing the day-to-day action in the engine room is Luke Tipping, whose technically assured cooking is on a roll, delivering dishes displaying a high degree of sophistication, a meticulous eye for detail and superb technical skills, all founded on top-class ingredients. Scallop ravioli arrives in a picturesque medley garnished with fennel and drizzled with a deeply-flavoured langoustine and pepper sauce, or the kitchen might apply its own contemporary and imaginative approach to a classic French idea, matching pickled onions, apple and turnip with chicken and duck liver parfait. Next up, an impeccably handled turbot fillet paired with crispy chicken wings and accompanied by baby leeks, oyster mushrooms and Jersey Royals shows that main-course combinations are just as intelligently thought through. Others bring eastern influences into play with outstanding results – perhaps Pyrenean lamb shank with aromatic cracked wheat, cumin, date purée, aubergine and feta. Presentation and technical pizzazz remain outstanding through to an imaginative take on Eton Mess involving glazed meringue, lemon pannacotta, and wild strawberry sorbet all garnished prettily with edible flowers. As well as the carte and set-price lunch, there's a seven-course tasting menu with a veggie version and optional wine flight.

Chef Andreas Antona, Luke Tipping **Owner** Andreas & Alison Antona **Seats** 70, Pr/dining room 20 **Times** 12-2.30/7-9.30, Closed BHs, D Sun **Prices** Fixed L 3 course £40, Tasting menu fr £85, Starter £14-£18, Main £24-£35, Dessert £10-£14 **Wines** 20 bottles over £30, 10 bottles under £30, 11 by glass **Parking** 12, On street **Notes** Tasting menu 7 course, Sunday L, Children welcome

DORRIDGE
Map 10 SP17

Hogarths Hotel

Modern British **NEW**

tel: 01564 779988 **Four Ashes Rd B93 8QE**
email: reception@hogarths.co.uk **web:** www.hogarths.co.uk
dir: M42 junct 4, exit onto A3400 Henley, 1st left onto Gale Ln, at T-junct left onto Four Ashes Rd

Mediterranean-influenced brasserie food in a stylish setting

A little Midlands village with a charming old church is the setting for Hogarths, a picturesque location that also manages to be handy for the NEC and the airport. Conferences and comedy nights are among the hotel's attractions, and so is a stylish-looking modern dining room with curvy white banquettes and lime green light fittings. Fresh Mediterranean-influenced brasserie food is the bill of fare, with quality produce in simple preparations. A fig, walnut and blue cheese tart dressed in balsamic reduction packs a good hit of flavour to begin with, as does treacle- and gin-cured salmon with sour cream and soda bread. The Inka charcoal grill works its magic for rib-eye steaks that come with the full set of onion rings, mushrooms and triple-cooked chips, or there's Spanish-themed hake on chorizo and saffron cassoulet. A citrussy take on baked Alaska to finish looks the business, with its meringue topping, lemon curd and lemon ice cream.

Chef Alex Alexandrov **Owner** Helena & Andy Hogarth **Seats** 80, Pr/dining room 100 **Times** 12-3/6-10 **Prices** Fixed L 2 course £15-£20, Fixed D 3 course £20-£30, Starter £5-£9, Main £10-£25, Dessert £5-£9, Service optional **Parking** 120 **Notes** Afternoon tea, Sunday L £29.95-£34, Vegetarian available, Children welcome

HOCKLEY HEATH
Map 10 SP17

Nuthurst Grange Hotel

Modern British v

tel: 01564 783972 **Nuthurst Grange Ln B94 5NL**
email: info@nuthurst-grange.co.uk **web:** www.nuthurst-grange.com
dir: Exit A3400, 0.5m S of Hockley Heath. Turn at sign into Nuthurst Grange Lane

Traditional and modern cooking amid private woodland

Nuthurst is one of those places that contrives to be a few minutes off the motorway (the M40), and yet a world away from bustling traffic. The long tree-lined avenue approach leads to a brick-built Victorian mansion in seven acres of private woodland, so allow plenty of time for exploring. The formal tone is proudly worn – it's a popular wedding venue – as is indicated by the gleaming silver carving trolley that lords it over the Kingswood dining room. A judicious balance of culinary modernism and traditional ideas is in evidence on the menus, describing an arc from lobster and crab cocktail with tomatoes and brown bread to creamed sea trout and mascarpone terrine with Parma ham crisps and gingerbread among the starters. Dishes have a lot going on in them but manage not to look crowded, as for duck breast with a pasty, roast parsnips, potato croquettes and roughly puréed

trompette mushrooms in Madeira jus. Artfully arranged desserts include pineapple soufflé with Valrhona salted caramel chocolate mousse and nutty florentines.

Nuthurst Grange Hotel

Chef Andrew Glover **Owner** Paul Hopwood **Seats** Pr/dining room 70 **Times** 12-2.30/7-9, Closed D Sun, 25-26 Dec, 1 Jan **Prices** Fixed L 2 course £19.95, Fixed D 3 course £39.95, Tasting menu fr £65, Service optional 10% **Wines** 14 by glass **Notes** Tasting menu with matching wines £100, Sunday L £29.95, Children welcome

See advert on page 539

MERIDEN
Map 10 SP28

BEST WESTERN PLUS Manor NEC Birmingham

Modern British, French

tel: 01676 522735 **Main Rd CV7 7NH**
email: reservations@manorhotelmeriden.co.uk **web:** www.manorhotelmeriden.co.uk
dir: M42 junct 6, A45 towards Coventry then A452 signed Leamington. At rdbt take B4102 signed Meriden, hotel on left

Smart upbeat cooking in a Midlands manor

The elegant Georgian Manor hotel in the village of Meriden strikes a neat balance between town and country: the rural setting is charming, yet the National Exhibition Centre and Drum are close to hand if you're doing business in the area. The Regency Restaurant has carved itself a niche in the local foodie scene with its up-to-date takes on classic dishes; it is an airy, traditionally styled space hung with paintings of English country scenes above smartly dressed tables laid with sparkling glasses and fresh flowers, and young, upbeat staff ensure it all ticks along nicely. Assured and unpretentious modern British cooking is the order of the day, starting with crab and scallop ravioli teamed with samphire and prawn bisque, followed by a piggy trio of pork tenderloin medallions, smoked pig's cheek and a trotter bonbon partnered with apricot and sage compôte, carrots, dauphinoise potato and thyme jus. The show closes with another well-matched trio – salted caramel parfait, white chocolate popcorn and a mini crème brûlée.

Times 12-3/6-10, Closed L Mon-Sat

Forest of Arden Marriott Hotel & Country Club

Modern British v

tel: 01676 522335 **Maxstoke Ln CV7 7HR**
email: ankush.sharma@marriotthotels.com **web:** www.marriottforestofarden.co.uk
dir: M42 junct 6 onto A45 towards Coventry, over Stonebridge flyover. After 0.75m left into Shepherds Ln. Left at T-junct. Hotel 1.5m on left

Good eating at a smart golfing hotel

A sprawling hotel with lots going on – golf and a spa for starters – the Forest of Arden Marriott is well-positioned for doing business in Brum, with the NEC and airport close to hand, and its Oaks Bar and Grill is a restaurant worth a trip in its

continued

MERIDEN *continued*

own right. Beneath a beamed, barn-style roof, there's a brightly-patterned carpet, leather banquettes, stylish olive green chairs and fashionably bare tables giving it a bright and breezy feel, and large floor-to-ceiling windows giving the bonus of views over the golf course. The kitchen deals in honest modern cooking without airs and graces, setting out with cider-steamed mussels with parsley and cream, followed by feather blade beef, braised to melting tenderness for six hours and served simply with mash and kale. To finish, apple and almond flapjack crumble is served with proper custard and apple crisps.

Chef Darcy Morgan **Seats** 192, Pr/dining room 18 **Times** 1-2.30/6.30-9.45 **Prices** Fixed D 3 course fr £32, Service optional **Wines** 16 by glass **Parking** 300 **Notes** Children welcome

▌ OLDBURY
Map 10 SO98

Saffron Restaurant

◉ Modern Indian

tel: 0121 552 1752 **909 Wolverhampton Rd B69 4RR**
email: info@saffron-online.co.uk
dir: *M5 junct 2. Follow A4123 (S) signs towards Harborne. Restaurant on right*

Smart modern setting for up-to-date Anglo-Indian fusion cooking

This contemporary Black Country Indian goes for a bold colour scheme involving scarlet and black chairs arranged in a chequerboard pattern at darkwood tables, plushly padded booths and statement wallpaper. The menu covers a lot of ground from tandoori staples and classics (Punjabi saag gosht or chicken tikka masala, for instance) to more refined, delicately spiced ideas built on quality, fresh ingredients. Catching the eye among starters is rabbit varuval, a South Indian speciality

teaming tender rabbit with onion, curry leaves, mustard seeds and a palate-tingling hit of chilli. The signature dishes show a kitchen that's happy to innovate in the fusion style, coming up with ideas such as pan-fried spiced red mullet with chickpea and spinach gâteau, sauced with cumin and coriander-scented beurre blanc. Among meatier propositions, try braised duck breast tossed in a smoky hickory sauce flavoured with Chinese five spice.

Chef Sudha Shankar Saha, Avijit Mondol **Owner** Abdul Rahman, A Momin **Seats** 96, Pr/dining room 30 **Times** 12-2.30/5.30-11, Closed D 25 Dec **Prices** Prices not confirmed, Service optional **Wines** 38 bottles under £30, 8 by glass **Parking** 25, On street **Notes** Sunday L, Vegetarian available, Children welcome

▌ SOLIHULL
Map 10 SP17

Hampton Manor

◉◉◉ *– see page 540*

▌ SUTTON COLDFIELD (ROYAL)
Map 10 SP19

BEST WESTERN PREMIER Moor Hall Hotel & Spa

◉◉ Modern British

tel: 0121 308 3751 **Moor Hall Dr, Four Oaks B75 6LN**
email: mail@moorhallhotel.co.uk **web:** www.moorhallhotel.co.uk
dir: *A38 onto A453 towards Sutton Coldfield, right at lights into Weeford Rd. Hotel 150yds on left*

Appealing modern cooking in country-house hotel

Although part of the Best Western stable, Moor Hall is a family-run country-house hotel within parkland a short distance from the city centre. It has two restaurants, prime of which is the panelled Oak Room in what was the dining room when the

Turners ◉◉◉

▌ BIRMINGHAM
Map 10 SP08

Modern British V

tel: 0121 426 4440 **69 High St, Harborne B17 9NS**
email: info@turnersrestaurantbirmingham.co.uk
dir: *Phone for directions*

Cooking up a gastronomic storm in a Birmingham suburb

On an innocuous row of shops on the busy high street of the Birmingham suburb of Harborne you'll find the smart grey frontage of this restaurant, and a glance inside reveals a stylish space with formally laid tables and a touch of class. This is chef-patron Richard Turner's place and his name is scored into the mirrors on the wall lest you forget. The menu format consists of a tasting menu and the 'Simply Turners' option, which is a sort of make-your-own menu of either three, four, five or six courses, plus a set-lunch option. The slick service adds to the impression that you're somewhere special. Richard's cooking is contemporary and refined, but the modern elements are restrained and subtle (no smoke and mirrors here), and the quality of the ingredients resonates from start to finish. A scallop dish includes céviche, salt-baked celeriac, apple, yogurt and horseradish in a creative interpretation of a modern classic, while pig's trotters come in a terrine with roast langoustine, buttermilk and oriental flavours. A fish option might be John Dory with crayfish

and crab, and a tasting of new season's lamb arrives with wild garlic, morels and lamb jus. Choose from a couple of dessert courses (or have both), with Yorkshire rhubarb starring in a crumble soufflé served with custard ice cream, and a strawberry offering such as Arctic roll with hibiscus jam. There are champagne cocktails and a bespoke beer selection, while the wine list has a good showing by the glass.

Chef Richard Turner **Owner** Richard Turner **Seats** 28 **Times** 12-2.30/6-9.30, Closed Sun-Mon, L Tue-Thu **Prices** Fixed L 3 course £32.50, Fixed D 3 course £55, Tasting menu £90 **Wines** 89 bottles over £30, 1 bottle under £30, 10 by glass **Parking** At rear **Notes** Children welcome

property was actually someone's home (the other is the informal Country Kitchen which offers a carvery and blackboard specials). The cooking is based on a repertory of contemporary ideas, producing starters of seared scallops with parsnip textures in honeyed jus, or lamb croquette in spiced tomato sauce with salad. Sound technique is applied to good-quality raw materials, and the menu flags items produced within a 40-mile radius. This is evident in slow-cooked pork belly with black pudding and pancetta, served with smoked garlic mash, or seared sea trout with charred chicory and baby gem in a spiky dressing of capers and pepper. The same care goes into puddings such as deliciously rich dark chocolate fondant with honeycomb and white chocolate ice cream.

Chef Charlotte Foster **Owner** Michael Webb **Seats** 70, Pr/dining room 30
Times 12-3.30/7-9.30, Closed L Mon-Sat, D Sun **Prices** Tasting menu fr £39, Starter £6-£9, Main £14.50-£23.50, Dessert £4.75-£5.50, Service optional **Wines** 13 bottles over £30, 38 bottles under £30, 10 by glass **Parking** 170 **Notes** Sunday L fr £21.50, Vegetarian available, Children welcome

New Hall Hotel & Spa
⊛⊛ Modern British

tel: 0121 378 2442 **Walmley Rd B76 1QX**
email: newhall@handpicked.co.uk **web:** www.handpickedhotels.co.uk/newhall
dir: *On B4148, E of Sutton Coldfield, close to M6 & M42 junct 9*

Modern fine dining in historic house

It is hard to imagine, but before Birmingham's suburban sprawl engulfed the village of Sutton Coldfield, this 800-year-old moat house stood in empty countryside. The hall hasn't actually been 'new' since the 14th century, and does business nowadays as an upmarket operation that on one hand flaunts its age in medieval beams, flagstones, and heraldic crests, and on the other, supplies 21st-century spa pampering with all the bells and whistles. It is all cushioned from the hurly-burly of modern Brum by 26 acres of fabulous grounds. The Bridge Restaurant is the top-end dining option, where mullioned stained-glass windows blend with a gently modern neutral decor as a setting for cooking that is rooted in the classics but tweaked for today's tastes with modern techniques and presentation. Ham hock and goose liver terrine is matched with poached cherries and chamomile jelly, ahead of crisp-skinned stone bass with spiced aubergine, fennel, sunblushed tomatoes and lemon, and a crab beignet. A vibrant finale delivers glazed lemon tart with raspberry sorbet, meringue and fresh raspberries.

New Hall Hotel & Spa

Chef Matthew Warburton **Owner** Hand Picked Hotels **Seats** 24, Pr/dining room 12
Times 12-2.30/7-9.30, Closed L Mon-Sat **Prices** Prices not confirmed, Service optional **Wines** 21 bottles under £30, 14 by glass **Parking** 60 **Notes** Sunday L, Vegetarian available, Children welcome

WALSALL

Map 10 SP09

Fairlawns Hotel & Spa

◉◉ Modern British V

tel: 01922 455122 **178 Little Aston Rd, Aldridge WS9 0NU**
email: reception@fairlawns.co.uk web: www.fairlawns.co.uk
dir: *Outskirts of Aldridge, 400yds from junct of A452 (Chester Rd) & A454*

Modern cooking in a characterful family-run hotel

Well placed for virtually anywhere you may need to be in the West Midlands, the spa hotel near Walsall is family-owned and run with plenty of individual character, a refreshing antidote to corporate anonymity. A sense of humour is in evidence in the interior signposting, while the dining room is a stylish venue, decorated with vivid paintings, wooden blinds and globe light fittings. An extensive Market Menu is supplemented by seafood specialities, and the style is modern British, but without too many oddball combinations. First up might be a twice-baked cauliflower cheese soufflé garnished with pancetta, its Mornay sauce perhaps overdoing the cheese note, or mussels in penne with a poached egg. Mains bring on well-timed roast stone bass on parsnip purée with onion rings, peas and baby gem in balsamic saucing, or a beef duo of slow-cooked shin and seared fillet with creamed celeriac and port-glazed shallots. Indulge yourself at the finishing line with a luscious treacle tart, served with mascarpone, lemon curd and a lemon and ginger coulis.

Chef Steve Kirkham, Paul Ingleby **Owner** John Pette **Seats** 80, Pr/dining room 100 **Times** 12-2/7-10, Closed 25-26 Dec, 1 Jan, Good Fri, Etr Mon, May Day, BH Mon, L Sat **Prices** Prices not confirmed, Service optional **Wines** 20 bottles over £30, 40 bottles under £30, 12 by glass **Parking** 120 **Notes** Sunday L, Children welcome

WOLVERHAMPTON

Map 10 SO99

Bilash

◉ Indian, Bangladeshi

tel: 01902 427762 **2 Cheapside WV1 1TU**
email: m@thebilash.co.uk
dir: *Opposite Civic Hall & St Peter's Church*

A happy mix of new and old ideas in longstanding Indian

In a quiet corner of the pedestrianised square overlooking St Peter's Church, Bilash has been pushing beyond the confines of mere curry for 30 years. The stylishly clean-cut interior works a colourful decor of caramel and burgundy high-backed leather seats at wooden tables set against pale lemon walls hung with modern Indian-themed pastel prints; a smart contemporary setting that reflects the kitchen's approach to its creative roll call of Bangladeshi and Indian regional dishes. Start with maacher shami kebab, a flat fishcake with lime, herbs and garam masala, served with tamarind sauce and excellent home-made chutneys, then follow with Goan tiger prawn masala – enormous tiger prawns marinated in spicy tomato paste and cooked with cumin, coriander, green chillies, roasted onions, curry leaves, mint and spring onions. Don't miss pukka Indian desserts such as rasmalai – an uber-sweet dumpling made from Indian paneer (cottage cheese) flavoured with cardamom and saffron, poached in sweetened cardamom-flavoured milk and served with chopped almonds, pistachios and saffron.

Chef Sitab Khan **Owner** Sitab Khan **Seats** 48, Pr/dining room 40 **Times** 12-2.30/5.30-10.30, Closed 25-26 Dec, 1 Jan, Sun **Prices** Fixed L 2 course £9.50-£14.95, Fixed D 3 course £24.95-£49.95, Tasting menu £35-£65, Starter £6.50-£12.90, Main £10.50-£28.90, Dessert £5.50-£7.90, Service optional **Wines** 4 bottles over £30, 12 bottles under £30, 5 by glass **Parking** 15, Civic car park **Notes** Pre-theatre D, Tasting menu with wine, Vegetarian available, Children welcome

Hampton Manor ◉◉◉

SOLIHULL

Map 10 SP17

Modern British V
tel: 01675 446080 **Swadowbrook Ln, Hampton-in-Arden B92 0EN**
email: info@hamptonmanor.eu web: www.hamptonmanor.eu
dir: *M42 junct 6 follow signs for A45 (Birmingham). At 1st rdbt, 1st exit onto B4438 (Catherine de Barnes Ln). Left into Shadowbrook Ln*

Imaginative contemporary cooking and bags of boutique style

The rather splendid Victorian manor house has connections to the family of former PM Sir Robert Peel (the man who put the first 'Bobbies' on the beat), and it remains a tranquil getaway from the nearby urban hubbub. The sleepy hamlet setting is only a few minutes from Solihull and Birmingham's NEC. They describe themselves as a restaurant with rooms, but with 15 stylish boutique bedrooms, luxe conference facilities and 45 acres of wooded grounds to explore, they're rather more than that. The glamorous interior design makes an impression with its bold colours and clever matching of old and new styles, not least in Peel's Restaurant, situated in the main manor house and overlooking the clock tower gardens, with its original fire place and striking chinoiserie decor. The kitchen is headed up by Robert Palmer and offers up some dazzling contemporary food served either à la carte or from four- and seven-course tasting menus. Things start with a bang with canapés

in the bar and a pre-starter of sweetcorn pannacotta with cheese beignet, before moving on to the menu proper and a starter of heritage beetroots with local Bosworth Ash goats' cheese and truffle. Next up, line-caught salt-cod combines with Cornish crab and Jerusalem artichoke purée, and Tiddenham duck breast with a terrine made with its confit leg. They've got their own kitchen garden to call upon to ensure a steady flow of seasonal vegetables, herbs and salads. The impressive technical skills on show continue into desserts such as a Valrhona chocolate number with two scoops of Parma Violets ice cream and cookie crumbs. The young and vivacious service team fit the vibe of the place, with a knowledgeable sommelier on hand to advise on the well put together wine list.

Chef Rob Palmer **Owner** Jan & Derrick Hill **Seats** 26, Pr/dining room 14 **Times** 6-9, Closed Sun-Mon, L all week **Prices** Fixed L 2 course £16-£20, Starter £9-£14, Main £18-£35, Dessert £9-£11, Service optional 10% **Wines** 226 bottles over £30, 38 bottles under £30, 12 by glass **Parking** 30 **Notes** Tasting menu 4/7 course, Afternoon tea, Children welcome

The Mount Hotel and Conference Centre

◉ Modern International NEW

tel: 01902 752055 & 752400 **Mount Rd, Tettenhall Wood WV6 8HL**
email: sales@themount.co.uk **web:** www.themount.co.uk
dir: *M54 junct 5, follow A41 down to Yew Tree Lane which becomes Mount Road, left at lights*

Buzzy brasserie cooking stately house style

The Mount sits on a sandstone ridge (hence its name) and is a stately Victorian mansion overlooking the canal, and equipped with rooms just made for opulent functions. What was the library has a sprung floor for hunt balls (and now weddings), but the dining room wears a more understated modern look, with grey walls, unclothed tables and views over the manicured lawns. Expect brasserie buzz rather than a country-house whispering gallery, and food that does a deft job of satisfying most modern tastes. Spiced crab and saffron tortellini with brown crab aïoli in shellfish bisque has an array of appetising flavours in it, while pickled quince and raisin purée sharpen up a slice of chicken liver pâté. Lamb two ways presents braised shoulder and fried rump on quinoa with a thoroughgoing Moroccan-spiced jus, though grilled steaks are the principal main-course draw. Chocolate and raspberry delice sprinkled with amaretti crumbs is a classy finisher.

Chef Craig Thomas **Owner** Mr Scott Bernard **Seats** 38, Pr/dining room
Times 12-3/6-10 **Wines** 8 bottles over £30, 16 bottles under £30, 9 by glass
Parking 120 **Notes** Sunday L £15.95-£17.95, Vegetarian available, Children welcome

WILTSHIRE

BEANACRE   Map 4 ST96

Beechfield House Hotel, Restaurant & Gardens

◉ Modern British

tel: 01225 703700 **SN12 7PU**
email: reception@beechfieldhouse.co.uk **web:** www.beechfieldhouse.co.uk
dir: *M4 junct 17, A350 S, bypass Chippenham, towards Melksham. Hotel on left after Beanacre*

Contemporary country-house dining

Beechfield House, built in 1878 as a private residence in the Venetian style, became a hotel in the 1960s and gently updated to meet 21st-century requirements. Soft classical music is just right for the handsome restaurant, with its chandelier, rug on the wooden floor, a large gilded mirror above the mantelpiece and Roman blinds at the windows. The expressive cooking follows a contemporary theme and keeps things fairly simple, turning out ham hock and cider terrine with pear and apricot chutney, then slowly roast shoulder of local lamb with root vegetables and a gratin of potato and sweet potato. A masterful handling of seafood brings on the likes of sautéed scallops with pancetta, cauliflower purée and truffle butter, and a main course of fish stew with mussels, chorizo and parmesan. There's a dab hand at desserts behind such offerings as pear and almond tart with deeply flavoured chocolate and single-malt ice cream.

Owner Chris Whyte **Seats** 70, Pr/dining room 20 **Times** 12-2/7-9.30, Closed 23-26 & 31 Dec, 1 Jan **Prices** Fixed L 2 course £15, Starter £6-£8.95, Main £16.95-£18.95, Dessert £6.50-£9.50 **Wines** 21 bottles over £30, 27 bottles under £30, 10 by glass **Parking** 70 **Notes** Sunday L £19.50-£21.50, Vegetarian available, Children welcome

BOX   Map 4 ST86

The Northey Arms

◉ British, European NEW

tel: 01225 742333 **Bath Rd SN13 8AE**
email: thenorthey@ohhcompany.co.uk **web:** www.ohhpubs.co.uk
dir: *Between juncts 17 & 18 of M4, on A4 between Bath & Corsham*

Comforting pub grub with a local flavour

Looking rather swish after top-to-toe renovation, this old stone-built inn has been brought up to full 21st-century spec with seagrass chairs, pine tables and boldly-patterned wallpaper in the split-level dining area and bar, and a clear focus on food. The kitchen is right on the money when it comes to local sourcing and fresh, forthright seasonal flavours. Locally-reared 32-day-aged steaks get star billing – perhaps a 14oz T-bone if you're feeling peckish – and come chargrilled with mushrooms, vine tomatoes, triple-cooked chips, and a choice of classic sauces. Otherwise, kick off with fishcakes with mango and chilli salsa, followed by pan-roasted lamb rump with ratatouille, rosemary potatoes, spinach and red wine jus. Fish is brought in daily from Looe to appear in ideas such as red mullet matched with saffron mash, glazed baby onions and roast red pepper sauce.

Chef Chris Alderson **Owner** Mark Warburton **Seats** 70 **Times** 12-10,
All-day dining, Closed 25-26 Dec, D 31 Dec, 1 Jan **Prices** Prices not confirmed,
Service optional **Wines** 19 bottles over £30, 38 bottles under £30, 17 by glass
Parking 40 **Notes** Sunday L, Vegetarian available, Children welcome

BRADFORD-ON-AVON   Map 4 ST86

The Muddy Duck

◉ Modern British

tel: 01225 858705 **Monkton Farleigh BA15 2QH**
email: dishitup@themuddyduckbath.co.uk **web:** www.themuddyduckbath.co.uk
dir: *M4 junct 18/A46 Batheaston/A363 to Bradford on Avon then turning to Monkton Farleigh & follow road to village*

Hearty modern dining in revamped pub

This wisteria-clad, stone-built 17th-century inn has been transformed in recent years from a simple local boozer into a switched-on dining pub. The traditional feel remains untouched – a walk-in inglenook, exposed beams and wooden floors make for a bar you'd be happy to perch at with a pint and some nibbles – but food is more of a driving force here these days. The kitchen deals in hearty modern pub grub, built on a bedrock of local produce and cooked with confidence to deliver well-defined flavours, as in a starter of confit chicken terrine and pâté with frozen grapes and sourdough toast, followed by slow-cooked, maple-glazed Wiltshire pork belly with pan-seared scallops and braised fennel. Fish might appear in the form of skate wing with braised butter beans, chorizo and salsa verde, while puddings can be as simple as good old rhubarb and custard or perhaps plum tarte Tatin with vanilla ice cream.

Chef Josh Roberts **Owner** Simon Blagden, Nigel Harris **Seats** 70
Times 12-2.30/6-9.30, Closed Xmas, D Sun **Prices** Prices not confirmed, Service optional **Wines** 19 bottles over £30, 32 bottles under £30, 12 by glass **Parking** 30
Notes Sunday L, Vegetarian available, Children welcome

BRADFORD-ON-AVON *continued*

The Three Gables

◉◉ Modern European V ◆ NOTABLE WINE LIST

tel: 01225 781666 **St Margaret St BA15 1DA**
email: info@thethreegables.com
dir: *M4 junct 18, A46 towards Bath, A363 Bradford-on-Avon, restaurant over Tower Bridge*

Mediterranean-influenced menu in a venerable greystone inn

The venerable greystone building opposite the town bridge looks slick indoors after an extensive restoration that brings contemporary style to the ancient exposed stonework of the first-floor dining room, which extends across the eponymous trio of gable windows. There's also a delightful patio garden at the back for alfresco dining. Co-owner (and wine expert, hence the fantastic list) Vito Scaduto takes care of things out front with unfailing Italian charm, while chef Marc Salmon brings a clear Mediterranean influence to bear on a finely-honed repertoire of contemporary dishes. Set-price lunch menus deliver stonking value – how about grilled mackerel with curried sweet potato and onion bhaji, followed by a posh take on sausage and mash, the sausage stuffed with truffled veal, with creamy champ mash and onion gravy? Trade up to the carte, and you might swap that for an assured treatment of lamb, the rump and pressed shoulder matched with potato and onion terrine, cured tomatoes and asparagus. Finish with white chocolate pannacotta with rhubarb crumble.

Chef Marc Salmon **Owner** Marc Salmon, Vito Scaduto **Seats** 55
Times 12-2/6.30-10, Closed 1-12 Jan, Sun-Mon **Prices** Fixed L 2 course £14, Fixed D 2 course £32.50, Starter £8.50-£13.50, Main £18.75-£25, Dessert £7.75-£9.25, Service optional **Wines** 200 bottles over £30, 50 bottles under £30, 16 by glass **Parking** Public car park **Notes** Children welcome

---

CALNE

Map 4 ST97

The White Horse

◉ Modern British

tel: 01249 813118 **Compon Bassett SN11 8RG**
email: info@whitehorse-comptonbassett.co.uk **web:** www.whitehorse-comptonbassett.co.uk
dir: *M4 junct 16 onto A3102, after Hilmarton village turn left to Compton Bassett*

A warm welcome and local produce

This charming old inn dates from the early 18th century and has had a long history of serving the community as bakery, grocery shop and, of course, the village pub. Today's inn gets the eating/drinking balance just right, so it's okay to prop up the bar and nurse a pint, or stick around and tuck into some unpretentious food. The menu may well be unpretentious, but it is not unimaginative. Free-range chicken liver parfait, for example, arrives with a Sauternes and chamomile jelly and brioche, while a main course fillet of sea bass is partnered by sweet Muscat risotto. There is a 'pub classics' menu, too, where home-made steak and kidney pie rubs shoulders with the house burger. For dessert, wild berry millefeuille with raspberry sorbet looks as pretty as a picture, and Sunday lunch is a traditional affair.

Chef Danny Adams **Owner** Danny & Tara Adams **Seats** 45, Pr/dining room 45
Times 12-9, All-day dining, Closed D Sun **Prices** Prices not confirmed, Service optional **Wines** 7 bottles over £30, 34 bottles under £30, 14 by glass **Parking** 45 **Notes** Sunday L, Vegetarian available, Children welcome

---

CASTLE COMBE

Map 4 ST87

The Bybrook at The Manor House, an Exclusive Hotel & Golf Club

◉◉◉ – *see below*

The Bybrook at The Manor House, an Exclusive Hotel & Golf Club ◉◉◉

CASTLE COMBE

Map 4 ST87

Modern British V ◆ NOTABLE WINE LIST

tel: 01249 782206 **SN14 7HR**
email: enquiries@manorhouse.co.uk **web:** www.manorhouse.co.uk
dir: *M4 junct 17, follow signs for Castle Combe via Chippenham*

Complex contemporary cooking in a pretty medieval village

The Manor House at the heart of the unspoilt medieval village of Castle Combe has been around since the 14th century, buffered by 365 acres of parkland. Nowadays, an 18-hole golf course draws those with an interest in stick swinging, and the high-flying contemporary country-house cooking in The Bybrook restaurant also provides a powerful attraction. The dining room is a sober setting exuding class with its mullioned windows, muted colours and pristine white linen, and the man heading up the kitchen is Richard Davies, whose face may be familiar to armchair cooks after appearances in the BBC's *Great British Menu*. His menus are built around well-thought-out and enterprising, though not deliberately startling, modern British ideas based, of course, on tip-top ingredients, a good deal of them sourced from the vicinity – the hotel's garden provides herbs and flowers to bring a dash of seasonal colour to proceedings. There's no stinting on the truffles in a first-course risotto teamed with crisp-coated chicken oyster beignets and parsley purée, while another delivers an on-trend, slow-cooked duck's egg with the assorted flavours and textures of pickled shimeji mushrooms, foie gras, celeriac velouté and pancetta. Next up, the robust flavour of pan-fried turbot fillet is matched with ceps, a fricassée of celeriac and pancetta and sherry jelly, while rump of lamb comes with cauliflower couscous, golden raisins and chocolate. The impressive technique and creativity continues with a dessert involving a capsule of mandarin cream with jasmine ice cream and raspberry meringue. While the spectacular wine list contains lots of exciting things for those with sufficient means, the sommelier has also pulled out a generous offering of good-value bottles.

Chef Richard Davies **Owner** Exclusive Hotels & Venues **Seats** 60, Pr/dining room 100 **Times** 12.30-2/7-9.30, Closed L Mon-Tue **Prices** Fixed L 2 course £25, Fixed D 3 course £62, Tasting menu £74 **Wines** 300 bottles over £30, 25 bottles under £30, 20 by glass **Parking** 100 **Notes** Tasting menu 7 course, Sunday L £35, Children 11 yrs+

COLERNE

Map 4 ST87

The Brasserie

◎◎ Modern British

tel: 01225 742777 **Lucknam Park Hotel & Spa SN14 8AZ**
email: brasserie@lucknampark.co.uk
dir: M4 junct 17, A350 towards Chippenham, then A420 towards Bristol for 3m. At Ford left to Colerne, 3m, right at x-rds, entrance on right

Smart brasserie in majestic country-house hotel

The second string to Lucknam Park's bow, The Brasserie offers a modernist, informal alternative to The Park Restaurant's fine-dinery. Located within the walled garden, with a wall of glass of its own, and right next-door to the spa, The Brasserie has a classy finish and serves up some pretty classy food, too – and there are 'healthy options' for those taking the spa detox thing seriously. There's an open kitchen, a wood-burning oven to confirm those brasserie credentials, and a team that knows what it's aiming for and keeps things simple and appealing. Start with crisp parmesan beignets, for example, with tomato salsa, avocado and herbs from the Lucknam Park gardens, or a Brinkworth blue cheese mousse with parsnip fritters, pear and walnut salad, and truffled honey vinaigrette. Slow-cooked pork belly might come in a main course with cumin sauerkraut, carrot purée, roast apple and sage, and to finish, there's the likes of satsuma, mango and pistachio in a creative trifle, or local farmhouses cheeses with chutney and crackers.

Times 7.30am-10pm, All-day dining

The Park Restaurant

◎◎◎ *– see page 544 and advert on page 545*

CORSHAM

Map 4 ST87

Guyers House Hotel

◎◎ Modern European, British

tel: 01249 713399 **Pickwick SN13 0PS**
email: enquiries@guyershouse.com **web:** www.guyershouse.com
dir: A4 between Pickwick & Corsham

Dazzling creativity in a much-changed Wiltshire farmhouse

Guyers House has been much tweaked and primped over the centuries since it began life as a simple stone farmhouse in the Restoration era. It's now a supremely elegant, peaceful country house in handsome grounds (including the de rigueur kitchen garden and orchard). A relaxing, narrow dining room looking over the lawns is patrolled by knowledgeable, friendly staff, and the menus have a real sense of creative elan to them. Begin with a fungal homage in the form of wild mushroom consommé with pickled girolles and mushroom jelly, glinting with gold leaf, or beetroot-cured salmon with orange and shallot salad. A dazzling fish course is perfectly timed brill fillets with smoked haddock raviolo, samphire, truffled cauliflower purée and a tuile dyed black with squid ink, while meat could be pork steak on merguez and bean cassoulet. The all-important chocolate and salted caramel combination comes as fondant and ice cream.

Chef Gareth John **Owner** Mr & Mrs Hungerford **Seats** 66, Pr/dining room 56 **Times** 12.30-2.30/7-9, Closed 30 Dec-3 Jan **Prices** Fixed L 2 course £22.50, Starter £7.50-£11.25, Main £18.95-£27.95, Dessert £7.95-£10.50, Service optional 10% **Wines** 9 bottles over £30, 24 bottles under £30, 5 by glass **Parking** 60 **Notes** Sunday L, Vegetarian available, Children welcome

The Methuen Arms

◎◎ British, Italian

tel: 01249 717060 **2 High St SN13 0HB**
email: info@themethuenarms.com **web:** www.themethuenarms.com
dir: M4 junct 17 onto A350 towards Chippenham, at rdbt exit onto A4 towards Bath. 1m past lights, at next rdbt turn sharp left onto Pickwick Rd, 0.5m on left

Gimmick-free appealing modern cookery in a Georgian pub

The Methuen Arms doesn't look in the least like a pub, being a Georgian building over three floors with a portico over the front door. Inside, though, real ales are dispensed at the bar, there are elm floorboards, rugs, log fires and softly neutral walls hung with local prints and etchings. 'No foams, towers or swipes,' declares the inn, promising instead simple, well-sourced and tasty food, aims it amply fulfils. Well-timed pan-fried scallops with saffron and parmesan risotto garnished with red watercress has been a notably accomplished starter, with another risotto, of leek and thyme, for chargrilled wood pigeon. Deep-fried haddock and chips and a burger are among main courses, but look elsewhere for more interest, a confident touch bringing on whole roast lemon sole say; complemented by a rich lobster and prawn sauce with crunchy broccoli tempura, and unusual pork Wellington with Jerusalem artichoke purée and wild mushrooms. Desserts can look as pretty as a picture, with a martini glass layered with vanilla pannacotta, poached rhubarb and prosecco and rhubarb jelly, and there may also be quince frangipane tart with cinnamon ice cream.

Chef Piero Boi **Owner** The Still family **Seats** 60, Pr/dining room 20 **Times** 12-3/6-10, Closed 25-26 Dec **Prices** Fixed L 2 course £17.50, Starter £5.50-£12.50, Main £13.50-£27.50, Dessert £6.50, Service optional **Wines** 29 bottles over £30, 37 bottles under £30, 14 by glass **Parking** 40 **Notes** Party menu 3 course £29.50, Early supper £17.50-£21.50, Sunday L £22.50-£26.50, Vegetarian available, Children welcome

CRICKLADE

Map 5 SU09

The Red Lion Inn

◎ Modern British

tel: 01793 750776 **74 High St SN6 6DD**
email: info@theredlioncricklade.co.uk **web:** www.theredlioncricklade.co.uk
dir: Just off A419 between Swindon & Cheltenham

Hearty food in a beer-oriented inn

It's hard to imagine a more enticing proposition than this 17th-century inn with its cosy beams, log fires and arsenal of real ales, including brews from its own Hop Kettle microbrewery. Food is taken as seriously as the beer, thanks to a kitchen that is truly passionate about local produce – the pub rears its own pigs, and veggies come fresh from locals' allotments. Take your pick from the bar for pub grub done right, or the contemporary country-chic dining room. Here the kitchen turns out switched-on, ingredients-led dishes such as pan-fried local wood pigeon with beetroot carpaccio, smoked potato purée and chervil, ahead of a three-way serving of wild rabbit (loin, confit leg and faggot) with celeriac purée, dauphinoise potato and baby vegetables. For pud, perhaps chocolate and griottine cherry sponge with chocolate sauce and home-made cookie dough ice cream.

Times 12-2.30/6.30-9, Closed 25-26 Dec, L all week, D Sun-Mon

The Park Restaurant ❀❀❀

COLERNE   Map 4 ST87

Modern British V ❦ NOTABLE WINE LIST

tel: 01225 742777 **Lucknam Park Hotel & Spa SN14 8AZ**
email: reservations@lucknampark.co.uk
web: www.lucknampark.co.uk
dir: *M4 junct 17, A350 to Chippenham, then A420 towards Bristol for 3m. At Ford left towards Colerne. In 4m right into Doncombe Ln, then 300yds on right*

Skilful, individualist cooking from a vastly experienced chef

Lucknam Park rises in Palladian splendour with its triple gable and portico entrance at the end of an immense tree-shaded drive in 500 acres of Wiltshire. The standard of upkeep throughout is reassuringly high, and the place boasts a Brasserie for informal dining, across the courtyard next to the spa. It also has the full-dress Park Restaurant, in a room shaped like an ark, but one equipped for the sailing with crystal chandelier and swagged coffee-coloured drapes. Crisply linened, well-spaced tables are attended by smoothly efficient staff, who bring a sense of occasion to a meal without pomposity. Hywel Jones is a vastly experienced chef who runs a tight ship, producing skilled and ambitious food with a high excitement factor. There is no clumsy copying of general trends here, and the innovative dishes reflect his ingenuity. An opener of poached plump Cornish langoustines topped with Exmoor's very own caviar, with light potato mousse and earthy gribiche dressing is an obvious winner, or there may be rose veal sweetbreads in pancetta with marinated salsify, given pungency with local truffles. A pairing of roast sea bass with maple-glazed chicken wing confers depth of flavour on both components by means of celeriac, chanterelles and confit baby onions, while loin and shoulder of Brecon lamb appears in spring array with peas and wild garlic, new season's morels, a smoky onion risotto and Wye Valley asparagus. Dessert might be a brandy snap filled with lemon and almond mousse, alongside a vanilla-poached peach, blood orange, and an improbably rich yogurt sorbet.

Chef Hywel Jones **Owner** Lucknam Park Hotels Ltd **Seats** 80, Pr/dining room 30 **Times** 12-3/6-10, Closed Mon, L Tue-Sat, D Sun **Prices** Fixed L 3 course £39, Fixed D 3 course £80, Tasting menu £105, Service optional **Wines** 8 bottles under £30, 12 by glass **Parking** 80 **Notes** Sunday L £39, Children 5 yrs+

DEVIZES
Map 4 SU06

The Peppermill
◎◎ British NEW

tel: 01380 710407 **4O Saint John's St SN1O 1BL**
email: philip@peppermilldevizes.co.uk **web:** www.peppermilldevizes.co.uk
dir: *In market place of town centre, opposite Santander Bank*

Unpretentious modern food in a lively venue

In a period building dating from the 15th century, The Peppermill is light, bright and contemporary on the inside. This family-run restaurant with rooms has style: six modern boutique bedrooms, a café where coffee is taken seriously, a wine bar with an excellent choice by the glass, and a restaurant that impresses with its contemporary, feel-good menu. Relaxed and informal service suits the mood of the place. In the evening you might start with BBQ-infused slow-roasted pork belly with carrot 'slaw', or potted shrimps with home-made brioche. Move on to a perfectly timed piece of swordfish with buttered cod cheeks and celeriac and vanilla purée, or 10oz rib-eye steak with triple-cooked chips and a choice of sauce. For dessert, the chocolate pot with home-made vanilla shortbread and sticky toffee pudding are just the job. At lunchtime, there are open sandwiches and wraps plus salads and light bites (a risotto for example), plus steaks, salmon and chicken cooked on the grill. It is a popular place so it's worth booking ahead.

Chef Leon Sheppard **Owner** Philip & Amanda O'Shea **Seats** 60, Pr/dining room 12
Times 12-2.30/5.30-9.30, Closed D Sun **Prices** Starter £4.95-£9.95, Main £13.95-£25.95, Dessert £4.50-£7.50 **Wines** 40 bottles over £30, 30 bottles under £30, 12 by glass **Parking** On street, Station Rd car park **Notes** Sunday L £6.50-£21, Vegetarian available, Children welcome

FONTHILL BISHOP
Map 4 ST93

The Riverbarn
◎ Modern British NEW

tel: 01747 820232 **SP3 5SF**
email: info@theriverbarn.org.uk **web:** www.theriverbarn.org.uk
dir: *1m off A303 signed to Fonthill Bishop, on B3089 between Chilmark & Hindon*

Local produce in a charming rural setting

Some parts of the cottagey Riverbarn date back 600 years or so and the place has served the community in various ways over the centuries. Today the property is in the safe hands of the Sutcliffe family and they're a winning team. The idyllic riverside setting and idyllic garden play their part in setting the mood, as does the charming service from mum and dad (Jill and Ian), with the simple decor and relaxed atmosphere recalling similar places across the Channel in France. The kitchen is the domain of sons Jonny and Tom, with the focus on local produce and evident modernity in the construction of dishes in starters such as mullet céviche with crispy mullet and pickled ginger, for example. Roast rump of Wilshire lamb is a fine main course, cooked just right, or go for hake from South Western waters. Finish with limoncello parfait with English raspberries and mint syrup.

Chef Jonny & Tom Sutcliffe **Owner** Ian & Jill Sutcliffe **Seats** 40
Times 12-2.30/6.30-9, Closed Xmas & New Year, Mon, D Sun, Tue & Wed (ex for B&B guests) **Prices** Fixed L 2 course £20, Fixed D 3 course £25, Starter fr £5.50, Main fr £14, Dessert fr £6 **Wines** 13 bottles over £30, 17 bottles under £30, 12 by glass **Parking** 30 **Notes** Sunday L, Vegetarian available, Children welcome

FOXHAM
Map 4 ST97

The Foxham Inn
◎ Modern British

tel: 01249 740665 **SN15 4NQ**
email: info@thefoxhaminn.co.uk **web:** www.thefoxhaminn.co.uk
dir: *Off B4069 between Sutton Benger & Lyneham*

Local pub with imaginative menu based on local produce

The family behind The Foxham are an industrious bunch, producing a range of jams, chutneys and sauces, as well as running this red-brick country inn and restaurant with its locally-sourced food and B&B accommodation. A passion for provenance runs right through the menu, and dishes list producers and regional affiliations. There are some bright ideas on the menu, too, with an appealing rusticity, and lots of big flavours. Start with Dorset snails with pancetta, chorizo and lentils in a dish guaranteed to quicken the pulse of a trencherman or woman, or there might be a savoury crème brûlée to catch the eye (made with leeks and Brinkworth blue cheese). Main courses might see breast of Tiddenham duck in a classic combo with braised red cabbage and dauphinoise potatoes, or pea risotto enriched with brie and elevated by shavings of Wiltshire truffles. Finish with bread-and-butter pudding with prune and Armagnac parfait.

Chef Neil Cooper **Owner** Neil & Sarah Cooper **Seats** 60
Times 12-2.30/7-11, Closed 1st 2 wks Jan, Mon **Prices** Fixed L 2 course £15-£18, Fixed D 3 course £28-£31, Tasting menu £35, Starter £6-£9, Main £12-£20, Dessert £6-£9 **Wines** 9 bottles over £30, 27 bottles under £30, 10 by glass **Parking** 16 **Notes** Sunday L £12-£24, Vegetarian available, Children welcome

HIGHWORTH

The Highworth
◎◎ Modern British NEW v

tel: 01793 762364 **1 Westrop SN6 7HJ**
email: info@thehighworth.com **web:** www.thehighworth.com
dir: *Phone for directions*

Technically complex, ambitious cooking in Georgian splendour

This handsome balustraded redbrick Georgian townhouse is the focal point of an appealing Cotswold market town with historic shopping streets and a listed building seemingly every which where you look. There is plenty of evidence of its past in the panelled walls and old fireplaces, but the dining room is done in understated modern style. Supplied partly from the concealed kitchen garden, the kitchen is aiming loftily with a style of British modernism that's high on technical skill and complexity, and described in contemporary menu-speak. That accounts for the garlic moss and rye soil that form the underlay for a presentation of quail that features the sliced breast, rolled confit leg and soft-boiled egg. Main course might be an alternating arrangement of breast of Downs lamb with parmesan pomme purée, dressed in tapenade and scattered with olives, a dish of striking impact, or perhaps a double-act of gilt-head bream and braised oxtail with peas and morels in parsley oil. More soil is hefted at dessert stage, this time of shortbread for a pear study that centres on delicately rendered millefeuille with matching mousse and sorbet.

Chef Chris Lovell **Owner** Bob Rae **Seats** 30, Pr/dining room 30 **Times** 12-2.30/7-9 Closed 25 Dec **Prices** Starter £6-£13, Main £14-£24, Dessert £6-£8.45, Service optional **Wines** 10+ bottles over £30, 10+ bottles under £30, 6 by glass **Parking** 20 **Notes** Sunday L £15.50-£17.95, Children welcome

HORNINGSHAM
Map 4 ST84

The Bath Arms at Longleat

Modern, Traditional British

tel: 01985 844308 **Longleat Estate BA12 7LY**
email: enquiries@batharms.co.uk **web:** www.batharms.co.uk
dir: A36 Warminster. At Cotley Hill rdbt 2nd exit (Longleat), Cleyhill rdbt 1st exit. Through Hitchcombe Bottom, right at x-rds. Hotel on the green

Charming boutique hotel with accomplished cooking

A creeper-covered stone building, The Bath Arms is in a picturesque village within the Longleat Estate. Local ales are dispensed in the friendly bar, with the restaurant a more formal-looking room with upmarket decor, chandeliers and sconces, and paintings on the walls. The kitchen takes pride in sourcing produce from within 50 miles of the estate and in keeping within broadly British parameters. Ham hock and chicken terrine with piccalilli or beetroot-cured salmon with horseradish mousse may precede game and ale pie in rich gravy with seasonal vegetables or pan-fried sea bream with sunblush tomatoes, samphire, rocket and sautéed potatoes, all technically correct and full of distinct flavours. Breads are made in-house, as are puddings such as rhubarb and coconut crumble with coconut ice cream, or Earl Grey pannacotta with blood orange sorbet.

Times 12-2.30/7-9

LITTLE BEDWYN
Map 5 SU26

The Harrow at Little Bedwyn

– see page 548

LOWER CHICKSGROVE
Map 4 ST92

Compasses Inn

Modern British

tel: 01722 714318 **SP3 6NB**
email: thecompasses@aol.com **web:** www.thecompassesinn.com
dir: Off A30 signed Lower Chicksgrove, 1st left onto Lagpond Ln, single-track lane to village

Broadly appealing menu in an ancient inn

Dating from the 14th century, this thatched country inn is a charming place, with its low beams and standing timbers, stone walls, wooden booths, log fires and a cheery, friendly atmosphere and informal, smiley staff. The menus are more cosmopolitan than the surroundings would suggest, and it's clear that a highly professional brigade is at the stoves. Starters range from grilled pickled mackerel with radish and fennel salad and dill dressing to a canonical version of foie gras and chicken liver terrine with apricot and ginger chutney. There are 'traditionals', such as beer-battered hake with chips and tartare sauce, but there is adventure elsewhere, for example in duck breast in a Szechuan pepper glaze with basmati rice, or accurately timed whole grilled Dover sole with lemon butter and herby gnocchi. Imaginative desserts stretch to ricotta and orange tart with cherry sorbet, and chocolate torte with mango ice cream.

Chef Dan Cousins, Ian Chalmers **Owner** Alan & Susie Stoneham **Seats** 50, Pr/dining room 14 **Times** 12-3/6-11, Closed 25-26 Dec, L Mon (Jan-Mar) **Prices** Starter £5.50-£8.25, Main £8.95-£22.50, Dessert £4.75-£6.50, Service optional **Wines** 2 bottles over £30, 28 bottles under £30, 8 by glass **Parking** 35 **Notes** Sunday L £10.50-£17.95, Vegetarian available, Children welcome

MALMESBURY
Map 4 ST98

Whatley Manor Hotel and Spa

– see page 549

PEWSEY
Map 5 SU16

Red Lion Freehouse

– see page 550 and advert on page 551

PURTON
Map 5 SU08

The Pear Tree at Purton

Modern British

tel: 01793 772100 **Church End SN5 4ED**
email: stay@peartreepurton.co.uk **web:** www.peartreepurton.co.uk
dir: From M4 Junct 16, follow signs to Purton. Turn right at Best One shop, hotel 0.25m on right

Conservatory dining in a former vicarage

Not a village pub as the name might suggest, but in fact a former vicarage turned into a country-house hotel. Situated in glorious gardens that extend to a meadow, wetlands and a vineyard, the place has been run by the same family for 25 years and is geared up to cater for business meetings, weddings, and anyone looking to escape to the country. The restaurant has made an impression with its take on contemporary British food, and the charm of its conservatory setting. There's no shortage of global flavours on the menu – as is the modern British way – so starters run to smoked chicken timbale fired up with wasabi and pickled ginger, or a chicken breast served satay style. There's a refinement to the kitchen's output: the anything-but-humble pear and celeriac soup (with horseradish cream and sage oil), and main-course roasted loin of cod with an accompanying rösti enriched with fresh crab. Finish with a nicely tart glazed lemon tart. Check out the cuvée Alix produces on the owners' own vineyard.

Chef Adam Conduit **Owner** Anne Young **Seats** 50, Pr/dining room 50
Times 12-2/7-9.15, Closed 26 Dec, D 25 Dec **Prices** Fixed L 2 course £15, Starter £6.50-£7.50, Main £14.50-£25.50, Dessert £7-£9, Service optional **Wines** 15 bottles over £30, 25 bottles under £30, 9 by glass **Parking** 30 **Notes** Afternoon tea £15, Sunday L £23, Vegetarian available, Children until 8.30

The Harrow at Little Bedwyn ❀❀❀

LITTLE BEDWYN Map 5 SU26

Modern British V 🍷 NOTABLE WINE LIST

tel: 01672 870871 **SN8 3JP**
email: office@theharrowatlittlebedwyn.com
web: www.theharrowatlittlebedwyn.com
dir: *Between Marlborough & Hungerford, well signed*

A shining beacon of quality food and wine in deepest Wiltshire

The Harrow sounds like a rustic gastro-pub and it does indeed look like many red-brick, creeper-clad Victorian country inns. That assessment, however, falls way short of the mark. Inside, it's another story. Tastefully modernised, its pale walls are hung with artwork, high-backed upholstered dining chairs are pulled up to white-clothed tables on the polished floorboards, and a double-sided wood burner adds a homely touch to the interconnecting dining rooms. It's a look that leaves no doubt that this is a place where food is taken seriously. Chef-patron Roger Jones has built up a remarkable network of suppliers over the years, buying only natural and free-range produce, much of it from artisan growers and traders. He has also set himself high culinary aspirations, pulling off some first-class work, as seen in a stunning starter of Pembroke lobster where two pieces of immaculately cooked tail are served in the shell, a claw is fried in a light, crisp coating and it's all enhanced by spiced Halen Mon sea salt, baby coriander leaves and a sweet lobster sauce. This is cooking that eschews silly fads and treats top-quality ingredients with intelligence, sensitivity and real skill. Next up, a crunchy crumb-coated bonbon is packed with moist pieces of duck and matched with earthy Puy lentils and

creamy mousse of rich foie gras balanced with the contrasting acidity of Pedro Ximenez sherry – a faultless dish where every element is there for a reason. A platter of intricate mini-desserts with a chocolate and passionfruit theme ends on a high note. Roger is something of an authority on wine and has assembled a remarkable 70-page list with expertise and enthusiasm, with suggested pairings for every dish.

Chef Roger Jones, John Brown **Owner** Roger & Sue Jones **Seats** 34
Times 12-3/7-11, Closed Xmas & New Year, Sun-Tue
Prices Tasting menu fr £50, Starter £15, Main £30, Dessert £9.50,
Service optional **Wines** 750 bottles over £30, 250 bottles under
£30, 20 by glass **Parking** On street **Notes** Fixed L 5 course with
wine £40, Gourmet menu 8 course £75, Children welcome

Whatley Manor Hotel and Spa @@@@

MALMESBURY   Map 4 ST98

Modern French V | NOTABLE WINE LIST

tel: 01666 822888 **Easton Grey SN16 0RB**
email: reservations@whatleymanor.com
web: www.whatleymanor.com
dir: *M4 junct 17, follow signs to Malmesbury, continue over 2 rdbts. Follow B4040 & signs for Sherston, hotel 2m on left*

Technically brilliant cooking in a luxury spa hotel

There's a genuine feeling of expectation as the gated entrance swings open into Whatley Manor's cobbled courtyards of honeystone Cotswold buildings – but that's as it should be, since Whatley Manor has long sat in the top flight of the UK's country-house hotels. Insulated from the real world by 12 acres of meadows, woodland, and fabulous gardens, Whatley is one of those places where absolute attention to detail drives every aspect of its operation. Built in the 18th century, the place was called Twatley Manor until the 1980s, when a judicious name change came with its conversion to a hotel and serious money was lavished on ensuring its rambling wood-panelled lounges sit seamlessly alongside a more contemporary aesthetic. A top-class spa takes care of the pampering side of things, while gastronomes will be getting all lathered up by the prospect of chef Martin Burge's astounding cooking in the Dining Room, a quietly refined, understated space of pale bamboo wood floors, buttermilk walls, and subtle lighting. Having honed his craft in the legendary kitchens of Pied à Terre, L'Ortolan and Raymond Blanc's Le Manoir aux Quat' Saisons, it should come as no surprise that the cooking is French-focused, contemporary, and looks jaw-droppingly

beautiful on the plate. Delivered via a trio of seven-course tasting menus, including a vegetarian version, phenomenal precision and luxury are there from the off in a composition involving caramelised foie gras dressed with compressed pear and ginger, and sticky Sauternes sauce. Produce is, naturally, as good as you can get, and flavours and textures come razor-sharp – perhaps Cornish turbot steamed and served with oyster and lime cannelloni, compressed cucumber and champagne-caviar sauce. Meat-based courses could focus on intensely flavoured, poached and roasted veal, partnered by slow-braised cheek, hazelnut textures, caramelised sweetbread and Madeira sauce – a bravura performance of technical fireworks. There's real finesse, too, in a dish marking the transition from savoury to sweet – black truffle ice cream dressed with creamed Roquefort, deep-fried Crottin goats' cheese and candied walnuts. A palate-cleansing play on clementine served with mandarin sorbet and juniper foam comes before a finale of tropical fruit with banana pannacotta, coconut ice cream and passionfruit curd. The wine list brims with interesting options, with a top-class sommelier to help you pinpoint the one for you. The Swiss chalet-style Le Mazot brasserie, meanwhile, offers everything from duck terrine with foie gras butter to a classic Swiss cheese fondue, or a steak cooked on a hot stone at the table.

Chef Martin Burge **Owner** Christian & Alix Landolt **Seats** 40, Pr/dining room 30 **Times** 7-10, Closed Mon-Tue, L all week
Prices Tasting menu £110 **Wines** 350 bottles over £30, 5 bottles under £30, 16 by glass **Parking** 120 **Notes** Tasting menu additional 10% service charge, Children 12 yrs+

RAMSBURY

Map 5 SU27

The Bell at Ramsbury

 Modern British, European

tel: 01672 520230 **The Square SN8 2PE**
email: reservations@thebellramsbury.com **web:** www.thebellramsbury.com
dir: M4 junct 14, A338 to Hungerford. B4192 towards Swindon. Left to Ramsbury

Ambitious cooking in made-over country inn

The 300-year-old Bell is the epitome of that modern phenomenon, the old village boozer reinvented as a smart contemporary food-oriented inn. Dazzlingly whitewashed outside, and made over in an almost Scandinavian-looking, pared-back contemporary style indoors, the place has an easy-going ambience that welcomes walkers and canine companions. The Shaker-style Café Bella tea room does cakes and snacks, while the bar sorts out real ale fans with a pint of Ramsbury Brewery's finest to go with pub classics like daily pies, burgers, and beer-battered fish and triple-cooked chips. Trade up to the more formal restaurant for more ambitious dishes built on local materials, bolstered by home-grown produce from the kitchen garden. Leek and mussel pâté with crisp breaded mussels and braised red peppers precedes venison (from the Ramsbury Estate) with celeriac mash, red cabbage and roasted carrots, or pan-fried duck breast with a bonbon of spiced leg meat, roasted tomatoes and couscous might appeal. For dessert, golden syrup adds depth to a crème brûlée paired with caramelised puff pastry and mandarin sorbet.

Times 12-3/6-9.30, Closed D Sun

ROWDE

Map 4 ST96

The George & Dragon

 Modern British, Mediterranean V

tel: 01380 723053 **High St SN10 2PN**
email: thegandd@tiscali.co.uk **web:** www.thegeorgeanddragonrowde.co.uk
dir: On A342, 1m from Devizes towards Chippenham

Tudor inn with Cornish seafood and more

This Tudor coaching inn stands on the main road through the unassuming village of Rowde, not far from Devizes. It's long had a solid reputation as a destination dining venue for the area, and is an attractively traditional country inn with lots of bare wood in furniture and floors. The daily-changing menu of modern pub food makes a fitting speciality of seafood hauled in from the boats at St Mawes, Cornwall. A simply grilled kipper on toast will satisfy anyone who skipped breakfast, but Cajun-spiced fishcakes with chilli dipping sauce are on hand too. A brochette of chargrilled scallops and black pudding slices may be taken as either starter or main, while the principal listing gets stuck into whole grilled lemon sole, mackerel with anchovy butter, or swordfish with rocket and parmesan. If seafood isn't your bag, beef fillet or rack of lamb may fit the bill, and it all finishes with chocolate and raspberry roulade, or 'ye olde lemon posset', its qualifier referring, we trust, to the historic nature of its recipe.

Chef Christopher Day **Owner** Christopher Day **Seats** 35 **Times** 12-3/7-11, Closed D Sun **Prices** Fixed L 2 course fr £16.50, Fixed D 3 course fr £19.50, Starter £6-£10, Main £10-£35, Dessert fr £6 **Wines** 4 bottles over £30, 4 bottles under £30, 9 by glass **Parking** 14 **Notes** Sunday L £19.50, Children welcome

Red Lion Freehouse

PEWSEY

Map 5 SU16

British

tel: 01980 671124 **East Chisenbury SN9 6AQ**
email: enquiries@redlionfreehouse.com **web:** www.redlionfreehouse.com
dir: Exit A303, at rdbt take A345 to Enford, right into East Chisenbury. Pub located on right

Top-class produce handled with great skill

A thatched pub in a pretty village in an Area of Outstanding Natural Beauty, you'll not stumble across the Red Lion by chance, so be sure to put SN9 6AQ into your Sat-Nav, or make sure you've got a good map reader on board, for this place is worth seeking out. It's run by Guy and Britt Manning with passion and enthusiasm, and when you hear that Guy learnt his trade at Wandsworth's Chez Bruce and the iconic Per Se in New York (where Britt was working on the pastry section), you'll gather it's rather the foodie destination. Every effort is made to maintain the pub feel of the place, with a relaxed atmosphere and some comforting pub grub and sandwiches up for grabs. Even when the chef pulls out all the stops, it's still the sort of flavour-focused, down-to-earth stuff that people actually want to eat. They grow veg in raised beds and in a greenhouse, keep their own chickens and pigs, and just about everything is made in-house. There's a Mediterranean spin to a starter of saffron-braised squid with crisp polenta and fennel salad, or go for a warm crab tart with dressed gem leaf salad. The simplicity and joy of sitting by the log-burner and tucking into roast rib of Wiltshire beef with hand-cut chips and béarnaise sauce is just what this place is all about. Skrei cod is a seasonal treat, served with ceps purée and sauce almondine, and, when it comes to dessert, choose between a classic crème brûlée or the more contemporary (and exotic) coconut and lime tapioca with compressed pineapple and mango and passionfruit sorbet. Stay in one of the five boutique rooms across the road, complete with beautiful views of the surrounding countryside.

Chef Guy & Brittany Manning **Owner** Guy & Brittany Manning **Seats** 45, Pr/dining room 25 **Times** 12-2.15/6-9, Closed D 24-25 Dec **Prices** Fixed L 2 course fr £18, Tasting menu fr £75, Starter £7-£10, Main £18-£30, Dessert £7-£10 **Wines** 31 bottles over £30, 19 bottles under £30, 20 by glass **Parking** 14 **Notes** Prix fixe menu 2 course £18, Sunday L £18-£25, Vegetarian available, Children welcome

Red Lion Freehouse
TROUTBECK GUEST HOUSE

East Chisenbury, Pewsey, Wiltshire SN9 6AQ
Tel: 01980 671124
Website: www.redlionfreehouse.com
Email: enquiries@redlionfreehouse.com

Situated in the heart of Wiltshire, *The Red Lion Freehouse* is a charming thatched pub dating back to Tudor times. Chef-owners Guy and Brittany Manning along with the team offer a warm welcome and encourage a relaxed atmosphere whether you are staying for the weekend in our boutique guest house or just popping in for a quick pint. The *Red Lion* is synonymous with seasonal, locally sourced produce and a home-made philosophy which includes everything from smoked and cured meats to the bitters used in cocktails.

Having held a Michelin star since 2012 and proudly achieving 3 AA rosettes, the *Red Lion* provides its guests with food, drink and accommodation of the highest standard. Located on the edge of Salisbury plain and just 15 minutes from World heritage site Stonehenge, it provides an ideal base from which to explore the stunning Wiltshire country side and beyond.

SALISBURY

Map 5 SU12

Salisbury Seafood & Steakhouse

Modern, Traditional International

tel: 01722 417411 & 424110 **206 Castle St SP1 3TE**
email: info@salisburyseafoodandsteakhouse.co.uk
web: www.salisburyseafoodandsteakhouse.co.uk
dir: From A36 at rdbt on Salisbury ring road, right onto Churchill Way East. At St Marks rdbt left onto Churchill Way North to next rdbt, left in Castle St

More than surf and turf in a stylish setting

The restaurant is part of the Milford Hall Hotel, an extended Georgian mansion in pretty gardens. It's a smartly appointed room, with a blond-wood floor, brown and cream high-backed dining chairs and one wall occupied by bottles of wine. You can dine very well on a seafood starter of pan-fried scallops with minted pea purée, crisp pancetta and balsamic syrup before a 28-day dry-aged steak with a choice of sauces: perhaps rib-eye with garlic and lime mayonnaise. But there's more to enjoy on the menu than surf and turf. Start with carpaccio with parmesan and rocket and go on to chargrilled butterflied chicken breast with lime and herb butter, chips, herb-grilled tomatoes and watercress, or pork, green pepper and mushroom stroganoff. Bring a meal to a happy conclusion with a dessert like apricot and frangipane tart with custard, or Baileys and orange cheesecake dusted with chocolate.

Chef Chris Gilbert **Owner** Simon Hughes **Seats** 55, Pr/dining room 20 **Times** 12-2/6-10 **Prices** Fixed D 3 course fr £24.95, Starter £6.25-£9.90, Main £11.50-£27, Dessert £5.95-£7.25, Service optional **Wines** 2 bottles over £30, 32 bottles under £30, 11 by glass **Parking** 60 **Notes** Sunday L £9.95-£15.95, Vegetarian available, Children welcome

SWINDON

Map 5 SU18

Chiseldon House Hotel

Modern European, British

tel: 01793 741010 **New Rd, Chiseldon SN4 ONE**
email: welcome@chiseldonhouse.com **web:** www.chiseldonhouse.com
dir: M4 junct 15, A346 signed Marlborough. After 0.5m turn right onto B4500 for 0.25m, hotel on right

Unfussy fine dining in a Regency manor house

The grand Regency manor house is a popular wedding venue, with the Marlborough Downs and attractive gardens providing a stunning backdrop, and the M4 handy for ease of access. The restaurant is a bright, opened-up dining room with smartly laid tables (white linen and all) and a cheerful service team. The cooking takes a fine-dining stance, with lots going on and an eye for presentation. A starter of pan-fried wood pigeon comes with rhubarb purée, crispy lardons and black pepper sauce, another pairing is poached pear with pickled walnuts and Oxford Blue cheese. Main-course stuffed neck of lamb is served with cannellini bean and leek confit and a minted jus, fishy mains depend on what has been landed at Brixham. For dessert, bitter chocolate tart comes with an Amaretto-flavoured pannacotta and toasted almonds.

Times 12-2/7-9

WARMINSTER

Map 4 ST84

The Bishopstrow Hotel & Spa

Modern British

tel: 01985 212312 **Borenam Rd BA12 9HH**
email: info@bishopstrow.co.uk **web:** www.bishopstrow.co.uk
dir: From Warminster take B3414 (Salisbury). Hotel signed

Modish British cooking in a light-filled elegant Regency house

Surrounded by 27 acres of grounds alongside the River Wylye, Bishopstrow is a creeper-clad Regency mansion that has been discreetly reinvented as a glossy country-house hotel with a cool contemporary spa. The tone throughout is airy and elegant, with neutral tones and light from full-length windows suffusing the dining rooms. The team in the kitchen put together vibrant contemporary menus, supported by top-class ingredients from the estate and local area. Pork and pigeon terrine with red onion marmalade, pickled beets and radishes is a typical starter. The main course might see Wiltshire lamb given a workout in the form of cutlet, shoulder and sausage matched with cumin cauliflower, and chard and gruyère gratin. Baileys pannacotta with chocolate fondue provides a suitably luscious finale, or you could go savoury with West Country cheeses.

Times 12-2/7-9.30

The Dove Inn

British, European

tel: 01985 850109 **Corton BA12 0SZ**
email: info@thedove.co.uk **web:** www.thedove.co.uk
dir: Off A36, Salisbury to Bath road, signed to Corton. Follow Station Road for 3m, pub on right

Something-for-everyone menu at the village pub

Fleeing the tourist throngs at Stonehenge, you might profitably escape to the Dove at Corton, a village pub that has been spruced up in light modern style, including the addition of a small conservatory, where dining extends from the main restaurant area and bar. On offer is a fairly large menu with something for everyone, from burgers and magnificent pies to sense-of-occasion Sunday lunches. The global classic cookbook is raided for proper crispy duck with hoi sin and pancakes or an Indian thali platter to start, and then canonical beef Stroganoff full of mushrooms, brandy and cream. If you're more of a modernist, you might opt for scallops with crisped Parma ham, followed by venison loin and bubble-and-squeak in chocolate and juniper jus, while satiating yourself in the gooiest way at the end with honeyed pecan pie and caramel ice cream.

Chef Bruno Fitas, Sarah Hoddinott **Owner** William Harrison-Allan **Seats** 60 **Times** 12-2.30/6-9, Closed 25 Dec **Prices** Starter £5.50-£8.95, Main £11.75-£21.95, Dessert £5.75-£6.95, Service optional **Wines** 11 bottles over £30, 15 bottles under £30, 5 by glass **Parking** 20 **Notes** Sunday L, Vegetarian available, Children welcome

WORCESTERSHIRE

BEWDLEY

Map 10 SO77

The Mug House Inn

Modern British

tel: 01299 402543 **12 Severnside North DY12 2EE**
email: drew@mughousebewdley.co.uk **web:** www.mughousebewdley.co.uk
dir: B4190 to Bewdley. On river, just over bridge on right

Inventive modern British pub cookery

Bewdley once boasted 71 licensed premises, and while the drinking scene may be somewhat curtailed these days, this old charmer remains. A mug house was the unvarnished name for a boozer in centuries gone by, and this Georgian example is an entirely pleasing place, with hanging baskets adorning the white façade, and views of river traffic on the Severn. Lively ideas start with king prawns dressed in crisp vodka and tonic-infused batter and spiked with sautéed shallots, chilli, garlic-smoked salt and sweet chilli and lime dipping sauce. They continue in a main-course assiette of pork that features roast loin, slow-roasted belly, pulled pork croquettes flavoured with sage and apple, and home-made black pudding served with onion and thyme purée, mustard mash, warm slaw and a red wine reduction. To finish, 'Pimm's Mess' is a mash-up of meringue, cream, Pimm's syrup, strawberries, mint and cucumber sorbet.

Chef Drew Clifford, Mark Rhoden **Owner** Drew Clifford **Seats** 26, Pr/dining room 12 **Times** 12-2.30/6.30-9, Closed D Sun **Prices** Fixed D 3 course fr £16.50, Starter £5.25-£6.95, Main £12.95-£29.50, Dessert £5.25-£7.95, Service optional **Wines** 1 bottle over £30, 26 bottles under £30, 10 by glass **Parking** Car park 100mtrs along river **Notes** Fixed D Mon-Thu only, Sunday L, Vegetarian available, Children 10 yrs+

Royal Forester Country Inn

🏵 Modern European

tel: 01299 266286 **Callow Hill DY14 9XW**
email: royalforesterinn@btinternet.com **web:** www.royalforesterinn.co.uk
dir: *Phone for directions*

Contemporary dining in medieval inn

This historic inn was built in 1411 but the interior of the Royal Forester is more a reflection of 21st-century tastes. There are ancient beams and exposed brick walls, certainly, and plenty of nooks and crannies, but with boutique bedrooms and a bar filled with tub chairs and sofas, it chimes with our times. The simple and smart restaurant is the setting for a menu of classically-inspired dishes featuring seafood shipped up from Cornwall and some items foraged by the chef himself. Start with the modern classic that is seared king scallops with local black pudding and cauliflower purée before moving on to spiced duck breast with a honey and anise jus. Steaks cooked on the grill are served with hand-cut chips, or find a willing accomplice and go for the roast rib of beef on the bone. Finish with a light lemon tart with Chantilly cream.

Chef Mark Hammond **Owner** Sean McGahern, Maxine Parker **Seats** 60, Pr/dining room 18 **Times** 12-3/6-9.30 **Prices** Fixed L 2 course £13.99, Fixed D 3 course £16.99, Starter £5-£10, Main £14-£26, Dessert £5-£6.50, Service optional **Wines** 14 bottles over £30, 34 bottles under £30, 6 by glass **Parking** 25 **Notes** Gourmet menu with wine £30 1st Tue of month, Sunday L £10-£15, Vegetarian available, Children welcome

▌ BROADWAY
Map 10 SP03

The Broadway Hotel

🏵 Traditional British

tel: 01386 852401 **The Green, High St WR12 7AA**
email: info@broadwayhotel.info **web:** www.cotswold-inns-hotels.co.uk/broadway
dir: *Follow signs to Evesham, then Broadway. Left onto Leamington Rd, hotel just off village green*

Nifty modern cooking in an atrium

The Broadway Hotel, overlooking the village green, has its roots in the 16th century, so Tattersalls Brasserie, in a contemporary, light-filled atrium, is a stark contrast to its traditional surroundings. The kitchen focuses on quality seasonal produce and has an assured sense of what will work, turning out appealing starters of seared scallops with chickpea and cauliflower curry and pickled cucumber, and seared mackerel fillet on crab bisque with diced roasted celeriac. Main courses maintain the momentum with Lighthorne lamb three ways (roast rump, slow-cooked shoulder and devilled kidney, all tender and full of flavour) with root vegetable gratin and rosemary sauce, a selection of steaks, and perhaps pan-fried hake fillet winningly accompanied by langoustine risotto and mousse, orange-braised fennel and a parsley fritter. Ambition doesn't falter with puddings of caramelised pineapple tart served with basil and mint syrup and basil ice cream.

Chef Eric Worger **Owner** Mr & Mrs Horton **Seats** 60 **Times** 12-3/7-9.30 **Prices** Prices not confirmed, Service optional **Wines** 3 bottles over £30, 23 bottles under £30, 13 by glass **Parking** 15 **Notes** Prix fixe 2/3 course £15.50/£18.50, Sunday L, Vegetarian available, Children welcome

Dormy House Hotel

🏵🏵 Modern British ⓥ

tel: 01386 852711 **Willersey Hill WR12 7LF**
email: reservations@dormyhouse.co.uk **web:** www.dormyhouse.co.uk
dir: *2m E of Broadway off A44, at top of Fish Hill turn for Saintbury/Picnic area. In 0.5m turn left, hotel on left*

Creative cooking in an impressive Cotswold house

Dormy House, a honeystone property perched above Broadway with views of the Cotswolds, has all the comforts of a contemporary hotel, with oak beams and panelling reminders of its 17th-century origins. The restaurant, an open-plan, airy room, has been given a modern look, and large windows give stunning views over the flower garden and beyond. Under chef Jon Ingram, the kitchen delivers full-flavoured, well-composed and uncluttered dishes that are distinctly in the contemporary British idiom. Watercress velouté is silky-smooth, rich and peppery, garnished with air-dried ham and a poached egg, or there may be treacled smoked salmon with Guinness bread and caviar cream for a touch of posh. At mains, roasted cod is a well-timed piece of fish, served on wilted cabbage in an excellent mussel and bacon jus, while beef fillet is gently poached and comes with salt beef hash and smoked onion marmalade for deeply resonant savoury and sweet notes. Dessert ideas are resoundingly successful too: unctuous honey and almond parfait sits on a thin layer of cobnut sponge with a spiced half plum.

Chef Jon Ingram **Owner** The Sorensen family **Seats** 75, Pr/dining room 14 **Times** 12.30-2.30/7-9.30, Closed L Mon-Sat **Prices** Service optional **Wines** 125 bottles over £30, 65 bottles under £30, 30 by glass **Parking** 70 **Notes** Sunday L £28, Children welcome

The Lygon Arms

🏵🏵 Modern British

tel: 01386 852255 **High St WR12 7DU**
email: thelygonarms@thehotelcollection.co.uk **web:** www.thehotelcollection.co.uk
dir: *From Evesham take A44 signed Oxford, 5m. Follow Broadway signs. Hotel on left*

Majestic Tudor hotel with 21st-century comforts

Fans of period dramas can live the dream at The Lygon Arms. This historic place has been offering up hospitality to weary travellers since the 16th century and has included Oliver Cromwell and Charles I as former visitors (doubtless not at the same time). The glorious honey-coloured exterior can't have changed much in all that time, but the interior – while keeping hold of a host of original features – is fit and ready for the modern traveller, whether that's for business or pleasure. The main restaurant occupies the Great Hall, an impressive space with a minstrels' gallery and no shortage of period charm, but rest assured a smart finish ensures comfort all round. The menu takes a contemporary approach while showing evident respect for classical ways. Start with breast of wood pigeon in the earthy company of Puy lentils, wild mushrooms and pancetta and move on to hake with lobster and razor clams, or a duo of mallard with a fig tarte Tatin. Finish with an intricate and elegant chocolate dessert.

Chef Ales Maurer **Owner** The Hotel Collection **Seats** 80, Pr/dining room 80 **Times** 12-2/7-9.30, Closed L Mon-Sat **Prices** Fixed D 3 course £39.50-£45, Starter £8.50-£13, Main £24.50-£34, Dessert £9.95-£11, Service optional **Wines** 14 bottles over £30, 48 bottles under £30, 24 by glass **Parking** 150 **Notes** Sunday L, Vegetarian available, Children welcome

BROADWAY *continued*

Russell's

◉◉ Modern British

tel: 01386 853555 **20 High St WR12 7DT**
email: info@russellsofbroadway.co.uk **web:** www.russellsofbroadway.co.uk
dir: *A44 follow signs to Broadway, restaurant on High St opposite village green*

Modern cooking in a paradise of honey-coloured stone

In a prime spot on the High Street of this pretty, touristy village, Russell's is smartly decked out in contemporary style, with a terrace to the front and a patio to the rear. The kitchen sources its materials from around the Cotswolds and uses them to good effect in its sharply inventive dishes. Pressed pig's head terrine, its meat falling apart at the touch of a fork, is a well-executed starter, served with warm red wine jus and chunks of salsify and turnips braised in red wine, an alternative to seared scallops with celeriac, prunes and Parma ham. Main courses are defined by their stimulating flavours and textures and imaginative compositions. Roast breast and confit leg of duck, for instance, is accompanied by juniper sauce, spicy pear and blackcurrant crumble and fondant potato, and fillets of stone bass with caponata, olives, parmesan polenta and trendy basil foam. Puddings are a wow and get heads turning: a light plum soufflé, say, with subtle Earl Grey pannacotta, a few poached plums and frothy almond foam.

Chef Neil Clarke **Owner** Andrew Riley **Seats** 60, Pr/dining room 14
Times 12-2.30/6-9.30, Closed BH Mon, 1 Jan, D Sun **Prices** Fixed L 2 course £16.50, Fixed D 2 course £16.50, Starter £7-£14, Main £15-£28, Dessert £7-£8, Service optional **Wines** 50 bottles over £30, 18 bottles under £30, 12 by glass **Parking** 7
Notes Sunday L £23.95-£26.95, Vegetarian available, Children welcome

---

▮ **BROMSGROVE** Map 10 SO97

The Vernon

◉ Modern European, British

tel: 01527 821236 **Droitwich Rd, Hanbury B60 4DB**
email: info@thevernonhanbury.com **web:** www.thevernonhanbury.com
dir: *A38 onto B4091 Hanbury Road, on junct with B4090*

Enticing cooking in revamped 18th-century inn

The 18th-century Vernon has been reinvented as a classy inn for the 21st century with sleek contemporary looks and boutique rooms should you want to stay over and give the menu a full workout. Lightwood furniture looks the part in the bar, while the restaurant sports wooden floors and chairs upholstered in coloured fabrics, and there's an extensive outdoor area. Up-to-date food based on fresh local produce does the job, too, starting with the likes of local Hartlebury asparagus jollied up with a crispy hen's egg, or warm crab and saffron savoury custard tart with watercress. Main courses could see rack and shoulder of lamb partnered with crushed Jersey Royals, carrots and pea and broad bean salsa verde, or roast smoked sea trout with crab and herb gnocchi, samphire and lemon. Leave room for puddings like peanut butter cheesecake with dark chocolate sorbet and caramel.

Chef Joseph Robert Watzlawek **Owner** Vernon Leisure Ltd **Seats** 73, Pr/dining room 24 **Times** 12-3/6-9.30 **Prices** Fixed L 2 course £16.95, Starter £5-£8, Main £9-£18, Dessert £5-£7, Service optional **Wines** 22 by glass **Parking** 50 **Notes** Sunday L, Vegetarian available, Children welcome

---

▮ **CHADDESLEY CORBETT** Map 10 SO87

Brockencote Hall Country House Hotel

◉◉◉ – *see opposite*

▮ **EVESHAM** Map 10 SP04

Wood Norton Hotel

◉ Modern British **NEW**

tel: 01386 765611 **Wood Norton WR11 4YB**
email: info@thewoodnorton.com **web:** www.thewoodnorton.com
dir: *M42 junct 3. Follow A435 towards Alcester, A46 Evesham. At Evesham Football Club rdbt 2nd exit onto A46. Evesham Country Park rdbt follow A44 Worcester, over 2 rdbts hotel on right*

Focused modern cooking in fabulous Victorian house

The hall was built in the late 19th century as an upmarket hunting lodge to attract European royalty, or such as was left of it. Interiors are fabulously rich, with chandeliers and wood panelling everywhere, and the dining room looks over the south terrace towards Bredon Hill and beyond. Low lighting creates a cocoon-like effect in the evenings, emphasised by acoustics that are more gentle murmurs than clamorous babble. The modern British repertoire is given a thorough workout for dishes that combine sharply focused flavour and thoughtful combination from the intricate likes of a starter of monkfish carpaccio with scallops, crispy seaweed and caramelised baby gem, to the assured simplicity of loin and belly of pork with apple purée, baby carrots and Savoy cabbage. Chocolate and cherry variations at dessert bring on chocolate crumble and poached cherries, with more of the fruit in parfait and sorbet forms.

Chef Paul Hudson **Owner** Wrigop Ltd **Seats** 60, Pr/dining room 140
Times 7-9.30, Closed L all week (ex special occasions) **Prices** Prices not confirmed, Service optional **Wines** 35 bottles over £30, 35 bottles under £30, 9 by glass
Parking 70 **Notes** Vegetarian available, Children welcome

▮ **KIDDERMINSTER** Map 10 SO87

The Granary Hotel & Restaurant

◉◉ Modern British

tel: 01562 777535 **Heath Ln, Shenstone DY10 4BS**
email: info@granary-hotel.co.uk **web:** www.granary-hotel.co.uk
dir: *On A450 between Worcester & Stourbridge. 2m from Kidderminster*

Smart, seasonal contemporary cooking in a boutique hotel

Close to the Midlands motorway arteries, yet nicely set in the countryside on the fringes of Kidderminster, the boutique-style Granary Hotel boasts its own market garden to supply the kitchen with the ultimate in low-mileage fruit and veg. The key players in the kitchen brigade have worked together for the best part of a decade, developing contemporary style of cooking that is all about working with the seasons and bringing great ingredients together in well-considered compositions. Given that the restaurant is about as far from the coast as it is possible to be in the UK, the team displays impressive dedication to sourcing fresh fish and seafood, and it is presented without fuss in a starter of sautéed king scallops in a classic pairing with crispy belly pork, sweet potato and apple. Main course brings a well-balanced combination of Barbary duck breast with glazed Parmentier potatoes, creamed cabbage, redcurrants and red wine jus. To finish, vanilla pannacotta gets a lift from fresh strawberries and crunchy honeycomb.

The Granary Hotel & Restaurant

Chef Anthony Phillips **Owner** Richard Fletcher **Seats** 60, Pr/dining room 16 **Times** 12-2.30/7-11, Closed L Mon, Sat, D Sun **Prices** Fixed L 2 course £12.95-£14.95, Fixed D 3 course £19.50-£22.50, Starter £6-£10.50, Main £15-£22.50, Dessert £5.25-£6.50, Service optional **Wines** 2 bottles over £30, 35 bottles under £30, 12 by glass **Parking** 95 **Notes** Sunday L £17.95, Vegetarian available, Children welcome

See advert on page 557

Stone Manor Hotel

@ Traditional **NEW**

tel: 01562 777555 **Stone DY10 4PJ**
email: enquiries@stonemanorhotel.co.uk **web:** www.stonemanorhotel.co.uk
dir: 2.5m from Kidderminster on A448, hotel on right

Modernist dishes and old-fashioned flambé shows

Having been devastated by fire, the manor was rebuilt in half-timbered style in the 1920s with requisitioned wood from the last British sailing-ship to go into battle, HMS Arethusa. Under new ownership now, its 25 acres of seductive gardens make it a covetable wedding venue, and in Fields restaurant, it has a space for appealing modern brasserie food with obvious roots in tradition. Flambé dishes cooked before your delighted eyes have been productively revived, so that beef fillet or chicken breast can be set alight with vodka or brandy. Before that, the more modernist likes of pork belly terrine with kiwi, raisins and sweet potato crisps in cider and ginger glaze might have set things on a course that continues with grey mullet and mussels with lemon and redcurrant couscous in saffron and parmesan cream. Finish with spiced plum crumble, served with sweet plum gnocchi, honeycomb and cinnamon crème fraîche.

Chef Paul Harris **Owner** Helena Hogarth **Seats** 60, Pr/dining room 26 **Times** 12-2/7-9.30 **Prices** Fixed L 2 course £15, Fixed D 3 course £26.95, Starter £8.95-£11.95, Main £14.95-£28.95, Dessert £6.95-£8.50, Service optional **Wines** 13 bottles over £30, 40 bottles under £30, 6 by glass **Parking** 300 **Notes** Sunday L £19.95, Vegetarian available, Children welcome

Brockencote Hall Country House Hotel ❀❀❀

CHADDESLEY CORBETT   Map 10 SO87

Modern British **V**
tel: 01562 777876 **DY10 4PY**
email: info@brockencotehall.com **web:** www.brockencotehall.com
dir: A38 to Bromsgrove, off A448 towards Kidderminster

Authoritative modern cookery in a grand Victorian manor house

The distinctly palatial Victorian manor house looks most striking when reflected in the waters of its ornamental lake, a principal feature of the 70 acres of landscaped gardens and parkland in which Brockencote Hall stands. The Chaddesley Restaurant is a stately vision of country-house luxury after recent refurbishment, its tables dressed in crisp linen and laid with elegant cutlery and glassware beneath a frosted-glass skylight, and provides a suitably elegant backdrop for bright, beautifully-presented food with a contemporary British tone. Adam Brown is in charge of the gastronomic show, and shows a clear fondness for regional produce, including foraged wild ingredients (the hall's grounds provide a cornucopia of seasonal goodies, including honey from their own hives), which he transforms with cutting-edge culinary technique into some exciting explorations of taste and texture. As you'd expect these days, there's a seven-course tasting option, but if you prefer to choose your own dishes, three-course market menus offer five choices at each stage.

Everything is there for a reason in Brown's compositions, witness a starter of confit duck ballotine that is spiked with little tart bursts of capers, offset with the sharpness of pickled cherries and cherry purée, and garnished with sweet walnuts. The construction of dishes shows a sound grasp of what works with what, partnering pan-fried halibut with various treatments of celeriac (purée, salt-baked and marinated), lovage and tender baby squid, or perhaps serving Goosnargh duck breast with nothing more outré than baby gem lettuce, beetroot and duck hearts. Technically impressive textural interplays shine once again at dessert, when apricots are delivered poached and in jelly, gel and mousse forms to contrast with vanilla pannacotta.

Chef Adam Brown **Owner** Eden Hotel Collection **Seats** 40, Pr/dining room 16 **Times** 12-2/6.45-9.45, **Prices** Fixed L 2 course £22.95, Fixed D 3 course £42.95-£59.95, Tasting menu £75, Service optional **Wines** 120 bottles over £30, 16 bottles under £30, 12 by glass **Parking** 50 **Notes** Afternoon tea £19.50, Sunday L £32.50, Children welcome

MALVERN
Map 10 SO74

L'Amuse Bouche Restaurant
◉◉ Modern French V

tel: 01684 572427 **51 Graham Rd WR14 2HU**
email: reservations@cotfordhotel.co.uk web: www.cotfordhotel.co.uk
dir: *From Worcester follow signs to Malvern on A449. Left into Graham Rd signed town centre, hotel on right*

Gentle French modernity with an episcopal past

Built in the mid-19th century in soft-focus Gothic as a summer bolt-hole for the Bishop of Worcester, complete with private chapel secure from the throngs of the devout, the Cotford Hotel is still in the rest-and-recreation business after all these years. The chapel is now L'Amuse Bouche restaurant, an attractive room with russet and gold wallpaper and a mirrored wall to give the illusion of space. The menu has moved in the direction of gentle French modernity. Loch Fyne scallops are flamed in anisette and served on a bed of wild mushrooms, samphire and tarragon with powdered pancetta, while mains deliver cider-braised pork belly stuffed with black pudding or, for the veggies, cranberry, apple and chestnut tart with cashews in basil cream sauce. To finish, dark chocolate mousse is laced with Amaretto and covered in raspberry foam, while the signature dessert is a banana Tatin scented with rosemary, served with clotted cream ice cream.

Chef Christopher Morgan **Owner** Christopher & Barbara Morgan **Seats** 40 **Times** 12-1.30/6-8.30, Closed L Mon-Sat **Prices** Starter £6-£9, Main £16.95-£23.95, Dessert £6.95, Service optional **Wines** 10 bottles over £30, 26 bottles under £30, 10 by glass **Parking** 15 **Notes** Pre-theatre menu, Sunday L £19.95-£24.95, Children welcome

The Cottage in the Wood Hotel
◉◉ Modern British ⚭ NOTABLE WINE LIST

tel: 01684 588860 **Holywell Rd, Malvern Wells WR14 4LG**
email: reception@cottageinthewood.co.uk web: www.cottageinthewood.co.uk
dir: *3m S of Great Malvern off A449, 500yds N of B4209, on opposite side of road*

Ambitious cooking in charming hotel

This former Georgian dower house sits in a spectacular location on a wooded hillside with panoramic views across the Severn Valley, so arrival while it is still light is advisable – unless you're stopping over for the night, in which case the view will be a stunning surprise in the morning. The family-run hotel is also home to the Outlook Restaurant, where tables by the windows are in demand. The kitchen turns out classically inspired food with gently contemporary leanings that suit the refined setting. Begin with a tarte fine of confit duck and rhubarb, flavoured with orange and ginger, or ravioli packed with crab and crayfish and dressed in crab bisque. Main courses are along similar lines, so bream and red mullet are brought together with cauliflower purée and pea and pancetta salad, and a meat option

might be pan-roasted poussin with an accompanying mushroom and leek pie. Finish with bitter chocolate tart with pistachio ice cream.

The Cottage in the Wood Hotel

Chef Dominic Pattin **Owner** The Pattin family **Seats** 70, Pr/dining room 20 **Times** 12.30-2/7-9.30 **Prices** Starter £5.45-£10.45, Main £11.95-£23.95, Dessert £2.95-£6.95, Service optional **Wines** 359 bottles over £30, 86 bottles under £30, 12 by glass **Parking** 40 **Notes** Pre-theatre D from 6pm, L menu Mon-Sat, Sunday L £18.95-£23.95, Vegetarian available, Children welcome

The Malvern
◉ Modern British

tel: 01684 898290 **Grovewood Rd WR14 1GD**
email: enquiries@themalvernspa.com web: www.themalvernspa.com
dir: *A4440 to Malvern. Over 2 rdbts, at 3rd turn left. After 6m, left at rdbt, over 1st rdbt, hotel on right*

Contemporary brasserie dining in the Malvern Hills

The very first spa resort in the town, The Malvern opened its doors back in 1910 to satisfy the demands of the Edwardian public. It's changed a bit since then. In fact, the interior is spellbindingly modern and capacious. The spa has all the bells and whistles you might imagine, and there's also a brasserie restaurant if you're seeking fulfillment of a different kind. It's a fresh-looking contemporary space with muted neutral tones, wooden tables and local artworks on the walls. The menu follows a bright and breezy brasserie-style format, so you might start with something very of the moment such as slow-cooked pork belly with black pudding, cauliflower purée, spaghetti crackling and sage jus, or go for the Asian flavours of Thai green mussels. Main-course baked lemon sole is served on the bone, and for dessert, caramel, banana and rum pannacotta comes with raisin purée, banana sorbet and vanilla-poached prunes.

Times 12-3/7-9.30

OMBERSLEY
Map 10 SO86

The Venture In Restaurant
◉◉ British, French

tel: 01905 620552 **Main Rd WR9 0EW**
dir: *From Worcester N towards Kidderminster on A449 (approx 5m). Left at Ombersley turn. Restaurant 0.75m on right*

Exceptional cooking in a crooked medieval house

Behind the half-timbered façade of this 15th-century property is a restaurant with bags of ancient character from its ceiling beams and standing timbers, with large brown leather-look dining chairs at the tables. Chef-patron Toby Fletcher stamps his own style on a modern Anglo-French repertory, carefully sourcing quality produce and handling it confidently and imaginatively. Chicken, guinea fowl and foie gras terrine has been a startlingly successful starter, its richness cut by oven-dried grapes, with a sherry vinegar and shallot dressing, with another option being steamed home-smoked haddock fillet with spinach, leeks and Mornay glaze. Effective, well-balanced combinations are also evident in main courses: perhaps pan-fried hake fillet on leek, saffron and tarragon risotto with an intense shellfish sauce, or seared pork fillet and confit belly with a Tatin of beetroot and goats' cheese and sage sauce. Extras like breads and petits fours are all of a standard, as are moreish puddings of Valrhona chocolate parfait with a delightful mango and passionfruit crumble.

Chef Toby Fletcher **Owner** Toby Fletcher **Seats** 32, Pr/dining room 32
Times 12-2/7-9.30, Closed 25 Dec-1 Jan, 2 wks summer & 2 wks winter, Mon, D Sun
Prices Fixed L 2 course fr £26, Fixed D 3 course fr £40, Service optional **Wines** 38 bottles over £30, 35 bottles under £30, 6 by glass **Parking** 15, On street
Notes Sunday L £30, Vegetarian available, Children 12 yrs+ D

UPTON UPON SEVERN   Map 10 SO84

White Lion Hotel

◉ Modern British, European

tel: 01684 592551 **21 High St WR8 OHJ**
email: info@whitelionhotel.biz **web:** www.whitelionhotel.biz
dir: *From A422 take A38 towards Tewkesbury. After 8m take B4104 for 1m, after bridge turn left to hotel*

Historic hotel with contemporary feel and flavour

The author Henry Fielding put up here while writing Tom Jones, and the White Lion also played a booze-fuelled part in the Civil War, but fascinating as the 16th-century inn's history may be, the place has stayed in tune with current trends without impacting on its immense character. Nowadays, the interior works a cheerfully updated look in the Pepperpot Brasserie, blending black timbered walls filled with blocks of yellow ochre, apricot, and terracotta colour with bare chunky oak tables and high-backed chairs. Food-wise, the deal is straightforward combinations and big-hearted flavours on a menu that has something for all-comers. Seared scallops are skewered on a rosemary sprig and matched with roast butternut squash purée and chorizo, ahead of a hearty plate of mustard- and herb-crusted roast rump of lamb served with bubble-and-squeak, celeriac purée and

rosemary jus. Baked apple crème brûlée with butterscotch sauce is a properly indulgent pudding.

Times 12-2/7-9.15, Closed 31 Dec-1 Jan, L few days between Xmas & New Year, D 24 Dec

EAST RIDING OF YORKSHIRE

BEVERLEY   Map 17 TA03

The Pipe and Glass Inn

◉◉ Modern British **v** ♦ NOTABLE WINE LIST

tel: 01430 810246 **West End, South Dalton HU17 7PN**
email: email@pipeandglass.co.uk
dir: *Just off B1248*

Superior modern cooking in stylish country inn

With its neat, creamy paintjob and red pantiles the 15th-century Pipe and Glass has been well cared for by its current owners and prepped to meet the demands of the discerning 21st-century visitor. It's still very much a pub – something the local community must be very grateful for – but it's also a dining destination in its own right, with a deserved reputation for contemporary British cuisine. The rustic bar has a smart finish with Chesterfield chairs and sofas, and a wood-burning stove, while the restaurant is dominated by horse-themed prints and chunky wooden tables. The industrious and creative team in the kitchen deliver arresting options such as a starter cheesecake made with Yellison goats' cheese and partnered with beetroot macaroon, golden beets and candied walnuts. It all seems entirely in keeping with the setting and chimes with the times. Carry on with slow-cooked, crispy shoulder of lamb (with devils on horseback and burnt onion purée) and finish with warm treacle tart with eggnog ice cream and nutmeg custard. The wine list is a cracker, too.

Chef James Mackenzie **Owner** James & Kate Mackenzie **Seats** 100, Pr/dining room 28 **Times** 12-2/6-9.30, Closed 25 Dec, 2 wks Jan, Mon (ex BHs), D Sun **Prices** Prices not confirmed, Service optional **Wines** 13 by glass **Parking** 60 **Notes** Sunday L, Children welcome

GOOLE
Map 17 SE72

The Lowther Hotel
◉ Modern British **NEW**

tel: 01405 767999 **Aire St DN14 5QW**
email: info@lowtherhotel.co.uk **web:** www.lowtherhotel.co.uk
dir: *M62 junct 36, 3rd exit at rdbt, then 1st exit at rdbt onto A614. Right onto Boothferry Rd, right onto Mariners St, left onto Stanhope St. At rdbt take 4th exit onto North St, right onto Aire St*

Modern cooking in a resurrected Regency hotel

Built near the docks in 1827 by Sir Edward Banks, who constructed London Bridge and Waterloo Bridge over the Thames, the renovated Lowther's industrial heritage is overlaid with a smart contemporary boutique look. Its Burlington Restaurant is a snappy modern brasserie-style space in tones of red and cream, with leather chairs and bare tables setting the tone for straightforward up-to-date food. Built around good quality seasonal ingredients that the kitchen sources from local farms and trusted suppliers, a starter of rainbow trout is served with caper mayonnaise, smoked pea purée and chervil, followed by Gressingham duck breast with pearl barley, beetroot, carrot, shallots and celeriac. If you're in the mood for fish, monkfish might come with purple kale, samphire, cauliflower purée and Parma ham. Dessert is a satisfying confection involving rhubarb and ginger cheesecake, orange sponge and gel, and rhubarb sorbet.

Chef Scott Braithwaite **Owner** Julie & Howard Duckworth **Seats** 32, Pr/dining room 30 **Times** 12-2/5-8.30, Closed L Mon-Sat, D Sun **Prices** Fixed D 3 course £24.95, Starter £3.95-£5.25, Main £9.95-£17.95, Dessert £3.95-£6.95 **Wines** 6 bottles over £30, 15 bottles under £30, 3 by glass **Parking** 15 **Notes** Sunday L £4.95-£8.95, Vegetarian available, Children welcome

WILLERBY
Map 17 TA03

BEST WESTERN Willerby Manor Hotel
◉ Modern European

tel: 01482 652616 **Well Ln HU10 6ER**
email: willerbymanor@bestwestern.co.uk **web:** www.willerbymanor.co.uk
dir: *M62/A63, follow signs for Humber Bridge, then signs for Beverley until Willerby Shopping Park. Hotel signed from rdbt next to McDonald's*

Solid brasserie cooking with borad appeal

In the tranquil East Riding of Yorkshire, only four miles from Hull, Willerby Manor is a thoroughly modern kind of establishment. Physiotherapy and sports rehabilitation are among the offerings, and dining takes place in a contemporary room combining wood tones and leafy green, with bare tables and attractive views over the gardens. A blackboard menu lists the many specials of the day, and the core of the operation is solid brasserie cooking and feel-good flavours. Sandwiches and wraps are inveigled in-between starters – salmon and asparagus quiche with champagne-dressed salad, or creamy mushroom pâté and Yorkshire Blue butter – and the main business. The last might be Cajun-rubbed pork medallions with couscous, battered courgettes and pineapple salsa, or sage gnocchi with chicken livers and wild garlic. Tropical flavours pour forth from a dessert of lychee bavarois with coconut ice cream and passionfruit jelly.

Chef David Roberts, Ben Olley **Owner** Alexandra Townend **Seats** 40, Pr/dining room 40 **Times** 10-10, All-day dining, Closed 25 Dec **Prices** Starter £6.10-£6.50, Main £6.25-£19.50, Dessert £4.65-£6.90, Service optional **Wines** 16 bottles under £30, 14 by glass **Parking** 200 **Notes** Sunday L £12-£15, Vegetarian available, Children welcome

NORTH YORKSHIRE

ALDWARK
Map 19 SE46

The Aldwark Arms
◉◉ Modern, Traditional British

tel: 01347 838324 **YO61 1UB**
email: peter@aldwarkarms.co.uk
dir: *Phone for directions*

Characterful Yorkshire country pub

Under the ownership of the Hardisty family since December 2013, The Aldwark got a smart refit, including a wood-burning stove. The welcoming character of this timbered pub in the Vale of York remains, with log-fires in winter, a kitchen garden terrace in kinder weather, hand-pumped ales and a plethora of locally-sourced produce. Expect an ambitiously extensive menu, bolstered by weekly specials, and there is much to entice. Seafoodies will be drawn to a starter of prawns, crayfish and white crabmeat stuffed into smoked salmon cornets, or there might be a tartlet of Mediterranean vegetables and goats' cheese with salad dressed in walnut oil. Main courses encompass favourites such as Thai green chicken curry or pasta carbonara, as well as sea bass in a Moroccan manner with chickpeas, courgettes and spinach. Game season turns up breast and confit leg of locally shot pheasant with bacon in port and juniper jus. Desserts are chalked up on the blackboards, and may include banoffee pie with vanilla ice cream.

Chef David Sandford, Jim Wilkinson **Owner** Peter, Ian & Andrew Hardisty **Seats** 74, Pr/dining room 12 **Times** 12-2/5.30-9 **Prices** Service optional **Wines** 3 bottles over £30, 27 bottles under £30, 8 by glass **Parking** 30 **Notes** Early bird 5.30-7pm 1-3 course £8.95-£16.95, Sunday L £10.95-£18.95, Vegetarian available, Children welcome

ARKENGARTHDALE
Map 18 NY90

Charles Bathurst Inn
◉ British

tel: 01748 884567 **DL11 6EN**
email: info@cbinn.co.uk **web:** www.cbinn.co.uk
dir: *B6270 to Reeth, at Buck Hotel turn N to Langthwaite, pass church on right, inn 0.5m on right*

Seasonal contemporary menus in a Dales inn

The CB, as it's familiarly known, is in Arkengarthdale – a tributary valley of celebrated Swaledale, five miles down the road from the lively market village of Reeth. It's named after a Georgian parliamentarian, and is done out with today's preferred light wood, with plenty of space between tables in the raftered dining room. Local farmers and fishermen supply much of the larder, which results in seasonally-changing menus of modern Yorkshire cooking. It's shown off to best effect on the Mirror Menu, where Whitby crab and avocado tian with lime and shallots comes with vivid saffron dressing, or a fine Scotch egg accompanied by home-made piccalilli and mustard-dressed saladings. After that, there may be a heartily sustaining casserole of local beef and Masham's Black Sheep ale, with a suet dumpling and leek mash, or salmon fillet with puréed celeriac and braised fennel. Look out for classically garnished roast grouse in the game season, and make space for desserts such as baked vanilla cheesecake with cranberry compôte.

Chef Gareth Bottomley **Owner** Charles Cody **Seats** 70, Pr/dining room 60 **Times** 12-2.30/6-9, Closed 25 Dec **Prices** Prices not confirmed **Wines** 15 bottles over £30, 20 bottles under £30, 10 by glass **Parking** 25 **Notes** Sunday L, Vegetarian available, Children welcome

ASENBY — Map 19 SE37

Crab Manor

◉◉ Modern British, European **V**

tel: 01845 577286 **Dishforth Rd YO7 3QL**
email: enquiries@crabandlobster.co.uk **web:** www.crabandlobster.co.uk
dir: A1(M) junct 49, on outskirts of village

Long-running non-minimalist seafood dining

Crab Manor is all about unique selling-points, with its mix of Georgian manor house, thatched lodge, Scandinavian pine-cabins and new garden rooms. Each of the guestrooms is themed to a different international style and, in the Crab & Lobster restaurant, it offers a dining operation that's also overflowing with personality. Again, there are various settings, from a garden terrace to a room hung in profusion with fishing nets and pots, saucepans and a military drum – understated minimalism be damned. Loyal supporters who have been packing the place for years come back for traditional seafood specialities cooked with flair and accuracy. Fresh plump blue-shelled mussels cram a hearty marinière, or might go Belgian with a preparation of cabbage, bacon and ale. Mains run to roast stone bass in bouillabaisse broth with chargrilled courgettes and baby fennel, or lobster thermidor that incorporates scallops and prawns. Ox cheek in port and Madeira pacifies the meat constituency, and it all ends with shortcrust lemon tart served with lemon curd ice cream, with added zing from orange and pink grapefruit segments.

Chef Steve Dean **Owner** Kymel Trading **Seats** 85, Pr/dining room 16 **Times** 12-2.30/7-9 **Prices** Fixed L 2 course £19-£22, Starter £5.50-£12, Main £13-£22.50, Dessert £7-£17, Service optional **Wines** 12 bottles over £30, 27 bottles under £30, 8 by glass **Parking** 80 **Notes** Sunday L, Children welcome

AUSTWICK — Map 18 SD76

The Traddock

◉◉ Modern British

tel: 01524 251224 **Settle LA2 8BY**
email: info@thetraddock.co.uk **web:** www.thetraddock.co.uk
dir: From Skipton take A65 towards Kendal, 3m after Settle turn right signed Austwick, cross hump back bridge, hotel 100yds on left

Modern British with Mediterranean undercurrents

To answer the question on all our lips, 'traddock' is a portmanteau word for a trading paddock, and became the nickname of the house when it was built on such a site in the 1740s. The Yorkshire Dales extend gloriously all around the characterful stone house, which has been appointed in opulent country-interiors style rather than rustic plain. A vigorous rendition of British modernism is the stock-in-trade, with overlays of various Mediterranean traditions. A white-truffled pumpkin and chestnut risotto is one way to start, or there might be salmon three ways – tartare, herbed ballotine and a gravad lax spin cured in beetroot, vodka and dill – garnished with Keta caviar. Pedigree meats for main include braised herb-stuffed shoulder of Old Spots pork with dauphinoise and roasted vegetables in sweet tomato sauce, while fish might be baked halibut in lemon and caper butter. Finish with properly rich sticky toffee pudding and vanilla ice cream.

Chef John Pratt **Owner** The Reynolds family **Seats** 36, Pr/dining room 16 **Times** 12-3/6.30-11 **Prices** Starter £4.95-£6.95, Main £14.95-£23.95, Dessert £5.90-£7.95, Service optional **Wines** 24 bottles over £30, 26 bottles under £30, 16 by glass **Parking** 20, On street **Notes** Afternoon tea, Sunday L £9.95-£17.95, Vegetarian available, Children welcome

AYSGARTH — Map 19 SE08

The Aysgarth Falls

◉ Modern British **NEW**

tel: 01969 663775 **DL8 3SR**
email: info@aysgarthfallshotel.com **web:** www.aysgarthfallshotel.com
dir: On A684 between Leyburn & Hawes

Imaginative cooking in traditional village inn

When you're exploring the Yorkshire Dales, schedule a pitstop at this traditional pub with rooms in the pretty village of Aysgarth, whether it's for a pint of locally brewed Black Sheep ale in the bar or for a meal in the contemporary restaurant overlooking the lovely garden and grounds. Modern British cooking is the deal here and there's plenty of ambition in the kitchen, right down to the striking presentation. Start with a well-timed line-caught east coast mackerel fillet with pickled kohlrabi, radish, cucumber and squid ink cracker, following on with a vibrant and well-executed main course of pan-roast venison, potato purée, swede and carrot, turnip, haggis fritter, beetroot, blackberry and heritage potatoes. Finish, perhaps, with forced Yorkshire rhubarb served with Earl Grey crème brûlée, poached rhubarb, rhubarb granita, red vein sorrel and ginger snap biscuit.

Chef Gavin Swift **Owner** Steve & Heather Swann **Seats** 45, Pr/dining room 14 **Times** 12-2.30/6-8.45 **Prices** Starter £4.50-£7.50, Main £10-£20, Dessert £1.50-£6.50, Service optional **Wines** 1 bottle over £30, 22 bottles under £30, 5 by glass **Parking** 25 **Notes** Sunday L £11-£19, Vegetarian available, Children welcome

BAINBRIDGE — Map 18 SD99

Yorebridge House

◉◉◉ – see page 560

BOLTON ABBEY — Map 19 SE05

The Burlington Restaurant

◉◉◉◉ – see page 561

The Devonshire Brasserie & Bar

◉ Traditional British

tel: 01756 710710 & 710441 **Bolton Abbey BD23 6AJ**
email: res@devonshirehotels.co.uk
dir: On B6160, 250yds N of junct with A59

Smart brasserie cooking in a top-class country hotel

The Devonshire Arms has a lot going for it, from its fabulous position on the 30,000-acre estate, the luxe bedrooms and high-end restaurant, but don't forget about the Brasserie & Bar. It sets the pace for a more informal experience, with colourfully upholstered chairs and local artworks displayed on the whitewashed walls, and generates a happy buzz. There are tables on the terrace too, to increase the feel-good factor. The menu deals in upscale modern brasserie food, with a Yorkshire flavour, so you might tuck into ham hock terrine with salt-baked beetroot and red wine mustard dressing, before cod with chorizo and crushed new potatoes, or fine pork belly with creamed sprouts and mash. There's creativity in desserts, too: perhaps set Yorkshire yogurt with apple compôte, cinnamon crumble and apple sorbet, or a version of rhubarb crumble with toasted almond ice cream.

Chef Adam Smith, Sean Pleasants **Owner** The Duke & Duchess of Devonshire **Seats** 60 **Times** 12-2.30/6-9.30 **Prices** Starter £5.95-£10, Main £14.50-£28, Dessert £6-£7.50 **Wines** 30 bottles over £30, 30 bottles under £30, 16 by glass **Parking** 40 **Notes** Sunday L fr £16.95, Vegetarian available, Children welcome

Yorebridge House 🏵🏵🏵

BAINBRIDGE Map 18 SD99

Modern British **V**  NOTABLE WINE LIST

tel: 01969 652060 **DL8 3EE**
email: enquiries@yorebridgehouse.co.uk
web: www.yorebridgehouse.co.uk
dir: *A648 to Bainbridge. Yorebridge House N of centre on right before river*

Refined cuisine and great wines

Yorebridge began life as a schoolhouse in the Victorian era, where the grim discipline must have been leavened a little by its tranquil riverside setting in a greystone Dales village. The entire surrounding countryside of the Dales National Park makes this a covetable place for a contemporary restaurant with rooms, and the place is decorated throughout to a high standard, with daylight pouring through windows and skylights into a dining space adorned with gilt-framed mirrors, chandeliers and potted plants. The fixed-price menus offer a version of country-house cooking that has some modernist touches, not least in the elegant presentations, but keeps a foot firmly planted on Yorkshire ground. Local goats' cheese comes in an earthy vegetal setting with mooli, baby turnips and candied walnuts, and the now traditional meaty treatment of scallops sees them teamed here with a slice of pig's brawn terrine, as well as smoked eel and puréed butternut squash. Big robust flavours are the hallmarks of main-course offerings too, with Jerusalem artichokes, crosnes and the scent of truffle the accompaniments for sea bass, while Gressingham duck comes with its gizzards, sweet potatoes and chicory. The vegetarian main might be accurately rendered potato gnocchi with kale, chestnuts

and the enriching note of Swaledale Blue cheese. Chocolate constructions are very much of the moment, so the appearance of a milk choc dome with popcorn and chocolate soil is quite to be expected, as is mandarin cheesecake with honeycomb, or a rhubarbed version of crème brûlée with gingerbread ice cream. A carefully assembled wine cellar has much to entice, opening with an imaginative selection by the glass, from Alsace Gewrztraminer to Mendoza Malbec.

Chef Daniel Shotton **Owner** Dave & Charlotte Reilly **Seats** 35, Pr/dining room 18 **Times** 12-3/7-9, **Prices** Fixed D 3 course £55 **Wines** 80 bottles over £30, 20 bottles under £30, 20 by glass **Parking** 30 **Notes** Sunday L £17.50-£22.50, Children welcome

The Burlington Restaurant ✿✿✿✿

BOLTON ABBEY Map 19 SE05

Modern British
tel: 01756 710441 & 718111 **BD23 6AJ**
email: res@devonshirehotels.co.uk
web: www.burlingtonrestaurant.co.uk
dir: *On B6160 to Bolton Abbey, 250 yds N of junct with A59 rdbt*

Innovative Yorkshire Dales cooking

A handsomely appointed spa hotel on the northern edge of the Duke of Devonshire's Bolton Abbey estate, The Devonshire Arms is in prime position to make the most of its glorious surroundings. The Dales National Park lies all about, its limestone gorges and tranquil villages providing fine walking country for more energetic patrons, or those with an eye for a decent holiday snap. Inside, a lively decorative tone banishes all thought of bland anonymity, and recent new investment has seen the upgrading of the spa and some of the guestrooms. Staff are classically trained, and understand that a careful balance of correct attention to detail and easy-going warmth is what impresses most. When it comes to food and drink, there are two options – either the informality of the Brasserie with its multi-coloured upholstery and menu of modern classics, or the principal dining room, the chandeliered Burlington and its conservatory extension. Here, against panoramic views over the countryside and the River Wharfe, Adam Smith pulls out all the stops for dynamic contemporary Yorkshire cooking full of innovation and intensity. A kitchen garden supplying vegetables, herbs, fruits and edible flowers is at the core of the operation (do pop in and have a look when you've a moment), and much else comes from the surrounding estate and from Dales growers and producers. Smith's output is sophisticated, finely worked, tirelessly inventive, but everything that comes your way has earned its place on the table. Peripheral details are stunning, from the witty canapés – cream cheese mini-meringues, lobster with pork crackling, a little duck burger – through to impressive home-made breads with smoked butter, and a pre-dessert of spearmint sorbet to refresh the senses in summer swelter. The main dishes are built up from complex layers of complementary flavours, and are notable for their freshness and clarity of intent. A first course comprising fresh mackerel, a roll of Whitby crab, compressed apple, cucumber and watermelon, segments of grapefruit, dashi syrup, and a

scattering of nasturtium petals is an essay in bracing, harmonious contrasts. The star of the main-course show is new season's lamb: delicately textured loin, cumin-scented, herb-crusted belly, and a crisp-coated ball of the sweetbread are accompanied by translucent ravioli filled with Botton cheddar, garden greens, shallots, and little chanterelles in a triumphant display. Textural contrasts are the theme of a dessert plate featuring intensely rich Amedei chocolate ganache, toffee tuiles, layered banana and hazelnuts, praline ice cream, and caramel sauce. This is an indisputably classy operation, matched by a huge wine list that comes with a knowledgeable and helpful sommelier.

Chef Adam Smith **Owner** The Duke & Duchess of Devonshire **Seats** 70, Pr/dining room 90 **Times** 7-9.30, Closed Xmas, New Year, Mon, L all week **Prices** Fixed D 3 course £65, Tasting menu £75 **Wines** 2000 bottles over £30, 20 bottles under £30, 30 by glass **Parking** 100 **Notes** ALC menu D, Vegetarian available, Children welcome

BOROUGHBRIDGE
Map 19 SE36

The Crown Inn
@@ Modern British V

tel: 01423 322300 **Roecliffe YO51 9LY**
email: info@crowninnroecliffe.co.uk **web:** www.crowninnroecliffe.com
dir: A1(M) junct 48, follow brown sign

Old coaching inn with up-to-date cooking

Hands-on owners Karl and Amanda Mainey have revamped The Crown with a perfectly-judged blend of traditional and contemporary touches. Within the venerable walls of the 16th-century coaching inn you'll find stone-flagged floors, chunky oak beams and roaring log fires, fashionably mismatched furniture and an atmosphere that radiates charm and hospitality. The kitchen takes top-class local produce and turns it all into generous, satisfying dishes that have both a clear regional flavour and unmistakably French accents. An impeccably seasonal springtime meal sets out with home-made ravioli stuffed with local rabbit and tarragon, supported by a glossy wild mushroom sauce and pecorino cheese, ahead of rump of new season lamb with crisp and buttery pommes Anna and a punchy pesto of capers and wild garlic. If you hanker for fish, how about hake steamed with king prawns over a stock of tomato, chorizo and mussels, and finished with a garlicky hit of aïoli? For pudding, there's a textbook rendition of classic tarte Tatin with home-made vanilla ice cream.

Chef Steve Ardern **Owner** Karl & Amanda Mainey **Seats** 60, Pr/dining room 20 **Times** 12-3.30/6-11 **Prices** Fixed L 2 course fr £18.95, Starter £4.50-£10.50, Main £13.95-£21.95, Dessert £6.95-£8.50, Service optional **Wines** 20 bottles over £30, 20 bottles under £30, 19 by glass **Parking** 30 **Notes** Sunday L £18.95-£21.95, Children welcome

BURNSALL
Map 19 SE06

The Devonshire Fell
@ Modern British

tel: 01756 729000 **BD23 6BT**
email: manager@devonshirefell.co.uk **web:** www.devonshirefell.co.uk
dir: On B6160, 6m from Bolton Abbey rdbt A59 junct

Simple modern cooking in a chic Dales hideaway

If you're wondering what the Yorkshire Dales have to do with the West Country, the name comes from the Duke and Duchess of Devonshire who reside hereabouts and run a mini-empire of switched-on, stylish bolt-holes. The place presents a sober face to the world, but inside, the Duchess has hit it with a contemporary boutique makeover that is all vibrant shades of lilac and blue, sensuous fabrics and attractive artwork in the funky bar and conservatory bistro. Informal, friendly service feeds into the easy-going vibe, while on the food front, please-all menus are driven by quality ingredients, with simple pubby classics such as fish and chips or steaks thrown into the mix. Otherwise, ham hock terrine with black pudding beignet and mustard mayonnaise might precede a piggy trio of pork fillet, cheek and belly with chive mash and carrots, or sea bream with ratatouille and salsa verde.

Times 12-2.30/6.30-9.30

CRATHORNE
Map 19 NZ40

Crathorne Hall Hotel
@@ Modern British

tel: 01642 700398 & 0845 072 7440 (Calls cost 7p per minute plus your phone company's access charge) **Crathorne TS15 0AR**
email: crathornehall@handpicked.co.uk
web: www.handpickedhotels.co.uk/crathorne-hall
dir: Off A19, 2m E of Yarm. Access to A19 via A66 or A1, Thirsk

Contemporary British style with clever combinations

A grandiose Edwardian pile built in 1906, Crathorne Hall was the largest and last to be built in North Yorkshire in the swan-song years of stately homes. While the decor and furnishings of the Leven Restaurant are a trip back to the early 20th century – oak half-panelled walls, heavy drapes at tall windows, oil paintings, and a gilt-edged coffered ceiling – it's fast forward to the 21st century in the kitchen. Here the style tends towards modern British sensibilities, with plenty of sound, classical technique on display. Tip-top produce, much of it sourced locally, is put to good use in well-considered dishes, starting with perfectly-timed scallops matched with chorizo, compressed apple and caper dressing. Next up, loin of lamb appears in a simple partnership with sautéed Jersey Royal potatoes and a fricassée of seasonal vegetables, or there might be pan-fried sea bass with red wine risotto, garlic purée and samphire. Puddings bring on more carefully considered combinations of flavour and texture, delivering velvety bitter chocolate tart with chocolate soil, pistachio ice cream and cherries.

Times 12.30-2.30/7-9.30

GOLDSBOROUGH
Map 19 SE35

Goldsborough Hall
@ British **NEW**

tel: 01423 867321 **Church St HG5 8NR**
email: info@goldsboroughhall.com **web:** www.goldsboroughhall.com
dir: 5 min E of Harrowgate, just off A59 between Harrowgate and A1(M)

Stately surroundings for contemporary-and-classic British cooking

Princess Mary, one of the Queen's aunts, lived in this 1620s stately home until she moved to Harewood House in 1929. By 2006 it was derelict, but Mark and Clare Oglesby bought it and set about restoring both the building and the grounds. The Dining Room is small – only 16 covers – with large, widely spaced, formally laid tables. In one corner sits a baby grand, antique furniture is dotted around, and the marble fireplace is a corker. White-gloved staff serve from the informal Garden menu, a seven-course taster, or the carte, source of inspiration for a typical meal of, say, salad of Whitby crab with Indian mango and tempura fennel, crispy ballotine of chicken with sunblushed tomato, asparagus and tarragon jus, and rhubarb pannacotta with poached rhubarb and ginger parkin. Meals may also be taken in the Princess Mary Drawing Room.

Chef Paul Richardson-Mackie **Owner** Mark & Clare Oglesby **Seats** 26, Pr/dining room 110 **Times** 12-10, All-day dining **Prices** Fixed D 3 course £35, Starter £6, Main £10.95, Dessert £6.95, Service optional **Wines** 40+ bottles over £30, 18 bottles under £30, 10 by glass **Parking** 50 **Notes** Fixed D 5 course £55, Afternoon tea, Vegetarian available, Children welcome

GRASSINGTON
Map 19 SE06

Grassington House
◉◉ Modern British

tel: 01756 752406 **5 The Square BD23 5AQ**
email: bookings@grassingtonhousehotel.co.uk **web:** www.grassingtonhousehotel.co.uk
dir: *A59 into Grassington, in town square opposite post office*

Modern European cooking amid the limestone hills

The stone-built Georgian house overlooks its cobbled village square amid the limestone hills of Wharfedale. Inside, the place has been subjected to all the tender loving care its architectural heritage requires, with a high level of elegance and comfort throughout. The crimson-toned No 5 dining room is the nerve-centre, extending into a conservatory space, and there's an outdoor terrace to capitalise on the surroundings. A new state-of-the-art, eco-friendly kitchen produces modern food with the accent on sharply etched flavours. First up might be a pairing of rare-breed pork belly and seared king scallops in toffee apple jus, or perhaps one of the sharing slates of nibbles. Daily fish specials are listed separately to the main menu, which deals in the likes of roast lamb rump with lamb-fat roasties, griddled aubergine and cumined pumpkin, or butternut and chestnut lasagne served with a leafy salad and parmesan. Imaginative side orders take in roast courgettes in honey, garlic and chilli, and the timed waits for desserts are rewarded with classic apple Tatin with vanilla cream, or chocolate fondant with salted caramel ice cream.

Chef John Rudden **Owner** Susan & John Rudden **Seats** 40 **Times** 12-2.30/6-9.30 **Prices** Fixed L 2 course £14.50, Fixed D 3 course £17.50, Tasting menu £39.50, Starter £4.50-£7.95, Main £12.95-£25.50, Dessert £5.50-£6.25, Service optional **Wines** 17 bottles over £30, 28 bottles under £30, 12 by glass **Parking** 20 **Notes** Fixed D 4 course Sun-Mon £39.50 per couple, Sunday L £16.50-£18.50, Vegetarian available, Children welcome

GUISBOROUGH
Map 19 NZ61

Gisborough Hall
◉◉ Modern British

tel: 01287 611500 **Whitby Ln TS14 6PT**
email: general.gisboroughhall@macdonald-hotels.co.uk **web:** www.gisborough-hall.co.uk
dir: *A171, follow signs for Whitby to Waterfall rdbt then 3rd exit into Whitby Lane, hotel 500yds on right*

Well-crafted interesting dishes in a Victorian mansion

On the edge of the North York Moors, the hall is an imposing Victorian-built, creeper-covered country-house hotel within well-kept grounds. Chaloner's restaurant is in what used to be the billiard room, a large space with pillars, a fireplace, white-patterned burgundy-coloured carpet and white upholstered seats at wooden-topped tables. The kitchen works around the abundance of Yorkshire's produce and puts a lot of effort into dishes that never seem overwrought. Roast breast of guinea fowl, for instance, perfectly cooked, is accompanied by a creditable Scotch egg made with fowl meat, together with mushroom ketchup, confit potatoes, kale and carrots, all elements working well together. A fish alternative might be steamed plaice fashionably partnered by chicken wings and quinoa, served with winkles, chicory and garlic. For starters, expect straightforward game terrine, or tea-smoked confit of mackerel with pickled cucumber and fennel. The kitchen clearly has an eye for presentation and an understanding of the balance of textures and flavours, seen in a theme on apple: mousse, strudel, poached and caramel.

Chef Jason Moore **Owner** Gisborough Estates Ltd **Seats** 90, Pr/dining room 33 **Times** 12.30-2.30/6.30-9.30, Closed L Mon-Sat **Prices** Fixed D 3 course £35-£48, Starter £6.75-£9.75, Main £18.50-£23.50, Dessert £6.75-£8.75, Service optional **Wines** 41 bottles over £30, 30 bottles under £30, 19 by glass **Parking** 180 **Notes** Sunday L £18.95-£22.95, Vegetarian available, Children welcome

HAROME
Map 19 SE68

The Star Inn
◉◉ Traditional, Modern British

tel: 01439 770397 **YO62 5JE**
email: reservations@thestaratharome.co.uk
dir: *From Helmsley take A170 towards Kirkbymoorside, after 0.5m turn right towards Harome. After 1.5m, inn 1st building on right*

Exhilarating Yorkshire inspired cooking in a thatched country inn

The thatched country pub in a moorland village just outside Helmsley is a perfect crooked house: it's hard to get pictures to hang straight on 14th-century walls, as you'll see. Comprising a comfortable rustic bar with candles, an old dining room with chunky tables, a real fire and knick-knacks galore, and a newer one with a bright, opulent, contemporary feel, The Star has it all, not forgetting genuinely friendly staff and Andrew Pern's Yorkshire-rooted country cooking, which places a high premium on big, rugged flavours. It doesn't come much more rugged than Stinking Bishop, the prime ingredient in a twice-baked soufflé served with smoked bacon salad and red wine shallots. That could be followed by roast rump of Ryedale lamb, pink and tender, with pan haggerty and pearl barley, all hedged about with rosemary-scented pan juices, or breaded Scarborough woof with brown shrimps, buttered samphire and duck egg gribiche. The exhilarating sense of novelty extends into desserts such as spiced fig Bakewell with superb chestnut and honey ice cream and a little jug of almond anglaise.

Chef Andrew Pern, Steve Smith **Owner** Andrew Pern **Seats** 70, Pr/dining room 10 **Times** 11.30-3/6.30-11, Closed L Mon, D Sun **Prices** Fixed L 2 course £20, Fixed D 3 course £25, Tasting menu £55-£80, Starter £8-£15, Main £19-£35, Dessert £6-£10 **Wines** 80 bottles over £30, 28 bottles under £30, 16 by glass **Parking** 30 **Notes** Chef's table for 6-8 people, Tasting menu 6-8 course, Sunday L £16-£35, Vegetarian available, Children welcome

HARROGATE
Map 19 SE35

Hotel du Vin & Bistro Harrogate
◉ British, Mediterranean

tel: 01423 856800 **Prospect Place HG1 1LB**
email: reception.harrogate@hotelduvin.com **web:** www.hotelduvin.com
dir: *A1(M) junct 47, A59 to Harrogate, follow town centre signs to Prince of Wales rdbt, 3rd exit, remain in right lane. Right at lights into Albert St, right into Prospect Place*

Fine food and wine in chic Georgian townhouse setting

The senses have always been well catered for by the renowned tea shops and Victorian spa in Harrogate, a tradition continued 21st -century-style by the local outpost of the HdV chain in a luxuriously converted terrace of eight Georgian townhouses opposite the 200-acre Stray common. As its name suggests, the Hotel du Vin brand takes a serious approach to the grape, so a snifter of one of the impressive array of wines available by the glass in the bar is a good move before settling into the slick Gallic-style bistro. The kitchen makes a virtue of simplicity and restraint, leaving the quality and freshness of the ingredients to speak for themselves. Chicken liver parfait with raisin chutney and toasted brioche makes a well-rendered version of a tried-and-tested starter, while superb steaks from the grill grab carnivores' attention at main course stage. On the fish front, there could be lemon sole Véronique, served with shallot and grape sauce.

Times 12-2/5.30-10

HARROGATE *continued*

Nidd Hall Hotel

◎◎ Modern British V

tel: 01423 771598 **Nidd HG3 3BN**
web: www.warnerleisurehotels.co.uk
dir: *A1(M) junct/A59 follow signs to Knaresborough. Continue through town centre & at Bond End lights turn left, then right onto B6165 signed Ripley & Pateley Bridge. Hotel on right in approx 4m*

Graceful modern cooking in a grand late-Georgian manor house

Built in the 1820s for a Bradford wool magnate, Nidd Hall is an early example of 19th-century pastiche, a glorious hodge-podge of architectural and stylistic references that take in everything from stained window panels to Tuscan columns. The colossal double-height fireplace and distant copper ceiling in the dining room give notice that the place was once grand enough to host the first meeting between Edward VIII and Mrs Simpson — possibly. Ancestral paintings and antlered heads surround you in the Terrace restaurant, the fine-dining option, which nonetheless manages a light decorative tone in keeping with the graceful version of modern British cooking on offer. Expect to find mandarin and chamomile fragrancing the confit duck and foie gras terrine, and then perhaps crispy noodles in seafood broth as a medium for main-course sea bass with mussels, or beetroot dauphinoise and black pudding teaming up with a pair of pork cuts, gingery fillet and slow-roasted belly. Desserts are just as inventive, serving date and port clafoutis with an apple and brandy shot, rum and raisin ice cream and mint foam.

Chef Kiran Selevarajan, Thomas Addison **Owner** Bourne Leisure **Seats** 42 **Times** 6.30-9.30, Closed Tue-Wed, L Mon, Thu-Sat **Prices** Prices not confirmed, Service optional **Wines** 11 by glass **Parking** 300 **Notes** Sunday L, No children

Rudding Park Hotel, Spa & Golf

◎◎ Modern British

tel: 01423 871350 **Rudding Park, Follifoot HG3 1JH**
email: reservations@ruddingpark.com web: www.ruddingpark.co.uk
dir: *A61 at rdbt with A658 follow signs 'Rudding Park'*

Brasserie menu in an elegant Regency era hotel

When you're ready for the whole country-house pampering package, Rudding Park fits the bill. It has its own golf course, glossy spa, and food that's worth a detour in the Clocktower Restaurant. The interior designer has come up trumps here to create vibrant, colourful spaces, from the long limestone bar, to the grand conservatory with a 400-year-old Catalonian olive tree, and the dining room with its eye-catching pink glass chandelier and elegantly understated contemporary looks. The kitchen team delivers skilful modern British cooking and local flavour via the 'food heroes' menu, which hauls in produce from a 75-mile radius, and a brasserie-style main menu setting out with seared scallops with salt and pepper squid, chorizo and roast red pepper gel. Next comes local venison with crispy bone marrow, chicory tart Tatin and pommes Anna, while two could sign up for an eight-bone rack of lamb

with celeriac dauphinoise, watercress and paloise sauce from the grill section. To finish, there could be apple and blackberry mousse with apple jelly and blackberry sorbet.

Chef Eddie Gray **Owner** Simon Mackaness & family **Seats** 110, Pr/dining room 14 **Times** 12-3/6-10 **Prices** Fixed L 2 course fr £30, Fixed D 3 course fr £39.50, Starter fr £9.50, Main fr £19.50, Dessert fr £9.50, Service optional **Wines** 84 bottles over £30, 28 bottles under £30, 11 by glass **Parking** 350 **Notes** Sunday L fr £25, Vegetarian available, Children welcome

Studley Hotel

◎◎ Pacific Rim

tel: 01423 560425 **28 Swan Rd HG1 2SE**
email: info@studleyhotel.co.uk web: www.orchidrestaurant.co.uk
dir: *Adjacent to Valley Gardens, opposite Mercer Gallery*

Smart hotel restaurant giving culinary tour of Asia

In the Studley Hotel's Orchid restaurant, a multinational brigade of chefs delivers authentic regional flavours in an eclectic Pan-Asian melting pot of cuisines from China, Indonesia, Japan, Korea, Malaysia, the Philippines, Thailand and Vietnam. Mango and darkwood interiors divided by Japanese lattice-style screens make for a classy contemporary setting, with a large TV screen providing a live video feed of the action in the kitchen. Express lunch menus offer stonking value, and if you want the chef to decide what you eat, a trio of set menu formulas bolsters the wide-ranging carte. Key ingredients are flown in regularly from Asia in the name of authenticity. A starter of sui yuk partners roasted belly pork with crunchy crackling and a sweet and savoury dip of yellow bean and honey, ahead of fried sea bass fillet with a spicy curry of Thai herbs, shredded lime leaves and coconut cream. Stick with the exotic theme for a dessert of Thai-style steamed banana and sticky rice cake cooked in a banana leaf and served with coconut ice cream.

Chef Kenneth Poon **Owner** Bokmun Chan **Seats** 72, Pr/dining room 20 **Times** 12-2/6-10, Closed 25-26 Dec, L Sat **Prices** Fixed L 2 course £10.95, Fixed D 3 course £24.90-£33.50, Starter £5.90-£8.20, Main £8.40-£22, Dessert £5.95-£8.95 **Wines** 15 bottles over £30, 26 bottles under £30, 12 by glass **Parking** 18, On street **Notes** Sunday L £16.90, Vegetarian available, Children welcome

van Zeller

◎◎ Modern British V

tel: 01423 508762 **8 Montpellier St HG1 2TQ**
email: info@vanzellerrestaurants.co.uk
dir: *Phone for directions*

Boldly defined culinary pyrotechnics

In the heart of the Montpellier quarter, Tom van Zeller's pace-setting contemporary cooking has taken Harrogate by storm. If you thought the town's principal business came in tea-cosies and cake-cases, think again. The discreet, narrow ash-grey frontage with its half-frosted windows and little balcony above does little to prepare the unsuspecting for the culinary pyrotechnics on display, and nor does the menu, which plays its descriptive cards close to its chest. Pigeon, beetroots and ketchup might be the prelude to salmon, bacon jam, avocado and watercress. When dishes arrive, it's easier to see why they defy easy summary. Everything comes as an arrangement of small discrete items, assembled in colourful, texturally diverse array like works of abstract art. Flavours are as boldly defined as the visuals, smoked eel given the sharp edges of apple, cucumber and goats' curd, rabbit the sweetness of carrot and marmalade, while a duck main course receives the rich autumnal range of spiced apple, hazelnuts, puntarelle and foie gras. Desserts too look for piercing assertive notes, as in passionfruit tart with cardamom.

Chef Tom van Zeller **Owner** Tom van Zeller **Seats** 34 **Times** 12-2/6-10, Closed 10 days Jan, Sun-Mon **Prices** Fixed L 3 course fr £35, Fixed D 3 course fr £50, Tasting menu fr £60, Service optional 12.5% **Wines** 6 bottles over £30, 6 bottles under £30, 9 by glass **Parking** Montpellier Hill **Notes** 10 course chef's menu fr £85, Children welcome

White Hart Hotel

◉◉ British

tel: 01423 505681 **2 Cold Bath Rd HG2 0NF**
email: reception@whitehart.net **web:** www.whitehart.net
dir: A59 to Harrogate. A661 3rd exit on rdbt to Harrogate. Left at rdbt onto A6040 for 1m. Right onto A61. Bear left down Montpellier Hill

Modern brasserie dishes in a Georgian landmark

Right by the Victorian Valley Gardens park, the White Hart is something of a Harrogate landmark, having provided bed and sustenance to travellers since the Georgian era. The Brasserie is its main eating space, a light room done out in on-trend sandy neutral colours with cheerful country-chic gingham curtains and upholstery. The kitchen cooks with the seasons in a menu packed with straightforward, up-to-date dishes such as monkfish cheek in a casserole with potato and Yorkshire chorizo, followed by wild venison haunch with spiced red cabbage, parsnips and red wine sauce. If you're up for fish, there could be butter-roasted fillet of stone bass with langoustine essence, ratte potatoes and sweet pepper. Puddings include regional delicacies such as Yorkshire ginger parkin, dolled up with winter spiced caramel and vanilla ice cream, as well as well as English burnt vanilla cream with boozy Agen prunes and shortcake. Alternatively, if you prefer honest-to-goodness comfort classics in a more casual setting, head for the Fat Badger pub in the same building.

Chef Richard Ferebee **Owner** Phil Barker **Times** 11.30-3.30/6-10 **Prices** Prices not confirmed **Notes** L expresss menu Mon-Fri 11.30-3.30, Sunday L

HAWNBY   Map 19 SE58

The Inn at Hawnby

◉ Modern British

tel. 01439 798202 **YO02 5QS**
email. info@innathawnby.co.uk **web.** www.innathawnby.co.uk
dir: From the S, A1 to Thirsk & Teeside exit A19/A168 for Scarborough onto A170. 1st left through Felixkirk. Through Boltby into Hawnby

Local cooking in an old grey moorland inn

The Youngs' old greystone country inn near Helmsley has the sweeping majesty of the North York Moors all around it, an inspiringly remote setting for walkers and gastronomes. A homely village pub atmosphere, complete with log fire, makes a cheering prospect, while the dining room looks more high-toned, with tables got up in double cloths, laid with quality settings and glassware. Jason Reeves keeps things on a local leash as far as possible, beginning with a pairing of ham hock terrine and a Scotched quail;s egg with pickled carrots and caper mayonnaise, and following with roast salmon, salade Niçoise and salsa verde, or a porcine assemblage of honeyed pork belly and pork-fat potatoes dressed in pomegranate and chimichurri. It can sometimes feel as though dishes would be more successful if they weren't striving so intently for complexity, but the prime materials are impeccable, and nobody is complaining at the arrival of textbook vanilla crème brûlée with a blowtorched top.

Chef Jason Reeves, Andrew Hall **Owner** Kathryn & David Young **Seats** 32, Pr/dining room 30 **Times** 12-2/7-9, Closed 25 Dec, L Mon-Tue (limited opening Feb-Mar please phone) **Prices** Starter £5-£7.25, Main £10.95-£18.95, Dessert £6-£9, Service optional **Wines** 15 bottles over £30, 11 bottles under £30, 12 by glass **Parking** 22 **Notes** Sunday L, Vegetarian available, Children welcome

---

HELMSLEY   Map 19 SE68

Black Swan Hotel

◉◉◉ – see page 566

Feversham Arms Hotel & Verbena Spa

◉◉ Modern British V

tel: 01439 770766 **1-8 High St YO62 5AG**
email: info@fevershamarmshotel.com **web:** www.fevershamarmshotel.com
dir: A1 junct 49 follow A168 to Thirsk, take A170 to Helmsley. Turn left at mini rdbt then right, hotel on right past church

Modern spa hotel with equally modern culinary ideas

The Feversham Arms has oodles of contemporary style behind its old stone frontage, with a restaurant of dark walls under its vaulted atrium and banquettes and designer-style seating at correctly set tables, an appropriate setting for sharp and sophisticated cooking built on fine regional ingredients. Seared scallop with warm apple jelly, black pudding and smoked roe emulsion seems entirely appropriate for a hotel in an affluent market town, and there might also be veal sweetbread with turnip and wood sorrel. Seasoning and timings are just so and flavour combinations well considered, seen in fillet of turbot served with an oxtail ravioli and Judas's ear (a mushroom), and fillet of pork Wellington with wild cabbage and a Taylor's tea and prune purée. There are 32-day aged steaks, too, served with triple-cooked chips, with good breads also part of the package. Tempting desserts have included chocolate and banana millefeuille, and Eton Mess with rhubarb and lemon.

Chef Norman Mackenzie **Owner** Feversham Arms Ltd **Seats** 65, Pr/dining room 24 **Times** 12-2.30/6.45-9.15 **Prices** Tasting menu fr £60, Starter £10-£15, Main £22-£32, Dessert £10, Service optional **Wines** 38 bottles under £30, 18 by glass **Parking** 50 **Notes** Tasting menu 6 course whole tables only, Sunday L £19.50-£25, Children welcome

---

The Pheasant Hotel

◉◉ Modern British V

tel: 01439 771241 **Mill St, Harome YO62 5JG**
email: reservations@thepheasanthotel.com **web:** www.thepheasanthotel.com
dir: Exit A170 signed Harome, hotel located opposite church

Skilful cooking by the village duck pond

Overlooking the duck pond in the pretty village of Harome, The Pheasant has been carved out of a blacksmith's, village shop and barns, all set around a courtyard of fruit trees. The flagstone-floored conservatory is mainly used for dining, with candles on neatly clothed tables lit after dark and where service is on the formal side. The cooking style is an updated British version of the classical French repertory, with an expert's skills behind judicious combinations. Expect dressed crab with a matching velouté, lemon sabayon, cucumber and seaweed sticks, followed by roast rump of beef with duxelle, pommes Anna and spinach purée. Dinner kicks off with an amuse-bouche – perhaps root vegetable velouté with ginger beer foam – before starters along the lines of seared scallops, perfectly cooked and seasoned, with rich braised lamb neck and cauliflower and truffle purée, or classic steak tartare with a hen's egg and beetroot, then braised pig cheeks boosted with squid, served with Alsace bacon and smoked butter mash. Satisfying puddings include rice pudding with damson jam.

Chef Peter Neville **Owner** Peter Neville, Jacquie Pern **Seats** 60, Pr/dining room 30 **Times** 12-2/6.30-9, Closed D 25 Dec **Prices** Prices not confirmed, Service optional **Wines** 67 bottles over £30, 20 bottles under £30, 12 by glass **Parking** 15 **Notes** Afternoon tea, Sunday L, Children welcome

---

HETTON   Map 18 SD95

The Angel Inn

◉◉◉ – see page 567

Black Swan Hotel ❀❀❀

HELMSLEY   Map 19 SE68

Modern British V

tel: 01439 770466 **Market Place YO62 5BJ**
email: enquiries@blackswan-helmsley.co.uk
web: www.blackswan-helmsley.co.uk
dir: *A170 towards Scarborough, on entering Helmsley hotel at end of Market Place, just off mini-rdbt*

Art on a plate in a gallery restaurant

Set in a trio of ancient houses spanning the centuries from Elizabethan to Georgian to Victorian, the Black Swan is still right at the heart of this lovely little market town in the 21st century, albeit with a rather neat boutique look these days to go with the old-world charm of its open fires and antiques. The Gallery restaurant (so named because it doubles up as a daytime gallery showcasing original artworks for sale) is where Patrick Bardoulet gets to show off his high level of skill and creative flair, sourcing the finest Yorkshire ingredients and turning them into dishes that wow with their clearly defined flavours and beautiful presentation. The setting is elegant, with tables wearing fine white linen, accessorised with sparkling glassware and soft background music. The front-of-house staff are delightfully unstuffy and well versed in the menus, which is handy since they read like a shopping list of ingredients. There's clear technical skill and innovation from the off: an amuse of lamb kofta with a shot glass of lemon jelly melting into warm chickpea purée precedes an opener starring veal sweetbreads with parsnip air, braised lettuce and cumin oil. Next up, loin and haunch of venison partnered with turnip cream, coffee sauce and lemon curd has superb depth and clarity of flavour, every component expertly handled, or there might be monkfish with bacon, butternut squash (puréed, roasted and pickled), razor clams and curried coconut. A finale of poached pear filled with dark chocolate sauce is complemented by tonka bean parfait, almonds and citrus tuile. The wine list offers plenty to explore if your budget allows.

Chef Patrick Bardoulet **Owner** John Jameson **Seats** 65, Pr/dining room 50 **Times** 12.30-2/7-9.30, Closed L Mon-Sat **Prices** Fixed D 3 course £29-£45, Tasting menu £65, Service optional **Wines** 166 bottles over £30, 39 bottles under £30, 19 by glass **Parking** 40 **Notes** Tasting menu 6 course, Market menu, Sunday L £24.95-£29.95, Children welcome

Black Horse Inn

◉◉ Modern, Traditional

tel: 01609 749010 & 749011 **7 Lumley Ln DL7 0SH**
email: gm@blackhorsekirkbyfleetham.com **web:** www.blackhorsekirkbyfleetham.com
dir: Exit A1 to Kirkby Fleetham, follow restaurant signs

Stylish pub cooking in a stone-built village inn

A short spin from the whirling traffic at Scotch Corner brings you to the north Yorkshire hamlet of Kirkby Fleetham, and its stone-built traditional inn, which pushes all the right buttons for a northern country hostelry, complete with stylishly furnished guestrooms. The main dining room, an elegant, ivory-coloured space under a low beamed ceiling, looks out over the back garden and lifts the Horse to an altogether higher level. A range of globally-inspired modern dishes is offered,

and if you find it hard to choose, the recommended way to begin is with one of the sharing-boards of 'bits and bobs', comprising different elements from the starter menu. There may be home-smoked mackerel with apple, beetroot and horseradish, chicken liver parfait with clementine marmalade, garlic and chilli king prawns with sesame toast, and more. Main courses span a range from Parma-wrapped chicken breast filled with smoked applewood cheddar in wild mushroom sauce, or pork belly with black pudding and mustard mash in cider jus. Finish with rhubarb and vanilla pannacotta with a pistachio tuile.

Black Horse Inn

Chef Lisa Miller **Owner** Phil Barker **Seats** 40, Pr/dining room 12 **Times** 12-2.30/5-9 **Prices** Fixed L 3 course £12.50-£15, Fixed D 3 course £12.50-£15, Starter £5-£9, Main £12-£27, Dessert £5-£8, Service optional **Wines** 21 bottles over £30, 27 bottles under £30, 10 by glass **Parking** 40 **Notes** Sunday L £13-£20, Vegetarian available, Children welcome

The Angel Inn ✿✿✿

British
tel: 01756 730263 **BD23 6LT**
email: info@angelhetton.co.uk **web:** www.angelhetton.co.uk
dir: 6m N Skipton, follow B6265 towards Grassington, left at duck pond & again at T-junct. The Angel up the hill on right

Forthright British cooking in a heritage country inn

The Angel was a drovers' inn about 500 years back, and must have presented as welcoming a sight to fatigued farmworkers then as it does to modern gastronomes today. Clad in red and green clambering foliage, it's a warren of little corners and crannies, with winter fires and cask ales to warm the cockles. Juliet Watkins acquired the place in the early 1980s, and set about coaxing it from the chicken-in-a-basket era to a brave new world in which a country pub offers inspired, imaginative cooking and decent wines. The erstwhile Francophile inclination of the kitchen has gradually given place to a more obviously home-grown version of modern thinking, founded on forthright flavours with no lip-service paid to left-field combinations. The signature starter for the past generation or two has been the little filo moneybag of seafood on rich lobster sauce, which Bruce Elsroth continues to honour, or there may be a classic of more recent vintage such as seared pigeon breast with beetroot compôte

and watercress in orange vinaigrette. A pairing of pot-roasted loin and panko-crumbed shoulder of local lamb with crushed peas and cherry tomatoes in rosemary jus needs more careful timing, but lacks nothing in quality of flavour, while seared halibut gains from an earthy setting on crushed Jerusalem artichokes in wild mushroom velouté. Finish with a textural homage to fine chocolate in the forms of nougatine, mousse, meringue shards and ice cream, served with coconut sorbet and honeycomb, or with a palate-sharpening lemon meringue pie in lemon custard with lime sorbet. Excellent home-made breads come with both plain and pesto butter.

Chef Bruce Elsworth **Owner** Juliet Watkins **Seats** 65, Pr/dining room 24 **Times** 12-2.30/6-10, Closed 25 Dec & 1 wk Jan, L Mon-Sat, D Sun **Prices** Tasting menu £55, Starter £7.25-£9.25, Main £13.95-£26.95, Dessert £6.95, Service optional **Wines** 107 bottles over £30, 35 bottles under £30, 21 by glass **Parking** 40 **Notes** Sat D 4 course £42, Sunday L £28, Vegetarian available, Children welcome

KNARESBOROUGH
Map 19 SE35

General Tarleton Inn
◉◉ Modern British

tel: 01423 340284 **Boroughbridge Rd, Ferrensby HG5 0PZ**
email: gti@generaltarleton.co.uk web: www.generaltarleton.co.uk
dir: *A1(M) junct 48 at Boroughbridge, take A6055 to Knaresborough. 4m on right*

Modern Yorkshire food with ambition

Not far from the castle, and with Harrogate barely five miles away, the GT is a country inn with character. It is decorated with an appealing mix of fine furnishings against exposed walls, roughcast stone offsetting the violet plush. Localism may be de rigueur up and down the country now, but when chef entitles his menus 'Food with Yorkshire Roots' here, he means it. Ambitious modern dishes in the restaurant compete with dependable bar food elsewhere, and the results look good. Beetroot-cured salmon with lemon gel and spring onion and horseradish cream is one way to start, a twice-baked wensleydale soufflé with tomato relish the regionally unimpeachable option. Suckling pig appears in as many guises as may be fitted on one plate – loin, belly, shoulder and black pudding with pear and dauphinoise – while the sole fish possibility on a meaty roll call of mains might be seared sea bass with truffle gnocchi and marinated artichoke. To round things off, treacle tart is got up not just with clotted cream, but Horlicks ice cream and peanut butter too.

Chef John Topham, Marc Williams **Owner** John & Claire Topham **Seats** 64, Pr/dining room 40 **Times** 12-1.45/6-9.15, Closed D 25-26 Dec, 1 Jan **Prices** Fixed L 2 course £16, Fixed D 3 course £19.50, Starter £6.20-£11.75, Main £14.95-£22.20, Dessert £5.20-£8, Service optional 10% **Wines** 62 bottles over £30, 18 bottles under £30, 12 by glass **Parking** 40 **Notes** Sunday L £22.50-£27, Vegetarian available, Children welcome

MALTON
Map 19 SE77

The Talbot Hotel
◉◉ British

tel: 01653 639096 **Yorkersgate YO17 7AJ**
email: reservations@talbotmalton.co.uk web: www.talbotmalton.co.uk
dir: *A46 Malton*

Distinctive modern cooking born and bred in Malton

Equidistant from Castle Howard and the Yorkshire Arboretum, The Talbot stands on a B-road running to the north of the River Derwent. It's a rugged but pastoral setting for an accomplished country-house hotel, in a house owned by the same family since the second George. A dining room done in pale green and gold, showcases contemporary cooking of distinctive flair. Dressing a Whitby crab involves adding lardo, fennel pollen and a sorrel sorbet as well as the more usual avocado, but the different layers work well together, as they do in a seasonal main course of Dales grouse roasted in hay, accompanied by its confit leg, mulled red cabbage, salt-baked veg and a bramble and juniper jus. A seafood pairing to conjure with offers wreckfish and crayfish with crispy buckwheat in a rich bisque sauce. The resourceful technical range extends into entertaining desserts such as milk chocolate ganache with rapeseed oil and aerated chocolate, damson sorbet and a caramelised plum.

Chef Jake Jones **Owner** Fitzwilliam Estate **Seats** 40, Pr/dining room 40 **Times** 12.30-2.30/6.30-9.30 **Prices** Fixed L 2 course £18, Tasting menu £65, Starter £8.95-£13.95, Main £18-£26.95, Dessert £7.50-£8.95, Service optional **Wines** 200 bottles over £30, 40 bottles under £30, 14 by glass **Parking** 40 **Notes** Thu Supper Club 2 main course with wine £30, Sunday L £18-£24, Vegetarian available, Children welcome

MASHAM
Map 19 SE28

Samuel's at Swinton Park
◉◉◉ *– see opposite*

Vennell's
◉◉ Modern British

tel: 01765 689000 **7 Silver St HG4 4DX**
email: info@vennellsrestaurant.co.uk
dir: *8m from A1 Masham exit, 10m N of Ripon*

Another of Masham's many assets

Not only is Masham home to the Black Sheep Brewery and an annual steam-engine rally, but the 2014 Tour de France peloton whistled through here. It's all happening. Just remember to pronounce it 'Massam'. Jon Vennell's self-named restaurant is another of the town's irresistible lures, the sort of neighbourhood eatery that, by punching above its weight, has become a destination for out-of-towners. Four dinners and one lunch a week keep things on a tight rein, and enable a style of cooking that's all about minute attention to detail. It might kick off with a serving of lightly poached salmon in an array of shoots and croûtons, alongside lemon jelly and a blob of chived crème fraîche, before mains bring on fine prime cuts such as rare-breed confit pork with beans and chorizo stewed in Pinot Noir, or turbot fillet with brown shrimps and capers in beurre blanc. Some of the local ale goes into a majestic suet pudding of beef and mushrooms, and desserts maintain the pace with lemon cheesecake in raspberry coulis.

Chef Jon Vennell **Owner** Jon & Laura Vennell **Seats** 30, Pr/dining room 16 **Times** 12-4/7.15-12, Closed 26-29 Dec, 1-14 Jan, 1 wk Sep, Mon-Tue, L Wed-Sat, D Sun **Prices** Fixed L 2 course £19.50, Dessert £3.49-£7.50, Service optional **Wines** 27 bottles over £30, 28 bottles under £30, 11 by glass **Parking** On street & Market Sq **Notes** ALC 2 course £24.50, Sunday L £19.50-£24.50, Vegetarian available, Children 4 yrs+

MIDDLESBROUGH
Map 19 NZ41

Chadwicks Inn Maltby
◉◉ Modern British Ⅴ

tel: 01642 590300 **High Ln, Maltby TS8 0BG**
email: info@chadwicksmaltby.co.uk
dir: *A19-A174(W)/A1045, follow signs to Yarm & Maltby, left at the Manor House, inn 500yds on left through village*

Ambitious modern cooking in a moorland country inn

Food is very much a focus at this traditional 19th-century inn on the edge of the moors. Have a drink in the bar, with its wood-burner and squashy sofas, and dine either in the red-walled snug or under beams in the relaxed and comfortable restaurant. A lunchtime and early-evening bistro menu dealing in the likes of ham hock terrine with a quail's egg and pineapple, then fish and chips, shifts up a couple of gears for the dinner menu, a slate of ambitiously enterprising dishes straight out of the 21st-century school. Start with seared scallops with local chorizo on butternut squash purée and go on to slowly cooked pork belly with sage-flavoured apple, celeriac and a black pudding Scotch egg. A grounding in the classics, suitably updated, is evident: a pressing of duck and goose liver, for example, with figs and turnip, then fillet of halibut with shellfish, caper and parsley butter and dauphinoise potatoes. Cheeses fly the Union Jack, and puddings include indulgent dark chocolate mousse, its richness cut by poached clementines and orange and caramel ice cream.

Chef Matthew Beadnall, Steve Lawford **Owner** Gary & Helen Gill, Lee Tolley **Seats** 47 **Times** 12-2.30/5-9.30, Closed 26 Dec, 1 Jan, Mon, D Sun **Prices** Fixed L 2 course £13.95, Starter £6.95-£9.50, Main £19-£26.50, Service optional **Wines** 29 bottles over £30, 23 bottles under £30, 7 by glass **Parking** 50 **Notes** Steak & wine night from £35 for 2, Bistro menu L & early eve, Sunday L £16.95-£19.95, Children welcome

NORTHALLERTON
Map 19 SE39

Solberge Hall

Modern British

tel: 01609 779191 **Newby Wiske DL7 9ER**
email: reservations@solbergehall.co.uk web: www.solbergehall.co.uk
dir: *A1(M) junct 51, follow A684 to Northallerton. After village of Ainderby Steeple turn right (signed Solberge Hall) for 2m*

Skilful brasserie cooking in a Georgian manor

Solberge Hall is a hit on the wedding circuit, which is no surprise given its Georgian charms and gloriously bucolic setting. You don't need to be participating in someone's big day, though, to rock up here, for no invitation is needed for lunch or dinner in the Garden Room Brasserie. The house has generous Georgian proportions throughout, not least in the brasserie with its whopping sash windows and high ceilings. The kitchen produces dishes that fit the brasserie moniker, but there's no lack of creativity on show in a repertoire that sees pan-seared scallops partnered with confit chicken wings and sweetcorn purée in a modern first course. Follow that with haunch of venison with parsnip textures and blackberry jus, or a Yorkshire sirloin matured for 28 days. Among desserts, blackberry Artic Roll competes with warm pecan tart with salted caramel ice cream and popcorn.

Chef Mark Wilson **Owner** West Register Hotels **Seats** 35, Pr/dining room 22 **Times** 12-2/7-9 **Prices** Fixed D 3 course £32.95, Service optional **Wines** 12 bottles over £30, 23 bottles under £30, 10 by glass **Parking** 95 **Notes** Sunday L £16.95-£19.95, Vegetarian available, Children welcome

OLDSTEAD
Map 19 SE57

The Black Swan at Oldstead

– see page 570

OSMOTHERLEY
Map 19 SE49

Cleveland Tontine

Modern European

tel: 01609 882671 **Staddlebridge DL6 3JB**
email: bookings@theclevelandtontine.co.uk web: www.theclevelandtontine.co.uk
dir: *Phone for directions*

Modern bistro cooking in revamped roadside restaurant with rooms

Built in 1804, this characterful roadside stopover was kept busy from day one by travellers overnighting from the London to Sunderland mail coach. Two centuries on, the place is still an enticing prospect after a contemporary refurbishment, and its atmospheric candlelit dining room with a monumental stone fireplace has lost none of its charm. The culinary style might best be described as modern British-meets-French-bistro, opening effectively with pan-seared scallops with truffled leeks, boudin blanc and chive butter sauce, followed by rose veal with crispy-crumbed crab and potato cakes, apple, and curry cream. If you're up for fish, try a creative pairing of pan-fried fillets of Dover sole with herb purée and frogs' leg Kiev. At dessert stage, a cappuccino brûlée is topped with foam and partnered by a rich caramel sponge and pistachio ice cream.

Chef James Cooper **Owner** Charles & Angela Tompkins **Seats** 88, Pr/dining room 50 **Times** 12-2.30/6.30-9, Closed D 25-26 Dec, 1 Jan **Prices** Starter £5.95-£10.95, Main £14.95-£33, Dessert £5-£10.95 **Wines** 48 bottles over £30, 39 bottles under £30, 16 by glass **Parking** 40 **Notes** Sunday L fr £26.95, Vegetarian available, Children welcome

Samuel's at Swinton Park

MASHAM
Map 19 SE28

Modern British **V**
tel: 01765 680900 **Swinton HG4 4JH**
email: enquiries@swintonpark.com web: www.swintonpark.com
dir: *Phone for directions*

Dynamic modern cooking in a glorious country estate

Swinton Park provides the opportunity to get a taste of *Downton Abbey*-style aristocratic life in a truly splendid house, originally built in the 1690s but added to over the years, and owned by the same family since the 1880s. Samuel's is the jewel in this sparkly crown, and it's headed-up by Simon Crannage, a man with prodigious talent and a passion for contemporary culinary goings on. The dining room is an unruffled space with an ornate ceiling and views over the lake and gardens. The menus include 'classic', 'tasting' and 'garden' versions, and, whichever you go for, you'll find refined, modern dishes that show acute technical skill and deliver balanced flavours. A first course based around heritage carrots (from the estate) allows the ingredients to shine, but still looks stunning, while roast breast of Yorkshire duck nearly steals the show with its tender meat and crisp skin (served with toasted quinoa, baked garden carrots and Madeira sauce). Among desserts, an espresso parfait comes with banana cream and dark chocolate mousse, not to mention some trendy

chocolate soil, and the cheese on offer stays loyal to Yorkshire with the likes of Swaledale Blue and Ribblesdale served with a bespoke chutney or jelly. A meal includes all the expected extras, from canapés to petits fours. There's a cookery school in the former Georgian stable block.

Chef Simon Crannage **Owner** Mr & Mrs Cunliffe-Lister **Seats** 60, Pr/dining room 20 **Times** 12.30-2/7-9.30, Closed L Mon (only Castle menu in bar) **Prices** Fixed L 2 course £22, Fixed D 3 course £55, Tasting menu £65, Service optional **Wines** 132 bottles over £30, 30 bottles under £30, 13 by glass **Parking** 80 **Notes** Sommelier pairing £28.50, Garden produce menu £52, Sunday L £28, Children 8 yrs+ D

PICKERING

Map 19 SE78

Fox & Hounds Country Inn

Modern British

tel: 01751 431577 **Main St, Sinnington YO62 6SQ**
email: fox.houndsinn@btconnect.com **web:** www.thefoxandhoundsinn.co.uk
dir: *In Sinnington centre, 3m W of Pickering, off A170*

Well-wrought pub food on the edge of the Moors

A stone-built country inn called the Fox & Hounds at the hub of its own little Yorkshire community on the edge of the North York Moors is distilled England. All is cosiness and cheer within, from the snug little bar with its wood-burner to the thickly carpeted dining room that looks on to the back garden. Well-wrought pub food based on fine prime materials, with chef's specials on the blackboard, are what everyone wants to see. Expect fried sea bass on pine nut fettuccine to start, or a twice-baked Lincolnshire Poacher soufflé with sweet-and-sour cherry tomatoes, and then gird your loins for three servings of lamb – a mini-rack, braised shoulder and a pie with tomatoes and rosemary – served with creamy, garlicky dauphinoise. Treacle tart and custard is as heritage British as it gets, give or take the odd garnishing of kumquat.

Chef Mark Caffrey **Owner** Mr & Mrs A Stephens **Seats** 36, Pr/dining room 10 **Times** 12-2/6.30-9, Closed 25-27 Dec **Prices** Starter £5.25-£8.95, Main £12.25-£23.95, Dessert £5.95-£7.95, Service optional **Wines** 9 bottles over £30, 32 bottles under £30, 9 by glass **Parking** 35 **Notes** Early D menu Sun-Fri 5.30-6.30pm £9.95, Light L wknd £9.95, Sunday L £23.95-£29.95, Vegetarian available, Children welcome

The White Swan Inn

Modern British

tel: 01751 472288 **Market Place YO18 7AA**
email: welcome@white-swan.co.uk **web:** www.white-swan.co.uk
dir: *Just beyond junct of A169/A170 in Pickering, turn right off A170 into Market Place*

Proud Yorkshire produce in a Tudor coaching inn

The Swan is a venerable stone-built coaching inn dating from the Tudor period, in a historic market town on the edge of the North York Moors. It's run with a clear eye to its role in the community, being a welcoming hostelry for locals, and a prime destination for regionally-sourced eating. The kitchen philosophy is all about feeding patrons on good Yorkshire produce that isn't overly mucked about with ('we don't do froths and smudges,' says chef). Rare-breed meats from the celebrated Ginger Pig butcher in nearby Levisham, local cheeses, fish from Whitby and veg from the allotment all feature proudly. Expect to start with ham hock terrine with a quail's egg, piccalilli and chargrilled toast, or potted crab with celeriac remoulade, before being spoiled for main-course choice. Will it be shallow-fried stone bass with kale and smoked salmon cream sauce, or rack of lamb with a Jersey Royal potato cake, minted new carrots and caper sauce? Puddings bring on the familiar likes of sticky toffee pudding, or maybe lemon meringue with pannacotta and lemon and poppy seed tuile.

Chef Darren Clemmit **Owner** The Buchanan family **Seats** 50, Pr/dining room 18 **Times** 12-2/6.45-9 **Prices** Starter £5.95-£8.95, Main £13.95-£25.95, Dessert fr £6.95, Service optional **Wines** 31 bottles over £30, 32 bottles under £30, 19 by glass **Parking** 45 **Notes** Fixed L/D menu on request, Sunday L, Vegetarian available, Children welcome

The Black Swan at Oldstead

OLDSTEAD

Map 19 SE57

Modern British **V**
tel: 01347 868387 **YO61 4BL**
email: enquiries@blackswanoldstead.co.uk **web:** www.blackswanoldstead.co.uk
dir: *A1 junct 49, A168, A19 S (or from York A19 N), then Coxwold, Byland Abbey*

Dazzling intrepid modern cooking on a family farmstead

Tucked into the southwestern corner of the North York Moors, Oldstead has been home to the Banks family for centuries. Tom Banks, in conjunction with a specialist produce gardener, oversees a terraced kitchen garden and orchard, as well as polytunnels out in the fields, to supply his stoves with the backbone of the menu's output. The compass needle is oriented unwaveringly towards the most ambitious and intrepid zone of present-day British modernism, with suggestions of Simon Rogan's L'Enclume at Cartmel and Sat Bains in Nottingham. The core of the operation is a tasting menu of nine courses, including intermediates, which offers a dazzling excursion through the repertoire, but every last detail on the carte is replete with ingenious care and panache as well. Butter-poached baby carrots from the garden with chestnuts, goats' curd and cream cheese add up to a memorable and well-considered composition, while softly unctuous crackled pork comes with the textural variations on cauliflower that others reserve for fish. At main, there can be majestic venison, the seared loin partnered by a stunningly

rich mini-shepherd's pie, fondant celeriac, blackberries and hazelnuts, or expertly timed halibut with exquisite mash, topped with shaved hen-of-the-wood, its aroma released as the jus is poured on at the table. Desserts may not always sound like dessert, but who cares when something as successful and innovative as parsnip cake with crab-apple and malt crumble comes your way?

Chef Tommy Banks **Owner** The Banks family **Seats** 40, Pr/dining room 12 **Times** 12-2/6-9, Closed 1 wk Jan, L Mon-Fri **Prices** Tasting menu fr £80, Service optional **Wines** 106 bottles over £30, 6 bottles under £30, 30 by glass **Parking** 25 **Notes** L Tasting menu 6 course £55, ALC menu £55, Fixed L £32, Sunday L fr £32, Children welcome

RICHMOND
Map 19 NZ10

The Frenchgate Restaurant and Hotel
◉◉ Modern British

tel: 01748 822087 & 07921 136362 **59-61 Frenchgate DL10 7AE**
email: info@thefrenchgate.co.uk web: www.thefrenchgate.co.uk
dir: *From A1 (Scotch Corner) to Richmond on A6108. After lights, 1st left into Lile Close (leading to Flints Terrace) for hotel car park. Or for front entrance continue to 1st rdbt, left into Dundas St. At T-junct left into Frenchgate*

Technical artistry on the plate and on the walls

Compounded of two original townhouses in photogenic Richmond, The Frenchgate is a modern boutique hotel with bags of character. Works by local artists are hung about the place, as well as some not so local. Can that really be an original Pissarro in the dining room? Yep. Uncovered wood surfaces lend the place an agreeably informal feel, and the whole thing is kept on a manageable scale, with just a few tables and a shortish menu, though filled out with appetisers and pre-desserts. Concentrated technical artistry is on show in a starter of quail's ballotine filled with wild mushroom mousse, alongside a pile of Puy lentils and a morel jelly with a quail egg set in it. Mains cover a spectrum from stone bass with razor clams in an emulsion sauce of brown crab, to mustard-crusted fillet and belly of local pork, appetisingly set off with crisp-fried kale and creamed Savoy, as well as mustard mash. Peach mousse with caramelised peach in its own coulis is a late-summer treat, only slightly overshadowed by over-assertive thyme ice cream.

Chef Robert Lacey **Owner** David & Luiza Todd **Seats** 24, Pr/dining room 24 **Times** 12-2/6-9.30 **Prices** Fixed D 3 course £34-£39, Service optional **Wines** 50 bottles over £30, 18 bottles under £30, 12 by glass **Parking** 12 **Notes** Pre-theatre menu, Tasting menu, Matching wine flights, Sunday L £15-£19, Vegetarian available, Children welcome

RIPON
Map 19 SE37

The Royal Oak
◉ Modern British

tel: 01765 602284 **36 Kirkgate HG4 1PB**
email: info@royaloakripon.co.uk web: www.royaloakripon.co.uk
dir: *In town centre*

Modern pub classics in an old coaching inn

A carefully renovated Georgian coaching inn in the centre of the pocket-sized city, not far from either the cathedral or the racing, The Royal Oak cuts a dash with its modern makeover of violet walls, bare-boarded split-level floors and log-burner. The pub ambience is retained with cask ales on draught, and a blackboard menu retailing conscientiously sourced local food. The styling is modern without being pretentious, and the well-rendered classic dishes full of appeal. Start with a fishcake and poached egg in mustard sauce with crisp pancetta, or crab, avocado and slow-roast tomato cocktail, before turning to trout with pea tortellini in shellfish cream sauce, or the signature offering of venison with chestnuts, turnips and beetroot, served with a portion of thyme-laced dauphinoise, in juniper jus. Desserts wheel out the big guns for sticky toffee pudding with peanut butter ice cream and blowtorched banana, or home-made cinnamon churros in chocolate sauce.

Chef Samantha Carlton **Owner** Adrian Sykes **Seats** 50 **Times** 12-9.30, All-day dining **Prices** Prices not confirmed, Service optional **Wines** 18 bottles under £30, 10 by glass **Parking** 4, Market car park **Notes** Sunday L, Vegetarian available, Children welcome

SCARBOROUGH
Map 17 TA08

Lanterna Ristorante
◉ Italian

tel: 01723 363616 **33 Queen St YO11 1HQ**
email: ralessio@lanterna-ristorante.co.uk
dir: *Phone for directions*

Convivial long-running Italian with classic cooking

It has been honoured by Italian newspaper La Stampa as 'the English temple of Italian cuisine', which seems an extraordinary accolade for an unassuming, albeit heartily convivial, place in Scarborough, but then Lanterna has been here for nigh on 40 years. Chef-patron, the tireless Giorgio Alessio, has been here since 1997, and undertook a major redecoration of the place in 2013, bringing in warm contrasting colour-schemes of reds and oranges, and sunny yellow and sky-blue, in the two dining rooms. The menu continues to fly the flag for simple, well-handled Italian cooking of the classic school: velvet crab with spaghetti and a creamy sauce, ravioli filled with ricotta and spinach in a tomato and basil sauce, fresh fish landed in Scarborough, and meaty options such as medallions of fillet steak served rare with garlic butter. Finish with a classic dessert like pannacotta flavoured with rum.

Chef Giorgio Alessio **Owner** Giorgio & Rachel Alessio **Seats** 35 **Times** 7-9.30, Closed 2 wks Oct, 25-26 Dec, 1 Jan, Sun, L all week **Prices** Starter £8.95-£36, Main £15.25-£49, Dessert £7.50-£11.50, Service optional **Wines** 35 bottles over £30, 36 bottles under £30, 5 by glass **Parking** On street, car park nearby **Notes** Vegetarian available, Children welcome

Palm Court Hotel
◉ Modern British

tel: 01723 368161 **St Nicholas Cliff YO11 2ES**
email: generalmanager@palmcourt-scarborough.co.uk
web: www.palmcourtscarborough.co.uk
dir: *In Scarborough town centre*

Modern dining in a Victorian hotel

Scarborough is enjoying something of a renaissance these days, and this grand old Victorian hotel has also moved with the times with a modern makeover sitting comfortably beside its elegant period features. Run by the same family for 30 years, it's a popular spot for the impeccably British institution that is afternoon tea, which should keep you ticking over until dinner in the elegant, neutral-toned restaurant, where tables swathed in floor-length linen sit beneath chandeliers. The kitchen doesn't try to reinvent the wheel here, relying on top-class local produce allied with tried-and-true culinary principles for its effect. Ham hock terrine with plum chutney and toasted brioche is a capably executed starter, followed by the simple comforts of roast belly pork with red cabbage, grain mustard mash and honey-glazed parsnips. Or there might be locally-landed cod matched with chorizo and red pepper vinaigrette, seafood pudding and spinach. Dessert is a refreshing duo of lemon tartlet and lemon curd sorbet.

Times 6-8.45, Closed 25 Dec, L all week

SCAWTON

Map 19 SE58

The Hare Inn

◎◎ Modern British NEW V

tel: 01845 597769 **YO7 2HG**
email: info@thehare-inn.com **web:** www.thehare-inn.com
dir: *1m from A170 between Helmsley & Thirsk*

Dynamic modern cooking in an old village inn

The Hare has the look of a proper moorland inn; a sturdy white-painted construction built to withstand the worst the climate can throw at it. It's very much a pub, with real ales at the pumps and a fire in the grate, and is an ideal spot to refuel while exploring the North York Moors. Look a little closer and you'll see quirky decorative touches here and there, and stick around to sample the food and you'll discover The Hare is a little dynamo of culinary endeavour. There's genuine contemporary flair on show, with creative dishes presented with style and cooked with precision (there's even a tasting menu). Start with scallops, cooked just-so, with nori and squid miso, or with smoked eel, apple and celeriac, and don't miss out on the hare, which comes as cannon, cutlets and bolognaise, with black pudding and carrots in various ways. There are lots of terrific local ingredients on show to enhance the sense of place. Finish with a modern construction of chocolate, mango and passionfruit.

Chef Paul Christopher Jackson **Owner** Frank Whitehead Ltd **Seats** 22
Times 12-2.30/6-9, Closed 3-24 Jan, Mon-Tue, D Sun **Wines** 20 bottles over £30, 8 bottles under £30, 12 by glass **Parking** 12 **Notes** Tasting menu L 4/5 course £20/£35, D 4/6/8 course £25-£65, Sunday L £13.95-£22.95, Children welcome

SUTTON-ON-THE-FOREST

Map 19 SE56

The Rose & Crown

◎ Modern British

tel: 01347 811333 **Main St YO61 1DP**
dir: *8m N of York towards Helmsley on B1363*

A local flavour in a 200-year-old inn

There's no shortage of period charm at The Rose & Crown, with the 200-year-old inn still packing a punch when it comes to period features (wooden floors, low-beamed ceilings and the like), but it is looking pretty spruce these days, fit-for-purpose as a 21st-century dining pub. The culinary output is focused on seasonal and local ingredients. Start, perhaps, with pan-seared king scallops with celeriac purée and truffle oil sitting on rocket leaves and thinly sliced Granny Smith apples, or a crispy pork croquette made with Old Spots pork, served with a shot of local cider. Main-course Yorkshire Dales lamb consists of braised confit and mint-glazed cutlet, partnered with minted new potatoes and an apple crisp, while a meat-free main course might be vegetable strudel. Local rhubarb is a seasonal treat, perhaps in a crème brûlée, with Yorkshire lemon curd ice cream. And if you want to end on a savoury note, what else but three local cheeses with biscuits?

Times 12-2.30/6-9, Closed Jan, Mon, D Sun

THIRSK

Map 19 SE48

The Black Lion & Bar Bistro

◎ Modern British V

tel: 01845 574302 **8 Market Place YO7 1LB**
email: info@blacklionthirsk.co.uk **web:** www.blacklionthirsk.co.uk
dir: *Phone for directions*

Traditional and modernist cooking in a revamped Yorkshire pub

A dramatic up-tick in The old Black Lion, easily found in the centre of the moorland market town of Thirsk, has produced an unmistakably modern venue. Rustic wood tables, plain half-panelled walls and a slate-tiled floor form a neutral backdrop to the well-supported buzzy ambience of the place. Menus change seasonally and are supplemented by blackboard specials, and the style mixes indelible British tradition with what is now equally indelible British modernism. A hearty bowl of Shetland mussels with smoked bacon in a cider broth with toasted sourdough is a good start, or there may be a modern reference dish such as scallops with pork belly and pea purée. For mains, daily fish specials and fine meats are treated with respect, as for thickly carved roast duck breast with Savoy cabbage, black pudding, duck-fat potatoes and a Chinese-spiced orange glaze. The homelier things are done well too, with Black Sheep ale going into the cod batter, and Sunday roasts arriving with all the required trimmings. Pannacotta in a Kilner jar is an improbable idea that works, its vanilla intensity counterpointed by sharp apple jelly, caramelised pistachios and a cloud of candyfloss.

Chef Harrison Barraclough **Owner** Paul Binnington **Seats** 100, Pr/dining room 20
Times 11.30-2.30/6.30-9, Closed D Sun-Mon **Prices** Fixed L 2 course £10-£16, Fixed D 3 course £15-£25, Tasting menu £40-£65, Starter £4.50-£7.95, Main £10.50-£22.50, Dessert £4.50-£5.50 **Wines** 2 bottles over £30, 20 bottles under £30, 10 by glass **Parking** 10 **Notes** Steak night Wed, Sunday L £7.50-£13, Children welcome

WEST WITTON
Map 19 SE08

The Wensleydale Heifer
◉ Modern British V

tel: 01969 622322 **Main St DL8 4LS**
email: info@wensleydaleheifer.co.uk **web:** www.wensleydaleheifer.co.uk
dir: On A684 (3m W of Leyburn)

Top-notch seafood and more in the heart of the Yorkshire Dales

Dining on super-fresh fish and seafood isn't the first thing that comes to mind when you're in the heart of the beautiful Yorkshire Dales National Park, but this chic 17th-century inn with boutique rooms draws foodies from far and wide for its piscine pleasures. Choose from the more casual fish bar, done out with rattan chairs and pale wood tables, and a smart restaurant, where Doug Hyde artwork hangs above chocolate leather chairs and linen-clothed tables. The wide-ranging menu offers something for all comers: king prawns are given an Asian spin with sweet chilli, sesame, coriander, crispy shallots, cashews, toasted coconut and Japanese yakiniku dipping sauce. Next up, salmon and crab are baked in a banana leaf and matched with Thai peanut curry sauce. It's not all about fish, either: the kitchen pleases carnivores too with prime slabs of locally-reared beef.

Chef David Moss **Owner** David & Lewis Moss **Seats** 70 **Times** 12-2.30/6-9.30 **Prices** Fixed L 2 course £19.75, Fixed D 3 course £21.75, Starter £8.50-£12.50, Main £16.25-£46, Dessert £7.50-£9, Service optional 10% **Wines** 31 bottles over £30, 26 bottles under £30, 13 by glass **Parking** 30 **Notes** Sunday L £21.75-£24.75, Children welcome

WHITBY
Map 19 NZ81

The Cliffemount Hotel
◉◉ Modern British

tel: 01947 840103 **Bank Top Ln, Runswick Bay TS13 5HU**
email: info@cliffemounthotel.co.uk **web:** www.cliffemounthotel.co.uk
dir: Exit A174, 8m N of Whitby, 1m to end

Simple but effective cooking in a clifftop hotel

Visitors to the ruined 13th-century abbey at Whitby, note that a mere five miles outside the town is the petite fishing village of Runswick Bay, where overlooking said bay from a windy perch is The Cliffemount. Indeed, the bluster off the sea is about as turbulent as things get in this sublimely peaceful spot, and the plainly decorated dining room enjoys the best of the views. The cooking keeps things reasonably simple but very effective. A large glass plate bearing a starter of grilled mackerel caught in the bay, with curried mussels and spring onion, makes the point eloquently, or there could be pork and apricot terrine with cranberry-clementine chutney. Fish is just as strong a suit at main, perhaps for well-timed hake with a croquette of brown shrimps in scampi bisque, while meat may be Gressingham duck breast with butternut purée and dauphinoise. Mulled plums are a delightful accompaniment to warm orange cake and vanilla ice cream, while local cheeses come with home-made cheddar biscuits and Black Sheep ale cake.

Chef David Spencer **Owner** Ian & Carol Rae **Seats** 50 **Times** 12-2.30/6-9 **Prices** Fixed D 3 course £25-£30, Tasting menu £29-£39, Starter £5-£11, Main £13-£25, Dessert £5-£8, Service optional **Wines** 3 bottles over £30, 24 bottles under £30, 10 by glass **Parking** 25 **Notes** Sunday L £11.95-£15.95, Vegetarian available, Children welcome

Estbek House
◉◉ Modern British

tel: 01947 893424 **East Row, Sandsend YO21 3SU**
email: info@estbekhouse.co.uk **web:** www.estbekhouse.co.uk
dir: From Whitby follow A174 towards Sandsend. Estbek House just before bridge next to Hart Inn

Fresh seafood by the sea near Whitby

Overlooking the North Sea just north of Whitby, Estbek House is perfectly positioned to source its materials from the chilly waters out front and the rolling moors behind (the North Yorks Moor National Park no less), and that's exactly what the kitchen team does. It all takes place in a handsome Regency house (Grade II listed) that operates as a restaurant with rooms of considerable charm. The smart restaurant has a soothing modernity and the staff are on the ball. Wild fish is the main passion here, hauled from local waters and prepared simply. Start with pan-seared scallops (from Shetland, but they grow 'em good up there) with pea purée and crisp Parma ham, and then it's into the main event, lemon sole, perhaps, expertly filleted and served with watercress sauce (or another sauce if you prefer) and dauphinoise potatoes and mixed veg. There's fish pie, too, plus local fillet steak glazed with Shiraz, and, for dessert, plum soup with ginger sorbet.

Chef Tim Lawrence **Owner** D Cross, T Lawrence **Seats** 40, Pr/dining room 20 **Times** 6-9, Closed 1 Jan-10 Feb, L all week **Prices** Starter £7.95-£10.45, Main £19.95-£36, Dessert £6.95-£8.95, Service optional **Wines** 100 bottles over £30, 20 bottles under £30, 12 by glass **Parking** 6 **Notes** Children welcome

YARM
Map 19 NZ41

Judges Country House Hotel
◉◉◉ – see page 574

YORK
Map 16 SE65

BEST WESTERN PLUS Dean Court Hotel
◉◉ Modern British

tel: 01904 625082 **Duncombe Place YO1 7EF**
email: sales@deancourt-york.co.uk **web:** www.deancourt-york.co.uk
dir: City centre, directly opposite York Minster

Contemporary Yorkshire cooking next to the Minster

Sitting on the corner of Petergate, the original principal thoroughfare through Roman York, Dean Court is an amalgam of Victorian buildings originally put up to house clergy at the celebrated Minster, adjacency to which is a powerful selling-point for today's privately run boutique hotel. Neither Gothic medievalism nor Victorian interior design have been carried through to the DCH dining room, which is a clean-lined, light-coloured contemporary haven adorned with decorative twigs. The modern styling gives a clue to the orientation of the cooking, where Yorkshire produce is put to effective use in offerings such as pigeon breast on beetroot risotto in blackcurrant jus, followed by sea bass and wilted spinach in shellfish bisque, or roast breast of guinea fowl with braised red cabbage in Madeira jus. The show-stopping sharing dish is rib of beef carved at the table and served with dauphinoise, and the show closes with variations on a theme of mango – brûlée, cheesecake and jelly.

Times 12.30-2/7-9.30, Closed 25 Dec eve, L Mon-Fri

YORK *continued*

The Churchill Hotel

◎◎ Modern British

tel: 01904 644456 **65 Bootham YO30 7DQ**
email: info@churchillhotel.com **web:** www.churchillhotel.com
dir: *On A19 (Bootham), W from York Minster, hotel 250yds on right*

Imaginative food and piano music

The set-up is all rather civilised in this Georgian mansion in its own grounds just a short walk from York Minster. The Churchill blends the airy elegance of its period pedigree with the sharp looks of a contemporary boutique city hotel in a dining room that looks through those vast arching windows (that the Georgians did so well) into the garden, where the trees are spangled in fairy lights. Laid-back live music floats from a softly-tinkling baby grand piano as the soundtrack to cooking that hits the target with its imaginative modern pairings of top-grade regional produce. Local wood pigeon, for example, is paired with black pudding bonbons, bitter chocolate and espresso jelly, while main-course saddle of venison might share a plate with Morteau sausage, choucroute, parsley root, and red wine salsify. To finish, duck eggs add extra oomph to a custard tart served with clementine, apricot and vanilla ice cream.

Times 11-2.30/5-9.30

Le Cochon Aveugle

◎◎ French **NEW** v

tel: 01904 640222 **37 Walmgate YO1 9TX**
email: cochonaveugle@gmail.com
dir: *Next to St Denys Church on Walmgate*

Contemporary French bistro that's a cut above

With no bar and just 16 covers, this converted shop in the centre of York deserves its 'small but perfectly formed' tag. With its black-and-white chequered floor, simple wooden furniture and linen napkins, there is an old-school French bistro feel to the place, although the contemporary cooking has considerably more flair and ambition than that. This is Joshua Overington's first solo venture, with partner Victoria running front-of-house, and the limitations of the tiny open kitchen means that only a fixed-price six-course tasting menu is served. The flavours may be classical, but the execution and presentation is thoroughly modern, as demonstrated in an arresting starter of grilled Yorkshire asparagus, quail's egg, lemon jam and parmesan. Mains are equally punchy – blow-torched mackerel turns up with salmon roe and a cauliflower farotto that uses spelt rather than traditional risotto rice, while spring lamb is paired with a light bean cassoulet and hazelnut crumble. For dessert, there may be Brillat-Savarin cheesecake, meringue and strawberry sorbet.

Chef Joshua Overington **Owner** Joshua Overington, Victoria Roberts **Seats** 18
Times 5.45-9, Closed 3 wks Jan, Sun-Mon, L all week **Prices** Tasting menu £35,
Service optional **Wines** 11 bottles over £30, 18 bottles under £30, 5 by glass
Parking On street, George St car park **Notes** Tasting menu 6 course, Children 8 yrs+

Judges Country House Hotel ❀❀❀

YARM	Map 19 NZ41

Modern British v **NOTABLE WINE LIST**

tel: 01642 789000 **Kirklevington Hall TS15 9LW**
email: enquiries@judgeshotel.co.uk **web:** www.judgeshotel.co.uk
dir: *1.5m from junct W A19, take A67 towards Kirklevington, hotel 1.5m on left*

Country-house cooking in glorious grounds

The present name derives from its use by Middlesbrough circuit judges in the 1970s and 1980s. When they relinquished it, it was acquired by its current owners, the Downs family, who have restored the 22 acres of grounds, including a woodland walk and walled kitchen garden, to something like their former splendour. The interiors are on the magnificent side too, with a conservatory extension at the front to capitalise on the garden views. A tented ceiling and gathered drapes create a stylish atmosphere to match. John Schwarz takes a scrupulous approach to the devising of dishes, insisting that everything on the plate is there for sound culinary reasons, not because it looks good or sounds exotic. The result is an accessible style of country-house cooking that fires on all cylinders. Yellison's goats' cheese turns up with textured beetroot variations and truffled honey dressing for an assertive starter, or there might be chunky game terrine with mooli and plum chutney. Fish is confidently handled in a main course that combines halibut with chorizo, broccoli and spinach, while grain-crusted venison is traditionally combined with apple, red cabbage and black pudding. Sunday lunch produces the treat of locally-reared beef in its pan juices with roasties and Yorkshire pudding. The sense of being thoroughly spoiled continues to the finishing-line, where warm Cluizel chocolate cake with hazelnut ice cream awaits alongside macadamia parfait with prunes and Earl Grey ice cream.

Chef John Schwarz **Owner** Mr M Downs **Seats** 60, Pr/dining room 50
Times 12-2/7-9.30, **Prices** Fixed L 2 course £27.45-£30.45, Fixed D 3 course £39.50, Starter £11.95-£14.95, Main £34.50-£41.50, Dessert £11.95-£18.95, Service optional **Wines** 107 bottles over £30, 28 bottles under £30, 12 by glass **Parking** 110 **Notes** Early bird menu, Sunday L £29.50, Children welcome

The Grand Hotel & Spa, York

◉◉ Modern British

tel: 01904 380038 **Station Rise YO1 6HT**
email: dining@thegrandyork.co.uk **web:** www.thegrandyork.co.uk
dir: *A1 junct 47, A59 signed York, Harrogate & Knaresborough. In city centre, near station*

Classic grills and creative modern ideas amid Edwardian splendour

Hard by the city's historic walls, the grand Edwardian edifice built as the headquarters of the North Eastern Railway has been stylishly repurposed as a luxury hotel, seamlessly blending palatial original features with 21st-century facilities, a swish spa down in the former vaults, and up-to-date dining in Hudsons, a smart, brasserie-style grill room. Straight-up steaks are sourced from a Yorkshire farm – a 10-oz rib-eye, for example, served with proper chips, Portobello mushrooms, confit tomato and Café de Paris butter – but the kitchen's imaginative modern repertoire appeals to a wider audience than the merely carnivorous. For starters, there's dressed Whitby crab, the rich brown meat leavened by sour apple jelly and sorrel sorbet, and sticking with a fishy theme, main-course stone bass with fennel, langoustines, herbs, buckwheat and bisque. Otherwise, pine-roasted wild venison with on-trend parsley root, choucroute, romanesco and juniper and orange jus might catch the eye, and to finish, more local flavour in the shape of Yorkshire ginger parkin dolled up with rhubarb, vanilla parfait and orange.

Chef Craig Atchinson **Owner** Splendid Hospitality Group **Seats** 60, Pr/dining room 32 **Times** 12.30-2.30/6.30-10 **Prices** Starter £6.50-£11.50, Main £14.95-£32.50, Dessert £7.95-£9.50, Service optional **Wines** 136 bottles over £30, 25 bottles under £30, 15 by glass **Parking** NCP Tanner Row **Notes** Sunday L £19.95-£24.95, Vegetarian available, Children welcome

The Grange Hotel

◉◉ Modern

tel: 01904 644744 **1 Clifton YO30 6AA**
email: info@grangehotel.co.uk **web:** www.grangehotel.co.uk
dir: *A19 (York/Thirsk road), approx 400yds from city centre*

Classy cooking in a city-centre hotel

Behind the pillared frontage of this classic 1829 townhouse is a designer-led interior of some panache, with inviting sofas, paintings on the walls, open fires and heavy curtains. The restaurant itself is divided into three distinct sections, all flamboyantly decorated, with walls and ceiling painted to create a tented effect, a horseracing mural, theatrical drapes at the windows in the red area and corners and alcoves with silver birch branches covered in twinkly lights. The cooking makes an impact, with the kitchen clearly taking a broad-based attitude, moving with the times and picking up ideas from near and far. How about 'pastrami' of salmon with wild garlic and micro salad, or another well-balanced starter of sliced smoked duck with figs, radishes and maple dressing? Diehards could go for a grilled steak as main course; others could opt for lamb loin and sweetbreads offset by pickled tomatoes and herby couscous. End with an attractively plated pudding such as hot chocolate fondant with white chocolate chip ice cream.

Chef Will Nicol **Owner** Jeremy & Vivien Cassel **Seats** 60, Pr/dining room 75 **Times** 12-2.30/6.30-9.30, Closed L Mon-Sat, D Sun **Prices** Prices not confirmed **Wines** 17 bottles over £30, 25 bottles under £30, 11 by glass **Parking** 26 **Notes** Brasserie early bird 3 course for 2 before 7pm, Sunday L, Vegetarian available, Children welcome

Guy Fawkes Inn

◉ Traditional British

tel: 01904 466674 **25 High Petergate YO1 7HP**
email: guyfawkesinn@gmail.com **web:** www.gfyork.com
dir: *A64 onto A1036 signed York & inner ring road. Over bridge into Duncombe Place, right into High Petergate*

Historic city-centre inn serving classic British food

The Gunpowder Plotter was born on this spot in 1570, in the shadow of York Minster, a fact which adds a frisson to the pub that has done business here for centuries. It is a darkly atmospheric, history-steeped den with an interior akin to stepping into an Old Master painting, with roaring log fires, wooden floors, gas lighting, cosy nooks and crannies, and cheerful service that suits the buzzy vibe. Menus change regularly to keep step with the seasons and daily chalkboard specials follow a hearty modern pub grub course, treating great local produce with honest, down-to-earth simplicity. Expect hearty main courses such as a porcine plateful of braised belly and seared loin of pork with a pig's cheek, black pudding and braising jus, pan-fried salmon with mussel and cockle chowder, or North Sea pollack with minted crushed peas and proper chips. And for afters, it's sticky toffee pudding with clotted cream.

Chef Adie Knowles **Owner** Phil Barker **Seats** 32 **Times** 12-4/5-8.45 **Prices** Fixed L 2 course £10, Starter £3.95-£13.50, Main £9.95-£21.95, Dessert £5.95-£7.95, Service optional **Wines** 8 bottles over £30, 18 bottles under £30, 11 by glass **Notes** Sunday L £10.95, Children welcome

Hotel du Vin & Bistro York

◉ European, French

tel: 01904 557350 **89 The Mount YO24 1AX**
email: info.york@hotelduvin.com **web:** www.hotelduvin.com
dir: *A1036 towards city centre, 6m. Hotel on right through lights*

Sturdy French domestic fare from HdV

The York billet of the HdV group is a late Georgian townhouse in the vicinity of the Minster's Gothic splendour and the city racecourse, a location none too subtly referenced in the equestrian pictures that adorn the bistro dining room. Bare tables and floor fit in with the unbuttoned ethos, and the menu offers sturdy French domestic fare with minimal flounce, much of which will be familiar with travellers who have hopped from one branch to another. Dressed crab on toasted baguette with radish in peppery mayonnaise might be the prelude to a robust fish main course such as roast cod on braised Puy lentils with button onions and pancetta, or calves' liver and bacon with mash, or the successful duck version of shepherd's pie. Lemon tart is perhaps a little sturdy, though offset with a decent raspberry sorbet.

Chef James Skinner **Owner** KSL **Seats** 80, Pr/dining room 24 **Times** 12-2.30/6-10.30 **Prices** Fixed L 2 course fr £14.95, Fixed D 3 course fr £16.95 **Wines** 50 bottles over £30, 20 bottles under £30, 18 by glass **Parking** 18 **Notes** Sun brunch 4 course with French market table, Sunday L fr £22.95, Vegetarian available, Children welcome

YORK *continued*

The Judge's Lodging

Modern British **NEW**

tel: 01904 638733 & 639312 **9 Lendal YO1 8AQ**
email: relax@judgeslodgingyork.co.uk **web:** www.judgeslodgingyork.co.uk
dir: *10 min walk from York train station*

All-day menu in a range of different spaces

The Georgian townhouse hard by the Minster has been creatively retooled as a modern hotel with a plethora of eating and drinking options. A cellar bar with original vaulted ceiling includes a glass box space, there are two sun terraces, a cask ale bar, and one consecrated to speciality gins and whiskies. Dining can be elegantly panelled or domestic-cosy, as you fancy, and the all-day menus trade in a wide range of international favourite dishes. Curtain raisers could be mushrooms fried with garlic and herbs in hollandaise, or chicken liver parfait wrapped in prosciutto with apricot and orange chutney. Choose your main act from a creative burger, the house fish pie (salmon, haddock and tiger prawns under cheesy mash), or succulent, accurately timed rib-eye in béarnaise with fat chips and rocket. Few will pass up the chance of a chocolate brownie with salted caramel ice cream, unless it's for rhubarb crème brûlée.

Chef David Ormsby **Owner** Thwaites Inns of Character **Seats** 100 **Times** 7.30am-10pm, All-day dining **Prices** Fixed L 2 course fr £12, Starter £4.95-£9, Main £9.75-£29, Dessert £4-£6.50 **Wines** 11 bottles over £30, 29 bottles under £30, 14 by glass **Parking** NCP, Marygate **Notes** Sunday L, Vegetarian available, Children welcome

Lamb & Lion Inn

Modern, Traditional British

tel: 01904 654112 **2-4 High Petergate YO1 7EH**
email: reservations@lambandlionyork.com **web:** www.lambandlionyork.com
dir: *A64 onto A1036. 3.5m, at rdbt 3rd exit, continue on A1036. 2m, right into High Petergate*

Solid English tradition with cosmopolitan touches in the old city walls

Seamlessly grafted into the ancient city walls of medieval York, its beer garden overlooked by the Minster, the Lamb & Lion makes a good fist of pleasing all comers, young and old, locals and visitors. As well as a traditional wood-panelled pub, it boasts a small parlour dining room of great character, with a high ceiling, open fire, carriage lanterns and seating on pews. The undisputed classic of the kitchen is a steak pie to be proud of, and Sunday roasts are a reliable draw too, offering topside or pork loin with Yorkshires and proper stock-pan gravy. Elsewhere, things get a trifle more cosmopolitan, with starters of red mullet on crab and coriander risotto, or crackled pork belly in cider vinegar caramel. Then comes coley fillet on paella, or a satisfying presentation of pot-roasted duck breast with herbed pommes Anna, braised red cabbage and a multitude of cherries. To finish, there's crème brûlée, given an old-English touch with quince, rhubarb fool with lemon biscotti, or white chocolate cheesecake in bourbon syrup.

Chef Katie Hoskins **Owner** Phil Barker **Seats** 40 **Times** 12-3/6-9 **Prices** Prices not confirmed, Service optional **Wines** 15 bottles under £30 **Parking** Marygate car park **Notes** Sunday L, Vegetarian available, Children welcome

Melton's Restaurant

Modern British

tel: 01904 634341 **7 Scarcroft Rd YO23 1ND**
email: greatfood@meltonsrestaurant.co.uk
dir: *South from centre across Skeldergate Bridge, restaurant opposite Bishopthorpe Road car park*

Long-running favourite with a well-judged menu

Melton's remains as popular as ever, and it's been going for over 20 years. It's bright and modern, with mirrors and murals on the walls, a wooden floor, banquettes and unclothed tables – all very unpretentious, with friendly but efficient service. The kitchen conscientiously uses Yorkshire produce, name-checking suppliers for dishes that are well thought out and carefully cooked. The menu of modern ideas offers plenty to enjoy – cep and field mushroom parfait with herb custard, parsley and garlic purée, say, or coley brandade with celeriac and truffle oil to start, followed by the full-throttle piggy flavours of belly pork, ham hock terrine, and pork and cep ballotine with soured cabbage and boulangère potatoes. If you're in the mood for fish, smoked haddock is matched with warm artichoke mousse, poached egg yolk, and leek and potato. The regional approach extends to cheeses and Yorkshire rhubarb with sablé biscuits and vanilla sabayon.

Chef Calvin Miller, Michael Hjort **Owner** Michael & Lucy Hjort **Seats** 30, Pr/dining room 16 **Times** 12-2/5.30-10, Closed 23 Dec-9 Jan, Sun-Mon **Prices** Fixed L 2 course fr £23, Tasting menu £40, Starter £7.10-£9.50, Main £16.70-£22.30, Dessert £7-£7.20, Service optional **Wines** 44 bottles over £30, 66 bottles under £30, 6 by glass **Parking** Car park opposite **Notes** Pre-theatre D, Early evening 2/3 course £23/£26, Vegetarian available, Children welcome

Middlethorpe Hall & Spa

Modern, Traditional British NOTABLE WINE LIST

tel: 01904 641241 **Bishopthorpe Rd, Middlethorpe YO23 2GB**
email: info@middlethorpe.com **web:** www.middlethorpe.com
dir: *A64 exit York West. Follow signs Middlethorpe & racecourse*

Seasonal modern British cooking in a 17th-century mansion

Middlethorpe Hall is part of the National Trust's portfolio of historic buildings, but this William and Mary-era property is a country-house hotel, not a museum. The majestic old building stands in 20 acres of primped gardens and parkland, while the interior designers have achieved a classy 18th-century look within – but there's a modern spa, too. The oak-panelled restaurant matches the smart and traditional mood of the house, with a refined formality that extends to the highly personable and professional service. The kitchen is happy to draw on contemporary ideas and offers up a fashionable surf and turf combination of diver-caught roasted scallop with sticky pork belly, kohlrabi and apple purée among first courses, or go for poached and roasted quail with truffles bringing a hint of luxury to the plate. Next up, there is an optional sorbet. Among main courses, pan-fried fillet of stone bass comes with cauliflower in various forms and Ebène caviar, and, to finish, Bramley apple soufflé is served with crumble and apple ice cream. The cracking wine list offers good advice on food and wine matching.

Chef Nicholas Evans **Owner** The National Trust **Seats** 60, Pr/dining room 56 **Times** 12.30-2/6.30-9.45, Closed 25 Dec, L 1 Jan, D 24 & 31 Dec **Prices** Fixed L 2 course fr £21.50, Fixed D 3 course fr £43, Tasting menu fr £99, Starter £10.50-£15.50, Main £21.50-£31.50, Dessert £8-£13.50 **Wines** 194 bottles over £30, 38 bottles under £30, 15 by glass **Parking** 70 **Notes** Gourmet menu 6 course, Sunday L fr £30, Vegetarian available, Children 6 yrs+

Oxo's on The Mount

◉◉ Modern European v

tel: 01904 619444 **The Mount Royale Hotel, 119 The Mount YO24 1GU**
email: info@oxosrestaurantyork.com
dir: *W on A1036, 0.5m after racecourse. Hotel on right after lights*

Yorkshire produce in modern European guise

Cobbled ingeniously together from a pair of Regency-era houses, The Mount Royale Hotel manages to create the atmosphere of a country-house venue within the confines of the city. Sitting proud on top of the Mount, one of the ancient approaches to medieval York, and just a canter from York racecourse, its softly-lit main dining room extends into an outdoor terrace called the Gazeover. The kitchen celebrates fine Yorkshire produce in contemporary dishes that pay a clear homage to French classics, getting off the mark with ham hock and parsley terrine with a quail's egg, and Wensleydale cheese and pineapple salad pointed with honey and mustard dressing. For mains, a prime piece of turbot is poached in butter and supported by Whitby crab and tarragon gnocchi, peas, samphire, and champagne butter sauce. Local meat fans might go for rump of Yorkshire lamb with dauphinoise potatoes, red wine-braised baby onions, butternut squash and redcurrant and rosemary jus. To finish, crème brûlée is tweaked with raspberry and saffron, and matched with macadamia shortbread and raspberry coulis.

Chef Russell Johnson **Owner** Richard Stuart Oxtoby **Seats** 70, Pr/dining room 18 **Times** 6-9.30, Closed L Mon-Sat **Prices** Starter £5.50-£12.50, Main £15.50-£28.95, Dessert £7.95-£8.95 **Wines** 6 bottles over £30, 30 bottles under £30, 16 by glass **Parking** 15 **Notes** Sunday L £17.95-£21.95, Children welcome

The Park Restaurant@Marmadukes Town House Hotel

◉◉◉ – *see below*

SOUTH YORKSHIRE

ROSSINGTON   Map 16 SK69

BEST WESTERN PREMIER *Mount Pleasant Hotel*

◉ Modern British

tel: 01302 868696 & 868219 **Great North Rd DN11 0HW**
email: reception@mountpleasant.co.uk **web:** www. mountpleasant.co.uk
dir: *S of Doncaster, adjacent to Robin Hood Airport, on A638 between Bawtry & Doncaster*

Sound country-house cooking in a tip-top hotel

This smart 18th-century country-house hotel squirrelled away in 100 acres of beautiful woodland feels miles from anywhere, yet it is on the outskirts of Doncaster. While the grand old house is traditional in many aspects of its cosy decor and formal-yet-friendly service, Mount Pleasant comes fully geared for the 21st century with a full complement of glossy spa, leisure and conference facilities. The kitchen sources its raw materials diligently and takes a broadly modern British line in its well-thought-out repertoire of comfort-oriented classics. A twice-baked Yorkshire cheese soufflé is well-rendered, ahead of slow-cooked shoulder of lamb with buttery mashed potato, roast Mediterranean vegetables and tomato jus, or you might go for fish in the shape of sea bass with minted fritters and garden pea broth. For pudding, salted caramel chocolate torte with caramel ice cream is as rich and indulgent as anyone could reasonably ask for.

Times 12-2/6.45-9.30, Closed 25 Dec

The Park Restaurant@Marmadukes Town House Hotel ◉◉◉

YORK   Map 16 SE65

Modern British **NEW** v

tel: 01904 640101 **4-5 St Peters Grove, Bootham YO30 6AQ**
email: reservations@marmadukesyork.com **web:** www.marmadukesyork.com
dir: *St Peters Grove, directly opposite St Peters School on Bootham, York*

Stunning views from an elegant restaurant

A Yorkshireman born and bred, Adam Jackson made his name in the area heading up the kitchen at The Black Swan in Oldstead. Opening his own restaurant was a logical career move, and not wanting to leave behind 'God's own county', he has set up shop on his own account in a smart hotel in a Victorian gentleman's townhouse just outside the city walls but within a short stroll of the Minster and city centre. The dining room occupies the modern conservatory extension and looks the part with its understated colour scheme, wooden floors and tables; it's an intimate dinner-only set-up, and with just 20 diners to cater for, good-humoured service strikes just the right balance of professional intent and chatty informality, and Jackson can ensure pin-point accuracy of flavours and textures in his imaginative contemporary cooking. Be prepared for a leisurely experience as it's all delivered via a regularly-changing six-course tasting menu that takes full account of local, seasonal produce. An earthy starter brings a platter of pulled pork with pickled vegetables, pease pudding and delicious home-baked bread, followed by tortellini, filled with pumpkin and peppers and helped along by shaved parmesan. Precisely handled monkfish wows with simple, vibrant Thai flavours of soy and sesame, while superb lamb is matched inventively with a clever spin on boulangère potatoes, which are transformed into liquid form and served as a jus, together with carrots and kohlrabi. Dessert is a fun take on a chocolate orange theme, or there might be apple crème brûlée. A concise, thoughtfully-composed wine list offers something to suit most pockets.

Chef Adam Jackson **Owner** Poisontip Ltd **Seats** 25 **Times** 7-8, Closed Sun-Mon, L all wk **Prices** Tasting menu £48, Service optional **Wines** 10 bottles over £30, 10 bottles under £30, 6 by glass **Parking** 20 **Notes** Children welcome

ROTHERHAM
Map 16 SK49

Hellaby Hall Hotel

Modern British

tel: 01709 702701 **Old Hellaby Ln, Hellaby S66 8SN**
email: reservations@hellabyhallhotel.co.uk **web:** www.hellabyhallhotel.co.uk
dir: *0.5m off M18 junct 1, onto A631 towards Maltby. Hotel in Hellaby – NB do not use postcode for Sat Nav*

Enterprising modern British cooking in a tasteful hotel

This hotel in pretty gardens has at its core a distinctive 17th-century manor of grey stone over three floors. The Carnelly Restaurant, spacious and airy, has white beams in the vaulted ceiling and floral yellow wallpaper on one wall contrasting with the otherwise subdued decor and darkwood furniture. A grounding in the classical French repertoire shines out of the cooking, with the kitchen following a more or less modern British route. Chicken and thyme ballotine is a first-rate rendition, complemented by pickled vegetables, another starter perhaps smoked haddock rillettes with arancini and pickled fennel salad. Clearly defined flavours are hallmarks, seen in main courses of tender honey-glazed pork shoulder in a rich sauce with apple purée, caramelised red cabbage and buttery mash, and pan-fried grey mullet with pancetta, mushroom risotto and confit shallots. For dessert, go for retro steamed syrup sponge with custard, or classic lemon tart with raspberry sorbet.

Chef Russ Mountford **Owner** Prima Hotels Ltd **Seats** 62, Pr/dining room 12
Times 6-9.15, Closed L all week **Prices** Fixed D 3 course fr £26.95, Service optional
Wines 4 bottles over £30, 8 bottles under £30, 4 by glass **Parking** 268
Notes Vegetarian available, Children welcome

SHEFFIELD
Map 16 SK38

Nonnas

Modern Italian NOTABLE WINE LIST

tel: 0114 268 6166 **535-541 Ecclesall Rd S11 8PR**
email: sheffield@nonnas.co.uk
dir: *From city centre onto Ecclesall Rd, large red building on left*

Italian mini-chain with exceptional modern cooking

Nonnas is a bustling, good-natured Italian restaurant with friendly staff, café-style marble-topped tables and green walls. Many of the staples are made in-house, from pasta to ice cream, using Yorkshire produce and ingredients flown in from the homeland, and the menu is a celebration of modern Italian cooking. This is an imaginative kitchen turning out properly cooked, highly original dishes. Rigatoni is sauced with duck leg braised in vin santo, with sausage and sage, and linguine with crab, chilli and fennel. Among accomplished secondi there might be the vivid combinations of Merlot-braised oxtail with beetroot mash and horseradish canederli (bread dumplings) and grilled sea bass fillet with borlotti bean and tomato stew and rosemary aïoli. Inspired puddings have included chocolate and beetroot cake with sweet beetroot and balsamic ripple ice cream alongside classic tiramisù.

Chef Ross Sayles **Owner** Maurizio Mori **Seats** 80, Pr/dining room 30
Times 12-3.15/5-9.30, Closed 25 Dec, 1 Jan, Mon **Prices** Tasting menu £25-£50,
Starter £4.50-£15, Main £9.50-£45, Dessert £5-£15 **Wines** 28 bottles over £30, 21 bottles under £30, 22 by glass **Parking** On street **Notes** Sun brunch, Vegetarian available, Children welcome

Rafters Restaurant

Modern British, European

tel: 0114 230 4819 **220 Oakbrook Rd, Nethergreen S11 7ED**
email: bookings@raftersrestaurant.co.uk **web:** www.raftersrestaurant.co.uk
dir: *5 mins from Ecclesall road, Hunters Bar rdbt*

Creative cooking in a leafy neighbourhood

After over 20 years as a dining hotspot in the city, Rafters continues to go from strength to strength. That seems to be the way with Rafters; the city won't be without it. Located on the first floor of a shop in a green part of Sheffield, there are leafy views to be had and some seriously good cooking to be enjoyed. The room has capacious windows and a smart finish, with richly upholstered, high-backed chairs and tables laid with white linen cloths. The cooking is modern and the menu is packed with interesting combinations. A starter of cumin-spiced scallops with cauliflower and golden raisins is the kitchen's version of a modern classic, or go for celeriac risotto with compressed apple and roasted hazelnuts. Main courses are equally on the money, with a duo of pork (fillet and belly) with butternut squash purée and sage gnocchi, or fillet of sea bass with courgette purée, crushed ratte potatoes and tapenade. Finish with an egg custard tart with forced rhubarb.

Chef Thomas Lawson **Owner** Alistair Myers, Thomas Lawson **Seats** 38
Times 12-2/7-8.30, Closed 25-26 Dec, 24-30 Aug, Mon-Tue, L Wed-Sat **Prices** Fixed
D 3 course £39-£42, Tasting menu £58-£63, Service optional **Wines** 44 bottles over £30, 23 bottles under £30, 12 by glass **Parking** On street **Notes** Sunday L £28-£34, Vegetarian available, Children 5 yrs+

Whitley Hall Hotel

Modern British

tel: 0114 245 4444 **Elliott Ln, Grenoside S35 8NR**
email: reservations@whitleyhall.com **web:** www.whitleyhall.com
dir: *A61 past football ground, then 2m, right just before Norfolk Arms, left at bottom of hill. Hotel on left*

Imaginative British cooking in a stunning country hotel

Surrounded by rolling countryside, Whitley Hall is a solid stone mansion dating from the 16th century (it has a priest's hole) with 20 acres of grounds including lakes and immaculate gardens. In surroundings like these, it's no wonder the place is a popular wedding venue. The restaurant may have a whiff of formality, but the kitchen keeps ahead of the game with a thoroughly modern menu, with gratifying results. Juxtaposing fruit with meat seems to be a favoured device, so pressed rabbit terrine comes with poached grapes and apricot purée and could be followed by duck breast with peaches, caramelised fennel purée, vanilla-infused mash and a lavender reduction. The team's confidence brings off even some unconventional-sounding combinations: fried pig's cheek, for instance, with a coriander pudding, fine beans and a devilled quail's egg, then seared monkfish liver accompanying tournedos of Shetland salmon served with spicy Puy lentils, braised vegetables and fig and apple chutney. Originality doesn't dry up among puddings, either: try vanilla crème brûlée with roast plums, plum ripple ice cream and gingerbread.

Times 12-2/7-9.30

WORTLEY
Map 16 SK39

The Wortley Arms

◉◉ Modern British V

tel: 0114 288 8749 **Halifax Rd S35 7DB**
email: enquiries@wortley-arms.co.uk
dir: M1 junct 36. Follow Sheffield North signs, right at Tankersley garage, 1m on right

Contemporary and classic food in a Georgian pub

The Wortley Arms is a traditional Georgian coaching inn with a reassuring interior of panelled walls, solid oak beams, open fires, hunting-themed pictures and a jumble of furniture – in short, an appealing spot for a pint of local ale and some straightforward modern gastro pub cooking. The kitchen keeps a clear focus on local ingredients and seasonality in its menus, which take in timeless pub staples (perhaps beer-battered fish and chips with home-made tartare sauce, or gammon steak with griddled pineapple) and up-to-date ideas, starting with pan-fried belly pork with pig's cheek and butternut squash purée or goats' cheese pannacotta with pickled beetroot and beetroot crisp. Mains are all about prime local materials, such as roast rack of lamb served with a hotpot of shoulder meat, parsnips and roast shallots, or venison haunch with Puy lentils, creamed cabbage and a shepherd's pie croquette. Comforting conclusions come courtesy of desserts like sticky toffee pudding with pistachio ice cream and butterscotch sauce or a more fancy rhubarb and custard millefeuille with rhubarb ripple ice cream.

Chef Andy Gabbitas **Owner** Andy Gabbitas **Seats** 80, Pr/dining room 12 **Times** 12-2.30/5-9, Closed D Sun **Prices** Starter £5.75-£10, Main £11-£26, Dessert £5.75-£6.95, Service optional **Wines** 5 bottles over £30, 24 bottles under £30, 8 by glass **Parking** 30 **Notes** Sunday L £10.50-£18.50, Children welcome

WEST YORKSHIRE

ADDINGHAM
Map 19 SE04

Craven Heifer

◉◉ Modern British

tel: 01943 830106 **Main St LS29 0PL**
email: info@wellfedpubs.co.uk **web:** www.thecravenheifer.com
dir: Follow Addingham signs. At major rdbt turn onto B6160. Hotel visable from following junct

Switched-on cooking in an ambitious gastro-pub

An old stone village inn, the Craven Heifer offers boutique rooms and compelling contemporary food on the fringes of the Yorkshire Dales. There's a proper bar complete with a welcoming fire in the cooler months and a menu of classy versions of pub classics. The main dining takes place in the restaurant, where seven-course taster and à la carte menus showcase the ambition of the kitchen's output. There's a genuine regional flavour here, combined with a passion for modern culinary ways, and a bit of playfulness too. Start with 'cheese & pickle', which is ravioli of peppered goats' cheese served with scorched baby gem lettuce and a sherry reduction, or 'ox salad' with its smoked beef and oxtail fritter. Move on to North Yorkshire red deer with home-made black pudding and candied ginger, or a fishy number that combines butter-roasted stone bass with sea vegetables and Shetland mussel stew. Desserts are no less inventive: 'apple & custard' arrives as an Earl Grey pannacotta, poached Granny Smith and cinder toffee.

Chef Mark Owens **Owner** Craig Minto **Seats** 41, Pr/dining room 16 **Times** 12-2/5.30-9, Closed 2 Jan, Mon **Prices** Tasting menu £39, Starter £6-£10, Main £13-£24, Dessert £6-£8, Service optional **Wines** 10 bottles over £30, 32 bottles under £30, 14 by glass **Parking** 20 **Notes** Early bird menu 2/3 course £12/£15, Sunday L £18, Vegetarian available, Children welcome

BINGLEY
Map 19 SE13

Five Rise Locks Hotel & Restaurant

◉ Modern British V

tel: 01274 565296 **Beck Ln BD16 4DD**
email: info@five-rise-locks.co.uk **web:** www.five-rise-locks.co.uk
dir: From A650 signed Bingley centre, turn right Park Rd. Beck Lane 300mtrs on left

Unfussy cooking in a family-run hotel

Built by a successful Victorian businessman in 1875, this one-time mill owner's family home is now a family-run hotel on a pleasingly intimate scale (just nine bedrooms), with a restaurant that's worth knowing about. Done out in a smart manner with high-backed leather chairs, linen-clad tables and a splendid burgundy and cream paint job, it offers views in daylight hours over the garden and Aire Valley. On the menu you'll find some appealing combinations such as warm goats' cheese and red onion confit served en croûte, or pigeon breast with rocket and beetroot salad to start. Next up, perhaps pan-fried calves' liver with crushed new potatoes, cabbage and onion confit, and, to finish, lemon posset or a selection of British cheeses.

Chef Steven Heaton, Richard Stoyle **Owner** Richard & Margaret Stoyle **Seats** 40, Pr/dining room 20 **Times** 12-2/6.30-9.15, Closed L Mon-Sat, D Sun (ex residents) **Prices** Fixed L 3 course £14.95, Fixed D 3 course fr £16.95, Starter £4.50-£7.95, Main £13.95-£24, Dessert £4.50-£5.95, Service optional **Wines** 4 bottles over £30, 26 bottles under £30, 10 by glass **Parking** 15 **Notes** Early bird menu 2 course Mon-Sat 6.30-7.30pm, Sunday L £14.95, Children welcome

BRADFORD
Map 19 SE13

Prashad

◉ Indian Vegetarian V

tel: 0113 285 2037 **137 Whitehall Rd, Drighlington BD11 1AT**
email: info@prashad.co.uk
dir: Follow A650 Wakefield Road then Whitehall Road

Indian vegetarian food of the highest order

When it comes to pukka Indian cooking, the competition in Bradford is strong, but Mrs Kaushy Patel's take on the vegetarian repertoire ensures a zealous local following beats a path to her door. Expect a bright and cheerful look, with one wall taken up by a huge mural of an Indian street scene. The all-in-one thali platter is a splendid way in to the vegetarian cuisine of the Gujarat, or you could head south for a spicy uttapam or masala dosa pancake served with spicy lentil soup and coconut chutney. Curries include chole-chick-peas cooked with whole cumin seeds in a tomato and onion sauce, which goes great with light-as-air puri bread and classic tarka dhal. Spicing is spot on throughout, and breads are cooked fresh to order.

Chef Kaushy & Minal Patel **Owner** M & DKM Patel **Seats** 75, Pr/dining room 10 **Times** 12-11, All-day dining, Closed 25 Dec, Mon, L Tue-Thu **Prices** Starter £5.35-£11.65, Main £11.85-£16.95, Dessert £2.99-£6.25, Service optional **Wines** 4 bottles over £30, 24 bottles under £30, 6 by glass **Parking** 26 **Notes** Children welcome

CLIFTON
Map 16 SE12

Black Horse Inn Restaurant with Rooms

Modern British, Mediterranean

tel: 01484 713862 **Westgate HD6 4HJ**
email: mail@blackhorseclifton.co.uk
dir: M62 junct 25, Brighouse, follow signs

Bold British flavours in a Yorkshire inn

This rambling 17th-century inn is nowadays more a smart restaurant with rooms than pub, although real ales are dispensed in the beamed bar. There are two dining rooms, one with darkwood furniture under a beamed ceiling, the other with double-clothed tables. The kitchen aims high, delivering ambitiously creative dishes without ignoring old favourites like beer-battered haddock with traditional accompaniments. Seared scallops are partnered by a ham hock, pork and leek pie along with pea shoots, tomato and broad bean salad, plus bacon and tomato jam, a busy but accomplished starter. Follow that with something like a winter warmer of ox cheek pie under a mash topping with root vegetable crisps, braised red cabbage and blueberry jus. Finish with a labour-intensive pudding such as strawberry and champagne jelly with basil pannacotta and foam and strawberry soup.

Times 12-2.30/5.30-9.30, Closed D 25-26 Dec, 1 Jan

HALIFAX
Map 19 SE02

Design House Restaurant

– see below

Holdsworth House Hotel

Traditional British

tel: 01422 240024 **Holdsworth Rd, Holmfield HX2 9TG**
email: info@holdsworthhouse.co.uk **web:** www.holdsworthhouse.co.uk
dir: From Halifax take A629 (Keighley road), in 2m right at garage to Holmfield, hotel 1.5m on right

Secluded manor house with well-crafted cooking

Built during the reign of Charles I, Holdsworth House looks fit for a king with its handsome creeper-covered façade and charming period interior. There's nothing dated about the elegant public spaces, sporting stylish furniture and luxurious fabrics, while the restaurant is the embodiment of sophistication with its burnished oak-panelled walls, oil paintings and mullioned windows. The kitchen is in tune with the rest of the operation, delivering food that is rooted in British (and Yorkshire) tradition but has a bit of style about it. Partridge off the Dales may find themselves potted in a first course with plum compôte, while Jerusalem artichokes are roasted in hay and served with goats' curd, winter truffles and trumpet mushrooms. The grill cooks up steaks, lamb rump, pork chop and the like, served traditionally, or go for roast monkfish tail with pommes Anna. For dessert, the kitchen's style is neatly summed by a dish of warm ginger beer cake with popcorn ice cream and spiced plums. Sunday lunches are classic affairs, and afternoon tea is the real deal.

Chef Martin Henley **Owner** Gail Moss, Kim Wynn **Seats** 45, Pr/dining room 120 **Times** 12-2/7-9.30, Closed D 25-26 Dec **Prices** Prices not confirmed, Service optional 10% **Wines** 29 bottles over £30, 47 bottles under £30, 11 by glass **Parking** 60 **Notes** Tasting menu 5 course, Sunday L, Vegetarian available, Children welcome

Design House Restaurant

HALIFAX
Map 19 SE02

Modern British

tel: 01422 383242 **Dean Clough, Arts & Business Centre HX3 5AX**
email: info@taste-lcc-co.uk
dir: Phone for directions

Witty high-concept dining in an old carpet factory

Built in the mid-19th century to house a carpet factory, Dean Clough Mills is a piece of Yorkshire industrial heritage, now repurposed as an arts, design and education complex. Tucked away inside is this sparkling-white modern brasserie with stone-flagged floors and laminate tables decorated with blown-glass apples. A picture window allows peeps into the kitchen, where a small team headed by Lee Marshall cooks as far outside the box as it can get, best experienced in the six-course tasting menu. 'Spring Harvest' is the counter-intuitive title of an opening dish centred on a crab bonbon in a sea of crumbled black olive, alongside vibrant spring baby veg, tomato jelly and a pungent mayonnaise of smoked garlic. Thematic concepts continue into subsequent courses, which take in 'Seaweed and Turf', featuring a wakame seaweed bhaji with beef sukiyami and soya jelly in miso soup, 'Captain Birdseye', a cod cheek with parsley nitro-cake and sweet pear jelly, and 'Golden Fleece', which offers lamb rump with thunderously strong jellies of pea and garlic, a saffron tuile and red wine jus for pouring. After a pre-dessert of many elements, the fashionable reworking of commercial confectionery brands continues with a homage to After Eights, a terrine of chocolate mint pannacotta with a little demi-tasse of frappuccino. Incidentals establish the interactive procedure, as with the onion velouté that must be poured over an amuse of murky-black cheddar charcoal custard which dissolves on contact. Breads come in a drawstring pouch, petits fours in a shallow terracotta planter submerged in chocolate-crumb soil. Staggeringly in the circumstances, canapés come as a simple dish of mixed olives in the bar.

Chef Lee Marshall **Owner** Lee Marshall **Seats** 70 **Times** 12-2/5.30-9, Closed 26 Dec-8 Jan, Sun-Mon, L Sat **Prices** Fixed L 2 course £7.95-£10.90, Fixed D 3 course £18.95-£21.95, Tasting menu fr £60, Service optional **Wines** 18 bottles over £30, 44 bottles under £30, 10 by glass **Parking** 50 **Notes** Vegetarian available, Children welcome

Shibden Mill Inn

🏵🏵 Modern British V

tel: 01422 365840 **Shibden Mill Fold, Shibden HX3 7UL**
email: enquiries@shibdenmillinn.com **web:** www.shibdenmillinn.com
dir: *From A58 into Kell Lane, after 0.5m left into Blake Hill. Inn at bottom of hill on left*

Adventurous flavours in a renovated corn mill

This 17th-century inn, once a mill (the millstream runs past), is an atmospheric old place with nooks and crannies, open fires, low beams, rustic-looking furniture and friendly but professional staff all creating an inviting and hospitable environment, helped along by candlelight in the evenings. The kitchen puts its shoulder to the wheel, turning out some inspired dishes that show a degree of complexity. Crab with beetroot, pickled carrots and courgettes, burned lime and crackers is an impressive starter with multiple layers, as is a main course of rolled and poached saddle of wild rabbit (cooked to perfection) served with langoustines, five spice, roast carrots, aged ham and light Jersey Royal soufflé. Seasonal game is a strength – partridge and chestnut pie, roast pheasant – and vegetarians are well looked after too. To finish, artisan Yorkshire cheeses are an alternative to a beautifully presented dessert: perhaps lemon tart with orange meringue, blood orange, pistachio and sorrel delivering great flavours.

Chef Darren Parkinson **Owner** Simon & Caitlin Heaton **Seats** 50, Pr/dining room 12
Times 12-2/6-9.30, Closed Xmas, D 24-26 Dec, 1 Jan **Prices** Fixed L 2 course £12-£13, Starter £6-£11, Main £9-£29, Dessert £4-£8, Service optional **Wines** 32 bottles over £30, 54 bottles under £30, 22 by glass **Parking** 60 **Notes** Sunday L £13.50-£17.10, Children welcome

See advert on page 582

HOLMFIRTH   Map 16 SE10

The Spiced Pear

🏵🏵 Modern British **NEW** V

tel: 01484 683775 **Sheffield Rd, New Mill HD9 7TP**
email: info@thespicedpearhepworth.co.uk
dir: *Phone for directions*

Switched-on modern food in a trendy venue

It may be out in the countryside, but there's nothing rustic or chintzy about either the interior or the food in this trendy contemporary package comprising a cocktail bar, restaurant and 1940s-themed tea shop. Expectations are raised when you learn that the chef-patron has served time with Raymond Blanc and grows most of the fresh seasonal produce himself, sourcing the rest from local artisan suppliers. Bare wooden tables, leather chairs and piano music drifting in from the bar set the scene, and you can expect on-trend culinary thinking that delivers plenty of big flavours. With the team going about their business in the open kitchen, things start with a full-bore duo of pan-seared scallops and crispy pig's cheek balanced by tart apple purée, a soy and chicken reduction, and Waldorf salad. Next up, venison haunch steak is marinated with blackberry and juniper, pan-seared and served up with a crisp venison-packed filo 'cigar', parsley root purée, spring veg and a cracking Pontefract liquorice sauce. Dessert is a zingy lemon tart and posset with raspberries.

Chef Timothy Bilton **Owner** Timothy & Adele Bilton **Seats** 80
Times 11-2/6-9.30, Closed Mon-Tue **Prices** Fixed L 2 course fr £21, Fixed D 3 course fr £25, Tasting menu fr £60, Starter £6-£14, Main £18-£32, Dessert £8-£9 **Wines** 40 bottles over £30, 40 bottles under £30, 23 by glass **Parking** 50 **Notes** Breakfast, Afternoon tea, Sunday L £25-£29, Children welcome

---

HUDDERSFIELD   Map 16 SE11

315 Bar and Restaurant

🏵🏵 Modern V

tel: 01484 602613 **315 Wakefield Rd, Lepton HD8 0LX**
email: info@315barandrestaurant.co.uk **web:** www.315barandrestaurant.co.uk
dir: *M1 junct 38 to Huddersfield*

Ambitious city-smart cooking in a reborn Yorkshire pub

This place brings a touch of metropolitan chic to Huddersfield. There's a buzz in the air throughout, with a sleek bar, a restaurant done out in restful neutral tones, with upholstered seats at correctly set tables and contemporary lighting, and a conservatory extension with vivid yellow-striped pillars. The menu bursts with bright, modern ideas. Crab and lobster mousse wrapped in nori with ginger, lime and coriander dressing makes an expressive starter, and there might be robustly flavoured duck liver and mushroom pâté with a salad of rocket, figs and parmesan. Main courses are no less original: fillet of sea bass, timed to the second, is served on a ginger-spiked compôte of rhubarb and white crabmeat with saffron potatoes and wilted lettuce, and duck breast on roast beetroot with blackberries, tondant potato and celeriac purée. Puddings are well executed and attractively presented, among them raspberry millefeuille on a base of lemon cake and cream topped with white chocolate, and chocolate cup filled with cherry compôte with brandy sabayon.

Chef Jason Neilson **Owner** Jason Neilson, Terry Dryden **Seats** 90, Pr/dining room 115
Times 12-9, All-day dining, Closed D Sun **Prices** Fixed L 2 course £15, Starter £5-£7.50, Main £12.50-£23.50, Dessert fr £6.25, Service optional **Wines** 18 by glass
Parking 97 **Notes** Sunday L £17.50-£19.95, Children welcome

---

ILKLEY   Map 19 SE14

Box Tree

🏵🏵🏵 – see page 583

Shibden Mill Fold
Shibden, Halifax

West Yorkshire HX3 7UL
Tel: 01422 365840
Fax: 01422 362971
Email: enquiries@shibdenmillinn.com
Website: www.shibdenmillinn.com

For over 350 years *The Shibden Mill Inn* has been at the heart of life in West Yorkshire's Shibden Valley. It's a magical place where generation after generation of locals have enjoyed time well spent with friends and family, sharing in life's special moments and shaping memories to last a life time.

The Inn's reputation for warm hospitality, premier 2 Rosette gastro dining and 5 Star Inn accommodation draws people to the Shibden Valley from far and wide, and the Mill has naturally become a popular choice for those wishing to savour a sumptuous weekend break or mid-week stay.

Stunning countryside walks are in easy reach, as too the bright lights and city centre shopping on offer in Leeds. From its unique location, The Shibden Mill offers easy access to the very best to be found in this delightful part of West Yorkshire.

Opening times for breakfast, morning coffee & cake, afternoon teas, lunch and dinner can be found on the food page of the website www.shibdenmillinn.com

LEEDS   Map 19 SE23

Jamie's Italian, Leeds

◉ Italian

tel: 0113 322 5400 **35 Park Row LS1 5JL**
email: leeds@jamiesitalian.com
dir: *300mtrs from station up Park Row, on left*

Italian tradition à la Jamie in a bank-turned-warehouse

A thoroughgoing makeover has transformed a once-grand banking temple into a warehouse eatery in the modern idiom, its original features still visible amid the girdering, tiling and brickwork. Sit up on high stools at a counter, or around cafeteria-style booth tables, for the Jamie-goes-to-Italy experience. Should the British affection for simple Italian food ever pall, the empire may come juddering to a halt, but thankfully no such disaffection is in evidence. And why would it be when a bowl of beautifully timed wild truffle risotto with aged parmesan is on hand, as well as pasta dishes built on luxuries like local lamb ragù, slow-cooked for 20 hours in red wine and rosemary, mixed into what the menu calls 'wriggly' pappardelle? With planks of antipasti, chillified arancini, or baked salmon with balsamic-roasted veg, there is plenty of versatility to the range, and nobody minds deserting Italian tradition to finish with a lump of chocolate brownie, Amaretto ice cream and caramelised amaretti popcorn.

Chef Ashley Thornton **Owner** Jamie Oliver **Seats** 200 **Times** 12-11, All-day dining, Closed 25-26 Dec **Prices** Starter £3.95-£6.95, Main £9.95-£23.95, Dessert £4.95-£5.45 **Wines** 10 bottles over £30, 19 bottles under £30, 17 by glass **Parking** On street **Notes** Vegetarian available, Children welcome

Malmaison Leeds

◉ Modern British

tel: 0113 398 1000 & 0844 693 0654 *(Calls cost 7p per minute plus your phone company's access charge)* **1 Swinegate LS1 4AG**
email: leeds@malmaison.com **web:** www.malmaison.com
dir: *City centre. 5 mins walk from Leeds railway station. On junct 16 of loop road, Sovereign St & Swinegate*

Vibrant cooking with global influences in a stylish city brasserie

The Malmaison group's Leeds branch has been carved out of an impressive building that used to be the headquarters of a tram company. In common with other hotels in the group, it is decorated and furnished to a high standard, creating the atmosphere of a contemporary boutique hotel. The brasserie is no exception, with plush leather booths and open fireplaces under its elegant ceiling. The cooking is built on a framework of quality ingredients, and talented professionals are clearly at work. So chicken liver parfait, rich and flavoursome, with figs might be followed by properly timed sea bass fillet with sautéed chorizo, black olives, mussel vinaigrette and new potatoes. Influences have been gathered from around the globe to add to the broad appeal, so veal bolognese with rigatoni might appear next to another main course of chicken tikka masala. End with a classic vanilla crème brûlée.

Chef Simon Silver **Owner** Malmaison **Seats** 85, Pr/dining room 12 **Times** 12-2.30/6-10 **Prices** Fixed L 2 course £19.95, Fixed D 3 course £24.95, Starter £5-£12.50, Main £14-£49, Dessert £6-£9 **Wines** 97 bottles over £30, 32 bottles under £30, 25 by glass **Parking** Criterion Place car park, Q Park **Notes** Sunday L £19.95, Vegetarian available, Children welcome

Box Tree ◉◉◉

ILKLEY   Map 19 SE14

Modern British, French v 🍷 NOTABLE WINE LIST

tel: 01943 608484 **35-37 Church St LS29 9DR**
email: info@theboxtree.co.uk
dir: *On A65 from Leeds through Ilkley, main lights approx 200yds on left*

Yorkshire culinary excellence since the early 1960s

It feels only right that the Box Tree, one of northern England's destination venues under successive owners since the early 1960s, should be housed in one of Ilkley's oldest buildings. From 1720, it was home to a succession of nearby Denton's gentleman farmers. The famous box trees out front were planted in the late-Victorian era and, after spells as antique shop and tea room, the restaurant of distinction was born. Decorated throughout to a very high standard, it has a particularly attractive lounge, with opulently upholstered furniture and portraits and seascapes on the walls. In November 2014, an extra dining room was opened on the first floor. Simon Gueller maintains the Box Tree's stellar reputation for cutting-edge food that utilises some of the advanced technical means that today's chefs love, but in a style that continues to make sense to aficionados of old-school haute cuisine. Every plate looks artfully composed and is often quite complex, but flavours shine forth, and every last ingredient is given its due. A menu gourmand with dishes culled from the carte is the enviable way to proceed, with four principal courses interspersed with a couple of foamy appetisers — caramelised onion with a gruyère straw at the outset, cranberry and champagne as pre-dessert. In between may come sturdily constructed duck terrine with warm apricot chutney and pear purée, followed by a fish such as sea bass with roast Jerusalem artichoke, confit tomato and puréed leek. The main meat business may be Scottish venison loin in tangy Cumberland sauce, garnished with braised red cabbage and roasted sprout leaves, and the finishing line heaves into view with a feather light rhubarb soufflé and vanilla ice cream.

Chef S Gueller, L Yates **Owner** R Gueller **Seats** 50, Pr/dining room 20 **Times** 12-2/7-9.30, Closed 27-31 Dec, 1-7 Jan, Mon, L Tue-Thu, D Sun **Prices** Fixed L 3 course £30, Fixed D 3 course £60, Tasting menu £75, Service optional 10% **Wines** 11 bottles over £30, 12 bottles under £30, 7 by glass **Parking** NCP, Ilkley town car park **Notes** Fixed L Fri-Sat, Sunday L £35, Children 10 yrs+ D

LEEDS *continued*

Salvo's Restaurant & Salumeria

Italian

tel: 0113 275 5017 & 275 2752 **115 Otley Rd, Headingley LS6 3PX**
email: dine@salvos.co.uk
dir: *On A660 2m N of city centre*

Popular Italian with a salumeria (deli-café)

Since it first opened its doors back in 1976, Salvo's has served the local Headingley community and built a deserved reputation. It's lively, family-friendly and family-run and will sort you out for some rustic and hearty regional Italian cooking. The Salumeria, which is a café-deli during the day and opens in the evening for musical soirees and the like, lies a few doors down from the restaurant. If you've come for a pizza because nothing else will do, the classics are all present and correct and you won't leave disappointed. But there is so much more: antipasti such as buffalo mozzarella with tomatoes and fresh basil, or Puglian sea bream fishcake layered with potatoes and pecorino cheese, pasta – perhaps tagliatelle with slow-cooked pork and beef ragù – and main courses run to the likes of twice-cooked belly pork with a sweet-and-sour confit of red peppers and capers.

Chef Giuseppe Schirripa, Geppino Dammone **Owner** John & Geppino Dammone **Seats** 88, Pr/dining room 20 **Times** 12-2/5.30-10.30, Closed 25-26 Dec, 1 Jan, L BHs **Prices** Fixed L 2 course fr £11.50, Fixed D 3 course fr £17.50, Starter £5-£9.95, Main £10-£28.50, Dessert £5.50-£12.95, Service optional **Wines** 9 bottles over £30, 33 bottles under £30, 6 by glass **Parking** On street, pay & display nearby **Notes** Sunday L fr £14.50, Vegetarian available, Children welcome

Thorpe Park Hotel & Spa

Modern British

tel: 0113 264 1000 **Century Way, Thorpe Park LS15 8ZB**
email: thorpepark@shirehotels.com **web:** www.restaurant-and-bar.co.uk/leeds/
dir: *M1 junct 46, follow signs off rdbt for Thorpe Park*

Unfussy contemporary cooking near the M1

Close to the M1 and with quick access into Leeds or out into the countryside, the modern Thorpe Park Hotel is a handy base for exploring the area while offering plenty of enticements to stick around. There's a spa, conference and leisure facilities, and, in the shape of the Restaurant & Bar, a drinking and dining option that makes the grade. The open plan and split-level dining room has a contemporary finish with pale wooden floor, artwork on the walls, and black leather-type chairs. The populist menu offers feel-good stuff such as crispy duck salad to start, or share an antipasti sharing plate. Move on to tiger prawn linguine, Yorkshire lamb shepherd's pie with pickled red cabbage and beetroot, or a steak cooked on the grill. Desserts are equally as comforting – warm treacle tart, say, with Pedro Ximenez and clotted cream.

Times 12-2/6.45-9.30

Town Hall Tavern

Modern British

tel: 0113 244 0765 **17 Westgate LS1 2RA**
email: info@townhalltavernleeds.co.uk
dir: *Located in city centre, opposite the Law Courts*

Refined pub fare in the city centre

This bustling city-centre pub looks like any old boozer from the outside, but the interior is stylish and comfortable. The cooking, too, is a cut above your standard pub norm, with an all-day menu offering a wide choice of appealing ideas. Grilled king prawns are served in tomato and garlic sauce hinting of chilli on top of a slice of toasted bread, and could precede pan-fried pork fillet on thyme jus with a notably good hash cake of pig's cheek, accompanied by contrasting sour cherries and poached apples. Pan-fried salmon fillet on rösti with prawns and creamy herb sauce is one of the signature dishes, and even a pub classic like cottage pie is lifted out of the ordinary, with the meat marinated in red wine and port. Desserts are taken seriously too: home-made peanut butter ice cream the perfect foil for a chocolate brownie.

Times 11.45-9, All-day dining, Closed 25-26 Dec, BH Mon

LIVERSEDGE
Map 16 SE12

Healds Hall Hotel & Restaurant

Modern British

tel: 01924 409112 **Leeds Rd WF15 6JA**
email: enquire@healdshall.co.uk **web:** www.healdshall.co.uk
dir: *M1 junct 40, A638. From Dewsbury take A652 signed Bradford. Left at A62. Hotel 50yds on right*

International favourites in a family-owned historic hotel

A short tootle from the M62, the stone-built Healds Hall is a family-owned hotel on a quietly grand scale, run with genuine Yorkshire hospitality and charm. Choose from a pair of eating spaces, the more informal Bistro with its conservatory extension, and Harringtons, the full-dress restaurant done in today's neutral tones. An extensive menu looks hither and thither for international favourite dishes such as crispy salt-and-pepper squid with garlic-lemon mayo, or Jamón Iberico de Bellota with chorizo and manchego. The best of the English repertoire turns up in the form of mains like pork and leek sausages with creamy mash, and salmon and herb fishcake with tartare, or you may wander into the realms of venison medallions with truffled artichoke risotto and morels in red wine sauce. A vegetarian tart comes laden with tomato, roast pepper, goats' cheese and basil, dressed in aged balsamic. Simple but satisfying puddings include treacle tart, and lemon crème brûlée with stewed rhubarb.

Chef Andrew Ward, David Winter **Owner** Mr N B & Mrs T Harrington **Seats** 46, Pr/dining room 30 **Times** 12-2/6-10, Closed 1 Jan, BHs, L Sat, D Sun (ex residents) **Prices** Fixed L 2 course £10.95, Fixed D 3 course £18.95-£28, Starter £4.95-£8.95, Main £11.50-£26.95, Dessert £4.95-£8.95, Service optional **Wines** 14 bottles over £30, 34 bottles under £30, 13 by glass **Parking** 90 **Notes** Sunday L £18.95-£24.95, Vegetarian available, Children welcome

OTLEY
Map 19 SE24

Chevin Country Park Hotel & Spa

Modern British

tel: 01943 467818 **Yorkgate LS21 3NU**
email: gm.chevin@crerarhotels.com **web:** www.crerarhotels.com
dir: *A658 towards Harrogate. Left at 1st turn towards Carlton, 2nd left towards Yorkgate*

Modern cooking in a Scandinavian-style log cabin

Surrounded by 44 acres of woodland and lakes, this spa hotel with a pool was built in the style of an Alpine log cabin, a theme that extends to the Lakeside Restaurant, where a wall of windows gives views over the patio and fishing lake. The industrious kitchen creates a daily-changing tasting menu as well as a carte, and there's also a steak and grill menu. Crab with avocado, parmesan beignets and gazpacho will get the taste buds zinging before main courses ranging from traditional rump of lamb with ratatouille and garlicky potatoes to seared sea bass fillet given a fillip from a rich crayfish emulsion accompanied by new potatoes, peas, broad beans and baby onions. Close attention is paid to desserts too, among which are individual coconut and cardamom pannacottas with tangy clementine sorbet.

Times 12-2.30/6-9

PONTEFRACT
Map 16 SE42

Wentbridge House Hotel
Modern British **V** NOTABLE WINE LIST

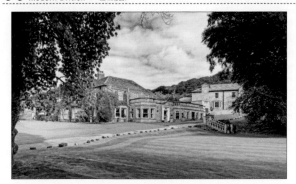

tel: 01977 620444 **The Great North Rd, Wentbridge WF8 3JJ**
email: info@wentbridgehouse.co.uk **web:** www.wentbridgehouse.co.uk
dir: *4m S of M62/A1 junct, 0.5m off A1*

Multi-influenced cooking in a Yorkshire manor house

Set in 20 acres of landscaped grounds in a West Yorkshire conservation village, Wentbridge is a stone-built grand manor house built at the turn of the 18th century. It had long associations with the Leatham family, luminaries of Barclays Bank, but became a country hotel in 1960. A degree of glossy formality prevails within, not least in the Fleur de Lys dining room, where candy-coloured upholstery creates a light, bright effect, and the cooking reaches out in all directions for its references. First up might be seared Shetland scallops with beans in truffled cappuccino for a majestic array of complementary elements. This may be followed by venison fillet with beetroot, cavolo nero and celeriac dauphinoise, or perfectly fresh cod Spanish-style with a stuffed red pepper, patatas bravas and aïoli. Main courses for sharing are quite the thing these days; if you can arrive at an agreement, go for classic Chateaubriand with choice of sauces, or duck à l'orange. To finish, there's zesty lemon tart with raspberry sorbet and a pistachio tuile, or perhaps a boozy baked Alaska bursting with cherries.

Chef Ian Booth **Owner** Mr G Page **Seats** 60, Pr/dining room 24
Times 7.15-9.30, Closed L Mon-Sat, D Sun, 25 Dec **Prices** Service optional
Wines 100 bottles over £30, 30 bottles under £30, 10 by glass **Parking** 100
Notes Sunday L £27.50, Children welcome

Find out more about how we assess for Rosette awards on page 9

WAKEFIELD
Map 16 SE32

Waterton Park Hotel
Modern, Traditional British **V**

tel: 01924 257911 **Walton Hall, The Balk, Walton WF2 6PW**
email: info@watertonparkhotel.co.uk **web:** www.watertonparkhotel.co.uk
dir: *3m SE off B6378. Exit M1 junct 39 towards Wakefield. At 3rd rdbt right for Crofton. At 2nd lights right & follow signs*

Sound flavour-packed cooking by a huge lake

The location of the Georgian hotel must be unique, as it stands on an island in a 26-acre lake, with a modern extension on the shore accessed via a bridge, which explains where the attractive Bridgeman restaurant gets its name from. Dishes are admirably understated and flavours are to the fore, with starters running from a salad of seared scallops with black pudding, poached apples and cauliflower foam, to carpaccio with parmesan shavings and horseradish dressing. Raw materials are conscientiously chosen and carefully cooked, demonstrated by main courses of Whitby cod steak in a walnut crust served with parsnip purée and white wine beurre blanc, and seared Gressingham duck breast with caramelised orange, pickled red cabbage and port-based gravy. Puddings make a fine finale, among them Yorkshire rhubarb crème brûlée with vanilla ice cream, and a duo of chocolate with espresso custard and chocolate drizzle.

Chef Armstrong Wgabi **Owner** The Kaye family **Seats** 50, Pr/dining room 40
Times 7-9.30, Closed D Sun **Prices** Prices not confirmed, Service optional **Wines** 10 by glass **Parking** 200 **Notes** Afternoon tea, Sunday L, Children welcome

WETHERBY
Map 16 SE44

Wood Hall Hotel
Modern British **V**

tel: 01937 587271 & 0845 072 7564 *(Calls cost 7p per minute plus your phone company's access charge)* **Trip Ln, Linton LS22 4JA**
email: woodhall@handpicked.co.uk **web:** www.handpickedhotels.co.uk/woodhall
dir: *From Wetherby take A661 (Harrogate road) N for 0.5m. Left to Sicklinghall/Linton. Cross bridge, left to Linton/Woodhall, right opposite Windmill Inn, 1.25m to hotel (follow brown signs)*

Classy cooking using local produce in an elegant country-house hotel

High on a hill, with fine views, this is the sort of country-house hotel where you'll want to linger. Dating from 1750, the property retains a number of original details, while furnishings and decor have been chosen with guests' comfort and well-being in mind. The Georgian Restaurant is as elegant as the other rooms, with its relaxing colour scheme, upholstered chairs and drapes at the windows. The rigorous pursuit of Yorkshire produce – beef from local farms, lamb from the moors, produce from the garden – eschews over-elaboration and unnecessary garnishes in favour of a simple approach, so the cooking is marked out by clear, distinct flavours. Raviolo of rabbit confit, with a sautéed scallop and gingery consommé is characteristic, as is duck terrine with fig and port jelly. A trio of beef (roast fillet, braised cheek and marrowbone croquette) with a rich jus is a typically well-conceived main course, with a fish option perhaps salmon 'pastrami' with beetroot and radish. End with an upbeat pudding like banana bavarois with caramelised fruit and peanut ice cream.

Chef Chris Pick **Owner** Hand Picked Hotels **Seats** 40, Pr/dining room 100
Times 12-2.30/7-9.30, Closed L Mon-Sat **Prices** Service optional **Wines** 50 bottles over £30, 10 bottles under £30, 18 by glass **Parking** 100 **Notes** Sunday L £25, Children welcome

CHANNEL ISLANDS
GUERNSEY

CASTEL
Map 24

Cobo Bay Hotel
◉◉ Modern, Traditional

tel: 01481 257102 & 07781 156757 **Coast Rd, Cobo GY5 7HB**
email: reservations@cobobayhotel.com **web:** www.cobobayhotel.com
dir: *From airport turn right, follow road to W coast at L'Erée. Turn right onto coast road for 3m to Cobo Bay. Hotel on right*

Superb views and admirable use of local produce

The view across the eponymous bay is seen at its best if you time it right for a sunset dinner at this west-facing beachside hotel. If you're lucky you can dine alfresco on the beach terrace, but if not it's no hardship to grab a table indoors in the smart contemporary restaurant. As you might hope in this wave-lapped setting, seafood is a strong suit here, arriving slithery fresh from local boats, and it is presented in straightforward contemporary combinations, along with a cornucopia of other top-quality locally-sourced produce. Courgette and red pepper soup is a well-made opener, or you might prefer to head straight for the fish – perhaps tempura monkfish or fritto misto with lemon and caper mayonnaise – then move on to pan-fried sea bass with pea and prawn risotto, garlic king prawns, and crab and lobster bisque. Banana tarte Tatin with caramel ice cream presses the comfort button at the end.

Times 12-2/6-9.30

ST MARTIN
Map 24

The Auberge
◉◉ Modern International

tel: 01481 238485 **Jerbourg Rd GY4 6BH**
email: dine@theauberge.gg
dir: *End of Jerbourg Rd at Jerbourg Point*

Locally led menu on a Guernsey clifftop

A clifftop position overlooking the neighbouring islands and the Channel through floor-to-ceiling windows certainly draws people to this sleek contemporary restaurant near St Peter Port. The garden and terrace for alfresco dining is a further attraction, but the main reason for a visit must of course be the food. Chef Daniel Green's cooking takes a lively and imaginative approach to the island's top-quality seasonal produce, and the resulting dishes are full of interest. The menu is big on fish and seafood, as in seared scallops with aromatic twice-cooked pork belly, or main course pan-roasted brill with warm tartare sauce and mussels deep-fried in panko breadcrumbs. Steak boards include onglet, fillet and Angus rump (served with chunky chips or French fries), or the whopping côte de boeuf for two to share. The fixed-price menu offers a value option at lunchtime and midweek evenings. Finish with a clever take on Eton Mess – a toffee and apple version with apple compôte, meringue, caramel brittle, whipped Guernsey cream and toffee sauce.

Chef Daniel Green **Owner** Liberation Group **Seats** 70, Pr/dining room 20
Times 12-2/6.30-10, Closed 25-26 Dec, D Sun **Prices** Prices not confirmed, Service optional **Wines** 30 bottles over £30, 26 bottles under £30, 12 by glass **Parking** 25
Notes Sunday L, Vegetarian available, Children welcome

La Barbarie Hotel
◉ Traditional British

tel: 01481 235217 **Saints Rd, Saints Bay GY4 6ES**
email: reservations@labarbariehotel.com **web:** www.labarbariehotel.com
dir: *At lights in St Martin take road to Saints Bay. Hotel on right at end of Saints Rd*

Unpretentious country-house cooking in a charming setting

The hotel's name comes from the story that, back in the 17th century, the owner of the house was kidnapped by Barbary Coast pirates. There is no such drama nowadays, the former priory transformed into a comfortable hotel with a soothing vibe and a restaurant that puts to good use the cornucopia of peerless fresh produce – fish, seafood, meat, cream and butter – supplied by Guernsey's coasts and meadows. La Barbarie's kitchen team clearly look to the nearby French mainland for their inspiration in the repertoire of simply cooked and presented dishes. A simple pairing of pan-fried scallops with black pudding, pancetta and apple sauce gets things off the blocks, followed by a classic combo of roast rack of new season lamb with shallot, port and rosemary sauce, dauphinoise potatoes, and fine green beans. Caramelised apple tart with a sharp palate-refreshing green apple sorbet brings things to a zingy close.

Chef Colin Pearson **Owner** La Barbarie Ltd **Seats** 70 **Times** 12-1.45/6-9, Closed mid Nov-mid Mar **Prices** Fixed L 2 course fr £11.45, Starter £6.45-£8.15, Main £12.45-£19.95, Dessert £5.45-£6.10, Service optional **Wines** 12 bottles over £30, 30 bottles under £30, 10 by glass **Parking** 60 **Notes** Early D £9.95, Fixed D 4 course £25.95, Sunday L £9.95-£20, Vegetarian available, Children welcome

Bella Luce Hotel, Restaurant & Spa
◉◉ French, Mediterranean V

tel: 01481 238764 **La Fosse GY4 6EB**
email: wakeup@bellalucehotel.com **web:** www.bellalucehotel.com
dir: *From airport, turn left to St Martin. At 3rd set of lights continue 30yds, turn right, straight on to hotel*

Sharp, modern cooking in a classy boutique hotel

With its 12th-century granite walls, bags of period charm and luxe boutique finish, Bella Luce really leaves a lasting impression. It's a class act. The Bar & Grill is the place for a cocktail or an upmarket sandwich or steak seared on the grill, but the main culinary action takes place in the restaurant where there's some sharp, classically-minded contemporary cooking going down. It's an elegant space with pristine tables and lots of character, looked over by a slick, professional team who leave nothing to chance. There's a good showing of local produce on the menu and a good deal of skill in the execution of dishes. Everything looks beautiful on the plate, too. Dressed Chancre crab comes with a Bloody Mary shot and coconut, while another starter sees belly of pork braised for eight hours and served with watercress salad and flavoured with lavender and honey. For mains, ox cheeks also get the braising treatment, served with creamed horseradish potato and sprouting greens, or go for plaice roasted on the bone and classically served with brown shrimps and a beurre noisette. Desserts are equally on the money.

Chef Seb Orzechowski, Seb Laskowy, Richard Waller, Chris Harworth **Owner** Luke Wheadon **Seats** 70, Pr/dining room 20 **Times** 12-2.30/6.30-9.30, Closed 2-22 Jan **Prices** Fixed L 2 course £20, Fixed D 3 course £25, Tasting menu £30-£40, Starter £5.50-£8.50, Main £12.50-£26, Dessert £6.95-£11.50 **Wines** 52 bottles over £30, 28 bottles under £30 **Parking** 38 **Notes** Afternoon tea £7, Champagne tea £20, Sunday L £20-£25, Children welcome

Hotel Jerbourg

◉ Modern British

tel: 01481 238826 **Jerbourg Point GY4 6BJ**
email: stay@hoteljerbourg.com **web:** www.hoteljerbourg.com
dir: *From airport turn left to St Martin, right at filter, straight on at lights, hotel at end of road on right*

Ocean views and classic seafood dishes

Magnificent views are a major pull at this modern hotel in lovely grounds out on the tip of the Jerbourg Peninsula. With the Atlantic lapping all around, thoughts are bound to turn to fish, so you will not be disappointed to see that the classic French repertoire is weighted in that direction. The kitchen resists the temptation to gild the lily, letting the sheer freshness and quality of prime piscine produce do the talking, serving Guernsey chancre crab with prawn and apple cocktail, ahead of turbot with crayfish and caviar butter sauce, or grilled brill fillet with sauté potatoes, spinach, and martini beurre blanc. Straight-up chargrilled steaks (entrecôte with dauphinoise potatoes and Roquefort sauce, say), or something requiring a touch more input from the kitchen — perhaps honey-glazed Barbary duck breast with potato rösti, asparagus and sherry vinegar jus — should keep the carnivores quiet. End with a classic crème brûlée.

Times 12-2.30/6.30-9.30, Closed 5 Jan-Mar

■ ST PETER PORT   Map 24

The Absolute End

◉ Modern, Traditional

tel: 01481 723822 **St Georges Esplanade GY1 2BG**
email: reservations@absoluteendrestaurant.com
dir: *Less than 1m from town centre. N on seafront road towards St Sampson*

Italian-accented fish restaurant overlooking the harbour

When you're above the harbour just outside St Peter Port you should be in the market for spanking fresh fish and seafood, and this unpretentious restaurant in converted fishermen's cottages comes up trumps with a repertoire of Italian-accented classics. A light-filled ground-floor room in olive green and white is supplemented by a terrace upstairs, and staff ensure a friendly tone to the proceedings. Reliable renditions of seared scallops with pea purée and crispy pancetta, and mains such as pan-fried brill fillet with potted mussels, crushed new potatoes and chives, all come up to snuff. Meat-eaters are not forgotten: herb-crusted rack of lamb, sauced with rosemary and red wine and served with dauphinoise potatoes, or chargrilled beef fillet with béarnaise and proper chips should keep them happy. Desserts such as sticky toffee pudding with butterscotch sauce will put a smile on everyone's face.

Chef Seamus Duggan **Owner** Seamus Duggan **Seats** 50, Pr/dining room 18
Times 12-2.30/6.30-late, Closed 25 Dec, 1 Jan, Sun **Prices** Starter £4.95-£9.50, Main £11.25-£22.95, Dessert £5.95-£6.95, Service optional **Wines** 15 bottles over £30, 30 bottles under £30, 4 by glass **Parking** On street **Notes** Vegetarian available, Children welcome

BEST WESTERN Hotel de Havelet

◉ Traditional British, International ᴠ

tel: 01481 722199 **Havelet GY1 1BA**
email: stay@dehaveletguernsey.com **web:** www.dehaveletguernsey.com
dir: *From airport follow signs for St Peter Port through St Martins. At bottom of 'Val de Terres' hill turn left at top of hill, hotel on right*

Sea views and classic no-nonsense cooking

The Georgian hotel is in a quiet spot surrounded by trees with sea and castle views and picture windows in the two restaurants to make the most of the vista. Both of the dining options are in the converted coach house (although there is bar food, too), with the Havelet Grill on the ground floor and the main Wellington Boot above. The latter is the main event, decorated in a traditional manner with neat tables and formal settings. There's nothing complicated about the food on offer, no bandwagons being jumped on, just classical cooking with a sure hand, and plenty of local ingredients. Start with beef carpaccio, which has at is heart some excellent meat, cut just right, and served with a rocket pesto. Next up, chargrilled lamb cutlets perfectly prepared, line-caught local sea bass, or perhaps an Egyptian-style beef ragoût showcasing the chef's roots. Finish with a well-made crème brûlée.

Chef Mohammed Ekamy **Owner** Hotel de Havelet Ltd (Mrs Karel Harris) **Seats** 100, Pr/dining room 20 **Times** 12-2/7-9.30, Closed L Mon-Sat **Prices** Fixed D 3 course fr £22, Starter £4.50-£7.50, Main £17.50-£25, Dessert £5.50-£8 **Wines** 10 bottles over £30, 20 bottles under £30, 5 by glass **Parking** 35 **Notes** Sunday L £17.50-£22.50, Children welcome

Mora Restaurant & Grill

◉ Modern Mediterranean

tel: 01481 715053 **The Quay GY1 2LE**
email: eat@mora.gg
dir: *Facing Victoria Marina*

Quayside seafood cooking with a Med twist

The old place on the quay in Guernsey's capital has been given a real decorative boost. Booth seating with jazzily patterned upholstery and dividers and lots of little framed pictures are the backdrop to cooking that now follows firmly modern Mediterranean lines. There's a happy buzz from strong local custom, which pours in for the likes of charred piquillo peppers filled with herbed ricotta in roast garlic dressing, or plates of local crab and prawns with Scottish smoked salmon. Seafood mains wrap cod in chorizo and accompany it with artichoke and tomato gnocchi, or team monkfish medallions with aubergine purée and green tapenade. The fish component of fish and chips encompasses bass, brill, scallops and battered prawns. Meat there is for those as wants it, including grilled steaks, with indulgent desserts like vanilla cheesecake and chocolate ice cream, or lemon tart and raspberry sorbet, to finish.

Chef Trevor Baines **Owner** Nello Ciotti **Seats** 90 **Times** 12-2.30/6-late, Closed 24 Dec, Jan, L 25 **Prices** Starter £6-£12.50, Main £12-£25, Dessert £5.95-£6.95, Service optional **Wines** 30 bottles over £30, 40 bottles under £30, 11 by glass **Parking** On pier **Notes** Brasserie menu, Sunday L £22.95, Vegetarian available, Children welcome

The Old Government House Hotel & Spa

◉ Indian

tel: 01481 724921 **St Ann's Place GY1 2NU**
email: governors@theoghhotel.com **web:** www.theoghhotel.com
dir: *At junct of St Julian's Av & College St*

Indian cooking at the old governor's residence

The beautiful white Georgian building was once the island governor's harbourside residence, though that's going back a fair while, as it was converted into a hotel as long ago as 1858. The red carpet that rolls out down the front steps sets the tone, and the magnificent interiors culminate in a dining room done in warm fuchsia tones and decorated with martial memorabilia and paintings. It's known now as the Curry Room, and serves authentic sub-continental food from an Indian chef. Expect marinated tandoori tiger prawns with cherry tomatoes, or a set of aubergine variations with minted yogurt, to start, followed by dynamically spiced main courses bursting with flavour, such as white fish and squid curry with mushroom and pea masala, butter chicken, or baby vegetable coconut curry for the veggies. Aromatic desserts include rosewater rice pudding with ginger snaps, or banana cake with coconut ice cream and masala caramel.

Times 12-2/7-11, Closed 25 & 31 Dec

ST SAVIOUR

Map 24

The Farmhouse Hotel

◎ Modern British, International

tel: 01481 264181 **Route des bas Courtils GY7 9YF**
email: enquiries@thefarmhouse.gg **web:** www.thefarmhouse.gg
dir: *From airport turn left. Approx 1m left at lights. 100mtrs, left, around airport runway perimeter. 1m, left at staggered junct. Hotel in 100mtrs on right*

Boutique hotel with resourceful cooking

The same family has owned this 15th-century farmhouse, now a boutique hotel, for three generations. Beams, stone floors and granite are reminders of the property's antiquity, superimposed today with a modern decor and comfortable furnishings. Eating outside is an attractive proposition, while the restaurant is in the oldest part of the building. Seasonality is central to the kitchen's output, bringing on shellfish in summer: perhaps scallops with a simple white wine sauce. Game is abundant in the colder months: partridge tortellini, say, with confit leg, leeks and basil, followed by roast goose with leg meat stuffing and a spot-on orange sauce. Otherwise, there might be boar's head with truffles, mushrooms and sauce gribiche, or fried fillet of cod with a smoked cod beignet, greens, fondant potatoes and parsley and caper beurre blanc, with a finale of chocolate and hazelnut tart, its pastry exemplary, with a hazelnut shard and vanilla crème fraîche.

Chef Nick Hawke **Owner** David & Julie Nussbaumer **Seats** 60, Pr/dining room 160 **Times** 12-2.30/6.30-9.30 **Prices** Service optional **Wines** 43 bottles over £30, 30 bottles under £30, 12 by glass **Parking** 80 **Notes** All day dining menu, Sunday L £19.50-£23.95, Vegetarian available, Children welcome

HERM

HERM

Map 24

White House Hotel

◎◎ European, Traditional British

tel: 01481 750000 **GY1 3HR**
email: hotel@herm.com **web:** www.herm.com
dir: *Close to harbour. Access by regular 20 min boat trip from St Peter Port, Guernsey*

Simple cooking and sea views in an island retreat

If you hanker for a simpler, slower pace of life, how about the pocket-sized, car- and pollution-free island of Herm? The island's only hotel – the White House – even takes the concept of getting away from it all a step further by dispensing with TVs, phones and clocks, but that doesn't mean you can totally kick back and relax in the restaurant, since old-school values require gentlemen to wear jackets and/or ties. As its name suggests, the Conservatory Restaurant is light and airy, and every table has a sea view. The kitchen doesn't try to reinvent the wheel, sticking to unfussy dishes that rely on the sheer quality of the raw materials and simple, accurate cooking for their effect. The contemporary European menu opens with an easy-on-the-eye composition of seared Guernsey scallops with Puy lentil and pancetta casserole, and truffled celeriac purée, before reaching out into the realms of duck breast teamed with Waldorf croquettes, roasted figs, Chantenay carrots and whisky jus. To finish, there's classic apple tarte Tatin with vanilla crème anglaise.

Times 12-2/7-9, Closed Nov-Apr

JERSEY

GOREY

Map 24

The Moorings Hotel & Restaurant

◎◎ Traditional

tel: 01534 853633 **Gorey Pier JE3 6EW**
email: reservations@themooringshotel.com **web:** www.themooringshotel.com
dir: *At foot of Mont Orgueil Castle*

Local food on the quayside

Smack on Gorey's picturesque harbour front, The Moorings has a continental feel with its pavement terrace overlooking the sea and ruins of Mont Orgueil Castle. Being rather closer to the French mainland than the UK, and with the smell of the sea in the air, it's no surprise to see Gallic influences underpin the menu, and plenty of splendid local seafood feature in both the bistro and Walkers Restaurant, a pretty space with neatly laid tables and a warm, summery colour scheme. It's not all about the bounty of the oceans, though, as the kitchen makes good use of the first-class ingredients from elsewhere in unfussy, clearly-focused dishes. Start with diver-caught scallops with truffled potatoes and pancetta crisp, followed by roast duck breast, glazed with marmalade and served with fondant potatoes and port jus. Fishy ideas might include pan-fried fillet of sea bass with crushed potatoes, scallops and sauce vièrge, and for pudding, a classic vanilla crème brûlée is done just right.

Chef Simon Walker **Owner** Simon & Joanne Walker **Seats** 65, Pr/dining room 35 **Times** 12-2/7-8.30 **Prices** Fixed L 2 course £13.50, Fixed D 3 course fr £24.50, Starter £9.20-£11.80, Main £19.95-£29.50, Dessert £6.50-£14.50, Service optional **Wines** 26 bottles over £30, 36 bottles under £30, 8 by glass **Notes** Sunday L £21.95, Vegetarian available, Children welcome

Sumas

◎◎ Modern British V

tel: 01534 853291 **Gorey Hill JE3 6ET**
email: info@sumasrestaurant.com **web:** www.sumasrestaurant.com
dir: *From St Helier take A3 E for 5m to Gorey. Before castle take sharp left. Restaurant 100yds up hill on left (look for blue blind)*

Inventive cooking and harbour views

Terrace tables at Sumas look out on boats bobbing in the harbour – or, at low tide, locals digging for clams in the sands of Gorey Bay. Inside, the space is fresh and clean, lined with a blue-and-white colour scheme and crisply clothed tables. It's a suitably airy, Mediterranean backdrop for the kitchen's contemporary, French-accented dishes. It is refreshing to see a goodly amount of seafood on the menu – we are in Jersey, after all – and a classic fish soup with croûtons and rouille is a good way to start at any time of year. But it's not all about fish, for this kitchen also seeks out the best the local land has to offer. The main course delivers roast loin of lamb wrapped in Serrano ham along with glazed sweetbreads, dauphinoise potato, pea purée and red wine sauce. For dessert, almond and vanilla pannacotta with green apple sorbet, salted caramel and vanilla sablé wraps things up on a high note, or you might finish with an entente cordiale of French and English cheeses.

Chef Patrice Bouffaut **Owner** Mrs Bults, Paul Dufty **Seats** 40
Times 12-2.30/6-9.30, Closed late Dec-mid Jan (approx), D Sun **Prices** Fixed L 2 course £12.50-£19, Fixed D 3 course £17.50-£23, Starter £6.75-£12, Main £14.50-£25.50, Dessert £6-£7.50, Service optional **Wines** 31 bottles over £30, 29 bottles under £30, 12 by glass **Parking** On street **Notes** Breakfast Sat-Sun, Sunday L £19-£23, Children welcome

---

| ROZEL | Map 24 |

Chateau la Chaire

◉◉ Traditional British, French V

tel: 01534 863354 **Rozel Bay JE3 6AJ**
email: res@chateau-la-chaire.co.uk **web:** www.chateau-la-chaire.co.uk
dir: From St Helier NE towards Five Oaks, Maufant, then St Martin's Church & Rozel. 1st left in village, hotel 100mtrs

Locally based cooking at the Pulpit

A chaire in French is a pulpit, this property having been named after an ecclesiastical-looking rock overhang. It was built for the botanist Samuel Curtis in the 1840s, after he'd earmarked the spot as a perfect location to establish a tropical garden. The interiors are all lush Victorian rococo, with cherubs sporting in the mouldings and walls of oak panelling in what are now the bar and dining room, though eating also extends into the conservatory and on to the terrace. The best of local materials — scallops, crab, pork, rabbit — are the backbone of Marcin Ciechomski's menus, which are squarely in the modern British mainstream. That crab turns up in cucumber gazpacho with lime sorbet and a crab-flavoured cracker, before chargrilled fillet and 'sticky shin' of Jersey beef, served with a hash brown and broccoli in Dijon mustard jus, or perhaps monkfish tail marinated in Merlot, with saffron risotto, aubergine purée and sauce vierge. Stay local for ice creams and cheeses, or wander off in the direction of peanut butter pannacotta and blackberry jam with berry sorbet.

Chef Marcin Ciechomski **Owner** Hatton Hotel Group **Seats** 60, Pr/dining room 28
Times 12-2/7-9.30 **Prices** Fixed L 3 course £16.95, Starter £7.95-£10.25, Main £19.25-£21.95, Dessert £6.95-£7.95 **Wines** 24 bottles over £30, 18 bottles under £30, 7 by glass **Parking** 30 **Notes** 'Taste of Jersey' tasting menu with/out wines, Sunday L £24.95, Children welcome

---

| ST BRELADE | Map 24 |

L'Horizon Beach Hotel and Spa

◉◉ Modern British

tel: 01534 743101 **St Brelade's Bay JE3 8EF**
email: lhorizon@handpicked.co.uk **web:** www.handpickedhotels.co.uk/lhorizon
dir: From airport right at rdbt towards St Brelade & Red Houses. Through Red Houses, hotel 300mtrs on right in centre of bay

Creative cooking and a touch of luxury on the beach

Built by a Victorian colonel who clearly knew a good spot when he saw one, L'Horizon has a contemporary finish within and offers maximum pampering in its spa and treatment rooms. Overlooking the bay, with pristine sand and shimmering sea out front, the view is a big draw, but it's the Grill restaurant that really puts this place on the map. It's a smart room with neutral colours and white linen on the tables, and a menu that makes excellent use of the island's bounty in bright, modern dishes. This is creative, contemporary stuff, with first courses such as scallops partnered with pig's cheek and lobster and crayfish tortellini, or garden and golden beets with ripple and crème fraîche. Among mains, turbot is served with gherkins and clams, and sea bass with a crab and vanilla sauce. Everything is presented with panache, and, given they call themselves the Grill, there's steak in the form of 28-day aged fillet with burnt shallot purée and horseradish creamed potatoes. Finish with apple soufflé with crumble and sorbet.

Chef Andrew Soddy **Owner** Julia Hands **Seats** 44, Pr/dining room 300
Times 6.30-10, Closed L Mon-Sat **Prices** Fixed L 2 course £20-£35.90, Fixed D 3 course £37, Starter £9.50-£11.50, Main £16.50-£28.50, Dessert £8.50-£15, Service optional **Wines** 33 bottles under £30, 19 by glass **Parking** 100 **Notes** Sunday L £28.95, Vegetarian available, Children welcome

---

Hotel La Place

◉ Modern British

tel: 01534 744261 & 748173 **Route du Coin, La Haule JE3 8BT**
email: andy@hotellaplacejersey.com **web:** www.hotellaplacejersey.com
dir: Off main St Helier/St Aubin coast road at La Haule Manor (B25). Up hill, 2nd left (to Red Houses), 1st right. Hotel 100mtrs on right

Modern bistro cooking near the harbour

Tucked away in a tranquil corner of Jersey close by St Aubin's harbour, the hotel started life as a huddle of rustic cottages around an original 17th-century farmhouse. A recent facelift has created a chic setting, particularly in the Retreat Restaurant, which sports a soft-focus seaside look involving high-backed Lloyd Loom chairs and pale wood tables set against a pastel palette of pale grey and cream. The cuisine is a harmonious blend of uncomplicated classics and gently modern European ideas built on plenty of the island's peerless produce. Start with a tried-and-true pairing of pan-fried scallops and crispy pancetta pointed up with tomato and red onion concasse. For mains, try the subtly spicy Portuguese chicken piri piri with French fries and a vibrant salad. To finish, white chocolate and orange add a lush veneer to a crème brûlée.

Times 6.30-9, Closed L all week

Ocean Restaurant at The Atlantic Hotel

◉◉◉◉ – see page 590

Oyster Box

◉◉ Modern British

tel: 01534 850888 **St Brelade's Bay JE3 8EF**
email: eat@oysterbox.co.uk
dir: On the beach just E of Fishermen's chapel

A beachside setting for spankingly fresh seafood and more

The views of St Brelade's Bay are unbeatable from the Oyster Box, whether you're dining alfresco on the terrace, or indoors in the cool, contemporary dining room with its floor-to-ceiling glass walls, wood and slate floors, high-backed wicker chairs at unclothed tables and an open-to-view kitchen. Local fish and seafood supply the main thrust of the menu — Jersey rock oysters from the Royal Bay of Grouville are hard to pass up as a starter. Carnivores are not ignored, however, and you'll find the likes of rabbit, smoked ham hock and foie gras terrine alongside seared tuna sashimi with toasted sesame, white radish and piquillo peppers. If you can resist the pleasures of grilled lobster with garlic butter and chancre crab with mayonnaise, there may be brill 'chop' served on the bone with spinach, Jersey Royals and brown shrimp béarnaise, or slow-cooked venison haunch with apple and potato gratin and caramelised red onion marmalade. For pudding, blood orange sorbet adds zip to a classic vanilla crème brûlée.

Chef Patrick Tweedie **Owner** Jersey Pottery **Seats** 100
Times 12-2.30/6-9.30, Closed 25-26 Dec, Mon (Jan-Mar), L Mon, D Sun (winter only)
Prices Fixed L 2 course £19, Fixed D 3 course £24, Starter £6-£12.25, Main £13.50-£27, Service optional **Wines** 55 bottles over £30, 50 bottles under £30, 25 by glass **Parking** Car park opposite **Notes** Sunday L £27.50, Vegetarian available, Children welcome

Ocean Restaurant at The Atlantic Hotel @@@@

ST BRELADE Map 24

Modern British V NOTABLE WINE LIST

tel: 01534 744101 **Le Mont de la Pulente JE3 8HE**
email: info@theatlantichotel.com
web: www.theatlantichotel.com
dir: *A13 to Petit Port, turn right into Rue de la Sergente & right again, hotel signed*

Top-class Jersey produce treated with skill

The boutique Atlantic Hotel lies amid exotic palm trees in a conservation area overlooking the wild dunes of St Ouen's Bay. The clean-lined structure dates from 1970, but with its white colonial-style shutters, a deep-blue pool straight out of a Hockney painting, a whiff of art deco in its low-slung white façade, and the La Moye golf course next door, you could be in 1930s Miami. For foodies, however, Mark Jordan's exciting cooking is the real draw. After learning his craft with a stellar cast of mentors in top-flight kitchens, he has headed up the Ocean Restaurant since 2004, establishing the venue as a gastronomic destination. With views out over the gardens towards the sea, and a soft-focus palette of blue, white and beige, comfortable hand-crafted furniture and modern artwork on the walls, it's a wonderfully light and airy setting for Jordan's effervescent contemporary ideas. You might get the show on the road with a tasting of duck miniatures with fig gel and toasted honey brioche, or risotto of Jersey squid and cauliflower with scallop carpaccio, each idea realised with masterful techniques that deliver explosions of distinct flavours. Whether you go for a fish or meat main course, you can be sure that the materials are all of exemplary quality — pan-roasted fillet

of Jersey sole, for example, supported by crushed Jersey Royals with crab, fennel and the lemon and caper kick of sauce Grenobloise. Or there could be an assiette of Jersey beef — all accurately timed and full of rich natural flavour — with lobster ravioli, beef consommé and dauphinoise cappuccino. The kitchen doesn't turn its back on vegetarians, with a dedicated menu alongside the regular carte, offering the likes of goats' cheese bonbon with pickled beetroot, candied walnuts and beetroot sorbet to start, followed by a baked tian of aubergine with garlic and thyme-roasted vegetables, black olives and salsa verde. Dessert ideas display the same thought-provoking flavours spiked with a sense of fun — glazed banana with vanilla cream, toffee popcorn and caramel ice cream, for example, while addicts of the cocoa bean will find deep satisfaction in a pavé made with Valrhona chocolate, with cocoa nib streusel and praline ice cream. Service is perfectly pitched, and the sommelier is a real pro too, guiding the way through a globetrotting list without neglecting those who are looking for a good choice by the glass.

Chef Mark Jordan **Owner** Patrick Burke **Seats** 60, Pr/dining room 60 **Times** 12.30-2.30/7-10, Closed Jan **Prices** Fixed L 2 course £20, Fixed D 3 course £55, Tasting menu £80 **Wines** 509 bottles over £30, 41 bottles under £30, 35 by glass **Parking** 60 **Notes** Fixed ALC 2/3 course £55/£65, Tasting menu 7 course, Sunday L £30, Children welcome

ST CLEMENT

Map 24

Green Island Restaurant

British, Mediterranean

tel: 01534 857787 **Green Island JE2 6LS**
email: info@greenisland.je
dir: *Phone for directions*

Great local seafood in bustling beach café

This laid-back beach café and restaurant stakes its claim to the title of most southerly eatery in the British Isles, so kick back and bask in its sun-kissed views over sandy Green Island bay. As you'd hope in this briny location, the emphasis is firmly on fish and shellfish, and the kitchen has the nous to treat them with a light touch to let the freshness and quality do the talking, as in an ultra-simple dish of freshly-landed sole meunière with Jersey potatoes and salad. If it's meat you're after, tarragon-crusted roast rack and braised shank of lamb with boulangère potatoes, garlicky flageolet beans and baby carrots, roasted root vegetables and garlic might be up for grabs, and to finish, a classic crème brûlée with sablé biscuits should strike a suitably Gallic note.

Chef Paul Insley **Owner** Alan M Winch **Seats** 40 **Times** 12-2.30/7-9.30, Closed Xmas, New Year, Jan-Feb, Mon, D Sun **Prices** Prices not confirmed, Service optional **Wines** 20 bottles over £30, 20 bottles under £30, 5 by glass **Parking** 20, Public car park adjacent **Notes** Fixed D £23.50 Tue-Thu, Sunday L, Vegetarian available, Children welcome

ST HELIER

Map 24

BEST WESTERN Royal Hotel

Modern European

tel: 01534 726521 **David Place JE2 4TD**
email: manager@royalhoteljersey.com **web:** www.morvanhotels.com
dir: *Follow signs for Ring Rd, pass Queen Victoria rdbt keep left, left at lights, left into Piersons Rd. Follow one-way system to Cheapside, Rouge Bouillon, at A14 turn to Midvale Rd, hotel on left*

Trendily presented food in a smart hotel

A hotel has been trading at this site since 1849. Nowadays, the Royal, centrally located in a quiet spot, has all the creature comforts travellers expect of a 21st-century version. In Seasons restaurant, a predominantly white colour scheme, with lightwood flooring, flowers on the tables and comfortable leather chairs, creates a coolly elegant atmosphere, appropriate surroundings for some polished cooking. Pink slices of duck breast fanned on a reduced jus, served with earthier leg confit, parsnip purée and roasted vegetables, is a well-considered main course, and could

follow something like grilled mackerel fillets, moist and bursting with flavour, cut by pickled vegetables. A decent choice of bread, all made on the premises, is offered, and puddings include nicely presented vanilla pannacotta flavoured with lavender accompanied by seasonal berries.

Times 6.30-9, Closed L all week

Bohemia Restaurant

— *see page 592*

Grand Jersey

see page 593

Hampshire Hotel

Mediterranean **NEW**

tel: 01534 724115 **53 Val Plaisant JE2 4TB**
email: info@hampshirehotel.je **web:** www.hampshirehotel.je
dir: *Phone for directions*

Contemporary setting and a local flavour

The four-square Hampshire Hotel has a contemporary restaurant sporting a colonial look with rattan chairs, ceiling fans and pot plants. There's a focus on Jersey produce in what is known as Christo's restaurant and no shortage of ambition when it comes to contemporary culinary ways. Among starters, that modern favourite of seared scallops (local ones from Bouley Bay, cooked just right) come with spring pea purée and wild rock samphire, or there might be local mussels cooked à la crème. Rack of spring lamb combines with minted and crushed Jersey Royals and wild garlic pesto in a winning combination, and wild duck (breast and confit leg) arrive in the creative company of a red cabbage mousse. There are simple steak options, too, and a terrific value daily menu, with desserts running to the likes of sticky toffee pudding. The short and to the point wine list is reasonably priced.

Chef Joe Baugh **Owner** Chris Robin **Seats** 100 **Times** 6.45-8.45, Closed L all week **Prices** Starter £5.95-£9.95, Main £10.95-£18.95, Dessert £5.95-£7.95, Service optional **Wines** 10 bottles under £30, 5 by glass **Parking** 28 **Notes** Vegetarian available, Children welcome

Ormer

— *see page 593*

Follow The AA online
twitter: @TheAA_Lifestyle
facebook: www.facebook.com/TheAAUK

Find us on Facebook

Bohemia Restaurant ❀ ❀ ❀ ❀

ST HELIER   Map 24

Modern French, British V

tel: 01534 880588 & 876500 **The Club Hotel & Spa, Green St JE2 4UH**
email: bohemia@huggler.com **web:** www.bohemiajersey.com
dir: *In town centre. 5 mins walk from main shopping centre*

Free-thinking creative cooking at a boutique spa hotel

When it comes to dining out, Jersey packs a punch. And when it comes to dining out in Jersey, Bohemia is a genuine heavyweight contender. The Club Hotel is a little slice of boutique heaven in the centre of St Helier, kitted out to meet the expectations of an urbane crowd, with a finish that is discreet and contemporary. The Bohemia sits well in this setting of refinement and recent refurbishment has only enhanced the place – the bar is now separated from the restaurant (to the benefit of both spaces) and the dining room itself looks sharp as a pin with its snazzy lighting, smart fabrics and precisely set, generously spaced tables. Steve Smith's arrival at the stoves has maintained the momentum here and kept Bohemia at the top of the culinary pecking order on the island, which is no surprise, given his pedigree at the highest level (including a much heralded stint in Melbourne). Diving into one of the tasting menus is the best way to get a handle on his cooking, but there are set lunch options, plus a 'classic menu' (a fixed-price carte) if you'd prefer three-course convention. Among the tasting options, the pescatorian is just that, putting glorious Jersey seafood in the spotlight, the vegetarian version is a class act, and the prestige really pushes the boat out. Each of the tasting menus comes with wine flight recommendations; Château Sigognac 2002, say, with a dish of Anjou pigeon that comes with the flavours and textures of beetroot, blackberry and liquorice. Steve Smith cooks in the modern vein, with a firm grasp of flavour combinations, and his forays into creativity are ambitious, but firmly rooted in good sense. First-rate technical skills are evident from the off with a course that fits into all the tasting menus – a light and earthy partnership of ceps and potato, sorrel and a quail's egg. An Asian influence is evident in some dishes (that time spent in Australia, perhaps?), such as one that combines local crab with pineapple, yuzu and wasabi. Everything looks beautiful on the plate, with the kitchen team's precision and eye for detail paying dividends for the customer. The classic menu might see meaty main courses of venison with pearl barley ragoût or turbot with oxtail and bone marrow. The contemporary ambition continues into desserts such as one that brings together rhubarb, champagne and hibiscus, or another that brings out comforting memories of Christmas via clementines, winter spices and oats.

Chef Steve Smith **Owner** Lawrence Huggler **Seats** 60, Pr/dining room 24 **Times** 12-2.30/6.30-10, Closed 24-30 Dec, Sun (ex Mother/Father's day), BH Mon **Prices** Fixed L 2 course £19.95, Fixed D 2 course £50-£59 **Wines** 120 bottles over £30, 19 bottles under £30, 24 by glass **Parking** 20, Opposite on Green Street **Notes** ALC 3 course £59, Surprise L/D menu 6 course £45/£49, Children welcome

Grand Jersey

British, French v

tel: 01534 722301 **The Esplanade JE2 3QA**
email: reception.grandjersey@handpicked.co.uk
web: www.handpickedhotels/grandjersey
dir: *Located on St Helier seafront*

Luxurious island cooking in a sprawling bayfront hotel

The rosette award for this establishment has been suspended due to a change of chef. Reassessment will take place in due course under the new chef. The view over the shimmering waters of St Aubin's Bay is undoubtedly the Grand's USP, and it is best enjoyed from the terrace or one of the sea-facing bedrooms. The sprawling hotel has a contemporary finish on the inside and is kitted out with a swish spa and a host of eating and drinking options. There's a champagne lounge with a boutique feel that makes a good starting point or finishing point to a visit (cocktails, coffee, and even afternoon tea). The main restaurant is the fine-dining Tassili, a diminutive space with dark and seductive decor, and a TV screen showing the goings-on at the pass. The modern tasting menus offer options from 'the land' or 'the land and sea' and deliver dishes made using up-to-date techniques. From the latter, you might start with Jersey lobster with a lobster 'Caesar' and jelly, plus avocado and Ebène caviar, before moving on to smoked salmon dish cut through with Asian flavours. The 'land' delivers a fashionable beetroot salad with goats' cream and fritters, with Ibérico ham and Marcona almonds, followed by a pork belly and braised cheek with chorizo and pork 'popcorn'. The creative ideas and contemporary technique continues into sweet courses such as a vanilla cheesecake with blackberry and Cassis textures, or pistachio and olive cake with an accompanying chocolate sorbet and macaroon. The cheese trolley may well catch your eye as it works its round.

Chef Nicolas Valmagna **Owner** Hand Picked Hotels **Seats** 24 **Times** 12-1.45/7-10, Closed Sun-Mon, L Tue-Thu **Prices** Fixed L 2 course £18.95, Fixed D 3 course £52, Tasting menu £60-£67, Starter £12-£18, Main £26-£34, Dessert £12-£15 **Wines** 70 bottles over £30, 14 bottles under £30, 16 by glass **Parking** 32, NCP **Notes** Children welcome

Ormer ❀❀❀

British, French v **NOTABLE WINE LIST**

tel: 01534 725100 **7-11 Don St JE2 4TQ**
email: book@ormerjersey.com
dir: *Phone for directions*

Shaun Rankin's sophisticated St Helier venture delivers the goods

If you think that Shaun Rankin's St Helier operation cuts a dash on the high street with its natty blue frontage, just wait until you get inside. A megabucks makeover retooled the dining room with art deco-style glam that could have been lifted straight from a 1920s ocean liner, all wooden floors, chandeliers, plush blue velvet buttoned banquettes and mustard yellow leather seats at darkwood tables simply decorated with small lamps. There's a lively ground-floor bar and a pavement terrace for people watching, but the ace in the hole is the roof garden and cigar terrace where you can round off a meal among lush plants and lemon trees. As always, Rankin's precise, assured creations start from the ground up, hauling in Jersey produce of peerless quality from land and sea, and showcasing the best the island has to offer in modern French dishes notable for their depth of natural flavour and beautiful presentation. A delicate starter brings together Jersey crab with coriander and mango in a crisp cannelloni, pointed up with the vivid notes of fresh pink grapefruit and grapefruit jelly, mango purée and chilli water vinaigrette. Next up, steak and chips, Rankin-style: flavour-packed feather blade is barbecued to perfection and delivered with crisp, fluffy duck fat chips, mushroom ketchup, seared baby gem lettuce and horseradish hollandaise. If something more subtle is required, how about John Dory partnered by roast baby fennel, marinated grapes, Pernod butter and star anise essence? An exemplary dessert matches popcorn, milk ice cream and salted caramel with an elegant take on chocolate brownie.

Chef Shaun Rankin **Owner** Shaun Rankin, Nick Bettany **Seats** 70, Pr/dining room 14 **Times** 12-2.30/6.30-10, Closed 25 Dec, Sun **Prices** Fixed L 2 course £19, Tasting menu £75, Starter £13-£16, Main £25-£30, Dessert £9 **Wines** 196 bottles over £30, 48 bottles under £30, 15 by glass **Parking** On street, Sand Street car park **Notes** Spring market D menu 3 course, Children welcome

ST HELIER *continued*

Restaurant Sirocco@The Royal Yacht

Modern British

tel: 01534 720511 **The Weighbridge JE2 3NF**
email: reception@theroyalyacht.com **web:** www.theroyalyacht.com
dir: *Adjacent to Weighbridge Park overlooking Jersey Harbour*

Bright Jersey cooking beneath purple bubbles

The wave-shaped balconies of this modern hotel on the harbour side help The Royal Yacht to match its setting. Inside all is blond wood and light airy design, and the dining options include an outdoor terrace, the informal Café Zephyr, and the top-drawer Restaurant Sirocco, where coffee-coloured napery, drapes in violet and yellow, and overhead lighting through a cluster of purple bubbles, complement the waterfront views. Vigorous Jersey cooking of great brio brightens the outlook even further, offering variations on a theme of beetroot with confit duck and foie gras, or lobster with chorizo, peas and parmesan gnocchi, to begin, and main courses such as accurately seared sea bass, with Jerusalem artichokes, asparagus and crab. Thoroughbred meats include lamb cannon given depth with smoked garlic and a langoustine, or beef fillet flambéed and Dianed at your table. Jersey Royals in the season are spun into a tempting, truffle-scented vegetarian main dish. A pannacotta and jelly platter is the texturally undemanding way to finish, or there could be pistachio cake and brittle with honey ice cream.

Chef Steve Walker **Owner** Lodestar Group, The Royal Yacht **Seats** 65, Pr/dining room 20 **Times** 12-4/7-10, Closed L Mon-Sat **Wines** 108 bottles over £30, 49 bottles under £30, 20 by glass **Parking** Car park **Notes** Tasting menu, Wkly rotating table d'hôte menu, Sunday L fr £22.50, Vegetarian available, Children welcome

See advert on opposite page

Greenhills Country Hotel

Mediterranean, British, French

tel: 01534 481042 **Mont de L'Ecole JE3 7EL**
email: reserve@greenhillshotel.com **web:** www.greenhillshotel.com
dir: *A1 signed St Peters Valley (A11). 4m, turn right onto E112*

Gently contemporary cooking of Jersey's fine produce

There is much to like about this relaxed country hotel dating from the 17th century with its riotously colourful gardens, heated outdoor pool and bags of traditional charm. The icing on the cake is the restaurant where tables are dressed in their best linen and the kitchen team turns out a wide-ranging menu taking in everything from a classic straight-up combo of fillet steak with wild mushrooms, chunky chips and grilled tomato, to more ambitious ideas along the lines of poached salmon fillet and prawns with vegetable paella and lobster and Noilly Prat sauce. Preceding this, Jersey scallops come in a tried-and-tested alliance with pancetta, capers and cauliflower purée. There's endeavour and comfort in equal measure for pudding, when that 1970s favourite tipple – advocaat – turns up in crème anglaise to go with sticky toffee pudding.

Chef Marcin Dudek **Owner** Seymour Hotels **Seats** 90, Pr/dining room 40 **Times** 12.30-2/7-9.30, Closed 21 Dec-12 Feb **Prices** Fixed L 2 course £13, Fixed D 3 course £29.50, Starter £5.50-£9.50, Main £11.50-£22.50, Dessert £4.25-£7.50, Service optional **Wines** 19 bottles over £30, 62 bottles under £30, 8 by glass **Parking** 45 **Notes** ALC specialities, Sunday L £21, Vegetarian available, Children welcome

---

Mark Jordan at the Beach

Anglo French

tel: 01534 780180 **La Plage, La Route de la Haule JE3 7YD**
email: bookings@markjordanatthebeach.com
dir: *A1 W from St Helier, left mini-rdbt towards St Aubins, follow sign 50mtrs on left*

Anglo-French fish dishes next to the beach

A suave, sea-breezy feel imbues Mark Jordan at the Beach, which is hardly surprising as only the promenade road separates it from the beach at St Peter. It comes into its own on sunny days when the sea sparkles, the more so for having a dining room where a signature chef gets to strut his stuff. It's a pleasant white-walled space with wicker chairs and fish pictures, which gives you all the clue you need as to what the forte is. The style is contemporary Anglo-French, as befits the location, seen in a starter of duck terrine with fig chutney and toasted brioche. Next up, a splendid piece of pan-fried cod, the flesh properly opalescent, is left to speak for itself, alongside crushed new potatoes, spinach, and beurre Nantais foam. You won't be neglected if you're dead set on meat, with the likes of honey-roasted duck breast with griottine cherries, caramelised red cabbage and fondant potato up for grabs. Dessert brings a perfectly-risen mint chocolate chip soufflé and chocolate ice cream.

Chef Mark Jordan, Tamas Varsanyi **Owner** Mark Jordan, Patrick Burke **Seats** 50 **Times** 12-2.30/6-9.30, Closed 9-23 Nov, Mon (winter), D Sun (winter) **Prices** Fixed L 2 course £19.50, Fixed D 3 course £27.50, Starter £7.50-£13.50, Main £14.50-£28.50, Dessert £6-£9.50, Service optional **Wines** 25 bottles over £30, 22 bottles under £30, 6 by glass **Parking** 16 **Notes** Sunday L £27.50, Vegetarian available, Children welcome

ST SAVIOUR
Map 24

Longueville Manor Hotel
❀❀❀ – see below

TRINITY
Map 24

Water's Edge Hotel
❀ Modern British

tel: 01534 862777 **Bouley Bay JE3 5AS**
email: info@watersedgejersey.com **web:** www.watersedgejersey.com
dir: 10-15 mins from St Helier, A9 N onto A8 then onto B31, follow signs to Bouley Bay

Sea views and cooking that aims high

Tucked into the cliffs of Bouley Bay a wave's lap from the briny, the Water's Edge is aptly named. The view from the restaurant is hard to beat, looking across an unbroken expanse of sea to the coast of France, and the food also merits serious attention. A new kitchen team took the reins in 2013 and has stamped its mark on the local foodie scene, hauling in the finest local produce and delivering it in well-executed, easy-on-the-eye dishes. Fish and seafood are naturally a strong suit – perhaps salmon tartare to start, ahead of braised shin of Jersey Angus beef which arrives with slices of fillet and foie gras, roasted baby beets, glazed carrots, sautéed leeks and horseradish duchess potatoes. The ambition continues to a well-crafted finale involving pear tarte Tatin and an unusual yet effective ice cream of Jersey Blue cheese and walnuts.

Times 12-2.30/6.30-9

SARK

SARK
Map 24

La Sablonnerie
❀ Modern, Traditional International

tel: 01481 832061 **Little Sark GY10 1SD**
email: reservations@sablonneriesark.com **web:** www.sablonneriesark.com
dir: On southern part of island. Horse & carriage transport to hotel

Uncomplicated ways with home-grown produce on a special island

Reaching this small hotel is quite an adventure: a horse-drawn carriage is sent to collect guests arriving on the ferry. The building itself is pretty ancient, with beams

Longueville Manor Hotel ❀❀❀

ST SAVIOUR
Map 24

Modern Anglo-French V 🍷 NOTABLE WINE LIST
tel: 01534 725501 **JE2 7WF**
email: info@longuevillemanor.com **web:** www.longuevillemanor.com
dir: From St Helier take A3 to Gorey, hotel 0.75m on left

Accomplished country-hotel cooking in an ancient house

Longueville has been around in one shape or another since the 14th century. Standing in 18 acres of immaculately maintained gardens and woodland, it has been Jersey's go-to place for a country-house hotel splurge since the Lewis family transformed the old pile into a hotel in 1949, running the show with warmth and immaculate attention to detail. A house full of character and history, then, right down to the 15th-century panelling in the Oak Room restaurant, which is recycled from oak chests taken as spoils of war from the Spanish Armada. The kitchen team has deep roots too, since Andrew Baird has been in residency here for over 20 years, gently evolving his Anglo-French culinary style in step with the times, without ever chasing ephemeral trends for tawdry effect. A Victorian kitchen garden supplies vegetables, herbs and salad leaves for menus that take full account of local fish, shellfish and the island's livestock, producing starters ranging from local crab with sweet pickled cucumber, melon, avocado and warm crab slaw, to roast free-range quail with glazed grapes, fig, ginger, orange and quail's egg. Main courses draw on classical culinary modes when partnering a two-way presentation of lamb (roast best end and braised shoulder) with potato gratin, baby globe artichoke and aubergine, or presenting delicately poached lemon sole with shellfish, baby vegetables and lobster sauce. However, there might also be a more modern marriage of fish and meat, matching grilled line-caught sea bass with confit chicken, tiger prawns and butternut squash. At the end, perhaps baked apple terrine with Jersey black butter bavarois, caramelised apples and Calvados ice cream, or French and British artisan cheeses resplendent on a trolley of 180-year-old French oak.

Chef Andrew Baird **Owner** Malcolm Lewis **Seats** 65, Pr/dining room 22
Times 12.30-2/7-10, **Prices** Fixed L 3 course £25, Fixed D 3 course £60-£66
Wines 300 bottles over £30, 69 bottles under £30, 25 by glass **Parking** 45
Notes Discovery menu with/without wine £80-£110, ALC 2/3 course, Sunday L £40-£46, Children welcome

and stone walls as evidence. In fine weather, take a table in the lovely garden, otherwise head for the main restaurant. Seafood draws the attention, from lobster (thermidor, say, or grilled with a lime and ginger butter glaze) to grilled fillets of sea bass served simply with bisque and croquette potatoes, or monkfish braised in sherry vinegar with brown shrimps and bacon. Meat dishes are no less interesting: perhaps caramelised duck breast with Sarladaise potatoes and a sage and green peppercorn jus. To start there might be perfectly seared scallops with pancetta and cauliflower purée, and to finish almond mousse with poached pears and caramel sauce, or passionfruit mousse with yogurt sorbet.

La Sablonnerie

Chef Colin Day **Owner** Elizabeth Perrée **Seats** 39 **Times** 12-2.30/7-9.30, Closed mid Oct-Etr **Prices** Fixed L 2 course £26.50, Fixed D 3 course £34.50, Tasting menu £39.50, Starter £9.80, Main £17.50, Dessert £9.50 **Wines** 16 bottles over £30, 50 bottles under £30, 6 by glass **Notes** Vegetarian meal on request, Sunday L, Vegetarian available, Children welcome

Stocks Hotel

◉◉ Modern British

tel: 01481 832001 & 832444 **GY10 1SD**
email: reception@stockshotel.com **web:** www.stockshotel.com
dir: *From Jersey or Guernsey via ferry to Sark harbour. Transfer to hotel approx 20 mins by foot, bicycle or carriage*

Fine classically focused dining in a secluded valley

Sitting in a quiet and picturesque valley – but then again just about everywhere on Sark is quiet and picturesque – Stocks is a smart hotel built around a farmhouse dating from the mid-1700s. It's done out in a traditional manner, and that goes for

the fine-dining restaurant, too. There's also a bistro by the swimming pool and an atmospheric bar. The main restaurant serves up plenty of local ingredients in bright, classically-focused modern dishes, with traditional lunches on Sundays. Rabbit loin is wrapped in Parma ham and roasted as a first course, served with apple and celeriac purée, and among main courses might be local sea bass partnered with braised celery, lobster sauce and chervil foam. Honey and Drambuie parfait is a dessert that shows good technical skills, served with a praline biscuit, and meals are preceded by canapés and breads served with excellent (and strong) local butter.

Stocks Hotel

Chef Vincent Haselton **Owner** Alex & Helen Magell **Seats** 60, Pr/dining room 12 **Times** 12-2.30/7-9, Closed 2 Jan-1 Mar **Prices** Fixed L 2 course £20-£35, Fixed D 3 course £35-£45, Tasting menu £70-£85, Starter £6.50-£10.50, Main £15.50-£25.50, Dessert £7.50-£12.50, Service optional **Wines** 57 bottles over £30, 24 bottles under £30, 6 by glass **Parking** 36, Bicycle spaces only **Notes** Champagne afternoon tea £49.50 for 2, Ride & dine £85 for 2, Sunday L £20-£35, Vegetarian available, Children welcome

ISLE OF MAN

DOUGLAS   Map 24 SC37

JAR Restaurant

◉◉ Modern, International, Pacific Rim
----

tel: 01624 663553 & 629551 **Admiral House Hotel, 12 Loch Promenade IM1 2LX**
email: jar@admiralhouse.com **web:** www.jar.co.im
dir: *Located 2 mins from Douglas Ferry Terminal. 20 mins from airport*

Sharp cooking using prime Manx produce in grand hotel

Set within the Victorian Admiral House Hotel, in a prime site on the promenade, JAR Restaurant has been given a clean, modern, spruced-up look. The menu opens with a selection of grazing-size dishes for sharing. Strong among them are sashimi, sushi and tempura rolls, taking in yellowfin tuna, teriyaki beef, smoked duck and squid with lime. Those who prefer the more conventional three-course route can opt for one of the 'small plates' for first course: perhaps beetroot-cured salmon and fennel salad, chicken, lime and coconut salad, or beef tartare. The kitchen buys only the best Manx produce and turns out dishes of bold combinations and vibrant flavours. Main courses run to roast cod fillet with squid ink, quinoa, spring onions and chilli, and roast monkfish with razor clams, chorizo and squid as well as more conventional roast duck breast with a parcel of leg meat, shallots and pak choi. End with lemon crème brûlée with raspberry sorbet.

Chef Karl Haworth **Owner** Branwell Ltd **Seats** 48 **Times** 12-2/6-10, Closed 26-30 Dec, Sun-Tue, L Sat **Prices** Prices not confirmed, Service optional **Wines** 34 bottles over £30, 12 bottles under £30, 7 by glass **Parking** Free parking opposite **Notes** Tasting menu, Vegetarian available, Children welcome

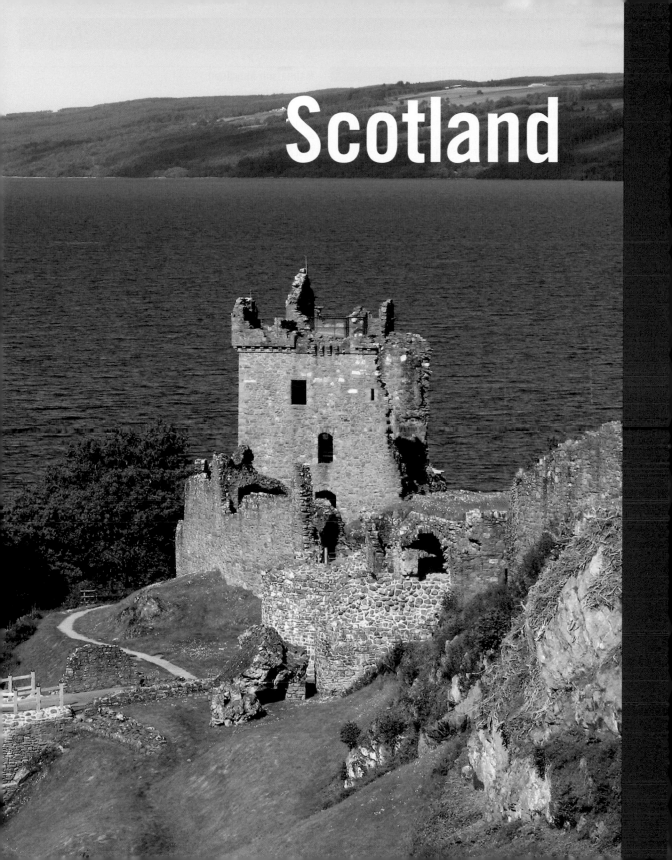

Scotland

CITY OF ABERDEEN

ABERDEEN   Map 23 NJ90

The Adelphi Kitchen

Modern British

tel: 01224 211414 & 07912 666256 **28 Adelphi AB11 5BL**
email: hello@theadelphikitchen.co.uk
dir: *Off Union St*

Switched-on barbecue restaurant with an upbeat vibe

Chris and Lynsey Tonner's restaurant in the Adelphi district of the city took a radical departure from its previous incarnation in 2013, emerging with the new moniker and a reinvented culinary concept. The latter has installed an open-pit barbecue in the kitchen to deliver impeccably-sourced local meat and seafood cooked 'dirty' — that's to say directly on the hot charcoal — with clear influences from those good ol' stateside barbecue-meisters and their racy Tex-Mex flavours. The place still has a buzz about it, with young, cheery staff keeping the mood casual and upbeat, and the kitchen sending out pan-fried scallops with tempura roe, asparagus, and smoked tomato and shellfish bisque sauce, followed by venison loin alongside potatoes with crispy chorizo, a mix of beetroots, confit cherry tomatoes and tomato jus. At dessert stage, sour cherry sorbet is a clever idea to cut through the richness of a double chocolate, bourbon and ginger brownie.

Chef Chris Tonner **Owner** Beetroot Restaurants Ltd **Seats** 37
Times 12-2.30/5-9.45, Closed 24-25 Dec, 1 Jan, Sun **Prices** Starter £6.50-£12, Main £14-£35, Dessert £6.50-£8, Service optional **Wines** 11 bottles over £30, 12 bottles under £30, 7 by glass **Parking** On street **Notes** Taster tray for 2 Tue £45, Vegetarian available, Children welcome

Fusion

Modern British **NEW**

tel: 01224 652959 **10 North Silver St AB10 1RL**
email: dining@fusionbarbistro.com
dir: *Phone for directions*

Funky spot for fizz and switched-on cooking

Blurring the line between bar and restaurant, Fusion is a big hit with Aberdeen's in-crowd. Get your meal on a roll with some bubbles in the funky Perrier-Jouët Champagne bar before heading upstairs to the Gallery restaurant, a chic spot to see and be seen in with its lime green seats, wooden floors and stencilled white walls. The creative modern British menu suits the upbeat vibe and has the capacity to excite with cleverly-tweaked ideas, as when loin of hare is combined with pheasant and thyme mousse and pointed up with cranberry mustard and herb brioche crumbs. A main-course duo of pork matches loin and confit belly with prune purée, sweet potato croquettes, silverskin onions and cider jus. Sloe gin pannacotta with pear sorbet and blueberry compôte is a good way to finish. Smiley staff keep it on the boil with pin-sharp service.

Chef Steven Murray **Owner** Mark Cavanagh **Seats** 50, Pr/dining room 25
Times 12-2.30/5-9.30, Closed Xmas (4 days), New Year (4 days), Sun-Mon, L Tue-Fri **Prices** Fixed D 3 course £29.95-£41.45, Tasting menu £45 **Wines** 14 bottles over £30, 15 bottles under £30, 11 by glass **Notes** Early supper/Sat L, Vegetarian available, Children welcome

Malmaison Aberdeen

Modern British

tel: 01224 327370 **49-53 Queens Rd AB15 4YP**
email: info.aberdeen@malmaison.com web: www.malmaisonaberdeen.com
dir: *A90, 3rd exit onto Queens Rd at 3rd rdbt, hotel on right*

Cool contemporary brasserie with theatre kitchen

Built from the solid granite that gives the city its moniker, the Aberdeen branch of the Malmaison group is suitably dashing, with boutique allure and a cool industrial-chic finish. The brasserie is at the heart of the operation, literally at the centre in this case, with exposed pipework on the high ceiling, and the rustic colours are moody, chic and reminiscent of the Scottish Highlands. The open-to-view kitchen reveals the Josper Grill, the source of a good deal of what follows. When it comes to red meat, you can pick out what you fancy through the glass partition. Start with chicken liver parfait with fig chutney and toasted brioche, or maybe a Thai roast pumpkin soup (there are no borders here). Next up, something from that Josper: a whopping T-bone, perhaps, or rib-eye, but there are other options such as smoked haddock fishcake with a warm poached egg, or a veggie risotto with pumpkin, tallegio, walnuts and sage. There are tasty-sounding burgers, too.

Chef John Burns **Owner** Malmaison **Seats** 90, Pr/dining room 30
Times 12-2.30/5.30-10.30, Closed D 25 Dec **Prices** Prices not confirmed **Wines** 26 bottles over £30, 16 bottles under £30, 27 by glass **Parking** 30 **Notes** Brunch £29.95, Sunday L, Vegetarian available, Children welcome

Maryculter House Hotel

Modern British

tel: 01224 732124 **South Deeside Rd, Maryculter AB12 5GB**
email: info@maryculterhousehotel.com web: www.maryculterhousehotel.com
dir: *Off A90 to S of Aberdeen and onto B9077. Hotel is located 8m on right, 0.5m beyond Lower Deeside Caravan Park*

Classical cooking in a characterful setting beside the River Dee

The location has connections to the Knights Templar and the house itself has bags of charm and character, standing on the banks of the River Dee (with fishing rights). The hotel's Priory restaurant doesn't lack period charm either, with stone walls and flickering candles, plus tables formally dressed for fine dining. There's an informal brasserie, too. The main event sees a menu of classically-minded dishes that might start with a confit duck and pear terrine served with a celeriac remoulade and mixed leaves dressed in a honey and mustard vinaigrette. Next up, main course might see salmon (as you might hope around here), pan-fried and partnered with wilted greens, fondant potato and a fishy chive cream. For dessert, a slice of dark chocolate tart with perfectly thin pastry comes with pistachio ice cream and chocolate truffles. There's a tasting menu, too, plus a slate of well-kept cheeses.

Chef Andrew Pavlantis **Owner** James Gilbert **Seats** 58, Pr/dining room 30
Times 6-9, Closed L all week **Prices** Fixed D 3 course £32-£38, Starter £5.95-£9.25, Main £11.50-£28.95, Dessert £5.95-£6.95, Service optional **Wines** 26 bottles over £30, 23 bottles under £30, 9 by glass **Parking** 60 **Notes** 7 course gourmet menu on certain dates, Brasserie 11am-9pm, Sunday L, Vegetarian available, Children welcome

Mercure Aberdeen Ardoe House Hotel & Spa

Modern Scottish, French

tel: 01224 860600 **South Deeside Rd, Blairs AB12 5YP**
email: h6626-dm@accor.com **web:** www.mercure.com
dir: *4m W of city off B9077*

19th-century hotel with 21st-century cooking

The soaring towers and grand gables of this old greystone house give a fine impression of an ancient castle, but actually it was built as a family home back in the 1870s. Three miles from the city centre and surrounded by 30 acres of grounds, these days it's a smart hotel with a spa and all modcons. The exterior may speak of traditional comfort, elegance and old-world grandeur, but indoors the designers have revamped the old girl with a jazzy contemporary look that carries through to the sleek new lines of Blair's Restaurant. The kitchen takes a contemporary path, turning out suitably unbuttoned and up-to-date dishes. These go from crispy salt and pepper-battered whitebait with lime and confit garlic aïoli, to main-course cod, crusted with chorizo and pimento and matched with spring onion and pea risotto and fennel and orange cream. Finish with rhubarb and custard pannacotta with poached rhubarb and shortbread.

Chef Richard Yearnshire **Owner** Accor UK **Seats** 100, Pr/dining room 25 **Times** 12.30-2.30/6.30-9.30 **Prices** Service optional **Wines** 15 bottles over £30, 15 bottles under £30, 17 by glass **Parking** 90 **Notes** Afternoon/high tea, Sunday L £25, Vegetarian available, Children welcome

Norwood Hall Hotel

Modern British

tel: 01224 868951 **Garthdee Rd, Cults AB15 9FX**
email: info@norwood-hall.co.uk **web:** www.norwood-hall.co.uk
dir: *Off A90, at 1st rdbt cross Bridge of Dee, left at rdbt onto Garthdee Rd (B&Q & Sainsburys on left) continue to hotel sign*

Victorian mansion showcasing fine Scottish produce

The interior of this 1881-built mansion is nothing short of stunning, all ornate fireplaces, stained-glass windows and an oak staircase. The restaurant has two areas, one panelled and hung with tapestries, the other more contemporary a word that also applies to the kitchen's style, with a strong Scottish element shining through. Ham hock terrine with red peppers and pineapple chutney is a stridently flavoured starter, while Marie Rose sauce is given a shot of whisky for crayfish tails, prawns and langoustines. Prime ingredients are carefully handled, as in rack of local lamb (three- or seven-bone), cooked to pink, served with red wine jus, dauphinoise, spinach and carrot purée, and in well-timed roast fillet of halibut in a parmesan crust with mussels, peas and warm tartare-style sauce. Cheeses are all Scottish, and puddings follow the route of lemon tart with caramel ice cream and Seville orange syrup.

Chef Kenny McMillian, Neil Ireland **Owner** Monument Leisure **Seats** 48, Pr/dining room 180 **Times** 12-2.30/6-9.45 **Prices** Prices not confirmed, Service optional **Wines** 46 bottles over £30, 24 bottles under £30, 12 by glass **Parking** 140 **Notes** Sunday L, Vegetarian available, Children 12 yrs+

Rock & Oyster

Modern British, Seafood **NEW**

tel: 01224 622555 **27-29 Union Ter AB10 1NN**
email: enquiries@rock-oyster.com
dir: *Phone for directions*

Innovative seafood cookery in a funky spot

This switched-on seafood restaurant has made quite a splash on the Aberdeen foodie scene since it opened in late 2013. Inside, colourful artwork enlivens a neutral contemporary space, and informal staff foster an unbuttoned ambience that sits well with the kitchen's thoroughly up-to-date take on fish-oriented cuisine. Fish is delivered daily to star in a main course of crisp-skinned sea bream served with shrimps, samphire and a sharp lemony risotto, or there could be a more thought-provoking pairing of halibut with scallop, guacamole and chicory. Diehard carnivores might go for a three-way serving of lamb (loin, belly and sweetbread) with spiced aubergine and confit tomato. Preceding this, velvety goats' cheese mousse arrives with marinated and salt-baked beetroot, and for pudding, there's a fresh, seasonal dish of condensed milk parfait with vanilla-poached rhubarb and rhubarb purée.

Chef Andrew Manson **Owner** Alasdair Cowie **Seats** 40 **Times** 5-10, Closed 25 Dec, 1 Jan, Sun-Mon, L Tue-Fri **Prices** Fixed D 3 course £27.65, Tasting menu £40-£80, Starter £7.25-£8.45, Main £17.95-£23.95, Dessert £6.95-£7.95 **Wines** 2 bottles over £30, 9 bottles under £30, 7 by glass **Parking** Denburn car park **Notes** Pre-theatre menu 5-6.30pm, Vegetarian available, Children welcome

The Silver Darling

French, Seafood

tel: 01224 576229 **Pocra Quay, North Pier AB11 5DQ**
email: silverdarling@hotmail.co.uk
dir: *At Aberdeen Harbour entrance*

Interesting ways with superbly fresh seafood

As befits its quayside location at the mouth of Aberdeen harbour, The Silver Darling has a firm focus on the bounty of the sea. The name is a colloquial reference to the herring that were once the bedrock of the local economy, and you can watch the trawlers come and go once you have ascended the spiral staircase to the luminous conservatory-style dining room perched atop a stocky granite building. The appetite for fish and seafood duly stimulated, the kitchen fulfills its part of the deal via a menu of French-accented contemporary ideas, with the odd foray into far-Eastern flavours. A clever starter sees mackerel served three ways — rillettes on toast, a little fishy burger, and pickled — accompanied by a stimulating mix of cucumber, fennel and dill, and apple and celery remoulade. Main course brings a splendid fillet of sea trout with Jerusalem artichoke purée, asparagus, and a turbocharged hit of vibrant Bois Boudran dressing. Desserts are impressive too — pannacotta is infused with vanilla seeds and served with rhubarb that has been poached or flavours a vibrant sorbet.

Chef Didier Dejean **Owner** Didier Dejean, Karen Murray **Seats** 50, Pr/dining room 8 **Times** 12-1.45/6.30-9.30, Closed Xmas-New Year, Sun, L Sat **Prices** Fixed L 2 course fr £19.50, Starter £9.50-£14.50, Main £16.50-£26.50, Dessert £8.50-£11.50 **Wines** 26 bottles over £30, 14 bottles under £30, 10 by glass **Parking** On quayside **Notes** ALC D only, Vegetarian available, Children welcome

ABERDEENSHIRE

BALLATER
Map 23 NO39

Loch Kinord Hotel
◉ Modern Scottish

tel: 01339 885229 **Ballater Rd, Dinnet AB34 5JY**
email: stay@lochkinord.com **web:** www.lochkinord.com
dir: *Between Aboyne & Ballater, on A93, in Dinnet*

Classical cooking in Royal Deeside

Built in rock-solid granite in the Victorian period, Loch Kinord is well placed for maximising time spent in Royal Deeside, whether that's the renowned fishing, a wee spot of whisky tasting, or simply walking in the glorious hills. There are homely lounges within where real fires keep you toasty, a small bar and a dining room done out with tartan wallpaper and plush red and gold carpets. There's a classical leaning to the kitchen's output, evident understanding of culinary ways, and a good showing of regional produce to inject a sense of place. Game terrine with red onion marmalade and toasted brioche is a typical starter, followed perhaps by rack of lamb with mustard and herb crust, the meat perfectly pink and tender, served with braised red cabbage and black pudding mash. Chocolate fondant oozes in all the right places and comes with a scoop of intensely flavoured vanilla ice cream.

Chef Maciej Jaworski **Owner** Andrew & Jenny Cox **Seats** 40 **Times** 6-9, Closed L all week **Prices** Fixed D 3 course £31.95-£37.95, Service optional **Wines** 7 bottles over £30, 20 bottles under £30, 6 by glass **Parking** 20 **Notes** Vegetarian available, Children welcome

BALMEDIE
Map 23 NJ91

Cock & Bull
◉ Modern Scottish, British Ⅴ

tel: 01358 743249 **Ellon Rd, Blairton AB23 8XY**
email: info@thecockandbull.co.uk **web:** www.thecockandbull.co.uk
dir: *6m N of Aberdeen on A90*

Big flavours at a distinctive country inn

The Cock & Bull is a pub of the gastro variety, a low-slung establishment built in the 19th century with all the incumbent character. There are wooden beams and real fires, but there's nothing stuck in the past about this particular pub: modern food and local artworks ensure that a visit is very much of our time. The art is for sale if it takes your fancy. Eat in either the conservatory dining room, cosy lounge in front of the fire, or the main restaurant, where traditional decor is gently updated to meet modern expectations. There's an all-day menu containing a good amount of regional goodies and modern-leaning ideas: black pudding Scotch egg, for example, with home-made brown sauce, or king scallops with autumn squash and coal oil. Next up, Gressingham duck leg confit, or the gourmet hot dog made with pulled pork, and, for dessert, dark chocolate fondant with honeycomb ice cream.

Chef Ryan Paterson **Owner** Rodger Morrison **Seats** 80, Pr/dining room 30 **Times** 10.30am-late, All-day dining, Closed 26 Dec, 2 Jan **Prices** Prices not confirmed, Service optional **Wines** 11 bottles over £30, 24 bottles under £30, 7 by glass **Notes** Sunday L, Children welcome

BANCHORY
Map 23 NO69

Raemoir House Hotel
◎◎ Modern, Traditional Scottish 🍷 NOTABLE WINE LIST

tel: 01330 824884 **Raemoir AB31 4ED**
email: hotel@raemoir.com **web:** www.raemoir.com
dir: A93 to Banchory then A980, hotel at x-rds after 2.5m

Modern country-house cooking in Royal Deeside

A couple of miles north of Banchory, perfectly placed for pilgrims on the whisky trail, the heart of Raemoir is a pair of buildings, an early Georgian hall house with a large greystone mansion in front of it. Flocked velvet wall-coverings, oil portraits of the ancestors and ornate gilt wood-framed mirrors establish a tone only befitting Royal Deeside in an elliptical dining room that was once the ballroom. Sashay instead now through menus of modern Scottish cooking, where global influences and cutting-edge technique produce starters of pork belly with a spiced bonbon of apple and black pudding in red wine jus, or panko-crumbed Crottin goats' cheese with huge green Gordal olives. The vegetarian main dish might be chickpea falafel with artichoke purée, while pedigree fish and meat are accorded respect in the form of cod with chorizo, cannellini beans, wilted greens and red pepper, or Ballater sirloin with button mushrooms, triple-cooked chips and béarnaise. For dessert, look no further than a warm chocolate brownie with crystallised nuts and passionfruit sorbet. Overnighters are rewarded with a sumptuous breakfast menu.

Chef Sam Ritchie **Owner** Neil & Julie Rae **Seats** 40, Pr/dining room 16 **Times** 12-2.30/5.30-9.30 **Prices** Starter £6-£13, Main £14-£28, Dessert £6-£10, Service optional **Wines** 62 bottles over £30, 22 bottles under £30, 12 by glass **Parking** 50 **Notes** Tasting menu, Fixed D 4 course £48, Sunday L £25-£32, Vegetarian available, Children 12 yrs+

CRATHES
Map 23 NO79

The Milton Brasserie
◎ Traditional British

tel: 01330 844566 & 844474 **AB31 5QH**
email: jay@miltonbrasserie.com
dir: On the A93, 15m W of Aberdeen, opposite Crathes Castle

Modern brasserie cooking in a cottage near the castle

Picturesquely sited near the castle at Crathes, not far from the Royal Deeside railway, The Milton is hardly a brasserie in the big-city sense. From the outside a charming whitewashed stone cottage, it has a countrified air within, complete with log-like pillars supporting a beamed ceiling and leathery, tweedy tones in the upholstery. The bill of fare, though, is more obviously in the modern idiom, starting with the likes of a fish and crab cake with fennel and dill chutney and russet-hued partan bree, as a prelude perhaps to lightly charred Barbary duck breast in Amarena cherry jus with cider fondant potato, or hake wrapped up in prosciutto with parsley risotto and a reduction of Noilly Prat. An individual cheesecake incorporating stewed rhubarb on a ginger biscuit base with rich custard ice cream is a neat way of combining two favourite dessert ideas, and there are Celtic cheeses with home-made oatcakes.

Chef Bob Miller **Owner** Jay Emmerson **Seats** 70, Pr/dining room 25 **Times** 12-3/6-9, Closed 25-26 Dec, 1-2 Jan, D Sun-Tue **Prices** Starter £4-£6.50, Main £12-£14, Dessert £4-£6.50, Service optional **Wines** 6 bottles over £30, 21 bottles under £30, 11 by glass **Parking** 70 **Notes** Sunday L, Vegetarian available, Children welcome

ELLON
Map 23 NJ93

Eat on the Green
◎◎ Traditional British, Scottish

tel: 01651 842337 **Udny Green AB41 7RS**
email: enquiries@eatonthegreen.co.uk
dir: A920 towards Udny Green/Ellon

Bright, modern cooking in a starry village inn

Craig Wilson is an enterprising chef and he's passionate about sharing his appreciation for fine Scottish ingredients. Ever fancied being a chef for the day? You can here, hands-on, as part of the team. There's also a champagne club, a chef's table (via a video link), and a private room on the first floor. And they even do afternoon tea. The two charming dining rooms are rich with local colour, with pictures of hereabouts and the chef in action, and tables dressed in sharp white linen. It's an atmospheric spot. The kitchen turns out some impressive modern dishes, presented with style, and delivering some spot-on flavours. A first-course tart has ultra-thin pastry and is packed with chorizo, pickled mushrooms and Mull cheddar, or there might be a pea risotto with crispy shallots and parmesan. Main-course Aberdeenshire pork hits the mark in a dish featuring both belly and fillet, served with a potato and pancetta terrine, plus an apple emulsion, confit of soya tomato and mushroom jus. Desserts such as vanilla pannacotta with strawberries and lemon curd are no less impressive.

Chef Craig Wilson **Owner** Craig & Lindsay Wilson **Seats** 82, Pr/dining room 16 **Times** 12-2/6-9, Closed 1st wk Jan, Mon-Tue, L Sat **Prices** Fixed L 2 course £23.95-£29.95, Fixed D 3 course £30-£59, Tasting menu £80-£115, Starter £5.50-£8.95, Main £23.95-£31.95, Dessert £7.95-£13.95, Service optional **Wines** 42 bottles over £30, 26 bottles under £30, 9 by glass **Parking** 7, On street **Notes** Tasting menu 8 course Wed-Fri 48hrs notice required, Sunday L £29.95-£34.95, Vegetarian available, Children welcome

INVERURIE
Map 23 NJ72

Macdonald Pittodrie House
◎◎ Modern, Traditional Scottish

tel: 01467 622437 **Chapel of Garioch, Pitcaple AB51 5HS**
email: pittodrie@macdonald-hotels.co.uk **web:** www.macdonald-hotels.com/pittodrie
dir: From A96 towards Inverness, pass Inverurie under bridge with lights. Turn left & follow signs

Gently modern cooking in a pastoral setting

A few miles off the main road, Pittodrie House has a wonderfully peaceful position, plus 2,000 acres to call its own. The building has its roots in the 15th century and there's a rugged grandeur to the place. Inside all is rich, warm decor and period detail, including the restaurant with its classical proportions and large oil canvases on the walls. It's a smart, classical setting for some gently modern Scottish cuisine. There's plenty of fine regional produce on the menu to add to the local flavour. Start with West Coast wild salmon and lobster tortellini with a frothy lobster bisque and spinach dressed with lobster oil, or there might be cream of cauliflower soup with truffle cream. Follow on with loin of Highland venison, the meat pink and tender, and served with celeriac both roasted and puréed, plus chestnuts and silky juniper-flavoured jus. Finish with blackberry parfait or a selection of British cheeses.

Chef Graham Campbell **Owner** Monument Leisure **Seats** 28, Pr/dining room 22 **Times** 12-3/7-9.30 **Prices** Fixed L 2 course £25-£35, Fixed D 3 course £49.50-£59.95, Tasting menu £60, Starter £9.95-£15.95, Main £19.95-£32.95, Dessert £8.95-£15.95, Service optional **Wines** 103 bottles over £30, 29 bottles under £30, 16 by glass **Parking** 300 **Notes** Afternoon tea £18.95, High tea £28.95, Sunday L £22.95-£25.95, Vegetarian available, Children welcome

KILDRUMMY   Map 23 NJ41

Kildrummy Inn

◉◉ Modern Scottish NEW

tel: 01975 571227 **AB33 8QS**
email: enquiries@kildrummyinn.co.uk **web:** www.kildrummyinn.co.uk
dir: *From Aberdeen inn on A97, 2m past Mossat junct, en-route to Cairngorm National Park*

Confident modern cooking in a rural inn

Kildrummy Inn has an authenticity that appeals to tourists and locals, while the output from its dynamic kitchen has put it on the foodie map. It's terrific value, too. There's a small bar kitted out with a tartan carpet and a stag theme, plus good local ales to choose from. The dining room consists of two traditional areas, one of which is a conservatory-style space, watched over by a friendly service team. Menus reveal classical sensibilities and a contemporary touch. Start with a terrine made with rillettes of confit chicken, looking pretty as a picture on a vibrant apricot purée, and topped with a crispy black pudding bonbon. Next up, beef appears fashionably in two ways – sirloin and slow-cooked featherblade – in a dish that marries flavours and textures with skill and craft. Flavours hit the mark when it comes to desserts, too, with a pannacotta alongside tropical fruit salsa and a suitably sharp lime sorbet. Excellent bread and a freebie courgette and parmesan velouté confirm the ambition of the kitchen.

Chef David Littlewood **Owner** David Littlewood, Nigel Hake **Seats** 30, Pr/dining room 12 **Times** 6-8.30, Closed Jan, Tue, L Mon, Wed-Sat **Prices** Fixed D 3 course £30, Service optional **Wines** 6 bottles over £30, 20 bottles under £30, 9 by glass **Parking** 20 **Notes** Sunday L £19-£23, Vegetarian available, Children welcome

OLDMELDRUM   Map 23 NJ82

Meldrum House Country Hotel & Golf Course

◉◉ Modern Scottish

tel: 01651 872294 **AB51 OAE**
email: enquiries@meldrumhouse.com **web:** www.meldrumhouse.com
dir: *11m from Aberdeen on A947 (Aberdeen to Banff road)*

Smart country-house hotel with a local flavour

Even if you're not a whizz with a niblick, Meldrum House is a good place to marinate in the luxury of a turreted baronial pile that has been around since the 13th century. It is a deeply traditional country-house hotel in 350 acres of wooded parkland, so there's plenty of breathing space to work up an appetite. The dining room strikes a traditional pose with its splendid proportions, ancestral portraits, real fire and burnished darkwood tables, and makes a grand setting for modern Scottish country-house cooking that puts local produce firmly on the agenda. You might set out on a rich note with wood pigeon paired with game confit and game sauce, or keep things light with a duo of scallops, langoustine and chilli ravioli. Next up, ballotine of slow-roasted pheasant with barley risotto, sweet potato purée and foie gras sauce is hard to resist in season, and, to finish, banoffee soufflé with spiced banana ice cream and toffee sauce is one alternative to Scottish cheeses with oatcakes and grape chutney.

Chef David Murray **Owner** Peter Walker **Seats** 40, Pr/dining room 16 **Times** 12-2/6.30-9 **Prices** Service optional **Wines** 8 by glass **Parking** 70 **Notes** Afternoon tea, Sunday L £31.50, Vegetarian available, Children welcome

PETERHEAD   Map 23 NK14

Buchan Braes Hotel

◉ Modern Scottish, European

tel: 01779 871471 **Boddam AB42 3AR**
email: info@buchanbraes.co.uk **web:** www.buchanbraes.co.uk
dir: *From Aberdeen take A90, follow Peterhead signs. 1st right in Stirling signed Boddam. 50mtrs, 1st right*

Bright, modern cooking in a contemporary hotel

The low-slung Buchan Braes won't win any architectural prizes, but it makes a spiffy contemporary hotel with its rural aspect (views of Stirling Hill), and up-to-date facilities that make it a hit for weddings and conferences. There's also the Grill Room restaurant, with its open kitchen, funky chandeliers, and warmly colourful decor. The modern Scottish cooking isn't all about the grill, although you might well opt for the chargrilled fillet with horseradish mash and oxtail and root vegetable broth. The kitchen also turns out pan-seared pigeon breast – nicely pink – with a potato and onion cake and claret jus, followed by baked loin of cod with baby spinach, creamy mash and Cullen skink sauce, or fillet of pork with slow-cooked belly. There's a pretty good showing of local ingredients all round. For dessert, perhaps a honeycomb Pavlova or rhubarb crumble with custard.

Chef Gary Christie **Owner** Kenneth Watt, Tony Jackson **Seats** 70, Pr/dining room 80 **Times** 11.45-2.30/6-9.30 **Prices** Fixed L 2 course £12.95, Fixed D 3 course £29.50, Starter £5.95-£9.50, Main £15.75-£23.50, Dessert £6.25, Service optional **Wines** 10 bottles over £30, 24 bottles under £30, 9 by glass **Parking** 100 **Notes** Sunday L £16.50-£23, Vegetarian available, Children welcome

STONEHAVEN   Map 23 NO88

The Tolbooth Restaurant

◉ Modern British, Seafood

tel: 01569 762287 **Old Pier, Stonehaven Harbour AB39 2JU**
email: enquiries@tolbooth-restaurant.co.uk
dir: *15m S of Aberdeen on A90, located in Stonehaven harbour*

Speciality seafood restaurant overlooking the harbour

There can't be many better spots than this in the UK for tucking into seafood. It's right on the harbour wall, with a local museum on the ground floor and the upstairs restaurant gives views over the boats coming and going from the safety of Stonehaven. The open-plan layout is contemporary and easy-going with the tables smartly dressed in linen cloths and a pleasing lack of airs and graces. What you eat depends on what has been landed that day, what's at its best, and everything is made on the premises. To start, crayfish Mornay, a daily special, is packed with flavour, or there might be hot-smoked monkfish with white asparagus and bois boudran dressing, or steamed Shetland mussels with a chunk of focaccia. Main-course hake is poached in Cabernet Sauvignon and served with sesame prawn bonbons, Puy lentils, pancetta and curly kale, and, for dessert, there is a fashionable salted-caramel tart with stem ginger ice cream and crème anglaise.

Chef Eddie Abbott **Owner** J Edward Abbott **Seats** 46 **Times** 12-4/6-12, Closed 1st 3 wks Jan, Mon-Tue, D Sun **Prices** Fixed L 2 course fr £15.95, Starter £7.50-£12.50, Main £17-£25, Dessert £6.50-£8.50, Service optional **Wines** 21 bottles over £30, 13 bottles under £30, 6 by glass **Parking** Public car park, 100 spaces **Notes** Sunday L £21.50-£26.50, Vegetarian available, Children welcome

ANGUS

FORFAR
Map 23 NO45

Drovers

🏵 Modern Scottish V

tel: 01307 860322 **Memus By Forfar DD8 3TY**
email: info@the-drovers.com
dir: *Forth Road bridge onto A823 then M90. Dundee through to Forfar onto A90, then B9128 Memus, Cortachy, The Glens*

Country inn serving rustic modern Scottish cooking

The Drovers is the kind of place you want to be stranded when the weather closes in. It's has a rural aspect amid the beautiful glens and a rustic solidity that suggests it's been around for a few years and the animal horns and antlers on the walls remind you that this is wild country. It's a very modern kind of pub that is as happy to serve you a pint as sit you down and serve up some smart, modern food. The restaurant positively buzzes with life at times and the service team cope with an easy charm. The menu makes good use of what lives and grows hereabouts and turns these fine ingredients into some rustic, modern Scottish food. Seared king scallops with roast pork belly, shallot and garlic purée and chestnut mushrooms is a positively contemporary first course, with the scallops cooked just-so and the balance of flavours spot on. Next up, roast monkfish is wrapped in Serrano ham and comes with Puy lentils, and venison steak is served in the company of celeriac and truffle purée.

Chef Eden Sinclair **Owner** John Dodd **Seats** 60, Pr/dining room 16
Times 12-2.30/5.30-9 **Prices** Fixed L 2 course £15-£22, Fixed D 3 course £20-£27, Starter £5-£8.50, Main £12-£22, Dessert £4.50-£8, Service optional **Wines** 11 bottles over £30, 18 bottles under £30, 7 by glass **Parking** 35 **Notes** Sunday L £8-£22, Children welcome

INVERKEILOR
Map 23 NO64

Gordon's

🏵🏵🏵 – see page 606

ARGYLL & BUTE

ARDUAINE
Map 20 NM71

Loch Melfort Hotel

🏵🏵 Modern British

tel: 01852 200233 **PA34 4XG**
email: reception@lochmelfort.co.uk web: www.lochmelfort.co.uk
dir: *On A816, midway between Oban & Lochgilphead*

Ambitious contemporary cooking and magnificent views

Tranquilly set in 17 acres of gardens, this country-house hotel was built in the late 19th century slap-bang on the shore of Asknish Bay with jaw-dropping views over to Jura and other islands. There's a pink-themed lounge bar with squishy sofas and a more informal bistro as well as the restaurant, where long windows catch the views. There are some instances of modern notions such as gels on the menu, but the kitchen generally sticks to traditions without straying into exaggerated flourishes. Thus, pheasant, duck, quail and black pudding go into a terrine set off by a port reduction and pear and saffron chutney, followed perhaps by braised shin of beef with pan-fried mignon of fillet served with girolles, roast shallots, potato cakes and red wine jus. Resourceful seafood dishes include grilled mackerel fillet with barigoule and fennel purée, and pan-fried fillet of sea bass with saffron potatoes, mussels, spinach and tapenade. To finish, fly the Scottish saltire with cranachan.

Chef Michael Knowles **Owner** Calum & Rachel Ross **Seats** 60, Pr/dining room 14
Times 6.30-9, Closed mid 2 wks Jan, midwk Nov-Mar, 1st 2wks Dec, L all week, D Tue-Wed (Nov-Mar) **Prices** Starter £10.25-£13.50, Main £17.95-£24.95, Dessert £6.95-£9.95, Service optional **Wines** 21 bottles over £30, 54 bottles under £30, 8 by glass **Parking** 65 **Notes** 4 course D £39.50, Vegetarian available, Children welcome

KILCHRENAN
Map 20 NN02

The Ardanaiseig Hotel

🏵🏵 Modern British V ★ NOTABLE WINE LIST

tel: 01866 833333 **by Loch Awe PA35 1HE**
email: marcel@ardanaiseig.com web: www.ardanaiseig.com
dir: *From A85 at Taynuilt onto B845 to Kilchrenan. Left in front of pub (road very narrow) signed 'Ardanaiseig Hotel' & 'No Through Road'. Continue for 3m*

Creative menu and high comfort in a stunning lochside hotel

During the 12-mile journey along a winding single-track road through glorious countryside anticipation rises. The Scottish baronial county house that waits at the end of the road will not disappoint, and its Gothic charms look even more intriguing if there's a mist covering the lawn. The location in lush gardens with a backdrop of Ben Cruachan rising from the waters of Loch Awe is second to none. The interior decoration is traditional and entirely in keeping, but with a contemporary spin and a touch of Gothic charm. The restaurant – candlelit in the evening – is a stylish space with striking artworks and tables dressed in pristine white linen cloths. The kitchen turns out bright modern dishes such as a starter of fillet of wild sea bass with textures of apple and celeriac remoulade, followed by slow-cooked Angus beef partnered with braised oxtail and a piece of seared foie gras. Finish with a deconstructed version of banoffee pie, or hot chocolate fondant with pistachio ice cream. There's a nine-course tasting menu if you fancy pushing the boat out.

Chef Colin Cairns **Owner** Bennie Gray **Seats** 40, Pr/dining room 20
Times 12-6.30/7-11 **Prices** Tasting menu £60, Starter £6-£12, Main £14-£24, Dessert £5-£12, Service optional **Wines** 91 bottles over £30, 10 bottles under £30, 9 by glass **Parking** 20 **Notes** ALC L menu £2-£25, Tasting menu 8 course, Sunday L £24, Children 5 yrs+

Taychreggan Hotel

🏵🏵 Modern British

tel: 01866 833211 & 833366 **PA35 1HQ**
email: info@taychregganhotel.co.uk web: www.taychregganhotel.co.uk
dir: *W from Crianlarich on A85 to Taynuilt, S for 7m on B845 (single track) to Kilchrenan*

Ambitious cooking with sublime loch views

The whitewashed 17th-century hotel lies a short drive from Oban, yet far from the madding crowd, on a peninsula jutting into Loch Awe, framed by timeless Highland landscapes – scenery that hasn't changed since herders swam their cattle across to stay here when the place was a lowly drovers' inn. A wall of floor-to-ceiling arched windows makes sure everyone gets that view in the restaurant, while the kitchen delivers the goods with its five-course set dinner menus built around a creative modern fusion of Scottish and French influences. It all begins with a soup – courgette, with perch and tarragon oil – ahead of a colourful composition involving tomato terrine with home-cured salmon, carrot purée, caviar, pickled cucumber, quail's egg and ruby chard. The main event stars Highland beef (roasted sirloin and slow-braised ox cheeks) with pearl barley, dauphinoise potato, wilted spinach, chargrilled courgettes and a rich red wine jus. Then it's time for something sweet – strawberries with vanilla pannacotta, mascarpone, puff pastry and crème fraîche sorbet – before a finale of oak-smoked brie on toast.

Times 7-8.45, Closed 3-21 Jan

LUSS
Map 20 NS39

The Lodge on Loch Lomond

◉◉ Traditional British, International

tel: 01436 860201 **G83 8PA**
email: res@loch-lomond.co.uk **web:** www.loch-lomond.co.uk
dir: N of Glasgow on A82

Fine Scottish dining above the loch

Perched on the edge of the loch, The Lodge could hardly be more guaranteed to induce a sense of tranquillity, the effect best enjoyed from Colquhoun's restaurant, which occupies a balcony built out on struts to give the impression that you are floating above the pristine glassy surface of the water. Glass-topped tables and tartan carpeting comprise the decorative order, and staff offer a discreetly attentive approach that exactly suits the surroundings. That must-have accoutrement of the modern restaurant kitchen, a Josper charcoal grill, rules the roost, turning out great Scotch sirloin accompanied by truffled mash and the likes of creamy peppercorn or paprika butter sauces. Prior to that could be monkfish tempura dressed in coconut, lime and ginger, or seared wood pigeon with shallot purée and an intense demi-glace dressing. Combinations of meat and shellfish, such as pork belly with garlic prawns, are less convincing, but desserts like chocolate and hazelnut brownie and toffee ice cream, or mango parfait with pineapple relish and coconut sorbet, are impressive, as are the Scottish cheeses served with chutney, apple and grapes.

Times 12-5/6-9

OBAN
Map 20 NM82

Coast

◉ Modern British

tel: 01631 569900 **104 George St PA34 5NT**
email: coastoban@yahoo.co.uk
dir: On main street in town centre

Vivacious brasserie cooking in a converted bank building

Next door to the art gallery, Coast is the very image of a modern brasserie, its granite frontage and expansive windows looking distinctly stately (it used to be a bank). The interior looks clean-lined and sharp, the unclothed tables simply laid, with a seasonally-changing menu of vivacious brasserie dishes offering something for everyone. Start with home-made chicken liver parfait with apple chutney, or enjoy the simplicity of chargrilled local langoustine dressed with garlic butter. Move on to pan-fried fillet of red gurnard (landed at Tarbert) with a mix of veg including salsify and fennel, anchovy fritter and chervil cream sauce, or haunch of Argyll venison with spiced red cabbage, pickled walnuts and a mash fired up with truffle and chives. Finish with apple and honeycomb parfait with toffee ice cream or a comforting sponge pudding such as a ginger version with spiced pears.

Chef Richard Fowler **Owner** Richard & Nicola Fowler **Seats** 46
Times 12-2/5.30-9.30, Closed 25 Dec, 2 wks Jan, Sun (Nov-Mar), L Sun **Prices** Fixed L 2 course £14.50, Fixed D 3 course £17.50, Starter £4.50-£10.95, Main £10.80-£25, Dessert £5.95, Service optional **Wines** 13 bottles over £30, 33 bottles under £30, 5 by glass **Parking** On street **Notes** Vegetarian available

Gordon's ❀❀❀

INVERKEILOR
Map 23 NO64

Modern Scottish
tel: 01241 830364 **Main St DD11 5RN**
email: gordonsrest@aol.com **web:** www.gordonsrestaurant.co.uk
dir: From A92 exit at signs for Inverkeilor (between Arbroath & Montrose)

Striking modern Scottish cookery in a coastal hamlet

The Watsons' hugely distinguished restaurant with rooms has put the snoozy coastal hamlet of Inverkeilor on the map of culinary destinations. It's a distinctly family affair, with Maria running things out front, son Garry increasingly taking care of the kitchen side of things, and the fleet-of-foot Gordon himself flitting between them. The place is hard to miss on the quiet high street, particularly after its spiffy, contemporary makeover bringing a clean-lined frontage and interior sporting designer thistle wallpaper and tartan upholstered seats at linen-swathed tables. The local fan base keeps the intimate dining room perennially busy, and fixed-price menus of high-definition modern Scottish cooking keep things focused with three choices at each stage. Dinner opens with perfectly seared scallops alongside crisp beignets and an indulgent purée of cauliflower, and an intense dressing of raisins and capers to bring it all together. An intermediate soup course offers the silky charms of a velouté of celeriac and Arbroath smokie, and then mains showcase local lamb – seared best end and confit shoulder – partnered by ravioli packed with minted pea purée and fresh peas, pistachio, butternut squash and lamb and tomato jus. Fishy compositions bring West Coast hake with an eclectic yet well-balanced array of spiced couscous, pak choi, baby leeks, mussels and coriander dressing. A finale stars Valrhona's finest gear in the forms of chocolate parfait that is ethereal in texture yet packs a big chocolate punch, together with bittersweet chocolate sorbet and dark and white chocolate sauces, all balanced by the fruitiness of pear poached in red wine syrup.

Chef Gordon & Garry Watson **Owner** Gordon & Maria Watson **Seats** 24, Pr/dining room 8 **Times** 12.30-1.45/7-9, Closed 3 wks Jan, Mon, L Sat, Tue, D Sun (in winter) **Prices** Fixed L 3 course fr £27, Service optional **Wines** 11 bottles over £30, 33 bottles under £30, 5 by glass **Parking** 6 **Notes** All bookings essential, 5 course D £55, Vegetarian available, Children 12 yrs+

Manor House Hotel

⚫ Scottish, European

tel: 01631 562087 **Gallanach Rd PA34 4LS**
email: info@manorhouseoban.com **web:** www.manorhouseoban.com
dir: *Follow MacBrayne Ferries signs, pass ferry entrance for hotel on right*

Traditional country-house dining by Oban harbour

Built for the Duke of Argyll in 1780, the Manor House sits in a suitably
commanding position overlooking the harbour at Oban. Half-panelled walls and
original oil paintings set the heightened tone in the low-ceilinged dining room, and
a lighting level to encourage intimacies prevails. Fine regional Scottish produce
receives its due celebration in menus that aim for a soft-focus country-hotel
approach (including intermediate courses of a soup such as celery and leek, then
lemon sorbet) rather than anything too wacky. Brilliantly timed salmon fillet
(crisp outside, soft within) comes on a chunky salsa of tomato, fennel and capers
for an inspired first course, after which the choice may take in guinea fowl breast
with pommes Parisienne and an assertively truffle-oiled jus gras, or rack of lamb
with honey-glazed veg and wilted spinach. A brisk chocolate kick is administered by
a hefty warm brownie with glossy fudge glaze and vanilla ice cream.

Chef Shaun Squire **Owner** Mr P L Crane **Seats** 34
Times 12-2/6.45-8.45, Closed 25-26 Dec **Prices** Starter £3.95, Main £8.95-£14,
Dessert £4.95, Service optional **Wines** 20 bottles over £30, 60 bottles under £30, 6
by glass **Parking** 18 **Notes** ALC L only, Fixed L(book)/D 4/5 course £31/£42, Sunday L
£31, Vegetarian available, Children 12 yrs+

PORT APPIN   Map 20 NM94

Airds Hotel and Restaurant

⚫⚫⚫ – see below

Airds Hotel and Restaurant ⚫⚫⚫

PORT APPIN   Map 20 NM94

Modern Scottish ⒱ 🍷 NOTABLE WINE LIST
tel: 01631 730236 **PA38 4DF**
email: airds@airds-hotel.com **web:** www.airds-hotel.com
dir: *From A828 (Oban to Fort William road), turn at Appin signed Port Appin. Hotel
2.5m on left*

Accomplished modern seasonal cooking by Loch Linnhe

The little hamlet of Port Appin sits on the shore of beautiful Loch
Linnhe in a setting of sublime tranquillity, with the brooding Morven
mountains as backdrop. Not far from the old ferry landing, Airds is
an intimate and luxurious country hotel with just 11 bedrooms – the
word 'boutique' springs to mind, although its interiors are completely
devoid of the stylistic affectation that the term sometimes implies.
The dining room is a long, tastefully furnished space with large
picture windows opening up views over the narrow road towards the
loch – naturally enough, the tables closest to the windows are the
ones to go for. High-class tableware, including napkins in tartan ties
and crisp linen, looks the part, and so does the seasonal modern
Scottish cooking. Dishes are intricately constructed and full of
imagination, with Asian and Mediterranean influences evident in first
courses such as a luxurious duo of langoustine and pan-seared foie
gras partnered with guava gel, morels and nori sponge and sauced
with Cointreau and shellfish butter, or a bold combination of smoked
salmon cannelloni with yuzu, cucumber, blue cheese bonbons and
oats. The eclectic approach continues with mains too: there's a lot
going on in a composition involving slow-cooked turbot, lamb hotpot,
pommes Anna, algae sponge, celeriac purée, textures of artichoke,
baby spinach and hazelnut jus, but everything makes sense, and
prime Scottish produce is always at the heart of it. To finish, there
could be a deconstructed carrot cheesecake comprising carrot
sorbet, roasted hazelnut gel, chocolate sponge, carrot ravioli,
butternut squash sugar and caramel tuile or the relatively simple
delights of pistachio soufflé with beetroot sorbet and orange
crème anglaise.

Chef Chris Stanley **Owner** Mr & Mrs S McKivragan **Seats** 32
Times 12-1.45/7.15-9.15, **Prices** Fixed L 3 course £18.95, Tasting menu £74,
Starter £3-£7, Main £7.50-£21, Dessert £4-£6, Service optional **Wines** 225
bottles over £30, 10 bottles under £30, 12 by glass **Parking** 20 **Notes** 5 course D
£55, Tasting menu 7 course, Sunday L £18.50, Children 8 yrs+

PORT APPIN *continued*

The Pierhouse Hotel

@ Seafood

tel: 01631 730302 & 730622 **PA38 4DE**
email: reservations@pierhousehotel.co.uk **web:** www.pierhousehotel.co.uk
dir: M8, A82 to Crianlarich & Fort William. At Ballachulish take A828 towards Oban. Turn
right in Appin for Port Appin & Lismore Ferry

Top-notch fish and seafood with stunning views

Tucked away on a quiet arm of Loch Linnhe where the little foot passenger ferry
shuttles across to Lismore Island, this waterside restaurant specialises in fish and
seafood. The brasserie-style dining room is a simple, magnolia-painted space –
after all, there's no point fretting over interior design when all eyes are turned
towards the peaks marching across the skyline above the loch. Oysters are hand-
picked from the Lismore oyster beds, mussels and langoustines come from Loch
Linnhe, and lobsters are kept in creels at the end of the pier where day boats drop
off fish at the door. There's no point faffing about with produce like that, so the
kitchen keeps it all simple: who could resist seared local scallops with artichoke
purée and Stornoway black pudding to start things off? The glorious simplicity and
freshness of the seafood platters is hard to ignore, and there's Drambuie crème
brûlée to send you home happy.

Chef Laura Milne **Owner** Nicholas & Nicolette Horne **Seats** 45, Pr/dining room 25
Times 12.30-2.30/6.30-9.30, Closed 25-26 Dec **Prices** Starter £4.95-£12.50, Main
£14.95-£39.95, Dessert £5.95-£8.95, Service optional **Wines** 4 bottles over £30, 27
bottles under £30, 5 by glass **Parking** 25 **Notes** Vegetarian available, Children
welcome

RHU
Map 20 NS28

Rosslea Hall Hotel

@ Modern International

tel: 01436 439955 **Ferry Rd G84 8NF**
email: enquiries@rossleahallhotel.co.uk **web:** www.rossleahallhotel.co.uk
dir: From Erskine Bridge A82 to Dumbarton to junct with A814 follow to Helensburgh.
Along water front 2m on left

Well-executed modern dishes and wonderful Clyde views

Views over the Firth of Clyde offer a stunning backdrop to this substantial, solid-
looking Victorian property, now a comfortable, stylish hotel. In the equally smart
restaurant, friendly but informed staff cut through any hint of formality projected by
correctly set clothed tables complete with candles and flowers. The kitchen works
around a tranche of modern ideas, producing, for instance, a well-conceived starter
of ham hock, parsley and potato terrine, served on a swipe of parsnip purée with
punchily spiced plums and port jelly. This might be followed by red onion tarte Tatin
successfully partnered by roasted beetroot and beetroot essence, or returning to the
classics for duck leg confit with Parmentier potatoes. Seasonality is seen in a
summery main course of pan-fried sea bass with a fricassée of peas, broad beans
and asparagus, served with gnocchi and vanilla cream, as it is in raspberry sorbet
as an accompaniment for raspberry and white chocolate cheesecake.

Chef James Quinn **Owner** BDL Select Hotel **Seats** 48, Pr/dining room 40
Times 12-3/6.30-9.30 **Prices** Fixed L 2 course £10.95-£17.95, Fixed D 3 course
£16.95-£29.95, Starter £3.95-£8.95, Main £10.95-£24.95, Dessert £3.95-£9.95,
Service optional **Wines** 8 bottles over £30, 28 bottles under £30, 6 by glass
Parking 60 **Notes** Afternoon tea £8.50, Sunday L £9.95-£15.95, Vegetarian
available, Children welcome

STRACHUR
Map 20 NN00

The Creggans Inn

@@ Modern British, French

tel: 01369 860279 **PA27 8BX**
email: info@creggans-inn.co.uk **web:** www.creggans-inn.co.uk
dir: A82 from Glasgow, at Tarbet take A83 towards Cairndow, left onto A815 to Strachur,
or by ferry from Gourock to Dunoon onto A815

Locally-sourced cooking on the shore of Loch Fyne

On the shores of Loch Fyne with pan-fried scallops, pea purée and a Parma ham
crisp on the menu – this must be heaven. The Creggans Inn is a whitewashed hotel
just across the road from the chilly waters of the loch, family run and full of life.
There's a bar and bistro with roaring fires and real ales, plus a restaurant – named
in honour of the loch, of course – which delivers a menu packed with gently modern
constructions, the ingredients drawn from local the waters and hills. Dinner is a
smart affair, with spruce waiting staff and classical music. If those scallops don't
catch your eye, start with slow-roast pork belly with apple purée and thyme jus, or
caramelised Golden Cross goats' cheese with beetroot carpaccio and pickled
walnuts. There's a soup or sorbet/granita next, followed by a main course such as
herb-crusted rack of Scotch lamb, or baked fillet of halibut, and desserts extend to
iced banana parfait with caramelised banana and chocolate sauce, or warm date
pudding with toffee sauce and coffee Chantilly cream.

Chef Lee Appleby **Owner** The MacLellan family **Seats** 35 **Times** 7-9, Closed 25-26
Dec, L all week **Prices** Prices not confirmed, Service optional **Wines** 6 by glass
Parking 25 **Notes** Fixed D 4 course £37, Vegetarian available, Children 8 yrs+

NORTH AYRSHIRE

DALRY
Map 20 NS24

Braidwoods

@@ Modern Scottish

tel: 01294 833544 **Drumastle Mill Cottage KA24 4LN**
email: keithbraidwood@btconnect.com
dir: 1m from Dalry on Saltcoats road

Creative cooking from a gifted husband-and-wife team

In a cottage in the middle of a field near Dalry, Braidwoods is a small,
unpretentious restaurant, its two rooms split by a central fireplace, with beams in
the low ceilings, close-set tables, an informal, relaxed atmosphere, and young and
helpful staff. Dinner, of three or four courses, could open with a well-balanced dish
of seared scallops on pea purée along with crispy chicken wings, or perhaps
beetroot-cured gravad lax on beetroot and clementine salad with a potato cake.
Main courses impress with their timing and presentation: melt-in-the-mouth roast
best end of local lamb on wilted spinach, with a mound of cauliflower purée topped
with confit neck fillet and a square of dauphinoise, all complemented by rosemary
jus, or grilled turbot fillet crowned with tapenade served on herb risotto and a rich
shellfish jus. Canapés make a great introduction to a meal, and puddings impress
too, among them Valrhona truffle cake with prune and Armagnac ice cream.

Times 12-1.45/7-9, Closed 25-26 Dec, 1st 3 wks Jan, 1st 2 wks Sep, Mon, L Tue
(Sun Etr-Sep), D Sun

SOUTH AYRSHIRE

AYR
Map 20 NS32

Enterkine Country House

◎◎ Modern British **V**

tel: 01292 520580 **Annbank KA6 5AL**
email: mail@enterkine.com **web:** www.enterkine.com
dir: 5m E of Ayr on B743

Well-crafted contemporary cooking in an elegant country house

Enterkine, dating from the 1930s, when it was built in the art deco style, is approached via a tree-lined avenue running through its 300 acres. Three sides of the restaurant have huge windows giving views of the estate; it's a handsome room, with high-backed upholstered chairs at clothed tables, a polished floor and swagged curtains. The menus have been carefully designed to maximise Ayrshire produce, although some items come from further afield: fillet of Orkney beef, for instance, with foie gras, parsnips, chanterelles and spinach. The kitchen adds a contemporary spin, producing starters of a tian of smoked salmon and langoustines with a quail's egg and chilli pineapple, and pork and ham hock terrine with wild mushrooms, red cabbage purée and truffled bean salad. Well-conceived main courses manage to balance traditional ideas with the more contemporary, so alongside loin of venison with red cabbage, shallots, celeriac and salsify might be halibut fillet with pancetta, brown shrimps, mousserons and samphire. Puddings make a satisfying conclusion: perhaps chocolate marquise with caramel ice cream.

Chef Paul Moffat **Owner** Mr Browne **Seats** 40, Pr/dining room 14 **Times** 12-2/7-9 **Prices** Fixed L 2 course £16.95, Fixed D 3 course £38-£45, Tasting menu £50-£75, Service optional **Wines** 7 bottles over £30, 18 bottles under £30, 13 by glass **Parking** 20 **Notes** Sunday L £18.95-£21.95, Children welcome

Fairfield House Hotel

◎◎ Modern International

tel: 01292 267461 **12 Fairfield Rd KA7 2AS**
email: reservations@fairfieldhotel.co.uk **web:** www.fairfieldhotel.co.uk
dir: From A77 to Ayr South. Follow signs for town centre. Left into Miller Rd. At lights turn left, then right into Fairfield Rd

Modern Scottish food overlooking the Firth of Clyde

The Glasgow tea merchant who built Fairfield House as his seaside retreat certainly bagged a lovely spot with views over the firth towards the Isle of Arran. Tastefully made over, the old girl's lofty plasterwork ceilings blend with a neutral modern look, while in Martin's Bar and Grill, orange and yellow tones prevail, and the conservatory opening on to an outdoor terrace basking in those island views is a real hot ticket when the sun's out. Confident modern Scottish cooking is the kitchen's forte, with pedigree Scots produce used as the bedrock of an appealing menu of big flavours. Cairngorm grouse is a good bet, particularly when it could appear in a starter comprising roast breast and a slow-cooked croquette partnered by celeriac and pearl barley risotto and girolles. Mains are equally eye-catching compositions, perhaps another two-way serving — venison this time — its roast loin matched with a steamed pudding, alongside root vegetable Parisienne and creamed potatoes. Finish with a chocolate fondant with coconut sorbet, tuile and jelly.

Chef John Main **Owner** The Martin family **Seats** 80, Pr/dining room 12 **Times** 11-9.30, All-day dining **Prices** Prices not confirmed, Service optional **Wines** 6 by glass **Parking** 50 **Notes** Vegetarian available, Children welcome

BALLANTRAE
Map 20 NX08

Glenapp Castle

◎◎◎ – see page 610

TROON
Map 20 NS33

Lochgreen House Hotel

◎◎◎ – see page 610

MacCallums of Troon

◎ International, Seafood

tel: 01292 319339 **The Harbour KA10 6DH**
dir: Phone for directions

Simple, fresh seafood on the harbourside

There should really only be one thing on your mind when dining at the Oyster Bar, given the proximity of the fishing boats in the harbour, and anyone seeking red meat or possessing a dietary requirement of any kind needs to give advance warning or risk disappointment. It's all about the bass, the turbot, the sole... for this is a seafood restaurant in a glorious harbourside setting within a converted pump house. They even have a fish and chip joint next door called the Wee Hurrie. The fish does the talking in a first course tempura turbot, with suitably thin and crisp batter and a perky garlic mayo to dip them into, and in a main course dish of lemon sole (two generous fillets) with two plump langoustines and garlic butter. It is simple stuff cooked with care, which is also true of desserts such as steamed date sponge pudding with salted caramel and hazelnut ice cream.

Chef Philip Burgess **Owner** John & James MacCallums **Seats** 43 **Times** 12-2.30/6.30-9.30, Closed Xmas, New Year, Mon, D Sun **Prices** Starter £4.95-£10.95, Main £10.95-£32.95, Dessert £4.95-£8.95, Service optional **Wines** 1 bottle over £30, 20 bottles under £30, 4 by glass **Parking** 12 **Notes** Sunday L, Children welcome

The Marine Hotel

◎ Modern British, Seafood

tel: 01292 314444 **Crosbie Rd KA10 6HE**
email: marine@thehotelcollection.co.uk **web:** www.thehotelcollection.co.uk
dir: A77, A78, A79 onto B749. Hotel on left after golf course

Unfussy cooking and fantastic coastal views

This imposing coastal hotel has 40 golf courses within striking distance and facilities aplenty to satisfy anyone who is not a lover of the game. It's also home to the Two Fat Ladies restaurant, which is part of a Glasgow-based group with three restaurants in the city. The dining room occupies a couple of spaces including a conservatory area, with views over Royal Troon golf course, and the atmosphere is on the refined side without being stuffy. There's a fishy theme at play in the decor, and while the menu does deal in the fruits of the sea, there are plenty of meaty options up for grabs. Start with smooth chicken liver parfait, for example, and move on to rump of lamb with herby creamed potatoes.

Times 12.30-2.30/5-10

Glenapp Castle ❀❀❀

BALLANTRAE | Map 20 NX08

Modern British v
tel: 01465 831212 **KA26 0NZ**
email: info@glenappcastle.com **web:** www.glenappcastle.com
dir: S through Ballantrae, cross bridge over River Stinchar, 1st right, castle gates in 1m, use entry system

Country-house cooking in the baronial style

Bearing a superficial resemblance to Balmoral, Glenapp is a Victorian architectural jeu d'esprit, its sandstone battlements and turrets standing ready to ward off assault by barbarous hordes. It was built in 1870 for the then Deputy Lord Lieutenant of Ayrshire, which only makes you wonder what kind of magnificence the Lord Lieutenant himself must have enjoyed. Inside, the place has been nurtured back into prime decorative fettle by the Cowan family, owners since 1994, and the expansive public rooms are richly furnished in the baronial style. Glorious views over the coastline to Arran and the hulking granite outcrop of Ailsa Craig are part of the allure of the dining room, where a regal deep crimson is the dominant hue, tables are smartly dressed, and the chandelier twinkles becomingly in the evenings. Tyron Ellul cooks a five-course set dinner menu (six if you count pre-dessert), with a pair of alternatives at main course. The opener is usually a soup, perhaps a lightly spiced butternut squash version with toasted seeds and a slick of good oil, with very often a terrine to follow, or else something like a serving of partridge breast with wild mushroom duxelles and a parmesan and thyme tart. Fish comes next, maybe sea trout from Loch Awe with roast turnip purée in jus gras, and the meat choice might be poached guinea fowl breast with confit garlic, or beef rib with a bonbon of braised meat and white onion purée. After the pre, the actual dessert arrives in the majestic form of banana soufflé with roasted banana ice cream, but there are Scottish cheeses with oatcakes and walnut bread for the less sweet-toothed.

Chef Tyron Ellul **Owner** Graham & Fay Cowan **Seats** 34, Pr/dining room 20 **Times** 12.30-2/6.30-9.30, Closed 3 Jan-25 Mar, Xmas **Prices** Fixed L 3 course £39.50, Tasting menu fr £65, Service optional **Wines** 115 bottles over £30, 9 by glass **Parking** 20 **Notes** Tasting menu D 6 course, Sunday L fr £29.50, Children 5 yrs+

Lochgreen House Hotel ❀❀❀

TROON | Map 20 NS33

Modern French
tel: 01292 313343 **Monktonhill Rd, Southwood KA10 7EN**
email: lochgreen@costley-hotels.co.uk **web:** www.lochgreenhouse.com
dir: From A77 follow Prestwick Airport signs, take B749 to Troon, hotel on left, 1m from junct

Modern cooking in a stunningly restored manor house

Built in 1905 for a wealthy lace mill owner, and run by the Costley family since 1989, Lochgreen House is a grand seaside mansion in 30 acres of woodland and immaculately tended gardens overlooking the Ayrshire coastline. It also rubs shoulders with the famous Royal Troon golf course, but you don't need to have any interest in the action on the venerable links to stay here, as the main draw is what is going on in the Tapestry restaurant. This is in an expansive extension overlooking the gardens at the rear of the house, where vast crystal chandeliers hang from a lofty beamed roof above well-spaced tables dressed in their best whites and plush tapestry-upholstered seats (spot the clue in the name). Head chef Andrew Costley likes to wave the flag for Scottish produce, which he puts to good use in his thoroughly accomplished modern cooking, delivering punchy, clearly delineated flavours and clever texture contrasts. A risotto of home-smoked haddock and leek with crumbled cheddar, a poached quail's egg and crisp potato galette could be one way to start, or there may be the luxury of butter-poached lobster tail with bouillabaisse sauce, saffron and croûtons. Next up, the Auld Alliance is alive and kicking in a classical dish matching a fillet of Ayrshire beef with boulangère potatoes, Café de Paris butter, garlic and shallots, or you might look to the East for line-caught sea bass with langoustine tempura, pak choi and carrots, all dressed with sesame and chilli. Desserts are perfectly conceived and impeccably balanced confections: perhaps milk chocolate and Baileys parfait with granola biscuit and honeycomb, or a classic apple tarte Tatin with caramelised milk ice cream.

Chef Andrew Costley, Iain Conway **Owner** Mr William Costley **Seats** 80, Pr/dining room 40 **Times** 12-2/7-10, **Prices** Fixed L 2 course fr £16.95, Fixed D 3 course fr £42.50, Starter £8.95-£12.95, Main £18-£28, Dessert £7-£10, Service optional **Wines** 70 bottles over £30, 40 bottles under £30, 11 by glass **Parking** 90 **Notes** Afternoon tea, Sunday L £20-£25, Vegetarian available, Children welcome

TURNBERRY
Map 20 NS20

Turnberry Resort, Scotland

◎◎ Traditional French

tel: 01655 331000 **Maidens Rd KA26 9LT**
email: turnberry@luxurycollection.com **web:** www.turnberryresort.co.uk
dir: From Glasgow take A77, M77 S towards Stranraer, 2m past Kirkoswald, follow signs for A719/Turnberry. Hotel 500mtrs on right

Classical dining at renowned coastal golf resort

The 1906 Restaurant of this luxurious golf-centric hotel is named after the year it opened. But before we get to food, there's a lot more to take in: the Turnberry sits on the glorious Ayrshire coast, with sweeping views across greens and fairways to the hump of Ailsa Craig. For those not bitten by the golfing bug, there's pampering in a top-notch spa, and the Grand Tea Lounge is resurrected for genteel afternoon teas. For the full-on dining experience, however, it's back to 1906, where the setting resembles a giant wedding cake, and the kitchen puts a luxury modern spin on Escoffier's classics. Foie gras gets its own section, starting perhaps with a brûlée with Sauternes-poached fruit, pumpernickel granola and gingerbread, then follow that with something from Escoffier's recipe book – perhaps honey-glazed duck suprême with braised chicory, baby turnips and pan juices. For a spot of table-side theatre, finish with a Grand Marnier-flambéed crêpe Suzette with orange and vanilla ice cream.

Chef Munur Kara **Owner** Trump Organization **Seats** 120, Pr/dining room 10 **Times** 7.06-10, Closed 8-22 Dec, L all week **Prices** Fixed D 3 course fr £45, Starter £7-£18, Main £18-£58, Dessert £7-£12, Service optional **Wines** 198 bottles over £30, 21 bottles under £30, 16 by glass **Parking** 200 **Notes** Brunch 1st & 3rd Sun of month, Vegetarian available, Children welcome

DUMFRIES & GALLOWAY

AUCHENCAIRN
Map 21 NX75

Balcary Bay Hotel

◎◎ Modern French, European

tel: 01556 640217 & 640311 **Shore Rd DG7 1QZ**
email: reservations@balcary-bay-hotel.co.uk **web:** www.balcary-bay-hotel.co.uk
dir: On A711 between Dalbeattie & Kirkcudbright. In Auchencairn follow signs to Balcary along shore road for 2m

Modern country-house cooking on the Solway coast

The solid-looking white hotel stands on the shore of the Solway Firth with views across the water to Heston Isle and the Lake District beyond. Soak up the views from the restaurant, with its predominantly blue and yellow colour scheme, a pleasant environment in which to enjoy some snappy cooking. The hotel might be in a secluded spot, but the kitchen team proves to be a forward-looking lot, turning out starters of hot-smoked trout with fennel and orange salad and a shallot and broad bean confit, and rolled pig's cheek in Parma ham with black pudding and cider jus. The daily-changing, set-price menu offers around five choices per course, with main courses extending from roast pheasant breast on Puy lentil stew with glazed shallots, carrot purée and game sauce to pan-fried beef fillet with spring onion mashed potato, roasted roots and gravy. Fish is imaginatively treated – perhaps grilled salmon fillet on a charred potato cake with candied beetroot and herb sauce – and to end might be lemon rum baba with thyme-poached apricots.

Chef Craig McWilliam **Owner** The Lamb family **Seats** 55 **Times** 12-2/7-8.30, Closed Dec-Jan, L Mon-Sat **Prices** Fixed D 3 course £40.75, Service optional **Wines** 54 bottles over £30, 43 bottles under £30, 12 by glass **Parking** 50 **Notes** Sunday L £25.75, Vegetarian available, Children welcome

GATEHOUSE OF FLEET
Map 20 NX55

Cally Palace Hotel

◎ Traditional **V**

tel: 01557 814341 **Cally Dr DG7 2DL**
email: info@callypalace.co.uk **web:** www.callypalace.co.uk
dir: From A74(M) take A75, at Gatehouse take B727. Hotel on left

Country-house dining using Scottish produce on the Solway coast

Although golf rules the roost in this Georgian country manor in 150 acres of parkland on the Solway coast, you don't need to have any interest at all in club swinging to have a great time here. Hiking and biking trails criss-cross the area, and there's every imaginable leisure activity for pampering or punishing yourself in readiness for dinner. Old-school opulence is the deal, with a pianist tinkling away in the background to add a softer note to proceedings in the formal restaurant. The kitchen delivers gently-modernised country-house cooking built on soundly-sourced Scottish produce, setting off with crispy confit duck leg with Puy lentil cassoulet and Bramley apple purée, followed by pan-fried venison haunch matched with dauphinoise potatoes, green beans, celeriac purée and grand veneur sauce. End with caramelised banana with passionfruit syrup and a lime tuile.

Chef Jamie Muirhead **Owner** McMillan Hotels **Seats** 110, Pr/dining room 25 **Times** 12-1/6.45-9, Closed 3 Jan-early Feb **Prices** Fixed L 2 course £14.95-£29.95, Starter £4.95-£9, Main £12-£25, Dessert £4.95-£9, Service optional **Wines** 35 bottles over £30, 55 bottles under £30, 11 by glass **Parking** 70 **Notes** Afternoon tea £15.95, Sunday L £12.95-£39.95, Children welcome

GRETNA
Map 21 NY36

Smiths at Gretna Green

◎◎ Modern British, International

tel: 01461 337007 **Gretna Green DG16 5EA**
email: info@smithsgretnagreen.com **web:** www.smithsgretnagreen.com
dir: From M74 junct 22 follow signs to Old Blacksmith's Shop. Hotel opposite

Imaginative cooking in sexy surroundings

An irregular-looking modernist hotel built in 2006, Smiths has certainly extended the options for those fleeing to the border with marriage on their minds, but makes a stylish, eye-catching stay even for those well on their way to a landmark anniversary. The Chainmail restaurant is split into cocooned areas that aim for a certain sexiness, with leather hangings, a mirrored wall, and silver-shirted staff who announce each dish as though it were a duchess arriving at a soirée. The thoughtfully constructed, imaginative menus are especially good at game, seen in a starter of heather-smoked hare with pickled pear purée and beetroot pannacotta, perhaps followed by venison loin with a faggot, a strip of liver, roasted celeriac and puréed chestnuts. Nori-wrapped salmon in crab and white bean chowder is one of the fish possibilities, while a revival of baked Alaska is a challenge requiring careful timing. Try carrot cake with cinnamon ice cream, and don't miss the excellent bread, which comes in a plant-pot.

Chef Phillip Woodcock **Owner** Alasdair Houston **Seats** 60, Pr/dining room 18 **Times** 12-9.30, All-day dining, Closed 25 Dec **Prices** Fixed L 2 course £10.50-£15, Fixed D 2 course £25-£35, Starter £6.50-£14.50, Main £11.50-£29.50, Dessert £6.50-£8.50, Service optional **Wines** 31 bottles over £30, 37 bottles under £30, 12 by glass **Parking** 115 **Notes** Tea time menu 3 course £10.95 4.30-6pm, Sunday L, Vegetarian available, Children welcome

Brodies

Modern British

tel: 01683 222870 **Holm St DG10 9EB**
email: whatscooking@brodiesofmoffat.co.uk **web:** www.brodiesofmoffat.co.uk
dir: *M74 junct 15 towards Selkirk, take 2nd right turn*

Bistro-style cooking in a contemporary setting

Starting the day as a coffee shop offering sandwiches, panini and light lunches, Brodies morphs into a wine bar and restaurant in the evening. Just off the high street, there's a contemporary sheen to the place that really pays off in the evening when it becomes quite a smart dining spot. The bistro-style menu offers some interesting stuff made with high quality ingredients. Kick off with a rustic tomato tarte Tatin, say, with melting goats' cheese and basil dressing, or a double-baked Lockerbie cheddar soufflé, and move on to a main course of smoked haddock with Parisienne potatoes. Pan-fried rib-eye arrives with chips stacked Jenga-style, plus onion rings, pea purée and mushroom fricassée, while a honey mascarpone pannacotta passes the wobble test. Sunday lunch is a classic affair.

Chef Russell Pearce **Owner** Russell & Danyella Pearce **Seats** 40 **Times** 10am-11pm, All-day dining, Closed 25-27 Dec, D Tue-Wed (Oct-Mar) **Prices** Starter £4.25-£5.50, Main £9.95-£16.95, Dessert £4.25-£6.50, Service optional **Wines** 2 bottles over £30, 21 bottles under £30, 18 by glass **Parking** On street **Notes** Early doors menu 5.30-7pm, Sunday L £14.95-£17.95, Vegetarian available, Children welcome

---

Hartfell House & The Limetree Restaurant

Modern British, Global

tel: 01683 220153 **Hartfell Crescent DG10 9AL**
email: enquiries@hartfellhouse.co.uk **web:** www.hartfellhouse.co.uk
dir: *Off High St at war memorial onto Well St & Old Well Rd. Hartfell Crescent on right*

Confident global cooking in a Victorian house

In a peaceful setting in an area of Outstanding Natural Beauty, Hartfell House is built of local stone and dates back to around 1850. Its period features are all perfectly intact, both outside and in. The residents' lounge is the place to linger over drinks either before or after dinner in the intimate Limetree Restaurant, which dazzles with gold cornices and ceiling roses. Non-residents would do well to book as this is a popular place to eat thanks to its eclectic menus informed by top-quality local produce. Malaysian spiced coconut milk soup with prawns, rice noodles, lime and coriander could precede loin of roe deer and Barony venison sausage with mushroom gratin dauphinoise, roast celeriac and carrots with thyme, and braised shallot sauce. For dessert you might well return to home territory with something like sticky gingerbread pudding with vanilla ice cream and treacle toffee sauce.

Chef Matt Seddon **Owner** Robert & Mhairi Ash **Seats** 26
Times 12.30-2.30/6.30-9, Closed Xmas, Mon, L Tue-Sat, D Sun **Prices** Fixed D 3 course £29, Service optional **Wines** 7 bottles over £30, 20 bottles under £30, 4 by glass **Parking** 6 **Notes** Sun L by arrangement, Sunday L £21-£24, Vegetarian available, Children welcome

Kirroughtree House

Modern British

tel: 01671 402141 **Minnigaff DG8 6AN**
email: info@kirroughtreehouse.co.uk **web:** www.kirroughtreehouse.co.uk
dir: *From A75 take A712, entrance to hotel 300yds on left*

Traditional country-house cooking with the shade of Robert Burns

Patrick Heron, a wealthy cattle-trader of the Whig persuasion, had Kirroughtree built as a country home in 1719, its most illustrious regular guest later in the century being Robert Burns, who used to sit on the staircase and give readings of his work to the family. A hotel since the early 1950s, the style is Scots baronial of unmimed magniloquence, the dual-winged dining room done in rich fabrics, swagged curtains and evening candlelight. The traditional country-house cooking pulls no punches, starting with chicken liver parfait and spiced plum chutney, or butternut squash risotto with sage butter, before proceeding to mint pesto-crusted rack of lamb with garlicky dauphinoise in a thin tomato and tarragon sauce, or salmon fillet with crushed potatoes in prawn and herb bisque. Finish with a fondant variation flavoured with coconut, its runny centre of white chocolate, served with a beautifully sweet-sharp cranberry sorbet.

Times 12-1.30/7-9, Closed 2 Jan-1 Feb

Knockinaam Lodge

– *see opposite*

Blackaddie House Hotel

Modern British

tel: 01659 50270 **Blackaddie Rd DG4 6JJ**
email: ian@blackaddiehotel.co.uk **web:** www.blackaddiehotel.co.uk
dir: *300mtrs off A76 on north side of Sanquhar*

Scottish country cooking with fish a strong suit

The stone-built house on the east bank of the River Nith feels like a natural place for the McAndrews to settle after a career that began in the glitzy world of five-star London hotels and a first, highly acclaimed independent place in Canterbury. The Scottish country location is perfect for sourcing top-drawer produce, with fish and seafood always a particular passion. Salt-cod brandade with French beans in shallot vinaigrette is the powerful, simple opener to a Gourmet Menu that might roll on with a fricassée of mussels, prawns and shrimps with leeks and caviar. Modern technique is acknowledged here and there, but not at the expense of firm classical underpinnings, producing a Scotch beef study that combines sautéed fillet, a sticky ragoût and beef terrine with accompanying greens, while salmon comes with roast chicory and crushed new potatoes in chive cream. To finish, lemon posset appears in parfait guise with raspberries, pistachios, honeycomb and meringue, and the selection of impeccable Scottish cheeses is served with home-made oatcakes.

Chef Ian McAndrew **Owner** Ian McAndrew **Seats** 20, Pr/dining room 20
Times 12-2/6.30-9 **Prices** Tasting menu £68, Service optional **Wines** 10 by glass **Parking** 20 **Notes** Gourmet tasting menu 7 course, Fixed D 4 course £55, Sunday L, Vegetarian available, Children welcome

Corsewall Lighthouse Hotel

◎ Modern Scottish V

tel: 01776 853220 **Corsewall Point, Kirkcolm DG9 0QG**
email: info@lighthousehotel.co.uk **web:** www.lighthousehotel.co.uk
dir: Take A718 from Stranraer to Kirkcolm, then follow B718 signed Lighthouse

A unique location with a true local flavour

Corsewall still earns its keep as a beacon for passing mariners heading into Loch Ryan, but it's also a hotel and restaurant. Needless to say the setting is something special, reached via a winding single-track road, with fabulous sea views towards Arran and Ailsa Craig waiting at the end. The accommodation and restaurant are in what used to be the keeper's living quarters and stores. There's a maritime theme in the restaurant, a traditionally-decorated room with bare wooden tables and a friendly, relaxed vibe. The menu keeps things relatively simple, so you might start with goats' cheese and red onion tartlet with a pesto dressing, before moving on to smoked haddock with a creamy Tobermory cheddar cheese sauce, or roast rack of Galloway lamb with a rich sherry, redcurrant and thyme reduction. Dessert extends to Amaretto and vanilla cheesecake with raspberry coulis.

Chef Andrew Downie **Owner** Kay & Pamela Ward **Seats** 28 **Times** 12-2.15/7-9.15 **Prices** Prices not confirmed, Service optional **Wines** 9 bottles over £30, 24 bottles under £30, 2 by glass **Parking** 20 **Notes** Fixed D 5 course £35-£39.75, Sunday L, Children welcome

The Buccleuch and Queensberry Arms Hotel

◎ Modern Scottish

tel: 01848 323101 & 330215 **112 Drumlanrig St DG3 5LU**
email: info@bqahotel.com **web:** www.bqahotel.com
dir: On A76 in centre of Thornhill

Hotel dining with a local flavour

The BQA to its friends, this family-run hotel has undergone an extensive refurbishment and emerged looking good and fit for purpose in the 21st century. There's a satisfying Scottish-ness to the place, which extends to the culinary output. The region's produce figures large on menus which show Pan-European leanings and no lack of ambition. A starter of smoked Solway haddock and butternut squash ravioli hits the spot, or go for the more exotic sesame prawn toast with pickled cauliflower mushroom and nori. Main-course local wild rabbit arrives in Wellington form, with truffle mash and roasted root vegetables, while Penrith chicken Kiev is enriched with black truffle and garlic butter. To finish, single origin chocolate fondant with salted caramel and vanilla ice cream competes with local cheeses. There's a classy bar menu, too, with ploughman's and a posh burger.

Chef Will Pottinger **Owner** The Sweerts de Landas family **Seats** 42, Pr/dining room 22 **Times** 10-10, All-day dining **Prices** Starter £4-£8, Main £14-£25, Dessert £4-£8, Service optional **Wines** 29 bottles over £30, 18 bottles under £30, 9 by glass **Parking** 100 **Notes** Sunday L £14, Vegetarian available, Children welcome

Knockinaam Lodge ◎◎◎

Modern Scottish V NOTABLE WINE LIST
tel. 01776 810471 **DG9 9AD**
email: reservations@knockinaamlodge.com **web:** www.knockinaamlodge.com
dir: From A77, follow signs to Portpatrick, then tourist signs to Knockinaam Lodge

Well-judged, classically-based cooking in splendid Galloway isolation

Knockinaam Lodge is the sort of country-house hotel where it's rather too easy to feel at home, which makes leaving quite a wrench. An out-of-the-way location helps to create a sense of anticipation on arrival, which is truly sated when you head along the single-track lane through beautiful countryside and the former Victorian hunting lodge comes into view. Within 30 acres of lush grounds, and its own private pebble beach and views across to Ireland on clear days, the house has history, too: Churchill and Eisenhower met here during WWII. Once through the door, log fires and an oak-panelled bar stocked with more than 120 single malt whiskies await. The smart, traditional dining room is the setting for the classically-inspired cooking of Tony Pierce, which may have its roots in traditional ways, but never seems out of step with our times. The dining experience starts with canapés and a snifter in one of the two lounges before you head into the restaurant and things begin with an amuse-bouche such as a black pudding and quail's egg number. The kitchen's modern Scottish output sees grilled fillet of impeccably prepared native brill served up with Dijon mustard and dill hollandaise, followed by roast cannon of Galloway lamb with juniper and port reduction, or slow roasted fillet of Speyside Angus beef partnered with spiced lentils and local carrots. There's a soup interlude between starter and main courses (cappuccino of turnip and thyme, say), and a palate-cleansing black grape juice before desserts such as an individual tarte Tatin, or warm gooey chocolate pudding with sour cherry ice cream. The wine list starts with an excellent slate of champagnes before heading off around the best addresses in France, with the rest of Europe and the New World getting due consideration.

Chef Anthony Pierce **Owner** David & Sian Ibbotson **Seats** 32, Pr/dining room 18 **Times** 12.30-2/7-9, **Prices** Service optional **Wines** 350 bottles over £30, 30 bottles under £30, 7 by glass **Parking** 20 **Notes** Fixed L 4 course £40, D 5 course £67.50, Sunday L £32.50, Children 12 yrs+

WEST DUNBARTONSHIRE

BALLOCH
Map 20 NS38

The Cameron Grill

✿✿ Modern British

tel: 01389 722582 & 755565 **Cameron House on Loch Lomond G83 8QZ**
email: reservations@cameronhouse.co.uk **web:** www.cameronhouse.co.uk
dir: M8 (W) junct 30 for Erskine Bridge. A82 for Crainlarich. 14m, at rdbt signed Luss, hotel on right

Classy grill in grand lochside hotel

In a splendid location on the banks of Loch Lomond, Cameron House pulls off a classy act with its stylish blend of tartans and luxurious contemporary looks. The decor in The Cameron Grill typifies the style with its dark and clubby masculinity: tobacco-brown leather chairs and banquettes, burnished dark wood, and a huge mural showing how clansmen caroused back in the day. It's not all about steak, but they are truly exceptional slabs of protein, cooked on a Josper grill, and it's all locally-reared stuff from Angus Limousin cattle bred at Cairnhill Farm in Ayrshire. If you're a touch peckish and up for some red meat action, take a 28-day aged rib-eye with onion rings, roasted shallots, plum tomato, blue cheese sauce and triple-cooked chips. Otherwise, start with scallops with pearl barley, bacon lardons and cauliflower purée and foam, then move on to roast cod with glazed chicken wings, wild mushrooms and red wine sauce. The hotel is also home to the fine-dining Martin Wishart at Loch Lomond.

Times 6.30-10, Closed L all week, D 26 Dec

Martin Wishart at Loch Lomond

✿✿✿ — see below

CLYDEBANK
Map 20 NS47

Beardmore Hotel

✿ Modern British

tel: 0141 951 6000 **Beardmore St G81 4SA**
email: info@beardmore.scot.nhs.uk **web:** www.thebeardmore.com
dir: M8 junct 19, follow signs for Clydeside Expressway to Glasgow road, then A814 (Dumbarton road), then follow Clydebank Business Park signs. Hotel on left

Intimate dining in a conference hotel

A hotel and conference centre next to the Jubilee hospital, about 10 miles out of Glasgow, the Beardmore is a multi-purpose hub for business meetings, fitness workouts and aspirational dining. That last takes place in a 'cosy wee' room with bare tables and floor, cream walls and a low-lit ambience only slightly ruffled by a soundtrack of piped pop. A newish spin on a modern classic produces a trio of scallops with crisp pancetta and three matching pyramids of a rather salty cauliflower pannacotta, amid the terrines and ballotines of the starter listing. The main event might be pork loin poached in sage butter alongside garlicky mash and apple purée in raisin-dotted jus, or cod with sautéed potatoes and confit fennel, sauced with dry sherry. Ecclefechan tart with toffee ice cream is a fine regional speciality, or there may be three variations on apple — Tatin, pannacotta and sorbet.

Times 6.30-10, Closed Sun, L all week

Martin Wishart at Loch Lomond ✿✿✿

BALLOCH
Map 20 NS38

Modern French V NOTABLE WINE LIST

tel: 01389 722504 **Cameron House on Loch Lomond G83 8QZ**
email: info@mwlochlomond.co.uk
dir: From A82, follow signs for Loch Lomond. Restaurant 1m after Stoneymullan rdbt on right

Refined, intelligent cooking on the shores of Loch Lomond

Cameron House is a castellated mansion on the banks of Loch Lomond with a physical presence and setting that is hard to beat. Expect five-star treatment and everything from a chic spa and posh lodges tucked away in the peaceful countryside. In this refined setting only a serious dining option will do, and since 2009 that's been the responsibility of Martin Wishart. Having made his Edinburgh restaurant into one of the top addresses in the UK, the move out here (where he previously worked) has resulted in another venue worthy of his reputation. Martin is not at the stoves — that's down to Graeme Cheevers — but the refined modern French cuisine on offer is redolent of the Wishart style. It all takes place in a handsome and rather contemporary dining room which looks rather dashing compared against today's favoured neutrality (think lime green banquettes and Regency stripes). There's a short à la carte, but the main attraction is the tasting menu, which comes in two sizes (six- or eight-course). From the six-course menu, you might start with miso-glazed Shetland salmon with toasted buckwheat, cucumber and dashi, followed by the luxurious pairing of Loch Fyne crab and foie gras with pickled carrots and apple. Flavours are clear and true and there's precision in the execution. Later on, roasted veal sweetbread arrives with caramelised onion, and mousseline made with Yukon Gold potatoes and Comté cheese. Among desserts, Valrhona dark chocolate finds its way into a soufflé (served with pistachio ice cream), while the selection of pasteurised and unpasteurised cheese is well worth checking out. The wine list covers regional France in detail without neglecting the rest of the world.

Chef Graeme Cheevers **Owner** Martin Wishart **Seats** 40
Times 12-2.30/6.30-10, Closed 25-26 Dec, 1 Jan, Mon-Tue, L Wed-Fri
Prices Fixed L 3 course £28.50, Tasting menu £75-£95 **Wines** 240 bottles over £30, 12 bottles under £30, 12 by glass **Parking** 150 **Notes** Tasting menu 6/8 course, Du Jour L 3 course, ALC menu £75, Sunday L, Children welcome

CITY OF DUNDEE

DUNDEE — Map 21 NO43

Castlehill Restaurant

◉◉ Contemporary Scottish NEW

tel: 01382 220008 **22-26 Exchange St DD1 3DL**
email: enquire@castlehillrestaurant.co.uk
dir: *From High St, travel down Castle St. Left into Exchange St. On left*

Dynamic contemporary cooking

The Scottish countryside and its abundant wildlife are recalled in the decor at this high-flying restaurant on Exchange Street, where earthy browns, stony greys and shimmering greens combine to provide a sense of place. There are the words of wise Scottish poets on the walls, too, and specially commissioned works of cast iron. It's smart and tasteful and void of cliché. The kitchen, under chef Adam Newth, makes the most of Scottish ingredients to produce refined and dynamic plates of contemporary food. Dishes such as first-course ravioli filled with ox cheek and served on a silky celeriac purée look beautiful on the plate and show some keen technical skills. Next up, a superb piece of turbot comes with warm potato salad and mussels, or go for guinea fowl cock-a-leekie with arancini. Desserts are no less impressive, including a summery concoction of berries and peppermint ice cream topped with a pink champagne granité, or warm chocolate pudding matched with honeycomb, bee pollen and Drambuie ice cream. The wine list is short but perfectly formed.

Chef Adam Newth **Owner** Paul McMillan **Times** 12-2.30/5.30-10, Closed Sun-Mon **Prices** Fixed L 2 course £14.95, Fixed D 3 course £36, Service optional **Wines** 14 bottles over £30, 9 bottles under £30, 13 by glass **Parking** On street **Notes** Vegetarian available, Children welcome

DoubleTree by Hilton Dundee

◉ Modern British

tel: 01382 641122 **Kingsway West DD2 5JT**
email: reception@doubletreedundee.co.uk **web:** www.doubletreedundee.co.uk
dir: *A90 at Landmark rdbt, west Dundee city centre*

Contemporary setting for modern and trad food

The original stone baronial mansion bristling with turrets was built to impress, but the whole place has been brought up to 21st-century spec with modern extensions, a smart leisure club, spanking new bedrooms and a classy conservatory restaurant. Looking into the hotel's six acres of lovely grounds and mature gardens, The Maze is named for the box hedge planting you see before you and offers an upmarket setting with linen-swathed tables and moody lighting at dinner. The kitchen steers a crowd-pleasing course with appealing menus of tried-and-trusted modern ideas. You could encounter chicken and duck rillettes with celeriac remoulade and focaccia croûton, ahead of braised blade of beef with pommes purée and a jus made from red wine, shallots and tarragon, or a Scottish steak cooked on the grill. Finish with a perky trifle made with raspberries and white chocolate and topped with a pistachio crumb.

Chef Raymond Sterpaio **Owner** BDL Management **Seats** 100, Pr/dining room 50 **Times** 12-10, All-day dining **Prices** Starter £6-£7, Main £12-£29, Dessert £7-£8, Service optional **Wines** 14 bottles over £30, 24 bottles under £30, 9 by glass **Parking** 150 **Notes** Fixed L/D on request, Sunday L, Vegetarian available, Children welcome

Malmaison Dundee

◉ British, French

tel: 0844 693 0661 *(Calls cost 5p per minute plus your phone company's access charge)*
44 Whitehall Crescent DD1 4AY
email: brasseriemgr.dundee@malmaison.com **web:** www.malmaison.com
dir: *Phone for directions*

Modern brasserie cooking in boutique style

The latest branch of the boutique Mal chain takes the score sheet to 13, and in this case it's a lucky number for the Dundonian dining scene. The setting is a majestic old hotel with a domed ceiling above a central wrought-iron staircase, reinvented with the Malmaison trademark sexy looks, which run through to the intimate candle lit brasserie's velour seats and darkly atmospheric colour scheme. The menu plays the modern brasserie game too, but isn't scared to step outside the European classics to set out with tuna tartare with avocado, pickled ginger, soy and lime dressing and wasabi. A main-course grilled double chicken breast is pointed up with a punchy lemon and caper dressing, while fans of red meat will no doubt be overjoyed to hear that there's a gold-standard Josper grill to make sure those dry-aged steaks are sizzled to perfection. A vanilla crème brûlée wraps things up on a classic note.

Times 12-2.45/5.30-10.30

CITY OF EDINBURGH

EDINBURGH — Map 21 NT27

Apex Waterloo Place Hotel

◉ Modern Scottish

tel: 0131 441 0440 & 523 1819 **23-27 Waterloo Place EH1 3BH**
email: edinburgh.reservations@apexhotels.co.uk **web:** www.apexhotels.co.uk
dir: *Phone for directions*

Clever contemporary food in slick setting

Grand Georgian proportions and elegant period features blending with a slick contemporary look give this hotel a classy edge, and the feel-good factor gets a further boost from a glossy spa and accomplished modern cooking in Elliot's Restaurant. The setting looks the part, mixing wooden floors, unclothed tables and curvy cream leather seats with corniced ceilings and soaring windows that flood the space with light. The kitchen deals in modern food that makes imaginative use of high-quality ingredients to come up with starters of Lanark Blue cheese pannacotta with roast pear purée, chicory, candied walnuts and walnut dressing, followed by Gressingham duck breast pointed up with satay glaze, pineapple purée, toasted cashews and hispi cabbage. Or you might go for a fish and meat combo of poached skate wing with glazed pork belly, cauliflower purée, salsify, morels and jus gras. Finish with burnt lemon custard with filo crisps and morello cherry sorbet.

Times 12-3/5.30-9.30

EDINBURGH *continued*

The Atelier

◎◎ Modern European NEW

tel: 0131 629 1344 **159-161 Morrison St EH3 8AG**
email: info@theatelierrestaurant.co.uk
dir: *In the centre of Haymarket, 0.2m from station*

Informal urban dining with concentrated flair

Snug in the heart of the Haymarket district, The Atelier is a culinary partnership of two ambitious and much-travelled chefs, whose vision of informal urban dining is realised here in the form of a laid-back, pared-down space with exposed rough stone walls and light wood kitchen-style tables. Colourful artwork relieves the neutrality and sets the tone for a culinary output that demonstrates accuracy, balance and flair. First up could be a serving of crisped pork belly bedded on deep-fried shredded leek, with braised chicory and red pepper jelly. Main-course fish dishes are replete with concentrated flavours, coley fillet in sauce vièrge gaining from crab bonbons and blasts of marine freshness from seaweed mash and kale. Sturdy hunks of meat such as venison haunch or 10oz rib-eye, seem to have raided the tuckshop for their accompaniments – cocoa nibs in the jus for the former, a revamped béarnaise of white chocolate and prosecco for the steak. If you've held off from chocolate thus far, sink into a chai-scented gâteau opéra and dark choc ice cream to finish, or else go for nougat parfait full of chewy bits, served with Granny Smith sorbet and mulled wine.

Chef Maciek Zielinski **Owner** Maciek Zielinski, Kamila Bogut **Seats** 32 **Times** 12-2.30/5.30-10.30 **Prices** Fixed L 2 course £15.90, Tasting menu £45-£55, Starter £14.50-£19.40, Main £13.50-£25.90, Dessert £6.75-£12.50, Service optional 10% **Wines** 13 bottles over £30, 23 bottles under £30, 14 by glass **Notes** Sunday L £15.90-£19.90, Vegetarian available, Children 5yrs+

Bia Bistrot

◎ British, French

tel: 0131 452 8453 **19 Colinton Rd EH10 5DP**
email: info@biabistrot.co.uk
dir: *From city centre at Holy corner turn right onto Colinton Rd*

Classy bistro fare that is tasty and well-crafted

The 'Bia' element of the name is the Gaelic for food, the 'Bistrot' part perhaps rather more self-evident, and it's the winning setting for the cooking of husband-and-wife team Roisin and Matthias Llorente. Their Irish/Scottish and French/Spanish ancestry seems to be a winning combination, too, with their bistrot serving up well-crafted and satisfying plates of food. It all takes place in a charming and easy-going environment, where wooden tables and smart leather seats stick to the 'bistrot' ethos. Lobster bisque of great depth of flavour comes with a salmon tortellini among first courses, or go for smoked haddock brandade with toasted rye bread. Main-course roasted rump of lamb is served with carrot purée and a textbook potato gratin, while a fishy main might be hake with broccoli purée and pan-fried polenta. Finish with a crêpe with caramelised apples and Chantilly cream, or British cheeses. There's a good value set lunch and early evening menu, too.

Chef Roisin & Matthias Llorente **Owner** Roisin & Matthias Llorente **Seats** 60, Pr/dining room 24 **Times** 12-2.30/5-10, Closed 1st 2 wks Jan, 2nd wk Jul, Sun-Mon **Prices** Fixed L 2 course £9.50, Fixed D 3 course £11, Starter £3.75-£6.50, Main £12.50-£19.75, Dessert £2-£7, Service optional **Wines** 8 bottles over £30, 16 bottles under £30, 9 by glass **Notes** Pre-theatre menu 5-6pm, Vegetarian available, Children welcome

Bistro Provence

◎ French

tel: 0131 344 4295 **88 Commercial St EH6 6LX**
email: reservations@bistroprovence.co.uk
dir: *Phone for directions*

Traditional Provençal cooking in the city centre

Michael Fons began his career, inauspiciously enough, working in a pizzeria in Marseille in the 1990s, but there has always been rather more to the British affection for Provence than pizza, and in 2013 he left a post at Gidleigh Park, Chagford, to open a restaurant homage to his native region in the Scottish capital. The city-centre venue, with its wide-windowed frontage, is done in impeccable modern style, with unclothed tables and white seating making a clean, neutral background for the Provençal specialities to come. You'd have something to say about it if there were no fish soup with rouille and garlic croûtons, and it's a relief to find there is, alongside baked scallops à la provençale, among 'Les Starters'. 'Les Mains' take in flambéed red mullet with braised fennel and peppers, and rosemaried lamb cutlets with polenta cake and piperade, sauced with sweet red Maury. To finish, there's traditional crème brûlée with cumin-flavoured langue de chat biscuits, or chocolate bavarois.

Chef Paul Malinen, Michael Fons **Owner** Michael Fons **Seats** 45, Pr/dining room 12 **Times** 12-3/6-10.30, Closed 1-10 Jan, Mon **Prices** Prices not confirmed **Wines** 16 bottles over £30, 11 bottles under £30, 11 by glass **Parking** 20 **Notes** Tasting menu 4 course, Special offer L menu £9.50, Vegetarian available, Children welcome

The Bon Vivant

◎ Contemporary European NEW

tel: 0131 225 3275 **55 Thistle St EH2 1DY**
email: info@bonvivantedinburgh.co.uk
dir: *Phone for directions*

Vibrant small-plate dining in a trendy spot

Tapas-style grazing and sharing is the drill at this trendy cocktail bar and eatery. Inside, artworks add splashes of brightness to a dark, moodily-lit space with candles in wax-covered bottles – it's very relaxed, with wooden tables and chairs, booths and banquettes to settle in with friends and work your way through a daily-changing roster of bright modern ideas. The kitchen takes its inspiration mainly from the Med, but global accents pop up here and there, so get started with crab cake with spicy seafood bisque mayonnaise, crispy squid with chilli jam, or crispy pork belly glazed with soy. The small-plate format isn't compulsory: larger servings deliver guinea fowl marinated in North African spices with tabbouleh, coriander yogurt, rose harissa and pomegranate, or perhaps salmon with crab crushed potatoes and cucumber and basil sauce vièrge. Finish with salted caramel and chocolate tart with passionfruit ice cream.

Chef Nico Ewert **Owner** Stuart McCluskey **Seats** 30 **Times** 12-10, All-day dining, Closed 25 Dec, 1 Jan **Prices** Starter £2-£6, Main £12-£18, Dessert £2-£5.50, Service optional 10% **Wines** 19 bottles over £30, 21 bottles under £30, 40 by glass **Notes** Vegetarian available, Children 5 yrs+

Café Royal

🌸 Modern Scottish

tel: 0131 556 1884 **19 West Register St EH2 2AA**
email: info@caferoyal.org.uk
dir: *Just off Princes St, close to Waverley Station, opposite Balmoral Hotel*

Victorian baroque grand dining

Edinburgh's Café Royal opened in the 1860s in premises originally conceived for the retailing of sanitary fittings. No bathtub, however luxurious, could quite have done justice to its Victorian-baroque scrolled and moulded interiors, which simply cry out to be the scene of grand dining with their gilt pillars, panelled ceilings and stained windows. These days, traditional Scots fare mingles with modern thinking on menus that open with oysters on mounds of crushed ice, but get into their stride with mussels in Thai broth, a sweetly alluring main course of duck breast and confit leg on sticky red cabbage with sweet potato purée in port jus. Fish might be straightforward baked cod with asparagus in hollandaise, or monkfish in Goan-style coconut curry. A layered torte of salted caramel on chocolate biscuit base is appealingly squishy, and well complemented by its benchmark vanilla ice.

Chef Anil Colasco **Seats** 40 **Times** 12-2.30/5-9.30 **Prices** Fixed L 3 course £35, Fixed D 3 course £45, Starter £6-£12, Main £17-£35, Dessert £6-£11 **Wines** 17 bottles over £30, 19 bottles under £30, 12 by glass **Notes** Pre-theatre Mon-Thu 5-6.45pm 2/3 course £14.95/£17.95, Sunday L, Vegetarian available, Children 5 yrs+

Calistoga Restaurant

🌸 Modern American 🍾 NOTABLE WINE LIST

tel: 0131 225 1233 **70 Rose St, North Ln EH2 3DX**
email: bookings@calistoga.co.uk
dir: *In North Lane off Rose St, between Frederick St & Castle St*

West Coast eating and drinking in a cobbled back alley

In a little cobbled back-crack between Princes and George Streets, Calistoga is a shrine to California's dynamic wine scene, and is named after one of its hotter regions. Wine references and bottles abound, as does a suitably laid-back West Coast mood, the menus naturally following suit with the likes of corn chowder and flat iron steaks. That chowder is rich and creamy, with carrots, butter beans, celery and potato floating about amid the sweetcorn, and might be followed by chilli-battered pollack with aubergine and sweet potato bake in dill sauce, or panko-crumbed pork with apple and red cabbage slaw and more sweet potato, this time as chunky fries. Dessert may be vanilla pannacotta with praline or there's a peanut butter and chocolate blondie with toffee sauce up for grabs. The wine list is an extended reminder of the versatility and ambitious reach of American viticulture.

Chef Alex MacKenzie **Owner** Gordon Minnis **Seats** 45, Pr/dining room 32 **Times** 12-2.30/5-10, Closed 26 Dec **Prices** Fixed L 2 course £12-£14, Fixed D 3 course fr £25, Starter £6-£12, Main £16-£28, Dessert £6-£10 **Wines** 27 bottles over £30, 86 bottles under £30, 13 by glass **Notes** Pre-theatre 2 course 5-6pm £12, Sunday L fr £12, Vegetarian available, Children welcome

Castle Terrace Restaurant

🌸🌸🌸 – *see below*

Castle Terrace Restaurant 🌸🌸🌸

EDINBURGH Map 21 NT27

Scottish, French Ⅴ 🍾 NOTABLE WINE LIST

tel: 0131 229 1222 **33-35 Castle Ter EH1 2EL**
email: info@castleterracerestaurant.com
dir: *Close to Edinburgh Castle, at the bottom of Lady Lawson St on Castle Terrace*

Refined, intelligent modern cooking with style near the Castle

Dominic Jack returned to his home city after stints at some top end addresses in the UK and France to work with his long-time friend Tom Kitchin at his eponymous restaurant. The two chefs share a passion for the 'from nature to plate' philosophy. Back in 2010, they set up Castle Terrace and Dominic became chef-patron at his own address. It's a soothingly contemporary place close to the castle, with a smart finish and a colour scheme that reflects the Scottish landscapes. There's a satisfying lack of pretension all round. Perhaps unsurprisingly, given the chef's past, the cooking treads a path between classical French ways and modern British thinking, delivering dishes that impress with their technical virtuosity and eye-catching delivery. Scottish ingredients steal the show, but this chef will also go the extra mile to ship something over from Rungis market in Paris if that's the best ingredient for the job. A range of menus include a set lunch option, another that celebrates the seasons, and a surprise tasting version that really showcases the talent in the kitchen. From the equally compelling à la carte menu, begin with a tartare of Scottish salmon served sushi style, or a risotto of organic spelt from Eden Valley served with crispy ox tongue and finely slice pork collar. Follow with North Sea hake partnered with a salt-cod brandade and a crispy tapenade croûton, or barbecued and braised shoulder of Ayrshire pork matched with its crispy belly and chickpeas. Desserts are no less compelling and inventive: pumpkin soufflé, say, with cinnamon and chocolate ganache and pumpkin sorbet. The wine list focuses on France without ignoring the rest of the world, with a terrific range of fine wines available by the glass.

Chef Dominic Jack **Owner** Dominic Jack, Mic & Tom Kitchin **Seats** 65, Pr/dining room 16 **Times** 12-2.15/6.30-10, Closed 20 Dec-19 Jan, Sun-Mon **Prices** Fixed L 3 course £28.50, Tasting menu £75, Starter £13-£19, Main £27-£42, Dessert £12-£14, Service optional 10% **Parking** NCP Castle Terrace **Notes** Children 5 yrs+

EDINBURGH *continued*

Chop Chop

Traditional Chinese

tel: 0131 221 1155 & 440 4708 **248 Morrison St, Haymarket EH3 8DT**
email: yin@chop-chop.co.uk
dir: *From Haymarket Station, restaurant 150yds up Morrison St*

Dumplings a go-go at a charming Chinese café

When Jian Wang opened in 1997, she intended to supply what she saw as a deficiency in Chinese catering in the UK – jiaozi, the traditional dumplings of her native Dongbei (in northeast China). That the dumplings won this charming café an accolade on Gordon Ramsay's *F-Word* speaks volumes about the commitment to authentic quality that drives the place. The red-and-yellow menus are essentially a dim sum format, featuring a myriad of little bites full of savoury intensity, textural variety and spice. Fried pork and prawn guo tie (pot-stickers) are little bombs of flavour, all the better for dipping in rice vinegar and soy, while the boiled items include beef and chilli, lamb and leek, and chicken. Other successful orders are crispy squid in sesame seeds and lemongrass, cumin-seeded lamb, and sides such as gingery bean sprout salad, and garlic-fried aubergine. Finish with Mongolian fried dumplings, non-traditionally filled with chocolate ice cream.

Chef Xuwei Yu **Owner** Jian Wang **Seats** 80 **Times** 12-2/5.30-10 **Prices** Starter £3-£7, Main £6-£12, Dessert £2-£7, Service optional 10% **Wines** 10 bottles under £30, 7 by glass **Parking** NCP **Notes** Unlimited banquet £20.25, Business L 4 dishes £7.50, Sunday L, Vegetarian available, Children welcome

Dalmahoy, A Marriott Hotel & Country Club

Modern, Traditional Scottish

tel: 0131 333 1845 **Kirknewton EH27 8EB**
email: mhrs.edigs.frontdesk@marriotthotels.com **web:** www.marriottdalmahoy.co.uk
dir: *Edinburgh City bypass (A720) turn onto A71 towards Livingston, hotel on left in 2m*

Golfing hotel with imaginative modern menu

An attractive stone-built country hotel near Livingston, Dalmahoy is dedicated to the single-minded pursuit of golf. Its dining room looks out over the greens, so there's no need to miss a single swing, and the split-level layout capitalises on the view. The style of cooking is modern Scottish, with local produce to the fore and a certain stateliness to the presentations. An imaginative spin on the pea and ham theme turns up in a starter of gently set pea pannacotta with wafers of crisp pancetta and a pea salad dressed in white truffle oil, or there may be gravad lax with Scotch whisky in the marinade, served with a potato scone and biting horseradish cream. Main course might produce a monkfish steak in haricot casserole, or quality Perthshire lamb rump with spiced beetroot purée, Lyonnaise potato and pearl barley risotto. If you've started with a pannacotta, finish with pasta, as in ingenious chocolate ravioli in red berry consommé.

Chef James Thomson **Owner** Marriott International **Seats** 150, Pr/dining room 18 **Times** 7-10, Closed L all week **Prices** Starter £6.50-£7.50, Main £17-£28.50, Dessert £7-£8.50, Service optional **Wines** 19 bottles over £30, 21 bottles under £30, 16 by glass **Parking** 350 **Notes** Sunday L, Vegetarian available, Children welcome

Divino Enoteca

Modern Italian, International 🍷 NOTABLE WINE LIST

tel: 0131 225 1770 **5 Merchant St EH1 2QD**
email: info@divinoedinburgh.com
dir: *Near National Museum of Scotland and The Grassmarket*

Exemplary Italian cooking and wines

Head down a dead-end street off the main drag and you'll be rewarded by this little cracker of an Italian restaurant and wine bar. It's a hip and happening venue with vibrant contemporary artworks on the walls, exposed brickwork and displays of wine bottles wherever you look: it's dark, moody, and a lot of fun. The kitchen's Italian output includes an excellent range of antipasti such as imported hams and salami, plus the more modern pan-fried scallops with smoked paprika polenta. Pasta options include ravioli of the day, or go for gnocchi with pancetta, clams and sautéed samphire. Pan-fried monkfish cheeks are served with salt-cod baccalà, confit lemon and braised leeks, grilled steak arrives in red wine sauce, and vegetarians can tuck into lasagne made with pumpkin and gorgonzola. Finish with white and dark truffles served with a glass of Pedro Ximenez. And while we're talking booze, the wine list excels when it comes to provincial Italy, with some terrific wine flight options on offer.

Chef Gavin Thompson **Owner** Tony Crolla **Seats** 85, Pr/dining room 14 **Times** 4-mdnt, All-day dining, Closed Sun, L Mon-Fri **Prices** Prices not confirmed, Service optional **Wines** 200 bottles over £30, 40 bottles under £30, 34 by glass **Parking** On street **Notes** Vegetarian available, Children welcome

The Dungeon Restaurant at Dalhousie Castle

Traditional European

tel: 01875 820153 **Bonnyrigg EH19 3JB**
email: info@dalhousiecastle.co.uk **web:** www.dalhousiecastle.co.uk
dir: *From A720 (Edinburgh bypass) take A7 south, turn right onto B704. Castle 0.5m on right*

Creative cuisine in a truly unique setting

Dalhousie Castle is a pukka 13th-century fortress in acreages of wooded parkland on the banks of the River Esk, so you know you're in for something a bit special when you're heading for The Dungeon Restaurant. Reality does not disappoint: the barrel-vaulted chamber comes with a full complement of romantic medieval candlelit vibes and enough weaponry – suits of armour, battleaxes and broadswords – to sort out the French all over again. Mentioning our cross-Channel cousins, the cooking here resurrects the Auld Alliance, with its roots in French classicism, and a bedrock of top-class Scottish ingredients. But the kitchen doesn't rely on the setting and fail-safe luxury ingredients for its effect: it's all brought together with skill and clever contemporary creativity. Smoked duck and foie gras cromesquis is matched with spiced bread and pear, ahead of pan-fried halibut and pork belly with parsley root purée and apple chutney. Dessert is winning confection of white chocolate and vanilla parfait with pistachio sponge, meringue and griottine cherries.

Chef Francois Giraud **Owner** Robert & Gina Parker **Seats** 45, Pr/dining room 100 **Times** 7-10, Closed L all week **Prices** Fixed D 3 course fr £49.50, Service optional **Wines** 52 bottles over £30, 43 bottles under £30, 10 by glass **Parking** 150 **Notes** ALC 5 course £49.50, Vegetarian available, Children welcome

L'Escargot Bleu

🏵 French, Scottish **NEW**

tel: 0131 557 1600 **56 Broughton St EH1 3SA**
email: contact@lescargotbleu.co.uk **web:** www.lescargotbleu.co.uk
dir: *On Broughton St, near Omni Centre*

French classics done right

L'Escargot Bleu is indeed blue – on the outside at least – while the interior strikes a bistro pose with its simple decor emboldened by vivid works of French pop art. And when it comes to snails, they are present and correct among les entrées. The bilingual menu deals in classic bistro dishes such as those snails, which are sourced from Barra in the Outer Hebrides, and in fact there's a Scottish flavour to a good deal of the kitchen's output. Start with seared scallops (from Skye) which arrive with spicy Puy lentils and crispy bacon, and move on to casserole of venison and beef cheeks with a rich red wine sauce, or pan-fried sea bass with Jerusalem artichokes and hollandaise. Desserts are as traditional as the crème brûlée which arrives without any unnecessary adornments. The two-course lunch and early-evening menu is a genuine bargain.

Chef Fred Berkmiller **Owner** Fred Berkmiller **Seats** 55, Pr/dining room 18 **Times** 12-2.30/5.30-10, Closed Xmas 1 wk, Sun (ex Aug Edinburgh festival) **Prices** Fixed L 2 course £12.90, Fixed D 3 course £25-£42, Starter £5.50-£12, Main £15-£25, Dessert £5.50, Service optional **Wines** 10 bottles over £30, 12 bottles under £30, 16 by glass **Notes** Early D menu 2 course £12.90, Vegetarian available, Children welcome

La Favorita

🏵 Modern Italian, Mediterranean

tel: 0131 554 2430 & 555 5564 **325-331 Leith Walk EH6 8SA**
email: dine@la-favorita.com
dir: *On A900 from Edinburgh to South Leith*

Vibrant Leith Italian venue with more than just giant pizzas

The Vittoria group's Leith pizzeria aims to provide upscale Italian food for a vibrant city crowd, seated at booth tables amid aquamarine walls. The menu core is an inspiring list of 14-inch pizza variations, from Zia Rosa (topped with chicken, sweet peppers and cherry tomatoes) to truffle-oiled sausage and mushroom Montanara, all cooked freshly in wood-fired ovens. A vast list of cured meats or vegetable antipasti, multi-ingredient pasta dishes and arborio risottos broadens the choice. Snack on polenta chips dipped in spicy salsa, or perhaps seafood bruschetta, to start. Those not in the market for pizza may opt for pancakes of scampi, prawns and crab in Cognac cream sauce, or a sweet-savoury risotto made with caramelised pears and taleggio. Traditional mains include steaks, veal chops and surf-and-turf options. Finish classically with pannacotta, tiramisù or ice creams. Cocktail pitchers help to get the party started, and there is a series of fixed-price deals for celebrations.

Chef Jarek Splawski **Owner** Tony Crolla **Seats** 120, Pr/dining room 30 **Times** 12-11, All-day dining, Closed 25-26 Dec **Prices** Fixed L 2 course £11.95, Starter £3.50-£13.95, Main £7.50-£25.95, Dessert £3.15-£11.95 **Wines** 4 bottles over £30, 26 bottles under £30, 7 by glass **Parking** On street **Notes** Sunday L, Vegetarian available, Children welcome

Field

🏵 Scottish **NEW** 🍷 NOTABLE WINE LIST

tel: 0131 667 7010 **41 West Nicolson St EH8 9DB**
email: dine@fieldrestaurant.co.uk
dir: *From Waverley Station, right onto Princes St, right onto South Bridge for 0.5m, right onto West Nicolson St*

Refined contemporary cooking in a minimalist setting

This dinky restaurant – just seven tables – takes a serious approach to matters of provenance, but the menu is not clogged up by endless lists of farms and artisan producers. With its minimalist colour scheme (white walls, wooden flooring and tables) and attention to detail where it matters – check out the small but perfectly formed wine list – Field offers modern Scottish food of some refinement. Begin with some scallops (from this part of the world of course), seared and served with a lightly spiced pumpkin purée, black pudding, gingerbread and pomegranate. Move on to a maple-glazed duck breast with Savoy cabbage enriched with pancetta and a duck sausage roll, or home-smoked sea trout with curried mussels. For dessert, the chocolate fondant oozes in all the right places, and comes with burnt marshmallow ice cream. There's a fixed-price menu available at lunchtimes and pre-theatre in the evening.

Chef Gordon Craig, Byron Kennedy **Owner** Gordon Craig, Rachel & Richard Conway **Seats** 22 **Times** 12-2/5.30-9, Closed Mon **Prices** Fixed L 2 course £11.95, Fixed D 3 course £14.95, Starter £4.95-£5.95, Main £10.95-£19, Dessert £5.95-£6.50, Service optional **Wines** 19 bottles over £30, 21 bottles under £30, 9 by glass **Parking** On street **Notes** Pre-theatre menu 5.30-6.45pm, Sunday L £8.95-£14.95, Vegetarian available, Children 5 yrs+

EDINBURGH continued

G&V Royal Mile Hotel

◉◉ Italian

tel: 0131 220 6666 & 240 1666 **1 George IV Bridge EH1 1AD**
email: info@gandvhotel.com **web:** www.quorvuscollection.com
dir: At corner of Royal Mile & George IV Bridge

Modern Italian cucina in a glamorous Royal Mile hotel

On the corner of George IV Bridge and Victoria Street (hence the G&V tag) stands this luxury designer-led boutique hotel. The interior looks as if it should be photographed for an Italian interior-design magazine, with a contemporary decor of striking colours. In the Cucina restaurant, colourful abstracts hang on vivid blue walls, banquettes are in bold grey and black fabrics and tables have red tops. Authentic, modern, seasonal Italian cooking is the orthodoxy here, with English subtitles on the menu for those who don't speak the lingo. Tagliatelle with pork ragù is a nicely balanced starter, or wander into the unknown with buffalo mozzarella with chocolate, prunes and candied chillies. Accurate cooking of top-quality produce is the norm, with main courses never so complex as to muddy flavours. Roast rump of lamb is accompanied by fennel, black olives and sun-dried tomatoes to make a most enjoyable main course, and likewise grilled swordfish in red wine dressing with cherry tomatoes and rocket. Fly the flag with puddings of tiramisù and Amaretto and chocolate fondant.

Chef Mattia Camorani **Owner** G&V Royal Mile Hotel **Seats** 90, Pr/dining room 40 **Times** 12.30-3/6-10, Closed D 25 Dec **Prices** Starter £7-£12, Main £18-£28, Dessert £5.50-£8, Service optional **Wines** 67 bottles over £30, 15 bottles under £30, 14 by glass **Notes** Pre-theatre 2/3 course 6-7pm £17/£21, Sunday L, Vegetarian available, Children welcome

Galvin Brasserie de Luxe

◉ French

tel: 0131 222 8988 **The Caledonian, A Waldorf Astoria Hotel, Princes St EH1 2AB**
email: brasserie.reservations@waldorfastoria.com
dir: On Rutland St off Lothian Rd at Caledonian Hotel

Timeless French brasserie dishes à la Galvin

The well-composed menu at the more accessible of the Galvin brothers' Edinburgh operations (the other being Pompadour) pleases diners hankering for a hit of cross-Channel classicism built on top-class Scottish produce. Housed in the luxurious Caledonian Waldorf Astoria, the setting also aims straight at the heart of Francophiles with its Parisian brasserie-styled looks: there are navy-blue banquettes, darkwood flooring and tables around a circular island seafood bar, and waiting staff in time-honoured black-and-white uniforms. As for the food, it's a trip to France without needing to fly: steak tartare, Burgundian snails, terrine of

chicken, ham hock and foie gras with sauce gribiche are all present and correct, while mains take in the rich flavours and textures of duck confit with boudin noir and red wine sauce, or pork cutlet with pommes mousseline and Agen prunes. Classic desserts include tarte Tatin with crème fraîche and rum baba with Chantilly.

Chef Jamie Knox **Owner** Chris & Jeff Galvin **Seats** 120, Pr/dining room 20 **Times** 12-2.30/6-10 **Prices** Fixed L 2 course £16.50, Fixed D 3 course £19.50, Starter £6.50-£12.50, Main £14-£19, Dessert £6-£7.50 **Wines** 41 bottles over £30, 21 bottles under £30, 16 by glass **Parking** 42 **Notes** Prix fixe menu before 7pm, Sunday L £14.50, Vegetarian available, Children welcome

The Gardener's Cottage

◉ British

tel: 0131 558 1221 **1 Royal Terrace Gardens, London Rd EH7 5DX**
email: eat@thegardenerscottage.co
dir: Access from London Road. Opposite No 1 Hillside Cresent

Carefully sourced Scottish garden cooking

William Playfair's gardens on the Royal Terrace at the foot of Calton Hill once included a path for the exiled French king to tread on his way to church, while this pleasant little house was home to the groundsman. With its blackboard menu propped up in the gravel outside, it makes an oasis of pastoral calm in the bustling city. Cosy up in wicker chairs at big communal tables for Scottish cooking that takes pride in its carefully sourced prime materials. That's clear from a starter of mutton and roe-deer meatballs in maltagliati pasta bound in rich creamy sauce with chopped nuts, and from a seafaring main course of turbot with winkles, strongly cured smoked bacon, apple and celeriac and a smoked yogurt dressing. Moist, substantial hazelnut cake comes with poached rhubarb and light sherry ice cream.

Chef Edward Murray, Dale Mailley **Owner** Edward Murray, Dale Mailley **Seats** 30, Pr/dining room 10 **Times** 12-2.30/5-9.30, Closed Xmas & New Year, Tue-Wed **Prices** Starter £5-£9, Main £14-£20, Dessert fr £6, Service optional 10% **Wines** 13 bottles over £30, 9 bottles under £30, 12 by glass **Parking** On street (charges apply 8.30-5) **Notes** Fixed D 6 course £35, Vegetarian available, Children welcome

La Garrigue

◉◉ Traditional French, Mediterranean 🍷 NOTABLE WINE LIST

tel: 0131 557 3032 **31 Jeffrey St EH1 1DH**
email: reservations@lagarrigue.co.uk **web:** www.lagarrigue.co.uk
dir: Halfway along Royal Mile towards Holyrood Palace, turn left at lights into Jeffrey St

Charming bistro with authentic South of France menu

La Garrigue is the name given to the wild, herb-scented expanses of scrubland in Provence and Languedoc in the south of France and chef-patron Jean-Michel Gauffre (who hails from down that way) has brought the honest rustic cooking of this region to his smart neighbourhood restaurant in Edinburgh's old town. Inside, there are vibrant artworks on lavender and purple walls, and chunky wooden tables and chairs made by the woodcarver and artist Tim Stead. The regional cooking style delivers full-bore flavours, using good local produce in authentic French country dishes done properly. The menu is a list of things you want to eat, starting with a fish soup with croûtons and rouille, tasting as if it has been flown in straight from the quayside of Marseille. Gauffre was born in the heartlands of cassoulet so you can rest assured that his take on the rich stew of belly pork, duck confit, Toulouse sausage and white beans is the real deal. Finish with baked cheesecake and cherry compôte, or a lavender crème brûlée.

Times 12-3/6.30-10.30, Closed 26-27 Dec, 1-2 Jan

Hadrian's

◉ Modern Scottish

tel: 0131 557 5000 & 557 2414 **The Balmoral Hotel, 1 Princes St EH2 2EQ**
email: hadrians.balmoral@roccofortehotels.com
dir: *Follow city centre signs. Hotel at east end of Princes St, adjacent to Waverley Station*

Classy brasserie in landmark hotel

This large, bustling brasserie-style restaurant is within The Balmoral Hotel but has its own street entrance. A cool, modern vibe is created by walnut flooring, darkwood tables and a colour scheme of lime green and, appropriately, shades of heather, while a mirror-lined wall reflects the light from the windows opposite. Scottish classics range from haggis, neeps and tatties to whisky pannacotta, and there's much to entice elsewhere on the menus. Pork belly with a scallop on a bed of tapenade is a masterly starter, and might be followed by a relatively simple main course of golden-skinned seared sea bream fillet on braised chicory with ratatouille. Sourdough bread is so good as to be moreish, and puddings run to visually attractive lemon meringue pie with grapefruit sorbet, crushed pistachios and an orange tuile.

Chef Jeff Bland **Owner** Rocco Forte Hotels **Seats** 100, Pr/dining room 26 **Times** 12-10.30, All-day dining **Prices** Prices not confirmed, Service optional **Wines** 8 by glass **Parking** Greenside Place NCP **Notes** Sunday L, Vegetarian available, Children welcome

Harvey Nichols Forth Floor Restaurant

◉ British, Modern European, International 🍷 NOTABLE WINE LIST

tel: 0131 524 8350 **30-34 St Andrew Square EH2 2AD**
email: forthfloor.reservations@harveynichols.com **web:** www.harveynichols.com/restaurants
dir: *Located on St Andrew Square at east end of George St, 2 min walk from Princes St*

City views and sharp modern Scottish cooking

Views of the castle – check – the Forth Bridge – check; the vista from the top floor of Harvey Nic's Edinburgh restaurant really does serve up the city on a plate. On the

top floor, of course, there's the usual brasserie and bar, and the more refined restaurant itself. The latter offers a slick contemporary dining room with white linen on the tables and burgundy-coloured leather seats to sink into, and on the menu is some sharp, contemporary cooking. The kitchen turns out smart seasonal dishes that don't lack for contemporary finesse and Scottish ingredients. Duck roulade with Calvados-soaked apricots, piccalilli purée and melba toast is a typically creative first course, grounded in classical technique, but not adverse to a bit of fun. Next up, perhaps venison cooked sous-vide and partnered with a shallot Tatin, or a superb piece of North Atlantic hake with creamed leeks and parsley potatoes (the ingredients really do the talking with that one). Finish with blackberry and apple soufflé.

Chef Stuart Muir **Owner** Harvey Nichols **Seats** 47, Pr/dining room 14
Times 12-3/6-10, Closed 25 Dec, 1 Jan, D Sun-Mon, 24 & 26 Dec, 2 Jan **Prices** Fixed L 2 course £28, Fixed D 3 course £33, Tasting menu £65-£95, Starter £8-£15, Main £16-£25, Dessert £8 **Wines** 264 bottles over £30, 35 bottles under £30, 16 by glass **Parking** 20 **Notes** Tasting menu 6 course, Afternoon tea £20 Sun-Fri 3-4pm, Sunday L £33, Vegetarian available, Children 12 yrs+

The Honours

◉◉ Modern French

tel: 0131 220 2513 **58a North Castle St EH2 3LU**
email: info@thehonours.co.uk **email:** www.thehonours.co.uk
dir: *In city centre*

Classic French brasserie food Wishart-style

Martin Wishart is a shining star of the Scottish (and indeed national) restaurant firmament, with his eponymous restaurant in Leith collecting awards aplenty. Here, though, he's bought his dedication to high quality and his attention to detail to the world of the French brasserie. There's a contemporary sheen to the place and a dedication to Scottish produce that delivers some feel-good food that proves the auld alliance is alive and well. A starter of crab cappuccino with rouille, croûtons and parmesan is a classy bowlful, or go for pressed duck and pistachio terrine with Morello cherries. Next up, there's grass-fed Scottish steaks cooked on the charcoal grill (T-bone, for example, with garlic and soy marinade), or ox cheeks à la bordelaise. There are shellfish, too (Cornish oysters, or hand-dived Orkney scallops), and fishy mains such as monkfish tail with crisp potato and Puy lentils. For dessert, rum cake competes with the soufflé du jour, and there are after dinner cocktails if you're in for the long haul.

Chef Paul Tamburrini **Owner** Martin Wishart **Seats** 65
Times 12-2.30/6-10, Closed Xmas, 1-3 Jan, Sun-Mon **Prices** Fixed L 2 course £18.50, Fixed D 3 course £22.50, Starter £8.25-£17, Main £16.75-£33, Dessert £2.75-£9.50, Service optional **Wines** 34 bottles over £30, 22 bottles under £30, 20 by glass **Parking** On street **Notes** Fixed D Tue-Fri 6-7pm, Vegetarian available, Children welcome

EDINBURGH *continued*

Hotel du Vin Edinburgh

◉ Modern British, French

tel: 0131 247 4900 **11 Bristo Place EH1 1EZ**
email: reception.edinburgh@hotelduvin.com **web:** www.hotelduvin.com
dir: *M8 junct 1, A720 (signed Kilmarnock/W Calder/Edinburgh W). Right at fork, follow A720 signs, merge onto A720. Take exit signed A703. At rdbt take A702/Biggar Rd. 3.5m. Right into Lauriston Pl which becomes Forrest Rd. Right at Bedlam Theatre. Hotel on right*

Bags of HdV style and sound brasserie cooking

The former city asylum is the setting for HdV's Edinburgh outpost. These days the setting is considerably more cheerful thanks to the group's trademark clubby look of well-worn leather seats and woody textures. There's a splendid tartan-clad whisky snug, plus a buzzy mezzanine bar overlooking the bistro, which offers the usual nods to France with its wine-related paraphernalia and hearty, rustic contemporary brasserie cooking that the group specialises in everywhere from Royal Tunbridge Wells to the Scottish capital. An Isle of Mull cheese soufflé is the signature starter, which you might follow with a classic plate of haggis, neeps and tatties, or perhaps hake paella.

Chef Gavin Lindsay **Owner** Hotel du Vin, Malmaison **Seats** 88, Pr/dining room 26 **Times** 12-2.30/5.30-10.30, Closed D 25 Dec **Prices** Fixed L 2 course fr £14.95, Fixed D 3 course fr £16.95, Starter £5.95-£10, Main £13.95-£29.50, Dessert £6.95-£8.95 **Wines** 150 bottles over £30, 75 bottles under £30, 20 by glass **Parking** NCP **Notes** Sun 4 course brunch, Sunday L fr £22.95, Vegetarian available, Children welcome

The Howard

◉◉ Modern Scottish, British, French

tel: 0131 557 3500 **34 Great King St EH3 6QH**
email: reception@thehoward.com **web:** www.thehoward.com
dir: *E on Queen St, 2nd left, Dundas St. Through 3 lights, right, hotel on left*

Quality Scottish cooking in an intimate hotel dining room

The Howard is very much in its Edinburgh element, a conversion of three 1820s townhouses on Great King Street in the heart of the New Town. Its 18 rooms are named after streets in the locality, and where other hotels have room service, the Howard has butlers, if you please. That the Atholl Restaurant seats a mere 14 covers is somehow in keeping with the tone of personalised solicitude, and its marble fireplace, smart table accoutrements and fresh flowers are a joy to behold. The modern Scottish cooking on offer is all about quality prime materials. Sautéed scallops are accompanied by black pudding, celeriac purée and a dressing of peppery rocket oil, or there might be velvety Jerusalem artichoke and leek soup garnished with cinnamon foam and garlic crisps. At main, delectably rich braised lamb shank comes with skirlie cake and puréed carrots in a rich jus, while Loch Etive salmon gets Shetland black potatoes and wilted spinach in a classic beurre blanc. Dessert is a highlight with correctly caramelised tonka bean crème brûlée.

Chef William Poncelet **Owner** Ricky Kapoor **Seats** 14, Pr/dining room 40 **Times** 12-2/6-9.30 **Prices** Fixed L 2 course £18-£21, Fixed D 3 course £28.50-£35, Tasting menu £65-£105, Starter £8.50-£11.20, Main £17.90-£28.95, Dessert £7.90-£9.95, Service optional **Wines** 50 bottles over £30, 10 bottles under £30, 10 by glass **Parking** 10 **Notes** Pre-theatre menu, Sunday L £18-£25, Vegetarian available, Children welcome

The Indian Cavalry Club

◉ Indian

tel: 0131 220 0138 **22 Coates Crescent EH3 7AF**
email: info@indiancavalryclub.co.uk
dir: *Few mins walk from Haymarket Railway Station & the west end of Princes St*

The West End's Indian star serving authentic flavours

Just a few minutes from the city's hub, this Indian restaurant has been going strong since it opened its doors in 1986. It's a comfortable, good-looking sort of place, with a contemporary decor of creamy tones and a wooden floor, with well-appointed tables and professional, well-drilled staff. The kitchen deploys sound techniques and quality ingredients to produce the authentic flavours of the sub-continent, taking great care with spicing and seasoning. Start with a lamb crêpe stuffed with tender meat in a sauce that bursts with flavour, or perhaps seafood soup, before tandoori chicken in a rich, piquant sauce with spicy yogurt. Try chargrilled fillet of sea bass and a sauce of your choice: one of lime and coconut, say, lightly sour and hot, from Goa. Vegetarian options, among them paneer palak (spinach and cottage cheese), get the thumbs up, as do naan and light and fluffy pilau rice, while desserts might run to gulab jamon in fruit syrup.

Chef M D Qayum, Biplob **Owner** Shahid Chowdhury **Seats** 120, Pr/dining room 50 **Times** 12-2/5.30-11.30 **Prices** Prices not confirmed **Wines** 9 bottles over £30, 23 bottles under £30, 2 by glass **Parking** On street **Notes** Sunday L, Vegetarian available, Children welcome

Kanpai Sushi

◉ Japanese

tel: 0131 228 1602 **8-10 Grindlay St EH3 9AS**
dir: *Joined to Lothian Road behind Usher Hall*

Classic Japanese food in Edinburgh's culture zone

Just around the corner from the Usher Hall and the Traverse Theatre, Kanpai is a diminutive but elegant sushi place that takes its name from the Japanese expression for 'Bottoms up!' As well as the sushi bar itself, there is an open kitchen counter where you can watch the kitchen brigade setting about its well-drilled artistry, and there is a soothing absence of the staff shouting that often animates Japanese venues. Attention to fine detail, and exemplary freshness are the hallmarks of wakame salad with soy and seaweed dressing, seared tuna in home-made miso, delicately battered squid tempura, melt-in-the-mouth nigiri scallops, white snow crab with onions in ponzu, and the moreish Kanpai special roll. This is an artfully presented king prawn wrapped in sticky rice, with sweet bean curd and avocado. Make sure to check out the list of sake and shochu spirits.

Chef Max Wang **Owner** Monica Wang **Seats** 45, Pr/dining room 8 **Times** 12-2.30/5-10.30, Closed Mon **Prices** Starter £2-£9.90, Main £7.90-£20.90, Dessert £4.20-£6.50, Service optional **Wines** 3 bottles over £30, 8 bottles under £30, 9 by glass **Parking** On street **Notes** Vegetarian available, Children 6 yrs+

The Kitchin

@@@@@ – see page 624

Locanda De Gusti

@@ Italian, Mediterranean, Seafood NEW

tel: 0131 346 8800 **102 Dalry Rd EH11 2DW**
dir: *5 min walk from Haymarket station*

A Neapolitan trattoria transported

Translating loosely as 'inn of taste', this Haymarket award-winner has more than a hint of an Italian domestic kitchen about it. Except, that is, the staff in their white steward's jackets bustling around the closely spaced tables, giving the place a truly professional feel. Using Italian artisanal products and Scotland's best meats, fish and seafood, the kitchen produces Southern Italian-Scottish cooking that Auld Reekie's citizens can't get enough of. Take, for example, mixed Scottish seafood feast, a starter full of the freshest squid, king prawns, langoustines, scallops and more, mixed with white wine and a kiss of chilli. Or there's a main course of linguine with grilled half lobster, Vesuvian and sun-dried tomatoes and, again, just a hint of chilli. From chef-patron Rosario's birthplace comes Neapolitan meatloaf stuffed with egg, parmesan, smoked mozzarella and ham, drowned (his word) in a rich tomato passata and basil sauce. Finish with cannolo Siciliano – crispy pastry filled with sweet cheese, infused with icing sugar. The wine list contains some real Italian gems.

Chef Rosario Sartore **Owner** Rosario Sartore **Seats** 30
Times 12-2.30/5-10.30, Closed Sun, L Mon-Wed **Prices** Fixed L 3 course £12.95, Starter £4.95-£8.95, Main £10.95-£19.95, Dessert £4.95-£7.95, Service optional **Wines** 10 by glass **Parking** On street **Notes** Fixed L Thu-Fri, Vegetarian available, Children welcome

Macdonald Holyrood Hotel

@ Modern Scottish NEW

tel: 0131 550 4500 **Holyrood Rd EH8 8AU**
email: holyrood@macdonald-hotels.co.uk **web:** www.macdonaldhotels.co.uk
dir: *Parallel to Royal Mile, near Holyrood Palace*

Stylish dining option in a modern hotel

A modern hotel on the receiving end of a recent £1.4 million makeover, Macdonald Holyrood is in fine fettle. Expect all mod cons including spa and business facilities. The hotel's restaurant is so up-to-the-minute it's even got an at-sign in its name – Rocca@Holyrood – and it's a winner with its elegant, contemporary finish and brasserie-style Italian(ish) menu. Scottish ingredients feature on a menu that covers modern Scottish and Italian bases, so you might start with bruschetta or a pizzetta, but equally there's ham hock terrine with piccalilli and seared scallops with black pudding and minted peas. There are steaks from grass-fed cattle, slow-braised beef in a luscious sauce, pasta options (wild mushroom pappardelle, say), and even beer-battered haddock with chips and tartare sauce. Finish with limoncello polenta cake or Scottish and Italian cheeses.

Chef Chris Shields **Owner** Macdonald Hotels **Times** 11.30-9.30, All-day dining **Prices** Fixed L 2 course fr £13.95, Fixed D 3 course fr £25, Starter £3-£9.95, Main £9-£25.50, Dessert £6.95-£8.95 **Wines** 10 bottles over £30, 17 bottles under £30, 6 by glass **Notes** Sunday L £10-£20, Children welcome

Malmaison Edinburgh

@ British, French

tel: 0131 468 5000 **One Tower Place, Leith EH6 7BZ**
email: edinburgh@malmaison.com **web:** www.malmaison.com
dir: *A900 from city centre towards Leith, at end of Leith Walk through 3 lights, left into Tower St. Hotel on right at end of road*

Dockside brasserie in the Mal boutique style

The first of the Malmaison boutique brand, Edinburgh's Mal occupies a renovated seamen's mission on the Forth waterfront in the old part of Leith. It's a perfect spot as the dockyards have been resurrected to house a trendy restaurant and bar zone, so there's a buzzy vibe about the place. The brasserie is a dark, clubby space with brown leather seating, ornate ironwork, deep burgundy walls, bold artwork, unclothed tables and candles and it all overlooks the Port of Leith (there's outdoor eating on the terrace too when the weather allows). On the menu is an impeccably contemporary and simple take on French brasserie food, which might start as classically as chicken liver parfait with spiced pear chutney and toasted brioche. The main course can be as unreconstructed as steaks or burgers, or those in the mood for fish could see immaculately-timed sea bass matched with chorizo, new potatoes and tomato and mussel dressing.

Chef Andrew McQueen **Owner** Malmaison **Seats** 60, Pr/dining room 60
Times 12-2.30/6-10.30 **Prices** Fixed D 3 course £22.50, Starter £5-£9.50, Main £12-£36, Dessert £6-£9 **Wines** 33 bottles over £30, 9 bottles under £30, 42 by glass **Parking** 45 **Notes** Sunday L £19.95, Vegetarian available, Children welcome

Norton House Hotel & Spa

@@@ – see page 625

Number One, The Balmoral

@@@ – see page 625

Ondine Restaurant

@@ Seafood ♦NOTABLE WINE LIST

tel: 0131 226 1888 **2 George IV Bridge EH1 1AD**
email: enquiries@ondinerestaurant.co.uk
dir: *In Edinburgh City Centre, just off the Royal Mile*

Contemporary seafood restaurant with ethical outlook

Ondine has earned a loyal following in a few short years, and it's not hard to see why: just off the Royal Mile, on George IV Bridge, it's a contemporary space with great views out over the old town, but sustainable seafood served amid an atmosphere of cheerful bustle is the main draw, and the sustainability ethos is not empty marketing speak. You could take a high seat at the central horseshoe-shaped crustacea bar, or park on a stripy banquette and get things under way with oysters – four types, no less, either as they come or cooked (tempura or grilled with Charentais sausage, perhaps) – or something like a classic fish and shellfish soup with the time-honoured accompaniments of rouille, gruyère and croûtons. Chef Roy Brett takes a sensibly restrained approach, so nothing is overworked and every molecule of flavour is extracted from the first-class piscine produce at his disposal. Thus main course might be simple crab gnocchi with lemon and garlic, sea bream curry, or good old-fashioned deep-fried haddock and chips with minted pea purée.

Chef Roy Brett **Owner** Roy Brett **Seats** 70, Pr/dining room 8
Times 12-3/5.30-10, Closed 1st wk Jan, Sun **Prices** Prices not confirmed, Service optional **Wines** 60 bottles over £30, 6 bottles under £30, 25 by glass **Parking** On street or Castle Terrace car park **Notes** Pre-theatre menu 2/3 course £22/£25 5.30-6.30pm, Vegetarian available, Children welcome

The Kitchin ❀❀❀❀❀

Scottish, French V ♦ NOTABLE WINE LIST

tel: 0131 555 1755 **78 Commercial Quay, Leith EH6 6LX**
email: info@thekitchin.com
dir: *In Leith, off Commercial St, opposite Scottish Executive building*

Benchmark modern Scottish cooking of great impact

Tom and Michaela Kitchin's restaurant opened on Leith's waterfront back in 2006 and has played its part in taking Edinburgh to the top of the UK's list of dining destinations. Their hard work and vision has given the city a restaurant that could hold its own in any of the world's top culinary hotspots. The one-time whisky warehouse with its generous proportions and urban patina seems made for the job of hosting such a contemporary and dynamic restaurant. A recent renovation that stripped everything out and started again with a blank canvas has resulted in an engaging space that combines the cast-iron pillars of the country's industrial past with its natural environment via shades of slate and heather. It's very much a restaurant of our times – smart but not stuffy, serious but not stern. Tom's background includes stints with the great and the good of classical French cuisine and this, combined with his passion for fine Scottish ingredients, has resulted in dishes of refinement and astonishing technical accomplishment. There is precision in the presentation, too, with everything looking stunning on the plate, but never at the expense of flavour. Take a dish called 'rockpool', for example, rich with squab lobster, crab, cockles, oysters and more, interspersed with foraged seaweed and finished with a pungent consommé, and topped with a fabulous seaweed 'cannelloni', or the superbly well-judged signature, a boned and rolled pig's head delivering intense flavour, but not at the expense of the roasted langoustine tail and garlic-flavoured cracked claws that sit alongside, all helped along with a salad of crispy ears and gem lettuce to add textural interest. Next up, second-to-none John Dory arrives with gnocchi, pumpkin purée and some lightly sautéed kale in a main course that allows the superb fish to shine, or there might be loin of roe deer with a beautifully silky juniper jus. The phenomenally high level of skill and sound judgement continues into dessert stage, where a yogurt pannacotta is served with an apple sorbet and sea

buckthorn from East Lothian, providing a perfectly judged balance of sweetness and sharpness, or another that combines pear and caramel to stunning effect. Every detail is considered here, nothing happens by chance and everything from the amuse-bouche (chilled beetroot velouté perhaps) and spectacular bread served with Scottish butter makes the experience memorable. It is worth saving room for cheese if at all possible, as when the trolley swings past there's a good chance you'll be hankering after its British-only cargo. The wine list favours France without ignoring the rest of the world and the selection by the glass means it's possible to drink something rather good without the need to stump up for a bottle.

Chef Tom Kitchin **Owner** Tom & Michaela Kitchin **Seats** 75, Pr/dining room 24 **Times** 12.15-2.30/6.30-10, Closed Xmas, New Year, 1st 2 wks Jan, Sun-Mon **Prices** Fixed L 3 course £28.50, Tasting menu £75, Starter £19.50-£22, Main £29-£40, Dessert £11, Service optional **Wines** 330 bottles over £30, 30 by glass **Parking** 30, On site parking evening only, all day Sat **Notes** Tasting menu 6 course, Celebration of the season menu, Children 5 yrs+

Norton House Hotel & Spa 🌸🌸🌸

EDINBURGH   Map 21 NT27

Modern Scottish, French

tel: 0131 333 1275 & 0845 072 7468 *(Calls cost 7p per minute plus your phone company's access charge)* **Ingliston EH28 8LX**
email: nortonhouse@handpicked.co.uk
web: www.handpickedhotels.co.uk/nortonhouse
dir: *M8 junct 2, off A8, 0.5m past Edinburgh Airport*

Outstanding modern Scottish cooking near the airport

An 1840-built mansion, Norton House is something of a rural retreat in 55 acres (which explains its popularity for weddings) although only a 20 minute drive from the city centre. There's a health club, spa and swimming pool as well as the full complement of conference facilities. Ushers restaurant, which takes its name from the Usher family of brewers who once lived here, is a discreetly elegant room, its walls decorated in a neutral tone, with brown leather seats at white-clothed tables and a patterned red carpet. This is the showcase of Graeme Shaw's cooking of astounding quality, seen, for example, in a creative and successful starter of three fat scallops with the contrasts of cucumber and lime mayonnaise and pickle, shards of potato bread adding another layer of texture, and in another of rabbit terrine with pickled vegetables, pear and gingerbread. Attention to detail and a breathtaking level of technical skill never falter. Smoked roe deer, accurately timed and tender, arrives under a juniper crumb on a bed of shredded sprouts, Morteau sausage adding an additional rich dimension, complemented by earthy chestnut and quince purée. Fish is no less impressive: a well-composed main course of monkfish, for instance, in curry sauce with pickled grapes, sweet potato and kale. Breads are enjoyable, incidentals such as canapés are well up to snuff, and an eye for attractive presentation is never more apparent than in desserts: perhaps Valrhona chocolate delice, rich and velvety and a joy to eat, with Amaretto ice cream and poached pears, or poached rhubarb with yogurt sorbet and goats' milk tapioca. A nine-course tasting menu, with matching wines an additional option, is also available.

Chef Graeme Shaw, Glen Bilins **Owner** Hand Picked Hotels **Seats** 22, Pr/dining room 40 **Times** 7-9.30, Closed Jan-Feb, Sun-Tue, L all week **Prices** Tasting menu £65-£90, Starter £9.50-£12.50, Main £20.50-£38, Dessert £7.50-£8.95, Service optional **Wines** 80 bottles over £30, 15 bottles under £30, 12 by glass **Parking** 100 **Notes** Tasting menu 8 course, Vegetarian available, Children welcome

Number One, The Balmoral 🌸🌸🌸

EDINBURGH   Map 21 NT27

Modern Scottish V 🍷 NOTABLE WINE LIST

tel: 0131 557 6727 **1 Princes St EH2 2EQ**
email: numberone@roccofortehotel.com **web:** www.restaurantnumberone.com
dir: *Follow city centre signs. Hotel at E end of Princes St, adjacent to Waverley Station*

Exquisite modern cooking in a majestic hotel

With its soaring clock tower (set three minutes fast to help you catch your train) looming above Waverley station, the landmark Balmoral hotel is one of the country's grand old railway hotels, though that classification rather belies its modern-day opulence. The public rooms establish a lavish tone with as much marble and fancy plasterwork as anyone could reasonably ask for, and the Number One restaurant looks pretty sharp after a refurbishment in 2015 added classy oak flooring to offset the dove-grey and gold banquettes and striking artworks on loan from the Royal College of Art that adorn its red lacquered walls. Executive chef Jeff Bland has reworked the menus in honour of the new look, but his tirelessly inventive culinary intelligence still drives dishes that are boldly but carefully conceived. Assertive flavours dovetail provocatively together, as is exquisitely demonstrated in a visually stunning first course of game pithivier, when a jug of partridge jus is poured into the pie to mingle with layers of partridge, foie gras and Savoy cabbage, its gamey richness offset by pickled root vegetables and a quenelle of silky carrot purée. Main course is an assiette of organic pork, each of the cuts delivering superb textures and depth of flavour, partnered with black pudding, sweet onion purée and apricot ketchup, the whole composition brought together with an anise-infused jus. Imaginative fishy ideas include lemon sole with cockles, grapes, celery and a classic Véronique sauce, and dessert concludes with a celebration of the humble apple, its focus a parfait of green apple matched sensuously with cinnamon doughnuts, caramel and fromage blanc ice cream.

Chef Jeff Bland, Brian Grigor **Owner** Rocco Forte Hotels **Seats** 60 **Times** 6.30-10, Closed 2 wks Jan, L all week **Prices** Fixed D 3 course £70, Tasting menu £79-£110, Starter £19.50, Main £37, Dessert £13.50, Service optional **Wines** 350 bottles over £30, 30 by glass **Parking** NCP & on street **Notes** Tasting menu 7/10 course, Scottish menu 4 course £75, Children welcome

EDINBURGH *continued*

One Square

🏵 Modern British

tel: 0131 221 6422 **Sheraton Grand Hotel & Spa, 1 Festival Square EH3 9SR**
email: info@onesquareedinburgh.co.uk **web:** www.onesquareedinburgh.co.uk
dir: *Off Lothian Road. Entrance to hotel from Festival Square*

Modern regional cooking in a trendy setting

The views of Edinburgh Castle certainly give a sense of place to One Square, a slick, modern dining option in the Sheraton Grand Hotel. The menu plays its part, too, serving up a good number of traditional dishes, albeit spruced up for the modern consumer. The restaurant and bar are sleek, contemporary spaces, with floor-to-ceiling windows and a cool, classy finish. The broad menu aims to satisfy all day long, so there are steak sandwiches, BLT, a posh burger and the like, but this kitchen can turn its hand to many things. Their version of partan bree is rich with crab and comes topped with fritters made from the brown meat, or go for monkish 'scampi' with a citrus mayonnaise. Next up, lamb Wellington with spiced carrot purée and burnt leek has the meat nicely pink, the pastry cooked just right, while a fishy main course sees sea bream partnered with Madras-spiced mussel broth. Finish with a warm apple and bramble tart.

Chef Craig Hart **Owner** Sheraton Grand **Seats** 90, Pr/dining room 40 **Times** 7am-11pm, All-day dining **Prices** Fixed L 2 course £16, Fixed D 3 course £20, Tasting menu £60, Starter £6.50-£13.50, Main £18-£32, Dessert £5.50-£10.50, Service optional 10% **Wines** 27 bottles over £30, 22 bottles under £30, 11 by glass **Parking** 125 **Notes** Unique dining experiences at The Pass or The Kitchen Table, Sunday L £29-£35, Vegetarian available, Children welcome

Plumed Horse

🏵🏵🏵 *– see opposite*

Pompadour by Galvin

🏵🏵🏵 *– see opposite*

Restaurant Mark Greenaway

🏵🏵🏵 *– see page 628*

Restaurant Martin Wishart

🏵🏵🏵🏵 *– see page 629*

Find out more about how we assess for Rosette awards on page 9

Rhubarb at Prestonfield House

🏵🏵 Traditional British 🍷 NOTABLE WINE LIST

tel: 0131 225 1333 **Priestfield Rd EH16 5UT**
email: reservations@prestonfield.com **web:** www.rhubarb-restaurant.com
dir: *Exit city centre on Nicholson St, onto Dalkeith Rd. At lights turn left into Priestfield Rd. Prestonfield on left*

Opulent surroundings for high-impact cooking

One of the city's most visually impressive dining rooms, Rhubarb at Prestonfield House is a real stunner with its richly glamorous decor of darkly opulent shades of red, period portraits and glinting chandeliers. It fits the bill in this 17th-century mansion, its restaurant named in honour of the Asian vegetable that Sir Alexander Dick brought to Scotland in 1746. The rest is history, and crumble. The kitchen neatly combines classical preparations with more contemporary ideas in a menu that has broad appeal. New season's asparagus (both white and green) star in a first course with morels and squat lobsters from Mull, or go for another that combines Gressingham duck meat and foie gras in a terrine and matches it with the creative combination of lime brioche and macerated blueberries. Among main courses, Peterhead cod is served en papillote with cider and tamarind paste and curried celery (plus some crab meat), and guinea fowl with its leg meat in an accompanying pastilla. There are classic Scottish steaks, too. For dessert, various textures of strawberry make a pretty picture on the plate, or go for tarte Tatin for two.

Times 12-2/6.30-10

Plumed Horse

Modern European **NOTABLE WINE LIST**

tel: 0131 554 5556 **50-54 Henderson St, Leith EH6 6DE**
email: contact@plumedhorse.co.uk **web:** www.plumedhorse.co.uk
dir: *From city centre N on Leith Walk, left into Great Junction St & 1st right into Henderson St*

Consistently impressive contemporary cuisine

Tony Borthwick's Plumed Horse has been at the sharp end of the Leith dining scene for a decade now and continues to offer refined and vibrant food that keeps customers coming back. It's a civilised space of striking artworks, calming shades of blue and pristine table settings. Choose from a fixed-price menu or the tasting option and expect dishes that impress with their sophistication and execution. The menu features some excellent Scottish ingredients at the heart of it all. Ballimore oysters (from Loch Fyne) are put to excellent use in a pannacotta opener alongside home-cured salmon flavoured with passionfruit, with the addition of a pink grapefruit and champagne jelly and two caviars. Another starter sees Dunsyre Blue cheese served up in a brioche tartlet with heirloom carrots four ways and topped with a walnut and cumin crumble. Flavours hit home and everything looks pretty as a picture on the plate. Among main courses, loin of rabbit with a truffle stuffing is partnered with sautéed kidney and chestnut gnocchi, while another

sees roast fillet of halibut dressed with a Gewürztraminer fumet. The level of refinement and attention to detail continues into desserts such as a salted caramel tart with beurre noisette ice cream and caramelised comice pears.

Chef Tony Borthwick, William Grubb **Owner** The Company of The Plumed Horse Ltd **Seats** 40 **Times** 12-2/7-9, Closed Xmas, New Year, 2 wks summer, 1 wk Etr, Sun-Mon **Prices** Fixed L 3 course £24.50, Fixed D 3 course £55, Tasting menu £69, Service optional **Wines** 229 bottles over £30, 32 bottles under £30, 16 by glass **Parking** On street **Notes** Tasting menu 8/9 course, Vegetarian available, Children 5 yrs+

Pompadour by Galvin

Modern French **V**

tel: 0131 222 8975 & 222 8777 **Waldorf Astoria Edinburgh, The Caledonian, Princes St EH1 2AB**
email: pompadour.reservations@waldorfastoria.com
web: www.galvinrestaurants.com
dir: *Situated on east end of Princess St, on Rutland St & Lothian Rd*

Haute cuisine Galvin-style comes to Edinburgh

The empire-building Galvin brothers came to town in 2012 and set up their high-end gastronomic flagship in the Caledonian Waldorf Astoria, a grand Victorian railway-era hotel once more resplendent after a megabucks refurbishment. 'The Pomp' – as locals affectionately know its grande dame of a restaurant – has been a byword for opulence since it opened its doors in 1925. The belle époque extravaganza was always considered to be the hottest ticket in town before the culinary opposition over in the rejuvenated Leith docks upped the ante, and it is still a contender. Looks-wise, none of the newcomers can trump its wedding cake plasterwork, delicate hand-painted panelling and peerless views of Edinburgh Castle perched upon its lofty crag. They've certainly nailed the luxurious service vibe too, with a full-works, classical French hierarchy as

professional, charming and efficient a team as you're ever likely to encounter, including a seriously knowledgeable sommelier to guide you through the oh-so French listings. Naturally, the Pompadour shows the same Francophile culinary direction as the Galvins' celebrated London establishments, delivering rich seasonal ingredients that sit together happily, prepared with razor-sharp technical ability and realised with haute cuisine flair. A procession of intricately presented dishes begins with a terrine of Ayrshire rabbit, ham hock and foie gras with a leek and hazelnut salad. Next up, a pavé of cod arrives with a delicate dressing of light curry and golden raisins, baby spinach and cauliflower purée, or two might sign up for a roast Chateaubriand with creamed spinach, potato millefeuille and confit garlic. Finally, Valrhona's exceptional Guanaja chocolate provides the basis for an exemplary mousse alongside mango sorbet and grilled mango.

Chef Fraser Allan **Owner** Chris & Jeff Galvin **Seats** 60, Pr/dining room 20 **Times** 6-10, Closed 2 wks Jan, Sun-Mon, L all week **Prices** Fixed D 3 course £29, Tasting menu £68, Starter £9.50-£21.50, Main £24.50-£34.50, Dessert £8.50-£10.50 **Wines** 229 bottles over £30, 6 bottles under £30, 28 by glass **Parking** 42 **Notes** Tasting menu 7 course, Children welcome

Restaurant Mark Greenaway ❀ ❀ ❀

Modern British 🍷 NOTABLE WINE LIST

tel: 0131 226 1155 **69 North Castle St EH2 3LJ**
email: bookings@rmgedinburgh.com
web: www.markgreenaway.com
dir: *Phone for directions*

Tautly controlled, imaginative dishes from a Scottish food ambassador

Mark Greenaway upped sticks to his current location right over the road from Martin Wishart's brasserie, The Honours, back in 2013 and is cooking up a storm. One of the leading lights of the Scottish culinary firmament, Greenaway has cooked for Scotland on the *Great British Menu*, and after stints in some pretty top-class kitchens, he has been doing his own thing since 2011, the current setting being one of classy, understated civility, with rich blue-grey walls and comfy chairs upholstered with swirly fabric at linen-swathed tables. Greenaway bangs the drum for Scotland's fine produce, showing off pedigree ingredients in dishes brimming with flair and imagination. If the budget is tight, come for the storming value Market menu (served at lunch or early evening), otherwise the carte offers six choices at each course, or if choosing is just too much work, leave it all up to the chef with an eight-course taster. There's lots going on in starters such as Loch Fyne crab 'cannelloni' with smoked cauliflower custard, lemon pearls, herb butter and baby coriander, but it's all thought through and works a treat. Main courses could deliver more labour-intensive compositions along the lines of 40-day aged Aberdeen Angus beef fillet with pommes dauphine, a pressing of osso buco, beetroot pickled shallots, watercress, aubergine purée and red wine jus, or a more orthodox meat-and-fish combo of monkfish wrapped in Parma ham with crispy chicken wings, baby turnip, confit carrots and brown butter jus. Greenaway has a thing for desserts, so expect complex variations on retro themes with a good dose of fun — baked Alaska, say, comprising salt-baked pineapple, green tea sponge, coconut meringue, lime espuma and vanilla ice cream.

Chef Mark Greenaway **Owner** Mark Greenaway, Nicola Jack
Seats 60 **Times** 12-2.30/5.30-10, Closed 25-26 Dec, 1-2 Jan, Sun-Mon **Prices** Prices not confirmed, Service optional **Wines** 67 bottles over £30, 25 bottles under £30, 13 by glass **Notes** Vegetarian available, Children 5 yrs+

Restaurant Martin Wishart ❀❀❀❀

Modern French **V** 🍷 NOTABLE WINE LIST

tel: 0131 553 3557 **54 The Shore, Leith EH6 6RA**
email: info@martin-wishart.co.uk
dir: *Off the A199*

Contemporary cooking from Scotland's culinary darling

Down by the waterside of Leith's docks is one of the UK's foremost dining destinations, a culinary colossus that has been at the forefront of Scotland's culinary renaissance since 1999. Martin Wishart worked with many of the big names of the classic and modern French school before it became his turn to inspire the next generation. Since opening here there has been expansion elsewhere to spread the message (Cameron House in Loch Lomond and a swish brasserie in the centre of Edinburgh called The Honours), but it is in Leith's refined and stylish venue with neutral shades and elegant table settings that the best work is done. Immaculate staff help to set the tone and prove that the attention to detail here covers all areas. If you're looking for a bargain come at lunch Tuesday to Friday, but really and truly this is the sort of place where you might want to consider pushing the boat out. There are three tasting menus to choose from — seafood and veggie versions alongside the regular one — and a concise fixed-price carte. Things get off to a flyer with bread served with Scottish butter that shows the kitchen possesses the confidence to do things simply and very, very well. Canapés don't let the side down, including warm cauliflower beignet subtly fired up by curry oil, and an impressive squid ink cracker with smoked salmon and avocado. Next up, Orkney scallop and black truffle arrive in a first course with a series of flawless purées (Jerusalem artichoke and sweet potato) and a hazelnut crumb, while another sees Gigha halibut arrive céviche style with the flavours of passiontruit and mango. The balance of flavours and textures in each dish is stunning. Borders roe deer is the central focus of a main course with smoky charred onions (BBQ they say) with braised lettuce and dates, or how about a pumpkin risotto off the veggie tasting menu, flavoured with walnut pesto and Lord of the Hundreds cheese? A pre-dessert of great visual impact arrives next; an apple and blackberry number with mousse, gel and a slab of meringue. When it comes to dessert, expect something rather special such as Ivoire white chocolate mousse with a 'milk sheet', ginger biscuit and rhubarb sorbet — white chocolate has never been so sophisticated. The wine list is a class act with a good number of glass and half-bottle options.

Chef Martin Wishart, Joe Taggart **Owner** Martin Wishart **Seats** 50, Pr/dining room 10 **Times** 12-2/6.30-10, Closed 25-26 Dec, 1 Jan, 2 wks Jan, Sun-Mon **Prices** Fixed L 3 course fr £28.50, Tasting menu fr £75, Service optional **Wines** 250 bottles over £30, 9 bottles under £30, 24 by glass **Parking** On street **Notes** Tasting menu 6 course, ALC 3 course £70, Children welcome

EDINBURGH *continued*

The Scran & Scallie

Traditional Scottish | NOTABLE WINE LIST

tel: 0131 332 6281 **1 Comely Bank Rd EH4 1DT**
email: info@scranandscallie.com
dir: *Located in Stockbridge behind Inverleith Park & Botanical Gdns*

Classy pub food from two stellar chefs

From the local maestros behind The Kitchin and Castle Terrace, Tom Kitchin and Dominic Jack's pub is done out in fashionable shabby-chic, with exposed brick walls and heritage artworks and fabrics. It's a popular place with bags of style and a relaxed mood, just the right sort of setting for a menu of rustic dishes combining refined modern classics with traditional preparations that might unjustly have fallen out of favour. 'From nature to plate,' the restaurant says. First up might be a solidly stuffed raviolo parcel of ham in watercress soup, or the bracing simplicity of half-a-dozen oysters. Main-course roasted monkfish swaddled in pancetta with Puy lentils is another classy little number, as an alternative to versions of pot-au-feu or the house fish pie. The feel-good factor continues into desserts such as sponge-topped apple tart with a rich crème anglaise served cold, or chocolate brioche pudding with pistachio ice cream.

Chef James Chapman, Tom Kitchin, Dominic Jack **Owner** Tom Kitchin, Dominic Jack **Seats** 70 **Times** 12-3.30/6-10.30, Closed 25 Dec **Prices** Fixed L 3 course £15, Starter £6-£12.50, Main £9.50-£22, Dessert £5.50-£8.50, Service optional **Wines** 26 bottles over £30, 22 bottles under £30, 33 by glass **Parking** On street **Notes** All-day dining Sat-Sun 12-10pm, Sunday L £16.50-£17.50, Vegetarian available, Children welcome

The Stockbridge Restaurant

Modern European

tel: 0131 226 6766 **54 Saint Stephen St EH3 5AL**
email: jane@thestockbridgerestaurant.com **web:** www.thestockbridgerestaurant.com
dir: *From A90 towards city centre, left Craigleith Rd B900, 2nd exit at rdbt B900, straight on to Kerr St, turn left onto Saint Stephen St*

Spirited flavours and assured cooking in distinctive surroundings

The Stockbridge is a charming restaurant, accessed down a flight of steps, in the affluent area it's named after. Dark-grey walls, some stone, are hung with vivid modern artwork and mirrors, and spotlights in the low ceiling create pools of light on crisply-clothed tables with upholstered chairs. The cooking goes from strength to strength, with the kitchen producing consistently well-conceived dishes from fine Scottish produce. Seared scallops with Serrano ham, butternut squash purée, apple salsa and caramelised walnuts, or chorizo and red pepper risotto flaked with parmesan are the sort of modern ideas that crop up among starters. A lot can go on

in main courses, but an assured touch means flavours are clean and well defined. Try perfectly cooked grilled halibut fillet served with crayfish and scallop mousse, braised beef cheeks, crushed potatoes, spinach and red wine jus, for instance, or roast duck breast with a foie gras boudin, a confit spring roll, chicory and potato terrine. A pre-dessert arrives before the real thing, which might be a theme on chocolate: rich brûlée, brownie, mousse and ice cream.

The Stockbridge Restaurant

Chef Jason Gallagher **Owner** Jason Gallagher, Jane Walker **Seats** 40 **Times** 7-9.30, Closed 1st 2 wks Jan, Mon, L all week (open on request only min 6 people) **Prices** Fixed L 2 course £12.95-£14.95, Fixed D 3 course £24.95-£28.95, Starter £7.95-£12.45, Main £17.95-£24.95, Dessert £6.45-£8.95, Service optional **Wines** 31 bottles over £30, 23 bottles under £30, 7 by glass **Parking** On street **Notes** Vegetarian available, Children until 8pm

Ten Hill Place Hotel

Modern, Traditional British **NEW**

tel: 0131 662 2080 **10 Hill Place EH8 9DS**
email: T@tenhillplace.com **web:** www.tenhillplace.com
dir: *Phone for directions*

On a cobbled street overlooking a quiet square

Can there be another hotel that uses its profits to help train the world's would-be surgeons? That is what this part-Georgian, part-new hotel owned by The Royal College of Surgeons of Edinburgh does – surely something to think about while enjoying a drink and listening to the pianist in the popular wine bar (Thursday to Sunday, with breaks, of course)? If you're thinking of trying Scotland's classic dish for the first time, then head for the elegantly decorated and furnished restaurant for a starter of haggis pastilla with neep (turnip) fondant, mashed potato and whisky jelly. Follow with braised and pressed pork belly with red onion purée, buttered mash and black pudding, or seared Scottish salmon with smoked haddock foam, Jersey Royals, burnt pickles and onions. Finish with vanilla pannacotta, rhubarb sorbet and jelly.

Chef Alan Dickson **Owner** Royal College of Surgeons **Seats** 54 **Times** 5-9.30, Closed Xmas, L all week **Prices** Starter £4.25-£6.50, Main £11-£21, Dessert £6-£7.50, Service optional **Wines** 1 bottle over £30, 22 bottles under £30, 21 by glass **Parking** 6, On street **Notes** Vegetarian available, Children welcome

Timberyard

– *see opposite*

21212

– *see page 632*

– see opposite
– see page 632

Timberyard ❀❀❀

Modern Scottish 🍾 NOTABLE WINE LIST

tel: 0131 221 1222 **10 Lady Lawson St EH3 9DS**
email: eat@timberyard.co **web:** www.timberyard.co
dir: *From Princes St, Lothian Rd (A700) left onto Castle Terrace,
right at rdbt, left onto Lady Lawson St, restaurant on right*

Creative modern cooking in a cool, casual setting

Anyone looking to get a handle on the restaurant zeitgeist need
look no further than Timberyard. In this old Victorian warehouse,
two generations of the Radford family have created a venue that
combines today's favoured urban rusticity with a philosophy based
around pride and passion for the ingredients. There's nothing
cynical about the people or the place. The main dining space
reflects the heritage of the building with whitewashed walls,
chunky floorboards and cast-iron pillars, and there are outside
tables in the south-facing courtyard. Ben Radford leads the line in
the kitchen with a forager's instinct and the focus on small
producers, with smoking and butchery taking place on the
premises, and their own veg patch to call upon. The menu is
structured such that you can go the small plate, tasting way or
keep a larger portion all to yourself. The ambition of the kitchen is
revealed from the get-go with the arrival of an amuse such as a
langoustine speared on a twig and topped with pretty flowers and
herbs, and the excellent sourdough bread which arrives in a tin
with whipped butter and dried sea buckthorn. Compelling flavour
combinations and simple but effective presentation is a
trademark: breast of guinea fowl (cooked just right) with celeriac,
broad beans, barley and delicately placed herbs and flowers, or a
main course of a superb piece of wild turbot with a slick of squid
ink and flavours that excite and impress. There are clever ideas
and dynamic flavours for dessert, too, such as burnt milk ice
cream with a host of chocolaty items and spiced bread crumbs.
The wine list sticks to Europe (including England and the East),
and they make lots of their own softies such as a delicious sea
buckthorn soda.

Chef Ben Radford **Owner** The Radford family **Seats** 72, Pr/dining
room 10 **Times** 12-2/5.30-9.30, Closed 1 wk Apr, Oct, Xmas, Sun-
Mon **Prices** Fixed L 2 course £23, Tasting menu £65, Starter £12-
£13, Main £21-£26, Dessert £10, Service optional **Wines** 150
bottles over £30, 10 bottles under £30, 13 by glass **Parking** Castle
Terrace NCP, On street **Notes** L 4 course £34, Tasting menu 8
course, Vegetarian available, Children welcome

21212 ❀❀❀❀

Modern French 🍷 NOTABLE WINE LIST

tel: 0131 523 1030 & 0845 222 1212 *(Calls cost 7p per minute plus your phone company's access charge)* **3 Royal Ter EH7 5AB**
email: reservation@21212restaurant.co.uk
web: www.21212restaurant.co.uk
dir: *Calton Hill, city centre*

Intense flavours and fun from a true culinary genius

When Paul Kitching and Katie O'Brien looked to Edinburgh to fulfil their ambition of opening a restaurant with rooms they struck exceedingly lucky with this sandstone property on Royal Terrace. It's a real classic with an exterior stolidity and great charisma once you cross the threshold. There is real personality on the inside, with contemporary design and classic elegance combining to create somewhere rather special. The four bedrooms have a high-end finish and there are quirky touches here and there. The high-ceilinged restaurant has ornate plasterwork and a classy finish with curvy banquettes, muslin-draped walls and windows looking out over Royal Terrace and the gardens beyond, while a glass partition separates diners from the open-to-view kitchen. Paul is one of the UK's most idiosyncratic chefs, right at the pointy tip of the cutting edge, and with Katie leading the line front-of-house with charm and efficiency, they form a potent partnership. If you're wondering what the name represents, the answer is the five-course menu format: a choice of two starters, two mains and two desserts, with one soup course and a cheese course in-between. That is the offering at lunch, but at dinner an extra dish has been added to the starter/main/dessert element, so it's really 31313. There's a sense of fun in the menu descriptions, which may well bamboozle, but Katie can enlighten and rest assured a good deal of thought has gone into every element. This is creative and dynamic modern food, where supremely good ingredients are cleverly worked into dishes that inspire and amaze. A first course called 'Winter Shellfish Warmer' combines smoked salmon, haddock infused with saffron, brown crab and caviar cream, plus a risotto flavoured with Beaufort cheese, Scottish roots and leek purée, into a dish that makes perfect sense in the eating. How about (and this is verbatim) 'Beef Fillet Cow Py, mooooolllliiii, H.P. P.P.P.P.P.Nuts'? 'Best End of Lamb, Corned Lancashire Hash'

needs less explanation, with additional elements such as prunes and bacon and bread sauce. Needless to say, there's no change of tack when it comes to desserts, not when 'Fig Rock & Rolls' are up for grabs, with a crispy crème brûlée, sweetcorn and cottage cheese. When it comes to deciding what to drink with this sort of food, it is worth seeking out the advice of the excellent sommelier.

Chef Paul Kitching **Owner** P Kitching, K O'Brien, J Revle
Seats 36, Pr/dining room 10 **Times** 12-1.45/6.45-9.30, Closed 2 wks Jan, 2 wks summer, Sun-Mon **Prices** Fixed L 2 course fr £22, Fixed D 3 course fr £49, Service optional **Wines** 245 bottles over £30, 9 bottles under £30, 6 by glass **Parking** On street
Notes Fixed D Tue-Thu 4/5 course £58/£69, Fri-Sat 5 course only, Vegetarian available, Children 5 yrs+

EDINBURGH *continued*

The Witchery by the Castle

Traditional Scottish **NOTABLE WINE LIST**

tel: 0131 225 5613 **Castlehill, The Royal Mile EH1 2NF**
email: mail@thewitchery.com **web:** www.thewitchery.com
dir: *Top of Royal Mile at gates of Edinburgh Castle*

Confident Scottish cooking in magnificent surroundings

This 16th-century merchant's house by the gates of the castle makes a strikingly atmospheric, even Gothic-looking restaurant. The Witchery itself is lined by carved oak panelling hung with tapestries under a heraldic-painted ceiling, while the Secret Garden dining room occupies an enclosed courtyard with a painted ceiling and doors leading to a terrace with terrific views. The cooking follows a contemporary route built on Scottish traditions, with the kitchen using quality native produce. Start with partridge with grilled potato terrine and burned onion mayonnaise and follow that with beef Rossini with Madeira jus, pommes Anna and spinach. Seafood gets a strong showing, from seared scallops with Ibérico ham and garlic butter to monkfish poached in olive oil with grilled kohlrabi, cumin-spiced lentils and curry velouté. Puddings are worth a punt: perhaps pineapple tarte Tatin with rum-flavoured caramel and coconut ice cream.

Chef Douglas Roberts **Owner** James Thomson **Seats** 110, Pr/dining room 60 **Times** 12-4/5.30-11.30, Closed 25 Dec **Prices** Prices not confirmed, Service optional **Wines** 12 by glass **Notes** Pre/post-theatre 2 course £15.95, Sunday L, Vegetarian available, Children 6 yrs+

FALKIRK

BANKNOCK Map 21 NS77

Glenskirlie House & Castle

Modern British

tel: 01324 840201 **Kilsyth Rd FK4 1UF**
email: macaloneys@glenskirliehouse.com **web:** www.glenskirliehouse.com
dir: *Follow A803 signed Kilsyth/Bonnybridge, at T-junct turn right. Hotel 1m on right*

Labour-intensive dishes in the modern British style

A castle for the 21st century, Glenskirlie is a bright white pile, kitted out with a conical-roofed turret here, a little step-gabling there, for the general idea. Set in central Scotland, not far from Falkirk, it's a country retreat that welcomes the wedding trade, and also has a range of eating options, from the informal Grill to a room for a private do, as well as the main dining room, an intimate space done in Victorian-style leaf-pattern wallpaper, that looks braw in the candlelit evenings. The menus have now taken a more obviously modern British turn, opening with complex constructions such as seared scallops with crab and lime mousse, pickled watermelon, lemon-rind purée and Jerusalem artichoke. Mains are no less labour-intensive, partnering venison loin with braised venison and potato terrine, celeriac fondant, smoked apple purée and wilted spring greens in red wine jus. Desserts spin variations on apple, or fashion banana into a parfait alongside caramelised banana, cinnamon pain perdu and nutty ganache.

Chef Daryl Jordan **Owner** John Macaloney, Colin Macaloney **Seats** 54, Pr/dining room 150 **Times** 12-2/6-9, Closed 26-27 Dec, 1-4 Jan **Prices** Fixed L 2 course £19.99, Fixed D 3 course fr £29.99, Starter £7.95-£13.95, Main £21.99-£28.99, Dessert £8.25-£8.95, Service optional **Wines** 50 bottles over £30, 25 bottles under £30, 11 by glass **Parking** 100 **Notes** Sunday L £24.99, Vegetarian available, Children welcome

Read all about our Wine Award winners on pages 17–19

POLMONT
Map 21 NS97

Macdonald Inchyra Hotel and Spa
Modern, Traditional

tel: 01324 711911 **Grange Rd FK2 0YB**
email: inchyra@macdonald-hotels.co.uk **web:** www.macdonald-hotels.co.uk
dir: *2 mins from M9 junct 5*

Brasserie-style cooking in a popular hotel

The solid-stone Inchyra is a smart hotel with a plush spa and all mod cons, making it a big hit on the wedding scene. It's also home to The Scottish Steak Club, a modern brasserie-style dining option done out in swathes of rich leather, animal prints and dark wood. They've got the relaxed mood just right, too, and the presence of a Josper grill in the kitchen suggests that detail has been attended to. The menu is a fashionable foray into brasserie-land, so prawn cocktail or shallot and goats' cheese tart might kick things off. Next up, a steak seems the way to go: rib-eye on the bone, perhaps, cooked pink as requested, and served with the classic accompaniments of fat-cut chips, vine tomatoes, watercress and a béarnaise sauce. There are plenty of non-steak options like pie of the day or jumbo scampi, plus more of that red meat fashioned into a burger. Finish with sticky toffee pudding or suchlike.

Times 12-9.45, All-day dining

FIFE

ANSTRUTHER
Map 21 N050

The Cellar
– see below

CUPAR
Map 21 N031

Ostlers Close Restaurant
Modern British V

tel: 01334 655574 **Bonnygate KY15 4BU**
dir: *In small lane off main street, A91*

Fabulous seasonal produce and skilled hand in the kitchen

Down a narrow alley just off the main street, this one-time scullery of a 17th-century Temperance hotel has been a favoured foodie bolt-hole since 1981. That's when James (Jimmy) and Amanda Graham bought the place, and their passion and dedication has put it well and truly on the map. With red-painted walls and linen-clad tables, it's an intimate space (just 26 covers), which is watched over by Amanda with a good deal of charm and enthusiasm. Jimmy's pleasingly concise, hand-written menus make the most of fruit, veg and herbs from the restaurant's garden (and polytunnel), and at the right time of year he can be found gathering wild mushrooms from the local woods. Seasonal Scottish produce takes centre stage, and you might spot an occasional Spanish influence amid the well-crafted modern repertoire. Dishes are packed with flavour, never over worked, with the ingredients given room to shine. Start, perhaps, with roast breast of Perthshire partridge with Stornoway black pudding mash and pork belly confit, before moving on to fillet of wild Scottish halibut (perfectly cooked) served with Pittenweem prawns, winter greens and saffron sauce. Vanilla pannacotta with a compôte of fruits, damson gin coulis and damson sorbet makes a fine and refreshing finale.

Chef James Graham **Owner** James & Amanda Graham **Seats** 26
Times 7-9.30, Closed 25-26 Dec, 1-2 Jan, 2 wks Apr, 2 wks Oct, Sun-Mon, L all week
Prices Starter £7.50-£12.50, Main £22-£26, Dessert £7.95, Service optional
Wines 23 bottles over £30, 44 bottles under £30, 6 by glass **Parking** On street, public car park **Notes** Fixed D 3 course Tue-Fri, Nov-May £30, Children 6 yrs+ D

The Cellar

ANSTRUTHER
Map 21 N050

Scottish, Modern British **NEW**
tel: 01333 310378 **24 East Green KY10 3AA**
email: thecellarrestaurant@outlook.com
dir: *Behind Scottish Fisheries Museum*

Dynamic contemporary cooking in an intimate setting

Just off the harbour front is a pretty cobbled courtyard leading to the 17th-century house that is home to The Cellar. The place was once a cooperage and smokery so it is fitting that it has been providing fine food for over 40 years. The current incumbent is chef-patron Billy Boyter, who returned from Edinburgh to his home town to take over the helm in April 2014 after heading up the kitchen at Number One, The Balmoral. The dining room has lots of period charm where bare stone walls, low ceilings with ancient beams, and an open fire create an intimate setting for Boyter to show off his considerable talents with a sophisticated modern British menu. Thoroughly grounded in classical technique, main course – 'duck, choucroute, celeriac, bramble' – delivers pink duck breast, its caramelised skin covered with bramble jam and hazelnuts, on a bed of choucroute beside superb purées of potato and celeriac. Fish cookery, too, is handled with real skill – an immaculately-timed, crisp-skinned fillet of stone bass is accompanied by curried giant couscous mixed with jewel-like pieces of red pepper, raisins and golden sultanas, and curried cauliflower purée. Before this, a croquette of pork cheek and mealy pudding (made with oatmeal, onions, suet and spices) is offset with lemon mayonnaise and pickled fennel, or crab with crème fraîche is matched with white turnip and borage leaf. Desserts end on a high note with ginger pannacotta paired with jelly, a doughnut and poached sticks of forced rhubarb, and vanilla-rich ice cream, or a knockout trio of rich chocolate crémeux, banana ice cream and lime curd.

Chef Billy Boyter **Owner** The Boyter family **Seats** 28
Times 12.30-1.45/6.30-9, Closed 25-26 Dec, 1 Jan, Mon-Tue, L Wed **Prices** Prices not confirmed, Service optional **Parking** On street **Notes** Sunday L, Vegetarian available, Children 5 yrs+

ELIE
Map 21 NO40

Sangsters
◉◉ Modern British

tel: 01333 331001 **51 High St KY9 1BZ**
dir: *From St Andrews on A917 take B9131 to Anstruther, right at rdbt onto A917 to Elie. (11m from St Andrews)*

Modern cooking on the village high street

Bruce and Jackie Sangster set up shop plumb in the middle of the main street of this unassuming Fife village, and set about wowing the locals with finely-crafted modern Scottish cooking that showcases plenty of local produce, including apples and herbs from the back garden. It all takes place in a smart dining room hung with landscape pictures, and furnished with crisply dressed tables and high-backed chairs. Dinner follows a four-course, fixed-price format, kicking off perhaps with seared Ross-shire scallops in a Thai-fragrant dressing of chilli, ginger, galangal and lemongrass, before an intermediate fish course, which could be steamed stuffed Loch Duart salmon, teamed with Arbroath smokie and Finnan haddock, in Sauternes and ginger sauce. Main course might be pork two ways, braised cheek and fillet stuffed with black pudding and apricot, with fennel, cabbage and braising juices, while mango and white chocolate parfait with tropical fruits and a sesame and poppy seed biscuit brings things to a close in style.

Times 12.30-1.30/7-8.30, Closed 25-26 Dec, Jan, 1st wk Nov, Mon (also Tue winter), L Tue-Sat, D Sun

PEAT INN
Map 21 NO40

The Peat Inn
◉◉◉ – *see page 636 and advert below*

ST ANDREWS
Map 21 NO51

The Adamson
◉◉ British

tel: 01334 479191 **127 South St KY16 9UH**
email: info@theadamson.com
dir: *Phone for directions*

Confident cooking in a classy modern brasserie

Once home to the pioneering photographer and physician, Dr John Adamson (hence the name), the handsome building is these days home to a chef who was runner-up in the 2013 edition of the BBC's *MasterChef: The Professionals* (well, it's not his home as such, but it is his place of work). The restaurant has a cool, rustic-chic finish, with exposed bricks, darkwood tables and a bar that serves up a nifty cocktail. The menu brings vim and vigour to the brasserie format with more than a touch of contemporary style and some high quality ingredients. Parmesan crème brûlée is a winning starter showing the ambition of this kitchen, with chargrilled Scottish squid with chorizo jam an appealing alternative. Braised blade of beef stars in a main course with haricot purée and sauce diablo, while a fishy option might be Atlantic sole with wilted spring greens and cockle burnt butter. The standard does not falter with desserts such as a great looking (and tasting) dish of bitter dark chocolate with salted caramel and banana.

Chef Scott Davies **Owner** Ken Dalton, Julie Lewis **Seats** 68
Times 12-3/5-10, Closed 25-26 Dec, 1 Jan **Prices** Fixed L 2 course £13-£18, Fixed D 3 course £16.50-£21.50, Starter £3.50-£14.50, Main £9.95-£34.50, Dessert £3.50-£7.95, Service optional **Wines** 16 bottles over £30, 18 bottles under £30, 12 by glass **Parking** On street **Notes** Chateaubriand to share £69, Sun L 2 sharing £29.50, Sunday L £9.50-£21.50, Vegetarian available, Children welcome

Ardgowan Hotel
◉ Steakhouse, Scottish **NEW**

tel: 01334 472970 **2 Playfair Ter, North St KY16 9HX**
email: info@ardgowanhotel.co.uk **web:** www.ardgowanhotel.co.uk
dir: *A91 onto A917. 100 mtrs from rdbt on left*

Accomplished cooking in golfing hotel

Built in 1847 and designed by the famous Scottish architect George Rae, this family-run hotel is a short walk from the world-famous golf course and university. The Playfair's Restaurant and Steakhouse is located under the reception area, below street level, and the configuration means that diners can often find themselves eating close to drinkers using the bar. It all makes for a relaxed atmosphere, although the linen-clothed tables in the restaurant add a touch of formality to proceedings in a room dotted with deer skulls and other county pursuit objects d'art. High-quality ingredients are treated simply and with confidence to conjure modern Scottish dishes. Among starters might be local pigeon breast with Stornaway Black Pudding, chutney and pomegranate dressing, while main courses bring on grilled Loch Tay salmon with a mushroom garni and truffled hollandaise sauce.

Chef Duncan McLachlan **Owner** Playfair Hotels **Seats** 45
Times 12-5/6-10, Closed Xmas, New Yr **Prices** Starter £3.95-£9.99, Main £9.95-£24.95, Dessert £4.95-£8.95, Service optional **Wines** 8 bottles over £30, 23 bottles under £30, 7 by glass **Parking** On street **Notes** Vegetarian available, Children welcome

The Peat Inn ❀❀❀

PEAT INN   Map 21 NO40

Modern British

tel: 01334 840206 **KY15 5LH**
email: stay@thepeatinn.co.uk **web:** www.thepeatinn.co.uk
dir: At junct of B940/B941, 6m SW of St Andrews

Virtuoso skills in a village institution

The Peat Inn has been around since the middle of the 18th century and offering hospitality in one shape or form for over 250 years. It still has the look of an old inn, and a traveller arriving unawares will feel they have struck lucky, for this is a restaurant with rooms of genuine refinement. If you need a bed for the night, they've got eight beautiful suites to choose from, but it's when it comes to matters of nourishment that the extent of your good fortune becomes apparent. Geoffrey and Katherine Smeddle have run the place since 2006 and have invested heart and soul to create a dining destination of the highest order. The newly refurbished restaurant consists of three dining areas and makes a sophisticated setting for Geoffrey's poised contemporary cooking. The local area provides much of what the kitchen needs, giving a genuine sense of place, and the four seasons are clearly represented over the course of a year. Modern culinary thinking is not eschewed, but there are no over-embellishments or show-boating either – each dish stands on its own two feet, the ingredients allowed to shine. Via tasting (including a vegetarian version) and à la carte menus, the kitchen turns out a first course such as honey-glazed breast of wild mallard with quince and cobnuts, or another where roast veal sweetbreads are matched with a rich sherry velouté. Main-course lemon sole is cooked on the

bone to maximise flavour, and arrives with lobster croquette and a champagne velouté, while an inspired veggie option might be risotto of spelt with blue cheese and truffle. To finish, hot mandarin soufflé with a dark chocolate and Grand Marnier sorbet catches the eye. The wine list, like everything else here, is a class act.

Chef Geoffrey Smeddle **Owner** Geoffrey & Katherine Smeddle **Seats** 50, Pr/dining room 14 **Times** 12.30-1.30/7-9, Closed 25-26 Dec, 1-14 Jan, Sun-Mon **Prices** Fixed L 3 course £19, Fixed D 3 course fr £45, Tasting menu fr £65, Starter fr £8, Main fr £14, Dessert fr £7.50, Service optional **Wines** 350 bottles over £30, 10 bottles under £30, 16 by glass **Parking** 24 **Notes** Tasting menu 6 course D, Chef's menu 4 course L, Vegetarian available, Children welcome

ST ANDREWS *continued*

Hotel du Vin St Andrews

French, British NEW

tel: 01334 472611 **40 The Scores KY16 9AS**
email: reception.standrews@hotelduvin.com **web:** www.hotelduvin.com
dir: *M90 junct 3, A92, A914, A91 to St Andrews. Left onto Golf Place, take first right*

Classic bistro dining in the old town

The latest outpost of the HdV brand has the usual broad appeal with its compelling mix of stylish boutique rooms, lively and informal bistro and stonking wine list. It's all happening in the old town a short walk from the renowned golf course. The bistro has burnished darkwood tables and panelled walls, rich leather seats and large windows that afford views over the city. The kitchen delivers the trademark menu of French impressionism, where Gallic and British classics sit side-by-side: Toulouse sausage and mash or haddock and chips? Shetland scallops might arrive as a first course dressed with sauce vièrge, and when it comes to main courses, the Josper oven turns out 28-day aged rib-eye (served with frites and a choice of sauce). Desserts show the same allegiances with treacle tart with clotted cream ice cream competing with tarte au citron. The wine list has strength in depth.

Chef Ross Edgar **Owner** Hotel de Vin, Malmaison **Seats** Pr/dining room 27
Times 12-2.30/5.30-10 **Prices** Fixed L 2 course fr £14.95, Fixed D 3 course fr £16.95, Starter £5.95-£12.95, Main £13.95-£42, Dessert £6.95-£8.95 **Wines** 105 bottles over £30, 41 bottles under £30, 22 by glass **Parking** 5, On street **Notes** Sun brunch 4 course with French market table, Sunday L fr £22.95, Vegetarian available, Children welcome

The Inn at Lathones

Modern European

tel: 01334 840494 **Largoward KY9 1JE**
email: stay@innatlathones.com **web:** www.innatlathones.com
dir: *5m SW of St Andrews on A915. In 0.5m before Largoward on left, just after hidden dip*

Imaginative, switched-on cooking in a characterful coaching inn

A cottagey white property in the hills above St Andrews, the 400-year-old former coaching inn is now a much-expanded hotel, its rooms around a central courtyard. A fireplace separates the bar from the restaurant in the original building. It is simply decorated, with plain walls, a beamed ceiling and bare wooden tables, vivid blue-upholstered dining chairs adding a colourful contrast. The cooking brings a switched-on, metropolitan-chic style to the area, seen in subtly flavoured crab crème brûlée with laverbread crisps and cucumber, then fillet of pork atop Savoy cabbage accompanied by confit belly and braised cheek, the plate dotted with bonbons of black pudding, baby apples, broad beans and carrots and a swipe of glossy Calvados sauce. More straightforward ideas work equally well: smoked ham hough, say, with a quail's egg, piccalilli and cheese, followed by seasonal roast partridge with red cabbage, Puy lentils, fondant potato and red wine jus. The pastry work is a strength too, judging by chocolate tart with a scoop of delicately flavoured parsnip ice cream, rich caramel sauce and cubes of banana bread.

Chef Chris Wright **Owner** Mr J White **Seats** 40, Pr/dining room 40
Times 6-9.30, Closed 24-26 Dec, 1st 2 wks Jan, L all week **Prices** Starter £4.50-£10.50, Main £15.50-£21.50, Dessert £3.95-£7.50, Service optional **Wines** 4 by glass **Parking** 35 **Notes** Vegetarian available, Children welcome

Road Hole Restaurant

– see page 638

Rocca Restaurant

– see page 639

Rufflets Country House

Modern British, European | NOTABLE WINE LIST

tel: 01334 472594 **Strathkinness Low Rd KY16 9TX**
email: reservations@rufflets.co.uk **web:** www.rufflets.co.uk
dir: *1.5m W of St Andrews on B939*

Family-owned hotel in exquisite grounds

The creeper-covered turreted mansion on the outskirts of the city has been in the same family ownership since 1952, sitting in 10 acres of exquisite gardens. Its name refers to the 'rough flat lands' that once comprised the local landscape. A recently refurbished red and white dining room at the back looks over the ambient greenery, and is split into two, so it can be converted into a more intimate space on quieter nights. The cooking is as modern as can be, trying out interesting approaches to top-drawer prime materials. First up might ham hough terrine garnished with sticks of apple, mango salsa and cider jelly, or perhaps scallops with a chicken wing and cubes of haggis. Main course might bring on vividly tinted saffron-poached cod in herb and pancetta crust with cauliflower foam, or pedigree Scotch beef fillet and ox cheek with dauphinoise in viscously rich foie gras jus. Desserts over-gild the lily a bit with spun sugar and the like, but underneath may well be damn fine pecan pie with cinnamon ice cream and caramelised banana.

Chef Grant MacNicol **Owner** Ann Murray-Smith **Seats** 60, Pr/dining room 130
Times 12.30-2.30/7-9.30 **Prices** Fixed L 2 course £13.50-£25, Fixed D 3 course £35-£45, Starter £3.50-£9.50, Dessert £5-£10, Service optional **Wines** 70 bottles over £30, 40 bottles under £30, 9 by glass **Parking** 50 **Notes** Sunday L, Vegetarian available, Children welcome

Russell Hotel

Scottish, International

tel: 01334 473447 **26 The Scores KY16 9AS**
email: enquiries@russellhotelstandrews.co.uk **web:** www.russellhotelstandrews.co.uk
dir: *From A91 lcft at 2nd rdbt into Golf Place, right in 200yds into The Scores, hotel in 300yds on left*

Scottish-Italian cooking in an intimate hotel dining room

A Victorian terraced townhouse on The Scores overlooking the bay makes a wonderfully relaxing bolt-hole for anyone, though golfing fanatics will particularly relish its proximity to the Old Course. A couple of minutes' walk and you're at the first tee. The small dining room is done in a mixture of sober grey and thistled wallpaper, with framed prints of the local scenery. It's a very intimate room, with low lighting in the evenings, and staff who aim to soothe with friendly conversation and assured knowledge. The cooking is modern Scottish with Italian inflections, with no alarming combinations. Smoked haddock with leek and goats' cheese croquettes and a salad of rocket, basil and walnuts is a gentle enough opener. Main courses include lemon- and herb-crusted cod in garlicky tomato sauce, pot-roasted pheasant with chestnut mushrooms and lardons, or roast loin of Grampian venison with pearl barley risotto, shaved parmesan and pesto.

Times 12-2/6.30-9.30, Closed Xmas

Road Hole Restaurant ✸✸✸

British, Modern Scottish

tel: 01334 474371 **The Old Course Hotel, Golf Resort & Spa KY16 9SP**
email: reservations@oldcoursehotel.co.uk
web: www.oldcoursehotel.co.uk
dir: *M90 junct 8 then A91 to St Andrews*

Stylish modern Scottish cooking overlooking the 17th hole

The Old Course in St Andrews is one of the oldest golf courses in the world, with the game first played here, quite incredibly, way back in the 1400s. The hotel of the same name is several hundred years older than that. It's an imposing presence towering over the famous Links, next to the famous 17th hole (the 'Road Hole'). There are a host of wining and dining options within this luxurious venue, the Road Hole Restaurant being the pick of the bunch. The elegant room of regal proportions has a sophisticated decor of panelled walls and muted colours, and acres of space between the well-dressed tables. The kitchen offers refined modern Scottish cuisine that seems entirely in keeping in this setting. Begin with a polished version of an old classic: Cullen skink as a creamy velouté with fresh as a daisy smoked haddock, confit shallot and pickled mustard seed. Another starter combines a pavé of foie gras with confit duck in a cromesquis, caramelised orange and cocoa granola, followed perhaps by a main course halibut with an Italian spin. There are appealing vegetarian options, too, such as a first course parmesan custard with smoked aubergine purée and Thai basil, followed by pithivier of squash and chickpeas with kohlrabi and pickled cucumber. The technical proficiency and all round good

sense continues in desserts such as heather honey parfait with rhubarb sorbet and ginger crumble, or the more exotic coconut soufflé with pineapple sorbet. The set lunch option is a very tempting offer, while the tasting menu is a good bet if you have time to spare.

Chef Martin Hollis, Craig McAllister **Owner** Kohler Company **Seats** 70, Pr/dining room 16 **Times** 12.30-2/7-9.30, Closed Mon-Tue, L Wed-Fri (Nov-Mar), Wed (Apr-Oct) **Prices** Fixed L 3 course £19.50, Starter £8-£14.50, Main £16-£36, Dessert £7.50-£9, Service optional **Wines** 185 bottles over £30, 15 bottles under £30, 11 by glass **Parking** 100 **Notes** Sunday L £19.50, Vegetarian available, Children 12 yrs+

ST ANDREWS *continued*

Sands Grill

◉ Steak, Seafood

tel: 01334 474371 & 468228 **The Old Course Hotel, Golf Resort & Spa KY16 9SP**
email: reservations@oldcoursehotel.co.uk
dir: *M90 junct 8 then A91 to St Andrews*

Locally-inspired brasserie-style cooking

The Old Course Hotel occupies an enviable spot overlooking the world-famous golf course and the coast beyond. It's a luxurious five-star affair with a spread of dining options, Sands Grill being the informal (relatively speaking) option, a contemporary brasserie-style venue done out with lots of butch black leather and dark wood, and kept ticking over by a slick and unstuffy service team. The kitchen plays a straight bat, delivering simple Mediterranean-inflected ideas. This could be a gratin of crab and prawn rigatoni to start, before excellent locally-sourced meats from the charcoal-fired Josper oven — Scotch Black Isle beef fillet, say, or rack of lamb with cottage pie, peas and broad beans. In the seafood department, high-rollers could splash out on grilled lobster with garlic and hazelnut butter, or tighter budgets could go for a more down-to-earth fishy main course such as breaded goujons of coley with hand-cut chips and brown shrimp butter.

Times 6-9.30, Closed L all week

The Seafood Restaurant

◉◉ Modern Seafood

tel: 01334 479475 **Bruce Embankment KY16 9AB**
email: standrews@theseafoodrestaurant.com
dir: *On A917 turn left along Golf Place*

Enlivening fish cookery between golf and sea

Less than 200 yards from the Old Course at St Andrews, the restaurant sits precariously balanced over the edge of the sea wall, with breathtaking views of the distant North Sea rollers. When the tide turns, the sea suddenly rushes in and rapidly submerges the rocks below. All of which explains why the internal decor of The Seafood contains next to nothing to distract the eye from the marine activity. Nothing, that is, except an open kitchen, where the kitchen team work assiduously at producing fish and seafood dishes that are as fresh and enlivening as the sea spray. Soused mackerel with charred cucumber, broccoli, almonds and buttermilk gives evidence of thinking outside the box, while a main course of herb-crumbed mustardy hake comes with earthy accompaniments of smoky Morteau sausage, shredded sprouts and sautéed potatoes. A perennially popular starter is smoked haddock rarebit with creamed leeks and pancetta in mustard dressing. This might set you up for an adventurous foray into the realms of gilt head bream and braised squid with foie gras in truffle cream. Simple satisfaction is delivered in a dessert pairing of coconut crème brûlée with lime sorbet.

Times 12-2.30/6.30-10, Closed 25-26 Dec, 1 Jan

Rocca Restaurant ◉◉◉

ST ANDREWS Map 21 NO51

Modern Italian, Scottish ⱽ
tel: 01334 472549 **Macdonald Rusacks Hotel, Pilmour Links KY16 9JQ**
email: info@roccarestaurant.com **web:** www.roccarestaurant.com
dir: *M90 junct 8, A91 to St Andrews. Turn left onto Golf Place, then right onto the links*

Inventive Scots-Italian food with ringside views of the golf

The seaside setting by West Sands beach is not the least enticement of the Macdonald group's Rusacks Hotel, and will be particularly appreciated by those impassioned about golf, which is the main draw. The Rocca dining room looks panoramically over the 18th fairway, allowing diners to see the conclusion of every game. A golfing concierge is on hand to keep you updated. The cooking takes a twin-track approach, combining a relatively straightforward Italian focus with intricately detailed Scottish modernism, and the unimpeachable quality of all prime materials adds high gloss to the operation. Evidence for this comes with an opening dish of flame-grilled mackerel, the fantastic flavour of the fish echoed in a tartare presentation alongside an ingenious cannelloni of crab in apple jelly, or the scallops with acorn-fed black ham and pumpkin gnocchi, seasoned with ginger and sage. At main course, Dornoch lamb cooked in hay appears in a comprehensive serving of the neck, loin, noisette and breadcrumbed sweetbread with cheesy potatoes and broad beans, while Orkney beef combines the fillet with braised short rib, helped along with smoked mash and porcini ketchup. Fish might be turbot from Scrabster, served with an oyster fritter, black quinoa and caviar. Nerveless technical ability produces a perfectly risen raspberry soufflé with raspberry ripple ice cream and sauce, or Braeburn apple cake with matching parfait in bay leaf custard.

Chef Davey Aspin **Owner** APSP Restaurants Ltd **Seats** 80, Pr/dining room 34 **Times** 12.30-2/6.30-9.30, Closed Sun (Oct-Mar), L Mon-Thu **Prices** Fixed L 2 course £19.50, Tasting menu £65, Starter £7-£13.50, Main £18-£30, Dessert £5.50-£9, Service optional 10% **Wines** 220 bottles over £30, 10 bottles under £30, 10 by glass **Parking** 23 **Notes** Children welcome

ST MONANS
Map 21 NO50

Craig Millar@16 West End

◉◉ Modern Scottish 🍷 NOTABLE WINE LIST

tel: 01333 730327 **16 West End KY10 2BX**
email: craigmillar@16westend.com
dir: *Take A959 from St Andrews to Anstruther, then W on A917 through Pittenweem. In St Monans to harbour then right*

Eclectic cooking with sweeping harbour views

Sweeping views of the Firth of Forth and St Monans harbour can get dramatic when winter waves surge over the sea wall, but all of the briny turmoil just serves to remind you of the business in hand here: serving fabulous fish and seafood with an exciting, modern spin. Large windows flood the uncluttered space with natural light, while unbuttoned service enhances the chilled out vibe. Chef-patron Craig Millar succeeds in blending fabulous Scottish produce with well-honed technique to deliver precise, Asian and European-influenced dishes in the modern idiom. Hand-dived scallops with Jerusalem artichoke purée, smoked bacon, nuts and seeds opens the show with a burst of intense flavour, while simplicity is the key in a main course of top-quality stone bass matched with couscous and satay sauce. Of course, it's not all about fish – braised ox cheek with Puy lentils and root vegetables should satisfy the carnivores at main course. On-the-money flavour combinations see chocolate tart matched with banana ice cream and salt caramel to finish.

Chef Craig Millar **Owner** Craig Millar **Seats** 35, Pr/dining room 25
Times 12.30-2/6.30-9, Closed 25-26 Dec, 1-2 Jan, 2 wks Jan, Mon-Tue **Prices** Fixed L 2 course fr £22, Fixed D 3 course fr £42, Tasting menu fr £60, Service optional **Wines** 77 bottles over £30, 11 bottles under £30, 7 by glass **Parking** 10 **Notes** Sunday L fr £26, Vegetarian available, Children 12 yrs+ D

CITY OF GLASGOW

GLASGOW
Map 20 NS56

Blythswood Square

◉◉ Modern British 🍷 NOTABLE WINE LIST

tel: 0141 248 8888 **11 Blythswood Square G2 4AD**
email: reserve@blythswoodsquare.com **web:** www. blythswoodsquare.com
dir: *Phone for directions*

Contemporary and classic cooking in former automobile headquarters

Built in 1821 as the grand headquarters for the Royal Scottish Automobile Club on leafy Blythswood Square, this imposing building has been injected with a good dollop of boutique style, plus a luxurious 21st-century spa for good measure, resulting in a hotel of real verve. A drink in the palatial Salon Lounge among fluted columns topped with gilt capitals makes a fine first impression, before heading into the restaurant in the former ballroom, where a stylish contemporary decor works a treat with the high ceilings and ornate plasterwork. The setting says switched-on and modern, and the good-looking food follows suit. Chicken liver parfait with prune chutney and toasted brioche sets out on a classic note, ahead of roast fillet of turbot with creamed spinach, grape fluid gel and white wine cream sauce. They've got a Josper grill too, which does justice to the excellent Scottish steaks (guest breeds are sourced from local farms), and it all ends with a creative spin on carrot cake, matched with crème fraîche sorbet, fizzy whipped lemon curd cream and ginger crumb.

Chef Martin Thliveros **Owner** Starwood Capital **Seats** 120, Pr/dining room 80
Times 12-2.30/6-10 **Prices** Fixed L 2 course £18.50, Fixed D 3 course £22, Starter £6-£12, Main £15-£33, Dessert £7-£12.50 **Wines** 34 bottles over £30, 10 bottles under £30, 13 by glass **Parking** On street **Notes** Pre-theatre menu, Sunday L, Vegetarian available, Children welcome

La Bonne Auberge

◉ French, Mediterranean

tel: 0141 352 8310 & 352 8300 **161 West Nile St G1 2RL**
email: info@higlasgow.com **web:** www.labonneauberge.co.uk
dir: *M8 junct 16, follow signs for Royal Concert Hall, hotel opposite*

Parisian style with imaginative menu in theatreland

This ever-popular venue looks for all the world like a French brasserie, with a predominantly red decor, lamps on wooden tables, banquettes and attentive and friendly staff wearing black waistcoats and long white aprons. The cooking might be based on the classic French repertoire, but the kitchen adds its own imaginative twists and turns. Begin with a rich chicken live pâté flavoured with garlic and port, served with spiced pear compôte and toasted brioche, before moving on to pork fillet wrapped in pancetta and partnered with white beans and chorizo, or Cajun-spiced cod fillet with spring onion mash and sweetcorn beurre blanc. Meats including BBQ pork loin and rib-eye steak are cooked on the grill. The lunchtime special might be croque monsieur followed by chocolate profiteroles, and is terrific value for money. For dessert, coconut and raspberry tart with pistachio ice cream hits the spot.

Chef Gerry Sharkey **Owner** Chardon Leisure Ltd **Seats** 90, Pr/dining room 100
Times 12-2.15/5-10 **Prices** Prices not confirmed **Wines** 6 bottles over £30, 15 bottles under £30, 10 by glass **Parking** NCP opposite **Notes** Pre-theatre menu £16.95 from 5pm, Sunday L, Vegetarian available, Children welcome

Cail Bruich

◉◉◉ – *see opposite*

Central Market

◉ Contemporary Scottish

tel: 0141 552 3530 **51 Bell St G1 1PA**
email: info@centralmarketglasgow.com
dir: *On Bell St next to Merchant Square*

Imaginative bistro-style cooking in buzzing ambience

This urban, industrial-chic café, restaurant and bar, makes a big impression with its huge windows soaring up to a mezzanine floor, cool decor of bare brick and white tiled walls, slate floors and horseshoe-shaped bar where oysters are displayed on ice. An open-to-view kitchen feeds into the buzz and there's plenty you'll want to eat all day long, from breakfast to a crowd-pleasing menu of modern Scottish bistro-style cooking. A starter of potted rabbit with quince, pickles and toasted sourdough is a dish that has its finger on the contemporary culinary pulse, while mains could dip into classic territory via steak tartare loaded with cornichons, capers and shallots and served with skinny fries. Alternatively, there might be well-handled fish – baked cod, say, with purple sprouting broccoli, kale and shellfish butter. Puddings like chocolate and beetroot brownie with clotted cream tick all the right boxes too.

Chef Andrew Lambert **Owner** Darren Scott **Seats** 56, Pr/dining room 30
Times 9.30am-10pm, All-day dining, Closed 25 Dec, 1 Jan **Prices** Fixed D 3 course £16, Starter £4.50-£8, Main £11-£17, Dessert £5-£8, Service optional **Wines** 10 bottles over £30, 26 bottles under £30, 11 by glass **Parking** On street, NCP **Notes** Breakfast menu, Vegetarian available, Children welcome

Gamba

⚜⚜ Scottish, Seafood

tel: 0141 572 0899 **225a West George St G2 2ND**
email: info@gamba.co.uk
dir: *On the corner of West Campbell St & West George St, close to Blythswood Sq*

Top-notch vibrant fish and seafood in the West End

This basement restaurant certainly wears its heart on its sleeve, with its name dropping a strong hint about its culinary raison d'être, gamba being Spanish for fat and juicy king prawns. This perennial favourite enjoys a well-deserved reputation as the go-to place for top-notch fish and seafood in the fashionable West End of the city. Warm colours, floors of dark wood and terracotta tiles, stylish fish-themed artwork and polished-wood tables create a decidedly warm feel, perfect for the Mediterranean- and Asian-influenced cooking. The kitchen is passionate about sourcing the best seasonal produce from the Scottish larder, with fish from sustainable stocks cooked with simplicity and flair. The menu might get under way with an oriental twist on fish soup with crab meat, stem ginger, coriander and prawn dumplings. It follows with a resolutely Scottish pairing of Isle of Gigha halibut with peat-smoked haddock, garden peas, leek, and a creamy sauce of scallops and chives. Standards stay high through to a dessert of frozen chocolate cake with mascarpone, caramel, and chocolate sauce.

Chef Derek Marshall **Owner** Mr D Marshall **Seats** 66
Times 12-2.30/5-10, Closed 25-26 Dec, 1st wk Jan, L Sun **Prices** Fixed L 2 course fr £21, Fixed D 3 course fr £23, Starter £6.50-£14.50, Main £11.50-£34, Dessert £7-£9.50, Service optional **Wines** 21 bottles over £30, 14 bottles under £30, 6 by glass **Parking** On street **Notes** Pre-theatre menu £21-£23, 3 course market menu with wine £30, Vegetarian available, Children welcome

---

AA RESTAURANT OF THE YEAR FOR SCOTLAND 2015–16

The Gannet

⚜⚜ Modern Scottish

tel: 0141 204 2081 **1155 Argyle St G3 8TB**
email: info@thegannetgla.com
dir: *Phone for directions*

Exciting modern Scottish bistro food with industrial styling

The West End is going through a period of exciting transition at the moment, and The Gannet, only open since late 2013, has been very much part of the metamorphosis. It's a very 21st-century venue, with hard-lined industrial styling, all exposed brickwork, wood floors and tiny cafe tables. The dining area is towards the back. Gannets are proverbially hungry, and the kitchen aims to fill you up with plates of deceptively simple modern bistro food that are full of galumphing flavours and sharp seasoning. An appealingly rough-and-ready approach to presentation produces an earthenware bowl loaded with golden-seared scallops, a crisp chicken wing and bits of squid in a green sauce of ramsons. That might be followed by well-rendered braised hogget alongside a slice of confit belly and potato terrine, braised fennel and a light cumin-fragrant jus, or maybe cod and asparagus in dashi stock with shiitakis and smoked eel. At the end comes a golden-yellow fondant with molten salt caramel centre, and a scoop of powerfully rich tonka bean ice cream, or perhaps a fine selection of farmhouse cheeses.

Chef Peter McKenna, Ivan Stein **Owner** Peter McKenna, Ivan Stein **Seats** 45, Pr/dining room 14 **Times** 12-2.30/5-9.45, Closed 25-26 Dec, 1st wk Jan, 1wk Jul, Mon **Prices** Starter £5-£9.50, Main £14-£18, Dessert £5, Service optional **Wines** 13 bottles over £30, 13 bottles under £30, 8 by glass **Parking** On street **Notes** Small plate menu 12-2.30 & 5-7pm £5-6.50, Sunday L, Vegetarian available, Children welcome

---

Cail Bruich ⚜⚜⚜

GLASGOW　　　　　　　　　　　　　　　**Map 20 NS56**

Modern British
tel: 0141 334 6265 **752 Great Western Rd G12 8QX**
email: info@cailbruich.co.uk
dir: *Phone for directions*

Artful modern cookery using the best of regional produce

The name means 'eat well' and you can be sure that is exactly what will happen when you pitch up in this high-flying West End bistro. Chef-patron Chris Charalambous is cooking up a storm right now, his output driven by a commitment to sourcing the finest seasonal materials from carefully-picked artisan suppliers. Cail Bruich is a family affair, with mum and dad serving out front, but there's nothing remotely homespun about this slick operation. The interior was completely reworked in 2015 and now looks the very image of a big-city eatery with its unclothed darkwood tables, red leather banquettes and low-slung copper lights. Nor was the makeover a purely cosmetic exercise, as the kitchen also got a load of new kit, including a charcoal-fired barbecue. The artfully-constructed modern European cooking is delivered via a trio of menu formats, from a well-priced market formula, trading up to the carte and a top-end six-course taster with an option for matching wines. Whichever you go for, there's a lively imagination at work realised with top-flight modern technique, as witnessed in an impressive starter of beef fillet tartare spiked with pickled shallot and fresh chives and served with smoked rye, whisky sauce and tarragon. Next up, a splendid fillet of Scrabster turbot stars in a clever main course, allied with smoked haddock risotto and grilled baby leeks, and sauced with a smoked butter emulsion, or there could be breast and boned leg of pheasant with spelt risotto, mushroom duxelle, roasted and puréed Jerusalem artichoke, kale, and truffle sauce. Dessert brings Valrhona's splendid Manjari chocolate in a decadent crémeux and lush sponge, accompanied by a riot of cherries in the forms of purée, sorbet and jelly.

Chef Chris Charalambous **Owner** Paul & Chris Charalambous **Seats** 48
Times 12-2.30/5.30-9.30, Closed Xmas, New Year, L Mon **Prices** Fixed L 2 course £15, Fixed D 3 course £25, Tasting menu £45-£55, Starter £6-£12, Main £16-£24, Dessert £7-£12, Service optional 10% **Wines** 27 bottles over £30, 12 bottles under £30, 10 by glass **Parking** On street **Notes** Sunday L £18-£25, Vegetarian available, Children welcome

GLASGOW continued

The Hanoi Bike Shop

◉ Vietnamese

tel: 0141 334 7165 **8 Ruthven Ln G12 9BG**
email: pho@thehanoibikeshop.co.uk **web:** www.thehanoibikeshop.co.uk
dir: *Phone for directions*

Stirring Vietnamese street food

Garage-chic, you might say, as this vibrant venture uses the machines as decoration alongside hanging lanterns which bring vivid colour to the space. It's the brainchild of the good people behind the long-running Ubiquitous Chip and its sister restaurant, Stravaigin. Down a little lane you'll find a hit of dazzling Vietnamese flavours, the joint spread over two buzzing floors, with staff in branded T-shirts working like troopers. It's got a chilled-out, canteen-style vibe which suits

the authentic street food menu, and sharing is the way to go. The menu gives the Vietnamese names of dishes followed by a detailed English translation, thus bahn thit lon trung are pork and coriander dumplings with a runny egg centre – packed with flavour – and ga nuong sua va xuai is a jelly fish salad with chargrilled chicken and mango. There are classic pho dishes, too, and a 'from the pot' section perhaps chargrilled chicken leg in a kaffir lime leaf and ginger sauce. Great fun.

The Hanoi Bike Shop

Chef Jesse Stevens **Owner** Colin Clydesdale, Carol Wright **Seats** 75, Pr/dining room 35 **Times** 12-12.30, All-day dining, Closed 25 Dec, 1 Jan, L 26 Dec **Prices** Prices not confirmed, Service optional **Wines** 2 bottles under £30, 4 by glass **Parking** On street **Notes** Sun brunch, Sunday L, Vegetarian available, Children welcome

Hotel du Vin at One Devonshire Gardens

◉◉◉ – *see below*

Hotel du Vin at One Devonshire Gardens ◉◉◉

GLASGOW	Map 20 NS56

French, European 🍷 NOTABLE WINE LIST

tel: 0141 339 2001 **1 Devonshire Gardens G12 0UX**
email: bistromer.glasgow@hotelduvin.com **web:** www.hotelduvin.com
dir: *M8 junct 17, follow signs for A82, after 1.5m turn left into Hyndland Rd*

Smart, creative cooking in an elegant townhouse hotel

More usually known for its straightforward renditions of French bistro cooking, the Hotel du Vin chain of boutique hotels has pulled out all the stops here at One Devonshire Gardens. The address has long been a major player in the Glasgow dining scene, and as the jewel in the crown of the HdV Group, it has maintained its culinary aspirations. The terrace of porticoed Victorian houses in a tree-lined street makes for an appealing hotel, furnished and decorated with panache. The Bistro – as the restaurant is named, in keeping with the rest of the group – is a rather grander room than its title denotes, done with burnished oak panelling, large bay windows, smartly-dressed tables and kept ticking smoothly over by clued-up, friendly staff. The kitchen displays a passion for its country's prime materials, which are handled with well-honed technical skills to produce sharp, modern dishes. In game season, roast breast of grouse with on-trend parsley root, braised endive, Serrano ham and hazelnut crumb may get things going, or perhaps pan-fried scallops

with squid ink noodles, oysters, cucumber and caviar. There's nothing fussy or gratuitously showy about main-course dishes such as roast loin of venison with braised red cabbage, chestnut purée and pommes dauphine, while hazelnut-crusted Barra monkfish arrives in a faultless balance of flavours and textures with lemon and garlic risotto nero and citrus dressing. Desserts such as amarena cherry soufflé with Valrhona chocolate sauce poured in at table, accompanied by almond ice cream, or a hybrid baked Alaska made with butterbeer (an imaginary Harry Potter tipple akin to butterscotch) ice cream, gingerbread and spiced wine syrup, provide an impressive finish.

Chef Barry Duff **Owner** KSL **Seats** 78, Pr/dining room 70
Times 12-2/5.30-10, Closed D 25 Dec **Prices Wines** 12 by glass **Parking** On street **Notes** Tasting menu 7 course, Sunday L £24.95, Vegetarian available, Children welcome

Malmaison Glasgow

@@ Modern French

tel: 0141 572 1001 **278 West George St G2 4LL**
email: info@thehonoursglasgow.co.uk **web:** www.malmaison.com
dir: *From George Square take St Vincent St to Pitt St. Hotel on corner with West George St*

Wishart wizardry comes to the Mal

The Glasgow Mal has made its home in a deconsecrated Greek Orthodox church, with all the architectural atmospherics that promises. In late 2014, the dining room, still in the vaulted former crypt, came under the aegis of Martin Wishart's restaurant venture, The Honours. Interior restyling has brought a sleek, low-lit contemporary look to the space, with red glass tables, circular banquette seating, and the strains of Paolo Nutini. A mix of traditional and modern French brasserie cooking is the draw, with favourites such as crab Marie Rose, or fine chicken liver parfait with apple and date chutney, to start, alongside less mainstream offerings like a tartare constructed of sea bream, anchovies, red pepper and crème fraîche. Select breeds and cuts of thoroughbred beef are the backbone of main courses, but useful diversions include rabbit in mustard sauce, or the sharply distinctive curry-dusted fillets of John Dory with leeks in a mussel-infused buttery sauce and Sauternes foam. Soufflé du jour is worth a look at dessert – a chocolate-crumbed mint version with a dollop of chocolate added at the last minute is a treat – or two might order a classic apple Tatin with cinnamon ice cream.

Chef Andrew Greenan **Owner** Malmaison **Seats** 106, Pr/dining room 56
Times 12-2.30/6-10 **Prices** Fixed L 2 course fr £18.50, Fixed D 3 course fr £22.50, Starter £7.95-£17, Main £16.95-£33, Dessert £7.50-£9.50 **Wines** 47 bottles over £30, 9 bottles under £30, 22 by glass **Parking** Q park Waterloo St **Notes** Sunday L fr £26.95, Vegetarian available, Children welcome

Mother India

@ Indian

tel: 0141 221 1663 & 221 1832 **28 Westminster Ter, Sauchiehall St G3 7RU**
email: info@motherindia.co.uk
dir: *From Kelvingrove Museum located on corner of Sauchiehall St & Kelvingrove St*

Long-running Indian landmark serving smart, interesting curries

This landmark restaurant has spawned a chain of outlets across Glasgow and Edinburgh since it launched here in 1990, and it continues to draw the crowds with its inventive, flavour-packed Indian food. Spread over three floors of a corner property near Kelvingrove Park, Mother India avoids cliché in its decor with prints of the city on the walls, wood panelling in the first-floor room, and an atmospheric cellar. Similarly, the menu takes a step away from curry-house standards to deliver some smart, broadly appealing dishes, with a few names and preparations that will be familiar to curry regulars. Start with chicken tikka pakoras, for example, which really hit the spot, served with spicy tomato chutney, following on with lamb mussallam with baby turnips and leeks, a dish slow-cooked to maximum effect. Desserts don't let the side down either; gulab jamon, perhaps, with an accompanying scoop of cardamom ice cream.

Times 12.30-2.30/5.30-10.30, Closed Xmas, New Year, L Mon-Thu

Number Sixteen

@ Modern International

tel: 0141 339 2544 & 07957 423615 **16 Byres Rd G11 5JY**
dir: *2 mins walk from Kelvinhall tube station, at bottom of Byres Rd*

Buzzy neighbourhood venue mixing interesting flavour combinations

This dinky neighbourhood restaurant on Glasgow's vibrant Byres Road has a strong local fan base who appreciate its unbuttoned vibe and the kitchen's creative approach to modern cooking. It is an elbow-to-elbow sort of space with a pocket-sized downstairs area, and a mini-mezzanine above, all decorated with colourful artwork, and kept ticking over by casually dressed, on-the-ball staff. The chefs

beavering away in the open-to-view kitchen aren't scared to experiment with novel flavour combinations, without losing sight of the seasons and the local supplies that come with them. A summer's lunch starts conventionally enough by bringing together a chicken liver and foie gras parfait with peach chutney and herb croûtons, before deploying a vibrant barrage of flavours in a main course of sea bream fillet with fennel, cucumber and olive salad, basil and almond gremolata, and pesto. Pudding delivers a subtly-flavoured combo of lavender pannacotta, poached plums and rhubarb.

Chef Gerard Mulholland **Owner** Gerard Mulholland, Joel Pomfret **Seats** 36, Pr/dining room 17 **Times** 12-2.30/5.30-9, Closed 25-26 Dec, 1-2 Jan **Prices** Fixed L 2 course £12.95, Starter £4.95-£7.50, Main £13.50-£16.95, Dessert £6.50, Service optional 10% **Wines** 8 bottles over £30, 25 bottles under £30, 6 by glass **Parking** On street **Notes** Sunday L £12.95-£15.95, Vegetarian available, Children welcome

Opium

@ Chinese, Oriental fusion

tel: 0141 332 6668 **191 Hope St G2 2UL**
email: eat@opiumrestaurant.co.uk
dir: *Phone for directions*

Asian fusion from a Hong Kong masterchef in the heart of the city

The name might evoke memories of a low point in Anglo-Chinese politics, but East and West are reconciled here in this pin-sharp, contemporary-styled Asian fusion restaurant in the pulsing heart of Glasgow. Big picture-windows allow light to flood into a slick space done out with dark wood and muted brown tones, where communal tables with high chairs share the space with conventional restaurant seating. Kwan Yu Lee learned his skills from virtual boyhood in Hong Kong, but has honed an on-trend mix of classical and modern Asian fusion dishes. An array of dim sum shows basic skills are not forgotten, with steamed salmon, fennel and chive dumplings with a ginger dipping sauce full of evocative aromas. Next up, try a bowl of noodles such as one packed with tenderloin of pork, fine beans and bean sprouts, flavoured with Shaoxing wine and oyster sauce. Finish with mango jelly with coulis and cream.

Chef Kwan Yu Lee **Owner** Trevor Lee **Seats** 54 **Times** 12-2.30/5-10 **Prices** Prices not confirmed, Service optional **Wines** 2 bottles over £30, 19 bottles under £30, 8 by glass **Notes** Pre-theatre 2/3 course menu, Sunday L, Vegetarian available, Children welcome

Ox and Finch

@ Modern British NEW v

tel: 0141 339 8627 **920 Sauchiehall St G3 7TF**
email: hello@oxandfinch.com
dir: *500mtrs E of Kelvingrove Art Gallery & Museum, near Hydro & SECC*

Hip new spot on Sauchiehall Street

Small plates are a big deal these days and here on Sauchiehall Street they're up for grabs in a venue with a trendy urban vibe which, judging by the speed tables are filled, has hit the proverbial nail on the head. The space has a fashionable industrial finish with brown leather banquettes and booths, and service is equally hip and casual (but by no means slack). Three or so plates per person will do the job for most, and sharing gives the opportunity to sample lots of them. The style is modern and rustic with European flavours dominating alongside some influences from Asia and North Africa. Crispy fried squid comes fresh as a daisy, served with orange and chilli salad while a perfectly-judged saffron aïoli, and baked beetroot with goats' curd is another winner. There's confit duck with Thai yellow curry and crispy rice, too, and among desserts charred baby pineapple looks a picture on the plate. For drinks, choose from craft beer or wines by the carafe.

Chef Daniel Spurr **Owner** Jonathan MacDonald **Seats** 70, Pr/dining room **Times** noon-mdnt, All-day dining, Closed 25-26 Dec, 1-2 Jan **Prices** Starter £2.75-£4.50, Main £6-£9.50, Dessert £4.50-£8.50, Service optional **Wines** 15 bottles over £30, 29 bottles under £30, 15 by glass **Parking** On street **Notes** Children welcome

GLASGOW *continued*

La Parmigiana

Italian, Mediterranean

tel: 0141 334 0686 **447 Great Western Rd, Kelvinbridge G12 8HH**
email: info@laparmigiana.co.uk **web:** www.laparmigiana.co.uk
dir: *Next to Kelvinbridge underground*

West End institution serving superior Italian fare

The blue-painted exterior of this West End stalwart conceals a calm and refined interior of red walls, bare wooden floor and purple-padded wooden seats at white-clothed tables, with friendly and knowledgeable staff adding to the congenial atmosphere. Bog-standard Italian fare this isn't, although fresh home-made pasta is a good bet – perhaps spinach and ricotta tortelli. Go for one of the shellfish starters like lobster ravioli with basil sauce, or chargrilled scallops with Jerusalem artichoke and beurre blanc. Progress perhaps to a well-rounded dish of tender, pink roast fillets of venison on polenta croûtons with a sauce of porcini and Italian sausage. The kitchen works its magic on top-drawer materials and treatments are never too complicated, so fillet of salmon is encased in puff pastry and served with lemony mustard sauce, and beef fillet is roasted and accompanied by a rich Barolo sauce. Fly the Italian flag with desserts like tiramisù, or vanilla pannacotta with matching ice cream.

Chef Peppino Camilli **Owner** Sandro & Stefano Giovanazzi **Seats** 50
Times 12-2.30/5.30-10.30, Closed 25-26 Dec, 1 Jan, D Sun **Prices** Prices not confirmed, Service optional **Wines** 35 bottles over £30, 15 bottles under £30, 8 by glass **Parking** On street **Notes** Pre-theatre 2/3 course 5.30-7pm £17.10/£19.90, Sunday L, Vegetarian available, Children welcome

Rogano

Scottish, Seafood V

tel: 0141 248 4055 **11 Exchange Place G1 3AN**
email: info@roganoglasgow.com
dir: *Phone for directions*

Art deco seafood restaurant 80 years young

Glasgow's longest-serving restaurant became an octogenarian in 2015, having been provisioning the city with fish and shellfish specialities since Cunard's luxury liner Queen Mary began its life on the Clyde. The perfectly preserved art deco interior is a delight in an era of stripped-to-the-bone minimalism, and the place is run with old-school Gallic courtesy and correctness. An often-starry clientele loyally returns for platters of fruits de mer, langoustines in garlic butter, and expertly rendered thermidor, the richly sauced lobster returned to its shell for gratinating, served with shoestring fries. There are inspired meat dishes too, not least an autumn starter of roast grouse on Puy lentils and girolles in balsamic jus, or the main-course venison loin wrapped in pancetta with its own pasty and pickled red cabbage. Tarte Tatin is done with as much panache as it is on the Boulevard St-Michel, its perfectly caramelised topping and sauce offset with subtle cinnamon ice cream, or there may be white chocolate cheesecake in a coulis of Perthshire raspberries.

Chef Gordon Provan **Owner** Lynnet Leisure **Seats** 70, Pr/dining room 16
Times 12-2.30/6-10.30, Closed 1 Jan **Prices** Fixed L 2 course £16.50, Fixed D 3 course £21.50, Tasting menu fr £45, Starter £6.50-£12, Main £20.50-£40, Dessert £6.50-£13.50 **Wines** 100 bottles over £30, 30 bottles under £30, 14 by glass **Parking** NCP car parks **Notes** Tasting menu 4 course with wine £80, Sunday L £16.50-£21.50, Children welcome

Shish Mahal

Indian

tel: 0141 339 8256 **60-68 Park Rd G4 9JF**
email: reservations@shishmahal.co.uk
dir: *From M8/A8 take exit towards Dumbarton. On Great Western Rd 1st left into Park Rd*

Long-standing Indian in a quiet part of the city

A Glaswegian institution since the 1960s, the Shish Mahal has seen generations of curry fans pass through its doors to sample Mr Ali's reliable classic Indian cooking. There's a smart modern feel to its warm Asian colour scheme, while leather seating and linen-clad tables do their bit to bolster the feel-good factor, and service is friendly and knowledgeable. The extensive menu explores familiar regional variations, taking in old favourites from the madras, vindaloo and bhuna stables, but there are plenty of intriguing ideas to broaden your horizons too. Lamb karahi is full of tender meat and vibrant, complex flavours, strong chilli heat as well as sweetly caramelised onion, coriander seed and garlic, and might be the follow-up to generously packed chicken pakoras in gram flour batter with raita and chutney, or prawns in garlic butter with pineapple. Finish with stickily satisfying gulab jamon in cardamom syrup.

Chef I Humayun **Owner** Ali A Aslam, Nasim Ahmed **Seats** 95, Pr/dining room 14
Times 12-2/5-11, Closed 25 Dec, L Sun **Prices** Fixed L 2 course £7.95, Starter £3.25-£8.95, Main £8.50-£17.95, Dessert £3.50-£4.95, Service optional **Wines** 2 bottles over £30, 18 bottles under £30, 1 by glass **Parking** Side street, Underground station car park **Notes** Fixed L 4 course, Vegetarian available, Children welcome

Stravaigin

◉ ◉ Modern International

tel: 0141 334 2665 **28-30 Gibson St, Kelvinbridge G12 8NX**
email: stravaigin@btinternet.com **web:** www.stravaigin.com
dir: *Next to Glasgow University. 200yds from Kelvinbridge underground*

Popular eatery with creative, multi-national flavour

The tagline of this switched-on stalwart of the Glasgow foodie scene – 'Think global, eat local' – neatly sums up its culinary ideology. Spread over two floors of café-bar and a basement restaurant, the operation goes for a quirky contemporary look. Reclaimed and reinvented pieces of modern art and interesting objets are set against rough stone walls, and beamed ceilings. This is the perfect foil to the consistently imaginative, flavour-driven cooking. The kitchen plunders Scotland's magnificent larder for its raw materials, which are allied with an eclectic approach to the world's cuisines. A starter of West Coast crab partnered with haddock wrapped in cucumber 'cannelloni', an apple and celeriac take on a Waldorf salad, and a spicy Indian-accented vadouvan oil all prove the point. Korean braised ox cheek with brown rice cake, kimchi, tempura oyster, and sesame-dressed cucumber and bean sprouts makes a similarly full-frontal attack on the taste buds, while desserts keep exploring interesting combos of flavour and texture with vanilla-poached rhubarb with pecan and brioche crumble and heather honey ice cream.

Chef Kenny Mackay **Owner** Colin Clydesdale, Carol Wright **Seats** 62 **Times** 11-11, All-day dining, Closed 25 Dec, 1 Jan, L 26 Dec **Prices** Starter £3.65-£7.50, Main £9.45-£23.45, Dessert £4.25-£9.95, Service optional **Wines** 6 bottles over £30, 40 bottles under £30, 23 by glass **Parking** On street, car park 100yds **Notes** Breakfast Mon-Fri, Brunch Sat-Sun, Sunday L £3.65-£23.45, Vegetarian available, Children welcome

---

WINNER OF THE AA WINE AWARD FOR SCOTLAND 2015–16

Ubiquitous Chip

◉ ◉ Scottish v ◗ NOTABLE WINE LIST

tel: 0141 334 5007 **12 Ashton Ln G12 8SJ**
email: reservations@ubiquitouschip.co.uk **web:** www.ubiquitouschip.co.uk
dir: *In West End, off Byres Rd. Adjacent to Hillhead underground station*

Iconic address for modern Scottish cooking

It's no surprise that the Chip has been in business since 1971: this trailblazing West End institution's success is due in part to its talent for keeping in step with the times without becoming a fickle follower of ephemeral trends. So, some dishes come and go, while others (the saltire-waving venison haggis, for example) have been around since year dot. Inside it's a warren of bars and dining areas, including a brasserie, the glass roofed, cobbled courtyard and a mezzanine, and all around are colourful murals and the buzz of contented customers. The cooking is imaginative – quirky, even – but always clear-headed and based on superb Scottish ingredients. Chickpea and roast garlic cake is pepped up with raisin salsa and toasted pistachios, while a hearty main course of wild pheasant breast gains depth from a flageolet bean cassoulet and buttered kale. If you're up for fish, lythe fillet (that's pollack to folk from south of the border) comes with samphire, smoked ham and spring onion velouté. For dessert, there's malt pannacotta with dark chocolate ganache.

Chef Andrew Mitchell **Owner** Colin Clydesdale **Seats** 110, Pr/dining room 45 **Times** 12-2.30/5-11, Closed 25 Dec, 1 Jan, L 26 Dec **Prices** Fixed L 2 course £15.95, Fixed D 3 course £19.95, Starter £6.45-£13.95, Main £15.95-£35, Dessert £5.95-£15, Service optional **Wines** 215 bottles over £30, 58 bottles under £30, 37 by glass **Parking** Lillybank Gardens (50mtrs) **Notes** Pre-theatre 2/3 course £15.95/£19.95 5-6.30pm Sun-Fri, Sunday L £15.95-£23.95, Children welcome

GLASGOW continued

Urban Bar and Brasserie

Modern British

tel: 0141 248 5636 **23-25 St Vincent Place G1 2DT**
email: info@urbanbrasserie.co.uk
dir: *In city centre between George Sq & Buchanan St*

Updated and interesting brasserie fare in a former bank

This sleek and modern bar-brasserie has capitalised on the grandiose architecture of a former bank (the erstwhile Scottish HQ of the Bank of England, no less), throwing in brown leather banquettes and chairs, smartly laid tables, and huge canvases of modern art to bring vibrant splashes of colour into the mix. Add in black-clad staff wearing long white aprons, and a bustling vibe, and you might be in a classic Parisian brasserie. The kitchen knows its stuff, producing a menu of Scotland-meets-Mediterranean ideas sprinkled with Asian flavours, a starter of smoked salmon with Thai jelly, cornichons and capers being typical of the style. Main courses can be as traditional as grilled lemon sole with tartare sauce and chips and as full-on as braised beef cheeks with parsnip purée, star anise gravy and crispy fennel. To finish, the addition of liquorice puts a novel spin on a crème brûlée.

Chef David Clunas **Owner** Alan Tomkins **Seats** 120, Pr/dining room 20 **Times** 12-10, All-day dining, Closed 25 Dec, 1 Jan **Prices** Fixed L 2 course £15.95, Fixed D 3 course £18.95, Starter £5.50-£11, Main £11.95-£29.95, Dessert £5.50-£7.95, Service optional **Wines** 20 bottles over £30, 20 bottles under £30, 8 by glass **Parking** NCP West Nile St **Notes** Pre-theatre, Sunday L £15.95-£18.95, Vegetarian available, Children 14 yrs+

Wee Lochan

Modern Scottish

tel: 0141 338 6606 **340 Crow Rd, Broomhill G11 7HT**
email: eat@an-lochan.com
dir: *Phone for directions*

Contemporary cooking in the leafy West End

The black frontage gives a distinguished look to a neighbourhood restaurant in the quiet, leafy reaches of the West End, its wide terrace allowing for pleasant outdoor dining in summer. Inside is light and airy, with black and white seating and a whole bunch of artworks for sale, from landscape prints to abstracts. The contemporary Scottish cooking scores many a hit with precise, defined flavours in thoughtfully composed dishes the inspiring norm. Start with a quartet of seared scallops with sliced chorizo, sauced with a buttery ribbon of herbs, lime and chilli, as a prelude to golden-skinned roast breast of guinea fowl garnished with a crisp bacon rasher, honey-glazed parsnips and mash in thyme-scented cider sauce. Desserts play to the gallery with an array of favoured flavours: perhaps dark chocolate delice, orange cake, hazelnut praline and honeycomb ice cream in orange anglaise.

Chef Rupert Staniforth **Owner** Aisla & Rupert Staniforth **Seats** 50
Times 12-3/5-10, Closed 25 Dec, 1-2 Jan **Prices** Fixed L 2 course £13.95, Fixed D 3 course £17.95, Starter £3.90-£9, Main £9-£18, Dessert £3-£5.70, Service optional **Wines** 12 bottles over £30, 30 bottles under £30, 18 by glass **Parking** On street (no charge) **Notes** Pre-theatre fixed menu, Sunday L £14.95-£17.95, Vegetarian available, Children welcome

HIGHLAND

CROMARTY

Map 23 NH76

The Factor's House

Modern British NEW

tel: 01381 600394 **Denny Rd IV11 8YT**
email: stay@thefactorshouse.com **web:** www.thefactorshouse.com
dir: *Phone for directions*

Daily-changing home-grown menu in a coastal hotel

This attractive red sandstone house with just three guest rooms once belonged to a merchant (hence the name) and stands in alluring grounds on a coastal inlet. Very much a two-handed operation by the Deakins – he runs front-of-house, she cooks – it features a wood-floored dining room with walls in burgundy and grey and tartan place mats on the tables. A daily-changing four-course dinner menu, including Scottish cheeses, is the offering, and there is real personality to the dishes. First up might be an odd but successful construction of smoked haddock and leek lasagne topped with a gratinated cheddar soufflé, to be followed by a much simpler, intensely flavoured rolled pork loin stuffed with spinach, accompanied by garlicky dauphinoise and a mound of braised red cabbage and apple. The dessert could then be rhubarb frangipane tart with poached home-grown rhubarb and a brandy snap basket of ginger ice cream.

Chef Fiona Deakin **Owner** Fiona & Graham Deakin **Seats** 10 **Times** 7-10, Closed 15 Dec-5 Jan, L all week **Prices** Prices not confirmed **Notes** Fixed D 4 course + coffee £37.50, Vegetarian available, Children 5 yrs+

DORNOCH

Map 23 NH78

Dornoch Castle Hotel

Modern Scottish

tel: 01862 810216 **Castle St IV25 3SD**
email: enquiries@dornochcastlehotel.com **web:** www.dornochcastlehotel.com
dir: *2m N of Dornoch Bridge on A9, turn right to Dornoch. Hotel in village centre opp Cathedral*

Medieval castle hotel with a true Scottish flavour

A 15th-century castle makes a dramatic and romantic setting for a hotel, and here a sympathetic updating and modernisation has managed to preserve original features. There's a courtyard and a well-stocked bar as well as a conservatory-style restaurant, where friendly staff, candlelight and gentle background music create a charming atmosphere. The kitchen works a modern vein without losing sight of regional traditions. Beautifully pan-fried pigeon breast is served in a stew of pancetta and Puy lentils to make a memorable starter. Scotland's lochs and coastline are the source of seafood – perhaps a cold mixed platter, or salmon fillet with braised fennel and lemony herb butter – while carnivores could try a well-composed dish of chargrilled pork chop on apple purée with a black pudding and potato cake, plus honey-roast carrots and parsnips. Finish with classic tarte Tatin.

Chef Brian Sangster **Owner** Colin & Ros Thompson **Seats** 75, Pr/dining room 25 **Times** 12-3/6-9.30, Closed 25-26 Dec, 2nd wk Jan **Prices** Starter fr £6.50, Main fr £16.95, Dessert fr £7.50, Service optional **Wines** 10 bottles over £30, 20 bottles under £30, 6 by glass **Parking** 12, On street (free) **Notes** Early D special menu, Sunday L £15-£18, Vegetarian available, Children welcome

FORT AUGUSTUS
Map 23 NH30

Inchnacardoch Lodge Hotel
Modern Scottish

tel: 01456 450900 **Inchnacardoch Bay PH32 4BL**
email: happy@inchhotel.com web: www.inchhotel.com
dir: *On A82. Turn right before entering Fort Augustus from Inverness*

Hearty regional cooking overlooking Loch Ness

A mid-Victorian hunting lodge overlooking Loch Ness, the Inch (as it's more monosyllabically known) did war service as an RAF base, but found its métier as a country-house hotel in the 1950s. Its hauntingly memorable location is on show through the picture windows, and is echoed in the pictures that adorn the dining room walls. The kitchen furnishes the kinds of hearty dishes to sate those of an outdoor persuasion, so a generous smoked salmon starter is further bolstered with a salmon fishcake, lime-spiked crème fraîche and tomato salsa. Main course might be roast rack of local lamb alongside a shepherd's pie, amid a plethora of vegetables and a handful of parsnip crisps, in redcurrant and rosemary gravy. Another option may be breast of corn-fed chicken glazed in Orkney cheddar and smoked bacon in an old-school creamy sauce of leeks, mushrooms, white wine and thyme. The final fortification arrives in the form of hot chocolate fondant with raspberry sauce and vanilla ice cream.

Chef John Starky **Seats** 24, Pr/dining room 6 **Times** 6.30-9.30, Closed L all week **Prices** Prices not confirmed **Wines** 4 bottles over £30, 5 bottles under £30, 3 by glass **Parking** 15 **Notes** Vegetarian available, Children welcome

Station Road
⚜️⚜️⚜️ – *see below*

FORT WILLIAM
Map 22 NN17

Inverlochy Castle Hotel
⚜️⚜️⚜️ – *see page 648*

GLENFINNAN
Map 22 NM98

The Prince's House
⚜️⚜️ Modern British

tel: 01397 722246 **PH37 4LT**
email: princeshouse@glenfinnan.co.uk web: www.glenfinnan.co.uk
dir: *From Fort William N on A82 for 2m. Turn left on to A830 Mallaig Rd for 15m to hotel*

Regionally-based cooking in a gorgeous historic region

Glenfinnan is where Bonnie Prince Charlie raised the Jacobite standard in 1745, as is attested by the stone monument that stands within its little walls against a gorgeous backdrop of loch, hills and viaduct. It would be hard to imagine a more splendid, or historically poignant spot for a retreat hotel, and Kieron and Ina Kelly's white-fronted house has charm in bucketloads. The dining room is hung with the Kellys' fine art collection, and extends into a small conservatory section with ravishing views over the glen. Kieron Kelly's cooking steps up to the regional plate with locally-grown produce, fish from Mallaig and venison from the surrounding hills. The four-course set menu might start with butternut squash soup, poured at the table over buttered leeks, beetroot crisps and crème fraîche, before salmon and halibut with asparagus in prawn butter, and then that venison, perhaps paired with wood pigeon in red wine and rowan berry jus. Dessert might transport you to sunnier climes with caramelised pineapple in passionfruit syrup, alongside lime and ginger sorbet and candied chillies.

Chef Kieron Kelly **Owner** Kieron & Ina Kelly **Seats** 30 **Times** 7-9, Closed Xmas, Oct-Mar, L all week **Prices** Prices not confirmed **Wines** 40 bottles over £30, 30 bottles under £30, 4 by glass **Parking** 18 **Notes** 4 course D £45, Vegetarian available, Children welcome

---

Station Road ⚜️⚜️⚜️

FORT AUGUSTUS
Map 23 NH30

Modern British v

tel: 01456 459250 **The Lovat, Loch Ness, Loch Ness Side PH32 4DU**
email: info@thelovat.com web: www.thelovat.com
dir: *On A82 between Fort William & Inverness*

Clever, creative cooking with loch views

At the southern end of Loch Ness, the Victorian-era Lovat hotel is run with environmentally friendliness in mind and offers stylish accommodation a brisk walk up the hill from the water's edge. Sensitive renovation has maintained the Victorian appeal of the building itself, while adding a bit of contemporary swagger. When it comes to eating, there are two options – brasserie and Station Road Restaurant – and you can be sure of some modern culinary excitement along the way. The man at the stoves in the restaurant is Sean Kelly, and he's an exponent of playful and thrilling cooking. Given the environmental considerations, you can rest assure that matters of food miles are taken into consideration. It all takes place in an oak-panelled dining room that gives views over the loch and provides an elegant setting for spirited food that they describe as 'fun dining', delivered via a five-course tasting menu (including a vegetarian version). The presentation of each dish is designed to stimulate and surprise, as with a duck liver parfait that is encased in a beetroot jelly and looks for all the world like a beetroot, until you cut into it to find the beautifully textured parfait within, or a crab mousse and watermelon number that uses moulds to create a pretty picture on the plate. A course named 'shepherd's pie, lamb titbits' (menu descriptions are brief and esoteric) offers up liver, loin and shoulder, each element cooked just right, alongside the powerfully flavoured pie. 'Cheese, nuts & chutney' arrives in a little box with the restaurant's name on it, and is a sweet not savoury course, while 'Kinder Surprise' displays sound technical skills.

Chef Sean Kelly **Owner** Caroline Gregory **Seats** 24, Pr/dining room 50 **Times** 7-9, Closed Nov-Mar, Sun-Wed, L all week **Prices** Prices not confirmed, Service optional **Wines** 25 bottles over £30, 35 bottles under £30, 13 by glass **Parking** 30 **Notes** Children 8 yrs+

INVERGARRY
Map 22 NH30

Glengarry Castle Hotel
Scottish, International

tel: 01809 501254 **PH35 4HW**
email: castle@glengarry.net **web:** www.glengarry.net
dir: *1m S of Invergarry on A82*

Traditional fare in a grand lochside hotel

If your knowledge of the lochs is a little shaky, note that Loch Oich, which the Glengarry overlooks, is situated between Loch Ness and Loch Lochy. The present building is a consummate slice of Victorian Scots baronial, built in the 1860s, and furnished throughout in the grand manner. Spotless white linen and quality glassware glow beneath the chandelier in the opulent dining room, where lightly modernised traditional fare is the order of the day. Pigeon breast and caramelised onion in port jus, all indulgent sticky-sweetness, could be the prelude to baked sea bass in a fragrant sauce of tomato, saffron and white wine, or chargrilled venison strip loin in juniper jus, served with a skirlie cake, the meat properly black-striped on the surface while pink in the middle. No whim need go unpandered to when there are desserts such as dark chocolate and ginger tart with white chocolate ice cream, and there are fine Scottish cheeses too.

Chef John McDonald **Owner** Mrs MacCallum & Sons **Seats** 40
Times 12-1.45/7-8.30, Closed mid Nov-mid Mar **Prices** Prices not confirmed
Wines 14 bottles over £30, 35 bottles under £30, 9 by glass **Parking** 30
Notes Vegetarian available, Children welcome

INVERGORDON
Map 23 NH77

The Birch Tree
British, French V

tel: 01349 853549 **Delny IV18 0NP**
email: thebirchtree@live.co.uk **web:** www.the-birch-tree.com
dir: *2m north of Tomich junct on left. Located at Delny Riding Centre*

Classy Scottish cookery at the Riding Centre

About a mile off the A9, amid fields crowded with horses from his parents' Delny Riding Centre, Barry Hartshorne's rural bistro lies in a village near Invergordon. The whole complex looks like the family home it is, the dining room smartly done in dark brown and cream, the kitchen on view through a small pass. Hartshorne mostly goes it alone back there, and the results are all the more impressive for that. Scottish ingredients predominate in cooking of distinct accuracy and class. A

Inverlochy Castle Hotel ❀❀❀

FORT WILLIAM
Map 22 NN17

Modern British V ⊞ NOTABLE WINE LIST
tel: 01397 702177 **Torlundy PH33 6SN**
email: info@inverlochy.co.uk **web:** www.inverlochycastlehotel.com
dir: *3m N of Fort William on A82, just past Golf Club, N towards Inverness*

Exceptional cooking and creativity in a grand castle

Inverlochy is the quintessential Victorian baronial castle, all castellated stone walls and turrets surrounded by 500 green acres overlooking its own loch. Pretty impressive then, and inside it just gets better: luxuriant furnishings and fittings, paintings, crystal chandeliers and open fires all add to an ambience of grandeur and opulence. Queen Victoria was particularly taken with the place, and maintaining the royal connections, some of the furniture in the three dining rooms was a gift from the King of Norway. You feel the need to put on the glad rags for dinner, and in any case, dining here without a jacket and tie, gentlemen, is not permitted. Given this stolidly traditional setting, Philip Carnegie's cooking is surprisingly modern, based on the finest native produce, and comes with an abundance of luxurious touches. The fixed-price dinner menu might kick off with roasted veal sweetbreads with macaroni gratin, ceps duxelle and white truffle, or caramelised scallops with pumpkin, salted almonds

and trompette mushrooms, a masterly contrast of flavours and textures. Main courses show the same commitment to tracking down the finest ingredients, brought together with bravura shows of technical expertise and an unerring confidence about palate-pleasing combinations. This could be roasted Ayrshire mallard served with its confit leg, curly kale, baby turnips and black pudding, or loin of monkfish with ras el hanout spices, sprouting broccoli and lightly-spiced Kinlochleven mussels. This is high-impact destination dining so you can expect to bow out with statement desserts: that might be a chocolate mousse (made with Valrhona's finest, naturellement) with pain d'épice ice cream, chestnut cream and orange, or a 10-minute wait for rhubarb soufflé with its sorbet.

Chef Philip Carnegie **Owner** Inverlochy Hotel Ltd **Seats** 40, Pr/dining room 20
Times 12.30-1.45/6.30-10, **Prices** Fixed L 2 course £28, Fixed D 3 course £67,
Tasting menu £85, Starter £16, Main £38, Dessert £13 **Wines** 240 bottles over
£30, 4 bottles under £30, 11 by glass **Parking** 20 **Notes** Children 8 yrs+

starter soufflé of Strathdon Blue stands in a pool of cheese and chive sauce, or there may be king scallop soup with squid-ink croûtons. At main, there's zingingly fresh fish, perhaps John Dory in smoked haddock velouté with brown shrimps and dill mash, as well as rump and belly of Ross-shire lamb, with broad beans and asparagus and minted pea croquette. Lemon tart is creamier than the norm, with a burnt sugar topping, and sharply offset with lemon parfait.

The Birch Tree

Chef Barry Hartshorne **Owner** Barry Hartshorne **Seats** 32 **Times** 12-2/6-10, Closed Mon-Tue, D Sun **Prices** Fixed L 2 course £14.95-£17.95, Starter £4.95-£9, Main £12.50-£18.95, Dessert £6, Service optional **Wines** 5 bottles over £30, 17 bottles under £30, 4 by glass **Parking** 18 **Notes** Sunday L £14.95-£17.95, Children welcome

INVERNESS
Map 23 NH64

Abstract Restaurant & Bar

◉◉ Modern French, European

tel: 01463 223777 **Glenmoriston Town House Hotel, 20 Ness Bank IV2 4SF** **email:** reception@glenmoristontownhouse.com **web:** www.glenmoristontownhouse.com **dir:** 2 mins from city centre, on river opposite theatre

Top Scottish produce in intimate restaurant by the river

Abstract is the restaurant at this luxury boutique hotel on the River Ness a few minutes' stroll from the city centre. There's also a brasserie and a bar with more than 250 bottles of Scotland's national drink. Abstract itself is an elegant room with a darkwood floor, brown high-backed leather-effect seats and slatted blinds at the windows. The kitchen has a modern outlook, occasionally reaching out beyond Europe to provide a diverse choice among its intelligently created dishes. Crab raviolo sitting on spinach and chopped tomato topped with rich, thick bisque purée is a distinctive starter that contrasts with another of tandoori-spiced roast pigeon with couscous. Main courses include cleverly constructed slow-cooked beef fillet, of superb quality, with small chunks of crispy bacon on mushroom purée with silky-smooth tarragon-flecked mash, and rapeseed-poached monkfish tail with braised endive and zesty lemon confit. A cheese trolley is wheeled around at the final stage, or opt for a novel dessert: perhaps a theme on strawberries and cream (sorbet and fruit, plus meringue, basil mousse and jelly and grated iced clotted cream).

Times 6-10, Closed Sun-Mon, L all week

Bunchrew House Hotel

◉◉ Scottish

tel: 01463 234917 **Bunchrew IV3 8TA** **email:** welcome@bunchrewhousehotel.com **web:** www.bunchrewhousehotel.com **dir:** 3m W of Inverness on A862 towards Beauly

A touch of Scottish baronial splendour

Bunchrew House, reached along a tree-lined drive, is a magnificent 17th-century mansion, complete with turrets and a pink façade, on the water's edge of the Beauly Firth. Take a stroll around the gardens, sit in front of a log fire in the drawing room or have a drink in the cocktail lounge before taking a seat in the restaurant, a long rectangular room with bay windows overlooking the sea, part-panelled walls, a ceiling in red and white and a gold fleur-de-lis design in the red carpet. An updated version of traditional Scottish cooking is the kitchen's view of its culinary world. The daily-changing menu might open with smooth, light chicken liver parfait alongside a dollop of fruity chutney and small pieces of excellent home-made soda bread. Follow that with wonderfully fresh and moist hake fillet topped with glossy chive butter on smooth mash flecked with pancetta along with black pudding wrapped in pancetta, cauliflower purée and grilled asparagus. For finale, choose layers of strawberries, cream and shortcake with refreshing basil ice cream.

Times 12-1.45/7-9, Closed 23-26 Dec

Loch Ness Country House Hotel

◉◉ Modern British

tel: 01463 230512 **Loch Ness Rd IV3 8JN** **email:** info@lochnesscountryhousehotel.co.uk **web:** www.lochnesscountryhousehotel.co.uk **dir:** On A82 (S), 1m from Inverness town boundary

Asian-influenced modern cooking for the monster-hunters

The greystone, bay-windowed Georgian house may not be on the lochside but, situated three miles out of Inverness, makes a good operational base for monster-hunters nonetheless. Its interiors are very classy, all stripes and tartan in the grand domestic manner, with dining going on in a pair of interlinked rooms done in restrained buffs and browns. Adam Dwyer is certainly plugged into modern food currents, and amalgamates an array of European and East Asian influences into his contemporary Scottish style. Dishes look crisply composed and full of appeal, as when a circle of home-made black pudding arrives topped with pink chicken liver and foie gras parfait, in turn crowned with apple and vanilla compôte. That could be followed by poached and fried sea bass with crab, samphire and pink fir apples in lemongrass consommé. Another Asian-inspired offering is shiitaki-coated roast pork loin and soy-braised shoulder with sesame pork toast, spiced crackling, puffed pork and pak choi in Chinese-spiced jus. The fragrant notes continue in desserts like basil pannacotta on gingerbread crumble with spiced toffee apple chunks and a ginger beer sorbet.

Chef Adam Dwyer **Owner** Loch Ness Hospitality Ltd **Seats** 42, Pr/dining room 16 **Times** 12-2.30/6-9 **Prices** Fixed L 2 course £12.95-£15.95, Fixed D 3 course £32.50-£40, Tasting menu £55-£65, Starter £5.50-£10.95, Main £13.95-£32, Dessert £6.50-£9.95, Service optional **Wines** 10 bottles over £30, 20 bottles under £30, 9 by glass **Parking** 50 **Notes** Afternoon tea, Sunday L £9.95-£18.95, Vegetarian available, Children welcome

INVERNESS *continued*

The New Drumossie Hotel

Modern Scottish

tel: 01463 236451 **Old Perth Rd IV2 5BE**
email: stay@drumossiehotel.co.uk web: www.drumossiehotel.co.uk
dir: *From A9 follow signs for Culloden Battlefield, hotel on left after 1m*

Confident, seasonal cooking at an art deco hotel

A few miles out of Inverness, the hotel is a sparkling-white art deco beauty, in acres of well-tended grounds framed by the Scottish Highlands — a setting that is balm to the soul. Its charm is due in no small part to the staff who treat guests with engaging politeness and feed them in a setting of well-oiled serenity in the Grill Room, where intricately-presented modern Scottish dishes are built on top-class raw materials. A starter of wood pigeon breast, seared nicely pink and matched with Stornoway Black Pudding, puréed and pickled beetroot, pickled vegetables and game jus shows the style. Mains include crispy pork belly with kale and leek mash, sweetcorn and aubergine purées, and apple and mirin jus. If something simple and sizzling from the grill appeals, there are impeccable Scottish rib-eye and sirloin steaks, with a choice of sauces that includes Arran mustard or whisky cream. Form stays true to the end with a confection of espresso pannacotta, dark chocolate and orange cream, toasted hazelnuts and banana bread mousse.

Chef Stewart Macpherson **Owner** Ness Valley Leisure **Seats** 90, Pr/dining room 30 **Times** 12.30-2/7-9.30 **Prices** Prices not confirmed **Wines** 13 by glass **Parking** 200 **Notes** Sunday L, Vegetarian available, Children welcome

Rocpool

Modern European

tel: 01463 717274 **1 Ness Walk IV3 5NE**
email: info@rocpoolrestaurant.com web: www.rocpoolrestaurant.com
dir: *On W bank of River Ness close to the Eden Court Theatre*

Riverside setting and smart modern cooking

This buzzy contemporary brasserie operation capitalises on its corner site on the banks of the River Ness, with sweeping windows on two sides to open up floodlit views of the river and castle at night. The interior is a cool exercise in contemporary design flair featuring lots of wood and a decor of natural tones. On the menu is an appealing cast of crowd-pleasing modern European dishes built on top-class Scottish produce, starting with hand-dived West Coast scallops with chorizo, its heat softened by spring onion crème fraîche and lemon, garlic and parsley butter. Next up, accurately-timed sirloin of rose veal arrives pink to celebrate early spring in the commendably seasonal company of pea and spinach risotto, asparagus and a warm dressing of feta cheese, mint and lemon. Elsewhere, there might be roast fillet of halibut with clams, cotechino sausage and polenta, spinach and fresh tomato confit. Dessert delivers a perfectly wobbly yogurt and vanilla pannacotta with the refreshing tropical flavours of roasted pineapple, and passionfruit and Malibu syrup.

Chef Steven Devlin **Owner** Steven Devlin **Seats** 55
Times 12-2.30/5.45-10, Closed 25-26 Dec, 1-3 Jan, Sun **Prices** Fixed L 2 course £15.95, Fixed D 2 course £17.95, Starter £3.95-£10.95, Main £12.95-£24.95, Dessert £6.95-£8.90, Service optional **Wines** 18 bottles over £30, 24 bottles under £30, 11 by glass **Parking** On street **Notes** Early D 5.45-6.45pm 2 course £17.95, Vegetarian available, Children welcome

---

KINGUSSIE Map 23 NH70

The Cross

Modern Scottish V NOTABLE WINE LIST

tel: 01540 661166 **Tweed Mill Brae, Ardbroilach Rd PH21 1LB**
email: relax@thecross.co.uk web: www.thecross.co.uk
dir: *From lights in Kingussie centre along Ardbroilach Rd, 300yds left onto Tweed Mill Brae*

Modern Scottish cooking in an old water mill

Surrounded by the wild beauty of the Cairngorm National Park, The Cross is tucked away in a peaceful spot with four acres to call its own. The Gynack Burn once powered the former tweed mill, but today the old stone building is the setting for more leisurely pursuits. It's a seductive location for a restaurant with rooms, and one that is matched by the authenticity of the interior — smart, for sure, but rustic and humble. The kitchen maintains the sense of place by using a good deal of produce from around these parts, and there's refinement to the dishes on the fixed-price and tasting menus. Begin with a tarte fine of foie gras and chicory, or West Coast scallops with Stornoway Black Pudding and compressed apples, and proceed

with the fashionably contemporary partnership of crispy sea bream with confit chicken, or the more classical Scottish grouse with crispy bacon and Savoy cabbage. End with passionfruit soufflé with coconut sorbet, or await the arrival of the cheese trolley. With a serious wine list and up to 40 malts, there's some good drinking to be had.

Chef David Skiggs **Owner** Derek & Celia Kitchingman **Seats** 30 **Times** 12-2.30/7-8.30, Closed Xmas & Jan (ex New Year) **Prices** Fixed L 3 course £25, Tasting menu £60, Service optional **Wines** 88 bottles over £30, 43 bottles under £30, 7 by glass **Parking** 12 **Notes** Afternoon tea £17, ALC D 3 course £55, Tasting menu 6 course, Sunday L, Children welcome

LOCHALINE
Map 20 NM64

The Whitehouse Restaurant
Modern British, Scottish

tel: 01967 421777 & 07884 361545 **PA80 5XT**
email: info@thewhitehouserestaurant.co.uk
dir: Take Corran Ferry on A82, on disembarking left towards Lochaline. Located in village

Vibrant, ingredient-led modern Scottish cooking

What you eat here will depend on the weather, the season and much more besides, for the ethos is all about locally-sourced ingredients from land and sea, and the kitchen works with what nature (and fishermen, farmers, foragers and shooters) provides on the day. The blackboard reveals all. This local bounty is turned into dishes that maintain integrity through simplicity, so you might start with creel-caught langoustine with a mayonnaise made with Scottish rapeseed, and move on to a large Highland crab salad with a gazpacho dressing. It's not all about seafood, though, with stag liver and kidney pan-seared and partnered with a jus made from Tomatin single malt, or local pork belly slow-cooked for 12 hours and served with apple and plum chutney. It all takes place near the ferry crossing to Mull in a simple white house (as promised), with no frills and fuss, just good food.

Chef Michael Burgoyne, Lee Myers **Owner** Jane Stuart Smith, Sarah Jones **Seats** 26 **Times** 12-3/6-9.30, Closed Nov-Mar, Sun-Mon **Prices** Fixed L 2 course fr £19.95, Fixed D 3 course fr £22.95, Starter £5.50-£15, Main £12-£28, Dessert £6-£10, Service optional **Wines** 9 bottles over £30, 17 bottles under £30, 5 by glass **Parking** 10 **Notes** Fixed D only before 5pm, Vegetarian available, Children welcome

MUIR OF ORD
Map 23 NH55

Ord House Hotel
British, French

tel: 01463 870492 **Ord Dr IV6 7UH**
email: admin@ord-house.co.uk **web:** www.ord-house.co.uk
dir: Off A9 at Tore rdbt onto A832. 5m, through Muir of Ord. Left towards Ullapool (A832). Hotel 0.5m on left

Comforting bistro cooking in a 17th-century house

Built for a laird in the 17th century, Ord House sits in 40 acres of woodland and gardens. It's decorated and furnished to reflect the age and style of the property, with log fires crackling away. The small-scale restaurant is on the first floor: pink carpet, polished wooden tables, cushioned wooden chairs and elevated views over the grounds and pond from curtained windows. The cooking leans towards the straightforward, with nothing too highfalutin, just spot-on flavours and fresh ingredients. Expect starters such as a salad of ham and cheddar with mixed leaves, tomatoes, a hard-boiled egg and croûtons, or smoked salmon pâté, then poached chicken breast stuffed with haggis in white wine sauce, or king prawn linguine in Mediterranean-style garlic sauce. Cap things off with classic crème brûlée or rich, sticky ginger pudding with ginger and brandy sauce.

Chef Eliza Allen **Owner** Eliza & John Allen **Seats** 26 **Times** 12-2/7-9, Closed Nov-end Feb **Prices** Starter £6.25-£9.50, Main £15.75-£21.25, Dessert £5.50-£6.95 **Wines** 9

bottles over £30, 37 bottles under £30, 4 by glass **Parking** 24 **Notes** Vegetarian available, Children welcome

NAIRN
Map 23 NH85

Boath House
⬤⬤⬤⬤ – see page 652

Golf View Hotel & Spa
Modern Scottish V

tel: 01667 452301 **Seabank Rd IV12 4HD**
email: golfview@crerarhotels.com **web:** www.golfviewhotel.co.uk
dir: Off A96 into Seabank Rd & continue to end

Modern Scottish cooking with golfing and sea views

The clue is in the name at a hotel that's another of Scotland's numerous places consecrated to the swinging of five-irons. In case you were under the impression there was only golf to look at, though, it enjoys a bracing seaside location, looking out over the Moray Firth not far from Inverness. Dining is in a choice of settings – the informal Links Brasserie with views of the greens, or the Fairways Restaurant, a more traditional half-panelled space with chandeliers and stripy drapes. A six-course fixed-price menu of modern Scottish food looks the best route to take, essaying a course from quail's egg hollandaise, through beetroot carpaccio with goats' cheese, to a demi-tasse of wild mushroom velouté, then on to a double-act of Highland venison and wood pigeon with rösti in game jus. A dessert such as plum crumble with ginger ice cream is followed by a taster serving of a single cheese, perhaps Dunsyre Blue with grape jelly.

Chef Saurav Kumar **Owner** Crerar Hotels **Seats** 70 **Times** 6.45-9, Closed L Mon-Sat **Prices** Tasting menu £32.95, Starter £7.95-£10.95, Main £12.95-£46.95, Dessert £4.95-£7.95, Service optional **Wines** 11 bottles over £30, 35 bottles under £30, 8 by glass **Parking** 30, Next to hotel on street **Notes** Steak night Thu, Tasting menu 6 course, Sunday L £9.95-£12.95, Children welcome

SPEAN BRIDGE
Map 22 NN28

Russell's at Smiddy House
⬤⬤ Modern Scottish

tel: 01397 712335 **Roy Bridge Rd PH34 4EU**
email: enquiry@smiddyhouse.com **web:** www.smiddyhouse.com
dir: In village centre, 9m N of Fort William, on A82 towards Inverness

Seasonal cooking amid elegant pastoral surroundings

Occupying a corner spot on the main road through the heart of Spean Bridge, the low-roofed, whitewashed building offers four smart bedrooms to stop over and spoil yourself with Glen Russell's seasonal Scottish cooking. Russell's, located on the ground floor in the 'Smiddyhouse', (once the village blacksmith's, hence the name) is an intimate, candelit spot where crisp linen-clothed tables are decked with sparkling glasses, quality china and fresh flowers. Well-presented modern Scottish cuisine makes good use of top-notch local materials, as in a starter of seared West Coast scallops partnered by Stornoway Black Pudding and two contrasting sauces of orange and butter. This paves the way for a well-wrought main course of saddle of Highland venison with a black pudding bonbon, mashed turnip, curly kale, carrots and a punchy whisky cream sauce, the whole dish dusted with toasted oatmeal. Exotic flavours are mustered at dessert stage for a finale involving marinated pineapple carpaccio layered with toasted coconut meringues, matched with vanilla ice cream and orange syrup.

Chef Glen Russell **Owner** Glen Russell, Robert Bryson **Seats** 38 **Times** 6-9, Closed 2 days a week (Nov-Apr), L Mon-Sat **Prices** Prices not confirmed **Wines** 14 bottles over £30, 20 bottles under £30, 7 by glass **Parking** 15 **Notes** Sunday L, Vegetarian available, Children welcome

Boath House ❀❀❀❀

NAIRN

Map 23 NH85

Modern British V 🍷 NOTABLE WINE LIST

tel: 01667 454896 **Auldearn IV12 5TE**
email: wendy@boath-house.com **web:** www.boath-house.com
dir: *2m E of Nairn on A96 (Inverness to Aberdeen road)*

Astonishing culinary intricacy in a restored Georgian manor

It's hard to imagine that this glorious Georgian property was looking worse for wear until it was taken over by Don and Wendy Matheson at the beginning of the 1990s. They not only restored it with stunning affect into the luxury retreat we see today, but they've created one of Scotland's finest dining destinations to boot. The gardens have received equal care and attention – Wendy just happens to be a garden designer – with 22 acres of pretty gardens, pristine lawns, wild woodland, trout lake and walled gardens to explore. They grow lots of things for the table in the walled garden, including vegetables and herbs, while bees do their bit for the environment and hens provide the eggs. The interior of the house is elegant and its period features are enhanced by chic fixtures and fittings. A meal starts with canapés in the elegant lounge. The dining room, like everywhere else, is pretty classy and French doors look out over the lawn and down to the lake. Charles Lockley has been at the stoves here for 18 years or so and has a trusted network of suppliers providing the very best regional produce to combine with what he grows or forages himself. His cooking is thrillingly contemporary without ever losing sight of the fact that these amazing ingredients need room to breathe, and the technical skill on show is impressive. Fixed-price lunch and dinner menus change on a daily basis with three- or six-course options in the evening. Dish descriptions may well be brief, but what follows is anything but sparse. Local game gets a good showing in an opener of pheasant and grouse with quail's egg, before a refined salmon course with crème fraîche and some Avruga caviar. Next up might be another local favourite in the form of roe deer with salsify and artichokes, or a fish course with halibut, truffle and celery. Everything looks beautiful on the plate and the composition of each dish shows a real eye for detail. Sweet courses might include a clever interpretation of rice pudding flavoured with nutmeg and served with quince and apple, or an impressive Macae chocolate

construction. The cheese course might be Black Bomber with prunes or Broon Coo brie with an oatmeal wafer. The wine list is a serious piece of work and afternoon tea a real treat if you find yourself around (and hungry) at the right time of day.

Chef Charles Lockley **Owner** Mr & Mrs D Matheson **Seats** 28, Pr/dining room 8 **Times** 12.30-1.15/7-Close, **Prices** Fixed L 2 course £24, Fixed D 3 course £45, Tasting menu £70, Service optional **Wines** 120 bottles over £30, 20 bottles under £30, 15 by glass **Parking** 25 **Notes** Tasting menu 6 course, Afternoon tea, Sunday L £24-£30, Children welcome

STRONTIAN
Map 22 NM86

Kilcamb Lodge Hotel & Restaurant

◉◉ Modern European, Scottish V

tel: 01967 402257 **PH36 4HY**
email: enquiries@kilcamblodge.co.uk **web:** www.kilcamblodge.co.uk
dir: Take Corran ferry off A82. Follow A861 to Strontian. 1st left over bridge after village

Traditional seafood specialities and modern Scottish cooking

The original Georgian house is the white-fronted bit in the middle, while two grey stone wings were clamped on in the Victorian era. Dr Fraser Darling, author of the *West Highland Survey*, called the place home just after the war, and its historical credentials are respected in the formal tone that distinguishes the main dining room, where crisp linens, abundant flowers and candlelight are the style. Less formal dining is on offer in the Driftwood Brasserie. A new departure is the speciality seafood menu, a daily-changing offering bought from a fishing-boat operating out of Tiree. Cracked crab claws with a dip, split langoustines in garlic butter, and seared trout with mustard mash are among its strengths, while the main menu deals in shredded duck leg with spiced onion, pak choi and a fried duck egg, followed by twice-cooked pork belly with burnt apple purée in whisky sauce, or spiced monkfish in green olive dressing with onion rings. Finish with date and toffee pudding and caramelised banana, or with the lighter option of pannacotta served with orange and star anise sorbet and chillified tropical fruit salsa.

Chef Gary Phillips **Owner** Sally & David Fox **Seats** 40 **Times** 12-2/5.30-9.30, Closed 1 Jan-1 Feb **Prices** Service optional **Wines** 53 bottles over £30, 16 bottles under £30, 10 by glass **Parking** 28 **Notes** Afternoon tea, Sunday L £19.50, Children 5 yrs+

TAIN
Map 23 NH78

The Glenmorangie Highland Home at Cadboll

◉◉ British, French

tel: 01862 871671 **Cadboll, Fearn IV20 1XP**
email: relax@glenmorangie.co.uk **web:** www.theglenmorangiehouse.com
dir: N on A9, at Nigg Rdbt turn right onto B9175 (before Tain) & follow signs for hotel

Dinner party dining in a magnificent Highland location

Set in fantastic grounds with a large walled garden and a tree-lined walk down to its own private beach, The Glenmorangie has appeal in spades. The namesake Distillery is nearby, making it something of a whisky lover's paradise (whisky tasting weekends prove a big pull), and as if that weren't enough, the French-influenced cuisine is out of the top drawer. Guests dine dinner-party-style here, at the long oak table. Seasonal produce might come straight from the walled garden to take a star turn in technically impressive creations on four-course, no-choice menus. Poached fillet of halibut with razor clams and mussels partnered with bok choy and champagne broth precedes a main course with real wow factor – a workout of local Peking duck involving truffled honey-glazed breast, leg rillettes and liver parfait with shallot purée, 'tattie' terrine, baby veg and duck jus. Dessert brings another tour de force of flavours and texture via banana (caramelised and parfait), dark chocolate and tonka bean ganache, peanut butter mousse, chocolate and peanut purée and passionfruit gel.

Chef David Graham, John Wilson **Owner** Glenmorangie Ltd **Seats** 30, Pr/dining room 12 **Times** 8-close, Closed Jan, L ex by prior arrangement **Prices** Prices not confirmed, Service optional **Wines** 43 bottles over £30, 10 bottles under £30, 15 by glass **Parking** 60 **Notes** 4 course D £55, D single sitting guests seated 7.30 for 8pm, Vegetarian available, Children 18 yrs+

THURSO
Map 23 ND16

Forss House Hotel

◉◉ Modern Scottish, British

tel: 01847 861201 **Forss KW14 7XY**
email: anne@forsshousehotel.co.uk **web:** www.forsshousehotel.co.uk
dir: On A836, 5m outside Thurso

Gentle country cooking in a Highland Georgian hotel

You can't get much further away from urban bustle in the mainland British Isles than the northern Highlands, where this Georgian country-house hotel luxuriates in splendid tranquillity below a waterfall on the River Forss, amid 20 acres of woodland. It was once the seat of the Radclyffe family, whose portraits hang in the dining room, many of them dating from before the house itself was built. Views of the gardens and riverside soothe the soul, even as the gentle Scottish country cooking seduces the taste buds. Plenty of pedigree Highland produce is on parade, naturally, with Scrabster scallops to start, in a winning combination with sweet shallot purée and parsley and caper dressing, while the main course might see Caithness lamb teamed with root veg dauphinoise and glazed red cabbage, or pan-roasted lemon sole accompanied by crushed potatoes mixed with Scrabster crab. Finish up with locally gathered mixed berries to garnish frozen strawberry mousse and crushed meringue, or with liquid-centred chocolate fondant with salt caramel ice cream and a coulis made from more of those berries.

Chef Ross Cameron **Owner** Ian & Sabine Richards **Seats** 26, Pr/dining room 14 **Times** 7-9, Closed 23 Dec-4 Jan, L all week **Prices** Starter £5.50-£7.50, Main £12.50-£24.50, Dessert £6.50-£7.50, Service optional **Wines** 7 bottles over £30, 18 bottles under £30, 4 by glass **Parking** 14 **Notes** Vegetarian available, Children welcome

TORRIDON
Map 22 NG95

The Torridon Restaurant

◉◉◉ – see page 654

WICK
Map 23 ND35

Mackay's Hotel

◉ Modern Scottish NEW

tel: 01955 602323 **Union St KW1 5ED**
email: info@mackayshotel.co.uk **web:** www.mackayshotel.co.uk
dir: Opposite Caithness General Hospital

Local produce in a cheerful hotel bistro

Situated on the shortest street in the world – the front door is located on Ebenezer Place – Mackay's Hotel is a local institution that has been run by the same family for 40 or so years. The hotel is also home to the No. 1 Bistro, a gently contemporary restaurant with a relaxed vibe. The kitchen makes good use of quality local ingredients with the suppliers name-checked on the menu, and there's a definite modernity to the output. Take an attractive starter of pan-fried hand-dived scallops, for example, which arrive in the company of smoked cauliflower purée, haggis bonbon and pickled shallots. Next up, baked Scrabster cod is an altogether more straightforward dish, with the flavoursome fish on creamy mash surrounded by herb and shellfish broth. Dessert brings forth a light iced passionfruit parfait with chocolate crumb and coconut and lime cream. There's a buzzy bar for real ales, cocktails and a terrific range of whiskies.

Chef Andrew Manson **Owner** Mr D Murray Lamont **Seats** 40, Pr/dining room 30 **Times** 12-2.30/5.30-9.30, Closed 24-25 Dec, 1-2 Jan **Prices** Fixed L 2 course £12.95, Fixed D 3 course £30, Tasting menu £50, Starter £4.95-£7.95, Main £10.95-£24.95, Dessert £3.95-£5.95 **Wines** 5 bottles over £30, 57 bottles under £30, 20 by glass **Notes** Sunday L £12.50-£14.95, Vegetarian available, Children welcome

NORTH LANARKSHIRE

CUMBERNAULD
Map 21 NS77

The Westerwood House & Golf Resort

◉ Modern Scottish

tel: 01236 457171 **1 St Andrews Dr, Westerwood G68 0EW**
email: stewartgoldie@qhotels.co.uk **web:** www.qhotels.co.uk
dir: *A80 junct signed Dullatur, from junct follow signs for hotel*

Confident modern cooking and top-drawer service

A sharply modern construction of brick and glass, Westerwood House is kitted out with business facilities and a snazzy spa, with the Campsie Hills creating a fine backdrop for its very own 18-hole golf course. And it all takes place a short distance outside of Glasgow. The restaurant – Flemings – matches the contemporary mood of the hotel and its colour scheme recalls the natural Scottish landscape. A modern-minded menu delivers the likes of céviche of halibut with candied lime and passionfruit pearls among first courses, followed by baked pork belly with honey-glazed figs and prunes soaked in Armagnac, or go for the simplicity of chargrilled Cairn Hill rib-eye. There's a tasting menu, too, with wine flight option. The creativity continues into desserts such as rhubarb crème brûlée matched with a liquorice ice cream, or another that combines orange and passionfruit in a soufflé.

Chef Stewart Goldie **Owner** Q Hotels **Seats** 180, Pr/dining room 60
Times 6.30-9.30, Closed Jan, Sun-Mon, L all week **Prices** Tasting menu fr £35, Starter £5.25-£9, Main £14-£28, Dessert £5.25-£8.25, Service optional 8%
Wines 21 bottles over £30, 23 bottles under £30, 12 by glass **Parking** 250
Notes Vegetarian available, Children welcome

SOUTH LANARKSHIRE

EAST KILBRIDE
Map 20 NS65

Macdonald Crutherland House

◉◉ British

tel: 01355 577000 **Strathaven Rd G75 0QZ**
email: general.crutherland@macdonald-hotels.co.uk **web:** www.macdonald-hotels.co.uk
dir: *Follow A726 signed Strathaven, straight over Torrance rdbt, hotel on left after 250yds*

Elegant hotel dining room with accomplished cooking

With the original parts of the building dating from the early 1700s, Crutherland House stands in nearly 40 acres of peaceful grounds. There are conference facilities aplenty these days, plus a spa in which to unwind and detox. The hotel is done out in a traditional manner, not least in the restaurant, with its panelled walls, paintings and well-spaced, burnished darkwood tables. The menu takes a comforting classical approach to culinary matters, with plenty of Scottish ingredients on show. Start with traditional smoked salmon from John Ross Jnr of Aberdeen, for example, or smoked haddock and leek fishcakes with lemon and parsley mayonnaise. Among main courses there are steaks cooked on the grill (21-day hung Scottish sirloin, maybe), or the likes of pan-roasted venison with dauphinoise potatoes, honey-glazed parsnips and blackberry jus. Among desserts, citrus tart competes with dark chocolate truffle cake with coffee anglaise and chocolate ice cream. There are Scottish cheeses, too.

Times 7-9, Closed L all week

The Torridon Restaurant ❀❀❀

TORRIDON
Map 22 NG95

British, French V ❖ NOTABLE WINE LIST

tel: 01445 791242 **By Achnasheen, Wester Ross IV22 2EY**
email: info@thetorridon.com **web:** www.thetorridon.com
dir: *From Inverness take A9 N, follow signs to Ullapool (A835). At Garve take A832 to Kinlochewe, take A896 to Torridon. Do not turn off to Torridon Village. Hotel on right after Annat*

A piece of loch-side Highland luxury

The Torridon estate covers 58 acres of some of the most compellingly wild and beautiful countryside in the UK. There's a farm on the estate, too, that's home to Highland cattle and Tamworth pigs, some of which will feature on the menu in the hotel's 1887 Restaurant. The setting by a sea loch is second to none and the house itself, a former Victorian hunting lodge, looks the part with its turrets and old-world solidity. It's stylish and elegant on the inside, where period features and traditional furnishing create a chic finish. The restaurant is similarly on point, the two interconnecting rooms lined with oak panels and blessed with spectacular views when the sun is up. Chef David Barnett and his team can call on the estate and their own kitchen garden for fresh, seasonal produce and what isn't on their doorstep is sourced with care and attention. The fixed-price, five-course menu offers a choice of two options at some of the courses,

but it's really a case of going with the flow and revelling in the skill and dedication of this brigade. In winter, proceedings might begin with mushroom cappuccino before Brahan Estate pheasant arrives in the form of a mousse, with salsify, tomato and walnuts. Next up, it's a choice between megrim sole (with artichokes and baby onions) or Dornoch lamb (with rosemary and celeriac), and whichever way you go you'll be sure to find careful execution and eye-catching presentation. The impressive modern Scottish output continues into desserts such as roasted plum with creamed cheese mousse and praline, and stump up a wee bit more cash to add a course of British and French cheeses. Like everything else here, the wine list is a class act.

Chef David Barnett **Owner** Daniel & Rohaise Rose-Bristow **Seats** 38, Pr/dining room 16 **Times** 12-2/6.45-9, Closed 2 Jan for 5 wks **Prices** Prices not confirmed, Service optional **Wines** 8 by glass **Parking** 20 **Notes** Fixed D 5 course £60, Children 10 yrs+

STRATHAVEN
Map 20 NS74

Rissons at Springvale

◉ Modern Scottish

tel: 01357 520234 & 521131 **18 Lethame Rd ML10 6AD**
email: info@rissons.co.uk **web:** www.rissonsrestaurant.co.uk
dir: *M74 junct 8, A71, through Stonehouse to Strathaven*

Modern Scottish bistro cooking in a comfortable restaurant with rooms

Centrally located near Strathaven's main shopping area, this restaurant with rooms is a popular dining destination. The restaurant, looking over the well-manicured garden, is smartly done out, a bright room with wooden floors, dark leather chairs and plain wooden tables; there's also a lounge with a wood-burning stove. Quality produce is cooked with attention to detail, and dishes are uncluttered by unnecessary flounces. Crisp-coated fishcake, moist and tasty within, is complemented by strips of soft dill-marinated mackerel and some pickled vegetables to make an enjoyable starter. Follow perhaps with pork belly on braised red cabbage surrounded by red wine sauce, accompanied by three haggis bonbons, parsnip purée and a couple of roast potatoes, or pan-fried salmon fillet with kedgeree. Cheeses are Scottish, and dessert might be excellent vanilla crème brûlée with home-made berry jam.

Chef Scott Baxter, Euan Munro **Owner** Scott & Anne Baxter **Seats** 40
Times 1-close/6-9.30, Closed New Year, 1 wk Jan, 1st wk Jul, Mon-Tue, L Wed-Sat, D Sun **Prices** Fixed L 2 course £15.95, Fixed D 3 course £18.95, Starter £4.50-£9.50, Main £12.50-£21.50, Dessert £5.50-£6.50, Service optional **Wines** 6 by glass **Parking** 10 **Notes** Early evening menu Wed-Fri, Sunday L £15.95-£18.95, Vegetarian available, Children welcome

EAST LOTHIAN

ABERLADY
Map 21 NT47

Ducks at Kilspindie

◉◉ Modern British ⭐ NOTABLE WINE LIST

tel: 01875 870682 **Main St EH32 0RE**
email: kilspindie@ducks.co.uk **web:** www.ducks.co.uk
dir: *A1 (Bankton junct) take 1st exit to North Berwick. At next rdbt 3rd exit onto A198 signed Longniddry, left towards Aberlady. At T-junct, facing river, right to Aberlady*

Creative cooking in smart restaurant with rooms

Malcolm Duck's place in the heart of a small village covers all the bases with its buzzy bar bistro, diminutive restaurant and smart, boutique-style accommodation. There are more than 20 golf courses in this neck of the woods, while anyone with a taste for whisky and Cuban cigars will find themselves in heaven here at Kilspindie. It matters not, though, if those pastimes don't appeal, for no excuse is needed to rock up to eat in Duck's Restaurant (or the more casual Duck's Bistro). The good-looking restaurant with its 10 tables and objets d'art (including a few relating to ducks) is matched by the attractiveness of what arrives on the plate. The kitchen turns out appealing contemporary combinations like a pig's head terrine with the accompanying flavours of parsnip and pear, while main-course plaice is perfectly cooked and partnered with cauliflower purée, quinoa and grilled baby leeks. Finish with spiced pear soufflé.

Times 12-3/6-10, Closed 25 Dec, Mon-Tue

GULLANE
Map 21 NT48

La Potinière

◉◉ Modern British

tel: 01620 843214 **Main St EH31 2AA**
dir: *5m from North Berwick on A198*

Well-considered cooking on the high street

A raspberry-painted exterior, with net curtains hanging in the windows, conceals a must-visit restaurant. It's a double-act operation with both Mary Runciman and Keith Marley at the stoves, and the small scale of the operation allows them to oversee every last detail, make everything in-house and time each dish to the second. Scrupulous sourcing means the menus change regularly, depending on what's best seasonally, with some produce grown in their own garden. The deal is just a couple of choices per course, kicking off with courgette and rosemary soup with apple crème fraîche, or twice-baked cheese soufflé with chives and tomato cream. A sense of balance and high levels of skill are evident in main courses: perhaps braised salmon partnered by crushed new potatoes with spring onion and smoked salmon, and tarragon and tomato sauce, or guinea fowl, its poached and seared breast teamed with confit leg, dauphinoise potatoes and a guinea fowl and mushroom jus. For dessert, vanilla pannacotta is contrasted with poached nectarine, raspberry sorbet and shortbread.

Chef Mary Runciman, Keith Marley **Owner** Mary Runciman **Seats** 24
Times 12.30-1.30/7-8.30, Closed Xmas, Jan, BHs, Mon-Tue, D Sun **Prices** Prices not confirmed, Service optional **Wines** 31 bottles over £30, 26 bottles under £30, 7 by glass **Parking** 10 **Notes** Fixed D 3/4 course £38/£43, Sunday L, Vegetarian available, Children welcome

NORTH BERWICK
Map 21 NT58

Macdonald Marine Hotel & Spa

◉◉ European

tel: 01620 897300 **Cromwell Rd EH39 4LZ**
email: sales.marine@macdonald-hotels.co.uk **web:** www.macdonaldhotels.co.uk/marine
dir: *From A198 turn into Hamilton Rd at lights then 2nd right*

Impressive Victorian pile with confident and accomplished cooking

On Scotland's majestic East Coast, the Marine Hotel is an upscale Grade II listed Victorian manor overlooking the East Lothian golf course. The Craigleith Restaurant surveys the action on the links through sweeping bay windows, while oak panelling, plush fabrics and chandeliers suspended from lofty ceilings convey a distinct sense of occasion. The service keeps things suitably friendly and relaxed. The kitchen is proud of what's on its doorstep and puts this splendid regional produce to good use, keeping up to speed with contemporary culinary goings on, while showing respect for classical thinking. Braised pork belly with white bean and chorizo casserole has a satisfyingly well-balanced richness, followed by an impeccably-timed fillet of sea bass partnered with king prawn and sweetcorn broth. Otherwise, the uncomplicated appeal of slow-braised beef cheeks with creamed potatoes and rosemary jus should hit the spot. To finish, classic crème brûlée is served with mango sorbet, or there might be the deep comfort of warm treacle tart with clotted cream.

Times 12.30-2.30/6.30-9.30

WEST LOTHIAN

LINLITHGOW
Map 21 NS97

Champany Inn

◉◉ Traditional British

tel: 01506 834532 & 834388 **Champany Corner EH49 7LU**
email: reception@champany.com
dir: *2m NE of Linlithgow. From M9 (N) junct 3, at top of slip road turn right. Champany 500yds on right*

Upmarket steakhouse in a characterful old mill

The Champany Inn deals in the polar opposite of fussy, faddy food and sticks to what it knows best: this is the destination of choice for fans of properly-hung, expertly-butchered and chargrilled slabs of Class-A meat. The rambling cluster of buildings dates from the 16th century, and focuses on the main circular restaurant in a former horse-powered flour mill, with its candlelit burnished wooden tables and bare-stone walls beneath a vaulted roof. Chicken liver parfait is a classic they do to perfection here, and it is all the better for a sharp Gewürztraminer jelly to cut its richness. Or you might start with hot-smoked salmon or cod from the Champany smokepot. But this is a mecca for beef, so the main event offers up your favourite cut – T-bone, porterhouse, rib-eye, Chateaubriand and all points in between – whacks it on a charcoal grill, and delivers the result timed to perfection. Quality of the raw materials is second to none, and consequently expensive. If you're on a budget, go for the more wallet-friendly Chop and Ale House.

Chef C Davidson, D Gibson **Owner** Mr & Mrs C Davidson **Seats** 50, Pr/dining room 30 **Times** 12.30-2/7-10, Closed 25-26 Dec, 1-2 Jan, Sun, L Sat **Prices** Fixed L 2 course fr £25.50, Fixed D 3 course fr £42.50, Starter £9.50-£17.50, Main £31-£49, Dessert £8.95 **Wines** 450 bottles over £30, 24 bottles under £30, 8 by glass **Parking** 50 **Notes** Vegetarian available, Children 8 yrs+

Livingston's Restaurant

◉◉ Modern British, European ᴠ

tel: 01506 846565 **52 High St EH49 7AE**
email: contact@livingstons-restaurant.co.uk **web:** www.livingstons-restaurant.co.uk
dir: *On high street opposite old post office*

Classic and modern cookery with frolicking rabbits on view

The address may technically be on Linlithgow's bustling high street, but access from a narrow alleyway at the back makes it feel a world away from the crowds, the more so when you see a family of rabbits frolicking on the lawn outside the window. A warm-hearted family-run place with a clean-lined look, all whitewashed walls and tiled floor, this is a popular spot for a productive mingle of modern and classic Scottish cookery. The former might set you up for a canter through the contemporary repertoire in the form of carrot and shiitaki terrine with miso gel, pickled mushrooms and a peanut and chilli spring roll, then pine nut-crusted venison fillet with its own haggis, artichokes and mash, or else stone bass with gnocchi in chicken jus and cep foam. If all that sounds a little too new-fangled, stick satisfyingly with chicken liver parfait and red onion marmalade, followed by cod with wilted greens in beurre noisette. Desserts might include a disassembled cranachan, or there are thoroughbred Scottish cheeses. Coffee comes with Mrs Livingston's home-made tablet.

Chef Ian Gourlay **Owner** The Livingston family **Seats** 60, Pr/dining room 15 **Times** 12-2.30/6-9.30, Closed 2 wks Jan, Mon **Prices** Fixed D 3 course £42.50, Starter £4.95-£6.50, Main £12.50-£19.95, Dessert £5.95-£7.50, Service optional **Wines** 32 bottles over £30, 29 bottles under £30, 6 by glass **Parking** NCP Linlithgow Cross, on street **Notes** Midwk menu offer 3 course £25, Sunday L £25, Children welcome

UPHALL
Map 21 NT07

Macdonald Houston House

◉◉ Traditional British, Modern Scottish

tel: 01506 853831 **EH52 6JS**
email: houstoun@macdonald-hotels.co.uk
web: www.macdonaldhotels.co.uk/our-hotels/macdonald-houstoun-house
dir: *M8 junct 3 follow Broxburn signs, straight over rdbt then at mini-rdbt turn right towards Uphall, hotel 1m on right*

Scottish cooking in an atmospheric tower restaurant

The white-painted house sits in a secluded spot surrounded by 22 acres of peaceful woodlands to the west of Edinburgh. It dates from the 16th century and Mary, Queen of Scots is said to be a past visitor. Recently redecorated, up in the tower the four rooms that make up the restaurant – Jeremy Wares at Houstoun House – sport deep burgundy walls, grand chandeliers and elegant unclothed tables lit by a single tall candle. The kitchen relies heavily on quality Scottish ingredients and presents them in a modern, unfussy style. You might start with thin onion and thyme tart and beetroot relish, or seared Skye scallops with red wine risotto and tomato pesto, before moving on to a traditional ashet (a pie) of ox cheek with creamy mash and root vegetables. The patriotic mood continues with a rich Caledonia burnt cream with rhubarb, or seasonal cranachan mess, amongst the desserts.

Chef Jeremy Wares, Chris Hazelton **Owner** Macdonald Hotels **Seats** 65, Pr/dining room 30 **Times** 6.30-9.30, Closed L all week **Prices** Fixed D 3 course £30, Starter £7.95-£9.50, Main £18-£24, Dessert £6.95-£9, Service optional **Wines** 60 bottles over £30, 16 bottles under £30, 13 by glass **Parking** 200 **Notes** Vegetarian available, Children welcome

MIDLOTHIAN

DALKEITH
Map 21 NT36

The Sun Inn

◉ Modern, Traditional

tel: 0131 663 2456 & 663 1534 **Lothian Bridge EH22 4TR**
email: thesuninn@live.co.uk **web:** www.thesuninnedinburgh.co.uk
dir: *Opposite Newbattle Viaduct on the A7 near Eskbank*

Winning menus in a popular gastro-pub

'Eat, drink, relax' exhorts the motto of this gastro-pub, and it's easy to comply, the last helped along by friendly, obliging staff and the conversion in 2008 of the old building that combines fabulous boutique bedrooms, and a good dose of rustic-chic style with the original oak beams, exposed stone and panelling. Expect welcoming log fires in winter, a bright patio in summer, and whatever the season, Scotland's larder forms the backbone of the kitchen's output. An eclectic menu, supported by blackboards name-checking local suppliers, delivers pub classics as well as inventive but not over-blown contemporary dishes. Pig's cheek with celeriac and cider purée with a baby toffee apple, for example, while mains could bring Scotch game pie with confit and rolled rabbit, pan-seared pigeon breast, prune purée, sprouts and bacon and horseradish mash. There's beer from the independent Stewart's of Edinburgh and a well-chosen wine list to complete the picture.

Chef Ian Minto, Barry Drummond **Owner** Bernadette McCarron **Seats** 90 **Times** 12-2/6-9, Closed 26 Dec, 1 Jan **Prices** Starter £5-£10, Main £13-£22, Dessert £5-£6.50, Service optional **Wines** 15 bottles over £30, 17 bottles under £30, 19 by glass **Parking** 75 **Notes** Early bird 2/3 course £11/£14 served 6-7pm, Sunday L £15-£18, Vegetarian available, Children welcome

MORAY

FORRES
Map 23 NJ05

Cluny Bank

@ Traditional European

tel: 01309 674304 **69 St Leonards Rd IV36 1DW**
email: info@clunybankhotel.co.uk **web:** www.clunybankhotel.co.uk
dir: From Forres High St turn down Tolbooth St beside Clocktower. At rdbt take 2nd exit (B9010), 500yds on left

Classical cooking and warm hospitality in a smart setting

A substantial Victorian mansion in lush, green gardens, Cluny Bank has traditionally-styled decor and a small, smart restaurant called Franklin's. It's the domain of chef-patron Lloyd Kenny, who is the sole hand in the kitchen (and the soul of the place, along with wife Julia out front). There is a lot of period charm to the restaurant and a definite air of sophistication. The menu is suitably classically focused, with the local Moray suppliers duly name-checked. You might kick off with mini oxtail suet pudding with a rich gravy, or pan-fried monkfish cheeks with shimeji mushroom fricassée and salsa verde, and follow on with a duo of pork – slow-cooked Ibérian black pig's cheek and Gables Farm loin – or grilled whole Dover sole. Chef likes to come out of the kitchen and his bonhomie is very welcome indeed, as are his desserts such as chocolate and rosemary pot with burnt caramel ice cream.

Chef Lloyd Kenny **Owner** Lloyd & Julia Kenny **Seats** 24 **Times** 6.30-8.45, Closed Sun, L all week **Prices** Starter £4.95-£9.95, Main £18.95-£26.95, Dessert £6.25, Service optional **Wines** 29 bottles over £30, 41 bottles under £30, 7 by glass **Parking** 10 **Notes** Vegetarian available, Children 8 yrs+

PERTH & KINROSS

AUCHTERARDER
Map 21 NN91

Andrew Fairlie@Gleneagles

@@@@ – see page 658

The Strathearn

@@ British, French | NOTABLE WINE LIST

tel: 01764 694270 **The Gleneagles Hotel PH3 1NF**
email: gleneagles.restaurant.reservations@gleneagles.com **web:** www.gleneagles.com
dir: Off A9 at exit for A823 follow signs for Gleneagles Hotel

Classical and modern cooking in art deco dining room

The vast hotel has a worldwide reputation for its championship golf courses and it has quite a reputation for cooking too, with Andrew Fairlie@Gleneagles as well as The Strathearn, a splendid art deco room with grand columns and moulded ceilings. A sense of drama is generated by the number of trolleys wheeled to the tables: fillet steak is flambéed, whole Dover sole is taken off the bone, roast meats are carved. If this creates the impression that the restaurant is in some time warp, think again: the kitchen is sharp enough to embrace the contemporary as well as the classics. Start with dressed crab accompanied by green apple jelly and tagliatelle, or wood pigeon with mooli choucroute, cherry purée and cocoa sesame crisp. Products are from the top drawer, and dishes are appealingly composed, main courses ranging from properly timed roast cod with black truffle, salsify and braised baby gem to guinea fowl ballotine with leg confit, girolles, sweetcorn, beetroot and potato espuma. Puddings could run to Grand Marnier soufflé with marmalade ice cream.

Chef Jonathon Wright **Owner** Diageo plc **Seats** 322 **Times** 12.30-2.30/7-10, Closed L Mon-Sat **Prices** Prices not confirmed, Service optional **Wines** 15 by glass **Parking** 300 **Notes** Sunday L, Vegetarian available, Children welcome

COMRIE
Map 21 NN72

Royal Hotel

@ Traditional Scottish

tel: 01764 679200 **Melville Square PH6 2DN**
email: reception@royalhotel.co.uk **web:** www.royalhotel.co.uk
dir: In main square, 7m from Crieff, on A85

Luxury small hotel with confident modern cooking

The 18th-century stone building on the main street of this riverside village is now a plush small-scale luxury hotel, with a peaceful library and lounge for pre-dinner drinks, where youthful staff take food orders, and a restaurant split into two areas linked by double doors. The kitchen's in the capable hands of David Milsom, who gives a gently modern tilt to his output without sacrificing tried-and-tested favourites. The seasonally-changing menu might open with fettuccine, cooked al dente, with a sauce of butternut squash, mushrooms and chestnuts, served with sage butter and parmesan shavings, or reassuringly familiar potted shrimps. Trustworthy sourcing is clear in pink slices of venison, of excellent quality, with black pudding clapshot, buttery spring greens and a port and redcurrant sauce, and in sea bass fillet with tomato tagliatelle. Standards are well maintained in puddings of vanilla pannacotta with chopped pineapple, and Eton Mess.

Chef David Milsom **Owner** Jerry & Teresa Milsom **Seats** 60, Pr/dining room 40 **Times** 12-2/6.30-9 **Prices** Starter £4.95-£7.95, Main £8.50-£22.50, Dessert £5.95, Service optional **Wines** 7 bottles over £30, 28 bottles under £30, 7 by glass **Parking** 18 **Notes** Sunday L £12.50-£24.50, Vegetarian available, Children welcome

Andrew Fairlie@Gleneagles ❀❀❀❀

AUCHTERARDER   Map 21 NN91

Modern French V ◆ NOTABLE WINE LIST

tel: 01764 694267 **The Gleneagles Hotel PH3 1NF**
email: reservations@andrewfairlie.co.uk
dir: *From A9 take Gleneagles exit, hotel in 1m*

Thrilling cooking at the hermetic heart of a golfing hotel

Andrew Fairlie was the winner of the first Roux Scholarship back in 1984 and his success stands as testament to the initiative that set so many chefs on the road to success. The legacy of that win can be seen in Fairlie's cooking today, as his passion for French cuisine runs deep, but more than anything it is the pursuit of excellence that shines through when dining chez Fairlie. The chef's appetite for the very best ingredients sourced from Scotland and France (mostly) is another distinguishing feature of this restaurant. It all takes place in the positively ginormous Gleneagles Hotel, built in 1924 to resemble a French château (funnily enough), with its proximity to the iconic golf course guaranteeing a steady stream of visitors to this picturesque part of Scotland. There's not much of a view to be had from the Andrew Fairlie restaurant – for a start it has no windows – but that matters not a jot, for the swish room is a refined setting for the culinary fireworks about to be unleashed. There are two menus to choose from: à la carte or dégustation. This is a kitchen that puts in the hours to maximise flavour, so Scrabster lobster shells are roasted over oak shavings from Islay whisky casks for five hours, with the meat then returned to the shell and lightly roasted, and dressed with a warm lime butter sauce and soft green herbs – the devil, as they say, is in the detail. In another first course, veal sweetbreads are caramelised and partnered with Jerusalem artichokes and parmesan in a happy marriage that reveals the pin-sharp technical know-how in the kitchen. A main course slow-cooked oxtail with seared foie gras proves to be another winning combination of flavours and textures, as is a dish of turbot, with asparagus and scallops both marinated and served as a velouté. Cheese precedes dessert, as is the French way. The high level of performance carries through into desserts such as rhubarb soufflé with pistachio sauce and vanilla ice cream, or another that sees orange and Cointreau combined in a mousse and served with honeyed citrus and mandarin sorbet. There are wine flight options for the carte and dégustation menus from a list that is big on Burgundy, Bordeaux and champagne. The service is slick and professional from start to finish.

Chef Andrew Fairlie **Owner** Andrew Fairlie **Seats** 54
Times 6.30-10, Closed 24-25 Dec, 3 wks Jan, Sun, L all week
Prices Prices not confirmed **Wines** 12 by glass **Parking** 300
Notes ALC 3 course £95, 6 course degustation £125,
Children 12 yrs+

FORTINGALL
Map 20 NN74

Fortingall Hotel

🏵 Modern Scottish

tel: 01887 830367 & 829012 **PH15 2NQ**
email: enquiries@fortingall.com **web:** www.fortingall.com
dir: *B846 from Aberfeldy for 6m, left signed Fortinghall for 3m. Hotel in village centre*

Well-balanced menu in Arts and Crafts village

A yew tree in the churchyard of this attractive village is reckoned to be between 3,000 and 9,000 years old, and as a result Fortingall is very much a destination for tourists, many of whom must end up at this Victorian country-house hotel. Dining takes place in two dining rooms, the main one done out in Arts and Crafts style, with a red carpet, an open fire, paintings on the walls and tartan-effect curtains. Dinner might open with skilfully made chicken and duck liver pâté served with home-made chutney and melba toast, before a main course such as rump of lamb sliced on tasty provençale vegetables with dauphinoise and a flavour-packed Madeira jus. Canapés are offered, breads are freshly baked and to round off a meal there may be a glass of silky white chocolate mousse topped with local raspberries.

Times 12-2/6.30-9

KILLIECRANKIE
Map 23 NN96

Killiecrankie Hotel

🏵🏵 Modern British V

tel: 01796 473220 **PH16 5LG**
email: enquiries@killiecrankiehotel.co.uk **web:** www.killiecrankiehotel.co.uk
dir: *Off A9 at Pitlochry, hotel 3m along B8079 on right*

Satisfying country-house cooking in tranquil Perthshire

Built for some blessed church minister back in 1840, the views across the Pass of Killiecrankie and the River Garry will soothe the troubled soul of any visitor. Surrounded by four acres of pretty gardens and woodland, this family-run hotel has charming traditional decor in its public rooms and restaurant. The team in the kitchen make the very best of this region's fine produce to deliver a fixed-price à la carte that comes with suggestions for two accompanying wines for each main course available by the bottle or half bottle. A flan of crayfish makes for a classic opener, with avocado, pink grapefruit and crème fraîche, or go for a trendy twice-baked goats' cheese brûlée with micro basil and red onion marmalade. Follow on with pan-fried fillet of Highland venison with a damson plum jus, or a lighter salad of poached salmon and prawns with lemon and herb mayonnaise. Plum and stem ginger tarte Tatin is a winning dessert, or maybe the selection of Scottish cheeses with oatcakes and crackers will catch your eye.

Chef Mark Easton **Owner** Henrietta Fergusson **Seats** 30, Pr/dining room 12
Times 6.30-8.30, Closed Jan-Feb, L all week **Prices** Prices not confirmed, Service optional **Wines** 32 bottles over £30, 47 bottles under £30, 9 by glass **Parking** 20
Notes Pre-theatre menu from 6.15pm Mon-Sat, 4 course D £42, Sunday L, Children welcome

KINCLAVEN
Map 21 NO13

Ballathie House Hotel

🏵🏵 Classic

tel: 01250 883268 **PH1 4QN**
email: info@ballathiehousehotel.com **web:** www.ballathiehousehotel.com
dir: *From A9, 2m N of Perth, take B9099 through Stanley & follow signs, or from A93 at Beech Hedge follow signs for Ballathie, 2.5m*

Modern country-house cooking by the Tay

The Ballathie Estate can accommodate eager beavers keen to try sled-dog racing or off-road cycling, or host the more sedate activities of walking and fishing, but head on over to the hotel for some rather more indulgent pastimes. The privately owned, turreted mansion overlooking the River Tay hosts a restaurant that impresses with its dedication to the ingredients sourced from the local landscape. The dining room has a classical elegance about it, with plenty of space between tables and views out across the verdant countryside. Traditional flavours combine with a moderated degree of invention to create dishes that seem entirely in keeping with the setting. Try pan-fried breast of partridge with little crumbed balls of confit leg meat and foie gras mousse, followed by roast rump of lamb with haggis bonbon and mint and parley salsa, or grilled halibut with herb crust and an aromatic chowder. Finish with dark chocolate cake with brown bread ice cream, or farmhouse cheeses with oatcakes. The bar serves up lunchtime snacks and nifty cocktails.

Times 12.30-2/7-9

MUTHILL
Map 21 NN81

Barley Bree Restaurant with Rooms

🏵🏵 British, French V

tel: 01764 681451 **6 Willoughby St PH5 2AB**
email: info@barleybree.com **web:** www.barleybree.com
dir: *A9 onto A822 in centre of Muthill*

Franco-Mediterranean cooking in a conservation village

This early 19th-century inn in a Perthshire conservation village, which once provided stabling for coach horses plying the Highland roads, has gone through a number of incarnations and names over the years, and settled into its present manifestation with the arrival of Fabrice and Alison Bouteloup in 2007. Now a modern day restaurant with rooms, its ancient brick and stone walls enhance the pleasingly come-as-you-are feel of the dining room. French and Mediterranean food traditions inform Fabrice's cooking, expressed through the medium of pedigree Scots produce. First up might be chicken and chorizo terrine with puréed trompettes and saffron-pickled cucumber, or peat-smoked haddock and a seared scallop with a gratin of courgette and potato in gremolata. Those lively openers lead on to saddle of venison with charred cabbage in truffle emulsion, or orientally inspired East Neuk monkfish tail dressed in red chilli and coriander, with orzo pasta and choi sum in Asian-spiced lobster bisque. For afters, seasonal berries come with white peach sorbet, rosé wine jelly and mint cream, while the crème brûlée is fragranced with rosemary.

Chef Fabrice Bouteloup **Owner** Fabrice & Alison Bouteloup **Seats** 35
Times 12-2/6.45-9, Closed Xmas, Mon-Tue, D Sun **Prices** Starter £7.50-£12.50, Main £21.50-£25, Dessert £7.50-£8.50 **Wines** 40 bottles over £30, 33 bottles under £30, 9 by glass **Parking** 12 **Notes** Sunday L £10.50-£13.50, Children welcome

Deans Restaurant

◉◉ Modern Scottish

tel: 01738 643377 **77-79 Kinnoull St PH1 5EZ**
email: deans@letseatperth.co.uk **web:** www.letseatperth.co.uk
dir: *On corner of Kinnoull St & Atholl St, close to North Inch & cinema*

Dazzling cooking in stylish restaurant

Deans really is a family-run joint, with Willie and Margot joined by their two sons at their ever-popular restaurant. It's right in the centre of town, in the heart of the action, and it delivers modern Scottish flavours in a vibrant and easy-going atmosphere. The red room provides a soothing respite if the weather is grim, with colourful prints adorning the walls and the darkwood tables left free of formal white linen. Willie Deans is a highly accomplished chef and his kitchen turns out some skilfully executed dishes such as a first course twice-baked Isle of Mull cheese soufflé of perfect consistency, with McSween's haggis, neeps and a whisky cream – a beautifully presented plate, too. A main course dish of loin of Ochil venison comes next, with a turnip and potato swirl, braised red cabbage, pear purée and a glossy, sticky jus. A fishy main might be fillets of halibut and sole with a leek and champagne sauce, and, for dessert, tuck into a caramel pannacotta with chocolate and orange truffle and caramel ice.

Chef Willie Deans **Owner** Mr & Mrs W Deans **Seats** 70 **Times** 12-3/6-10, Closed 1st 2 wks Jan, Mon **Prices** Fixed L 2 course fr £12.50, Fixed D 3 course fr £20, Starter £4.95-£10.50, Main £14-£25, Dessert £5-£12.50, Service optional **Wines** 23 bottles over £30, 36 bottles under £30, 14 by glass **Parking** Multi-storey car park (100 yds) **Notes** Pre-theatre menu Tue-Fri 6-9pm, Sunday L, Vegetarian available, Children welcome

Murrayshall House Hotel & Golf Course

◉◉ Modern British

tel: 01738 551171 **New Scone PH2 7PH**
email: info@murrayshall.co.uk **web:** www.murrayshall.co.uk
dir: *From Perth A94 (Coupar Angus) turn right signed Murrayshall before New Scone*

Polished cooking amid the rolling Lowland acres

With not one but two golf courses, Murrayshall doesn't do anything by halves. It's a grand old house dating from the 17th century and sitting in a whopping 350-acre estate (plenty of room for those fairways), and extended over the years (or centuries) to make room for all the facilities of a first-class hotel. The main dining option is the Old Masters restaurant, which is a series of elegant spaces with views over the green Perthshire landscape, and watched over by dapper staff. The menu is rich with Scottish ingredients, from salmon to scallops, and haggis to steaks, while cooking techniques combine both contemporary and traditional elements. Start with pork, cider and foie gras pie, which is really a terrine, served with pickled

vegetables, and move on to braised veal with turnip and haggis mash, or a clever chicken creation with tattie scone and mushroom and red wine sauce. There's rib-eye steak cooked on the grill, too, and desserts such as Amaretto crème brûlée with almond shortbread.

Times 12-2.30/7-9.45, Closed 26 Dec, L Sat-Mon

Pig'Halle

◉ French

tel: 01738 248784 **South St PH2 8PG**
email: info@pighalle.co.uk
dir: *Beside Salutation Hotel*

Pork, and more, in buzzy French bistro

On a busy street in the centre of Perth, Pig'Halle has been given a Parisian look, with a map of the Métro embossed on a large mirror, wine memorabilia, some banquette seating and red-upholstered round-backed chairs at darkwood tables. It's an atmospheric, buzzy sort of place, people drawn by the bistro-style cooking and the France-inspired menu. As its punning name suggests, pork is a theme, from a starter of melt-in-the-mouth belly with black pudding, sautéed spiced pear and apple and tomato salsa, a beautifully composed dish, to a full-blooded main course of confit trotter with spinach, celeriac remoulade and chips. Elsewhere, seek out Gallic classics such as frogs' legs, or sole Véronique with wilted spinach and crushed potatoes, and don't ignore the board of specials: there could be a flavour-packed duo of venison (braised shoulder pie), and collops fanned over a rich ragoût of pancetta and Puy lentils). Well-executed desserts might include tarte Tatin and creamy chocolate and Amaretto tart.

Chef Herve Tabourel **Owner** Herve & Paula Tabourel **Seats** 40 **Times** 12-3/5.30-9.30 **Prices** Fixed L 2 course fr £11.90, Fixed D 3 course fr £17.90, Starter £5-£8.50, Main £11-£42, Dessert £5-£8, Service optional **Wines** 6 bottles over £30, 26 bottles under £30, 11 by glass **Parking** Canal St car park **Notes** Pre-theatre 5.30-6.45pm 2/3 course £13.90/£16.90, Sunday L £11.90-£25, Vegetarian available, Children welcome

The Roost Restaurant

◉ British, Modern French

tel: 01738 812111 **Forgandenny Rd, Bridge of Earn PH2 9AZ**
email: enquiries@theroostrestaurant.co.uk
dir: *M90 junct 9, Bridge of Earn. Follow brown tourist signs*

Modern French cooking with fine Scottish ingredients

A husband-and-wife operation in a single-storey building resembling a farmyard outhouse, The Roost is smart as can be inside, with crisply clad tables and a plethora of pictures and mirrors. The cooking has shifted gently in the direction of the modern French mode of late, but still using thoroughbred Scottish ingredients, including some from the Roost's own kitchen garden. Nothing could be more obviously à la mode than a starter of seared Rougié foie gras with hibiscus purée and grape jam, or for that matter a salad of pigeon, bacon and boudin noir with artichoke crisps in Marsala dressing. At main, there could well be sensitively handled halibut with saffron tagliatelle, brown shrimps, baby fennel and samphire in shellfish sauce, or perhaps loin of red deer with a shallot tart in medlar and juniper jus. Finish with rhubarb vacherin adorned with pistachios.

Chef Tim Dover **Owner** Tim & Anna Dover **Seats** 24 **Times** 12-2/6.45-9, Closed 25 Dec, 1-18 Jan, Mon, D Tue-Wed, Sun **Prices** Fixed L 2 course £19.50, Fixed D 3 course £37.85-£49.85, Tasting menu fr £75, Starter £5.75-£7.75, Main £14.95-£15.25, Dessert £6.50-£7.50, Service optional **Wines** 19 bottles over £30, 20 bottles under £30, 10 by glass **Parking** 6 **Notes** ALC L menu, Tasting menu with wine £100, Sunday L £21.95-£24.95, Vegetarian available, Children welcome

63@Parklands

◎◎ Modern European V

tel: 01738 622451 **2 St Leonards Bank PH2 8EB**
email: info@63atparklandshotel.com **web:** www.63atparklands.com
dir: *Adjacent to Perth station, overlooking South Inch Park*

Taking up the slack when Tay Street is closed

A little way out of the city centre, the Parklands Hotel is home to the sister restaurant of the original on Tay Street, this place being open for dinner on the days – Thursday to Monday – when Tay Street isn't. The surroundings here are distinctly more pastoral, in a manor house in fine gardens overlooking South Inch Park. The format is a five-course fixed-price menu, with two or three choices at most stages. Proceedings might open with grilled smoked mackerel with Beaufort cheese crumble in winter minestrone, or more robustly with wild hare in celeriac velouté, before an intervening soup turns up. A three-way option for main might encompass halibut fillet with roast chicken and scallop cream and fragrant rice, Highland venison with haggis cannelloni, bittersweet cabbages and neeps, or the standby classic, Angus beef fillet in béarnaise. Cheeses precede the dessert alternatives, which could be poached rhubarb in pink peppercorn sabayon with white chocolate mousse, or a chilled exotic broth of mango, pineapple and anise with coconut sorbet and a passionfruit madeleine.

Chef Graeme Pallister **Owner** Scott & Penny Edwards **Seats** 32, Pr/dining room 22 **Times** 7-9, Closed 25 Dec-5 Jan, Tue-Wed, L all week **Prices** Fixed D 3 course £39.50-£47.50, Service optional **Wines** 30 bottles over £30, 45 bottles under £30, 8 by glass **Parking** 25 **Notes** Children welcome

63 Tay Street

◎◎ Modern Scottish V 🍷NOTABLE WINE LIST

tel: 01738 441451 **63 Tay St PH2 8NN**
email: info@63taystreet.com
dir: *In town centre, on river*

Attractive, imaginative cooking by the River Tay

Graeme Pallister's popular local restaurant occupies part of the ground floor of an imposing stone building on the Tay riverside. A shipboard feel is created by means of porthole mirrors, and the decor is all about stripped-back elegance, with an uncovered floor, good napery and claret-hued seating. 'Local, honest, simple' is the stated motto, although a restaurant chef's idea of 'simple' may not necessarily accord with yours. Dishes look attractive, as with a shallow, crisp-coated, twice-baked Roquefort soufflé, with sweetly poached pear and cobnuts, or a fish main course such as Scrabster cod and West Coast mussels bedded on gently curried green lentils, a dish that has enough innate sea-fresh flavour to throw a red wine sauce into relief. Meat might be an imaginative fusion assemblage of spatchcock quail with pickled plum, cavolo nero and merguez sausage, while the highly original garnish for sublime white chocolate and pistachio mousse and vanilla ice cream is a hot sweet wonton filled with soft banana, the whole garnished with candied orange peel. Don't miss the fine breads.

Chef Graeme Pallister **Owner** Scott & Penny Edwards, Graeme Pallister **Seats** 38 **Times** 12-2/6-9, Closed Xmas, New Year, 1st wk Jul, Sun-Mon, L Tue-Wed **Prices** Fixed L 2 course £19-£25, Fixed D 3 course £42-£48.50, Tasting menu £55, Starter £6.50, Main £13.50-£18, Dessert £5.50-£7, Service optional **Wines** 125 bottles over £30, 49 bottles under £30, 7 by glass **Parking** On street **Notes** Pre-theatre, express menu 2/3 course £19.50/£24.50, Children welcome

Tabla

◎ Indian V

tel: 01738 444630 **173 South St PH2 8NY**
email: thirmalreddy@yahoo.com
dir: *Phone for directions*

Zesty Indian home cooking in the city centre

'The guest is God,' declares the menu, but don't let it go to your head. Start nibbling on ambrosia, and you'll miss out on the richly satisfying, traditional Indian home cooking of the Kumar family's central Perth eatery. The ambience has more personality than many a formula Indian, with exposed stone walls, full-drop windows and a glass panel looking into the kitchen. Indian music featuring the eponymous tabla drums plays softly. A vegetable pakora of crisp potato nuggets filled with carrots, peas and coriander seeds served with a tomato salsa-style dressing, is an appetiser for a classic main course of murgh balti, a delicate, fragrantly-spiced dish of tender chicken in a sauce of tomato, chickpeas, ginger and garlic. A full listing of vegetarian dishes is prominent on the menu. Finish with sticky gulab jamon dumplings flavoured with cardamom and rose water.

Chef Praveen Kumar **Owner** Praveen Kumar & Saroo **Seats** 42 **Times** 12-2.30/5-10.30, Closed L Sun **Prices** Fixed L 2 course £9.95, Fixed D 3 course £16.95, Starter £4.95-£6.95, Main £8.95-£14.95, Dessert £3.95-£4.95 **Wines** 4 bottles over £30, 4 bottles under £30, 3 by glass **Parking** On street **Notes** Pre-theatre 2 course fr £13.95, Tapas menu L £9.95, D £14.95, Children welcome

---

PITLOCHRY   Map 23 NN95

Fonab Castle Hotel

🏵🏵🏵 *see page 662*

Green Park Hotel

◎ British

tel: 01796 473248 **Clunie Bridge Rd PH16 5JY**
email: bookings@thegreenpark.co.uk **web:** www.thegreenpark.co.uk
dir: *Turn off A9 at Pitlochry, follow signs for 0.25m through town, turn left at Clunie Bridge Rd*

Country-house cooking with magnificent views

The Green Park has one of those dining rooms where the injunction to 'bag a table by the window' is worth heeding, the reward being prime views over Loch Faskally, with the forests and mountains as backdrop. It's a long room with a chintzy feel, where tables are clad in floor-length coverings, respectably spaced and individually adorned with blooms. A gentle version of country-house cooking is in the offing, so avocado mousse is garnished with Serrano ham, shaved parmesan and dried tomato, while main courses run to braised rose veal osso buco with basil mash, in a dressing of tomatoes, olive oil and herbs, or a seafood assemblage of poached salmon, prawns, mackerel and anchovies with saffron mayonnaise and salad. Finish up with moreish gingerbread pudding served with a moat of caramel sauce and a garnish of banana ice cream.

Times 12-2/6.30-8.30

PITLOCHRY *continued*

Knockendarroch Hotel & Restaurant

◉◉ Modern Scottish

tel: 01796 473473 **Higher Oakfield PH16 5HT**
email: bookings@knockendarroch.co.uk **web:** www.knockendarroch.co.uk
dir: *On entering town from Perth, 1st right (East Moulin Road) after railway bridge, then 2nd left, last hotel on left*

Resourceful cooking at elegantly appointed hotel

A handsome sandstone house in a wooded setting, Knockendarroch has country-house comforts and a diminutive restaurant that delivers classy modern Scottish food. It's all very traditional within, with warming fires in the cooler months, ornate cornicing, chandeliers and the like, and a genuine hospitality runs right through the place. The kitchen makes good use of high-quality regional produce to deliver well-crafted and refined dishes. A starter of wood pigeon, for example, its breast beautifully pink, comes with parsnip purée and a smoked bacon rösti, while main courses might see loin of Perthshire lamb partnered with pommes dauphinoise, Jerusalem artichoke purée and an excellent haggis samosa. A fishy main might be hake with a sweetcorn pancake and zingy sunblushed tomato and chorizo salsa, and, for dessert, there might be lemon meringue pie with nicely zesty lemon curd, toasted marshmallows and golden pastry crumb.

Chef Graeme Stewart **Owner** Struan & Louise Lothian **Seats** 24
Times 5.30-8.30, Closed mid Nov-mid Jan, L all week **Prices** Fixed D 3 course £38, Service optional **Wines** 8 bottles over £30, 25 bottles under £30, 5 by glass **Parking** 12 **Notes** Pre-theatre D Jun-Oct, Vegetarian available, Children 10 yrs+

ST FILLANS Map 20 NN62

The Four Seasons Hotel

◉◉ Modern British v

tel: 01764 685333 **Loch Earn PH6 2NF**
email: info@thefourseasonshotel.co.uk **web:** www.thefourseasonshotel.co.uk
dir: *From Perth take A85 W, through Crieff & Comrie. Hotel at west end of village*

Breathtaking loch views and appealing modern cooking

Perched on the edge of Loch Earn, The Four Seasons has a location to die for with its breathtaking southwesterly views over the water and wooded hills. The hotel dates from the 19th century, with modifications made over the years to fine-tune the place for modern sensibilities. Country-house chintz has definitely been chucked out in this stylish bolt-hole, particularly in the waterside Meall Reamhar restaurant, where colourful seats contrast with cool white walls hung with original artwork and those stunning views as a backdrop to a modern British menu, built on spectacular Scottish ingredients brought together in inventive pairings. Kick off with (perfectly) seared hand-dived scallops matched with crisp air-cured bacon, Granny Smith jam, smoked morcilla black pudding and cauliflower pannacotta, or carpaccio of venison with beetroot and horseradish dressing. Next up, Pata Negra pork and pig's cheek is served with truffled mash and a chilli and sherry vinegar sauce, and seared turbot and king scallop come in the company of pea and pancetta risotto. Finish with a creative mango and chilli parfait with coconut truffle and punch sorbet.

Chef David Errington **Owner** Andrew Low **Seats** 40, Pr/dining room 20
Times 12-2.30/6-9.30, Closed Jan-Feb & some wkdays Mar, Nov & Dec
Prices Tasting menu £42, Service optional **Wines** 61 bottles over £30, 52 bottles under £30, 8 by glass **Parking** 30 **Notes** Sunday L £15.95-£20.95, Children welcome

---

Fonab Castle Hotel ◉◉◉

PITLOCHRY Map 23 NN95

Modern Scottish v
tel: 01796 470140 **Foss Rd PH16 5ND**
email: reservations@fonabcastlehotel.com **web:** www.fonabcastlehotel.com
dir: *Pitlochry A9 take Foss Rd junct. Hotel 1st on left*

Bold Scottish cooking and a treasure trove of single malts

Fonab is a castellated pile of reddish stone with a conical corner turret and handsome gables, looking for all the world as though it features in a Walter Scott novel. Although built around a core of sweeping staircases and panelled interiors, its present-day refurbishment has ingeniously conjured a modern country-house hotel from the place, with glassed-in views over Loch Faskally from both the Brasserie and the upmarket Sandeman restaurant, the latter so named in honour of the port-shipping family who once owned the house. A display of pedigree single malts and gins adds distinction. Paul Burns' culinary style suits the ambience with its bold contemporary approach, producing dishes that are full of striking combinations but avoiding an excess of technical ostentation. A six-course tasting menu, with optional wine selections, offers a comprehensive tour of Burns' abilities. After an appetiser of Isle of Skye scallop dusted with scallop roe and paired with parsnip purée comes the luxury of lobster with shaved truffle, saffron-poached potato and heritage tomato dressing. That is followed by pressed foie gras terrine with pain d'épice crumb, Madeira jelly, fig chutney and pomegranate. Then the main business arrives: melt-in-the-mouth tender beef fillet, poached sous-vide then roasted, and supported by a beignet of shoulder meat, cauliflower purée, morels, fondant potato and Madeira jus. You might then move on to a bravura dessert of whipped white chocolate with champagne-poached rhubarb and ginger granola that will bring down the curtain.

Chef Paul Burns **Owner** Mr & Mrs Clark **Times** , **Prices** Tasting menu £70 **Wines** 114 bottles over £30, 36 bottles under £30, 15 by glass **Parking** 50 **Notes** Fixed menu 5 course £50, Tasting menu 7 course, Sunday L, Children welcome

EAST RENFREWSHIRE

UPLAWMOOR
Map 20 NS45

Uplawmoor Hotel

Modern Scottish

tel: 01505 850565 **66 Neilston Rd G78 4AF**
email: info@uplawmoor.co.uk web: www.uplawmoor.co.uk
dir: *M77 junct 2, A736 signed Barrhead & Irvine. Hotel 4m beyond Barrhead*

Modern and traditional cooking in a former coaching inn

This long whitewashed building has been greatly expanded and upgraded since its humble 1750 beginnings as a one-room coaching inn. Nowadays it's very much the hub of the village, with its popular restaurant in a rectangular blue-carpeted room with white walls and darkwood furniture under a beamed ceiling. The kitchen bakes its own bread and works around fresh local produce, steering a course between the traditional and more esoteric notions. Starters of Cullen skink or chicken liver pâté with onion and orange marmalade might appear next to seared scallops with black pudding and crispy bacon in balsamic dressing. Main courses come from the familiar mould of chicken Kiev, beef Stroganoff, and seared salmon fillet in a creamy leek and white wine sauce with Lyonnaise potatoes and green beams. End with a tried-and-tested dessert like banana split or sherry trifle.

Chef Alan Muir **Owner** Stuart & Emma Peacock **Seats** 30
Times 12-3/6-9.30, Closed 26 Dec, 1 Jan, Mon-Thu, L Fri-Sat **Prices** Fixed D 3 course £21-£25, Starter £5-£9, Main £10-£25, Dessert £5.50-£6.50, Service optional **Wines** 1 bottle over £30, 15 bottles under £30, 8 by glass **Parking** 40 **Notes** Early evening menu 5.30-7pm, Sunday L, Vegetarian available, Children 12 yrs+

SCOTTISH BORDERS

EDDLESTON
Map 21 NT24

The Horseshoe Restaurant with Rooms

Modern Scottish NOTABLE WINE LIST

tel: 01721 730225 **Edinburgh Rd EH45 8QP**
email: reservations@horseshoeinn.co.uk web: www.horseshoeinn.co.uk
dir: *On A703, 5m N of Peebles*

Voguish Scottish cookery in a roadside restaurant with rooms

Centuries ago, the single-storey, cottage-like roadside premises housed a blacksmith's, but time transformed them into a village inn, and now distinctly more upmarket restaurant with rooms. Beneath low ceilings, a striking decorative approach features mottled wallpaper, Romanesque interior pillars and dark-red carpeting. Soft lighting in the main dining area creates an intimate feel, with smartly dressed staff doing their descriptive bit as dishes are delivered. They carry voguish Scottish cookery founded on top-drawer ingredients. First up could be a marbled terrine of rabbit, prune and potato with a serving of Stornoway Black Pudding and rather assertive piccalilli, before mains such as poached cod with mussels, chervil gnocchi and artichokes, or roast haunch of Highland red deer with cavolo nero and parsnips in black pepper jus, with a mini-cottage pie full of Morteau sausage. Dessert might be dark chocolate delice with orange purée and honeycomb. Cheeses come with apricot chutney, quince and oat biscuits.

Chef Alistair Craig **Owner** Border Steelwork Structures Ltd **Seats** 40, Pr/dining room 14 **Times** 12-2.30/7-9, Closed 2 wks Jan, 2 wks Jul, Mon-Tue **Prices** Fixed D 3 course £35-£45, Tasting menu fr £55, Service optional **Wines** 153 bottles over £30, 40 bottles under £30, 10 by glass **Parking** 20 **Notes** Sunday L £22.50-£27.50, Vegetarian available, Children 5 yrs+

JEDBURGH
Map 21 NT62

The Ancrum Cross Keys

Modern British NEW

tel: 01835 830242 **Ancrum TD8 6XH**
email: crosskeysdining@gmail.com
dir: *4m N of Jedburgh, off A68*

Dynamic contemporary cooking in a village pub

A 200-year-old tavern in the centre of the village, the Cross Keys is a country pub that still functions as such – the atmospheric front bar with its early 20th-century gantry is even listed – but head into the informal restaurant, with its views into the kitchen, and you'll find dishes served on earthenware plates and wooden boards that are positively racy. There's a Scottish flavour to the culinary goings on, but also creativity and some decidedly modern ideas. Start with leg and breast of partridge, for example, each element cooked just right and served with poached pear, burdock root and apple jelly. Everything looks attractive on the plate, and flavours and textures are deftly managed. Next up, saddle of venison comes as a main course in the earthy company of liver, chestnuts and black trumpet mushrooms, or try the loin and cheek of monkfish with saffron gnocchi and onion purée. The imaginative partnerships continue with desserts such as the dark chocolate tart with its accompanying marshmallow, sweet pumpkin purée and malt parfait.

Chef David Malcolm **Owner** John Henderson **Seats** 24 **Times** 12-3/6-9.30, Closed 25 Dec, 1 Jan, Mon **Prices** Tasting menu £55, Starter £5-£9, Main £15-£21, Dessert £3-£7 **Wines** 4 bottles over £30, 18 bottles under £30, 12 by glass **Parking** 5, Free village parking **Notes** Sunday L £13-£21, Vegetarian available, Children welcome

KELSO
Map 21 NT73

The Cobbles Freehouse & Dining

Modern British

tel: 01573 223548 **7 Bowmont St TD5 7JH**
email: info@thecobbleskelso.co.uk
dir: *A6089 from Edinburgh, turn right at rdbt into Bowmont St. Restaurant in 0.3m*

Modern menu in a lively pub setting

Tucked just off the town's main square, The Cobbles is an old inn which has successfully negotiated the minefield that is the pub/restaurant dynamic. It satisfies both needs. The bar has loads of atmosphere, especially on a Friday night when there's live music, and sells the owner's own Tempest ales (brewed down the road). There are bar snacks such as wraps and burgers on offer, but in the dapper restaurant – that expands into the upstairs function space during the busier summer months – you'll find Scottish-inspired dishes that impress. West Coast scallops come with a pecan crumb, black pudding and cauliflower purée, plus dinky shallot rings, while a main-course confit pork belly number hits all the right buttons. There are steaks, too, sourced from Scottish herds, and served with a host of accompaniments including caramelised vegetables and garlic mushrooms. Finish with an ace dark chocolate fondant with cherry purée and an almond streusel.

Chef Daniel Norcliffe **Owner** Annika & Gavin Meiklejohn **Seats** 35, Pr/dining room 30 **Times** 12-2.30/5.45-9, Closed 25 Dec **Prices** Service optional **Wines** 4 bottles over £30, 26 bottles under £30, 7 by glass **Parking** Free parking behind restaurant **Notes** Sunday L £10.95-£20.95, Vegetarian available, Children welcome

KELSO *continued*

The Roxburghe Hotel & Golf Course

◉◉ Modern British

tel: 01573 450331 **Heiton TD5 8JZ**
email: hotel@roxburghe.net **web:** www.roxburghe.net
dir: *From A68, 1m N of Jedburgh, take A698 for 5m to Heiton*

Impressive country setting for fine modern Scottish cooking

Owned by the Duke of Roxburghe, who takes a hands-on approach to running this grand Jacobean country-house hotel, the turreted pile is tucked in woodland close to the River Teviot on the Duke's vast estate. If you're not a roughy toughy outdoor type, there's pampering on hand in the health and beauty salon. But first and foremost, this is prime huntin' shootin' fishin' territory, so the estate provides a good deal of what turns up on the menu. The impressive dining room delivers ducal finery in spades, with its views over the manicured lawns, plush fabrics, horse-racing prints, crisp linen tablecloths, and a tartan carpet to remind you that you're north of the border. Thankfully the kitchen is not stuck in the past, turning out modernist ideas starting with a risotto of Orkney girolles and goats' cheese, followed by Eyemouth with saffron and squid ink linguine, langoustines and trompette de mort mushrooms. To finish, green apple sorbet makes a zingy foil to moist pumpkin cake with crunchy pumpkin seeds.

Times 12.30-2/7-9.30

MELROSE
Map 21 NT53

Burt's Hotel

◉◉ Modern Scottish, British 🍷 NOTABLE WINE LIST

tel: 01896 822285 **Market Square TD6 9PL**
email: enquiries@burtshotel.co.uk **web:** www.burtshotel.co.uk
dir: *A6091, 2m from A68, 3m S of Earlston. Hotel in market square*

Contemporary cooking at an old favourite

Owned and run by the Henderson family for over 40 years, this handsome 18th-century inn is rooted into Melrose life. It stands on the picturesque market square, a short stroll from the River Tweed, and sports a hunting, shooting and fishing theme that extends through the traditionally decorated restaurant and the bustling bar, where you'll find winter log fires, hearty grub, Scottish ales, and a mere 90 malt whiskies to tick off. The kitchen moves with the times, turning out modern Scottish dishes prepared from quality locally-sourced produce. Yellow split pea and ham soup is a heart-warming classic, or modernists might go for seared scallops with confit potato, truffle mayonnaise and pancetta sauce. This being Scotland, you're never far from game, so follow with venison served with boulangère potatoes, spiced red cabbage and pearl vegetable jus, or pan-fried salmon fillet with chorizo and tiger prawn risotto and herb salad. Finish with an assiette of apple, comprising a nutty crumble, a moist sponge, apple strudel ice cream and vanilla crème anglaise.

Chef Trevor Williams **Owner** The Henderson family **Seats** 50, Pr/dining room 25 **Times** 12-2/7-9, Closed 26 Dec, 5-12 Jan, L Mon-Fri **Prices** Starter £5-£9.95, Main £14.50-£25.50, Dessert £7.50-£8.50, Service optional **Wines** 33 bottles over £30, 27 bottles under £30, 8 by glass **Parking** 40 **Notes** Sunday L £17.95-£23.50, Vegetarian available, Children 10 yrs+

PEEBLES
Map 21 NT24

Macdonald Cardrona Hotel, Golf & Spa

◉ Modern British

tel: 01896 833600 **Cardrona EH45 8NE**
email: general.cardrona@macdonald-hotels.co.uk **web:** www.macdonald-hotels.co.uk
dir: *From Edinburgh on A701 signed Penicuik/Peebles. Then A703, at 1st rdbt beside garage turn left onto A72, hotel 3m on right*

Gently modern and ravishing country views

Amassed on the banks of the River Tweed, the Cardrona is a swish modern hotel with a championship golf course and luxe spa. It's also home to Renwicks restaurant, where a wall of glass serves up views of the green fairways and rolling Border hills beyond. There's a good deal of regional produce on the menu and the cooking is straightforward and gently modern. A roulade of confit duck leg with Asian slaw and oriental dressing looks beyond the border county for its inspiration, but equally there might be locally-smoked haddock with a savoury pannacotta and lemon and caper dressing. Main course might see outdoor reared pork (fillet and braised belly) partnered with Stornoway Black Pudding and an apple purée, or seared rib-eye with a red onion and feta tart. Desserts run to warm chocolate brownie with caramelised pistachio and pistachio ice cream.

Times 12.30-2/6.30-9.45

ST BOSWELLS
Map 21 NT53

Dryburgh Abbey Hotel

◉ Modern, Traditional British

tel: 01835 822261 **TD6 0RQ**
email: enquiries@dryburgh.co.uk **web:** www.dryburgh.co.uk
dir: *From A68 to St Boswells. Take B6404 for 2m. Take B6356 for about 2m to hotel*

Classic-meets-modern dishes in Walter Scott country

Overlooking the River Tweed and the Abbey, where Sir Walter Scott is buried, this baronial-style hotel is surrounded by wooded grounds. The broad-based menu will have something to appeal to all comers, with starters ranging from smoked duck with rhubarb chutney and segments of orange to a traditional prawn cocktail. Much of the fresh produce comes from the hotel's own gardens, and the kitchen assembles dishes with intelligence, resulting in effective main courses of tender pork belly with crispy crackling, broad bean ragout, sauté potatoes and black pudding, and chunky cod fillet with chorizo, potatoes crushed with olive oil, green beans and tomatoes. Other main courses can be as familiar as fish pie, as can desserts of sticky toffee pudding with butterscotch sauce and vanilla ice cream.

Chef Mark Wilkinson **Owner** Dryburgh Abbey Hotel Limited **Seats** 78, Pr/dining room 40 **Times** 7-9, Closed L all week **Prices** Starter £4.50-£6.25, Main £9.95-£21.95, Dessert £4.95-£9.50, Service optional **Wines** 36 bottles over £30, 20 bottles under £30, 11 by glass **Parking** 50 **Notes** Vegetarian available, Children welcome

STIRLING

ABERFOYLE
Map 20 NN50

Macdonald Forest Hills Hotel & Resort

◎ Modern Scottish

tel: 01877 389500 **Kinlochard FK8 3TL**
email: general.foresthills@macdonald-hotels.co.uk
web: www.macdonald-hotels.co.uk/foresthills
dir: 4m from Aberfoyle on B829

Modern cooking in a happening resort hotel

Twenty-five acres of mature gardens run down to the shore of Loch Ard at this white-painted mansion. In the restaurant, a curved wall of floor-to-ceiling windows gives magnificent views over the gardens and loch; tables are of bare wood, high-backed chairs are either upholstered or leather, and staff are friendly and talkative. 'Keep it simple' might be the kitchen's mantra. A commendable sense of restraint characterises its output so flavours are undiluted by an over abundance of ingredients. Brie and red onion tart with herb salad is an effective starter, contrasting with the relative complexity of seared cod fillet atop a pancake rolled around creamed smoked mackerel. Braised lamb shoulder, of beautifully tender meat, comes with rosemary jus, buttery mash, cabbage and baby onions, alongside another sensibly composed main course of seared salmon fillet with ratatouille and wilted spinach. Finish with satsuma crème brûlée with decadent chocolate chip cookies.

Chef David Robertson **Owner** Macdonald Hotels **Seats** 70, Pr/dining room 20 **Times** 6.30-9.30, Closed L Mon-Sat **Prices** Fixed D 3 course fr £35, Service optional **Wines** 80 bottles over £30, 10 bottles under £30, 14 by glass **Parking** 50 **Notes** Sunday L £15-£19.50, Vegetarian available, Children welcome

CALLANDER
Map 20 NN60

Roman Camp Country House Hotel

◎◎◎ – see page 666

FINTRY
Map 20 NS68

Culcreuch Castle Hotel & Estate

◎ Traditional Scottish NEW v

tel: 01360 860555 **Kippen Rd G63 OLW**
email: info@culcreuch.com **web:** www.culcreuch.com
dir: Please phone for directions

Dining room or dungeon dining at an ancestral castle

The castle has been the ancestral home of the clan Galbraith for over 700 years, but only got its start in the world as a hotel around 30 years ago. Standing in 1600 acres of grounds, including a picturesque loch, it has all the medieval accoutrements that could be desired. These include a thick-walled dungeon for aperitifs and simpler dining, and a high-ceilinged, half-panelled dining room on the first floor, adorned with oil paintings and a roaring fire. If you're lucky, one of the resident ghosts may put in an appearance. Country-house cooking with some imaginative touches is the approach, producing scallops with chorizo, black olives and apple, or a ballotine of smoked chicken, ham and foie gras with pineapple chutney, and mains such as Indian-spiced monkfish, the cheek meat in a samosa, on coriander purée dotted with broad beans and sweetcorn. The signature dessert is pear and popcorn millefeuille on almond purée with liquorice cake and caramel ice cream.

Chef Paul O'Malley **Owner** The Kim family **Seats** 22, Pr/dining room 30 **Times** 12-2.30/5-9, Closed 25-26 Dec, 1st 2wks Jan **Prices** Fixed D 3 course £36, Starter £4-£6.50, Main £10-£17.50, Dessert £4.50, Service optional **Wines** 5 bottles over £30, 21 bottles under £30, 7 by glass **Parking** 60 **Notes** Children welcome

STIRLING
Map 21 NS79

The Stirling Highland Hotel
⊛ British, European

tel: 01786 272727 **Spittal St FK8 1DU**
email: stirling@thehotelcollection.co.uk web: www.thehotelcollection.co.uk
dir: *In road leading to Stirling Castle – follow Castle signs*

Commanding valley views and confident cooking in an old school

A grand old Victorian property just down the hill from Stirling's historic castle, The Stirling Highland Hotel was built in the 1850s as a school and there are references to the building's former life throughout – take a pre-dinner sharpener in the Headmaster's Study, before moving into Scholar's Restaurant. The eating takes place in three third-floor dining rooms of generous Victorian proportions, with vaulted ceilings, large windows and smartly laid out tables. The menu takes a modern approach to some familiar ideas, so a first-course smoked haddock kedgeree is breaded and deep-fried, and served with curried mayonnaise and a quail's egg, and guinea fowl arrives in a main course filled with prune mousse and partnered with a fondant potato, Savoy cabbage and butternut squash purée. There's a similarly contemporary approach to desserts, as when rhubarb gets the trio treatment – crumble, fool and sorbet.

Times 7-9.45, Closed L all week

STRATHYRE
Map 20 NN51

Creagan House
⊛⊛ French, Scottish

tel: 01877 384638 **FK18 8ND**
email: eatandstay@creaganhouse.co.uk web: www.creaganhouse.co.uk
dir: *0.25m N of village, off A84*

17th-century Trossachs farmhouse with good food

The views alone make a visit worthwhile to this welcoming 17th-century farmhouse in a village at the head of Loch Lubnaig. Dinner is served in the stately baronial-style dining room, with its vaulted ceiling and grand stone fireplace. The surroundings contrast with the contemporary-style country-house cooking, built on irreproachable local produce – meat from Perthshire farms, fish from Scottish ports, eggs from their own hens, and as much fruit and vegetables as possible grown in the garden. Typical starters are seared Mull scallops topping creamed clams, leeks and mushrooms, and a filo parcel of braised oxtail with Jerusalem artichoke crostini, mushrooms and truffle. Ingredients are sensibly and skilfully handled, so dishes are never short of interest: fillet of turbot, for instance, comes with a pan-fried pâté of lobster, scallop and crab and vermouth sauce, and loin of local venison on beetroot and pearl barley risotto gets a gin and juniper sauce. Finish with a selection of well-kept Scottish cheeses or one of the home-made desserts.

Chef Gordon Gunn **Owner** Gordon & Cherry Gunn **Seats** 15, Pr/dining room 6 **Times** 7.30-8.30, Closed 28 Oct-17 Mar, Wed-Thu, L all week (ex parties) **Prices** Fixed D 3 course fr £37.50, Service optional **Wines** 44 bottles over £30, 27 bottles under £30, 7 by glass **Parking** 15 **Notes** Vegetarian available, Children 10 yrs+

Roman Camp Country House Hotel ⊛⊛⊛

CALLANDER
Map 20 NN60

Modern French **V**
tel: 01877 330003 **FK17 8BG**
email: mail@romancamphotel.co.uk web: www.romancamphotel.co.uk
dir: *N on A84 through Callander, Main St turn left at East End into drive*

Scottish modernist cooking of inventive energy

Look southwards across the meadows from the hotel gardens, and the conspicuous earthwork jutting from the landscape is what remains of the ancient encampment that gives the place its name. Despite being in the centre of the Trossachs town of Callander, once you are in the grounds here, you'll feel comfortably a good hundred miles from urban settlement. Deriving from an early 17th-century manor house built for the Earls of Moray, it has been a hotel since the 1930s, and is full of period furnishings and old-fashioned comfort. The elliptical dining room is a particular joy, washed in natural light during the day, intimately enclosed in evenings when the curtains are drawn and the fire lit. Modern Scottish cooking of great inventive energy flows forth from a small brigade led by Ian McNaught, seen at its most expressive in the four-course set menu. That might run from Skye scallops with black pudding, Serrano ham and mandarin gel, via watercress soup with a confit egg yolk, to breast and pressed leg of Goosnargh duck with a peanut flapjack and artichokes, before the final flourish brings on a top-drawer tripartite chocolate array, served with malted pearl barley ice cream. The carte offers a sensible three choices per course, keeping things focused for crab raviolo in bouillabaisse, then a duo of braised pig's cheek and roasted langoustines with sweet-and-sour apricot purée. At the close of business comes a trio of citric dazzlements – lemon parfait, orange sorbet and lime curd – or a selection of farmhouse cheeses with toasted fig and walnut bread and membrillo. Reckoning in appetisers such as foie gras custard with cherry jelly and Sauternes foam, the whole operation exudes finely detailed class.

Chef Ian McNaught **Owner** Eric Brown **Seats** 120, Pr/dining room 36 **Times** 12-2/7-9, **Prices** Fixed L 3 course £28.50-£30, Tasting menu £55, Starter £11.50-£23, Main £24-£35, Dessert £11-£15, Service optional **Wines** 180 bottles over £30, 15 bottles under £30, 16 by glass **Parking** 80 **Notes** Tasting menu 4 course, Sunday L £28.50-£30, Children welcome

SCOTTISH ISLANDS

ISLE OF HARRIS

TARBERT (TAIRBEART)　　　　　Map 22 NB10

Hotel Hebrides

◎ Modern Scottish

tel: 01859 502364 **Pier Rd HS3 3DG**
email: stay@hotel-hebrides.com **web:** www.hotel-hebrides.com
dir: *To Tarbert via ferry from Uig (Isle of Skye); or ferry from Ullapool to Stornaway, A859 to Tarbert; or by plane to Stornaway from Glasgow, Edinburgh or Inverness*

Seafood specialities overlooking the incoming ferries

The modern boutique hotel is the focal point of a village of some 500 souls on the Isle of Harris. Guests roll in on the ferry from Skye, overseen by diners in the Pierhouse seafood restaurant, where a bare floor boarded look keeps things simple and informal, though the staff all sport rather fetching lime green ties. Fish and shellfish are the strongest suits, ranging from bowls of generously crammed chowder to main dishes of seared megrim sole in citrus and caper beurre blanc with samphire, and rainbow trout with kale in salsa verde. Meat sticklers might set a course via fried chicken livers on toasted brioche with blackberry and rosemary jus to roast Hebridean lamb rack with minted mash, before all are reunited for biscuit-based Belgian chocolate torte, served with Amaretto cream streaked with berry coulis, or lemon meringue cheesecake with forest fruit compôte.

Chef Graham Smith **Owner** Mr & Mrs Macleod **Seats** 35 **Times** 12-4/6-9, Closed Nov-Mar **Prices** Fixed L 2 course fr £12.95, Starter £4.95-£12.95, Main £10.95-£35, Dessert £4.95-£6.95, Service optional **Wines** 8 bottles over £30, 10 bottles under £30, 4 by glass **Parking** 30 **Notes** Sunday L £12.95-£15.95, Vegetarian available, Children welcome

ISLE OF MULL

FIONNPHORT　　　　　Map 20 NM32

Ninth Wave Restaurant

◎ Modern British, Pacific Rim **NEW** v

tel: 01681 700757 **PA66 6BL**
email: enquiries@ninthwaverestaurant.co.uk
dir: *Near end of Ross of Mull, just before village of Fionnphort (A849) where the ferry to Iona departs, turn off signed*

Creative cooking in a remote island location

On the southern tip of Mull where ferries shuttle across to tiny Iona, John and Carla Lamont's pocket-sized restaurant is about as remote as they come. It's a stylish contemporary space on a seven-acre croft with a kitchen garden for fresh produce. Fish and seafood are caught from John's own boat every day, while Carla mans the stoves. The dinner-only affair seats just 18 lucky diners, who can expect skilfully-cooked menus full of ambitious and inventive ideas. To start, langoustine and crab won ton dumplings come in a spicy Thai-style coconut milk and kaffir lime broth, while pan-fried sea bream is partnered creatively by a deep-fried courgette blossom stuffed with fish and sea urchin. Elsewhere, crab and smoked Applewood cheese are united in a soufflé-style cheesecake, and to finish, blackberries from the croft turn up in a dark chocolate tart with bramble jelly and semi-fredo.

Chef Carla Lamont **Owner** Carla & John Lamont **Seats** 18 **Times** 7-12, Closed Mon-Tue, L all week **Prices** Fixed D 3 course fr £46, Service optional **Wines** 14 bottles over £30, 18 bottles under £30, 2 by glass **Parking** 10 **Notes** 4/5 course D £54/£64, Children 12 yrs+

TIRORAN　　　　　Map 20 NM42

Tiroran House Hotel

◎◎◎ – *see page 669*

TOBERMORY　　　　　Map 22 NM55

Highland Cottage

◎◎ Modern Scottish, International

tel: 01688 302030 **24 Breadalbane St PA75 6PD**
email: davidandjo@highlandcottage.co.uk **web:** www.highlandcottage.co.uk
dir: *Opposite fire station. Main St up Back Brae, turn at top by White House. Follow road to right, left at next junct into Breadalbane St*

Inspired local cooking in a charming island hotel

The Curries' salmon-hued small hotel in Tobermory's conservation area, not far from the fishing pier, is a jewel of a place. The charming interiors, replete with squashy sofas, interesting books and well-chosen ornaments, are a delight, and the place is cleverly laid out to lead you from the bar and conservatory into the suavely furnished dining room. Jo Currie cooks, and does a splendid job of showcasing Mull produce, as well as much from the mainland. A starter risotto is a demonstration dish, both for its flawless timing and the savoury intensity of its locally-smoked haddock, topped for the final flourish with a perfect poached egg. Loin of superlative lamb might come next, the tender, richly flavoured meat supported by potato and turnip gratin and a concentrated redcurrant and rosemary gravy, or there may be bracingly fresh sea bass with braised leeks, in tomato, olive and caper butter. Cranachan gains from a peaty malt flavour to the oatmeal, as well as an intense raspberry hit, or go for the tang of lemon posset, served with buttery home-made shortbread.

Times 7-9, Closed Nov-Mar, L all week

SHETLAND

SCALLOWAY　　　　　Map 24 HU43

Scalloway Hotel

◎◎ Modern Scottish v

tel: 01595 880444 **Main St ZE1 0TR**
email: info@scallowayhotel.com **web:** www.scallowayhotel.com
dir: *7m from Lerwick on west mainland on A970*

Creative cooking in an unpretentious setting in the far north

The bounty of the Atlantic is landed practically on the doorstep of this family-run hotel on the waterfront of the Shetlands former capital. It's an unpretentious place with a genuine community feel that opens its arms to all-comers, from oil rig workers to passing ships' crews, making the bar a convivial haunt for casual dishes along the lines of fish pie with parsley mash or haddock and chips done right. The restaurant presents itself very nicely with linen tablecloths and quality glasses and there are some bright ideas on a seasonal menu that showcases the islands' produce – local lamb, for starters, its seared belly and crisp lamb 'bacon' served with Jerusalem artichoke purée, followed by lemon sole with crushed Shetland Black potatoes, caramelised salsify and crab and tarragon butter sauce. Desserts are no less creative: pear tarte Tatin with five spice ice cream and almond shards, or perhaps chocolate fondant with cranberry ice cream. If you want to slacken your belt and stop over, simple bedrooms are decorated with locally-spun tweed, woollen carpets and art.

Chef Ciaran Lack **Owner** P McKenzie **Seats** 36 **Times** 12-3/5-9, Closed Xmas, New Year **Prices** Starter £5-£11, Main £15-£25, Dessert £6-£7.50, Service optional **Wines** 23 bottles over £30, 22 bottles under £30, 10 by glass **Parking** 10 **Notes** Sunday L, Children welcome

ISLE OF SKYE

COLBOST — Map 22 NG24

The Three Chimneys & The House Over-By

see opposite

ISLEORNSAY — Map 22 NG71

Duisdale House Hotel

@@ Modern Scottish

tel: 01471 833202 **Sleat IV43 8QW**
email: info@duisdale.com **web:** www.duisdale.com
dir: *7m N of Armadale ferry & 12m S of Skye Bridge on A851*

Modern Scottish seasonal cooking in remotest southern Skye

With bags of boutique style and a dreamy location by the Sound of Sleat, Duisdale House has a lot going for it. The garden is a treat, too, especially if you're a fan of rhododendrons, but it's the restaurant that really catches the eye. Occupying a conservatory and a rich-red room with a real fire and stylish fixtures and fittings, the restaurant focuses on seasonal, regional ingredients and the cooking is in the modern vein. It's the kind of place that likes to satisfy with additional bits and bobs, such as canapés, including a haggis bonbon, and amuse-bouche such as smoked ham hock with piccalilli. Hand-dived scallops are familiar enough in these parts, but here they come in a first course with white onion purée, grapefruit, syboes (spring onion) and bacon (or at least a bacon 'dust'). Main-course fillet and cheek of Lochaber pork is an equally satisfying construction, with potato fondant, Savoy cabbage, celeriac and a rich, glossy jus. To finish, enjoy another complex array of flavours in a dish of banana mousse with dark chocolate, pineapple and yogurt.

Times 12-2.30/6.30-9

Hotel Eilean Iarmain

@@ Traditional Scottish

tel: 01471 833332 **Sleat IV43 8QR**
email: hotel@eileaniarmain.co.uk **web:** www.eileaniarmain.co.uk
dir: *Mallaig & cross by ferry to Armadale, 8m to hotel or via Kyle of Lochalsh*

Spectacular sea views and consummate cooking

The hotel is very much a part of this small community, with Gaelic spoken and regular ceilidh nights in the bar, while the owners also run a small distillery and art gallery next door. The whitewashed property is in a fabulous spot overlooking the Sound of Sleat, across to the Knoydart Hills on the mainland beyond. A warm welcome awaits once you cross the threshold, and quite likely a roaring log fire, too, and the place is done out with traditional charms to the fore. The restaurant has views over the water and looks smart with tables dressed in white linen and flickering candles, while the culinary output is rather more contemporary than you might imagine. Start with a savoury pannacotta (goats' cheese, garlic and chive) with beetroot purée and pickled carrots, before moving on to oven-roasted loin of estate venison with mini fondant potato, sautéed kale and a glossy red wine sauce. Finish with a dark chocolate sphere with white chocolate and honey ganache, Cointreau mousse, raspberry jelly and honeycomb crumble.

Chef Alistair Kelly **Owner** Lady Lucilla Noble **Seats** 40, Pr/dining room 22
Times 12-2.30/6.30-8.45 **Prices** Fixed D 3 course £39.95-£42.50, Tasting menu £45, Starter £9.95-£11.95, Main £17.95-£24.95, Dessert £4.95-£8.50, Service optional
Wines 14 bottles over £30, 21 bottles under £30, 7 by glass **Notes** Sunday L, Vegetarian available, Children welcome

Kinloch Lodge

@@@ *– see page 670*

Toravaig House Hotel

@@ Modern Scottish

tel: 01471 820200 **Knock Bay, Sleat IV44 8RE**
email: info@skyehotel.co.uk **web:** www.skyehotel.co.uk
dir: *From Skye Bridge, left at Broadford onto A851, hotel 11m on left. Or from ferry at Armadale take A851, hotel 6m on right*

Plush island retreat with modern Scottish cooking

With views over the 14th-century Knock Castle and the Sound of Sleat, the whitewashed Toravaig House serves up an enviable Skye vista. The hotel has classy interiors, with high quality fixtures and fittings, and it's run with passion and attention to detail by owners Anne Gracie and Ken Gunn. The restaurant — the Iona — is an equally smart space, with candlelight bringing a cosy glow in the evenings. The cooking takes a modern Scottish path, in keeping with the majestic surroundings, and makes good use of regional produce. Island scallops, for example, come in a creative combination with confit carrot, mustard dressing and smoked cheddar, with another option being roast breast of quail with a Mediterranean spin with polenta and chorizo. There's a soup course next, or rather a nifty wild mushroom velouté, followed by a main course such as West Coast turbot with razor clams, or Barbary duck breast with pearl barley and caramelised shallots. These are well-crafted plates of food. Finish with Blairgowrie raspberries with white chocolate and oregano oil.

Times 12.30-2.30/6.30-9.30

Tiroran House Hotel ❀❀❀

TIRORAN   Map 20 NM42

Modern Scottish
tel: 01681 705232 **PA69 6ES**
email: info@tiroran.com **web:** www.tiroran.com
dir: *Phone for directions*

Outstanding cooking in a secluded country house

The long and winding road that takes you out to the Tiroran House Hotel from the ferry terminal serves to introduce you to the stunning landscape and heighten expectation of what lies ahead. Once you arrive, the white-painted house doesn't disappoint, perched on a wooded hillside with views over the loch, and you'll find restful country-house comfort within. Another thing to look forward to is a warm welcome from Lawrence Mackay, who will likely be wearing a kilt as he hosts the dinner service with considerable charm. Given the location it is likely you'll be staying over in one of the traditional bedrooms. The restaurant, consisting of two diminutive elegant dining rooms, with views across the lawn to the loch, is a civilised and soothing spot to enjoy the contemporary and inspiring cooking of Craig Ferguson. Craig and his team have a kitchen garden to call upon for a lot of the fresh stuff, plus a host of trusted suppliers on the island, and you can expect a menu that has classical foundations without ever feeling stuck in the past. Begin with an array of well-made canapés before a first-course such as a plump wild mushroom tortellino served with a boneless quail breast, a swipe of trompette purée and some pickled trompettes, or the local heroes that are creel-caught langoustines. There's complexity in a main course dish of fillet of Forres pork with gels and purées adding little hits of apple and parsley, while, among desserts, there are more wonderfully judged flavours in a salted caramel tart with its accompanying lavender ice cream. Wine is another passion of mine host, and the list has plenty of enticing options at reasonable prices.

Chef Craig Ferguson, Alex Dashwood-Baker **Owner** Laurence & Katie Mackay **Seats** 26, Pr/dining room 16 **Times** 7.15-10, Closed Dec-Feb, L all week **Prices** Prices not confirmed, Service optional **Wines** 10 bottles over £30, 17 bottles under £30, 4 by glass **Parking** 14 **Notes** ALC Mon-Sat £48, Sun supper £36, Vegetarian available, Children welcome

The Three Chimneys & The House Over-By

COLBOST   Map 22 NG24

Modern British 🍷 NOTABLE WINE LIST
tel: 01470 511258 **IV55 8ZT**
email: eatandstay@threechimneys.co.uk **web:** www.threechimneys.co.uk
dir: *5m W of Dunvegan take B884 signed Glendale. On left beside loch*

Exceptional cooking in a wild, romantic setting

The Rosette award for this establishment has been suspended due to a change of chef. Reassessment will take place in due course under the new chef. Elemental landscapes are one good reason to visit Skye, but there's also Eddie and Shirley Spear's restaurant, which over the last 30 years has made its mark, on both the local economy and on the island's culinary reputation. Fashioned from two crofters' cottages, there are also classy bedrooms next door as staying over is a good option – you're hardly likely to be just passing by this remote foodie destination. The decor reflects a sense of place, boosted by stunning views over land and loch, and that same sense of the island's identity is reflected in the cooking. It's delivered via sensibly short lunch and dinner menus (three options per course) alongside an eight-course tasting extravaganza, which you could tackle at a kitchen table up close to the action. You might kick off with a starter that owes a debt to Morocco: Boer goat glazed with the island's own Talisker whisky alongside cinnamon pastilla, spiced couscous, cucumber and mint, followed by a rather more saltire-waving main course of blade and tongue of Black Isle beef with tattie scones, celery and apple remoulade, Dunsyre Blue cheese and pickled walnuts. Fish dishes might star red mullet and mackerel from Mallaig matched with Anna potato, fennel confit and slaw, and saffron aïoli. Sweet courses might include Medjool date cake soufflé, for example, with Pedro Ximenez and golden raisin ice cream, and hot toffee sauce. The wine list is a fine piece of work, and even more reason to book one of those charming bedrooms.

Chef Scott Davies **Owner** Eddie & Shirley Spear **Seats** 40 **Times** 12.15-1.45/6.15-9.30, Closed 1 Dec-23 Jan, L Nov-Mar **Prices** Fixed L 3 course £38-£50, Fixed D 3 course £65, Tasting menu £90-£110, Service optional **Wines** 105 bottles over £30, 12 bottles under £30, 25 by glass **Parking** 12 **Notes** Tasting menu 7 course, Sun L Jun-Aug, Sunday L, Vegetarian available, Children 5yrs L/8yrs D

Cuillin Hills Hotel

@@ Modern Scottish

tel: 01478 612003 **IV51 9QU**
email: info@cuillinhills-hotel-skye.co.uk **web:** www.cuillinhills-hotel-skye.co.uk
dir: 0.25m N of Portree on A855

Creative and classic dining with breathtaking views

The restaurant at this country-house hotel looks out over Portree Bay to the Cuillin mountains – no wonder it's called 'The View'. The breathtaking panorama is visible from every single table in the dining room, which means arrival during daylight hours is advisable. The hotel was built as a hunting lodge for the Macdonalds back in the 1880s and sits in 15 acres of mature grounds. The place has a stylish country-chic finish throughout. The restaurant has expanded into what was the brasserie, with a single menu offering creative modern dishes alongside some updated classics, and an excellent showing of regional seafood. A first course terrine of confit chicken is pointed up by an array of pickled vegetables and silky apricot purée, while another purée of blood orange accompanies Barbary duck breast. Portree Bay langoustines, Carbost oysters and Loch Eisort mussels are the very best the local waters have to offer. For traditionalists, there's all the comfort of breaded haddock with tartare sauce and the burger with Orkney cheddar. Finish with a sharp lemon posset with raspberry gel.

Chef Daniel Flemming **Owner** Wickman Hotels **Seats** 40 **Times** 12–2/6.30–9 **Prices** Service optional **Wines** 25 bottles over £30, 36 bottles under £30, 8 by glass **Parking** 56 **Notes** Sunday L £14.95, Vegetarian available, Children welcome

Loch Bay Seafood Restaurant

@ British Seafood

tel: 01470 592235 **MacLeod Ter IV55 8GA**
email: lochbay@gmail.com
dir: 4m off A850 by B886

Satisfying straightforward seafood cookery by the bay

With room only for a couple of dozen diners at a time, Loch Bay is a diminutive institution around these parts, a place of simplicity and integrity. Its position right by the loch shore, in a row of 18th-century fishermen's cottages, sets the tone for the fishy delights that lie within. David and Alison Wilkinson run the place with hands-on enthusiasm and passion – she's out front, he's at the stoves – and the menu is driven by what comes out of the local waters. It's humble and rustic within, with a wood-burning stove, pictures of the area and wooden tables. Start with razor clams – or spoots as they call them round these parts – fresh as a daisy and grilled with garlic and herb sauce, or the lobster and leek risotto might catch your eye. Main-course Dover sole comes with excellent triple-cooked chips, and Loch Bay king prawns are a good choice if they're available. Vanilla and Drambuie pannacotta with passionfruit ends things on a high.

Chef David Wilkinson **Owner** David & Alison Wilkinson **Seats** 23 **Times** 6.30–9, Closed mid Oct–Etr, Sun–Tue, L all week **Prices** Prices not confirmed, Service optional **Wines** 10 bottles over £30, 30 bottles under £30, 8 by glass **Parking** 6 **Notes** Vegetarian menu on request, Children 8 yrs+ D

Ullinish Country Lodge

@@@ – see opposite

Kinloch Lodge @@@

French, Scottish V NOTABLE WINE LIST

tel: 01471 833214 & 833333 **Sleat IV43 8QY**
email: reservations@kinloch-lodge.co.uk **web:** www.kinloch-lodge.co.uk
dir: 1m off main road, 6m S of Broadford on A851, 10m N of Armadale

Accomplished Scottish cooking in the Macdonald ancestral home

Kinloch Lodge is the ancestral home of the high chief of the Clan Donald and was turned into a hotel and restaurant by the current incumbents, Godfrey and Claire Macdonald. Lady Claire is a renowned cookery writer with over a dozen books to her name. The white-painted house has an understated charm and a setting beside Na Dal sea loch that is positively breathtaking. The interior is a sanctuary away from the real world, too, with a modest elegance in its public rooms, where a log fire crackles in the grate and sofas await to enjoy a cup of tea, a glass of something stronger, or maybe just a doze. The restaurant has been the domain of Marcello Tully since 2007 and he has cemented the reputation of Kinloch Lodge house as a dining destination with his French-inflected modern Scottish cuisine offered via a daily-changing menu and tasting option. The dinner menu kicks off with a 'soupçon' such as roast red pepper and black olive before a first course proper OF salmon (steamed and home-cured) with warm beetroot mousse and sautéed leeks. Next up it is Marcello's special – local skate wing stuffed with lobster mousse, maybe – and then a choice of meat or fish: Fort Augustus venison fillet with apple and parsnip purée, chorizo and another purée of leaf spinach and local herbs, or local sea bream with coriander and vanilla sauce. Finally, choose between a sweet course such as smooth passionfruit parfait with Knockraich yogurt sorbet, or go for Scottish and French cheeses off the trolley (or go large and have them both).

Chef Marcello Tully **Owner** Lord & Lady Macdonald **Seats** 55, Pr/dining room 12 **Times** 12–2/6–9, **Prices** Fixed L 3 course £32.99, Tasting menu fr £80, Service optional **Wines** 300 bottles over £30, 16 by glass **Parking** 50 **Notes** Fixed L 4 course £37.99, Fixed D 5 course £70, Sunday L £32.99–£37.99, Children welcome

Ullinish Country Lodge  ❀ ❀ ❀

STRUAN   Map 22 NG33

Modern French **V**
tel: 01470 572214 **IV56 8FD**
email: ullinish@theisleofskye.co.uk **web:** www.theisleofskye.co.uk
dir: *9m S of Dunvegan on A863*

Electrifying cooking in a Skye hideaway

The breathtaking views alone make the considerable effort of travelling to Ullinish worthwhile, with lochs on three sides and the rugged beauty of the Black Cuillins and MacLeod's Tables marching across the skyline. The white-painted restaurant with rooms (there are just four guest rooms, so you won't have to share the space with too many others) dates from the 18th century, and is done out in a traditional style with tartan carpet in the intimate restaurant, where service is relaxed, friendly and polished. A daily 'link van' collects meat, seafood and garden produce from a network of the island's small suppliers and delivers them to the kitchen, where the team works its wizardry. Dinner menus keep a tight focus, offering two choices at each stage, and there's clearly considerable talent at play here when it comes to balancing flavours. Starters might be diver-caught scallops with crispy chicken wing, pink grapefruit, cauliflower and raisins, or skilfully handled quail breast partnered with full-flavoured confit leg, sweetcorn in various guises, burnt onion,

tarragon and mushrooms, all beautifully presented and working in harmony. At main course stage, spanking-fresh brill could be matched with truffle macaroni, borage, baby onions, courgettes and sharp little hits of capers, while the meaty alternative might see loin of Orbost Estate lamb partnered with a croquette of its shank, Gentleman's Relish, broad beans and celeriac. Cheese comes French-style before pudding, supported by oatcakes and the imaginative accompaniments of wine purée, iced grapes and celery cress, while the finale presents a dilemma – is it to be cranachan soufflé with raspberry sorbet or a composition involving sour cherry, dark chocolate and green apple?

Chef Richard Massey **Owner** Brian & Pam Howard **Seats** 22
Times 7.30-8.30, Closed 24 Dec-31 Jan, L all week **Prices** Prices not confirmed, Service optional **Wines** 36 bottles over £30, 40 bottles under £30, 16 by glass
Parking 10 **Notes** 4 course D £55, Children 16 yrs+

Wales

ISLE OF ANGLESEY

BEAUMARIS
Map 14 SH67

Bishopsgate House Hotel

Traditional Welsh

tel: 01248 810302 **54 Castle St LL58 8BB**
email: hazel@bishopsgatehotel.co.uk **web:** www.bishopsgatehotel.co.uk
dir: *From Menai Bridge onto A545 to Beaumaris. Hotel on left in main street*

Reliable cookery on the Beaumaris waterfront

The cheery mint-green façade of Bishopsgate House stands out from the neighbours along the Georgian terrace overlooking Beaumaris Green and the peaks of Snowdonia across the Menai waterfront. The intimate, low-ceilinged restaurant is full of old-world charm and enjoys a strong following with locals who know they can rely on the kitchen's quietly confident cooking, as well as a healthy showing of top-class local produce. Straightforward crowd-pleasing menus set out with braised pork belly with apple purée and white pudding, while brandy and herbs add extra interest to a chicken liver pâté served with onion marmalade and brioche. Next up, a fresh piece of hake is crusted with lemon and herbs and served with creamed leeks, or if you're in the mood for a meaty main course, there might be pan-fried loin of lamb with a mustard and herb crust and honey and rosemary jus. Finish with pecan tart and honeycomb ice cream.

Times 12.30-2.30/6.30-9.30, Closed L Mon-Sat

Ye Olde Bulls Head Inn

— *see opposite*

LLANFACHRAETH
Map 14 SH38

Black Lion Inn

Modern, Traditional British **NEW**

tel: 01407 730718 **Llanfaethlu LL65 4NL**
email: mari.faulkner@blacklionanglesey.co.uk **web:** www.blacklionanglesey.com
dir: *From A55 junct 3, signed A5 Valley. Right at lights onto A5025 for 6m*

Revamped pub with a local flavour

The gloriously rural 17th-century Black Lion was derelict before new owners took over and revitalised the place to meet contemporary expectations. Today's whitewashed inn has a cosy bar and dining spaces including a modern extension, with traditional features such as slate floors and Welsh fabrics (used as artworks) ensuring a sense of place, and there are also two smart bedrooms. There are real ales on tap, but it's very much a dining pub, with the kitchen putting local supplies to good use – they grow their own salads and veg, too. Y Cwt Caws goats' cheese and red pepper pannacotta has just the right amount of wobble, served with a balsamic reduction and peppery leaves, and main courses include beer-battered haddock and chips or soft and melting pork belly with black pudding fritter and maple cream sauce. Finish with Welsh cheeses or a seasonal fruit tart.

Chef Wayne Roberts **Owner** Leigh & Mari Faulkner **Seats** 80, Pr/dining room 30 **Times** 12-2.30/6-8.30, Closed 10 days Jan, Mon-Tue (Nov-Apr), L Wed **Prices** Starter £4.95-£8.95, Main £10.95-£25.95, Dessert £5.95-£7.95, Service optional **Wines** 7 by glass **Parking** 30 **Notes** Sunday L, Vegetarian available, Children welcome

MENAI BRIDGE
Map 14 SH57

Sosban & The Old Butcher's Restaurant

— *see page 676*

CARDIFF

CARDIFF
Map 9 ST17

Bully's

French, European

tel: 029 2022 1905 **5 Romilly Crescent CF11 9NP**
email: info@bullysrestaurant.co.uk
dir: *5 mins from city centre*

Lively modern cooking in busy but relaxed restaurant

Bully's is a busy-looking restaurant, virtually every inch of its walls covered with pictures, mirrors and other paraphernalia, and Russell Bullimore tirelessly adds and changes things. The kitchen relies on Welsh providers for its materials and devises menus that show a clear grounding in the French repertoire while pulling in ideas from near and far. Timing is ever well judged, seen in starters of seared scallops fragrant with vanilla essence, accompanied by Puy lentils and fine beans, and pan-fried foie gras cut by caramelised pineapple. Sauces are well considered: a glossy one of marjoram for a main course of pink rump of lamb with rainbow chard, creamed leeks and sautéed potatoes, one of peanuts and star anise for succulent pork tenderloin with pak choi and Parmentier potatoes. Puddings are worth a punt too, among them crisp-based mango tarte Tatin with peach and vanilla ice cream, and canonical honey and orange crème brûlée.

Times 12-2/6.30-9, Closed 22-27 Dec, 1st wk Jan, D Sun

Moksh

Indian **NEW** v

tel: 029 2049 8120 **Ocean Building, Bute Crescent CF10 5AN**
email: enquiries@moksh.co.uk
dir: *M4 junct 33, A4232, exit Cardiff Bay before Butetown tunnels. 1st exit rdbt. Located in Mermaid Quay*

Creative techno cooking, Indian style

Contemporary Indian fusion cooking is nothing new, but this kitchen takes it to the next level by throwing elements of molecular wizardry into the mix. The setting is suitably modern, with glass screens separating chunky unclothed tables beneath a trippy night sky ceiling, and the food has a sense of fun. 'Einstein in India' starts things off by throwing the kitchen sink at a dish comprising whisky smoke-scented king prawn tikka, a sous-vide Lucknowi lamb chop with 'candy floss', Hyderabadi mince cupcake and a chicken kebab with tikka masala spheres and 'disappearing' Bombay mix. By comparison, Ratnagiri mango lamb is almost mainstream, the lamb cooked in a balanced sweet and spicy sauce of coconut milk and mango pulp. Dessert is another innovative idea – a crisp tikka masala samosa alongside white chocolate and saffron mousse cake with coconut ice cream and applewood smoke.

Chef Stephen Gomes **Owner** Stephen Gomes **Seats** 53 **Times** 12-2.30/6-11, Closed 25 Dec **Prices** Fixed L 2 course £10-£15, Tasting menu £38, Starter £5-£8, Main £12-£19, Dessert £3-£6, Service optional **Wines** 6 bottles over £30, 19 bottles under £30, 5 by glass **Notes** Vegetarian tasting menu £30, Children welcome

Ye Olde Bulls Head Inn

　　　　　　　　　Map 14 SH67

Modern British

tel: 01248 810329 **Castle St LL58 8AP**
email: info@bullsheadinn.co.uk **web:** www.bullsheadinn.co.uk
dir: *Town centre, main street*

Dynamically detailed cooking in a historic inn

Built following the restoration of Edward IV's reign in the 1470s, the Bulls Head stands a cannonball shot away from the Castle. It has borne witness to many of the key events in British history, having headquartered Parliamentary forces during the Civil War, and served as one of the early Quaker meeting houses, not to mention played host to notables both literary and political over the stretching centuries. It's still going strong as a place of convivial resort, stronger than ever arguably, dividing its catering operations between a slate-floored brasserie with bar counter, and the Loft restaurant, where the gentle fawn colour-scheme is enlivened with curlicue patterning, and Hefin Roberts' dynamic cooking is full of innovation and fine detail. The fashion for menu-writing that simply barks out the main ingredient at you is sidestepped in favour of full disclosure, and everything promised in the description is present and correct on the immaculately presented plates. Some dishes are at heart simple enough in conception, perhaps an opening caramelised red onion tart, accompanied by a mousse of Crottin de Chavignol and a scattering of toasted pine nuts, while others take off into culinary orbit for blow-torched pork belly with blanched leeks, garlic cream and gin-soaked raisins to bring a riot of complex flavours. Main courses conjure unexpected depths out of the best Welsh meats — beef fillet, cannon and salt-baked shoulder of lamb, rare-breed pork in jus lie — but it's hard to overlook the fish options that include precision-timed fillet of poached sea trout with fennel risotto, kohlrabi and preserved lemon in ginger velouté. And even desserts come roaring out of the creative traps with apple and lime cheesecake, dehydrated apple sponge and basil ice cream.

Chef Hefin Roberts **Owner** D Robertson, K Rothwell **Seats** 45
Times 7-9.30, Closed 25-26 Dec, 1 Jan, Sun-Mon, L all week
Prices Fixed D 3 course £47.50, Service optional **Wines** 65 bottles over £30, 35 bottles under £30, 4 by glass **Parking** 10
Notes Vegetarian available, Children 7 yrs+

CARDIFF continued

Park House

◉◉ British, International V NOTABLE WINE LIST

tel: 029 2022 4343 **20 Park Place CF10 3DQ**
email: enquiries@parkhouserestaurant.co.uk
dir: Opposite Cardiff Museum

Contemporary cooking in a Gothic revival architectural masterpiece

Chef Jonathan Edwards presides over one of the most enjoyable places to eat in Cardiff. Housed in an example of the Welsh capital's fine pieces of Gothic architectural extravagance and overlooking the gardens of the National Museum of Wales, the restaurant is done out in hues of pink and peach to jolly up the background of oak panelling. The kitchen turns out an ambitious menu that delivers well-defined flavours from premium ingredients, and doesn't shy away from some pretty inventive pairings, as seen in a starter of lobster and crab ravioli with spiced chilli ketchup and lemongrass-scented tea. Next up, Cornish turbot is sent out in the bracing company of Hafod cheddar leeks, buttered spinach, morel mushroom cream and smoked bacon gnocchi, while caramelised Kelmscott pork might appear with brown shrimp, Bramley apples and summer cabbage. A chocolate platter involving a rich pavé and 'pulled' chocolate with a peppermint macaroon and spearmint sorbet rounds off a polished act. The wine list is put together with real authority.

Chef Jonathan Edwards **Owner** Adam & Claire Pledger **Seats** 80, Pr/dining room 40 **Times** 11-4/6-11, Closed 25-26 Dec & some BHs, Mon-Tue, D Sun **Prices** Fixed L 2 course £18, Starter £12-£14, Main £26-£36, Dessert £10-£12, Service optional 8% **Wines** 600 bottles over £30, 80 bottles under £30, 15 by glass **Parking** NCP 50 mtrs **Notes** Pre-theatre ALC D menu 25% discount, Sunday L fr £25, No children

Park Plaza Cardiff

◉ British, European V

tel: 029 2011 1111 & 2011 1103 **Greyfriars Rd CF10 3AL**
email: lagunarestaurant@parkplazahotels.co.uk **web:** www.lagunakitchenandbar.com
dir: Located on Greyfriars Rd inside Park Plaza Hotel

Generous brasserie cooking in the city centre

Right in the heart of the Welsh capital, not far from the castle and the Millennium Stadium, this contemporary hotel is all about boutique style, with original modern artworks here and there. A floor-to-ceiling wine wall divides the bar from the Laguna restaurant, where a sleek wood-surfaced tone predominates, and the generously portioned brasserie food is deservedly popular. Start with an appetising salad of Perl Las blue cheese with pear, candied walnuts and chicory, or a Thai fishcake glazed in smoked chilli with roast pineapple. These could be preambles to pork comme il faut – soft belly with a brittle crackling stick, pumpkin purée and dauphinoise. If it's fish you're after, look to roast cod on saffroned fennel risotto. Round things off with a proper baked Alaska in whisky anglaise, or an enjoyably rich crème brûlée made with Jersey cream, served with milk chocolate shortbread.

Chef Justin Llewellyn **Owner** Martin Morris **Seats** 110, Pr/dining room 140 **Times** 12-2.30/5.30-9.30, Closed 25-26 Dec **Prices** Fixed L 2 course £12.95-£26.90, Starter £4.95-£8.95, Main £9.95-£28.95, Dessert £4.95-£8.95 **Wines** 44 bottles over £30, 38 bottles under £30, 9 by glass **Parking** NCP **Notes** Pre-theatre £15.95, Afternoon tea £17.50-£25.95, Sunday L £16.95-£19.95, Children welcome

Sosban & The Old Butcher's Restaurant ❀❀❀

MENAI BRIDGE   Map 14 SH57

Modern **NEW** V

tel: 01248 208131 **Trinity House, 1 High St LL59 5EE**
email: eat@sosbanandtheoldbutchers.com
dir: A55 E, junct 9 straight on, Britania Bridge. Exit A55 at junct 8a, right at T-junct A5 to Menai Bridge. At rdbt 2nd exit onto B5420. Left at x-rds, A545 High St

Progressive contemporary dining on the high street

This one-time butcher's shop is now a thrillingly modern restaurant run by a husband-and-wife team who have brought contemporary cuisine to Menai Bridge. The unassuming shop front gives no clue as to the culinary adventures that await within. The dining room is adorned with striking modern artworks and there are original slate panels and various bits and bobs from the building's days in the meat trade. Well-spaced tables are smartly dressed and the friendly service sets the tone. There is no menu as such, so it is simply a case of trusting in the chef and going with the flow, or as they themselves say, 'forget the menu, savour the experience'. It turns out you're in very safe hands. Things kick off with an amuse-bouche such as tender Anglesey asparagus with raisin purée, caper butter and peanuts in a multi-layered and audaciously successful partnership. Presentation seldom fails to impress, and the baking is

up to the mark, too, with soda bread and parmesan biscuits hitting the spot. Pork cheek arrives meltingly soft with burnt apple, crisp broccoli and sage powder in a miniature reinterpretation of a Sunday roast, with every flavour hitting the mark. Next up, 'slightly' salted cod has a crisp skin and is served with mushroom purée and wild garlic, plus burnt onion and a flavourful chicken jus. A pre-dessert is up next (strawberry lollipop, say), before a dessert course proper such as a powerfully flavoured ginger pannacotta with rhubarb and strawberry purée, almonds, pistachios and strawberry sorbet.

Chef Stephen Owen Stevens **Owner** Stephen & Bethan Stevens **Seats** 16 **Times** 7-11, Closed Xmas, New Year, Jan, Sun-Wed **Prices** Tasting menu £43.70-£50, Service optional **Wines** 13 bottles over £30, 23 bottles under £30, 5 by glass **Parking** On street, car park **Notes** Children welcome

CARMARTHENSHIRE

LAUGHARNE
Map 8 SN31

The Corran Resort & Spa

◉◉ Modern British, Welsh **NEW**

tel: 01994 427417 **East Marsh SA33 4RS**
email: info@thecorran.com **web:** www.thecorran.com
dir: *Phone for directions*

Welsh coastal cooking in a boutique spa hotel

Amid the coastal marshland of Carmarthenshire, The Corran is a stylish spa hotel within three miles of both Laugharne Castle, and the Boathouse, home of the unofficial Welsh laureate, Dylan Thomas. Fashioned from a mix of 16th-century farm buildings and modern amenities, it boasts a spacious, glass-fronted restaurant overlooking the garden and sun terrace, run by helpful and knowledgeable staff. Plentiful local produce of land and sea finds its way on to menus that under-sell dishes which come as all the more of a pleasant surprise when they arrive. Salmon cured in black treacle with pickles and salad vies for attention with generously stuffed short-rib ravioli in mushrooms and Marsala to begin. After those come Indian-styled John Dory with sag aloo in curried velouté, topped with coconut foam, fried Dover sole with fennel in Pernod butter, or else a beef steak comprised of fillet, cheek and hotpot, given extra dimension with rich artichoke purée. A combination of chocolate ganache, passionfruit curd and honeycomb adds up to an array of sweet temptations, or there may be textbook Bakewell tart with clotted cream.

Chef Justin Heasman **Owner** Peter Burnett **Seats** 70, Pr/dining room 30 **Times** 12-2.30/6-9 **Prices** Starter £5.50-£7.50, Main £12.50-£28.50, Dessert £4.75-£9, Service optional **Wines** 7 bottles over £30, 27 bottles under £30, 21 by glass **Notes** Sun brunch, Afternoon tea, Sunday L £16.95-£19.95, Vegetarian available, Children welcome

The Cors Restaurant

◉◉ Modern

tel: 01994 427219 **Newbridge Rd SA33 4SH**
email: nick@thecors.co.uk
dir: *A40 from Carmarthen, left at St Clears & 4m to Laugharne*

Charming restaurant in Dylan Thomas country

Chef-proprietor Nick Priestland has taken a lovely Victorian rectory and transformed it into a one-off, idiosyncratic restaurant with rooms. Just off Laugharne's main street in Dylan Thomas country, the trees, shrubs, ponds, and modern sculptures in the magical bog garden ('cors' is Welsh for bog) are unmissable when lit up at night, while the moody interior has a Gothic edge with its claret-hued walls, wrought-iron seats and stained-glass windows; an atmospheric setting for unaffected, precise cooking that trumpets the virtues of excellent local ingredients. Full-on flavours are more important here than fancy presentation, thus smoked haddock brûlée certainly grabs the attention at the start of a summer's dinner, before roast rack of Welsh lamb arrives with the punchy flavours of a rosemary and garlic crust, dauphinoise potatoes and caramelised onion gravy, and it all ends happily with a summer fruit Pavlova.

Times 7-9.30, Closed 25 Dec, Sun-Wed, L all week

LLANDEILO
Map 8 SN62

The Plough Inn

◉ Modern International

tel: 01558 823431 **Rhosmaen SA19 6NP**
email: info@ploughrhosmaen.com **web:** www.ploughrhosmaen.com
dir: *On A40 1m N of Llandeilo towards Llandovery. From M4 onto A483 at Pont Abraham*

Modern and traditional dishes in a refurbed boutique hotel

The contemporary boutique hotel is in the beautiful Towy Valley, on the edge of the Brecon Beacons and not far from the National Botanic Garden of Wales. Within light tones predominate in both the inviting bar and the raftered dining room. Informal, warm-hearted service sets the tone, and there's a menu of modern Welsh cooking to supplement the more obvious favourites such as beer-battered fish and chips, or peppered steaks with onion rings. Slow-cooked pig's cheek with roasted shallots in pearl barley broth is a particularly warming way to start, with mains such as bream fillet alongside pea and coriander risotto, or pot-roasted, locally-shot partridge with creamed Savoy cabbage in rosemary jus, to follow. Desserts to fire the imagination include a spin on baked Alaska, with mixed berry ice cream and peach sauce, or pannacotta with tonka biscotti, blood orange sorbet and pistachio soil.

Chef Chris Lovell **Owner** Andrew Roberts **Seats** 190, Pr/dining room 30 **Times** 11.30-3.30/5.30-9.30, Closed 26 Dec **Prices** Fixed L 2 course £14.45, Starter £5.45-£8.95, Main £11.95-£49.95, Dessert £5.95-£15, Service optional **Wines** 6 bottles over £30, 32 bottles under £30, 11 by glass **Parking** 70 **Notes** Sunday L £16.70-£18.95, Vegetarian available, Children welcome

LLANELLI
Map 8 SN50

Sosban Restaurant

◉◉ British, French

tel: 01554 270020 **The Pumphouse, North Dock SA15 2LF**
email: ian@sosbanrestaurant.com **web:** www.sosbanrestaurant.com
dir: *Phone for directions*

Informal brasserie cooking in a former hydraulic station

The Victorian pump house building on Llanelli's North Docks has been reinvented as a powerhouse on the local culinary scene. With its landmark 90 foot high castellated stone tower it's not hard to find. Once inside, the expansive industrial-chic skeleton of the building impresses with arched windows looking out to sea, Welsh slate floors, and classy bare wooden tables. The team toiling away at the stoves inside an open-to-view kitchen turns out a French-accented brasserie-style repertoire with a broad appeal, offering carefully-conceived, on-trend dishes – flavour-packed pork rillettes, paired with sweet pear chutney, pickles and crisp toast to start, followed by roast loin of Gower lamb with the Mediterranean glow of ratatouille, pesto and tomatoes. Otherwise, fish fans might go for wild sea bass matched simply with crushed potatoes, spinach and chive beurre blanc, or turbot with the defiantly Welsh accompaniments of cockles, laverbread sauce and curly kale. To finish, a textbook chocolate fondant with raspberry ripple ice cream hits the spot, or you might go for a savoury ending with the all-Welsh cheeseboard.

Chef Sian Rees, Ian Wood **Owner** Robert Williams & Partners **Seats** 90, Pr/dining room 20 **Times** 12-2.45/6-9.45, Closed 25 Dec, 1 Jan, D Sun **Prices** Fixed L 2 course fr £15.50, Fixed D 3 course fr £18.50, Starter £4.50-£9.50, Main £14.50-£28.50, Dessert £4.50-£8 **Wines** 49 bottles over £30, 34 bottles under £30, 14 by glass **Parking** 100 **Notes** Fixed D until 6.45pm, Sunday L £15.50-£18.50, Vegetarian available, Children welcome

NANTGAREDIG
Map 8 SN42

Y Polyn
◉◉ Modern British

tel: 01267 290000 **SA32 7LH**
email: ypolyn@hotmail.com
dir: *Follow brown tourist signs to National Botanic Gardens, Y Polyn signed from rdbt in front of gardens*

Unpretentious cooking from an industrious country-pub kitchen

Mark and Sue Manson make no bones about the approach at their hospitable country pub, saying: 'We're not trying to win any prizes for innovative cooking'. However, they deserve plaudits for their single-minded commitment to hard graft. The kitchen is commendably industrious in its work with excellent local prime materials, and while Sue may disavow any striving for fashionable novelty in her cooking, there is a pleasing freshness to the menu. Start with crispy ham hock bonbons in a pool of vividly flavoursome parsley sauce with a poached egg and shards of Carmarthen ham. Main course stars pan-fried brill fillet with a supporting cast of pea purée, wilted baby spinach and brown butter breadcrumbs, or there could be rump and confit breast of splendid salt marsh lamb with celeriac purée and onion soubise. At the end comes a skilfully-made blackberry baked Alaska, or fine Welsh cheeses served with wheat wafers and walnut chutney.

Chef Susan Manson **Owner** Mark & Susan Manson **Seats** 40
Times 12-2/7-9, Closed Mon, D Sun **Prices** Fixed L 2 course £13.50, Fixed D 3 course £35-£39, Starter £6.50-£9.50, Main £13.50-£18.50, Dessert £7.50, Service optional **Wines** 25 bottles over £30, 51 bottles under £30, 9 by glass **Parking** 25 **Notes** ALC prices for L only, Sunday L £20-£25, Vegetarian available, Children welcome

NEWCASTLE EMLYN
Map 8 SN34

Gwesty'r Emlyn Hotel
◉ Welsh

tel: 01239 710317 **Bridge St SA38 9DU**
email: reception@gwestremlynhotel.co.uk **web:** www.gwestremlynhotel.co.uk
dir: *In town centre*

Welsh ingredients in a revamped coaching inn

This 300-year-old one-time coaching inn looks the part with its four-square façade and archway, and there is plenty of period charm within, but it's had a bit of a makeover to sport a gently contemporary look, albeit one which won't scare the horses. The restaurant, called Bwyty'r Bont, has warm, neutral tones and smartly upholstered chairs and nary a stiff linen tablecloth in sight. The menu is short and to the point and offers up a good amount of Welsh produce, while the relaxed and friendly service team suit the mood to a Tee. Start with a slice of barbecue pork belly served on thin slices of crusty bread and pea purée, or a trio of Welsh 'tasters' that includes Glamorgan sausage and cockles with bacon and laverbread. Next up, medallions of Welsh beef with roasted root veg and garlic mash, or grilled fillet of turbot with sauce vièrge.

Chef Ian Williams, Italo Veritis, Rhydian Jones **Owner** Mr & Mrs Davies **Seats** 60, Pr/dining room 8 **Times** 12-2.30/6-9, Closed L Sun **Prices** Fixed L 2 course fr £10.95, Fixed D 3 course fr £29.95, Service optional **Wines** 9 bottles over £30, 28 bottles under £30, 14 by glass **Parking** 120 **Notes** Sun L in function suite £10.95-£18, Vegetarian available, Children welcome

CEREDIGION

ABERAERON
Map 8 SN46

Ty Mawr Mansion
◉◉ Modern British, Welsh

tel: 01570 470033 **Cilcennin SA48 8DB**
email: info@tymawrmansion.co.uk **web:** www.tymawrmansion.co.uk
dir: *4m from Aberaeron on A482 to Lampeter road*

Food from within ten miles of a handsome Georgian mansion

In a lofty position above the Aeron Valley, this stone-built Georgian mansion is tucked away in 12 acres of gorgeous grounds. Inside, it is an authentically-restored gem right down to its heritage colour schemes – sunny yellows lighten the feel, while lavender walls combine with darkwood floors and blue and white Regency-striped chairs at bare wooden tables in the rather splendid restaurant. Lots of hotels go on about their organic and local ingredients, but in this case it is not empty bluster: most of the materials come from within a ten-mile radius, including organic produce from Cilcennin village's farms on the doorstep, while the coast (four miles distant) supplies the fishy stuff. Start, perhaps, with seared Cardigan Bay scallops with cauliflower risotto, chorizo and tempura caper berries, then move on via a sorbet, to pan-seared fillet and confit belly of local pork served with crackling, parsnip purée and pan juices. For pudding there may be duck egg tart with garden rhubarb in the form of compôte and sorbet.

Times 7-9, Closed 26 Dec-7 Jan, Sun, L all week, D Mon

EGLWYS FACH
Map 14 SN69

Plas Ynyshir Hall Hotel
◉◉◉◉ – *see opposite*

LAMPETER
Map 8 SN54

The Falcondale Hotel & Restaurant
◉◉ Modern British V

tel: 01570 422910 **Falcondale Dr SA48 7RX**
email: info@thefalcondale.co.uk **web:** www.thefalcondale.co.uk
dir: *1m from Lampeter take A482 to Cardigan, turn right at petrol station, follow for 0.75m*

Fine Welsh produce cooked in a lovely rural setting

An Italianate mansion built in verdant countryside, Falcondale has 14 acres all to itself. It's the kind of country-house hotel that delivers peace and quiet and that getting-away-from-it-all vibe, with elegant and refined public spaces that bring about nothing more than the desire for another G&T and a read of the paper. The dining room has a traditional finish, but a dash of contemporary style, too, so the tables are left unclothed and a happy hum pervades. The cooking reveals classical roots, but this is gently modernised stuff, and good use is made of the regional bounty. Haloumi cheese from the Cothi Valley is served in a first course with salted beet, horseradish and a Cabernet Sauvignon dressing, while another starter might be pork belly with black pudding and caramelised apple. Loin of venison stars in a main course with Gorwydd cheese gnocchi, enoki mushrooms and a chocolate and onion sauce, and a fishy main might be fillet of plaice with dauphine potatoes, braised fennel and lemongrass sauce. Finish with fig tarte Tatin.

Chef Dafydd Davies **Owner** Chris & Lisa Hutton **Seats** 36, Pr/dining room 20
Times 12-2/6.30-9 **Prices** Fixed L 2 course fr £15.95, Fixed D 3 course fr £40, Service optional **Wines** 57 bottles over £30, 65 bottles under £30, 18 by glass **Parking** 60 **Notes** Tasting menu 7 course (pre-booked), Sunday L fr £27.50, Children welcome

Plas Ynyshir Hall Hotel ✿ ✿ ✿ ✿

EGLWYS FACH   Map 14 SN69

Modern British 🍷 NOTABLE WINE LIST

tel: 01654 781209 **SY20 8TA**
email: ynyshir@relaischateaux.com **web:** www.ynyshir-hall.co.uk
dir: *On A487, 6m S of Machynlleth*

Daring contemporary cooking amid birdsong and ancient trees

The term 'destination hotel' is particularly apt for this tranquil country house, since Plas Ynyshir Hall is not the sort of place you simply stumble upon. Secreted away in splendid gardens within a 1,000-acre RSPB reserve on the Dovey Estuary, the place has been around since the 15th century and was once owned by Queen Victoria, who planted many of the now mature trees to encourage birdlife to the estate. These days, the sound of birdsong helps soothe away modern life's nerve-frazzling effects, and the kitchen's masterful cooking boosts the feeling of spiritual well-being further still. In charge of the whole show since 1989, Rob and Joan Reen have made a deeply personal contribution to the illustrious history of the hall, establishing it firmly as one of the gastronomic magnets of Wales, and running every aspect of the enterprise with solicitous care and attention. A lavender-hued dining room is easy on the eye, with Rob Reen's vibrant paintings adorning the walls, and head chef Gareth Ward's culinary magic playing the lead role. Ward headed west to Wales after a three-year stint at Sat Bains in Nottingham, and brings with him that inventive and forward-looking chef's ethos of weaving intricate combinations of flavours, texture and temperature. Ingredients are of the highest possible order: Welsh lamb and Wagyu beef, fish from Cardigan Bay and local rivers, produce from the hall's own gardens and foraged wild ingredients form the basis of minimally worded eight and eleven-course tasting menus. Opening the show, 'Not French onion soup' is made from Japanese dashi stock flavoured with onion oil, diced tofu, pickled shallots, sea vegetables, onion and miso purée and brown butter croûtons, while mackerel comes in a vibrant sea-fresh partnership with elderflower, cucumber and green strawberry. Elsewhere, artichokes might come puréed, pickled, and roasted in butter and dashi, then matched with smoked bone marrow and parsley. That might be counterpointed by the full-bore savoury impact of melt-in-the-mouth Welsh Wagyu beef in a complex three-part presentation: in a 'burger' with shallots and sesame seeds, glazed with soy sauce and Marmite and matched with pickled shiitaki mushrooms, and in a deeply-flavoured beef 'fudge'. After that, Ynyshir ricotta with pickled pineapple, ham and rocket provides a crossover dish before desserts such as a fun take on the theme of a 'Walnut Whip', or a Cox's Apple workout with the fruit served as a terrine, purée and tart with buttermilk custard and wood sorrel granita.

Chef Gareth Ward **Owner** Rob & Joan Reen, John & Jen Talbot **Seats** 30, Pr/dining room 16 **Times** 12-2/7-9, Closed Jan **Prices** Tasting menu £55, Service optional **Wines** 260 bottles over £30, 23 bottles under £30, 18 by glass **Parking** 15 **Notes** Fixed L 5/8 course £35/£80, Fixed D 8/11 course £80/£90, Sunday L £35, Children welcome

CONWY

ABERGELE
Map 14 SH97

The Kinmel Arms

◉◉ Modern British, French

tel: 01745 832207 **The Village, St George LL22 9BP**
email: info@thekinmelarms.co.uk web: www.thekinmelarms.co.uk
dir: *From A55 junct 24a to St George. E on A55, junct 25. 1st left to Rhuddlan, then 1st right into St George. Take 2nd right*

Energetically creative coastal cooking

A stone-built village inn at St George on the north Wales coast, about 15 minutes' drive from Llandudno, The Kinmel is a hive of activity. An art gallery and studio have been added, which makes sense as there's much to inspire in the surrounding landscapes, but the most powerful draw is still the energetically creative cooking, which uses a welter of premium Welsh and Borders produce in imaginative ways. The backdrop to it all is an elegant dining room arrayed in crisp linen, gleaming stemware and candlelight, where pigeon breasts and salt-baked parsnip with granola, or mackerel with beetroot variations, pickled mooli, and oyster and cucumber sauce, are among the alluring ways to begin. Roll on with breast and pressed leg of guinea fowl with choucroute in sauce allemande, or perhaps a relatively traditional serving of sea bass in vermouth with sprouting broccoli and puréed celeriac. Dessert could be as complex as pear delice with walnut ice cream, pickled pear purée and walnut brittle, or as straightforward as a regally risen passionfruit soufflé.

Chef Chad Huges, Heddwen Wheeler **Owner** Tim & Lynn Watson **Seats** 70, Pr/dining room 10 **Times** 12-3/6-11.30, Closed 25 Dec, 1-2 Jan, Sun-Mon **Prices** Fixed L 2 course £15-£27, Fixed D 3 course £19-£32, Dessert £6-£7, Service optional **Wines** 37 bottles over £30, 52 bottles under £30, 15 by glass **Parking** 60 **Notes** Vegetarian available, Children welcome

BETWS-Y-COED
Map 14 SH75

Craig-y-Dderwen Riverside Hotel

◉ Traditional, International

tel: 01690 710293 **LL24 OAS**
email: info@snowdoniahotel.com web: www.snowdoniahotel.com
dir: *A5 to Betws-y-Coed, cross Waterloo Bridge, take 1st left*

Modern Welsh cooking in a beautiful riverside setting

Built in the 1890s for an industrialist, the partly timbered house became a favourite bolt-hole, and perhaps inspiration too, for Sir Edward Elgar. A hotel since the twenties, it has been carefully restored to offer the full country-house package, complete with conservatory dining room views of a riverside teeming with wildlife (do look out for the otters). Dishes boldly mix and match ingredients, and while the performance is not perfectly consistent, there is plenty to celebrate. Begin with sardines with a hollandaise sauce and tomato brioche, or cockles and mussels in a creamy leek sauce, and move on to confit duck leg with dauphinoise potatoes and an orange and Cointreau sauce. To finish, pecan tart arrives in the company of rum and raisin ice cream, while the cheese selection is a slate of Welsh options.

Chef Paul Goosey **Owner** Martin Carpenter **Seats** 82, Pr/dining room 40 **Times** 12-2.30/6.30-9, Closed 2 Jan-1 Feb **Prices** Prices not confirmed, Service optional **Wines** 50 bottles over £30, 60 bottles under £30, 7 by glass **Parking** 50 **Notes** Sunday L, Vegetarian available, Children welcome

Llugwy River Restaurant@Royal Oak Hotel

◉ Modern British, Welsh

tel: 01690 710219 **Holyhead Rd LL24 OAY**
email: royaloakmail@btopenworld.com web: www.royaloakhotel.net
dir: *On A5 in town centre, next to St Mary's church*

Former coaching inn with quality Welsh cuisine

Cappuccino-coloured walls with yellow sconces and ceiling chandeliers characterise the restaurant at this Victorian coaching inn, with dining chairs in a stripy fabric pulled up at lightwood tables on a patterned carpet, all brightly comfortable. The kitchen staunchly supports local suppliers and assembles a concise menu that buzzes with interest, often displaying Eastern influence. As well as chicken liver parfait with red onion marmalade, starters may run to scallop carpaccio with lime sabayon, mango jelly and pea shoots. Main courses vary from a duo of lamb (roast rump and faggot) with bubble-and-squeak, ratatouille and red wine jus to grilled sea bass with Thai-spiced risotto and green curry cream. Game shows up in season – perhaps whole roast partridge with parsnip purée, red cabbage and fig tart – and to end there may be tiramisù with coffee ice cream.

Chef Dylan Edwards **Owner** Royal Oak Hotel Ltd **Seats** 60, Pr/dining room 20 **Times** 12-3/6.30-9, Closed 25-26 Dec, Mon-Tue, L Wed-Sat, D Sun **Prices** Fixed L 2 course fr £11.95, Fixed D 3 course £25-£30, Service optional **Wines** 6 bottles over £30, 28 bottles under £30, 11 by glass **Parking** 100 **Notes** Sunday L £11.95-£15.95, Vegetarian available, Children welcome

CAPEL CURIG
Map 14 SH75

Bryn Tyrch Inn

◉ Modern Welsh NEW

tel: 01690 720223 & 07855 762791 **LL24 OEL**
email: info@bryntyrchinn.co.uk web: www.bryntyrchinn.co.uk
dir: *On A5 at top end of village*

Charming old inn with mountain views

The old whitewashed roadside inn with a stunning Snowdonia backdrop offers sanctuary to walkers, climbers and families alike. It's an egalitarian kind of place without pretention, and universally friendly service. The interior has plenty of charm and updates to the decor are entirely in keeping with the setting – original features remain but there's nothing tired or stuffy about the place. Eat in the bar or the terrace dining room and expect simple, homely stuff based on a good amount of regional produce. There's some modernity in the kitchen's output, with tempura king prawns with a Japanese-style chilli sauce on offer, or go local with smoked salmon, trout and mackerel roulade served with pickled vegetables and melba toast. Main-course Welsh rump steak is served in the classic manner, while Anglesey sea bass comes with locally-grown cauliflower and samphire and chive potatoes. Finish with lemon posset.

Chef Peter Mills **Owner** Neil & Rachel Roberts **Seats** 100, Pr/dining room 20 **Times** 12-9, All-day dining, Closed 15-27 Dec **Prices** Starter £6-£7, Main £13-£25, Dessert £5.50-£6, Service optional **Wines** 10 bottles over £30, 20 bottles under £30, 8 by glass **Parking** 40 **Notes** Sunday L £10.95-£15.95, Vegetarian available, Children welcome

---

CONWY   Map 14 SH77

Castle Hotel Conwy

◎◎ Modern British, International

tel: 01492 582800 **High St LL32 8DB**
email: mail@castlewales.co.uk web: www.castlewales.co.uk
dir: *A55 junct 18, follow town centre signs, cross estuary (castle on left). Right then left at mini-rdbts onto one-way system. Right at Town Wall Gate, right onto Berry St then High St*

Modern British dining in a local landmark

Conwy is a UNESCO World Heritage Site and, when it comes to matters of history, the town's Castle Hotel can hold its own. Occupying the site of a Cistercian abbey, with a Victorian bell-gabled façade of local green granite and red Ruabon bricks, it's been a coaching inn since the 15th century. Its period appeal is not preserved in aspic, with boutique styling throughout and a reputation as a local dining destination. Dawsons Restaurant & Bar, with its courtyard garden and stylish decor, offers modern British menus that deliver brasserie-style dishes and classic comfort options. Start with a sharing plate of charcuterie or smooth chicken liver parfait with rich prune chutney, and move on to twice-cooked sticky pork belly (with caramelised apples and red onions), or Conwy mussels in cider and spring onion sauce. There are posh fish and chips, burgers and steaks, too, and desserts such as apple and brandy tarte Tatin. A slate of Welsh cheeses includes Perl Las and Caws Llyn, served with savoury palmiers and red grape and sultana chutney.

Chef Andrew Nelson **Owner** The Lavin family **Seats** 70 **Times** 12-9.30, All-day dining, Closed D 25 Dec **Prices** Starter £3.90-£9.95, Main £12.55-£22.95, Dessert £1.95-£14.95 **Wines** 19 bottles over £30, 25 bottles under £30, 16 by glass **Parking** 36 **Notes** Small plates menu spring & summer, Sunday L, Vegetarian available, Children welcome

---

The Groes Inn

◎ Traditional British, Welsh

tel: 01492 650545 **Tyn-y-Groes LL32 8TN**
email: reception@groesinn.com web: www.groesinn.com
dir: *On B5106, 3m from Conwy*

Historic inn serving simple pub grub

Once a stopping point for weary stagecoach passengers, the 16th-century Groes is said to be Wales's first licensed house. The white-fronted inn has all the expected beamed ceilings and roaring fires, plus some interesting paraphernalia you probably wouldn't expect such as Victorian portraits, a collection of military hats and some historic cooking utensils. Try a pint or bottle of the inn's own Groes ale – a light ale with citrus tones. Food can be taken in the welcoming bar, cosy restaurant, airy conservatory or the garden, which has wonderful views. Fresh pub cooking using classic combinations defines the kitchen's output. Start with a smooth chicken liver pâté with toast and chutney before oven-baked whole rainbow trout, which slides off the bone, served with fennel and king prawns, carrots and roasted new potatoes with lemon and dill butter. Poached pears with cider ice cream provides a satisfying finish.

Times 12-2.15/6.30-9

DEGANWY   Map 14 SH77

Quay Hotel & Spa

◎◎ Modern European V

tel: 01492 564100 & 564165 **Deganwy Quay LL31 9DJ**
email: reservations@quayhotel.com web: www.quayhotel.com
dir: *M56, A494, A55 junct 18, straight across 2 rdbts. At lights bear left into The Quay. Hotel/Restaurant on right*

Steaks and seafood on the Conwy estuary

A stylish boutique hotel on the Conwy estuary, the Quay is a north Welsh destination for getting away from it all. Within striking distance of Snowdonia, it offers golf and spa treatments in the modern way, and boasts a smart eatery, the Grill Room, upholstered in muted greens and lilacs. Locally-landed fish and seafood are a strong draw, naturally, with oysters in shallots and red wine vinegar, crab croquettes with capers and 'tartare hollandaise', or mussels either Thai-style or marinière to get things going. A charcoal-fired oven ensures more sizzle for the steaks, which come in various cuts, all aged for 28 days, or stay fishy with monkfish medallions with butter-poached langoustines in shellfish bisque. The slapstick kitchen antics depicted on the dessert menu shouldn't be deemed to indicate that any less care has been taken over your hot apple crumble soufflé, served with apple and toffee ripple ice cream. High rollers may opt for the five-course tasting menu with wine flight.

Chef Sue Leacy **Owner** Inspire Ltd **Seats** 120, Pr/dining room 40 **Times** 12-3/6.30-9.30 **Prices** Prices not confirmed, Service optional **Wines** 18 bottles over £30, 40 bottles under £30, 19 by glass **Parking** 110 **Notes** Sunday L, Children welcome

---

LLANDUDNO   Map 14 SH78

Bodysgallen Hall and Spa

◎◎◎ *see page 682*

Dunoon Hotel

◎ Traditional British

tel: 01492 860787 **Gloddaeth St LL30 2DW**
email: reservations@dunoonhotel.co.uk web: www.dunoonhotel.co.uk
dir: *Exit promenade at War Memorial by pier onto Gloddaeth St. Hotel 200 yds on right*

Local ingredients and unpretentious British cooking

The restaurant here, accessed from the hotel lobby, is full of old-world charm, with oak-panelled walls, brass fittings and chandeliers, and flowers and linen napery on the tables; formally-attired staff are relaxed and attentive. The cooking style is more likely to reassure than to startle with modernism, with the kitchen clearly attempting to keep its customer base happy, so dishes are technically accurate and nicely presented without being showy. Among the starters, tarts – perhaps a warm one of pea and parmesan, and smoked fish – maybe locally smoked salmon and trout in silky-smooth risotto, get a decent showing among starters. Main courses run to Conwy Valley pheasant as roast breast and braised leg with pancetta-based gravy, mash and parsnip crisps, venison Wellington and perhaps seared fillet of prosciutto-wrapped monkfish on a bed of creamed leeks. For pudding, look no further than vanilla crème brûlée with plum compôte.

Chef Leighton Thomas **Owner** Rhys & Charlotte Williams **Seats** 80 **Times** 12-2/6.15-8.15, Closed mid Dec-1 Mar **Prices** Prices not confirmed, Service optional **Wines** 23 bottles over £30, 97 bottles under £30, 8 by glass **Parking** 20 **Notes** ALC menu 5 course £28.50, Pre-theatre D menu, Sunday L, Vegetarian available, Children welcome

LLANDUDNO *continued*

Empire Hotel & Spa

◉ Modern British

tel: 01492 860555 **Church Walks LL30 2HE**
email: reservations@empirehotel.co.uk **web:** www.empirehotel.co.uk
dir: *From Chester, A55 junct 19 for Llandudno. Follow signs to Promenade, turn right at war memorial & left at rdbt. Hotel 100yds on right*

Traditional brasserie cooking in an impressive Victorian spa hotel

Just off the promenade, the impressive white painted Victorian hotel with its portico entrance has been successfully refurbished to blend modern decorative garnishing, including spa facilities, with the 19th-century foundation of the place. The Watkins restaurant is named after a wine business that once flourished on the premises, and is done in clean, stylish fashion with ornate light fixtures and mirror panels. The kitchen turns out an essentially traditional bill of fare, with classic brasserie dishes much in evidence. Start with a fishcake of smoked and fresh salmon served with tartare sauce, or smooth chicken liver pâté with Cumberland dressing and crostini, as a prelude to well-seasoned loin of lamb with red cabbage, good roasties and rosemary jus, or perhaps a king prawn curry with basmati. Finish with cherry and almond tart, or Baileys-laced chocolate cheesecake on raspberry coulis. A short list of reasonably priced wines contains a decent choice by the glass.

Chef Michael Waddy, Jerome Ngugi **Owner** Len & Elizabeth Maddocks, Elyse Waddy **Seats** 110 **Times** 12.30-2/6.30-9.30, Closed 22-30 Dec, L Mon-Sat **Prices** Fixed D 3 course £23.95, Service optional 10% **Wines** 8 bottles over £30, 40 bottles under £30, 10 by glass **Parking** On street **Notes** Sunday L £16.25, Vegetarian available, Children welcome

Imperial Hotel

◉ Modern, Traditional British

tel: 01492 877466 **The Promenade LL30 1AP**
email: reception@theimperial.co.uk **web:** www.theimperial.co.uk
dir: *A470 to Llandudno*

Grand hotel cooking with views of the sea

The wedding cake stucco façade of the Imperial is a landmark on Llandudno's seafront. On a balmy day, alfresco dining on the terrace with a splendid backdrop of the bay is on the cards, a view which remains constant indoors, seen through the huge picture windows of Chantrey's Restaurant. The kitchen turns out menus of classically-inflected modern cooking featuring a sound showing of fine Welsh produce: slow-braised ham hock with pear and cider jelly, salt and pepper crackling and home-made herb brioche might open the show, while labour-intensive mains

Bodysgallen Hall and Spa ◉◉◉

LLANDUDNO   Map 14 SH78

Modern British v ⬧NOTABLE WINE LIST
tel: 01492 584466 **LL30 1RS**
email: info@bodysgallen.com **web:** www.bodysgallen.com
dir: *A55 junct 19, A470 towards Llandudno. Hotel 2m on right*

Ambitious, refined cooking in a grand National Trust property

When only the full-dress stately home experience will do, Bodysgallen never fails to deliver the goods – the old girl has been owned by the National Trust since 2008, after all. The 17th-century pile is buffered from the real world by 200 acres of parkland, rose gardens and geometrically precise parterres, and the view from its lofty perch is one that stays with you forever, sweeping across the skyline to Snowdonia, Conwy Castle and the Isle of Anglesey. You step into a genteel world of antiques, oil paintings, dark oak panelling and stone-mullioned windows, yet this is no stuffy country house, thanks to the efforts of charming staff, who strike all the right notes – obliging, courteous and always on the ball. Located in the Main Hall, the dining room is a refined and elegant space, with grand period character and views over the verdant countryside, and the unbuttoned approach means that, while smart dress is preferred, gentlemen are spared jacket and tie order. The cooking matches the upscale setting with its ambition and refinement, and there is a

finely judged modernity to starters such as a lightly poached yolk of duck egg, anointed in green garlic velouté at the table, alongside warm potato terrine and a garnish of new season's Wye Valley asparagus. An optional palate-sharpening sorbet intervenes (perhaps lemon and thyme) before the main event, which might be fillets of butter-poached John Dory with hand-made macaroni in langoustine butter, accompanied by infant greens of broccoli, courgette and spinach, or saddle of rabbit with tarragon boudin blanc in wild mushroom sauce. Dynamic desserts such as salted banana parfait with a Szechuan-peppered banana crisp end the show. The blue-blooded wine list does justice to the tremendous cooking.

Chef Adam Middleton, Richard Connor **Owner** The National Trust **Seats** 60, Pr/dining room 40 **Times** 12.30-1.45/7-9.30, Closed 24-26 Dec, L Mon **Prices** Fixed L 2 course £19.95-£25, Fixed D 3 course £43-£49 **Wines** 6 bottles under £30, 8 by glass **Parking** 40 **Notes** Pre-theatre D, Tasting menu on request, Sunday L £27, Children 6 yrs+

run to loin of Welsh lamb wrapped in leek mousse and prosciutto with crispy lamb breast, pea purée, Anna potato and rosemary jus. Desserts bring on classic crème brûlée with roasted pineapple, or a more ambitious warm pear, sultana and almond financier with toffee ice cream and pear and sultana compôte.

Chef Arwel Jones, Joanne Williams **Owner** Greenclose Ltd **Seats** 150, Pr/dining room 30 **Times** 12.30-3/6-9 **Prices** Starter £6.50-£8.50, Main £19.50-£25.75, Dessert £6.50-£8.50, Service optional **Wines** 37 bottles over £30, 87 bottles under £30, 15 by glass **Parking** 20, Promenade pay & display **Notes** Sunday L £16-£20, Vegetarian available, Children welcome

The Lilly Restaurant with Rooms

◉ Modern Welsh

tel: 01492 876513 **West Pde, West Shore LL30 2BD**
email: thelilly@live.co.uk **web:** www.thelilly.co.uk
dir: *Just off A546 at Llandudno, follow signs for the Pier, beach front on right*

Modern Welsh cooking overlooking the sea

Located in the sedate West Shore part of the town, and with unrestricted views over the coastline and restless sea, The Lilly is a family-run restaurant with rooms that covers a lot of bases. There's the Madhatters Brasserie (referencing the area's associations with C S Lewis) with its grill menu and sandwiches, but the main culinary destination is the flamboyantly decorated restaurant. With only 10 tables and lavish furnishings, the restaurant is the setting for menus that combine creativity with comforting familiarity. Kick off with scallops with a crab Scotch egg and sweetcorn purée, and move on to a duo of Welsh lamb (rump and braised shoulder), or go for posh fish and chips with tartare dressing. There's fillet steak, too with traditional accompaniments and bordelaise sauce, and, for dessert, a classic lemon tart delivers a satisfying sharpness.

Times 12-3/6-9, Closed Mon-Tue, L Wed-Sat, D Sun

St George's Hotel

◉ Modern, Traditional, Welsh

tel: 01492 877544 & 862184 **The Promenade LL30 2LG**
email: info@stgeorgeswales.co.uk **web:** www.stgeorgeswales.co.uk
dir: *A55, exit at Glan Conwy for Llandudno. A470 follow signs for seafront (distinctive tower identifies hotel)*

Patriotic Welsh cooking in a grand seafront hotel

Llandudno's prom is the place to be for splendid sunsets and sweeping views across the bay, and St George's Hotel sits centre stage among a grand line-up of seafront buildings. The place is a timeless slice of Victorian wedding cake grandeur, with an irresistible terrace to head for on balmy days, although the floor-to-ceiling windows of the restaurant within allow you to enjoy the same views when the weather isn't playing ball. Balancing trends with tradition, the kitchen brings together excellent local ingredients with confident simplicity: smoked mackerel with horseradish cream, beetroot, and garlic crostini is a typical starter. Lamb is always a good bet in these parts, especially when it is served as a main course of slow-cooked rump and breast with fresh peas, pearl barley and mint sauce jelly, or there may be roast cod loin with mussels, courgette and saffron cream. To finish, the addition of coconut and lemongrass give pannacotta an exotic spin.

Chef Gwyn Roberts **Owner** Anderbury Ltd **Seats** 110, Pr/dining room 12 **Times** 12-2.30/6.30-9.30 **Prices** Fixed L 2 course £17-£24, Fixed D 3 course £20-£30, Starter £6-£12, Main £12-£21, Dessert £6-£12, Service optional **Wines** 10 bottles over £30, 10 bottles under £30, 10 by glass **Parking** 36 **Notes** Pre-theatre menu, Sunday L £18-£23, Vegetarian available, Children welcome

RUTHIN

Ruthin Castle Hotel

◉ Modern British **NEW**

tel: 01824 702664 **Castle St LL15 2NU**
email: reservations@ruthincastle.co.uk **web:** www.ruthincastle.co.uk
dir: *From town square take road towards Corwen for 100yds*

Pan-European influenced cooking beneath chandeliers

In its nigh-on 750-year existence, Ruthin Castle has been many things including, from 1923 to 1950, a clinic for treating obscure internal diseases. In the early 60s the castle was incorporated into today's richly furnished hotel. Enjoy a pre-dinner drink in the octagonal, panelled Library Bar (which offers its own menu, by the way), then aim for Bertie's restaurant, named after Edward VII, a frequent visitor. Don't expect a huge choice, for the menu lists only four dishes for each course. Nonetheless even a total of just 12 dishes still permits plenty of permutations, one being braised rabbit boudin, followed by grilled fillet of cod with smoked bacon and potato chowder, and a rhubarb and custard dessert. Themed medieval dinners are popular here.

Chef Michael Cheetham, Lee Jones, Johnathon Goodman **Owner** Prima Hotel Group **Seats** 70, Pr/dining room **Times** 12-3/6-9 **Prices** Fixed L 2 course £14.95-£19.95, Fixed D 3 course £29.95-£46.95, Starter £5.50-£7.50, Main £23-£25.50, Dessert £5.50-£8.50, Service optional **Wines** 57 bottles over £30, 27 bottles under £30, 15 by glass **Notes** Afternoon tea £17.50, Sunday L, Vegetarian available, Children before 7pm

ABERSOCH Map 14 SH32

Porth Tocyn Hotel

◉◉ Modern British ▮ NOTABLE WINE LIST

tel: 01758 713303 **Bwlch Tocyn LL53 7BU**
email: bookings@porthtocynhotel.co.uk **web:** www.porthtocynhotel.co.uk
dir: *2m S of Abersoch, through Sarn Bach & Bwlch Tocyn. Follow brown signs*

Well-established country house with first-class cooking

Three generations of the Fletcher-Brewer family have run Porth Tocyn since 1948, converting a lowly terrace of lead miners' cottages and building the place up into the comfy, relaxed and unstuffy small-scale country house we see today. You can see why they put down such deep roots: who would want to move on from that spectacular view of Cardigan Bay with the peaks of Snowdonia rising in the distance? Inside, all is homely, relaxed and unstuffy, with a lived-in patina in its interconnecting antique-filled lounges. Vast picture windows in the smart restaurant capitalise on that remarkable panorama across the bay, while Louise Fletcher-Brewer oversees the kitchen team as it cooks up an assured repertoire that

continued

ABERSOCH *continued*

combines traditional values with more modern sensibilities. Carefully-sourced local, seasonal produce underpins it all, starting with the likes of pan-fried tournedos of hare with black pudding bonbons, sweet potato purée and port jus, followed by pan-fried, herb-crusted cannon of Welsh lamb teamed with carrot and cumin purée, green beans, toasted almonds, crushed potatoes and redcurrant and port jus. Finish with a comfort food classic — warm treacle tart with Chantilly cream.

Chef L Fletcher-Brewer, Ian Frost **Owner** The Fletcher-Brewer family **Seats** 50 **Times** 12.15-2.30/7.15-9, Closed mid Nov, 2 wks before Etr, occasional low season **Prices** Fixed D 3 course £46 **Wines** 26 bottles over £30, 71 bottles under £30, 6 by glass **Parking** 50 **Notes** Light lunches Mon-Sat, Sunday L £26, Vegetarian available, Children 6 yrs+ D

CAERNARFON
Map 14 SH46

Seiont Manor Hotel
◉◉ Modern British V

tel: 01286 673366 & 0845 072 7550 *(Calls cost 7p per minute plus your phone company's access charge)* **Llanrug LL55 2AQ**
email: seiontmanor@handpicked.co.uk **web:** www.handpickedhotels.co.uk/seiontmanor
dir: *From Bangor follow signs for Caernarfon. Leave Caernarfon on A4086. Hotel 3m on left*

Compelling cooking in farmhouse hotel

Positioned between Snowdonia National Park and the Menai Strait, Seiont Manor has upscaled rather dramatically since its days as a working farmstead. It's a rather handsome old stone property finished to a high standard and up-to-speed for meeting the needs of the 21st-century visitor (elegant bedrooms, fetching public areas), and it all sits in 150 acres of lush grounds with the River Seiont flowing through. The Llwyn y Brain dining room — a civilised place with a smart finish — is the setting for dishes that show a touch of refinement and ambition. A first course delivers the taste of the sea in the shape of lobster bisque with seared scallop, buttered langoustine and a salmon samosa, while main-course venison comes in the inventive company of smoked potato and chocolate sauce. There are good cooking skills on show and a creative take on regional ingredients; local sewin trout, for example, prepared confit-style with vanilla, and served with fennel purée and garlic 'whizz'. A dessert of pistachio and orange cake ends things on a high.

Chef Richard Williams **Owner** Hand Picked Hotels **Seats** 55, Pr/dining room 30 **Times** 12-2/7-9.30 **Prices** Fixed L 2 course £12.95-£18.95, Fixed D 3 course £37, Service optional **Wines** 104 bottles over £30, 6 bottles under £30, 18 by glass **Parking** 60 **Notes** ALC 3 course £49, Sunday L £14.95-£19.95, Children welcome

CRICCIETH
Map 14 SH53

Bron Eifion Country House Hotel
◉ Modern British, Welsh

tel: 01766 522385 **LL52 0SA**
email: enquiries@broneifion.co.uk **web:** www.broneifion.co.uk
dir: *A497, between Porthmadog & Pwllheli*

Modern Welsh cooking in a Victorian summer residence

The luxuriantly creeper-clad house stands on the Llyn Peninsula, and has the dual charm of ravishing gardens and a stone's-throw proximity to the beach at Criccieth. Built as a private summer residence in 1883, it was conceived with rest and relaxation in mind, and retains that reputation today. A majestic staircase, oak panelling and comfortable country-house furniture give the right impression, though the Garden Room restaurant aims for a more contemporary look, with bare tables and windows all around. Modern Welsh cooking is what to expect, with a

lengthy roll call of dishes utilising many of the favoured ingredients of the present. Seared scallops with crisp pancetta, pea purée and tempura-battered quail's egg is a modern classic with a tweak, and could be the prelude to roast duck breast in duck stock and plum sauce with potato gratin, sweet-and-sour cabbage and a white vegetable purée. End on a high with strawberry cheesecake mousse, served with dried strawberries and sorbet.

Chef Jason Hughes **Owner** John & Mary Heenan **Seats** 150, Pr/dining room 24 **Times** 12-2/6.30-9 **Prices** Starter £6-£9, Main £15-£19, Dessert £6-£8, Service optional **Wines** 20 bottles over £30, 28 bottles under £30, 6 by glass **Parking** 50 **Notes** Gourmand menu 8 course £65, Sunday L £16.95-£19.95, Vegetarian available, Children welcome

DOLGELLAU
Map 14 SH71

Bwyty Mawddach Restaurant
◉ Modern British

tel: 01341 421752 **Pen Y Garnedd, Llanelltyd LL40 2TA**
email: enquiries@mawddach.com
dir: *A470 Llanelltyd to A496 Barmouth, restaurant 0.2m on left after primary school*

Confident modern British cooking in barn conversion

When it comes to barn conversions, this one is rather impressive. Ifan Dunn saw the potential in the old granite building on the family farm and turned into a snazzy modern restaurant. The setting is pretty special, too, with views over the Mawddach Estuary and Cader Idris (the second highest mountain in Wales), and a glass wall ensures a good view for all inside. The cool, contemporary interior, spread over two floors, has a vaulted ceiling upstairs and slate floors on the ground floor. The cooking fits the bill amongst all this rustic-chic modernity, with some bright ideas and lots of regional ingredients. Start with celeriac soup with salted almonds, celery and apple, or a linguine rich with slow-cooked local pork. Next up, torched salmon fillet with brown butter and capers, or dry-aged Welsh Black rib-eye steak accompanied by triple-cooked chips, and, for dessert, apple and shot cake crumble with Douglas fir pine ice cream.

Chef Ifan Dunn **Owner** Roger, Will & Ifan Dunn **Seats** 75 **Times** 12-2.30/6.30-9, Closed 26 Dec, 1 wk Jan, 1 wk Apr, 2 wks Nov, Mon-Tue, D Sun, Wed **Prices** Starter £6.50-£9, Main £14.50-£21, Dessert £6.50-£8, Service optional **Wines** 8 bottles over £30, 19 bottles under £30, 7 by glass **Parking** 20 **Notes** Sunday L £20.95-£23.95, Vegetarian available, Children welcome

Penmaenuchaf Hall Hotel
◉◉ Modern British 🍷 NOTABLE WINE LIST

tel: 01341 422129 **Penmaenpool LL40 1YB**
email: relax@penhall.co.uk **web:** www.penhall.co.uk
dir: *From A470 take A493 (Tywyn/Fairbourne), entrance 1.5m on left by sign for Penmaenpool*

Modern British cooking in a Snowdonia garden room

Within the Snowdonia National Park, the greystone Penmaenuchaf Hall is surrounded by manicured gardens acting as a counterpoint to the wooded wildness of the surrounding hills. There are spectacular views from the Victorian-era house to Cader Idris and the Mawddach Estuary, and, with 21 acres all to itself, there's plenty of opportunity to get close to nature. The traditionally elegant, conservatory-style Llygad yr Haul restaurant offers a menu that reveals the kitchen's intentions to pay homage to the local landscape out of the window by featuring Welsh produce, but there's no lack of contemporary creative flair either. The Rhug Estate provides its organic pork belly, which is given the confit treatment, and served with onion and bacon compôte, crisp potato and truffle salad, and its lamb, too, the rump arriving with Mediterranean-style accompaniments. Seared brill comes in the meaty company of oxtail (plus braised gem lettuce and red wine sauce), while, to finish, bread-and-butter pudding is made with croissants and peach Melba is a deconstructed version. The wine list has lots to catch the eye and prices that won't scare the horses.

Chef J Pilkington, T Reeve **Owner** Mark Watson, Lorraine Fielding **Seats** 36, Pr/dining room 20 **Times** 12-2/7-9.30 **Prices** Fixed L 2 course fr £19.25, Fixed D 3 course fr £27.50, Starter £9, Main £27-£32, Dessert £9-£13.25, Service optional **Wines** 52 bottles over £30, 67 bottles under £30, 6 by glass **Parking** 36 **Notes** Sunday L fr £21.25, Vegetarian available, Children 6 yrs+

MALLWYD
Map 14 SH81

Tafarn y Brigand's Inn
◉ Contemporary **NEW**

tel: 01650 511999 **SY20 9HJ**
email: bookings@brigandsinn.com **web:** www.brigandsinn.com
dir: *Phone for directions*

Charming old inn for contemporary cooking

This 15th-century roadside inn has been revamped and spruced up to meet contemporary expectations, but its period features remain present and correct. There are cosy fires, real ales at the pumps, stylish bedrooms, and a bilingual menu that sees regional produce put to good use in modern preparations. The present-day favourite of seared scallops arrive with glistening caramelisation in the company of a smooth pea purée, pressing of pork belly and a shard of smoked bacon. The main course might deliver an Indian-inspired ginger-braised ox cheek or the more Mediterranean looking roasted hake with herb gnocchi and fricassée of leeks, peas and baby onions. Finish with warm treacle tart with poached rhubarb and ginger sauce or the selection of Welsh cheeses with home-made chutney and bara brith. Lunch is a slightly simpler affair, still showing the same passion for local provenance.

Chef Jon Beck **Owner** Frank Wilson **Seats** 40, Pr/dining room 50 **Times** 12-3/6-9 **Prices** Prices not confirmed **Notes** Afternoon tea, Sunday L, Vegetarian available, Children welcome

PORTHMADOG
Map 14 SH53

Royal Sportsman Hotel
◉◉ Modern British, Welsh

tel: 01766 512015 **131 High St LL49 9HB**
email: enquiries@royalsportsman.co.uk **web:** www.royalsportsman.co.uk
dir: *At rdbt junct of A497 & A487*

Contemporary cooking in a buzzy old coaching inn

The four-square hotel has been holding court on this spot since 1862, when it made its debut as a coaching inn. Today it's very much a 21st-century version of the same, with smart bedrooms, buzzy bar and fireside lounge, plus a restaurant that delivers some rather good stuff. There's a Welsh flavour to the culinary proceedings in the traditionally-decorated dining room, where regional ingredients form the basis of the contemporary cuisine. There's also a 'classics' menu that makes good use of local produce, too. On the main menu, pig's cheek and foie gras terrine sets the standard, with golden raisins flavoured with jasmine to cut though the richness. Main-course rump of Welsh spring lamb is a super piece of meat, with accompanying tapenade, tomatoes and baby courgettes, or there might be pan-fried monkfish with Arborio rice, chorizo, squid and a citrus velouté. There's no shortage of zesty flavours amongst desserts, with the likes of black cherry frozen parfait with green apple sorbet, or dark chocolate fondant with wild blackberries and pistachio.

Chef Russell Croston **Owner** Aby Quddus **Seats** 60 **Times** 12-2.30/6-9 **Prices** Prices not confirmed, Service optional **Wines** 4 bottles over £30, 20 bottles under £30, 11 by glass **Parking** 17, On street **Notes** Sunday L, Vegetarian available, Children welcome

PORTMEIRION
Map 14 SH53

The Hotel Portmeirion
◉◉ Modern Welsh

tel: 01766 770000 & 772324 **Minffordd LL48 6ET**
email: hotel@portmeirion-village.com **web:** www.portmeirion-village.com
dir: *Off A487 at Minffordd*

Lively modern Welsh cooking in a fantasy Italianate village

The fantasy Italianate village on the north Wales coast, created by Sir Clough Williams-Ellis over half a century, was conceived around the ruin of what is now the hotel. When the whole place began to materialise in 1926, the hotel, then unlicensed, was its focal point. It's still a gem, with views over the Dwyryd estuary and the hills beyond. A gracefully curving dining room was added in 1931. Fresh, lively, modern Welsh cooking enhances the whole experience no end, in the form of starters such as sautéed langoustines with smoked apple purée, pink grapefruit and celery, before the main business follows on with crisp-skinned sea bass served with crab tortellini and pak choi in a sauce combining the various piquancies of fennel, lemongrass and coriander, or lamb loin with goats' cheese dauphinoise, provençale veg and pesto. Fashionable rhubarb gets a dessert outing in a parfait topped with a little stick of candyfloss, plus a bright pink sorbet and a custard-filled doughnut.

Times 12-2.30/6.30-9.30, Closed 2 wks Nov

PWLLHELI
Map 14 SH33

Plas Bodegroes
◉◉ Modern British

tel: 01758 612363 **Nefyn Rd LL53 5TH**
email: gunna@bodegroes.co.uk
dir: *On A497, 1m W of Pwllheli*

Seasonal cooking in a scene of pastoral contentment

The Chowns' restaurant with rooms has been a fixture of the northwest Wales dining scene since the 1980s. A picture of pastoral contentment greets the eye, especially in spring and summer, when lavender scents the air, lambs bleat in the meadows, and jays chase each other amid the rhododendrons. The dining room is no dour oak-panelled retreat, but a fresh, airy space with mint-green walls hung with small artworks, a bare wood floor and elegant high-backed chairs. Chris Chown has always made a virtue of cooking to the seasons, and achieves positive results without recourse to undue complexity or technological boffinry. A fine smoked haddock tart with lemon-dressed fennel and watercress salad is an appealing opener, its pastry excellent, the filling beautifully balanced. Main courses might deliver firm-flavoured local pork loin with a broad bean and bacon fricassée and wild garlic purée, or sea bass in the Asian style, with crab, ginger and pak choi in lemongrass sauce. A satisfying chocolate trio to finish comprises dark mousse, a chocolate-pastried tart and a quenelle of white chocolate ice cream.

Chef Chris Chown, Hugh Bracegirdle **Owner** Mr & Mrs C Chown **Seats** 40, Pr/dining room 24 **Times** 12.30-2.30/7-9.30, Closed Dec-Feb, Mon, L Tue-Sat, D Sun **Prices** Fixed D 3 course £48.50, Service optional **Wines** 190 bottles over £30, 121 bottles under £30, 45 by glass **Parking** 20 **Notes** Sunday L £24.50, Vegetarian available, Children welcome

MONMOUTHSHIRE

ABERGAVENNY
Map 9 SO21

Angel Hotel

◎ Modern, Traditional British, International

tel: 01873 857121 **15 Cross St NP7 5EN**
email: mail@angelabergavenny.com **web:** www.angelabergavenny.com
dir: *From A40 & A465 junct follow town centre signs, S of Abergavenny, past stations*

Old inn with a brasserie-style menu

This hotel in the heart of the town was a posting inn in the first half of the 19th century, and its Georgian façade and spacious interiors are in fine fettle today. There's a contemporary finish to the generously proportioned internal spaces, with modern art and warm colours throughout. The same brasserie-style menu is up for grabs in the Foxhunter Bar or Oak Room restaurant, with lunchtime sandwiches and steaks cooked on the grill. This is a kitchen, though, that can cover a lot of ground to bring you fresh crab and mango salad or Tuscan bean and pasta soup to start, followed by rack of lamb – pink and tender – served with a little pan of shepherd's pie, or tiger prawns piri-piri style. Finish with a simple chocolate pot with pistachios and vanilla ice cream, or pear and apple crumble with crème anglaise.

Chef Wesley Hammond **Owner** Caradog Hotels Ltd **Seats** 80, Pr/dining room 120 **Times** 12-2.30/6-9.30, Closed 25 Dec, D 24-30 Dec **Prices** Fixed L 3 course £25, Fixed D 3 course £25, Starter £6.80-£12.80, Main £10.80-£28, Dessert £2-£7.80, Service optional **Wines** 47 bottles over £30, 47 bottles under £30, 10 by glass **Parking** 30 **Notes** Afternoon tea £21.80, Sunday L £21-£25, Vegetarian available, Children welcome

The Hardwick

◎◎ Modern British

tel: 01873 854220 **Old Raglan Rd NP7 9AA**
email: info@thehardwick.co.uk
dir: *Phone for directions*

Compellingly simple cooking in revamped country pub

Hard at work in a revamped old inn just outside Abergavenny is a chef with a wealth of experience at the sharp end the restaurant biz. Those heady London days behind him, Stephen Terry draws on all his knowledge to deliver simply inspiring food that is rooted in its environment. The rustic-chic charms of the restaurant and stylish contemporary bedrooms all add to the appeal of the place, with a pervading attitude among the staff that they're here to make sure you have a great time. Suppliers are nurtured and appreciated, their wares turned into unpretentious and mood-enhancing stuff such as a starter of meatloaf (made from Welsh pedigree pork) with melted Swiss cheese, onion marmalade and pickles, or a salad of hot chorizo and castelfranco radicchio. Dry-aged rib-eye is a superb piece of meat cooked just right (served with triple-cooked chips and melting Hardwick butter), while another main course matches shoulder of Brecon lamb with deep-fried polenta and salsa verde. Set lunches and grilled sandwiches fit the bill during the day, while Sunday lunch is a cut above the norm as you might expect. The wine list has lots to offer at sensible prices.

Times 12-3/6.30-10, Closed 25 Dec

Llansantffraed Court Hotel

◎◎ Modern British, Welsh **🍷 NOTABLE WINE LIST**

tel: 01873 840678 **Old Raglan Rd, Llanvihangel Gobion, Clytha NP7 9BA**
email: reception@llch.co.uk **web:** www.llch.co.uk
dir: *M4 junct 24/A449 to Raglan. At rdbt take last exit to Clytha. Hotel on right in 4.5m*

Ambitious Welsh modernism in a William and Mary mansion

A handsome brick-built William and Mary house in rural Monmouthshire, LLCH (as the web address has it) stands in 20 acres of trimly kept lawns with mature trees and a walled kitchen garden, within sight of the Tudor church of St Bridget's. Any sudden whirring you hear will be a 'copter landing on the helipad. A low-ceilinged raftered dining room, the Court, is elegantly presented, with well-spaced tables dressed in good napery, and the culinary ambition here has entered lift-off with a range of multi-course tasters (five, seven or nine courses with wine selections) supplementing the principal carte. A page of proudly attributed local suppliers inspires confidence. The results can be seen in seared langoustines with a 'risotto' of diced potato and smoked bacon, followed by roast breast and confit leg of Gressingham duck supported by roasted baby beetroot and beetroot purée, parsnips (roasted and crisps), and wild mushrooms. To finish, there's a switched-on array of tangerine soufflé and jelly with confit peel, almonds and candied citrus ice cream.

Chef Mike Hendry **Owner** Mike Morgan **Seats** 50, Pr/dining room 35 **Times** 12-2/7-9 **Prices** Fixed L 2 course £15, Fixed D 3 course £30-£35, Tasting menu £50-£85, Starter £6-£11, Main £15-£24, Dessert £6-£9, Service optional **Wines** 78 bottles over £30, 52 bottles under £30, 130 by glass **Parking** 300 **Notes** Tasting menu 7 course with matched wines, Sunday L £30, Vegetarian available, Children welcome

Restaurant 1861

◎◎ Modern British, European **v**

tel: 0845 388 1861 *(Calls cost 7p per minute plus your phone company's access charge)*
& 01873 821297 **Cross Ash NP7 8PB**
web: www.18-61.co.uk
dir: *On B4521, 9m from Abergavenny, 15m from Ross-on-Wye, on outskirts of Cross Ash*

Modern European cooking in a converted Victorian pub

The Kings' converted pub out in the wilds at Cross Ash, a little to the northeast of Abergavenny, was built in the year it's named after. After beginning his career with the Roux brothers, Simon King has gone native in Wales, and 1861 is in many ways a celebration of what the region has to offer, including a constant supply of fine vegetables grown by Kate King's dad. The culinary style applies techniques from the European, notably French, traditions in modern combinations that are unmistakably appealing. Smoked and confit goose with agrodolce cherries, or proper fish soup with saffron rouille and garlic croûtons, might kick things off. Mains include good seasonal game such as pheasant fricasséed in grain mustard cream, stuffed trotter in truffled Madeira sauce, or richly treated fish like sea bass in red wine, or hake with langoustine fritters in creamy champagne sauce. It's worth the wait for one of the hot desserts, perhaps a banoffee soufflé with chocolate poured in, or go modishly vegetal with acorn pannacotta and pumpkin ice cream.

Chef Simon King **Owner** Simon & Kate King **Seats** 40 **Times** 12-2/7-9, Closed 1st 2 wks Jan, Mon, D Sun **Prices** Fixed L 2 course fr £22, Fixed D 3 course fr £35, Tasting menu fr £55, Starter £8-£13.50, Main £20-£24, Dessert £7.25-£8.50, Service optional **Wines** 39 bottles over £30, 39 bottles under £30, 7 by glass **Parking** 20 **Notes** Tasting menu 7 course, Sunday L £22-£25, Children welcome

Walnut Tree Inn

◎◎◎ – *see opposite*

Walnut Tree Inn ❀❀❀

ABERGAVENNY   Map 9 SO21

WINNER OF THE AA WINE AWARD FOR WALES 2015–16

Modern British 🍷 NOTABLE WINE LIST

tel: 01873 852797 **Llandewi Skirrid NP7 8AW**
email: mail@thewalnuttreeinn.com
web: www.thewalnuttreeinn.com
dir: *3m NE of Abergavenny on B4521*

Blissfully unfussy and focused cooking by a culinary mastermind

When you eat at the Walnut Tree you're in the capable hands of Shaun Hill, one of the UK's truly exceptional chefs. During the decade spent putting Ludlow on the culinary map at his much-lauded Merchant House, Hill often popped over the Marches border to eat in the Walnut Tree in its glory days under Franco Taruschio. The place dropped off the gastronomic radar after the Italian chef moved on, so Hill set about resurrecting it to its rightful place on the foodie destination map in 2008. He's still at the stoves most days. The whitewashed inn goes for an unaffected rustic look enlivened with contemporary local art as a backdrop to some finely-tuned cooking. Never one for chasing ephemeral culinary fads and trends, Shaun Hill prefers to keep it real, sourcing the best ingredients he can lay his hands on and unleashing his formidable, seemingly effortless technical skills on making it all look deceptively simple. Plaice with sautéed leeks and a shrimp and dill croquette is an assured starter, while main-course sea bass with octopus, chorizo and paprika sauce is another straight-talking combo. For something more fortifying, there may be a full-blooded skirt of beef with oxtail and bone marrow crust, which delivers a punch to knock your socks off. Desserts keep the good ideas flowing: dark chocolate and raspberry torte, or perhaps plum soup with honey ice cream. The intriguing wine list promises bottles from small artisan winemakers, and while staff are impeccably helpful and attentive, they don't faff about with constant wine top ups. A couple of cottages in the grounds allow you to stay over and fill your boots.

Chef Shaun Hill **Owner** Shaun Hill, William Griffiths **Seats** 70, Pr/dining room 26 **Times** 12-2.30/7-10, Closed 1 wk Xmas, Sun-Mon **Prices** Prices not confirmed, Service optional **Wines** 50 bottles over £30, 40 bottles under £30, 8 by glass **Parking** 30 **Notes** Vegetarian available, Children welcome

LLANGYBI
Map 9 ST39

The White Hart Village Inn
◉◉ Modern British

tel: 01633 450258 & 07748 114838 **Old Usk Rd NP15 1NP**
email: enquiries@thewhitehartvillageinn.com
dir: *M4 junct 25 onto B4596 Caerleon road, through town centre on High St, straight over rdbt onto Usk Rd continue to Llangybi*

Impressive gastro-pub cooking in a smart village inn

The handsomely revamped 16th-century White Hart is the hub of Llangybi and stands close to the Roman settlement of Caerleon in the beautiful Usk Valley. Rich in history and atmosphere, the traditional bar has low-slung windows, black-painted beams, original Tudor plasterwork and a blazing fire in the grand inglenook fireplace, while the more contemporary dining areas are the setting for some top-notch gastro-pub food. Regional produce is at the heart of the imaginative menus and daily-changing blackboards, plus a six-course tasting menu that gives evidence of serious intent. The chefs are confident exponents of the modern British style, turning out accurately-cooked ideas with punchy, well-balanced flavours – wood pigeon with foie gras, ras el hanout spices and shallot barley, say, followed by roast mallard served with sweet-and-sour aubergine, potato, sweetcorn and hazelnut, or pollack with confit potato, chestnuts, sprout tops and mussels. To finish, crème brûlée could come with a creative twist of lemon and stem ginger. The individual mini-loaves of bread are spot-on – served hot from the oven for great texture and flavour.

Chef Adam Whittle **Owner** Michael Bates **Seats** 46, Pr/dining room 36
Times 12-3/6-9.30, Closed Mon (ex BHs), D Sun **Prices** Fixed L 2 course £15.95-£18.95, Fixed D 3 course £19.95, Tasting menu £45, Starter £5.95-£10.25, Main £12.95-£23.95, Dessert £5.95-£8.95, Service optional **Wines** 12 bottles over £30, 21 bottles under £30, 13 by glass **Parking** 30 **Notes** Fixed L/D Tue-Thu, Tasting menu 6 course Tue-Sat, Sunday L £18.95-£23.95, Vegetarian available, Children welcome

MONMOUTH
Map 10 SO51

Bistro Prego
◉◉ Modern Italian

tel: 01600 712600 **7 Church St NP25 3BX**
email: enquiries@pregomonmouth.co.uk **web:** www.pregomonmouth.co.uk
dir: *Travelling N A40 at lights left turn, T-junct left turn, 2nd right, hotel at rear of car park*

Buzzy bistro with an Italian edge

This simple and welcoming little bistro with rooms in the heart of Monmouth's old town has cornered a strong local fan base, won over by its no-nonsense approach. The food here is all about sourcing top-class local ingredients and bringing them together without undue fuss or fashionable flim-flam, whether you pop by for a light snack or lunch – perhaps crispy sweetbreads with tartare sauce, followed by slow-roasted pork belly with wild garlic bubble-and-squeak – or dinner, when the kitchen turns out a more involved bistro offering. As you may have spotted in the name, a strongly Italophile vein courses through it all: the menu skips with flair and imagination from a starter of vincisgrassi – baked pasta with porcini mushrooms and Parma ham – to a local wild boar chop with roasted beetroot, Swiss chard and red wine jus. For pudding, you can't go wrong with rhubarb and apple crumble with vanilla ice cream, or there might be a refreshing finale of pineapple carpaccio with mint, pomegranate and elderflower sorbet.

Chef Stephen Robbins **Owner** Stephen Robbins, Tom David, Sue Howell **Seats** 66
Times 12-2.15/6.30-9.15, Closed 24-26 & 31 Dec, 1 Jan **Prices** Starter £4-£8, Main £8-£22, Dessert £4-£7, Service optional 10% **Wines** 18 bottles over £30, 37 bottles

under £30, 18 by glass **Parking** Pay & display at rear of restaurant **Notes** Pre-theatre from 6pm bookings only, Sunday L £16.50, Vegetarian available, Children welcome

The Inn at Penallt
◉◉ Modern British

tel: 01600 772765 **Penallt NP25 4SE**
email: enquiries@theinnatpenallt.co.uk **web:** www.theinnatpenallt.co.uk
dir: *From Monmouth on B4293 towards Trellech. After 2m turn left signed Penallt, at village x-rds turn left, 0.3m on right*

Straightforward, honest cooking in the Wye Valley

There are country views, stone walls, real ales, comfy rooms, good food – it's a classic. The locals know how lucky they are. The diminutive village is home to this 17th-century inn with its robust exterior and slate, wood and roaring fires within. Few rural establishments have the dedication displayed here to sourcing food from both sides of the nearby border. There's a smarter dining room out back if you don't fancy the bonhomie of the bar. Kick things off with a starter of smoked duck breast with poached pear, walnuts and blue cheese sauce, or carpaccio of Welsh beef. Follow on with the blade of that same beef, served with dauphinoise potatoes and a red wine and thyme reduction, or fillet of Anglesey sea bass with a truffle and saffron beurre blanc, and finish with treacle tart with lemon and ginger ice cream.

Chef Peter Hulsmann **Owner** Andrew & Jackie Murphy **Seats** 28, Pr/dining room 28
Times 12-2.30/6-9, Closed Mon, L Tue, D Sun **Prices** Fixed L 2 course £16.95, Starter £5.95-£9.95, Main £13.95-£25.95, Dessert £6.95, Service optional **Wines** 25 bottles over £30, 43 bottles under £30, 9 by glass **Parking** 26 **Notes** Wed evening meal & drink £10.95, Thu steak & wine £16.95, Sunday L £16.95-£24.95, Vegetarian available, Children welcome

ROCKFIELD

Map 9 SO41

The Stonemill & Steppes Farm Cottages

Modern British, European, International

tel: 01600 716273 **NP25 5SW**
email: bookings@thestonemill.co.uk **web:** www.thestonemill.co.uk
dir: A48 to Monmouth, B4233 to Rockfield. 2.6m from Monmouth town centre

Clearly focused European cooking in a 16th-century cider mill

A beautifully converted barn in a 16th-century mill complex with self-catering bed and breakfast cottages, just a few miles west of Monmouth, and within striking distance of the Wye Valley and the Forest of Dean, provides the impressive setting for accomplished ingredients-led cooking. Inside it's a riot of oak beams and vaulted ceilings, with chunky rustic tables around an ancient stone cider press. The kitchen's modern approach makes sound use of fresh regional and Welsh produce to deliver accurately cooked and simply presented modern European ideas. Natural flavours shine through in a starter of mushroom soup with white truffle oil and sea salt. The same straight-up approach to flavour combinations results in an impressively piggy main course of slow-cooked pork belly and roast pork tenderloin with mustard creamed potatoes, spring greens and Calvados sauce. A well-matched pairing of dark chocolate iced parfait with Grand Marnier cream brings things to a close, or you might go for a savoury finish via a slate of Welsh cheeses with oatcakes and apple and plum chutney.

Chef Richard Birchall, Jordan Simons **Owner** Mrs M L Decloedt **Seats** 56, Pr/dining room 12 **Times** 12-2/6-9, Closed 25-26 Dec, 2 wks Jan, Mon, D Sun **Prices** Fixed L 2 course £14.95, Fixed D 3 course £20.95, Starter £6.95-£8.95, Main £16.95-£24.95, Dessert £5.95, Service optional **Wines** 10 bottles over £30, 36 bottles under £30, 7 by glass **Parking** 40 **Notes** Sunday L £16.50-£18.50, Vegetarian available, Children welcome

SKENFRITH

Map 9 SO42

The Bell at Skenfrith

Modern British, Welsh **NOTABLE WINE LIST**

tel: 01600 750235 **NP7 8UH**
email: enquiries@skenfrith.co.uk **web:** www.skenfrith.co.uk
dir: N of Monmouth on A466 for 1m. Left on B4521 towards Abergavenny, 3m on left

Simple modern pub food by the Monnow

The Bell gleams white amid the fields, not far from the Monnow riverbank, a 17th-century coaching inn togged up in fashion-conscious style inside. The original slate-flagged floor is retained, but the dining room, a vision in buttermilk yellow with French doors on to the garden, is refreshingly light and airy. A menu of simple modern pub food founded on reliable ingredients pulls off most of the tasks it sets itself. Asparagus in hollandaise is garnished with half a smoked salmon Scotch egg as an appealing start, which might precede seared bream with citrus-poached fennel, buttered samphire and saffron potatoes in sauce vièrge, or a three-way serving of local duck as pink breast, tenderly shredded leg and a meat-boosted potato cake in red wine jus. Finish with creamy lemon tart and blackcurrant sorbet, or boozily rich prune and Armagnac pudding with toffee sauce and clotted cream.

Chef Marc Montgomery **Owner** Richard Ireton **Seats** 60, Pr/dining room 40 **Times** 12-2.30/7-9.30 **Prices** Fixed L 2 course fr £22, Starter £5.95-£9.25, Main £12.95-£23.95, Dessert £6.50-£8.50 **Wines** 13 bottles over £30, 44 bottles under £30, 16 by glass **Parking** 35 **Notes** Sunday L £22-£28, Vegetarian available, Children welcome

USK

Map 9 SO30

Newbridge on Usk

Traditional British

tel: 01633 451000 & 410262 **Tredunnock NP15 1LY**
email: newbridgeonusk@celtic-manor.com **web:** www.celtic-manor.com
dir: A449 to Usk exit through town & turn left after bridge through Llangibby. After approx 1m Cwrt Bleddyn Hotel on right, turn left opposite hotel up lane. Drive through village of Tredunnock, down hill, inn on banks of River Usk

Pastoral riverside setting for contemporary cooking

On a bend in the Usk, with views of the river, this restaurant with rooms is in a peaceful spot surrounded by well-tended gardens. The property dates back 200 years, so expect the usual beams, fireplaces and wooden floors, while the two-level restaurant has a rustic charm. The kitchen is assiduous about its sourcing (Welsh lamb and cheeses, fish from Brixham, chicken from the Wye Valley, for instance), and its menu ticks some cosmopolitan boxes. A duo of lamb comes as shoulder in ras el hanout and as seared rump, served with spinach and kale dotted with almonds, and pan-fried wild sea bass fillet is coated in Parma ham and accompanied by globe artichokes and watercress. Flavours are clear, witness starters of glazed belly of pork, nicely sticky, with black pudding and apple salad, and crab risotto with a spicy tomato foam and parmesan crisp. Puddings like rich dark chocolate mousse with ginger parfait, or banana crème brûlée are followed by petits fours with coffee.

Chef Gavin McDonagh **Owner** Celtic Manor Resorts **Seats** 90, Pr/dining room 16 **Times** 12-2.30/7-10 **Prices** Fixed L 2 course fr £15.95, Starter £5.95-£11.25, Main £15.95-£23.50, Dessert £6.25-£7.95, Service optional **Wines** 20 bottles over £30, 20 bottles under £30, 9 by glass **Parking** 60 **Notes** Early bird D menu offer, Sunday L fr £24.95, Vegetarian available, Children welcome

USK continued

The Three Salmons Hotel

◉◉ ◉ Modern Welsh

tel: 01291 672133 **Bridge St NP15 1RY**
email: general@threesalmons.co.uk
dir: *M4 junct 24/A449, 1st exit signed Usk. On entering town hotel on main road*

Brasserie cooking of appealing simplicity

This black and white coaching inn has been a feature of Usk for the past three centuries. Set amid the fine walking and fishing country of south Wales, its present-day incarnation is pared-down stylish, with a clean-lined contemporary look, best seen in the uncluttered dining room, where well-spaced unclothed tables and wooden blinds at the windows create a laid-back feel. The Three Salmons is one of those places that runs its own kitchen garden, and the rest of the produce is sourced just as discerningly for brasserie cooking that highlights its quality. An opening dish of ham hock with black pudding, apple and a Scotch quail's egg makes that clear. Mains might follow on with a suitably robust treatment of hake, which comes with confit chicken wing, a giant oyster mushroom and dauphinoise in lemon butter. Calves' liver is tenderly timed, and matched with crisp smoked bacon, spinach and creamy mash, and meals end in populist fashion with chocolate fondant and ginger ice cream, or crème caramel with poached pear.

The Three Salmons Hotel

Chef James Bumpass **Owner** T Strong, B Dean, P Clarke, J Bumpass **Seats** 55, Pr/dining room 80 **Times** 12-2.30/6.30-9.30 **Prices** Prices not confirmed, Service optional **Wines** 39 bottles over £30, 61 bottles under £30, 14 by glass **Parking** 80 **Notes** Afternoon tea £13, Sunday L, Vegetarian available, Children welcome

WHITEBROOK	Map 4 SO50

The Whitebrook

◉◉ ◉ – *see below*

The Whitebrook ◉◉◉

WHITEBROOK	Map 4 SO50

British, French **v**
tel: 01600 860254 **NP25 4TX**
email: info@thewhitebrook.co.uk **web:** www.thewhitebrook.co.uk
dir: *From Monmouth take B4293 towards Trellech, in 2.7m left towards Whitebrook, continue for 2m*

Modern metropolitan cooking in the Wye Valley

The verdant wildness of the Wye Valley that surrounds The Whitebrook offers the potential of a stunning natural larder, an opportunity not missed by chef-patron Chris Harrod. Mr Harrod arrived in Wales having worked with Raymond Blanc and headed up highly regarded kitchens, and his coming has returned this spot between Monmouth and Tintern Abbey to the top table. The one-time drovers' inn dates from the 17th century and reveals its vintage here and there, but the finish is cool and contemporary in the rustic-chic manner. In keeping with the setting, the service is devoid of stuffiness. The Whitebrook is a restaurant with rooms that offers a classy getaway, but first-and-foremost it's a cracking restaurant. Chris Harrod and his kitchen team forage in the valley for the likes of pennywort, wild onion and bitter cress, and what ingredients aren't picked by hand are sourced from the region with due diligence. A la carte and tasting menus are on offer, including excellent vegetarian versions, with the lunchtime offering particularly excellent value. The cooking may well be pin-sharp and modern, but flavour leads the way, with well-judged combinations such as hand-dived scallops in the fashionable company of pork belly, plus chestnuts, celery and apple, or Golden Cenarth cheese dumpling partnered with salt-baked turnip, duck gizzard and woodland sorrel. Follow on with Wye Valley duck breast with caraway cabbage, onion purée and smoked bacon, or wild sea bass with chard, foraged fennel and oyster mushrooms from the valley. Foraged herbs bring a local flavour from start to finish, with mugwort featuring in a dessert of crown prince pumpkin and white chocolate. The wine list, sorted by style, has organic and biodynamic possibilities.

Chef Chris Harrod **Owner** Chris Harrod **Seats** 32 **Times** 12-2/7-9, Closed 1st 2 wks Jan, Mon **Prices** Fixed L 2 course £25, Fixed D 3 course fr £54, Tasting menu fr £67, Service optional 10% **Wines** 105 bottles over £30, 42 bottles under £30, 13 by glass **Parking** 20 **Notes** Sunday L fr £35, Children 12 yrs+

NEWPORT

NEWPORT   Map 9 ST38

Le Patio at the Manor House

◉ Modern French

tel: 01633 413000 **The Celtic Manor Resort, Coldra Woods NP18 1HQ**
email: bookings@celtic-manor.com **web:** www.celtic-manor.com
dir: *M4 junct 24, B4237 towards Newport. Hotel 1st on right*

French country cooking in a Welsh golf resort

If you're splashing out on a golfing week at the sprawling Celtic Manor Resort, you can ring the changes by eating in a different venue every day you're there. Tucked away in the historic part of the old manor house, Le Patio is the place to head for when you need a hit of hearty French country cooking, served in an informal glass-roofed extension done out with bare blond-wood tables and wicker seats. Starters are as simple as onion soup with croûtons and gruyère, or confit pork terrine with almonds, herbs and sweet garlic served with plum and ginger chutney and onion bread, while mains take in regional classics such as beef bourguignon with mash, bouillabaisse with rouille and toasted garlic bread, and Alsatian chicken slow-cooked in Riesling with cream, lardons, mushrooms and served with sweet potato purée. End with cinnamon and apple bavarois with apple sorbet.

Times 6.30-10, Closed L all week

Rafters

◉ Modern British

tel: 01633 413000 **The Celtic Manor Resort, Coldra Woods NP18 1HQ**
email: bookings@celtic-manor.com **web:** www.celtic-manor.com
dir: *M4 junct 24, B4237 towards Newport. Hotel 1st on right*

Grill classics at the 19th hole

There are views over the Ryder Cup course from Rafters, a classy grill restaurant on the Celtic Manor Resort. It's within the Twenty Ten Clubhouse (2010 being the year the cup came to town), and with its high beamed ceiling, smart, modern look and those views, there's a lot to like. The kitchen makes a play for Welsh ingredients and, with it being a grill restaurant and all, there are locally-reared steaks aged for 21 days as the star attraction. They come with hickory-infused chips and soused red onion salad, but it you're not in the mood for the red stuff, other main course options might include grilled sea bass with kohlrabi and a pea and spinach velouté, or twice-baked goats' cheese soufflé with roasted chestnuts and butternut squash purée. Kick off with smoked haddock rarebit with crab and sweetcorn fritters, or a classy prawn cocktail, and finish with apple and caramel trifle with cider granité.

Times 12-2.30/6-10, Closed D Mon-Wed (Oct-Mar)

Terry M at The Celtic Manor Resort

◉◉◉ – *see page 692*

PEMBROKESHIRE

HAVERFORDWEST   Map 8 SM91

Wolfscastle Country Hotel
◉◉ Modern British, Welsh

tel: 01437 741225 **Wolf's Castle SA62 5LZ**
email: info@wolfscastle.com **web:** www.wolfscastle.com
dir: *From Haverfordwest take A40 towards Fishguard. Hotel in centre of Wolf's Castle*

Modern classic cooking in a historic location

Local legend has it that the great Welsh rebel leader Owain Glyn Dwr may be buried in the field alongside this old stone country hotel next to the castle of the same name. Standing on a promontory overlooking the confluence of two rivers, it makes the most of its historic location with a conservatory extension to the principal restaurant. It's all got up in grey-toned minimal garb, with unclothed tables and a menu of modern classic dishes that have gained in confidence and flair. A double act of pork belly and scallop with puréed cauliflower in chicken jus is a well-rendered version of the familiar reference dish, or there might be potted pulled duck with red onion marmalade and cornichons. Accurately cooked fillet and short rib of Welsh Black beef is a triumph, served with the gentling textures of roast garlic mash and puréed spinach, while hake appears Spanish-style with prawn and chorizo paella and charred fennel. Finish with rich chocolate fondant, served with salted caramel ice cream and orange jelly.

Wolfscastle Country Hotel

Times 12-2/6-9, Closed 24-26 Dec

Terry M at The Celtic Manor Resort ❀❀❀

NEWPORT   Map 9 ST38

Modern British
tel: 01633 413000 **Coldra Woods NP18 1HQ**
email: terrym@celtic-manor.com **web:** www.celtic-manor.com
dir: *From M4 junct 24 take B4237 towards Newport, turn right after 300yds*

Outstanding cooking at a world-class golfing hotel

Terry M is a truly elegant space with pristine white walls, darkwood flooring, slinky gold lighting, shimmering crystal bead chandeliers, and high-backed ivory leather chairs. It's the kind of space that promises a memorable experience, and such hopes are borne out by scrupulously professional yet unstuffy service and the kitchen's high-flying culinary output. Tim McDougall delivers refined dishes which impress with respect for classical ways while delivering lashings of contemporary va-va-voom. Prime Welsh ingredients are given prominence on menus that run to a six-course tasting version, an excellent value express lunch, and three-course outings that might get under way with hand-dived scallops alongside chicken boudin and white beans, or a torchon of duck liver cooked in port and served with a walnut wafer. At main-course stage, die-hards might go for a timeless trio of Welsh beef rib with potato galette and truffle butter jus, or for modernists, perhaps red mullet fillet with rocket and passionfruit sauce and roasted vegetables. It all ends with plenty of oohing and aahing with the arrival of dramatic desserts like chocolate bavarois with blood orange salad and grapefruit mousse, or a perfectly risen plum soufflé with pain d'épices ice cream.

Chef Tim McDougall **Owner** Celtic Manor Resort **Seats** 50, Pr/dining room 12 **Times** 12-2.30/7-9.30, Closed 1-14 Jan, Mon-Tue **Prices** Fixed L 2 course £15.95-£22.95, Fixed D 3 course fr £49.50, Tasting menu £70, Service optional **Wines** 195 bottles over £30, 40 bottles under £30, 12 by glass **Parking** 1000 **Notes** Tasting menu 7 course, Sunday L fr £32.50, Vegetarian available, Children 13 yrs+

NARBERTH
Map 8 SN11

The Grove
◉◉◉ – see page 694 and advert on page 695

NEWPORT
Map 8 SN03

Llys Meddyg
◉◉ British

tel: 01239 820008 & 821050 **East St SA42 0SY**
email: contact@llysmeddyg.com **web:** www.llysmeddyg.com
dir: A487 to Newport, located on the Main Street, through the centre of town

Accomplished cooking in a former coaching inn

Llys Meddyg is an attractive package when you want to explore the Pembrokeshire Coast National Park. The handsome Georgian townhouse is easy to spot in the centre of Newport village: converted from a coaching inn, it now earns a crust as a comfortable, smartly-done-out restaurant with rooms. There's a cosy stone-walled cellar bar with flagstones, ceiling beams and a wood-burner, a lovely kitchen garden for pre-dinner drinks, and an elegant restaurant hung with art. The kitchen champions local produce, sustainably sourced whenever possible, and goes foraging to boost the repertoire with nature's seasonal bounty, turning up pennywort to partner home-smoked salmon served with horseradish cream and lemon jelly. Main courses ally precision with a lack of pretension: confit leg and roast breast of pheasant, perhaps, with cannellini bean and vegetable consommé, or pan-fried sea bass accompanied by tomato, pearl onions, crab bisque, nuts and spices. A winter pudding might see mulled pear served with cinnamon doughnut, or a savoury finish with Welsh cheeses is good whatever the season.

Chef Mathew Smith **Owner** Ed & Louise Sykes **Seats** 30, Pr/dining room 14
Times 6-9, Closed L all week (ex summer L kitchen garden) **Prices** Fixed D 3 course £25, Tasting menu £55, Starter £6.95 £11.95, Main £14.50 £26.50, Dessert £7.95 £9.95, Service optional **Wines** 4 by glass **Parking** 8, On street **Notes** Vegetarian available, Children welcome

PEMBROKE
Map 8 SM90

BEST WESTERN Lamphey Court Hotel & Spa
◉ Modern British

tel: 01646 672273 **Lamphey SA71 5NT**
email: info@lampheycourt.co.uk **web:** www.lampheycourt.co.uk
dir: M4 then A477 to Pembroke. Left at Milton for Lamphey, hotel on right on entering village

Homely cooking in a grandiose Georgian mansion

As Georgian mansions go, Lamphey Court is a bit of an eye-popper, a great white whale of an edifice with massive columns fronting a portico entrance that wouldn't have disgraced a Roman temple. Built in 1823, it's now been equipped with a decidedly very 21st-century spa and gym, and if you're looking to get plenty of exercise while you're here, the Pembrokeshire Coastal Path isn't far distant, while the national park is all around. The kitchen turns out homely food with one or two flourishes of modern Britishism. Start with smoked trout and horseradish cream, or one of the trendy sharing platters of tapas or Italian charcuterie, and then set about confit duck leg on spiced red cabbage in redcurrant jus, pulled pork and sweet chilli burger or herb-crusted roast salmon in warm dill yogurt sauce. Favourite puddings include apple and blackberry crumble, or honey and lemon cheesecake.

Times 12-2.30/6.15-10

PORTHGAIN
Map 8 SM83

The Shed
◉ Traditional British, Mediterranean

tel: 01348 831518 **SA62 5BN**
email: caroline@theshedporthgain.co.uk **web:** www.theshedporthgain.co.uk
dir: 7m from St Davids. Off A487

Fresh seafood and laid-back ambience on the harbour

Seafood is king at this simple beach hut-style 'fish and chip bistro' right on the quayside in the dinky fishing village of Porthgain. The place sells its own-caught and local, sustainable fresh fish and seafood from a counter during the warmer months, and sitting outdoors with a glass of wine, you couldn't ask for a more delightfully unaffected venue. Indoors, gingham tablecloths, whitewashed walls and fish-related art all add up to a laid-back setting for unpretentious dishes that let the sheer quality and freshness of the raw materials do the talking. Proper beer-battered fish and chips gets its own menu, otherwise tiger prawns are pan-fried with lashings of garlic butter and parsley, then spanking-fresh hake is matched with poppy seeds, cucumber pickle salad and coriander yogurt. End with dark chocolate and Tia Maria torte with coffee crunch ice cream and espresso sauce.

Chef Rob & Caroline Jones **Owner** Rob & Caroline Jones **Seats** 60
Times 12-3/5.30-9, Closed Nov-Apr (open only wknds except half term & Xmas hols), D Tue (off peak) **Prices** Starter £4.95-£7.50, Main £10.95-£21.50, Dessert £3.50-£6.50, Service optional **Wines** 2 bottles over £30, 24 bottles under £30, 7 by glass **Parking** On village street **Notes** Sunday L, Vegetarian available, Children welcome

The Grove 🌹🌹🌹

Modern British 🍷 NOTABLE WINE LIST

tel: 01834 860915 **Molleston SA67 8BX**
email: info@thegrove-narberth.co.uk
web: www.thegrove-narberth.co.uk
dir: *From A40, take A478 to Narberth. Continue past castle &
Herons Brook, turn right bottom of hill*

Tireless attention to detail in a beautifully restored country house

When the main house was built in the late 17th century, next to an
original Plantagenet longhouse (which still survives), this site was
a key stopping-point on the London to St David's coach-route. The
present owners have restored the property from near-dereliction to
its current splendour, not least the grounds, which are watched
over by venerable old oaks and beeches. Inside has been done in
pastel-shaded country interiors style, with daring splotches of
purple in the lounge, and a soothing air pervading the smartly
appointed dining room. Duncan Barham heads up a kitchen that
recognises no limits to its reach, producing an extensive menu that
makes the attention to detail in each dish all the more impressive.
Positive seasoning and considered combinations are the hallmarks
of successful showings such as flawlessly timed scallops with pork
belly, the dish adorned with soft-pickled vegetables and hot jellies,
all spiked with soy and dashi. One moment, Italy is in the kitchen's
sights, as for bresaola with goats' curd and plum, the next it's
Morocco, in ras el hanout-spiced quail on tabbouleh. Preseli
Bluestone lamb is the star of a main that offers the rump and
heart against a slew of broad beans, peas and wild garlic, while
fish might be John Dory stuffed with olives, or monkfish on lentil
dhal. Variations on a banana theme make for a memorable dessert
plate of gâteau, mousse, poached and rum-soaked slices, along
with salted caramel ice cream, while pineapple in multiple guises
appears with a cardamom-spiked crème caramel. Fine British
cheeses come with fig preserve, and an authoritative modern wine
list under the custody of an expert sommelier puts the gilding on
the gingerbread.

Chef Duncan Barham, Peter Whaley **Owner** Neil Kedward, Zoe Agar
Seats 70, Pr/dining room 25 **Times** 12-2.30/6-9.30, **Prices** Fixed L
2 course £23, Tasting menu £78, Service optional **Wines** 250
bottles over £30, 23 bottles under £30, 18 by glass **Parking** 42
Notes ALC 3 course £54, Tasting menu 7 course, Sunday L £25,
Vegetarian available, Children welcome

Cwtch

◉ Modern British

tel: 01437 720491 **22 High St SA62 6SD**
email: info@cwtchrestaurant.co.uk
dir: *A487 St Davids, restaurant on left before Cross Square*

Big taste of Wales in the smallest city

If your Welsh isn't up to scratch, the name is pronounced 'cutsh' and it has all the cosseting connotations of hug, snug, and cosy. The restaurant lives up to its name as far as the ambience goes, with three small dining rooms spread over two floors, and done out with the pared-back simplicity of whitewashed stone walls, sturdy beams and foodie books for diners to leaf through. The cooking takes a similarly restrained approach, leaving peerless Pembrokeshire produce to do the talking. Open with a chunky terrine of ham hock, apricot and pistachio with sourdough toast, followed by a soul-soothing main course of slow-roasted pork belly with onion gravy, apple sauce, black pudding and crackling. Fishy options might run to hake fillet with sweetcorn, smoked pancetta and cockle chowder and red pepper tapenade. Round things off with puddings that fly the red dragon, such as sticky toffee bara brith pudding with vanilla ice cream.

Chef Nic Mascall **Owner** Jackie & John Hatton-Bell **Seats** 50, Pr/dining room **Times** 6-10, Closed 25-26 Dec, Jan, Mon-Tue (Nov-Mar), L Mon-Sat (Oct-Apr), D Sun (Oct-Apr) **Prices** Fixed D 3 course £26-£30, Service optional **Wines** 6 bottles over £30, 23 bottles under £30, 9 by glass **Parking** On street, car park **Notes** Early evening offer 6-6.45pm 2/3 course £22/£26, Sunday L £20-£24, Vegetarian available, Children welcome

SAUNDERSFOOT — Map 8 SN10

AA RESTAURANT OF THE YEAR FOR WALES 2015–16

Coast Restaurant

◎◎ Modern British

tel: 01834 810800 **Coppel Hall Beach SA69 9AJ**
email: reservations@coastsaundersfoot.co.uk web: www.coastsaundersfoot.co.uk
dir: *Phone for directions*

Emblematic modern structure on the Pembrokeshire shoreline

If you were looking for an emblematic 21st-century restaurant venue, you couldn't go far wrong with Coast. A purpose-built curvaceous wood structure, it stands on the Pembrokeshire shore, with just the sea and sky before it. Huge picture windows allow for relaxed contemplation, and the interior scene is all simple bare tables, banquettes strewn with cushions, and an atmosphere of serenely informal professionalism. The seafood-strong menu construction is exactly of the moment too, built from local materials and with more flexibility than the old three-course format ever allowed. A Nibbles list offers temptations such as tankards of prawns, crispy pigs' ears and apple sauce, or houmous dusted with smoked paprika, before you get into the full starter menu. A broad swathe of heterogeneous choice ranges from crab with mango, wasabi yogurt and coriander to griddled squid with pink grapefruit and shaved fennel, and mains follow up with the likes of halibut, lentils and cauliflower in garam masala, or 28-day dry-aged rib-eye with peppercorn butter. Finish with marmalade baked Alaska and bloodorange.

Chef Will Holland **Owner** Neil Kedward, Zoe Agar **Seats** 64
Times 12-2.30/6-9.30, Closed Mon-Tue (Nov-Feb), D Sun (Nov-Feb) **Prices** Fixed L 2 course £18, Fixed D 3 course £24, Starter £8-£14, Main £14-£26, Dessert £9-£12
Wines 29 bottles over £30, 9 bottles under £30, 17 by glass **Parking** Pay & display before 6pm **Notes** Tasting menu 6 course, Fixed L/D autumn/winter only, Sunday L, Vegetarian available, Children welcome

St Brides Spa Hotel

◎ Modern British

tel: 01834 812304 **St Brides Hill SA69 9NH**
email: reservations@stbridesspahotel.com web: www.stbridesspahotel.com
dir: *A478 onto B4310 to Saundersfoot. Hotel above harbour*

Pleasingly unfussy food and fabulous sea views

The coastal views of Saundersfoot harbour and Carmarthen Bay from its clifftop perch are reason enough to pay this laid-back spa hotel a visit, and after a restorative hit of pampering treatments, the kitchen soothes the palate via a brace of wide-ranging menus. The outdoor terrace is the place to be when the weather plays ball, but when the Welsh climate does its thing, there's the Gallery bar for a menu of simple classics based on top-class regional produce, and the Cliff Restaurant, where the chefs crank things up a notch to deliver some vibrant, unpretentious cooking. A simple but effective combo of chorizo with roasted potato cake and charred red pepper starts things off, followed by halibut wrapped in pancetta with roasted garlic mash and parsley jus. To finish, roasted figs come with mascarpone ice cream and cinnamon toast.

Chef Toby Goodwin **Owner** Andrew & Lindsey Evans **Seats** 100, Pr/dining room 50
Times 11-close, All-day dining **Prices** Starter £6.50-£8, Main £16-£24, Dessert £6.25-£7.25, Service optional **Wines** 104 bottles over £30, 79 bottles under £30, 14 by glass **Parking** 60 **Notes** All day Gallery menu, Sunday L, Vegetarian available, Children welcome

SOLVA — Map 8 SM82

Crug Glâs Country House

◎ Modern British **NEW**

tel: 01348 831302 **Abereiddy SA62 6XX**
email: janet@crug-glas.co.uk web: www.crug-glas.co.uk
dir: *From St Davids take A487 to Fishguard. 1st left after Carnhedryn, house signed*

Unflashy cooking in a country restaurant with rooms

Five plush bedrooms and 600 acres of rolling farmland to buffer guests from the outside world make Crug Glâs an inviting prospect. Hands-on owners Janet and Perkin Evans have renovated the interiors using local materials to achieve a neat balance of smart modernity without trampling on the house's history – the place dates from the 12th century, after all. At the end of the day, kick off the walking boots and settle into the formal Georgian dining room for Janet's traditional country-house cooking. Pembrokeshire's finest produce forms the backbone of menus that aim to comfort rather than challenge. Cream of celeriac and apple soup gets a lift from curry oil and parsnip crisps, followed by pan-fried pheasant breast with chestnut-stuffed cabbage, dauphinoise potatoes, parsnip purée and an aromatic sauce of apple and Black Mountain liqueur. Finish with a salted caramel and chocolate slice.

Chef Janet Evans **Owner** Janet Evans **Seats** 35, Pr/dining room 16
Times 12-2.30/6.30-8.30, Closed 25-26 Dec **Prices** Fixed L 2 course fr £19, Starter £5-£9, Main £16.50-£30, Dessert £5.50-£8, Service optional **Wines** 5 bottles over £30, 16 bottles under £30, 7 by glass **Notes** Sunday L, Vegetarian available, Children welcome

POWYS

BRECON
Map 9 SO02

Peterstone Court

◉ Modern British, European

tel: 01874 665387 **Llanhamlach LD3 7YB**
email: info@peterstone-court.com **web:** www.peterstone-court.com
dir: *1m from Brecon on A40 to Abergavenny*

Excellent local food on the edge of the Brecon Beacons

With it Georgian proportions and position in the Brecon Beacons National Park (by the River Usk), Peterstone Court has a lot going for it. It's an ideal base for exploring the landscape, but, really and truly, it's the perfect escape for a bit of pampering. There's a suitably contemporary feel to the place on the inside and a classy finish that includes a swish bar and a spa offering treatments and all that jazz (and a seasonal heated outdoor pool). But, best of all, there's the Conservatory Restaurant, which serves up some nifty modern food based on regional ingredients. A starter of beetroot tarte Tatin shows the way, or go for some trendy surf 'n' turf in the shape of crisp pork belly with garlic king prawns. Among main courses, Glaisfer Farm provides lamb, pork and chicken (the former served as a trio of rack, breast and hotpot), or there might be roast wild rabbit with fondant potato and game jus. Finish with white chocolate cheesecake with raspberry coulis and coconut ice cream.

Times 12-2.30/6-9.30

BUILTH WELLS
Map 9 SO05

Caer Beris Manor Hotel

◉ Modern European

tel: 01982 552601 **LD2 3NP**
email: caerberis@btinternet.com **web.** www.caerberis.com
dir: *From town centre follow A483/Llandovery signs. Hotel on left on edge of town*

Fusion cooking comes to a Welsh feudal estate

Drenched in a violently colourful history, the Caer Beris estate traces its lineage back to the Welsh feudal kings of late antiquity. Towards the end of the 19th century, a captain in the Hussars remade it into a private sporting estate, but retained such features as the medieval panelling in the dining room. Sitting in 27 acres of parkland bordered by the River Irfon, it's clearly enjoying its present day incarnation as a destination country hotel, the contrasts of time emphasised in the modern seating and tableware that offset the panelling and stone fireplace in the 1896 dining room. Spencer Ralph brings with him a CV overflowing with experience gained in the crucibles of fusion cooking in the southern hemisphere, so expect the likes of pressed duck terrine with poached rhubarb, prune compôte and pickled ginger to start, followed by salmon on roast beets and fennel dressed in red wine jus and tarragon oil, or classic Welsh lamb navarin with sweet potato dauphinoise and turnip remoulade. A cockle-warming dessert then turns up in the shape of pear and honey tart with nutmeg ice cream and hot toddy syrup.

Times 12-2.30/6.30-9.30

CRICKHOWELL
Map 9 SO21

The Bear

◉ Modern British, International

tel: 01873 810408 **High St NP8 1BW**
email: bearhotel@aol.com **web:** www.bearhotel.co.uk
dir: *Town centre, off A40 (Brecon road). 6m from Abergavenny*

Vibrant modern cooking in a medieval pub

The old stagecoach doesn't run past here any more, but an enduring testament to the last time it did is present in the form of a Victorian timetable in the bar. The Bear goes back further than that, though, to the reign of Henry III in the 1430s, when it must have been as much a local beacon as it is now, at the heart of the Brecon Beacons National Park. Its traditional interiors and ancient arched cellar where the beers are kept are all part of the deal, as is vibrant modern food with the emphasis on regionally-sourced ingredients. Start with shredded duck à la Peking with plum sauce, sesame seeds and salad, before going on to squid-ink linguine with Cornish crab dressed in coriander and chilli, or confit lamb shoulder cooked for half a day, with pink fir-apples and garlic in rosemary jus. Simple but effective desserts include seasonal baked figs in Marsala, with matching ice cream.

Times 12-2/7-9.30, Closed 25 Dec, L Mon-Sat, D Sun

HAY-ON-WYE
Map 9 SO24

Old Black Lion Inn

◉ Modern British, Italian

tel: 01497 820841 **26 Lion St HR3 5AD**
email: info@oldblacklion.co.uk **web:** www.oldblacklion.co.uk
dir: *1m off A438. From TIC car park turn right along Oxford Rd, pass NatWest Bank, next left (Lion St), hotel 20yds on right*

Well-judged, appealing cooking in a historic inn

Dating from the 17th century, the whitewashed inn has bags of character, with beams in low ceilings and stone fireplaces. You can eat in the bar or in the more sedate next-door dining room. The inn has earned something of a local reputation for its fish specials, among them perhaps roast fillet of cod with an interesting sauce of ginger and onion, served with wilted greens and crushed potatoes. Quality shines out of ingredients — roast loin of lamb and mushroom-stuffed breast, for instance, with sherry-glazed vegetables and lamb jus — and dishes are notable for their sensible combinations. A starter of ham hock terrine with mustard and piccalilli sounds straightforward enough, but the kitchen puts thought and effort into all its output, so it may also present seared scallops with crispy speck, broccoli purée, roast almonds and paprika and pimento oil. End with white chocolate parfait partnered by raspberry coulis or delve into the past with jam-topped rice pudding.

Chef Maximillion Evilio **Owner** Dolan Leighton **Seats** 40, Pr/dining room 20
Times 12 2.30/6.30 9.30, Closed 24-26 Dec **Prices** Fixed L 2 course £12, Starter £4.95-£7.50, Main £12.50-£24.50, Dessert £5.75-£5.95, Service optional **Wines** 10 bottles over £30, 19 bottles under £30, 9 by glass **Parking** 10, On street nearby **Notes** Sunday L, Vegetarian available, Children welcome

HAY-ON-WYE *continued*

The Swan-at-Hay Hotel

🏵 British, French

tel: 01497 821188 **Church St HR3 5DQ**
email: stay@swanathay.co.uk **web:** www.swanathay.co.uk
dir: *In town centre, on Brecon Road opposite cinema bookshop*

Alluring menus in a family-run hotel

The Swan is a family-run hotel of grey stone with flower-bordered lawns to the rear, with relaxed and welcoming service in the bistro-style dining room even when it's busy. Local produce is at the core of the kitchen's business, and the concise menu is an appealing slate of contemporary ideas, among them toothsome Gloucestershire Old Spots and cider rillettes with red onion marmalade, and seasonal roast Craswall partridge (from just a few miles away) with Calvados jus, dauphinoise and honey-roast parsnips. Bresaola is cured in-house and teamed with parmesan and cracked black pepper, and might be followed by one of the fish offerings: perhaps fillet of Loch Duart salmon with rosemary-spiked potatoes, broccoli and orange-flavoured beurre blanc. End with a memorable pudding such as hot chocolate fondant, its centre oozing liquid, with a scoop of vanilla ice cream and raspberry coulis, or a platter of local cheeses.

Times 12-3/6.30-9

KNIGHTON   Map 9 SO27

Milebrook House Hotel

🏵 Modern, Traditional **V**

tel: 01547 528632 **Milebrook LD7 1LT**
email: hotel@milebrookhouse.co.uk **web:** www.milebrookhouse.co.uk
dir: *2m E of Knighton on A4113 (Ludlow)*

Quality British food on the Welsh-English border

When the legendary explorer and travel writer Sir Wilfred Thesiger returned from a stint on a camel in the sands of Arabia's Empty Quarter, he came back to recharge the batteries in Milebrook, an idyllic Georgian mansion in the Marches hills. It's a comfortingly traditional place, much-loved by shooting parties, with a handy kitchen garden to provide fresh seasonal fruit and veg, and a skilled hand in the kitchen to track down the best local suppliers and deliver country-house classics cooked with flair and imagination. Seared breast of local pigeon with crispy chorizo, caramelised apple and watercress is the sort of thing to expect, followed by pan-fried pork fillet wrapped in prosciutto with potato purée, sautéed courgettes and honey and wholegrain mustard sauce. Desserts such as lemon posset with whimberry jelly hit the spot, or there are artisan cheeses from both sides of the border.

Chef Katie Marsden **Owner** Mr & Mrs R T Marsden **Seats** 40, Pr/dining room 16
Times 12-2/6.30-9, Closed L Mon **Prices** Fixed L 2 course £15-£18, Fixed D 3 course £29-£33, Starter £5.25-£7.75, Main £16.50-£21.75, Dessert £6.50-£7, Service optional **Wines** 6 bottles over £30, 36 bottles under £30, 8 by glass **Parking** 24
Notes Sunday L, Children 8 yrs+

LLANDRINDOD WELLS   Map 9 SO06

The Metropole

🏵 Modern British **V**

tel: 01597 823700 **Temple St LD1 5DY**
email: info@metropole.co.uk **web:** www.metropole.co.uk
dir: *In centre of town off A483, car park at rear*

Stylish spa hotel with sound modern cooking using regional fare

Run by the same family since Queen Victoria's reign, The Metropole has long been a local landmark with its soaring turrets, opening in the town's heyday as a spa resort. Today's hotel offers 21st-century spa treatments. It also has a couple of dining options, with an informal brasserie, and the Radnor and Miles Restaurant, which takes a slightly more formal approach, with white linen-clad tables and high-backed leather chairs. There's a regional flavour to the menu, with plenty of game in season, and lamb, beef and chicken cooked on the grill. Smoked haddock, shallot and watercress soup with summer truffle oil is a simple enough starter, delivering good flavours, but you might also begin with a pressing of Gressingham duck and foie gras with apples and sloe gin. Next up, grilled sea bass – soft flesh, crispy skin – or Welsh ham hock pot-au-feu with cassoulet, and, for dessert, a riff on rhubarb.

Chef Nick Edwards **Owner** Justin Baird-Murray **Seats** 46, Pr/dining room 250
Times 12-2.15/6-9.30 **Prices** Starter £5.50-£6.25, Main £10.75-£22, Dessert £4.50-£6.95 **Wines** 4 bottles over £30, 29 bottles under £30, 9 by glass **Parking** 150
Notes Sunday L £13.45-£16.95, Children welcome

LLANFYLLIN   Map 15 SJ11

Seeds

🏵 Modern British

tel: 01691 648604 **5-6 Penybryn Cottages, High St SY22 5AP**
dir: *In village centre. Take A490 N from Welshpool, follow signs to Llanfyllin*

Accurate cooking in an intimate, relaxed setting

When you don't require your food to push any culinary boundaries or arrive with froths and gels, try Seeds, a superbly relaxing little bistro with an intimate ambience (there are just 20 seats) in a 500-year-old terrace, run by an amiable husband-and-wife team and their welcoming and unstuffy staff. Mellow jazz floats around the artworks and curios decorating the low-beamed, slate-floored dining room as chef-patron Mark Seager works the stoves of a bijou kitchen, turning out simple, tasty classic bistro dishes. Starters can be as simple as warm black pudding salad with blackcurrant sauce or home-made chicken liver pâté with chutney and toast, while mains take in the likes of rack of Welsh fillet steak with brandy and cream sauce, or grilled sea bass fillet served on roasted cherry tomatoes with balsamic. Desserts follow a similar vein of classic comfort – perhaps bread-and-butter pudding with cream, or classic crème brûlée.

Chef Mark Seager **Owner** Felicity & Mark Seager **Seats** 20
Times 11-2/7-9, Closed 24-25 Dec, 1 wk Oct, Sun-Tue (Sun-Wed winter, may vary) **Prices** Fixed D 3 course £27.95-£31.70, Starter £4.95-£6.95, Main £8.95-£18.95, Dessert £5.45-£6.95, Service optional **Wines** 16 bottles over £30, 70 bottles under £30, 3 by glass **Parking** Free town car park, on street **Notes** Pre-music festival menu Jun-Jul, Vegetarian available, Children welcome

LLANWDDYN
Map 15 SJ01

Lake Vyrnwy Hotel & Spa
Modern British

tel: 01691 870692 **Lake Vyrnwy SY10 0LY**
email: info@lakevyrnwyhotel.co.uk web: www.lakevyrnwy.com
dir: *On A4393, 200yds past dam turn sharp right into drive*

Interesting menus, breathtaking views

Birdwatching, fishing and hill walking are all possibilities at this stylish Victorian hotel with lovely views over the lake, and where better to end a day than with dinner in the conservatory restaurant. Local produce is the backbone of the kitchen's output, some from the estate itself. A well-composed starter brings scallops with apple, a celery and walnut salad and crisp celery ribbons, or you might begin with a full-bore partnership of pan-fried quail breast with apple and brandy purée, candied walnuts and balsamic, followed by roast duck breast with cider-braised potato, baby gem lettuce, sweet caramelised onions and a red cabbage purée full of mulled fruit spiciness. Fish, too, is handled deftly, perhaps roast halibut with samphire, pink grapefruit and basil sauce, buttered spinach and a prawn raviolo. Pudding brings things to a happy conclusion with lemon curd tart with sweet basil mousse.

Chef David Thompson **Owner** The Bisiker family **Seats** 85, Pr/dining room 220 **Times** 12-2/6.45-9.15 **Prices** Fixed D 2 course £27.50, Service optional **Wines** 29 bottles over £30, 55 bottles under £30, 10 by glass **Parking** 80 **Notes** Fixed 5 course D £39.95, Sunday L £22.50, Vegetarian available, Children welcome

LLANWRTYD WELLS
Map 9 SN84

Carlton Riverside
Modern British

tel: 01591 610248 **Irfon Crescent LD5 4SP**
email: carltonriverside@hotmail.co.uk web: www.carltonriverside.com
dir: *In town centre beside bridge*

Confident cooking and river views

Picture windows give views over the River Irfon from the dining room of this restaurant with rooms, making visits during daylight hours rather special, while, as night falls, the lights are dimmed and the mood becomes a little more intimate. It's not a large room, seating only 20 or so, with a contemporary, country-style finish.

Service is relaxed and personable. The kitchen is the domain of the long-running chef-patron, and she ensures the best stuff comes her way, much of it from around this neck of the woods. There's a light touch to a first-course cod loin, topped with a parmesan and lemon crust, and served with a butter sauce, or go for the earthiness of wild mushrooms on grilled brioche. Next up, fillet of sea bass is partnered with squid ink noodles, courgette ribbons and a cracking lobster sauce, and rump of Welsh lamb is roasted and arrives with creamed leeks and Madeira jus. The technical proficiency of the kitchen is confirmed by a banana soufflé into which white chocolate sauce is poured.

Chef Mary Ann Gilchrist **Owner** Dr & Mrs Gilchrist **Seats** 20 **Times** 7-9, Closed Xmas, Sun, L all week **Prices** Tasting menu £37.50, Starter £6-£8, Main £15.95-£25, Dessert £6-£9, Service optional **Wines** 13 bottles over £30, 35 bottles under £30, 4 by glass **Parking** Car park opposite **Notes** Vegetarian available, Children welcome

Lasswade Country House
Modern British

tel: 01591 610515 **Station Rd LD5 4RW**
email: info@lasswadehotel.co.uk web: www.lasswadehotel.co.uk
dir: *Exit A483 into Irfon Terrace, right into Station Rd, 350yds on right*

Organic focus in an Edwardian country house

Run with great charm by owners Roger and Emma Stevens, this grand Edwardian house sits at the edge of the Victorian spa town with 360-degree views of the Cambrian Mountains and Brecon Beacons. It's a soothing spot, and when you add the chef-proprietor's skilled modern British cooking into the deal, the whole package is an inviting prospect. After pre-dinner drinks in the homely lounge, it all takes place in a traditional-style dining room kitted out with burnished mahogany furniture. Driven by a passion for sourcing organic and sustainable produce from Wales and the Marches area, Roger keeps combinations straightforward, timings accurate, and interweaves flavours intelligently. Expect daily-changing dinner menus to get going with home-smoked trout fillets matched with potato and radish salad, and lemon and thyme oil, followed, perhaps, by a plate of that splendid Cambrian mountain lamb, comprising roast rump, braised breast and sautéed kidneys in grain mustard and tomato sauce with leek soufflé and Madeira wine reduction.

Times 7.30-9.30, Closed 25-26 Dec, L all week

LLYSWEN
Map 9 SO13

Llangoed Hall
— see page 700

Find out more about how we assess for Rosette awards on page 9

RHONDDA CYNON TAFF

MISKIN
Map 9 ST08

Miskin Manor Country Hotel

◉◉ Modern, Traditional British **v**

tel: 01443 224204 **Pendoylan Rd CF72 8ND**
email: info@miskin-manor.co.uk **web:** www.miskin-manor.co.uk
dir: M4 junct 34, exit onto A4119, signed Llantrisant, hotel 300yds on left

Inventive modern British cooking in tranquil setting

The manor, in 25 acres of colourful grounds, dates from the 1860s, with 21st-century facilities including meeting rooms, a swimming pool, spa and gym, with a bistro serving drinks and light lunches. The main event takes place in the Meisgyn Restaurant, an elegant room with leaded windows hung with curtains, oak panelling and wrought-iron dining chairs at tables set with quality napery. The kitchen team man the stoves, sourcing farm-fresh Welsh produce and making everything in-house, from bread to petits fours. The style is very much of our day, with scallops glazed in miso, seared and accompanied by sesame purée, baby turnips and verjus cream, competing with a plainer starter of beef tartare with mayonnaise and pickles. Fillet of sea bass is imaginatively served with coconut broth, coconut and coriander gnocchi and razor clams, and roast pheasant might appear in season, with juniper jus, poached figs and parsnip with cavolo nero. End with something like dark chocolate and hazelnut tart with a raspberry marshmallow, crème fraîche ice cream and chocolate sauce.

Chef David Owen **Owner** Mr & Mrs Rosenberg **Seats** 50, Pr/dining room 30 **Times** 12-2.30/6-10, Closed D 25-26 Dec **Prices** Fixed L 2 course £17.95, Fixed D 3 course £23.95, Starter £5.95-£8.50, Main £21.95-£25.95, Dessert £6.95, Service optional **Wines** 16 bottles over £30, 27 bottles under £30, 12 by glass **Parking** 200 **Notes** Sunday L £16.50-£20.50, Children welcome

PONTYCLUN
Map 9 ST08

La Luna

◉ Modern International

tel: 01443 239600 **79-81 Talbot Rd, Talbot Green CF72 8AE**
email: info@la-lunarestaurant.com
dir: M4 junct 34, follow signs for Llantrisant, turn left at 2nd lights

Relaxed bistro dining near the shops

The family-run La Luna is an unpretentious venue that covers a lot of bases, whether you're after a bite to eat while out shopping (it's opposite a retail park), or fancy a cocktail and tapas in the first-floor lounge bar. The place has an easy-going atmosphere and a contemporary finish, which fits the kitchen's sunny Med-style, brasserie-inspired output. A starter of chargrilled king prawns with samphire and slow-roasted tomatoes and peppers shows the style, with the simplicity of seafood cocktail, pasta options, and Welsh steaks cooked on the grill adding to its broad appeal. Medallions of Welsh sirloin might find their way into a stroganoff, with confit potatoes, parsnips and onions. Desserts run to the likes of raspberry crème brûlée or bread-and-butter pudding with rum and toffee sauce. There's an early evening menu, too, and some fair-weather outside tables.

Times 12-3/6-10, Closed 24 Dec, 1 Jan & BHs, Mon, D Sun

Llangoed Hall ❀❀❀

LLYSWEN
Map 9 SO13

Modern British **v**
tel: 01874 754525 **LD3 0YP**
email: enquiries@llangoedhall.co.uk **web:** www.llangoedhall.co.uk
dir: On A470, 2m from Llyswen towards Builth Wells

Refined contemporary dining in a grand country house

Llangoed Hall has 17 acres of the Wye Valley all to itself including pristine lawns, manicured gardens, a kitchen garden and maze, while glorious views over rolling countryside and the Black Mountains add to the sense of tranquillity. There's been a property on this spot since 1632 with today's grand stone mansion completed just after World War I. The interior has a luxurious traditional finish with original features and fine furniture creating a sophisticated old-school atmosphere; one impressive feature is a gallery designed by Clough Williams-Ellis (of Portmeirion fame). The restaurant is suitably genteel and refined, the tables draped in pristine floor-length linen and the walls hung with artworks that are the real deal. Nick Brodie and his team in the kitchen make good use of the hotel's organic kitchen garden – ensuring the seasonal and local boxes are ticked – and what doesn't come from their own land is sourced with due diligence. Choose from the à la carte or tasting menu (including a cracking veggie version) and expect polished modern British cuisine. A first course dish of steamed cock crab shows a creative touch with its use of buttermilk, mango and salted peanuts, while celeriac is poached with truffles and partnered with beetroot, rye and hazelnuts. The presentation of each plate is a visual treat. Tiddenham duck breast stars in a main course with its liver and heart (plus bitter leaves, pommes purée and rhubarb), or go for halibut with sea vegetables, chanterelles à la grecque and Ibérico gnocchi. There's no lack of invention among desserts either; a fig dish, say, with parfait, carpaccio and caramelised fruit, with the flavours of Amaretto and almonds running through. The concern for environmental matters that runs through this business extends to the impressive wine list.

Chef Nick Brodie **Owner** Llangoed Ltd, Calum C Milne **Seats** 30, Pr/dining room 16 **Times** 12.30-2.30/6.30-10.30, **Prices** Tasting menu £65-£115, Starter £18-£22.50, Main £28-£39.50, Dessert £10-£17, Service optional 10% **Wines** 100 bottles over £30, 25 bottles under £30, 6 by glass **Parking** 130 **Notes** Tasting menu 7(veg)/10 course, Sunday L £15-£45, Children welcome

Llechwen Hall Hotel

◉ Modern Welsh

tel: 01443 742050 **Llanfabon CF37 4HP**
email: reservations@llechwenhall.co.uk **web:** www.llechwen.co.uk
dir: A470 N towards Merthyr Tydfil. 3rd exit at large rdbt then 3rd exit at mini rdbt, hotel signed 0.5m on left

Scenic, historical setting for unfussy cooking

On the top of a hill, reached via a winding drive, this white-rendered hotel is surrounded by its own attractive grounds. A comfortable lounge area overlooks the garden. The low-ceilinged, heavily beamed restaurant, is recently extended and has plenty of atmosphere with its whitewashed walls hung with oils and candles flickering on bare wooden tables. Smartly-dressed staff provide relaxed and with-it service. The kitchen is ahead of the game when it partners pan-fried and sautéed scallops with confit chorizo cassoulet and aïoli and turns out a main course of roast rump of local lamb with honey-roast salsify, herby and garlicky mash and delightful, sticky onion jus. Another well-considered main course might be pan-fried sea bass fillet with seafood bisque and crushed potatoes. Conclude with bara brith-and-butter pudding with Penderyn whisky-infused custard, or baked Welsh cake cheesecake with strawberry preserve.

Chef Paul Trask **Owner** Ramish Gor **Seats** 60, Pr/dining room 300 **Times** 12-2/7-9 **Prices** Prices not confirmed, Service optional **Wines** 2 bottles over £30, 30 bottles under £30, 4 by glass **Parking** 100 **Notes** Sunday L, Vegetarian available, Children welcome

SWANSEA

Patricks with Rooms

◉ Modern British **NEW**

tel: 01792 360199 **638 Mumbles Rd SA3 4EA**
email: reception@patrickswithrooms.com **web:** www.patrickswithrooms.com
dir: Exit M4 junct 42, 5m from Swansea City. From Swansea, with sea on left, over mini rdbt at White Rose pub. Restaurant 0.5 m on right

Satisfying seasonal cooking on the bay side

Large windows make the most of the sea views at this easy-going contemporary restaurant with rooms overlooking Swansea Bay. Inside, the dining room has a relaxed, informal ambience that suits its minimalist contemporary looks – stark white walls broken up by bright artworks and smart tablecloths laid with good quality cutlery. The kitchen team takes provenance seriously, heading out on foraging trips for laverbread and berries and hauling in the best local materials for a menu that sets out with pressed duck terrine, its richness balanced by a vibrant compôte of spiced plums, orange and cranberry. Forthright seasonal flavours define a main course of roast rack of lamb partnered with root vegetable rösti, parsnip purée, bacon, and red wine and rosemary jus. For dessert, pannacotta is flavoured with star anise and paired with mince pie ice cream. The home-made breads are excellent too.

Chef Patrick Walsh, Dean Fuller **Owner** Catherine & Patrick Walsh, Sally & Dean Fuller **Seats** 75 **Times** 12-2.20/6.30-9.50, Closed 25-26 Dec, 1 Jan **Prices** Fixed L 3 course £23, Starter £4.80-£7.80, Main £16.80-£21, Dessert £6.90-£8.80, Service optional **Wines** 5 bottles over £30, 21 bottles under £30, 15 by glass **Parking** On street, car park opposite **Notes** Afternoon tea £17, Sun brunch, Vegetarian available, Children welcome

Fairyhill

◉◉ Modern British V ♦ NOTABLE WINE LIST

tel: 01792 390139 **SA3 1BS**
email: postbox@fairyhill.net **web:** www.fairyhill.net
dir: M4 junct 47, take A483 then A484 to Llanelli, Gower, Gowerton. At Gowerton follow B4295 for approx 10m

Elegant country-house hotel in lovely setting with real local flavour

This period country house in its hugely tranquil location hits the sweet spot between old-school formality and contemporary good taste. You're in safe hands, and you know it. There are 24 acres of grounds to explore, with streams, waterfalls and woods, and plenty of luxurious spaces within. The restaurant makes excellent use of the produce from the region and delivers a refined experience that doesn't feel in the least bit stuffy. The smart modern British cooking might see you start with Perl Las beignets with walnuts and poached pear, or head off further south for pan-seared stuffed baby squid with tomato fondue, chorizo and capers. Main-course Welsh pork belly comes in a fashionable partnership with Caldey Island lobster, while dessert brings forth iced lemon parfait with blackcurrant and mint. If you're staying the night in one of the stylish bedrooms you'll have good cause to dive into the phenomenally good wine list with gusto.

Chef Paul Davies, David Whitecross **Owner** Mr Hetherington, Mr Davies **Seats** 60, Pr/dining room 40 **Times** 12-2/7-9, Closed 26 Dec, 1-25 Jan, Mon-Tue (Nov-Mar) **Prices** Fixed L 2 course £20, Fixed D 3 course £45, Starter £10, Main £25, Dessert £10, Service optional **Wines** 120 bottles over £30, 50 bottles under £30, 10 by glass **Parking** 45 **Notes** Afternoon tea £20-£27.50, Sunday L £27.50, Children 8 yrs+

The Dragon Hotel

◉ Modern European

tel: 01792 657100 & 657159 **The Kingsway Circle SA1 5LS**
email: enquiries@dragon-hotel.co.uk **web:** www.dragon-hotel.co.uk
dir: M4 junct 42, A483 follow signs for city centre A4067. After lights at Sainsbury's right onto The Strand then left into Kings Ln. Hotel straight ahead

A touch of modern style in the heart of Swansea

The Dragon is breathing fire after a megabucks renovation has brought everything up to full contemporary spec, making the most of its location in the thick of Swansea's town-centre action. Built on a bedrock of local produce, the straightforward modern European cooking is in tune with the setting. Keenly-priced two- or three-course dinner menus, bolstered by a carte, are served in the contemporary Piano Restaurant and typically get going with wild mushroom risotto with spinach and goats' cheese, then move on to rump steak with blue cheese butter, slow-roasted tomatoes and chips. Dessert might be iced gingerbread parfait with dark chocolate sauce. If you're here for lunch, similar fare is served in the buzzy Dragon Brasserie, a breezy modern venue with exposed industrial ducting and spotlights above bare darkwood tables and ringside seats looking through full-length windows onto the busy street.

Chef Hayley James, Mark Turner **Owner** Dragon Hotel Ltd **Seats** 65, Pr/dining room 80 **Times** 12-2.30/6-9.30 **Prices** Fixed L 2 course fr £12.50, Fixed D 3 course fr £24.95, Starter £5.75-£7.50, Main £10.25-£17.95, Dessert £5.75-£7.50, Service optional **Wines** 6 bottles over £30, 33 bottles under £30, 13 by glass **Parking** 50, NCP **Notes** Tasting menu, Pre-theatre menu by reservation only, Sunday L £12.50-£16.95, Vegetarian available, Children welcome

SWANSEA *continued*

Hanson at the Chelsea Restaurant

◉◉ Modern Welsh, French

tel: 01792 464068 **17 St Mary St SA1 3LH**
email: andrew_hanson@live.co.uk
dir: *In small lane between St Mary Church & Wine St*

Appealing bistro cooking in a popular city-centre venue

Andrew Hanson's unassuming-looking restaurant is tucked away down a narrow side street in the city centre, making it among other things a rather popular lunchtime venue. It looks like a classic modern bistro inside with clothed tables pressed in cheek by jowl, blackboard menus and small framed pictures against a delicate yellow colour-scheme. The service tone is as relaxed and friendly as can be, and the cooking an appealing mix of local produce and French influences, with the emphasis on fish and seafood, but not forgetting fine Welsh lamb. Potted chicken rillettes matched with pistachio and thyme butter, fig chutney and toasted sourdough makes for a hearty opener, followed by a time-honoured main-course combination of calves' liver, button mushrooms, shallots, Alsace bacon and Madeira sauce, and potato purée. Fish cookery is handled sensitively too, perhaps serving roast monkfish with home-made pappardelle, mussels and clams, parsley and parmesan, or pan-fried Dover sole with piquant lemon and parsley butter. Finish with vanilla pannacotta with raspberry coulis, or brioche bread-and-butter pudding with honey and whisky.

Chef Andrew Hanson, Gareth Sillman, Nathan Kirby **Owner** Andrew & Michelle Hanson **Seats** 50, Pr/dining room 20 **Times** 12-2/7-10, Closed 25-26 Dec, BHs, Sun **Prices** Fixed L 2 course £13.95, Fixed D 3 course £20, Starter £3.95-£8.95, Main £11.95-£23.50, Dessert £5.95 **Wines** 8 by glass **Notes** Vegetarian available, Children welcome

---

TORFAEN

CWMBRAN
Map 9 ST29

The Parkway Hotel & Spa

◉ Modern European NEW

tel: 01633 871199 & 486312 **Cwmbran Dr NP44 3UW**
email: enquiries@parkwayhotel.co.uk **web:** www.parkwayhotelandspa.com
dir: *M4 junct 25a & 26, A4051 follow Cwmbran-Llantarnam Park signs. Right at rdbt, right for hotel*

Modern hotel with unfussy menu and carvery

The single-storey Parkway is a 20th-century property with a whopping 70 bedrooms, spa facilities aplenty and enough space to cater for conferences and weddings. When it comes to dining, there's quite a lot going on, from afternoon tea, bar meals served in the lounge and Ravellos Restaurant with its à la carte menu and carvery options. The warmly decorated dining room is the setting for simple dishes along the lines of smooth duck liver pâté with date and grape compôte, or Perl Las cheese with pickled pear and candied walnuts. Move on to roast salmon with a bouillabaisse garnish, or a roast carved to order and served with roast potatoes and a choice of vegetables. Finish with chocolate cheesecake with cookie crumb or vanilla pannacotta partnered with an orange jelly and dark chocolate.

Chef Clive Williams **Owner** Lana de Savary **Seats** 85, Pr/dining room **Times** 6.30-10, Closed L Mon-Sat **Prices** Fixed D 3 course £21.95, Starter £4.50-£8, Main £12-£22.50, Dessert £4.50-£7, Service optional **Parking** 250 **Notes** Sunday L £19.95, Vegetarian available, Children welcome

---

VALE OF GLAMORGAN

HENSOL
Map 9 ST07

Llanerch Vineyard

◉ Modern British NEW

tel: 01443 222716 **CF72 8GG**
email: info@llanerch-vineyard.co.uk **web:** www.llanerch-vineyard.co.uk
dir: *M4 junct 34, follow brown tourist signs to Llanerch Vineyard*

Local produce and home-grown wine

Around 22 acres of south-facing slopes of the Ely Valley have been planted with vines since 1986, and you can raise a glass to the committed and industrious owners while dining in their restaurant or bistro. There's a lot going on: wander around the vineyard, stay over in a boutique bedroom, or partake of a cookery class. The easy-going bistro offers simple stuff all day such as Welsh rarebit, sandwiches or a gourmet burger, while the ante is upped in the evening restaurant. It's an unpretentious spot with cheerful service and views over the vines. The menu focuses on regional produce and shows some creativity when it comes to flavour combinations. There's celeriac soup, say, with poached pears and watercress, or pan-seared pollack with fennel velouté. Welsh meats figure large – Duffryn Bach lamb rump with an accompanying Wellington, or haunch of Bwlch venison with orange-scented red cabbage – and desserts run to a zesty glazed pineapple number. To wash all this down is – what else? – Welsh wine.

Chef Michael Hudson **Owner** Ryan Davies **Seats** 40 **Times** 12-4/6.30-9, Closed 24 Dec-13 Jan, L Mon-Sat, D Sun **Prices** Starter £5-£9, Main £17-£28, Dessert £5-£9, Service optional **Wines** 30 bottles over £30, 20 bottles under £30, 10 by glass **Parking** 400 **Notes** Afternoon tea, Sunday L £17.50-£22.50, Vegetarian available, Children welcome

Vale Resort

◉ Modern British

tel: 01443 667800 **Hensol Park CF72 8JY**
email: sales@vale-hotel.com **web:** www.vale-hotel.com
dir: *M4 junct 34, exit signed Pendoylan, turn 1st right twice, then 1st left before white house on bend. Hotel on right*

Huge valley resort with plenty of options

The Resort luxuriates in no less than 650 acres of the Vale of Glamorgan, but is only 15 minutes' drive from Cardiff. Rugby fans might spot members of the Welsh national team cooling their heels after a match, but the place is vast enough for everybody to get pleasantly lost in. A bright airy room, the Vale Grill, with white walls and well-spaced tables is one dining option, or there's a linen-clad restaurant, La Cucina, as well as a champagne bar. Up-to-date British cooking is the principal draw in the Grill, moving from a pairing of marbled ham hock and black pudding roulade in plenty of mustard from twin dressings of remoulade and vinaigrette, to roast pheasant breast with braised red cabbage and a savoury bread pudding in redcurrant jus. A smooth-textured cheesecake to finish gains depth from mulled wine syrup and forthright cinnamon ice cream.

Chef Daniel James **Owner** The Leekes family **Seats** 80, Pr/dining room 50 **Times** 6.30-11, Closed L all week **Prices** Prices not confirmed **Parking** 500 **Notes** Sunday L, Vegetarian available, Children welcome

PENARTH
Map 9 ST17

Restaurant James Sommerin

◉◉◉ *– see opposite*

LLANARMON DYFFRYN CEIRIOG
Map 15 SJ13

The Hand at Llanarmon

◉ Modern European

tel: 01691 600666 **Ceiriog Valley LL20 7LD**
email: reception@thehandhotel.co.uk **web:** www.thehandhotel.co.uk
dir: *Leave A5 at Chirk onto B4500 signed Ceiriog Valley, continue for 11m*

Modern European cooking in a whitewashed Ceiriog inn

A whitewashed country inn buried in the sumptuous Ceiriog Valley, The Hand makes a concerted effort to come up to rustic expectations inside, with dozing dogs toasting themselves before the open fires, plenty of chunky furniture and brass ornaments, and a photographic gallery of the area in days gone by. A stuffed fox stands sentinel in the hallway. The kitchen turns out some impressive renditions of modern European food, beginning with braised beef and tomato risotto, or confit duck with Perl Lâs cheese, walnuts and almonds, and continuing with sensitively cooked, crisp-skinned mullet fillet with creamed leeks, peas, gem lettuce and a heap of mash. Welsh lamb is naturally a strong point, especially when it comes with McArdle's black pudding from Chirk, and a fruity redcurrant and red wine sauce. Finish in heartwarming fashion with oat-topped Bramley apple and gooseberry crumble, served with decent custard, or Welsh cheeses and oatcakes.

Chef Grant Mulholland **Owner** Jonathan & Jackie Greatorex **Seats** 40 **Times** 12-2.20/6.30-8.45 **Prices** Fixed L 2 course £14.50, Starter £4.50-£6.50, Main £9-£22.50, Dessert £5.75-£7.25, Service optional **Wines** 5 bottles over £30, 30 bottles under £30, 7 by glass **Parking** 15 **Notes** Sunday L £15-£21.50, Vegetarian available, Children welcome

ROSSETT
Map 15 SJ35

BEST WESTERN Llyndir Hall Hotel

◉ Traditional British NEW

tel: 01244 571648 **Llyndir Ln LL12 0AY**
email: llyndirhallhotel@feathers.uk.com **web:** www.feathers.uk.com
dir: *Phone for directions*

Country-house hotel with gently modern menus

A country-house hotel with function spaces for weddings, meetings and events, Llyndir Hall is a handsome house that boasts swanky spa facilities. There are five acres of landscaped gardens, too, and do check out the sculptures as you take a stroll. The hotel is home to a bright and contemporary restaurant looking out over the grounds. Expect classic dishes and a modern twist or two along the way. Slow-braised pork cheek is soft and tender in a first course with carrot and caraway purée and chargrilled asparagus, with main courses running to pan-seared sea bass with sautéed scallops and salsa verde, plus steaks cooked on the grill and served with classic sauces. For dessert, strawberry millefeuille has plenty of full-on fruity flavour.

Chef Tom Burge **Owner** Topland **Seats** Pr/dining room **Times** 6.30-9.30 **Prices** Starter £5.25-£6.75, Main £14.95-£24.50, Dessert £5.50, Service optional **Wines** 5 bottles over £30, 24 bottles under £30 **Notes** Vegetarian available

Restaurant James Sommerin ◉◉◉

PENARTH
Map 9 ST17

Modern British NEW v
tel: 029 2070 6559 **The Esplanade CF64 3AU**
email: info@jamessommerinrestaurant.co.uk
web: www.jamessommerinrestaurant.co.uk
dir: *Phone for directions*

Dazzling displays of contemporary cuisine

James Sommerin's name is familiar to anyone who's up to speed with the Welsh foodie scene as the erstwhile head chef of The Whitebrook. And now here he is on Penarth's seafront as chef-patron of a snazzy restaurant with rooms with his name above the door and cracking views of the Severn Estuary. Indoors, it's a picture of understated contemporary style with white linen tablecloths, curvy grey velours seats, creamy banquettes, local artists' work on the walls and the de rigueur window on to the cheffy action in the kitchen. Sommerin uses pin-sharp technique to sculpt flavours and textures in some refined and precisely-engineered cooking that takes the finest, locally-sourced materials as its starting point. To experience the results, choose between a carte and five- or seven-course tasting menus; if you want to go the whole hog, there's a 14-course tasting extravaganza at the chef's table inside the kitchen. Things get going with intricate amuses, among them a golden croquette of pig's head

with pickled celeriac and apple matchsticks, and a little jar of sweetcorn purée with slithers of haddock and salty bacon shavings. Following this, a breathtaking display of creative ideas, from an opener of cauliflower slivers bound together with a creamy truffle-infused cauliflower velouté partnered by wild mushrooms and fresh thyme, to suprême and confit thigh of guinea fowl with sweetcorn purée, pearl barley, sprout leaves, smoked bacon foam and truffle jus. Things conclude with a brace of desserts, one subjecting chocolate and cherries to a thorough workout, counterpointed by vanilla yogurt mousse, the other a grown-up take on a fig roll served with raisin purée, nougatine shards and Grand Marnier ice cream.

Chef James Sommerin **Owner** James & Louise Sommerin **Seats** 65, Pr/dining room 12 **Times** 12-2.30/7-9.30, Closed 1 wk Jan, Mon **Prices** Fixed L 2 course £27, Tasting menu £55-£85, Service optional **Wines** 100+ bottles over £30, 15 bottles under £30, 14 by glass **Parking** On street **Notes** Tasting menu 5/7/10 course, Chefs table £150, Afternoon tea, Children welcome

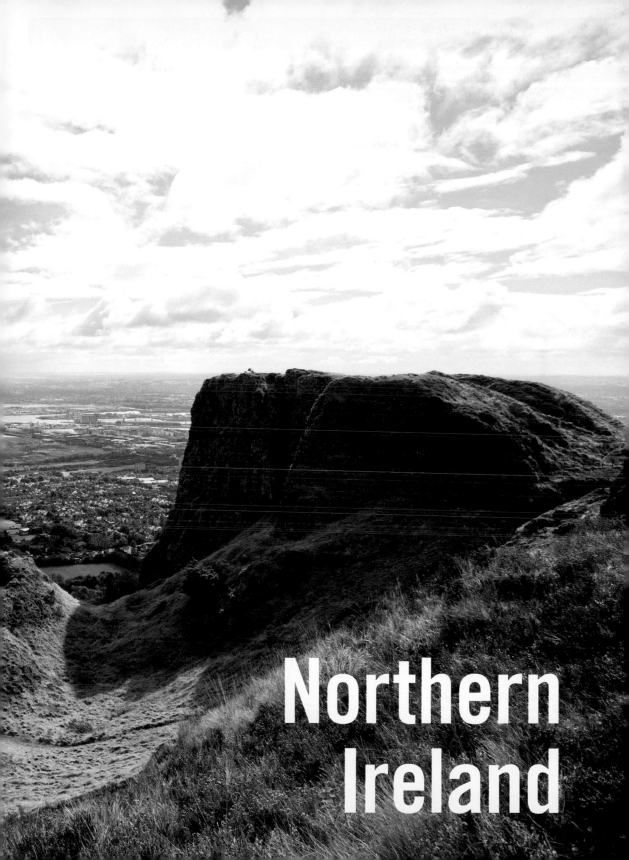

Northern Ireland

NORTHERN IRELAND
COUNTY ANTRIM

BALLYMENA — Map 1 D5

Galgorm Resort & Spa

◉◉◉ – *see opposite and advert on page 708*

BUSHMILLS — Map 1 C6

Bushmills Inn Hotel

◉ Modern Irish with a twist **v**

---

tel: 028 2073 3000 **9 Dunluce Rd BT57 8QG**
email: mail@bushmillsinn.com **web:** www.bushmillsinn.com
dir: *2m from Giant's Causeway on A2 in Bushmills after crossing river*

Locally-based cooking near the Giant's Causeway

Although there are peat fires and nooks and crannies, the word 'inn' is a bit of an understatement, as this is an upmarket boutique hotel (with a helipad!). In the restaurant, wooden partitions create booths around tables, and there's an extension with a distinctive beamed ceiling. High-class culinary standards are evident in what appears on the plate, and the menu is brimful of attention-grabbing ideas, among them pheasant boudin with poached pears and cherry jus, then pink-roast haunch of venison with roasted root vegetables, parsnip purée and roasting juices. Lovers of seafood could opt for crab salad with a poached quail's egg, chicory, julienne and lemon mayonnaise, followed by pan-fried hake fillet with cockle and mussel beurre blanc. End with a delightful coffee and orange theme with coffee cake and meringue with candied orange, jelly and blood orange and burned orange ice cream.

Chef Gordon McGladdery, Donna Thompson **Owner** Alan Dunlop **Seats** 120
Times 12-5/6-9.30 **Prices** Starter £5.45-£8.85, Main £14-£24, Dessert £5-£7.95,
Service optional **Wines** 47 bottles over £30, 39 bottles under £30, 8 by glass
Parking 70 **Notes** Sunday L fr £13.85, Children welcome

BELFAST

BELFAST — Map 1 D5

Beatrice Kennedy

◉ Modern, Traditional Irish, International **v**

---

tel: 028 9020 2290 **44 University Rd BT7 1NJ**
email: reservations@beatricekennedy.co.uk
dir: *Adjacent to Queens University*

Modern bistro food in the university district

The name is nothing to do with the famous family across the pond, but simply the last resident of this Victorian-era townhouse before it was converted to a restaurant. There's a real buzz to the place and a relaxed bistro-style attitude all round, from the cordiality of the welcome to the warmth of the decor. Located in the university district, there's a pre-theatre menu for anyone on a budget or in a rush for curtain up, and a bespoke veggie menu if required. The menu casts a wide net with dishes that show a Pan-European approach and a few Asian influences. Start, say, with wonderfully tender crispy beef with curried lentils and spiced tomato relish, or smoked cod with a soft egg and black pudding beignet. Next up, there's more curry flavour in a roast monkfish dish (served with a shellfish wonton). Round it all off with pecan pie with Chantilly cream.

Chef Jim McCarthy **Owner** Jim McCarthy **Seats** 75, Pr/dining room 25
Times 12.30-3/5-10.30, Closed 24-26 Dec, 1 Jan, Etr, Mon, L Tue-Sat **Prices** Fixed L
3 course £18.50, Fixed D 3 course £25-£30, Tasting menu £35, Starter £5-£9, Main
£15-£20, Dessert £6, Service optional **Wines** 6 bottles over £30, 25 bottles under
£30, 4 by glass **Parking** On street **Notes** Pre-theatre menu 5-7pm £14.95, 6 course
£40, Sunday L £18.50, Children welcome

Café Vaudeville

◉ French

---

tel: 028 9043 9160 **25-39 Arthur St BT1 4GQ**
email: info@cafevaudeville.com
dir: *Phone for directions*

Big-flavoured brasserie dishes in a historic city-centre building

The city-centre building has the moneyed look of the former bank it once was, but Café Vaudeville is now a glamorous bar and restaurant. There's a touch of Art Nouveau bling to the interior, with the appropriately named Luxebar and a 'coffee dock' serving boulangerie-style snacks. The restaurant to the rear has a domed ceiling and coloured lights that change to set the mood. The menu deals in modern Irish small plates and sharing options alongside traditionally sized main courses, with punchy flavours on offer. Baby back ribs are marinated with chilli and tamarind, slow-cooked and finished on the chargrill, followed by a rib-sticking main course of pork belly slow-cooked for 18 hours with Guinness, served with potato mash, chorizo baked beans and apple purée. Finish with perfectly executed chocolate fondant cake with a liquid centre, served with honeycomb ice cream.

Times 12-3/5-9, Closed Sun

Deanes at Queens

◉◉ Modern British, Irish

---

tel: 028 9038 2111 **1 College Gardens BT9 6BQ**
email: deanesatqueens@michaeldeane.co.uk
dir: *From city centre go towards Queens University then 1st left onto College Gardens, restaurant 1st on right*

Vibrant brasserie dining near the university

The eponymous Mr Deane has several establishments around the city, including this lively bar and grill joint in a buzzy, popular spot in the heart of the University Quarter with views over the Botanic Gardens. Refurbishment in early 2014 has resulted in a stylish, contemporary space of chrome and glass, with a feature fireplace and terrace tables. The cooking matches the modernity of the setting, delivering a genuine Irish flavour and come creative combinations. An opener of crispy venison shoulder is gloriously tender, partnered with root veg and berry and brown bread crumble, while another sees Portavogie crab packed into a terrine with potato and cheddar and served with gazpacho and avocado. An excellent piece of roast cod stars in a main course (with scallops, crab and potato purée), or go for Mourne Blackface lamb with a Mediterranean spin. To finish, choose between the likes of chocolate truffle tart or warm almond cake with caramelised pear and granola, or go savoury with the French and Irish cheeses.

Times 12-3/5.30-10, Closed 25-26 Dec, D Sun

EIPIC

◉◉◉ – *see page 709*

Galgorm Resort & Spa ✿✿✿

BALLYMENA   Map 1 D5

Modern British **V** 🍷 NOTABLE WINE LIST

tel: 028 2588 1001 **136 Fenaghy Rd, Galgorm BT42 1EA**
email: reservations@galgorm.com **web:** www.galgorm.com
dir: *1m from Ballymena on A42, between Galgorm & Cullybackey*

Ambitious contemporary cooking and river views

This upscale country resort hotel stands in 163 acres of parkland with the River Maine flowing through. Add luxurious bedrooms, a swish spa, posh conference and wedding facilities, and three dining venues, and you have a package to keep most people happy. The aptly named River Room Restaurant is the top dining option, with the river floodlit at night to create an alluring atmosphere and its floor-to-ceiling windows ensuring that everyone gets a gander of the watery views. The kitchen sources its ingredients diligently from a network of local suppliers (and as you'd hope with all those acres out there, there's room for a kitchen garden) and under the direction of Jonnie Boyd, transforms the haul into vibrant contemporary dishes with a clear seasonal focus. Things get off the mark with a well-crafted starter of pan-seared sea bass with salsify, shrimps, charred cucumber and sea beets, proving that the simple ideas can provide a truly great experience. Next up, top-quality venison with smoked beetroot, cocoa nibs, chicory, fondant potato and game jus shows well-considered balancing of flavours and textures. Fish courses, too, show real flair and sensitivity towards the balance of components and their impact on the palate — perhaps monkfish partnered by salsify, shiitaki mushrooms, langoustines and squid ink tagliatelle. Desserts are a high point,

especially when white pannacotta comes with the tart contrast of rhubarb sorbet, grenadine-poached sorbet, and coconut and ginger biscuits. Everything, from the excellent home-made bread and inventive canapés to the superb petits fours is crafted with impressive attention to detail. Supporting it all is a wine list put together with authority and knowledge.

Chef Israel Robb, Jonnie Boyd **Owner** Nicholas & Paul Hill **Seats** 50
Times 12-2.30/6.30-9.30, Closed Mon-Tue, L Wed-Sat
Prices Starter £7.50-£9, Main £22-£24, Dessert £6-£7.50
Wines 200 bottles over £30, 54 bottles under £30, 12 by glass
Parking 200 **Notes** Sunday L £25.95-£29.95, Children welcome

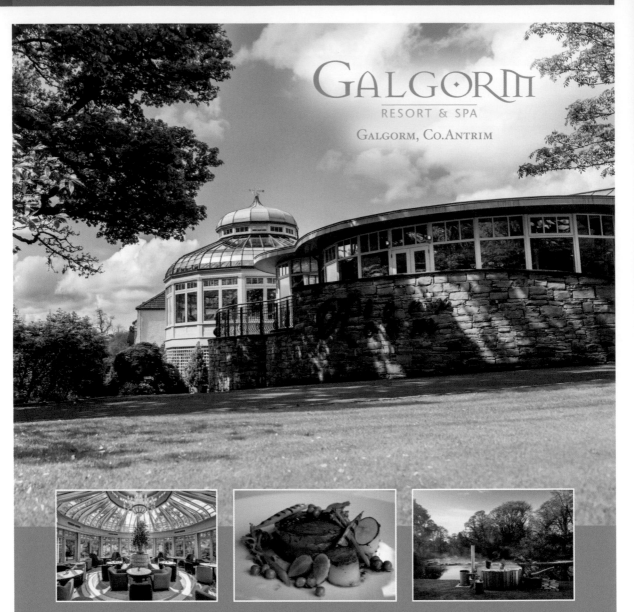

BELFAST *continued*

James Street South Restaurant & Bar

◉◉ Modern European

tel: 028 9043 4310 **21 James Street South BT2 7GA**
email: info@jamesstreetsouth.co.uk **web:** www.jamesstreetsouth.co.uk
dir: *Located between Brunswick St & Bedford St*

Serious city-slicker cooking in a sharp venue

Tucked away behind City Hall, this capacious red-brick former linen mill is the hub of Niall McKenna's empire, home to the flagship James Street South Restaurant as well as the Bar & Grill and cookery school. Pristine linen-clad tables and unchallenging, contemporary colours make a serene and understated setting for refined, French-accented food. David Gillmore heads up the kitchen, deploying well-honed French techniques in a blend of classical and contemporary ideas that show a sense of adventure, as witnessed in a starter of coffee-roasted carrots pointed up with crème fraîche and tarragon vinegar caramel. Regional ingredients take a leading role, such as the local monkfish, John Dory and hake that form the backbone of a signature Irish Sea bouillabaisse, or the Baronscourt Estate venison that is partnered with turnip and a mushroom 'cottage pie'. Bargain lunch and pre- and post-theatre options help keep things affordable, and there are tasting menus with matching wines if you're going for broke. To finish, dark chocolate and black cherries make for an intense version of clafoutis.

Chef David Gillmore **Owner** Niall & Joanne McKenna **Seats** 60, Pr/dining room 40 **Times** 12-2.45/5.45-10.45, Closed 1 Jan, Etr Mon, 12-15 Jul, 25-26 Dec, Sun **Prices** Fixed L 2 course fr £15.50, Starter £7-£9.50, Main £15.50-£25, Dessert £5-£9.50, Service optional **Wines** 35 bottles over £30, 40 bottles under £30, 11 by glass **Parking** On street **Notes** Pre-theatre menu Mon-Sat 2/3 course, Vegetarian available, Children welcome

The Merchant Hotel

◉◉ Modern European V

tel: 028 9023 4888 **16 Skipper St, Cathedral Quarter BT1 2DZ**
email: thegreatroom@merchanthotel.com **web:** www.themerchanthotel.com
dir: *In city centre, 2nd left at Albert clock onto Waring St. Hotel on left*

Magnificent grand setting for inventive contemporary cooking

The Victorian former headquarters of Ulster Bank is a building on a grand scale and these days the beneficiaries are those that rock up to eat, drink or sleep at this decidedly swanky hotel. There are cool boutique bedrooms, bars (including a happening jazz one), and, in The Great room, a fine-dining restaurant. The latter is a stunning space filled with marble columns and plasterwork under a glass-domed ceiling, with banquettes and chairs upholstered in rich red. The kitchen makes sense

continued

EIPIC ✿✿✿

BELFAST   Map 1 D5

Modern European V
tel: 028 9033 1134 **36-40 Howard St BT1 6PF**
email: info@michaeldeane.co.uk
dir: *At rear of City Hall. Howard St on left opposite Spires building*

Classy and confident cooking chez Michael Deane

Michael Deane is an elder statesman of the Northern Irish dining scene, with a little empire around the city (EIPIC, Meat Locker, Love Fish, Deanes Deli, Deanes at Queens, Deane and Decano) providing the kind of food people want to eat. Here in the Howard Street flagship, head chef Danni Barry directs the kitchen's efforts, returning to the Deane fold after a stint with Simon Rogan at L'Enclume. The place has mellowed in recent years, becoming less serious about the fripperies that come at the high end of eating out. Don't go thinking it is rough-and-ready, though, for this is a classy operation, with neatly laid, linen-dressed tables on a dark tiled floor and dark toned walls. The bargain three-course prix-fixe menu is a good entry point for those on a budget, and a flexible carte offers four, five or six courses of contemporary cooking, which has at its core excellent regional produce that arrives on the plate with its integrity intact. The concepts are not fanciful, simply focused on flavour and executed with a high degree of skill — witness a duck yolk cooked at 63 degrees and served simply with vibrant asparagus, peas and lettuce foam, or grilled langoustines matched with salt-baked and puréed celeriac, and sea greens. Flawless fish cookery brings pan-fried cod in herb butter with Jerusalem artichoke purée, pickled grapes and sea beets, while the flavours are turned up to 11 in a harmonious dish of roast chicken with braised morels, a vibrant purée of spinach and wild garlic, truffled mash spiked with crisp chicken skin, and an intense jus. Veggies are well served by a six-course taster.

Chef Michael Deane, Simon Toye, Danni Barry **Owner** Michael Deane **Seats** 30, Pr/dining room 50 **Times** 12-3/5.30-10, Closed 6-26 Jan, 8-31 Jul, 25 Dec, BHs, Sun-Tue, L Wed-Thu, Sat **Prices** Fixed L 3 course £30, Tasting menu £40-£60 **Wines** 76 bottles over £30, 25 bottles under £30, 8 by glass **Parking** On street (after 6pm), car park Clarence St **Notes** Children welcome

BELFAST *continued*

of it all with a classical-meets-modern repertoire where tip-top regional produce is treated with respect. Portavogie lobster and scallops might provide the filling for first-course ravioli, paired with poached langoustine and shellfish bisque, while seared foie gras comes with fig marmalade, fresh almonds and brioche. Next up, perhaps seared wild venison loin with glazed chicory, roast swede and sour cherry marmalade, or roast cod fillet with white crab bonbon, buttered curly kale and salt-cod brandade. To finish, try Valrhona dark chocolate and peanut fondant with banana sorbet.

Chef John Paul Leake **Owner** The Merchant Hotel **Seats** 85, Pr/dining room 18 **Times** 12-2.30/6-10, Closed L Sat **Prices** Fixed L 2 course £19.50, Fixed D 3 course £26.50, Tasting menu £70-£90, Starter £6.50-£10.50, Main £19.50-£28.50, Dessert £8.50-£15.50 **Wines** 106 bottles over £30, 52 bottles under £30, 13 by glass **Parking** On street **Notes** Pre-theatre 2/3 course £18.50/£22.50, Sunday L £25.50-£29.50, Children welcome

OX

◉◉ Modern Irish **NEW**

tel: 028 9031 4121 **1 Oxford St BT1 3LA**
email: info@oxbelfast.com
dir: *Near Queensbridge Beacon of Hope statue in Belfast city centre*

Skilful modern cooking in stunning riverside location

Overlooking the River Lagan in the heart of Belfast, OX is a collaboration between local boy Stephen Toman and Frenchman Alain Kerloc'h, who worked together in Paris under the legendary Alain Passard. The stylishly minimalistic dining room with its open kitchen and mezzanine area makes for an unpretentious, almost retro setting for what is thoroughly contemporary food that often elevates vegetables to star billing. The cooking's light, modern touch keeps things simple and fresh, using top-notch ingredients in skilfully delivered dishes such as a delicate starter of scallops, white bean bisque and lemongrass. A spring meal might feature a well-judged rump of Mourne lamb teamed with chicory, black olive and spinach, before ending with a wonderfully fresh and just-made jasmine crème brûlée with plum sorbet. For those diners eager to sample more dishes, the tasting menus – including one for vegetarians – are a popular choice for the table. A conscientiously chosen wine list adds the final gloss to this quality operation.

Chef Stephen Toman **Owner** Stephen Toman, Alain Kerloc'h **Seats** 40 **Times** 12-2.30/6-9.30, Closed Last 2 wks Jul, Xmas, New Year, BHs, Sun-Mon **Prices** Fixed D 3 course £20, Tasting menu fr £45, Starter £4.50-£9.50, Main £15.50-£25, Dessert £6.50 **Wines** 43 bottles over £30, 18 bottles under £30, 12 by glass **Parking** Car park nearby **Notes** Tasting menu 5 course, Vegetarian available, Children welcome

Shu

◉◉ Modern Irish

tel: 028 9038 1655 **253-255 Lisburn Rd BT9 7EN**
email: eat@shu-restaurant.com
dir: *From city centre take Lisburn Rd (lower end). Restaurant in 1m, on corner of Lower Windsor Avenue*

Contemporary Irish cooking with a buzz and good service

The name suggests an Asian influence, but this a thoroughly European kind of restaurant, with classical French thinking as the foundation of the sharp, modern cooking on show. (Shu, by the way, is the ancient Egyptian god of atmosphere). Situated in a Victorian terrace in trendy Lisburn, the airy space with an open-to-view kitchen is served by a smartly turned-out team. There is, however, an Asian flavour in one or two dishes on the menu – witness a starter of salt and chilli squid served with classic dipping sauces of sweet chilli, wasabi mayonnaise, and soy, garlic and chilli. Otherwise, start with something like foie gras and chicken liver parfait with apple and chilli jelly, and toasted walnut and raisin bread. Main-course wood pigeon is scented with the smoky note of Lapsang Souchong, and comes with

celeriac purée, deep-fried kale, and beetroot, while a fishy main might be roast cod with crushed potatoes, brassicas and sauce nero. For pudding, vanilla cheesecake is matched with textures of blood orange and almond praline.

Chef Brian McCann **Owner** Alan Reid **Seats** 100, Pr/dining room 24 **Times** 12-2.30/6-10, Closed 25-26 Dec, 1 Jan, 12-13 Jul, Sun **Prices** Fixed L 2 course £13.25, Fixed D 3 course £28.25-£30.50, Starter £4.75-£9, Main £12.50-£23, Dessert £5.75, Service optional **Wines** 35 bottles over £30, 49 bottles under £30, 18 by glass **Parking** 4, On street **Notes** Vegetarian available, Children welcome

COUNTY DOWN

BANGOR
Map 1 D5

The Boathouse Restaurant

◉◉◉ – *see opposite*

COMBER
Map 1 D5

The Old Schoolhouse Inn

◉◉ Modern British **NEW** ᵥ

tel: 028 9754 1182 **100 Ballydrain Rd BT23 6EA**
email: info@theoldschoolhouseinn.com **web:** www.theoldschoolhouseinn.com
dir: *Phone for directions*

Lively modern Irish inspiration by the Lough

Ensconced in the Down countryside by Strangford Lough, though only 20 minutes' drive out of Belfast, The Old Schoolhouse has been under the tutelage of the same family for over 30 years. It's an elegant conversion of the original school building, with a chef at the stoves who began his career as a 17-year-old under the London aegis of Marco Pierre White. As at many another rural venue, the kitchen grows much of its own produce, which forms the foundation of modern Irish cooking that's full of lively inspiration. Seafood is a strong suit, perhaps for crab with a smoked mackerel fishcake, beetroot and apple, or in scallops teamed with pork belly, Alsace bacon and butter beans. Duck from a local farm is served as breast and a roll of confit leg and shredded potato, with creamed cabbage and puréed carrot aromatised with star anise, while mussels are given a main-course marinière spin with Armagh cider, shallots and buckwheat. The signature dessert is high-powered chocolate marquise with intense vanilla ice cream, cocoa nibs and honeycomb.

Chef Will Brown **Owner** Will Brown **Seats** 50, Pr/dining room 30 **Times** 12-10.30, All-day dining, Closed Mon **Prices** Fixed L 2 course fr £14, Fixed D 3 course fr £18, Tasting menu fr £45, Starter £4.95-£8.50, Main £12-£23.50, Dessert £7-£9, Service optional **Wines** 26 bottles over £30, 27 bottles under £30, 11 by glass **Parking** 30 **Notes** Sunday L £18.50-£23.50, Children welcome

CRAWFORDSBURN
Map 1 D5

The Old Inn

◉◉ Modern European

tel: 028 9185 3255 **15 Main St BT19 1JH**
email: info@theoldinn.com **web:** www.theoldinn.com
dir: *From Belfast along A2, past Belfast City Airport. Continue past Holywood & Belfast Folk & Transport museum. 2m after museum left at lights onto B20 for 1.2m*

Revamped restaurant in a historical old inn

The Old Inn is an apt moniker when the oldest – and thatched – part of the building dates from the 17th century. These days it's a lavishly decorated and furnished hotel with a high level of glitz, not least the restaurant, where a circular recess hung with lights has been set in the ornate ceiling. This is a busy dining venue, drawing people not just with the decor but for the modern European-style cooking built on prime local produce. Scallops, as fresh as can be, are served with no more than wilted salad and mayonnaise to make a delightful starter, or there might be the earthier flavours of Clonakilty black pudding with crispy pancetta, a poached egg and roast tomatoes. Timings are impeccable, seen in chicken breast with artichokes, root vegetables and a well-considered sauce, and monkfish dusted in black olives with chorizo, spinach and sunblush tomato fettuccine. Canapés and breads are of a standard, as are puddings along the lines of chocolate delice with salted caramel ice cream.

Chef Nick Clough **Owner** Paul & Garvan Rice **Seats** 134, Pr/dining room 50 **Times** 12-9.30, All-day dining, Closed 25 Dec **Prices** Fixed L 2 course £8.95, Fixed D 3 course £26, Starter £4.90-£10.50, Main £12-£23, Dessert £4.95-£7, Service optional 10% **Wines** 8 bottles over £30, 38 bottles under £30, 11 by glass **Parking** 80 **Notes** Sizzler menu £12.50, Sunday L £9-£13, Vegetarian available, Children welcome

DUNDRUM
Map 1 D5

Mourne Seafood Bar

🏵 Seafood

tel: 028 4375 1377 **10 Main St BT33 0LU**
email: bob@mourneseafood.com
dir: On main road from Belfast to The Mournes, on village main street

Fresh fish and shellfish at the foot of the Mourne mountains

With a sister establishment in Belfast, the Dundrum branch of Mourne seafood is in a refreshingly peaceful location. At the foot of the Mourne mountains, with a nature reserve close by, it is dedicated of course to fish and shellfish, much of which comes from the proprietors' own seafood beds. The daily-changing menu offers its wares in a broad range of styles, from salt-and-chilli squid with garlic mayo, scallop linguine and wilted greens, or smoked mackerel pâté in lettuce cups to start, and then temptations such as grilled lobster or battered fish and chips with mushy peas following on. Accompaniments are always designed to suit the main items, so expect chorizo, chickpeas and tomato with hake, mustard mash and a poached egg

with smoked haddock, or leeks and hollandaise with Glenarm salmon. If you're not of the fish persuasion, there are sirloin steaks with fat chips and béarnaise sauce.

Chef Dominic Gribben **Owner** Bob & Joanne McCoubrey **Seats** 75, Pr/dining room 20 **Times** 12.30-9.30, All-day dining, Closed 25 Dec, Mon-Thu (winter) **Prices** Starter £4.50-£8, Main £9.50-£17, Dessert £4.50, Service optional **Wines** 6 bottles over £30, 12 bottles under £30, 5 by glass **Parking** On street **Notes** Fixed D menu Sat only, Sunday L, Vegetarian available, Children welcome

NEWCASTLE
Map 1 D5

Brunel's Restaurant at The Anchor Bar

🏵 Modern Irish **NEW**

tel: 028 4372 3951 **9 Bryansford Rd BT33 0HJ**
email: reservations@brunelsrestaurant.co.uk
dir: Top of Main St, follow road to right. Restaurant immediately on right above The Anchor Bar, accessed via red front door

Modern Irish brasserie food with bracing sea views

Brunel's is a first-floor venue above the ever-popular Anchor Bar, just off the Newcastle seafront. While the bar is skilfully crafted from reclaimed wood, naked light fixtures dangle above unclothed tables for the minimal look, softened by candlelight in the evenings, Craft beers and a decent wine list are among the attractions, as are the knowledgeable, friendly service team who deliver satisfying plates of modern Irish brasserie food, with seafood a trump card. Start with butter-poached langoustines and roast carrots, garnished with buttermilk froth and gingerbread crumb, and follow it perhaps with roast coley and chorizo risotto, with capers and pine nuts in a sherry dressing. Rump of Mourne mountain lamb is a fine cut that doesn't need the distraction of hazelnut purée, but does gain a little from

continued

The Boathouse Restaurant 🏵🏵🏵

BANGOR
Map 1 D5

Modern International **NEW**
tel: 028 9146 9253 **1a Seacliff Rd BT20 5HA**
email: info@theboathouseni.co.uk
dir: Down Main St just after the marina & below the pier

Creative, complex cooking by the marina

Housed in the dinky stone-built Victorian harbourmaster's office by the marina, the Castel brothers' charming pint-sized restaurant certainly punches above its weight. Spread over two floors with views of yachts bobbing at anchor, vaulted ceilings and local art on whitewashed stone walls, the place hums with the sound of contented diners, and no wonder, since the exciting cooking here brings in roving gourmets from far and wide. Joery Castel is the man at the stoves, turning out contemporary European dishes that bring together top-class local produce with displays of technological fireworks, delivered via daily-changing menus inspired from far and wide. Castel hails from Holland, and since the Dutch have a thing for Indonesian and Malaysian food, things get off the mark with the Far-Eastern fire of a grilled Malaysian-style boneless chicken leg with satay sauce, barbecued and fresh cucumber, serundeng (a mix of grated coconut, peanuts and spices), atjar tjampoer (a pickled vegetable condiment) and crispy rice. Next up, we revert to

European mode in a complex main course involving pan-fried halibut with charred langoustine, crispy Parma ham, potato croquette, carrot purée and roast carrot brunoise, parsley gel and potato sauce – a virtuoso combination of bold flavours. Meat-based ideas might bring a more orthodox partnership: a perfectly handled noisette of dry-aged Glenarm lamb with dauphinoise potato, ratatouille, wild garlic, and black olive jus. Dessert returns to multi-faceted complexity with a composition of spiced carrot cake with candied carrots, counterpointed by the citrus tang of lemon mascarpone, plus dehydrated white chocolate crunch, orange gel and candied hazelnuts.

Chef Joery Castel **Owner** Jasper & Joery Castel **Seats** 36
Times 12.30-2.30/5.30-9.30, Closed Mon-Tue **Prices** Fixed L 2 course fr £16, Fixed D 3 course £32.50-£35, Tasting menu £45-£55, Service optional **Wines** 10 by glass **Notes** Sunday L, Vegetarian available, Children welcome

NEWCASTLE *continued*

its marine accompaniments of sea beets and samphire. Chocolate fondant is inspiringly rich in flavour with a good oozy filling, and comes with the sharpening touch of black cherry sorbet.

Chef Paul Cunningham **Owner** Paul Cunningham **Seats** 50, Pr/dining room 25 **Times** 12-3/6-9.30, Closed Mon-Tue **Prices** Prices not confirmed, Service optional **Wines** 10 bottles over £30, 20 bottles under £30, 10 by glass **Parking** Free at Donard Park **Notes** Early bird Wed-Fri 6-7.30pm 2/3 course £14.95/£16.95, Sunday L, Vegetarian available, Children welcome

NEWTOWNARDS
Map 1 D5

Balloo House

◉ Traditional European

tel: 028 9754 1210 **1 Comber Rd, Killinchy BT23 6PA**
email: info@balloohouse.com **web:** www.balloohouse.com
dir: *A22 from Belfast, through Dundonald. 6m from Comber*

Lively bistro and serene dining room in a venerable old house

The man in charge here is Danny Millar and he's somewhat of a TV star these days with stints on the BBC's *Saturday Kitchen* and *Great British Menu*. But you'll usually find him behind the stoves at this old coaching inn and former farmhouse close to Strangford Lough. A major refurbishment in late 2014 has accentuated its original historical features with the additions of darkwood panelling and peacock blue and tan leather booth seating which creates an intimate atmosphere. When it comes to the menu, the kitchen offers the best of Irish and European tradition, with a contemporary touch and some Pan-Asian flavours to spice things up. Wild mushroom risotto gets the ball rolling followed by roast cod with char siu pork, or Irish rose veal with truffle and parmesan polenta. For dessert, try passionfruit crème brûlée with pineapple salsa and biscotti biscuit or brownie mousse with poached cherries and vanilla ice cream.

Chef Danny Millar, Grainne Donnelly **Owner** Balloo Inns Ltd **Seats** 80, Pr/dining room 30 **Times** 12-9, All-day dining, Closed 25 Dec **Prices** Fixed L 2 course £13.95, Fixed

D 3 course £18.95, Starter £3.95-£7.95, Main £9.95-£20.95, Dessert £3.50-£5.95, Service optional **Wines** 15 bottles over £30, 45 bottles under £30, 9 by glass **Parking** 60 **Notes** Sunday L £22.95, Vegetarian available, Children welcome

COUNTY FERMANAGH

ENNISKILLEN
Map 1 C5

Lough Erne Resort

◉◉◉ *– see opposite*

Manor House Country Hotel

◉ Irish, European

tel: 028 6862 2200 **Killadeas BT94 1NY**
email: info@manorhousecountryhotel.com **web:** www.manorhousecountryhotel.com
dir: *On B82, 7m N of Enniskillen*

Contemporary cooking and lough views

The colonel who rebuilt this old manor in the 1860s brought some craftsmen over from Italy to spruce up the interior, and you can still see some of their handiwork in today's property. There's a modern extension, a golf course and much more besides, but there's no taking away from the view down to Lough Erne. The fine-dining action takes place in the Belleek Restaurant, housed in a conservatory extension that gets the very best of the view. Wherever you sit, the finish is smart and genteel, watched over by a formal service team. The menu has a genuine local flavour and a contemporary European spin, as seen in seared Donegal Bay scallops with gremolata and a parsnip and vanilla purée, or roast rack of Fermanagh lamb partnered with lemon-glazed sweetbreads and colcannon. Sunday lunch is a traditional affair, while desserts are a creative bunch.

Chef Rory Carville **Owner** Liam & Mary McKenna **Seats** 90, Pr/dining room 350 **Times** 12.30-3/6-10, Closed L Mon-Fri, D Sun **Prices** Fixed D 3 course £35, Service optional **Wines** 20 bottles over £30, 40 bottles under £30 **Parking** 300 **Notes** Sunday L £18.95, Vegetarian available, Children welcome

COUNTY LONDONDERRY

LIMAVADY
Map 1 C6

The Lime Tree

◉ Traditional Mediterranean

tel: 028 7776 4300 **60 Catherine St BT49 9DB**
email: info@limetreerest.com
dir: *Enter Limavady from Derry side. Restaurant on right on small slip road*

Long-running restaurant showcasing the pick of the province

The Lime Tree is a pint-sized neighbourhood restaurant in the town centre, its simply painted walls hung with vibrant artwork. There's plenty to enjoy here, not least a menu that holds much of interest, particularly for lovers of seafood, all ocean-fresh and cooked just so. Main courses have taken in seafood thermidor (nuggets of plaice, monk, salmon, hake and cod in a rich cheese and brandy sauce) and fillets of lemon sole stuffed with crabmeat in creamy chive sauce, preceded perhaps by a signature starter of crab cakes. Meat-eaters, meanwhile, can choose chicken liver pâté with Cumberland sauce, then duck confit cut by classic orange sauce served with champ. Themed evenings such as Spanish are successes, and puddings can be as decadent as gooey chocolate brownie with creamy vanilla ice cream and chocolate sauce.

Chef Stanley Matthews **Owner** Mr & Mrs S Matthews **Seats** 30 **Times** 12-1.30/5.30-9, Closed 25-26 Dec, 12 Jul, Sun-Mon, L Sun-Wed **Prices** Fixed D 3 course fr £20, Starter £4.60-£7.95, Main £14.50-£22.50, Dessert £5.50-£5.95, Service optional **Wines** 9 bottles over £30, 29 bottles under £30, 6 by glass **Parking** On street **Notes** Vegetarian available, Children welcome

Roe Park Resort

Modern, Traditional

tel: 028 7772 2222 **BT49 9LB**
email: reservations@roeparkresort.com **web:** www.roeparkresort.com
dir: *On A6 (Londonderry-Limavady road), 0.5m from Limavady. 8m from Derry airport*

Traditional dining in a relaxed resort hotel

Built as a country mansion in the 18th century, surrounded by 150 acres of grounds beside the River Roe, Roe Park has been extended in recent years into a vast modern golfing and leisure resort. Just one of several dining options here, Greens Restaurant is a stylish, split-level space offering mostly traditional cooking with the odd modern twist. Start, perhaps, with confit duck rillette with toasted sourdough, beetroot and orange relish, moving on to fillet of Irish beef with potato croquette, confit garlic, button mushrooms and jus, or grilled salmon supreme with oriental noodles and a ginger and soy dressing. If cheesecake is your thing, there's a daily-changing selection of flavours, or you may want to go down the comfort route with the steamed banana and ginger pudding with fresh cream and sauce anglaise.

Chef Frank Kivlehan **Owner** Mr Conn, Mr McKeever, Mr Wilton **Seats** 160, Pr/dining room 50 **Times** 12-3/6.30-9 **Prices** Prices not confirmed, Service optional **Wines** 8 by glass **Parking** 250 **Notes** Sunday L, Vegetarian available, Children welcome

---

LONDONDERRY Map 1 C5

Browns Restaurant and Champagne Lounge

Modern Irish V

tel: 028 7134 5180 **1 Bonds Hill, Waterside BT47 6DW**
email: eat@brownsrestaurant.com
dir: *Phone for directions*

On-the-money modern Irish cooking

Situated on the edge of the city centre by Lough Foyle, Browns has quickly garnered a loyal local following since it opened its doors in 2009. Get in the mood with a glass of bubbly on a squidgy sofa in the champagne lounge, then head for one of the white linen-swathed tables in the dining room, where toffee-hued walls and leather seating, stripy banquettes, and pale wooden floors add up to a sharp contemporary look. Driven by well-sourced local ingredients and unfussy execution, the kitchen turns out an appealing roll-call of modern Irish ideas, with fish and seafood a strong suit. Pan-seared scallops are matched with braised pork cheek, honey and soy sauce, and apple and star anise purée, ahead of roast fillet of monkfish with cauliflower served crispy and in a curried cream sauce. To finish, Turkish Delight, chocolate cookies and ginger cream put a novel spin on crème brûlée.

Chef Ian Orr **Owner** Ian Orr **Seats** 60 **Times** 12-3/5.30-10, Closed 3 days Xmas, Mon, L Sat, D Sun **Prices** Prices not confirmed, Service optional **Wines** 35 bottles over £30, 51 bottles under £30, 14 by glass **Parking** On street **Notes** Tasting menu 6 course, Early bird £19.95 Tue-Sat, Sunday L, Children welcome

---

Lough Erne Resort 🏵🏵🏵

ENNISKILLEN Map 1 C5

Modern, Traditional V NOTABLE WINE LIST

tel: 028 6632 3230 **Belleek Rd BT93 7ED**
email: info@lougherneresort.com **web:** www.lougherneresort.com
dir: *A46 from Enniskillen towards Donegal, hotel in 3m*

Dynamic modern Irish cooking at a luxury resort hotel

Fully loaded with a sybaritic Thai spa and a golf course designed by Nick Faldo, this glossy purpose-built resort hotel on its own 60-acre peninsula jutting into the eponymous lough deserves every one of its five stars. When it comes to fine dining, the Catalina restaurant (named after the World War II seaplanes that were based on the lough and commemorated in framed photos) is an expansive space with vaulted ceilings and views of the course and water through its arched windows, and dressed up with smart linen and swagged drapes for a refined and traditional backdrop to Noel McMeel's dynamic modern cooking. With Irish flavours leaping out from every skilfully rendered dish, the results are never less than stimulating. First up, wonderful pork belly is served with butternut squash and maple purée, and offset with the delicate pickled tang of shimeji mushrooms, or you might start with a terrine of braised and roasted chicken wrapped in bacon and matched with roast mushroom purée, smoked bacon cream and onion seeds. Main courses are equally well conceived, serving superb rump of Lough Erne lamb with burnt onion, Jerusalem artichoke, black onion powder, tasty fingerling potatoes, and molasses and mint jus, or bringing together pickled mushrooms, mandarin, orange, butternut purée, crispy puffed rice and coriander shoots to support a splendid fillet of baked stone bass. An intense bitter chocolate delice with caramelised pecan, yellowman (a chewy toffee-like honeycomb) and honeycomb ice cream, or a beautifully-risen banana soufflé with white chocolate custard, double chocolate ice cream and peanut brittle make for decadent finishers. Charming staff are the icing on the cake, attentive without ever being intrusive, and well briefed on the menu.

Chef Noel McMeel **Owner** Castle Hume Leisure Ltd **Seats** 75, Pr/dining room 30 **Times** 1-2.30/6.30-10, Closed L Mon-Sat **Prices** Fixed L 2 course £19.50, Fixed D 3 course fr £45, Tasting menu £75 **Wines** 70 bottles over £30, 36 bottles under £30, 13 by glass **Parking** 200 **Notes** Sunday L £19.50-£24, Children welcome

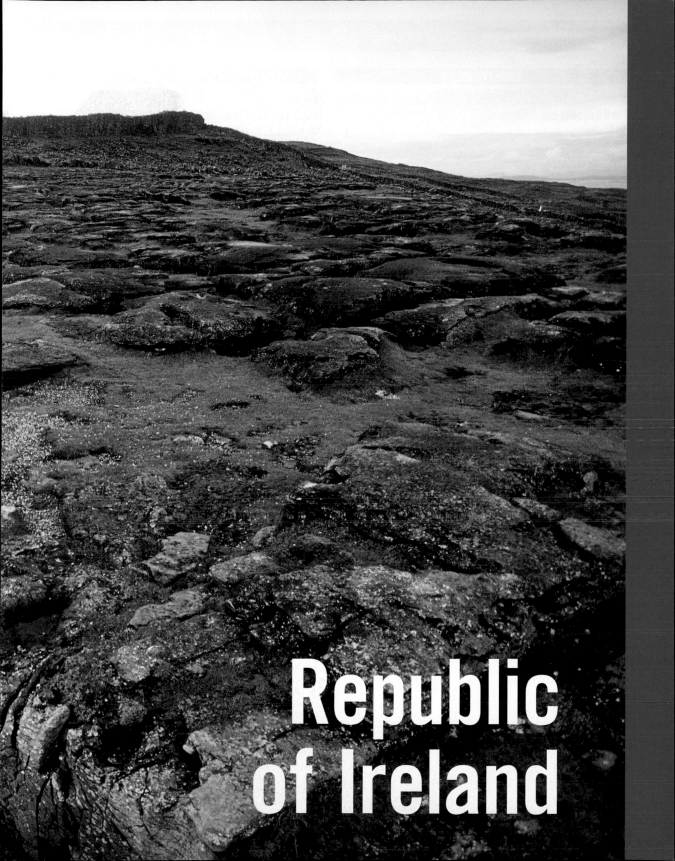

Republic
of Ireland

COUNTY CARLOW

LEIGHLINBRIDGE — Map 1 C3

Lord Bagenal Inn

◉ Modern Irish **NEW**

tel: 059 9774000 **Main St**
email: info@lordbagenal.com **web:** www.lordbagenal.com
dir: *M9 junct 6, R448 left onto R705, hotel on right*

Unpretentious dishes in a riverside hotel

Back in 1979, the original roadside restaurant was almost killed off by the advent of a new motorway, but the enterprising owners built a hotel on the site to keep passing trade coming to their door. The place wears a distinctly contemporary face these days, and its restaurant fits the bill with a smartly refurbished look to go with appealingly unpretentious cooking. A please-all menu offers a mixed bag of oriental, international and modern Irish dishes made with a good showing of local ingredients, starting with classic chicken liver parfait topped with golden raisins set in Pedro Ximenez jelly and served in time-honoured fashion with toasted brioche. Main course showcases plaice fresh from Duncannon served simply with lemon and herb butter, champ potatoes and seasonal vegetables, and things end with the comfort of sticky toffee and pecan pudding with caramel sauce.

Chef Shein Than **Owner** James Kehoe **Seats** Pr/dining room
Times 12-2.30/6-9.30, Closed 25 Dec, St Stephens Day **Prices** Fixed L 2 course €21-€30, Fixed D 3 course €25-€40, Starter €4-€11, Main €12.50-€28, Dessert €5, Service optional **Wines** 70 bottles over €30, 30 bottles under €30, 8 by glass **Parking** 100 **Notes** Sunday L €25, Vegetarian available, Children welcome

TULLOW — Map 1 C3

Mount Wolseley Hotel, Spa & Country Club

◉ Modern European

tel: 059 9180100 & 9151674
email: info@mountwolseley.ie **web:** www.mountwolseley.ie
dir: *N7 from Dublin. In Naas, take N9 towards Carlow. In Castledermot left for Tullow*

Modern Irish cooking on an ancestral estate

The Wolseleys of Staffordshire came to Ireland in the 17th century and fought on King William's side in 1690. They remained in possession of this estate until long after independence, but it was redeveloped by new owners the Morrisseys in the 1990s as a sumptuous hotel and country club, with plenty of golf. In keeping with the chic surroundings, the place encompasses a stylish split-level dining room overlooking a garden courtyard, where smartly attired staff attend at equally well turned-out tables. Seafood is a forte, as is demonstrated by a starter of gin-cured salmon with pickled cucumber and a wasabi and cucumber emulsion. Meatier appetites are assuaged by a main course of roast chicken breast with butternut squash purée, fondant potato, and chorizo and barley jus. Finish with the signature lemon posset, served alongside confit orange and shortbread.

Times 12.30-2.30/6-9.30, Closed 24-26 Dec, L Mon-Sat

COUNTY CAVAN

CAVAN — Map 1 C4

Radisson Blu Farnham Estate Hotel

◉ European, Modern International

tel: 049 4377700 **Farnham Estate**
email: info.farnham@radissonblu.com **web:** www.farnhamestate.com
dir: *From Dublin take N3 to Cavan. From Cavan take Killeshandra road for 4km*

Irish produce, French-influenced cooking

With lakes, rivers and ancient oak forests all around on this massive 1,300-acre, 16th-century estate, you're never short of outdoor pursuits to work up a keen appetite at Farnham, a historic stately home that has morphed into an upmarket country hotel offering the full corporate package of spa, golf, wedding and meeting facilities. Clever use of plush drapes and screens helps to soften the capacious space that is the Botanica Restaurant, and a friendly service team is well-versed in the ins and outs of each dish. The kitchen places its faith in local ingredients, bringing it all together with French-inspired flair. Spicy tiger prawns, orange and dill-infused salmon, and smoked mackerel rillettes make up a seafood platter, then roast rack and slow-cooked rump of local lamb is delivered with aubergine caviar and buttery potato mash. Dessert could be a riff on lemon, in the shape of a zesty tart, madeleines, and jelly.

Times 1-3/7-9.15, Closed L Mon-Sat

COUNTY CLARE

BALLYVAUGHAN — Map 1 B3

Gregans Castle

◉◉◉ – see opposite

DOOLIN — Map 1 B3

Cullinan's Seafood Restaurant & Guest House

◉◉ Modern French

tel: 065 7074183
email: info@cullinansdoolin.com **web:** www.cullinansdoolin.com
dir: *Located in Doolin town centre R479*

Artistically presented seafood and meat by the River Aille

The Cullinans' guesthouse in rural Clare overlooks the Aille River meadow, the sumptuous views captured by floor-to-ceiling windows on two sides of the dining room. It's an unquestionably charming setting, but it is chef-proprietor James Cullinan's skilful French-influenced modern cooking that is the showstopper. Cream leather seating and linen-clad tables make for a smart setting, and dishes are presented with a certain artistry and deliver on freshness, flavour and accuracy. The kitchen's confident, supremely professional knack with seafood might bring forth a rich and creamy chowder, followed by butter-roasted hake topped with gremolata, and matched with asparagus fricassée, mussels and scallion, and smoked haddock velouté. If you're moving on to meat for main, you might encounter roasted rack and mini shepherd's pie of superlative Burren lamb, served with baby peas, roast garlic and thyme jus, or Irish beef fillet with beer-braised onions, mushroom duxelles, French beans and a Burgundy wine reduction. Finish self-indulgently with a choc-fest trio of chocolate, orange and pistachio marquise, chocolate millefeuille and ice cream.

Chef James Cullinan **Owner** James & Carol Cullinan **Seats** 24 **Times** 6-9, Closed Nov-Mar, Wed, Sun (excl BH wknds), L all week **Prices** Fixed D 3 course €31.50, Starter €6.50-€9.95, Main €21.50-€28.50, Dessert €6.95-€8.75, Service optional **Wines** 7 bottles over €30, 17 bottles under €30, 7 by glass **Parking** 20 **Notes** Vegetarian available, Children 4 yrs+

LAHINCH
Map 1 B3

Moy House

◉◉ Modern French **V**

tel: 065 7082800
email: moyhouse@eircom.net **web:** www.moyhouse.com
dir: *Located 1km from Lahinch on the Miltown Malbay road*

Seasonal cooking with panoramic views of the bay

The gleaming white hotel on the Clare coast was the ancestral home of the Fitzgerald family, having originally been built for Sir Augustine of that ilk in the mid-Georgian era. Standing proud in 15 acres of grounds overlooking the bay at Lahinch, it's full of period character inside, from the roughcast stone walls of the entrance hall to the country-interiors style of the lounge, though the dining room with its minimalist modern chandeliers and panoramic views from the headland is in more contemporary style. As is the food, which draws on unimpeachable local supply lines for four-course seasonal dinner menus that have much to entice. First up might be potato-filled agnolotti pasta with sauce soubise, garnished with the glorious Burren smoked salmon and shredded spring onion, then locally reared beef with mushroom duxelles, wilted spinach and confit garlic in sauce bordelaise. After a pause for a cheese such as Tipperary's wonderful Cashel Blue with port-poached apple and candied walnuts, things are rounded off with moist almond cake and lemon curd.

Chef Matthew Strefford **Owner** Antoin O'Looney **Seats** 35, Pr/dining room 22
Times 7-8.30, Closed Jan-Mar, Nov-Dec, Sun-Mon (off peak) **Prices** Tasting menu €60, Service optional **Wines** 4 bottles under €30, 4 by glass **Parking** 50 **Notes** Fixed D 5 course €60 (reservation req), Children welcome

LISDOONVARNA
Map 1 B3

Sheedy's Country House Hotel

◉◉ Modern Irish

tel: 065 7074026
email: info@sheedys.com **web:** www.sheedys.com
dir: *20m from Ennis on N87*

Flavour-led cooking in a small rural hotel

Chef-patron John Sheedy is the latest in a long line of Sheedys who have run the family business since the 18th century. The small-scale country-house hotel is the oldest house in the village, which lies on the fringes of The Burren close by the coast, and exudes the sort of family-run, unpretentious tradition that keeps a loyal fan base returning again and again. It goes without saying, then, that John Sheedy has long-established local supply lines to support his passion for authentic ingredients: the kitchen garden provides fresh herbs and vegetables to supplement local organic meat and fish landed at nearby Doolin. Full-on, clearly defined flavours are what to expect in a repertoire of uncomplicated modern dishes, such as rillettes of rabbit with dried plum and brandied chutney, followed by roast rack of Burren lamb with a crisp crust of parsley and mustard, served with confit shoulder, spinach, and a ragoût of broad beans and tomato concasse. A classic lemon posset with raspberry coulis and sorbet and langue de chat biscuits makes a creamy, crunchy and refreshing finish.

Chef John Sheedy **Owner** John & Martina Sheedy **Seats** 28
Times 6.30-8.30, Closed mid Oct-mid Mar, 1 day a wk (Mar-Apr) **Prices** Starter €8.90-€12.50, Main €18.50-€28, Dessert €7.80-€9.50, Service optional **Wines** 10 bottles over €30, 8 bottles under €30, 2 by glass **Parking** 25 **Notes** Vegetarian available, Children 8 yrs+

Gregans Castle ◉◉◉

BALLYVAUGHAN
Map 1 B3

Modern Irish, European
tel: 065 7077005
email: stay@gregans.ie **web:** www.gregans.ie
dir: *On N67, 5km S of Ballyvaughan village*

Outstanding contemporary food at a little house in The Burren

Despite the name, it isn't actually a castle, but let's not quibble over terminology as Gregans is a luxurious hideaway filled with antiques and period Georgian elegance that is unlikely to disappoint. It's set in The Burren, whose wild and beautiful landscapes surely inspired the fantastical settings in the novels of Tolkien and C S Lewis – they both popped in for a bit of a break from the worlds of hobbits and Narnia. The restaurant is a romantic and refined room where picture windows open on to a view across the gardens to Galway Bay. Candlelight flickers in the evening, and as the summer sun sets, diners are treated to an eerie light show as the dying rays ignite the grey limestone rocks. And if it's a light show you're after, there are some fireworks on the plate too, for David Hurley's sharp modern cooking is out of the top drawer. The local landscape provides a good deal of the ingredients and the cooking techniques of the kitchen team favour modernist culinary thinking, setting out along the lines of cured foie gras with blood orange, celery and gingerbread, all combining to form a hugely satisfying whole with well-judged flavours and bags of invention. Next up, wild Irish venison might be partnered productively with Jerusalem artichoke, pickled pear and truffle, or steamed wild turbot served up with leek, wild garlic, potato gnocchi and hazelnuts. Among desserts, there could be dark chocolate truffle cake with white chocolate, passionfruit and coconut, or an invigorating combination of blackcurrant soufflé and sorbet with buttermilk custard. An extremely fine global wine list includes organic and biodynamic wines.

Chef David Hurley **Owner** Simon Haden **Seats** 50, Pr/dining room 30
Times 6-9, Closed Nov-mid Feb, Sun, Wed (ex Sun BHs), L all week **Prices** Fixed D 3 course €70, Tasting menu €85 **Wines** 50 bottles over €30, 40 bottles under €30, 8 by glass **Parking** 20 **Notes** Tasting menu 9 course, Vegetarian available, Children 6 yrs+

LISDOONVARNA *continued*

Wild Honey Inn

◉◉ Modern Irish

tel: 065 7074300 **Kincora**
email: info@wildhoneyinn.com **web:** www.wildhoneyinn.com
dir: *N18 from Ennis to Ennistymon. Continue through Ennistymon towards Lisdoonvarna, located on the right at edge of town*

Simple cooking done right

Wild Honey has been around since 1860, and although a makeover in recent years has grafted on a smart contemporary sheen, this convivial family-run inn oozes heaps of cosy character. The bar is utterly unpretentious with its pubby tables and 'first come first served' no bookings policy, so you'd best arrive early to dig into the kitchen's no-nonsense modern bistro cooking. Driven by the splendid larder of the rugged West Coast, the culinary emphasis is on wild, free-range and seasonal ingredients, delivered in a hearty repertoire that is simplicity itself. A confident hand at the stoves delivers well-defined flavours, whether it's a starter of scallops with crispy chicken wings, roasted carrots and carrot purée, or wild halibut served with cockles and mussels, peas, broad beans, and fennel velouté. Meatier fare might run to marinated lamb neck fillet with pearl barley, root vegetables, wild garlic, and red wine jus, while comforting desserts, such as warm toffee pudding with toffee sauce and salted caramel ice cream, or classic vanilla crème brûlée, complete the picture.

Chef Aidan McGrath **Owner** Aidan McGrath, Kate Sweeney **Seats** 50, Pr/dining room 40 **Times** 1-3.30/5-9, Closed Jan-Feb, Mon-Tue, L Wed-Fri **Prices** Starter €5-€11.50, Main €14.50-€27.90, Dessert €7.90-€8.50 **Notes** Restricted opening Oct-Dec & Mar, Sunday L, Vegetarian available, Children 4 yrs+

■ **NEWMARKET-ON-FERGUS**   Map 1 B3

Carrygerry Country House

◉ Modern Irish **NEW**

tel: 061 360500 **Carrygerry**
email: info@carrygerryhouse.com **web:** www.carrygerryhouse.com
dir: *Phone for directions*

Family-owned country hotel by the Shannon

Dating back to the 1790s, Carrygerry is a cream-coloured country house covered in contrasting shades of creeper, its elegant dining room extending into a conservatory space overlooking the Shannon estuary. On a clear day, you can see the local airport's control tower. It's a family-owned place run with welcoming warmth, and trades in traditional country-house cooking using much artisan and organic produce. The signature starter is a well-laden bowl of creamy seafood chowder, a satisfying prelude to the likes of lamb rump with roasted veg in port and redcurrant jus, or herb-crusted cod bedded on prawn risotto. Vegetarian main course might be a large baked flat cap mushroom filled with tomato, pine nuts and spinach in pesto dressing. Finish with feather-light sticky toffee pudding with banana ice cream and bittersweet toffee sauce, or Irish cheeses served with home-made fruity chutney.

Chef Niall Ennis **Owner** Niall & Gillian Ennis **Seats** 50 **Times** 6-10, Closed Xmas, Sun-Mon **Prices** Starter €6-€9, Main €16.50-€27, Dessert €6-€9, Service optional **Wines** 12 bottles over €30, 20 bottles under €30, 8 by glass **Parking** 25 **Notes** Sunday L fr €29, Vegetarian available, Children welcome

---

Dromoland Castle

◉◉ Traditional Irish, European ⱴ

tel: 061 368144
email: sales@dromoland.ie **web:** www.dromoland.ie
dir: *From Ennis take N18, follow signs for Shannon/Limerick. 7m follow Quin. Newmarket-on-Fergus sign. Hotel 0.5m. From Shannon take N18 towards Ennis*

Classical haute cuisine in a spectacular castle

It's a castle to be sure. Turrets and ramparts are present and correct at this top-end country-house hotel, with a golf course on the vast estate, a spa within its 15th-century walls, and plenty of good eating to be had. The Fig Tree restaurant is the informal dining option and there's a plush cocktail bar too, but the main deal is the Earl of Thomond restaurant, located in a spectacular room filled with antiques and oak-panelled period character and a resident harpist to soothe the soul. The cooking fits the bill with its unmistakably French accent and top-notch produce drawn from the estate itself and local suppliers. Roast pigeon breasts are served on a grilled polenta cake with pea purée, pickled Jerusalem artichoke and port sauce, followed by pan-fried John Dory fillets matched with saffron remoulade, capers, leeks and cucumber, and chilli and sage butter. Service is formal (expect a cloche or two) and everything looks wonderful on the plate. For dessert, mandarin ice cream is a foil to warm rhubarb crumble tart.

Chef David McCann **Owner** Dromoland Castle Holdings Ltd **Seats** 80, Pr/dining room 40 **Times** 7-10, Closed L all week (ex private bookings) **Prices** Starter €13-€19, Main €31-€37, Dessert €11-€15 **Wines** 210 bottles over €30, 14 bottles under €30, 10 by glass **Parking** 140 **Notes** Children welcome

---

COUNTY CORK

■ **BALLINGEARY**   Map 1 B2

Gougane Barra Hotel

◉ Irish, French

tel: 026 47069 **Gougane Barra**
email: info@gouganebarrahotel.com **web:** www.gouganebarrahotel.com
dir: *Off R584 between N22 at Macroom & N71 at Bantry. Take Keimaneigh junct for hotel*

Tried-and-true country cooking in hauntingly beautiful setting

The Cronin family has owned property in hauntingly beautiful Gougane Barra since Victorian times, when its potential as an idyllic retreat was first fully realised, though the present hotel dates back only to the 1930s. Those views over the lake towards the mountains of Cork look especially magnificent from the ample windows of the dining room, where fine seasonal artisan produce takes centre-stage. There are no airs and graces to the cooking, just careful presentation in tried-and-true formulas that never lack for support. Dingle Bay smoked salmon, or a double-act of Clonakilty black and De Róiste white pudding, with bacon and apple sauce, might fire the starting-gun, before grilled cutlets of exemplary West Cork lamb with colcannon and port gravy make their appearance. Fish could be herb-crusted hake with creamed leeks and peas in prawn sauce, with flourless pear frangipane and butterscotch ice cream to round things off in style.

Times 12.30-2.30/6-8.30, Closed 20 Oct-10 Apr, L Mon-Sat (ex group bookings)

BALLYCOTTON	Map 1 C2

Bayview Hotel

◎◎ Modern Irish, French

tel: 021 4646746
email: res@thebayviewhotel.com **web:** www.thebayviewhotel.com
dir: *At Castlemartyr on N25 (Cork-Waterford road) turn onto R632 to Garryvoe, then follow signs for Shanagarry & Ballycotton*

Imaginative contemporary cooking and sea views

Bayview Hotel has a prime position above the bay and the harbour, and expansive windows through which you can admire the whole, lovely panorama as you eat. It's a gently contemporary space with muted colour tones, looked over by a charming service team who are pretty much all local. There's a lot of local influence here, in fact, with a passion for the fruits of the countryside and sea around these parts. The seafood is landed down the road, farmers deliver their wares to the door, and the chef and his team know how to make the very best of them in creative, clearly-focused dishes. Start with the humble mackerel, perhaps, which comes three ways on a slate plate – pickled, smoked and pan-fried – with cucumber jelly, wasabi cream, mango mayonnaise and sesame crisps. Next up, roast rack and braised shank of lamb – nice and pink, perfectly rested – comes with spaghetti squash purée, glazed carrots and ras el hanout, and to finish, a well-made lemon tart hits the spot.

Times 1-3/7-9, Closed Nov-Apr, L Mon-Sat

BALLYLICKEY	Map 1 B2

Seaview House Hotel

◎◎ Modern, Traditional v

tel: 027 50073 & 50462
email: info@seaviewhousehotel.com **web:** www.seaviewhousehotel.com
dir: *3m N of Bantry towards Glengarriff, 70yds off main road, N71*

Polished cooking in a smart country-house hotel

The grand white-painted Seaview has the promised vista over Bantry Bay, glimpsed through the trees in the pretty gardens, but all the better from the first- and second-floor bedrooms. The restaurant is done out in a traditional manner, traversing three well-proportioned rooms, one of which is a conservatory with lush garden views. There's a good deal of local produce on the menu – crabs out of the bay, perhaps, or lamb from west Cork – and everything is handled with care and attention to detail. Start, perhaps, with a light and flavourful scallop mousse, served with a vermouth sauce and topped with the scallop roe. Next up, a superb piece of sole, grilled on the bone which is removed before service, and partnered with a caper butter served in a pot, plus mashed potatoes, wilted spinach, broccoli and cauliflower. Chocolate mousse with white chocolate sauce is a typical dessert.

Chef Eleanor O'Donavon **Owner** Kathleen O'Sullivan **Seats** 50
Times 12.30-1.45/7-9.30, Closed Nov-Mar, L Mon-Sat **Prices** Fixed L 3 course €30, Fixed D 3 course €45, Starter €5-€9.50, Main €25, Dessert €4.50-€6.50 **Wines** 10 by glass **Parking** 32 **Notes** Sunday L €30, Children welcome

BALTIMORE
Map 1 B1

Rolfs Country House
French, European

tel: 028 20289
email: info@rolfscountryhouse.com **web:** www.rolfscountryhouse.com
dir: *Into Baltimore, sharp left, follow restaurant signs, up hill*

Continental classics in a heavenly spot

Set in beautiful sub-tropical gardens overlooking Baltimore Harbour to Roaringwater Bay and Carbery's 100 islands, it is hardly surprising that the Haffner family have put down roots at their delightful 10-room hotel since 1979. Johannes Haffner is the current incumbent at the stoves, and he runs the culinary side of the operation with his sister Frederica. They bring dedication to ensure that produce is locally grown, reared and caught, organic whenever possible, and pastries and breads are all home-baked. The beamed and stone-walled restaurant provides a cosy and informal setting for a classic European repertoire: local mussels come with white wine, garlic and herb cream sauce, while fresh crab arrives with salad leaves from the garden and Marie Rose sauce. At main course, a brace of de-boned quail are flambéed with Cognac and matched with apricots and cream sauce, and to finish, there's caramelised apple tarte Tatin with cream.

Chef Johannes Haffner **Owner** Johannes Haffner **Seats** 50, Pr/dining room 14 **Times** 6-9.30, Closed Xmas, Mon-Tue (winter) **Prices** Fixed D 3 course €35, Starter €4.50-€13, Main €18-€29, Dessert €6.50-€9.50 **Wines** 21 bottles over €30, 16 bottles under €30, 12 by glass **Parking** 45 **Notes** Sunday L, Vegetarian available, Children welcome

CORK
Map 1 B2

Maryborough Hotel & Spa
Modern International ᴠ

tel: 021 4365555 **Maryborough Hill, Douglas**
email: info@maryborough.ie **web:** www.maryborough.com
dir: *From Jack Lynch Tunnel take 2nd exit signed Douglas. Right at 1st rdbt, follow Rochestown road to fingerpost rdbt. Left, hotel on left 0.5m up hill*

Contemporary country-house cooking in a luxury hotel

There's a whiff of glamour at this Georgian country-house hotel, with later additions tacked on, surrounded by 14 acres of well-maintained gardens and woodland. Refurbishment has given a sharp look to the bar and restaurant, called Bellini's, giving it a modern glossy sheen. Fresh, locally-sourced produce is the kitchen's stock-in-trade, with the long menu a list of bright and modern ideas. Thai-style salmon and cod patties served with lime aïoli and a rice noodle crisp, and terrine of confit duck, with herby pistachio crumble and beetroot and raspberry purée, are the sort of cleverly conceived starters to expect. Quality and accurate timings never fail to impress, seen in intricate main courses of rolled belly pork with spicy ribs, smoked apple, sweet cabbage and apple jus, and roast salmon steak stuffed with fennel mousse served with beetroot and salsify salad. Desserts end assertively with perhaps Baileys parfait with mocha syrup.

Chef Gerry Allen **Owner** Dan O'Sullivan **Seats** 170, Pr/dining room 60 **Times** 12.30-10, All-day dining, Closed 24-26 Dec **Prices** Fixed L 2 course fr €25, Fixed D 3 course fr €39, Starter €6.50-€12.30, Main €18.50-€27.50, Dessert €6.20-€8, Service optional **Wines** 15 bottles over €30, 13 bottles under €30, 8 by glass **Parking** 300 **Notes** Sunday L, Children welcome

DURRUS
Map 1 B2

Blairscove House & Restaurant
International

tel: 027 61127
email: mail@blairscove.ie **web:** www.blairscove.ie
dir: *R591 from Durrus to Crookhaven, in 1.5m restaurant on right through blue gate*

Buffet dining in a converted barn

On a promontory overlooking peaceful Dunmanus Bay, Blairscove is a west Cork country hotel brimming with charm. The main house is Georgian, and the accommodation and restaurant occupy a pretty development facing a lilypond, in what were the piggery, stables and barn. With its soaring ceiling and narrow windows, through which hay was once dispensed to the livestock, the dining room is full of character, not least from striking modern artworks, and so is the catering operation itself. Stroll over to the buffet, cruise-ship fashion, and help yourself to an array of hors d'oeuvres, before ordering from the main menu for the principal dish. That could be a half-rack of new season's lamb with its smoked sweetbreads, served with aubergine gratin in tomatoey sauce choron, or tuna poached in olive oil with toasted pine nuts and basil, with a vegetarian option of grilled aubergine and spiced chickpeas in walnut dressing, served with labneh. Then it's back to serve-yourself for puddings such as glazed frangipane tart, fruit salad or crème brûlée.

Chef Ronald Klötzer **Owner** P & S De Mey **Seats** 75, Pr/dining room 48 **Times** 6.30-9.30, Closed Nov-17 Mar, Sun-Mon, L all week **Prices** Fixed D 3 course €58, Service optional **Wines** 14 bottles over €30, 27 bottles under €30, 5 by glass **Parking** 30 **Notes** Vegetarian available, Children welcome

GARRYVOE
Map 1 C2

Garryvoe Hotel

◉ Modern Irish

tel: 021 4646718 **Ballycotton Bay, Castlemartyr**
email: res@garryvoehotel.com **web:** www.garryvoehotel.com
dir: *From N25 at Castlemartyr (Cork-Rosslare road) take R632 to Garryvoe*

Modern Irish cooking in a grand seafront hotel

Right on the seafront overlooking Ballycotton Bay, the Garryvoe is something of a local institution, but one that has moved with the times, modernising and aggrandising in the process. The high-ceilinged dining room naturally makes the most of those Cork coastal views, with well-spaced tables set with high-class accoutrements. The cooking might be described as modern Irish, but with no inhibitions about featuring retro dishes too. Start with crab croquette with chilli jam, citrus crab millefeuille and celeriac in wild mushroom bisque, moving on to a classic main course such as roast rump of local lamb with creamed cabbage and root veg in red wine reduction. The finale could be chocolate fondant with pistachio ice cream and raspberry coulis.

Times 1-2.30/6.30-8.45, Closed 24-25 Dec, L Mon-Sat

GOLEEN
Map 1 A1

The Heron's Cove

◉ Traditional Irish

tel: 028 35225 **The Harbour**
email: suehill@eircom.net **web:** www.heronscove.com
dir: *In Goleen village, turn left to harbour*

Unbroken sea views, super-fresh seafood and more

This delightful restaurant with rooms sits in an idyllic spot on Goleen harbour near to Mizen Head, where the lonely Fastnet Rock lighthouse beams out across the Atlantic at Ireland's most south westerly point. This is an exceptionally easy-going, friendly place, where you can eat out to sublime sea views on the balcony overlooking the tiny inlet in summer, and the kitchen takes time to source the best local ingredients that are the backbone of its output. The menu is as straightforward and untussy as its surroundings; typical starters are moules marinières, or crab cakes with wasabi mayonnaise, while main course could bring a local fish and meat combo of seared Dunmanus Bay scallops with Goleen lamb chops, creamy smoked bacon sauce, rosemary jus and potato cake, or roast leg of duck with Calvados and red cabbage. At the end, apricots and Cointreau add an indulgent note to bread-and-butter pudding in creamy custard.

Chef Irene Coughlan **Owner** Sue Hill **Seats** 30 **Times** 7-9.30, Closed Xmas, Oct-Apr (only open for pre-bookings), L all week (ex private functions) **Prices** Fixed D 3 course fr €27.50, Starter €5.50-€11.95, Main €16.75-€27.50, Dessert €6.95, Service optional **Wines** 25 bottles over €30, 35 bottles under €30, 2 by glass **Parking** 10 **Notes** Vegetarian available, Children welcome

KINSALE
Map 1 B2

The White House

◉ Traditional, International

tel: 021 4772125 **Pearse St, The Glen**
email: info@whitehouse-kinsale.ie **web:** www.whitehouse-kinsale.ie
dir: *Located in town centre*

Broadly appealing menu in a gastronomic hub

The White House has been in the hospitality game since the mid-19th century, and occupies a prime site in the centre of a town that holds a renowned Gourmet Festival every autumn. That means there's plenty to live up to in the gastronomic stakes, and the kitchen here rises to the occasion with a resourceful repertoire of modern Irish dishes that draws inspiration from far and wide, but is also a dab hand at Irish stews, fish pies and the like. Baked cod fillet is coated in Cajun spices for a satisfying main course accompanied by ratatouille topped with melted cheese. Local mussels make a fine starter, with a creamy dressing of white wine, garlic and lemongrass, and favourite puddings take in apple and cinnamon crumble with well-churned vanilla ice cream, or passionfruit and mango cheesecake.

Times 12-10, All-day dining, Closed 25 Dec

MALLOW
Map 1 B2

Springfort Hall Country House Hotel

◉ Modern, Irish

tel: 022 21278 & 30620
email: stay@springfort-hall.com **web:** www.springfort-hall.com
dir: *N20 onto R581 at Two Pot House, hotel 500mtrs on right*

Modern dining in a Georgian country house

The kitchen team in this immaculately-preserved Georgian country house certainly aren't scared of a bit of domestic hard graft: no corners are cut here — meat and fish is smoked in-house and everything is made from scratch from fresh, judiciously-sourced local produce. The setting for all of this laudable culinary endeavour is the palatial Lime Tree Restaurant, where all the detail of the original ornate plasterwork is picked out in gold paint and a crystal chandelier hangs above pristine white linen-clothed tables on polished timber flooring. The kitchen deals in a broadly modern Irish style of cookery, sending out ideas such as black pudding and glazed pork belly with pickled leeks, apple purée and cider jelly, followed by seared wild venison with butternut squash purée, Savoy cabbage, pickled mushrooms and candied pumpkin seeds.

Times 12-9.30, All-day dining, Closed 25-26 Dec

SHANAGARRY
Map 1 C2

Ballymaloe House

◉◉ Traditional Irish 🍷 NOTABLE WINE LIST

tel: 021 4652531
email: res@ballymaloe.ie **web:** www.ballymaloe.com
dir: *From R630 at Lakeview rdbt, left onto R631, left onto Cloyne. Continue for 2m on Ballycotton Rd*

Fabulous food in a classic country-house setting

Ivan and Myrtle Allen were way, way ahead of the curve some 50 years ago when they opened a restaurant in their farmhouse. No-one had heard the term 'farm to fork', nobody was doing anything quite like it. Fast forward to 2014 and there is a cookery school and hotel accommodation, and the idea of fresh produce brought to the table in double-quick time and served simply just seems normal. The place is still run by the Allen family (sadly, Ivan died in 1998) and its reputation has spread internationally. The restaurant is supplied by the farm and walled garden and the kitchen team have a wealth of superb foodstuffs to work with. The four dining rooms are traditional and comfortable. Cod landed at nearby Ballycotton might appear in a first course with salsa verde, while another starter combines a salad of garden leaves with Crozier blue cheese, pear and walnuts. Main-course Gubbeen ham is baked with Saint-Véran (a white Burgundy) and comes with pommes boulangère and spinach, and there's a pre-theatre menu, too.

Chef Gillian Hegarty **Owner** The Allen family **Seats** 110, Pr/dining room 50 **Times** 1-1.30/7-9.30, Closed Xmas, 6 Jan-6 Feb, Mon-Tue (Feb), L Wed (Feb), D Sun (Feb) **Prices** Fixed D 2 course fr €50, Service optional **Wines** 300 bottles over €30, 20 bottles under €30, 18 by glass **Parking** 100 **Notes** Fixed D 5 course €60-€75, Sunday L, Vegetarian available, Children 7 yrs+ D

COUNTY DONEGAL

DONEGAL
Map 1 B5

Harvey's Point Hotel

Modern, Irish

tel: 074 9722208 **Lough Eske**
email: stay@harveyspoint.com **web:** www.harveyspoint.com
dir: *From Donegal 2m towards Lifford, left at Harvey's Point sign, follow signs, take 3 right turns to hotel gates*

Contemporary Irish cooking overlooking Lough Eske

It was the heavenly setting that brought the Swiss family Gysling here to the shore of Lough Eske in the Donegal Hills to build their sprawling luxurious hotel complex in the late 1980s. Its Harvey's Restaurant has been made over recently, with an open kitchen allowing diners to follow the cheffy action, while the split-level layout democratically allows everyone to bask in those splendid lough views through a wall of full-length windows. The kitchen uses pedigree Irish produce to produce imaginative contemporary dishes realised with impressive technical ability. Lobster opens proceedings in a relatively traditional mode, delivering the luxurious crustacean encased in tortellini topped with shaved parmesan, truffle and lobster foam. Main-course grilled sea trout comes with a crab croquette and pearl barley in parsley sauce, or there may be venison loin with broccoli purée, red wine-braised salsify and poached plum. Proceedings come to a close with a tasting of orange, comprising a moist and spongy Tunisian orange cake with orange sorbet and millefeuille.

Chef Marc Gysling **Owner** Marc & Deirdre Gysling **Seats** 120 **Times** 12.30-9.30, All-day dining, Closed Sun-Tue (Nov-Apr), Sun, Wed (Jun-Oct) **Prices** Fixed L 2 course €19-€24, Fixed D 3 course €49-€55, Starter €8-€12, Main €25-€32, Dessert €8-€12, Service optional **Wines** 70 bottles over €30, 17 bottles under €30, 17 by glass **Parking** 200 **Notes** Sunday L €29-€35, Vegetarian available, Children welcome

The Red Door Country House

Modern, Traditional European

tel: 074 9360289 **Fahan, Inishowen**
email: info@thereddoor.ie **web:** www.thereddoor.ie
dir: *In Fahan village, church on right, The Red Door signed on left*

Confident modern Irish cooking by a lough

If it's a deal breaker, rest assured the front door is indeed red. With views over Lough Swilly, this country house is popular for weddings and business meetings, but also has a restaurant run by a hands-on team who bake their own bread and do a good deal of the meat butchery themselves. The series of dining rooms – including a sun room – have traditional finishes, with polished teak tables and smart linen napery. The menu shows a passion for the produce of this part of the world, along with sound classical training and some bright modern thinking. Seared scallops with Haven Smokehouse salmon comes with pickled cucumber, cumin-scented beetroot and courgette jelly in a smart first course, followed perhaps by rack of Donegal lamb with ratatouille and boulangère potatoes, or roast wild Irish hake served on the bone. To finish, strawberry and white chocolate mousse, or tarte Tatin with apple parfait and crème anglaise.

Times 12-4/5-close, Closed Mon-Wed, L Thu-Fri

DUNFANAGHY
Map 1 C6

Arnolds Hotel

Traditional

tel: 074 9136208 **Main St**
email: enquiries@arnoldshotel.com **web:** www.arnoldshotel.com
dir: *On N56 from Letterkenny, hotel on left on entering the village*

Good Irish cooking on the coast

In a village overlooking Sheephaven Bay, with Killahoey Beach a stroll away, Arnolds Hotel has been welcoming guests since 1922. It's a friendly, comfortable and comforting place, with open fires in the winter, and a restaurant capitalising on those coastal views. The kitchen takes a fuss-free approach, relying on quality raw materials and sound technique to make the most of flavours. To start there may be steamed mussels in garlic and dill cream, or balls of mushroom risotto coated in oatmeal, fried and dressed with white truffle and parmesan. Fish is well handled, seen in baked fillet of turbot served simply on pea purée with red pesto, or there might be honey-glazed roast duckling on rösti with a rich orange sauce, or fillet steak with grilled mushrooms, mustard mash and a bourbon and pepper cream. Desserts are of the home-baked variety, including Arnolds Hotel Pavlova.

Times 6-9.30, Closed Nov-Apr (excl New Year)

LETTERKENNY
Map 1 C5

Radisson Blu Hotel Letterkenny

Modern Irish

tel: 074 9194444 **Paddy Harte Rd**
email: info.letterkenny@radissonblu.com **web:** www.radissonblu.ie/hotel-letterkenny
dir: *N14 into Letterkenny. At Polestar Rdbt take 1st exit, to hotel*

Unpretentious cooking in a modern hotel

A modern hotel of glass and steel, this outpost of the Radisson Blu group is in the centre of Letterkenny. The Port Bar & Grill can sort you out for steak sandwich or burger, but the TriBeCa Restaurant catches the eye. The bright and smart dining room has a large screen showing the action in the kitchen, which whets the appetite for the likes of duck confit with braised red cabbage and apple and cinnamon purée that is to come. The menu takes inspiration from modern brasserie cooking to deliver the likes of salad of Clonakilty black pudding with sauté potatoes and poached egg, followed by glazed rump of Slaney Valley lamb (with roasted sweet potatoes and pea purée), or sirloin steak with an accompanying red onion tarte Tatin. Finish with white chocolate crème brûlée or Irish cheeses.

Chef Collette Langan **Owner** Paul Byrne **Seats** 120, Pr/dining room 320 **Times** 12.30-3.30/6-9.30, Closed L Mon-Sat **Prices** Fixed D 3 course €19.95-€27.50, Starter €4.50-€9.95, Main €13.95-€24.95, Dessert €5.95-€10.95, Service optional **Wines** 4 bottles over €30, 20 bottles under €30, 6 by glass **Parking** 150 **Notes** Early bird menu 6-7pm €19.95, Fixed L 2/3 course Sun only, Sunday L €12.95-€23.95, Vegetarian available, Children welcome

MOVILLE
Map 1 C6

Redcastle Hotel, Golf & Spa Resort

Modern, International

tel: 074 9385555 **Inishowen Peninsula**
email: info@redcastlehotel.com **web:** www.redcastlehotel.com
dir: *On R238 between Derby & Greencastle*

Traditionally based Irish cooking with loughside views

The Redcastle estate can trace its lineage all the way back to a 16th-century proprietor called Cathal O'Doherty. At one point, it was owned by a Pennsylvania farming family, but today it makes a superbly located northwestern seafront hotel in the modern boutique style. A terrace overlooking Lough Foyle is a covetable place for a sundowner, informal eating is offered in the Captain's Bar, or repair to the Edge dining room for some traditionally-based Irish cooking with modern flourishes. Start with a tartlet of Cooleeney camembert and fennel marmalade with crispy bacon, cranberries and tarragon, or smoked chicken Caesar with all the trimmings. Mains might take an oriental theme for roast cod with pak choi, mussels and ginger, and lemongrass jelly, or else aim to fortify by means of slow-braised lamb shank with roast celeriac and champ on tomato fondue. Conclude with Irish cheeses, or blackberry Bakewell sponge with cardamom custard and blackberry sorbet.

Chef Gordon Smyth **Owner** Pisona Developments **Seats** 120
Times 12-4/6-9.30, Closed 25 Dec **Prices** Prices not confirmed, Service optional
Wines 16 bottles over €30, 11 bottles under €30, 6 by glass **Parking** 360 **Notes** Early bird offer off peak, Sunday L, Vegetarian available, Children welcome

---

| RATHMULLAN | Map 1 C6 |

Rathmullan House

◎◎ Modern Irish

tel: 074 9158188
email: info@rathmullanhouse.com **web:** www.rathmullanhouse.com
dir: R245 Letterkenny to Ramelton, over bridge right onto R247 to Rathmullan. On entering village turn at Mace shop through village. Gates of hotel on right

Modern Irish cooking overlooking the lough

A grand white-painted late-Georgian house on the Fanad peninsula in the far northwest, overlooking Lough Swilly, Rathmullan was once home to one of Ireland's banking dynasties, but was acquired by the Wheeler family in 1962. It's beautifully maintained, with attractive, colourful interiors and a dining room recently restyled as the Cook and Gardener. Antique tables now bare all where once they went linened, though the tented ceiling stays. Menus are now à la carte, and the new name reflects the links between the kitchen and the hotel's own walled garden where much of the produce is grown. Modern Irish cooking draws, like its British counterpart, on other culinary traditions, so expect Gubbeen chorizo with a wild mushroom risotto cake in apple sauce, as a prelude to monkfish with Lyonnaise potatoes, lemon aïoli and kalamata tapenade, or free-range chicken breast with potato gratin and braised Puy lentils. More traditional notes are sounded in pork shoulder with colcannon, and there are Irish cheeses, as well as apple-treacle tart, to finish.

Chef Michael Harley **Owner** The Wheeler family **Seats** 70, Pr/dining room 30
Times 1-2.30/7-8.45, Closed Jan-mid Feb, Xmas **Prices** Fixed L 2 course €20-€35, Fixed D 3 course €33-€60, Starter €8-€15, Main €16-€27.50, Dessert €8-€11.50
Wines 20 bottles over €30, 15 bottles under €30, 10 by glass **Parking** 40
Notes Vegetarian available, Children welcome

DUBLIN

| DUBLIN | Map 1 D4 |

Ashling Hotel, Dublin

◎ Irish, European

tel: 01 6772324 **Parkgate St**
email: info@ashlinghotel.ie **web:** www.ashlinghotel.ie
dir: Close to River Liffey, opposite Heuston Station

Skilfully turned-out modern cooking near Dublin Zoo

The Ashling is a large, modern and glitzy hotel near Phoenix Park and Dublin Zoo, where Chesterfields Restaurant occupies a spacious, softly lit room with plushly upholstered dining chairs and a busily patterned carpet. The kitchen has some success with its combinations of flavours and textures, and dishes are noted for their accurate timings. This is shown in seared scallops with pancetta crisps, cauliflower purée and hollandaise, for instance, then roast breast of guinea fowl with crisp gnocchi, sautéed curly kale and Madeira jus. Prime native produce is the stock-in-trade, among it carpaccio of wild Wicklow venison with raspberry

vinaigrette and a pomegranate and pine nut salsa, and line-caught fillet of cod in Parma ham served with spinach and brown shrimp ravioli, fine beans and lemon cream. Irish farmhouse cheeses bring up the rear along with puddings along the lines of autumn berry Eton Mess and classic crème brûlée.

Chef Gary Costello **Owner** Foxfield Inns Ltd **Seats** 180
Times 12.30-2.30/6-9.30, Closed 24-26 Dec **Prices** Fixed L 2 course €11.95-€16.95, Fixed D 3 course €25-€29, Starter €5.25-€10.50, Main €14.50-€29, Dessert €6.50-€9, Service optional **Wines** 8 bottles over €30, 8 bottles under €30, 6 by glass **Parking** 80 **Notes** Sunday L €14.95-€19.95, Vegetarian available, Children welcome

---

Balfes at The Westbury Hotel

◎ Contemporary Irish **NEW**

tel: 01 6463353 **Grafton St**
email: reserve@balfes.ie
dir: Phone for directions

Buzzy all-day dining venue with creative menu

The second dining option at the Westbury Hotel (after the main restaurant named after Oscar Wilde), Balfes is an all-day operation that takes its inspiration from Paris and New York. With its own street entrance, and pavement tables, it's an affable place with white walls, dark leather seats and a long bar counter down one end. Kick off in the morning with an omelette or blueberry pancakes with maple syrup or pop in for a lunch of roast sea trout with yuzu salt, asparagus and citrus hollandaise. The Josper oven turns out grilled gambas, served with harissa aïoli, and breast of free-range chicken partnered with chorizo and white bean cassoulet. A long list of cocktails, draught and bottled beers, and a serviceable wine list fit the bill whatever time of day you're passing. For dessert, Josper grilled pineapple with coconut competes for your attention with chocolate fondant with almond ice cream.

Chef Cathal Dunne **Owner** Doyle Collection **Seats** 140 **Times** 12-10.30, All-day dining, Closed 25 Dec, Good Fri **Prices** Fixed L 2 course €14-€50, Fixed D 3 course €25-€46, Starter €7-€15, Main €16-€29, Dessert €7.50 **Wines** 24 bottles over €30, 4 bottles under €30, 8 by glass **Parking** St Stephen's Green **Notes** Sunday L €10.50-€29, Vegetarian available, Children welcome

---

Castleknock Hotel & Country Club

◎ European, International

tel: 01 6406300 **Porterstown Rd, Castleknock**
email: info@chcc.ie **web:** www.castleknockhotel.com
dir: M50 from airport. Exit at junct 6 (signed Navan, Cavan & M3) onto N3, becomes M3. Exit at junct 3. At top of slip road 1st left signed Consilla (R121). At T-junct left. 1km to hotel

Contemporary dining in a country club setting

Just 15 minutes from the centre of Dublin, Castleknock is a country club with plenty of pizazz. The green fairways of the 18-hole golf course blanket the grounds, while inside it is classy and pristine, with all the spa facilities you can imagine. There are several eating and drinking options, the pick of the bunch being the Park Restaurant, with its elegant finish. There are floor-to-ceiling windows with swagged curtains, richly-coloured walls and large artworks, plus burnished darkwood tables. Steak has long been the mainstay of the kitchen's output, but there is a lot more going on besides, and a heap of regional produce to ensure a local flavour. Confit of wild Wicklow rabbit with apple gel, hazelnuts, Granny Smith apple and watercress is a creative first course, followed perhaps by roast rump of Cooley lamb – a fine piece of meat, soft and tender – and served with broad beans, feta and a warm potato salad.

Chef Neil Kearns **Owner** FBD Hotels & Resorts **Seats** 65, Pr/dining room 400
Times 12.30-3/5.30-10, Closed 24-26 Dec **Prices** Fixed L 2 course €27.50, Fixed D 3 course €25-€37.50, Starter €7.50-€13.50, Main €18.50-€28.95, Dessert €7.50-€9.50 **Wines** 12 by glass **Parking** 200 **Notes** Fixed 4 course D 2 people with wine €69, Sunday L €27.50, Vegetarian available, Children welcome

DUBLIN *continued*

The Cellar Restaurant

@@ Modern Irish

tel: 01 6030600 & 6030630 **Merrion Hotel, Upper Merrion St**
email: info@merrionhotel.com
dir: *Top Upper Merrion Street, opp Government buildings*

Modern Irish cooking down below

Down below the gleaming-white expanses of the Merrion Hotel, The Cellar is where to come for modern Irish cooking. If you're expecting crepuscular gloom down here, think again. A vision of white-linened tables and fresh flowers is in prospect, and the cooking starts as it means to go on, with a bracing salad of quinoa, pomegranate, feta and spinach, dressed in cider vinegar. An alternative way to begin might be with dashi-seasoned calamari with fennel salad and citrus aïoli, and then mains wheel out the big guns of tradition for 28-day dry-aged rib-eye in Café de Paris butter with broccoli hollandaise, or a whole black sole from Kilmore Quay with garlicky spinach in lemon and caper beurre noisette. Or mix it up modern-style for seared halibut with lardo, charred cauliflower, salsify and broad beans in beurre rouge. Desserts with attitude include a chocolate-orange crémeux made with Valrhona, along with hazelnuts and a buttermilk and coconut sorbet. A fixed-price lunch deal comes with the full regalia of appetisers and pre-desserts.

Chef Ed Cooney **Times** 12.30-2/6-10, Closed L Sat **Prices** Prices not confirmed **Parking** Merrion Sq **Notes** Sun brunch 12.30-2.30pm, Vegetarian available, Children welcome

Crowne Plaza Dublin Northwood

@ Asian Fusion, International

tel: 01 8628888 **Northwood Park, Santry Demesne, Santry**
email: info@crowneplazadublin.ie **web:** www.cpdublin.crowneplaza.com
dir: *M50 junct 4, left into Northwood Park, 1km, hotel on left*

East-West fusion food near the airport

It's just a short jaunt via the complimentary shuttle-bus from Dublin airport to the Crowne Plaza, which sits regally amid 85 acres of mature woodland in Northwood Park. The whole place is done in swish contemporary style, including the Touzai restaurant, where east-meets-west for a menu of creative fusion cooking. That could mean prawn and rice noodle salad in Thai dressing to start, and then nasi goreng with chicken and seafood, or pork ribs with spring onion dressing and champ. Wok dishes come in starter or main sizes, but if you're determined to stay west, look to ham hock terrine with sourdough bread and piccalilli, and cod gratinated in mozzarella with saffron orzo. Mix it up for dessert with a lemongrass brûlée and vanilla ice cream.

Chef Logan Irwin **Owner** Tifco Ltd **Seats** 156, Pr/dining room 15 **Times** 5.30-10, Closed 25 Dec, L all week **Prices** Fixed D 3 course €24.95-€45, Starter €5.50-€11.95, Main €12.95-€28.95, Dessert €6.50-€9.95 **Wines** 34 bottles over €30, 17 bottles under €30, 15 by glass **Parking** 360 **Notes** Vegetarian available, Children welcome

Crowne Plaza Hotel Dublin – Blanchardstown

@ Italian, European, International

tel: 01 8977777 **The Blanchardstown Centre**
email: info@cpireland.crowneplaza.com **web:** www.cpireland.ie
dir: *M50 junct 6 (Blanchardstown)*

Italian dining in a funky modern venue

The Blanchardstown branch of the Crowne Plaza empire fits the bill, whether you're suited and booted for business, or dropping by to refuel after a hit of retail therapy in the shops and boutiques of the nearby Blanchardstown Centre. The Forchetta

restaurant works a loud and proud contemporary look with bold floral wallpaper and bare darkwood tables – it's a buzzy, breezy setting that suits the crowd-pleasing modern Italian menu. The usual suspects from the world of pizza and pasta are all present and correct, or you might ignore convention and start with a fish soup involving mussels, clams, prawns, salmon and cod in a tomato and white wine broth, and follow with a chargrilled Irish steak, or lamb shank roasted in red wine, garlic and rosemary. Puddings are Italian classics – pannacotta or tiramisù, for example.

Chef Jason Hayde **Owner** Tifco Hotels **Seats** 100, Pr/dining room 45 **Times** 12-2.30/6-9.30, Closed 24-25 Dec **Prices** Fixed L 2 course €19.95-€35, Fixed D 3 course €24.95-€55, Starter €7-€10.50, Main €10.50-€26.95, Dessert €6, Service optional **Wines** 20 bottles over €30, 27 bottles under €30, 6 by glass **Parking** 200 **Notes** Carvery L served Sanctuary Bar, Vegetarian available, Children welcome

Fahrenheit Restaurant

@ Modern Irish

tel: 01 8332321 & 8523263 **Clontarf Castle Hotel, Castle Av, Clontarf**
email: mwoods@clontarfcastle.ie **web:** www.clontarfcastle.ie
dir: *From Dublin city. O'Connell St, head south onto O'Connell St lower, left onto Abbey St lower, continue onto R105 at Clontarf Rd left onto Castle Ave, left after 500mtrs*

Modern Irish cookery in a boutique castle

Ten minutes out of the city centre, Dublin's Clontarf Castle Hotel is a beguiling mix of ancient structure and modern boutique luxiness. Dating from the 12th century, it served as headquarters for the English army's quartermaster-general during Cromwell's rampages, but achieved its present apogee on reopening as an upmarket hotel in 1998. The Fahrenheit Grill is the destination restaurant, a dramatic showcase room for some striking modern Irish cookery. Kick off with a breakfast salad of crisp-fried egg, bacon and Clonakilty black pudding, or scallops and pork belly with sweet potato purée. Move on to substantial main courses such as breast and confit leg of duck with carrot purée in vanilla and cardamom jus, or cod with a cassoulet of chorizo, white beans and tomato, and saffron mash. It all concludes with Bramley apple crumble and salted caramel ice cream, wild honey parfait with macerated figs, or lemon pannacotta with blackberry compôte.

Chef Stuart Heeney **Owner** Gerry Houlihan **Seats** 90, Pr/dining room 20 **Times** 5.30-10, Closed L all week (private pre-booked only) **Prices** Prices not confirmed, Service optional **Wines** 15 bottles over €30, 38 bottles under €30, 13 by glass **Parking** 200 **Notes** Early bird 2/3 course €19.20/€24, Table d'hôte menu 3 course, Vegetarian available, Children welcome

Radisson Blu St Helens Hotel

@ Traditional Italian, International

tel: 01 218 6000 & 218 6032 **Stillorgan Rd**
email: talavera@radissonblu.com **web:** www.radissonblu.ie/sthelenshotel-dublin
dir: *On N11 Stillorgan dual carriageway*

Regional and classic Italian cooking in a grand house

This grand old house dates from the middle of the 17th century but has all the expected 21st-century mod cons of a Radisson Blu. There's a restaurant called Talavera, which serves up smart Italian food in a series of rooms with either traditional country-house decor or rather more contemporary chic. There's also an all-day Orangery Bar for a cocktail or afternoon tea. The main restaurant focuses on the cooking of Lombardy, from whence the chef hails, and there's a tasting menu which includes a risotto – of course – and maybe osso buco as the star attraction. Otherwise you might start with a classic carpaccio, or spaghetti with tomato sauce and a generous amount of seafood (mussels, squid and prawns). Move on to noisettes of lamb with a fresh mint dressing and chorizo-flavoured mash, or pan-fried brill with asparagus confit, tomatoes and capers. Finish with rhubarb tart or tiramisù.

Chef Giancarlo Anselmi **Owner** Cosgrave Developments **Seats** 120, Pr/dining room 96 **Times** 5.30-9.30 **Prices** Prices not confirmed, Service optional **Wines** 12 bottles over €30, 3 bottles under €30, 11 by glass **Parking** 220 **Notes** Sunday L, Vegetarian available, Children welcome

Restaurant Patrick Guilbaud

⊛⊛⊛⊛ – see page 726

Roganstown Hotel and Country Club

⊛ European

tel: 01 8433118 **Naul Rd, Sword**
email: info@roganstown.com **web:** www.roganstown.com
dir: Phone for directions

Modern cooking in a golfing resort

A sprawling resort with golf, spa and conference facilities, Roganstown is also home to the impressive McLoughlins Restaurant. Located in a wood-panelled room within the hotel (the original part of the structure was a farmhouse in a former life), there's plenty of room between well-dressed tables. The kitchen seeks out first-class ingredients and delivers a menu that has ambition and a contemporary feel. A first-course dish of lightly smoked scallops (nicely seared) arrive under a cloche to make an impression, served with a silky purée of minted peas and some pickled vegetables. Next up, among main courses, suckling pig cutlets are tender and moist, coming with a 'Pomme William', braised red cabbage and sweet potato purée, while a fishy main might be pan-fried salmon with a shellfish velouté. There are modern cooking techniques on show, not least in a dessert of saffron-poached pear with textures of raspberry.

Chef Iain McFadden **Owner** Ian McGuiness **Seats** 100, Pr/dining room 30 **Times** 12.30-4.30/5-10, Closed Xmas, Mon-Tue, L Wed-Sat **Prices** Fixed D 3 course €24.95-€30, Service optional **Wines** 3 bottles over €30, 22 bottles under €30, 8 by glass **Notes** Sunday L €19.95-€24.95, Vegetarian available, Children welcome

The Shelbourne Dublin, a Renaissance Hotel

⊛⊛ Traditional Irish, European

tel: 01 6634500 **27 St Stephen's Green**
email: rhi.dubbr.dts@renaissancehotels.com **web:** www.theshelbourne.ie
dir: M1 to city centre, along Parnell St to O'Connell St towards Trinity College, 3rd right into Kildare St, hotel on left

Grand modern hotel with seafood, steaks and modernist dishes too

In a sign that all bases are covered, the Shelbourne retains a 'genealogy butler', to research your family background, should you decide to delve into who you think you are. This grand modern hotel is in a prime location on St Stephen's Green, the expansive garden square at the heart of the capital, offering a range of eating and drinking options culminating in the tip-top Saddle Room. Here a menu of modern brasserie dishes specialises in seafood (including generously loaded platters) and majestic 32-day aged beef (two of you might set about a pound of Chateaubriand). Modernists might look further afield to the likes of seared foie gras in Banyuls with fig compôte, or Knockdrinna goats' cheese with pickled courgette in beetroot emulsion. Mains might include rabbit loin wrapped in Alsace bacon with kale and puréed carrots, or roast halibut with baby leeks in chilled oyster cream. A five-course taster offers a tour of the more adventurous dishes, while puddings take a traditional line for rhubarb crumble, or blackberry mousse with caramelised apple.

Chef Garry Hughes **Owner** Renaissance Hotels **Seats** 120, Pr/dining room 20 **Times** 12.30-2.30/5.45-10.30 **Prices** Fixed L 2 course €21.95-€24.95, Fixed D 3 course €29.95-€42, Tasting menu €65, Starter €7.95-€20, Main €17.95-€56, Dessert €8.95-€15.95 **Wines** 100 bottles over €30, 10 bottles under €30, 12 by glass **Parking** Valet parking **Notes** Pre-theatre menu 2/3 course 6-7pm, Sunday L €24.95-€29.95, Vegetarian available, Children welcome

The Talbot Hotel Stillorgan

⊛ Traditional Mediterranean, International

tel: 01 2001800 & 2001822 **Stillorgan Rd**
email: info@stillorganpark.com **web:** www.stillorganpark.com
dir: On N11 follow signs for Wexford, pass RTE studios on left, through next 5 sets of lights. Hotel on left

Gently modern cooking in a spa hotel

A hotel with a spa and wedding packages among its attractions, Stillorgan Park is also home to the Purple Sage restaurant, with its breezy vibe and contemporary finish. There are plenty of nooks and crannies in the split-level room if you're after a bit of privacy. The menu takes a gently modern tack, nothing too wacky, and with classic combinations at the heart of the action. Pan-fried venison sausage, for example, might turn up with root vegetable purée and cranberry compôte, or a smoked trout and prawn mousse. Grilled breast of pheasant with a chestnut and apricot stuffing is a wintery main course, or go for roasted monkfish with black truffle and a fresh herb risotto. For dessert, lemon and lime frangipane tart served with vanilla ice cream has a satisfying tartness, and there are Irish cheeses, too.

Chef Enda Dunne **Owner** Des Pettitt **Seats** 140, Pr/dining room 60 **Times** 12-2.30/5.45-10.15, Closed 25 Dec, L Sat, D Sun-Mon **Prices** Prices not confirmed, Service optional **Wines** 5 bottles over €30, 20 bottles under €30, 14 by glass **Parking** 300 **Notes** Early bird menu 2/3 course €21/€25, Sunday L, Vegetarian available, Children welcome

The Westbury Hotel

⊛⊛ Modern Irish

tel: 01 6791122 **Grafton St**
email: westbury@doylecollection.com **web:** www.doylecollection.com
dir: Adjacent to Grafton St, half way between Trinity College & St Stephen's Green

Crowd-pleasing cooking in a swish hotel

This prestigious city-centre hotel has a fine-dining restaurant that is dedicated to Oscar Wilde with a bust of the writer and poet, and references continuing into the artworks dotted around the swishly decorated and furnished room. Waterford crystal chandeliers above tables laid with crisp white linen, sparkling silver and glassware, make a glossy setting for a wide-ranging menu of comfort-oriented modern brasserie dishes. The kitchen picks the cream of Ireland's produce and showcases it in a Dublin Bay prawn cocktail with Marie Rose sauce and guacamole. Otherwise, kick off with Carlingford Lough oysters or Irish smoked salmon with caper berries and lemon crème fraîche. Staying in seafood mode, main course delivers well-timed stone bass matched with sauce vierge and baby fennel, or you might go for meaty mains – perhaps a steak or herb-crusted rack of lamb from the grill, or duck confit with pickled Puy lentils and parsnip purée. Puddings are a strong suit when they include an authentic rendition of classic crema Catalana, or vanilla pannacotta with poached rhubarb.

Times 6.30-10.30, Closed Sun-Mon, L all week

Restaurant Patrick Guilbaud ✿✿✿✿

DUBLIN   Map 1 D4

Modern French V

tel: 01 6764192 **Merrion Hotel, 21 Upper Merrion St,**
email: info@restaurantpatrickguilbaud.ie
web: www.restaurantpatrickguilbaud.ie
dir: *Opposite government buildings, next to Merrion Hotel*

Outstanding French cooking at the pre-eminent Dublin address

Paris-born Monsieur Guilbaud opened his restaurant in 1981 with the aim of bringing haute cuisine to Dublin at a time when it probably seemed like a 'brave' move. Bravery is rewarded sometimes and that is very much the case here, for Restaurant Patrick Guilbaud has been at the forefront of Irish fine dining ever since. The smart Merrion Hotel is the second location for the restaurant, having moved here in the late 1990s, and it seems like a natural fit. The swish Georgian townhouse hotel has a luxurious traditional interior, but Restaurant Patrick Guilbaud is rather more contemporary in its demeanour – colourful artworks with soothingly neutral colour tones, watched over by a professional and engaging service team. The kitchen is headed up by Guillaume Lebrun, as has always been the case, and he delivers modern French food of craft and creativity. There's nothing here to shake the foundations of classic French cuisine, but the kitchen's output is modern and in touch with our times. Choose between the sizable à la carte or four- and eight-course dégustation menus. Start with blue lobster ravioli, which arrives in a coconut-scented lobster cream with toasted almonds and a split curry dressing, or go for grilled scallops from Castletownbere in County Cork, served with

bacon and cabbage. The quality of the ingredients used is impressive throughout, as is presentation, which is never less than eye-catching. Main course offers paupiette of black sole with sweet garden peas, tomato dashi and minted Viennoise, or roast Brittany squab pigeon, which is partnered with spelt cooked in a rich consommé, violet artichokes and spicy Speculoos biscuit. A classic fillet of Irish beef with roast foie gras and Madeira and truffle jus will satisfy traditionalists. Vegetarians fare very well here indeed, with a number of bespoke options such as truffle baked potato tortellini with sweet pea and truffle emulsion up for grabs. The same level of skill and creativity is attained at dessert stage, where an assiette of Valrhona chocolate is hard to ignore (served with salted caramel ganache and praline ice cream), with raspberry rose with sheep's yogurt sorbet a lighter option. The cheese course is perhaps unsurprisingly a journey through the very best of France and Ireland. The wine list covers the whole world while ensuring that France stays centre stage.

Chef Guillaume Lebrun **Owner** Patrick Guilbaud, Guillaume Lebrun, Stéphane Robin **Seats** 80, Pr/dining room 25 **Times** 12.30-2.15/7.30-10.15, Closed 25 Dec, 1st wk Jan, Sun-Mon **Prices** Fixed L 2 course €40, Tasting menu €98-€185, Service optional **Wines** 1200 bottles over €30, 20 by glass **Parking** in square **Notes** ALC menu 2/3/4 course €85/€105/€130, Children welcome

COUNTY DUBLIN

KILLINEY
Map 1 D4

Fitzpatrick Castle Hotel
Modern European

tel: 01 2305400
email: info@fitzpatricks.com **web:** www.fitzpatrickcastle.com
dir: *From Dun Laoghaire port turn left, on coast road right at lights, left at next lights. Follow to Dalkey, right at Ivory pub, immediate left, up hill, hotel at top*

Country-house cooking with views over Dublin Bay

The castellated house was built in the 18th century, and has had something of a martial career, being successively owned by a parade of army officers, the scene of fighting during the Easter Rising, and having troops stationed here during World War II. Things are rather calmer now, as befits the tranquil prospect of its perch overlooking Dublin Bay. A range of hospitable dining venues includes the Grill, housed in the former dungeon, where wine-red banquettes and exposed stone walls are the background for a menu of well-wrought modern brasserie cooking. There's no wild experimentation here, just good honest preparations of prime materials. Expect rosemary-scented seared scallops on an underlay of wilted spinach, as the prelude to pistachio-crusted rack of lamb on champ, or monkfish with minted pea purée in saffron sauce. Finish with frozen winter berries and coconut ice cream.

Chef Phil Whittal **Owner** Eithne Fitzpatrick **Seats** 75 **Times** 6-9.30, Closed 25 Dec, L Mon-Sat **Prices** Prices not confirmed, Service optional **Wines** 7 bottles over €30, 12 bottles under €30, 11 by glass **Parking** 200 **Notes** Sunday L, Vegetarian available, Children welcome

COUNTY GALWAY

BARNA
Map 1 B3

The Pins at The Twelve
International, Modern Irish

tel: 091 597000 **Barna Village**
email: enquire@thetwelvehotel.ie
dir: *Coast road Barna village, 10 mins from Galway*

Eclectic dining in a design-led venue

Part of the boutique-style Twelve Hotel, gastronomes will be pleased to learn that The Pins is actually an unusual amalgam of bar, bakery, bistro and pizzeria. If you want to keep things simple, the Dozzina pizzeria turns out authentic Neapolitan-style thin and crispy pizzas made in an oven hewn from Vesuvian stone, but you can put the kitchen through its paces via a menu of uncomplicated modern gastro pub: – dishes that champions regional suppliers. Start with something like a terrine of pork belly, pistachio and black pudding with pear compôte, followed by pan-seared hake with gratinated oyster, fondant potato, creamed leeks and prawn bisque, or slow-braised lamb shank with coriander couscous, grilled vegetables, apricot purée and toasted almonds. Dessert might be bread-and-butter pudding with caramel sauce. For more ambitious contemporary cooking, trade up to the Upstairs@West Restaurant.

Chef Martin O'Donnell **Owner** Fergus O'Halloran **Seats** 140, Pr/dining room 20 **Times** breakfast-10, All-day dining **Prices** Fixed L 2 course €22, Fixed D 3 course €25, Starter €5.50-€13, Main €12.50-€24, Dessert €5.50-€9, Service optional **Wines** 300 bottles over €30, 60 bottles under €30, 35 by glass **Parking** 120 **Notes** BBQ menu options private functions, Pre-theatre menu, Sunday L €12-€22, Vegetarian available, Children welcome

Upstairs@West, The Twelve
Modern Irish NOTABLE WINE LIST

tel: 091 597000 **Barna Village**
email: west@thetwelvehotel.ie **web:** www.thetwelvehotel.ie
dir: *Coast road Barna village, 10 mins from Galway*

Well-conceived modern dishes in a seaside hotel

A boutique hotel with bags of contemporary swagger, The Twelve is in a coastal area just a short distance from the centre of Galway. There's a lot going on: a cool bar, a bakery selling artisan breads and cakes, a pizza place, and not forgetting the stylish bedrooms. The main dining action takes place in the Upstairs restaurant, which is focused on seasonal regional produce and wines from around the world. Billed as 'small plates' or 'large plates', kick off with Marty's Killarly harbour mussels in a Pernod and shallot reduction, served with a home-made seaweed soda farl, or go for the crisp pork belly with Connemara scallops, apple purée and cider reduction. Those larger plates follow the same path, delivering appealing plates with bang-on flavours and a contemporary flourish; Glin Valley chicken, maybe, with Colcannon gnocchi and chicken foam, or a côte de boeuf for two to share, with triple-cooked chips and Cashel Blue béarnaise. Finish with a lemon and lavender pudding with whiskey wine gums and lemon sherbet, and the artisan Irish cheeses are well worth checking out.

Chef Martin O'Donnell **Owner** Fergus O'Halloran **Seats** 94, Pr/dining room 100 **Times** 1-4/6-10, Closed Mon-Tue, L Wed-Fri **Prices** Tasting menu €30-€40, Starter €7-€14, Main €17-€33, Dessert €7-€10, Service optional **Wines** 300 bottles over €30, 60 bottles under €30, 35 by glass **Parking** 120 **Notes** Gourmet menu 5 course with wine, Wine tutorials, Sunday L €8-€20, Vegetarian available, Children welcome

CASHEL
Map 1 A4

Cashel House
Traditional Irish, French

tel: 095 31001
email: res@cashel-house-hotel.com **web:** www.cashel-house-hotel.com
dir: *S of N59. 1m W of Recess*

A heavenly location and top-notch regional produce

Standing at the head of Cashel Bay in 50 acres of delightful, gardens, Cashel House is a gracious 19th-century country house that has been in the hands of the McEvilly family since 1968. When you have worked up a serious appetite on the local golf courses and woodland walks, the restaurant offers a repertoire of French-accented classics, served in either an airy conservatory extension, or a polished traditional setting amid antiques and artworks. Connemara's lakes, rivers, hillsides and the fishermen out in the bay supply the kitchen with the finest produce it could wish for, which is handled simply and with the confidence to let the flavours do the

continued

CASHEL *continued*

talking. A puff pastry parcel containing quail breast wrapped in ham with a creamy brandy sauce sets the ball rolling, before a sorbet (champagne, perhaps), then pan-fried monkfish comes with tomato, saffron and coriander concasse, or there could be roast rack of Connemara lamb with Guinness and honey sauce. White and dark chocolate terrine with orange liqueur sauce makes a fine finale.

Chef Arturo Tillo **Owner** Kay McEvilly & family **Seats** 70, Pr/dining room 20 **Times** 12.30-2.30/6.30-9, Closed 2 Jan-12 Feb **Prices** Fixed D 3 course fr €35, Starter €6-€24, Main €15.50-€38, Dessert €7.50-€12.50 **Wines** 5 by glass **Parking** 30 **Notes** 5 course D €55, Sunday L, Vegetarian available, Children welcome

CLIFDEN   Map 1 A4

Abbeyglen Castle Hotel

French, International

tel: 095 21201 **Sky Rd**
email: info@abbeyglen.ie **web:** www.abbeyglen.ie
dir: *N59 from Galway towards Clifden. Hotel 1km from Clifden on Sky Rd*

Fresh local produce in a charming old property

The crenallated Victorian fantasy of Abbeyglen Castle basks in views sweeping from Connemara's Twelve Bens mountains to the shores of Clifden Bay. Ensconced in 12 acres of lovely grounds, it is just a five-minute walk from the bustle and cosy pubs of Clifden village, but you might find it hard to drag yourself away from its classic country-house comforts. In the restaurant at dinner, the decor is bold and bright with artworks on cherry-red walls, crystal chandeliers, and a pianist tinkles away on a grand piano. Expect classic cooking built on excellent local materials. As you'd hope, given the closeness to the briny, fish and seafood makes a good showing – fresh oysters, seafood chowder, or poached salmon with hollandaise – while meat could turn up as slow-roasted suckling pig teamed with braised belly pork, apple chutney, celeriac crisps and a grain mustard reduction. Puddings finish slap in the comfort zone with the likes of chocolate bread-and-butter pudding or rhubarb crumble with crème anglaise.

Times 7-9, Closed 6-31 Jan, L all week

GALWAY   Map 1 B3/4

Ardilaun Hotel & Leisure Club

Modern International

tel: 091 521433 **Taylor's Hill**
email: info@theardilaunhotel.ie **web:** www.theardilaunhotel.ie
dir: *1m from city centre, towards Salthill on west side of city, near Galway Bay*

Country-house cooking near the Bay

Built in the early Victorian era for the Persse family, one of whose scions co-founded the Abbey Theatre in Dublin, Ardilaun is a grandiose townhouse set in several acres of grounds not far from the Bay. Alternatives of bistro or full-on restaurant dining keep things flexible, with the main dining room offering cooking in the European country-house manner. Baked pepper stuffed with mushrooms and saffron risotto, with pesto dressing, is a labour-intensive starter, and might be the gateway to ling fillet on dill and lemon mash in lobster and spring vegetable broth, or a classic Angus sirloin with sautéed pied de mouton mushrooms, pearl onions and confit garlic. Bayonne ham-wrapped chicken breast filled with a sage and onion farce, sauced with Shiraz and juniper, is a satisfying mix of elements, and proceedings end with the likes of coconut cheesecake, rum-raisin ice cream and roasted pineapple in a sauce of Malibu.

Chef David O'Donnell **Owner** The Ryan family **Seats** 180, Pr/dining room 380 **Times** 1-2.30/6.30-9.15, Closed 23-26 Dec, L Mon-Sat **Prices** Fixed L 2 course €14.50, Fixed D 3 course €28, Starter €8.75-€10.50, Main €17.25-€52, Dessert €6.95-€7.95 **Wines** 62 bottles over €30, 9 bottles under €30, 9 by glass **Parking** 300 **Notes** Meal deal in Bistro 2/3 course €24/€27.50, Sunday L €9.95-€23, Vegetarian available, Children welcome

The G Hotel

Modern Irish

tel: 091 865200 **Wellpark, Dublin Rd**
email: info@theg.ie **web:** www.theghotel.ie
dir: *Phone for directions*

Modern Irish brasserie cooking in a postmodern experience hotel

That gnomic initial is the clue to the style – a Force 10 postmodern experience hotel with interiors by avante-garde milliner Philip Treacy. Gendered lounges are in blue for boys, and screaming pink with black-and-white concentric circles for girls. Hard reflective surfaces are offset by pillbox views of the wild western coast, while Gigi's restaurant is done in full-throttle collisions of purple and pink, leafy green and sky blue, and then some. You might think the contemporary Irish brasserie cooking would struggle to keep up, but there's plenty of vivacity here too, from laden sharing boards of charcuterie or seafood, or starters such as king scallops with smoked bacon and caper noisette, to outstanding main-course proteins like Wexford beef rib-eye with oxtail cannelloni, or roast sea bass in clam and mussel broth with saffron whipped potatoes. Sign up for Dinner and A Movie, and as soon as you've finished your cookies-and-cream cheesecake with winter berry and star-anise compôte, you can glide through to the EYE cinema for a 3D treat.

Times 12.30-3/5.30-10, Closed 23-26 Dec, L Mon-Sat

Glenlo Abbey Hotel

Modern French **NEW**

tel: 091 519600 **Kentfield, Bushypark**
email: info@glenloabbey.ie **web:** www.glenloabbeyhotel.ie
dir: *2m from Galway City Centre on N59 to Clifden*

Country-house dining in Pullman carriages from the Orient Express

Float four miles or so upstream on the River Corrib from Galway to find Glenlo, a grandiose country house built in the early Georgian era. Its private abbey was never quite finished or consecrated, but stands as a monument to good intentions. The house itself has architectural diversion enough, but the twin railway carriages from the Orient Express that have been fashioned into its dining room are something to see. It's a splendid design concept, and makes an elegant setting for the traditionally based European cooking on offer. A seafood path might take you from seared king scallops on onion soubise with watercress pesto to potato-scaled turbot en papillote in a capered white wine sauce. Otherwise, go for Bluebell Falls goats' cheese mousse with beetroot, then venison loin with wild mushrooms and rowanberries. For afters, the stonkingly rich chocolate pudding is well matched with a sharp-tasting blackcurrant sorbet.

Owner Lalco Hospitality **Seats** 66, Pr/dining room 30 **Times** 6.30-9.30, Closed Sun-Tue (Oct-Apr), L all week **Prices** Prices not confirmed **Wines** 58 bottles over €30, 32 bottles under €30, 8 by glass **Parking** 150 **Notes** Vegetarian available, Children welcome

Park House Hotel & Restaurant

Modern Irish, International

tel: 091 564924 **Forster St, Eyre Square**
email: restaurant@parkhousehotel.ie **web:** www.parkhousehotel.ie
dir: *In city centre/Eyre Sq*

Appealing menu in bustling city-centre hotel

Standing just off the city's Eyre Square and built of striking pink granite, Park House has been offering high standards of food and accommodation for well over 35 years. Its celebrated Park Restaurant – where paintings of old Galway help keep the past alive – fairly bustles at lunchtime and mellows in the evening. Endearing classical design – in reds and golds with banquette seating and chairs and closely-set tables – suits the surroundings, likewise the traditionally-inspired cooking is classically underpinned, while making good use of traceable local ingredients on a menu with broad appeal. Orange- and honey-glazed breast of duckling with a peppercorn sauce, for instance, or prime fillet steak au poivre to Dublin Bay prawns thermidor. Finish with profiteroles, apple pie or Pavlova.

Chef Robert O'Keefe, Martin Keane **Owner** Eamon Doyle, Kitty Carr **Seats** 145, Pr/dining room 45 **Times** 12-3/6-10, Closed 24-26 Dec **Prices** Prices not confirmed, Service optional **Wines** 12 bottles over €30, 43 bottles under €30, 7 by glass **Parking** 40, Adjacent to hotel **Notes** Early evening menu 2/3 course with tea/coffee €28/€32, Sunday L, Vegetarian available, Children welcome

RECESS (SRAITH SALACH)   Map 1 A4

Lough Inagh Lodge
◉◉ Irish, French

tel: 095 34706 & 34694 **Inagh Valley**
email: inagh@iol.ie **web:** www.loughinaghlodgehotel.ie
dir: From Galway take N344. After 3.5m hotel on right

Spectacular scenery and Irish country-house cooking

Dating from 1880, when it was built as a fishing lodge, this boutique hotel is in a lovely spot on the shore of Lough Inagh surrounded by wild mountains. There's an oak-panelled bar, a library with a log fire, and a restaurant where silver and glassware reflect candlelight and an oval window gives wonderful views. Chatty and attentive staff are happy to make recommendations about the set-price dinner menu, which might open with air-dried lamb and beef with a warm chickpea croquette and red onion marmalade, or mussels steamed with white wine and garlic. A modern spin is given to traditional Irish cuisine, along with the more classical, and fresh native produce is evident. Main courses are commendably free of frills and flounces. Precisely cooked duck breast, sliced and fanned on the plate, in a sauce of plum purée hinting of star anise, for instance, is served with fondant potato and well-timed seasonal vegetables, or baked lobster with a simple lemon butter. End with luscious chocolate pudding with raspberry sorbet and slices of poached orange.

Times 7-8.45, Closed mid Dec-mid Mar

COUNTY KERRY

DINGLE (AN DAINGEAN)   Map 1 A2

Coastguard Restaurant
◉ Modern Irish

tel: 066 9150200 **Dingle Skellig Hotel, & Peninsula Spa**
email: reservations@dingleskellig.com **web:** www.dingleskellig.com
dir: N86 from Tralee (30km). Hotel on harbourside on left

Modern Irish cooking and Dingle Bay views

It isn't possible to get much further west on the European continent than this spot. The Dingle Skellig Hotel is a sprawling establishment right on the coast with glorious views all round. A family-friendly sort of place, there's a kids' club, leisure facilities, a room for teenagers to hang out, plus a spa for the grown-ups.The main dining option is the Coastguard Restaurant (food is also available in the bar, bistro and cocktail lounge), with its stunning view over the bay through capacious picture windows.The kitchen works with the excellent produce around these parts, with locally landed fish and West Kerry lamb stealing the show. The modern Irish repertoire runs to a classic combination of pan-fried scallops with local black pudding, pea purée and Parma ham crisps, each element cooked correctly, followed by seared breast of duckling with a confit fig and sautéed fennel. Finish with orange and rhubarb crème brûlée.

Times 6.30-9.15, Closed Jan

Gormans Clifftop House & Restaurant
◉ Modern, Traditional

tel: 066 9155162 & 083 0033133 **Glaise Bheag, Ballydavid (Baile na nGall)**
email: info@gormans-clifftophouse.com **web:** www.gormans-clifftophouse.com
dir: R559 to An Mhuirioch, turn right at T-junct, N for 3km

Clifftop cracker with splendid local produce

The stone-built house perching on the clifftops above Smerwick harbour on the northwestern tip of the Dingle Peninsula has been owned by the Gorman family since the 18th century, which might explain why chef-proprietor Vincent Gorman has a passion for sourcing as much as possible of his materials from the local farms and ports. Simplicity is the key to this delightful restaurant with rooms: there's nothing to get in the way of the dining room's sweeping views across the Atlantic, produce is spankingly fresh and the concise menu offers five choices at each stage. You might start with locally-smoked organic salmon served with a simple salad and horseradish cream, and follow with a hearty Kerry lamb stew with root vegetables and potatoes, or pan-fried hake fillet with roasted cherry tomatoes, lemon butter and fresh herbs. To finish, there could be mango parfait with passionfruit and mango syrup.

Chef Vincent Gorman **Owner** Sile & Vincent Gorman **Seats** 30 **Times** 7-8, Closed Oct-Mar, Sun, L all week **Prices** Prices not confirmed, Service optional **Wines** 10 bottles over €30, 17 bottles under €30, 6 by glass **Parking** 25 **Notes** Vegetarian available, Children welcome

KENMARE   Map 1 B2

Park Hotel Kenmare
◉◉ Classic Irish NEW

tel: 064 664 1200
email: info@parkkenmare.com **web:** www.parkkenmare.com
dir: Phone for directions

Classy cooking in opulent surroundings

Set against a backdrop of the Cork and Kerry Mountains, with stunning views over Kenmare Bay, this landmark Victorian hotel dates from 1897 and the opulence extends to the dining room with its high ceilings and picture windows overlooking the well-tended gardens. Fine crystal glassware, gleaming silver cutlery and polished silver cloches, combined with formal service from immaculately attired staff, add an air of traditional elegance to a meal here and the cooking suits the grand surroundings. Top-notch ingredients sourced from the surrounding area dominate the menu, starting with attractively presented Kenmare Bay scallops teamed with pork cheek croquette and spiced carrot. Main course might bring a super-fresh fillet of halibut accompanied by roasted cauliflower, brown shrimps, bulgar wheat, brown butter and a sweet and fruity caper and raisin puree. A well-flavoured dessert of 'Kir Royale' blackcurrant mousse and champagne sorbet is one satisfying way to end a meal. A comprehensive and carefully chosen wine list offers some notable bottles at prices to match.

Chef James Coffey **Owner** John & Francis Brennan **Seats** 70 **Times** 7-9, Closed 27 Nov-23 Dec, 2 Jan-4 Mar, Sun, L all week **Prices** Prices not confirmed **Wines** 450 bottles over €30, 6 by glass **Parking** 60 **Notes** Table d'hôte 5 course D €70, Vegetarian available, Children welcome

KENMARE *continued*

Sheen Falls Lodge

◉◉ Modern European V

tel: 064 6641600 **Sheen Falls Lodge**
email: info@sheenfallslodge.ie **web:** www.sheenfallslodge.ie
dir: *From Kenmare take N71 to Glengarriff. Take 1st left after suspension bridge. 1m from Kenmare*

French, European cooking by cascading waters

Not far from the Rings of both Kerry and Beara, Sheen Falls is a stately country house that makes the most of its location. The River Sheen cascades past as it falls towards the bay, and the hotel's drape-framed picture windows overlook floodlit surrounding woodland. A refined tone of soft lighting and piano accompaniment is maintained in La Cascade restaurant, which is enhanced by helpful, informative staff. Home-smoked salmon, superb seafood and organic produce distinguish the output. This takes a classical French line with soft-textured duck liver parfait to start, copiously garnished with caramelised figs, quince and red fruit compôte, or else lobster bisque with brandy and saffron crème fraîche, before main courses that might feature perfectly timed fish, perhaps roast halibut with provençal vegetables in bouillabaisse sauce. Meats might include rack and shoulder of Kerry lamb with mint foam and gnocchi, or a double act of pork belly and duck breast in cider sauce. A shortbread-based lemon tart with blackcurrant sorbet closes the deal, unless you can be tempted by a tasting of Irish farmhouse cheeses.

Chef Philip Brazil **Owner** Palladium Hotels & Resorts **Seats** 120, Pr/dining room 40 **Times** 7-9.30, Closed 2 Jan-1 Feb, L all week **Prices** Starter €14.50-€18.50, Main €26.50-€36.50, Dessert €11.50-€12.50, Service optional **Wines** 16 by glass **Parking** 75 **Notes** Children welcome

---

KILLARNEY   Map 1 B2

The Brehon Killarney

◉ Modern European NEW V

tel: 064 6630700 **The Brehon Hotel, Muckross Rd**
email: info@thebrehon.com **web:** www.thebrehon.com
dir: *Enter Killarney follow signs for Muckross Road (N71). Hotel on left 0.3m from town centre*

Bold contemporary cooking of vim and vigour

Brehon was the name for the body of law that governed Ireland in ancient times. It gave its subjects an obligation of hospitality, so it seems a logical name for a hotel. By contrast Danu, after whom the main dining room here is named, was a pagan earth-goddess, mother of the Celtic pantheon. The kitchen brings us fast-forwarding up to the present day with contemporary Irish cooking of ingenuity and impressive depth. That translates as organic Clare Island salmon cured in orange and vodka, accompanied by salmon tartare, ribbons of pickled cucumber and horseradish cream, as a prelude to pinkly seared lamb rump in a jus infused with Douglas fir needles, served with a dollop of buttery colcannon threaded with vivid green kale and seasoned with smoked paprika. Finish with a faithful interpretation of crème brûlée, its velvety smoothness matched by home-made biscotti.

Chef Mr Chad Byrne **Owner** Patrick O'Donoghue & family **Seats** 100, Pr/dining room 100 **Times** 6.30-9, Closed L all week **Prices** Fixed L 2 course €28-€32, Fixed D 3 course €35-€40, Starter €6.50-€9.50, Main €20-€28, Dessert €8-€10, Service optional **Wines** 6 bottles over €30, 21 bottles under €30, 8 by glass **Parking** 250 **Notes** Children welcome

Cahernane House Hotel

◉◉ Modern European, International

tel: 064 6631895 **Muckross Rd**
email: info@cahernane.com **web:** www.cahernane.com
dir: *From Killarney follow signs for Kenmare, then from Muckross Rd over bridge. Hotel signed on right. Hotel 1m from town centre*

Modern country-house cooking in a tranquil setting

Ringed by peaks in the heart of the Killarney National Park, Cahernane was once the seat of the Earls of Pembroke, and sits in a peaceful private estate just a short stroll from the shores of Lough Leane. Reached via an impressive avenue of mature trees, the 17th-century house is a deeply traditional place replete with original fireplaces, intricate ceilings and ancestral oil portraits – a style that makes for a sense of occasion when dining in the Herbert Room Restaurant to a backdrop of the lake and immaculately kept grounds. The food is weighted towards classical and traditional themes enlivened with flashes of modern flair, so things kick off with pan-fried quail with date and orange purée, citrus emulsion and home-made chutney, while a well-thought-out main course sees roast saddle of venison partnered with celeriac remoulade, butternut squash purée and a juniper-infused jus. To finish, natural yogurt sorbet makes an intelligent counterpoint to the richness of praline crème brûlée. For a more casual mood, there's bistro fare in the old wine cellar bar.

Times 12-2.30/7-9.30, Closed Jan-Feb, L all week (ex by arrangement), D Sun

---

The Lake Hotel

◉ Traditional European V

tel: 064 6631035 **On the Shore, Muckross Rd**
email: info@lakehotel.com **web:** www.lakehotelkillarney.com
dir: *2km from town centre on N71 Muckross Rd*

Lough views and successful modern cooking

The Lake Hotel earns its name, as it's bang on the shore of Lough Lein, with glorious views over water and mountains. The hotel has been much extended over the years, and The Castlelough Restaurant, built as part of the original 1820 house, has itself seen total refurbishment while retaining its high ceilings, cornicing and vast windows catching those views. The kitchen works around a slate of modern ideas based on classical traditions, using the area's tip-top ingredients. An assiette of duck, for instance, comes as terrine, smoked, with hazelnuts and orange, and warm pithivier, and a plate of smoked fish as salmon blini, sea trout with lemon and caviar dressing, and haddock fishcake with caper aïoli. Main courses can seem more mainstream, as in chicken breast with fondant potato, pea purée, and leek and mushroom ragout, although roast saddle of rabbit partnered by monkfish and served with black pudding, carrots and a savoury jus brings an interesting interpretation of surf 'n' turf.

Chef Noel Enright **Owner** The Huggard family **Seats** 100, Pr/dining room 65 **Times** 6.30-9, Closed Dec-Jan, L all week **Prices** Fixed L 2 course €16-€32, Fixed D 3 course €38, Tasting menu €20-€39, Starter €6-€9, Main €15-€28, Dessert €8-€10.50, Service optional **Wines** 37 bottles over €30, 12 bottles under €30, 6 by glass **Parking** 150 **Notes** Children welcome

KILLORGLIN
Map 1 A2

Carrig House Country House & Restaurant

Modern Irish, European

tel: 066 9769100 **Caragh Lake**
email: info@carrighouse.com **web:** www.carrighouse.com
dir: N70 to Killorglin

Fine dining with expansive lough views

Carrig is a lovingly restored Victorian country manor in acres of colourful woodland gardens with views across Caragh Lake to the Kerry Mountains. Inside, the genteel house is done out in period style, with turf fires sizzling in cosy, chintzy lounges, while the dining room is the very image of 19th-century chic; all William Morris wallpapers, swagged curtains, polished floorboards, and formally laid tables. The cooking, on the other hand, takes a more up-to-date approach, lining up superb local ingredients and sending them to finishing school: crab could get a fashionable three-way treatment as ravioli, soup and pasty, and might be followed by Skeganore duck breast with vanilla and lime potato purée, and sweet port and brandy jus. Finish with prune and Armagnac crème brûlée.

Times 7-9

TRALEE
Map 1 A2

Ballyseede Castle

Traditional European

tel: 066 7125799
email: info@ballyseedecastle.com **web:** www.ballyseedecastle.com
dir: On N21 just after N21/N22 junct

Appealing well-conceived food in a castle hotel

The castle is indeed that, crenallated and turreted, dating from the late 16th century, surrounded by 30 acres of woodland. It's now a deluxe hotel offering the full-on country-house experience (weddings are also popular). The O'Connell Restaurant looks like something in a stately home, a gracefully curved room with luxurious drapes at the windows, columns, oil paintings and a chandelier. 'Resplendent grandeur' heads the menu, but the cooking is more down-to-earth than that might suggest, the kitchen clearly taking a contemporary outlook on matters culinary. Starters make an impact, from breaded monkfish cheeks and prawns with home-made tomato and caraway seed ketchup and tartare sauce, to braised belly pork with a black pudding croquette, crackling, fried apple and a sticky jus. Top-quality native produce is used throughout, evident in well-conceived, unfussy main courses: perhaps pan-fried salmon fillet with a creamy sauce of leeks, peas, dill and saffron, or roast duck confit glazed in honey and orange with a jus of port, grapes and orange. End with something like chocolate parfait and butterscotch sauce.

Times 12.30-2.30/7-9, Closed Jan-3 Mar, L Mon-Sat

COUNTY KILDARE

STRAFFAN
Map 1 C/D4

The K Club

Traditional French

tel: 01 6017200 **River Room**
email: sales@kclub.ie **web:** www.kclub.ie
dir: From Dublin take N4, exit for R406, hotel on right in Straffan

Classy, contemporary food in a five-star hotel

The architect was aiming for the French château look, and by jove he got it! That was back in 1832, and today his vision performs as a five-star hotel as if built for the job. It is a luxurious place with a swanky spa, golf course and no stone left unturned in the pursuit of indulgence. There are dining options aplenty, not least of which is the River Restaurant, with its commanding views of the Liffey and the hotel's formal gardens. Tables are generously spaced and smartly laid, with grand floral displays making a statement in their own right. The cooking is classically minded and built on solid regional foundations. Roast breast of wood pigeon in the company of its confit leg shows sound technique, served with artichoke purée and a jus rich with Madeira. For mains, loin of Wicklow venison is no less impressive, with red rhubarb compôte, ceps and an oozing chunk of local honeycomb. Warm poached Comice pear filled with a chocolate frangipane, plus a chocolate sauce and pear as sorbet and foam, is a satisfying finale.

Chef Finbar Higgins **Owner** Dr Michael Smurfit **Seats** 110, Pr/dining room 30 **Times** 1-3/7-9.15 **Prices** Prices not confirmed, Service optional **Wines** 250 bottles over €30, 10 by glass **Parking** 300 **Notes** Vegetarian available, Children welcome

COUNTY KILKENNY

THOMASTOWN
Map 1 C3

Kendals Brasserie

French, European

tel: 056 7773000 **Mount Juliet Hotel**
email: info@mountjuliet.ie
dir: M7 from Dublin, N9 towards Waterford, exit at junct 9/Danesfort for hotel

A taste of France beside the golf course

Kendals is housed in a converted stable block of Mount Juliet Hotel, a light-filled, airy space under a pitched wooden ceiling, its rafter-hung with fabric, with modern chandeliers, a soaring stone fire surround and tables decorated with fresh flowers. The kitchen concentrates on the style of French brasserie classics, updated to suit the tastes of our days with some input from other cuisines, so goats' cheese mousse appears with pistachios, black grapes, beetroot and raisins, while chicken parfait is partnered by duck rillettes and accompanied by salted grapes and watercress. Main courses follow in similar mould: fillet of hake with bean cassoulet, a chorizo and leek sausage and mussels, and pan-fried pork cutlet with apple jus, black pudding, kale and pommes purée. Menus are bilingual, so among puddings expect cheesecake à la vanille with blood orange jelly and sorbet.

Chef Cormac Rowe **Owner** Tetrarch Capital **Seats** 70 **Times** 6-9.30, Closed Mon & Wed (seasonal) **Prices** Starter €6.50-€11.50, Main €17.50-€31, Dessert €3.50-€11, Service optional **Wines** 38 bottles over €30, 25 bottles under €30, 10 by glass **Parking** 200 **Notes** Early bird menu 6-7pm 3 course €28, Vegetarian available, Children welcome

THOMASTOWN *continued*

The Lady Helen Restaurant

⚘⚘⚘ – *see below*

COUNTY LAOIS

BALLYFIN

Ballyfin Demesne

⚘⚘ Modern European **NEW** V

tel: 057 875 5866
email: info@ballyfin.com **web:** www.ballyfin.com
dir: *M7 junct 18, follow signs to Mountrath. In Mountrath turn right at lights, follow Ballyfin Rd for 8km. Entrance gate on left via intercom*

Dazzling French-inspired cooking amid Regency opulence

Possibly Ireland's most opulent Regency house, standing in over 600 acres, Ballyfin makes a grand country hotel, with only 20 guest rooms, so you won't need to feel shoehorned in. Loaded with 18th-century artworks and antiques inside, it's had its ornate plaster mouldings carefully restored, and the high-ceilinged dining room gazes out over the terrace towards a temple folly where a water feature cascades. A walled garden supplies the kitchen with plenty of produce, as do the resident bees, and lucky human residents are regaled with menus of French-inspired contemporary cooking of considerable dazzle. A trio of scallops comes with soused and puréed cauliflower in a caper-dotted shellfish dressing to start, prior to salted cod with langoustine cannelloni in truffled beurre blanc, or magisterial Kilkenny

duck with date purée, roasted carrots and spinach in a glossy orange jus. The signature dessert is a traditional nutmegged egg custard tart garnished with shards of meringue and rhubarb sorbet. Quality canapés and home-made breads add lustre to the occasion, as does an enterprising, well-written wine list.

Chef Michael Tweedie **Owner** Mr Krehbiel **Seats** 39, Pr/dining room 39
Times 6.30-9.30 Closed Jan-14 Feb, L all week **Prices** Prices not confirmed
Parking Valet parking **Notes** L residents only 1-3pm Children 9 yrs+

COUNTY LEITRIM

MOHILL   Map 1 C4

Lough Rynn Castle

⚘⚘ Modern, Traditional Irish V

tel: 071 9632700
email: enquiries@loughrynn.ie **web:** www.loughrynn.ie
dir: *N4 (Dublin to Sligo), hotel 8km off N4 & 2km from Mohill*

Contemporary flavours in a peaceful location

The 200-year-old ancestral home of Lord Leitrim was built to impress: Lough Rynn Castle sits in 300 acres of idyllic Ireland beside the eponymous lough, complete with its own championship golf course. The Sandstone Restaurant is an intimate space in the converted stables that makes a feature of its bare stone walls (hence the name), and comes plushly furnished with well-upholstered high-backed chairs and linen-clothed tables. The kitchen lives up to the fine-dining expectations of the setting, taking care in sourcing the finest County Leitrim ingredients, and putting it all together with skill and imagination in an ambitious repertoire of contemporary European-accented dishes. Crab cannelloni arrives with seared scallops, the

The Lady Helen Restaurant ⚘⚘⚘

THOMASTOWN   Map 1 C3

Modern Irish V
tel: 056 7773000 **Mount Juliet Hotel,**
email: info@mountjuliet.ie **web:** www.mountjuliet.com
dir: *M7 from Dublin, N9 towards Waterford, exit at junct 9/Danesfort for hotel*

Cooking of artistry and impact in a manor-house hotel

If you want to play at being aristocracy, a stay at Mount Juliet should do the trick. The imposing Georgian manor-house hotel stands in a lushly sprawling estate whose expanses keep guests occupied with such pursuits as river and lake fishing, woodland strolls, stick swinging around a golf course designed by Jack Nicklaus, plus shooting, archery and spa pampering. For foodies, the main attraction lies in the Lady Helen dining room, an opulent space with splendid plasterwork ceilings, views over the grounds, and a fashionably muted beige decor. The tone of service is gently formal, but staff are friendly and keen, and have a good knowledge of what's on the menus. Suppliers and sources are credited in the preamble, from Wexford seafood to wild game, with the option of choosing from the carte or signing up to a seven-course taster or 10-course surprise blowout. Simple menu descriptions don't tell the full story of what's going on in Cormac Rowe's labour-intensive and minutely-detailed compositions. For example, one starter comprises lobster in

two preparations – the tail simply poached and quenelles of claw meat bound with a fresh herb dressing – served with tubes of cucumber filled with lightly-pickled cucumber, fresh and pickled radish, tomatoes and baby gem lettuce. Main course brings turbot of exemplary quality and depth of flavour partnered with a decadent slice of foie gras, earthy Beluga lentils and a cumin-scented carrot purée. The multi-faceted approach continues into a dessert that plays with variations on a strawberry theme, the fruit presented in vanilla-poached meringues in macerated, dried and fresh forms with a sorbet of wild strawberries from the estate and crunchy candied pistachios.

Chef Cormac Rowe **Owner** Tetrarch Capital **Seats** 60, Pr/dining room 80
Times 6.30-9.45, Closed Sun & Tue, L all week **Prices** Fixed D 3 course fr €75, Tasting menu €75-€99, Service optional **Wines** 10 by glass **Parking** 200
Notes Children welcome

crunch of samphire, a scallop and watermelon gel, and seafood foam, followed by a two-way serving of lamb-seared loin with basil jus, and braised knuckle in filo pastry – with celeriac purée, sautéed courgettes and potato croquettes. The curtain comes down with an apple and olive oil timbale with iced beetroot parfait, violet and beetroot foam, olive oil jelly and pistachio cream.

Chef Clare O'Leary **Owner** Hanly Group, Alan Hanly **Seats** 90, Pr/dining room 10 **Times** 12-2.30/7-9, Closed L Mon-Sat **Prices** Fixed L 2 course €14, Starter €9.50-€13.50, Main €27.50-€29.50, Dessert €9.50-€18.50, Service optional **Wines** 12 by glass **Notes** Fixed D 4 course €44, Sunday L €14-€27, Children welcome

COUNTY LIMERICK

LIMERICK   Map 1 B3

Limerick Strand Hotel

◉ Irish Contemporary

tel: 061 421800 **Ennis St**
email: info@strandlimerick.ie **web:** www.strandlimerick.ie
dir: *On the Shannon side of Sarsfield Bridge, on River Shannon*

Contemporary Irish brasserie food by the river

A new-build hotel by the side of the river has all the mod cons, including a bright, airy dining room with full-drop windows, the better to view what The Pogues once hailed as 'the broad majestic Shannon'. Sourcing from within the county supplies a menu of populist brasserie dishes, with an Irish contemporary gloss on international ideas. Start with two slices of duck roulade zinged up with five spice on ginger- and sesame-dressed saladings with kumquat marmalade. That could lead to a brace of sea bass fillets saltimbocca-style, wrapped in Parma ham and sage leaves, or chicken breast with truffle-oiled mash in wild mushroom and tarragon cream. The chocolate marquise packs a mighty punch, and is nicely offset with a sharp raspberry sauce. Good breads, light brown soda and sourdough, come with intensely anchovied tapenade.

Chef Tom Flavin **Owner** John Malone **Seats** 120, Pr/dining room 450 **Times** 6-10, Closed L Mon-Sat **Prices** Fixed D 2 course fr €25.95, Starter €8.95-€10.50, Main €17.95-€24.95, Dessert €4.95-€8, Service optional **Parking** 200 **Notes** Sunday L €23.95-€28.95, Vegetarian available, Children welcome

COUNTY LOUTH

CARLINGFORD   Map 1 D4

Ghan House

◉◉ Modern Irish

tel: 042 9373682
email: info@ghanhouse.com **web:** www.ghanhouse.com
dir: *M1 junct 18 signed Carlingford, 5mtrs on left after 50kph speed sign in Carlingford*

Creative dining by the lough

The white-painted Ghan House has stood majestically by Carlingford Lough since Georgian times and is close (but not too close) to buildings that have been here a lot longer than that – some back to the 13th century. It really is on the water's edge, within its own pretty walled garden complete with a veg patch to fuel the kitchen.

The restaurant – traditional dining room and drawing room – has views over the Mourne Mountains and the garden, and a team in the kitchen who make just about everything in-house. There are modern touches and classic partnerships along the way. Local sea scallops, for example, might turn up in the company of white beans, chorizo from the Gubbeen smokehouse and mojo verde, or you could go for the warming comfort of roast parsnip soup with curried crème fraîche. Among main courses, saddle of Wicklow venison is partnered with celeriac and beetroot, with a kick of ginger, and rump of Slane Valley lamb with a sage and bacon rissole and onion ash. Finish with Grand Marnier parfait and chocolate tart.

Chef Stephane Le Sourne **Owner** Joyce & Paul Carroll **Seats** 50, Pr/dining room 34 **Times** 1-3/6-10, Closed 24-26 & 31 Dec, 1-2 Jan, 1 day a wk (varies), L Mon-Sat (open by arrangement & most Sun), D 1 day a wk (varies) **Prices** Fixed L 2 course €21.50, Fixed D 3 course €39.50, Tasting menu €33-€53, Service optional **Wines** 14 bottles over €30, 40 bottles under €30, 14 by glass **Parking** 24 **Notes** Tasting menu 6 course Mon-Thu 6-7.45pm, D 4 course €45, Sunday L €29.50, Vegetarian available, Children welcome

DROGHEDA   Map 1 D4

Scholars Townhouse Hotel

◉◉ Modern Irish **NEW**

tel: 041 9835410 **King St**
email: info@scholarshotel.com **web:** www.scholarshotel.com
dir: *Follow West St (Main St) to St Lawrences Gate. Turn left, up the hill. On left*

Lively modern cooking in a Victorian former monastery

Originally built as a Christian Brothers monastery in 1867 by George Ashlin and EW Pugin, Scholars was fully renovated by the McGowan family on acquisition in 2005. The extraordinary interiors demonstrate the Victorian instinct for not leaving any square inch unoccupied, the panelled walls crammed with landscape pictures, and potted plants, lamps and elliptical mirrors everywhere you look. Ceiling frescoes of the Battle of the Boyne in the interlinked dining rooms furnish a historical note that is thrown into relief by the lively modern Irish cooking. Start with salt-and-vinegar lemon sole and crispy mussels with smoked potato salad, or maybe foie gras parfait with pistachio butter and chocolate oil, before pedigree main-course meats bring on rump and braised shoulder of Kerry lamb dressed with garlic purée and mint jelly in red wine jus, or chicken breast and maple-syrup wings with sage and onion polenta and truffled feta terrine. Praline soufflé with pumpkin ice cream and hazelnuts is interesting, rhubarb and apple trifle an emphatic success.

Chef Michael Hunter **Owner** Martin & Patricia McGowan **Seats** 75, Pr/dining room 36 **Times** 12-9.30, All-day dining, Closed 25-26 Dec **Prices** Fixed L 3 course €25, Fixed D 3 course €35, Starter €7.95-€13.95, Main €15.95-€35.95, Dessert €7.95-€12.95, Service optional **Wines** 46 bottles over €30, 12 bottles under €30, 15 by glass **Parking** 30 **Notes** Sunday L €14.95-€25, Vegetarian available, Children welcome

Follow The AA online

twitter: @TheAA_Lifestyle
facebook: www.facebook.com/TheAAUK

Find us on Facebook

COUNTY MAYO

BALLINA
Map 1 B4

Belleek Castle
◉◉ Modern Irish V

tel: 096 22400 & 21878 **Belleek**
email: info@belleekcastle.com web: www.belleekcastle.com
dir: *In Belleek woods N of Ballina*

Irish regional cooking with a foothold in tradition

Built in the 1820s on the site of a medieval abbey, Belleek is more manor house than your actual castle, but altogether splendid even so. The retired naval officer who transformed it into a hotel in 1970 added touches of the nautical here and there to the medieval styling, resulting in a glorious hodgepodge. With Killala and Moy seafood on hand, fine game and in-house dry-ageing of beef, not to mention gathering of wild plants from the forest, it's clear that the kitchen is well placed to deliver the goods. The style is sophisticated, but retains a foothold in tradition, offering first the house pie of pork in pork-fat pastry with orange and ginger marmalade, or a bowl of forest and hedgerow soup, all wild mushrooms, nettle pesto and garlic. Seafood could be Mulranny trout in lemon and dill, or turbot in capers and champagne, while the beef fillet in flamed in Jameson's and served with a peppery jus. At the end comes caramel cheesecake with peanut ice cream and blueberries, or lemon and passionfruit tart.

Chef Stephen Lenahan **Owner** Paul Marshal Doran **Seats** 55, Pr/dining room 30 **Times** 1-3/5.30-9.30, Closed Xmas & Jan **Prices** Fixed L 3 course €28.50-€39, Fixed D 3 course €29.50-€35, Tasting menu €49.50-€65.50, Starter €8.90-€12.90, Main €16.90-€32.50, Dessert €8.90-€12.90, Service optional **Wines** 57 bottles over €30, 7 bottles under €30, 5 by glass **Parking** 90 **Notes** Early bird menu 3 course €29.50, Tasting menu 5/8 course, Sunday L fr €20, Children welcome

Mount Falcon Estate
◉◉ Traditional French

tel: 096 74472 **Foxford Rd**
email: info@mountfalcon.com web: www.mountfalcon.com
dir: *On N26, 6m from Foxford & 3m from Ballina. Hotel on left*

Polished cooking using exemplary local materials

The grand baronial-style house stands in 100 acres of grounds, with pristine lawns and woodland, and a helipad if you plan to arrive in style. The hotel on the banks of River Moy is popular with golfers, who are drawn to the top courses that pepper the landscape in these parts. The dining option is the Kitchen Restaurant, so named as it takes up the kitchen and pantry area of this splendid old house, and it looks good with its linen-clad tables and food-related prints on the walls. The chef hails from Paris and there's a definite French classicism to his output, as well as a genuine appreciation of the top-quality produce available in this part of Ireland. The 100-acre estate makes a contribution to the menu, too. Start perhaps with a winning combo of Wicklow pigeon and 'Kelly's' black pudding, the pigeon marinated in cocoa liqueur, the black pudding in a crisp croquette, plus root parsley purée, parsley steam cake, cocoa jelly and a grand veneur sauce – refined and complex stuff. Main course might deliver corn-fed chicken cooked sous-vide with truffle spätzle, confit black lard and lavender jus.

Times 6.30-9, Closed 25 Dec, L Mon-Sat

BELMULLET
Map 1 A5

The Talbot Hotel
◉ Modern Irish

tel: 097 20484 **Barrack St**
email: info@thetalbothotel.ie web: www.thetalbothotel.ie
dir: *Phone for directions*

Contemporary cooking amid boutique glamour

Sprinkled with boutique fairy dust, The Talbot has a stylish look and a friendly attitude. The bar still functions as such with live music at weekends ensuring the place still has lots of energy to go with all the style. The main dining option – The Barony Restaurant – looks plush and glam with its colourful fabrics and sparkling chandeliers, and there's a small terrace for an alfresco lunch or early dinner. The kitchen seeks out good regional ingredients and delivers a menu that matches the tone of the place for contemporary attitude. Start with smoked duck breast in a salad with seasonal leaves, roasted walnuts and orange segments dressed in a walnut vinaigrette, and move on to pan-seared sea bass (with a nicely crispy skin) served on a cassoulet flavoured with a mild chorizo. For dessert, rum crème brûlée comes with a caramelised banana.

Chef Brendan Conmy **Owner** Tom & Orla Talbot **Seats** 60, Pr/dining room 12 **Times** 6.30-9 **Prices** Fixed L 3 course €20, Fixed D 3 course €35, Starter €5.90-€11.90, Main €15.90-€24.90, Dessert €6.50, Service optional **Parking** On street **Notes** Reduced hrs out of season, Sunday L €21.30-€37.70, Vegetarian available, Children welcome

CONG
Map 1 B4

The George V Dining Room
◉◉ Traditional European, International

tel: 094 9546003 **Ashford Castle**
email: ashford@ashford.ie web: www.ashford.ie
dir: *In Cross, turn left at church onto R345 signed Cong. Turn left at hotel sign & continue through castle gates*

A touch of class in a magnificent castle

The main restaurant at Ashford Castle was built by the then owners of the hotel – a certain Guinness family – to host a reception for the Prince of Wales (later King

George V) back in 1906. The doubtless luxury of that time is not lost today, for this house on the shores of Lough Corrib lives up to its billing: a magnificent 13th-century castle with a glorious interior, set in 350 acres of parkland. It's the kind of place where you dress up for dinner. The elegantly adorned George V Dining Room with its Waterford crystal chandeliers and oak panels is the setting for classic menus with an Irish flavour. There is contemporary flair in a starter of seared prawn tails with apple cider jelly and a swipe of cauliflower purée. Main courses run to perfectly pink rump of lamb and fillet of John Dory with bisque sauce, while slow-roasted rib of beef is served from a carving trolley at the table. There's a tasting menu option with optional wine flight. End with an accomplished cherry soufflé with orange oil ice cream.

Times 7-9.30, Closed L all week

The Lodge at Ashford Castle

◉ Contemporary Irish **NEW** v

tel: 094 9545400 **Ashford Estate**
email: reception@thelodgeatashfordcastle.com **web:** www.thelodgeatashfordcastle.com
dir: *Phone for directions*

Creative Irish cooking and lough views

On the Ashford Castle Estate (one-time home of the Guinness family), The Lodge is grander than you might imagine and has been extended over the years. The original Victorian building hosts the Quay Bar and Brasserie and the main dining option, Wilde's, which offers glorious views over Lough Corrib from its first-floor setting. There's a gently contemporary elegance to the decor over the three spaces that make up the restaurant. The kitchen aims to impress with its ambitious contemporary output (including a tasting menu) and local suppliers are name-checked on the menu. Killary Fjord mussels are cooked in squid ink batter and matched with a liquorice mayonnaise, while beef tartare comes with a hen's egg, wood sorrel and horseradish. 'Wilde's Wild Fish' is a main course dish of turbot with monk's beard and Caesar sauce, and, to finish, rum baba gets a hit from its accompanying wasabi ice cream.

Chef Jonathan Keane **Owner** Red Carnation Hotels **Seats** 60, Pr/dining room 50 **Times** 1-3/6.30-9.30, Closed 24-26 Dec, L Mon-Sat **Prices** Fixed L 3 course €28, Tasting menu €75, Starter €8-€16, Main €20-€31, Dessert €8-€12 **Wines** 40 bottles over €30, 3 bottles under €30 **Parking** 50 **Notes** Sunday L €28, Children welcome

Mulranny Park Hotel

◉◉ Modern

tel: 098 36000
email: info@mulrannyparkhotel.ie **web:** www.mulrannyparkhotel.ie
dir: *R311 from Castlebar to Newport onto N59. Hotel on right*

Country-house splendour on the Atlantic coast

It may be hard to envisage now, but this was once the railway station hotel for Mulranny, opened by Great Western Railways in the 1890s. It was only a few short years later that it offered the luxury of hot running water too. Now a sumptuous country-house operation, it offers sweeping views over the Atlantic from the Nephin dining room, where swagged drapes and linened tables set the tone, with more informal eating in the Waterfront Bar. Modern Irish cooking is the stock-in-trade, founded on pedigree local ingredients. A duo of Keem Bay smoked salmon and barbecued fresh salmon with honey-mustard aïoli, pickled cucumber and red onion dressing might start proceedings, with complex but effective main dishes extending from seared duck magret with black pudding mousse, braised spiced red cabbage and puréed parsnips in veal jus to roast Curran blue trout with chorizo and baby

leek orzo and sauce gribiche. Tempting finishers include pear and almond frangipane tart, served warm with crème anglaise and rum and raisin ice cream.

Chef Chamila Manawatta **Owner** Tom Bohan, Tom Duggan **Seats** 100, Pr/dining room 50 **Times** 6.30-9, Closed Jan **Prices** Fixed D 3 course €45, Starter €6-€9.50, Main €24-€30, Dessert €6-€12, Service optional **Wines** 6 bottles over €30, 14 bottles under €30, 3 by glass **Parking** 200 **Notes** Vegetarian available, Children welcome

Hotel Westport Leisure, Spa & Conference

◉ Modern Irish, British, European

tel: 098 25122 **Newport Rd**
email: reservations@hotelwestport.ie **web:** www.hotelwestport.ie
dir: *N5 to Westport. Right at end of Castlebar St, 1st right before bridge, right at lights, left before church. Follow to end of street*

Exemplary local produce at a riverside hotel

Heavenly scenery frames this expansive family-run hotel and spa set in seven acres of mature woodland. And with miles of walking and cycling on the Great Western Greenway close to hand, there's no excuse for failing to bring a keen appetite to table. After a top-to-tail refurbishment, the place is looking pretty nifty, with plush carpets and seating beneath an ornate ceiling, while views overlooking the Carrowbeg River are timeless. Expect a bedrock of straightforward modern ideas built on the finest local, seasonal materials – perhaps home-cured organic Clare Island salmon with cucumber jelly, shaved fennel and lemon oil, followed by the simplicity of roast rib of beef with horseradish jus and pan juices, or grilled fillet of wild Atlantic hake matched with roast vegetables and salsa verde. Finish with rich chocolate fondant with pistachio ice cream, or bow out on a savoury note with Irish artisan cheeses.

Chef Stephen Fitzmaurice **Owner** Cathal Hughes **Seats** 120, Pr/dining room 45 **Times** 1-2.30/6-9.30 **Prices** Fixed L 2 course €21.50-€26.50, Fixed D 3 course €35-€40, Tasting menu €35-€40, Service optional **Wines** 20 bottles over €30, 31 bottles under €30, 10 by glass **Parking** 220 **Notes** Afternoon tea, Sunday L €21.50-€26.50, Vegetarian available, Children welcome

Knockranny House Hotel

◉◉ Modern International

tel: 098 28600
email: info@khh.ie **web:** www.knockrannyhousehotel.ie
dir: *On N5 (Dublin to Castlebar road), hotel on left before entering Westport*

Inventive modern Irish cooking in the tranquil west

The Noonans' tranquil spa hotel makes the most of its Mayo situation, with stunning views every which way, but none more calming to the senses than over Clew Bay. Inside comes with all the accoutrements of an upscale hotel, including a full-dress dining room, La Fougère, which eschews modern minimalism in favour of immaculate table linen and glassware. The kitchen draws on thoroughbred west Irish produce, including saladings from Knockranny's own organic garden, and the team in the kitchen are adept at the art of combining tastes and textures. That may be seen in a first course pairing of rare-breed pork belly with a seared langoustine, hazelnuts and lime-spiked squash purée. Mains offer the choice of extravagantly worked fish dishes such as John Dory in lobster velouté with lemon and dill gnocchi, smoked eel and puréed fennel, or pedigree meats like loin and shoulder of rose veal with smoked pommes Anna in sauce chasseur. Nor does the invention flag at dessert, certainly not in complex creations such as spiced pineapple with lime parfait, minted lime sponge, mango sorbet and passionfruit jelly.

Times 6.30-9.30, Closed Xmas, L Mon-Sat (open selected Sun)

COUNTY MEATH

DUNBOYNE
Map 1 D4

Dunboyne Castle Hotel & Spa

◉◉ Modern European

tel: 01 8013500
email: ediaz@dunboynecastlehotel.com **web:** www.dunboynecastlehotel.com
dir: In Dunboyne take R157 towards Maynooth. Hotel on left

Classy contemporary European cooking in a regal setting

The main structure was built in the mid-1800s and looks suitably regal, with later tasteful development extending the space to the sprawling property seen today. It's all very contemporary on the inside, with a swish spa and modern meeting rooms, while the business of eating takes place in The Ivy restaurant. The modern European cooking is based on high-quality produce sourced with due diligence and cooked with skill. Seared quail breast with duck foie gras, a deep-fried quail's egg, soubise and orange gel is an effective starter, or there might be cured mackerel with lemon crème fraîche, pickled carrot, pear and mustard relish and a potato crisp. Everything looks good on the plate and flavour combinations are well considered, not least in a main course of loin of venison wrapped in Parma ham with bitter chocolate and port sauce, red cabbage, salsify, candied beetroot and potato gratin. Turbot might star among main courses, in a parmesan crust with lime and coriander oil, curried cauliflower, cauliflower and coconut purée and potato noodles. A dessert of tarte Tatin with custard and vanilla ice cream brings down the curtain in style.

Chef John Nagle **Owner** Danceglen Ltd **Seats** 154 **Times** 1-3/6.30-9.30, Closed L Mon-Sat **Prices** Fixed D 3 course €29.95, Starter €7-€12, Main €17-€30, Dessert €6.50-€10 **Wines** 30 bottles over €30, 29 bottles under €30, 12 by glass **Parking** 360 **Notes** Early bird Sun-Thu all evening & Fri 6-7.30pm €21.95/€26.95, Sunday L €20-€23, Vegetarian available, Children welcome

KILMESSAN
Map 1 D5

The Station House Hotel

◉ European, Mediterranean

tel: 046 9025239 & 9025565
email: info@stationhousehotel.ie **web:** www.stationhousehotel.ie
dir: From Dublin N3 junct 6 to Dunshaughlin, R125 to Kilmessan

Extensive menu in converted railway station

The last train rumbled past in the 1960s and the former station house has found a new lease of life as a country-house hotel. These days there are traditionally decorated bedrooms – even a suite in the old signal box – and a restaurant occupying the one-time waiting room. The Signal Restaurant has smart, linen-clad tables and a broad menu that keeps things relatively simple and classical. A starter, for example, of wild mushroom and garlic risotto might kick things off, or go for roasted quail, scented with rosemary, de-boned and served with roast chestnuts and red wine sauce. Next up, there are main courses such as baked fillet of salmon with a tomato and basil sauce, or a grilled Irish fillet steak with peppercorn sauce. Desserts run to caramel mousse with toffee sauce or baked apple strudel with crème anglaise.

Times 12.30-4.30/5-10.30

NAVAN
Map 1 D4

Bellinter House

◉◉ Modern European NEW v

tel: 046 9030900
web: www.bellinterhouse.com
dir: M3 junct 7 Dublin to Cavan. Follow Kilmessa signs straight over 2 rdbts left at Tara Na Ri pub

Sharp modern food in a Palladian mansion

This rather grand house, as it goes, designed in the Palladian style back in the middle of the 18th century, now operates as a country-house hotel. Popular on the wedding and corporate scene, there are elegant gardens on the River Boyne and an interior that combines period charm with 21st-century boutique glamour. The restaurant is called Eden and is related to the place of the same name in the Temple Bar area of Dublin. Down in the vaulted basement, there's a slick contemporary finish to the space and a menu to match, with service that is both cheerful and professional. The kitchen's output is focused on regional produce and there's evident technical ability on show. Dublin Bay prawns make an appearance alongside a tomato and chilli aïoli, snappy sesame tuile and punchy pickled cucumber, with main courses running to a rack of tender Slaney lamb with a nicely judged salsa and pommes Anna, or baked fillets of sea bass with crab and fennel croquette. Finish with a good-looking Pina Colada millefeuille.

Chef Francoise Herpin **Owner** Jay Bourke, John Reynolds **Seats** 120, Pr/dining room 20 **Times** 12-3/6-10, Closed 24-25 Dec, L Mon-Sat **Prices** Fixed L 2 course €25, Fixed D 3 course €43, Service optional **Wines** 8 bottles over €30, 8 bottles under €30, 8 by glass **Notes** Afternoon tea, Sunday L €25-€30, Children welcome

SLANE
Map 1 D4

Conyngham Arms Hotel

◉ Traditional European NEW

tel: 041 988 4444 **Main St**
email: info@conynghamarms.ie **web:** www.conynghamarms.ie
dir: Phone for directions

Smart village inn with unfussy food

This 18th-century coaching inn is still a refuge for weary travellers on the road to here or there, and it can put on a rather nice wedding these days too. It's also home to a smart brasserie-style restaurant offering straightforward food from breakfast through to dinner. There's a decent amount of Irish produce on the menu, including goods from the owners' bakery and coffee shop in the village. Chicken liver parfait is made in-house and arrives encased in butter with lightly pickled cucumber and carrot to cut through the richness. Next up, lamb shanks come with creamy mash and a red wine jus, and locally-sourced chicken is chargrilled and served atop a well-made asparagus risotto. There's a burger or sirloin steak, too, and desserts extend to a nicely tart lemon tart or chocolate fudge cake.

Chef Killian O'Donohoe **Owner** Trish Conroy **Seats** 35, Pr/dining room 30 **Times** 12-9, All-day dining **Prices** Starter €5.50-€9.50, Main €10-€23.50, Service optional **Wines** 2 by glass **Parking** On street **Notes** Sunday L, Vegetarian available

Tankardstown

◎◎ Modern Irish

tel: 041 9824621
email: info@tankardstown.ie **web:** www.tankardstown.ie
dir: M1 exit 10, N51 (Navan-Slane road), take turn directly opposite main entrance to Slane Castle, signed Kells. Continue for 5km

Modern Irish cooking in a classy rustic setting

Tankardstown is a much-extended Georgian manor house that is geared up for weddings and business gatherings, and it does not want for country charm. In this idyllic spot, there is also an excellent dining proposition in the shape of the Brabazon restaurant. Situated in the one-time cow shed, expect a smart rustic finish with lots of exposed stonework, a central fireplace and pretty terrace. The setting may be traditional, but the food displays more contemporary leanings. The kitchen can call on the walled organic garden for fresh supplies (they have their own chickens, too), and a newly installed smoker brings a potent aroma to proceedings. The menu – including a tasting version – is filled with dishes that reflect modern ideas and cooking techniques. Start with house-cured bacon and radish tops with celeriac and ash, and move on to fillet of hake with cauliflower, pollen and squid ink. A meaty main course might be hay-smoked duck breast with a mini Wellington, and finish with a deconstructed classic such as poached apple with crumble, sorbet and cider sabayon.

Chef Robert Krawczyk **Owner** Patricia & Brian Conroy **Seats** 70
Times 12.30-3.30/6-8.30, Closed 3 days Xmas, Mon-Tue, L Wed-Sat **Prices** Tasting menu €45-€65, Service optional **Wines** 20 bottles over €30, 9 bottles under €30, 9 by glass **Notes** Fixed 3 course menu for larger groups, Sunday L €25-€30, Vegetarian available, Children welcome

COUNTY MONAGHAN

CARRICKMACROSS
Map 1 C4

Shirley Arms Hotel

◎ Modern Irish V

tel: 042 9673100 **Main St**
email: reception@shirleyarmshotel.ie **web:** www.shirleyarmshotel.ie
dir: N2 to Derry, take Ardee Rd to Carrickmacross

Modern Irish brasserie food in a handsome Georgian house

The market town of Carrickmacross can boast a tradition of producing fine lace, some of it seen in the Duchess of Cambridge's wedding outfit, as well as being the inspiration for Patrick Kavanagh's poetry. It's also home to this handsome stone-built hotel, once called White's, a name that lives on in its principal dining room, which is kitted out in checkered upholstery with wood dividers and big floral pictures. Here, the order of the day is modern Irish brasserie food that sweeps over a broad arc from Thai beef salad with peanuts and julienne veg, or prawn and courgette risotto dressed in lemon and chilli, to start, closely followed by the likes of herb-crusted hake fillet on ratatouille in basil velouté, lamb shank with mustard mash in red wine jus, or a classic surf-and-turf pairing of fillet steak and lobster in garlic butter.

Chef Micheál Muldoon **Owner** Jim McBride **Seats** 90, Pr/dining room 150
Times 12-3/5-9.30, Closed Good Fri, 25-26 Dec **Wines** 2 bottles over €30, 10 bottles under €30, 3 by glass **Parking** 150 **Notes** Fixed seasonal menu Mon-Thu, Sunday L €22-€30, Children welcome

GLASLOUGH
Map 1 C5

The Lodge at Castle Leslie Estate

◎◎ Traditional Irish, International

tel: 047 88100 **The Lodge, Castle Leslie Estate**
email: info@castleleslie.com **web:** www.castleleslie.com
dir: M1 junct 14 N Belfast signed Ardee/Derry. Follow N2 Derry Monaghan bypass, then N12 to Armagh for 2m, left N185 to Glaslough

Modern country-house cooking in splendid isolation

The Castle Leslie Estate extends over 1,000 acres, sprinkled with ancient woodlands and lakes, and boasts two plush bolt-holes – the Castle and The Lodge – operating as separate country-house hotels, each with a distinct identity. The boutique-style Lodge comes with a luxury spa, and Snaffles, a large, stylish contemporary restaurant with a hand-carved ceiling, oak beams, a glass wall opening the space up to country views, and a baby grand piano to add to the refined atmosphere. The kitchen keeps its finger on the pulse of culinary trends, turning out up-to-date country-house cooking. Lough Neagh smoked eel gets things under way, matched intelligently with beetroot risotto, foam and crème fraîche. Then Fermanagh Saddleback pork gets a workout, arriving as rolled roasted fillet and slow-cooked belly with black pudding soufflé, apple, red cabbage, and caramelised onion mash. If you're up for fish, there might be pan-fried turbot with carrot gratin and Muscat butter sauce. Finish with coffee and caramel macaroon with praline sauce and vanilla ice cream.

Chef Andrew Bradley **Owner** Samantha Leslie **Seats** 110, Pr/dining room 50
Times 6-9.30, Closed 24-27 Dec, L all week **Prices** Prices not confirmed, Service optional **Wines** 27 bottles over €30, 37 bottles under €30, 14 by glass **Parking** 200 **Notes** Tasting menu, Vegetarian available, Children welcome

COUNTY ROSCOMMON

ROSCOMMON
Map 1 B4

Kilronan Castle Estate & Spa

◉◉ Modern French

tel: 071 9618000 & 086 0210542 **Ballyfarnon**
email: enquiries@kilronancastle.ie **web:** www.kilronancastle.ie
dir: M4 to N4, exit R299 towards R207 Droim ar Snámh/Drumsna/Droim. Exit R207 for R280, turn left Keadue Road R284

Modern country house cooking amid Victorian Gothic grandeur

Kilronan certainly looks like an authentic medieval castle complete with a business-like crenallated turret, but it is actually a mere pastiche, dating from the early 19th century. After a thorough restoration in 2006 that carefully preserved its period character, it now trades as an upmarket hotel with luxurious spa and leisure facilities. The interior sports the full-dress Victorian Gothic look, a style which works to particularly impressive effect in the Douglas Hyde restaurant, where clubby oak panelling and a magnificent carved fireplace combine with crystal chandeliers, heavy swagged drapes and linen-swathed tables. Perhaps unsurprisingly, given the grand setting, the kitchen looks to French classicism for its inspiration, spiked here and there with oriental notes. A starter of quail Benedict sees a brace of quail breasts served atop wilted spinach on a toasted muffin and pointed up with a well-made hollandaise sauce, while main course sea bass fillets come with Dublin Bay prawns, prawn mousseline, and a deeply-flavoured reduction of fish stock and dry Vermouth. Dessert is an elaborate millefeuille layered with creamy 'pannacotta' parfait.

Times 1-3.30/6-10, Closed L Mon-Sat (ex group requests)

COUNTY SLIGO

ENNISCRONE
Map 1 B5

Waterfront House

◉ Modern European NEW

tel: 096 37120 **Sea Front, Cliff Rd**
email: relax@waterfronthouse.ie **web:** www.waterfronthouse.ie
dir: Phone for directions

Globetrotting seafood cookery plus sunsets

The white-fronted hotel with red-framed windows is situated on the 'wild Atlantic way' that is the Sligo coast, where spectacular sunsets are the norm. Customers dine in a light-filled, wood-floored room with views over the miles of beach, its homely ambience offset with napkins and staff neckties in daring lime-green. Seafood is very much to the fore, with tasting banquets on the first Friday of the month, and not everything is necessarily trad. Start with panko-crumbed calamari and spiced houmous with coconut-sumac dressing if you will, and there are Spanish and east Asian stylings too. Otherwise, a serving of sautéed mushrooms with St Tola goats' cheese on toast might precede accurately cooked whole Dover sole fillets with crab, scallops and prawns in nut butter, or Mayo lamb rump in port and redcurrants. Finish with mint Pavlova sandwiching chocolate ganache, a scoop of orange ice cream on the side.

Chef Aiden Hennigan **Owner** Jennifer Scott **Seats** 70
Times 12.30-3.30/5-9, Closed Mon-Wed (Nov-Apr) **Prices** Fixed L 2 course €17.50-€20, Fixed D 3 course €24.50-€35, Starter €5-€15, Main €14.95-€27.95, Dessert €4.95-€9.95, Service optional **Wines** 8 bottles over €30, 18 bottles under €30, 18 by glass **Parking** 20 **Notes** Daily specials 1 starter, 2 main €25 (usually seafood), Sunday L €17.50-€25, Vegetarian available, Children welcome

SLIGO
Map 1 B5

Radisson Blu Hotel & Spa Sligo

◉ Modern Irish, Mediterranean

tel: 071 9140008 & 9192400 **Rosses Point Rd, Ballincar**
email: info.sligo@radissonblu.com **web:** www.radissonblu.ie/sligo
dir: From N4 into Sligo to main bridge. Take R291 on left. Hotel 1.5m on right

Technically ambitious cooking for the Yeats fans

Sligo is W B Yeats country, and the Radisson Blu is ideally placed to cater for the annual pilgrimage of devotees who come to see the places the poet loved. It's a classy modern hotel, designed in boutique manner with plenty of vivid colour, notably reds and purples in the Classiebawn dining room. Here, the bill of fare is contemporary Irish cooking of notable technical ambition. Try a deconstructed egg for starters, the yolk crisped, the breadcrumbed white poached in red ale, dressed in horseradish crème fraîche. That might lead on to Ballinasloe lamb, the rack smoked over turf and heather, the shoulder herb-crusted, served with polenta and garlicky mash in minted jus with a jelly of Sheep Dip Irish whiskey. Then an inventive dessert turns up, perhaps gingerbread and candied peel crème brûlée with a baby pear poached in mulled wine.

Chef Joe Shannon **Owner** Radisson Blu **Seats** 120, Pr/dining room 60
Times 6-9.45, Closed L Pre-bookings only **Prices** Fixed D 3 course €31.50-€48, Starter €6.50-€10.50, Main €18.50-€28.50, Dessert €6.50-€9.50 **Wines** 6 bottles over €30, 6 bottles under €30, 7 by glass **Parking** 600 **Notes** Seasonal early bird menu, Vegetarian available, Children welcome

Sligo Park Hotel & Leisure Club

◉ Modern Irish NEW

tel: 071 9190400 **Pearse Rd**
email: sligo@leehotels.com **web:** www.sligopark.com
dir: On N4 to Sligo, junct 52 (Sligo S) Carrowroe/R287. Follow signs for Sligo (R287), 1m on right

Simple Irish fare in a contemporary hotel restaurant

Covering all the bases, Sligo Park is both business- and family-friendly, and with everything from full-on leisure facilities and surrounding verdant countryside, there's plenty of opportunity to build up an appetite. The dining option is the Hazelwood Restaurant, which has a warm contemporary finish of fuchsia and mauve, and views out over walled gardens. The service team offers bags of charm. The kitchen stays true to Irish produce and delivers classic dishes with a few modern touches here and there. A dressed crab and pineapple roll, for example, comes with goats' cheese beignet and sweet tomato salsa, and there's an oriental flavour to a main course honey-glazed duck breast. Dry-aged steak comes with hand-cut chunky chips, crispy onion tempura and a whiskey cream sauce and desserts might offer up a classic crème brûlée done just right. The wine list offers a decent selection by the glass.

Chef Chris Friel **Owner** RJ Kidney & Co **Seats** 120, Pr/dining room 340
Times 1-2.15/6.30-9, Closed L Mon-Sat **Prices** Fixed D 3 course €32, Service optional **Wines** 14 bottles over €30, 19 bottles under €30, 10 by glass **Parking** 200 **Notes** Sunday L €20-€24, Vegetarian available, Children welcome

COUNTY TIPPERARY

CLONMEL   Map 1 C3

Hotel Minella

⚜ Traditional V

tel: 052 612 2388
email: reservations@hotelminella.ie **web:** www.hotelminella.com
dir: *S of river in town*

Country cooking in an extended Georgian hotel

The garden runs down to the banks of the River Suir and those are the Comeragh Mountains looming in the background – a charming spot. The hotel has extended out from an original Georgian mansion and doesn't lack for facilities. The restaurant is at ground-floor level in the original house, so has plenty of character and a traditional, period feel, as well as views across the garden to the river. The kitchen team keep things simple with a good choice of unchallenging fare with a local flavour. Two crisp and golden fishcakes might get the ball rolling, packed with a decent amount of fish and herbs, and served with home-made tartare sauce and dressed salad leaves. Next up, roast rack of lamb comes nicely pink and in the company of a redcurrant and rosemary sauce, plus accurately cooked vegetables. For dessert, a wobbly pannacotta is flavoured with a mix of berries.

Chef Christopher Bray **Owner** John & Elizabeth Nallen **Seats** 120, Pr/dining room 60 **Times** 1-3/6.30-9.30 **Prices** Fixed L 3 course €28-€35, Fixed D 3 course €35-€45, Service optional **Wines** 6 bottles over €30, 6 bottles under €30, 10 by glass **Notes** Sunday L €28-€35, Children welcome

THURLES   Map 1 C3

Inch House Country House & Restaurant

⚜ Irish

tel: 050 451348 & 51261
email: mairin@inchhouse.ie **web:** www.inchhouse.ie
dir: *6.5km NE of Thurles on R498*

Splendid ingredients cooked simply in a Georgian manor

Quite the enterprise, Inch House is the hub of a working farm run by the Egan family, which is not only a rather lovely country-house hotel, but a hive of activity. They run the hotel and farm the land, but they also make preserves and chutneys which you can enjoy at home. There's plenty of comfort to be had at Inch House, though, with swish bedrooms and a relaxed service style that makes you feel like part of the family (almost). Needless to say the land provides a lot of the ingredients – they make their own black pudding, too – and what isn't home-grown won't have travelled very far. This is country-house cooking. Warm Gortnamona goats' cheese with a walnut and crumb crust is a simple enough starter, the cheese gently warmed through and served with salad from the garden and the house's red onion marmalade. Next up, suprême of chicken wrapped in bacon with a mushroom sauce, and for dessert, a berry crème brûlée.

Chef John Barry **Owner** John & Nora Egan **Seats** 50 **Times** 6-9.15, Closed Xmas & New Year, Sun-Mon, L all week **Prices** Fixed D 3 course €35, Starter €7-€12, Main €18-€30, Dessert €5-€10, Service optional **Wines** 8 bottles over €30, 10 bottles under €30, 2 by glass **Parking** 50 **Notes** ALC Sat, Vegetarian available, Children 3 yrs+

COUNTY WATERFORD

ARDMORE   Map 1 C2

Cliff House Hotel

⚜⚜⚜⚜ – *see page 740*

WATERFORD   Map 1 C2

Bistro at the Tower

⚜ Modern Irish, European

tel: 051 862300 **The Mall**
email: events@thw.ie **web:** www.towerhotelwaterford.com
dir: *City centre, main N25. Located at end of Merchants Quay*

Seafood-led menu at a smart city-centre hotel

Part of an Irish-Spanish group of upmarket venues, the Tower is a smart hotel and leisure centre on the Mall in Waterford, a comfortable haven of mod cons with an ancient turret. Its principal dining room, the Bistro, has an inspired, vividly colourful design influenced by the pacific calm of the nearby Marina. With so many fishing villages hereabouts, it comes as no surprise to find that fish and seafood are strong suits. A meal might begin with seafood chowder, or fishcakes in Thai sweet chilli sauce, as a means of whetting the appetite for salmon fillet with egg noodles and stir-fried veg, or a mixed grill of seafood with chorizo in lemon butter. Meatheads need look no further than grilled Irish Angus steak of impeccable pedigree, with garlic potatoes in Jameson's and peppercorn sauce. Finish with chocolate fondant, served with fudge sauce and honeycomb ice cream.

Chef John Moore, Ray Kelly **Owner** FBD Hotels & Resorts **Seats** 80, Pr/dining room 70 **Times** 12.30-2.30/6.30-9.30, Closed 25-26 Dec, L Mon-Sat (open on request) **Prices** Fixed L 2 course €15.50-€18.50, Fixed D 3 course €20-€25, Starter €5-€6.95, Main €17-€22, Dessert €5.95-€7.95, Service optional **Wines** 12 bottles over €30, 26 bottles under €30, 4 by glass **Parking** 90 **Notes** Pre-theatre menu with wine 2 people €59, Sunday L €14.50-€23.50, Vegetarian available, Children welcome

Faithlegg House Hotel & Golf Resort

⚜ Modern Irish, French

tel: 051 382000 **Faithlegg**
email: liammoran@fhh.ie **web:** www.faithlegg.com
dir: *From Waterford follow Dunmore East Rd then Cheekpoint Rd*

Modern country-house cooking in an 18th-century hotel

The original mansion, built in the 1780s, opened as a country-house hotel in 1998 after immaculate restoration. It has its own 18-hole golf course and leisure centre, while the high-ceilinged restaurant looks over the garden from what was a pair of drawing rooms. The cooking makes an impact, based as it is on native produce and a range of neat ideas. Boudin of black pudding with blue cheese foam, perry sorbet and Irish stout jus is a novel but effective starter. Move on to tea-smoked salmon fillet on mussel and saffron stew with pickled red onion flavoured with dill, or grilled loin and roast haunch steak of venison with roast celeriac and curly kale cream. End loyally with Irish artisan cheeses or Baileys crème brûlée.

Times 1-2.30/6-9.30, Closed 25 Dec, L pre-book only

Cliff House Hotel

Modern Irish V

tel: 024 87800 & 87803
email: info@thecliffhousehotel.com
web: www.thecliffhousehotel.com
dir: *N25 to Ardmore. Hotel at the end of village via The Middle Road*

Tirelessly innovative-Irish cooking overlooking the ocean

The jewel of the Cliff Collection hospitality group is this modern hotel perched on the cliff in the Waterford fishing community of Ardmore. It's a wild and windswept, not to say magically enchanting, location for a spa break that's far enough away from airport and ferry to allow you to feel you've been beamed out of the present world of care. Family-run with personable warmth and charm, it's a great place to go fishing, kayaking, whale-watching – anything really. Waves crash on the sandy beach, while inside you could be bobbing about in the pool, or settling into a tub chair in the House Restaurant, where panoramic views of the ocean and headland are pretty much guaranteed to soothe the spirits. Dutch-born Martijn Kajuiter arrived here in 2007, and set the kitchen on a firm upward trajectory, bringing in home-grown talent to help him realise his clean-lined, tirelessly innovative Irish cooking. Dishes look artfully arranged in the contemporary fashion, but where this approach can often lead to not much more than the sum of their parts, here a persuasive sense of balance created by everything working together is achieved, and the results are often sensational. Pigeon as a starter has become commonplace, but here a Red Label squab receives its full due, the breast and leg appearing with foie gras in an array of black rice, chestnuts and chervil root, variously dressed with woodruff oil, Cabernet Sauvignon vinegar and a rich pigeon jus. Scallops, both seared and céviche, are tricked out with Jerusalem artichoke, sea spinach, pink peppercorns, black garlic and caviar. Thoroughbred Irish produce from land and sea brings class to main courses that might team up grilled halibut with fennel, beech mushrooms and brown shrimps with watercress oil and lard, while an almost classical treatment for roasted stuffed veal striploin sees it paired with its sweetbreads alongside shallots and gnocchi in thyme-infused veal jus. Even at dessert stage, the same determination to attain impact through resourceful multi-layering brings on crème and savarin of rhubarb with custard ice cream, gin-and-tonic candyfloss and cardamom in ginger cream. Chocolate is 65%-solids organic gear done every which way – ganache, crème, caramelised – bedazzled with 24-karat gold-flecked olive oil, apricot and sea salt, with white coffee ice cream. Half-a-dozen pedigree cheeses exercise their own allure, and don't stint on accompaniments of quince jelly, salad, crackers, walnut bread and a scone.

Chef Martijn Kajuiter, Stephen Hayes, Darren Mulvihill
Owner Valshan Ltd **Seats** 64, Pr/dining room 20
Times 6.30-10, Closed Xmas, Sun-Mon (occasional Tue), L all
week **Prices** Tasting menu fr €95 **Wines** 100 bottles over €30,
3 bottles under €30, 12 by glass **Parking** 30 **Notes** Tasting menu
8 course, ALC menu 3 course €75, Children welcome

COUNTY WEXFORD

GOREY
Map 1 D3

Amber Springs Hotel

◉ Modern European

tel: 053 9484000 **Wexford Rd**
email: info@ambersprings.ie **web:** www.ambersprings.ie
dir: N11 junct 23, 500mtrs from Gorey by-pass at junct 23

Modern hotel with food to match

This contemporary hotel in historic Gorey opened in 2006 and has something for everyone, whether you're tying the knot, planning a spot of down time in the spa, setting up a corporate team building session, or just looking to de-stress by the coast and eat well. The latter is taken care of by Kelby's Bistro, a clean-cut, neutral modern space up on the first floor, where sweeping picture windows open up views across the gardens to fields beyond. Straightforward, easy-going comfort food is the deal here, with much of the seasonal produce – particularly beef – provided by the owners' farm, as in a main course of dry-aged Angus sirloin steak served with onion and truffle purée, smoked butter hollandaise, and cherry tomatoes. This might come book-ended by crispy deep-fried lemon and pepper calamari with a spicy kick from mango and chilli purée, and glazed chocolate mousse with pistachio ice cream to finish.

Times 1-3/6-9, Closed 25-26 Dec, L Mon-Sat

Ashdown Park Hotel

◉ Mediterranean, European

tel: 053 9480500 **Station Rd**
email: info@ashdownparkhotel.com **web:** www.ashdownparkhotel.com
dir: On approach to Gorey town take N11 from Dublin. Take left signed for Courtown. Hotel on left

Crowd-pleasing menu in an elegant setting

With sandy beaches and golf courses nearby, this modern hotel on a grand scale, within walking distance of the centre of Gorey, has plenty of attractions of its own. There's a spa and conference facilities, for a start, plus some 22 acres of grounds to explore. It is also home to the Rowan Tree Restaurant, where tables are dressed up in crisp white linen, and the kitchen turns out some pleasingly straightforward dishes based on good local ingredients, including some things from the grounds. Start with a Caesar salad with croûtons, smoked bacon and parmesan, or prawn and pineapple skewers with an Asian dressing. Next up, rump of Wexford lamb is roasted and served with buttered cabbage and thyme jus, or there might be a duo of cod and rainbow trout with braised leeks and almond and dill butter, and for dessert, something like mango cheesecake with blackcurrant coulis.

Times 12.30-3/5.30-9, Closed 24-26 Dec, L Mon-Fri

Marlfield House

◉◉ Classical

tel: 053 9421124 **Courtown Rd**
email: info@marlfieldhouse.ie **web:** www.marlfieldhouse.com
dir: N11 junct 23, follow signs to Courtown. Turn left for Gorey at Courtown Road Rdbt, hotel 1m on the left

Grand hotel dining in the heart of Wexford

If you hanker after a touch of country-house luxury and you're in the southeast of Ireland, head on over to Marlfield House. It's been a while since the Earls of Courtown held grand house parties in this opulent Regency-era home, but you can get a taste of it in today's smart and luxurious hotel. The dining room consists of more than one handsomely decorated space, leading into an impressive conservatory, while murals and mirrors are interspersed with huge windows which open on to the immaculate garden. The kitchen garden plays its part in delivering first-rate seasonal produce, and the chefs do the rest. The contemporary Mediterranean-inflected menu might see you starting with crab and lemon crumble with roast beetroot salad, or pan-roasted quail with ragoût of fennel, peppers and thyme jus. Next up, seared North Atlantic monkish with a cassoulet of saffron potatoes, or pan-fried rib-eye of Wexford beef, and for dessert, buttermilk pannacotta with Wexford berries, sesame seed tuile and toasted almond flakes.

Times 12.30-2.30/7-9, Closed Xmas, Jan-Feb, Mon-Tue (Mar-Apr, Nov-Dec), L Mon-Sat

Seafield Golf & Spa Hotel

◉◉ Modern Irish, French

tel: 053 942 4000 **Ballymoney**
email: reservations@seafieldhotel.com **web:** www.seafieldhotel.com
dir: M11 exit 22

Smart contemporary cooking in a modern spa hotel

We've Italian designers to thank for the super-cool finish within this luxe spa and golf hotel on the cliffs above the sea, with not a hint of old-school formality or corporate banality. This place is glamorous and no mistake. The high-end finish extends to the restaurant, which has not an iota of stuffiness. A huge bronze female centaur keeps watch over the dining room, where lighting and music levels are kept soft, and the decor is in cool black, from the marble walls to the chandeliers. The food matches the venue for modernity and creativity, but keeps true to the spirit of its locale with a good showing of regional ingredients. There's real technical proficiency on show, and plenty of creative thinking. Take a starter of jasmine-cured monkfish, for example, with octopus carpaccio and smoked mint jelly, or a main-course fillet of Tipperary beef with an oxtail terrine, warm parsley jelly and wild mushroom gratin. Everything looks beautiful on the plate, not least a dessert such as orange-infused crème brûlée with a few extra surprises.

Chef Susan Leacy **Owner** Seafield Hotel Ltd **Seats** 90, Pr/dining room 40
Times 6-9.30, Closed L all week **Prices** Starter €9.95-€11.50, Main €18.95-€31.95, Dessert €9.50-€10.25 **Wines** 36 bottles over €30, 6 bottles under €30, 12 by glass **Parking** 100 **Notes** Vegetarian available, Children welcome

ROSSLARE
Map 1 D2

Beaches Restaurant at Kelly's Resort Hotel

◉◉ Traditional European

tel: 053 9132114
email: info@kellys.ie **web:** www.kellys.ie
dir: From N25 take Rosslare/Wexford road signed Rosslare Strand

Beachside resort hotel with modern cooking

The Beaches restaurant is aptly named, as it sits on five miles of golden sands in Rosslare. The Kelly family have run their resort hotel since 1895 – why move when you can work in a setting like this? – and the venue is set up to capitalise on the views, bathed in light through good-sized windows, and with restful pastel hues, white linen on the tables, and a mini gallery of original artworks on the walls. Local produce is as good as it gets, and the kitchen has the experience and confidence to treat it all simply and let the sheer quality do the talking in simple contemporary dishes. Confit duck arrives in an unfussy combo with spiced pears and baked plums with five spice, while local goose from an artisan producer is roasted and pointed up with chestnut stuffing, braised ham, caramelised pear and glazed pearl onions. Yogurt and lime pannacotta with raspberry sorbet provides a refreshing finale.

Times 1-2/7.30-9, Closed mid Dec-mid Feb

ROSSLARE *continued*

La Marine Bistro

🌸 Modern

tel: 053 9132114 **Kelly's Resort Hotel & Spa**
email: info@kellys.ie
dir: *From N25 take Rosslare/Wexford road signed Rosslare Strand*

Bistro-style cooking at a smart seaside resort hotel

The more casual stand-alone restaurant of Kelly's Resort Hotel is an easy-going venue with views of the chefs at work in the open kitchen. The shipshape French bistro theme suits the beachside setting to a T, as does its menu of classic Gallic bistro fare, which is all built on the eminently solid foundations of spankingly fresh local produce. Top-class fish and seafood comes but a short way from Kilmore Quay to be treated simply and sent out in ideas such as monkfish medallions with warm saffron and garlic mayonnaise, or scallops with creamy spiced Puy lentils and coconut crème fraîche. Meat eaters are not sent home hungry either – there may be roast rack of lamb with gratin dauphinoise and redcurrant sauce, and to finish, pear, chocolate and almond pithivier or well-chosen local cheeses.

Times 12.30-2/6.30-9, Closed mid Dec-Feb

WEXFORD
Map 1 D3

Whitford House Hotel Health & Leisure Club

🌸 Traditonal European

tel: 053 9143444 **New Line Rd**
email: info@whitford.ie **web:** www.whitford.ie
dir: *From Rosslare ferry port take N25. At Duncannon Rd rdbt right onto R733, hotel immediately on left. 1.5m from Wexford*

Traditionally-based cooking in a family-run hotel

A family-run boutique hotel since the 1960s, not far from the town centre and within reach of the Rosslare ferry, Whitford House is a haven of contemporary creature comforts. State-of-the-art spa facilities and a little cocktail bar are among the various ways to indulge yourself, but best of all is the Seasons dining room. Primrose-coloured walls and gaily striped upholstery make an uplifting impression, and the cooking sticks to a traditionally based route, but with plenty of style. Start in Mediterranean fashion with a puff pastry tart piled with roasted tomatoes, mozzarella and basil, served with a balsamic-dressed salad of rocket, pine nuts and parmesan, before going on to slow-roast lamb rump in its own juices, or steamed salmon on spinach, sauced with white wine. Comforting pudding options include strawberry Pavlova, sherry trifle or sticky toffee pudding and butterscotch sauce, and there are great Irish cheeses, served with Gubbeen cheese crackers.

Times 12.30-3/7-9, Closed 24-27 Dec, L Mon-Sat, D Mon-Thu (out of season)

COUNTY WICKLOW

DELGANY
Map 1 D3

Glenview Hotel

🌸🌸 Modern Irish, European **V**

tel: 01 2873399 **Glen O' the Downs**
email: sales@glenviewhotel.com **web:** www.glenviewhotel.ie
dir: *From Dublin city centre follow signs for N11, past Bray on N11 S'bound, exit 9. From airport, M50 S onto N11 S, junct 9*

Imaginative seasonal cooking and lush valley views

The Woodlands Restaurant at this hotel is up on the first floor to maximise the view over the Glen o' the Downs, and it is an impressive vista. There are large arched windows to make the best of the views over the treetops and down the valley, and inside all is soothing pastel shades and sparkling glassware. The chef has Indian heritage and there are one or two Asian touches on the menu, but the food is mostly what is loosely termed modern Irish cooking. A starter of pan-fried scallops with shellfish bisque is a winning combination, or there might be confit duck leg croquettes served with a spiced apple purée. To follow, Wicklow lamb comes in a fashionable three-way construction, with an array of vegetables, and Kilmore Quay cod is flavoured with Goan spices and served with quail's egg and red onion chutney. For dessert, pannacotta with fresh strawberries is a summer treat.

Chef Sandeep Pandy **Owner** Paddy Crean **Seats** 80, Pr/dining room 36 **Times** 12.30-2.30/5.30-9.30, Closed L Mon-Sat **Prices** Fixed L 2 course €19.50-€24.50, Fixed D 3 course €28.50-€29.50 **Wines** 20 bottles over €30, 19 bottles under €30, 13 by glass **Parking** 150 **Notes** Sunday L €29, Children welcome

ENNISKERRY
Map 1 D3

Powerscourt Hotel

🌸🌸 Modern European

tel: 01 2748888 **Powerscourt Estate**
email: info@powerscourthotel.com **web:** www.powerscourthotel.com
dir: *N11 to R117 Enniskerry, follow signs for Powerscourt Gardens*

Upscale dining in a Palladian hotel

With a sweeping Palladian mansion at its heart, the Powerscourt resort has a couple of golf courses, a luxurious spa and classy bedrooms. There's also an Irish pub called McGills, but the main event food-wise is the swish and glamorous Sika Restaurant. There are glorious mountain views from its third-floor dining room, a space decorated with an upscale finish while maintaining plenty of the room's original character. There's a chef's table, too. The food is contemporary Irish inasmuch as it takes first-class regional produce and applies both modern and classical techniques. Take a starter of pan-fried scallops, for example, with Jerusalem artichokes, pancetta and apple balsamic jus, or a main course dish of Atlantic halibut with parsnip purée, brown shrimps and a vermouth cream. A meaty main course might be Challans duck breast served with its confit leg, plus Savoy cabbage, black pudding and a pickled garlic jus. Desserts are no less creative and well crafted; lemon tart with toasted almond ice cream, for example, or apple fondant with a Granny Smith sorbet.

Times 1-2.30/6-10, Closed L Mon-Sat

MACREDDIN
Map 1 D3

BrookLodge Hotel & Macreddin Village

 Modern Irish

tel: 0402 36444
email: info@brooklodge.com **web:** www.brooklodge.com
dir: *N11 to Rathnew, R752 to Rathdrum, R753 to Aughrim, follow signs to Macreddin Village*

Dramatic dining venue, organic and wild food

Looking every inch the luxurious country-house retreat, the BrookLodge hotel is the heart of the purpose-built Macreddin Village. The upmarket operation comprises an 18-hole golf course and spa, a pub and brewery, café, bakery, smokehouse, and Italian restaurant. The Strawberry Tree (dinner-only) is the top foodie option of the whole set-up, a strikingly opulent setting, spreading through three grand rooms with mirrored ceilings reflecting twinkling modern chandeliers, bare burnished mahogany tables, and gilt-framed mirrors on midnight-blue walls. Given its status as Ireland's first certified organic restaurant, provenance of seasonal ingredients is king, so if it's not wild or foraged, it's sourced from certified organic producers, with herbs and soft fruit grown in the estate's own walled garden. The kitchen brings all of this peerless produce together creatively, showing its skill in simple dishes such as wild wood pigeon terrine with strawberry and green pepper jam, followed by guinea fowl with dried fruit compote, or organic Irish Angus beef roasted in a crust of Irish turf for that true touch of terroir.

Times 7-9.30, Closed 24-26 Dec, Mon, L all week

NEWTOWN MOUNT KENNEDY
Map 1 D3

Druids Glen Resort

Modern V

tel: 01 2870800
email: reservations@druidsglenresort.com **web:** www.druidsglenresort.com
dir: *Follow M50 south from airport. Follow M11/N11 through Kilmacanogue, junct 12 signed Newtown Mount Kennedy, follow signs*

Simple brasserie dishes and two golf courses

Druids Glen boasts not just one, but two championship golf courses, plus the full package of spa pampering and leisure facilities in its acreages of landscaped grounds, with the Wicklow hills thrown in as a backdrop. Naturally, the place does a brisk trade in weddings and conferences, and when you have finished tying the knot, team building or whacking balls around, there's classy modern cooking to be had in the main dining room. Stylishly revamped in muted hues of blue and grey, with velvet booths, and a feature fire set in a huge granite hearth, the place now goes by the name of Hugo's Restaurant, and is the arena for the kitchen's French-accented modern Irish repertoire. To views over the famous Druids Glen course, tee off with a three-way treatment of salmon – confit, rillettes and a smoked brûlée

with avocado foam, cucumber jelly and shaved fennel, then follow on with fillet of Atlantic cod with lobster ravioli, celeriac boulangère, and a fennel and lobster emulsion. Finish with strawberry crème brûlée with wild strawberry sorbet.

Chef Malek Hamidouche **Owner** Flinns, Lappins, Hurleys **Seats** 170, Pr/dining room 22 **Times** 1-2.30/5.30-10, Closed L Mon-Sat **Prices** Fixed L 2 course €26, Fixed D 3 course €45-€50, Starter €7-€12.95, Main €19.75-€29.50, Dessert €6.50-€8.50, Service optional **Wines** 51 bottles over €30, 14 bottles under €30, 12 by glass **Parking** 400 **Notes** Afternoon tea, Sunday L, Children welcome

RATHNEW
Map 1 D3

Hunter's Hotel

Traditional Irish, French

tel: 0404 40106 **Newrath Bridge**
email: reception@hunters.ie **web:** www.hunters.ie
dir: *N11 exit at Wicklow/Rathnew junct. 1st left onto R761. Restaurant 0.25m before village*

Classical Irish cooking in an ancestral family hotel

Great venerability resides not just in the stones of Hunter's, Ireland's oldest coaching inn, but in the ownership, which has passed through generations of the Gelletlie family since 1825. Barely half-an-hour from the Dun Laoghaire ferry, it sits in riotously colourful gardens, its dining room a vision of crisp linen, mahogany and fine living. A small team of dedicated, volubly friendly staff runs the show. Expect daily-changing menus of classically informed Irish cooking, starting with spanking-fresh crab tian in dill mayonnaise, and progressing via an intermediate course (perhaps leek and potato soup or lime and ginger sorbet) to the likes of crisply roasted breast and leg of duckling with blueberry sauce and pommes purée, or a loaded seafood brochette in curry dressing. Strawberry pannacotta to finish comes in a cocktail glass, lifted with a portion of balsamic-marinated strawberries, or you might be tempted by a selection of Ireland's new generation of artisan cheeses.

Chef Mark Barry **Owner** Richard & Tom Gelletlie **Seats** 54, Pr/dining room 30 **Times** 12.45-3/7.30-9, Closed 3 days Xmas **Prices** Prices not confirmed, Service optional **Wines** 4 by glass **Parking** 30 **Notes** Afternoon tea €12, Sunday L, Children welcome

Tinakilly Country House & Restaurant

Modern Irish

tel: 0404 69274
email: reservations@tinakilly.ie **web:** www.tinakilly.ie
dir: *From Dublin Airport follow N11/M11 to Rathnew. Continue on R750 towards Wicklow. Hotel entrance approx 500mtrs from village on left*

Modernised country-house cooking overlooking the Irish Sea

The distinguished grey Italianate Victorian mansion was built in 1883 for an engineer who pioneered the laying of the undersea telegraph connecting the British Isles to north America. Clad in climbing foliage, it gazes fondly out over the Irish Sea. An L-shaped dining room with high ceilings and vibrant green walls contains a mix of antique and modern furniture as well as bare and clothed tables, and makes a diverting setting for the modernised country-house cooking on offer. Ingredients are well-chosen and the timing and seasoning of dishes does them justice, as for an opening pairing of scallops and the famous Clonakilty black pudding from County Cork, with butternut purée and pea shoots. Mains offer fine local meats such as herb-crusted Wicklow lamb rack in a provençal medium of chargrilled ratatouille veg and tomato fondue, or freshest fish such as Parma ham-wrapped cod with braised fennel, baby leeks and champ. A tarte Tatin variant made with pineapple is a success, the triumph ratified by its accompanying unabashedly boozy rum and raisin ice cream.

Times 12.30-4/6.30-8.30, Closed 24-26 & 31 Dec, 1-2 Jan, L Mon-Sat

KEY TO ATLAS

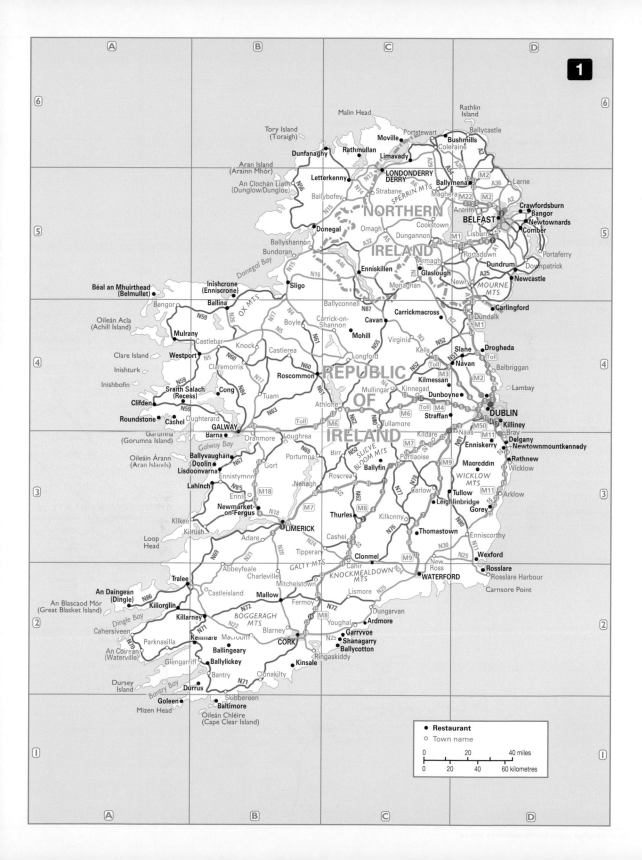

Legend

M6	Motorway/toll motorway
S H S	Motorway junction full/restricted. Service area
A33	Primary route single/dual carriageway
A34	Other A road single/dual carriageway
B3400	B road
	Unclassified road
V	Vehicle ferry
C	Fast vehicle ferry or catamaran
● **Oundle**	Restaurant
● **Glasgow**	AA Restaurant of the Year
○ Spalding	Town/Village name
	National boundary
ESSEX	English county name & boundary
CONWY	Welsh county name & boundary
MORAY	Scottish county name & boundary
	National Park

ISLES OF SCILLY

Bryher · Tresco · St Martin's · Higher Town · New Grimsby · Hugh Town · St Mary's · ISLES OF SCILLY (ST MARY'S) · Middle Town · Old Town · St Agnes

SV

SW

Lundy

Hartland Point · Hartland · Morwenstow · Kilkhampton · Bude · Stratto · Bude Bay · Widemouth Bay · Crackington Haven · Week St Mary · Boscastle · Tintagel · Delabole · Camelford · Lau · Port Isaac · Polzeath · Pendoggett · St Tudy · Bolventor · BODMIN MOOR · Harlyn · Rock · Blisland · Porthcothan · Padstow · WadeBridge · St Cleer · Mawgan Porth · St Mawgan · CORNWALL · Bodmin · Watergate Bay · NEWQUAY · St Columb Major · Lanivet · Dobwalls · Newquay · West Pentire · Roche · Bugle · St Blazey · Liskeard · St Keyne · Perranporth · Summercourt · Lostwithiel · Golant · Pelynt · St Agnes · Ladock · St Stephen · St Austell · Fowey · Polperro · Looe · Porthtowan · Marazanvose · Grampound · Polruan · Talland Bay · Portreath · St Day · Carnon Downs · Pentewan · Mevagissey · St Ives Bay · Gwithian · Truro · Tregony · Gorran Haven · St Ives · Redruth · Portloe · Zennor · Camborne · Lelant · Hayle · A393 · St Just-in-Roseland · Veryan · St Just · Penryn · Portscatho · Marazion · Falmouth · St Mawes · Penzance · Newlyn · Constantine · Mawnan Smith · Land's End · Sennen · St Buryan · Praa Sands · Helston · Gweek · Manaccan · Porthcurno · Treen · Mousehole · Mount's Bay · Porthleven · St Keverne · Mullion · Coverack · Cadgwith · Lizard · Lizard Point

For continuation pages refer to numbered arrows

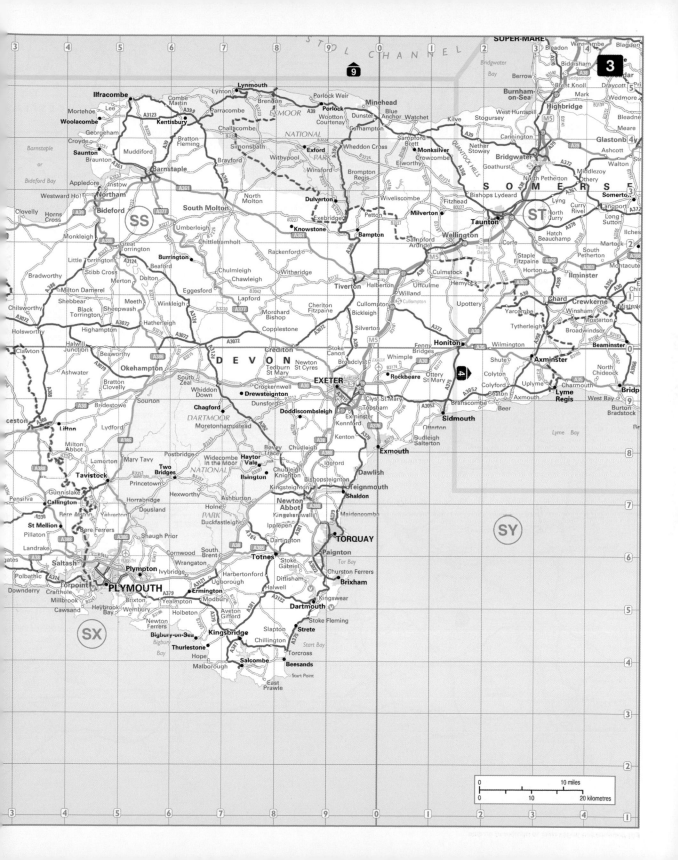

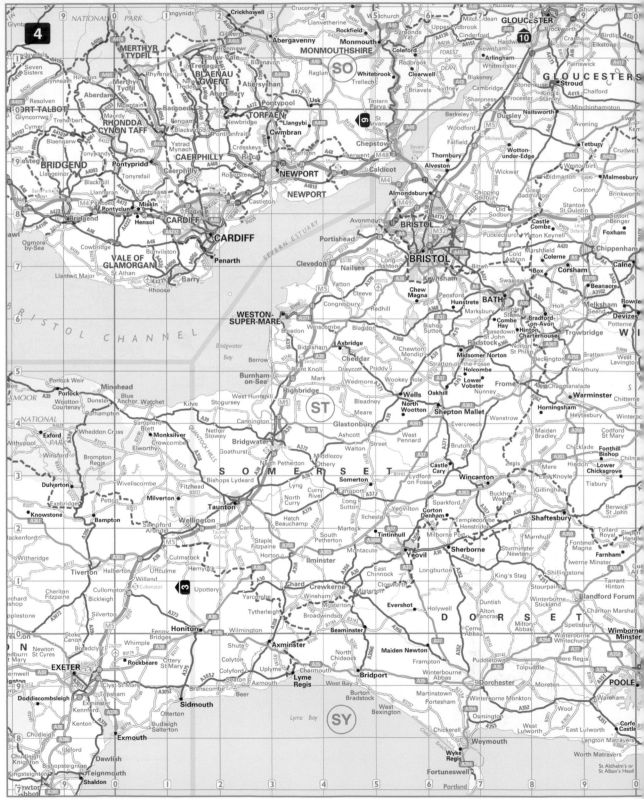

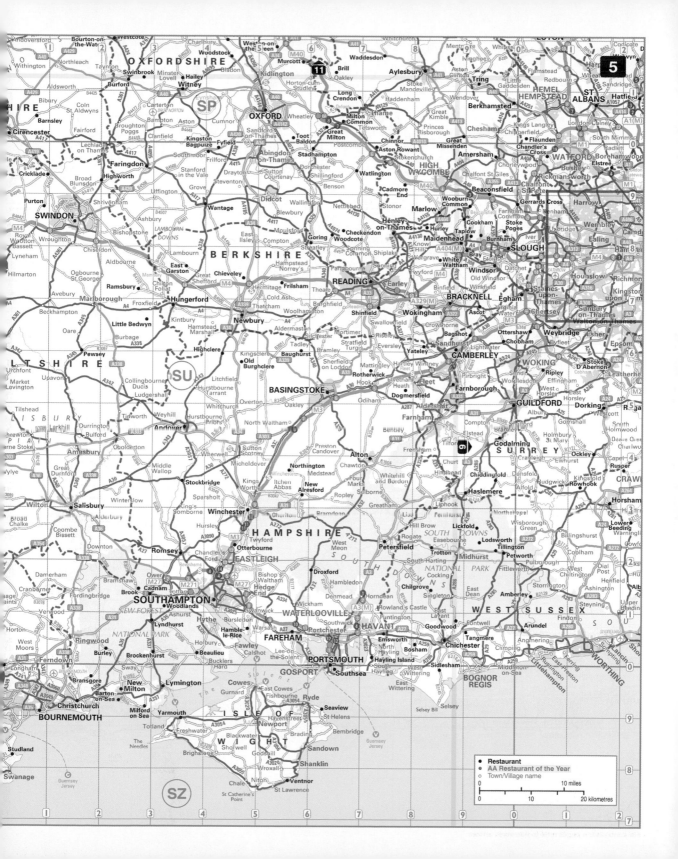

For continuation pages refer to numbered arrows

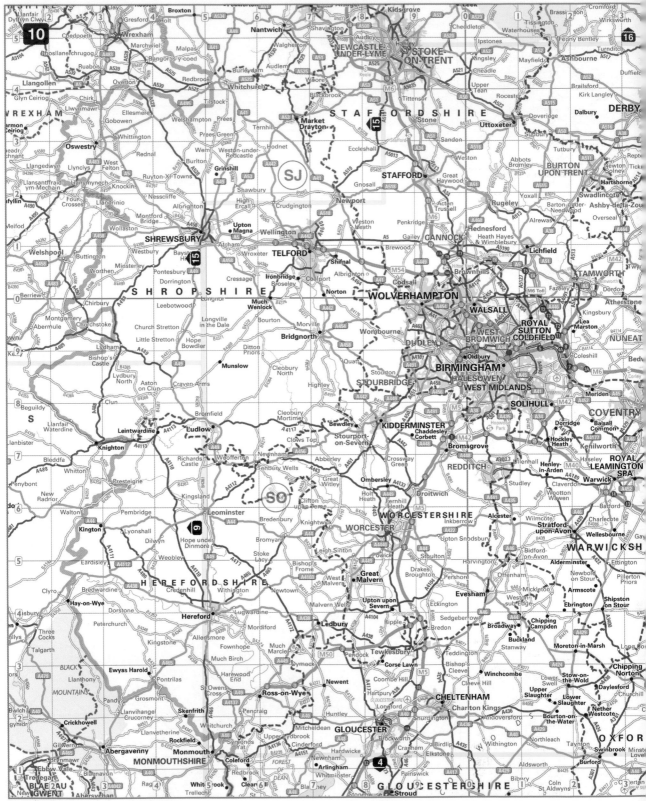

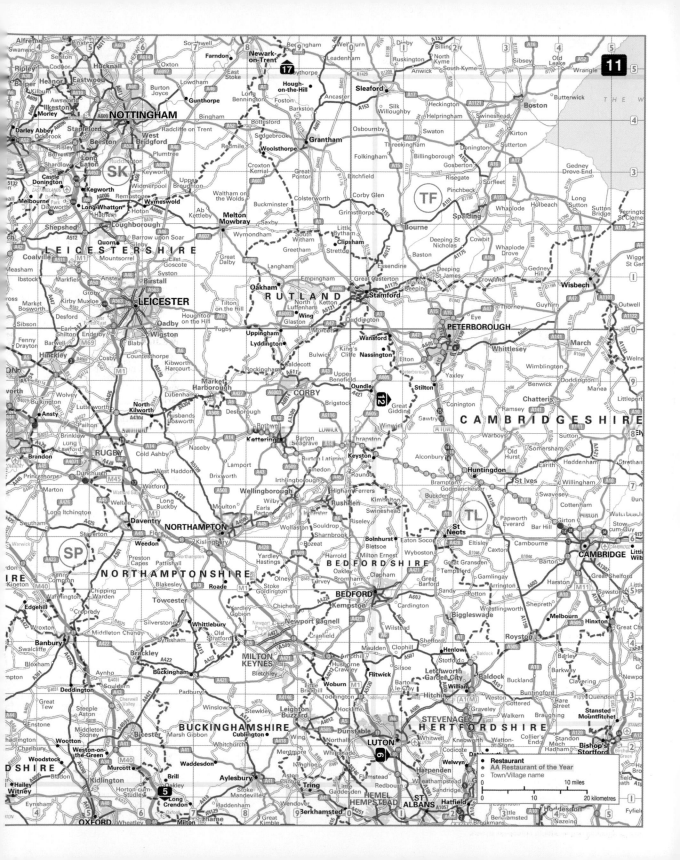

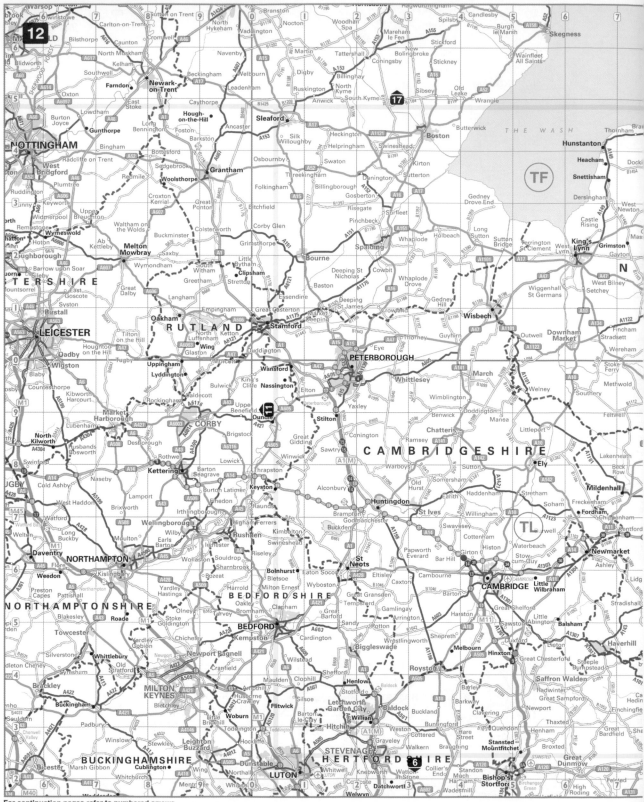

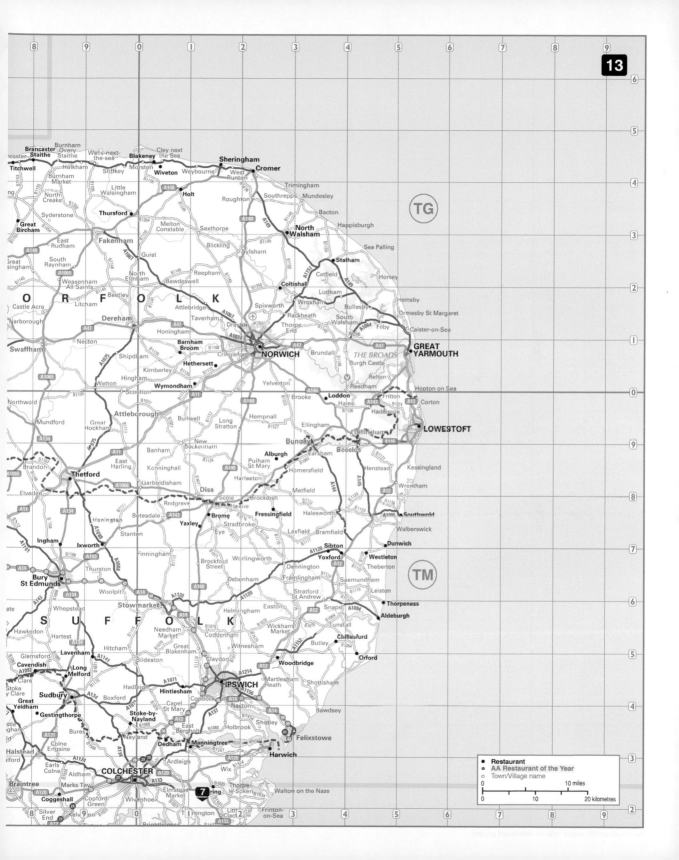

14

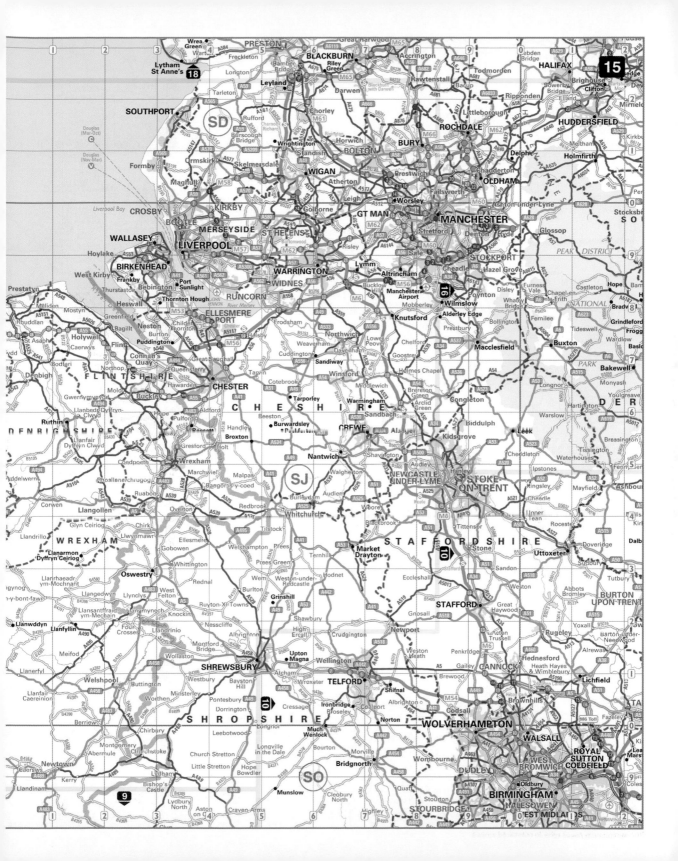

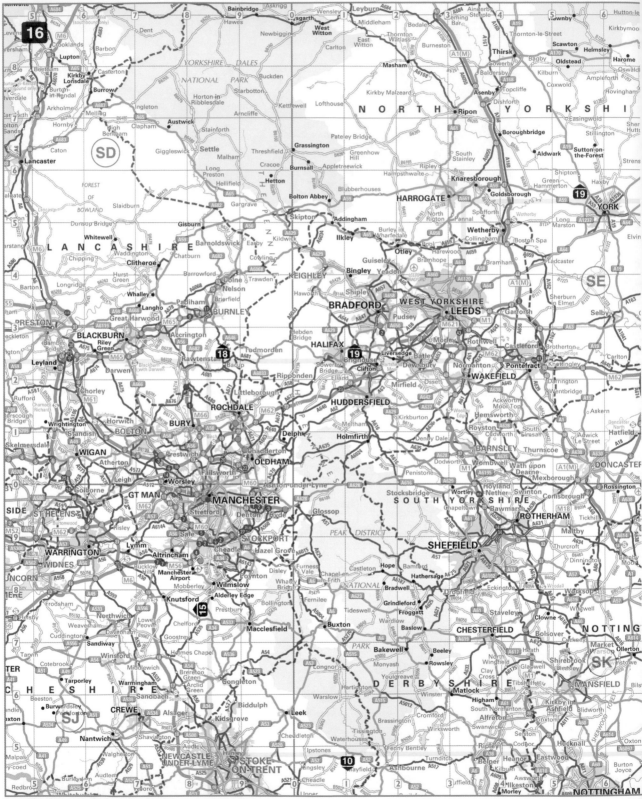

Restaurant
AA Restaurant of the Year
Town/Village name

0   10 miles
0   10   20 kilometres

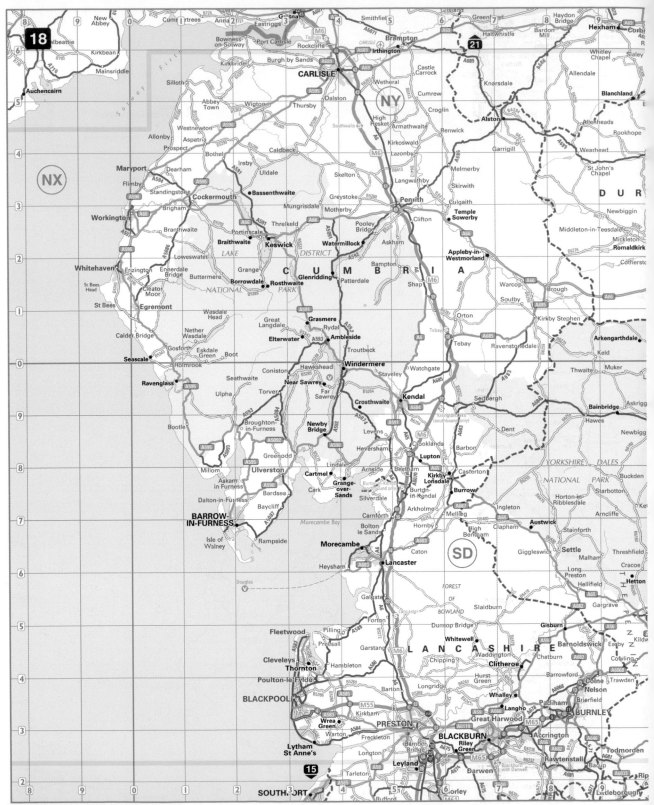

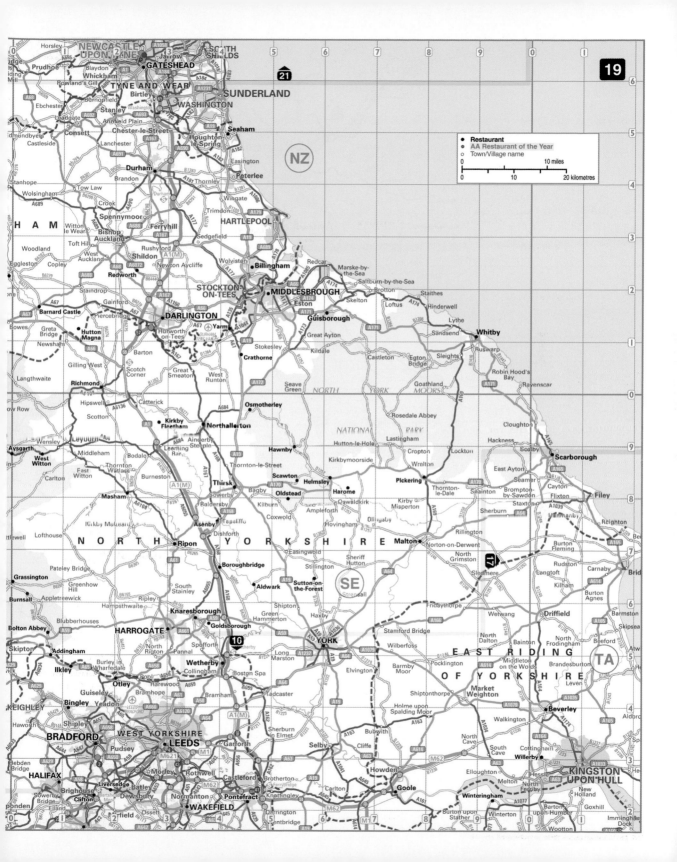

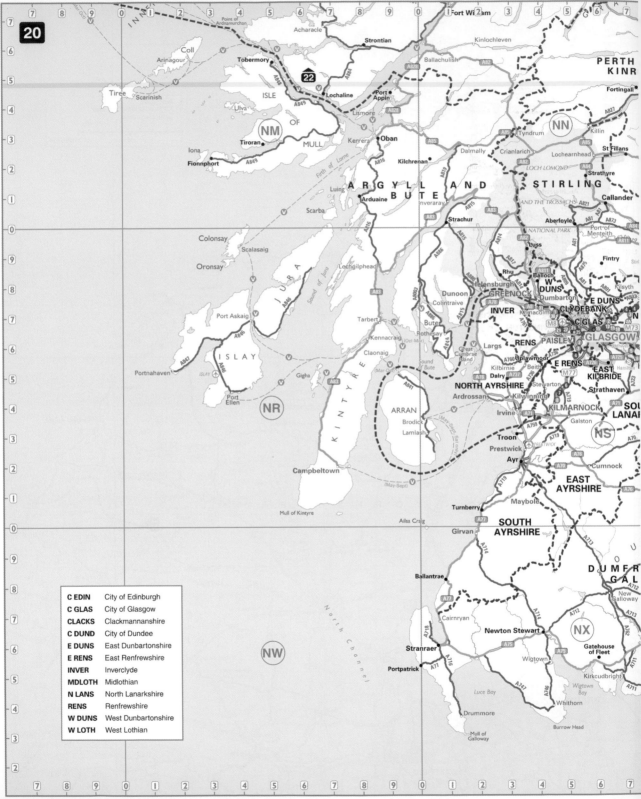

C EDIN	City of Edinburgh
C GLAS	City of Glasgow
CLACKS	Clackmannanshire
C DUND	City of Dundee
E DUNS	East Dunbartonshire
E RENS	East Renfrewshire
INVER	Inverclyde
MDLOTH	Midlothian
N LANS	North Lanarkshire
RENS	Renfrewshire
W DUNS	West Dunbartonshire
W LOTH	West Lothian

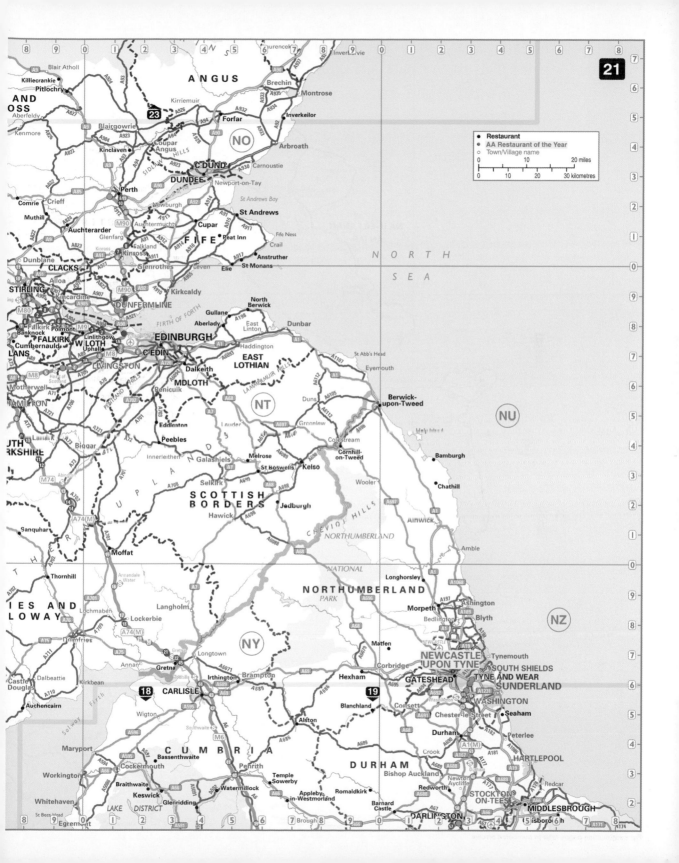

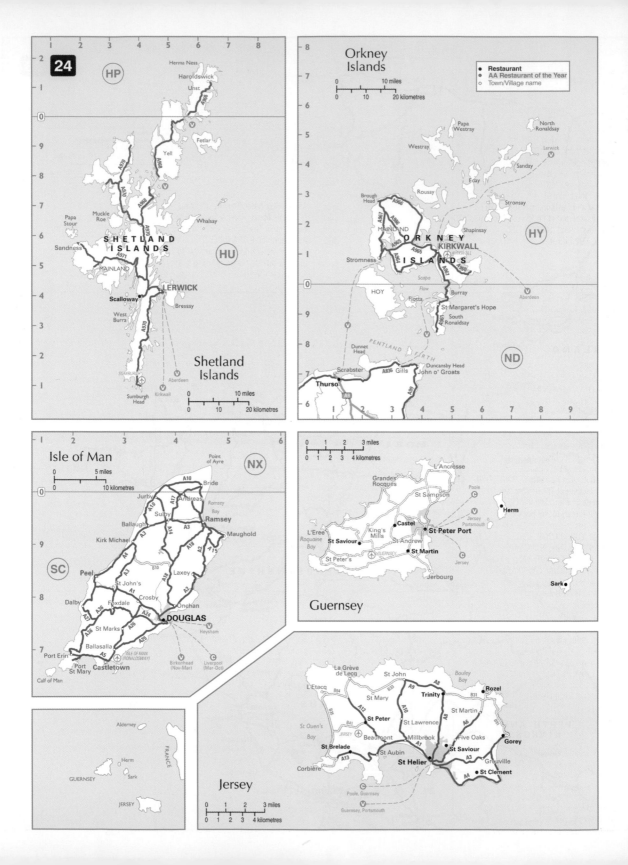

24

Shetland Islands

Orkney Islands

Isle of Man

Guernsey

Jersey

Index of Restaurants

Acknowledgments

The Automobile Association wishes to thank the following photographers and organisations for their assistance in the preparation of this book.

Abbreviations for the picture credits are as follows – (t) top; (b) bottom; (l) left; (r) right; (c) centre; (AA) AA World Travel Library

Front & Back Cover: © A. Astes / Alamy

England Opener AA/James Tims;
London Opener AA/James Tims;
Scotland Opener AA/Jonathan Smith;
Wales Opener AA/Mari Sterling;
Northern Ireland Opener AA/Chris Hill
Republic of Ireland Opener AA/Stephen Hill

003 Courtesy of Restaurant Mark Greenaway; 004 Courtesy of L'Ortolan, Shinfield; 008 Courtesy of Stravaigin, Glasgow; 010 Courtesy of Daniel Clifford © Adrian Franklin; 011 Courtesy of Midsummer House Restaurant, Cambridge; 012 Courtesy of Robin Hutson; 013 Courtesy of Belmond Le Manoir aux Quats' Saisons; 014-015 AA/James Tims; 014l Courtesy of House of Tides, Newcastle-upon-Tyne; 014r Courtesy of Tredwell's, London; 015l Courtesy of The Gannet, Glasgow; 015r Courtesy of Coast Restaurant, Saundersfoot; 016 Simon Burt/Alamy; 018-019 AA/James Tims; 018tl Courtesy of The Sun Inn, Dedham; 018bl Courtesy of The Sun Inn, Dedham; 018r Courtesy of The Sun Inn, Dedham; 019l Courtesy of Ubiquitous Chip, Glasgow; 019r Courtesy of Walnut Tree Inn, Abergavenny; 020 Valentyn Volkov/Alamy; 021 Image Source/Alamy; 022 YAY Media AS/Alamy; 024-025 Courtesy of JW Steakhouse; 027 Greg Blomberg/Alamy; 028 Courtesy of Northcote Restaurant; 029 Courtesy of Northcote Restaurant; 030 Courtesy of Northcote Restaurant; 030-031 Courtesy of Northcote Restaurant; 031 Courtesy of Northcote Restaurant; 032 Courtesy of Northcote Restaurant; 033 Courtesy of Northcote Restaurant; 253 AA/James Tims; 308 AA/Sarah Montgomery; 383 AA/James Tims; 384 AA/Sarah Montgomery; 671 AA/Stephen Whitehorne.

Every effort has been made to trace the copyright holders, and we apologise in advance for any unintentional omissions or errors. We would be pleased to apply any corrections in a following edition of this publication.